Looking for ways to integrate the Web into your curriculum?

ClassZone

classzone.com

ClassZone, McDougal Littell's textbook-companion Web site, is the solution! Online teaching support for you and engaging, interactive content for your students!

ClassZone is your online guide to ***The Language of Literature***

- Web links to help guide student's research
- Interactive activities for practice and comprehension
- Internet tutorial to help students conduct research on the Web
- Standardized test practice
- Teacher Center for classroom planning

Log on to ClassZone at classzone.com

With the purchase of ***Language of Literature***, you have immediate access to ClassZone.

Teacher Access Code

MCDKLMLHLPIHU

Use this code to create your own user-name and password. Then, access both teacher only and student resources.

Student Access Code

MCDB7CIJVTGHL

Give this code to your class. Each student creates a unique username and password to access resources for students.

McDougal Littell

THE LANGUAGE OF LITERATURE

TEACHER'S EDITION

Grade 10

McDougal Littell
A HOUGHTON MIFFLIN COMPANY
Evanston, Illinois • Boston • Dallas

ISBN 0-618-17039-1

Printed in the United States of America.

1 2 3 4 5 6 – DWO – 05 04 03 02

Senior Consultants

The senior consultants guided the conceptual development for *The Language of Literature* series. They participated actively in shaping prototype materials for major components, and they reviewed completed prototypes and/or completed units to ensure consistency with current research and the philosophy of the series.

Arthur N. Applebee Professor of Education, State University of New York at Albany; Director, Center for the Learning and Teaching of Literature; Senior Fellow, Center for Writing and Literacy

Andrea B. Bermúdez Professor of Studies in Language and Culture; Director, Research Center for Language and Culture; Chair, Foundations and Professional Studies, University of Houston-Clear Lake

Sheridan Blau Senior Lecturer in English and Education and former Director of Composition, University of California at Santa Barbara; Director, South Coast Writing Project; Director, Literature Institute for Teachers; Former President, National Council of Teachers of English

Rebekah Caplan Senior Associate for Language Arts for middle school and high school literacy, National Center on Education and the Economy, Washington, D.C.; served on the California State English Assessment Development Team for Language Arts; former co-director of the Bay Area Writing Project, University of California at Berkeley

Peter Elbow Emeritus Professor of English, University of Massachusetts at Amherst; Fellow, Bard Center for Writing and Thinking

Susan Hynds Professor and Director of English Education, Syracuse University, Syracuse, New York

Judith A. Langer Professor of Education, State University of New York at Albany; Co-director, Center for the Learning and Teaching of Literature; Senior Fellow, Center for Writing and Literacy

James Marshall Professor of English and English Education; Chair, Division of Curriculum and Instruction, University of Iowa, Iowa City

Contributing Consultants

Linda Diamond Executive Vice President, Consortium on Reading Excellence (CORE); co-author of *Building a Powerful Reading Program*

Lucila A. Garza ESL Consultant, Austin, Texas

Jeffrey N. Golub Assistant Professor of English Education, University of South Florida, Tampa

William L. McBride, Ph.D. Reading and Curriculum Specialist; former middle and high school English instructor

Sharon Sicinski-Skeans, Ph.D. Assistant Professor of Reading, University of Houston-Clear Lake; primary consultant on *The InterActive Reader*

T4

THE LANGUAGE OF LITERATURE

Experience the Language of Literature

I want to change people's minds...

I want to love what I do...

I want to make a statement...

Experience

THE LANGUAGE OF LITERATURE

Experience the Language of Literature

The Language of Literature provides students with high-interest selections and a variety of opportunities to interact with the literature, analyze what they read, and enjoy the experiences that great literature has to offer.

I want to see the world...

Skillfully Crafted Instruction

A variety of skills and strategies "bookend" each selection to support students before and after they read and help them connect to the literature.

Interactive Strategies

Critical reading, writing, and thinking strategies are interwoven throughout the text to help students build comprehension and develop their writing skills.

Solid Literary Analysis

Students learn how to analyze literature from a number of genres, interpret a variety of literary themes, and apply the analyses to their own experiences.

Flexible Ongoing Assessment

Assessment options in both print and electronic formats are integrated with the selections to help students be better prepared and more successful.

Experience the possibilities. Experience success. Experience *The Language of Literature*.

I want to create a memory...

Literature

Skillfully Crafted Instruction

Specific reading and literary strategies appear before each selection and are mirrored at the end to give students a complete literature experience.

I want to try new things...

Connect to Your Life helps students identify with the characters, plots, and themes and relate what they read to their own lives.

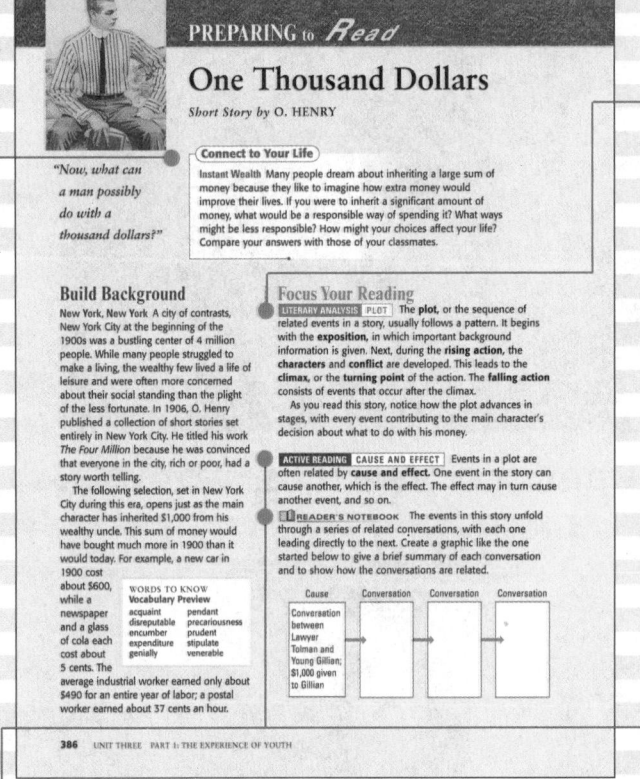

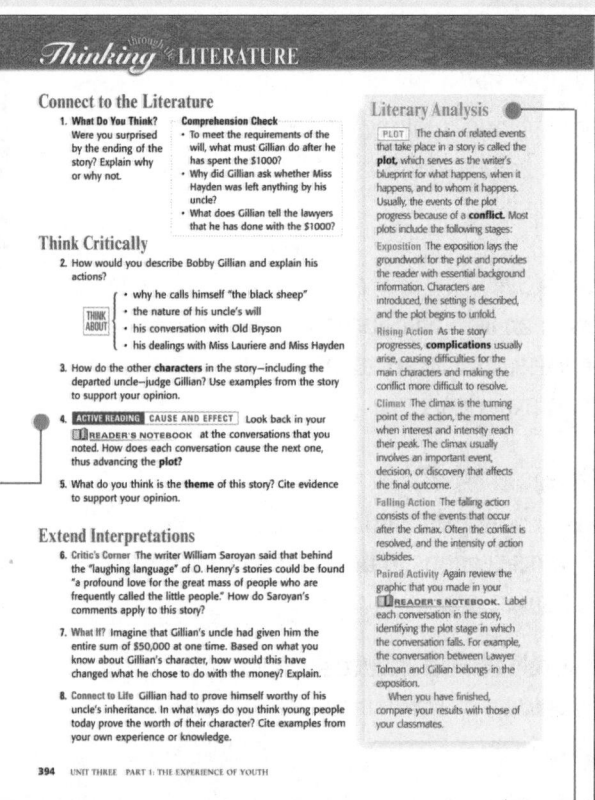

PREPARING to *Read*

One Thousand Dollars

Short Story by O. HENRY

"Now, what can a man possibly do with a thousand dollars?"

Connect to Your Life

Instant Wealth Many people dream about inheriting a large sum of money because they like to imagine how extra money would improve their lives. If you were to inherit a significant amount of money, what would be a responsible way of spending it? What ways might be less responsible? How might your choices affect your life? Compare your answers with those of your classmates.

Build Background

New York, New York A city of contrasts, New York City at the beginning of the 1900s was a bustling center of 4 million people. While many people struggled to make a living, the wealthy few lived a life of leisure and were often more concerned about their social standing than the plight of the less fortunate. In 1906, O. Henry published a collection of short stories set entirely in New York City. He titled his work *The Four Million* because he was convinced that everyone in the city, rich or poor, had a story worth telling.

The following selection, set in New York City during this era, opens just as the main character has inherited $1,000 from his wealthy uncle. This sum of money would have bought much more in 1900 than it would today. For example, a new car in 1900 cost about $600, while a newspaper and a glass of cola each cost about 5 cents. The average industrial worker earned only about $490 for an entire year of labor; a postal worker earned about 37 cents an hour.

WORDS TO KNOW
Vocabulary Preview

acquaint	pendant
disreputable	precariousness
encumber	prudent
expenditure	stipulate
genially	venerable

Focus Your Reading

LITERARY ANALYSIS PLOT The **plot**, or the sequence of related events in a story, usually follows a pattern. It begins with the **exposition**, in which important background information is given. Next, during the **rising action**, the **characters** and **conflict** are developed. This leads to the **climax**, or the **turning point** of the action. The **falling action** consists of events that occur after the climax.

As you read this story, notice how the plot advances in stages, with every event contributing to the main character's decision about what to do with his money.

ACTIVE READING CAUSE AND EFFECT Events in a plot are often related by **cause and effect.** One event in the story can cause another, which is the effect. The effect may in turn cause another event, and so on.

READER'S NOTEBOOK The events in this story unfold through a series of related conversations, with each one leading directly to the next. Create a graphic like the one started below to give a brief summary of each conversation and to show how the conversations are related.

Cause	Conversation	Conversation	Conversation
Conversation between Lawyer Tolman and Young Gillian; $1,000 given to Gillian	→	→	

386 UNIT THREE PART 1: THE EXPERIENCE OF YOUTH

The **Active Reading** strand prepares students to focus on a concept they will encounter in the selection and incorporates graphic organizers through the **Reader's Notebook**. Students are then asked to review their notes and journal entries from their **Reader's Notebook**.

Literary Analysis provides the definitions of specific literary terms and supports those definitions with literary examples.

Thinking through the LITERATURE

Connect to the Literature

1. **What Do You Think?** Were you surprised by the ending of the story? Explain why or why not.

Comprehension Check
- To meet the requirements of the will, what must Gillian do after he has spent the $1000?
- Why did Gillian ask whether Miss Hayden was left anything by his uncle?
- What does Gillian tell the lawyers that he has done with the $1000?

Think Critically

2. How would you describe Bobby Gillian and explain his actions?

THINK ABOUT
- why he calls himself "the black sheep"
- the nature of his uncle's will
- his conversation with Old Bryson
- his dealings with Miss Lauriere and Miss Hayden

3. How do the other **characters** in the story—including the departed uncle—judge Gillian? Use examples from the story to support your opinion.
4. ACTIVE READING CAUSE AND EFFECT Look back in your READER'S NOTEBOOK at the conversations that you noted. How does each conversation cause the next one, thus advancing the **plot?**
5. What do you think is the **theme** of this story? Cite evidence to support your opinion.

Extend Interpretations

6. **Critic's Corner** The writer William Saroyan said that behind the "laughing language" of O. Henry's stories could be found "a profound love for the great mass of people who are frequently called the little people." How do Saroyan's comments apply to this story?
7. **What If?** Imagine that Gillian's uncle had given him the entire sum of $50,000 at one time. Based on what you know about Gillian's character, how would this have changed what he chose to do with the money? Explain.
8. **Connect to Life** Gillian had to prove himself worthy of his uncle's inheritance. In what ways do you think young people today prove the worth of their character? Cite examples from your own experience or knowledge.

Literary Analysis

PLOT The chain of related events that take place in a story is called the **plot**, which serves as the writer's blueprint for what happens, when it happens, and to whom it happens. Usually, the events of the plot progress because of a **conflict.** Most plots include the following stages:

Exposition The exposition lays the groundwork for the plot and provides the reader with essential background information. Characters are introduced, the setting is described, and the plot begins to unfold.

Rising Action As the story progresses, **complications** usually arise, causing difficulties for the main characters and making the conflict more difficult to resolve.

Climax The climax is the turning point of the action, the moment when interest and intensity reach their peak. The climax usually involves an important event, decision, or discovery that affects the final outcome.

Falling Action The falling action consists of the events that occur after the climax. Often the conflict is resolved, and the intensity of action subsides.

Paired Activity Again review the graphic that you made in your READER'S NOTEBOOK. Label each conversation in the story, identifying the plot stage in which the conversation falls. For example, the conversation between Lawyer Tolman and Gillian belongs in the exposition.

When you have finished, compare your results with those of your classmates.

394 UNIT THREE PART 1: THE EXPERIENCE OF YOUTH

Key literary concepts such as Plot and Conflict "bookend" the selection. The concepts are introduced before reading and reinforced and practiced after reading.

Crafted

Interactive Strategies

Interwoven support increases comprehension, improves writing skills, and makes the literature experience more meaningful.

The InterActive Reader™ consumable worktext takes core selections from the main anthology and breaks them down into manageable reading chunks to increase comprehension.

Students receive **focused instruction** on specific reading skills and have the opportunity to **mark up** the text with their own notes.

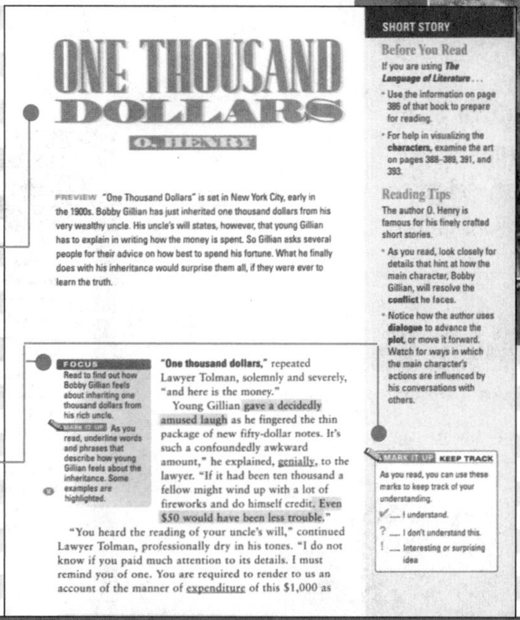

SHORT STORY

ONE THOUSAND DOLLARS

O. HENRY

PREVIEW "One Thousand Dollars" is set in New York City, early in the 1900s. Bobby Gillian has just inherited one thousand dollars from his very wealthy uncle. His uncle's will states, however, that young Gillian has to explain in writing how the money is spent. So Gillian asks several people for their advice on how best to spend his fortune. What he finally does with his inheritance would surprise them all, if they were ever to learn the truth.

Before You Read

If you are using *The Language of Literature* . . .

- Use the information on page 386 of that book to prepare for reading.
- For help in visualizing the **characters**, examine the art on pages 388–389, 391, and 393.

Reading Tips

The author O. Henry is famous for his finely crafted short stories.

- As you read, look closely for details that hint at how the main character, Bobby Gillian, will resolve the **conflict** he faces.
- Notice how the author uses **dialogue** to advance the **plot**, or move it forward. Watch for ways in which the main character's actions are influenced by his conversations with others.

FOCUS Read to find out how Bobby Gillian feels about inheriting one thousand dollars from his rich uncle.

MARK IT UP As you read, underline words and phrases that describe how young Gillian feels about the inheritance. Some examples are highlighted.

"One thousand dollars," repeated Lawyer Tolman, solemnly and severely, "and here is the money."

Young Gillian gave a decidedly amused laugh as he fingered the thin package of new fifty-dollar notes. It's such a confoundedly awkward amount," he explained, genially, to the lawyer. "If it had been ten thousand a fellow might wind up with a lot of fireworks and do himself credit. Even $50 would have been less trouble."

"You heard the reading of your uncle's will," continued Lawyer Tolman, professionally dry in his tones. "I do not know if you paid much attention to its details. I must remind you of one. You are required to render to us an account of the manner of expenditure of this $1,000 as

MARK IT UP KEEP TRACK

As you read, you can use these marks to keep track of your understanding.

✓ ___ I understand.

? ___ I don't understand this.

! ___ Interesting or surprising idea

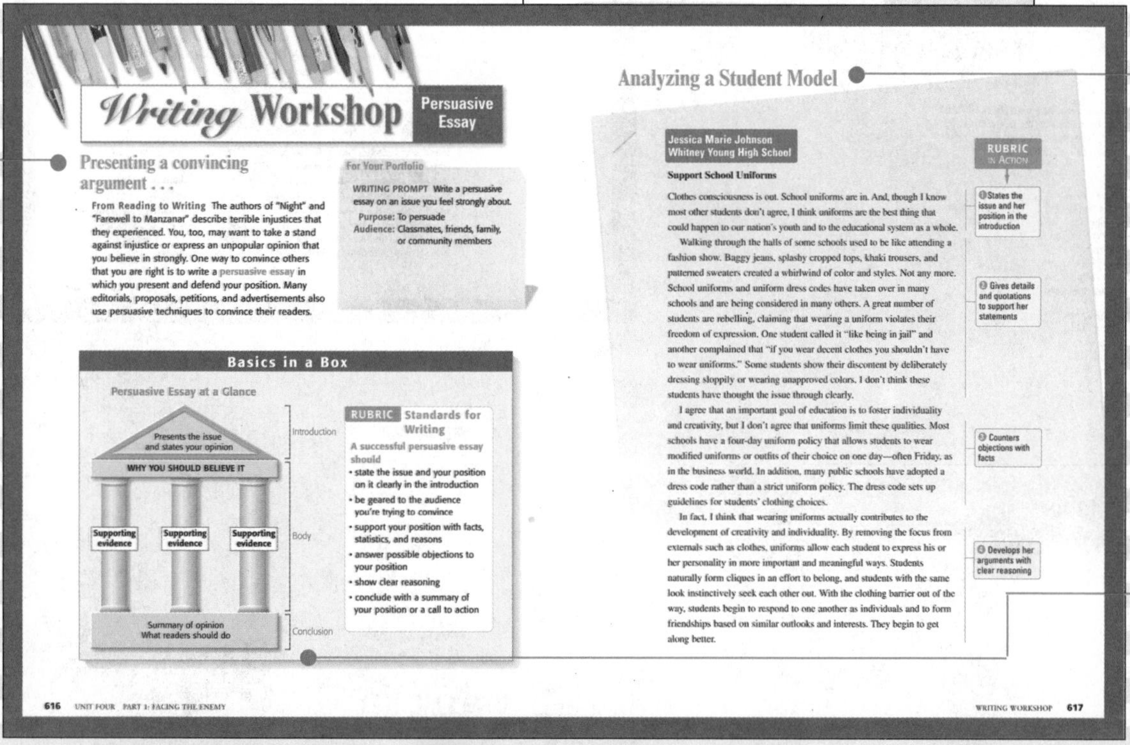

Writing Workshop

Persuasive Essay

Presenting a convincing argument . . .

From Reading to Writing The authors of "Night" and "Farewell to Manzanar" describe terrible injustices that they experienced. You, too, may want to take a stand against injustice or express an unpopular opinion that you believe in strongly. One way to convince others that you are right is to write a persuasive essay in which you present and defend your position. Many editorials, proposals, petitions, and advertisements also use persuasive techniques to convince their readers.

For Your Portfolio

WRITING PROMPT Write a persuasive essay on an issue you feel strongly about.

Purpose: To persuade

Audience: Classmates, friends, family, or community members

Basics in a Box

Persuasive Essay at a Glance

RUBRIC Standards for Writing

A successful persuasive essay should

- state the issue and your position on it clearly in the introduction
- be geared to the audience you're trying to convince
- support your position with facts, statistics, and reasons
- answer possible objections to your position
- show clear reasoning
- conclude with a summary of your position or a call to action

Analyzing a Student Model

Jessica Marie Johnson
Whitney Young High School

Support School Uniforms

Clothes consciousness is out. School uniforms are in. And, though I know most other students don't agree, I think uniforms are the best thing that could happen to our nation's youth and to the educational system as a whole.

Walking through the halls of some schools used to be like attending a fashion show. Baggy jeans, splashy cropped tops, khaki trousers, and patterned sweaters created a whirlwind of color and styles. Not any more. School uniforms and uniform dress codes have taken over in many schools and are being considered in many others. A great number of students are rebelling, claiming that wearing a uniform violates their freedom of expression. One student called it "like being in jail" and another complained that "if you wear decent clothes you shouldn't have to wear uniforms." Some students show their discontent by deliberately dressing sloppily or wearing unapproved colors. I don't think these students have thought the issue through clearly.

I agree that an important goal of education is to foster individuality and creativity, but I don't agree that uniforms limit these qualities. Most schools have a four-day uniform policy that allows students to wear modified uniforms or outfits of their choice on one day—often Friday, as in the business world. In addition, many public schools have adopted a dress code rather than a strict uniform policy. The dress code sets up guidelines for students' clothing choices.

In fact, I think that wearing uniforms actually contributes to the development of creativity and individuality. By removing the focus from externals such as clothes, uniforms allow each student to express his or her personality in more important and meaningful ways. Students naturally form cliques in an effort to belong, and students with the same look instinctively seek each other out. With the clothing barrier out of the way, students begin to respond to one another as individuals and to form friendships based on similar outlooks and interests. They begin to get along better.

RUBRIC IN ACTION

1 States the issue and her position in the introduction

2 Gives details and quotations to support her statements

3 Counters objections with facts

4 Develops her arguments with clear reasoning

616 UNIT FOUR PART 1: FACING THE ENEMY

WRITING WORKSHOP 617

Literary, professional, and student models show skills in context and provide a wide range of practice opportunities in literary analysis.

Graphic organizers visually represent specific writing lessons.

Writing Workshops, prompted by the literature, build skills and establish rubrics for different types of writing.

Interactive

Solid Literary Analysis

Students compare and contrast ideas as they learn to interpret and analyze literature within a variety of themes and genres.

Comparing Literature shows students how to compare and contrast two literature selections from different genres or cultures.

Assessment practice prepares students for standardized tests with a compare-and-contrast focus.

Comparing Literature

Love and Marriage Across Cultures

Marriage Is a Private Affair	Love Must Not Be Forgotten
Short Story by CHINUA ACHEBE	*Short Story by* ZHANG JIE

What's the Connection?

Love at the Crossroads Every society in some way seeks to set standards for love and marriage. Often, tension exists between what a society or culture expects and what the individual wants. In choosing a spouse, an individual may face pressures from family, friends, community members, or public opinion.

In the following two selections, you will read about characters who are torn between their personal desires and the traditions and expectations of society. While both stories focus on individuals, they also reflect the conflicts and tensions of the societies portrayed.

A Chinese bride and groom in traditional wedding attire.

Points of Comparison

Analyzing Similar Problems in Different Cultures In this unit, you have read about conflicts that arise when two cultures meet, or when one culture changes. In the pages that follow, you will analyze and compare the problems of characters who challenge cultural traditions and social expectations in an attempt to find love and fulfillment.

Critical Thinking: Analyze and Compare

The first step in analysis is to define the parts of the whole. To analyze the problems of characters who seek love in a changing world, it will help you to develop a kind of graphic called an **analysis frame.** This frame will help you break each problem into parts. To begin, think about the ways in which the standards of our own society might present obstacles for a person in search of an ideal mate. Continue to identify other potential obstacles to love and marriage. The analysis frame shown has been started for you.

Problem: Finding an Ideal Mate
↓
Obstacle 1: Expectations of family and friends
↓
(blank)

READER'S NOTEBOOK As you read the following stories, note the various obstacles faced by the main characters, which contribute to their problems. At each Points of Comparison, you will be asked to create a separate analysis frame for the story you have read.

LOVE AND MARRIAGE ACROSS CULTURES 187

Students are taught how to use **critical thinking skills** to make connections, analyze, and compare selections.

Comparing Literature: Assessment Practice

In writing assessments, you will often be asked to analyze and compare two literary works with similar themes like "Marriage Is a Private Affair" and "Love Must Not Be Forgotten." You are now going to practice writing an essay with this kind of focus.

PART 1 Reading the Prompt

You will often be asked to write in response to a prompt like the one below. In such situations, you first need to read the prompt carefully. Then you should read it again, searching for key words that help you identify the purpose of the essay and decide how to approach it.

Writing Prompt
"Marriage Is a Private Affair" and "Love Must Not Be Forgotten" both explore the problems of individuals seeking love and fulfillment in a changing culture. In an essay, analyze the problem faced by a main character in each story. Compare the way in which each main character challenges the traditions and expectations of his or her society. To what degree does each succeed? Include evidence from the selection to support your analysis.

STRATEGIES IN ACTION

1. I need to write an essay that will **analyze**—or break down—the problems faced by the main characters.
2. I have to **compare** how the main characters challenge their society.
3. I need to include **examples** or **quotations** from the stories.

PART 2 Planning an Analysis Essay

- Devise a graphic like the one shown to help organize your analysis.
- For each main character, break down the problem that he or she faces by listing the various obstacles to love and marriage. (Refer to the charts you developed on pages 187, 194, and 209.)
- Look for similarities and differences among the problems, the obstacles, and the characters' responses to the obstacles.

Marriage Is a Private Affair	Love Must Not Be Forgotten
Problem:	Problem:
Obstacles:	Obstacles:
Character's Response:	Character's Response:

PART 3 Drafting Your Essay

Introduction Identify the main problem of each character. Describe how each character responds to the problem.

Organization For each character, you will need to break the problem down, discussing one obstacle at a time. You probably will find it helpful to discuss one story in its entirety, then the other.

Make sure that you draw comparisons between the characters and their situations. Include examples.

Conclusion
End your essay with a clear statement that compares and contrasts the problems faced by the two characters and their responses.

LOVE AND MARRIAGE ACROSS CULTURES 211

I want a challenge...

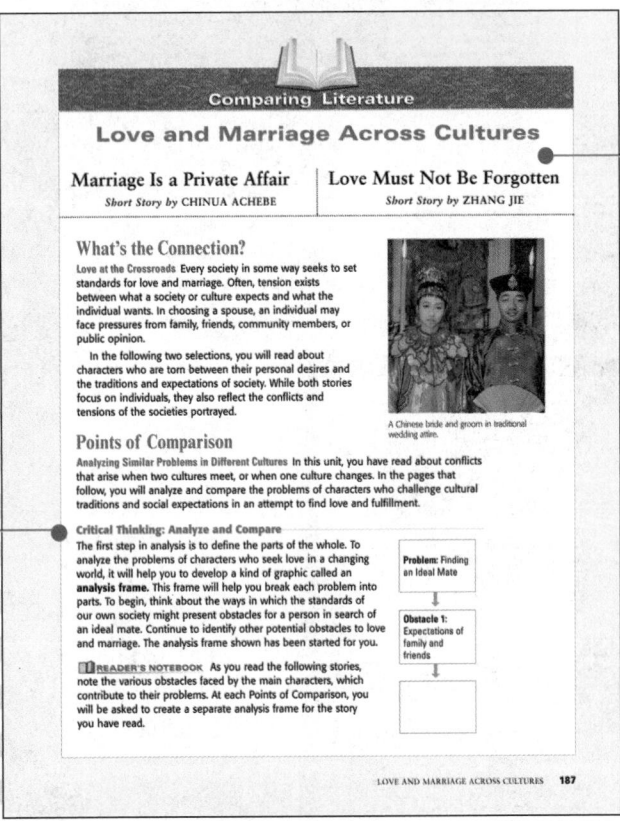

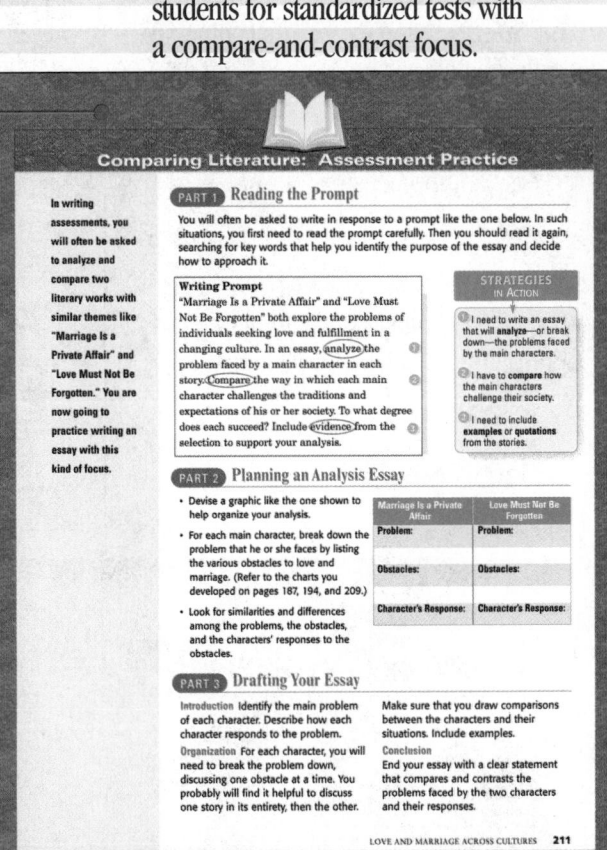

Literary

Flexible, Ongoing Assessment

A variety of assessment options meets the needs of a broad range of students as they acquire essential skills and prepare for standardized tests.

Assessment practice and strategies are supported in each unit of the *Pupil's Edition.*

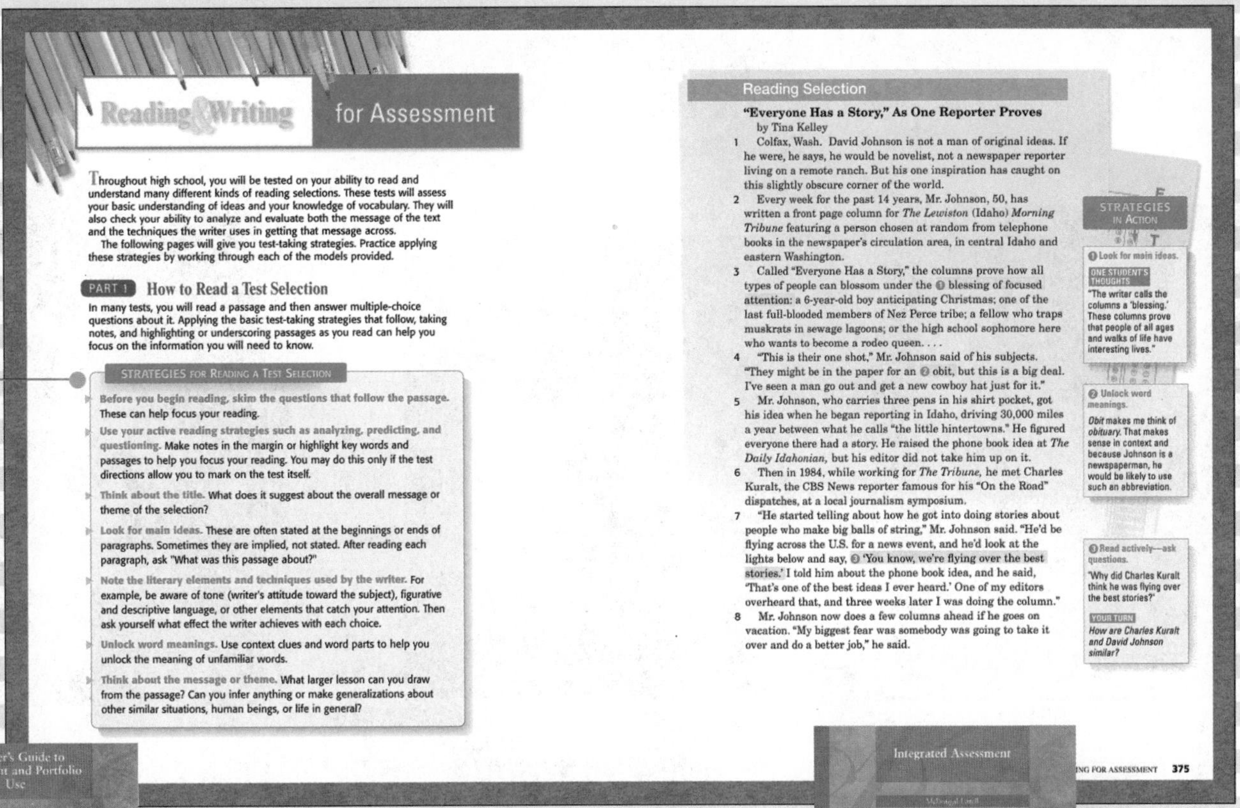

Reading & Writing for Assessment

Throughout high school, you will be tested on your ability to read and understand many different kinds of reading selections. These tests will assess your basic understanding of ideas and your knowledge of vocabulary. They will also check your ability to analyze and evaluate both the message of the text and the techniques the writer uses in getting that message across.

The following pages will give you test-taking strategies. Practice applying these strategies by working through each of the models provided.

PART 1 How to Read a Test Selection

In many tests, you will read a passage and then answer multiple-choice questions about it. Applying the basic test-taking strategies that follow, taking notes, and highlighting or underscoring passages as you read can help you focus on the information you will need to know.

STRATEGIES FOR READING A TEST SELECTION

- **Before you begin reading, skim the questions that follow the passage.** These can help focus your reading.
- **Use your active reading strategies such as analyzing, predicting, and questioning.** Make notes in the margin or highlight key words and passages to help you focus your reading. You may do this only if the test directions allow you to mark on the test itself.
- **Think about the title.** What does it suggest about the overall message or theme of the selection?
- **Look for main ideas.** These are often stated at the beginnings or ends of paragraphs. Sometimes they are implied, not stated. After reading each paragraph, ask "What was this passage about?"
- **Note the literary elements and techniques used by the writer.** For example, be aware of tone (writer's attitude toward the subject), figurative and descriptive language, or other elements that catch your attention. Then ask yourself what effect the writer achieves with each choice.
- **Unlock word meanings.** Use context clues and word parts to help you unlock the meaning of unfamiliar words.
- **Think about the message or theme.** What larger lesson can you draw from the passage? Can you infer anything or make generalizations about other similar situations, human beings, or life in general?

Reading Selection

"Everyone Has a Story," As One Reporter Proves
by Tina Kelley

1 Colfax, Wash. David Johnson is not a man of original ideas. If he were, he says, he would be novelist, not a newspaper reporter living on a remote ranch. But his one inspiration has caught on this slightly obscure corner of the world.

2 Every week for the past 14 years, Mr. Johnson, 50, has written a front page column for *The Lewiston* (Idaho) *Morning Tribune* featuring a person chosen at random from telephone books in the newspaper's circulation area, in central Idaho and eastern Washington.

3 Called "Everyone Has a Story," the columns prove how all types of people can blossom under the ❶ blessing of focused attention: a 6-year-old boy anticipating Christmas; one of the last full-blooded members of Nez Perce tribe; a fellow who traps muskrats in sewage lagoons; or the high school sophomore here who wants to become a rodeo queen. . . .

4 "This is their one shot," Mr. Johnson said of his subjects. "They might be in the paper for an ❷ obit, but this is a big deal. I've seen a man go out and get a new cowboy hat just for it."

5 Mr. Johnson, who carries three pens in his shirt pocket, got his idea when he began reporting in Idaho, driving 30,000 miles a year between what he calls "the little hintertowns." He figured everyone there had a story. He raised the phone book idea at *The Daily Idahonian,* but his editor did not take him up on it.

6 Then in 1984, while working for *The Tribune,* he met Charles Kuralt, the CBS News reporter famous for his "On the Road" dispatches, at a local journalism symposium.

7 "He started telling about how he got into doing stories about people who make big balls of string," Mr. Johnson said. "He'd be flying across the U.S. for a news event, and he'd look at the lights below and say, ❸ 'You know, we're flying over the best stories.' I told him about the phone book idea, and he said, 'That's one of the best ideas I ever heard.' One of my editors overheard that, and three weeks later I was doing the column."

8 Mr. Johnson now does a few columns ahead if he goes on vacation. "My biggest fear was somebody was going to take it over and do a better job," he said.

STRATEGIES IN ACTION

❶ Look for main ideas.

ONE STUDENT'S THOUGHTS

"The writer calls the columns a 'blessing.' These columns prove that people of all ages and walks of life have interesting lives."

❷ Unlock word meanings.

Obit makes me think of *obituary.* That makes sense in context and because Johnson is a newspaperman, he would be likely to use such an abbreviation.

❸ Read actively—ask questions.

"Why did Charles Kuralt think he was flying over the best stories?"

YOUR TURN

How are Charles Kuralt and David Johnson similar?

...ING FOR ASSESSMENT 375

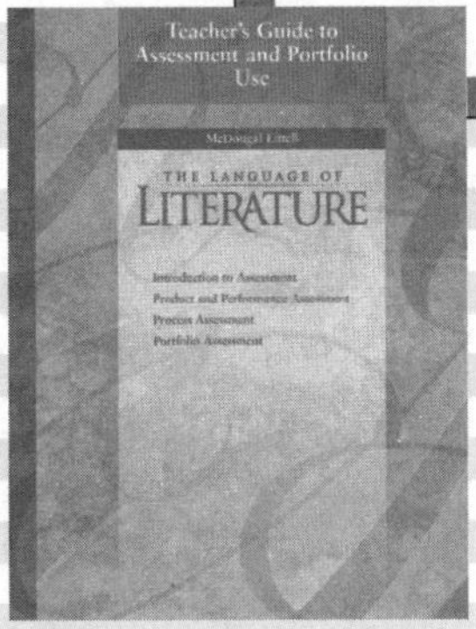

The Teacher's Guide to Assessment and Portfolio Use includes portfolio assessment, writing rubrics, and other forms of open-ended assessment.

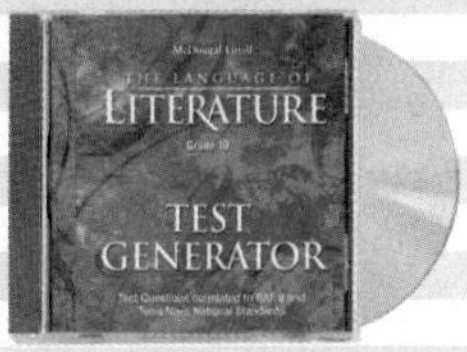

The **Test Generator CD-ROM** contains a variety of pre-made tests and a test bank of items that allows teachers to create customized tests.

The **Formal Assessment** and **Integrated Assessment** booklets provide selection tests, part tests, a mid-year test, and end-of-year tests, writing rubrics, and practice questions for standardized tests.

Assessment

THE LANGUAGE OF LITERATURE

Time-Saving Teaching Support

The Language of Literature Comprehensive Teacher's Edition

The annotated *Teacher's Edition* serves as a complete reference tool for the classroom. Each page contains a wealth of information that includes a lesson overview, teaching strategies, background information, and references to ancillary materials.

The InterActive Reader™

The Interactive Reader™ is a consumable worktext that reinforces active reading strategies, encourages writing during reading, and increases comprehension by breaking down core selections from *The Language of Literature* anthology into manageable reading chunks. The *Teacher's Guide* contains complete lesson plans for each selection, activities, mini-lessons, and graphic organizers.

The Reading Toolkit

The Reading Toolkit is a valuable collection of teacher tools, mini-lessons, copymasters, and transparencies that helps teachers diagnose students' abilities and provides them with guidelines for direct instruction in reading comprehension skills and strategies.

Literature Connections

Each *Literature Connections* volume contains a complete novel or play with five to eight theme-related readings that represent a variety of genres. Each title is supported by a *Teacher's SourceBook* that includes background material, author biographies, discussion starters, and suggested essay questions.

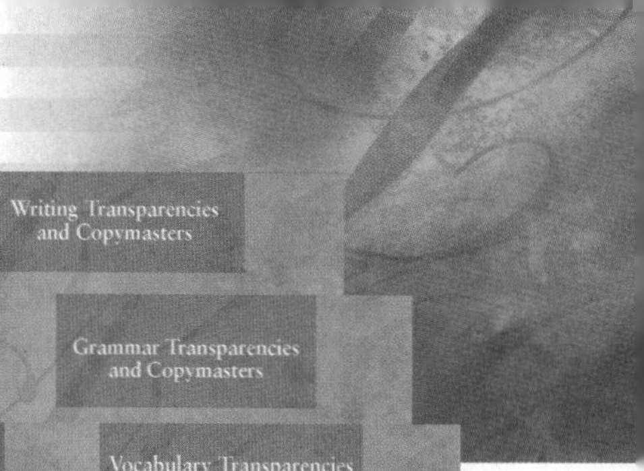

Unit Resource Books

The *Unit Resource Books,* one per unit, provide additional skills work and extensions of activities and exercises. Contents include a family and community involvement section; a selection summary; SkillBuilders in active reading, literary analysis, vocabulary, grammar, and spelling; a selection quiz; a Writing Workshop; a reflect and assess segment; and answer keys.

Resource Management Guide

This organizational guide helps teachers match ancillary materials to each selection.

Lesson Planning Guide

This booklet helps teachers organize resources, keep track of daily objectives and activities, and track standards met.

Formal Assessment

This booklet offers selection tests, part tests, a mid-year test, an end-of-year test, writing rubrics, and standardized test practice questions.

Integrated Assessment

Features of this booklet include Unit Integrated Assessments, an End-of-Year Integrated Assessment, and a record of student thinking and planning.

Teacher's Guide to Assessment and Portfolio Use

This guide includes portfolio assessment, writing rubrics, and other forms of open-ended assessment.

English Learners/Students Acquiring English Resources

The Language of Literature offers solid support for the English Learner.

EL/SAE Spanish Study Guide

EL/SAE Teacher's SourceBook for Language Development

Skills Transparencies and Copymasters

A variety of transparencies and copymasters help teachers enhance their lessons in the following areas:

Writing
Grammar
Vocabulary
Communications
(includes Fine Art transparencies)
Literary Analysis
Reading and Critical Thinking

THE LANGUAGE OF LITERATURE

Integrated Technology

Literature in Performance

This video series helps students compare written selections to film adaptations of literature. Featured performers include well-known actors such as John Heard in "The Cask of Amontillado," LeVar Burton in "Almos' a Man," Anjelica Huston in "A Rose for Emily," and Orson Welles in "Macbeth." The *Video Resource Book* provides activities that motivate students to think critically about what they have viewed.

Audio Library

Professional recordings of selections from the anthology help students develop strategies for critical listening. These audio CDs enrich the literary experience for all students and provide extra support to less-proficient readers, students acquiring English, and auditory learners.

Electronic Teacher Tools

This easy-to-use CD-ROM contains all print support materials for *The Language of Literature* in one place, allowing teachers to browse, preview, and print ancillary pages when needed.

Test Generator

This CD-ROM contains a variety of pre-made tests and a test bank of items that allows teachers to create customized tests. The program provides tools that walk the user through the searching and editing steps and help correlate the tests to national and state standards.

NetActivities

This CD-ROM contains extension activities for each Author Study in the text and offers additional information about featured authors through links to related Web sites.

I want to share ideas...

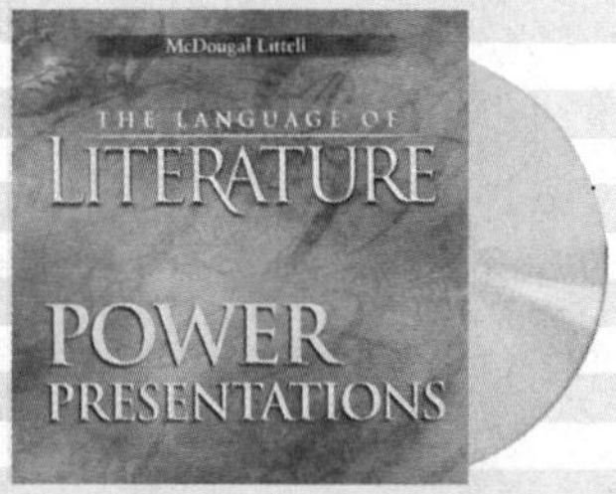

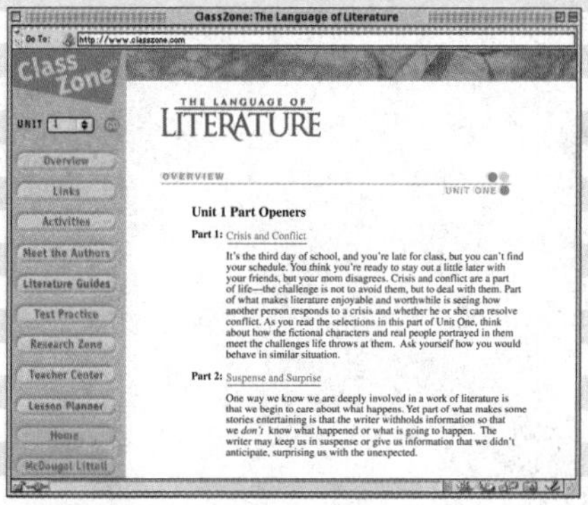

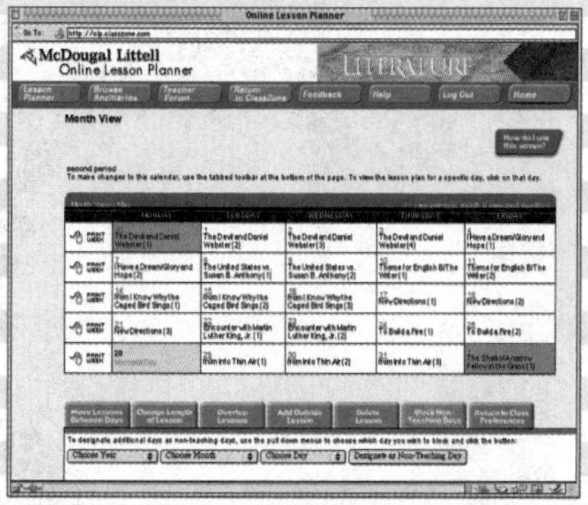

Power Presentations

This CD-ROM contains PowerPoint® presentations that are tied to the Writing Workshops found in the *Pupil's Edition*.

Electronic Library

This CD-ROM collection lets teachers customize instruction by choosing the works of a favorite author from over 200 additional pieces of classic literature.

classzone.com

ClassZone is an online guide to *The Language of Literature* that provides access to a variety of Internet resources. This companion Web site offers links correlated to the textbook, an Internet research tutorial, vocabulary flipcards and other activities, author background, spelling practice, a *Teacher Center* and access to the *Online Lesson Planner.*

Online Lesson Planner

The *Online Lesson Planner* allows teachers to conveniently create, edit, and customize lesson plans on the Internet. Lessons can be modified to incorporate activities from the *Teacher's Edition* or customized to meet specific classroom needs. A correlation feature allows the plans to be correlated to specific state standards or guidelines.

McDougal Littell

THE LANGUAGE OF LITERATURE

EMILY DICKINSON
AMY TAN
WALT WHITMAN
EDNA ST. VINCENT MILLAY
MAYA ANGELO
ROBERT FROST
KURT VONNEGUT, JR.
O. HENRY
LEO TOLSTOY
GABRIELA MISTRAL
SIR THOMAS MALORY
ALICE WALKER
CORETTA SCOTT KING
AGATHA CHRISTIE
LANGSTON HUGHES
STEPHEN CRANE
SANDRA CISNEROS
ISABEL ALLENDE
CHINUA ACHEBE
MARK TWAIN
GUY DE MAUPASSANT
CARL SANDBURG
NIKKI GIOVANNI
TIM O'BRIEN
RAY BRADBURY
EDGAR ALLAN POE
ANTON CHEKHO
PABLO NERUDA
WILLIAM SHAKESPEAR
JOHN STEINBECK
DORIS LESSING

McDougal Littell

THE LANGUAGE OF LITERATURE

Arthur N. Applebee

Andrea B. Bermúdez

Sheridan Blau

Rebekah Caplan

Peter Elbow

Susan Hynds

Judith A. Langer

James Marshall

McDougal Littell

A HOUGHTON MIFFLIN COMPANY

Evanston, Illinois • Boston • Dallas

Acknowledgments

Unit One

Delacorte Press/Seymour Lawrence: "Harrison Bergeron," from *Welcome to the Monkey House* by Kurt Vonnegut, Jr. Copyright © 1961 by Kurt Vonnegut, Jr. Used by permission of Delacorte Press/Seymour Lawrence, a division of Bantam Doubleday Dell Publishing Group, Inc.

Brandt & Brandt Literary Agents: "Searching for Summer," from *The Green Flash* by Joan Aiken. Copyright © 1969 by Joan Aiken. Reprinted by permission of Brandt & Brandt Literary Agents, Inc.

"By the Waters of Babylon" by Stephen Vincent Benét, from *Selected Works of Stephen Vincent Benét,* published by Holt, Rinehart & Winston, Inc. Copyright © 1937 by Stephen Vincent Benét. Copyright renewed © 1955 by Rosemary Carr Benét. Reprinted by permission of Brandt & Brandt Literary Agents, Inc.

Beacon Press: "The Sun," from *New and Selected Poems* by Mary Oliver. Copyright © 1992 by Mary Oliver. Reprinted by permission of Beacon Press, Boston.

Simon & Schuster: "There Will Come Soft Rains" by Sara Teasdale, from *Collected Poems of Sara Teasdale.* Copyright © 1937 by Macmillan Publishing Company. Reprinted with the permission of Simon & Schuster.

Viking Penguin and Penguin Books Canada: "The Thrill of the Grass," from *The Thrill of the Grass* by W. P. Kinsella. Copyright © 1984 by W. P. Kinsella. Used by permission of Viking Penguin, a division of Penguin Putnam Inc., and Penguin Books Canada Limited.

Continued on page 1274

ISBN 0-618-17040-5

Printed in the United States of America.

1 2 3 4 5 6 7 8 9 – DWO – 06 05 04 03 02 01

iv

Senior Consultants

The senior consultants guided the conceptual development for *The Language of Literature* series. They participated actively in shaping prototype materials for major components, and they reviewed completed prototypes and/or completed units to ensure consistency with current research and the philosophy of the series.

Arthur N. Applebee Professor of Education, State University of New York at Albany; Director, Center for the Learning and Teaching of Literature; Senior Fellow, Center for Writing and Literacy

Andrea B. Bermúdez Professor of Studies in Language and Culture; Director, Research Center for Language and Culture; Chair, Foundations and Professional Studies, University of Houston-Clear Lake

Sheridan Blau Senior Lecturer in English and Education and former Director of Composition, University of California at Santa Barbara; Director, South Coast Writing Project; Director, Literature Institute for Teachers; Former President, National Council of Teachers of English

Rebekah Caplan Senior Associate for Language Arts for middle school and high school literacy, National Center on Education and the Economy, Washington, D.C.; served on the California State English Assessment Development Team for Language Arts; former co-director of the Bay Area Writing Project, University of California at Berkeley

Peter Elbow Emeritus Professor of English, University of Massachusetts at Amherst; Fellow, Bard Center for Writing and Thinking

Susan Hynds Professor and Director of English Education, Syracuse University, Syracuse, New York

Judith A. Langer Professor of Education, State University of New York at Albany; Co-director, Center for the Learning and Teaching of Literature; Senior Fellow, Center for Writing and Literacy

James Marshall Professor of English and English Education; Chair, Division of Curriculum and Instruction, University of Iowa, Iowa City

Contributing Consultants

Linda Diamond Executive Vice President, Consortium on Reading Excellence (CORE); co-author of *Building a Powerful Reading Program*

Lucila A. Garza ESL Consultant, Austin, Texas

Jeffrey N. Golub Assistant Professor of English Education, University of South Florida, Tampa

William L. McBride, Ph.D. Reading and Curriculum Specialist; former middle and high school English instructor

Sharon Sicinski-Skeans, Ph.D. Assistant Professor of Reading, University of Houston-Clear Lake; primary consultant on *The InterActive Reader*

v

Multicultural Advisory Board

The multicultural advisors reviewed literature selections for appropriate content and made suggestions for teaching lessons in a multicultural classroom.

Julie A. Anderson, English Department Chairperson, Dayton High School, Dayton, Oregon

Vikki Pepper Ascuena, Meridian High School, Meridian, Idaho

Dr. Joyce M. Bell, Chairperson, English Department, Townview Magnet Center, Dallas, Texas

Linda F. Bellmore, Livermore High School, Livermore, California

Dr. Eugenia W. Collier, Author; lecturer; Chairperson, Department of English and Language Arts; Teacher of Creative Writing and American Literature, Morgan State University, Maryland

Dr. Bill Compagnone, English Department Chairperson, Lawrence High School, Lawrence, Massachusetts

Kathleen S. Fowler, President, Palm Beach County Council of Teachers of English, Boca Raton Middle School, Boca Raton, Florida

Jan Graham, Cobb Middle School, Tallahassee, Florida

Barbara J. Kuhns, Camino Real Middle School, Las Cruces, New Mexico

Patricia J. Richards, Prior Lake, Minnesota

Janna Rigby, Clovis High School, Clovis, California

Continued on page 1285

Teacher Review Panels

The following educators provided ongoing review during the development of the tables of contents, lesson design, and key components of the program.

CALIFORNIA

Steve Bass, 8th Grade Team Leader, Meadowbrook Middle School, Ponway Unified School District

Cynthia Brickey, 8th Grade Academic Block Teacher, Kastner Intermediate School, Clovis Unified School District

Continued on page 1286

Manuscript Reviewers

The following educators reviewed prototype lessons and tables of contents during the development of *The Language of Literature* program.

David Adcox, Trinity High School, Euless, Texas

Carol Alves, English Department Chairperson, Apopka High School, Apopka, Florida

Jacqueline Anderson, James A. Foshay Learning Center, Los Angeles, California

Continued on page 1287

vi

Student Board

The student board members read and evaluated selections to assess their appeal for 10th-grade students.

Marcus Allen, Southeast High School, North Carolina

Jayme Charak, Niles North High School, Illinois

Alisia Darby, McCallum High School, Texas

RonAmber Deloney, Roosevelt High School, Texas

Amy Doblestein, Shades Valley Resource Learning Center, Alabama

Quoleshna Z. Elbert, Lincoln College Preparatory Academy, Missouri

Katrina Gorski, Loudon County High School, Virginia

Rafael Gutierrez, Garner High School, North Carolina

Geoffrey L. Harvey, Phineas Banning High School, California

Karina Hernandez, Waltrip High School, Texas

Ellen Hooper, Casa Roble High School, California

Sunita Juneja, Strongsville High School, Ohio

Scott McGregor, Broadneck High School, Maryland

Katherine McGuire, Lyons Township High School, Illinois

Tim Mosher, Clarkston North High School, New York

Emily Myers, Union High School, Grand Rapids, Michigan

Eulizer Nazario, Mission Bay High School, California

Jacob Parks, Newton High School, Kansas

Ronnie G. Pigao, Phineas Banning High School, California

Wendy Pomales, Boston High School, Massachusetts

Josh Raub, Lakeview High School, Minnesota

Jessica Reynolds, Eastern Hills High School, Texas

Kevin Schatzman, Miami Killian Sr. High School, Florida

Stephanie Stone, John Marshall High School, Texas

Sabrina Van Damme, Choctawhatchee High School, Florida

Cynthia Villicana, Phineas Banning High School, California

Adriana M. Zuniga, San Marcos High School, Texas

vii

The Language of Literature

Overview

UNIT ONE The Challenge of Change

Part 1 The Price of Progress

GENRE FOCUS
Fiction
Nonfiction

SKILL FOCUS
Writing Workshop: Opinion Statement
Grammar: Parts of Speech
Vocabulary: Understanding Context Clues

Part 2 Cultural Crossroads

LITERARY FOCUS
Theme

SKILL FOCUS
Writing Workshop: Focused Description
Grammar: Parts of Speech
Vocabulary: Analyzing Word Parts

UNIT TWO In the Name of Love

Part 1 Ties that Bind

GENRE FOCUS
Poetry

SKILL FOCUS
Writing Workshop: Poetry
Grammar: The Sentence and Its Parts
Vocabulary: Analogies

Part 2 Mysteries of the Heart

GENRE FOCUS
Drama

SKILL FOCUS
Writing Workshop: Problem-Solution Essay
Grammar: The Sentence and Its Parts
Vocabulary: Using Word Origins to Understand Meanings

UNIT THREE The Search for Identity

Part 1 The Experience of Youth

LITERARY FOCUS
Plot

SKILL FOCUS
Writing Workshop: Career Search Report
Grammar: Verbs and Verbals
Vocabulary: Understanding Idioms and Figurative Language

Part 2 The Power of Heritage

LITERARY FOCUS
Author's Perspective

SKILL FOCUS
Communication Workshop: Oral History
Grammar: Verbs and Verbals
Vocabulary: Denotation and Connotation

UNIT FOUR Lessons of History

Part 1 Facing the Enemy

LITERARY FOCUS
Irony

SKILL FOCUS
Writing Workshop: Persuasive Essay
Grammar: Phrases
Vocabulary: Reference Aids—Foreign Terms

Part 2 Tests of Conviction

LITERARY FOCUS
Point of View

SKILL FOCUS
Grammar: Phrases
Vocabulary: Words with Mulitple Meanings

Part 3 The Tragedy of Julius Caesar

GENRE FOCUS
Shakespearean Drama

SKILL FOCUS
Writing Workshop: Cause-and-Effect Essay
Grammar: Phrases

UNIT FIVE Discovering the Truth

Part 1 Simple Truths

LITERARY FOCUS
Symbolism and Figurative Language

SKILL FOCUS
Writing Workshop: Interpretive Essay
Grammar: Clauses
Vocabulary: Analyzing Word Parts—Affixes

Part 2 Appearance vs. Reality

LITERARY FOCUS
Realism

SKILL FOCUS
Writing Workshop: Autobiographical Incident
Grammar: Clauses
Vocabulary: Using Context Clues for Specialized Vocabulary

UNIT SIX The Making of Heroes

Part 1 Unsung Heroes

LITERARY FOCUS
Style

SKILL FOCUS
Communication Workshop: Multimedia Presentation
Grammar: Special Sentence Structures
Vocabulary: Context Clues—Synonyms, Definitions, and Antonyms

Part 2 The Heroic Tradition

GENRE FOCUS
Myths and Legends

SKILL FOCUS
Writing Workshop: Research Report
Grammar: Special Sentence Structures
Vocabulary: Developing a Stronger Vocabulary

Student Resource Bank

Reading Handbook
Writing Handbook
Communication Handbook
Grammar Handbook
Glossary of Literary Terms
Glossary of Words to Know in English and Spanish

Literature Connections

Each of the books in the *Literature Connections* series combines a novel or play with related readings—poems, stories, plays, personal essays, articles—that add new perspectives on the theme or subject matter of the longer work.

Listed below are some of the most popular choices to accompany the Grade 10 anthology:

Great Expectations by Charles Dickens

The Chosen by Chaim Potok

Fahrenheit 451 by Ray Bradbury

Farewell to Manzanar by Jeanne Wakatsuki Houston and James D. Houston

Kaffir Boy by Mark Mathabane

A Midsummer Night's Dream by William Shakespeare

A Place Where the Sea Remembers by Sandra Benítez

A Tale of Two Cities by Charles Dickens

A Separate Peace by John Knowles

The Underdogs by Mariano Azuela

West with the Night by Beryl Markham

When Rain Clouds Gather by Bessie Head

THE LANGUAGE OF
LITERATURE

Reading Strategies

ix

Ray Bradbury Author Study

NETACTIVITIES: Author Exploration

GENRE FOCUS: NONFICTION

READING AND WRITING SKILLS

xi

xii

UNIT TWO

In the Name of Love

xiii

xiv

UNIT THREE

The Search for Identity

xv

Part 2 The Power of Heritage 451

xvi

UNIT FOUR

Lessons of History 540

xvii

xviii

xix

UNIT FIVE

Discovering the Truth

xx

xxi

Detail of *The Arming & Departure of the Knights of the Round Table on the Quest for the Holy Grail* (1895–1896), Sir Edward Coley Burne-Jones. From the *Holy Grail Tapestry Series*. Birmingham City Council Museums and Art Gallery, England.

UNIT SIX

xxii

xxiii

Student *Resource Bank*

xxiv

Selections by Genre

Fiction

Romance

Nonfiction

xxv

Poetry

xxvi

Drama

Electronic Library

The *Electronic Library* is a CD-ROM that contains additional fiction, nonfiction, poetry, and drama for each unit in *The Language of Literature.* Here is a sampling from the titles included in Grade 10.

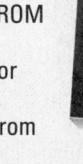

The Stolen Bacillus
H. G. Wells

Half a Day
Naguib Mahfouz

The Spring Returns
Petrarch

Leaving Crete
Sappho

The Story of Pyramus and Thisbe
Ovid

Intimate
Gabriela Mistral

Verotchka
Anton Chekhov

A Doll's House
Henrik Ibsen

To Imagination
Emily Brontë

The Stamp Collection
Karel Čapek

To Posterity
Bertolt Brecht

The Silver Mine
Selma Lagerlöf

A Hunger Artist
Franz Kafka

Tartuffe
Molière

The Birthmark
Nathaniel Hawthorne

The Myth of Sisyphus
Albert Camus

from **The Apology**
Plato

The Lady of Moge
Ursula K. Le Guin

Eldorado
Edgar Allan Poe

Prometheus
Johann Wolfgang von Goethe

xxvii

Special Features in This Book

Author Study

Learning the Language of Literature

The Active Reader: Skills and Strategies

Comparing Literature

Reading for Information

xxviii

Writing Workshops

Communication Workshops

Building Vocabulary

Assessment Pages

1

Realms of the Imagination

Look at the words on the poster at the right. "Imagine a world where dreams come true . . . and magic is real." Which of us hasn't imagined a world like that, or a world where space travel is an everyday occurrence, or where scientists can re-create the age of the dinosaurs?

We all love to visit the world of the imagination. This is the reason we watch movies and television shows. It is also the reason we read literature. With writers such as Ray Bradbury and Kurt Vonnegut, Jr., we can travel to the future, while Shakespeare and Malory can transport us to the past. Other writers, such as Alice Walker, Tim O'Brien, and Sandra Cisneros, introduce us to worlds closer to home. As you will see, good literature feeds the imagination.

A scene from *Star Trek: Voyager*, a television show.

"I think that science fiction and fantasy offer the liveliest, freshest approaches to many of our problems today, and I always hope to write in this vivid and vigorous form. . . ."

—Ray Bradbury
Contemporary writer

MERLIN
IMAGINE A WORLD
WHERE DREAMS
COME TRUE...
AND MAGIC IS REAL.

A poster for the television movie *Merlin.*

Young Arthur pulls Excalibur from the stone.

"When I was nine, I took siege with King Arthur's fellowship of knights. . . . The magic happened. . . . Perhaps a passionate love for the English language opened to me from this one book [Malory's *Morte d'Arthur*]"

—John Steinbeck
Nobel Prize–winning writer

- **Why do some stories capture the imagination of generations of readers?**
- **What kinds of stories most appeal to you?**
- **How can you find excitement and relevance in literature you read?**

The answers lie on the next few pages.

Get Involved with the Literature

Think about an activity that you do well, whether it's playing the piano or throwing a baseball. How did you learn to master and appreciate that activity? While you no doubt learned from others, you probably learned the most by doing the activity yourself. Just about any activity is richer and more interesting when you are actively involved. The same is true with literature. Good readers don't simply absorb the words; they become actively engaged with what they read.

Your Reader's Notebook

Almost any kind of notebook can be used to help you interact with literature. Use your Reader's Notebook to keep track of what's going on inside your mind as you read. Here are three ways to interact.

READING MODEL

Alongside "The Interlopers" are the spoken comments made by two tenth-grade students, Robert Wingader and Thanh-Thuy Nguyen (tăn to͞o ē wĭn), while they were reading the story. Their comments provide a glimpse into the minds of readers actively engaged in the process of reading. You'll notice that in the cours of reading, Robert and Thuy (to͞o ē) quite naturally used the Strategies for Reading that were introduced on page 5. You'll also note that these readers responded differently to the story—no two readers think the same way.

To benefit most from this model of active reading, read the story first, jotting down your own responses in your reading log. Then read Robert's and Thuy's comments and compare their processes of reading with your own.

THE INTERLOPERS

Sak

Robert: I've heard of the Carpathians, but I don't know where they are.
CONNECTING / QUESTIONING

Thuy: At first I thought he was hunting, but now I think it's like a game to him. He's hunting another man.
CLARIFYING

Robert: Why is the land so jealously guarded?
QUESTIONING

In a forest of mixed growth somewhere on the eastern spurs of the Carpathians, a man stood one winter night watching and listening, as though he waited for some beast of the woods to come within the range of his vision, and, later, of his rifle. But the game for whose presence he kept so keen an outlook was none that figured the sportman's calendar as lawful and proper for the chase; Ulrich von Gradwitz patrolled the dark forest in quest of a human enemy

The forest lands of Gradwitz were of wide extent and well stocked with game; the narrow strip of precipitous woodland that lay on its outskirt was not remarkable for the game it harbored or the shooting it afforded, but it was the most jealously guarded of a its owner's territorial possessions. A famous lawsuit, in the days of his grandfather, had wrested it from the illegal possession of a neighboring family of petty landowners; the dispossessed party had never acquiesced in the judgment of the Courts, and a long series of poaching affrays and similar scandals had embittered the relationship between the families for three generations. The neighbor feud had

8 READING MODEL

❶ Record Your Thoughts

In your READER'S NOTEBOOK, jot down ideas, responses, connections, and questions before, while, and after you read a selection. (See "Strategies for Reading," page 7.) Summarize important passages, and include sketches and charts, too, if they will help. If you wish, compare your ideas with those of a classmate.

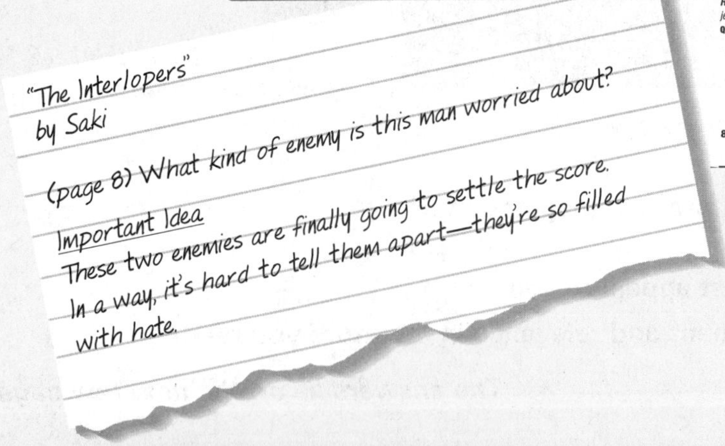
"The Interlopers"
by Saki
(page 8) What kind of enemy is this man worried about?
Important Idea
These two enemies are finally going to settle the score.
In a way, it's hard to tell them apart—they're so filled
with hate.

❷ Improve Your Reading Skills

Complete the specific READER'S NOTEBOOK activity on the first page of each literature lesson. This activity will help you apply an important skill as you read the selection.

❸ Collect Ideas for Writing

Be aware of intriguing themes, passages, and thoughts of your own as you read or complete follow-up activities. In a special section of your READER'S NOTEBOOK, jot down anything that may later be a springboard to your own writing.

grown into a personal one since Ulrich had come to be head of his family; if there was a man in the world whom he detested and wished ill to it was Georg Znaeym, the inheritor of the quarrel and the tireless game-snatcher and raider of the disputed border-forest. The feud might, perhaps, have died down or been compromised if the personal ill-will of the two men had not stood in the way; as boys they had thirsted for one another's blood, as men each prayed that misfortune might fall on the other, and this wind-scourged winter night Ulrich had banded together his foresters to watch the dark forest, not in quest of four-footed quarry, but to keep a lookout for the prowling thieves whom he suspected of being afoot from across the land boundary. The roebuck, which usually kept in the sheltered hollows during a storm wind, were running like driven things tonight, and there was movement and unrest among the creatures that were wont to sleep through the dark hours. Assuredly there was a disturbing element in the forest, and Ulrich could guess the quarter from whence it came.

He strayed away by himself from the watchers whom he had placed in ambush on the crest of the hill, and wandered far down the steep slopes amid the wild tangle of undergrowth, peering through the tree trunks and listening through the whistling and skirling of the wind and the restless beating of the branches for sight or sound of the marauders. If only on this wild night, in this dark, lone spot, he might come across Georg Znaeym, man to man, with none to witness—that was the wish that was uppermost in his thoughts. And as he stepped around the trunk of a huge beech, he came face to face with the man he sought.

The two enemies stood glaring at one another for a long silent moment.

Each had a rifle in his hand, each had hate in his heart and murder uppermost in his mind. The chance had come to give full play to the passions of a lifetime. But a man who has been brought up under the code of a restraining civilization cannot easily nerve himself to shoot down his neighbor in cold blood and without word spoken, except for an offense against his hearth and honor. And before the moment of hesitation had given way to action a deed of Nature's own violence overwhelmed them both. A fierce shriek of the storm had been answered by a splitting crash over their heads, and ere they could leap aside a mass of falling beech tree had thundered down on them. Ulrich von Gradwitz found himself stretched on the ground, one arm numb beneath him and the other held almost as helplessly in a tight tangle of forked branches, while both legs were pinned beneath the fallen

Thuy: *I picture Ulrich and Georg as having rocky childhoods. These two guys hated each other and were very competitive.*
EVALUATING

Thuy: *Ulrich is hunting not for animals but for people who are trespassing. That's the game for him*
CLARIFYING

Robert: *This is a very dense forest; the vegetation is so thick that walking must be difficult.*
VISUALIZING

Thuy: *He's got vengeance in his eyes; he wants to murder Georg. He's bloodthirsty!*
CLARIFYING

Robert: *It's ironic that Ulrich found Georg just as he had hoped. Seems unrealistic. I'm reminded that so many wars are just about land. Murder seems too harsh a penalty for a land dispute.*
EVALUATING / CONNECTING

Thuy: *I'm beginning to think I know where the story is going. I think they'll be caught and then both might die. Or, they might not hate each other in the end and have to work together to save their lives.*
PREDICTING

THE INTERLOPERS 9

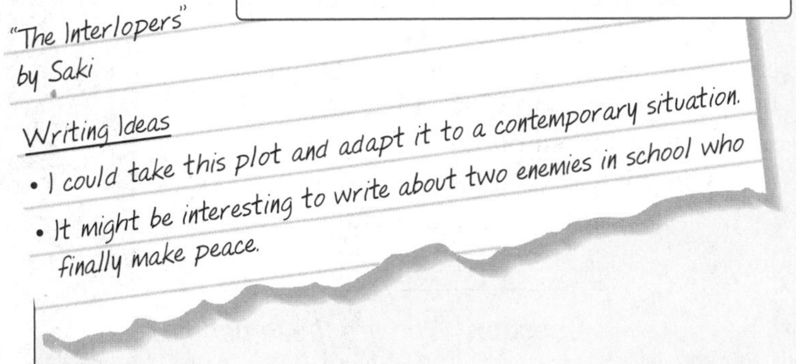
"The Interlopers"
by Saki
Writing Ideas
• I could take this plot and adapt it to a contemporary situation.
• It might be interesting to write about two enemies in school who finally make peace.

Your Working Portfolio

Artists and writers keep portfolios in which they store works in progress or the works they are most proud of. Your portfolio can be a folder, a box, or a notebook—the form doesn't matter. Just make sure to keep adding to it—with drafts of your writing experiments, summaries of your projects, and your own goals and accomplishments as a reader and writer. Later in this book, on the Reflect and Assess pages, you will choose your best or favorite work to place in a ***Presentation Portfolio.***

5

Become an Active Reader

The strategies you need to become an active reader are already within your grasp. In fact, you use them every day to make sense of the images and the events in your world. Whether watching a movie or interpreting a photograph, you already know how to employ such strategies.

Take a look at this puzzling photograph. Read the comments alongside it, made by one student. As you will see, this student used four different strategies—Question, Clarify, Predict, and Connect—to understand and interpret the situation shown in the photograph. These and the other reading strategies listed on the next page can help you interact with literature as well.

Question *Who are these people? Where are they? What could have caused such massive destruction?*

Clarify *The man is holding her gown so it doesn't drag. They're trying not to spoil their wedding clothes.*

Predict *I wonder what kind of wedding ceremony will take place.*

6

Connect *This reminds me of photos from European cities after bombing in World War II.*

Strategies for Reading

Following are specific reading strategies that are introduced and applied throughout this book. Use them when you read and interact with the various literature selections. Occasionally **monitor** how well the strategies are working for you and, if desired, modify them to suit your needs.

PREDICT Try to figure out what will happen next and how the selection might end. Then read on to see how accurate your guesses were.

VISUALIZE Visualize characters, events, and setting to help you understand what's happening. When you read nonfiction, pay attention to the images that form in your mind as you read.

CONNECT Connect personally with what you're reading. Think of similarities between the descriptions in the selection and what you have personally experienced, heard about, and read about.

QUESTION Question what happens while you read. Searching for reasons behind events and characters' feelings can help you feel closer to what you are reading.

CLARIFY Stop occasionally to review what you understand, and expect to have your understanding change and develop as you read on. Reread and use resources to help you clarify your understanding. Also watch for answers to questions you had earlier.

EVALUATE Form opinions about what you read, both while you're reading and after you've finished. Develop your own ideas about characters and events.

On the next page, you will see how two readers applied these strategies to the story "The Interlopers."

Go Beyond the Text If you really become an active reader, your involvement doesn't stop with the last line of the text. Decide what else you'd like to know. Discuss your ideas with others, do some research, or jump on the Internet.

More Online
www.mcdougallittell.com

Alongside "The Interlopers" are the spoken comments made by two tenth-grade students, Robert Wingader and Thanh-Thuy Nguyen (tän to͞o ē wĭn), while they were reading the story. Their comments provide a glimpse into the minds of readers actively engaged in the process of reading. You'll notice that in the course of reading, Robert and Thuy (to͞o ē) quite naturally used the Strategies for Reading that were introduced on page 7. You'll also note that these readers responded differently to the story—no two readers think the same way.

To benefit most from this model of active reading, read the story first, jotting down your own responses in your reading log. Then read Robert's and Thuy's comments and compare their processes of reading with your own.

THE INTERLOPERS

Saki

Robert: *I've heard of the Carpathians, but I don't know where they are.*
CONNECTING / QUESTIONING

Thuy: *At first I thought he was hunting, but now I think it's like a game to him. He's hunting another man.*
CLARIFYING

Robert: *Why is the land so jealously guarded?*
QUESTIONING

In a forest of mixed growth somewhere on the eastern spurs of the Carpathians, a man stood one winter night watching and listening, as though he waited for some beast of the woods to come within the range of his vision, and, later, of his rifle. But the game for whose presence he kept so keen an outlook was none that figured in the sportman's calendar as lawful and proper for the chase; Ulrich von Gradwitz patrolled the dark forest in quest of a human enemy.

The forest lands of Gradwitz were of wide extent and well stocked with game; the narrow strip of precipitous woodland that lay on its outskirt was not remarkable for the game it harbored or the shooting it afforded, but it was the most jealously guarded of all its owner's territorial possessions. A famous lawsuit, in the days of his grandfather, had wrested it from the illegal possession of a neighboring family of petty landowners; the dispossessed party had never acquiesced in the judgment of the Courts, and a long series of poaching affrays and similar scandals had embittered the relationships between the families for three generations. The neighbor feud had

8 READING MODEL

grown into a personal one since Ulrich had come to be head of his family; if there was a man in the world whom he detested and wished ill to it was Georg Znaeym, the inheritor of the quarrel and the tireless game-snatcher and raider of the disputed border-forest. The feud might, perhaps, have died down or been compromised if the personal ill-will of the two men had not stood in the way; as boys they had thirsted for one another's blood, as men each prayed that misfortune might fall on the other, and this wind-scourged winter night Ulrich had banded together his foresters to watch the dark forest, not in quest of four-footed quarry, but to keep a lookout for the prowling thieves whom he suspected of being afoot from across the land boundary. The roebuck, which usually kept in the sheltered hollows during a storm wind, were running like driven things tonight, and there was movement and unrest among the creatures that were wont to sleep through the dark hours. Assuredly there was a disturbing element in the forest, and Ulrich could guess the quarter from whence it came.

He strayed away by himself from the watchers whom he had placed in ambush on the crest of the hill, and wandered far down the steep slopes amid the wild tangle of undergrowth, peering through the tree trunks and listening through the whistling and skirling of the wind and the restless beating of the branches for sight or sound of the marauders. If only on this wild night, in this dark, lone spot, he might come across Georg Znaeym, man to man, with none to witness—that was the wish that was uppermost in his thoughts. And as he stepped around the trunk of a huge beech, he came face to face with the man he sought.

The two enemies stood glaring at one another for a long silent moment.

Each had a rifle in his hand, each had hate in his heart and murder uppermost in his mind. The chance had come to give full play to the passions of a lifetime. But a man who has been brought up under the code of a restraining civilization cannot easily nerve himself to shoot down his neighbor in cold blood and without a word spoken, except for an offense against his hearth and honor. And before the moment of hesitation had given way to action a deed of Nature's own violence overwhelmed them both. A fierce shriek of the storm had been answered by a splitting crash over their heads, and ere they could leap aside a mass of falling beech tree had thundered down on them. Ulrich von Gradwitz found himself stretched on the ground, one arm numb beneath him and the other held almost as helplessly in a tight tangle of forked branches, while both legs were pinned beneath the fallen

Thuy: *I picture Ulrich and Georg as having rocky childhoods. These two guys hated each other and were very competitive.*
EVALUATING

Thuy: *Ulrich is hunting not for animals but for people who are trespassing. That's the game for him.*
CLARIFYING

Robert: *This is a very dense forest; the vegetation is so thick that walking must be difficult.*
VISUALIZING

Thuy: *He's got vengeance in his eyes; he wants to murder Georg. He's bloodthirsty!*
CLARIFYING

Robert: *It's ironic that Ulrich found Georg just as he had hoped. Seems unrealistic. I'm reminded that so many wars are just about land. Murder seems too harsh a penalty for a land dispute.*
EVALUATING / CONNECTING

Thuy: *I'm beginning to think I know where the story is going. I think they'll be caught and then both might die. Or, they might not hate each other in the end and have to work together to save their lives.*
PREDICTING

THE INTERLOPERS 9

mass. His heavy shooting boots had saved his feet from being crushed to pieces, but if his fractures were not as serious as they might have been, at least it was evident that he could not move from his present position till someone came to release him. The descending twigs had slashed the skin of his face, and he had to wink away some drops of blood from his eyelashes before he could take in a general view of the disaster. At his side, so near that under ordinary circumstances he could almost have touched him, lay Georg Znaeym, alive and struggling, but obviously as helplessly pinioned down as himself. All around them lay a thick-strewn wreckage of splintered branches and broken twigs.

Thuy: *This is a bloody scene. It's like you're watching a movie when the tree falls. It reminds me of* Jurassic Park.
CONNECTING

Robert: *This reminds me of another story that I read in which a character is trapped by circumstances in nature. The tree falling seems unlikely but convenient for the author.*
CONNECTING / EVALUATING

Relief at being alive and exasperation at his captive plight brought a strange medley of pious thank offerings and sharp curses to Ulrich's lips. Georg, who was nearly blinded with the blood which trickled across his eyes, stopped his struggling for a moment to listen, and then gave a short, snarling laugh.

"So you're not killed, as you ought to be, but you're caught, anyway," he cried; "caught fast. Ho, what a jest, Ulrich von Gradwitz snared in his stolen forest. There's real justice for you!"

Thuy: *Georg's laughing at the guy he hates. He's thinking, "You're getting what you deserve. Even if you're not dying, at least you're in pain." It seems like he's taking some joy in that—I really don't like this guy.*
CLARIFYING / EVALUATING

And he laughed again, mockingly and savagely.

"I'm caught in my own forest land," retorted Ulrich. "When my men come to release us, you will wish, perhaps, that you were in a better plight than caught poaching on a neighbor's land, shame on you."

Georg was silent for a moment; then he answered quietly.

"Are you sure that your men will find much to release? I have men, too, in the forest tonight, close behind me, and they will be here first and do the releasing. When they drag me out from under these branches, it won't need much clumsiness on their part to roll this mass of trunk right over on the top of you. Your men will find you dead under a fallen beech tree. For form's sake I shall send my condolences to your family."

"It is a useful hint," said Ulrich fiercely. "My men had orders to follow in ten minutes' time, seven of which must have gone by already, and when they get me out—I will remember the hint. Only as you will have met your death poaching on my lands, I don't think I can decently send any message of condolence to your family."

Robert: *All the bickering about whose men are going to find them seems pointless and feeble.*
EVALUATING

"Good," snarled Georg, "good. We fight this quarrel out to the death, you and I and our foresters, with no cursed interlopers to come between us. Death . . . to you, Ulrich von Gradwitz."

"The same to you, Georg Znaeym, forest thief, game snatcher."

Thuy: *This reminds me of* The Inferno *by Dante and how only God can damn you and cause your death. Georg is thinking he's God—or at least as powerful as God—by damning Ulrich.*
CONNECTING / CLARIFYING

Both men spoke with the bitterness of possible defeat before them, for each knew that it might be long before his men would

10 READING MODEL

seek him out or find him; it was a bare matter of chance which party would arrive first on the scene.

Both had now given up the useless struggle to free themselves from the mass of wood that held them down; Ulrich limited his endeavors to an effort to bring his one partially free arm near enough to his outer coat pocket to draw out his wine flask. Even when he had accomplished that operation, it was long before he could manage the unscrewing of the stopper or get any of the liquid down his throat. But what a heaven-sent draft it seemed! It was an open winter, and little snow had fallen as yet, hence the captives suffered less from the cold than might have been the case at that season of the year; nevertheless, the wine was warming and reviving to the wounded man, and he looked across with something like a throb of pity to where his enemy lay, just keeping the groans of pain and weariness from crossing his lips.

"Could you reach this flask if I threw it over to you?" asked Ulrich suddenly; "there is good wine in it, and one may as well be as comfortable as one can. Let us drink, even if tonight one of us dies."

"No, I can scarcely see anything; there is so much blood caked around my eyes," said Georg, "and in any case I don't drink wine with an enemy."

Ulrich was silent for a few minutes and lay listening to the weary screeching of the wind. An idea was slowly forming and growing in his brain, an idea that gained strength every time that he looked across at the man who was fighting so grimly against pain and exhaustion. In the pain and languor that Ulrich himself was feeling the old fierce hatred seemed to be dying down.

"Neighbor," he said presently, "do as you please if your men come first. It was a fair compact. But as for me, I've changed my mind. If my men are the first to come, you shall be the first to be helped, as though you were my guest. We have quarreled like devils all our lives over this stupid strip of forest, where the trees can't even stand upright in a breath of wind. Lying here tonight, thinking, I've come to think we've been rather fools; there are better things in life than getting the better of a boundary dispute. Neighbor, if you will help me to bury the old quarrel I—I will ask you to be my friend."

Georg Znaeym was silent for so long that Ulrich thought, perhaps, he had fainted with the pain of his injuries. Then he spoke slowly and in jerks.

Thuy: *I'm having a hard time telling the difference between the two men. I need to keep them straight in my mind.*
MONITORING

Robert: *It's a good thing that Ulrich finally saw past the feud.*
EVALUATING

Thuy: *When Ulrich drinks the wine he feels warm and some relief from his suffering. It's the first time he feels pity toward his enemy.*
CLARIFYING

Thuy: *Ulrich does have some human characteristics; I don't hate him as much as I used to.*
EVALUATING

Robert: *It's pitiful that Georg wouldn't accept Ulrich's offer. It's hard to believe that he's that uneasy about drinking wine with his enemy.*
EVALUATING

Thuy: *Ulrich calls Georg "neighbor," which contradicts "enemy." He's almost like a friend now.*
CLARIFYING

Thuy: *Now I know why they hate each other and have been quarreling all this time—it's because of the forest. They see now that they have been fools in the past because of this.*
CLARIFYING / EVALUATING

THE INTERLOPERS 11

Thuy: The whole village knows about the feud. It would be a big surprise if they came back to the village as friends.
CLARIFYING / PREDICTING

"How the whole region would stare and gabble if we rode into the market square together. No one living can remember seeing a Znaeym and a von Gradwitz talking to one another in friendship. And what peace there would be among the forester folk if we ended our feud tonight. And if we choose to make peace among our people, there is none other to interfere, no interlopers from outside. . . . You would come and keep the Sylvester night beneath my roof, and I would come and feast on some high day at your castle. . . . I would never fire a shot on your land, save when you invited me as a guest; and you should come and shoot with me down in the marshes where the wildfowl are. In all the countryside there are none that could hinder if we willed to make peace. I never thought to have wanted to do other than hate you all my life, but I think I have changed my mind about things too, this last half-hour. And you offered me your wine flask. . . . Ulrich von Gradwitz, I will be your friend."

Robert: All feuds should be settled like this; gangs, for instance, could make peace and avoid futile battles.
EVALUATING / CONNECTING

For a space both men were silent, turning over in their minds the wonderful changes that this dramatic reconciliation would bring about. In the cold, gloomy forest, with the wind tearing in fitful gusts through the naked branches and whistling around the tree trunks, they lay and waited for the help that would now bring release and succor to both parties. And each prayed a private prayer that his men might be the first to arrive, so that he might be the first to show honorable attention to the enemy that had become a friend.

Robert: I wonder how Georg's and Ulrich's men will react to the ending of the feud.
QUESTIONING

Thuy: At first, each man wanted his own people to come first so the other would be killed, but now, each wants to be first to save the other's life. They both want to be first to show their friendship.
CLARIFYING

Presently, as the wind dropped for a moment, Ulrich broke silence.

"Let's shout for help," he said; "in this lull our voices may carry a little way."

"They won't carry far through the trees and undergrowth," said Georg, "but we can try. Together, then."

Robert: They're finally working together to save themselves.
CLARIFYING

The two raised their voices in a prolonged hunting call.

"Together again," said Ulrich a few minutes later, after listening in vain for an answer halloo.

"I heard something that time, I think," said Ulrich.

"I heard nothing but the pestilential wind," said Georg hoarsely.

There was silence again for some minutes, and then Ulrich gave a joyful cry.

Robert: I wonder whose men these are.
QUESTIONING

"I can see figures coming through the wood. They are following in the way I came down the hillside."

Both men raised their voices in as loud a shout as they could muster.

12 READING MODEL

Border Patrol (1951), Andrew Wyeth. Private collection.

"They hear us! They've stopped. Now they see us. They're running down the hill towards us," cried Ulrich.

"How many of them are there?" asked Georg.

"I can't see distinctly," said Ulrich; "nine or ten."

"Then they are yours," said Georg; "I had only seven out with me."

"They are making all the speed they can, brave lads," said Ulrich gladly.

"Are they your men?" asked Georg. "Are they your men?"

"No," said Ulrich with a laugh, the idiotic chattering laugh of a man unstrung with hideous fear.

"Who are they?" asked Georg quickly, straining his eyes to see what the other would gladly not have seen.

"*Wolves.*" ❖

Thuy: *Why "hideous fear"? If men are coming, it doesn't matter who they are.*
QUESTIONING

Thuy: *Now I see. Now they're going to die together. I like the ending.*
CLARIFYING / EVALUATING

THE INTERLOPERS **13**

The Challenge of Change

In Unit One, students will read selections which explore various ways in which people, relationships, places, and societies change over time. This unit contains two parts, and selections in both parts contribute to the unit theme by examining how a variety of characters are affected by great changes in their lives.

Part 1

The Price of Progress Selections in Part 1 emphasize the effects of technological progress on characters in a number of settings. For example, in "Searching for Summer," ordinary men and women must live in a world which is always overcast because bombs have altered the atmosphere.

Part 2

Cultural Crossroads Selections in Part 2 emphasize the changes in individuals and their relationships that are caused by cultural differences. For example, in "Fish Cheeks," a Chinese-American girl must reconcile her Chinese heritage with her desire to become accepted in American society.

THE CHALLENGE OF CHANGE

There is

nothing permanent

except

change.

HERACLITUS

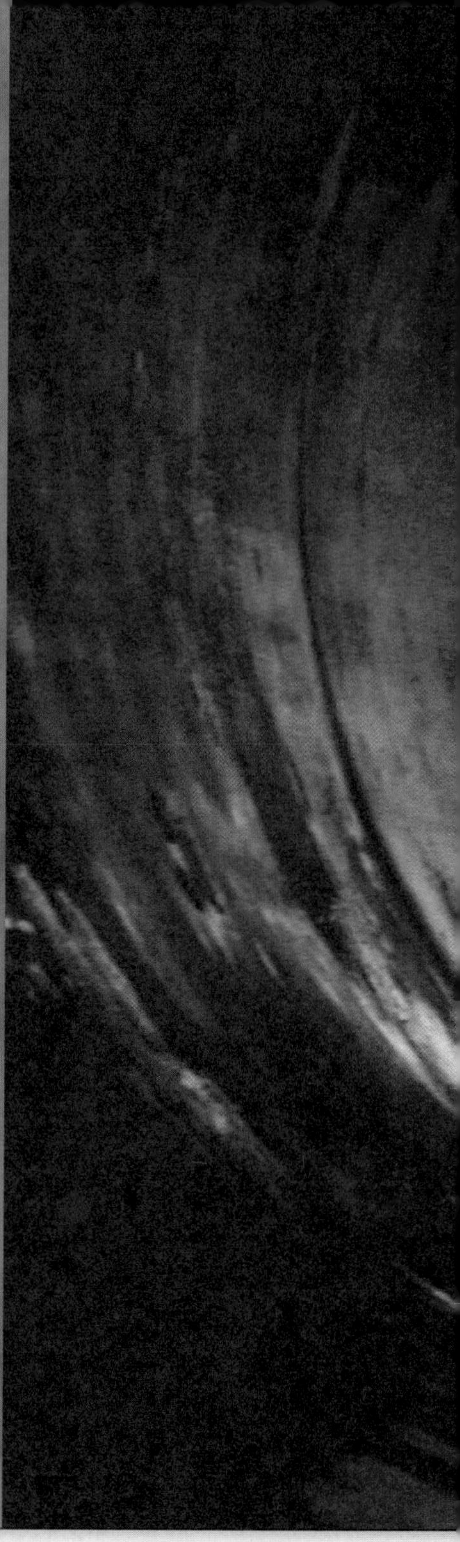

Chicago Tribune photo by Heather Stone.

Mini Lesson Viewing and Representing

Finished section of the Deep Tunnel in the upper-Des Plaines water system in Chicago, Illinois.

Photograph by Heather Stone

ART APPRECIATION

Instruction Heather Stone uses light to capture the essence of a common structure. The piercing light at the top right of the picture draws the eye directly into the tunnel. Stone's use of artificial light dramatizes reality and also accentuates the form of the tunnel. In addition, taking the picture while operating engineer Joe Burba walks through it allows the viewer to comprehend the size of the tunnel relative to a known quantity. Stone probably took many photographs experimenting with the light until she achieved the desired effect.

Ask: How does the use of the spotlights affect your perception of the tunnel?

Possible Response: The two spotlights enable the viewer to see the full shape and depth of tunnel.

Making Connections

To help students explore the connections between the art, the quotation, and the unit theme, have them consider the following questions:

Ask: Why do you think people write stories about change?
Possible Response: because the world and the people who inhabit it are constantly changing; because people constantly need to adapt to a changing world, and writing and reading about it might help us adapt better

Ask: What do you think Heraclitus meant by this statement? What is your reaction to his statement?
Possible Response: The only thing we can count on is change; things will never stop changing. It is a permanent part of the human condition.

Ask: Why do you think this photograph was chosen to depict the theme of change? Students should support their opinions with specific details from it.
Possible Response: The photograph has a futuristic look and shows the use of technology.

Ask: What kind of stories and experiences might you expect to read about in this unit?
Possible Response: stories about people, nature, technology, or societies that change in some important way

Conduct a class discussion in which students discuss a particular experience of their own through which they learned that nothing stays the same.
Possible Response: Responses will vary.

VIDEODISC **LaserLinks**
Unit Overview Chart
See Teacher's SourceBook p. 4 for bar codes.

PART 1 SKILLS TRACE

Features and Selections	Literary Analysis	Reading and Critical Thinking	Writing Opportunities
Learning the Language of Literature Fiction **The Active Reader**	Plot, 17	Reading Fiction, 19	
SHORT STORY Harrison Bergeron **Difficulty Level:** ***Average***	Theme, 20, 27 Science Fiction, 27	Making Inferences, 20, 27	Glampers's Report, 28 Warden's Address, 28
SHORT STORY Searching for Summer **Difficulty Level:** ***Easy*** **Literary Link:** The Sun	Character, 30, 39 Fantasy, 39	Identifying Characters' Motives, 30, 39 Test Practice, 38	Evening Dialogue, 40 Story Outline, 40
SHORT STORY By the Waters of Babylon **Difficulty Level:** ***Average*** **Literary Link** There Will Come Soft Rains **Building Vocabulary**	Plot, 42, 53 Point of View, 53	Sequence, 42, 53	Journals of the Dead, 54 Debate Dialogue, 54 Informal Assess., 52
SHORT STORY A Sound of Thunder **Difficulty Level:** ***Average***	Foreshadowing, 71, 82 Review: Science Fiction, 82	Predicting, 71, 82 Informal Assess., 81	Advertisement, 83 Incident Report, 83
INTERVIEW Interview with Ray Bradbury **Difficulty Level:** ***Easy***	Primary Sources: Interview, 84		
SHORT STORY There Will Come Soft Rains **Difficulty Level:** ***Average***	Setting, 86, 93 Point of View, 93	Visualizing, 86, 93 Test Practice, 90	House Monologue, 94 Appliance Argument, 94
SHORT STORY The Pedestrian **Difficulty Level:** ***Average***	Description, 95, 101 Review: Character, 101	Sensory Details, 95, 101 Choosing a Summary, 100	Citizen Profile, 103 Critical Review, 103
The Author's Style Author Study Project	Analysis of Style, 102		Imitating Style, 102 Changing Style, 102
Learning the Language of Literature: Nonfiction **The Active Reader**	Nonfiction, 104	Reading Nonfiction, 106	
ESSAY Dial Versus Digital **Difficulty Level:** ***Average***	Expository Essay, 107, 110	Analyzing Structure, 107, 110 Fact and Opinion, 110	Tech Paragraph, 111 Invented Terms, 111
ESSAY Once More to the Lake **Difficulty Level:** ***Challenging*** **Literary Link** A Letter from E. B. White	Personal Essay, 112, 121	Identifying Comparison and Contrast, 112, 121	Vacation Essay, 122 Slide Show, 122 Newspaper Editorial, 122 Author Activity, 123 Test Practice, 119

LEGEND **DLS – Daily Language SkillBuilder**
CCL – Cross Curricular Link
Green type – Teacher's Edition

Speaking and Listening Viewing and Representing	Inquiry and Research	Grammar, Usage, and Mechanics	Vocabulary
News at Six, 28 Video Viewing, 28 Art Appreciation, 25	Public Opinion, 28	Proper Nouns, 29 DLS, 20 Parts of Speech, 26 Proper Nouns, 28	Context Clues, 28 Context Clues, 22 Figurative Language, 24
Story Illustrations, 40 Radio Advertisement, 40 Art Appreciation, 31, 36 Dramatic Presentation, 34	Nuclear Fallout, 40	Grammar in Context, 41 DLS, 30 Proper Adjectives, 37 Punctuating Adjectives, 40	Idioms, 40 Using a Dictionary, 32
Journey Map, 54 Artifact Collection, 54 Art Connection, 54 Art Appreciation, 43, 44, 48	News Reel, 54 Film Study, 54	Pronouns, 54 DLS, 42 Pronouns, 50 Pronouns, 54	Context Clues, 56 Prefixes, 49
Butterfly Drawing, 83 Video Adaptation, 83 Viewing and Representing, 78 Newscast, 80	Science, 83 Astronomy, 83	DLS, 71	Assessment Practice, 83 Context Clues, 72 Word Origins, 75
Future Set Design, 94 Readers Theater, 94 Art Appreciation, 91	Political Climate, 94 Poetry Connection, 94	Action Verbs, 94, 94 DLS, 86 Compound Adjectives, 92	
Panel Discussion, 103 Comic-Book Version, 103 Viewing and Representing, 99	TV of the Past, 103	DLS, 95	Context Clues, 96 Prefixes, 98
Speaking and Listening, 102 Movie-Trailer Storyboard, 103			
Personal Interviews, 111 Progress Presentation, 111 Art Connection, 111 Art Appreciation, 109	Inquiry and Research, 111	DLS, 107 Nouns Used as Adjectives, 111	
Travel Advertisement, 122 Cross-Generational Presentation, 122 Art Appreciation, 114, 118	Vacation Spots, 122	Active and Passive Voice, 123 DLS, 112 Adverbs, 120, 122	Word Meaning, 122 Synonyms and Antonyms, 113 Word Origins, 117

UNIT ONE
PART 1 SKILLS TRACE

Features and Selections	Literary Analysis	Reading and Critical Thinking	Writing Opportunities
MEMOIR Montgomery Boycott **Difficulty Level:** ***Average*** **Literary Link:** Sit-Ins	Memoir, 124, 133	Cause and Effect, 124, 133 Test Practice, 132	Historic Diary, 134 Newspaper Editorial, 134
Real World Link A Eulogy to Dr. Martin Luther King, Jr.		Primary Source: Persuasive Rhetoric, 136	
Writing Workshop: **Opinion Statement** **Assessment Practice**		Analyzing a Student Model, 139	Opinion Statement, 141 Refining Topic Sentences, 142

UNIT ONE
PART 2 SKILLS TRACE

Features and Selections	Literary Analysis	Reading and Critical Thinking	Writing Opportunities
Learning the Language of Literature Theme **The Active Reader**	Theme, 145	Drawing Conclusions, 147	
SHORT STORY No Witchcraft for Sale **Difficulty Level:** ***Challenging***	Theme and Character, 148, 156	Drawing Conclusions, 148, 156 Test Practice, 155	Letter, 157 Medicine Man Dialogue, 157
SHORT STORY The Son from America **Difficulty Level:** ***Average*** **Literary Link:** Grudnow	Plot and Theme, 159, 167	Making Predictions, 159, 167 Test Practice, 165	Lentshin Newsletter, 168 Literary Review, 168 Old World Sketches, 168
ESSAY Through the One-Way Mirror The Border: A Glare of Truth **Difficulty Level:** ***Average***	Theme in Nonfiction, 170, 178	Comparison and Contrast, 170, 178 Predicting, 173 Informal Assess., 177	Border Interview, 179 Image Analysis, 179 Heritage Essay, 179
Real World Link *from* To Make a Nation: How Immigrants Are Changing America **Building Vocabulary**		Magazine Article: Distinguishing Fact and Opinion, 181	
Comparing Literature: **Love and Marriage Across Cultures**		Analyze and Compare, 187	
SHORT STORY Marriage Is a Private Affair **Difficulty Level:** ***Average***	Cultural Conflict, 188, 194	Cultural Characteristics, 188, 194 Informal Assess., 193	Okeke's Letter, 195
SHORT STORY Love Must Not Be Forgotten **Difficulty Level:** ***Challenging***	Cultural Setting, 196, 209	Identifying Cultural Characteristics, 196, 209	Monologue, 210 Character Profile, 210 Test Practice, 210
Comparing Literature: **Assessment Practice**		Reading the Prompt, 211	Analysis Essay, 211
Writing Workshop: **Focused Description** **Assessment Practice**		Analyzing a Student Model, 213	Focused Description, 215 Word Choice, 216
Reflect and Assess: **The Challenge of Change**		Interpreting Theme, 219 Analyzing Nonfiction, 219	Responses to Change, 218 Building Your Portfolio, 219

LEGEND **DLS – Daily Language SkillBuilder**
CCL – Cross Curricular Link
Green type – Teacher's Edition

Speaking and Listening Viewing and Representing	Inquiry and Research	Grammar, Usage, and Mechanics	Vocabulary
Storytelling, 134 Historical Exhibit, 134 Speech for the Ages, 134 News Photography, 125	A Dark Day in History, 134 We Shall Overcome, 134	Adverbs, 135 Active Versus Linking Verbs, 130 Adverbs, 134	Context Clues, 126
	Activity Link: Montgomery Boycott, 137 Inquiry and Research, 137		
Picturing Text Structure, 139		Pronoun-Antecedent, 142 Revising and Editing, 143	
Oral Tale, 157 Bar Graph, 157 Editorial Page, 157 Art Appreciation, 151	Alternative Medicine, 157 Colonialism in Southern Africa, 157	Adverbs, 158, 158 DLS, 148 Active Verbs, 154 Parts of Speech, 156	Meaning Clues, 157 Prefixes, 149
A Son's Portrait, 168 A Son's Scrapbook, 168 Personal Interview, 168 Art Appreciation, 161 Presenting a Persuasive Argument, 166	World Religions, 168	Nouns, Tone, and Mood, 169 DLS, 159 Proper and Common Nouns, 168	Related Words, 168 Context Clues, 160 Word Origins, 164
Visual Essay, 179 Illustrated Map, 179 Art Appreciation, 172	Inquiry and Research, 179	Abstract, Concrete Nouns, 180 DLS, 170 Capitalization, 176 Abstract, Concrete Nouns, 180	Context Clues, 179 Context Clues, 171, 175
	Activity Link: The Border, 182 Inquiry and Research, 182		Analyzing Word Parts, 183
Persuasive Writing and Speaking, 195	Marrying for Love, 195	DLS, 188 Demonstrative Pronouns, 191	Assessment Practice, 195 Thesaurus, 189 Word Origins, 192
Art Connection, 210 Art Appreciation, 198, 205, 208 Dramatic Reading, 203	Cultural Revolution, 210	DLS, 196 Pronouns, 200 Pronoun Case, 202	Assessment Practice, 210 Context Clues, 197 Word Origins, 206
		Subject-Verb Agreement, 216 Revising and Editing, 217	
Graphing the Causes of Change, 218			

RESOURCE MANAGEMENT GUIDE PART 1

To introduce the theme/literary period of this unit, use Fine Art Transparencies T17–19 in the Communications Transparencies and Copymasters.

	Unit Resource Book	Assessment	Integrated Technology and Media	Additional Support: Literary Analysis Transparencies
Harrison Bergeron *pp. 20–29*	• Summary p. 4 • Active Reading p. 5 • Literary Analysis p. 6 • Words to Know p. 7 • Grammar p. 8 • Selection Quiz p. 9	• Selection Test, Formal Assessment pp. 7–8 Test Generator	Audio Library Video: Literature in Performance, Video Resource Book pp. 3–9	• Plot T1
Searching for Summer *pp. 30–41*	• Summary p. 10 • Active Reading p. 11 • Literary Analysis p. 12 • Words to Know p. 13 • Grammar p. 14 • Selection Quiz p. 15	• Selection Test, Formal Assessment pp. 9–10 Test Generator	Audio Library LaserLinks, Teacher's SourceBook p. 6 Research Starter www.mcdougallittell.com	• Character T2
By the Waters of Babylon *pp. 42–55*	• Summary p. 16 • Active Reading p. 17 • Literary Analysis p. 18 • Grammar p. 19 • Selection Quiz p. 20	• Selection Test, Formal Assessment pp. 11–12 Test Generator	Audio Library LaserLinks, Teacher's SourceBook pp. 7–8	
A Sound of Thunder *pp. 71–85*	• Summary p. 22 • Active Reading p. 23 • Literary Analysis p. 24 • Words to Know p. 25 • Selection Quiz p. 26	• Selection Test, Formal Assessment pp. 13–14 Test Generator	Audio Library Video: Literature in Performance, Video Resource Book pp. 11–16 Research Starter www.mcdougallittell.com NetActivities	
There Will Come Soft Rains *pp. 86–94*	• Summary p. 27 • Active Reading p. 28 • Literary Analysis p. 29 • Selection Quiz p. 30	• Selection Test, Formal Assessment pp. 15–16 Test Generator	Audio Library NetActivities	• Setting T3
The Pedestrian *pp. 95–103*	• Summary p. 31 • Active Reading p. 32 • Literary Analysis p. 33 • Selection Quiz p. 34	• Selection Test, Formal Assessment pp. 17–18 Test Generator	Audio Library Research Starter www.mcdougallittell.com NetActivities	
Dial Versus Digital *pp. 107–111*	• Summary p. 35 • Active Reading p. 36 • Literary Analysis p. 37 • Selection Quiz p. 38	• Selection Test, Formal Assessment pp. 19–20 Test Generator	Audio Library	• Types of Nonfiction T4
Once More to the Lake *pp. 112–123*	• Summary p. 39 • Active Reading p. 40 • Literary Analysis p. 41 • Words to Know p. 42 • Grammar p. 43 • Selection Quiz p. 44	• Selection Test, Formal Assessment pp. 21–22 Test Generator	Audio Library	• Types of Nonfiction T4

T = Transparency C = Copymaster

	Reading and Critical Thinking Transparencies	Grammar Transparencies and Copymasters	Vocabulary Transparencies and Copymasters	Writing Transparencies and Copymasters	Communications Transparencies and Copymasters
	• Making Inferences T7	• Daily Language SkillBuilder T1 • Parts of Speech C62	• Personal Word List C17 • Context Clues C18 • Figurative Language C19	• Writing Process T1, T2 • Elaboration T10 • Point of View T23	• Evaluation Matrix: Film/Video T7 • Evaluating Roles in Groups T8 • Impromptu Speaking: Dialogue, Role-Play, Debate T13
	• Cluster Diagram T48	• Daily Language SkillBuilder T1 • Proper Adjectives C71	• Word Meanings C20	• Writing Process T1, T2 • The Uses of Dialogue T24	• Evaluation Matrix: Commercial T6 • Dramatic Reading T12
	• Chronological Order T11	• Daily Language SkillBuilder T2 • Personal and Reflexive Pronouns C153	• Prefixes C21 • Figurative Language C22	• Effective Language T13 • Sensory Word List T14 • The Uses of Dialogue T24	• Impromptu Speaking: Dialogue, Role-Play, Debate T13
	• Predicting Outcomes T2	• Daily Language SkillBuilder T2	• Context Clues C23 • Word Origins C24	• Point of View T23 • Achieving Conciseness T21	• Evaluation Matrix: Film/Video T7
	• Organizational Chart: Horizontal T51	• Daily Language SkillBuilder T3 • Compound Adjectives C73		• Writing Structure T6, T8 • Point of View T23 • Persuasive Essay C30	• Dramatic Reading T12 • Verbal Strategies T14
	• Organizational Chart: Horizontal T51	• Daily Language SkillBuilder T3	• Context Clues C25 • Prefixes C26	• Writing Structure T10, T11 • Extending Sentences T19 • Opinion Statement C25	• Evaluating Roles in Groups T8
	• Cause and Effect T1 • Analyzing Text Structure T17	• Daily Language SkillBuilder T4	• Conditional Words C27	• Achieving Unity T7 • Opinion Statement C25	• Interviewing T9 • Formal Presentations T10
	• Venn Diagram T50	• Daily Language SkillBuilder T4 • Position of Adverbs C75	• Synonyms and Antonyms C28 • Word Origins: Latin Roots C29	• Writing Structure T5, T6, T8 • Figurative Language and Sound Devices T15 • Showing, Not Telling T22 • Opinion Statement C25	• Formal Presentations T10

UNIT ONE, PART 1 CONTINUED

	Unit Resource Book	Assessment	Integrated Technology and Media	Additional Support: Literary Analysis Transparencies
Montgomery Boycott *pp. 124–135*	• Summary p. 45 • Active Reading p. 46 • Literary Analysis p. 47 • Words to Know p. 48 • Grammar p. 49 • Selection Quiz p. 50	• Selection Test, Formal Assessment pp. 23–24 Test Generator	Audio Library LaserLinks, Teacher's SourceBook pp. 11–12	• Types of Nonfiction T4

Writing Workshop: Opinion Statement

Unit One Resource Book
- Prewriting p. 51
- Drafting and Elaboration p. 52
- Peer Response Guide pp. 53–54
- Revising, Editing, and Proofreading p. 55
- Student Models pp. 56–61
- Rubric for Evaluation p. 62

Writing Coach

Writing Transparencies and Copymasters T11, T20, C25

Teacher's Guide to Assessment and Portfolio Use

Unit Assessment
- Unit One, Part 1 Test, Formal Assessment pp. 25–26
- Test Generator
- Unit One Integrated Test, Integrated Assessment pp. 1–6

Unit Technology
- ClassZone www.mcdougallittell.com
- Electronic Teacher Tools
- Electronic Library

UNIT ONE PART 2

To introduce the theme/literary period of this unit, use Fine Art Transparencies T17–19 in the Communications Transparencies and Copymasters.

	Unit Resource Book	Assessment	Integrated Technology and Media	Additional Support: Literary Analysis Transparencies
No Witchcraft for Sale *pp. 148–158*	• Summary p. 63 • Active Reading p. 64 • Literary Analysis p. 65 • Words to Know p. 66 • Grammar p. 67 • Selection Quiz p. 68	• Selection Test, Formal Assessment pp. 27–28 Test Generator	LaserLinks, Teacher's SourceBook pp. 13–14 Research Starter www.mcdougallittell.com	• Theme: Influences of Character, Setting, and Plot T5
The Son From America *pp. 159–169*	• Summary p. 69 • Active Reading p. 70 • Literary Analysis p. 71 • Words to Know p. 72 • Grammar p. 73 • Selection Quiz p. 74	• Selection Test, Formal Assessment pp. 29–30 Test Generator	Audio Library LaserLinks, Teacher's SourceBook p. 15	• Theme: Influences of Character, Setting, and Plot T5
Through the One-Way Mirror **The Border: A Glare of Truth** *pp. 170–180*	• Summary p. 75 • Active Reading p. 76 • Literary Analysis p. 77 • Words to Know p. 78 • Grammar p. 79 • Selection Quiz p. 80	• Selection Test, Formal Assessment pp. 31–32 Test Generator	Audio Library Research Starter www.mcdougallittell.com	• Theme: Influences of Character, Setting, and Plot T5
Marriage Is a Private Affair *pp. 188–195*	• Summary p. 82 • Active Reading p. 83 • Literary Analysis p. 84 • Words to Know p. 85 • Selection Quiz p. 86	• Selection Test, Formal Assessment pp. 33–34 Test Generator	Audio Library LaserLinks, Teacher's SourceBook p. 16	
Love Must Not Be Forgotten *pp. 196–210*	• Summary p. 87 • Active Reading p. 88 • Literary Analysis p. 89 • Words to Know p. 90 • Selection Quiz p. 91 • Comparing Literature p. 92	• Selection Test, Formal Assessment pp. 35–36 Test Generator	Audio Library LaserLinks, Teacher's SourceBook p. 17	• Setting T3

Writing Workshop: Focused Description

Unit One Resource Book
- Prewriting p. 93
- Drafting and Elaboration p. 94
- Peer Response Guide pp. 95–96
- Revising, Editing, and Proofreading p. 97
- Student Models pp. 98–103
- Rubric for Evaluation p. 104

Writing Coach

Writing Transparencies and Copymasters T11, T20, C26

Teacher's Guide to Assessment and Portfolio Use

Unit Assessment
- Unit One, Part 2 Test, Formal Assessment pp. 37–38
- Test Generator
- Unit One Integrated Test, Integrated Assessment pp. 1–6

Unit Technology
- ClassZone www.mcdougallittell.com
- Electronic Teacher Tools
- Electronic Library

T = Transparency C = Copymaster

	Reading and Critical Thinking Transparencies	Grammar Transparencies and Copymasters	Vocabulary Transparencies and Copymasters	Writing Transparencies and Copymasters	Communications Transparencies and Copymasters
	• Cause and Effect T1	• Action and Linking Verbs C68	• Context Clues C30	• Generating Ideas T1 • Writing Structure T6, T7, T11 • Opinion Statement C25	• Dramatic Reading T12 • Nonverbal Strategies T15

STUDENTS ACQUIRING ENGLISH

The **Spanish Study Guide,** pp. 1–30, includes language support for the following pages:

- Family and Community Involvement (per unit)
- Selection Summaries and Vocabulary
- Active Reading
- Literary Analysis

	Reading and Critical Thinking Transparencies	Grammar Transparencies and Copymasters	Vocabulary Transparencies and Copymasters	Writing Transparencies and Copymasters	Communications Transparencies and Copymasters
	• Organizational Chart: Horizontal T51	• Daily Language SkillBuilder T5	• Prefixes C31	• Organizing Your Writing T11 • Levels of Language T12 • The Uses of Dialogue T24	• Dramatic Reading T12 • Verbal Strategies T14
	• Predicting Outcomes T2	• Daily Language SkillBuilder T5 • Common and Proper Nouns C65	• Context Clues C32 • Word Origins C33	• Levels of Language T12 • Achieving Conciseness T21 • Opinion Statement C25	• Interviewing T9 • Formal Presentations T10
	• Compare and Contrast T15	• Daily Language SkillBuilder T6 • Abstract and Concrete Nouns C64 • Capitalization I C162	• Context Clues C34 • Figurative Language C35	• Varying Sentence Openers and Closers T18 • Interpretive Essay C33	
	• Locating Material in the Library I T27 • Notetaking T40	• Daily Language SkillBuilder T6 • Demonstrative Pronouns C67	• Using a Thesaurus C36 • Word Origins C37	• Generating Ideas T1 • Effective Language T13	
	• Notetaking T40	• Daily Language SkillBuilder T7 • Pronoun Case C149 • Reflexive and Intensive Pronouns C154	• Word Origins C38	• Writing Structure T6, T8 • Figurative Language and Sound Devices T15	• Formal Presentations T10

STUDENTS ACQUIRING ENGLISH

The **Spanish Study Guide,** pp. 31–46, includes language support for the following pages:

- Family and Community Involvement (per unit)
- Selection Summaries and Vocabulary
- Active Reading
- Literary Analysis

UNIT ONE
DAILY LANGUAGE SKILLBUILDERS

Selection	SkillBuilder Sentences	Suggested Answers
Harrison Bergeron	**1.** the only way humans can explore the future are through there imagination and reasoning **2.** Many science fiction storyes is set in the future	**1.** **T**he only way humans can explore the future **is** through **their** imagination and reasoning**.** **2.** Many science fiction **stories are** set in the future**.**
Searching for Summer	**1.** "Whose ringing that bell anyways, she asked."	**1.** "**Who's** ringing that bell**, anyway?"** she asked**.**
	2. Mrs. Maybury don't know the answer to your question, replied Ben.	**2.** **"M**rs. Maybury **doesn't** know the answer to your question**,"** replied Ben.
By the Waters of Babylon	**1.** John is real brave to explore a dangerously place all alone. **2.** Our teacher asked "which of the legends that Johns people believed were disproved by his journey"?	**1.** John is **really** brave to explore a **dangerous** place all alone. **2.** Our teacher asked**, "W**hich of the legends that John**'s** people believed were disproved by his journey**?"**
A Sound of Thunder	**1.** Michael Crichton writed jurassic park a novel about a present day theme park with real dinosaurs. **2.** H. G. wells was another author that wroted about time travel in the book the time machine.	**1.** Michael Crichton **wrote** <u>**J**urassic **P**ark</u>**,** a novel about a present**-**day theme park with real dinosaurs. **2.** H. G. **W**ells was another author **who wrote** about time travel in the book <u>**T**he **T**ime **M**achine</u>.
There Will Come Soft Rains	**1.** A story beginning "On monday August 19 2002 in sunnyvale california the time was two-twenty three p,m." is an example of how science fiction writers create suspence. **2.** Bradbury isnt opposed to technology: in fact he supports nasa, Americas Space Program.	**1.** A story beginning "On **M**onday**,** August 19**,** 2002**,** in **S**unnyvale**, C**alifornia**,** the time was **two twenty-three p.m.**" is an example of how science fiction writers create **suspense**. **2.** Bradbury **isn't** opposed to technology**;** in fact**,** he supports **NASA**, America**'s** **s**pace **p**rogram.

UNIT ONE
DAILY LANGUAGE SKILLBUILDERS

Selection	SkillBuilder Sentences	Suggested Answers
The Pedestrian	**1.** "How much hours of television do each of you watch every night, asked Mrs. Garza?	**1.** "How **many** hours of television **does** each of you watch every night**?"** asked Mrs. Garza.
	2. "I watch only one hour every night, I watch the evening news and then jeopardy" reply Bill.	**2.** "I watch only one hour every night**.** I watch the evening news and then **J**eopardy**,**" **replied** Bill.
Dial Versus Digital	**1.** "In our class, we read two book by Isaac Asimov one was about a robot and the other was about black holes", I said.	**1.** "In our class, we read two book**s** by Isaac Asimov**. O**ne was about a robot**,** and the other was about black holes**,"** I said.
	2. Jim said. "I liked the book about the robots. Who looked exactly like humans."	**2.** Jim said**,** "I liked the book about the robots **w**ho looked exactly like humans."
Once More to the Lake	**1.** Outboard motors move boats more swift, then inboard motors does.	**1.** Outboard motors move boats more **swiftly than** inboard motors **do**.
	2. E. B. White was real pleased to return back to the Lake.	**2.** E. B. White was **really** pleased to return to the **l**ake.
No Witchcraft for Sale	**1.** "Which character in the story does you like better" asked Joe. Gideon or did you like Teddy?	**1.** "Which character in the story **did** you like better**?"** asked Joe. **"**Gideon or Teddy?**"**
	2. Well, Lee answered, "at first I liked Teddy best but eventually I came to respect Gideon more.	**2.** **"**Well,**"** Lee answered, "at first I liked Teddy **better,** but eventually I came to respect Gideon more.**"**
The Son from America	**1.** "I was born in the United States my parents immigrated to the U.S. and never learned to speak without an accent," said Julio.	**1.** "I was born in the United States**. M**y parents immigrated to the U.S. and never learned to speak without an accent," said Julio.
	2. "Did you ever visit there native country," asked Marie.	**2.** "Did you ever visit **their** native country**?"** asked Marie.

DAILY LANGUAGE SKILLBUILDERS

Selection	SkillBuilder Sentences	Suggested Answers
Through the One-Way Mirror The Border: A Glare of Truth	**1.** "I prefer Mora's essay, said Monica, because its more persinal than Atwoods." **2.** I don't agree said Roy." I prefer Atwood's essay, it gives you more information about American culture, perceptions about americans, and information about canadian culture."	**1.** "I prefer Mora's essay," said Monica, "because it's more **personal** than Atwood's." **2.** "I don't agree," said Roy. "I prefer Atwood's essay. **I**t gives you more information about American **and Canadian** culture**s** and perceptions about **A**mericans."
Marriage Is a Private Affair	**1.** To take action aginst another Family Member is usually not a wise thing to do, Nnaemeka told Nene. **2.** neither his father or the elder in the Village was happy to hear of Nnaemekas decision.	**1.** "To take action **against** another **f**amily **m**ember is usually not a wise thing to do," Nnaemeka told Nene. **2.** **N**either his father **nor** the elder in the **v**illage was happy to hear of Nnaemeka's decision.
Love Must Not Be Forgotten	**1.** "My Mother, Zhong Yu, was a wonderful writer and I has all of her works" Shanshan told the new Librarian. **2.** Shanshan was a Teenager during the Cultural Revolution in china when criticism of her mothers work begins	**1.** "My **m**other, Zhong Yu, was a wonderful writer**,** and I **have** all of her works**,**" Shanshan told the new **l**ibrarian. **2.** Shanshan was a **t**eenager during the Cultural Revolution in **C**hina when criticism of her mother's work **began.**

INTEGRATING GRAMMAR AND LITERATURE: GRAMMAR PLANNER

	Unit One	Unit Two	Unit Three	Unit Four	Unit Five	Unit Six
Grammar Focus by Unit	Parts of Speech	The Sentence and Its Parts	Verbs and Verbals	Phrases	Clauses	Special Sentence Structures

The Language of Literature offers several options for integrating grammar instruction and literature.

- Each unit has a specific grammar focus. The grammar focus for this unit is highlighted on the planning chart. Categories of grammar skills for this unit are shown in red.
- The Pupil's Edition includes instructive features entitled *Grammar in Context*. The instruction in these features arises from the selections and relates to the grammar focus for each unit.
- The Writing Workshops in the Pupil's Edition include grammar tips that help students produce error-free drafts.
- Mini Lessons in the Teacher's Edition complement the instruction in the *Grammar in Context* features. Additional Mini Lessons relate to the grammar focus for each unit as well as to the literature.
- Daily Language SkillBuilders in the Teacher's Edition provide students with ongoing proofreading practice and reinforce punctuation, spelling, grammar and usage, and capitalization.
- Grammar Copymasters and Transparencies, which may be used independently or in conjunction with Mini Lessons in the Teacher's Edition, present grammar in a traditional, systematic sequence.

PE instruction shown in black
TE Mini Lessons shown in green

Part 1

Parts of Speech

Overview
"Harrison Bergeron," p. 26
"By the Waters of Babylon," p. 54
"By the Waters of Babylon," p. 54
"Dial Versus Digital," p. 111

Proper and Common Nouns
"Harrison Bergeron," p. 29
"Harrison Bergeron," p. 28

Possessives (Nouns)
Writing Workshop, p. 143

Action vs. Linking Verbs
"Montgomery Boycott," p. 130

Modifiers: Adjectives and Adverbs
"Searching for Summer," p. 41
"Once More to the Lake," p. 120
"Montgomery Boycott," p. 135
"Montgomery Boycott," p. 134

Proper Adjectives
"Searching for Summer," p. 37

Compound Adjectives
"There Will Come Soft Rains," p. 92

Position of Adverbs
"Once More to the Lake," pp. 122–123

Using Clauses

Sentence Fragments
Writing Workshop, p. 143

Verb Usage

Active and Passive Voice
"Once More to the Lake," p. 123

Pronoun Usage

Pronoun Agreement with Antecedent
Writing Workshop, p. 143

Pronouns: Personal and Reflexive
"By the Waters of Babylon," pp. 50–51

Using Modifiers

Avoiding Double Negatives
Writing Workshop, p. 143

End Marks and Commas

Commas in a Series
"Searching for Summer," p. 41
"Searching for Summer," p. 41

Style

Verb Choices (Choosing Precise Verbs)
"There Will Come Soft Rains," p. 94
"There Will Come Soft Rains," p. 94

Part 2

Parts of Speech

Overview
The Son from America, p. 169
"No Witchcraft for Sale," p. 156

Abstract and Concrete Nouns
"Through the One-Way Mirror," "The Border: A Glare of Truth," p. 180
"Through the One-Way Mirror," "The Border: A Glare of Truth," p. 180

Proper and Common Nouns
"The Son from America," p. 168

Demonstrative Pronouns
"Marriage Is a Private Affair," p. 191

Modifiers: Adjectives and Adverbs
"No Witchcraft for Sale," p. 158
"No Witchcraft for Sale," p. 158

Parts of the Sentence

Run-on Sentences
Writing Workshop, p. 217

Verb Usage

Verb Tenses
Writing Workshop, p. 217

Active and Passive Voice
"No Witchcraft for Sale," p. 154

Pronoun Usage

Correct Case
"Love Must Not Be Forgotten," p. 202

Pronouns: Reflexive and Intensive
"Love Must Not Be Forgotten," p. 200

Capitalization

"Through the One-Way Mirror," "The Border: A Glare of Truth," p. 176

PART 1 The Price of Progress

How do you view progress? Do you believe that we are moving inevitably toward a better life, aided by electronic wizardry, or are you worried about what might be lost along the way as our world changes rapidly? This part of Unit One features stories of people who must contend with forces of change. In various ways the selections challenge you to determine the price of progress.

ACTIVITY

Create two illustrations—one suggesting progress and the other suggesting the opposite of progress. Then compare your illustrations with those of other class-mates and discuss what the images reveal about your views of progress.

16

LEARNING the Language of Literature

Fiction is narrative writing that springs from a writer's imagination, though it may be based on actual events and real people. Although one purpose of fiction is to entertain, it can also provide important insights into human nature. The two major types of fiction are **short stories,** brief works that can usually be read in a sitting, and **novels,** longer and generally more complex narratives. Both short stories and novels share the elements of **plot, character, setting, theme,** and **point of view.** Use the following passages from Saki's "The Interlopers" to learn more about the elements of fiction.

Plot

The word ***plot*** refers to the chain of related events that take place in a story. In most plots, events are set in motion by **conflicts**—struggles between or within characters. Most plots include the following stages:

Element	Definition
exposition	provides needed background information
rising action	the part of the plot in which the conflict intensifies
climax	the turning point of the action, when the reader's interest is at its highest point
falling action or dénouement	the action after the climax, in which the conflict is often resolved

PLOT

A famous lawsuit, in the days of his grandfather, had wrested it [a woodland] from the illegal possession of a neighboring family of petty landowners; the dispossessed party had never acquiesced in the judgment of the Courts, and a long series of poaching affrays and similar scandals had embittered the relationships between the families for three generations.

YOUR TURN What conflict is introduced in the passage at the right?

Character

Characters are the individuals, real or imaginary, who take part in the action of stories. The characters who are at the center of a story's action are called **main characters;** less important ones are **minor characters.** Characters that grow or change as the plot unfolds are called **dynamic characters,** while **static characters** remain unchanged. The development of characters in fiction is known as **characterization.** There are four basic methods of characterization: physical description; a character's own speech, thoughts, feelings, and actions; the speech, thoughts, feelings, and actions of other characters; and a narrator's comments.

YOUR TURN In this passage, what techniques of characterization has Saki used?

CHARACTER

Each had a rifle in his hand, each had hate in his heart and murder uppermost in his mind. The chance had come to give full play to the passions of a lifetime. But a man who has been brought up under the code of a restraining civilization cannot easily nerve himself to shoot down his neighbor in cold blood.

OVERVIEW

Objectives

- understand the following literary terms:
  - plot
  - character
  - setting
  - theme
  - point of view
- analyze the elements of fiction and identify their characteristics
- analyze techniques used in characterization, theme, and point of view

Teaching the Lesson

This lesson analyzes terms related to the elements of fiction and shows how they are used in one type of fiction, the short story.

Introducing the Concepts

Have students bring up both fiction and nonfiction works that they've read. Ask them what differences they noted between the two genres. Then, ask students to name a novel and a short story they have read. Ask them to identify differences and similarities between the two.

Presenting the Concepts

Plot

Have students discuss the different types of conflicts encountered in stories they have read so far. As students suggest stories and conflicts, ask them to describe the climax of the story they name.

YOUR TURN The passage introduces a conflict between three generations of two families over the ownership of a woodland. The conflict is intensified by a lawsuit, scandals, and poaching.

Character

Have students mention memorable characters that they have read about in class. If they have been introduced to the terms for character development, ask students to relate these terms to the characters and the qualities that made them memorable.

YOUR TURN The techniques of characterization Saki uses in the passage are a character's actions and a narrator's comments.

Making Connections

Setting
Ask students to identify other stories in which setting plays a major part in the conflict. Discuss how natural elements, such as snowstorms, tornadoes, or floods, intensify the conflict in a story.

Theme
Caution students that a theme is not just a comment on life, people, or society that a story makes. It is also not a subject such as true love or traditional family values. Taking these as suggestions of what a theme is not, ask students to identify themes from literature and film that they found inspiring.

YOUR TURN You can infer that the theme will be a variation on the passage's last clause: "there are better things in life than getting the better of a boundary dispute."

Point of View
Remind students that one way to identify a first-person point of view is that the narrator describes the action in his or her own words, using first-person pronouns such as *I, me,* and *us.* In third-person point of view, the narrator refers to all characters with third-person pronouns such as *he, she,* and *they.*

YOUR TURN Clues that help identify the third-person limited point of view are the use of third-person pronouns (his, he) and the awareness of Ulrich's thoughts but not the man's.

Setting
The **setting** of a story is the time and place in which the events occur. The place can be real or imaginary, and the time can be a particular time of day, a season, a period of history, or even the future. Setting plays an important part in some stories, having a major effect on what happens to the characters. In other stories, the settings are only backdrops. In "The Interlopers," the setting serves as the scene of a key conflict between man and nature.

Theme
A **theme** is a central idea or message in a work of literature. It is not the work's subject but a perception about life or human nature that the writer wants to communicate. Themes are seldom stated directly; usually they must be inferred. A theme can be revealed by the ways characters change during a story and the conflicts they experience, statements in which the narrator or a character says something important about life, or by a work's title.

YOUR TURN From the passage at the right, what can you infer about a possible theme of the story?

THEME

"We have quarreled like devils all our lives over this stupid strip of forest, where the trees can't even stand upright in a breath of wind. Lying here tonight, thinking, I've come to think we've been rather fools; there are better things in life than getting the better of a boundary dispute."

Point of View
The term **point of view** refers to the relationship between a narrator and the events he or she describes. When a story's narrator is a character participating in the story's action, the story is said to be written from a **first-person point of view.** In a story told from a **third-person point of view,** on the other hand, a narrator outside the action describes the events and characters. This point of view can be subdivided into **third-person omniscient,** in which the narrator is "all-knowing," able to see into the minds of all the characters, and **third-person limited,** in which the narrator perceives events only as an observer or only through the eyes of one character. A narrator whose viewpoint is limited to that of a single character will describe only that character's feelings and only the events that the character witnesses.

YOUR TURN What clues in this passage can help you identify the point of view from which the story is told?

POINT OF VIEW

Ulrich was silent for a few minutes and lay listening to the weary screeching of the wind. An idea was slowly forming and growing in his brain, an idea that gained strength every time that he looked across at the man who was fighting so grimly against pain and exhaustion.

Fiction has the capacity to entertain and the power to illuminate through compelling plots, strong characterization, detailed descriptions of setting, and universal themes. Though each story is unique, the reading strategies outlined here can help you get the most from any work of fiction you read.

Reading Fiction

Strategies for Using Your READER'S NOTEBOOK

As you read, take notes to
- **connect** your personal experiences to the feelings, motives, and actions of the characters you are reading about
- record any phrases, passages, images, or ideas that you find interesting
- write down any **questions** you have about plot, character, setting, theme, or point of view

1 Strategies for Understanding Plot

- Note the cause-and-effect links between events.
- Identify the main conflict, but also take note of the minor difficulties and problems that characters encounter.

2 Strategies for Analyzing Characters

- In a chart like this one, record examples of the methods of characterization that the writer uses. Note which characters are dynamic and which are static.
- Look for clues to each character's motives and actions. **Evaluate** the character's personality, and **predict** what he or she will do next.
- Watch for signs of internal conflict—that is, emotional or psychological conflict within characters.

"The Interlopers"

Character	Ulrich
Words & actions	"I've come to think we've been rather fools."
Thoughts	
Appearance	
What others think	

3 Strategies for Visualizing Setting

- Look for specific adjectives and details that convey the place and time of the story.
- Use the writer's descriptions to help you **visualize,** or "see," the characters in that setting.
- **Evaluate** the effects the setting may have on the characters and on the plot of the story.

4 Strategies for Recognizing Themes

- Note any sentences or ideas that you find especially interesting. They might be clues to a theme.
- Observe how characters change and what lessons they learn during the story.
- **Question** whether a title offers any clues to a theme.

5 Strategies for Determining Point of View

- Observe the pronouns the narrator uses. *I, me,* and *us* signal a first-person point of view; *he, she,* and *they,* a third-person point of view.
- If the story is told from a third-person point of view, **question** whether an omniscient narrator is supplying information that no single observer could know, or if the information is limited to what an outside observer or a single character might see and hear.

Need More Help?

Remember that active readers use the essential reading strategies explained on page 7: **visualize, predict, clarify, question, connect, evaluate, monitor.**

OVERVIEW

Objectives

- understand fiction by analyzing elements of plot, character, setting, theme, and point of view
- identify elements of fiction and use them to predict, visualize, question, and evaluate a story

Teaching the Lesson

Reading Fiction

The strategies on this page will help students learn and apply specific skills for identifying the elements of plot, character, setting, theme, and point of view in works of fiction.

Presenting the Strategies

Help students understand the elements of fiction by applying them to a simple children's story they are familiar with, such as "The Three Little Pigs," "The Tale of Peter Rabbit," or a story they have previously read in class.

Strategies for Using Your Reader's Notebook

Have students make two columns in their Reader's Notebook for writing responses that link their own personal experiences (either similar or contrasting) with a character's experiences. The columns should be headed "[name of the character]'s Experiences" and "My Experiences."

1 Strategies for Understanding Plot

Explain to students that a key word in a cause-and-effect relationship is the word *because.* At any point in the story, have students pause to complete the following frame:________________ is occurring because ________________.

2 Strategies for Analyzing Characters

Remind students that, in addition to actions, characterization can occur principally through what a character says or thinks, what other characters say about that character, and what the author or narrator says about the character.

3 Strategies for Visualizing Setting

Remind students that minimal reference to concrete physical details of sight, sound, and smell will often go a long way in suggesting a setting or atmosphere. Have them close their eyes to visualize the setting in the story, then ask them to list concrete details in the setting they've just visualized.

4 Strategies for Recognizing Themes

When they finish the story, have students describe the main character at the beginning of the story and that same character at the end of the story. What did the character learn? How does the title relate to the story? Students should apply these questions to a story and state the theme in one sentence.

5 Strategies for Determining Point of View

Have students select two passages from the story: a dramatic scene with dialogue and a narrative passage without dialogue. Then have students list all the details they can find that indicate the point of view the author is using.

OVERVIEW

This selection is included in the **Grade 10 InterActive Reader.**

Objectives

1. understand and appreciate **science fiction (Literary Analysis)**
2. understand the **theme** of the story **(Literary Analysis)**
3. **make inferences (Active Reading)**

Summary

The year is 2081; George and Hazel Bergeron are living in a society in which everyone is equal. Citizens who are stronger, more attractive, or more intelligent are forced to wear "handicaps" that bring them down to an "average" level. Although most people are resigned to this system, the Bergerons' genius son Harrison resists by plotting to overthrow the government. Consequently, he is imprisoned. George and Hazel see their son on TV during his escape from jail. Harrison throws off his handicaps and dances with a ballerina, also freed from her handicap. Because they are too beautiful and too talented for society, they must be eliminated; both are shot by the Handicapper General, Diana Moon Glampers.

Thematic Link

Vonnegut portrays a society in which everyone has to be equal; for this they have paid a high price: the elimination of all individual differences; everyone is average.

5-Minute Warm-Up

Daily Language SkillBuilder

Have students **proofread** the display sentences on page 15i and write them correctly. The sentences also appear on Transparency 1 of **Grammar Transparencies and Copymasters.**

Mini Lesson **Preteaching Vocabulary**

If you would like to preteach the WORDS TO KNOW for this selection, use the Mini Lesson on pp. 22–23.

"The year was 2081, and everybody was finally equal."

Harrison Bergeron

Short Story by KURT VONNEGUT, JR.

Connect to Your Life

Equal Is as Equal Does Can you think of a time when you've had to hide your skills for someone else's sake? Maybe you gave a wrong answer in class, just to avoid looking too smart in front of friends. Or perhaps you let a friend beat you at a video game. Discuss the advantages and disadvantages of covering up your strengths to pretend as though you are "equal" to someone else. Use examples to support your opinion.

Build Background

What's Your Handicap? If you've played golf or run a footrace, you might know the term "handicap." It's a way to even up the game so that good, average, and poor players can compete as equals. In a footrace, for example, faster runners might handicap themselves by giving slower runners a head start. In golf, where players win by completing the course with the fewest number of strokes, better golfers sometimes start the game with a handicap of extra strokes. In "Harrison Bergeron," people are given handicaps in daily life, so that no one will be any stronger, smarter, or better-looking than anyone else.

WORDS TO KNOW
Vocabulary Preview

calibrated	symmetry
consternation	synchronizing
cower	vague
hindrance	vigilance
luminous	wince

Focus Your Reading

LITERARY ANALYSIS | **THEME** Stories often have a central idea or message, also known as the **theme.** Theme gives meaning to the story by providing some insight into life or human nature. The first lines of "Harrison Bergeron" give you a clue to the story's theme:

The year was 2081, and everybody was finally equal. They weren't only equal before God and the law. They were equal every which way.

As you read, think about how the issue of equality relates to the theme of the story.

ACTIVE READING | **MAKING INFERENCES** **Inferences** are logical guesses based on clues in the text and on common sense. Read the following sentence from "Harrison Bergeron":

It wasn't clear at first as to what the bulletin was about, since the announcer, like all announcers, had a serious speech impediment.

In that society, all news announcers have speech impediments, which would make them unfit for the job by today's standards. From this clue, you can infer that people in that society are not hired according to their strengths.

READER'S NOTEBOOK As you read this story, jot down at least five inferences you can make about the main characters and the society. Fill in a chart like the one shown.

Clue		Inference
All announcers have speech impediments.	→	People are not hired for their strengths.
	→	

LESSON RESOURCES

UNIT ONE RESOURCE BOOK, pp. 4–9

ASSESSMENT RESOURCES

Formal Assessment, pp. 7–8

Teacher's Guide to Assessment and Portfolio Use

Test Generator

SKILLS TRANSPARENCIES AND COPYMASTERS

Literary Analysis

- Theme, T1 (for Activity, p. 27)

Reading and Critical Thinking

- Making Inferences, T17 (for Think Critically, item 4, p. 27)

Grammar

- Parts of Speech, C62 (for Mini Lesson, p. 26)

Vocabulary

- Context Clues, C18 (for Mini Lesson, p. 22)
- Figurative Language, C19 (for Mini Lesson, p. 24)

Writing

- Writing Process, T1, T2 (for Writing Option 2, p. 28)
- Elaboration, T10 (for Writing Option 1, p. 28)
- Point of View, T23 (for Inquiry & Research, p. 28)

Communications

- Evaluation Matrix: Film/Video, T7 (for Activities & Explorations 2, p. 28)
- Evaluating Roles in Groups, T8 (for Inquiry and Research, p. 28)
- Impromptu Speaking: Dialogue, Role-Play, Debate T13 (for Activities & Explorations 1, p. 28)

INTEGRATED TECHNOLOGY

Audio Library

Video: Literature in Performance

- *Harrison Bergeron.* See **Video Resource Book,** pp. 3–9.

Visit our website:
www.mcdougallittell.com

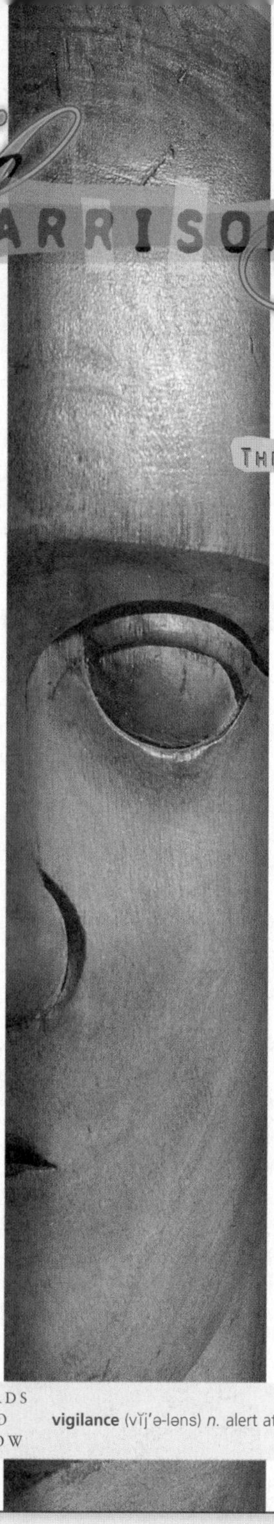

Harrison Bergeron

Kurt Vonnegut, Jr.

The year was 2081, and everybody was finally equal. They weren't only equal before God and the law. They were equal every which way. Nobody was smarter than anybody else. Nobody was better looking than anybody else. Nobody was stronger or quicker than anybody else. All this equality was due to the 211th, 212th, and 213th Amendments to the Constitution, and to the unceasing vigilance of agents of the United States Handicapper General.

Some things about living still weren't quite right, though. April, for instance, still drove people crazy by not being springtime. And it was in that clammy month that the H-G men took George and Hazel Bergeron's fourteen-year-old son, Harrison, away.

It was tragic, all right, but George and Hazel couldn't think about it very hard. Hazel had a perfectly average intelligence, which meant she couldn't think about anything except in short bursts. And George, while his intelligence was way above normal, had a little mental handicap radio in his ear. He was required by law to wear it at all times. It was tuned to a government transmitter.[1] Every twenty seconds or so, the transmitter would send out some sharp noise to keep people like George from taking unfair advantage of their brains.

Detail of *The Spirit of Our Time* (about 1920), Raoul Hausmann. Assemblage with wigmaker's dummy head, 12 ¾″ high. Collections Musée National d'Art Moderne, Centre Georges Pompidou, Paris.

1. **transmitter:** an electronic device for broadcasting radio signals.

WORDS TO KNOW

vigilance (vĭj′ə-ləns) *n.* alert attention; watchfulness

21

TEACHING THE LITERATURE

Customizing Instruction

Less Proficient Readers

Ask students to consider these questions as they read:

- Who are the main characters?
- What is the setting of the story?
- What is the major conflict of the story?

Students Acquiring English

Tell students that Vonnegut uses many idioms and slang words in this story. Suggest that they keep a list of words or phrases that cause them difficulty as they read. Then discuss these problem phrases as a class.

Use **Spanish Study Guide** for additional support, pp. 4–6.

Gifted and Talented

Have students investigate how our society helps people who have handicaps or disabilities.

BLOCK SCHEDULING: MANAGING TIME

If your schedule requires that you cover the lesson objectives in a shorter time, use . . .

- Preparing to Read, p. 20
- Thinking Through the Literature, p. 27
- Vocabulary in Action, p. 28
- Grammar in Context, p. 29

If you want to take advantage of longer class time, use . . .

- TE Teaching Options: Preteaching Vocabulary, pp. 22–23; Vocabulary Strategy, p. 24; Viewing and Representing, p. 25
- Choices & Challenges and Author Activity, pp. 28–29

Reading and Analyzing

Reading Skills and Strategies: PREVIEW

Briefly summarize the events of the story, without revealing the ending. Have students examine the images and study the active reading questions.

Literary Analysis THEME

The theme is the author's central message, which often reveals the writer's view of life. To help students discover the theme of this story, ask them to think about what happens to the central characters as the story progresses. Have the characters changed? Have they learned anything? What is the conflict of the story? Answers to these questions may provide clues to the story's theme.

Use **Unit One Resource Book** p. 6 for more practice.

ACTIVE READING

A VISUALIZE The dancers probably looked like amateurs with no particular talent.

Active Reading MAKING INFERENCES

Explain that making inferences, logical guesses based on clues in the text and common sense, is an important reading skill because it helps the reader anticipate the events of the plot. Point out some of the clues like the ones given below, and guide students to make inferences about them.

Use **Unit One Resource Book** p. 5 for more practice.

ACTIVE READING

B MAKE INFERENCES The ballerinas would have been excellent dancers without their handicaps.

George and Hazel were watching television. There were tears on Hazel's cheeks, but she'd forgotten for the moment what they were about.

On the television screen were ballerinas.

A buzzer sounded in George's head. His thoughts fled in panic, like bandits from a burglar alarm.

"That was a real pretty dance, that dance they just did," said Hazel.

"Huh?" said George.

"That dance—it was nice," said Hazel.

"Yup," said George. He tried to think a little about the ballerinas. They weren't really very good—no better than anybody else would have been, anyway. They were burdened with sashweights[2] and bags of birdshot,[3] and their faces were masked, so that no one, seeing a free and graceful gesture or a pretty face, would feel like something the cat drug in. George was toying with the vague notion that maybe dancers shouldn't be handicapped. But he didn't get very far with it before another noise in his ear radio scattered his thoughts.

"Huh?" said George.

A ACTIVE READING

VISUALIZE Imagine the dancers with their masks and handicaps. What do you think their dance looks like?

George winced. So did two out of the eight ballerinas.

Hazel saw him wince. Having no mental handicap herself, she had to ask George what the latest sound had been.

"Sounded like somebody hitting a milk bottle with a ball peen hammer,[4]" said George.

"I'd think it would be real interesting, hearing all the different sounds," said Hazel, a little envious. "All the things they think up."

"Um," said George.

"Only, if I was Handicapper General, you know what I would do?" said Hazel. Hazel, as a matter of fact, bore a strong resemblance to the Handicapper General, a woman named Diana Moon Glampers. "If I was Diana Moon Glampers," said Hazel, "I'd have chimes on Sunday—just chimes. Kind of in honor of religion."

"I could think, if it was just chimes," said George.

"Well—maybe make 'em real loud," said Hazel. "I think I'd make a good Handicapper General."

"Good as anybody else," said George.

"Who knows better'n I do what normal is?" said Hazel.

"Right," said George. He began to think glimmeringly about his abnormal son who was now in jail, about Harrison, but a twenty-one-gun salute in his head stopped that. 1

"Boy!" said Hazel, "that was a doozy, wasn't it?"

It was such a doozy that George was white and trembling, and tears stood on the rims of his red eyes. Two of the eight ballerinas had collapsed to the studio floor and were holding their temples.

ACTIVE READING

MAKE INFERENCES What inference can you make about the ballerinas from this description? B

"All of a sudden you look so tired," said Hazel. "Why don't you stretch out on the sofa, so's you can rest your handicap bag on the pillows, honeybunch." She was referring to the

2. **sashweights:** lead weights used in some kinds of windows to keep them from falling shut when raised.
3. **birdshot:** tiny lead pellets made to be loaded in shotgun shells.
4. **ball peen hammer:** a hammer with a head having one flat side and one rounded side.

WORDS TO KNOW

vague (vāg) *adj.* unclear; hazy
wince (wĭns) *v.* to shrink or flinch involuntarily, especially in pain

22

Teaching Options

Mini Lesson Preteaching Vocabulary

USING CONTEXT CLUES Ask students to review the list of WORDS TO KNOW. Remind them that they can often understand the meaning of an unfamiliar word by examining the context in which a word is used. Use the model sentence to show how context clues provide inferences to word meaning.

Model Sentence

The loud knock on the door forced him to *cower* in fear behind the wall.

Instruction

- Write the model sentence on the chalkboard.
- Ask a volunteer to summarize the meaning of the sentence.
- Have students infer meanings of the word cower from the meaning of the sentence.
- Ask a volunteer to use the word *cower* in another sentence.

forty-seven pounds of birdshot in a canvas bag, which was padlocked around George's neck. "Go on and rest the bag for a little while," she said. "I don't care if you're not equal to me for a while."

George weighed the bag with his hands. "I don't mind it," he said. "I don't notice it any more. It's just a part of me."

2 "You been so tired lately—kind of wore out," said Hazel. "If there was just some way we could make a little hole in the bottom of the bag, and just take out a few of them lead balls. Just a few."

"Two years in prison and two thousand dollars fine for every ball I took out," said George. "I don't call that a bargain."

"If you could just take a few out when you came home from work," said Hazel. "I mean—you don't compete with anybody around here. You just set around."

"If I tried to get away with it," said George, "then other people'd get away with it—and pretty soon we'd be right back to the dark ages again, with everybody competing against everybody else. You wouldn't like that, would you?"

"I'd hate it," said Hazel.

"There you are," said George. "The minute people start cheating on laws, what do you think happens to society?"

If Hazel hadn't been able to come up with an answer to this question, George couldn't have supplied one. A siren was going off in his head.

3 "Reckon it'd fall all apart," said Hazel.

"What would?" said George blankly.

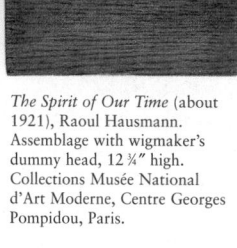

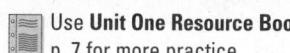

The Spirit of Our Time (about 1921), Raoul Hausmann. Assemblage with wigmaker's dummy head, 12 ¾″ high. Collections Musée National d'Art Moderne, Centre Georges Pompidou, Paris.

"Society," said Hazel uncertainly. "Wasn't that what you just said?"

"Who knows?" said George.

The television program was suddenly interrupted for a news bulletin. It wasn't clear at first as to what the bulletin was about, since the announcer, like all announcers, had a serious speech impediment.[5] For about half a minute, and in a state of high excitement, the announcer tried to say, 4

"Ladies and gentlemen—"

He finally gave up, handed the bulletin to a ballerina to read.

"That's all right—" Hazel said of the announcer, "he tried. That's the big thing. He tried to do the best he could with what God gave him. He should get a nice raise for trying so hard."

"Ladies and gentlemen—" said the ballerina, reading the bulletin. She must have been extraordinarily beautiful, because the mask she wore was hideous. And it was easy to see that she was the strongest and most graceful of all the dancers, for her handicap bags were as big as those worn by two-hundred-pound men.

And she had to apologize at once for her voice, which was a very unfair voice for a woman to use. Her voice was a warm, luminous, timeless

5. **speech impediment** (ĭm-pĕd′ə-mənt): a physical defect that prevents a person from speaking normally.

WORDS TO KNOW **luminous** (lo͞o′mə-nəs) *adj.* bright; brilliant

Customizing Instruction

Students Acquiring English

1 Help students understand Hazel's language by explaining the contractions she uses ('em = them; better'n = better than) and the term *doozy,* which means "big one."

2 Point out the nonstandard usage of *them.* Explain that *those* would be the grammatically correct word in this context. *Them* is a pronoun and should not be used as a demonstrative adjective.

3 Help students understand the meaning of *reckon.* First, explain that Hazel has left off the subject of the sentence, "I." Then, tell them that *reckon* means "believe" or "think."

Less Proficient Readers

4 Use the following question to help students understand why the television broadcast announcer spoke hesitatingly.

- Why was the television announcer excited?

Answer: He had just learned that Harrison Bergeron had escaped from jail.

Exercises Read the following sentences. Ask students to use context clues to determine the meanings of the italicized terms.

1. Is that thermometer *calibrated* in degrees Celsius or Fahrenheit?
2. When the nurse pricks my finger at the doctor's office, I always *wince.*
3. The pearl bracelet was *luminous* in the sunlight.
4. The comedian's *consternation* was obvious when his monologue was interrupted by a police chase through the theater.
5. I have a *vague* idea of what you are talking about, but I need more information before I can proceed.
6. Leave your backpack at home because it will be a *hindrance* to you in the crowded room.
7. That architect always balances the elements of her designs to preserve *symmetry.*
8. Let's agree to guard the house with *vigilance.*
9. The swimmers stayed in formation, *synchronizing* their strokes perfectly.

Use **Unit One Resource Book** p. 7 for more practice.

A lesson on context clues appears on page 56 in the Pupil's Edition.

Reading and Analyzing

ACTIVE READING

A PREDICT Harrison may try to change the system and free people from their handicaps.

Reading Skills and Strategies: QUESTIONING

B Students should monitor their reading strategies and make modifications when understanding breaks down. Encourage students to question what happens and what is said as they read. Ask them what the author means when he says, "In the race of life, Harrison carried three hundred pounds."

Possible Response: Harrison's handicap must keep him from excelling. He must be like everyone else.

Literary Analysis: ELEMENTS OF SCIENCE FICTION

The setting of a science fiction story often helps to explain the events of the plot. Ask students to describe the setting of this story and how it contributes to the plot.

Answer: It is set in April 2081 in a society that has been equalized to the point that the lives of the characters are dull, uninteresting, and highly regulated.

melody. "Excuse me—" she said, and she began again, making her voice absolutely uncompetitive.

"Harrison Bergeron, age fourteen," she said in a grackle[6] squawk, "has just escaped from jail, where he was held on suspicion of plotting to overthrow the government. He is a genius and an athlete, is under-handicapped, and should be regarded as extremely dangerous."

A **ACTIVE READING**

PREDICT What do you think will happen now that Harrison has escaped?

1 A police photograph of Harrison Bergeron was flashed on the screen—upside down, then sideways, upside down again, then right side up. The picture showed the full length of Harrison against a background calibrated in feet and inches. He was exactly seven feet tall.

"I AM THE EMPEROR!"

The rest of Harrison's appearance was Halloween and hardware. Nobody had ever born heavier handicaps. He had outgrown hindrances faster than the H-G men could think them up. Instead of a little ear radio for a mental handicap, he wore a tremendous pair of earphones, and spectacles with thick wavy lenses. The spectacles were intended to make him not only half blind, but to give him whanging headaches besides.

Scrap metal was hung all over him. Ordinarily, there was a certain symmetry, a military neatness to the handicaps issued to strong people, but Harrison looked like a walking junkyard. In the race of life, Harrison carried three hundred pounds. B

And to offset his good looks, the H-G men required that he wear at all times a red rubber ball for a nose, keep his eyebrows shaved off, and cover his even white teeth with black caps at snaggle-tooth random.

"If you see this boy," said the ballerina, "do not—I repeat, do not—try to reason with him."

There was the shriek of a door being torn from its hinges.

Screams and barking cries of consternation came from the television set. The photograph of Harrison Bergeron on the screen jumped again and again, as though dancing to the tune of an earthquake. 2

George Bergeron correctly identified the earthquake, and well he might have—for many was the time his own home had danced to the same crashing tune. . . . "That must be Harrison!" said George.

The realization was blasted from his mind instantly by the sound of an automobile collision in his head.

When George could open his eyes again, the photograph of Harrison was gone. A living, breathing Harrison filled the screen.

Clanking, clownish, and huge, Harrison stood in the center of the studio. The knob of the uprooted studio door was still in his hand. Ballerinas, technicians, musicians, and announcers cowered on their knees before him, expecting to die.

"I am the Emperor!" cried Harrison. "Do you hear? I am the Emperor! Everybody must do what I say at once!" He stamped his foot and the studio shook.

---

6. **grackle:** a blackbird with a harsh, unpleasant call.

WORDS TO KNOW

calibrated (kăl′ə-brā′tĭd) *adj.* marked with measurements **calibrate** *v.*
hindrance (hĭn′drəns) *n.* something that interferes with an activity; obstacle
symmetry (sĭm′ĭ-trē) *n.* a similarity between the two sides of something; balance
consternation (kŏn′stər-nā′shən) *n.* a confused amazement or fear
cower (kou′ər) *v.* to draw back in fear; cringe

24

Teaching Options

Mini Lesson Vocabulary Strategy

FIGURATIVE LANGUAGE: SIMILES **Instruction** A simile is a figure of speech that compares two things that are basically unlike yet have something in common. A simile states this by means of the word *like* or *as.* Remind students that they can rely on context to determine the meaning of unfamiliar words. Write these examples of similes on the chalkboard and discuss them with students:

The baby was as happy as a lark.
She felt like a bird in paradise.

Practice Point out the simile on page 25: *"The bar snapped like celery."* Ask students to visualize a stalk of celery snapping—how easy is it to snap celery? What sound does it make? Then ask them what Vonnegut is saying with this simile.

Answer: Harrison snaps the bar easily. He is exceptionally powerful.

Ask students to write a simile to describe each of these scenes:

- students eating lunch in the cafeteria are like . . .
- runners racing on a track are like . . .
- a student excited about a report card is . . . . as a . . .

Use **Vocabulary Transparencies and Copymasters,** p. 19.

A lesson on figurative language appears on page 419 in the Pupil's Edition.

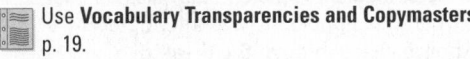

The Mad Painter [Il pittore matto] (1981–1982), Enzo Cucchi. Oil on canvas, 119½″ × 83¾″. Solomon R. Guggenheim Museum, New York. Exxon Corporation Purchase Award with additional funds contributed by the Junior Associates, 1982. Photo by David Heald copyright © The Solomon R. Guggenheim Foundation, New York (FN 82.2927).

"Even as I stand here—" he bellowed, "crippled, hobbled, sickened—I am a greater ruler than any man who ever lived! Now watch me become what I *can* become!"

Harrison tore the straps of his handicap harness like wet tissue paper, tore straps guaranteed to support five thousand pounds.

Harrison's scrap-iron handicaps crashed to the floor.

Harrison thrust his thumbs under the bar of the padlock that secured his head harness. The bar snapped like celery. Harrison smashed his headphones and spectacles against the wall.

He flung away his rubber-ball nose, revealed a man that would have awed Thor, the god of thunder.

"I shall now select my Empress!" he said, looking down on the cowering people. "Let the first woman who dares rise to her feet claim her mate and her throne!"

A moment passed, and then a ballerina arose, swaying like a willow. 3

Harrison plucked the mental handicap from her ear, snapped off her physical handicaps with marvelous delicacy. Last of all, he removed her mask.

She was blindingly beautiful. "Now—" said Harrison, taking her hand, "shall we show the people the meaning of the word dance? Music!" he commanded.

The musicians scrambled back into their chairs, and Harrison stripped them of their handicaps, too. "Play your best," he told them, "and I'll make you barons and dukes and earls."

The music began. It was normal at first—cheap, silly, false. But Harrison snatched two musicians from their chairs, waved them like batons as he sang the music as he wanted it

Customizing Instruction

Less Proficient Readers

1 Help students understand that the photograph is flipped around three times before appearing right side up because the person displaying the photograph is not very good at his or her job. Remind students that they can use clues such as these to make inferences.

2 Make sure students understand that what is happening is not actually an earthquake but Harrison's footsteps. Ask students to find the clue that tells them that *earthquake* is being used figuratively.

Answer: The words *as though*

What kind of figurative language is this?

Answer: A simile

3 Have students suggest why the ballerina decides to join Harrison.

Possible Responses: She is beautiful and intelligent and sees her match in Harrison; she wants to be Empress.

Mini Lesson Viewing and Representing

The Mad Painter [Il pittore matto] **by Enzo Cucchi**

ART APPRECIATION

Instruction Artists rely on elements of art and principles of design to help them express their ideas and feelings. Cucchi paid close attention to color as an element and movement as a principle in *The Mad Painter.*

Application Have students describe the mood conveyed by the colors in this painting. Have them point out lines and shapes that make them think of movement. What other aspects of the painting reflect the meaning of Vonnegut's story?

Possible Response: The colors convey an angry, powerful mood. Curved lines in the man's garment and wavy lines in the background suggest movement. The white masklike shape makes this figure seem extraordinary.

Reading and Analyzing

Reading Skills and Strategies: PREDICT

A Have students predict how the H-G will respond to Harrison's defiant behavior.

Possible Responses: The H-G will execute Harrison; the H-G will put Harrison back in prison.

Literary Analysis THEME

B Ask students to share their thoughts about the theme, or Vonnegut's message.

Possible Responses: It is important to take a stand against what you believe is wrong; believing in yourself will enable you to do amazing things.

After they finish the story, ask students if they would state the theme differently.

Possible Responses: Yes, because the deaths of Harrison and the dancer give the story a pessimistic turn.

Active Reading MAKING INFERENCES

Have students look back through the story for details about the ballerina who danced with Harrison. Ask students to make inferences about her character and support their inferences with text evidence.

Possible Response: If she didn't have to wear a handicap, she would have been a talented ballerina. By accepting Harrison's offer to dance, she shows she is willing to defy the system, and to accept the consequences.

Literary Analysis: SCIENCE FICTION

After students have read the story, ask them why this selection is considered science fiction.

Possible Responses: The story comments on present-day society by examining an imagined future society.

played. He slammed them back into their chairs.

The music began again and was much improved.

Harrison and his Empress merely listened to the music for a while—listened gravely, as though synchronizing their heartbeats with it.

They shifted their weights to their toes.

Harrison placed his big hands on the girl's tiny waist, letting her sense the weightlessness that would soon be hers.

And then, in an explosion of joy and grace, into the air they sprang!

Not only were the laws of the land abandoned, but the law of gravity and the laws of motion as well.

They reeled, whirled, swiveled, flounced, capered, gamboled,[7] and spun.

They leaped like deer on the moon.

The studio ceiling was thirty feet high, but each leap brought the dancers nearer to it.

It became their obvious intention to kiss the ceiling.

They kissed it.

And then, neutralizing gravity with love and pure will, they remained suspended in air inches below the ceiling, and they kissed each other for a long, long time.

A It was then that Diana Moon Glampers, the Handicapper General, came into the studio with a double-barreled ten-gauge shotgun. She fired twice, and the Emperor and the Empress were dead before they hit the floor.

Diana Moon Glampers loaded the gun again. She aimed it at the musicians and told them they had ten seconds to get their handicaps back on.

It was then that the Bergerons' television tube burned out.

Hazel turned to comment about the blackout to George. But George had gone out into the kitchen for a can of beer.

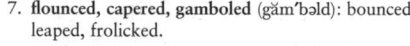

George came back in with the beer, paused while a handicap signal shook him up. And then he sat down again. "You been crying?" he said to Hazel.

"Yup," she said.

"What about?" he said.

"I forget," she said. "Something real sad on television."

"What was it?" he said.

"It's all kind of mixed up in my mind," said Hazel.

"Forget sad things," said George.

"I always do," said Hazel.

"That's my girl," said George. He winced. There was the sound of a riveting[8] gun in his head.

"Gee—I could tell that one was a doozy," said Hazel.

"You can say that again," said George.

"Gee—" said Hazel, "I could tell that one was a doozy." ❖ **B**

---

7. **flounced, capered, gamboled** (găm′bəld): bounced, leaped, frolicked.
8. **riveting** (rĭv′ĭ-tĭng) **gun:** a power tool used to hammer the bolts (called rivets) used in construction work to fasten metal beams or plates together.

WORDS TO KNOW **synchronizing** (sĭng′krə-nī′zĭng) *v.* matching the timing of **synchronize** *v.*

26

Teaching Options

Mini Lesson Grammar

DETERMINING PARTS OF SPEECH

Instruction Remind students that a *noun* is a word that names a person, place, thing, or idea; a *verb* is a word that expresses action or a state of being; and an *adjective* is a word that modifies a noun. Point out that some words, such as *jump,* can be dual parts of speech. Write the following sentence on the chalkboard:

In (an ideal) society, everyone is (equal).

Practice Have students copy the following sentence. Ask them to underline the nouns once and the verbs twice. Then have them put parentheses around each adjective.

(Beautiful) ballerinas were burdened with sashweights and bags of birdshot.

Use **Grammar Transparencies and Copymasters,** p. 61.

Use McDougal Littell's ***Language Network,*** Chapter 1, for more instruction in parts of speech.

Connect to the Literature

1. **What Do You Think?** What is your response to the story's ending? Discuss it with your classmates.

Comprehension Check
- Why does Harrison's father, George, have difficulty thinking about anything for very long?
- What is the purpose of all the gear Harrison wears?
- What does Diana Moon Glampers do to Harrison? Why?

Think Critically

2. What do you think Harrison's rebellion reveals about his **character** and his values? Support your opinion with references to the text.

3. Do you feel sorry for George and Hazel Bergeron, or do you find fault with the way they respond to events? Explain your answer.

THINK ABOUT
- George's handicap
- Hazel's "perfectly average intelligence"
- their comments about their son

4. **ACTIVE READING** **MAKING INFERENCES** Based on the chart you made in your **READER'S NOTEBOOK**, what conclusions can you draw about the society in which the characters live?

5. What do you think Vonnegut might be trying to say about today's society and the role a government can play in achieving equality among people? Use examples from the story to support your opinion.

Extend Interpretations

6. **What If?** Imagine that Diana Moon Glampers had missed and that Harrison and the ballerina escaped. How might the story's **plot** have changed? Write your response in your **READER'S NOTEBOOK**.

7. **Connect to Life** The United States has often been called the land of opportunity. This suggests that individuals are free to pursue their dreams to the best of their abilities, which may differ greatly. At the same time, our Declaration of Independence states that all people are created equal. In what ways is there a tension between equality and opportunity in our nation today?

Literary Analysis

THEME The **theme** of a story is its central message. It expresses an attitude or insight into life or human nature. To identify the theme of a story, you must draw inferences from clues. One way to uncover the theme is to consider what happens to the main characters. For example, Harrison's death and the subsequent responses of his parents suggest that Vonnegut is criticizing both the society, the government, and the parents.

Activity Look back through the story. List phrases, sentences, or events that provide clues to the theme. Pay attention to the relationship between the phrases Vonnegut uses and the events he writes about. You may find that his use of humor is not entirely lighthearted. Then write a sentence stating the theme in your own words. Compare your theme statement with those of your classmates.

SCIENCE FICTION Stories that tell about the future by blending scientific data and theory with the author's creative imagination are called **science fiction.** Most science fiction comments in some way on present-day society. In "Harrison Bergeron," the author imagines a future society in which competition and inequality have been eliminated.

Paired Activity Work with a partner and look for elements of science fiction in the story. Keep track of these elements, and when you are done, discuss your results with a larger group.

GUIDING STUDENT RESPONSE

Connect to the Literature

1. **What Do You Think?**
Students may feel that the ending gives a depressing view of our future.

Comprehension Check
- He wears a device that emits a loud, unpleasant sound about every 20 seconds.
- The heavy gear handicaps his bright mind, subdues his strength, and disguises his good looks.
- She kills him because he demonstrates his physical and mental superiority by rejecting governmental attempts to handicap him.

Use Selection Quiz in **Unit One Resource Book,** p. 9.

Think Critically

2. Possible Responses: He has a strong and fiercely independent character and values freedom and the rights of the individual. For example, he says, "Even as I stand here—crippled, hobbled, sickened—I am a greater ruler than any man who ever lived! Now watch me become what I *can* become!" He believes no imposed handicaps can truly shape his personality.
3. Possible Responses: Students may feel that George and Hazel are victims of a society in which no one can excel. George's handicap prevents him from using his true intelligence, Hazel lacks the intelligence to rebel.
4. Have students support their responses with evidence from the text. This society is oppressive and controlling, ruling its citizens by crushing their individuality and making them afraid. Its belief in equality has brought about mediocrity.
5. Possible Responses: Their society has gone to extremes to control exceptional individuals. No one is better off or more talented than anyone else. When Vonnegut says at the beginning of the story that the 211th, 212th, and 213th Constitutional Amendments enacted the handicapping movement, he is using irony to imply that passing too many laws will erode the basic rights and freedoms that the Constitution is supposed to ensure.

Extend Interpretations

What If? Students' responses should demonstrate a basic understanding of the characters of Harrison and the ballerina. They are strong characters who might be able to change the course set by the society.

Connect to Life Students will need to discuss what is meant by equality and how it may affect the opportunities available to each individual. How much does achieving your dreams depend on the individual; how much on the laws of the land?

Literary Analysis

Theme Students may find many clues to the theme, such as the numerous amendments to the Constitution, the irony that April still was not springlike, Hazel's inability to think of anything except in short bursts, the lack of competition, the lack of beauty. Thematic statements may focus on the importance of individuality, how society can benefit from individual differences, or Vonnegut's implied criticism of excessive governmental regulations.

Choices & CHALLENGES

Writing Options

1. Glampers's Report In order to satisfy her superiors, Diana Moon Glampers must make a complete report of events that led her to shoot Harrison. Write the official report. Explain events from her point of view. Include her rationale for her extreme action.

2. Warden's Address Alarmed by Harrison's escape, the head of the prison delivers a speech to the heads of state, urging them to clamp down on inequality. Write the speech, detailing the warden's concerns and suggestions. Place the report in your **Working Portfolio.**

Activities & Explorations

1. News at Six With three or four classmates, create a TV news report on Harrison Bergeron's escape and death. Divide up the roles of news reporter, Diana Moon Glampers, and various eyewitnesses. Present your telecast before your class. ~ **SPEAKING AND LISTENING**

2. Video Viewing View the video excerpt of *Harrison Bergeron* provided with this program. In a small group, discuss how the filmmakers changed the setting and content of the story. Decide whether you think the changes are in keeping with the theme of the story. ~ **VIEWING AND REPRESENTING**

VIDEO **Literature in Performance**

Inquiry & Research

Public Opinion Should sports teams hold tryouts so that only the best are chosen or should the coaches let anyone play? Should the choir make people audition? In other words, where should schools draw the line between recognizing excellence and achieving equality? With your classmates, conduct a survey of public opinion about no-cut policies for school teams or clubs. Prepare a questionnaire and then interview other students in your school. Discuss your findings. What can you infer from the results?

Vocabulary in Action

EXERCISE A: CONTEXT CLUES Write the Word to Know that best completes the meaning of each sentence.

1. In Vonnegut's vision of the future, intelligent people hear loud noises in fitted radios that hurt their ears and make them ________.
2. The ballerina is very strong and beautiful. She seems ________, or glowing with an inner light.
3. As Harrison and the ballerina dance, they begin ______ their movements.
4. Harrison Bergeron does not let the handicaps he is fitted with be a ________ to him.
5. If Diana Moon Glampers approached you with a shotgun, would you ________ and tremble in fear?

EXERCISE B: SYNONYMS On your paper, write the Word to Know that belongs in each group of synonyms.

1. dismay, terror, ________
2. equilibrium, ________, proportion
3. ________, gradated, measured
4. acuity, ________, diligence
5. indistinct, unclear, ________

Building Vocabulary
For an in-depth study of context clues, see page 56.

WORDS TO KNOW					
	calibrated	cower	luminous	synchronizing	vigilance
	consternation	hindrance	symmetry	vague	wince

Writing Options

1. **Glampers's Report** Student responses will vary but should contain detailed reasons why Diana Moon Glampers shot Harrison. The report may be written in the first person.
2. **Warden's Address** Remind students that the warden is trying to persuade the heads of state to act on his suggestions. Tell them that literary elements such as repetition and parallel structure are often used in speeches to reinforce meaning. Suggest that students include such elements in their speeches.

Activities & Explorations

1. **News at Six** Make sure each group member contributes to the presentation by assuming a particular role or task. You may want to set a time limit, such as five minutes, to encourage students to focus their telecasts.
2. **Video Viewing** Students need to discuss the theme and then examine whether the film supports it.

Inquiry & Research

Public Opinion Help students write questions that are objective and unbiased. Emphasize that an unbiased questionnaire will yield the best results; a biased questionnaire may influence people's responses. Have students create a chart or graph showing a numerical breakdown of their findings.

Vocabulary in Action

Exercise A
1. wince
2. luminous
3. synchronizing
4. hindrance
5. cower

Exercise B
1. consternation
2. symmetry
3. calibrated
4. vigilance
5. vague

Mini Lesson **Grammar**

PROPER NOUNS

Instruction All nouns name persons, places, or things. Proper nouns name specific persons, places, and things, while common nouns name general persons, places, and things. Proper nouns are capitalized. Common nouns are not capitalized unless they begin a sentence.

Practice Write the following passage on the chalkboard. Have students identify the nouns. Then discuss which nouns are common and which are proper.

People like Harrison Bergeron are threatening to agents who must uphold the laws of society. By declaring himself the Emperor, Harrison risks the wrath of Diana Moon Glampers, the Handicapper General. *(Common nouns: People, agents, laws, society, wrath. Proper nouns: Harrison Bergeron, Emperor, Diana Moon Glampers, Handicapper General)*

Use **Unit One Resource Book,** p. 8.
Use **Grammar Transparencies and Copymasters,** p. 65.

Use McDougal Littell's ***Language Network,*** Chapter 1, for more instruction in proper nouns.

Grammar in Context: Proper Nouns

In the short story "Harrison Bergeron," Kurt Vonnegut invents proper nouns that help create satire.

> **"Harrison Bergeron, age fourteen," she said in a grackle squawk, "has just escaped from jail, where he was held on suspicion of plotting to overthrow the government."**

A **proper noun** names a specific person, place, or thing. In the example, Vonnegut has created a proper noun that alludes to a quality of the character it names. The name *Bergeron* contains the French word *berger,* which means "shepherd." Harrison is a sort of shepherd who tries to lead people away from the evil influence of the handicapper general.

Apply to Your Writing In fiction writing, using carefully chosen proper nouns can help you suggest character traits and convey a satirical or realistic tone.

WRITING EXERCISE Replace the underlined words with proper nouns of your own creation. Try to convey a particular tone or attitude with each proper noun. Remember to capitalize each name.

Example: ***Original*** The dance company danced the same routine every night.
Rewritten The Lead-Footed Leapers danced the same routine every night.

1. The Bergerons' house is neat, small, and exactly like every other house on the street.
2. The television set, manufactured by a national company, produces a wavy picture and static-filled sound.
3. The announcer garbles half of every sentence.
4. The jail looms gray and forbidding.
5. When the orchestra plays the song, Harrison and the ballerina spring into the air.

Grammar Handbook
Nouns, p. 1182.

Kurt Vonnegut, Jr.

1922–

Other Works
The Sirens of Titan
Mother Night
Cat's Cradle
God Bless You, Mr. Rosewater
Jailbird
Slaughterhouse Five

Serious Humor Kurt Vonnegut began writing short stories in the late 1940s, and he achieved quick success. Because so many of his stories deal with science and social criticism, he has been dubbed a science fiction writer, although he has never liked that designation. For Vonnegut, no subject is off-limits. He writes about the brutality in human nature and our fears of technology, war, and politics. Although he deals with devastatingly serious topics, his writing is easy to read. He often attacks his subjects with dark humor and wild absurdities.

Real Life into Fiction Vonnegut's life has not always been easy. His mother died while he was home on leave from the army during World War II. He was a prisoner of war in Dresden, Germany, when that city was leveled by bombing; he witnessed great destruction during the war and immediately afterward. In 1958, his sister died of cancer. Many of these wrenching experiences have found their way into Vonnegut's fiction.

Critical Arrival Although Vonnegut has always been popular, he has not always been critically praised. In the 1970s that changed. He is now regarded as one of the most important writers of the late 20th century. "Harrison Bergeron" was published in a 1968 collection of Vonnegut stories called *Welcome to the Monkey House.*

Author Activity

Look for book reviews of Vonnegut's work from the early part of his career (before 1970) and the later part (after 1970). How did critics' reactions change over time? Bring copies of at least two contrasting reviews to class and discuss them with your classmates.

Grammar in Context

WRITING EXERCISE Answers will vary. Possible answers are shown.

1. The Bergerons' house is neat, small, and exactly like every other house on Normal Avenue.
2. The television set, manufactured by Fuzzyvision, Inc., produces a wavy picture and static-filled sound.
3. Stanley Slurrings garbles half of every sentence.
4. Hopeless House Jail looms gray and forbidding.
5. When the orchestra plays "Leap for the Stars," Harrison and the ballerina spring into the air.

Author Activity

Students' findings will vary. Most reviews from before 1970 will be more critical and negative than later reviews.

HARRISON BERGERON 29

OVERVIEW

Objectives

1. understand and appreciate a **short story (Literary Analysis)**
2. understand static and dynamic **characters (Literary Analysis)**
3. **identify characters' motives (Active Reading)**

Summary

At some unspecified time in the future, after "the bomb," the sun appears only rarely in places; a permanent cloud belt keeps the sky gray and the land barren. Newlyweds Lily and Tom plan to find a bit of sun while they are on their honeymoon in the south of England. After their scooter breaks down in Molesworth, they meet Mr. Noakes, an unscrupulous businessman who claims that if he could find a sunlit place, he would develop it and make his fortune. While returning a lost handbag, Lily and Tom find a miraculous sunlit place at the end of a dark, wooded path; it is the Hatching's cottage, where they stay for a few blissful days with the kind old woman and her son, working in an amazingly green garden and enjoying the rare blue sky and the sight of stars. When they return to the village, Mr. Noakes is curious about their suntans. To protect the peaceful golden place they found, Lily and Tom say they were elsewhere and head north, pretending to return to where they had found sunlight.

5-Minute Warm-Up

Daily Language SkillBuilder

Have students **proofread** the display sentences on page 15i and write them correctly. The sentences also appear on Transparency 1 of **Grammar Transparencies and Copymasters.**

Mini Lesson **Preteaching Vocabulary**

If you would like to preteach the WORDS TO KNOW for this selection, use the Mini Lesson, p. 32.

"How could the sky ever have been blue? You might as well say, 'In the days when the grass was pink.'"

Searching for Summer

Short Story by JOAN AIKEN

Connect to Your Life

Aftermath of a Disaster Every year, people all over the world experience natural and technological disasters, such as tornadoes or oil spills. Sometimes communities can recover from them fairly quickly. Others have effects that last for years. Think of a disaster that you have experienced or heard about. How lasting were the effects? What adjustments did the community or nation have to make as a result? Discuss your reply with a partner.

Build Background

Nuclear Anxiety Joan Aiken wrote "Searching for Summer" in the 1950s, setting the story in a future "eighties," perhaps the 1980s or the 2080s. At the time of publication, the memory of the 1945 atomic bombing of Hiroshima and Nagasaki in Japan remained fresh in the minds of many. People lived with the lurking threat of nuclear war. As a result of nuclear weapons testing, radioactive matter, also known as fallout, would rain down from the sky, polluting the environment. The weapons themselves were growing more advanced and powerful all the time, and no one knew exactly what would happen to the earth in the event of a nuclear war. Many writers, artists, and filmmakers explored this issue in their work, imagining the possible outcomes of a nuclear disaster.

WORDS TO KNOW
Vocabulary Preview

indomitable
omen
unavailing
voluble
withered

VIDEODISC **LaserLinks: Background for Reading**
Geographical Connection

Focus Your Reading

LITERARY ANALYSIS CHARACTER **Characters** are the people who participate in the action of a story or other literary work. In many stories, characters undergo some sort of change as the **plot** unfolds. Such characters are called **dynamic characters,** as opposed to **static characters,** who remain the same. As you read the following story, think about whether the characters change, and if so, how they change. How is this change or lack of change significant to the story?

ACTIVE READING IDENTIFYING CHARACTERS' MOTIVES A character's **motive** is the intention or desire that causes him or her to act in a particular way. Understanding why characters act as they do can help you to understand the events of a story.

READER'S NOTEBOOK As you read this story, complete a graphic like the one shown with your ideas about the motives of Mr. Noakes, Lily, Tom, and Mrs. Hatching.

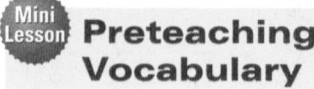

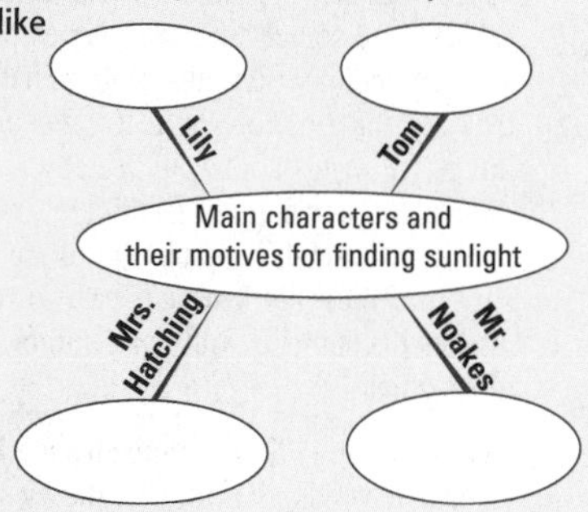

LESSON RESOURCES

UNIT ONE RESOURCE BOOK, pp. 10–15

ASSESSMENT RESOURCES
Formal Assessment, pp. 9–10
Teacher's Guide to Assessment and Portfolio Use
Test Generator

SKILLS TRANSPARENCIES AND COPYMASTERS

Literary Analysis
- Character, T2 (for Activity, p. 39)

Reading and Critical Thinking
- Cluster Diagram, T48 (for Reader's Notebook, p. 30)

Grammar
- Proper Adjectives, C71 (for Mini Lesson, p. 37)

Vocabulary
- Word Meanings, C20 (for Mini Lesson, p. 32)

Writing
- Writing Process, T1, T2 (for Writing Option 2, p. 40)
- The Uses of Dialogue, T24 (for Writing Option 1, p. 40)

Communications
- Evaluation Matrix: Commercial, T6 (for Activities & Explorations 2, p. 40)
- Dramatic Reading, T12 (for Mini Lesson, p. 34)

INTEGRATED TECHNOLOGY

Audio Library
LaserLinks
- Geographical Connection: Southern England, See **Teacher's SourceBook,** p. 6.

Internet: Research Starter
Visit our website:
www.mcdougallittell.com

Searching for Summer

Joan Aiken

The Mysterious Bird (1917), Charles Burchfield. Watercolor and pencil on paper, 20¾″ × 17¾″, Delaware Art Museum, Wilmington, bequest of John L. Sexton, 1955.

31

TEACHING THE LITERATURE

Customizing Instruction

Less Proficient Readers
Ask students to discuss how rainy or overcast weather affects their everyday lives.

Set a Purpose In reading the story students should notice how the lack of sunlight affects the characters' everyday lives and what they do.

Mini Lesson Viewing and Representing

The Mysterious Bird **by Charles Burchfield**

ART APPRECIATION Charles Burchfield uses energetic, expressionistic techniques, yet the subject—an unpaved rural road—is highly realistic.

Instruction Explain to students that this road was probably similar to many of the roads near the small Ohio town where Burchfield lived in 1917.

Application Ask students the following questions: How do the foreground and the background of the painting differ from each other? What kind of mood does each create?

Possible Response: The yellow foreground looks bright and sunny, perhaps representing hope. The background is gray and cloudy, creating a more ominous mood than the foreground.

Reading and Analyzing

Reading Skills and Strategies: PREVIEW

Briefly summarize the story, emphasizing the importance of the setting. Ask students to think about the title while they examine the images and read the called-out quotes.

Literary Analysis CHARACTER

Dynamic characters undergo some sort of change as the plot of a story unfolds. Static characters do not change. In this selection, students should note how characters do or do not change.

Use **Unit One Resource Book** p. 12 for more practice.

Active Reading

IDENTIFYING CHARACTERS' MOTIVES

Ask students to think about why the characters act in a particular way. The characters' motives may not be directly stated, but they can be inferred from the characters' actions or speech.

Ask students to pay particular attention to the newlyweds, Mr. Noakes, and Mrs. Hatching.

Use **Unit One Resource Book** p. 11 for more practice.

Lily wore yellow on her wedding day. In the eighties people put a lot of faith in omens and believed that if a bride's dress was yellow her married life would be blessed with a bit of sunshine.

It was years since the bombs had been banned, but still the cloud never lifted. Whitish gray, day after day, sometimes darkening to a weeping slate color or, at the end of an evening, turning to smoky copper, the sky endlessly, secretively brooded.

Old people began their stories with the classic, fairy-tale opening: "Long, long ago, when I was a liddle un, in the days when the sky was blue . . ." and children, listening, chuckled among themselves at the absurd thought, because, *blue,* imagine it! How could the sky ever have been *blue?* You might as well say, "In the days when the grass was pink."

Stars, rainbows, and all other such heavenly sideshows had been permanently withdrawn, and if the radio announced that there was a blink of sunshine in such and such a place, where the cloud belt had thinned for half an hour, cars and buses would pour in that direction for days in an unavailing search for warmth and light.

After the wedding, when all the relations were standing on the church porch, with Lily shivering prettily in her buttercup nylon, her father prodded the dour[1] and withered grass on a grave—although it was August, the leaves were hardly out yet—and said, "Well, Tom, what are you aiming to do now, eh?"

"Going to find a bit of sun and have our honeymoon in it," said Tom. There was a general laugh from the wedding party.

"Don't get sunburned," shrilled Aunt Nancy.

"Better start off Bournemouth[2] way. Paper said they had a half-hour of sun last Wednesday week," Uncle Arthur weighed in heavily.

"We'll come back brown as—as this grass," said Tom, and ignoring the good-natured teasing from their respective families, the two young people mounted on their scooter, which stood ready at the churchyard wall, and chugged away in a shower of golden confetti. When they were out of sight, and the yellow paper had subsided on the gray and gritty road, the Whitemores and the Hoskinses strolled off, sighing, to eat wedding cake and drink currant[3] wine, and old Mrs. Hoskins spoiled everyone's pleasure by bursting into tears as she thought of her own wedding day when everything was so different.

Meanwhile Tom and Lily buzzed on hopefully across the gray countryside, with Lily's veil like a gilt banner floating behind. It was chilly going for her in her wedding things, but the sight of a bride was supposed to bring good luck, and so she stuck it out, although her fingers were blue to the knuckles. Every now and then they switched on their portable radio and listened to the forecast. Inverness had seen the sun for ten minutes yesterday, and Southend[4] for five minutes this morning, but that was all.

"Both those places are a long way from here," said Tom cheerfully. "All the more reason we'd find a nice bit of sunshine in these parts somewhere. We'll keep on going south. Keep your eyes peeled, Lil, and tell me if you see a blink of sun on those hills ahead."

But they came to the hills and passed them, and a new range shouldered up ahead and then slid away behind, and still there was no flicker

1. **dour** (do͝or): gloomy; forbidding.
2. **Bournemouth** (bôrn′məth): a British seaside resort.
3. **currant:** a berry used to make jams, jellies, and wines.
4. **Inverness . . . Southend:** resort towns in the north and south of the British Isles.

WORDS TO KNOW
omen (ō′mən) *n.* a thing or event supposed to foretell good or evil; a sign
unavailing (ŭn′ə-vā′lĭng) *adj.* useless; ineffective
withered (wĭ*th*′ərd) *adj.* shriveled or shrunken, as if from lack of water or food

32

Teaching Options

Mini Lesson: Preteaching Vocabulary

USING A DICTIONARY Have students use a dictionary to find precise meanings for the WORDS TO KNOW. Ask them to write the definitions in a notebook that they use for new vocabulary words. As they encounter the WORDS TO KNOW in their reading, have them check their definitions. If they have more than one definition for a word, they should use the context to determine the best definition.

Use **Unit One Resource Book** p. 13 for additional support.

or patch of sunshine to be seen anywhere in the gray, winter-ridden landscape. Lily began to get discouraged, so they stopped for a cup of tea at a drive-in.

"Seen the sun lately, mate?" Tom asked the proprietor.

He laughed shortly. "Notice any buses or trucks around here? Last time I saw the sun was two years ago September; came out just in time for the wife's birthday."

"It's stars I'd like to see," Lily said, looking wistfully at her dust-colored tea. "Ever so pretty they must be."

"Well, better be getting on I suppose," said Tom, but he had lost some of his bounce and confidence. Every place they passed through looked nastier than the last, partly on account of the dismal light, partly because people had given up bothering to take a pride in their boroughs.[5] And then, just as they were entering a village called Molesworth, the dimmest, drabbest, most insignificant huddle of houses they had come to yet, the engine coughed and died on them.

How could the sky ever have been *blue?*

"Can't see what's wrong," said Tom, after a prolonged and gloomy survey.

"Oh, Tom!" Lily was almost crying. "What'll we do?"

"Have to stop here for the night, s'pose." Tom was short-tempered with frustration. "Look, there's a garage just up the road. We can push the bike there, and they'll tell us if there's a pub[6] where we can stay. It's nearly six anyway."

They had taken the bike to the garage, and the man there was just telling them that the only pub in the village was the Rising Sun, where Mr. Noakes might be able to give them a bed, when a bus pulled up in front of the petrol[7] pumps.

"Look," the garage owner said, "there's Mr. Noakes just getting out of the bus now. Sid!" he called.

But Mr. Noakes was not able to come to them at once. Two old people were climbing slowly out of the bus ahead of him: a blind man with a white stick, and a withered, frail old lady in a black satin dress and hat. "Careful now, George," she was saying, "mind ee be careful with my son William."

"I'm being careful, Mrs. Hatching," the conductor said patiently, as he almost lifted the unsteady old pair off the bus platform. The driver had stopped his engine, and everyone on the bus was taking a mild and sympathetic interest, except for Mr. Noakes just behind who was cursing irritably at the delay. When the two old people were on the narrow pavement, the conductor saw that they were going to have trouble with a bicycle that was propped against the curb just ahead of them; he picked it up and stood holding it until they had passed the line of petrol pumps and were going slowly off along a path across the fields. Then, grinning, he put it back, jumped hurriedly into the bus, and rang his bell.

"Old nuisances," Mr. Noakes said furiously. "Wasting public time. Every week that palaver[8] goes on, taking the old man to Midwick Hospital Outpatients and back again. I know what *I'd* do with 'em. Put to sleep, that sort ought to be."

Mr. Noakes was a repulsive-looking

---

5. **boroughs:** towns or districts.
6. **pub:** a British term for a small tavern. Pubs in small towns sometimes serve meals and rent rooms to travelers.
7. **petrol:** a British term for gasoline.
8. **palaver** (pə-lăv′ər): useless chatter.

Customizing Instruction

Students Acquiring English
Students may be unfamiliar with the British idioms. Suggest they use context clues to help them understand their meanings.

Use **Spanish Study Guide** for additional support, pp. 7–9.

BLOCK SCHEDULING: MANAGING TIME

If your schedule requires that you cover the lesson objectives in a shorter time, use . . .
- Preparing to Read, p. 30
- Thinking Through the Literature, p. 39
- Vocabulary in Action, p. 40
- Grammar in Context, p. 41

If you want to take advantage of longer class time, use . . .
- TE Teaching Options: Preteaching Vocabulary, p. 32; Viewing and Representing, pp. 31, 36; Speaking and Listening, p. 34; Multicultural Link, p. 35; Standardized Test Practice, p. 38
- Choices & Challenges, pp. 40–41

Reading and Analyzing

Reading Skills and Strategies: PREDICT

A Ask students to predict whether Tom and Lily will find sunlight. Ask them to explain the reasons for their predictions.

Possible Response: Students may have a sense that Tom and Lily are different; they seem optimistic and innocent.

Reading Skills and Strategies: VISUALIZE

B Ask students to visualize Mrs. Hatching and William using the details given in the story.

Possible Response: Both Mrs. Hatching and William are old and move slowly. Mrs. Hatching is withered and frail, dresses in black satin, and is quite talkative. William is blind, quiet, and dependent on his mother and uses his hands to "see."

individual, but when he heard that Tom and Lily wanted a room for the night, he changed completely and gave them a leer that was full of false goodwill. He was a big, red-faced man with wet, full lips, bulging pale-gray bloodshot eyes, and a crop of stiff greasy black hair. He wore tennis shoes.

"Honeymooners, eh?" he said, looking sentimentally at Lily's pale prettiness. "Want a bed for the night, eh?" and he laughed a disgusting laugh that sounded like thick oil coming out of a bottle, heh-heh-heh-heh, and gave Lily a tremendous pinch on her arm. Disengaging herself as politely as she could, she stooped and picked up something from the pavement. They followed Mr. Noakes glumly up the street to the Rising Sun.

A While they were eating their baked beans, Mr. Noakes stood over their table grimacing at them. Lily unwisely confided to him that they were looking for a bit of sunshine. Mr. Noakes's laughter nearly shook down the ramshackle building.

"Sunshine! Oh my gawd! That's a good 'un! Hear that, Mother?" he bawled to his wife. "They're looking for a bit of sunshine. Heh-heh-heh-heh-heh-heh! Why," he said, banging on the table till the baked beans leaped about, "if I could find a bit of sunshine near here, permanent bit that is, dja know what I'd do?"

The young people looked at him inquiringly across the bread and margarine.

"Lido,[9] trailer site, country club, holiday camp—you wouldn't know the place. Land around here is dirt cheap; I'd buy up the lot. Nothing but woods. I'd advertise—I'd have people flocking to this little dump from all over the country. But what a hope, what a hope, eh? Well, feeling better? Enjoyed your tea? Ready for bed? Heh-heh-heh-heh, bed's ready for you."

Avoiding one another's eyes, Tom and Lily stood up.

"I—I'd like to go for a bit of a walk first, Tom," Lily said in a small voice. "Look, I picked up that old lady's bag on the pavement; I didn't notice it till we'd done talking to Mr. Noakes, and by then she was out of sight. Should we take it back to her?"

"Good idea," said Tom, pouncing on the suggestion with relief. "Do you know where she lives, Mr. Noakes?"

"Who, old Ma Hatching? Sure I know. She lives in the wood. But you don't want to go taking her bag back, not this time o' the evening you don't. Let her worry. She'll come asking for it in the morning."

"She walked so slowly," said Lily, holding the bag gently in her hands. It was very old, made of black velvet on two ring handles, and embroidered with beaded roses. "I think we ought to take it to her, don't you, Tom?"

"Oh, very well, very well, have it your own way," Mr. Noakes said, winking at Tom. "Take that path by the garage; you can't go wrong. I've never been there meself, but they live somewhere in that wood back o' the village; you'll find it soon enough."

They found the path soon enough, but not the cottage. Under the lowering[10] sky they walked forward endlessly among trees that carried only tiny and rudimentary leaves, wizened and poverty-stricken.[11] Lily was still wearing her wedding sandals, which had begun to blister her. She held onto Tom's arm, biting her lip with the pain, and he looked down miserably at her bent brown head; everything had turned out so differently from what he had planned. 1

By the time they reached the cottage Lily

9. **lido** (lī'dō): a British term for a public outdoor swimming pool.
10. **lowering** (lou'ər-ĭng): dark and threatening.
11. **rudimentary . . . poverty-stricken:** leaves that are imperfectly formed and shriveled up from lack of sunlight.

Teaching Options

Mini Lesson

Speaking and Listening

DRAMATIC PRESENTATION

Instruction Help students prepare a dramatic presentation of the conversation Mr. Noakes has with Lily and Tom at the Rising Sun. Working in groups, ask students to list the characteristics of Lily, Tom, and Mr. Noakes that they feel are important to portray.

Present Student groups can decide how they will present the dramatic interpretation. Student audience members can evaluate how the performance increases their appreciation and understanding of the characters in Aiken's story.

could hardly bear to put her left foot to the ground, and Tom was gentling her along: "It can't be much farther now, and they'll be sure to have a bandage. I'll tie it up, and you can have a sit-down. Maybe they'll give us a cup of tea. We could borrow an old pair of socks or something. . . ." Hardly noticing the cottage garden, beyond a vague impression of rows of runner beans, they made for the clematis-grown[12] porch and knocked. There was a brass lion's head on the door, carefully polished.

"Eh, me dear!" It was the old lady, old Mrs. Hatching, who opened the door, and her exclamation was a long-drawn gasp of pleasure and astonishment. "Eh, me dear! 'Tis the pretty bride. See'd ye s'arternoon when we was coming home from hospital."

"Who be?" shouted a voice from inside.

"Come in, come in, me dears. My son William'll be glad to hear company; he can't see, poor soul, nor has this thirty year, ah, and a pretty sight he's losing this minute—"

"We brought back your bag," Tom said, putting it in her hands, "and we wondered if you'd have a bit of plaster[13] you could kindly let us have. My wife's hurt her foot—"

My wife. Even in the midst of Mrs. Hatching's voluble welcome the strangeness of these words struck the two young people, and they fell quiet, each of them, pondering, while Mrs. Hatching thanked and commiserated, all in a breath, and asked them to take a seat on the sofa and fetched a basin of water from the scullery,[14] and William from his seat in the chimney corner demanded to know what it was all about.

"Wot be doing? Wot be doing, Mother?"

" 'Tis a bride, all in's finery," she shrilled back at him, "an's blistered her foot, poor heart." Keeping up a running commentary for William's benefit she bound up the foot, every now and then exclaiming to herself in wonder over the fineness of Lily's wedding dress, which lay in yellow nylon swathes around the chair. "There, me dear. Now us'll have a cup of tea, eh? Proper thirsty you'm fare to be, walking all the way to here this hot day." B

Hot day? Tom and Lily stared at each other and then around the room. Then it was true, it was not their imagination, that a great dusty golden square of sunshine lay on the fireplace wall, where the brass pendulum of the clock at every swing blinked into sudden brilliance? That the blazing geraniums on the windowsill housed a drove of murmuring bees? That, through the window, the gleam of linen hung in the sun to whiten suddenly dazzled their eyes? 2

"The sun? Is it really the sun?"

"The sun? Is it really the sun?" Tom said, almost doubtfully.

"And why not?" Mrs. Hatching demanded. "How else'll beans set, tell me that? Fine thing if sun were to stop shining." Chuckling to herself she set out a Crown Derby tea set, gorgeously colored in red and gold, and a baking of saffron[15] buns. Then she sat down and, drinking her own tea, began to question the two of them about where they had come from, where they were going. The tea was

12. **clematis-grown:** covered with a flowering vine.
13. **plaster:** a British term for an adhesive bandage.
14. **scullery:** a small room in which dishwashing and other kitchen chores are done.
15. **saffron:** made with a cooking spice that imparts an orange-yellow color to foods.

WORDS TO KNOW **voluble** (vŏl'yə-bəl) *adj.* in or with a long flow of words; talkative

Customizing Instruction

Students Acquiring English

1 Explain to students that the term *poverty-stricken* is being used figuratively here. Explain that *poverty-stricken* usually applies to humans and means "very poor or lacking material things." Ask students why Aiken might have used this expression to describe the leaves.

Possible Response: Just as a poverty-stricken person is deprived of things he or she needs, the leaves are deprived of the sunlight that they need.

Multiple Learning Styles

Auditory Learners

2 To help students compare and contrast the sunlit cottage to the gray skies over the rest of England, ask them to discuss what kind of music might go with each setting. What sounds do they associate with gray skies and gloom? What sounds do they associate with sunlight?

Have students bring in samples of music to go with each of the two settings. They may play or sing their own music or bring in recorded songs. Have them play their selections for the class, and have the class discuss how each piece relates to the setting.

Multicultural Link: Ceremonial Colors

Although this story is set in the future, wearing yellow is a wedding custom from the past. Ancient Roman brides traditionally wore bright yellow veils that fully covered their faces. In almost all cultures, brides wear a particular color for their wedding. Often this traditional color has symbolic value. In most Western cultures, the bride wears white, which symbolizes purity. In many Asian cultures, however, the preferred color is red, the color associated with joy and good fortune. Traditional Chinese brides wear red *quipaos*, silk dresses with high necks and slit skirts. Hindu brides also have a preference for red, and the traditional Hindu wedding garment is a red silk sari with an intricate gold border.

Reading and Analyzing

Literary Analysis: SETTING

A Have students list any images and descriptions used to describe the cottage. Ask students to compare the setting at the cottage with the setting elsewhere in the story. Have them analyze the relevance of the setting to the meaning of the text.

Possible Response: Rows of runner beans are outside the cottage, bees hover over blazing geraniums on the windowsill, and the gleam of linen hung in the sun to dry dazzles their eyes. The cottage is teeming with life, and sunshine is abundant. The rest of the world is covered in a dull, gray haze. Sunshine occurs very seldom in the rest of the world.

Literary Analysis: FANTASY

B A fantasy often shows extravagant imagination. Ask students to discuss how the characters and the setting exceed the bounds of reality.

Possible Response: It is unrealistic that the sun always shines at Mrs. Hatching's cottage and that no one else knows about it.

tawny[16] and hot and sweet; the clock's tick was like a bird chirping; every now and then **A** a log settled in the grate; Lily looked sleepily around the little room, so rich and peaceful, and thought, I wish we were staying here. I wish we needn't go back to that horrible pub. . . . She leaned against Tom's comforting arm.

"Look at the sky," she whispered to him. "Out there between the geraniums. Blue!"

Embrace II (1981), George Tooker. Egg tempera on gesso panel, 18″ × 24″, private collection.

"And ee'll come up and see my spare bedroom, won't ee now?" Mrs. Hatching said, breaking off the thread of her questions—which indeed was not a thread, but merely a savoring[17] of her pleasure and astonishment at this unlooked-for visit—"Bide here, why don't ee? Mid as well. The lil un's fair wore out. Us'll do for ee better 'n rangy old Noakes; proper old scoundrel 'e be. Won't us, William?"

"Ah," William said appreciatively. "I'll sing ee some o' my songs."

A sight of the spare room settled any doubts. The great white bed, huge as a prairie, built up with layer upon solid layer of mattress, blanket, and quilt, almost filled the little shadowy room in which it stood. Brass rails shone in the green dimness. "Isn't it quiet," Lily whispered. Mrs. Hatching, silent for the moment, stood looking at them proudly, her bright eyes slowly moving from face to face. Once her hand fondled, as if it might have been a baby's downy head, the yellow brass knob.

And so, almost without any words, the matter was decided.

Three days later they remembered that they must go to the village and collect the scooter which must, surely, be mended by now.

They had been helping old William pick a basketful of beans. Tom had taken his shirt off, and the sun gleamed on his brown back; Lily was wearing an old cotton print which Mrs. Hatching, with much chuckling, had shortened to fit her.

It was amazing how deftly, in spite of his blindness, William moved among the beans, feeling through the rough, rustling leaves for the stiffness of concealed pods. He found twice as many as Tom and Lily, but then they, even

16. **tawny:** tan in color.
17. **savoring:** full appreciation or enjoyment.

Teaching Options

Mini Lesson Viewing and Representing

***Embrace II* by George Tooker**

ART APPRECIATION Explain to students that George Tooker paints in the difficult medium of egg tempera in which pigments are suspended in egg yolk to form a paint that adheres well to dry plaster.

Instruction Direct students' attention to the woman's head tilting back, allowing the sun to bathe her face. Ask students what mood is created by the rolling hills in the background.

Possible Response: The gently rolling hills create a calm, serene feeling.

Application Ask students how the couple in the painting might remind the viewer of Lily and Tom.

Possible Response: The couple's happiness and peacefulness are reminiscent of Lily and Tom's when they are staying at the sunlit cottage.

on the third day, were still stopping every other minute to exclaim over the blueness of the sky. At night they sat on the back doorstep while Mrs. Hatching clucked inside as she dished the supper, "Starstruck ee'll be! Come along in, do-ee, before soup's cold; stars niver run away yet as I do know."

"Can we get anything for you in the village?" Lily asked, but Mrs. Hatching shook her head.

"Baker's bread and suchlike's no use but to cripple thee's innardses wi' colic.[18] I been living here these eighty year wi'out troubling doctors, and I'm not faring to begin now." She waved to them and stood watching as they walked into the wood, thin and frail beyond belief, but wiry, indomitable, her black eyes full of zest. Then she turned to scream menacingly at a couple of pullets[19] who had strayed and were scratching among the potatoes.

Almost at once they noticed, as they followed the path, that the sky was clouded over.

B "It *is* only there on that one spot," Lily said in wonder. "All the time. And they've never even noticed that the sun doesn't shine in other places."

"That's how it must have been all over the world, once," Tom said.

At the garage they found their scooter ready and waiting. They were about to start back when they ran into Mr. Noakes.

"Well, well, well, well, *well!*" he shouted, glaring at them with ferocious good humor. "How many wells make a river, eh? And where did you slip off to? Here's me and the missus was just going to tell the police to have the
1 rivers dragged. But hullo, hul*lo*, what's this? Brown, eh? Suntan? Scrumptious," he said, looking meltingly at Lily and giving her another tremendous pinch. "Where'd you get it, eh? That wasn't all got in half an hour, *I* know. Come on, this means money to you and me; tell us the big secret. Remember what I said; land around these parts is dirt cheap."

Tom and Lily looked at each other in horror. They thought of the cottage, the bees humming among the runner beans, the sunlight glinting in the red-and-gold teacups. At night, when they had lain in the huge sagging bed, stars had shone through the window, and the whole wood was as quiet as the inside of a shell.

"Oh, we've been miles from here," Tom lied 1
hurriedly. "We ran into a friend, and he took us right away beyond Brinsley." And as Mr. Noakes still looked suspicious and unsatisfied, he did the only thing possible. "We're going back there now," he said. "The sunbathing's grand." And opening the throttle, he let the scooter go. They waved at Mr. Noakes and chugged off toward the gray hills that lay to the north.

"My wedding dress," Lily said sadly. "It's on our bed."

They wondered how long Mrs. Hatching would keep tea hot for them, who would eat all the pasties.[20]

"Never mind, you won't need it again," Tom comforted her.

At least, he thought, they had left the golden place undisturbed. Mr. Noakes never went into the wood. And they had done what they intended; they had found the sun. Now they, too, would be able to tell their grandchildren, when beginning a story, "Long, long ago, when we were young, in the days when the sky was blue . . ." ❖

---

18. **cripple . . . colic** (kŏl'ĭk): give yourself a bad case of indigestion.
19. **pullets:** young hens.
20. **pasties** (păs'tēz): a British term for meat pies.

WORDS TO KNOW **indomitable** (ĭn-dŏm'ĭ-tə-bəl) *adj.* not easily discouraged, defeated, or subdued

37

Customizing Instruction

Less Proficient Readers

1 Use the following questions to guide students to understand the ending of the story.

- Why do Lily and Tom leave the cottage?

Possible Response: to go into the village to get their scooter after it has been repaired

- What makes Mr. Noakes believe that Tom and Lily have found sunlight?

Possible Response: Lily and Tom are suntanned.

- Why does Mr. Noakes want Lily and Tom to tell him where the sunlight is?

Possible Response: so he can turn the place into a resort

- Why don't Lily and Tom go back to the cottage after Mr. Noakes sees them?

Possible Response: They are afraid he will follow them and disrupt the peacefulness of the cottage.

Mini Lesson Grammar

PROPER ADJECTIVES Remind students that a proper adjective is formed from a proper noun and thus requires a capital letter. Write the following example on a transparency.

Proper Noun: Shakespeare
Proper Adjective: Shakespearean actor

Then, display the following sentence on a transparency and underline the proper adjectives as shown.

Joan Aiken, the daughter of the American poet Conrad Aiken, wrote a series of books that presented alternative English histories.

Practice Have students use proper nouns from the text to create five proper adjectives.

Possible Response: English cottage, August leaves, Molesworth bus, Rising Sun baked beans, Crown Derby tea set

Use **Grammar Transparencies and Copymasters,** p. 71.

Use McDougal Littell ***Language Network,*** Chapters 1 and 10, for more instruction in proper adjectives.

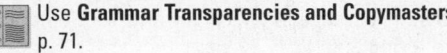

LITERARY LINK

Reading and Analyzing

Active Reading: COMPARE AND CONTRAST

Read Mary Oliver's "The Sun" aloud to students. Ask them to compare Oliver's image of the sun to the treatment of the sun in "Searching for Summer."

Possible Response: The sun is absent in the short story while Oliver exults in the sun's rays.

Literary Analysis: MOOD

Ask students to think about the image of a "rumpled sea." What might the poet mean by this image? What kind of mood does it evoke?

Possible Response: She is evoking an image of waves and comparing them to the rumples found in clothes and bedcovers; the term *rumpled* gives the image and the poem a familiar, informal mood.

Literary Analysis: FIGURATIVE LANGUAGE

Ask students why the speaker says that the sun "reaches out."

Possible Response: The rays of the sun seem to stretch out toward people; the speaker thinks of the sun as a benevolent power.

The Sun

Mary Oliver

Have you ever seen
anything
in your life
more wonderful

than the way the sun,
every evening,
relaxed and easy,
floats toward the horizon

and into the clouds or the hills,
or the rumpled sea,
and is gone—
and how it slides again

out of the blackness,
every morning,
on the other side of the world,
like a red flower

streaming upward on its heavenly oils,
say, on a morning in early summer,
at its perfect imperial distance—
and have you ever felt for anything

such wild love—
do you think there is anywhere, in any language,
a word billowing enough
for the pleasure

that fills you,
as the sun
reaches out,
as it warms you

as you stand there,
empty-handed—
or have you too
turned from this world—

or have you too
gone crazy
for power,
for things?

19 imperial: of great size; majestic.

Teaching Options

✓ Assessment Standardized Test Practice

CHOOSING THE MAIN IDEA For some standardized tests, students will be asked to choose the main idea of a passage. Remind students that the statement of the main idea should reflect the most important idea of the passage. Read aloud or write the following question on the chalkboard:

Which of the following statements best summarizes the passage in which Lily and Tom dine at the Rising Sun?

A. While Lily and Tom eat, Mr. Noakes reveals to them his desire to find a sunny place and turn it into a resort.

B. Lily and Tom eat baked beans with bread and margarine. They are happy to be together.

C. Mr. Noakes is loud and intrusive.

Lead students through the process of choosing the statement. Consider each choice. Point out that, while all of the statements contain accurate information about the story, the best statement should include the most important information. For that reason, **A** is the best choice.

Connect to the Literature

1. **What Do You Think?** Write a sentence that expresses your feelings about the outcome of the story.

Comprehension Check
- What is the setting of this story?
- Why are Tom and Lily driving around the country on their scooter?
- What is Mr. Noakes like?
- What do Tom and Lily find when they return Mrs. Hatching's handbag?

Think Critically

2. What words and phrases would you use to describe the **setting** of the story?

3. ACTIVE READING UNDERSTANDING CHARACTERS' MOTIVES Look at the characters' motives you recorded in your READER'S NOTEBOOK. Compare Lily and Tom's motives for finding a bit of sunlight with those of Mr. Noakes.

4. Why do you think the sun shines only over the Hatchings's cottage?

5. Do you think Tom and Lily do the right thing in not going back to the cottage? Explain your opinion.

6. What **themes,** or messages, do you see in this story?

THINK ABOUT
- the disastrous events alluded to at the beginning of the story
- why sunshine is important to Tom and Lily
- which **characters** are presented positively and which negatively

Extend Interpretations

7. **Critic's Corner** Student reviewer Jayme Charak remarked, "The story went to the heart. It was a sweet story and makes you think about the future." How does this reaction compare with your own?

8. **Comparing Texts** In the poem "The Sun," how does Mary Oliver's depiction of the sun differ from the sun as described in Joan Aiken's story? How is it similar?

9. **Connect to Life** Think of situations in your own community or elsewhere in which there has been a conflict between some people's desire to protect places of natural beauty and other people's desire to develop those places for economic gain. How should such conflicts be resolved?

Literary Analysis

CHARACTER The **characters** of a literary work are the individuals that participate in the action. In many stories, one or more characters undergo a change. These are called **dynamic characters,** whereas those who do not change are called **static characters.** Dynamic characters generally change by learning a major lesson or altering a **character trait,** or consistent part of their personality.

Activity Fill out a chart like the one started below, in which you identify each of the story's four main characters as dynamic or static. Explain your answer for each character.

Character	Dynamic or static?	Why?
Lily		
Tom		

FANTASY **Fantasy** is a type of fiction that contains events, places, or other details that could not exist in the real world. The characters in a fantasy are often realistic, but they have experiences that overstep the bounds of reality. The purpose of fantasy may be to delight and amuse or it might make a serious comment on reality. **Science fiction** is also a form of fantasy, as they both include strong imaginary components.

Cooperative Learning Activity In a small group, make a list of examples from the story that show how this story illustrates the definition of fantasy. Share your list with another group and discuss your responses.

GUIDING STUDENT RESPONSE

Connect to the Literature

1. **What Do You Think?**
Students will probably agree that Tom and Lily acted nobly, especially since Mr. Noakes wanted to personally profit from what had belonged to everyone, the sun.

Comprehension Check
- The story is set in England in the future, where the skies are always cloudy.
- They are looking for sunlight on their honeymoon.
- Mr. Noakes is disgusting and loud and greedy.
- Tom and Lily find sunlight.

Use Selection Quiz
Unit One Resource Book, p. 15.

Think Critically

2. Possible Responses: bleak, gray, sunless, and cold
3. Possible Response: Lily and Tom want to experience the sun. Mr. Noakes, however, wants to exploit the sun.
4. They seem to have lived in peace and harmony with nature.
5. Students will agree that Tom and Lily had to protect the Hatchings.
6. Possible Responses: We need to be careful how we treat each other and the environment. We need to be responsible for our actions.

Extend Interpretations

Critic's Corner Student responses often show that they are as concerned about the environment as Tom and Lily seem to be in the story.

Comparing Texts Aiken focuses on describing life without the sun. Oliver is enthralled by the sun's beauty and warmth. Students can imagine that Tom and Lily might have recited Oliver's poem once they had arrived at the Hatchings's cottage.

Connect to Life Ask students to focus on particular areas within their community. Underline the unit's theme and our dilemma in today's world.

Literary Analysis

Character When the students have completed the chart, ask them to explain their results by referring to specific passages in the story.

Fantasy Students will notice Tom and Lily's journey to the sun, the sunlit oasis that no one else knows about, and Mrs. Hatching's innocence.

Writing Options

1. **Evening Dialogue** When writing the dialogue, students should consider whether Lily and Tom believe Mr. Noakes is still following them or is waiting for them to return to Molesworth.
2. **Story Outline** Students should consider what constant heat would do to people's health and the environment.

Activities & Explorations

1. **Story Illustrations** You might have students sequence and arrange the illustrations so that they "tell" the story in pictures. Assign students or small groups brief scenes or events to illustrate.
2. **Radio Advertisement** Students can use Mr. Noakes's own words as a guide for this activity. Their advertisements should reflect details provided in the story and by Mr. Noakes's character.

Inquiry & Research

Nuclear Fallout Students may want to concentrate on the effects on humans, or the effects on the environment.

Vocabulary in Action

1. voluble
2. omen
3. indomitable
4. withered
5. unavailing

Choices & CHALLENGES

Writing Options

1. Evening Dialogue Write a dialogue Tom and Lily might have in the evening after leaving Molesworth, discussing whether they will ever return to the Hatchings's cottage.

2. Story Outline Write an outline for a story like "Searching for Summer," but one in which the sun burns constantly and clouds are rare. Use the outline below as a model.

Writing Handbook
See pages 1155–1156: Narrative Writing.

- **I. Scene 1: early morning**
  - **A. The sun rises.**
  - **B. Birds sit weakly in the trees.**
  - **C. Mr. Jones fills the bathtub with ice.**
- **II. Scene 2: classroom**
  - **A. Children rush from the car to an air-conditioned school.**
  - **B. Teacher closes the classroom blinds.**

Activities & Explorations

1. Story Illustrations Prepare a set of illustrations for "Searching for Summer." Include pictures of the main characters, various landscapes, and a caption for each of the pictures. Then show your illustrations to the class and read the captions. ~ **ART**

2. Radio Advertisement Imagine that Mr. Noakes has discovered the sunshine over the Hatchings's home. With a partner, create and present to the class a radio commercial that Mr. Noakes might put together to advertise the area as a tourist attraction. ~ **SPEAKING AND LISTENING**

Inquiry & Research

Nuclear Fallout Atomic and nuclear explosions have created terrible environmental damage, both at the time of explosion and through fallout, or the descent of radioactive particles after such an explosion. Research the effects of fallout as experienced in Japan after World War II, in the Ukraine with the 1986 accident at Chernobyl, or at various nuclear testing sites. How much does Aiken's world resemble a real-life nuclear aftermath? How is it different? Write a short research paper about your findings.

More Online: Research Starter
www.mcdougallittell.com

Ruined nuclear reactor at Chernobyl.

Vocabulary in Action

EXERCISE: IDIOMS Write the vocabulary word that is suggested by each set of idioms below.

1. run off at the mouth, have the gift of gab, be a chatterbox, talk till the cows come home
2. a black cat crossing your path, gathering clouds, a feeling in one's bones, seeing the handwriting on the wall
3. be a lion, have an iron will, never say die, not be a pushover
4. waste away, curl up and die, dry up and blow away, be a shadow of a former self
5. cry over spilt milk, close the barn door after the horse is stolen, carry water in a sieve

Building Vocabulary
Several Words to Know in this lesson contain prefixes and suffixes. For an in-depth lesson on word parts, see page 856.

WORDS TO KNOW		
	indomitable	voluble
	omen	withered
	unavailing	

Teaching Options

Mini Lesson Grammar

PUNCTUATING ADJECTIVES

Instruction When two or more adjectives precede a noun and work together to modify it, they are often separated by hyphens.

Example: The sunlight danced around the rims of the red-and-gold teacups.

When a series of adjectives modifies one noun, those adjectives are usually separated by commas.

Example: Lily clutched the old woman's bag, finding its surface velvety, worn, and strangely comforting.

Exercises Have students punctuate the following sentences:

1. The gray blue sky was completely overcast by the time they reached town. *(Insert a hyphen between* gray *and* blue.*)*
2. The sun shown on the runner beans, which were fragrant warm and stiff. *(Insert commas after* fragrant *and* warm.*)*

Grammar in Context: Adjectives

In "Searching for Summer," Joan Aiken uses adjectives to help convey the impact of an unexpected patch of sunlight in the midst of a gray, desolate world.

> **Then it was true, it was not their imagination, that a great dusty golden square of sunshine lay on the fireplace wall, where the brass pendulum of the clock at every swing blinked into sudden brilliance?**

You may recall that an **adjective** is a word that modifies a noun or pronoun. Joan Aiken has carefully chosen adjectives that help a reader imagine how extraordinary sunlight is in the world of her story.

Apply to Your Writing Choosing adjectives carefully can help you

- create a specific mood or tone
- create vivid images in your readers' minds
- add information about a place or character

Punctuation Tip: When you use more than one adjective, you may need to use commas or hyphens.

WRITING EXERCISE The sentences below describe the Hatchings's beautiful world. Supply your own adjectives to complete the sentences.

Example: _____ ivy curls around a tree behind the house.
Green-and-white-striped ivy curls around a tree behind the house.

1. Sunlight gives a _____ gleam to the clock on the mantle.
2. Tom and Lily take one look at the _____ spare room and decide to stay.
3. The young couple revel in the _____ days and _____ nights.
4. Despite their age and physical problems, Mrs. Hatching and William are _____ people.

Grammar Handbook
Adjectives, p. 1188

Joan Aiken
1924–

Other Works
The Windscreen Weepers and Other Tales of Horror and Suspense
The Haunting of Lamb House
Morningquest

In Her Fathers' Footsteps The daughter of the American poet Conrad Aiken, Joan Aiken grew up in England, where her parents settled before she was born. After her parents divorced, her mother married another writer, Martin Armstrong. "I knew I was going to be a writer," Joan explains, "like Conrad, like Martin, whose books were to be seen around the house."

A Career Begun In 1945, Aiken met and married Ronald Brown and also began having her poems and stories published in magazines. Her first book of fiction for young adults, *All You've Ever Wanted and Other Stories,* appeared in 1953. Widowed about two years later and needing to support her two children, she became an editor for *Argosy* magazine but continued to write in her spare time.

Literature of the Imagination Joan Aiken has devoted much of her career to writing richly imaginative literature for children and young adults. These stories create worlds of fantasy, mystery, and humor—"what I would have liked to read as a child," she says. In the 1960s she won critical acclaim for a series of books that present alternative histories of England. *The Wolves of Willoughby Chase* (1962), the first in the series, explores what England might have been like if a different royal family had come to power in the 1700s. The series also includes *Black Hearts in Battersea* (1964) and *Night Birds on Nantucket* (1966). Themes of fantasy, mystery, and history also carry through into Aiken's books for adults. Her novel *Mansfield Revisited* was written as a sequel to Jane Austen's *Mansfield Park.*

Grammar in Context

WRITING EXERCISE Answers will vary. Possible answers are shown.

1. Sunlight gives a golden gleam to the clock on the mantle.
2. Tom and Lily take one look at the peaceful, well-furnished spare room and decide to stay.
3. The young couple revel in the warm, sunny days and cool, starry nights.
4. Despite their age and physical problems, Mrs. Hatching and William are generous, cheerful people.

Use **Unit One Resource Book,** p. 14.
Use **Grammar Transparencies and Copymasters,** p. 73.

Use McDougal Littell ***Language Network,*** Chapter 11, for more instruction in punctuating adjectives.

OVERVIEW

This selection is included in the **Grade 10 InterActive Reader.**

Objectives

1. understand and appreciate a **fantasy short story (Literary Analysis)**
2. understand **plot** development **(Literary Analysis)**
3. recognize **sequence** of events **(Active Reading)**

Summary

Ancient laws forbid the People of the Hills to cross the great river and enter the Place of the Gods. According to legend, the Great Burning that once occurred there has poisoned the earth. Nonetheless, John, a priest's son, dreams that he must journey to the Place of the Gods as his rite of passage. He waits for signs that point the way to the Place of the Gods and then begins his journey. After an arduous eight days, John reaches the great river and builds a raft to cross it. Once across, he explores the Place of the Gods—actually the ruins of New York City. He observes the remains of statues, skyscrapers, and homes. During his night in the city, John dreams of life as it was in the Place of the Gods before and during the Great Burning. John realizes that the gods were merely human beings who "ate knowledge too fast." He returns home resolved to study their writings and rebuild their city.

Thematic Link

In this story, a young man comes to realize that a past society paid a steep price for knowledge and progress: annihilation.

5-Minute Warm-Up

Daily Language SkillBuilder

Have students **proofread** the display sentences on page 15i and write them correctly. The sentences also appear on Transparency 2 of **Grammar Transparencies and Copymasters.**

PREPARING to *Read*

By the Waters of Babylon

Short Story by STEPHEN VINCENT BENÉT

"It is there that the spirits live . . . it is there that there are the ashes of the Great Burning."

Connect to Your Life

Through These Doors Think about events that mark the passage from childhood to adulthood in your own life. Are you considered an adult upon graduating from high school? Are there cultural or religious rituals that mark this important transition? Discuss any rites of passage that you have experienced. How did you change as a result, and what knowledge did you gain?

Build Background

Rites of Passage Most cultures have rites of passage to mark the journey from childhood to adulthood or from one role in life to another. Commonly, the participants in a rite of passage stop their normal activities, separate from their community in some way, and concentrate on gaining new knowledge or insights to prepare for their new roles. When the process is completed, the participants return to society and take up their new role in the community. In the selection you are about to read, John, the main character, goes on a journey that becomes a rite of passage and gives him new knowledge.

By the Waters of Babylon The title of this selection is based upon a passage from Psalm 137: "By the waters of Babylon we sat down and wept, when we remembered thee, O Zion." This psalm was composed when Jewish people were enslaved by the Babylonians around 600 B.C. The psalm expresses the Jews' longing for their homeland. Babylon was the largest city of the ancient world, a center of culture, learning, and world trade.

Focus Your Reading

LITERARY ANALYSIS PLOT The **plot** is the chain of related events that take place in a story. Usually, the events of a plot progress because of a **conflict,** or struggle between opposing forces. In the following selection, the main character decides to take a journey, though, as this passage indicates, such a journey is against the ancient laws of his people:

> ***It is forbidden to cross the great river and look upon the place that was the Place of the Gods. . . . We do not even say its name.***

As you read, pay attention to the conflicts that John must face on his journey and what he learns from them.

ACTIVE READING SEQUENCE When you read, it helps to pay close attention to the sequence of events. In this story, the main events follow chronological order; that is, the events are arranged in the order of their occurrence. As you read the story, look for signal words and phrases, such as *after a time, then,* and *when,* that mark the order of events.

READER'S NOTEBOOK Create a chart like the one started, and as you read keep track of important events in the story. In each box, describe an event and tell what the narrator learns from it.

Narrator's journey

Event: Narrator learns:	→	Event: Narrator learns:

LESSON RESOURCES

UNIT ONE RESOURCE BOOK, pp. 16–20

ASSESSMENT RESOURCES

Formal Assessment, pp. 11–12

Teacher's Guide to Assessment and Portfolio Use

Test Generator

SKILLS TRANSPARENCIES AND COPYMASTERS

Literary Analysis

- Plot, T1 (for Paired Activity, p. 53)

Reading and Critical Thinking

- Chronological Order, T11 (for Think Critically, item 2, p. 53)

Grammar

- Personal and Reflexive Pronouns, C153 (for Mini Lessons, pp. 50 and 54)

Vocabulary

- Prefixes, C21 (for Mini Lesson, p. 49)

Writing

- Effective Language, T13 (for Writing Option 2, p. 54)
- The Uses of Dialogue, T24 (for Writing Option 2, p. 54)

Communications

- Impromptu Speaking: Dialogue, Role-Play, Debate, T13 (for Inquiry & Research 1 and 2, p. 54)

INTEGRATED TECHNOLOGY

Audio Library

LaserLinks

- Literary Connection: The Biblical Babylon
- Geographical Connection: Tracing John's Journey

See **Teacher's SourceBook,** p. 7.

Visit our website:
www.mcdougallittell.com

BY THE WATERS OF BABYLON

STEPHEN VINCENT BENÉT

Starburst, Colin Hay.

The north and the west and the south are good hunting ground, but it is forbidden to go east. It is forbidden to go to any of the Dead Places except to search for metal, and then he who touches the metal must be a priest or the son of a priest. Afterwards, both the man and the metal must be purified. These are the rules and the laws; they are well made. It is forbidden to cross the great river and look upon the place that was the Place of the Gods—this is most strictly forbidden. We do not even say its name, though we know its name. It is there that spirits live, and demons—it is there that there are the ashes of the Great Burning. These things are forbidden—

TEACHING THE LITERATURE

Customizing Instruction

Students Acquiring English
Students may have difficulty with the description of John's journey. Explain that the journey is a series of challenges that John has to meet as he proceeds to the Place of the Gods. Tell them to notice what he learns each time.

Use **Spanish Study Guide** for additional support, pp. 10–12.

Less Proficient Readers
Set a Purpose Have students read to see where John goes on his journey.

Gifted and Talented
Ask students to read Psalm 137 and discuss why they think Benét alluded to it in his title. How does reading the psalm affect their understanding of the story?

Mini Lesson Viewing and Representing

***Starburst* by Colin Hay**

ART APPRECIATION Hay, a Scottish artist, enjoys creating futuristic architectural landscapes such as this one.

Instruction Point out the two main elements in the painting, the moon and stars of the natural landscape that contrast with the architectural structures. Ask students to identify features of the painting that portray the fantasy of the story.

Possible Response: The buildings seem futuristic. Yet, they seem very old, because they are beginning to crumble.

Have students compare the architectural structures in the painting with those described in the story.

Possible Response: The structures in the painting resemble the barren Dead Places. There are no people visible in or near the desolate buildings. The structures show deterioration while the natural elements continue to exist unchanged.

Reading and Analyzing

Reading Skills and Strategies: PREVIEW

After briefly summarizing the stages of John's journey, discuss the art images and called-out quotations. Build Background could help students understand the story's plot.

Active Reading SEQUENCE

Have students brainstorm words and phrases that signal the order of events. Make a list of these words on the chalkboard so students can refer to it as they read.

Possible Response: *Just before, next, finally, immediately, at last,* and *then* are just a few examples.

Use **Unit One Resource Book** p. 17 for more practice.

Literary Analysis: CONFLICT

Plot, a chain of related events in a story, may be advanced by either external or internal conflict. External conflict is a struggle between a character and an outside force, such as society, nature, or another character. Internal conflict is a struggle within a character's mind. It may occur when the character has to make a difficult decision or deal with opposing feelings. After reading the opening passages, students may want to predict whether the conflict in this story will be primarily internal or external.

Hills (1914), Man Ray. Oil on canvas, 10⅛″ × 12″, Munson-Williams-Proctor Institute, Museum of Art, Utica, New York, museum purchase.

they have been forbidden since the beginning of time.

My father is a priest; I am the son of a priest. I have been in the Dead Places near us, with my father—at first, I was afraid. When my father went into the house to search for the metal, I stood by the door, and my heart felt small and weak. It was a dead man's house, a spirit house. It did not have the smell of man, though there were old bones in a corner. But it is not fitting that a priest's son should show fear. I looked at the bones in the shadow and kept my voice still.

Then my father came out with the metal—a good, strong piece. He looked at me with both eyes, but I had not run away. He gave me the metal to hold—I took it and did not die. So he knew that I was truly his son and would be a priest in my time. That was when I was very young—nevertheless, my brothers would not have done it, though they are good hunters.

After that, they gave me the good piece of meat and the warm corner by the fire. My father watched over me—he was glad that I should be a priest. But when I boasted or wept without a reason, he punished me more strictly than my brothers. That was right.

After a time, I myself was allowed to go into the dead houses and search for metal. So I learned the ways of those houses—and if I saw bones, I was no longer afraid. The bones are light and old—sometimes they will fall into dust if you touch them. But that is a great sin.

I was taught the chants and the spells—I was taught how to stop the running of blood from a wound and many secrets. A priest must know many secrets—that was what my father said. If the hunters think we do all things by chants and spells, they may believe so—it does not hurt them. I was taught how to read in the old books and how to make the old writings—that was hard and took a long time. My knowledge made me happy—it was like a fire in my heart. Most of all, I liked to hear of the Old Days and the stories of the gods. I asked myself many questions that I could not answer, but it was good to ask them. At night, I would lie awake and listen to the wind—it seemed to me that it was the voice of the gods as they flew through the air.

We are not ignorant like the Forest People—our women spin wool on the wheel; our priests wear a white robe. We do not eat grubs from

Teaching Options

Mini Lesson: Viewing and Representing

***Hills* by Man Ray**

ART APPRECIATION Man Ray (1890–1976), an American painter, is well-known for his surreal paintings in which both real and dreamlike images are combined.

Instruction This landscape reflects Ray's use of unexpected colors and stark shapes. What effect do the colors in this painting have on its mood?

Possible Response: The yellowish skies and dark hills suggest an unsettling and ominous mood. The stark colors and bold lines create a desolate landscape without much detail.

the tree; we have not forgotten the old writings, although they are hard to understand. Nevertheless, my knowledge and my lack of knowledge burned in me—I wished to know more. When I was a man at last, I came to my father and said, "It is time for me to go on my journey. Give me your leave."

He looked at me for a long time, stroking his beard; then he said at last, "Yes. It is time." That night, in the house of the priesthood, I asked for and received purification. My body hurt, but my spirit was a cool stone. It was my father himself who questioned me about my dreams.

He bade me look into the smoke of the fire and see—I saw and told what I saw. It was what I have always seen—a river, and, beyond it, a great Dead Place and in it the gods walking. I have always thought about that. His eyes were stern when I told him—he was no longer my father but a priest. He said, "This is a strong dream."

"It is mine," I said, while the smoke waved and my head felt light. They were singing the star song in the outer chamber, and it was like the buzzing of bees in my head.

He asked me how the gods were dressed, and I told him how they were dressed. We know how they were dressed from the book, but I saw them as if they were before me. When I had finished, he threw the sticks three times and studied them as they fell.

"This is a very strong dream," he said. "It may eat you up."

"I am not afraid," I said and looked at him with both eyes. My voice sounded thin in my ears, but that was because of the smoke.

He touched me on the breast and the forehead. He gave me the bow and the three arrows.

"Take them," he said. "It is forbidden to travel east. It is forbidden to cross the river. It is forbidden to go to the Place of the Gods. All these things are forbidden."

"All these things are forbidden," I said, but it was my voice that spoke and not my spirit. He looked at me again.

"My son," he said. "Once I had young dreams. If your dreams do not eat you up, you may be a great priest. If they eat you, you are still my son. Now go on your journey." 1

I went fasting, as is the law. My body hurt but not my heart. When the dawn came, I was out of sight of the village. I prayed and purified myself, waiting for a sign. The sign was an eagle. It flew east.

Sometimes signs are sent by bad spirits. I waited again on the flat rock, fasting, taking no food. I was very still—I could feel the sky above me and the earth beneath. I waited till the sun was beginning to sink. Then three deer passed in the valley, going east—they did not wind me or see me. There was a white fawn with them—a very great sign.

"This is a very strong dream," he said. "It may eat you up."

I followed them, at a distance, waiting for what would happen. My heart was troubled about going east, yet I knew that I must go. My head hummed with my fasting—I did not even see the panther spring upon the white fawn. But, before I knew it, the bow was in my hand. I shouted, and the panther lifted his head from the fawn. It is not easy to kill a panther with one arrow, but the arrow went through his eye and into his brain. He died as he tried to spring—he rolled over, tearing at the ground. Then I knew I was meant to go east—I knew that was my journey. When the night came, I made my fire and roasted meat.

Customizing Instruction

Less Proficient Readers

1 To help students understand how John's childhood prepared him to undertake his rite of passage, ask them to notice what special knowledge John was taught as a priest's son.

Possible Response: John learned to enter the Dead Places and search for metal. He also learned chants, spells, healing practices, reading, and writing.

BLOCK SCHEDULING: MANAGING TIME

If your schedule requires that you cover the lesson objectives in a shorter time, use . . .

- Preparing to Read, p. 42
- Thinking Through the Literature, p. 53
- Grammar in Context, p. 54

If you want to take advantage of longer class time, use . . .

- TE Teaching Options: Viewing and Representing, pp. 43, 44, 48; Vocabulary Strategy, p. 49; Multicultural Link, p. 47; Workplace Link, p. 46; Informal Assessment, p. 52
- Choices & Challenges and Author Activity, pp. 54–55

Reading and Analyzing

Literary Analysis PLOT

(A) Most plots include an exposition, which lays the groundwork for the plot and gives the reader necessary background information. Ask students to discuss what they have learned so far about the narrator and his way of life.

Possible Responses: He is the son of a priest; he is braver than his brothers; he is intelligent enough to read and write; his people are somewhat superstitious and are not technologically advanced.

Use **Unit One Resource Book,** p. 18 for more practice.

Literary Analysis: POINT OF VIEW

(B) Remind students that a first-person narrative is told from the point of view of one of the characters involved in the story. Ask them what effect the first-person point of view and John's song of this story have on the reader.

Possible Response: The narrator's vocabulary is too limited to name much of what he sees, so the reader must read carefully and use his or her imagination to understand.

Reading Skills and Strategies: PREDICTING

Challenge students to predict how John's journey will affect his understanding of his people's stories and legends.

Possible Response: The journey will reveal that some of the stories and legends, although they serve a teaching purpose, are not literally true any longer.

It is eight suns' journey to the east, and a man passes by many Dead Places. The Forest People are afraid of them, but I am not. Once I made my fire on the edge of a Dead Place at night, and next morning, in the dead house, I found a good knife, little rusted. That was small to what came afterward, but it made my heart feel big. Always when I looked for game, it was in front of my arrow, and twice I passed hunting parties of the Forest People without their knowing. So I knew my magic was strong and my journey clean, in spite of the law.

Toward the setting of the eighth sun, I came to the banks of the great river. It was half a day's journey after I had left the god road—we do not use the god roads now, for they are falling apart into great blocks of stone, and the forest is safer going. A long way off, I had seen the water through trees, but the trees were thick. At last, I came out upon an open place at the top of a cliff. There was the great river (A) below, like a giant in the sun. It is very long, very wide. It could eat all the streams we know and still be thirsty. Its name is Ou-dis-sun, the Sacred, the Long. No man of my tribe had seen it, not even my father, the priest. It was magic, and I prayed.

Then I raised my eyes and looked south. It was there, the Place of the Gods.

How can I tell what it was like—you do not know. It was there, in the red light, and they were too big to be houses. It was there with the red light upon it, mighty and ruined. I knew that in another moment the gods would see me. I covered my eyes with my hands and crept back into the forest.

Surely, that was enough to do, and live. Surely it was enough to spend the night upon the cliff. The Forest People themselves do not come near. Yet, all through the night, I knew that I should have to cross the river and walk in the places of the gods, although the gods ate me up. My magic did not help me at all, and yet there was a fire in my bowels, a fire in my mind. When the sun rose, I thought, "My journey has been clean. Now I will go home from my journey." But, even as I thought so, I knew I could not. If I went to the Place of the Gods, I would surely die, but, if I did not go, I could never be at peace with my spirit again. It is better to lose one's life than one's spirit, if one is a priest and the son of a priest.

Nevertheless, as I made the raft, the tears ran out of my eyes. The Forest People could have killed me without fight, if they had come upon me then, but they did not come. When the raft was made, I said the sayings for the dead and painted myself for death. My heart was cold as a frog and my knees like water, but the burning in my mind would not let me have peace. As I pushed the raft from the shore, I began my death song—I had the right. It was a fine song.

"I am John, son of John," I sang. "My
people are the Hill People.
They are the men.
I go into the Dead Places, but I am not slain.
I take the metal from the Dead Places, but
I am not blasted.
I travel upon the god roads and am not
afraid. E-yah! I have killed the panther; I
have killed the fawn!
(B) *E-yah! I have come to the great river. No* 1
man has come there before.
It is forbidden to go east, but I have gone,
forbidden to go on the great river, but I
am there.
Open your hearts, you spirits, and hear my
song.
Now I go to the Place of the Gods; I shall
not return.
My body is painted for death and my limbs
weak, but my heart is big as I go to the
Place of the Gods!"

Teaching Options

Workplace Link: Using Visual Aids

Instruction Being able to use visual aids to interpret information, as well as having the ability to create visual aids in order to help others acquire and understand information, is an important workplace skill. Useful visual aids include charts, graphs, displays, posters, and diagrams.
Have students note how John tries to use the things he sees on his journey to come to conclusions about the ruined civilization of the past. Ask them to imagine how John will begin to teach his people about the things he has learned during his search for knowledge.

Application Have students imagine that they are trying to teach a person from the past or from the imagined future about an aspect of present-day civilization. Ask them to create a visual aid they could use to help the person understand that aspect of culture or technology.

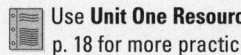

All the same, when I came to the Place of the Gods, I was afraid, afraid. The current of the great river is very strong—it gripped my raft with its hands. That was magic, for the river itself is wide and calm. I could feel evil spirits about me, in the bright morning; I could feel their breath on my neck as I was swept down the stream. Never have I been so much alone—I tried to think of my knowledge, but it was a squirrel's heap of winter nuts. There was no strength in my knowledge anymore, and I felt small and naked as a new-hatched bird—alone upon the great river, the servant of the gods.

2

Yet, after a while, my eyes were opened, and I saw. I saw both banks of the river—I saw that once there had been god roads across it, though now they were broken and fallen like broken vines. Very great they were, and wonderful and broken—broken in the time of the Great Burning when the fire fell out of the sky. And always the current took me nearer to the Place of the Gods, and the huge ruins rose before my eyes.

I do not know the customs of rivers—we are the People of the Hills. I tried to guide my raft with the pole, but it spun around. I thought the river meant to take me past the Place of the Gods and out into the Bitter Water of the legends. I grew angry then—my heart felt strong. I said aloud, "I am a priest and the son of a priest!" The gods heard me—they showed me how to paddle with the pole on one side of the raft. The current changed itself—I drew near to the Place of the Gods.

When I was very near, my raft struck and turned over. I can swim in our lakes—I swam to the shore. There was a great spike of rusted metal sticking out into the river—I hauled myself up upon it and sat there, panting. I had saved my bow and two arrows and the knife I found in the Dead Place, but that was all. My raft went whirling downstream toward the Bitter Water. I looked after it, and thought if it had trod me under, at least I would be safely dead. Nevertheless, when I had dried my bowstring and restrung it, I walked forward to the Place of the Gods.

It felt like ground underfoot; it did not burn me. It is not true what some of the tales say, that the ground there burns forever, for I have been there. Here and there were the marks and stains of the Great Burning, on the ruins, that is true. But they were old marks and old stains. It is not true either, what some of our priests say, that it is an island covered with fogs and enchantments. It is not. It is a great Dead Place—greater than any Dead Place we know. Everywhere in it there are god roads, though most are cracked and broken. Everywhere there are the ruins of the high towers of the gods.

How shall I tell what I saw? I went carefully, my strung bow in my hand, my skin ready for danger. There should have been the wailings of spirits and the shrieks of demons, but there were not. It was very silent and sunny where I had landed—the wind and the rain and the birds that drop seeds had done their work—the grass grew in the cracks of the broken stone. It is a fair island—no wonder the gods built there. If I had come there, a god, I also would have built.

IT IS NOT TRUE WHAT SOME OF THE TALES SAY . . .

How shall I tell what I saw? The towers are not all broken—here and there one still stands, like a great tree in a forest, and the birds nest high. But the towers themselves look blind, for the gods are gone. I saw a fish hawk, catching fish in the river. I saw a little dance of white butterflies over a great heap of broken stones and columns. I went there and looked about me—there was a carved stone with cut letters,

Customizing Instruction

Multiple Learning Styles

Auditory Learners

1 Invite students to sing John's ballad. They can make up their own melodies or accompaniments.

Students Acquiring English

2 Ask students to interpret the words *I could feel their breath on my neck.* Point out that a person's skin is often said to "crawl" when danger is near. Ask volunteers if there is a similar idiom in their native language and, if so, to translate it directly into English.

Less Proficient Readers

Use the following questions to help students to understand John's journey.

- Where has the narrator traveled?
  Answer: John has traveled to the Place of the Gods.
- Why did he want to go there?
  Possible Response: A powerful vision compelled him.

Set a Purpose Have students read on to find out what happens to John in the Place of the Gods.

Multicultural Link: Rites of Passage

Like the Hill People to whom the narrator of the story belongs, many cultures all over the world have rites of passage for young people becoming adults. Benét's description of John's rite of passage strongly resembles some Native American practices that require young men to go on solitary journeys, guided by portents and spiritual signs. For instance, young Sioux undertake vision quests, during which they pray, fast, and endure other forms of deprivation in hopes of inducing a vision. Young Papago travel alone into the desert on a quest for a power-giving dream. In Australia, Aborigine boys go on solitary "walkabouts," desert journeys lasting several days, during which they must be completely self-sufficient.

Reading and Analyzing

Reading Skills and Strategies: CLARIFYING

A Ask students to use the details in this paragraph to explain the Place of the Gods.

Possible Response: The pigeons, towers, roads, cats, and dogs suggest a modern city.

Literary Analysis: FORESHADOWING

B Read aloud the following sentence: "The wild dogs are more dangerous, for they hunt in a pack, but them I did not meet till later." Have students discuss how this sentence advances the plot.

Possible Response: The sentence foreshadows a frightening event. It advances the plot by heightening suspense; the reader knows the narrator will encounter the dogs later.

1 *Toto* (1988), Jimmy Lee Sudduth. Paint with mud on wood, 31¾″ × 24″, from *American Self-Taught,* by Frank Maresca and Roger Ricco, published by Knopf, 1993.

broken in half. I can read letters, but I could not understand these. They said UBTREAS. There was also the shattered image of a man or a god. It had been made of white stone, and he wore his hair tied back like a woman's. His name was ASHING, as I read on the cracked half of a stone. I thought it wise to pray to ASHING, though I do not know that god.

A How shall I tell what I saw? There was no smell of man left, on stone or metal. Nor were there many trees in that wilderness of stone. There are many pigeons, nesting and dropping in the towers—the gods must have loved them, or, perhaps, they used them for sacrifices. There are wild cats that roam the god roads, green-eyed, unafraid of man. At night they wail like demons, but they are not demons. The wild dogs are more dangerous, for they hunt in a pack, but them I did not meet till later. Everywhere there are the carved stones, carved with magical numbers or words.

I went north—I did not try to hide myself. When a god or a demon saw me, then I would die, but meanwhile I was no longer afraid. My hunger for knowledge burned in me—there was so much that I could not understand. After a while, I knew that my belly was hungry. I could have hunted for my meat, but I did not hunt. It is known that the gods did not hunt as we do—they got their food from enchanted boxes and jars. Sometimes these are still found in the Dead Places—once, when I was a child and foolish, I opened such a jar and tasted it and found the food sweet. But my father found out and punished me for it strictly, for, often, that food is death. Now, though, I had long gone past what was forbidden, and I entered the likeliest towers, looking for the food of the gods. 2

I found it at last in the ruins of a great temple in the mid-city. A mighty temple it must have been, for the roof was painted like the sky at night with its stars—that much I could see, though the colors were faint and dim. It went down into great caves and tunnels—perhaps they kept their slaves there. But when I started to climb down, I heard the squeaking of rats, so I did not go—rats are unclean, and there must have been many tribes of them, from the

Teaching Options

Mini Lesson: Viewing and Representing

***Toto* by Jimmy Lee Sudduth**

ART APPRECIATION Sudduth is not only an artist, but also a blues musician and a storyteller. Most of his paintings depict the people and places of rural Alabama.

Instruction Sudduth uses a combination of mud, sugar, water, and natural pigments to create his plywood paintings. Ask students why Sudduth might prefer to work with materials such as these.

Possible Response: Sudduth might prefer simple materials because they give an unfinished, "raw" look to his painting.

Application Ask students how Sudduth's depiction of a dog relates to their impression of the dogs in the story.

Possible Response: The openmouthed dog in the painting is sinister and threatening, just like the wild dogs that try to attack John in the story.

squeaking. But near there, I found food, in the heart of a ruin, behind a door that still opened. I ate only the fruits from the jars—they had a very sweet taste. There was drink, too, in bottles of glass—the drink of the gods was strong and made my head swim. After I had eaten and drunk, I slept on the top of a stone, my bow at my side.

When I woke, the sun was low. Looking down from where I lay, I saw a dog sitting on his haunches. His tongue was hanging out of his mouth; he looked as if he were laughing. He was a big dog, with a gray-brown coat, as big as a wolf. I sprang up and shouted at him, but he did not move—he just sat there as if he were laughing. I did not like that. When I reached for a stone to throw, he moved swiftly out of the way of the stone. He was not afraid of me; he looked at me as if I were meat. No doubt I could have killed him with an arrow, but I did not know if there were others. Moreover, night was falling.

I looked about me—not far away there was a great, broken god road, leading north. The towers were high enough, but not so high, and while many of the dead houses were wrecked, there were some that stood. I went toward this god road, keeping to the heights of the ruins, while the dog followed. When I had reached the god road, I saw that there were others behind him. If I had slept later, they would have come upon me asleep and torn out my throat. As it was, they were sure enough of me; they did not hurry. When I went into the dead house, they kept watch at the entrance—doubtless they thought they would have a fine hunt. But a dog cannot open a door, and I knew, from the books, that the gods did not like to live on the ground but on high.

I had just found a door I could open when the dogs decided to rush. Ha! They were surprised when I shut the door in their faces—it was a good door, of strong metal. I could hear their foolish baying beyond it, but I did not stop to answer them. I was in darkness—I found stairs and climbed. There were many stairs, turning around till my head was dizzy. At the top was another door—I found the knob and opened it. I was in a long small chamber—on one side of it was a bronze door that could not be opened, for it had no handle. Perhaps there was a magic word to open it, but I did not have the word. I turned to the door in the opposite side of the wall. The lock of it was broken, and I opened it and went in.

Within, there was a place of great riches. The god who lived there must have been a powerful god. The first room was a small anteroom—I waited there for some time, telling the spirits of the place that I came in peace and not as a robber. When it seemed to me that they had had time to hear me, I went on. Ah, what riches! Few, even, of the windows had been broken—it was all as it had been. The great windows that looked over the city had not been broken at all, though they were dusty and streaked with many years. There were coverings on the floors, the colors not greatly faded, and the chairs were soft and deep. There were pictures upon the walls, very strange, very wonderful—I remember one of a bunch of flowers in a jar—if you came close to it, you could see nothing but bits of color, but if you stood away from it, the flowers might have been picked yesterday. It made my heart feel strange to look at this picture—and to look at the figure of a bird, in some hard clay, on a table and see it so like our birds. Everywhere

WITHIN, THERE WAS A PLACE OF GREAT RICHES.

Customizing Instruction

Multiple Learning Styles

Visual Learners

1 Ask students to visualize and describe the background or surroundings for "Toto."

Less Proficient Readers

2 Have students tell what John means when he observes that he "had long gone past what was forbidden."

Possible Response: Defying the laws of his people, John has traveled east, crossed the great river, and entered the Place of the Gods.

Mini Lesson Vocabulary Strategy

PREFIXES: Ante-

Instruction The prefix *ante-* means "earlier" or "in front of." It comes from the Latin word *ante* meaning "before." When John walks into the anteroom of the apartment, he is entering a small room that leads to (or comes in front of) the rest of the rooms. Other words that use the prefix *ante-* are *antecedent, antebellum,* and *antedate.*

Activity Have students find the meanings of *antecedent, antebellum,* and *antedate.* Ask them to use each word in a sentence. Ask students to describe how they can use knowledge of the prefix *ante-* to remember the meanings of these words.

Use **Vocabulary Transparencies and Copymasters,** pp. 7, 21, 26, 31.

A lesson on affixes appears on p. 856 in the Pupil's Edition.

Reading and Analyzing

Literary Analysis: POINT OF VIEW

A Ask students how the first-person point of view is important to this passage.

Possible Responses: It adds humor; it emphasizes just how much life changed after the Great Burning, because John doesn't recognize any of the modern conveniences he encounters.

Literary Analysis PLOT

B John journeys out of his body and sees the Place of the Gods as it was in the past, before and during the Great Burning. Ask students how John's vision advances the plot.

Possible Response: It describes the lives of the "gods" and reveals the story of their destruction.

Active Reading SEQUENCE

C Call on volunteers to describe, in chronological order, the Great Burning and the Destruction.

Possible Response: Weapons, perhaps bombs, fell from the sky. People scattered and ran to escape–but only a few succeeded. Fallout from the weapons poisoned the earth and the people who had not been hit. The towers of the city began to fall. The last survivor died.

there were books and writings, many in tongues that I could not read. The god who lived there must have been a wise god and full of knowledge. I felt I had a right there, as I sought knowledge also.

A Nevertheless, it was strange. There was a washing place but no water—perhaps the gods washed in air. There was a cooking place but no wood, and though there was a machine to cook food, there was no place to put fire in it. Nor were there candles or lamps—there were things that looked like lamps, but they had neither oil nor wick. All these things were magic, but I touched them and lived—the magic had gone out of them. Let me tell one thing to show. In the washing place, a thing said "Hot," but it was not hot to the touch—another thing said "Cold," but it was not cold. This must have been a strong magic, but the magic was gone. I do not understand—they had ways—I wish that I knew.

It was close and dry and dusty in the house of the gods. I have said the magic was gone, but that is not true—it had gone from the magic things, but it had not gone from the place. I felt the spirits about me, weighing upon me. Nor had I ever slept in a Dead Place before—and yet, tonight, I must sleep there. When I thought of it, my tongue felt dry in my throat, in spite of my wish for knowledge. Almost I would have gone down again and faced the dogs, but I did not.

I had not gone through all the rooms when the darkness fell. When it fell, I went back to the big room looking over the city and made fire. There was a place to make fire and a box with wood in it, though I do not think they cooked there. I wrapped myself in a floor covering and slept in front of the fire—I was very tired.

Now I tell what is very strong magic. I woke in the midst of the night. When I woke, the fire had gone out, and I was cold. It seemed to me that all around me there were whisperings and voices. I closed my eyes to shut them out. Some will say that I slept again, but I do not think that I slept. I could feel the spirits drawing my spirit out of my body as a fish is drawn on a line.

Why should I lie about it? I am a priest and the son of a priest. If there are spirits, as they say, in the small Dead Places near us, what spirits must there not be in that great Place of the Gods? And would not they wish to speak? After such long years? I know that I felt myself drawn as a fish is drawn on a line. I had stepped out of my body—I could see my body asleep in front of the cold fire, but it was not I. I was drawn to look out upon the city of the gods.

It should have been dark, for it was night, but it was not dark. Everywhere there were lights—lines of light—circles and blurs of light—ten thousand torches would not have been the same. The sky itself was alight—you could barely see the stars for the glow in the sky. I thought to myself "This is strong magic" and trembled. There was a roaring in my ears like the rushing of rivers. Then my eyes grew used to the light and my ears to the sound. I knew that I was seeing the city as it had been when the gods were alive. 1

That was a sight indeed—yes, that was a sight: I could not have seen it in the body—my body would have died. Everywhere went the gods, on foot and in chariots—there were gods beyond number and counting, and their chariots blocked the streets. They had turned night to day for their pleasure—they did not sleep with the sun. The noise of their coming and going was the noise of many waters. It was magic what they could do—it was magic what they did.

I looked out of another window—the great vines of their bridges were mended, and the god roads went east and west. Restless, restless, were the gods and always in motion! They burrowed tunnels under rivers—they flew in the air. With unbelievable tools they did giant

Teaching Options

Mini Lesson Grammar

PRONOUNS: PERSONAL AND REFLEXIVE Remind students that personal pronouns are subjects of sentences or objects of verbs or objects of prepositional phrases. The form of a personal pronoun used as a subject (I, you, he, she, it, we, they) usually differs from its form when used as an object (me, you, him, her, it, us, them). Write these examples on the chalkboard.

"*I* shared the fruit bar with Maria." (subject)

"Maria shared the fruit bar with *me*." (object)

Reflexive pronouns refer back to the subject of a sentence. They end in *-self* or *-selves* (myself, yourself, itself, himself, herself, ourselves, yourselves, themselves). Stress that reflexive pronouns should not be used as subjects of sentences or objects of verbs or prepositions. They are used to indicate that the subject receives the action of the verb. (I hurt *myself*.)

"Velma and *I* chose the video." (correct)

"Velma and *myself* chose the video." (incorrect)

Practice Ask students to revise the following sentences. Then have them work in cooperative groups to orally identify and correct any errors in pronoun usage. Students should take turns leading the discussion for each sentence.

1. Before his journey to the Place of the Gods, John purified *hisself*. *(himself)*

2. The enemies of the People of the Hills hid

works—no part of the earth was safe from them, for, if they wished for a thing, they summoned it from the other side of the world. And always, as they labored and rested, as they feasted and made love, there was a drum in their ears—the pulse of the giant city, beating and beating like a man's heart.

Were they happy? What is happiness to the gods? They were great; they were mighty; they were wonderful and terrible. As I looked upon them and their magic, I felt like a child—but a little more, it seemed to me, and they would pull down the moon from the sky. I saw them with wisdom beyond wisdom and knowledge beyond knowledge. And yet not all they did was well done—even I could see that—and yet their wisdom could not but grow until all was peace.

B Then I saw their fate come upon them, and that was terrible past speech. It came upon them as they walked the streets of their city. I have been in the fights with the Forest People—I have seen men die. But this was not like that. When gods war with gods, they use weapons we do not know. It was fire falling out of the sky and a mist that poisoned. It was the time of the Great Burning and the Destruction. They ran about like ants in the streets of their city—poor gods, poor gods! Then the towers began to fall. A few escaped—yes, a few. The legends tell it. But, even after the city had become a Dead Place, for many years the poison was still in the ground. I saw it happen; I saw the last of them die. It was darkness over the broken city, and I wept.

All this, I saw. I saw it as I have told it, though not in the body. When I woke in the morning, I was hungry, but I did not think first of my hunger, for my heart was perplexed and confused. I knew the reason for the Dead Places, but I did not see why it had happened. It seemed to me it should not have happened, with all the magic they had. I went through the house looking for an answer. There was so much in the house I could not understand—and yet I am a priest and the son of a priest. It was like being on one side of the great river, at night, with no light to show the way.

Then I saw the dead god. He was sitting in his chair, by the window, in a room I had not entered before, and for the first moment, I thought that he was alive. Then I saw the skin on the back of his hand—it was like dry leather. The room was shut, hot and dry—no doubt that had kept him as he was. At first I was afraid to approach him—then the fear left me. He was sitting looking out over the city—he was dressed in the clothes of the gods. His age was neither young nor old—I could not tell his age. But there was wisdom in his face and great sadness. You could see that he would have not run away. He had sat at his window, watching his city die—then he himself had died. But it is better to lose one's life than one's spirit—and you could see from the face that his spirit had not been lost. I knew that, if I touched him, he would fall into dust—and yet, there was something unconquered in the face.

WERE THEY HAPPY? WHAT IS HAPPINESS TO THE GODS?

That is all of my story, for then I knew he was a man—I knew then that they had been men, neither gods nor demons. It is a great knowledge, hard to tell and believe. They were men—they went a dark road, but they were men. I had no fear after that—I had no fear going home, though twice I fought off the dogs and once I was hunted for two days by the Forest People. When I saw my father again, I

Customizing Instruction

Students Acquiring English

1 Point out the word *tongues* and explain that it is a poetic way of saying "languages." Invite students to say aloud a word or words for "languages" in their primary languages.

Less Proficient Readers

Have students describe John's experiences during his first day in the Place of the Gods.

Possible Response: He explores, eats some food, is chased by dogs, and finds refuge in an apartment.

Set a Purpose: Have students read on to find out what happens to John after he goes to sleep in the apartment.

theirselves in the forest. *(themselves)*

3. John's father taught *he* well. *(him)*
4. Does John's rite of passage impress *yourself?* *(you)*
5. John found food in one of the buildings and ate *itself. (it)*

Use **Grammar Transparencies and Copymasters,** pp. 39, 153.

Use McDougal Littell's ***Language Network,*** Chapters 1 and 8, for more instruction and practice in pronouns.

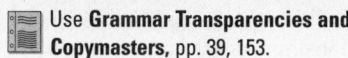

Reading and Analyzing

Literary Analysis: AUTHOR'S PURPOSE

(A) Ask students why they think Benét wrote about a great annihilation similar to a nuclear holocaust.

Possible Responses: He wanted to warn readers that the weapons societies are building can be the means of their destruction. He wanted to persuade people to change their attitude toward war and life in general in order to avoid a fate like the one described in the story.

LITERARY LINK

(B) Use the following questions to help students analyze and understand the poem.

1. What do you think is Teasdale's attitude toward humankind?
   Possible Response: Humans are an unimportant blip in history; humans are dangerous to nature and therefore will not be missed after they are gone.
2. How would you interpret Teasdale's message about war?
   Possible Response: She sees war as leading to the end of civilization; war is pointless self-destruction because, when it is over, nature will continue as it always has.

Sara Teasdale (1884–1933)

Teasdale won a Pulitzer Prize for her poetry collection *Love Songs* in 1917. She was a contemporary of Benét and became acquainted with many leading American writers during her life in New York City. Other collections of her works include *Flame and Shadow* and *Strange Victory.*

prayed and was purified. He touched my lips and my breast; he said, "You went away a boy. You come back a man and a priest." I said, "Father, they were men! I have been in the Place of the Gods and seen it! Now slay me, if it is the law—but still I know they were men."

He looked at me out of both eyes. He said, "The law is not always the same shape—you have done what you have done. I could not have done it my time, but you come after me. Tell!"

I told, and he listened. After that, I wished to tell all the people, but he showed me otherwise. He said, "Truth is a hard deer to hunt. If you eat too much truth at once, you may die of the truth. It was not idly that our fathers forbade the Dead Places." He was right—it is better the truth should come little by little. I have learned that, being a priest. Perhaps, in the old days, they ate knowledge too fast.

Nevertheless, we make a beginning. It is not for the metal alone we go to the Dead Places now—there are the books and the writings. They are hard to learn. And the magic tools are broken—but we can look at them and wonder. At least, we make a beginning. And, when I am chief priest, we shall go beyond the great river. We shall go to the Place of the Gods—the place newyork—not one man but a company. We shall look for the images of the gods and find the god ASHING and the others—the gods Lincoln and Biltmore[1] and Moses.[2] But they were men who built the city, not gods or demons. They were men. I remember the dead man's face. They were men who were here before us. We must build again. ❖ (A)

1. **Biltmore:** the name of a famous hotel in New York City.
2. **Moses:** Robert Moses (1888–1981), a New York City public official whose name appears on many bridges and other structures built during his administration.

LITERARY LINK

There Will Come Soft Rains

Sara Teasdale

There will come soft rains and the
  smell of the ground,
And swallows circling with their
  shimmering sound;

And frogs in the pools singing at
  night,
And wild plum-trees in tremulous
  white;

Robins will wear their feathery fire
Whistling their whims on a low
  fence-wire; (B)

And not one will know of the war,
  not one
Will care at last when it is done.

Not one would mind, neither bird
  nor tree
If mankind perished utterly;

And Spring herself, when she woke
  at dawn,
Would scarcely know that we were
  gone.

Teaching Options

Assessment Informal Assessment

You can informally assess students' understanding of the selection by having them write a journal entry that John might make to himself about his experience in the Place of the Gods. Have students describe the things John sees and the conclusions he draws about the Place of the Gods before the Great Burning.

RUBRIC

3 Full Accomplishment Response includes a description of the important things John sees and shows a full understanding of the conclusions he reaches about civilization before the Great Burning.

2 Substantial Accomplishment Response includes a description of most of the important things John sees and shows a general understanding of the conclusions he reaches about civilization before the Great Burning.

1 Little or Partial Accomplishment Response includes minimal description of the things John sees and shows little understanding of the conclusions he reaches about civilization before the Great Burning.

Connect to the Literature

1. **What Do You Think?** At what point in the story did you begin to figure out what the Place of the Gods was? Explain how you reached your conclusion.

Comprehension Check
- When and where does the story take place?
- Why does John travel to the Place of the Gods?
- What does John discover when he arrives at his destination?

Think Critically

2. **ACTIVE READING** **RECOGNIZING SEQUENCE** Review the chart that you made in your **READER'S NOTEBOOK**, which identified events and what the narrator learned from them. Which events do you think contribute the most to the narrator's coming of age? Explain your reasoning.
3. Why do you think it is forbidden for anyone but a priest to visit the Dead Places? Explain your opinion.
4. How would you describe John as a **character?**

   THINK ABOUT
   - the way that he uses language
   - his determination to finish his journey and complete his rite of passage
   - the importance he gives to knowledge
   - what he means by "It is better to lose one's life than one's spirit" (page 46)
   - his statement "We must build again"
5. How does the **title** of this selection add to your understanding of Benét's story?
6. What do you think is the **theme,** or message, of the story? Support your ideas with evidence from the story.

Extend Interpretations

7. **Comparing Texts** How does the world described in the poem "There Will Come Soft Rains" on page 52 compare with the world described in "By the Waters of Babylon"?
8. **Connect to Life** Do you think it is dangerous for a person or a society to have too much knowledge? Support your opinion.

Literary Analysis

PLOT The **plot** of a story is the writer's blueprint for what happens, when it happens, and to whom it happens. Typically, most include the following stages:

Exposition This stage provides groundwork for the plot. Characters are introduced, the setting is described, and conflicts are identified.
Rising Action As the story progresses, complications usually arise, causing difficulties for the main characters.
Climax This is the turning point of the story, the moment when interest and intensity reach their peak. Usually, an important discovery or decision is made.
Falling Action This stage consists of events that occur after the climax. Often, the conflict is resolved.

Paired Activity With a partner, review the sequence of events that you listed in your **READER'S NOTEBOOK.** Classify the events according to the plot stages described above. Then compare your results with those of your classmates.

POINT OF VIEW The term **point of view** refers to the kind of narrator used in a literary work. In the **first-person point of view,** the narrator is a character in the story who tells everything in his own words. "By the Waters of Babylon" is told in the first person.

Activity Rewrite a key passage from the story using a different point of view. For example, what if the narrator had been John's father or someone outside of the action?

GUIDING STUDENT RESPONSE

Connect to the Literature

1. **What Do You Think?**
   Students may say after John's dream or when he first saw the dead god.

Comprehension Check
- The story takes place in the future, in the ruins of New York City.
- John travels to the Place of the Gods because of a powerful dream and as a rite of passage to manhood and priesthood.
- John discovers that the gods were human beings.

Use Selection Quiz
Unit One Resource Book, p. 20.

Think Critically

2. Possible Response: The discovery of the mummified body contributes most to the narrator's coming of age because this discovery shows him that some of his culture's legends are historically inaccurate.
3. Possible Responses: The Dead Places are considered dangerous; the Hill People think that the Dead Places are inhabited by powerful spirits.
4. Possible Response: John is intelligent, courageous, spiritual, adventurous, and determined.
5. Possible Responses: Benét is drawing a parallel between Babylon and New York City in the 20th century; like Babylon, New York City is part of the rise and fall of history. No matter how developed a civilization is, its survival is not ensured.
6. Possible Responses: Too much progress inevitably leads to destruction; war will destroy the world as we know it.

Extend Interpretations

Comparing Texts Teasdale's poem and Benét's short story both agree that war will destroy our civilization.

Connect to Life Students may want to think of the effect of too much knowledge in specific areas: warfare, medicine, business, astronomy, for example.

Literary Analysis

Plot Exposition: events through narrator's starting out alone on journey to Dead Places
Rising Action: events through vision of the city before and after Great Burning

Climax: realization that mummified body is that of a man, not a god

Falling Action: events following climax

Point of View Rewritten passages should use the different point of view consistently. Details included should reflect accurately what the new narrator would observe and describe.

Writing Options

1. **Journals of the Dead** Responses will vary. Journal entries could describe the war that destroys New York City, the conditions leading up to the war, or the man's daily life.
2. **Debate Dialogue** Both John and the priest should give reasons for their opinions. Before students begin writing, have them review the rules of punctuation for dialogue.

Activities & Explorations

1. **Journey Map** Assign researchers to look for events and details from the story and artists to create the map. All students should contribute ideas. Completed maps should accurately depict the territory in which John lives and travels according to story details.
2. **Artifact Collection** Students can create artifact cards naming each object, stating its function, and explaining its composition. However, these cards should be written from John's perspective; therefore, often the name, function, and/or composition will not be correct. Students should try to see the objects from John's point of view before they begin.

Art Connection

Students may have visualized more details or the ruins of specific buildings in New York City.

Inquiry & Research Germany's aggression was making Europe very uneasy. World War II was about to begin.

Writing Options

1. **Journals of the Dead** Compose a series of journal entries that the dead man sitting at the window might have left in his safe, to be found by someone like John.

2. **Debate Dialogue** Imagine that a powerful priest of the Hill People is against John's making public the insights he gained on his journey. Write a dialogue of the debate between John and the priest about whether the people should learn the truth about the gods. Begin by listing the reasons that you think John and the priest would give.

Activities & Explorations

1. **Journey Map** With a group of classmates, develop a map that shows the territory in which John lives and travels. Be sure to show the sites of important events in John's journey. Add other details to make your map complete.
~ GEOGRAPHY

2. **Artifact Collection** Put together a collection of artifacts that John might have brought back from his visit to the Place of the Gods. Present your collection to the class as John might have presented it to the people of his village.
~ SPEAKING AND LISTENING

Inquiry & Research

1. **News Reel** Benét published "By the Waters of Babylon" in 1937. Find out about world events and the general public mood of that time to learn what might have prompted him to write such a story. Present your findings to the class as a script for a movie newsreel or as a series of news headlines or articles.

2. **Film Study** View the film *The Gods Must Be Crazy,* in which people from a primitive culture make unexpected contact with modern society. Compare and contrast the film and the Benét story.

Art Connection

Does the painting *Starburst* on page 43 reflect your own image of the Place of the Gods? Explain your answer.

Starburst, Colin Hay.

Grammar in Context: Pronouns

In the excerpt below, Benét uses pronouns to establish the narrative point of view. A **pronoun** is a word used in place of a noun or another pronoun.

> **He asked me how the gods were dressed, and I told him how they were dressed. We know how they were dressed from the book. . . .**

Benét's use of first-person pronouns *(me, I, we)* shows that the story is being told from the point of view of one of the characters. The reader experiences events only through that character's eyes and mind. The use of the pronouns *him* and *they* in place of "my father" and "the gods" makes the writing smoother and more concise. How would the story be different if it were told from a third-person point of view (*"His father* asked *him,* . . . and *he* told *his father* . . .")?

WRITING EXERCISE Rewrite the sentences below, changing first-person pronouns to third-person pronouns. Where appropriate, replace repeated nouns with pronouns.

Example: ***Original*** I go with my father to get metal and hold a piece of the metal.
Rewritten He goes with his father to get metal and holds a piece of it.

1. I dream about walking in the Dead Places and about returning to tell my people all about the Dead Places.
2. I tell my father that I have decided to leave.
3. My father gives me a blessing and wishes me well.
4. I wonder about the buildings—who made the buildings and how the buildings were destroyed.

Grammar Handbook
Pronouns, p. 1183

Teaching Options

Mini Lesson Grammar

PRONOUNS

Instruction A pronoun is a word that can be used to replace a noun. Often, using pronouns improves the flow in a sentence. A personal pronoun, which refers to a person, has gender, number, and case. The case indicates how a personal pronoun is used in a sentence. The person of a personal pronoun indicates its gender and number.

Practice Have students work in cooperative groups to complete the writing exercise included with the Grammar in Context feature on the Pupil's page. Suggest they refer to page 1183 of their Grammar Handbooks if they would like additional information about personal pronouns.

Use **Unit One Resource Book,** p. 19.

Use **Grammar Transparencies and Copymasters,** pp. 39, 153.

Use McDougal Littell ***Language Network,*** Chapters 1 and 8, for more instruction in pronouns.

Stephen Vincent Benét

1898–1943

Other Works

The Devil and Daniel Webster
Ballads and Poems
Selected Works of Stephen Vincent Benét

Born to Books Stephen Vincent Benét was the most famous member of a writing family that also included his brother William and his sister Laura. Benét was born in Bethlehem, Pennsylvania, and grew up on various army bases in California and in other parts of the country. As a boy he was studious, and his main companions were the books in the family library. A love of poetry came naturally to him because his father often read poetry aloud and would discuss its form and content with his children. Benét studied literature at Yale University and at the Sorbonne in Paris, France. There he met Rosemary Carr, who worked for the Paris edition of the *Chicago Tribune.* Benét and Carr eventually married, and they collaborated on various literary pieces.

A Proud American Benét was deeply patriotic, and much of his writing is based on American history and folklore. With his wife, he wrote *A Book of Americans* (1933), a collection of historical sketches for younger readers. He was best known for his poetry and short stories, but he also wrote many other kinds of works, including novels and scripts for radio and film. He even wrote an operetta. Based on Washington Irving's classic tale "The Legend of Sleepy Hollow," it was nationally broadcast on the radio in 1937.

Versatile Writer Among Benét's best-known works are the humorous short story "The Devil and Daniel Webster" (1937), for which he received an O. Henry Memorial Prize, and *John Brown's Body* (1928), a long narrative poem about the Civil War, based on information that Benét culled from military records in his father's library. The poem won Benét the first of his two Pulitzer Prizes. The second came for *Western Star* (1943), another long poem about the history of America, which was to have been the first volume in a series. The series remained unfinished at the time of Benét's death.

Author Activity

A noted historian, Henry Steele Commager, said that Benét "loved his country passionately, gave his life to singing her beauty and glory." Find passages from Benét's *America*, his *We Stand United*, or another work that illustrates how Benét viewed the United States, its people, and its history.

LaserLinks: Background for Reading
Literary Connection
Geographical Connection

Grammar in Context

WRITING EXERCISE

ANSWERS

1. He dreams about walking in the Dead Places and about returning to tell his people all about them.
2. He tells his father that he has decided to leave.
3. His father gives him a blessing and wishes him well.
4. He wonders about the buildings—who made them and how they were destroyed.

Author Activity

The passages that students quote should support their assertions.

Building Vocabulary

Objectives

- expand vocabulary through discussion
- examine the context of a word to deduce its meaning
- understand the variety of context clues used to determine word meaning

VOCABULARY EXERCISE

1. "skillfully"; contrast clue
2. "cringed" or "shrank away"; inference clue
3. "delicious"; comparison clue
4. "great joy"; cause-and-effect clue
5. "twisting" or "winding"; inference clue

Meaning Through Context

Do you pause when you come across an unfamiliar word or phrase, or do you continue reading? Doing both might be a good idea—first pausing and thinking about a possible meaning, then reading for clues in the following sentences. Try using this method to figure out the meaning of the highlighted words in the excerpt at the right.

In Vonnegut's vision of the future, smart people must wear radios that interrupt their thoughts, serving as an "equalizing" handicap. This is made clear by the **context** in which *mental handicap radio* occurs—especially by the last sentence of the excerpt, which describes how the handicap works.

> **And George, while his intelligence was way above normal, had a little mental handicap radio in his ear.**
> **. . . It was tuned to a government transmitter. Every twenty seconds or so, the transmitter would send out some sharp noise to keep people like George from taking unfair advantage of their brains.**
> —Kurt Vonnegut, "Harrison Bergeron"

Strategies for Building Vocabulary

In the example above, a type of context clue known as a description clue helped you understand an unfamiliar expression. Here are some other types of context clues.

❶ Comparison and Contrast Clues Sometimes the idea expressed by an unfamiliar word may be compared or contrasted with the idea expressed by a word that you know. A comparison clue can take the form of a simile (a comparison containing *like* or *as*), as in the sentence "Those summer days stayed in his memory indelibly, like pictures carved in stone." Here, the simile comparing the memories to stone carvings can help you see that *indelibly* means "in a way impossible to erase."

A contrast clue illuminates the meaning of an unfamiliar word by contrasting it with the idea expressed by another word. Words that signal contrasts include *although, but, however, in spite of, yet,* and *in contrast.* How does the contrast with *moved on* clarify the meaning of *mesmerized* in the sentence "He stood momentarily mesmerized by the Dead Place, but the barking dog broke the spell and he moved on"?

❷ Cause-and-Effect Clues When the cause of an action is stated by means of an unfamiliar word, a clue to its meaning may be found in the effect. Some words that signal cause-and-effect relationships are *because, since, consequently, therefore, when,* and *as a result.* Notice how the words that follow *as a result* clarify the meaning of *boycott* in this sentence: "People began a boycott of the city bus system, and as a result, the buses traveled empty while many people walked to work."

❸ Inference Clues Sometimes you can infer the meaning of a word by considering the main idea of the passage in which it occurs. How does the main idea of the following passage allow you to infer the meaning of *consternation:* "There was the shriek of a door being torn from its hinges. Screams and barking cries of consternation came from the television set. The photograph of Harrison Bergeron on the screen jumped again and again, as though dancing to the tune of an earthquake."

EXERCISE Define the underlined words in these sentences. In each case, tell what kind of context clue helped you understand the word's meaning.

1. William moved deftly in spite of his blindness.
2. The prisoners cowered before the emperor, expecting to die. He studied them grimly while his soldiers gripped their swords.
3. The pie was as delectable as the mouthwatering creations his mother used to make.
4. Scoring the winning goal filled her with jubilation.
5. The path to the Dead Place was tortuous. It wound through forests and zigzagged through narrow valleys.

The Thrill of the Grass

W. P. Kinsella

Like other sports, the game of baseball has changed over the years. A major change occurred in 1965 when the city of Houston built its Astrodome, the first indoor baseball stadium. This stadium featured a nylon, grasslike carpet called AstroTurf® that served as a substitute for natural grass. Over the next few decades, variations of this artificial turf, which is padded and covers an asphalt surface, came to be used in other stadiums. People who support the use of artificial turf note that it holds up well in any weather and requires little maintenance. Critics, however, point out that its hard surface causes injuries and makes the ball bounce in unusual ways. They also regret the loss of natural grass, which they associate with pleasant memories of baseball in years past.

"The Thrill of the Grass" deals with the issue of artificial turf and the strong feelings that it elicits from fans. The story is set during the baseball strike of 1981, when, for 49 days, major-league players refused to play while they awaited a new contract.

VIDEODISC **LaserLinks: Background for Reading**
Cultural Connection

Possible Objectives

You can use this selection to achieve one or more of the following objectives:

- enjoy silent sustained reading (Option One)
- read and analyze literature with a group (Option Two)
- use the Reader's Notebook to formulate questions about literature (Option Three)
- write in response to literature (Option Three)

Summary

When a strike turns the summer of 1981 into a season without major league baseball, a lone fan visits an empty stadium. He longs to be inside, and as he walks along the fence, he discovers a door he is able to unlock. Once inside, he gazes at the prickly artificial turf that covers the field. As he muses about its ugliness, an idea forms and ripens in his mind. The man visits another avid baseball fan—a prominent man he has seen in a seat near his. He invites the man to meet him at the empty ballpark. That night, the businessman watches his new friend cut out a square of artificial turf and replace it with real sod. Then the two men plan a return trip. Night after night, they bring more friends, returning to the stadium with rakes, hoes, hoses, and sod. In this way, the fans rebuild the park of their dreams, just in time for the strike to end.

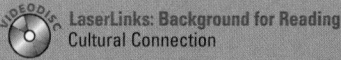

Reading the Selection

Option One
Silent Sustained Reading

You might set aside time each week for independent reading. During this time, you and your students would read for enjoyment. "The Thrill of the Grass" can be read independently in about 30 minutes. If you want to encourage students to read for pleasure, you might forego assignments related to the selection. Should you want to make assignments, Options Two and Three offer suggestions.

Option Two
Shared Reading Groups

You may assign students to groups or allow them to choose their own. Students can read the selection together, alternately reading sections aloud, or they can read independently and meet to cooperate in a project that portrays some element of the story.

Possible Projects

- Students can work in pairs to play the roles of radio sportscasters reporting on the unusual activities of the baseball fans in "The Thrill of the Grass." Suggest that partners first skim the story and note major actions they will report. After rehearsing the interchange, students can deliver their broadcasts to classmates.
- Students can write a continuation of the story by creating the scene that dramatizes the players' return to the stadium after the strike ends. How do the players react when they discover the natural grass? Will they support the change? Students' narratives should include both dialogue and action.
- Students can list and define baseball terminology as they encounter it in the story, helping those in the group who know less about baseball.

Busch Stadium (1982), Jim Dow. Three-panel panorama from 8″ × 10″ color negatives.

1981: the summer the baseball players went on strike. The dull weeks drag by, the summer deepens, the strike is nearly a month old. Outside the city the corn rustles and ripens in the sun.

Summer without baseball: a disruption to the psyche.[1] An unexplainable aimlessness engulfs me. I stay later and later each evening in the small office at the rear of my shop. Now, driving home after work, the worst of the rush hour traffic over, it is the time of the evening I would normally be heading for the stadium.

I enjoy arriving an hour early, parking in a far corner of the lot, walking slowly toward the stadium, rays of sun dropping softly over my shoulders like tangerine ropes, my shadow gliding with me, black as an umbrella. I like to watch young families beside their campers, the mothers in shorts, grilling hamburgers, their men drinking beer. I enjoy seeing little boys dressed in the home team uniform, barely toddling, clutching hotdogs in upraised hands.

I am a failed shortstop. As a young man, I saw myself diving to my left, graceful as a toppling tree, fielding high grounders like a cat leaping for butterflies, bracing my right foot and tossing to first, the throw true as if a steel ribbon connected my hand and the first baseman's glove. I dreamed of leading the American League in hitting—being inducted into the Hall of Fame. I batted .217 in my senior year of high school and averaged 1.3 errors per nine innings.

I know the stadium will be deserted; nevertheless I wheel my car down off the freeway, park, and walk across the silent lot, my footsteps rasping and mournful. Strangle-grass and creeping charlie are already inching up through

1. **psyche** (sī′kē): the human spirit or soul.

Option Three

Reader's Notebook

Provide the following direction to students before they read.

The story is rich with internal description focusing on the narrator's thoughts, memories, and feelings. Before they read, ask students to notice these reflective moments. Each time students encounter a moment in the story where the narrator describes a past moment or feeling, instruct them to write a brief summary of that internal moment in their Reader's Notebook. Students should number these moments consecutively as they encounter them.

After they read the story, ask students to evaluate the narrator's motivations for his actions. Why does the narrator feel so compelled to act as he does? What aspects of his past experience and feelings have motivated him to take such a risk?

Have students discuss their evaluations in class. Assist in the discussion by noting similarities and differences in the interpretations of the narrator's motives. After the discussion, students can add to or modify their evaluations.

THE THRILL OF THE GRASS 59

After Reading

Possible Activities

Independent Activities

- Have students return to the story to gather descriptive details about the baseball stadium as a setting. Have them draw a schematic design of the field in their Reader's Notebook. They should note the physical details of the field and stadium, the details about the fans who generally watch from behind first base side, and the details about the fans who watch from behind third base.
- Have students review the Learning the Language of Literature and Active Reader, pages 17–19. They can note which skills and strategies they used while reading the selection.

Discussion Activities

- Use the details formulated by students' notes as the basis for a discussion about whether the author is attempting to characterize a basic distinction between two fundamentally different types of human beings in the world. In what ways are people either "first base types" or "third base types"? What details suggest that differences in values, attitudes, and approaches to life are represented by which side of the field a person occupies? Ask students to clarify these characteristics and then have them decide which side of the field they would choose.
- Discuss the possible meanings the author might be implying with the word *thrill* in the story's title, "The Thrill of the Grass."

Assessment Opportunities

- You can assess students' comprehension of the story by asking them to explain the narrator's motives for replacing the stadium's artificial turf with grass. In their explanation, ask students to discuss at least two personal experiences the narrator refers to and show how these experiences seem to motivate his actions.
- You can use any of the discussion questions as essay questions.
- You can have students turn any one of their Reader's Notebook entries into an essay.

the gravel, surreptitious, surprised at their own ease. Faded bottle caps, rusted bits of chrome, an occasional paper clip, recede into the earth. I circle a ticket booth, sun-faded, empty, the door closed by an oversized padlock. I walk beside the tall, machinery-green, board fence. A half mile away a few cars hiss along the freeway; overhead a single-engine plane fizzes lazily. The whole place is silent as an empty classroom, like a house suddenly without children.

It is then that I spot the door-shape. I have to check twice to be sure it is there: a door cut in the deep green boards of the fence, more the promise of a door than the real thing, the kind of door, as children, we cut in the sides of cardboard boxes with our mother's paring knives. As I move closer, a golden circle of lock, like an acrimonious[2] eye, establishes its certainty.

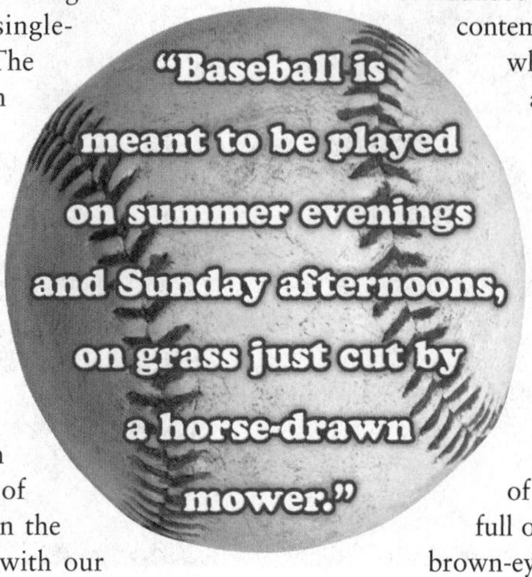

"Baseball is meant to be played on summer evenings and Sunday afternoons, on grass just cut by a horse-drawn mower."

I stand, my nose so close to the door I can smell the faint odour of paint, the golden eye of a lock inches from my own eyes. My desire to be inside the ballpark is so great that for the first time in my life I commit a criminal act. I have been a locksmith for over forty years. I take the small tools from the pocket of my jacket, and in less time than it would take a speedy runner to circle the bases I am inside the stadium. Though the ballpark is open-air, it smells of abandonment; the walkways and seating areas are cold as basements. I breathe the odours of rancid popcorn and wilted cardboard.

The maintenance staff were laid off when the strike began. Synthetic grass does not need to be cut or watered. I stare down at the ball diamond, where just to the right of the pitcher's mound, a single weed, perhaps two inches high, stands defiant in the rain-pocked dirt.

The field sits breathless in the orangy glow of the evening sun. I stare at the potato-coloured earth of the infield, that wide, dun[3] arc, surrounded by plastic grass. As I contemplate the prickly turf, which scorches the thighs and buttocks of a sliding player as if he were being seared by hot steel, it stares back in its uniform ugliness. The seams that send routinely hit ground balls veering at tortuous angles, are vivid, grey as scars.

I remember the ballfields of my childhood, the outfields full of soft hummocks[4] and brown-eyed gopher holes.

I stride down from the stands and walk out to the middle of the field. I touch the stubble that is called grass, take off my shoes, but find it is like walking on a row of toothbrushes. It was an evil day when they stripped the sod from this ballpark, cut it into yard-wide swathes,[5] rolled it, memories and all, into great green-and-black cinnamon-roll shapes, trucked it away. Nature temporarily defeated. But Nature is patient.

Over the next few days an idea forms within me, ripening, swelling, pushing everything else into a corner. It is like knowing a new,

2. **acrimonious** (ăk′rə-mō′nē-əs): harsh; bitter.
3. **dun:** brownish gray.
4. **hummocks:** low, rounded hills.
5. **swathes** (swŏths): strips as wide as the blade of a mowing machine.

wonderful joke and not being able to share. I need an accomplice.

I go to see a man I don't know personally, though I have seen his face peering at me from the financial pages of the local newspaper, and the *Wall Street Journal,* and I have been watching his profile at the baseball stadium, two boxes to the right of me, for several years. He is a fan. Really a fan. When the weather is intemperate, or the game not close, the people around us disappear like flowers closing at sunset, but we are always there until the last pitch. I know he is a man who attends because of the beauty and mystery of the game, a man who can sit during the last of the ninth with the game decided innings ago, and draw joy from watching the first baseman adjust the angle of his glove as the pitcher goes into his windup.

He, like me, is a first-base-side fan. I've always watched baseball from behind first base. The positions fans choose at sporting events are like politics, religion, or philosophy: a view of the world, a way of seeing the universe. They make no sense to anyone, have no basis in anything but stubbornness.

I brought up my daughters to watch baseball from the first-base side. One lives in Japan and sends me box scores from Japanese newspapers, and Japanese baseball magazines with pictures of superstars politely bowing to one another. She has a season ticket in Yokohama;[6] on the first-base side.

"Tell him a baseball fan is here to see him," is all I will say to his secretary. His office is in a skyscraper, from which he can look out over the city to where the prairie rolls green as mountain water to the limits of the eye. I wait all afternoon in the artificially cool, glassy reception area with its yellow and mauve chairs, chrome and glass coffee tables. Finally, in the late afternoon, my message is passed along.

"I've seen you at the baseball stadium," I say, not introducing myself.

"Yes," he says. "I recognize you. Three rows back, about eight seats to my left. You have a red scorebook and you often bring your daughter . . . "

"Granddaughter. Yes, she goes to sleep in my lap in the late innings, but she knows how to calculate an ERA[7] and she's only in Grade 2."

"One of my greatest regrets," says this tall man, whose moustache and carefully styled hair are polar-bear white, "is that my grandchildren all live over a thousand miles away. You're very lucky. Now, what can I do for you?"

"I have an idea," I say. "One that's been creeping toward me like a first baseman when the bunt sign is on.[8] What do you think about artificial turf?"

"Hmmmf," he snorts, "that's what the strike should be about. Baseball is meant to be played on summer evenings and Sunday afternoons, on grass just cut by a horse-drawn mower," and we smile as our eyes meet.

"I've discovered the ballpark is open, to me anyway," I go on. "There's no one there while the strike is on. The wind blows through the high top of the grandstand, whining until the pigeons in the rafters flutter. It's lonely as a ghost town."

"And what is it you do there, alone with the pigeons?"

"I dream."

"And where do I come in?"

"You've always struck me as a man who dreams. I think we have things in common. I

---

6. **Yokohama** (yō′kə-hä′mə): a large city in Japan.
7. **ERA:** earned run average for a baseball pitcher; that is, the average number of earned runs—runs scored without the aid of an error—a pitcher allows every nine innings.
8. **when the bunt sign is on:** when the coach has signaled the batter to tap at the pitched ball instead of swinging at it.

THE THRILL OF THE GRASS 61

think you might like to come with me. I could show you what I dream, paint you pictures, suggest what might happen . . . "

He studies me carefully for a moment, like a pitcher trying to decide if he can trust the sign his catcher has just given him.

"Tonight?" he says. "Would tonight be too soon?"

"Park in the northwest corner of the lot about 1:00 A.M. There is a door about fifty yards to the right of the main gate. I'll open it when I hear you."

He nods.

I turn and leave.

The night is clear and cotton warm when he arrives. "Oh, my," he says, staring at the stadium turned chrome-blue by a full moon. "Oh, my," he says again, breathing in the faint odours of baseball, the reminder of fans and players not long gone.

"Let's go down to the field," I say. I am carrying a cardboard pizza box, holding it on the upturned palms of my hands, like an offering.

When we reach the field, he first stands on the mound, makes an awkward attempt at a windup, then does a little sprint from first to about half-way to second. "I think I know what you've brought," he says, gesturing toward the box, "but let me see anyway."

I open the box, in which rests a square foot of sod, the grass smooth and pure, cool as a swatch of satin, fragile as baby's hair.

"Ohhh," the man says, reaching out a finger to test the moistness of it. "Oh, I see."

We walk across the field, the harsh, prickly turf making the bottoms of my feet tingle, to the left-field corner where, in the angle formed by the foul line and the warning track, I lay down the square foot of sod. "That's beautiful," my friend says, kneeling beside me, placing his hand, fingers spread wide, on the verdant[9] square, leaving a print faint as a veronica.[10]

I take from my belt a sickle-shaped blade, the kind used for cutting carpet. I measure along the edge of the sod, dig the point in and pull carefully toward me. There is a ripping sound, like tearing an old bed sheet. I hold up the square of artificial turf like something freshly killed, while all the time digging the sharp point into the packed earth I have exposed. I replace the sod lovingly, covering the newly bared surface.

"A protest," I say.

"But it could be more," the man replies.

"I hoped you'd say that. It could be. If you'd like to come back . . . "

"Tomorrow night?"

"Tomorrow night would be fine. But there will be an admission charge . . . "

"A square of sod?"

"A square of sod two inches thick . . . "

"Of the same grass?"

"Of the same grass. But there's more."

"I suspected as much."

"You must have a friend . . . "

"Who would join us?"

"Yes."

"I have two. Would that be all right?"

"I trust your judgment."

"My father. He's over eighty," my friend says. "You might have seen him with me once or twice. He lives over fifty miles from here, but if I call him, he'll come. And my friend . . . "

"If they pay their admission, they'll be welcome . . . "

"And *they* may have friends . . . "

"Indeed they may. But what will we do with this?" I say, holding up the sticky-backed square of turf, which smells of glue and fabric.

9. **verdant** (vûr′dnt): covered with green growth.

10. **a print faint as a veronica** (və-rŏn′ĭ-kə): a simile referring to the image of Jesus' face supposedly left on the handkerchief offered to him by Saint Veronica for wiping away his blood on the way to the crucifixion.

Stretching at First (about 1976), John Dobbs. Oil on canvas, 36″ × 40″, collection of Gilbert Kinney, Washington, D.C.

THE THRILL OF THE GRASS **63**

"We could mail them anonymously to baseball executives, politicians, clergymen."

"Gentle reminders not to tamper with Nature."

We dance toward the exit, rampant with excitement.

"You will come back? You'll bring others?"

"Count on it," says my friend.

They do come, those trusted friends, and friends of friends, each making a live, green deposit. At first, a tiny row of sod squares begins to inch along toward left-centre field. The next night even more people arrive, the following night more again, and the night after there is positively a crowd. Those who come once seem always to return accompanied by friends, occasionally a son or young brother, but mostly men my age or older, for we are the ones who remember the grass.

Night after night the pilgrimage continues. The first night I stand inside the deep green door, listening. I hear a vehicle stop; hear a car door close with a snug thud. I open the door when the sound of soft-soled shoes on gravel tells me it is time. The door swings silent as a snake. We nod curt greetings to each other. Two men pass me, each carrying a grasshopper-legged sprinkler. Later, each sprinkler will sizzle like frying onions as it wheels, a silver sparkler in the moonlight.

During the nights that follow, I stand sentinel-like at the top of the grandstand, watching as my cohorts arrive. Old men walking across a parking lot in a row, in the dark, carrying coiled hoses, looking like the many wheels of a locomotive, old men who have slipped away from their homes, skulked down their sturdy sidewalks, breathing the cool, grassy, after-midnight air. They have left behind their sleeping, grey-haired women, their immaculate bungalows, their manicured lawns. They continue to walk across the parking lot, while occasionally a soft wheeze, a nibbling, breathy sound like an old horse might make, divulges their humanity.

They move methodically toward the baseball stadium which hulks against the moon-blue sky like a small mountain. Beneath the tint of starlight, the tall light standards which rise above the fences and grandstand glow purple, necks bent forward, like sunflowers heavy with seed.

My other daughter lives in this city, is married to a fan, but one who watches baseball from behind third base. And like marrying outside the faith, she has been converted to the third-base side. They have their own season tickets, twelve rows up just to the outfield side of third base. I love her, but I don't trust her enough to let her in on my secret.

I could trust my granddaughter, but she is too young. At her age she shouldn't have to face such responsibility. I remember my own daughter, the one who lives in Japan, remember her at nine, all knees, elbows and missing teeth—remember peering in her room, seeing her asleep, a shower of well-thumbed baseball cards scattered over her chest and pillow.

I haven't been able to tell my wife—it is like my compatriots and I are involved in a ritual for true believers only. Maggie, who knew me when I still dreamed of playing professionally myself—

Maggie, after over half a lifetime together, comes and sits in my lap in the comfortable easy chair which has adjusted through the years to my thickening shape, just as she has. I love to hold the lightness of her, her tongue exploring my mouth, gently as a baby's finger

"Where do you go?" she asks sleepily when I crawl into bed at dawn.

I mumble a reply. I know she doesn't sleep well when I'm gone. I can feel her body rhythms change as I slip out of bed after midnight.

"Aren't you too old to be having a change of life," she says, placing her toast-warm hand on my cold thigh.

I am not the only one with this problem.

"I'm developing a reputation," whispers an affable man at the ballpark. "I imagine any number of private investigators following any number of cars across the city. I imagine them creeping about the parking lot, shining pen-lights on licence plates, trying to guess what we're up to. Think of the reports they must prepare. I wonder if our wives are disappointed that we're not out discoing with frizzy-haired teenagers?"

Night after night, virtually no words are spoken. Each man seems to know his assignment. Not all bring sod. Some carry rakes, some hoes, some hoses, which, when joined together, snake across the infield and outfield, dispensing the blessing of water. Others cradle in their arms bags of earth for building up the infield to meet the thick, living sod.

I often remain high in the stadium, looking down on the men moving over the earth, dark as ants, each sodding, cutting, watering, shaping. Occasionally the moon finds a knife blade as it trims the sod or slices away a chunk of artificial turf, and tosses the reflection skyward like a bright ball. My body tingles. There should be symphony music playing. Everyone should be humming "America the Beautiful."

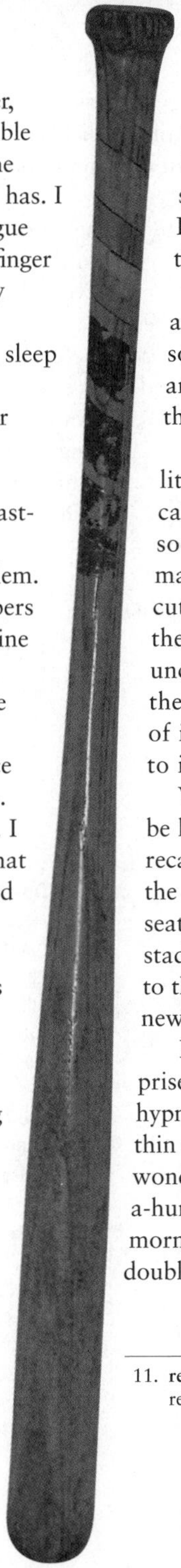

Toward dawn, I watch the men walking away in groups, like small patrols of soldiers, carrying instead of arms, the tools and utensils which breathe life back into the arid ballfield.

Row by row, night by night, we lay the little squares of sod, moist as chocolate cake with green icing. Where did all the sod come from? I picture many men, in many parts of the city, surreptitiously cutting chunks out of their own lawns in the leafy midnight darkness, listening to the uncomprehending protests of their wives the next day—pretending to know nothing of it—pretending to have called the police to investigate.

When the strike is over, I know we will all be here to watch the workouts, to hear the recalcitrant[11] joints crackling like twigs after the forced inactivity. We will sit in our regular seats, scattered like popcorn throughout the stadium, and we'll nod as we pass on the way to the exits, exchange secret smiles, proud as new fathers.

For me, the best part of all will be the surprise. I feel like a magician who has gestured hypnotically and produced an elephant from thin air. I know that I am not alone in my wonder. I know that rockets shoot off in half-a-hundred chests—the excitement of birthday mornings, Christmas eves, and hometown doubleheaders, boils within each of my

11. **recalcitrant** (rĭ-kăl′sĭ-trənt): showing stubborn resistance.

THE THRILL OF THE GRASS **65**

conspirators. Our secret rites[12] have been performed with love, like delivering a valentine to a sweetheart's door in that blue-steel span of morning just before dawn.

Players and management are meeting around the clock. A settlement is imminent. I have watched the stadium covered square foot by square foot until it looks like green graph paper. I have stood and felt the cool odours of the grass rise up and touch my face. I have studied the lines between each small square, watched those lines fade until they were visible to my eyes alone, then not even to them.

What will the players think, as they straggle into the stadium and find the miracle we have created? The old-timers will raise their heads like ponies, as far away as the parking lot, when the thrill of the grass reaches their nostrils. And, as they dress, they'll recall sprawling in the lush fields of childhood, the grass as cool as a mother's hand on a forehead.

"Goodbye, goodbye," we say at the gate, the smell of water, of sod, of sweat, small perfumes in the air. Our secrets are safe with each other. We go our separate ways.

Alone in the stadium in the last chill darkness before dawn, I drop to my hands and knees in the centre of the outfield. My palms are sodden. Water touches the skin between my spread fingers. I lower my face to the silvered grass, which, wonder of wonders, already has the ephemeral[13] odours of baseball about it. ❖

12. **rites:** ceremonies.

13. **ephemeral** (ĭ-fĕm′ər-əl): short-lived; passing quickly.

W. P. Kinsella
1935–

Other Works
The Dixon Cornbelt League and Other Baseball Stories
Box Socials
Shoeless Joe
The Alligator Report
The Iowa Baseball Confederacy
The Further Adventures of Slugger McBatt

Slow Beginnings Success did not come easily to William Patrick Kinsella. Born in Edmonton, Alberta, Canada, Kinsella says that he always thought of himself as a writer, though he wrote more than 50 stories before getting published. He also worked at various odd jobs, such as running his own pizza restaurant, managing a credit agency, and driving a taxicab. Kinsella did not begin college until he was in his 30s.

A True Fan Kinsella grew up loving the game of baseball, though he was a poor player himself. He penned his first baseball story, a murder mystery called "Diamond Doom," when he was in the eighth grade. Kinsella published his first collection of baseball stories, *Shoeless Joe Jackson Comes to Iowa,* in 1980. He expanded the title story into his award-winning novel *Shoeless Joe* (1982), which garnered much attention when it was adapted and produced as the 1989 Hollywood movie *Field of Dreams.*

Author Activity

Hollywood's Take View the film *Field of Dreams,* based on Kinsella's novel *Shoeless Joe.* Then present an oral movie review similar to those provided by television movie critics. In your review, include comparisons with "The Thrill of the Grass."

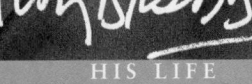

Author Study

Ray Bradbury

OVERVIEW

"Here's a teller of tales . . . who wanted to celebrate things . . . even the dark things because they have meaning."

—Ray Bradbury, suggesting his own epitaph

Social Critic for the Future

A major writer of fantasy and science fiction, Ray Bradbury explores the future, outer space—and the human heart. He has lived to see much science fiction become science fact. Yet Bradbury's work presents very human themes. His most chilling stories comment on the human consequences of progress and often reflect on the ironies of life. Explore the life, work, and passions of a remarkable figure who has been called the world's greatest living science fiction writer.

1920–

SHAPED BY THE FUTURE Ray Bradbury was born in 1920 in Waukegan, Illinois, a town north of Chicago. From an early age, his spongelike mind was directed toward fantasy by the popular culture of his day. He was a fan of movies, radio, comics, museums, traveling circuses, and science fiction magazines. At the age of 12, the Century of Progress exhibit in Chicago captured his interest. However, a more realistic setting—the public library—would also leave permanent impressions on his imagination. Bradbury

HIS LIFE

1920 Is born Aug. 22 in Waukegan, Illinois

1923 Is "profoundly affected" by film *Hunchback of Notre Dame*

1932 Attempts first lengthy writing

1934 Moves with family to Los Angeles

1920 — 1925 — 1930

HIS TIMES

1920 *New York Times* editorial predicts multistage rockets will never reach the moon.

1926 First liquid-fuel rocket is flown.

1930 The planet Pluto is discovered.

OVERVIEW

Objectives

- appreciate the craft of one of America's premier science fiction and fantasy writers
- understand the contribution popular culture made to Bradbury's growth as a writer
- gain information about Bradbury's fiction by reading about his life

This Author Study offers a unique opportunity for students to focus on the work of Ray Bradbury. Students can gather information about his life, gaining insight into the real person behind his famous literary work.

PREVIEW

Using Text Organizers

Have students preview the article, noting the basic text organizers: title, subheads, captions, and time line. Ask students to describe the information they would expect to find in each section. Have students use the subheads to create a graphic organizer. As they read, have them categorize information from the article under the appropriate heading. Remind students that when they do independent research, they should use text organizers to locate and organize information.

Geography

A The Chicago and Northwestern Railway connects Waukegan to both Chicago and Minneapolis. The train station is at the very edge of the bluff and is used in Bradbury's stories of Green Town (his fictional name for Waukegan). The area's deep ravines, particularly the one closest to Bradbury's home in Waukegan, added an air of darkness and mystery to his childhood and to his Green Town stories.

LIFE AND TIMES

Magic

A Ray Bradbury credits magic as an early influence on his imagination. He loved the magic shows that traveling carnivals brought to his hometown. One night a magician named Mr. Electrico, with his electric chair and flaming blue hair, passed his flaming sword over Bradbury in the crowd of one of these traveling magic shows, and said, "Live forever!" Bradbury spent the next few days getting to know the magician. Mr. Electrico told him that they had been friends in another lifetime and that Bradbury had been a close comrade who had died in Mr. Electrico's arms during World War I. Bradbury developed his skills as a magician and practiced illusions from an early age. When his writing career began—at age 12—he used his powers of illusion and the inspiration Mr. Electrico had given him.

Radio

B An important influence on Bradbury's fiction and life was network radio and the radio dramas of the 1920s and 1930s. When his family moved to Tucson, Arizona, Bradbury got a job in local radio reading comic strips to children. In return, the station gave him free movie tickets, which stoked his love for the movies. Later, as a teenager in Los Angeles, he became friends with the comedian George Burns. He would watch Burns and Gracie Allen perform their radio program. Once, he and a high school classmate were invited to be the audience for a particular episode of *The Burns and Allen Show* that was broadcast to the East Coast. In addition, as a budding writer—and typist—he was assigned by Burns to type the radio program's scripts!

constantly checked out what he called "all those gorgeous books," many by early science fiction writers such as H. G. Wells and Jules Verne. These writers inspired him **A** to begin writing outer-space adventure stories of his own.

Educated in a Library In 1934, Bradbury moved with his family to Los Angeles. By age 15, he was sending stories for publication to national magazines, though with no success at first. At this time, most science fiction was viewed as popular but lightweight entertainment.

After finishing high school in 1938, Bradbury sold newspapers on Los Angeles street corners, continuing to write in his spare time. That same year, his first short story was published in a little-known, local magazine. Unpaid but encouraged, he submitted his stories to the well-established **B** *Weird Tales* magazine. He sharpened his storytelling craft, though he had no formal schooling after high school. About his background, Bradbury once said, "I never went to college, so I raised and educated myself in a library."

Reading the fiction of serious writers like John Steinbeck and Ernest Hemingway influenced Bradbury's maturing style. After selling his first story, "The Pendulum," in 1941, he was ready to take more definite steps toward a profession. At age 22, he quit selling newspapers and began living entirely off his income from writing.

A Soaring Career

From 1942 to 1945, Bradbury sold a story each month to *Weird Tales*. His work was also reaching a wider, more literary audience in such national magazines as *The Saturday Evening Post* and *The New Yorker*. In 1947, he published his first book, *Dark Carnival*, a collection of horror tales. In 1950, *The Martian Chronicles*, his book about Earth colonists on Mars, received critical acclaim. The work reflects what Bradbury has expressed as a basic theme of his writing: "Science ran too far ahead of us too quickly, and the people

Bradbury's 1950 book became the basis for a popular 1980 TV miniseries.

- 1938 Has first story published in amateur magazine
- 1942 Begins selling stories to *Weird Tales*
- 1947 Wins first writing award; has first book published
- 1950 *The Martian Chronicles* published
- 1953 Has *Fahrenheit 451* published

1940 — 1945 — 1950 — 1955

- 1942 First fission chain reaction leads to atomic-bomb creation.
- 1945 U.S. drops atomic bombs on Japan.
- 1946 First automatic digital electronic computer is developed.
- 1952 U.S. explodes first hydrogen bomb.
- 1957 Soviet launch of the satellite *Sputnik* starts space race.

Sputnik

got lost in a mechanical wilderness." Many readers, themselves surrounded by rapid technological change, agreed with this view.

In 1953, Bradbury published *Fahrenheit 451*, which many consider his most important book. It depicts a future government that controls its people by eliminating mental stimulation. Some critics (C) have compared *Fahrenheit 451* with George Orwell's *1984* and Aldous Huxley's *Brave New World*, novels that warn of controlling trends in society.

Most of the themes of Bradbury's work come out of his childhood. Because of that, he is considered the most autobiographical science fiction writer. He claims to possess an extraordinary memory of the events of his life, including every book he's read and every film he's seen. His attachment to the memory of Waukegan is legendary. Features of his hometown are reworked into the fictional Green Town found in several of his stories.

"FUN WITH IDEAS" Ray Bradbury's distinguished career includes other types of writing. His plays, many of them adaptations of his stories, have been staged since 1960. He has written screenplays and television scripts, including 42 he produced for a cable network's *Ray Bradbury Television Theatre* from 1985 to 1990. In addition, he helped design Spaceship Earth for Epcot Center in Disney World and contributed to the design of public spaces in Los Angeles and San Diego.

However, it is writing that remains most important to Bradbury. Since his childhood,

LITERARY *Contributions*

Ray Bradbury's work has been recognized for bringing the literary craft to the field of science fiction. Here are some of Bradbury's more than 500 works. (D)

Novels

Fahrenheit 451 (1953)
Something Wicked This Way Comes (1962)
A Graveyard for Lunatics (1990)
Green Shadows, White Whale (1992)

Short-Story Collections

Dark Carnival (1947)
The Martian Chronicles (1950)
The Illustrated Man (1951)
The Golden Apples of the Sun (1953)
The October Country (1955)
Dandelion Wine (1957)
A Medicine for Melancholy (1960)
I Sing the Body Electric (1969)
Long After Midnight (1976)
The Toynbee Convector (1988)
Quicker Than the Eye (1996)
Driving Blind (1997)

Plays

The Wonderful Ice-Cream Suit (1972)
Pillar of Fire (1975)

1963 **Is nominated for Academy Award for documentary film script**

1965 **Has a story in *Fifty Best American Short Stories: 1916–1965***

1971 **Moon crater named Dandelion in honor of *Dandelion Wine***

1960 1965 1970 1975

1961 **Soviet cosmonaut becomes first human in outer space.**

1969 **Three-stage rocket lands astronauts on the moon; the *Times* retracts its 1920 editorial.**

1971 **Microchip is invented.**

LIFE AND TIMES

Utopia

(C) Bradbury intends his frightening description of future human society in *Fahrenheit 451* to be a warning. This reverse-utopian fictional society, also found in the novels 1984 and *Brave New World,* is called a dystopia. A dystopia is an imaginary place where the conditions of life are extremely bad. A dystopia is the opposite of a utopia. Literary utopian societies began with Sir Thomas More's *Utopia,* which first presents this perfect society as a vision of a mythic and unattainable nowhere (the word utopia literally means "no-place"). Some of the social organization and customs of More's Utopians came from Amerigo Vespucci's descriptions of Indians in his *New World* and *Four Voyages.* However, on More's island of Utopia all property is communal, slaves perform the menial work, and, although More says the Utopians hate war, they nonetheless go to battle.

Science Fiction & the Cold War

(D) Films containing flying saucers were a product of the Cold War of the 1950s and 60s. Science fiction films concern social chaos, and the conflicts they present are between institutions of society, or between society and some alien being. Science fiction films gained great popularity in the 1950s with movies like *Destination Moon* (based on a Robert Heinlein novel), which accurately forecast the Apollo moon missions, and *The Thing* (1951), which reflected American anxiety about the Russian atomic bomb falling from the sky.

LIFE AND TIMES

The French New Wave

A French filmmaker François Truffaut had been associated with the French New Wave of the late 1950s and 1960s. The New Wave was a period of cinema history during which French directors began making a new kind of quirky, realistic movie. The films of the French New Wave were shot with hand-held (and often shaky) cameras and used actors speaking and looking directly at the camera. The purpose was to make the audience aware of the films *as films,* a constructed art form, and themselves *as an audience,* rather than draw the audience into a narrative duplication of reality where they could lose themselves in the story. The French New Wave was an homage to classic Hollywood film, yet it also revolutionized the style of American movies of the late 1960s and 1970s.

François Truffaut

B Truffaut was already internationally renowned when he bought the rights to *Fahrenheit 451.* As a young man, he had been so in love with books that he would steal money to buy them. Like Bradbury, Truffaut had a great love of movies, and he often left school to sneak into them. Truffaut was later sent to a reformatory for stealing, which he used as the subject of his first film, *The 400 Blows (Les Quatre cents coups).* For *Fahrenheit 451,* he considered casting Paul Newman in the role of Montag before settling on the German actor Oskar Werner. Although *Fahrenheit 451* was not critically successful when released, the visual quality of Truffaut's ending sequence, showing pages of burning books, particularly impressed Bradbury. A distinction of Truffaut's film is that no written words are shown until the final credits.

he has written for hours almost daily. Although a leading figure in science fiction writing, Bradbury himself has never driven an automobile and did not fly in an airplane until after he was 70 years old. Yet, he believes that humankind has a "manifest destiny in space"; he is a strong advocate for space flight. (In 1971 the *Apollo 15* crew named a moon crater Dandelion Crater in honor of Bradbury's book *Dandelion Wine.*)

While much of his writing reveals someone wrestling with problems that affect human existence, Bradbury tries not to weigh down his work. "I write for fun," he has said. "You can't get too serious. I don't pontificate [express opinions] in my work. I have fun with ideas."

More Online: Author Link
www.mcdougallittell.com

A Bradbury on Screen

Ray Bradbury's first connection to Hollywood came in 1952, when he wrote the screenplay for his short story "The Fog Horn." This resulted in the 1953 monster film *The Beast from 20,000 Fathoms.* Soon after, Bradbury developed the concept for a film that came to be known as *It Came from Outer Space.* To experience the three-dimensional special effects of the film, viewers wore specially tinted glasses like those shown here. **B** In 1966, French filmmaker François Truffaut filmed Bradbury's novel *Fahrenheit 451.*

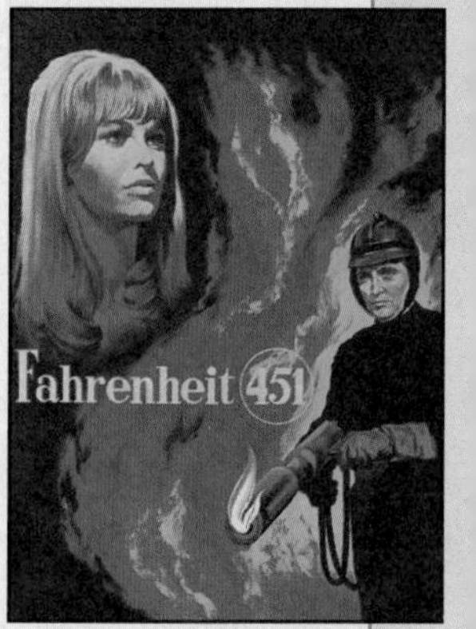

Poster for movie version of *Fahrenheit 451,* 1966

***It Came from Outer Space,* 1953**

3-D glasses enabled 1950s moviegoers to experience "realistic" special effects.

1977 **Receives Life Achievement Award at World Fantasy Convention**

1989 **Receives Grand Master Award from Science Fiction Writers of America**

Bradbury in Waukegan

1996 **Returns to Waukegan Public Library to publicize latest book**

1980 | 1985 | 1990 | 1995

1976 **Two U.S. *Viking* spacecraft land on Mars to search for life.**

1981 **First manned space shuttle orbits Earth for 54 hours.**

1983 ***Pioneer 10* becomes first spacecraft to leave the solar system.**

1990 **Hubble Space Telescope is launched.**

1997 **Martian probe *Sojourner* transmits startling images to Earth.**

1998 **The Hubble finds a planet outside our solar system.**

"The Monster, at the first motion, lunged forward with a terrible scream."

A Sound of Thunder

Short Story by RAY BRADBURY

Connect to Your Life

Time Travel If traveling through time were possible, what era would you most like to visit? Would you want to travel back to the past or ahead into the future? Would you want to travel just a few dozen years, or would you travel hundreds, a thousand, or even more years? Share your thoughts in a class discussion.

Build Background

The Fourth Dimension Time travel has been a popular idea in science fiction ever since the British author H. G. Wells wrote his short novel *The Time Machine* in 1895. In his novel, Wells suggested that in addition to the three dimensions of length, height, and width, there was a fourth dimension of duration, or time. Wells speculated that if a machine could be invented to move along the fourth dimension, travel backward and forward in time would be possible.

Science fiction writers since Wells's time have continued to use time travel as a basis for many adventures. Films such as *Back to the Future* popularized the notion of time travel. The story that follows is set in the future, yet the characters travel back into the distant past.

WORDS TO KNOW
Vocabulary Preview

annihilate	revoke
expendable	sheathed
infinitesimally	subliminal
primeval	taint
resilient	undulate

Focus Your Reading

LITERARY ANALYSIS FORESHADOWING Bradbury uses **foreshadowing** to prepare a reader for events and plot twists that will occur later in a story. This technique creates **suspense**—excitement or tension—and prepares the reader for what is to come. Often, a reader can pick up on foreshadowing just by knowing how stories work. Sometimes foreshadowing is apparent when a character makes an unusual statement or issues a strong warning. For example, in Bradbury's story a man named Travis, a guide on a dinosaur hunt, has this exchange with another character:

"So be careful. Stay on the Path. Never step off!"
"I see," said Eckels.

Watch for other examples of foreshadowing as you read Bradbury's story.

ACTIVE READING PREDICTING **Prediction** involves using text clues to make a reasonable guess about what will happen in a story. Sometimes your predictions will miss the mark. Other times, you'll recognize foreshadowing or other clues in a story and be able to make accurate predictions. Reread the exchange in the Literary Analysis section. What clue could help you predict what will happen later?

READER'S NOTEBOOK As you read, create a chart like this one to record your predictions together with the clues on which you based them.

What Will Happen Next?	
Text Clues	Predictions

OVERVIEW

This selection is included in the **Grade 10 InterActive Reader.**

Objectives

1. understand and appreciate **science fiction (Literary Analysis)**
2. recognize **foreshadowing (Literary Analysis)**
3. **predict** events in a plot **(Active Reading)**

Summary

It is 2055, the day after an important election in which democracy wins out over dictatorship. Eckels signs up with Time Safari, Inc., to travel 60 million years into the past to hunt dinosaurs. Travis, the safari guide, points out an antigravity path and warns everyone to stay on it so that nothing, not even a blade of grass, is changed. He explains that even a small change in history could have a magnified effect. When confronted with a real dinosaur, Eckels panics and accidentally leaves the path. Upon returning to the present, Eckels learns that the dictator Deutscher has defeated the candidate for democracy in the presidential election. Eckels discovers a dead butterfly stuck to his muddy shoe; he has changed history. Travis aims his rifle at Eckels and fires.

Thematic Link

While they had viewed the time travel safari as progress, the hunters discover that a small misstep in the past can exact a heavy price in the present.

5-Minute Warm-Up

Daily Language SkillBuilder

Have students **proofread** the display sentences on page 15i and write them correctly. The sentences also appear on Transparency 2 of **Grammar Transparencies and Copymasters.**

Mini Lesson Preteaching Vocabulary

If you would like to preteach the WORDS TO KNOW for this selection, use the Mini Lesson, p. 72.

LESSON RESOURCES

UNIT ONE RESOURCE BOOK, pp. 22–26

ASSESSMENT RESOURCES
Formal Assessment, pp. 13–14
Teacher's Guide to Assessment and Portfolio Use
Test Generator

SKILLS TRANSPARENCIES AND COPYMASTERS
Reading and Critical Thinking
- Predicting Outcomes, T2 (for Think Critically, item 4, p. 82)

Vocabulary
- Context Clues, C23 (for Mini Lesson, p. 72)
- Word Origins, C24 (for Mini Lesson, p. 75)

Writing
- Achieving Conciseness, T21 (for Writing Options 1 and 2, p. 83)
- Point of View, T23 (for Writing Option 2, p. 83)

Communications
- Evaluation Matrix: Film/Video, T7 (for Activities & Explorations 2, p. 83)

INTEGRATED TECHNOLOGY
Audio Library
Video: Literature in Performance
- *A Sound of Thunder.* See **Video Resource Book,** pp. 11–16.

Internet: Research Starter
Visit our website:
www.mcdougallittell.com

TEACHING THE LITERATURE

Reading and Analyzing

Reading Skills and Strategies: PREVIEW

Briefly frame the setting of the story by summarizing the sequence of events without revealing the powerful ending. Have students focus their attention on the behavior of Eckels as the story unfolds and examine how his behavior contrasts with that of tour leaders.

Active Reading PREDICTING

In order to have a basis for predicting what might happen in this story, have students read the quotations and study the pictures. Then students can put their predictions in a table. Allow time to discuss briefly how students' predictions compare to the events of the story and to make new predictions.

Use **Unit One Resource Book** p. 23 for more practice.

Literary Analysis FORESHADOWING

Foreshadowing provides hints or clues to future events in a story. Bradbury uses foreshadowing to add suspense and prepare the reader for events to come. Suggest that students add a column to their tables for clues provided through foreshadowing that help them confirm or contradict their predictions.

Use **Unit One Resource Book** p. 24 for more practice.

A Sound of Thunder

RAY BRADBURY

The sign on the wall seemed to quaver under a film of sliding warm water. Eckels felt his eyelids blink over his stare, and the sign burned in this momentary darkness:

TIME SAFARI, INC.
SAFARIS TO ANY YEAR IN THE PAST.
YOU NAME THE ANIMAL.
WE TAKE YOU THERE.
YOU SHOOT IT.

A warm phlegm gathered in Eckels's throat; he swallowed and pushed it down. The muscles around his mouth formed a smile as he put his hand slowly out upon the air, and in that hand waved a check for ten thousand dollars to the man behind the desk.

"Does this safari guarantee I come back alive?"

"We guarantee nothing," said the official, "except the dinosaurs." He turned. "This is Mr. Travis, your Safari Guide in the Past. He'll tell you what and where to shoot. If he says no shooting, no shooting. If you disobey instructions, there's a stiff penalty of another ten thousand dollars, plus possible government action, on your return."

Eckels glanced across the vast office at a mass and tangle, a snaking and humming of wires and steel boxes, at an aurora[1] that flickered now orange, now silver, now blue. There was a sound like a gigantic bonfire burning all of Time, all the years and all the parchment calendars, all the hours piled high and set aflame.

A touch of the hand and this burning would, on the instant, beautifully reverse itself. Eckels remembered the wording in the advertisements to the letter. Out of chars and ashes, out of dust and coals, like golden salamanders, the old years, the green years, might leap; roses sweeten the air, white hair turn Irish-black, wrinkles vanish; all, everything fly back to seed, flee death, rush down to their beginnings, suns rise in western skies and set in glorious easts, moons eat themselves opposite to the custom, all and everything cupping one in another like Chinese boxes,[2] rabbits into hats, all and everything returning to the fresh death, the seed death, the green death, to the time before the beginning. A

1. **aurora:** a light that changes colors.
2. **Chinese boxes:** a series of boxes, each of which fits neatly inside the next larger one.

Teaching Options

Mini Lesson Preteaching Vocabulary

CONTEXT CLUES The context in which a word is used can provide clues about its meaning. Students can sometimes make inferences about a word's meaning based on other words or phrases in the same sentence. Use the model sentence to demonstrate this process.

Model Sentence

The bombs <u>*annihilated*</u> all life in the city, <u>killing</u> even the grass and trees.

Instruction

- Write the model sentence on the chalkboard, and underline the new word and the clue as shown.
- Have students infer the meaning of the word *annihilate* from the context of the sentence.
- Ask a volunteer to use the word *annihilate* in a sentence.

touch of a hand might do it, the merest touch of a hand.

"Unbelievable." Eckels breathed, the light of the Machine on his thin face. "A real Time Machine." He shook his head. "Makes you think. If the election had gone badly yesterday, I might be here now running away from the results. Thank God Keith won. He'll make a fine President of the United States."

"Yes," said the man behind the desk. "We're lucky. If Deutscher had gotten in, we'd have the worst kind of dictatorship. There's an anti-everything man for you, a militarist, anti-Christ, anti-human, anti-intellectual. People called us up, you know, joking but not joking. Said if Deutscher became President they wanted to go live in 1492. Of course it's not our business to conduct Escapes, but to form Safaris. Anyway, Keith's President now. All you got to worry about is—"

"Shooting my dinosaur," Eckels finished it for him.

"A *Tyrannosaurus rex*. The Tyrant Lizard, the most incredible monster in history. Sign this release. Anything happens to you, we're not responsible. Those dinosaurs are hungry."

Eckels flushed angrily. "Trying to scare me!"

"Frankly, yes. We don't want anyone going who'll panic at the first shot. Six Safari leaders were killed last year, and a dozen hunters. We're here to give you the severest thrill a *real* hunter ever asked for. Traveling you back sixty million years to bag the biggest game in all of Time. Your personal check's still there. Tear it up."

Mr. Eckels looked at the check. His fingers twitched.

"Good luck," said the man behind the desk. "Mr. Travis, he's all yours."

They moved silently across the room, taking their guns with them, toward the Machine, toward the silver metal and the roaring light.

First a day and then a night and then a day and then a night, then it was day-night-day-night-day. A week, a month, a year, a decade! A.D. 2055. A.D. 2019. 1999! 1957! Gone! The Machine roared.

They put on their oxygen helmets and tested the intercoms.

Eckels swayed on the padded seat, his face pale, his jaw stiff. He felt the trembling in his arms, and he looked down and found his hands tight on the new rifle. There were four other men in the Machine. Travis, the Safari Leader; his assistant, Lesperance; and two other hunters, Billings and Kramer. They sat looking at each other, and the years blazed around them.

"Can these guns get a dinosaur cold?" Eckels felt his mouth saying.

"If you hit them right," said Travis on the helmet radio. "Some dinosaurs have two brains, one in the head, another far down the spinal column. We stay away from those. That's stretching luck. Put your first two shots into the eyes, if you can, blind them, and go back into the brain."

The Machine howled. Time was a film run backward. Suns fled, and ten million moons fled after them. "Think," said Eckels. "Every hunter that ever lived would envy us today. This makes Africa seem like Illinois."

The Machine slowed; its scream fell to a murmur. The Machine stopped.

The sun stopped in the sky.

The fog that had enveloped the Machine blew away, and they were in an old time, a very old time indeed, three hunters and two Safari Heads with their blue metal guns across their knees.

"Christ isn't born yet," said Travis. "Moses has not gone to the mountain to talk with God. The Pyramids are still in the earth, waiting to be cut out and put up. *Remember* that. Alexander, Caesar, Napoleon, Hitler—none of them exists."

The man nodded.

Customizing Instruction

Less Proficient Readers

Discuss the concept of time travel with students. Have students keep these questions in mind as they read:

- Who are the characters in the story?
- What is the setting when the characters are in their present day?
- Where and when in time do the time travelers go?
- What conflict does time travel create?

Students Acquiring English

Ask students to stop reading and summarize events at regular intervals. Point out changes in time as they occur.

Use **Spanish Study Guide** for additional support, pp. 13–15.

Gifted and Talented

Ask students to use clues from the selection to analyze what kind of person Travis is.

- page 74—smart—he understands how individuals can affect history; authoritative—he gives orders well.
- page 78—calm—he tries to stop Eckels from panicking; brave—He doesn't run from the dinosaur.
- page 80—a harsh judge—he is very critical of Eckels.
- page 81—a killer—he shoots Eckels to avenge the society they knew.

Exercises Ask students to read each of the following sentences and look for clues about the meaning of the underlined word.

1. The new puppy is <u>resilient</u>, rebounding from all kinds of bumps and scrapes.
2. The <u>infinitesimal</u> differences in the twins' facial structure were barely noticeable.
3. Once in its cocoon, the caterpillar was <u>sheathed</u> in a protective material around its entire body.
4. The flag <u>undulated</u> in the breeze while the water's surface rippled.
5. Some advertisers include <u>subliminal</u> messages in their advertising that cause us to have certain subconscious associations with their products.

Use **Unit One Resource Book** p. 25 for more practice.

A lesson on context clues appears on p. 56 in the Pupil's Edition.

Reading and Analyzing

Literary Analysis: SCIENCE FICTION

A Ask students to speculate about what an antigravity metal might be. What can they hypothesize about its use, based on their own scientific knowledge?

Possible Response: Gravity is the force that draws objects toward Earth, so an antigravity metal would probably be immune to that force. An antigravity path would float in the air and keep those walking on it from disturbing the ground.

Reading Skills and Strategies: QUESTION

B Pause to have students formulate questions about Time Safari, Inc. Why do the travelers really need to be so careful? Consider Travis's explanation of how careful they are.

Possible Response: Disturbing or changing anything in the past would have drastic effects on the travelers' present life.

"That"—Mr. Travis pointed—"is the jungle of sixty million two thousand and fifty-five years before President Keith."

He indicated a metal path that struck off into green wilderness, over streaming swamp, among giant ferns and palms.

"And that," he said, "is the Path, laid by Time Safari for your use. It floats six inches above the earth. Doesn't touch so much as one grass blade, flower, or tree. It's an antigravity
A metal. Its purpose is to keep you from touching this world of the past in any way. Stay on the Path. Don't go off it. I repeat. *Don't go off.* For *any* reason! If you fall off, there's a penalty. And don't shoot any animal we don't okay."

"Why?" asked Eckels.

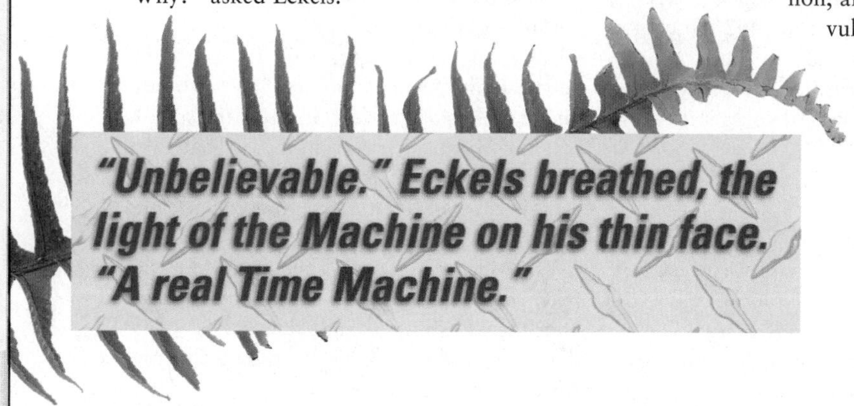
"Unbelievable," Eckels breathed, the light of the Machine on his thin face. "A real Time Machine."

They sat in the ancient wilderness. Far birds' cries blew on a wind, and the smell of tar and an old salt sea, moist grasses, and flowers the color of blood.

"We don't want to change the Future. We don't belong here in the Past. The government doesn't *like* us here. We have to pay big graft to keep our franchise.[3] A Time Machine is finicky business. Not knowing it, we might kill an important animal, a small bird, a roach, a flower even, thus destroying an important link in a growing species."

"That's not clear," said Eckels.

"All right," Travis continued, "say we accidentally kill one mouse here. That means all the future families of this one particular mouse are destroyed, right?"

"Right."

"And all the families of the families of the families of that one mouse! With a stamp of your foot, you annihilate first one, then a dozen, then a thousand, a million, a *billion* possible mice!"

"So they're dead," said Eckels. "So what?"

"So what?" Travis snorted quietly. "Well, what about the foxes that'll need those mice to survive? For want of ten mice, a fox dies. For want of ten foxes, a lion starves. For want of a lion, all manner of insects, vultures, infinite billions of life forms are thrown into chaos and destruction. Eventually it all 1 boils down to this: fifty-nine million years later, a caveman, one of a dozen on the *entire world,* goes hunting wild boar or saber-toothed tiger for food. But you, friend, have *stepped* on all the tigers in that region. By stepping on *one* single mouse. So the caveman starves. And the caveman, please note, is not just *any* expendable man, no! He is an *entire future nation.* From his loins would have sprung ten sons. From *their* loins one hundred sons, and thus onward to a civilization. Destroy this one man, and you destroy a race, a people, an entire history of life. It is comparable to slaying some of Adam's grandchildren. The

3. **graft to keep our franchise:** money paid as a bribe to officials in return for their approval of the business.

WORDS TO KNOW
annihilate (ə-nī′ə-lāt′) *v.* to destroy completely; wipe out
expendable (ĭk-spĕn′də-bəl) *adj.* dispensable; unnecessary

74

Teaching Options

BLOCK SCHEDULING: MANAGING TIME

If your schedule requires that you cover the lesson objectives in a shorter time, use . . .
- Preparing to Read, p. 71
- Thinking Through the Literature, p. 82
- Vocabulary in Action, p. 83

If you want to take advantage of longer class time, use . . .
- TE Teaching Options: Preteaching Vocabulary, pp.72–73; Cross-Curricular Link, p. 76; Vocabulary Strategy, p. 75; Viewing and Representing, p. 78; Speaking and Listening, p. 80; Informal Assessment, p. 81;
- Choices & Challenges, p. 83

stomp of your foot, on one mouse, could start an earthquake, the effects of which could shake our earth and destinies down through Time, to their very foundations. With the death of that one caveman, a billion others yet unborn are throttled in the womb. Perhaps Rome never rises on its seven hills. Perhaps Europe is forever a dark forest, and only Asia waxes healthy and teeming. Step on a mouse, and you crush the Pyramids. Step on a mouse, and you leave your print, like a Grand Canyon, across Eternity. Queen Elizabeth might never be born; Washington might not cross the Delaware; there might never be a United States at all. So be careful. Stay on the Path. *Never* step off!"

"I see," said Eckels. "Then it wouldn't pay for us even to touch the *grass?*"

"Correct. Crushing certain plants could add up infinitesimally. A little error here would multiply in sixty million years, all out of proportion. Of course maybe our theory is wrong. Maybe Time *can't* be changed by us. Or maybe it can be changed only in little subtle ways. A dead mouse here makes an insect imbalance there, a population disproportion later, a bad harvest further on, a depression, mass starvation, and, finally, a change in *social* temperament in far-flung countries. Something much more subtle, like that. Perhaps only a soft breath, a whisper, a hair, pollen on the air, such a slight, slight change that unless you looked close you wouldn't see it. Who knows? Who really can say he knows? We don't know. We're guessing. But until we do know for certain whether our messing around in Time *can* make a big roar or a little rustle in history, we're being careful. This Machine, this Path, your clothing and bodies, were sterilized, as you know, before the journey. We wear these oxygen helmets so we can't introduce our bacteria into an ancient atmosphere."

"How do we know which animals to shoot?"

"They're marked with red paint," said Travis. "Today, before our journey, we sent Lesperance here back with the Machine. He came to this particular era and followed certain animals."

"Studying them?"

"Right," said Lesperance. "I track them through their entire existence, noting which of them lives longest. Very few. How many times they mate. Not often. Life's short. When I find one that's going to die when a tree falls on him, or one that drowns in a tar pit, I note the exact hour, minute, and second. I shoot a paint bomb. It leaves a red patch on his side. We can't miss it. Then I correlate our arrival in the Past so that we meet the Monster not more than two minutes before he would have died anyway. This way, we kill only animals with no future, that are never going to mate again. You see how *careful* we are?"

"But if you came back this morning in Time," said Eckels eagerly, "you must've bumped into *us,* our Safari! How did it turn out? Was it successful? Did all of us get through—alive?"

Travis and Lesperance gave each other a look.

"That'd be a paradox," said the latter. "Time doesn't permit that sort of mess—a man meeting himself. When such occasions threaten, Time steps aside. Like an airplane hitting an air pocket. You felt the Machine jump just before we stopped? That was us passing ourselves on the way back to the Future. We saw nothing. There's no way of telling *if* this expedition was a success, *if we* got our monster, or whether all of us—meaning *you,* Mr. Eckels—got out alive."

Eckels smiled palely.

"Cut that," said Travis sharply. "Everyone on his feet!"

They were ready to leave the Machine.

The jungle was high and the jungle was broad

WORDS TO KNOW **infinitesimally** (ĭn′fĭn-ĭ-tĕs′ə-mə-lē) *adv.* in steps so small as to be immeasurable or incalculable

75

Customizing Instruction

Multiple Learning Styles
Visual or Spatial Learners

1 Have students create a sequence chain to illustrate the food chain Travis is describing. Sequence chains should contain events in the order shown.

- A mouse is accidentally killed in the past.
- Future families of this particular mouse are destroyed.
- All subsequent families of the mouse are destroyed.
- For want of ten mice, a fox starves to death.
- For want of ten foxes, a lion starves.
- For want of a lion, insects, vultures, and billions of life forms starve.
- Fifty-nine million years later, a caveman starves.
- An entire future nation is eliminated.

Mini Lesson Vocabulary Strategy

RESEARCHING WORD ORIGINS

Instruction The word *annihilate* stems from the Latin *annihilare,* which means "to reduce to nothing."

Application Have students work in cooperative groups to research the origins of the WORDS TO KNOW. Each group should together find a word origin for one word and then should make up a riddle that has the word as the answer. The riddle should suggest the meaning and the origin of the word.

Example: Which word comes from the Latin *annihilare,* which means "to reduce to nothing"? Groups can then solve each other's riddles and use the new word in a sentence.

Use **Vocabulary Transparencies and Copymasters,** p. 24.

A lesson on word origins appears on p. 356 in the Pupil's Edition.

Reading and Analyzing

Reading Skills and Strategies: VISUALIZE

A Have students note descriptive passages of *Tyrannosaurus rex* and select the most effective passages. They should be prepared to defend choices. Does Bradbury's description help the reader visualize the dinosaur? How does the description add to the suspense of the story?

Possible Response: Words that create a powerful image include *striding, towering, piston, thick, warrior,* etc. The description helps create and explain Eckels's fatal response.

Active Reading PREDICTING

B Ask students to predict whether or not Eckels is right when he says the dinosaur cannot be killed. Why or why not?

Possible Response: Eckels is probably going into shock and does not know what he's saying. The safari guides have shot and killed dinosaurs before.

and the jungle was the entire world forever and forever. Sounds like music and sounds like flying tents filled the sky, and those were pterodactyls[4] soaring with cavernous gray wings, gigantic bats of delirium and night fever.[5] Eckels, balanced on the narrow Path, aimed his rifle playfully.

1 "Stop that!" said Travis. "Don't even aim for fun, blast you! If your guns should go off—"

Eckels flushed. "Where's our *Tyrannosaurus?*"

Lesperance checked his wristwatch. "Up ahead. We'll bisect his trail in sixty seconds. Look for the red paint! Don't shoot till we give the word. Stay on the Path. *Stay on the Path!*"

They moved forward in the wind of morning.

"Strange," murmured Eckels. "Up ahead, sixty million years, Election Day over. Keith made President. Everyone celebrating. And here we are, a million years lost, and they don't exist. The things we worried about for months, a lifetime, not even born or thought of yet."

Illustration copyright © Douglas Henderson. From *The Complete T-Rex* by John Horner and Don Lessem, published by Simon & Schuster.

"Safety catches off, everyone!" ordered Travis. "You, first shot, Eckels. Second, Billings. Third, Kramer."

2 "I've hunted tiger, wild boar, buffalo, elephant, but now, this is *it,*" said Eckels. "I'm shaking like a kid."

"Ah," said Travis.

Everyone stopped.

Travis raised his hand. "Ahead," he whispered. "In the mist. There he is. There's His Royal Majesty now."

The jungle was wide and full of twitterings, rustlings, murmurs, and sighs.

Suddenly it all ceased, as if someone had shut a door.

Silence.

A sound of thunder.

Out of the mist, one hundred yards away, came *Tyrannosaurus rex.*

---

4. **pterodactyls** (tĕr′ə-dăk′təlz): extinct flying reptiles having a wingspan of up to 40 feet.
5. **bats . . . fever:** the sort of bats that appear in nightmares and visions caused by drugs or illness.

Teaching Options

Cross Curricular Link Science

DINOSAURS The excavation of dinosaur fossils has fascinated both scientists and collectors since the first dinosaur bones were discovered in the early 1800s. In 1841, Sir Richard Owen first proposed the name *Dinosauria* for the giant extinct animals. Since that time, dinosaur remains have been found all over the world, and with each dig come new discoveries. While it is not possible to go on a safari hunt for live dinosaurs, as Eckels did, it is possible to go on a dinosaur dig. The question remains, should dinosaur digs be for scientific purposes only, or should the digs be opened up to amateur dinosaur enthusiasts who can pay the price?

"It," whispered Eckels. "It . . ."

"Sh!"

It came on great oiled, resilient, striding legs. It towered thirty feet above half of the trees, a great evil god, folding its delicate watchmaker's claws close to its oily reptilian chest. Each lower leg was a piston, a thousand pounds of white bone, sunk in thick ropes of muscle, sheathed over in a gleam of pebbled skin like the mail of a terrible warrior. Each thigh was a ton of meat, ivory, and steel mesh. And from the great breathing cage of the upper body those two delicate arms dangled out front, arms with hands which might pick up and examine men like toys, while the snake neck coiled. And the head itself, a ton of sculptured stone, lifted easily upon the sky. Its mouth gaped, exposing a fence of teeth like daggers. Its eyes rolled, ostrich eggs, empty of all expression save hunger. It closed its mouth in a death grin. It ran, its pelvic bones crushing aside trees and bushes, its taloned feet clawing damp earth, leaving prints six inches deep wherever it settled its weight. It ran with a gliding ballet step, far too poised and balanced for its ten tons. It moved into a sunlit arena warily, its beautifully reptilian hands feeling the air.

"Why, why," Eckels twitched his mouth. "It could reach up and grab the moon."

"Sh!" Travis jerked angrily. "He hasn't seen us yet."

"It can't be killed." Eckels pronounced this verdict quietly, as if there could be no argument. He had weighed the evidence, and this was his considered opinion. The rifle in his hands seemed a cap gun. "We were fools to come. This is impossible."

"Shut up!" hissed Travis.

"Nightmare."

"Turn around," commanded Travis. "Walk

WORDS TO KNOW

resilient (rĭ-zĭl′yənt) *adj.* capable of bouncing or springing back to an original shape after being stretched, bent, or compressed

sheathed (shēthd) *adj.* enclosed in a protective covering **sheathe** *v.*

Customizing Instruction

Less Proficient Readers

Ask students the following questions about Eckels:

1 What does Eckels do that irritates Travis just before they see the dinosaur?

Possible Response: He aims his gun at some pterodactyls.

2 How do you know Eckels is afraid of the dinosaur even before he sees it?

Possible Response: He says he is shaking like a kid.

3 What conclusion does Eckels reach when he sees the size of the dinosaur?

Possible Response: He says that the dinosaur cannot be killed and they were fools to come.

Reading and Analyzing

Active Reading PREDICTING

A Have students predict whether Eckels harms anything when he steps off the path, and whether his actions will have an impact on the future.

Possible Response: Travis has warned the hunters repeatedly to stay on the path and has explained the food chain in detail, perhaps foreshadowing that someone, possibly Eckels, will harm something, and it will affect the future.

Reading Skills and Strategies: QUESTION

B Ask students to meet with a partner and discuss why the hunters don't want their picture taken with the dinosaur.

Possible Response: Like Eckels, the hunters are overwhelmed and sickened by the dinosaur. They just want to forget the entire experience.

quietly to the Machine. We'll remit one-half your fee."

"I didn't realize it would be this *big*," said Eckels. "I miscalculated, that's all. And now I want out."

"It *sees* us!"

1 "There's the red paint on its chest!"

The Tyrant Lizard raised itself. Its armored flesh glittered like a thousand green coins. The coins, crusted with slime, steamed. In the slime, tiny insects wriggled, so that the entire body seemed to twitch and undulate, even while the monster itself did not move. It exhaled. The stink of raw flesh blew down the wilderness.

"Get me out of here," said Eckels. "It was never like this before. I was always sure I'd come through alive. I had good guides, good safaris, and safety. This time, I figured wrong. I've met my match and admit it. This is too much for me to get hold of."

"Don't run," said Lesperance. "Turn around. Hide in the Machine."

"Yes." Eckels seemed to be numb. He looked at his feet as if trying to make them move. He gave a grunt of helplessness.

"Eckels!"

He took a few steps, blinking, shuffling.

"Not *that* way!"

The Monster, at the first motion, lunged forward with a terrible scream. It covered one hundred yards in six seconds. The rifles jerked up and blazed fire. A windstorm from the beast's mouth engulfed them in the stench of slime and old blood. The Monster roared, teeth glittering with sun.

Eckels, not looking back, walked blindly to the edge of the Path, his gun limp in his arms, stepped off the Path, and walked, not knowing it, in the jungle. His feet sank into green moss. His legs moved him, and he felt alone and remote from the events behind. A

The rifles cracked again. Their sound was lost in shriek and lizard thunder. The great level of the reptile's tail swung up, lashed sideways. Trees exploded in clouds of leaf and branch. The Monster twitched its jeweler's hands down to fondle at the men, to twist them in half, to crush them like berries, to cram them into its teeth and its screaming throat. Its boulder-stone eyes leveled with the men. They saw themselves

WORDS TO KNOW **undulate** (ŭn'jə-lāt') *v.* to move in waves or in a smooth, wavelike motion

78

Teaching Options

Mini Lesson Viewing and Representing

Instruction *Tyrannosaurus rex,* shown in the image above, lived 65 to 97 million years ago. Adult tyrannosaurs were more than 47 feet (14 meters) long, with skulls more than 4 feet long. These meat eaters walked about on powerful hind legs, but their forelimbs were small and useless. A tyrannosaur's jaws could contain up to 60 teeth, some longer than a human hand. Have students note that the image of *Tyrannosaurus rex* shown above differs from the one on page 77.

Application Ask students to compare the mood of the two images. How do the movement and position of the dinosaur contribute to the mood? Does one image fit their vision of the story more than the other?

Possible Response: The dinosaur in the image above looks as if it is about to lunge forward. The mood is terrifying, exciting, and calls for an immediate response.

mirrored. They fired at the metallic eyelids and the blazing black iris.

Like a stone idol, like a mountain avalanche, *Tyrannosaurus* fell. Thundering, it clutched trees, pulled them with it. It wrenched and tore the metal Path. The men flung themselves back and away. The body hit, ten tons of cold flesh and stone. The guns fired. The Monster lashed its armored tail, twitched its snake jaws, and lay still. A fount of blood spurted from its throat. Somewhere inside, a sac of fluids burst. Sickening gushes drenched the hunters. They stood, red and glistening.

The thunder faded.

The jungle was silent. After the avalanche, a green peace. After the nightmare, morning.

Billings and Kramer sat on the pathway and threw up. Travis and Lesperance stood with smoking rifles, cursing steadily.

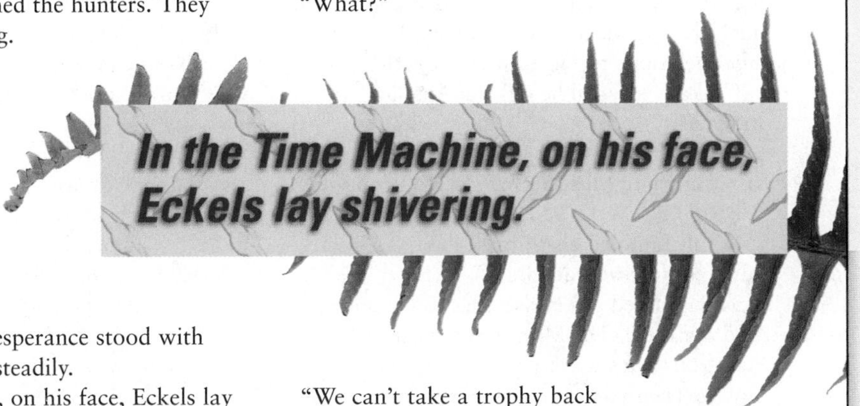

In the Time Machine, on his face, Eckels lay shivering.

In the Time Machine, on his face, Eckels lay shivering. He had found his way back to the Path, climbed into the Machine.

Travis came walking, glanced at Eckels, took cotton gauze from a metal box, and returned to the others, who were sitting on the Path.

"Clean up."

They wiped the blood from their helmets. They began to curse too. The Monster lay, a hill of solid flesh. Within, you could hear the sighs and murmurs as the furthest chambers of it died, the organs malfunctioning, liquids running a final instant from pocket to sac to spleen, everything shutting off, closing up forever. It was like standing by a wrecked locomotive or a steam shovel at quitting time, all valves being released or levered tight. Bones cracked; the tonnage of its own flesh, off balance, dead weight, snapped the delicate forearms, caught underneath. The meat settled, quivering.

Another cracking sound. Overhead, a gigantic tree branch broke from its heavy mooring, fell. It crashed upon the dead beast with finality.

"There." Lesperance checked his watch. "Right on time. That's the giant tree that was scheduled to fall and kill this animal originally." He glanced at the two hunters. "You want the trophy picture?"

"What?"

"We can't take a trophy back to the Future. The body has to stay right here where it would have died originally, so the insects, birds, and bacteria can get at it, as they were intended to. Everything in balance. The body stays. But we *can* take a picture of you standing near it."

The two men tried to think, but gave up, shaking their heads. **B**

They let themselves be led along the metal Path. They sank wearily into the Machine cushions. They gazed back at the ruined Monster, the stagnating mound, where already strange reptilian birds and golden insects were busy at the steaming armor.

A sound on the floor of the Time Machine stiffened them. Eckels sat there, shivering.

"I'm sorry," he said at last.

"Get up!" cried Travis.

Customizing Instruction

Multiple Learning Styles

Interpersonal Learners Ask students to form cooperative groups and discuss Eckels's behavior on the dinosaur hunt. What could he have done differently? Could he have done anything to save himself once he stepped off the path?

Possible Response: Eckels should have gone straight back to the time machine when Travis told him to do so. Once he strayed off the path, there was nothing he could have done to save himself.

Less Proficient Readers

1 Ask students why there was red paint on one of the dinosaurs.

Answer: The dinosaur was going to die.

Reading and Analyzing

Reading Skills and Strategies: SUMMARIZE

A Ask students to summarize the changes the time travelers encounter when they return.

Possible Response: The air is different, the man and the desk have changed, the words on the sign are spelled differently.

Reading Skills and Strategies: QUESTION

B Ask students to formulate a question to help them interpret the end of the story; what motivates Travis to shoot Eckels?

Possible Response: Travis shoots Eckels because he is angry that the future has changed because Eckels stepped off the path. Judging by Travis's character, he has probably killed before.

Eckels got up.

"Go out on that Path alone," said Travis. He had his rifle pointed. "You're not coming back in the Machine. We're leaving you here!"

Lesperance seized Travis's arm. "Wait—"

"Stay out of this!" Travis shook his hand away. "This fool nearly killed us. But it isn't *that* so much, no. It's his *shoes!* Look at them! He ran off the Path. That *ruins* us! We'll forfeit! Thousands of dollars of insurance! We guarantee no one leaves the Path. He left it. Oh, the fool! I'll have to report to the government. They might revoke our license to travel. Who knows *what* he's done to Time, to History!"

"Take it easy; all he did was kick up some dirt."

"How do we *know?*" cried Travis. "We don't know anything! It's all a mystery! Get out there, Eckels!"

Eckels fumbled his shirt. "I'll pay anything. A hundred thousand dollars!"

Travis glared at Eckels's checkbook and spat. "Go out there. The Monster's next to the Path. Stick your arms up to your elbows in his mouth. Then you can come back with us."

"That's unreasonable!"

"The Monster's dead, you idiot. The bullets! The bullets can't be left behind. They don't belong in the Past; they might change anything. Here's my knife. Dig them out!"

The jungle was alive again, full of the old tremorings and bird cries. Eckels turned slowly to regard the primeval garbage dump, that hill of nightmares and terror. After a long time, like a sleepwalker he shuffled out along the Path.

He returned, shuddering, five minutes later, his arms soaked and red to the elbows. He held out his hands. Each held a number of steel bullets. Then he fell. He lay where he fell, not moving.

"You didn't have to make him do that," said Lesperance.

"Didn't I? It's too early to tell." Travis nudged the still body. "He'll live. Next time he won't go hunting game like this. Okay." He jerked his thumb wearily at Lesperance. "Switch on. Let's go home."

1492. 1776. 1812. **1**

They cleaned their hands and faces. They changed their caking shirts and pants. Eckels was up and around again, not speaking. Travis glared at him for a full ten minutes.

"Don't look at me," cried Eckels. "I haven't done anything."

"Who can tell?"

"Just ran off the Path, that's all, a little mud on my shoes—what do you want me to do—get down and pray?"

"We might need it. I'm warning you, Eckels, I might kill you yet. I've got my gun ready."

"I'm innocent. I've done nothing!"

1999. 2000. 2055.

The Machine stopped.

"Get out," said Travis.

The room was there as they had left it. But not the same as they had left it. The same man sat behind the same desk. But the same man did not quite sit behind the same desk.

Travis looked around swiftly. "Everything okay here?" he snapped.

"Fine. Welcome home!"

Travis did not relax. He seemed to be looking at the very atoms of the air itself, at the way the sun poured through the one high window.

"Okay, Eckels, get out. Don't ever come back."

Eckels could not move.

"You heard me," said Travis. "What're you *staring* at?"

Eckels stood smelling of the air, and there was a thing to the air, a chemical taint so subtle, so slight, that only a faint cry of his **A**

WORDS TO KNOW
revoke (rĭ-vōk') *v.* to cancel or withdraw
primeval (prī-mē'vəl) *adj.* belonging to the earliest times or ages
taint (tānt) *n.* a trace of something that harms, spoils, or corrupts

Teaching Options

Mini Lesson: Speaking and Listening

NEWSCAST Instruction Television or radio newscasts not only present the day's major news events, but also regular features, such as sports and weather reports. Most newscasts have two main anchors, along with special sports and weather reporters. Newscasts also have reporters who broadcast live from a news event.

Prepare Have students form groups to plan and present a newscast describing the story. If possible, have students videotape their news stories. Suggest that the groups choose one of two options: the future as it is before the safari or the alternate future Eckels creates when he steps on the butterfly. The newscast should report on the election and other aspects of contemporary life. Suggest that students view a television newscast before planning their own, paying close attention to the newscast's structure and presentation.

Present Have students present a newscast from the future describing the story. Groups can view each other's newscast.

BLOCK SCHEDULING This activity is particularly well suited for longer class periods.

subliminal senses warned him it was there. The colors, white, gray, blue, orange, in the wall, in the furniture, in the sky beyond the window, were . . . were . . . And there was a *feel.* His flesh twitched. His hands twitched. He stood drinking the oddness with the pores of his body. Somewhere, someone must have been screaming one of those whistles that only a dog can hear. His body screamed silence in return. Beyond this room, beyond this wall, beyond this man who was not quite the same man seated at this desk that was not quite the same desk . . . lay an entire world of streets and people. What sort of world it was now, there was no telling. He could feel them moving there, beyond the walls, almost, like so many chess pieces blown in a dry wind. . . .

A

But the immediate thing was the sign painted on the office wall, the same sign he had read earlier today on first entering.

Somehow, the sign had changed:

TYME SEFARI INC.
SEFARIS TU ANY YEER EN THE PAST.
YU NAIM THE ANIMALL.
WEE TAEKYUTHAIR.
YU SHOOT ITT.

Eckels felt himself fall into a chair. He fumbled crazily at the thick slime on his boots. He held up a clod of dirt, trembling, "No, it *can't* be. Not a *little* thing like that. No!"

Embedded in the mud, glistening green and gold and black, was a butterfly, very beautiful and very dead.

"Not a little thing like *that!* Not a butterfly!" cried Eckels.

It fell to the floor, an exquisite thing, a small thing that could upset balances and knock down a line of small dominoes and then big dominoes and then gigantic dominoes, all down the years across Time. Eckels's mind whirled. It *couldn't* change things. Killing one butterfly couldn't be *that* important! Could it?

His face was cold. His mouth trembled, asking: "Who—who won the presidential election yesterday?"

The man behind the desk laughed. "You joking? You know very well. Deutscher, of course! Who else? Not that fool weakling Keith. We got an iron man now, a man with guts!" The official stopped. "What's wrong?"

Eckels moaned. He dropped to his knees. He scrabbled at the golden butterfly with shaking fingers. "Can't we," he pleaded to the world, to himself, to the officials, to the Machine, "can't we take it *back;* can't we *make* it alive again? Can't we start over? Can't we—"

He did not move. Eyes shut, he waited, shivering. He heard Travis breathe loud in the room; he heard Travis shift his rifle, click the safety catch, and raise the weapon.

B

There was a sound of thunder. ❖

WORDS TO KNOW

subliminal (sŭb-lĭm'ə-nəl) *adj.* below the threshold of conscious perception; subconscious

Customizing Instruction

Less Proficient Readers

1 Have students turn back to page 73. Compare the years the Time Machine passed on its way back in time with the years it passes on its return trip. Ask students to discuss why the years have changed.

Possible Response: The years have changed because what Eckels has done in the past has changed the future.

Assessment Informal Assessment

ALTERNATIVE ENDING Informally assess students' understanding of the selection by having them imagine an alternative ending in which Travis is arrested for murdering Eckels. Students' writing could include testimony by Lesperance and the other hunters who tell what has happened.

RUBRIC

3 **Full Accomplishment** Response reflects a full understanding of the events and characters in the story.

2 **Substantial Accomplishment** Response shows a general understanding of the events in the story, but may not fully reflect an understanding of the characters.

1 **Little or Partial Accomplishment** Response shows little understanding of the events or the characters in the story.

GUIDING STUDENT RESPONSE

Connect to Literature

1. What Do You Think?
Students may be surprised by the ending, although some may have predicted that Travis would kill Eckels.

Comprehension Check

- Time Safari, Inc., offers trips back in time to hunt dinosaurs.
- Eckels steps off the antigravity path and accidentally kills a butterfly.
- Small details have changed, such as the spelling on the sign, the feel of the air, and the man sitting behind the desk.

Use Selection Quiz
Unit One Resource Book, p. 26.

Think Critically

2. Possible Responses: cowardly; selfish; unthinking; full of bravado but empty of real substance; a thrill seeker; insincere; rich.
3. Possible Responses: Time Safari, Inc., is only out to make money. Even though Travis seems to care about obeying the laws, it is only so Time Safari, Inc., can keep its license. If Time Safari, Inc., cared about people, it wouldn't offer safaris where hunters or guides are sometimes killed.
4. Possible Responses: Check student notebooks to be sure students understood the assignment.
5. Possible Responses: Even the most insignificant action can have huge repercussions; individuals have the power to change the course of history.

Thinking through the LITERATURE

Connect to the Literature

1. **What Do You Think?** What was your reaction to the "sound of thunder" at the end of the story?

Comprehension Check
- What kind of business does Time Safari, Inc. operate?
- What does Eckels do that has such far-reaching consequences?
- What is different when Eckels returns to his own time?

Think Critically

2. How would you describe Eckels?

THINK ABOUT
- his reasons for going on a safari
- his response to the tyrannosaurus
- his attitude about stepping off the path

3. How would you characterize the business practices of Time Safari, Inc.?

4. ACTIVE READING PREDICTING How accurate were the **predictions** you made in your READER'S NOTEBOOK? Discuss with classmates the details that either helped or misled you.

5. In your opinion, what **theme,** or message, is Bradbury conveying through the story?

THINK ABOUT
- the society Eckels returns to as compared with the society depicted at the beginning of the story
- the significance of the butterfly

Extend Interpretations

6. **Critic's Corner** In a review of *Dinosaur Tales,* the collection of Bradbury stories that contains "A Sound of Thunder," the critic Andrew Andrews remarks that Bradbury "gets to you—in simple ways he shows you how to marvel over these awesome, startling creatures." What was your reaction to Bradbury's portrayal of the dinosaurs in the story?

7. **Connect to Life** Recall the ideas you discussed about time travel before you read the story. Why do you think time travel has become such a popular topic of stories and movies?

Literary Analysis

FORESHADOWING **Foreshadowing** is a device a writer uses to prepare a reader for an event that happens later in the story. The use of foreshadowing also adds suspense. Foreshadowing takes the form of hints—bits of information that suggest to the reader what is coming. Writers provide foreshadowing by creating a **mood** that prepares a reader emotionally for what is to come, by including facts and details that provide clues, by revealing **character traits** that determine future action, or by describing events that suggest what might happen later.

Paired Activity Now that you know the outcome of the story, review it with a partner to find additional foreshadowing that you may have missed. Make a chart like the one below to record your results. When you have listed three or four hints and outcomes, discuss the story's title. How might it work as an example of foreshadowing?

Hint	Outcome
"If you disobey instructions . . ."	Eckels disobeys instructions.

REVIEW SCIENCE FICTION
Science fiction is prose writing in which the writer explores possibilities of the future, using known scientific information as well as his or her imagination. When considering the difference between fantasy and science fiction, Bradbury once explained that science fiction "could happen." Why do you think "A Sound of Thunder" qualifies as science fiction?

Extend Interpretations

Critic's Corner Students should find Bradbury's description of the dinosaur to be credible.

Connect to Life Students may respond that the idea of time travel is intriguing because it offers the chance to relive a special moment or occasion or to change an unhappy event. People are also curious about their future.

Literary Analysis

Set the stage for the paired activity by reading aloud the opening paragraphs of the selection asking students to listen and identify words that help build the eerie and ominous **mood** of the selection.

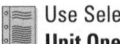

Writing Options

1. Adventure Advertisement Write persuasive copy for a poster or magazine advertisement inviting hunters to venture across time to hunt prehistoric creatures. Try to convince readers that this adventure is worth the high price and that it is important for them to responsibly follow every rule.

2. Incident Report Writing as Travis, compose a two-paragraph report to your superiors in which you describe the main incident from the story, what you presume are its consequences, and how you propose to make sure nothing like this happens again.

Activities & Explorations

1. Butterfly Drawing Create a fanciful picture of a butterfly in which you visually convey the notion—presented in the story through prose—that the butterfly contains within it the seeds of history. For example, you might include pictures on the wings. ~ **ART**

2. Video Adaptation As you view the clip from the film of "A Sound of Thunder," compare the way the dinosaur appears with the way you imagined it as you read. What did you find scarier, the tyrannosaurus you imagined or the one you viewed? Discuss your responses with other students. ~ **VIEWING AND REPRESENTING**

VIDEO **Literature in Performance**

Inquiry & Research

Science Have you ever heard of the "butterfly effect"—the notion that the flapping of a butterfly's wings can change the weather? With a partner, research the connections between the butterfly effect and chaos theory, which offers a scientific explanation of apparently random or irregular behavior of systems in nature. Then, in an oral report for your classmates, explain how the story reflects these scientific theories.

Astronomy With a partner, research the nature of time in outer space, and how space travel is travel through time as well.

More Online: Research Starter
www.mcdougallittell.com

VIDEODISC **LaserLinks:**
Background for Reading
Literary Connection
Science Connection

Vocabulary in Action

EXERCISE: ASSESSMENT PRACTICE On your paper, write the letter of the word that is the best synonym for each boldfaced word.

1. **infinitesimally:** (a) lastingly, (b) microscopically, (c) happily
2. **undulate:** (a) hover, (b) ripple, (c) surrender
3. **revoke:** (a) repeat, (b) modify, (c) repeal
4. **primeval:** (a) wicked, (b) ancient, (c) best
5. **resilient:** (a) elastic, (b) shiny, (c) weak
6. **expendable:** (a) difficult, (b) costly, (c) nonessential
7. **annihilate:** (a) demolish, (b) confuse, (c) restore
8. **taint:** (a) purity, (b) rotation, (c) contamination
9. **subliminal:** (a) instinctive, (b) underground, (c) inhuman
10. **sheathed:** (a) exposed, (b) surrounded, (c) beautified

Building Vocabulary

For an in-depth lesson on the denotation and connotation of words, see page 494.

Writing Options

1. **Adventure Advertisement** Have students write advertisements that are vivid and full of intriguing details. Advertisements should also include warnings to hunters that they must follow the rules. **To make this assignment more challenging**, students should not use any of the details Bradbury used in the advertisement in the story.
2. **Incident Report** Have students write incident reports that contain some false details. For example, Travis would not say that he killed Eckels. The better incident reports will include all relevant details from the story.

Activities & Explorations

1. **Butterfly Drawing** Encourage to promote artistic creativity.
2. **Video Adaptation** See Literature in Performance Teachers Resource Book for suggestions on comparing the text and the video.

Inquiry & Research

Science/Astronomy Have students work individually or cooperatively to research the butterfly effect and chaos theory. Students can present reports orally. Allow graphic media options.

Vocabulary in Action

Answers

1. b
2. b
3. c
4. b
5. a
6. c
7. a
8. c
9. a
10. b

Teaching the Literature

Build Background

Though Bradbury is primarily known as a creative writer of fiction, poetry, and plays, he has also written a book of essays on the craft of writing. Called *Zen in the Art of Writing,* the book contains essays (and poems) that describe Bradbury's writing process, advice to writers on cultivating their muse, and the joy he felt when writing some of his best-known works.

Bradbury's primary advice to young writers is to sit down and write 1,000 to 2,000 words a day for the next 20 years of their lives. He wrote in this manner for ten years before he produced a story he considered good.

He also describes a writing process he developed as a young man as one of word association. Each morning, he sits at the typewriter and writes down a word or series of words that come into his mind. From this, he develops a story around the word or words. He also advises writers to relax, but as a corollary to this suggestion, he adds that relaxation comes from the work of writing. Once one's truth is put down on the page through the hard work of writing, relaxation comes.

Teaching Nonfiction: Skills and Strategies

MAIN IDEA/SUPPORTING DETAILS

Helping students understand main ideas and supporting details allows them to conclude what an author considers important. Students will be able to recognize explicitly stated main ideas, infer main ideas not directly stated, and identify details that support the main idea.

In this interview Bradbury expands on his ideas about writing. Ask students what Bradbury considers most important in his life.

Possible Responses: He considers writing and his family the most important things in his life. Money and material possessions mean little to him.

Have students identify supporting details that back up their answer.

Possible Responses: He doesn't need to spend money on expensive restaurants or on entertainment. He also states directly that "Money is not important." He also says that he writes everyday except weekends, which are for his family.

Interview with Ray Bradbury

Preparing to Read

Build Background

With the authority acquired from more than 60 years of constant story production, Bradbury often speaks frankly to young writers and students about the art of writing. Because of this, he is usually a good source for colorful quotes on the subject of writing and the way he approaches it. In this interview, the writer promotes "the old-fashioned virtues of hard, constant labor."

Focus Your Reading

PRIMARY SOURCES | INTERVIEW

An **interview** is a recorded conversation of questions and answers with a person having firsthand or expert knowledge on some subject. A good interviewer will be prepared with background knowledge on the interviewee. In addition, a good interviewer is armed with two essentials:

- a list of questions, most of which require thoughtful responses
- the flexibility to let the conversation stray if the interviewee goes off in an unexpected, interesting direction

Interview by
FRANK FILOSA

Do you write every day?

Every day of my life except weekends, which are for the family: my wife and my four lovely daughters.

Could you describe a typical day, your process of writing?

I do a first draft as passionately and as quickly as I can. I believe a story is only valid when it is immediate and passionate; when it dances out of your subconscious.[1] If you interfere in any way, you destroy it. There's no difference between a short story and life. Surprise is where creativity comes. Allow your subconscious[1] to come out into the light and say what it has to say. Let your characters have their way. Let your secret life be lived. Then at your leisure, in the succeeding weeks, months or years, you let the story cool off, and then, instead of rewriting, you relive it. If you try to rewrite, which is a cold exercise, you'll wind up with all kinds of Band-aids on your story, which people can see. It's very important that a story have a skin around it just as we have a skin. A story must have the same sort of life we have though it is shorter. It has this fantastic entity[2] to itself, a need to run to its end, and you just have to let it go.

1. **subconscious:** the part of the mind below the level of conscious awareness.
2. **entity:** unique existence.

You wrote, "Success is a continuing process. Failure is a stoppage. The man who keeps moving and working does not fail."
The average young person you meet today seems to have the motto, "If at first you don't succeed, stop right there." They want to start at the top of their profession and not to learn their art on the way up. That way they miss all the fun. If you write a hundred short stories and they're all bad, that doesn't mean you've failed. You fail only if you stop writing. I've written about 2,000 short stories; I've only published about 300, and I feel I'm still learning. Any man who keeps working is not a failure. He may not be a great writer, but if he applies the old-fashioned virtues of hard, constant labor, he'll eventually make some kind of career for himself as a writer.

Isn't this hard to do for most people? The rent has to be paid. You have to do mundane[3] things like eat. In your teens you sold newspapers, and between editions you wrote, but didn't you have to give up most of the things people feel they have to have?
Depends on what you have to have.

You can get along on a very small amount of money. You can give up clothes. You can give up movies and theater. You can eat Kraft Dinner every day of your life. I'm a student of Kraft Dinner. I'm a specialist in Campbell's Tomato Soup. You can go to the market today, and for a few cents you can have a banquet. I still love Campbell's Tomato Soup. This is a free plug for them, and I hope they send me a free can of soup. I'm the cheapest freeloader in the history of mankind. My idea of a real meal is to sit down with a can of tomato soup, a couple glasses of milk, and a half a pound of crackers. I went through a record of expenses I kept during my first year of marriage. At that time I was making about $30 a week writing, and my wife was making $35 at a job to support us so I could get my writing done. We'd go down to Ocean Park at night and have a couple of hot dogs and a Coke. We'd go through the penny arcade, and for 32 cents we'd have a magnificent evening. If you have someone who cares about you, it's very easy to give up things. If you're alone, you buy things to compensate for[4] your loneliness.

Money is not important. The material things are not important. Getting the work done beautifully and proudly is important. If you do that, strangely enough, the money will come as a just reward for work beautifully done. A tape recorder, an automobile, they don't really belong to you. What really belongs to you? Yourself, you. That's all you'll ever have. I am ruthless with anyone around me who doesn't think or create always at the top of his form.

3. **mundane:** ordinary; day-to-day.
4. **compensate for:** make up for.

INTERVIEW WITH RAY BRADBURY 85

OVERVIEW

Objectives

1. understand and appreciate a **short story (Literary Analysis)**
2. understand the importance of **setting (Literary Analysis)**
3. **visualize** setting **(Active Reading)**

Summary

Inside the only house left intact amid the ruins of the city, electronic voices announce the routine events of the day as if the inhabitants were still living there. On a charred wall outside the house are the ghostly images of each family member, their shadows captured on the walls by an atomic blast. One night, a storm-tossed tree limb crashes through a window and inadvertently starts a fire. Although the house swings into full operation, it cannot stop the fire. The house burns until only one wall stands and one electronic voice continues to announce the day's date.

Thematic Link

This science fiction piece describes a future in which technology has progressed to such a point that humans seem almost unnecessary.

5-Minute Warm-Up

Daily Language SkillBuilder

Have students **proofread** the display sentences on page 15i and write them correctly. The sentences also appear on Transparency 3 of **Grammar Transparencies and Copymasters.**

There Will Come Soft Rains

Short Story by RAY BRADBURY

"Today is August 4, 2026."

Connect to Your Life

Progress or Danger? One reason cellular phones have become popular is that they enable people to make business calls while commuting; unfortunately, that practice has led to a sharp increase in automobile accidents. Millions of people find helpful information on the Internet; however, some people fear that criminals will have access to their personal financial information. Overall, do you think that technology provides more benefits or poses more hazards? Discuss your ideas with a classmate.

Build Background

Technology: No Guarantee At first, electrically powered machines assisted people only in their workplaces. Around the turn of the 20th century, however, with the spread of electricity, machines started to appear in people's homes. For example, the electric washing machine was invented in 1901, the electric vacuum cleaner in 1907, and the electric toaster in 1909.

Science fiction writers of this time began writing of ideal situations in which people were freed from time-consuming everyday tasks by various appliances. Writers imagined self-sufficient machine beings, acting as servants; in 1921, a writer coined the word *robot.* On the surface, the idea of being freed from daily chores had great appeal. However, as writers probed the idea more deeply, it became apparent that technological advancement did not necessarily guarantee social progress.

Focus Your Reading

LITERARY ANALYSIS SETTING Every story has a **setting**—a time and place for its action. For science fiction writers, setting has no boundaries. Ray Bradbury is known for bringing together the fantastic and the ordinary, as he does in this early sentence from "There Will Come Soft Rains": "'Today is August 4, 2026,' said a second voice from the kitchen ceiling, 'in the city of Allendale, California.'"

The story takes place in the future, on what begins as an ordinary day. As you read, look for signs suggesting how this place differs from today's world. Also, pay close attention to the progression of time.

ACTIVE READING VISUALIZING When you **visualize,** you use your imagination to form pictures in your mind. The more precise the **details** a writer supplies, the better a reader is able to visualize a story's **setting, characters,** and **events.**

READER'S NOTEBOOK As you read the story, fill in a chart like this one. Record each time of day. Jot down any words or phrases that help you "see" both ordinary and unusual happenings.

Time of Day	What Seems Ordinary?	What Seems Unusual?

LESSON RESOURCES

UNIT ONE RESOURCE BOOK, pp. 27–30

ASSESSMENT RESOURCES

Formal Assessment, pp. 15–16

Teacher's Guide to Assessment and Portfolio Use

Test Generator

SKILLS TRANSPARENCIES AND COPYMASTERS

Literary Analysis
- Setting, T3 (for Activity, p. 93)

Reading and Critical Thinking
- Organizational Chart: Horizontal, T51 (for Reader's Notebook, p. 86)

Grammar
- Compound Adjectives, C73 (for Mini Lesson, p. 92)

Writing
- Point of View, T23 (for Literary Analysis, p. 93)
- Persuasive Essay, C30 (for Writing Option 2, p. 94)

Communications
- Dramatic Reading, T12 (for Activities & Explorations 2, p. 94)
- Verbal Strategies, T14 (for Activities & Explorations 2, p. 94)

INTEGRATED TECHNOLOGY

Audio Library

Net Activities

Visit our website:
www.mcdougallittell.com

Blue Floor (1990), Roy Lichtenstein. 12-color lithograph/woodblock/screen-print, 57 ¾" × 83 ½". Copyright 1990 © Estate of Roy Lichtenstein/Gemini G.E.L., Los Angeles, California.

THERE WILL COME SOFT RAINS

RAY BRADBURY

In the living room the voice-clock sang, *Tick-tock, seven o'clock, time to get up, time to get up, seven o'clock!* as if it were afraid that nobody would. The morning house lay empty. The clock ticked on, repeating and repeating its sounds into the emptiness. *Seven-nine, breakfast time, seven-nine!*

In the kitchen the breakfast stove gave a hissing sigh and ejected from its warm interior eight pieces of perfectly browned toast, eight eggs sunnyside up, sixteen slices of bacon, two coffees, and two cool glasses of milk.

"Today is August 4, 2026," said a second voice from the kitchen ceiling, "in the city of Allendale, California." It repeated the date three times for memory's sake. "Today is Mr. Featherstone's birthday. Today is the anniversary of Tilita's marriage. Insurance is

Customizing Instruction

Less Proficient Readers

Have students keep these questions in mind as they read.

- How does the author show that different electronic voices are speaking?
  Answer: Italics and quotation marks are used
- How does the author make the story suspenseful?
  Answer: The reader wonders what has happened to the people.

Set a Purpose: Have students read on to discover what happens in the house and what has happened to its human inhabitants.

Students Acquiring English

Because the specific words "atomic blast" are not used on these pages, help students understand the clues throughout the story that indicate the events that have taken place.

Possible Response: The house is standing "alone in a city of rubble and ashes." (p. 88)

Use **Spanish Study Guide** for additional support, pp. 16–18.

BLOCK SCHEDULING: MANAGING TIME

If your schedule requires that you cover the lesson objectives in a shorter time, use . . .

- Preparing to Read, p. 86
- Thinking Through the Literature, p.93

If you want to take advantage of longer class time, use . . .

- TE Teaching Options: Viewing and Representing, pp. 91; Cross Curricular Link, p. 88; Standardized Test Practice, p. 90
- Choices & Challenges, pp. 94

Reading and Analyzing

Reading Skills and Strategies: PREVIEW

Briefly summarize the plot and explain that there are no human characters in the story. Have students look through the text and discuss the image on the opening page as well as the title. If necessary, discuss the background material on technology. Ask students to note the italicized phrases, paying particular attention to the progression of time. Have students read to find out how technology and time play an important role in the story.

Literary Analysis SETTING

Remind students that setting is more than time and place. The setting creates atmosphere, contributes to the story's emotional effect, and affects the plot of the story. As students read, have them analyze the relevance of setting and time frame to the text's meaning. Students should make note of descriptive words or phrases that reveal the setting to be unexpected, unusual, or futuristic.

Use **Unit One Resource Book** p. 29 for more exercises.

Active Reading VISUALIZING

Bradbury helps the reader visualize the scene clearly in the first few paragraphs. Ask students how the author effectively creates the opening scene in the household and how long it takes to realize that something is very unusual. **Possible Response:** The step-by-step announcements of the "voice-clock" indicate a normal morning routine. Something already seems odd in the first paragraph.

Use **Unit One Resource Book** p. 28 for more exercises.

payable, as are the water, gas, and light bills."

Somewhere in the walls, relays[1] clicked, memory tapes glided under electric eyes.

Until this day, how well the house had kept its peace.

Eight-one, tick-tock, eight-one o'clock, off to school, off to work, run, run, eight-one! But no doors slammed, no carpets took the soft tread of rubber heels. It was raining outside. The weather box on the front door sang quietly: "Rain, rain, go away; rubbers, raincoats for today . . ." And the rain tapped on the empty house, echoing.

Outside, the garage chimed and lifted its door to reveal the waiting car. After a long wait the door swung down again.

At eight-thirty the eggs were shriveled and the toast was like stone. An aluminum wedge scraped them into the sink, where hot water whirled them down a metal throat which
1 digested and flushed them away to the distant sea. The dirty dishes were dropped into a hot washer and emerged twinkling dry.

Nine-fifteen, sang the clock, *time to clean.*

Out of warrens[2] in the wall, tiny robot mice darted. The rooms were acrawl with the small cleaning animals, all rubber and metal. They thudded against chairs, whirling their mustached runners, kneading the rug nap, sucking gently at hidden dust. Then, like mysterious invaders, they popped into their burrows. Their pink electric eyes faded. The house was clean.

Ten o'clock. The sun came out from behind the rain. The house stood alone in a city of rubble and ashes. This was the one house left standing. At night the ruined city gave off a radioactive glow which could be seen for miles.

Ten-fifteen. The garden sprinklers whirled up in golden founts, filling the soft morning air with scatterings of brightness. The water pelted windowpanes, running down the charred west side where the house had been burned evenly free of its white paint. The entire west face of the house was black, save for five places. Here the silhouette[3] in paint of a man mowing a lawn. Here, as in a photograph, a woman bent to pick flowers. Still farther over, their images burned on wood in 2
one titanic instant, a small boy, hands flung into the air; higher up, the image of a thrown ball, and opposite him a girl, hands raised to catch a ball which never came down.

The five spots of paint—the man, the woman, the children, the ball—remained. The rest was a thin charcoaled layer.

The gentle sprinkler rain filled the garden with falling light.

Until this day, how well the house had kept its peace. How carefully it had inquired, "Who goes there? What's the password?" and, getting no answer from lonely foxes and whining cats, it had shut up its windows and drawn shades in an old-maidenly preoccupation with self-protection which bordered on a mechanical paranoia.[4]

It quivered at each sound, the house did. If a sparrow brushed a window, the shade snapped up. The bird, startled, flew off! No, not even a bird must touch the house!

The house was an altar with ten thousand attendants, big, small, servicing, attending, in choirs. But the gods had gone away, and the ritual of the religion continued senselessly, uselessly.

Twelve noon.

A dog whined, shivering, on the front porch.

The front door recognized the dog voice and 3
opened. The dog, once huge and fleshy, but now

1. **relays:** devices that automatically turn switches in electric circuits on and off.
2. **warrens:** passageways or burrows.
3. **silhouette** (sĭl′o͞o-ĕt′): a shadowlike image of the outline of a person's shape.
4. **paranoia** (păr′ə-noi′ə): an irrational fear of danger or misfortune.

Teaching Options

Cross Curricular Link Science

TECHNOLOGY Computer-aided engineering and information systems have made significant contributions to society. Computer-aided design, or CAD, is a system used to design items like circuits, clothing patterns, and machine parts. CAD systems feature video monitors and interactive graphics-input devices and can be integrated with computer-aided manufacturing, or CAM, to increase productivity. In addition to manufacturing and design, computer-based information systems, or CIS, are able to perform calculations and correlations at complex levels exceeding human ability. Information systems also have begun to mimic human cognitive processes.

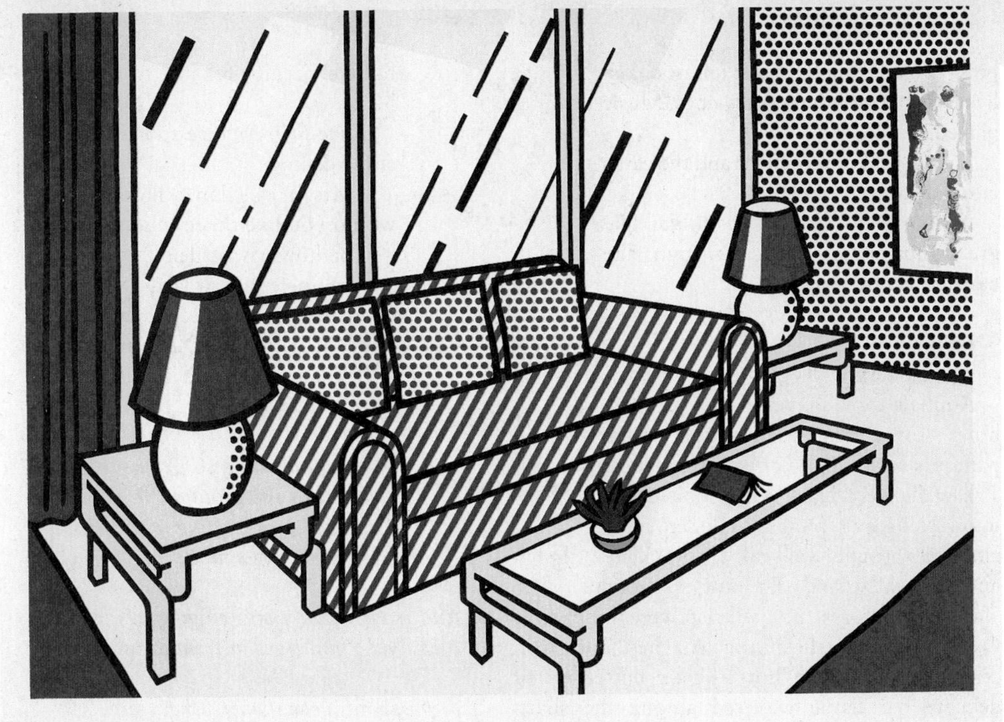

Red Lamps (1990), Roy Lichtenstein. 11-color lithograph/woodblock/screenprint, 57 ¼″ × 78 ¾″.

gone to bone and covered with sores, moved in and through the house, tracking mud. Behind it whirred angry mice, angry at having to pick up mud, angry at inconvenience.

For not a leaf fragment blew under the door but what the wall panels flipped open and the copper scrap rats flashed swiftly out. The offending dust, hair, or paper, seized in miniature steel jaws, was raced back to the burrows. There,
3 down tubes which fed into the cellar, it was dropped into the sighing vent of an incinerator which sat like evil Baal[5] in a dark corner.

The dog ran upstairs, hysterically yelping to each door, at last realizing, as the house realized, that only silence was here.

It sniffed the air and scratched the kitchen door. Behind the door, the stove was making pancakes which filled the house with a rich baked odor and the scent of maple syrup.

The dog frothed at the mouth, lying at the door, sniffing, its eyes turned to fire. It ran wildly in circles, biting at its tail, spun in a frenzy, and died. It lay in the parlor for an hour.

Two o'clock, sang a voice. 3

Delicately sensing decay at last, the regiments of mice hummed out as softly as blown gray leaves in an electrical wind.

Two-fifteen.

The dog was gone.

In the cellar, the incinerator glowed suddenly and a whirl of sparks leaped up the chimney.

Two thirty-five.

Bridge tables sprouted from patio walls. Playing cards fluttered onto pads in a shower of

5. **Baal** (bā′əl): an idol worshiped by certain ancient peoples of the Middle East.

Customizing Instruction

Students Acquiring English

1 Review the author's use of metaphor when he mentions the "metal throat." Point out that the throat he is referring to is the garbage disposal pipe "swallowing" the food.

Use **Spanish Study Guide** for additional support, pp. 16–18.

Less Proficient Readers

2 Ask students why the silhouettes of the family are located on the side of the house.

Possible Response: The atomic blast burned off the white paint on the side of the house, except where the people were standing and blocking the house.

Gifted and Talented

The story reveals some of the effects of an atomic explosion. Students may want to do some research to explain these and other effects more specifically.

Less Proficient Readers

3 Use the following to help students understand what has happened to the dog.

- Why is the dog very thin and covered in sores?
  Possible Response: It is dying from the effects of radioactive exposure and starvation.
- What happens to the dog's remains?
  Possible Response: The mechanical mice have odor sensors. When they detect the faint smell of decay, they dispose of the dog's body in the incinerator.

Reading and Analyzing

Literary Analysis SETTING

A In the description of the nursery, the author uses a great deal of sensory imagery. Ask students to cite specific passages and explain why Bradbury has appealed to the senses.

Possible Responses: The hum of bees, the meadowlike carpet, and the scent of animals are a few images that the author uses to bring life into the empty nursery.

Reading Skills and Strategies: QUESTION

B Students should question why there is so much activity, if there are no humans present.

Possible Response: The mechanical things no longer need humans to make them function.

There will come soft rains and the smell of the ground

pips. Martinis manifested[6] on an oaken bench with egg-salad sandwiches. Music played.

But the tables were silent and the cards untouched.

At four o'clock the tables folded like great butterflies back through the paneled walls.

Four-thirty.

The nursery walls glowed.

Animals took shape: yellow giraffes, blue lions, pink antelopes, lilac panthers cavorting in crystal substance. The walls were glass. They looked out upon color and fantasy. Hidden films clocked through well-oiled sprockets, and the walls lived. The nursery floor was woven to resemble a crisp, cereal meadow. Over this ran aluminum roaches and iron crickets, and in the hot still air butterflies of delicate red tissue wavered among the sharp aroma of animal spoors! There was the sound like a great matted yellow hive of bees within a dark bellows, the lazy bumble of a purring lion. And there was the patter of okapi[7] feet and the murmur of a fresh jungle rain, like other hoofs, falling upon the summer-starched grass. Now the walls dissolved into distances of parched weed, mile on mile, and warm endless sky. The animals drew away into thorn brakes and water holes. **A**

It was the children's hour.

Five o'clock. The bath filled with clear hot water.

Six, seven, eight o'clock. The dinner dishes manipulated like magic tricks, and in the study a *click*. In the metal stand opposite the hearth where a fire now blazed up warmly, a cigar popped out, half an inch of soft gray ash on it, smoking, waiting. **B**

Nine o'clock. The beds warmed their hidden circuits, for nights were cool here.

Nine-five. A voice spoke from the study ceiling:

"Mrs. McClellan, which poem would you like this evening?" **B**

The house was silent.

The voice said at last, "Since you express no preference, I shall select a poem at random." Quiet music rose to back the voice. "Sara Teasdale. As I recall, your favorite. . . .

"There will come soft rains and the smell of the ground,
And swallows circling with their shimmering sound;

And frogs in the pools singing at night,
And wild plum trees in tremulous[8] white;

Robins will wear their feathery fire,
Whistling their whims on a low fence-wire;

And not one will know of the war, not one
Will care at last when it is done.

Not one would mind, neither bird nor tree,
If mankind perished utterly;

And Spring herself, when she woke at dawn
Would scarcely know that we were gone."

The fire burned on the stone hearth and the cigar fell away into a mound of quiet ash on its tray. The empty chairs faced each other between the silent walls, and the music played.

6. **manifested:** appeared.
7. **okapi** (ō-kä′pē): an antelope-like hoofed mammal of the African jungle.
8. **tremulous** (trĕm′yə-ləs): trembling.

Teaching Options

Assessment Standardized Test Practice

PERCEIVING CAUSE-AND-EFFECT RELATIONSHIPS

In standardized testing, students will be asked to choose a cause-and-effect relationship. Help students understand the difference between the two terms then read aloud or write on the chalkboard the following question.

Which of the following statements does NOT reflect a cause-and-effect relationship?

A. The dog expects the humans to feed it, so it returns to the house.

B. The water supply is exhausted, therefore the house cannot adequately fight the fire.

C. The dog gives a familiar whine at the door, then the house lets it in.

D. The window shades of the house flap, and birds land on the windowsill.

Lead students through the process of locating the inaccurate cause-and-effect relationship. Consider each choice. Point out that the first three statements contain accurate interpretations of a cause-and-effect relationship from the story. The last statement shows an inaccurate relationship from the story. Explain that the bird landing on the windowsill is not related to the window shade flapping. For that reason, **D** is the correct choice.

Yellow Vase (1990), Roy Lichtenstein. 11-color lithograph/woodblock/screenprint, 55½″ × 84½″.

At ten o'clock the house began to die.

The wind blew. A falling tree bough crashed through the kitchen window. Cleaning solvent, bottled, shattered over the stove. The room was ablaze in an instant!

"Fire!" screamed a voice. The house lights flashed, water pumps shot water from the
1 ceilings. But the solvent spread on the linoleum, licking, eating, under the kitchen door, while the voices took it up in chorus: "Fire, fire, fire!"

The house tried to save itself. Doors sprang tightly shut, but the windows were broken by the heat and the wind blew and sucked upon the fire.

The house gave ground as the fire in ten billion angry sparks moved with flaming ease from room to room and then up the stairs. While scurrying water rats squeaked from the walls, pistoled their water, and ran for more. And the wall sprays let down showers of mechanical rain.

But too late. Somewhere, sighing, a pump shrugged to a stop. The quenching rain ceased. The reserve water supply which had filled baths and washed dishes for many quiet days was gone.

The fire crackled up the stairs. It fed upon Picassos and Matisses[9] in the upper halls, like delicacies, baking off the oily flesh, tenderly crisping the canvases into black shavings.

Now the fire lay in beds, stood in windows, changed the colors of drapes!

And then, reinforcements.

From attic trapdoors, blind robot faces peered down with faucet mouths gushing green chemical.

The fire backed off, as even an elephant must at the sight of a dead snake. Now there were twenty snakes whipping over the floor, killing the fire with a clear cold venom of green froth.

But the fire was clever. It had sent flame outside the house, up through the attic to the

9. **Picassos and Matisses:** paintings by the famous 20th-century artists Pablo Picasso (päb′lō pĭ-kä′sō) and Henri Matisse (äN-rē′ mə-tēs′).

Customizing Instruction

1 Students Acquiring English

Help students understand the word *solvent*. Explain that many kinds of household solvents contain alcohol, turpentine, or kerosene, which are highly flammable.

Multiple Learning Styles

Visual Learners

Have students draw a schematic view of the house, either a cross section or a floor plan, to aid in understanding where the sequence of events takes place.

Gifted and Talented

Have students write a description of the characters and events on August 3, 2026.

Mini Lesson Viewing and Representing

Yellow Vase **by Roy Lichtenstein**

ART APPRECIATION

The American artist Roy Lichtenstein, considered a pop artist, is easily recognized by his stark use of lines reminiscent of comic book illustrations.

Application Based on the details in the picture, have students suggest reasons why this particular piece of art complements the genre of science fiction.

Possible Response: There is an ordinary but unreal quality to the piece. The patterns and lines are unexpected and unusual. The style of the picture has an op-art, futuristic look; the furniture and other elements in the picture are not portrayed in a natural manner.

THERE WILL COME SOFT RAINS 91

Reading and Analyzing

Reading Skills and Strategies: EVALUATING

A Remind students that personification is a device used to make an object, animal, or idea exhibit human qualities. Point out examples of the author's use of personification as it relates to the house. Then have students evaluate how effectively personification provides human qualities where there is no human life.

Possible Response: The author uses personification throughout the entire story. On this page, for example, the house shudders, the stove cooks at a psychopathic rate, and pieces of furniture resemble skeletons.

Literary Analysis SETTING

B Ask students how the setting has changed by the end of the story and how it has remained the same.

Possible Response: The setting has changed dramatically because the house has been almost completely destroyed by the fire. Parts of the setting have remained unchanged. It is the same time of day as in the beginning of the story and a singular, calm voice announces the date to no one.

pumps there. An explosion! The attic brain which directed the pumps was shattered into bronze shrapnel on the beams.

The fire rushed back into every closet and felt of the clothes hung there.

The house shuddered, oak bone on bone, its bared skeleton cringing from the heat, its wire, its nerves revealed as if a surgeon had torn the skin off to let the red veins and capillaries quiver in the scalded air. Help, help! Fire! Run, run! Heat snapped mirrors like the first brittle winter ice. And the voices wailed Fire, fire, run, run, like a tragic nursery rhyme, a dozen voices, high, low, like children dying in a forest, alone, alone. And the voices fading as the wires popped their sheathings like hot chestnuts. One, two, three, four, five voices died.

In the nursery the jungle burned. Blue lions roared, purple giraffes bounded off. The panthers ran in circles, changing color, and ten million animals, running before the fire, vanished off toward a distant steaming river. . . .

Ten more voices died. In the last instant under the fire avalanche, other choruses, oblivious,[10] could be heard announcing the time, playing music, cutting the lawn by remote-control mower, or setting an umbrella frantically out and in the slamming and opening front door, a thousand things happening, like a clock shop when each clock strikes the hour insanely before or after the other, a scene of maniac confusion, yet unity; singing, screaming, a few last cleaning mice darting bravely out to carry the horrid ashes away! And one voice,

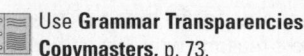

Girl with Tear III (1977), Roy Lichtenstein. Oil and magna on canvas, 46″ × 40″. Copyright © Estate of Roy Lichtenstein/Leo Castelli Gallery, New York.

with sublime[11] disregard for the situation, read poetry aloud in the fiery study, until all the film spools burned, until all the wires withered and the circuits cracked.

The fire burst the house and let it slam flat down, puffing out skirts of spark and smoke. **A**

In the kitchen, an instant before the rain of fire and timber, the stove could be seen making breakfasts at a psychopathic[12] rate, ten dozen eggs, six loaves of toast, twenty dozen bacon strips, which, eaten by fire, started the stove working again, hysterically hissing!

The crash. The attic smashing into kitchen and parlor. The parlor into cellar, cellar into sub-cellar. Deep freeze, armchair, film tapes, circuits, beds, and all like skeletons thrown in a cluttered mound deep under.

Smoke and silence. A great quantity of smoke.

Dawn showed faintly in the east. Among the ruins, one wall stood alone. Within the wall, a last voice said, over and over again and again, even as the sun rose to shine upon the heaped rubble and steam:

"Today is August 5, 2026, today is August 5, 2026, today is . . ." ❖ **B**

10. **oblivious** (ə-blĭv′ē-əs): paying no attention; heedless.
11. **sublime:** splendid.
12. **psychopathic** (sī′kə-păth′ĭk): insane.

Teaching Options

Mini Lesson Grammar

COMPOUND ADJECTIVES Remind students that a compound adjective is a modifier made up of more than one word. When two or more words serve together as a single modifier before a noun, a hyphen forms the modifying words into a unit. *(She created a well-organized project.)* When a compound adjective follows the noun, or the adjective ends in "ly," no hyphen is needed. *(Her project was well organized.)* Write the following sentence on the chalkboard.

"She was the only French speaking person at the convention."

Underline the compound adjective as shown. Have students determine whether the compound adjective should contain a hyphen or if the hyphen is unnecessary. *(The hyphen is necessary because the modifier precedes the noun.)*

Use **Grammar Transparencies and Copymasters,** p. 73.

Use McDougal Littell ***Language Network,*** Chapter 11, for more instruction in compound adjectives.

Connect to the Literature

1. **What Do You Think?** If you were to think back to this story in the days and weeks to come, what image do you think would most likely come to your mind?

Comprehension Check
- What unusual qualities and appliances does the house have?
- What has happened outside the house?
- What finally destroys the house?

Think Critically

2. Only as the story progresses do you learn something of what has happened outside the McClellan home. What effect do you think this delay creates?
3. What do you think has happened to the former inhabitants of the house?

   THINK ABOUT
   - the announcements that the voice in the kitchen ceiling makes
   - the duties the house performs
   - the silhouettes on the side of the house
4. ACTIVE READING VISUALIZING Review the information you recorded in your READER'S NOTEBOOK. What description led you to think that something very out of the ordinary had happened outside the home?
5. What effect does Bradbury create by including the Teasdale poem in his story?

   THINK ABOUT
   - the message, or **theme,** of each selection
   - the **settings** of the poem and story

Extend Interpretations

6. **What If?** Suppose the mechanical house were programmed to detect early signs of nuclear fallout. What warning do you think it might have issued, or what defensive action might it have taken?
7. **Connect to Life** Think about the discussion you had for Connect to Your Life, on page 86, about the benefits and dangers of technology. Has the story changed your opinion? Why or why not?

Literary Analysis

SETTING **Setting** is the time and place of the action of a story. Setting may also include details of a story's social and cultural environment. In "There Will Come Soft Rains," you quickly learn the basic time and place of the story. From the voice from the kitchen ceiling, you also get hints that the story is set in a routine, middle-class environment:

"Today is Mr. Featherstone's birthday. Today is the anniversary of Tilita's marriage. Insurance is payable, as are the water, gas, and light bills."

These details suggest that the day should have been an ordinary one for the McClellan family. It is against this typical American social setting that Bradbury contrasts the annihilation of atomic war. This contrast gives the story its power.

Activity Review "There Will Come Soft Rains," paying special attention to the passage of time. Note the details about setting provided in the passages that follow each time announcement. How does this add to your understanding of the events that took place before the story began?

POINT OF VIEW The perspective from which a story is told is called **point of view. Third-person** point of view occurs when a narrator outside the action describes events and characters. How does the third-person narrator of "There Will Come Soft Rains" maintain interest in a story where there are no human characters? Explain.

GUIDING STUDENT RESPONSE

Connect to the Literature

1. **What Do You Think?**
   Students may imagine their own homes functioning without anyone.

Comprehension Check
- Devices with voices, a stove that cooks and serves breakfast, and mechanical mice represent unusual qualities.
- The city has been destroyed by an atomic blast, but the house is left standing.
- A fire set off by a storm-blown branch breaks a window and spills flammable cleaning fluid on the stove.

Use Selection Quiz **Unit One Resource Book,** p. 30.

Think Critically

2. The reader realizes something is wrong, and the delay builds suspense.
3. The announcements show that the homeowners lived efficient, time-ordered lives. Since there is no response to the voices, something is wrong. The house performs all routine duties. The silhouettes burned into the side of the house indicate that the family was killed in an instantaneous fiery flash by an atomic blast.
4. The house is left standing alone amid rubble and ashes; the city gives off a radioactive glow at night; the images left on the charred wall.
5. By using Teasdale's poem, Bradbury reiterates his central theme of concern for mankind's future.
   The theme of each selection shows that time marches forward with or without the existence of humans.
   The setting of each selection reflects calm acceptance of the theme.

Extend Interpretations

What If? Students might mention that perhaps the house had a special shelter to protect its inhabitants.
Connect to Life Ask students to support their opinions with reasons.

Literary Analysis

Activity The passage of time would have been given by a living narrator; however, no one has survived.
Point of View Interest is heightened because despite the lack of a human narrator, we do learn information. It seems mechanically dispensed.

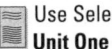

Choices & CHALLENGES

Writing Options

1. House Monologue Imagine that the attic "brain" has developed human understanding. The house now realizes what has happened to its inhabitants. Replace the house's "spoken" monologue in the story with a new one that reflects the house's knowledge of its critical situation.

2. Appliance Argument Write a persuasive essay expressing your views on whether the technological devices in "There Will Come Soft Rains" could improve people's lives. Cite evidence to support your arguments. Put your persuasive essay in your **Working Portfolio.**

Writing Handbook
See pages 1161–1162: Persuasive Writing.

Activities & Explorations

1. Future Set Design Design a diorama of the McClellan home. Create cutaway sections to show the hidden devices. ~ **ART**

2. Readers Theater In a Readers Theater presentation, performers read aloud, using a work of literature as a script. Divide Bradbury's story into time periods, and assign a reader to each section. Before performing, decide what tones of voice are appropriate to the narration and automated machines of the story. ~ **PERFORMING**

Inquiry & Research

1. Political Climate Bradbury's story was written in 1950–51 and reflects some common fears of the time. What was making Americans nervous? Find out about the international political climate of the period and how that might have contributed to the development of this story. Report what you find to the class.

2. Poetry Connection Find out about Sara Teasdale and the circumstances behind her writing the poem "There Will Come Soft Rains." Compare and contrast Bradbury's and Teasdale's basic themes.

Grammar in Context: Action Verbs

In "There Will Come Soft Rains," Ray Bradbury's use of action verbs allows the reader to form a clear image of what happens to eggs and toast that go uneaten in an empty house in the year 2026.

> **An aluminum wedge scraped them into the sink, where hot water whirled them down a metal throat which digested and flushed them away to the distant sea.**

Bradbury's strong verbs convey the cold efficiency of the robot-operated house. The verb *digested* makes it sound as if the house were a living organism. Think about how much less lively the writing would be if Bradbury had used *moved* instead of *scraped, washed* instead of *whirled, received* instead of *digested,* and *sent* instead of *flushed.*

Apply to Your Writing Using strong action verbs can help you

- make your writing more vivid and lively
- describe events more effectively
- give the reader clues to characters' qualities and appearances

WRITING EXERCISE Substitute an action verb for the underlined verb in each sentence.

Example: ***Original*** The cleaning mice went across the carpet and into the kitchen.

Rewritten The cleaning mice whirred across the carpet and into the kitchen.

1. The sprinklers put water on the garden.
2. A radioactive glow came from the ruined city.
3. The dog fell on the floor and died.
4. A falling tree limb broke the kitchen window.
5. Fire moved through the rooms of the house.

Connect to the Literature Write down four action verbs that appear on page 92. What sort of mood do these verbs create? Why might Bradbury have chosen them?

Writing Options

1. **House Monologue** Students might imagine sad, angry, or frightened emotional states.
2. **Appliance Argument** Students may make suggestions that have to do with their schoolwork.

Activities and Explorations

1. **Future Set Design** Suggest using materials, like cardboard, that are easy to cut, so that interior spaces can be shown. Dioramas should include all rooms mentioned in the story.
2. **Readers Theater** Have students perform a choral reading of the story. Allow time for them to plan and rehearse their reading. Encourage the performers to work together in building to a dramatic climax of frenzied voices and descriptions of action to portray the chaos of the fire.

Inquiry & Research

1. **Political Climate** To approach this question, suggest students locate both print and nonprint using text and information technical resources, including databases and the Internet.
   Possible Response: Soviet Communists threatened the West with statements such as: "we will bury you."
2. **Poetry Connection** Students may discover that both author and poet reflected the concerns and fears of their times.

Grammar in Context

Exercise Answers will vary. Possible answers are shown.

1. The sprinklers sprayed water on the garden.
2. A radioactive glow oozed from the ruined city.
3. The dog collapsed on the floor and died.
4. A falling tree limb smashed the kitchen window.
5. Fire raged through the rooms of the house.

Teaching Options

Mini Lesson Grammar

ACTION VERBS

Instruction Action verbs express physical or mental action. Using action verbs can strengthen sentences. When students are writing about lively or intense events, the use of action verbs will make their sentences more effective.

Practice Work through the first assignment in the Grammar in Context exercises with the class. Encourage students to come up with several action verbs to replace the verb *put*. Have students say the sentence aloud, inserting their action verb at the appropriate point. Evaluate the effect of each of the new sentences. Students can complete the exercises independently.

Use **Grammar Transparencies and Copymasters,** p. 68.

Use McDougal Littell ***Language Network,*** Chapter 1, for more instruction in action verbs.

The Pedestrian

Short Story by RAY BRADBURY

"The lone car turned a corner quite suddenly and flashed a fierce white cone of light upon him."

Connect to Your Life

Walking Habits In the story you are about to read, Leonard Mead is the pedestrian, out walking one night "for air, and to see, and just to walk." As he walks he passes a number of homes, wondering what TV programs the people inside are watching. When you yourself take a walk, is it merely to get somewhere? Or do you ever walk just to "get away from it all"? Jot down a description of the kind of walking you do.

Build Background

It's a TV World By the mid-1990s, 99 percent of households in the United States had a television, and 38 percent had more than one. There were 776 televisions for every 1,000 Americans, the world's highest ratio. It was determined that each American TV was on for an average of 51 to 52 hours per week, or more than 7 hours per day. Ray Bradbury anticipated such statistics as far back as 1951, when he wrote this story—except that he imagined that TV viewing would not reach such a high level until well into the 21st century!

Focus Your Reading

LITERARY ANALYSIS DESCRIPTION Bradbury brings "The Pedestrian" to life through **description**—writing that helps a reader picture the **scenes, events,** and **characters** in a story. Description often involves the use of precise language and the composing of vivid and original phrases. These are found in this sample passage:

> ***There was a good crystal frost in the air; it cut the nose and made the lungs blaze like a Christmas tree inside.***

Think about the effects created by the descriptive details you encounter in the story.

ACTIVE READING RECOGNIZING SENSORY DETAILS **Sensory details** are references to sight, smell, hearing, taste, and touch. In appealing to the five senses, they help readers to more fully experience what is happening. Notice the senses Bradbury calls to mind in this passage from the story:

> ***During the day it was a thunderous surge of cars, . . . as the scarab-beetles, a faint incense puttering from their exhausts, skimmed homeward to the far directions.***

READER'S NOTEBOOK As you read this story, record some sensory details that help you experience Leonard Mead's night in the city. Here's an example:

Sensory Details	
Phrase or Sentence	**Sense(s) Appealed to**
"patterns of frosty air . . . like the smoke of a cigar"	sight

OVERVIEW

Objectives

1. understand and appreciate a **short story (Literary Analysis)**
2. evaluate the author's use of **description (Literary Analysis)**
3. recognize **sensory details (Active Reading)**

Summary

Every day in the year 2053, Leonard Mead takes his evening walk, enjoying the fresh air, the solitude, and the silence. One evening his peaceful reveries are interrupted by a patrol car, the first sign of activity Mead has seen in the 10 years he has been taking his ritual evening walk. A metallic voice from inside the car commands Mead to put his hands in the air and then questions him. Mead explains he is walking, "for air, and to see, and just to walk," but his reasons fail to satisfy the voice. Mead is ordered into the computer-operated patrol car. The story ends with Mead in the back seat of the car as it winds through the dark, deserted streets on its way to a psychiatric center for "regressive" tendencies.

Thematic Link

In this story, Bradbury suggests that the price of an electronically enhanced world may be that simple pleasures will be viewed with suspicion.

5-Minute Warm-Up

Daily Language SkillBuilder

Have students **proofread** the display sentences on page 15j and write them correctly. The sentences also appear on Transparency 3 of **Grammar Transparencies and Copymasters.**

LESSON RESOURCES

UNIT ONE RESOURCE BOOK, pp. 31–34

ASSESSMENT RESOURCES
Formal Assessment, p. 17
Teacher's Guide to Assessment and Portfolio Use
Test Generator

SKILLS TRANSPARENCIES AND COPYMASTERS
Reading and Critical Thinking
- Organizational Chart: Horizontal, T51 (for Reader's Notebook, p. 95)

Vocabulary
- Context Clues, C25 (for Mini Lesson, p. 96)
- Prefixes, C26 (for Mini Lesson, p. 98)

Writing
- Writing Structure, T10, T11 (for Writing Option 2, p. 103)
- Extending Sentences, T19 (for Applications, p. 102)
- Opinion Statement, C25 (for Writing Option 2, p. 103)

Communications
- Evaluating Roles in Groups, T8 (for Activities & Explorations 1, p. 103)

INTEGRATED TECHNOLOGY
Audio Library
Net Activities
Internet: Research Starter
Visit our website:
www.mcdougallittell.com

TEACHING THE LITERATURE

Reading and Analyzing

Literary Analysis: PREVIEW

Before students begin reading, give them a brief summary of the story. Ask students to preview the story by viewing the images and thinking about the title. Point out the ominous mood that has been set.

Active Reading

RECOGNIZING SENSORY DETAILS

Have students identify the sensory details the author uses in the fourth paragraph to illustrate the chilly autumn evening.

Possible Responses: "good crystal frost"; "made the lungs blaze like a Christmas tree"; "listened to the faint push of his soft shoes through autumn leaves"; and "smelling its rusty smell."

Use **Unit One Resource Book,** p. 32 for additional support.

Literary Analysis DESCRIPTION

Descriptive language helps to set the mood of a story. Ask students to point out descriptive phrases in the first two paragraphs and think about what kind of mood is being set.

Possible Response: "misty evening," "dark windows," "walking through a graveyard," "whisperings and murmurs." Such phrases create a feeling of spookiness or loneliness.

Use **Unit One Resource Book,** p. 33 for additional support.

The Pedestrian

Ray Bradbury

To enter out into that silence that was the city at eight o'clock of a misty evening in November, to put your feet upon that buckling concrete walk, to step over grassy seams and make your way, hands in pockets, through the silences, that was what Mr. Leonard Mead most dearly loved to do. He would stand upon the corner of an intersection and peer down long moonlit avenues of sidewalk in four directions, deciding which way to go, but it really made no difference; he was alone in this world of A.D. 2053, or as good as alone, and with a final decision made, a path selected, he would stride off, sending patterns of frosty air before him like the smoke of a cigar.

Sometimes he would walk for hours and miles and return only at midnight to his house. And on his way he would see the cottages and homes with their dark windows, and it was not unlike walking through a graveyard where only the faintest glimmers of firefly light appeared in flickers behind the windows. Sudden gray phantoms seemed to manifest upon inner room walls where a curtain was still undrawn against the night, or there were whisperings and murmurs where a window in a tomblike building was still open.

Mr. Leonard Mead would pause, cock his head, listen, look, and march on, his feet

Teaching Options

Mini Lesson Vocabulary Strategy

USING CONTEXT CLUES

Instruction Remind students that while reading they can sometimes understand the meaning of an unfamiliar word by looking at the word in its context. Use the model sentence to demonstrate the strategy of using context clues to determine meaning.

Model Sentence

Susie experienced *intermittent* problems with her telephone line. Sometimes she heard static, and sometimes she didn't.

Instruction

- Write the model sentence on the chalkboard.
- Ask a volunteer to summarize the meaning of the sentence.
- Have students come up with an approximate definition of the word based on the meaning of the sentence.
- Ask a volunteer to use the word *intermittent* in a new context.

Activity Read the following sentences. Ask the students to use context clues to determine the meanings of the italicized words.

1. He wiped the scrape with an *antiseptic* to avoid infection.

Night Shadows (1921), Edward Hopper. Etching, 6⅞″ × 8¼″. Sheldon Memorial Art Gallery, University of Nebraska-Lincoln, F. M. Hall Collection (1951.H-333).

making no noise on the lumpy walk. For long ago he had wisely changed to sneakers when strolling at night, because the dogs in intermittent[1] squads would parallel his journey with barkings if he wore hard heels, and lights might click on and faces appear and an entire street be startled by the passing of a lone figure, himself, in the early November evening.

On this particular evening he began his journey in a westerly direction, toward the hidden sea. There was a good crystal frost in the air; it cut the nose and made the lungs blaze like a Christmas tree inside; you could feel the cold light going on and off, all the branches filled with invisible snow. He listened to the faint push of his soft shoes through autumn leaves with satisfaction, and whistled a cold quiet whistle between his teeth, occasionally picking up a leaf as he passed, examining its skeletal pattern in the infrequent lamplights as he went on, smelling its rusty smell.

"Hello, in there," he whispered to every house on every side as he moved. "What's up tonight on Channel 4, Channel 7, Channel 9? Where are the cowboys rushing, and do I see

1. **intermittent:** appearing from time to time.

Customizing Instruction

Less Proficient Readers
Explain that the story, set in the future, seems simple and peaceful at the start. Have students pay special attention to events or other details that suggest something may be wrong.

Set a Purpose Have students read to discover what goes wrong during Mr. Mead's walk.

Students Acquiring English
As it is never directly stated, students may not understand that Mr. Mead is alone because all of the people are indoors watching television. Ask students to explain what Mr. Mead asks at each house.

Answer: He wants to know about the evening's programs.

Then ask students what all of the people except Mr. Mead are doing.

Answer: Everyone is watching television.

Use **Spanish Study Guide** for additional support, pp. 19–21.

Gifted and Talented
Mention to students that Bradbury's story illustrates one of the greatest challenges facing modern civilization: maintaining a balance between society's need for order and an individual's need for freedom. Ask students to think of examples of government rules that could be construed as interfering with personal freedom. Have them debate whether the rules are reasonable or whether they undermine freedom.

2. After baby Alex was born, his five-year-old sister, Lori, began to exhibit *regressive* behavior such as crawling and kicking her heels.

Use **Vocabulary Transparencies and Copymasters,** p. 25.

A lesson on context clues appears on p. 56 in the Pupil's Edition.

Reading and Analyzing

Reading Skills and Strategies: QUESTION

A Have students discuss why the voice replies "no profession" when Mead says he is a writer.

Possible Response: In this society, Mead's profession does not conform to what most people are doing.

Reading Skills and Strategies: EVALUATE

Ask students to examine the author's view of what man will be like in the future. Ask them if they agree or disagree with this view.

Literary Analysis: CHARACTER

B Ask students how Mead's career as a writer reveals his character and his place in society. How might his character differ if he were employed in the computer or television industry?

Possible Response: As a writer, Mead is out of step with the rest of society. If he were employed in the television or computer industry, he would likely be a valued, accepted member of society. He would think like everyone else.

the United States Cavalry over the next hill to the rescue?"

The street was silent and long and empty, with only his shadow moving like the shadow of a hawk in midcountry. If he closed his eyes and stood very still, frozen, he could imagine himself upon the center of a plain, a wintry, windless Arizona desert with no house in a thousand miles, and only dry river beds, the streets, for company.

"What is it now?" he asked the houses, noticing his wrist watch. "Eight-thirty P.M.? Time for a dozen assorted murders? A quiz? A revue? A comedian falling off the stage?"

Was that a murmur of laughter from within a moon-white house? He hesitated, but went on when nothing more happened. He stumbled over a particularly uneven section of sidewalk. The cement was vanishing under flowers and grass. In ten years of walking by night or day, for thousands of miles, he had never met another person walking, not one in all that time.

He came to a cloverleaf intersection which stood silent where two main highways crossed the town. During the day it was a thunderous surge of cars, the gas stations open, a great insect rustling and a ceaseless jockeying for position as the scarab-beetles, a faint incense puttering from their exhausts, skimmed homeward to the far directions. But now these highways, too, were like streams in a dry season, all stone and bed and moon radiance.

He turned back on a side street, circling around toward his home. He was within a block of his destination when the lone car turned a corner quite suddenly and flashed a fierce white cone of light upon him. He stood entranced, not unlike a night moth, stunned by the illumination, and then drawn toward it.

A metallic voice called to him:

"Stand still. Stay where you are! Don't move!"

He halted.

"Put up your hands!"

"But—" he said.

"Your hands up! Or we'll shoot!"

The police, of course, but what a rare, incredible thing; in a city of three million, there was only one police car left, wasn't that correct? Ever since a year ago, 2052, the election year, the force had been cut down from three cars to one. Crime was ebbing; there was no need now for the police, save for this one lone car wandering and wandering the empty streets.

"Your name?" said the police car in a metallic whisper. He couldn't see the men in it for the bright light in his eyes.

"Leonard Mead," he said.

"Speak up!"

"Leonard Mead!"

"Business or profession?"

"I guess you'd call me a writer."

"No profession," said the police car, as if talking to itself. The light held him fixed, like a museum specimen, needle thrust through chest. **A**

"You might say that," said Mr. Mead. He hadn't written in years. Magazines and books didn't sell any more. Everything went on in the tomblike houses at night now, he thought, continuing his fancy. The tombs, ill-lit by television light, where the people sat like the dead, the grey or multicolored lights touching their faces, but never really touching *them*. **B**

"No profession," said the phonograph voice, hissing. "What are you doing out?"

"Walking," said Leonard Mead.

"Walking!"

"Just walking," he said simply, but his face felt cold.

"Walking, just walking, walking?"

"Yes, sir."

Teaching Options

Mini Lesson Vocabulary Strategy

UNDERSTANDING PREFIXES in-, inter-, un-

Instruction The word *intermittent* contains the prefix *inter-*, which means "between." The definition for *intermittent*, "appearing from time to time," indicates that something that is intermittent has a "between" time that is somehow different from the rest of the time. Intermittent rainfall means that it rains, then it doesn't rain, then it rains again. Explain that the prefixes *in-* and *un-* both mean "not." Remind students that *in-* sometimes has a different meaning. Provide simple examples such as *incomplete* and *unsympathetic* to illustrate how the prefixes function in a word.

Activity Help students use knowledge of the prefix *inter-* as well as *in-* and *un-* to comprehend the meanings of words that begin with these prefixes. Have them work in pairs to determine the meaning of *interchangeable, intermediary, injustice, incalculable, unbecoming,* and *unrelenting.* Ask students to use each word in a sentence and to show how they used the knowledge of the prefix to arrive at the meaning of the word. Then have students check their results against a dictionary.

Use **Vocabulary Transparencies and Copymasters,** p 26.

A lesson on affixes appears on p. 856 in the Pupil's Edition.

Flying Man with Briefcase No. 2816932 (1983), Jonathan Borofsky. Painted Gatorfoam, 94½″ × 24½″ × 1″. Copyright © 1983 Jonathan Borofsky/Gemini G.E.L., Los Angeles, California.

Customizing Instruction

Less Proficient Readers

Have students keep these questions in mind to guide them through the action.

- To whom is Mead asking questions?

Answer: the houses he passes

- Why is Mead surprised to see a police car?

Answer: The city has only one, so the odds that he would see it are slim.

- Why does the car make Mead stop?

Answer: His behavior is so unusual that it is suspicious.

Students Acquiring English

Explain that the expression "cloverleaf intersection" refers to a place where several highways cross each other. From above the circular ramps going onto and coming off the highway look like a cloverleaf.

Mini Lesson Viewing and Representing

Instruction The two illustrations on this page and on p. 97 help to emphasize the mood the author has created in this story.

Application Ask students what feelings the drawings evoke in them. Have them point out the elements of the drawings that help create these feelings.

Possible Responses: In the first drawing, the artist contrasts dark and light creating an ominous, lonely feeling. The use of scratchy lines could be interpreted as "cold." In the second illustration, the figure has no specific identity. He, like Mead in the story, could represent any man.

Reading and Analyzing

Reading Skills and Strategies: CLARIFY

A Ask students to explain the "crime" Mead has committed. Have them point out the facts that prove his "guilt."

Possible Response: Mead's crime is that he is different from the rest of society. The voice finds Mead suspicious because he is a writer, he desires fresh air despite the fact that his home has air conditioning, he does not own a television set, and he is not married.

"Walking where? For what?"

"Walking for air. Walking to see."

"Your address!"

"Eleven South Saint James Street."

"And there is air in your house, you have an air *conditioner,* Mr. Mead?"

"Yes."

"And you have a viewing screen in your house to see with?"

"No."

"No?" There was a crackling quiet that in itself was an accusation.

"Are you married, Mr. Mead?"

"No."

"Not married," said the police voice behind the fiery beam. The moon was high and clear among the stars and the houses were gray and silent.

"Nobody wanted me," said Leonard Mead with a smile.

"Don't speak unless you're spoken to!"

Leonard Mead waited in the cold night.

"Just *walking,* Mr. Mead?"

"Yes."

"But you haven't explained for what purpose."

"I explained; for air, and to see, and just to walk."

"Have you done this often?"

"Every night for years."

The police car sat in the center of the street with its radio throat faintly humming.

"Well, Mr. Mead," it said.

"Is that all?" he asked politely.

"Yes," said the voice. "Here." There was a sigh, a pop. The back door of the police car sprang wide. "Get in."

"Wait a minute, I haven't done anything!"

"Get in."

"I protest!"

"Mr. Mead."

He walked like a man suddenly drunk. As he passed the front window of the car he looked in. As he had expected, there was no one in the front seat, no one in the car at all.

"Get in."

He put his hand to the door and peered into the back seat, which was a little cell, a little black jail with bars. It smelled of riveted steel. It smelled of harsh antiseptic;[2] it smelled too clean and hard and metallic. There was nothing soft there.

"Now if you had a wife to give you an alibi," said the iron voice. "But—"

"Where are you taking me?"

The car hesitated, or rather gave a faint whirring click, as if information, somewhere, was dripping card by punch-slotted card under electric eyes. "To the Psychiatric Center for Research on Regressive Tendencies.[3]" **A**

"Just *walking,* Mr. Mead?"

He got in. The door shut with a soft thud. The police car rolled through the night avenues, flashing its dim lights ahead.

They passed one house on one street a moment later, one house in an entire city of houses that were dark, but this one particular house had all of its electric lights brightly lit, every window a loud yellow illumination, square and warm in the cool darkness.

"That's *my* house," said Leonard Mead.

No one answered him.

The car moved down the empty river-bed streets and off away, leaving the empty streets with the empty sidewalks, and no sound and no motion all the rest of the chill November night. ❖

2. **antiseptic:** a substance used to kill germs.
3. **Regressive Tendencies:** habits of acting in ways that belong to a more primitive stage of development.

Teaching Options

Assessment Standardized Test Practice

CHOOSING THE BEST SUMMARY For some standardized tests, students will be asked to choose the best summary of a passage. To provide students with some help in choosing the best summary, read aloud or write on the chalkboard the following question.

Which of the following statements best summarizes the short story "The Pedestrian"?

A. A man goes for a walk on a brisk fall night.

B. A man is questioned by a police patrol.

C. In A.D. 2053, taking a walk is so unusual that a man is taken into police custody for doing so.

Lead students through the process of choosing the best summary. Consider each choice. Point out that all of the statements contain accurate information about the story, but the best summary should include the most important information. For that reason, **C** is the best choice.

Connect to the Literature

1. **What Do You Think?** Do you think Leonard Mead will ever again walk his city's streets? Explain.

Comprehension Check
- What interrupts Leonard's walk one November night?
- What makes him appear suspicious to the police?
- Where is he taken at the end of the story?

Think Critically

2. ACTIVE READING RECOGNIZING SENSORY DETAILS Review the examples of sensory details that you recorded in your READER'S NOTEBOOK. Which passage do you think best conveys Leonard Mead's separation from others?

3. What are your impressions of Leonard's world of 2053?

THINK ABOUT
- what Leonard hasn't seen in ten years of nightly walks
- what passes for "normal" night behavior in the city
- the condition of the city's sidewalks

4. Of Leonard's several responses to the police car, which do you think gets him into the most trouble? Why?

5. Would you call Leonard a rebel? Why or why not?

6. What kind of statement about TV do you think Bradbury tries to make?

Extend Interpretations

7. **Critic's Corner** According to Bradbury's biographer David Mogan, "The Pedestrian" is science fiction that comments on present-day irritations with society and technology by portraying a future in which the problems are exaggerated. On the basis of the selections you've read in this Author Study, what would you say are some of Bradbury's specific concerns about the modern world? Defend your views with evidence from the selections.

8. **Connect to Life** Bradbury's science fiction stories have been termed "warning fictions." Which of the three stories in this Author Study do you feel holds the most powerful warning for readers of your generation? Explain the reasons for your choice.

Literary Analysis

DESCRIPTION **Description** is the process by which a writer creates a word picture of a scene, event, or character. Good descriptive writing appeals to the senses, helping the reader to see, hear, smell, taste, or feel the subject being described. It relies on vivid and precise language.

In the following passage, Bradbury reveals the impersonal, insensitive way that Leonard Mead is being observed:

And on his way he would see the cottages and homes with their dark windows, and it was not unequal to walking through a graveyard where only the faintest glimmers of firefly light appeared in flickers behind the windows.

Paired Activity With a partner, choose three or four more examples of description that you found particularly well crafted. Discuss how each example contributes to the mood of the story.

REVIEW CHARACTER The individuals who participate in the action of a literary work are called **characters.** The most important characters are main characters, and the less prominent ones are minor characters. "The Pedestrian" has an unusual cast of characters. Briefly review the story. How much do you feel you know about the story's main character? Explain. The robot voices in the police car can be considered minor characters. What human traits do you feel they imitate, if any?

GUIDING STUDENT RESPONSE

Connect to the Literature

1. **What Do You Think?**
Students may feel that Mead will walk the streets again, because he has not yet given in to the system.

Comprehension Check
- a police car
- he is out walking alone at night
- the Psychiatric Center for Research on Regressive Tendencies

Use Selection Quiz **Unit One Resource Book,** p. 34.

Think Critically

2. Encourage students to support their choices.
3. Possible Response: It's bleak and deserted; no one ventures outdoors. Instead everyone is inside watching television.
4. Students may feel that Mead's profession gets him into the most trouble.
5. He is a rebel because he defies society's norms by walking and by not owning a television. He is not a rebel, but merely a throw-back to an earlier day and age.
6. Possible Response: Bradbury thinks that television has led to an isolated, fragmented society and a redefinition of what is "normal."

Extend Interpretations

Critic's Corner Students will notice that Bradbury seems concerned about the role technology will play in our lives. It may curtail our freedoms; we may become totally dependent on technology.

Connect to Life Students should be encouraged to explain their choices and even select passages that they feel were especially powerful.

Literary Analysis

Paired Activity Ask students to choose the words that are crucial to the descriptive passages and to explain why they are so important.

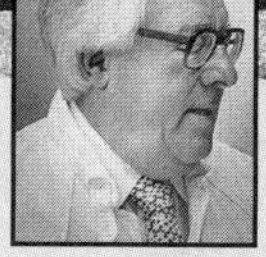

THE AUTHOR'S STYLE

Bradbury's Compelling Compositions

A piece of literature's **style** is the particular way in which it is written. Style is not so much *what* is said as *how* it is said. It is the writer's uniquely individual way of communicating ideas. Critics have noted that Bradbury's style conveys urgency, excitement, "a sense of breathless wonder," and a hint of sadness. The qualities that make up his style come from a variety of techniques.

Key Aspects of Bradbury's Style

- short phrases that form one long sentence and lend a flowing, almost poetic quality to his lines
- use of sensory details and frequent use of **similes**—comparisons that use the word *like* or *as* ("teeth like daggers")—and more direct comparisons called **metaphors** ("watchmaker's claws")
- use of rhythm and repetition
- intriguing beginnings that capture readers' interest

Analysis of Style

At the right are excerpts from each of the Bradbury stories you have read. Study the list above, and then read each excerpt carefully. Complete the following activities:

- A • Find examples of each stylistic device in the three paragraphs.
- B • Find examples of other devices you see at work in each excerpt.
- C • The term *poetic* is sometimes used to describe Bradbury's prose. Which lines do you consider most poetic? Support your answer.

Applications

1. **Speaking and Listening** Alone or with a group, read aloud each excerpt at the right in an attempt to reveal the characteristics that the critics have noted. As a class, discuss the differences in mood and intensity you hear among these oral interpretations.
2. **Imitating Style** Choose one of the stories and add to it somewhere another paragraph that you have created using Bradbury's style. Share your work by reading it to the class.
3. **Changing Style** Rewrite one of the excerpts in a simpler way. Be sure to keep the same idea. Then read your versions and the originals aloud and compare them. Discuss the differences in effect with your classmates.

from A Sound of Thunder

Out of chars and ashes, out of dust and coals, like golden salamanders, the old years, the green years, might leap; roses sweeten the air, white hair turn Irish-black, wrinkles vanish; all, everything fly back to seed, flee death, rush down to their beginnings, suns rise in western skies and set in glorious easts, moons eat themselves opposite to the custom, all and everything cupping one in another like Chinese boxes, rabbits into hats, all and everything returning to the fresh death, the seed death, the green death, to the time before the beginning.

from There Will Come Soft Rains

In the last instant under the fire avalanche, other choruses, oblivious, could be heard announcing the time, playing music, cutting the lawn by remote-control mower, or setting an umbrella frantically out and in the slamming and opening front door, a thousand things happening, like a clock shop when each clock strikes the hour insanely before or after the other, a scene of maniac confusion, yet unity; singing, screaming, a few last cleaning mice darting bravely out to carry the horrid ashes away!

from The Pedestrian

To enter out into that silence that was the city at eight o'clock of a misty evening in November, to put your feet upon that buckling concrete walk, to step over grassy seams and make your way, hands in pockets, through the silences, that was what Mr. Leonard Mead most dearly loved to do.

The Author's Style

Beyond the fantastic settings and situations that make up his fiction is the consideration of his style, making the fantastic vivid and memorable. Students will be made aware of Bradbury's style through the "Key Aspects of Bradbury's Style" chart and then find examples of the four points in the excerpts in the right margin.

Analysis of Style

A First activity

phrases into long sentences: The excerpts from "A Sound of Thunder," "There Will Come Soft Rains," and "The Pedestrian" each contain one long sentence made up of short, poetic phrases.

sensory details and figurative language: "A Sound of Thunder": "out of dust . . . , like golden salamanders, the old years, the green years, might leap . . ."; "There Will Come Soft Rains": "like a clock shop when each clock strikes the hour insanely before or after the other . . ."

rhythm and repetition: "A Sound of Thunder": "Out of chars and ashes, out of dust and coals . . ."; "There Will Come Soft Rains": " . . . singing, screaming, a few last cleaning mice darting bravely . . ."; "The Pedestrian": "To enter out into that silence . . . to put your feet upon that . . . walk, to step over grassy seams . . ."

intriguing beginnings: "There Will Come Soft Rains": Reading "In the last instant under the fire avalanche," one immediately wonders what might happen next; "The Pedestrian": "To enter out into that silence . . ." directs the reader to enter the story.

B Second activity

other examples: "A Sound of Thunder": use of stark contrasts such as white hair and Irish-black; contradictions such as "moons eat themselves" and "suns rise in western skies"; "There Will Come Soft Rains": use of references to music such as "choruses," "heard," "music," "slamming," "strikes," "unity," and "singing"

C Third activity

Poetic lines include the opening of "A Sound of Thunder" because of the simile, the rhythmic phrasing, and the close of that passage: "all and everything returning to fresh death, the seed death, the green death. . . ."

Applications

1. **Speaking and Listening** Have students use the following criteria to critique oral interpretation. The student
   - makes and supports a valid interpretation of how the character might voice those lines
   - uses voice (volume and tone) to establish mood and convey meaning
   - uses movement and gestures to establish mood and convey meaning
   - uses facial expressions to establish mood and convey meaning
2. **Imitating Style** Remind students to revisit the Key Aspects box on the page before beginning their paragraphs.
3. **Changing Style** Have students go through the entire writing process for this activity—prewriting, drafting, editing, and publishing. Encourage them to choose manageable sections of no more than 20 lines.

Writing Options

1. Citizen Profile Create a short profile of an "average" citizen of Leonard Mead's world of 2053. You might review the story for details of the characteristics, listing them in a graphic like the one below.

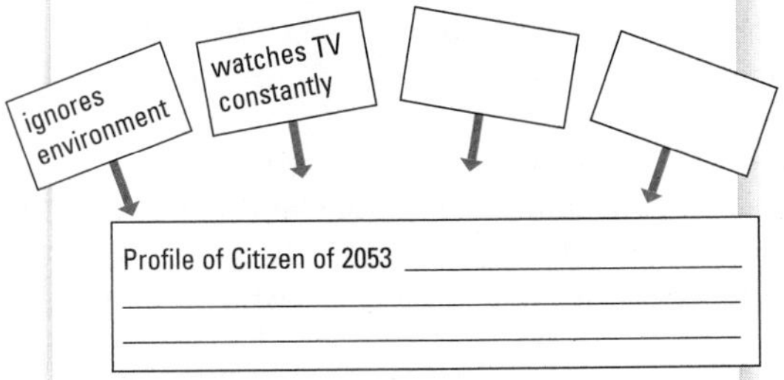

2. Critical Review Write a review of "The Pedestrian." Address the importance of science in the story. Also offer your opinion of how closely the world of Leonard Mead matches your view of the not-so-distant future. Put your review in your **Working Portfolio.**

Activities & Explorations

1. Panel Discussion In the mid-1960s, Bradbury adapted "The Pedestrian" for the stage. With a small group, hold a panel discussion in which you examine the following questions: What are the differences between a one-character story and a play? What are the different ways that character is revealed in the two genres? Which genre do you think you prefer? ~ **SPEAKING AND LISTENING**

2. Comic-Book Version Working in teams, depict scenes from "The Pedestrian" in comic-book form. Display your drawings in a single class book. ~ **ART**

Inquiry & Research

TV of the Past In small groups, investigate typical programming in TV's early days and compare it to typical programming today.

Create and present to your class a storyboard for a **trailer**—a short filmed movie advertisement—to be used as a preview for a film of a story by Ray Bradbury. A **storyboard** is a series of rough, cartoonlike drawings, often on posterboards, that depicts scenes of a film, trailer, television show, or the like. The storyboard represents a number of decisions that ultimately provide the guide for the finished product on film.

Launching the Project Choose teams to take the project to the stage of actual storyboard creation. After a group has selected one of Bradbury's stories, it can select scenes for consideration for the trailer.

Organizing the Trailer A trailer should be a teaser, creating interest in the film by revealing some essential information about the setting and costuming and some fragmented information about plot.

Preparing the Storyboard Divide your group into new teams for the actual creation of the storyboard. Sketches can be created by the group's better illustrators; however, if equipment is available, you may use computer software to create images from the Bradbury tale you've selected. Eventually, transfer all the scenes of your storyboard to chart paper or large posterboard sheets. Also, remember that your trailer can run no more than two minutes. Estimate the running time for each of your sketched scenes.

More Online: Research Starter
www.mcdougallittell.com

Author Study Project

MOVIE-TRAILER STORYBOARD

Drawing can be an intimidating project for students who are not artistically inclined. Suggest that students review previews that they have seen recently at the movies and discuss what they think the movie will be about and whether they will like the movie. Students who fear drawing can practice tracing characters from a simply drawn cartoon in the newspaper. Use these steps to lead students into the actual storyboard creation.

VIDEO SOURCES

Suggest students watch a video version of one of Bradbury's stories such as *Something Wicked This Way Comes, The Illustrated Man,* or *Fahrenheit 451* as a resource both for contributing to their understanding of Bradbury's work as well as for their storyboard project.

MULTIMEDIA PROJECT

Students can turn their storyboard projects into actual trailers by using a home video camera. The groups for the storyboard project can assign roles among themselves as camera operator, director, production designer, costume and prop manager, and actors. The fantastic quality of Bradbury's stories will require students to use their imaginations in creating simple sets to stand in for the fantastic images.

OVERVIEW

Objectives
- understand the major types of nonfiction:
  - autobiography
  - biography
  - memoir
  - essay
  - personal essay
- understand how writers of nonfiction shape information for their own purposes
- identify biases and attitudes in nonfiction writing

Teaching the Lesson

This lesson analyzes both terms related to nonfiction writing and the major types of nonfiction writing.

Introducing the Concepts
Ask students to contrast and compare types of factual writing. For example, how is a newspaper article different from a speech? How is an advertisement similar to a movie review? Ask them to discuss how nonfiction is different from fiction.

Presenting the Concepts
Autobiography
Emphasize to students the differences between autobiography, which is usually formal in style and covers the entire life or a great portion of the life of a writer, and journals, letters, and diaries, which are usually highly informal in style and cover a shorter period of a writer's life.

YOUR TURN We learn that the writer feels embarrassed by her Chinese heritage and the effect it might have on Robert.

Biography
Ask students to name some of the biographies they have read. Ask them what made the biographies memorable. Ask if students detected any biases of the writer in the biographies.

YOUR TURN Words such as "confident," "painstaking," "crucial," and "most famous" reveal the writer's respectful and admiring attitude toward Nelson Mandela.

Nonfiction

Nonfiction is prose writing about real people, places, and events. Unlike fiction, nonfiction is mainly written to convey factual information, although writers of nonfiction shape information in accordance with their own purposes and attitudes. Nonfiction includes a diverse range of writing: newspaper articles, cookbooks, letters, movie reviews, speeches, true-life adventure stories, advertising, and more. Nonfiction can be a good source of information, but readers frequently have to examine it more carefully than fiction in order to detect biases, notice gaps in the information, and identify errors in logic. Use the following passages to learn about some of the major types of nonfiction.

Autobiography
An **autobiography** is a writer's account of his or her own life and is, in almost every case, told from the first-person point of view. Generally, an autobiography focuses on the most significant events and people in the writer's life over a period of time and on the ways in which those events and people affected the writer. Shorter autobiographical narratives include such private writings as **journals, diaries,** and **letters.** An **autobiographical essay,** another type of short autobiographical work, focuses on a single person or event in the writer's life.

YOUR TURN From the excerpt at the right—part of an autobiographical essay—what do you learn about the writer's feelings about her heritage?

AUTOBIOGRAPHY

When I found out that my parents had invited the minister's family over for Christmas Eve dinner, I cried. What would Robert think of our shabby *Chinese* Christmas? What would he think of our noisy *Chinese* relatives who lacked proper American manners?

—Amy Tan, "Fish Cheeks"

Biography
A **biography** is an account of a person's life written by another person. The writer of a biography usually researches his or her subject in order to present accurate information. The best biographers strive for honesty and balance in their accounts of their subjects' lives, highlighting weaknesses as well as strengths, failures as well as achievements. Remember, though, that every writer has attitudes and feelings that can influence the way he or she writes about a subject.

YOUR TURN In this excerpt from a biographical essay, what words and phrases reveal the writer's attitude toward Nelson Mandela?

BIOGRAPHY

After more than two decades in prison, confident that on some crucial issues a leader must make decisions on his own, Mandela decided on a new approach. And after painstaking preliminaries, the most famous prisoner in the world was escorted, in the greatest secrecy, to the State President's office to start negotiating not only his own release but also the nation's transition from apartheid to democracy.

—Andre Brink, "Nelson Mandela"

Memoir

A **memoir** is a form of autobiographical writing in which a writer focuses on his or her involvement with noted people, significant events, or both. Memoirs are usually anecdotal or intimate in tone, giving the reader insight into the impact of historical events on people's lives. The focus of a memoir is usually on newsworthy people and events that the writer has known at first hand.

YOUR TURN The excerpt at the right tells of events on the day after Rosa Parks was arrested for refusing to surrender her seat on a bus to a white person. E. D. Nixon and Ralph Abernathy were civil rights leaders. As you read the excerpt, look for characteristics of a memoir.

MEMOIR

The first we knew about it [the Montgomery bus boycott] was when Mr. Nixon called my husband early in the morning of Friday, December 2. He had already talked to Ralph Abernathy. After describing the incident, Mr. Nixon said, "We have taken this type of thing too long. I feel the time has come to boycott the buses."

—Coretta Scott King, "Montgomery Boycott"

Essay

An **essay** is a brief work of nonfiction that deals with a single subject. Some essays are **formal;** in these, writers systematically develop their ideas in an impersonal manner. Others are **informal,** perhaps including anecdotes and humor. Two common types of essay are the persuasive essay and the expository essay. In a **persuasive essay** a writer tries to convince you to share a belief, to agree with a position, or to take some action. The primary purpose of an **expository essay** is to convey or explain information.

YOUR TURN Read this excerpt from an expository essay. What explanation is the writer offering?

ESSAY

Clockwise is the turning direction of the hands of a clock, and counterclockwise is the opposite of that. Since throughout the day we often stare at clocks (dial clocks that is), we have no trouble in following directions or descriptions that include those words.

But if dial clocks disappear, so will the meaning of those words for anyone who never has stared at anything but digitals.

—Isaac Asimov, "Dial Versus Digital"

Personal Essay

A **personal essay** is an essay that expresses a writer's thoughts, feelings, and opinions on a subject. This type of essay allows a writer to explore the meaning of events and issues in his or her own life. Personal essays tend to be written in an informal, conversational style.

YOUR TURN As you read this excerpt, look for clues as to the essay's subject and the author's attitude toward the subject.

PERSONAL ESSAY

One summer, along about 1904, my father rented a camp on a lake in Maine and took us all there for the month of August. We all got ringworm from some kittens . . . and my father rolled over in a canoe with all his clothes on; but outside of that the vacation was a success and from then on none of us ever thought there was any place in the world like that lake in Maine.

—E. B. White, "Once More to the Lake"

Making Connections

Memoir

Suggest to students that the subject of a memoir is often viewed through the writer's memory, and memory often suggests an intimate tone.

YOUR TURN Characteristics of a memoir found in the passage are the focus on Martin Luther King, Jr., and the historic Montgomery bus boycott as remembered by someone who was involved in the events.

Essay

Be sure that students understand the difference between editorials and essays. In order to clarify the difference, present students with an idea, such as the revolution in information technology. Ask them how they might develop this idea into a letter to the editor. How would an expository essay explaining the use of a Web navigator be different from the letter?

YOUR TURN The writer notes the meaning of *clockwise* and *counterclockwise* and explains that these words will not make sense to anyone who has never seen a dial clock.

Personal Essay

Alert students to the fact that personal essays are focused on a writer's personal opinions and so are different from memoirs or journals, which focus on people and personal views on events.

YOUR TURN The essay's subject is on childhood vacations, particularly one on a lake in Maine where the subject experienced happy childhood times.

OVERVIEW

Objectives

- analyze, evaluate, and appreciate narrative nonfiction
- organize information into charts as the basis for clarifying, visualizing, and questioning a writer's attitude, motive, and purpose

Teaching the Lesson

Reading Nonfiction

The strategies on this page will help students learn and apply strategies for understanding significant elements of nonfiction.

Presenting the Strategies

To help students understand the forms of nonfiction, have them envision themselves as professional writers.

1 Strategies for Analyzing an Autobiography or a Biography

Remind students to read autobiographies and biographies critically. Writers can be biased, excluding details or events that could be damaging to the image they wish to present.

2 Strategies for Understanding a Memoir

Explain that one indicator of bias in any piece of writing, including a memoir, is whether or not the writer explores both sides of an issue. Encourage students to look for evidence that indicates whether the writer is presenting only one side of the story or more than one side.

3 Strategies for Evaluating an Essay

In order to evaluate the strength of an argument, it is essential to know whether the argument is based on fact or opinion. Have students read several paragraphs of an essay, analyzing each sentence to determine whether it is fact or opinion, and then create a tally sheet to visualize the basis of the argument's reasoning as either factual or opinionated.

4 Strategies for Appreciating a Personal Essay

Have students think about what they already know about the essay and what they expect to learn from the essay. As they read it, students should determine the writer's purpose and theme.

The Active Reader: Skills and Strategies

Nonfiction writing is our primary form of written communication. Many of the strategies you use in reading fiction can also be used in reading narrative nonfiction. In addition, the reading strategies explained here can help.

Reading Nonfiction

1 Strategies for Analyzing an Autobiography or a Biography

- Keep track of the sequence of events, perhaps using a chart like this one. **Evaluate** events' effects on the subject of the work.

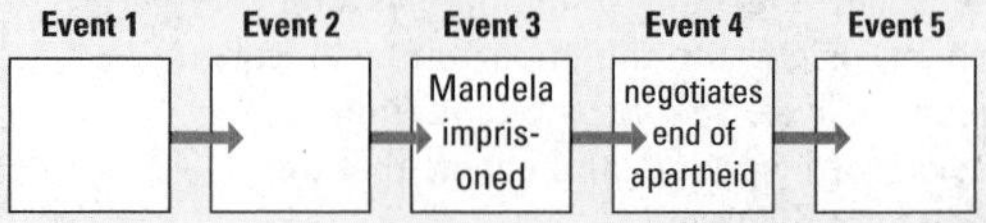

- Form judgments about the work's subject. **Clarify** what qualities contributed to his or her success (or failure).
- When reading an autobiography, **question** what the events included—and the writer's attitude toward them—reveal about the writer.
- When reading a biography, analyze the writer's attitude toward the subject. Notice whether the account is favorable, negative, or balanced.

2 Strategies for Understanding a Memoir

- **Connect** to the memoir by using your prior knowledge. What insights into events or time periods that you already know about does the writer give?
- **Visualize** the people and events described in the memoir.
- Be alert for evidence of a bias in the writing.
- Consider the writer's motives: Is he or she primarily sharing personal experiences or interpreting historical events?

3 Strategies for Evaluating an Essay

- Distinguish between facts and opinions on a chart like this one. A fact can be proved or disproved. An opinion expresses a belief that cannot be proved or disproved. Opinions supported by facts are still opinions.

Fact	The cabin is located 50 feet from the lake.
Opinion	The cabin is comfortable.
Opinion Supported by Facts	With its modern plumbing, the cabin is very comfortable.

- **Clarify** your understanding by summarizing main ideas as you read.
- Try to determine the writer's purpose for writing the essay.
- When reading a persuasive essay, **evaluate** the writer's ideas and reasoning.

4 Strategies for Appreciating a Personal Essay

- Set purposes to guide your reading. Try to **predict** what information the work will provide.
- **Connect** the writer's comments to your own experiences.

Need More Help?

Remember that active readers use the essential reading strategies explained on page 7: **visualize, predict, clarify, question, connect, evaluate, monitor.**

"There are no good substitutes for clockwise *or* counterclockwise.*"*

Dial Versus Digital

Essay by ISAAC ASIMOV

Connect to Your Life

Fast Forward! Computers, video games, software, telephones, fax machines, televisions—what will they be like 10 or 20 years from now? Will the technological wonders of today be collecting dust in a closet? Think about some of the changes in technology that you have witnessed in your own lifetime. How have they affected you? Do you think progress in technology always improves the quality of life? Discuss your opinions with other classmates.

Build Background

The Great Explainer Isaac Asimov earned the nickname "The Great Explainer" for his remarkable ability to explain even the most difficult scientific concepts in a way that almost everyone can understand. In his hundreds of books and essays, Asimov delves into every aspect of science and technology, from the solar system to algebra to nuclear fusion. He also expresses his personal opinion on these subjects, especially when they cause him to worry about the effect that progress will have on the future. In "Dial Versus Digital," he worries that digital clocks will change more than just how we tell time.

Focus Your Reading

LITERARY ANALYSIS EXPOSITORY ESSAY An **expository essay** explains a particular subject with the purpose of helping the reader understand the subject more thoroughly. Like other types of essays, it gives information and often reveals the opinions of the writer, as the following passage from this essay shows:

> ***And yet there will be a loss in the conversion of dial to digital, and few people seem to be worrying about it.***

As you read this essay, look for explanations of how the disappearance of dial clocks could affect our future.

ACTIVE READING ANALYZING TEXT STRUCTURE Writers always choose a **structure**, or pattern of organization, to present their information. Nonfiction writers can choose from a variety of structures and usually pick the one that best fits their purpose for writing. In "Dial Versus Digital," for example, Asimov uses the **cause-and-effect** structure. He begins by discussing a cause—the loss of the dial clock—and proceeds by examining the effects that are likely to occur.

READER'S NOTEBOOK Create a chart like the one shown to help you identify each effect that the author predicts.

Digital clocks are replacing dial clocks.		
EFFECT	EFFECT	EFFECT

OVERVIEW

This selection is included in the **Grade 10 InterActive Reader.**

Objectives

1. understand the characteristics of an **expository essay (Literary Analysis)**
2. analyze the **text structure** of an essay **(Active Reading)**

Summary

Isaac Asimov sees unanticipated consequences in the shift from dial clocks to digital clocks. Chief among them is a loss of common reference terms such as "clockwise" and "counterclockwise," and "o'clock" for determining position. Asimov is also worried that the 60-minute hour does not translate easily into the base ten system that anchors a digital timepiece. He concludes that a complete switch to digital clocks will present some real problems.

Thematic Link

Even technological progress in timepiece design can extract an unanticipated price.

5-Minute Warm-Up

Daily Language SkillBuilder

Have students **proofread** the display sentences on page 15j and write them correctly. The sentences also appear on Transparency 4 of **Grammar Transparencies and Copymasters.**

LESSON RESOURCES

UNIT ONE RESOURCE BOOK, pp. 35–38

ASSESSMENT RESOURCES
Formal Assessment, pp. 19–20
Teacher's Guide to Assessment and Portfolio Use
Test Generator

SKILLS TRANSPARENCIES AND COPYMASTERS
Literary Analysis
- Types of Nonfiction, T4 (for Expository Essay, p. 110)

Reading and Critical Thinking
- Cause and Effect, T1 (for Active Reading, p. 107)
- Analyzing Text Structure, T17 (for Think Critically, item 4, p. 110)

Writing
- Achieving Unity, T7 (for Writing Option 1, p. 111)
- Opinion Statement, C25 (for Writing Option 1, p. 111)

Communications
- Interviewing, T9 (for Activities and Explorations 1, p. 111)
- Formal Presentations, T10 (for Activities & Explorations 2, p. 111)

INTEGRATED TECHNOLOGY
Audio Library
Visit our website:
www.mcdougallittell.com

DIAL VERSUS DIGITAL 107

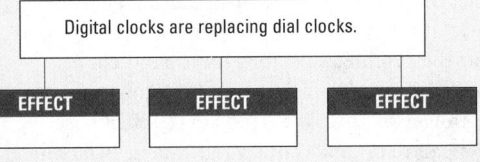

TEACHING THE LITERATURE

Reading and Analyzing

Reading Skills and Strategies:
PREVIEW

Give students a brief summary of the essay and ask them to preview the Preparing to Read page. Have them predict what Asimov will say about the conversion from dial to digital.

Active Reading
ANALYZING TEXT STRUCTURE

Asimov structures this essay by presenting the cause, the replacement of dial clocks with digital clocks, and then exposes three noticeable effects. As they read, students should look for signals that Asimov is describing an effect.

Use **Unit One Resource Book,** p. 36 for additional support.

Literary Analysis EXPOSITORY ESSAY

Ask students to explain how this essay provides specific information.

Possible Response: Asimov provides details on how the terms *clockwise* and *counterclockwise* are used by various people.

Use **Unit One Resource Book,** p. 37 for additional support.

ACTIVE READING

RECOGNIZE CAUSE AND EFFECT

He uses transition terms such as *here is another example,* or *here is still another point.*

ACTIVE READING

CONNECT **Possible Response:** in a sport a player may be assigned to a position equivalent to 11 on the clock face.

Dial versus Digital

Isaac Asimov

There seems no question but that the clock dial, which has existed in its present form since the Seventeenth Century and in earlier forms since ancient times, is on the way out. More common today are digital clocks, which mark off the hours, minutes, and seconds in changing numbers.

This certainly seems an advance in technology. People no longer will have to interpret the meaning of "the big hand on the 11 and the little hand on the 5"; digital clocks will indicate at once that it is 4:55.

And yet there will be a loss in the conversion of dial to digital, and few people seem to be worrying about it.

When something turns, it can turn in just one of two ways, either clockwise or counterclockwise, and we all know which is which. Clockwise is the turning direction of the hands of a clock, and counterclockwise is the opposite of that. Since throughout the day we often stare at clocks (dial clocks that is), we have no trouble in following directions or descriptions that include those words.

But if dial clocks disappear, so will the meaning of those words for anyone who never has stared at anything but digitals. There are no good substitutes for *clockwise* or *counterclockwise.* The nearest you can come is by a consideration of your hands. If you clench your fists with your thumbs pointing at your chest and look at your forefingers, you will see that the forefinger of your right hand curves counterclockwise from knuckle to tip, while the forefinger of your left hand curves clockwise. You can then talk about a right-hand twist and a left-hand twist. But people don't stare at their hands the way they stare at clocks, and this will never be an adequate substitute.

Nor is this a minor matter. Astronomers define the north pole and south pole of any rotating body in such terms. If you are hovering above a pole of rotation and the body is rotating counterclockwise, it is the north pole; if it is rotating clockwise, it is the south pole. Astronomers also speak of direct motion and retrograde motion, by which they mean counterclockwise and clockwise, respectively.

ACTIVE READING

RECOGNIZE CAUSE AND EFFECT Asimov has just finished discussing the first effect of the switch from dial to digital. Look ahead. How does Asimov signal the next effects?

Here is another example. Suppose you are looking through a microscope at some object on a slide, or through a telescope at some view in the sky. In either case you may wish to point out something to a colleague. "Notice that object at 11 o'clock," you may say—or 5 o'clock, or 2 o'clock, or whatever.

Everyone knows the location of any number from 1 to 12 on the clock dial and easily can use such a reference to find an object.

Once the dial is gone, location by *o'clock* also will be gone, and there is no good substitute. Of course, you can use directions instead: northeast, southwest by south, and so on. However, this would assume you always know which direction is north. Or, if you are arbitrary[1] and decide to let north be straight ahead or straight up regardless of its real location, it still remains true that very few people are as familiar

Teaching Options

Cross Curricular Link **History**

TIMEPIECES The earliest timekeeping device was the sundial, which made use of the shifting position of a shadow as the day progresses. The clepsydra, or water clock, used the gradual flow of water or another liquid to measure time. Invented in perhaps the 14th century B.C., the clepsydra remained in use for centuries. Galileo used a mercury clepsydra in his experiments. Not until the late Middle Ages was the mechanical clock developed. Using weights as a source of energy, early clocks lost up to half an hour per day. Medieval clockmakers strove to improve accuracy. A Dutch invention, the pendulum, was used in clocks to ensure regular movement. Springs began to replace weights, leading to smaller, portable clocks and watches.

Today, the atomic clock, driven by the electromagnetic radiation of certain elements, is our most precise timekeeper, accurate to within one second in tens of thousands, even millions of years.

ACTIVE READING

CONNECT In what other situations might you use a clock face to point out the location of something?

with a compass as they are with a clock face.

Here's still another point. When children are learning to count, once they master the first few numbers, they quickly get the whole idea. You go from 0 to 9 and 0 to 9 over and over again. In other words, you go from 0 to 9, then from 10 to 19, then from 20 to 29, and so on until you reach 90 to 99, and then you pass on to 100, when the whole thing starts again. It is very systematic, and once you learn it you never forget.

Time is different. Since the early Sumerians[2] couldn't handle fractions very well, they chose 60 as their base because it can be divided evenly in a number of ways. Ever since, we have continued to use 60 in certain applications, the chief of which is in the measurement of time. Thus, there are 60 minutes to an hour.

If you are using a dial, that doesn't matter. You simply note the position of the hands, and they automatically become a measure of time: "half past 5," "a quarter past 3," "a quarter to 10," and so on. You see time as space and not as numbers.

In a digital clock, however, time is measured only as numbers, so you go from 1:01 to 1:59 and then move directly to 2:00. It introduces an irregularity in the number system that is going to insert an unnecessary stumbling block into education. Just think: 5.50 is halfway between 5 and 6 if we measure length or weight or money or anything but time. In time, 5:50 is nearly 6; it is 5:30 that is halfway between 5 and 6.

What shall we do about all this? I can think of nothing. There is an odd conservatism[3] among people that will make them fight to the death against making time decimal and having 100 minutes to the hour.

But even so, what can be done about the lost meaning of *clockwise, counterclockwise,* and *o'clock* as points of reference? It will be a pretty problem for our descendants. ❖

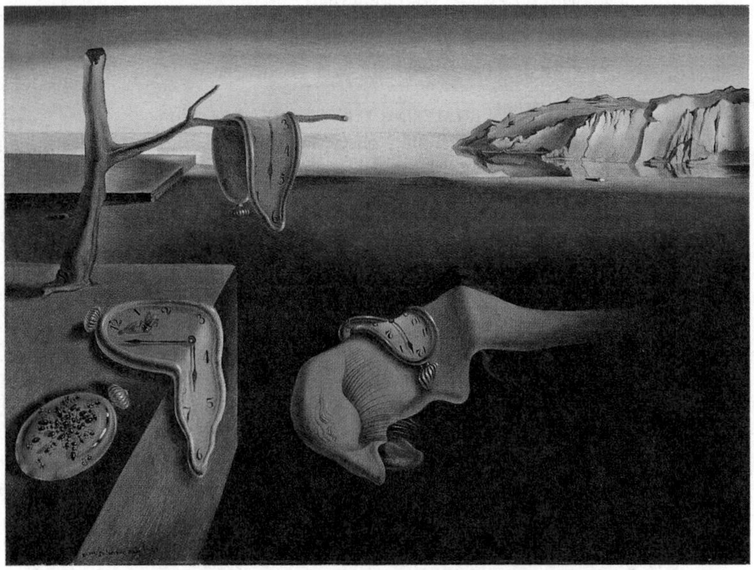

The Persistence of Memory [Persistence de la mémoire] (1931), Salvador Dali. Oil on canvas, 9½" × 13". The Museum of Modern Art, New York. Given anonymously. Photograph © 1998 The Museum of Modern Art, New York.

1. **arbitrary** (är′bĭ-trĕr′ē): making a choice on the basis of what is convenient rather than what is reasonable or natural.
2. **Sumerians** (so͞o-mîr′ē-ənz): the people of one of the earliest human civilizations, which flourished from 5,000 to 4,000 years ago in the Middle East.
3. **conservatism** (kən-sûr′və-tĭz′əm): unwillingness to change.

Customizing Instruction

Less Proficient Readers

Have students keep these questions in mind as they read.

- What is the main argument?

Answer: The switch from dial to digital clocks will cause some problems.

- What two technologies is the author comparing?

Answer: dial clock faces and digital clock faces

- What examples does the author use to explain his argument?

Answer: The use of *clockwise* and *counterclockwise* to indicate direction of rotation; the use of *o'clock* to indicate position; the difference between the numbering system for time (base 60) and almost all other operations (base 10)

Students Acquiring English

Explain to students that the basic conflict Asimov is discussing is the transition from clocks that use a dial and hands to clocks that use a digital readout. If necessary, illustrate by showing students a dial watch or clock and a digital watch or clock.

Use **Spanish Study Guide** for additional support, pp. 22–24.

Gifted and Talented

Have students think of some other recent shifts in technology, such as from typewriter to computer, and have them explain what might have been lost or might be lost in that shift.

Mini Lesson Viewing and Representing

Persistence of Memory **by Salvador Dalí**

ART APPRECIATION The Spanish artist Salvador Dalí (1904–1989) was recognized for his great skill in drawing and painting. In the 1920s, Dalí moved to Paris, studied Freud, and was an important contributor to the artistic movement known as surrealism.

Instructions Surrealism was an artistic and literary movement that united the conscious and unconscious realms of experience, or the world of fantasy and dreams with the world of reality. In his paintings, Dalí often presented everyday items in the process of unusual, sometimes disturbing, transformation. Ask students how this painting evokes these elements of surrealism.

Possible Response: The melting clocks show time, a real and exacting element of everyday life, as a fantastical dream component sliding away as if time were elusive and had no meaning. The clocks are definitely undergoing an unusual transformation.

GUIDING STUDENT RESPONSE

Connect to the Literature

1. **What Do You Think?**
   Possible Responses: Students may think that they are convincing because he has presented both simple and complex effects.

Comprehension Check
- the change from dial clocks to digital clocks
- We may not be able to tell people to turn clockwise or counterclockwise, or use positions of numbers on the clock face to indication direction.
- The 60-minute clashes with the base 10 digital numerical system. Children can no longer simply memorize the positions on the dial to deal with this confusing discrepancy.

Use Selection Quiz in **Unit One Resource Book,** p. 38.

Think Critically

2. Students may be able to imagine different, more modern terminology.
3. Students may feel that Asimov has mounted enough evidence to make it clear that he is arguing against the digital clock.
4. Remind students to analyze the cause-and-effect text structure and how it influences understanding. Possible Response: The author wants to keep the reader's attention and interest, which means that simpler or more interesting facts are presented early in the essay. Then the author gradually introduces more complicated ideas.
5. **Possible Responses:** With new technology there are losses as well as gains; the price of progress can be the loss of a useful point of reference.

Thinking through the LITERATURE

Connect to the Literature

1. **What Do You Think?** Did you find Asimov's examples convincing? Explain your response.

Comprehension Check
- What is the technological change that worries the author?
- How might this change affect the way we give directions?
- How could it affect the way children learn to tell time?

Think Critically

2. Do you agree that "there are no good substitutes" for the words *clockwise* and *counterclockwise?* Why or why not?
3. Do you think the author is arguing against the use of digital clocks? Explain your judgment.

   THINK ABOUT
   - his opinion of digital clocks
   - the **tone** he uses in his conclusion

4. ACTIVE READING ANALYZING TEXT STRUCTURE Study the **cause-effect** chart that you created in your READER'S NOTEBOOK. Notice how Asimov organizes information about the effects, beginning with the most immediate and obvious ones. How does this structure affect your understanding or interest?
5. What do you think is the **theme,** or most important message, of the essay?

Extend Interpretations

6. **Critic's Corner** One critic has said that Asimov is "thankfully, a teacher first and a scientist second." How would you explain this quotation? Find details from the essay that support this statement.
7. **Connect to Life** What do you think is gained or lost when progress in modern technology changes the way we live? List examples of recent changes and their effects to support your opinion.

Literary Analysis

EXPOSITORY ESSAY In an **expository essay,** a writer wants to explain something or give information about a topic. In this essay, for example, Asimov gives information about two different types of clocks.

Activity Review the selection to look for ways that Asimov involves the reader. For example, in key places he uses the pronoun *you,* as if the reader were actually performing actions. Find other examples of the techniques Asimov uses to involve the reader.

ACTIVE READING FACT AND OPINION A **fact** is a statement about something that has happened or something that can be observed. A fact can be proven to be correct; for example, Asimov writes:

When something turns, it can turn in just one of two ways, either clockwise or counterclockwise.

On the other hand, **opinions, judgments,** feelings, or beliefs can be expressed by using words and phrases such as *I think, it seems, always, never, probably, most, all,* or *none.* For example, Asimov expresses this opinion:

And yet there will be a loss in the conversion of dial to digital, and few people seem to be worrying about it.

With a partner, go back through the essay and make a list of both facts and opinions that Asimov has used to help you understand his concerns about clocks. When you are done, compare your list with other classmates'.

Extend Interpretations

Critic's Corner Ask students whether Asimov's vocabulary and approach would have been appropriate for an audience of scientists. Ask students to give examples of words and comparisons from the essay that make his writing accessible to and understandable for the nonscientist.

Connect to Life Students should be able to respond with a variety of examples. They may want to get the opinions of their parents or grandparents.

Literary Analysis

Activity Asimov also uses the pronoun *we;* in addition, at the end of the essay, he asks the reader questions. He seems to be sharing his thoughts directly with the reader.

Choices & CHALLENGES

Writing Options

1. Tech Paragraph Basing your answer on recent advances in technology, do you agree or disagree that the effects of progress are usually positive? Write your opinion in an expository paragraph and place it in your **Working Portfolio.**

Writing Handbook
See page 1158: Cause and Effect.

2. Invented Terms Develop two new words that you think would be adequate substitutes for *clockwise* and *counterclockwise.* Then write a set of directions in which you use your new words.

Activities & Explorations

1. Personal Interviews Interview six or seven older adults on the impact that modern technology has had on them. What difference has it made in your life? Share your findings with classmates. ~ **SPEAKING AND LISTENING**

2. Progress Presentation In an oral report, tell how specific inventions have changed our lives. Use visual aids to help your classmates understand your information. ~ **SPEAKING AND LISTENING**

Inquiry & Research

Find out more about the history of timepieces and what kinds of instruments were used to tell time before the dial clock. Draw simple sketches to illustrate some of these instruments. Then share your findings with other classmates and discuss the following question: What kind of timepiece might eventually replace the digital clock?

Art Connection

Take another look at Dali's painting *The Persistence of Memory* on page 109. What do you think is the connection between the painting and "Dial versus Digital"?

Isaac Asimov

1920–1992

Other Works
The Robots of Dawn
Robot Dreams
Frontiers
The Subatomic Monster
The Disappearing Man and Other Mysteries
Computer Crimes and Capers

A Working Youth Isaac Asimov was born in Russia, and came with his parents to the United States when he was just three. His parents owned a candy store, where Asimov worked from ages 9 to 22. He and his family always worked long hours and kept the store open seven days a week. Asimov had no time for extracurricular activities, but his years in the candy store gave him two qualities that would affect his whole life–a strong work ethic and a fascination for science fiction. Asimov once said that he always kept "candy-store hours."

Prolific Writer In his lifetime, the "Great Explainer" wrote over 470 books in addition to countless essays and magazine articles. He did all his own research and typing and wrote constantly, 7 days a week, 12 hours a day. He even taught himself to type 90 words a minute so that he could keep up with his busy work schedule.

Leader in Science Fiction According to many critics, Asimov wrote some of the best science-fiction stories ever published. He first discovered this genre in magazines that were for sale in his family's store. His father thought magazines were unsuitable reading material, but he allowed his son to read a science-fiction magazine only because it had the word *science* in the title. At age 17, Asimov wrote his own science-fiction story, and eventually he originated many of the classic ideas used by other science-fiction writers, including concepts involving robots and robotics.

Writing Options

1. **Tech Paragraph** Students should use specific examples to support their opinion.
2. **Invented Terms** Guide students by suggesting everyday tasks that might involve the concept of clockwise, such as changing a tire, opening a combination lock, or unlocking a door.

Activities & Explorations

1. **Personal Interviews** Have students interview adults of varying ages and technological knowledge. Before each interview, students should write out possible questions and be prepared to suggest examples of current technologies such as computers, cellular phones, and fax machines. To record these interviews, students should take notes or use tape recorders, then present the report in class.
2. **Progress Presentation** Have students focus on one or two inventions common to daily life, then use pictures, illustrations, and library research material to explain the impact of these inventions. Encourage students to look at everyday inventions such as lightbulbs, radios, or telephones.

Inquiry & Research

You might have students check resources on astronomy and navigation, as these fields have had a strong impact on the development of accurate timepieces.

Art Connection

Possible Response: Dali's painting seems to portray the death of clocks.

Mini Lesson Grammar

NOUNS USED AS ADJECTIVES Remind students that words can function as different parts of speech, depending on their use in a sentence. Nouns like *dial* and *base* become adjectives when they are used to modify other nouns. Examples: <u>*dial*</u> clock, <u>*base*</u> ten.

Model Sentence
He painted his room <u>sky</u> blue and his <u>window</u> frame white.

Instruction
- Write the model sentence on the chalkboard.
- Underline the nouns used as adjectives as shown.

Use McDougal Littell's ***Language Network,*** Chapter 9, for more instruction in nouns used as adjectives.

OVERVIEW

This selection is included in the **Grade 10 InterActive Reader.**

Objectives

1. understand and appreciate a **personal essay (Literary Analysis)**
2. identify **comparison and contrast (Active Reading)**

Summary

Feeling nostalgic about his childhood summers at a lake in Maine, White returns there with his son. When the boy sneaks out on the first morning to explore the shore by boat, just as White himself once did, White begins to feel that his son is White himself as a boy. By extension, he feels as though he is his father. This dual existence is both strange and fascinating. Throughout this time at the lake, the author reminisces about many of his experiences there as a child and reflects on how things have both changed and remained the same.

Thematic Link

Returning to the lake where he spent his childhood summers, White finds that progress has not destroyed the things he cherished about the place, only altered them in small ways. Time, however, has exacted its price on him; he is older and closer to death.

5-Minute Warm-Up

Daily Language SkillBuilder

Have students **proofread** the display sentences on page 15j and write them correctly. The sentences also appear on Transparency 4 of **Grammar Transparencies and Copymasters.**

PREPARING to *Read*

Once More to the Lake

Essay by E. B. WHITE

"I wondered how time would have marred this unique, this holy spot—"

Connect to Your Life

Childhood Revisited Think of a special place from childhood that you would like to revisit. Jot down specific details that this place brings to mind and describe what you would hope to find if you returned there.

Build Background

Essayist for the Ages Although well-known for his classic children's books, such as *Stuart Little* and *Charlotte's Web*, E. B. White may be best known for his essays, which appeared for many years in *The New Yorker* magazine. He once described the essayist as a writer "sustained by the childish belief that everything he thinks about, everything that happens to him, is of general interest." Few writers have been able to capture the wonders of everyday life as well as White has. In the following essay, a simple visit to a lake becomes a moving experience as White recalls his own childhood.

WORDS TO KNOW
Vocabulary Preview

haunt
indelible
languidly
petulant
tentatively

Focus Your Reading

LITERARY ANALYSIS PERSONAL ESSAY A **personal essay** is a brief nonfiction work that expresses the writer's thoughts, feelings, and opinions on events and issues in his or her own life. As you read this essay, look for details about White's own views and recollections. What do you learn about him as a person?

ACTIVE READING IDENTIFYING COMPARISON AND CONTRAST **Comparison and contrast** is a device used by a writer to identify similarities and differences between two things. In the essay you are about to read, White compares his childhood vacations in Maine with a vacation in the present with his own son. When comparing two different times, writers use certain words or phrases to signal comparison and contrast.

Compare: *same, just as, still, always*
Contrast: *since, difference, now, nowadays, in those days, more, not so much*

READER'S NOTEBOOK As you read this story, jot down characteristics of the lake during White's childhood and the lake as it is in the present. Then make a Venn diagram like the one here to show the differences and similarities.

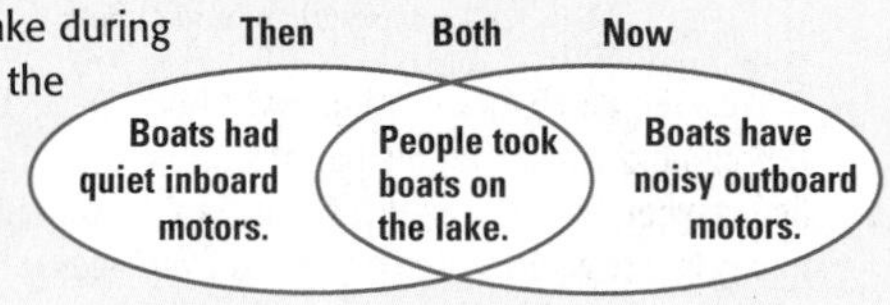
Then
Both
Now
Boats had quiet inboard motors.
People took boats on the lake.
Boats have noisy outboard motors.

LESSON RESOURCES

UNIT ONE RESOURCE BOOK, pp. 39–44

ASSESSMENT RESOURCES
Formal Assessment, pp. 21–22
Teacher's Guide to Assessment and Portfolio Use
Test Generator

SKILLS TRANSPARENCIES AND COPYMASTERS

Literary Analysis
- Types of Nonfiction, T4 (for Cooperative Learning Activity, p. 121)

Reading and Critical Thinking
- Venn Diagram, T50 (for Reader's Notebook, p. 112)

Grammar
- Position of Adverbs, C75 (for Mini Lesson, p. 122)

Vocabulary
- Synonyms and Antonyms, C28 (for Mini Lesson, p. 113)
- Word Origins: Latin Roots, C29 (for Mini Lesson, p. 117)

Writing
- Writing Structure, T5, T6, T8 (for Writing Option 1, p. 122)
- Figurative Language and Sound Devices, T15 (for Writing Option 1, p. 122)
- Opinion Statement, C25 (for Writing Option 3, p. 122)
- Showing, Not Telling, T22 (for Writing Option 2, p. 122)

Communications
- Formal Presentations, T10 (for Activities & Explorations 2, p. 122)

INTEGRATED TECHNOLOGY
Audio Library
Visit our website:
www.mcdougallittell.com

Once More to the Lake

E. B. White

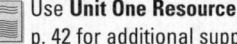

Illustration by Gary Head.

113

Customizing Instruction

Students Acquiring English
Describe the lake setting. Point out in the United States, people like to vacation near water during the summer in places where the weather is pleasant. Have students share places where they have enjoyed vacationing.

Use **Spanish Study Guide** for additional support, pp. 25–27.

Mini Lesson Preteaching Vocabulary

SYNONYMS AND ANTONYMS

Instruction Call students' attention to the list of WORDS TO KNOW. Remind them that they can sometimes understand the meaning of an unfamiliar word by examining context clues. One kind of context clue is a synonym or antonym, used instead of the unknown word.

Model Sentence

She was surprised that Jack sang so *tentatively*; at rehearsal he had sung confidently and without hesitation.

Instruction

- Write the model sentence on the chalkboard.
- Ask a volunteer to summarize the meaning of the sentence.
- Have students use the antonyms *confidently* and *without hesitation* to guess the meaning of *tentatively*.
- Ask a second volunteer to use the word *tentatively* in a sentence.

Use **Unit One Resource Book** p. 42 for additional support.

A lesson on synonyms and antonyms as context clues appears on p. 1000 in the Pupil's Edition.

TEACHING THE LITERATURE

Reading and Analyzing

Literary Analysis: PREVIEW

Briefly summarize the story emphasizing its personal, reflective nature. Ask students to study the images and the title. Discuss the Build Background feature on p. 112, then ask them to predict what the story will be about.

Literary Analysis PERSONAL ESSAY

A personal essay provides an opportunity for a writer to explore the meaning of events and issues in his or her own life. The author's purpose for writing can vary. He or she might give an opinion, persuade, or simply narrate an interesting event. As students read White's essay, ask them to try to determine his main purposes for writing.

Use **Unit One Resource Book,** p. 41 for more practice.

Active Reading

IDENTIFYING COMPARISON AND CONTRAST

Two things are compared to discover their similarities, or are contrasted to discover their differences.

In this selection, White is contrasting the sea that he is now used to as an adult with the lake where he spent his youth. Have students list the characteristics of the ocean, and at the end of the essay, contrast these with the characteristics of the lake.

Use **Unit One Resource Book,** p. 40 for more practice.

ACTIVE READING

QUESTION He is now the father with a son at the same lake where he had enjoyed summers with his father.

August 1941

One summer, along about 1904, my father rented a camp[1] on a lake in Maine and took us all there for the month of August. We all got ringworm[2] from some kittens and had to rub Pond's Extract on our arms and legs night and morning, and my father rolled over in a canoe with all his clothes on; but outside of that the vacation was a success and from then on none of us ever thought there was any place in the world like that lake in Maine. We returned summer after summer—always on August 1 for one month. I have since become a salt-water man, but sometimes in summer there are days when the restlessness of the tides and the fearful cold of the seawater and the incessant wind that blows across the afternoon and into the evening make me wish for the placidity of a lake in the woods. A few weeks ago this feeling got so strong I bought myself a couple of bass hooks and a spinner and returned to the lake where we used to go, for a week's fishing and to revisit old haunts.

I took along my son, who had never had any fresh water up his nose and who had seen lily pads only from train windows. On the journey over to the lake I began to wonder what it would be like. I wondered how time would have marred this unique, this holy spot—the coves and streams, the hills that the sun set behind, the camps and the paths behind the camps. I was sure that the tarred road would have found it out, and I wondered in what other ways it would be desolated. It is strange how much you can remember about places like that once you allow your mind to return into the grooves that lead back. You remember one thing, and that suddenly reminds you of another thing. I guess I remembered clearest of all the early mornings, when the lake was cool and motionless, remembered how the bedroom smelled of the lumber it was made of and of the wet woods whose scent entered through the screen. The partitions in the camp were thin and did not extend clear to the top of the rooms, and as I was always the first up I would dress softly so as not to wake the others, and sneak out into the sweet outdoors and start out in the canoe, keeping close along the shore in the long shadows of the pines. I remembered being very careful never to rub my paddle against the gunwale[3] for fear of disturbing the stillness of the cathedral.

The lake had never been what you would call a wild lake. There were cottages sprinkled around the shores, and it was in farming country although the shores of the lake were quite heavily wooded. Some of the cottages were owned by nearby farmers, and you would live at the shore and eat your meals at the farmhouse. That's what our family did. But although it wasn't wild, it was a fairly large and undisturbed lake and there were places in it that, to a child at least, seemed infinitely remote and primeval.

I was right about the tar: it led to within half a mile of the shore. But when I got back there, with my boy, and we settled into a camp near a farmhouse and into the kind of summertime I had known, I could tell that it

1. **camp:** a summer cottage.
2. **ringworm:** a contagious skin disease caused by a fungus that produces itchy, ring-shaped patches.
3. **gunwale** (gŭn′əl): the upper edge of the side of a boat.

WORDS TO KNOW **haunt** (hônt) *n.* a place visited frequently

Teaching Options

Mini Lesson: Viewing and Representing

Morning of Life **by David Ericson**

ART APPRECIATION The American artist David Ericson (1869–1946) began his art career by painting the people and scenes from his surroundings in northern Minnesota. This painting is one of several of Ericson's son, David.

Instruction Have students note the clear colors and the soft outlines the artist uses. Ask them the following questions: What time of day does the painting evoke? What is the mood of the painting?

Possible Responses: It evokes dawn; the painting is tender and nostalgic.

Application Ask students how this painting reflects the tone of the essay.

Possible Response: The look of morning light reminds us of White exploring the lake in the morning. The hazy quality is evocative of the happy, hazy quality of childhood memories.

was going to be pretty much the same as it had been before—I knew it, lying in bed the first morning, smelling the bedroom and hearing the boy sneak quietly out and go off along the shore in a boat. I began to sustain the illusion that he was I, and therefore, by simple transposition, that I was my father. This sensation persisted, kept cropping up all the time we were there. It was not an entirely new feeling, but in this setting it grew much stronger. I seemed to be living a dual existence. I would be in the middle of some simple act, I would be picking up a bait box or laying down a table fork, or I would be saying something, and suddenly it would be not I but my father who was saying the words or making the gesture. It gave me a creepy sensation.

ACTIVE READING

QUESTION Why does White think of himself in terms of his father?

We went fishing the first morning. I felt the same damp moss covering the worms in the bait can, and saw the dragonfly alight on the tip of my rod as it hovered a few inches from the surface of the water. It was the arrival of this fly that convinced me beyond any doubt that everything was as it always had been, that the years were a mirage and that there had been no years. The small waves were the same, chucking the rowboat under the chin as we fished at anchor, and the boat was the same boat, the same color green and the ribs broken in the same places, and under the floorboards the same freshwater leavings and débris—the dead hellgrammite,[4] the wisps of moss, the rusty discarded fishhook, the dried blood from yesterday's catch. We stared silently at the tips of our rods, at the dragonflies that came and went. I lowered the tip of mine into the water, tentatively, pensively dislodging the fly, which darted two feet away, poised, darted two feet back, and came to rest again a little farther up the rod. There had been no years between the ducking of this dragonfly and the other one—the one that was part of memory. I looked at the boy, who was silently watching his fly, and it was my hands that held his rod, my eyes watching. I felt dizzy and didn't know which rod I was at the end of.

Morning of Life (1907), David Ericson. Oil on canvas, 27″ × 22¼″, collection of the Tweed Museum of Art, University of Minnesota, Duluth, gift of Mrs. E. L. Tuohy.

We caught two bass, hauling them in briskly as though they were mackerel, pulling them over the side of the boat in a businesslike manner without any landing net, and stunning

4. **hellgrammite:** the larva of an insect, often used as fish bait.

WORDS TO KNOW

tentatively (tĕn′tə-tĭv-lē) *adv.* hesitantly; uncertainly

Customizing Instruction

Less Proficient Readers

Have students keep the following questions in mind to help them understand what White and his son do at the lake and how White is affected by this trip.

- What does White's son do that White himself did at the lake when he was a child?

Answer: He sneaks off by himself in the early morning to explore the lake shore.

- What do White and his son do together on the first day?

Answer: They go fishing.

Reading and Analyzing

Literary Analysis: TONE

A Diction is an author's choice of words. His choice of words contributes to the tone of the selection. Ask students what White's choice of the words "Summertime, oh, summertime" lends to the paragraph.
Possible Responses: It makes the paragraph seem songlike and poetic.

Literary Analysis PERSONAL ESSAY

Have students write a brief description of the author's personality as it is revealed in this personal essay. Have them consider the following questions.
- Why does he go back to the lake?
- What does he think about while he is at the lake with his son?

ACTIVE READING

B EVALUATE Possible Response: The summer reminds him of the pleasant, simpler times of his childhood.

ACTIVE READING

C COMPARE AND CONTRAST The motors have different sounds; the inboard was quiet, but the newer outboard motors make irritable sounds and disturb the peace of the lake.

them with a blow on the back of the head. When we got back for a swim before lunch, the lake was exactly where we had left it, the same number of inches from the dock, and there was only the merest suggestion of a breeze. This seemed an utterly enchanted sea, this lake you could leave to its own devices for a few hours and come back to, and find that it had not stirred, this constant and trustworthy body of water. In the shallows, the dark, water-soaked sticks and twigs, smooth and old, were undulating in clusters on the bottom against the clean ribbed sand, and the track of the mussel was plain. A school of minnows swam by, each minnow with its small individual shadow, doubling the attendance, so clear and sharp in the sunlight. Some of the other campers were in swimming, along the shore, one of them with a cake of soap, and the water felt thin and clear and unsubstantial. Over the years there had
1 been this person with the cake of soap, this cultist, and here he was. There had been no years.

Up to the farmhouse to dinner through the teeming, dusty field, the road under our sneakers was only a two-track road. The middle track was missing, the one with the marks of the hooves and the splotches of dried, flaky manure. There had always been three tracks to choose from in choosing which track to walk in; now the choice was narrowed down to two. For a moment I missed terribly the middle alternative. But the way led past the tennis court, and something about the way it lay there in the sun reassured me; the tape had loosened along the back line, the alleys were green with plantains and other weeds, and the net (installed in June and removed in September) sagged in the dry noon, and the whole place steamed with midday heat and hunger and emptiness. There was a choice of pie for dessert, and one was blueberry and one was apple, and the waitresses were the same country girls, there having been no passage of time, only the illusion of it as in a dropped curtain—the waitresses were still fifteen; their hair had been washed, that was the only difference—they had been to the movies and seen the pretty girls with the clean hair.

Summertime, oh, summertime, pattern of life **A**
indelible, the fade-proof lake, the woods unshatterable, the pasture with the sweet fern and the juniper forever and ever, summer without end; this was the background, and the life along the shore was the design, the cottagers with their innocent and tranquil design, their tiny docks with the flagpole and the American flag floating against the white clouds in the blue sky, the little paths over the roots of the trees leading from camp to camp and the paths leading back to the outhouses and the can of lime for sprinkling, and at the souvenir counters at the store the miniature birch-bark canoes and the postcards that showed things looking a little better than they looked. This was the American family at play, escaping the city heat, wondering whether the newcomers in the camp at the head of the cove were "common" or "nice," wondering whether it was true that the people who drove up for Sunday dinner at the farmhouse were turned away because there wasn't enough chicken.

ACTIVE READING

EVALUATE Why do you think the summer means so much to White? **B**

It seemed to me, as I kept remembering all this, that those times and those summers had been infinitely precious and worth saving. There had been jollity and peace and goodness. The arriving (at the beginning of August) had been

WORDS TO KNOW **indelible** (ĭn-dĕl′ə-bəl) *adj.* impossible to remove or eliminate; permanent

Teaching Options

BLOCK SCHEDULING: MANAGING TIME

If your schedule requires that you cover the lesson objectives in a shorter time, use . . .
- Preparing to Read, p. 112
- Thinking Through the Literature, p. 121
- Vocabulary in Action, p. 122
- Grammar in Context, p. 123

If you want to take advantage of longer class time, use . . .
- TE Teaching Options: Preteaching Vocabulary, p. 113; Vocabulary Strategy, p. 117; Viewing and Representing, p. 114, 118; Standardized Test Practice, p. 119
- Choices & Challenges and Author Activity, pp. 122–123.

so big a business in itself, at the railway station the farm wagon drawn up, the first smell of the pine-laden air, the first glimpse of the smiling farmer, and the great importance of the trunks and your father's enormous authority in such matters, and the feel of the wagon under you for the long ten-mile haul, and at the top of the last long hill catching the first view of the lake after eleven months of not seeing this cherished body of water. The shouts and cries of the other campers when they saw you, and the trunks to be unpacked, to give up their rich burden. (Arriving was less exciting nowadays, when you sneaked up in your car and parked it under a tree near the camp and took out the bags and in five minutes it was all over, no fuss, no loud wonderful fuss about trunks.)

Peace and goodness and jollity. The only thing that was wrong now, really, was the sound of the place, an unfamiliar nervous sound of the outboard motors. This was the note that jarred, the one thing that would sometimes break the illusion and set the years moving. In those other summertimes all motors were inboard; and when they were at a little distance, the noise they made was a sedative, an ingredient of summer sleep. They were one-
2 cylinder and two-cylinder engines, and some were make-and-break and some were jump-spark, but they all made a sleepy sound across the lake. The one-lungers throbbed and fluttered, and the twin-cylinder ones purred and purred, and that was a quiet sound, too. But now the campers all had outboards. In the daytime, in the hot mornings, these motors made a petulant, irritable sound; at night, in the still evening when the afterglow lit the water, they whined about one's ears like mosquitoes. My boy loved our rented outboard, and his great desire was to achieve single-handed mastery over it, and authority, and he soon learned the trick of choking it a little (but not too much), and the adjustment of the needle valve. Watching him I would remember the things you could do with the old one-cylinder engine with the heavy flywheel, how you could have it eating out of your hand if you got really close to it spiritually. Motorboats in those days didn't have clutches, and you would make a landing by shutting off the motor at the proper time and coasting in with a dead rudder. But there was a way of reversing them, if you learned the trick, by cutting the switch and putting it on again exactly on the final dying revolution of the flywheel, so that it would kick back against compression and begin reversing. Approaching a dock in a strong following breeze, it was difficult to slow up sufficiently by the ordinary coasting method, and if a boy felt he had complete mastery over his motor, he was tempted to keep it running beyond its time and then reverse it a few feet from the dock. It took a cool nerve, because if you threw the switch a twentieth of a second too soon you would catch the flywheel when it still had speed enough to go up past center, and the boat would leap ahead, charging bull fashion at the dock.

ACTIVE READING

COMPARE AND CONTRAST (C) What point does White make in comparing the inboard motors with the outboard motors?

We had a good week at the camp. The bass were biting well and the sun shone endlessly, day after day. We would be tired at night and lie down in the accumulated heat of the little bedrooms after the long hot day and the breeze would stir almost imperceptibly outside and the smell of the swamp drift in through the rusty screens. Sleep would come easily and in the morning the red squirrel would be on the roof, tapping out his gay routine. I

WORDS TO KNOW

petulant (pĕch′ə-lənt) *adj.* showing unreasonable annoyance over little things

Customizing Instruction

Gifted and Talented

1 Remind students that White is constantly maintaining two images: one of the past and one of the present. Ask them to search for passages that reflect this duality.

Based on their findings, ask them to hypothesize about what seems to change and what remains the same.

Possible Response: White realizes that nature and the human condition remain the same, despite the changes that "progress" have brought.

Auditory Learners

2 Point out to students that the boat motors are described with words that appeal to the sense of sound. Ask them to find words that make this appeal.

Possible Responses: *throbbed, fluttered, purred, whined.*

Mini Lesson Vocabulary Strategy

RESEARCHING WORD ORIGINS: LATIN ROOTS

Instruction The word *tentatively* is based on the Latin root, a variant of *temptare,* which means "to test, feel, try, or tempt." When White tentatively lowers the tip of his fishing rod into the water on p. 115, he is just testing to see what the dragonfly will do. Other words based on this same root are *tentacle, attempt, tempt,* and *temptress.* Explain to students that knowing basic root words such as this can help them interpret the meanings of unfamiliar words.

Activity Have students work in pairs to research the Latin root and origins of *constant* and *unsubstantial.* Then have them find other words with the same root.

Answer: *constare–com* thoroughly + *stare* to stand; *substantia–substare* be present–*sub* under + *stare*

Possible words: instant; distant; instantaneous; instance; distance

Use **Vocabulary Transparencies and Copymasters,** p. 29.

A lesson on using word origins to understand meanings appears on p. 356 in the Pupil's Edition.

Reading and Analyzing

Active Reading CLARIFY

A White's son is enjoying the same summer activities that he had enjoyed.

Reading Skills and Strategies: VISUALIZE

B Have students visualize the thunderstorm at the lake as White describes it. Have them discuss how White's description compares to their own recollections of thunderstorms.

From the Potomac River Series, 1991, Diana Suttenfield. Mary Bell Galleries, Chicago.

118

Teaching Options

Mini Lesson Viewing and Representing

From the Potomac River Series **by Diana Suttenfield**

ART APPRECIATION Ask students to study the image. Explain that Suttenfield was greatly influenced by European masters, especially the Impressionists. Suttenfield lives in the country and draws upon its landscapes for her subjects.

Instruction Have students point out examples of the artist's use of light and dark and the soft, hazy lines and discuss how these affect the mood of the painting.

Possible Response: The light over the river contrasts with the dark, hazy woods, making the river seem safe and peaceful and giving the woods a mysterious, sinister quality.

Application Ask students whether the mood of the painting is similar to the mood at the lake White revisits.

Possible Response: The painting has the same dreamlike quality that the essay does. Also, the dark foreground gives the painting a mood of impending doom that is picked up in the last sentence of the essay.

kept remembering everything, lying in bed in the mornings—the small steamboat that had a long rounded stern like the lip of a Ubangi,[5] and how quietly she ran on the moonlight sails, when the older boys played their mandolins and the girls sang and we ate doughnuts dipped in sugar, and how sweet the music was on the water in the shining night, and what it had felt like to think about girls then. After breakfast we would go up to the store and the things were in the same place—the minnows in a bottle, the plugs and spinners disarranged and pawed over by the youngsters from the boys' camp, the Fig Newtons and the Beeman's gum. Outside, the road was tarred and cars stood in front of the store. Inside, all was just as it had always been, except there was more Coca-Cola and not so much Moxie and root beer and birch beer and sarsaparilla. We would walk out with the bottle of pop apiece and sometimes the pop would backfire up our noses and hurt. We explored the streams, quietly, where the turtles slid off the sunny logs and dug their way into the soft bottom; and we lay on the town wharf and fed worms to the tame bass. Everywhere we went I had trouble making out which was I, the one walking at my side, the one walking in my pants.

ACTIVE READING

CLARIFY How does White's son remind him of himself? A

B One afternoon while we were there at that lake a thunderstorm came up. It was like the revival of an old melodrama that I had seen long ago with childish awe. The second-act climax of the drama of the electrical disturbance over a lake in America had not changed in any important respect. This was the big scene, still the big scene. The whole thing was so familiar, the first feeling of oppression and heat and a general air around camp of not wanting to go very far away. In midafternoon (it was all the same) a curious darkening of the sky, and a lull in everything that had made life tick; and then the way the boats suddenly swung the other way at their moorings with the coming of a breeze out of the new quarter, and the premonitory rumble. Then the kettledrum, then the snare, then the bass drum and cymbals, then crackling light against the dark, and the gods grinning and licking their chops in the hills. 1 Afterward the calm, the rain steadily rustling in the calm lake, the return of light and hope and spirits, and the campers running out in joy and relief to go swimming in the rain, their bright cries perpetuating the deathless joke about how they were getting simply drenched, 2 and the children screaming with delight at the new sensation of bathing in the rain, and the joke about getting drenched linking the generations in a strong indestructible chain. And the comedian who waded in carrying an umbrella.

When the others went swimming, my son said he was going in, too. He pulled his dripping trunks from the line where they had hung all through the shower and wrung them out. Languidly, and with no thought of going in, I watched him, his hard little body, skinny and bare, saw him wince slightly as he pulled up around his vitals the small, soggy, icy garment. As he buckled the swollen belt, suddenly my groin felt the chill of death. ❖

5. **Ubangi** (yōō-băng′gē): a woman of a people living near the Ubangi River in Africa, with pierced lips enlarged by saucerlike disks.

WORDS TO KNOW

languidly (lăng′gwĭd-lē) *adv.* without vigor or energy; listlessly

Customizing Instruction

Students Acquiring English

1 Describe situations in which some animals would lick their chops such as the following: a begging dog; a cat about to get its dinner; a predator about to pounce on its prey.

Less Proficient Readers

2 Help students understand how the joke about getting drenched links the generations.

Possible Response: It forms a chain because through the years, every time the campers have swum in the rain, chances are someone has made that same joke.

Assessment Standardized Test Practice

POINT OF VIEW For some standardized tests, students will be required to submit a writing sample. The sample must demonstrate good organization and good grammar and spelling skills. Have students write an essay from the point of view of the son, in which he describes the trip to the lake and makes observations about his father.

RUBRIC

3 **Full Accomplishment** The essay is consistently from the son's point of view, contains observations about the father, and is based on details in "Once More to the Lake." It is well organized and contains no grammar or spelling errors.

2 **Substantial Accomplishment** The point of view is consistent. The essay contains some observations about the father, but it is not entirely based on details from "Once More to the Lake." It contains a few grammar or spelling errors or lacks coherent organization.

1 **Little or Partial Accomplishment** The point of view is inconsistent, the essay contains very few observations about the father. The essay has serious grammar and spelling errors and lacks coherent organization.

Reading and Analyzing

Reading Skills and Strategies: CONTRASTING

A Ask how White's description of the lake in the essay "Once More to the Lake" is different from his description in this letter.

Possible Responses: His description of the lake in the essay is much more personal. He describes the lake as having "placidity," calling it "this holy spot." In the letter he only describes the lake in terms of "freshwater life . . . very different from saltwater."

Reading Skills and Strategies: MAKING INFERENCES

B Have students use evidence from the text to determine what questions White was asked.

Possible Responses: Why did he go back to the lake? Where did he get the "idea of time"? Did he have a title from the start? What is his writing process? Does he have any tricks or shortcuts?

A Letter from E. B. White

I'm not an expert on what goes on under my hood, but I'll try to answer your questions.

When I wrote "Once More to the Lake," I was living year round in this place on the coast of Maine and contributing a monthly department to Harper's.[1] I had spent many summers as a boy on Great Pond—one of the Belgrade Lakes. It's only about 75 miles from here and one day I felt an urge to revisit the lake and have a week of freshwater life, which is very different from saltwater. (A) So I went over with my small son and we did some fishing. I simply started with a desire to see again and experience again what I had seen and experienced as a boy. During our stay over there, the "idea of time" naturally insinuated itself into my thoughts, because my son was the age I had been in the previous life at the lake, and so I felt a sort of mixed-up identity. I don't recall whether I had the title from the start. Probably not. I don't believe the title had anything to do with the composing process. The "process" is probably every bit as mysterious to me as it is to some of your students—if that will make them feel any better.

Sorry I can't be more explicit.[2] Writing, (B) for me, is simply a matter of trying to find out and report what's going on in my head and get it down on paper. I haven't any devices, shortcuts, or tricks.

1. **contributing . . . Harper's:** writing a regular feature for the magazine *Harper's Bazaar.*
2. **explicit:** clear and detailed.

Teaching Options

Mini Lesson Grammar

ADVERBS

Instruction Adverbs modify verbs, adjectives, and other adverbs. They provide information about when, where, how often, or to what degree. Adverbs are often formed by adding *-ly* to adjectives; however, adding *-ly* to a noun often forms an adjective.

Practice Write the following words on the chalkboard. Have students identify the words as adjectives or adverbs. For the adverbs, have students describe how the word would modify a verb.

freely (adverb; in what manner)
stubbornly (adverb; in what manner)
friendly (adjective)
periodically (adverb; how often)
motherly (adjective)

Use **Unit One Resource Book,** p. 43 for additional support.

Use **Grammar Transparencies and Copymasters,** p. 75.

Use McDougal Littell ***Language Network,*** Chapter 9, for more instruction in using adverbs.

Thinking through the LITERATURE

Connect to the Literature

1. **What Do You Think?** What scene from the essay stands out most in your mind? Why?

Comprehension Check
- Why does White take a vacation at this particular lake?
- Which change at the lake bothers White the most?
- When does White feel a "chill of death"?

Think Critically

2. Why do you think this return trip to the lake is so important to White?

THINK ABOUT
- what he remembers about this childhood place
- the fact that he brings his son with him
- details in the first paragraph

3. What insights does White seem to gain from this experience?

THINK ABOUT
- his identification with his son
- his identification with his father
- what has changed and what has stayed the same over time

4. What do you make of White's phrase "the chill of death" in the last sentence of the essay? Explain your response.

5. **ACTIVE READING** **IDENTIFYING COMPARISON AND CONTRAST** In this essay, White talks about the similarities as well as the differences between the lake of his childhood and the lake now. Which do you think are more important to White, the similarities or the differences? Refer to your Venn diagram as well as the text in explaining your opinion.

6. What insights about "Once More to the Lake" do you gain from reading "A Letter from E. B. White"?

Extend Interpretations

7. **Critic's Corner** White's friend and *New Yorker* colleague James Thurber once praised him for "those silver and crystal sentences which have a ring like nobody else's sentences in the world." In your opinion, which sentences in the essay might be described this way?

8. **Connect to Life** In this essay, written more than half a century ago, White suggests that there is a "strong indestructible chain" linking the generations. Do you believe such a chain exists today? Explain your opinion.

Literary Analysis

PERSONAL ESSAY A brief piece of nonfiction that expresses the writer's thoughts, feelings, and opinions on events and issues from his or her own life is called a **personal essay.** For E. B. White, the personal essay was a favorite form of writing. Personal essays sometimes include elements of **autobiography,** a form of writing in which a person tells the story of his or her own life. Some personal essays, however, focus more on reflections or ideas than on a narrative of events. Many deal with both.

Cooperative Learning Activity With a small group, look at the essay and examine how much White uses personal reflection as compared to the narration of events. Construct a pie chart like the one below, showing the approximate proportion of reflection to narration. Discuss how this proportion contributes to the essay's total effect and how the piece might be different if White had used less personal reflection.

GUIDING STUDENT RESPONSE

Connect to the Literature

1. **What Do You Think?**
Students should enjoy sharing their responses.

Comprehension Check
- because this is the lake where he spent every August as a child
- the noise of the outboard motors
- when his son puts on a cold, wet bathing suit

Use **Unit One Resource Book,** p. 44 for additional support.

Think Critically

2. Possible Responses: The lake meant a lot to him as a child and he wants to re-create the pleasure he had there and share it with his son; he is trying to recapture his past by going back.
3. Possible Responses: He learns that the more things change, the more they stay the same; he understands that as people grow older, they assume different roles.
4. Possible Responses: It refers to his own mortality and the fact that he has grown older and closer to death; it refers to the death of his childhood.
5. Possible Response: The similarities are more important to White because they take him back to his childhood and make him feel the way his son feels. For example, the way a dragonfly hovers over the water makes him feel that "there had been no years."
6. Students may enjoy knowing that White went to the lake just to enjoy being with his son. He was a typical father.

Extend Interpretations

Critic's Corner Students should explain their choice of sentences.

Connect to Life Students may respond that such a chain does still exist. However, some students may not agree because families are structured so differently today. Students should support their opinions with details from the story and examples from their lives.

Literary Analysis

Cooperative Learning Activity In this selection, White wants to reveal his feelings about his experiences. His personal reflections are crucial to this purpose. Therefore, he uses more reflections of his experiences than narration of events.

ONCE MORE TO THE LAKE 121

Writing Options

1. **Vacation Essay** Essays should include a detailed account of White's son's activities in "Once More to the Lake" and should reflect an understanding of the content of the essay and the way a young boy would view a week at the lake.
2. **Slide Show Script** Students should consider the order in which White might arrange the slides; they could be arranged chronologically or from favorite to least favorite. Remind students that the narration of a slide show would be informal and possibly humorous.
3. **Newspaper Editorial** Remind students that editorials should contain opinions supported by facts, details, and examples.

Activities & Explorations

1. **Travel Advertisement** In planning their advertisements, students could consider the reasons the lake appeals to White and his son. You might want to have students work in small groups to complete this activity.
2. **Cross-generational Presentation** Students might begin preparing by making a chart that compares and contrasts their family activity in the past and in the present. Encourage students to use photographs or other visual aids in their presentations.

Inquiry & Research

Vacation Spots Students might check library resources or the Internet or ask older relatives or neighbors where they used to go for vacation when they were small. Then, drawing conclusions from the information gathered, students could consider whether it would be possible to take that same vacation today.

Vocabulary in Action

Exercise A: Word Meaning

1. c
2. e
3. d
4. b
5. a

Writing Options

1. **Vacation Essay** Draft an essay that White's son might have written in school when asked to describe his summer vacation. Make sure to include the son's observations of his father.
2. **Slide Show Script** Prepare the script that White might have used to give a slide presentation to his neighbors after his return home.
3. **Newspaper Editorial** Suppose developers are planning to clear away the cottages and build high-rise condominiums around this lake. Write an editorial for the local newspaper, opposing or approving of the plan. Place the entry in your **Working Portfolio.**

Writing Handbook
See pages 1161–1162: Persuasive Writing.

Activities & Explorations

1. **Travel Advertisement** Create an illustrated travel brochure advertising the place described in this essay. Scan the essay for details about the lake in Maine and its surroundings in the present day. Draw pictures of the lake, including captions and text to convince travelers to choose your spot for their next vacation. ~ **ART**
2. **Cross-Generational Presentation** Think of some activity or tradition that has been repeated for more than one generation in your family or community. How has this activity remained the same? How has it changed? Make a presentation in which you describe to your class the history of this event. ~ **SPEAKING AND LISTENING**

Inquiry & Research

Vacation Spots With increased technology and the development of rural areas, family vacations in America have changed over the past 100 years; people drive more cars, use more motorboats, and in some regions must travel farther to find quiet, secluded areas. Research tourism in the United States at the beginning of the century and now. Write a short report about the changes that have occurred as well as the things that have remained constant.

Vocabulary in Action

EXERCISE A: WORD MEANING For each phrase in the first column, write the letter of the synonymous phrase in the second column.

1. languidly loiter	a. permanent pigment
2. tentatively tell	b. cross character
3. Harold's haunt	c. listlessly linger
4. petulant person	d. Harry's hangout
5. indelible ink	e. doubtfully disclose

EXERCISE B With a partner, try creating music that helps to convey the meanings of three of the Words to Know. You could clap out a rhythm, hum a tune, or use a musical instrument.

Building Vocabulary
For an in-depth study of synonyms, see page 1000.

WORDS TO KNOW		
	haunt indelible languidly	petulant tentatively

Mini Lesson Grammar

POSITION OF ADVERBS **Instruction** Remind students that adverbs, such as *recently*, *quickly*, and *nearly*, often modify the action of verbs. Adverbs are often positioned near the verbs they modify. Write the following sentence on the chalkboard. "I looked at the boy, who was silently watching the fly, and it was my hands that held his rod, my eyes watching."
Underline the adverb as shown. Explain that it modifies "watching" and answers the question "How?"

Grammar in Context: Active and Passive Voice

E. B. White uses both the active and the passive voice in this sentence from "Once More to the Lake."

> **Some of the cottages were owned by nearby farmers, and you would live at the shore and eat your meals at the farmhouse.**

Verbs in the **active voice,** like those shown in blue type, emphasize the people or things performing actions (you *would live, eat*). They create lively, energetic images, like those in a movie. Verbs in the **passive voice,** like the one shown in red type, emphasize the people or things that are acted upon (cottages *were owned*). The images they create are more like photographs or still lifes. Experienced writers make use of both voices to convey precise shades of meaning in their writing.

Usage Tip: You can use passive voice when the subject of the sentence is not known, or when you want to shift emphasis to another word.

WRITING EXERCISE Rewrite each sentence, changing the voice of the verb from active to passive or vice versa. Briefly explain how your revision changed the focus of the sentence.

Example: ***Original*** The shoreline is dotted with cottages. (passive)
Rewritten Cottages dot the shoreline. (active, shifts emphasis to the cottages)

1. Some of the farmers serve hot meals.
2. The camp is already rented out.
3. Cars have worn away the middle track of the road.
4. The whir of outboard motors breaks the silence.
5. The ocean is stirred up by strong winds.

Connect to the Literature Skim White's essay for sentences in which he uses the passive voice. How does the use of this voice help create a sense of time's standing still?

Grammar Handbook Active and Passive Voice, p. 1187

E. B. White

1899–1985

Other Works
One Man's Meat
The Points of My Compass
The Elements of Style
Charlotte's Web
Poems and Sketches of E. B. White

Rise to Success In addition to being regarded as one of the 20th century's finest essayists, E. B. White has been acclaimed as a poet, humorist, and children's author. Born in Mount Vernon, New York, Elwyn Brooks White attended Cornell University, where he edited the college newspaper. In 1922, after serving in World War I and then completing his education at Cornell, he briefly worked as a reporter for the *Seattle Times* and served as mess boy on a ship to Alaska. On returning to the New York area, White began submitting his writing to the then-new magazine *The New Yorker.* He soon joined the *New Yorker* staff and remained associated with the magazine for the rest of his writing career.

A Man for All Seasons The subject matter of White's essays is extremely varied—everything "from the tremor of a leaf in the afternoon sun to the malaise of modern man," as one critic observed. Often he wrote about rural Maine, where he vacationed as a child and as an adult.

Celebrated Accomplishments White is well-known for the 1959 edition of *The Elements of Style,* a writing manual that he coauthored with his former college professor William Strunk, Jr. He also collaborated with his wife, Katherine, in editing the 1941 anthology *A Subtreasury of American Humor.* His many literary awards include a Pulitzer Prize special citation.

Author Activity

White Retrospective At the library, look up some of White's essays from his years at *The New Yorker.* Choose one and, in your own words, summarize the essay and explain how it fits the definition of a personal essay on page 105.

Grammar in Context

WRITING EXERCISE Answers to item 2 may vary.

1. Hot meals are served by some of the farmers. (passive, shifts emphasis from the farmers to the meals)
2. Summer tourists have already rented out the camp. (active, specifies the doers of the renting)
3. The middle track of the road has been worn away by cars. (passive, shifts emphasis from the cars to the road)
4. The silence is broken by the whir of outboard motors. (passive, shifts emphasis from the sound of the motors to the silence)
5. Strong winds stir up the ocean. (active, shifts emphasis from the ocean to the winds)

Author Activity

White Retrospective Students may need to go to the local library to find magazines from the 1930s–1970s. Find out the process for locating older magazines at the local library (filling out a request form, locating microfiche or microfilm, etc.) and explain it to students before they begin the activity.

Practice Have students copy the following sentences. Ask them to underline the adverb and indicate the verb it modifies and what question it answers.

1. The road leading up to the lake had been paved recently.
   Answer: paved; "When?"
2. The shores of the lake were heavily wooded.
   Answer: wooded; "To what extent?"
3. White and his son fished happily at the lake that first morning.
   Answer: fished; "How?"
4. When White and his son were fishing, a dragonfly darted nearby.
   Answer: darted; "Where?"
5. The sun shone endlessly during the week White and his son visited the lake.
   Answer: shone; "To what extent?"

Use **Grammar Transparencies and Copymasters,** p 75.

Use McDougal Littell's ***Language Network,*** Chapters 1 and 9, for more instruction and practice in adverbs.

ONCE MORE TO THE LAKE 123

OVERVIEW

Objectives

1. understand and appreciate a **memoir (Literary Analysis)**
2. recognize **cause and effect (Active Reading)**

Summary

In this excerpt from *My Life with Martin Luther King*, Coretta Scott King, the wife of the civil rights leader, recalls the events in 1955 that sparked the bus boycott in Montgomery, Alabama. Segregation laws at that time still forced black passengers to sit in the back of public buses. In addition, they had to stand if a white person needed their seat. However, on December 1, 1955, a woman passenger named Rosa Parks, too tired to stand, refused a bus driver's command to give up her seat to a white man. She was immediately arrested. Quickly, the news spread and the African-American leaders proposed a peaceful protest, a boycott of all public buses. On Monday, December 5, the Montgomery buses ran almost totally empty, because African Americans walked or rode their bicycles to work. The boycott was an overwhelming success and that night Martin Luther King, Jr., was chosen president of the protest movement. In a televised speech, King advocated nonviolent protests that set the tone for the civil rights movement he had helped to launch.

Thematic Link

In order to achieve equality, African Americans in Montgomery were willing to pay the price for progress by boycotting their chief means of transportation.

Mini Lesson **Preteaching Vocabulary**

If you would like to preteach the WORDS TO KNOW for this selection, use the Mini Lesson pp. 126–127.

Editor's Note: This selection contains racial epithets that are essential to the power and accuracy of the author's portrayal of the Montgomery bus boycott. For this reason, it is the author's specific wish that the language remain unaltered in this book.

"Our concern was not to put the bus company out of business, but to put justice in business."

Montgomery Boycott

Memoir by CORETTA SCOTT KING

Connect to Your Life

Liberty and Justice for All What do you know about the civil rights movement and two of its key participants, Rosa Parks and Martin Luther King, Jr.? Share your knowledge with your classmates in a class discussion.

Build Background

Times of Protest In the 1890s and early decades of the 20th century, many states, especially in the South, passed laws to ensure segregation, the complete separation of the races in public places. These so-called Jim Crow laws—named after a character in an old song—discriminated against African Americans. After World War II, opponents of these laws challenged their legality. In 1954 the Supreme Court, reversing an earlier decision, declared that it was unconstitutional to force whites and blacks to attend separate schools. Soon afterward, African Americans in Montgomery, Alabama, began the bus boycott that is the subject of the following selection.

A pivotal event in the civil rights movement, the Montgomery boycott first brought to national attention the Reverend Martin Luther King, Jr., the writer's husband. King's eye-opening efforts of nonviolent protest helped inspire many others in the struggle for civil rights. In 1960, for example, African-American students in Greensboro, North Carolina, initiated a new protest strategy, the sit-in, when they risked arrest for insisting on being served at a local segregated lunch counter.

WORDS TO KNOW
Vocabulary Preview

coercion	exposé
coherently	militant
degrading	oppression
devoid	perpetuation
exaltation	radiant

VIDEODISC **LaserLinks: Background for Reading**
Historical Connection

Focus Your Reading

LITERARY ANALYSIS **MEMOIR** A **memoir** is a work of nonfiction that is based on a writer's memory of key events and people in his or her life. In this selection, Coretta Scott King shares her memory of her husband's involvement in a history-making event, as illustrated by this passage:

> ***Our greatest concern was how we were going to reach the fifty thousand people of Montgomery, no matter how hard we worked.***

As you read, notice how Mrs. King blends historical reporting with her own private memories.

ACTIVE READING **CAUSE AND EFFECT** Events in real life are often related by **cause and effect,** which means that one event is the reason that another event happens. The first event is the **cause;** the events produced by the cause are the **effects.** "Montgomery Boycott" reports a now-famous incident from the civil rights movement in which Mrs. Rosa Parks refused to give up her seat on a bus. Her one act produced many important effects.

READER'S NOTEBOOK As you read the selection, look for evidence of the different effects caused by Mrs. Parks's decision. Notice how different people and groups in Montgomery responded to her action. Jot down your findings on a diagram like this one.

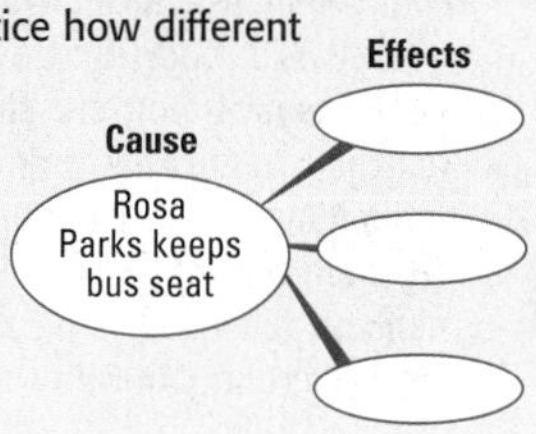

LESSON RESOURCES

UNIT ONE RESOURCE BOOK, pp. 45–50

ASSESSMENT RESOURCES

Formal Assessment, pp. 23–24

Teacher's Guide to Assessment and Portfolio Use

Test Generator

SKILLS TRANSPARENCIES AND COPYMASTERS

Literary Analysis

- Types of Nonfiction, T4 (for Cooperative Learning Activity, p. 113)

Reading and Critical Thinking

- Cause and Effect, T1 (for Think Critically, item 2, p. 133)

Grammar

- Action and Linking Verbs, C68 (for Mini Lesson, p. 130)

Vocabulary

- Context Clues, C30 (for Mini Lesson, p. 126)

Writing

- Generating Ideas, T1 (for Writing Option 1, p. 134)
- Writing Structure, T6, T7, T11 (for Writing Options 1 and 2, p. 134)
- Opinion Statement, C25 (for Writing Option 2, p. 134)

Communications

- Dramatic Reading, T12 (for Activities & Explorations 1, p. 134)
- Nonverbal Strategies, T15 (for Activities & Explorations 2, p. 134)

INTEGRATED TECHNOLOGY

Audio Library

LaserLinks

- The Montgomery Bus Boycott
- The Civil Rights Movement

See **Teacher's SourceBook,** pp. 11–12.

Visit our website: www.mcdougallittell.com

MONTGOMERY BOYCOTT

CORETTA SCOTT KING

NOTICE
IT IS REQUIRED BY LAW UNDER
PENALTY OF FINE OF $5.00 TO $25.00
THAT WHITE AND NEGRO PASSENGERS MUST
OCCUPY THE RESPECTIVE SPACE OR SEATS
INDICATED BY SIGNS IN THIS VEHICLE
COLORED
BANK

At one time, signs ordering the segregation of black and white passengers were posted on buses and trains in the South. This photograph was taken the day the Supreme Court banned segregation on public transportation. UPI/Bettmann Newsphotos.

Customizing Instruction

Less Proficient Readers

Ask students to make a list of the selection's events. Suggest they list events in the order of their occurrence.

Set a Purpose Have students read this selection to find out how the events of 1955 in Montgomery, Alabama, changed people's lives. Students should interpret possible influences of the historical context on King's memoir.

Students Acquiring English

Explain to students what is meant by the term *civil rights* in this selection.

Answer: Those rights given to citizens, especially equal treatment of all people and equal protection under the law.

Use **Spanish Study Guide** for additional support, pp. 28–30.

Gifted and Talented

You might ask students to read or view other accounts of the Montgomery bus boycott and compare them with this account. Ask them what differences exist between the accounts. What hypothesis can they offer to explain these differences?

Mini Lesson Viewing and Representing

NEWS PHOTOGRAPHY During the 1950s and 1960s, photographs and television news footage showed viewers in America and around the world the struggles and triumphs of the civil rights movement.

Instruction Remind students to read the caption, and to study the photograph for details, paying special attention to the position of the people.

Application Ask students to examine the photograph to find ways in which the photographer has used irony to illustrate this civil rights triumph.

Possible Responses: The obvious happiness of the people as one of them points to a symbol of their oppression—the "colored" sign indicating that these African American passengers are not sitting in their designated section.

TEACHING THE LITERATURE

Reading and Analyzing

Reading Skills and Strategies: PREVIEW

Briefly summarize the events described in the essay, pointing out how the days of the week help give structure to the memoir. Discuss the called-out quotations from King's speech, as well as terms such as *civil disobedience, boycott, march,* and *protest.* Ask students to notice as they read how one event leads to another.

Active Reading CAUSE AND EFFECT

Point out to students that the same event can be both an effect and a cause. As students read the selection, have them think of the Montgomery bus boycott as an effect and write down the cause.

Possible Response: Rosa Parks's arrest; Injustice

Use **Unit One Resource Book** p. 46 for additional support.

Literary Analysis MEMOIR

A memoir is an account of important events and key people in the writer's life. As students read, have them keep a list of the key people and of the key events in this selection.

Possible Responses: people—Rosa Parks, E. D. Nixon, Martin Luther King, Jr.; events—Mrs. Parks's refusal to give up her seat, the organization of the boycott, King's speech

Use **Unit One Resource Book** p. 47 for additional support.

Of all the facets of segregation in Montgomery, the most degrading were the rules of the Montgomery City Bus Lines. This northern-owned corporation outdid the South itself. Although seventy percent of its passengers were black, it treated them like cattle—worse than that, for nobody insults a cow. The first seats on all buses were reserved for whites. Even if they were unoccupied and the rear seats crowded, blacks would have to stand at the back in case some whites might get aboard; and if the front seats happened to be occupied and more white people boarded the bus, black people seated in the rear were forced to get up and give them their seats. Furthermore—and I don't think northerners ever realized this—blacks had to pay their fares at the front of the bus, get off, and walk to the rear door to board again. Sometimes the bus would drive off without them after they had paid their fare. This would happen to elderly people or pregnant women, in bad weather or good, and was considered a joke by the drivers. Frequently the white bus drivers abused their passengers, calling them . . . black cows, or black apes. Imagine what it was like, for example, for a black man to get on a bus with his son and be subjected to such treatment.

There had been one incident in March 1955, when fifteen-year-old Claudette Colvin refused to give up her seat to a white passenger. The high school girl was handcuffed and carted off to the police station. At that time Martin served on a committee to protest to the city and bus-company officials. The committee was received politely—and nothing was done.

The fuel that finally made that slow-burning fire blaze up was an almost routine incident. On December 1, 1955, Mrs. Rosa Parks, a forty-two-year-old seamstress whom my husband aptly described as "a charming person with a radiant personality," boarded a bus to go home after a long day working and shopping. The bus was crowded, and Mrs. Parks found a seat at the beginning of the black section. At the next stop more whites got on. The driver ordered Mrs. Parks to give her seat to a white man who boarded; this meant that she would have to stand all the way home. Rosa Parks was not in a revolutionary frame of mind. She had not planned to do what she did. Her cup had run over. As she said later, "I was just plain tired, and my feet hurt." So she sat there, refusing to get up. The driver called a policeman, who arrested her and took her to the courthouse. From there Mrs. Parks called E. D. Nixon, who came down and signed a bail bond for her.

Mr. Nixon was a fiery Alabamian. He was a Pullman porter[1] who had been active in A. Philip Randolph's Brotherhood of Sleeping Car Porters, and in civil rights activities. Suddenly he also had had enough; suddenly, it seemed, almost every African American in Montgomery had had enough. It was spontaneous combustion.[2] Phones began ringing all over the black section of the city. The Women's Political Council suggested a one-day boycott of the buses as a protest. E. D. Nixon courageously agreed to organize it.

The first we knew about it was when Mr. Nixon called my husband early in the morning of Friday, December 2. He had already talked to Ralph Abernathy.[3] After describing the incident, Mr. Nixon said, "We have taken this type

1. **Pullman porter:** a railroad employee who serves people in a Pullman car; that is, a passenger car with seats that can be converted into beds.
2. **spontaneous combustion** (spŏn-tā′nē-əs kəm-bŭs′chən): literally, the situation that occurs when something bursts into flames on its own, without the addition of heat from an outside source.
3. **Ralph Abernathy** (1926–1990): a minister who became a close colleague of Martin Luther King, Jr., and an important civil rights leader.

WORDS TO KNOW

degrading (dĭ-grā′dĭng) *adj.* tending to lower one's dignity; insulting **degrade** *v.*
radiant (rā′dē-ənt) *adj.* bright; glowing

126

Teaching Options

Mini Lesson Preteaching Vocabulary

CONTEXT CLUES Instruction Activity Write the following sentences on the chalkboard. Instruct students to complete each sentence with the most appropriate WORD TO KNOW.

1. The sun's ________ beams shone through the curtains. *(radiant)*
2. Despite efforts to make them surrender, the strikers remained ________. *(militant)*
3. Hearing the choir sing so beautifully left the audience with a feeling of ________ *(exaltation)*
4. The reporter wrote a(n) ________ detailing the bus line's scandalous segregationist practices. *(exposé)*
5. Henry felt the bus line's practices ________ him. *(degraded)*
6. The Bill of Rights has helped encourage the ________ of individual freedom in the United States. *(perpetuation)*
7. The man slumped in his seat was ________ of energy. *(devoid)*

. . . blacks had to pay their fares at the front of the bus, get off, and walk to the rear door to board again.

of thing too long. I feel the time has come to boycott the buses. It's the only way to make the white folks see that we will not take this sort of thing any longer."

Martin agreed with him and offered the Dexter Avenue Church as a meeting place. After much telephoning, a meeting of black ministers and civic leaders was arranged for that evening. Martin said later that as he approached his church Friday evening, he was nervously wondering how many leaders would really turn up. To his delight, Martin found over forty people, representing every segment of African-American life, crowded into the large meeting room at Dexter. There were doctors, lawyers, businessmen, federal-government employees, union leaders, and a great many ministers. The latter were particularly welcome, not only because of their influence, but because it meant that they were beginning to accept Martin's view that "religion deals with both heaven and earth. . . . Any religion that professes to be concerned with the souls of men and is not concerned with the slums that doom them, the economic conditions that strangle them, and the social conditions that cripple them, is dry-as-dust religion." From that very first step, the Christian ministry provided the leadership of our struggle, as Christian ideals were its source.

Martin told me after he got home that the meeting was almost wrecked because questions or suggestions from the floor were cut off. However, after a stormy session, one thing was clear: however much they differed on details, everyone was unanimously for a boycott. It was set for Monday, December 5. Committees were organized; all the ministers present promised to urge their congregations to take part. Several thousand leaflets were printed on the church mimeograph machine, describing the reasons for the boycott and urging all blacks not to ride buses "to work, to town, to school, or anyplace on Monday, December 5." Everyone was asked to come to a mass meeting at the Holt Street Baptist Church on Monday evening for further instructions. The Reverend A. W. Wilson had offered his church because it was larger than Dexter and more convenient, being in the center of the black district.

Saturday was a busy day for Martin and the other members of the committee. They hustled around town talking with other leaders, arranging with the black-owned taxi companies for special bulk fares and with the owners of private automobiles to get the people to and from work. I could do little to help because Yoki[4] was only two weeks old, and my physician, Dr. W. D. Pettus, who was very careful, advised me to stay in for a month. However, I was kept busy answering the telephone, which rang continuously, and coordinating from that central point the many messages and arrangements.

Our greatest concern was how we were going to reach the fifty thousand black people of Montgomery, no matter how hard we worked. The white press, in an outraged exposé, spread

4. **Yoki:** nickname of the Kings' daughter Yolanda.

WORDS TO KNOW
exposé (ĕk'spō-zā') *n.* an account that reveals something negative to the public

Customizing Instruction

Students Acquiring English
Explain to students that a *boycott* is a protest in which people abstain from buying a product or using a service.

Gifted and Talented
Explain to students that Martin Luther King, Jr., was greatly influenced by the Indian leader, Mohandas Gandhi. Have students read about Gandhi to better understand which aspects of his philosophy King used as a civil rights leader.

Multiple Learning Styles
Auditory Learners
If possible, play audiotapes of Martin Luther King, Jr., speaking so that students hear the cadence of his speech and can appreciate his eloquence and skilled delivery.

8. Through ________, he forced people to accept his views. *(coercion)*
9. The people longed for freedom from their tyrant's ________. *(oppression)*
10. Logical and organized, his speech ________ expressed the group's agenda. *(coherently)*

Use **Unit One Resource Book** p. 48 for additional support.

A lesson on context clues appears on p. 56 in the Pupil's Edition.

Reading and Analyzing

Literary Analysis: HISTORICAL FACT AND PERSONAL OPINION

A Ask students to examine Coretta Scott King's description of the hours leading up to the boycott, beginning with Martin reading the paper late Sunday night. Ask them to make two lists: one containing verifiable historical facts and the other containing Coretta Scott King's personal opinions and observations.

Possible Responses: Historical facts—the paper's report about the boycott, boycotts had failed in other cities, the buses were empty

Personal opinion—Martin's state of mind, inner struggle, and their doubts about the possibility of success

Reading Skills and Strategies: QUESTION

B Ask students what King means when he says, "He who accepts evil without protesting against it is really cooperating with it." Do they agree or disagree?

the word for us in a way that would have been impossible with only our own resources.

As it happened, a white woman found one of our leaflets, which her black maid had left in the kitchen. The irate woman immediately telephoned the newspapers to let the white community know what the blacks were up to. We laughed a lot about this, and Martin later said that we owed them a great debt.

On Sunday morning, from their pulpits, almost every African-American minister in town urged people to honor the boycott.

A Martin came home late Sunday night and began to read the morning paper. The long articles about the proposed boycott accused the NAACP[5] of planting Mrs. Parks on the bus—she had been a volunteer secretary for the Montgomery chapter—and likened the boycott to the tactics of the White Citizens Councils.[6] This upset Martin. That awesome conscience of his began to gnaw at him, and he wondered if he was doing the right thing. Alone in his study, he struggled with the question of whether the boycott method was basically unchristian. Certainly it could be used for unethical ends. But, as he said, "We were using it to give birth to freedom . . . and to urge men to comply with the law of the land. Our concern was not to put the bus company out of business, but to put justice in business." He recalled Thoreau's[7] words, "We can no longer lend our cooperation to an evil system," and he thought, B "He who accepts evil without protesting against it is really cooperating with it." Later Martin wrote, "From this moment on I conceived of our movement as an act of massive noncooperation. From then on I rarely used the word 'boycott.' "

Serene after his inner struggle, Martin joined me in our sitting room. We wanted to get to bed early, but Yoki began crying and the telephone kept ringing. Between interruptions we sat together talking about the prospects for the success of the protest. A We were both filled with doubt. Attempted boycotts had failed in Montgomery and other cities. Because of changing times and tempers, this one seemed to have a better chance, but it was still a slender hope. We finally decided that if the boycott was sixty percent effective we would be doing all right, and we would be satisfied to have made a good start.

A little after midnight we finally went to bed, but at five-thirty the next morning we were up and dressed again. The first bus was due at six o'clock at the bus stop just outside our house. We had coffee and toast in the kitchen; then I went into the living room to watch. Right on time, the bus came, headlights blazing through the December darkness, all lit up inside. I shouted, "Martin! Martin, come quickly!" He ran in and stood beside me, his face lit with excitement. There was not one person on that usually crowded bus!

We stood together waiting for the next bus. It was empty too, and this was the most heavily traveled line in the whole city. Bus after empty bus paused at the stop and moved on. We were so excited we could hardly speak coherently. Finally Martin said, "I'm going to take the car and see what's happening other places in the city."

He picked up Ralph Abernathy and they cruised together around the city. Martin told me about it when he got home. Everywhere it was the same—a few white people and maybe one or two blacks in otherwise empty buses. Martin

5. **NAACP:** the National Association for the Advancement of Colored People, a prominent civil rights organization.
6. **White Citizens Councils:** groups that formed, first in Mississippi and then throughout the South, to resist the 1954 Supreme Court decision to desegregate the schools.
7. **Thoreau** (thə-rō'): Henry David Thoreau (1817–1862), American writer whose famous essay "Civil Disobedience" helped inspire the ideas of nonviolent resistance used in the civil rights movement.

WORDS TO KNOW **coherently** (kō-hîr'ənt-lē) *adv.* in a manner that shows clear thinking and makes sense

Teaching Options

BLOCK SCHEDULING: MANAGING TIME

If your schedule requires that you cover the lesson objectives in a shorter time, use . . .
- Preparing to Read, p. 124
- Thinking Through the Literature, p. 133
- Vocabulary in Action, p. 134

If you want to take advantage of longer class time, use . . .
- TE Teaching Options: Preteaching Vocabulary, pp. 126–127; Viewing and Representing, p. 125; Multicultural Link, p. 129; Cross Curricular Link, p. 131; Standardized Test Practice, p. 132
- Choices & Challenges and Author Activity, pp. 134–135

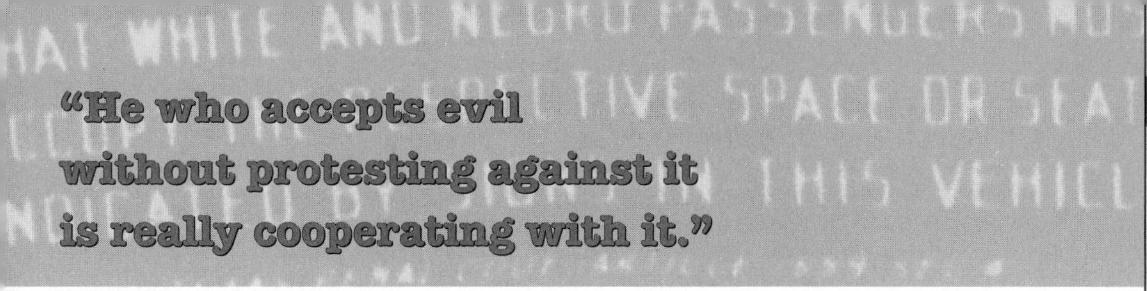

"He who accepts evil without protesting against it is really cooperating with it."

and Ralph saw extraordinary sights—the sidewalks crowded with men and women trudging to work; the students of Alabama State College walking or thumbing rides; taxicabs with people clustered in them. Some of our people rode mules; others went in horse-drawn buggies. But most of them were walking, some making a round-trip of as much as twelve miles. Martin later wrote, "As I watched them I knew that there is nothing more majestic than the determined courage of individuals willing to suffer and sacrifice for their freedom and dignity."

Martin rushed off again at nine o'clock that morning to attend the trial of Mrs. Parks. She was convicted of disobeying the city's segregation ordinance and fined ten dollars and costs. Her young attorney, Fred D. Gray, filed an appeal. It was one of the first clear-cut cases of an African American being convicted of disobeying the segregation laws—usually the charge was disorderly conduct or some such thing.

The leaders of the Movement called a meeting for three o'clock in the afternoon to organize the mass meeting to be held that night. Martin was a bit late, and as he entered the hall, people said to him, "Martin, we have elected you to be our president. Will you accept?"

Fear was an invisible presence at the meeting, along with courage and hope. Proposals were voiced to make the organization, which the leaders decided to call the Montgomery Improvement Association, or MIA, a sort of secret society, because if no names were mentioned it would be safer for the leaders. E. D. Nixon opposed that idea. "We're acting like little boys," he said. "Somebody's name will be known, and if we're afraid, we might just as well fold up right now. The white folks are eventually going to find out anyway. We'd better decide now if we are going to be fearless men or scared little boys."

That settled that question. It was also decided that the protest would continue until certain demands were met. Ralph Abernathy was made chairman of the committee to draw up the demands.

Martin came home at six o'clock. He said later that he was nervous about telling me he had accepted the presidency of the protest movement, but he need not have worried, because I sincerely meant what I said when I told him that night: "You know that whatever you do, you have my backing."

Reassured, Martin went to his study. He was to make the main speech at the mass meeting that night. It was now six-thirty and—this was the way it was usually to be—he had only twenty minutes to prepare what he thought might be the most decisive speech of his life. He said afterward that thinking about the responsibility and the reporters and television cameras, he almost panicked. Five minutes wasted and only fifteen minutes left. At that moment he turned to prayer. He asked God "to restore my balance and be with me in a time when I need Your guidance more than ever."

How could he make his speech militant enough to rouse people to action and yet devoid of hate and resentment? He was determined to do both.

WORDS TO KNOW

militant (mĭl′ĭ-tənt) *adj.* showing a fighting spirit; aggressive
devoid (dĭ-void′) *adj.* completely lacking; empty

Customizing Instruction

Less Proficient Readers
Ask students the following questions to assess their understanding of the story.

- What details tell us whether the bus boycott was successful?

Possible Responses: empty buses; crowded sidewalks

- What was the outcome of Rosa Parks's trial?

Possible response: She was found guilty of disobeying segregation laws.

Multicultural Link Boycott

PROTEST LEADERS The tactic of staging a boycott is an old one. The first victim of this practice was Captain Charles Cunningham Boycott, a rent collector for the Earl of Erne in County Mayo, Ireland. In the 1880's after two years of bad potato crops, Boycott raised the rents so high that the tenant farmers ostracized him. They refused to talk to him or sell him goods. In the end, Boycott was forced to flee to England. In India in 1921, Mohandas Gandhi began to organize a series of boycotts in which the Indian people refused to buy cloth from their British rulers. Gandhi encouraged Indians to spin their own material. In fact, he himself practiced spinning two hours every day and made the spinning wheel a symbol of his National Congress Party. In 1930 Gandhi led another boycott against the British-controlled salt mines and ocean salt fields. Although it was against British law, he encouraged thousands to gather their own salt from the sea.

Reading and Analyzing

Reading Skills and Strategies: CLARIFY

Ask students to clarify how King distinguishes his movement from other interest groups like the White Citizens Councils and the Ku Klux Klan.

Possible Response: The latter two promote injustice and advocate the supremacy of one group, while King's group works for justice and equality for all; King's group is nonviolent while the other movements often resort to violent measures.

Literary Analysis: FIGURATIVE LANGUAGE

A Explain to students that King is using personification when he speaks of the "birth of justice." Ask students why he might use this figure of speech in this case.

Possible Responses: to emphasize that justice would be something new; to capitalize on the positive connotations that *birth* has

Martin and Ralph went together to the meeting. When they got within four blocks of the Holt Street Baptist Church, there was an enormous traffic jam. Five thousand people stood outside the church listening to loudspeakers and singing hymns. Inside it was so crowded, Martin told me, the people had to lift Ralph and him above the crowd and pass them from hand to hand over their heads to the platform. The crowd and the singing inspired Martin, and God answered his prayer. Later Martin said, "That night I understood what the older preach-

Dr. Martin Luther King, Jr. (*left*), and Coretta Scott King in their early days as civil rights activists. Culver Pictures.

Teaching Options

Mini Lesson Grammar

LINKING VERBS Remind students that a subject is a noun and a predicate is a verb. Two types of verb are active and linking. Common linking verbs are *be, become, seem, appear, taste, smell, sound, feel,* and *look.* Linking verbs describe a condition, usually linking the subject to a predicate noun or adjective. Write the following sentence on the chalkboard. Underline the verb as shown.

The geese <u>seemed</u> fat and ready for the hard journey. (linking verb)

Have students identify the subject of *seemed* (geese). Explain that "fat and ready for the hard journey" is the condition of the geese. Their action is to fly south.

Use **Grammar Transparencies and Copymasters,** p. 68.

Use McDougal Littell's ***Language Network,*** Chapters 1 and 6, for more instruction in verbs.

"... we are tired. Tired of being segregated and humiliated; tired of being kicked about by the brutal feet of oppression."

ers meant when they said, 'Open your mouth and God will speak for you.'"

First the people sang "Onward, Christian Soldiers" in a tremendous wave of five thousand voices. This was followed by a prayer and a reading of the Scriptures. Martin was introduced. People applauded; television lights beat upon him. Without any notes at all he began to speak. Once again he told the story of Mrs. Parks, and rehearsed some of the wrongs black people were suffering. Then he said,

> *But there comes a time when people get tired. We are here this evening to say to those who have mistreated us so long, that we are tired. Tired of being segregated and humiliated; tired of being kicked about by the brutal feet of oppression.*

The audience cheered wildly, and Martin said,

> *We have no alternative but to protest. We have been amazingly patient . . . but we come here tonight to be saved from that patience that makes us patient with anything less than freedom and justice.*

Taking up the challenging newspaper comparison with the White Citizens Councils and the Klan,[8] Martin said,

> *They are protesting for the perpetuation of injustice in the community; we're protesting for the birth of justice . . . their methods lead to violence and lawlessness. But in our protest there will be no cross-burnings, no white person will be taken from his home by a hooded Negro mob and brutally murdered . . . We will be guided by the highest principles of law and order.* (A)

Having roused the audience for militant action, Martin now set limits upon it. His study of nonviolence and his love of Christ informed his words. He said,

> *No one must be intimidated to keep them from riding the buses. Our method must be persuasion, not coercion. We will only say to the people, "Let your conscience be your guide." . . . Our actions must be guided by the deepest principles of the Christian faith. . . . Once again we must hear the words of Jesus, "Love your enemies. Bless them that curse you. Pray for them that despitefully use you." If we fail to do this, our protest will end up as a meaningless drama on the stage of history and its memory will be shrouded in the*

8. **Klan:** the Ku Klux Klan, a secret society trying to establish white power and authority by unlawful and violent methods directed against African Americans and other minority groups.

WORDS TO KNOW

oppression (ə-prĕsh'ən) *n.* unjust or cruel exercise of power or authority
perpetuation (pər-pĕch'o͞o-ā'shən) *n.* a long-lasting continuation
coercion (kō-ûr'zhən) *n.* the use of power or threats to force someone to do something

131

Customizing Instruction

Gifted and Talented

Ask students to analyze the characteristics of clearly-written text in Dr. King's prose style, looking for examples of parallelism, imagery, and allusion. Students should examine syntax and word choice. One especially complex sentence is ". . . we come here tonight to be saved from that patience that makes us patient with anything less than freedom and justice."

Cross Curricular Link History

CIVIL RIGHTS ACTS After years of sit-ins, marches, and nonviolent resistance, the civil rights movement gained momentum; as a result, two important pieces of civil rights legislation were enacted by the mid-1960s. The Civil Rights Act of 1964 guaranteed equal voting rights, prohibited segregation or discrimination in public accommodations, and discrimination for employment based on sex, and established the Equal Employment Opportunity Commission. The Fair Housing Act of 1968 prohibited discrimination in housing.

Martin Luther King, Jr., the most respected and eloquent civil rights leader of the 1960s, was assassinated in 1968. Nevertheless, his nonviolent fight against injustice continued under the leadership of Ralph Abernathy and the young Jesse Jackson.

Reading and Analyzing

Reading Skills and Strategies:
EVALUATE

Ask students to evaluate how effectively Coretta Scott King has depicted the events.

Possible Response: Students may note that understanding the Kings' inner turmoil and doubts helps create a moving memoir.

ugly garments of shame. . . . We must not become bitter and end up by hating our white brothers. As Booker T. Washington[9] *said, "Let no man pull you so low as to make you hate him."*

Finally, Martin said,

If you will protest courageously, and yet with dignity and Christian love, future historians will say, "There lived a great people—a black people—who injected new meaning and dignity into the veins of civilization." This is our challenge and our overwhelming responsibility.

As Martin finished speaking, the audience rose cheering in exaltation. And in that speech my husband set the keynote and the tempo of the Movement he was to lead, from Montgomery onward. ❖

9. **Booker T. Washington** (1856–1915): African-American educator and writer.

LITERARY LINK

SIT-INS

Margaret Walker

Greensboro, North Carolina, in the Spring of 1960

You were our first brave ones to defy their
  dissonance of hate
With your silence
With your willingness to suffer
Without violence
Those first bright young to fling names across pages
Of new southern history
With courage and faith, convictions, and intelligence
The first to blaze a flaming path for justice
And awaken consciences
Of these stony ones.

Come, Lord Jesus, Bold Young Galilean[1]
Sit Beside this Counter, Lord, with Me!

1. **Galilean** (găl′ə-lē′ən): a term used as a synonym for Jesus, because Galilee was the center of Jesus' ministry.

WORDS TO KNOW

exaltation (ĕg′zôl-tā′shən) *n.* the act of glorifying, praising, or honoring

Teaching Options

Mini Lesson: Standardized Test Practice

CHOOSING THE MAIN IDEA For some standardized tests, students will be asked to choose the main idea of a passage. To provide students with some help in choosing the main idea, read aloud or write on the chalkboard the following question.

Application: Which of the following statements best states the main idea of the paragraph beginning on p. 131 with "No one must be intimidated . . ." and ending on p. 132 with ". . . make you hate him"?

A. People must be forced to ride the buses.

B. The protesters must be careful to avoid violence or force.

C. The protesters should love their enemies.

D. History has proved that change comes slowly.

Lead students through the process of choosing the best main idea. Point out that **A** is contradictory to the message of the paragraph, while **C** is a supporting idea. The main idea should express the overall meaning of the passage. For that reason, **B** is the best choice.

Connect to the Literature

1. **What Do You Think?** What went through your mind while reading the selection? Describe your thoughts.

Comprehension Check
- What did the African-American leaders in Montgomery do to protest Mrs. Parks's arrest?
- Why was the first day of the boycott a success?
- What method of protest did Dr. King recommend?

Think Critically

2. ACTIVE READING CAUSE AND EFFECT Review the cause-and-effect diagram that you made in your READER'S NOTEBOOK as you read the selection. What do you think were the most important effects of Rosa Parks's decision not to give up her bus seat?

3. Do you think the phrase "spontaneous combustion" is a good description of the events leading up to the boycott?

THINK ABOUT
- Rosa Parks's motivation for challenging the system
- how segregation had affected the African-American community

4. What does the selection suggest about the character, goals, and principles of Martin Luther King, Jr.?

5. What is your opinion of Rosa Parks and her accomplishments? Explain your opinion.

6. Based on your understanding of "Montgomery Boycott," what qualities do you think were valued by the early participants in the civil rights movement?

Extend Interpretations

7. **Comparing Texts** Compare and contrast the ways in which "Montgomery Boycott" and the poem "Sit-Ins" depict the actions and motivations of civil rights protesters. Cite evidence from the poem, as well as from the memoir.

8. **Connect to Life** Do you think a boycott is an effective and fair means of protest? Use examples to explain your reasoning.

Literary Analysis

MEMOIR A **memoir** is a type of nonfiction that focuses on a person's life. In some cases, *memoir* is simply another word for **autobiography,** a work that tells about the personal experiences of the author. In other cases, however, a memoir can be a **biography** or a **biographical sketch.** For example, people can write memoirs about famous friends or family members. A biographical memoir usually blends the writer's knowledge of the subject with other sources of information about the subject. Mrs. King's memoir combines elements of biography and autobiography.

Cooperative Learning Activity In a small group, review "Montgomery Boycott" to decide where Mrs. King is likely to have gathered her information. For example, a statement such as "Martin came home late Sunday night," probably came from her own memory. But other statements probably required outside sources of information, such as interviews or newspaper accounts. Create a chart, like the one shown, to record information. For each statement recorded, decide whether it is likely to have come from Mrs. King's memory or from other sources.

Sources of Information

Statement/Information	Memory	Other Sources
"Martin came home late Sunday night."	✓	

GUIDING STUDENT RESPONSE

Connect to the Literature

1. **What Do You Think?**
Students may say that it seems incredible that segregation laws were still enforced until the 1960s, 100 years after the Civil War ended.

Comprehension Check
- They organized a boycott of public buses.
- The buses were all or nearly empty.
- Dr. King called for nonviolent resistance, or civil disobedience.

Use **Unit One Resource Book** p. 50 for additional support.

Think Critically

2. Ask students to distinguish between immediate, specific effects like Rosa Parks's detention in jail and more far-reaching effects like the call for a boycott and the formation of the Montgomery Improvement Association.
3. Yes, an individual's response sparked the community to take action.
4. Most students will mention his dedication to nonviolence and his religious faith.
5. Students should be able to support their response with details from the memoir.
6. Early participants believed in group cooperation and solidarity, a willingness to make personal sacrifices and a belief in a cause.

Extend Interpretations

Comparing Texts Encourage students to compare and contrast the viewpoints of the authors. Coretta Scott King is an active participant in the origin of the movement; Margaret Walker writes later, both as a follower of King's ideals and as a participant in the ongoing struggle. Students might note the allusions to Christian ideals and the imagery of fire present in "Montgomery Boycott" and in "Sit-Ins."

Connect to Life Responses will vary. Students might address issues of today that might elicit boycotts: pollution, intolerance, job losses. Encourage students to define *boycott* precisely and to think through the effects of any proposed boycott.

Literary Analysis

Cooperative Learning Activity Each member of the learning circle should contribute a statement and indicate whether it is historical fact or whether it reflects personal interpretation. Students may want to comment on the balance of the two sources of information that are synthesized in this memoir. Students should evaluate sources including how the writer's motivation may affect credibility.

Writing Options

1. **Historic Diary** Student responses will vary. Encourage students to imagine and record her feelings, as well as her surroundings and her observations.
2. **Newspaper Editorial** Remind students that the purpose of an editorial is to persuade. Being aware of both sides of an argument helps the writer construct an effective editorial.

Activities and Explorations

1. **Storytelling** Remind students to think of how their presentations must be tailored to the needs and expectations of the young audience. Appropriate vocabulary and length, vivid details, and graphics will add to the story.
2. **Historical Exhibit** If possible, ask students to search out images used by media sources sympathetic to the boycott and contrast those images with those used by anti-boycott media sources.
3. **Speech for the Ages** Encourage students to do research on Dr. King's life to help them understand the timing and significance of their selections.

Inquiry & Research

1. **A Dark Day** Students may look at the words of Robert Kennedy.
2. **We Shall Overcome** Time lines should show the civil rights legislation of 1964 and 1968.

Choices & CHALLENGES

Writing Options

1. **Historic Diary** Write the diary entry Rosa Parks might have written just after her famous bus ride and arrest. Expand on ideas touched upon in the selection and in your discussions.
2. **Newspaper Editorial** Write an editorial on the Montgomery boycott that might have appeared the day after it began. In your editorial, consider the reasons both for and against the boycott. Then recommend a course of action. Use a diagram like the one below to jot down notes for writing. Place the editorial in your **Working Portfolio.**

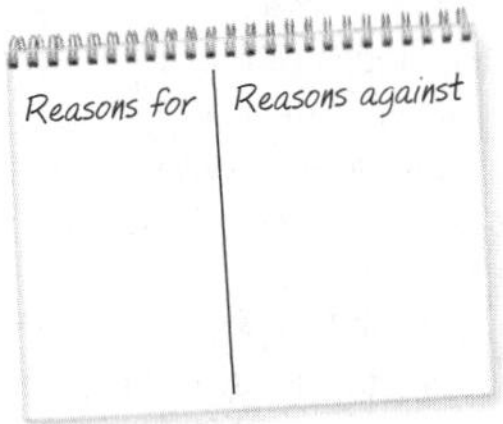

Activities & Explorations

1. **Storytelling** Retell the story of the boycott as if you were presenting it to an audience of young children celebrating Martin Luther King Day. If possible, make arrangements to tell your story to an appropriate audience. ~ **SPEAKING AND LISTENING**
2. **Historical Exhibit** Find and photocopy news stories and magazine articles that reported the Montgomery boycott when it happened. Use them in a "Moments in History" bulletin-board display or exhibit. ~ **VIEWING AND REPRESENTING**
3. **Speech for the Ages** Bring to class and play a recording of a speech by Martin Luther King, Jr. Explain when and where he made the speech and why it is significant. ~ **SPEAKING AND LISTENING**

Inquiry & Research

1. **A Dark Day in History** Martin Luther King, Jr., was assassinated on April 4, 1968. Find out how another national leader reacted to King's death and was able to offer words of comfort to others.

Real World Link To begin your research, read Robert Kennedy's speech about King on pages 136–137.

2. **We Shall Overcome** Research and prepare a time line that identifies and briefly describes events in the civil rights movement. You might begin with the Montgomery boycott or with the 1954 Supreme Court decision in *Brown v. Board of Education of Topeka, Kansas.*

Martin Luther King,, Jr., leads protest march from Selma to Montgomery, 1965.

Vocabulary in Action

EXERCISE: ASSESSMENT PRACTICE On your paper, indicate whether the following pairs of words are synonyms or antonyms.

1. degrading–humiliating
2. radiant–dim
3. exposé–tribute
4. oppression–injustice
5. coherently–sensibly
6. militant–meek
7. devoid–full
8. perpetuation–halt
9. coercion–intimidation
10. exaltation–glorification

Building Vocabulary

For an in-depth lesson on word origins, see page 356.

Teaching Options

Mini Lesson Grammar

ADVERBS

Instruction Adverbs modify verbs, adjectives, and other adverbs. They provide information about when, where, how often, or to what degree. Adverbs are often formed by adding *-ly* to adjectives; however, adding *-ly* to a noun often forms an adjective.

Practice Write the following words on the chalkboard. Have students identify the words as adjectives or adverbs. For the adverbs, have students describe how the word would modify a verb.

freely (adverb; in what manner)
stubbornly (adverb; in what manner)
friendly (adjective)
periodically (adverb; how often)
motherly (adjective)

Use **Unit One Resource Book** p. 49 for additional support.

Use **Grammar Transparencies and Copymasters,** p. 70.

Use McDougal Littell's ***Language Network,*** Chapter 9, for more instruction in using adverbs.

Grammar in Context: Adverbs

In the excerpt from "Montgomery Boycott," Coretta Scott King frequently uses adverbs to add detail. An **adverb,** as you may recall, is a word that modifies a verb, an adjective, or another adverb.

time
[E. D. Nixon] had already talked to Ralph Abernathy.

degree degree
However much they differed on details,

manner
everyone was unanimously for a boycott.

As the labels above the sentences show, adverbs can supply information about when, to what degree, or in what manner things are done. They can also tell where and how often events occur.

Usage Tip: Be sure not to use an adjective when an adverb is called for. Example: He ran quickly (not quick).

WRITING EXERCISE Supply an adverb to complete each sentence.

Example: Dr. King _____ decided to attend the meeting. (When?)
Dr. King later decided to attend the meeting.

1. White bus drivers _____ treated black riders with contempt. (How often?)
2. Dr. King waited _____ for the other leaders, wondering if they would show up. (In what manner?)
3. People who could not get into the church waited _____. (Where?)
4. Dr. King said that blacks had been _____ patient about trying to change unjust laws. (To what degree?)
5. Now he recommended that people protest _____. (In what manner?)

Grammar Handbook
Adverbs, p. 1188

Coretta Scott King
1927–

Other Works
The Words of Martin Luther King, Jr.

Struggle for Equality As a child in Heiberger, Alabama, Coretta Scott had to walk five miles a day to a one-room schoolhouse while white children rode past her on a school bus. That experience and others made her determined to struggle for racial equality. Recognizing education as the key to winning that struggle, she studied hard and eventually won a scholarship to Antioch College in Ohio, where her sister Edythe had been the first African-American student on campus.

Fateful Encounter After graduation, Coretta Scott moved to Boston to study music and there met Martin Luther King, Jr., then a graduate student at Boston University, whose dreams of fighting for racial equality coincided with her own. The two were married in 1953.

Civil-Rights Champion Over the years, Coretta Scott King has shown great determination and courage in her fight for civil rights. In 1956 her home was bombed; in 1968 her husband was assassinated in Memphis, Tennessee. Nevertheless, on the day before her husband's funeral, she led a march of striking Memphis garbage collectors, and the next year she published *My Life with Martin Luther King, Jr.,* the book from which "Montgomery Boycott" is taken. Since then, she has remained a tireless champion in the struggle for racial justice, most notably as founder and chief executive officer of the Martin Luther King, Jr., Center for Nonviolent Social Change in Atlanta, Georgia.

Author Activity

With a partner, investigate recent efforts to reopen the case of Martin Luther King's assassination. Find out what Mrs. King and her children have to say about the murder of Dr. King and the handling of the original investigation.

GUIDING STUDENT RESPONSE

Vocabulary in Action

1. synonyms
2. antonyms
3. antonyms
4. synonyms
5. synonyms
6. antonyms
7. antonyms
8. antonyms
9. synonyms
10. synonyms

Grammar in Context

WRITING EXERCISE Answers will vary. Possible answers are shown.

1. White bus drivers frequently treated black riders with contempt.
2. Dr. King waited anxiously for the other leaders, wondering if they would show up.
3. People who could not get into the church waited outside.
4. Dr. King said that blacks had been amazingly patient about trying to change unjust laws.
5. Now he recommended that people protest courageously.

Author Activity

Encourage students to use appropriate print and information including library resources and the Internet to learn the most recent results of the investigation into the assassination of Martin Luther King, Jr. The report was made public in August l998 by the Attorney General of the United States.

Real WORLD Link

Internet Feature Article

Objectives
- analyze a persuasive speech
- identify the rhetorical techniques of ethical appeal, repetition, and parallelism
- determine the purpose of a speech based on textual evidence
- become aware of rhetorical techniques in other texts

Connecting to the Literature
The excerpts from King's speech delivered at the Holt Street Baptist Church (p. 131) contain the same rhetorical devices used by Robert Kennedy in "A Eulogy to Dr. Martin Luther King, Jr."

Reading for Information

Tell students that Robert F. Kennedy was President John Kennedy's brother and served as the attorney general during President Kennedy's term in office. Robert F. Kennedy was himself assassinated, dying on June 6, 1968.

In answering the questions regarding rhetoric, students will be analyzing the characteristics of clearly-written text. They should note patterns of organization, syntax, and word choice.

1 He says that he, too, experienced the death of a family member. President John Kennedy was the family member, killed on November 22, 1963.

2 Possible Response: The repetition is effective because it provides a clear outline of how Americans should not react toward this act of violence. Other examples of repetition include: love, compassion, justice; prayer; black, white.

3 Other examples of parallelism include the series of infinitives in paragraph four; the series of clauses beginning "It is not . . ." in paragraph nine; the series of verb phrases beginning with "want" in paragraph ten.

Real WORLD Link — Primary Source

A Eulogy to Dr. Martin Luther King, Jr.

BY ROBERT F. KENNEDY

On April 4, 1968, hundreds of African Americans gathered for what they thought would be an exciting political event. A presidential candidate, Robert Kennedy, was coming to speak to them. Before he was to deliver his speech, however, Kennedy was informed that Martin Luther King, Jr., had been assassinated earlier that day. He nevertheless went to the rally, where he found the people upbeat in anticipation of his appearance. Realizing that they were unaware of the tragic event, he began his speech with the following words.

I have bad news for you, for all of our fellow citizens, and people who love peace all over the world, and that is that Martin Luther King was shot and killed tonight.

Martin Luther King dedicated his life to love and to justice for his fellow human beings, and he died because of that effort.

In this difficult day, in this difficult time for the United States, it is perhaps well to ask what kind of a nation we are and what direction we want to move in. For those of you who are black—considering the evidence there evidently is that there were white people who were responsible—you can be filled with bitterness, with hatred, and a desire for revenge. We can move in that direction as a country, in great polarization—black people amongst black, white people amongst white, filled with hatred toward one another. ❶

Or we can make an effort, as Martin Luther King did, to understand and to comprehend, and to replace

136

Reading for Information

Has a teacher, a coach, a politician, or a community leader ever given a speech that inspired you? If so, he or she may have used some of the **rhetorical techniques**—ways of using language persuasively—that Kennedy used in this address.

PERSUASIVE RHETORIC
Kennedy sensed that there might be an intense reaction to the news of the assassination. In his speech, he used certain rhetorical techniques to persuade the crowd to remain calm.

YOUR TURN Use the questions and activities below to help you explore Kennedy's persuasive techniques.

❶ The **ethical appeal** is a persuasive technique in which the speaker appeals to the audience's sense of right, justice, and virtue. For example, Kennedy says:

> "We can move in that direction as a country, in great polarization—black people amongst black, white people amongst white, filled with hatred . . . Or we can make an effort . . . to understand and to comprehend, and to replace that violence, that stain of bloodshed . . . with an effort to understand with compassion and love."

Kennedy is appealing to the audience's sense of ethics in order to persuade them to his point of view. What does Kennedy say in the next paragraph that may reveal how he identifies with the situation?

1 that violence, that stain of bloodshed that has spread across our land, with an effort to understand with compassion and love.

For those of you who are black and are tempted to be filled with hatred and distrust at the injustice of such an act, against all white people, I can only say that I feel in my own heart the same kind of feeling. I had a member of my family killed, but he was killed by a white man. But we have to make an effort in the United States, we have to make an effort to understand, to go beyond these rather difficult times.

My favorite poet was Aeschylus. He wrote, "In our sleep, pain which cannot forget falls drop by drop upon the heart until, in our own despair, against our will, comes wisdom through the awful grace of God."

2 What we need in the United States is not division; what we need in the United States is not hatred; what we need in the United States is not violence or lawlessness but love and wisdom, and compassion toward one another, and a feeling of justice towards those who still suffer within our country, whether they be white or they be black.

So I shall ask you tonight to return home, to say a prayer for the family of Martin Luther King, that's true, but more importantly to say a prayer for our own country, which all of us love—a prayer for understanding and that compassion of which I spoke.

3 We can do well in this country. We will have difficult times. We've had difficult times in the past. We will have difficult times in the future. It is not the end of violence; it is not the end of lawlessness; it is not the end of disorder.

But the vast majority of white people and the vast majority of black people in this country want to live together, want to improve the quality of our life, and want justice for all human beings who abide in our land.

Let us dedicate ourselves to what the Greeks wrote so many years ago: to tame the savageness of man and to make gentle the life of this world.

Let us dedicate ourselves to that, and say a prayer for our country and for our people.

2 **Repetition** of words or phrases is a rhetorical device used to emphasize concepts or ideas. An example is Kennedy's repetition of the phrase "what we need in the United States is not." How effective do you think this device is? Identify at least two additional examples of repetition in the speech.

3 **Parallelism** is a form of repetition in which similar grammatical structures are used to emphasize ideas or concepts. For example, Kennedy's "We can do well in this country. . . We will . . . We've had . . . We will . . ." shows the use of parallelism. Parallel sentence structures also create a rhythm that helps to call attention to the point being made. Find two additional examples of parallelism in the speech, and explain how they emphasized Kennedy's ideas.

Inquiry & Research

Activity Link: "Montgomery Boycott," p. 124

With a partner, go back through Kennedy's speech, and point out passages that you find particularly moving. How do you think Kennedy's audience might have reacted to these passages?

Mini Lesson Inquiry & Research

The Inquiry & Research activity on this page links to the Inquiry & Research section of Choices and Challenges (p. 134) that follows the excerpt from "Montgomery Boycott."

Instruction Have students locate other speeches given by civic, political, or religious leaders and analyze them for the rhetorical devices of ethical appeal, repetition, and parallelism. Their analyses should also consider the characteristics of clearly written text, including patterns of organization, syntax, and word choice. Students may locate appropriate information by using periodicals, book indexes, databases, and the Internet.

Practice Have students identify words or phrases that

- appeal to the reader's sense of right, justice, and virtue (ethical appeal).
- emphasize concepts effectively (repetition).
- use similar grammatical structures to emphasize ideas (parallelism).

Objectives
- write an Opinion Statement
- use a written text as a model for writing
- revise a draft to refine topic sentences
- check for correct pronoun-antecedent agreement

Introducing the Workshop

A Opinion Statement Opinions are a common part of everyday conversation. Ask students to think about two or three opinions that they or their friends have expressed in the last twenty-four hours. When you ask them to consider how they supported their opinions, they will recognize that in conversation they do not always rely on facts and logical reasoning. However, in the editorial pages of a newspaper, convincing opinions are supported with concrete reasons and evidence.

Have students discuss the kinds of topics that writers typically address in editorials. Remind students that in writing an opinion statement they, too, will be able to express an opinion and attempt to persuade readers to agree with their view.

Basics in a Box

B Using the Graphic Like the pillars that support a roof, the strength of reasoning and evidence offered to support an opinion can determine whether the opinion stands.

C Presenting the Rubric To better understand the assignment, students can refer to the Standards for Writing a Successful Opinion Statement. You may wish to discuss with them the complete rubric, which describes several levels of proficiency. Explain that students' opinion statements will be assessed according to these standards.

Use McDougal Littell's ***Language Network,*** Chapter 15, for more instruction on elaborating to support opinions.

To engage students visually, use **Power Presentation** 1, Opinion Statement.

Writing Workshop — Opinion Statement

Expressing your opinion . . .

A

From Reading to Writing The opinions of Kurt Vonnegut and W. P. Kinsella come through clearly in their stories. Mary Oliver expresses her views throughout her poem "The Sun." All writers express their opinions directly or indirectly. Some writers, however, create an **opinion statement,** an essay or article specifically designed to express an opinion or persuade. Opinion pieces often appear in newspapers and magazines.

For Your Portfolio

WRITING PROMPT Write an opinion statement on a topic you feel strongly about.

Purpose: To persuade, to share an opinion

Audience: Readers of your school or local newspaper, your classmates

Basics in a Box

B

Opinion Statement at a Glance

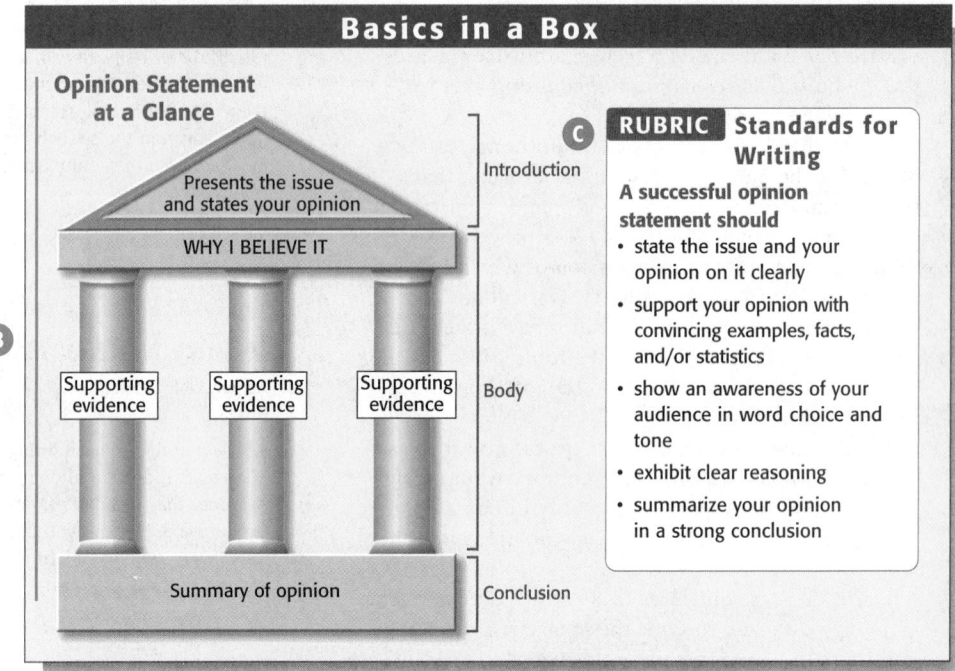

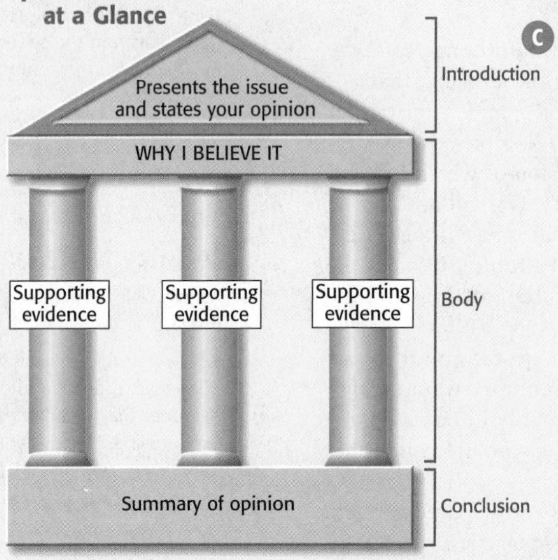

C

RUBRIC Standards for Writing

A successful opinion statement should
- state the issue and your opinion on it clearly
- support your opinion with convincing examples, facts, and/or statistics
- show an awareness of your audience in word choice and tone
- exhibit clear reasoning
- summarize your opinion in a strong conclusion

LESSON RESOURCES

USING PRINT RESOURCES

Unit One Resource Book
- Prewriting, p. 51
- Drafting, p. 52
- Peer Response, pp. 53–54
- Revising, Editing, and Proofreading, p. 55
- Student Models, pp. 56–61
- Rubric, p. 62

Writing Transparencies and Copymasters
- Writing Process Transparencies, pp. 1–4
- Writing Style Transparencies, pp. 12–24
- Writing Template Copymasters, p. 25

USING MEDIA RESOURCES

LaserLinks
Writing Springboards
See Teacher's SourceBook p. 64 for bar codes.

Writing Coach CD-ROM

Visit our website:
www.mcdougallittell.com

Analyzing a Student Model

Aina Calabrese
Southwest High School

Buckle Up!

On a warm June evening nearly a year ago, my 21-year-old neighbor got into his sports car and took off for his girlfriend's house. He never got there. When she saw him later that evening, he was in the intensive care unit of the local hospital, barely clinging to life after a car accident. His doctors say that he has permanent brain damage and probably will never be able to return to work or live on his own. The doctors also say that his injuries would have been much less severe if he had been wearing a safety belt.

Our state is not one of those that have a law requiring motorists to wear safety belts. I strongly believe that the state legislature should pass such a law as soon as possible. I also believe that people should make it their personal rule to buckle up as soon as they get into a car.

Statistics show that fewer than 20 percent of American motorists use safety belts regularly. If everyone wore a safety belt, as many as 16,000 lives would be saved a year and severe injuries would be greatly reduced. According to the National Highway Traffic Safety Administration (NHTSA), wearing safety belts reduces the likelihood of serious or fatal injuries by 40 to 55 percent. NHTSA surveys also show that more people wear safety belts in areas that have safety-belt laws.

Wearing safety belts would not only save lives and reduce injuries, but it would also save society a great deal of money. Traffic accidents cost approximately $8.5 billion per year. By reducing accidents, the use of safety belts would lower this amount. The medical benefits paid by insurance companies would decrease, resulting in lower vehicle insurance premiums. Companies would also lose less money due to employee absences.

Although no one can argue with these statistics, not everyone agrees with me. Opponents of safety-belt laws say that the laws violate the individual's freedom of choice. They say it is not the role of government to protect people from themselves and the consequences of their actions.

An individual's actions often affect other people as well, however. My neighbor's choice not to wear a safety belt, for example, not only ruined his life, but also devastated his family.

The individual's freedom of choice is not an absolute freedom, though. People do not live in isolation. We are part of an interconnected society

RUBRIC IN ACTION

1. This writer begins with a powerful anecdote illustrating the issue.
   Other Options:
   - State your opinion directly.
   - Ask a question.
2. States her opinion clearly and succinctly
3. Uses facts and statistics to support her opinions
   Other Options:
   - Cite expert opinions.
   - Give examples.
4. Addresses opposing arguments

Teaching the Lesson

Analyzing the Model

"Buckle Up!"

D The student model provides reasons and evidence to support the opinion that a law requiring motorists to wear seat belts is needed.

Have students read the student model. Point out that the writer draws the reader into the essay with an anecdote about a friend.

Students can take turns reading aloud the Rubric in Action. Point out key words and phrases in the student model that correspond to the elements mentioned in the Rubric in Action.

1. Ask students to suggest an alternative opening based on the other options suggested.
   Possible Response: Imagine losing a friend or family member in a traffic accident because he or she wasn't wearing a seat belt.
2. Ask students why stating her opinion after telling the anecdote is effective.
   Possible Response: The writer has captured the reader's attention and interest by telling the anecdote first.
3. Ask students how the use of statistics affects their opinion of the writer.
   Possible Response: By citing statistics that have been researched, the writer enhances her credibility.
4. Ask students why presenting an opposing argument can be effective.
   Possible Response: It shows the writer has carefully considered opposing views and refuted them with sound reasoning and evidence.

Mini Lesson: Viewing and Representing

PICTURING TEXT STRUCTURE

Instruction Reasoning and evidence to support an opinion are important parts of effective persuasive writing. However, the structure of the text—its unity and logical coherence—also contributes to effectiveness. Some writers begin with their strongest evidence while others save the best for last.

Activity Have students analyze the text structure of the student model by creating a graphic organizer. The graphic should indicate how the student writer has organized the essay. Students might first reread the model and make notes to summarize important ideas.

Anecdote illustrating consequences of not wearing safety belts
↓
States opinion that wearing seat belts should be mandatory
↓
Supporting evidence including facts and statistics
↓
States opposing view and refutes it with reasons and examples
↓
Summarizes opinion

5. Point out how thoroughly the writer discusses and develops her reasons. Here, the writer claims that not wearing a seat belt affects not only the individual but "society as a whole." The writer then discusses what those effects to society are, supporting her generalization with specific examples.
6. Have students identify the transition phrases in this paragraph and explain how they work.
   Possible Response: "In addition" shows the continuation of a reason stated previously. "On the other hand" indicates contrast.
7. Have students compare the second paragraph of the model where the writer's opinion is first stated with this last paragraph where the opinion is restated.
   Possible Response: In the beginning, the writer says "I believe," which is a much more tentative expression. In the end, however, the writer states her opinion firmly and clearly, and urges readers to "speak out" and "buckle up."

that will function well only if we all consider other people's needs as well as our own. In deciding to do as we please, we have to think about other individuals' right to do the same. Our lives are not ours to take reckless chances with when our deaths will bring terrible pain to our families and friends. Putting on a safety belt is such a simple thing to do. Using a device that has been proven to save lives does not restrict people's freedom, but just shows their good sense.

An individual's choice not to wear a safety belt can affect not just his or her family and friends, but also society as a whole. I already mentioned increased costs to insurance companies and businesses. Injured motorists who require long-term care can also become a financial burden on society. My neighbor is a good example. His medical costs have been so high that his benefits will soon run out. Since he is unable to take care of himself and his family cannot afford to pay for private nursing care, he will have to go into a state-supported nursing home.

❺ Continues her arguments

In addition to paying these monetary costs, society also loses the productivity and unique contributions of each person who is killed or severely injured in an automobile accident. Society cannot tell people how to develop their individual talents. On the other hand, people have a responsibility to use those talents to make a contribution to society. Throwing away our lives because we don't want to insert a metal buckle into a holder is turning our backs on our social responsibility.

❻ Uses transitions to keep the arguments clear and logical

The evidence showing that safety belts reduce traffic deaths and the severity of injuries could not be clearer. It is also clear that people wear safety belts if there are laws requiring their use. There is no question that the benefits to society from the use of safety belts far outweigh the individual's freedom of choice in this matter. So speak out to support laws requiring the use of safety belts. And until those laws are passed—and afterwards, too—be safe, be responsible, and buckle up.

❼ Ends with a summary and strong statement of opinion

Writing Your Opinion Statement

❶ Prewriting

As you begin to think about your opinion statement, **list** a few issues you have strong feelings about. What are your views about school policies, social problems, sports, or modern art and music? **Recall** the last time you were really pleased by an event or learned about something that made you angry or disappointed. See the **Idea Bank** in the margin for more suggestions. After you select an issue to write about, follow the steps below.

Planning Your Opinion Statement

1. **Think about your opinion on the issue.** What aspects of the issue particularly concern you? How can you best state your opinion about it?
2. **Evaluate why you hold your belief.** What reasons convinced you to form your opinion? What reasons will be convincing to your audience? How can you answer opposing beliefs?
3. **Research the issue.** Where can you find examples, facts, and statistics that support your opinion? Which evidence is strongest?
4. **Consider the tone of your writing.** Do you want to present a serious, scholarly essay? Would you influence your audience more by adopting a humorous or satirical tone?

❷ Drafting

Don't recite other people's opinions. . . . Tell me what you know.
Ralph Waldo Emerson

As you start putting your opinion in writing, just follow your thoughts where they take you. Remember, part of drafting is clarifying and refining your ideas. You can organize and fine-tune your work later in the writing process. As you draft, keep in mind that you eventually will have to **state your opinion** clearly and succinctly and **present examples, facts, and statistics** that support it. You might consider using an especially strong or striking example or fact to introduce your writing.

As you draft your arguments, be sure you have used valid reasoning. Especially watch out for these illogical arguments:

Circular reasoning—simply restating a point without providing evidence *(This is the best plan because it is better than the others.)*

Over-generalization—making a statement that is too broad to prove *(No one would vote for that candidate.)*

For more on faulty reasoning see **Communication Handbook,** pp. 1175–1176.

Ask Your Peer Reader

- How would you restate the issue I'm writing about?
- How would you summarize my opinion?
- What are my most convincing reasons?
- What other facts support my position?
- What information, if any, is unclear or unneeded?

IDEA Bank

1. Your Working Portfolio
Look for ideas in the **Writing Options** you completed earlier in this unit:
- **Warden's Address,** p. 28
- **Tech Paragraph,** p. 111
- **Newspaper Editorial,** p. 122
- **Newspaper Editorial,** p. 134

2. Debugging
With a small group of classmates, talk about issues that bug you.

3. Media Quest
Look through newspapers or weekly newsmagazines for articles or columns on issues that you feel strongly about.

Have a question?

See the **Writing Handbook**
Persuasive Writing, pp. 1161–1162

Guiding Student Writing

Prewriting

Choosing an Issue

If after reading the Idea Bank students are having difficulty choosing an issue, suggest they try the following:
- Think about something that you would like to change in your school or community.
- Read the editorials in several different newspapers, including school publications.
- Examine some aspect of popular culture that you react strongly to, either positively or negatively. Use it as a takeoff point for expressing your opinion.

Planning the Opinion Statement

1. Students might spend a few minutes freewriting about their issue in order to uncover specific aspects of the issue that bother them.
2. Students can work in pairs to analyze each other's reasons. Have students take two positions, one "For" and one "Against" the opinion. Then let students articulate their reasons for each belief.
3. Have students use the library and the Internet to find information to support their opinion. Depending on the issue, some students may wish to conduct their own research as well. Remind students to also seek facts and reasons that support the opposing view so they can refute objections.
4. Suggest that students first state the goal of the writing, then choose a tone that would best accomplish this goal.

Drafting

Suggest that students make a checklist for the components of the opinion statement—facts, statistics, examples, observations, anecdotes, and quotations— and check them off as they are included in their drafts. Remind them to also state opposing arguments and refute them with facts and examples.

If students need help organizing their essay, you might share with them the following guidelines:

I. Statement of opinion
II. Supporting evidence
III. Statement of opposing arguments and evidence to refute them
IV. Conclusion

Revising

REFINING TOPIC SENTENCES

In the example, point out that all of the supporting sentences discuss the monetary savings that would result from using seat belts to reduce injuries. The paragraph is more effective when this point is clearly stated in the topic sentence.

Suggest that students reread their draft one paragraph at a time. On a separate sheet of paper, have them number each paragraph and summarize the paragraph's main idea in fresh language. They can then analyze these new sentences for their effectiveness and work them into the draft to replace or enhance currently existing topic sentences.

Editing and Proofreading

PRONOUN-ANTECEDENT AGREEMENT

Remind students that agreement in *number* means singular pronouns must refer to singular nouns and plural pronouns must refer to plural nouns:

his book; *Emilio's* book
their books; *Emilio's* and *Lisa's* books

Agreement in *gender* means that masculine and feminine pronouns must refer to masculine and feminine antecedents, respectively:

his book; *Emilio's* book;
her book; *Lisa's* book

Notice in the preceding examples that the pronouns and antecedents have another form of agreement. They are all in the third person.

In the example paragraph in the text, point out that the plural pronoun *their* refers to the plural noun *people.* The first person pronoun *our* refers to the first person pronoun *we.*

Students should check pronoun-antecedent agreement as a part of providing an error-free final draft.

Reflecting

Have students write a brief note addressing what they learned in the process of writing an opinion statement. Students can clip these evaluations to their opinion statement and place both in their working portfolios.

Need revising help?

Review the **Rubric,** p. 138

Consider **peer reader** comments

Check **Revision Guidelines,** p. 1145

❸ Revising

TARGET SKILL ▶ REFINING TOPIC SENTENCES Your opinions will be most convincing to readers if your writing is well organized. One way to stay on track is to make sure each paragraph includes a good topic sentence and that all the details in the paragraph relate to its topic sentence.

> Wearing safety belts would *[not only]* save lives and reduce injuries*[, but it would also save society a great deal of money.]* Traffic accidents cost approximately $8.5 billion per year. By reducing accidents, the use of safety belts would lower this amount. The medical benefits paid by insurance companies would decrease, resulting in lower vehicle insurance premiums. Companies would also lose less money *[due to employee absences]*.

Perplexed by pronouns?

See the **Grammar Handbook,** pp. 1183–1184

Publishing IDEAS

- Invite students to hear you read your opinion statement. Perhaps put up an announcement with the time and place on the school bulletin board. Ask for discussion about the issue.
- Send your opinion statement to a newspaper as a letter to the editor.

More Online: Publishing Options
www.mcdougallittell.com

❹ Editing and Proofreading

TARGET SKILL ▶ PRONOUN-ANTECEDENT AGREEMENT When you focus on stating your opinion and supporting it clearly, you might overlook issues such as making pronouns and their antecedents agree. Errors in pronoun agreement baffle readers and weaken your arguments, though. Make sure that pronouns agree with their antecedents in number, gender, and person.

> Society cannot tell people how to develop ~~its~~ *[their]* individual talents. On the other hand*[,]* people have a responsibility to use those talents to make a contr*[i]*bution to society. Throwing away our lives because we don't want to insert a metal buckle into a holder is like turning ~~their~~ *[our]* backs on our social responsibility.

❺ Reflecting

FOR YOUR WORKING PORTFOLIO What did you learn about the issue you wrote about? How did your opinion on it change or become stronger? Save your opinion statement in your **Working Portfolio.**

Assessment Practice Revising & Editing

Read this paragraph from the first draft of an opinion statement. The underlined sections may include the following kinds of errors:

- **double negatives**
- **incorrect possessive forms**
- **lack of pronoun-antecedent agreement**
- **sentence fragments**

For each underlined section, choose the revision that most improves the writing.

What does one get when you buy an organic tomato? (1) Was it grown using chemical fertilizers? Was the tomatos' DNA (2) genetically altered to make it less perishable? Under current consumer laws. You can't find out the answers to these questions for sure. (3) Yet people have the right to know what's in their food. (4) The organic food industry doesn't seem to agree. Since it doesn't regulate labeling. (5) Government guidelines for the organic food industry are a good idea. Without them, consumers cannot hardly know (6) what they are getting when they buy "organic" food.

1. **A.** What does one get when they buy an organic tomato?
   B. What does one get when we buy an organic tomato?
   C. What do you get when you buy an organic tomato?
   D. Correct as is
2. **A.** tomato's DNA
   B. tomatos's DNA
   C. tomatos dna
   D. Correct as is
3. **A.** Under current consumer laws; you can't find out the answers to these questions for sure.
   B. Under current consumer laws, you can't find out the answers to these questions for sure.
   C. You can't find out the answers to these questions for sure. Especially under current consumer laws.
   D. Correct as is
4. **A.** your food
   B. our food
   C. his or her food
   D. Correct as is
5. **A.** The organic food industry doesn't seem to agree: since it doesn't regulate labeling.
   B. The organic food industry doesn't seem to agree, since it doesn't regulate labeling.
   C. Since it doesn't regulate labeling. The organic food industry doesn't seem to agree.
   D. Correct as is
6. **A.** cannot hardly know
   B. can't not know
   C. cannot know
   D. Correct as is

Need extra help?

See the **Grammar Handbook**
Possessive Nouns, p. 1182
Pronoun Agreement, p. 1183
Correcting Sentence Fragments, p. 1199

Assessment Practice

Briefly review with students the kinds of errors that the passage may contain. Encourage students to read the entire passage before they correct the errors.

Answers:
1. C; **2.** A; **3.** B; **4.** D; **5.** B; **6.** C

WRITING WORKSHOP 143

PART 2 Cultural Crossroads

The phrase *cultural crossroads* has two distinct meanings. On the one hand, it can refer to an intersection of two or more cultures—an intersection that may produce mutual enrichment, conflict, or misunderstanding. On the other hand, it can refer to a critical turning point within a single culture. For example, a traditional society may reach a crossroads when it seeks to adopt modern ways of living. As you read this part of Unit One, consider which meaning best applies to each selection.

ACTIVITY

Working with a partner, find two or three news stories dealing with cultural crossroads. For example, a newspaper might have a report about a conflict between two cultural groups, or a newscast might feature a story about a culture in the process of change. Discuss your findings with your classmates.

144

Theme is the central idea in a work of literature. It is a perception about life or human nature that the writer shares with the reader. You've probably heard fables that spelled out the theme as the moral of the story. For instance, "Slow and steady wins the race" is the moral of "The Tortoise and the Hare." In all other forms of fiction, the theme is not so directly stated; you have to infer it from **character, plot,** and **setting.**

Theme should not be confused with the subject of a story. Rather, theme is an insight or idea about the subject. For example, the subject of "Searching for Summer" (page 30) is a future world without sunshine. The story dramatizes what the writer Joan Aiken imagines such a society might be like. It is up to the reader to infer the theme, a statement about what this lack of sunshine means for human beings. Here are some ways to look for clues to the theme.

Theme Expressed Through Setting

By giving details about time and place, the setting of a story can provide important clues to the theme. For example, descriptions of setting in "Searching for Summer" show the negative effects of a lack of sunshine: "Whitish gray, day after day, sometimes darkening to a weeping slate color." Into this gloom come the contrasting yellow of Lily's wedding dress and the newlyweds' hope of finding a sunny place to honeymoon. Tom and Lily's journey takes them and the reader deeper into the setting.

YOUR TURN In the passage at the right, what are the effects of the cloud cover on the landscape and the people?

SETTING CLUES

Every place Tom and Lily passed through seemed nastier than the last, partly on account of the dismal light, partly because people had given up bothering to take pride in their boroughs. And then, just as they were entering a village called Molesworth, the dimmest, drabbest, most insignificant huddle of houses they had come to yet, the car engine coughed and died.

—Joan Aiken, "Searching for Summer"

Theme Expressed Through Character

The characters in "Searching for Summer" are carefully crafted to represent aspects of the theme. At one extreme is the repulsive Mr. Noakes, who wants to make money off the sunshine. At the other extreme are kindly Mrs. Hatching and her blind son, William, who have the blue sky and the sun. In between are Lily and Tom, whose hope and persistence get rewarded, not Mr. Noakes's greed. It is their act of protecting the Hatching cottage that points toward the theme.

YOUR TURN Read the passage at the right. Why is it important to Tom and Lily that the cottage remain undisturbed?

CHARACTER CLUES

"But hullo, hullo, what's this? Brown, eh? Suntan? Scrumptious," [Mr. Noakes] said . . . "Where'd you get it, eh? That wasn't all got in half an hour, I know. Come on, this means money to you and me; tell us the big secret . . ."

Tom and Lily looked at each other in horror. They thought of the cottage, the bees humming among the runner beans, the sunlight glinting in the red-and-gold teacups. At night . . . stars had shone through the window, and the whole wood was quiet as the inside of a shell.

—Joan Aiken, "Searching for Summer"

LEARNING the Language of LITERATURE

OVERVIEW

Objectives

- understand the relevance of theme expressed through:
  - setting
  - character
  - plot
- identify thesis or theme in nonfiction

Teaching the Lesson

This lesson analyzes theme in fiction and nonfiction and shows how setting, character, and plot influence theme.

Introducing the Concepts

Have students recall stories and essays they have read so far and discuss the themes. Ask students to say what made the themes memorable.

Presenting the Concepts

Theme Expressed Through Setting

Discuss with students how a setting may imply an idea within a story. Ask them to suggest locales (examples: New York City, an alley at night, the attic of an old house) which, by themselves, communicate ideas.

YOUR TURN Remind students to analyze the relevance of the setting to the meaning of the passage. The cloud cover causes people to lose pride in where they live and causes the landscape to look dreary.

Theme Expressed Through Character

Alert students to the fact that characters' names often suggest their personalities and, hence, may say something about ideas the author intends them to represent.

YOUR TURN It is important that the cottage remain undisturbed because it represents beauty and life to Tom and Lily.

Theme Expressed Through Plot

Remind students that plot is the unfolding of events in a story and that a plot revolves around conflicts in a story. A writer will often provide hints at a theme in how the characters resolve their conflicts.

YOUR TURN Possible Response: It is better to protect a treasure for future generations than to make an immediate profit.

Theme in Nonfiction

Discuss with students works of nonfiction in which a thesis is implied rather than stated. What kinds of clues suggest the implied thesis of a particular work?

YOUR TURN Possible Response: Asimov's theme is supported by specific examples, such as the lack of reference for "clockwise" if all clocks are digital.

Theme Expressed Through Plot

Since the characters' actions drive the plot, the decisions that they make, including the outcomes of those decisions, often express a theme, or insight about life. Tom and Lily's lie to Mr. Noakes about where they've been is intended to keep the cottage a secret. Their decision suggests that places where the sun shines are natural treasures that need to be protected from humans, not exploited for profit. Only a few people, like Tom and Lily and the Hatchings, can be trusted, since humans had caused the problem in the first place. The story ends very much as it begins, with a reference to future generations.

PLOT CLUES

At least, [Tom] thought, they had left the golden place undisturbed. Mr. Noakes never went into the wood. And they had done what they intended; they had found the sun. Now they, too, would be able to tell their grandchildren, when beginning a story, "Long, long ago, when we were young, in the days when the sky was blue . . . "

—Joan Aiken, "Searching for Summer"

YOUR TURN Add together what you know about the setting (the effects of the lack of sun), character (how Tom and Lily choose to act), and plot (the unfolding of events). Then, write a sentence stating your interpretation of the story's theme. Try stating the theme as a moral to the story or a warning for the future.

Theme in Nonfiction

In narrative forms of nonfiction, such as autobiography and biography, theme is very similar to what it is in fiction, a perception about life that must be inferred from the events and the development of a person's life. In nonnarrative forms of nonfiction, such as news reports, articles, and essays, the theme is the main idea or opinion that a writer wants a reader to understand.

The theme of an essay is often called a **thesis** and is more directly stated than the theme of a story. For example, in his essay "Dial Versus Digital" (page 107), Isaac Asimov states his theme in the third paragraph: "And yet there will be a loss in the conversion of dial to digital, and few people seem to be worrying about it." Asimov sees a problem, and he wants people to be worried about it. The rest of his essay consists of alarming examples to prove his thesis, or theme.

NONFICTION CLUES

When something turns, it can turn in just one of two ways, either clockwise or counterclockwise, and we all know which is which. . . . But if dial clocks disappear, so will the meaning of those words for anyone who never has stared at anything but digitals. There are no good substitutes for *clockwise* or *counterclockwise.*

—Isaac Asimov, "Dial Versus Digital"

YOUR TURN How does the example in the passage at the right support Asimov's theme? Discuss your response with a classmate.

Whether you read about real or imaginary people and events, recognizing themes can give you valuable insights into human nature. Use the strategies here to help you draw conclusions about themes in the works you read.

Drawing Conclusions

When you draw a conclusion, you combine text information with prior knowledge. After you have looked at all the events and details in a selection, you're ready to make a logical conclusion about the meaning of these details—just like a judge weighing evidence. Use the following strategies to help you draw conclusions about the theme of a selection.

1 Strategies for Drawing Conclusions about Theme

- Use a graphic like the one below to gather clues about setting, character, and plot that hint at a deeper meaning.

Setting	Effects of no sunshine: drab, gray landscape
Character	Tom and Lily learn how precious the sun is.
Plot	They decide to protect the cottage from Mr. Noakes.
Theme	

- **Connect** the experiences discussed in the piece of writing to your own experiences.
- Most themes in literature are implied. **Draw conclusions** from the details to make general statements about characters, events, and setting.

2 Using Setting to Determine Theme

- Think about why the writer chose a particular setting. Ask yourself if the same events could have happened elsewhere or at another time.
- **Draw conclusions** about how the setting affects the characters, the plot, or the overall atmosphere of the story.

3 Using Character to Determine Theme

- Pay close attention to the characters, roles, actions, and motives.
- Determine what ideas about life or human nature a character's personality and values reveal.
- Apply your own **generalizations** about human nature as you read.

4 Using Plot to Determine Theme

- Identify the **conflict.** A writer's choice of conflict and the way the conflict is resolved may be clues to a theme.
- **Draw conclusions** from a character's actions, the results of these actions, and the things a character learns from the actions.

5 Strategies for Recognizing Theme in Nonfiction

- In autobiographies and other forms of narrative nonfiction, look at important events and **draw conclusions** about a person's values.
- In news reports, articles, and essays, look for a strong statement at the beginning or the end that expresses the main idea or thesis.

Need More Help?

Remember that active readers use the essential reading strategies explained on page 7: **visualize, predict, clarify, question, connect, evaluate, monitor.**

OVERVIEW

Objectives

- draw conclusions about theme
- organize information into different forms, such as charts, for determining theme

Teaching the Lesson

Drawing Conclusions

The strategies on this page will help students learn and apply the skill of drawing conclusions about theme in fiction and nonfiction.

Presenting the Strategies

Make sure students understand how to draw a conclusion by using an example from their everyday life or by giving them a hypothetical set of facts they can use to draw a conclusion.

1 Strategies for Drawing Conclusions About Theme

Have students complete the graphic by drawing a conclusion about Theme from the information provided concerning Setting, Character, and Plot.

Possible Response: Life without sunshine is symbolic death.

2 Using Setting to Determine Theme

Encourage students to use their instinctive response to a setting as a basis for making a judgment. For example, if a setting is dismal and dark, students' instinctive response will probably not be cheerful. Such a response is a good indicator of the feeling the writer intended in choosing details of setting.

3 Using Character to Determine Theme

Ask students to respond to a character as if he or she were someone they just met. What kind of an impression does the character create? What details or actions contribute to that impression? What conclusions can be drawn from the impression?

4 Using Plot to Determine Theme

Be sure that students understand that plot is not the same thing as theme. Readers should think about the type of conflict the writer chooses and how the characters approach the conflict.

5 Strategies for Recognizing Theme in Nonfiction

Point out that a person's values can be indicated by what a person desires, what a person is committed to achieving, and what a person is willing to sacrifice.

OVERVIEW

Objectives
1. understand and appreciate a **short story (Literary Analysis)**
2. analyze characters to understand the **theme (Literary Analysis)**
3. draw **conclusions** about characters **(Active Reading)**

Summary
The Farquars are a white family in Southern Rhodesia whose only child, Teddy, is a special favorite of their African cook, Gideon. Gideon watches sadly as the boy becomes like a white man who expects black people, including Gideon, to obey him. One day, when a snake spits venom into Teddy's eyes, Gideon runs into the bush and comes back with a root to save the boy's eyesight. When an interested scientist inquires after the root, the Farquars ask Gideon for samples of the root, citing the benefit to others of a new medicine. Gideon feels betrayed and refuses to cooperate, leading the others on a long hike—a wild goose chase—to "discover" common blue flowers. After a time, the Farquars and Gideon seem to reconcile, but a rift remains between the African cook and his employers.

Thematic Link
A man reaches a **crossroads** between two cultures and must decide between his loyalty to his African heritage and his employer.

5-Minute Warm-Up

Daily Language SkillBuilder

Have students **proofread** the display sentences on page 15j and write them correctly. The sentences also appear on Transparency 5 of **Grammar Transparencies and Copymasters.**

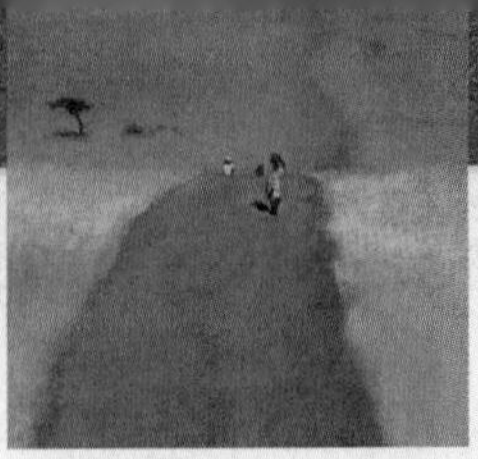

PREPARING to *Read*

No Witchcraft for Sale

Short Story by DORIS LESSING

"No one can live in Africa . . . without learning very soon that there is an ancient wisdom of leaf and soil and season."

Connect to Your Life

Clash of Cultures Think of an incident in which people from different cultures or races have misjudged or misunderstood one another. Perhaps you have personally experienced such a misunderstanding, or perhaps you have read about one. In a small group, describe the incident, offering your explanation of what happened.

Build Background

Colonial Africa Africa has long been a setting for misunderstanding and confrontation between cultures and races. In the 1800s and early 1900s, most African countries became colonies of European powers. Although many of the African countries had been strong kingdoms with well-developed economies and cultures, they came to be dominated politically, economically, and culturally by their European rulers.

In the 1890s, the region that would become Southern Rhodesia (and eventually Zimbabwe) fell under British control. A land of great beauty and mineral wealth, Southern Rhodesia had a large population of British settlers that for decades dominated the country, both as a British colony and, after 1965, as an independent nation. Following a sometimes violent struggle, the black majority gained control of the country—in 1980 renaming it Zimbabwe, after the ancient African capital city of the region. "No Witchcraft for Sale" takes place in Southern Rhodesia during the time of white rule.

WORDS TO KNOW
Vocabulary Preview
anecdote
annul
distasteful
efficacy
indifferently

VIDEODISC **LaserLinks:**
Background for Reading
Geographical Connection

Focus Your Reading

LITERARY ANALYSIS **THEME AND CHARACTER** A **theme** is an important idea or message conveyed by a work of fiction. One way to discover the theme is to study the **characters** in the story. By examining conflicts between characters and the changes that main characters undergo, you can often detect a central idea. As you read this story, look for details about the characters and their relationships that will help you to understand Lessing's message.

ACTIVE READING **DRAWING CONCLUSIONS** To **draw conclusions,** you need to put together various pieces of information—from your reading and what you already know—to make logical statements. To draw a conclusion about a **character,** for example, you put together evidence about what that character says or does. In this story, Gideon, an African, is a servant to the Farquars, white colonists in Southern Rhodesia. Consider what the passage below reveals about Gideon's view of his world.

> ***Gideon, who was watching, shook his head wonderingly, and said: "Ah, missus, these are both children, and one will grow up to be a baas [master], and one will be a servant."***

READER'S NOTEBOOK As you read, keep track of how Gideon and Mrs. Farquar interact. In a chart similar to the one below, note what each character does or says.

Character	Action	Speech
Gideon		
Mrs. Farquar		

LESSON RESOURCES

UNIT ONE RESOURCE BOOK, pp. 63–68

ASSESSMENT RESOURCES
Formal Assessment, pp. 27–28
Teacher's Guide to Assessment and Portfolio Use
Test Generator

SKILLS TRANSPARENCIES AND COPYMASTERS
Literary Analysis
- Theme: Influences of Character, Setting, and Plot, T5 (for Paired Activity, p. 156)

Reading and Critical Thinking
- Organizational Chart: Horizontal, T51 (for Reader's Notebook, p. 148)

Grammar
- Action and Linking Verbs, C68 (for Mini Lesson, p. 154)

Vocabulary
- Prefixes, C31 (for Mini Lesson, p. 149)

Writing
- Organizing Your Writing, T11 (for Activities & Explorations 3, p. 157)
- Levels of Language, T12 (for Writing Option 2, p. 157)

Communications
- Dramatic Reading, T12 (for Activities & Explorations 1, p. 157)
- Verbal Strategies, T14 (for Activities & Explorations 1, p. 157)

INTEGRATED TECHNOLOGY
LaserLinks
- Geographical Connection: Zimbabwe
- Health Connection: Medicinal Plants

See **Teacher's SourceBook,** pp. 13–14.
Internet: Research Starter
Visit our website:
www.mcdougallittell.com

Conjur Woman (1975), Romare Bearden. Collage on board, 46″ × 36″, private collection, courtesy of Sheldon Ross Gallery, Birmingham, Michigan. Copyright © Romare Bearden Foundation/Licensed by VAGA, New York.

No Witchcraft for Sale

Doris Lessing

149

TEACHING THE LITERATURE

Customizing Instruction

Less Proficient Readers

Set a Purpose As students make their way through the story, they might find it helpful to read key paragraphs aloud and make observations about the relationships between key characters such as Gideon and Teddy or Gideon and Mrs. Farquar.

Students Acquiring English

Ask students what they think the word *witchcraft* means. Explain that in the context of this story, it does not have to do with supernatural ceremonies, but rather with the secret knowledge of the medicinal uses of herbs.

Use **Spanish Study Guide** for additional support, pp. 31–33.

Gifted and Talented

Have interested students examine and discuss the role of religion in the relationship between Gideon and the Farquars.

Mini Lesson Preteaching Vocabulary

USING PREFIXES Call students' attention to the list of WORDS TO KNOW. Remind them that sometimes they can understand the meaning of an unfamiliar word by examining its prefix. Use the model sentence to demonstrate the strategy of applying prefixes to determine word meanings.

Model Sentence

Because Cynthia didn't like country music, she found the idea of going to a square dance *distasteful*.

Instruction

- Write the model sentence on the chalkboard.
- Ask a volunteer to summarize the meaning of the sentence.
- Have students use the meaning of the prefix to infer meanings for the word *distasteful*.
- Ask a volunteer to use the word *distasteful* in a sentence.

Use **Unit One Resource Book,** p. 66 for more practice.

A lesson on affixes appears on page 856 in the Pupil's Edition.

Reading and Analyzing

Reading Skills and Strategies: PREVIEW

Have students look through the story. Discuss the image on the opening page as well as the title. If necessary, discuss the background material on colonial Africa. Ask how the images and the title suggest a clash of cultures. As they begin to read, have students look for the source of this clash.

Active Reading

DRAWING CONCLUSIONS

As students read the story, have them use information that they read to draw conclusions about the characters of Teddy, Mrs. Farquar, and Gideon. Have them try to fill in the table on p. 148 with at least one piece of information from each page for each character.

Use **Unit One Resource Book,** p. 64 for more practice.

Literary Analysis

THEME AND CHARACTER

In fiction, writers often reveal their own ideas about the way the world works and the ways that people interact within that world. These ideas can be understood as the theme of a short story or novel. A writer often expresses these ideas through his or her characters.

As they read, ask students to think about the theme of the story.

Use **Unit One Resource Book,** p. 65 for more practice.

ACTIVE READING

A EVALUATE Teddy does not show much respect for Gideon.

The Farquars had been childless for years when little Teddy was born; and they were touched by the pleasure of their servants, who brought presents of fowls and eggs and flowers to the homestead when they came to rejoice over the baby, exclaiming with delight over his downy golden head and his blue eyes. They congratulated Mrs. Farquar as if she had achieved a very great thing, and she felt that she had—her smile for the lingering, admiring natives was warm and grateful.

Later, when Teddy had his first haircut, Gideon the cook picked up the soft gold tufts from the ground and held them reverently in his hand. Then he smiled at the little boy and said: "Little Yellow Head." That became the native name for the child. Gideon and Teddy were great friends from the first. When Gideon had finished his work, he would lift Teddy on his shoulders to the shade of a big tree, and play with him there, forming curious little toys from twigs and leaves and grass, or shaping animals from wetted soil. When Teddy learned to walk, it was often Gideon who crouched before him, clucking encouragement, finally catching him when he fell, tossing him up in the air till they both became breathless with laughter. Mrs. Farquar was fond of the old cook because of his love for her child.

There was no second baby; and one day Gideon said: "Ah, missus, missus, the Lord above sent this one; Little Yellow Head is the most good thing we have in our house." Because of that "we" Mrs. Farquar felt a warm impulse towards her cook; and at the end of the month she raised his wages. He had been with her now for several years; he was one of the few natives who had his wife and children in the compound and never wanted to go home to his kraal,[1] which was some hundreds of miles away. Sometimes a small piccanin[2] who had been born the same time as Teddy, could be seen peering from the edge of the bush, staring in awe at the little white boy with his miraculous fair hair and Northern blue eyes. The two little children would gaze at each other with a wide, interested gaze, and once Teddy put out his hand curiously to touch the black child's cheeks and hair.

Gideon, who was watching, shook his head wonderingly, and said: "Ah, missus, these are both children, and one will grow up to be a baas,[3] and one will be a servant"; and Mrs. Farquar smiled and said sadly, "Yes, Gideon, I was thinking the same." She sighed. "It is God's will," said Gideon, who was a mission boy.[4]

"Gideon, look at me!" And Gideon would laugh and say: "Very clever, Little Yellow Head."

The Farquars were very religious people; and this shared feeling about God bound servant and masters even closer together.

Teddy was about six years old when he was given a scooter, and discovered the intoxications of speed. All day he would fly around the homestead, in and out of flowerbeds, scattering squawking chickens and irritated dogs, finishing with a wide dizzying arc into the kitchen door. There he would cry: "Gideon, look at me!" And Gideon would laugh and say: "Very clever, Little Yellow Head." Gideon's youngest son, who was now a herdsboy, came especially up from the compound to see the scooter. He was afraid to come near it, but Teddy showed off in

1. **kraal** (krôl): a native village in southern Africa.
2. **piccanin** (pĭk′ə-nĭn′): a native child (the term *piccanin* is usually considered offensive).
3. **baas:** boss.
4. **mission boy:** a boy educated at a school run by Christian missionaries.

Teaching Options

BLOCK SCHEDULING: MANAGING TIME

If your schedule requires that you cover the lesson objectives in a shorter time, use . . .
- Preparing to Read, p. 148
- Thinking Through the Literature, p. 156
- Vocabulary in Action, p. 157
- Grammar in Context, p. 158

If you want to take advantage of longer class time, use . . .
- TE Teaching Options: Preteaching Vocabulary, p. 149; Viewing and Representing, p. 151; Multicultural Link, p. 152; Standardized Test Practice, p. 155; Inquiry & Research, p. 157
- Choices & Challenges and Author Activity, pp. 157–158

front of him. "Piccanin," shouted Teddy, "get out of my way!" And he raced in circles around the black child until he was frightened and fled back to the bush.

"Why did you frighten him?" asked Gideon, gravely reproachful.

Teddy said defiantly: "He's only a black boy," and laughed.

Then, when Gideon turned away from him without speaking, his face fell. Very soon he slipped into the house and found an orange and brought it to Gideon, saying: "This is for you." He could not bring himself to say he was sorry; but he could not bear to lose Gideon's affection either. Gideon took the orange unwillingly and sighed. "Soon you will be going away to school, Little Yellow Head," he said wonderingly, "and then you will be grown up." He shook his head gently and said, "And that is how our lives go." He seemed to be putting a distance between himself and Teddy, not because of resentment, but in the way a person accepts something inevitable. The baby had lain in his arms and smiled up into his face: the tiny boy had swung from his shoulders and played with him by the hour. Now Gideon would not let his flesh touch the flesh of the white child. He was kind, but there was a grave formality in his voice that made Teddy pout and sulk away. Also, it made him into a man: with Gideon he was polite, and carried himself formally, and if he came into the kitchen to ask for something, it was in the way a white man uses towards a servant, expecting to be obeyed.

ACTIVE READING

EVALUATE How does Teddy view Gideon? **A**

But on the day that Teddy came staggering into the kitchen with his fists to his eyes, shrieking with pain, Gideon dropped the pot full of hot soup that he was holding, rushed to the child, and forced aside his fingers. "A snake!" he exclaimed. Teddy had been on his scooter and had come to a rest with his foot on the side of a big tub of plants. A tree snake, hanging by its tail from the roof, had spat full into his eyes. Mrs. Farquar came running when she heard the commotion. "He'll go blind," she sobbed, holding Teddy close against her. "Gideon, he'll go blind!" Already the eyes, with perhaps half an hour's sight left in them, were swollen up to the size of fists: Teddy's small white face was distorted by great purple oozing protuberances.[5] Gideon said: "Wait a minute, missus, I'll get some medicine." He ran off into the bush.

Mrs. Farquar lifted the child into the house and bathed his eyes with permanganate.[6] She had scarcely heard Gideon's words; but when she saw that her remedies had no effect at all, and remembered how she had seen natives with no sight in their eyes because of the spitting of a snake, she began to look for the return of her cook, remembering what she heard of the efficacy of native herbs. She stood by the window, holding the terrified, sobbing little boy in her arms, and peered helplessly into the bush. It was not more than a few minutes before she saw Gideon come bounding back, and in his hand he held a plant.

"Do not be afraid, missus," said Gideon, "this will cure Little Yellow Head's eyes." He stripped the leaves from the plant, leaving a small white fleshy root. Without even washing it, he put the root in his mouth, chewed it vigorously, and then held the spittle there while he took the child forcibly from Mrs. Farquar.

5. **protuberances** (prō-to͞o′bər-ən-səz): bulges or swellings.

6. **permanganate** (pər-măng′gə-nāt′): a solution of the chemical potassium permanganate, formerly used as an antidote to snake poison.

WORDS TO KNOW

efficacy (ĕf′ĭ-kə-sē) *n.* the power to produce a desired effect; effectiveness

Customizing Instruction

Less Proficient Readers

Use the following questions to help students understand the conflict between Gideon and Teddy.

- What does Teddy say that makes Gideon turn away?

  Possible Response: He says that the boy he frightened was "only a black boy."
- What kind of apology does Teddy make to Gideon? Is it a full apology?

  Possible Response: He brings Gideon an orange; he does not say he is sorry.
- How does Gideon's behavior toward Teddy change as a result of this conflict?

  Possible Response: He becomes formal and distant with Teddy.

Set a Purpose Encourage students to think about how the relationship between Teddy and Gideon continues to change throughout the story.

Students Acquiring English

Explain to students that the idiom "his face fell" is not meant to be taken literally, but means "a disappointed look appeared on his face."

Mini Lesson Viewing and Representing

Conjur Woman **by Romare Bearden,** p. 149

ART APPRECIATION Encourage students to investigate the source of *Conjur Woman,* focusing on the life of the artist. Romare Bearden (1914–1988) grew up in New York City during the Harlem Renaissance. Bearden specialized in collages, which are notable for their striking colors and dramatic juxtapositions of images.

Instruction Ask what images are being juxtaposed in the collage.

Possible Response: There are a variety of details, many of them drawn from the natural world, such as a snake, birds, and tropical plants. There is also a collage of a human face.

Application The images depicted in the collage are of many different styles and do not necessarily go together in an orderly or easy-to-understand fashion. What might be the purpose of this style? How is it relevant to this story?

Possible Response: The confusing way in which these elements are presented might be seen as similar to the practices of a "witch doctor," or herbal healer, which are mysterious and confusing to outsiders.

Reading and Analyzing

Reading Skills and Strategies: PREDICTION

A After they have read the scene in which Gideon saves Teddy's eyesight, have students predict how Gideon's relationship with the Farquars might change. Ask students to provide evidence to support their predictions.
Possible Response: Teddy and his parents might grow to have a deeper respect for Gideon and his abilities.

Literary Analysis: SETTING

Ask students how the emergency caused by the snake reveals the differences between Gideon's and the Farquars' attitudes toward the "bush."
Possible Response: Gideon obviously knows his way in the "bush," and knows how to use natural resources. For the Farquars, the "bush" is more mysterious, perhaps even hostile, because they lack Gideon's knowledge and understanding of it.

The Ukimwi Road (1994), John Harris.

He gripped Teddy down between his knees, and pressed the balls of his thumbs into the swollen eyes, so that the child screamed and Mrs. Farquar cried out in protest: "Gideon, Gideon!" But Gideon took no notice. He knelt over the writhing child, pushing back the puffy lids till chinks of eyeball showed, and then he spat hard, again and again, into first one eye, and then the other. He finally lifted Teddy gently into his mother's arms, and said: "His eyes will get better." But Mrs. Farquar was weeping with **A** terror, and she could hardly thank him: it was impossible to believe that Teddy could keep his sight. In a couple of hours the swellings were gone: the eyes were inflamed and tender but Teddy could see. Mr. and Mrs. Farquar went to Gideon in the kitchen and thanked him over and over again. They felt helpless because of their gratitude: it seemed they could do nothing to express it. They gave Gideon presents for his wife and children, and a big increase in wages, but these things could not pay for Teddy's now completely cured eyes. Mrs. Farquar said: "Gideon, God chose you as an instrument for His goodness," and Gideon said: "Yes, missus, God is very good."

Now, when such a thing happens on a farm, it cannot be long before everyone hears of it. Mr. and Mrs. Farquar told their neighbors and the story was discussed from one end of the district to the other. The bush is full of secrets. No one can live in Africa, or at least on the veld,[7] without learning very soon that there is an ancient wisdom of leaf and soil and season—and, too, perhaps most important of all, of the darker tracts of the human mind—which is the

1

7. **veld** (vĕlt): an open, grass-covered plain of southern Africa.

Teaching Options

Multicultural Link — Health

HERBAL CURES Cultures around the world use herbal medicine in the treatment of illness. Scientists in places such as India, China, Ethiopia, and Uganda have found locally grown plants to have medicinal effects on conditions such as tuberculosis, malaria, cardiovascular disease, and cancer. The growth of alternative, or natural, medicine in industrialized countries has resulted almost entirely from the interests of consumers.

black man's heritage. Up and down the district people were telling anecdotes, reminding each other of things that had happened to them.

"But I saw it myself, I tell you. It was a puff-adder bite. The kaffir's[8] arm was swollen to the elbow, like a great shiny black bladder. He was groggy after a half a minute. He was dying. Then suddenly a kaffir walked out of the bush with his hands full of green stuff. He smeared something on the place, and next day my boy was back at work, and all you could see was two small punctures in the skin."

The scientist explained how humanity might benefit if this new drug could be offered for sale.

This was the kind of tale they told. And, as always, with a certain amount of exasperation, because while all of them knew that in the bush of Africa are waiting valuable drugs locked in bark, in simple-looking leaves, in roots, it was impossible to ever get the truth about them from the natives themselves.

The story eventually reached town; and perhaps it was at a sundowner party, or some such function, that a doctor, who happened to be there, challenged it. "Nonsense," he said. "These things get exaggerated in the telling. We are always checking up on this kind of story, and we draw a blank every time."

Anyway, one morning there arrived a strange car at the homestead, and out stepped one of the workers from the laboratory in town, with cases full of test-tubes and chemicals.

Mr. and Mrs. Farquar were flustered and pleased and flattered. They asked the scientist to lunch, and they told the story all over again, for the hundredth time. Little Teddy was there too, his blue eyes sparkling with health, to prove the truth of it. The scientist explained how humanity might benefit if this new drug could be offered for sale; and the Farquars were even more pleased: they were kind, simple people, who liked to think of something good coming about because of them. But when the scientist began talking of the money that might result, their manner showed discomfort. Their feelings over the miracle (that was how they thought of it) were so strong and deep and religious, that it was distasteful to them to think of money. The scientist, seeing their faces, went back to his first point, which was the advancement of humanity. He was perhaps a trifle perfunctory: it was not the first time he had come salting the tail of[9] a fabulous bush-secret.

Eventually, when the meal was over, the Farquars called Gideon into their living-room and explained to him that this baas, here, was a big Doctor from the Big City, and he had come all that way to see Gideon. At this Gideon seemed afraid; he did not understand; and Mrs. Farquar explained quickly that it was because of the wonderful thing he had done with Teddy's eyes that the Big Baas had come.

Gideon looked from Mrs. Farquar to Mr. Farquar, and then at the little boy, who was showing great importance because of the occasion. At last he said grudgingly: "The Big Baas want to know what medicine I used?" He spoke incredulously, as if he could not believe

8. **kaffir's** (kăf′ərz): belonging to a black African (usually considered offensive).

9. **salting the tail of:** trying to capture (from the childhood belief that birds can be caught by putting salt on their tail).

WORDS TO KNOW
anecdote (ăn′ĭk-dōt′) *n.* a short account of an interesting or humorous incident
distasteful (dĭs-tāst′fəl) *adj.* unpleasant; disagreeable

Customizing Instruction

Less Proficient Readers

1 Have students explain why the Farquars are in Gideon's debt.

Answer: Gideon has saved the eyesight of their child.

Set a Purpose Have students read on to find out how the drug used to heal Teddy causes a conflict between the Farquars and Gideon and how the conflict is resolved.

Gifted and Talented

Ask students to describe the benefits and the drawbacks of using physical evidence as the only yardstick of evaluating truth or reality. Invite students to outline two contrasting viewpoints—one that defends the strict use of physical evidence and excludes unproved native remedies, and one that defends the realm of the mysterious or alternative medicine. You might organize a panel discussion or debate to allow students to present the "case" for each position.

Reading and Analyzing

ACTIVE READING

A DRAW CONCLUSIONS Possible Response: The relationship has been amiable up to now but is not very deeply trusting.

Literary Analysis: CONFLICT

B Remind students that there are two kinds of conflict—internal and external. Ask them what kind of conflict is taking place in this passage.
Possible Response: The conflict is an external conflict between Gideon and the Farquars.

ACTIVE READING

C PREDICT Students will likely predict that, because Gideon is not even trying to find the root, he won't find it.

Reading Skills and Strategies: EVALUATE

D Have students evaluate the relationship between Teddy and Gideon at the end of the story.
Possible Response: They have grown further into their roles of master and servant. However, they have also acquired some distance on the root incident, and can now joke comfortably on the matter. In this respect, they have come to terms with their differences.

ACTIVE READING

DRAW CONCLUSIONS
What can you conclude about the relationship between Gideon and the Farquars? A

his old friends could so betray him. Mr. Farquar began explaining how a useful medicine could be made out of the root, and how it could be put on sale, and how thousands of people, black and white, up and down the continent of Africa, could be saved by the medicine when that spitting snake filled their eyes with poison. Gideon listened, his eyes bent on the ground, the skin of his forehead puckering in discomfort. When Mr. Farquar had finished he did not reply. The scientist, who all this time had been leaning back in a big chair, sipping his coffee and smiling with skeptical good-humor, chipped in and explained all over again, in different words, about the making of drugs and the progress of science. Also, he offered Gideon a present.

B There was silence after this further explanation, and then Gideon remarked indifferently that he could not remember the root. His face was sullen and hostile, even when he looked at the Farquars, whom he usually treated like old friends. They were beginning to feel annoyed; and this feeling annulled the guilt that had been sprung into life by Gideon's accusing manner. They were beginning to feel that he was unreasonable. But it was at that moment that they all realized he would never give in. The magical drug would remain where it was, unknown and useless except for the tiny scattering of Africans who had the knowledge, natives who might be digging a ditch for the municipality in a ragged shirt and a pair of patched shorts, but who were still born to healing, hereditary healers, being the nephews or sons of the old witch doctors whose ugly masks and bits of bone and all the uncouth properties of magic were the outward signs of real power and wisdom.

The Farquars might tread on that plant fifty times a day as they passed from house to garden, from cow kraal[10] to mealie[11] field, but they would never know it.

But they went on persuading and arguing, with all the force of their exasperation; and Gideon continued to say that he could not remember, or that there was no such root, or that it was the wrong season of the year, or that it wasn't the root itself, but the spit from his mouth that had cured Teddy's eyes. He said all these things one after another, and seemed not to care they were contradictory. He was rude and stubborn. The Farquars could hardly recognize their gentle, lovable old servant in this ignorant, perversely obstinate[12] African, standing there in front of them with lowered eyes, his hands twitching his cook's apron, repeating over and over whichever one of the stupid refusals that first entered his head.

But they went on persuading and arguing, with all the force of their exasperation.

And suddenly he appeared to give in. He lifted his head, gave a long, blank angry look at the circle of whites, who seemed to him like a circle of yelping dogs pressing around him, and said: "I will show you the root."

They walked single file away from the homestead down a kaffir path. It was a blazing

10. **cow kraal:** a livestock enclosure or corral.
11. **mealie:** corn.
12. **perversely obstinate:** stubbornly and wrongly insistent on having one's own way.

WORDS TO KNOW
indifferently (ĭn-dĭf′ər-ənt-lē) *adv.* in a way showing no particular interest or concern
annul (ə-nŭl′) *v.* to do away with or make invalid; cancel

154

Teaching Options

Mini Lesson Grammar

ACTIVE VERBS Instruction Discuss with students the advantages of using active versus passive verbs. Active verbs add life and specificity to writing, while passive verbs tend to be dull and vague.
Exercise Have students read each pair of sentences and explain which sentence contains the active verb.

1. The wind blew gritty, thick dust in their faces. *(active)*
   The thick dust was blown in their faces by the wind. *(passive)*
2. The Farquars might tread on that plant fifty times a day. *(active)*
   The plant might be tread on fifty times a day by the Farquars. *(passive)*
3. He picked up a handful of blue flowers from the grass. *(active)*
   A handful of blue flowers were picked up by him. *(passive)*

Use **Grammar Transparencies and Copymasters,** p. 135 for more support.

Use McDougal Littell's ***Language Network,*** Chapter 6, for more instruction in active and passive verbs.

December afternoon, with the sky full of hot rain-clouds. Everything was hot: the sun was like a bronze tray whirling overhead, there was a heat shimmer over the fields, the soil was scorching underfoot, the dusty wind blew gritty and thick and warm in their faces. It was a terrible day, fit only for reclining on a verandah[13] with iced drinks, which is where they would normally have been at that hour.

From time to time, remembering that on the day of the snake it had taken ten minutes to find the root, someone asked: "Is it much further, Gideon?" And Gideon would answer over his shoulder, with angry politeness: "I'm looking for the root, baas." And indeed, he would frequently bend sideways and trail his hand among the grasses with a gesture that was insulting in its perfunctoriness. He walked them through the bush along unknown paths for two hours, in that melting destroying heat, so that the sweat trickled coldly down them and their heads ached. They were all quite silent: the Farquars because they were angry, the scientist because he was being proved right again; there was no such plant. His was a tactful silence.

ACTIVE READING

C **PREDICT** Do you think Gideon will find the root?

At last, six miles from the house, Gideon suddenly decided they had had enough; or perhaps his anger evaporated at that moment. He picked up, without an attempt at looking anything but casual, a handful of blue flowers from the grass, flowers that had been growing plentifully all down the paths they had come.

He handed them to the scientist without looking at him, and marched off by himself on the way home, leaving them to follow him if they chose.

When they got back to the house, the scientist went to the kitchen to thank Gideon: he was very very polite, even though there was an amused look in his eyes. Gideon was not there. Throwing the flowers casually into the back of his car, the eminent visitor departed on his way back to his laboratory.

Gideon was back in his kitchen in time to prepare dinner, but he was sulking. He spoke to Mr. Farquar like an unwilling servant. It was days before they liked each other again.

The Farquars made inquiries about the root from their laborers. Sometimes they were answered with distrustful stares. Sometimes the natives said: "We do not know. We have never heard of the root." One, the cattle boy, who had been with them a long time, and had grown to trust them a little, said: "Ask your boy in the kitchen. Now, there's a doctor for you. He's the son of a famous medicine man who used to be in these parts, and there's nothing he cannot cure." Then he added politely: "Of course, he's not as good as the white man's doctor, we know that, but he's good for us."

After some time, when the soreness had gone from between the Farquars and Gideon, they began to joke: "When are you going to show us the snake-root, Gideon?" And he would laugh and shake his head, saying, a little uncomfortably: "But I did show you, missus, have you forgotten?"

Much later, Teddy, as a schoolboy, would come into the kitchen and say: "You old rascal, Gideon! Do you remember that time you tricked us all by making us walk miles all over the veld for nothing? It was so far my father had to carry me!"

And Gideon would double up with polite laughter. After much laughing, he would suddenly straighten himself up, wipe his old eyes, and look sadly at Teddy, who was grinning mischievously at him across the kitchen: "Ah, Little Yellow Head, how you have grown! Soon you will be grown up with a farm of your own . . ." ❖ D

13. **verandah** (və-răn′də): a long porch.

Customizing Instruction

Less Proficient Readers

Use the following questions to help students understand Gideon's actions.

- Does Gideon give the medicinal root to the Farquars and the scientist?
  Answer: No
- How does Gideon express his refusal to cooperate?
  Answer: He pretends not to understand what the Farquars and the scientist are talking about. He finally leads them on a long trek through the bush, pretending to give them what they want, but giving them something very different.
- Why are the Farquars angry with Gideon?
  Answer: They think he has been uncooperative and stubborn.
- What do the Farquars learn about Gideon from the cattle boy?
  Answer: They learn that Gideon is the son of a famous and respected native healer.

Assessment Standardized Test Practice

CHOOSING THE BEST SUMMARY For some standardized tests, students will be asked to choose the best summary of a passage. To provide students with some help in choosing the best summary, read aloud or write on the chalkboard the following question.

Which of the following statements best describes the conflict between Teddy and Gideon?

A. Teddy wants to be friends with Gideon, so he gives him an orange.

B. After Teddy has offended Gideon, he gives him an orange; however, he is too proud to make a full apology.

C. Gideon is angry with Teddy because Teddy mistreated one of the native African children.

Lead students through the process of choosing the best summary. Consider each choice. Point out that, while all of the statements contain accurate information about the story, the best summary should include the most important information. For that reason, **B** is the best choice.

Connect to the Literature

1. **What Do You Think?** Guidelines for student response: Students should cite specific events or moments in the text. Some will say that the scene where Gideon saves Teddy's vision has strong suspense and a positive outcome.

Comprehension Check

- Teddy is temporarily blinded by snake venom.
- Gideon applies the pulp of a medicinal root to Teddy's eyes.
- Gideon gives the scientist a bundle of common blue flowers, which are not the medicinal herb.

Use Selection Quiz in **Unit One Resource Book,** p. 68.

Think Critically

2. Students may note that although Mrs. Farquar is friendly toward Gideon, she is also ignorant of his background and condescending. They may note that Gideon is very respectful toward Mrs. Farquar, while not being entirely honest.
3. Responses will vary. Students may include the following points:
   - The whites have more power than the blacks, who work for them.
   - The title suggests that some things are too valuable to sell.
   - The plant is effective against snake poison, although there is no scientific explanation as to why.
   - Gideon is motivated by his strong cultural beliefs.
4. Students should give evidence from the text to support their responses.
5. Responses will vary. Students may feel that with greater awareness and sensitivity, the Farquars might have broached the subject of the root differently with Gideon.

Extend Interpretations

What If? Possible response: Gideon would have lost his integrity by trading the wisdom of his people for a price.

Connect to Life Responses will vary; some students will point to historical figures, such as civil rights leaders.

Connect to the Literature

1. **What Do You Think?** Which part of this story evoked the strongest response in you? Describe your reaction to that part of the story and compare it to your classmates' responses.

Comprehension Check

- What happens to Teddy's eyes?
- How is Teddy saved from blindness?
- What does Gideon give the scientist?

Think Critically

2. **ACTIVE READING** **DRAWING CONCLUSIONS** Look at the details about Gideon and Mrs. Farquar that you entered in your READER'S NOTEBOOK. What conclusions can you draw about each **character?** How do those conclusions help you to understand the **conflict** between them?
3. Do you think Gideon was justified in his refusal to share his knowledge of the medicinal plant? Why or why not?

   THINK ABOUT
   - the relationship between the whites and the blacks
   - the **title** of the story
   - the plant's effectiveness against snake poison
   - what you think motivates Gideon's actions
4. The Farquars believe themselves to be people of good will. Do you agree with them? Support your opinion.
5. Do you think the cultural and racial misunderstandings in this story could have been avoided? Use examples from the story to support your opinion.

Extend Interpretations

6. **What If?** Imagine that Gideon had cooperated with the white scientist by revealing his people's secret herbal treatments. How would that have changed your judgment of his **character?**
7. **Connect to Life** In this story, Gideon stands up for his own dignity and the dignity of his culture. Think of other instances you know of in which an individual has taken a stand to protect his or her rights or culture. How successful do you think such actions can be in influencing people's attitudes?

Literary Analysis

THEME AND CHARACTER Writers of fiction use their stories to convey messages and insights about life and human nature. The message, or **theme,** of any story can often be understood by reflecting upon what happens to the central **characters**. For example, in this story, the author examines the reasons for the distrust and misunderstandings between races and cultures by focusing on the interaction between Gideon and Mrs. Farquar. Gideon's transformation from a dutiful servant to a quietly defiant healer helps the reader understand Lessing's message.

Paired Activity With a partner, study the action and speech of Teddy and the scientist. Use two diagrams, each like the one shown, to record significant details and your own conclusions about each character. In what ways do you think these two characters contribute to the cultural clashes in this story? Share your ideas with your classmates. Then expand your discussion to consider how all of Lessing's characters and their interaction help you understand the author's theme.

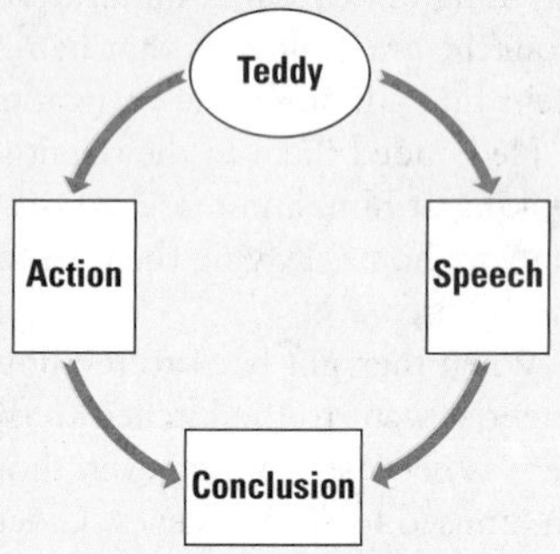

Teaching Options

Mini Lesson Grammar

PARTS OF SPEECH **Instruction** Remind students that there are many different parts of speech: nouns, verbs, adjectives, adverbs, pronouns, prepositions, conjunctions, and interjections. Review with students the function of each part of speech. Then remind them that words should be classified primarily by what function they perform in a sentence, and that many words can be used as more than one part of speech. The word *place*, for example, can be used as a noun (This is the *place*) or a verb (*Place* the glass on the table).

Exercise Have students tell whether the underlined word is a noun or a verb.

1. "They gave Gideon presents for his wife and children . . ." (*noun*)
2. ". . . the next day my boy was back at work. . ." (*noun*)
3. "The scientist explained how society might benefit . . ." (*verb*)

Use **Grammar Transparencies and Copymasters,** p. 62.

Use McDougal Littell's ***Language Network,*** Chapter 1, for more instruction in parts of speech.

Writing Options

1. Letter from the Author Assume the identity of Doris Lessing and write a letter to her publisher in which she explains the story's theme. Also explain which characters reflect values that she supports.

2. Medicine Man Dialogue Write a dialogue between Gideon and his son in which Gideon explains why he did not give the scientist the healing root.

Activities & Explorations

1. Oral Tale Prepare an oral tale that Gideon might tell his neighbors about his "helping" the scientist, and tell it to your classmates. ~ **SPEAKING AND LISTENING**

2. Bar Graph Create a bar graph in which you rate each character's power in society, with the longest bar representing the most powerful character. Then explain your ratings to the class. ~ **VIEWING AND REPRESENTING**

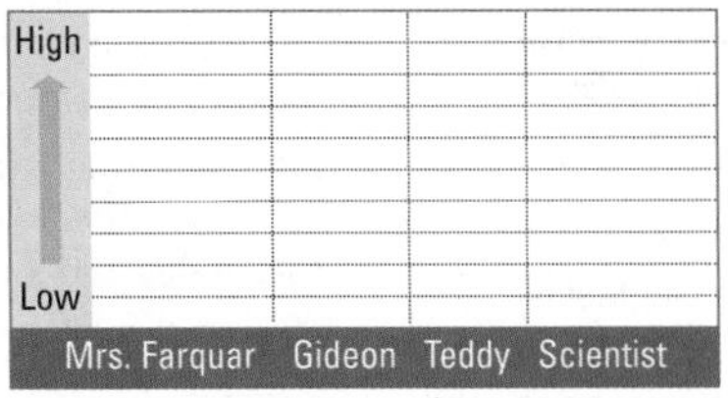

3. Editorial Page In a small group, work to develop a newspaper editorial page focusing on the events in this story. Include an editorial presenting the paper's position on whether Gideon was right to keep his secret. Express other points of view about Gideon's decision in letters to the editor from doctors, snakebite victims, and traditional healers. ~ **JOURNALISM**

Inquiry & Research

Alternative Medicine With a partner, research the medicinal properties of plants native to your part of the country. Present your findings by displaying a sample or picture of each plant along with an explanation of its medicinal use.

More Online: Research Starter
www.mcdougallittell.com

Vocabulary in Action

EXERCISE: MEANING CLUES Answer the following questions.

1. Is a **distasteful** activity one that is popular, one that is difficult, or one that is unappealing?
2. Are you most likely to react **indifferently** to a remark that angers you, that bores you, or that surprises you?
3. Is an **anecdote** a story that is amusing, that is boring, or that is instructional?
4. Would a medicine known for its **efficacy** have a reputation for working well, for being expensive, or for having side effects?
5. In an effort to **annul** the effects of an insulting remark you made, would you repeat it, add to it, or say you were kidding?

Building Vocabulary

Several Words to Know in this lesson contain prefixes and suffixes. For an in-depth lesson on word parts, see page 856.

Mini Lesson Inquiry & Research

COLONIALISM IN SOUTHERN AFRICA This story takes place in Southern Rhodesia, which is now the country of Zimbabwe. Have students research the history of Zimbabwe and its path to statehood. What relationship did the European colonists have with the native Zimbabweans? Interested students can compare Zimbabwe's history with that of other southern African countries such as Namibia, Botswana, and especially South Africa. Encourage students to generate their own relevant, interesting, and researchable questions.

Students should begin their research by looking for appropriate print and nonprint resources including bibliographic databases or the Internet. Have them draw conclusions from the information gathered and present their findings in a written or oral report.

Literary Analysis

Paired Activity Student conclusions will vary. They should include at least two or three examples of the speech and action of each character, and the conclusion should follow logically from the examples.

Writing Options

1. **Letter from the Author** Lessing's letter might discuss the cultural gap between colonial and native cultures in Africa, demonstrated in the relationship between a white family and their black African servant. Gideon is probably the character that Lessing identifies with the most.
2. **Medicine Man Dialogue** Gideon might explain to his son that some wisdom is beyond monetary value and should not be given away to those who may not understand it.

Activities & Explorations

1. **Oral Tale** Students' tales should reflect an understanding of the events of the story and of Gideon's point of view.
2. **Bar Graph** Student responses will vary; students may or may not consider Gideon the least powerful character in the story.
3. **Editorial Page** Encourage students to consider as many points of view as possible (such as doctors, snakebite victims, and traditional healers) before drafting their response. Students should support their positions with evidence and with rational arguments.

Inquiry & Research

Have students begin their research by looking in books on the plant life of your region.

Vocabulary in Action

Exercise: MEANING CLUES

1. unappealing
2. that bores you
3. amusing
4. for working well
5. say you were kidding

Grammar in Context

WRITING EXERCISE

Answers will vary. Possible answers are shown.

1. While learning to walk, Teddy would inevitably fall, but Gideon was there to catch him.
2. One day, Gideon sees Teddy riding his scooter rapidly around Gideon's youngest son.
3. Once Teddy stops his scooter near a tree snake, which spits poison into his eyes.

Author Activity

Another Dimension The title of the futuristic series is *Children of Violence* (1952–1969). In order, the books are *Martha Quest, A Proper Marriage, A Ripple from the Storm, Landlocked,* and *The Four-Gated City.* These books are about a heroine named Martha Quest, who, like Doris Lessing, struggles to come to terms with her identity by confronting the racism of the British class system in Africa. The novels conclude with a narrowly avoided Apocalypse-style ending in the year 2000.

Grammar in Context: Using Adverbs to Clarify Actions

Notice how in "No Witchcraft for Sale" Doris Lessing uses adverbs to provide information about Gideon.

> **At last he said grudgingly: "The Big Baas want to know what medicine I used?"**
>
> **He would frequently bend sideways and trail his hand among the grasses. . . . Gideon suddenly decided they had had enough.**

In these sentences, adverbs reveal important characteristics of Gideon. The reader can feel his emotions, see him in action, and imagine his thoughts. **Usage note**: The placement of an adverb can change the meaning of a sentence. Position it carefully.

WRITING EXERCISE Supply an adverb to clarify the verb in each sentence. Use an adverb of the type named in parentheses.

Example: Gideon _____ lifts Teddy on his shoulders and carries him around the yard. (time)
Gideon often lifts Teddy on his shoulders and carries him around the yard.

1. While learning to walk, Teddy would _____ fall, but Gideon was there to catch him. (manner)
2. One day, Gideon sees Teddy riding his scooter _____ around Gideon's youngest son. (manner)
3. _____ Teddy stops his scooter near a tree snake, which spits poison into his eyes. (time)

Grammar Handbook
Adverbs, p. 1188

LaserLinks: Background for Reading
Health Connection

Doris Lessing

1919–

Other Works
Going Home
African Stories
This Was the Old Chief's Country
The Golden Notebook
Under My Skin
Volume One of My Autobiography, to 1949

A Different Childhood Born to British parents in Persia, Doris Lessing grew up in Southern Rhodesia, where her family went to farm when she was about five. Her childhood was fairly solitary, and she spent most of her time reading or walking outdoors. "The storms, the winds, the silences of the bush; the sunlit or rain-whipped mountains; fields of maize miles long; sunflowers that turned their heads after the sun; cotton plants with their butterfly-like pink and white flowers—these, and the neighbors, were my education," she said.

African Themes Lessing left school at 14 and worked as a nursemaid and telephone operator in Salisbury, Southern Rhodesia, until she married at the age of 19. In 1949, after two failed marriages, she moved to England, which remains her place of residence. Not long afterward, Lessing published her first novel, *The Grass Is Singing* (1950), and the story collection *This Was the Old Chief's Country* (1951). These stories were based on her intimate knowledge of Southern Rhodesia, especially the problems between blacks and whites. Because of her outspoken criticism of racism and her radical political sympathies, Lessing was banned from her homeland and South Africa. Nonetheless, her works have been praised for their honest portrayal of colonial Africa and its mysterious, often harsh, natural beauty.

Contemporary Masterpiece Another major theme in Lessing's writing is the role of women in modern society. *The Golden Notebook* (1962), an experimental novel about a woman coming to terms with her personal relationships and her role in the world, is widely regarded as her masterpiece.

Author Activity

Another Dimension Some of Lessing's best-known works are her science fiction novels. Find out the subject matter and title of her five-novel science fiction series.

Teaching Options

Mini Lesson Grammar

ADVERBS Remind students that words modifying verbs are called adverbs. Used in this manner, adverbs clarify verbs, offering more information about *when* or *how* something is done. Adverbs usually follow the verb they modify, but occasionally precede them. Use the model sentence to demonstrate the place and purpose of adverbs.

Model Sentence
The students *always* write *carefully.*

Exercises Write the following sentences on the board. Ask students to identify the adverbs.

1. Teddy always says such horrible things. *(always)*
2. Gideon spoke angrily to Mrs. Farquar. *(angrily)*
3. The snake rose up suddenly and spat in Teddy's eyes. *(suddenly)*

Use **Grammar Transparencies and Copymasters,** p. 75.

Use McDougal Littell's ***Language Network,*** Chapter 9, for more instruction and practice in adverbs.

PREPARING to *Read*

The Son from America

Short Story by ISAAC BASHEVIS SINGER

"Berl removed the straw, and the son saw that the boot was full of gold coins."

Connect to Your Life

Strangers in a Strange Land What kinds of changes do you think people go through when they immigrate to the United States and adapt to a new way of life? How might their departure from their native lands affect the family and friends they leave behind? Use a chart like the one shown to explore the answers to these questions. Share personal experiences of immigration, if possible, in a small group.

Effects on Immigrants	Effects on Those Left Behind
Need to find a job	

Build Background

Jewish Immigrants Millions of eastern European Jews immigrated to the United States near the beginning of the 20th century, often fleeing religious persecution or seeking a better way of life. Life in America at the time bore little resemblance to the life these immigrants had left behind. In the "old country"—particularly in rural villages—change occurred slowly, if at all, and people lived simply, as their ancestors before them had lived. In the United States, however, change was occurring at a rapid pace as economic and urban development transformed the nation and its people.

To meet the challenge of living in a new country, immigrants learned English, found jobs, and often became assimilated, or absorbed, into mainstream American culture. In order to fit in, some abandoned the cultural and religious traditions that had formerly shaped their lives. However, as they adapted to their newfound freedom and relative prosperity, most tried to maintain the feeling of community they had left behind. Typically, they settled among other Jews from the same towns or regions in eastern Europe. They also formed social groups, or societies, that raised money to help support those still living in their native villages.

VIDEODISC **LaserLinks: Background for Reading**
Cultural Connection

WORDS TO KNOW
Vocabulary Preview

abdicate	hinterland
benediction	illegible
contour	raspingly
flax	recite
heretic	thatched

Focus Your Reading

LITERARY ANALYSIS PLOT AND THEME

Plot refers to the chain of related events that take place in a story. In many stories, the outcome of the plot—the way in which the central **conflict** or misunderstanding is resolved—helps to reveal the writer's **theme,** or message. As you read this story, consider how the twists and turns of the plot contribute to the story's theme.

ACTIVE READING MAKING PREDICTIONS

A **prediction** is a reasonable guess about what will happen next. To make predictions about the outcome of this story, consider the following as you read:

- the description of the **setting**
- specific details about the **characters**
- important statements made by the characters
- the **title** of the selection

READER'S NOTEBOOK Before you begin reading, reflect upon the story's title and predict what you think will happen. As you read, jot down new predictions, based upon what you learn about the characters and their setting.

LESSON RESOURCES

UNIT ONE RESOURCE BOOK, pp. 69–74

ASSESSMENT RESOURCES
Formal Assessment, pp. 29–30
Teacher's Guide to Assessment and Portfolio Use
Test Generator

SKILLS TRANSPARENCIES AND COPYMASTERS
Literary Analysis
- Theme: Influences of Character, Setting, and Plot, T5 (for Paired Activity, p. 167)

Reading and Critical Thinking
- Predicting Outcomes, T2 (for Think Critically, item 2, p. 167)

Grammar
- Common and Proper Nouns, C65 (for Mini Lesson, p. 168)

Vocabulary
- Context Clues, C32 (for Mini Lesson, p. 160)
- Word Origins, C33 (for Mini Lesson, p. 164)

Writing
- Levels of Language, T12 (for Writing Option 1, p. 168)
- Achieving Conciseness, T21 (for Writing Option 3, p. 168)
- Opinion Statement, C25 (for Writing Option 2, p. 168)

Communications
- Interviewing, T9 (for Activities and Explorations 3, p. 168)
- Formal Presentations, T10 (for Activities & Explorations 2, p. 168)

INTEGRATED TECHNOLOGY
Audio Library
LaserLinks
- Cultural Connection: Village Life in Poland
- Storyteller: Susan Stone Tells "Yossele, the Holy Miser"

See **Teacher's SourceBook,** p. 15.

Visit our website:
www.mcdougallittell.com

OVERVIEW

Objectives

1. understand and appreciate a **short story (Literary Analysis)**
2. recognize and appreciate **plot and theme (Literary Analysis)**
3. **make predictions** about the outcome of the story **(Active Reading)**

Summary

Old Berl and his wife Berlcha live in the tiny Polish village of Lentshin in a one-room hut. Every month they receive a check from their son Samuel, who went to America 40 years ago. One morning Samuel returns home, and his joyful parents prepare a special Sabbath feast. After dinner, Samuel learns that his parents have not spent any of the money he sent. They explain that their garden and animals supply all their needs. Samuel also learns that Lentshin has no thieves, no homeless people, and no need for the additional money he has raised. Unlike the cities of America, this remote Jewish village in Poland needs nothing.

Thematic Link

A man who has achieved success in America returns to the "old country" to help his parents and their village. He finds that he must reexamine his assumptions as he reaches a **cultural crossroads.**

5-Minute Warm-Up

Daily Language SkillBuilder

Have students **proofread** the display sentences on page 15j and write them correctly. The sentences also appear on Transparency 5 of **Grammar Transparencies and Copymasters.**

Mini Lesson **Preteaching Vocabulary**

If you would like to preteach the WORDS TO KNOW for this selection, use the Mini Lesson, p. 160.

TEACHING THE LITERATURE

Reading and Analyzing

Reading Skills and Strategies: PREVIEW

Have students scan the selection before they begin reading, paying attention to the prereading page and the artwork. Ask them to discuss what they think the selection will be about.

Active Reading: PREDICTING

Predicting the events of a story is like using clues to solve a puzzle. Have students use the "clues" on this page—the title and the first three paragraphs—to predict what might happen that would involve Berl and the son from America.

Possible Responses: Students might think that some catastrophe will befall the town or that the money will be stolen. They might also think that Berl and Berlcha will hear something from their son.

Use **Unit One Resource Book,** p. 70 for more practice.

Literary Analysis: THEME AND PLOT

The theme of a short story is its main message or idea—often a perception about life, human nature, or values. Ask students to make notes, as they read, about the values of Berl and Berlcha, the villagers of Lentshin, and Samuel.

Plot is the series of events that happen in the story. Have students keep a summary of the events of the story in their Reader's Notebook.

The Son from America

Isaac Bashevis Singer

The village of Lentshin was tiny—a sandy marketplace where the peasants of the area met once a week. It was surrounded by little huts with thatched roofs or shingles green with moss. The chimneys looked like pots. Between the huts there were fields, where the owners planted vegetables or pastured their goats.

In the smallest of these huts lived old Berl, a man in his eighties, and his wife, who was called Berlcha (wife of Berl). Old Berl was one of the Jews who had been driven from their villages in Russia and had settled in Poland. In Lentshin, they mocked the mistakes he made while praying aloud. He spoke with a sharp "r." He was short, broad-shouldered, and had a small white beard, and summer and winter he wore a sheepskin hat, a padded cotton jacket, and stout boots. He walked slowly, shuffling his feet. He had a half acre of field, a cow, a goat, and chickens.

The couple had a son, Samuel, who had gone to America forty years ago. It was said in Lentshin that he became a millionaire there. Every month, the Lentshin letter carrier brought old Berl a money order and a letter that no one could read because many of the words were English. How much money Samuel sent his parents remained a secret. Three times a year, Berl and his wife went on foot to Zakroczym[1] and cashed the money orders there. But they never seemed to use the money. What for? The garden, the

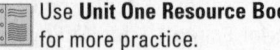

1. **Zakroczym** (zä-krô′chəm).

WORDS TO KNOW

thatched (thăcht) *adj.* covered with plant stalks or leaves **thatch** *v.*

Teaching Options

Mini Lesson: Preteaching Vocabulary

USING CONTEXT CLUES Call students' attention to the list of WORDS TO KNOW. Remind them that sometimes they can understand the meaning of an unfamiliar word by examining the context in which the word is used. Use the model sentence to demonstrate the strategy of using context clues that provide **inferences** to word meaning.

Model Sentence

In English class, students were required to stand in front of the class and *recite* from memory an entire poem.

Instruction

- Write the model sentence on the chalkboard.
- Ask a volunteer to summarize the meaning of the sentence.
- Have students use the meaning of the sentence to **infer** meanings for the word *recite*.
- Ask a volunteer to use the word *recite* in a sentence.

Use **Unit One Resource Book,** p. 72 for more practice.

A lesson on context clues appears on p. 56 in the Pupil's Edition.

The Grey House (1917), Marc Chagall. Thyssen-Bornemisza Museum, Madrid, Spain, Nimatallah/Art Resource, New York. Copyright © 1996 Artists Rights Society (ARS), New York/ADAGP, Paris.

Customizing Instruction

Less Proficient Readers

Help students become engaged with the story by having them read the first two paragraphs silently. Ask students to describe Berl and his life in the village. Then ask students, as they read, to watch for any change or interruption in his way of living.

Students Acquiring English

Point out to students that this story is set in Poland, and that some place names and words may be unfamiliar, even to English speakers.

Use **Spanish Study Guide** for additional support, pp. 34–36.

Multiple Learning Styles

Visual Learners

Ask students to describe or sketch Berl, adding details about his age, facial expression, and dress. Students might also sketch his thatched-roof hut and the little village of Lentshin.

Gifted and Talented

Tell students that Isaac Bashevis Singer is famous for using elements of oral storytelling in his writing. Have students listen in their minds and note details about Singer's writing that contribute to the storytelling quality of the story. Have them give examples from the text with their response.

Mini Lesson Viewing and Representing

The Grey House **by Marc Chagall**

ART APPRECIATION Marc Chagall [1887–1985] was born in Russia. His artistic style is often surreal, dreamlike, and highly imaginative. Many of his subjects are drawn from the Jewish village life and folklore of his boyhood.

Instruction Ask students to discuss the town depicted in the painting above. Who might live where?

Possible Response: The church (note cross on top) is in the center of what looks like the wealthier part of town. The gray house is far more modest and seems to be on the edge of town, perhaps in the part of town where poor folks or peasants live.

Application Do you think the house is really as large as shown, in comparison to the church? What might the artist be trying to say about the house?

Possible Response: The gray house is in the foreground of the painting, which, with the painter's use of perspective, makes it look bigger than the church. Its place in the foreground seems to indicate its importance to the artist. While many would consider the town's church as its most distinguishing structure, the artist decided to highlight the humble house. Its prominence may reflect his childhood perception of "home" as being the single most important place in the town.

Reading and Analyzing

Reading Skills and Strategies: VISUALIZATION

Ask students to identify descriptive details that seem particularly vivid in describing life in Lentshin. Have them draw or describe the mental pictures they are visualizing.

Literary Analysis: CHARACTER DEVELOPMENT

A An author creates and reveals a character through evidence: description, action, or dialogue. Ask students to identify evidence of how characters are revealed in the story. For instance, what do we learn from the description of the actions and dialogue that take place when Samuel returns home?
Possible response: Samuel shows affection for his parents, revealed by action (he hugs and kisses them both) and dialogue ("Mother, it's me, your son."). The parents are surprised and glad to see their son, shown in dialogue, (Berl addresses his wife by name for the first time in years) and actions (Berlcha weeps and almost forgets that she must hurry to make supper before sundown, when the Sabbath starts).

cow, and the goat provided most of their needs. Besides, Berlcha sold chickens and eggs, and from these there was enough to buy flour for bread.

No one cared to know where Berl kept the money that his son sent him. There were no thieves in Lentshin. The hut consisted of one room, which contained all their belongings: the table, the shelf for meat, the shelf for milk foods, the two beds, and the clay oven. Sometimes the chickens roosted in the woodshed and sometimes, when it was cold, in a coop near the oven. The goat, too, found shelter inside when the weather was bad. The more prosperous villagers had kerosene lamps, but Berl and his wife did not believe in newfangled gadgets. What was wrong with a wick in a dish of oil? Only for the Sabbath[2] would Berlcha buy three tallow candles at the store. In summer, the couple got up at sunrise and retired with the chickens. In the long winter evenings, Berlcha spun flax at her spinning wheel, and Berl sat beside her in the silence of those who enjoy their rest.

1

Once in a while when Berl came home from the synagogue after evening prayers, he brought news to his wife. In Warsaw there were strikers who demanded that the czar abdicate. A heretic by the name of Dr. Herzl[3] had come up with the idea that Jews should settle again in Palestine. Berlcha listened and shook her bonneted head. Her face was yellowish and wrinkled like a cabbage leaf. There were bluish sacks under her eyes. She was half deaf. Berl had to repeat each word he said to her. She would say, "The things that happen in the big cities!"

Here in Lentshin nothing happened except usual events: a cow gave birth to a calf, a young couple had a circumcision party,[4] or a girl was born and there was no party. Occasionally, someone died. Lentshin had no cemetery, and the corpse had to be taken to Zakroczym. Actually, Lentshin had become a village with few young people. The young men left for Zakroczym, for Nowy Dwor, for Warsaw, and sometimes for the United States. Like Samuel's, their letters were illegible, the Yiddish[5] mixed with the languages of the countries where they were now living. They sent photographs in which the men wore top hats and the women fancy dresses like squiresses.[6]

Berl and Berlcha also received such photographs. But their eyes were failing, and neither he nor she had glasses. They could barely make out the pictures. Samuel had sons and daughters with Gentile[7] names—and grandchildren who had married and had their own offspring. Their names were so strange that Berl and Berlcha could never remember them. But what difference do names make? America was far, far away on the other side of the ocean, at the edge of the world. A Talmud[8] teacher who came to Lentshin had said that Americans walked with their heads down and their feet up. Berl and Berlcha could not grasp this. How was it possible? But since the teacher said so, it must be true. Berlcha pondered for some time, and then she said,

2. **the Sabbath:** a weekly day of rest and worship for Jews, beginning at sundown Friday and ending at sundown Saturday.
3. **Dr. Herzl** (hĕrt′səl): Theodor Herzl, an Austrian writer and journalist who, in response to anti-Jewish feeling in Europe in the late 1800s, called for the establishment of a Jewish state.
4. **circumcision party:** a party following the Jewish ceremony called *brith milah* (brĭt′ mē-lä′), in which a baby boy is circumcised and given a Hebrew name on the eighth day after birth.
5. **Yiddish:** a language—containing elements of German, Hebrew, and several other languages—spoken by Jews in central and eastern Europe and by their descendants in other countries.
6. **squiresses:** wives of country gentlemen (squires).
7. **Gentile** (jĕn′tīl′): not Jewish (usually applied to people and things Christian).
8. **Talmud** (täl′mo͝od): the writings that are the basis of Jewish civil and religious law.

WORDS TO KNOW

flax (flăks) *n.* a plant that is the source of the fibers used to make linen
abdicate (ăb′dĭ-kāt′) *v.* to give up an office or position
heretic (hĕr′ĭ-tĭk) *n.* a person who disagrees with accepted beliefs, particularly those of a religious group
illegible (ĭ-lĕj′ə-bəl) *adj.* unreadable

Teaching Options

BLOCK SCHEDULING: MANAGING TIME

If your schedule requires that you cover the lesson objectives in a shorter time, use . . .
- Preparing to Read, p. 159
- Thinking Through the Literature, p. 167
- Vocabulary in Action, p. 168
- Grammar in Context, p. 169

If you want to take advantage of longer class time, use . . .
- TE Teaching Options: Preteaching Vocabulary p. 160; Viewing and Representing, p. 161; Cross Curricular Link, p. 163; Standardized Test Practice, p. 165; Vocabulary Strategy, p. 164; Speaking and Listening, p. 166
- Choices & Challenges and Author Activity, pp. 168–169

"One can get accustomed to everything."

And so it remained. From too much thinking—God forbid—one may lose one's wits.

One Friday morning, when Berlcha was kneading the dough for the Sabbath loaves, the door opened and a nobleman entered. He was so tall that he had to bend down to get through the door. He wore a beaver hat and a cloak bordered with fur. He was followed by Chazkel, the coachman from Zakroczym, who carried two leather valises with brass locks. In astonishment Berlcha raised her eyes.

The nobleman looked around and said to the coachman in Yiddish, "Here it is." He took out a silver ruble and paid him. The coachman tried to hand him change, but he said, "You can go now."

When the coachman closed the door, the nobleman said, "Mother, it's me, your son Samuel—Sam."

Berlcha heard the words and her legs grew numb. Her hands, to which pieces of dough were sticking, lost their power. The nobleman hugged her, kissed her forehead, both her cheeks. Berlcha began to cackle like a hen, "My son!" At that moment Berl came in from the woodshed, his arms piled with logs. The goat followed him. When he saw a nobleman kissing his wife, Berl dropped the wood and exclaimed, "What is this?"

The nobleman let go of Berlcha and embraced Berl. "Father!"

For a long time Berl was unable to utter a sound. He wanted to recite holy words that he had read in the Yiddish Bible, but he could remember nothing. Then he asked, "Are you Samuel?"

"Yes, Father, I am Samuel."

"Well, peace be with you." Berl grasped his son's hand. He was still not sure that he was not being fooled. Samuel wasn't as tall and heavy as this man, but then Berl reminded himself that Samuel was only fifteen years old when he had left home. He must have grown in that faraway country. Berl asked, "Why didn't you let us know that you were coming?"

"Didn't you receive my cable?" Samuel asked.

Berl did not know what a cable was.

Berlcha had scraped the dough from her hands and enfolded her son. He kissed her again and asked, "Mother, didn't you receive a cable?"

"What? If I lived to see this, I am happy to die," Berlcha said, amazed by her own words. Berl, too, was amazed. These were just the words he would have said earlier if he had been able to remember. After a while Berl came to himself and said, "Pescha, you will have to make a double Sabbath pudding in addition to the stew."

It was years since Berl had called Berlcha by her given name. When he wanted to address her, he would say, "Listen," or "Say." It is the young or those from the big cities who call a wife by her name. Only now did Berlcha begin to cry. Yellow tears ran from her eyes, and everything became dim. Then she called out, "It's Friday—I have to prepare for the Sabbath." Yes, she had to knead the dough and braid the loaves. With such a guest, she had to make a larger Sabbath stew. The winter day is short, and she must hurry.

Her son understood what was worrying her, because he said, "Mother, I will help you."

Berlcha wanted to laugh, but a choked sob came out. "What are you saying? God forbid."

Customizing Instruction

Multiple Learning Styles

Visual Learners

1 Using the description of the hut's contents, have students draw up a bird's-eye view of Berl and Berlcha's hut, positioning all of their belongings and adding details such as windows and a door.

Less Proficient Readers

Help students understand a major plot development in the story after they finish both pages. Ask them to explain what event has interrupted Berl and Berlcha's normal routine.

Possible Response: After decades of absence, Berl and Berlcha's son Samuel, now a tall, well-dressed, apparently wealthy American, has unexpectedly arrived for a visit.

Cross Curricular Link History

IMMIGRANTS IN NEW YORK Samuel, the "son from America," is an imaginary character, but 12 million real immigrants traveled to America, entering through New York's Ellis Island immigration center during the decades between 1892 and 1924. Among this vast number of immigrants were many Jews from countries in Eastern Europe, including Russia and Poland, fleeing repression and poverty. Many settled in New York City, populating neighborhoods like Manhattan's Lower East Side, where they worked in the thriving garment industry (often for low wages) and lived in crowded tenements.

By 1920, immigrants began to face increasing prejudice and hostility. Opposition to newcomers resulted in a 1924 law establishing national-origin quotas and reducing the flow of immigrants from southern and eastern European countries.

Reading and Analyzing

Reading Skills and Strategies: QUESTIONING

Ask students to write down three questions about Samuel and his parents that occur to them as they read the text on pages 164 and 165.

Possible Responses: Why does Berlcha weep when her son offers to bake bread? What will happen between Samuel and his parents? What will happen to the money sent by Samuel?

Le juif en vert [Jew in green] (1914), Marc Chagall. Oil on cardboard 38⅜″ × 30¾″, private collection, Geneva, Switzerland. Copyright © 1996 Artists Rights Society (ARS), New York/ADAGP, Paris.

The nobleman took off his cloak and jacket and remained in his vest, on which hung a solid-gold watch chain. He rolled up his sleeves and came to the trough. "Mother, I was a baker for many years in New York," he said, and he began to knead the dough.

"What! You are my darling son who will say Kaddish[9] for me." She wept raspingly. Her strength left her, and she slumped onto the bed.

Berl said, "Women will always be women." And he went to the shed to get more wood. The goat sat down near the oven; she gazed with surprise at this strange man—his height and his bizarre clothes.

The neighbors had heard the good news that Berl's son had arrived from America, and they came to greet him. The women began to help Berlcha prepare for the Sabbath. Some laughed; some cried. The room was full of people, as at a wedding. They asked Berl's son, "What is new in America?"

And Berl's son answered, "America is all right."

"Do Jews make a living?"

"One eats white bread there on weekdays."

"Do they remain Jews?"

"I am not a Gentile."

After Berlcha blessed the candles, father and son went to the little synagogue across the street. A new snow had fallen. The son took large steps, but Berl warned him, "Slow down."

In the synagogue the Jews recited "Let Us Exult" and "Come, My Groom." All the time, the snow outside kept falling. After prayers, when Berl and Samuel left the Holy Place, the village was unrecognizable. Everything was covered in snow. One could see only the contours of the roofs and the candles in the windows. Samuel said, "Nothing has changed here."

Berlcha had prepared gefilte fish,[10] chicken

9. **Kaddish** (kä'dĭsh): a Jewish prayer recited by mourners after the death of a close relative.

10. **gefilte** (gə-fĭl'tə) **fish:** a traditional Jewish food made from finely chopped fish.

WORDS TO KNOW

raspingly (răs'pĭng-lē) *adv.* in a harsh manner; gratingly

contour (kŏn'to͝or') *n.* an outline of a shape

164

Teaching Options

Mini Lesson Vocabulary Strategy

RESEARCHING WORD ORIGINS

Instruction The word *synagogue* comes from the Greek prefix *syn-* ("with," "together with") and the Greek root *agein* ("to drive or lead"), and means "bringing or leading together." Another form of the prefix *syn-* is *sym-*. Common words that use the *syn-/sym-* prefix include *sympathy* (*sym-* + *pathos,* "feelings, emotion, experience," meaning "feeling or experiencing together with another person") and *synonym* (*syn* + *onyma,* "name," meaning "a word having the same, or nearly the same, meaning as another").

Practice Have students work in pairs to research the word origins of other *syn-/sym-* related words, such as *symphony, symbiosis, symmetrical, symptom, syndrome, synergy,* or *synthesis.* Have them describe how they can use knowledge of the *syn-/sym-* prefix to remember the meanings of these and other related words.

Use **Vocabulary Transparencies and Copymasters,** p. 33.

A lesson on researching word origins appears on p. 356 in the Pupil's Edition.

soup with rice, meat, carrot stew. Berl recited the benediction over a glass of ritual wine. The family ate and drank, and when it grew quiet for a while, one could hear the chirping of the house cricket. The son talked a lot, but Berl and Berlcha understood little. His Yiddish was different and contained foreign words.

After the final blessing Samuel asked, "Father, what did you do with all the money I sent you?"

Berl raised his white brows. "It's here."

"Didn't you put it in a bank?"

"There is no bank in Lentshin."

"Where do you keep it?"

Berl hesitated. "One is not allowed to touch money on the Sabbath, but I will show you." He crouched beside the bed and began to shove something heavy. A boot appeared. Its top was stuffed with straw. Berl removed the straw, and the son saw that the boot was full of gold coins.
1 He lifted it.

"Father, this is a treasure!" he called out.

"Well."

"Why didn't you spend it?"

"On what? Thank God, we have everything."

"Why didn't you travel somewhere?"

"Where to? This is our home."

The son asked one question after the other, but Berl's answer was always the same: they wanted for nothing. The garden, the cow, the goat, the chickens provided them with all they needed. The son said, "If thieves knew about this, your lives wouldn't be safe."

"There are no thieves here."

2 "What will happen to the money?"

"You take it."

Slowly, Berl and Berlcha grew accustomed to their son and his American Yiddish. Berlcha could hear him better now. She even recognized his voice. He was saying, "Perhaps we should build a larger synagogue."

"The synagogue is big enough," Berl replied.

"Perhaps a home for old people."

"No one sleeps in the street."

The next day after the Sabbath meal was eaten, a Gentile from Zakroczym brought a paper—it was the cable. Berl and Berlcha lay down for a nap. They soon began to snore. The goat, too, dozed off. The son put on his cloak and his hat and went for a walk. He strode with his long legs across the marketplace. He stretched out a hand and touched a roof. He wanted to smoke a cigar, but he remembered it was forbidden on the Sabbath. He had a desire to talk to someone, but it seemed that the whole of Lentshin was asleep. He entered the synagogue. An old man was sitting there, reciting psalms. Samuel asked, "Are you praying?"

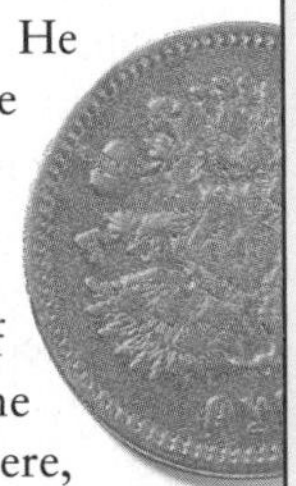

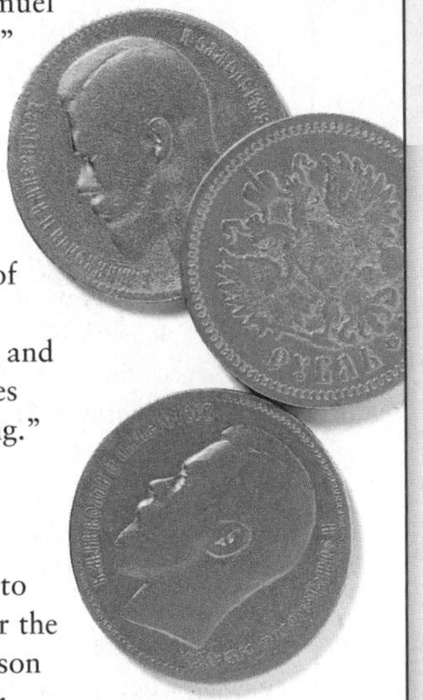

"What else is there to do when one gets old?"

"Do you make a living?"

The old man did not understand the meaning of these words. He smiled, showing his empty gums, and then he said, "If God gives health, one keeps on living."

Samuel returned home. Dusk had fallen. Berl went to the synagogue for the evening prayers, and the son remained with his mother. The room was filled with shadows.

Berlcha began to recite in a solemn singsong, "God of Abraham, Isaac, and Jacob, defend the poor people of Israel and Thy name. The Holy Sabbath is departing; the welcome week is coming to us. Let it be one of health, wealth, and good deeds."

"Mother, you don't need to pray for wealth,"

WORDS TO KNOW
benediction (bĕn′ĭ-dĭk′shən) *n.* a blessing
recite (rĭ-sīt′) *v.* to say out loud something memorized

165

Customizing Instruction

Less Proficient Readers

Help students understand the irony in the situation of Samuel's discovery that his parents and the villagers of Lentshin do not feel that they need anything. Ask students the following questions:

1 What are purposes for which Samuel assumes that his parents might have wanted to use additional money?
Answer: to buy things for themselves or to travel

2 Why is Berl's offering the money back to Samuel amusing?
Answer: Samuel already has far more money than Berl, so he clearly does not need it. It's amusing, because it is the opposite of what you might expect.

Assessment Standardized Test Practice

ANALYZING AND EVALUATING TEXT For some standardized tests, students will be asked to analyze and evaluate the meaning of specific passages of text. To provide students with practice in choosing the most accurate interpretation of a passage, read aloud or write on the chalkboard the following question:

Which of the following statements best describes Berl's attitude toward Samuel's offer of money?

A. He is uninterested, having no purpose for additional funds.
B. He is insulted, telling his son not to offer again.
C. He is hurt, thinking Samuel is judging him to be a failure.
D. He is grateful, knowing his son means to be generous.

Lead students through the process of choosing the best summary. Have them consider each choice. Point out that since the author does not characterize Berl's feelings by direct description, the reader must infer Berl's attitude from what he says (dialogue) and what he does (actions). Only one choice, **A**, fits both what Berl says and what he does in response to his son's offer of money.

Reading and Analyzing

Reading Skills and Strategies: DRAWING CONCLUSIONS

Have students draw conclusions about the conditions of life in America based on the evidence of Samuel's actions and words. What can you conclude about Samuel's life in the United States?

Possible Response: Samuel wears fur (he is relatively rich); he helps his mother bake bread (in America, baking is a profession, not a domestic task); he assumes that money should be spent (poor people need money to live in America); he worries about thieves (robbery is relatively common in America).

LITERARY LINK

Reading Skills and Strategies: CONNECTING

A Have students read the poem "Grudnow" and point out how Pastan's poem connects with the story.

Possible Response: The selections both include characters who have lived in Russia and Poland.

Ask students to evaluate the characters' opinions of their European homeland.

Possible Response: In the short story, Samuel finds that his parents lead a simple and quiet, but satisfying, existence in their homeland. The grandfather of the speaker in the poem reflects that his home town is desolate.

Samuel said. "You are wealthy already."

Berlcha did not hear—or pretended not to. Her face had turned into a cluster of shadows.

In the twilight Samuel put his hand into his jacket pocket and touched his passport, his checkbook, his letters of credit. He had come here with big plans. He had a valise filled with presents for his parents. He wanted to bestow gifts on the village. He brought not only his own money but funds from the Lentshin Society in New York, which had organized a ball for the benefit of the village. But this village in the hinterland needed nothing. From the synagogue one could hear hoarse chanting. The cricket, silent all day, started again its chirping. Berlcha began to sway and utter holy rhymes inherited from mothers and grandmothers:

Thy holy sheep
In mercy keep,
In Torah and good deeds;
Provide for all their needs,
Shoes, clothes, and bread
And the Messiah's tread. ❖

Translated by the author and Dorothea Straus

LITERARY LINK

GRUDNOW

LINDA PASTAN

A

When he spoke of where he
came from,
my grandfather could have been
clearing his throat
of that name, that town
sometimes Poland, sometimes Russia,
the borders penciled in
with a hand as shaky as his.
He left, I heard him say,
because there was nothing there.

I understood what he meant
when I saw the photograph
of his people standing
against a landscape emptied
of crops and trees, scraped raw
by winter. Everything
was in sepia, as if the brown earth
had stained the faces,
stained even the air.

I would have died there, I think
in childhood maybe
of some fever,
my face pressed for warmth
against a cow with flanks
like those of the great-aunts
in the picture. Or later
I would have died of history
like the others, who dug
their stubborn heels into that earth,
heels as hard as the heels
of the bread my grandfather tore
from the loaf at supper. He always
sipped his tea through a cube of sugar
clenched in his teeth, the way
he sipped his life here, noisily,
through all he remembered
that might have been sweet in
Grudnow.

WORDS TO KNOW

hinterland (hĭn'tər-lănd') *n.* a region far from large cities

Teaching Options

Mini Lesson Speaking and Listening

PRESENTING A PERSUASIVE ARGUMENT Prepare In small groups, have students discuss the positive and negative aspects of the lives of those who emigrated from little eastern European villages like Lentshin. Then ask them to prepare a dramatic "debate" between Berl or Berlcha and the grandfather in Linda Pastan's "Grudnow." To prepare for the debate, ask students to think about the positive and negative aspects of traditional village life (example: the village is free of crime and homelessness, but the young men seem to be leaving).

Present Have students elect two representatives to portray Berl or Berlcha and the grandfather in the debate. After each side has presented its case, students in the audience might question the characters about their positions.

Connect to the Literature

1. **What Do You Think?** How did you react to the outcome of the story? Jot down some of your first thoughts.

Comprehension Check
- How do Berl and Berlcha live?
- Why didn't Berl spend the money Samuel had sent him?
- What plan did Samuel have for Lentshin?

Think Critically

2. **ACTIVE READING** **PREDICTING** Compare the predictions you made in your READER'S NOTEBOOK about the outcome of the **plot.** Were your predictions correct? At what points in the story were you able to make predictions?

3. What are your impressions of Berl and Berlcha?

   THINK ABOUT
   - the description of their home and community
   - their understanding of the world
   - their reasons for not spending the money their son has sent
   - the role of tradition and religion in their life

4. What are your impressions of their son, Samuel?

   THINK ABOUT
   - why he returns to Lentshin
   - how he has adapted to life in his new country
   - how he reacts to his parents' life

5. How would you explain what Samuel has realized by the end of the story?

Extend Interpretations

6. **Comparing Texts** Would you say that the grandfather in the poem "Grudnow" has more in common with Samuel or with Samuel's parents? Why?

7. **Critic's Corner** In awarding Singer its prize for literature, the Nobel Prize committee praised his "impassioned narrative art which, with roots in a Polish-Jewish cultural tradition, brings universal human conditions to life." Would you say that "The Son from America" deals with universal human conditions? Explain your answer.

8. **Connect to Life** Do aspects of life in Lentshin exist anywhere in the United States today? Cite details from the story as you share your opinion with classmates.

Literary Analysis

PLOT AND THEME The **theme** or message of a story is often developed through the **plot,** which is the writer's blueprint for what happens, when it happens, and to whom it happens. Through the action of the story and the resolution of **conflict,** a writer may reveal a truth about human behavior or an observation about the human condition. In this story, the plot takes a number of unexpected turns, which suggest a great deal about what Singer values in life.

Paired Activity With a partner, create a chart similar to the one below. List important events from the story's plot. Then consider the outcomes of these events. What theme, or themes, do these outcomes suggest?

Event	Outcome
1. Son moves to America.	1. Son makes money as a baker.
2.	2.
3.	3.
Theme:	

GUIDING STUDENT RESPONSE

Connect to the Literature

1. **What Do You Think?** Students may register surprise at the outcome. Good responses might note the differences between our modern values or needs and the perceived needs of Berl and Berlcha.

Comprehension Check
- They live very simply, without electricity or other modern conveniences.
- They didn't need the money to live as they were accustomed.
- He wanted to use his wealth to help—and change—his parents' village: build a new synagogue, provide a home for the elderly.

Think Critically

2. Answers will vary. Students may be surprised at Berl's lack of interest in Samuel's attempts to give them money, or at the fact that the money actually plays a very small role in the story.
3. Berl and Berlcha are simple peasants in a tiny village with little education or knowledge of the world. However, they feel that they lack nothing and their faith makes them content.
4. Possible response: Samuel is a well-intentioned and kind son who genuinely wants to help his parents and their village. He does not have exactly the same values as his parents, but he respects their faith and sees how they are content in their way of life.
5. Samuel has reevaluated his own ideas about the necessity of money or progress.

Literary Analysis

Paired Activity Students should describe the development of the plot in their charts. Student charts will vary, but should include some of the following events: Samuel returns to Lentshin; Samuel offers to bake bread for his mother; Berl shows Samuel the unspent money. Suggested themes should include the idea that some people require very little wealth to live happily.

Extend Interpretations

Comparing Texts Answers may vary. Students may feel that the views of the grandfather of the poem are more like Samuel's than his parents'. Both Samuel and the grandfather left to go to America in search of wealth and opportunity.

Critic's Corner Possible Response: The story touches on universal elements that include aspects of leaving home, a son's care for his parents, whether "progress" truly makes people's lives better, traditions of faith, respect for differences in values, and so on.

Connect to Life Possible Response: Some American religious communities—specifically the Amish and some Mennonites—reject modern technology and materialism. There are many non-American workers who immigrate temporarily or permanently in order to seek better opportunities.

Writing Options

1. **Lentshin Newsletter** Student responses will vary but should contain specific details and observations from Samuel's point of view.
2. **Literary Review** If possible, have students read book reviews in newspapers and other sources as models to help them structure their own reviews.
3. **Old World Sketches** Have students use details from the story and then embellish them. Some students may wish to draw pencil sketches to illustrate their written sketches.

Activities and Explorations

1. **A Son's Portrait** Students who draw the mature Samuel should consider details of his dress and appearance as revealed in the story.
2. **A Son's Scrapbook** Samuel is in many ways a tourist who might be interested in visiting sites he remembers from childhood and photographing them.
3. **Personal Interview** Have students think of four or five questions before the actual interview.

Inquiry & Research

Encourage students to use appropriate print and nonprint resources to find information about the history of Judaism and how these rituals have come about. Remind students that they may use technical resources such as databases and the Internet.

Vocabulary in Action

ANSWERS

Exercise A	Exercise B
1. b	1. c
2. c	2. c
3. d	3. a
4. c	4. b
5. c	5. b

Choices & CHALLENGES

Writing Options

1. **Lentshin Newsletter** Imagine that you are Samuel. Write a newsletter article for the Lentshin Society magazine, describing your trip to Lentshin, Poland. Be sure to explain why you have returned to New York with the money that the society has raised for the village.

2. **Literary Review** Write a review of this story, telling what you liked or didn't like about Singer's storytelling techniques.

3. **Old World Sketches** Write character sketches of Berl and Berlcha. Use quotations from the story to help you describe the characters' appearance, their home, and how they live and relate to each other. Place the entry in your **Working Portfolio.**

Writing Handbook
See page 1153: Description.

Activities & Explorations

1. **A Son's Portrait** Draw or paint a portrait of Samuel as seen through his parents' eyes. ~ **ART**

2. **A Son's Scrapbook** Work with two classmates to create a scrapbook of Samuel's trip to Lentshin. Use old photos, art reproductions, bits of writing or clippings, and drawings of your own to depict the most important aspects of his visit. Include captions explaining how the images reflect Samuel's encounters and realizations. ~ **VIEWING AND REPRESENTING**

3. **Personal Interview** Conduct an interview with someone you know who has immigrated to America. Then summarize what you have learned about this person's experiences. ~ **SPEAKING AND LISTENING**

Inquiry & Research

World Religions Research the Jewish celebration of the Sabbath. Look for information on the symbolism of candles, bread, and wine and on the traditional laws governing behavior on the Sabbath, some of which are mentioned in the story. Present your findings to your classmates in an oral report.

Vocabulary in Action

EXERCISE A: RELATED WORDS On your paper, write the letter of the word in each group that does not belong with the other words.

1. (a) matted, (b) detonated, (c) thatched, (d) shingled
2. (a) appoint, (b) abdicate, (c), gesticulate, (d) rule
3. (a) contour, (b) size, (c) shade, (d) consternation
4. (a) preach, (b) lecture, (c) percussively, (d) recite
5. (a) club moss, (b) flax, (c) quartz, (d) elm

EXERCISE B: ASSESSMENT PRACTICE Write the letter of the antonym of each boldfaced word below.

1. **illegible:** (a) knowledgeable, (b) advisable, (c) discernible
2. **heretic:** (a) cynic, (b) valet, (c) adherent
3. **raspingly:** (a) melodically, (b) repeatedly, (c) marginally
4. **hinterland:** (a) allowance, (b) metropolis, (c) villain
5. **benediction:** (a) benefit, (b) slander, (c) diction

Building Vocabulary
For an in-depth study on context clues, involving antonyms and synonyms, see page 1000.

WORDS TO KNOW					
	abdicate	contour	heretic	illegible	recite
	benediction	flax	hinterland	raspingly	thatched

Teaching Options

Mini Lesson **Grammar**

PROPER AND COMMON NOUNS

Instruction: Nouns can be classified as "proper" or "common."

Proper nouns name particular persons, places, things, or ideas. They are always capitalized. Write the following words on the chalkboard:

Chicago
Kennedy
Antarctica
White House

Common nouns are less specific. They identify people, places, things, or ideas in general. Write the following words on the chalkboard:

city
season
continent
painting style

Have students correct the nouns in the following sentences.

Grammar in Context: Using Nouns to Establish Tone and Mood

Notice the simple nouns Singer uses to describe Berl and Berlcha's home in "The Son from America."

> **The hut consisted of one room, which contained all their belongings: the table, the shelf for meat, the shelf for milk foods, the two beds, and the clay oven.**

You may recall that a **noun** is a word that refers to a person, place, or thing. The nouns in this sentence help to convey the simple outlook and lifestyle of Berl and Berlcha. How would the tone of the sentence be different if *hut* were replaced with *house* or if *meat* were replaced with *steaks?*

WRITING EXERCISE Change the underlined nouns in these sentences so that they refer to life in a wealthy modern city instead of life in a rural town.

Example: ***Original*** Their furniture includes two stools and a table covered with oilcloth.
Rewritten Their furniture includes two armchairs and a sofa covered with velvet.

1. In the marketplace, peasants buy flour and eggs.
2. His father has a goat, some chickens, and a cow.
3. Berl wears boots and a jacket made of cotton.
4. At night, Berlcha takes out her spinning wheel and makes thread out of flax.

Grammar Handbook
Nouns, p. 1182

VIDEODISC **LaserLinks: Background for Reading**
Storyteller

Isaac Bashevis Singer

1904–1991

Other Works
Gimpel the Fool and Other Stories
In My Father's Court
Yentl the Yeshiva Boy
Shosha
The Collected Stories of Isaac Bashevis Singer

Early Years One of the world's foremost Yiddish-language authors, Isaac Bashevis Singer was born in a tiny village in rural Poland and spent most of his youth in Warsaw, the country's capital. His father and both of his grandfathers were rabbis, so he received a traditional religious education. Singer was very close with his older brother, I. J. Singer, a writer who rejected some traditional beliefs and supported the modernization of Judaism. "I was fascinated both with my brother's rationalism and with my parents' mysticism," he once remarked, and both interests are evident in his writings. He also said that he preferred "to write about the world which I knew, which I know best." As a result, much of his fiction is set in the Polish-Jewish communities of his boyhood, which no longer exist.

A Writer's Journey In the 1920s, while working in Warsaw as a proofreader for a Yiddish literary journal edited by his brother, Singer began writing and publishing his own stories and book reviews. In 1932 he became coeditor of *Globus,* a literary magazine in which he published portions of what would become his first novel, *Satan in Goray.* The complete novel appeared in 1935, the same year that Singer left for America to join his brother, who had emigrated the year before. He settled in New York City and began writing articles, book reviews, and short stories for the *Daily Forward,* a Yiddish newspaper.

World Renown Over the course of his career, Singer won a great number of honors and awards for his writing, including the 1978 Nobel Prize in literature. He always wrote in Yiddish, his native tongue, even though he learned English and even collaborated on English translations of his works. Singer once said, "When I was a boy, they called me a liar . . . for telling stories. Now they call me a writer. It's more advanced, but it's the same thing." He also believed that "every experience becomes important when it's told, not before."

Author Activity

Storyteller Singer Read at least two other stories by Singer, paying close attention to his style. Based on your readings, what generalizations can you make about Singer's style and subject matter?

Grammar in Context

WRITING EXERCISE Answers will vary. Possible responses are shown.

1. In the mall, shoppers buy dresses and shoes.
2. His father has a car, some tools, and a lawn mower.
3. Berl wears sneakers and a vest made of leather.
4. At night, Berlcha takes out her blender and makes smoothies out of strawberries.

Author Activity

Three popular stories of Singer's are "Gimpel the Fool," "Zlateh the Goat," and "Yentl." Remind students that "Yentl" was made into a movie with Barbra Streisand playing the title character. In making generalizations about Singer's work, students may point out that his works often are deceptively simple, almost like parables, Aesop's fables, or other simple-seeming stories. They carry a lot of meaning although they don't appear to be very complicated.

Exercises

1. Berl and berlcha lived in a ramshackle hut on the edge of their village. *(Berlcha)*
2. Their son samuel had lived in New york for many Years. *(Samuel; York; years)*
3. He decided to visit, bringing gifts, a checkbook, and Letters of Credit. *(letters; credit)*
4. Berlcha fixed her son a festive meal of Gefilte fish and soup. *(gefilte)*
5. They shared a glass of ritual wine and tried to converse in yiddish. *(Yiddish)*

Use **Unit One Resource Book,** p. 73 for additional support.

Use **Grammar Transparencies and Copymasters,** p. 65.

Use McDougal Littell's ***Language Network,*** Chapter 1, for more instruction and practice in proper and common nouns.

THE SON FROM AMERICA **169**

OVERVIEW

These selections are included in the **Grade 10 InterActive Reader.**

Objectives

1. understand and appreciate an **essay (Literary Analysis)**
2. understand the **theme** of each **nonfiction** selection **(Literary Analysis)**
3. recognize the use of **comparison and contrast (Active Reading)**

Summary

Relying on wry humor and clever descriptive language, the Canadian author Margaret Atwood considers how Canadians and Americans view themselves and each other as neighbors and allies on the world stage of nations. While Canadians are fascinated with America's policies and culture, the Yanks seem barely aware of Canada as a separate nation. Author Pat Mora, born in the Texas border town of El Paso but now living in America's heartland, writes in a more personal style. Separated from her native region and her family's Mexican roots, she sees even more clearly how she has been shaped by this border culture.

Thematic Link

As women who live outside of mainstream American society, each author examines her own culture by comparing it with another. Both draw important conclusions about the role of language and perception in shaping identity at the **cultural crossroads.**

5-Minute Warm-Up

Daily Language SkillBuilder

Have students **proofread** the display sentences on page 15k and write them correctly. The sentences also appear on Transparency 6 of **Grammar Transparencies and Copymasters.**

Through the One-Way Mirror

Essay by MARGARET ATWOOD

The Border: A Glare of Truth

Essay by PAT MORA

Connect to Your Life

Borderline Views Think about life in your community or neighborhood. What are the boundaries that define different neighborhoods? How often do you cross these boundaries to go into the next town or another neighborhood? With a partner, jot down what you have noticed about the borders that separate the two communities or neighborhoods and what life is like on the other side.

Build Background

Long Borders Our nation shares borders with two major countries, Canada to the north and Mexico to the south. Those who live along the border are part of a border culture, often characterized by a blending of two traditions and two languages. Our border with Canada has long been a peaceful one, although after the Civil War many Canadians feared that the United States would expand its borders. With the exception of French-speaking Quebec, the United States and Canada share English as an official language as well as historic ties with Great Britain, Ireland, France, and Scandinavia. This historic legacy helps explain the cultural similarities between the two countries.

In contrast, our southern border's geographic location has often been contested by Mexico, whose people were among the original settlers of the Southwest. In fact, Texas was part of Mexico until 1836; it became part of the United States in 1845. Fighting along the border continued until the United States declared war on Mexico to settle the dispute. In 1848, Mexico signed a treaty giving up land that became California, Nevada, and Utah, and parts of Arizona, Colorado, New Mexico, and Wyoming. These historic events help explain why the Spanish language and many Mexican traditions and customs play a significant role along the Mexican border.

Focus Your Reading

LITERARY ANALYSIS THEME IN NONFICTION Sometimes the **theme,** or message, of a nonfiction selection is directly stated. Other times it is implied, or stated indirectly. As a reader of nonfiction, you can gain insight into the theme of a work by looking for passages that reveal or hint at the writer's opinion. As you read the following two selections, look for details or passages that offer clues to the theme of the selections.

ACTIVE READING COMPARISON AND CONTRAST In both of the following essays, the authors rely on **comparison and contrast** to organize their material and create a text structure. In a comparison, the similarities of two or more objects, persons, events, stories, or, in this case, cultures are examined. Similarities are often indicated by words such as *all, each, both, likewise, also, just,* and *as.* When two or more things are contrasted, the differences are examined. Differences are often indicated by these words: *on the other hand, however, different, whereas,* and *even though.*

READER'S NOTEBOOK Create charts like the ones shown to record the similarities and differences each author uses to develop and organize her essay.

Life in U. S.	Life in Canada

Life in El Paso	Life in Ohio

LESSON RESOURCES

UNIT ONE RESOURCE BOOK, pp. 75–80

ASSESSMENT RESOURCES

Formal Assessment, pp. 31–32

Teacher's Guide to Assessment and Portfolio Use

Test Generator

SKILLS TRANSPARENCIES AND COPYMASTERS

Literary Analysis

- Theme: Influences of Character, Setting, and Plot, T5 (for Paired Activity, p. 178)

Reading and Critical Thinking

- Compare and Contrast, T15 (for Think Critically, item 2, p. 178)

Grammar

- Capitalization I, C162 (for Mini Lesson, p. 176)
- Abstract and Concrete Nouns, C64 (for Mini Lesson, p. 180)

Vocabulary

- Context Clues, C34 (for Mini Lesson, p. 171)
- Figurative Language, C35 (for Mini Lesson, p. 175)

Writing

- Varying Sentence Openers and Closers, T18 (for Writing Option 2, p. 179)
- Interpretive Essay, C33, (for Writing Option 3, p. 179)

INTEGRATED TECHNOLOGY

Audio Library

Internet: Research Starter

Visit our website: www.mcdougallittell.com

THROUGH THE ONE-WAY

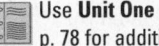

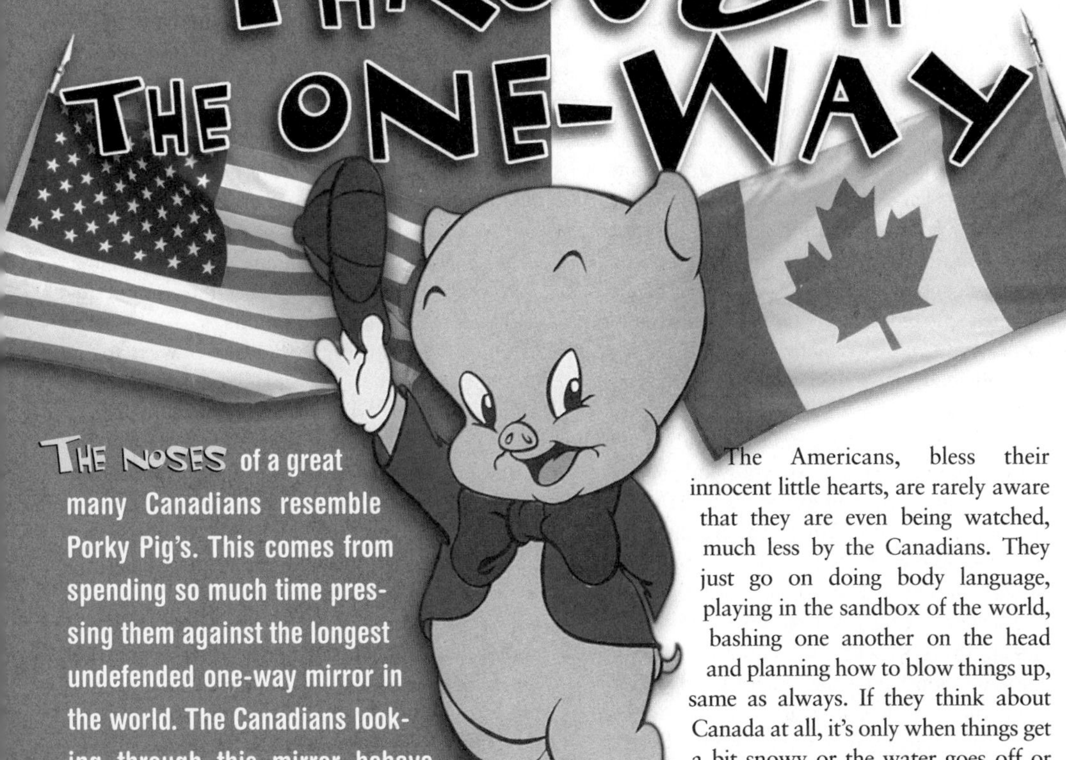

THE NOSES of a great many Canadians resemble Porky Pig's. This comes from spending so much time pressing them against the longest undefended one-way mirror in the world. The Canadians looking through this mirror behave the way people on the hidden side of such mirrors usually do: they observe, analyze, ponder, snoop and wonder what all the activity on the other side means in decipherable human terms.

The Americans, bless their innocent little hearts, are rarely aware that they are even being watched, much less by the Canadians. They just go on doing body language, playing in the sandbox of the world, bashing one another on the head and planning how to blow things up, same as always. If they think about Canada at all, it's only when things get a bit snowy or the water goes off or the Canadians start fussing over some piddly detail, such as fish.[1] Then they regard them as unpatriotic; for Americans don't really see Canadians as foreigners, not like the

1. **some piddly . . . fish:** a reference to the occasional clashes between U.S. and Canadian fishers over the boundaries of their fishing territories.

MIRROR

Margaret Atwood

WORDS TO KNOW **analyze** (ăn'ə-līz') *v.* to study carefully by separating into parts

171

TEACHING THE LITERATURE

Customizing Instruction

Less Proficient Readers
Have students keep these questions in mind as they read:
- Why did this writer choose this particular topic for her essay?
- Am I enjoying this essay? Why or why not?

Students Acquiring English
Have students look through the essays for references to place names and languages. Discuss the role that language plays in relationships between Americans and Canadians, and between Americans and Mexicans, in bridging differences and in sustaining them.

Use **Spanish Study Guide** for additional support, pp. 37–40.

Gifted and Talented
In this essay, Atwood refers to several political and historical events, such as the flight to Canada of American draft-dodgers in the Vietnam War, and the recognition of Cuba and China. As they read this essay, have students make note of these events and find out more about American and Canadian policy and behavior in these matters. Then ask them to explain whether their findings support or refute Atwood's commentary.

Mini Lesson: Preteaching Vocabulary

USING CONTEXT CLUES Call students' attention to the WORDS TO KNOW. Remind them that sometimes they can understand the meaning of an unfamiliar word by examining the context in which the word is used. Use the model sentence to demonstrate the strategy of using context clues that provide inferences to word meaning.

Model Sentence

Emily couldn't study because of the *raucous* laughter coming from the loud television, which probably had a laugh track.

Instruction
- Write the model sentence on the chalkboard.
- Ask a volunteer to summarize the meaning of the sentence.
- Have students use the meaning of the sentence to **infer** meanings for the word *raucous.*
- Ask a volunteer to use the word *raucous* in a sentence.

Use **Unit One Resource Book,** p. 78 for additional support.

A lesson on context clues appears on p. 56 in the Pupil's Edition.

TEACHING THE LITERATURE

Reading and Analyzing

Literary Analysis: PREVIEW

Have students preview both selections. Discuss with them the images on the opening spreads and the titles of each selection. Have students find and discuss the other images in the selections. Discuss with students the Build Background feature on p. 170, then ask them to predict what the selections will be about.

Active Reading COMPARING AND CONTRASTING

As students prepare to identify similarities and differences about life in each area to record in their Reader's Notebooks, suggest that they first just jot down any details they find. Later, they can scan the two columns to see whether each detail points out a similarity between the two cultures or a difference.

Use **Unit One Resource Book,** p. 76 for additional support.

Literary Analysis THEME IN NONFICTION

After students read the opening paragraphs of each essay, have them write down what they believe the theme is. After they have read each essay, ask students whether their predictions were accurate and why.

Possible Responses: Atwood: Canadians are more interested in Americans than vice versa, which is troublesome. Mora: Language and traditions are important because they keep a culture alive.

Use **Unit One Resource Book,** p. 77 for additional support.

Mexicans, unless they do something weird like
speak French or beat the New York Yankees at
baseball. Really, think the Americans, the Canadians
1 are just like us, or would be if they could.

Or we could switch metaphors and call the border the longest undefended backyard fence in the world. The Canadians are the folks in the neat little bungalow, with the tidy little garden and the duck pond. The Americans are the other folks, the ones in the sprawly mansion with the bad-taste statues on the lawn. There's a perpetual party, or something, going on there—loud music, raucous laughter, smoke billowing from the barbecue. Beer bottles and Coke cans land among the peonies. The Canadians have their own beer bottles and barbecue smoke, but they tend to overlook it. Your own mess is always more forgivable than the mess someone else makes on your patio.

The Canadians can't exactly call the police—they suspect that the Americans are the police—and part of their distress, which seems permanent, comes from their uncertainty as to whether or not they've been invited. Sometimes they do drop by next door, and find it exciting but scary. Sometimes the Americans drop by their house and find it clean. This worries the Canadians. They worry a lot. Maybe those Americans want to buy up their duck pond, with all the money they seem to have, and turn it into a cesspool or a water-skiing emporium.

It also worries them that the Americans don't seem to know who the Canadians are, or even where, exactly, they are. Sometimes the Americans call Canada their backyard, sometimes their front yard, both of which imply ownership. Sometimes they say they are the Mounties and the Canadians are Rose Marie.[2] (All these things have, in fact, been said by American politicians.) Then they accuse the Canadians of being paranoid and having an identity crisis. Heck, there is no call for the Canadians to fret about their identity, because everyone knows they're Americans, really. If the Canadians disagree with that, they're told not to be so insecure.

One of the problems is that Canadians and Americans are educated backward from one another. The Canadians—except for the Québecois,[3] one keeps saying—are taught about the rest of the world first and Canada second. The Americans are taught about the United States first, and maybe later about other places, if they're of strategic importance. The Vietnam War draft dodgers got more culture shock in Canada than they did in Sweden. It's not the clothing that is different, it's those mental noises.

Of course, none of this holds true when you get close enough, where concepts like "Americans" and "Canadians" dissolve and people are just people, or anyway some of them are, the ones you happen to approve of. I, for instance, have never met any Americans I didn't like, but I only get to meet the nice ones. That's what the businessmen think too, though they have other individuals in mind. But big-scale national mythologies have a way of showing up in things like foreign policy, and at events like international writers' congresses, where the Canadians often find they have more to talk about with the Australians, the West Indians, the New Zealanders[4] and even the once-loathed snooty Brits, now declining into humanity with the dissolution of empire, than they do with the impenetrable and mysterious Yanks.

But only sometimes. Because surely the Canadians understand the Yanks. Shoot, don't they see Yank movies, read Yank mags, bobble

2. **Mounties . . . Rose Marie:** a reference to the 1926 operetta *Rose Marie* (later the basis of a popular film starring Nelson Eddy and Jeanette MacDonald), in which the main characters are a Royal Canadian Mounted Policeman and the woman he loves.

3. **Québecois** (kā'bĕ-kwä'): the French-speaking residents of the Canadian province of Quebec.

4. **Australians . . . New Zealanders:** peoples whose countries were, like Canada, once part of the British Empire.

WORDS TO KNOW

raucous (rô'kəs) *adj.* loud and disorderly; boisterous

impenetrable (ĭm-pĕn'ĭ-trə-bəl) *adj.* impossible to understand; incapable of being pierced

172

Teaching Options

Mini Lesson: Viewing and Representing

Porky Pig **by Frederick Bean "Tex" Avery**

ART APPRECIATION Born in Taylor, Texas, "Tex" Avery (1908–1980) began drawing comic strips in high school. After studying at the Art Institute of Chicago, he moved to California to take advantage of opportunities offered by the growing film industry. He was soon hired by one of the early pioneers in the animation field, Walter Lantz. Later he was a leading artist at Warner Brothers and MGM during the 1930s and 1940s, an era considered the Golden Age of Hollywood cartoon comedy.

Instruction Point out to students that a cheerful Porky Pig is positioned between the American and Canadian flags. Ask what significance they think this image has for people on either side of the border.

Possible Response: Americans see Porky Pig as an American creation. To Canadians, Porky Pig represents another aspect of American culture they can admire but never consider theirs.

around to Yank music and watch Yank telly, as well as their own, when there is any?

Sometimes the Canadians think it's their job to interpret the Yanks to the rest of the world; explain them, sort of. This is an illusion: they don't understand the Yanks as much as they think they do, and it isn't their job.

But, as we say up here among God's frozen people, when Washington catches a cold, Ottawa sneezes. Some Canadians even refer to their capital city as Washington North and wonder why we're paying those guys in Ottawa when a telephone order service would be cheaper. Canadians make jokes about the relationship with Washington which the Americans, in their thin-skinned, bunion-toed way, construe as anti-American (they tend to see any nonworshipful comment coming from that gray, protoplasmic fuzz outside their borders as anti-American). They are no more anti-American than the jokes Canadians make about the weather: it's there, it's big, it's hard to influence, and it affects your life.

Of course, in any conflict with the Dreaded Menace, whatever it might be, the Canadians would line up with the Yanks, probably, if they thought it was a real menace, or if the Yanks twisted their arms or other bodily parts enough or threatened a "scorched-earth policy" (another real quote). Note the qualifiers. The Canadian idea of a menace is not the same as the U.S. one. Canada, for instance, never broke off diplomatic relations with Cuba, and it was quick to recognize China. Contemplating the U.S.-Soviet growling match, Canadians are apt to recall a line from Blake[5]: "They became what they beheld."

Certainly both superpowers suffer from the imperial diseases once so noteworthy among the Romans, the British and the French: arrogance and myopia. But the bodily-parts threat is real enough, and accounts for the observable wimpiness and flunkiness of some Ottawa politicians. Nobody, except at welcoming-committee time, pretends this is an equal relationship.

Americans don't have Porky Pig noses. Instead they have Mr. Magoo eyes, with which they see the rest of the world. That would not be a problem if the United States were not so powerful. But it is, so it is. ❖

5. **Blake:** the British poet and artist William Blake.

Thinking Through the Literature

1. **Comprehension Check** What is the "one-way mirror"?
2. ACTIVE READING | COMPARE AND CONTRAST Examine the list of details about life in the United States and life in Canada that you compiled in your READER'S NOTEBOOK. What do you think are the most important similarities and differences?
3. Why do you think Atwood uses Mr. Magoo to describe the Americans and Porky Pig to describe the Canadians?
4. What does Atwood really think about Americans and Canadians? Cite evidence from her essay to support your opinion.

WORDS TO KNOW

construe (kən-stro͞o') *v.* to interpret
myopia (mī-ō'pē-ə) *n.* nearsightedness

173

Customizing Instruction

Less Proficient Readers

1 Help students follow the essay by pointing out two of the essay's primary metaphors. The first metaphor compares the U.S.-Canadian border to a one-way mirror through which Canadians view Americans. The second metaphor compares Canada and America to neighbors separated by a fence.

Students Acquiring English

Help students understand the following idioms: *drop by,* meaning to visit unexpectedly; *having an identity crisis,* meaning uncertainty about what is important about you and *snooty,* meaning snobbish or conceited.

Thinking Through the Literature

1. **Comprehension Check** The "one-way mirror" is the border between Canada and the United States that allows Canadians to look out.
2. Some similarities are language and historical ties to Britain. Some differences: Canadians are more interested in Americans than vice-versa; Americans are taught first about the United States, while Canadians are taught first about the world.
3. Possible Response: Canadians get a turned-up nose as a result of pressing up against the glass and looking at the Americans. Mr. Magoo can barely see, much like Americans who are completely unaware of anyone else.
4. Good responses will note that Atwood compliments and notes the eccentricities of both countries.

Use **Unit One Resource Book,** p. 80 for additional support.

A lesson on context clues appears on page 179 in the Pupil's Edition.

BLOCK SCHEDULING: MANAGING TIME

If your schedule requires that you cover the lesson objectives in a shorter time, use . . .
- Preparing to Read, p. 170
- Thinking Through the Literature, p. 178
- Vocabulary in Action, p. 179
- Grammar in Context, p. 180

If you want to take advantage of longer class time, use . . .
- TE Teaching Options: Preteaching Vocabulary p. 171; Viewing and Representing, p. 172, Vocabulary Strategy, p. 175, Informal Assessment, p. 177
- Choices & Challenges, p 179

Reading and Analyzing

Reading Skills and Strategies: CLARIFYING

A Point out that Pat Mora suggests that smell, one of the five senses, evokes her heritage. What senses can students connect to their heritage?

Possible Response: Accept all reasonable answers that include one or more of the five senses: sight, smell, taste, hearing, touch. Students should give explanations or examples from their heritage in their response.

Reading Skills and Strategies: MAKING CONNECTIONS

B Have students explain what Pat Mora means when she says that "learning another language is renaming the world."

Possible Response: Words in another language can create different images or perceptions of the world.

The Border
A Glare of Truth

Pat Mora

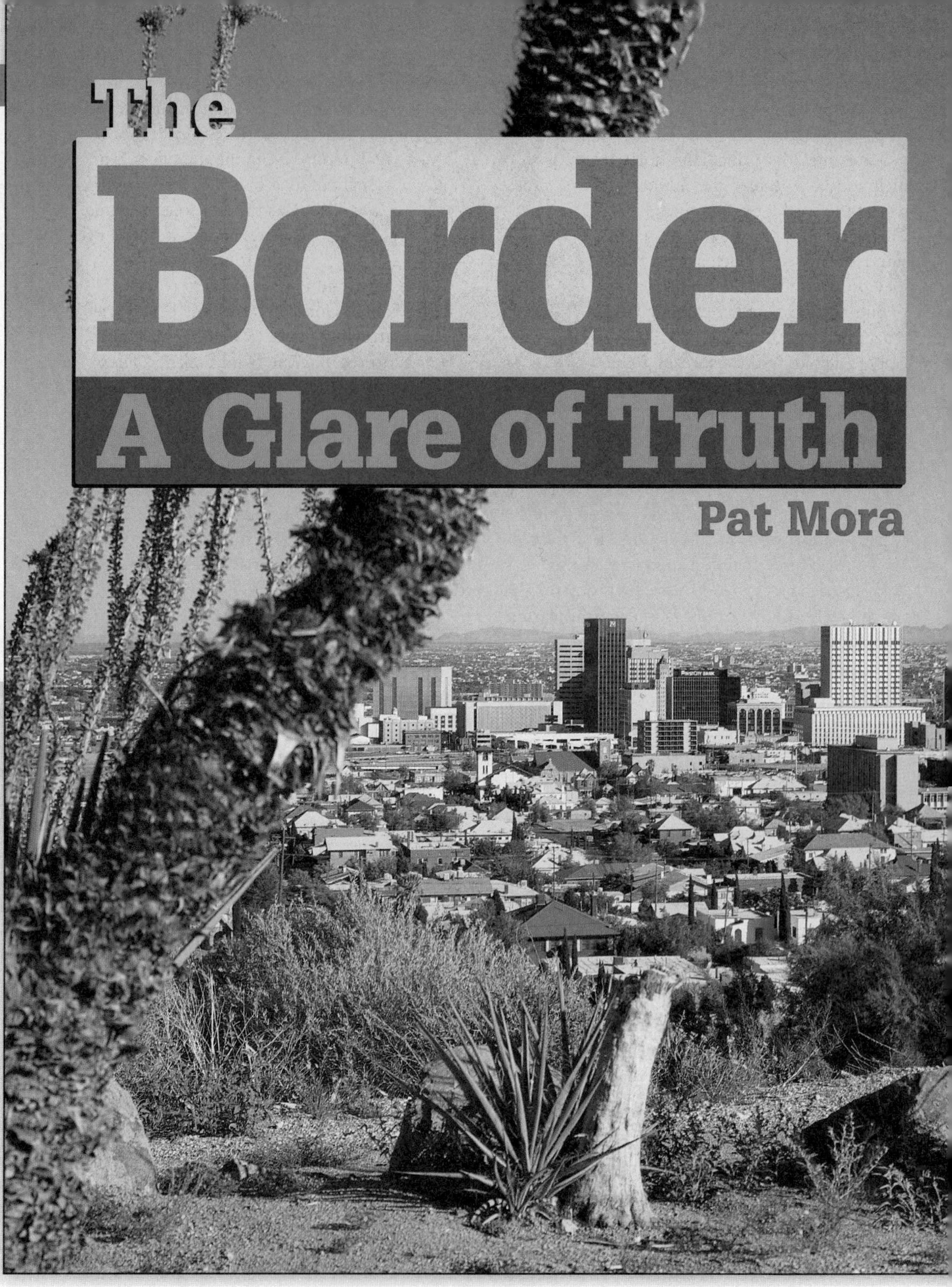

I moved away for the first time from the U.S.-Mexican border in the fall of 1989. Friends were sure I'd miss the visible evidence of Mexico's proximity found in cities such as my native El Paso. Friends smiled that I'd soon be back for good
A Mexican food, for the delicate taste and smell of cilantro,[1] for soft tortillas freshly made. There were jokes about care packages flying to the Midwest.

Although most of my adult home and work life had been spent speaking English, I was prepared to miss the sound of Spanish weaving in and out of my days like the warm aroma from a familiar bakery. I knew I'd miss the pleasure of moving back and forth between two languages—a pleasure that can deepen human understanding and increase our versatility conceptually as well as linguistically. 1

And indeed, when I hear a phrase in Spanish in a Cincinnati restaurant, my head turns quickly. I listen, silently wishing to be part of that other conversation, if only for a few moments, to feel Spanish in my mouth. I'm reading more poetry in Spanish, sometimes reading the lines aloud to myself, enjoying sounds I don't otherwise hear. Recently I heard a voice on National Public Radio say that learning another language is renaming the world. B What an interesting perception. Because language shapes as well as reflects our reality, exploring it allows us to see and to explore our world anew, much as experiencing the world with a young child causes us to pause, savor.

I smile when my children, who were too busy when they were younger, now inform me that when they visit they hope we'll be speaking Spanish. They have discovered as I did that languages are channels, sometimes to other people, sometimes to other views of the world, sometimes to other aspects of ourselves. So we struggle with irregular verbs, laughing together. 2

Is it my family—children, parents, siblings, niece, nephews—that I miss in this land of leaves so unlike my bare desert? Of course, but

1. **cilantro** (sē-län′trô) *Spanish:* coriander—an herb whose leaves are used as a seasoning.

WORDS TO KNOW
proximity (prŏk-sĭm′ĭ-tē) *n.* closeness
versatility (vûr′sə-tĭl′ĭ-tē) *n.* an ability to do many things well

Customizing Instruction

Students Acquiring English
Ask students about their experiences trying to become bilingual. How does it feel to move back and forth between two languages, as the author does?

1 Discuss the phrase "increase our versatility conceptually as well as linguistically." In essence, this means that we are flexible both in our speech and in our thinking. Help students understand that Mora is pointing to the fundamental connection between thought and language.

Less Proficient Readers
2 Use the following question to help students understand why the author misses living in a bilingual environment.

- Why does the author smile when her children tell her they want to speak Spanish when they visit?

Possible Response: She is happy that her children understand the importance of their Spanish heritage, but amused that they have changed their attitude in adulthood.

Mini Lesson Vocabulary Strategy

USING CONTEXT CLUES TO DETERMINE MEANING OF FIGURATIVE LANGUAGE

Instruction Context clues not only provide insight into the meaning of unfamiliar words, they can also help students determine the meaning of figurative language. Examples of figurative language include similes and metaphors.

Have students reread the first sentence of the second paragraph of this essay: "Although most of my adult home and work life had been spent speaking English, I was prepared to miss the sound of Spanish weaving in and out of my days like the warm aroma from a familiar bakery." Then have them identify context clues that help them understand the figurative meaning of this sentence. For example, the word *like* helps the reader identify the simile comparing the sound of Spanish to a warm aroma.

Practice Have students identify other examples of figurative language in this essay. Then have them list the context clues that help them determine meaning.

Use **Vocabulary Transparencies and Copymasters,** p. 35.

A lesson on using context clues to determine meaning of figurative language appears on p. 56 in the Pupil's Edition.

Reading and Analyzing

Literary Analysis: FIGURATIVE LANGUAGE

Discuss with students how figurative language—simile, metaphor, and personification, for example—give texture and depth to writing. Ask them to explain what comparisons are being made by the following figures of speech.

- "a sturdy, elastic web"—a metaphor for the connection by telephone
- "prevalent as scorpions"—a simile that compares a deadly insect to poverty

Literary Analysis: TONE

Ask students to compare and contrast the tones of the two essays, or the authors' attitudes toward their subjects. Are the essays nostalgic, sarcastic, satirical, bitter, humorous, idealistic, cynical, wistful, or something else? If students were to write an essay comparing their own culture to another, what tone do they think they might adopt, and why?
Possible Response: The tone of Atwood's essay is humorous and satirical, while the tone of Mora's essay is nostalgic, wistful, and proud.

Literary Analysis THEME IN NONFICTION

A Have students discuss the last paragraph in terms of theme. Ask them to identify one sentence in this paragraph that states the theme.

Possible Response: "What I miss about the sights and sounds of the border is, I've finally concluded, its stern honesty" states the theme because it answers the main question in the essay: What do I miss most about the border?

my family, although miles away, is with me daily. The huge telephone bills and the steady stream of letters and cards are a long-distance version of the web of caring we once created around kitchen tables. Our family web just happens to stretch across these United States, a sturdy, elastic web steadily maintained by each in his or her own way.

Oh, I miss the meals seasoned with that family phrase, "Remember the time when . . . ?" But I've learned through the years to cherish our gatherings when I'm in the thick of them, to sink into the faces and voices, to store the memories and stories like the industrious Ohio squirrel outside my window stores her treasures.

I've enjoyed this furry, scurrying companion as I've enjoyed the silence of bare tree limbs against an evening sky, updrafts of snow outside our third-floor window, the ivory light of cherry blossoms. I feel fortunate to be experiencing the geographical center of this country, which astutely calls itself the Heartland. If I'm hearing the "heart," its steady, predictable rhythms, what am I missing from this country's southern border, its margin?

Is it other rhythms? I remember my mixed feelings as a young girl whenever my father selected a Mexican station on the radio, feelings my children now experience about me. I wanted so to *be an American,* which in my mind, and perhaps in the minds of many on the border, meant (and means) shunning anything from Mexico.

But as I grew I learned to like dancing to those rhythms. I learned to value not only the rhythms but all that they symbolized. As an adult, such music became associated with celebrations and friends, with warmth and the sharing of emotions. I revel in a certain Mexican passion not for life or about life, but *in* life—a certain intensity in the daily living of it, a certain abandon in such music, in the hugs, sometimes in the anger. I miss the *chispas,* "sparks," that spring from the willingness, the habit, of allowing the inner self to burst through polite restraints. Sparks can be dangerous but, like risks, are necessary.

I brought cassettes of Mexican and Latin American music with us when we drove to Ohio. I'd roll the car window down and turn the volume up, taking a certain delight in sending such sounds like mischievous imps across fields and into trees. Broadcasting my culture, if you will.

Foreign Spooks

Released full blast into the autumn air
from trumpets, drums, flutes,
the sounds burst from my car like confetti
riding the first strong current.
The invisible imps from Peru, Spain,
Mexico grin as they spring from guitars,
harps, hand claps, and violins,
they stream across the flat fields of Ohio,
hide in the drafts of abandoned gray barns,
and the shutters of stern, white houses,
burrow into cold cow's ears and the crackle
of dry corn, in squirrel fur, pond ripple,
tree gnarl,
owl hollow, until the wind sighs

and they open their wide, impudent
mouths, and together con gusto[2]
startle sleeping farm wives,
sashaying raccoons, and even
the old harvest moon.

2. **con gusto** (kôn gōōs'tô) *Spanish:* with pleasure.

WORDS TO KNOW
astutely (ə-stōōt'lē) *adv.* with keen perceptiveness; wisely
impudent (ĭm'pyə-dənt) *adj.* bold and shameless

176

Teaching Options

Mini Lesson Grammar

CAPITALIZATION The following words should always be capitalized: the first word of a sentence, proper nouns such as names and places, proper adjectives formed from proper nouns and the pronoun "I." Write the following sentence on the chalkboard, and ask students to rewrite it correctly, then discuss.
"i think pat mora's essay gives an interesting picture of the experience of a spanish speaker in the united states."
"I think Pat Mora's essay gives an interesting picture of the experience of a Spanish speaker in the United States."

Practice Have students correct the faulty capitalization in the following sentences.

1. The u.s.-mexican border is a place where diverse Cultures meet. (*Capitalize U.S., Mexican; use lower case for cultures.*)
2. When Mora moved to cincinnati, ohio, her parents remained in el Paso. (*Capitalize Cincinnati, Ohio,* and *El*)

Use **Grammar Transparencies and Copymasters,** p. 162.

Use McDougal Littell's ***Language Network,*** Chapter 10, for more instruction in capitalization.

On my first return visit to Texas, I stopped to hear a group of *mariachis* playing their instruments with proud gusto. I was surprised and probably embarrassed when my eyes filled with tears not only at the music, but at the sight of wonderful Mexican faces. The musicians were playing for some senior citizens. The sight of brown, knowing eyes that quickly accepted me with a smile, the stories in those eyes and in the wrinkled faces were more delicious than any *fajitas* or *flan*[3].

When I lived on the border, I had the privilege accorded to a small percentage of our citizens: I daily saw the native land of my grandparents. I grew up in the Chihuahua desert, as did they, only we grew up on different sides of the Rio Grande. That desert—its firmness, resilience, and fierceness, its whispered chants and tempestuous dance, its wisdom and majesty—shaped us as geography always shapes its inhabitants. The desert persists in me, both inspiring and compelling me to sing about her and her people, their roots and blooms and thorns.

The desert is harsh, hard as life, no carpet of leaves cushions a walk, no forest conceals the shacks on the other side of the sad river. Although a Midwest winter is hard, it ends, melts into rich soil yielding the yellow trumpeting of daffodils. But the desert in any season can be relentless as poverty and hunger, realities prevalent as scorpions in that stark terrain. Anthropologist Renato Rosaldo, in his provocative challenge to his colleagues, *Culture and Truth,* states that we live in a world "saturated with inequality, power, and domination."

The culture of the **A** border illustrates this truth daily, glaringly. Children go to sleep hungry and stare at stores filled with toys they'll never touch, with books they'll never read. Oddly, I miss that clear view of the difference between my comfortable life and the lives of so many who also speak Spanish, value family, music, celebration. In a broader sense, I miss the visible reminder of the difference between my insulated, economically privileged life and the life of most of my fellow humans. What I miss about the sights and sounds of the border is, I've finally concluded, its stern honesty. The fierce light of that grand, wide Southwest sky not only filled me with energy, it revealed the glare of truth. ❖

3. **fajitas** (fä-hē'täs) . . . **flan** (flän) *Spanish:* two popular Mexican foods—the first a dish of grilled meat wrapped in tortillas, the second a custard dessert.

WORDS TO KNOW **prevalent** (prĕv'ə-lənt) *adj.* widespread; common

Customizing Instruction

Less Proficient Readers
As they read, have students make a list of things Mora misses about her bilingual culture. Tell them that each paragraph includes at least one thing they can add to their lists.

Possible Responses:
- speaking Spanish more often
- being in the center of her family "web"
- dancing to Mexican music
- listening to Mexican music
- Mexican food
- the Chihuahua desert
- the clear view the border gives of poverty, hunger, and illiteracy

Students Acquiring English
Have students look up the meaning of the following words and write down the definitions: *siblings, shunning, imps, gusto, resilience, tempestuous, provocative, stern.* Encourage them to write a sentence using each word correctly.

Answers: brothers and sisters; avoiding, rejecting; mischievous creatures; energy, flair; flexibility, durability; stormy; calling up a feeling or thought, enticing; serious, unforgiving

Multiple Learning Styles
Visual Learners

Have students create a diorama or drawing of the border between Mexico and the United States, based on Mora's description of the desert and the people.

✓ Assessment Informal Assessment

EVALUATING THE ESSAYS Have students work together in groups to answer the following questions. Tell them to support their answers with evidence from the text and from their own experience.

A. What is the theme of each essay?
B. What is the tone of each essay?
C. How is figurative language used in each essay?
D. Do you agree with all the points made by the authors? Why or why not?
E. Why do you think the authors chose to write about their subjects in essay form? How would their subjects be different as stories or poems?

RUBRIC

3 Full Accomplishment Group's response answers all five questions and provides logical support. The response demonstrates a full understanding of all aspects of both essays.

2 Substantial Accomplishment Group's response answers all five questions and provides some logical support. The response demonstrates a substantial understanding of most aspects of both essays.

1 Little or Partial Accomplishment Group's response does not answer all five questions and/or lacks logical support. The response demonstrates little understanding of the essays.

GUIDING STUDENT RESPONSE

Connect to the Literature

1. What Do You Think?
Students may mention how Mora feels about her family being from a country much less powerful than her own. Mora is a person very attuned to the physical world: she misses the sights of the desert, the sounds of music, the smells and tastes of her favorite foods. She is compassionate and sees clearly the differences between her life in the United States and the world where her own roots go deep.

Comprehension Check

- Acceptable answers include speaking Spanish and hearing Spanish spoken; regular personal contact with her family; the "sparks" of everyday life—the passion, the hugs, the occasional outbursts of anger; the desert.
- Both Mora and her grandparents grew up in the Chihuahua desert, although her grandparents grew up in Mexico and Mora grew up in El Paso.

Think Critically

2. Responses will vary. Some responses will include Mora's feelings about the weather and terrain of the two places and her feelings about the personal differences such as language and family.
3. Possible Response: Learning a different language has given Mora a whole new way of experiencing the world. Hearing even a few words can take her back in memory. She loves the sounds and rhythms of Mexican and other Latin American music; additionally, the music symbolizes for her the warmth of friends and the sharing of emotions. Every day, Mexican life is lived intensely. Emotions readily burst to the surface.
4. Possible Response: She makes it clear that it is the contrast with her new life that allows her to see her old life more clearly. She points this out by describing not only her feelings about Ohio, but her feelings on returning for visits to El Paso and to Mexico.
5. Answers will vary, but should include the idea that the Mexican-Texan border exposes the privileged Americans to the poverty and struggle on the other side; it allows no one side to hide from the other.

Thinking through the LITERATURE

Connect to the Literature

1. **What Do You Think?** What impressions of the author did you form as a result of reading this essay?

Comprehension Check

- Describe three things that Mora remembers affectionately about her life in El Paso.
- How does the desert link Mora to the native land of her grandparents?

Think Critically

2. **ACTIVE READING** **COMPARISON AND CONTRAST** Compare the chart you created in your **READER'S NOTEBOOK** with a classmate's chart. Discuss what you think are the most important similarities and differences between life in El Paso and life in Ohio.

3. How does Mora's heritage enrich her life?

   THINK ABOUT
   - her views about language
   - what she values about Mexican and Latin American music
   - what she means by the "Mexican passion not for life or about life but *in* life"

4. Do you think that Mora could have come to the same conclusions about her heritage if she had not moved away from El Paso? Explain your opinion.

5. What do you think Mora means by the title "The Border: A Glare of Truth"?

   THINK ABOUT
   - her view of the desert and its influence on culture
   - what she means by the "stern honesty" of the border
   - the diversity represented by the "culture of the border"

Extend Interpretations

6. **Comparing Texts** Study how each author has organized the information in her essay. Though both Atwood and Mora rely on **comparison and contrast,** they do so in different ways. Do you think one way is more helpful to the reader than another? Explain your opinion.

7. **Connect to Life** In what ways do you think it would be difficult to live next to the United States? Explain your opinion.

Literary Analysis

THEME IN NONFICTION The **theme** is the message of a nonfiction selection. It is not the same as the subject, although in nonfiction, it often has something to do with the subject. Rather, the theme reveals the writer's understanding of life, or human nature. For example, in "The Border," Pat Mora's subject is culture, and her theme reveals what she thinks about cultural differences.

Paired Activity With a partner, review Atwood's essay, identifying clues that suggest her perceptions of Canadian and American cultural differences. Then write a sentence that states Atwood's theme. Compare it with those of your classmates. Next, review Mora's selection by studying examples of what she misses from her border culture. Use this list to help you write a sentence that states her theme.

Atwood's Perceptions	What Mora Misses
• Canadians are in "the neat little bungalow"; Americans are in "the sprawly mansion."	• Speaking and hearing Spanish

Extend Interpretations

Comparing Texts In analyzing text structures, students should note that the organization of Atwood's essay has a more traditional compare-and-contrast structure, moving back and forth between Canadian and American attributes. Mora's essay flows more loosely from one trait of border culture to the next, while offering relatively few examples about life in Ohio. The contrast exists in the form of a standing implication that life in Ohio is different from life at the Mexican border. Student opinions about the effectiveness of these two techniques will vary, but should include rational support.

Connect to Life Accept all reasonable, well-supported responses. The student is expected to draw upon his/her own background to provide a connection to texts.

Literary Analysis

Paired Activity Remind students to check to make sure that their sentences state an idea or message and do not merely identify a subject.

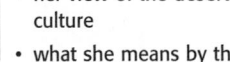

Writing Options

1. Border Interview Imagine that a television news station has decided to interview Mora and Atwood together. Write the interview between the newscaster and the two guests. In your interview, have the authors address the advantages and disadvantages of life on the border. If possible, include direct quotations from both essays.

2. Image Analysis In describing Americans, Atwood wrote, "Americans don't have Porky Pig noses. Instead, they have Mr. Magoo eyes, with which they see the rest of the world." Write an analysis of what you think she means by this image.

Writing Handbook
See page 1159: Analysis.

3. Heritage Essay Write a personal essay in which you describe a significant cultural tradition in your life that makes you reflect on the importance of ethnic ties. Place the entry in your **Working Portfolio.**

Activities & Explorations

1. Visual Essay Both selections have many images that appeal to the sense of sight. Working with a partner or a small group, choose one of the essays and create illustrations that tell the essay's story in pictures or cartoons.
~ **VIEWING AND REPRESENTING**

2. Illustrated Map Choose either of our geographic neighbors and design a map that shows its border with the United States. Be sure to include major border cities.
~ **GEOGRAPHY**

Inquiry and Research

Over the course of the 20th century, millions of people have immigrated to the United States. Find out more facts about our nation's recent immigrants and their countries of origin.

Real World Link
Begin your research by reading the magazine article on page 181.

More Online: Research Starter
www.mcdougallittell.com

Vocabulary in Action

EXERCISE A: CONTEXT CLUES Find the word that is used incorrectly in each sentence below. Rewrite the sentence, replacing the incorrect word with a Word to Know.

1. Atwood's article is about how the people of two neighboring countries can misunderstand one another as they try to cower one another's attitudes.
2. Canadians see Americans as loud, delicate, and tasteless.
3. Relations between the United States and the former Soviet Union included an element of influenza, according to Atwood.
4. She says that Americans prevail any criticism as anti-American.
5. Even though Americans and Canadians are so similar, they remain an unavailable mystery to one another.

EXERCISE B: MEANING CLUES Choose the Word to Know that is the best solution for each riddle.

1. I happen often in many places.
2. I have many talents.
3. I describe a clever way of doing things.
4. I am extremely rude.
5. I am nearer than you think.

Building Vocabulary
For an in-depth discussion on how to expand your vocabulary, see page 1102.

WORDS TO KNOW					
	analyze	construe	impudent	prevalent	raucous
	astutely	impenetrable	myopia	proximity	versatility

Writing Options

1. **Border Interview** Remind students that a good interviewer asks open-ended questions.
2. **Image Analysis** Points might include: Unlike Canadians, we look *out* at the world and don't see much. Canadians look *into* our world with a combination of envy and bewilderment.
3. **Heritage Essay** Ask students to think about which elements of their lives are *different* from most of the people they know. The elements that differ are more likely to come from ethnic roots.

Activities & Explorations

1. **Visual Essay** Some visual images include: In Margaret Atwood's essay: Porky Pig and Mr. Magoo, Mounties, mirror, fence. In Pat Mora's essay: the bare desert, a family around a kitchen table, wrinkled faces of old people.
2. **Illustrated Map** You might want to make this a cooperative activity.

Inquiry & Research

Suggest that students focus their research on specific aspects of immigration.

Vocabulary in Action

EXERCISE A: CONTEXT CLUES

1. Atwood's article is about how the people of the two neighboring countries can misunderstand one another as they try to analyze one another's attitudes.
2. Canadians see Americans as loud, raucous, and tasteless.
3. Relations between the United States and the former Soviet Union included an element of myopia, according to Atwood.
4. She says that Americans construe any criticism as anti-American.
5. Even though Americans and Canadians are so similar, they remain an impenetrable mystery to one another.

EXERCISE B: MEANING CLUES

1. prevalent
2. versatility
3. astutely
4. impudent
5. proximity

Grammar in Context

WRITING EXERCISE Answers will vary. Possible responses are shown.

1. At the border there is evidence of the nearness of Mexico, such as fresh tortillas, lively music, and Spanish voices.
2. When Pat Mora moved to Cincinnati, she missed her family—all the children, parents, sisters and brothers, nieces and nephews.
3. Mora and her family engage in long-distance communication through long telephone calls and letters and frequent post cards.

Grammar in Context: Abstract and Concrete Nouns

Pat Mora uses abstract and concrete nouns to describe living on the U.S.-Mexican border.

> **The culture of the border illustrates this truth daily, glaringly. Children go to sleep hungry and stare at stores filled with toys they'll never touch, with books they'll never read.**

Abstract nouns, like those shown in blue type, name things that cannot be perceived with the senses. **Concrete nouns,** like those shown in red type, name objects that can be seen, heard, smelled, touched, or tasted. Often writers follow abstract nouns that express general concepts (like *culture* and *truth)* with concrete nouns that illustrate or clarify those concepts.

WRITING EXERCISE In each sentence, supply a group of words containing concrete nouns that illustrate the concept named by the underlined abstract noun.

Example: An intense longing _____ envelops her now that she is away from home.

An intense longing for her scratched-up desk, battered green stapler, and bright blue pencil holder envelops her now that she is away from home.

1. At the border there is evidence of the nearness of Mexico, such as _____.
2. When Pat Mora moved to Cincinnati, she missed her family—all the _____.
3. Mora and her family engage in long-distance communication through _____.

Margaret Atwood
1939–

Other Works
The Circle Game
Lady Oracle
Surfacing
The Handmaid's Tale
Cat's Eye

Canada's Treasure Margaret Atwood, a poet, novelist, essayist, critic, and short-story writer, has been called "a national heroine of the arts." Her novels, which have won worldwide critical acclaim, typically focus on female characters who search for identity in a confusing and often threatening world. A number of her books have become best-sellers, earning her a loyal audience. As reporter Judy Klemesrud notes, "People follow her on the streets and in stores." A frequent guest on Canadian television and radio, she is one of her country's most visible writers.

Wilderness Roots Born in the city of Ottawa in Ontario, Canada, Atwood spent much of her childhood in wilderness regions, where she accompanied her scientist father on long field trips. Atwood grew up in a highly educated family that encouraged her to think for herself. She began writing poetry at age 5; when she was 16, she realized that writing was all she wanted to do.

Pat Mora
1942–

Other Works
Chants
Borders
Communion
Agua Santa/Holy Water

On the Border In her poetry, short stories, and essays, Pat Mora portrays the cultural diversity and visual beauty of the Southwest and the harmony that can exist between nature and human beings. Mora has spent most of her life in El Paso, where she was born. (Her four grandparents had migrated from Mexico to El Paso to escape a revolution.) She has said that when she was young, she spoke Spanish at home with her grandmother and aunt, but she did not always want her school friends to know that she spoke Spanish. After receiving a master's degree from the University of Texas at El Paso, Mora pursued a career in teaching.

The Value of Heritage In 1986, Mora received a Kellogg National Fellowship to study ways of preserving cultures. She explains, "I am interested in how we save languages and traditions. What we have inside of our homes and our families is a treasure chest that we don't pay attention to."

Teaching Options

Mini Lesson Grammar

ABSTRACT AND CONCRETE NOUNS Remind students that concrete nouns are people, places, or things that can be perceived with the senses. Abstract nouns, on the other hand, cannot be perceived with the senses. Abstract nouns are concepts or ideas rather than objects.

Exercise Write the following words on the chalkboard and ask students to identify them as abstract or concrete nouns:

love *(abstract)*
telephone *(concrete)*
Mexico *(concrete)*
travel *(abstract)*
tortilla *(concrete)*
envy *(abstract)*
yard *(concrete)*
mirror *(concrete)*
Porky Pig *(concrete)*
admiration *(abstract)*

Use **Unit One Resource Book,** p. 79 for additional support.

Use **Grammar Transparencies and Copymasters,** p. 64.

from To Make a Nation:
How Immigrants Are Changing America

BY PENNY LOEB, DORIAN FRIEDMAN, MARY C. LORD, DAN MCGRAW AND KUKULA GLASTRIS

❶ More than 8.6 million immigrants entered the United States during the 1980s, an influx which has impacted the United States. economically, politically, and socially.

Communities across America are grappling with what many politicians, pundits, and talk-show hosts refer to simply as the "immigrant problem." In the 1980s, the nation absorbed more than 8.6 million newcomers, mostly from Asia, Latin America, and the Caribbean. . . .

❷ To better understand who the new immigrants are and what impact they have on the nation, *U.S. News* conducted a computer analysis of 12.5 million recently released census records. Reporters also interviewed dozens of immigrants and local government officials in eight communities across the nation. The results reveal a somewhat surprising picture of the newest Americans—those who arrived between 1980 and 1990. Principal findings of the *U.S. News* study:

❸
- Far from being uneducated huddled masses, a majority of recent immigrants have high-school educations; the exceptions are Mexicans and Indochinese refugees. More than half those from nations such as the Philippines have bachelor's degrees.
- Contrary to popular opinion, immigrants do not rob citizens of jobs but either expand employment niches or take jobs few Americans want.
- Most newcomers do not rely on welfare. Though public assistance increased much faster for a few immigrant groups than for citizens, overall only about 4 percent of new immigrants received welfare aid.
- While only 20 percent of recent immigrants boast incomes higher than the average U.S. citizen, they catch up. After a decade in this country, immigrants, on average, took home salaries comparable to those of nonimmigrant Americans.
- There is no significant difference in political opinions between immigrants and American-born citizens. While immigrants are more apt to register as independents, both immigrants and native-born citizens hold nearly identical beliefs on issues such as crime and welfare, a comparison of polling data from the University of Chicago shows.

Reading for Information

When you read a magazine article, are you able to sort facts from opinions? How do you know whether the facts you're reading are accurate?

DISTINGUISHING FACT AND OPINION

A **fact** is a statement that can be proved to be correct or incorrect. Because statements of fact can sometimes be incorrect, it is important for readers to consider the source of the information and judge its **reliability,** or dependability. A reliable source for statistics on population growth would be the U.S. Census Bureau, for example.

An **opinion** is a statement of someone's beliefs, judgments, or feelings—things that are not factual. An opinion cannot be proved or disproved, and for this reason it is sometimes referred to as a **nonfact.** Words like *terrible, wonderful, always, never, probably, most, all,* and *none* often signal opinions; so do phrases such as *I think, I believe,* and *it seems.*

YOUR TURN To help you distinguish facts and opinions in this magazine article, use the activities below.

❶ Is there a sentence in the first paragraph that expresses an opinion? Explain how you know.

❷ **Judging Reliability** How accurate do you think the "findings" of the *U.S. News* study are? Explain your opinion.

❸ Write an opinion of your own, based on the facts contained in this excerpt.

Real WORLD Link

Magazine Article

Objectives
- distinguish facts from nonfacts
- evaluate sources of information
- identify trends and draw conclusions from data

Connecting to the Literature
The excerpt from the magazine article "To Make a Nation: How Immigrants Are Changing America" presents immigration statistics along with insights into the impact immigrants have on the nation. The article is linked to the essays by Margaret Atwood and Pat Mora (p. 179).

Reading for Information

In addition to citing facts from reliable sources, articles should be clearly organized. This excerpt presents facts in an organized way to contradict the popular notion of an "immigrant problem." Remind students that they can use the graph on page 182 as well as other text organizers to help them locate and categorize information.

1 No, the sentences all present information that can be verified.
2 The facts seem reliable, given that *U.S. News* used computer analysis of 12.5 million census records and interviewed dozens of immigrants and local government officials.
3 Students' opinions should be based on these facts:
   - The majority of immigrants have high school educations.
   - Immigrants expand employment niches rather than reduce them.
   - Few immigrants receive welfare.
   - After a decade, immigrants earn salaries comparable to non-immigrants.
   - Immigrants share the political concerns of native-born Americans.

Interpreting Graphs

4 Each bar represents a country.

5 Mexico was the source of the greatest number of immigrants.

6 Mexico's 2.1 million immigrants comprise 24 percent of the total immigrants.

Spotting Trends

The bar graph shows the total number of immigrants from each country in descending order. Since more than half of the total number of immigrants are already represented on the chart, the 30th country would probably be the source of less than 100,000 immigrants.

1990 U.S. Immigration Census Profile

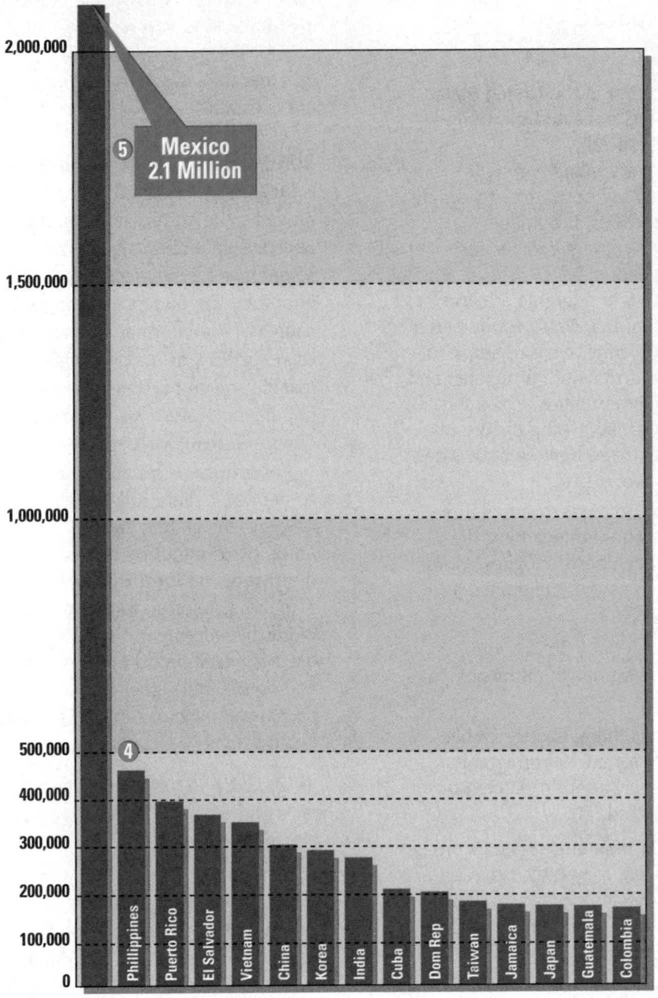

6 Total immigrants to the United States (1980–90)

Interpreting Graphs

The bar graph at the left shows how the top 15 countries of origin contributed to the total of 8.6 million immigrants to the United States in 1980–1990.

YOUR TURN Use the questions below to help you interpret the graph.

4. What does each bar represent?
5. Which country was the source of the greatest number of immigrants?
6. Although Mexico's bar looks huge in the graph, what percentage of the 8.6 million total immigrants actually came from that country?

Spotting Trends If the bar graph were expanded to include the top 30 countries of origin, would you expect the 30th country to have been the source of more than 100,000 or less than 100,000 immigrants?

Inquiry & Research

Activity Link: "The Border: A Glare of Truth," p. 170

Update this bar graph with the most recent immigration statistics. Use the Internet, or a recently published encyclopedia or almanac. Compare the statistics you find with the 1980–1990 figures. Have there been any major shifts in the rankings of countries of origin?

Mini Lesson Inquiry & Research

The Inquiry & Research activity on this page links to the Inquiry & Research section of Choices and Challenges (p. 179), which asks students to find out more facts about the United States's recent immigrants and their countries of origin.

Instruction Demonstrate to students how they can find statistical information using reference materials, almanacs, periodicals, databases, and the Internet.

Practice Have students find statistical information concerning U. S. immigration and create a bar graph reflecting the statistics found in their research. Instruct them to compare that information with the information presented in the bar graph on page 182 and to draw conclusions about major shifts in U. S. immigration by observing changes in the total number of immigrants, the countries from which immigrants came, the degree of disparity in the number of immigrants coming from different countries, and any regional trends in immigration.

Word Parts and Meaning

> This was said so seriously and so **bluntly** that Nene could not find speech immediately. In the **cosmopolitan** atmosphere of the city it had always seemed to her something of a joke that a person's tribe could determine whom he married.
> —Chinua Achebe, "Marriage Is a Private Affair"

Have you ever opened up a word to see how it works? A word may be composed of several parts that serve specific functions in shaping the word's meaning. Consider the words in blue type on the right.

Bluntly is made up of two parts: the base word *blunt*, meaning "frank" or "abrupt," and *-ly*, a suffix that makes an adverb of manner. *Cosmopolitan* is made up of three parts: the Greek roots *cosm* ("world") and *polit* ("citizen") and *-an*, a suffix that makes an adjective. Together, the parts of *cosmopolitan* form a word that means "sophisticated" or "worldly." Recognizing the parts of a word can often help you determine the word's meaning.

Strategies for Building Vocabulary

When you encounter an unfamiliar word, see if it has recognizable parts. A **base word,** such as *blunt*, can stand alone. A **root,** such as *cosm*, cannot stand alone—other roots or affixes need to be added to it. An **affix,** like *-ly* in *bluntly*, is attached to a base word or a root to change its meaning or function. An **affix** at the beginning of a word is called a **prefix;** one at the end is called a **suffix.**

❶ Roots and Affixes An understanding of word parts can help you decipher unfamiliar words. See if you can use the following information to determine the meaning of *dissuasion:*

Prefix	Root	Suffix
dis-	*suas*	*-ion*
"away"	"urge"	"a process of"

The root *suas* comes from the Latin *suadere*, meaning "to urge." The prefix *dis-* means "away"; the suffix *-ion* means "a process of." Therefore, the word *dissuasion* refers to a process of urging someone away from doing something.

❷ Word Families Words containing the same root are usually related in meaning. Knowing the root can help you understand other words in the same word family. For example, the word *efficacy* contains the Latin root *fic,* which means "do" or "make." The idea of doing can be seen in the definition of *efficacy*—"the power to produce a desired effect"—and the same idea is involved in the meanings of other words in the *fic* family, such as *efficient, proficient,* and *sufficient.*

❸ Learning the Roots Use these charts to help you learn several Greek and Latin roots.

Greek Root	Meaning	Example
derm	skin	dermatology, dermatitis
gen	birth, race	generation, genetics
gram	something written	diagram, grammatical
hydr	water	hydrogen, hydroelectric
pan	all, entire	panorama, pandemic
psych	mind, soul	psychology, psychic

Latin Root	Meaning	Example
centr	center	central, concentric
cred, credit	believe	credit, credible
fer	bear, carry	transfer, infer
fug, fugit	flee	fugitive, refuge
pos, posit	place, put	position, impose
sign	sign, mark	insignificant, signify

EXERCISE Identify the roots in these words, as well as the meanings of the roots and of the words. Then use each word correctly in a sentence.

1. composition
2. ungrammatical
3. centrifugal
4. proficient
5. epidermis

Building Vocabulary

Objectives

- research word origins to help understand meanings
- apply meanings of roots in order to understand them
- use reference materials such as a dictionary, glossary, or thesaurus to determine precise word meanings

VOCABULARY EXERCISE

Students' sentences will vary.

1. Latin root *posit,* meaning "place" or "put"; "a putting together of parts to form a whole"; The painting's composition was striking.
2. Greek root *gram,* meaning "something written"; "not adhering to the rules of grammar"; The ungrammatical beginning to the novel intrigued me.
3. Latin roots *centr,* meaning "center," and *fug,* meaning "flee"; "moving away from a center"; The centrifugal force of the merry-go-round scared Sam.
4. Latin root *fic,* meaning "do" or "make"; "having an ability to do something well"; Ben is a proficient reader.
5. Greek root *derm,* meaning "skin"; "the outer layer of the skin"; Martha has a severe rash on her epidermis.

Possible Objectives

You can use this selection to achieve one or more of the following objectives:

- enjoy silent sustained reading (Option One)
- read and analyze literature with a group (Option Two)
- use the Reader's Notebook to formulate questions about literature (Option Three)
- write in response to literature (Option Three)

Summary

In this autobiographical selection, Amy Tan recalls a Christmas Eve when she was 14 years old. Her parents invited the minister's family for holiday dinner, including their son, Robert, the boy she claimed to love at the time. Tan describes the strangeness of the Chinese foods her mother prepared for the celebration on this day, a menu that included prawns, squid, and fungi, among other things. Tan also makes clear the anxieties she felt at the presence of Robert in the midst of her family celebration. As the evening advances, so does her embarrassment, which leads to an eventual state of despair. She cringes at the table manners of her Chinese relatives in the presence of their American guests, whose cultural tradition and eating habits are so different. Her father belches loudly at the end of the meal and explains that belching is a Chinese custom that communicates polite satisfaction. Tan, in the midst of her burning desire to impress the boy and win his acceptance, is left stunned and ashamed. It isn't until the guests leave that she gains wisdom and perspective offered by her mother, who tells her that on the inside she will always remain Chinese, regardless of her wishes to be American on the outside. This statement represents an act of love that Tan carries with her throughout life.

ON YOUR OWN

The Chinese-American experience is the focus of Amy Tan's writing, both in fiction and nonfiction. Born in California, the daughter of Chinese immigrants, she often tells about the difficulty of growing up with roots in one culture while living in another. Her writing describes the embarrassing moments, painful misunderstandings, and mixed feelings that are a result of dual loyalty. In this selection, Tan remembers an awkward Christmas Eve dinner.

Fish Cheeks

Amy Tan

I fell in love with the minister's son the winter I turned fourteen. He was not Chinese, but as white as Mary in the manger. For Christmas I prayed for this blond-haired boy, Robert, and a slim new American nose.

When I found out that my parents had invited the minister's family over for Christmas Eve dinner, I cried. What would Robert think of our shabby *Chinese* Christmas? What would he think of our noisy *Chinese* relatives who lacked proper American manners? What terrible disappointment would he feel upon seeing not a roasted turkey and sweet potatoes but *Chinese* food?

On Christmas Eve I saw that my mother had outdone herself in creating a strange menu. She was pulling black veins out of the backs of fleshy prawns. The kitchen was littered with appalling mounds of raw food: A slimy rock cod with bulging fish eyes that pleaded not to be thrown into a pan of hot oil. Tofu, which looked like stacked wedges of rubbery white sponges. A bowl soaking dried fungus back to life. A plate of squid, their backs crisscrossed with knife markings so they resembled bicycle tires.

Um den Fisch [Around the fish] (1926), Paul Klee. Oil on canvas, 18 3/8″ × 25 1/8″, The Museum of Modern Art, New York, Abby Aldrich Rockefeller Fund, photo copyright © 1995 The Museum of Modern Art, New York.

And then they arrived—the minister's family and all my relatives in a clamor of doorbells and rumpled Christmas packages. Robert grunted hello, and I pretended he was not worthy of existence.

Dinner threw me deeper into despair. My relatives licked the ends of their chopsticks and reached across the table, dipping them into the dozen or so plates of food. Robert and his family waited patiently for platters to be passed to them. My relatives murmured with pleasure when my mother brought out the whole steamed fish. Robert grimaced. Then my father poked his chopsticks just below the fish eye and plucked out the soft meat. "Amy, your favorite," he said, offering me the tender fish cheek. I wanted to disappear.

At the end of the meal my father leaned back and belched loudly, thanking my mother for her fine cooking. "It's a polite Chinese custom to show you are satisfied," explained my father to our astonished guests. Robert was looking down at his plate with a reddened face. The minister managed to muster up a

Reading the Selection

Option One

Silent Sustained Reading

You might set aside time each week for independent reading. During this time, you and your students would read for enjoyment. "Fish Cheeks" can be read independently in about 15 minutes. If you want to encourage students to read for pleasure, you might forego assignments related to the selection. Should you want to make assignments, Options Two and Three offer suggestions.

Option Two

Shared Reading Groups

Students can read the selection together, alternately reading sections aloud, or they can read independently and meet to cooperate in a project that portrays some element of the story.

Possible Projects

- Have students focus on the descriptions and names of Chinese foods in the text to create a menu for the Christmas Eve meal that is served. Each student in the group can create a menu of the traditional celebration meal served in their homes during the holidays to compare and contrast.
- Students can outline a sequel to this story based on Tan's newfound wisdom gained at the end. Have students set their sequel on Christmas Eve one year later, assuming that the same meal is served to the same guests. Will the narrator's attitude be different? If so, how will her attitude affect her actions? If not, how will her actions be affected?
- Students can write advice to the narrator in a "Dear Amy" letter in which they share an embarrassing experience of their own and offer a line of reasoning that will reassure, instruct, and or help the narrator deal with her feelings in this situation.

FISH CHEEKS **185**

Option Three
Reader's Notebook

Provide the following direction to students before they read.

Begin by summarizing the conflict that exists for Tan in "Fish Cheeks." Ask students to draw a line down the center of a page in their Reader's Notebook, creating a column labeled *PRIDE* and a column labeled *SHAME.* Instruct students to read the selection and to make notes in the appropriate column regarding Tan's attitude and feelings toward her Chinese heritage. When they complete the story, have them reread the mother's comment about the difference between what Tan is on the inside and what she is on the outside. Ask students to consider whether Tan's feelings about her heritage seem to be based more on internal or more on external factors.

Students can write a brief analysis in their Reader's Notebook of Tan's conflict and their own ideas about whether she resolves that conflict.

Possible Activities
Independent Activities

- Have students review the story and note details that indicate Tan's internal, emotional response to the events. When they finish, ask students to assume Tan's character and write in their Reader's Notebook as they think she might write on this Christmas Eve. Instruct students to describe their feelings in two "Dear Diary" entries, one before the guests arrive and one after they depart.
- Have students review the Learning the Language of Literature and Active Reader on pages 104–106. They can note which skills and strategies they used while reading the selection.

quiet burp. I was stunned into silence for the rest of the night.

After everyone had gone, my mother said to me, "You want to be the same as American girls on the outside." She handed me an early gift. It was a miniskirt in beige tweed. "But inside you must always be Chinese. You must be proud you are different. Your only shame is to have shame."

And even though I didn't agree with her then, I knew that she understood how much I had suffered during the evening's dinner. It wasn't until many years later—long after I had gotten over my crush on Robert—that I was able to fully appreciate her lesson and the true purpose behind our particular menu. For Christmas Eve that year, she had chosen all my favorite foods.

Amy Tan
1952–

Other Works
The Joy Luck Club
The Kitchen God's Wife

Cultural Struggles Amy Tan was not always the proud Chinese American that she is now. She recalls dreaming, when she was young, of making her features look more Western by having plastic surgery. It was not until she made her first trip to China in 1987 that Tan could truly accept both the Chinese and American cultures as her own.

Changing Directions Though Tan won a writing contest at the age of eight, her identity as a writer was also slow in coming. In fact, she did not plan on a literary career. After two years of postgraduate study at the University of California in Berkeley, Tan worked for several years as a consultant to programs for children with disabilities. She then became a reporter for a medical publication and eventually a freelance technical writer. Later, Tan turned to playing jazz piano and writing fiction.

From Book to Film After getting some of her stories published in magazines, Tan combined the stories with others to form a novel called *The Joy Luck Club.* The book became a bestseller and was made into a movie. It portrays the cultural and generational gaps between four young Chinese-American women and their mothers.

Author Activity
Read On Tan's famous novel *The Joy Luck Club* (1989) has enjoyed wide success. Read additional stories about Chinese-American life from this collection.

Discussion Activities
- Have students discuss how Tan's age was a contributing factor to her emotional response. Why did Robert's presence add to this reaction? Would her and Robert's responses be different if they were 8, 18, or 28 years old?
- Discuss why the author chose the title "Fish Cheeks."

Assessment Opportunities
- You can assess student comprehension of the story by evaluating the conflict analysis students wrote in their Reader's Notebooks.
- You can use any of the discussion questions as essay questions.
- You can have students develop any one of their Reader's Notebook entries into an essay.

Comparing Literature

Love and Marriage Across Cultures

Marriage Is a Private Affair
Short Story by CHINUA ACHEBE

Love Must Not Be Forgotten
Short Story by ZHANG JIE

What's the Connection?

Love at the Crossroads Every society in some way seeks to set standards for love and marriage. Often, tension exists between what a society or culture expects and what the individual wants. In choosing a spouse, an individual may face pressures from family, friends, community members, or public opinion.

In the following two selections, you will read about characters who are torn between their personal desires and the traditions and expectations of society. While both stories focus on individuals, they also reflect the conflicts and tensions of the societies portrayed.

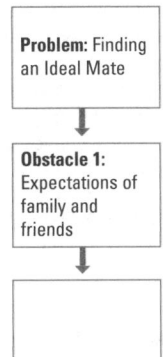

A Chinese bride and groom in traditional wedding attire.

Points of Comparison

Analyzing Similar Problems in Different Cultures In this unit, you have read about conflicts that arise when two cultures meet, or when one culture changes. In the pages that follow, you will analyze and compare the problems of characters who challenge cultural traditions and social expectations in an attempt to find love and fulfillment.

Critical Thinking: Analyze and Compare

The first step in analysis is to define the parts of the whole. To analyze the problems of characters who seek love in a changing world, it will help you to develop a kind of graphic called an **analysis frame.** This frame will help you break each problem into parts. To begin, think about the ways in which the standards of our own society might present obstacles for a person in search of an ideal mate. Continue to identify other potential obstacles to love and marriage. The analysis frame shown has been started for you.

Problem: Finding an Ideal Mate
↓
Obstacle 1: Expectations of family and friends
↓
(blank)

READER'S NOTEBOOK As you read the following stories, note the various obstacles faced by the main characters, which contribute to their problems. At each Points of Comparison, you will be asked to create a separate analysis frame for the story you have read.

Comparing Literature
LOVE AND MARRIAGE ACROSS CULTURES

OVERVIEW

This feature gives students an opportunity to compare, analyze, and form opinions about two short stories. The focus of this comparison is the problems that arise across cultures in choosing a spouse.

Teaching Option
Because each story is accompanied by its own introductory and response pages, teachers have the option of pairing the stories or teaching them individually. Used in conjunction with the Comparing Literature Assessment Practice on page 211, the stories may help students prepare for literature-based writing assessments.

What's the Connection?

To highlight the concept that a social code influences individual values, choices, and behaviors in life, ask students to identify elements of the social codes that influence their lives. Encourage students to focus on standards of behavior and social expectations that govern specific actions, such as how close we stand to someone during conversation, standards for conduct at public events, standards for conduct on a date, and so forth. Then have students discuss the degree to which this code is inherent or overt. Ask them to name situations in which they openly challenged the social code. What was the result of their actions?

Points of Comparison
Have students consider the deeper value choices that can stand in opposition to the dominant values of the social group and may lead to an individual's banishment or ostracism. These situations often involve personal beliefs and convictions that cannot be easily compromised without the individual feeling unsatisfied for giving up his or her personal conviction or values. Issues such as religious beliefs, the choice of whom to date or marry, the choice of what career to pursue, involve elements of personal happiness.

Critical Thinking: Analyze and Compare
Other possible obstacles to marriage might include expectations of society as a whole. The level of your education and your socioeconomic status may also prevent you from meeting the ideal mate.

LOVE AND MARRIAGE ACROSS CULTURES 187

OVERVIEW

Objectives

1. understand and appreciate a **short story (Literary Analysis)**
2. understand and recognize **cultural conflict (Literary Analysis)**
3. understand **cultural characteristics (Active Reading)**

Summary

Nnaemeka travels from the Nigerian capital of Lagos to his village to explain to his father, Okeke, that he cannot marry the bride who has been chosen for him. Instead, he has become engaged to Nene, a girl who is from another tribe and follows modern ways. Heartbroken, Okeke vows never to see the girl, and for eight years he has nothing to do with his son. Then Nene writes to her father-in-law, asking him to allow his grandsons to visit. Touched, Okeke is filled with remorse, fearing he will die before making amends for his coldness.

Thematic Link

In this story, two cultures—modern and urban, rural and traditional—meet and clash.

5-Minute Warm-Up

Daily Language SkillBuilder

Have students **proofread** the display sentences on page 15k and write them correctly. The sentences also appear on Transparency 6 of **Grammar Transparencies and Copymasters.**

Marriage Is a Private Affair

Short Story by CHINUA ACHEBE

"You don't really mean that he will object to your marrying me on that account?"

Connect to Your Life

Marry Who? Marriage customs vary greatly throughout the world. In some cultures, people's marriages are traditionally arranged by their parents; in others, the partners make up their own minds. Discuss what you know about arranged marriages. What purpose do they serve? What advantages and disadvantages might they have?

Build Background

Nigerian Crossroads This story takes place in the West African country of Nigeria, a land of great cultural diversity. Centuries-old traditions continue to govern life in Nigerian villages, where parents often play a decisive role in choosing mates for their children. In the cities, however, modern practices have displaced many of the village traditions, including the role of parent as matchmaker. The tension between old and new ways of living sometimes creates conflict within families, especially between generations.

The following story focuses on a conflict between a father and son about the choice of the son's marriage partner. Both men are Ibo (ē′bō), members of one of Nigeria's largest ethnic groups. The son, like many of his contemporaries, has moved away from the village of his birth and lives in a city—in this case, Lagos (lā′gŏs), the economic and commercial center of the nation, with a population of 1.4 million. In the villages of Nigeria, the Ibo live apart from other peoples, maintaining their traditional way of life. In Lagos, ethnic groups, cultures, and religions mingle freely.

WORDS TO KNOW **Vocabulary Preview**

commiserate	dissuasion	perfunctorily	remorse
cosmopolitan	forsaken	persevere	theological
deference	homily		

LaserLinks: Background for Reading
Cultural Connection

Focus Your Reading

LITERARY ANALYSIS | **CULTURAL CONFLICT** The plot of every story is constructed around **conflict,** or the struggle between opposing forces. In some stories, struggles occur as a result of cultural differences; these **cultural conflicts** arise from differences in values, beliefs, or customs.

As you read the following story, look for examples of conflicts arising from cultural friction.

ACTIVE READING | **IDENTIFYING CULTURAL CHARACTERISTICS** In order to understand the conflict in this story, you will need to pay close attention to the cultural context. The following passage, for example, shows a tension between city ways and tribal ways of life.

In the cosmopolitan atmosphere of the city it had always seemed to her something of a joke that a person's tribe could determine whom he married.

READER'S NOTEBOOK As you read, take notes on the cultural characteristics of the village and the city. Use a chart like the one shown.

Culture of the City	Culture of the Village
People can marry across cultural and ethnic lines.	

LESSON RESOURCES

UNIT ONE RESOURCE BOOK, pp. 82–86

ASSESSMENT RESOURCES

Formal Assessment, pp. 33–34

Teacher's Guide to Assessment and Portfolio Use

Test Generator

SKILLS TRANSPARENCIES AND COPYMASTERS

Reading and Critical Thinking

- Locating Material in the Library I, T27 (for Inquiry & Research, p. 195)
- Notetaking, T40 (for Reader's Notebook, p. 188)

Grammar

- Demonstrative Pronouns, C67 (for Mini Lesson, p. 191)

Vocabulary

- Using a Thesaurus, C36 (for Mini Lesson, p. 189)
- Word Origins, C37 (for Mini Lesson, p. 192)

Writing

- Generating Ideas, T1 (for Inquiry & Research, p. 195)
- Effective Language, T13 (for Writing Options, p. 195)

INTEGRATED TECHNOLOGY

Audio Library

LaserLinks

- Author Background: Chinua Achebe
- Cultural Background: Marriage in Nigeria

See **Teacher's SourceBook,** p. 16.

Visit our website:
www.mcdougallittell.com

MARRIAGE Is a Private Affair

Chinua Achebe

"Have you written to your dad yet?" asked Nene[1] one afternoon as she sat with Nnaemeka[2] in her room at 16 Kasanga Street, Lagos.

"No. I've been thinking about it. I think it's better to tell him when I get home on leave!"

"But why? Your leave is such a long way off yet—six whole weeks. He should be let into our happiness now."

Nnaemeka was silent for a while and then began very slowly as if he groped for his words: "I wish I were sure it would be happiness to him."

"Of course it must," replied Nene, a little surprised. "Why shouldn't it?"

"You have lived in Lagos all your life, and you know very little about people in remote parts of the country."

"That's what you always say. But I don't believe anybody will be so unlike other people that they will be unhappy when their sons are engaged to marry."

"Yes. They are most unhappy if the engagement is not arranged by them. In our case it's worse—you are not even an Ibo."

This was said so seriously and so bluntly that Nene could not find speech immediately. In the cosmopolitan atmosphere of the city it had always seemed to her something of a joke that a person's tribe could determine whom he married.

At last she said, "You don't really mean that he will object to your marrying me simply on that account? I had always thought you Ibos were kindly disposed to other people."

"So we are. But when it comes to marriage, well, it's not quite so simple. And this," he added, "is not peculiar to the Ibos. If your father were alive and lived in the heart of Ibibioland, he would be exactly like my father."

"I don't know. But anyway, as your father is

1. **Nene** (nā'nā).
2. **Nnaemeka** (ən-nä'ä-mā'kä).

WORDS TO KNOW **cosmopolitan** (kŏz'mə-pŏl'ĭ-tn) *adj.* worldly; sophisticated

189

TEACHING THE LITERATURE

Customizing Instruction

Less Proficient Readers
To aid their comprehension, have students ask themselves the following questions as they read.

- Who are the main characters?
  Answer: Nnaemeka, Nene, and Okeke
- How are the main characters related to one another?
  Answer: Okeke is Nnaemeke's father; Nene is Nnaemeke's fiancée and, later, wife
- What is the cause of the main conflict in the story?
  Answer: Nnaemeke does not marry the woman Okeke has picked out for him; instead, he marries Nene.

Students Acquiring English
With the aid of the phonetic transcriptions, have students practice pronouncing the characters' names before they begin reading. Spanish speakers may notice that these Nigerian names include vowels similar to those in Spanish.

Use **Spanish Study Guide** for additional support, pp. 41–43.

Gifted and Talented
Have students discuss how clashes between contemporary and traditional culture continue to take place here today. Have students read other works dealing with the subject and compare them with "Marriage Is a Private Affair." Suggest that they start with "The Son from America" (pp. 159–169).

Mini Lesson: Preteaching Vocabulary

USING A THESAURUS Call students' attention to the list of WORDS TO KNOW. Remind them that they can often understand the meaning of an unfamiliar word by discovering other, simpler words that have similar meanings.

Example
Words related to *cosmopolitan: sophisticated, worldly, broad-minded, urbane*

Instruction
Have students use a thesaurus to find synonyms for the WORDS TO KNOW. After writing down the synonyms, have students give a definition in their own words that accurately explains each of the WORDS TO KNOW.

Use **Unit One Resource Book,** p. 85 for additional support.

Reading and Analyzing

Reading Skills and Strategies:
PREVIEW

Have students look at Preparing to Read, page 188. Ask them to consider the title, the image, and the quote beneath the image. Ask students to predict what the story will be about, based on these items. Before students read, give them a brief summary of the story.

Literary Analysis

CULTURAL CONFLICT

The chief conflict in this story is over a clash of cultures. Students should recognize the distinctive characteristics of the cultures. Ask students to identify the values, beliefs, and customs on both sides that are the source of this conflict.

Possible Response: The traditional culture values marriages that are arranged by the parents and remain within the tribe; the modern culture values marriages based on love.

Use **Unit One Resource Book,** p. 84 for additional support.

Active Reading

IDENTIFYING CULTURAL CHARACTERISTICS

As students read, have them keep two lists, one of characteristics of the culture of Okeke's village and the other of characteristics of the culture of Lagos.

Use **Unit One Resource Book,** p. 83 for additional support.

so fond of you, I'm sure he will forgive you soon enough. Come on then, be a good boy and send him a nice lovely letter . . ."

"It would not be wise to break the news to him by writing. A letter will bring it upon him with a shock. I'm quite sure about that."

"All right, honey, suit yourself. You know your father."

As Nnaemeka walked home that evening, he turned over in his mind different ways of overcoming his father's opposition, especially now that he had gone and found a girl for him. He had thought of showing his letter to Nene but decided on second thoughts not to, at least for the moment. He read it again when he got home and couldn't help smiling to himself. He remembered Ugoye[3] quite well, an Amazon[4] of a girl who used to beat up all the boys, himself included, on the way to the stream, a complete dunce at school.

I have found a girl who will suit you admirably—Ugoye Nweke, the eldest daughter of our neighbor, Jacob Nweke. She has a proper Christian upbringing. When she stopped schooling some years ago, her father (a man of sound judgment) sent her to live in the house of a pastor where she has received all the training a wife could need. Her Sunday school teacher has told me that she reads her Bible very fluently. I hope we shall begin
1 *negotiations when you come home in December.*

On the second evening of his return from Lagos Nnaemeka sat with his father under a cassia tree. This was the old man's retreat where he went to read his Bible when the parching December sun had set and a fresh, reviving wind blew on the leaves.

"Father," began Nnaemeka suddenly, "I have come to ask for forgiveness."

"Forgiveness? For what, my son?" he asked in amazement.

"It's about this marriage question."

"Which marriage question?"

"I can't—we must—I mean it is impossible for me to marry Nweke's daughter."

"Impossible? Why?" asked his father.

"I don't love her."

"Nobody said you did. Why should you?" he asked.

"Marriage today is different . . ."

"Look here, my son," interrupted his father, "nothing is different. What one looks for in a wife are a good character and a Christian background."

Nnaemeka saw there was no hope along the present line of argument.

"Moreover," he said, "I am engaged to marry another girl who has all of Ugoye's good qualities, and who . . ."

His father did not believe his ears. "What did you say?" he asked slowly and disconcertingly.

"She is a good Christian," his son went on, "and a teacher in a girls' school in Lagos."

"Teacher, did you say? If you consider that a qualification for a good wife, I should like to point out to you, Emeka, that no Christian woman should teach. St. Paul in his letter to the Corinthians says that women should keep silence." He rose slowly from his seat and paced forwards and backwards. This was his pet subject, and he condemned vehemently those church leaders who encouraged women to teach in their schools. After he had spent his emotion on a long

3. **Ugoye** (o͞o-gō′yā).
4. **Amazon:** an exceptionally tall, strong woman.

Teaching Options

BLOCK SCHEDULING: MANAGING TIME

If your schedule requires that you cover the lesson objectives in a shorter time, use . . .
- Preparing to Read, p. 188
- Thinking Through the Literature, p. 194
- Vocabulary in Action, p. 195

If you want to take advantage of longer class time, use . . .
- TE Teaching Options: Preteaching Vocabulary p. 189; Grammar, p. 191; Vocabulary Strategy, p. 192; Informal Assessment, p. 193, Speaking and Listening, p. 195
- Choices & Challenges, p. 195

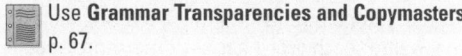

Wooing (1984), Varnette Honeywood. Collage. Copyright © 1984 Varnette P. Honeywood.

homily, he at last came back to his son's engagement, in a seemingly milder tone.

"Whose daughter is she, anyway?"

"She is Nene Atang."

"What!" All the mildness was gone again. "Did you say Neneataga; what does that mean?"

"Nene Atang from Calabar.[5] She is the only girl I can marry." This was a very rash reply, and Nnaemeka expected the storm to burst. But it did not. His father merely walked away into his room. This was most unexpected and perplexed Nnaemeka. His father's silence was infinitely more menacing than a flood of threatening speech. That night the old man did not eat.

When he sent for Nnaemeka a day later, he applied all possible ways of dissuasion. But the young man's heart was hardened, and his father eventually gave him up as lost.

"I owe it to you, my son, as a duty to show you what is right and what is wrong. Whoever put this idea into your head might as well have cut your throat. It is Satan's work." He waved his son away.

"You will change your mind, Father, when you know Nene."

"I shall never see her" was the reply. From that night the father scarcely spoke to his son. He did not, however, cease hoping that he would realize how serious was the danger he was heading for. Day and night he put him in his prayers.

Nnaemeka, for his own part, was very deeply affected by his father's grief. But he kept hoping that it would pass away. If it had occurred to him that never in the history of his people had a man married a woman who spoke a different tongue, he might have been less optimistic. "It has never been heard," was the verdict of an old man speaking a few weeks later. In that

5. **Calabar:** a seaport in southeastern Nigeria.

WORDS TO KNOW

homily (hŏm'ə-lē) *n.* a tedious, moralizing lecture; sermon
dissuasion (dĭ-swā'zhən) *n.* the persuading of someone not to perform an action

Customizing Instruction

Students Acquiring English

1 Explain that *negotiation* is the process of reaching an agreement or contract. Point out that in the story, *negotiations* refer to financial arrangements for a marriage. In many cultures, money or property is exchanged as a condition of marriage.

Mini Lesson Grammar

DEMONSTRATIVE PRONOUNS The pronouns *this, that, these,* and *those* are demonstrative pronouns for persons or things. *This* and *these* refer to persons or things that are near in space or time. *That* and *those* refer to persons or things that are farther away in space or time.

Model Sentence

The child pointed to the red balloon. "*This* is the balloon I want, Dad, not *that* other one," she said.

Exercise Read the following sentences aloud or write them on the chalkboard. Have students determine which demonstrative pronoun should be used in each sentence.

1. After you left, he took all *these/those* candy wrappers you left on the floor and threw them away.
2. "I knew I should have studied for *this/that* test yesterday," said Sam reflectively.
3. "After my daughter left *this/that* house, she went to college and studied all *these/those* things she had always wanted to," the man said.

Answers: 1. those; 2. that; 3. this, those

Use **Grammar Transparencies and Copymasters,** p. 67.

Use McDougal Littell's ***Language Network,*** Chapter 1, for more instruction in demonstrative pronouns.

Reading and Analyzing

Active Reading: SUMMARIZE

A Have students summarize the conversation among Okeke and other men of the village.

Possible Response: One man comments that such a marriage has not been heard of before. Others see it as a sign of the end of the world. It is suggested that Okeke see a native doctor. He refuses, and the conversation turns to gossip about a woman who tricked her herbalist.

Active Reading: EVALUATE

B Have students suggest what they think Nnaemeke's father was trying to win. Then ask if they feel the father truly won something.

Possible Response: Most students will interpret the text to mean that Nnaemeke's father was successful in forgetting his son. In a larger sense, though, Nnaemeke's father has lost something very important—his relationship with his son.

short sentence he spoke for all of his people. This man had come with others to commiserate with Okeke[6] when news went round about his son's behavior. By that time the son had gone back to Lagos.

"It has never been heard," said the old man again with a sad shake of his head.

"What did Our Lord say?" asked another gentleman. "Sons shall rise against their fathers; it is there in the Holy Book."

"It is the beginning of the end," said another.

The discussion thus tending to become theological, Madubogwu, a highly practical man, brought it down once more to the ordinary level.

"Have you thought of consulting a native doctor about your son?" he asked Nnaemeka's father.

"He isn't sick" was the reply.

A "What is he then? The boy's mind is diseased, and only a good herbalist[7] can bring him back to his right senses. The medicine he requires is *Amalile*, the same that women apply with success to recapture their husbands' straying affection."

"Madubogwu is right," said another gentleman. "This thing calls for medicine."

"I shall not call in a native doctor." Nnaemeka's father was known to be obstinately ahead of his more superstitious neighbors in these matters. "I will not be another Mrs. Ochuba. If my son wants to kill himself, let him do it with his own hands. It is not for me to help him."

"But it was her fault," said Madubogwu. "She ought to have gone to an honest herbalist. She was a clever woman, nevertheless."

"She was a wicked murderess," said Jonathan, who rarely argued with his neighbors because, he often said, they were incapable of reasoning. "The medicine was prepared for her husband, it was his name they called in its preparation, and I am sure it would have been perfectly beneficial to him. It was wicked to put it into the herbalist's food and say you were only trying it out."

Six months later, Nnaemeka was showing his young wife a short letter from his father:

> *It amazes me that you could be so unfeeling as to send me your wedding picture. I would have sent it back. But on further thought I decided just to cut off your wife and send it back to you because I have nothing to do with her. How I wish that I had nothing to do with you either.*

When Nene read through this letter and looked at the mutilated picture, her eyes filled with tears, and she began to sob.

"Don't cry, my darling," said her husband. "He is essentially good-natured and will one day look more kindly on our marriage." But years passed, and that one day did not come.

For eight years, Okeke would have nothing to do with his son, Nnaemeka. Only three times (when Nnaemeka asked to come home and spend his leave) did he write to him.

"I can't have you in my house," he replied on one occasion. "It can be of no interest to me where or how you spend your leave—or your life, for that matter."

The prejudice against Nnaemeka's marriage was not confined to his little village. In Lagos, especially among his people who worked there,

6. **Okeke** (ō-kā'kā).
7. **herbalist** (ûr'bə-lĭst): a person who is expert in the use of medicinal herbs.

WORDS TO KNOW
commiserate (kə-mĭz'ə-rāt') *v.* to express sorrow or pity for another's trouble
theological (thē'ə-lŏj'ĭ-kəl) *adj.* having to do with the study of God and religion

192

Teaching Options

Mini Lesson Vocabulary

RESEARCHING WORD ORIGINS

Instruction Tell students that the word *homily* is based on the Greek word *homilia*, which means "conversation" or "instruction." Explain to students that the meaning of *homily* has become more specialized, and a homily is now a sermon or a long, moralizing lecture.

Practice Have students work in groups to find the origins of the words *deference, perfunctory,* and *persevere*. After students find the word origins, ask them whether each word has become more specific or less specific than its original.

Answers: deference, Latin *deferre*, to bring down—more specific; perfunctory, Latin *perfunctus*, to get rid of—less specific; persevere, Latin *perseverare*, strict or severe—more specific

Use **Vocabulary Transparencies and Copymasters,** pp. 11, 79.

A lesson on researching word origins appears on p. 356 in the Pupil's Edition.

it showed itself in a different way. Their women, when they met at their village meeting, were not hostile to Nene. Rather, they paid her such excessive deference as to make her feel she was not one of them. But as time went on, Nene gradually broke through some of this prejudice and even began to make friends among them. Slowly and grudgingly they began to admit that she kept her home much better than most of them.

B The story eventually got to the little village in the heart of the Ibo country that Nnaemeka and his young wife were a most happy couple. But his father was one of the few people in the village who knew nothing about this. He always displayed so much temper whenever his son's name was mentioned that everyone avoided it in his presence. By a tremendous effort of will he had succeeded in pushing his son to the back of his mind. The strain had nearly killed him, but he had persevered and won.

Then one day he received a letter from Nene, and in spite of himself he began to glance through it perfunctorily until all of a sudden the expression on his face changed and he began to read more carefully.

> *. . . Our two sons, from the day they learnt that they have a grandfather, have insisted on being taken to him. I find it impossible to tell them that you will not see them. I implore you to allow Nnaemeka to bring them home for a short time during his leave next month. I shall remain here in Lagos . . .*

The old man at once felt the resolution he had built up over so many years falling in. He was telling himself that he must not give in. He tried to steel his heart against all emotional appeals. It was a reenactment of that other struggle. He leaned against a window and looked out. The sky was overcast with heavy black clouds, and a high wind began to blow, filling the air with dust and dry leaves. It was one of those rare occasions when even Nature takes a hand in a human fight. Very soon it began to rain, the first rain in the year. It came down in large sharp drops and was accompanied by the lightning and thunder which mark a change of season. Okeke was trying hard not to think of his two grandsons. But he knew he was now fighting a losing battle. He tried to hum a favorite hymn, but the pattering of large raindrops on the roof broke up the tune. His mind immediately returned to the children. How could he shut his door against them? By a curious mental process he imagined them standing, sad and forsaken, under the harsh angry weather—shut out from his house.

That night he hardly slept, from remorse—and a vague fear that he might die without making it up to them. ❖ 1

WORDS TO KNOW	
	deference (dĕf'ər-əns) *n.* courteous regard or respect
	persevere (pûr'sə-vîr') *v.* to persist in the face of difficulties
	perfunctorily (pər-fŭngk'tə-rĭ-lē) *adv.* in a careless, uninterested way
	forsaken (fôr-sā'kən) *adj.* abandoned **forsake** *v.*
	remorse (rĭ-môrs') *n.* a deep sense of guilt over a wrong one has done

Customizing Instruction

Less Proficient Readers

1 Ask students what has changed Okeke's feelings.

Possible response: his grandsons' desire to see him and his desire to see them

Assessment Informal Assessment

ALTERNATIVE ENDING To informally assess students' understanding of the story, have them imagine an alternative version in which Nnaemeka follows his father's wishes and marries the tribal woman he does not love. Students could write a diary by Nnaemeka where he debates whether or not he made the right decision.

RUBRIC

3 **Full Accomplishment** Response reflects a full understanding of the events in the story and the character of Nnaemeka.

2 **Substantial Accomplishment** Response shows a general understanding of the events but may not fully reflect the character of Nnaemeka.

1 **Little or Partial Accomplishment** Response shows little understanding of the events or of the character of Nnaemeka.

GUIDING STUDENT RESPONSE

Connect to the Literature

1. **What Do You Think?**
Responses will vary. Students may choose Nene for her tolerance, Nnaemeka for his wish to do right by all of those he loves, or even Okeke for his adherence to his principles.

Comprehension Check

- He tries to arrange a marriage for Nnaemeka.
- Nene is not of the tribe; she works as a teacher; Okeke has not arranged the marriage himself.
- Okeke ends his unwavering disapproval of his son's marriage once he considers his grandsons.

Use **Unit One Resource Book,** p. 86 for additional support.

Think Critically

2. Possible Response: Okeke is upset and disappointed at his son's open flouting of tradition. His attitude changes in the end as his love for his family, especially for his grandsons, finally outweighs his traditional beliefs.
3. Answers will vary. Students should point to examples of Nnaemeka's behavior to support their opinions.
4. Answers will vary. Students should point to examples of Nene's behavior to support their opinions.
5. Answers will vary, but should include the idea that people in the city are at least somewhat accustomed to dealing with cultural differences, whereas the people in the village have led a much more culturally isolated existence.
6. Possible Response: The title suggests in matters where personal freedom and tradition conflict, personal freedom should win out.

Thinking through the LITERATURE

Connect to the Literature

1. **What Do You Think?** Which character do you think is the most sympathetically portrayed? Explain your reaction.

Comprehension Check
- What does Nnaemeka's father try to do for him in the village while Nnaemeka works in Lagos?
- Why does Okeke oppose Nnaemeka's choice of a wife?
- What happens at the end of the story?

Think Critically

2. How would you explain Okeke's reaction to his son's marriage, and his change of attitude at the end of the story?

THINK ABOUT
- the cultural traditions that influence Okeke
- how he feels about his son's actions
- how he is affected by Nene's letter

3. How well do you think Nnaemeka handles his father's opposition to his marriage?
4. What is your opinion of Nene's personality and judgment?
5. **ACTIVE READING** **IDENTIFYING CULTURAL CHARACTERISTICS** Look over the chart of cultural characteristics you created for your **READER'S NOTEBOOK.** In your opinion, what is the most important difference between Nnaemeka's city life and Okeke's village life? Explain.
6. How do you think the story's **title** relates to its **theme?**

Extend Interpretations

7. **Critic's Corner** The critic G. D. Killam has said about Achebe's work, "Through it all the spirit of man and the belief in the possibility of triumph endures." Do you think this comment applies in any way to "Marriage Is a Private Affair"? Explain your response.
8. **Connect to Life** What do you think is gained and lost when a society changes from traditional ways of life to modern ways?
9. **Points of Comparison** Review the analysis frame graphic that you created to identify different kinds of obstacles to finding an ideal mate. Now make a second frame analyzing the obstacles in this story. How do the obstacles you identified compare with the various obstacles revealed in this story?

Literary Analysis

CULTURAL CONFLICT When customs or socially influenced beliefs push people in different directions, cultural conflict often occurs. The conflict may happen when two different cultures come in contact, or it may occur when a culture changes. In this story, conflict arises around changing marriage customs as well as the contact between urban and rural cultures in Nigeria. For example, Nene faces prejudice among the Ibo women in Lagos:

Their women, when they met at their village meeting, were not hostile to Nene. Rather, they paid her such excessive deference as to make her feel she was not one of them.

Paired Activity Review the story once more with a partner, and identify each place in which cultural conflict occurs. List the incident and think about the beliefs motivating the people on each side of the conflict. Compare your results with those of other students.

Extend Interpretations

Critic's Corner Student responses should refer specifically to the text. Possible Response: The fact that Okeke eventually chooses to acknowledge his son's marriage and children shows the triumph of spirit that G. D. Killam meant.

Connect to Life Responses should include examples from both the text and the real world.

Points of Comparison Student responses should include specific references to their earlier analysis frames and compare text events to their own experiences or the experiences of others.

Literary Analysis

Paired Activity Paired students should make written notes of the incidents and motivations and refer to them in group discussions.

Choices & CHALLENGES

Writing Options

Okeke's Letter Write a letter that Okeke might send in response to Nene's letter. Your letter should reflect the father's personality and feelings.

Inquiry & Research

Marrying for Love When did romantic love become a basis for marriage? What countries are associated with the origins of romantic love as we know it? Do library research to learn the answers to these or other questions about the origins of modern Western marriage customs. Give an oral report on your findings.

Vocabulary in Action

EXERCISE A: ASSESSMENT PRACTICE For each group of words below, write the letter of the word that is an antonym of the boldfaced word.

1. **perservere:** _______
   (a) praise, (b) quit, (c) accept
2. **dissuasion:** _______
   (a) improvement, (b) silence, (c) encouragement
3. **remorse:** _______
   (a) attraction, (b) improvement, (c) satisfaction
4. **cosmopolitan:** _______
   (a) provincial, (b) widespread, (c) elegant
5. **perfunctorily:** _______
   (a) thoroughly, (b) naturally, (c) wisely

EXERCISE B: MEANING CLUES Read each title below and write the vocabulary word, not used in Exercise A, that you might expect to find in a magazine article with that title.

1. "Sermons to Live By"
2. "The Tragedy of America's Cast-Off Pets"
3. "How to Help When a Loved One Hurts"
4. "Prayer in the Schools: The Debate Goes On"
5. "The Wisdom of Age: Honoring Our Elderly"

WORDS TO KNOW			
	commiserate	forsaken	remorse
	cosmopolitan	homily	theological
	deference	perfunctorily	
	dissuasion	persevere	

Chinua Achebe

1930–

Other Works
Arrow of God
A Man of the People
Beware, Soul Brother, and Other Poems
Anthills of the Savannah
Things Fall Apart

The Stories of His People Chinua Achebe is one of contemporary Africa's most famous authors. A member of the Ibo people of eastern Nigeria, Achebe was born in the village of Ogidi, where his father taught at a Christian mission school. As a child, Achebe learned both the Ibo and the English languages. He first considered a writing career while a student at Nigeria's University of Ibadan. "I read some appalling European novels about Africa," he explains, "... and realized that our story could not be told for us by anyone else."

Political Years During the Nigerian civil war of 1967–1970, Achebe supported the independence effort of Biafra, a predominately Ibo region in eastern Nigeria. He served on diplomatic missions representing Biafra. After the fall of Biafra, Achebe took a university position in Nigeria. He has devoted his life to teaching and writing ever since.

Literary Legacy Although fluent in Ibo, Achebe usually writes in English. He is generally regarded as the most accomplished of the African novelists who write in English. In addition to novels and short stories, Achebe has written children's books and collections of essays and poetry. "Marriage Is a Private Affair" is from *Girls at War and Other Stories,* published in 1973.

VIDEODISC **LaserLinks: Background for Reading**
Author Background

Writing Options

Okeke's Letter Student responses should take into account both Okeke's initial disapproval and his final change of heart.

Inquiry & Research

Students should locate appropriate print resources, including books on European cultural history. Remind students to consult nonprint resources including databases and the Internet.

Vocabulary in Action

Exercise A: ASSESSMENT PRACTICE
1. b
2. c
3. c
4. a
5. a

Exercise B: MEANING CLUES
1. homily
2. forsaken
3. commiserate
4. theological
5. deference

Mini Lesson: Speaking and Listening

PERSUASIVE WRITING AND SPEAKING

Instruction Have students break up into pairs. One person will write a persuasive argument to be spoken for two or three minutes in favor of Nnaemeke's marriage to Nene. The other student will write an argument of similar length against the marriage.

Have each pair present its arguments to the class. Listeners can evaluate each speaker's message to decide which side (for or against the marriage) made the more persuasive presentation.

MARRIAGE IS A PRIVATE AFFAIR 195

OVERVIEW

Objectives

1. understand and appreciate a **short story (Literary Analysis)**
2. recognize elements of **cultural setting (Literary Analysis)**
3. identify **cultural characteristics (Active Reading)**

Summary

As the narrator, Shanshan, ponders her hesitation to marry a handsome suitor, she reflects on her late mother, Zhong Yu, and her life of unfulfilled love. The narrator knew that her mother's early and brief marriage had lacked love, but from her mother's diary, she has learned that her mother did love a man of strong character and firm political convictions. Although he was married—out of duty to another family—his devotion to her mother never flagged. The lovers enjoyed only a single stroll, in which they never even clasped hands. The narrator knows, however, that her mother died happy to have known true love. Mindful of her mother's admonition to never marry for the wrong reason, Shanshan decides it is better to remain single than to enter a loveless marriage.

Thematic Link

A revolutionary culture intersects with an ancient one. Faced with traditions from both, an individual still struggles to fulfill her own desires.

5-Minute Warm-Up

Daily Language SkillBuilder

Have students **proofread** the display sentences on page 15k and write them correctly. The sentences also appear on Transparency 7 of **Grammar Transparencies and Copymasters.**

"For a republic thirty is still young. But a girl of thirty is virtually on the shelf."

Love Must Not Be Forgotten

Short Story by ZHANG JIE

Connect to Your Life

What Makes a Marriage? Think about married couples that you know. Based on your observations, what qualities are essential to a good marriage? Discuss your ideas with a group of classmates.

Build Background

Chinese Cultural Revolution In the 1960s and 1970s, when this selection takes place, many institutions of Chinese life, including marriage, were subjected to intense questioning. Since 1949, Mao Zedong (sometimes spelled Mao Tse-tung) and his Communist forces had been in control of China. By the mid 1960s Mao felt that new blood was needed to keep the ideals of Communism alive, so he implemented the Cultural Revolution in 1966. For the next three years, groups of young students and other radicals removed and replaced older Communist Party leaders. Many leaders were executed; others were sent to prison or to the countryside to be "re-educated" in communist thought.

Despite sweeping political changes, many Chinese customs were slow to change. For example, centuries-old traditions dictated that marriages be arranged by the couple's families when the prospective spouses were still young children. Although new laws enacted by the Communists allowed individuals to choose their own marriage partners, marrying for love was still frowned upon because communist teachings encouraged individuals to suppress personal desires for the greater social good.

WORDS TO KNOW
Vocabulary Preview

ardent	heretic
atonement	naiveté
aversion	parry
censure	renounce
coyness	wistful

LaserLinks: Background for Reading
Cultural Connection

Focus Your Reading

LITERARY ANALYSIS CULTURAL SETTING The time and place of a short story's action is called the **setting.** Setting can also include the social and cultural environment in which the action of a story takes place. In the story you are about to read, the author provides many clues about the story's **cultural setting,** such as the following passage:

> ***It was clear from the tear-stained pages of Mother's diary that he had been harshly denounced; but the steadfast old man never knuckled under to the authorities.***

As you read this story, look for other examples of the story's cultural setting.

ACTIVE READING IDENTIFYING CULTURAL CHARACTERISTICS The culture of China during the time of this story strongly influences the plot and the characters' attitudes and motivations. To understand the characters and events, you need to pay attention to what the story reveals about the traditions, political institutions, and beliefs and values of Chinese culture.

READER'S NOTEBOOK As you read, take notes on the cultural characteristics of China that are revealed in the story.

LESSON RESOURCES

UNIT ONE RESOURCE BOOK, pp. 87–91

ASSESSMENT RESOURCES

Formal Assessment, pp. 35–36
Teacher's Guide to Assessment and Portfolio Use
Test Generator

SKILLS TRANSPARENCIES AND COPYMASTERS

Literary Analysis
- Setting, T3 (for Cooperative Learning Activity, p. 209)

Reading and Critical Thinking
- Notetaking, T40 (for Reader's Notebook, p. 196)

Grammar
- Pronoun Case, C149 (for Mini Lesson, p. 202)
- Reflexive and Intensive Pronouns, C154 (for Mini Lesson, p. 200)

Vocabulary
- Word Origins, C38 (for Mini Lesson, p. 206)

Writing
- Writing Structure, T6, T8 (for Writing Option 1, p. 210)

Communications
- Formal Presentations, T10 (for Inquiry & Research, p. 210)

INTEGRATED TECHNOLOGY

Audio Library
LaserLinks
- Cultural Connection: China's Cultural Revolution. See **Teacher's SourceBook,** p. 17.

Visit our website:
www.mcdougallittell.com

Love Must Not Be Forgotten

Zhang Jie

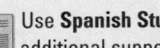

Red Peonies (1929), Ch'i Pai-Shih. Arthur M. Sackler Museum, Harvard University.

I am thirty, the same age as our People's Republic. For a republic thirty is still young. But a girl of thirty is virtually on the shelf.

Actually, I have a bona fide[1] suitor. Have you seen the Greek sculptor Myron's Discobolus? Qiao Lin[2] is the image of that discus thrower. Even the padded clothes he wears in winter fail to hide his fine physique. Bronzed, with clear-cut features, a broad forehead and large eyes, his appearance alone attracts most girls to him.

But I can't make up my mind to marry him. I'm not clear what attracts me to him, or him to me.

---

1. **bona fide** (bō′nə fīd): authentic; genuine.
2. **Qiao Lin** (chou′lĭn′).

TEACHING THE LITERATURE

Customizing Instruction

Less Proficient Readers
Have students ask themselves the following questions as they read the story.
- Who are the main characters?
  Answer: the narrator and her mother, Zhong Yu
- What is the narrator's problem?
  Answer: She is not sure she wants to marry her suitor.
- What was Zhong Yu's problem?
  Answer: She could not marry the man she loved.

Students Acquiring English
Tell students that the idiom "on the shelf" means, in this country, "destined to remain single." Explain to students that remaining single will be an important issue throughout this story.

Use **Spanish Study Guide** for additional support, pp. 44–46.

Gifted and Talented
The narrator's mother is a successful and well-known Chinese writer. Have students find out more about how professional and private life changed for women in Maoist China. Then have them discuss these changes as they are or are not reflected in this story.

Mini Lesson Preteaching Vocabulary

USING CONTEXT CLUES Call students' attention to the list of WORDS TO KNOW. Remind them that sometimes they can understand the meaning of an unfamiliar word by examining the context in which the word is used. Use the model sentence to demonstrate the strategy of using context clues to make **inferences** about word meanings.

Model Sentence

The ruling party imprisoned the *heretic* for his dissenting statements.

Instruction

Write the model sentence on the chalkboard. Have students use the meaning of the sentence to infer the meaning of the word *heretic*.

Possible response: Someone who disagrees with the ruling group.

Ask a volunteer to use the word *heretic* in a sentence.

Possible response: The heretic had to keep his opinions secret.

Use **Unit One Resource Book,** p. 90, for additional support.

A lesson on using context clues appears on p. 56 in the Pupil's Edition.

Reading and Analyzing

Reading Skills and Strategies: PREVIEW

Have students look through the story. Have them examine the art, the called-out quotes, and the title. Point out the mix of romantic and political messages in these elements. Then have students read the Build Background feature on p. 196. Ask them to predict what the story will be about. Before students read the story, give them a brief summary.

Active Reading

IDENTIFYING CULTURAL CHARACTERISTICS

After they read the opening paragraph, ask students what conclusions they can reach about marriage in China in 1979, when the story begins.

Possible Response: It is typical for women to marry at a younger age than 30.

Use **Unit One Resource Book,** p. 88 for additional support.

Literary Analysis **CULTURAL SETTING**

The story takes place in Communist China. As they read, ask students to keep a list of elements of that cultural setting that have a direct influence on the relationship detailed in the story. Students should consider and interpret the possible influences of historical contexts on the selection.

Possible Responses: The man Zhong Yu loves has married someone else out of obligation to a man who died for the Party; he is later killed in the Cultural Revolution.

Use **Unit One Resource Book,** p. 89 for additional support.

I know people are gossiping behind my back, "Who does she think she is, to be so choosy?"

1 To them, I'm a nobody playing hard to get. They take offense at such preposterous behavior.

Of course, I shouldn't be captious.[3] In a society where commercial production still exists, marriage like most other transactions is still a form of barter.

I have known Qiao Lin for nearly two years, yet still cannot fathom whether he keeps so quiet from aversion to talking or from having nothing to say. When, by way of a small intelligence test, I demand his opinion of this or that, he says "good" or "bad" like a child in kindergarten.

Once I asked, "Qiao Lin, why do you love me?" He thought the question over seriously for what seemed an age. I could see from his normally smooth but now wrinkled forehead that the little grey cells in his handsome head were hard at work cogitating.[4] I felt ashamed to have put him on the spot.

Finally he raised his clear childlike eyes to tell me, "Because you're good!"

Loneliness flooded my heart. "Thank you, Qiao Lin!" I couldn't help wondering, if we were to marry, whether we could discharge our duties to each other as husband and wife. Maybe, because law and morality would have bound us together. But how tragic simply to comply with law and morality! Was there no stronger bond to link us?

How tragic simply to comply with law and morality! Was there no stronger bond to link us?

When such thoughts cross my mind, I have the strange sensation that instead of being a girl contemplating marriage I am an elderly social scientist.

Perhaps I worry too much. We can live like most married couples, bringing up children together, strictly true to each other according to the law. . . . Although living in the seventies of the twentieth century, people still consider marriage the way they did millennia ago, as a means of continuing the race, a form of barter or a business transaction in which love and marriage can be separated. As this is the common practice, why shouldn't we follow suit?

But I still can't make up my mind. As a child, I remember, I often cried all night for no rhyme or reason, unable to sleep and disturbing the whole household. My old nurse, a shrewd though uneducated woman, said an ill wind had blown through my ear. I think this judgment showed prescience,[5] because I still have that old weakness. I upset myself over things which really present no problem, upsetting other people at the same time. One's nature is hard to change.

I think of my mother too. If she were alive, what would she say about my attitude to Qiao Lin and my uncertainty about marrying him?

My thoughts constantly turn to her, not because she was such a strict mother that her ghost is still watching over me since her death. No, she was not just my mother but my closest

3. **captious** (kăp′shəs): quick to find fault; quibbling.

4. **cogitating** (kŏj′ĭ-tā′tĭng): thinking carefully; pondering.

5. **prescience** (prē′shē-əns): knowledge of things before they happen; foresight.

WORDS TO KNOW **aversion** (ə-vûr′zhən) *n.* a strong, definite dislike

Teaching Options

Mini Lesson Viewing and Representing

Red Peonies **by Ch'i Pai-shih,** p. 197

ART APPRECIATION Born to a poor peasant family in the Hunan Province, Ch'i Pai-shih (1863–1957) became a leading artist of the People's Republic of China. At the age of eight, he was apprenticed to a carpenter because he was a delicate child and unable to work with his family in the fields. He became a master carver and successfully taught himself other arts. *Red Peonies,* completed in 1929, is a vibrant example of Ch'i Pai-shih's style.

Instructions: Ch'i Pai-shih was known for quick, confident brush strokes in a somewhat abstract style. Point out the use of massive, vibrant flowers that fill almost half of the hanging scroll and are set off by leaves rendered in ink and paint. A poem and two red artist's seals at the lower right provide balance.

Application Ask students to give adjectives describing the mood of the painting. How might the painting be different without the calligraphy in the bottom right-hand corner?

Possible Responses: Adjectives: lush, romantic, quiet, passionate. Without the calligraphy the painting might look imbalanced, or it might look more dynamic, as though the flowers are about to slide down the panel.

friend. I loved her so much that the thought of her leaving me makes my heart ache.

She never lectured me, just told me quietly in her deep, unwomanly voice about her successes and failures, so that I could learn from her experience. She had evidently not had many successes—her life was full of failures.

During her last days she followed me with her fine, expressive eyes, as if wondering how I would manage on my own and as if she had some important advice for me but hesitated to give it. She must have been worried by my naiveté and sloppy ways. She suddenly blurted out, "Shanshan,[6] if you aren't sure what you want, don't rush into marriage—better live on your own!"

Other people might think this strange advice from a mother to her daughter, but to me it embodied her bitter experience. I don't think she underestimated me or my knowledge of life. She loved me and didn't want me to be unhappy.

"I don't want to marry, mum!" I said, not out of bashfulness or a show of coyness. I can't think why a girl should pretend to be coy. She had long since taught me about things not generally mentioned to girls.

"If you meet the right man, then marry him. Only if he's right for you!"

"I'm afraid no such man exists!"

"That's not true. But it's hard. The world is so vast, I'm afraid you may never meet him." Whether I married or not was not what concerned her, but the quality of the marriage.

"Haven't you managed fine without a husband?"

"Who says so?"

"I think you've done fine."

"I had no choice. . . ." She broke off, lost in thought, her face wistful. Her wistful lined face reminded me of a withered flower I had pressed in a book.

"Why did you have no choice?"

"You ask too many questions," she parried, not ashamed to confide in me but afraid that I might reach the wrong conclusion. Besides, everyone treasures a secret to carry to the grave. Feeling a bit put out, I demanded bluntly, "Didn't you love my dad?"

"No, I never loved him."

"Did he love you?"

"No, he didn't."

"Then why get married?"

She paused, searching for the right words to explain this mystery, then answered bitterly, "When you're young, you don't always know what you're looking for, what you need, and people may talk you into getting married. As you grow older and more experienced, you find out your true needs. By then, though, you've done many foolish things for which you could kick yourself. You'd give anything to be able to make a fresh start and live more wisely. Those content with their lot will always be happy, they say, but I shall never enjoy that happiness." She added, self-mockingly, "A wretched idealist, that's all I am." **2**

Did I take after her? Did we both have genes which attracted ill winds?

"Why don't you marry again?"

"I'm afraid I'm still not sure what I really want." She was obviously unwilling to tell me the truth.

I cannot remember my father. He and Mother split up when I was very small. I just recall her telling me sheepishly that he was a fine handsome fellow. I could see she was ashamed of having judged by appearances and made a futile choice. She told me, "When I can't sleep at night, I force myself to sober up by recalling all those

6. **Shanshan** (shän′shän′).

WORDS TO KNOW

naiveté (nä′ēv-tā′) *n.* lack of sophistication; childlike innocence
coyness (coi′nĭs) *n.* the pretense of being more modest and innocent than one really is
wistful (wĭst′fəl) *adj.* full of wishful longing; sad
parry (păr′ē) *v.* to turn aside or avoid (a question) with a clever reply

Customizing Instruction

Students Acquiring English

1 Explain to students that "playing hard to get" means rejecting advances repeatedly so the suitor will try harder. Ask students who speak languages other than English to describe similar expressions in their first languages.

Less Proficient Readers

2 Ask students why Zhong Yu married a man she did not love. Ask students to keep this in mind as they learn her real story.

Possible responses: She was young and didn't know what she wanted; people may have talked her into getting married; he was handsome.

BLOCK SCHEDULING: MANAGING TIME

If your schedule requires that you cover the lesson objectives in a shorter time, use . . .

- Preparing to Read, p. 196
- Thinking Through the Literature, p. 209
- Vocabulary in Action, p. 210

If you want to take advantage of longer class time, use . . .

- TE Teaching Options: Preteaching Vocabulary p. 197; Viewing and Representing, p. 198, 205, 208; Multicultural Link, p. 201; Speaking and Listening, p. 203; Cross Curricular Link, p. 204, Vocabulary Strategy, p. 206; Standardized Test Practice, 210

Reading and Analyzing

ACTIVE READING

A CLARIFY **Possible Response:** She sees her mother as so fascinating that any man she loved would have to love her, and the happy couple would have made for a happy household.

Active Reading

IDENTIFY CULTURAL CHARACTERISTICS

B What does the lover's decision to marry tell you about Chinese culture? **Possible Responses:** Students should recognize distinct characteristics of the Chinese culture. The lover's decision shows the importance of duty. It also shows that marriage is not necessarily an individual matter, but one of family and society as he chose his wife not because of her personality, but because she was the daughter of a man who saved his life.

ACTIVE READING

C IDENTIFY CULTURAL CHARACTERISTICS **Possible Response:** The events show that personal feelings often play a secondary role to concerns of tradition, honor, and obligation.

stupid blunders I made. Of course it's so distasteful that I often hide my face in the sheet for shame, as if there were eyes watching me in the dark. But distasteful as it is, I take some pleasure in this form of atonement."

I was really sorry that she hadn't remarried. She was such a fascinating character, if she'd married a man she loved, what a happy household ours would surely have been. Though not beautiful, she had the simple charm of an ink landscape. She was a fine writer too. Another author who knew her well used to say teasingly, "Just reading your works is enough to make anyone love you!"

ACTIVE READING

CLARIFY Why does the narrator think that her mother should have remarried? **A**

She would retort, "If he knew that the object of his affection was a white-haired old crone, that would frighten him away."

At her age, she must have known what she really wanted, so this was obviously an evasion. I say this because she had quirks which puzzled me.

For instance, whenever she left Beijing on a trip, she always took with her one of the twenty-seven volumes of Chekhov's[7] stories published between 1950 and 1955. She also warned me, "Don't touch these books. If you want to read Chekhov, read that set I bought you." There was no need to caution me. Having a set of my own why should I touch hers? Besides, she'd told me this over and over again. Still she was on her guard. She seemed bewitched by those books.

So we had two sets of Chekhov's stories at home. Not just because we loved Chekhov, but to parry other people like me who loved Chekhov. Whenever anyone asked to borrow a volume, she would lend one of mine. Once, in her absence, a close friend took a volume from her set. When she found out, she was frantic and at once took a volume of mine to exchange for it.

Ever since I can remember, those books were on her bookcase. Although I admire Chekhov as a great writer, I was puzzled by the way she never tired of reading him. Why, for over twenty years, had she had to read him every single day?

Sometimes, when tired of writing, she poured herself a cup of strong tea and sat down in front of the bookcase, staring raptly at that set of books. If I went into her room then, it flustered her, and she either spilt her tea or blushed like a girl discovered with her lover.

I wondered: Has she fallen in love with Chekhov? She might have if he'd still been alive.

When her mind was wandering just before her death, her last words to me were: "That set. . . ." She hadn't the strength to give it its complete title. But I knew what she meant. "And my diary . . . 'Love Must Not Be Forgotten'. . . . Cremate them with me." **1**

I carried out her last instruction regarding the works of Chekhov, but couldn't bring myself to destroy her diary. I thought, if it could be published, it would surely prove the most moving thing she had written. But naturally publication was out of the question.

At first I imagined the entries were raw material she had jotted down. They read neither like stories, essays, a diary or letters. But after reading the whole I formed a hazy impression, helped out by my imperfect memory. Thinking it over, I finally realized that this was no lifeless manuscript I was holding, but an anguished, loving heart. For over twenty years one man had occupied her heart, but he was not for her. She used these diaries as a substitute for him, a means of pouring out her feelings to him, day after day, year after year.

7. **Chekhov's** (chĕk′ôfs): Anton Chekhov (1860–1904; also spelled Chekov), a Russian author, whose short stories were first published in Chinese in the 1950s.

WORDS TO KNOW

atonement (ə-tōn′mənt) *n.* the act of making up for a serious error, sin, or wrong

Teaching Options

Mini Lesson Grammar

REFLEXIVE AND INTENSIVE PRONOUNS Remind students that these pronouns are formed by adding *-self* or *-selves* to common pronouns. Reflexive pronouns reflect action back on the subject. Intensive pronouns add emphasis but are not essential to meaning.

Write the following examples on the chalkboard.

Reflexive: The children helped themselves to the cookies in the jar.

Intensive: We went to the state basketball championship ourselves.

Exercise: Have students identify the underlined pronoun as reflexive or intensive.

I could not stop myself from buying the new video. *(reflexive)*

Jacqueline herself is running for president of the Student Council. *(intensive)*

The guests helped themselves to dessert. *(reflexive)*

Have you asked the governor himself about this bill? *(intensive)*

Use **Grammar Transparencies and Copymasters,** p. 154.

Use McDougal Littell ***Language Network,*** Chapter 1, for more instruction on reflexive and intensive pronouns.

No wonder she had never considered any eligible proposals, had turned a deaf ear to idle talk whether well-meant or malicious. Her heart was already full, to the exclusion of anybody else. "No lake can compare with the ocean, no cloud with those on Mount Wu."[8] Remembering those lines I often reflected sadly that few people in real life could love like this. No one would love me like this.

I learned that towards the end of the thirties **2** when this man was doing underground work for the Party[9] in Shanghai, an old worker had given his life to cover him, leaving behind a helpless wife and daughter. Out of a sense of duty, of gratitude to the dead and deep class feeling, he had unhesitatingly married the girl. **B** When he saw the endless troubles caused by "love" of couples who had married for "love," he may have thought, **C** "Thank Heaven, though I didn't marry for love, we get on well, able to help each other." For years, as man and wife they lived through hard times.

ACTIVE READING

IDENTIFY CULTURAL CHARACTERISTICS What do these events reveal about the values of Chinese culture?

He must have been my mother's colleague. Had I ever met him? He couldn't have visited our home. Who was he?

In the spring of 1962, Mother took me to a concert. We went on foot, the theatre being quite near.

A black limousine pulled up silently by the pavement. Out stepped an elderly man with white hair in a black serge tunicsuit. What a striking shock of white hair! Strict, scrupulous, distinguished, transparently honest—that was my impression of him. The cold glint of his flashing eyes reminded me of lightning or swordplay. Only ardent love for a woman really deserving his love could fill cold eyes like those with tenderness.

He walked up to Mother and said, "How are you, Comrade Zhong Yu?[10] It's been a long time."

"How are you!" Mother's hand holding mine suddenly turned icy cold and trembled a little.

They stood face to face without looking at each other, each appearing upset, even stern. Mother fixed her eyes on the trees by the roadside, not yet in leaf. He looked at me. "Such a

Forbidden Fruit, Simon Ng. Reprinted with the permission of Simon & Schuster Books for Young Readers, an imprint of Simon & Schuster Children's Publishing Division. From *Tales from Gold Mountain: Stories of the Chinese in the New World,* a Groundwood Book/Douglas & McIntyre. Text Copyright © 1989 by Paul Yee, illustrations Copyright © 1989 by Simon Ng.

8. **Mount Wu:** a high mountain in southern China.
9. **the Party:** the Communist Party.
10. **Zhong Yu** (jŏng′yo͞o′).

WORDS TO KNOW **ardent** (är′dnt) *adj.* displaying great warmth of feeling; passionate

201

Customizing Instruction

Less Proficient Readers

1 To help students understand the importance of Zhong Yu's diary to the story, ask them the following questions.

- What did Zhong Yu ask her daughter to do when she died?
  Answer: cremate her with her diary and her set of books by Chekhov
- What did her daughter do with Zhong Yu's request and why?
  Answer: Shanshan cremated the Chekhov books but did not burn her mother's diary because she thought it could be published and would be the most moving thing Zhong Yu had written.
- What name did Zhong Yu give her diary?
  Answer: "Love Must Not Be Forgotten"

Students Acquiring English

2 Explain to students that "underground work" is illegal work done in secrecy, especially work hidden from the government.

Multicultural Link: Traditions

DUTY AND OBLIGATION Ancient traditions remain at the heart of modern Chinese life. These traditions are based on the Buddhist virtues of austerity and enlightenment and the Confucian ideals of unselfishness, courage, and honor. Confucianism has strict rules about behavior toward the living and toward departed ancestors. According to one tradition, it is a man's duty to marry the widow or the daughter of a man who has saved his life, and this duty must come before everything else. To Confucius, a person's inner virtues can only be fully realized through such "ritual propriety" of this kind.

Reading and Analyzing

Literary Analysis: CHARACTER

A Ask students what Shanshan's rude comment that her mother is lacking in beauty reveals about Shanshan's character.

Possible Response: She is frank and feisty; she isn't always willing to show devotion to her mother.

B Ask students to describe the qualities that attracted Zhong Yu to the man she loved.

Possible Responses: his strength of character, intelligence, courage, political convictions, or their common literary and artistic tastes

big girl already. Good, fine—you take after your mother."

Instead of shaking hands with Mother he shook hands with me. His hand was as icy as hers and trembling a little. As if transmitting an electric current, I felt a sudden shock. Snatching my hand away I cried, "There's nothing good about that!"

A "Why not?" he asked with the surprised expression grown-ups always have when children speak out frankly.

I glanced at Mother's face. I did take after her, to my disappointment. "Because she's not beautiful!"

He laughed, then said teasingly, "Too bad that there should be a child who doesn't find her own mother beautiful. Do you remember in '53, when your mum was transferred to Beijing, she came to our ministry to report for duty? She left you outside on the verandah,[11] but like a monkey you climbed all the stairs, peeped through the cracks in doors, and caught your finger in the door of my office. You sobbed so bitterly that I carried you off to find her."

"I don't remember that." I was annoyed at his harking back to a time when I was still in open-seat pants.[12]

"Ah, we old people have better memories." He turned abruptly and remarked to Mother, "I've read that last story of yours. Frankly speaking, there's something not quite right about it. You shouldn't have condemned the heroine. . . . There's nothing wrong with falling in love, as long as you don't spoil someone else's life. . . . In fact, the hero might have loved her too. Only for the sake of a third person's happiness, they had to renounce their love. . . ."

A policeman came over to where the car was parked and ordered the driver to move on. When the driver made some excuse, the old man looked around. After a hasty "Goodbye" he strode to the car and told the policeman, "Sorry. It's not his fault, it's mine. . . ."

I found it amusing watching this old cadre[13] listening respectfully to the policeman's strictures.[14] When I turned to Mother with a mischievous smile, she looked as upset as a first-form[15] primary schoolchild standing forlornly in front of the stern headmistress. Anyone would have thought she was the one being lectured by the policeman.

The car drove off, leaving a puff of smoke. Very soon even this smoke vanished with the wind, as if nothing at all had happened. But the incident stuck in my mind.

Analyzing it now, he must have been the man whose strength of character won Mother's heart. That strength came from his firm political convictions, his narrow escapes from death in the revolution, his active brain, his drive at work, his well-cultivated mind. Besides, strange to say, he and Mother both liked the oboe. Yes, she must have worshipped him. She once told me that unless she worshipped a man, she couldn't love him even for one day. B

But I could not tell whether he loved her or not. If not, why was there this entry in her diary?

"This is far too fine a present. But how did you know that Chekhov's my favorite writer?"

11. **verandah** (və-răn′də): a partly enclosed porch.
12. **open-seat pants:** pants with a slit down the back, worn by young children.
13. **cadre** (kăd′rē): a member of a tightly knit revolutionary party or military group.
14. **strictures** (strĭk′chərz): rules or remarks setting limits or making restrictions.
15. **first-form:** first-grade.

WORDS TO KNOW **renounce** (rĭ-nouns′) *v.* to give up, especially as a matter of principle

Teaching Options

Mini Lesson Grammar

PRONOUN CASE Instruction: Review the three cases of pronouns:

- Nominative case indicates the pronoun is a subject or subject complement; examples include *I, you,* or *she.*
- Objective case indicates the word is an object of a verb or preposition; examples include *me, him,* or *them.*
- Possessive case indicates ownership; examples include *my, its,* or *your.*

Practice Have students find each pronoun in the following sentences and identify its case.

His tutoring was very helpful to me. *(His-possessive; me-objective)*

They tried to get us to go there, but we stuck to our earlier plan. *(They-nominative; us-objective; we-nominative; our-possessive)*

It was easy for us to get them to cancel their previous engagement. *(It-nominative; us-objective; them-objective; their-possessive)*

Use **Grammar Transparencies and Copymasters,** p. 149.

Use McDougal Littell's ***Language Network,*** Chapter 8, for more instruction in pronoun cases.

"You said so."

"I don't remember that."

"I remember. I heard you mention it when you were chatting with someone."

So he was the one who had given her the *Selected Stories of Chekhov.* For her that was tantamount[16] to a love letter.

Maybe this man, who didn't believe in love, realized by the time his hair was white that in his heart was something which could be called love. By the time he no longer had the right to love, he made the tragic discovery of this love for which he would have given his life. Or did it go deeper than that?

This is all I remember about him.

How wretched Mother must have been, deprived of the man to whom she was devoted! To catch a glimpse of his car or the back of his head through its rear window, she carefully figured out which roads he would take to work and back. Whenever he made a speech, she sat at the back of the hall watching his face rendered hazy by cigarette smoke and poor lighting. Her eyes would brim with tears, but she swallowed them back. If a fit of coughing made him break off, she wondered anxiously why no one persuaded him to give up smoking. She was afraid he would get bronchitis again. Why was he so near yet so far?

He, to catch a glimpse of her, looked out of the car window every day, straining his eyes to watch the streams of cyclists, afraid that she might have an accident. On the rare evenings on which he had no meetings, he would walk by a roundabout way to our neighborhood, to pass our compound gate. However busy, he would always make time to look in papers and journals for her work.

> *We agreed to forget each other. But I deceived you, I have never forgotten.*

His duty had always been clear to him, even in the most difficult times. But now confronted by this love he became a weakling, quite helpless. At his age it was laughable. Why should life play this trick on him?

Yet when they happened to meet at work, each tried to avoid the other, hurrying off with a nod. Even so, this would make Mother blind and deaf to everything around her. If she met a colleague named Wang, she would call him Guo[17] and mutter something unintelligible.

It was a cruel ordeal for her. She wrote:

We agreed to forget each other. But I deceived you, I have never forgotten. I don't think you've forgotten either. We're just deceiving each other, hiding our misery. I haven't deceived you deliberately, though; I did my best to carry out our agreement. I often stay far away from Beijing, hoping time and distance will help me to forget you. But on my return, as the train pulls into the station, my head reels. I stand on the platform looking around intently, as if someone were waiting for me. Of course there is no one. I realize then that I have forgotten nothing. Everything is unchanged. My love is like a tree the roots of which strike deeper year after year—I have no way to uproot it.

At the end of every day, I feel as if I've forgotten something important. I may

16. **tantamount** (tăn′tə-mount′): equal in effect or value.

17. **Guo** (gwō): The Chinese characters for this family name are similar to those for the name *Wang*.

Customizing Instruction

Less Proficient Readers

Set a Purpose

Have students read to find out what happened to the man Zhong Yu loved.

Mini Lesson Speaking and Listening

DRAMATIC READING Prepare Help students prepare a dramatic reading of one or more of Zhong Yu's diary entries. Have them list characteristics of Zhong Yu that are revealed by her writing. Then have them describe the qualities of a monologue that would represent these characteristics. Have them consider tone of voice, pitch, volume, and the speed with which Zhong Yu would speak. Have them also consider facial expressions, posture, and gestures that might effectively convey her personality.

Present Students can decide how to present the monologue. Students should be able to justify their choice of verbal and nonverbal performance techniques by referring to their interpretations of the text. Audience members should evaluate how the performance increases their appreciation and understanding of Zhong Yu, and of the story in general.

LOVE MUST NOT BE FORGOTTEN 203

Reading and Analyzing

Guide for Reading

ACTIVE READING

A CLARIFY Possible Responses: The man was married to someone else; Zhong Yu and the man she loved placed duty and honor ahead of individual emotional needs.

Active Reading: SUMMARIZING

B Ask students to summarize what happened to Zhong Yu's true love. **Possible Response:** He was killed during the Cultural Revolution for questioning the prevailing political theory.

wake with a start from my dreams wondering what has happened. But nothing has happened. Nothing. Then it comes home to me that you are missing! So everything seems lacking, incomplete, and there is nothing to fill up the blank. We are nearing the ends of our lives, why should we be carried away by emotion like children? Why should life submit people to such ordeals, then unfold before you your lifelong dream? Because I started off blindly, I took the wrong turning, and now there are insuperable[18] *obstacles between me and my dream.*

Yes, Mother never let me go to the station to meet her when she came back from a trip, preferring to stand alone on the platform and imagine that he had met her. Poor mother with her greying hair was as infatuated as a girl.

ACTIVE READING

CLARIFY Why was the mother unable to fulfill her dream? **A**

Not much space in the diary was devoted to their romance. Most entries dealt with trivia: Why one of her articles had not come off; her fear that she had no real talent; the excellent play she missed by mistaking the time on the ticket; the drenching she got by going out for a stroll without her umbrella. In spirit they were together day and night, like a devoted married couple. In fact, they spent no more than twenty-four hours together in all. Yet in that time they experienced deeper happiness than some people in a whole lifetime. Shakespeare makes Juliet say, "I cannot sum up half my sum of wealth." And probably that is how Mother felt.

B He must have been killed in the "cultural revolution." Perhaps because of the conditions then, that section of the diary is ambiguous and obscure. Mother had been so fiercely attacked for her writing, it amazed me that she went on keeping a diary. From some veiled allusions I gathered that he had queried the theories advanced by that "theoretician" then at the height of favor, and had told someone, "This is sheer Rightist[19] talk." It was clear from the tear-stained pages of Mother's diary that he had been harshly denounced; but the steadfast old man never knuckled under to the authorities. His last words were, "When I go to meet Marx,[20] I shall go on fighting my case!" **B**

That must have been in the winter of 1969, because that was when Mother's hair turned white overnight, though she was not yet fifty. And she put on a black arm band. Her position then was extremely difficult. She was criticized for wearing this old-style mourning, and ordered to say for whom she was in mourning. **1**

"For whom are you wearing that, mum?" I asked anxiously.

"For my lover." Not to frighten me she explained, "Someone you never knew."

"Shall I put one on too?" She patted my cheeks, as she had when I was a child. It was years since she had shown me such affection. I often felt that as she aged, especially during these last years of persecution, all tenderness had left her, or was concealed in her heart, so that she seemed like a man.

She smiled sadly and said, "No, you needn't wear one."

Her eyes were as dry as if she had no more tears to shed. I longed to comfort her or do something to please her. But she said, "Off you go."

I felt an inexplicable dread, as if dear Mother had already half left me. I blurted out, "Mum!"

Quick to sense my desolation, she said gently, "Don't be afraid. Off you go. Leave me alone for a little."

---

18. **insuperable** (ĭn-so͞oʹpər-ə-bəl): impossible to overcome; insurmountable.
19. **Rightist:** belonging to a conservative or reactionary politics.
20. **Marx:** Karl Marx (1818–1883), a German economic philosopher revered by communists.

Teaching Options

Cross Curricular Link History

CULTURAL REVOLUTION In 1966, Mao Zedong initiated what came to be known as the Great Proletarian Cultural Revolution. It was designed to prevent the growth of class differences and the restoration of capitalism. Mao's "Little Red Book," which contained quotations from his writings, was widely distributed. Followers also wore little pins that bore his portrait, and statues of Mao were raised near important buildings. During this period, writers like Shanshan's mother were often persecuted for being "too personal." Zhang Jie herself left China in 1989 after the government cracked down on "Western thinking" among students and intellectuals.

A painting in the class-education exhibition, Niutung People's Commune No. 4 (about 1970), Niutung People's Commune Spare-Time Art Group.

Customizing Instruction

Less Proficient Readers

1 Ask students how Zhong Yu reacted when she learned her true love had been executed.

Possible Responses: Her hair turned white overnight; she put on a black armband.

Mini Lesson Viewing and Representing

A painting in the class-education exhibition, **by the Niutung People's Commune Spare-Time Art Group**

ART APPRECIATION Painted around 1970 by peasants during the Great Proletarian Cultural Revolution, this revolutionary art was meant "for uniting and educating the people and for attacking and destroying the enemy." These lines accompany the painting:

Dancing are the Chinling Mountains, Laughing is the Weishui River,
The revolutionary committee has been set up. Revisionism is on the run; our rivers and mountains will be red forever.

Instruction This painting was done by a group, rather than an individual.

Application Ask students what the method used to create the painting, its subject, and its execution have in common with the story.

Possible response: the subordination of the individual to the requirements of society

Reading and Analyzing

Active Reading: CLARIFYING

A Ask students to clarify what the narrator means when she says her mother had a "locked heart."

Possible Response: Although her heart was full of love for the man, this love was secretly and carefully protected.

ACTIVE READING

B **EVALUATE** **Possible Responses:** The mother's devotion to her beloved is emotionally moving and profound; such devotion is tragically misplaced.

I was right. She wrote:

You have gone. Half my soul seems to have taken flight with you.

I had no means of knowing what had become of you, much less of seeing you for the last time. I had no right to ask either, not being your wife or friend. . . . So we are torn apart. If only I could have borne that inhuman treatment for you, so that you could have lived on! You should have lived to see your name cleared and take up your work again, for the sake of those who loved you. I knew you could not be a counter-revolutionary. You were one of the finest men killed. That's why I love you—I am not afraid now to avow it.

Snow is whirling down. . . . This whiteness covers up your blood and the scandal of your murder.

I have never set store by my life. But now I keep wondering whether anything I say or do would make you contract your shaggy eyebrows in a frown. I must live a worthwhile life like you and do some honest work for our country. Things can't go on like this—those criminals will get what's coming to them.

I used to walk alone along that small asphalt road, the only place where we once walked together, hearing my footsteps in the silent night. . . . I always paced to and fro and lingered there, but never as wretchedly as now. Then, though you were not beside me, I knew you were still in this world and felt that you were keeping me company. Now I can hardly believe that you have gone.

At the end of the road I would retrace my steps, then walk along it again. Rounding the fence I always looked back, as if you were still standing there waving goodbye. We smiled faintly, like casual acquaintances, to conceal our undying love. That ordinary evening in early spring, a chilly wind was blowing as we walked silently away from each other. You were wheezing a little because of your chronic bronchitis. That upset me. I wanted to beg you to slow down, but somehow I couldn't. We both walked very fast, as if some important business were waiting for us. How we prized that single stroll we had together, but we were afraid we might lose control of ourselves and burst out with "I love you"—those three words which had tormented us for years. Probably no one else could believe that we never once even clasped hands!

> *I must live a worthwhile life like you and do some honest work for our country.*

No, Mother, I believe it. I am the only one able to see into your locked heart. **A**

Ah, that little asphalt road, so haunted by bitter memories. We shouldn't overlook the most insignificant spots on earth. For who knows how much secret grief and joy they may hide.

No wonder that when tired of writing, she would pace slowly along that little road behind our window. Sometimes at dawn after a sleepless night, sometimes on a moonless, windy evening. Even in winter during howling gales which hurled sand and pebbles against the windowpane. . . . I thought this was one of her

Teaching Options

Mini Lesson Vocabulary

RESEARCHING WORD ORIGINS Explain to students that sometimes knowing a word origin can help them understand a word's current meaning. Use the model to demonstrate using a word's origin to assist in understanding its current meaning.

Model

Wistful–Old English *wistly,* intently

Instruction

- Write the model on the chalkboard.
- Have students look at the definition of wistful on p. 199 and discuss how its meaning is similar to and different from the meaning of its origin word.

Practice

Have students use a dictionary to look up the word origins of *atone, coy, parry,* and *renounce* and write them down using the model format. When students have finished, discuss with the class how the current meanings of the words are similar to and different from the meanings of the origin words.

Use **Vocabulary Transparencies and Copymasters,** p. 38.

A lesson on researching word origins appears on p. 356 in the Pupil's Edition.

eccentricities, not knowing that she had gone to meet him in spirit.

She liked to stand by the window too, staring at the small asphalt road. Once I thought from her expression that one of our closest friends must be coming to call. I hurried to the window. It was a late autumn evening. The cold wind was stripping dead leaves from the trees and blowing them down the small empty road.

She went on pouring out her heart to him in her diary as she had when he was alive. Right up to the day when the pen slipped from her fingers. Her last message was:

I am a materialist,[21] *yet I wish there were a Heaven. For then, I know, I would find you there waiting for me. I am going there to join you, to be together for eternity. We need never be parted again or keep at a distance for fear of spoiling someone else's life. Wait for me, dearest, I am coming—*

I do not know how Mother, on her death bed, could still love so ardently with all her heart. To me it seemed not love but a form of madness, a passion stronger than death. If undying love really exists, she reached its extreme. She obviously died happy, because she had known true love. She had no regrets.

ACTIVE READING

B **EVALUATE** What is your opinion of the mother's devotion to her loved one?

Now these old people's ashes have mingled with the elements. But I know that, no matter what form they may take, they still love each other. Though not bound together by earthly laws or morality, though they never once clasped hands, each possessed the other completely. Nothing could part them. Centuries to come, if one white cloud trails another, two grasses grow side by side, one wave splashes another, a breeze follows another . . . believe me, that will be them.

Each time I read that diary "Love Must Not Be Forgotten" I cannot hold back my tears. I often weep bitterly, as if I myself experienced their ill-fated love. If not a tragedy it was too laughable. No matter how beautiful or moving I find it, I have no wish to follow suit!

Thomas Hardy[22] wrote that "the call seldom produces the comer, the man to love rarely coincides with the hour for loving." I cannot censure them from conventional moral standards. What I deplore is that they did not wait for a "missing counterpart" to call them.

If everyone could wait, instead of rushing into marriage, how many tragedies could be averted!

When we reach communism,[23] will there still be cases of marriage without love? Maybe, because since the world is so vast, two kindred spirits may be unable to answer each other's call. But how tragic! However, by that time, there may be ways to escape such tragedies.

Why should I split hairs? 1

Perhaps after all we are responsible for these tragedies. Who knows? Maybe we should take the responsibility for the old ideas handed down from the past. Because if someone never marries, that is a challenge to these ideas. You will be called neurotic, accused of having guilty secrets or having made political mistakes. You may be regarded as an eccentric who looks down on ordinary people, not respecting age-old customs—a heretic. In short they will trump up endless vulgar and futile charges to ruin

21. **materialist** (mə-tîr′ē-ə-lĭst): here, a person who believes that the physical world is the only reality.
22. **Thomas Hardy** (1840–1928): a British author.
23. **When we reach communism:** When we reach the ideal state by following communist principles.

WORDS TO KNOW

censure (sĕn′shər) *v.* to criticize severely; to blame
heretic (hĕr′ĭ-tĭk) *n.* a person who holds controversial opinions that do not conform to the prevailing opinions of a society, religion, or group

Customizing Instruction

Students Acquiring English

1 Tell students that the idiom "split hairs" means to make trivial distinctions. Ask students to volunteer any similar expressions in their first language.

Reading and Analyzing

Literary Analysis CULTURAL SETTING

A Have a volunteer read aloud the last two sentences of the story. Ask students how Shanshan's argument for allowing people to live single reflects the cultural setting of this story.

Possible Response: Shanshan shifts her focus from the individual to the group, making her final argument rest on the benefits this very personal decision will have for the larger society.

New Look of a Village (about 1970), Niutung People's Commune Spare-Time Art Group.

your reputation. Then you have to knuckle under to those ideas and marry willy-nilly. But once you put the chains of a loveless marriage around your neck, you will suffer for it for the rest of your life.

I long to shout: "Mind your own business! Let us wait patiently for our counterparts. Even waiting in vain is better than willy-nilly marriage. To live single is not such a fearful disaster. I believe it may be a sign of a step forward in culture, education and the quality of life." ❖ **A**

Translated by Gladys Yang

Teaching Options

Mini Lesson: Viewing and Representing

New Look of a Village **by Niutung People's Commune Spare-Time Art Group**

ART APPRECIATION Point out to students that this painting was done by the same commune that did the painting on p. 205.

Application Ask students what this painting suggests to them about the ideal village in Communist China.

Possible Responses: All the houses are the same; the people move and work in groups; agriculture is the main occupation.

Activity Arrange students in small groups. Instruct each group to produce a drawing representing the group's idea of an ideal community. Groups may use a computer graphics program to portray their agreed ideal. When the groups have finished, have them present their drawings and discuss the process by which the group arrived at its idea of an ideal community. Have them evaluate the difficulty of having a group agree on an ideal.

Connect to the Literature

1. **What Do You Think?** What is your response to the mother's life story?

Comprehension Check
- What decision does the narrator face?
- What advice does her mother give her?
- What prevented the mother and her lover from marrying?

Think Critically

2. How do you think the **narrator** is affected by her mother's advice and experiences?

THINK ABOUT
- the narrator's feelings about her relationship with Qiao Lin
- the narrator's views on love and marriage
- how the narrator says she is viewed by society

3. Do you think the mother and the man she loved made the right choices about their relationship? Explain your opinion.
4. ACTIVE READING IDENTIFYING CULTURAL CHARACTERISTICS Look over the notes on cultural characteristics that you created for your READER'S NOTEBOOK. In your opinion, to what extent were the lives of the narrator and her mother affected by their culture? Give evidence from your notes and from the story to support your response.
5. Do you agree or disagree with the mother that it is better to live on one's own than to rush into marriage? Use examples from the story to support your opinion.
6. Predict the narrator's future. Will she marry, and if so, will she be happy? Explain why or why not.

Extend Interpretations

7. **Comparing Texts** What advice do you think the mother in this story would have given Okeke in "Marriage Is a Private Affair" when he rejected his son's decision to marry Nene?
8. **Connect to Life** Do you think that our society puts pressures on people to get married? Discuss your views with your classmates.
9. **Points of Comparison** Look at the analysis frames that you developed on pages 187 and 194. Make a third frame for this story, identifying the obstacles to love. How do these obstacles in this story compare with the various obstacles to love identified on your previous charts?

Literary Analysis

CULTURAL SETTING The **setting** is the time and place of the action of a story. However, a setting does not only consist in the physical location. It also includes the cultural environment in which the events unfold. In some stories, setting is not very important; the events could happen almost anywhere at almost anytime. In other stories, such as this one, the events are greatly influenced by the cultural setting.

Cooperative Learning Activity Working with a group, review the selection. Identify each major event in the story and discuss to what extent the event is influenced by the cultural setting. Consider whether the event could have occurred at some other place or time. Record your findings on a table like the one shown below.

Major event	Influenced by cultural setting? Why or why not?
Mother's loved one marries another woman.	Yes—he did it out of duty, gratitude to the dead, and class feeling.

GUIDING STUDENT RESPONSE

Connect to the Literature

1. **What Do You Think?**
Responses will vary. Some students will find it a very tragic or a beautiful story.

Comprehension Check
- Whether or not she should marry
- She should marry the man who is right for her.
- He was already married to someone else.

Use **Unit One Resource Book,** p. 91 for additional support.

Think Critically

2. Answers may vary. The narrator is uncertain about her mother's advice at first, but eventually she decides to take her mother's advice and wait.
3. Some will think that the mother and her beloved made a mistake, that he should have married her instead. Others will appreciate the sense of honor and self-sacrifice shown by the two. Students should support their responses.
4. Student responses should include an awareness of the importance of duty in Chinese culture and the communist focus on the good of the whole society.
5. Student opinions will vary, but should include examples from the story.
6. Possible Responses: Shanshan will marry the right man and be happy; she will not marry because the odds of finding the right person are very slim.

Literary Analysis

Cooperative Learning Activity Student charts should include major events in the story, including those that are not culturally influenced. For example, the death of the narrator's mother was not described as being culturally or societally influenced.

Extend Interpretations

Comparing Texts Possible Response: She would have advised him to let his son marry whom he wished because it is better to marry the person who is right than to follow the dictates of a culture and be unhappy.

Connect to Life Student answers will vary. They should, however, include examples from their own knowledge or experience of society.

Points of Comparison Student responses will vary, but they should include a comparison of the events described in the text with their own experiences or those of others. Similarities should include a sense of familial duty and obedience. Students should also mention that the parent-child relationships in the two stories are very different; in one story, the parent represents societal barriers, while in the other, the parent has herself defied these barriers.

Writing Options

1. **Mother's Monologue** Students should include the mother's hopes that her daughter will wait to marry until she knows who she is and who is right for her.
2. **Character Profile** Remind students that information about a character can be obtained from what the character says and does, what other characters say about the character, and what the narrator says about the character.

Inquiry & Research

Students might want to follow up their research on the Cultural Revolution with some research on the changes occurring in China today and the transition between communism and an industrial market economy.

Art Connection

Student responses will vary, but should include mention of the fact that in communism, individual needs are often subordinate to group well-being. Students should refer to examples of this in the story.

Vocabulary in Action

ASSESSMENT PRACTICE

1. c
2. b
3. c
4. b
5. a
6. b
7. c
8. a
9. b
10. a

Choices & CHALLENGES

Writing Options

1. Mother's Monologue Write a monologue in which the mother describes her feelings toward her daughter.

2. Character Profile Write a character evaluation of any prominent figure in the selection. First, provide an objective description of the character, and then state your opinion of that character. Base your statements on details in the selection.

Inquiry & Research

Cultural Revolution China's Cultural Revolution had wide-ranging effects on the country. Use current books as well as magazine and newspaper articles from the period to investigate ways in which the Cultural Revolution affected common people. Present your findings in an oral report.

Art Connection

The painting on page 208 shows workers at a political meeting in China. What does this painting tell you about the power of the Communist government over the lives of the characters in this selection?

Vocabulary in Action

EXERCISE: ASSESSMENT PRACTICE Determine the relationship between each pair of boldfaced words below. On your paper, write the letter of the choice that shows the most similar relationship.

1. **renounce** : **accept** :: (a) agree : approve (b) despise: disapprove (c) abandon : join
2. **wistful** : **sad** :: (a) warm : hot (b) bashful : shy (c) cheerful : gloomy
3. **atonement** : **sin** :: (a) question : answer (b) fact : opinion (c) apology : insult
4. **naiveté** : **worldliness** :: (a) beauty : youth (b) simplicity : complexity (c) love : marriage
5. **parry** : **question** :: (a) dodge : bullet (b) donate : gift (c) suffer : injury
6. **coyness** : **modesty** :: (a) intelligence : foolishness (b) bravado : courage (c) cowardice : fear
7. **censure** : **opponent** :: (a) advise : counselor (b) ridicule : mockery (c) praise : hero
8. **ardent** : **fond** :: (a) hilarious : funny (b) cool : icy (c) wicked : evil
9. **heretic** : **society** :: (a) criminal : prison (b) outlaw : community (c) voter : democracy
10. **aversion** : **dislike** :: (a) passion : fondness (b) innocence : guilt (c) elm : tree

Building Vocabulary
For an in-depth study of analogies, see page 263.

Zhang Jie
1937–

Other Works
As Long as Nothing Happens, Nothing Will
Heavy Wings

Pursuing a Dream Zhang Jie has been one of China's most highly acclaimed and, at times, controversial authors. Brought up in poverty and forced by the government to pursue college studies in economics instead of in literature as she had dreamed, Zhang Jie developed a strong sensitivity to injustices within the Communist system. After college Zhang Jie was directed to become a statistician, and during the Cultural Revolution, she, like many other college graduates, was sent to southern China to work in a factory. Finally, in 1976, Zhang Jie was able to move to Beijing and begin a writing career. Her first story, published in 1978, won her the first of many writing awards. By the early 1980s, Zhang Jie was a best-selling writer in her homeland. With "Love Must Not Be Forgotten," she became the first Chinese author in years to write about romantic love, marriage, and the role of women.

Teaching Options

Assessment **Standardized Test Practice**

POINT OF VIEW You can informally assess students' understanding of the selection by asking them to write about the events of the story from the point of view of a character other than the narrator, either as Qiao Lin or the old man. The events should be written as if they were the diary entries of these characters.

RUBRIC

3 **Full Accomplishment** Response reflects a full understanding of the events in the story and the characters as well.

2 **Substantial Accomplishment** Response shows a general understanding of the events in the story but does not fully reflect the characters.

1 **Little or Partial Accomplishment** Response reflects little understanding of the events in the story or of the characters.

Comparing Literature: Assessment Practice

In writing assessments, you will often be asked to analyze and compare two literary works with similar themes like "Marriage Is a Private Affair" and "Love Must Not Be Forgotten." You are now going to practice writing an essay with this kind of focus.

PART 1 Reading the Prompt

You will often be asked to write in response to a prompt like the one below. In such situations, you first need to read the prompt carefully. Then you should read it again, searching for key words that help you identify the purpose of the essay and decide how to approach it.

> **Writing Prompt**
> "Marriage Is a Private Affair" and "Love Must Not Be Forgotten" both explore the problems of individuals seeking love and fulfillment in a changing culture. In an essay, analyze the problem faced by a main character in each story. ❶ Compare the way in which each main character challenges the traditions and expectations of his or her society. ❷ To what degree does each succeed? Include evidence from the selection to support your analysis. ❸

STRATEGIES IN ACTION

❶ I need to write an essay that will **analyze**—or break down—the problems faced by the main characters.

❷ I have to **compare** how the main characters challenge their society.

❸ I need to include **examples** or **quotations** from the stories.

PART 2 Planning an Analysis Essay

- Devise a graphic like the one shown to help organize your analysis.
- For each main character, break down the problem that he or she faces by listing the various obstacles to love and marriage. (Refer to the charts you developed on pages 187, 194, and 209.)
- Look for similarities and differences among the problems, the obstacles, and the characters' responses to the obstacles.

Marriage Is a Private Affair	Love Must Not Be Forgotten
Problem:	Problem:
Obstacles:	Obstacles:
Character's Response:	Character's Response:

PART 3 Drafting Your Essay

Introduction Identify the main problem of each character. Describe how each character responds to the problem.

Organization For each character, you will need to break the problem down, discussing one obstacle at a time. You probably will find it helpful to discuss one story in its entirety, then the other. Make sure that you draw comparisons between the characters and their situations. Include examples.

Conclusion
End your essay with a clear statement that compares and contrasts the problems faced by the two characters and their responses.

PART 1 Reading the Prompt

Model the process of reading a prompt:

- Read through the prompt in its entirety.
- List key words of the assignment on the board ("analyze," "compare," and "include evidence").
- Define each key word using the Strategies in Action to show how students can restate the prompt in their own words.

PART 2 Planning an Analysis Essay

- Students can use the chart they have been filling out for the two stories (referenced on pages 187, 194, and 209).
- Suggest that students expand their charts by adding several obstacles that each character confronts.
- By adding a third column to their graphics labeled "Similarities and Differences," students can increase their understanding of the comparison.

PART 3 Drafting Your Essay

Introduction Suggest that students define the problems associated with an individual who, seeking personal satisfaction, comes into conflict with a governing social code. Encourage students to use this opening to lead into a description of each character's problem and response to that problem.

Organization Remind students that they should make sure their analyses are parallel, which means that obstacles discussed for story A are discussed in the same order for story B. It is probably best to begin with similarities. This should help maintain a smooth, parallel organization and flow. Differences can then be dealt with last, since they will not be parallel.

Conclusion Encourage students to conclude by restating the general difference or similarity between the problems and/or responses of the characters. Students should support their general statement with a summary of reasons or evidence already presented in the body of the essay. Remind students not to introduce new points or evidence in the conclusion.

Suggest students leave some time for revising their essays so they can produce an error-free final draft.

LOVE AND MARRIAGE ACROSS CULTURES 211

Objectives
- write a Focused Description
- use a written text as a model for writing
- revise a draft to improve word choice
- check for subject-verb agreement

Introducing the Workshop

(A) Focused Description Explain that writers use focused description to convey a precise, detailed account. Literary writers and journalists employ focused descriptions to create a vivid sense of "present" that puts readers as close as possible to the actual experience of the moment or scene being described.

Have students cite examples of vivid, focused description from their recent reading in which they felt as if they were "present" in the moment being described. What effect does this have on the reader? How do the details make the writing come alive? Point out that through writing a focused description students will also be able to create a detailed "present" in which readers feel like they are actually on the scene witnessing an event or viewing the scene or object being described.

Basics in a Box

(B) Using the Graphic Just as the graphic indicates, the elements of a focused description appeal to all the senses to create a vivid picture in the reader's mind. The graphic suggests the kinds of sensory details students can use to write an effective description.

(C) Presenting the Rubric To better understand the assignment, students can refer to the Standards for Writing a Successful Focused Description. You may wish to discuss with them the complete rubric, which describes several levels of proficiency. If you plan to assess student writing according to these standards, inform students so they will be aware of your expectations. Let them know about any additional standards you may set.

Use McDougal Littell's ***Language Network,*** Chapter 19, for more instruction on writing a focused description.

To engage students visually, use **Power Presentation** 2, Focused Description.

Writing Workshop — Focused Description

Creating a vivid description . . .

From Reading to Writing In Isaac Bashevis Singer's story "The Son from America," the main characters' simple lives are shown through singular details: a goat who lives in their one-room hut, an oil dish that serves as their lamp. Through **focused description,** authors like Singer can create vivid settings and help readers grasp some aspects of the characters' inner lives. Similarly, lawyers, police officers, doctors, and reporters also rely on focused descriptions in their work to communicate experiences or problems to others. (A)

For Your Portfolio

WRITING PROMPT Write a focused description of a scene or situation.

Purpose: To convey a vivid picture that helps the reader share your experience

Audience: Classmates, friends, or people who know about the scene or situation you are describing

Basics in a Box

Focused Description at a Glance (B)

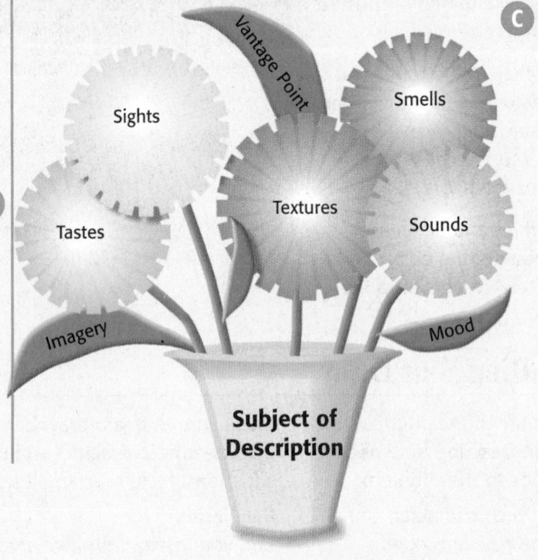

(C) **RUBRIC Standards for Writing**

A successful description should
- focus on a person, place, or object
- convey a clear sense of purpose
- use sensory details and precise words to create a vivid picture, establish a mood, or express emotion
- include figurative language or dialogue when appropriate
- use a consistent method of organization such as spatial order, order of importance, or order of impression

LESSON RESOURCES

USING PRINT RESOURCES

Unit One Resource Book
- Prewriting, p. 91
- Drafting, p. 92
- Peer Response, pp. 93–94
- Revising, Editing, and Proofreading, p. 95
- Student Models, pp. 96–101
- Rubric, p. 102

Writing Transparencies and Copymasters
- Writing Process Transparencies, pp. 1–4
- Writing Style Transparencies, pp. 12–24
- Writing Template Copymasters, p. 26

USING MEDIA RESOURCES

LaserLinks
Writing Springboards
See Teacher's SourceBook p. 64 for bar codes.

Writing Coach CD-ROM

Visit our website:
www.mcdougallittell.com

Analyzing a Student Model

Katie Eskra
Evanston Township High School

RUBRIC IN ACTION

Miles of Aisles in Wisconsin

We were driving along Highway 42, coming home from Aspen Bay. My parents were talking in the front seat, probably about what they had to do the next day. I wanted to have an argument with my sister, but I looked over and she was reading a book. I think it was about people pretending to kill other people on Halloween or something, but I'm not sure. It was one of those books you can read in about half an hour and then can't remember the plot the next day. I had decided just to look out the window at the snow and trees and occasional silo when my mom remembered we had forgotten to go to the store that morning. We were out of milk and a few other things, and we wanted to get some cake mix for that night. We're always making cakes for no particular reason when we're in Wisconsin. A huge grocery store appeared down the road, so we pulled into the lot. (D) Suddenly a wave of sadness and depression washed over me.

> ❶ The writer opens with details that describe her mood and situation.
> **Other Options:**
> - Open with dialogue.
> - Bring the reader directly into the main setting you want to describe.

> ❷ Introduces the store as the focus. The writer also names the mood the store evokes.

The store looked normal enough at first glance, and yet there seemed to be a forlorn and forgotten aura surrounding it. The building was in the middle of nowhere, but it looked ready to accommodate great hordes of people if they ever decided to show up. I think it got lost on the way to a big city and ended up where it was by accident. The parking lot was an enormous expanse of asphalt, neatly plowed and divided precisely by thick yellow lines into countless spaces. There were only four or five cars in the lot, all dilapidated and rusting and about twenty years old. One of the license plates read ILUVWI, though it was hard to read because of the big scratches in the metal. We parked next to one of the scrap heaps and all decided to go inside.

> ❸ Includes specific details to show the parking lot

The automatic doors opened promptly, and we stepped into an area with numerous shopping carts standing in perfect lines against the wall. Most of them had bits of paper or wrappers in them, but we chose one that didn't. A second set of doors opened, and we pushed our cart through into a colossal, artificially lit room. The fluorescent lights on

> ❹ Uses spatial order of organization—from outside to inside the store

Teaching the Lesson

Analyzing the Model

"Miles of Aisles in Wisconsin"

(D) In this student model, descriptive detail enables readers to visualize a grocery store that strikes the narrator as a lonely, unusual place. The writer's choice of certain words and details helps establish this distinct mood.

Have students read the model, then discuss how the winter setting contributes to the mood. Ask students to describe emotions typically associated with winter.

Possible Responses: Winter suggests barrenness and isolation, which supports the writer's main theme. Loneliness and sadness are typically associated with winter.

Students can take turns reading aloud the Rubric in Action. Point out key words and phrases in the student model that correspond to the elements mentioned in the Rubric in Action.

1. Have students suggest an alternative opening based on the other options listed.
   Possible Response: As we pulled our family car into the enormous parking lot of a huge grocery store, an enormous sadness washed over me.
2. Point out how the writer begins her description of the grocery store by stating how she feels when she first sees the store. The writer then describes the store from the outside.
3. Ask students to identify details that contribute to the mood.
   Possible Response: Images, such as "dilapidated and rusting" twenty-year-old cars, license plates with "big scratches in the metal," and "scrap heaps" all contribute to the forlorn mood.
4. Discuss how the writer uses movement to keep the description from being static and passive.
   Ask students to look again at the opening paragraph and to explain how the strategy of a moving point of view is working in both places.
   Possible Responses: In both places, the writer is in transit–first in the car and now from the parking lot into the store. This moving point of view creates a sense of unfolding action that keeps the reader moving toward a destination.

Mini Lesson: Viewing and Representing

PICTURING TEXT STRUCTURE

Instruction Choosing a subject and carefully selecting the details and words to describe it are important parts of writing an effective focused description. However, organizing and structuring those details to create a certain impression are just as important.

Activity Have students analyze the text structure of the student model by creating a graphic organizer or other visual representation of that structure. The graphic students create should indicate how the student writer has organized the elements of her essay. Students might first reread the model, then talk with a partner and make notes about how each paragraph relates to the whole description.

Introduces the setting and the narrator's feelings of sadness → Describes the outside of the grocery store → Describes the inside of the grocery store → Describes the people in the store → Narrator's sadness lifts as she leaves the store

5. Ask students to evaluate how successful these details are in creating a sense of "present moment" that puts readers in the scene.
   Possible Response: The details—the cracked and dirty floor, the clatter of the grocery cart hitting a bump, and the "layer of dust that came off on our hands—" appeal to more than one sense, creating an opportunity for readers to experience the moment.
6. Point out that words and phrases such as "suspiciously," "slowly," "all herself," "cheap magazines," and "none of them looked up" reinforce the sense of loneliness and boredom.

the ceiling far above our heads seemed pathetic in the immensity of the store. The walkways were long and foreboding, and we decided to get what we needed as fast as possible and leave.

We bravely attacked every aisle in search of what we needed, but there were no signs indicating what kind of food was in each row so it took us quite a while. The cement floor was cracked and dirty, and every time the cart hit a bump it let out a clatter that echoed faintly in our ears. The food all seemed to come in gigantic bulk packages and was organized neatly and efficiently. Many of the cans were dented or rusty, however, and everything in the store was covered with a thin layer of dust that came off on our hands when we touched anything. We came across one other shopper who was stooped over, searching furtively through her handbag in the cereal aisle. We didn't stop to ask what she was doing.

5 Uses sensory details to describe sight and sound

Finally we found what we needed and quickly made our way to the front of the store. The checkout lady peered at us suspiciously over her thick reading glasses and put down her magazine with a sigh when she saw we actually wanted to buy something. She checked our purchases through slowly, then bagged them all herself. There were six other women sitting at the other registers, doing their nails or reading cheap magazines. None of them looked up as we paid for our groceries and prepared to leave the store.

6 Describes the women with details that support the writer's sadness

"Have a nice day," the lady mumbled, not expecting us to hear, as we walked out the door.

"You too," I replied over the lump in my throat.

My mood lifted as we crossed the parking lot and climbed back into our car. Soon we were on the highway, heading away from that strange, sad place—so big and so empty.

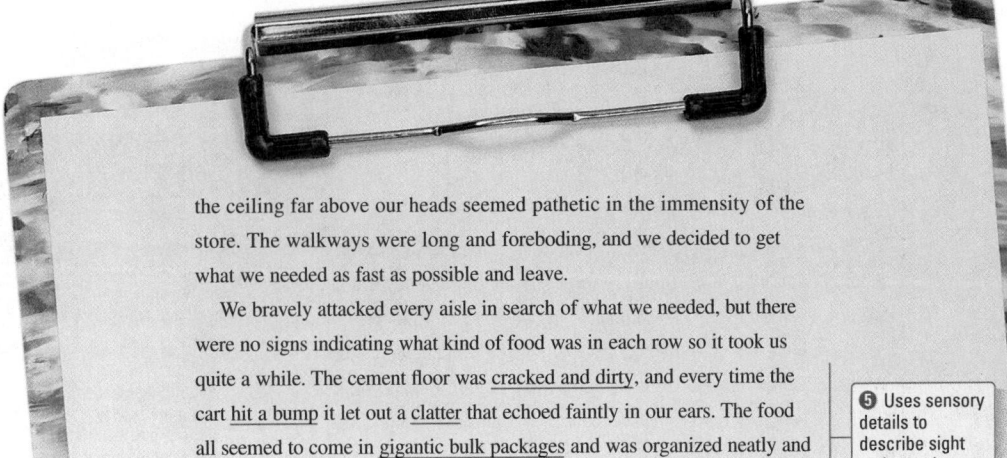

Writing Your Focused Description

❶ Prewriting

You can observe a lot by watching.
Yogi Berra, baseball player and manager

To find a subject for your description, you might try **recalling** a time when you found something so interesting you couldn't wait to describe it to your friends. Make a **list** of places—both strange and familiar—that you find fascinating. Or think of interesting or unusual people you know. See the **Idea Bank** in the margin for more suggestions. After you select a subject to describe, follow the steps below.

Planning Your Focused Description

1. **Decide your purpose.** Why are you describing this particular thing? Do you want to write to someone you care about to show why something is important to you? to make a person vivid and memorable? to create a particular mood? to recreate a scary event?
2. **Gather information through your senses.** Because careful observation is the key to powerful descriptive writing, you need to gather as many sensory details as possible. Close your eyes and imagine the smells, sounds, or textures you associate with the person, place, object, or event. What colors or shapes help describe your subject?
3. **Identify your audience.** What do your readers know about your subject? What part of your description might need some background information? What additional information do your readers need?

❷ Drafting

Begin writing even if you have not refined your purpose or chosen a specific focus. Keep going. Your focus will become clearer as you develop and refine your ideas.

Start by stating the most important aspect of your subject and providing details that support the subject and contribute to the overall effect. Use **sensory language** to convey a mood clearly. Words like *dilapidated, rusty, cracked, dirty, clatter,* and *searching furtively* all contribute to the forlorn feel of the store in the student model. **Show** what you are describing. If you include people, use **actions** or **dialogue** to let them reveal themselves.

You may choose an **organization** before you begin your draft, or you may order and rearrange your details in a later draft. At some point, however, you must

Ask Your Peer Reader

- What do you think my purpose is for describing this subject?
- Which details help you imagine my subject most clearly?
- What else would you like to know about my subject?

IDEABank

1. Your Working Portfolio
Look for ideas in the **Writing Options** you completed earlier in this unit.
- **Old World Sketches,** p. 168
- **Heritage Essay,** p. 179

2. Time Out
Sit quietly for 5 to 10 minutes in a park or on a busy street corner. Look for a writing topic by jotting down details of what you see, hear, and smell.

3. Post Cards
Recall interesting or unusual places you have seen or heard about. Try to picture these places as they might appear on a post card. Write about the place for which you have the most vivid mental picture.

Have a question?

See the **Writing Handbook**
Descriptive Writing, pp. 1153–1154

Guiding Student Writing

Prewriting

Choosing a Subject

If after reading the Idea Bank students are having difficulty choosing their subjects, suggest they try the following:
- Look through photo albums at home in search of particularly memorable moments or past experiences. Bring photos to class to recall specific details.
- Think about a special event, such as a vacation, a party, a sports event, or an awards ceremony. Describe your emotions and recall details of the setting.
- Choose someone that stands out in your memory and list several sensory details about them. What makes these people unique? In what setting would they feel comfortable?

Planning the Focused Description

1. Students might work in pairs to discuss their subjects. Have them explain to their partner why their subject is important to them.
2. Have students imagine the object or scene as if they were stepping into an old photograph or movie. Then, as they explore the scene, have them picture and record what they see, hear, smell, taste, and feel.

Drafting

Organizing the Draft

The student model represents one approach to organizing a focused description. Discuss the advantages of using a moving point of view that leads readers gradually closer to the object, as in the student model. Then discuss the effects of the other organizational methods listed in the text.

Invite students to consider themselves directors of their focused descriptions. What detail will the reader get first? When should the camera zoom in on a small detail? When does the camera pan around the room absorbing the entire scene? Does the first shot focus on a small item and then pull back for a bigger picture? Suggest that students experiment with different organizational patterns to see which works best for their focused description.

Revising

WORD CHOICE

Point out that the example shows how the writing was revised to make the descriptions more specific. Discuss the impact of these revisions.

Have students choose one paragraph in their drafts to complete this activity. Explain that they should circle all the adjectives and nouns and underline all the verbs in the paragraph. Then, have them revise where appropriate to use more concrete and specific words. You might also have students use a thesaurus as they search for the right words. When they finish revising this paragraph, have them reread their entire focused description to look for ways to make their details more specific.

Editing and Proofreading

SUBJECT-VERB AGREEMENT

Remind students that agreement errors can occur during revision when words in sentences are being added and deleted. Agreement errors are also common when the subject and verb are separated by phrases and clauses.

In the example, the writer changed *shoppers* to its singular form, so the singular verb *was* is needed instead of the plural *were.* The word *handbags* was changed to the singular form, *her handbag,* to agree with the singular antecedent *shopper.*

To help students find agreement errors in their own writing, you might ask them to first underline the subject of each sentence. Then have them check to see that singular subjects have singular verbs, and that plural subjects take plural verbs. Students should check subject-verb agreement as part of producing an error-free final draft.

Reflecting

In addition to answering the questions in the text, you might ask students to discuss their revision process. Was the revision process as productive as it could have been? Did their final draft differ significantly from earlier drafts? Ask students to focus their comments on what they accomplished or failed to accomplish in making revisions. Have students add these self-evaluations to their working portfolios.

choose a method of organization in order to create a clear, well-ordered description. There are three common methods for organizing a description:

- **Spatial order**
  Arrange details from bottom to top, left to right, inside to outside, and so on.
- **Order of importance**
  Present the most significant detail first. Other, less important details follow. Or begin with the least important details and work up to the most important ones.
- **Order of impression**
  Arrange details according to what first catches your attention. Then descibe details you notice later. This type of organization can give a "you are there" quality to your description.

Need revising help?

Review the **Rubric,** p. 212

Consider **peer reader** comments

Check **Revision Guidelines,** p. 1145

❸ Revising

TARGET SKILL ▶ WORD CHOICE Apt word choices add punch to your descriptions. Vague or abstract words can leave the image fuzzy for the reader. Try adding concrete words to leave a stronger impression.

> There were ~~not many~~ *only four or five* cars ~~around,~~ *in the lot* all ~~ugly~~ *dilapidated and rusting* and about twenty years old. One of the license plates *read ILUVWI, though it* was hard to read because of the big scratches in the metal.

Stumped by subject-verb agreement?

See the **Grammar Handbook,** pp. 1200–1202

❹ Editing and Proofreading

TARGET SKILL ▶ SUBJECT-VERB AGREEMENT During revision, if you change the number of your subject, don't forget to match your verb to the subject. Below, the writer changed the singular subject, then matched the verb and details.

> We came across ~~other shoppers who were~~ *one shopper who was* stooped over, searching furtively through ~~handbags~~ *her handbag* in the cereal aisle. ~~and peeking into the frozen foods.~~

Publishing IDEAS

- Submit your description to the school literary magazine or newspaper.
- Send your description to an e-mail buddy.

More Online: Publishing Options
www.mcdougallittell.com

❺ Reflecting

FOR YOUR WORKING PORTFOLIO How did writing a focused description help you see something in a new way? What lessons do you have for yourself about writing based on what you did here? Attach your answer to your finished work. Save your focused description in your **Working Portfolio.**

Option

Managing the Paper Load

Before turning in final drafts, have students write a brief statement describing the revisions they made. You might evaluate your students' revision strategies as a featured aspect of their final grade.

Assessment Practice Revising & Editing

Read this paragraph from the first draft of a focused description. The underlined sections may include the following kinds of errors:

- **vague word choice**
- **lack of subject-verb agreement**
- **inconsistent verb tenses**
- **run-on sentences**

For each underlined section, choose the revision that most improves the writing.

> Standing alone on stage behind the curtain, I feel funny (1). I can hear the audience settling down and growing quiet. The stage manager and the lighting operator sits (2) in the darkened electronics booth. The actors are ready. My senses have become sharper I can smell (3) the sticky greasepaint on my face. My neck burned (4) with the heat from the stage lights. The house lights dim the curtain begins to rise (5). It catches slightly on the way up; so does my pulse. Suddenly the curtain is up, and the show has begun (6).

1. **A.** nervous and excited.
   B. indifferent and tired.
   C. some emotion inside.
   D. something strange.

2. **A.** sat
   B. sit
   C. sitting
   D. Correct as is

3. **A.** sharper. I can smell
   B. sharper I can smell,
   C. sharper, I can smell
   D. Correct as is

4. **A.** burn
   B. has burnt
   C. burns
   D. Correct as is

5. **A.** The house lights dim, the curtain begins to rise.
   B. The house lights dim, curtain begins to rise.
   C. The house lights dim, and the curtain begins to rise.
   D. Correct as is

6. **A.** the curtain is up. And the show has begun.
   B. the curtain is up, the show had begun.
   C. the curtain is up the show has begun.
   D. Correct as is

Need extra help?

See the **Grammar Handbook**
Verb Tense, p. 1186
Correcting Run-on Sentences, p. 1199
Subject-Verb Agreement, pp. 1200–1202

Assessment Practice

Using the first question as a model, guide students in evaluating the choices and choosing the correct answer.

B. This choice is incorrect because the adjectives *indifferent* and *tired* conflict with the mood established in the rest of the paragraph.

C. This choice is incorrect because it is too vague. It hasn't stated which emotion the narrator is feeling.

D. This choice is also incorrect because it is too vague.

A. This is the best choice because it replaces the vague adjective *funny* with more specific adjectives, *nervous* and *excited.* These adjectives fit the mood of the rest of the paragraph.

Answers:
1. A; **2.** B; **3.** A; **4.** C; **5.** C; **6.** D

OBJECTIVES
- reflect on and assess student understanding of the unit
- compare text events with experiences of students and other readers
- provide examples of themes that cross texts
- compare across texts elements of texts such as conflicts and characterization
- assess and build portfolios

Reflecting on Theme

OPTION 1

A successful response will
- select at least two changes from the unit's selections and at least one from the student's personal experience.
- arrange changes in a chart with two columns labeled "Welcome Changes" and "Unwelcome Changes."
- underline changes toward which student has strongest feelings.
- evaluate student's attitude toward change, based on information in chart.

OPTION 2

A successful response will
- identify what the student believes to be at least three major causes of cultural change.
- arrange causes of cultural change into a pie chart with the most important or most common cause occupying the largest section of the pie chart.
- compare the pie chart with those of the other students and discuss similarities and differences.

OPTION 3

A successful response will
- list characters and authors from the unit who the student believes would agree with the Heraclitus quotation.
- list characters and authors from the unit who the student believes would disagree with the Heraclitus quotation.
- place the student in one of the lists.

The Challenge of Change

The selections in this unit show many dimensions of change, from changes that mark an individual's life to ones that affect an entire culture. How has your own understanding of change been affected by the selections? Explore this question by completing one or more of the options in each section.

Chicago Tribune photo by Heather Stone.

Reflecting on Theme

OPTION 1

Charting Responses to Change Look at the illustrations you made in the activity from page 16, showing your ideas about progress. With these in mind, would you say you are a person who welcomes change, or do you tend to regard it with caution? Make a two-column chart, with one column labeled "Welcome Changes" and the other labeled "Unwelcome Changes." Fill in the chart by listing, in the appropriate columns, some changes that are presented in this unit's selections, as well as ones that you have faced in your own life. Underline the entries that you have the strongest feelings about. Then write an evaluation of your own attitude toward change.

OPTION 2

Graphing the Causes of Change Work with a partner to create a pie chart showing what you believe to be the major causes of cultural change affecting individuals and societies. To identify the causes, consider the changes presented in this unit's selections and reflect on your own experiences with cultural change. Consider also the news stories you found for the activity on page 144. Remember that the largest section of your chart should represent the most important or most common cause of change. Compare your pie chart with those of your classmates, and discuss their similarities and differences.

OPTION 3

Evaluating a Quotation Consider the quotation from the philosopher Heraclitus at the beginning of this unit: "There is nothing permanent except change." Which of the characters and authors in this unit might agree with this statement? Which might disagree? Make two lists of characters and authors—one list showing those who would agree, the other showing those who would disagree. Include yourself in one of the lists.

Self ASSESSMENT

READER'S NOTEBOOK

Which of the selections in this unit might have the greatest influence on you in the future—those dealing with the price of progress (Part 1) or those examining cultural issues (Part 2)? Create a list of the selection titles, arranging them in their order of impact.

Self Assessment

Ask students which they believe will affect their future more: the price we must pay for progress or cultural issues? Then ask students which stories in this unit had the greatest effect on them. Ask students whether those stories dealt with the price of progress or cultural issues.

Reviewing Literary Concepts

OPTION 1

Interpreting Theme Review at least four selections from this unit and for each one, write down a sentence stating the theme in your own words. Then consider what each selection suggests about the author's attitude toward change. Record your comments in a chart like the one shown. Discuss your responses with your classmates.

Selection	Theme	Author's Attitude Toward Change
The Thrill of the Grass	By working together in small ways, people can resist change.	Some things, like baseball, should not be changed.

OPTION 2

Analyzing Nonfiction All of the nonfiction selections in this unit deal in one way or another with the concept of technological or cultural change. Choose three nonfiction pieces from the unit that you find most interesting. What does each have to say about change? Then review the definitions of fiction on pages 17–18 and of nonfiction on pages 104–105. What is it about each piece that makes it nonfiction rather than fiction? Use details from the selections to support your response. Compare your responses with those of your classmates.

Self ASSESSMENT

READER'S NOTEBOOK
Imagine that a rich, eccentric patron of your school is offering a $5,000 prize to students who show mastery of the following terms. There is a catch, however—you have only 15 minutes to review the terms. To help you use your time efficiently, divide the terms into three categories: those you don't need to review, those you need to review only briefly, and those for which you require extensive review. Then spend 15 minutes reviewing the necessary terms (and hope that you find that rich patron!).

theme	expository essay
science fiction	personal essay
character	memoir
fantasy	autobiography
plot	biography
point of view	theme
foreshadowing	nonfiction
setting	cultural conflict
description	cultural setting

Building Your Portfolio

- **Writing Options** Imagine that you are applying for a job and your prospective employer has asked to see a writing sample. Review your Writing Options for this unit, paying particular attention to any that reflect the world of work, such as an advertisement, a newsletter article, or an editorial. Choose the one that you feel would most impress an employer. Write a note explaining your choice. Then add the piece and the note to your **Presentation Portfolio.**
- **Writing Workshops** In this unit you wrote an Opinion Piece on a topic you feel strongly about. You also wrote a Focused Description of a scene or situation. Reread these pieces and decide which is a stronger example of your writing. Explain your choice in a note attached to the preferred piece. Place the piece in your **Presentation Portfolio.**
- **Additional Activities** Think back to any of the assignments you completed under **Activities & Explorations** and **Inquiry & Research.** Which activity or piece of writing would you most like to expand into a larger project? Write a note explaining your choice, and add it, along with your record of the original work, to your portfolio.

Self ASSESSMENT

Presentation Portfolio. Review the pieces that you have chosen to include. Do they have anything in common? What do they suggest about your strengths and interests as a writer?

Setting GOALS

As you worked through the activities in this unit, you probably became more aware of your strengths and weaknesses in reading and writing skills. After reviewing the work that you did for this unit, create a list of skills that you would like to work on in the next unit.

Reviewing Literary Concepts

OPTION 1

Use the Unit 1 Resource Book, p. 105, to provide students a ready-made, full-depth chart for recording their four selections, their themes, and the authors' attitudes toward change.

OPTION 2

A successful response will
- select three nonfiction pieces from Unit 1.
- explain what each piece has to say about change.
- explain what makes each piece nonfiction, using examples for support.

Building Your Portfolio

Students will use their Presentation Portfolios to file what they consider their highest quality work—the very best in their Working Portfolios.

For more information on using writing and assessing portfolios, see the *Teacher's Guide to Assessment and Portfolio Use,* p. 53.

The *Electronic Library* is a CD-ROM that contains additional fiction, nonfiction, poetry, and drama for each unit in *The Language of Literature.*

These are the additional selections found in Unit 1 of the *Electronic Library.*

Yehuda Amichai
The Diameter of the Bomb

H. G. Wells
The Stolen Bacillus

Naguib Mahfouz
Half a Day

Witi Ihimaera
His First Ball

Italo Calvino
Santa's Children

Encourage students to select one of the longer works described to read silently with comprehension over a period of time.

UNIT ONE Extend Your *Reading*

LITERATURE CONNECTIONS

Fahrenheit 451

RAY BRADBURY

This classic science fiction novel, first published in 1953, depicts a terrifying future in which reading is banned and the job of firemen is to burn books. The novel follows the progress of Guy Montag, a fireman who becomes curious about the books he is destroying. A searing attack on censorship, the book is also fiercely critical of the dehumanizing effects of mass media, commercialism, and modern technology.

These thematically related readings are provided along with *Fahrenheit 451:*

Afterword to the Novel
RAY BRADBURY

The Portable Phonograph
WALTER VAN TILBURG CLARK

"You Have Insulted Me"
KURT VONNEGUT, JR.

Burning a Book
WILLIAM STAFFORD

A Summer's Reading
BERNARD MALAMUD

The Paterson Public Library
JUDITH ORTIZ COFER

The Phoenix
SYLVIA TOWNSEND WARNER

And Even *More* . . .

Things Fall Apart

CHINUA ACHEBE

Set in an Ibo village in Nigeria in the late 1800s, the story of Okonkwo unfolds like a Greek tragedy as traditional Ibo customs are challenged by new European ways. Achebe's first novel, *Things Fall Apart* was published in England in 1958. Critics both within and outside of Africa consider it a classic. The book is also part of the *Literature Connections* series published by McDougal Littell.

Books

Brave New World
ALDOUS HUXLEY
In this nightmarish future world, the government controls all aspects of human life, aided by science and technology. The book is also part of the *Literature Connections* series published by McDougal Littell.

The Time Machine
H.G. WELLS
The inventor of a time machine travels to a distant future, where he discovers two races of people, the childlike Eloi and the hideous Morlocks.

LITERATURE CONNECTIONS

Picture Bride

YOSHIKO UCHIDA

Yoshiko Uchida tells the story of Hana Omiya, a Japanese woman who comes to the United States as a "picture bride"—a woman whose marriage is arranged by family members through an exchange of photographs. The novel follows Hana's experiences, beginning with her arrival in San Francisco in 1917 and continuing through her family's relocation to a Japanese internment camp in Utah in 1943. Her expectations of life in the United States change constantly, causing her to adapt to America on her own terms.

These thematically related readings are provided along with *Picture Bride*:

***from* City in the Sun**
PAUL BAILEY

***from* Farewell to Manzanar**
JEANNE WAKATSUKI HOUSTON AND JAMES D. HOUSTON

No Speak English
SANDRA CISNEROS

A Migration Created by a Burden of Suspicion
DIRK JOHNSON

Breaking Silence for My Father
JANICE MIRIKITANI

Clothes
CHITRA BANERJEE DIVAKARUNI

The Heart of a Woman
GEORGIA DOUGLAS JOHNSON

Having Our Say: The Delany Sisters' First 100 Years
SARAH LOUISE DELANY AND ANNIE ELIZABETH DELANY
Two African-American sisters share stories about their remarkable lives, each of which spanned over 100 years.

An Island Like You: Stories from the Barrio
JUDITH ORTIZ COFER
Stories about Puerto Rican teenagers who are often caught between the traditions of their heritage and the new ways of life in the United States.

Other Media

Isaac Bashevis Singer: Isaac in America
Documentary on the life and works of Nobel prize-winning storyteller Isaac Bashevis Singer. In the words of the subject: "It's a masterpiece. I'm in it, but it's still a masterpiece." Monterey Home Video.
(VIDEOCASSETTE)

Eyes on the Prize
An award-winning series on the civil rights movement in the United States. News footage and eyewitness accounts help to chronicle the struggle for equality from 1954 to 1965. PBS Video.
(VIDEOCASSETTE)

A Necklace of Raindrops and Other Stories by Joan Aiken
Caedmon.
(AUDIOCASSETTE)

Chinua Achebe Reads
American Audio Prose Library
(AUDIOCASSETTE)

EXTEND YOUR READING 221

UNIT TWO

In the Name of Love

The selections in Unit Two explore aspects of love—the emotional and sometimes unreasoning ties it forms and the life-affecting impact it can make. The unit is divided into two parts to more fully explore the effects of emotional ties, both painful and exhilarating, on a variety of characters.

Part 1

Ties that Bind Through fiction, nonfiction, and poetry, this part emphasizes the endurance of love over time, separation, and other difficulties. For example, in "Those Winter Sundays," the speaker recognizes as an adult the quiet, faithful acts of love his father had done many years earlier, despite the speaker's indifference at the time.

Part 2

Mysteries of the Heart This part emphasizes the destructive power of possessive and romantic love. For example, in "The Californian's Tale," a man, unable to face his wife's death, has pretended for 19 years that she is only away on a visit and will soon return.

The Lovers (Somali Friends) (1950), Lois Mailou Jones. Casein on canvas, The Evans-Tibbs Collection, Washington, D.C.

Mini Lesson Viewing and Representing

The Lovers (Somali Friends)
by Lois Mailou Jones

ART APPRECIATION

Instruction Lois Mailou Jones (1905–1998) was born in Boston. In 1930 she became a professor of design and painting at Howard University—a position she held until retirement in 1977. Jones had more than 60 solo exhibitions of her work and was noted as among the first African-American women artists to explore African themes in their paintings.

Ask: Why do you think the artist called the people in this painting both "lovers" and "friends"?

Possible Response: The relationship between the two people is one of lovers, but possibly the artist painted the subjects using models, which to her were friends.

In the Name of Love

Great literature, past or present, is the expression of great knowledge of the human heart.

Edith Hamilton
German-born educator, writer, and classical scholar
1867–1963

Making Connections

To help students explore the connections between the art, the quotation, and the unit theme, have them consider the following questions:

Ask: **Do you think that love is an important theme to explore? Why?**
Possible Response: Yes. Love, positive or destructive, is arguably the reason behind the great majority of our actions.

Edith Hamilton had a lifelong interest in Greek and Roman society. The quotation from her comes from her book *The Greek Way* (1930).
Ask: **Paraphrase Edith Hamilton's statement.**
Possible Response: All first-class written works express the emotions of the writer; the purpose of writing is to express one's feelings; the most important themes to write about involve human emotions.

Ask: **How do you think the two subjects of this painting feel about each other? Why do you think so?**
Possible Responses: They know one another well, because they are looking into one another's eyes and standing close together; they trust one another, because their expressions are open and not defensive or frightened.

Ask: **What kinds of stories and experiences might you expect to read about in this unit?**
Possible Response: various relationships involving love—romantic love, love between parents and children, or love between friends

UNIT TWO
PART 1 SKILLS TRACE

Features and Selections	Literary Analysis	Reading and Critical Thinking	Writing Opportunities
Learning the Language of Literature Poetry	Poetry, 225		
The Active Reader: Skills and Strategies		Reading Poetry, 227	
POETRY Piano Those Winter Sundays **Difficulty Level:** ***Average***	Imagery, 228, 231 Speaker, 231	Visualizing, 228, 231	Childhood Poem, 232 Image Dictionary, 232
POETRY Sonnet 18 Sonnet 30 **Difficulty Level:** ***Challenging***	Sonnet Structure, 233, 236	Strategies for Reading Sonnets, 233, 236 Test Practice, 238	Speaker Profile, 237 Not-love Poem, 237
SHORT STORY Sweet Potato Pie **Difficulty Level:** ***Average*** Literary Link Salvador Late or Early	Characterization, 239, 252 Dialect, 252	Sequence of Events, 239, 252 Test Practice, 248	Charley's Journal, 253 Family Poem, 253
POETRY Simile Moon Rondeau Woman **Difficulty Level:** ***Average*** Building Vocabulary	Figurative Language, 255, 260	Understanding Comparisons, 255, 256, 258, 260 Test Practice, 262	His Poem, 261 Love Letter, 261
Real World Link		Magazine Article: Reading A Feature Article, 276	
Writing Workshop: Poetry Assessment Practice		Analyzing a Student Model, 278	Poem, 280 Adding Detail, 281

UNIT TWO
PART 2 SKILLS TRACE

Features and Selections	Literary Analysis	Reading and Critical Thinking	Writing Opportunities
Learning the Language of Literature Drama	Drama, 284		
The Active Reader: Skills and Strategies		Reading Drama, 286	
DRAMA The Bear **Difficulty Level:** ***Average***	Farce, 287, 300 Drama, 300	Visualizing, 287, 300	Analysis, 301 Drama Review, 301 Test Practice, 301

LEGEND **DLS – Daily Language SkillBuilder**
CCL – Cross Curricular Link
Green type – Teacher's Edition

Speaking and Listening Viewing and Representing	Inquiry and Research	Grammar, Usage, and Mechanics	Vocabulary
Choral Reading, 232 Art Appreciation, 230		Sentence Fragments, 232	
Comparative Description, 237 Rock Sonnet, 237 Author Activity, 238 Art Appreciation, 235	Earlier English, 237	Rhetorical Questions, 237 DLS, 233 Rhetorical Questions, 237	
Set Building, 253 Public Service Announcement, 253 Working the Fields, 253 Art Appreciation, 242	Harlem Heritage, 253 Harlem Renaissance, 253	Compound Verbs, 254 DLS, 239 Parallel Compound Predicates, 254	Context Clues, 253 Context Clues, 240
Poetic Pictures, 261 Multimedia Presentation, 261 She Wanted to Be, 261 Author Activity, 262 Art Appreciation, 257 Poetry and Song, 261	Dictionary Explorations, 261	DLS, 255 Objects of Prepositions, 258	Analogies, 263
Discussion, 276	Activity Link: A Case of Cruelty, 276 Inquiry and Research, 276		
		Punctuation, 281 Revising and Editing, 282	
Scene in Performance, 301 Set Design, 301 Sequel to the Play, 301 Author Activity, 302 Art Appreciation, 289, 292, 296 Dramatic Reading, 297	Czarist Russia, 301	Kinds of Sentences, 302 DLS, 287 Sentence Types, 298	Context Clues, 301 Context Clues, 288 Word Meanings and Spelling, 290

PART 2 SKILLS TRACE

Features and Selections	Literary Analysis	Reading and Critical Thinking	Writing Opportunities
SHORT STORY The Californian's Tale **Difficulty Level: *Challenging***	Historical Setting, 303, 311 Review: Foreshadowing, 311	Interpreting the Relationship Between Setting and Characters, 303, 311	Love Letter, 312 Alternative Solutions, 312 Comic Scene, 312 Informal Assess., 310
Real World Link Gold Is Found and a Nation Goes Wild		Historical Background: Chronological Order, 314	
SHORT STORY Brigid **Difficulty Level: *Average***	Conflict, 316, 326 Review: Characterization, 326 Author Activity, 328	Analyzing Motivation, 316, 326	Character Sketch, 327 Imaginary Conversation, 327 Problem-Solution Essay, 327 Informal Assess., 324
SHORT STORY Lalla **Difficulty Level: *Easy***	Point of View, 329, 343	Predicting, 329, 343 Test Practice, 342	Movie Title, 344 Lalla's List, 344 Telephone Talk, 344
POETRY Love Without Love The Taxi **Difficulty Level: *Average***	Metaphor and Simile, 346, 349	Paraphrasing, 346, 349	Poetic Images, 350 Journal, 350
POETRY Tonight I Can Write... / Puedo Escribir Los Versos **Difficulty Level: *Average*** Building Vocabulary	Repetition, 351, 354 Review: Figurative Language, 354	Interpreting Comparisons, 351, 354	Paragraph, 355 Personal Poem, 355
Writing Workshop: **Problem-Solution Essay** Assessment Practice		Analyzing a Student Model, 365	Problem-Solution Essay, 367 Sentence Combining, 368
Reflect and Assess: **In the Name of Love**	Understanding Metaphor and Simile, 371		Comparing Love's Emotions, 370 Evaluating Love Relationships, 370 Building Your Portfolio, 371
Reading and Writing for Assessment		How to Read a Test Selection, 374 How to Answer Multiple-Choice Questions, 377	How to Respond in Writing, 378

LEGEND **DLS – Daily Language SkillBuilder**
CCL – Cross Curricular Link
Green type – Teacher's Edition

Speaking and Listening Viewing and Representing	Inquiry and Research	Grammar, Usage, and Mechanics	Vocabulary
Expressive Painting, 312 Dramatic Presentation, 312 Miners' Dialogue, 312 Art Appreciation, 305, 308 Reading Aloud, 309	The California Gold Rush, 312	Placement of Adjectives, 313 DLS, 303 Placement of Adjectives, 312	Context Clues, 304 Suffixes and Prefixes, 307
Activity Link: The Californian's Tale Share a Story, 315	Activity Link: The Californian's Tale, 315 Inquiry and Research, 315		
Eulogy for Owen, 327 Abstract Painting, 327 Radio Play, 327 Art Connection, 327 Art Appreciation, 319, 322 Nonverbal Cues, 323	Life in Ireland, 327	Compound Sentences, 328 DLS, 316 Identifying Sentence Structures, 325 Compound Sentences, 327	Reference Materials to Determine Precise Meanings, 320
Values Poster, 344 Future Conversation, 344 Art Appreciation, 334, 340	Exploring England, 344	Complex Sentences, 345 DLS, 329 Coordinating Conjunctions, 344	Context Clues, 344 Word Origins, 330
Sketch of a Poem, 350 TV Talk Show, 350 Art Appreciation, 348	The Look of Love, 350	DLS, 346	
Dramatic Monologue, 355 Mood Music, 355 Choral Reading, 355		DLS, 351	Word Origins, 356 Denotation and Connotation, 352
Picturing Text Structure, TE 365		Run-ons, 368 Revising and Editing, 369	
Portraying Love's Agony and Ecstasy, 370 Appreciating the Sonnet, 371			
		How to Revise and Edit a Test Selection, 379	

UNIT TWO

RESOURCE MANAGEMENT GUIDE PART 1

To introduce the theme/literary period of this unit, use Fine Art Transparencies T20–22 in the Communications Transparencies and Copymasters.

	Unit Resource Book	Assessment	Integrated Technology and Media	Additional Support: Literary Analysis Transparencies
Piano **Those Winter Sundays** *pp. 228–232*	• Active Reading p. 4 • Literary Analysis p. 5	• Selection Test, Formal Assessment pp. 39–40 Test Generator	Audio Library	• Poetry: Imagery T9
Shakespeare Sonnet 18 **Millay Sonnet 30** *pp. 233–238*	• Active Reading p. 6 • Literary Analysis p. 7 • Grammar p. 8	• Selection Test, Formal Assessment p. 41 Test Generator	Audio Library LaserLinks, Teacher's SourceBook p. 19	• Poetry: Sound Devices T8
Sweet Potato Pie *pp. 239–254*	• Summary p. 9 • Active Reading p. 10 • Literary Analysis p. 11 • Words to Know p. 12 • Grammar p. 13 • Selection Quiz p. 14	• Selection Test, Formal Assessment pp. 43–44 Test Generator	Audio Library Research Starter www.mcdougallittell.com	• Character T2
Simile **Moon Rondeau** **Woman** *pp. 255–262*	• Active Reading p. 15 • Literary Analysis p. 16	• Selection Test, Formal Assessment pp. 45–46 Test Generator	Audio Library	• Symbols and Figurative Language T21

Writing Workshop: Poetry

Unit Two Resource Book
- Prewriting p. 18
- Drafting and Elaboration p. 19
- Peer Response Guide pp. 20–21
- Revising, Editing, and Proofreading p. 22
- Student Models pp. 22–28
- Rubric for Evaluation p. 29

Writing Coach

Writing Transparencies and Copymasters T11, T20, C27

Teacher's Guide to Assessment and Portfolio Use

Unit Assessment

- Unit Two, Part 1 Test, Formal Assessment pp. 47–48

Test Generator

- Unit Two Integrated Test, Integrated Assessment pp. 7–12

Unit Technology

ClassZone www.mcdougallittell.com

Electronic Teacher Tools

Electronic Library

T = Transparency   C = Copymaster

	Reading and Critical Thinking Transparencies	Grammar Transparencies and Copymasters	Vocabulary Transparencies and Copymasters	Writing Transparencies and Copymasters	Communications Transparencies and Copymasters
	• Visualizing T8	• Sentence Fragments C126		• Sensory Word List T14 • Figurative Language and Sound Devices T15 • Poem C27	• Dramatic Reading T12 • Verbal Strategies T14
	• Locating Information Using Print References T32	• Daily Language SkillBuilder T7 • Rhetorical Questions C174		• Figurative Language and Sound Devices T15 • Poem C27	• Reading Aloud T11 • Dramatic Reading T12 • Verbal Strategies T14
		• Daily Language SkillBuilder T8 • Compound Predicates I C86	• Context Clues C39	• Generating Ideas T1 • Sensory Word List T14 • Poem C27	• Evaluation Matrix: Commercial T6 • Impromptu Speaking: Dialogue, Role-Play, Debate T13
	• Organizational Chart: Horizontal T51	• Daily Language SkillBuilder T8 • Objects of Prepositions C94		• Sensory Word List T14 • Figurative Language and Sound Devices T15 • Poem C27	

STUDENTS ACQUIRING ENGLISH

The **Spanish Study Guide,** pp. 47–61, includes language support for the following pages:

- Family and Community Involvement (per unit)
- Selection Summaries and Vocabulary
- Active Reading
- Literary Analysis

RESOURCE MANAGEMENT GUIDE PART 2

To introduce the theme/literary period of this unit, use Fine Art Transparencies T20–22 in the Communications Transparencies and Copymasters.

	Unit Resource Book	Assessment	Integrated Technology and Media	Additional Support: Literary Analysis Transparencies
The Bear *pp. 287–302*	• Summary p. 30 • Active Reading p. 31 • Literary Analysis p. 32 • Words to Know p. 33 • Grammar p. 34 • Selection Quiz p. 35	• Selection Test, Formal Assessment pp. 49–50 Test Generator	Audio Library LaserLinks, Teacher's SourceBook p. 22 Research Starter www.mcdougallittell.com	• Drama: Stage Directions T11
The Californian's Tale *pp. 303–313*	• Summary p. 36 • Active Reading p. 37 • Literary Analysis p. 38 • Words to Know p. 39 • Grammar p. 40 • Selection Quiz p. 41	• Selection Test, Formal Assessment pp. 51–52 Test Generator	Audio Library LaserLinks, Teacher's SourceBook p. 23	• Setting T3
Brigid *pp. 316–328*	• Summary p. 42 • Active Reading p. 43 • Literary Analysis p. 44 • Grammar p. 45 • Selection Quiz p. 46	• Selection Test, Formal Assessment pp. 53–54 Test Generator	Audio Library	• Plot: Conflict T12
Lalla *pp. 329–345*	• Summary p. 47 • Active Reading p. 48 • Literary Analysis p. 49 • Words to Know p. 50 • Grammar p. 51 • Selection Quiz p. 52	• Selection Test, Formal Assessment pp. 55–56 Test Generator	Audio Library LaserLinks, Teacher's SourceBook pp. 24–25 Research Starter www.mcdougallittell.com	• Point of View T17
Love Without Love **The Taxi** *pp. 346–350*	• Active Reading p. 53 • Literary Analysis p. 54	• Selection Test, Formal Assessment p. 57 Test Generator	Audio Library	• Symbols and Figurative Language T21
Tonight I Can Write .../ Puedo Escribir Los Versos ... *pp. 351–355*	• Active Reading p. 55 • Literary Analysis p. 56	• Selection Test, Formal Assessment pp. 59–60 Test Generator	Audio Library	• Symbols and Figurative Language T21

Writing Workshop: Problem–Solution Essay

Unit Two Resource Book
- Prewriting p. 58
- Drafting and Elaboration p. 59
- Peer Response Guide pp. 60–61
- Revising, Editing, and Proofreading p. 62
- Student Models pp. 63–68
- Rubric for Evaluation p. 69

Writing Coach

Writing Transparencies and Copymasters T11, T20, C28

Teacher's Guide to Assessment and Portfolio Use

Unit Assessment
- Unit Two, Part 2 Test, Formal Assessment pp. 61–62
- Test Generator
- Unit Two Integrated Test, Integrated Assessment pp. 7–12

Unit Technology
- ClassZone www.mcdougallittell.com
- Electronic Teacher Tools
- Electronic Library

T = Transparency   C = Copymaster

Reading and Critical Thinking Transparencies	Grammar Transparencies and Copymasters	Vocabulary Transparencies and Copymasters	Writing Transparencies and Copymasters	Communications Transparencies and Copymasters
• Visualizing T8	• Daily Language SkillBuilder T9 • Sentence Types C119	• Word Meanings and Spellings C40	• Effective Language T13 • Opinion Statement C25 • Interpretive Essay C33	
• Noting Details T9	• Daily Language SkillBuilder T9 • Placement of Adjectives C74	• Context Clues C41 • Prefixes C42	• Effective Language T13 • Showing Not Telling T22	• Impromptu Speaking: Dialogue, Role-Play, Debate T13
• Organizational Chart: Horizontal T51	• Daily Language SkillBuilder T10 • Identifying Sentence Structures C121 • Compound Sentences C123	• Using Reference Materials C43	• Identifying Writing Variables T2 • Topic Sentences and Thesis Statements T6 • Problem-Solution C28	• Nonverbal Strategies T15 • Reading Aloud T11
• Predicting Outcomes T2	• Daily Language SkillBuilder T10 • Coordinating Conjunctions C77	• Word Origins C44	• Persuasive Essay C30 • Effective Language T13	• Dramatic Reading T12 • Impromptu Speaking: Dialogue, Role-Play, Debate T13
• Paraphrasing and Summarizing C41	• Daily Language SkillBuilder T11		• Sensory Word List T14 • Figurative Language and Sound Devices T15	• Interviewing T9 • Impromptu Speaking: Dialogue, Role-Play, Debate T13
• Organizational Chart: Horizontal T51	• Daily Language SkillBuilder T11	• Denotation and Connotation C45	• Figurative Language and Sound Devices T15 • Poem C27	• Dramatic Reading T12 • Verbal Strategies T14 • Nonverbal Strategies T15

STUDENTS ACQUIRING ENGLISH

The **Spanish Study Guide,** pp. 62–79, includes language support for the following pages:

- Family and Community Involvement (per unit)
- Selection Summaries and Vocabulary
- Active Reading
- Literary Analysis

DAILY LANGUAGE SKILLBUILDERS

Selection	SkillBuilder Sentences	Suggested Answers
Sonnet 18 Sonnet 30	**1.** Understanding the rhyme scheme of a sonnet can help you understand their meaning. **2.** Although Shakespeare wrote many sonnets in England. The first sonnets was written in italy.	**1.** Understanding the rhyme scheme of a sonnet can help you understand **its** meaning. **2.** Although Shakespeare wrote many sonnets in England**, t**he first sonnets **were** written in **I**taly.
Sweet Potato Pie	**1.** Everyone should do their best to help brothers and sisters. **2.** Rachel feels its her responsibility too help Cathy succeed.	**1.** Everyone should do **his or her** best to help brothers and sisters. **2.** Rachel feels **it's** her responsibility **to** help Cathy succeed.
Simile Moon Rondeau Woman	**1.** "I like to write poems that has rhymes," said James but I'm to shy too read them outloud." **2.** "I use to be shy like you," said Mary, "but I took a speech class now I enjoy speaking to crowds."	**1.** "I like to write poems that **have** rhymes," said James, **"**but I'm **too** shy **to** read them **out loud**." **2.** "I **used** to be shy like you," said Mary, "but I took a speech class. **N**ow I enjoy speaking to crowds."

UNIT TWO
DAILY LANGUAGE SKILLBUILDERS

Selection	SkillBuilder Sentences	Suggested Answers
The Bear	**1.** My Grandfather lived in russia, just like Smirnov, said Joseph. "I'd like to visit the town where he was born." **2.** "My Aunt and my cousin took a trip to Moscow last year," said Mary. "I think they visited checkhov's grave."	**1.** "My **g**randfather lived in **R**ussia, just like Smirnov," said Joseph. "I'd like to visit the town where he was born." **2.** "My **a**unt and my cousin took a trip to Moscow last year," said Mary. "I think they visited **Chekhov's** grave."
The Californian's Tale	**1.** Hard-working Miners, who discovered gold, had a wonderful opportunity to make alot of money. **2.** There is a small town in california called sutter's Mill, where the Gold Rush of 1849 begun.	**1.** Hard-working **m**iners who discovered gold had a wonderful opportunity to make **a lot** of money. **2.** There is a small town in **C**alifornia called **S**utter's Mill, where the Gold Rush of 1849 **began**.
Brigid	**1.** Parents often argues about what is best for they're children. **2.** People in small towns sometimes worry, about what other people says about them.	**1.** Parents often **argue** about what is best for **their** children. **2.** People in small towns sometimes worry about what other people **say** about them.

UNIT TWO
DAILY LANGUAGE SKILLBUILDERS

Selection	SkillBuilder Sentences	Suggested Answers
Lalla	**1.** jane barney and lalla traveled with there mother to carwheal in cornwall. **2.** When his mother told him about moving barney said he wouldnt mind starting at a new school.	**1.** **J**ane**,** **B**arney**,** and **L**alla traveled with **their** mother to **C**arwheal in **C**ornwall. **2.** When his mother told him about moving**,** **B**arney said he **wouldn't** mind starting at a new school.
Love Without Love The Taxi	**1.** The lover found an old letter turning the pages of a book. **2.** Lying on the table, he forgot the poem.	**1.** **Turning the pages of a book,** the lover found an old letter. **2.** He forgot the poem **that was lying** on the table.
Tonight I Can Write.../ Puedo Escribir Los Versos...	**1.** Each of the partners in a relationship have an obligation to the other. **2.** The poet's love for she is more great than her love for he.	**1.** Each of the partners in a relationship **has** an obligation to the other. **2.** The poet's love for **her** is **greater** than her love for **him**.

INTEGRATING GRAMMAR AND LITERATURE: GRAMMAR PLANNER

	Unit One	Unit Two	Unit Three	Unit Four	Unit Five	Unit Six
Grammar Focus by Unit	Parts of Speech	The Sentence and Its Parts	Verbs and Verbals	Phrases	Clauses	Special Sentence Structures

The Language of Literature offers several options for integrating grammar instruction and literature.

- Each unit has a specific grammar focus. The grammar focus for this unit is highlighted on the planning chart. Categories of grammar skills for this unit are shown in red.
- The Pupil's Edition includes instructive features entitled *Grammar in Context*. The instruction in these features arises from the selections and relates to the grammar focus for each unit.
- The Writing Workshops in the Pupil's Edition include grammar tips that help students produce error-free drafts.
- Mini Lessons in the Teacher's Edition complement the instruction in the *Grammar in Context* features. Additional Mini Lessons relate to the grammar focus for each unit as well as to the literature.
- Daily Language SkillBuilders in the Teacher's Edition provide students with ongoing proofreading practice and reinforce punctuation, spelling, grammar and usage, and capitalization.
- Grammar Copymasters and Transparencies, which may be used independently or in conjunction with Mini Lessons in the Teacher's Edition, present grammar in a traditional, systematic sequence.

PE instruction shown in black
TE Mini Lessons shown in green

Part 1

Parts of the Sentence

Compound Verbs
"Sweet Potato Pie," p. 254

Parallel Compound Predicates
"Sweet Potato Pie," p. 254

Using Phrases

Identifying Objects of Prepositions
"Simile," "Moon Rondeau," pp. 258–259

Using Clauses

Sentence Fragments
Writing Workshop, p. 282
"Piano," "Those Winter Sundays," p. 232

Subject-Verb Agreement

Writing Workshop, p. 282

End Marks and Commas

Commas with Nonessential Clauses and Phrases
Writing Workshop, p. 282

Other Uses of Commas
Writing Workshop, p. 282

Sentence Types
The Bear, pp. 298–299

Style

Rhetorical Questions
"Sonnet 18," "Sonnet 30," p. 237
"Sonnet 18," "Sonnet 30," p. 237

Parallel Structure
Writing Workshop, p. 282

Part 2

Parts of Speech

Placement of Adjectives
"The Californian's Tale," p. 313
"The Californian's Tale," p. 312

Coordinating Conjunctions
"Lalla," pp. 344–345

Parts of the Sentence

Run-on Sentences
Writing Workshop, p. 369

Using Clauses

Identifying Sentence Structures
"Brigid," p. 325

Compound Sentences
"Brigid," p. 328
"Brigid," p. 327

Complex Sentences
"Lalla, p. 345

Pronoun Usage

Pronoun Agreement with Antecedent
Writing Workshop, p. 369

PART 1 Ties that Bind

The writers who created the original Star Trek series for television imagined an entire race of people—the Vulcans—defined by their logic and absence of emotion. For the Vulcans, love's passions posed a threat to reason. In this part of Unit Two, you will read selections that would certainly puzzle the Vulcans. Here, you will encounter a variety of ties created by love.

ACTIVITY

Think about a loving relationship in your own life. List various feelings that you experience in that relationship. Then create a bar graph that shows the relative frequencies of these feelings. For example, the longest bar might be used to represent contentment, while the shortest bar might be used to represent anger. As you read, compare your experience of love with those described in the selections.

224

LEARNING the Language of Literature

Poetry is something that most people recognize when they see it, even if they cannot define the term *poetry* precisely. In poetry, unlike prose, the look and sound of the words are inseparable from a poem's meaning. The word *poet* comes from the Greek word *poiētēs*, meaning "one who makes or fashions," and writing a poem involves a careful choice and crafting of language. Reading a poem, too, is different from reading prose; it is an experience that involves all the senses. As the French poet Paul Valéry said, "Prose [is] walking, poetry dancing."

Form

The **form** of a poem is the physical arrangement of the words on the page. This includes the length and placement of the lines and the way they are grouped into **stanzas.** Some poetry is written in strict formal patterns. Other poetry, known as **free verse,** is not. Poets choose forms that help them convey their ideas.

YOUR TURN Look at the two excerpts at the right. Which is an example of free verse? Explain your answer.

FORM

Love can not fill the thickened lung with breath,
Nor clean the blood, nor set the fractured bone;
Yet many a man is making friends with death
Even as I speak, for lack of love alone.

—Edna St. Vincent Millay, "Sonnet 30"

she spun herself into a web
and   looking for a place to rest
turned to him
but he stood straight
declining to be her corner

—Nikki Giovanni, "Woman"

Sound Devices

Poets use a variety of techniques to produce special qualities of sound. **Alliteration, assonance, consonance,** and **rhyme** involve repetition of sounds.

- **Alliteration** is a repetition of initial consonant sounds in nearby words (as in "to **j**iggle and **j**ump for **j**oy").
- **Assonance** is a repetition of vowel sounds within words (as in "a gr**ee**d as d**ee**p as the s**ea**").
- **Consonance** is a repetition of consonant sounds within or at the end of words (as in "of flee**t** foo**t** and sou**nd** mi**nd**").
- **Rhyme** is a repetition of final sounds in two or more words (as in "a st**ray** g**ray** t**ray**"). The **rhyme scheme** of a poem is the pattern formed by the rhymes at the end of the lines.

Onomatopoeia is the use of words—like *snort, clank,* and *whir*—that sound like what they refer to.

YOUR TURN Find and identify examples of sound devices in the excerpt at the right.

SOUND DEVICES

There will come soft rains and the
smell of the ground,
And swallows circling with their
shimmering sound;

And frogs in the pools singing at night,
And wild plum-trees in tremulous white;

Robins will wear their feathery fire
Whistling their whims on a low fence-wire;

—Sara Teasdale, "There Will Come Soft Rains"

LEARNING the Language of LITERATURE

OVERVIEW

Objectives
- understand the following literary terms:
  - form
  - sound devices
  - rhythm
  - figurative language
- identify and analyze poetic devices

Teaching the Lesson

This lesson analyzes the forms and devices used in poetry and identifies terms used in the analysis of poetry.

Introducing the Concepts
Introduce poetry by comparing a poem to the lyrics of a popular song. Ask students to provide lyrics, and then discuss ways in which poetry differs from the song lyric.

Presenting the Concepts
Form
Emphasize that modern poetry is seldom rhymed. Discuss with students the concepts of free verse: Free verse may use rhyme, especially half rhyme and internal rhyme, but no pattern of rhyme is established; free verse is rhythmic and is usually divided into stanzas, which may or may not be regular.

YOUR TURN Nikki Giovanni's "Woman" is an example of free verse. No formal or regular pattern of rhythm or rhyme is used in her poem. Millay's poem is written in sonnet form.

Sound Devices
Emphasize to students that they will probably not be able to hear the sound devices used in poetry on hearing a poem read the first time. Suggest they read each poem out loud at least three times.

YOUR TURN Alliteration—"will wear their feathery fire . . .Whistling their whims"; Assonance—"come soft"; Rhyme—ground/sound, night/white, fire/wire; Onomatopoeia—"Whistling"

Making Connections

Rhythm
Remind students that a sonnet is written in lines of iambic pentameter. Show them that an iamb is two syllables, the first one unstressed and the second stressed. Remind them that pentameter means that there are five iambs per line in a sonnet.

YOUR TURN Possible Response: The poem's meter shows what ideas are emphasized when reading the poem; the stressed syllables tend to fall on the most important words and therefore reinforce the poem's meaning.

Figurative Language
Have students come up with examples of similes and metaphors from their reading. Remind students that metaphor establishes a closer relationship than a simile between the unlike things being compared.

YOUR TURN Possible Response: The simile shows the extraordinary closeness of a relationship between two people.

Personification
Suggest to students that when a speaker of a poem uses personification, it sometimes suggests a parallel with a speaker's own emotions.

YOUR TURN Possible Response: The speaker is hesitant and ill-at-ease, for his or her house is not a place of comfort to wake up to on cold mornings.

Rhythm is the pattern, or beat, of stressed and unstressed syllables in a line of poetry. When a rhythm is repeated throughout a poem, it is known as the poem's **meter.** Poets use rhythm to highlight the musical quality of language and to emphasize ideas and feelings. In the following line from Shakespeare's "Sonnet 18," the stressed syllables are marked (´) and the unstressed syllables are marked (˘):

Shăll Í cŏmpáre thĕe tó ă súmmĕr's dáy?

YOUR TURN Tap out the pattern of stressed and unstressed syllables in the excerpt from Millay's "Sonnet 30" at the right. How does the poem's meter help you read the lines?

RHYTHM

Love is not all: it is not meat nor drink
Nor slumber nor a roof against the rain;
Nor yet a floating spar to men that sink
And rise and sink and rise and sink again;

—Edna St. Vincent Millay, "Sonnet 30"

Figurative Language
Most poets try to create word pictures in their poems that help readers see, hear, feel, smell, and even taste the experiences they present. Such word pictures are called **imagery.** One technique poets use to create strong imagery is **figurative language,** which conveys meanings beyond the literal meanings of the words. Similes and metaphors are kinds of figurative language involving comparisons between things that have something in common.

- In a **simile** (such as "My life is like an open book"), a word such as *like* or *as* signals the comparison.
- A **metaphor** (such as "Jealousy is a green-eyed monster") is a direct comparison, with no signal word.

YOUR TURN How does the simile in this excerpt help you understand the relationship between the speaker and the person addressed?

SIMILE

What did we say to each other
that now we are as the deer
who walk in single file

—N. Scott Momaday, "Simile"

Personification is a type of figurative language in which animals, inanimate objects, or ideas are given human qualities (as in "The teakettle ordered us back to the kitchen").

YOUR TURN What does the personification in the excerpt at the right tell you about the speaker's frame of mind?

PERSONIFICATION

I'd wake and hear the cold splintering,
breaking.
When the rooms were warm, he'd call,
and slowly I would rise and dress,
fearing the chronic angers of that house,

—Robert Hayden, "Those Winter Sundays"

The Active Reader: Skills and Strategies

A poet doesn't create a poem just by writing an essay and dividing it into short lines. A poem therefore shouldn't be read in the same way an essay is read. Reading poetry requires paying attention not only to the meanings of the words but also to what their sound and arrangement on the page conveys. The strategies on this page will help you learn to read and enjoy poetry.

Reading Poetry

Strategies for Using Your READER'S NOTEBOOK

As you read, take notes to
- record striking or memorable images or uses of language
- analyze the poem's meter and rhyme
- explore your reactions to the poem's message

1 Strategies for Examining Form
- Look at the poem before you read it. **Question** whether the lines and stanzas form a regular pattern on the page.
- As you read the poem, first aloud and then to yourself, listen for rhythmic patterns. Ask yourself if you hear a regular beat.
- Pause in your reading where punctuation marks appear, not necessarily at the ends of lines. In poetry, the end of a line does not always indicate the end of a thought.

2 Strategies for Appreciating Sound
- Read the poem aloud several times.
- Identify the sound devices—alliteration, assonance, consonance, rhyme, and onomatopoeia—that the poet uses.
- Determine whether the poem has a rhyme scheme.
- **Monitor** your reactions to hearing the poem. Do the sounds calm you, make you sad, or cause you to feel other emotions?

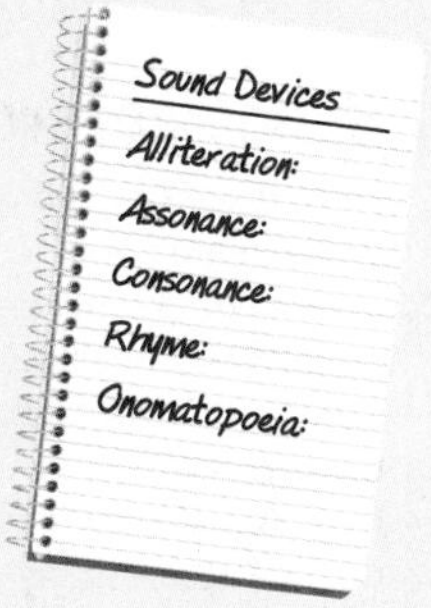

3 Strategies for Understanding Figurative Language
- Identify the types of figurative language that the poet uses.
  - **Visualize** the objects, ideas, or people compared in similes and metaphors. Try using a Venn diagram like the one at the right to chart the similarities and differences.
  - Analyze how the similes, metaphors, and personifications you encounter change or **clarify** your understanding of the poem.

"Simile"
The speaker and the person addressed are compared with deer.

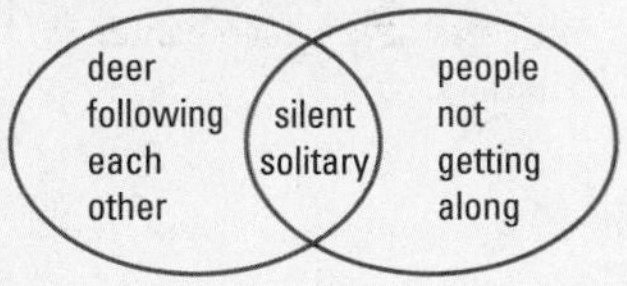

4 Strategies for Determining Meaning
- **Question** whether the title offers any clues about the poem's message.
- **Connect** your personal memories and feelings with what you read. They may provide you with insights into the poem's meaning.
- Summarize the idea or feeling the poem leaves you with.

Need More Help?

Remember that active readers use the essential reading strategies explained on page 7: **visualize, predict, clarify, question, connect, evaluate, monitor.**

OVERVIEW

Objectives
- understand how form, sound, and figurative language contribute to the meaning of a poem
- identify patterns of language and sound, using Venn diagrams to clarify understanding

Teaching the Lesson

The strategies on this page will help students learn and apply specific skills for identifying elements of form, sound devices, and figurative language that contribute to the meaning of a poem.

Presenting the Strategies

Help students understand the elements of poetry by applying them to a simple children's poem or nursery rhyme they are familiar with or a poem they have read previously in class.

Strategies for Using Your Reader's Notebook

Have students list the images they find striking in a poem and then briefly describe the aspect of the image that they find most intriguing or interesting.

1 Strategies for Examining Form

Be sure students understand that the visual, graphic elements of a poem—the arrangement of words on the page, the white space that surrounds the words, and the punctuation within and between lines—create a structure that indicates relationships between words and ideas in poetry.

2 Strategies for Appreciating Sound

Encourage students to read a poem aloud at different tempos or speeds—especially slower tempos—in order to hear the full, resonant sound of the words. You may want to play professional recordings of poems to let students hear the distinction of an oral interpretation.

3 Strategies for Understanding Figurative Language

Explain to students that not all similes and metaphors will require a Venn diagram analysis but that creating Venn diagrams can help enhance their skill at interpreting figurative language.

4 Strategies for Determining Meaning

Each new reading of a poem can bring new meaning and feeling. Have students read a poem at least three times. After each reading, have students write a summary of the main idea. Encourage students to let their summaries grow and change since initial meanings are often times not the deepest meanings.

OVERVIEW

These selections are included in the **Grade 10 InterActive Reader.**

Objectives

1. understand and appreciate two **poems (Literary Analysis)**
2. analyze sensory **imagery (Literary Analysis)**
3. **visualize** images and setting **(Active Reading)**

Summary

When the speaker in "Piano" listens to a woman sing, he is transported back to his youth. He remembers sitting under the piano while his mother played and sang on Sunday evenings in the winter. The speaker cannot respond to the woman's singing in the present because he is overwhelmed by the childhood memory. The speaker in Hayden's "Those Winter Sundays" recalls his father rising early in the bitter cold—even on Sundays—to start a fire and warm the house before his father awakened him. He spoke indifferently to this man who warmed the house and polished his shoes, because he didn't understand that these were acts of love.

Thematic Link

The speakers in both poems reflect on the **ties that bind** them through their powerful childhood memories.

Reading Skills and Strategies: PREVIEW

Have students preview the selection. Ask students what the poems' titles and the images throughout the selection suggest to them. Discuss with students the Build Background feature on p. 228. Ask students how they think these poems fit the theme "Ties That Bind." Before students begin reading, give them a brief summary of the selection.

PREPARING to *Read*

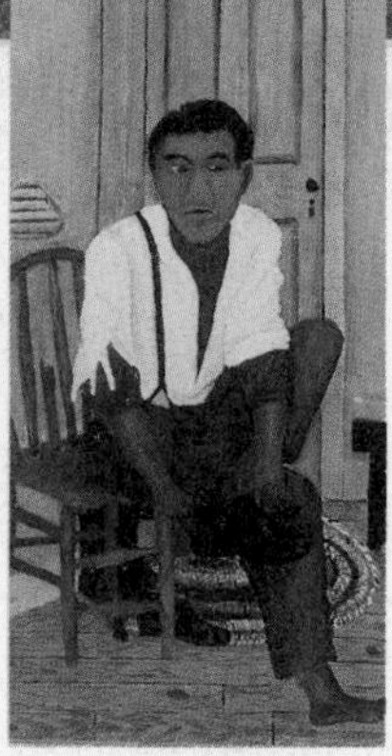

Piano

Poetry by D. H. LAWRENCE

Those Winter Sundays

Poetry by ROBERT HAYDEN

Connect to Your Life

Childhood Memories Recall a routine household activity from your childhood that now evokes strong feelings in you. Perhaps your mother read to you at night, your father patiently helped you with homework, or your grandmother baked a weekly pie. Create a simple chart, like the one shown here, to record sensations that you associate with that memory. Fill in all applicable boxes.

Build Background

Early Years The two poems that you are about to read draw upon the poets' memories of their own childhood. D. H. Lawrence, the son of a coal miner and his cultured wife, grew up in the late 19th century near Nottingham, England. Robert Hayden, born in 1913, was raised by poor, hard-working foster parents in Detroit, Michigan. Each poet, coincidentally, examines a parent's legacy by recalling activities of long-ago winter Sundays.

Focus Your Reading

LITERARY ANALYSIS | IMAGERY When writers use words and phrases to re-create vivid sensory experiences for the reader, they are making use of **imagery.** Although most imagery appeals to the visual sense, imagery may also appeal to the senses of smell, hearing, taste, or touch. In this passage from "Those Winter Sundays," the experience of bitter cold is made vivid by imagery:

Sundays too my father got up early
and put his clothes on in the blueblack cold,

As you read the following poems, pay attention to how each poet's use of imagery affects you as a reader.

ACTIVE READING | VISUALIZING **Visualizing,** the act of mentally picturing something you read, can help you understand and appreciate the imagery in poetry. Certain questions can help you to visualize what you read:

- Where and when does the poem take place?
- Are there people portrayed? If so, who are they and what do they look like?
- What details in the **setting** of the poem trigger your own mental pictures?

READER'S NOTEBOOK As you read these two poems, develop your own mental pictures of the characters and the scenes that are described. Make a list of the images that you can most easily visualize.

LESSON RESOURCES

UNIT TWO RESOURCE BOOK, pp. 4–5

ASSESSMENT RESOURCES

Formal Assessment, pp. 39–40

Teacher's Guide to Assessment and Portfolio Use

Test Generator

SKILLS TRANSPARENCIES AND COPYMASTERS

Literary Analysis

- Poetry: Imagery, T9 (for Literary Analysis, p. 231)

Reading and Critical Thinking

- Visualizing, T8 (for Active Reading, p. 228)

Grammar

- Sentence Fragments, C126 (for Mini Lesson, p. 232)

Writing

- Sensory Word List, T14 (for Writing Option 2, p. 232)
- Figurative Language and Sound Devices, T15 (for Writing Option 1, p. 232)

Communications

- Dramatic Reading, T12 (for Activities & Explorations, p. 232)
- Verbal Strategies, T14 (for Activities & Explorations, p. 232)

INTEGRATED TECHNOLOGY

Audio Library

Visit our website:
www.mcdougallittell.com

Reading and Analyzing

GUIDE FOR READING

A The mental picture is one of a young child enjoying the comfort of being near his mother while she sings and plays the piano for him.

Piano

D. H. Lawrence

Softly, in the dusk, a woman is singing to me;
Taking me back down the vista of years, till I see
A child sitting under the piano, in the boom of the
    tingling strings
And pressing the small, poised feet of a mother who
    smiles as she sings.

In spite of myself, the insidious mastery of song
Betrays me back, till the heart of me weeps to belong
To the old Sunday evenings at home, with winter outside
And hymns in the cozy parlour, the tinkling piano
    our guide.

So now it is vain for the singer to burst into clamour
With the great black piano appassionato. The glamour
Of childish days is upon me, my manhood is cast
Down in the flood of remembrance, I weep like a child
    for the past.

Guide for Reading

2 vista (vĭs'tə): a passage affording a distant view.

What mental picture do you form when reading this stanza? **A**

5 insidious (ĭn-sĭd'ē-əs): working subtly and gradually; treacherous.

9 vain: useless.

10 appassionato (ə-pä'sē-ə-nä'tō): an Italian word meaning "with deep emotion," used as a musical direction.

Thinking Through the Literature

1. **Comprehension Check** What is being recalled in this poem?
2. **ACTIVE READING** **VISUALIZING** Look back at the list of **images** from "Piano" in your **READER'S NOTEBOOK**. Compare the mental pictures that you formed with those formed by your classmates. What details in the poem contributed to those mental pictures?
3. Why does the **speaker**—the voice that talks to the reader—"weep like a child for the past"?

   THINK ABOUT
   - what he means by "the glamour of childish days"
   - what he values about "the old Sunday evenings at home"
4. Why does the speaker say that "now it is vain for the singer to burst into clamour"?

   THINK ABOUT
   - why the woman might be singing to him
   - the difference between his situations now and in the past

TEACHING THE LITERATURE

Customizing Instruction

Less Proficient Readers

Have students keep these questions in mind as they read the poems.

- Who is the speaker in each poem?
  Answer: "Piano"—the grown-up child who used to sit at his mother's feet; "Those Winter Sundays"—the grown-up child whose father used to warm the house and polish his shoes
- What image does each speaker convey about his parent?
  Possible Response: "Piano"—a small, elegant, musical, loving mother; "Those Winter Sundays"—a quiet, hardworking, loving man

Students Acquiring English

To help students use punctuation marks as a guide to comprehension, model how to read the poems aloud, accenting the pauses and run-on lines.

Use **Spanish Study Guide** pp. 50–52 for additional support.

Thinking Through the Literature

1. The speaker is recalling the Sunday evenings he spent listening to his mother play the piano.
2. Students should list at least three details from the poem.
3. Possible Response: The speaker weeps for the past because he misses his childhood days.
4. Possible Response: because he is overwhelmed by the memory of his mother and cannot concentrate on the singer's music

Reading and Analyzing

Literary Analysis IMAGERY

A As students read the poems, have them jot down any images in their Reader's Notebook. Have students put a star in front of an image that includes a sense other than sight.

Possible Responses: "Piano"—woman's singing, boom of tingling strings, pressing the feet, cozy parlour; "Those Winter Sundays"—blueblack cold, hear the cold, the father's call.

Use **Unit Two Resource Book,** p. 5 for more practice.

Active Reading VISUALIZING

Have students visualize the setting in each of the poems as they read. How do the settings differ?

Possible Response: The setting in "Piano" is a cozy parlour that is warm in contrast to the cold outside. The setting in "Those Winter Sundays" is a cold house that is probably not as elegant.

Use **Unit Two Resource Book,** p. 4 for more practice.

Reading Skills and Strategies: CLARIFYING

B Ask students why they think no one ever thanked the speaker's father and why the speaker spoke indifferently to him.

Possible Responses: The father may have been intimidating and his son may have been afraid of him; his son may have been too young to realize and appreciate the sacrifices his father made for him.

ACTIVE READING

C **CONNECT** Whether or not students have experienced severe cold, their answers should describe physical sensations of cold that they remember or that they imagine.

Sunday Morning Breakfast (1943), Horace Pippin. Private collection, courtesy of Galerie St. Etienne, New York.

Those Winter Sundays

ROBERT HAYDEN

Sundays too my father got up early
A and put his clothes on in the blueblack cold,
then with cracked hands that ached
from labor in the weekday weather made
B banked fires blaze. No one ever thanked him.

I'd wake and hear the cold splintering, breaking.
When the rooms were warm, he'd call,
and slowly I would rise and dress,
fearing the chronic angers of that house,

Speaking indifferently to him,
who had driven out the cold
and polished my good shoes as well.
What did I know, what did I know
of love's austere and lonely offices?

Guide for Reading

What do you think the "blueblack cold" feels like? **C**

9 chronic (krŏn′ĭk): lasting or recurring for a long time.

14 austere (ô-stîr′): stern; severe; **offices:** duties; ceremonies.

Teaching Options

Mini Lesson: Viewing and Representing

***Sunday Morning Breakfast* by Horace Pippin**

ART APPRECIATION Horace Pippin served in World War I and was wounded, leaving his right arm partially paralyzed. After returning home to Pennsylvania, Pippin eventually discovered he could clasp a paintbrush in his deadened right hand, then use his left arm to push the hand and brush across the canvas. His first painting took him three years to finish. Pippin painted memories of his childhood and of war, events from the lives of Abraham Lincoln and John Brown, and stories from the Bible.

Instruction Have students note the chipped walls in the painting, the plain furnishings, and the torn curtain and shirt. Point out how the sparkle of the yellows and whites and the burning stove add touches of brightness.

Application Have students meet in cooperative groups and discuss the mood in the painting based on its details. Have them compare the father in the painting to the father in "Those Winter Sundays."

Connect to the Literature

1. **What Do You Think?** Jot down three words or phrases describing the sensations you experienced while reading "Those Winter Sundays."

Comprehension Check
- What time is recalled in this poem?
- What does the father do for his son?
- How does the child react to his father?

Think Critically

2. **ACTIVE READING** **VISUALIZING** Look back to the list of **images** from "Those Winter Sundays" in your **READER'S NOTEBOOK**. Read aloud the words and phrases from the poem that helped you to form mental pictures. What image is the strongest one for you?

3. What is your opinion of the **speaker?**

THINK ABOUT
- the speaker's observations in lines 5 and 10
- the question that ends the poem
- the possible reason that the speaker recalls this memory

4. What lessons might be learned from this poem? Explain your answer.

Extend Interpretations

5. **Comparing Texts** Compare and contrast the speakers' attitudes toward their childhood in "Piano" and "Those Winter Sundays."

6. **Connect to Life** What feelings or memories from your own life did these poems awaken?

Literary Analysis

IMAGERY The use of words and phrases to create sensory experiences for readers is called **imagery.** Images can appeal to one or more of the five senses: sight, hearing, taste, smell, and touch. For example, "A child sitting under the piano" appeals to the sense of sight; "the boom of the tingling strings" appeals to the senses of hearing and touch; and "pressing the small, poised feet" appeals to the senses of sight and touch.

Paired Activity With a partner, list three more images from "Piano" and three from "Those Winter Sundays," naming the sense or senses to which each image appeals. Then discuss which poem, in your opinion, uses imagery more effectively.

SPEAKER The **speaker** is the voice in a poem that "talks" to the reader, similar to the narrator in fiction. The speaker is not necessarily the same as the poet, although in some cases it may be. Sometimes, a poet will create a speaker with a distinct identity in order to achieve a certain effect.

Activity Identify the speakers in "Piano" and "Those Winter Sundays." Consider what the poems say explicitly about them as children and what is implied about them as adults. What can you infer about the speakers and their present perspective? For each poem, fill out a graphic like the one shown to help you organize your ideas.

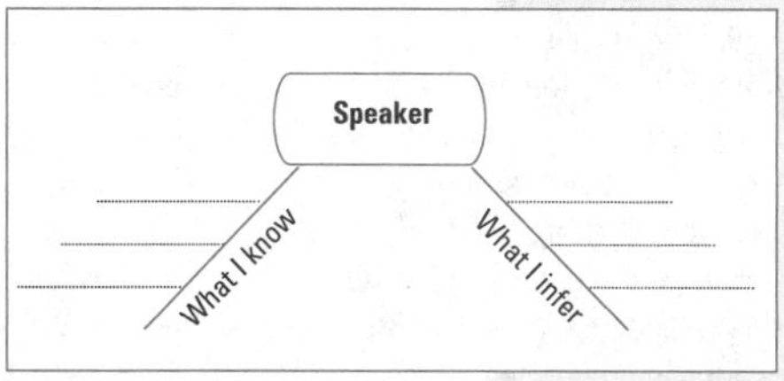

GUIDING STUDENT RESPONSE

Connect to the Literature

1. **What Do You Think?**
Possible Responses: quiet; feeling cranky in the early morning; gratefulness toward father; a feeling of regret for the past.

Comprehension Check
- The speaker recalls the Sunday winter dawns of his childhood.
- The father starts a fire so it will be warm when his son awakens. He also shines his son's good shoes.
- He speaks to him indifferently and does not thank him.

Think Critically

2. Possible Responses: Students could cite "cracked hands that ached," "the cold splintering, breaking," "polished my good shoes."
3. Possible Responses: The speaker is young and does not understand his father's struggles. Perhaps this memory is recalled because the speaker is now a father and can better recognize how a parent's love is expressed.
4. Possible Responses: Children should try to appreciate what their parents or other adults do for them and try to be considerate and appreciative; people sometimes show love through actions instead of words.

Extend Interpretations

Comparing Texts In general, the speakers have different attitudes toward their childhood. The speaker in "Piano" is so fond of his mother and his childhood that her memory brings him to tears. The speaker in "Those Winter Sundays" is trying to understand his father's actions as well as his own. There was anger in his house, which is not mentioned in "Piano." However, both speakers recognize the love their parents gave them when they were children.

Connect to Life Elicit responses from students who are willing to share memories from their own childhoods.

Literary Analysis

Imagery Student responses will vary; possible responses include the following:

"Piano"
woman singing—hearing; in the dusk—sight; the boom of the strings—hearing, touch

"Those Winter Sundays"
blueblack cold—touch, sight; cracked hands—touch; blazing fires—sight, touch

Speaker Students should support this inference with text evidence. Students may find it useful to pay special attention to verb tenses, especially in "Piano."

Writing Options

1. **Childhood Poem** To get students started, have them note down images that their memory evokes and consider how their memory makes them feel.
2. **Image Dictionary** To make this assignment less challenging, students can complete it in groups.

Activities & Explorations

Choral Reading Students may want to listen to choral readings of these poems or other familiar poems before performing.

Choices & CHALLENGES

Writing Options

1. **Childhood Poem** Use the chart you created for Connect to Your Life on page 228 as the starting point for a poem about your childhood memory. Include vivid imagery that appeals to different senses. Place the poem in your **Working Portfolio.**

2. **Image Dictionary** Create a dictionary of sensory images. Under the headings "Sight," "Hearing," "Touch," "Taste," and "Smell," record words and phrases from your reading, including those encountered in "Piano" and "Those Winter Sundays."

Activities & Explorations

Choral Reading With a small group, prepare a choral reading of one of these poems. Discuss what emotions should be expressed, where pauses should fall, and which words or phrases should be given emphasis. Then practice your reading aloud. ~ **SPEAKING AND LISTENING**

D. H. Lawrence

1885–1930

Other Works
The Complete Short Stories of D. H. Lawrence
The Complete Poems of D. H. Lawrence

Coal Miner's Son David Herbert Lawrence grew up in poverty in the coal-mining district of Nottinghamshire, England. His father was a hard-working, hard-drinking coal miner; his mother, to whom he was deeply attached, was a former schoolteacher who instilled in her son a love of learning and culture. A sickly but intellectually gifted child, Lawrence attended school on scholarships and after graduation became a schoolteacher himself, writing fiction and poetry in his spare time.

His Path to Fame Lawrence's first poems were published when a girlfriend submitted them to a magazine whose editor was impressed with Lawrence's efforts. With the editor's help, Lawrence was able to publish his first novel, *The White Peacock,* in 1911. He went on to produce a string of critically acclaimed novels, many of which focus on male-female relationships with a frankness that shocked the public of his day. Aside from being one of the most celebrated novelists of the 20th century, Lawrence has long been recognized as a first-rate poet. "Piano," a famous example of his poetic craftsmanship, was written in 1918, seven years after his mother died.

Robert Hayden

1913–1980

Other Works
Angle of Ascent: New and Selected Poems
Collected Prose
Robert Hayden: Collected Poems

The Making of a Poet Robert Hayden grew up in Detroit, Michigan, where he was raised by foster parents who made great sacrifices to insure his education. Their efforts were also encouraged by Hayden's natural mother, who occasionally sent him books to read. Hayden began writing poems in elementary school, although for years he doubted that he could make a career of it. In 1936 he was employed by the Federal Writers' Project to research African-American history and folklore. Soon afterward, he began working part-time for an African-American weekly paper whose editor helped him publish his first book of poetry, *Heart-Shape in the Dust* (1940).

An Academic Life In 1941, Hayden enrolled in graduate school at the University of Michigan, where one of his most inspiring professors was the British poet W. H. Auden. Eventually becoming a professor himself, Hayden taught for over 20 years at Fisk University in Nashville, Tennessee. As his reputation as a scholar grew, so did his fame as a poet. "Those Winter Sundays," one of his best-known shorter poems, was first collected in the volume *A Ballad of Remembrance,* published in 1962.

Teaching Options

Mini Lesson Grammar

SENTENCE FRAGMENTS Instruction A sentence fragment fails to express a complete, independent thought. Unlike a complete sentence, a sentence fragment lacks a subject or a verb or it begins with a subordinating conjunction, such as *although* or *when.* Write the following sentence fragment on the board:

"A child sitting under the piano."

Have students identify the subject in the sentence. *(child)* Ask if the subject has a verb *(no)*

Have a volunteer revise the fragment so that it is a complete sentence.

Exercises Have students copy the following sentence fragments and decide why each is not a sentence. Then, ask students to rewrite each of the fragments so that it is a complete sentence.

1. Takes him back to his childhood. *(lacks a subject)*
2. While his father loved him. *(begins with a subordinate word)*
3. The woman singing beside him. *(lacks a verb)*

Use **Grammar Transparencies and Copymasters,** p. 126.

Use McDougal Littell's ***Language Network,*** Chapter 5, for more instruction in sentence fragments.

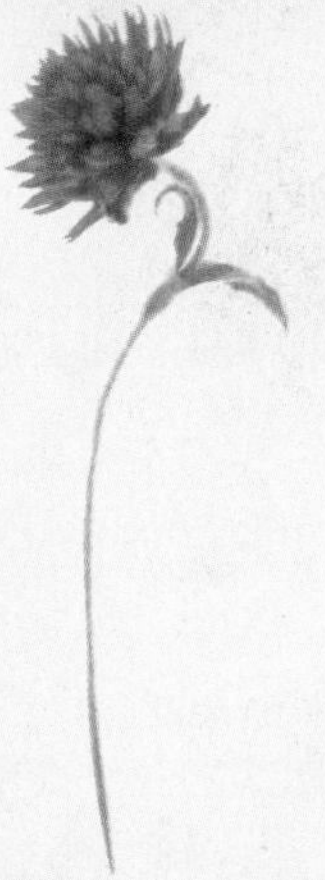

Sonnet 18

Poetry by
WILLIAM SHAKESPEARE

Sonnet 30

Poetry by
EDNA ST. VINCENT MILLAY

Connect to Your Life

What Is Love? Poets, like songwriters, often make use of comparisons when describing love. Love may be compared to an illness or a fire or even a balloon drifting in the air. With a partner, come up with different comparisons to describe love or a beloved person. You may use lyrics from popular music or any other phrases that come to mind. Share your best responses with your classmates. Then discuss what the comparisons reveal about people's attitudes towards love.

Build Background

Sonnet Origins Poets have often explored the topic of love in **sonnets,** which are 14-line poems that have been a popular form of expression for many centuries. The sonnet originated in Italy; in fact, the word sonnet comes from the Italian for "little song." The form was first popularized by the Italian poet Petrarch (1304–1374), who wrote a famous sonnet sequence, or series, expressing his love for a woman named Laura. From Italy, the form spread to France, Spain, and England, where many poets, including William Shakespeare, experimented with the form. Shakespeare's 154 sonnets are widely regarded as the finest in English. Like Petrarch's, Shakespeare's sonnets often focus on romantic love; they also address the love between friends. Since Shakespeare's day, many English-language poets have tried their hand at writing sonnets. Among them is the 20th-century American poet Edna St. Vincent Millay.

Focus Your Reading

LITERARY ANALYSIS | **SONNET STRUCTURE** The **structure** of the **sonnet** is reflected by the **rhyme scheme,** or the pattern of rhyme in a poem. Poets use rhyme not only to please the ear but also to mark units of thought.

To identify a poem's rhyme scheme, you assign a letter of the alphabet to each rhymed sound at the end of the line. The example below, from another Shakespeare sonnet, illustrates an *abab* rhyme scheme. Note that *fled* rhymes with *dead* and that *bell* rhymes with *dwell.*

No longer mourn for me when I am dead	a
Than you shall hear the surly sullen bell	b
Give warning to the world that I am fled	a
From this vile world, with vilest worms to dwell.	b

The **English,** or **Shakespearean, sonnet** is characterized by the fixed rhyme scheme *abab cdcd efef gg.* This type of sonnet is divided into three **quatrains,** or groups of four rhymed lines, and one **couplet,** or rhymed pair of lines. Each group of lines usually corresponds to a unit of thought in the poem. The **couplet** provides commentary on the subject developed in the preceding three quatrains.

ACTIVE READING | **STRATEGIES FOR READING SONNETS** The following strategies can help you to understand a **sonnet** and to recognize how the **structure** contributes to its meaning:

1. Identify the **rhyme scheme** and the major units of thought.
2. In your own words, describe the situation, problem, or question that is introduced at the beginning of the poem.
3. Identify the **turning point,** if there is one.
4. Find out how the situation is clarified, the problem resolved, or the question answered.
5. Summarize the message of the poem in your own words.

READER'S NOTEBOOK As you read the following sonnets, apply the five strategies described above. Record the results of each task.

OVERVIEW

Objectives

1. understand and appreciate two **poems (Literary Analysis)**
2. understand **sonnet structure** by examining **rhyme scheme (Literary Analysis)**
3. implement **strategies for reading sonnets (Active Reading)**

Summary

The speaker in Shakespeare's "Sonnet 18" compares his beloved to a summer's day. He concludes that she is more lovely and gentle, and more enduring—an eternal summer that will not fade and will always be fair. He thinks he has immortalized his beloved with this sonnet. The speaker in "Sonnet 30" notes that although love is not necessary for life, many men lose the will to live because they lack love. She says she may someday be pressed to give up love for survival, yet she does not think she would.

Thematic Link

In these two sonnets, the speakers explore the depth and intensity of the ties that bind them to their loves.

5-Minute Warm-Up

Daily Language SkillBuilder

Have students **proofread** the display sentences on page 223i and write them correctly. The sentences also appear on Transparency 7 of **Grammar Transparencies and Copymasters.**

LESSON RESOURCES

UNIT TWO RESOURCE BOOK, pp. 6–8

ASSESSMENT RESOURCES
Formal Assessment, p. 39
Teacher's Guide to Assessment and Portfolio Use
Test Generator

SKILLS TRANSPARENCIES AND COPYMASTERS

Literary Analysis
- Poetry: Sound Devices, T8 (for Cooperative Learning Activity, p. 236)

Reading and Critical Thinking
- Locating Information Using Print References, T32 (for Inquiry and Research, p. 237)

Grammar
- Rhetorical Questions, C174 (for Mini Lesson, p. 237)

Writing
- Figurative Language and Sound Devices, T15 (for Writing Option 2, p. 237)
- Poem, C27 (for Writing Option 2, p. 237)

Communications
- Dramatic Reading, T12 (for Activities & Explorations 1, p. 237)
- Verbal Strategies, T14 (for Activities & Explorations 1, p. 237)
- Reading Aloud, T11 (for Author Activities, p. 238)

INTEGRATED TECHNOLOGY
Audio Library
LaserLinks
- Author Background: William Shakespeare. See **Teacher's SourceBook,** p. 19.

Visit our website:
www.mcdougallittell.com

SONNETS 18/30 **233**

TEACHING THE LITERATURE

Reading and Analyzing

Reading Skills and Strategies: PREVIEW

Have students preview the selection. Have students find and discuss the images on pp. 234–235 and the poems' titles. Discuss with students the Build Background feature on p. 233. Ask students to predict what the sonnets will be about. Before students begin reading, give them brief summaries of the two poems.

Active Reading READING SONNETS

Remind students to monitor their reading strategies as they read the sonnets. Have students summarize the meaning of each quatrain and the couplet in "Sonnet 18," as below. Then have students do the same for "Sonnet 30."

Possible Response:

Quatrain 1 **how she is better than a summer's day**

Quatrain 2 **a summer's day's faults**

Quatrain 3 **how she does not have those faults**

Couplet **she will be immortalized by the poem**

Use **Unit Two Resource Book** p. 6 for more practice.

Literary Analysis SONNET STRUCTURE

Remind students that a sonnet's structure is dependent on its rhyme scheme. Arrange students into small groups, then have each group write its own sonnet, adhering strictly to the English sonnet rhyme scheme (*abab cdcd efef gg*). Tell students that subject matter and even sense are not important for this exercise; they merely need to stick to the rhyme scheme. When the groups have finished their sonnets, have them share them with the class, and have the class comment on whether each sonnet adheres to the proper rhyme scheme.

Use **Unit Two Resource Book** p. 7 for more practice.

Sonnet 18

William Shakespeare

Shall I compare thee to a summer's day?
Thou art more lovely and more temperate:
Rough winds do shake the darling buds of May,
And summer's lease hath all too short a date:
Sometime too hot the eye of heaven shines,
And often is his gold complexion dimmed;
And every fair from fair sometime declines,
By chance or nature's changing course untrimmed;
But thy eternal summer shall not fade,
Nor lose possession of that fair thou owest;
Nor shall Death brag thou wander'st in his shade,
When in eternal lines to time thou growest:
  So long as men can breathe, or eyes can see,
  So long lives this, and this gives life to thee.

2 temperate (tĕm′pər-ĭt): moderate; mild.

8 untrimmed: stripped of beauty.

10 thou owest (ō′əst): you own; you possess.

Thinking Through the Literature

1. **Comprehension Check** What basic comparison is made in this poem?
2. What words would you use to describe how the **speaker** feels about the person being addressed? Support your opinion with details from the poem.
3. ACTIVE READING STRATEGIES FOR READING SONNETS Refer to what you recorded in your READER'S NOTEBOOK. How did your analysis of this sonnet's **structure** help you to understand the poem?

   THINK ABOUT
   - the question raised in the first line
   - the **rhyme scheme**
   - the main point of each **quatrain** and **couplet**

Thinking Through the Literature

1. **Comprehension Check** The speaker compares his beloved to a summer's day.
2. Possible Response: The speaker truly loves this woman. When he compares her to a summer day, he concludes that she is more lovely and gentle than the summer day. He believes her beauty is immortal.
3. Student responses should show recognition of the different units of thought delineated by the poem's structure: the comparison with a summer's day; the suggestion that most beauty fades over time; the statement that the subject's beauty is, however, immortal; and the statement in the final couplet that this poem shall lend her immortality.

Lovers III (1990), Eng Tay. Edition 175, intaglio. Published by Tapir Editions, New York.

Sonnet 30

Edna St. Vincent Millay

Love is not all: it is not meat nor drink
Nor slumber nor a roof against the rain;
Nor yet a floating spar to men that sink
And rise and sink and rise and sink again;
Love can not fill the thickened lung with breath,
Nor clean the blood, nor set the fractured bone;
Yet many a man is making friends with death
Even as I speak, for lack of love alone.
It well may be that in a difficult hour,
Pinned down by pain and moaning for release,
Or nagged by want past resolution's power,
I might be driven to sell your love for peace,
Or trade the memory of this night for food.
It well may be. I do not think I would.

3 spar: a pole used to support a ship's sails.

11 want: need.

Customizing Instruction

Less Proficient Readers

Point out that even experts in literature often must read a poem several times to fully understand. Encourage students to grasp whatever meaning they can at first reading. Challenge them to learn what they can about the speakers' feelings for their loved ones.

Students Acquiring English

Use **Spanish Study Guide** pp. 53–55 for additional support.

Mini Lesson: Viewing and Representing

Lovers III by Eng Tay

ART APPRECIATION Eng Tay was born and raised in Malaysia, though he has lived in New York City for the last two decades. An internationally recognized printmaker and artist, Tay's works are characterized by a quiet play of color harmonies.

Instruction Have students note that there are two central figures in the painting, though at first glance there may only seem to be one. Ask students why Tay might have blurred the boundary between the two figures. What does this suggest about the relationship between the lovers?

Possible Response: He wanted to portray the figures as very close. They depend greatly on one another.

Application Based on the details in the painting, have students suggest whether the relationship depicted in the painting is more like that expressed in "Sonnet 18" or in "Sonnet 30."

Possible Response: The relationship depicted in the painting is more like the relationship in "Sonnet 30" because the speaker of "Sonnet 30" seems extremely attached to and dependent on her lover.

GUIDING STUDENT RESPONSE

Connect to the Literature

1. **What Do You Think?**
Students may refer to any lines from the poem. They may be stirred to think more about love; they might be saddened, or have other responses.

Comprehension Check

- Millay says that love is not food, drink, shelter, or medicine—the material things a person needs to stay alive.
- Many people are dying from lack of love.

Think Critically

2. Possible Response: The speaker is referring to people's physical needs.
3. Responses will vary. Students should show some recognition of the poem's setup: in the first quatrain she contrasts love with life essentials, such as food and medicine; in the second quatrain she continues this line, then refutes it, saying that men die all the time for lack of love, as opposed to the lack of other physical needs; finally, she says that it's possible she would exchange love for one of these essentials, but she thinks not. Students may note that the poem's content does not hold as firmly to the structure as does Shakespeare's sonnet.
4. Possible Response: The speaker believes love is more important than anything else.

Connect to the Literature

1. **What Do You Think?** Which lines of Millay's "Sonnet 30" did you find most memorable? Describe your response to those lines.

Comprehension Check

- What does Millay say that love is *not?*
- How would you paraphrase what she says in lines 7 and 8?

Think Critically

2. Consider all the details that the speaker uses to explain why "Love is not all." In your opinion, what do these details have in common?
3. ACTIVE READING STRATEGIES FOR READING SONNETS
Refer to your READER'S NOTEBOOK. How did your analysis of this **sonnet's structure** help you to understand the poem?

THINK ABOUT
- the statement in the poem's first line
- the **rhyme scheme**
- the main point of each **quatrain** and **couplet**

4. What seems to be the speaker's overall opinion of love?

Extend Interpretations

5. **Comparing Texts** Do you think Shakespeare's "Sonnet 18" and Millay's "Sonnet 30" follow the same structure? Explain, using your knowledge of sonnet structure and details from the poems.
6. **Connect to Life** Do you think these poems convey attitudes about love that are still common today? Draw upon the discussion from Connect to Your Life on page 233 to support your opinion.

Literary Analysis

SONNET STRUCTURE In addition to the **rhyme scheme, sonnet structure** is also determined by the sound pattern. **Sonnets** usually follow a regular **rhythm** called **meter.** The meter of a poem is like the beat of a song. Each unit of meter is known as a **foot.** In English, the most commonly used type of metrical foot is an **iamb,** which is an unstressed syllable followed by a stressed syllable (˘ ´).

Two terms are used to identify the meter of a line of poetry. The first word describes the main type of metrical foot in the line. The second word describes the number of feet in the line: **trimeter** (three feet), **tetrameter** (four feet), **pentameter** (five feet), and so on. Thus, the meter of a poem might be **iambic trimeter** or **iambic pentameter.** The following example from Millay's sonnet illustrates iambic pentameter, the most common pattern. Note the iambic pattern of unstressed, followed by stressed, syllables. Also note that each line consists of five iambs (pentameter).

Nŏr yét ă flóatĭng spár tŏ mén thăt sínk

Ănd rísé ănd sínk ănd ríse ănd sínk ăgaín;

Cooperative Learning Activity Work in a small group to identify the metrical pattern of Shakespeare's and Millay's sonnets.

Extend Interpretations

Comparing Texts Possible Responses: Yes, because they both follow the same rhyme scheme; no, because Shakespeare develops his idea in three quatrains and a final couplet, while Millay develops an idea in lines 1–6, refutes it in lines 7–8, and resolves the question in the remaining lines.
Connect to Life Responses will vary. Students should refer to points from the discussion they had before reading the poems.

Literary Analysis

Sonnet Structure Students' metrical markings should show that both poems are written in iambic pentamer, although there are words or groups of words that do not fall into this meter, such as the first four words of the Millay sonnet. Explain to students that scansion, as this exercise is called, is sometimes subject to disagreement.

Writing Options

1. Speaker Profile Create a personality profile of one of the speakers in the two poems. Use details from the poem to support your opinion of the speaker's personality.

2. Not-love Poem Write a sonnet or another poem in which, like Millay, you express your own view of love by defining what it is not. Place the entry in your **Working Portfolio.**

Activities & Explorations

1. Comparative Description Prepare a "weather report" that is not about the weather at all but about the qualities of a person whom you know well. In your report, try to imitate some of the techniques used by Shakespeare to make comparisons. Present your report to the class, using any visual materials that will enhance your presentation. ~ **SPEAKING AND LISTENING**

2. Rock Sonnet Turn either sonnet into a song and perform it before the class. ~ **MUSIC**

Inquiry & Research

Earlier English Shakespeare wrote almost 500 years ago. Study his sonnet for words or expressions that are no longer commonly used. Then create a list of those terms and try to come up with a modern substitute for each one, looking up in the dictionary words that are unfamiliar to you. Compare your results with those of your classmates.

Grammar in Context: Rhetorical Questions

Consider this line from Shakespeare's "Sonnet 18." Do you think the speaker expects an answer to his question?

"Shall I compare thee to a summer's day?"

This question is actually a rhetorical question. It is asked not to get an answer but to create an effect. A writer who uses a rhetorical question usually does so because the question is more striking and dramatic than a statement would be.

Statement	Rhetorical Question
• Never was such nonsense written.	• Was ever such nonsense written?
• There will never be an end to this.	• Will there ever be an end to this?
• I shall compare thee to a summer's day.	• Shall I compare thee to a summer's day?

Usage Tip: You can often turn a statement into a rhetorical question by switching the positions of the subject and a helping verb or by replacing the subject with an interrogative pronoun, such as *who* or *what.*

WRITING EXERCISE Rewrite each statement as a rhetorical question.

Example: ***Original*** No one has evoked more poignantly than Shakespeare the quickness of beauty's fading.

Rewritten Who has evoked more poignantly than Shakespeare the quickness of beauty's fading?

1. It has never been easy to express powerful feelings.
2. We stumble and stutter every time we try.
3. I don't know who could express such feelings better than a poet.
4. There aren't any sonnets that surpass Shakespeare's.

Connect to the Literature Try changing a line of "Sonnet 18" (other than the first) into a rhetorical question. Do you think your change improves the poem, or do you like the line better as a statement? Explain your answer.

Writing Options

1. **Speaker Profile** To make this assignment less difficult, have students create a profile for each speaker in cooperative groups.
2. **Not-love Poem** To get students started, have them discuss their view of love with a partner.

Activities & Explorations

1. **Comparative Description** To get students started, have them meet in cooperative groups and come up with weather terms that could also describe a person, such as "sunny," "like a thundering storm front," and "cold and icy."
2. **Rock Sonnet** Students may compose their own music or set the sonnet to music that already exists.

Inquiry and Research

Earlier English Students may want to consult other annotated texts. Suggest that students use the *Oxford English Dictionary* or an unabridged dictionary.

Grammar in Context

WRITING EXERCISE Answers may vary.

1. Has it ever been easy to express powerful feelings?
2. Don't we stumble and stutter every time we try?
3. Who could express such feelings better than a poet?
4. Are there any sonnets that surpass Shakespeare's?

Mini Lesson Grammar

RHETORICAL QUESTIONS

For use with Grammar in Context, page 237.

Instruction Tell students that questions asked in poetry and literature often do not require answers but simply emphasize ideas that readers can be expected to agree with. These questions are called rhetorical questions.

Write the following question on the board:

"Shall I compare thee to a summer's day?"

Note how Shakespeare's question in "Sonnet 18" is rhetorical; he doesn't expect readers to answer it.

Practice Have students copy each of the following sentences. Have them meet in cooperative groups and rewrite each sentence as a rhetorical question.

1. Love is not all.
   Possible Response: Is love all?
2. I might be driven to sell your love for peace.
   Possible Response: Might I be driven to sell your love for peace?
3. Summer's lease has all too short a date.
   Possible Response: Does summer's lease have too short a date?

Use **Unit Two Resource Book,** p. 8 for additional support.

Author Activity

Shall I Compare Thee to Another Sonnet?

Students can find Shakespeare's collected sonnets in a variety of anthologies; *The Riverside Shakespeare* provides full annotation for each of Shakespeare's works and may be helpful to students.

Rhyme and Rhythm

Millay's poetry collections include *A Few Figs from Thistles, Second April, The Harp Weaver and Other Poems, The Buck in the Snow,* and *Wine from These Grapes.*

William Shakespeare

1564–1616

Other Works

Romeo and Juliet
Julius Caesar
Macbeth
As You Like It
Twelfth Night

The Bard of Avon The son of a merchant, William Shakespeare grew up in the market town of Stratford-upon-Avon, England, where he attended the local grammar school. In 1582 he married Anne Hathaway, who later gave birth to three children. Shakespeare probably moved to London in the 1580s and began a career as an actor with the Lord Chamberlain's Men, London's leading theater company. In the 1590s he began writing plays for the group. Great acclaim followed, under both Queen Elizabeth I and her successor, King James I, who became the theater company's patron. From then on known as the King's Players, the group performed mainly at London's Globe Theatre, where Shakespeare was a part owner.

The Bard's Legacy When he died, Shakespeare was able to leave his heirs a large inheritance. Of course, Shakespeare's greatest legacy was his writing–over 150 sonnets and over 35 dramas that are generally regarded as the world's finest. These include tragedies such as *Hamlet* and *King Lear* and comedies such as *The Taming of the Shrew* and *A Midsummer Night's Dream.*

Author Activity

Shall I Compare Thee to Another Sonnet? Find a collection of Shakespeare's sonnets and choose one that you like. Then compare it with Sonnet 18. With a group, share your chosen sonnets and discuss what they all have in common.

VIDEODISC **LaserLinks: Background for Reading**
Author Background

Edna St. Vincent Millay

1892–1950

Other Works

A Few Figs from Thistles
The Harp-Weaver and Other Poems
Conversation at Midnight

Vassar Girl Makes Good Edna St. Vincent Millay was still a student when she burst on the literary scene in 1912 with her poem "Renascence." After graduating from Vassar College, she settled in Greenwich Village, a New York City neighborhood then enjoying its heyday as a center for poets and artists. Millay quickly became one of Greenwich Village's social lions, admired as much for her offbeat, romantic lifestyle as for her skill with the pen. Though Millay lived the life of a nonconformist, her well-crafted verse usually conformed to poetic traditions of the past. She was one of the few poets of her day who did not abandon rhyme and meter, and her sonnets are still considered masterpieces.

In Times of Change In 1923, Millay became the first woman to win the Pulitzer Prize in poetry. Her work reflected many of the social changes that swept through the United States during that era and won her international acclaim. "Love is not all," which appears as Sonnet 30 in her *Collected Sonnets* (1941), was first published in her sonnet sequence *Fatal Interview* (1931).

Author Activity

Rhyme and Rhythm Look for poems other than sonnets by Millay and read them with an ear for the rhyme and meter. Choose a few and read them aloud. How much variety do you find in the form of the poems? Compare your findings with those of your classmates.

Teaching Options

Assessment Standardized Test Practice

COMPARE AND CONTRAST You can informally assess students' understanding of the selections by having them write a brief essay in which they compare and contrast how the speakers in "Sonnet 18" and "Sonnet 30" view love. Students should use details from the sonnets to back up their assertions.

RUBRIC

3 **Full Accomplishment** Response reflects a full understanding of the sonnets and uses specific details to support its claim.

2 **Substantial Accomplishment** Response shows a general understanding of the sonnets and uses some details to support its claim.

1 **Little or Partial Accomplishment** Response shows little or partial understanding of the sonnets and uses few or no details to support its claim.

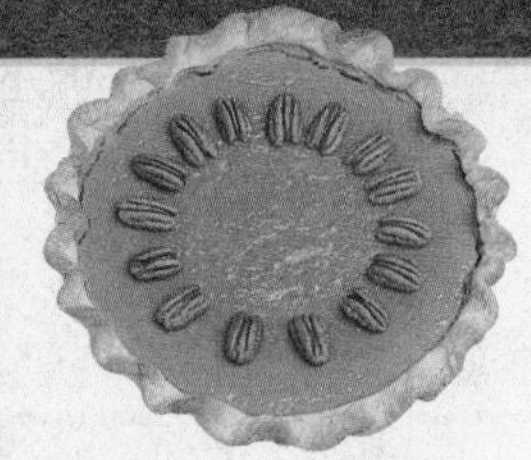

Sweet Potato Pie

Short Story by EUGENIA COLLIER

"Whenever I come to Harlem I feel somehow as if I were coming home—"

Connect to Your Life

All in the Family Think about the relationship between the oldest and youngest siblings in a family. What qualities are typical of that relationship? In your opinion, who has it easier, the oldest or the youngest? Why? Discuss your ideas on the matter with your classmates.

Build Background

One Family, Two Worlds In "Sweet Potato Pie," the narrator recalls two very different settings: the sharecropper's shanty where he grew up with his family and his eldest brother's home in Harlem. Sharecropping, or tenant farming, is a system in which a person or family works someone else's farm in exchange for a share of the profits. Traditionally, sharecroppers have been very poor. In the United States, sharecropping arose after the Civil War and declined as modern, mechanized farming was introduced. Sharecropping is still a way of life in other parts of the world.

From the late 19th century through World War II, millions of African Americans left farms and small towns in the South to seek economic opportunity in Northern big cities. The first wave of this movement, ending in the 1920s, was known as the Great Migration. Cities such as Chicago, Detroit, and New York grew considerably in size. In the 1920s Harlem, a part of New York City, became the world's largest urban black community. Though crowded and generally poor, Harlem became a focus of African-American culture, music, and art.

WORDS TO KNOW
Vocabulary Preview

boisterous	nuance
edifice	panorama
entity	reminiscence
gaunt	reverently
impersonal	sultry

Focus Your Reading

LITERARY ANALYSIS **CHARACTERIZATION** **Characterization** refers to the techniques used by a writer to develop characters. Writers portray characters through a combination of physical description; the speech, thoughts, feelings, or actions of the characters; and direct commentary by the narrator. In this passage from the story you are about to read, the author characterizes the narrator's brother Charley by his speech:

> ***"Lucky for you, you got a* mind. *And that's something ain't everybody got."***

As you read the following story, pay special attention to the main characters and the author's methods of characterization.

ACTIVE READING **SEQUENCE OF EVENTS** Many fiction writers make use of **flashback,** or an account of something that took place before the beginning of a story. Often, a flashback interrupts a story's **sequence of events** to provide information about the past. To help the reader keep track of the time order of events, writers use tense changes as well as signal words and phrases, especially at the beginning of paragraphs. Such phrases from this story include the following: *one day, years later, the war came along,* and *when we were young.*

READER'S NOTEBOOK As you read, keep track of the chronological order of events by constructing a timeline similar to the one shown.

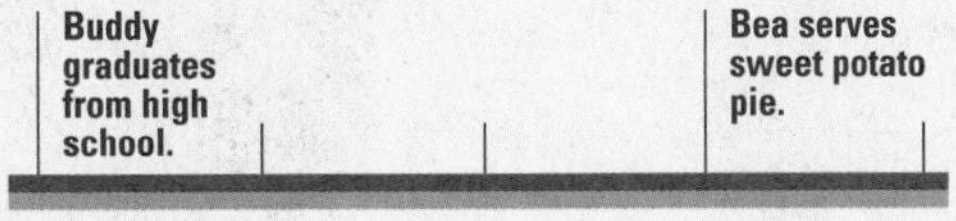
Buddy graduates from high school.
Bea serves sweet potato pie.

OVERVIEW

Objectives

1. understand and appreciate a **short story (Literary Analysis)**
2. analyze **characterization (Literary Analysis)**
3. analyze text for **sequence of events (Active Reading)**

Summary

This story is told in flashback, looking back to events earlier in the evening and to events from the speaker's childhood. Buddy is the youngest of five children, and his oldest brother is Charley. Through his family's help, Buddy became the first in his family to earn a college degree, and has achieved success as a college professor. Today, Buddy visits Charley in Harlem whenever he can, enjoying the family, food, and recollections of old times. Charley clearly loves Buddy, but tries to hide their relationship from the world, so that the world will not think less of Buddy.

Thematic Link

While Buddy is successful, he is proud of the **ties that bind** him to the brother who raised him. His brother Charley is proud of him, but wants to hide those ties from the world—Charley doesn't want people perceiving his brother the way he himself is perceived.

Editor's Note This selection has been edited slightly to delete material that may be considered objectionable.

5-Minute Warm-Up

Daily Language SkillBuilder

Have students **proofread** the display sentences on page 223i and write them correctly. The sentences also appear on Transparency 8 of **Grammar Transparencies and Copymasters.**

Mini Lesson Preteaching Vocabulary

If you would like to preteach the WORDS TO KNOW for this selection, use the Mini Lesson, p. 240.

LESSON RESOURCES

UNIT TWO RESOURCE BOOK, pp. 9–14

ASSESSMENT RESOURCES
Formal Assessment, pp. 41–43
Teacher's Guide to Assessment and Portfolio Use
Test Generator

SKILLS TRANSPARENCIES AND COPYMASTERS
Literary Analysis
- Character, T2 (for Cooperative Learning Activity, p. 252)

Grammar
- Compound Predicates I, C86 (for Mini Lesson, p. 254)

Vocabulary
- Context Clues, C39 (for Mini Lesson, p. 240)

Writing
- Generating Ideas, T1 (for Writing Option 1, p. 253)
- Sensory Word List, T14 (for Writing Option 2, p. 253)
- Poem, C27 (for Writing Option 2, p. 253)

Communications
- Evaluation Matrix: Commercial, T6 (for Activities & Explorations 2, p. 253)
- Impromptu Speaking: Dialogue, Role-Play, Debate T13 (for Inquiry & Research, p. 253)

INTEGRATED TECHNOLOGY
Audio Library
Internet: Research Starter
Visit our website:
www.mcdougallittell.com

TEACHING THE LITERATURE

Reading and Analyzing

Reading Skills and Strategies: PREVIEW

Have students preview the selection. Have students look through the selection, then ask students what the title, the images, and the called-out quotes in the story suggest. Discuss with students the Build Background feature on p. 239, and ask them to jot down questions that they would like to have answered as they read the story. Before students begin reading, give them a brief summary of the selection.

Active Reading SEQUENCE OF EVENTS

Have students list each event in the story in their Reader's Notebook. As students read, they should analyze the development of the plot. They should note which events are flashbacks and the signal words used to indicate that time has passed.

Discuss how the information provided in each flashback helps students understand the main characters' actions.

Use **Unit Two Resource Book** p. 10 for more practice.

Literary Analysis CHARACTERIZATION

Characterization refers to the techniques the author uses to develop the characters. You can often tell what a character is like by his or her physical description; what he or she says, does, and thinks; how other characters react to this character; and what the narrator says about the character. As they read, have students make mental notes of character traits as revealed through the above methods.

Use **Unit Two Resource Book** p. 11 for more practice.

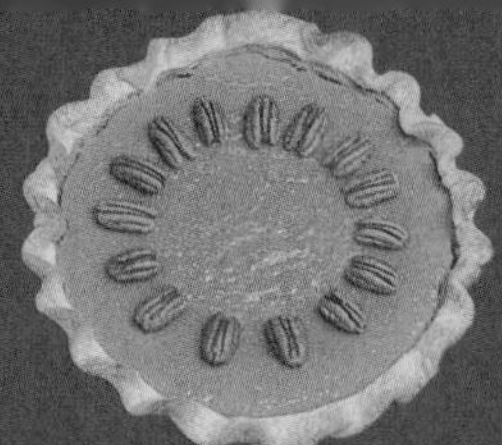

Sweet

Eugenia Collier

From up here on the fourteenth floor, my brother Charley looks like an insect scurrying among other insects. A deep feeling of love surges through me. Despite the distance, he seems to feel it, for he turns and scans the upper windows, but failing to find me, continues on his way. I watch him moving quickly—gingerly, it seems to me—down Fifth Avenue and around the corner to his shabby taxicab. In a moment he will be heading back uptown.

Picture by Christopher Myers from *Harlem: A Poem* by Walter Dean Myers. Published by Scholastic Press, a division of Scholastic Inc. Illustration copyright © 1997 by Christopher Myers. Reprinted by permission of Scholastic Inc.

240

Teaching Options

Mini Lesson Preteaching Vocabulary

USING CONTEXT CLUES Call students' attention to the list of WORDS TO KNOW. Remind them that sometimes they can understand the meaning of an unfamiliar word by examining the context in which the word is used. Use the model sentence to demonstrate the strategy of using context clues to provide inferences to word meaning.

Model Sentence Big cities are crowded, polluted, *boisterous* places.

Instruction

- Write the model sentence on the board.
- Ask a volunteer to summarize the meaning of the sentence.
- Have students use the meaning of the sentence to infer meanings for the word *boisterous*.
- Ask a volunteer to use the word *boisterous* in a sentence.

Use **Unit Two Resource Book** p. 12 for more practice.

A lesson on using context clues appears on page 56 in the Pupil's Edition.

Potato Pie

Customizing Instruction

Less Proficient Readers

Have students keep these questions in mind as they read.

- What is the setting of the story?
  Answer: in the present, a New York hotel room; earlier in the evening, at Charley's apartment in Harlem; in Buddy's childhood, their sharecropper cabin
- What is the relationship between the narrator and Charley?
  Answer: They are brothers.
- How does the narrator feel about Charley?
  Answer: He loves and respects him.

Students Acquiring English

Students new to English may encounter slight difficulty when reading dialect. Encourage them to work in pairs and take turns reading the dialogue out loud to one another. They can then share ideas about the meaning of particularly difficult sentences.

Use **Spanish Study Guide** for additional support, pp. 56–58.

Gifted and Talented

When students finish reading, have them find more information about sharecroppers, the Great Migration, and Harlem. Ask them to compare the setting of the story with their findings.

BLOCK SCHEDULING: MANAGING TIME

If your schedule requires that you cover the lesson objectives in a shorter time, use . . .

- Preparing to Read, p. 239
- Thinking Through Literature, p. 252
- Vocabulary in Action, p. 253
- Grammar in Context, p. 254

If you want to take advantage of longer class time, use . . .

- TE Teaching Options: Preteaching Vocabulary p. 240; Viewing and Representing, p. 242; Standardized Test Practice, p. 248
- Choices & Challenges, p. 253

Reading and Analyzing

Reading Skills and Strategies: CLARIFYING

A Ask students to explain why the narrator's parents only come "into sharp focus" on special occasions. Why aren't more memories of his parents available?

Possible Response: The narrator's parents were very poor and worked in the fields from very early in the morning until late at night. He remembers them mainly from special occasions when they were not working.

B Ask students what they think the narrator means when he says Lil and Charley "rode herd on the rest of us while Pa and Mama toiled in fields not their own."

Possible Response: The narrator means Lil and Charley took care of the younger children while their parents worked in fields owned by someone else.

I turn from the window and flop down on the bed, shoes and all. Perhaps because of what happened this afternoon or maybe just because I see Charley so seldom, my thoughts hover over him like hummingbirds. The cheerful, impersonal tidiness of this room is a world away from Charley's walk-up flat in Harlem and a hundred worlds from the bare, noisy shanty[1] where he and the rest of us spent what there was of childhood. I close my eyes, and side by side I see the Charley of my boyhood and the Charley of this afternoon, as clearly as if I were looking at a split TV screen. Another surge of love, seasoned with gratitude, wells up in me.

As far as I know, Charley never had any childhood at all. The oldest children of sharecroppers never do. Mama and Pa were shadowy figures whose voices I heard vaguely
1 in the morning when sleep was shallow and whom I glimpsed as they left for the field before I was fully awake or as they trudged wearily into the house at night when my lids were irresistibly heavy.

They came into sharp focus only on special occasions. One such occasion was the day when
A the crops were in and the sharecroppers were paid. In our cabin there was so much excitement in the air that even I, the "baby," responded to it. For weeks we had been running out of things that we could neither grow nor get on credit. On the evening of that day we waited anxiously for our parents' return. Then we would cluster around the rough wooden table—I on Lil's lap or clinging to Charley's neck, little Alberta nervously tugging her plait,[2] Jamie crouched at Mama's elbow, like a panther about to spring, and all seven of us silent for once, waiting. Pa would place the money on the table—gently, for it was made from the sweat of their bodies and from their children's tears. Mama would count it out in little piles, her dark face stern and, I think now, beautiful. Not with the hollow beauty of well-modeled features but with the strong radiance of one who has suffered and never yielded.

"This for store bill," she would mutter, making a little pile. "This for c'llection. This
for piece o'gingham[3] . . ." and so on, stretching 2
the money as tight over our collective needs as Jamie's outgrown pants were stretched over my bottom. "Well, that's the crop." She would look up at Pa at last. "It'll do." Pa's face would relax, and a general grin flitted from child to child. We would survive, at least for the present.

The other time when my parents were solid entities was at church. On Sundays we would don our threadbare Sunday-go-to-meeting clothes and tramp, along with neighbors similarly attired, to the Tabernacle Baptist Church, the frail edifice of bare boards held together by who knows what, which was all that my parents ever knew of security and future promise.

Being the youngest and therefore the most likely to err, I was plopped between my father and my mother on the long wooden bench. They sat huge and eternal like twin mountains at my sides. I remember my father's still, black profile silhouetted against the sunny window, looking back into dark recesses of time, into some dim antiquity,[4] like an ancient ceremonial mask. My mother's face, usually sternly set, changed with

1. **shanty:** shack.
2. **plait:** braid.
3. **piece o'gingham** (ə-gĭng′əm)**:** piece of a type of cotton cloth with a checked pattern.
4. **antiquity** (ăn-tĭk′wĭ-tē)**:** ancient time.

WORDS TO KNOW
impersonal (ĭm-pûr′sə-nəl) *adj.* showing no emotion or signs of personality
entity (ĕn′tĭ-tē) *n.* a being
edifice (ĕd′ə-fĭs) *n.* building; structure

242

Teaching Options

Mini Lesson Viewing and Representing

Spring Planting **by Jonathan Green**

ART APPRECIATION Tell students that Jonathan Green captured the essence of his Gullah heritage in his work. The Gullahs are African Americans of the Sea Islands and tidewater area of South Carolina and Georgia. They are noted for their pride, dignity, and strong religious faith.

Application Ask students whether the workers in the painting are like Buddy's parents. Why or why not?

Possible Responses: The workers in the painting are like Buddy's parents in that they may be sharecroppers working a field. They are both facing the house in the background and seem to be working toward it. This may suggest their desire to finish their work and go home. Buddy's parents also worked very long days and spent little time with their family.

Spring Planting (1988), Jonathan Green. Oil on masonite, 24″ × 32″.
Collection of Shigeki Masui. Photograph by Tim Stamm.

the varying nuances of her emotion, its planes shifting, shaped by the soft highlights of the sanctuary, as she progressed from a subdued "amen" to a loud "Help me, Jesus" wrung from the depths of her gaunt frame.

My early memories of my parents are associated with special occasions. The contours[5] of my everyday were shaped by Lil and Charley, the oldest children, who rode herd on the rest of us while Pa and Mama toiled in fields not their own. Not until years later did I realize that Lil and Charley were little more than children themselves.

B

Lil had the loudest, screechiest voice in the county. When she yelled, "Boy, you better git yourself in here!" you *got* yourself in there. It was Lil who caught and bathed us, Lil who fed us and sent us to school, Lil who punished us when we needed punishing and comforted us when we needed comforting. If her voice was loud, so was her laughter. When she laughed, everybody laughed. And when Lil sang, everybody listened.

Charley was taller than anybody in the world, including, I was certain, God. From his shoulders, where I spent considerable time in the earliest years, the world had a different perspective. I looked down at tops of heads rather than at the undersides of chins. As I

5. **contours** (kŏn′to͝orz′): outlines.

WORDS TO KNOW

nuance (no͞o′äns′) *n.* subtle or slight variation
gaunt (gônt) *adj.* thin and bony

243

Customizing Instruction

Less Proficient Readers

1 Have students explain what the narrator means when he says his parents were "shadowy figures," and that their money "was made from the sweat of their bodies and from their children's tears."

Possible Response: The narrator refers to his parents as "shadowy figures" because they were only home when it was dark and he was asleep. His parents worked hard for their money so it was made "from the sweat of their bodies." Because his parents worked so long and were not home for their children, the money was made from "their children's tears."

Students Acquiring English

2 Explain to students that characters in this story speak in a dialect. Help students understand the following passage in dialect.

"This for c'llection. This for piece o' gingham . . ."

Answer: This is for the collection. This is for a piece of gingham.

Reading and Analyzing

Reading Skills and Strategies: CLARIFYING

A Ask students to explain why Buddy's success in school is a personal triumph for his brothers and sisters.
Possible Response: Buddy's siblings had to leave school to work and support the family. Because they helped Buddy stay in school, they each shared in his success in getting through school.

Reading Skills and Strategies: QUESTIONING

B Ask students what they think Buddy means when he says, "I realized in that moment that I wasn't necessarily the smartest–only the youngest."
Possible Response: Buddy is referring to his brothers' and sisters' potential. He attributes his success more to his circumstances than to his intelligence.

grew older, Charley became more father than brother. Those days return in fragments of splintered memory: Charley's slender, dark hands whittling a toy from a chunk of wood, his face thin and intense, brown as the loaves Lil baked when there was flour. Charley's quick fingers guiding a stick of charred kindling over a bit of scrap paper, making a wondrous picture take shape—Jamie's face or Alberta's rag doll or the spare figure of our bony brown dog. Charley's voice low and terrible in the dark, telling ghost stories so delightfully dreadful that later in the night the moan of the wind through the chinks in the wall sent us scurrying to the security of Charley's pallet,[6] Charley's sleeping form.

Some memories are more than fragmentary. I can still feel the *whap* of the wet dishrag across my mouth. Somehow I developed a stutter,
1 which Charley was determined to cure. Someone had told him that an effective cure was to slap the stutterer across the mouth with a sopping wet dishrag. Thereafter, whenever I began, "Let's g-g-g—," *whap!* from nowhere would come the ubiquitous[7] rag. Charley would always insist, "I don't want hurt you none, Buddy—" and *whap* again. I don't know when or why I stopped stuttering. But I stopped.

Already laid waste by poverty, we were easy prey for ignorance and superstition, which hunted us like hawks. We sought education feverishly—and, for most of us, futilely, for the sum total of our combined energies was required for mere brute survival. Inevitably each child had to leave school and bear his share of the eternal burden.

Eventually the family's hopes for learning fastened on me, the youngest. I remember—I *think* I remember, for I could not have been more than five—one frigid day Pa huddled on a rickety stool before the coal stove, took me on his knee and studied me gravely. I was a skinny little thing, they tell me, with large, solemn eyes.

Charley was determined that I would break the chain of poverty, that I would "be somebody."

"Well, boy," Pa said at last, "if you got to depend on your looks for what you get out'n this world, you just as well lay down right now." His hand was rough from the plow, but gentle as it touched my cheek. "Lucky for you, you got a *mind*. And that's something ain't everybody got. You go to school, boy, get yourself some learning. Make something out'n yourself. Ain't nothing you can't do if you got learning."

Charley was determined that I would break the chain of poverty, that I would "be somebody." As we worked our small vegetable garden in the sun or pulled a bucket of brackish water from the well, Charley would tell me, "You ain gon be no poor farmer, Buddy. You gon be a teacher or maybe a doctor or a lawyer. One thing, bad as you is, you ain gon be no preacher." 2

I loved school with a desperate passion, which became more intense when I began to realize what a monumental struggle it was for my parents and brothers and sisters to keep me there. The cramped, dingy classroom became a

6. **pallet:** a narrow bed.
7. **ubiquitous** (yo͞o-bĭk′wĭ-təs): seemingly everywhere.

battleground where I was victorious. I stayed on top of my class. With glee I outread, outfigured, and outspelled the country boys who mocked my poverty, calling me "the boy with eyes in back of his head"—the "eyes" being the perpetual[8] holes in my hand-me-down pants.

As the years passed, the economic strain was eased enough to make it possible for me to go on to high school. There were fewer mouths to feed, for one thing. Alberta went North to find work at sixteen; Jamie died at twelve.

A I finished high school at the head of my class. For Mama and Pa and each of my brothers and sisters, my success was a personal triumph. One by one they came to me the week before commencement, bringing crumpled dollar bills and coins long hoarded, muttering, "Here, Buddy, put this on your gradiation clothes." My graduation suit was the first suit that was all my own.

On graduation night our cabin (less crowded now) was a frantic collage of frayed nerves. I thought Charley would drive me mad.

"Buddy, you ain pressed out them pants right. . . . Can't you git a better shine on them shoes? . . . Lord, you done messed up that tie!"

Overwhelmed by the combination of Charley's nerves and my own, I finally exploded. "Man, cut it out!" Abruptly he stopped tugging at my tie, and I was afraid I had hurt his feelings. "It's okay, Charley. Look, you're strangling me. The tie's okay."

Charley relaxed a little and gave a rather sheepish chuckle. "Sure, Buddy." He gave my shoulder a rough joggle. "But you gotta look good. You *somebody.*"

My valedictory address[9] was the usual idealistic, sentimental nonsense. I have forgotten what I said that night, but the sight of Mama and Pa and the rest is like a lithograph[10] burned on my memory; Lil, her round face made beautiful by her proud smile; Pa, his head held high, eyes loving and fierce; Mama radiant. Years later when her shriveled hands were finally still, my mind kept coming back to her as she was now. I believe this moment was the apex[11] of her entire life. All of them, even Alberta down from Baltimore—different now, but united with them in her pride. And Charley, on the end of the row, still somehow the protector of them all. Charley, looking as if he were in the presence of something sacred.

As I made my way through the carefully rehearsed speech, it was as if part of me were standing outside watching the whole thing—their proud, work-weary faces, myself wearing the suit that was their combined strength and love and hope: Lil with her lovely, low-pitched voice, Charley with the hands of an artist, Pa and Mama with who knows what potential lost with their sweat in the fields. I realized in that moment that I wasn't necessarily the smartest—only the youngest. B

And the luckiest. The war came along, and I exchanged three years of my life (including a fair amount of my blood and a great deal of pain) for the GI Bill[12] and a college education. Strange how time can slip by like water flowing through your fingers. One by one the changes came—the old house empty at last, the rest of us scattered; for me, marriage, graduate school, kids, a professorship, and by now a thickening waistline and thinning hair. My mind spins off the years, and I am back to this afternoon and today's Charley—still long and lean, still gentle-eyed, still my greatest fan, and still determined to keep me on the ball. 3

8. **perpetual** (pər-pĕch′o͞o-əl): eternal; constant.

9. **valedictory** (văl′ĭ-dĭk′tə-rē) **address:** a farewell speech delivered at graduation, usually by the top student in the class.

10. **lithograph:** a print produced by treating an image area to retain ink while the nonimage areas are treated to repel ink.

11. **apex** (ā′pĕks): highest point.

12. **GI Bill:** federal legislation passed after World War II to help veterans pay for college.

Customizing Instruction

Less Proficient Readers

1 Use the following questions to help students understand why Charley hits Buddy with a dishrag.

- What is Charley hoping to do when he hits Buddy with the wet dishrag?
  Possible Response: Charley is trying to cure Buddy of his stuttering.
- Is Charley a cruel person?
  Possible Response: No, he really does not want to hurt Buddy. He wants to improve Buddy's speech.

Students Acquiring English

2 Ask students to give the meaning of this sentence in Standard English.
Possible Response: However, because you are as bad as you are, you will never be a preacher.

3 Help students understand what Buddy means when he says "my mind spins off the years."
Possible Response: He means he stops thinking about the past and returns his thoughts to the present.

Reading and Analyzing

Reading Skills and Strategies: CLARIFYING

A Ask students to explain why Buddy doesn't tell Charley and Bea that he will be in town and visiting. What does he mean when he says he does not want to "be company"?

Possible Response: Buddy doesn't want Charley and Bea to go to a lot of trouble getting ready for his visit or to act formally, as they would for "company."

Reading Skills and Strategies: COMPARE AND CONTRAST

B Ask students to compare Charley now to the way the narrator describes him when they were children. In what ways is he the same? How has he changed?

Possible Response: Charley remains the protective older brother, even when he and Buddy are grown. He loves Buddy and treats him like a celebrity. Even though Buddy is an adult, Charley still explains things to him patiently. Charley is older now, drives a taxicab, and has a family of his own.

A I didn't tell Charley I would be at a professional meeting in New York and would surely visit; he and Bea would have spent days in fixing up, and I would have had to be company. No, I would drop in on them, take them by surprise before they had a chance to stiffen up. I was eager to see them—it had been so long. Yesterday and this morning were taken up with meetings in the posh Fifth Avenue hotel—a place we could not have dreamed in our boyhood. Late this afternoon I shook loose and headed for Harlem, hoping that Charley still came home for a few hours before his evening run. Leaving the glare and glitter of downtown, I entered the subway that lurks like the dark, inscrutable *id*[13] beneath the surface of the city. When I emerged, I was in Harlem.

Whenever I come to Harlem I feel somehow as if I were coming home—to some mythic ancestral home. The problems are real, the people are real—yet there is some mysterious epic quality about Harlem, as if all black people began and ended there, as if each had left something of himself. As if in Harlem the very heart of Blackness pulsed its beautiful, tortured rhythms. Joining the throngs of people that saunter Lenox Avenue late afternoons, I headed for Charley's apartment. Along the way I savored the panorama of Harlem—women with shopping bags trudging wearily home; little kids flitting saucily through the crowd; groups of adolescent boys striding boldly along—some boisterous, some ominously silent; tables of merchandise spread on the sidewalks with hawkers singing their siren songs of irresistible 1 bargains; a blaring microphone sending forth waves of words to draw passersby into a restless bunch around a slender young man whose eyes have seen Truth; defeated men standing around on street corners or sitting on steps, heads down, hands idle; posters announcing Garvey Day;[14] "Buy Black" stamped on pavements; store windows bright with things African; stores still boarded up, a livid scar from last year's rioting. There was a terrible tension in the air; I thought of how quickly dry timber becomes a roaring fire from a single spark.

I mounted the steps of Charley's building—old and in need of paint, like all the rest—and pushed the button to his apartment. The graffiti on the dirty wall recorded the fantasies of past visitors. Some of it was even a dialogue of sorts. . . .

B "Well . . . it's Buddy!" roared Charley as I arrived on the third floor. "Bea! Bea! Come here, girl, it's Buddy!" And somehow I was simultaneously shaking Charley's hand, getting clapped on the back, and being buried in the fervor of Bea's gigantic hug. They swept me from the hall into their dim apartment.

". . . Buddy, what you doing here? Whyn't you tell me you was coming to New York?" His face was so lit up with pleasure that in spite of the inroads of time, he still looked like the Charley of years gone by, excited over a new litter of kittens.

"The place look a mess! Whyn't you let us know?" put in Bea, suddenly distressed.

"Looks fine to me, girl. And so do you!"

And she did. Bea is a fine-looking woman, plump and firm still, with rich brown skin and thick black hair.

"Mary, Lucy, look, Uncle Buddy's here!" Two neat little girls came shyly from the TV. Uncle Buddy was something of a celebrity in this house.

I hugged them heartily, much to their

13. **id:** according to the theories of Sigmund Freud, part of the mind associated with instinct and primitive needs.

14. **Garvey Day:** a special day in Harlem commemorating Jamaican-born Marcus Garvey (1887–1940), who moved to New York and became a highly influential activist, calling for economic independence for blacks and advocating a "back to Africa" movement.

WORDS TO KNOW

panorama (păn′ə-răm′ə) *n.* an unobstructed view of a wide area
boisterous (boi′stər-əs) *adj.* loud, noisy, and unrestrained

> Whenever I come to Harlem I feel somehow as if I were coming home—to some mythic ancestral home.

discomfort. "Charley, where you getting all these pretty women?"

We all sat in the warm kitchen, where Bea was preparing dinner. It felt good there. Beautiful odors mingled in the air. Charley sprawled in a chair near mine, his long arms and legs akimbo.[15] No longer shy, the tinier girl sat on my lap, while her sister darted here and there like a merry little water bug. Bea bustled about, managing to keep up with both the conversation and the cooking.

I told them about the conference I was attending, and, knowing it would give them pleasure, I mentioned that I had addressed the group that morning. Charley's eyes glistened.

"You hear that, Bea?" he whispered. "Buddy done spoke in front of all them professors!"

"Sure I hear," Bea answered briskly, stirring something that was making an aromatic steam. "I bet he weren't even scared. I bet them professors learnt something, too."

We all chuckled. "Well anyway," I said, "I hope they did."

We talked about a hundred different things after that—Bea's job in the school cafeteria, my Jess and the kids, our scattered family.

"Seem like we don't git together no more, not since Mama and Pa passed on," said Charley sadly. "I ain't even got a Christmas card from Alberta for three-four year now."

"Well, ain't no two a y'all in the same city. An' everybody scratchin' to make ends meet," Bea replied. "Ain't nobody got time to git together."

"Yeah, that's the way it goes, I guess," I said.

"But it sure is good to see you, Buddy. Say, look, Lil told me bout the cash you sent the children last winter when Jake was out of work all that time. She sure 'preciated it."

"Lord, man, as close as you and Lil stuck to me when I was a kid, I owed her that and more. Say, Bea, did I ever tell you about the time—" and we swung into the usual reminiscences.

They insisted that I stay for dinner. Persuading me was no hard job: fish fried golden, ham hocks and collard greens, corn bread—if I'd *tried* to leave, my feet wouldn't have taken me. It was good to sit there in Charley's kitchen, my coat and tie flung over a chair, surrounded by soul food and love.

"Say, Buddy, a couple months back I picked up a kid from your school."

"No stuff."

"I axed him did he know you. He say he was in your class last year."

"Did you get his name?"

"No, I didn't ax him that. Man he told me you were the best teacher he had. He said you were one smart cat!" **2**

"He told you that cause you're my brother."

"Your *brother*—I didn't tell him I was your brother. I said you was a old friend of mine."

I put my fork down and leaned over. "What you tell him *that* for?"

Charley explained patiently as he had explained things when I was a child and had missed an obvious truth. "I didn't want your

15. **akimbo** (ə-kĭm′bō): bowed outward.

WORDS TO KNOW **reminiscence** (rĕm′ə-nĭs′əns) *n.* pleasant memory or recollection

247

Customizing Instruction

Students Acquiring English

1 Ask students what is meant by "a blaring microphone sending forth waves of words to draw passersby into a restless bunch around a slender young man whose eyes have seen Truth."

Possible Response: This passage is referring to someone calling out religious messages over a microphone.

Multiple Learning Styles

Visual Learners

Ask students to collaborate on a mural illustrating Charley's building and its surroundings, based on the details given in the story. Students can draw on the chalkboard or on a large piece of paper hung on the wall.

Students Acquiring English

2 Help students understand dialect such as the following:

> "No, I didn't ax him that. Man he told me you were the best teacher he had. He said you were one smart cat!"

Answer: No, I didn't ask him that. He told me you were the best teacher he had. He said you were very smart!

Reading and Analyzing

Literary Analysis: CONFLICT

Ask students to identify the conflict at the end of the story. How is the conflict resolved?

Possible Response: Charley and Buddy engage in a conflict at the end of the story when Charley refuses to let Buddy take the sweet potato pie into the hotel because it is in a brown paper bag. The conflict is resolved when Charley carries the pie into the hotel for Buddy, so that Buddy can maintain his appearance as a respectable professional.

Literary Analysis CHARACTERIZATION

What do the argument between Buddy and Charley and its resolution reveal about Charley's character?

Possible Response: Charley wants to make sure that Buddy's appearance is appropriate, but he also wants to make sure that Buddy has the things he wants.

Looking Along Broadway Towards Grace Church (1981), Red Grooms. Mixed media, 71″ × 63 ¾″ × 28 ¾″. Courtesy Marlborough Gallery, New York. Copyright © 2000 Red Grooms/Artists Rights Society (ARS), New York.

students to know your brother wasn't nothing but a cab driver. You *somebody.*"

"You're a nut," I said gently. "You should've told that kid the truth." I wanted to say, I'm proud of you, you've got more on the ball than most people I know, I wouldn't have been anything at all except for you. But he would have been embarrassed.

Bea brought in the dessert—homemade sweet potato pie! "Buddy, I must of knew you were coming! I just had a mind I wanted to make sweet potato pie."

There's nothing in this world I like better than Bea's sweet potato pie! "Lord, girl, how you expect me to eat all that?"

The slice she put before me was outrageously big—and moist and covered with a light, golden crust—I ate it all.

"Bea, I'm gonna have to eat and run," I said at last.

Charley guffawed. "Much as you et, I don't 1
see how you gonna *walk,* let alone *run.*" He went out to get his cab from the garage several blocks away.

Teaching Options

Assessment Standardized Test Practice

CHOOSING THE BEST SUMMARY For some standardized tests students will be asked to choose the best summary of a passage. To provide students with help in choosing the best summary, read aloud or write on the board the following question:

Which of the following best summarizes Charley and Buddy's conversation about Buddy's former student?

A. Charley picked up a former student of Buddy's, who said Buddy was the best teacher he ever had. Charley doesn't tell the student that he is Buddy's brother because he doesn't want the boy to know Buddy has a brother who is a taxicab driver.

B. Charley tells Buddy he picked up one of his students in his cab a few months back. Charley forgot to ask the boy his name.

C. Charley picked up a former student in his cab who said Buddy was "one smart cat." Charley and the student made pleasant conversation.

Lead students through the process of choosing the best summary. Consider each choice. Point out that while all of the statements contain accurate information about the story, the best summary should include the most important information. For this reason, **A** is the best choice.

Bea was washing the tiny girl's face. "Wait a minute, Buddy, I'm gon give you the rest of that pie to take with you."

"Great!" I'd eaten all I could hold, but my *spirit* was still hungry for sweet potato pie.

Bea got out some waxed paper and wrapped up the rest of the pie. "That'll do you for a snack tonight." She slipped it into a brown paper bag.

I gave her a long goodbye hug. "Bea, I love you for a lot of things. Your cooking is one of them!" We had a last comfortable laugh together. I kissed the little girls and went outside to wait for Charley, holding the bag of pie reverently.

In a minute Charley's ancient cab limped to the curb. I plopped into the seat next to him, and we headed downtown. Soon we were assailed[16] by the garish lights of New York on a sultry spring night. We chatted as Charley skillfully managed the heavy traffic. I looked at his long hands on the wheel and wondered what they could have done with artists' brushes.

We stopped a bit down the street from my hotel. I invited him in, but he said he had to get on with his evening run. But as I opened the door to get out, he commanded in the old familiar voice, "Buddy, you wait!"

For a moment I thought my coat was torn or something. "What's wrong?"

"What's that you got there?"

I was bewildered. "That? You mean this bag? That's a piece of sweet potato pie Bea fixed for me."

"You ain't going through the lobby of no big hotel carrying no brown paper bag."

"Man, you *crazy!* Of course I'm going—Look, Bea fixed it for me—*That's my pie—*"

Charley's eyes were miserable. "Folks in that hotel don't go through the lobby carrying no brown paper bags. That's *country.* And you can't neither. You *somebody,* Buddy. You got to be *right.* Now gimme that bag."

"I want that pie, Charley. I've got nothing to prove to anybody—"

I couldn't believe it. But there was no point in arguing. Foolish as it seemed to me, it was important to him.

"You got to look *right,* Buddy. Can't nobody look dignified carrying a brown paper bag."

So finally, thinking how tasty it would have been and how seldom I got a chance to eat anything that good, I handed over my bag of sweet potato pie. If it was that important to him—

I tried not to show my irritation. "Okay, man—take care now." I slammed the door harder than I had intended, walked rapidly to the hotel, and entered the brilliant, crowded lobby.

"That Charley!" I thought. Walking slower now, I crossed the carpeted lobby toward the elevator, still thinking of my lost snack. I had to admit that of all the herd of people who jostled each other in the lobby, not one was carrying a brown paper bag. Or anything but expensive attaché cases or slick packages from exclusive shops. I suppose we all operate according to the symbols that are meaningful to us, and to Charley a brown paper bag symbolizes the humble life he thought I had left. I was *somebody.*

I don't know what made me glance back, but I did. And suddenly the tears of laughter, toil, and love of a lifetime burst around me like fireworks in a night sky.

For there, following a few steps behind, came Charley, proudly carrying a brown paper bag full of sweet potato pie. ❖

16. **assailed:** attacked.

WORDS TO KNOW

reverently (rĕv′ər-ənt-lē) *adv.* with great respect
sultry (sŭl′trē) *adj.* warm and humid

Customizing Instruction

Students Acquiring English

1 Explain to students that *guffawed* means "laughed."

Less Proficient Readers

Use the following questions to help students understand the ending.

- Why won't Charley let Buddy take the sweet potato pie into the hotel?
  Possible Response: The pie is in a brown paper bag, and Charley doesn't think the bag fits his brother's image as a professional.
- Why does Buddy agree to leave the pie in the cab even though he really wants it?
  Possible Response: Buddy doesn't want to argue with the brother he loves.
- Why does Charley carry the pie into the hotel himself?
  Possible Response: He feels it's okay for him, a cabdriver, to carry a brown paper bag, but not for his brother, because Buddy is somebody important. At the same time, he wants Buddy to have the pie.

Reading and Analyzing

Reading Skills and Strategies: COMPARING

Ask students to compare Salvador with Charley in "Sweet Potato Pie."

Possible Response: Both boys are very poor. Both accept responsibility for the welfare of their siblings.

Salvador Late or Early

Sandra Cisneros

Salvador with eyes the color of caterpillar, Salvador of the crooked hair and crooked teeth, Salvador whose name the teacher cannot remember, is a boy who is no one's friend, runs along somewhere in that vague direction where homes are the color of bad weather, lives behind a raw wood doorway, shakes the sleepy brothers awake, ties their shoes, combs their hair with water, feeds them milk and corn flakes from a tin cup in the dim dark of the morning.

Salvador, late or early, sooner or later arrives with the string of younger brothers ready. Helps his mama, who is busy with the business of the baby. Tugs the arms of Cecilio, Arturito, makes them hurry, because today, like yesterday, Arturito has dropped the cigar box of crayons, has let go the hundred little fingers of red, green, yellow, blue, and nub of black sticks that tumble and spill over and beyond the asphalt puddles until the crossing-guard lady holds back the blur of traffic for Salvador to collect them again.

Salvador inside that wrinkled shirt, inside the throat that must clear itself and apologize each time it speaks, inside that forty-pound body of boy with its geography of scars, its history of hurt, limbs stuffed with feathers and rags, in what part of the eyes, in what part of the heart, in that cage of the chest where something throbs with both fists and knows only what Salvador knows, inside that body too small to contain the hundred balloons of happiness, the single guitar of grief, is a boy like any other disappearing out the door, beside the schoolyard gate, where he has told his brothers they must wait. Collects the hands of Cecilio and Arturito, scuttles off dodging the many schoolyard colors, the elbows and wrists crisscrossing, the several shoes running. Grows small and smaller to the eye, dissolves into the bright horizon, flutters in the air before disappearing like a memory of kites.

Street Corner Shop, Colin Middleton. Christie's Images.

Customizing Instruction

Less Proficient Readers

Ask the following questions to help students visualize Salvador:

- The author says Salvador has eyes the color of a caterpillar. What color is a caterpillar?
  Possible Response: Green, gray, dark brown, or black
- The author says Salvador lives in an area where the homes are the color of bad weather. What color is bad weather?
  Possible Response: Gray

Students Acquiring English

Help students understand what the author means when she says Salvador's body has a "geography of scars." In this passage, she means Salvador's body is covered with scars as a map or a globe is covered with distinct regions and features.

GUIDING STUDENT RESPONSE

Connect to the Literature

1. **What Do You Think?**
Students might feel that Charley is a very loving and admirable brother, or they might feel that he has an exaggerated sense of the difference between himself and his brother.

Comprehension Check
- Buddy loves his family and respects them a great deal.
- Charley acts as Buddy's protector and advisor. He is a father-figure to Buddy.
- Buddy escapes poverty by staying in school and graduating from college and graduate school.
- Buddy does not tell Charley he is coming to visit because he does not want Charley and Bea to go to a lot of trouble preparing for his visit.

Use Selection Quiz
Unit Two Resource Book, p. 14.

Think Critically

2. Possible Response: Charley took care of Buddy when they were children and takes great pride in his younger brother's accomplishments. Buddy regards Charley with great love and respect, and is aware of the sacrifices made for him.
3. Possible Response: Charley learned to become responsible at a very young age because he needed to take care of his younger siblings. As the youngest, Buddy was given the opportunity to remain in school, in part because he had fewer family responsibilities and in part because the family had fewer mouths to feed when he was in high school.
4. Possible Response: The narrator feels as if he's going home when he visits Harlem because it seems like the ancestral home of black people.
5. Some students may think they'd feel proud of Buddy and glad they could help him. Others may say they'd feel jealous or ashamed.
6. Possible Response: The author's use of flashback is very effective. Understanding the narrator's past helps us understand why he and Charley act the way they do now.

Thinking through the LITERATURE

Connect to the Literature

1. **What Do You Think?**
What is your reaction to Charley when he comes after Buddy at the end of the story?

Comprehension Check
- What does Buddy think of his family?
- What part does Charley play in Buddy's childhood?
- How does Buddy escape poverty?
- Why doesn't Buddy tell Charley of his plans to visit?

Think Critically

2. How would you describe the relationship between Buddy and Charley? Cite evidence to support your answer.
3. How did their family life help to shape Buddy's and Charley's lives and personalities?

THINK ABOUT
- their respective positions in the family birth order
- the family's livelihood
- Buddy's comment that "Charley never had any childhood at all"

4. Why do you think the **narrator** feels that visiting Harlem is somehow like going home?
5. If you were Charley, how would you feel about your life compared with Buddy's?
6. ACTIVE READING **SEQUENCE OF EVENTS** Refer to the timeline of events in your READER'S NOTEBOOK. In your opinion, how effective is the author's use of **flashback**? Explain.

Extend Interpretations

7. **Comparing Texts** In her character sketch, "Salvador Late or Early" on page 250, Sandra Cisneros describes Salvador, a young boy. Which of the characters in "Sweet Potato Pie" do you think Salvador most resembles? Explain your answer.
8. **Connect to Life** At the end of the story Buddy states, "I suppose we all operate according to the symbols that are meaningful to us." What **symbols** are important in your life, and what do they represent? For example, a car might represent freedom or success.

Literary Analysis

CHARACTERIZATION To develop characters, writers rely on the techniques of **characterization.** There are four basic methods of characterization:
- physical description
- a character's own thoughts, words, or actions
- the thoughts, words, or actions of other characters about or toward a character
- the narrator's own direct comments about a character

Cooperative Learning Activity In a small group, choose one of the characters from "Sweet Potato Pie" to study. Create a chart like the one at the bottom of the page, showing the author's methods of developing each character. Compare your charts with those of other groups. Which methods of characterization does Collier use most in this story?

DIALECT The regional variation of a language spoken by a particular group is called a **dialect.** Dialects vary in pronunciation, vocabulary, colloquial expressions, sentence structure, and grammatical construction. Writers use dialect to establish setting and to develop characters. In Collier's story, the characters speak a Southern African-American dialect.

Paired Activity With a partner, look for examples of dialect in "Sweet Potato Pie" and read them aloud. Discuss how the author's use of dialect contributes to this story.

Character	How character looks	What character thinks, says, or does	How others respond to character	What narrator says about character
Buddy				

Extend Interpretations

Comparing Texts Salvador most resembles Charley because he, like Charley, must care for his younger brothers. He is very poor and forced to act responsibly at a very young age.

Connect to Life Student symbols will vary. Have students list at least three symbols that are important to them, and give a coherent explanation of their meanings.

Literary Analysis

Characterization Make a chart on the chalkboard for the whole class in which different groups compile their own entries.

Dialect Some students may feel self-conscious about reading dialect aloud, while others may be inclined to exaggerate. Encourage them to be respectful when reading dialect.

Writing Options

1. Charley's Journal Imagine that Charley, too, recorded his impressions of the evening with his brother. Write a diary entry that makes use of details from the story to show what Charley saw and felt.

2. Family Poem Write a poem describing one of the family scenes from this story. Use details provided in the story, and invent any other details necessary to round out the scene and make it believable. Place the poem in your **Working Portfolio.**

Writing Handbook
See pages 1153–1154: Descriptive Writing.

Activities & Explorations

1. Set Building Design a stage set for this story, depicting either the sharecropper's shanty or Charley's flat in Harlem. Look back over the story for clues about the setting, and decide which details to show on stage. Then create either a model or drawing of your set and display it for your class. ~ **ART/THEATER**

2. Public Service Announcement Create a 60-second TV or radio commercial that shows Buddy urging high-school students to stay in school. In writing Buddy's script, make use of what you learn from the story. When you have finished, perform your commercial for the class.
~ **SPEAKING AND LISTENING**

Inquiry & Research

Harlem Heritage Research the history of Harlem as a center of African-American culture. Investigate one element of Harlem culture, such as music or art. Then develop an oral presentation on the subject for your class. Make use of any audio-visual aids that will help you communicate with your audience.

More Online: Research Starter
www.mcdougallittell.com

Art Connection

Working the Fields The paintings of Jonathan Green depict the Gullah people, a group of African Americans who inhabit the coastal islands of South Carolina where he grew up. What does this painting, *Spring Planting,* make you think about the life of a farmer?

Vocabulary in Action

EXERCISE A: CONTEXT CLUES On your paper, write the Word to Know that best completes each sentence.

1. From the apartment's picture window, the narrator could see a _______ of Harlem street life below.
2. The narrator's _______ of his childhood shows how family members can remain devoted to one another even in the midst of poverty and hard times.
3. Summer nights in New York are often _______, especially in August.
4. The hotel had a prestigious address and was quite an imposing _______.
5. Collier uses dialogue and description to convey every subtle _______ of her characters' personalities.

EXERCISE B: ASSESSMENT PRACTICE

On your paper, write the letter of the word that is a synonym of each boldfaced word.

1. **gaunt:** (a) short, (b) thin, (c) fat
2. **boisterous:** (a) silent, (b) angry, (c) noisy
3. **impersonal:** (a) friendly, (b) emotionless, (c) passionate
4. **entity:** (a) being, (b) detective, (c) taxpayer
5. **reverently:** (a) respectfully, (b) insolently, (c) brutally

WORDS TO KNOW				
boisterous	entity	impersonal	panorama	reverently
edifice	gaunt	nuance	reminiscence	sultry

Mini Lesson Inquiry & Research

HARLEM RENAISSANCE In the 1920s, African-American culture in Harlem blossomed in a movement known as the Harlem Renaissance. Primarily a literary movement, it also included developments in the visual arts and music. Artists, musicians, and writers gathered and shared ideas, stimulating new confidence and racial pride. Students may wish to do their oral presentation on a single writer, artist, or musician from this era.

Students should generate researchable questions. They should locate appropriate print and nonprint information using text and technical resources including on-line databases and the Internet. Their reports should reflect the conclusions drawn from the information gathered.

Writing Options

1. **Charley's Journal** To help students start writing, have them reread the story and list the events they want to include in the journal.
2. **Family Poem** To help students get started, ask them to select a scene in the story that is meaningful to them. Then, have them think about how this scene could be expressed in a poem. Remind them that they can invent details to supplement the scene if necessary.

Activities & Explorations

1. **Set Building** Students' designs should demonstrate an understanding of the story's setting.
2. **Public Service Announcement** Encourage students to videotape their commercials. Students should begin by rereading the story and listing any details that they want to include in the commercial, such as Buddy persevering even though he was very poor. The final product should demonstrate an understanding of the story.

Inquiry & Research

Harlem Heritage Students may want to focus on a single figure, such as an artist, musician, or political figure. Encourage students to choose a variety of subject matters so that the class presentations can provide students with a broad range of material on Harlem culture.

Art Connection

Working the Fields The life of a farmer includes a lot of silent hard work, where family members work side by side.

Vocabulary in Action

Exercise A
1. panorama
2. reminiscence
3. sultry
4. edifice
5. nuance

Exercise B
1. b
2. c
3. b
4. a
5. a

Grammar in Context: Compound Verbs

In "Sweet Potato Pie," Eugenia Collier uses a compound verb to describe the actions of the narrator, Buddy, when he was a child.

> **With glee I outread, outfigured, and outspelled the country boys who mocked my poverty.**

A **compound verb** consists of two or more verbs that have the same subject and are joined by a conjunction. Think about the choices Collier made in writing the sentence above and about the effects of those choices.

Choice	Effect
• Use of three verbs rather than one • Use of verbs containing the same prefix *(out-)*	• Emphasizes that Buddy did better than his classmates in every subject • Creates rhythm and emphasis

Apply to Your Writing You can use compound verbs to combine ideas and to create rhythms in your own writing. Compound verbs can also help you convey sequences of events.

WRITING EXERCISE Combine each pair of sentences to form a single sentence containing a compound verb.

Punctuation Tip: In a series containing three or more elements, use a comma after each element except the last one.

Example: ***Original*** Charley protects his youngest brother, Buddy. Charley also guides and encourages him.
Rewritten Charley protects, guides, and encourages his youngest brother, Buddy.

1. On payday Mama gathers the money on the table. Then she counts it and divides it.
2. Lil punishes the younger children. But she also comforts them.
3. After Pa studies Buddy's face, he ponders. Then he decides.
4. On graduation night, Charley nags Buddy. Charley criticizes him; he also fusses at him.
5. While Buddy makes his graduation speech, his family members beam. They also sit proudly and look respectful.

Grammar Handbook
Punctuation, p. 1203

Eugenia Collier
1928–

Other Works
Breeder and Other Stories
Spread My Wings

Upbringing and Education Eugenia Collier was born in Baltimore, Maryland, which is still her home. The daughter of a physician and a teacher, she graduated with honors from Howard University in 1948 and earned her master of arts from Columbia University in 1950. She went on to become a professor of English.

Stepping Stones Collier wrote that when she discovered "the richness, the diversity, the beauty of my black heritage," it helped her determine her personal and professional goals. After five years as a caseworker in the Baltimore Department of Public Welfare, Collier turned to teaching college. Later, she started writing, and in 1969, she received the Gwendolyn Brooks Award for Fiction from *Negro Digest* for her story "Marigolds."

Publication Soon after she received the award, anthologies and magazines began to carry Collier's work. Her stories attempt to convey something about the lives of a segment of society that Collier felt was not well represented in contemporary fiction. Along with her poems and articles, her stories have appeared in *Negro Digest, TV Guide, Black World,* the *New York Times,* and other journals.

Grammar in Context

WRITING EXERCISE Answers may vary slightly.

1. On payday Mama gathers, counts, and divides the money on the table.
2. Lil punishes but also comforts the younger children.
3. After Pa studies Buddy's face, he ponders and decides.
4. On graduation night Charley nags, criticizes, and fusses at Buddy.
5. While Buddy makes his graduation speech, his family members beam, sit proudly, and look respectful.

Teaching Options

Mini Lesson Grammar

PARALLEL COMPOUND PREDICATES For use with Grammar in Context. Remind students that a compound predicate is made of two or more verbs or verb phrases joined by a conjunction. Each verb that is part of a compound predicate must be in the same form or tense. For example, a verb may be in either the present tense (plain form), the past tense (ending with *-ed*), past participle (verb with *have, has,* or *had*), or present participle (ending with *-ing*) form.

Model Sentence
Each child had to leave school and bear his share of the eternal burden.

Instruction
- Write the model sentence on the board.
- Underline the verbs as shown. Explain that *leave* and *bear* are parallel.
- Have students identify that they are both in the present tense.

Use **Unit Two Resource Book,** p. 13.
Use **Grammar Transparencies and Copymasters,** p. 86.

Use McDougal Littell's ***Language Network,*** Chapter 2, for more instruction in parallel compound predicates.

Simile

Poetry by
N. SCOTT MOMADAY

Moon Rondeau

Poetry by
CARL SANDBURG

Woman

Poetry by
NIKKI GIOVANNI

Mondrian Dancing (1984–1985), Susan Rothenberg. Oil on canvas, 78¼″ × 91″. St. Louis (Missouri) Art Museum. Purchase: Funds given by the Shoenberg Foundation, Inc.

Connect to Your Life

The Nature of Love Poets often rely on nature to communicate their ideas about love. In Shakespeare's "Sonnet 18," for example, the speaker's beloved is compared to a summer's day. If a poet were to write about you, what aspect of nature might you be compared to? Write an impromptu poem that draws a comparison between you and an object or event in nature. Let your imagination run free.

Build Background

Nature's Gifts The poet William Blake once expressed his desire "to see a World in a Grain of Sand / And a heaven in a Wild Flower." In the hands of poets, the objects of the natural world—plant, mineral, and animal—can take on a significance limited only by one's imagination. To a poet, a blade of grass, the smell of leaf mold, or the movement of deer may evoke original thought. Each of the following three poems makes use of objects in the natural world to explore the mysteries of romantic relationships.

Focus Your Reading

LITERARY ANALYSIS FIGURATIVE LANGUAGE Words or phrases known as **figurative language** communicate ideas beyond the ordinary, literal meanings of the words. These lines from the poem "Woman" provide an example:

she wanted to be a robin singing
through the leaves

In all likelihood, the woman does not really want to be transformed into a bird, but this passage does tell you about her personality and her desires. As you read the poems that follow, look carefully at the use of figurative language.

ACTIVE READING UNDERSTANDING COMPARISONS Poets often make **comparisons** in order to convey meaning or emotion in fresh and interesting ways. In the poem "Moon Rondeau," the poet compares love with a door. Like a door, love can open the way to new experiences and new vistas.

READER'S NOTEBOOK As you read the following poems, look for comparisons. For each poem, create a chart like the one shown to track the comparisons that you find. First identify the two things being compared. Then jot down a few words or a phrase that describes the meaning or emotions that the comparison evokes.

Item 1	Item 2	Suggested Meaning
love	door	Love can open the way to new experiences.

OVERVIEW

Objectives

1. understand and appreciate three **poems (Literary Analysis)**
2. interpret **figurative language (Literary Analysis)**
3. **understand comparisons (Active Reading)**

Summary

All three poems discuss the nature of relationships. In "Simile," the poet likens the wariness of lovers (who have probably quarreled) to vigilant deer. In "Moon Rondeau," two lovers compare their love to a door that opens on a beautiful spring evening. They see the moon as an emblem of their love. The poem "Woman" describes a woman who imagines herself transformed into a blade of grass, a robin, a web, a book, and a bulb—but her man will not go along with her. Finally, the woman decides that she must hold on to her own identity, regardless of what the man does or thinks.

Thematic Link

In the relationships in these poems, the ties that bind are sometimes strained, sometimes full of promise, sometimes misplaced.

5-Minute Warm-Up

Daily Language SkillBuilder

Have students **proofread** the display sentences on page 223i and write them correctly. The sentences also appear on Transparency 8 of **Grammar Transparencies and Copymasters.**

LESSON RESOURCES

UNIT TWO RESOURCE BOOK, pp. 15–16

ASSESSMENT RESOURCES

Formal Assessment, pp. 45–46

Teacher's Guide to Assessment and Portfolio Use

Test Generator

SKILLS TRANSPARENCIES AND COPYMASTERS

Literary Analysis

- Symbols and Figurative Language, T21 (for Activity, p. 260)

Reading and Critical Thinking

- Organizational Chart: Horizontal, T51 (for Reader's Notebook, p. 255)

Grammar

- Objects of Prepositions, C94 (for Mini Lesson, p. 258)

Writing

- Sensory Word List, T14 (for Writing Option 1, p. 261)
- Figurative Language and Sound Devices, T15 (for Writing Option 1, p. 261)
- Poem, C27 (for Writing Option 1, p. 261)

INTEGRATED TECHNOLOGY

Audio Library

Visit our website:
www.mcdougallittell.com

TEACHING THE LITERATURE

Reading and Analyzing

Reading Skills and Strategies: PREVIEW

Have students preview the selection. Ask students to study the poems' titles and the images on pp. 257–259, and have them make predictions about the poems' settings and the speakers. Discuss with students the Build Background feature on p. 255. Before students begin reading, give them brief summaries of the poems.

Active Reading UNDERSTANDING COMPARISONS

Encourage students to read the poems line by line when looking for comparisons, because figures of speech can be easy to overlook.

Use **Unit Two Resource Book,** p. 15 for more practice.

Literary Analysis FIGURATIVE LANGUAGE

Point out to students that when people use the word *literally* in a sentence, they are generally making the point that they are not using figurative language, but speaking literally.

Use **Unit Two Resource Book,** p. 16 for more practice.

Thinking Through the Literature

1. Students may say that the poem is quiet, pensive, or tentative.
2. Possible Responses: wariness, fear, or caution
3. The speaker may feel hopeful or may feel nervous that the relationship will not succeed.
4. Student responses will vary, but should include a discussion of the value and difficulties of argument in a relationship.

Simile

N. Scott Momaday

What did we say to each other
that now we are as the deer
who walk in single file
with heads high
with ears forward
with eyes watchful
with hooves always placed on
firm ground
in whose limbs there is latent flight

8 **latent** (lāt'nt): present but not active; potential.

Thinking Through the Literature

1. How would you describe the **mood,** or feeling, of this poem?
2. ACTIVE READING UNDERSTANDING COMPARISONS Review the chart that you completed in your READER'S NOTEBOOK for this poem. What human emotions and experiences are evoked by comparing the two people to deer?

   THINK ABOUT
   - the relationship between the speaker and the person being addressed
   - the physical description of the deer
   - what is suggested by the first line of the poem
3. How do you think the **speaker** feels about the future of the relationship he is describing? Explain your opinion.
4. Is it possible for two people to remain close without sometimes quarreling? Share your opinions with classmates.

BLOCK SCHEDULING: MANAGING TIME

If your schedule requires that you cover the lesson objectives in a shorter time, use . . .
- Preparing to Read, p. 255
- Thinking Through the Literature, p. 260

If you want to take advantage of longer class time, use . . .
- TE Teaching Options: Viewing and Representing, p. 257; Speaking and Listening, p. 261; Standardized Test Practice, p. 262;
- Choices & Challenges and Author Activity, pp. 261–262

Corn Maiden (1982), David Dawangyumptewa. Photo Copyright © 1987 by Jerry Jacka.

Customizing Instruction

Less Proficient Readers

Set a Purpose Have students read to find out how the speaker of each poem feels about the relationship he or she describes.

Students Acquiring English

Explain to students that poets do not always use conventional punctuation and capitalization. "Simile" is one long question, despite the lack of end punctuation. "Moon Rondeau," however, is fully punctuated and should be read with the usual pauses and inflections indicated by punctuation. "Woman" is completely without punctuation or capitalization, but it is easier to understand if each stanza is read as if it were a sentence.

Use **Spanish Study Guide** for additional support, pp. 59–61.

Gifted and Talented

In these poems about love relationships, the poets compare love, relationships, or people to concrete objects rather than abstract concepts. Have students discuss why this might be. Invite them to think about what kind of abstract concepts might be used in such a comparison, and consider which approach they think is more effective.

Mini Lesson Viewing and Representing

Corn Maiden **by David Dawangyumptewa**

ART APPRECIATION In the watercolor painting *Corn Maiden,* Hopi artist David Dawangyumptewa portrays the Corn Maiden legend of his people. In the top center, the sun shines in the starry sky. Below the sun are stylized clouds, which bring rain. The two Corn Maidens, symmetrically opposite each other, signify ripeness and plenty. The painting is stylized—that is, designed according to an artificial pattern rather than imitating nature.

Instruction Ask students to analyze the composition of the painting. How do the elements of the painting work together?

Possible Responses: The presence of the sun, stars, moon, and clouds in the sky at the same time suggests the cyclical nature of the universe.

Application Ask students what connection they see between the painting and the poem "Simile."

Possible Response: Both use simple natural images; one could say that the painter and the poet both turn to nature in their search for meaning. Both are created by Native Americans.

Reading and Analyzing

Literary Analysis: FREE VERSE

Remind students that free verse uses neither rhyme nor fixed meter. Instead, it is written in lines of irregular length, and it often more clearly reflects natural speech patterns.

Have students read one of the three poems in this selection aloud. Ask them whether it is in free verse and how they can tell.

Possible Response: All three poems are written in free verse. The absence of fixed meter, the absence of rhyme, the irregular line lengths, and the irregular stanza lengths indicate that these poems are in free verse.

Active Reading: VISUALIZE

There are five pairs of images used in "Woman," one in each of the first five stanzas. Have students describe each of these image pairs, and discuss how it helps describe what the woman wants.

Possible Response: Answers will vary for each image. Overall, the images imply that she wants him to help give her a place and a purpose.

Thinking Through the Literature

1. Two sweethearts look at the moon and declare that all lovers, such as they, own the moon.
2. Possible Response: The two are very whimsical and creative; together they seem very comfortable and in love with nature, as well as each other.
3. Possible Response: People in love sometimes feel so aware of themselves and nothing else that they think the world revolves around them. This sense of importance and specialness is reflected in the rapturous quality of the rest of the poem as well.

Mondrian Dancing (1984–1985), Susan Rothenberg. Oil on canvas, 78 ¼″ × 91″. St. Louis (Missouri) Art Museum. Purchase: Funds given by the Shoenberg Foundation, Inc.

Moon Rondeau

Carl Sandburg

1

"Love is a door we shall open together."
So they told each other under the moon
One evening when the smell of leaf mould
And the beginnings of roses and potatoes
Came on a wind.

Late in the hours of that evening
They looked long at the moon and called it
A silver button, a copper coin, a bronze wafer,
A plaque of gold, a vanished diadem,
A brass hat dripping from deep waters.

"People like us,
us two,
We own the moon."

3 leaf mould: a mixture of decomposed leaves and other organic material.

9 diadem (dī'ə-dĕm'): a crown.

Thinking Through the Literature

1. **Comprehension Check** What happens in this poem?
2. **ACTIVE READING** **UNDERSTANDING COMPARISONS** Refer to the chart you made for this poem in your **READER'S NOTEBOOK**. In this poem, the two people in love compare the moon to six different objects. What do these comparisons suggest about the couple and their relationship?
3. How do you interpret the poem's last three lines, and how do those lines help you to understand the rest of the poem?

Teaching Options

Mini Lesson Grammar

OBJECTS OF PREPOSITIONS Prepositions show the relationship of a noun (the object of the preposition) to another part of the sentence. Often, prepositions orient things or people in time and space. The object of a preposition is the noun that the preposition connects to the sentence. Write the following sentence on the board, underlining the prepositions and their objects and placing the prepositional phrases in brackets:

Just [after the 7th-inning stretch], the batter hit the ball [into the stands] and ran triumphantly [around the bases].

Remind students to identify the preposition first, then find the noun that is its object; modifiers like articles and adjectives may come between the preposition and its object.

WOMAN

Nikki Giovanni

she wanted to be a blade
of grass amid the fields
but he wouldn't agree
to be the dandelion

she wanted to be a robin singing
through the leaves
but he refused to be
her tree

she spun herself into a web
and looking for a place to rest
turned to him
but he stood straight
declining to be her corner

she tried to be a book
but he wouldn't read

she turned herself into a bulb
but he wouldn't let her grow

she decided to become
a woman
and though he still refused
to be a man
she decided it was all
right

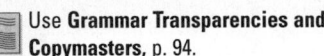

White Breeze (1995), Jonathan Green. Oil on canvas, 48″ × 60″. Collection of Gilbert and Elizabeth Ney. Photograph by Tim Stamm.

Customizing Instruction

Less Proficient Readers

1 Explain that a rondeau is a lyrical poem of French origin with a particular structure and rhyme scheme; it is also the name of a type of medieval French song. Although "Moon Rondeau" does not have a rhyme scheme, it is certainly a lyrical poem, and it seems likely that Sandburg had this form in mind when writing and titling the poem.

Exercises Have students copy the following sentences. Ask them to underline the prepositions and objects and place the prepositional phrase within brackets.

1. I have often compared myself to a tiger, but never to a deer.
   Answer: to a tiger; to a deer
2. When two people quarrel about a problem, reconciling can be difficult.
   Answer: about a problem
3. Last night the moon passed behind a cloud, but it was so bright that the light shone through the cloud cover and into my bedroom.
   Answer: behind a cloud; through the cloud cover; into my bedroom
4. I would rather live alone in the woods than in the bustling, anonymous city.
   Answer: in the woods; in the bustling, anonymous city
5. She imagined that she was a blade of grass growing on a hillside.
   Answer: of grass; on a hillside

Use **Grammar Transparencies and Copymasters,** p. 94.

Use McDougal Littell's ***Language Network,*** Chapter 3, for more instruction in objects of prepositions.

GUIDING STUDENT RESPONSE

Connect to the Literature

1. **What Do You Think?**
Students may admire her for choosing to be secure in her own identity; others might be confused about what she wants and be unsure of what to think about her.

Comprehension Check
- The man refuses to become her complement or support.
- To stand on her own.

Think Critically

2. Encourage students to think about each "transformation" separately. Why might the woman want to become a blade of grass, a robin, or a spider? Ask students what each stanza tells us about the woman's aspirations.
3. Student responses will vary, but may suggest that the poem is about both love and independence; when love disappoints, then one must become independent.
4. Students may suspect that she is happy to be rid of the man, or they may think that she is resigned to being alone, but still wishes he were there.

Thinking through the LITERATURE

Connect to the Literature

1. **What Do You Think?** What do you think of the woman in this poem?

Comprehension Check
- What happens each time the woman tries to forge a relationship with the man?
- What does she decide in the end?

Think Critically

2. ACTIVE READING UNDERSTANDING COMPARISONS After reviewing the chart that you completed in your READER'S NOTEBOOK for this poem, discuss what each of the comparisons suggests about the woman and her relationship with the man. Which comparison do you think is the most revealing?

THINK ABOUT
- what the woman ("she") wants from the man ("he")
- what the poem suggests about the man's personality
- what the woman learns from her experience
- the meaning of the poem's last **stanza**

3. Do you think this poem is mainly about love or about independence? Support your answer with evidence from the poem.
4. How do you think the woman now feels about her relationship with the man? Explain.

Extend Interpretations

5. **Comparing Texts** In terms of **mood,** which of the two preceding poems, "Moon Rondeau" and "Simile," is most like "Woman"? Give details from the poems to support your answer.
6. **Comparing Texts** Which of the three poems makes the most effective use of **figurative language** drawn from nature? Support your answer with examples from the poems.
7. **Connect to Life** Of the three poems, which most nearly reflects your own attitude about love relationships? Explain your answer.

Literary Analysis

FIGURATIVE LANGUAGE Poets use **figurative language** to convey ideas beyond the literal meanings of the words. When the couple in Sandburg's poem describes the moon as a "vanished diadem," the poet is not telling the reader that there is an actual crown in the sky, but suggesting that the moon is in its waning crescent stage. His use of this image lends the moon an elegance that it would not have, had he described it literally. Figurative language also includes specific **figures of speech,** such as **simile** and **metaphor.** A simile is a stated comparison using the words *like* or *as:* "now we are as the deer." A metaphor is an exaggerated comparison that does not use the words *like* or *as:* "Love is a door we shall open together."

Activity Identify other examples of similes and metaphors or other figurative language in the poems. Then choose one poem and think of new comparisons for an extension of that poem. Try to retain the spirit of the original poem.

FREE VERSE Poetry that does not contain regular patterns of **rhyme** and **meter** is known as **free verse.** The lines in free verse often flow more naturally than rhymed, metrical lines do. Therefore, they achieve a rhythm more like everyday human speech.

Paired Activity With a partner, take turns reading the three poems aloud. In what ways does each poem resemble everyday speech? Discuss your responses.

Extend Interpretations

Comparing Texts Students should use specific detail in making their comparisons.

Comparing Texts Student responses will vary, but should demonstrate an understanding of the figurative language and its effects.

Connect to Life If possible, encourage students to make connections to the emotional content and mood of the poem they choose. Some students may be reluctant to discuss their own attitudes about love relationships.

Literary Analysis

Figurative Language Students may find more examples of metaphor than simile in these poems. Encourage students to brainstorm ideas for figures of speech before they begin writing.

Free Verse Encourage students to experiment with their methods of reading the poems aloud; they might read first in a very stylized, rhythmic fashion and then in a manner that sounds more like everyday speech.

Choices & CHALLENGES

Writing Options

1. His Poem "Woman" is told from "her" point of view. How might "he" see the relationship? Write a poem modeled on "Woman," from the man's perspective. Place the entry in your **Working Portfolio.**

2. Love Letter Choose one of the three poems and write a letter from one character in the poem to the other. Think of what the poem tells you about the couple's relationship and use it as a basis for your letter.

Activities & Explorations

1. Poetic Pictures Choose one poem and create an illustration or series of illustrations to convey an idea or emotion suggested by the poem. ~ **ART**

2. Multimedia Presentation Using a computer with appropriate software, create a multimedia presentation to accompany one of the poems. Use graphics, sound effects, and music to capture the mood and meaning of the poem.
~ **VIEWING AND REPRESENTING**

Inquiry & Research

Dictionary Explorations Look up the **etymology,** or word origins, of *metaphor* and *simile.* How do the origins of these terms help you to understand and remember their meaning? Then look up the word *rondeau.* What do the different meanings suggest about the relationship between poetry and song?

Art Connection

She Wanted to Be What connection do you see between the woman and the sky in this painting? In light of this connection, what similarity do you see between the painting and the poem "Woman"?

N. Scott Momaday
1934–

Other Works
The Way to Rainy Mountain
Angle of Geese and Other Poems
The Names: A Memoir

Inspired by Heritage N. Scott Momaday's poetry and prose reflect his deeply felt love for his Kiowa Indian ancestry. His father, a member of the Kiowa tribe, was one of the finest Native American artists of his day; his mother was a writer and a teacher. When asked how his heritage affected his work, Momaday told an interviewer, "When I was growing up on the reservations of the Southwest, I saw people who were deeply involved in their traditional life, in the memories of their blood. They had, as far as I could see, a certain strength and beauty that I find missing in the modern world at large. I like to celebrate that involvement in my writing."

Literary Achievement Momaday has received a number of honors and awards for his writing, including the Pulitzer Prize for fiction in 1969 for his novel *House Made of Dawn.* Momaday has since published several books of poetry and fiction, as well as essays and articles on preserving the environment. Momaday says, "I sometimes think [writing] is a very lonely sort of work. But when you get into it, it can be exhilarating, tremendously fulfilling and stimulating."

Author Activity

Kiowa Values How does Momaday's experiences growing up as a Kiowa resonate in his writing? Read some additional pieces of his writing and look for evidence of his Kiowa upbringing. Share your findings in class.

Mini Lesson Speaking and Listening

POETRY AND SONG Poetry is closely connected to song. The ancient Greeks, for instance, sang their epics and lyrics. Although modern written poetry may seem to have lost its obvious connection to music, remind students that the rhythm we hear when we read poetry aloud is similar to the rhythm they hear in contemporary songs.

Instruction Ask students to bring in examples of popular songs. Choose one song and transcribe its lyrics together as a class. Have students read the words as poetry, without the music. Ask students what is lost without the music. What is gained?

Possible Response Students may notice a loss of emotion when the words are read without the music. Generally, words are easier to recognize and analyze when they are studied apart from the music, so students may notice that they understand complex lyrics more readily without music.

Writing Options

1. **His Poem** Students may write their poems either as a response to the woman's desires, or as a poem about how men seek and find independence. Tell students that they may write their poems either as free verse or in rhyme and meter.
2. **Love Letter** Encourage students to imagine the relationship before, during, and after the poem. Students should allow their imaginations free reign.

Activities & Explorations

1. **Poetic Pictures** Using the artwork in this section, point out that the illustrations may be representational or abstract. Encourage students to write captions for their illustrations to help identify their content.
2. **Multimedia Presentation** This activity is appropriate for small groups. Encourage students to use information from the author biographies in their presentations.

Inquiry & Research

Dictionary Explorations Students may need some assistance deciphering the etymological notation in the dictionary definitions. Refer to the mini lesson on page 330 for more practice. Some students may wish to look in the *Oxford English Dictionary* for extensive etymological information.

Art Connection

She Wanted to Be Students should note that the woman in the painting almost seems to become a part of the sky, like the woman in the poem, who imagines herself becoming a part of nature.

Author Activity

Kiowa Values Momaday wrote a mythic history of the Kiowas, entitled *The Way to Rainy Mountain* (1969). A novel, *The Ancient Child,* and a book of essays, *Ancestral Voices: Conversations with N. Scott Momaday,* both appeared in 1989. Encourage students to read about the Kiowa people in encyclopedia entries and history books.

Author Activity

What's Poetry Before reading Sandburg's definitions, have students compose their own definition of poetry.

Author Activity

Spoken Verse Encourage students to experiment with their performances. Remind students that Giovanni began writing in the 1960s, and that she was influenced by Amiri Baraka and James Baldwin. Encourage students to read selections by these authors as well.

Carl Sandburg

1878–1967

Other Works

Selected Poems of Carl Sandburg
Honey and Salt
The American Songbag
Good Morning, America
Abraham Lincoln

Jack of All Trades Sandburg was born in Galesburg, Illinois, to Swedish parents. He finished grammar school at age 13 and started driving a milk wagon. Over the coming years, he held a long series of jobs, among them harvesting ice, washing dishes, and working for a tinsmith. After serving in the Spanish-American War (April–August 1898), Sandburg attended Lombard College in Galesburg, where he captained the basketball team and edited the college newspaper. After college, he continued from job to job, with stints as a salesman, fireman, pamphleteer, and newspaperman.

Rise to Fame In 1914, Sandburg published a group of poems in *Poetry* magazine, and two years later, his first book of poems, *Chicago Poems.* With those two publications, Sandburg embarked on his path to widespread fame. Over the next 50 years, he wrote poetry, history, biography, and fiction; his biography of Abraham Lincoln is considered one of the great works of the 20th century. Sandburg had a deep, rich voice and traveled widely to read his poetry, sometimes accompanying himself on the guitar.

The Good Life Despite his fame, Sandburg continued to lead a modest life, wanting most "to be out of jail, . . . to eat regular, . . . to get what I write printed, . . . a little love at home, . . . [and] to sing every day." Sandburg won two Pulitzer Prizes, one in poetry and one in history.

Author Activity

What's Poetry? In his book *Good Morning, America,* Sandburg provides 38 definitions of poetry. Look them up and discuss them with your class. How do they fit the poems you have read?

Nikki Giovanni

1943–

Other Works

Black Feeling, Black Talk/Black Judgement
Cotton Candy on a Rainy Day
Those Who Ride the Night Winds
Conversations with Nikki Giovanni
Truth Is on Its Way

Young Militant Nikki Giovanni's maternal grandmother was one of the great inspirations of her life. She was outspoken and proud of her race, and Giovanni grew up to be like her grandmother. In college, she became an activist in the black political movements of the 1960s, and her first volumes of poems combine militant rage with skillful wordplay. These volumes established Giovanni as a leading voice among contemporary African-American poets. In the early 1970s, after the birth of her son Tommy, her work became more introspective, turning from the political to the personal. She began to concentrate and sharpen her powers as a poet, writing of themes such as family love, loneliness, and frustration. Black pride, however, continues to echo throughout her poetry.

Storyteller Another important aspect of Giovanni's poetry is its sound and rhythm. "I come from a long line of storytellers," she once said. Her grandfather was a Latin scholar and her mother a lover of literature; both loved telling stories. "I appreciated the quality and the rhythm of the telling of the stories," Giovanni said. It was important to her to use language in ways that could be spoken aloud. She has made numerous recordings of her poetry.

Author Activity

Spoken Verse Locate a recording of Giovanni reading her own poetry. Listen to the rhythm and accents she gives her poems. Then select one poem and rehearse your own performance of it.

Teaching Options

Assessment Standardized Test Practice

ALTERNATIVE ENDING You can assess your students' ability to analyze and critically evaluate their understanding of the poems by asking them to write a sequel to "Simile," "Moon Rondeau," or "Woman" in paragraph form. What might happen to the characters after the end of the poem?

RUBRIC

3 **Full Accomplishment** Response reflects a full understanding of the characters and theme of the poem.

2 **Substantial Accomplishment** Response shows a general understanding of the characters and theme of the poem.

1 **Little or Partial Accomplishment** Response shows little or no understanding of the characters or theme of the poem.

The Importance of Comparison

Comparison is an important aspect of thinking. When you see how an object can be compared to other objects, your understanding of the object is enriched. Literature provides many examples of comparisons, or analogies; two are shown on the right.

Shakespeare could simply have said that his beloved was beautiful, and Sandburg could have described the moon as shiny and round. By using comparisons, however, they were able to make their descriptions more insightful and vivid.

Shall I compare thee to a summer's day?
Thou art more lovely and more temperate:
—William Shakespeare, "Sonnet 18"

Late in the hours of that evening
They looked long at the moon and called it
A silver button, a copper coin, a bronze wafer,
A plaque of gold, a vanished diadem,
A brass hat dripping from deep waters.
—Carl Sandburg, "Moon Rondeau"

Strategies for Building Vocabulary

Literature is not the only place where analogies can be found. They are also found in tests, in problems that ask you to identify similarities in the relationships expressed by pairs of words. Analogy problems are often stated like this:

CHRONIC : RECURRING :: (A) gymnast : agile, (B) irritation : fury, (C) gratitude : appreciation, (D) sporadic : ongoing

This problem may be restated as "*Chronic* is to *recurring* as ___?___ is to ___?___." To solve such a problem, use the following strategies.

❶ Find the Relationship Figure out the relationship expressed by the first two words before thinking about the analogy as a whole. In the example above, the capitalized words are synonyms, or words with like meanings. Therefore, you need to find a pair of synonyms among the choices. The correct answer is C—*gratitude* and *appreciation* are synonyms. The other pairs of words express different kinds of relationships.

Sometimes analogy problems are set up so that you need determine only the last word in each analogy, as in the following example:

MUSICIAN : HORN :: carpenter : ________
(A) house, (B) hammer, (C) carpentry, (D) music

❷ Kinds of Analogies The pairs of words in analogies can express a variety of kinds of relationships. The chart below shows several of the most common.

EXERCISE Complete each analogy by choosing a word from the following list. Identify the kind of relationship on which the analogy is based.

convalescence	**medicine**	**diligence**
irresistible	**amateur**	**fruit**
adamant	**inevitability**	**diminished**

1. CONVICTION : BELIEF :: dedication : ________
2. PLACID : AGITATED :: professional : ________
3. TRANSCEND : TRANSCENDENCE :: convalesce : ________
4. OCCASIONAL : INTERMINABLE :: attractive : ________
5. RETRIEVER : DOG :: apple : ________

Types of Relationships in Analogies

Type	Example	Relationship
Part to whole	BRANCH : TREE	is a part of
Synonyms	PLAUSIBLE : BELIEVABLE	means the same as
Antonyms	INDIFFERENCE : CONCERN	means the opposite of
Cause to effect	STARVATION : EMACIATION	results in or leads to
Object to purpose	LADDER : CLIMBING	is used for
Degree of intensity	TROTTING : GALLOPING	is less (or more) intense than
Grammar	INDIGNANT : INDIGNATION	is grammatically related to
Item to category	MARS : PLANET	is a type or example of

Building Vocabulary

Objectives
- complete analogies
- identify the kind of relationship in an analogy

EXERCISE
1. diligence: synonym
2. amateur: antonym
3. convalescence: cause to effect
4. irresistible: degree of intensity
5. fruit: item to category

Possible Objectives

You can use this selection to achieve one or more of the following objectives:

- enjoy silent sustained reading (Option One)
- read and analyze literature with a group (Option Two)
- use the Reader's Notebook to formulate questions about literature (Option Three)
- write in response to literature (Option Three)

Summary

The veterinarian James Herriot recalls Mrs. Donovan, an elderly woman who used to walk miles throughout Darrowby with her small terrier. When Mrs. Donovan's dog died, the old woman declared she would never have another dog. However, when Herriot found an emaciated, sore-covered golden retriever surviving in a filthy shed, Mrs. Donovan took the dog and transformed it into a happy, healthy pet. Whenever the old woman saw Herriot, she always exclaimed, "Mr. Herriot, haven't I made a difference to this dog!"

A Case of Cruelty

James Herriot felt very strong ties to animals of all kinds. For years he worked as a veterinarian, treating both pets and farm animals in a rural part of the English county of Yorkshire. Recognizing that his experiences might make for good reading, he eventually began to put them down on paper. Herriot won fame with a series of books about the veterinary practice he shared with his partner, Siegfried, in a village called Darrowby. "A Case of Cruelty," from that series, recounts an experience involving the "small animal" side of their practice.

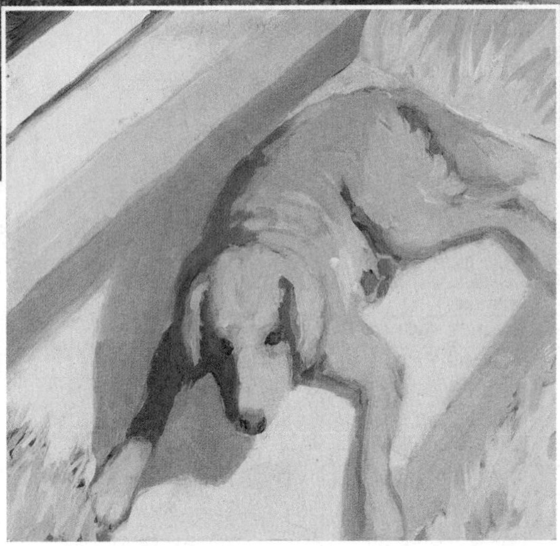

Golden Retriever (1972), Fairfield Porter. Oil on wood panel, 14⅛" × 15⅛", The Parrish Art Museum, Southampton, New York, gift of the Estate of Fairfield Porter (1980.10.124). Photo by Jim Strong, Inc.

James Herriot

The silvery haired old gentleman with the pleasant face didn't look the type to be easily upset, but his eyes glared at me angrily, and his lips quivered with indignation.

"Mr. Herriot," he said. "I have come to make a complaint. I strongly object to your callousness in subjecting my dog to unnecessary suffering."

"Suffering? What suffering?" I was mystified.

"I think you know, Mr. Herriot. I brought my dog in a few days ago. He was very lame, and I am referring to your treatment on that occasion."

I nodded. "Yes, I remember it well . . . but where does the suffering come in?"

"Well, the poor animal is going around with his leg dangling, and I have it on good authority that the bone is fractured and should have been put in plaster immediately." The old gentleman stuck his chin out fiercely.

"All right, you can stop worrying," I said. "Your dog has a radial paralysis[1] caused by a blow on the ribs, and if you are patient and follow my treatment he'll gradually improve. In fact I think he'll recover completely."

"But he trails his leg when he walks."

"I know—that's typical, and to the layman it does give the appearance of a broken leg. But he shows no sign of pain, does he?"

1. **radial paralysis:** loss of movement in the lower part of the leg.

WORDS TO KNOW

indignation (ĭn′dĭg-nā′shən) *n.* anger aroused by something unjust, mean, or unworthy
callousness (kăl′əs-nĭs) *n.* emotional hardness; lack of feeling

Reading the Selection

Option One
Silent Sustained Reading

You might set aside time each week for independent reading. During this time, you and all of your students would read for enjoyment. "A Case of Cruelty" will appeal to many students and can be read independently in about 25 minutes. If you want to encourage students to read for pleasure, you might forgo assignments related to the selection. Should you want to make assignments, Options Two and Three offer suggestions.

Option Two
Shared Reading Groups

You may assign students to groups or allow them to choose their own. Students can read the selection together, alternately reading sections aloud, or they can read independently and meet to cooperate in a project that portrays some element of the story.

Possible Projects

- Students can view an episode on videocassette of *All Creatures Great and Small,* the PBS television series based on Herriot's books. Have students compare the episode to "A Case of Cruelty" in an oral review. Suggest that students begin with a brief summary of the episode, giving the title and their general opinion of the episode.
- Students can create a pamphlet titled "How to Care for a Dog." In the pamphlet, students should list the *do's* and *don'ts* of dog care based on the treatment of the animals in the selection. Students should include examples from the selection to illustrate each point.

Option Three
Reader's Notebook

Provide the following direction to students before they read:

Ask students to share their own stories about the pets they have had or have known. Then have students make predictions about "A Case of Cruelty" based on the story's title alone.

Tell students to read the selection, pausing at the end of column two, page 267. At that point, students should adjust their predictions. What is Mrs. Donovan feeling? What will happen next? Have them write any questions they would like to ask Herriot or Mrs. Donovan.

At the end of the story, students will return to their predictions. Ask them to note whether any of their predictions came true. Was the story predictable? What parts of the story did they enjoy most? In what way is the title ironic?

Have students describe a memorable experience in their Reader's Notebook that they have had with an animal. Have students compare their writing with Herriot's recollection.

Herriot's style abounds with lively, detailed descriptions of his characters and Roy, the golden retriever. Have students incorporate similar details to their writing.

"No, he seems quite happy, but this lady seemed to be absolutely sure of her facts. She was adamant."

"Lady?"

"Yes," said the old gentleman. "She is very clever with animals, and she came around to see if she could help in my dog's convalescence. She brought some excellent condition powders[2] with her."

"Ah!" A blinding shaft pierced the fog in my mind. All was suddenly clear. "It was Mrs. Donovan, wasn't it?"

"Well . . . er, yes. That was her name."

Old Mrs. Donovan was a woman who really got around. No matter what was going on in Darrowby—weddings, funerals, house-sales—you'd find the dumpy little figure and walnut face among the spectators, the darting, black-button eyes taking everything in. And always, on the end of its lead, her terrier dog.

When I say "old," I'm only guessing, because she appeared ageless; she seemed to have been around a long time, but she could have been anything between fifty-five and seventy-five. She certainly had the vitality of a young woman because she must have walked vast distances in her dedicated quest to keep abreast of events. Many people took an uncharitable view of her acute curiosity, but whatever the motivation, her activities took her into almost every channel of life in the town. One of these channels was our veterinary practice.

Because Mrs. Donovan, among her other widely ranging interests, was an animal doctor. In fact I think it would be safe to say that this facet of her life transcended all the others.

She could talk at length on the ailments of small animals, and she had a whole armory of medicines and remedies at her command, her two specialities being her miracle-working condition powders and a dog shampoo of unprecedented value for improving the coat. She had an uncanny ability to sniff out a sick animal, and it was not uncommon when I was on my rounds to find Mrs. Donovan's dark, gypsy face poised intently over what I had thought was my patient, while she administered calf's foot jelly[3] or one of her own patent nostrums.[4]

She could talk
at length on the ailments
of small animals.

~

I suffered more than Siegfried because I took a more active part in the small animal side of our practice. I was anxious to develop this aspect and to improve my image in this field, and Mrs. Donovan didn't help at all. "Young Mr. Herriot," she would confide to my clients, "is all right with cattle and such like, but he don't know nothing about dogs and cats."

And of course they believed her and had implicit faith in her. She had the irresistible mystic appeal of the amateur, and on top of that there was her habit, particularly endearing in Darrowby, of never charging for her advice, her medicines, her long periods of diligent nursing.

Older folk in the town told how her husband, an Irish farm worker, had died many years ago and

2. **condition powders:** medicines for keeping an animal in good condition.
3. **calf's foot jelly:** meat gelatin made by boiling calves' feet; an old-fashioned, nutritious remedy.
4. **patent nostrums** (păt′nt nŏs′trəmz): nonprescription medicines whose effectiveness has not been proven scientifically; quack remedies.

WORDS TO KNOW

adamant (ăd′ə-mənt) *adj.* remaining firm despite the pleas or reasoning of others; stubbornly unyielding
convalescence (kŏn′və-lĕs′əns) *n.* the gradual return to health and strength after an illness or an injury
transcend (trăn-sĕnd′) *v.* to move above and beyond; to be greater than
mystic (mĭs′tĭk) *adj.* showing supernatural powers; spiritual; inspiring mystery or wonder

how he must have had a "bit put away" because Mrs. Donovan had apparently been able to indulge all her interests over the years without financial strain. Since she inhabited the streets of Darrowby all day and every day, I often encountered her, and she always smiled up at me sweetly and told me how she had been sitting up all night with Mrs. So-and-so's dog that I'd been treating. She felt sure she'd be able to pull it through.

There was no smile on her face, however, on the day when she rushed into the surgery[5] while Siegfried and I were having tea.

"Mr. Herriot!" she gasped. "Can you come? My little dog's been run over!"

I jumped up and ran out to the car with her. She sat in the passenger seat with her head bowed, her hands clasped tightly on her knees.

"He slipped his collar and ran in front of a car," she murmured. "He's lying in front of the school half way up Cliffend Road. Please hurry."

I was there within three minutes, but as I bent over the dusty little body stretched on the pavement, I knew there was nothing I could do. The fast-glazing eyes, the faint, gasping respirations, the ghastly pallor of the mucous membranes[6] all told the same story.

"I'll take him back to the surgery and get some saline[7] into him, Mrs. Donovan," I said. "But I'm afraid he's had a massive internal hemorrhage.[8] Did you see what happened exactly?"

She gulped. "Yes, the wheel went right over him."

Ruptured liver, for sure. I passed my hands under the little animal and began to lift him gently, but as I did so, the breathing stopped, and the eyes stared fixedly ahead.

Mrs. Donovan sank to her knees, and for a few moments she gently stroked the rough hair of the head and chest. "He's dead, isn't he?" she whispered at last.

"I'm afraid he is," I said.

She got slowly to her feet and stood bewilderedly among the little group of bystanders on the pavement. Her lips moved, but she seemed unable to say any more.

I took her arm, led her over to the car and opened the door. "Get in and sit down," I said. "I'll run you home. Leave everything to me."

I wrapped the dog in my calving overall[9] and laid him in the boot[10] before driving away. It wasn't until we drew up outside Mrs. Donovan's house that she began to weep silently. I sat there without speaking till she finished. Then she wiped her eyes and turned to me.

"Do you think he suffered at all?"

"I'm certain he didn't. It was all so quick—he wouldn't know a thing about it."

She tried to smile. "Poor little Rex, I don't know what I'm going to do without him. We've traveled a few miles together, you know."

"Yes, you have. He had a wonderful life, Mrs. Donovan. And let me give you a bit of advice—you must get another dog. You'd be lost without one."

She shook her head. "No, I couldn't. That little dog meant too much to me. I couldn't let another take his place."

"Well I know that's how you feel just now, but I wish you'd think about it. I don't want to seem callous—I tell everybody this when they lose an animal, and I know it's good advice."

"Mr. Herriot, I'll never have another one." She shook her head again, very decisively. "Rex was my faithful friend for many years, and I just want to remember him. He's the last dog I'll ever have."

---

5. **surgery:** in Britain, a general term for a physician's or veterinarian's office.
6. **mucous membranes:** thin layers of tissue lining the nose, mouth, and other body passages.
7. **saline** (sā'lēn'): a salt solution used to stem the effects of blood loss.
8. **internal hemorrhage** (hĕm'ər-ĭj): excessive bleeding inside the body.
9. **calving overall:** a special heavy overall worn by the veterinarian assisting in the birth of a calf.
10. **boot:** British term for the trunk of a car.

After Reading

Possible Activities

Independent Activities

- Have students expand the description of a memorable experience with an animal they wrote about in their Reader's Notebook into a nonfiction narrative. Remind students to include all necessary plot elements and make their narratives as entertaining as possible.
- Students can write an editorial for the Darrowby paper on the discovery of Roy in the garden shed. Remind students that editorials usually have a persuasive purpose. Ask them to suggest a remedy that would limit or eliminate cruelty to animals.

Discussion Activities

- Use the questions formulated by students as the start of a discussion.
- Have students compare and contrast the life of the dogs in the poem "Eight Puppies" with the experiences Roy probably had as a puppy.
- Ask students how they would describe Mrs. Donovan. Have them consider the following points before the discussion begins: her opinion about Herriot's treatment of local pets; her presence at every community event; her reaction to the death of her terrier; and her dedication and actions toward Roy.

Assessment Opportunities

- You can assess student comprehension of the story by evaluating the questions students formulate in their Reader's Notebook.
- You can use any of the discussion questions as essay questions.
- You can have students turn any one of their Reader's Notebook entries into an essay.

A CASE OF CRUELTY 267

I often saw Mrs. Donovan around the town after this, and I was glad to see she was still as active as ever, though she looked strangely incomplete without the little dog on its lead. But it must have been over a month before I had the chance to speak to her.

It was on the afternoon that Inspector Halliday of the R.S.P.C.A.[11] rang me.

"Mr. Herriot," he said. "I'd like you to come and see an animal with me. A cruelty case."

"Right, what is it?"

"A dog, and it's pretty grim. A dreadful case of neglect." He gave me the name of a row of old brick cottages down by the river and said he'd meet me there.

Halliday was waiting for me, smart and business-like in his dark uniform, as I pulled up in the back lane behind the houses. He was a big, blond man with cheerful blue eyes, but he didn't smile as he came over to the car.

"He's in here," he said and led the way towards one of the doors in the long, crumbling wall. A few curious people were hanging around, and with a feeling of inevitability I recognized a gnome-like brown face. Trust Mrs. Donovan, I thought, to be among those present at a time like this.

We went through the door into the long garden. I had found that even the lowliest dwellings in Darrowby had long strips of land at the back as though the builders had taken it for granted that the country people who were going to live in them would want to occupy themselves with the pursuits of the soil; with vegetable and fruit growing, even stock keeping[12] in a small way. You usually found a pig there, a few hens, often pretty beds of flowers.

But this garden was a wilderness. A chilling air of desolation hung over the few gnarled apple and plum trees standing among a tangle of rank grass as though the place had been forsaken by all living creatures.

Halliday went over to a ramshackle wooden shed with peeling paint and a rusted corrugated iron roof. He produced a key, unlocked the padlock and dragged the door partly open. There was no window, and it wasn't easy to identify the jumble inside; broken gardening tools, an ancient mangle, rows of flower pots and partly used paint tins.[13] And right at the back, a dog sitting quietly.

I didn't notice him immediately because of the gloom and because the smell in the shed started me coughing, but as I drew closer, I saw that he was a big animal, sitting very upright, his collar secured by a chain to a ring in the wall. I had seen some thin dogs, but this advanced emaciation reminded me of my textbooks on anatomy; nowhere else did the bones of pelvis, face and rib cage stand out with such horrifying clarity. A deep, smoothed out hollow in the earth floor showed where he had lain, moved about, in fact lived, for a very long time.

The sight of the animal had a stupefying effect on me; I only half took in the rest of the scene—the filthy shreds of sacking scattered nearby, the bowl of scummy water.

"Look at his back end," Halliday muttered.

I carefully raised the dog from his sitting position and realized that the stench in the place was not entirely due to the piles of excrement. The hindquarters were a welter of pressure sores which had turned gangrenous,[14] and strips of sloughing tissue[15] hung down from them. There were similar sores along the sternum[16] and ribs. The coat, which seemed to be a dull yellow, was matted and caked with dirt.

11. **R.S.P.C.A.:** the Royal Society for the Prevention of Cruelty to Animals.
12. **stock keeping:** keeping farm animals.
13. **tins:** British term for cans.
14. **gangrenous** (găng′grə-nəs): infected with gangrene, which is the death or decay of body tissue due to loss of blood supply.
15. **sloughing** (slŭf′ĭng) **tissue:** dead body tissue separating from the surrounding living tissue.
16. **sternum:** the breastbone, from which the ribs branch off.

WORDS TO KNOW

rank (răngk) *adj.* growing abundantly or excessively

Old Farmhouse (1872), Edward Henry Fahey, RI. Watercolor and bodycolor, heightened with gum arabic, 13¾″ × 9¾″, Anthony Reed Gallery, London.

The inspector spoke again. "I don't think he's ever been out of here. He's only a young dog—about a year old—but I understand he's been in this shed since he was an eight-week-old pup. Somebody out in the lane heard a whimper, or he'd never have been found."

I felt a tightening of the throat and a sudden nausea which wasn't due to the smell. It was the thought of this patient animal sitting starved and forgotten in the darkness and filth for a year. I looked again at the dog and saw in his eyes only a calm trust. Some dogs would have barked their heads off and soon been discovered, some would have become terrified and vicious, but this was one of the totally undemanding kind, the kind which had complete faith in people and accepted all their actions without complaint. Just an occasional whimper perhaps as he sat interminably in the empty blackness which had been his world and at times wondered what it was all about.

"Well, Inspector, I hope you're going to throw the book at whoever's responsible," I said. Halliday grunted. "Oh, there won't be much done. It's a case of diminished responsibility. The owner's definitely simple. Lives with an aged mother who hardly knows what's going on either. I've seen the fellow, and it seems he threw in a bit of food when he felt like it, and that's about all he did. They'll fine him and stop him keeping an animal in the future but nothing more than that."

"I see." I reached out and stroked the dog's head, and he immediately responded by resting a paw on my wrist. There was a pathetic dignity about the way he held himself erect, the calm eyes regarding me, friendly and unafraid. "Well, you'll let me know if you want me in court."

"Of course, and thank you for coming along." Halliday hesitated for a moment. "And now I expect you'll want to put this poor thing out of his misery right away."

I continued to run my hand over the head and ears while I thought for a moment. "Yes . . . yes, I suppose so. We'd never find a home for him in this state. It's the kindest thing to do. Anyway, push the door wide open will you so that I can get a proper look at him."

In the improved light I examined him more thoroughly. Perfect teeth, well-proportioned limbs with a fringe of yellow hair. I put my stethoscope on his chest, and as I listened to the slow, strong thudding of the heart, the dog again put his paw on my hand.

I turned to Halliday, "You know, Inspector,

A CASE OF CRUELTY 269

inside this bag of bones there's a lovely healthy golden retriever. I wish there was some way of letting him out."

As I spoke, I noticed there was more than one figure in the door opening. A pair of black pebble eyes were peering intently at the big dog from behind the inspector's broad back. The other spectators had remained in the lane, but Mrs. Donovan's curiosity had been too much for her. I continued conversationally as though I hadn't seen her.

"You know, what this dog needs first of all is a good shampoo to clean up his matted coat."

"Huh?" said Halliday.

"Yes. And then he wants a long course of some really strong condition powders."

"What's that?" The inspector looked startled.

"There's no doubt about it," I said. "It's the only hope for him, but where are you going to find such things? Really powerful enough, I mean." I sighed and straightened up. "Ah well, I suppose there's nothing else for it. I'd better put him to sleep right away. I'll get the things from my car."

When I got back to the shed, Mrs. Donovan was already inside examining the dog despite the feeble remonstrances[17] of the big man.

"Look!" she said excitedly, pointing to a name roughly scratched on the collar. "His name's Roy." She smiled up at me. "It's a bit like Rex, isn't it, that name?"

"You know, Mrs. Donovan, now you mention it, it is. It's very like Rex, the way it comes off your tongue." I nodded seriously.

She stood silent for a few moments, obviously in the grip of a deep emotion, then she burst out.

"Can I have 'im? I can make him better, I know I can. Please, please let me have 'im!"

"Well I don't know," I said. "It's really up to the inspector. You'll have to get his permission."

Halliday looked at her in bewilderment, then he said: "Excuse me, Madam," and drew me to one side. We walked a few yards through the long grass and stopped under a tree.

"Mr. Herriot," he whispered, "I don't know what's going on here, but I can't just pass over an animal in this condition to anybody who has a casual whim. The poor beggar's had one bad break already—I think it's enough. This woman doesn't look a suitable person . . ."

I held up a hand. "Believe me, Inspector, you've nothing to worry about. She's a funny old stick, but she's been sent from heaven today. If anybody in Darrowby can give this dog a new life it's her."

Halliday still looked very doubtful. "But I still don't get it. What was all that stuff about him needing shampoos and condition powders?"

"Oh never mind about that. I'll tell you some other time. What he needs is lots of good grub, care and affection, and that's just what he'll get. You can take my word for it."

"All right, you seem very sure." Halliday looked at me for a second or two then turned and walked over to the eager little figure by the shed.

I had never before been deliberately on the lookout for Mrs. Donovan: she had just cropped up wherever I happened to be, but now I scanned the streets of Darrowby anxiously day by day without sighting her. I didn't like it when Gobber Newhouse got drunk and drove his bicycle determinedly through a barrier into a ten-foot hole where they were laying the new sewer and Mrs. Donovan was not in evidence among the happy crowd who watched the council workmen[18] and two policemen trying to get him out; and when she was nowhere to be seen when they had to fetch the fire engine to

17. **remonstrances** (rĭ-mŏn′strəns-ĭz): protests; complaints; objections.

18. **council workmen:** construction workers for the local government, here putting in the new sewer.

the fish and chip shop the night the fat burst into flames, I became seriously worried.

Maybe I should have called round to see how she was getting on with that dog. Certainly I had trimmed off the necrotic tissue[19] and dressed the sores before she took him away, but perhaps he needed something more than that. And yet at the time I had felt a strong conviction that the main thing was to get him out of there and clean him and feed him, and nature would do the rest. And I had a lot of faith in Mrs. Donovan—far more than she had in me—when it came to animal doctoring; it was hard to believe I'd been completely wrong.

It must have been nearly three weeks, and I was on the point of calling at her home, when I noticed her stumping briskly along the far side of the market place, peering closely into every shop window exactly as before. The only difference was that she had a big yellow dog on the end of the lead.

I turned the wheel and sent my car bumping over the cobbles till I was abreast of her. When she saw me getting out, she stopped and smiled impishly, but she didn't speak as I bent over Roy and examined him. He was still a skinny dog, but he looked bright and happy, his wounds were healthy and granulating[20] and there was not a speck of dirt in his coat or on his skin. I knew then what Mrs. Donovan had been doing all this time; she had been washing and combing and teasing at that filthy tangle till she had finally conquered it.

As I straightened up, she seized my wrist in a grip of surprising strength and looked up into my eyes.

"Now, Mr. Herriot," she said. "Haven't I made a difference to this dog!"

"You've done wonders, Mrs. Donovan," I said. "And you've been at him with that marvelous shampoo of yours, haven't you?"

She giggled and walked away, and from that

> I had a lot of faith in Mrs. Donovan—far more than she had in me.

day I saw the two of them frequently but at a distance, and something like two months went by before I had a chance to talk to her again. She was passing by the surgery as I was coming down the steps, and again she grabbed my wrist.

"Mr. Herriot," she said, just as she had done before. "Haven't I made a difference to this dog!"

I looked down at Roy with something akin to awe. He had grown and filled out, and his coat, no longer yellow but a rich gold, lay in luxuriant shining swathes over the well-fleshed ribs and back. A new, brightly studded collar glittered on his neck, and his tail, beautifully fringed, fanned the air gently. He was now a golden retriever in full magnificence. As I stared at him, he reared up, plunked his forepaws on my chest and looked into my face, and in his eyes I read plainly the same calm affection and trust I had seen in that black, noisome[21] shed.

"Mrs. Donovan," I said softly, "he's the most beautiful dog in Yorkshire." Then, because I knew she was waiting for it. "It's those wonderful condition powders. Whatever do you put in them?"

"Ah, wouldn't you like to know!" She bridled[22] and smiled up at me coquettishly and indeed she was nearer being kissed at that moment than for many years.

---

19. **necrotic tissue:** tissue in which the cells have died through injury or disease.
20. **granulating:** healing by forming fleshy new growth and tiny new blood vessels.
21. **noisome** (noi′səm): foul; disgusting.
22. **bridled:** lifted the head and drew in the chin, like a horse restrained by its bridle.

WORDS TO KNOW
coquettishly (kō-kĕt′ĭsh-lē) *adv.* in a flirtatious manner

Portrait of Fridel Battenberg (1920), Max Beckmann. Oil on canvas, 97 cm × 48.5 cm, Kunstmuseum Hannover (Germany) mit Sammlung Sprengel. Copyright © 1996 Artists Rights Society (ARS), New York/VG Bild-Kunst, Bonn, Germany.

I suppose you could say that that was the start of Roy's second life. And as the years passed, I often pondered on the beneficent providence which had decreed that an animal which had spent his first twelve months abandoned and unwanted, staring uncomprehendingly into that unchanging, stinking darkness, should be whisked in a moment into an existence of light and movement and love. Because I don't think any dog had it quite so good as Roy from then on.

His diet changed dramatically from odd bread crusts to best stewing steak and biscuit, meaty bones and a bowl of warm milk every evening. And he never missed a thing. Garden fêtes,[23] school sports, evictions, gymkhanas[24]—he'd be there. I was pleased to note that as time went on, Mrs. Donovan seemed to be clocking up an even greater daily mileage. Her expenditure on shoe leather must have been phenomenal, but of course it was absolute pie[25] for Roy—a busy round in the morning, home for a meal then straight out again; it was all go.

Mrs. Donovan didn't confine her activities to the town center; there was a big stretch of common land down by the river where there were seats, and people used to take their dogs for a gallop, and she liked to get down there fairly regularly to check on the latest developments on the domestic scene. I often saw Roy loping majestically over the grass among a pack of assorted canines, and when he wasn't doing that, he was submitting to being stroked or patted or generally fussed over. He was handsome, and he just liked people; it made him irresistible.

It was common knowledge that his mistress had bought a whole selection of brushes and combs of various sizes with which she labored over his coat.

23. **fêtes** (fāts): outdoor parties; festivals.

24. **gymkhanas** (jĭm-kä′nəz): sporting events in which gymnastics, horse-jumping, or other contests are held.

25. **pie:** slang for something highly desirable; a treat.

Some people said she had a little brush for his teeth, too, and it might have been true, but he certainly wouldn't need his nails clipped—his life on the roads would keep them down.

Mrs. Donovan, too, had her reward; she had a faithful companion by her side every hour of the day and night. But there was more to it than that; she had always had the compulsion to help and heal animals, and the salvation of Roy was the high point of her life—a blazing triumph which never dimmed.

I know the memory of it was always fresh because many years later I was sitting on the sidelines at a cricket match, and I saw the two of them; the old lady glancing keenly around her, Roy gazing placidly out at the field of play, apparently enjoying every ball. At the end of the match I watched them move away with the dispersing crowd; Roy would be about twelve then, and heaven only knows how old Mrs. Donovan must have been, but the big golden animal was trotting along effortlessly, and his mistress, a little more bent perhaps and her head rather nearer the ground, was going very well.

When she saw me, she came over, and I felt the familiar tight grip on my wrist.

"Mr. Herriot," she said, and in the dark probing eyes the pride was still as warm, the triumph still as bursting new as if it had all happened yesterday.

"Mr. Herriot, haven't I made a difference to this dog!" ❖

James Herriot

1916–1995

Other Works

All Things Wise and Wonderful
The Lord God Made Them All
Every Living Thing

First Career James Herriot, whose real name was James Alfred Wight, was only 13 when he decided to become a vet. After training in Scotland, he settled in England and in 1938 began working in Yorkshire. "The life of a country vet was dirty, uncomfortable, sometimes dangerous," he once told an interviewer. "It was terribly hard work and I loved it."

Rising to the Challenge For over 25 years Herriot kept coming home from work and telling his wife about interesting on-the-job experiences, always promising to write a book about them. One day she finally challenged him, observing that vets of 50 do not write first books. "Well, that did it," Herriot later explained. "I stormed out and bought some paper and taught myself to type." The result was *If Only They Could Talk,* published in England in 1970 and followed two years later by *It Shouldn't Happen to a Vet.* For his first American edition Herriot joined the two books together under the title *All Creatures Great and Small* (1972), and the new version became a bestseller. Three similar books followed.

Author Activity

Quite a Character Herriot's books are filled with colorful characters such as Mrs. Donovan. Find one of his books and read a chapter or two. Then write a short description of the characters you encounter and share it with your class.

Inquiry & Research

Research reported cases of cruelty to animals.

Real World Link
Begin your research by reading the magazine article on page 276.

LaserLinks: Background for Reading
Biographical Connection
Social Studies Connection

WORDS TO KNOW

placidly (plăs'ĭd-lē) *adv.* in an undisturbed manner; quietly; calmly

Eight Puppies

GABRIELA MISTRAL

Between the thirteenth and the fifteenth day
the puppies opened their eyes.
Suddenly they saw the world,
anxious with terror and joy.
They saw the belly of their mother,
saw the door of their house,
saw a deluge of light,
saw flowering azaleas.

They saw more, they saw all,
the red, the black, the ash.
Scrambling up, pawing and clawing
more lively than squirrels,
they saw the eyes of their mother,
heard my rasping cry and my laugh.

And I wished I were born with them.
Could it not be so another time?
To leap from a clump of banana plants
one morning of wonders—
a dog, a coyote, a deer;
to gaze with wide pupils,
to run, to stop, to run, to fall,
to whimper and whine and jump with joy,
riddled with sun and with barking,
a hallowed child of God, his secret, divine servant.

Translated by Doris Dana

Ocho Perritos

GABRIELA MISTRAL

Los perrillos abrieron sus ojos
del treceavo al quinceavo día.
De golpe vieron el mundo,
con ansia, susto y alegría.
Vieron el vientre de la madre,
la puerta suya que es la mía,
el diluvio de la luz,
las azaleas floridas.

Vieron más: se vieron todos,
el rojo, el negro, el ceniza,
gateando y aupándose,
más vivos que las ardillas;
vieron los ojos de la madre
y mi grito rasgado, y mi risa.

Y yo querría nacer con ellos.
¿Por qué otra vez no sería?
Saltar de unos bananales
una mañana de maravilla,
en can, en coyota, en venada;
mirar con grandes pupilas,
correr, parar, correr, tumbarme
y gemir y saltar de alegría,
acribillada de sol y ladridos
hija de Dios, sierva oscura y divina.

Still Life with Three Puppies (1888), Paul Gauguin. Oil on wood, 36⅛″ × 24⅝″,
The Museum of Modern Art, New York, Mrs. Simon Guggenheim Fund.
Photo Copyright © 1995 The Museum of Modern Art, New York.

EIGHT PUPPIES 275

Real WORLD Link

Internet Feature Article

Objectives
- identify facts in a feature article
- identify elements that engage the reader
- summarize main ideas
- identify the "five W's"

Connecting to the Literature
Like Roy in James Herriot's "A Case of Cruelty" (p. 264), Champ in "An Angry Public Backs Champ" suffers at the hand of his owner. Concerned neighbors band together to rescue the dog.

Reading for Information

While readers' empathy is focused on Champ, the facts presented in this feature article outline his owner's abusive behavior and the concerned community's reactions to save Champ.

1 Champ will not be going home with the abusive owner who beat and stomped him.

2 who: Kevin Deschene
what: beat and stomped Champ; Deschene was convicted
when: in November when Jim Molloy took pictures
how: Jim Molloy's photographs helped convict Deschene
why: animal lovers are outraged; animal cruelty is a crime

AN ANGRY PUBLIC BACKS CHAMP

❶ Every dog has his day, and Champ finally is going to have a nice one. As a result, thousands of dog lovers can breathe a bit easier; the 18-month-old German shepherd mix won't be going home to Kevin Deschene, the owner who beat him and stomped him.

❷ Champ's plight became known after Jim Molloy, 31, Deschene's next-door neighbor in Lowell, Mass., took a series of photographs in November of Deschene savagely abusing the dog. The pictures helped convict Deschene, 19, of animal cruelty, for which he was sentenced to six months in jail and fined $500.

But Deschene's family, insisting that Kevin had done no wrong, promised a court battle to regain custody of the dog from the Lowell Humane Society. Outraged animal lovers, all with a higher opinion of the dog than of Kevin, rebelled, deluging the Humane Society with 3,700 letters and submitting petitions bearing 21,000 signatures demanding that Champ be protected. Hundreds of the letter writers—some of them offering to pay long-distance shipping charges—wanted to adopt Champ themselves.

Allan Davidson, executive director of the Lowell Humane Society, showed up for a May 4 hearing in Lowell District Court with the letters and petitions—but without Champ. "I put the dog in a safe house, sort of a witness protection program," Davidson said. "I would have faced contempt charges rather than turn the dog over."

As it turned out, Davidson's precautions were unnecessary. At the last minute, the Deschenes decided not to contest custody of Champ. The family, it seemed, had more pressing legal matters to attend to. On the day of the hearing, Barbara Deschene, Kevin's mother, was arrested for alleged welfare fraud, and his sister Kim, 22, was charged with intimidating witness Molloy by shouting obscenities and throwing eggs at his home.

In the meantime, Davidson has picked out a new home for Champ, about 30 miles from Lowell. Since the dog still harbors ill will toward men, Davidson says he will be living in "a female-only household, where there are four cats, some horses, another dog, and 18 acres of land."

Kevin, now serving his time in a less hospitable environment—a House of Correction—will not be as fortunate.

Reading for Information

How would you react if you witnessed an unjust action taking place, such as someone abusing an animal? In this feature article, a witness decides to take action to save an animal—and goes above and beyond the expected response.

READING A FEATURE ARTICLE
Feature articles usually involve the direct presentation of facts with limited analysis or interpretation. In addition to informing readers, features should also be engaging.

YOUR TURN Use the questions and activities below to help you read the feature article.

❶ **Summarizing Main Ideas**
Feature articles often begin by summarizing the main idea. What key information does the first paragraph contain?

❷ An effective news article usually deals with the "five W's"—*who, what, where, when,* and *why* (and sometimes *how*). Additionally, facts, descriptions, quotations, and other details draw readers into the human side of events. For example, the detail that the event occurred in Lowell, Massachusetts, is the *where* of the account. Identify the other W's throughout the article.

Inquiry & Research

Activity Link: "A Case of Cruelty," p. 273
How does your community deal with abused animals? How does it treat animal abusers? Discuss these questions with your classmates, and compare the information you gather with that given in the article.

Mini Lesson Inquiry & Research

The Inquiry & Research activity on this page links to the research asked for in the Inquiry & Research section at the end of "A Case of Cruelty," page 273.

This activity may be treated as either a class discussion or an assignment for students to produce a feature article.

Instruction If a feature article is assigned, remind students to include the "five W's"—*who, what, where, when,* and *why* (and sometimes *how*) in their articles. As they do the Inquiry & Research activity, students will need to contact local animal shelters and police stations. Encourage students to use striking or dramatic facts to engage readers immediately in their opening paragraphs.

Practice Have students work in pairs to collaborate in writing their feature article. When they finish, have pairs exchange articles and identify the "five W's" in each other's work.

Writing Workshop — Poetry

Expressing your ideas and feelings in verse . . .

A **From Reading to Writing** People have many mistaken ideas about what **poetry** should look and sound like. A poem is not just a jingle or a simple rhyme. It can take any form and may be written on any subject. Some poems, like D. H. Lawrence's "Piano," capture an experience and tell a brief story. Others make surprise observations. Poems often present small scenes that take place in memory or imagination or in the world. In writing a poem, poets condense an experience into well-chosen sensory words that embody the meaning of the experience and make it come alive for readers.

For Your Portfolio

WRITING PROMPT Write a poem that describes an experience, an idea, a place, a person, or a feeling.

Purpose: To express yourself
Audience: Your classmates, friends, or family

Basics in a Box

Poetry at a Glance

B

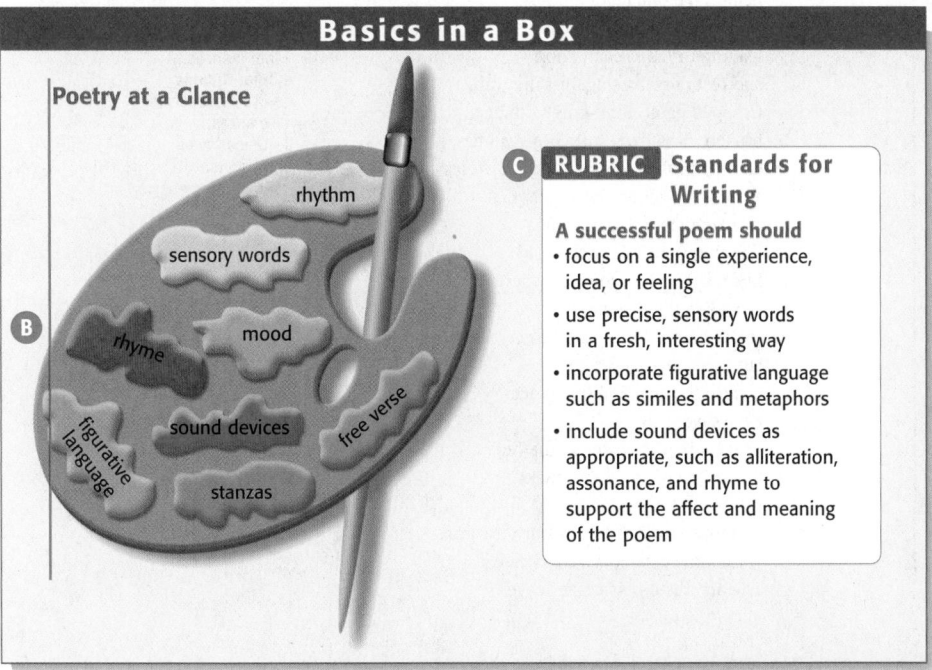

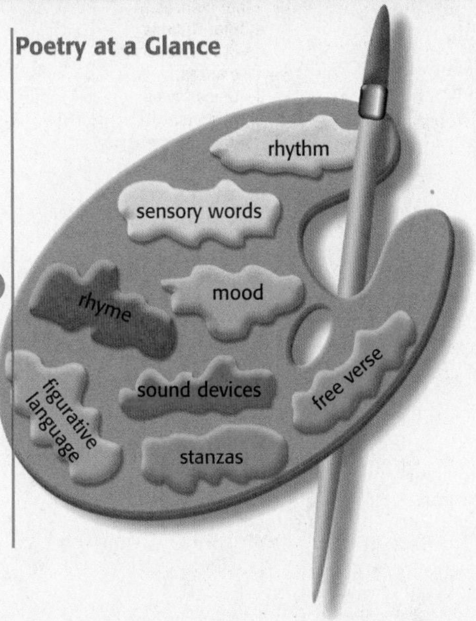

C **RUBRIC Standards for Writing**

A successful poem should

- focus on a single experience, idea, or feeling
- use precise, sensory words in a fresh, interesting way
- incorporate figurative language such as similes and metaphors
- include sound devices as appropriate, such as alliteration, assonance, and rhyme to support the affect and meaning of the poem

LESSON RESOURCES

USING PRINT RESOURCES
Unit Two Resource Book
- Prewriting, p. 18
- Drafting, p. 19
- Peer Response, pp. 20–21
- Revising, Editing, and Proofreading, p. 23
- Student Models, pp. 24–28
- Rubric, p. 29

Writing Transparencies and Copymasters
- Writing Process Transparencies, pp. 1–4
- Writing Style Transparencies, pp. 12–24
- Writing Template Copymasters, p. 27

USING MEDIA RESOURCES
LaserLinks
Writing Springboards
See Teacher's SourceBook p. 64 for bar codes.

Writing Coach CD-ROM

Visit our website:
www.mcdougallittell.com

Objectives
- write a Poem
- use a written text as a model for writing
- revise a draft to add detail
- use punctuation correctly

Introducing the Workshop

A **Poetry** Remind students that modern poetry is very different from the poetry of previous centuries and also from the poetry of nursery rhymes that most of us recall from childhood. Rather than emphasizing the rhyme as a structural sound pattern, modern poetry creates a unified structure by means of other sound devices, such as alliteration, assonance, and repetition of vowel and syllable sounds within lines.

Ask students to name their favorite poets and poems. Read aloud in class some examples of both the older style of rhyming poetry and the modern style of unrhymed poetry. Have students comment and name features they find appealing. What similarities are there between the poems and musical lyrics? Ask students to look at the lyrics of their favorite songs and identify poetic devices. Point out that writing a poem gives students the opportunity to express their thoughts and feelings, and to share those thoughts and feelings with others.

Basics in a Box

B **Using the Graphic** Like the colors on a painter's palette, the details in a poem are blended and intensified to create an overall meaning. The graphic suggests the elements that students can use to draft a successful poem.

C **Presenting the Rubric** To better understand the assignment, students can refer to the Standards for Writing a Successful Poem. You may wish to discuss with them the complete rubric, which describes several levels of proficiency.

Use McDougal Littell's ***Language Network,*** Chapter 24, for more instruction in writing poetry.

To engage students visually, use **Power Presentation** 3, Poetry.

Teaching the Lesson

D Analyzing the Model "Through Whispers in the Wind"; "Perspective"; "In the Steel City"

Three student models present examples of poems that begin with closely observed aspects of the concrete world and end with an emotional meaning. Students can take turns reading aloud the poems and the Rubric in Action. Point out key words and phrases in the student models that correspond to the elements mentioned in the Rubric in Action.

"Through Whispers in the Wind"

1. Ask students to describe why the alliteration of the w sound is appropriate to represent the wind.
   Possible Response: The soft sound mimics the sound of gentle wind.
2. Ask students to explain how love is like an open door.
   Possible Response: The image of an open door suggests possibility and hope.

"Perspective"

1. Have students suggest an alternative structure based on the other options listed.
   Possible Response: The poem could be divided into three stanzas—the first stanza focusing on the description of the auction house, the second on climbing the gutters to watch the wind roll across the grassy field, and the third on the interaction between elements in the setting and their effect on the speaker.

Analyzing Student Models

D

Sheila Schmitt
Litchfield High School

Through Whispers in the Wind

Out the door
with the wind whispering
in my ear,
for the first time
in love

RUBRIC IN ACTION

❶ Uses alliteration to help re-create the sound of the wind

❷ Offers a fresh, vivid image of love as a door opening

Nathan Fellman
Kent School

Perspective

It was our place in the springtime
behind the old auction house.
We'd sit on the back steps
leading to the French doors
and rest ourselves against the wall.
Chipped paint, blue-gray with age,
broken glass from little boys' games,
and the broken gutters hanging uselessly.
We used to climb those gutters
to watch the tall grass field.
The wind made it crawl
like a caterpillar going nowhere.
Tracks in the distance
created a border for the field,
but no train would ever
disturb the peace in that place.
Hours we'd sit
amused by the waves of the field
that rolled off over the tracks.
When we sat too long,
a rooster reminded us of our intrusion,
but no one else bothered to care.
The air was too sweet to leave.

❶ This writer creates a sense of unity by not dividing his poem into stanzas.
Other Options:
- Create separate stanzas.
- Use a rhyme scheme.

❷ Uses an unexpected, concrete simile to express the sense of wind in the grass

Mara Noëlle Scanlon
Greensburg Central Catholic High School

In the Steel City

Pap-pap had the greenest thumb
in all the North Hills
of Pittsburgh, though
anything green was admired
there. A gray man
in a gray city, he once
spit melon seeds
from his kitchen window
and grew three juicy
beauties. Tiny roses
climbed around the patio
and a patch of gold and fuchsia
waved wildly on the lawn.
A plumber at fourteen,
he knew the city's slimy depths
and said the world was full
of jackasses, but he coddled
his mums like newborn lambs
and knelt to breathe
the wet black earth.

When the city steps became
impossible, Pap-pap
packed up Grandma
and their green brocade sofa,
settling with his battered pipe
and history books in his
brown corduroy armchair. He'd left
his heart buried in the strawberry bed,
waiting for spring in strangers'
young hands. There was
no plot of begonias
in the russet-hued apartment,
packed with modern conveniences;
he wilted, sick and finally old.

Father's Day brought
pots of purple daisies
and a balcony window box
where tomatoes formed
on splintered wooden rods.
Listless hands grew dirty again;
Pap-pap thrived
in the warm summer rain.

❶ Draws the reader into the poem by using simple, direct language

❷ Uses repetition and assonance to create a contrast

❸ Breaks lines within sentences for emphasis

❹ Creates a vivid image with a striking simile

❺ Includes precise, sensory words

❻ Uses a well-chosen metaphor

❼ Chooses words carefully *(wilted)* to draw a parallel between Pap-pap and his plants

"In the Steel City"

2. Explain that assonance is the repetition of vowel sounds within words. Ask students to identify the repetitions of words and sounds, both beginning sounds and internal sounds, used in these lines.
   Possible Response: The poet repeats the word "gray" in lines five and six; the words "spit" and "seeds" repeat the same beginning consonant sound; "kitchen window" and "juicy beauties" repeat the same internal vowel sounds.
4. Have students describe the literal act that underlies this comparison.
   Possible Response: Pap-pap treats his flowers with a great tenderness.
6. Ask students to predict how they think Pap-pap will fare in his new environment based on the metaphor of leaving "his heart buried in the strawberry bed."
   Possible Response: Pap-pap may wither and die if he can no longer continue to garden.
7. Point out that although Pap-pap has recovered his health and once again thrives as he works with plants, the larger parallel suggested here has to do with the cycles of nature, life, and death. Just as a plant has its "annual" season, so does a human have a "lifetime."

Guiding Student Writing

Prewriting

CHOOSING A TOPIC

If after reading the Idea Bank students are having difficulty choosing their topics, suggest they try the following:

- Sit at a window, in a park, or in a yard and observe the world that passes by. Focus on specific movements and small actions. Use your observations as the basis for a poem.
- Look at photographs of your childhood as well as photographs of the lives of older family members. Look for little stories that could be the basis for a poem.
- Observe objects in nature, such as flowers, plants, animals, trees, rivers, ponds, sky, stars, moon, sun. Use the details of your observation as the basis for a poem.

Planning the Poem

2. Encourage students to look for actions and objects that best express the emotions they wish to convey. They may begin by naming the emotion, then describing the object or action that best expresses that emotion.
3. Have students write each image on the top of a page and then respond to it by letting language freely follow in response. After developing several images, they can choose the one that has the most potential as a starting point.

Drafting

Since poetry is such an aural art form meant to be heard as much as read, encourage students to read aloud as they compose their poems, constantly listening to the sounds of words and revising or generating new sounds accordingly. Students can also read their poems aloud to a partner. Have partners give thoughtful comments about the images and sounds in the poem.

IDEABank

1. Your Working Portfolio
Look for ideas in the **Writing Options** you completed earlier in this unit:

- **Childhood Poem**, p. 232
- **Not-love Poem**, p. 237
- **Family Poem**, p. 253
- **His Poem**, p. 261

2. And Then She Said . . .
Listen carefully to people's conversations at school, at home, and in the streets. Choose a line of dialogue as the basis for your poem.

3. Borrowed Beginning
Choose a line from a poem, book, or movie that you like. Use it as the first line of your own poem

Writing Your Poem

1 Prewriting

Anything is good material for poetry. Anything.
William Carlos Williams, American poet

Poems often grow out of a word or phrase that captures the writer's imagination because of its sound, rhythm, or meaning. Try just sitting quietly and letting feelings, memories, and words run through your mind. **Jot down** words and ideas that interest you, specifically those that describe sounds, sights, tastes, smells, and feelings. See the **Idea Bank** in the margin for more suggestions. After you choose a topic for your poem, follow the steps below.

Planning Your Poem

1. **Freewrite about your topic.** Read over the notes you made in searching for a topic. Circle interesting words, images, and details. Make a web to explore your associations with those details, or begin a new freewrite. Which details do you want to include in your poem?
2. **Identify the mood you want to express.** Examine your feelings about the topic: Do you feel happy, sad, thoughtful, amused, angry? Focus on creating additional images and details that reinforce that mood.
3. **Choose a starting point.** Which word, line, or image draws you most strongly? Which seems to lead to other interesting images and ideas? Look for one powerful line that can be the focus of your poem.

2 Drafting

Play with ideas and words that come to mind as you think about your topic. Let your language flow freely. Read your writing aloud and listen to the sounds and rhythms of your words. Explore sound devices such as **alliteration** (**l**ife-**l**ong), **assonance** (gr**ee**dy sch**e**mer), and **rhyme** (st**ay** aw**ay**). Also try using **figurative language—simile, metaphor, and personification**—comparisons that help readers see your subject in a new way.

Also consider the overall **mood** of your poem. Choose words whose positive or negative **connotations** emphasize that mood. For example, you might use the word *cabin* to create one kind of mood and the word *shack* to create another. Experiment with different structures, too. Rhythm, rhyme, and stanza breaks can give your poem a more formal feel.

Read your draft aloud to yourself and listen to the words you have written. Think about how you might begin to shape the poem by changing words, line breaks, and punctuation.

Ask Your Peer Reader

- What is the overall mood of my poem?
- Which images appeal to you the most? Why?

❸ Revising

TARGET SKILL ▶ ADDING DETAIL The success of a poem depends largely on the clarity and concreteness of the picture it paints. Add precise, concrete details to make your poem an experience for all the senses.

> *blue-gray with age,*
> Chipped paint, ^ broken glass
>
> from little boys' games,
>
> and the gutters hanging uselessly.
>
> We used to climb those gutters
>
> *tall grass*
> to watch ~~the~~ ^ field.
>
> *crawl*
> The wind made it ~~look as~~
> *like a caterpillar going nowhere*
> ~~though it were crawling.~~
> ^

❹ Editing and Proofreading

TARGET SKILL ▶ USING PUNCTUATION In a poem, a sentence may end in the middle of a line or may extend for several lines. Use the standard rules for punctuating sentences to make sure your lines are not misread.

> Pap-pap had the greenest thumb
>
> in all the North Hills
>
> of Pittsburgh ^ though
>
> anything green was admired
>
> there ⊙ a gray man
>
> in a gray city ^ he once
>
> spit melon seeds
>
> from his kitchen window . . .

❺ Reflecting

FOR YOUR WORKING PORTFOLIO What did you discover about your feelings or your topic while writing your poem? What techniques would you like to try in your next poem? Attach your answer to your poem. Save your poem in your **Working Portfolio.**

Need revising help?

Review the **Rubric**, p. 277

Consider **peer reader** comments

Check **Revision Guidelines**, p. 1145

Puzzled by punctuating poetry?

See the **Grammar Handbook**, pp. 1203–1204

Publishing IDEAS

- Publish your poem in your school literary magazine.
- Read your poem aloud at a class poetry circle. Record the readings on videotape or audiotape.

More Online: Publishing Options
www.mcdougallittell.com

Revising

ADDING DETAIL

To help students sharpen their revision skills, have them take all of the noun phrases and verb phrases from their draft and list them horizontally as column heads. Then, in each column, they can list modifiers that paint a more specific picture. Students may want to use a thesaurus to include precise modifiers. Encourage them to use details that appeal to more than one sense.

Editing and Proofreading

USING PUNCTUATION

A volunteer might first read the example aloud without any punctuation. Discuss the problems with this type of reading. Then have the same person read the poem again with punctuation. Explain that punctuation—commas, periods, exclamation marks, and dashes—indicate where the reader should pause or indicate how the poem might be read. Punctuation can also clarify the meaning the writer intends to communicate to the reader.

Have students read their poems aloud to a partner. Listen for places where punctuation is needed. Students might also experiment with different types of punctuation and then read their poems to their partner with various types of punctuation.

Even though punctuation in poetry may be unusual, encourage students to strive for an error-free final draft of their poems.

Reflecting

Encourage students to express what they discovered about their feelings and the subjects they wrote about. What particular aspects of themselves or their world did they discover? Have students add these self-evaluations to their working portfolios.

Assessment Practice

Encourage students to read the complete paragraph before they answer the questions. Then model how they can eliminate incorrect choices for the first question.

A. This choice is incorrect because *publishing* is in the progressive tense and shows ongoing action. *Publishing* must be used with a helping verb.

B. This choice is incorrect because the verb is in the infinitive form.

C. This choice is incorrect because *publishers* is a noun and the sentence needs a verb.

D. This is the correct choice. *Publish* is in the present tense and so are the verbs in the rest of the paragraph.

Answers:
1. D; **2.** B; **3.** A; **4.** B; **5.** C; **6.** A

Assessment Practice Revising & Editing

Read this opening from the first draft of a student essay. The underlined sections may include the following kinds of errors:

- **sentence fragments**
- **comma errors**
- **lack of parallel structure**
- **lack of subject-verb agreement**

For each underlined section, choose the revision that most improves the writing.

My friend Charles and I publish (1) a monthly literary magazine. Our magazine, called Fresh Words showcases (2) student poetry and prose. Running a magazine take (3) a lot of work. As editors, we read submissions, choose the pieces we will publish, and are inputting the student work (4). Charles is a good sketch artist and designer. He adds illustrations. Decides how each page should look. (5) We truly enjoy creating the magazine and, students seem to enjoy reading it (6).

1. **A.** publishing
B. to publish
C. publishers
D. Correct as is

2. **A.** Our magazine called Fresh Words, showcases
B. Our magazine, called Fresh Words, showcases
C. Our magazine called, Fresh Words, showcases
D. Correct as is

3. **A.** takes
B. took
C. taken
D. Correct as is

4. **A.** reading submissions, choosing the pieces we will publish, and inputting the student work.
B. read submissions, choose the pieces we will publish, and input the student work.
C. are reading submissions, choose the pieces we will publish, and inputting the student work.
D. Correct as is

5. **A.** He adds illustrations, decides how each page should look.
B. He adds illustrations and how each page should look.
C. He adds illustrations and decides how each page should look.
D. Correct as is

6. **A.** We truly enjoy creating the magazine, and students seem to enjoy reading it.
B. We truly enjoy creating, the magazine, and students seem to enjoy reading it.
C. We truly enjoy creating the magazine, and, students seem to enjoy reading it.
D. Correct as is

Need extra help?

See the **Grammar Handbook**
Punctuation Chart, pp. 1203–1204
Subject-Verb Agreement, pp. 1200–1201
Writing Complete Sentences, p. 1199

PART 2 Mysteries of the Heart

Consider the Roman god of love, Cupid. Young, beautiful, mischievous—even cruel—he shoots his arrows of love, and the results are almost always unpredictable. His characteristics reflect love's mysterious powers. As you will see in this part of Unit Two, love can have a profound impact, for better or worse, on people's lives.

ACTIVITY

With a group of classmates, create a brief glossary of expressions that convey the strange, wonderful, and even frightful effects of love. You may want to include phrases such as *love-crazed* and *head over heels in love,* as well as expressions that you have heard at home or through the media. Define each expression, and give an example of its use. After reading these selections, you may have ideas for additions to the glossary.

283

OVERVIEW

Objectives
- analyze the use of dramatic elements in a play
- identify the terms for the elements of drama: character, dialogue, stage directions, and plot
- identify types of character and dialogue in a play
- understand the uses of stage direction and plot

Teaching the Lesson

This lesson analyzes drama and the elements of drama and examines the use of character, dialogue, stage directions, and plot as elements of a dramatic work.

Introducing the Concepts

Have students mention past school plays they have attended or performed in. Ask them what made the experience memorable and then relate their experiences to the concepts of the dramatic elements.

Presenting the Concepts

Character

Have students come up with examples of major and minor characters from stories they have read. Ask them to compare character development in the stories to character development and presentation in plays they have seen or read.

YOUR TURN Possible Response: Mrs. Popov would be the protagonist because the playwright reveals more detail about her and her relationships. The details allow the reader to identify with her. Her speeches drive the conflict and action in the excerpt while Smirnov's dialogue reveals his conflicts with her and therefore identifies him as the antagonist in the play.

Dialogue

Remind students that dialogue in drama carries the story line and reveals character and so must sound like, or approximate, everyday speech. Alert them, however, that dramatic dialogue is a heightened form of ordinary speech and eliminates many of ordinary speech's pauses and repetitions.

YOUR TURN Possible Response: The soliloquy reveals that Mrs. Popov considers herself a faithful and forgiving wife who intends to isolate herself from society, not out of love for her dead husband, but out of a kind of pride.

Drama is broadly defined as any story told in dialogue form that is performed by actors for an audience. In fact, the word *drama* comes from the Greek word *dran,* meaning "to do" or "to act." Today, drama includes movies, TV shows, live stage productions, and radio plays. Dramatic works can be poetry or prose, comedy or tragedy, fiction or fact, a one-person show or a cast of thousands. You can also enjoy these works as literature, visualizing the action and characters as you read. Dramas share the common elements of character, dialogue, stage directions, and plot. Use the following passages from *The Bear* by Anton Chekhov to learn more about these dramatic elements.

Character

In drama, as in fiction, the story revolves around **main characters,** with **minor characters** contributing to the action. **Round** (or **dynamic**) characters change during the course of the story, while **flat** (or **static**) characters remain the same. Audiences usually identify with the central character, or **protagonist.** Opposing the protagonist is the **antagonist.** The struggle between them creates the conflict in the story. Characters known as **foils** have qualities that offer a striking contrast to the traits of other characters.

YOUR TURN Read the excerpt at the right. Compare the traits of the two main characters. Would you choose Mrs. Popov or Smirnov to be the protagonist? the antagonist?

CHARACTER

Smirnov. . . . Tell me frankly, did you ever see a sincere, faithful, true woman? You know you didn't. . . . You'll never find a constant woman, not in a month of Sundays, you won't, not once in a blue moon!

Mrs. Popov. Well, I like that! Then who is true and faithful in love to your way of thinking? Not men by any chance?

Smirnov. Yes, madam. Men.

Mrs. Popov. *Men!* (*gives a bitter laugh*) Men true and faithful in love! That's rich, I must say. (*vehemently*) . . . If it comes to that, the best man I've ever known was my late husband. . . . I loved him passionately. . . . And—what do you think? This best of men was shamelessly deceiving me all along the line!

Dialogue

Dialogue, or conversation between characters, conveys everything in drama, from plot details to character revelations. In addition to dialogue between two or more characters, drama uses other types of speech: the **monologue,** a long, uninterrupted speech by one character that reveals his or her thoughts and feelings; the **soliloquy,** in which the character is alone and speaks his or her private thoughts aloud as if the audience were not there; and the **aside,** a short speech delivered directly to the audience as if the other characters could not hear it.

YOUR TURN What does this soliloquy reveal about Mrs. Popov's feelings, motives, and possible future actions?

DIALOGUE

Mrs. Popov (*looking at the snapshot* [*of her deceased husband*]). Now you shall see how I can love and forgive, Nicholas. My love will only fade when I fade away myself, when this poor heart stops beating. (*laughs, through tears*) Well, aren't you ashamed of yourself? I'm your good, faithful little wifie; I've locked myself up, and I'll be faithful to the grave, while you—aren't you ashamed, you naughty boy? You deceived me, and you used to make scenes and leave me alone for weeks on end.

Stage Directions

Stage directions, usually printed in italics and set off in parentheses, are the playwright's instructions for how the play should be staged and performed. They often provide background information on characters, historical periods, and actions occurring before the play begins. They are also used to describe **scenery,** or **setting**—the physical environment that suggests a specific time or place. In addition, they tell the actors how to play their parts and specify lighting, costumes, music, sound effects, and **props**—or objects, like furniture, used in a performance. In television or films, directions include camera angles and shots.

YOUR TURN In this passage, what information do the stage directions give about costumes, props, and the actors' performances?

STAGE DIRECTIONS

Mrs. Popov (*with a vicious laugh*). He likes me! He dares to say he likes me! (*points to the door*) I won't detain you.

Smirnov (*puts down the revolver without speaking, picks up his peaked cap and moves off; near the door he stops, and for about half a minute the two look at each other without speaking; then he speaks, going up to her hesitantly*). Listen. Are you still angry? I'm absolutely furious myself, but you must see—how can I put it? The fact is that, er, it's this way, actually—(*shouts*) Anyway, can I help it if I like you? (*clutches the back of a chair, which cracks and breaks*)

Plot

The **plot** in a drama is a series of related events that usually begin with a problem or conflict that intensifies, reaches a peak, and is eventually resolved. Conflict can be **external,** pitting one character against another person or an outside force, or **internal,** involving a struggle within a character. The elements of plot—**exposition, rising action, climax, falling action,** and **resolution**—are discussed on pages 17–18. Dramatic plots are often divided into **scenes,** each scene establishing a different place or time. Longer plays are divided into **acts,** with an act comprising a number of related scenes. *The Bear* is a one-act play composed of 11 scenes.

David Suchet (Smirnov) and Pauline Collins (Mrs. Popov) in *The Bear;* Royal Court Theater, 1978.

YOUR TURN Read the passage at the right. Does the conflict appear to be internal, external, or both? Explain your choice.

PLOT

Smirnov. . . . I've gone all sloppy, soft, and sentimental. Kneeling like an imbecile, offering my hand! Disgraceful! Scandalous! I haven't been in love for five years, I swore not to, and here I am crashing head over heels, hook, line, and sinker! I offer you my hand. Take it or leave it. (*gets up and hurries to the door*).

Mrs. Popov. Just a moment.

Smirnov (*stops*). What is it?

Mrs. Popov. Oh, never mind, just go away. But wait. No, go, go away. . . . Oh, if you knew how furious I am!

Making Connections

Stage Directions

Discuss with students the effects that the set and setting (time and locale) can have on performance, character, and ideas in the play. Remind them that some directors of plays ignore an author's stage directions and recreate the play in another time or block the actors' actions differently from the stage directions' suggestions. Suggest to them recent movies based on Shakespearean plays that set *Hamlet* in the 19th century and set *Richard III* in a speculative 1930s-era Fascist England.

YOUR TURN Possible Response: The stage directions inform the reader that Smirnov wears a peaked hat (costume), holds a revolver, and cracks a chair's back (props). In addition, the actors are directed to perform in certain ways: Mrs. Popov is to laugh viciously and point Smirnov toward the door while Smirnov is to put down his revolver, put on his hat, move toward the door, pause, approach Mrs. Popov, and grip a chair's back until he breaks it.

Plot

Suggest to students that the number of acts a playwright uses in the play often depends on the number and complexity of the play's conflicts.

YOUR TURN Possible Response: The conflicts in the passage are both internal and external. The internal conflict is shown in the indecision and hesitation in both characters' speeches while an external conflict is shown through the characters' bickering about Smirnov's exit (which, when expanded, suggests the conflict over the marriage proposal).

OVERVIEW

Objectives
- understand how to read stage directions and apply them to elements of character, setting, dialogue, and plot in drama
- use charts and graphics to diagram plot conflicts, and to compare and contrast characters

Teaching the Lesson

The strategies on this page will help students learn and apply specific skills for identifying the elements of character, dialogue, setting, and plot in drama.

Presenting the Strategies
Help students understand the elements of drama by applying them to a film or television program they are familiar with or to a play they have previously read in class.

Strategies for Using Your Reader's Notebook
Instead of writing stage directions verbatim, encourage students to record only the key words that suggest important aspects of character, dialogue, setting, or conflict.

1 Strategies for Exploring Characters
A sample completion of the chart could look like this:

Character 1:
- Will not let himself get distracted from his goals
- Is very serious about playing basketball
- Hates to lose

Character 2:
- Knows that his sister needs help
- Wants to do the best thing for his family
- Likes to help others

Shared Traits:
- Both are devoted to a cause.
- Both have strong desires to succeed at what they do.

2 Strategies for Understanding Dialogue
First have students make a list of a character's thoughts and feelings as they infer them from the stage directions. Then have students list details from the dialogue that further support those conclusions.

The Active Reader: Skills and Strategies

Drama, as literature, can be as exciting as any novel. Memorable characters, exotic settings, and surprising plots match the best in prose fiction. To get the most from any play you read, try the reading strategies explained here.

Reading Drama

Strategies for Using Your READER'S NOTEBOOK
As you read, take notes to
- record stage directions that are key to understanding plot or character
- note any dialogue you think is particularly revealing or interesting
- **connect** your personal experiences to the events in the drama
- write down any questions you have about setting, plot, or characters

1 Strategies for Exploring Characters
- **Visualize** the characters as you read the stage directions, which often describe a character's appearance and reactions.
- **Evaluate** the characters' actions and words, and **question** what motivates them.
- Create a simple graphic like this one to compare and contrast the two main characters.
- Notice changes in characters.

Character 1	Shared Traits	Character 2

2 Strategies for Understanding Dialogue
- Analyze the writer's use of monologues and asides to reveal a character's motives, feelings, and conflicts.
- Note how the stage directions help you understand the action and the characters' thoughts and feelings.
- Read the play aloud, alone or with others.

3 Strategies for Visualizing Drama
- Read the stage directions, and sketch the sets and scenery described.
- Identify the time period and location of the play.
- **Evaluate** how setting influences the play's mood and tone.

4 Strategies for Examining Plot
- Read the opening stage directions for any background to the action.
- Identify the main conflict. Diagram the **external** and **internal conflicts** of the characters, as in the chart at right.
- Note at what points the conflict intensifies, reaches a peak, and resolves.
- **Evaluate** whether the ending is a satisfactory resolution to the conflict.

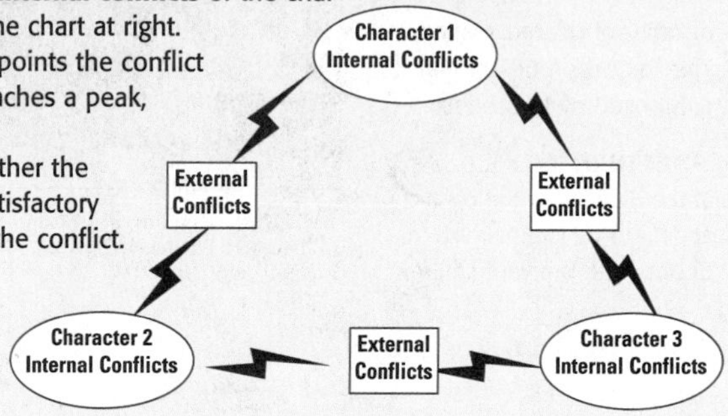

Need More Help?
Remember that active readers use the essential reading strategies explained on page 7: **visualize, predict, clarify, question, connect, evaluate, monitor.**

3 Strategies for Visualizing Drama
Have students incorporate elements from the time period and location of the play into their sketches of sets and scenery. They might consult encyclopedias for additional clues on the period and locale.

4 Strategies for Examining Plot
Have students extend a line from each oval and rectangle in their conflict diagram. On that line, students will summarize the forces, ideas, or elements of character that are in conflict.

The Bear

Drama by ANTON CHEKHOV (chĕk′ôf)

"She'll get no chivalry from me!"

Connect to Your Life

Battle Lines What does the phrase "battle of the sexes" mean to you? In a class discussion, share your definition of the term and your opinions about it. Also describe examples of the battle of the sexes from books, movies, plays, or television shows.

Build Background

The Russian Gentry In the following one-act comedy, the battle of the sexes takes place on a country estate in 19th-century Russia. The two combatants are both members of what was then Russia's privileged land-owning class. One is a woman who would describe herself as a genteel widow with delicate sensibilities, while the other is an outspoken gentleman farmer whose hot temper makes him seem like a bear, or a crude, insensitive person. Like others of his class, he is educated enough to know French—considered a language of refinement by upper-class Russians of the day—but he pokes fun at those who insist on speaking it. Far more at home with the "manly" pursuits of his class, such as riding, dueling, and managing his farm, he seems out of place in the widow's elegant drawing room, the formal room for receiving guests that is the setting of the play's "battle."

WORDS TO KNOW
Vocabulary Preview
emancipation
futile
languish
liberty
sniveling

Focus Your Reading

LITERARY ANALYSIS FARCE A **farce** is a humorous play that typically involves ridiculous situations and physical comedy. Characters are often **stereotypes;** that is, they conform to a fixed pattern or lack complexity as characters. They frequently display exaggerated behavior or language, as the character Smirnov does in these lines from *The Bear:*

> ***Oh, I'm so furious! I could pulverize the whole world, I'm in such a rage. I feel quite ill.***

As you read, be aware of the elements of farce in Chekhov's play.

ACTIVE READING VISUALIZING A work of drama is primarily written to be performed—it must be interpreted by a director, actors, set designers and others. When you read a drama, you do not have access to this collaboration of talents. Instead, you must **visualize** the setting and the action. While reading, picture the events described and form an image of each major character. Try to "hear" the words as each character speaks. As well as visualizing what is revealed through **dialogue,** pay attention to the **stage directions,** which describe the scenery and props. The stage directions also provide hints to the performers—and the readers—on how the characters look, move, and speak.

READER'S NOTEBOOK As you read, make notes describing the image you have formed of each of the major characters and of the play's setting.

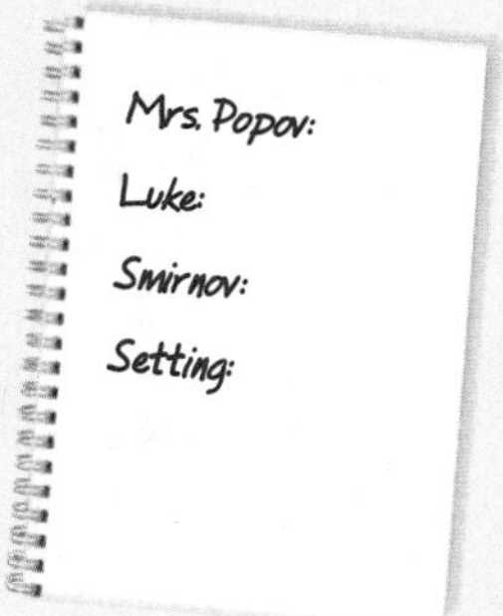

VIDEODISC **LaserLinks: Background for Reading**
Visual Vocabulary

OVERVIEW

Objectives

1. understand and appreciate **drama (Literary Analysis)**
2. understand the term **farce (Literary Analysis)**
3. **visualize** setting and action **(Active Reading)**

Summary

In this humorous one-act play, Mrs. Popov, a young widow, continues to mourn one year after her husband's death. Gregory Smirnov, a landed gentleman, suddenly comes to collect on a debt of her late husband's. The two aristocrats argue over the debt. The conflict escalates until Smirnov challenges Mrs. Popov to a duel. She accepts. As Mrs. Popov fetches the pistols, Smirnov marvels at her spirit. When she returns, pistols at the ready, he declares his love. At first, she resists, but then she returns his affection.

Thematic Link

Smirnov and Mrs. Popov begin as combatants but end as lovers in this play that illustrates the **mysteries of the heart**.

Editor's Note This selection has been edited slightly to delete material that may be considered objectionable.

5-Minute Warm-Up

Daily Language SkillBuilder

Have students **proofread** the display sentences on page 223j and write them correctly. The sentences also appear on Transparency 9 of **Grammar Transparencies and Copymasters.**

LESSON RESOURCES

UNIT TWO RESOURCE BOOK, pp. 30–35

ASSESSMENT RESOURCES
Formal Assessment, pp. 49–50
Teacher's Guide to Assessment and Portfolio Use
Test Generator

SKILLS TRANSPARENCIES AND COPYMASTERS
Literary Analysis
- Drama: Stage Directions, T11 (for Drama, p. 300)

Reading and Critical Thinking
- Visualizing, T8 (for Think Critically, item 2, p. 300)

Grammar
- Sentence Types, C119 (for Mini Lesson, p. 298)

Vocabulary
- Word Meanings and Spellings, C40 (for Mini Lesson, p. 290)

Writing
- Effective Language, T13 (for Writing Options 3, p. 301)
- Opinion Statement, C25 (for Writing Option 2, p. 301)
- Interpretive Essay, C33 (for Writing Option 1, p. 301)

INTEGRATED TECHNOLOGY
Audio Library
LaserLinks
- Drama Connection: Scenes from "The Bear." See **Teacher's SourceBook,** p. 22.

Internet: Research Starter
Visit our website:
www.mcdougallittell.com

TEACHING THE LITERATURE

Reading and Analyzing

Reading Skills and Strategies: PREVIEW

Have students preview the selection. Discuss with students the Build Background feature on p. 287. Before students begin reading, give them a brief summary of the story. Have students make predictions about how the images and the title will connect to what they already know about the play based on the summary.

Active Reading VISUALIZING

Help students locate stage directions, usually in italics, throughout the text. Note that directions are often sparse. Directors and set designers use their imaginations to fill out the directions.

Use **Unit Two Resource Book,** p. 31 for more practice.

Literary Analysis FARCE

Review with students the Literary Analysis feature on p. 287. Ask students to mention contemporary examples of farce in popular culture.

Possible Responses: *The Simpsons*; films by Mel Brooks; some films starring Eddie Murphy

Discuss the use of stereotyping and exaggeration in comedy. How do Luke's first lines and Mrs. Popov's reply suggest that the play will be a farce?

Possible Responses: Luke describes his mistress's exaggerated behavior: she hasn't set foot outdoors for a year; Mrs. Popov responds in overly dramatic fashion: "My life's finished."

Use **Unit Two Resource Book,** p. 32 for more practice.

The Bear
A Farce in One Act
by Anton Chekhov
Cast of Characters
Mrs. Helen Popov, a young widow with dimpled cheeks, a landowner
Gregory Smirnov, a landowner in early middle age
Luke, Mrs. Popov's old manservant
The action takes place in the drawing room of Mrs. Popov's country house.

Scene 1

(Mrs. Popov, *in deep mourning, with her eye fixed on a snapshot, and* Luke)

Luke. This won't do, madam; you're just making your life a misery. Cook's out with the maid picking fruit, every living creature's happy, and even our cat knows how to enjoy herself—she's parading round the yard trying to pick up a bird or two. But here you are cooped up inside all day like you was in a convent cell[1]—you never have a good time. Yes, it's true. Nigh on twelve months it is since you last set foot outdoors.

Mrs. Popov. And I'm never going out again; why should I? My life's finished. He lies in his grave; I've buried myself inside these four walls—we're both dead.

Luke. There you go again! I don't like to hear such talk, I don't. Your husband died and that was that—God's will be done, and may he rest in peace. You've shed a few tears and that'll

1. **convent cell:** a small room occupied by an individual nun in a convent, a community of nuns living under strict religious vows.

Teaching Options

Mini Lesson Preteaching Vocabulary

USING CONTEXT CLUES Call students' attention to the list of WORDS TO KNOW. Remind them that sometimes they can understand the meaning of an unfamiliar word by examining the context in which the word is used. Use the model sentence to demonstrate the strategy of using context clues that provide inferences to word meaning.

Model Sentence

The young man apologized for taking the *liberty* of speaking out of turn.

Instruction

- Write the model sentence on the board.
- Ask a volunteer to rephrase the sentence, guessing at the meaning of *liberty*.
- Have students use the sentence to infer the meaning of the word *liberty*.
- Ask a volunteer to use the word *liberty* in a sentence.

Use **Unit Two Resource Book** p. 33 for more practice.

A lesson on using context clues appears on p. 56 in the Pupil's Edition.

Portrait of the Pianist, Conductor, and Composer A. G. Rubinstein (1881), Ilya Efimovich Repin. Oil on canvas, 80 cm × 62.3 cm, The State Tretyakov Gallery, Moscow, acquired by P. M. Tretyakov from the artist.

Customizing Instruction

Less Proficient Readers

Have students keep these questions in mind as they read:

- Who are the characters in the play?
  Answer: Luke, Mrs. Popov, and Smirnov.
- Who comes to visit, and why?
  Answer: Mr. Smirnov, to collect a debt.
- Where is the play set?
  Answer: In the drawing room of Mrs. Popov's country house.

Students Acquiring English

Explain to students that "deep mourning" is a term referring to the expressions of grief that follow the death of a loved one. Point out that Mrs. Popov has continued this behavior long past the usual time period.

Use **Spanish Study Guide** for additional support, pp. 62–64.

Gifted and Talented

Encourage students to find hints of serious themes in this play, such as grief, misunderstanding, and the unpredictability of emotion. Have them record these themes as they read. When they have finished reading the play, have them discuss why Chekhov might have chosen to use a humorous play to discuss such serious subjects.

Mini Lesson Viewing and Representing

Portrait of the Pianist, Conductor, and Composer A. G. Rubinstein **by Ilya Efimovich Repin**

ART APPRECIATION Repin (1844–1930) was a leading realist painter who depicted social scenes and also produced many portraits. Rubenstein (1829–1894) was the founder of the Petersburg Conservatory, a school for musicians. This painting was commissioned for a portrait gallery of distinguished figures in Russian culture.

Instruction Have students discuss the realism and detail they see in the painting. Ask them what the painter's purpose is.

Possible Responses: to give the most accurate portrayal of Rubinstein possible; to portray Rubinstein without glamorizing him

Reading and Analyzing

Reading Skills and Strategies: VISUALIZE

Help students become directors by asking them to imagine how they would cast Mrs. Popov and Luke. What physical qualities would they look for in the actors? In addition to her dimpled cheeks, what other details would students add to the description of Mrs. Popov? Ask students what physical qualities they would look for in an actor who would portray Luke.

Literary Analysis: CHARACTERS AND STEREOTYPES

In drama, characters and their motivations usually drive the plot. We learn about characters through their words and actions. In a farce, characters are often stereotypes—that is, recognizable types of people whose words and behavior reinforce our expectations. Ask students to list characteristics of Mrs. Popov and Smirnov that reflect stereotypes of feminine and masculine behavior. What aspects of their characters seem stereotyped?

Possible Response: Mrs. Popov is a stereotypical female role, one with exaggerated devotion to her late husband and radical, irrational mood swings. Smirnov has the exaggerated characteristics of a boorish man, being entirely rude, impatient, inflammatory, and, in the end, passionate.

ACTIVE READING

(A) **VISUALIZE** **Possible Response:** Mrs. Popov is a gaunt, elegant woman dressed in a long black dress, with her hair pulled back. Luke is wearing a butler's uniform and is very neatly groomed.

do; it's time to call it a day—you can't spend your whole life a-moaning and a-groaning. The same thing happened to me once, when my old woman died, but what did I do? I grieved a bit, shed a tear or two for a month or so, and that's all she's getting. Catch me wearing sackcloth and ashes[2] for the rest of my days; it'd be more than the old girl was worth! (*sighs*) You've neglected all the neighbors—won't go and see them or have them in the house. We never get out and about, lurking here like dirty great spiders, saving your presence. The mice have been at my livery[3] too. And it's not for any lack of nice people either—the county's full of 'em, see. There's the regiment stationed at Ryblovo, and them officers are a fair treat; a proper sight for sore eyes they are. They have a dance in camp of a Friday, and the brass band plays most days. This ain't right, missus. You're young, and pretty as a picture with that peaches-and-cream look, so make the most of it. Them looks won't last forever, you know. If you wait another ten years to come out of your shell and lead them officers a dance, you'll find it's too late.

Mrs. Popov (*decisively*). Never talk to me like that again, please. When Nicholas died, my life lost all meaning, as you know. You may think I'm alive, but I'm not really. I swore to wear this mourning and shun society till my dying day, do you hear? Let his departed spirit see how I love him! Yes, I realize you know what went on—that he was often mean to me, cruel and, er, unfaithful even; but I'll be true to the grave and show him how much I can love. And he'll find me in the next world just as I was before he died.

Luke. Don't talk like that—walk round the garden instead. Or else have Toby or Giant harnessed and go and see the neighbors.

Mrs. Popov. Oh dear! (*weeps*)

Luke. Missus! Madam! What's the matter? For heaven's sake!

Mrs. Popov. He was so fond of Toby—always drove him when he went over to the Korchagins' place and the Vlasovs'. He drove so well too! And he looked so graceful when he pulled hard on the reins, remember? Oh Toby, Toby! See he gets an extra bag of oats today.

Luke. Very good, madam.

(*A loud ring.*)

ACTIVE READING

VISUALIZE What picture have you formed in your mind of Mrs. Popov and Luke?

Mrs. Popov (*shudders*). Who is it? Tell them (A) I'm not at home.

Luke. Very well, madam. (*goes out*)

Scene 2

(Mrs. Popov, *alone*)

Mrs. Popov (*looking at the snapshot*). Now you shall see how I can love and forgive, Nicholas. My love will only fade when I fade away myself, when this poor heart stops beating. (*laughs, through tears*) Well, aren't you ashamed of yourself? I'm your good, faithful little wifie; I've locked myself up, and I'll be faithful to the grave, while you—aren't you ashamed, you naughty boy? You deceived me, and you used to make scenes and leave me alone for weeks on end.

Scene 3

(Mrs. Popov *and* Luke)

Luke (*comes in, agitatedly*). Someone's asking for you, madam. Wants to see you—

2. **sackcloth and ashes:** rough, scratchy clothing and ashes worn as symbols of mourning.
3. **livery:** a servant's uniform.

Teaching Options

Mini Lesson Vocabulary Strategy

WORD MEANINGS AND SPELLING

Instruction Words may have suffixes, prefixes, and roots (the original core of a word). Point out that knowing the meaning of a word will help us identify each of these parts and aid us in spelling the word. Remind students that we figure out meanings of words both through context and through the use of a dictionary.

Model Sentence

He drew a *symmetrical* picture.

Instruction

- Write the model sentence on the chalkboard.
- Explain to students that the word *symmetrical* means "having matching or equal parts, of equal measure."
- Ask students to find a root between a prefix *(sym-)* and a suffix *(-cal).* Remind them that applying the meaning of prefixes, roots, and suffixes can help them understand the word.
- If students have difficulty, ask them to look up the word *meter*.

Use **Vocabulary Transparencies and Copymasters.**

Mrs. Popov. Then I hope you told them I haven't received visitors since the day my husband died.

Luke. I did, but he wouldn't listen—his business is very urgent, he says.

Mrs. Popov. *I am not at home!*

Luke. So I told him, but he just swears and barges straight in, drat him. He's waiting in the dining room.

Mrs. Popov (*irritatedly*). All right, ask him in here then. Aren't people rude?

(Luke *goes out.*)

Mrs. Popov. Oh, aren't they all a bore? What do they want with me; why must they disturb my peace? (*sighs*) Yes, I see I really shall have to get me to a nunnery.[4] (*reflects*) I'll take the veil;[5] that's it.

Scene 4

(Mrs. Popov, Luke *and* Smirnov)

Smirnov (*coming in, to* Luke). You're a fool, my talkative friend. . . . (*seeing* Mrs. Popov, *with dignity*) May I introduce myself, madam? Gregory Smirnov, landed gentleman[6] and lieutenant of artillery retired. I'm obliged to trouble you on most urgent business.

Mrs. Popov (*not holding out her hand*). What do you require?

Smirnov. I had the honor to know your late husband. He died owing me twelve hundred roubles[7]—I have his two IOUs. Now I've some interest due to the land bank tomorrow, madam, so may I trouble you to let me have the money today?

Mrs. Popov. Twelve hundred roubles—How did my husband come to owe you that?

Smirnov. He used to buy his oats from me.

Mrs. Popov (*sighing, to* Luke). Oh yes—Luke, don't forget to see Toby has his extra bag of oats. (Luke *goes out. To* Smirnov.) Of course I'll pay if Nicholas owed you something, but I've nothing on me today, sorry. My manager will be back from town the day after tomorrow, and I'll get him to pay you whatever it is then, but for the time being I can't oblige. Besides, it's precisely seven months today since my husband died, and I am in no fit state to discuss money.

Smirnov. Well, I'll be in a fit state to go bust with a capital B if I can't pay that interest tomorrow. They'll have the bailiffs[8] in on me.

Mrs. Popov. You'll get your money the day after tomorrow.

Smirnov. I don't want it the day after tomorrow; I want it now.

Mrs. Popov. I can't pay you now, sorry.

Smirnov. And I can't wait till the day after tomorrow.

Mrs. Popov. Can I help it if I've no money today?

Smirnov. So you can't pay then?

Mrs. Popov. Exactly.

Smirnov. I see. And that's your last word, is it?

Mrs. Popov. It is.

Smirnov. Your last word? You really mean it?

Mrs. Popov. I do.

Smirnov (*sarcastic*). Then I'm greatly obliged to you; I'll put it in my diary! (*shrugs*) And people expect me to be cool and collected! I met the local excise man[9] on my way here just now. "My dear Smirnov," says he, "why are you always losing your temper?" But how can I

4. **get me to a nunnery:** go and live in a convent. This is probably a reference to a line from Shakespeare's *Hamlet* in which Hamlet angrily tells his girlfriend, "Get thee to a nunnery."
5. **veil:** the outer covering of a nun's headdress and, by extension, the life of a nun.
6. **landed gentleman:** a land owner. In Russia before the Russian Revolution, only a few people owned land.
7. **roubles:** units of Russian money; often spelled *rubles.*
8. **bailiffs:** assistants or deputies to the police chief.
9. **excise man:** tax man.

Customizing Instruction

Less Proficient Readers

Use the following questions to help students understand the characters and action.

- Why does Gregory Smirnov invade Mrs. Popov's solitude?
  Answer: He is hoping to collect money that Mrs. Popov's late husband owed him
- What do Smirnov and Mrs. Popov begin to fight about?
  Answer: Smirnov needs the money immediately, but Mrs. Popov says she cannot pay him right away.

BLOCK SCHEDULING: MANAGING TIME

If your schedule requires that you cover the lesson objectives in a shorter time, use . . .

- Preparing to Read, p. 287
- Thinking Through the Literature, p. 300
- Vocabulary in Action, p. 301
- Grammar in Context, p. 302

If you want to take advantage of longer class time, use . . .

- TE Teaching Options: Preteaching Vocabulary, p. 288; Viewing and Representing, pp. 289, 296; Speaking and Listening, p. 297; Cross Curricular Links, p. 294; Standardized Test Practice, p. 301
- Choices & Challenges and Author Activity, pp. 301–302

Reading and Analyzing

Literary Analysis: SETTING

In a drama, the stage contains one or more *sets* that establish the play's setting. Often, as in this play, the setting is an interior room. Ask students to examine dialogue and stage directions to put together a description of the set.

Response: Student descriptions should include the information that Mrs. Popov's drawing room contains a door, a window, at least one chair, and a snapshot of Mrs. Popov's late husband. Students should also assume that the drawing room has other furniture as well.

ACTIVE READING

A VISUALIZE **Possible Responses:** Large, burly, and unkempt, with a booming voice and broad, sudden gestures.

help it, I ask you? I'm in desperate need of money! Yesterday morning I left home at crack of dawn. I call on everyone who owes me money, but not a soul forks out. I'm dog tired. I spend the night in some . . . awful place. Then I fetch up here, fifty miles from home, hoping to see the color of my money, only to be fobbed off[10] with this "no fit state" stuff! How *can* I keep my temper?

Mrs. Popov. I thought I'd made myself clear. You can have your money when my manager gets back from town.

Smirnov. It's not your manager I'm after; it's you. What the blazes, pardon my language, do I want with your manager?

Mrs. Popov. I'm sorry, my dear man, but I'm not accustomed to these peculiar expressions and to this tone. I have closed my ears. (*hurries out*)

Scene 5

(Smirnov, *alone*)

Smirnov. Well, what price that! "In no fit state!" Her husband died seven months ago, if you please! Now have I got my interest to pay or not? I want a straight answer—yes or no? All right, your husband's dead, you're in no fit state and so on and so forth, and your blasted manager's hopped it. But what am I supposed to do? Fly away from my creditors by balloon, I take it! Or go and bash the old brain-box against a brick wall? I call on Gruzdev—not at home. Yaroshevich is in hiding. I have a real old slanging match[11] with Kuritsyn and almost chuck him out of the window. Mazutov has the bellyache, and this creature's "in no fit state." Not one of the swine will pay. This is what comes of being too nice to them and behaving like some sniveling no-hoper or old

1 woman. It doesn't pay to wear kid gloves with this lot! All right, just you wait—I'll give you something to remember me by! You don't make a monkey out of me, blast you! I'm staying here—going to stick around till she coughs up. Pah! I feel well and truly riled today. I'm shaking like a leaf, I'm so furious—choking I am. Phew, . . . I really think I'm going to pass out! (*shouts*) Hey, you there!

Scene 6

(Smirnov *and* Luke)

Luke (*comes in*). What is it?

Smirnov. Bring me some kvass[12] or water, will you?

(Luke *goes out*)

Smirnov. What a mentality, though! You need money so bad you could shoot yourself, but she won't pay, being "in no fit state to discuss money," if you please! There's female logic for you and no mistake! That's why I don't like talking to women. Never have. Talk to a woman—why, I'd rather sit on top of a powder magazine![13] Pah! It makes my flesh creep, I'm so fed up with her, her and that great trailing dress! Poetic creatures they call 'em! Why, the very sight of one gives me cramp in both legs, I get so aggravated.

Scene 7

(Smirnov *and* Luke)

Luke (*comes in and serves some water*). Madam's unwell and won't see anyone.

10. **fobbed off:** put off with a trick or an excuse.
11. **slanging match:** the exchange of angry, abusive language.
12. **kvass** (kväs): Russian beer.
13. **powder magazine:** a room in which gun powder and other explosives are stored in a fort or on a ship.

WORDS TO KNOW

sniveling (snĭv'əl-ĭng) *adj.* whining

Teaching Options

Mini Lesson: Viewing and Representing

A Room in the Brasovo Estate **by Stanislav Iulianovich Zhukovskii**

ART APPRECIATION Have students investigate the source of *A Room in the Brasovo Estate,* including information about the painter. Their research should disclose that S. I. Zhukovskii (1873–1944) was born near Warsaw, Poland, and studied art in Moscow. He gained recognition in the 1910s for paintings of the interiors of country estates—paintings that showed the estate owners' possessions, but not the owners themselves.

Instruction Encourage students to identify and discuss the amount of detail in Zhukovskii's painting. Ask them what they think the artist's purpose was.

Possible Response: to examine and display the way that wealthy landowners lived

Application Ask students how this room resembles and differs from Mrs. Popov's room as they have imagined it.

Possible Response: Students may remark that they had visualized the room to be shaped like the set of a stage.

A Room in the Brasovo Estate (1916), Stanislav Iulianovich Zhukovskii. Oil on canvas, 80 cm × 107 cm, The State Tretyakov Gallery, Moscow, accessioned from the People's Commissariate of Foreign Affairs, 1941.

Customizing Instruction

Students Acquiring English

1 Explain to students that "to wear kid gloves" means "to treat gently" and that "this lot" means "this group of people"—in this case, debtors. Ask students to reword Smirnov's remark "It doesn't pay to wear kid gloves with this lot!" in standard English.

Possible Response: It doesn't do any good to treat these people gently!

Gifted and Talented

2 Ask students to discuss the subtle change in attitude and tone that seems to overtake Smirnov in Scene 7 when he says, "A fine specimen I am, I must say—dust all over me. . . ." Point out that in drama readers should look for changes in character as possible foreshadowing of future actions. Have students discuss why this change takes place. What might it foreshadow?

Smirnov. You clear out!

(Luke *goes out*)

Smirnov. "Unwell and won't see anyone." All right then, don't! I'm staying put, chum, and I don't budge one inch till you unbelt.[14] Be ill for a week, and I'll stay a week; make it a year, and a year I'll stay. I'll have my rights, lady! As for your black dress and dimples, you don't catch me that way—we know all about those dimples! (*shouts through the window*) Unhitch, Simon; we're here for some time—I'm staying put. Tell the stable people to give my horses oats. And you've got that animal tangled in the reins again, you great oaf! (*imitates him*) "I don't care." I'll give you don't care! (*moves away from the window*) How ghastly—it's unbearably hot, no one will pay up, I had a bad night, and now here's this female with her long black dress and her states. I've got a headache. How about a glass of vodka? That might be an idea. (*shouts*) Hey, you there!

ACTIVE READING

VISUALIZE What impression do you have of Smirnov's appearance, voice, and mannerisms?

Luke (*comes in*). What is it?

Smirnov. Bring me a glass of vodka.

(Luke *goes out*)

Smirnov. Phew! (*sits down and looks himself over*) A fine specimen I am, I must say—dust all over me, my boots dirty, unwashed, hair unbrushed, straw on my waistcoat. I bet the little woman took me for a burglar. (*yawns*) It's not exactly polite to turn up in a drawing room in this rig! Well, anyway, I'm not a guest here; I'm collecting money. And there's no such thing as correct wear for the well-dressed creditor. **2**

14. **unbelt:** take off a belt designed to hold money; in this case, to pay what is due.

Reading and Analyzing

Literary Analysis: CONFLICT

A Remind students that conflict between characters lies at the heart of any drama—whether comedy, farce, or tragedy. In a farce, the conflict, while deeply serious, is nevertheless treated as comedy and is often disguised by a conflict of a lighter nature. Ask students to name the surface conflict between Mrs. Popov and Smirnov.

Possible Response: Smirnov wants his payment immediately, and Mrs. Popov cannot or will not pay him right away.

Have students reread Smirnov's and Mrs. Popov's speeches on pages 294 and 295. Then ask them what deeper conflict might be disguised by the argument over money. Remind them to look for the resolution of the conflicts as they read the rest of the story.

Possible Response: their mutual mistrust of the opposite sex

ACTIVE READING

B **EVALUATE** Student responses will vary. They may think that Smirnov is obnoxious and sexist, or that he is simply a bitter person.

Luke (*comes in and gives him the vodka*). This is a liberty, sir.

Smirnov (*angrily*). What!

Luke. I, er, it's all right, I just—

Smirnov. Who do you think you're talking to? You hold your tongue!

Luke (*aside*). Now we'll never get rid of him, botheration take it! It's an ill wind brought him along.

(Luke *goes out*)

Smirnov. Oh, I'm so furious! I could pulverize the whole world, I'm in such a rage. I feel quite ill. (*shouts*) Hey, you there!

Scene 8

(Mrs. Popov *and* Smirnov)

Mrs. Popov (*comes in, with downcast eyes*). Sir, in my solitude I have grown unaccustomed to the sound of human speech, and I can't stand shouting. I must urgently request you not to disturb my peace.

Smirnov. Pay up and I'll go.

Mrs. Popov. As I've already stated quite plainly, I've no ready cash. Wait till the day after tomorrow.

A **Smirnov.** I've also had the honor of stating quite plainly that I need the money today, not the day after tomorrow. If you won't pay up now, I'll have to put my head in a gas oven tomorrow.

Mrs. Popov. Can I help it if I've no cash in hand? This is all rather odd.

Smirnov. So you won't pay up now, eh?

Mrs. Popov. I can't.

Smirnov. In that case I'm not budging; I'll stick around here till I do get my money. (*sits down*) You'll pay the day after tomorrow, you say? Very well, then I'll sit here like this till the day after tomorrow. I'll just stay put exactly as I am. (*jumps up*) I ask you—have I got that interest to pay tomorrow or haven't I? Think I'm trying to be funny, do you?

Mrs. Popov. Kindly don't raise your voice at me, sir—we're not in the stables.

Smirnov. I'm not discussing stables; I'm asking whether my interest falls due tomorrow. Yes or no?

Mrs. Popov. You don't know how to treat a lady.

Smirnov. Oh yes I do.

Mrs. Popov. Oh no you don't. You're a rude, ill-bred person. Nice men don't talk to ladies like that.

Smirnov. Now, this *is* a surprise! How do you want me to talk then? In French, I suppose? (*in an angry, simpering voice*) *Madame, je voo pree.* You won't pay me—how perfectly delightful. Oh, *pardong*, I'm sure—sorry you were troubled! Now isn't the weather divine today? And that black dress looks too, too charming! (*bows and scrapes*)

Mrs. Popov. That's silly. And not very clever.

Smirnov (*mimics her*). "Silly, not very clever." I don't know how to treat a lady, don't I? Madam, I've seen more women in my time than you have house sparrows. I've fought three duels over women. There have been twenty-one women in my life. Twelve times it was me broke it off; the other nine got in first. Oh yes! Time was I slobbered, mooned around, bowed and scraped and practically crawled on my belly. I loved; I suffered; I sighed at the moon; I languished; I melted; I grew cold. I loved passionately, madly, in every conceivable fashion, . . . burbling nineteen to the dozen about women's emancipation and wasting half my

WORDS TO KNOW
liberty (lĭb′ər-tē) *n.* an action that is too bold or forward
languish (lăng′gwĭsh) *v.* to suffer with longing
emancipation (ĭ-măn′sə-pā′shən) *n.* a setting free from restraint or controls

Teaching Options

Cross Curricular Link History

CLASS DIVISIONS Czarist Russian society was divided into clearly demarcated classes: the landed gentry, who constituted only a small fraction of the population; the peasants, who were the vast majority; and a small but increasingly influential merchant class. Before 1861, the peasants were serfs who were practically owned by the landowners; after their emancipation, some peasants were able to improve their circumstances, but the aristocracy retained most political and economic power until the 1917 revolution.

Class divisions have been important in many societies. In England before World War I, a land-inheriting upper class dominated both the working class and a middle class that consisted of professionals and merchants. In India, the Hindu caste system, a very complex and rigid social hierarchy, persisted in practice even after it was outlawed upon independence in 1947. In many Latin American nations, small numbers of very wealthy families own much of the land, a situation that has created chronic social unrest.

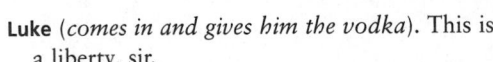

substance[15] on the tender passion. But now—no thank you very much! I can't be fooled anymore; I've had enough. Black eyes, passionate looks, crimson lips, dimpled cheeks, moonlight, "Whispers, passion's bated breathing"[16]—I don't give a tinker's cuss[17] for the lot now, lady. Present company excepted, all women, large or small, are simpering, mincing, gossipy creatures. They're great haters. They're eyebrow deep in lies. They're futile; they're trivial; they're cruel; they're outrageously illogical. And as for having anything upstairs (*taps his forehead*)—I'm sorry to be so blunt, but the very birds in the trees can run rings round your average bluestocking.[18] Take any one of these poetical creations. Oh, she's all froth and fluff, she is; she's half divine; she sends you into a million raptures. But you take a peep inside her mind, and what do you see? A common or garden crocodile! (*clutches the back of a chair, which cracks and breaks*) And yet this crocodile somehow thinks its great lifework, privilege and monopoly is the tender passion—that's what really gets me! But damn and blast it, and crucify me upside down on that wall if I'm wrong—does a woman know how to love any living creature apart from lap dogs? Her love gets no further than sniveling and slobbering. The man suffers and makes sacrifices, while she just twitches the train of her dress and tries to get him squirming under her thumb; that's what her love adds up to! You must know what women are like, seeing you've the rotten luck to be one. Tell me frankly, did you ever see a sincere, faithful, true woman? You know you didn't. Only the old and ugly ones are true and faithful. You'll never find a constant woman, not in a month of Sundays you won't, not once in a blue moon!

ACTIVE READING

B **EVALUATE** What do you think of Smirnov's opinions about women?

Mrs. Popov. Well, I like that! Then who is true and faithful in love to your way of thinking? Not men by any chance?

Smirnov. Yes, madam. Men.

Mrs. Popov. *Men!* (*gives a bitter laugh*) Men true and faithful in love! That's rich, I must say. (*vehemently*) What right have you to talk like that? Men true and faithful! If it comes to that, the best man I've ever known was my late husband, I may say. I loved him passionately, with all my heart as only an intelligent young woman can. I gave him my youth, my happiness, my life, my possessions. I lived only for him. I worshiped him as an idol. And—what do you think? This best of men was shamelessly deceiving me all along the line! After his death I found a drawer in his desk full of love letters, and when he was alive—oh, what a frightful memory!—he used to leave me on my own for weeks on end, he carried on with other girls before my very eyes, he was unfaithful to me, he spent my money like water, and he joked about my feelings for him. But I loved him all the same, and I've been faithful to him. What's more, I'm still faithful and true now that he's dead. I've buried myself alive inside these four walls, and I shall go round in these widow's weeds[19] till my dying day.

Smirnov (*with a contemptuous laugh*). Widow's weeds! Who do you take me for? As if I didn't know why you wear this fancy dress and bury yourself indoors! Why, it sticks out a mile! Mysterious and romantic, isn't it? Some army

15. **substance:** wealth or fortune.
16. **bated breathing:** breathing held in, due to excitement or fear. Smirnov is quoting the first lines of a well-known lyric by A. A. Fet.
17. **a tinker's cuss:** the smallest degree or amount.
18. **bluestocking:** a woman having intellectual or literary interests.
19. **widow's weeds:** the black mourning clothes of a widow.

WORDS TO KNOW **futile** (fyo͞ot'l) *adj.* serving no useful purpose

Customizing Instruction

Less Proficient Readers

Help students understand the play by asking them the following questions.

- Why does Smirnov refuse to leave?
  Answer: He wants his money first.
- What is Smirnov's opinion of women?
  Answer: He thinks they are shallow, insincere, and cruel.
- How did Mrs. Popov's husband treat her?
  Answer: He cheated on her, spent her money, and made fun of her feelings.

Students Acquiring English

1 Explain to students that *burbling* means "bubbling" or "gurgling" and that "nineteen to the dozen" is an expression meaning "excessively" or "to a great degree."

Cross Curricular Link French

FRENCH LANGUAGE IN RUSSIA During much of the Czarist period, the Russian aristocracy spoke mainly French. Russian was considered the language of the serfs until the Russian-language poetry of Alexander Pushkin became popular in the 1820s and the native Russian language began to gain acceptance among the upper class. Later in the 19th century, Chekhov and the novelist Leo Tolstoy (1828–1910) customarily used French for the characters they intended to present as snobs.

Reading and Analyzing

Reading Skills and Strategies: PARAPHRASE

Students should monitor their reading strategies and make modifications when understanding breaks down. Have students paraphrase or explain in their own words what happens in Scene 9. Ask students to write their paraphrases in their Reader's Notebook.

Possible Response: Smirnov frightens Luke, and Mrs. Popov tells Smirnov to leave and insults him. He challenges her to a duel, and she accepts. Smirnov is impressed by her spirit and decides that he likes her.

Literary Analysis: CHARACTERIZATION

Ask students what the contrast between Luke's reaction to Smirnov's threats and Mrs. Popov's reaction to Smirnov's threats tells us about her character.

Possible Response: She has more courage and resolve than Luke does, and she is not fooled by Smirnov's bravado.

Portrait of M. K. Oliv (1895), Valentin Aleksandrovich Serov. Oil on canvas, 88 cm × 68.5 cm, The State Russian Museum, St. Petersburg, accessioned from I. A. Mamontov, 1904.

cadet or hack poet[20] may pass by your garden, look up at your windows and think: "There dwells Tamara,[21] the mysterious princess, the one who buried herself alive from love of her husband." Who do you think you're fooling?

1 **Mrs. Popov** (*flaring up*). *What!* You dare to take that line with me!

Smirnov. Buries herself alive—but doesn't forget to powder her nose!

Mrs. Popov. You dare adopt that tone!

Smirnov. Don't you raise your voice to me, madam;
2 I'm not one of your servants. Let me call a spade a spade. Not being a woman, I'm used to saying what I think. So stop shouting, pray.

Mrs. Popov. It's you who are shouting, not me. Leave me alone, would you mind?

Smirnov. Pay up, and I'll go.

Mrs. Popov. You'll get nothing out of me.

Smirnov. Oh yes I shall.

Mrs. Popov. Just to be awkward, you won't get one single copeck.[22] And you can leave me alone.

20. **hack poet:** a poet who writes shallow or ordinary verse, usually just to make a living.
21. **Tamara:** a reference to the heroine of the poem "Tamara" by Russian Romantic poet Mikhail Lermontov.
22. **copeck:** a Russian coin of little value, similar to a penny.

Teaching Options

Mini Lesson Viewing and Representing

Portrait of M. K. Oliv **by Valentin Aleksandrovich Serov**

ART APPRECIATION This portrait of a young Russian married woman is notable for its interplay of deep shadows and light, in the manner of Rembrandt. Serov (1865–1911) remarked about the subject of his 1895 oil painting, "She resembles a young mouse peeking out of a dark corner with two sharp eyes."

Instruction Point out the interplay of light and shadow and how the artist has placed his subject in the shadows, except for her face. Ask students to explain why they agree or disagree with Serov's description of his subject.

Application Ask students whether the portrait resembles Mrs. Popov as they have imagined her.

Possible Response: No. The figure in the painting seems shy and retiring, while Mrs. Popov is self-assured and assertive.

Smirnov. Not having the pleasure of being your husband or fiancé, I'll trouble you not to make a scene. (*sits down*) I don't like it.

Mrs. Popov (*choking with rage*). Do I see you sitting down?

Smirnov. You most certainly do.

Mrs. Popov. Would you mind leaving?

Smirnov. Give me my money. (*aside*) Oh, I'm in such a rage! Furious I am!

Mrs. Popov. I've no desire to bandy words with cads,[23] sir. Kindly clear off! (*pause*) Well, are you going or aren't you?

Smirnov. No.

Mrs. Popov. No?

Smirnov. No!

Mrs. Popov. Very well then! (*rings*)

Scene 9

(*The above and* Luke)

Mrs. Popov. Show this gentleman out, Luke.

Luke (*goes up to* Smirnov). Be so good as to leave, sir, when you're told, sir. No point in—

3 **Smirnov** (*jumping up*). You hold your tongue! Who do you think you're talking to? I'll carve you up in little pieces.

Luke (*clutching at his heart*). Heavens and saints above us! (*falls into an armchair*) Oh, I feel something terrible—fair took my breath away, it did.

Mrs. Popov. But where's Dasha? Dasha! (*shouts*) Dasha! Pelegeya! Dasha! (*rings*)

Luke. Oh, they've all gone fruit picking. There's no one in the house. I feel faint. Fetch water.

Mrs. Popov. Be so good as to clear out!

Smirnov. Couldn't you be a bit more polite?

Mrs. Popov (*clenching her fists and stamping*). You uncouth oaf! You have the manners of a bear! Think you own the place? Monster!

Smirnov. What! You say that again!

Mrs. Popov. I called you an ill-mannered oaf, a monster!

Smirnov (*advancing on her*). Look here, what right have you to insult me?

Mrs. Popov. All right, I'm insulting you. So what? Think I'm afraid of you?

Smirnov. Just because you look all romantic, you can get away with anything—is that your idea? This is dueling talk!

Luke. Heavens and saints above us! Water!

Smirnov. Pistols at dawn!

Mrs. Popov. Just because you have big fists and the lungs of an ox, you needn't think I'm scared, see? Think you own the place, don't you!

Smirnov. We'll shoot it out! No one calls me names and gets away with it, weaker sex or no weaker sex.

Mrs. Popov (*trying to shout him down*). You coarse lout!

Smirnov. Why should it only be us men who answer for our insults? It's high time we dropped that silly idea. If women want equality, let them . . . have equality! I challenge you, madam! 4

Mrs. Popov. Want to shoot it out, eh? Very well.

Smirnov. This very instant!

Mrs. Popov. Most certainly! My husband left some pistols; I'll fetch them instantly. (*moves hurriedly off and comes back*) I'll enjoy putting a bullet through that thick skull. . . . (*goes out*)

Smirnov. I'll pot[24] her like a sitting bird. I'm not one of your sentimental young puppies. She'll get no chivalry from me!

---

23. **bandy . . . cads:** exchange words with scoundrels.

24. **pot:** shoot.

Customizing Instruction

Students Acquiring English

Help students understand these idioms:

1 "take that line"
Answer: take that sort of approach

2 "call a spade a spade"
Answer: speak frankly

3 "hold your tongue"
Answer: stop talking

4 "it's high time"
Answer: It's time for something to happen, if not already past that time.

Encourage students to find similar idioms in their first languages. Remind students that they can understand the main idea of a character's speech without understanding every single idiom.

Mini Lesson Speaking and Listening

DRAMATIC READING

Instruction Explain to students that in dramatic reading actors take roles and read their characters' dialogue aloud while looking at the script. Unlike a full-fledged performance, a dramatic reading does not rely on scenery, costumes, props, lighting, sound effects, or the movements of the actors. Its emphasis is on the actors' oral interpretation of the characters. Students should justify their choice of verbal and nonverbal performance techniques by referring to their interpretations of the text.

Application Ask three volunteers to prepare and perform a dramatic reading of several scenes, preferably following Scene 6. Encourage the rest of the class (the audience) to listen to the actors as they bring the characters to life. Invite class discussion afterward, focusing on the question, "What did you learn about the play from listening to the dramatic reading that you did not get from reading?"

Reading and Analyzing

Literary Analysis FARCE

Have students discuss the play's ending. Ask them what elements of farce we can see in the ending.

Possible Response: the sudden reversal of action—from duel to embrace—is farcical and exaggerated; the characters' disjointed and ridiculous words are often at odds with their behavior.

ACTIVE READING

A PREDICT Have students write down their answers to this question before they read scene 10. When students have finished reading the play, have them compare their predictions with the outcome.

Reading Skills and Strategies: CLARIFYING

B Ask students why Toby gets no oats today.

Possible Response: To Mrs. Popov, Toby represents her husband and his interests. Once she abandons her mourning and embraces Smirnov, she also abandons her empty faithfulness to her husband.

Luke. Kind sir! (*kneels*) Grant me a favor; pity an old man and leave this place. First you frighten us out of our wits; now you want to fight a duel.

Smirnov (*not listening*). A duel! There's true women's emancipation for you! That evens up the sexes with a vengeance! I'll knock her off as a matter of principle. But what a woman! (*mimics her*) ". . . I'll put a bullet through that thick skull." Not bad, eh? Flushed all over, flashing eyes, accepts my challenge! You know, I've never seen such a woman in my life.

Luke. Go away, sir, and I'll say prayers for you till the day I die.

Smirnov. There's a regular woman for you, something I do appreciate! A proper woman—not some namby-pamby, wishy-washy female, but a really red-hot bit of stuff, a regular pistol-packing little spitfire. A pity to kill her, really.

1

Luke (*weeps*). Kind sir—do leave. Please!

Smirnov. I definitely like her. Definitely! Never mind her dimples; I like her. I wouldn't mind letting her off what she owes me, actually. And I don't feel angry anymore. Wonderful woman!

Scene 10

(*The above and* Mrs. Popov)

Mrs. Popov (*comes in with the pistols*). Here are the pistols. But before we start would you mind showing me how to fire them? I've never had a pistol in my hands before.

ACTIVE READING

A **PREDICT** What do you think will be the outcome of the duel?

Luke. Lord help us! Mercy on us! I'll go and find the gardener and coachman. What have we done to deserve this? (*goes out*)

Smirnov (*examining the pistols*). Now, there are several types of pistol. There are Mortimer's special dueling pistols with percussion caps.[25] Now, yours here are Smith and Wessons, triple action with extractor,[26] center-fired. They're fine weapons, worth a cool ninety roubles the pair. Now, you hold a revolver like this. (*aside*) What eyes, what eyes! She's hot stuff all right!

Mrs. Popov. Like this?

Smirnov. Yes, that's right. Then you raise the hammer and take aim like this. Hold your head back a bit; stretch your arm out properly. Right. And then with this finger you press this little gadget; and that's it. But the great thing is—don't get excited, and do take your time about aiming. Try and see your hand doesn't shake.

Mrs. Popov. All right. We can't very well shoot indoors; let's go in the garden.

Smirnov. Very well. But I warn you, I'm firing in the air.

Mrs. Popov. Oh, this is the limit! Why?

Smirnov. Because, because—That's my business.

Mrs. Popov. Got cold feet, eh? I see. Now don't shilly-shally, sir. Kindly follow me. I shan't rest till I've put a bullet through your brains. . . . Got the wind up, have you? 2

Smirnov. Yes.

Mrs. Popov. That's a lie. Why won't you fight?

Smirnov. Because, er, because you, er, I like you.

Mrs. Popov (*with a vicious laugh*). He likes me! He dares to say he likes me! (*points to the door*) I won't detain you.

Smirnov (*puts down the revolver without speaking, picks up his peaked cap and moves off; near the door he stops, and for about half a minute the two look at each other without speaking; then he speaks, going up to her hesitantly*). Listen. Are you still angry? I'm

25. **percussion caps:** small powder caps used to set off some older guns.

26. **extractor:** the part of a gun that pulls the shell case out of the chamber so that it may be ejected after firing.

Teaching Options

Mini Lesson Grammar

SENTENCE TYPES Remind students that there are four sentence types: declarative, interrogative, imperative, and exclamatory. The type of a sentence may determine its end punctuation. A declarative sentence makes a statement and ends with a period. An interrogative sentence asks a question and ends with a question mark. An exclamatory sentence is emphatic and ends in an exclamation point. An imperative sentence gives a command and ends with a period or (if it is also emphatic) an exclamation point.

Model Sentences

Her husband died last year. *(declarative)*

When did her husband die? *(interrogative)*

Your husband never paid the debt! *(exclamatory)*

Pay the debt! *(imperative)*

Instruction

Point out to students that interrogative sentences do not follow normal word order (subject, verb, object). Instead, they follow question word order, with the verb and subject inverted. Point out that imperative sentences contain the command form of the verb and lack a "subject." Instead, the subject *(you)* is implied in the verb.

absolutely furious myself, but you must see—how can I put it? The fact is that, er, it's this way, actually—(*shouts*) Anyway, can I help it if I like you? (*clutches the back of a chair, which cracks and breaks*) . . . fragile stuff, furniture! I like you! Do you understand? I, er, I'm almost in love.

Mrs. Popov. Keep away from me; I loathe you.

Smirnov. God, what a woman! Never saw the like of it in all my born days. I'm sunk! Without trace! Trapped like a mouse!

Mrs. Popov. Get back or I shoot.

Smirnov. Shoot away. I'd die happily with those marvelous eyes looking at me; that's what you can't see—die by that dear little velvet hand. Oh, I'm crazy! Think it over and make your mind up now, because once I leave this place we shan't see each other again. So make your mind up. I'm a gentleman and a man of honor, I've ten thousand a year, I can put a bullet through a coin in midair and I keep a good stable. Be my wife.

Mrs. Popov (*indignantly brandishes the revolver*). A duel! We'll shoot it out!

Smirnov. I'm out of my mind! Nothing makes any sense. (*shouts*) Hey, you there—water!

Mrs. Popov (*shouts*). We'll shoot it out!

Smirnov. I've lost my head, fallen for her like some damfool boy! (*Clutches her hand. She shrieks with pain.*) I love you! (*kneels*) I love you as I never loved any of my twenty-one other women—twelve times it was me broke it off; the other nine got in first. But I never loved anyone as much as you. I've gone all sloppy, soft and sentimental. Kneeling like an imbecile, offering my hand! Disgraceful! Scandalous! I haven't been in love for five years, I swore not to, and here I am crashing head over heels, hook, line and sinker! I offer you my hand. Take it or leave it. (*gets up and hurries to the door*)

Mrs. Popov. Just a moment.

Smirnov (*stops*). What is it?

Mrs. Popov. Oh, never mind, just go away. But wait. No, go, go away. I hate you. Or no—don't go away. Oh, if you knew how furious I am! (*throws the revolver on the table*) My fingers are numb from holding this beastly thing. (*tears a handkerchief in her anger*) Why are you hanging about? Clear out!

Smirnov. Good-bye.

Mrs. Popov. Yes, yes, go away! (*shouts*) Where are you going? Stop. Oh, go away then. I'm so furious! Don't you come near me, I tell you.

Smirnov. (*going up to her*). I'm so fed up with myself! Falling in love like a schoolboy! Kneeling down! It's enough to give you the willies! (*rudely*) I love you! Oh, it's just what the doctor ordered, this is! There's my interest due in tomorrow, hay making's upon us—and *you* have to come along! (*takes her by the waist*) I'll never forgive myself. 3

Mrs. Popov. Go away! You take your hands off me! I, er, hate you! We'll sh-shoot it out!

(*A prolonged kiss*)

Scene 11

(*The above,* Luke *with an axe, the gardener with a rake, the coachman with a pitchfork and some workmen with sundry sticks and staves*)

Luke (*seeing the couple kissing*). Mercy on us! (*pause*)

Mrs. Popov (*lowering her eyes*). Luke, tell them in the stables—Toby gets no oats today. B

Curtain

Translated by Ronald Hingley

Customizing Instruction

Students Acquiring English

Help students understand these difficult idioms and nonsense phrases.

1 "namby-pamby" (weak and indecisive); "wishy-washy" (indecisive; lacking character)

2 "shilly-shally" (procrastinate; waste time)

3 "give you the willies" (give you a feeling of uneasiness)

Encourage students to hear the humor of these phrases as they read. Ask students to supply similar silly phrases from their first languages.

Exercises Have students copy the following sentences. Ask them to identify the sentences as one of the four sentence types and to provide end punctuation.

1. Smirnov walked into the room *(declarative; period)*
2. Why can't you pay the debt now *(interrogative; question mark)*
3. Stay away *(imperative; exclamation point or period)*
4. Please open the door, Luke *(imperative; period)*
5. Mrs. Popov ran to her room and looked for the pistols *(declarative; period)*
6. You are an absurd, rude, and annoying man *(exclamatory; exclamation point or declarative; period)*

Use **Unit Two Resource Book,** p. 34.

Use **Grammar Transparencies and Copymasters,** p. 119.

Use McDougal Littell's ***Language Network,*** Chapter 4, for more instruction in sentence types.

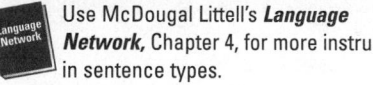

GUIDING STUDENT RESPONSE

Connect to the Literature

1. What Do You Think?
Students should be able to explain their ratings by referring to specific passages.

Comprehension Check

- He wants to collect a debt owed by her late husband.
- She intends to have a duel with Smirnov.
- They suddenly fall in love.

Use Selection Quiz
Unit Two Resource Book, p. 35.

Think Critically

2. Encourage students to sketch their image both in pictures and in words. Consider pairing for comparison students who are describing the same or nearly the same image, or images, from the same scene.
3. Students may feel that he is insensitive and boorish, or they might feel that he is simply full of hot air. Encourage students to refer to all available information on Smirnov's attitude—not only Smirnov's speeches in Scene 8, but also his attempt to explain why he is attracted to Mrs. Popov.
4. Possible Response: Smirnov's bark is worse than his bite; he is not really as mean as he pretends to be.
5. Students might describe Mrs. Popov as a fickle, moody, and quick-tempered woman.
6. Some students will feel that both Mrs. Popov and Smirnov are moody, irrational, and quick-tempered. Others might think that they represent opposing male and female stereotypes.
7. Possible Response: Luke provides a voice of reason in contrast with Smirnov's bluster and Mrs. Popov's affectations. Toby, the horse, stands in for the late Mr. Popov—first indulged, finally put aside in favor of Smirnov.

Connect to the Literature

1. Rate this comedy on a scale of 1 to 10, with 10 representing "very funny" and 1 representing "not funny at all." Share your response.

Comprehension Check

- Why does Smirnov come to Mrs. Popov's house?
- Why does Mrs. Popov fetch her husband's pistols?
- How do Smirnov and Mrs. Popov finally resolve their differences?

Think Critically

2. **ACTIVE READING VISUALIZING** Review the notes in your READER'S NOTEBOOK. What images of the **set** and **characters** did you form as you read the play? Sketch or briefly describe one of those images, and compare it with a classmate's.
3. What is your opinion of Smirnov's attitude toward women? Cite examples from the play to support your opinion.
4. Do you think that Smirnov is really a bear, as the title implies? Explain your answer.
5. How would you describe Mrs. Popov?

   THINK ABOUT
   - how she responded to her husband's death
   - what her marriage was really like
   - why she agrees to the duel
   - her change of heart at the end of the play
6. Of the sayings "Birds of a feather flock together" and "Opposites attract," which do you think is more appropriate to the romance in *The Bear?* Explain your answer.
7. In a well-made play, even **minor characters** contribute to its success. In your opinion, what do Luke and the horse, Toby, contribute to this play?

Extend Interpretations

8. **Critic's Corner** A student reviewer, Cynthia Villicana, found Chekhov's play to be interesting because it is "romantic and funny at the same time." How does her judgment of the play compare with your own?
9. **Connect to Life** Do you think men or women most often win the battle of the sexes? Explain your reasoning.

Literary Analysis

FARCE A **farce** is a play that prompts laughter through ridiculous situations, exaggerated behavior and language, and physical comedy. Characters are often **stereotypes;** that is, they conform to a fixed pattern or are defined by a single trait. In *The Bear,* for example, Luke might be seen as a stereotype of a loyal but critical servant who tells his superior more than she wants to hear.

Paired Activity With a partner, create a chart like the one shown, citing examples of ridiculous situations, exaggerated behavior and language, and physical comedy in *The Bear.* Would you say that the main characters are stereotypes? Why or why not?

Ridiculous Situations	Exaggerated Behavior/Language	Physical Comedy

DRAMA As you know, **dialogue** and **stage directions** are two essential components of drama. How did the dialogue and stage directions in *The Bear* influence the images that you formed of the **characters?** Review the notes that you compiled in your READER'S NOTEBOOK. Put a *D* next to those notes that seem a direct result of the dialogue; put an *S* next to those that were produced by the stage directions. When finished, discuss how stage directions influence your understanding of dialogue. Use examples from the play to support your opinion.

Extend Interpretations

Critic's Corner Students should be prepared to support their opinion by referring to specific events or passages from the text.

Connect to Life Encourage students to think about who "wins" in the play and how they define "winning" in the battle of the sexes.

Literary Analysis

Farce Student charts should refer to specific examples from the text, and use them to support their responses.

Drama Possible Response: The stage directions, which are slight, generally serve to clarify the dialogue, such as entrances and exits, and the fact that Mrs. Popov is crying at the beginning of the play. Sometimes they give emphasis to dialogue, such as when Smirnov breaks the chair.

Writing Options

1. Analysis of the Combatants Why do you think the two main characters in *The Bear* fall in love? Write an analysis that explains their behavior, citing details from the play to support your ideas.

Writing Handbook
See page 1159: Analysis.

2. Drama Review Imagine that you are a theater critic. Write a review of *The Bear* that focuses on your opinion of the play itself, though you may also include imaginary details about the quality of the production.

3. Modern Scene Write your own dramatic scene, set in modern times, involving the battle of the sexes. See if you can work in various elements of farce.

Activities & Explorations

1. Scene in Performance Working with two classmates, select a scene from *The Bear* and perform it in front of the rest of the class. As you prepare and rehearse your scene, pay particular attention to Chekhov's stage directions. ~ **PERFORMING**

2. Set Design Sketch a set design for a production of this play. You may wish to conduct historical research to make your set as accurate as possible. ~ **ART**

3. Sequel to the Play With a group of classmates, stage a sequel to *The Bear,* set at the wedding reception after the two main characters marry. Improvise dialogue and action in keeping with the characters' earlier portrayals. Guests at the reception can share stories about the couple's odd courtship. ~ **SPEAKING AND LISTENING**

Inquiry & Research

Czarist Russia Research the society in which this play is set. In particular, find out more about the class system that prevailed in Russia from 1861 until the Russian Revolution of 1917. Present your findings to the class in an oral report.

More Online: Research Starter
www.mcdougallittell.com

Members of the Russian nobility in the 19th century.

Vocabulary in Action

EXERCISE: CONTEXT CLUES Write the word that best completes each sentence.

1. That ill-mannered man overstepped his bounds and took the ______ of asking a woman out on a date just one week after her husband's funeral!
2. Giving him a book on etiquette would be ______, since rude people don't see any point to politeness.
3. "Why," he might whine, "should I ______ with desire instead of just asking for what I want?"
4. Overwhelmed by his rudeness, the woman cried, "You inconsiderate, ______ idiot!"
5. One who wants ______ from the restrictions imposed by good manners will find that there is a price to pay for such freedom.

WORDS TO KNOW
emancipation, futile, languish, liberty, sniveling

Building Vocabulary
For an in-depth study of word origins, see page 183 or page 356.

Writing Options

1. **Analysis of the Combatants** Students might focus on how the characters' attitudes toward each other change and discuss the character traits that suggest compatibility. How does interaction between the characters lead to their final embrace?
2. **Drama Review** Remind students that reviewers are always faced with the dilemma of how much to reveal about the play's plot.
3. **Modern Scene** Encourage students to use some devices found in *The Bear:* seemingly opposite personality types; stereotyping; absurd twists of plot.

Activities & Explorations

1. **Scene in Performance** Encourage students to add stage directions to Chekhov's. If possible, have one student act as a director to coordinate rehearsals and interpret stage directions. Adding furniture or other props may help students to execute the stage directions.
2. **Set Design** Point out that set designers of period plays or movies spend days in research libraries looking at contemporary paintings, sketches, or photographs to get ideas for sets and props. Suggest that students search for books on 19th- and early 20th-century art, set design, theater, costumes, and furniture—preferably focused on Russia or Europe.
3. **Sequel to the Play** Suggest that students limit the speaking roles in this play to the three main characters of *The Bear* and four or five additional characters.

Inquiry & Research

Czarist Russia Students may want to begin their research by looking at books about the Russian Revolution and reading about the conditions that led up to it.

Vocabulary in Action

Exercise: Context Clues
1. liberty
2. futile
3. languish
4. sniveling
5. emancipation

Assessment Standardized Test Practice

ANALYZING VIEWPOINT You can assess students' understanding of the selection by having them summarize what happens in the play from the viewpoint of Smirnov, Mrs. Popov, or Luke. Have students imagine that they are one of these three characters and ask them to write a letter to a cousin in Moscow, explaining what occurred in the play.

RUBRIC

3 Full Accomplishment Response reflects a full understanding of the events in the play and of the character.

2 Substantial Accomplishment Response shows a general understanding of the events in the play and of the character.

1 Little or Partial Accomplishment Response shows little understanding of the events in the play and of the character.

Grammar in Context

WRITING EXERCISE

Answers will vary. Possible answers are shown.

1. Why should I go out again? *(declarative; interrogative; the speaker is using a rhetorical question to express a determination to stay.)*
2. He was so fond of Toby. *(exclamatory; declarative; the speaker is stating a simple fact.)*
3. You should be ashamed of yourself! *(interrogative; exclamatory; the speaker is being harshly critical.)*
4. Won't you come in, please? *(imperative; interrogative; the question is more polite than the command.)*
5. Don't expect me to take you seriously. *(interrogative; imperative; the speaker sounds more arrogant and less sarcastic.)*

Author Activity

Students might be interested in the film *Vanya on 42nd Street* (directed by Louis Malle and available on video). The film depicts a small company rehearsing Chekhov's *Uncle Vanya*.

Grammar in Context: Kinds of Sentences

In this excerpt from *The Bear,* Chekhov uses four different kinds of sentences.

> **Mrs. Popov.** Would you mind leaving?
> **Smirnov.** Give me my money. *(aside)* Oh, I'm in such a rage! Furious I am!
> **Mrs. Popov.** I've no desire to bandy words with cads, sir.

Sentence	Kind
Would you mind leaving?	Interrogative
Give me my money.	Imperative
Oh, I'm in such a rage!	Exclamatory
Furious I am!	Exclamatory
I've no desire to bandy words with cads, sir.	Declarative

A **declarative sentence** makes a statement. An **interrogative sentence** asks a question. An **imperative sentence** gives a command. An **exclamatory sentence** expresses strong emotion.

In the passage above, the imperative and exclamatory sentences show that Smirnov is upset. Mrs. Popov, who is trying to remain calm, uses interrogative and declarative sentences.

WRITING EXERCISE Identify the type of each sentence. Then rewrite it as a different type of sentence, indicating what type you have rewritten it as. Tell how your change affects the tone of the sentence. Do not use any of the sentence types more than twice.

Example: ***Original*** Would you mind leaving? (interrogative)

Rewritten Leave! (exclamatory [and imperative]; the speaker is angry and may be shouting.)

1. There's no reason for me to go out again.
2. How fond he was of Toby!
3. Aren't you ashamed of yourself?
4. Come in, please.
5. Do you expect me to take you seriously?

Grammar Handbook

The Sentence and Its Parts, p. 1192

Anton Chekhov

1860–1904

Other Works
Uncle Vanya
The Three Sisters
The Cherry Orchard
Stories of Russian Life
The Brute and Other Farces

Dr. Chekhov One of his country's greatest authors, Anton Chekhov was born to a poor family in Taganrog in the south of Russia. After finishing high school, Chekhov enrolled in medical school in Moscow, but since his family needed his financial support, he began writing comical sketches and selling them to popular newspapers and journals. Although Chekhov obtained his degree in 1884, he practiced medicine only sporadically throughout his writing career.

A Master of the Stage By 1887 Chekhov had published three story collections and was beginning to experiment with drama, producing *The Bear* and several more one-act farces, as well as full-length plays. The first performance of one of these plays, *The Seagull,* received such poor reviews that Chekhov nearly stopped writing drama; however, a successful restaging at the Moscow Art Theater turned the criticism around. In the next few years Chekhov wrote three more plays for which he is best remembered: *Uncle Vanya, The Three Sisters,* and *The Cherry Orchard.* Chekhov died of tuberculosis in 1904.

Author Activity

Chekhov the Dramatist Find out more about Chekhov's contributions to the theater. Prepare a class presentation of this information and, if possible, share with the class various photographs from stage productions of his plays.

VIDEODISC **LaserLinks: Background for Reading**
Drama Connection

PREPARING to *Read*

"It was a lonesome land!"

The Californian's Tale

Short Story by MARK TWAIN

Connect to Your Life

No Place Like Home What do you think makes a house a home? Is a home created by its comfortable furnishings or the personal touches in its decoration? Is it created by the feelings of the people who live there or by the way guests are welcomed? For five minutes, do some focused freewriting about what it takes to make a house a home.

Build Background

Gold Rush The comforts of home have a special significance for the characters in "The Californian's Tale," who live in a lonely environment in the aftermath of the California Gold Rush. Gold was first discovered in 1848 at Sutter's Mill east of Sacramento. During 1849 alone, more than 80,000 so-called "forty-niners", mostly men, rushed to the California territory to prospect, or hunt, for gold in the region's many rivers and creeks. By 1850 California had grown so much that it was admitted as a state in the Union.

Once the precious ore became harder to find, many Gold Rush "boom" towns turned into ghost towns. Some veteran prospectors, however, did remain to continue their search for gold or to try their hand at farming.

California Gold Camps

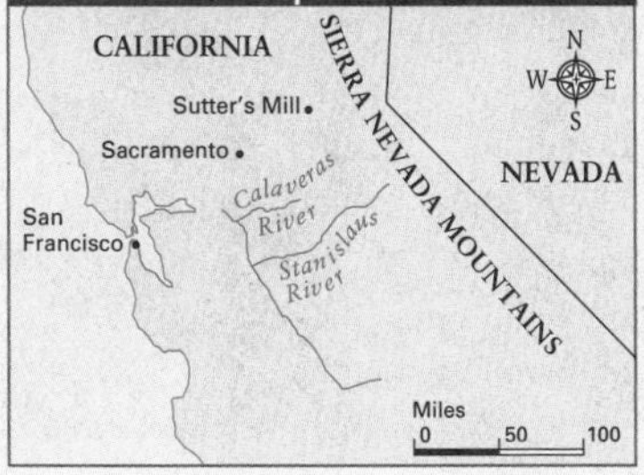

WORDS TO KNOW
Vocabulary Preview

balmy	furtive	predecessor	sever
boding	grizzled	sedate	supplicating
desolation	imploring		

Focus Your Reading

LITERARY ANALYSIS **HISTORICAL SETTING** As you know, **setting** is the time and place of the action of a story. **Historical setting** refers to a particular historical period, such as the aftermath of the California Gold Rush in "The Californian's Tale." The isolation of the frontier is illustrated by the following passage:

> ***It was a lovely region, woodsy, balmy, delicious, and had once been populous, long years before, but now the people had vanished and the charming paradise was a solitude.***

As you read, consider how the geographical location and historical time frame prompt the development of the **plot** and create a **mood,** or atmosphere, within the story.

ACTIVE READING **INTERPRETING THE RELATIONSHIP BETWEEN SETTING AND CHARACTERS**

The **setting** of a story may also give the reader insights into the **characters.** To understand the characters in Twain's story, you need to understand how the lonely frontier environment has influenced their lives. Similarly, Henry's cozy cottage, which offers such a welcome relief to the hard frontier life, helps the reader to understand why Henry values his wife so highly.

READER'S NOTEBOOK As you read, note relevant details about the frontier surroundings and Henry's cottage. Consider what insight each part of the story's setting gives into the characters and their lives.

VIDEODISC **LaserLinks: Background for Reading**
Historical Connection

OVERVIEW

This selection is included in the **Grade 10 InterActive Reader.**

Objectives

1. understand and appreciate a **short story (Literary Analysis)**
2. connect story to **historical setting (Literary Analysis)**
3. **interpret the relationship between setting and characters (Active Reading)**

Summary

The narrator meets an ex-miner named Henry who invites him into his isolated, rose-clad cottage, a delightful home full of lovely feminine touches. Henry praises his young wife and begs the narrator to stay three days until her return. On the night of her scheduled return, three friends celebrate with Henry until the hour she is to arrive, and then they drug Henry and put him to bed. They explain that Henry's wife disappeared 19 years before, and the miner lost his mind. Since then, his friends hold this party each year to help Henry through the anniversary of his young wife's disappearance.

Thematic Link

Sympathetic friends understand the **mysteries of the heart** that keep alive a man's illusion about his departed wife.

5-Minute Warm-Up

Daily Language SkillBuilder

Have students **proofread** the display sentences on page 223j and write them correctly. The sentences also appear on Transparency 9 of **Grammar Transparencies and Copymasters.**

Mini Lesson **Preteaching Vocabulary**

If you would like to preteach the WORDS TO KNOW for this selection, use the Mini Lesson, p. 304.

LESSON RESOURCES

UNIT TWO RESOURCE BOOK, pp. 36–41

ASSESSMENT RESOURCES
Formal Assessment, pp. 51–52
Teacher's Guide to Assessment and Portfolio Use
Test Generator

SKILLS TRANSPARENCIES AND COPYMASTERS
Literary Analysis
- Setting, T3 (for Cooperative Learning Activity, p. 311)

Reading and Critical Thinking
- Noting Details, T9 (for Reader's Notebook, p. 303)

Grammar
- Placement of Adjectives, C74 (for Mini Lesson, p. 312)

Vocabulary
- Context Clues, C41 (for Mini Lesson, p. 304)
- Prefixes, C42 (for Mini Lesson, p. 307)

Writing
- Effective Language, T13 (for Writing Options, p. 312)
- Showing, Not Telling, T22 (for Writing Option 1, p. 312)

Communications
- Impromptu Speaking: Dialogue, Role-Play, Debate, T13 (for Activities & Explorations 2 and 3, p. 312)

INTEGRATED TECHNOLOGY
Audio Library
LaserLinks
- Historical Connection: The Gold Rush. See **Teacher's SourceBook,** p. 23.

Internet: Research Starter
Visit our website:
www.mcdougallittell.com

TEACHING THE LITERATURE

Reading and Analyzing

Literary Analysis

HISTORICAL SETTING

As they read the first page of the story, have students identify elements of historical setting and what type of conflict might occur in such a setting.

Possible Responses:

- post-gold rush desolation; struggle with loneliness and the difficulty of wilderness survival
- gold miners lost their wealth; difficulty of disappointed hopes

Ask students what sort of mood these details create.

Possible Response: peaceful but lonely and perhaps despairing

Use **Unit Two Resource Book** p. 38 for more practice.

Active Reading

INTERPRETING THE RELATIONSHIP BETWEEN SETTING AND CHARACTERS

As students read the story, point out the list of the little domestic touches that make Henry's house seem so pleasant to the narrator. Ask students what Henry's attitude toward these details reveals about him. What does the narrator's response to them reveal about Henry?

Possible Response: That Henry so adores these furnishings suggests that he is proud of both his wife and his home. The narrator's response indicates his weariness of rough living and his appreciation of simple niceties.

Use **Unit Two Resource Book** p. 37 for more practice.

The Californian's Tale

Mark Twain

Thirty-five years ago I was out prospecting on the Stanislaus,[1] tramping all day long with pick and pan and horn, and washing a hatful of dirt here and there, always expecting to make a rich strike, and never doing it.

1. **Stanislaus:** a river in California where gold was mined.

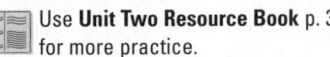

Old-Time Cabin, Maynard Dixon. Courtesy of Museum of Art, Brigham Young University. Copyright © Museum of Art, Brigham Young University, all rights reserved.

304

Teaching Options

Mini Lesson: Preteaching Vocabulary

USING CONTEXT CLUES Call students' attention to the list of WORDS TO KNOW. Remind them that they can frequently find clues about the words' meaning in the context in which they are used. Use the model sentence to demonstrate the strategy of using context clues to provide **inferences** to word meaning.

Model Sentence

It was a lovely region, woodsy, balmy, and delicious.

Instruction

- Write the model sentence on the chalkboard.
- Ask a volunteer to summarize the meaning of the sentence.
- Have students use the meaning of the sentence to **infer** meanings for the word *balmy.*
- Ask a volunteer to use the word *balmy* in a sentence.

Use **Unit Two Resource Book** p. 39 for more practice.

A lesson on using context clues appears on p. 56 in the Pupil's Edition.

At last, in the early part of the afternoon, when I caught sight of a human creature, I felt a most grateful uplift.

It was a lovely region, woodsy, balmy, delicious, and had once been populous, long years before, but now the people had vanished and the charming paradise was a solitude. They went away when the surface diggings gave out. In one place, where a busy little city with banks and newspapers and fire companies and a mayor and aldermen had been, was nothing but a wide expanse of emerald turf, with not even the faintest sign that human life had ever been present there. This was down toward Tuttletown.[2] In the country neighborhood thereabouts, along the dusty roads, one found at intervals the prettiest little cottage homes, snug and cozy, and so cobwebbed with vines snowed thick with roses that the doors and windows were wholly hidden from sight—sign that these were deserted homes, forsaken years ago by defeated and disappointed families who could neither sell them nor give them away. Now and then, half an hour apart, one came across solitary log cabins of the earliest mining days, built by the first gold miners, the predecessors of the cottage builders. In some few cases these cabins were still occupied; and when this was so, you could depend upon it that the occupant was the very pioneer who had built the cabin; and you could depend on another thing, too—that he was there because he had once had his opportunity to go home to the States rich, and had not done it; had rather lost his wealth, and had then in his humiliation resolved to sever all communication with his home relatives and friends, and be to them thenceforth as one dead. Round about California in that day were scattered a host of these living dead men—pride-smitten poor fellows, grizzled and old at forty, whose secret thoughts were made all of regrets and longings—regrets for their wasted lives, and longings to be out of the struggle and done with it all.

It was a lonesome land! Not a sound in all those peaceful expanses of grass and woods but the drowsy hum of insects; no glimpse of man or beast; nothing to keep up your spirits and make you glad to be alive. And so, at last, in the early part of the afternoon, when I caught sight of a human creature, I felt a most grateful uplift. This person was a man about forty-five years old, and he was standing at the gate of one of those cozy little rose-clad cottages of the sort already referred to. However, this one hadn't a deserted look; it had the look of being lived in and petted and cared for and looked after; and so had its front yard, which was a garden of flowers, abundant, gay, and flourishing. I was invited in, of course, and required to make myself at home—it was the custom of the country.

It was delightful to be in such a place, after long weeks of daily and nightly familiarity with

2. **Tuttletown:** a mining town near the Stanislaus River.

WORDS TO KNOW

balmy (bä′mē) *adj.* soothingly fragrant; mild and pleasant
predecessor (prĕd′ĭ-sĕs′ər) *n.* someone who came before and has been succeeded or replaced by another
sever (sĕv′ər) *v.* to cut or break off
grizzled (grĭz′əld) *adj.* streaked with or partly gray

Customizing Instruction

Less Proficient Readers

Set a Purpose
Have students read to find out why this cottage is so well tended.

Students Acquiring English

Discuss with students the background material on the California Gold Rush (page 314), and explain that this story takes place just after the Gold Rush had died down.

Use **Spanish Study Guide** for additional support, pp. 65–67.

Gifted and Talented

Tell students that Mark Twain, while he considered himself a foe of sentimentality, also succumbed to it in some of his works. Ask students to think about whether "The Californian's Tale" is sentimental or realistic. Encourage them to support their opinions with details from the selection.

Possible Responses: The story is sentimental in its exaggerated picture of a lover's grief and its manipulation of readers' emotions; it is realistic in showing a man possessed by illusion.

Mini Lesson: Viewing and Representing

Old-Time Cabin **by Maynard Dixon**

ART APPRECIATION Dixon portrayed not the melodramatic "Wild West" but rather the reality of day-to-day life in the old West. This painting is one of many he created during a sojourn in Utah in 1933.

Instruction Point out the use of light and shadow in this painting. Ask students how the front wall of the cabin in the foreground contrasts with the rest of the cabin, as well as with the surrounding grass and sky. What might it signify?

Possible Response: The front of the cabin is covered in dark shadow while the rest of the painting is bathed in sunlight, suggesting that frontier life had both a bright, positive side (light) as well as a darker, negative dimension (shadow).

Application Ask students whether the cabin resembles their mental image of the cabin that the narrator comes across, and why or why not.

Possible Response: No, because the cabin in the story is covered in roses and has a well-tended front yard full of flowers. The cabin in the painting lacks these things.

Reading and Analyzing

Literary Analysis: CHARACTER

A Point out that Twain uses words in this passage related to food *(fasting, famishing, nourishment, feast)* for describing the narrator's response to finding a home with the comforts of a woman's touch. Ask students what this comparison suggests to them about the narrator's feelings.

Possible Response: It suggests a starvation and desperate hunger for civilized things that is finally satisfied. The narrator "eats it up" because he has been starved for these comforts.

Reading Skills and Strategies: CLARIFYING

B Ask students to explain the meaning of Henry's statement about his wife's house-keeping—"you can't find out the law of it." What "law" is he referring to?

Possible Response: The law he refers to seems to be the underlying reason that certain arrangements of objects are pleasing to the senses.

Reading Skills and Strategies: QUESTIONING

C Ask students what makes the narrator feel a "sense of profanation" at the thought of using the towels.

Possible Response: The towels are so "clean and white" that the narrator feels too impure to use them.

miners' cabins—with all which this implies of dirt floor, never-made beds, tin plates and cups, bacon and beans and black coffee, and nothing of ornament but war pictures from the Eastern illustrated papers tacked to the log walls. That was all hard, cheerless, materialistic desolation, but here was a nest which had aspects to rest the tired eye and refresh that something in one's nature which, after long fasting, recognizes, when confronted by the belongings of art, howsoever cheap and modest they may be, that it has unconsciously been famishing and now has found nourishment. I could not have believed that a rag carpet could feast me so, and so content me; or that there could be such solace to the soul in wallpaper and framed lithographs,[3] and bright-colored tidies[4] and lamp mats, and Windsor chairs,[5] and varnished whatnots,[6] with seashells and books and china vases on them, and the score of little unclassifiable tricks and touches that a woman's hand distributes about a home, which one sees without knowing he sees them, yet would miss in a moment if they were taken away. The delight that was in my heart showed in my face, and the man saw it and was pleased; saw it so plainly that he answered it as if it had been spoken.

"All her work," he said, caressingly; "she did it all herself—every bit," and he took the room in with a glance which was full of affectionate worship. One of those soft Japanese fabrics with which women drape with careful negligence the upper part of a picture frame was out of adjustment. He noticed it, and rearranged it with cautious pains, stepping back several times to gauge the effect before he got it to suit him. Then he gave it a light finishing pat or two with his hand, and said: "She always does that. You can't tell just what it lacks, but it does lack something until you've done that—you can see it yourself after it's done, but that is all you know; you can't find out the law of it. It's like the finishing pats a mother gives the child's hair after she's got it combed and brushed, I reckon. I've seen her fix all these things so much that I can do them all just her way, though I don't know the law of any of them. But she knows the law. She knows the why and the how both; but I don't know the why; I only know the how."

He took me into a bedroom so that I might wash my hands; such a bedroom as I had not seen for years: white counterpane,[7] white pillows, carpeted floor, papered walls, pictures, dressing table, with mirror and pincushion and dainty toilet things; and in the corner a washstand, with real chinaware bowl and pitcher, and with soap in a china dish, and on a rack more than a dozen towels—towels too clean and white for one out of practice to use without some vague sense of profanation.[8] So my face spoke again, and he answered with gratified words:

"All her work; she did it all herself—every bit. Nothing here that hasn't felt the touch of

3. **lithographs:** prints made by a process in which portions of a flat surface are treated either to retain or to repel ink.
4. **tidies:** decorative coverings for the arms or headrest of a chair or sofa.
5. **Windsor chairs:** wooden chairs with high-spoked backs, outward-slanting legs, and saddle seats.
6. **whatnots:** a set of light, open shelves for displaying ornaments.
7. **counterpane:** bedspread.
8. **profanation:** the showing of contempt for something regarded as sacred.

WORDS TO KNOW

desolation (dĕs'ə-lā'shən) *n.* the state of being empty, deserted, or forlorn; barrenness; loneliness

306

Teaching Options

BLOCK SCHEDULING: MANAGING TIME

If your schedule requires that you cover the lesson objectives in a shorter time, use . . .
- Preparing to Read, p. 303
- Thinking Through the Literature, p. 311
- Vocabulary in Action, p. 312
- Grammar in Context, p. 313

If you want to take advantage of longer class time, use . . .
- TE Teaching Options: Preteaching WORDS TO KNOW, p. 304; Viewing and Representing, pp. 305, 308; Vocabulary Strategy, p. 307; Speaking and Listening, p. 309; Informal Assessment, p. 310
- Choices & Challenges and Author Activity, pp. 312–313

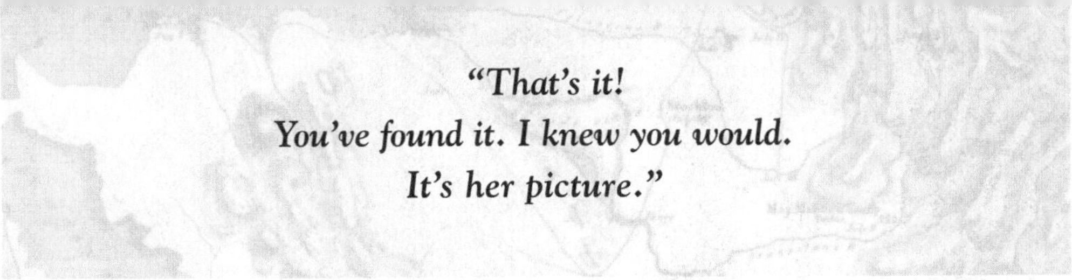

"That's it!
You've found it. I knew you would.
It's her picture."

her hand. Now you would think—But I mustn't talk so much."

By this time I was wiping my hands and glancing from detail to detail of the room's
2 belongings, as one is apt to do when he is in a new place, where everything he sees is a comfort to his eye and his spirit; and I became conscious, in one of those unaccountable ways,
1 you know, that there was something there somewhere that the man wanted me to discover for myself. I knew it perfectly, and I knew he was trying to help me by furtive indications with his eye, so I tried hard to get on the right track, being eager to gratify him. I failed several times, as I could see out of the corner of my eye without being told; but at last I knew I must be looking straight at the thing—knew it from the pleasure issuing in invisible waves from him. He broke into a happy laugh, and rubbed his hands together, and cried out:

"That's it! You've found it. I knew you would. It's her picture."

I went to the little black-walnut bracket[9] on the farther wall, and did find there what I had not yet noticed—a daguerreotype case.[10] It contained the sweetest girlish face, and the most beautiful, as it seemed to me, that I had ever seen. The man drank the admiration from my face, and was fully satisfied.

"Nineteen her last birthday," he said, as he put the picture back; "and that was the day we were married. When you see her—ah, just wait till you see her!"

"Where is she? When will she be in?"

"Oh, she's away now. She's gone to see her people. They live forty or fifty miles from here. 3
She's been gone two weeks today."

"When do you expect her back?"

"This is Wednesday. She'll be back Saturday, in the evening—about nine o'clock, likely."

I felt a sharp sense of disappointment.

"I'm sorry, because I'll be gone then," I said, regretfully.

"Gone? No—why should you go? Don't go. She'll be so disappointed."

She would be disappointed—that beautiful creature! If she had said the words herself they could hardly have blessed me more. I was feeling a deep, strong longing to see her—a longing so supplicating, so insistent, that it made me afraid. I said to myself: "I will go straight away from this place, for my peace of mind's sake."

"You see, she likes to have people come and stop with us—people who know things, and can talk—people like you. She delights in it; for she knows—oh, she knows nearly everything herself, and can talk, oh, like a bird—and the books she reads, why, you would be astonished. Don't go; it's only a little while, you know, and she'll be so disappointed."

I heard the words, but hardly noticed them, I was so deep in my thinkings and strugglings. He left me, but I didn't know. Presently he was

9. **bracket:** a small shelf.

10. **daguerreotype** (də-gâr'ə-tīp') **case:** a frame-like case holding an early type of photograph.

WORDS TO KNOW

furtive (fûr'tĭv) *adj.* shifty; having a hidden motive or purpose

supplicating (sŭp'lĭ-kāt'ĭng) *adj.* humbly or sincerely asking, begging, or praying
supplicate *v.*

Customizing Instruction

Less Proficient Readers

1 Ask students to pause here and predict what the "something" might be that the man wishes the narrator to discover. Then have them read on to discover what the something is.
Answer: a picture of the man's wife
Discuss whether the answer is what students expected.

Students Acquiring English

2 Tell students that *apt* means "likely."

3 Explain that in this context, "She's gone to see her people" means she is visiting her relatives and family.

Multiple Learning Styles

Visual Learners
As they read, have students draw a story map, drawing and labeling a box to represent each scene.

Mini Lesson Vocabulary Strategy

SUFFIXES AND PREFIXES

Instruction The word *predecessor* applies the prefix *pre-* (which means before) to the Latin root word *decessor* (which means someone who leaves). Remind students that they can apply the meanings of prefixes and roots to understand the meanings of words.

Practice Have students work in pairs to create a list of words that use the prefix *pre-*. Ask them to write a definition and a sentence using each word, then to describe how the prefix influences the word's meaning.

Possible Responses:
Word prefix
Definition a syllable or syllables attached to the beginning of a word
Sentence A *prefix* can change the meaning of a word.
Influence *pre-* means that it goes at the beginning of the word.

Use **Vocabulary Transparencies and Copymasters,** p. 42.

A lesson on suffixes and prefixes appears on p. 856 in the Pupil's Edition.

Reading and Analyzing

Active Reading

INTERPRETING THE RELATIONSHIP BETWEEN SETTING AND CHARACTER

A Ask students what aspects of the setting might make the man so eager for the narrator's company.

Possible Response: The isolation might prevent him from meeting many different people, making the narrator a welcome novelty.

Literary Analysis: FORESHADOWING

B Ask students what might be foreshadowed by the two miners' weeping at the letter and Henry's constant worrying that something has happened to his wife.

Possible Responses: She is not going to show up; something bad has happened to her.

Literary Analysis: SUSPENSE

Ask students to find details that add suspense to the action.

Possible Responses: The narrator's frequent glances at his watch; Henry's constant questions; Henry's peering down the road; Charley's reassurances

Into the Past (1941), Hananiah Harari. Oil on canvas, 15″ × 12⅞″, Richard York Gallery, New York.

back, with the picture case in his hand, and he held it open before me and said:

A "There, now, tell her to her face you could have stayed to see her, and you wouldn't."

That second glimpse broke down my good resolution. I would stay and take the risk. That night we smoked the tranquil pipe, and talked till late about various things, but mainly about her; and certainly I had had no such pleasant and restful time for many a day. The Thursday followed and slipped comfortably away. Toward twilight a big miner from three miles away came—one of the grizzled, stranded pioneers—and gave us warm salutation, clothed in grave and sober speech. Then he said:

"I only just dropped over to ask about the little madam, and when is she coming home. Any news from her?"

"Oh yes, a letter. Would you like to hear it, Tom?"

"Well, I should think I would, if you don't mind, Henry!"

Henry got the letter out of his wallet, and said he would skip some of the private phrases, if we were willing; then he went on and read the bulk of it—a loving, sedate, and altogether

WORDS TO KNOW **sedate** (sĭ-dāt′) *adj.* serenely deliberate, composed, and dignified

308

Teaching Options

Mini Lesson: Viewing and Representing

Into the Past **by Hananiah Harari**

ART APPRECIATION This oil painting by Harari (1912–) recaptures the atmosphere of earlier times through a collage of items including an old, stamped envelope, a postcard of an old building, and antique photographs of a child and a woman in 19th-century dress.

Instruction Point out that the items in the painting are arranged inside a picture frame. Ask how this depiction reinforces the idea that memory itself is a "creative" act.

Possible Response: Usually, a work of art goes inside a picture frame. Setting the objects from the past inside the frame suggests that the same process goes into our arrangement of things past as goes into the creation of a work of art.

Application Ask students to recall the details of Henry's devotion to objects relating to his wife. Ask them how Henry's reverence for those objects relates to the painting.

Possible Response: Henry has used the objects to construct a memory of his wife that has replaced the reality of her absence. This collection of objects is similar to those in the painting, also serving as a reminder that, in this case, helps Henry sustain the illusion that his wife is alive.

charming and gracious piece of handiwork, with a postscript full of affectionate regards and messages to Tom, and Joe, and Charley, and other close friends and neighbors.

As the reader finished, he glanced at Tom, and cried out:

"Oho, you're at it again! Take your hands away, and let me see your eyes. You always do that when I read a letter from her. I will write and tell her."

3 "Oh no, you mustn't, Henry. I'm getting old, you know, and any little disappointment makes me want to cry. I thought she'd be here herself, and now you've got only a letter."

"Well, now, what put that in your head? I thought everybody knew she wasn't coming till Saturday."

"Saturday! Why, come to think, I did know it. I wonder what's the matter with me lately? Certainly I knew it. Ain't we all getting ready for her? Well, I must be going now. But I'll be on hand when she comes, old man!"

Late Friday afternoon another gray veteran tramped over from his cabin a mile or so away, and said the boys wanted to have a little gaiety and a good time Saturday night, if Henry thought she wouldn't be too tired after her journey to be kept up.

"Tired? She tired! Oh, hear the man! Joe, *you* know she'd sit up six weeks to please any one of you!"

1 When Joe heard that there was a letter, he asked to have it read, and the loving messages in it for him broke the old fellow all up; but he said he was such an old wreck that *that* would happen to him if she only just mentioned his name. "Lord, we miss her so!" he said.

Saturday afternoon I found I was taking out my watch pretty often. Henry noticed it, and said, with a startled look:

"You don't think she ought to be here so soon, do you?"

I felt caught, and a little embarrassed; but I laughed, and said it was a habit of mine when I was in a state of expectancy. But he didn't seem quite satisfied; and from that time on he began to show uneasiness. Four times he walked me up the road to a point whence we could see a long distance; and there he would stand, shading his eyes with his hand, and looking. Several times he said:

"I'm getting worried, I'm getting right down worried. I know she's not due till about nine o'clock, and yet something seems to be trying to warn me that something's happened. You don't think anything has happened, do you?"

I began to get pretty thoroughly ashamed of him for his childishness; and at last, when he repeated that imploring question still another time, I lost my patience for the moment, and spoke pretty brutally to him. It seemed to shrivel him up and cow[11] him; and he looked so wounded and so humble after that, that I detested myself for having done the cruel and unnecessary thing. And so I was glad when Charley, another veteran, arrived toward the edge of the evening, and nestled up to Henry to hear the letter read, and talked over the preparations for the welcome. Charley fetched out one hearty speech after another, and did his best to drive away his friend's bodings and apprehensions. 2

"Anything *happened* to her? Henry, that's pure nonsense. There isn't anything going to happen to her; just make your mind easy as to that. What did the letter say? Said she was well, didn't it? And said she'd *be* here by nine o'clock, didn't it? Did you ever know her to fail of her word? Why, you know you never did. Well, then, don't you fret; she'll be here, and that's absolutely certain, and as sure as you are

11. **cow:** to intimidate; to frighten with threats or a show of force.

WORDS TO KNOW
imploring (ĭm-plôr′ĭng) *adj.* begging; making an urgent appeal **implore** *v.*
boding (bō′dĭng) *n.* a warning or omen about the future, especially of evil **bode** *v.*

309

Customizing Instruction

Students Acquiring English

1 Discuss the idiom "broke the old fellow all up." Explain that the expression means "made him cry." Ask students who speak languages other than English to describe similar expressions in their first languages.

Multiple Learning Styles

Interpersonal Learners

2 Encourage students to discuss the emotions displayed in the narrator's flare-up at Henry. Ask them to consider their own feelings about Henry's behavior and whether they think the narrator was justified in getting angry.

Mini Lesson: Speaking and Listening

READING ALOUD Use this Mini Lesson to prepare students for the Miner's Dialogue activity on p. 312. Reading aloud is a skill that is not practiced as often now as it was in frontier days.

Instruction The main task in reading aloud is to convey the mood or emotional tone of the work. Readers convey mood by using emphasis, volume, and pauses to highlight certain passages. Changes in the rate of reading also affect mood. A faster rate may suggest joy or excitement or fear. A slower rate is usually more appropriate for a serious piece.

Voice quality and tone, as well as facial expressions and gestures, can also convey meaning to listeners.

Present Have students keep these guidelines in mind as they present the interpretive readings of the story aloud in class, such as the dialogue responses to Henry's wife's letter. After a reading, have the speakers tell what mood, tone, and meaning they were trying to express, and have the listeners tell what mood, tone, and meaning were communicated. Students should justify their choice of verbal and nonverbal performance techniques by referring to their interpretation of the text.

Reading and Analyzing

Reading Skills and Strategies: PREDICT

A When the men have their last drink, the narrator is scolded for taking the wrong glass of the two that remain. The last glass is reserved for Henry. Ask students why they think this is so.

Possible Responses: It may be a special glass; the drink might be drugged.

Reading Skills and Strategies: VISUALIZE

B The final scene is somewhat dramatic in that Henry reaches an emotional climax before tension is resolved by his peaceful sleep. Ask students to visualize Henry's face during the final dialogue when he says he is "sick with fear." Have them write a brief description of Henry's face and how it might appear in these final moments.

Possible Response: His face looks frenzied with his forehead wrinkled and jaws clenched; then, as he begins to fall asleep, his face relaxes and he looks dreamy-eyed.

born. Come, now, let's get to decorating—not much time left."

Pretty soon Tom and Joe arrived, and then all hands set about adorning the house with flowers. Toward nine the three miners said that as they had brought their instruments they might as well tune up, for the boys and girls would soon be arriving now, and hungry for a good, old-fashioned breakdown.[12] A fiddle, a banjo, and a clarinet—these were the instruments. The trio took their places side by side, and began to play some rattling dance music, and beat time with their big boots.

It was getting very close to nine. Henry was standing in the door with his eyes directed up the road, his body swaying to the torture of his mental distress. He had been made to drink his wife's health and safety several times, and now Tom shouted:

"All hands stand by! One more drink, and she's here!"

A Joe brought the glasses on a waiter,[13] and served the party. I reached for one of the two remaining glasses, but Joe growled, under his breath:

"Drop that! Take the other."

Which I did. Henry was served last. He had hardly swallowed his drink when the clock began to strike. He listened till it finished, his face growing pale and paler; then he said:

B "Boys, I'm sick with fear. Help me—I want to lie down!"

They helped him to the sofa. He began to nestle and drowse, but presently spoke like one talking in his sleep, and said: "Did I hear horses' feet? Have they come?"

One of the veterans answered, close to his ear: "It was Jimmy Parrish come to say the party got delayed, but they're right up the road a piece, and coming along. Her horse is lame, but she'll be here in half an hour."

"Oh, I'm *so* thankful nothing has happened!"

He was asleep almost before the words were out of his mouth. In a moment those handy men had his clothes off, and had tucked him into his bed in the chamber where I had washed my hands. They closed the door and came back. Then they seemed preparing to leave; but I said: "Please don't go, gentlemen. She won't know me; I am a stranger."

They glanced at each other. Then Joe said:

"She? Poor thing, she's been dead nineteen years!"

"Dead?"

"That or worse. She went to see her folks half a year after she was married, and on her way back, on a Saturday evening, the Indians captured her within five miles of this place, and she's never been heard of since."

"And he lost his mind in consequence?"

"Never has been sane an hour since. But he only gets bad when that time of the year comes round. Then we begin to drop in here, three days before she's due, to encourage him up, and ask if he's heard from her, and Saturday we all come and fix up the house with flowers, and get everything ready for a dance. We've done it every year for nineteen years. The first Saturday there was twenty-seven of us, without counting the girls; there's only three of us now, and the girls are all gone. We drug him to sleep, or he would go wild; then he's all right for another year—thinks she's with him till the last three or four days come round; then he begins to look for her, and gets out his poor old letter, and we come and ask him to read it to us. Lord, she was a darling!" ❖

12. **breakdown:** a noisy, energetic American country dance.

13. **waiter:** a tray.

Teaching Options

Assessment Informal Assessment

You can informally assess students' understanding of the selection by having them write a journal entry in the first-person voice of one of Henry's friends, recounting the events of the story and giving the journal writer's views about Henry, Henry's wife, and the strange annual ritual. If students wish, they may read their journal entries aloud or exchange them with partners to read and compare.

RUBRIC

3 Full Accomplishment The journal entry shows a full understanding of the events and characters in the story.

2 Substantial Accomplishment The journal entry shows a general understanding of the events and characters in the story.

1 Little or Partial Accomplishment The journal entry shows little or no understanding of the events and characters in the story.

Connect to the Literature

1. **What Do You Think?** Were you surprised by the outcome of this story? Explain why or why not.

Comprehension Check
- What causes the narrator to stay for a few days at Henry's cottage?
- Why does Henry think his friends are planning a party?
- Why do his friends really hold a party?
- What happened to Henry's wife?

Think Critically

2. How would you describe Henry?

THINK ABOUT
- Henry's expectation of his wife's return
- the anxiety that Henry experiences on Saturday night

3. ACTIVE READING | INTERPRETING DETAILS ABOUT SETTING Review the notes in your READER'S NOTEBOOK about the relationship between the story's **setting** and **characters.** How does the setting—the cottage and its frontier surroundings—help you to understand the characters in the story?

4. Why do you think the narrator becomes so fascinated by Henry's wife?

THINK ABOUT
- the narrator's description of the cottage and the wife's photograph
- what Henry says about her
- the type of life the narrator has led

5. Do you think the miners exercise good judgment in staging a welcome home party for Henry's wife year after year? Why or why not?

Extend Interpretations

6. **The Writer's Style** Mark Twain wrote for the ear, capturing the voices of his characters like no other author of his time. In small groups, take turns reading aloud the **dialogue** from the story. What do you notice about Twain's use of dialogue?

7. **Connect to Life** Why do you think some people are attracted by a life of isolation in remote surroundings? Does such a lifestyle appeal to you at all? Why or why not?

Literary Analysis

HISTORICAL SETTING The term **historical setting** is used to describe the time and place of the action of a story that takes place in a particular historical period. The story's historical setting is crucial to "The Californian's Tale."

The frontier setting contributes to the story's **plot.** For example, the tough nature of life in the aftermath of the Gold Rush accounts for the disappearance of Henry's wife.

The setting also establishes a **mood,** or atmosphere, that enables the reader to understand the loneliness of the **characters** and their need for companionship.

Cooperative Learning Activity Consider what would have to change in order to rewrite "The Californian's Tale" with a different historical setting. With a small group of classmates, discuss other possible historical settings for this story. Try to come up with one alternative setting that would allow you to maintain the mood and basic plot structure of Twain's narrative.

REVIEW FORESHADOWING **Foreshadowing** is a writer's use of hints or clues to indicate events that will occur later in a narrative. This technique often creates **suspense.** In "The Californian's Tale," for example, the crying of Henry's friends upon hearing the wife's letter foreshadows the ending of the story. With a partner, find three more examples of foreshadowing in "The Californian's Tale." Which of them—if any—did you recognize as foreshadowing when you first read the story? What effect did they have on you?

GUIDING STUDENT RESPONSE

Connect to the Literature

1. **What Do You Think?**
Student responses will vary, but should include an explanation of why the student was or was not surprised.

Comprehension Check
- The narrator decides to stay because of Henry's insistence and his growing fascination with Henry's wife.
- Henry believes his friends hold the party as a welcome home celebration for his returning wife.
- Henry's friends really hold the party in order to help Henry get through the anniversary of his wife's disappearance.
- While returning from a visit to her parents, Henry's wife was captured by Indians and never heard from again.

Use Selection Quiz
Unit Two Resource Book, p. 41.

Think Critically

2. Possible Response: Henry is a childishly devoted husband who has never been able to accept the disappearance of his wife.
3. Students should analyze the relevance of the setting to the text's meaning. Possible Responses: The isolation and danger of the frontier setting may explain the characters' intense devotion and commitment to each other.
4. Possible Response: The narrator's roving, prospecting life has isolated him from women and comfort for a long time. Henry's wife represents a level of comfort and attractiveness that the narrator is not accustomed to.
5. Possible Responses: Yes—they are helping Henry bear grief which he wouldn't otherwise survive; no—they are keeping an illusion alive rather than helping Henry face reality.

Extend Interpretations

The Writer's Style Possible Response: Twain's characters' manner of speaking is as important as what they say. Their speech is also very idiomatic, giving it a natural sound and flow.

Connect to Life Possible Response: People may choose to live in isolation because they are disillusioned with society, because they are introverted, or because they like the quiet of nature. Students' own preferences and experiences will vary.

Literary Analysis

Historical Setting Students' alternatives to the story's setting should include examples of details that would replace those in frontier California.

Review Foreshadowing Possible examples of foreshadowing:

p. 305: "Round about California . . . and done with it all."

p. 309: Tom cries at hearing the letter

p. 309: Henry begins to show uneasiness

pp. 309–310: Constant references to time when she should arrive

p. 310: Joe growls at the narrator to take the other drink.

Writing Options

1. **Love Letter** Challenge students to study the dialogue and diction in Twain's story and try to replicate it in their letters, while also bearing in mind the woman's charm and graciousness.
2. **Alternative Solutions** Have students evaluate each solution by considering how comforting its effect on the grieving person would be.
3. **Comic Scene** Students may write their scenes either in narrative form or in dramatic play form.

Activities & Explorations

1. **Expressive Painting** Encourage students to reread the passages that describe their chosen settings and to make rough annotated sketches.
2. **Dramatic Presentation** After assigning roles, students might first do a dramatic reading of the story, each reading the dialogue of his or her given character. Through this reading, students may determine where the given dialogue is sufficient and where extra dialogue needs to be filled in.
3. **Miners' Dialogue** Student actors should review the story beforehand. One member of the group might summarize the events and record the group's ideas for extending the story, while another member checks the accuracy of the character portrayals. See the Mini Lesson on page 309.

Inquiry & Research

The California Gold Rush Encourage students to locate appropriate print and nonprint information, including biographies, histories of the West, histories of the California Gold Rush, encyclopedias, and specialized history journals. They should also consult technical resources including on-line databases and the Internet.

Vocabulary in Action

1. d	6. a
2. b	7. a
3. c	8. c
4. b	9. b
5. d	10. c

Choices & CHALLENGES

Writing Options

1. **Love Letter** Write the wife's letter that Henry has treasured for so many years. Be sure to incorporate the details about the letter's content that the story provides.

2. **Alternative Solutions** What other solutions might the miners have come up with to help Henry through the anniversary of his wife's disappearance? Write down a list of possible solutions and briefly evaluate each one. Place the list in your **Working Portfolio.**

3. **Comic Scene** Imagine that Henry's wife actually returns, 19 years after leaving. Write a comic scene in which Henry and his wife are reunited but find it difficult to adjust to the changes in each other. Be sure to include the wife's explanation for her absence.

Activities & Explorations

1. **Expressive Painting** Create a painting of either the landscape described at the beginning of the story or the interior of Henry's house. Try to capture the mood of either setting. ~ **ART**

2. **Dramatic Presentation** Working in a small group, write and perform a script for a dramatic presentation of "The Californian's Tale." In your stage directions, include information about sets, costumes, and props. ~ **PERFORMING**

James Marshall

3. **Miners' Dialogue** What happens after the story ends? Get together with three other classmates and continue the conversation among the narrator, Tom, Charley, and Joe, with each student acting out a role. Talk over what happened that night, tell stories about past gatherings, and share impressions of the wife. ~ **SPEAKING AND LISTENING**

Inquiry & Research

The California Gold Rush Find out more about the start of the California Gold Rush. Who were John Sutter and James Marshall? What is ironic about the fates that befell the two men?

Real World Link As a starting point to your research, read the magazine article on page 314.

Vocabulary in Action

EXERCISE: ASSESSMENT PRACTICE Write the letter of the word that is not similar in meaning to the other words in each numbered set.

1. (a) calm (b) sedate (c) controlled (d) disturbed
2. (a) forefather (b) follower (c) ancestor (d) predecessor
3. (a) sever (b) cut (c) join (d) amputate
4. (a) mild (b) irritating (c) balmy (d) refreshing
5. (a) supplicating (b) seeking (c) appealing (d) denying
6. (a) cheerfulness (b) emptiness (c) bleakness (d) desolation
7. (a) memory (b) prediction (c) boding (d) foretelling
8. (a) old (b) grizzled (c) young (d) aged
9. (a) deceitful (b) open (c) mysterious (d) furtive
10. (a) imploring (b) pleading (c) commanding (d) begging

Building Vocabulary
For an in-depth lesson on analogies, see page 263.

Teaching Options

Mini Lesson Grammar

PLACEMENT OF ADJECTIVES For use with Grammar in Context, p. 313. An adjective is a word that describes a noun or pronoun. Point out that adjectives usually appear *before* the noun or pronoun they modify. Also note that sometimes, for variety, for emphasis, or for added detail, a writer might put an adjective both *before and after* the noun or pronoun it modifies.

Model Sentence

"It was a lovely region, woodsy, balmy, delicious . . ."

Discuss how these adjectives add descriptive information to the noun.

Practice Ask students to write a paragraph describing the setting of "The Californian's Tale," placing adjectives both before and after nouns or pronouns to add descriptive information.

Use **Unit Two Resource Book** p. 40.
Use **Grammar Transparencies and Copymasters,** p. 74.

Use McDougal Littell's ***Language Network,*** Chapter 9, for more instruction in adjective placement.

Grammar in Context: Placement of Adjectives in a Sentence

In the following sentence Twain varies the placement of adjectives to create special emphasis.

> **It was a lovely region, woodsy, balmy, delicious, and had once been populous, long years before, but now the people had vanished and the charming paradise was a solitude.**

Adjectives can appear either before or after the nouns they modify. Expert writers choose where to place adjectives with an eye to the particular effects they are trying to create. Note the positions of the four adjectives shown in blue in the sentence above. By placing one of the adjectives before the noun *region* and the other three adjectives after it, Twain emphasizes the first adjective, *lovely,* using the other three adjectives to explain why the region is lovely. How would the emphasis be different if all four adjectives were placed before the noun?

WRITING EXERCISE Change the placement of the underlined adjectives in each sentence. Explain briefly how your revision affects the sound, rhythm, or emphasis of the sentence.

Example: *Original* I came across a cluster of cottage homes, snug and cozy.

Rewritten I came across a cluster of snug and cozy cottage homes. (adds emphasis to *snug* and *cozy*)

1. Scattered about central California were poor, proud, dirty, disappointed fellows.
2. I'd spent recent weeks with some of these coarse miners, cold and callous.
3. The bedroom was a delightful, dainty, white, and clean room.
4. The loving, gracious letter brought me close to tears.
5. I learned the truth about our fragile, widowed, and deluded host.

Grammar Handbook
Adjectives, p. 1188

Mark Twain
1835–1910

Other Works
The Adventures of Tom Sawyer
The Adventures of Huckleberry Finn
The Innocents Abroad
A Connecticut Yankee in King Arthur's Court

Heading West Mark Twain—whose real name was Samuel Clemens—grew up in the Mississippi River port of Hannibal, Missouri. Before becoming a writer, Twain worked first as a printer and then as a steamboat pilot on the Mississippi, but when the river was closed to commercial traffic during the Civil War, he headed west to prospect for gold. He supported himself by writing for local newspapers, adopting his pen name from a riverman's term for water two fathoms deep, or just deep enough for safe navigation.

International Fame Although Twain never struck it rich in the western mines, he did successfully mine his western experiences to win fame and fortune as a writer. In 1865, one of his California tall tales, "The Celebrated Jumping Frog of Calaveras County," was published in a New York newspaper. The story became an immediate hit, launching a writing career that earned him international acclaim. Twain's two most famous books, *The Adventures of Tom Sawyer* and *The Adventures of Huckleberry Finn,* drew their inspiration from his own wild and spirited boyhood along the Mississippi River. He is also remembered for his satires, his humorous tall tales, his travel sketches, and his public lectures.

Author Activity

Troubled Years Twain's own wife, Livy, died only a few years after he wrote "The Californian's Tale." Find out what other tragedies and troubles befell Twain in his later years.

VIDEODISC **LaserLinks: Background for Reading**
Author Background

Grammar in Context

WRITING EXERCISE Answers and explanations will vary. Possible answers are shown.

1. Scattered about central California were poor, proud fellows, dirty and disappointed. (improves the rhythm of the sentence by dividing the adjectives into pairs, each beginning with the same consonant sound)
2. I'd spent recent weeks with some of these coarse, cold, callous miners. (creates a strong rhythm by grouping three adjectives that begin with a hard *c* sound)
3. The bedroom was a delightful room, dainty, white, and clean. (emphasizes *delightful,* with *dainty, white,* and *clean* serving to explain why the room is delightful)
4. The letter, loving and gracious, brought me close to tears. (adds emphasis to *loving* and *gracious*)
5. I learned the truth about our fragile host, widowed and deluded. (emphasizes *fragile,* with *widowed* and *deluded* serving to explain why the host is fragile)

Author Activity

Troubled Years In the last 20 years of his life, Mark Twain suffered from depression. He invested in many get-rich-quick schemes that failed and was deeply in debt following a U.S. financial crisis in 1893, although he later regained much of his wealth from book income and money earned on lecture tours. In 1896, his favorite daughter, Susy, died, followed by the deaths of his wife, Olivia, in 1904, and his youngest daughter, Jean, in 1909. After growing progressively more pessimistic, Twain died on April 21, 1910.

Real WORLD Link

Internet Feature Article

Objectives
- recognize chronological order
- make inferences based on time lapses between events
- identify cause and effect

Connecting to the Literature
The setting of "The Californian's Tale" is several years later than the historical events outlined in "Gold Is Found and a Nation Goes Wild." Both writings explore the hopes and disappointments of fortune hunters.

Reading for Information

Tell students that historical narratives are written in chronological order, the order in which the events occurred. By presenting information in this way, the reader can establish cause and effect relationships.

1 A time line can assist in recognizing relationships between events. A possible time line might include the following dates and events:

1834: Sutter comes to America.
1848: Sutter begins building a sawmill.
1848 (January 24): Marshall finds a gold nugget.
1848 (January 28): Sutter and Marshall test the nugget for gold.
1848 (summer): People rush to Sutter's land.
1848 (winter): Polk confirms reports of gold.
1849 (late): California's population jumps from 20,000 to 100,000.
1852: Sutter declares bankruptcy.
1878: Sutter dies.

Gold Is Found and a Nation Goes Wild

In the process of building Sutter's Mill, pictured above, James Marshall discovered gold there in 1848.

❶ John August Sutter was a short, fat, kindly man whom everyone in California knew for his hospitality. He had come to America from Switzerland in 1834, and catching the western fever, had traveled across the plains to Oregon. In time he arrived in the Sacramento Valley, where the Mexican governor welcomed his plan to develop the country and granted him some land. Sutter built a fort, and gathering Indians, Hawaiians, and white settlers around him, established a colony called New Helvetia, which he ruled like a feudal baron.[1]

❷ Early in 1848, he began building a sawmill on his property, along the south fork of the American River. On the morning of January 24, a mechanic from New Jersey named James Marshall saw something glint in the water. Stepping down into the ditch, he picked up a shiny nugget, and all day he and the camp housekeeper at the mill boiled the bit of metal in a kettle of lye. When it failed to tarnish, Marshall gathered

1. **feudal** (fyo͞od′ l) **baron:** a nobleman and landholder in medieval Europe.

Reading for Information

Do you sometimes find reading about historical events confusing? Some descriptions of eventful periods are so involved that a reader can become overwhelmed with details. To begin to make sense of historical writing, readers often need to establish the correct order, or chronology, of events.

CHRONOLOGICAL ORDER
Writers make choices about how they organize the information they present. One way of structuring a historical account is to present events in **chronological order**—the order in which they occurred.

YOUR TURN To help you recognize the chronological order in this historical article, use the questions and activities below.

❶ **Constructing a Time Line** A time line is a graphic device that can help you establish chronological order. It can also help you analyze the relationships between historical events during a particular era. Make a time line of the events described in this article, beginning with the year of Sutter's arrival in the United States. Refer to the dates and other references to time in the article as you complete the time line.

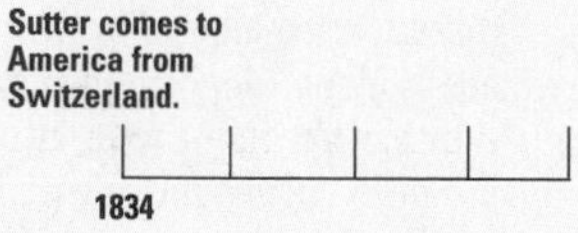
Sutter comes to America from Switzerland.
1834

more of the glistening flakes and specks, wrapped them in a rag, and on January 28 took them to the fort. Sutter examined them. "Yes, it looks like gold," he agreed. "Come, let us test it."

Gold it was indeed, and the two men were unable to keep their secret. Laborers at the fort heard the rumor first and deserted their work; then the report spread to nearby settlements and on to the coast. By summer whole towns were emptied by a fevered rush to Sutter's land. Men abandoned their families, left homes and trades, jumped ships in the harbors. In Monterey, wrote the alcalde,[2] "A whole platoon of soldiers from the fort left only their colors behind," and he added that some people were going even on crutches, and one had been carried to the mines on a litter.

Six months later a report to Congress by President Polk confirmed the news to the world, and the greatest gold rush in history was on. From the East an army of Americans stampeded for California, crossing the plains in wagons, on mules, and afoot, following every route that the pioneers had blazed. Others went around Cape Horn by ship or hurried across the continent at Panama or Mexico. At the diggings they were joined by Australians, Peruvians, pigtailed Chinese, and men from every land that had heard ❸ the news. By the end of 1849, California's population had jumped from 20,000 to nearly 100,000, and the biggest waves of newcomers were still to arrive.

The discovery that made fortunes for many ruined Sutter. There was neither law nor force to restrain the prospectors. They overran his land, butchered his cattle, and destroyed everything that he had labored to build. By 1852 he was bankrupt. Afterward he pleaded for redress, and California granted him a pension of $250 a month. But it ended in 1878, and the man who had once been known for his open-armed hospitality died two years later in a little town in Pennsylvania, still petitioning Congress for the return of his lost acres. James Marshall, who had discovered the gold, fared even worse. He died in poverty, selling his autograph to support himself.

2. alcalde (ăl-käl′ dē): mayor or chief official.

❷ A time line can be used to gauge the intervals of time separating events. Determine how much time passed between the discovery of gold in California and President Polk's report to Congress. What might the length of the interval indicate about communication and transportation in the 1800s?

❸ A time line may also provide clues to possible cause-and-effect relationships between events. Between January 1848 and the end of 1849, California's population swelled dramatically. Examine your time line. What event probably caused that population explosion?

Examining Your Time Line Review the entries in your time line. To be sure you've covered the important events, check the entries against the information in the article. You may want to illustrate your time-line entries with simple sketches.

Inquiry & Research

Activity Link: "The Californian's Tale," p. 312

As "The Californian's Tale" and this article illustrate, fortune seekers were just as likely to find misfortune as to become rich in the Gold Rush. Review your research about John Sutter or James Marshall. Share your favorite story about one of these men with your classmates.

2 Almost a year lapsed between the discovery of gold and President Polk's report to Congress. Students can infer that communication lines between the east and west coasts were undeveloped since it took six months for the news from California to reach Washington.

3 President Polk's report to Congress confirms the discovery of gold in California.

Mini Lesson Inquiry & Research

The Inquiry & Research activity links on this page to the Inquiry & Research activity section of Choices & Challenges following "The Californian's Tale," page 312.

Instruction Discuss the effect that sudden wealth might have on a person's life. In what ways could such an occurrence have both a positive and negative dimension? As students find factual information about Sutter and Marshall, encourage them to think about the emotional impact the events had in each man's life.

Practice Encourage students to draft their favorite stories about John Sutter and James Marshall and then revise them by adding factual and descriptive detail. They might also choose to read their stories aloud in role-play.

OVERVIEW

Objectives

1. understand and appreciate a **short story (Literary Analysis)**
2. identify internal and external **conflict (Literary Analysis)**
3. **analyze motivation (Active Reading)**

Summary

Owen and his wife quarrel when she mentions his "half-witted" sister Brigid. Owen's wife complains that Brigid's presence makes it difficult for their daughters to attract husbands, but Owen insists that he will not let his sister be put away. He then goes to check on Brigid. When his wife later walks to Brigid's house, she discovers her husband lying dead. Brigid does not understand that her brother has suffered a stroke and died. In the moments that follow, the wife comes to the conclusion that she has failed her husband. She resolves to take Brigid home with her to live.

Thematic Link

After Owen's death, the **mysteries of the heart** move his wife to care for his sister.

5-Minute Warm-Up

Daily Language SkillBuilder

Have students **proofread** the display sentences on page 223j and write them correctly. The sentences also appear on Transparency 10 of **Grammar Transparencies and Copymasters.**

Fire and Water (1927), Winifred Nicholson. Copyright © artist's family.

Brigid

Short Story by MARY LAVIN

"I could cry sometimes myself when I think about her."

Connect to Your Life

Home Care What should people do when a family member is too old or disabled to take care of himself or herself? Some feel that the elderly and disabled should remain with their families, whatever the cost. Others believe that the needs of such people are better met in special homes where they will be cared for by professionals. What do you think? With a small group of classmates, discuss the pros and cons of each option.

Build Background

Rural Ireland This story is set in Ireland, a rainy, largely agricultural land. Irish farms are small by American standards, and most farm families struggle to support themselves. "Brigid" takes place in the 1930s or 1940s, when farmers were typically poor. Farms like the one in the story often lacked electricity, indoor plumbing, and many of the other conveniences we associate with modern life.

Despite the poverty—or perhaps because of it—Irish farming families remained close-knit, with children expected to care for aging parents and for other relatives unable to care for themselves. As author Joe McCarthy noted in the 1960s, "The bonds of an Irish family are deep between brothers and sisters and their uncles, aunts, and grandparents. . . . It is a disgrace for a family to let old relatives live alone, and a scandalous shame to put a granduncle or an aged aunt among strangers in a nursing home or public institution."

Focus Your Reading

LITERARY ANALYSIS **CONFLICT**

"Brigid" opens with an argument between a married couple:

> ***"What harm is a sup of rain?" he said.***
>
> ***"That's you all over again," she said. "What harm is anything, as long as it doesn't affect yourself?"***

This kind of **conflict,** in which characters struggle against each other, is an example of **external conflict.** However, conflict may also be **internal,** occurring within a character. As you read "Brigid," look for examples of conflict and consider whether each conflict is external or internal.

ACTIVE READING **ANALYZING MOTIVATION** Understanding a character's **motivation**—the driving force behind his or her thoughts, feelings, and actions—is often the key to understanding an entire story.

READER'S NOTEBOOK As you read "Brigid," use two diagrams like the one shown below to record the motivation of Owen and his wife for the things they say and do. Identify the moment at which the motivation and behavior of Owen's wife radically changes.

Character: Owen	
Action/Statement	**Motivation**
• Owen goes to check on Brigid	
•	
•	
•	

LESSON RESOURCES

UNIT TWO RESOURCE BOOK, pp. 42–46

ASSESSMENT RESOURCES

Formal Assessment, pp. 51–52

Teacher's Guide to Assessment and Portfolio Use

Test Generator

SKILLS TRANSPARENCIES AND COPYMASTERS

Literary Analysis

- Plot: Conflict, T12 (for Paired Activity, p. 326)

Reading and Critical Thinking

- Organizational Chart: Horizontal, T51 (for Reader's Notebook, p. 316)

Grammar

- Identifying Sentence Structures, C121 (for Mini Lesson, p. 325)
- Compound Sentences, C123 (for Mini Lesson, p. 327)

Vocabulary

- Using Reference Materials, C43 (for Mini Lesson, p. 320)

Writing

- Identifying Writing Variables, T2 (for Writing Option 1, p. 327)
- Problem-Solution, C28 (for Writing Option 3, p. 327)

Communications

- Nonverbal Strategies, T15 (for Mini Lesson, p. 323)

INTEGRATED TECHNOLOGY

Audio Library

Visit our website: www.mcdougallittell.com

Brigid

MARY LAVIN

The rain came sifting through the air and settled like a bloom on the fields. But under the trees it fell in single heavy drops, noisily, like cabbage water running through the holes of a colander.[1]

1. **colander** (kŭl′ən-dər): a bowl-shaped, perforated kitchen utensil for draining off liquid and rinsing food.

TEACHING THE LITERATURE

Customizing Instruction

Less Proficient Readers

Have students keep these questions in mind as they read:

- Who are the main characters in the story?
  Answer: Owen, his wife, and his sister Brigid
- What is the main conflict in the story?
  Answer: Owen wants to keep Brigid in her cottage, but his wife wants to put her in an institution.

Gifted and Talented

Throughout the story, Owen's daughters are present, although their presence is not necessarily physical. As students read the story, have them keep track of the daughters and their role in what is happening. Then, when they have finished reading, ask them to write a paragraph explaining the daughters' role in the story.

Possible Response: Owen's wife tries to use the future happiness and well-being of her daughters to persuade her husband to put Brigid away. The reasons she claims, however, may not be the same as her actual reasons. It is possible that she wants her daughters not to "fail" at love as she later comes to feel she has failed.

BLOCK SCHEDULING: MANAGING TIME

If your schedule requires that you cover the lesson objectives in a shorter time, use . . .

- Preparing to Read, p. 316
- Thinking Through the Literature, p. 326
- Grammar in Context, p. 328

If you want to take advantage of longer class time, use . . .

- TE Teaching Options: Viewing and Representing, pp. 319, 322; Vocabulary Strategy, p. 320; Speaking and Listening, p. 323; Informal Assessment, p. 324
- Choices and Challenges and Author Activity, pp. 327–328

Reading and Analyzing

Reading Skills and Strategies:
PREVIEW

Have students preview the selection. Have students find and discuss the title, images, and the first italicized quotation in the selection. Discuss with students the Build Background feature on p. 316. Before students begin reading, give them a brief summary of the story.

Active Reading
ANALYZING MOTIVATION

Characters have motivations not only for actions, but also for attitudes and thoughts. As students read, have them look for the motivations behind Owen's refusal to put Brigid in a home and for his wife's insistence that they do so.

Possible Response: Owen made a promise to his mother that he would never send Brigid away; his wife is concerned that Brigid's proximity will keep suitors away from her daughters.

Use **Unit Two Resource Book,** p. 43 for additional support.

Literary Analysis: CONFLICT

As students read, have them identify the main external conflict between the two main characters and the internal conflict within each that fuels their external conflict.

Possible Response: The external conflict is their constant argument over what to do with Brigid. The wife's internal conflict is her concern that her daughters will never marry; the man's internal conflict lies in his simultaneous desire to please his wife and his desire to care for Brigid as he promised his mother he would.

Use **Unit Two Resource Book,** p. 44 for additional support.

The house was in the middle of the trees.

"Listen to that rain!" said the woman to her husband. "Will it never stop?"

"What harm is a sup[2] of rain?" he said.

"That's you all over again," she said. "What harm is anything, as long as it doesn't affect yourself?"

"How do you mean, when it doesn't affect me? Look at my feet. They're sopping. And look at my hat. It's soused."[3] He took the hat off and shook the rain from it onto the spitting bars of the grate.

"Quit that," said the woman. "Can't you see you're raising ashes?"

"What harm is ashes?"

"I'll show you what harm," she said, taking down a plate of cabbage and potato from the shelf over the fire. "There's your dinner destroyed with them." The yellow cabbage was lightly sprayed with ash.

1 "Ashes is healthy, I often heard said. Put it here!" He sat down at the table, taking up his knife and fork, and indicating where the plate was to be put by tapping the table with the handle of the knife. "Is there no bit of meat?" he asked, prodding the potato critically.

"There's plenty in the town, I suppose."

"In the town? And why didn't somebody go to the town, might I ask?"

"Who was there to go? You know as well as
2 I do there's no one here to be traipsing in and out every time there's something wanted from the town."

"I suppose one of our fine daughters would think it the end of the world if she was asked to go for a bit of a message? Let me tell you they'd get husbands for themselves quicker if they were seen doing a bit of work once in a while."

"Who said anything about getting husbands for them?" said the woman. "They're time enough getting married."

"Is that so? Mind you now, anyone would think that you were anxious to get them off your hands with the way every penny that comes into the house goes out again on bits of silks and ribbons for them."

"I'm not going to let them be without their bit of fun just because you have other uses for your money than spending it on your own children!"

"What other uses have I? Do I smoke? Do I drink? Do I play cards?"

"You know what I mean."

"I suppose I do." The man was silent. He left down his fork. "I suppose you're hinting at poor Brigid again?" he said. "But I told you forty times, if she was put into a home[4] she'd be just as much of an expense to us as she is in the little house above there." He pointed out of the window with his fork.

"I see there's no use in talking about it," said the woman. "All I can say is God help the girls, with you, their own father, putting a drag on them so that no man will have anything to do with them after hearing about Brigid."

"What do you mean by that? This is something new. I thought it was only the bit of bread and tea she got that you grudged the poor thing. This is something new. What is this?"

"You oughtn't to need to be told, a man like you that saw the world, a man that traveled like you did, a man that was in England and London."

"I don't know what you're talking about." He took up his hat and felt it to see if the side he had placed near the fire was dry. He turned the other side toward the fire. "What are you trying to say?" he said. "Speak plain!"

2. **sup:** a small quantity of liquid.
3. **soused** (soust): soaking wet; drenched.
4. **home:** here, a residential institution where people are cared for.

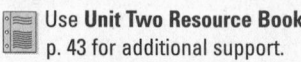

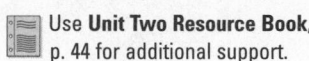

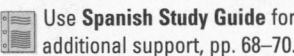

Rebecca (about 1947), Raphael Soyer. Oil on canvas, 26″ × 20″, courtesy of Forum Gallery, New York.

Customizing Instruction

Students Acquiring English

1 Point out to students the nonstandard usage in Owen's sentence "Ashes is healthy." Ask them to rephrase the sentence in standard English.

Answer: "Ashes are healthy."

Explain to students that the characters in this story speak in a dialect that varies from standard English, most prominently in its use of singular verb forms when plural verb forms are expected.

Use **Spanish Study Guide** for additional support, pp. 68–70.

2 Explain to students that *traipsing* means "walking about."

Mini Lesson Viewing and Representing

Rebecca **by Raphael Soyer**

ART APPRECIATION Russian-born artist Raphael Soyer (1899-1987) has a subdued, realistic style that expresses an intimate sympathy for people. For much of his career, Soyer portrayed the ordinary people of New York City going about their daily tasks.

Instruction Point out the unpretentious pose and expression of the woman in this painting. Ask students to identify details that suggest her "ordinary person" status.

Possible Responses: Her fingers and her face look unposed and unglamorous.

Her eyes look tired, perhaps from overwork.

Both her hands and face seem overly "fleshy" and not at all comfortable with the attention they are being given.

Application Ask students to compare the figure in the painting with characteristics of Brigid presented in the story, focusing on any details that seem to connect one to the other.

Possible Responses: The woman has an empty expression on her face suggesting she's not a deeply thinking person, quite like Brigid.

The figure in the painting is holding a flower, which connects to the flowers that Owen's wife once gave Brigid.

Reading and Analyzing

Reading Skills and Strategies: CLARIFYING

A Discuss Owen's claim that Brigid's lifestyle has nothing to do "with anybody but the poor creature herself." Owen says that whatever Brigid's situation is, it is "her own trouble." Have students clarify what this means.

Possible Response: Owen claims that a person's life is nobody's concern except his or her own. "Her own trouble" means that her business is her business and nobody else's.

Reading Skills and Strategies: CONNECTING

Ask students to imagine what it would be like to be in Owen's situation. How would it feel to have to decide whether to commit a brother, sister, or parent to permanent institutional care?

Possible Responses: Student responses will vary; some students will have personal experience in this matter, and may be sensitive about it.

Reading Skills and Strategies: EVALUATING

B Given that Owen's wife seems to have little success changing her husband's mind, consider her use of the claim that Owen will "be sorry one of these days when [Brigid is] found dead in the chair." Ask students whether this seems like persuasive reasoning based on a logical appeal to facts, or an emotional appeal that plays on feelings.

Possible Response: It seems to be an emotional appeal coming from a sense of exasperation.

"Is any man going to marry a girl when he hears her aunt is a poor half-witted creature, soft 1 in the head, and living in a poke of a hut, doing nothing all day but sitting looking into the fire?"

A "What has that got to do with anybody but the poor creature herself? Isn't it her own trouble?"

"Men don't like marrying into a family that has the like of her in it."

"Is that so? I didn't notice that you were put off marrying me, and you knew all about poor Brigid. You used to bring her bunches of primroses. And one day I remember you pulling the flowers off your hat and giving them to her when she started crying over nothing. You used to say she was a harmless poor thing. You used to say you'd look after her."

"And didn't I? Nobody can say I didn't look after her. Didn't I do my best to have her taken into a home, where she'd get proper care? You can't deny that."

"I'm not denying it. You never gave me peace or ease since the day we were married. But I wouldn't give in. I wouldn't give in then, and I won't give in now, either. I won't let it be said that I had hand or part in letting my own sister be put away."

"But it's for her own good." This time the woman's voice was softer, and she went over and turned the wet hat again on the fender.[5] "It's nearly dry," she said, and she went back to the table and took up the plate from which he had eaten and began to wash it in a basin of water at the other end of the table. "It's for her own good. I'm surprised you can't see that; you, a sensible man, with two grown-up daughters. B You'll be sorry one of these days when she's found dead in the chair—the Lord between us and all harm—or falls in the fire and gets scorched to death—God preserve us from the like! I was reading, only the other day, in a paper that came round something from the shop, that there was a case like that up in the Midlands."

"I don't want to hear about it," said the man, shuffling his feet. "The hat is dry, I think," he said, and he put it on his head and stood up.

"That's the way you always go on. You don't want to listen to anything unpleasant. You don't want to listen to anything that's right. You don't want to listen because you know what I'm saying is true and you know you have no answer to it."

"You make me tired," said the man; "it's always the one story in this house. Why don't you get something else to talk about for a change?"

The woman ran to the door and blocked his way.

"Is that your last word?" she said. "You won't give in?"

"I won't give in. Poor Brigid. Didn't my mother make me promise I'd never have hand or part in putting the poor creature away? 'Leave her alone,' my mother used to say, 'she's doing no harm to anyone.' "

"She's doing harm to our daughters," said the woman, "and you know that. Don't you?" She caught his coat and stared at him. "You know the way Matty Monaghan[6] gave up Rosie after dancing with her all night at a dance in the Town Hall last year. Why did he do that, do you suppose? It's little you know about it at all! You don't see Mamie crying her eyes out some nights after coming in from a walk with the girls and hearing bits of talk from this one and that one, and putting two and two together, and finding out for herself the talk that goes on among the men about girls and the kind of homes they come from!"

"There'd be a lot more talk if the poor creature was put away. Let me tell you that, if you don't know it for yourself! It's one thing to have

5. **fender:** a metal screen in front of a fireplace to keep hot coals and ashes from falling out.

6. **Monaghan** (mŏn′ə-hăn).

Teaching Options

Mini Lesson Vocabulary Strategy

USING REFERENCE MATERIALS TO DETERMINE PRECISE WORD MEANINGS

Instruction In a dictionary, more than one sense or meaning is listed for most words. Meanings are usually numbered and listed from most common to least common, showing subtle but often important differences. For instance, the word *soft* is used to describe Brigid—she's said to be "soft in the head" and "a bit soft." Yet, *soft* has as many as thirteen different meanings listed in a college dictionary.

Exercises Have students use a dictionary to look up the underlined word in each of the following sentences from "Brigid." Instruct them to write down the definition that is most appropriate for the word as it is used in the sentence.

1. ". . . even then it was thought she was only slow, that she'd grow out of it."

Possible Response: not smart or clever

2. "But she'd be so happy in a home!"

Possible Response: an institution

3. "He was cutting across the field . . ."

Possible Response: taking a shorter course

Use **Vocabulary Transparencies and Copymasters,** p. 43.

a poor creature, doing no one any harm, living quiet, all by herself, up at the end of a boreen[7] where seldom or never anyone gets a chance of seeing her. It's another thing altogether to have her taken away in a car and everyone running to the window to see the car pass and talking about her and telling stories from one to another till in no time at all they'd be letting on she was twice as bad as she is, and the stories about her would be getting so wild that none of us could go down the streets without being stared at as if we were all queer!"

"You won't give in?" his wife asked once more.

"I won't give in."

"Poor Mamie. Poor Rosie." The woman sighed. She put the plate up on the dresser.

Owen shuffled his feet. "If you didn't let it be seen so plain that you wanted to get them off, they might have a better chance. I don't know what they want getting married for, in any case. They'd be better off to be interested in this place, and raise a few hens, and make a bit of money for themselves so they could be independent and take no notice of people and their gossip!"

"It's little you know about anything, that's all I have to say," said the woman.

Owen moved to the door.

"Where are you going now?"

"There's no use in my telling you and drawing down another stream of abuse on myself when I mention the poor creature's name."

The woman sighed and then stood up and walked over to the fire.

"If that's where you're going you might as well take over these clean sheets." She took down a pair of sheets from where they were airing on the shelf over the fire. "You can't say but I look after her, no matter what," she said.

"If you remembered her the way I do," said the man, "when she was only a little bit of a child, and I was growing up and going to school, you'd know what it feels like to hear talk of putting her in a home. She used to have lovely hair. It was like the flossy heads of the dandelions when they are gone past their best. No one knew she was going to be a bit soft[8] until she was toddling around and beginning to talk, and even then it was thought she was only slow, that she'd grow out of it."

"I know how you feel," said the woman. "I could cry sometimes myself when I think about her. But she'd be so happy in a home! We could visit her any time we wanted. We could hire a car and drive over to see her, all of us, on a fine Sunday now and again. It would be some place to go. And it would cost no more than it costs to keep her here."

"You don't want to listen to anything unpleasant. You don't want to listen to anything that's right."

She didn't know whether he had heard the end of the sentence because he had gone out through the yard and was cutting across the field, with his ash plant[9] in his hand.

"He was cutting across the field with the ash plant in his hand when we were starting off on our walk," said Rosie, when she and Mamie

7. **boreen** (bôr-ēn′): a narrow country lane.

8. **a bit soft:** simple-minded; mentally slow.

9. **ash plant:** a walking stick made from a young ash tree.

Customizing Instruction

Less Proficient Readers

Ask students the following questions to help them understand the conflict between Owen and his wife.

- What does Owen's wife want for her daughters?
  Answer: She wants them to be happy and to find suitable husbands.
- In her view, what keeps her daughters from achieving this?
  Answer: Brigid is scaring away potential husbands.

Students Acquiring English

1 Explain to students that one meaning for *poke* is "a sack." Then ask students what "living in a poke of a hut" might mean.

Possible Response: living in a house that is very small

Reading and Analyzing

Reading Skills and Strategies: PREDICT

A Ask students to predict what they think has happened to Owen.

Possible Answers: He's gone off on a long walk; he's gotten into an accident; he's gone to visit Brigid.

Literary Analysis: CHARACTER

B Ask students to analyze Owen's wife's justification for going inside to see Brigid. What does she mean that it would be "unnatural" not to? What does this suggest about her character?

Possible Response: It means that it would impolite or inconsiderate not to greet Brigid and that, in spite of her desire to put Brigid in a home, she has at least a certain amount of care and concern for Brigid. She seems to have very human feelings about Brigid's well-being.

Literary Analysis: SETTING

Ask students to analyze the relevance of the setting to the text's meaning. At this point in the story, the setting is bathed in darkness. It is dark outside, and Brigid's cottage is lit only by a faintly flickering firelight. Ask students what effect the darkness creates and what it might represent.

Possible Response: The darkness creates an effect of mystery and unease. It could represent the wife's inability to figure out what has happened to Owen.

Fire and Water (1927), Winifred Nicholson. Copyright © artist's family.

Teaching Options

Mini Lesson: Viewing and Representing

Fire and Water **by Winifred Nicholson**

ART APPRECIATION Winifred Nicholson (1893–1981) was a distinguished artist and thinker in the 1920s and 1930s. According to one art critic, Nicholson's "life of paintings led to a deeper exploration of the colours at the edge of the rainbow."

Instruction Point out that red is considered a "warm" color that draws the viewer in closer to a painting, while blue is considered a "cool" color that tends to create distance. Ask students to explain how these perceptions work in expressing the fire's intensity in this painting.

Possible Response: The warm red and yellow tones draw the viewer closer to the source of heat, creating a deeper intensity.

Application Ask students to compare the fire in the painting with the fire in Brigid's house as Owen's wife first sees it.

Possible Response: The fire in the painting is much more intense and gives off much more light.

Then ask students to compare the intensity of the fire in the painting with the emotional intensity of the scene in the story.

Possible Response: The hot, reddish and yellowish tones of the painting bring to mind the same level of intensity as the tense, harried search for Owen.

came in to their supper and her mother asked her if she had seen their father out in the yard.

A "He was going up to your Aunt Brigid then," said their mother. "Did you not see him after that?"

"That was three hours ago," said Mamie, looking worried. "He wouldn't be over there all this time. Would he? He must be doing something for Aunt Brigid—chopping wood or mending something. He wouldn't be just sitting over there all this time."

"Ah, you wouldn't know what he'd be doing," the mother said, and the girls looked at each
1 other. They knew then there had been words between their father and mother while they were out.

"Maybe one of you ought to run over and see what's keeping him?" said their mother.

"Oh, leave him alone," said Mamie. "If he wants to stay over there, let him! He'll have to be home soon anyway to put in the calves. It's nearly dark."

But soon it was very dark, and the calves were still out. The girls had gone out again to a dance, and it was beginning to rain when Owen's wife put on her coat and went across the field herself and up the boreen to Brigid's.

How can she sit there in the dark? she thought, when she didn't see a light in the window. But as she got nearer she saw there was a faint glow from the fire on the hearth. She felt sure Owen wasn't there. He wouldn't be there without lighting a lamp, or a bit of a
B candle! There was no need to go in. She was going to turn back, but it seemed an unnatural thing not to call to the door and see if the poor creature was all right.

Brigid was the same as ever, sitting by the fire with a silly smile and not looking up till she was called three or four times.

"Brigid, did you see Owen?" his wife asked without much hope of a reply.

Brigid looked up. "Owen is a queer man," she said. That was all the answer she gave.

"So he was here! What time did he leave?"

Brigid grumbled something.

"What are you saying, Brigid?"

"He wouldn't go home," Brigid said. "I told him it was time to go home for his tea, but he wouldn't answer me. 'Go home,' I said, 'go home, Owen.' "

The other woman couldn't see her in the dark. The fire was flickering too irregularly to see by its light.

"When did he go? What time was it? Did you notice?"

Brigid could be difficult sometimes. Was she going to be difficult now?

"He wouldn't go home," Brigid said again.

Suddenly Owen's wife saw his ash plant lying on the table.

"Is he still here?" she said, sharply, and she glanced back at the door. "I didn't see him in the yard! I didn't hear him!"

"He wouldn't speak to me," Brigid said again stubbornly.

The other woman couldn't see her in the dark. The fire was flickering too irregularly to see by its light.

Customizing Instruction

Students Acquiring English

1 Explain that the expression "there had been words" means that there had been an argument.

Multiple Learning Styles

Visual Learners

Suggest that students draw a map of the area in which story events occur. Have them indicate the house, the village, the boreen, Brigid's house, and the fields, and ask them to consider how the close proximity of everything helps explain Owen's wife's concern about her husband's absence.

Possible Response: Given that there aren't many places to go, Owen's absence would seem significant.

Mini Lesson: Speaking and Listening

NONVERBAL CUES Speakers in all face-to-face situations convey important information nonverbally, through gesture, posture, facial expression, tone of voice, and eye contact. For example, an authority figure such as a parent or teacher can effectively communicate an unspoken message with just a certain expression or movement of the eyes. In social conversation, we are often unaware of the gestures and nonverbal cues that convey important information.

Instruction Divide the class into groups of four. In each group, assign two students to read the opening dialogue in "Brigid" aloud (just the conversational exchange, not the narrative) while the other two observe the dialogue and take note of the nonverbal cues the speakers use in the exchange.

Present Give students an opportunity to study the dialogue to decide how they will use nonverbal cues to convey emotion, attitude, and other essential information. After the first pair presents the dialogue, have them trade roles with the observing pair and repeat the activity. When groups are finished, reconvene the whole class for a discussion of how nonverbal cues were used and to what effect.

Reading and Analyzing

Literary Analysis: THEME

A What does the wife's sudden decision to take Brigid into her house suggest?
Possible Response: It suggests that the concern and care Owen's wife has had for her husband can now only be expressed through concern and care for Brigid, or that she has seen how her earlier attitude was a selfish one, and she wants to make up for it.

Literary Analysis: CONFLICT

B Ask students to summarize the internal conflict that Owen's wife expresses in this paragraph.
Possible Response: She is torn by a sense of having failed her husband, realizing it is now too late to correct her actions or ask forgiveness of him.

Active Reading
ANALYZING MOTIVATION

C Ask students what Owen's wife's realization that her husband had to divert his love to Brigid suggests about her real motivation for wishing to send Brigid away.
Possible Response: She has been jealous of her husband's devoted attention to Brigid. This now seems like her actual motivation for her long-standing desire to put Brigid away.

"But where is he? Is there anything the matter with him?" She ran to the door and called out into the dark. But there was no answer. She stood there trying to think. She heard Brigid talking to herself, but she didn't trouble to listen. She might as well go home, she thought. Wherever he was, he wasn't here. "If he comes back, Brigid, tell him I was here looking for him," she said. "I'll go home through the other field."

Brigid said something then that made her turn sharply and look at her.

"What did you say?"

"I told him to get up. I told him that his head was getting scorched. But he wouldn't listen to me."

"Tell him yourself," said Brigid, and then she seemed to be talking to herself again. And she was leaning down in the dark before the fire.

"Why don't you talk?" she said. "Why don't you talk?"

Owen's wife began to pull out the old settle bed[10] that was in front of the fire, not knowing why she did it, but she could feel the blood pounding in her ears and behind her eyes.

"He fell down there and he wouldn't get up!" Brigid said. "I told him to get up. I told him that his head was getting scorched. But he wouldn't listen to me. He wouldn't get up. He wouldn't do anything."

Owen's wife closed her eyes. All of a sudden she was afraid to look. But when she looked, Owen's eyes stared up at her, wide open, from where he lay on his back on the hearth.

"Owen!" she screamed, and she tried to pull him up.

His shoulders were stiff and heavy. She caught his hands. They were cold. Was he dead? She felt his face. But his face was hot, so hot she couldn't put her hand on it. If he was dead he'd be cold. She wanted to scream and run out of the house, but first she tried to drag him as far as she could from the ashy hearth. Then suddenly feeling the living eyes of Brigid watching her, and seeing the dead eyes staring up from the blistered red face, she sprang up, knocking over a chair, and ran out of the house, and ran screaming down the boreen.

Her screams brought people running out to their doors, the light streaming out each side of them. She couldn't speak, but she pointed up the hill and ran on. She wanted to get to the pump.

It was dark at the pump, but she could hear people running the way she had pointed. Then when they had reached the cottage, there was no more running, but great talking and shouting. She sat down at the side of the pump, but there was a smell off her hands and desperately she bent forward and began to wash them under the pump, but when she saw there was hair stuck to her fingers she wanted to scream again, but there was a great pain gathering in her heart, not yet the pain of loss, but the pain of having failed; failed in some terrible way.

I failed him always, she thought, from the very start. I never loved him like he loved me; **B**

10. **settle bed:** a long bench used both as a seat and as a bed.

Teaching Options

Assessment **Informal Assessment**

You can informally assess students' understanding of the selection by having them write a paragraph explaining the change that Owen's wife undergoes immediately after her husband's death.

RUBRIC

3 Full Accomplishment The paragraph reflects a full understanding of the change undergone by Owen's wife.

2 Substantial Accomplishment The paragraph reflects a general understanding of the change undergone by Owen's wife.

1 Little or Partial Accomplishment The paragraph displays little or no understanding of the change undergone by Owen's wife.

not even then, long ago, the time I took the flowers off my hat. It wasn't for Brigid, like he thought. I was only making myself out to be what he imagined I was. I didn't know enough about loving to change myself for him. I didn't even know enough about it to keep him loving me. He had to give it all to Brigid in the end.

He gave it all to Brigid; to a poor daft thing that didn't know enough to pull him back from the fire or call someone when he fell down in a stroke. If it was anyone else was with him, he might have had a chance.

Oh, how had it happened? How could love be wasted and go to loss like that?

It was like the way the tossy balls of cowslips[11] they used to make as children were forgotten and left behind in the fields, till they were trodden into the muck by the cattle and the sheep.

Suddenly she thought of the heavy feet of the neighbors tramping the boards of the cottage up in the fields behind her, and rising up, she ran back up the boreen.

"Here's the poor woman now," someone said, as she thrust past the crowd around the door.

They began to make a way for her to where, on the settle bed, they had laid her husband. But instead she parted a way through the people and went toward the door of the room off the kitchen.

"It's Brigid I'm thinking about," she said. "Where is she?"

"Something will have to be done about her now all right," someone said.

"It will," she said, decisively, and her voice was as true as a bell.

She had reached the door of the room.

"That's why I came back," she said, looking around her defiantly. "She'll need proper minding[12] now. To think she hadn't the strength to run for help or pull him back a bit from the fire." She opened a door.

Sitting on the side of the bed, all alone, she saw Brigid.

"Get your hat and coat, Brigid," she said. "You're coming home with me." ❖

11. **tossy balls of cowslips:** strung-together flowers and stems of cowslips. A cowslip is a wildflower that grows in Britain and Ireland.

12. **minding:** tending; watching; caring for.

Customizing Instruction

Less Proficient Readers

To help students understand the story, ask them the following questions.

- What happens to Owen when he goes to see Brigid?
  Answer: He probably suffers a stroke or heart attack and falls down too close to the fire; he dies.
- Why does Brigid not help him?
  Answer: She does not understand what has happened.
- At the end of the story, what does Owen's wife decide to do about Brigid?
  Answer: She takes Brigid into her own home.

Mini Lesson **Grammar**

IDENTIFYING SENTENCE STRUCTURES

Explain to students that there are four grammatical types of sentences—**simple, compound, complex**, and **compound-complex**.

A **simple sentence** contains one independent clause and no dependent clauses:

The fire burned brightly through the night.

A **compound sentence** contains two or more independent clauses and no dependent clauses:

One sister likes to dance, / and the other sister likes to watch.

A **complex sentence** contains one independent clause and at least one dependent clause:

Mother doesn't like the rain / because it makes the air so damp and hard to breathe.

A **compound-complex sentence** contains two or more independent clauses and at least one dependent clause:

I will eat almost anything / when I'm hungry, / but I sometimes regret it later.

Practice Ask students to find one example of each sentence type in the story.

Use **Grammar Transparencies and Copymasters,** p. 121.

Use McDougal Littell's ***Language Network,*** Chapter 4, for more instruction in identifying sentence structures.

GUIDING STUDENT RESPONSE

Connect to the Literature

1. What Do You Think?
Possible Responses: frustration with Owen or with his wife; sadness at Owen's death and at Brigid's fate

Comprehension Check
- She wants Brigid to be put in an institution.
- Owen falls down and dies.
- She decides to take Brigid home to live with her.

Use Selection Quiz
Unit Two Resource Book, p. 46.

Think Critically

2. Possible Responses: Yes—she was unable to selflessly love Owen; no—she served Owen faithfully enough throughout their marriage.

3. Possible Response: Owen is a committed, devoted man who has strong integrity and a very clear sense of his purpose in life. He is strong-willed with an individual mind; he thinks for himself and bristles at the idea of social conventions pressuring people to act in certain ways.

4. Possible Response: Owen is motivated by a lifelong devotion to his sister and the promise he made his mother. Owen's wife initially claims to be motivated by concern for her daughters' need to find husbands. After Owen's death, however, it becomes clear that she wishes to address her failure to love Owen as he loved her. This is a believable change of heart following a traumatic experience.

5. Possible Responses: we are closer to her than any other character—so much so that we identify with her and her name is not important; the author wants to emphasize her role as a wife more than her presence as her own individual.

Thinking through the LITERATURE

Connect to the Literature

1. **What Do You Think?** What was your strongest emotion as you read this story? Share your thoughts with a classmate.

Comprehension Check
- At the beginning of the story, what does Owen's wife want to have happen to Brigid?
- What occurs when Owen goes to check on Brigid?
- What decision does Owen's wife make at the end of the story?

Think Critically

2. Do you agree with Owen's wife in her assessment that she "failed" Owen? Explain your answer.

3. What is your impression of Owen's **character**?

THINK ABOUT
- the way he takes care of Brigid
- his assertion to his wife that he "won't give in"
- his comments about his daughters
- the promise that he made to his mother (page 320)

4. **ACTIVE READING** ANALYZING MOTIVATION Review the charts in your READER'S NOTEBOOK and describe the **motivation** of Owen and his wife in their respective attitudes toward Brigid at the beginning of the story. What motivates Owen's wife in her attitude toward Brigid after Owen's death? Explain whether you find her change in attitude believable.

5. Why do you think the author does not reveal the name of Owen's wife?

Extend Interpretations

6. **What If?** If Owen had not died, how do you think he and his wife might have resolved their **conflict** over Brigid?

7. **Critic's Corner** Novelist and reviewer Jean Stubbs said that Lavin "invites us to contemplate with her the infinite sadness and beauty of the world, the divine inconsequence of life." Do you think "Brigid" supports this description of Lavin's writing? Explain your answer, citing details from the story.

8. **Connect to Life** At the end of the story, Owen's wife says, "I didn't even know enough about loving to change myself for him." Do you think people should make changes in themselves for those they love? Why or why not?

Literary Analysis

CONFLICT **Conflict** is the struggle between opposing forces. **External conflict** occurs when a character is pitted against an outside force, such as another character, a physical obstacle, or an aspect of nature or society. **Internal conflict** happens when the struggle takes place within a character. "Brigid" contains examples of external conflict. At the beginning of the story, Owen and his wife argue about food, the weather, and money, though it becomes clear that the real source of conflict between them is Brigid. The story also features internal conflict, as Owen's wife wrestles with her feelings of guilt at letting her late husband down.

Conflict	External or Internal	Resolution

Paired Activity With a classmate, review the external and the internal conflicts in the story, filling in a chart like the one above. For each one, identify the opposing forces, and state how the conflict is resolved, if at all.

REVIEW CHARACTERIZATION As you know, there are four basic methods of characterization, which are described in detail on page 252. Find passages from the story that illustrate Lavin's various methods of characterization. Which method does she use the most? How does her use of characterization influence your understanding and feelings about Brigid?

Extend Interpretations

What If? Students may think that Owen and his wife could reach a compromise about caring for Brigid.

Critic's Corner Possible Responses: The story does reflect both beauty and sadness—beauty, that Owen's wife could transform into a loving woman, and sadness, that it takes the death of her husband to trigger that transformation. It shows the "divine inconsequence of life" in its detailing of everyday happenings: the eating of a meal, the drying of a hat by the fire, or the washing of a dish.

Connect to Life Have students compare the text events with their own or other readers' experiences.

Literary Analysis

Conflict Encourage students to go through the story one page at a time when looking for the conflicts. Remind them that the resolutions may not occur for several pages.

Characterization Students may note that Lavin uses mostly dialogue with some action. Toward the end, she tells the reader what Owen's wife is thinking. We know Brigid almost entirely through what others say of her, which makes her fairly remote to the reader.

Choices & CHALLENGES

Writing Options

1. Character Sketch Write a character sketch of Owen's wife based on what is revealed about her in the story.

2. Imaginary Conversation Compose the conversation in which Owen's wife tells her daughters what happened and explains that she will be taking care of Brigid.

3. Problem-Solution Essay What is the best form of care for people who are too old or disabled to look after themselves? If they are put in special homes, should the government provide financial support for those who do not have enough money? Draft a problem-solution essay in which you consider solutions to this social problem. Place the draft in your **Working Portfolio.**

Writing Handbook
See page 1159: Problem-Solution.

Activities & Explorations

1. Eulogy for Owen Imagine that you are Owen's wife. Deliver a eulogy for Owen in which you express your feelings about him and give voice to your regrets. ~ **SPEAKING AND LISTENING**

2. Abstract Painting Think about the emotions you had as you read this story. Create an abstract painting that expresses one or more of your feelings. ~ **ART**

3. Radio Play Rewrite a scene from this story in the form of a radio dramatization. Include descriptive passages for a narrator to read aloud. If possible, tape-record your performance of the scene. ~ **PERFORMING**

Inquiry & Research

Life in Ireland Find out more about rural life in Ireland during the first half of the 20th century. Write a brief report describing housing, schooling, occupations, and working conditions.

Art Connection

Look at the painting on page 319. How does this portrait match the image you formed of Brigid as you read the story? Do you think the mood of the painting suits the story? Why or why not?

Writing Options

1. **Character Sketch** Instruct students to study the dialogue and actions of Owen's wife to capture the essence of her character in their sketches.
2. **Imaginary Conversation** Remind students to take into account the mother's realization and change of heart at the end of the story.
3. **Problem-Solution Essay** Students may wish to use examples from this story or from their own experience to support their arguments.

Activities & Explorations

1. **Eulogy for Owen** Encourage students to reread the passages that describe or represent Owen's personality and character. Remind students that values, attitudes, and personal determination are powerful aspects of character.
2. **Abstract Painting** Students may wish to skim the story again to create a list of emotional responses.
3. **Radio Play** Remind students to use techniques such as tone of voice, pitch, volume, and rate of speech to suit their particular characters.

Inquiry & Research

Life in Ireland Have students form groups and prepare oral reports. Suggest that they assign roles—such as obtaining research materials and compiling information—within their groups once they've agreed on topics. All group members should take part in presenting information to the class.

Art Connection

Refer students to the Viewing and Representing activity on p. 319.

Mini Lesson Grammar

COMPOUND SENTENCES A compound sentence contains two or more independent clauses and no dependent clauses.

Model Sentence

The fire burns in the hearth, / but the ashes fly everywhere.

Practice Ask students to write two simple sentences and then combine the simple sentences into a compound sentence. Have them repeat this for five pairs of sentences.

Possible Response: John studied hard for Algebra. He knew it would pay off.
John studied hard for Algebra, **and** he knew it would pay off.

Use **Grammar Transparencies and Copymasters,** p. 123.

Use McDougal Littell's ***Language Network,*** Chapter 4, for more instruction in compound sentences.

Choices & CHALLENGES

Grammar in Context: Compound Sentences

In this excerpt from "Brigid," compound sentences appear in the narrator's report of a conversation between the main characters, a married couple.

> "I wouldn't give in then, and I won't give in now, either. **I won't let it be said that I had hand or part in letting my own sister be put away."**
>
> **"But it's for her own good."** This time the woman's voice was softer, and she went over and turned the wet hat again on the fender.

A **compound sentence** consists of two or more independent clauses—clauses that can stand alone as sentences—joined together. The compound sentences in the passage above, each of which contains two independent clauses, are shown in blue. The first compound sentence shows a connection between the past and the present. The second compound sentence provides two details about the sentence of dialogue that precedes it—the manner in which the sentence was spoken and the action that accompanied the speaking of it.

WRITING EXERCISE Combine each group of sentences into a single compound sentence, using the coordinating conjunction that makes the most sense. (Use *but* three times and *and, for,* and *nor* once each. For two of the groups, the correct conjunctions are shown in parentheses to give you a hint.) Change or eliminate underlined phrases as necessary when you combine sentences.

Example: *Original* You don't want to listen to anything unpleasant. You don't want to listen to anything that's right.

Rewritten You don't want to listen to anything unpleasant, *and* you don't want to listen to anything that's right.

1. The rain thoroughly soaks the fields. Under the trees it only drips.
2. Owen's wife wants to put Brigid in a home. Owen refuses. He loves his sister. *(but, for)*
3. She doesn't want Owen to visit Brigid so often. She does not like spending money on Brigid. *(nor)*
4. Owen doesn't answer. His face shows nothing. His wife knows his thoughts.

Mary Lavin
1912–1996

Other Works
The Shrine and Other Stories
A Family Likeness and Other Stories

Home in Ireland Although she was born in Massachusetts, Mary Lavin lived most of her life in Ireland and wrote about Ireland in virtually all of her fiction. The daughter of an Irish couple who spent a few years in America, Lavin immigrated to Ireland when she was nine and attended a convent school in the Irish capital of Dublin. Four years later, her father became the manager of the Bective estate in Ireland's County Meath. Lavin's first collection of short stories, published in 1942, was called *Tales from Bective Bridge*.

"Controlled Revelation" With her stories being published on both sides of the Atlantic Ocean, Lavin became one of Ireland's foremost short story writers. "Mary Lavin is a great artist," said the eminent British critic V. S. Pritchett: "We are excited by her sympathy, her acute knowledge of the human heart, her truthfulness and, above all, by the controlled revelation of untidy powerful emotion." "Brigid," which was first published in *Dublin Magazine* (1944), was later included in the Dell anthology, *Great Irish Short Stories* (1964).

Author Activity

Power of Place Most of Lavin's fiction is set in Ireland, the country she lived in for most of her life. How important do you think the rural Irish setting is in "Brigid"? Discuss your thoughts with a small group of classmates.

Grammar in Context

WRITING EXERCISE

1. The rain thoroughly soaks the fields, but under the trees it only drips.
2. Owen's wife wants to put Brigid in a home, but Owen refuses, for he loves his sister.
3. She doesn't want Owen to visit Brigid so often, nor does she like spending money on Brigid.
4. Owen doesn't answer, and his face shows nothing, but his wife knows his thoughts.

Author Activity

Encourage students to analyze the importance of the rural Irish setting for this story by imagining how the story would be different if it were given an urban setting. What might be different about the characters? Their values? The relationships between people, especially outside the family? Their assumptions about life? Use these questions to highlight the characteristics and contributions of the rural setting to the story.

PREPARING to *Read*

Lalla

Short Story by ROSAMUNDE PILCHER

"I know what I'm going to do with my life."

Connect to Your Life

Value Scale When you set a goal for your life or make another important decision, you probably base that decision on your values, the ideals or beliefs that are most important to you. Think about the values that you would consider when setting a goal or making a major decision. List five values that are important to you, then rank them from one to five, with one being the most important.

Build Background

Town and Country In the selection you are about to read, Lalla, the main character, makes several life decisions based on her values. One choice she faces is whether to live in the cosmopolitan capital city of London or in a rural village in the county of Cornwall, on the remote southwest coast of England.

Cornwall is popular with tourists and artists for its rugged beauty. The county occupies a long, narrow peninsula that juts into the Atlantic Ocean. The area is mainly rural, with small farming villages scattered through the inland countryside and picturesque fishing towns along the coast.

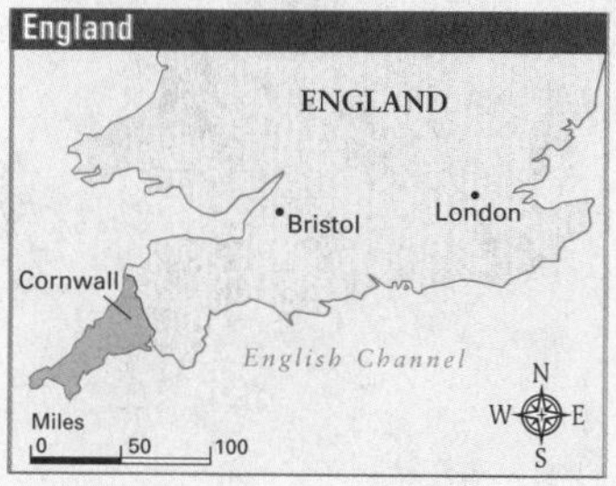

WORDS TO KNOW **Vocabulary Preview**

benign, bereft, decipher, enmity, impeccably, ludicrous, resignation, trepidation, unnervingly, vacillating

Focus Your Reading

LITERARY ANALYSIS **POINT OF VIEW** "Lalla" is told from the **point of view** of the title character's sister, a young girl named Jane. This **narrator** describes characters and relates events as she sees and understands them. As a result, the reader is given insight into Jane's thoughts and feelings, as in the following example:

> ***"But . . ." I started and then stopped. I wasn't like Lalla. I wanted to make friends.***

Such comments reveal the narrator's attitudes and values. As you read, look for other clues about Jane's values.

ACTIVE READING **PREDICTING** Many stories open with **exposition,** background information that usually introduces the **characters,** describes the **setting,** and **summarizes** significant events that took place before the story's action begins. On the basis of a story's exposition, it is often possible to make **predictions** about events that occur later in the narrative. In "Lalla," the exposition tells us about Lalla and her family and explains why they must make a significant change in their life.

READER'S NOTEBOOK As you read the story, pause at the first break marked by extra spacing and a large capital letter (on page 332). Make a prediction about what you think will happen to Lalla. At the next break (on page 334), review your earlier prediction and revise it, if necessary. Continue making and revising predictions at each break in the story.

VIDEODISC **LaserLinks: Background for Reading**
Geographical Connection
Visual Vocabulary

OVERVIEW

Objectives

1. understand and appreciate a **short story (Literary Analysis)**
2. identify **point of view (Literary Analysis)**
3. make **predictions** based on exposition **(Active Reading)**

Summary

Jane tells the story of her beautiful sister, Lalla, who is horrified to leave London and move to rural Cornwall after their father dies. Lalla meets and falls in love with Godfrey Howard. Though Godfrey is a veterinary student in Bristol, he and Lalla write letters and spend their holidays together. At a dance given by a friend, Lalla meets the wealthy Allan Sutton. She moves to London and eventually becomes engaged to Allan. The next Easter, however, Lalla breaks her engagement to Allan and leaves behind her glamorous city life. She returns home to Godfrey and to the companionship and warmth that she did not have in London.

Thematic Link

Lalla learns that sometimes what appears to be love is not, and that **the mysteries of the heart** will often lead a person back to family and friends that were left behind.

5-Minute Warm-Up

Daily Language SkillBuilder

Have students **proofread** the display sentences on page 223k and write them correctly. The sentences also appear on Transparency 10 of **Grammar Transparencies and Copymasters.**

LESSON RESOURCES

UNIT TWO RESOURCE BOOK, pp. 47–52

ASSESSMENT RESOURCES
Formal Assessment, pp. 55–56
Teacher's Guide to Assessment and Portfolio Use
Test Generator

SKILLS TRANSPARENCIES AND COPYMASTERS
Literary Analysis
- Point of View, T17 (for Cooperative Learning Activity, p. 343)

Reading and Critical Thinking
- Predicting Outcomes, T2 (for Think Critically, item 3, p. 343)

Grammar
- Coordinating Conjunctions, C77 (for Mini Lesson, p. 344)

Vocabulary
- Word Origins, C44 (for Mini Lesson, p. 330)

Writing
- Persuasive Essay, C30 (for Writing Option 1, p. 344)
- Effective Language, T13 (for Writing Option 3, p. 344)

Communications
- Dramatic Reading, T12 (for Activities & Explorations 2, p. 344)
- Impromptu Speaking: Dialogue, Role-Play, Debate, T13 (for Activities & Explorations 2, p. 344)

INTEGRATED TECHNOLOGY
Audio Library
LaserLinks
- Geographical Connection: London and Cornwall
- Visual Vocabulary

See **Teacher's SourceBook,** p. 24.

Internet: Research Starter
Visit our website:
www.mcdougallittell.com

Mini Lesson **Preteaching Vocabulary**

If you would like to preteach the WORDS TO KNOW for this selection, use the Mini Lesson, p. 330.

TEACHING THE LITERATURE

Reading and Analyzing

Reading Skills and Strategies: PREVIEW

Have students preview the selection. Ask students what the title, the images, and the highlighted quotations throughout the story suggest to them. Discuss with students the Build Background feature on p. 329, and then give them a brief summary of the story.

Active Reading PREDICTING

At the end of the first page, Jane says that "there were no boundaries to our new territory." She is speaking particularly of physical boundaries, but characters can also encounter social and emotional boundaries. Have students make a list of boundaries, physical and otherwise, that Jane, Lalla, and their family might cross as the story develops. Have students compare their lists with what actually occurs as they read the rest of the story.

Use **Unit Two Resource Book** p. 48 for more practice.

Literary Analysis POINT OF VIEW

Have students construct a chart that lists Jane's observations about her sister and what those observations reveal about Jane's attitudes toward her sister.

Possible Responses:

Observations	Attitudes
Lalla keeps asking questions about the move.	Jane thinks Lalla is selfish.
Lalla won't consider being friends with the Roystons.	Jane wishes Lalla were more friendly.
Lalla is beautiful.	Jane is envious of her beauty.

Use **Unit Two Resource Book** p. 49 for more practice.

Lalla

Rosamunde Pilcher

There was a Before and After. Before was before our father died, when we lived in London, in a tall narrow house with a little garden at the back. When we went on family skiing holidays every winter and attended suitable—and probably very expensive—day schools.

Portrait of Amber (1991), Charles Warren Mundy. Oil on canvas, 8″ × 10″, private collection.

Mini Lesson Preteaching Vocabulary

RESEARCHING WORD ORIGINS Call students' attention to the list of WORDS TO KNOW. Explain that many words in English have their origins in other languages. Write the history of the word *vacillating* on the board:

Lat. *vacillare*, "to waver."

Explain that the abbreviation *Lat.* stands for Latin. Point out that in every dictionary is a list of these abbreviations. Have students find the list if they have dictionaries. Then explain that the word in italics is the Latin word from which the English word came, and that following this is the original meaning of the Latin word. Note that students may find that the current meaning of a word and the original meaning are quite different.

Practice Have students work in pairs to look up the origins of the WORDS TO KNOW. Point out that in order to find some origins, students will have to determine the root word (for example: *bereft: bereave; decipher, cipher; resignation, resign*).

Use **Unit Two Resource Book** p. 50 for more practice.

A lesson on word origins appears on p. 356 in the Pupil's Edition.

Our father was a big man, outgoing and immensely active. We thought he was immortal, but then most children think that about their father. The worst thing was that Mother thought he was immortal too, and when he died, keeling over on the pavement between the insurance offices where he worked, and the company car into which he was just about to climb, there followed a period of ghastly limbo. Bereft, uncertain, lost, none of us knew what to do next. But after the funeral and a little talk with the family lawyer, Mother quietly pulled herself together and told us.

We were living in the country and there were no boundaries to our new territory.

At first we were horrified. "Leave London? Leave school?" Lalla could not believe it. "But I'm starting 'O' levels[1] next year."

"There are other schools," Mother told her.

"And what about Jane's music lessons?"

"We'll find another teacher."

"I don't mind about leaving school," said Barney. "I don't much like my school anyway."

Mother gave him a smile, but Lalla persisted in her inquisition.[2] "But where are we going to *live?*"

"We're going to Cornwall."

And so it was After. Mother sold the lease of the London house and a removals firm[3] came and packed up all the furniture and we traveled, each silently thoughtful, by car to Cornwall. It was spring, and because Mother had not realized how long the journey would take, it was dark by the time we found the village and, finally, the house. It stood just inside a pair of large gates, backed by tall trees. When we got out of the car, stiff and tired, we could smell the sea and feel the cold wind.

"There's a light in the window," observed Lalla.

"That'll be Mrs. Bristow," said Mother, and I knew she was making a big effort to keep her voice cheerful. She went up the little path and knocked at the door, and then, perhaps realizing it was ludicrous to be knocking at her own door, opened it. We saw someone coming down the narrow hallway towards us—a fat and bustling lady with grey hair and a hectically flowered pinafore.[4]

"Well, my dear life," she said, "what a journey you must have had. I'm all ready for you. There's a kettle on the hob[5] and a pie in the oven."

The house was tiny compared to the one we had left in London, but we all had rooms to ourselves, as well as an attic for the dolls' house, the books, bricks,[6] model cars and paintboxes we had refused to abandon, and a ramshackle shed alongside the garage where we could keep our bicycles. The garden was even smaller than the London garden, but this didn't matter because now we were living in the country and there were no boundaries to our new territory.

1. **'O' levels:** in Britain, a series of secondary-school examinations given before students can advance to higher studies.
2. **inquisition** (ĭn′kwĭ-zĭsh′ən): a lengthy series of questions.
3. **removals firm:** chiefly British term for a moving company.
4. **pinafore** (pĭn′ə-fôr): an apron.
5. **hob:** a warming shelf, especially on the back or side of a fireplace.
6. **bricks:** chiefly British term for building blocks.

WORDS TO KNOW

bereft (bĭ-rĕft′) *adj.* suffering the death of a loved one; deprived of someone or something important

ludicrous (lo͞o′dĭ-krəs) *adj.* laughably absurd; ridiculous

Customizing Instruction

Less Proficient Readers

Encourage students to discuss an event in their lives which divided their lives into "Before" and "After." Ask students to read about "Before" at the start of the story and then predict what "After" will be like.

Possible Responses: Jane will learn to like the country; Lalla will be unhappy.

Then have them read on to find out both how the narrator's life changes after her father's death and how her sister's life changes.

Students Acquiring English

This story is filled with British idioms and vocabulary, many of which are defined in the footnotes. Before students read the story, go over the footnotes with them.

Use **Spanish Study Guide** for additional support, pp. 71–73.

Gifted and Talented

Have students trace the social pressures of status and wealth experienced by Jane and her family. Have them pay attention to the ways these pressures affect choices made by Lalla. When students have finished reading the story, have them discuss these social pressures, their impact on Lalla, and their importance to the story.

BLOCK SCHEDULING: MANAGING TIME

If your schedule requires that you cover the lesson objectives in a shorter time, use . . .

- Preparing to Read, p. 329
- Thinking Through the Literature, p. 343
- Vocabulary in Action, p. 344
- Grammar in Context, p. 345

If you want to take advantage of longer class time, use . . .

- TE Teaching Options: Preteaching Vocabulary, p. 330; Cross Curricular Link, p. 332; Viewing and Representing, pp. 334, 340; Standardized Test Practice, p. 342
- Choices & Challenges, p. 344

Reading and Analyzing

Literary Analysis: CHARACTER

A Ask students what this paragraph reveals about the character of the narrator, both physically and emotionally.
Possible Response: She is short and stocky, with unruly hair. She feels that she is, and always will be, less attractive than Lalla.

Reading Skills and Strategies: VISUALIZING

B Have students describe the attributes of a "strong and roomy" tree house.
Possible Response: Thick floors, strong walls/banisters, wide enough that several children could sit in at once.

Active Reading PREDICTING

C Ask students to predict how the relationship between Jane and Barney and the Roystons will develop. Remind them to support their predictions with text evidence.
Possible Responses: They will eventually become friends; they will remain foes throughout their childhood.

We explored, finding a wooded lane which led down to a huge inland estuary[7] where it was possible to fish for flounder from the old sea wall.[8] In the other direction, a sandy right-of-way[9] led past the church and over the golf links[10] and the dunes to another beach—a wide and empty shore where the ebb tide[11] took the ocean out half a mile or more.

The Roystons, father, mother and two sons, lived in the big house and were our landlords. We hadn't seen them yet, though Mother had walked, in some trepidation, up the drive to make the acquaintance of Mrs. Royston, and to thank her for letting us have the house. But Mrs. Royston hadn't been in, and poor Mother had had to walk all the way down the drive again with nothing accomplished.

"How old are the Royston boys?" Barney asked Mrs. Bristow.

"I suppose David's thirteen and Paul's about eleven." She looked at us. "I don't know how old you lot are."

"I'm seven," said Barney, "and Jane's twelve and Lalla's fourteen."

"Well," said Mrs. Bristow. "That's nice. Fit in nicely, you would."

"They're far too young for me," said Lalla. "Anyway, I've seen them. I was hanging out the washing for Mother, and they came down the drive and out of the gate on their bicycles. They didn't even look my way."

"Come now," said Mrs. Bristow, "they're probably shy as you are."

"We don't particularly want to know them," said Lalla.

"But . . ." I started and then stopped. I wasn't like Lalla. I wanted to make friends. It would be nice to know the Royston boys. They had a tennis court; I had caught a glimpse of it through the trees. I wouldn't mind being asked to play tennis.

But for Lalla, of course, it was different. Fourteen was a funny age, neither one thing nor the other. And as for the way that Lalla looked! Sometimes I thought that if I didn't love her, and she wasn't my sister, I should hate her for her long, cloudy brown hair, the tilt of her nose, the amazing blue of her eyes, the curve of her pale mouth. During the last six months she seemed to have grown six inches.

I was short and square and my hair was too curly and horribly tangly. The awful bit was, I couldn't remember Lalla ever looking the way I looked, which made it fairly unlikely that I should end up looking like her. **A**

A few days later Mother came back from shopping in the village to say that she had met Mrs. Royston in the grocer's and we had all been asked for tea.

Lalla said, "I don't want to go."

"Why not?" asked Mother.

"They're just little boys. Let Jane and Barney go."

"It's just for tea," pleaded Mother.

She looked so anxious that Lalla gave in. She shrugged and sighed, her face closed in resignation.

We went, and it was a failure. The boys didn't want to meet us any more than Lalla wanted to meet them. Lalla was at her coolest, her most

7. **estuary** (ĕs′cho͞o-ĕr′ē): the wide part of a river where its currents meet the tides of an ocean or sea.
8. **sea wall:** a wall or embankment built to shelter the coast from storms or erosion.
9. **right-of-way:** a path or road on which the public is allowed to cross private property.
10. **golf links:** a golf course.
11. **ebb tide:** the outgoing tide.

WORDS TO KNOW
trepidation (trĕp′ĭ-dā′shən) *n.* a state of alarm or dread; apprehension; anxiety
resignation (rĕz′ĭg-nā′shən) *n.* the act of giving up; submission

Teaching Options

Cross Curricular Link Geography

LONDON London has been one of the world's largest and busiest cities for centuries. The city boasts many famous museums, art galleries, parks, and cathedrals. It also offers a wide variety of job opportunities, fine shops, and exciting night life. London was founded in southeast England on the River Thames by the Romans in the 1st century A.D. It has been continuously inhabited since then, and as a result displays architecture from the Roman occupation up to the present. London is a busy, thriving city; it is a center of finance, shipping, and government—it is the capital of the United Kingdom of Great Britain and Northern Ireland. London claims extensive shopping districts, celebrated parklands, famous monuments, and world-class museums.

remote. I knocked over my teacup, and Barney, who usually chatted to everybody, was silenced by the superiority of his hosts. When tea was over, Lalla stayed with the grown-ups, but Barney and I were sent off with the boys.

"Show Jane and Barney your tree house," Mrs. Royston told them as we trailed out of the door.

B They took us out into the garden and showed us the tree house. It was a marvelous piece of construction, strong and roomy. Barney's face was filled with longing. "Who built it?" he asked.

"Our cousin Godfrey. He's eighteen. He can build anything. It's our club, and you're not members."

C They whispered together and went off, leaving us standing beneath the forbidden tree house.

1 When the summer holidays came, Mother appeared to have forgotten about our social debt to the Royston boys, and we were careful not to remind her. So their names were never raised, and we never saw them except at a distance, cycling off to the village or down to the beach. Sometimes on Sunday afternoons they had guests and played tennis on their court. I longed to be included, but Lalla, deep in a book, behaved as though the Roystons didn't exist. Barney had taken up gardening, and, with his usual singlemindedness, was concentrating on digging himself a vegetable patch. He said he was going to sell lettuces, and Mother said that maybe he was the one who was going to make our fortune.

It was a hot summer, made for swimming. Lalla had grown out of her old swimsuit, so Mother made her a cotton bikini out of scraps. It was pale blue, just right for her tan and her long, pale hair. She looked beautiful in it, and I longed to look just like her. We went to the beach most days and often saw the Royston boys there. But the beach was so vast that there was no necessity for social contact, and we all avoided each other.

Until one Sunday. The tide came in during the afternoon that day, and Mother packed us a picnic so we could set off after lunch. When we got to the beach, Lalla said she was going to swim right away, but Barney and I decided we would wait. We took our spades and went down to where the outgoing tide had left shallow pools in the sand. There we started the construction of a large and complicated harbor. Absorbed in our task, we lost track of time, and never noticed the stranger approaching. Suddenly a long shadow fell across the sparkling water.

I looked up, shading my eyes against the sun. He said "Hello" and squatted down to our level.

"Who are you?" I asked.

"I'm Godfrey Howard, the Roystons' cousin. I'm staying with them."

Illustration by
Robbin Gourley

Customizing Instruction

Less Proficient Readers

Make sure students have grasped the main events of the story by asking them the following questions.

Where did the family move to from London?

Answer: a house near the sea in Cornwall

Who is narrating this story?

Answer: Jane, Lalla's younger sister

How are the children adjusting to their new home?

Possible Response: Jane and Barney seem to like Cornwall, but Lalla is less positive; they haven't made friends with the Royston boys.

Students Acquiring English

1 Explain to students that the "social debt" referred to is the family's obligation to ask Mrs. Royston and her sons over for tea, in return for Mrs. Royston's invitation to them. Ask why the children would not remind their mother about the social debt.

Possible Response: Their first visit with the Roystons was so awkward they do not want to repeat it.

LALLA 333

Reading and Analyzing

Literary Analysis: PLOT

A Point out that as Godfrey's attention turns from Jane to Lalla, the plot also takes a turn. Ask students to predict what direction the plot might take from here on.

Possible Responses: The plot might center on the relationship between Godfrey and Lalla; it might deal with Godfrey's helping the family make friends in the neighborhood.

Literary Analysis: CHARACTER

B Ask students what Jane's reaction to Lalla's and Godfrey's separation from the group reveals about her.

Possible Response: Jane is not an insecure person. She is mature enough to realize that her sister and Godfrey wanting to be together, apart from the others, is natural.

Literary Analysis POINT OF VIEW

Point out to students that since the story is told from Jane's point of view, we have to infer other characters' feelings from her observations. Ask students how the description of the day at the beach would be different if Lalla were the narrator.

Possible Response: The description would focus more on Godfrey, and would give us direct insight into what Lalla is feeling in regard to Godfrey.

1 Barney suddenly found his tongue. "Did you build the tree house?"

"That's right."

"How *did* you do it?"

Godfrey began to tell him. I listened and wondered how any person apparently so nice could have anything to do with those hateful Royston boys. It wasn't that he was particularly good-looking. His hair was mousey, his nose too big and he wore spectacles. He wasn't even very tall. But there was something warm and friendly about his deep voice and his smile.

"Did you go up and look at it?"

Barney went back to his digging. Godfrey looked at me. I said, "They wouldn't let us. They said it was a club. They didn't like us."

"They think you don't like them. They think you come from London and that you're very grand."

This was astonishing. "Grand? *Us?*" I said indignantly. "We never even pretended to be grand." And then I remembered Lalla's coolness, her pale, unsmiling lips. "I mean—Lalla's older—it's different for her." His silence at this was encouraging. "I wanted to make friends," I admitted.

A He was sympathetic. "It's difficult sometimes. People are shy." All at once he stopped, and looked over my shoulder. I turned to see what had caught his attention and saw Lalla coming towards us across the sand. Her hair lay like wet silk over her shoulders, and she had knotted her red towel around her hips like a sarong.[12] As she approached, Godfrey stood up. I said, introducing them the way Mother introduced people, "This is Lalla."

"Hello, Lalla," said Godfrey.

"He's the Roystons' cousin," I went on quickly. "He's staying with them."

"Hello," said Lalla.

Godfrey said, "David and Paul are wanting to play cricket. It's not much good playing cricket with just three people and I wondered if you'd come and join us?"

"Lalla won't want to play cricket," I told myself. "She'll snub him and then we'll never be asked again."

But she didn't snub him. She said, uncertainly, "I don't think I'm much good at cricket."

"But you could always try?"

"Yes." She began to smile, "I suppose I could always try."

And so we all finally got together. We played a strange form of beach cricket invented by Godfrey, which involved much lashing out at the ball and hysterical running. When we were too hot to play any longer, we swam. The Roystons had a couple of wooden surfboards, and they let us have turns, riding in on our stomachs on the long, warm breakers of the flood tide.[13] By five o'clock we were ready for tea, and we collected our various baskets and haversacks[14] and sat around in a circle on the sand. Other people's picnics are always much nicer than one's own, so we ate the Royston sandwiches and chocolate biscuits, and they ate Mother's scones with loganberry jam in the middle.

We had a last swim before the tide turned, and then gathered up our belongings and walked slowly home together. Barney and the two Roystons led the way, planning the next day's activities, and I walked with Godfrey and Lalla. But gradually, in the natural manner of events, they fell behind me. Plodding up and over the springy turf of the golf course, I listened to their voices.

"Do you like living here?"

12. **sarong:** a skirtlike garment formed by wrapping cloth around the waist.

13. **flood tide:** the incoming tide.

14. **haversacks** (hăv′ər-săks′): supply bags carried over one shoulder, popular with hikers.

Teaching Options

Mini Lesson: Viewing and Representing

First Sail **by Charles Warren Mundy**

ART APPRECIATION "I attempt to use as few brush strokes as possible, making each one really count," explains the artist. In this painting, Mundy has used a few simple, broad brush strokes on the girl's dress and on the water to emphasize the sunny pleasantness of the scene.

Instruction Ask students to describe the mood in the picture and what they feel provides the mood.

Possible Responses: Students may cite the effect of color and the relaxed postures of the subjects.

Instruction Ask how the mood in the picture reflects the mood in the story now that the main characters have made new friends.

Possible Responses: The people in the picture appear relaxed and happy, and are enjoying each others' company. The characters in the story have finally gotten past the uncomfortable part of getting to know each other and finally enjoy spending time together.

First Sail (1993), Charles Warren Mundy. Oil on canvas, 30″ × 40″, private collection.

"It's different from London."

"That's where you lived before?"

"Yes, but my father died, and we couldn't afford to live there any more."

"I'm sorry, I didn't know. Of course, I envy your living here. I'd rather be at Carwheal than anywhere else in the world."

"Where do you live?"

"In Bristol."

"Are you at school there?"

"I've finished with school. I'm starting college in September. I'm going to be a vet."

"A vet?" Lalla considered this. "I've never met a vet before."

He laughed. "You haven't actually met one yet."

I smiled to myself in satisfaction. They sounded like two grown-ups talking. Perhaps a grown-up friend of her own was all that Lalla had needed. I had a feeling that we had crossed another watershed.[15] After today, things would be different. B

15. **watershed:** a critical point that marks a division or a change of course; a turning point.

Customizing Instruction

Less Proficient Readers

Explain to students what the sea terms *breakers, flood tide*, and *tide turned* mean:

Breakers are waves that break into foam against the shore.

Flood tide is the rising tide.

Tide turned means that the incoming tide started to ebb (as here), or that the outgoing tide began to flood again.

Ask students to describe how the movement of the sea affects the actions of the children.

Answer: They surf and play in the water, but when the tide turns they leave the beach.

Students Acquiring English

1 Explain to students that "found his tongue" means that he began to speak. Ask students what causes Barney to "find his tongue."

Answer: Barney is fascinated by the tree house, and he knows that Godfrey built it.

Reading and Analyzing

Reading Skills and Strategies: CLARIFYING
Have students clarify the nature of the relationship between Lalla and Godfrey.
Possible Response: They are in love.

Literary Concept: CHARACTER
A Ask students what this sentence tells the reader about Godfrey.
Possible Response: He is determined to finish school; he has ambition. He is not rich.

Active Reading PREDICTING
B Ask students to predict what will happen at the dance. Remind them to base their predictions on text evidence.
Possible Response: At the dance Lalla will meet and be attracted to another young man.

1 The Roystons were now our friends. Our relieved mothers—for Mrs. Royston, faced with our unrelenting enmity, had been just as concerned and conscience-stricken as Mother—took advantage of the truce, and after that Sunday we were never out of each other's houses. Through the good offices[16] of the Roystons, our social life widened, and Mother found herself driving us all over the county to attend various 2 beach picnics, barbecues, sailing parties and teenage dances. By the end of the summer we had been accepted. We had dug ourselves in. Carwheal was home. And Lalla grew up.

She and Godfrey wrote to each other. I knew this because I would see his letters to her lying on the table in the hall. She would take them upstairs to read them in secret in her room, and we were all too great respecters of privacy ever to mention them. When he came to Carwheal, which he did every holiday, to stay with the Roystons, he was always around first thing in the morning on the first day. He said it was to see us all, but we knew it was Lalla he had come to see.

He now owned a battered second-hand car. A lesser man might have scooped Lalla up and taken her off on her own, but Godfrey was far too kind, and he would drive for miles, to distant coves and hilltops, with the whole lot of us packed into his long-suffering car, and the boot[17] filled with food and towels and snorkels and other assorted clobber.[18]

But he was only human, and often they would drift off on their own and walk away from us. We would watch their progress and let them go, knowing that in an hour or two they would be back—Lalla with a bunch of wild flowers or some shells in her hand, Godfrey sunburned and tousled—both of them smiling and content in a way that we found reassuring and yet did not wholly understand.

Lalla had always been such a certain person, so positive, so unveering from a chosen course, that we were all taken by surprise by her vacillating indecision as to what she was going to do with her life. She was nearly eighteen, with her final exams over and her future spread before her like a new country observed from the peak of some painfully climbed hill.

Mother wanted her to go to university.

"Isn't it rather a waste of time if I don't know what I'm going to do at the end of it? How can I decide now what I'm going to do with the rest of my life? It's inhuman. Impossible."

"But darling, what do you want to do?"

"I don't know. Travel, I suppose. Of course, I could be really original and take a typing course."

"It might at least give you time to think things over."

This conversation took place at breakfast. It might have continued forever, reaching no satisfactory conclusion, but the post arrived as we sat there over our empty coffee cups. There was the usual dull bundle of envelopes, but, as well, a large square envelope for Lalla. She opened it idly, read the card inside and made a face. "Goodness, how grand, a proper invitation to a proper dance."

"How nice," said Mother, trying to decipher the butcher's bill. "Who from?"

"Mrs. Menheniot," said Lalla.

We were all instantly agog, grabbing at the invitation in order to gloat over it. We had once been to lunch with Mrs. Menheniot, who lived with Mr. Menheniot and a tribe of junior Menheniots in a beautiful house on the Fal.[19] For

16. **offices:** kind acts performed to help someone else.
17. **boot:** British term for the trunk of a car.
18. **clobber:** British slang for clothing or equipment.
19. **Fal:** a river in western Cornwall.

WORDS TO KNOW
enmity (ĕn′mĭ-tē) *n.* the hatred between enemies; antagonism; hostility
vacillating (văs′ə-lāt′ĭng) *adj.* swinging indecisively from one course of action or opinion to another **vacillate** *v.*
decipher (dĭ-sī′fər) *v.* to read or interpret something unclear; to figure out

some unspecified reason they were very rich, and their house was vast and white with a pillared portico[20] and green lawns which sloped down to the tidal inlets of the river.

"Are you going to go?" I asked.

Lalla shrugged. "I don't know."

"It's in August. Perhaps Godfrey will be here and you can go with him."

"He's not coming down this summer. He has to earn money to pay his way through college."

She would not make up her mind whether or not she would go to Mrs. Menheniot's party and probably never would have come to any decision if it had not been for the fact that, before very long, I had been invited too. I was really too young, as Mrs. Menheniot's booming voice pointed out over the telephone when she rang Mother, but they were short of girls and it would be a blessing if I could be there to swell the numbers. When Lalla knew that I had been asked as well, she said of course we would go. She had passed her driving test, and we would borrow Mother's car.

We were then faced with the problem of what we should wear, as Mother could not begin to afford to buy us the sort of evening dresses we wanted. In the end she sent away to Liberty's[21] for yards of material, and she made them for us, beautifully, on her sewing machine. Lalla's was pale blue lawn and in it she looked like a goddess—Diana the Huntress perhaps. Mine was a sort of tawny-gold, and I looked quite presentable in it, but of course not a patch on[22] Lalla.

When the night of the dance came, we put on our dresses and set off together in Mother's Mini,[23] giggling slightly with nerves. But when we reached the Menheniots' house, we stopped giggling because the whole affair was so grand as to be awesome. There were floodlights and car parks[24] and hundreds of sophisticated-looking people all making their way towards the front door.

Indoors, we stood at the foot of the crowded staircase, and I was filled with panic. We knew nobody. There was not a single familiar face. Lalla whisked a couple of glasses of champagne from a passing tray and gave me one. I took a sip, and at that very moment a voice rang out above the hubbub. "Lalla!" A girl was coming down the stairs, a dark girl in a strapless satin dress that had very obviously not been made on her mother's sewing machine.

20. **pillared portico** (pĭl′ərd pôr′tĭ-kō′): a porch with a roof supported by columns.

21. **Liberty's:** a London store especially famous for the fabric it sells.

22. **not a patch on:** not nearly as good as.

23. **Mini** (mĭn′ē): a small, fairly inexpensive, popular British car.

24. **car parks:** British term for parking lots.

Illustration by Robbin Gourley

Customizing Instruction

Less Proficient Readers

1 Ask students how Jane's family's relationship with the Roystons has changed.

Answer: With the help of Godfrey, the young people have all become friends.

2 Ask how this new friendship helps Lalla's family adjust to life in Cornwall.

Answer: The Roystons include their tenants in their active social life, and the newcomers are accepted by their other new neighbors.

Set a Purpose Have students read to find out what important choices Lalla makes about her life.

Reading and Analyzing

Reading Skills and Strategies: CLARIFYING

A Ask students why the unexpected arrival of Godfrey upsets Jane.

Possible Responses: Jane is fond of Godfrey and is worried that he will be hurt if he learns that Lalla is with Allan; she is afraid Godfrey will be embarrassed and feel out of place; she is afraid Godfrey will no longer want to date Lalla when he sees her with Allan.

Literary Analysis: CHARACTER

B Ask students what this passage tells them about Lalla's values.

Possible Response: She prefers the big city; she is interested in wealth and appearances.

Literary Analysis: PLOT

C Students should analyze the plot development at this point. Have students note how the author speeds up the pace and condenses story events here. Tremendous changes occur in Lalla's life in the space of three sentences. Ask students to describe these changes.

Possible Response: Lalla moves to London. She gets a job as a secretary in a magazine office, but soon becomes a model.

Lalla looked up. "Rosemary!"

She was Rosemary Sutton from London. She and Lalla had been at school together in the old days. They fell into each other's arms and embraced as though this was all either of them had been waiting for. "What are you doing? I never thought I'd see you here. How marvelous. Come and meet Allan. You remember my brother Allan, don't you? Oh, this is exciting."

Allan was so good-looking as to be almost unreal. Fair as his sister was dark, impeccably turned out. Lalla was tall, but he was taller. He looked down at her, and his rather wooden features were filled with both surprise and obvious pleasure. He said, "But of course I remember." He smiled and laid down his glass. "How could I forget? Come and dance."

I scarcely saw her again all evening. He took her away from me, and I was bereft, as though I had lost my sister forever. At one point I was rescued by Mrs. Menheniot herself, who dragooned[25] some young man into taking me to supper, but after supper even he melted away. I found an empty sofa in a deserted sitting-out room,[26] and collapsed into it. It was half-past-twelve, and I longed for my bed. I wondered what people would think if I put up my feet and had a little snooze.

Somebody came into the room and then withdrew again. I looked up and saw his retreating back view. I said, "Godfrey." He turned back. I got up off the sofa, back on to my aching feet.

"What are you doing here? Lalla said you were working."

"I am, but I wanted to come. I drove down from Bristol. That's why I'm so late." I knew why he had wanted to come. To see Lalla. "I didn't expect to see you."

"They were short of girls, so I got included."

We gazed glumly at each other, and my heart felt very heavy. Godfrey's dinner jacket looked as though he had borrowed it from some larger person, and his bow tie was crooked. I said, "I think Lalla's dancing."

"Why don't you come and dance with me, and we'll see."

I thought this a rotten idea but didn't like to say so. Together we made our way towards the ballroom. The ceiling lights had been turned off, and the disco lights now flashed red and green and blue across the smoky darkness. Music thumped and rocked an assault on our ears, and the floor seemed to be filled with an unidentifiable confusion of people, of flying hair and arms and legs. Godfrey and I joined in at the edge, but I could tell that his heart wasn't in it. I wished that he had never come. I prayed that he would not find Lalla.

But of course, he saw her, because it was impossible not to. It was impossible to miss Allan Sutton as well. They were both so tall, so beautiful. Godfrey's face seemed to close up.

"Who's she with?" he asked.

"Allan Sutton. He and his sister have come down from London. Lalla used to know them."

I couldn't say any more. I couldn't tell Godfrey

I couldn't say any more. I couldn't tell Godfrey to go and claim her for himself.

25. **dragooned** (drə-go͞ond′): compelled by threats or force. The term is used humorously here.

26. **sitting-out room:** a room used by those not dancing.

WORDS TO KNOW **impeccably** (ĭm-pĕk′ə-blē) *adv.* flawlessly; perfectly

338

to go and claim her for himself. I wasn't even certain by then what sort of a reception she would have given him. And anyway, as we watched them, Allan stopped dancing and put his arm around Lalla, drawing her towards him, whispering something into her ear. She slipped her hand into his, and they moved away towards the open French window.[27] The next moment they were lost to view, swallowed into the darkness of the garden beyond.

At four o'clock in the morning Lalla and I drove home in silence. We we not giggling now. I wondered sadly if we would ever giggle together again. I ached with exhaustion, and I was out of sympathy with her. Godfrey had never even spoken to her. Soon after our dance he had said goodbye and disappeared, presumably to make the long, lonely journey back to Bristol.

She, on the other hand, had an aura of happiness about her that was almost tangible. I glanced at her and saw her peaceful, smiling profile. It was hard to think of anything to say.

It was Lalla who finally broke the silence. "I know what I'm going to do. I mean, I know what I'm going to do with my life. I'm going back to London. Rosemary says I can live with her. I'll take a secretarial course or something, then get a job."

"Mother will be disappointed."

B "She'll understand. It's what I've always wanted. We're buried down here. And there's another thing; I'm tired of being poor. I'm tired of homemade dresses and never having a new car. We've always talked about making our fortunes, and as I'm the eldest, I might as well make a start. If I don't do it now, I never will."

I said, "Godfrey was there this evening."

"Godfrey?"

"He drove down from Bristol."

She did not say anything, and I was angry. I wanted to hurt her and make her feel as bad as I felt. "He came because he wanted to see you. But you didn't even notice him."

"You can scarcely blame me," said Lalla, "for that."

C And so she went back to London, lived with Rosemary, and took a secretarial course, just as she said she would. Later, she got a job on the editorial staff of a fashionable magazine, but it was not long before one of the photographers spied her potential, seduced her from her typewriter, and started taking pictures of her. Soon her lovely face smiled at us from the cover of the magazine.

"How does it feel to have a famous daughter?" people asked Mother, but she never quite accepted Lalla's success, just as she never quite accepted Allan Sutton. Allan's devotion to Lalla had proved unswerving and he was her constant companion.

"Let's hope he doesn't marry her," said Barney, but of course eventually, inevitably, they decided to do just that. "We're engaged!" Lalla rang up from London to tell us. Her voice sounded, unnervingly, as though she was calling from the next room.

"Darling!" said Mother, faintly.

"Oh, do be pleased. Please be pleased. I'm so happy and I couldn't bear it if you weren't happy, too."

So of course Mother said that she was pleased, but the truth was that none of us really liked Allan very much. He was—well—spoilt. He was conceited. He was too rich. I said as much to Mother, but Mother was loyal to Lalla.

---

27. **French window:** a type of window that extends to the floor.

WORDS TO KNOW

unnervingly (ŭn-nûrv′ĭng-lē) *adv.* in a way that causes someone to become nervous or upset; disturbingly

Customizing Instruction

Students Acquiring English

1 Explain to students the meaning of the sentence "Godfrey's face seemed to close up."

Answer: He removed all expression from his face, so that no one would know what he was thinking by looking at him.

Have students explain why Godfrey would react in such a way to seeing Lalla.

Possible Response: Godfrey sees how beautiful Lalla looks with Allan Sutton, how she might be attracted to the lifestyle that Allan represents, and how he may no longer appeal to her.

Reading and Analyzing

Literary Analysis: SETTING

A Point out that the time is Easter—a traditional time of renewal—and the weather "makes one feel young again." Have students discuss what these details suggest.
Possible Response: The characters' lives may take a new direction; Lalla may become more like her younger self, who loved being with Godfrey.

Literary Analysis POINT OF VIEW

B Have students use the details of this paragraph to describe Jane's feelings about Godfrey.
Possible Response: She admires him for his self-assurance, wisdom, and attractiveness.
Ask what these feelings might suggest about Jane's hopes regarding Godfrey.
Possible Response: She may hope that Godfrey will finally succeed in his relationship with Lalla.

Literary Analysis: CHARACTER

C Allan says that Lalla's decision came as "a bolt from the blue" and he thought she was "just tired." What do these comments suggest about Allan's character?
Possible Response: He isn't very perceptive; he isn't sensitive to Lalla's feelings.
Ask students to speculate about how these character traits might have influenced Lalla's decision to break off the engagement.
Possible Response: She may have decided that she was unable to marry a man who could not understand her.

She said, "*Things* mean a lot to Lalla. I think they always have. I mean, possessions and security. And perhaps someone who truly loves her."

I said, "Godfrey truly loved her."

"But that was when they were young. And perhaps Godfrey couldn't give her love."

"He could make her laugh. Allan never makes her laugh."

"Perhaps," said Mother sadly, "she's grown out of laughter."

And then it was Easter. We hadn't heard from Lalla for a bit and didn't expect her to come to Carwheal for the spring holiday. But she rang up, out of the blue, and said that she hadn't been well and was taking a couple of weeks off. Mother was delighted, of course, but concerned about her health.

By now we were all more or less grown-up. David was studying to be a doctor, and Paul had a job on the local newspaper. I had achieved a place at the Guildhall School of Music, and Barney was no longer a little boy but a gangling teenager with an insatiable appetite. Still, however, we gathered for the holidays, and that Easter Godfrey abandoned his sick dogs and ailing cows to the ministrations[28] of his partner and joined us.

A It was lovely weather, almost as warm as summer. The sort of weather that makes one feel young again—a child. There was scented thyme on the golf links, and the cliff walks were starred with primroses and wild violets. In the Roystons' garden the daffodils blew in the long grass beneath the tree house, and Mrs. Royston put up the tennis net and swept the cobwebs out of the summer house.

It was during one of these sessions that Godfrey and I talked about Lalla. We were in the summer house together, sitting out while the others played a set.

"Tell me about Lalla."

"She's engaged."

"I know. I saw it in the paper." I could think of nothing to say. "Do you like him—Allan Sutton, I mean?"

I said "Yes," but I was never much good at lying.

Godfrey turned his head and looked at me. He was wearing old jeans and a white shirt, and I thought that he had grown older in a subtle way. He was more sure of himself and somehow more attractive. **B**

He said, "That night of the Menheniots' dance, I was going to ask her to marry me."

"Oh, Godfrey."

"I hadn't even finished my training, but I thought perhaps we'd manage. And when I saw her, I knew that I had lost her. I'd left it too late."

On the day that Lalla was due to arrive, I took Mother's old car into the neighboring town to do some shopping. When the time came to return home, the engine refused to start. After struggling for a bit, I walked to the nearest garage and persuaded a kindly, oily man to come and help me. But he told me it was hopeless.

We walked back to the garage, and I telephoned home. But it wasn't Mother who answered the call, it was Godfrey.

I explained what had happened. "Lalla's train is due at the junction in about half an hour and we said someone would meet her."

There was a momentary hesitation, then Godfrey said, "I'll go. I'll take my car."

When I finally reached home, exhausted from carrying the laden grocery bags from the bus stop, Godfrey's car was nowhere to be seen.

28. **ministrations** (mĭn′ĭ-strā′shənz): services performed to aid someone or something.

Teaching Options

Mini Lesson Viewing and Representing

The Cove **by Fairfield Porter**

ART APPRECIATION Fairfield Porter (1907–1975), an American painter who lived most of his life on Great Spruce Head Island, Maine, painted many landscapes and seascapes. He was also a prominent writer on art. In this painting, Porter uses soft pastels to depict a quiet landscape of green and gold.

Application Have students imagine that the figure in the painting is Godfrey. Ask how the painting seems to express his feelings about losing Lalla. Be sure students consider the stance of the figure in the painting.

Possible Response: The figure in the painting is alone and therefore there is a sense of loneliness, of abandon. Because the figure is walking away from the viewer, there is a sense of the figure walking away from something, just as Godfrey feels that he is walking away from Lalla.

The Cove (1964), Fairfield Porter. Oil on canvas, 37″ × 53½″, The Metropolitan Museum of Art, New York, bequest of Arthur M. Bullowa, 1993 (1993.406.7). Copyright © 1995 The Metropolitan Museum of Art.

A short time later the telephone rang. But it wasn't Lalla, explaining where they were, it was a call from London and it was Allan Sutton.

"I have to speak to Lalla."

His voice sounded frantic. I said cautiously, "Is anything wrong?"

"She's broken off our engagement. I got back from the office and found a letter from her and my ring. She said she was coming home. She doesn't want to get married."

I found it in my heart to be very sorry for him. "But Allan, you must have had *some* idea."

1 "None. Absolutely none. It's just a bolt from the blue. I know she's been a bit off-color lately, but I thought she was just tired." C

"She must have her reasons, Allan," I told him, as gently as I could.

"Talk to her, Jane. Try to make her see sense."

He rang off at last. I put the receiver back on the hook and stood for a moment, gathering

Customizing Instruction

Students Acquiring English

1 Explain to students that "a bolt from the blue" is something completely unexpected.

Ask students why Lalla's breaking off the engagement was a "bolt from the blue" to Allan.

Possible Response: Allan had thought that Lalla loved him, and was very surprised that she said she didn't want to marry him and that she left London.

Reading and Analyzing

Active Reading POINT OF VIEW

A Ask students what events have caused Jane's eyes to become full of tears.

Possible Responses: Her desire for Lalla and Godfrey to become a couple has been realized; her desire for a return to close relations with Lalla has been realized; her desire for Lalla's happiness and self-assurance has been realized.

Literary Analysis: PLOT

B Explain to students that in this paragraph, the story reaches its resolution. Ask students to describe the plot development by identifying the resolution.

Possible Response: Lalla has returned to the people she loves and who love her: Godfrey and her family.

Literary Analysis: CHARACTER

C Ask students what they think Lalla has found out about herself.

Possible Responses: She has realized that she values her family and home; material things and social prestige won't make her happy; she values being with people with whom she can talk and who are sensitive to her feelings.

my wits about me and assessing this new and startling turn of events. I found myself caught up in a tangle of conflicting emotions. Enormous sympathy for Allan; a reluctant admiration for Lalla, who had had the courage to take this shattering decision; but, as well, a sort of rising excitement.

Godfrey. Godfrey and Lalla. Where were they? I knew then that I could not face Mother and Barney before I had found out what was going on. Quietly, I opened the door and went out of the house, through the gates, down the lane. As soon as I turned the corner at the end of the lane, I saw Godfrey's car parked on the patch of grass outside the church.

B It was a marvelously warm, benign sort of evening. I took the path that led past the church and towards the beach. Before I had gone very far, I saw them, walking up over the golf links towards me. The wind blew Lalla's hair over her face. She was wearing her London high-heeled boots so was taller than Godfrey. They should have appeared ill-assorted, but there was something about them that was totally right. They were a couple, holding hands, walking up from the beach as they had walked innumerable times, together.

I stopped, suddenly reluctant to disturb their intimacy. But Lalla had seen me. She waved and then let go of Godfrey's hand and began to run towards me, her arms flailing like windmills.

"Jane!" I had never seen her so exuberant.

"Oh, Jane." I ran to meet her. We hugged each other, and for some stupid reason my eyes were full of tears. **A**

"Oh, darling Jane . . ."

"I had to come and find you."

"Did you wonder where we were? We went for a walk. I had to talk to Godfrey. He was the one person I could talk to."

"Lalla, Allan's been on the phone."

"I had to do it. It was all a ghastly mistake."

"But you found out in time. That's all that matters."

"I thought I was going after what I wanted. I thought I had what I wanted, and then I found out that I didn't want it at all. Oh, I've missed you all so much. There wasn't anybody I could talk to." **C**

Over her shoulder I saw Godfrey coming, tranquilly, to join us. I let go of Lalla and went to give him a kiss. I didn't know what they had been discussing as they paced the lonely beach, and I knew that I never would. But still, I had the feeling that the outcome could be nothing but good for all of us.

I said, "We must go back. Mother and Barney don't know about anything. They'll be thinking that I've dissolved into thin air, as well as the pair of you."

"In that case," said Godfrey, and he took Lalla's hand in his own once more, "perhaps we'd better go and tell them."

And so we walked home, the three of us. In the warm evening, in the sunshine, in the fresh wind. ❖

WORDS TO KNOW **benign** (bĭ-nīn') *adj.* mild; gentle

Teaching Options

Assessment Standardized Test Practice

DRAWING AN INFERENCE For some standardized tests, students will be asked to draw an inference supported with text evidence. To provide students with some help in choosing the best inference, read aloud or write on the board the following question.

Which of the following best explains Jane's comment, "I had the feeling that the outcome could be nothing but good for all of us."

A. Jane is glad that Lalla has broken off her engagement because she never liked Allan.

B. Jane sees that Lalla has matured and has learned to value her family, her love for Godfrey, and her life in Cornwall.

C. Jane has always hoped that Lalla and Godfrey would continue their relationship.

Lead students through the process of choosing the best inference. Consider each choice. Point out that, while all of the statements apply to the story, the best inference should include all pertinent information. For that reason, **B** is the best choice.

Thinking through the LITERATURE

Connect to the Literature

1. **What Do You Think?** What was your reaction to the story? Discuss your reaction with a classmate.

Comprehension Check
- Why does Lalla's family move to Cornwall?
- As teenagers, how do Lalla and Godfrey feel about each other?
- Who is Allan Sutton?
- Why does Lalla move to London?

Think Critically

2. Do you think Lalla makes a wise choice in the end? Why or why not?

3. ACTIVE READING PREDICTING Review the **predictions** that you made in your READER'S NOTEBOOK. How close were your predictions to what actually happens? To what extent do you think the story's **exposition** provides clues about Lalla's future behavior? Explain your answer.

4. In what ways, if any, do you think Lalla's **character** and values change as she gets older? Use examples from the story to support your opinion.

THINK ABOUT
- her reaction to moving to Cornwall
- her relationships with Godfrey and Allan
- her comments to Jane after the Menheniots' dance
- her final decision

5. How does Jane's view of her older sister affect what you think of Lalla?

Extend Interpretations

6. **Critic's Corner** A magazine editor once noted, "When Rosamunde Pilcher writes about people, in crisis or at peace, falling in or out of love, discovering new life or accepting death, readers see themselves . . . or their children . . . or their parents." Do you agree? Explain.

7. **Connect to Life** What values do you think are most important for people to consider when they choose a mate?

Literary Analysis

POINT OF VIEW Point of view refers to the type of **narrator** used in a story. The short story "Lalla" uses a **first-person point of view,** in which the narrator is a character in the story who tells everything in her own words. This narrator, Lalla's sister Jane, describes characters and relates events as she sees and understands them.

Cooperative Learning Activity Working in a small group, review the story and take notes about Jane's judgment of the following characters and settings: Lalla, Godfrey, Allan, Jane herself, Cornwall, London. Then consider how Jane's point of view influences your own judgment of the characters, events, and places in the story. What do you learn about Jane's values as a result of your reading?

Lalla: Sometimes aloof ("Lalla was at her coolest, her most remote," page 332)
Godfrey:

GUIDING STUDENT RESPONSE

Connect to the Literature

1. **What Do You Think?**
Student responses will vary. Some students will say that they found the story heartwarming; others might find it overly sweet.

Comprehension Check
- Her father has died.
- They enjoy one another's company.
- He is a rich and handsome man from London, and the brother of Lalla's former schoolmate.
- She wants to return to city life and to find work.

Use Selection Quiz
Unit Two Resource Book, p. 52.

Think Critically

2. Possible Response: Yes, because she finally chose in favor of love and family, instead of the more superficial values of money and appearances.
3. Student predictions will vary; students may think that the exposition suggests early the difficulty of doing without the expensive things that life in London has to offer.
4. Possible Responses: As a teen, Lalla values the excitement of city life. She resents leaving London and returns at the first opportunity. After a while, though, the allure of sophisticated city life appeals to her less, and she comes to value her family and close friends in Cornwall more.
5. Possible Response: Seeing Lalla through Jane's eyes gives us more distance than we would have if Lalla were the story's narrator. This way, Lalla seems older and more glamorous.

Extend Interpretations

Critic's Corner Student responses will vary, but should include details from the story and their own experience or perspective.

Connect to Life Student responses will vary, but may use Godfrey and Allan as points of reference.

Literary Analysis

Point of View Students should cite specific commentary by Jane.

Writing Options

1. **Movie Title** Have students share their movie titles with the class.
2. **Lalla's List** Remind students that the list should reflect Lalla's growing dissatisfaction with her glamorous life in London and with the social world Allan represents.
3. **Telephone Talk** Suggest that students first decide whether Lalla will be frank or gentle with Allan.

Activities & Explorations

1. **Values Poster** Suggest that students brainstorm with partners to generate ideas for images appropriate to each character. Encourage students to review the story for ideas.
2. **Future Conversation** Before students create their conversations, review with the class the personality traits of the characters and the roles they played in the story.

Inquiry & Research

Exploring England As students research London and Cornwall, have them take into account how life might have changed in these places in the last few decades.

Vocabulary in Action

Exercise A

1. resignation
2. bereft
3. vacillating
4. enmity
5. benign
6. unnervingly
7. trepidation
8. ludicrous
9. decipher
10. impeccably

Writing Options

1. Movie Title Imagine that this story is being turned into a television movie. Write a proposal for a new title that will attract viewers. Be sure to explain your reasoning.

2. Lalla's List Create the two lists of pros and cons Lalla might have made before she decided to return to Cornwall. On one list, show the benefits and problems of staying with Allan. On the other, analyze the advantages and disadvantages of returning to Godfrey.

3. Telephone Talk Write a script for a telephone conversation between Lalla and Allan in which she explains why she is leaving him and moving back to Cornwall.

Activities & Explorations

1. Values Poster Create a poster. One side should include images that represent Allan's values; the other side should represent Godfrey's values. ~ **ART**

2. Future Conversation With three or four other classmates, act out an imaginary conversation that takes place 10 years after the story. Choose among the roles of Lalla, Godfrey, Jane, Mother, and Allan, and reminisce about "the old days." In the role of your character, talk about what happened and why you made the decisions you did. ~ **SPEAKING AND LISTENING**

Inquiry & Research

Exploring England Find out more information about London and Cornwall. Then, in the light of your findings, discuss which of these two locations you would prefer to live in.

More Online: Research Starter
www.mcdougallittell.com

Vocabulary in Action

EXERCISE A: CONTEXT CLUES Write the word that is closest in meaning to the italicized word or phrase in each sentence.

1. Allan spoke with *grudging acceptance* of Lalla's engagement to Godfrey.
2. Jane knew she would feel *very lonely* after Lalla got married.
3. Mother was exasperated with Lalla for *changing her mind* so often about the wedding plans.
4. For Lalla's sake, Godfrey and Allan put aside their *intense dislike* for each other.
5. On the wedding day the weather turned sunny and *mild.*
6. Before the ceremony, Uncle Peter spoke *distressingly* to Godfrey about the responsibilities of married life.
7. Remembering Uncle Peter's advice, Godfrey felt some *anxiety* about getting married.
8. Aunt Fran arrived wearing a *very silly* green feathered hat.
9. Allan missed the wedding because he could not *figure out* the map Barney sent him.
10. The ceremony went exactly as planned, and the organist played the wedding music *without a single mistake.*

EXERCISE B With a partner, take turns using facial expressions and/or body gestures to act out the meaning of three Words to Know each and guessing what word is being shown.

Building Vocabulary
For an in-depth lesson on context clues, see page 56.

WORDS TO KNOW					
	benign	decipher	impeccably	resignation	unnervingly
	bereft	enmity	ludicrous	trepidation	vacillating

Mini Lesson Grammar

COORDINATING CONJUNCTIONS For use with Grammar in Context. Coordinating conjunctions can connect two independent clauses. The most common coordinating conjunctions are *and, but, or, nor, for, yet,* and *so.*

Write the following sentence on the board:

Godfrey lived in Bristol, but he often visited Cornwall.

Point out that a comma precedes a coordinating conjunction between two independent clauses, unless the two clauses are very short.

Practice Have students connect the following pairs of independent clauses with a coordinating conjunction, using the correct punctuation.

1. Lalla moved to London. She began working as a model.
   Possible Response: Lalla moved to London, and she began working as a model.
2. Jane told Godfrey she liked Allan. She was lying.
   Possible Response: Jane told Godfrey she liked Allan, but she was lying.
3. Jane did not like Allan. She did not like his lifestyle.

Grammar in Context: Complex Sentences

In "Lalla," Rosamunde Pilcher uses complex sentences to show how events are related in time.

> When the night of the dance came, we put on our dresses and set off together in Mother's Mini.
>
> As soon as I turned the corner at the end of the lane, I saw Godfrey's car parked on the patch of grass outside the church.

A **complex sentence** consists of one independent clause and one or more subordinate clauses. An independent clause can stand alone as a sentence; a subordinate clause cannot. In the sentences above, the independent clauses are shown in blue, and the subordinate clauses are shown in red.

In a complex sentence, the independent clause expresses the main idea of the sentence. The subordinate clause or clauses express ideas that are less important than, but related to, the main idea. In the examples above, the subordinate clauses indicate the times at which the events related in the independent clauses took place. Subordinate clauses can also be used to express relationships of cause, condition, manner, place, and purpose.

Usage Tip: Subordinate clauses begin with subordinating conjunctions. These include *although, as soon as, because, than, that, when,* and *where.*

WRITING EXERCISE Rewrite each pair of sentences as a single complex sentence by turning the first sentence into a subordinate clause beginning with the conjunction shown in parentheses. Use a comma to separate the two clauses.

Example: ***Original*** The father dies. The family moves to Cornwall. *(after)*

Rewritten After the father dies, the family moves to Cornwall.

1. Mother goes to the Roystons' house to introduce herself. Mrs. Royston isn't home. *(when)*
2. Mrs. Royston learns that Mother has come to visit. She invites the family over for tea. *(as soon as)*
3. Mrs. Royston chats with Mother. The children go to see the tree house. *(while)*
4. Lalla meets Allan Sutton at the dance. She has been close friends with Godfrey Royston. *(until)*
5. Lalla breaks her engagement with Allan. She starts spending time with Godfrey again. *(after)*

Grammar Handbook

The Structure of Sentences, p. 1198

Rosamunde Pilcher

1924–

Other Works
The Shell Seekers
The Blue Bedroom and Other Stories
September
Flowers in the Rain and Other Stories

Writer from Cornwall Although she now lives in Scotland, Rosamunde Pilcher grew up in Cornwall, the setting of her story "Lalla." She joined the Women's Royal Naval Service during World War II and became a writer soon after the war ended. From 1949 to 1987 she published more than 20 romantic novels. Though her work was largely ignored by British critics, some of it was well received in America. Praise from the *New York Times* for her novel *Sleeping Tiger* (1967) brought Rosamunde Pilcher to the attention of *Good Housekeeping* magazine, which has since published many of her stories. Nevertheless, it was not until *The Shell Seekers* appeared in 1987 that she found herself treated as a serious novelist.

Fighting for Respect Pilcher accepts being called a writer of "light fiction," but she dislikes the label "romantic fiction" and the contempt that often goes with it. After winning respect with *The Shell Seekers,* she commented, "All my life I've had people coming up and saying, 'Sat under the hair dryer and read one of your little stories, dear. So clever of you. Wish I had the time to do it myself.' . . . And now I'm hoping that nobody will ever, ever say that again."

Grammar in Context

WRITING EXERCISE

1. When Mother goes to the Roystons' house to introduce herself, Mrs. Royston isn't home.
2. As soon as Mrs. Royston learns that Mother has come to visit, she invites the family over for tea.
3. While Mrs. Royston chats with Mother, the children go to see the tree house.
4. Until Lalla meets Allan Sutton at the dance, she has been close friends with Godfrey Royston.
5. After Lalla breaks her engagement with Allan, she starts spending time with Godfrey again.

Possible Response: Jane did not like Allan, and she did not like his lifestyle.

Use **Unit Two Resource Book,** p. 51.

Use **Grammar Transparencies and Copymasters,** p. 77.

Use McDougal Littell's ***Language Network,*** Chapter 1, for more instruction and practice in coordinating conjunctions.

LALLA 345

OVERVIEW

Objectives

1. understand and appreciate two **poems (Literary Analysis)**
2. analyze **metaphor and simile (Literary Analysis)**
3. understand how to **paraphrase (Active Reading)**

Summary

Highlighting the different forms of love, the speaker in "Love Without Love" seeks a higher, gentler, more exalted love than a romantic, passionate one. He compares this love to a bird in an extended metaphor. In "The Taxi," the speaker is riding in a taxi away from her beloved. The poem presents images of the night, streets, and passing lamps as the speaker is whisked farther and farther away.

Thematic Link

Both poems deal with different yet equally potent kinds of love. "Love Without Love" describes a calm, tranquil, accepting love, while "The Taxi" describes a frantic, tormented love.

5-Minute Warm-Up

Daily Language SkillBuilder

Have students **proofread** the display sentences on page 223k and write them correctly. The sentences also appear on Transparency 11 of **Grammar Transparencies and Copymasters.**

PREPARING to *Read*

Love Without Love

Poetry by LUIS LLORÉNS TORRES
(lo͞o-ĕs′ yô-rĕns′ tô′rĕs)

The Taxi

Poetry by AMY LOWELL

"Love me that way, flying over everything."

Connect to Your Life

Images of Love In a small group, identify images that suggest romantic love in our culture. For example, you might think of a movie scene with two people on a moonlit walk or a television commercial that portrays a man and a woman nestled before a fireplace. Then discuss what these images reveal about our views of romantic love. Use a chart like the one shown to keep track of your images and what they reveal. Share your findings with your classmates.

Romantic Love in Our Culture

Image	What It Reveals
a man and a woman on a moonlit walk	• peacefulness of love • love removed from the harsh realities of ordinary life

Build Background

Love Poetry The following two poems use vivid, unexpected images to convey the poets' ideas about romantic love. The first poem is by Luis Lloréns Torres, a famous Puerto Rican poet who began publishing his verse in 1899 and was noted for his love poems and his patriotic verse. The second poem is by Amy Lowell, an American poet who won fame just a few years after Lloréns Torres. This poem reflects Lowell's interest in **imagism,** a literary movement that stressed the importance of using clear, precise images in poetry.

Focus Your Reading

LITERARY ANALYSIS | METAPHOR AND SIMILE A **simile** is a direct comparison, using the words *like* or *as,* between two unlike things that have something in common. A **metaphor** is a similar form of comparison, but without the use of *like* or *as.* In "Love Without Love," for example, the speaker refers to "the dog of my heart," which is a metaphor. As you read the two poems, note the poets' use of these forms of figurative language. Ask yourself how each poet's use of metaphor and simile contributes to the main ideas of each poem.

ACTIVE READING | PARAPHRASING One strategy that can help you understand a poem more fully is to **paraphrase** it—that is, to restate parts or all of the poem in your own words. When you paraphrase, you will often need to use more words than the poet, as shown by the example below. Your paraphrase should attempt to convey the meaning of the events, emotions, and attitudes suggested by the poem.

READER'S NOTEBOOK As you read these poems, identify lines that seem particularly significant to the poem or whose meaning is not completely clear to you. Paraphrase these lines, using a chart like the one shown to the right.

Poem: "Love Without Love"

Line:	Paraphrase:
Suddenly I've felt you flying through my soul . . .	Unexpectedly I have your presence, as if you were moving through me.

LESSON RESOURCES

UNIT TWO RESOURCE BOOK, pp. 53–54

ASSESSMENT RESOURCES

Formal Assessment, p. 57

Teacher's Guide to Assessment and Portfolio Use

Test Generator

SKILLS TRANSPARENCIES AND COPYMASTERS

Literary Analysis

- Symbols and Figurative Language, T21 (for Paired Activity, p. 349)

Reading and Critical Thinking

- Paraphrasing and Summarizing, C41 (for Think Critically, item 4, p. 349)

Writing

- Sensory Word List, T14 (for Writing Option 1, p. 350)
- Figurative Language and Sound Devices, T15 (for Writing Options 1and 2, p. 350)

Communications

- Interviewing, T9 (for Activities & Explorations 2, p. 350)
- Impromptu Speaking: Dialogue, Role-Play, Debate, T13 (for Activities & Explorations 2, p. 350)

INTEGRATED TECHNOLOGY

Audio Library

Visit our website: www.mcdougallittell.com

Love Without Love

Luis Lloréns Torres

I love you, because in my thousand and one nights of dreams,
I never once dreamed of you.
I looked down paths that traveled from afar,
but it was never you I expected.
Suddenly I've felt you flying through my soul
in quick, lofty flight,
and how beautiful you seem way up there, far
from my always idiot heart!
Love me that way, flying over everything.
And, like the bird on its branch, land in my arms
only to rest,
then fly off again.
Be not like the romantic ones who,
in love, set me on fire.
When you climb up my mansion,
enter so lightly, that as you enter
the dog of my heart will not bark.

Translated by Julio Marzán

Thinking Through the Literature

1. Think about the **image** from this poem that stands out the most to you. What does this image make you think of?
2. What does the **speaker's** choice of images say to you about his attitude toward his relationship with his loved one?

THINK ABOUT
- the image of the bird flying through his soul in lines 5–6
- the speaker's reference to his "idiot heart" in line 8
- the contrast between his beloved and "the romantic ones" in line 13
- the speaker's request in lines 15–16

3. What does the **title** of the poem mean to you?
4. Compare and contrast your ideas about love with those of the speaker.

TEACHING THE LITERATURE

Customizing Instruction

Less Proficient Readers
As students read each poem, have them ask themselves the following questions.
- What sort of mood does the poem convey?
  Possible Response: "Love Without Love"—happy, dreamy, peaceful; "The Taxi"— unhappy, desperate, painful
- How does the narrator feel about being separated from his or her lover?
  Possible Response: "Love Without Love"—undisturbed; "The Taxi"—anguished, desperate

Students Acquiring English
Explain to students that these poems present two different approaches to love: the first is passionless and calm, while the second is passionate and perturbed.

Use **Spanish Study Guide** for additional support, pp. 74–76.

Gifted and Talented
Encourage interested students to read more poems by Torres and Lowell. How do the themes of the other poems compare to those on these pages?

Thinking Through the Literature

1. Possible Responses: the bird—a wedding dove; the "dog of my heart"—a watchdog
2. Possible Response: He values its tranquillity and safety.
3. Student responses will vary, but might suggest that this speaker is looking for love without romance, which is often equated with love.
4. Student responses will vary. Encourage students to first articulate for themselves the speaker's views of love and then their own before they compare the two.

Reading and Analyzing

Reading Skills and Strategies:
PREVIEW
Have students preview the selection. Discuss the titles of the poems, the images, and the Build Background feature on p. 346. Before students begin reading, give them brief summaries of the two poems.

Active Reading: PARAPHRASING
Students should monitor their reading strategies and make modifications. Remind them that paraphrasing is helpful in understanding poetry. Have students paraphrase lines 14–16 of "Love Without Love" and lines 11–12 of "The Taxi." Discuss the differences between the two attitudes conveyed in the two sets of lines.
Possible Responses: "Love Without Love"—"When you enter my heart, please do not call up strong, passionate feelings"; "The Taxi"—"Why should I leave you, since it only causes me pain?" The first set of lines indicates a desire for a lack of passion; the second indicates strong passion.

Use **Unit Two Resource Book** p. 53 for more practice.

Literary Analysis
METAPHOR AND SIMILE
Have students find one simile and one metaphor from each of the two poems.
Possible Response:
"Love Without Love"—simile: ". . . like the bird on its branch, land in my arms"; metaphor: "When you climb up my mansion"
"The Taxi"—simile: "The world beats dead/Like a slackened drum"; metaphor: "the sharp edges of the night"

Use **Unit Two Resource Book** p. 54 for more practice.

THE TAXI

AMY LOWELL

When I go away from you
The world beats dead
Like a slackened drum.
I call out for you against the jutted stars
And shout into the ridges of the wind.
Streets coming fast,
One after the other,
Wedge you away from me,
And the lamps of the city prick my eyes
So that I can no longer see your face.
Why should I leave you,
To wound myself upon the sharp edges of the night?

Times Square, New York City No. 2 (1990), Robert Gniewek. Oil on linen, 38" × 60", courtesy of Louis K. Meisel Gallery, New York. Photo by Steve Lopez.

Teaching Options

Mini Lesson: Viewing and Representing

Times Square, New York City No. 2 **by Robert Gniewek**

ART APPRECIATION The works of Robert Gniewek (1951–) usually combine photography and paint. The photorealist uses New York City as his palette. His first step in creating art is taking photographs. Once he has a photo, he uses paint to "push reality over the edge." *Times Square* is an extraordinary nightscape of light-splashed images and reflections.

Application Ask students how the light in this painting "pricks" a viewer's eyes. In what other ways does the art reflect the poem?

Possible Responses: The light pricks the eyes because it is hard and glaring. The unfocused light on the streets indicates rapid motion; the sharp, cold edges of the buildings suggest the sharp edges of the night.

Application Have students collect used photographs (perhaps from magazines), or take new photos. Have them each select a photograph and add paint to it so that the finished work reflects an emotion or state of mind—for example, love, fear, comfort, or loneliness.

Connect to the Literature

1. **What Do You Think?** What questions would you like to ask the speaker in "The Taxi"?

Think Critically

2. Based on the **images** used in this poem, how would you describe the speaker's feelings about love?

   THINK ABOUT
   - the sound a slackened drum would make, as described in lines 2–3
   - her sense of the streets wedging her loved one away from her in line 8
   - the last two lines, where she compares leaving her loved one to being wounded

3. Do you think "The Taxi" is a good **title** for this poem? Explain your reasoning.

4. **ACTIVE READING** **PARAPHRASING** Look back at the lines you paraphrased in your READER'S NOTEBOOK. Compare your **paraphrases** with those of your classmates. What lines were the most difficult to paraphrase? Did you find it easier to paraphrase one of the poems, or did both present a similar level of difficulty?

Extend Interpretations

5. **Comparing Texts** Compare and contrast the **speakers'** attitudes toward love in "Love Without Love" and "The Taxi."

6. **Connect to Life** Which speaker's view of love appeals more to you? Explain your choice.

Literary Analysis

METAPHOR AND SIMILE

Metaphors and **similes** are forms of **figurative language** that make comparisons between things that are basically unlike but have something in common. For example, Lowell compares the wind with a solid, physical obstacle in the metaphor "the ridges of the wind." Unlike a metaphor, a simile states the comparison between two things directly by using the word *like* or *as*. Identify one simile and at least one metaphor in each poem. What ideas are being communicated in each of these examples of figurative language?

Paired Activity Explain the metaphor in lines 5–9 of "Love Without Love." How does the image of love expressed in this metaphor compare with some of the images you identified and discussed for Connect to Your Life on page 346?

METAPHOR	SIMILE
is	like *or* as

GUIDING STUDENT RESPONSE

Connect to Literature

1. **What Do You Think?**
   Possible Responses: Do you still love the person you just left? Why did you leave?

Think Critically

2. Possible Responses: Love is a major part of the speaker's life; the speaker has a strong need to be with her beloved.
3. Possible Responses: Yes, because it helps readers visualize the speaker's location; no, because the taxi has not that much to do with the actual love.
4. Encourage students to discuss any differing interpretations that are evident in different paraphrases of particular lines.

Extend Interpretations

Comparing Texts Possible Response: The speaker in "Love Without Love" seeks refuge from passion and heated emotion in quiet, secure love, while the speaker in "The Taxi" is very passionate and heated, although she is in pain. Both speakers may be said to recognize the pain that often accompanies passion.

Connect to Life Student responses will vary, but should include specific reasons.

Literary Analysis

Metaphor and Simile Ask students to recall their idea of romantic love. Some students will have no experience with romantic love, and may feel uncomfortable discussing it. Encourage them to draw on books or films they have read or seen.

Writing Options

1. **Poetic Images** Have the students look for images that connect people. For instance, they might use clasped hands, a bicycle built for two, a shared taxi ride, and so forth.
2. **Journal of the Perfect Day** Have students review the poem for ideas about what the speaker might consider to be a perfect day.

Activities & Explorations

1. **Sketch of a Poem** If possible, draw an example for the students. For example, you might draw a dog guarding a heart.
2. **TV Talk Show** The questions should be prewritten and approved to avoid any embarrassment in class.

Inquiry & Research

The Look of Love Collect old magazines for students to use. Share the finished products and have students discuss why they selected the pictures they did.

Writing Options

1. Poetic Images The images in "The Taxi" convey feelings about love by describing the pain of being separated from a loved one. Develop a list of images that the speaker might use to convey how she feels when she is with her loved one.

2. Journal of the Perfect Day Write a journal entry in which the speaker of "Love Without Love" records a perfect day with his loved one.

Activities & Explorations

1. Sketch of a Poem Create a sketch showing a figurative expression from one of the poems in a literal way. For example, you might show a night scene that literally has sharp edges. ~ **ART**

2. TV Talk Show Stage a television talk show in which the host interviews four classmates posing as the couples represented in "Love Without Love" and "The Taxi." Have the host and members of the audience ask the couples about their views of love and the relationship they have or want. ~ **SPEAKING AND LISTENING**

Inquiry & Research

The Look of Love Look through books and magazines for images of love. Then put together a photographic essay that contrasts the ideas of love expressed in these two poems.

Luis Lloréns Torres

1878–1944

Other Works
Poems in *The Puerto Rican Poets*
Poems in *Inventing a Word*

Poet and Leader One of Puerto Rico's most respected modern poets, Luis Lloréns Torres said the goal of the poet "consists of the presentation in a sensitive manner of scenes and landscapes of the ideal world . . . existing in every poet's imagination." Lloréns Torres took up writing poetry when he was studying law in Spain. He was still in Spain when he published his first book of verse, *At the Foot of the Alhambra,* in 1899. On returning to Puerto Rico, he served in the Puerto Rican legislature and joined with other political leaders who supported independence from the United States. Lloréns Torres also founded and edited the *Antilles Journal,* a literary journal that was highly respected in Puerto Rico and the rest of Latin America. In the journal, he published his own poetry along with works by other leading Latin American writers. Lloréns Torres's association with the *Antilles Journal,* as well as subsequent work, won him a place as a major poet of Latin America.

Amy Lowell

1874–1925

Other Works
Sword Blades and Poppy Seeds
What's O'Clock

Imagist Approach A member of an illustrious American family, Amy Lowell was the sister of a noted astronomer, the granddaughter of the founder of Lowell, Massachusetts, and a descendant of the famous American poet James Russell Lowell (1819–1891). She spent much of her early adulthood involved in civic activities. Then, deciding to become a poet herself, Lowell spent ten years studying the craft before she published her first collection of poems, *A Dome of Many-Colored Glass,* in 1912. Soon afterward, while visiting England, she met the American poet Ezra Pound (1885–1972) and adopted his theories of imagism. Pound wanted poetry to rely on clear, concrete images and the patterns of ordinary speech. Such images in "The Taxi" as the world beating dead "like a slackened drum" and the lights of the city pricking the speaker's eyes reflect this imagist approach.

"The night is shattered, and she is not with me."

Tonight I Can Write . . . / Puedo Escribir Los Versos . . .

Poetry by PABLO NERUDA (nĕ-ro͞o′də)

Connect to Your Life

Nature's Mirror The natural world can sometimes seem to hold up a mirror to your emotions. For example, if you are in a bad mood on a rainy day, you may think that the weather reflects how you feel. In a small group, discuss how elements in nature may seem to reflect various human emotions. Together, brainstorm a list of images from nature that suggest feelings such as sadness, love, or regret. Share your ideas with the rest of the class.

Build Background

Comparisons in Poetry Poets often illuminate human emotions and experiences by drawing comparisons to the natural world. In this unit, for example, you have seen how Luis Lloréns Torres describes his loved one in terms of a bird. Frequently, poets employ **figures of speech,** such as **similes** and **metaphors,** to make their comparisons. Another common figure of speech is **personification,** which attributes human qualities to an object, animal, or idea. In the following poem, various figures of speech are used to express the emotions felt by the speaker.

Focus Your Reading

LITERARY ANALYSIS REPETITION A striking feature of "Tonight I Can Write . . ." is the poet's use of **repetition**—a literary technique in which a sound, word, phrase, or line is repeated for emphasis. As you read the poem, pay attention to the effect of Neruda's use of repetition. In particular, look for ways in which the poet repeats lines with slight changes, as in the following examples:

I no longer love her, that's certain, but how I loved her. (line 23)
I no longer love her, that's certain, but maybe I love her. (line 27)

ACTIVE READING INTERPRETING COMPARISONS In this poem, the speaker makes use of comparisons to suggest his own emotion. For example, he **personifies** the night, stating that "blue stars shiver in the distance." This statement reveals more about his own feelings than about the night. As you read, pay attention to descriptions of the natural world and what they suggest about the speaker's emotions and experience.

READER'S NOTEBOOK Complete a chart like the one below. In the first column, list each image from nature that you find. In the second column, describe the human emotions or experiences that are suggested by that image.

Image from nature	Suggested human emotions or experiences

OVERVIEW

This selection is included in the **Grade 10 InterActive Reader.**

Objectives

1. understand and appreciate a **poem (Literary Analysis)**
2. identify **repetition** as a literary technique **(Literary Analysis)**
3. **interpret comparisons (Active Reading)**

Summary

The speaker of the poem writes of a lost love and of the poetic words he can now use to describe his past relationship. He writes of his feelings for her and weighs his need to accept that she is gone against his longing for her love.

Thematic Link

This poem deals with the contradictory and mysterious feelings that accompany the loss of love.

5-Minute Warm-Up

Daily Language SkillBuilder

Have students **proofread** the display sentences on page 223k and write them correctly. The sentences also appear on Transparency 11 of **Grammar Transparencies and Copymasters.**

LESSON RESOURCES

UNIT TWO RESOURCE BOOK, pp. 55–56

ASSESSMENT RESOURCES

Formal Assessment, pp. 59–60

Teacher's Guide to Assessment and Portfolio Use

Test Generator

SKILLS TRANSPARENCIES AND COPYMASTERS

Literary Analysis

- Symbols and Figurative Language, T21 (for Figurative Language, p. 354)

Reading and Critical Thinking

- Organizational Chart: Horizontal, T51 (for Reader's Notebook, p. 351)

Vocabulary

- Denotation and Connotation, C45 (for Mini Lesson, p. 352)

Writing

- Figurative Language and Sound Devices, T15 (for Writing Option 2, p. 355)
- Poem, C27 (for Writing Option 2, p. 355)

Communications

- Dramatic Reading, T12 (for Activities & Explorations, p. 355)
- Verbal Strategies, T14 (for Activities & Explorations, p. 355)
- Nonverbal Strategies, T15 (for Activities & Explorations, p. 355)

INTEGRATED TECHNOLOGY

Audio Library

Visit our website:
www.mcdougallittell.com

TEACHING THE LITERATURE

Reading and Analyzing

Reading Skills and Strategies: PREVIEW

Have students preview the selection. Discuss with students the Build Background feature on p. 351. Before students begin reading, give them a brief summary of the poem. Ask students to study the images and the title of the poem.

Literary Analysis REPETITION

Review the Focus Your Reading feature on repetition on p. 351. Ask students to look at lines 6 and 9 and analyze the text structure. Have them explain how the lines are alike, yet different.

Possible Response: Both lines follow the same grammatical structure, and most of the words are identical. However, line 6 suggests that the woman was not constant in her love and the man was, while line 9 suggests the opposite.

Use **Unit Two Resource Book** p. 56 for more practice.

Active Reading
INTERPRETING COMPARISONS

Ask students to complete the comparison chart suggested in Focus Your Reading, p. 351. When they have finished, ask them what is the most commonly recurring image.

Answer: night

Ask students why the poet might have relied so heavily on this image for this poem.

Possible Response: The darkness of night corresponds to the darkness of the speaker's emotional state.

Use **Unit Two Resource Book** p. 55 for more practice.

TONIGHT *I Can Write . . .*

PABLO NERUDA

Tonight I can write the saddest lines.

Write, for example, 'The night is shattered
and the blue stars shiver in the distance.'

The night wind revolves in the sky and sings.

Tonight I can write the saddest lines.
I loved her, and sometimes she loved me too.

Through nights like this one I held her in my arms.
I kissed her again and again under the endless sky.

She loved me, sometimes I loved her too.
How could one not have loved her great still eyes.

Tonight I can write the saddest lines.
To think that I do not have her. To feel that I have lost her.

To hear the immense night, still more immense without her.
And the verse falls to the soul like dew to the pasture.

What does it matter that my love could not keep her.
The night is shattered and she is not with me.

This is all. In the distance someone is singing. In the distance.
My soul is not satisfied that it has lost her.

My sight searches for her as though to go to her.
My heart looks for her, and she is not with me.

The same night whitening the same trees.
We, of that time, are no longer the same.

I no longer love her, that's certain, but how I loved her.
My voice tried to find the wind to touch her hearing.

Another's. She will be another's. Like my kisses before.
Her voice. Her bright body. Her infinite eyes.

I no longer love her, that's certain, but maybe I love her.
Love is so short, forgetting is so long.

Because through nights like this one I held her in my arms
my soul is not satisfied that it has lost her.

Though this be the last pain that she makes me suffer
and these the last verses that I write for her.

Translated by W. S. Merwin

352

Teaching Options

Mini Lesson Vocabulary Strategy

DENOTATION AND CONNOTATION Explain to students that *denotation* refers to the literal, dictionary definition of a word and that *connotation* refers to the subtle shades of meaning that are attached to a word.

Write the model sentences on the chalkboard.

Model Sentences

The thin man crossed the street.
The gaunt man crossed the street.

Explain that, while both *thin* and *gaunt* mean "lean" in a denotative sense, they have quite different connotations. *Thin* is fairly neutral and carries little judgment, but *gaunt* carries with it a sense of illness or starvation.

Exercises Have students read the following sentences. Have students choose the word with the most appropriate connotations.

1. Herbert was fond of gazing into Lucinda's ________ eyes. *(bright; reflective)*
2. The dog ________ quickly from the hornets' nest. *(departed; fled)*
3. The child ________ each time her mother pulled through a tangle with the hairbrush. *(complained; whined)*

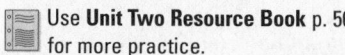

PUEDO *Escribir Los Versos . . .*

PABLO NERUDA

Puedo escribir los versos más tristes esta noche.

Escribir, por ejemplo: 'La noche está estrellada,
y tiritan, azules, los astros, a lo lejos.'

El viento de la noche gira en el cielo y canta.

Puedo escribir los versos más tristes esta noche.
Yo la quise, y a veces ella también me quiso.

En las noches como ésta la tuve entre mis brazos.
La besé tantas veces bajo el cielo infinito.

Ella me quiso, a veces yo también la quería.
Cómo no haber amado sus grandes ojos fijos.

Puedo escribir los versos más tristes esta noche.
Pensar que no la tengo. Sentir que la he perdido.

Oir la noche inmensa, más inmensa sin ella.
Y el verso cae al alma como al pasto el rocío.

Qué importa que mi amor no pudiera guardarla.
La noche está estrellada y ella no está conmigo.

Eso es todo. A lo lejos alguien canta. A lo lejos.
Mi alma no se contenta con haberla perdido.

Como para acercarla mi mirada la busca.
Mi corazón la busca, y ella no está conmigo.

La misma noche que hace blanquear los mismos arboles.
Nosotros, los de entonces, ya no somos los mismos.

Ya no la quiero, es cierto, pero cuánto la quise.
Mi voz buscaba el viento para tocar su oído.

De otro. Será de otro. Como antes de mis besos.
Su voz, su cuerpo claro. Sus ojos infinitos.

Ya no la quiero, es cierto, pero tal vez la quiero.
Es tan corto el amor, y es tan largo el olvido.

Porque en noches como ésta la tuve entre mis brazos,
mi alma no se contenta con haberla perdido.

Aunque éste sea el último dolor que ella me causa,
y éstos sean los últimos versos que yo le escribo.

Customizing Instruction

Less Proficient Readers

Have students ask themselves the following questions as they read the poem.

- What has happened to the relationship between the speaker and the woman referred to in the poem?
  Answer: It has ended.
- How does the speaker feel about the way the relationship turned out?
  Possible Response: He regrets the passing of their love.

Students Acquiring English

If you have students who are fluent in Spanish, have them read the original Spanish version of the poem aloud. Then have them point out and explain any parts of the translation with which they disagree. Invite them to suggest better translations.

Use **Spanish Study Guide** for additional support, pp. 77–79.

Gifted and Talented

Invite students to locate poems from different cultures and different historical periods in which a speaker bewails a lost love or an unhappy romance. Have them compare the attitudes and modes of expression in these poems with those of "Tonight I Can Write."

4. Gertrude had stayed up late studying, and felt terribly ________ the next day at school. *(sluggish; inactive)*

5. Arthur zipped up his parka against the ________ air. *(cold; frigid)*

Answers: **1.** bright; **2.** fled; **3.** whined; **4.** sluggish; **5.** frigid

Use **Vocabulary Transparencies and Copymasters,** p. 45.

GUIDING STUDENT RESPONSE

Connect to the Literature

1. **What Do You Think?** Students should explain their answers in detail.

Comprehension Check
- He has lost his beloved.
- Aspects of nighttime, darkness, cold, and distance are most prominent.

Think Critically

2. Possible Response: The speaker may feel cold and shattered and distant from the one he loves; the night reminds him of other nights when he held her.
3. Possible Responses: He remembers her so fondly and remembers her so lovingly that he must love her; he no longer loves her, but he wishes that he could.
4. Student responses will vary.
5. Possible Response: This poem explores the mysteries of love relationships. The speaker seems unsure and struggles to make sense of the complexity of love relationships, and his own conflicting feelings about this love.

Thinking through the LITERATURE

Connect to the Literature

1. **What Do You Think?** Which lines of "Tonight I Can Write . . ." are the most memorable for you? Why?

Comprehension Check
- Why is the speaker's soul "not satisfied"?
- What aspects of nature are most prominent in the poem?

Think Critically

2. **ACTIVE READING** **INTERPRETING COMPARISONS** Review the chart that you created in your READER'S NOTEBOOK. What do the **images** from nature reveal about the speaker's emotions and experience?

   THINK ABOUT
   - why the speaker says "The night is shattered and the blue stars shiver"
   - what you learn about the speaker's relationship with the woman
   - why the night feels "still more immense without her"
   - what this night reminds him of

3. Do you think the **speaker** still loves the woman? Support your opinion.
4. Reread the last two lines of the poem. What is your opinion of the speaker's conclusion?
5. How do you think "Tonight I Can Write . . ." relates to the **theme** of this part of the unit, "Mysteries of the Heart"? Explain.

Extend Interpretations

6. **Comparing Texts** Do you think this poem has more in common with Amy Lowell's "Taxi" (page 348) or with N. Scott Momaday's "Simile" (page 256)? Cite details to support your evaluation.
7. **Connect to Life** Why do you think so many poems and songs are about love and its loss? Discuss this question with your classmates, using examples of songs or other poems about lost love that you find particularly memorable.

Literary Analysis

REPETITION **Repetition** is a literary technique in which sounds, words, phrases, or lines are repeated for emphasis or unity. In "Tonight I Can Write . . ." Neruda repeats the first line three times to emphasize the speaker's sorrow and to help unify the poem.

Paired Activity With a partner, make a list of other repeated words, phrases, or lines. Then discuss how each instance of repetition affects your understanding of the speaker's feelings. Why do you think Neruda sometimes repeats part of a line and then adds new information?

REVIEW **FIGURATIVE LANGUAGE** Review the poem and identify each **metaphor, simile,** or **personification.** Then create one metaphor, one simile, and one personification of your own to compare your feelings to objects in nature.

Extend Interpretations

Comparing Texts Student responses will vary, but should include specific references to the poems.

Connect to Life Refer students to the other poems in this unit for this discussion.

Literary Analysis

Repetition Encourage students to read the poem aloud in order to analyze the text structure and how it affects their understanding of the poem.

Review Figurative Language Encourage students to read the poem line by line, stopping at the end of each couplet to examine it for figurative language.

Writing Options

1. **Lovelorn Paragraph** Draft a paragraph that explains the speaker's situation. Include details or quotations from the poem. Then share your writing with a classmate and compare your explanations.
2. **Personal Poem** Express your own ideas about love and loss in a poem. Try to include images from nature as well as repetition and figurative language to help emphasize and unify your ideas.

Activities & Explorations

Dramatic Monologue In a dramatic monologue, give the other side of the story for the poem. In other words, assume the identity of the loved one in the poem and express your feelings and ideas about the relationship described by the speaker. ~ **PERFORMING**

Inquiry & Research

Mood Music Find a contemporary song that reveals some of the same emotions conveyed by "Tonight I Can Write . . ." Share the song with your classmates and discuss how it relates to the poem.

Pablo Neruda

1904–1973

Other Works
Residence on Earth
Elemental Odes
The Heights of Macchu Picchu
Extravagaria

Early Success Pablo Neruda, the pen name of Ricardo Eliezer Neftalí Reyes y Basoalto, was drawn to poetry at an early age, even though his working-class family scoffed at his literary ambitions. He began publishing poems at the age of 15. When just 20, he won celebrity throughout his native Chile with *Twenty Love Poems and a Song of Despair* in which "Tonight I Can Write . . ." first appeared.

Political Poetry After Neruda served in his nation's diplomatic corps—an honor then commonly granted to talented Latin American writers—he shifted the focus of his poetry to political and social criticism. In the early 1970s, Neruda supported Chile's socialist leader Salvador Allende and served as his nation's ambassador to France. When the poet received the 1971 Nobel Prize in literature, the event was celebrated as a national holiday in his homeland. Neruda produced more than 40 volumes of poetry, translations, and verse drama during his literary career.

Author Activity

With Hindsight In later life, Neruda renounced much of his earlier work. Find out why and report your findings back to the class. Then discuss what you think about Neruda's verdict.

Writing Options

1. **Lovelorn Paragraph** The speaker's situation can be given a background that is only hinted at in the actual poem. Remind students that their explanation should not change the relationship established in the poem.
2. **Personal Poem** To make the assignment more challenging, give students a set number of similes, metaphors, and images that they must include. This activity can be done as a pair-share activity.

Activities & Explorations

Dramatic Monologue It will be easier to write the monologue if the student first imagines a background for the loved one.

Inquiry & Research

Mood Music To make the assignment more challenging, have students write and perform their own song based on the poem.

Author Activity

With Hindsight Suggest that, in addition to sources on Neruda, students find information on the Spanish civil war and 20th-century Chilean politics.

Mini Lesson: Speaking and Listening

CHORAL READING Have students volunteer to prepare a choral reading of the poem. Have them assign certain lines for individual readers and others for the group. Let them perform their reading for the class. Have the class discuss how the reading affected their perception of the poem.

Building Vocabulary

Objectives
- identify the root of a word
- understand the concept of word family and word history

EXERCISE
Students should research word origins to help them understand the meanings of the words. Knowing a word's history also helps them remember a word's meaning.

Possible Responses

1. predecessor—one who precedes another in time
   root: *cess* from *cedere,* to go
   The chairperson was handed the gavel by her predecessor.
   related word: successful or decease
2. significant—full of meaning; important
   root: *sign* from *signum,* sign
   The team's first victory was the most significant.
   related word: signal
3. implore—to beg
   root: *plor* from *plorare,* to cry out
   The student implored the teacher to give him credit.
   related word: deplore
4. seismograph: an instrument that records the intensity and duration of earthquakes
   root: *seismos-,* earthquake, functions as a root word
   The seismograph accurately recorded the earthquake.
   related word: seismology
5. creditable: worthy of praise
   root: *credit* from *credere,* to trust or believe
   The creditable child turned in the missing wallet, money and all.
   related word: discredit

Ancient Roots

The English language is like a city with a long history—if you dig below the modern surface, you find remains of former civilizations. In English, some of the most important remains are Greek and Latin; these two languages underlie many of the words we use every day. Take a look, for example, at the excerpt on the right. The highlighted words would look familiar to citizens of ancient Rome.

> **It was a lovely region, woodsy, balmy, delicious, and had once been populous, long years before, but now the people had vanished and the charming paradise was a solitude.**
>
> —Mark Twain, "The Californian's Tale"

The word *delicious* is a descendant of the Latin word *dēliciōsus. Populous* and *solitude* come from the Latin words *populōsus* and *sōlitūdō*. In each case, the meanings of the modern English word and the ancient Latin word are just about the same.

Strategies for Building Vocabulary

The words *delicious, populous,* and *solitude* are modeled closely on their ancient Latin sources. Familiarizing yourself with word origins can help you determine and remember the meanings of unfamiliar words.

❶ **Word Families** The core of the word *solitude* is the Latin root *sol,* meaning "alone"—a root that also appears in a number of other English words, such as *soliloquy* and *solitary*. Because these words contain the same root, they are related in meaning. You can often figure out the meanings of words in such a "word family" if you know the meaning of the root they share. The chart below shows several members of the *sol* family. Note the shared element in their meanings.

English Words Containing the Latin Root *Sol*

Word	Meaning
desolation	a state of being abandoned; loneliness
sole	only
soliloquy	a speech by a character alone on stage
solitaire	a card game played by one person
solitary	living or going without others
solitude	a state of being alone
solo	a performance by single individual

❷ **Spelling** Recognizing roots and word families can also help you spell words correctly. For example, *pictograph, phonograph,* and *geography* all contain the Greek root *graph.* Knowing how to spell the root makes it easier to figure out how to spell the words that contain it.

❸ **Word Histories** If a word has an interesting history, or etymology, knowing that history can help you remember the word's meaning. Consider the word *dragoon,* meaning "to compel by threats or force." This word comes from the French word *dragon* and was originally a noun denoting a kind of firearm (one that "breathed fire" like a dragon). Later, it was used to refer to a soldier armed with that type of gun. Then, in the 17th and 18th centuries, when European monarchs frequently used these soldiers to keep their subjects in line, the word came to be used as a verb in the way it is today. If you remember *dragoon*'s history, you will have no trouble remembering its meaning.

EXERCISE Identify the root of each word and tell what the root means. Then write the word's meaning, a sentence containing the word, and at least one related word. Use a dictionary if you need help.

1. predecessor
2. significant
3. implore
4. seismograph
5. creditable

Bill Cosby's talent lies in his ability to share, in a humorous way, experiences that we all know or understand. From childhood tales like "Tonsils" and "Cool Covers" on his early comedy albums to later routines about his growing family to his portrayal of Dr. Huxtable on *The Cosby Show*, his best comedy has always flowed out of real-life situations. His is the art of drawing people closer together by showing us how much we have in common.

In this excerpt from *Love and Marriage*, Cosby relates a story that, despite its humorous treatment, still rings true—how hurt pride and disappointment can make us do crazy things.

from Love and Marriage

Bill Cosby

During my last year of high school, I fell in love so hard with a girl that it made my love for Sarah McKinney seem like a stupid infatuation with a teacher. Charlene Gibson was the Real Thing and she would be Mrs. Charlene Cosby, serving me hot dogs and watching me drive to the hoop and giving me the full-court press for the rest of my life.

In tribute to our great love, I was moved to give Charlene something to wear. A Temple[1] T-shirt didn't seem quite right and neither did my Truman button.[2] What Charlene needed was a piece of jewelry; and I was able to find the perfect one, an elegant pin, in my mother's dresser drawer.

1. **Temple:** Temple University in Philadelphia, Pennsylvania, which Cosby attended.
2. **Truman button:** a button supporting the candidacy of Harry Truman (1884–1972) who became president after the death of Franklin Roosevelt in 1945 and ran for the office on his own in 1948.

ON YOUR OWN

Possible Objectives

You can use this selection to achieve one or more of the following objectives:

- enjoy silent sustained reading (Option One)
- read and analyze literature with a group (Option Two)
- use the Reader's Notebook to formulate questions about literature; write in response to literature (Option Three)

Summary

In this autobiographical reflection on his high school days, Bill Cosby tells the story of swiping his mother's jewelry to give to a girl he thought he loved. After ten days, however, the girl dumps him and keeps the pin. He attempts to regain it—because he wants to "punish" Charlene—but she says she lost it, leading Cosby to call her mother to get it back. Since getting the pin wasn't enough to repay Charlene for dumping him, he plots to return the favor by dumping her.

In a telephone conversation, he tries but fails to lure Charlene into his trap, thus motivating him to seek "full revenge." His strategy is to escort a girl prettier than Charlene to a party in order to rouse Charlene's jealousy. When he confronts Charlene at the party, she is fully aware of his strategy and, instead of being victimized by Cosby's revenge, confounds him with a simple question: Are you ever gonna grow up?

Reading the Selection

Option One
Silent Sustained Reading

You might set aside time each week for independent reading. During this time, you and your students would read for enjoyment. Remind students that they should always establish a purpose for reading, even if that purpose is enjoyment. "Love and Marriage" can be read independently in about 30 to 45 minutes. If you want to encourage students to read for pleasure, you might forego assignments related to the selection. Should you want to make assignments, Options Two and Three offer suggestions.

Option Two
Shared Reading Groups

You may assign students to groups or allow them to choose their own. Students can read the selection together, alternately reading sections aloud, or they can read independently and meet to cooperate in a project that portrays some element of the story.

Possible Projects

- Students can find evidence supporting answers to the question: Does Bill Cosby get what he deserves in the end?
- Students can divide their groups in half, with one half writing the instructions for "How NOT TO Win a Girlfriend or Boyfriend" and the other half writing instructions for "How TO Win a Girlfriend or Boyfriend." Both groups should base their instructions on examples taken from the story. When they finish, have groups compare their responses.
- Students can isolate the references to athletics in the story and create a portrait of Bill Cosby as an athlete.

Ten days after I had made this grand presentation, Charlene dumped me; but, sentimentalist that she was, she kept the pin. When I confessed my dark deed to my mother, she didn't throw a brick at me, she merely wanted to have the pin back, a request that I felt was not unreasonable since I had stolen it. Moreover, retrieving the pin was important to me, but for a romantic reason: I wanted to punish Charlene. Paying back the person with whom you have recently been in love is one of life's most precious moments.

"I want that pin back," I said to Charlene on the phone.

"I can't do that," she replied.

"Why not?"

"Because I lost it."

"You *lost* it?"

"That's what I just said."

"How could you *lose* it?"

"Easy. First I had it, then I didn't."

And so, I went to her house, where her mother said she wasn't home. Nervously I told her mother why I needed the pin returned and she understood without saying I had done anything wrong. Of course, she didn't have the world's sharpest judgment because she still thought I was a wonderful person. In fact, all the mothers of the girls

Germantown High School, Philadelphia, Pennsylvania, where Bill Cosby attended school.

Germantown Historical Society, Pennsylvania.

who rejected me thought I was a wonderful person; I would have made a fine father to those girls.

"Mrs. Gibson," I said, "Charlene told me she lost the pin. I'm not saying I don't believe her, but I don't."

"Just one minute, William," she said, and she turned and went upstairs. Moments later, she returned with the pin. And then I went home and waited for the satisfaction of Charlene calling me to say:

How dare you go to my house and ask my mother for that pin!

But no call from her came.

Probably because she's ashamed of lying to me, I told myself; *but maybe because she truly likes me and wants to keep the pin for that reason.*

I was convincing myself that Charlene wanted to have an elegant token of me and that now I should call *her* to rekindle this wondrous love-hate relationship, for Charlene and I had been meant for each other: she was a liar and I was a thief. Two such people, who had been so deeply in love, should have had a chance to keep torturing each other. . . . We had been too close for our relationship to end with her dumping me. We had to get back together so I could dump *her.*

All these thoughts went through my head as I sat with my hand on the phone, wanting to get into a fight with Charlene for old times' sake. Shakespeare said that the lunatic and the lover are the same, but he was wrong: the lunatic has more sense than the man who wanted to call Charlene so that he could hang up on her. However, I had to be very careful to keep her from hanging up on *me* or else she would have been two ahead of me, with no overtime to play.

Finally, after the kind of reasoning that made Napoleon invade Russia,[3] I picked up the phone.

"I think you owe me an apology."

"Oh, is that what you think?"

"Hello, Charlene," I said, at least beginning well by getting her name right.

"Yes," she coldly replied, neatly falling into my trap.

"I think you owe me an apology."

"Oh, is that what you think?"

"It certainly is."

Note how cleverly I was preparing her for the kill.

"So that's the way you feel?" I said. "That no apology is necessary?"

"That's the way I feel; I just said it. You have some problem with English?"

"No, I'm just checking to see if you really want to keep the reputation of being a dishonest person and lying about having something that belonged to somebody else."

"You stole the pin from your mother and you're calling *me* dishonest?"

3. **Napoleon invade Russia:** Napoleon's invasion of Russia in 1812 was a major military disaster that resulted in the decimation of his army.

Option Three
Reader's Notebook

Provide the following direction to students before they read:

Draw students' attention to the initial situation that is described in the first three pages of "Love and Marriage" and to the characters as they are portrayed by the narrator. In particular, ask students to focus as they read and write on the motives of each character in this conflict.

Tell students to read the story, pausing at the section break in the middle of column two on page 360. At that point, students should summarize the motives of both the narrator and Charlene in their Reader's Notebook. Have them put an asterisk by those motives that, in their opinion, express genuine concern for the other person and those that express largely self-interest.

At the end of the story, students will return to their notes. Ask them to write a brief analysis of each character's motives in their Reader's Notebooks.

LOVE AND MARRIAGE 359

After Reading

Possible Activities

Independent Activities

- Have gifted students skim over the story looking for details that suggest the narrator's tongue-in-cheek tone in recounting this incident. Ask them to write in their Reader's Notebook the extent to which the author exaggerates his own attitude simply for humorous effect.

Discussion Activities

- Have students find examples of the narrator's humor. What makes these passages humorous? How does humor help minimize humiliating situations?
- Discuss the question that Charlene asks the narrator at the end of the story: Will he ever grow up? The narrator's answer is, of course, that he has. Who is correct?

Assessment Opportunities

- You can assess student comprehension of the story by evaluating the analysis of each character's motivations as students formulated them in their Reader's Notebooks.
- You can use any of the discussion questions as essay questions.
- You can have students develop any one of their Reader's Notebook entries into an essay.

"But you didn't *know* I stole it. And it meant something special to me."

"I didn't *ask* you to give it to me," she said.

"But you *lied* about losing it."

"No, I didn't. I didn't know where it was."

"Your mother went right upstairs and found it."

"Just the way *you* found it in your mother's drawer."

My appetite for humiliation was clearly boundless as I pressed on in a conversation that revealed new dimensions in male dumbness.

"Put your mother on the phone," I said.

"Put *your* mother on the phone," she said, "and I'll ask her how it feels to have a crazy son."

"Crazy, huh? It just so happens that I was crazy in love with you. Have you already forgotten our plans to have children?"

"Well, start without me. I'm definitely not having them if they're yours."

"And that's just fine with me."

"Me too."

"Look, Charlene . . . I don't think we should end this by being angry with each other."

"Yeah, I guess not."

"I know that you're in love with someone else this week and I wish you the best."

"Coming from you, that means nothing to me."

"Look, Charlene, I think we should end this by being friends. I think we should end it so . . . well, so if you ever want to call me and ask me a question, like how to break a zone defense or something, I'll be happy to give you the answer."

Now note how cleverly I was luring her into a position where I could dump her last and make her feel sorry she had ever known me, a sentiment she already may have felt.

"I don't think I'll be calling you," she said.

"So that's the way you feel?"

"Why do I have to tell you everything twice? I think I've told you enough."

And then she hung up. She hadn't even said good-bye—once.

Should I call her back to slam her with my own good-bye? I asked myself.

No, I decided. I would find the revenge that she deserved for messing around with my heart, the only part of my body that I could never get into shape.

The revenge I devised had a simple splendor: I would find a girl who was prettier than Charlene, entice her into a relationship, and then flaunt this relationship to Charlene, who would promptly jump off a cliff. And so, with both the dedication and the mental balance of Captain Ahab chasing Moby Dick,[4] I began my great hunt. The following day, I began pursuing a gorgeous girl I'll call Artemis, after the Greek Goddess of Virginity. For many months, boys had been throwing themselves at Artemis like tacklers trying to bring down Jim Brown.[5] Nonetheless, on this day, I summoned the courage to approach her and say, "Hi, I'm Bill Cosby and I was wondering if you're going to John Thomas's party on Friday night."

She looked at me silently for a moment, but I knew that she knew who I was because I had played varsity basketball on nights when the

4. **Captain Ahab . . . Moby Dick:** In Herman Melville's *Moby Dick,* Captain Ahab was obsessed to the point of madness with chasing a white whale; his obsession led to his death and the deaths of nearly his entire crew.

5. **Jim Brown:** a star football player of the 1950s and 1960s; considered to be one of the greatest running backs of all time.

girls had come out of hiding.

"No, I'm not going," she said.

And suddenly I feared that her refusal to go with me would get back to Charlene and make her heart sing.

"But we've been talking about going, haven't we?" said one of several girls who made up Artemis' entourage.[6]

Fixing me with a cool look, she said, "What time's the party?"

"Eight o'clock," I replied.

"Okay, I'll go with you."

"Yeah, we'll go with you," said one of her friends.

"Right, we'll go," said a third.

"Could I talk to you alone for a minute?" I said to Artemis.

"I guess so," she said, clearly falling for me.

Taking her hand, I led her away from the entourage and said, "Look, I want to go to the party with *you,* not a field hockey team."

"They're my friends."

"And I'm glad you have them. But can't you give them a night off and go just with *me?*"

"I thought you were going steady with Charlene."

"Yeah, I was, but *she* wasn't, so I released her. And a lucky thing too 'cause it made room for you. Listen, you want to come and watch track practice this afternoon?"

"Not really."

"I do the high jump."

"I'm sure you do."

"And I'll be jumping just for you."

"The way you jumped for Charlene?"

"Charlene was just a high hurdle compared to you."

And not sounding like an idiot was a high hurdle for me too, but this divine female was heady stuff.

"Okay, then," she said, "you'll pick me up on Friday around eight?"

"You bet," I said, wondering how I was going to pick her up in a trolley.

When Friday came, however, I was able to pick her up in a car driven by my friend Ed Ford, who'd agreed to double date because he couldn't believe that Artemis had fallen off her pedestal and into the depths occupied by me.

"I still don't see her going with *you,*" said Ed as we drove to her house. "Maybe she's gonna become a nun and has to do some kinda suffering."

"You just don't understand women," I said. "She *knows* I'm using her to pay back Charlene, and she's doing it 'cause women hate each other. But the funny thing is, I'm also falling in love with her."

"And when she dumps you, who you gonna use to punish *her?*" said Ed. "Lena Horne?[7] Man, you're over your head in beauty."

6. **entourage** (ŏn′to͞o-räzh′): group of followers.

7. **Lena Horne** (lē′nə hôrn): a U.S. singer noted for both her enormous vocal talent as well as her great beauty.

LOVE AND MARRIAGE **361**

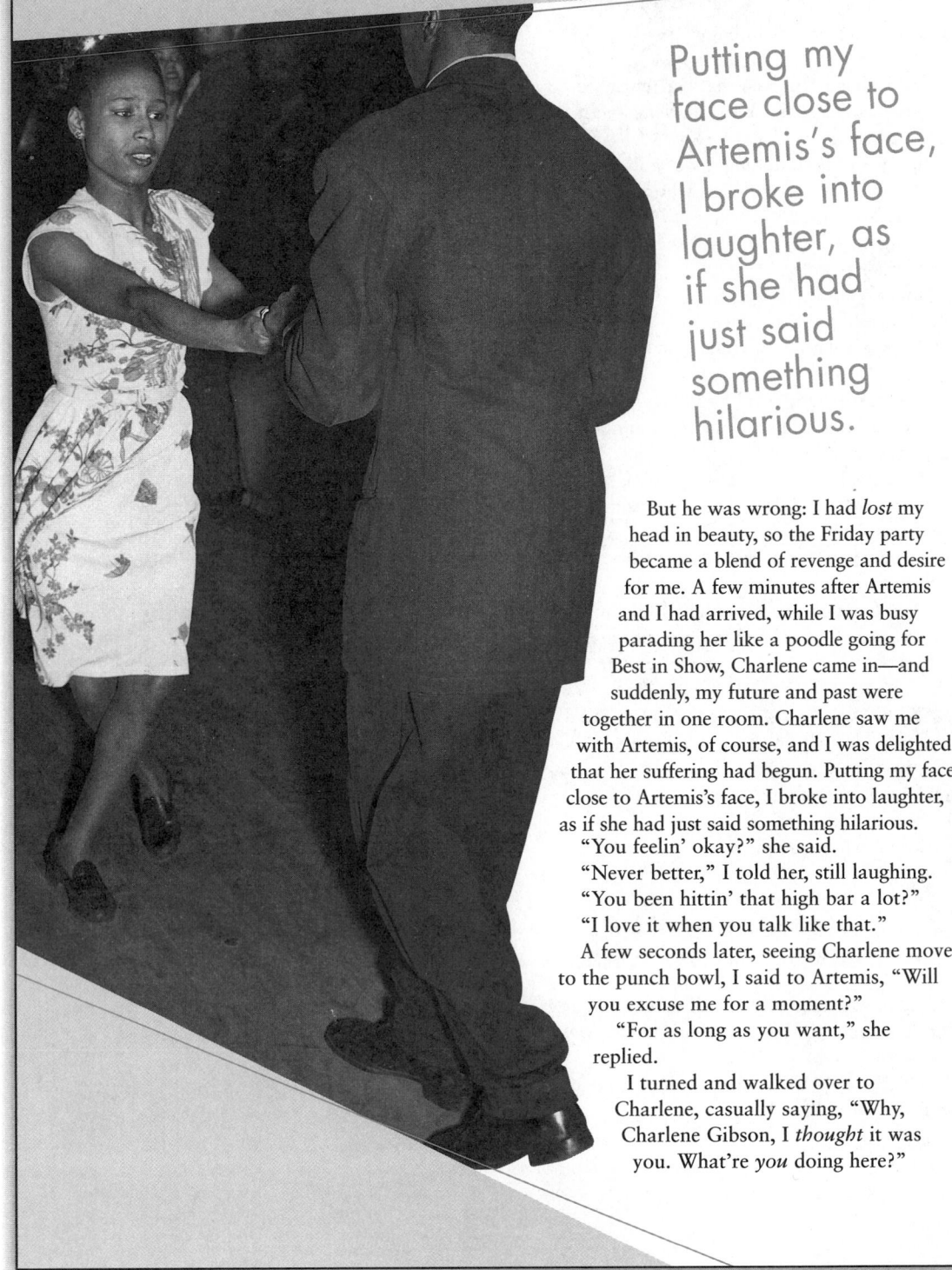

Putting my face close to Artemis's face, I broke into laughter, as if she had just said something hilarious.

But he was wrong: I had *lost* my head in beauty, so the Friday party became a blend of revenge and desire for me. A few minutes after Artemis and I had arrived, while I was busy parading her like a poodle going for Best in Show, Charlene came in—and suddenly, my future and past were together in one room. Charlene saw me with Artemis, of course, and I was delighted that her suffering had begun. Putting my face close to Artemis's face, I broke into laughter, as if she had just said something hilarious.

"You feelin' okay?" she said.

"Never better," I told her, still laughing. "You been hittin' that high bar a lot?"

"I love it when you talk like that."

A few seconds later, seeing Charlene move to the punch bowl, I said to Artemis, "Will you excuse me for a moment?"

"For as long as you want," she replied.

I turned and walked over to Charlene, casually saying, "Why, Charlene Gibson, I *thought* it was you. What're *you* doing here?"

"Making a big mistake," she said. "Artemis and *you?* Since when did she start doing social work with thieves?"

"Glad you're having fun, Charlene."

"What're you gonna steal for *her?* Your mother's *watch?*"

"Have some pink and white mints. They'll really clear your head."

"I know you, Bill Cosby. You're just rentin' that girl to make me feel bad. I thought you wanted to be friends."

"Well, I did," I said, suddenly wishing that I had chosen a more gracious revenge.

"I thought you wanted me to be able to ask you questions."

"Well . . . yeah."

"Okay, here's one: Are you ever gonna grow up?"

It was a simple true-false question, the kind on which I usually guessed, and so I took a guess now: "I certainly am."

Often through the years, I have thought of Charlene's question; and I now know the answer is that no man ever grows up in the eyes of a woman—or ever grows familiar with the rules for dealing with her. Sigmund Freud[8] once said, "What do women want?" The only thing I have learned in fifty-two years is that women want men to stop asking dumb questions like that. ❖

---

8. **Sigmund Freud** (sĭg′mənd froid): an Austrian doctor who developed the theory and practice of psychoanalysis.

Bill Cosby

1937–

Other Works
Fatherhood

Versatility with a Smile Actor, author, comic, educator—Bill Cosby is very funny, but he is also multifaceted. In the early 1960s, Cosby toured the country and made albums as a comic. His first acting job was playing a secret agent in the espionage series *I Spy,* which ran from 1965 to 1968. He was the first African American to have a starring dramatic role on network television, and his fine work earned him three Emmy Awards. His animated program *Fat Albert and the Cosby Kids* won him a new generation of viewers, and the role of Dr. Heathcliff Huxtable on *The Cosby Show* broadened his popularity further. In 1984, Cosby was inducted into the Television Hall of Fame.

Values Education Cosby is justifiably proud of his education, which is why the credits for *The Cosby Show* list him as William H. Cosby, Jr., Ed.D. Cosby left high school without earning his diploma, but passed his equivalency exam while in the U.S. Navy. Once out of the military, Cosby won an athletic scholarship to Temple University in Philadelphia, but he left during his sophomore year to pursue his comedy career. He later resumed his studies at the University of Massachusetts and was awarded a doctorate degree in education in 1977. Cosby and his wife, Camile, are active in promoting education among African Americans. In 1988 they donated $20 million to Spelman College in Atlanta.

Author Activity

Art Imitates Life Select a segment from one of Cosby's works that typifies his humor. Share your choice with your classmates, either by reading aloud or by playing an audio or video recording. Discuss the basis of Cosby's appeal.

LOVE AND MARRIAGE 363

Writing Workshop
Problem-Solution Essay

Objectives
- write a Problem-Solution Essay
- use a written text as a model for writing
- revise a draft to combine sentences
- correct run-on sentences

Introducing the Workshop

A Problem-Solution Essay Explain to students that in a problem-solution essay, the writer presents a detailed solution to an existing problem. Identifying and solving problems are practical skills with many applications in business, school, and the community. Ask students to describe instances in their lives when they have encountered a problem and proposed a solution. Ask them to comment on how successful they were in convincing others to support the changes they proposed.

Discuss some of the general features of a convincing solution to a problem. Point out that by writing a problem-solution essay, students will be able to present a solution to an existing problem.

Basics in a Box

B Using the Graphic As suggested by the graphic, the introduction states and analyzes an existing problem. The "light bulb," or body of the essay, provides readers with an enlightened solution to the problem. The conclusion restates the problem and explains the benefits of the solution.

C Presenting the Rubric To better understand the assignment, students can refer to the Standards for Writing a Successful Problem-Solution Essay. You may wish to discuss with them the complete rubric, which describes several levels of proficiency.

Use McDougal Littell's ***Language Network,*** Chapter 23, for more instruction on writing a problem-solution essay.

To engage students visually, use **Power Presentation** 4, Problem-Solution Essay.

Writing Workshop
Problem-Solution Essay

Recommending a course of action. . .

A

From Reading to Writing The story "Lalla" is about a young woman who solves a problem: Which man should she marry, and what kind of life should she lead? Fiction dealing with problems compels interest because life also has many problems and conflicts. One way to deal with these difficulties is to analyze the problem and explore possible solutions. **Problem-solution** writing can be found in places ranging from newspaper editiorials to personal letters.

For Your Portfolio

WRITING PROMPT Write a problem-solution essay that examines a problem that deeply interests you.

Purpose: To inform, to persuade
Audience: Anyone interested in the problem you are addressing

Basics in a Box

Problem-Solution Essay at a Glance

B

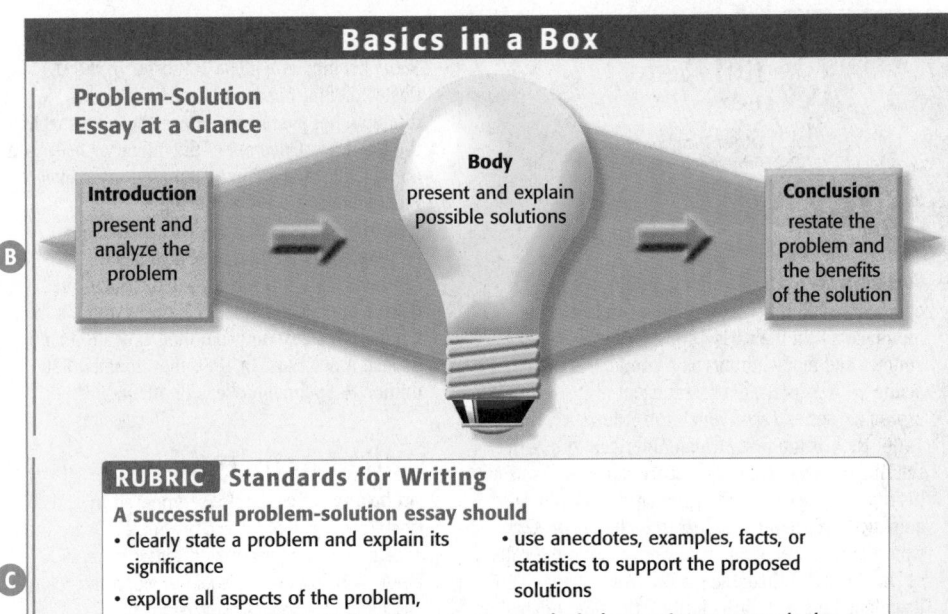

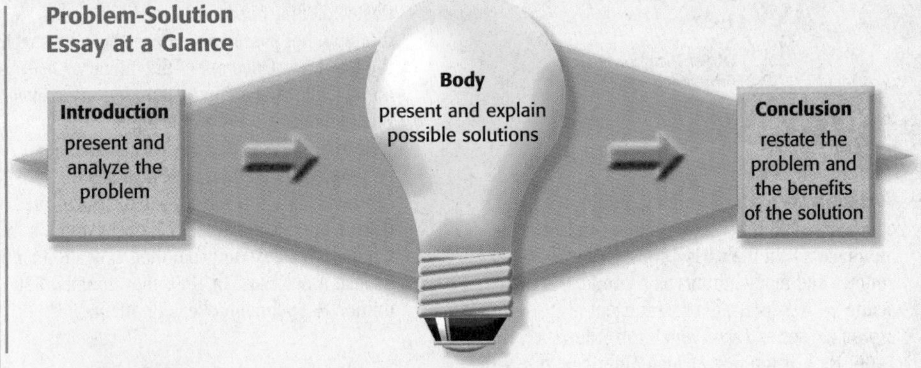
Introduction
present and analyze the problem
Body
present and explain possible solutions
Conclusion
restate the problem and the benefits of the solution

C

RUBRIC Standards for Writing

A successful problem-solution essay should
- clearly state a problem and explain its significance
- explore all aspects of the problem, including its causes and effects
- offer one or more reasonable solutions and explain how to put them into effect
- use anecdotes, examples, facts, or statistics to support the proposed solutions
- use logical reasoning to persuade the audience

LESSON RESOURCES

USING PRINT RESOURCES
Unit Two Resource Book
- Prewriting, p. 58
- Drafting, p. 59
- Peer Response, pp. 60–61
- Revising, Editing and Proofreading, p. 62
- Student Models, pp. 63–68
- Rubric, p. 69

Writing Transparencies and Copymasters
- Writing Process Transparencies, pp. 1–4
- Writing Style Transparencies, pp. 12–24
- Writing Template Copymasters, p. 28

USING MEDIA RESOURCES
LaserLinks
Writing Springboards
See Teacher's SourceBook p. 64 for bar codes.
Writing Coach CD-ROM
Visit our website:
www.mcdougallittell.com

Analyzing a Student Model

Raleigh Postiglione
Whitney Young High School

RUBRIC IN ACTION

High School Cliques in Today's Society

Today, high school is not only a steppingstone to higher education but it is a time for teenagers to create themselves, meet new people, and begin discovering and nurturing their talents. However, such obstacles as cliques can hamper this progress. A clique is a small group of people who socialize mainly among themselves and exclude others. Whether these cliques are based on appearance, wealth, or race, they can harm both their own members and those excluded from them. Cliques thrive on ignorance and prejudice and restrict academic performance and social interaction. They can have permanent psychological effects.

> ❶ Defines the problem and explains why it is significant

D

On an academic level, cliques inhibit such activities as group work and class discussion. In the classroom, it is extremely important to have an environment where students can feel comfortable and safe. Otherwise, it will be difficult for them to reach their full potential. A teacher's job is to promote interaction among all students in order to expose them to new ideas. When only a few students dominate the group and ridicule or reject others, there can be no open exchange of ideas in the classroom.

> ❷ Explores one aspect of the problem

Cliques also create social obstacles. From as early as kindergarten, cliques gradually begin to form, and they can grow tighter and more selective as the years pass. This is why it is so important for parents to instill open-mindedness in their children from an early age. Kids who view the world through biased eyes are often the cause of cliques. Young children have great potential to be independent thinkers and caring souls, but they can also be very fragile. For example, at a magnet school where students come from all over the city and from many different backgrounds, some children may judge and reject others on the basis of physical appearance, fashion, or other trivial matters. This kind of rejection can snowball and continue for years.

> ❸ Identifies a possible cause of another aspect of the problem

Though it is hard to believe that rejection from a few teenagers could permanently scar an individual, it happens. A high school student looks on this rejection not as mere dislike from a bunch of kids but as cruel rejection by his or her peers, those who should provide support and understanding. If a person is sensitive and vulnerable, this reaction from fellow classmates can be traumatic and make it difficult to reach one's full academic and personal potential. Growing up is tough, but there is often

> ❹ Uses transitional words to clarify the connections between ideas

Teaching the Lesson

Analyzing the Model

"High School Cliques in Today's Society"

D The writer addresses a school problem and, after analyzing its causes and effects, suggests a solution that has ramifications which extend into the larger social world beyond school.

After students read the model, they can take turns reading aloud the Rubric in Action. Point out key words and phrases in the student model that correspond to the elements mentioned in the Rubric in Action.

1. Have students suggest an alternative opening.
   Possible Response: The writer might begin with a classroom scene where cliques are having a negative effect.
2. Have students label the specific aspect of the problem that this paragraph addresses.
   Possible Response: Academic problems occur because students are too intimidated by cliques to freely exchange ideas during class discussions and group work.
3. Ask students what the writer sees as the possible cause of cliques.
   Possible Response: The writer thinks that cliques begin early in life—perhaps as early as kindergarten—and continue because children learn bias and begin to reject others on the basis of trivial differences, such as wealth, race, fashion, or physical appearance.

Mini Lesson Viewing and Representing

PICTURING TEXT STRUCTURE

Instruction Stating the problem and offering clear solutions is an important part of writing a problem-solution essay. However, structural signals are also needed so that readers do not get confused about which sections define the problem and which propose solutions.

Activity Have students analyze the text structure of the student model by creating a graphic organizer. The graphic should illustrate how the student writer organized his problem-solution essay. Before students create a graphic organizer for the model, they might first work in pairs to discuss what the writer accomplished in each paragraph of the essay.

I. Defines the problem: high school cliques
II. Explains its causes and effects
- **A. Cliques thrive on prejudice and bias**
- **B. Cliques inhibit learning and create social obstacles**
- **C. Cliques have negative psychological effects on the people they exclude**

III. Proposes solutions
- **A. Classroom teacher's role**
- **B. School assemblies**

IV. Summarizes reasons to adopt solutions

5. Point out that nearly two thirds of the essay is used to establish the problem, with less than one third focusing on a solution. The writer decides the proportion of focus on problem and solution, depending on the topic and the audience. Ask students why they think this writer chose to focus primarily on the problem rather than the solution. **Possible Response:** Establishing the seriousness of the problem is the first step in solving it. If the audience fails to recognize the problem or its effects, even the best solution is unlikely to work.
6. Discuss the merits and drawbacks, if any, of the second solution. Ask volunteers who have a wide variety of friendships to share their experiences. **Possible Response:** One advantage of such an assembly would be to raise student awareness of the problem. One drawback is that no one can be forced to befriend others.

comfort in knowing that others can relate to your problems and that everyone is basically in the same boat. Cliques isolate some students and leave them to fend for themselves. High school is a jungle. The fittest survive, and those who cannot conform and fit in somewhere are left in the dust.

Even those who do "fit in" may feel the negative effects of being in a clique later in life. Being in a select group of friends from whom you never fear rejection and humiliation leaves you with little experience in coping with the real world. Cliques are present not only in high school but in the workplace and the social world as well. Just because you may have been accepted among one group does not necessarily mean you will receive as warm a welcome in a different setting.

Although many students would like to eliminate cliques, it may not be possible for students alone to bring their different social circles together. A push from teachers is necessary. Teachers cannot control whom their students associate with at lunch and on weekends, but they can promote positive interaction in their classrooms. It is a teacher's duty not just to lecture to a nameless group of students but to some extent to guide students' social interaction. For instance, in my sophomore English Literature class, my teacher puts us in groups of four several times a week. To complete the work, we must cooperate and listen to everyone's comments. Whether students are reluctant or not, the teacher should consciously pair a "bookworm" with a "jock" and a "prep" with a "rebel." This shows people that though they may dress differently and like different things, deep down they all want to have friends and be respected and liked.

❺ Offers one solution to the problem and supports it with a specific example

Outside the classroom, teachers, students, and counselors could sponsor assemblies at which student leaders tell of personal experiences with cliques and encourage everyone to reach out to others. Many schools have sponsored anti-clique programs in which students make a real attempt to befriend a large variety of people.

❻ This writer gives a second possible solution and tells how to put it into effect.

Other Options:
- Elaborate on the first solution with facts or statistics.
- Discuss the merits and drawbacks of the first solution.

In a world where everyone must strive to overcome prejudice and bias of some sort, there is no place for cliques. Good friendships are one thing, but elite, discriminating kids are another. To achieve a more open-minded society, it must be instilled in children early to be respectful and understanding of all people and never to prejudge. At the time, a high school clique may not appear to be a big deal, but its effects can last late into life. Students should avoid cliques, give everyone a chance, and perceive the world as it is: an ever-changing society made up of unique individuals who must be appreciated and respected for who and what they are.

❼ Concludes by using valid reasoning to persuade the audience to adopt the proposed solutions

Writing Your Problem-Solution Essay

❶ Prewriting

Man is a problem-solving animal. . .

Joyce Carol Oates, American writer

Begin by thinking of a meaningful problem. **Brainstorm** problems that you have discussed with your friends lately. **Recall** current school, community, national, and international problems. See the **Idea Bank** in the margin for more suggestions. After you have selected a problem in need of a solution, follow the steps below.

Planning Your Problem-Solution Essay

1. **Think about the problem.** Why do you think it is a serious problem? What are its causes and effects?
2. **Brainstorm possible solutions.** How might the problem be solved? Consider drawing a cluster map to display possible solutions.
3. **Consider each solution and eliminate impractical ones.** Does one solution stand out as the best solution? Will people support it? Will it draw political and economic backing?
4. **Identify your audience.** Who will read your essay? What do they already know and feel about the problem? How can you address their concerns?
5. **Research necessary supporting facts.** What kinds of data will help support the solution to the problem? Do you need to do research, consult experts, or examine your own thoughts?

❷ Drafting

As you begin drafting, don't be too concerned about form or completeness. You can perfect your writing later. You may want to try the following organization:

- **Identify** the problem and explain why it is significant.
- **Explain** the causes and effects of the problem, giving facts, statistics, examples, or quotations to support your points.
- **Explain and support** the proposed solutions. Address any concerns or objections your audience may have.
- **Conclude** by describing how to achieve the solutions.

Ask Your Peer Reader

- How would you define the problem I describe?
- Which information did you find most and least convincing?
- What information is missing or unclear?

IDEA Bank

1. Your Working Portfolio
Build on one of the **Writing Options** you completed earlier in this unit:

Alternative Solutions, p. 313

Problem-Solution Essay, p. 327

2. Issues and Answers
Read the letters to the editor in a local newspaper. What issues are people concerned about? What reasonable solutions can you offer?

3. Problem Interview
Ask several people to name a personal, local, national, and international problem that concerns them. Chart their answers and choose one problem to write about.

Guiding Student Writing

Prewriting

Choosing a Problem

If after reading the Idea Bank students are having difficulty choosing a problem, suggest they try the following:

- List problems you confront on your job that need solutions.
- Focus on social problems in your community, such as unemployment, latchkey kids, after-school programs, deteriorating schools and parks, or ethnic conflicts.
- Focus on problems confronted by teenagers, or think of problems for which teenagers could be part of the solution, such as helping younger children learn to read or working with elderly shut-ins.

Planning the Problem-Solution Essay

1. Point out that, as students begin to jot down the causes of a problem and its effects, they will also inadvertently run into potential solutions.
3. Have students work in pairs to discuss solutions. Have them list pluses and minuses for each solution and use this analysis to choose the best solution.

Drafting

Some students will be comfortable with drafting to see where their ideas take them. Others might prefer working from an outline based on the four headings suggested in the text.

Still other students, rather than attempting too much in their first draft, might find it helpful to break down the essay into a series of paragraphs. In part one, students focus solely on identifying the problem, perhaps using research and expert testimony to do so. In part two they explain the causes and effects of the problem. In part three they explain and support the solutions and refute objections. In the final part, they write their conclusion.

Revising

SENTENCE COMBINING

Point out that in the unrevised example, the word *although* is added to signal a contrast between the ideas expressed in sentences one and two, and the word *but* is added to show contrast between the ideas expressed in sentences four and five.

Discuss the logical relationships suggested by the subordinating conjunction *because* and by the conjunctive adverb *therefore*. Then have students read their drafts one paragraph at a time and examine each sentence in relation to the sentence that follows and precedes it. Instruct them to identify logical relationships that exist between sentences and ideas, then combine sentences by using conjunctions that make these relationships clear.

Editing and Proofreading

RUN-ONS

Explain that a run-on sentence occurs when two independent clauses—groups of words that can stand alone because they have a subject and a verb—are joined without the proper punctuation marks or conjunctions.

Direct students' attention to the sample paragraph. Discuss three ways a run-on sentence could be corrected: by adding a period after the first sentence; by adding a comma and a coordinating conjunction between the two clauses; by adding a semicolon between the independent clauses. Have students explain why the best way to correct the first run-on is by adding the word *but* preceded by a comma. Then ask a volunteer to justify the way the second run-on sentence was corrected in the example.

Have students use the Editing and Proofreading instruction to help them produce error-free final drafts.

Reflecting

Have students write brief notes addressing the question in the text. Then have them clip their responses to their essays and place both in their working portfolios.

Need revising help?

Review the **Rubric,** p. 364

Consider **peer reader** comments

Check **Revision Guidelines,** p. 1145

3 Revising

TARGET SKILL ▶ SENTENCE COMBINING Using too many short sentences makes your writing choppy and often doesn't show the logical relationship between ideas. In a problem-solution essay, you may want to join sentences with words such as *because, therefore, although,* and *but.*

> Many students would like to eliminate cliques. It may not be possible for students alone to bring their different social circles together. A push from teachers is necessary. Teachers cannot control whom their students associate with at lunch and on weekends. They can promote positive interaction in their classroom.

Rattled by run-ons and fragments?

See the **Grammar Handbook,** p. 1199

4 Editing and Proofreading

TARGET SKILL ▶ RUN-ONS Run-on sentences—two or more sentences written as though they were one—can confuse your readers. Correct run-ons by rewriting long sentences as two separate sentences, by joining them with a semicolon or coordinating conjunction, or by making one of the sentences into a subordinate clause.

> Growing up is tough there is often comfort in knowing that others can relate to your problems and that everyone is basically in the same boat. Cliques isolate some students and leave them to fend for themselves. High school is a jungle, the fittest survive and those who cannot conform and fit in somewhere are left in the dust.

Publishing IDEAS

- Send your essay as a letter to the editor of a school or local newspaper.
- E-mail your essay to a friend. If it deals with a larger problem, E-mail it to a list of people with interest in the issue.

More Online: Publishing Options
www.mcdougallittell.com

5 Reflecting

FOR YOUR WORKING PORTFOLIO How did writing your essay help you find a solution to the problem? Attach your answer to your finished work. Save your problem-solution essay in your **Working Portfolio.**

Assessment Practice Revising & Editing

Read this paragraph from the first draft of a problem-and-solution essay. The underlined sections may include the following kinds of errors:

- **correctly written sentences that should be combined**
- **lack of pronoun-antecedent agreement**
- **run-on sentences**
- **spelling errors**

For each underlined section, choose the revision that most improves the writing.

Some teenagers feel shy. This isn't unusual. (1) Some shy teenagers are afraid of appearing aukward (2) in front of their peers. Others worry that they (3) don't have anything interesting to say. "For me, being in a room full of strangers is scary," explains one high school student. "What if people don't like me what if nobody says anything to me (4)?" Most teenagers will probly (5) overcome their shyness as they get older. However, there are techniques teens can use to help themselves (6), such as striking up a conversation with a new student.

1. **A.** Some teenagers feel shy, this isn't unusual.
B. Some teenagers feel shy this isn't unusual.
C. It isn't unusual for teenagers to feel shy.
D. Correct as is

2. **A.** awkward
B. akward
C. alkward
D. Correct as is

3. **A.** we
B. them
C. us
D. Correct as is

4. **A.** "What if people don't like me, what if nobody says anything to me?"
B. "What if people don't like me? What if nobody says anything to me?"
C. "What if people don't like me. what if nobody says anything to me?"
D. Correct as is

5. **A.** probably
B. probabley
C. probley
D. Correct as is

6. **A.** himself
B. ourselves
C. theirselves
D. Correct as is

Need extra help?

See the **Grammar Handbook**
Correcting Run-on Sentences, p. 1199
Pronoun Agreement, p. 1183

Assessment Practice

Before students begin the exercise, you may wish to briefly review the types of errors that the passage may contain. Encourage students to read all the choices carefully before they select the correct answer to each question.

Answers:
1. C; **2.** A; **3.** D; **4.** B; **5.** A; **6.** D

Objectives
- reflect on and assess student understanding of the unit
- compare text events with experiences of students and other readers
- provide examples of themes that cross texts
- compare across texts elements of texts such as conflicts and characterization
- assess and build portfolios

Reflecting on Theme

OPTION 1

A successful response will
- select from the unit one selection that comes closest to the student's own experience of love.
- select from the unit one selection that is furthest removed from the student's own experience of love.
- explain why the student has chosen the two selections rather than others in the unit.

OPTION 2

A successful response will
- create a collage comprising images and words that suggest the student's views on the extremes of love.
- explain the collage
- examine whether the student's view of love was changed by the readings.

OPTION 3

A successful response will
- be one or two full paragraphs long.
- explain which relationship portrayed in the unit demonstrates the purest kind of love.

Self-Assessment
Ask students to identify the conceptions of love that they had before they read the selections in this unit. Have students explain how characters or situations in this unit affected their perceptions of love.

In the Name of Love

Have the selections in this unit changed your opinions about love or deepened your understanding of its effects? What new things have you learned as a reader and writer? Explore these questions by completing one or more of the options in each of the following sections.

Reflecting on Theme

OPTION 1

Comparing Love's Emotions Review the activity on page 224, which asked you to create a bar graph identifying the different feelings that you have experienced in a love relationship. Then review the selections in the unit to identify which one comes closest to your own experience of love; also identify the selection that seemed furthest removed from your experience. Write a note explaining why you have chosen those two selections instead of other selections in the unit. Consider how the selections that you have chosen affect your own understanding of love.

OPTION 2

Portraying Love's Agony and Ecstasy As you saw in this unit, love can lead people to great happiness or to the depths of misery. Consider which selections in the unit depict the agony of love, which portray its ecstasy, and which, if any, capture both extremes. You may also find it helpful to review the glossary of expressions you created in the activity on page 283. Then create a collage with images and words that suggest your own views about the extremes of love. Your images may also be based on love relationships described in the selections. Share your collage with a small group of classmates. Explain how your collage represents your views, and discuss whether your opinions of love were changed by your readings.

OPTION 3

Evaluating Love Relationships This unit includes selections about family love, romantic love, and even the love of animals. Review the different loving relationships portrayed in the selections of this unit. In your judgment, which relationship demonstrates the purest kind of love? Explain your choice in one or two paragraphs.

Self ASSESSMENT

READER'S NOTEBOOK

Put together your reflections about love by creating two lists, one titled "What Love Is" and one titled "What Love Is Not." Each list may consist of words or phrases, references to characters from the selections, or brief descriptions of people and events from your own life. Then consider how your ideas about love have changed or developed as a result of the readings from this unit. Circle or highlight elements on your list that show any change in your thinking.

Reviewing Literary Concepts

OPTION 1

Understanding Metaphor and Simile After reviewing the definitions of *metaphor* and *simile* on pages 260 and 349, search through the selections in this unit to find at least five metaphors or similes that you find interesting or memorable. Create a chart like the one shown. Compare your chart with those created by other students.

Selection	Metaphor/ Simile	Things Compared	Feeling Produced
"Tonight I Can Write. . ."	"The night is shattered and she is not with me." (metaphor)	The night is being compared with something that can be broken, such as a piece of fine china or a fragile glass.	sadness; an overwhelming sense of loss

OPTION 2

Appreciating the Sonnet Review the information about the sonnet on pages 233 and 236. Then work with a partner to create a poster, pamphlet, or multimedia display about the sonnet. Include information about its history, offer your own definitions of *sonnet* and related terms, and present a variety of sonnets. You may include decorative art and present recordings of sonnet readings.

Self ASSESSMENT

READER'S NOTEBOOK

Create a test to measure other students' understanding of the following terms. One section of your test might require that students match terms with their definitions. Another section might include excerpts of poems, along with questions focused on how the terms can be applied to the poetry. Take a test created by one of your classmates, and note any terms that give you trouble. Work with classmates to clarify the meaning of these terms.

imagery	simile
speaker	metaphor
sonnet structure	free verse
rhyme scheme	farce
rhythm	historical setting
meter	mood
iambic pentameter	foreshadowing
characterization	conflict
dialect	point of view
figurative language	narrator
	repetition

Building Your Portfolio

- **Writing Options** For several Writing Options, you've written poems of your own in response to poems in this unit. Write a note about one of your poems. How well does it stand on its own? What would you change, if anything? What about this experience can help your writing of other poems? Add the poem and the note to your **Presentation Portfolio.**
- **Writing Workshops** In one Workshop you wrote a Poem about an experience, idea, place, person, or feeling. In another you wrote an Essay outlining a problem and proposing a solution. Reread these pieces and decide which one is the more successful piece of writing. Explain your choice in a note attached to your chosen piece. Place the writing in your **Presentation Portfolio.**
- **Additional Activities** Reflect upon any of the assignments you completed under **Activities & Explorations** and **Inquiry & Research.** Which activity proved the most difficult? Keep a record of any assignments that you would like to work on further in the future.

Self ASSESSMENT

Presentation Portfolio

Think about the pieces you have just added to your portfolio. How do they compare with the items you added previously? Are your choices beginning to reveal any preferences you may have for certain types of writing or activities?

Setting GOALS

Set a new challenge for yourself to turn a weakness into a strength or to come to a new appreciation of certain genres of literature. For example, if you have struggled with poetry in the past, set a goal to improve in that area.

Reviewing Literary Concepts

OPTION 1

Use the Unit 2 Resource Book, page 70, to provide students a ready-made, full-depth chart for recording their metaphors and similes.

OPTION 2

A successful response will
- create a poster, pamphlet, or multimedia display about the sonnet.
- include information about the sonnet's history, offer definitions of *sonnet* and related terms, and present a variety of sonnets.

To expand this activity, have students write and present their own sonnets.

Building Your Portfolio

Students will use their Presentation Portfolios to file what they consider their highest quality work—the very best projects and activities from their Working Portfolios.

For more information on using writing and assessing portfolios, see the *Teacher's Guide to Assessment and Portfolio Use* beginning on page 53.

The *Electronic Library* is a CD-ROM that contains additional fiction, nonfiction, poetry, and drama for each unit in *The Language of Literature.*

These are the additional selections found in Unit 2 of the *Electronic Library.*

Nicholasa Mohr
A Thanksgiving Celebration

Tu Fu
The Return

Alfonsina Storni
One More Time

Petrarch
The Spring Returns

Sappho
Leaving Crete

Ovid
The Story of Pyramus and Thisbe

Isak Dinesen
The Ring

Luigi Pirandello
War

Gabriela Mistral
Intimate

Serafín and Joaquín Alvarez Quintero
A Sunny Morning

Horacio Quiroga
Three Letters . . . and a Footnote

Anton Chekhov
Verotchka

Encourage students to select one of the longer works described as an opportunity to read silently over a sustained period of time.

UNIT TWO Extend Your *Reading*

LITERATURE CONNECTIONS

A Midsummer Night's Dream

WILLIAM SHAKESPEARE

Love and magic rule the world of this fanciful comedy set in ancient Athens and a nearby wood. The fair maiden Hermia loves Lysander, but her father insists that Demetrius be her mate. To escape a forced marriage, Hermia runs away with Lysander to the woods, followed by Demetrius (who is madly in love with Hermia) and Helena (Hermia's friend who is hopelessly in love with Demetrius). Unknowingly, the lovers enter the kingdom of fairies, where love potions and magical transformations are the order of the night.

These thematically related readings are provided along with *A Midsummer Night's Dream*:

A Midsummer Night's Dream
BY NORRIE EPSTEIN

The Song of Wandering Aengus
BY WILLIAM BUTLER YEATS

The Sweet Miracle/El Dulce Milagro
BY JUANA DE IBARBOUROU, TRANSLATED BY ALICE STONE BLACKWELL

April Witch
BY RAY BRADBURY

Come And Be My Baby
BY MAYA ANGELOU

Love's Initiations, *from* Care of the Soul
BY THOMAS MOORE

The Sensible Thing
BY F. SCOTT FITZGERALD

***from* Love and Marriage**
BY BILL COSBY

And Even *More* . . .

Cold Sassy Tree

OLIVE ANN BURNS

Fourteen-year-old Will Tweedy lives in a small Southern town where everything is everyone else's business. The adventures begin when Mr. Blakeslee elopes with Miss Love, a Yankee woman half his age. Will narrates this tale of love, death, coming of age, and family ties.

Books

Breeders and Other Short Stories
EUGENIA COLLIER
A collection of uplifting stories about African-American life.

Honey and Salt
CARL SANDBURG
Vibrant, whimsical verse about life, love, and death by one of America's most celebrated poets.

All Creatures Great and Small
JAMES HERRIOT
The author writes a true story of his experiences as a country veterinarian in northern England.

LITERATURE CONNECTIONS

Jane Eyre

CHARLOTTE BRONTE

In 19th-century England, Jane is an orphan, a teacher, and a governess. She is fiercely independent and moral in spirit—qualities that are tested and that ultimately bring her the happiness she has searched for. The heroine claims her right to feel strong emotions and to act on her own convictions.

These thematically related readings are provided along with *Jane Eyre*:

Sonnet 141
BY WILLIAM SHAKESPEARE

Beauty: When the Other Dancer Is the Self
BY ALICE WALKER

The Governess
BY DANIEL POOL

The Little Governess
BY KATHERINE MANSFIELD

I see, I see the crescent moon
BY ANNA AKHMATOVA, TRANSLATED BY RICHARD MCKANE

Signs and Symbols
BY VLADIMIR NABOKOV

A Home for Hope
BY RON ARIAS

Seventh House
BY R.K. NARAYAN

In the Evening
BY ANNA AKHMATOVA, TRANSLATED BY DANIEL WIESSBORT

A Marriage Proposal
ANTON CHEKHOV

Lomov and Natalia may get married—if they can ever stop arguing.

The Way to Rainy Mountain
N. SCOTT MOMADAY

A retelling of Kiowa myths, told to the author by his grandmother, with illustrations by his father, Al Momaday.

Other Media

Carl Sandburg: Poet of the People
Born of illiterate immigrants, this democratic poet led a life of hard work and gritty adventure, rising to fame and honor. Narrated by Hugh Downs. Aims.
(VIDEOCASSETTE)

Pablo Neruda
Library Video Company.
(VIDEOCASSETTE)

N. Scott Momaday Reads
American Audio Prose Library.
(AUDIOCASSETTE)

All Things Bright and Beautiful
Listen for Pleasure.
(AUDIOCASSETTE)

EXTEND YOUR READING 373

OVERVIEW

The Reading and Writing for Assessment feature provides practice in taking standardized tests. As students work through this lesson, they will learn strategies for reading comprehension questions, multiple-choice questions, and essay and short-answer questions. Boxed strategies located alongside the text will help guide students through the activities. These strategies model processes students can use as they take standardized tests.

This feature is based on and will help to prepare students for state assessments, including end-of-course assessments. It will also prepare students for the reading comprehension questions used on such college board examinations as the Scholastic Aptitude Test (SAT) and the American College Test (ACT).

Objectives

- understand and apply strategies for reading a test selection
- recognize literary techniques in a test selection
- understand and apply strategies for answering multiple-choice questions about a test selection
- respond to a writing prompt and present ideas in a logical order
- understand and apply strategies for revising and proofreading a test response

Reading & Writing for Assessment

Throughout high school, you will be tested on your ability to read and understand many different kinds of reading selections. These tests will assess your basic understanding of ideas and your knowledge of vocabulary. They will also check your ability to analyze and evaluate both the message of the text and the techniques the writer uses in getting that message across.

The following pages will give you test-taking strategies. Practice applying these strategies by working through each of the models provided.

PART 1 How to Read a Test Selection

In many tests, you will read a passage and then answer multiple-choice questions about it. Applying the basic test-taking strategies that follow, taking notes, and highlighting or underscoring passages as you read can help you focus on the information you will need to know.

STRATEGIES FOR READING A TEST SELECTION

- **Before you begin reading, skim the questions that follow the passage.** These can help focus your reading.
- **Use your active reading strategies such as analyzing, predicting, and questioning.** Make notes in the margin or highlight key words and passages to help you focus your reading. You may do this only if the test directions allow you to mark on the test itself.
- **Think about the title.** What does it suggest about the overall message or theme of the selection?
- **Look for main ideas.** These are often stated at the beginnings or ends of paragraphs. Sometimes they are implied, not stated. After reading each paragraph, ask "What was this passage about?"
- **Note the literary elements and techniques used by the writer.** For example, be aware of tone (writer's attitude toward the subject), figurative and descriptive language, or other elements that catch your attention. Then ask yourself what effect the writer achieves with each choice.
- **Unlock word meanings.** Use context clues and word parts to help you unlock the meaning of unfamiliar words.
- **Think about the message or theme.** What larger lesson can you draw from the passage? Can you infer anything or make generalizations about other similar situations, human beings, or life in general?

Reading Selection

"Everyone Has a Story," As One Reporter Proves

by Tina Kelley

1 Colfax, Wash.—David Johnson is not a man of original ideas. If he were, he says, he would be a novelist, not a newspaper reporter living on a remote ranch. But his one inspiration has caught on in this slightly obscure corner of the world.

2 Every week for the past 14 years, Mr. Johnson, 50, has written a front page column for *The Lewiston* (Idaho) *Morning Tribune* featuring a person chosen at random from telephone books in the newspaper's circulation area, in central Idaho and eastern Washington.

3 Called "Everyone Has a Story," the columns prove how all types of people can blossom under the ❶ blessing of focused attention: a 6-year-old boy anticipating Christmas; one of the last full-blooded members of the Nez Perce tribe; a fellow who traps muskrats in sewage lagoons; or the high school sophomore here who wants to become a rodeo queen. . . .

4 "This is their one shot," Mr. Johnson said of his subjects. "They might be in the paper for an ❷ obit, but this is a big deal. I've seen a man go out and get a new cowboy hat just for it."

5 Mr. Johnson, who carries three pens in his shirt pocket, got his idea when he began reporting in Idaho, driving 30,000 miles a year between what he calls "the little hintertowns." He figured everyone there had a story. He raised the phone book idea at *The Daily Idahonian,* but his editor did not take him up on it.

6 Then in 1984, while working for *The Tribune,* he met Charles Kuralt, the CBS News reporter famous for his "On the Road" dispatches, at a local journalism symposium.

7 "He started telling about how he got into doing stories about people who make big balls of string," Mr. Johnson said. "He'd be flying across the U.S. for a news event, and he'd look at the lights below and say, ❸ 'You know, we're flying over the best stories.' I told him about the phone book idea, and he said, 'That's one of the best ideas I ever heard.' One of my editors overheard that, and three weeks later I was doing the column."

8 Mr. Johnson now does a few columns ahead if he goes on vacation. "My biggest fear was somebody was going to take it over and do a better job," he said.

STRATEGIES IN ACTION

❶ Look for main ideas.

ONE STUDENT'S THOUGHTS

"The writer calls the columns a 'blessing.' These columns prove that people of all ages and walks of life have interesting lives."

❷ Unlock word meanings.

Obit makes me think of *obituary.* That makes sense in context and because Johnson is a newspaperman, he would be likely to use such an abbreviation.

❸ Read actively—ask questions.

"Why did Charles Kuralt think he was flying over the best stories?"

YOUR TURN

How are Charles Kuralt and David Johnson similar?

Teaching the Lesson

Begin by previewing the text. Note the title and identify the subject of the reading selection. Read through the questions and prompts at the end of the text. Ask students what they will need to look for as they read.

1 The main idea of a paragraph is the idea that determines the subject matter of the paragraph. Encourage students to look for the one idea in a paragraph that is supported by all the details. As they read each detail in a paragraph, they should ask themselves, "What idea does this detail describe or relate to?"

2 Students can sometimes unlock meanings of shortened words by determining from which larger word a shortened word is taken. If students run across an unfamiliar word that looks like part of a larger word that they know, they should substitute the larger word for the smaller. If the larger word makes sense in the context, students can then infer that the smaller word is a shortened version of the larger, and has the same meaning.

3 **Possible Response:** He thought that the most interesting stories were those of the people not ordinarily covered in news stories.

Encourage students to come up with their own questions about the selection.

YOUR TURN They are both interested in stories about ordinary people.

4 The writer explains the expression "million-dollar rains" by describing the increase in wheat production that they bring. Students can sometimes find explanations of figurative language within a selection.

YOUR TURN Possible Response: to give the reader an impression of the area inhabited by the people interviewed by Mr. Johnson

5 Use the following questions to help students unlock the meanings of unfamiliar words:

- Does the sentence or paragraph offer any clues to the word's meaning?
- Does the sentence restate or extend information provided earlier in the selection?

6 Making notes about characters, events, and ideas can help students analyze them and understand them better.

YOUR TURN Possible Response: He likes getting a general idea of the people living around him.

Customizing for Less Proficient Readers

7 Reading comprehension tests often assess students' ability to recognize main ideas in a test selection. Use the following questions to guide less proficient readers to recognize main ideas.

- How does Mr. Hayes feel about being included in a story?

Possible Response: delighted

- What main idea from earlier in the selection does Mr. Hayes's attitude support?

Possible Response: People get excited about being featured in the paper.

YOUR TURN The people interviewed by Mr. Johnson feel that it is an important event.

9 The Palouse, the region of Idaho and Washington that Mr. Johnson covers for the newspaper is not an area where a journalist can work from press releases. The steep, undulating hills continue for 30 to 60 miles from here, waiting for ❹ "million-dollar rains," as they are known around here, which can push wheat production up to 150 bushels an acre. Homes, towns and major breaking news stories are all far apart.

10 Mr. Johnson said he saw the column as a human geography project. He remembers spreading out several years' worth of columns when compiling a book of them. "I thought, geez, this is pretty much what people were like in *The Lewiston Tribune* area in the late 1980's."

11 His selection process is not entirely random. Subjects have to live in a home with a phone and they have to be willing to talk. Often, Mr. Johnson does get turned down.

12 "I always felt someday I'll call an ax murderer, and it'll be the greatest story I'll never get," Mr. Johnson said. But he does not ❺ hanker much for the big story that would get him to a city or a larger paper. At 50, he lives with his wife, two daughters, three horses and six dogs on 117 acres near Princeton. His paper has a circulation of 30,000, in an area where about 150,000 live.

13 "It's a noisy newspaper," he said, and he likes it that way.

Recently he drove out past where North Palouse Road turns to gravel near Colfax, to meet Chiquita, a white Andalusian horse who might be Sarah McKnight's ticket to becoming Rodeo Queen of the Palouse Empire Fair in September.

14 ❻ "Ah, that's the hook on the story," he said when Sarah, 16, mentioned her goal. It takes her seven hours to wash and groom the $1,500 horse, which she bought with her wages from Taco Time. Her boyfriend, whom she said is "cowboy kind of quiet," answered the phone at Sarah's house when Mr. Johnson called, but she immediately took over.

15 Before leaving the corral, she introduced Jim Hayes, the 84-year-old widower who owns the land where Chiquita boards. The rancher explained that Sarah is too easy on the horse, adding: "Horses are kind of like women. They're all nice and some are nicer." He hugged the girl, who calls him Grandpa.

16 "I'll tell you what, Mr. Johnson," Mr. Hayes called after the reporter, who was heading back to town. ❼ "Why don't we see about a subscription to *The Lewiston Tribune* for a while?"

❹ Note literary elements like use of figurative language.

"The 'million-dollar rains' must be called that because of the money farmers earn from increased wheat production."

YOUR TURN

Why does the writer devote a paragraph to this description of the Palouse?

❺ Use context clues to unlock word meanings.

"*Hanker* must mean want or look forward to."

❻ Read actively—analyze.

"The subjects Johnson writes about are not what most journalists would call 'news.'"

YOUR TURN

If the writer had asked Johnson why he writes his column, what might Johnson have said?

❼ Look for main ideas.

"Like most subjects of Johnson's column, Mr. Hayes seems really tickled to be included."

YOUR TURN

What main idea of the selection is supported by the quotation at the end?

376

Check Your Understanding

Have students use the following questions to test their understanding of the selection before they answer the questions in their texts.

- What were the main ideas in the selection?
- How does the writer encourage readers to care about the information she presents?
- What structure does the writer use for the selection?
- Did the selection answer all your questions about the subject? If not, what questions remain unanswered?

PART 2 How to Answer Multiple-Choice Questions

Use the strategies in the box and notes in the side column to help you answer the questions below and on the following pages.

Based on the selection you have just read, choose the best answer for each of the following questions.

1. What does the title, "Everyone Has a Story," mean?
   - **A.** Stories can be found everywhere.
   - **B.** Everyone likes a story.
   - **C.** Each person's life is unique and special.
   - **D.** Everyone wants to tell his or her own story to the world.
2. Johnson chooses people at random from the telephone book because
   - **A.** he wants to be fair.
   - **B.** he wants to prove that everyone really does have a story.
   - **C.** he didn't have a better idea.
   - **D.** his editor told him to do it that way.
3. Why is Johnson's column printed on the front page of *The Lewistown Morning Tribune?*
   - **A.** The paper doesn't have enough news stories.
   - **B.** The readers requested the front page.
   - **C.** The paper wants to show readers that their stories are worthy of attention.
   - **D.** All of the above
4. Which of the following details from the selection helps the writer to show that Johnson is a humble person?
   - **A.** Johnson calls the small towns "little hintertowns."
   - **B.** Johnson said that his biggest fear was that someone would do his column better than he did.
   - **C.** Johnson says sometimes subjects refuse to be interviewed.
   - **D.** Johnson carries three pens in his shirt pocket.
5. When Johnson said that he saw his column as a "human geography project," he probably meant that
   - **A.** driving all over the Palouse helped him learn the geography of the area.
   - **B.** his column accurately reflects what people were like in that area in the late 1980s.
   - **C.** readers of the newspaper could learn about the area's geography by reading his column.
   - **D.** finding people to interview is like finding a place on a map.

STRATEGIES FOR ANSWERING MULTIPLE-CHOICE QUESTIONS

- **Ask questions** that help you eliminate some of the choices.
- **Pay attention** to choices such as "all of the above" or "none of the above." To eliminate them, all you need to find is one answer that doesn't fit.
- **Skim your notes.** Details you noticed as you read may provide answers.

STRATEGIES IN ACTION

Pay attention to choices such as all of the above.

ONE STUDENT'S THOUGHTS

"We are never told anything about readers requesting front page coverage. *I can eliminate choice B.*"

YOUR TURN

What choice reflects the overall message of this piece?

Ask questions. What choice makes the most sense?

ONE STUDENT'S THOUGHTS

"Driving around would teach Johnson about physical geography, not human geography. I can eliminate choice A."

YOUR TURN

What other choices don't make sense?

Guiding Student Response

Multiple-Choice Questions

1. C
2. B
3. C

YOUR TURN Choice **C** most nearly reflects the overall message of the piece. Although the reason that the column is on the first page is never stated or hinted at in the selection, the message of the selection emphasizes the importance of each person's story.

4. B
5. B

YOUR TURN Choices C and D also do not make sense. The column is not about physical geography, so readers could not learn about that subject from it. Finding a place on a map is a search for a specific, predetermined location, but finding people to interview is open-ended and random.

Short-Answer Question

The primary message of this story is that everyone has an interesting story to tell. In the title and in paragraph 3, the writer states that Johnson "proves" this to be true.

YOUR TURN In the title, in paragraph 3, and in paragraph 9 the writer states her own opinions. The first two could be statements of the selection's theme.

Essay Question

Possible Response to Prompt

The writer of this selection uses figurative language to sympathetically portray Mr. Johnson and the people he interviews.

The writer's own expression expresses her feelings that these people are something beautiful, and her inclusion of many of their colorful expressions shows her interest in and love of their means of expressing themselves.

By describing the people in her article favorably and using their colorful mode of speech, the writer shows her sympathy for and appreciation of them.

YOUR TURN "all types of people can blossom"; "This is their one shot"; "It's a noisy newspaper"; "cowboy kind of quiet"; "horses are kind of like women"

PART 3 How to Respond in Writing

You may also be asked to write answers to questions about a reading passage. **Short-answer questions** usually ask you to answer in a sentence or two. **Essay questions** require a fully developed piece of writing.

Short-Answer Question

STRATEGIES FOR RESPONDING TO SHORT-ANSWER QUESTIONS

- **Identify the key words** in the writing prompt that tell you the ideas to discuss. Make sure you know what is meant by each.
- **State your response directly** and to the point.
- **Support your ideas** by using evidence from the selection.
- **Use correct grammar.**

Sample Writing Prompt

Answer the following question in one or two sentences.

What is the primary message or theme of this selection? Does the writer tell us what her message is? If so, where?

STRATEGIES IN ACTION

Support your ideas by using evidence from the selection.

ONE STUDENT'S THOUGHTS

"The last two questions of the prompt suggest that I can find the writer's message by looking in the selection—somewhere, she must come right out and say what her message is."

YOUR TURN

Find the passages in the selection where the writer states her own opinion. Then decide which of these passages could be a statement of the selection's theme.

Essay Question

STRATEGIES FOR ANSWERING ESSAY QUESTIONS

- **Look for direction words** in the writing prompt, such as *essay, analyze, describe,* or *compare and contrast* that tell you how to respond directly to the prompt.
- **List the points** you want to make before beginning to write.
- **Write an interesting introduction** that presents your main point.
- **Develop your ideas** by using evidence from the selection that supports the statements you make. Present the ideas in a logical order.
- **Write a conclusion** that summarizes your points.
- **Check your work** for correct grammar.

Sample Writing Prompt

This selection contains many figurative expressions like "too tired to spit" and "cowboy kind of quiet." How does the writer use figurative language to show her sympathy to Johnson and the people in his area? Write an essay in which you analyze the use of figurative language and tone in this selection.

Look for direction words.

ONE STUDENT'S THOUGHTS

"The directions tell me to *analyze* the writer's *figurative* language. To do that, I will have to give examples of figurative language from the selection. Then I will have to explain how my examples show the writer's sympathy for Johnson and the people in the Palouse area."

YOUR TURN

Make a list of the figurative expressions in the selection.

PART 4 How to Revise and Edit a Test Selection

Here is a student's first draft in response to the writing prompt at the bottom of page 378. Read it and answer the multiple-choice questions that follow.

> Sympathetic to Johnson and other people living in the Palouse area, figurative expressions are used by the writer of this selection to create a sympathetic tone. For example, many people who live in this area work on farms and ranches. The writer includes expressions that remind the reader of this, like "cowboy kind of quiet," and "million dollar rains." She seems to depict Johnson as a farmer that has a crop of people, tending them and helping them to "blossom under the blessing of focused attention." She also include quotations that show how people "blossom" because of Johnson's column, like "I've seen a man go out and get a new cowboy hat just for it."

1. What is the BEST way to rewrite the sentence in lines 1–3 ("Sympathetic to Johnson . . . sympathetic tone.")?

A. Creating a sympathetic tone, the writer of this selection shows her sympathy to Johnson, by using figurative expressions, and other people living in the Palouse area.

B. The writer of this selection uses figurative expressions to create a tone sympathetic to Johnson and other people living in the Palouse area.

C. Using figurative expressions to create tone, the writer of this selection sympathizes with Johnson and other people living in the Palouse area.

D. Figurative expressions help the writer to create a tone that is sympathetic to Johnson, and also help the writer to create a tone sympathetic to other people living in the Palouse area.

2. What is the BEST change, if any, to make to the sentence in lines 6–9 ("She seems . . . focused attention.")?

A. Change *that* to *who.*

B. Change *that* to *whom.*

C. Change *that* to *which.*

D. Make no change.

3. What is the BEST change, if any, to make to the sentence in lines 9–11 ("She also . . . 'just for it.' ")?

A. Change the verb to *including.*

B. Change the verb to *includes.*

C. Change the verb to *had included.*

D. Make no change.

STRATEGIES FOR REVISING, EDITING, AND PROOFREADING

- **Read the passage carefully.**
- **Note the parts that are confusing or don't make sense.** What kinds of errors would that signal?
- **Look for errors** in grammar, usage, spelling, and capitalization. Common errors include:
  - run-on sentences
  - sentence fragments
  - lack of subject-verb agreement
  - unclear pronoun antecedents
  - lack of transition words

Answers
1. B
2. A
3. B

Check Your Understanding

Have students reread their own responses to the short-answer and essay questions. Then have students use the following questions to guide themselves as they revise and edit their own work.

- Have I responded directly to the direction words in the writing prompt?
- Have I supported my ideas with evidence from the selection?
- Have I presented my ideas in a logical order?
- Have I included an introduction and a conclusion?
- Have I used correct grammar?

READING AND WRITING FOR ASSESSMENT 379

The Search for Identity

In Unit Three, students will read selections which explore ways in which the past affects people in the present. This unit contains two parts, both of which contribute to the unit theme by examining the lessons of youth and the effects of heritage as components of one's identity.

Part 1

The Experience of Youth Selections in Part 1 emphasize the lessons and difficult decisions faced in youth. For example, the girl in "The Opportunity" makes a difficult decision to turn down a once-in-a-lifetime opportunity to act in a Broadway play because she thinks the play is terrible.

Part 2

The Power of Heritage Selections in Part 2 emphasize the power that family, culture, and tradition exercise over characters. For example, in "Everyday Use" a woman realizes which of her two daughters truly understands, shares, and will perpetuate family traditions.

UNIT THREE

The Search for IDENTITY

"Who in the world am I? Ah, that's the great puzzle!"

LEWIS CARROLL

Allées Piétonnières (1995), Jean-Pierre Stora. The Grand Design, Leeds, England/Superstock.

Mini Lesson Viewing and Representing

Allées Piétonnières
by Jean-Pierre Stora

ART APPRECIATION

Instruction French artist Jean-Pierre Stora (1933–1996) painted *Allées Piétonnières* (Pedestrian Walkways) in 1995. The people in the painting appear to be moving in different directions at various speeds, some walking quickly while others are moving slowly or even standing still. The walkways appear to be rings in a circle, producing a mazelike effect. By showing people moving in different directions and at varying speeds along what appears to be a maze, Stora may have been commenting on people's difficult search for their identity.

Ask: What overall mood do you think this painting conveys?

Possible Response: The mood is mysterious because the people in the painting have no faces. The lack of facial expressions gives the work an anonymous feel, which may support the artist's idea that people are searching for their identity.

Making Connections

To help students explore the connections between the art, the quotation, and the unit theme, have them consider the following questions:

Ask: **What is meant by Lewis Carroll's quote?**
Possible Response: Like a great puzzle, one's own identity is difficult to figure out and consists of many pieces.

Ask: **What kinds of stories and experiences might you expect to read about in this unit?**
Possible Response: These selections may deal with youth, learning about oneself, cultural heritage, and family relationships across generations.

Ask: **How do you think this painting represents the themes of this unit?**
Possible Response: Stora's painting shows people walking, seemingly looking or possibly searching—searching for their identity.

UNIT THREE
PART 1 SKILLS TRACE

Features and Selections	Literary Analysis	Reading and Critical Thinking	Writing Opportunities
The Search for Identity The Experience of Youth			
Learning the Language of Literature Plot	Plot, 383		
The Active Reader: Skills and Strategies		Linking Ideas Within Texts, 385	
SHORT STORY One Thousand Dollars **Difficulty Level:** ***Average***	Plot, 386, 394 Test Practice, 393	Cause and Effect, 386, 394	Gillian's Profile, 395 Gossip Column, 395 Cause-and-Effect Analysis, 395
SHORT STORY Initiation **Difficulty Level:** ***Average***	Internal Conflict 397, 407 Review: Climax and Plot, 407	Sequence of Events, 397, 407 Test Practice, 406	Court Script, 408 Analysis, 408
Real World Link *from* Letters Home		Primary Source: Analyzing a Letter, 410	
AUTOBIOGRAPHY Getting a Job *from* I Know Why the Caged Bird Sings **Difficulty Level:** ***Average*** Building Vocabulary	Narrative Nonfiction, 411, 417	Cause and Effect, 411, 417 Test Practice, 416	Job Description, 418 Inspirational Narrative, 418
Comparing Literature: The Immigrant Experience	Comparing and Contrasting Poems, 432	Establishing a Basis of Comparison, 432	
POETRY Exile **Difficulty Level:** ***Challenging***	Narrative Poetry, 433, 437 Test Practice, 436	Poetic Elements, 433, 437	Travel Poem, 438
POETRY Lost Sister **Difficulty Level:** ***Challenging***	Cultural and Literary Symbol, 439, 442	Poetic Elements, 439, 442 Test Practice, 441	Letters Home, 443 New Title, 443
Comparing Literature: Assessment Practice		Reading the Prompt, 444	Comparison-Contrast Essay, 444
Writing Workshop: Career Search Report Assessment Practice		Analyzing a Student Model, 446	Career Search Report, 448

UNIT THREE
PART 2 SKILLS TRACE

Features and Selections	Literary Analysis	Reading and Critical Thinking	Writing Opportunities
The Power of Heritage			
Learning the Language of Literature Author's Perspective	Author's Perspective, 452		
The Active Reader: Skills and Strategies		Determining Author's Purpose, 454 Evaluating What You Read, 454	

LEGEND DLS – Daily Language SkillBuilder
CCL – Cross Curricular Link
Green type – Teacher's Edition

Speaking and Listening Viewing and Representing	Inquiry and Research	Grammar, Usage, and Mechanics	Vocabulary
Art Appreciation, 380			
Cartoon Scene, 395 Dramatic Dialogue, 395 Art Appreciation, 391 Speaking and Listening, 392	Men of Fortune, 395	Verbs and Diction, 396 DLS, 386 Verbs, 395 Verb Choice, 396	Meaning Clues, 395 Precise Word Meanings, 388 Root Word Meanings, 390
TV Talk Show, 408 Fashion Update, 408 Art Connection, 408 Art Appreciation, 398, 401 Speaking and Listening, 405	Initiation in Publishing, 408	Verb Tenses, 409 DLS, 397 Verb Tenses, 408	Context Clues, 408 Context Clues, 402 Word Origins, 404
	Activity Link: Initiation, 410 Inquiry and Research, 410		
Civil Rights, 418 Author Activity, 418 Dramatic Reading, 412 Art Appreciation, 414		DLS, 411 Helping Verbs, 418	Assessment Practice, 418 Analogies, 415 Idioms and Figurative Language, 419
Radio Play, 438 Storyboard, 438 Dramatic Reading, 434	Escape to Freedom, 438 Author Activity, 438	DLS, 433 Modal Forms of Verbs, 435	
Cultural References, 443 Chinese Immigration, 443 Art Appreciation, 440		DLS, 439 Verbs, 443	
		Logical Order of Details, 449 Correct Verb Forms, 449 Revising and Editing, 450	

PART 2 SKILLS TRACE

Features and Selections	Literary Analysis	Reading and Critical Thinking	Writing Opportunities	
MEMOIR A Celebration of Grandfathers **Difficulty Level:** ***Average***	Author's Perspective and Tone, 455, 460 Review: Style, 460	Author's Purpose, 455, 460 Informal Assess., 458	Character Sketch, 461 Living History, 461	
POETRY Fifth Grade Autobiography **Difficulty Level:** ***Average*** Remembered **Difficulty Level:** ***Average***	Imagery, 462, 466 Review: Personification, 466	Analyzing Effects of Word Choice, 462, 466 Test Practice, 465	Diary Entry, 467 Photo Poem, 467	
SHORT STORY The Study of History **Difficulty Level:** ***Average***	Characterization, 468, 479 Test Practice, 478	Making Inferences About Characters, 468, 479	Letters of Love, 480 Autobiographical Tale, 480	
Real World Link Were You Born That Way?		Magazine Article: Taking Notes, 482		
ESSAY Teacher Who Changed My Life **Difficulty Level:** ***Easy*** Building Vocabulary	Audience, 484, 491	Fact from Nonfact, 484, 491 Informal Assess., 489	Character Sketch, 492 Oral History Notes, 492	
AUTHOR STUDY Alice Walker				
SHORT STORY Everyday Use **Difficulty Level:** ***Average***	Conflict / Resolution, 503, 513	Drawing Conclusions, 503, 513 Test Practice, 512	Memo, 514 Sequel, 514 Comparison, 514	
POETRY Women Poem at Thirty-Nine **Difficulty Level:** ***Average***	Diction, 516, 520	Denotation / Connotation, 516, 520 Test Practice, 519		
ESSAY In Search of Our Mothers' Gardens **Difficulty Level:** ***Average***	Author's Perspective, 522, 527	Main Idea, 522, 527 Generalizations, 527 Test Practice, 526		
The Author's Style Author Study Project	Analysis of Style, 528		Imitating Style, 528 Changing Style, 528 Personal Response, 529 Praise Poem, 529	
Communication Workshop: Oral History		Analyzing a Professional Model, 531	Oral History, 532	
Reflect and Assess: The Search for Identity	Plot Structure, 537	Classifying Experiences of Youth, 536 Analyzing Author's Perspective, 537	Nominating a Guest Speaker, 536 Building Your Portfolio 537	

LEGEND **DLS – Daily Language SkillBuilder**
CCL – Cross Curricular Link
Green type – Teacher's Edition

Speaking and Listening Viewing and Representing	Inquiry and Research	Grammar, Usage, and Mechanics	Vocabulary
Storytelling, 461 Art Appreciation, 456	Tales of Taos, 461 Demographic Survey, 461	DLS, 455 Verbs, 461	Word Origins, 459
Character Portrait, 467 Speaker's Eulogy, 467 Dramatic Reading, 464		DLS, 462 Figurative Language, 467	
Storyboard, 480 Art Appreciation, 472, 474	Nature and Nurture, 480	Precise Verbs, 481 DLS, 468 Verb Choices, 476 Gerunds and Gerund Phrases, 480	Test Practice, 480 Context Clues, 470 Meaning of Roots, 473
	Activity Link: The Study of History, 483 Inquiry and Research, 482		
Monologue, 492 Qualities List, 492 Photo Essay, 492 Author Activity, 493 Viewing and Representing, 490	A Nation Torn, 492	Participles, 493 DLS, 484 Verb Tenses, 492	Test Practice, 492 Context Clues, 486 Meanings of Roots, 488 Denotation and Connotation, 494
Story Quilt, 514 Reader's Theater, 514 Oral History, 514 Family Art, 514 Art Connection, 514 Art Appreciation, 504, 508 Analyzing a Performance Review, 513	Sharecropping System, 514 Black Pride Movement, 514	Active and Passive Voice, 515 DLS, 503 Active and Passive Voice, 514	Context Clues, 506 Analogies, 510
		DLS, 516 Inactive Verbs, 518	
		DLS, 522 Possessives, 528	Context Clues, 524
Speaking and Listening, 528 Unsung Heroes, 529 Quilt Display, 529	Women's Voices, 529 Celebrating the Cultural Arts, 529		
		Unity and Coherence, 534 Punctuating Materials, 534 Revising and Editing, 535	

UNIT THREE
RESOURCE MANAGEMENT GUIDE
PART 1

To introduce the theme/literary period of this unit, use Fine Art Transparencies T23–25 in the Communications Transparencies and Copymasters.

	Unit Resource Book	Assessment	Integrated Technology and Media	*Additional Support* Literary Analysis Transparencies
One Thousand Dollars *pp. 386–396*	• Summary p. 4 • Active Reading p. 5 • Literary Analysis p. 6 • Words to Know p. 7 • Grammar p. 8 • Selection Quiz p. 9	• Selection Test, Formal Assessment pp. 63–64 Test Generator	Audio Library	• Plot T1
Initiation *pp. 397–409*	• Summary p. 10 • Active Reading p. 11 • Literary Analysis p. 12 • Words to Know p. 13 • Grammar p. 14 • Selection Quiz p. 15	• Selection Test, Formal Assessment pp. 65–66 Test Generator	Audio Library	• Plot: Conflict T12
Getting a Job *from* **I Know Why the Caged Bird Sings** *pp. 411–418*	• Summary p. 16 • Active Reading p. 17 • Literary Analysis p. 18 • Words to Know p. 19 • Selection Quiz p. 20	• Selection Test, Formal Assessment pp. 67–68 Test Generator	Audio Library Research Starter www.mcdougallittell.com	• Types of Nonfiction T4
Exile *pp. 433–438*	• Active Reading p. 22 • Literary Analysis p. 23	• Selection Test, Formal Assessment pp. 69–70 Test Generator	Audio Library LaserLinks, Teacher's SourceBook p. 27	• Poetry: Form T7
Lost Sister *pp. 439–443*	• Active Reading p. 24 • Literary Analysis p. 25 • Comparing Literature p. 26	• Selection Test, Formal Assessment p. 71 Test Generator	Audio Library	• Symbols and Figurative Language T21

Writing Workshop: Career Search Report

Unit Three Resource Book
- Prewriting p. 27
- Drafting and Elaboration p. 28
- Peer Response Guide pp. 29–30
- Revising, Editing, and Proofreading p. 31
- Student Models pp. 32–37
- Rubric for Evaluation p. 38

Writing Coach

Writing Transparencies and Copymasters T11, T20, C29

Teacher's Guide to Assessment and Portfolio Use

Unit Assessment
- Unit Three, Part 1 Test, Formal Assessment pp. 73–74

Test Generator

- Unit Three Integrated Test, Integrated Assessment pp. 13–18

Unit Technology

ClassZone www.mcdougallittell.com

Electronic Teacher Tools

Electronic Library

T = Transparency C = Copymaster

Reading and Critical Thinking Transparencies	Grammar Transparencies and Copymasters	Vocabulary Transparencies and Copymasters	Writing Transparencies and Copymasters	Communications Transparencies and Copymasters
• Sequencing T13	• Daily Language SkillBuilder T12 • Using Verbs: Principal Parts C129 • Verb Choice C137	• Using Reference Materials C46 • Meanings of Roots C47	• Achieving Coherence T8 • Cause and Effect C31	• Impromptu Speaking: Dialogue, Role-Play, Debate T13
• Chronological Order T11 • Sequence Chain T49	• Daily Language SkillBuilder T12 • Verb Tenses I C127	• Context Clues C48 • Word Origins C49	• Achieving Unity T7 • The Uses of Dialogue T24	• Evaluating Roles in Groups T8 • Interviewing T9 • Impromptu Speaking: Dialogue, Role-Play, Debate T13
• Cause and Effect T1 • Notetaking T40	• Daily Language SkillBuilder T13 • Auxiliary Verbs C69	• Analogies C50	• Effective Language T13 • Levels of Language T12 • Showing, Not Telling T22	• Formal Presentations T10
• Organizational Chart: Horizontal T51	• Daily Language SkillBuilder T13 • Modal Forms of Verbs C136		• Writing Process T1–4 • Figurative Language and Sound Devices T15 • Poem C27	• Dramatic Reading T12
• Organizational Chart: Horizontal T51	• Daily Language SkillBuilder T14		• Writing Process T1–4 • Sensory Word List T14	

STUDENTS ACQUIRING ENGLISH

The **Spanish Study Guide,** pp. 80–97, includes language support for the following pages:
- Family and Community Involvement (per unit)
- Selection Summaries and Vocabulary
- Active Reading
- Literary Analysis

UNIT THREE
RESOURCE MANAGEMENT GUIDE
PART 2

To introduce the theme/literary period of this unit, use Fine Art Transparencies T23–25 in the Communications Transparencies and Copymasters.

	Unit Resource Book	Assessment	Integrated Technology and Media	Additional Support: Literary Analysis Transparencies
A Celebration of Grandfathers *pp. 455–461*	• Summary p. 39 • Active Reading p. 40 • Literary Analysis p. 41 • Selection Quiz p. 42	• Selection Test, Formal Assessment pp. 75–76 Test Generator	Audio Library Research Starter www.mcdougallittell.com	• Author's Perspective T13
Fifth Grade Autobiography Remembered *pp. 462–467*	• Active Reading p. 43 • Literary Analysis p. 44	• Selection Test, Formal Assessment pp. 77–78 Test Generator	Audio Library	• Poetry: Imagery T9
The Study of History *pp. 468–481*	• Summary p. 45 • Active Reading p. 46 • Literary Analysis p. 47 • Words to Know p. 48 • Grammar p. 49 • Selection Quiz p. 50	• Selection Test, Formal Assessment pp. 79–80 Test Generator	Audio Library LaserLinks, Teacher's SourceBook p. 28	• Character T2
The Teacher Who Changed My Life *pp. 484–493*	• Summary p. 51 • Active Reading p. 52 • Literary Analysis p. 53 • Words to Know p. 54 • Grammar p. 55 • Selection Quiz p. 56	• Selection Test, Formal Assessment pp. 81–82 Test Generator	Audio Library LaserLinks, Teacher's SourceBook p. 29 Research Starter www.mcdougallittell.com	• Style, Voice, Diction, Purpose T22
Everyday Use *pp. 503–515*	• Summary p. 58 • Active Reading p. 59 • Literary Analysis p. 60 • Words to Know p. 61 • Grammar p. 62 • Selection Quiz p. 63	• Selection Test, Formal Assessment pp. 83–84 Test Generator	Audio Library NetActivities	• Plot: Conflict T12
Women **Poem at Thirty-Nine** *pp. 516–521*	• Active Reading p. 64 • Literary Analysis p. 65	• Selection Test, Formal Assessment pp. 85–86 Test Generator	Audio Library NetActivities	• Style, Voice, Diction, Purpose T22
***from* In Search of Our Mothers' Gardens** *pp. 522–529*	• Summary p. 66 • Active Reading p. 67 • Literary Analysis p. 68 • Words to Know p. 69 • Selection Quiz p. 70	• Selection Test, Formal Assessment pp. 87–88 Test Generator	Research Starter www.mcdougallittell.com NetActivities	• Author's Perspective T13

Communication Workshop: Oral History	Unit Assessment	Unit Technology
Unit Three Resource Book • Conducting Your Interview p. 71 • Planning and Drafting p. 72 • Peer Response Guide pp. 73–74 • Revising, Editing, and Proofreading p. 75 • Student Model p. 76 • Rubric for Evaluation p. 77	• Unit Three, Part 2 Test, Formal Assessment pp. 89–90 • Mid-Year Test, Formal Assessment pp. 91–99 Test Generator • Unit Three Integrated Test, Integrated Assessment pp. 13–18	ClassZone www.mcdougallittell.com Electronic Teacher Tools Electronic Library

T = Transparency C = Copymaster

Reading and Critical Thinking Transparencies	Grammar Transparencies and Copymasters	Vocabulary Transparencies and Copymasters	Writing Transparencies and Copymasters	Communications Transparencies and Copymasters
• Determining Author's Purpose and Audience T19 • Organizing and Interpreting Information on Statistical Tables T35	• Daily Language SkillBuilder T14 • Commonly Confused Verbs C138	• Word Meanings C51	• Generating Writing Ideas T1 • Elaboration T10	• Impromptu Speaking: Dialogue, Role-Play, Debate T13
	• Daily Language SkillBuilder T15 • Figurative Language C180		• Figurative Language and Sound Devices T15 • Poem C27	• Evaluating Roles in Groups T8 • Verbal Strategies T14
• Making Inferences T7 • Cluster Diagram T48	• Daily Language SkillBuilder T15 • Gerunds and Gerund Phrases C105 • Verb Choice C176	• Context Clues C52 • Word Origins C53	• Writing Process T1–4 • Writing Structure T8, T10, T11 • Point of View T23 • Autobiographical Incident C34	
• Fact vs. Opinion T3	• Daily Language SkillBuilder T16 • Verb Tenses II C128	• Context Clues C54 • Word Origins C55	• Showing, Not Telling T22 • Elaboration T10	• Dramatic Reading T12 • Nonverbal Strategies T15
• Drawing Conclusions T4	• Daily Language SkillBuilder T16 • Active and Passive Voice C135	• Context Clues C56 • Analogies C57	• Levels of Language T12 • Effective Language T13	• Interviewing T9 • Dramatic Reading T12 • Impromptu Speaking: Dialogue, Role-Play, Debate T13
• Organizational Chart: Horizontal T51	• Daily Language SkillBuilder T17 • Inactive Verbs: *To Be* C177			
• Main Idea and Supporting Details T12	• Daily Language SkillBuilder T17 • Possessive Nouns C66	• Context Clues C58	• Varying Sentence Openers and Closers T18 • Poem C27	

STUDENTS ACQUIRING ENGLISH

The **Spanish Study Guide,** pp. 98–118, includes language support for the following pages:

- Family and Community Involvement (per unit)
- Selection Summaries and Vocabulary
- Active Reading
- Literary Analysis

UNIT THREE

DAILY LANGUAGE SKILLBUILDERS

Selection	SkillBuilder Sentences	Suggested Answers
One Thousand Dollars	**1.** Do you think William Sydney Porter, known better by his pen name O. Henry liked surprises. **2.** After being accused of robing the First National bank in Austin Texas he fled to Honduras in central America.	**1.** Do you think William Sydney Porter, known better by his pen name O. Henry**,** liked surprises**?** **2.** After being accused of **robbing** the First National **B**ank in Austin**,** Texas**,** he fled to Honduras in **C**entral America.
Initiation	**1.** If you was in the same position as Millicent" would you have been making the same choice." Lee asked her frend Joanie. **2.** "I don't know" joanie answered, it took a lot of currage"	**1.** "If you **were** in the same position as Millicent**,** would you **have made** the same choice**?**" Lee asked her **friend** Joanie. **2.** "I don't know**,**" **J**oanie answered**. "I**t took a lot of courage."
Getting a Job	**1.** "it wasnt fair that Maya Angelou can't get a job just because she was black, said Lola. **2.** "I agree. Raul answer—"it seems like the discrimination she is experiencing made her even more determined.	**1.** "**It wasn't** fair that Maya Angelou **couldn't** get a job just because she was black**,"** said Lola. **2.** "I agree**,"** Raul **answered. "I**t seems like the discrimination she **experienced** made her even more determined**."**
Exile	**1.** I wonder, what it would be like to leave you're home in the middle of the night," wondered Joe. Ill bet Alvarez was scared." **2.** "Its a good thing her family was with her. Eleanor said."" At least she wasnt travel alone."	**1.** **"**I wonder what it would be like to leave **your** home in the middle of the night," wondered Joe. **"I'll** bet Alvarez was scared." **2.** "**It's** a good thing her family was with her**,"** Eleanor said**.** "At least she **wasn't traveling** alone."

DAILY LANGUAGE SKILLBUILDERS

Selection	SkillBuilder Sentences	Suggested Answers
Lost Sister	**1.** I reluctant to leave the united States for another countrie **2.** My freind Suzanne miss her Grandmother in China.	**1.** I **am** reluctant to leave the **U**nited States for another **country.** **2.** My **friend** Suzanne **misses** her **g**randmother in China.
A Celebration of Grandfathers	**1.** Living in a small agricultural community, a person feels close to the earth and in control of their world. **2.** Anayas memoir is about his grandfather, that was a wise, strong man.	**1.** Living in a small agricultural community, a person feels close to the earth and in control of **his or her** world. **2.** Anaya**'s** memoir is about his grandfather, **who** was a wise, strong man.
Fifth Grade Autobiography Remembered	**1.** Poet's sometimes remember there past in their work. **2.** Getting to know ones Grandfather is often a wonderfull experience.	**1.** **Poets** sometimes remember **their** past in their work. **2.** Getting to know one**'s** **g**randfather is often a **wonderful** experience.
The Study of History	**1.** Last Summer, Jeremiahs grandfather, a navajo, taught him how make fry bread. **2.** Maria, who's Mother emigrated from Italy to the United States when she was a child. Plans to take her daughter to Italy next year to visit her relatives.	**1.** Last **s**ummer, Jeremiah**'s** grandfather, a **N**avajo, taught him how **to** make fry bread. **2.** Maria, **whose m**other emigrated from Italy to the United States **as a child, p**lans to take her daughter to Italy next year to visit her relatives.

DAILY LANGUAGE SKILLBUILDERS

Selection	SkillBuilder Sentences	Suggested Answers
The Teacher Who Changed My Life	**1.** A teacher can exerts a powerful influence on students lives **2.** students must take advantage of oportunities to learn.	**1.** A teacher can **exert** a powerful influence on students**'** lives. **2.** **S**tudents must take advantage of **opportunities** to learn.
Everyday Use	**1.** The south were a good place to grow tobacco cause of it's rich soil said uncle Joe. **2.** In many towns the women gathers and held quilting bees.	**1.** "The **S**outh **was** a good place to grow tobacco **because** of **its** rich soil," said **U**ncle Joe. **2.** In many towns the women **gathered** and held quilting bees.
Women Poem at Thirty-Nine	**1.** Alice Walker learn a great deal from her parents. **2.** The women in Walker's mothers generation were real strong.	**1.** Alice Walker **learned** a great deal from her parents. **2.** The women in Walker's mother**'s** generation were **really** strong.
In Search of Our Mother's Gardens	**1.** Many woman of the past were very strong. **2.** Walkers mother enjoyed planting flower's.	**1.** Many **women** of the past were very strong. **2.** Walker**'s** mother enjoyed planting **flowers**.

INTEGRATING GRAMMAR AND LITERATURE: GRAMMAR PLANNER

Grammar Focus by Unit	Unit One	Unit Two	Unit Three	Unit Four	Unit Five	Unit Six
	Parts of Speech	The Sentence and Its Parts	Verbs and Verbals	Phrases	Clauses	Special Sentence Structures

The Language of Literature offers several options for integrating grammar instruction and literature.

- Each unit has a specific grammar focus. The grammar focus for this unit is highlighted on the planning chart. Categories of grammar skills for this unit are shown in red.
- The Pupil's Edition includes instructive features entitled *Grammar in Context*. The instruction in these features arises from the selections and relates to the grammar focus for each unit.
- The Writing Workshops in the Pupil's Edition include grammar tips that help students produce error-free drafts.
- Mini Lessons in the Teacher's Edition complement the instruction in the *Grammar in Context* features. Additional Mini Lessons relate to the grammar focus for each unit as well as to the literature.
- Daily Language SkillBuilders in the Teacher's Edition provide students with ongoing proofreading practice and reinforce punctuation, spelling, grammar and usage, and capitalization.
- Grammar Copymasters and Transparencies, which may be used independently or in conjunction with Mini Lessons in the Teacher's Edition, present grammar in a traditional, systematic sequence.

PE instruction shown in black
TE Mini Lessons shown in green

Part 1

Parts of Speech
Helping Verbs
"Getting a Job," p. 418

Using Clauses
Sentence Fragments
Writing Workshop, p. 450

Verb Usage
Verb Tenses
"Initiation," p. 409
"Initiation," pp. 408–409

Using Verbs (Principal Parts)
"One Thousand Dollars," p. 395

Forming Tenses with Irregular Verbs
"One Thousand Dollars, p. 396
Writing Workshop, p. 450

Using Verbs: Voice
"Lost Sister," p. 443

Modal Forms of Verbs
"Exile," p. 435

Using Modifiers
Avoiding Misplaced and Dangling Modifiers
Writing Workshop, p. 450

Capitalization
Writing Workshop, p. 450

Part 2

Parts of Speech
Possessives
from *In Search of Our Mothers' Gardens,* p. 528
Communication Workshop, p. 535

Using Phrases
Participles
"The Teacher Who Changed My Life," p. 493

Gerunds and Gerund Phrases
"The Study of History," pp. 480–481

Verb Usage
Verb Tenses
"The Teacher Who Changed My Life," pp. 492–493

Verb Choices
"One Thousand Dollars," p. 396

Active and Passive Voice
"Everyday Use," p. 515
"Everyday Use," pp. 514–515

Commonly Confused Verbs
"A Celebration of Grandfathers," p. 461

Using Modifiers
Comparative and Superlative Modifiers
Communication Workshop, p. 535

Avoiding Double Negatives
Communication Workshop, p. 535

Other Punctuation
Punctuating Dialogue
Communication Workshop, p. 535

Style
Verb Choices (Choosing Precise Verbs)
"The Study of History," p. 481
"The Study of History," pp. 476–477

Inactive Verbs: To Be
"Women," "Poem at Thirty-Nine," p. 518

Figurative Language
"Fifth Grade Autobiography," "Remembered, " p. 467

PART 1 The Experience of Youth

Young or old, we all talk about experiences from our younger days. Though we continue to learn throughout our lives, youth is a time when our experiences shape our values and our understanding of the world. In this part of Unit Three, you will explore the ways in which early experiences shape and influence the lives of young people.

ACTIVITY

Interview a classmate about an early experience that had a strong influence on him or her. Record the results of your interview, and then have the same classmate interview you. Share with the rest of the class what both of you learned from the interviews. In discussion, consider why different kinds of events influence people as strongly as they do.

The Sheridan Theatre (1937), Edward Hopper. Oil on canvas, 17⅛″ × 25¼″. Collection of The Newark (New Jersey) Museum (40.118). The Newark Museum/Art Resource, New York.

382

LEARNING the Language of Literature

Plot refers to the chain of related events that take place in a story. Think of the plot as a blueprint for how the story unfolds: what happens, where it happens, how and when it happens, and to whom it happens. Usually, the events of a plot progress because of a **conflict,** or struggle between opposing forces. Although many types of plots exist, most follow these stages: **exposition, rising action, climax,** and **falling action.** Use the following passages to learn more about the elements of plot.

Exposition

The **exposition** lays the groundwork for the plot by providing the reader with essential background information. Characters are introduced and the plot begins to unfold. The **setting**—the time and place in which the events occur—also is described during the exposition. Although the exposition generally appears at the opening of a story, it may also occur later in the narrative.

YOUR TURN Read this passage and determine what details provide essential background information for the story. Share your ideas in a class discussion.

EXPOSITION

Thirty-five years ago I was out prospecting on the Stanislaus, tramping all day long with pick and pan and horn, and washing a hatful of dirt here and there, always expecting to make a rich strike, and never doing it. It was a lovely region, woodsy, balmy, delicious, and had once been populous, long years before, but now the people had vanished and the charming paradise was a solitude.

—Mark Twain, "The Californian's Tale"

PLOT AT A GLANCE

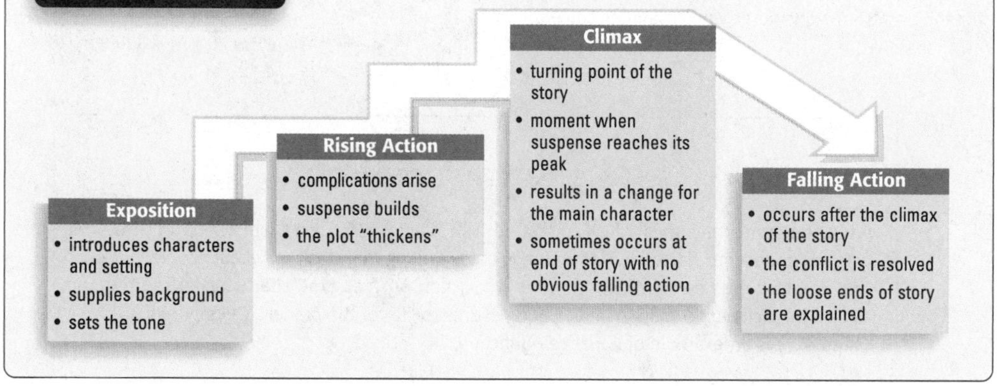

Exposition
• introduces characters and setting
• supplies background
• sets the tone
Rising Action
• complications arise
• suspense builds
• the plot "thickens"
Climax
• turning point of the story
• moment when suspense reaches its peak
• results in a change for the main character
• sometimes occurs at end of story with no obvious falling action
Falling Action
• occurs after the climax of the story
• the conflict is resolved
• the loose ends of story are explained

OVERVIEW

Objectives

- understand the following literary terms:
  - exposition
  - rising action
  - climax
  - falling action
  - narrative nonfiction
- analyze details for how they contribute background information to a story
- analyze actions in terms of conflict and climax

Teaching the Lesson

This lesson analyzes terms related to plot in fiction and narrative nonfiction and shows how actions in a story are structured in terms of exposition, rising action, climax, and falling action.

Introducing the Concepts

Have students recount stories they are familiar with from literature and film that involve exciting conflicts and satisfying resolutions. Ask them to describe what makes a story satisfying.

Presenting the Concepts

Exposition

Point out that sometimes exposition involves an author explaining the background necessary to understand a situation, but most often this information is conveyed indirectly. Usually, the characters' dialogue and actions provide details and clues about what is to come.

YOUR TURN The narrator is recalling events from years ago: he was a gold miner who didn't strike it rich but who seems to have enjoyed the beauty of the isolated setting where he searched for gold.

Rising Action
Have students discuss examples of conflict from stories they have read in class. What kinds of conflict are more predominant—internal or external?

YOUR TURN Owen's wife cannot find her husband and begins to feel nervous anxiety.

Climax
Explain that the climax of a story is almost always a dramatic scene that does not include exposition.

YOUR TURN The turning point is Lalla's decision to break off the engagement.

Falling Action
Point out that the falling action or dénouement of a plot is usually short. Sometimes, if the tension of the conflict has been drawn out to the very last moment, the falling action may not even occur until the final sentence of the story.

Narrative Nonfiction
Since fictional technique involves bringing readers close to the living moment of a character's experience, nonfiction can be greatly enhanced by the same technique. When reading narrative nonfiction, have students identify the fictional elements they recognize.

Rising Action

As the story progresses, complications usually arise, causing difficulties for the main characters. Key conflicts become more difficult to resolve. As the characters struggle to find solutions to the conflict, **suspense,** or tension, builds.

YOUR TURN What conflict is evident in the excerpt at the right?

RISING ACTION THROUGH CONFLICT

"But where is he? Is there anything the matter with him?" She [Owen's wife] ran to the door and called out into the dark. But there was no answer. . . . She stood there trying to think. . . . She might as well go home, she thought. Wherever he was, he wasn't here. "If he comes back, Brigid, tell him I was here looking for him," she said. "I'll go home through the other field."

Brigid said something then that made her turn sharply and look at her.

"What did you say?"

"Tell him yourself," said Brigid.

—Mary Lavin, "Brigid"

Climax

The **climax** is the turning point of the action. It is the moment when the story's intensity—and the reader's interest—reaches its highest point. The climax of the story usually involves an important event, decision, or discovery that affects the final outcome.

YOUR TURN In this passage, what important decision signals the turning point or climax of the story?

CLIMAX

A short time later the telephone rang. But it wasn't Lalla, explaining where they were, it was a call from London and it was Allan Sutton.

"I have to speak to Lalla."

His voice sounded frantic. I said cautiously, "Is anything wrong?"

"She's broken off our engagement. I got back from the office and found a letter from her and my ring. She said she was coming home. She doesn't want to get married."

—Rosemunde Pilcher, "Lalla"

Falling Action

The **falling action** consists of the events that occur after the climax. Often, the conflict is resolved, and the intensity of the action subsides. Sometimes this phase of the plot is referred to as the **dénouement**, from a French word that means "untying." It is during this stage that the plot is untangled, with any lingering questions answered and mysteries solved.

Narrative Nonfiction

While the term *plot* is most often associated with fiction, it also is a characteristic of some types of nonfiction. **Narrative nonfiction** is prose writing that deals with real people, places, and events. It uses elements typically found in fiction, such as **plot, character,** and **setting** to present factual information and to bring events to life for the reader. "Getting a Job" (page 411) is an example of narrative nonfiction.

The Active Reader: Skills and Strategies

Just as builders rely on blueprints to guide their work, writers of both fiction and nonfiction rely on an overall structure to make their ideas clear. Your job as a reader is to clarify the relationships among ideas and events in a written text—and the strategies here can help.

Linking Ideas Within Texts

Determining chronological order, recognizing cause-and-effect relationships, and identifying comparisons and contrasts can help readers to spot the related ideas or events in a text.

1 Understanding Chronological Order

- **Chronological order,** or time order, is the sequence in which events occur.
- In nonfiction, look for clue words that signal shifts in time. Examples of clue words are *before, during, after, first, second, next,* and *last.*
- Be aware that a writer may interrupt the chronological flow of events by using a flashback to provide background information.
- Use a graphic like the one shown for "Brigid" to keep track of each event as it is introduced.

Beginning Event

Event 1
Owen and his wife quarrel.

↓

Event 2

↓

Final Outcome

Event 3

2 Recognizing Cause-and-Effect Relationships

- A **cause** is an event or action that directly results in another event or action. An **effect** is the direct outcome of an event.
- Be aware that many nonfiction works are structured to show cause-and-effect relationships between major events or ideas.

> Clue words that signal cause: *because, since, therefore, if/then*
> Clue words that signal effect: *brought about, led to, as a result, consequently*

- Keep in mind that, in fiction, cause-and-effect relationships are often the key to understanding how a plot advances, what motivates characters, and how a conflict begins.
- Remember that a single cause may have several effects. In turn, each of those effects may be the cause of yet another effect.

3 Making Comparisons and Contrasts

- **Comparisons** and **contrasts** are devised by writers to show similarities and differences among things, persons, events, and written works.
- Clue words are helpful in making comparisons and contrasts, as well as in analyzing cause and effect.

> Comparison clue words: *all, each, both, similar, likewise, same*
> Contrast clue words: *on the other hand, however, different, even though*

- As you read, **question** how one idea or event is similar to or different from another.
- In fiction, compare and contrast characters or compare and contrast one particular character at the beginning and at the end of a story.
- Use graphic organizers such as charts and Venn diagrams to make both comparisons and contrasts.

Need More Help?

Remember that active readers use the essential reading strategies explained on page 7 **visualize, predict, clarify, question, connect, evaluate, monitor.**

The Active Reader: Skills and Strategies

OVERVIEW

Objectives

- recognize how cause-and-effect relationships, chronological order, and comparisons and contrasts link related ideas or events
- use graphics, including charts and Venn diagrams, to organize information

Teaching the Lesson

The strategies on this page will help students learn and apply skills that can be used to link related ideas in both fiction and nonfiction.

Presenting the Strategies

Help students understand the basic logic of each strategy by giving examples drawn from everyday life.

1 Understanding Chronological Order
Point out that transition words and phrases such as *now, then,* and *I remember* will indicate whether a section of narrative is situated in the present of the story or in the past.

A sample completion of the chart could look like this:

Event 1
Owen and his wife quarrel.
Event 2
Owen dies.
Event 3
Owen's wife brings Brigid home with her.

2 Recognizing Cause-and-Effect Relationships
To help students understand cause-and-effect relationships, describe a story full of action such as "No Witchcraft for Sale." Have students identify an action that causes an effect (By refusing to tell people how he heals Teddy's sight, Gideon upsets the Farquars; the cause is refusing to tell, the effect is the upset.)

3 Making Comparisons and Contrasts
Have students create three Venn diagrams in which they compare and contrast one character with three others.

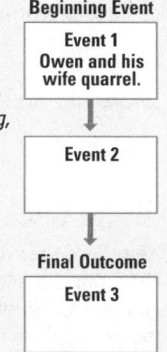

OVERVIEW

This selection is included in the Grade 10 InterActive Reader.

Objectives

1. understand and appreciate a **short story (Literary Analysis)**
2. analyze **plot** development **(Literary Analysis)**
3. analyze **cause and effect** in fiction **(Active Reading)**

Summary

A dismayed Bobby Gillian must decide what to do with the $1,000 that his deceased uncle willed to him. Furthermore, he has to account for what he does with the money. Having lived well on an allowance from his very wealthy uncle, he is not accustomed to keeping such records. He asks the advice of several people, but in the end decides to give the money to Miss Hayden, his uncle's ward, whom he loves. When he learns that he will inherit an additional $50,000 if he has spent the $1,000 unselfishly, or wisely, he claims that he has lost the money at the races. This act allows Miss Hayden to inherit the entire sum.

Thematic Link

The youthful Gillian has already learned from experience and observation that money does not ensure happiness or good character.

Editor's Note This selection has been edited slightly to delete material that may be considered objectionable.

5-Minute Warm-Up

Daily Language SkillBuilder

Have students **proofread** the display sentences on page 381i and write them correctly. The sentences also appear on Transparency 12 of **Grammar Transparencies and Copymasters.**

Mini Lesson Preteaching Vocabulary

If you would like to preteach the WORDS TO KNOW for this selection, use the Mini Lesson, p. 388.

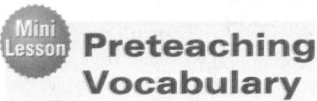

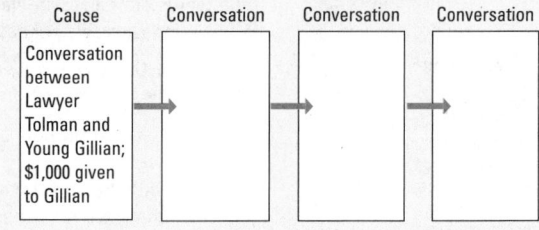

One Thousand Dollars

Short Story by O. HENRY

"Now, what can a man possibly do with a thousand dollars?"

Connect to Your Life

Instant Wealth Many people dream about inheriting a large sum of money because they like to imagine how extra money would improve their lives. If you were to inherit a significant amount of money, what would be a responsible way of spending it? What ways might be less responsible? How might your choices affect your life? Compare your answers with those of your classmates.

Build Background

New York, New York A city of contrasts, New York City at the beginning of the 1900s was a bustling center of 4 million people. While many people struggled to make a living, the wealthy few lived a life of leisure and were often more concerned about their social standing than the plight of the less fortunate. In 1906, O. Henry published a collection of short stories set entirely in New York City. He titled his work *The Four Million* because he was convinced that everyone in the city, rich or poor, had a story worth telling.

The following selection, set in New York City during this era, opens just as the main character has inherited $1,000 from his wealthy uncle. This sum of money would have bought much more in 1900 than it would today. For example, a new car in 1900 cost about $600, while a newspaper and a glass of cola each cost about 5 cents. The average industrial worker earned only about $490 for an entire year of labor; a postal worker earned about 37 cents an hour.

WORDS TO KNOW
Vocabulary Preview

acquaint	pendant
disreputable	precariousness
encumber	prudent
expenditure	stipulate
genially	venerable

Focus Your Reading

LITERARY ANALYSIS PLOT The **plot,** or the sequence of related events in a story, usually follows a pattern. It begins with the **exposition,** in which important background information is given. Next, during the **rising action,** the **characters** and **conflict** are developed. This leads to the **climax,** or the **turning point** of the action. The **falling action** consists of events that occur after the climax.

As you read this story, notice how the plot advances in stages, with every event contributing to the main character's decision about what to do with his money.

ACTIVE READING CAUSE AND EFFECT Events in a plot are often related by **cause and effect.** One event in the story can cause another, which is the effect. The effect may in turn cause another event, and so on.

READER'S NOTEBOOK The events in this story unfold through a series of related conversations, with each one leading directly to the next. Create a graphic like the one started below to give a brief summary of each conversation and to show how the conversations are related.

Cause	Conversation	Conversation	Conversation
Conversation between Lawyer Tolman and Young Gillian; $1,000 given to Gillian →	→	→	

LESSON RESOURCES

UNIT THREE RESOURCE BOOK, pp. 4–9

ASSESSMENT RESOURCES
Formal Assessment, pp. 63–64
Teacher's Guide to Assessment and Portfolio Use
Test Generator

SKILLS TRANSPARENCIES AND COPYMASTERS
Literary Analysis
- Plot, T1 (for Literary Analysis, p. 386)

Reading and Critical Thinking
- Sequencing, T13 (for Reader's Notebook, p. 386)

Grammar
- Using Verbs: Principal Parts, C129 (for Mini Lesson, p. 395)
- Verb Choice, C137 (for Mini Lesson, p. 396)

Vocabulary
- Using Reference Materials, C46 (for Mini Lesson, p. 388)
- Meanings of Roots, C47 (for Mini Lesson, p. 390)

Writing
- Achieving Coherence, T8 (for Writing Option 3, p. 395)
- Cause and Effect, C31 (for Writing Option 3, p. 395)

Communications
- Impromptu Speaking: Dialogue, Role-Play, Debate, T13 (for Activities & Explorations 2, p. 395)

INTEGRATED TECHNOLOGY
Audio Library
Visit our website:
www.mcdougallittell.com

ONE THOUSAND DOLLARS

O. HENRY

"One thousand dollars," repeated Lawyer Tolman, solemnly and severely, "and here is the money."

Young Gillian gave a decidedly amused laugh as he fingered the thin package of new fifty-dollar notes.

TEACHING THE LITERATURE

Customizing Instruction

Less Proficient Readers
Students can follow the plot of the story by paying close attention to what the characters do and say. Suggest that they notice the use of dialogue, since the plot advances through the conversations.

Set a Purpose Have students read to learn more about Gillian and the other characters he encounters.

Students Acquiring English
Explain that a will is a legal document that gives instructions about how a person wants his or her possessions distributed after he or she dies. Explain that wills can have very detailed and complicated instructions. Have students keep a list of questions about Uncle Gillian's will as the story progresses.

Use **Spanish Study Guide** pp. 83–85 for additional support.

Gifted and Talented
Have students write a script based on the story. Invite them to incorporate actual dialogue from the story.

BLOCK SCHEDULING: MANAGING TIME

If your schedule requires that you cover the lesson objectives in a shorter time, use . . .

- Preparing to Read, p. 386
- Thinking Through the Literature, p. 394
- Vocabulary in Action, p. 395
- Grammar in Context, p. 396

If you want to take advantage of longer class time, use . . .

- TE Teaching Options: Preteaching Vocabulary, p. 388; Vocabulary Strategy, p. 390; Viewing and Representing, p. 391 Speaking and Listening, p. 392; Standardized Test Practice, p. 393;
- Choices & Challenges and Author Activity, pp. 395–396

ONE THOUSAND DOLLARS 387

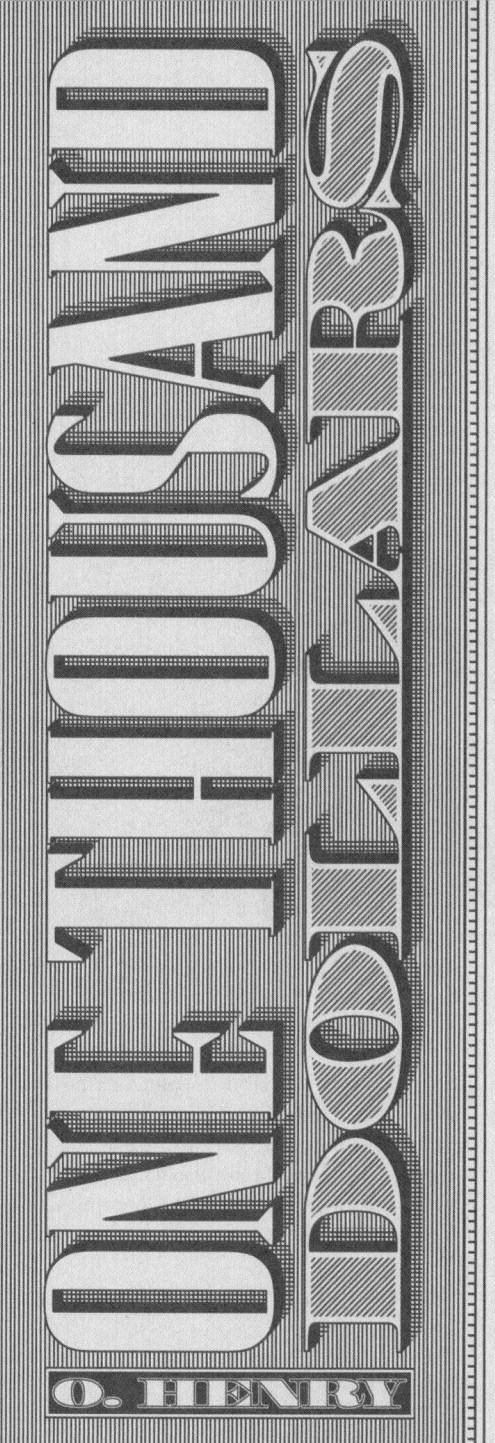

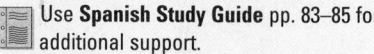

Reading and Analyzing

Reading Skills and Strategies:
PREVIEW
Briefly summarize the story emphasizing that the structure is based on a series of conversations with individual characters. Ask students to look for details that might explain the surprise ending.

Literary Analysis PLOT

Review the four stages of plot: exposition, rising action, climax, and falling action. Emphasize the importance of exposition in understanding how the plot unfolds. O. Henry immediately introduces the conflict, followed by the development of the exposition, in which more characters are introduced.

Use **Unit Three Resource Book** p. 6 for more practice.

Active Reading CAUSE AND EFFECT

A cause-and-effect relationship often shows how one event can cause another that is the effect. Then this effect can cause the next event. This relationship, a causal chain, structures the plot of this story.

Use **Unit Three Resource Book** p. 5 for more practice.

"It's such a confoundedly awkward amount," he explained, genially, to the lawyer. "If it had been ten thousand a fellow might wind up with a lot of fireworks and do himself credit. Even $50 would have been less trouble."

"You heard the reading of your uncle's will," continued Lawyer Tolman, professionally dry in his tones. "I do not know if you paid much attention to its details. I must remind you of one. You are required to render to us an account of the manner of expenditure of this $1,000 as soon as you have disposed of it. The will stipulates that. I trust that you will so far comply with the late Mr. Gillian's wishes."

"You may depend upon it," said the young man, politely, "in spite of the extra expense it will entail. I may have to engage a secretary. I was never good at accounts."

Gillian thrust the package of notes into his coat pocket and went to his club. There he hunted out one whom he called Old Bryson.

Old Bryson was calm and forty and sequestered.[1] He was in a corner reading a book, and when he saw Gillian approaching he sighed, laid down his book and took off his glasses.

"Old Bryson, wake up," said Gillian. "I've a funny story to tell you."

"I wish you would tell it to some one in the billiard-room," said Old Bryson. "You know how I hate your stories."

"This is a better one than usual," said Gillian, rolling a cigarette; "and I'm going to tell it to you. It's too sad and funny to go with

1. **sequestered:** solitary; alone.

WORDS TO KNOW
genially (jēn′yə-lē) *adv.* in a friendly manner
expenditure (ĭk-spĕn′də-chər) *n.* an act of spending
stipulate (stĭp′yə-lāt′) *v.* to state as a condition; specify

388

Teaching Options

Mini Lesson Preteaching Vocabulary

USING REFERENCE MATERIALS TO DETERMINE PRECISE WORD MEANINGS **Instruction** Explain that the dictionary definition of a word is called its *denotation*, while the emotions or attitudes associated with the word are its *connotation*. Some synonyms, like *genially* and *graciously*, may be very similar in denotation but have distinct connotations. Begin the following chart on the board to compare the connotations of the two words.

Exercises Have students use a thesaurus and dictionary to complete charts of their own, comparing each of the WORDS TO KNOW with a synonym chosen from the thesaurus.

Word	Denotation	Connotation
genially	in a sympathetic or kindly way	friendliness; cheerfulness
graciously	in a tactful or merciful way	politeness

Use **Unit Three Resource Book** p. 7 for more practice.

Courtesy Cluett, Peabody & Co., Inc.

the rattling of billiard balls. I've just come from my late uncle's firm of legal corsairs.[2] He leaves me an even thousand dollars. Now, what can a man possibly do with a thousand dollars?"

"I thought," said Old Bryson, showing as much interest as a bee shows in a vinegar cruet, "that the late Septimas Gillian was worth something like half a million."

"He was," assented Gillian, joyously, "and that's where the joke comes in. He's left his whole cargo of doubloons to a microbe. That is, part of it goes to the man who invents a new bacillus[3] and the rest to establish a hospital for doing away with it again. There are one or two trifling bequests on the side. The butler and the housekeeper get a seal ring and $10 each. His nephew gets $1,000."

"You've always had plenty of money to spend," observed Old Bryson.

"Tons," said Gillian. "Uncle was the fairy godmother as far as an allowance was concerned."

"Any other heirs?" asked Old Bryson.

"None." Gillian frowned at his cigarette and kicked the upholstered leather of a divan uneasily. "There is a Miss Hayden, a ward of my uncle, who lived in his house. She's a quiet thing—musical—the daughter of somebody who was unlucky enough to be his friend. I forgot to say that she was in on the seal ring and $10 joke, too. I wish I had been. Then I could have had two bottles of brut,[4] tipped the waiter with the ring and had the whole business off my hands. Don't be superior and insulting, old Bryson—tell me what a fellow can do with a thousand dollars."

2. **corsairs** (kôr′sârz′): pirates.

3. **bacillus** (bə-sĭl′əs): bacterium.

4. **brut** (bro͞ot): very dry (that is, not sweet) champagne.

Customizing Instruction

Less Proficient Readers

Use the following questions to help students understand Gillian's dilemma.

- Why isn't Gillian happy about inheriting $1,000 from his uncle?
  Possible Response: He thinks the amount is awkward—too much to spend easily and quickly, but too little to make him rich.
- What rule does Gillian have to follow when he decides how to spend the money?
  Possible Response: He has to tell his uncle's lawyers exactly how he spent all of it.

Set a Purpose Have students read to see what ideas other characters have about how Gillian could use his $1,000.

Students Acquiring English

Phrases and terms that may need some clarification: *vinegar cruet*—glass bottle holding vinegar for table use; *cargo of doubloons*—all his money; *trifling bequests*—small gifts from the will; *divan*—a small sofa; *ward*—a child or dependent person in the care of an adult who is not a relative.

Multiple Learning Styles

Kinesthetic

Have a student read the passage from "Gillian thrust the package of notes . . ." to " 'There is a Miss Hayden . . .' " aloud. Then have other students pantomime the body language and other nonverbal expressions that would make the characters of Gillian and Old Bryson come to life.

ONE THOUSAND DOLLARS **389**

Reading and Analyzing

Literary Analysis: CHARACTER

The character of Gillian is revealed by what he says, as well as what others say and think about him. Ask students to note the details that help define Gillian.

Possible Response: He is a carefree and irresponsible young man who is used to getting what he wants. He is good-natured, even flippant. Old Bryson doesn't like or respect Gillian.

Active Reading CAUSE AND EFFECT

A Ask students what effect the conversation with Old Bryson has on Gillian.

Possible Response: As a result, Gillian decides to pay Miss Lauriere a visit.

Reading Skills and Strategies: CLARIFYING

B Ask students to clarify Old Bryson's character by noticing what the narrator reveals, as well as what he says.

Possible Response: Old Bryson could be offensive; his suggestions seem sarcastic and reveal his dislike of Gillian.

Reading Skills and Strategies: CONNECTING

The early 20th century was the beginning of a new way of life in America. Industrial development resulted in many people moving from rural, agricultural areas to urban areas. Ask students to tell about where and how some of their ancestors lived during this period.

ACTIVE READING

C QUESTION Old Bryson thinks that Gillian is rather spoiled and irresponsible.

Old Bryson rubbed his glasses and smiled. And when Old Bryson smiled Gillian knew that he intended to be more offensive than ever.

"A thousand dollars," he said, "means much or little. One man may buy a happy home with it and laugh at Rockefeller.[5] Another could send his wife South with it and save her life. A thousand dollars would buy pure milk for one hundred babies during June, July, and August and save fifty of their lives. You could count upon a half hour's diversion with it at faro[6] in one of the fortified art galleries. It would furnish an education to an ambitious boy. I am told that a genuine Corot[7] was secured for that amount in an auction room yesterday. You could move to a New Hampshire town and live respectably for two years on it.

"You could rent Madison Square Garden for one evening with it, and lecture your audience, if you should have one, on the precariousness of the profession of heir presumptive."[8]

A "People might like you, Old Bryson," said Gillian, always unruffled, "if you wouldn't moralize. I asked you to tell me what I could do with a thousand dollars."

B "You?" said Bryson, with a gentle laugh, "Why, Bobby Gillian, there's only one logical thing you could do. You can go buy Miss Lotta Lauriere a diamond pendant with the money, and then take yourself off to Idaho and inflict your presence upon a ranch. I advise a sheep ranch, as I have a particular dislike for sheep."

ACTIVE READING

C **QUESTION** How do you think Old Bryson feels about Gillian?

"Thanks," said Gillian, rising. "I thought I could depend on you, Old Bryson. You've hit on the very scheme. I wanted to chuck the money in a lump, for I've got to turn in an account for it, and I hate itemizing."

Gillian phoned for a cab and said to the driver: "The stage entrance of the Columbine Theatre."

Miss Lotta Lauriere was assisting nature with a powder puff, almost ready for her call at a crowded matinee, when her dresser mentioned the name of Mr. Gillian.

"Let it in," said Miss Lauriere. "Now, what is it, Bobby? I'm going on in two minutes."

"Rabbit-foot your right ear a little," suggested Gillian, critically. "That's better. It won't take two minutes for me. What do you say to a little thing in the pendant line. I can stand three ciphers[9] with a figure in front of 'em."

"Oh, just as you say," carolled Miss Lauriere. "My right glove, Adams. Say, Bobby, did you see that necklace Della Stacey had on the other night? Two thousand two hundred dollars it cost at Tiffany's. But, of course—pull my sash a little to the left, Adams." 1

"Miss Lauriere for the opening chorus!" cried the call boy without.

Gillian strolled out to where his cab was waiting.

"What would you do with a thousand dollars if you had it?" he asked the driver.

"Open a s'loon," said the cabby promptly and huskily. "I know a place I could take money in with both hands. It's a four-story brick on a corner. I've got it figured out. Second story . . . chop suey; third floor—manicures and foreign missions; fourth floor—pool-room. If you was thinking of putting up the cap"—

"Oh, no," said Gillian, "I merely asked from curiosity. I take you by the hour. Drive till I tell you to stop."

5. **Rockefeller:** John D. Rockefeller, who built a great oil-refining corporation in the late 1800s and became the first American billionaire.
6. **faro** (fâr'ō): a gambling game played with cards.
7. **Corot** (kô-rō'): painting by Jean Baptiste Camille Corot, a 19th-century French artist known for his landscapes.
8. **heir** (âr) **presumptive:** one who is expected to inherit the estate of another.
9. **ciphers** (sī'fərz): zeroes.

WORDS TO KNOW

precariousness (prĭ-kâr'ē-əs-nĭs) *n.* insecurity; uncertainty

pendant (pĕn'dənt) *n.* a piece of jewelry made to hang from a necklace or bracelet

390

Teaching Options

Mini Lesson: Vocabulary Strategy

APPLYING ROOT WORD MEANINGS

Instruction Gillian tells Lawyer Tolman, "You will find there a memorandum, sir, . . . of the vanished dollars." Tell students that the definition of *memorandum* is a note regarding something that needs to be remembered. The root *memor-* means *mindful, remembering.* Remind students that they can apply the meaning of roots to comprehend unfamiliar words.

Practice Have students write sentences using the following words in which *memo* is the root component: *memoir, memorabilia, memorial.* Have them use dictionaries if needed to determine precise word meaning and usage.

Use **Vocabulary Transparencies and Copymasters,** p. 47.

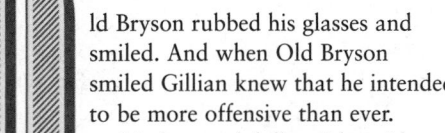

Femme à sa Toilette [Actress in her dressing room] (about 1879), Edgar Degas. Oil on canvas, 33 ⅝″ × 29 ¾″. The Norton Simon Foundation, Pasadena, California.

Customizing Instruction

Less Proficient Readers

1 Help students understand that something Miss Lauriere says causes Gillian to change his mind about buying a diamond necklace for her. Ask them to find the passage.

Possible Response: In the passage beginning "Oh, just as you," she hints that she wants a more expensive necklace like she saw another woman wearing.

Students Acquiring English

Words that may need clarification: *heir presumptive*–someone who expects to inherit most of a person's possessions; *cap*–slang for "capital," the money needed to start a business.

Mini Lesson: Viewing and Representing

Femme à sa Toilette **by Edgar Degas**

ART APPRECIATION This 1879 painting by the French Impressionist painter Edgar Degas was one of many portraying actresses and dancers. Degas, working with pastels, rendered the motion of ballerinas, actresses, and even race horses with a vibrancy unequaled in his day. He also became a friend and supporter of the American Impressionist Mary Cassatt.

Instruction Point out the soft, flowing shapes of the woman's clothing and hair. Ask what the artist has made the focus of attention.

Possible Response: Students may say the standing figure of the woman or the face of the woman reflected in the mirror.

Application Discuss the tension created by portraying the woman's back and face at the same time. Ask students how this makes the image more intimate or more mysterious. How might this woman be like Miss Lauriere?

Possible Response: Like Miss Lauriere, this woman seems very concerned with her appearance.

Reading and Analyzing

Literary Analysis: THEME

Ask students to think about what lessons Gillian learned about life that resulted from his conversations with each character.

Possible Response: Gillian seems to learn more from the people with the least amount of money: the cabby, the pencil vendor, Miss Hayden. Money seems to breed greed and a disagreeable character.

Literary Analysis PLOT

A Ask students to identify the climax or turning point of the story.

Possible Response: The climax occurs when Gillian picks up the envelope before the lawyer does, then tears the envelope to pieces.

ACTIVE READING

B **CAUSE AND EFFECT** He hoped to find out if Miss Hayden had inherited a sum of money from his uncle.

ACTIVE READING

C **CLARIFY** He cared for her.

Eight blocks down Broadway Gillian poked up the trap[10] with his cane and got out. A blind man sat upon a stool on the sidewalk selling pencils. Gillian went out and stood before him.

"Excuse me," he said, "but would you mind telling me what you would do if you had a thousand dollars?"

"You got out of that cab that just drove up, didn't you?" asked the blind man.

"I did," said Gillian.

"I guess you are all right," said the pencil dealer, "to ride in a cab by daylight. Take a look at that, if you like."

He drew a small book from his coat pocket and held it out. Gillian opened it and saw that it was a bank deposit book. It showed a balance of $1,785 to the blind man's credit.

Gillian returned the book and got into the cab.

"I forgot something," he said. "You may drive to the law offices of Tolman & Sharp, at ——, Broadway."

Lawyer Tolman looked at him hostilely and inquiringly through his gold-rimmed glasses.

"I beg your pardon," said Gillian cheerfully, "but may I ask you a question? It is not an impertinent[11] one, I am sure. Was Miss Hayden left anything by my uncle's will besides the ring and the $10?"

ACTIVE READING

B **CAUSE AND EFFECT** What do you think caused Gillian to return to the lawyer's office?

"Nothing," said Mr. Tolman.

"I thank you very much, sir," said Gillian, and out he went to his cab. He gave the driver the address of his late uncle's home.

Miss Hayden was writing letters in the library. She was small and slender and clothed in black. But you would have noticed her eyes. Gillian drifted in with his air of regarding the world as inconsequent.[12]

"I've just come from old Tolman's," he explained. "They've been going over the papers down there. They found a"—Gillian searched his memory for a legal term—"they found an amendment or a postscript or something to the will. It seems that the old boy loosened up a little on second thoughts and willed you a thousand dollars. I was driving up this way and Tolman asked me to bring you the money. Here it is. You'd better count it to see if it's right." Gillian laid the money beside her hand on the desk.

Miss Hayden turned white. "Oh!" she said, and again "Oh!" Gillian half turned and looked out the window.

"I suppose, of course," he said, in a low voice, "that you know I love you."

"I am sorry," said Miss Hayden, taking up her money.

"There is no use?" asked Gillian, almost light-heartedly.

"I am sorry," she said again.

"May I write a note?" asked Gillian, with a smile. He seated himself at the big library table. She supplied him with paper and pen, and then went back to her secretaire.[13]

Gillian made out his account of his expenditure of the thousand dollars in these words:

ACTIVE READING

C **CLARIFY** What do these comments reveal about Gillian's feelings toward Miss Hayden?

"Paid by the black sheep, Robert Gillian, $1,000 on the account of eternal happiness, owed by Heaven to the best and dearest woman on earth." **1**

Gillian slipped his writing into an envelope, bowed and went his way.

His cab stopped again at the office of Tolman & Sharp.

"I have expended the thousand dollars," he said, cheerily, to Tolman of the gold glasses, "and I have come to render account of it, as I agreed. There is quite a feeling of summer in the air—do you not think so, Mr. Tolman?" He tossed a white envelope on the lawyer's table. "You will find there a memorandum, sir, of the

10. **poked up the trap:** pushed open the door in the roof of the cab (to tell the driver that he wanted to stop).
11. **impertinent:** rude.
12. **inconsequent:** unimportant.
13. **secretaire** (sĕk′rə-târ′): a desk with a small bookcase on top.

Teaching Options

Mini Lesson: Speaking and Listening

Have the class use the script written by gifted and talented students in performing a scene or the entire selection as a play (see Customizing Instruction, p. 387). Call for volunteers who wish to audition for particular parts. Set up groups, one for each character. Have auditioning students read the parts for a particular character that they wish to play to the group. Have each group select the student who will play the part. Then have visual learners design scenes and arrange chairs, small tables, and other items that would serve as props in the classroom.

BLOCK SCHEDULING This activity is particularly well-suited for longer class periods.

modus operandi[14] of the vanished dollars."

Without touching the envelope, Mr. Tolman went to a door and called his partner, Sharp. Together they explored the caverns of the immense safe. Forth they dragged as trophy of their search a big envelope sealed with wax. This they forcibly invaded, and wagged their venerable heads together over its contents. Then Tolman became spokesman.

"Mr. Gillian," he said, formally, "there was a codicil[15] to your uncle's will. It was intrusted to us privately, with instructions that it be not opened until you furnished us with a full account of your handling of the $1,000 bequest in the will. As you have fulfilled the conditions my partner and I have read the codicil. I do not wish to encumber your understanding with its legal phraseology, but I will acquaint you with the spirit of its contents.

"The codicil promises that in the event that your disposition of the $1,000 demonstrates that you possess any of the qualifications that deserve reward, much benefit will accrue to you. Mr. Sharp and I are named as the judges, and I assure you that we will do our duty strictly according to justice—with liberality.[16] We are not at all unfavorably disposed toward you, Mr. Gillian. But let us return the letter of the codicil. If your disposal of the money in question has been prudent, wise, or unselfish, it is in our power to hand you over bonds to the value of $50,000 which have been placed in our hands for that purpose. But if—as our client, the late Mr. Gillian, explicitly provides—you have used this money as you have used money in the past—I quote the late Mr. Gillian—in reprehensible dissipation[17] among disreputable associates—the $50,000 is to be paid to Miriam Hayden, ward of the late Mr. Gillian, without delay. Now, Mr. Gillian, Mr. Sharp and I will examine your account in regard to the $1,000. You submit it in writing, I believe. I hope you will repose confidence in our decision."

Mr. Tolman reached out for the envelope. Gillian was a little the quicker in taking it up. He tore the account and its cover leisurely into strips and dropped them into his pocket.

"It's all right," he said, smiling. "There isn't a bit of need to bother you with this. I don't suppose you'd understand these itemized bets, anyway. I lost the thousand dollars on the races. Good-day to you, gentlemen." **A**

Tolman & Sharp shook their heads mournfully at each other when Gillian left, for they heard him whistling gayly in the hallway as he waited for the elevator. ❖

---

14. **modus operandi** (mō′dəs ŏp′ə-răn′dē): method of functioning.
15. **codicil** (kŏd′ə-sĭl): a supplement to a will.
16. **liberality** (lĭb′ə-răl′ĭ-tē): generosity.
17. **reprehensible dissipation** (rĕp′rĭ-hĕn′sə-bəl dĭs′ə-pā′shən): shameful loose living.

Detail from an illustration by J. C. Leyendecker (1917). Two oils on canvas, 28″ × 21″. Photo courtesy of the Archives of the American Illustrators Gallery, New York. Copyright © ASaP of Holderness, NH 03245, U.S.A.

WORDS TO KNOW

venerable (vĕn′ər-ə-bəl) *adj.* worthy of respect by virtue of age or dignity
encumber (ĕn-kŭm′bər) *v.* to burden
acquaint (ə-kwānt′) *v.* to inform; familiarize
prudent (pro͞od′nt) *adj.* characterized by good judgment
disreputable (dĭs-rĕp′yə-tə-bəl) *adj.* having a bad reputation; not respectable

Customizing Instruction

Less Proficient Readers

Use the following questions to help students understand what Gillian does at the lawyer's office.

- What had Gillian written in the note for the lawyer?
  Possible Response: He wrote that he had given the money to Miss Hayden.
- What was supposed to happen if Gillian used the $1,000 unselfishly?
  Possible Response: He was supposed to receive $50,000.
- Why did Gillian tear up the note before the lawyer could read it?
  Possible Response: He wanted Miss Hayden to receive the $50,000.

Students Acquiring English

1 Clarify for some students that the term "black sheep" is used to describe a member of a family or group who does not live by the moral expectations of the family or group.

Have one student read the lawyer's speech aloud. After each sentence, stop and ask a volunteer to explain the meaning of the sentence in more ordinary language.

Mini Lesson Standardized Test Practice

DESCRIBE CHARACTER IN A LITERARY SELECTION

For some standardized tests, students will be asked to describe a character. Ask students to describe Bobby Gillian by completing the statement below; encourage students to develop an explanation that uses details from the story.

- Bobby Gillian shows that he has been misunderstood by his uncle and others because he . . .

Lead students through the process of selecting details that show he has been misunderstood.

RUBRIC

3 **Full Accomplishment** Student presents details from the story that explain the character of Bobby Gillian.

2 **Substantial Accomplishment** Student presents some thoughts about Bobby Gillian's character, but development may be lacking.

1 **Little or Partial Accomplishment** Student does not have enough evidence to evaluate the character of Bobby Gillian.

GUIDING STUDENT RESPONSE

Connect to the Literature

1. **What Do You Think?**
Students should understand that Gillian does not want the money, and that he is unselfish.

Comprehension Check
- He must give a written account of how he used the money.
- He was thinking about giving his inheritance to her.
- He says he lost it gambling on the races.

Use Selection Quiz **Unit Three Resource Book,** p. 9.

Think Critically

2. Gillian's actions reveal that he is caring and sensitive. He is not as concerned with money as other members of his family.
3. The other characters consider him different and irresponsible.
4. Each conversation leads to the next. The causal chain is evident.
5. Love can inspire great generosity; appearances can be deceiving.

Thinking through the LITERATURE

Connect to the Literature

1. **What Do You Think?** Were you surprised by the ending of the story? Explain why or why not.

Comprehension Check
- To meet the requirements of the will, what must Gillian do after he has spent the $1,000?
- Why did Gillian ask whether Miss Hayden was left anything by his uncle?
- What does Gillian tell the lawyers that he has done with the $1,000?

Think Critically

2. How would you describe Bobby Gillian and explain his actions?

THINK ABOUT
- why he calls himself "the black sheep"
- the nature of his uncle's will
- his conversation with Old Bryson
- his dealings with Miss Lauriere and Miss Hayden

3. How do the other **characters** in the story—including the departed uncle—judge Gillian? Use examples from the story to support your opinion.
4. **ACTIVE READING** **CAUSE AND EFFECT** Look back in your **READER'S NOTEBOOK** at the conversations that you noted. How does each conversation cause the next one, thus advancing the **plot?**
5. What do you think is the **theme** of this story? Cite evidence to support your opinion.

Extend Interpretations

6. **Critic's Corner** The writer William Saroyan said that behind the "laughing language" of O. Henry's stories could be found "a profound love for the great mass of people who are frequently called 'the little people'." How does Saroyan's comment apply to this story?
7. **What If?** Imagine that Gillian's uncle had given him the entire sum of $50,000 at one time. Based on what you know about Gillian's character, how might this have changed what he chose to do with the money? Explain.
8. **Connect to Life** Gillian had to prove himself worthy of his uncle's inheritance. In what ways do you think young people today prove the worth of their character? Cite examples from your own experience or knowledge.

Literary Analysis

PLOT The chain of related events that take place in a story is called the **plot,** which serves as the writer's blueprint for what happens, when it happens, and to whom it happens. Usually, the events of the plot progress because of a **conflict.** Most plots include the following stages:

Exposition The exposition lays the groundwork for the plot and provides the reader with essential background information. Characters are introduced, the setting is described, and the plot begins to unfold.

Rising Action As the story progresses, **complications** usually arise, causing difficulties for the main characters and making the conflict more difficult to resolve.

Climax The climax is the turning point of the action, the moment when interest and intensity reach their peak. The climax usually involves an important event, decision, or discovery that affects the final outcome.

Falling Action The falling action consists of the events that occur after the climax. Often the conflict is resolved, and the intensity of action subsides.

Paired Activity Again review the graphic that you made in your **READER'S NOTEBOOK.** Label each conversation in the story, identifying the plot stage in which the conversation falls. For example, the initial conversation between Lawyer Tolman and Gillian belongs in the exposition.

When you have finished, compare your results with those of your classmates.

Extend Interpretations

Critic's Corner O. Henry portrays Miss Hayden in a sympathetic manner. She seems innocent and unaffected by the wealth around her.

What If? Complete responses will consider Gillian's impulsiveness and his feelings for Miss Hayden.

Connect to Life Students should compare the text events with their own or others' experiences. Students may describe how young people handle work, money, and other responsibilities. They may cite when teens resist peer pressure and temptations to break rules.

Literary Analysis

Plot Students may want to give details from each stage of the plot.

Choices & CHALLENGES

Writing Options

1. Gillian's Profile Write a personality profile of Bobby Gillian. Use details from the story to support your analysis of his character.

2. Gossip Column Write an entry in a newspaper column that describes what happened to Miss Hayden in the year that followed her inheritance.

3. Cause-and-Effect Analysis Think about a decision you have made that had significant effects. Describe what caused your decision and the effects that followed. Use a chart like the one shown to organize your thoughts.

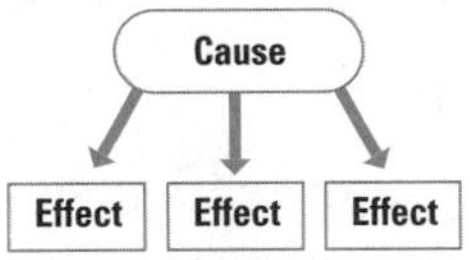

Writing Handbook
See page 1158: Cause and Effect.

Activities & Explorations

1. Cartoon Scene Create a cartoon strip that focuses on one of the conversations in the story. Include actual dialogue in the thought balloons. Try to capture the spirit of the characters. ~ **ART**

2. Dramatic Dialogue With a classmate, role-play a conversation between Bobby Gillian and Old Bryson in which Gillian explains why he decided to let Miss Hayden inherit the money. ~ **SPEAKING AND LISTENING**

Inquiry & Research

Men of Fortune During the era in which this story takes place, the top leaders of business and industry often gained national prominence due to their vast wealth and influence. Investigate one of the following men from that era: John D. Rockefeller, Andrew Carnegie, Cornelius Vanderbilt, or J. P. Morgan. Explain how your subject became wealthy and whether he used his wealth to help others.

Andrew Carnegie

Vocabulary in Action

EXERCISE A: MEANING CLUES On your paper, write the Word to Know that is closest in meaning to the underlined word in each sentence.

1. The terms of the will require that the inheritor follow a particular rule.
2. The inheritor has to explain his spending of his inheritance.
3. The lawyers are happy to familiarize young Gillian with the meaning of the will.
4. Mr. Gillian hoped his nephew would be wise and exercise good judgment.
5. He suspected, however, that his nephew would spend the money in the company of corrupt men.

EXERCISE B: WORD KNOWLEDGE On your paper, create a word web for each of the following words: *encumber, genially, pendant, precariousness,* and *venerable*. Write three synonyms and a definition in each web.

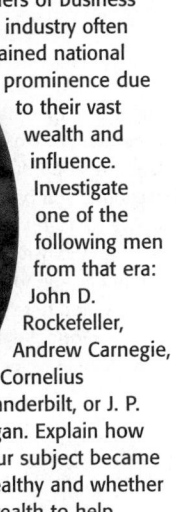

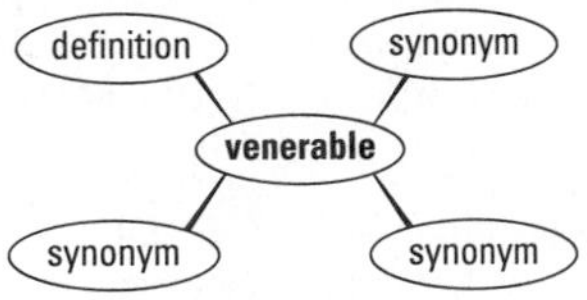

Building Vocabulary
For an in-depth lesson on using semantic mapping to build your vocabulary, see page 1102.

WORDS TO KNOW					
	acquaint	encumber	genially	precariousness	stipulate
	disreputable	expenditure	pendant	prudent	venerable

Writing Options

1. **Gillian's Profile** Remind students to use Gillian's words and actions as well as other characters' responses and reactions to him to support their writing.
2. **Gossip Column** Remind students that a gossip column should answer the journalistic questions *who, what, where, when, why*, and *how*.
3. **Cause-and-Effect Analysis** Students can consider decisions that affect school/grades, friends, family, jobs, money, and so on.

Activities & Explorations

1. **Cartoon Scene** Suggest to students that they reread passages, visualizing in detail the characters' actions, facial expressions, attitudes, and tone.
2. **Dramatic Dialogue** Have students consider the nature of Miss Hayden and Gillian's relationship in the past that would be consistent with their conversation in the story.

Inquiry & Research

Students should also investigate how the legacy of these men continues to enrich our lives.

Vocabulary in Action

EXERCISE A

1. stipulate
2. expenditure
3. acquaint
4. prudent
5. disreputable

EXERCISE B

Answers will vary. Accept any webs that demonstrate students' understanding of the meanings of the relevant WORDS TO KNOW.

Mini Lesson Grammar

USING VERBS: PRINCIPAL PARTS Instruction Write the following forms of the verbs *look* and *eat* on the board:

Present	Past	Present Participle	Past Participle
look	looked	is looking	have looked
eat	ate	is eating	have eaten

Explain to students that the principal parts of a verb include the present and past tenses, and the present and past participles.

Have students look up and write the principal parts of the following irregular verbs:

1. begin
   Response: begin, began, is beginning, have begun
2. know
   Response: know, knew, is knowing, have known
3. drive
   Response: drive, drove, is driving, have driven
4. tear
   Response: tear, tore, is tearing, have torn
5. swim
   Response: swim, swam, is swimming, have swum

Use **Unit Three Resource Book,** p. 8.

Use **Grammar Transparencies and Copymasters,** p. 129.

Use McDougal Littell's ***Language Network,*** Chapter 6, for more instruction in the principal parts of verbs.

Grammar in Context

WRITING EXERCISE Answers will vary. Possible answers are shown.

1. You must obey all the rules.
2. The old man hid where nobody could see him.
3. You could waste the money on a good time.
4. She knows all about your rude behavior.

Author Activity

In "The Last Leaf," a young woman recovers from a life-threatening illness, but the friend who secretly gave her inspiration dies as a result of what he did to help her. In "The Gift of the Magi," a husband and wife each sell a most treasured possession to buy a surprise Christmas present for the other—only to find that the gifts they chose for each other are useless without their treasures. In "The Ransom of Red Chief," two kidnappers hold a young boy for ransom, but end up paying his father to take him back because he is so wild no one can stand to be around him.

Grammar in Context: Verbs and Diction

In "One Thousand Dollars," young Gillian mocks the lawyer Tolman by speaking to him in a formal tone.

> **"I have expended the thousand dollars, . . . and I have come to render account of it, as I agreed."**

Diction, sometimes called level of language, is an outgrowth of word choice—for instance, a decision to use formal or informal words. Writers vary their diction to suit particular situations. In the passage above, O. Henry created the formal tone partly through the use of carefully chosen verbs. Gillian might have announced, informally, "I spent the money, and here's how." But his imitation of the lawyer's formal diction shows the reader his attitude toward the lawyer.

WRITING EXERCISE Rewrite each sentence, changing the diction from formal to informal. Pay special attention to finding a less formal verb.

Usage Tip: Make sure each verb agrees with its subject in number.

Example: ***Original*** The documents stipulate the procedure for making the expenditure.

Rewritten The papers explain how to pay the money.

1. You must comply with the totality of the regulation.
2. The elderly gentleman sequestered himself where no personage could discern his presence.
3. You could squander the funds on light entertainment.
4. She is well acquainted with your impolite conduct.

Grammar Handbook Subject-Verb Agreement, p.1200

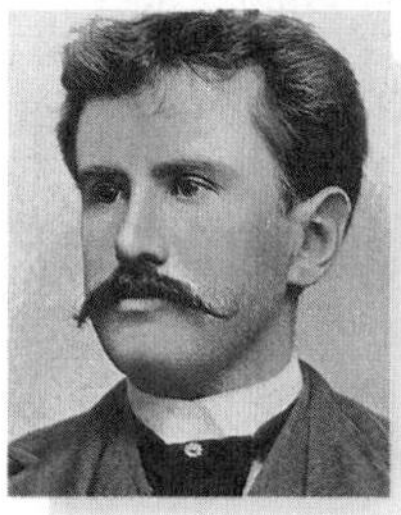

O. Henry

1862–1910

Other Works

The Four Million
The Trimmed Lamp and Other Stories of the Four Million
Whirligigs
The Voice of the City: Further Stories of the Four Million

A Writer's Beginnings O. Henry was the pen name of William Sydney Porter. Born in Greensboro, North Carolina, he was brought up by his grandmother and aunt after the death of his mother. At age 15, he left school to work as a clerk in his uncle's drugstore.

Texas Trouble In 1882, O. Henry moved to Texas, where he worked as a ranch hand, a clerk, a bookkeeper, a draftsman, a newspaper owner, and a reporter. Eventually, he became a bank teller at the First National Bank in Austin. After leaving this position, he was accused of taking $5,000 from the bank to cover some of his personal debts. He may have been innocent, but rather than stand trial, he fled to Honduras in Central America. More than a year later, he did return home to visit his dying wife. He was tried and sent to prison for three years, where he began to write short stories under the pen name O. Henry.

The Toast of New York City After his release from prison, O. Henry eventually settled in New York City—his beloved "Bagdad-on-the-Subway"—where he devoted his time and his energies to writing. He had a gift for finding a story in the little details of everyday life, and he often walked around with a notebook, ready to jot down impressions and ideas. As he observed, "There are stories in everything." O. Henry's stories, notable for their surprise endings, became even more famous after his death. At the time of his death, he had written over 600 short stories.

Author Activity

Tales with a Twist O. Henry's short stories often take an intriguing turn at the end. Read at least two other stories of his, such as "The Last Leaf," "The Gift of the Magi," or "The Ransom of Red Chief." Compare the endings of these stories with the ending of "One Thousand Dollars."

Mini Lesson Grammar

VERB CHOICE Instruction Write the following sets of verbs and meanings on the chalkboard or transparency:

to set: set, set, set—the subject puts or places something else

to sit: sit, sat, sat—the position or movement of the subject itself

to lay: lay, laid, laid—the subject puts or places something else

to lie: lie, lay, lain—the position or movement of the subject itself

Point out that the first verb in each pair is an action that is performed. Then explain that the second verb in each set indicates the position or movement of the subject itself. Read the following sentences:

Derrick (set, sat) the plate on the table. (*Identify the "something."*)

The dog (set, sat) attentively until its master called. (*Ask if the dog performed an action or positioned itself.*)

Use **Grammar Transparencies and Copymasters,** p. 137.

Use McDougal Littell's ***Language Network,*** Chapter 6, for more instruction in verbs.

Initiation

Short Story by SYLVIA PLATH

"Millicent had waited a long time for acceptance, longer than most."

Connect to Your Life

Pressure to Conform Most teenagers feel the pressure to be like their peers in order to gain acceptance. The attraction of belonging to a group is strong, whether it is a casual circle of friends, a team, or a club. Discuss situations in which peer pressure and the need to belong to a group influence the choices that an adolescent makes. In your judgment, what are appropriate ways of responding to such pressure?

Build Background

Sorority Sisters In "Initiation" the main character feels peer pressure to join a high school sorority, a highly selective social club for girls that is much like a fraternity for boys. To gain admittance, individuals must be approved by the members of the sorority. Also, recruits must often undergo a series of humiliating tasks to prove their worth, a process of initiation known as hazing. Today high school sororities and fraternities are rare; however, they still play an important role in the social life of many colleges and universities.

WORDS TO KNOW
Vocabulary Preview

calculating	fanfare
comradeship	gnome
conclusively	prestige
disinherited	spontaneous
exclusive	vivacious

Focus Your Reading

LITERARY ANALYSIS INTERNAL CONFLICT In fiction, **conflict,** which can either be external or internal, is crucial to the development of **plot.** An **internal conflict** occurs when a character has to make a difficult decision or resolve an inner struggle. In this story, the main character, Millicent, struggles with loyalties divided between a sorority and her friend Tracy. This internal conflict is illustrated by the following passage:

> ***Then there was another thing that bothered her. Leaving Tracy on the outskirts. . . . Millicent had seen it happen before.***

As you read, look for evidence of Millicent's internal conflict.

ACTIVE READING SEQUENCE OF EVENTS To make sense of the **plot** of a story, you need to follow the **sequence of events,** or the order in which events happen. Sometimes the flow of a story is interrupted by a **flashback,** an account of past events that can help readers understand a character's present situation. This story begins on a Friday, but the flashback relates information about the events of the previous week.

READER'S NOTEBOOK As you read the following story, keep track of the chronology, or time order, of events. Fill out a chart like this one to record information about what happens in each stage of the plot.

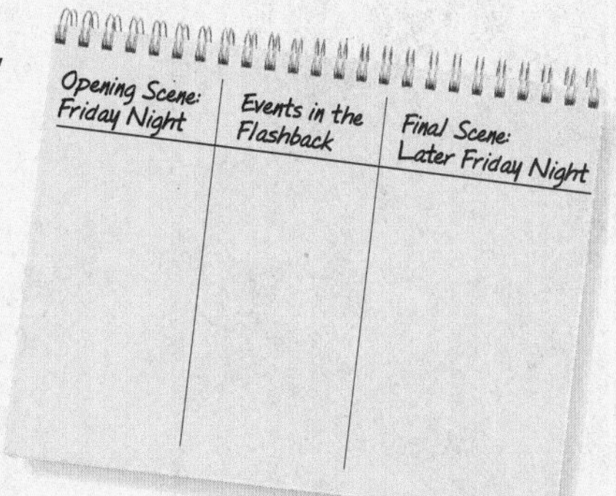

OVERVIEW

Objectives

1. understand and appreciate a **short story (Literary Analysis)**
2. identify **internal conflict (Literary Analysis)**
3. analyze **sequence of events (Active Reading)**

Summary

Though Millicent would like to be true to her friend Tracy, she also wants to join the high school social sorority. To become a member she must complete a series of tasks that are a part of the initiation process. During the process, several incidents make her realize that the girls in the sorority are exclusive and superficial. In addition, she encounters an interesting rider on a bus, who talks about heather birds, mythological birds that are wild and free. As a result of their conversation, she reevaluates her interest in the sorority; ultimately, she asserts herself and declines their invitation to become a member.

Thematic Link

Young people often feel pressure from their peers to conform. Asserting oneself in the face of pressure is important for youths to experience.

5-Minute Warm-Up

Daily Language SkillBuilder

Have students **proofread** the display sentences on page 381i and write them correctly. The sentences also appear on Transparency 12 of **Grammar Transparencies and Copymasters.**

LESSON RESOURCES

UNIT THREE RESOURCE BOOK, pp. 10–15

ASSESSMENT RESOURCES
Formal Assessment, pp. 65–66
Teacher's Guide to Assessment and Portfolio Use
Test Generator

SKILLS TRANSPARENCIES AND COPYMASTERS
Literary Analysis
- Plot: Conflict, T12 (for Paired Activity, p. 407)

Reading and Critical Thinking
- Chronological Order, T11 (for Sequence of Events, p. 397)
- Sequence Chain, T49 (for Reader's Notebook, p. 397)

Grammar
- Verb Tenses I, C127 (for Mini Lesson, p. 408)

Vocabulary
- Context Clues, C48 (for Mini Lesson, p. 402)
- Word Origins, C49 (for Mini Lesson, p. 404)

Writing
- The Uses of Dialogue, T24 (for Writing Option 1, p. 408)
- Achieving Unity, T7 (for Writing Option 2, p. 408)

Communications
- Evaluating Roles in Groups, T8 (for Mini Lesson, p. 405)
- Interviewing, T9 (for Activities & Explorations 1, p. 408)
- Impromptu Speaking: Dialogue, Role-Play, Debate, T13 (for Activities & Explorations 2, p. 408)

INTEGRATED TECHNOLOGY
Audio Library
Visit our website:
www.mcdougallittell.com

Mini Lesson **Preteaching Vocabulary**

If you would like to preteach the WORDS TO KNOW for this selection, use the Mini Lesson, pp. 402–403.

TEACHING THE LITERATURE

Reading and Analyzing

Reading Skills and Strategies: PREVIEW

Summarize the story, emphasizing the dilemma of the main character. Preview the story by discussing the images, the title, and the called-out quotations.

Active Reading SEQUENCE OF EVENTS

Students can track the sequence of events by noting what happens as they read the selection. Point out that the first and last events happen on a Friday. The rest of the story is told as a flashback about the previous week's events. The sequence is revealed through the days of the week.

Use **Unit Three Resource Book** p. 11 for more practice.

Literary Analysis INTERNAL CONFLICT

Point out that internal conflict takes place in a character's mind. One way to look for an internal conflict in a narrative is to find the character's thoughts. Have students keep a list of Millicent's thoughts as they read to help them understand her internal conflicts.

Use **Unit Three Resource Book** p. 12 for more practice.

Teaching Options

Mini Lesson: Viewing and Representing

Illustration by Emma Barron

ART APPRECIATION

Instruction Point out the use of light and darkness in this portrait. Ask how the use of shadow makes the girl seem mysterious.

Possible Response: The artist's use of the subject's hair, hiding the left side of the subject's face, creates mystery because the viewer cannot make out all the details of her face.

Application Based on the details of the portrait, ask students how this image connects to the story's character Millicent.

Possible Response: Initiations are often secretive. The subject of the portrait has her fingers to her lips, perhaps keeping a secret.

INITIATION

SYLVIA PLATH

The basement room was dark and warm, like the inside of a sealed jar, Millicent thought, her eyes getting used to the strange dimness. The silence was soft with cobwebs, and from the small, rectangular window set high in the stone wall there sifted a faint bluish light that must have been coming from the full October moon. She could see now that what she was sitting on was a woodpile next to the furnace.

Millicent brushed back a strand of hair. It was stiff and sticky from the egg that they had broken on her head as she knelt blindfolded at the sorority altar a short while before. There had been a silence, a slight crunching sound, and then she had felt the cold, slimy egg-white flattening and spreading on her head and sliding down her neck. She had heard someone smothering a laugh. It was all part of the ceremony.

There really was no doubt now that she would get in.

Then the girls had led her here, blindfolded still, through the corridors of Betsy Johnson's house and shut her in the cellar. It would be an hour before they came to get her, but then Rat Court would be all over and she would say what she had to say and go home.

For tonight was the grand finale, the trial by fire. There really was no doubt now that she would get in. She could not think of anyone who had ever been invited into the high school sorority and

Customizing Instruction

Less Proficient Readers
Ask students to note incidents that help persuade Millicent to decline the invitation to join the sorority.

Students Acquiring English
Discuss the concept of initiation into sororities and fraternities in the United States. Ask if students know of similar initiation rituals elsewhere. Explain that nearly all cultures have some form of ritual for young people crossing the threshold to adulthood. Students should recognize the distinctive and shared characteristics of cultures.

Use **Spanish Study Guide** for additional support, pp. 86–88.

Gifted and Talented
Invite students to discuss how a good friend like Tracy might have argued against joining a sorority.

BLOCK SCHEDULING: MANAGING TIME

If your schedule requires that you cover the lesson objectives in a shorter time, use . . .
- Preparing to Read, p. 397
- Thinking Through the Literature, p. 407
- Vocabulary in Action, p. 408
- Grammar in Context, p. 409

If you want to take advantage of longer class time, use . . .
- TE Teaching Options: Preteaching Vocabulary, pp. 402–403; Viewing and Representing, pp. 398, 401; Multicultural Link, p. 400; Vocabulary Strategy, p. 404; Speaking and Listening, p. 405; Standardized Test Practice, p. 406
- Choices & Challenges, p. 408

Reading and Analyzing

Reading Skills and Strategies: PREDICTING

Have students predict what will happen at the end of the story. They should support their predictions with text evidence.

Possible Responses: Millicent will fail the initiation; Millicent will join the sorority; Millicent will decline to join the sorority.

What clues have they already been given about the main character to support their prediction?

Possible Responses: Millicent feels rebellious, conforming will be difficult for her; Millicent wants to join the sorority very much; Millicent is close to Tracy and won't want to abandon her.

Literary Analysis: CHARACTER

A Ask students what the interchange between Tracy and Millicent reveals about each girl's character.

Possible Response: Tracy knows that her relationship with Millicent is bound to change. Millicent, on the other hand, believes that nothing will come between her and Tracy. Tracy is doubtful about the future of their friendship.

Literary Analysis: FIGURATIVE LANGUAGE

B Have students identify the extended metaphor and discuss how the image is maintained.

Possible Response: Millicent is comparing herself to a princess beginning in the last paragraph on p. 400.

Have students look for repetition of this metaphor as they read.

failed to get through initiation time. But even so, her case would be quite different. She would see to that. She could not exactly say what had decided her revolt, but it definitely had something to do with Tracy and something to do with the heather birds.

What girl at Lansing High would not want to be in her place now? Millicent thought, amused. What girl would not want to be one of the elect,[1] no matter if it did mean five days of initiation before and after school, ending in the climax of Rat Court on Friday night when they made the new girls members? Even Tracy had been wistful when she heard that Millicent had been one of the five girls to receive an invitation.

A "It won't be any different with us, Tracy," Millicent had told her. "We'll still go around together like we always have, and next year you'll surely get in." 3

"I know, but even so," Tracy had said quietly, "you'll change, whether you think you will or not. Nothing ever stays the same."

And nothing does, Millicent had thought. How horrible it would be if one never changed . . . if she were condemned to be the plain, shy Millicent of a few years back for the rest of her life. Fortunately there was always the changing, the growing, the going on.

It would come to Tracy, too. She would tell Tracy the silly things the girls had said, and Tracy would change also, entering eventually into the magic circle. She would grow to know the special ritual as Millicent had started to last week.

"First of all," Betsy Johnson, the vivacious blonde secretary of the sorority, had told the five new candidates over sandwiches in the school cafeteria last Monday, 4 "first of all, each of you has a big sister. She's the one who bosses you around, and you just do what she tells you."

"Remember the part about talking back and smiling," Louise Fullerton had put in, laughing. She was another celebrity in high school, pretty and dark and Vice-President of the Student Council. "You can't say anything unless your big sister asks you something or tells you to talk to someone. And you can't smile, no matter how you're dying to." The girls had laughed a little nervously, and then the bell had rung for the beginning of afternoon classes.

It would be rather fun for a change, Millicent mused, getting her books out of her locker in the hall, rather exciting to be part of a closely knit group, the exclusive set at Lansing High. Of course, it wasn't a school organization. In fact, the principal, Mr. Cranton, wanted to do away with initiation week altogether, because he thought it was undemocratic and disturbed the routine of school work. But there wasn't really anything he could do about it. Sure, the girls had to come to school for five days without any lipstick on and without curling their hair, and of course everybody noticed them, but what could the teachers do?

Millicent sat down at her desk in the big study hall. Tomorrow she would come to school, proudly, laughingly, without lipstick, with her brown hair straight and shoulder length, and then everybody would know, even the boys would know, that she was one of the elect. Teachers would smile helplessly, thinking perhaps: So now they've picked Millicent Arnold. I never would have guessed it.

B A year or two ago, not many people would have guessed it. Millicent had waited a long time for acceptance, longer than most. It was as if she had been sitting for years in a pavilion[2] outside a dance floor, looking in through the windows at the golden interior, with the lights clear and the air like honey, wistfully watching the gay couples

1. **elect:** elite group; "in" crowd.
2. **pavilion** (pə-vĭl′yən): a small roofed structure in a garden or park.

WORDS TO KNOW
vivacious (vĭ-vā′shəs) *adj.* lively; spirited
exclusive (ĭk-sklo͞o′sĭv) *adj.* tending to exclude others; select

Teaching Options

Multicultural Link **Rites of Passage**

Many cultures mark a child's passage into adulthood with initiation rites. Like a Jewish bar or bat mitzvah, these rites publicly declare a child's coming-of-age and the beginning of adult responsibilities. Apache girls have a coming-of-age ceremony called the Sunrise Dance. This four-day event involves feasting, gift giving, chants, dances, and other entertainment. The girls who are being honored wear a deerskin costume that is a copy of that worn by White Painted Woman, the mythological mother of all the Apache.

Young men also have initiation rites. Among the Aruntas, an Aborigine people, young men have more than one coming-of-age ceremony. During the first ceremony, which takes place while the boy is still a child, he is snatched from the women of his family. The men toss him into the air while the women sing and dance. His relatives paint special patterns on his body to help him grow up more quickly. Then he goes to live in the men's camp.

waltzing to the never-ending music, laughing in pairs and groups together, no one alone.

But now at last, amid a week of fanfare and merriment, she would answer her invitation to enter the ballroom through the main entrance marked "Initiation." She
1 would gather up her velvet skirts, her silken train, or whatever the disinherited princesses wore in the story books, and come into her rightful kingdom. . . . The bell rang to end study hall.

"Millicent, wait up!" It was Louise Fullerton behind her, Louise who had always before been very nice, very polite, friendlier than the rest, even long ago, before the invitation had come.

"Listen," Louise walked down the hall with her to Latin, their next class, "are you busy right after school today? Because I'd like to talk to you about tomorrow."

"Sure. I've got lots of time."

"Well, meet me in the hall after
5 home room then, and we'll go down to the drugstore or something."

Bauhaus Stairway (1932), Oskar Schlemmer. Oil on canvas, 63⅞" × 45". The Museum of Modern Art, New York. Gift of Philip Johnson. Photograph copyright © 1998 The Museum of Modern Art.

Walking beside Louise on the way to the drugstore, Millicent felt a surge of pride. For all anyone could see, she and Louise were the best of friends.

"You know, I was so glad when they voted you in," Louise said.

Millicent smiled. "I was really thrilled to get the invitation," she said frankly, "but kind of sorry that Tracy didn't get in, too."

Tracy, she thought. If there is such a thing as a best friend, Tracy has been just that this last year.

"Yes, Tracy," Louise was saying, "she's a nice girl, and they put her up on the slate, but . . . well, she had three blackballs against her."

"Blackballs? What are they?" 2

"Well, we're not supposed to tell anybody outside the club, but seeing as you'll be in at the end of the week I don't suppose it hurts." They were at the drugstore now.

WORDS TO KNOW
fanfare (făn′fâr′) *n.* showy display or celebration
disinherited (dĭs′ĭn-hĕr′ĭ-tĭd) *adj.* deprived of a rightful inheritance **disinherit** *v.*

Customizing Instruction

Gifted and Talented

1 Ask students to contrast what Millicent thought would be the benefits of belonging to a sorority with the reality of belonging.

Students Acquiring English

2 Explain that *blackball* is a term used to describe a negative vote excluding someone from membership in an organization.

Less Proficient Readers

3 Help students recognize that Millicent's conversation with Tracy is a flashback. Ask them how Plath has indicated this.

Possible Response: The conversation is written in past perfect tense.

4 Ask students when Millicent has lunch with Betsy Johnson and the other candidates.

Answer: Monday

5 Ask students when Millicent goes to the drugstore with Louise Fullerton.

Answer: that same Monday afternoon

Mini Lesson: Viewing and Representing

ART APPRECIATION Oskar Schlemmer, a German born artist, lived from 1888–1943 during a period of artistic upheaval and experimentation. His work can be identified by its attention to forms, often simplified in detail.

Instruction Point out the highly geometric, sleek shapes in this painting. Have students describe the painting's overall tone and emotional effect.

Possible Response: The tone is muted and cool; the effect is one of distance and alienation because the viewer sees primarily the backs and profiles of the figures in the painting. The subjects appear to be clones of one another because of their similarities.

Application Have students imagine that Millicent is about to turn the corner and come down the staircase. How does she look? What other connections can be made between the art and the story?

Possible Response: Students might imagine Millicent as a more multidimensional and colorful figure than the others represented here.

Reading and Analyzing

Reading Skills and Strategies: EVALUATING

A Have students evaluate the sorority's selection process, including the tradition of blackballing. Ask them if they think it is fair for voters to cast an anonymous ballot, or if all should be held accountable for their choices.

Possible Response: Blackballing is unfair, but an anonymous ballot is the only way to ensure that people will express their true opinions.

Literary Analysis: PLOT

Discuss with students how a story's plot moves through a series of stages: from exposition, where the basic situation is presented, to rising action, climax, and eventually to falling action and resolution. Ask students to imagine a diagram which would visually present these stages.

Possible Responses: Student might draw an inverted "V" diagram on the board that represents this pattern.

Literary Analysis INTERNAL CONFLICT

B Have students explain why Millicent suddenly feels rebellious.

Possible Response: As a gopher, Millicent has been stripped of her individuality, and her instinct is to rebel. The initiation process seems to demean her individuality, and she suddenly finds herself seriously doubting the value of sorority membership.

"You see," Louise began explaining in a low voice after they were seated in the privacy of the booth, "once a year the sorority puts up all the likely girls that are suggested for membership . . ."

Millicent sipped her cold, sweet drink slowly, saving the ice cream to spoon up last. She listened carefully to Louise, who was going on, ". . . and then there's a big meeting, and all the girls' names are read off and each girl is discussed."

"Oh?" Millicent asked mechanically, her voice sounding strange.

"Oh, I know what you're thinking," Louise laughed. "But it's really not as bad as all that. They keep it down to a minimum of catting.[3] They just talk over each girl and why or why not they think she'd be good for the club. And then they vote. Three blackballs eliminate a girl."

"Do you mind if I ask you what happened to Tracy?" Millicent said.

Louise laughed a little uneasily. "Well, you know how girls are. They notice little things. I mean, some of them thought Tracy was just a bit *too* different. Maybe you could suggest a few things to her."

"Like what?"

"Oh, like maybe not wearing knee socks to school, or carrying that old bookbag. I know it doesn't sound like much, but well, it's things like that which set someone apart. I mean, you know that no girl at Lansing would be seen dead wearing knee socks, no matter how cold it gets, and it's kiddish and kind of green to carry a bookbag."

"I guess so," Millicent said.

"About tomorrow," Louise went on. "You've drawn Beverly Mitchell for a big sister. I wanted to warn you that she's the toughest, but if you get through all right it'll be all the more credit for you."

"Thanks, Lou," Millicent said gratefully, thinking, this is beginning to sound serious. Worse than a loyalty test, this grilling over the coals. What's it supposed to prove anyway? That I can take orders without flinching? Or does it just make them feel good to see us run around at their beck and call?

"All you have to do really," Louise said, spooning up the last of her sundae, "is be very meek and obedient when you're with Bev and do just what she tells you. Don't laugh or talk back or try to be funny, or she'll just make it harder for you, and believe me, she's a great one for doing that. Be at her house at seven-thirty."

And she was. She rang the bell and sat down on the steps to wait for Bev. After a few minutes the front door opened and Bev was standing there, her face serious.

"Get up, gopher," Bev ordered.

There was something about her tone that annoyed Millicent. It was almost malicious.[4] And there was an unpleasant anonymity[5] about the label "gopher," even if that was what they

3. **catting:** petty, nasty gossip.
4. **malicious** (mə-lĭsh′əs): spiteful; cruel.
5. **anonymity** (ăn′ə-nĭm′ĭ-tē): lack of recognition as an individual.

"Well, you know how girls are. They notice little things. I mean,

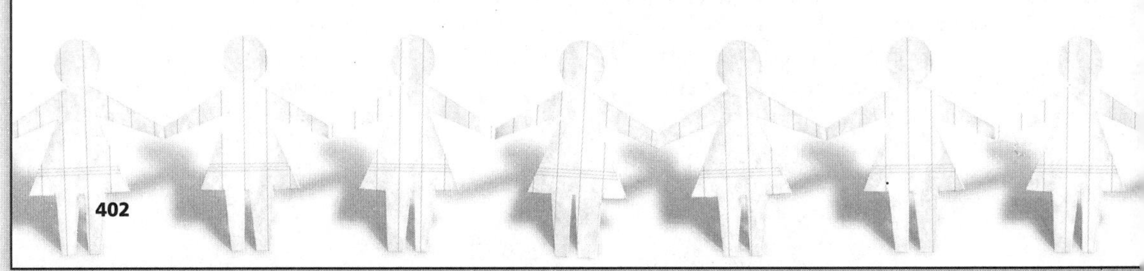

402

Teaching Options

Mini Lesson: Preteaching Vocabulary

CONTEXT CLUES Call students' attention to the list of WORDS TO KNOW. Use the model sentence to demonstrate how they can use context clues to infer the meaning of an unfamiliar word. Remind students that they will need to find the relevant material in the surrounding words and sentences.

Model Sentence

Betsy Johnson, the *vivacious* blond secretary of the sorority, spoke energetically with the new candidates at lunch.

Instruction

- Write the model sentence on the chalkboard.
- Ask a volunteer to read the sentence and identify the relevant words that provide inferences to the meaning of the italicized word. Circle the context clues and ask how they helped determine word meaning.

Possible Response: *vivacious* could mean full of energy; the context clue *spoke energetically* indicates that she spoke with a great deal of enthusiasm.

always called the girls being initiated. It was degrading, like being given a number. It was a denial of individuality.

B Rebellion flooded through her.

"I said get up. Are you deaf?"

Millicent got up, standing there.

"Into the house, gopher. There's a bed to be made and a room to be cleaned at the top of the stairs."

Millicent went up the stairs mutely. She found Bev's room and started making the bed. Smiling to herself, she was thinking: How absurdly funny, me taking orders from this girl like a servant.

Bev was suddenly there in the doorway. "Wipe that smile off your face," she commanded.

There seemed something about this relationship that was not all fun. In Bev's eyes, Millicent was sure of it, there was a hard, bright spark of exultation.[6]

On the way to school, Millicent had to walk behind Bev at a distance of ten paces, carrying her books. They came up to the drugstore, where there already was a crowd of boys and girls from Lansing High waiting for the show.

The other girls being initiated were there, so Millicent felt relieved. It would not be so bad now, being part of the group.

"What'll we have them do?" Betsy Johnson asked Bev. That morning Betsy had made her "gopher" carry an old colored parasol through the square and sing "I'm Always Chasing Rainbows."

"I know," Herb Dalton, the good-looking basketball captain, said.

A remarkable change came over Bev. She was all at once very soft and coquettish.[7]

"You can't tell them what to do," Bev said sweetly. "Men have nothing to say about this little deal."

"All right, all right," Herb laughed, stepping back and pretending to fend off a blow.

"It's getting late." Louise had come up. "Almost eight-thirty. We'd better get them marching on to school."

The "gophers" had to do a Charleston step[8] all the way to school, and each one had her own song to sing, trying to drown out the other four. During school, of course, you couldn't fool around, but even then, there was a rule that you mustn't talk to boys outside of class or at lunch time . . . or any time at all after school. So the sorority girls would get the most popular boys to go up to the "gophers" and ask them out, or try to start them talking, and sometimes a "gopher" was taken by surprise and began to say something before she could catch herself. And then the boy reported her and she got a black mark.

Herb Dalton approached Millicent as she was getting an ice cream at the lunch counter that noon. She saw him coming before he spoke to her, and looked down quickly, thinking: He is too princely, too dark and smiling. And I am

6. **exultation** (ĕk′səl-tā′shən): triumphant joy.
7. **coquettish** (kō-kĕt′ĭsh): flirtatious.
8. **Charleston step:** a step used in a dance popular in the 1920s.

some of them thought Tracy was just a bit *too* different . . ."

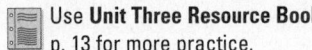

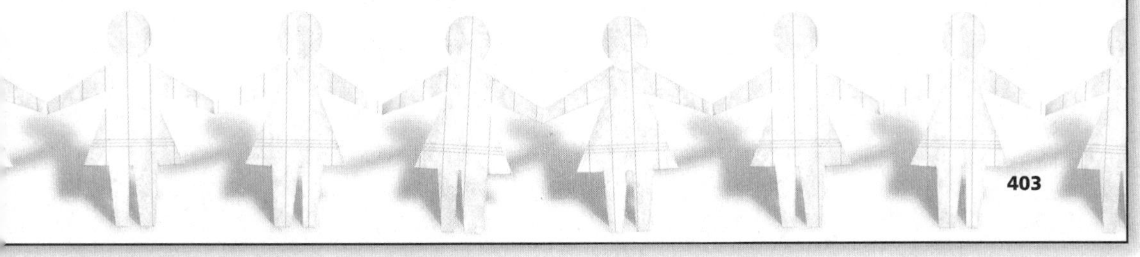

Customizing Instruction

Less Proficient Readers

Use the following questions to check students' understanding.

- What does Louise tell Millicent about the sorority selection process?
  Possible Response: She tells her that the girls are judged and then voted upon.
- How does Bev treat Millicent?
  Possible Response: She treats her like a slave, having her make Bev's bed, carry her books, and keep quiet.
- What do Millicent and the other initiates have to do?
  Possible Response: They have to do whatever they're told. They cannot wear makeup or curl their hair, and they are not allowed to talk to boys.

Set a Purpose Have students read to find out what happens to Millicent and the other initiates.

Students Acquiring English

Explain to students that a "gopher" is someone who performs tedious tasks. Have students keep track of the kinds of duties that Millicent must perform as a "gopher."

Exercises Read the following sentences. Ask students to use context clues to help them infer the meaning of the italicized word.

1. Although membership was small, Millicent hoped to be part of the *exclusive* set at Lansing High.
2. After a week of *fanfare* and merriment, she would enter the ballroom.
3. The *disinherited* princess no longer wore fine silk dresses.
4. Bev wore a *calculating* smile that suggested she was plotting something unpleasant.
5. The man looked something like a *gnome* or a cheerful leprechaun.
6. Millicent broke out into *spontaneous* laughter at the man's comment.
7. She enjoyed the *comradeship* she found among her new companions on the bus.
8. Millicent thought that belonging to the sorority would give her enough *prestige* to talk to anyone.
9. Millicent's coronation would label her *conclusively* as one of the select.

Use **Unit Three Resource Book** p. 13 for more practice.

A lesson on context clues appears on p. 56 in the Pupil's Edition.

Reading and Analyzing

Reading Skills and Strategies: MAKING CONNECTIONS

A Ask students if they agree with Millicent's statement that the girls who were outsiders now "scoffed at the initiation antics as childish and absurd to hide their secret envy."

Possible responses: Yes, because people are always jealous of those who have more status; no, because the initiation antics really are childish and absurd.

Literary Analysis: SYMBOL

B Have students explain what they think the man on the bus represents to Millicent.

Possible Response: He represents freedom, imagination, individuality.

Literary Analysis: CLIMAX

C Remind students that the climax of a story is its turning point, the moment when interest and intensity reach their peak. It usually involves an important event, decision, or discovery that affects the final outcome. Have students identify the climax in "Initiation."

Possible Response: The climax occurs when Millicent realized that "you didn't have to belong to a club to feel related to other human beings."

much too vulnerable.[9] Why must he be the one I have to be careful of?

I won't say anything, she thought, I'll just smile very sweetly.

She smiled up at Herb very sweetly and mutely. His return grin was rather miraculous. It was surely more than was called for in the line of duty.

"I know you can't talk to me," he said, very low. "But you're doing fine, the girls say. I even like your hair straight and all."

Bev was coming toward them, then, her red mouth set in a bright, calculating smile. She ignored Millicent and sailed up to Herb.

"Why waste your time with gophers?" she caroled gaily. "Their tongues are tied, but completely."

Herb managed a parting shot. "But that one keeps *such* an attractive silence."

Millicent smiled as she ate her sundae at the counter with Tracy. Generally, the girls who were outsiders now, as Millicent had been, (A) scoffed at the initiation antics as childish and absurd to hide their secret envy. But Tracy was understanding, as ever.

"Tonight's the worst, I guess, Tracy," Millicent told her. "I hear that the girls are taking us on a bus over to Lewiston and going to have us performing in the square."

"Just keep a poker face outside," Tracy advised. "But keep laughing like mad inside."

Millicent and Bev took a bus ahead of the rest of the girls; they had to stand up on the way to Lewiston Square. Bev seemed very cross about something. Finally she said, "You were talking with Herb Dalton at lunch today."

"No," said Millicent honestly.

"Well, I *saw* you smile at him. That's practically as bad as talking. Remember not to do it again."

Millicent kept silent.

"It's fifteen minutes before the bus gets into town," Bev was saying then. "I want you to go up and down the bus asking people what they eat for breakfast. Remember, you can't tell them you're being initiated."

Millicent looked down the aisle of the crowded bus and felt suddenly quite sick. She thought: How will I ever do it, going up to all those stony-faced people who are staring coldly out of the window . . .

"You heard me, gopher."

"Excuse me, madam," Millicent said politely to the lady in the first seat of the bus, "but I'm taking a survey. Could you please tell me what you eat for breakfast?"

"Why . . . er . . . just orange juice, toast and coffee," she said.

"Thank you very much." Millicent went on to the next person, a young businessman. He ate eggs sunny side up, toast and coffee.

By the time Millicent got to the back of the bus, most of the people were smiling at her. They obviously know, she thought, that I'm being initiated into something.

Finally, there was only one man left in the corner of the back seat. He was small and jolly, with a ruddy, wrinkled face that spread into a beaming smile as Millicent approached. In his brown suit with the forest-green tie he looked something like a gnome or a cheerful leprechaun. (B)

"Excuse me, sir," Millicent smiled, "but I'm taking a survey. What do you eat for breakfast?"

"Heather birds' eyebrows on toast," the little man rattled off. (C)

9. **vulnerable:** defenseless.

WORDS TO KNOW

calculating (kăl′kyə-lā′tĭng) *adj.* crafty; cunning

gnome (nōm) *n.* an imaginary dwarflike creature that lives underground

404

Teaching Options

Mini Lesson: Vocabulary Strategy

RESEARCHING WORD ORIGINS: *PRAESTIGIAE*

Instruction The word *prestige* is based upon the Latin word *praestigiae,* which means *conjuror's tricks.* It is also related to the word *praestringere,* which combines *in front* of with *to bind tight.* When membership in the sorority is described as providing "prestige value," it means that membership is a show, a presentation of one's self to others.

Practice Have students work in pairs to research the word origins of the meaning of *prestidigitation* and *prestigious* in order to understand their meanings. Then have them use each word in a sentence. Ask students to describe how they can use knowledge of the root word *praestigiae* to remember the meanings of these words. As they read, have students use reference materials to research and record the word origins of five words from the selection. Where applicable, they should list words related with a common root.

Use **Vocabulary Transparencies and Copymasters,** p. 49.

A lesson on word origins appears on p. 356 in the Pupil's Edition.

So many people were shut up tight inside themselves like boxes, yet they would open up, unfolding quite wonderfully, if only you were interested in them.

"*What?*" Millicent exclaimed.

"Heather birds' eyebrows," the little man explained. "Heather birds live on the
2 mythological moors and fly about all day long, singing wild and sweet in the sun. They're bright purple and have *very* tasty eyebrows."

Millicent broke out into spontaneous laughter. Why, this was wonderful, the way she felt a sudden comradeship with a stranger.

"Are you mythological, too?"

"Not exactly," he replied, "but I certainly hope to be some day. Being mythological does wonders for one's ego."

The bus was swinging into the station now; Millicent hated to leave the little man. She wanted to ask him more about the birds.

And from that time on, initiations didn't bother Millicent at all. She went gaily about Lewiston Square from store to store asking for broken crackers and mangoes, and she just laughed inside when people stared and then brightened, answering her crazy questions as if she were quite serious and really a person of consequence.[10] So many people were shut up tight inside themselves like boxes, yet they would open up, unfolding quite wonderfully, if
3 only you were interested in them. And really, you didn't have to belong to a club to feel related to other human beings.

One afternoon Millicent had started talking with Liane Morris, another of the girls being initiated, about what it would be like when they were finally in the sorority.

"Oh, I know pretty much what it'll be like," Liane had said. "My sister belonged before she graduated from high school two years ago."

"Well, just what *do* they do as a club?" Millicent wanted to know.

"Why, they have a meeting once a week . . . each girl takes turns entertaining at her house . . ."

"You mean it's just a sort of exclusive social group . . ."

"I guess so . . . though that's a funny way of putting it. But it sure gives a girl prestige value. My sister started going steady with the captain of the football team after she got in. Not bad, I say."

No, it wasn't bad, Millicent had thought, lying in bed on the morning of Rat Court and listening to the sparrows chirping in the gutters. She thought of Herb. Would he ever have been so friendly if she were without the sorority label? Would he ask her out (if he ever did) just for herself, no strings attached?

---

10. **consequence:** importance.

WORDS TO KNOW	
	spontaneous (spŏn-tā′nē-əs) *adj.* occurring or acting without a plan; impulsive
	comradeship (kŏm′răd-shĭp′) *n.* companionship
	prestige (prĕ-stēzh′) *n.* high status; esteem

Customizing Instruction

Less Proficient Readers

Have students describe the man on the bus.

Possible Response: He is "small and jolly," smiling and friendly. He is wearing a brown suit and a green tie. He is a free spirit.

How do these details seem significant?

Possible Response: He seems happy to be different; he makes Millicent think about the value of being different.

Students Acquiring English

1 Explain to students that heather is a hardy shrub with a bell-like flower that grows on the British Isles. If possible, show students a picture of moors covered in blooming heather.

2 Help students understand the meaning of *mythological*. Explain that something that is mythological does not exist in a literal sense. Have volunteers give examples of myths and famous mythological beings (Zeus, Pegasus, etc.).

Multiple Learning Styles

Visual and Spatial Learners

Invite students to draw or paint a picture of the man on the bus and the heather birds, based on the descriptions they have read.

Mini Lesson: Speaking and Listening

Instruction A panel discussion has a moderator to keep the discussion focused while the rest of the class will ask the panel questions and raise issues for discussion.

Prepare Assign six students the panelist roles of Louise, Betsy, Beverly, Liane, Millicent, and Tracy. Assign a seventh student the role of moderator. Have the panelists and the moderator meet to discuss their characters and roles. Have the rest of the class think of questions they would like to ask the panel. Encourage them to ask Millicent, Liane, and Tracy their reasons for joining a sorority. Ask Louise, Betsy, and Bev what the sorority does as a club.

Present During the discussion, remind the panelists to stay in character. Help the moderator guide the discussion and keep everyone on task.

BLOCK SCHEDULING This activity is particularly well suited for longer class periods.

Reading and Analyzing

Reading Skills and Strategies: EVALUATING

Have students evaluate Millicent's encounter with the strange man on the bus. Do they think that she would have decided against joining the sorority if she had not met him?

Possible Response: Without this encounter, she might have joined the sorority, but eventually, being an individualist, she would have quit the club or refused to conform to its expectations.

Literary Analysis: THEME

Theme, the central idea in a work of literature, should not be confused with the subject of a work. It is a perception about life or human nature that the writer shares with the reader. Ask students to jot down a sentence that states the theme of this selection and then discuss the different interpretations.

Possible Response: Human beings often feel more comfortable belonging to a group, being like everyone else; the price of this membership is the loss of personal freedom and identity.

A Ask students if they think Millicent will become friends with everybody, including Tracy, and why or why not.

Possible Response: No, because the girls in the sorority will take Millicent's decision as an insult. They will be angry with her and view her refusal to join as a betrayal of their trust. Yes. They will admire her individualistic nature.

Then there was another thing that bothered her. Leaving Tracy on the outskirts. Because that is the way it would be; Millicent had seen it happen before.

Outside, the sparrows were still chirping, and as she lay in bed Millicent visualized them, pale gray-brown birds in a flock, one like the other, all exactly alike.

And then, for some reason, Millicent thought of the heather birds. Swooping carefree over the moors, they would go singing and crying out across the great spaces of air, dipping and darting, strong and proud in their freedom and their sometime loneliness. It was then that she made her decision.

Seated now on the woodpile in Betsy Johnson's cellar, Millicent knew that she had come triumphant through the trial of fire, the searing period of the ego which could end in two kinds of victory for her. The easiest of which would be her coronation[11] as a princess, labeling her conclusively as one of the select flock.

The other victory would be much harder, but she knew that it was what she wanted. It was not that she was being noble or anything. It was just that she had learned there were other ways of getting into the great hall, blazing with lights, of people and of life.

It would be hard to explain to the girls tonight, of course, but she could tell Louise later just how it was. How she had proved something to herself by going through everything, even Rat Court, and then deciding not to join the sorority after all. And how she could still be friends with everybody. Sisters with everybody. Tracy, too. **A**

The door behind her opened and a ray of light sliced across the soft gloom of the basement room.

"Hey, Millicent, come on out now. This is it." There were some of the girls outside.

"I'm coming," she said, getting up and moving out of the soft darkness into the glare of light, thinking: This is it, all right. The worst part, the hardest part, the part of initiation that I figured out myself.

But just then, from somewhere far off, Millicent was sure of it, there came a melodic fluting, quite wild and sweet, and she knew that it must be the song of the heather birds as they went wheeling and gliding against wide blue horizons through vast spaces of air, their wings flashing quick and purple in the bright sun.

Within Millicent another melody soared, strong and exuberant,[12] a triumphant answer to the music of the darting heather birds that sang so clear and lilting over the far lands. And she knew that her own private initiation had just begun. ❖

---

11. **coronation:** crowning.
12. **exuberant** (ĭg-zo͞o′bər-ənt): full of unrestrained joy.

WORDS TO KNOW

conclusively (kən-klo͞o′sĭv-lē) *adv.* unquestionably; decisively

Teaching Options

Assessment Standardized Test Practice

CHOOSING THE BEST SUMMARY For some standardized tests, students will be asked to choose the best summary of a passage. To provide students with some help in choosing the best summary, read aloud or write on the chalkboard the following question:

Which of the following statements best summarizes the realization Millicent experiences after her conversation with the man on the bus?

A. She realizes that most people are friendly and that she can be friendly, too.

B. She realizes that she doesn't need to belong to a special club in order to be special herself.

C. She realizes that she likes Tracy more than the girls who belong to the sorority.

D. She realizes that many people are withdrawn and shy.

Lead students through the process of choosing the best summary. Consider each choice. Point out that, while all of the statements contain accurate information about what Millicent experiences, the best summary should include the most important information. For that reason, **B** is the best choice.

Connect to the Literature

1. **What Do You Think?** What do you think of Millicent at the end of the story? Support your opinion.

Comprehension Check
- What tasks did Millicent have to perform as part of the hazing process?
- Why wasn't Millicent's friend Tracy asked to join the sorority?
- What happens on the bus that helps Millicent make her decision?

Think Critically

2. What is Millicent's **motivation** for not joining the sorority?

THINK ABOUT
- her relationships with Tracy and Bev
- the tasks required of her during initiation week
- what she finds out about being in a sorority
- the effect of her conversation with the older man on the bus

3. Do you think Herb will have any interest in Millicent when she is not in the sorority? Why or why not?

4. How do you explain the meaning of the last sentence in the story?

5. ACTIVE READING SEQUENCE OF EVENTS With a partner, review the events that you recorded in your READER'S NOTEBOOK. How do you think your understanding of these events is influenced by the author's use of a **flashback?**

Extend Interpretations

6. **What If?** Imagine that Millicent had joined the sorority with the belief that she could persuade the others to invite Tracy to join. What would this have suggested about Millicent's **character?**

7. **Connect to Life** "Initiation" takes place in the early 1950s. Do you think this story is dated, or does its **theme,** or message, still apply today? Explain your reasoning.

Literary Analysis

INTERNAL CONFLICT **Conflict,** the struggle between opposing forces, is the basis of **plot** in most narrative literature. **Internal conflict** occurs when the struggle takes place within a character. In this story, Millicent experiences internal conflict in the process of deciding whether to join the sorority.

Paired Activity Working with a partner, return to the chart in your READER'S NOTEBOOK. What do you think were the most significant events that influenced Millicent's internal conflict and her decision to reject membership in the sorority? Cite evidence from the story to support your opinion.

SYMBOL A **symbol** is a person, place, or thing that stands for something beyond itself. In literature, objects and images are often used to symbolize abstract ideas. What do you think the heather birds symbolize for Millicent in the story?

REVIEW CLIMAX AND PLOT Where do you think the **climax** of the **plot** occurs in this story? How can you tell?

GUIDING STUDENT RESPONSE

Connect to the Literature

1. **What Do You Think?**
Students may feel respect for her strength to assert herself in the face of peer pressure.

Comprehension Check
- She has to obey the orders of an unpleasant member, sing in the public square, ask the people on the bus about their breakfast, ask in shops for broken crackers and mangoes, have a raw egg broken on her head, and remain alone in a gloomy, dark basement.
- According to one club member, Tracy is too different from the acceptable norm. She wears knee socks, for example, and carries a book bag.
- She talks to a man who gives her a bit of wisdom in the form of fantastic talk about birds.

Use Selection Quiz **Unit Three Resource Book,** p. 15.

Think Critically

2. Possible Response: She realizes the importance of being herself. She also reevaluates the friendships that are valuable to her.
3. Possible Response: No, because Herb never paid any attention to Millicent before she became a candidate for the club. He would not risk ridicule by dating either Millicent or Tracy. Yes, he admires her individuality.
4. Possible Response: It means that Millicent's true initiation—the independent thought and action required of an honest, moral individual—is not ending with this one action, but just beginning.
5. Possible Response: The events in the flashback form the real heart of the story; it adds interest and drama to understand what happened to motivate Millicent to change her mind.

Extend Interpretations

What If? Possible Response: Millicent would have seemed a weaker character who succumbed to peer pressure.

Connect to Life Possible Response: Reading today's newspapers, we see numerous examples of college students submitting to unreasonable and even dangerous hazing, sometimes resulting in death. This sort of "initiation" takes subtler forms in all sorts of organizations.

Literary Analysis

Internal Conflict In discussing Millicent's internal conflict, students should consider how the conflict is addressed and resolved. Students may note that before she talks to the man on the bus, she is having doubts about joining the sorority.

Symbol The birds symbolize freedom and individuality.

Review Climax and Plot Students may cite Millicent's encounter with the little man on the bus as the definitive climax because "from that time on initiations didn't bother Millicent at all."

Writing Options

1. **Rat Court Script** As a prewriting exercise, have students write a character sketch of Millicent. They may include directions for Millicent's actions in their script.
2. **Sorority Sister Analysis** Millicent is the same age as the other girls, and apparently in the same socio-economic group. She is interested in dating and enjoying herself, as they are. However, she is strong and individualistic, where they are more readily influenced by peer pressure.

Activities & Explorations

1. **TV Talk Show** To help students see the complexity of the situation, have the students playing Bev and Louise switch parts with the students playing Millicent and the host midway through the talk show. Urge students to do realistic role-playing when they defend the sorority, perhaps using examples from their own experience involving the value of being part of a group and conforming to certain norms.
2. **Fashion Update** Suggest that students draw the outfits that the girls would wear to the same function, such as a football game or out on a date. Encourage them to add color and texture to their drawings.

Inquiry & Research

Initiation in Publishing Suggest that students look in an autobiographical dictionary for basic information about Sylvia Plath before looking in a biography or other more specialized source.

Art Connection

Possible Response: These students have similar hairstyles and body types. Their portrayal conveys a sense of conformity and a loss of individuality.

Vocabulary in Action

Exercise A

1. a
2. b
3. c
4. c
5. c

Exercise B

1. vivacious
2. disinherited
3. fanfare
4. calculating
5. gnome

Choices & CHALLENGES

Writing Options

1. **Rat Court Script** Imagine what Millicent does and says at Rat Court. Write a script to portray the scene.
2. **Sorority Sister Analysis** Write an analysis of Millicent's character in which you compare and contrast her to the girls in the sorority. In what ways is she similar to the sorority girls? In what ways is she different? Use a Venn diagram like the one shown to organize your thoughts.

Writing Handbook
See page 1157: Compare and Contrast.

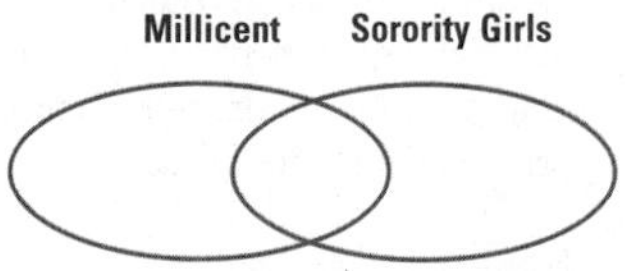

Activities & Explorations

1. **TV Talk Show** In a group of four, stage a talk show in which Louise and Bev argue in favor of sororities in high school and Millicent argues against them. One member can play the role of the host. The rest of the class can play the part of the audience.
~ **SPEAKING AND LISTENING**
2. **Fashion Update** Imagine Millicent, Tracy, Louise, and Bev in a contemporary high school. Design an outfit for each of them that conveys each girl's personality and social standing.
~**ART**

Inquiry and Research

Initiation in Publishing At the age of 20, Sylvia Plath submitted this story to *Seventeen* magazine. It was published in 1953. Find out more about Sylvia Plath's early successes in publishing.

Real World Link Before conducting your research, read the letter on page 410 to learn more about Plath's experience in getting this story published.

Art Connection

Notice the rounded, robot-like figures in the painting on page 401. What feelings are conveyed by the artist's rendering of the students at the Bauhaus school? How well do you think the painting evokes the setting of Millicent's school?

Vocabulary in Action

EXERCISE A: CONTEXT CLUES Note each boldfaced word. On your paper, write the letter of the phrase that best completes the sentence.

1. Students with **prestige** among their classmates are (a) held in high regard, (b) not respected, (c) totally ignored.
2. Millicent broke into **spontaneous** laughter at the man's strange story because (a) she knew what he was going to say, (b) she was not expecting such an odd response, (c) she had been in a silly mood all day.
3. An **exclusive** sorority might (a) welcome large numbers of new members, (b) open membership to male students, (c) try to restrict membership.
4. If the girls voted **conclusively** to accept Millicent, the sorority would (a) reject her immediately, (b) have to take another vote, (c) not need to vote again on the issue.
5. Girls who joined the sorority for **comradeship** hoped to (a) be left alone, (b) antagonize others, (c) make friends.

EXERCISE B: MEANING CLUES On your paper, write the Word to Know that best completes each title.

1. How to Be a Spirited and ________ Hostess
2. The Dashed Hopes of the ________ Heir
3. Parades, Celebrations, and Other Forms of ________
4. The Devious and ________ Plots of Caesar Carrington
5. The ________: A Creature of Folklore

WORDS TO KNOW				
calculating	conclusively	exclusive	gnome	spontaneous
comradeship	disinherited	fanfare	prestige	vivacious

Mini Lesson Grammar

VERB TENSES Instruction A verb tense is the form taken by a verb to show when, and under what conditions, something happens. Present, past, and future are the most familiar verb tenses: I *am* a student; I *was* a student; I *will be* a student. Remind students that there are many tenses, including the present perfect, past perfect, and progressive tenses. It is important for verbs in a sentence to agree in tense. Write the following sentences on the chalkboard. Underline the verbs as shown.

"She <u>thought</u> that Tracy is still her friend. She <u>will hope</u> the experience with the sorority <u>didn't cause</u> permanent harm to their friendship."

Activity Have students offer suggestions to rewrite the sentence so that all the verbs are in agreement with each other. For example: "She <u>thought</u> that Tracy <u>was</u> still her friend. She hoped the experience with the sorority <u>didn't cause</u> permanent harm to their friendship."

Practice Have students correct the verb tenses in the following sentences.

1. Millicent wants to join the sorority, but she worried about having left her friend Tracy behind.

   Possible Response: Millicent wanted to join the sorority, but she worried about leaving her friend Tracy behind.

Grammar in Context: Verb Tenses

In the following sentence from "Initiation," Sylvia Plath uses several verb tenses as Tracy makes a prediction about her friend Millicent.

> present / past perfect
> **"I know, but even so," Tracy had said quietly,**
> future / present future
> **"you'll change, whether you think you will or not."**

By changing the tense of a verb, you can indicate whether something is happening now, has happened in the past, or will happen in the future. In the example above, Sylvia Plath uses a tense known as the **past perfect tense.** This tense is used to indicate that an action occurred before some other action in the past.

WRITING EXERCISE Rewrite each sentence, following the directions in parentheses to change the tenses of the verbs.

Example: ***Original*** She will decide what to do when the clock strikes midnight. (Change two verbs to past tense.)

Rewritten She decided what to do when the clock struck midnight.

1. Millicent is planning what to say when the other girls welcome her into the sorority. (Change two verbs to past tense.)
2. She is invited to join the club because she has changed. (Change one verb to past tense and another to past perfect tense.)
3. "Bev is your big sister," Betsy said, "and you have to obey her every command." (Change two verbs to future tense.)

Sylvia Plath
1932–1963

Other Works
Ariel
Winter Trees
The Bell Jar
Collected Poems

Pressures of Achievement Few modern writers can match the early successes of Sylvia Plath. By the age of eight, Plath had experienced two extraordinary events—the publication of her first poem and her father's unexpected death—both of which would have long-lasting effects. Even before she entered college, Plath had drawings, stories, and poems published in national publications. She attended Smith College on a scholarship, where she continued to publish steadily and win honors for her work. By age 21, she was named a guest editor at *Mademoiselle* magazine after winning the magazine's College Fiction Contest.

Creative Dedication The glittering triumphs of early success, however, proved difficult to sustain. While still in college, Plath suffered a serious mental breakdown. After treatment, she returned to Smith, graduated with top honors, and was awarded the prestigious Fulbright scholarship which allowed her to study in England at Cambridge University. In England, Plath met the poet Ted Hughes, whom she later married. He observed that her drive to express herself and to define herself through her poetry picked up momentum over the years, until it reached almost a frenzied state.

Triumph for Poetry Plath's poems are intensely personal and complex; through her poetry she explored the painful dilemmas of her own life as poet, wife, mother, and daughter. Her only novel, *The Bell Jar* (1963), was based upon her personal experience of mental breakdown. In 1963, after battling years of depression, she took her own life. As a critic observed, her final poems are a "triumph for poetry at the moment that they are a defeat for their author." Even after her premature death, her reputation continued to grow, and in 1982 her work *Collected Poems* was awarded the Pulitzer Prize.

Grammar in Context

Writing Exercise

1. Millicent was planning what to say when the other girls welcomed her into the sorority.
2. She was invited to join the club because she had changed.
3. "Bev will be your big sister," Betsy says, "and you will have to obey her every command."

2. Betsy Johnson is the club secretary and will volunteer her cellar for the final initiation ritual.
   Possible Response: Betsy Johnson was the club secretary and volunteered her cellar for the final initiation ritual.
3. After the man on the bus talks about the heather birds, Millicent will have felt very cheerful.
   Possible Response: After the man on the bus talked about the heather birds, Millicent felt very cheerful.
4. "You did exactly as I say for the rest of the week," Bev snaps.
   Possible Response: "You will do exactly as I say for the rest of the week," Bev snapped.

Use **Unit Three Resource Book** p. 14 for additional support.

Use **Grammar Transparencies and Copymasters,** p. 127.

Use McDougal Littell's ***Language Network,*** Chapter 6, for more instruction in verb tenses.

Real WORLD Link

Primary Source

Objectives
- recognize internal conflict
- infer a main idea

Connecting to the Literature
Sylvia Plath's short story "The Initiation" (p. 397) tells of Millicent's desire to be accepted into an exclusive group of friends. Plath's desire for her work to be accepted is reflected in the quote "Millicent had waited a long time for acceptance, longer than most" (p. 400).

Reading for Information

Plath's own internal conflict is revealed when she writes to her mother "I never even cherished the smallest hope of getting one of the third prizes" [from *Seventeen*], and "this news makes me feel that I am maybe not destined to deteriorate after all."

1 Plath is surprised. Since her estimated time for a response had passed, she no longer thought about the entry. When Plath says that she is "maybe not destined to deteriorate," she reveals her insecurity in her ability to be a good writer.

2 Plath states that she loves her mother, wants to "lay more laurels" at her feet, and credits her mother for giving her the "heredity and the incentive to be mentally ambitious." The relationship seems close and loving.

from *Letters Home*

On Getting "Initiation" Published, by Sylvia Plath

October 6, 1952

Dear Mummy,

❶ Wow! Speak of appropriate psychological moments for getting unexpected good news, this was one. I wandered lazily downstairs just before lunch today and glanced casually in my mailbox. Two letters from you. I opened the little one first, looked at it, puzzled for a few minutes before it suddenly dawned on me what the contents were. I never even cherished the smallest hope of getting one of the third prizes [from *Seventeen* for "Initiation"] this year—as you know, I figured out the relative deadline for their decision by my other story and had long since given up thinking about it.

This news makes me feel that I am maybe not destined to deteriorate, after all. . . .

Sylvia Plath, her mother, and her brother, pictured above in 1949.

❷ Your last big morale-building letter was most appreciated. You are the most wonderful mummy that a girl ever had, and I only hope I can continue to lay more laurels at your feet. Warren and I both love you and admire you more than anybody in the world for all you have done for us all our lives. For it is you who has given us the heredity and the incentive to be mentally ambitious. Thank you a million times!

Your very own Sivvy

Reading for Information

Letters Home is a collection of letters Sylvia Plath wrote to her mother from 1950 to 1963. The letter reprinted here was written after she had won second prize ($200) for "Initiation" in *Seventeen's* short story contest. It provides details that shed light on the writer's personal life and its relationship to her writing.

ANALYZING A LETTER
A letter is a **primary source** because it offers firsthand information about a topic. From the personal details in letters, you can often gain insight into an individual's thoughts and emotions. You may also get a detailed account of an event.

YOUR TURN Use the activities below to analyze the letter.

❶ How does Plath react to the news that her story has won a prize? What clues suggest Plath's feelings about her writing?

❷ From this passage, how would you describe Plath's relationship with her mother?

Inquiry & Research

Activity Link: "Initiation" p. 408
Beginning with the publication of "Initiation," create a time line of Plath's published works. Refer to the Internet, encyclopedia articles, published letters, and critical reviews for information.

More Online: Research Starter
www.mcdougallittel.com

410

Mini Lesson: Inquiry & Research

The Inquiry & Research activity on this page links to the Inquiry & Research section of Choices and Challenges (p. 408).

Instruction The time between events can be graphically depicted by creating a time line. In gathering information to include on the time line, encourage students to take notes indicating the title and date of each of Plath's publications. Information for beginning the time line can be found in Plath's biographical background (p. 409).

Practice Students may use reference print or nonprint sources including the Internet to complete the time line. Have students draw conclusions about Plath's writing career based on patterns they observe in her publishing history.

PREPARING to *Read*

Getting a Job

from I Know Why the Caged Bird Sings

Autobiography by MAYA ANGELOU

". . . in the struggle lies the glory."

Connect to Your Life

On the Job Think about a part-time or summer job that you have had in the past or one that you hope to have in the future. How would you feel if you were denied the job because of your race, religion, ethnic background, or something else that had nothing to do with your qualifications? How would you respond to such a situation?

Build Background

Job Discrimination "Getting a Job" takes place in San Francisco in the 1940s during a period when more and more jobs were opening up to American women because so many men were overseas fighting in World War II. However, despite these new opportunities for women, racial prejudice still limited the types of employment open to African Americans.

The following selection is an excerpt from *I Know Why the Caged Bird Sings,* the first in a series of autobiographical works written by Maya Angelou. Angelou, born Marguerite Johnson, was raised by her grandmother in Arkansas, but at the age of 12 she moved to San Francisco to live with her mother.

WORDS TO KNOW
Vocabulary Preview

ascend	haphazardly
charade	haughty
comprehend	hypocrisy
dexterous	ostensibly
diametrically	terse

Focus Your Reading

LITERARY ANALYSIS NARRATIVE NONFICTION An autobiography can be classified as a work of **narrative nonfiction,** which tells a true story about real people, places, and events. As such, it has many of the same elements that a fictional narrative has. Angelou, for example, creates a vivid **setting,** as illustrated by this description of her room:

My room had all the cheeriness of a dungeon and the appeal of a tomb.

As you read this selection, look for evidence of other fictional elements, such as **plot** and **conflict,** that Angelou uses to bring events to life.

ACTIVE READING IDENTIFYING CAUSE AND EFFECT IN NONFICTION When reading narrative nonfiction, you often get a better understanding of events if you pause to consider their **cause-and-effect** relationships. The following sentence illustrates such a relationship:

***Women had replaced men on the streetcars as conductors and motormen* [cause], *and the thought of sailing up and down the hills of San Francisco in a dark-blue uniform . . . caught my fancy* [effect].**

The first condition—women working as streetcar conductors—caused the effect: Angelou imagined herself doing such work.

READER'S NOTEBOOK As you read this selection, jot down at least three causes that led Marguerite to seek the job of streetcar conductor. Then list at least three effects that this experience had on her life.

OVERVIEW

This selection is included in the **Grade 10 InterActive Reader.**

Objectives

1. understand elements of **narrative nonfiction (Literary Analysis)**
2. **identify cause and effect in nonfiction (Active Reading)**

Summary

The narrator, Maya Angelou, is a fifteen-year-old African-American girl living in San Francisco with her mother during the 1940s. Because many men are overseas fighting in World War II, many previously unavailable jobs are now open to women. Angelou wants a job as a conductor on a cable car. Her mother reminds her that the company doesn't hire African Americans. Through sheer determination, Angelou gets the job, and puts up with split shifts and long hours. By the end of her account, when she returns to high school, she sees that her experience has moved her even further away from the values and preoccupations of her peers.

Thematic Link

Angelou's experience shapes her youth and strengthens her self-confidence.

Editor's Note

This excerpt has been edited slightly to delete material that may be considered objectionable.

5-Minute Warm-Up

Daily Language SkillBuilder

Have students **proofread** the display sentences on page 381i and write them correctly. The sentences also appear on Transparency 13 of **Grammar Transparencies and Copymasters.**

Mini Lesson **Preteaching Vocabulary**

If you would like to preteach the WORDS TO KNOW for this selection, use the Mini Lesson, p. 415.

LESSON RESOURCES

UNIT THREE RESOURCE BOOK, pp. 16–20

ASSESSMENT RESOURCES

Formal Assessment, pp. 67–68

Teacher's Guide to Assessment and Portfolio Use

Test Generator

SKILLS TRANSPARENCIES AND COPYMASTERS

Literary Analysis
- Types of Nonfiction, T4 (for Cooperative Learning Activity, p. 417)

Reading and Critical Thinking
- Cause and Effect, T1 (for Identifying Cause and Effect in Nonfiction, p. 411)
- Notetaking, T40 (for Reader's Notebook, p. 411)

Grammar
- Auxiliary Verbs, C69 (for Mini Lesson, p. 418)

Vocabulary
- Analogies, C50 (for Mini Lesson, p. 415)

Writing
- Levels of Language, T12 (for Writing Option 1, p. 418)
- Effective Language, T13 (for Writing Option 2, p. 418)
- Showing, Not Telling, T22 (for Writing Option 2, p. 418)

Communications
- Formal Presentations, T10 (for Inquiry & Research, p. 418)

INTEGRATED TECHNOLOGY

Audio Library

Internet: Research Starter

Visit our website:
www.mcdougallittell.com

Getting a Job

TEACHING THE LITERATURE

Reading Skills and Strategies: PREVIEW

Briefly summarize the story, analyzing and pointing out the cause-and-effect relationship of the events of the story. Discuss the advertisements on the opening page, the title of the story, and the background material on job discrimination.

Active Reading CAUSE AND EFFECT

Events in the story often cause a change in a character's attitude toward himself or herself, toward another character, or toward life. The result of the event is called the effect. Ask students to track and analyze how each event or difficulty affects Marguerite.

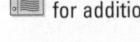

Use **Unit Three Resource Book** p. 17 for additional support.

Literary Analysis ELEMENTS OF NARRATIVE NONFICTION

Although this is a nonfiction account, it includes elements of fiction—plot, conflict, and setting. Students should note the exposition, rising action, climax, falling action, and resolution of the plot.

Use **Unit Three Resource Book** p. 18 for additional support.

Maya Angelou

My room had all the cheeriness of a dungeon and the appeal of a tomb. It was going to be impossible to stay there, but leaving held no attraction for me, either. . . .

The answer came to me with the suddenness of a collision. I would go to work. Mother wouldn't be difficult to convince; after all, in school I was a year ahead of my grade and Mother was a firm believer in self-sufficiency. In fact, she'd be pleased to think that I had that much gumption,[1] that much of her in my character. (She liked to speak of herself as the original "do-it-yourself girl.")

Once I had settled on getting a job, all that remained was to decide which kind of job I was most fitted for. My intellectual pride had kept me from selecting typing, shorthand or filing as subjects in school, so office work was ruled out. War plants and shipyards demanded birth certificates, and mine would reveal me to be fifteen, and ineligible for work. So the well-paying defense jobs were also out. Women had replaced men on the streetcars as

1. **gumption:** initiative; boldness.

Teaching Options

Mini Lesson Speaking and Listening

DRAMATIC READING Instruction Make the following points about dramatic readings:

- Focus on a specific scene
- Include details that reveal character and conflict
- Consider characters' tone

Prepare Ask students to prepare a dramatic presentation based on Marguerite's repeated efforts to be employed at the Market Street Railway Company. Help them work in cooperative groups to make valid interpretations of her conversations with the receptionist and the organizations that were reluctant to help her. Encourage students to consider how Marguerite's character traits can be conveyed through choice of words, voice, and posture. Then have them do the same for the other characters.

Present Students should justify their choice of verbal and nonverbal performance techniques by referring to their analysis and interpretations of the text. Student groups can decide how they will present the dramatic reading. Students who are audience members should evaluate how the performance increases their appreciation and understanding of Marguerite's quest to get a job.

conductors and motormen, and the thought of sailing up and down the hills of San Francisco in a dark-blue uniform, with a money changer at my belt, caught my fancy.

Mother was as easy as I had anticipated. The world was moving so fast, so much money was being made, so many people were dying in Guam,[2] and Germany, that hordes of strangers became good friends overnight. Life was cheap and death entirely free. How could she have the time to think about my academic career?

To her question of what I planned to do, I replied that I would get a job on the streetcars. She rejected the proposal with: "They don't accept colored people on the streetcars."

I would like to claim an immediate fury which was followed by the noble determination to break the restricting tradition. But the truth is, my first reaction was one of disappointment. I'd pictured myself, dressed in a neat blue serge suit, my money changer swinging jauntily at my waist, and a cheery smile for the passengers which would make their own work day brighter.

From disappointment, I gradually ascended the emotional ladder to haughty indignation, and finally to that state of stubbornness where the mind is locked like the jaws of an enraged bulldog.

I would go to work on the streetcars and wear a blue serge suit. Mother gave me her support with one of her usual terse asides, "That's what you want to do? Then nothing beats a trial but a failure. Give it everything you've got. I've told you many times, 'Can't do is like Don't Care.' Neither of them have a home."

Translated, that meant there was nothing a person can't do, and there should be nothing a human being didn't care about. It was the most positive encouragement I could have hoped for.

In the offices of the Market Street Railway Company, the receptionist seemed as surprised to see me there as I was surprised to find the interior dingy and the décor drab. Somehow I had expected waxed surfaces and carpeted floors. If I had met no resistance, I might have decided against working for such a poor-mouth-looking concern. As it was, I explained that I had come to see about a job. She asked, was I sent by an agency, and when I replied that I was not, she told me they were only accepting applicants from agencies.

The classified pages of the morning papers had listed advertisements for motorettes[3] and conductorettes and I reminded her of that. She gave me a face full of astonishment that my suspicious nature would not accept.

"I am applying for the job listed in this morning's *Chronicle* and I'd like to be presented to your personnel manager." While I spoke in supercilious[4] accents, and looked at the room as if I had an oil well in my own backyard, my armpits were being pricked by millions of hot pointed needles. She saw her escape and dived into it.

"He's out. He's out for the day. You might call tomorrow and if he's in, I'm sure you can see him." Then she swiveled her chair around on its rusty screws and with that I was supposed to be dismissed.

"May I ask his name?"

She half turned, acting surprised to find me still there.

"His name? Whose name?"

"Your personnel manager."

2. **Guam:** a U.S. island territory that was a scene of fierce fighting during World War II.

3. **motorettes:** female streetcar drivers.

4. **supercilious** (so͞o′pər-sĭl′ē-əs): disdainful; haughty.

WORDS TO KNOW
ascend (ə-sĕnd′) *v.* to rise; climb
haughty (hô′tē) *adj.* proud; arrogant
terse (tûrs) *adj.* brief; concise

413

Customizing Instruction

Less Proficient Readers

Have students think about the following questions as they read the selection.

- Who is the main character? What does she want?
  Answer: the narrator; a job as a streetcar conductor
- What steps does she take to get what she wants?
  Answer: She applies in person, seeks the help of Negro organizations, and visits the streetcar company's offices incessantly.
- Do you admire her determination, or do you think she is foolish to keep fighting the racial prejudice that prevented African Americans from getting certain jobs?

Gifted and Talented

Students may be interested to find out that women held jobs in defense plants, building munitions and defense vehicles and even fielded professional baseball teams. Encourage students to hypothesize what happened to these women when the war was over and the men came home and were ready to take their jobs back. Students can then share findings with the class once the selection has been read.

BLOCK SCHEDULING: MANAGING TIME

If your schedule requires that you cover the lesson objectives in a shorter time, use . . .

- Preparing to Read, p. 411
- Thinking Through the Literature, p. 417

If you want to take advantage of longer class time, use . . .

- TE Teaching Options: Preteaching Vocabulary p. 415; Viewing and Representing, p. 414; Speaking and Listening, p. 412; Standardized Test Practice, p. 416
- Choices & Challenges and Author Activity, p. 418

Reading and Analyzing

Reading Skills and Strategies: PREDICTING
Have students predict what they think is going to happen to Marguerite. Ask whether they believe she will get a job as a conductorette on the streetcar.
Possible Response: Yes, she will get the job because she is fiercely determined to do so.

Literary Analysis: CONFLICT
Have students meet in small groups to identify and discuss the various conflicts Marguerite experiences. Remind them that there are two kinds of conflict—internal and external.
Possible Response: Marguerite experiences internal conflict when she becomes discouraged in her quest. There are several external conflicts: between Marguerite and the receptionist, between Marguerite and the white conductorette, between Marguerite and the Negro organizations, and between Marguerite and those with racist views.

We were firmly joined in the hypocrisy to play out the scene.

"The personnel manager? Oh, he's Mr. Cooper, but I'm not sure you'll find him here tomorrow. He's . . . Oh, but you can try."

"Thank you."

"You're welcome."

And I was out of the musty room and into the even mustier lobby. In the street I saw the receptionist and myself going faithfully through paces that were stale with familiarity, although I had never encountered that kind of situation before and, probably, neither had she. We were like actors who, knowing the play by heart, were still able to cry afresh over the old tragedies and laugh spontaneously at the comic situations.

The miserable little encounter had nothing to do with me, the me of me, any more than it had to do with that silly clerk. The incident was a recurring dream, concocted years before by stupid whites and it eternally came back to haunt us all. The secretary and I were like Hamlet and Laertes[5] in the final scene, where, because of harm done by one ancestor to another, we were bound to duel to the death. Also because the play must end somewhere.

1 I went further than forgiving the clerk, I accepted her as a fellow victim of the same puppeteer.

On the streetcar, I put my fare into the box and the conductorette looked at me with the usual hard eyes of white contempt. "Move into the car, please move on in the car." She patted her money changer.

Her Southern nasal accent sliced my meditation and I looked deep into my thoughts. All lies, all comfortable lies. The receptionist was not innocent and neither was I. The whole charade we had played out in that crummy waiting room had directly to do with me, Black, and her, white.

I wouldn't move into the streetcar but stood on the ledge over the conductor, glaring. My mind shouted so energetically that the announcement made my veins stand out, and my mouth tighten into a prune.

I WOULD HAVE THE JOB. I WOULD BE A CONDUCTORETTE AND SLING A FULL MONEY CHANGER FROM MY BELT. I WOULD.

The next three weeks were a honeycomb of determination with apertures[6] for the days to go in and out. The Negro organizations to whom I appealed for support bounced me back and

5. **Hamlet and Laertes** (lā-ûr'tēz): characters who kill each other in a sword fight in the last scene of Shakespeare's *Hamlet*.

6. **apertures** (ăp'ər-chərz): openings.

WORDS TO KNOW

hypocrisy (hĭ-pŏk'rĭ-sē) *n.* a pretense of being what one is not; falsehood
charade (shə-rād') *n.* an ill-disguised pretense

Teaching Options

Mini Lesson Viewing and Representing

ART APPRECIATION
Instruction This photograph reveals a loaded streetcar on a typical work day in the 1940s.
Application Ask students to share their observations about the work scene based on the photograph.
Possible Response: Many peopled depended on the streetcar for transportation; most of the passengers are white males. It would be difficult to get a ticket from everyone.

forth like a shuttlecock on a badminton court. Why did I insist on that particular job? Openings were going begging that paid nearly twice the money. The minor officials with whom I was able to win an audience thought me mad. Possibly I was.

Downtown San Francisco became alien and cold, and the streets I had loved in a personal familiarity were unknown lanes that twisted with malicious intent. Old buildings, whose gray rococo façades housed my memories of the Forty-Niners, and Diamond Lil, Robert Service, Sutter and Jack London,[7] were then imposing structures viciously joined to keep me out. My trips to the streetcar office were of the frequency of a person on salary. The struggle expanded. I was no longer in conflict only with the Market Street Railway but with the marble lobby of the building which housed its offices, and elevators and their operators.

During this period of strain Mother and I began our first steps on the long path toward mutual adult admiration. She never asked for reports and I didn't offer any details. But every morning she made breakfast, gave me carfare and lunch money, as if I were going to work. She comprehended the perversity of life, that in the struggle lies the joy. That I was no glory seeker was obvious to her, and that I had to exhaust every possibility before giving in was also clear.

On my way out of the house one morning she said, "Life is going to give you just what you put in it. Put your whole heart in everything you do, and pray, then you can wait." Another time she reminded me that "God helps those who help themselves." She had a store of aphorisms[8] which she dished out as the occasion demanded. Strangely, as bored as I was with clichés, her inflection gave them something new, and set me thinking for a little while at least. Later when asked how I got my job, I was never able to say exactly. I only knew that one day, which was tiresomely like all the others before it, I sat in the Railway office, ostensibly waiting to be interviewed. The receptionist called me to her desk and shuffled a bundle of papers to me. They were job application forms. She said they had to be filled

7. **Forty-Niners . . . Jack London:** Forty-niners were people who flocked to northern California in the gold rush of 1849; Diamond Lil was a colorful character of the gold-rush era; Robert Service was a Canadian poet who wrote about life in the mining camps of the 1897 Klondike gold rush; John Sutter owned the California ranch where gold was discovered in 1848; Jack London was a writer who grew up in the San Francisco area and joined the Klondike gold rush.

8. **aphorisms** (ăf'ə-rĭz'əmz): proverbs.

WORDS TO KNOW
comprehend (kŏm'prĭ-hĕnd') *v.* to understand
ostensibly (ŏ-stĕn'sə-blē) *adv.* apparently; supposedly

Customizing Instruction

Less Proficient Readers

1 Discuss the phrase "fellow victims of the same puppeteer." Explain that the author is saying that both whites and blacks are victims of racism.

Next, to help students understand how cause and effect works in the narrative, ask them the following questions:

- Why are there jobs available on the streetcars?
- Why does Marguerite believe she might now get one of these jobs?

Possible Response: The men who would ordinarily have these jobs are fighting in the war. Thus, Marguerite believes she has an opportunity, in spite of her sex and race.

What does Marguerite's mother do? How do her actions affect Marguerite?
Possible Response: Her mother supports her by preparing her food, giving her money and advice, and later picking her up from work when she gets the job. The effect is that Marguerite feels fortified and supported in her struggle to achieve her goal.

Set a Purpose Have students predict whether Marguerite will enjoy the job once she gets it.

Mini Lesson: Preteaching Vocabulary

ANALOGIES Instruction Introduce analogies to students by telling them to think of mathematical equations, in which the quantities on either side of the equal sign are the same. Word analogies are much the same. They compare two pairs of words that have the same relationship. The words may be antonyms or synonyms, or there may be another logical connection between them. Understanding how to use analogies helps build vocabulary and logical thinking skills.
Write the following analogies on the chalkboard:
Ascend is to climb as eat is to consume. (synonyms)
Haughty is to humble as simple is to complicated. (antonyms)
Terse is to statement as boring is to speech. (shows relationship between adjectives/nouns)

Practice Have students work in pairs to create analogy statements for the following: *hypocrisy, charade, comprehend, ostensibly, dexterous, haphazardly,* and *diametrically*. Encourage them to use a dictionary and a thesaurus. Remind students that the parts of speech and word order in each pair of words must match.

Use **Vocabulary Transparencies and Copymasters**, p. 50.

A lesson on analogies appears on p. 263 in the Pupil's Edition.

Reading and Analyzing

Reading Skills and Strategies: EVALUATING
How do students react to the fact that Marguerite lied about her age and her former work experience in order to be eligible for the job?
Possible Response: Students may or may not agree that lying was acceptable. Many may feel that special circumstances existed which excused her behavior.

Reading Skills and Strategies: CONNECTING
Ask students why they think Marguerite now feels alienated when she returns to school. Why haven't her independence, money, and new clothes made her "a part of the gay life" of her contemporaries, as she had hoped? Ask students to describe moments when they have felt different from their peers.
Possible Response: Because of her experiences, Marguerite has gained more than material possessions. She has become an adult, wise and independent. Her struggles to overcome racism and her own internal conflicts have caused her to mature in a way that her peers have not.

Literary Analysis: DESCRIPTION
Have students list the descriptive details they remember from the narrative. Ask them how these details increase the power of the narrative.
Possible Response: Descriptive details such as the musty lobby, the nasal accent of the conductorette, the old buildings, the blue serge suit, and "swinging on the back of the rackety trolley" allow the reader to experience the events as the author remembers them.

in triplicate. I had little time to wonder if I had won or not, for the standard questions reminded me of the necessity for dexterous lying. How old was I? List my previous jobs, starting from the last held and go backward to the first. How much money did I earn, and why did I leave the position? Give two references (not relatives).

Sitting at a side table my mind and I wove a cat's ladder of near truths and total lies. I kept my face blank (an old art) and wrote quickly the fable of Marguerite Johnson, aged nineteen, former companion and driver for Mrs. Annie Henderson (a White Lady) in Stamps, Arkansas.

I was given blood tests, aptitude tests, physical coordination tests, and Rorschachs,[9] then on a blissful day I was hired as the first Negro on the San Francisco streetcars.

Mother gave me the money to have my blue serge suit tailored, and I learned to fill out work cards, operate the money changer and punch transfers. The time crowded together and at an End of Days I was swinging on the back of the rackety trolley, smiling sweetly and persuading my charges to "step forward in the car, please."

For one whole semester the street cars and I shimmied up and scooted down the sheer hills of San Francisco. I lost some of my need for the Black ghetto's shielding-sponge quality, as I clanged and cleared my way down Market Street, with its honky-tonk homes for homeless sailors, past the quiet retreat of Golden Gate Park and along closed undwelled-in-looking dwellings of the Sunset District.

My work shifts were split so haphazardly that it was easy to believe that my superiors had chosen them maliciously. Upon mentioning my suspicions to Mother, she said, "Don't worry about it. You ask for what you want, and you pay for what you get. And I'm going to show you that it ain't no trouble when you pack double."

She stayed awake to drive me out to the car barn at four thirty in the mornings, or to pick me up when I was relieved just before dawn. Her awareness of life's perils convinced her that while I would be safe on the public conveyances,[10] she "wasn't about to trust a taxi driver with her baby."

When the spring classes began, I resumed my commitment with formal education. I was so much wiser and older, so much more independent, with a bank account and clothes that I had bought for myself, that I was sure that I had learned and earned the magic formula which would make me a part of the gay life my contemporaries led.

Not a bit of it. Within weeks, I realized that my schoolmates and I were on paths moving diametrically away from each other. They were concerned and excited over the approaching football games, but I had in my immediate past raced a car down a dark and foreign Mexican mountain. They concentrated great interest on who was worthy of being student body president, and when the metal bands would be removed from their teeth, while I remembered sleeping for a month in a wrecked automobile and conducting a streetcar in the uneven hours of the morning. ❖

9. **Rorschachs** (rôr'shäks'): psychological tests in which people are asked to interpret a set of inkblots.
10. **conveyances** (kən-vā'ən-səz): means of transportation.

WORDS TO KNOW
dexterous (dĕk'stər-əs) *adj.* skillful; clever
haphazardly (hăp-hăz'ərd-lē) *adv.* in an aimless or random manner
diametrically (dī'ə-mĕt'rĭ-klē) *adv.* in complete opposition

Teaching Options

Assessment Standardized Test Practice

CHOOSING THE BEST SUMMARY For some standardized tests, students will be asked to choose the best summary of a passage. To provide students with some help in choosing the best summary, read aloud or write on the chalkboard the following question:
What is the best summary of the narrative?

A. Marguerite wants a job as a conductor on a streetcar, and she gets one.

B. Marguerite wants a job as a conductor on a streetcar. Though she encounters many obstacles because of her race, she is persistent and eventually gets the job.

C. Marguerite's mother lives in San Francisco. Marguerite's mother supports her in her goal to get a job. Her mother fixes Marguerite breakfast each morning and gives her lunch money and carfare.

Lead students through the process of choosing the best summary. Consider each choice. Point out that, while all of the statements contain accurate information about what Marguerite experiences, the best summary should include the most important information. For that reason, **B** is the best choice.

Connect to the Literature

1. **What Do You Think?** What is your judgment of Marguerite? Jot down words and phrases that describe your view of her.

Comprehension Check
- Why does Marguerite initially decide to get a job?
- How does the receptionist respond to Marguerite?
- How does Marguerite's mother encourage her?

Think Critically

2. **ACTIVE READING** **IDENTIFYING CAUSE AND EFFECT IN NONFICTION** Review the **causes** and the **effects** that you identified in your **READER'S NOTEBOOK**. What do you think is the most important cause that led Marguerite to seek her job? What effect of the job is likely to have made the most impact on her life?

3. In your opinion, why does Marguerite finally get the job?

4. What do you think of the mother's attitude toward her daughter and toward life?

THINK ABOUT
- the advice that the mother gives
- why the mother "never asked for reports"
- how the mother responds to Marguerite's split work shifts

5. What do you think are the personal qualities that helped Marguerite to become a conductorette? Do you think these qualities are helpful for any person who is job hunting?

Extend Interpretations

6. **Comparing Texts** Identify another person or **character** that you have read about in this text who might be able to match Marguerite's determination. Compare and contrast how those qualities come through in each selection.

7. **Connect to Life** Explain the meaning of each of the following **aphorisms,** or wise sayings, that Marguerite's mother used to give her daughter advice, and discuss how each one could apply to your life:
- "Nothing beats a trial but a failure."
- "Life is going to give you just what you put into it."
- "You ask for what you want, and you pay for what you get."

Literary Analysis

NARRATIVE NONFICTION A work of **narrative nonfiction** tells a story about real-life events, people, and places. It uses elements typically found in fictional narratives to present factual information and to bring the events to life for the reader. For example, the **"plot"** of "Getting a Job" consists of the events that led Angelou to her job as streetcar conductor. In storylike fashion, her account has a beginning, middle, and end. The author takes pains to create vivid **settings** in which the action takes place, from her room to the offices of the Market Street Railway Company to the hills of San Francisco. Like a fictional narrative, Angelou's story depends upon **conflict,** which is portrayed through **dialogue** and **description.**

Cooperative Learning Activity In a group, review the elements of fiction described on pages 17–18. Then choose a passage from this selection to illustrate each fictional term that you think can be applied to Angelou's text. For example, you can choose a particularly vivid description to show how Angelou creates setting. Read each passage aloud and explain how it illustrates a technique normally associated with fiction that can also be used by writers of nonfiction.

GUIDING STUDENT RESPONSE

Connect to the Literature

1. **What Do You Think?**
Students will note that she is determined, proud, and hardworking.

Comprehension Check
- She is bored, is a year ahead in school, and wants to make some money.
- She reacts to Marguerite with surprise and doesn't take her seriously. Eventually, she treats her with a cool, formal politeness.
- She first encourages Marguerite and she doesn't ask too many questions. She also helps her by taking her to and from work at inconvenient hours.

Use Selection Quiz **Unit Three Resource Book** p. 20.

Think Critically

2. Students may respond that the challenge was the most important cause. The most important effect, perseverance can pay off.
3. Possible Response: Her decision to try and her determination are the most important factors.
4. Possible Response: Her attitude is strong and supportive, and her advice is sound.
5. Possible Response: Her determination is the key to getting the job. Patience is important, as is her attention to her appearance.

Extend Interpretations

Comparing Texts Class discussion may prove lively as students share why they have chosen a specific character.

Connect to Life
- Possible Response: We learn from our failures as well as our successes, but we learn nothing if we don't try at all.
- Possible Response: Nothing is free; everything worthwhile involves effort.
- Possible Response: Everything in life has a value and a price. If we want something we must be willing—and able—to pay the price.

Literary Analysis

Narrative Nonfiction Remind students that narrative nonfiction has many of the same elements that a fictional narrative has. Ask students to list the elements of fiction before beginning this activity. Students should describe and analyze the development of plot and identify conflicts and their resolutions. They should also analyze the relevance of setting to the text's meaning.

Choices & CHALLENGES

Writing Options

1. Ideal Job Description Write a job description for a job that you would like to have. Include requirements about age, qualifications, experience, and salary. Model your description on the "Help Wanted" ads in the newspaper. Place your job description in your **Working Portfolio.**

2. Inspirational Narrative Think of a person you know or have read about who, like Marguerite, has overcome obstacles with his or her personal determination. Write a narrative in which you tell about that person's struggle.

Writing Handbook
See pages 1155–1156: Narrative Writing.

Inquiry & Research

Civil Rights Research and prepare an oral report on the civil rights laws that Congress passed in the 1960s. Which laws would now be applied to the kind of job discrimination that Angelou encountered? How are those laws enforced today?

More Online: Research Starter
www.mcdougallittell.com

Vocabulary in Action

EXERCISE: ASSESSMENT PRACTICE On your paper, indicate whether each of the following pairs of words are *Synonyms* or *Antonyms*. Words to Know are shown in boldfaced type.

1. systematically—**haphazardly**
2. **comprehend**—know
3. fraudulence—**hypocrisy**
4. **terse**—lengthy
5. humble—**haughty**
6. **dexterous**—clumsy
7. misrepresentation—**charade**
8. **ascend**—drop
9. evidently—**ostensibly**
10. **diametrically**—oppositely

Maya Angelou
1928–

Other Works
I Know Why the Caged Bird Sings
Even the Stars Look Lonesome
"On the Pulse of Morning"
Wouldn't Take Nothin' for My Journey Now

A Southern Childhood Marguerite Johnson, now better known as Maya Angelou, acquired her nickname of Maya from her brother, who called her "My" or "Mine." She was not yet five when her parents divorced, and she and her brother went to live in Stamps, Arkansas, where her father's mother owned a small grocery store. There she experienced the poverty of the Great Depression. In 1940, after her mother remarried, she moved to San Francisco where, in addition to working as a streetcar conductor, she studied dance and drama.

Multiple Talents After high school, she worked as a cook, a waitress, a dancer, and a singer. In the late 1950s, she performed in off-Broadway plays, joined the Harlem Writers Guild, and served as the northern coordinator of Martin Luther King's Southern Christian Leadership Conference. In 1963, she taught music and drama in the newly independent African nation of Ghana.

Writing Fame Encouraged by writer friends like James Baldwin and Jules Feiffer, Angelou wrote the autobiography of her early years, published in 1970 as *I Know Why the Caged Bird Sings.* A resounding success, it prompted several more installments, including *The Heart of a Woman* (1981), which chronicles Angelou's activist years in New York, and *All God's Children Need Traveling Shoes* (1986), about her time in Africa. Also a talented poet, she was invited by Bill Clinton to create and read a poem at his 1993 inauguration as president.

Author Activity

Powerful Poetry Find out more about Maya Angelou's role at the 1993 presidential inauguration. What poem did she recite? Obtain a copy of the poem, and rehearse and present an oral recitation.

Writing Options

1. **Ideal Job Description** Remind students to balance elements of the ideal job, such as pay and satisfaction. A job that is ideal for the summer between junior and senior years would be very different from that to which a student might devote years of college study.
2. **Inspirational Narrative** Help your students brainstorm to find someone they actually know who has overcome obstacles. Help them see that what looks like a small barrier to an outsider may have taken great grit to conquer. Such things as learning to read as an adult, gaining the courage to beat depression, or overcoming a disability would make effective narratives.

Inquiry & Research

Civil Rights Students will note that the Civil Rights Act of 1964 prevents discrimination based on race, religion, or gender.

Vocabulary in Action

EXERCISE

1. antonym
2. synonym
3. synonym
4. antonym
5. antonym
6. antonym
7. synonym
8. antonym
9. synonym
10. synonym

Author Activity

Powerful Poetry At President Clinton's inauguration in 1993, Maya Angelou read a poem that had been especially written for the occasion—"On the Pulse of Morning." The long poem is a call for hope, diversity, and equality. Since then, she has been a national celebrity. The last poet to appear at a presidential inauguration was Robert Frost, who read his poem "The Gift Outright" at John F. Kennedy's inauguration.

Mini Lesson Grammar

HELPING VERBS A verb phrase has two parts—the main verb and a helping verb. Helping verbs include the following: *be* (all forms), *has, have, had, shall, will, can, may, should, would, could, might, must, do, did,* and *does*. Write the following sentence on the chalkboard:

"He is going to the movie with Janice, so he can reassure her in case she gets scared."

Have students underline the helping verbs in the sentence. *(is, can)* Discuss how a helping verb "helps" another verb to express time, attitude, or possibility. Explain that negative modifiers and adverbs sometimes come between the helping verb and the main verb. (Example: He **is** not going to the movie.)

Practice Have students work in cooperative groups to find five sentences in the selection that use helping verbs. Ask them to underline the helping verbs and circle the main verbs.

Use **Grammar Transparencies and Copymasters,** p. 69.

Use McDougal Littell's ***Language Network,*** Chapter 6, for more instruction in helping verbs.

Don't Be So Literal

Does figurative language cause you to freeze like a deer in headlights? Do idioms drive you up a wall? If you're told you have a green thumb, do you check your hand? If so, then you are being too literal. Frequently, words are used in an imaginative way and not meant to be understood literally. Consider the two examples on the right.

> **"Put your whole heart in everything you do, and pray, then you can wait."**
> —Maya Angelou, "Getting a Job"
>
> **I gradually ascended the emotional ladder to haughty indignation, and finally to that state of stubbornness where the mind is locked like the jaws of an enraged bulldog.**
> —"Getting a Job"

The expression "put your whole heart in" does not refer to a heart transplant. Instead, it is a more colorful way of saying "put forth all your effort." It's an example of an **idiom,** an expression whose meaning differs from the combined meanings of its words. In the second example, Angelou uses a vivid comparison to convey her stubbornness. "The mind is locked like the jaws of an enraged bulldog" is **figurative language,** language in which words are used in nonliteral ways to create particular effects.

Strategies for Building Vocabulary

Because idioms and figurative language don't mean what they might appear to, they may sometimes be difficult to understand. The strategies below will help you make sense of them.

❶ Idioms When you encounter an idiom that is unfamiliar, you can often figure it out from its **context,** the words that surround it. When reading the following example, think about the context of the highlighted idiom:

> **Millicent realized that she and all the other girls were in the same boat. They all had to endure five days of initiation. They all had to get bossed around by a "big sister." And they all had to go through the final trial by fire.**

The three sentences that follow the idiom give you example clues by indicating particular ways in which the girls are "in the same boat." They help to clarify that the idiom means "in the same situation."

❷ Similes and Metaphors Two of the most common kinds of figurative language are similes and metaphors. In a **simile** the word *like* or *as* is used to compare two things. In a **metaphor** one thing is said to *be* another. To make sense of these figures of speech, think about how the things being compared are alike. In the following example, how is the man like a gnome or leprechaun?

> **He was small and jolly, with a ruddy, wrinkled face . . . In his brown suit with the forest-green tie he looked something like a gnome or a cheerful leprechaun.**
> —Sylvia Plath, "Initiation"

If a figure of speech contains an unfamiliar word, you can try to determine the meaning of the unfamiliar word by analyzing its parts. Study the metaphor in the following excerpt.

> **The incident was a recurring dream, concocted years before by stupid whites and it eternally came back to haunt us all.**
> —"Getting a Job"

If you know the meanings of the prefix *re-* ("again") and the word *occurring,* you can guess that *recurring* means "happening repeatedly."

EXERCISE Identify each idiom, simile, and metaphor in this passage.

> **Like a sick old man, my car wheezed and coughed down the street. My mechanic told me to keep a stiff upper lip, but I knew my car was a lemon.**

Building Vocabulary

Objectives

- identify and explain the use of idioms and figurative language
- use context to determine the meaning of idioms and figurative language

VOCABULARY EXERCISE

1. like a sick old man = simile
2. keep a stiff upper lip = idiom
3. my car was a lemon = metaphor or idiom

Possible Objectives

You can use this selection to achieve one or more of the following objectives:

- enjoy silent sustained reading (Option One)
- read and analyze literature with a group (Option Two)
- use the Reader's Notebook to formulate questions about literature (Option Three)
- write in response to literature (Option Three)

Summary

In this short story set in New York City, Mrs. Wilson is puzzled by her 16-year-old daughter, Elise, who is suddenly uninterested in good grades or attending college. The mother lives modestly and works at a low-paying office job while encouraging her daughter to prepare for a realistic career. Elise, however, insists with great certainty that she is going to be an actress. One day, while baby-sitting, she is noticed by a powerful agent who claims Elise is perfect for a role in a Broadway play, and Elise agrees to an audition.

At the theater, there is a huge crowd of actors, all being thanked and dismissed except for Elise. She is invited to read and is impressive enough that she is offered the part. She is given the script and asked to meet the next day to sign a contract.

That night Elise reads the play and is completely distraught, claiming that the play "stinks." The next day, she rejects the contract stating that she doesn't like the play but doesn't reveal her instinct that the play is horrible. The producer, director, playwright, and agent all react scornfully, yet Elise confidently and quietly returns to baby-sitting, having let a once-in-a-lifetime opportunity slip away. Mrs. Wilson later reads reviews of the play in the newspaper and discovers that it closed after five performances. In a moment of profound love, she comes to trust and accept her daughter's instinctive judgment.

ON YOUR OWN

In "The Opportunity," a young woman is given an unexpected chance to fulfill her dream of becoming an actress. As you will see, her opportunity leads to a surprising turn of events.

THE OPPORTUNITY

John Cheever

Mrs. Wilson sometimes thought that her daughter Elise was dumb. Elise was her only daughter, her only child, but Mrs. Wilson was not so blinded by love that the idea that Elise might be stupid did not occasionally cross her mind. The girl's father had died when she was eight, Mrs. Wilson had never remarried, and the girl and her mother lived affectionately and closely. When Elise was a child, she had been responsive and lively, but as she grew into adolescence, as her body matured, her disposition changed, and some of the wonderful clarity of her spirit was lost. At sixteen she seemed indolent,[1] and to have developed a stubborn indifference to the hazards and rewards of life. She was a beautiful girl with dark hair and a discreet and striking grace, but Mrs. Wilson sometimes thought sadly that there was a discrepancy[2] between Elise's handsome brow and what went on behind it. Her face and her grace were almost never matched by anything she had to say. She would sit for an hour on the edge of her bed, staring at nothing. "What are you thinking

1. **indolent** (ĭn′də-lənt): lazy.
2. **discrepancy** (dĭ-skrĕp′ən-sē): inconsistency.

Johanna IV (1985), Franz Gertsch. Mixed media on board, 29½″ × 29½″. Courtesy Louis K. Meisel Gallery, New York.

Reading the Selection

Option One
Silent Sustained Reading

You might set aside time each week for independent reading. During this time, you and your students would read for enjoyment. "The Opportunity" can be read independently in about 30 to 45 minutes. If you want to encourage students to read for pleasure, you might forego assignments related to the selection. Should you want to make assignments, Options Two and Three offer suggestions.

Option Two
Shared Reading Groups

You may assign students to groups or allow them to choose their own. Students can read the selection together, alternately reading sections aloud, or they can read independently and meet to cooperate in a project that portrays some element of the story.

Possible Projects
- Have students use descriptions of Elise presented in the story to construct two different versions of her opportunity: one as it would be perceived by her mother and one as it would be perceived by Gloria Hegel.
- Have students compare the portrayal of a life in the theater that Mrs. Wilson presents to Elise early in the story with the reality that Elise experiences when she attends the audition.
- Students can write a description of what they imagine the secret thoughts of Elise Wilson to be.

Option Three

Reader's Notebook

Ask students to pause at the section break in column two on page 422 to summarize their impressions of Elise. Then have them write a prediction about the outcome of the story in their Reader's Notebook. What do they expect will happen to Elise in the end?

At the end of the story, have students write a paragraph comparing their initial prediction with the actual outcome of the story. Then, have them skim through the story and make a list of details that either supported their prediction or diverged from it. If the actual outcome diverged from their prediction, ask students to isolate the exact place where it diverged. Have them comment on the predictability of Elise.

If they prefer the outcome they initially predicted over the actual outcome, invite students to rewrite the story in their Reader's Notebook.

about?" Mrs. Wilson would ask; "what's on your mind, Elise?" Elise's answer, when she made it, was always the same. "Nothing. I don't know. I wasn't thinking about anything."

Mrs. Wilson worked as a secretary. They lived in a three-room walk-up over a grocery store. They were poor. Elise, in her first two years at high school, had got brilliant grades, and Mrs. Wilson had hoped to get her a college scholarship, but in her third year Elise's grades slumped, and she barely passed into the senior class. She didn't seem to mind. She said she didn't care. Mrs. Wilson gave up the idea of a scholarship and decided that Elise should take a commercial course[3] in her senior year and go to work when she graduated. She made the decision regretfully but with a clear eye on the future, for Mrs. Wilson had no rich relatives or any other expectations of help beyond her own ability to work and save. She told Elise her plans, early in the summer after school had closed.

"I really didn't want to go to college," Elise said.

"Well I'm glad it isn't too much of a disappointment, dear," Mrs. Wilson said. "I'll go over next week and see about enrolling you in the commercial course."

"I don't want to take a commercial course," Elise said.

"Why not, dear?"

"It would be a waste of my time," Elise said. "Why should I take a commercial course? What good would that do me? I'm going to be an actress. A commercial course would be a waste of time. I'm going on the stage."

"When did you decide this?"

"Oh, a long time ago," Elise said.

Mrs. Wilson struggled to hold her temper. She felt that she had had more than her share of loneliness and hard work since her husband's death, and to have these burdens increased with the worries of an indolent and stage-struck girl made her feel desperate and tired. She waited until this feeling had passed. Then she began, patiently, to describe to the girl the difficulties of the theater. Thousands of experienced, beautiful, and talented actresses were out of work. Even those who did work, didn't work often, and only a few of the thousands in the profession made an annual salary as big as a file clerk's. When Mrs. Wilson had finished, Elise said nothing.

"Well, what are you thinking, dear?" Mrs. Wilson asked. "What's on your mind?"

"Nothing," Elise said. "I don't know. I wasn't thinking about anything." She yawned. "I guess I'll go to bed." She kissed her mother good night, and went into her room. It also seemed to Mrs. Wilson that Elise needed a lot of sleep. She couldn't remember the needs of her own youth, but it seemed to her that Elise spent an awful lot of time sleeping.

Elise spent a month in the country with her grandmother that summer. This was her vacation. When she returned to New York in August, she took up again the job as baby-sitter that had occupied most of her spare time during the winter, and all of her time when she was not in school. She worked regularly for a young couple named Cogswell, who had two girls and a baby boy. She took the children to the park, gave them their meals, their baths, and if the Cogswells were having guests for cocktails, as they often did, she stayed with the children until the guests had left. She gave half of the salary she got for this to her mother and spent the other half on orange drinks, frankfurters, candy bars, ice cream, rental-library fees, and silver bracelets. She had twenty-two silver bracelets and dreamed of having fifty. When she had

3. **a commercial course:** classes focusing on secretarial or bookkeeping skills.

finished at the Cogswells, she would walk slowly home. She would eat supper with her mother and sometimes, as the autumn approached, Mrs. Wilson would bring up the question of Elise's future.

"Elise, dear, I wish you'd think seriously about taking that commercial course," she'd say.

"But Mother. I've told you that I think it's a waste of time," Elise would say quietly. Then Elise would disappear into her room and, it seemed to Mrs. Wilson, into the dark continent of adolescence. There was an Amherst and a Williams[4] pennant over her bed, but the other walls were covered with photographs that she had cut out of *Life* magazine. This gallery depressed Mrs. Wilson. If the pictures had made any sense, or if there had been any connection between one picture and another, she wouldn't have minded so much, but the pictures had been chosen indiscriminately, or along mysterious lines of discrimination. Overlapping a portrait of a Doberman pinscher was a picture of some Chinese refugees walking along a bank of the Yangtze River. Next to these was a picture of the Casino at Nice, Rex Barney,[5] a wedding in Chicago, the damage done by a tornado in Oklahoma, and the coronation of a chief in Africa.

Illustration by John Hyatt.

Late in August the Cogswells had a large cocktail party, and Elise stayed late at their apartment that day. At seven o'clock, she took the children into the living room to say good night to their parents and the guests, and when she had returned with them to the nursery, she thought she heard herself being discussed by one of the guests. Elise was changing the baby's diaper when Mrs. Cogswell came into the nursery and said that one of the guests was a theatrical agent, and that she wanted to talk with Elise. Mrs. Cogswell was very excited at this turn of events, but Elise finished folding and pinning the diaper before she spoke. "All right," she said.

She returned to the living room with Mrs. Cogswell and was introduced to Gloria Hegel, the agent. The party was breaking up. Miss

4. **Amherst . . . Williams:** colleges in Massachusetts.
5. **Rex Barney:** a pitcher for the Brooklyn Dodgers from 1943 to 1950.

After the Reading

Possible Activities

Independent Activities

- Have gifted students skim over the story and jot down details about the photographs Elise has on her walls. Then, ask them to write in their Reader's Notebook a paragraph on what these photos reveal about Elise. What type of people did Elise choose to place on her walls? Why do you think the author included this detail about Elise?
- Have students review the Learning the Language of Literature and Active Reader, pages 383–385. They can note which skills and strategies they used while reading the selection.

Discussion Activities

- Use students' predictions about the outcome of the story as a starting point for discussion about the wisdom of Elise's final decision. Did Elise make the right decision? Explain.
- Discuss whether Elise's mother was right or wrong in allowing Elise to make her own decision about accepting the role in the play.

Assessment Opportunities

- You can assess student comprehension of the story by asking students to discuss the strength of Elise's character as reflected in her ability to stand by her decisions, even when they are at odds with those of the adults in her life.
- You can use any of the discussion questions as essay questions.
- You can have students develop any one of their Reader's Notebook entries into an essay.

THE OPPORTUNITY **423**

Hegel drew Elise down beside her on the sofa and stared at her intently. "Darling," she said. "Tom Leary has just written a new play and the lead is for a girl of about your age and they've been trying to cast it all summer and they haven't been able to find anyone—*anyone.* I know what they want. I've talked with Tommy, and the minute I saw you walk into this room I knew you were it. Now, have you ever thought of going on the stage?"

"I've decided that I would," Elise said.

"Have you ever had any experience?"

"No."

"Can you come down to my office tomorrow afternoon?"

"You'll have to ask Mrs. Cogswell."

"Of course you can," Mrs. Cogswell said. "Isn't this exciting?"

Miss Hegel gave Elise her address and made an appointment with her for three, and after she had left, both the Cogswells told Elise that she was the biggest agent in New York, and they named six or seven movie stars she had handled. Mr. Cogswell mixed another shaker of drinks, and the couple seemed more excited than the girl. When Elise's work was finished, she walked home slowly and told her mother the news.

"I may have a job, Ma," she said.

"That's nice," Mrs. Wilson said. "Baby-sitting?"

"On the stage," Elise said.

"Now, you've got to get this idea of going on the stage out of your head," Mrs. Wilson said.

"But this agent said that she thought she could get me a part," Elise said quietly. "I didn't ask her. She asked me. Her name is Gloria Hegel. She's kind of funny looking. She was at the Cogswells. I'm going to see her tomorrow."

"Well, there's nothing to get excited about, is there?" Mrs. Wilson said.

"I'm not excited," Elise said.

For her interview with Miss Hegel, Elise dressed, as she dressed for everything, in a long, voluminous[6] skirt and a pair of worn ballet slippers. She put on all her silver bracelets, and if it had been raining, she would have put on her head a scarf that had ELISE ELISE ELISE ELISE written on it. It wasn't raining. It was a hot day at the end of summer. One of Elise's many physical gifts was that she could appear cool, even in the most sustained heat. When she came into Miss Hegel's office that afternoon, she looked composed and fresh. Miss Hegel was wearing a hat and talking on the telephone. She made a broad gesture of welcome to Elise, scowled at the telephone, and nodded for Elise to sit down. She made it clear that Elise stood much higher in her estimation than the person she was talking with. "I know, darling, I know," she kept saying impatiently into the telephone, "I know, darling, but I'm busy now and you'll have to call me later." She slammed the receiver into its cradle and swung around to Elise.

"I have the most exciting news for you, darling," she said. "I talked with Harry Belber this morning and I told him about you, and you're just what they want. I was afraid the fact that you don't have any experience would count against you, but Harry told me that it doesn't make any difference, that Ben Traveler would rather teach a beginner what to do than teach somebody what not to do, and that what they're looking for is the kind of fresh, unspoiled charm you have. They want me to bring you over to the theater this afternoon." She glanced at her watch. "Of course, we can't be sure you're going to get the part, but there's an awfully good chance you will and this office is one hundred percent behind you. The play is going to be a hit—I know that—it's just what the audiences want, and if you get the part we'll

6. **voluminous** (və-lo͞o′mə-nəs): full; ample.

sign a year's contract and after you've been on Broadway for a year I'll take you out to the coast. Cigarette?"

"No, thank you," Elise said. "I don't smoke."

"The play is called *The Devil's Eye* and it's by Tom Leary," Miss Hegel said. "He has had eight hits on Broadway and twenty-six screen credits. You don't have to worry about your author. Ben Traveler is going to direct it, and I guess I don't have to tell you that he's one of the best-known directors on Broadway. Harry Belber's going to produce it. He has never produced a show before, but his grandfather left him millions and millions of dollars from that abrasive business[7] and the production is budgeted at a hundred and fifty thousand. After all, a producer never does anything but send out for sandwiches, anyhow. When you go over to the theater this afternoon they'll expect you to walk on, and if they like your looks they'll ask you to read a few lines. Do you think you'll have any trouble? Stage fright, I mean?"

"No," Elise said.

"Good, darling," Miss Hegel said. She settled back in her chair and gave Elise a thorough, nearly accusatory look. "Your hair's all right," she said, "and Jack's going to be over at the theater to put on your make-up. Let's go."

When they got to the theater, Elise was surprised to find a crowd in the lobby. At first she thought that there must be a matinee and that the men and women had come out for a cigarette, and then she realized that they, like herself, were looking for work. An elderly man was speaking to the crowd. "Mr. Belber and Mr. Traveler are terribly sorry," he was saying, "but all the parts for this one are cast." The crowd began to turn away. "Mr. Belber and Mr. Traveler want to thank you very much, and they're both very sorry that you've come all the way over here for nothing, but all the parts for this one are cast. Mr. Belber and Mr. Traveler want to thank you very much . . ." The crowd started out, and Miss Hegel took Elise into the theater.

The auditorium was dark, and except for three men she could see sitting in the front row, the place was empty. The stage was set and lighted for a play that was still running, and the sense of contrived[8] illusion, given by the darkness and the lighted set and the sense that to be in a theater at that unusual hour was a privilege, a mark of importance, pleased and excited the girl. The set was familiar. It represented a comfortable living room. The furniture was covered with sheets, as if the tenants had gone away for the summer, but the rest of the set was as it would be that night when the audience arrived. Miss Hegel led Elise down a side aisle and through a box to the back of the stage. Waiting behind the set were thirty or forty more actresses, and adding these to the crowd in the lobby, Elise had not known there were so many. A man put on her stage make-up in a dressing room, and she returned to wait with the others. As their names were called, they would walk onto the set. The conversations they had with the powers in the front row didn't vary much. "How do you do, Miss Hodge," the director would say. "We're very glad you came over, but I'm afraid there's nothing for you in this. Thank you very much. How do you do, Miss Beverly. We're very glad you came over, but I'm afraid there's nothing for you in this. Thank you very much. How do you do, Miss Griswold . . ."

The outward indifference with which they took their chance and lost was the first that

7. **abrasive business:** a company that manufactures substances used for grinding, smoothing, and polishing (such as those on the surface of sandpaper).

8. **contrived:** planned; artificial.

THE OPPORTUNITY 425

Elise had seen of the theater's good humor, and the openness with which these women talked to her while she waited was her first experience with the theater's peculiar kindliness. Then it was her turn. She walked onto the stage. The number of bright, colored lights directed on it surprised her. She looked out into the dark auditorium, but with the light against her eyes she could see no one there.

"How do you do, Miss Wilson," someone said. "We're very glad you came over. Now, will you please come forward a little? The light's better there. Thank you. How old are you, Miss Wilson?"

"Sixteen."

"Have you ever had any experience?"

"No."

"Would you take a few steps, please."

"Yes." She walked toward the wings. She could see Gloria smiling broadly.

"Thank you, thank you," the voice from the dark said. "Now will you say something for us, Miss Wilson."

"What would you like me to say?"

"Anything."

"'The quality of mercy is not strained,'" she said. "'It droppeth as the gentle rain from heaven upon the . . .'"

"That's enough, thank you, Miss Wilson. I think we've heard enough. Now I wonder if you'd go through a scene for us? Gloria has a copy of the script. You can look it over, and in about fifteen minutes we'll want you to come on again and go through a speech."

"All right," she said.

"Thank you very much."

She walked off the set. Gloria embraced her excitedly and led her back to one of the dressing rooms. The speech she was expected to read was made by a young girl to her stepmother. In it, she refused to enter into a marriage her stepmother had arranged for her. "You can't make me marry Rickey," it began. "No one can make me marry Rickey. . . ." Elise read it once to herself, and then read it twice aloud to Gloria. Then she was called back to the stage, and she walked onto the set.

"Where shall I stand?" she asked.

"A little more toward center."

"Here?"

"That will do."

"Shall I begin now?"

"Yes."

"You can't make me marry Rickey," she began. "No one can make me marry Rickey. . . ."

When she had finished the speech she relaxed, as if reading it had taken something out of her. She looked toward the dark. From there she heard excited whispering, in which the words "wonderful, wonderful" were repeated. Then she saw Gloria beckoning to her wildly from the wings, and she walked off the set. "They love you!" Gloria said. "They love you; you've got the part. They want to see you in the office." Backstage was empty, Elise noticed. All the others had gone. Miss Hegel led her up some back stairs to an office, and Mr. Belber, Mr. Traveler, and Mr. Leary came in.

The three men seemed to her kind, witty, and rich. Their conservative clothes, their gray hair, and the heavy-framed glasses they all wore made her think of the directors of a trust company. When the introductions were finished, they told her they wanted her for the part and would give her a copy of the play to read that night. Rehearsals would begin in three days. They would discuss the contract with Miss Hegel in the morning and sign it at noon. Miss Hegel would have to get Elise an Equity card[9] and see about entering her in the professional children's school. They agreed to meet at noon, and Elise and Miss Hegel left and got a taxi.

9. **Equity card:** a card indicating membership in the actors' union.

426 UNIT THREE PART 1

The Sheridan Theatre (1937), Edward Hopper. Oil on canvas, 17⅛″ × 25¼″.
Collection of The Newark (New Jersey) Museum (40.118).
The Newark Museum/Art Resource, New York.

"I'm not going to sign a run-of-the-play contract," Miss Hegel said, as they drove across town. "I'm only going to let them have you for a year. Then I'll take you out to the coast for two years. Then back to Broadway for another play. Then back to the coast. Then back here for a musical. Can you sing? Can you dance?"

"Not much," Elise said.

"Well, you can learn," Gloria said. "Back here for a musical with a television show on the side, and then back to the coast again, and you won't even be twenty-three years old." She began to talk about hundreds and thousands of dollars and, absorbed in these calculations, she said goodby to Elise absentmindedly. Elise walked home.

It was after six, and Mrs. Wilson was waiting.

"I think I've got it, Ma," Elise said. "Miss Hegel's going to ask for five hundred a week, but she doesn't think I'll get more than three-fifty. They gave me a copy of the play. I've got to read it tonight."

Mrs. Wilson sat down. If the poor woman had ever allowed herself to expect anything, the shock might not have been so great, but because she had contented herself with the thought of a hard life, the prospects of Broadway and Hollywood staggered her. Elise got her mother a glass of water and sat on the arm of her chair until she had recovered.

"Well, I thought we might go out tonight and

THE OPPORTUNITY 427

have dinner in a restaurant for a celebration," Mrs. Wilson said, "but if you have to read the play tonight I guess we'd better put off our celebration. I suppose there'll be a lot of work to it, as well as money and excitement."

Mrs. Wilson cooked the dinner, and when they had finished and washed the dishes, Elise went into her room to read the play, and Mrs. Wilson sat down with some sewing. She was intensely excited, but she was proud of the composure[10] they were both showing. If anyone should look into their apartment, they would not know that night was unlike any other. It was hot. All the familiar sounds of that neighborhood on a late summer night came through the open windows. From the other room, she could hear Elise turning the pages of the play. She had been sewing and the girl had been reading for about three hours, when she heard Elise get up from her desk and come to the door. She looked up and saw that Elise had been crying.

"Is it a sad play, dear?" Mrs. Wilson asked.

"No." Elise ran to her mother, knelt on the floor beside her chair, and put her face in her mother's lap. She began to cry again.

"But what's the matter, dear?" Mrs. Wilson asked. "Tell me. Tell me what's the matter?"

"It stinks," Elise said.

"What do you mean, dear?"

"I mean the play stinks," Elise cried. She lifted her swollen face and looked at her mother. "I can't be in it, I just can't be in it, Mother. I wouldn't be in such an awful play, I don't care how much they paid me. It's worse than any movie I ever saw; it's even worse than the comic books. It stinks." She put her face in her mother's lap and sobbed for a while. Then she lifted her head again.

"You see, it's about this old actress who lives in a big country house in the fashionable part of Maryland," she said. "That's what it says right in the play. 'In the fashionable part of Maryland.' Well, I'm her stepdaughter and she wants me to marry a rich man named Rickey, and I want to marry a farmer named Joel. And in the end it turns out that Joel was rich all the time." She sobbed a little at the thought of this; then went on: "On top of this, there's this zany family living in the house, the same zany family that they've had in every play and movie since the flood. There's a crazy old man in the cellar who thinks he's making atomic bombs, and a punchy prize fighter who thinks he's Thomas Edison[11] and there's an Englishman with a monocle and a cane that explodes and a parrot that talks with a French accent and in one scene I have to come out of a grandfather clock making noises like a cuckoo."

"Well, as you describe it, it doesn't sound very good, I'll admit," Mrs. Wilson said judiciously, "but do you think we're the ones to judge whether or not a play is good? After all, Mr. Leary has written eight very successful plays, and you told me Miss Hegel said that Mr. Traveler had directed many successful plays. Surely Mr. Belber wouldn't want to invest a hundred and fifty thousand dollars in something that hasn't any merit."

"I don't understand that," Elise said. "I just know the play stinks."

"But how can you be so sure, dear?" Mrs. Wilson asked.

"I can be sure of what I like and what I don't like, can't I?" Elise asked. "I'm not going to come out of a grandfather clock making noises like a cuckoo for anybody. I don't like the play. I don't want to be in it."

"Perhaps if you sleep on it . . ."

"I don't have to sleep on it."

"Well, let's go to bed and sleep on it," Mrs. Wilson said. "We're both tired."

But Mrs. Wilson couldn't sleep. She didn't know what to do. She couldn't force the girl to take the part, but at the same time, to see

10. **composure:** self-control.

11. **Thomas Edison:** a renowned American inventor.

inexperience refuse a promise of so much money and pleasure gave her a painful wrench. She heard Elise sigh in the dark, and thinking that the girl might be wakeful, too, she went into her room—but Elise, as soon as she had got into bed, had fallen into the deep sleep of youth. Mrs. Wilson noticed on the walls photographs of Rex Barney, the late Mrs. Harvey Cushing, Henry Wallace, Valentina, Montgomery Clift, Stanton Griffis, and Jackie Robinson.[12]

In the morning, Mrs. Wilson left for her office without waking Elise, so that she would not be tempted to influence the girl's decision. Elise would have to decide, and Mrs. Wilson wanted, if she could, to keep out of it; but her curiosity and suspense increased as the morning went on, and at ten o'clock she called the apartment and asked Elise if she had made up her mind. "I made up my mind last night," Elise said. Then Mrs. Wilson went back to her shorthand notes and her typewriter, her posture chair and her green steel desk, with the realization that she would spend most of the rest of her life in their company. She could expect a pension when she was a white-haired woman of sixty-five. Perhaps then she could retire modestly to New Jersey. She was thankful that the span of hopeful excitement had been so brief.

Elise's appointment was for noon. When she got down to the theater, Mr. Belber, Mr. Traveler, and Mr. Leary were waiting. Gloria Hegel was there. As soon as Elise stepped into the office, Gloria began to talk. Elise didn't have a chance to say anything until she'd finished. Then she spoke.

"I can't sign the contract," she said.

"What do you mean, darling, what do you mean you can't sign it?" Gloria asked. "I've been over this contract with a fine-tooth comb and you couldn't do any better. You couldn't get a better contract anywhere."

"I don't want to sign it," the girl said.

"But why, darling, why?"

"I read the play last night. I don't want to be in it."

"Do you know anything about this, Gloria?" the producer asked.

"I don't know what's in her head," Gloria said. "I don't know what she's talking about."

"I just don't want to be in it," Elise said.

"If you don't want to be in it, you don't have to be in it," the playwright said. He got her meaning long before the others.

"Now just a minute, Tom," Mr. Belber said. "Take it easy."

"If she doesn't want to be in my play, she doesn't have to be in my play," Tom Leary shouted. "I've never seen such effrontery.[13] I never wanted her for the part, anyhow. She's too young. She hasn't had any experience. She's too tall."

"Shut up, Tom," the producer said. Then he turned to Elise. "I don't understand you, Miss Wilson," he said quietly. "Is there something about the contract that isn't satisfactory or is there something, some line in your part that you want changed?"

For the first time during the proceedings the girl seemed to lose her poise. She sat stiffly at the table with her hands folded and her head down, and it cost her an effort to speak.

"It just isn't one speech, Mr. Belber," she said. "It's the whole play. I don't like it."

"If she doesn't want to be in my play, she doesn't have to be in my play," Leary shouted. "Get her out of here. Get somebody else. Get the

12. **Mrs. Harvey Cushing . . . Jackie Robinson:** people in the news in the late 1940s and early 1950s—Mrs. Harvey Cushing was a philanthropist and art collector, Henry Wallace was vice-president of the United States from 1941 to 1945 and an unsuccessful presidential candidate in 1948, Valentina was a famous Italian fashion designer, Montgomery Clift was a rising American movie star, Stanton Griffis was a U.S. diplomat, and Jackie Robinson was the first African-American baseball player in the modern major leagues.

13. **effrontery:** insulting boldness.

THE OPPORTUNITY 429

brat out of here. I've got sensibilities just the same as she has. Telephone Hollywood. Get Dolores Random. Get anybody. Get her out of here."

Elise stood. They were all watching. "I'm sorry it turned out this way," she said. "It was very good of you to offer me the chance." She opened the door and went out. Gloria followed and stopped her in the hall. "Is this really what you mean, darling?" she asked. "Are you really turning down this job because you think it isn't any good?"

"Yes," Elise said.

"You little punk," Gloria said. Elise started down the stairs. Gloria shouted after her, "You brat, you baby-sitter, you . . . fool."

Elise telephoned Mrs. Cogswell from a drugstore and asked if she could come back to work. Mrs. Cogswell was delighted. An hour later, Elise was absentmindedly pushing a baby carriage down First Avenue, eating a strawberry ice-cream cone, and smiling at the delivery boys from the grocery store.

Either through forgetfulness or disappointment, Elise never mentioned her experience in the theater again. But Mrs. Wilson couldn't put the experience out of her mind as easily as her daughter, and she began to read eagerly the theater page of the morning paper in order to follow the fortunes of the play.

The beginning of rehearsals was announced. Elise's part was taken by someone from Hollywood. When the company went to Wilmington for the opening, Mrs. Wilson thought of the train ride that she and Elise might have taken, their hotel suite there, and the excitement of an opening. A week later, when the company went to Philadelphia, she made the trip vicariously.[14] She had never been to Philadelphia, but her vision of that city was clear. A week after the opening in Philadelphia, she went to

14. **vicariously** (vī-kâr′ē-əs-lē): in imagination, by picturing the experiences of those actually taking part.

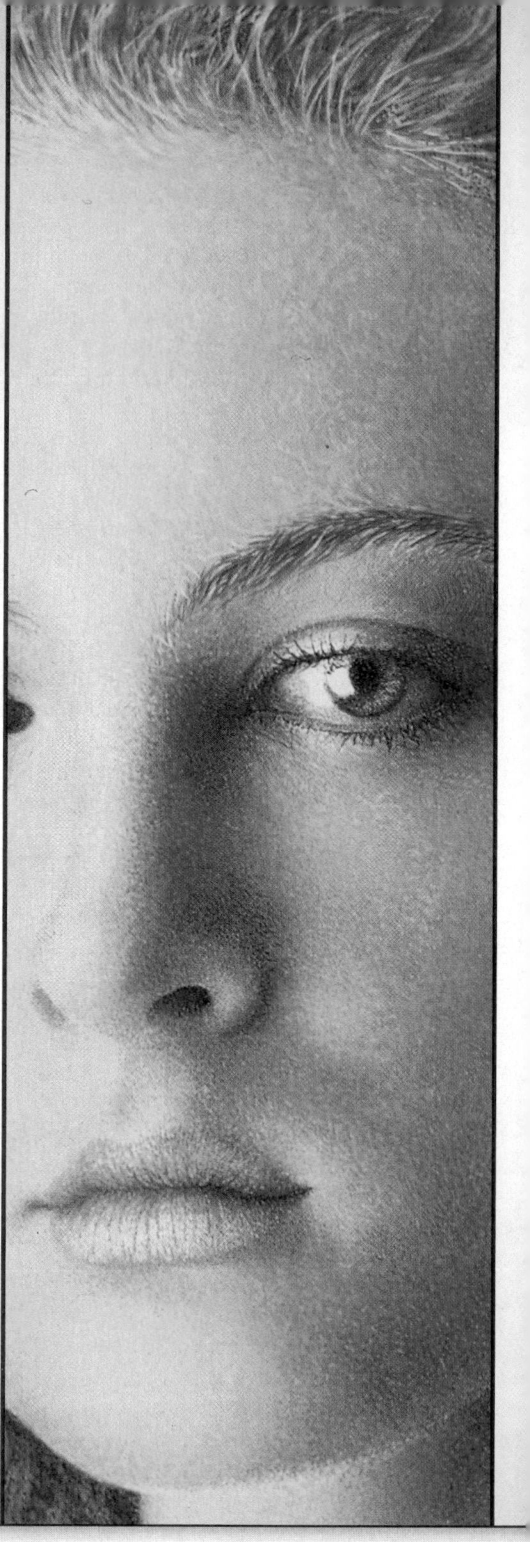

Detail of *Johanna IV* (1985), Franz Gertsch. Mixed media on board, 29½″ × 29½″. Courtesy Louis K. Meisel Gallery, New York.

Times Square and bought a trade paper to read a review of the play. It was late and the sidewalk was crowded, but she opened the paper, standing in the middle of the sidewalk, and read the review in the light from the newsstand.

Scorn, ridicule, abuse, and disgust were heaped on the playwright and his associates, but this vituperation[15] was, in a sense, wasted, for at the bottom of the notice Mrs. Wilson read that the play had closed in Philadelphia after five performances. Mr. Belber was returning to his grandfather's abrasive business, and Mr. Traveler and Mr. Leary had gone to their farms. She read the review twice to make sure, and then threw the paper into an ashcan and took a subway home. Elise was sitting in her room, surrounded by her pictures. A text on double-entry bookkeeping was open in front of her, but she wasn't studying, she was staring at nothing. Mrs. Wilson looked at her daughter with profound love, for she knew that there was some connection between the beauty of the girl's face and the beauty of her judgments. ❖

15. **vituperation** (vī-to͞o′pə-rā′shən): harsh condemnation; abusive words.

John Cheever

1912–1982

Other Works

The Enormous Radio and Other Stories
The Housebreaker of Shady Hill and Other Stories
The Wapshot Chronicle
The Stories of John Cheever

Unexpected Opportunity Ironically, the origins of John Cheever's literary career can be traced to his expulsion from prep school. At age 17, Cheever wrote a short story titled "Expelled" based upon his dismissal from Thayer Academy, a prestigious school in his home state of Massachusetts. The story was published by the *New Republic,* and a literary career was born. In his early years of writing, Cheever lived in poverty in New York City. After years of honing his storytelling skills, he became a regular contributor to the *New Yorker,* a magazine famous for the quality of its fiction. His first collection of short stories, *The Way Some People Live,* was published in 1942.

A Brilliant Observer In the 1950s Cheever's reputation continued to grow as he published three more volumes of short stories and his first novel, *The Wapshot Chronicle,* which garnered a National Book Award. His fiction typically examines the life and morals of suburban America, using humor and irony to portray the disappointments and tragedies hidden beneath the appearance of success. Because of his ability to use seemingly insignificant events as a means of unmasking truths about his characters, he was praised as the "Chekhov of the suburbs."

Recognized Master Cheever continued to publish steadily in the 1960s and 1970s and came to be regarded as a master of the short story. *The Stories of John Cheever,* published in 1978, became one of the few short-story anthologies ever to make the *New York Times* bestseller list; that same collection earned the Pulitzer Prize and the National Book Critics Circle Award. Two of his earlier stories, "The Country Husband" (1956) and "The Embarkment for Cythera," (1964) won the O. Henry Award. According to one admiring critic, Cheever "won fame as a chronicler of mid-century manners, but his deeper subject was life and death."

Author Activity

Read two more stories by Cheever; then, in an oral report, compare and contrast the setting of those stories with that of "The Opportunity." If Cheever were writing today, where do you think his stories would be set?

THE OPPORTUNITY 431

Comparing Literature
THE IMMIGRANT EXPERIENCE

OVERVIEW

This feature gives students an opportunity to compare, evaluate, and form opinions about two poems. The focus of this comparison is the physical and emotional impact of leaving one's home and emigrating to a new country.

Teaching Option

Because each poem is accompanied by its own introductory and response pages, teachers have the option of pairing the poems or teaching them individually. Used in conjunction with the Comparing Literature Assessment Practice on page 444, the poems may help students prepare for literature-based writing assessments.

What's the Connection?

Have students discuss why people might choose to leave their homeland and immigrate to a new and unknown country. (*Religious, political, or ethnic persecution; dangerous and threatening conditions of war; unfavorable or depressed economic conditions; poverty; unemployment; limited opportunities and a desire to seek a better life elsewhere are all reasons to leave one's own country.*)

Encourage students whose ancestors immigrated to the United States to share their stories and describe their ancestors' reasons for immigrating. Ask students whether they would consider emigrating today from the United States to another country. Why or why not?

Points of Comparison

Explain that one's search for personal identity within one's native culture is somewhat simpler than the search for identity in an unfamiliar environment. People could possibly remain torn between two cultural traditions, their own native culture and the culture of their new homeland. Ask students to name some challenges that might confront an immigrant in a new country. Suggest that students recall stories they've read in the textbook that reflect individuals struggling for identity, either within their own culture or within a new and different culture.

Possible Responses: Immigrants face challenges involving language, finding work, succeeding at school, finding housing, and possibly facing discrimination and prejudice.

Critical Thinking: Establishing a Basis of Comparison

The chart will provide students with a device for constructing a side-by-side comparison of the two poems.

Comparing Literature

The Immigrant Experience

Exile

Poetry by JULIA ALVAREZ

Lost Sister

Poetry by CATHY SONG

What's the Connection?

Coming to America You are about to read two poems on the subject of immigrating to the United States. Although one is drawn from a poet's own experiences and the other is about an invented character, both seek to convey the physical and emotional impact of leaving one's home and adapting to a new country.

Because the United States is a nation of immigrants, most of us are familiar with stories of immigration. In reading about people who have taken the bold step of leaving a familiar environment to find a new home in the United States, we may be reminded of our own family's origins. Such stories are part of our shared national heritage.

Immigrants arrive at Ellis Island, New York.

Points of Comparison

Comparing and Contrasting Poems In this unit so far, you have studied the experience of young people as they search for personal identity. The next two poems tell about that search when it takes place in a new land. In the pages that follow, you will compare and contrast these two poems, making judgments about their similarities and differences.

Critical Thinking: Establishing a Basis of Comparison

To compare and contrast two works of literature, you need to establish a basis of comparison. The chart shown will help you focus on three basic aspects of each poem—the content, the form, and the language—that can serve as your basis of comparison. Use the chart as a guide for your exploration.

Poetic Elements	"Exile"	"Lost Sister"
Content subject matter/speaker/setting/conflict/characters/plot		
Form physical arrangement/pattern/structure/use of stanzas		
Language word choice/imagery/figurative language/symbols		

READER'S NOTEBOOK. As you read the following two poems, note any observations that come to mind about the content, form, and language used. Add other descriptors to the chart as necessary.

PREPARING to *Read*

Exile

Poetry by JULIA ALVAREZ

"We stood awhile, marveling at America, / both of us trying hard to feel luckier than we felt. . . ."

Connect to Your Life

Change of Place What would it be like to be uprooted from your home and to arrive in a strange new country? With a group, brainstorm a list of ways in which your life might change if you emigrated to another country. Then discuss how you might cope with these changes.

Build Background

Dominican Dictatorship In 1930, Rafael Trujillo (tro͞o-hē′ ō) seized power in the West Indian country of the Dominican Republic. In the following 31 years, he led the country under a harsh dictatorship. While Trujillo did bring about economic improvements, he severely limited the freedom of his people. Opponents of his rule were brutally silenced; many were imprisoned or killed.

Julia Alvarez grew up in the Dominican Republic. In 1960, her family was forced to flee the country and emigrate to the United States because her father had been involved in a failed plot to overthrow Trujillo. The poem "Exile" opens in Ciudad Trujillo, the capital city that Trujillo renamed after himself. The capital's name was changed back to its original Santo Domingo after the dictator was assassinated in 1961.

VIDEODISC **LaserLinks: Background for Reading** Art Gallery

Focus Your Reading

LITERARY ANALYSIS NARRATIVE POETRY The following poem tells a story about one person's experience of immigration. This **narrative poem,** like a short story, has **characters,** a **setting,** and a **plot,** as well as other narrative elements. Notice how the opening lines of "Exile" tell of a particular event and introduce Papi and the speaker:

The night we fled the country, Papi,
you told me we were going to the beach.

You may find it helpful to read the poem aloud so that you can appreciate its storytelling elements.

ACTIVE READING RECOGNIZING POETIC ELEMENTS Compared with prose, poetry is a very economical form of writing; it uses relatively few words to express meaning and feeling. The building blocks of poetry—the **poetic elements**—can be broken down into **form, language,** and **content.** *Form* refers to the arrangement or pattern of the poem, such as the placement of lines and the grouping of lines in **stanzas.** The *language* of poetry is highly concentrated. Poets choose each word with great care and often make use of **imagery, figures of speech,** and **symbols.** *Content* refers to what a poem is about, or its subject matter. To appreciate the content of "Exile," try to imagine what it would feel like to be in the speaker's situation.

READER'S NOTEBOOK As you read "Exile," pay attention to its form, language, and content. Fill in the appropriate boxes in the chart that you created on page 432.

OVERVIEW

Objectives

1. understand characteristics of **narrative poetry (Literary Analysis)**
2. recognize **poetic elements (Active Reading)**

Summary

In this poem, the narrator recalls her family's risky escape from the Dominican Republic. Fortunately, they arrive safely in New York City, where one day she and her father gaze at a department store window displaying an American father and daughter outfitted for the beach. In the window's reflection, Alvarez and her father also see their own "too formal" image.

Thematic Link

The poem tells the story of a profound experience from Alvarez's childhood.

5-Minute Warm-Up

Daily Language SkillBuilder

Have students **proofread** the display sentences on page 381i and write them correctly. The sentences also appear on Transparency 13 of **Grammar Transparencies and Copymasters.**

LESSON RESOURCES

UNIT THREE RESOURCE BOOK, pp. 22–23

ASSESSMENT RESOURCES
Formal Assessment, pp. 69–70
Teacher's Guide to Assessment and Portfolio Use
Test Generator

SKILLS TRANSPARENCIES AND COPYMASTERS
Literary Analysis
- Poetry: Form, T7 (for Paired Activity, p. 437)

Reading and Critical Thinking
- Organizational Chart: Horizontal, T51 (for Reader's Notebook, p. 432)

Grammar
- Modal Forms of Verbs, C136 (for Mini Lesson, p. 435)

Writing
- Writing Process, T1–4 (for Writing Options, p. 438)
- Figurative Language and Sound Devices, T15 (for Writing Options, p. 438)
- Poem, C27 (for Writing Options, p. 438)

Communications
- Dramatic Reading, T12 (for Activities & Explorations 1, p. 438)

INTEGRATED TECHNOLOGY
Audio Library
LaserLinks
- Art Gallery: Alone. See **Teacher's SourceBook,** p. 27.

Visit our website:
www.mcdougallittell.com

TEACHING THE LITERATURE

Reading and Analyzing

Reading Skills and Strategies: PREVIEW

Have students look over the poem before they read. Ask them to consider how the title, the italicized quotation, and the two art pieces might be connected. Then have students read the Connect to Your Life and Build Background features.

Active Reading

RECOGNIZING POETIC ELEMENTS

Review with students the basic elements of poetry, which can be broken down into form, language, and content. Students should identify and describe these elements as they come across them in the poem.

Use **Unit Three Resource Book** p. 22 for additional support.

Literary Analysis

NARRATIVE POETRY

Ask students to identify the characters and the settings of this poem, then ask them to describe the events of the plot as they unfold.

Use **Unit Three Resource Book** p. 23 for additional support.

EXILE

Julia Alvarez

Ciudad Trujillo, New York City, 1960

The night we fled the country, Papi,
you told me we were going to the beach,
hurried me to get dressed along with the others,
while posted at a window, you looked out

at a curfew-darkened Ciudad Trujillo,
speaking in worried whispers to your brothers,
which car to take, who'd be willing to drive it,
what explanation to give should we be discovered . . .

On the way to the beach, you added, eyeing me.
The uncles fell in, chuckling phony chuckles,
What a good time she'll have learning to swim!
Back in my sisters' room Mami was packing

a hurried bag, allowing one toy apiece,
her red eyes belying her explanation:
a week at the beach so Papi can get some rest.
She dressed us in our best dresses, party shoes.

Something was off, I knew, but I was young
and didn't think adult things could go wrong.
So as we quietly filed out of the house
we wouldn't see again for another decade,

I let myself lie back in the deep waters,
my arms out like Jesus' on His cross,
and instead of sinking down as I'd always done,
magically, that night, I could stay up,

floating out, past the driveway, past the gates,
in the black Ford, Papi grim at the wheel,
winding through back roads, stroke by difficult stroke,
out on the highway, heading toward the coast.

5 Ciudad Trujillo (syo͞o-däd′ tro͞o-hē′yō): the capital of the Dominican Republic. (In 1961, the city was renamed Santo Domingo.)

Teaching Options

Mini Lesson

Speaking and Listening

DRAMATIC READING

Instruction Help students prepare a dramatic reading of the poem by considering such elements as tone, volume, diction, and body language.

Prepare In small cooperative groups members can assume the voice of the different characters and of the poet. Readings should represent a valid interpretation of the text. Italicized passages should be noted carefully.

Present Student groups can decide how they will present the dramatic reading. They should justify their choice of verbal and nonverbal performance techniques by referring to their analysis and interpretation of the text. Students who are audience members should evaluate how the performance increases their appreciation and understanding of narrative poetry.

BLOCK SCHEDULING This activity is particularly well suited for longer class periods.

Illustration by
Meredith Nemirov.

Past the checkpoint, we raced towards the airport,
my sisters crying when we turned before
the family beach house, Mami consoling,
there was a better surprise in store for us!

She couldn't tell, though, until . . . until we were there.
But I had already swum ahead and guessed
some loss much larger than I understood,
more danger than the deep end of the pool.

At the dark, deserted airport we waited.
All night in a fitful sleep, I swam.
At dawn the plane arrived, and as we boarded,
Papi, you turned, your eyes scanned the horizon

as if you were trying to sight a distant swimmer,
your hand frantically waving her back in,
for you knew as we stepped inside the cabin
that a part of both of us had been set adrift.

Weeks later, wandering our new city, hand in hand,
you tried to explain the wonders: escalators
as moving belts; elevators: pulleys and ropes;
blond hair and blue eyes: a genetic code.

Customizing Instruction

Less Proficient Readers

As they read the poem, have students ask themselves the following questions:

- Is an adult or a child telling the story?
  Answer: a young woman remembers the events of her family's escape from the Dominican Republic when she was a child.
- Why does the poet keep referring to swimming throughout the poem?

Possible Response: The sea separates her from her homeland and is recalled in the display in the department store window.

Students Acquiring English

Discuss the figurative language in the sixth stanza. Explain to students that the girl is not literally floating. Help students understand why the author might have chosen this image to depict the girl's state of mind.

Possible Responses: to illustrate the girl's feeling of lack of control; to link her feelings to the father's story about going to the beach

Use **Spanish Study Guide** for additional support, pp. 92–94.

Gifted and Talented

Have students write a narrative poem about an important event in their own lives or in the lives of people they have known. They may illustrate the poem or perform a reading. Their poem should reflect the various elements of narrative poetry.

Mini Lesson Grammar

MODAL FORMS OF VERBS A modal—such as *can, could, had better, may, might, must, ought to, shall, should, will,* or *would*—is an auxiliary that expresses a speaker's attitudes, or "moods." In a sentence, a modal is followed immediately by the simple form of a verb. Often, the distinctions between modals are subtle. *Should,* for example, indicates a mild obligation, while *must* a strong obligation or necessity. Write the following sentence on the chalkboard:

I should go to the library this weekend.

Practice Have students underline the modal auxiliaries in the following sentences, and discuss what attitude, or "mood," they communicate.

1. I ought to help my little brother do his homework.
Answer: Attitude: advisability, obligation

2. You can use my car tomorrow.
Answer: Attitude: informal permission

3. I would like to go to the movie.
Answer: Attitude: preference

Use **Grammar Transparencies and Copymasters,** p. 136.

Use McDougal Littell's ***Language Network***, Chapter 6, for more instruction in modal forms of verbs.

Reading and Analyzing

Reading Skills and Strategies: EVALUATING

Have students evaluate the narrator's mood at the end of the poem.
Possible Responses: uncertain; apprehensive

Literary Analysis: SETTING

Ask students how the settings of the poem—first the Dominican Republic and then New York—influence and reinforce the narrator's feelings.
Possible Response: The dark Dominican Republic setting reinforces the narrator's sense of loss; the bright New York setting, full of strange things and people, emphasizes the narrator's feelings of disconnection.

Literary Analysis: SYMBOL

Discuss with students the two families in the poem: Alvarez's family and the family in the Macy's display window. Ask students to explain what the second family symbolizes to the poet.
Possible Response: The display window family symbolizes the strangeness of this new place and the narrator's feelings of alienation.

The Promenade, Fifth Avenue (1986), Bill Jacklin. Oil on canvas, 96″ × 72″. Courtesy Marlborough Gallery, New York. Copyright © Bill Jacklin.

We stopped before a summery display window
at Macy's, *The World's Largest Department Store,*
to admire a family outfitted for the beach:
the handsome father, slim and sure of himself,

so unlike you, Papi, with your thick mustache,
your three-piece suit, your fedora hat, your accent.
And by his side a girl who looked like Heidi
in my storybook waded in colored plastic.

We stood awhile, marveling at America,
both of us trying hard to feel luckier
than we felt, both of us pointing out
the beach pails, the shovels, the sandcastles

no wave would ever topple, the red and blue boats.
And when we backed away, we saw our reflections
superimposed, big-eyed, dressed too formally
with all due respect as visitors to this country.

Or like, Papi, two swimmers looking down
at the quiet surface of our island waters,
seeing their faces right before plunging in,
eager, afraid, not yet sure of the outcome.

54 fedora hat: a soft felt hat with a fairly wide brim and a crease in the crown.

55 Heidi: a Swiss girl who is the title character of a famous children's book by Johanna Spyri.

Teaching Options

Assessment Standardized Test Practice

DESCRIBE PLOT, SETTING, CHARACTER, AND MOOD
You can informally assess students' understanding of the selection by having them describe or summarize details that reveal their comprehension of the poetic elements.

RUBRIC

3 **Full Accomplishment** Response reflects a full understanding of the poetic elements.
2 **Substantial Accomplishment** Response shows a general understanding of the poetic elements but lacks development.
1 **Little or Partial Accomplishment** Response shows little understanding of the poetic elements.

Connect to the Literature

1. **What Do You Think?** Jot down three words or phrases to describe your reaction to this poem.

Comprehension Check
- What kind of trip do the characters take?
- Where does the second half of the poem take place?

Think Critically

2. What is your impression of Papi and his relationship to the **speaker?** Cite details from the poem to support your judgment.
3. How would you describe the speaker's emotions during the night her family "fled the country"?

   THINK ABOUT
   - what the adults say and do
   - her ignorance of the family's destination
   - the comparisons that she draws to swimming
4. Describe the speaker's reaction to the department store window. What does her reaction tell you about her feelings toward her new home?
5. In the last stanza, the speaker uses a **simile,** comparing Papi and herself to "two swimmers." Why do you think the poem concludes with this simile?
6. **ACTIVE READING** RECOGNIZING POETIC ELEMENTS In a small group, compare the chart in your READER'S NOTEBOOK with those of your classmates. Then appoint a person to read the poem aloud again. Working together, add elements you might have missed when you first read the poem. Share your ideas about what you think are the most important or interesting poetic elements in "Exile."

Extend Interpretations

7. **Connect to Life** What aspects of your own experience can help you to understand how the speaker feels as she looks at the store window? How do you think her experience compares with that of most immigrants to this country?
8. **Points of Comparison** Again review the chart in your READER'S NOTEBOOK that you used to identify the **poetic elements** in "Exile." Now that you have analyzed one poem, has your understanding or appreciation of any of the elements changed?

Literary Analysis

NARRATIVE POETRY Poetry that tells a story is called **narrative poetry.** Like a short story, a narrative poem includes **characters, setting, plot,** and **point of view,** all of which combine to develop a **theme.** In this poem, the events of the family's journey are told in **chronological order,** as they might be in a short story. There are even snippets of **dialogue,** as shown by the underlined words in these lines:

On the way to the beach, you added,
eyeing me.
The uncles fell in, chuckling
phony chuckles,
What a good time she'll have
learning to swim!

Paired Activity Imagine that the speaker is telling a friend about the same experiences described in the poem. Working with a partner, write her story in prose. Then compare and contrast the prose version and the poem. Discuss what a narrative poem can do that a prose story cannot.

GUIDING STUDENT RESPONSE

Connect to the Literature

1. **What Do You Think?**
   Students may note a sad or reflective mood.

Comprehension Check
- They leave their home under cover of night to take a plane.
- New York City, the family's new home

Think Critically

2. Possible Response: Papi is the speaker's father, a man whom she loves and trusts. She obeys him without question, even though she senses something is not quite right.
3. Possible Response: Her feelings are mixed. A "week at the beach" sounds like fun, but the actions of the adults—her mom's tears, her uncles' phony chuckles, the limit of one toy apiece, the drive through winding back roads, turning off before the beach house and going instead to the airport—add to a feeling of danger and risk. While she is apprehensive, she is also trusting.
4. Possible Response: She is fascinated but distant. She finds America interesting but alien, not homelike.
5. Possible Response: Because they are both faced with the same challenge: to dive into this new world together. Throughout the poem, the image of swimming is one that brings up mixed feelings for the narrator.
6. Students may want to discuss the characters.

Extend Interpretations

Connect to Life Students may understand the feeling of displacement. They may understand that many people experience a similar feeling.
Points of Comparison Students should be able to discuss the poetic elements and rely on the poems to support their opinions.

Literary Analysis

Narrative Poetry Students may have a lively discussion comparing the two genres and discussing the power of each.

Writing Options

Travel Poem Ask your students to first decide on the journey they want to write about, then to think back to how they *felt* about it. Their feelings may be clear, or they may be ambivalent. The most interesting stories are often about something that is both exciting and scary, or sad and hopeful. Help students brainstorm some images and unrealistic elements that reflect these feelings. Then suggest that they weave the metaphorical elements into their narrative of what happened on the journey, much as Alvarez does in her poem.

Activities & Explorations

1. **Radio Play** Scriptwriters will need to invent believable dialogue and sound effects and to avoid "dead air." Remind students to keep narration to a minimum, allowing exciting, interesting scenes to carry the story.
2. **Exile Storyboard** Remind your storyboard creators that the poem is seen from the point of view of a little girl. The adults tower over her, sometimes picking her up or protecting her, and are sometimes shadowy and puzzling. She is at the center of the action—this could be visually depicted either by showing her acting out the story, or by showing the story through her eyes.

Inquiry & Research

Escape to Freedom Accounts of World War II political refugees may increase students' interest in the historic period. Before beginning their research, students should generate relevant, interesting, and researchable questions. They can locate appropriate print and nonprint information using text resources and technical resources including on-line databases and the Internet, and draw conclusions from information gathered. Remind them to use text organizers to categorize information as they conduct their independent research.

Choices & CHALLENGES

Writing Options

Travel Poem Write a narrative poem about a journey you have made or that you would like to make. Use narrative elements such as characterization, setting, plot, and conflict.

Activities & Explorations

1. **Radio Play** Write and produce a radio play of the Alvarez family's escape from the Dominican Republic. Base the script on the events described in the poem. Use sound effects to create suspense and enhance the listener's sense of place and event. ~ **SPEAKING AND LISTENING**
2. **Exile Storyboard** Draw a storyboard in which you lay out the plot of "Exile" in a series of rough sketches, showing the same events that are described in the poem. ~ **VIEWING AND REPRESENTING**

1.
Papi awakens narrator.
2.

Inquiry & Research

Escape to Freedom History is full of examples of people who have been forced to leave their homelands for political reasons. Investigate the story of one such person and write a short report about his or her life.

Julia Alvarez

1950–

Other Works
Homecoming
How the Garcia Girls Lost Their Accents
In the Time of the Butterflies
The Other Side/El Otro Lado

American-born Immigrant Julia Alvarez was born in New York City but lived the first ten years of her life in the Dominican Republic. Her Dominican parents had previously immigrated to the United States, but three weeks after their daughter's birth, they returned to their homeland, where the family lived on the property of Alvarez's grandparents. In 1960, after her father became involved in a plot to overthrow Dominican dictator Rafael Trujillo, the family fled to the United States. Alvarez spent the rest of her childhood in New York City.

A Quest for Understanding Alvarez continues to be influenced by the immigration experience. "I write out of who I am," she says, "and the questions I need to figure out. A lot of what I have worked through has had to do with coming to this country and losing a homeland and a culture." Although she was 10 when she fled the Dominican Republic, she remembers nothing of it. "I think it's the pivotal day of my life," she says, "and I can't remember anything that happened."

Contemporary Author Alvarez is best known for her semi-autobiographical novel, *How the Garcia Girls Lost Their Accents*, published in 1991. The novel tells the story of a Dominican family that immigrated to New York. Fifteen interconnected stories focus on the four Garcia sisters who, in addition to facing the usual difficulties of growing up, must learn to live in a new culture with its unfamiliar language. Alvarez has since published two other novels and has published several volumes of poetry. Her fiction, nonfiction, and verse have appeared in numerous magazines and literary journals. She currently teaches literature and creative writing at Middlebury College in Vermont, where she has been since 1988.

Author Activity

Research the Internet for more information about Julia Alvarez and her work. Find out about her latest publications and activities.

Author Activity

Alvarez has always had a passion for stories. Although she sometimes felt isolated as an immigrant, books provided a new world for her, in which she was always welcome. The fact that she was in a country where she was surrounded by books, and where women were encouraged to develop their talents, was an important influence that eventually led to her becoming an author. *Homecoming*, *How the Garcia Girls Lost Their Accents*, and *In the Time of the Butterflies* are just a few of her most widely known works.

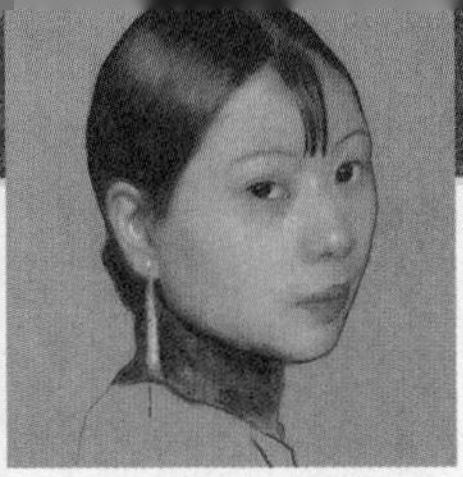

PREPARING to *Read*

Lost Sister

Poetry by CATHY SONG

"There is a sister across the ocean, who relinquished her name. . . ."

Connect to Your Life

Women of the World Think about various situations that might prompt a woman to immigrate to the United States. What part might the social conditions in her native country play in her decision to leave? How do you think the experience of an immigrant woman in the United States might differ from that of an immigrant man? In class discussion share what you know about the lives of female immigrants. Draw upon personal experience, or share what you have read or have seen in films or television shows.

Build Background

Women in China In "Lost Sister," Cathy Song contrasts the traditional life of women in China with that of a Chinese woman who has emigrated to the United States. For many centuries, Chinese marriages were arranged when the partners were children. Before marriage, a girl was subservient to the adults in her family; afterward, when she moved into her husband's family's home, she was subservient to her husband, his male relations, and his older female relations. Only after having children did she gain some measure of authority.

In some parts of China, it was considered essential for a girl to have small feet if she was to be married, so female children were subjected to the practice of foot binding—the tight wrapping of the feet to stunt their growth—between the ages of five and seven. Because this process bent the feet, breaking the bones of the insteps, the girls would hobble for the rest of their lives.

Focus Your Reading

LITERARY ANALYSIS CULTURAL AND LITERARY SYMBOL A **symbol** is a person, place, or object that has some meaning beyond itself. By using symbols, a writer can communicate complex ideas or emotions. A **cultural symbol** is one that has a shared meaning across an entire culture. A rose, for example, is commonly used as a symbol of romantic love in our culture. A **literary symbol,** by contrast, has a meaning that is specific to a work of literature, a meaning suggested by the context of the work. In "Lost Sister," jade is used as both a cultural and a literary symbol.

In China,
even the peasants
named their first daughters
Jade—

As you read the poem, consider the possible symbolic meanings of jade.

ACTIVE READING RECOGNIZING POETIC ELEMENTS Just as you did with "Exile," pay attention to the use of poetic elements in this poem. You may notice that Cathy Song tells her story in a less direct manner than that used by Alvarez. Song relies more on **figurative language** and **symbols** to convey her meaning. Also, her poem does not have a **plot** in the usual sense, though it does convey **conflict.**

READER'S NOTEBOOK As you read, record your observations about "Lost Sister" on the chart that you began on page 432.

OVERVIEW

Objectives

1. understand and appreciate a **poem (Literary Analysis)**
2. identify **cultural and literary symbols (Literary Analysis)**
3. recognize **poetic elements (Active Reading)**

Summary

The poem explores the feelings of a Chinese woman who escaped the restrictions of her homeland but feels lost in the West.

Thematic Link

The poet realizes the importance of her roots in searching for her identity.

5-Minute Warm-Up

Daily Language SkillBuilder

Have students **proofread** the display sentences on page 381j and write them correctly. The sentences also appear on Transparency 14 of **Grammar Transparencies and Copymasters.**

LESSON RESOURCES

UNIT THREE RESOURCE BOOK, pp. 24–25

ASSESSMENT RESOURCES

Formal Assessment, pp. 71–72
Teacher's Guide to Assessment and Portfolio Use
Test Generator

SKILLS TRANSPARENCIES AND COPYMASTERS

Literary Analysis
- Symbols and Figurative Language, T21 (for Paired Activity, p. 442)

Reading and Critical Thinking
- Organizational Chart: Horizontal, T51 (for Reader's Notebook, p. 439)

Grammar
- Emphatic Verb Forms, C133 (for Mini Lesson, p. 443)

Writing
- Writing Process, T1–4 (for Writing Options 1 and 2, p. 443)

INTEGRATED TECHNOLOGY

Audio Library
Visit our website:
www.mcdougallittell.com

TEACHING THE LITERATURE

Reading and Analyzing

Reading Skills and Strategies: PREVIEW

Give a brief summary of the poem, and have students look at the title and the picture. Reading the Connect to Your Life and Build Background features can also provide helpful information.

Active Reading

RECOGNIZING POETIC ELEMENTS

Instruct students to find in the poem an example of each of these poetic elements: figurative language, symbol, and conflict.

Use **Unit Three Resource Book** p. 24 for more practice.

Literary Analysis

CULTURAL AND LITERARY SYMBOL

Jade functions as both a cultural and a literary symbol in the poem. Jade is a cultural symbol of value or preciousness. So the peasants name their first daughters Jade. Jade is a literary symbol for China. The sister who goes to America dilutes jade green with the blue of the ocean she has crossed.

Use **Unit Three Resource Book** p. 25 for more practice.

Lost Sister

CATHY SONG

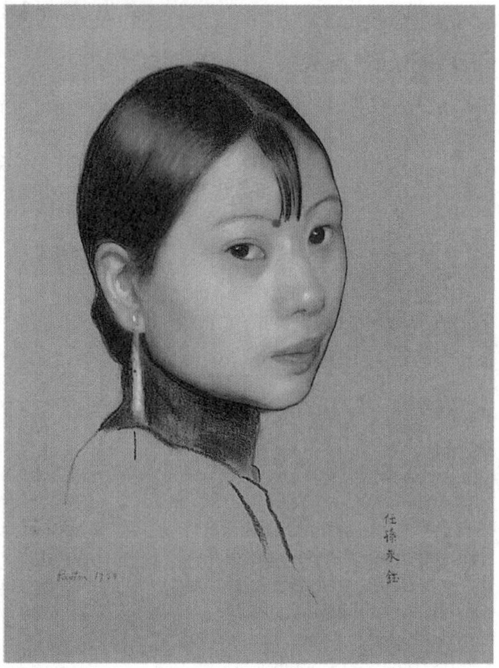

Portrait of Miss Jen Sun-ch'ang (1934), William McGregor Paxton. Courtesy Robert Douglas Hunter.

1

In China,
even the peasants
named their first daughters
Jade—
the stone that in the far fields
could moisten the dry season,
could make men move mountains
for the healing green of the inner hills
glistening like slices of winter melon.

And the daughters were grateful:
they never left home.
To move freely was a luxury
stolen from them at birth.
Instead, they gathered patience,
learning to walk in shoes
the size of teacups,
without breaking—
the arc of their movements
as dormant as the rooted willow,
as redundant as the farmyard hens.
But they traveled far
in surviving,
learning to stretch the family rice,
to quiet the demons,
the noisy stomachs.

19 dormant (dôr′mənt): inactive.

20 redundant (rĭ-dŭn′dənt): needlessly repetitive.

Teaching Options

Mini Lesson: Viewing and Representing

Portrait of Miss Jen Sun-ch'ang **by William McGregor Paxton**

ART APPRECIATION Paxton (1869–1941) was an esteemed portraitist of the Boston School of painting. Paxton usually painted elegant women, with richly furnished parlors or carefully contrived studio settings as backgrounds. He also used color to great effect. This work represents something of a departure for Paxton, as there is no background and the colors are muted, with the exception of the young woman's green earring.

Application Ask students why they think this painting was chosen to accompany this poem.

Possible Response: The green earring brings to mind the frequent mentions of jade in the poem, and might be seen as the young woman's way of connecting herself to China, like the fermented roots, the jade link handcuffed to her wrist, Mah-Jongg tiles, and the firecrackers.

2

There is a sister
across the ocean,
who relinquished her name,
diluting jade green
with the blue of the Pacific.
Rising with a tide of locusts,
she swarmed with others
to inundate another shore.
In America,
there are many roads
and women can stride along with men.

But in another wilderness,
the possibilities,
the loneliness,
can strangulate like jungle vines.
The meager provisions and sentiments
of once belonging—
fermented roots, Mah-Jongg tiles and firecrackers—
set but a flimsy household
in a forest of nightless cities.
A giant snake rattles above,
spewing black clouds into your kitchen.
Dough-faced landlords
slip in and out of your keyholes,
making claims you don't understand,
tapping into your communication systems
of laundry lines and restaurant chains.

You find you need China:
your one fragile identification,
a jade link
handcuffed to your wrist.
You remember your mother
who walked for centuries,
footless—
and like her,
you have left no footprints,
but only because
there is an ocean in between,
the unremitting space of your rebellion.

28 relinquished (rĭ-lĭng'kwĭsht): gave up; abandoned.

29 diluting (dĭ-lo͞o'tĭng): lessening the strength or purity of.

33 inundate (ĭn'ŭn-dāt'): overwhelm as if by a flood; overflow.

43 Mah-Jongg (mä'zhŏng'): a game of Chinese origin, played with tiles resembling dominoes.

64 unremitting (ŭn'rĭ-mĭt'ĭng): continuing without interruption; unceasing.

Customizing Instruction

Gifted and Talented

Have students reread the similes in lines 19 and 20, which compare Chinese daughters to other living things. Invite students to write their own similes about young American women.

Less Proficient Readers

Have students ask themselves the following questions as they read the poem:

- How much freedom do women in China have?
  Answer: very little
- How much freedom do women have in America?
  Answer: a great deal
- What difficulties might an immigrant woman have in America?

Possible Responses: loneliness; a sense of severance from her homeland; cultural confusion

Students Acquiring English

Draw students' attention to the phrase "fragile identification" in line 54. Explain that *fragile* means "weak or easily broken" and *identification* means, in this case, a person's sense of self. Explain that her loss of identity is an important idea in the poem, as it applies to someone who has left her homeland for an unfamiliar place.

Use **Spanish Study Guide** for additional support, pp. 95–97.

Assessment Standardized Test Practice

EVALUATE AND MAKE JUDGMENTS On some standardized tests, students will be required to evaluate and make judgments. Ask students to write evaluations of the life of a woman in China in comparison to that of a woman in the United States, using details from the poem. In their opinion, is one lifestyle easier than another?

RUBRIC

3 Full Accomplishment Answer displays full understanding of how the lives of women differ. Their opinion should be supported with details from the poem.

2 Substantial Accomplishment Answer displays a general understanding of how the lives of women differ. Their opinion is evident, but not well supported.

1 Little or Partial Accomplishment Answer displays little understanding of how the lives of women differ. Their opinion is unsupported.

LOST SISTER 441

GUIDING STUDENT RESPONSE

Connect to the Literature

1. What Do You Think?
Students may sense a mood of sadness or loss.

Comprehension Check
- to rebel against the repression of women in China and gain new freedom
- loneliness and the difficulty of adjusting to a strange culture

Think Critically

2. Possible Response: Jade signified powerful qualities. The speaker feels that traditional Chinese families simultaneously revered and repressed their daughters, perhaps regarding them as a treasure to be locked away.
3. Possible Response: The immigrant woman has freedom and equal opportunities, but the choices can be overwhelming to someone from a different culture. For different reasons each woman, the mother and the immigrant have lost their identity.
4. Students may point to examples of the figurative language, similes, and personification.

Thinking through the LITERATURE

Connect to the Literature

1. **What Do You Think?** What kind of mood did this poem leave you with? Explain your response to a classmate.

Comprehension Check
- Why did the sister go to America?
- What difficulties does the sister face in America?

Think Critically

2. How does the **speaker** feel about the traditional life of Chinese women, as described in the first part of the poem?

   THINK ABOUT
   - the significance of the name Jade (lines 1–9)
   - the speaker's description of the lives of daughters (lines 10–25)

3. What conclusions can you reach about the life of the immigrant Chinese woman, as described in the second part of the poem?

   THINK ABOUT
   - the "many roads" she can take (lines 35–36)
   - the use of the word "strangulate" (line 40)
   - the comparison between the "footless" mother and the immigrant daughter with "no footprints" (lines 57–61)

4. **ACTIVE READING** RECOGNIZING POETIC ELEMENTS Review the chart in your READER'S NOTEBOOK. What do you think are the most important or interesting **poetic elements** used by Song? Discuss your answer with your classmates.

Extend Interpretations

5. **Different Perspectives** How might the poem be different if the immigrant described were male instead of female? Explain your reasoning.
6. **Connect to Life** How do you think the feelings expressed in this poem are similar to or different from those of other immigrant women from different times and places? Explain your opinion.
7. **Points of Comparison** Look again at the chart in your READER'S NOTEBOOK. Compare the information that you recorded for "Lost Sister" and "Exile." What do you think are the most important differences between the two poems? Cite evidence from the poems to support your judgment.

Literary Analysis

CULTURAL AND LITERARY SYMBOLS A person, place, or object with meaning beyond itself is known as a **symbol. Cultural symbols** are things with symbolic meaning for people in a particular culture. The stone jade, for example, is a cultural symbol in China, where carved jade objects and jewelry are equated with such abstract values as toughness, durability, and moral and physical beauty. **Literary symbols** are things that are given symbolic meaning within the context of specific literary works. In this poem, for example, jade has a symbolic meaning that is specific to the experience of the immigrant sister.

Paired Activity With a partner, review the three references to jade in "Lost Sister." Study the context for each reference, as found in lines 1–9, 26–30, and 53–56. What does jade symbolize in the poem? Consider what it means in Chinese culture and what it represents about the experience of the immigrant sister.

Extend Interpretations

Different Perspectives Students may feel that the role of the male is similar across cultures, and, therefore, males might not have as much trouble with their identity in new cultures.

Connect to Life Students may bring personal observations to a classroom discussion. Increased freedom and opportunities will probably affect most women.

Points of Comparison Check charts to ensure that students have recorded observations about the content, form, and language of both poems, so that they have a basis on which to compare the two.

Literary Analysis

Cultural and Literary Symbols Students should focus their responses using the term *literary symbol.* Remind students that jade is also a cultural symbol for the Chinese.

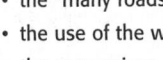

Choices & CHALLENGES

Writing Options

1. Letters Home Imagine that you are the woman portrayed in the second part of the poem. Write two letters to a sister in China—one conveying your thoughts shortly after leaving home, the other describing your feelings after living in America for a while. Be sure to express your feelings about immigration.

2. New Title Compose an alternative title for the poem, providing an explanation of the title's meaning and the reasons you think it appropriate.

Inquiry & Research

1. Cultural References Research some of the poem's references to Chinese or Chinese-American life, and share your findings with your classmates in an oral report. For example, you might report on foot binding, rice, Mah-Jongg (also spelled *mahjong*), firecrackers, or the businesses in which Chinese immigrants to the United States have traditionally found jobs.

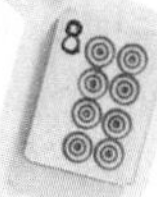

2. Chinese Immigration There is a long history of Chinese immigration to the United States, going back as early as the 1860s, when many Chinese came over to help build the Central Pacific Railroad. Research the history of Chinese Americans and create a poster display of your findings.

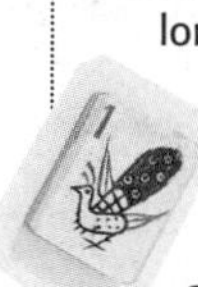

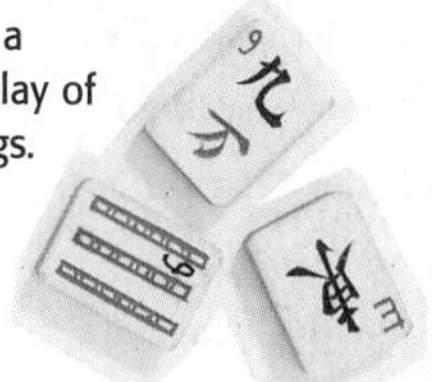

Mah-Jongg game pieces

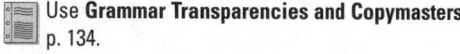

Cathy Song

1955–

Other Works
Picture Bride
Frameless Windows, Squares of Light
School Figures

Bouquet of Poems In 1982 Cathy Song's first poetry collection, *Picture Bride,* was published as the winner of the Yale Series of Younger Poets competition, a contest open to any American writer under the age of 40 who has not previously published a volume of poetry. Many of the poems in the book, like "Lost Sister," chronicle aspects of the Chinese-American experience. Noting that *Picture Bride* is divided into sections named for different flowers, the contest judge, Richard Hugo, compared Song's poems to "flowers—colorful, sensual and quiet—offered almost shyly as bouquets to those moments in life that seemed minor but in retrospect count the most."

Poet and Teacher Song was born and raised in Hawaii and attended the University of Hawaii and Wellesley College; she earned her master's degree at Boston University. In addition to publishing poems in a number of anthologies and literary journals, she has coedited the anthology *Sister Stew: Fiction and Poetry by Women.* She now lives and teaches in Honolulu, Hawaii.

Author Activity

Read some additional poems by Cathy Song in *Picture Bride.* Choose your favorite poem and read it aloud to your class. Then compare and contrast it to "Lost Sister."

Writing Options

1. **Letters Home** For the first letter, have students examine the first part of the poem for ideas about why the woman might have left China and how she might feel to have gotten away. For the second letter, have students examine the second part of the poem for ideas about the woman's experiences in America.
2. **New Title** Responses should be well supported and reveal an understanding of the poem's intent.

Inquiry & Research

1. **Cultural References** This activity can be handled well in a cooperative learning situation.
2. **Chinese Immigration** Some students may also want to investigate the demographics of Chinese Americans.

Mini Lesson Grammar

USING VERBS: VOICE Explain to students that *voice* refers to the relationship of a verb to its subject. If a verb is in active voice, its subject performs an action. Write the following sentences on the chalkboard:

The poet describes jade.

Jade is described by the poet.

Point out to students that the subject of the first sentence does the action, making the verb active. Point out that the subject of the second sentence receives the action, making the verb passive.

Practice Have students rewrite the following sentences, changing verbs from passive to active voice.

1. Hundreds of paper lanterns were seen by my sister. *(My sister saw hundreds of paper lanterns.)*
2. Rice was eaten by the peasant family. *(The peasant family ate rice.)*
3. You were given a jade link bracelet by your mother. *(Your mother gave you a jade link bracelet.)*

Use **Grammar Transparencies and Copymasters,** p. 134.

Use McDougal Littell's ***Language Network,*** Chapter 6, for more instruction and practice in voice.

PART 1 Reading the Prompt
Model the process of reading a prompt:

- Read through the prompt in its entirety.
- List key words of the assignment on the chalkboard ("Compare and contrast"; "content, form, and language"; and "evidence").
- Define each key word using Strategies in Action to show how students can restate the prompts in their own words.

PART 2 Planning a Comparison-Contrast Essay

- Students can use the chart they have been filling out for the two poems (referenced on page 432).
- Suggest that students expand their graphic by adding several specific characteristics of each speaker's personal situation and obstacles revealed in the poem. These characteristics and obstacles can be elaborated to develop the essay.
- Encourage students to first compare and contrast the content of the poems because content ideas are the most prominent aspects of these two poems. Students may then turn their attention to discussing form and language as secondary points.

PART 3 Drafting Your Essay
Introduction Suggest that students open with a powerful, dramatic hook, such as an anecdote or a rhetorical question that will emphasize the experiences described by the speakers in these poems. Using such an emotional appeal can grab and engage readers' attention.
Organization Suggest that students create an outline using the detail they included in their graphics. Once they have established a structure for their essays, have them add appropriate transition words on the outline to signal the logical relationships between ideas and examples.
Conclusion Suggest that students conclude by referring again to the hook they used to open the essay. Such a technique for framing the essay can tighten its unity and give readers a sense of closure.

Comparing Literature: Assessment Practice

In writing assessments, you will often be asked to compare and contrast two literary works like "Exile" and "Lost Sister." You are now going to practice writing an essay with this kind of focus.

PART 1 Reading the Prompt

You will be often be required to write in response to a prompt like the one below. Your first step should be to read the entire prompt carefully. Then you should read through it again, looking for key words.

Writing Prompt

"Exile" is a poem based upon the emigration of the speaker and her family from the Dominican Republic to the United States. "Lost Sister" is about the differences between Chinese women in China and the lost sister, a Chinese woman who has immigrated to America. Compare and contrast (1) the two poems in terms of their (2) content, form, and language. Give evidence (3) from the poems to support your analysis.

STRATEGIES IN ACTION

1. I have to **compare and contrast** two poems about immigrants.
2. I have to base my comparison on the **content, form, and language** of the two poems.
3. I need to include **details, examples,** or **quotations** from the poems to support my opinion.

PART 2 Planning a Comparison-Contrast Essay

- Identify the basis of comparison. (Refer to the chart you developed on page 432.)
- Create a graphic like the one shown to help in planning your comparison-contrast essay.
- Determine how the poems are alike and different. (Review the information on the chart that you completed for both poems.)
- State similarities and differences as precisely as possible.

Poetic Elements	"Exile"	"Lost Sister
Content subject matter/speaker/setting/conflict/characters/plot		
Form physical arrangement/pattern/structure/use of stanzas		
Language word choice/imagery/figurative language/symbols		
Summary Similarities Between Poems: Differences:		

PART 3 Drafting Your Essay

Introduction Begin by introducing your topic and identifying the basis of your comparison. Briefly identify major similarities and differences. Be specific.
Organization Analyze each selection individually or take one element of poetry at a time and discuss its role in both poems. Use signal words, such as *similarly, also, like, but, unlike,* and *while* to call attention to similarities and differences. Use examples from the poems to illustrate your points.
Conclusion Wrap up your essay with a summary of the major differences and similarities.
Writing Handbook
See page 1157: Compare and Contrast.

Writing Workshop | Career Search Report

Researching a career...

From Reading to Writing In John Cheever's short story, "The Opportunity," Elise envisions a career as an actress, but her mother chides her to "get this idea of going on the stage out of your head." Career decisions are among the most important decisions people make. You can begin thinking about your own career by researching jobs that interest you. Writing a **career search report** can help you examine your goals and uncover facts about a particular career.

For Your Portfolio

WRITING PROMPT Write a career search report in which you examine your career goals and explore a career that interests you.

Purpose: To learn about a particular career
Audience: Yourself, other students, or your career guidance counselor

Basics in a Box

Career Search Report at a Glance

Introduction
Gives information about yourself and your interests

→

Body

Examines Possible Career
Responsibilities
Education
Salary/Benefits
Employment Outlook
Advancement

→

Conclusion
Summarizes what you learned

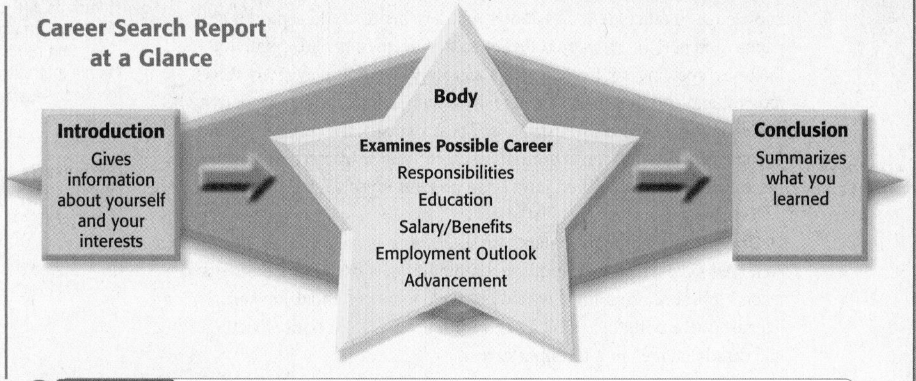

C RUBRIC Standards for Writing

A successful career search report should

- discuss your career goals
- describe your talents, skills, and interests
- focus on one or more specific careers
- report on factual aspects of each career
- mention sources of factual information
- examine the advantages and disadvantages of each career and weigh their importance to you

WRITING WORKSHOP **445**

Writing Workshop
Career Search Report

Writing Workshop
Career Search Report

Objectives
- write a Career Search Report
- use a written text as a model for writing
- revise a draft to order details logically
- use correct verb tense and forms

Introducing the Workshop

A Career Search Report Have students brainstorm about the people they have interacted with in the last 24 hours and then have them name the different kinds of jobs these people hold. If students include television characters and personalities, the list grows even larger. Next, ask them to brainstorm a list of television character "careers" they are familiar with. In addition, career possibilities can be guided by one's dreams and interests.

Discuss with students how they most enjoy spending their time, then imagine ways they could channel those interests into a career. Point out that through writing a Career Search Report, students will be able to learn more about a specific career or careers. This information can help them decide whether or not the career is one they would like to pursue further.

Basics in a Box
B Using the Graphic As the graphic suggests, the elements of a Career Search Report work together to introduce personal interests as well as present in-depth information about career possibilities. The graphic offers suggestions for elements that students can focus on as they draft their reports.

C Presenting the Rubric To better understand the assignment, students can refer to the Standards for Writing a Successful Career Search Report. You may wish to discuss with them the complete rubric, which describes several levels of proficiency. Be sure students know that their career search reports will be assessed according to how well they meet the standards for a successful report.

Use McDougal Littell's ***Language Network***, Chapter 28, for more instruction on interviewing strategies.

To engage students visually, use **Power Presentation** 5, Career Research Report.

LESSON RESOURCES

USING PRINT RESOURCES
Unit Three Resource Book
- Prewriting, p. 27
- Drafting, p. 28
- Peer Response, pp. 29–30
- Revising, Editing, and Proofreading, p. 31
- Student Models, pp. 32–37
- Rubric, p. 38

Writing Transparencies and Copymasters
- Writing Process Transparencies, pp. 1–4
- Writing Style Transparencies, pp. 12–24
- Writing Template Copymasters, p. 29

USING MEDIA RESOURCES
LaserLinks
Writing Springboards
See Teacher's SourceBook p. 64 for bar codes.

Writing Coach CD-ROM
Visit our website:
www.mcdougallittell.com

Teaching the Lesson

Analyzing the Model

"Designing a Career"

D The student model describes and analyzes the advantages and disadvantages of two very different career choices: teaching and screenwriting.

Explain that these two careers offer a sharp contrast in a number of respects. These contrasts help the writer analyze and evaluate two very distinct careers.

After students read the model, they can take turns reading aloud the Rubric in Action. Point out key words and phrases in the student model that correspond to the elements mentioned in the Rubric in Action.

1. Have students suggest an alternative opening based on the other option listed.
   Possible Response: The writer might eliminate the first paragraph altogether and simply start with paragraph two.
2. Ask students to point out similarities and differences between the two careers.
   Possible Response: Similarities: both involve creativity; both require dedication, education, and skill. Differences: teaching is oriented toward helping others; screenwriting is oriented toward producing a product.
4. Ask students to describe how the chart presents two important aspects of this career: time involved and rewards involved.
   Possible Response: Time is shown in terms of weekly and yearly schedules; rewards are shown in terms of personal and financial rewards.

Analyzing a Student Model

Laurel Eskra
Evanston Township High School

Designing a Career

Some people know from a young age what profession they will choose later in life. A biology teacher here at my high school told me, "I knew from the age of five that I would end up teaching!" For these people, life is less complicated than it is for those of us who have not yet pinned down precise career goals. Without clear goals, we may feel intimidated and confused by the huge variety and number of possible jobs. We find ourselves evaluating exactly where we'd like to be in five years, ten years, and eventually thirty years.

The search for a career is also a search for identity. For me, I know that I am interested in education and the arts. I believe I would find it stimulating to be either a teacher of young children or a screenwriter. These two very different professions interest me because of the mystery involved in each. Teachers are dedicated, respected, and intelligent adults who spread their knowledge to others in a classroom. As a teacher, I would aspire to be patient and help many people. In contrast, screenwriters are creativity factories, spewing out brilliant plots and storylines for televisions shows, movies, and commercials. I have really begun to admire the productivity and creativity of these professionals. These two specific professions have become intriguing to me. Through research, I have learned more about these careers and identified how I can prepare myself for each.

D

Teaching

The educational requirements for a teaching license vary from state to state. All states, however, require completion of a bachelor's degree and a teacher training program. I would not have to worry about job security, because there will always be a need for teachers. I see both advantages and disadvantages in a teaching career.

Advantages and Disadvantages of Teaching

Advantages	Disadvantages
Schedule—two-month vacation in summer	**Work load**—more than 40 hours/week plus grading and preparation time
Personal rewards—helping others, exercising and developing creativity and courage	**Low pay**—$37,900 on average *(Occupational Outlook Handbook)*

RUBRIC IN ACTION

1. This writer opens with a relevant anecdote.
   Another Option:
   • State the purpose of the paper directly.
2. Briefly mentions her personal interests and focuses on two jobs that reflect those interests
3. Presents the thesis statement
4. Presents factual information about teaching and credits the sources of information

Screenwriting

A more whimsical career choice is that of a screenwriter. Screenwriters develop original fiction and nonfiction scripts for radio and television broadcasts as well as for advertisements. The requirements for becoming a screenwriter include a degree in communications, journalism, or English, as well as solid writing skills. This is a very competitive career, but the need for screenwriters is expected to increase slightly over the next decade. The following chart shows the advantages and disadvantages of this career for me.

⑤ Elaborates on second career—screenwriting

Advantages and Disadvantages of Screenwriting

Advantages	Disadvantages
Schedule—freedom to set own schedule	**Competition**—hard career to break into
Salary—about $16,000 for 30-minute prime-time script *(American Almanac of Jobs and Salaries)*	**Working environment**—often noisy, crowded rooms
Personal rewards—excitement and challenge of using creativity and being original	

Through my research into teaching and screenwriting, I discovered many important facts. Both careers could be rewarding to me for different reasons. As a teacher, I would be rewarded by knowing that I am helping others learn. As a screenwriter, I would have more money and freedom. Both careers would be outlets for my creativity, and I find both intriguing. Screenwriting is a dream career that is harder to get into. Teaching is a more down-to-earth career offering the opportunity to reach out to students. Though there are certain aspects about both that I find disenchanting, they both seem important, interesting, and rewarding. Having either as my official profession later in life would be thrilling as well as an honor.

⑥ Concludes by summarizing advantages and disadvantages of each career

5. Ask students which aspects of screenwriting are presented in sharpest contrast with those of teaching.

   Possible Response: A specific talent and skill is required for screenwriting—solid writing skills. Also, screenwriting is highly competitive in a way that teaching is not.

6. Point out how the student writer brings her own values to bear in the final paragraph. Ask students to summarize the advantages the writer cites.

   Possible Response: Teaching presents the personal reward of helping others. It is creative and down-to-earth. Screenwriting presents the personal rewards of money and freedom. It is creative and more of a dream career.

Guiding Student Writing

Prewriting

Choosing a Career

If after reading the Idea Bank students are having difficulty choosing their careers, suggest they try the following:

- Make a list of adults you most admire. For each person, list the characteristics you admire and the person's career. Use these as a basis for exploring career possibilities.
- Browse through recent newspapers and magazines looking specifically for the careers of people involved in news stories.
- Visit your school's counseling center. Examine literature and catalogs that provide various career options.

Planning the Career Search Report

1. Have students take a personal inventory in which they list the following: values they feel strongest about, characteristics of people they most admire, what they would most like to accomplish in life, what kind of family life they would like. Encourage them to use this thinking to articulate their long-range goals.
2. Have students make three separate columns on a sheet of paper with the following headings: Talents, Skills, and Interests. After students complete this self-assessment, have them list careers for which their talents, skills, or interests are most suited.
3. **and 4.** Encourage students to thoroughly chart information about the careers they are most interested in as they research. Creating a "template" and then using it to make a one-page chart for each career can help them be thorough. Instruct them to record the source of their information, including page numbers.
5. Have students use the two charts they created for numbers 2 to 4 to match careers with their personal goals and skills.

Drafting

Although there is no one correct way to approach drafting, explain to students that the structure of the student model has features that might be useful to follow. Have students attempt to break down the larger task of their Career Search Report into smaller pieces by creating headings that will guide their focus in each section. Then, with these headings in place, they can develop their points systematically with details and discussion.

IDEA Bank

1. Your Working Portfolio
Build on this **Writing Option,** which you completed earlier in this unit:
- **Ideal Job Description,** p. 418

2. Classified Information
Skim the classified ads in your Sunday newspaper to see which careers seem most in demand. Choose one of these careers to research.

3. Who You Know
Think of all the people you know who have interesting jobs. Talk to a few of them about their jobs. Choose one or two of those jobs to research.

Writing Your Career Search Report

❶ Prewriting

Browse through the *Occupational Outlook Handbook* to find out about careers you might research. This book contains information on hundreds of job titles. See the **Idea Bank** in the margin for more ideas. After you have found one or two careers to research, follow the steps below.

Planning Your Career Search Report

1. **Examine your goals.** Take a good look at yourself. What are you looking for in a job or career? What are your most important goals?
2. **Examine your talents, skills, and interests.** What do you do well? What activities do you enjoy most? Make a list of your skills, and then think about which skills you'd like to use on the job. For which of the jobs and careers your choose to research are your skills most suited?
3. **Research the careers.** Books such as the *Occupational Outlook Handbook* can help you learn more about the careers that interest you. You might also interview people in the careers you are exploring. Another way to learn about these careers is to contact professional, trade, or union associations that represent them. These groups often produce brochures about job opportunities.
4. **Record your findings.** Make a chart for possible careers in which you list the responsibilities, education or training required, the outlook for employment, and possible salaries. As you learn more about the careers, note the advantages and disadvantages of each. Be sure to record the sources of any factual information in your chart.
5. **Match careers with your goals and skills.** How well do the careers that you identified match your goals and skills? Choose the career that best suits you and use it as the subject of your report.

❷ Drafting

You might begin by presenting **information about yourself** or **facts about the career** you are considering. Just let your thoughts flow as you draft, but be sure at some point to state the career you are exploring and to discuss your career goals, skills, and interests. Also examine the **advantages** and **disadvantages** of the career in light of your goals and skills and sum up what you learned about yourself, the career, and its suitability for you.

Ask Your Peer Reader

- What are my career goals? How does the career I described reflect those goals?
- How well does my career choice suit my skills?
- What additional information about each career would be helpful?

❸ Revising

TARGET SKILL ▶ LOGICAL ORDER OF DETAILS As you revise your career report, check to see that the ideas in each paragraph are presented in an order that makes sense. Use transitions such as *next, since, in contrast,* and *on the other hand* to show clear relationships between ideas.

> These two very different professions interest me because of the mystery involved in each. Teachers are dedicated, respected, and intelligent adults who spread their knowledge to others in a classroom. [As a teacher, I would aspire to be patient and help many people.] ^In contrast, Screenwriters are creativity factories, spewing out brilliant plots and storylines for television shows, movies, and commercials.

❹ Editing and Proofreading

TARGET SKILL ▶ CORRECT VERB FORMS Using incorrect verb forms in your career search report can confuse your reader. When you proofread, check each verb to make sure you have used the correct tense and form.

> I have really ~~began~~ ^begun to admire the productivity and creativity of these professionals. These two specific professions ~~has~~ ^have become intrigu~~e~~ing to me.

❺ Reflecting

FOR YOUR WORKING PORTFOLIO What did you discover about your career goals while writing this report? How did this report change your ideas about the career you chose? Attach your answers to your finished work. Save your career search report in your **Working Portfolio.**

Need revising help?

Review the **Rubric**, p. 445

Consider **peer reader** comments

Check **Revision Guidelines**, p. 1145

Publishing IDEAS

- Contribute your report to an ongoing career file in the classroom or in the school career counselor's office.
- Post your report to a school Web site or career search Web site.

More Online: Publishing Options
www.mcdougallittell.com

Revising

LOGICAL ORDER OF DETAILS

As students revise their paragraphs, remind them that their writing will make more sense if they group related ideas together. For instance, in the sample paragraph in the text, the last sentence presents information about the qualities necessary in a teacher; therefore, it should be placed directly after sentence two, which discusses other qualities successful teachers need.

Editing and Proofreading

CORRECT VERB FORMS

Consistency in tense and verb form is essential in effective writing. Often, if there is more than one verb in a sentence, problems can arise. Errors occur when tenses and forms shift needlessly.

Write the following example on the chalkboard. Discuss the error in verb forms, and explain how to proofread for and correct such errors.

Incorrect: The coach ordered the players to do push-ups and was explaining how victory requires discipline.

Correct: The coach **ordered** the players to do push-ups and **explained** how victory requires discipline.

Explain that when revising longer passages, it is necessary to pay attention to the verb tense that is initially established and not to lose track of it as the passage progresses.

In the first sentence in the example from the text, the past participle form *begun* is needed to form the present perfect tense have *begun.* In the second sentence the plural verb *have* is needed to agree with the plural subject *professions.*

Remind students that using correct verb forms is part of producing an error-free final draft.

Reflecting

Encourage students to write a brief response to the questions. You might also ask them to evaluate which parts of their analysis were most effective and which were least effective. Have students clip their responses to their career search reports and place both in their working portfolios.

WRITING WORKSHOP 449

Assessment Practice

Before students begin the exercise, you may wish to briefly review the kinds of errors that the passage contains. Then demonstrate how students can eliminate incorrect choices for the first question.

A. This choice is incorrect because a comma will not correct the sentence fragment. A conjunction is needed to correctly join the first sentence with the fragment.

B. This choice is incorrect because it contains a sentence fragment.

D. This choice can be eliminated because of the sentence fragment.

C. This is the correct choice because the coordinating conjunction *and* correctly joins the two verbs *have loved* and *felt*.

Answers:
1. C; **2.** C; **3.** A; **4.** C; **5.** B

Assessment Practice Revising & Editing

Read this paragraph from the first draft of a student essay. The underlined sections may include the following kinds of errors:

- **sentence fragments**
- **incorrect verb forms**
- **capitalization errors**
- **misplaced modifiers**

For each underlined section, choose the revision that most improves the writing.

> It's no surprise that veterinary medicine is the career that interests me most. I've always loved animals. Felt I could communicate with them. (1) To become a veterinarian, carefully I must choose the right school. (2) I will take a variety of courses, concentrating on Biology, Chemistry, and Math. (3) I will chose (4) my medical specialty by my third year in college. After I earn my undergraduate degree, I plan to attend one of the 31 veterinary medical colleges in the United States. I know a little about helping injured and sick animals from volunteering at the local animal shelter. I look forward to learning more about how to treat animals in school. (5)

1. **A.** I've always loved animals, felt I could communicate with them.
   B. I've always loved animals, communicate with them.
   C. I've always loved animals and felt I could communicate with them.
   D. Correct as is

2. **A.** To become a veterinarian carefully, I must choose the right school.
   B. To carefully become a veterinarian, I must choose the right school.
   C. To become a veterinarian, I must carefully choose the right school.
   D. Correct as is

3. **A.** biology, chemistry, and math
   B. Biology, Chemistry, and math
   C. biology, chemistry, and Math
   D. Correct as is

4. **A.** I will chosen
   B. I will be chosen
   C. I will choose
   D. Correct as is

5. **A.** I look forward in school to learning more about how to treat animals.
   B. I look forward to learning more in school about how to treat animals.
   C. I look forward to, in school, learning more about how to treat animals.
   D. Correct as is

Need extra help?

See the **Grammar Handbook**
Correcting Fragments, p. 1199
Phrases, p. 1206
Verb Tense, p. 1186

PART 2 The Power of Heritage

How would you define heritage? Would you describe it in terms of ethnic or racial background? Is it shaped by family, religious, or cultural traditions? In this part of Unit Three, you will read about characters and real people who come to important realizations about their heritage and its power. You will also be asked to explore your own heritage.

ACTIVITY

Create a pie graph showing the different aspects of your own heritage. Use separate labels, such as "Family," "Religion," "Social Groups," and "Ethnic Background" to identify each piece of your heritage pie. The sizes of the pieces should reflect the relative importance of each aspect of your heritage. The largest piece should represent the most important aspect; the smallest should represent the least important.

451

OVERVIEW

Objectives
- understand the following:
  - author's perspective
  - interpretation of experience
  - tone
  - cultural context
  - portrayal of individuals
- analyze tone and identify an author's attitudes, values, and beliefs
- infer an author's perspective from tone and cultural context

Teaching the Lesson

This lesson analyzes elements of nonfiction and fiction that reflect the author's beliefs and values and indicate his or her perspective.

Introducing the Concepts
Point out that an author's perspective is not different from a person's perspective. Ask students to brainstorm examples of public figures from current events and name details that indicate their perspectives on particular issues.

Presenting the Concepts
Author's Perspective in Nonfiction
In nonfiction, an explicit thesis statement will often indicate the author's perspective. Encourage students to look for an explicit thesis sentence as a starting place in determining the author's perspective.

The Interpretation of Experience
Point out that our interpretations are frequently governed by our values, beliefs, and attitudes, all of which are subjective rather than objective.

YOUR TURN The first passage best reveals Angelou's perspective. She may have included both interpretations to contrast the limitations of the narrow view with the possibilities in the larger view.

Tone
Name a recent local event with which students are familiar. Have two groups of students cooperate to create interpretations of the event. The first group should present a humorous interpretation; the second group should present a serious interpretation.

Author's Perspective

Author's Perspective is a unique combination of ideas, attitudes, feelings, values, and beliefs that make up the way a writer looks at the world. According to E. B. White, "Every writer, by the way he uses language, reveals something of his spirit, his habits, his capacities, his bias." Of course, we each have a perspective, too, complete with our own biases—personal preferences and prejudices—that color that perspective.

Author's Perspective in Nonfiction

An author's perspective is easier to detect in nonfiction than in fiction. For example, Isaac Asimov's essay "Dial Versus Digital" (page 107) is basically a one-sided argument in favor of dial clocks. Such a stand against digital clocks may sound strange coming from a science fiction writer, but therein lies a lesson for the reader. Don't make assumptions about an author's perspective. Base your judgment on what a writer says or implies in his or her work.

The Interpretation of Experience

In autobiographical nonfiction, writers' interpretations of events in their lives offer a key to their perspectives. For example, in "Getting a Job" (page 411), Maya Angelou explores two different interpretations of her experience with the receptionist at the Market Street Railway Company.

YOUR TURN Read the two passages at the right. Which passage best reveals Angelou's adult beliefs and values—in other words, her perspective? Why do you think she included both her interpretations of the event?

THE INTERPRETATION OF EXPERIENCE

1 The miserable little encounter had nothing to do with me, the me of me, any more than it had to do with that silly clerk. The incident was a recurring dream, concocted years before by stupid whites and it eternally came back to haunt us all. . . .
I went further than forgiving the clerk, I accepted her as a fellow victim of the same puppeteer.

2 All lies, all comfortable lies. The receptionist was not innocent and neither was I. The whole charade we had played out in that crummy waiting room had directly to do with me, Black, and her, white.

—Maya Angelou, "Getting a Job"

Tone

The attitude that a writer takes toward a particular subject is called **tone**. The tone of a literary work can vary greatly, ranging from a serious tone to a humorous tone, as in the excerpt from Bill Cosby's *Love and Marriage* (page 357). Tone reveals a writer's values and feelings in a very personal way. Imagine how different Bill Cosby's tone would be if he had written about his failure with Charlene right after it happened, instead of years later. Humor is often just a matter of perspective.

Cultural Context

The behavior, beliefs, institutions, art, and values of a community or time period make up a culture. For some writers, culture plays an important part in defining their perspective. For instance, Margaret Atwood tries to be fair, if not objective, in her essay, "Through the One-Way Mirror" (page 170): she criticizes both Canadians and Americans. But something in her tone reveals strong feelings about Americans that stem, at least in part, from her perspective as a Canadian.

YOUR TURN Read the passage at the right from Atwood's essay. How is Atwood's perspective influenced by her culture? What is her tone in the passage? Point out words that reveal her tone.

TONE AND CULTURAL CONTEXT

The Americans, bless their innocent little hearts, are rarely aware that they are even being watched, much less by the Canadians. . . If they think about Canada at all, it's only when things get a bit snowy or the water goes off or the Canadians start fussing over some piddly detail, such as fish. Then they regard them as unpatriotic; for Americans don't really see Canadians as foreigners, . . . Really, think the Americans, the Canadians are just like us, or would be if they could.

—Margaret Atwood, "Through the One-Way Mirror"

Portrayal of Individuals

The way various individuals are presented in most nonfiction is also an important clue to the author's perspective. In "A Celebration of Grandfathers" (page 455), Rudolfo Anaya celebrates all grandfathers by praising his own grandfather.

YOUR TURN In the passage at the right, what can you infer about Anaya's own values? Point out words that reveal those values.

PORTRAYAL OF INDIVIDUALS

I grew up speaking Spanish, and oh! how difficult it was to learn English. Sometimes I would give up and cry out that I couldn't learn. Then he would say *"Ten paciencia."* Have patience. *Paciencia*, a word with the strength of centuries . . . "You have to learn the language of the Americanos," he said. "Me, I will live my last days in my valley. You will live in a new time."

—Rudolfo A. Anaya, "A Celebration of Grandfathers"

Author's Perspective in Fiction

Most writers keep their personal opinions out of their fiction. Their perspectives are given directly only in interviews, in nonfiction they write themselves, or in articles about them written by someone else. Still, readers can sometimes infer an author's perspective from elements in a story—such as plot, character, and theme—and from the tone and cultural context of a story.

YOUR TURN Read Mark Twain's description of Tuttletown from "The Californian's Tale" (page 303). What does it suggest about Twain's perspective on the California Gold Rush?

FICTION

In some few cases these cabins were still occupied; and when this was so, you could depend upon it that the occupant was the very pioneer who had built the cabin; that he was there because he had once had his opportunity to go home to the States rich, and had not done it; had rather lost his wealth, and had then in his humiliation resolved to sever all communication with his home relatives and friends, and be to them thenceforth as one dead.

—Mark Twain, "The Californian's Tale"

Making Connections

Cultural Context

Explain to students that culture more often than not is transparent in our lives, creating perspectives of which we are largely unaware. Cultural attitudes toward men and women, for instance, have a large influence on our beliefs and actions. Remind students that as they read they should look for and recognize both the shared and distinctive characteristics of cultures.

YOUR TURN Atwood feels as if Canadian culture has been slighted by the Americans. Her tone is anguished resentment, revealed by words that include "little hearts"; "fussing . . . piddly detail"; "unpatriotic"; and "just like us."

Portrayal of Individuals

Just as in everyday life, the way we describe another person reveals a great deal about our attitude and judgment toward that person.

YOUR TURN Anaya values his Spanish heritage and the wisdom of his grandfather, revealed in the quotations of words spoken by his grandfather.

Author's Perspective in Fiction

Explain that an author's perspective will be more subtly and indirectly suggested in fiction. Personal opinions are often conveyed largely through an author's "camera angles" or choices of what he or she wishes to bring into focus.

YOUR TURN This passage suggests Twain's belief that the people who pursued the California Gold Rush were driven by a sense of "all or none" desperation.

OVERVIEW

Objectives
- determine an author's reasons for writing a text
- evaluate how well an author achieves his or her purpose

Teaching the Lesson

The strategies on this page will help students learn how to determine an author's purpose by questioning the text and monitoring their own reactions.

Presenting the Strategies
Help students understand purpose by bringing in magazines to discuss how purpose lies behind selected examples of advertising.

1 Determining the Author's Purpose Students can sometimes determine a writer's purpose for writing nonfiction by finding the thesis, which is usually stated in the opening paragraphs. Often times, however, they will have to read an entire piece to determine the writer's purpose, especially in fiction.

2 Evaluating What You Read Point out that each of the questions listed implicitly contains the evaluative criteria that can be used to make a judgment about a piece of writing. Have students use these questions to create a checklist of "Evaluative Criteria."

The Active Reader: Skills and Strategies

Why do you think Mark Twain wrote "The Californian's Tale"? Did he have more than one reason? These questions are at the heart of an author's purpose. The strategies here can help you better understand such purposes as you read.

Purposes for Writing

1 Determining Author's Purpose
Author's purpose refers to the reasons an author has for writing something. Usually, an author has one of these four basic purposes in mind: to entertain; to inform or explain; to persuade or influence; to express emotions, thoughts, or ideas.

Most writing, however, is complex enough to have more than one purpose. For example, Twain probably wrote "The Californian's Tale" to entertain, but he also may have wanted to inform readers about the bleaker side of the California Gold Rush.

- **Understanding the Author's Message** Don't assume that there is only one level of interpretation of a story. A humorous story, for example, may actually have a serious message beneath its surface.
- **Understanding the "How"** Awareness of an author's purpose sometimes suggests *how* to read. If you realize that an author is trying to inform you, you will pay close attention to the details he or she provides.

Strategies for Determining Purpose
Look for direct statements of purpose in the introduction. (In nonfiction, the purpose is often part of the **thesis statement.**) Or, you may have to **infer** the purpose from the theme, from what you already know about the genre or the author, or from your own response to the writing.
Monitor your own reaction to a piece of writing. Are you entertained? Are you learning something? Are you being persuaded to believe something or to take action?
Analyze any facts in the piece. How are they used—to explain, to support an argument, to add realism to a story?

2 Evaluating What You Read
Evaluating how well the author achieves his or her purpose is the next step. Ask yourself the following questions, and be prepared to support your opinion with evidence:
- If the purpose was to entertain, did I enjoy the selection? Was the language appropriate to the purpose, and were effective literary techniques used?
- If the purpose was to explain, did I understand the subject? Was the information presented thoroughly and logically?
- If the author was trying to persuade, was I convinced? Did I feel that the opinion was supported with sound reasons and sufficient evidence?
- If the purpose was to create a certain mood or share personal experiences, beliefs, or feelings, did I understand why the author felt as he or she did?

Need More Help?

Remember that active readers use the essential reading strategies explained on page 7: **visualize, predict, clarify, question, connect, evaluate, monitor.**

PREPARING to *Read*

A Celebration of Grandfathers

Memoir by RUDOLFO A. ANAYA

"Simple lessons from a simple man."

Connect to Your Life

Generation to Generation Think about the elderly people in your life—perhaps relatives, neighbors, or friends of your family. How would you describe their values and view of the world? In what ways are these different from the values and worldview of your own generation? Discuss your thoughts with a small group of classmates, giving examples of the different attitudes and values of the two generations.

Build Background

Pride of Place Rudolfo Anaya's Mexican-American heritage and the landscape of New Mexico, the state in which he was born and still resides, are important elements in most of the author's writing. This southwestern state is a place of geographical contrasts. Central New Mexico is part of the Rocky Mountains, and Taos—the Native American pueblo settlement in northern New Mexico that Anaya believes was home to his ancestors—is near the highest mountain in the state, Wheeler Peak. In sharp contrast, the eastern portion of the state is an extension of the Great Plains. It was on this flat terrain, along the Pecos River, that Anaya's grandfather settled and worked the land. Until the late 1940s, the life described in Anaya's story was still quite common, but after World War II, as more people moved to New Mexico, many of the small agricultural villages were deserted.

Focus Your Reading

LITERARY CONCEPT **AUTHOR'S PERSPECTIVE AND TONE** The language and details a writer chooses help to create **tone,** the attitude a writer displays toward a subject. The tone of a work can help you recognize and understand an **author's perspective**—what the author thinks and believes. As you read this memoir, think about how Anaya's attitude toward his grandfather reflects his own beliefs and ideas.

ACTIVE READING **IDENTIFYING AUTHOR'S PURPOSE** The author's purpose refers to a writer's main reason for writing. Generally, a writer of nonfiction writes for one or more of the following purposes: to inform; to express ideas, opinions, and feelings; to analyze; to persuade; or to entertain. To help you determine Anaya's purpose(s) in writing this memoir, look for the following as you read:

- facts about places or people (inform)
- comments the author makes about the facts he has reported (express ideas, opinions, and feelings)
- statements that explain how a subject is defined or how it works (analyze)
- statements that seem to be trying to convince you of something (persuade)
- passages that you find particularly enjoyable (entertain)

READER'S NOTEBOOK As you read the selection, jot down any statements that appear to indicate the author's purpose(s).

OVERVIEW

This selection is included in the **Grade 10 InterActive Reader.**

Objectives

1. understand and appreciate a **memoir (Literary Analysis)**
2. analyze and appreciate **author's perspective and tone (Literary Analysis)**
3. **identify author's purpose (Active Reading)**

Summary

As a young boy in New Mexico, Anaya learned that his elders were strong in their beliefs and created wise paths for the young to follow. Anaya's grandfather, a farmer, taught young Anaya to appreciate the natural cycles of the earth, including death. After Anaya's grandfather died, Anaya looked back on the simplicity of his grandfather's wisdom. Today, he wonders how he can make the values of his grandfather's generation fit into his world today.

Thematic Link

Anaya writes his memoir in honor of his grandfather and his grandfather's generation. Anaya preserves the **power of** his **heritage** by celebrating his grandfather's wisdom.

5-Minute Warm-Up

Daily Language SkillBuilder

Have students **proofread** the display sentences on page 381j and write them correctly. The sentences also appear on Transparency 14 of **Grammar Transparencies and Copymasters.**

LESSON RESOURCES

UNIT THREE RESOURCE BOOK, pp. 39–42

ASSESSMENT RESOURCES

Formal Assessment, pp. 75–76

Teacher's Guide to Assessment and Portfolio Use

Test Generator

SKILLS TRANSPARENCIES AND COPYMASTERS

Literary Analysis
- Author's Perspective, T13 (for Paired Activity, p. 460)

Reading and Critical Thinking
- Determining Author's Purpose and Audience, T19 (for Think Critically, item 6, p. 460)
- Organizing and Interpreting Information on Statistical Tables, T35 (for Inquiry & Research 2, p. 461)

Grammar
- Commonly Confused Verbs, C138 (for Mini Lesson, p. 461)

Vocabulary
- Word Meanings, C51 (for Mini Lesson, p. 459)

Writing
- Generating Writing Ideas, T1 (for Writing Option 2, p. 461)
- Elaboration, T10 (for Writing Option 1, p. 461)

Communications
- Impromptu Speaking: Dialogue, Role-Play, Debate, T13 (for Activities & Explorations, p. 461)

INTEGRATED TECHNOLOGY

Audio Library

Internet: Research Starter

Visit our website:
www.mcdougallittell.com

A CELEBRATION OF GRANDFATHERS 455

TEACHING THE LITERATURE

Reading and Analyzing

Reading Skills and Strategies: PREVIEW

Summarize the memoir, emphasizing the author's perspective. The opening image helps students visualize the strength that Anaya's grandfather always demonstrates. Students should pay particular attention to the italicized Spanish expressions.

Active Reading

IDENTIFYING AUTHOR'S PURPOSE

Discuss the various purposes an author may have for writing: to inform, express ideas, opinions, feelings, analyze, persuade, or entertain. Identifying the author's purpose helps the reader understand why certain details have been included.

Use **Unit Three Resource Book** p. 40 for additional support.

Literary Analysis

AUTHOR'S PERSPECTIVE AND TONE

Have students list any details from the story that reflect the author's attitude toward his grandfather and other elderly people. Students should realize that these details affect the tone of the memoir.

Use **Unit Three Resource Book** p. 41 for additional support.

A Celebration

Teaching Options

Mini Lesson: Viewing and Representing

ART APPRECIATION Instruction Have students note details about the farmer in the painting: his clothes, his tools, his posture, etc. Ask them what they can tell about the farmer.

Possible Response: The bent-over farmer in the painting laboriously works the soil with simple tools. Without the aid of modern technology, he relies solely on his physical condition and manual dexterity.

Application Considering the details in the painting, ask students what similarities they see between the farmer in the painting and Anaya's grandfather.

Possible Response: The position of the man and the endless view of the field show the careful, painstaking, patient nature of the man's work. The figure also seems rooted in the earth, a part of nature's cycle.

# of Grandfathers

Rudolfo A. Anaya

Campesino [Farmer] (1976), Daniel Desiga. Oil on canvas, 50 ½″ × 58 ½″. Collection of Alfredo Aragón. Courtesy UCLA at the Armand Hammer Museum of Art and Cultural Center, Los Angeles.

"Buenos días le de Dios, abuelo." God give you a good day, grandfather. This is how I was taught as a child to greet my grandfather, or any grown person. It was a greeting of respect, a cultural value to be passed on from generation to generation, this respect for the old ones.

The old people I remember from my childhood were strong in their beliefs, and as we lived daily with them, we learned a wise path of life to follow. They had something important to share with the young, and when they spoke, the young listened. These old *abuelos* and *abuelitas*[1] had worked the earth all their lives, and so they knew the value of nurturing, they knew the sensitivity of the earth. . . . They knew the rhythms and cycles of time, from the preparation of the earth in the spring to the digging of the *acequias*[2] that brought the water to the dance of harvest in the fall. They shared good times and hard times. They helped each other through the epidemics and the personal tragedies, and they shared what little they had when the hot winds burned the land and no rain came. They learned that to survive one had to share in the process of life. . . .

My grandfather was a plain man, a farmer from the valley called Puerto de Luna on the Pecos River. He was probably a descendant of those people who spilled over the mountain from Taos, following the Pecos River in search of farmland. There in that river valley he settled and raised a large family.

1. *abuelos* (ä-bwĕ′lôs) . . . *abuelitas* (ä-bwĕ-lē′täs) *Spanish:* grandfathers . . . grannies.
2. *acequias* (ä-sĕ′kyäs) *Spanish:* irrigation ditches.

Customizing Instruction

Less Proficient Readers

Have students keep these questions in mind as they read.

- How does Anaya feel about his grandfather?
  Possible Response: respectful, admiring
- How does Anaya feel about elderly people?
  Possible Response: They have things to teach us.
- What kind of influence has Anaya's grandfather had on him?
  Possible Response: Anaya tries to lead the kind of generous, nurturing life that his grandfather led.

Students Acquiring English

To help students understand the author's description of his grandfather in the story, explain that he uses words such as *plain* and *simple* in a positive way. He means that his grandfather was what he appeared to be and did not pretend to be something else. Have students read to find other descriptive words.

Use **Spanish Study Guide** for additional support, pp. 98–100.

Gifted and Talented

To give students a deeper understanding of the life of Anaya's grandfather, have them find out more information about the climate and soil conditions of the Puerto de Luna valley on the Pecos River.

BLOCK SCHEDULING: MANAGING TIME

If your schedule requires that you cover the lesson objectives in a shorter time, use . . .

- Preparing to Read, p. 455
- Thinking Through the Literature, p. 460

If you want to take advantage of longer class time, use . . .

- TE Options: Viewing and Representing, p. 456; Vocabulary Strategy, p. 459; Informal Assessment, p. 458
- Choices & Challenges p. 461

A CELEBRATION OF GRANDFATHERS 457

Reading and Analyzing

Reading Skills and Strategies: CLARIFYING

A Ask students what they think Anaya means when he says of patience, "*Paciencia,* a word with the strength of centuries, a word that said that someday we would overcome . . . "

Possible Response: Anaya means that with the strength and patience, one can overcome any obstacle if given enough time.

Literary Analysis: DICTION

B Ask students why they think Anaya uses sentence fragments such as "Simple lessons from a simple man."

Possible Response: Anaya uses fragments for emphasis. The fragments are also short and to the point.

Reading Skills and Strategies: PARAPHRASING

C Have students express the following passage in their own words:

"But this process is something to be faced, not something to be hidden away by false images."

Possible Response: Society needs to face the reality of aging.

ACTIVE READING

D **QUESTION** The grandfather's most important attributes are his wisdom, strength, patience, and knowledge about nature. This author believes that the values of the older generation are well worth learning.

ACTIVE READING

E **EVALUATE** Students may want to discuss the place "old values" have in today's world.

Bearded and walrus-mustached, he stood five feet tall, but to me as a child he was a giant. I remember him most for his silence. In the summers my parents sent me to live with him on his farm, for I was to learn the ways of a farmer. My uncles also lived in that valley, there where only the flow of the river and the whispering of the wind marked time. For me it was a magical place.

I remember once, while out hoeing the fields, I came upon an anthill, and before I knew it I was badly bitten. After he had covered my welts with the cool mud from the irrigation ditch, my grandfather calmly said: "Know where you stand." That is the way he spoke, in short phrases, to the point.

One very dry summer, the river dried to a trickle; there was no water for the fields. The young plants withered and died. In my sadness and with the impulse of youth I said, "I wish it would rain!" My grandfather touched me, looked up into the sky and whispered, "Pray for rain." In his language there was a difference. He felt connected to the cycles that brought the rain or kept it from us. His prayer was a meaningful action, because he was a participant with the forces that filled our world; he was not a bystander.

A young man died at the village one summer. A very tragic death. He was dragged by his horse. When he was found, I cried, for the boy was my friend. I did not understand why death had come to one so young. My grandfather took me aside and said: "Think of the death of the trees and the fields in the fall. The leaves fall, and everything rests, as if dead. But they

1 loom again in the spring. Death is only this nall transformation in life."

These are the things I remember, these fleeting images, few words.

I remember him driving his horse-drawn wagon into Santa Rosa in the fall when he brought his harvest produce to sell in the town. What a tower of strength seemed to come in that small man huddled on the seat of the giant wagon. One click of his tongue and the horses obeyed, stopped or turned as he wished. He never raised his whip. How unlike today, when so much teaching is done with loud words and threatening hands.

I would run to greet the wagon, and the wagon would stop. "*Buenos días le de Dios, abuelo,*" I would say. . . . "*Buenos días te de Dios, mi hijo,*"[3] he would answer and smile, and then I could jump up on the wagon and sit at his side. Then I, too, became a king as I rode next to the old man who smelled of earth and sweat and the other deep aromas from the orchards and fields of Puerto de Luna.

We were all sons and daughters to him. But today the sons and daughters are breaking with the past, putting aside *los abuelitos.* The old values are threatened, and threatened most where it comes to these relationships with the old people. If we don't take the time to watch and **D** feel the years of their final transformation, a part of our humanity will be lessened.

ACTIVE READING

QUESTION What things about his grandfather strike Anaya as being most important, and what does this tell you about the **author's perspective?**

I grew up speaking Spanish, and oh! how difficult it was to learn English. Sometimes I would give up and cry out that I couldn't learn. Then he would say, "*Ten paciencia.*" Have patience. *Paciencia,* a word with the strength of centuries, a word that said that someday we would overcome. . . . "You have to learn the language of the Americanos," he said. "Me, I will live my last days in my valley. You will live in a new time." **A**

A new time did come; a new time is here. How will we form it so it is fruitful? We need to

3. ***mi hijo*** (mē ē'hô) *Spanish:* my boy.

Teaching Options

Assessment Informal Assessment

MAKE INFERENCES AND DRAW CONCLUSIONS

You can informally assess students' understanding of the selection by having them write a paragraph in which they make inferences about the importance Anaya places on preserving old values. Students should use examples from the selection to draw conclusions about the author's perspective.

RUBRIC

3 **Full Accomplishment** Response reflects the ability to make inferences from passages in the text in order to draw a conclusion about the author's perspective on the importance of preserving old values.

2 **Substantial Accomplishment** Response draws a general conclusion about the author's perspective on preserving old values.

1 **Little or Partial Accomplishment** Response shows little understanding of the author's perspective.

know where we stand. We need to speak softly and respect others, and to share what we have. We need to pray not for material gain, but for rain for the fields, for the sun to nurture growth, for nights in which we can sleep in peace, and for a harvest in which everyone can share. Simple lessons from a simple man. These lessons he learned from his past, which was as deep and strong as the currents of the river of life.

He was a man; he died. Not in his valley but nevertheless cared for by his sons and daughters and flocks of grandchildren. At the end, I would enter his room, which carried the smell of medications and Vicks. Gone were the aroma of the fields, the strength of his young manhood. Gone also was his patience in the face of crippling old age. Small things bothered him; he shouted or turned sour when his expectations were not met. It was because he could not care for himself, because he was returning to that state of childhood, and all those wishes and desires were now wrapped in a crumbling, old body.

"Ten paciencia," I once said to him, and he smiled. "I didn't know I would grow this old," he said. . . .

I would sit and look at him and remember what was said of him when he was a young man. He could mount a wild horse and break it, and he could ride as far as any man. He could dance all night at a dance, then work the *acequia* the following day. He helped the neighbors; they helped him. He married, raised children. Small legends, the kind that make up every man's life.

He was ninety-four when he died. Family, neighbors, and friends gathered; they all agreed he had led a rich life. I remembered the last years, the years he spent in bed. And as I remember now, I am reminded that it is too easy to romanticize[4] old age. Sometimes we forget the pain of the transformation into old age, we forget the natural breaking down of the body. . . . My grandfather pointed to the leaves falling from the tree. So time brings with its transformation the often painful wearing-down process. Vision blurs, health wanes; even the act of walking carries with it the painful reminder of the autumn of life. But this process is something to be faced, not something to be hidden away by false images. Yes, the old can be young at heart, but in their own way, with their own dignity. They do not have to copy the always-young image of the Hollywood star. . . .

I returned to Puerto de Luna last summer to join the community in a celebration of the founding of the church. I drove by my grandfather's home, my uncles' ranches, the neglected adobe washing down into the earth from whence it came. And I wondered, how might the values of my grandfather's generation live in our own? What can we retain to see us through these hard times? I was to become a farmer, and I became a writer. As I plow and plant my words, do I nurture as my grandfather did in his fields and orchards? The answers are not simple.

ACTIVE READING

EVALUATE How do you feel about the "old values" Anaya describes?

"They don't make men like that anymore," is a phrase we hear when one does honor to a man. I am glad I knew my grandfather. I am glad there are still times when I can see him in my dreams, hear him in my reverie. Sometimes I think I catch a whiff of that earthy aroma that was his smell. Then I smile. How strong these people were to leave such a lasting impression.

So, as I would greet my *abuelo* long ago, it would help us all to greet the old ones we know with this kind and respectful greeting: *"Buenos días le de Dios."* ❖

4. **romanticize:** view in an unrealistic or sentimental way.

Customizing Instruction

Students Acquiring English

1 Help students understand the term *transformation* in this passage.

Possible Response: Transformation means to undergo change. Anaya's grandfather means that death is one of the changes that is part of life.

Multiple Learning Styles

Visual Learners

Anaya's grandfather lived in the valley of Puerto de Luna near the Pecos River. Have students locate Puerto de Luna on a map of Mexico. Ask them to find Santa Rosa, the town to which Anaya's grandfather drove his horse-drawn wagon to sell his produce.

Mini Lesson Vocabulary Strategies

RESEARCHING WORD ORIGINS Instruction The word *adobe* comes to English through Spanish and refers to sun-dried brick or a building made of these bricks. Many Spanish words have become part of the English language. Have students research *rodeo, pueblo,* and *canyon* as an aid to understanding Spanish influences on the English language.

Practice Have students work in pairs to find the meanings of the Spanish origins for *rodeo, pueblo,* and *canyon*. Ask them to use each word in a sentence. Invite students to identify any other words in the English language with Spanish origins.

Possible Responses: *rodeo–rodear,* to surround. We saw some excellent horsemanship at the rodeo. *pueblo–pueblo,* village; people. The ancient pueblo is now uninhabited. *canyon–caña,* a tube. The canyon was wider than we had expected.

Use **Vocabulary Transparencies and Copymasters,** p. 51.

A lesson on understanding foreign words appears on p. 584 in the Pupil's Edition.

GUIDING STUDENT RESPONSE

Connect to the Literature

1. **What Do You Think?**
   Students may point out that he was both loving and tough.

Comprehension Check

- Anaya's grandfather was a farmer.
- as a transformation similar to the seasonal transformation of plants
- He returned to join the community in a celebration of the founding of the church.

Use Selection Quiz
Unit Three Resource Book, p. 42.

Think Critically

2. Students may point out that the grandfather understood the natural cycles and lived in harmony with them.
3. Possible Response: Anaya's grandfather taught him to be patient and strong; he taught him to cherish his family and the earth.
4. He felt at peace because the grandfather had completed his cycle.
5. Possible Response: The physical setting of a farm taught the grandfather to be patient and nurturing; the cultural setting of isolation from mainstream America allowed the grandfather to retain his traditional values.
6. The author is concerned about the present and wants his readers to remember the importance of time-honored values.

Connect to the Literature

1. **What Do You Think?** What is your impression of the author's grandfather?

Comprehension Check

- What did Anaya's grandfather do for a living?
- How did the grandfather describe death to Anaya?
- Why did the author return to Puerto de Luna?

Think Critically

2. What do you think Anaya means when he says that his grandfather was "a participant with the forces that filled our world," rather than a bystander?
3. What are the most important lessons you think the author has learned from his grandfather?
4. How do you think Anaya felt about his grandfather's "final transformation"?

   THINK ABOUT
   - the description of the grandfather when he was active
   - the conditions of the grandfather's final days
   - the lessons he taught Anaya about death and about nature
   - the author's comment that the process of aging is "something to be faced"

5. To what extent do you think the physical and cultural **setting** helped to shape the grandfather's values? Explain your answer.
6. ACTIVE READING AUTHOR'S PURPOSE Looking at the notes in your READER'S NOTEBOOK, what do you consider to be the **author's purpose** or purposes in writing this **memoir**? How successful do you think he is in achieving his goals? Explain your answer.

Extend Interpretation

7. **What If?** If Rudolfo Anaya had remained on the farm, do you think the questions he asks at the end of the story would be different? Would it be easier to keep his grandfather's values alive? Explain your answers.
8. **Connect to Life** Do you think the things Anaya learned from his grandfather are relevant to your life today? Why or why not?

Literary Analysis

AUTHOR'S PERSPECTIVE AND TONE

An **author's perspective** is the set of beliefs, feelings, and attitudes he or she displays in a work of literature. One element that helps you to understand an author's perspective is **tone**—the attitude an author takes toward a subject. The language and details that an author chooses help create the tone, which might be playful, serious, bitter, angry, or detached, among other possibilities.

Paired Activity Working with a classmate, agree on two or three adjectives that best describe the tone of this piece. Then note in a brief paragraph what you consider to be Anaya's perspective and tone in this memoir. Consider his thoughts and feelings on modern society, the lessons to be learned from his grandfather's generation, and the ways in which the elderly should be treated. In what ways do you think the tone of the piece contributes to Anaya's perspective?

STYLE **Style**—the way in which a piece of literature is written—may also contribute to the author's perspective. Elements such as **word choice, sentence length, imagery,** and use of **dialogue** contribute to an author's personal style. In this selection, for example, Anaya sometimes uses short, simple sentences, a stylistic technique that helps to convey the "simple lessons" he learned from his grandfather. Review the selection again and identify other elements of Anaya's style. How do you think these elements of style contribute to the author's perspective?

Extend Interpretations

What If? No, the life his grandfather lived does not exist anymore; yes, Anaya would still live in the small agricultural community.

Connect to Life Encourage students to react to this piece and to respond to each other's thoughts about what is relevant in their life today.

Literary Analysis

Author's Perspective and Tone The author's serious tone underlines his basic concern about the lessening of humanity in today's world.

Style Anaya uses a fairly simple vocabulary; he incorporates fragments of dialogue into his memoir; his imagery evokes the Southwestern landscape; he also makes use of Spanish terms.

Choices & CHALLENGES

Writing Options

1. Character Sketch Write a brief character sketch in which you describe what you consider to be the most important qualities of Anaya's grandfather.

2. Living History Questions Choose an elderly relative or neighbor from whom you have learned valuable lessons. Write a list of questions that you would ask to elicit his or her life story in an oral history. Place the list of questions in your **Working Portfolio.**

Activities & Explorations

Storytelling Anaya describes some of his grandfather's accomplishments as "small legends." Select one detail of the grandfather's life or create another "small legend"—perhaps focusing on the accomplishments of a relative—and relate it to the class as if you were a village storyteller responsible for keeping the legends alive.
~ **SPEAKING AND LISTENING**

Inquiry & Research

1. Tales of Taos Anaya explains that his grandfather's ancestors probably came from Taos. Research the rich history of New Mexico, focusing on the parts of the state described in the story. Present your findings in a written or multimedia report.

2. Demographic Survey As developments in healthcare increase life expectancy, the population of the United States includes more and more elderly people. Obtain information from the U.S. Census Bureau about the country's future demographics (statistics on human population). Create a chart like the one below, showing predicted changes over the next 50 years.

More Online: Research Starter
www.mcdougallittell.com

Decade	Average Age of Population	Number of People over 100
2000–2009		
2010–2019		
2020–2029		
2030–2039		
2040–2049		

Rudolfo A. Anaya
1937–

Other Works
Bless Me, Ultima
Heart of Aztlán
Tortuga
The Legend of La Llorona

Write from the Heart Anaya's writing springs from who he is and where he came from. Born and raised in New Mexico, where he still resides, Anaya focuses on his New Mexican background. A fascination with the oral tradition of Spanish *cuentos* (stories) and the mystical elements within these tales has also influenced his work, leading to his translation of a group of tales in *Cuentos: Tales from the Hispanic Southwest.* Anaya is best known for his first novel, *Bless Me, Ultima,* the story of a boy growing up in a small village in New Mexico.

Life and Literature Though the son of a laborer, Anaya was sent during the summer to learn farming from his grandfather. He later attended the University of New Mexico, where he earned a B.A. and M.A. in English and an M.A. in guidance and counseling. Anaya went on to work as a public school teacher, counselor, and university professor. His novels have received numerous honors and have been translated into several other languages. In 1992, he and his wife, Patricia Lawless, established a literary prize, the Premio Aztlán, for new Hispanic writers.

Writing Options

1. **Character Sketch** To launch this option, encourage students to work cooperatively to locate passages that reveal the grandfather's qualities.
2. **Living History Questions** Have students use the questions to interview an elderly relative or neighbor.

Activities & Explorations

Storytelling Encourage students to give dramatic tellings of their legends, using body language, gestures, tone, pitch, and volume to bring the tale to life.

Inquiry & Research

1. **Tales of Taos** Encourage students to read about New Mexico before it became a state.
2. **Demographic Survey** Encourage students to predict how increases in life expectancy will affect families, the economy, and our values.

Mini Lesson Grammar

COMMONLY CONFUSED VERBS Some verbs are close in meaning or appearance and are often confused. For example, *adapt* means to adjust or make suitable, and *adopt* means to accept or receive as one's own. Write the following sentence on the chalkboard and discuss the verb.

Anaya became a writer and <u>adapted</u> to a changing world.

Working in pairs, students can refer to the dictionary for the definitions for each of the following pairs of commonly confused verbs: *rob/steal, can/may,* and *adhere/cohere.*

Practice Select the correct verb in each sentence below.

1. If he (*can/may*), Anaya would like to live by his grandfather's values. (*can*)
2. Anaya believes we should not (*rob/steal*) the elderly of their dignity. (*rob*)
3. The grandfather's community showed a strong sense of loyalty and (*adherence/coherence*). (*coherence*)

Use **Grammar Transparencies and Copymasters,** p. 138.

Use McDougal Littell's ***Language Network,*** Chapter 6, for more instruction on troublesome verb pairs.

A CELEBRATION OF GRANDFATHERS 461

OVERVIEW

Objectives

1. understand and appreciate two **contemporary poems (Literary Analysis)**
2. analyze **imagery** in each poem **(Literary Analysis)**
3. **analyze the effects** of **word choice (Active Reading)**

Summary

Both Rita Dove and Naomi Shihab Nye use poetry to express the joy and meaning found in everyday life. In "Fifth Grade Autobiography," Dove describes a childhood fishing trip with her grandparents. The poet uses details from a photo to bring the memory to life. Nye's poem "Remembered" uses imagery to express her insights and emotions about a man who longs for remembrance. Nye's poem, like Dove's, draws primarily upon autobiographical experiences.

Thematic Link

In "Fifth Grade Autobiography" and "Remembered," two poets remember people who played important roles in their lives.

5-Minute Warm-Up

Daily Language SkillBuilder

Have students **proofread** the display sentences on page 381j and write them correctly. The sentences also appear on Transparency 15 of **Grammar Transparencies and Copymasters.**

PREPARING to *Read*

Fifth Grade Autobiography

Poetry by RITA DOVE

Remembered

Poetry by NAOMI SHIHAB NYE

"You won't forget me now, / will you?"

Connect to Your Life

Childhood Memories In your mind, travel back to a time in your life when you shared a memorable occasion with one or more of your relatives. Recall as many of the details of the day as you can, trying to picture the people and events. What sounds, smells, and tastes do you associate with the memory? Share your memories and impressions with a classmate.

Build Background

Life Celebrated Both Rita Dove and Naomi Shihab Nye are well known for poetry that celebrates ordinary lives, finding joy and meaning in the details of the everyday. Much of the work of both poets is autobiographical, as can be seen in the poems that follow. There are differences in the places and the lives they describe; Dove is African American, while Nye's heritage is Palestinian. However, there are also strong parallels between their experiences, insights, and emotions. Dove once noted that her poems "are poems about humanity," and Nye stated, "For me the primary source of poetry has always been local life, . . . our own ancestry sifting down to us through small essential daily tasks."

Focus Your Reading

LITERARY ANALYSIS | **IMAGERY** **Imagery** refers to words or phrases that help the reader imagine sensory experiences. Most images are visual, but imagery may also appeal to the senses of hearing, smell, taste, or touch. In the poem "Remembered," for example, Naomi Shihab Nye writes that "the fire remembered all the crackling music it knew," an image that focuses on the sound of the fire. Sometimes an image can appeal to more than one sense. As you read these poems, look for images and notice which senses they appeal to.

ACTIVE READING | **ANALYZING THE EFFECTS OF WORD CHOICE** A writer's **word choice,** or **diction,** includes both **vocabulary** (individual words) and **syntax** (the order or arrangement of words). It can be described in terms such as **formal** or **informal,** and **literal** or **figurative.** Modern poetry often makes use of informal language drawn from the vocabulary and speech patterns of everyday life. The poems you are about to read both include examples of figurative language, but they also often employ informal vocabulary in simple prose. For example, look at the first two lines of "Fifth Grade Autobiography":

I was four in this photograph fishing
with my grandparents at a lake in Michigan.

As you read, pay close attention to the poets' diction. Why do you think the poets chose such words? What feelings and ideas do the words suggest to you?

READER'S NOTEBOOK Note examples of informal diction in each poem—words, phrases, or sentences that seem to reflect the speech patterns of everyday life. Consider what the effect of such language is on an **audience.**

LESSON RESOURCES

UNIT THREE RESOURCE BOOK, pp. 43–44

ASSESSMENT RESOURCES

Formal Assessment, pp. 77–78

Teacher's Guide to Assessment and Portfolio Use

Test Generator

SKILLS TRANSPARENCIES AND COPYMASTERS

Literary Analysis

- Poetry: Imagery, T9 (for Paired Activity, p. 466)

Grammar

- Figurative Language, C180 (for Mini Lesson, p. 467)

Writing

- Point of View, T23 (for Writing Option 1, p. 467)
- Figurative Language and Sound Devices, T15 (for Writing Option 2, p. 467)
- Poem, C27 (for Writing Option 2, p. 467)

Communications

- Evaluating Roles in Groups, T8 (for Mini Lesson, p. 464)
- Verbal Strategies, T14 (for Mini Lesson, p. 464)

INTEGRATED TECHNOLOGY

Audio Library

Visit our website:
www.mcdougallittell.com

Fifth Grade Autobiography

Rita Dove

I was four in this photograph fishing
with my grandparents at a lake in Michigan.
My brother squats in poison ivy.
His Davy Crockett cap
sits squared on his head so the raccoon tail
flounces down the back of his sailor suit.

My grandfather sits to the far right
in a folding chair,
and I know his left hand is on
the tobacco in his pants pocket
because I used to wrap it for him
every Christmas. Grandmother's hips
bulge from the brush, she's leaning
into the ice chest, sun through the trees
printing her dress with soft
luminous paws.

I am staring jealously at my brother;
the day before he rode his first horse, alone.
I was strapped in a basket
behind my grandfather.
He smelled of lemons. He's died—

but I remember his hands.

4 Davy Crockett cap: a raccoon-skin cap of the kind worn by the pioneer and folk hero Davy Crockett in a hugely popular series of Walt Disney TV shows in the 1950s.

16 luminous (lo͞oʹmə-nəs): shining with light.

Thinking Through the Literature

1. What is your sense of the emotions expressed in this poem? Discuss them with a classmate.
2. How do you think the **speaker** feels about her grandparents?
   THINK ABOUT
   - what prompts the speaker's memories
   - the **details** she uses to describe her grandparents
3. What do you think is the significance of the fact that the speaker can remember her grandfather's hands?
4. In your opinion, how does the **title** relate to the content of the poem? Explain your answer.

TEACHING THE LITERATURE

Customizing Instruction

Less Proficient Readers
Remind students that in poetry, the end of a line is not always the end of a thought. Point out that students must read to the end of the sentence. Read aloud the first stanza of "Fifth Grade Autobiography" to help students hear where pauses for punctuation belong.

Students Acquiring English
These two poems are autobiographical, because they describe people and events that are particularly memorable or significant in the author's life.

Use **Spanish Study Guide** for additional support, pp. 101–103.

Gifted and Talented
Throughout the selections, both authors describe people they have known. Ask students to pick a character from each selection and imagine a conversation between the two individuals, drawing on the details to flesh out the dialogue.

Thinking Through the Literature

1. Students may sense emotions of security and love.
2. The photograph brings back memories of family; she remembers the details that speak of the bond between them.
3. His hands are symbols of his strength.
4. Possible Response: Autobiographies are a typical grade school assignment.

BLOCK SCHEDULING: MANAGING TIME

If your schedule requires that you cover the lesson objectives in a shorter time, use . . .
- Preparing to Read, p. 462
- Thinking Through the Literature, pp. 463, 466

If you want to take advantage of longer class time, use . . .
- TE Teaching Options: Speaking and Listening, p. 464; Standardized Test Practice, p. 465
- Choices & Challenges, p. 467

Reading and Analyzing

Reading Skills and Strategies: PREVIEW

Have students look through both poems, noting any obvious connections. Discuss the titles of both pieces and the Build Background feature on life celebrated.

Active Reading

ANALYZING THE EFFECTS OF WORD CHOICE

Word choice can contribute to the mood of the poem and also reveal the feelings of the poet. Students should focus on the details in each of these poems in order to determine the overall effect.

Use **Unit Three Resource Book,** p. 43 for more practice.

Literary Analysis IMAGERY

Images—words or phrases that appeal to sight, taste, touch, smell, or hearing—create in the reader feelings that are similar to the feelings felt by the poet.

Use **Unit Three Resource Book,** p. 44 for more practice.

Remembered

Naomi Shihab Nye

He wanted to be remembered so he gave people things
they would remember him by. A large trunk, handmade of
ash and cedar. A tool box with initials shaped of scraps.
A tea kettle that would sing every morning,
antique glass jars to fill with crackers, noodles, beans.
A whole family of jams he made himself from the figs and berries
that purpled his land.

He gave these things unexpectedly. You went to see him
[1] and came home loaded. You said "Thank you" till your lips
grew heavy with gratitude and swelled shut.
Walking with him across the acres of piney forest,
you noticed the way he talked to everything, a puddle, a stump,
the same way he talked to you.
[2] "I declare you do look purty sittin' there in that field
reflectin' the light like some kind of mirror, you know what?"
As if objects could listen.
As if earth had a memory too.

At night we propped our feet by the fireplace
and laughed and showed photographs and the fire remembered
all the crackling music it knew. The night remembered
how to be dark and the forest remembered how to be mysterious
and in bed, the quilts remembered how to tuck up under our chins.
Sleeping in that house was like falling down a deep well,
rocking in a bucket all night long.

In the mornings we'd stagger away from an unforgettable breakfast
of biscuits—he'd lead us into the next room
ready to show us something or curl another story into our ear.
He scrawled the episodes out in elaborate longhand
and gave them to a farmer's wife to type.

3 ash and cedar: woods used in making trunks and chests—ash because of its strength, and cedar because of its pleasant aroma.

Teaching Options

Mini Lesson: Speaking and Listening

DRAMATIC READING

Prepare Help students prepare a dramatic reading of the poem. Have them work in cooperative groups, considering the speaker's tone, pitch, volume, pace, posture, and hand gestures. They should justify their choices of verbal and nonverbal performance techniques by referring to their interpretation of the text.

Present Student groups can decide who presents the dramatic reading and how it will be presented. Student audience members can evaluate how the performance increases their appreciation and understanding of the poem.

BLOCK SCHEDULING This activity is particularly well suited for longer class periods.

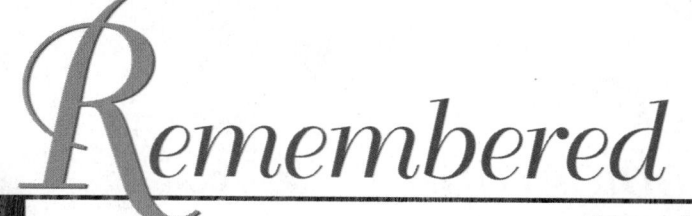

Stories about a little boy and a grandfather,
chickens and prayer tents, butter beans and lightning.
He was the little boy.
Some days his brain could travel backwards easier than it could
sit in a chair, right there.

When we left he'd say "Don't forget me! You won't forget me now,
will you?" as if our remembering could lengthen his life.
I wanted to assure him, there will always be a cabin in our blood
only you live in. But the need for remembrance silenced me,
a ringing rising up out of the soil's centuries, the ones
who plowed this land, whose names we do not know.

Photo by Art Gore, from *Images of Yesterday.*

Customizing Instruction

Students Acquiring English

1 Help students understand "You said 'Thank you' till your lips grew heavy with gratitude and swelled shut."

Possible Response: The speaker means the man gave people so much that they said "Thank you" until it seemed useless to keep repeating it.

Less Proficient Readers

2 Remind students that dialect is a variety of a language particular to a region or social group. For example, after reading the following passage, students may want to discuss how use of dialect helps contribute to the poem. "I declare you do look purty sittin' there in that field reflectin' the light like some kind of mirror, you know what?"

Possible Response: Dialect is used to show the man's personality.

Assessment Standardized Test Practice

CHOOSING THE BEST SUMMARY For some standardized tests, students will be asked to choose the best summary. To provide students with some help in choosing the best summary, read aloud or write on the chalkboard the following question: Which one of the following statements best summarizes "Fifth Grade Autobiography"?

A. A photograph of her grandparents, her brother, and herself taken during a fishing trip at a lake in Michigan brings back memories of feeling loved and secure.

B. A photograph of her grandparents and her brother and herself brings back memories of her grandfather's tobacco and her grandmother's dress.

C. A photograph taken during a fishing trip at a lake in Michigan makes her remember when her brother wore a Davy Crockett hat and squatted in poison ivy.

D. A photograph of her grandfather sitting in a folding chair and her grandmother leaning on an ice chest remind her of her childhood.

Lead students through the process of choosing the best summary. While all of the statements contain accurate information about the poem, the best summary should include the most important information. For that reason, **A** is the best choice.

GUIDING STUDENT RESPONSE

Connect to the Literature

1. What Do You Think?
A sense of sadness or regret

Comprehension Check

- The man gives things away because he wants people to remember him.
- She wants to remember him, but she is aware of all the others long forgotten who have died before him.

Think Critically

2. Students may feel that he is eccentric, but also that he has a special connection to nature. He seems special.
3. Use of the first-person singular and plural suggests that the poet knew him personally.
4. Possible Response: There will be a special place in their memories for him.
5. Possible Response: "The ones" refers to the people who have been forgotten, the people who have been gone so long that no one remembers their names.
6. Many students will point to the use of dialect in "Remembered." Others will point to the simple "down home" details included in "Fifth Grade Autobiography."

Connect to the Literature

1. **What Do You Think?** What feelings does this poem trigger in you?

Comprehension Check

- Why does the man in "Remembered" give things away?
- Why doesn't the speaker answer the man when she leaves?

Think Critically

2. What is your impression of the man described in "Remembered"?

   THINK ABOUT
   - the gifts he gives people
   - his habit of talking to inanimate objects
   - the stories he tells

3. What do you think is the relationship between the **speaker** and the man in the poem? Explain your answer.
4. Analyze the meaning of the phrase "there will always be a cabin in our blood that only you live in."
5. In your opinion, what is the significance of "the ones . . . whose names we do not know"?
6. ACTIVE READING ANALYZING THE EFFECTS OF WORD CHOICE Review the words, phrases, and sentences you jotted down in your READER'S NOTEBOOK. In your opinion, which of the two poems uses the **informal diction** of everyday speech to the better effect? Support your response.

Extend Interpretation

7. **Different Perspectives** What different ideas about the nature of remembering do you think are expressed in the two poems? Give examples to support your answer.
8. **Comparing Texts** Which person do you think is more similar to the grandfather portrayed in Rudolfo Anaya's "A Celebration of Grandfathers," the grandfather in Dove's poem or the man in Nye's poem? Explain your answer.
9. **Connect to Life** Do the people or events in these two poems remind you of anyone or anything in your life? Write a paragraph or two about a person you know or a time you spent that is similar in some respect to one of the two poems.

Literary Analysis

IMAGERY **Imagery** refers to those words and phrases that help the reader imagine sensory experiences, such as sight, hearing, smell, taste, or touch. Because sight is the most highly developed sense for the majority of people, most images are visual. A writer can also appeal to the senses of hearing, smell, taste, or touch. Writers can also use imagery that appeals to more than one sense. Typically, poets use imagery to evoke underlying ideas, feelings, and emotions.

Paired Activity Working with a classmate, analyze the imagery in each poem, using a chart like the one shown. Does one of the poems appeal to a certain sense more than the other does? What underlying ideas, feelings, or emotions do the images evoke?

Sense	Word/Phrase
Sight	". . . figs and berries / that purpled his land."
Hearing	
Smell	
Taste	
Touch	

REVIEW PERSONIFICATION **Personification** is a figure of speech in which human qualities are attributed to an object, animal, or idea. What examples of personification can you see in the third stanza of "Remembered"? What effect do these examples of personification have on your understanding of the poem?

Extend Interpretations

Different Perspectives Students should be able to compare and contrast the idea of remembering presented in these two poems.
Comparing Texts Before answering, students can discuss the question in cooperative groups.
Connect to Life Generate a discussion in which students brainstorm some memorable childhood moments that included other family members or a neighbor.

Literary Analysis

Imagery Students should support their opinions by finding passages that appeal to a certain sense or images that help evoke emotions.
Personification There are four uses of personification: "the fire remembered . . . ," "the night remembered . . . ," "the forest remembered . . . ," and "the quilts remembered."

Choices & CHALLENGES

Writing Options

1. Diary Entry Imagine you are the speaker of "Remembered." Write a diary entry in which you recall your visit to the man described in the poem.

2. Photo Poem Think of a photograph that captures a memorable moment of your childhood. Write a poem about the people and events in the photograph.

Activities & Explorations

1. Character Portrait Draw or paint a portrait of one of the people described in the two poems. Try to make your portrait reflect the subject's personality. ~ **ART**

2. Speaker's Eulogy Assuming the identity of one of the two speakers, deliver a eulogy in honor of either the grandfather in "Fifth Grade Autobiography" or the man in "Remembered." ~ **SPEAKING AND LISTENING**

Rita Dove

1952–

Other Works
Thomas and Beulah
Museum
Fifth Sunday
Through the Ivory Gate
Grace Notes

Eager Learner As a child in Akron, Ohio, Rita Dove would "rush into the local public library with the same eagerness other children reserved for the candy store." Her enthusiasm blossomed into academic success. Educated at Miami University in Ohio and the University of Iowa, Dove also studied drama and poetry in Germany as a Fulbright Scholar. She taught English at Arizona State University for eight years and is currently the Commonwealth Professor of English at the University of Virginia.

Working Poet Dove is best known for *Thomas and Beulah,* a collection of poems based on the lives of her grandparents, which earned her a Pulitzer Prize in 1987. In 1993, she became the youngest person and the first African American to be named Poet Laureate of the United States. In addition to several books of poetry, Dove has written short stories, a novel, and a play.

Poetry to the People Dove has said that she wants to "bring poetry into everyday discourse . . . make it more of a household word." In pursuit of this goal, she travels and does readings.

Naomi Shihab Nye

1952–

Other Works
Words under the Words
Hugging the Jukebox
Sitti's Secrets

World Traveler Though she was born in St. Louis, when Arab-American poet Naomi Shihab Nye was 14, she and her family moved to Jerusalem to live near their Palestinian relatives. Several years later the family returned to the United States, settling in San Antonio, Texas, where Nye still lives. Her experience overseas and the diverse heritage of her family (she has a Palestinian father and American mother) have helped Nye to see common strands in the lives of widely varied people.

Writing as a Way of Life Nye's first full-length collection, *Different Ways to Pray,* earned the poet her first major award, the Voertman Poetry Prize, in 1980. Her interest in diverse cultures found another outlet in the editing of *This Same Sky,* a collection of poems for young people from 129 poets in 68 countries. A short-story writer, children's book author, and songwriter as well as a poet, Nye has worked as a visiting writer in schools for more than 20 years. She once said that she feels poetry is "basic to our lives and to education."

Writing Options

1. **Diary Entry** To help students get started, let cooperative groups review the details of the poem prior to writing.
2. **Photo Poem** Encourage students to talk about the photo with a family member.

Activities & Explorations

1. **Character Portrait** Students can begin by listing the details of the character they choose.
2. **Speaker's Eulogy** Explain that a eulogy is a speech in praise of someone who has died. Read a sample eulogy for the students, or play a recording of one.

Mini Lesson Grammar

FIGURATIVE LANGUAGE Figurative language describes ordinary things in a new way. Poets often use figurative language such as similes, metaphors, and personification to compare one thing to another. A simile is a comparison of unlike things using the word *like* or *as.* A metaphor compares two unlike things without using *like* or *as.* In personification, an object, animal, or idea exhibits human qualities.

Discuss the following simile:

> "Sleeping in that house was like falling down a deep well, rocking in a bucket all night long."

Practice Ask students to identify the simile, metaphor, or personification in the following sentences.

1. She wants to assure the man that they will always have the cabin in their blood. *(metaphor)*
2. The fire in the cabin remembered all the crackling music it knew. *(personification)*
3. They slept like logs in the cabin. *(simile)*

Use **Grammar Transparencies and Copymasters,** p. 180.

Use McDougal Littell's ***Language Network,*** Chapter 15, for more instruction in figurative language.

OVERVIEW

Objectives

1. understand and appreciate a **short story (Literary Analysis)**
2. analyze **characterization (Literary Analysis)**
3. **make inferences about characters (Active Reading)**

Summary

A young Irish boy, Larry Delaney, speculates who he would be if his parents had married other people. To satisfy his curiosity, Larry learns more about one of his mother's suitors and then he visits Mrs. O'Brien, who had almost married Larry's father. When she asks him how he would like to have her for a mother, he feels a new appreciation for his own family and for his heritage.

Thematic Link

Confronting what he might have been if his parents had married other people, a young boy begins to appreciate the **power of heritage** when he sees how his parents have affected his lifestyle and identity.

Editor's Note This selection has been edited slightly to delete material that may be considered objectionable.

5-Minute Warm-Up

Daily Language SkillBuilder

Have students **proofread** the display sentences on page 381j and write them correctly. The sentences also appear on Transparency 15 of **Grammar Transparencies and Copymasters.**

Mini Lesson Preteaching Vocabulary

If you would like to preteach the WORDS TO KNOW for this selection, use the Mini Lesson, pp. 470–471.

PREPARING to *Read*

The Study of History

Short Story by FRANK O'CONNOR

"I was fascinated by the problem of who I would have been if I hadn't been me."

Connect to Your Life

Quirks of Fate What would your life have been like if your ancestors had made different decisions before you were born? For example, what if your family had decided to settle in a different country? What if your mother had chosen a different mate, so that you had a different father? Imagine a different set of circumstances in your family background. Then freewrite for five minutes about who you might be or what your life might be like.

Build Background

Fiction and Reality The boy who would come to be known as Frank O'Connor often daydreamed about who he might have been if his family background had been different. Born Michael Francis O'Donovan in 1903, O'Connor grew up in Barrackton, a slum on the outskirts of Cork in southwestern Ireland. He shared a close bond with his mother, and he adopted her maiden name when he decided to write under a pseudonym.

Not only did O'Connor write two autobiographies; he also wrote autobiographical fiction about a boy named Laurence ("Larry") Delaney. Larry appears in a number of O'Connor's short stories, and like the author himself, he is an only child who is sometimes frustrated by the sharp contrasts between the rich and the poor in Cork. Naive and full of insecurities, he is often embarrassed by the commonness of his parents. Larry Delaney is the main character in the story you are about to read.

WORDS TO KNOW
Vocabulary Preview

biased	exasperated	saucy
brooding	impertinent	uncanny
complacently	incredulously	
contemptuously	ordained	

Focus Your Reading

LITERARY ANALYSIS CHARACTERIZATION O'Connor brings the **characters** in "The Study of History" to life through his methods of **characterization.** This includes the following techniques: physical description; the speech, thoughts, feelings, and actions of a character; the responses of other characters to a character; the narrator's direct comments about a character.

Because the story is told from a **first-person point of view,** the narrator, Larry, is the only character whose thoughts and feelings are revealed to us directly, as in this example:

> . . . *I felt wretched and guilty and I didn't know why.*

As you read, be aware of how the author develops characters. In particular, notice how the thoughts and feelings of the first-person narrator help reveal Larry's personality.

ACTIVE READING MAKING INFERENCES ABOUT CHARACTERS

To build a rounded picture of a **character,** readers must **make inferences,** or logical guesses, on the basis of **details** revealed about that character. For example, Larry's reluctance to talk to Mrs. O'Brien, whom he wishes to see, might indicate his shyness. As you read "The Study of History," pay attention to the details that O'Connor uses in describing his characters. What do these details tell you about the characters' personalities, attitudes, and family backgrounds?

READER'S NOTEBOOK Note details about each character in a cluster diagram like the one shown below.

LaserLinks: Background for Reading
Historical Connection

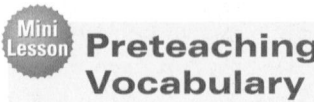

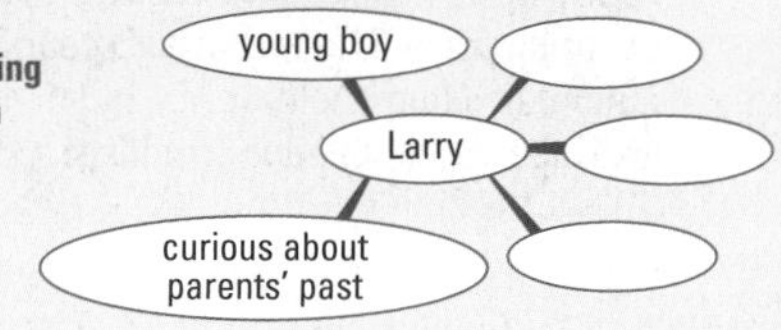

LESSON RESOURCES

UNIT THREE RESOURCE BOOK, pp. 45–50

ASSESSMENT RESOURCES

Formal Assessment, pp. 79–80

Teacher's Guide to Assessment and Portfolio Use

Test Generator

SKILLS TRANSPARENCIES AND COPYMASTERS

Literary Analysis

- Character, T2 (for Cooperative Learning Activity, p. 479)

Reading and Critical Thinking

- Making Inferences, T7 (for Think Critically, item 3, p. 479)
- Cluster Diagram, T48 (for Reader's Notebook, p. 468)

Grammar

- Gerunds and Gerund Phrases, C105 (for Mini Lesson, p. 480)
- Verb Choice, C176 (for Mini Lesson, p. 476)

Vocabulary

- Context Clues, C52 (for Mini Lesson, p. 470)
- Word Origins, C53 (for Mini Lesson, p. 473)

Writing

- Writing Process, T1–4 (for Writing Options, p. 480)
- Writing Structure, T8, T10, T11 (for Writing Options, p. 480)

INTEGRATED TECHNOLOGY

Audio Library

LaserLinks

- Historical Connection: The Ireland of Frank O'Connor. See **Teacher's SourceBook,** p. 28.

Visit our website:
www.mcdougallittell.com

The Study of History

Frank O'Connor

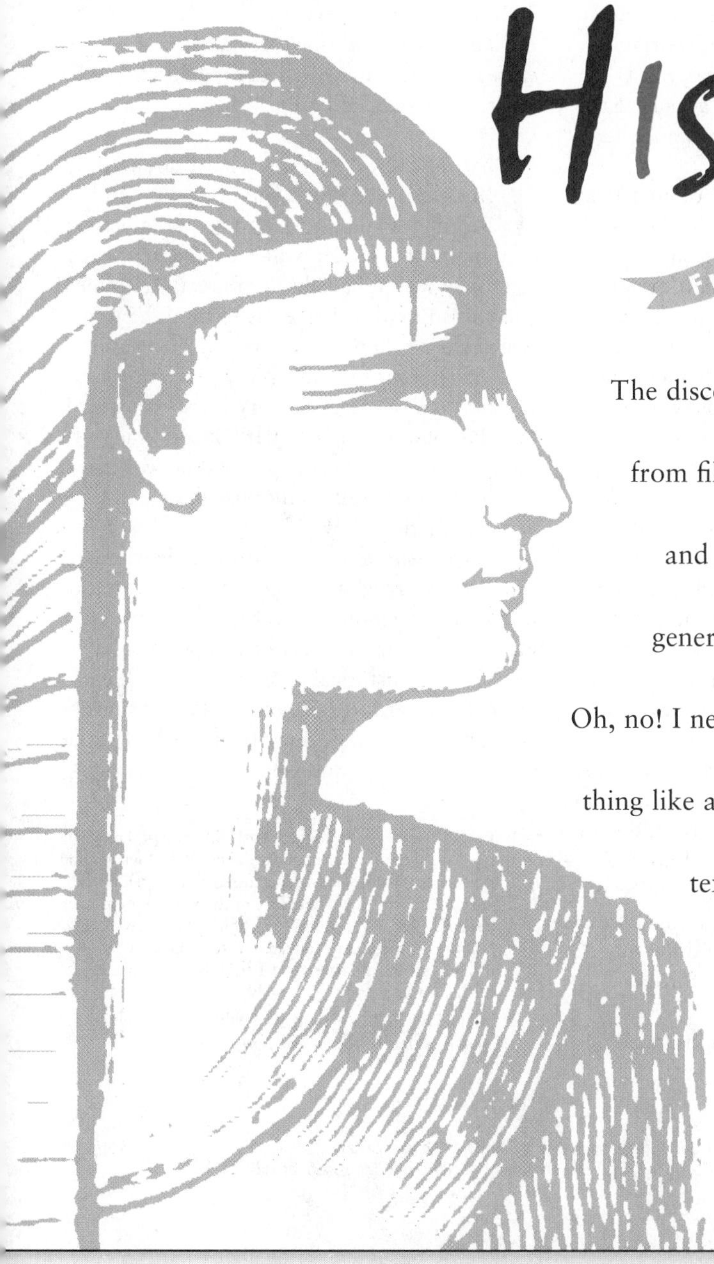

The discovery of where babies came from filled my life with excitement and interest. Not in the way it's generally supposed to, of course. Oh, no! I never seem to have done anything like a natural child in a standard textbook. I merely discovered the fascination of history.

TEACHING THE LITERATURE

Customizing Instruction

Less Proficient Readers
Invite students to discuss what they have learned or inherited from their families. Ask them how these traits have shaped their characters. Have students read on to learn what Larry finds interesting about the past.

Students Acquiring English
Since the story takes place in Ireland, the dialogue reflects the characters' dialect. Point out that *ye* means "you," and *'tis* means "it is." The selection contains footnotes throughout that refer to Irish words and expressions. Remind students to read the footnotes carefully.

Use **Spanish Study Guide** for additional support, pp.104–106.

Gifted and Talented
Ask students to analyze, as they read, what lends humor to the selection.

BLOCK SCHEDULING: MANAGING TIME

If your schedule requires that you cover the lesson objectives in a shorter time, use . . .
- Preparing to Read, p. 468
- Thinking Through the Literature, p. 479
- Vocabulary in Action, p. 480
- Grammar in Context, p. 481

If you want to take advantage of longer class time, use . . .
- TE Teaching Options: Preteaching Vocabulary, pp. 470–471; Viewing and Representing, pp. 472, 474; Vocabulary Strategy, p. 473; Standardized Test Practice, p. 478
- Choices & Challenges and Author Activity, pp. 480–481

THE STUDY OF HISTORY 469

Reading and Analyzing

Reading Skills and Strategies: PREVIEW

Remind students that they are expected to establish a purpose for reading such as to discover or interpret. Summarize the selection reminding students that Larry's conversations lead to a realization. Discuss the image on the opening page as well as the title. Ask students what they think the author means by "history."

Active Reading MAKING INFERENCES ABOUT CHARACTERS

Tell students that making inferences is "reading between the lines," or making logical guesses based on information in the text and common sense. Readers combine clues in the text with what they already know from their experience to figure out what is not directly stated. Students should look for details that help them make inferences about the characters.

Use **Unit Three Resource Book** p. 46 for more practice.

Literary Analysis CHARACTERIZATION

Characterization is the method the author uses to bring his characters to life. There are four basic methods: physical description; the character's speech, thoughts, feelings, or actions; and the speech, thoughts, feelings, and actions of other characters; or the narrator's own direct comments.

Discuss with students how the first-person point of view of this story affects characterization.

Use **Unit Three Resource Book** p. 47 for more practice.

Up to this, I had lived in a country of my own that had no history, and accepted my parents' marriage as an event ordained from the creation; now, when I considered it in this new, scientific way, I began to see it merely as one of the turning points of history, one of those apparently trivial events that are little more than accidents but have the effect of changing the destiny of humanity. 1 I had not heard of Pascal, but I would have approved his remark about what would have happened if Cleopatra's nose had been a bit longer.[1]

It immediately changed my view of my parents. Up to this, they had been principles, not characters, like a chain of mountains guarding a green horizon. Suddenly a little shaft of light, emerging from behind a cloud, struck them, and the whole mass broke up into peaks, valleys, and foothills; you could even see whitewashed farmhouses and fields where people worked in the evening light, a whole world of interior perspective. Mother's past was the richer subject for study. It was extraordinary the variety of people and settings that woman had had in her background. She had been an orphan, a parlormaid, a companion, a traveler; and had been proposed to by a plasterer's apprentice, a French chef who had taught her to make superb coffee, and a rich and elderly shopkeeper in Sunday's Well.[2] Because I liked to feel myself different, I thought a great deal about the chef and the advantages of being a Frenchman, but the shopkeeper was an even more vivid figure in my imagination because he had married someone else and died soon after—of disappointment, I had no doubt—leaving a large fortune. The fortune was to me what Cleopatra's nose was to Pascal: the ultimate proof that things might have been different.

"How much was Mr. Riordan's fortune, Mummy?" I asked thoughtfully.

"Ah, they said he left eleven thousand," Mother replied doubtfully, "but you couldn't believe everything people say."

That was exactly what I could do. I was not prepared to minimize a fortune that I might so easily have inherited.

"And weren't you ever sorry for poor Mr. Riordan?" I asked severely.

"Ah, why would I be sorry, child?" she asked with a shrug. "Sure, what use would money be where there was no liking?"

That, of course, was not what I meant at all. My heart was full of pity for poor Mr. Riordan who had tried to be my father; but, even on the low level at which Mother discussed it, money would have been of great use to me. I was not so fond of Father as to think he was worth eleven thousand pounds, a hard sum to visualize but more than twenty-seven times greater than the largest salary I had ever heard of—that of a Member of Parliament. One of the discoveries I was making at the time was that Mother was not only rather hardhearted but very impractical as well.

But Father was the real surprise. He was a brooding, worried man who seemed to have no proper appreciation of me and was always wanting me to go out and play or go upstairs and read, but the historical approach changed him like a character in a fairy tale. "Now let's talk about the ladies Daddy nearly married," I would say; and he would stop whatever he was doing

1. **Pascal** (pă-skăl′) **. . . longer:** The 17th-century French philosopher and mathematician Blaise Pascal wrote that if Cleopatra's nose had been shorter (not longer, as the narrator says), "the whole face of the world would have been changed." Cleopatra (69–30 B.C.), a queen of Egypt famous for her beauty, affected history through her romances with the Roman leaders Julius Caesar and Mark Antony.
2. **in Sunday's Well:** on Sunday's Well Road, a street in the wealthier part of the city of Cork.

WORDS TO KNOW
ordained (ôr-dānd′) *adj.* established by authority or fate **ordain** *v.*
brooding (bro͞od′ĭng) *adj.* having a moody or depressed disposition **brood** *v.*

Teaching Options

Mini Lesson Preteaching Vocabulary

USING CONTEXT CLUES Students can determine the meaning of an unfamiliar word by examining the context in which the word is used. Use the model sentence to demonstrate the strategy of using context clues to determine meaning.

Model Sentence

The jury felt that the testimony of the defendant's mother was *biased,* so they did not believe it.

Instruction

- Write the model sentence on the chalkboard.
- Ask a volunteer to summarize the meaning of the sentence.
- Have students use the meaning of the sentence to infer the meaning of the word *biased.*
- Ask a volunteer to use the word *biased* in a sentence.

Exercises Read the following sentences. Ask the students to use context clues to infer the meanings of the italicized words.

1. "You have *brooded* over your bad test grade for too long," Mohammed said to Samantha. "It's time to stop dwelling on the bad grade and start studying harder so that you can do better on the next test."
2. Juan believes that most people are too *complacent* about air pollution. He believes everyone should be more concerned about the quality of the air they breathe.

and give a great guffaw. "Oh, ho, ho!" he would say, slapping his knee and looking slyly at Mother, "you could write a book about them." Even his face changed at such moments. He would look young and extraordinarily mischievous. Mother, on the other hand, would grow black.

"You could," she would say, looking into the fire. "Daisies!"

"'The handsomest man that walks Cork!'" Father would quote with a wink at me. "That's what one of them called me."

"Yes," Mother would say, scowling. "May Cadogan!"

"The very girl!" Father would cry in astonishment. "How did I forget her name? A beautiful girl! 'Pon my word, a most remarkable girl! And still is, I hear."

"She should be," Mother would say in disgust. "With six of them!"

"Oh, now, she'd be the one that could look after them! A fine head that girl had."

"She had. I suppose she ties them to a lamppost while she goes in to drink and gossip."

That was one of the peculiar things about history. Father and Mother both loved to talk about it but in different ways. She would only talk about it when we were together somewhere, in the Park or down the Glen, and even then it was very hard to make her stick to the facts, because her whole face would light up and she would begin to talk about donkey carriages, or concerts in the kitchen, or oil lamps, and though nowadays I would probably value it for atmosphere, in those days it sometimes drove me mad with impatience. Father, on the other hand, never minded talking about it in front of her, and it made her angry—particularly when he mentioned May Cadogan. He knew this perfectly well, and he would wink at me and make me laugh outright, though I had no idea of why I laughed, and, anyway, my sympathy was all with her.

"But, Daddy," I would say, presuming on his high spirits, "if you liked Miss Cadogan so much, why didn't you marry her?"

At this, to my great delight, he would let on to be filled with doubt and distress. He would put his hands in his trousers pockets and stride to the door leading into the hallway.

> *"'The handsomest man that walks Cork!'"*
> Father would quote with a wink at me.
> *"That's what one of them called me."*

"That was a delicate matter," he would say, without looking at me. "You see, I had your poor mother to think of."

"I was a great trouble to you," Mother would say, in a blaze.

"Poor May said it to me herself," he would go on as though he had not heard her, "and the tears pouring down her cheeks. 'Mick,' she said, 'that girl with the brown hair will bring me to an untimely grave.'"

"She could talk of hair!" Mother would hiss. "With her carroty mop!" 2

"Never did I suffer the way I suffered then, between the two of them," Father would say with deep emotion as he returned to his chair by the window.

"Oh, 'tis a pity about ye!" Mother would cry in an exasperated tone and suddenly get up and go into the front room with her book to escape his teasing. Every word that man said she took literally. Father would give a great guffaw of delight, his hands on his knees and his eyes on the ceiling, and wink at me again. I would

WORDS TO KNOW **exasperated** (ĭg-zăs'pə-rā'tĭd) *adj.* made impatient or angry; annoyed **exasperate** *v.*

Customizing Instruction

Less Proficient Readers

1 Ask students to explain the comparison between Pascal's remark about Cleopatra's nose and Larry's discovery about his parents' past.

Possible Response: According to Pascal, if Cleopatra's nose had been less beautiful, Roman leaders might not have fallen in love with her and history would have been very different. Similarly, Larry realizes that had his parents married different people, his world would also be very different.

Students Acquiring English

2 Explain that when Larry's mother describes May Cadogan's hair as "carroty," she means that it is bright orange like a carrot. Explain that the description is meant to be unflattering.

3. The snobbish man *contemptuously* refused to drink the cheap wine his hosts offered him.
4. Dad told Tim three times to turn off the water. Finally, he grew *exasperated* and shouted, "Stop wasting the water!"
5. The *impertinent* child insulted his grandmother by saying he thought her oatmeal cookies tasted like sawdust.
6. "You're going where?" Maya asked *incredulously* after her best friend told her she was spending the summer in New Zealand.
7. Bob felt that his marriage to Tammy was so perfect that it must have been *ordained* by fate.
8. Lucy was often described as *saucy.* Some people thought Lucy's sometimes outrageous behavior was disrespectful; others looked upon her more kindly and said she was merely high-spirited.
9. Kim has the *uncanny* ability to predict who is calling on the telephone even before she answers it.

Use **Unit Three Resource Book** p. 48 for more exercises.

A lesson on context clues appears on p. 56 in the Pupil's Edition.

Reading and Analyzing

Active Reading

MAKING INFERENCES ABOUT CHARACTERS

A Ask students to make inferences regarding Larry's and his mother's personalities based on the scene that takes place in the front room.

Possible Response: Larry and his mother are both sensitive. Larry's mother is sensitive to her husband's teasing, and Larry is sensitive to his mother's feelings.

Reading Skills and Strategies: EVALUATING

B Larry says that his solemn politeness "probably scared the wits out of" the boys. Ask students why Larry might feel this way.

Possible Response: Larry's solemn politeness sharply contrasts with the rough speech of Gussie and the other boys. When he mentions scaring the wits out of the boys, he means that his formal demeanor probably shocked them.

Jimmy O'D (about 1925), Robert Henri. Oil on canvas, 24″ × 20″, Collection of the Montclair (New Jersey) Art Museum, museum purchase, Picture Buying Fund (26.1).

laugh with him, of course, and then grow wretched because I hated Mother's sitting alone in the front room. I would go in and find her in her wicker chair by the window in the dusk, the book open on her knee, looking out at the Square. She would always have regained her composure when she spoke to me, but I would have an uncanny feeling of unrest in her and stroke her and talk to her soothingly as if we had changed places and I were the adult and she the child. **A**

But if I was excited by what history meant to them, I was even more excited by what it meant to me. My potentialities were double theirs. **2** Through Mother I might have been a French boy called Laurence Armady or a rich boy from Sunday's Well called Laurence Riordan. Through Father I might, while still remaining a Delaney, have been one of the six children of the mysterious and beautiful Miss Cadogan. I was fascinated by the problem of who I would have been if I hadn't been me, and, even more, by the problem of whether or not I would have known that there was anything wrong with the arrangement. Naturally, I tended to regard Laurence Delaney as the person I was intended

WORDS TO KNOW

uncanny (ŭn-kăn′ē) *adj.* strange; eerie; weird

Teaching Options

Mini Lesson **Viewing and Representing**

***Jimmy O'D* by Robert Henri**

ART APPRECIATION Robert Henri was born Robert Henry Cozad in Cincinnati in 1865. He was strongly influenced by Thomas Eakins, an American painter of the previous generation. Henri first went to Ireland in 1913. He spent every summer there, from 1923 until his death in 1929, painting many portraits of Irish children. *Jimmy O'D* dates from about 1925.

Instruction Henri painted his portraits with broad, fast brush strokes because he felt portraits must be painted quickly in order to capture the subject's personality. Ask students what personality traits they see in this portrait.

Possible Response: Some students may see thoughtfulness or sensitivity. Others may see wariness or toughness.

Application Ask students whether their image of Larry Delaney resembles the boy in this portrait and have them explain their responses.

to be, and so I could not help wondering whether as Laurence Riordan I would not have been aware of Laurence Delaney as a real gap in my make-up.

I remember that one afternoon after school I walked by myself all the way up to Sunday's Well, which I now regarded as something like a second home. I stood for a while at the garden gate of the house where Mother had been working when she was proposed to by Mr. Riordan, and then went and studied the shop itself. It had clearly seen better days, and the cartons and advertisements in the window were dusty and sagging. It wasn't like one of the big stores in Patrick Street, but at the same time, in size and fittings, it was well above the level of a village shop. I regretted that Mr. Riordan was dead, because I would have liked to see him for myself instead of relying on Mother's impressions, which seemed to me to be biased. Since he had, more or less, died of grief on Mother's account, I conceived of him as a really nice man; lent him the countenance and manner of an old gentleman who always spoke to me when he met me on the road; and felt I could have become really attached to him as a father. I could imagine it all: Mother reading in the parlor while she waited for me to come home up Sunday's Well in a school-cap and blazer, like the boys from the Grammar School,[3] and with an expensive leather
3 satchel instead of the old cloth school bag I carried over my shoulder. I could see myself walking slowly and with a certain distinction, lingering at gateways and looking down at the river; and later I would go out to tea in one of the big houses with long gardens sloping to the water, and maybe row a boat on the river along with a girl in a pink frock. I wondered only whether I would have any awareness of the National School[4] boy with the cloth school bag who jammed his head between the bars of a gate and thought of me. It was a queer, lonesome feeling that all but reduced me to tears.

But the place that had the greatest attraction of all for me was the Douglas Road, where Father's friend Miss Cadogan lived, only now she wasn't Miss Cadogan but Mrs. O'Brien. Naturally, nobody called Mrs. O'Brien could be as attractive to the imagination as a French chef or an elderly shopkeeper with eleven thousand pounds, but she had a physical reality that the other pair lacked. As I went regularly to the library at Parnell Bridge, I frequently found myself wandering up the road in the direction of Douglas and always stopped in front of the long row of houses where she lived. There were high steps up to them, and in the evening the sunlight fell brightly on the house fronts till they looked like a screen. One evening as I watched a gang of boys playing ball in the street outside, curiosity overcame me. I spoke to one of them. Having been always a child of solemn and unnatural politeness, I probably scared the wits out of them. B

"I wonder if you could tell me which house Mrs. O'Brien lives in, please?" I asked.

"Hi, Gussie!" he yelled to another boy. "This fellow wants to know where your old one lives."

This was more than I had bargained for. Then a thin, good-looking boy of about my own age detached himself from the group and came up to me with his fists clenched. I was feeling distinctly panicky, but all the same I studied him closely. After all, he was the boy I might have been.

"What do you want to know for?" he asked suspiciously.

Again, this was something I had not anticipated.

---

3. **Grammar School:** a private school.

4. **National School:** a public school funded by the government.

WORDS TO KNOW **biased** (bī'əst) *adj.* marked by an unfair preference; prejudiced

Customizing Instruction

Multiple Learning Styles

Spatial or Graphic Learners

1 Invite students to create portraits of the different possible Larrys as the narrator might imagine them: the real Laurence Delaney, Laurence Riordan, Laurence Armady, and Laurence Delaney, son of May Cadogan.

Less Proficient Readers

2 Ask students the following questions to make sure they understand why Larry is intrigued by the past:

- What fact about his parents most interests Larry?
  Answer: He is fascinated by the idea that they might have married other people.
- Why is Larry interested in Mrs. O'Brien?
  Answer: She is an old sweetheart of Larry's father, and Larry wonders what he would have been like if she had been his mother.

Students Acquiring English

3 Point out that the word *satchel* means bookbag or backpack. In this passage, the leather satchel costs more than the cloth school bag.

Mini Lesson Vocabulary Strategy

APPLYING MEANINGS OF ROOTS

Instruction The word *incredulously* derives from the Latin prefix *in-*, meaning "not," and the root word *credere,* meaning "to believe." When Gussie asks, "What's that?" *incredulously,* he cannot believe what he is hearing. Other words based on this root are *credence, incredible, credo,* and *credulous.*

Practice Have students work in pairs to find the meaning of *credence, incredible, credo,* and *credulous.* They may use a dictionary to determine the precise meaning and usage. Ask them to use each word in a sentence. Ask them to describe how they can use knowledge of the root word *credere* to remember the meanings of these words.

Use **Vocabulary Transparencies and Copymasters,** p. 53.

Reading and Analyzing

Literary Analysis CHARACTERIZATION

A Ask students what the speech of the O'Brien family reveals about their character.

Possible Response: Their speech contains slang and nonstandard usage suggesting that the family is not as "proper" as Larry's and may be less educated.

B Ask students to identify descriptive words and phrases that the narrator uses to comment on Gussie's manners and personality.

Possible Responses: "pointing me out to her in a manner I had been brought up to regard as rude"; "bawled"

Reading Skills and Strategies: QUESTIONING

C Ask students why Larry feels "terror" at the prospect of meeting Mrs. O'Brien.

Possible Response: He really doesn't know what to say to her or what reasonable explanation he can give for coming to see her.

"My father was a great friend of your mother," I explained carefully, but, so far as he was concerned, I might as well have been talking a foreign language. It was clear that Gussie O'Brien had no sense of history.

"What's that?" he asked incredulously.

At this point we were interrupted by a woman I had noticed earlier, talking to another over the railing between the two steep gardens. She was small and untidy looking and occasionally rocked the pram[5] in an absent-minded way as though she only remembered it at intervals.

"What is it, Gussie?" she cried, raising herself on tiptoe to see us better.

B "I don't really want to disturb your mother, thank you," I said, in something like hysterics, but Gussie anticipated me, actually pointing me out to her in a manner I had been brought up to regard as rude.

"This fellow wants you," he bawled.

2 "I don't really," I murmured, feeling that now I was in for it. She skipped down the high flight of steps to the gate with a laughing, puzzled air, her eyes in slits and her right hand arranging her hair at the back. It was not carroty as Mother described it, though it had red lights when the sun caught it.

"What is it, little boy?" she asked coaxingly, bending forward.

C "I didn't really want anything, thank you," I said in terror. "It was just that my daddy said you lived up here, and, as I was changing my book at the library, I thought I'd come up and inquire. You can see," I added, showing her the book as proof, "that I've only just been to the library."

"But who is your daddy, little boy?" she asked, her gray eyes still in long, laughing slits. "What's your name?"

"My name is Delaney," I said. "Larry Delaney."

"Not *Mike* Delaney's boy?" she exclaimed wonderingly. "Well, sure, I should have known it from that big head of yours." She passed her hand down the back of my head and laughed. "If you'd only get your hair cut, I wouldn't be long recognizing you. You wouldn't think I'd know the feel of your old fellow's head, would you?" she added roguishly. **1**

"No, Mrs. O'Brien," I replied meekly.

"Why, then indeed I do, and more along with it," she added in the same saucy tone, though the meaning of what she said was not clear to me. "Ah, come in and give us a good look at you! That's my eldest, Gussie, you were talking to," she added, taking my hand. Gussie trailed behind us for a purpose I only recognized later.

"Ma-a-a-a, who's dat fella with you?" yelled a fat little girl who had been playing hopscotch on the pavement.

"That's Larry Delaney," her mother sang over her shoulder. I don't know what it was about that woman but there was something about her high spirits that made her more like a regiment than a woman. You felt that everyone should fall into step behind her. "Mick Delaney's son from Barrackton. I nearly married his old fellow once. Did he ever tell you that, Larry?" she added slyly. She made sudden swift transitions from brilliance to intimacy that I found attractive.

"Yes, Mrs. O'Brien, he did," I replied, trying to sound as roguish as she, and she went off into a delighted laugh, tossing her red head.

"Ah, look at that now! How well the old divil didn't forget me! You can tell him I didn't forget him either. And if I married him, I'd be your mother now. Wouldn't that be a queer old three and fourpence?[6] How would you like me for a mother, Larry?"

5. **pram:** a baby carriage.

6. **a queer old three and fourpence:** slang expression meaning "an odd thing."

WORDS TO KNOW

incredulously (ĭn-krĕj'ə-ləs-lē) *adv.* in a manner expressing skepticism or disbelief

saucy (sô'sē) *adj.* disrespectful in a bold or high-spirited way, pert

474

Teaching Options

Mini Lesson: Viewing and Representing

Spring in St. John's Wood **by Dame Laura Knight**

ART APPRECIATION The British artist Laura Knight (1877–1970) was well-known during her lifetime and was the first artist to be made a Dame of the British Empire. A realistic painter, Knight painted such diverse subjects as landscapes and villages; scenes from the ballet, theater, and circus; and the trials of Nazi war criminals at Nuremberg.

Instruction St. John's Wood is a residential neighborhood in the northwestern part of London. While today it is much more urban than this 1933 painting shows, St. John's Wood has always possessed a quiet air and a neighborhood feeling.

Application Ask students what features of this painting convey a sense of calm.

Possible Response: Students might note that the subdued colors, the orderly lawns, and the deep shadows all suggest a quiet setting.

Application Ask students the following questions, and have them explain their answers: In what kind of setting do you imagine "The Study of History" to take place? How is it similar to what you see in *Spring in St. John's Wood*?

Spring in St. John's Wood (1933), Dame Laura Knight. Oil on canvas, 51¾" × 45½", Board of Trustees of the National Museums and Galleries on Merseyside, Walker Art Gallery, Liverpool, Great Britain.

Customizing Instruction

Less Proficient Readers

1 Ask students whom Mrs. O'Brien refers to when she says "old fellow."
Answer: Larry's father

Students Acquiring English

2 Explain that the expression *in for it* means "in trouble." Larry is afraid Mrs. O'Brien will be angry at him for disturbing her.

Explain the discrepancy between the name "Mike Delaney" and "Mick Delaney" by telling students that *Mick*, like *Mike*, is a nickname for *Michael*. Explain that the phrase *dat fella* is a dialectal version of "that fellow." This speech pattern helps develop the character.

Reading and Analyzing

Literary Analysis CHARACTERIZATION

A Explain to students that authors can use setting to develop characters. Ask what the details of Gussie's room reveal about him.

Possible Response: The unmade cots and the scribbles on the wall suggest that Gussie is careless and untidy. The air rifle and model airplanes suggest that he has the interests of many active boys.

Reading Skills and Strategies: EVALUATING

B Ask students to evaluate Larry's description of Gussie as "spoiled" and "calculating." Is Larry's description accurate? Why or why not?

Possible Responses: Yes, Gussie is unfriendly and goes to the house with Larry hoping to get something. Gussie also whines for a sixpence and suggests that the two go to the sweetshop only because he wants Larry to buy him sweets. No, it is natural for Gussie to behave badly if he's jealous over the attention his mother is paying Larry.

Active Reading

MAKING INFERENCES ABOUT CHARACTERS

C Ask students to make inferences about Mrs. O'Brien's personality based on the details of Larry's encounter with her.

Possible Response: She is fun, energetic, forceful, disorganized . . . and she has a good sense of humor.

"Very much, thank you," I said complacently.

"Ah, go on with you, you would not," she exclaimed, but she was pleased all the same. She struck me as the sort of woman it would be easy enough to please. "Your old fellow always said it: your mother was a *most* superior woman, and you're a *most* superior child. Ah, and I'm not too bad myself either," she added with a laugh and a shrug, wrinkling up her merry little face.

In the kitchen she cut me a slice of bread, smothered it with jam, and gave me a big mug of milk. "Will you have some, Gussie?" she asked in a sharp voice as if she knew only too well what the answer would be. "Aideen," she said to the horrible little girl who had followed us in, "aren't you fat and ugly enough without making a pig of yourself? Murder the Loaf we call her," she added smilingly to me. "You're a polite little boy, Larry. Is the book for your mother?"

"Who wants to read that blooming old stuff?"

Gussie said contemptuously.

"Oh, no, Mrs. O'Brien," I replied. "It's my own."

"You mean you can read a big book like that?" she asked incredulously, taking it from my hands and measuring the length of it with a puzzled air.

"Oh, yes, I can."

"I don't believe you," she said mockingly. "Go on and prove it!"

There was nothing I asked better than to prove it. I felt that as a performer I had never got my due, so I stood in the middle of the kitchen, cleared my throat, and began with great feeling to enunciate one of those horribly involved opening paragraphs you found in children's books of the time. "On a fine evening in Spring, as the setting sun was beginning to gild the blue peaks with its lambent[7] rays, a rider, recognizable as a student by certain niceties[8] of attire, was slowly, and perhaps regretfully, making his way . . ." It was the sort of opening sentence I loved.

"I declare!" Mrs. O'Brien interrupted in astonishment. "And that fellow there is one age with you, and he can't spell *house*. How well you wouldn't be down at the library, you caubogue,[9] you! . . . That's enough now, Larry," she added hastily as I made ready to entertain them further.

"Who wants to read that blooming[10] old stuff?" Gussie said contemptuously.

Later, he took me upstairs to show me his air rifle and model airplanes. Every detail of the room is still clear to me: the view into the back garden with its jungle of wild plants where Gussie had pitched his tent (a bad site for a tent as I patiently explained to him, owing to the danger from wild beasts); the three cots still unmade; the scribbles on the walls; and Mrs. O'Brien's voice from the kitchen telling Aideen to see what was wrong with the baby, who was screaming his head off from the pram outside the front door. Gussie, in particular, fascinated me. He was spoiled, clever, casual; good-looking, with his mother's small clean features; gay and calculating. I saw

7. **lambent:** flickering lightly on a surface.
8. **niceties:** fine points or details.
9. **caubogue** (kô-bōg′): simpleton; bumpkin (from the Irish *cábóg*).
10. **blooming:** in Ireland and Britain, a slang word used to add intensity to a statement.

WORDS TO KNOW

complacently (kəm-plā′sənt-lē) *adv.* in a contented, unconcerned manner

contemptuously (kən-tĕmp′cho͞o-əs-lē) *adv.* in a way that shows one's low opinion of someone or something; scornfully

Teaching Options

Mini Lesson Grammar

VERB CHOICES Remind students vivid action verbs make sentences interesting and memorable. Good verbs *show* the action; they don't merely *tell* about it. Write the following sentence on the chalkboard:

Larry Delaney walked into the room.

Explain to students that the verb *walked* conveys nothing more than the fact that Larry, who was once outside of the room, is now inside the room. Show students how substituting *raced* for *walked* conveys that Larry is in a hurry. Ask students to think of other synonyms for *walk* that might reveal more about Larry and the situation he is in.

Practice Have students copy the following sentences. Ask them to form groups and work together to come up with descriptive action verbs to replace the underlined verbs. Tell them they may use a thesaurus if they wish. When they are finished, ask them to explain to the class what additional information the verbs they have chosen provide for the reader.

1. "Guess what? My parents are taking me to India next summer to meet my relatives!" said Jaseil.

Possible Responses: Exclaimed, shouted, and gushed would all convey Jaseil's excitement.

that when I left and his mother gave me a sixpence.[11] Naturally I refused it politely, but she thrust it into my trousers pocket, and Gussie dragged at her skirt, noisily demanding something for himself.

"If you give him a tanner,[12] you ought to give me a tanner," he yelled.

"I'll tan you," she said laughingly.

"Well, give up a lop[13] anyway," he begged, and she did give him a penny to take his face off her, as she said herself, and after that he followed me down the street and suggested we should go to the shop and buy sweets. I was simple-minded, but I wasn't an out-and-out fool, and I knew that if I went to a sweetshop with Gussie, I should end up with no sixpence and very few sweets. So I told him I could not buy sweets without Mother's permission, at which he gave me up altogether as a sissy or worse.

It had been an exhausting afternoon but a very instructive one. In the twilight I went back slowly over the bridges, a little regretful for that fast-moving, colorful household, but with a new appreciation of my own home. When I went in, the lamp was lit over the fireplace and Father was at his tea.

"What kept you, child?" Mother asked with an anxious air, and suddenly I felt slightly guilty, and I played it as I usually did whenever I was at fault—in a loud, demonstrative, grown-up way. I stood in the middle of the kitchen with my cap in my hand and pointed it first at one, then at the other.

"You wouldn't believe who I met!" I said dramatically.

"Wisha,[14] who, child?" Mother asked.

"Miss Cadogan," I said, placing my cap squarely on a chair and turning on them both again. "Miss May Cadogan. Mrs. O'Brien as she is now."

"Mrs. O'Brien?" Father exclaimed, putting down his cup. "But where did you meet Mrs. O'Brien?"

"I said you wouldn't believe it. It was near the library. I was talking to some fellows, and what do you think but one of them was Gussie O'Brien, Mrs. O'Brien's son. And he took me home with him, and his mother gave me bread and jam, and she gave me *this.*" I produced the sixpence with a real flourish.

2

"Well, I'm blowed!" Father gasped, and first he looked at me, and then he looked at Mother and burst into a loud guffaw.

"And she said to tell you she remembers you too, and that she sent her love."

"Oh, by the jumping bell of Athlone!"[15] Father crowed and clapped his hands on his knees. I could see he believed the story I had told and was delighted with it, and I could see, too, that Mother did not believe it and that she was not in the least delighted. That, of course, was the trouble with Mother. Though she would do anything to help me with an intellectual problem, she never seemed to understand the need for experiment. She never opened her mouth while Father cross-questioned me, shaking his head in wonder and storing it up to tell the men in the factory. What pleased him most was Mrs. O'Brien's remembering the shape of his head, and later, while Mother was out of the kitchen,

C

11. **sixpence:** a coin worth six British pennies.
12. **tanner:** another term for a sixpence.
13. **lop:** chunk; piece.
14. **wisha:** in Ireland, an introductory interjection meaning "Well!" or "Indeed!"
15. **by the jumping bell of Athlone** (ăth-lōn′): a humorous exclamation. Athlone is a town in central Ireland.

Customizing Instruction

Less Proficient Readers

1 Ask the following questions to make sure that students understand what happens when Larry meets Mrs. O'Brien:

- How would you summarize what Larry does at Mrs. O'Brien's house?
  Possible Response: Larry eats bread and jam, impresses Mrs. O'Brien with his reading skills, and looks at Gussie's room.
- How does Mrs. O'Brien feel about Larry and how does she demonstrate these feelings?
  Possible Response: She likes him, she is impressed by him, she tells him so, and she offers him money.

Set a Purpose Have students read on to discover how Larry's parents react to his visit to Mrs. O'Brien.

Students Acquiring English

2 Explain that *with a real flourish* means "with a showy gesture that reflects delight and pride," *blowed* means "astonished," and *guffaw* means a "huge laugh."

2. Upon arriving in India, Jaseil got on a train to Bombay.
Possible Responses: Hopped on and jumped on would convey excitement.

3. The train went down the tracks toward Bombay.
Possible Responses: Roared and raced would convey speed; chugged would convey a lack of speed.

4. When Jaseil arrived in Bombay, he met his relatives.
Possible Responses: Embraced, hugged, and greeted would convey friendliness and enthusiasm.

5. While in India, Jaseil had many interesting foods such as *nan*, a type of bread; *kulsi*, a type of ice cream; and papaya, a fruit.
Possible Responses: Devoured or enjoyed suggests that he likes the food; sampled suggests that he had many foods from which to choose.

Use **Grammar Transparencies and Copymasters,** p. 176.

Use McDougal Littell's ***Language Network,*** Chapter 6, for more instruction and practice in verbs.

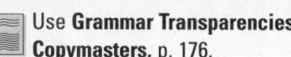

Reading and Analyzing

Literary Analysis: THEME

A Remind students that theme is the central idea or message in a work of literature. It tells the author's perception about life or human nature. The theme can often be determined by examining how the main character changes during the story. Discuss how Larry changes and how this change reflects "the power of heritage."

Possible Responses: Larry recognizes the power and importance of his heritage.

Reading Skills and Strategies: SUMMARIZING

B Ask students to summarize Larry's reaction to his visit with Mrs. O'Brien.

Possible Response: At first Larry enjoys thinking about what his life would have been like had his father married May Cadogan. He realizes that he would have been a very different boy, perhaps like Gussie. The thought of being someone else upsets him.

Reading Skills and Strategies: CONNECTING

Ask students to think about how their lives would be different if their parents had made different choices.

I caught him looking in the mirror and stroking the back of his head.

But I knew too that for the first time I had managed to produce in Mother the unrest that Father could produce, and I felt wretched and guilty and didn't know why. This was an aspect of history I only studied later.

That night I was really able to indulge my passion. At last I had the material to work with. I saw myself as Gussie O'Brien, standing in the bedroom, looking down at my tent in the garden, and Aideen as my sister, and Mrs. O'Brien as my mother, and, like Pascal, I re-created history. I remembered Mrs. O'Brien's laughter, her scolding, and the way she stroked my head. I knew she was kind—casually kind—and hot-tempered, and recognized that in dealing with her I must somehow be a different sort of person. Being good at reading would never satisfy her. She would almost compel you to be as Gussie was: flattering, impertinent, and exacting. Though I couldn't have expressed it in those terms, she was the sort of woman who would compel you to flirt with her. **B**

Then, when I had had enough, I deliberately soothed myself as I did whenever I had scared myself by pretending that there was a burglar in the house or a wild animal trying to get in the attic window. I just crossed my hands on my chest, looked up at the window, and said to myself: "It is not like that. I am not Gussie O'Brien. I am Larry Delaney, and my mother is Mary Delaney, and we live in Number 8, Wellington Square. Tomorrow I'll go to school at the Cross, and first there will be prayers, and then arithmetic, and after that composition."

For the first time the charm did not work. I had ceased to be Gussie, all right, but somehow I had not become myself again, not any self that I knew. It was as though my own identity was a sort of sack I had to live in, and I had deliberately worked my way out of it, and now I couldn't get back again because I had grown too big for it. I practiced every trick I knew to reassure myself. I tried to play a counting game; then I prayed, but even the prayer seemed different, as though it didn't belong to me at all. I was away in the middle of empty space, divorced from mother and home and everything permanent and familiar. Suddenly I found myself sobbing. The door opened, and Mother came in in her nightdress, shivering, her hair over her face.

"You're not sleeping, child," she said in a wan and complaining voice.

I snivelled, and she put her hand on my forehead.

"You're hot," she said. "What ails you?"

I could not tell her of the nightmare in which I was lost. Instead, I took her hand, and gradually the terror retreated, and I became myself again, shrank into my little skin of identity, and left infinity and all its anguish behind.

"Mummy," I said, "I promise I never wanted anyone but you." ❖

WORDS TO KNOW **impertinent** (ĭm-pûr'tn-ənt) *adj.* rude; insolent

Teaching Options

Assessment Standardized Test Practice

You can assess students' understanding of the characters by asking them to describe Larry and his mother and father. Students will need to demonstrate an understanding of the methods of characterization.

RUBRIC

3 **Full Accomplishment** Response describes the characters' appearance, speech, behavior, and other characters' comments.

2 **Substantial Accomplishment** Response describes each character in general, but may not utilize the components of characterization.

1 **Little or Partial Accomplishment** Response shows little understanding of character development.

Connect to the Literature

1. **What Do You Think?** Did you find this story humorous? serious? both? Explain your answer.

Comprehension Check
- How does Larry's mother react when his father talks about old sweethearts?
- Why does Larry go to Mrs. O'Brien's house?
- What scares Larry on the night of his visit to Mrs. O'Brien?

Think Critically

2. Do you think Larry would be happy as Mrs. O'Brien's son? Why or why not?

3. **ACTIVE READING** **MAKING INFERENCES ABOUT CHARACTERS** Look again at the cluster diagram you made in your READER'S NOTEBOOK. What **inferences** can you make about young Larry Delaney's personality, on the basis of **details** about him in the story?

THINK ABOUT
- how he spends his free time
- his relationship with each of his parents
- why he fantasizes about a different family background
- his encounter with Gussie and Mrs. O'Brien

4. What seems to be the **narrator's** attitude toward his own childhood? Support your response with details from the story.

5. Frank O'Connor once said that storytelling "doesn't deal with problems; it doesn't have any solutions to offer; it just states the human conditions." What do you think the writer is trying to say about the human condition in this story?

Extend Interpretations

6. **Different Perspectives** How do you think Gussie might describe Larry's visit to Mrs. O'Brien?

7. **Connect to Life** Which do you feel is more influential in determining what kind of person a child becomes—biological factors (inherited genes) or environmental factors (culture, friendships, economic status, and so forth)? Explain your opinion.

Literary Analysis

CHARACTERIZATION

Characterization consists of the techniques that a writer uses to develop **characters.** There are four basic methods of characterization:

1. physical description
2. a character's speech, thoughts, feelings, and actions
3. the speech, thoughts, feelings, and actions of other characters
4. the narrator's direct comments about the character.

O'Connor uses all four techniques to bring the characters in "The Study of History" to life.

Cooperative Learning Activity As Larry tells this story from a **first-person point of view,** the reader is told the narrator's thoughts and feelings directly. How important do you think this is for the reader's understanding of Larry's **character?** Working with a few classmates, review the end of the story (starting at "That night I was really able . . ." on page 478). Discuss how this part of the story would be different if the reader did not know Larry's thoughts and feelings.

GUIDING STUDENT RESPONSE

Connect to the Literature

1. What Do You Think?
Be sure that students give reasons for their opinion.

Comprehension Check
- Larry's mother becomes upset and jealous.
- Larry is curious about the woman his father might have married, and he wonders what his life would be like if she were his mother.
- Larry becomes confused about who he is.

Use Selection Quiz
Unit Three Resource Book, p. 50.

Think Critically

2. Possible Responses: Yes, because Mrs. O'Brien would spoil him and amuse him; no, because he needs a more sensitive and intellectual environment than she could give him.

3. Possible Responses: He is intelligent; he has a vivid imagination; he is curious; he loves his mother; he is in awe of his father; he is quick to judge other people; he is slightly egotistical; he is proud of his accomplishments.

4. Possible Responses: The narrator is amused yet nostalgic when he describes his parents' relationship; he seems to miss the naiveté and nerve he had as a child; he feels fortunate to have his parents.

5. Possible Responses: Many facets of our lives depend on accidental factors; every experience has a positive and a negative side; our parents are an important part of who we are.

Extend Interpretations

Different Perspectives Students may suggest that Gussie would see Larry as an arrogant show-off. He would be jealous of Larry and angry with his mother for paying so much attention to Larry.

Connect to Life Be sure that students explain their opinions.

Literary Analysis

Characterization The story is essentially an epiphany; students will understand the importance of the first-person point of view.

Writing Options

1. **Letters of Love** A list of details about each character will help students write the love letters.
2. **Autobiographical Tale** Encourage students to use at least one of the methods of characterization to develop the characters in their tales.

Activities & Explorations

Storyboard This activity provides opportunities for students with different learning styles to work cooperatively. One student may record the group's ideas, while another organizes the ideas to make sure they show the plot of the story. A third student can assign drawing tasks and monitor the group to make sure everyone is working toward the same goal.

Inquiry & Research

Nature and Nurture Students need to read print material, especially accessible in weekly news magazines. They can also locate nonprint information using technical resources such as on-line databases and the Internet.

Vocabulary in Action

1. c
2. b
3. a
4. a
5. c
6. b
7. c
8. b
9. a
10. c

Choices & CHALLENGES

Writing Options

1. **Letters of Love** Write several love letters that Michael Delaney and May Cadogan might have exchanged. Alternatively, write a love letter in which Mr. Riordan proposes marriage to Larry's mother, then write her response.
2. **Autobiographical Tale** Write about an autobiographical incident that, like Larry Delaney's story, deals with a turning point in your life. If you prefer, write from the point of view of the person you might have become if the circumstances of your birth had been different, using as a springboard the freewriting you did for the Connect to Your Life on page 468.

Activities & Explorations

Storyboard Plan a film version of "The Study of History" by designing and drawing a storyboard—a series of sketches showing the sets and the positions of the actors in one or more scenes of the story.

Inquiry & Research

Nature and Nurture As more and more developments are made in the field of genetic research, scientists continue to explore how both heredity and the environment we live in affect our lives. Find out more about this ongoing scientific debate.

Real World Link Begin your research by reading the magazine article on page 482.

Dolly the sheep was the first genetically cloned animal, born in 1997.

Vocabulary in Action

EXERCISE: ASSESSMENT PRACTICE On a separate piece of paper, write the letter of the **antonym** of each boldfaced word below.

1. **brooding:** (a) reserved, (b) moody, (c) lighthearted
2. **uncanny:** (a) artificial, (b) familiar, (c) mysterious
3. **exasperated:** (a) calm, (b) confused, (c) disturbed
4. **impertinent:** (a) polite, (b) minor, (c) fearful
5. **incredulously:** (a) surprisingly, (b) densely, (c) trustfully
6. **ordained:** (a) explained, (b) prohibited, (c) decreed
7. **biased:** (a) stubborn, (b) crooked, (c) fair
8. **contemptuously:** (a) cruelly, (b) respectfully, (c) disgustingly
9. **complacently:** (a) argumentatively, (b) falsely, (c) dishonestly
10. **saucy:** (a) tasteless, (b) wishful, (c) shy

Building Vocabulary
A number of the Words to Know in this lesson contain prefixes and suffixes. For an in-depth lesson on word parts, see page 856.

Teaching Options

Mini Lesson Grammar

GERUNDS AND GERUND PHRASES Explain that a gerund is a type of verbal. Remind students that verbals are words that look like verbs but that function as some other part of speech. A gerund always ends in *-ing* and functions as a noun. Write the following sentence on the chalkboard:

Larry enjoys <u>reading.</u>

Explain that *reading* is a gerund. Although it looks like a verb, it functions as a noun in this sentence. It is an activity, a thing. It serves as the direct object of the sentence.

Explain that a gerund phrase consists of a gerund and any modifiers or complements it may have. The entire phrase acts as a noun. Write the following sentence on the chalkboard as an example:

Larry enjoys <u>listening to his parents' stories.</u>

Explain that in the sentence above, the entire phrase functions as a direct object.

Practice Ask students to underline the gerunds or gerund phrases in these sentences and to state whether the gerund or gerund phrase functions as a subject, a direct object, or an object of a preposition.

Grammar in Context: Precise Verbs

In the following excerpt from "The Study of History," Frank O'Connor's use of vivid verbs brings to life the narrator's first encounter with Mrs. O'Brien.

> **"This fellow wants you," he bawled.**
> **"I don't really," I murmured, feeling that now I was in for it. She skipped down the high flight of steps to the gate. . . .**

Later Mrs. O'Brien gives the narrator a coin.

> **Naturally I refused it politely, but she thrust it into my trousers pocket, and Gussie dragged at her skirt, noisily demanding something for himself.**

Writers can be more concise by using precise verbs rather than combinations of vague verbs and adverbs. Imagine how the passages above would be different if O'Connor had used *said loudly* instead of *bawled* and *forcefully put* instead of *thrust*. By using precise verbs, he gave his writing vigor and a playful tone.

WRITING EXERCISE Rewrite each sentence, replacing the underlined words with vivid verbs.

Example: ***Original*** She comes quickly down the stairs and immediately leaves through the gate.

Rewritten She hurtles down the stairs and dashes through the gate.

1. Learning about his parents' history drastically changes the narrator's view of his life.
2. Mr. Delaney laughs broadly and loudly hits his knee.
3. He really bothers Mrs. Delaney with his reminiscences; she menacingly says her responses through clenched teeth.
4. Larry waits awhile at the gate and looks steadily at the house he might have lived in.
5. All of the activity at the O'Briens' house tires out Larry.

Connect to the Literature Look at the verbs used in the description of Mr. Delaney's reaction to Larry's account of his visit with Mrs. O'Brien (page 477, second column). How are the verbs suited to Mr. Delaney's personality?

Grammar Handbook Verbs, p. 1185

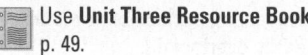

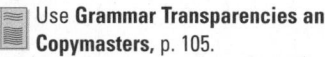

Frank O'Connor

1903–1966

Other Works
Domestic Relations
An Only Child

Escape into Books Frank O'Connor grew up in a troubled, impoverished home, but he found refuge in the imaginary world of literature. He was an avid reader as a young boy and by the time he was 12 had already begun to pursue his life's work as a writer, creating an anthology of his own biographies, poems, and essays on Irish history.

Passion for Writing For many years, O'Connor worked as a librarian in Cork and in Dublin, an occupation that gave him time to write. Eventually he became one of Ireland's most influential literary figures, producing everything from poetry to novels, travel books to literary criticism. O'Connor is best known for his intimate and realistic short stories, however. According to James Matthews, O'Connor's biographer, "Only when he had a story banging around in the echo chamber of his mind was Frank O'Connor really alive." His passion for writing is evident not only in his work but also in his writing habits: he was known to revise his stories over and over again, even after they were published.

Author Activity

Alter Ego Find and read another O'Connor story in which Larry Delaney is the narrator. What new insights does the story give into Larry's character?

Grammar in Context

WRITING EXERCISE Answers will vary. Possible answers are shown.

1. Learning about his parents' history transforms the narrator's view of his life.
2. Mr. Delaney guffaws and slaps his knee.
3. He exasperates Mrs. Delaney with his reminiscences; she hisses her responses through clenched teeth.
4. Larry lingers at the gate and stares at the house he might have lived in.
5. All of the activity at the O'Briens' house exhausts Larry.

Connect to the Literature Possible Response: Verbs such as *gasped, burst, crowed,* and *clapped* emphasize that Mr. Delaney becomes loud and enthusiastic when his former girlfriends are being discussed.

Author Activity

Alter Ego As an only child, Larry Delaney seems insecure; he perceives the difference between the rich and the poor while growing up in Cork. He struggles with the fact that his parents are just common people.

Exercises

1. Making model airplanes is one of Gussie's favorite hobbies.
   Answer: *Making model airplanes; subject*
2. Larry enjoys daydreaming about his parents' past.
   Answer: *daydreaming about his parents' past; direct object*
3. Reading is not Gussie's idea of a good time.
   Answer: *Reading; subject*
4. Larry's father takes great delight in teasing his wife.
   Answer: *teasing his wife; object of a preposition*
5. Larry thinks turning down Mr. Riordan's marriage proposal was impractical.
   Answer: *turning down Mr. Riordan's marriage proposal; direct object*
6. Not knowing what to say to Mrs. O'Brien makes Larry nervous.
   Answer: *Not knowing what to say to Mrs. O'Brien; subject*

Use **Unit Three Resource Book,** p. 49.

Use **Grammar Transparencies and Copymasters,** p. 105.

Use McDougal Littell's ***Language Network,*** Chapter 3, for more instruction and practice on gerunds.

Real WORLD Link

Magazine Article

Objectives
- take notes as a means of organizing information
- outline the main idea and supporting details in an article containing technical information
- paraphrase information to support a conclusion
- identify information to support a conclusion
- summarize an article containing technical information

Connecting to the Literature
Frank O'Connor's character Larry Delaney would have been interested in current DNA research that seems to indicate a strong genetic influence on behavior. His musings about "who I would have been if I hadn't been me" led him to explore a bit of his parents' history.

Reading for Information
Technical information is more easily understood when concrete examples are used to illustrate complex ideas. Students can readily identify the similarities in the identical twins raised by different families because they are concretely specific.

1 Student outlines will vary. Suggest that students write a sentence for each paragraph as their main heading and add a few sentences that include details for their subheadings.

Were You Born That Way?

Text by George Howe Colt;
Reporting by Anne Hollister

1 Does the key to who we are lie in our genes or in our family, friends, and experiences? In one of the most bitter scientific controversies of the 20th century—the battle over nature and nurture—a wealth of new research has tipped the scales overwhelmingly toward nature. Studies of twins and advances in molecular biology have uncovered a more significant genetic component to personality than was previously known. Far from a piece of putty, say biologists, my daughter is more like a computer's motherboard,[1] her basic personality hardwired into infinitesimal squiggles of DNA. As parents, we would have no more influence on some aspects of her behavior than we had on the color of her hair. And yet new findings are also shedding light on how heredity and environment interact.

2 The moment the scales began to tip can be traced to a 1979 meeting between a steelworker named Jim Lewis and a clerical worker named Jim Springer. Identical twins separated five weeks after birth, they were raised by families 80 miles apart in Ohio. Reunited 39 years later, they would have strained the credulity[2] of the editors of *Ripley's Believe It or Not.* Not only did both have dark hair, stand six feet tall, and weigh 180 pounds, but they spoke with the same inflections, moved with the same gait, and made the same gestures. Both loved stock car racing and hated baseball. Both married women named Linda, divorced them, and married women named Betty. . . . Their scores on personality tests were as close as if one person had taken the same test twice.

Identical twins raised in different families are a built-in research lab for measuring the relative contributions of nature

1. **motherboard:** the main board of a computer, usually containing the circuitry.
2. **credulity** (krĭ-do͞oʹlĭ-tē): the tendency to believe.

Reading for Information

DNA is the microscopic material that carries the hereditary information that determines aspects of your physical appearance. But are your personality and behavior also predetermined, or are they shaped by life experiences? Scientists refer to this question as the "nature vs. nurture" debate. A science article like this one is filled with complex ideas and technical terms. This requires that readers sift through details to uncover the important information.

TAKING NOTES

Note taking is an effective way to collect and organize the information that you read. There are three basic note-taking techniques:
- **outlining** (listing main ideas and adding numbered supporting details); **topic outlines** include the use of letters and numbers for points and subpoints of a topic; **sentence outlines** use complete sentences for the main ideas and details
- **paraphrasing** (restating the main ideas in your own words)
- **summarizing** (condensing an article's main ideas into shorter paragraphs, sentences, or phrases)

YOUR TURN Use the questions and activities below as you take notes on this article.

1 **Outlining Key Points** Use the sentence outline format shown here as you take notes on the rest of the article. Record only key points; don't try to write down every word.

Mini Lesson Inquiry & Research

The Inquiry & Research activity on this page links to the Inquiry & Research section of Choices and Challenges (p. 480).

Instruction Point out that, although research indicates a strong genetic influence on behavior, the article also states that "critics accuse researchers of confusing correlation with causation. . ." This subtle point suggests that definitive conclusions cannot be drawn about how genetic factors work or the role they play, thus creating a plausible skepticism that is being too easily overlooked.

Practice Using their notes and summaries, have students brainstorm support for each side of the nature vs. nurture issue. Then, have them work in small groups to share their ideas and formulate a position, including the possibility that the group does not reach a consensus. When each group is ready, conduct discussion in a roundtable format, with groups presenting their positions in turn before the table is opened for discussion.

and nurture. The Jims became one of 7,000 sets of twins studied by the Minnesota Center for Twin and Adoption Research, one of half a dozen such centers in this country. Using psychological and physiological tests to compare the relative similarity of identical and fraternal[3] twins, these
❸ centers calculate the "heritability" of behavioral traits—the degree to which a trait in a given population is attributable to genes rather than to the environment. . . .

Studies of twins have produced an impressive list of attributes or behaviors that appear to owe at least as much to heredity as to environment. It includes alienation, extroversion,[4] traditionalism, leadership, career choice, risk aversion, attention deficit disorder, religious conviction, and vulnerability to stress. One study even concluded that happiness is 80 percent heritable—it depends little on wealth, achievement or marital status. . . . Critics accuse researchers of confusing correlation with causation, yet they admit the data suggest a strong genetic influence on behavior. Far less clear is how it all works. Is there a gene for becoming an astronaut? For enjoying symphonies? . . .

The human body has 100 trillion cells, each equipped with a complete set of DNA distributed among 23 pairs of chromosomes. (DNA is microscopic yet sizable: If set out in a continuous strand, the DNA from a single cell would be six feet long.) Each cell's DNA is made up of some three
❹ billion nucleic components. Most of these seem to be nonfunctioning—"junk" DNA, biologists call them—but about 3 percent are working genes. The total number of working genes is believed to be 80,000, give or take 20,000. The task: to pinpoint the one-in-three-billion bit that might contribute to a particular behavior. . . .

By the year 2005, scientists are expected to have mapped the entire sequence of the human genome.[5] . . . Within a few decades, people who feel ill will go to physician-geneticists who will run DNA scans to check the relevant genes, make pinpoint diagnoses, and prescribe drugs targeted to precise genetic needs. This will be true for depression, phobias, and life-threatening obesity, as well as for less crippling traits. Just as Mary Poppins had a magic bottle from which she dispensed spoonfuls of strawberry-flavored liquid to cure Michael's fussiness, parents may supply a pill to embolden their shy child before the school dance.

3. **fraternal:** referring to a set of twins who develop from two separate eggs, rather than from one egg.
4. **extroversion:** interest in others.
5. **genome** (jē′nōm′): a complete set of chromosomes with its associated genes.

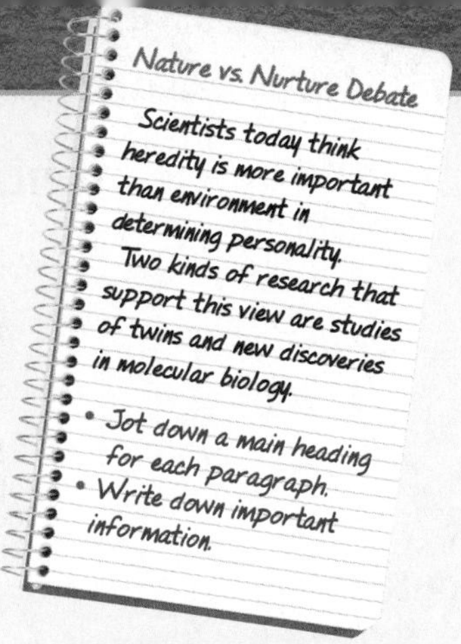

Nature vs. Nurture Debate
Scientists today think heredity is more important than environment in determining personality.
Two kinds of research that support this view are studies of twins and new discoveries in molecular biology.
• Jot down a main heading for each paragraph.
• Write down important information.

❷ **Paraphrasing** Notice the peculiar similarities of Jim Lewis's and Jim Springer's lives. In your notes, explain in your own words how the information about these long-separated twins supports one side of the nature vs. nurture debate.

❸ **Direct Quotes** When you want to quote from an article directly, use quotation marks. What information in this paragraph might it be helpful to record word for word?

❹ Why is it difficult to find evidence of behavioral traits in DNA? Be sure to cover this information in your notes.

Summarizing Review the explanation of summarizing given on the previous page. Then refer to your notes as you write a brief summary of this article.

Inquiry & Research

Activity Link: "The Study of History," p. 480

Larry Delaney in "The Study of History" wondered how he came to be the person he is. What do you think shapes a personality? Use your notes as a quick reference source for a class discussion on the nature vs. nurture issue.

2 The similarities in physical and behavioral traits between the two men is so striking that they might be attributed to genetic influences rather than environmental influences.

3 Technical scientific information might be quoted.

4 It is difficult because each of the body's 100 trillion cells has a complete set of DNA, made up of three billion nucleic components.

Summarizing

Remind students that a summary contains only the most important details. It also should not include any personal opinions.

REAL WORLD LINK 483

OVERVIEW

Objectives

1. understand and appreciate an **essay (Literary Analysis)**
2. recognize the effect of **audience (Literary Analysis)**
3. **distinguish fact from nonfact (Active Reading)**

Summary

Nicholas Gage describes how the power of the written word transformed a meek immigrant boy into an award-winning writer. Gage recalls how he came to the United States as a nine-year-old Greek refugee who spoke no English. Four years later, he met his teacher and mentor, Miss Marjorie Hurd, who asked young Gage to write about his escape from war-torn Greece, the death of his mother, and his stay in a refugee camp. His essay won a medal in a national writing contest. Eventually, Gage went on to study journalism and has since won many awards and honors for his writing. He notes that none of these honors would have been possible without the guidance of Miss Hurd, who remains important in his life.

Thematic Link

A Greek refugee realizes the **power of heritage** when he is exposed to the literary wealth of his native country and encouraged to write his family's story.

5-Minute Warm-Up

Daily Language SkillBuilder

Have students **proofread** the display sentences on page 381k and write them correctly. The sentences also appear on Transparency 16 of **Grammar Transparencies and Copymasters.**

Mini Lesson Preteaching Vocabulary

If you would like to preteach the WORDS TO KNOW for this selection, use the Mini Lesson, pp. 486–487.

"What are all you goof-offs doing here?' she bellowed at the would-be journalists."

The Teacher Who Changed My Life

Essay by NICHOLAS GAGE

Connect to Your Life

Life Changers Think of the various people who have influenced the course of your life. When you look back, 10 or 20 years from now, which of these people do you think will have made a lasting impression on you? Jot down your thoughts about one of these people.

Build Background

War Refugee Nicholas Gage was born in 1939 in Lia, a mountain village in northwestern Greece. Nicholas lived his early years with his mother, Eleni, and four older sisters. His father, Christos, had left his impoverished village to find work in the United States, eventually settling in Worcester, Massachusetts. Before World War II began, his father had been able to return home for extended visits, but the war and the German occupation of Greece made such travel impossible.

After World War II, Eleni and her five children found themselves caught in Greece's bitter civil war between the Communists and the royalists, those who supported rule by the king. In 1947 the Communists took control of Lia, blocking all exit opportunities. In the spring of 1948, the Communists began retreating into nearby Albania, taking the village children with them. Eleni made secret arrangements for the family to flee, but her plan was only partially successful. Though Nicholas and three sisters escaped, one daughter and the mother were left behind. Eventually, Nicholas and his three sisters were able to join their father in the United States.

WORDS TO KNOW
Vocabulary Preview

authoritarian	mentor
catalyst	mortify
emphatically	muse
formidable	tact
hone	void

Focus Your Reading

LITERARY ANALYSIS AUDIENCE The **audience** for a piece of writing is the person or persons intended to read it. "The Teacher Who Changed My Life" was first published in a newspaper magazine supplement intended for a general American readership. As you read, consider how Gage's sense of the audience he is writing for helps determines the **content, style,** and **purpose** of his essay.

ACTIVE READING DISTINGUISHING FACT FROM NONFACT Gage's essay contains verifiable **facts**—statements that can be proved—both about the civil war he fled in Greece and about his experiences in the United States. However, a personal essay includes more than just basic facts. The strength of Gage's essay arises from his recollection of his **feelings** and **opinions** about events and people in his life. Such elements in a personal essay can be described as **nonfact;** although they are true, they cannot be objectively verified in the way that facts can. As you read "The Teacher Who Changed My Life," be aware of the relationship between verifiable facts and the author's account of his personal reactions to his experiences.

READER'S NOTEBOOK Record examples of **fact and nonfact** in Gage's essay, using a chart like the one shown.

Fact	Nonfact
Gage arrived in the United States in 1949.	He felt "very lucky" to have come to the United States.

VIDEODISC **LaserLinks: Background for Reading**
Historical Connection

LESSON RESOURCES

UNIT THREE RESOURCE BOOK, pp. 51–56

ASSESSMENT RESOURCES
Formal Assessment, pp. 81–82
Teacher's Guide to Assessment and Portfolio Use
Test Generator

SKILLS TRANSPARENCIES AND COPYMASTERS

Literary Analysis
- Style, Voice, Diction, Purpose, T22 (for Paired Activity, p. 491)

Reading and Critical Thinking
- Fact vs. Opinion, T3 (for Think Critically, item 4, p. 491)

Grammar
- Verb Tenses II, C128 (for Mini Lesson, p. 492)

Vocabulary
- Context Clues, C54 (for Mini Lesson, p. 486)
- Word Origins, C55 (for Mini Lesson, p. 488)

Writing
- Showing, Not Telling, T22 (for Writing Option 1, p. 492)
- Elaboration, T10 (for Writing Option 2, p. 492)

Communications
- Dramatic Reading, T12 (for Activities & Explorations 1, p. 492)

INTEGRATED TECHNOLOGY

Audio Library
LaserLinks
- Historical Connection: The Greek Civil War, 1947–1949. See **Teacher's SourceBook,** p. 29.

Internet: Research Starter
Visit our website:
www.mcdougallittell.com

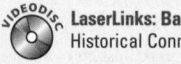

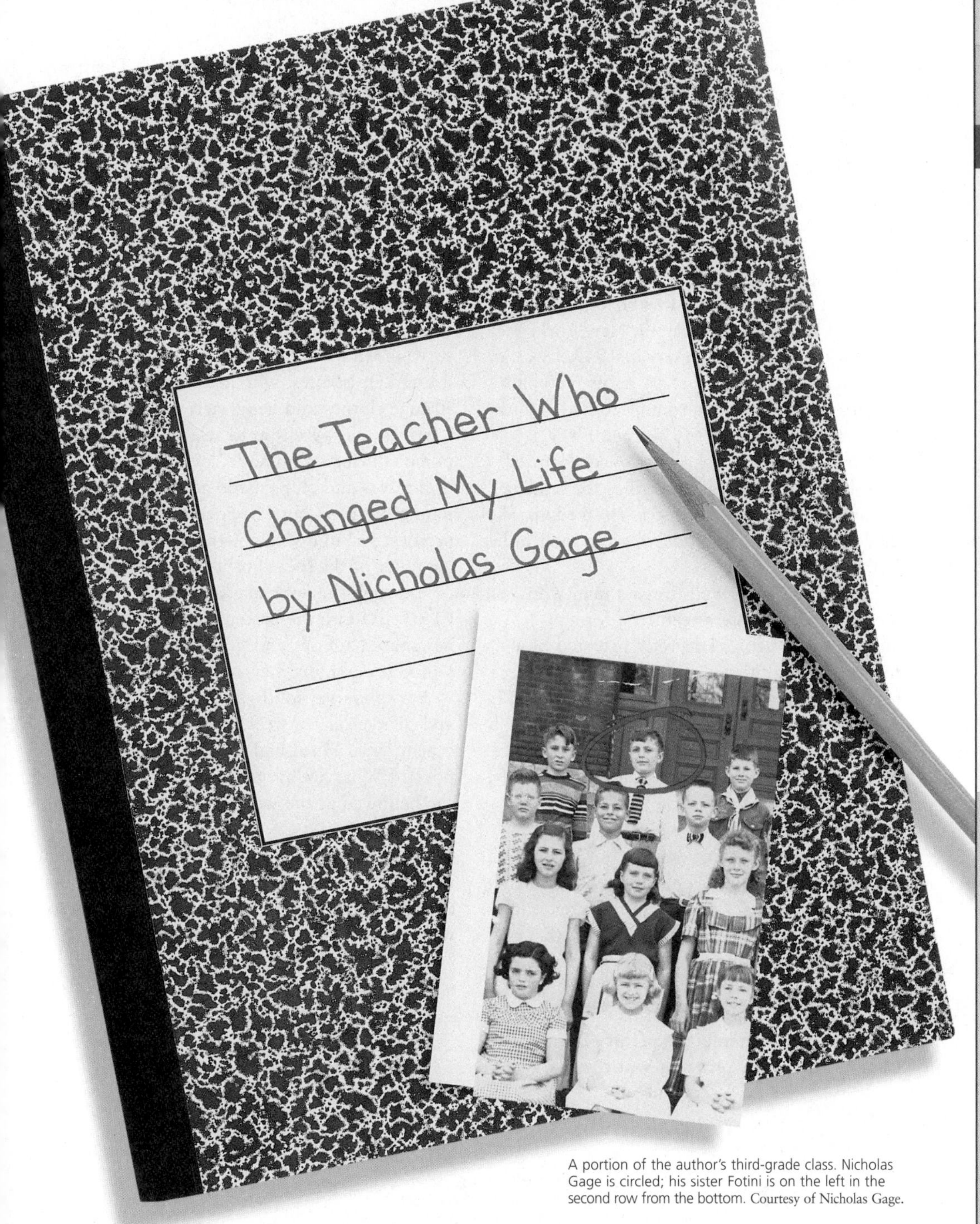
The Teacher Who
Changed My Life
by Nicholas Gage

A portion of the author's third-grade class. Nicholas Gage is circled; his sister Fotini is on the left in the second row from the bottom. Courtesy of Nicholas Gage.

TEACHING THE LITERATURE

Customizing Instruction

Less Proficient Readers

Help students understand the story's overall organization by discussing shifts in sequence and by pointing out that there is a story within the essay.

Set a Purpose Have students adjust their purpose for reading to find out about the hardships Gage endured.

Students Acquiring English

For students who are unfamiliar with our school system, it might be helpful to discuss the differences between junior high and senior high school.

Use **Spanish Study Guide** pp. 107–109 for additional support.

Gifted and Talented

In Greek mythology, the Muses were the patron goddesses of the arts, who were called upon to inspire creativity and skill. Ask students to point out ways in which Miss Hurd was Gage's "muse."

BLOCK SCHEDULING: MANAGING TIME

If your schedule requires that you cover the lesson objectives in a shorter time, use . . .

- Preparing to Read, p. 484
- Vocabulary in Action, p. 492
- Grammar in Context, p. 493

If you want to take advantage of longer class time, use. . .

- TE Teaching Options: Preteaching Vocabulary, pp. 486–487; Vocabulary Strategy, p. 488; Informal Assessment, p. 489
- Choices & Challenges and Author Activity, pp. 492–493

Reading and Analyzing

Reading Skills and Strategies: PREVIEW

Summarize the essay and discuss the title, pointing out that it suggests the author's purpose for writing the essay. If necessary, discuss the background material on war refugees.

Active Reading DISTINGUISHING FACT FROM NONFACT

Facts can be verified, while nonfacts are often expressions of feelings and opinions responding to the facts. Words such as *seem, think, feel, imagine, and wonder* often signal nonfact information.

Use **Unit Three Resource Book** p. 52 for more practice.

Literary Analysis AUDIENCE

Point out that a writer's audience helps determine the essay's content, style, and purpose. Gage's selection was first published in a newspaper magazine supplement and written for a general American readership. Students may want to discuss how the intended audience affects the content of the first two paragraphs.

Possible Response: To appeal to an American audience, Gage begins by showing his appreciation for the United States. He also supplies background information on the conflict that prompted his flight from Greece.

Use **Unit Three Resource Book** p. 53 for more practice.

The person who set the course of my life in the new land I entered as a young war refugee—who, in fact, nearly dragged me onto the path that would bring all the blessings I've received in America—was a salty-tongued, no-nonsense schoolteacher named Marjorie Hurd. When I entered her classroom in 1953, I had been to six schools in five years, starting in the Greek village where I was born in 1939.

When I stepped off a ship in New York Harbor on a gray March day in 1949, I was an undersized 9-year-old in short pants who had lost his mother and was coming to live with the

1 father he didn't know. My mother, Eleni Gatzoyiannis,[1] had been imprisoned, tortured and shot by Communist guerrillas for sending me and three of my four sisters to freedom. She died so that her children could go to their father in the United States.

The portly, bald, well-dressed man who met me and my sisters seemed a foreign, <u>authoritarian</u> figure. I secretly resented him for not getting the whole family out of Greece early enough to save my mother. Ultimately, I would grow to love him and appreciate how he dealt with becoming a single parent at the age of 56, but at first our relationship was prickly, full of hostility.

As Father drove us to our new home—a tenement in Worcester, Mass.—and pointed out the huge brick building that would be our first school in America, I clutched my Greek notebooks from the refugee camp, hoping that my few years of schooling would impress my teachers in this cold, crowded country. They didn't. When my father led me and my 11-year-old sister to Greendale Elementary School, the grim-faced Yankee principal put the two of us in a class for the mentally retarded. There was no facility in those days for non-English-speaking children.

By the time I met Marjorie Hurd four years later, I had learned English, been placed in a normal, graded class and had even been chosen for the college preparatory track in the Worcester public school system. I was 13 years old when our father moved us yet again, and I entered Chandler Junior High shortly after the beginning of seventh grade. I found myself surrounded by richer, smarter and better-dressed classmates, who looked askance at my strange clothes and heavy accent. Shortly after I arrived, we were told to select a hobby to pursue during "club hour" on Fridays. The idea of hobbies and clubs made no sense to my immigrant ears, but I decided to follow the prettiest girl in my class—the blue-eyed daughter of the local Lutheran minister. She led me through the door marked "Newspaper Club" and into the presence of Miss Hurd, the newspaper adviser and English teacher who would become my <u>mentor</u> and my <u>muse</u>.

A <u>formidable</u>, solidly built woman with salt-and-pepper hair, a steely eye and a flat Boston accent, Miss Hurd had no patience with layabouts. "What are all you goof-offs doing here?" she bellowed at the would-be journalists. "This is the Newspaper Club! We're going to put out a *newspaper*. So if there's anybody in this room who doesn't like work, I suggest you go across to the Glee Club now, because you're going to work your tails off here!" 2

I was soon under Miss Hurd's spell. She did indeed teach us to put out a newspaper, skills I

1. **Eleni Gatzoyiannis** (ĕ-lĕ′nē gät′zô-yän′ĭs).

WORDS TO KNOW

authoritarian (ə-thôr′ĭ-târ′ē-ən) *adj.* expecting or demanding absolute obedience.
mentor (mĕn′tôr′) *n.* a wise and trusted teacher
muse (myo͞oz) *n.* a guiding spirit or source of inspiration
formidable (fôr′mĭ-də-bəl) *adj.* inspiring awe, fear, or wonder

Teaching Options

Mini Lesson: Preteaching Vocabulary

CONTEXT CLUES Call students' attention to the list of WORDS TO KNOW. Use the model sentence to demonstrate how they can use context clues to infer the meaning of an unfamiliar word. Context clues are not labeled and they will need to find the relevant material in the surrounding words and sentences.

Model Sentence Writing a research paper can be a <u>formidable</u> assignment until you break it into smaller tasks.

Instruction

- Write the model sentence on the chalkboard.
- Ask a volunteer to read the sentence and identify the relevant words that provide inferences to the meaning of the underlined word. Ask what the meaning of the underlined word could be. Circle the context clues and ask how they helped determine word meaning.

Possible Response: *formidable* could mean huge and overwhelming; the context clue *break it into smaller tasks* indicates a task that is large and could be a lot to handle.

Exercises

Read the following sentences. Ask students to use context clues to help them infer the meaning of the underlined word.

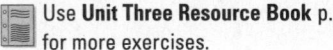

Passport photo of Nicholas Gage and three of his sisters. Courtesy of Nicholas Gage.

honed during my next 25 years as a journalist. Soon I asked the principal to transfer me to her English class as well. There, she drilled us on grammar until I finally began to understand the logic and structure of the English language. She assigned stories for us to read and discuss; not tales of heroes, like the Greek myths I knew, but stories of underdogs—poor people, even immigrants, who seemed ordinary until a crisis drove them to do something extraordinary. She also introduced us to the literary wealth of Greece—giving me a new perspective on my war-ravaged, impoverished homeland. I began to be proud of my origins.

One day, after discussing how writers should write about what they know, she assigned us to compose an essay from our own experience. Fixing me with a stern look, she added, "Nick, I want you to write about what happened to your family in Greece." I had been trying to put those painful memories behind me and left the assignment until the last moment. Then, on a warm spring afternoon, I sat in my room with a yellow pad and pencil and stared out the window at the buds on the trees. I wrote that the coming of spring always reminded me of the last time I said goodbye to my mother on a green and gold day in 1948.

I kept writing, one line after another, telling how the Communist guerrillas occupied our village, took our home and food, how my mother started planning our escape when she learned that the children were to be sent to re-education camps[2] behind the Iron Curtain[3] and

2. **re-education camps:** camps where people were forced to go to be indoctrinated with Communist ideas and beliefs.
3. **behind the Iron Curtain:** on the Communist side of the imaginary divide between the democracies of Western Europe and the Communist dictatorships of Eastern Europe; in this case, the camps were in Albania.

WORDS TO KNOW **hone** (hōn) *v.* to sharpen

Customizing Instruction

Less Proficient Readers

Ask students to summarize how Miss Hurd has affected Gage's life to this point in the story.

Possible Response: She has helped him learn English, introduced him to literature, and taught him to be proud of his origins.

Set a Purpose Have students read on to find out how Gage feels that Miss Hurd's class continued to affect his life in later years.

Students Acquiring English

1 Define *guerrillas* as "members of a rebel military force."

2 Define *salt-and-pepper hair* as "black hair that is turning white."

1. I didn't want to hurt my friend's feelings, so I used tact when I told her that her new dress didn't suit her.
2. "No, you may not go out until all your homework is done!" the father emphatically told his daughter.
3. Please don't sing "Happy Birthday" to me in the cafeteria. It would mortify me!
4. Not being able to button his old jeans was the catalyst that finally made Trent start exercising.
5. When Jason started his new job, he asked one of his more experienced colleagues to be his mentor.
6. When Cassie's best friend moved away, she felt a great void in her life.
7. Max is a very authoritarian boss. He fired one of his employees just for being five minutes late for work.
8. Some fashion designers have a favorite model who acts as a muse, inspiring them to create fabulous clothes.
9. This knife is dull! I need to hone it.

Use **Unit Three Resource Book** p. 54 for more exercises.

A lesson on context clues appears on p. 56 in the Pupil's Edition.

Reading and Analyzing

Reading Skills and Strategies: EVALUATING
Ask students whether President Reagan's decision to seek an arms agreement was indeed a fitting memorial to the author's mother.
Possible Response: Yes, the author's mother died crying out for her children. The arms agreement was intended to ensure that wars would never again separate children and parents; no, the arms agreement might allow bad regimes to stay in power.

Reading Skills and Strategies: SUMMARIZING
Have students summarize how Gage became successful.
Possible Response: He spent four years at Boston University, where he won the Hearst Award and scholarships to Columbia's Graduate School of Journalism.

Reading Skills and Strategies: CLARIFYING
A Ask students what Gage means by "she would alternately bully and charm each one with her own special brand of tough love until the spark caught fire."
Possible Response: Because she truly cared about her students, she would do whatever it took to get them to do their best.

Reading Skills and Strategies: CONNECTING
Miss Hurd has become an honorary member of Nick's family. Ask students if their families have "honorary" members. Ask them to share what these people mean to them.

how, at the last moment, she couldn't escape with us because the guerrillas sent her with a group of women to thresh wheat in a distant village. She promised she would try to get away on her own, she told me to be brave and hung a silver cross around my neck, and then she kissed me. I watched the line of women being led down into the ravine and up the other side, until they disappeared around the bend—my mother a tiny brown figure at the end who stopped for an instant to raise her hand in one last farewell.

For the first time I began to understand the power of the written word. A secret ambition took root in me.

I wrote about our nighttime escape down the mountain, across the minefields and into the lines of the Nationalist soldiers, who sent us to a refugee camp. It was there that we learned of our mother's execution. I felt very lucky to have come to America, I concluded, but every year, the coming of spring made me feel sad because it reminded me of the last time I saw my mother.

I handed in the essay, hoping never to see it again, but Miss Hurd had it published in the school paper. This mortified me at first, until I saw that my classmates reacted with sympathy and tact to my family's story. Without telling me, Miss Hurd also submitted the essay to a contest sponsored by the Freedoms Foundation at Valley Forge, Pa., and it won a medal. The Worcester paper wrote about the award and quoted my essay at length. My father, by then a "five-and-dime-store chef," as the paper described him, was ecstatic with pride, and the Worcester Greek community celebrated the honor to one of its own.

For the first time I began to understand the power of the written word. A secret ambition took root in me. One day, I vowed, I would go back to Greece, find out the details of my 1
mother's death and write about her life, so her grandchildren would know of her courage. Perhaps I would even track down the men who killed her and write of their crimes. Fulfilling that ambition would take me 30 years.

Meanwhile, I followed the literary path that Miss Hurd had so forcefully set me on. After junior high, I became the editor of my school paper at Classical High School and got a part-time job at the Worcester *Telegram and Gazette.* Although my father could only give me $50 and encouragement toward a college education, I managed to finance four years at Boston University with scholarships and part-time jobs in journalism. During my last year of college, an article I wrote about a friend who had died in the Philippines—the first person to lose his life working for the Peace Corps—led to my winning the Hearst Award for College Journalism. And the plaque was given to me in the White House by President John F. Kennedy.

For a refugee who had never seen a motorized vehicle or indoor plumbing until he was 9, this was an unimaginable honor. When the Worcester paper ran a picture of me standing next to President Kennedy, my father rushed out to buy a new suit in order to be properly dressed to receive the congratulations of the Worcester Greeks. He clipped out the photograph, had it laminated in plastic and carried it in his breast pocket for the rest of his life to show everyone he met. I found the much-worn photo in his

WORDS TO KNOW
mortify (môr'tə-fī') *v.* to cause to feel shame or humiliation
tact (tăkt) *n.* the sensitivity to say and do what is appropriate when dealing with other people

Teaching Options

Mini Lesson: Vocabulary Strategy

APPLYING MEANING OF ROOTS: *MORTIFY*
Instruction The word *mortify* is based on the Latin root *mort,* which means *death.* When Nick's essay appears in the school paper, he is initially mortified—feeling as though he will die from embarrassment. Other words based on the same root are *mortality, mortician,* and *mortuary.*
Practice Have students work in pairs to find the meaning of *mortality, mortician*, and *mortuary.* They may use a dictionary to help determine the precise meaning and usage. Ask them to use each word in a sentence. Ask them to explain how they can use knowledge of the root word *mort* to remember the meanings of these words.

Use **Vocabulary Transparencies and Copymasters,** p. 55.

pocket on the day he died 20 years later.

In our isolated Greek village, my mother had bribed a cousin to teach her to read, for girls were not supposed to attend school beyond a certain age. She had always dreamed of her children receiving an education. She couldn't be there when I graduated from Boston University, but the person who came with my father and shared our joy was my former teacher, Marjorie Hurd. We celebrated not only my bachelor's degree but also the scholarships that paid my way to Columbia's Graduate School of Journalism. There, I met the woman who would eventually become my wife. At our wedding and at the baptisms of our three children, Marjorie Hurd was always there, dancing alongside the Greeks.

By then, she was Mrs. Rabidou, for she had married a widower when she was in her early 40s. That didn't distract her from her vocation of introducing young minds to English literature, however. She taught for a total of 41 years and continually would make a "project" of some balky student in whom she spied a spark of potential. Often these were students from the most troubled homes, yet she would alternately bully and charm each one with her own special brand of tough love until the spark caught fire. She retired in 1981 at the age of 62 but still avidly follows the lives and careers of former students while overseeing her adult stepchildren and driving her husband on camping trips to New Hampshire.

A

Miss Hurd was one of the first to call me on Dec. 10, 1987, when President Reagan, in his television address after the summit meeting with Gorbachev,[4] told the nation that Eleni Gatzoyiannis's dying cry, "My children!" had helped inspire him to seek an arms agreement "for all the children of the world."

"I can't imagine a better monument for your mother," Miss Hurd said with an uncharacteristic catch in her voice.

Although a bad hip makes it impossible for her to join in the Greek dancing, Marjorie Hurd Rabidou is still an honored and enthusiastic guest at all our family celebrations, including my 50th birthday picnic last summer, where the shish kebab was cooked on spits, clarinets and *bouzoukis*[5] wailed, and costumed dancers led the guests in a serpentine line around our Colonial farmhouse, only 20 minutes from my first home in Worcester.

My sisters and I felt an aching void because my father was not there to lead the line, balancing a glass of wine on his head while he danced, the way he did at every celebration during his 92 years. But Miss Hurd was there, surveying the scene with quiet satisfaction. Although my parents are gone, her presence was a consolation, because I owe her so much.

She would alternately bully and charm each one with her own special brand of tough love until the spark caught fire.

This is truly the land of opportunity, and I would have enjoyed its bounty even if I hadn't walked into Miss Hurd's classroom in 1953. But she was the one who directed my grief and

4. **summit meeting with Gorbachev** (gôr′bə-chôf′): a high-level meeting between U.S. president Ronald Reagan and Mikhail Gorbachev, the last premier of the Soviet Union.

5. ***bouzoukis*** (bŏŏ-zōō′kēz): traditional Greek stringed instruments resembling mandolins.

WORDS TO KNOW

void *n.* a feeling of loss; emptiness

Customizing Instruction

Less Proficient Readers

Have students explain what Gage's father does with the photograph of his son with President Kennedy and what this detail tells the reader about the father.

Possible Response: He carries the photo with him at all times and shows it to people he meets. He is intensely proud of his son.

Students Acquiring English

1 To help students understand the strength of Gage's ambition as indicated by the phrase "took root in me," encourage them to visualize a tree's roots—how solidly they are lodged in the ground and how much strength it takes to pull them out.

Gifted and Talented

Have students discuss how much Gage really owes to Miss Hurd for his success as an investigative reporter and writer: Would his ability have come to the fore anyway, even without Miss Hurd's help? Or do we need a catalyst to spark our creative talents?

Assessment Informal Assessment

CAUSE AND EFFECT You can informally assess students' understanding of the selection by having students perceive the cause-and-effect relationship implied in the following quotation:

Miss Hurd and Nicholas Gage are talking at Gage's 50th birthday party. The conversation turns to Gage's experiences in Miss Hurd's classroom and how they affected him later.

RUBRIC

3 **Full Accomplishment** Students accurately and concisely bring out specific details from the essay that show how Gage's experiences in Miss Hurd's classroom affected him.

2 **Substantial Accomplishment** Students describe events from the essay, but they do not clearly express the effect Miss Hurd had on the author.

1 **Little or Partial Accomplishment** Students have difficulty expressing events from the essay.

Reading and Analyzing

Literary Analysis: ESSAY

Ask students what the final paragraph tells about the author's purpose for writing this essay.

Possible Response: He is writing to express his gratitude to Miss Hurd while she is still alive.

Reading Skills and Strategies: CONNECTING

Ask students if anyone has been a catalyst for change in their lives, even if in just a small way.

Pictured at left, Marjorie Hurd Rabidou and Nicholas Gage. Copyright © Eddie Adams / SYGMA. At right, Nicholas Gage and his family at the harbor in Piraeus, Greece, ready to set out for the United States. Courtesy of Nicholas Gage.

pain into writing, and if it weren't for her, I wouldn't have become an investigative reporter and foreign correspondent, recorded the story of my mother's life and death in *Eleni* and now my father's story in *A Place for Us,* which is also a testament to the country that took us in. She was the catalyst that sent me into journalism and indirectly caused all the good things that came after. But Miss Hurd would probably deny this emphatically.

A few years ago, I answered the telephone and heard my former teacher's voice telling me, in that won't-take-no-for-an-answer tone of hers, that she had decided I was to write and deliver the eulogy at her funeral. I agreed (she didn't leave me any choice), but that's one assignment I never want to do. I hope, Miss Hurd, that you'll accept this remembrance instead. ❖

WORDS TO KNOW

catalyst (kăt'l-ĭst) *n.* something that causes change or action
emphatically (ĕm-făt'ĭ-klē) *adv.* forcefully; strongly

Teaching Options

Mini Lesson: Viewing and Representing

Instruction Have students study the early photograph of Gage and his sisters, as well as the photos on pages 485 and 490. Ask students what they can tell from the expressions on the children's faces. Ask what details in the pictures help them better understand Gage's experience as a newcomer to this country.

Possible Response: The children look serious and sad. They probably feel alone and afraid, because they've lost their mother and everything is new and unfamiliar to them.

Application Ask students to study the two photos on page 490, then think of adjectives that describe the mood of each one. Ask volunteers for their adjectives, and write them on the chalkboard in two columns headed *Adult Nick* and *Young Nick*. Have students discuss the two lists and give reasons for their choices.

Possible Response: Young Nick: tense, serious, anxious; Adult Nick: happy, prosperous, relaxed, confident. Young Nick is on the brink of a frightening journey to a new land. Adult Nick is a successful writer, fulfilling the goals he dreamed of as a young student.

Connect to the Literature

1. **What Do You Think?** What words and phrases sum up your response to this selection? Discuss them with a classmate.

Comprehension Check
- Why did Gage and his sisters come to the United States?
- What did Miss Hurd ask Gage to write about?
- What career did Gage pursue?
- How does Miss Hurd continue to play a role in the author's life?

Think Critically

2. What do you think were the most important effects that Miss Hurd had on the author's life?

THINK ABOUT
- the hardships of Nicholas Gage's childhood
- Miss Hurd's essay assignment
- their friendship

3. Gage says that Miss Hurd would probably deny that she "was the catalyst that sent [him] into journalism and indirectly caused all the good things that came after." Why do you think he says this?

THINK ABOUT
- what you learned about her personality and teaching style
- how she might view his tribute to her influence

4. **ACTIVE READING** DISTINGUISHING FACT FROM NONFACT
Review the notes in your READER'S NOTEBOOK. What are the basic **facts** that the essay presents about the author's experiences in his homeland after World War II? What do you learn about the way the author felt about these events? To what extent do you think the facts presented in Gage's essay give weight to his account of the feelings and opinions he had in his youth?

5. What personal qualities do you think helped Nicholas Gage to succeed in his adopted homeland?

Extend Interpretations

6. **Comparing Texts** Compare and contrast the influence of Miss Hurd on Nicholas Gage with the influence of the grandfather on Rudolfo Anaya in "A Celebration of Grandfathers" (page 455).

7. **Connect to Life** Would you want Miss Hurd for your teacher? Give reasons for your answer.

Literary Analysis

AUDIENCE Every writer has some sense of the **audience** for whom he or she is writing. Gage's essay was written for a general audience and published in a newspaper supplement. To gain insight into the relationship between Gage and his audience, imagine that he considered the following questions while he was writing the essay:
- Why will readers want to read this essay?
- How do I want them to feel after reading the essay?
- What does the general public already know about the situation in Greece after World War II?
- What more do I want them to know and why?
- What details would they find most interesting?
- How can I make the information easy for readers to follow?
- What kind of language will be most appropriate?

The **details** Gage includes, the level of **diction** he uses, and the attitude he expresses toward his subject are all influenced by his sense of who his readers—or audience—would be.

Paired Activity How might Gage's account differ if he had chosen a different audience? Imagine, for example, that he was writing for a Greek audience who knew about the civil war in their own land but were unaware of aspects of life in the United States that might take an immigrant by surprise. Discuss with a partner how writing for this different audience might change the focus of Gage's essay.

GUIDING STUDENT RESPONSE

Connect to the Literature

1. **What Do You Think?**
Students may feel inspired or reflective.

Comprehension Check
- They wanted to escape the Communist guerrillas in Greece during a civil war.
- She asked him to write about what happened to his family in Greece.
- Gage became a journalist and an author.
- She attends family events and is a good friend.

Use Selection Quiz
Unit Three Resource Book p. 56.

Think Critically

2. Possible Responses: Her affirmation of his writing ability may have been the most important effect. Miss Hurd helped Gage come to terms with the hardships of his life. She encouraged him to take pride in his past. She helped him develop his talent and continued her encouragement throughout Gage's adulthood.
3. Possible Responses: Miss Hurd's tough, no-nonsense style might make it difficult for her to accept Gage's praise. She might also feel that Gage was downplaying his own talent.
4. Students should be careful to distinguish facts from opinions. They should evaluate the credibility of information sources including how the writer's motivation may affect credibility.
Possible Responses: Communist guerrillas occupied his village, sending children to reeducation camps. They sent his mother to thresh wheat so she could not escape with them, then executed her for sending her children away. Readers learn that Gage felt sad about the loss of his mother and that in the beginning he resented his father for not saving the whole family. He wanted to find her killers. Students may say that the facts justify Gage's feelings.
5. Possible Response: Students might say that Gage succeeded because he valued education and set goals for himself.

Extend Interpretations

Comparing Texts
Possible Responses:
Similarities
- Both adults shape the lives and values of young boys.
- Both elicit lasting respect and gratitude.

Differences
- Miss Hurd decided to take Nicholas under her wing, whereas the grandfather was related to Rudolfo.
- Gage pursued the career for which Miss Hurd prepared him, whereas Rudolfo became a writer instead of a farmer.

Connect to Life Students answering yes might point out that she tried to bring out the best in her students. Those answering no might find Miss Hurd's teaching style too intimidating and her demands too exacting.

Literary Analysis

Audience The content of the essay would include facts and nonfacts about life in the U.S. The essay would then have a different purpose.

Writing Options

1. **Character Sketch** Students may wish to use dialogue or a telling anecdote to profile their character.
2. **Oral History Notes** Have students recall specific details and events that show the person's lasting impression. Students may wish to use as a starting point the thoughts they jotted down for Connect to Your Life on page 484.

Activities & Explorations

1. **Father's Monologue** In performing their monologues, students might like to use a prop, such as the laminated photograph of Gage and John F. Kennedy.
2. **Qualities List** Have students recall the best teachers they have had and the characteristics they liked most about them. One group member can record the three or four most important characteristics, based on the group's discussion. Students can review the selection for details about Miss Hurd, then decide which criteria these examples illustrate.
3. **Photo Essay** Students might cluster photographs around certain character traits, revealing the subject's personality. They might display photographs chronologically, perhaps under the heads "Before" and "After," showing the subject's influence over time.

Inquiry & Research

A Nation Torn Ask students to share their summaries in an oral report or a visual display.

Students' written summaries should include main ideas and supporting details.

Vocabulary in Action

1. f
2. i
3. b
4. h
5. j
6. c
7. e
8. a
9. g
10. d

Choices & CHALLENGES

Writing Options

1. **Character Sketch** Describe either Nicholas Gage or Miss Hurd in a character sketch. Include details from the selection.
2. **Oral History Notes** Think of a person who has had a great impact on your life. Write the introductory notes for an oral history in which you explain what effect that person has had on your life. Place the notes in your **Working Portfolio.**

Activities & Explorations

1. **Father's Monologue** Imagine that you are the author's father. Perform a dramatic monologue in which you tell the story of your son's life and explain your feelings about him. ~ **PERFORMING**
2. **Qualities List** Work with a small group to list the characteristics you think are necessary in a good teacher. Then evaluate Miss Hurd in terms of those characteristics, citing evidence from the selection to support your evaluation. Share your findings with the rest of the class. ~ **SPEAKING AND LISTENING**
3. **Photo Essay** Create a photo essay about someone who has influenced your life. Include captions that explain what the photographs depict. ~ **VIEWING AND REPRESENTING**

Inquiry & Research

A Nation Torn Find out more about the bitter civil war that was waged in Greece after World War II. What was the outcome of the war? Summarize your findings in a short written report.

More Online: Research Starter
www.mcdougallittell.com

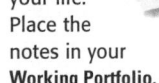

A young boy sits in the ruins of his home during the Greek Civil War.

Vocabulary in Action

EXERCISE: ASSESSMENT PRACTICE Match each word on the left with the word on the right that is most nearly opposite in meaning. Use each word only once.

1. authoritarian	a. fullness
2. mentor	b. opponent
3. muse	c. flatter
4. formidable	d. weakly
5. hone	e. awkwardness
6. mortify	f. lenient
7. tact	g. result
8. void	h. unimpressive
9. catalyst	i. pupil
10. emphatically	j. dull

Building Vocabulary

For an in-depth lesson on context clues involving antonyms and synonyms, see page 1000.

WORDS TO KNOW				
	authoritarian	formidable	mortify	void
	catalyst	hone	muse	
	emphatically	mentor	tact	

Mini Lesson Grammar

VERB TENSES Remind students that the tense of a verb tells when the action in the sentence takes place. For example, the past tense tells that the action took place in the past, while the future tense expresses an action that will occur. Remind students that the present tense either names an action that occurs regularly or expresses a general truth. Then write the sentences on the chalkboard.

"Gage sees the United States as the land of opportunity."

"Miss Hurd gave young Nick a sense of his potential and the confidence to develop it."

"Gage's work will inspire young people today."

Underline the verbs as shown. Have students identify the verb tenses and explain what each tense tells about the time that an action takes place.

Next point out to students that the perfect tenses of verbs name actions that occurred at an indefinite time. Write on the chalkboard the examples below.

"Gage has written a work of extraordinary power."

"Nick had been ashamed of his origins, until Miss Hurd revealed to him the literary richness of ancient Greece."

Explain that the verb *has written* is in the present perfect tense, which names an action that happened at an indefinite time in the past or an action that happened in the past and is still

Grammar in Context: Participles

In this excerpt, Nicholas Gage uses participles in describing his 50th birthday party.

> **My sisters and I felt an aching void because my father was not there to lead the line, balancing a glass of wine on his head while he danced, the way he did at every celebration during his 92 years. But Miss Hurd was there, surveying the scene with quiet satisfaction.**

A **participle** is a verb form that functions as an adjective, modifying a noun or pronoun. In this passage, Gage uses three participles in the course of creating a lively description. The participle *aching* modifies the noun *void, balancing* modifies *father,* and *surveying* modifies *Miss Hurd.* Notice how each participle is associated with a different person or group, establishing a nice balance.

There are two kinds of participles: **present participles** and **past participles.** Present participles end in *-ing;* past participles of many verbs end in *-d* or *-ed.* The following diagram shows how one of the participles in the example was formed.

VERB: *ache* → PRESENT PARTICIPLE: *aching* → PARTICIPLE + NOUN: *aching void*

WRITING EXERCISE Rewrite each sentence, adding a participle that modifies the underlined word. Use at least two past participles.

Usage Tip: Remember that a participle always modifies a noun or pronoun.

Example: ***Original*** Miss Hurd was a teacher.

Rewritten Miss Hurd was an inspiring teacher.

1. Everyone jumped at the sound of Miss Hurd's voice.
2. It was difficult to write about my family's experience.
3. Miss Hurd often gave me suggestions.
4. I felt very proud when I opened the newspaper and saw my story.

Grammar Handbook Participles and Participial Phrases, p. 1196

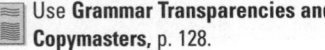

Nicholas Gage

1939–

Other Works
Eleni
Hellas: A Portrait of Greece
A Place for Us

Journalistic Career Miss Hurd's influence helped launch Nicholas Gage (originally Nikola Gatzoyiannis) on a remarkable career as an investigative reporter. For the *Boston Herald Traveler* he exposed shocking conditions at a school for the mentally retarded; for the *Wall Street Journal* he reported on organized crime in both the United States and Great Britain. In 1970 Gage was recruited by the *New York Times.* While there, he wrote news stories on a number of controversial issues, including drug trafficking and government corruption in Latin America and an attempt to sell New York's Metropolitan Museum of Art a fake vase for a million dollars. During this time he also wrote two novels, as well as nonfiction about his native Greece.

Search for Justice In 1980 Gage retired from journalism to devote all his time to researching a book about his mother. His investigations led him to the man responsible for his mother's death, whom he considered killing. In the end, however, he refused to exact vengeance, realizing that to do so would be to "become like him, purging myself as he did of all humanity or compassion."

Author Activity

Read excerpts from *Eleni,* Nicholas Gage's 1983 book about his mother, or view the 1985 movie adaptation on videocassette. Then summarize the book or film in an oral report to classmates.

Grammar in Context

WRITING EXERCISE Answers will vary. Possible answers are shown.

1. Everyone jumped at the sound of Miss Hurd's commanding voice.
2. It was difficult to write about my family's terrifying experience.
3. Miss Hurd often gave me encouraging suggestions.
4. I felt very proud when I opened the newspaper and saw my published story.

Author Activity

Encourage students to make a story map of events as they read or watch *Eleni.* When they plan their summaries, they can refer to these maps to determine the key events in the narrative.

happening now. The verb *had been ashamed* is in the past perfect tense. This tense names an action that happened before another action or event in the past.

Practice Have students copy the following sentences. Ask them to underline the verbs and identify their tense.

1. Nick's mother made a plan for her children's escape.
   Answer: *made; past*
2. Gage will always value the friendship of Miss Hurd.
   Answer: *will value; future*
3. Nick had experienced great loss before he landed in the United States at age nine.
   Answer: *had experienced; past perfect*
4. Winning a prize inspires the young Nick to pursue his dream.
   Answer: *inspires; present*
5. Gage's teacher has observed him for years and years.
   Answer: *has observed; present perfect*

Use **Grammar Transparencies and Copymasters,** p. 128.

Use McDougal Littell's ***Language Network,*** Chapter 6, for more instruction on verb tenses.

THE TEACHER WHO CHANGED MY LIFE **493**

Building Vocabulary

Objectives
- expand vocabulary through wide and varied reading
- rely on context to determine the meaning of multiple-meaning words
- distinguish between denotative and connotative meanings of words

VOCABULARY EXERCISE
Word choice in chart will vary.

Synonyms and Shades of Meaning

Changing a single word in a sentence can affect the tone of a passage or alter its entire meaning. Read the excerpt on the right from "The Teacher Who Changed My Life," and think about the narrator's use of the word *portly* to describe his father.

> **The portly, bald, well dressed man who met me and my sisters seemed a foreign, authoritarian figure.**
> —Nicholas Gage, "The Teacher Who Changed My Life"

The author could have used any one of several synonyms for *portly*. *Fat*, *chubby*, *plump*, and *stout* all have the same **denotation,** or literal meaning. However, these words also have implied meanings, or **connotations,** which differ. *Fat* carries negative connotations that are too derogatory for the father. *Chubby* and *plump* have too-pleasant connotations to apply to someone who seems like an "authoritarian figure." *Stout* lacks the implications of stateliness and dignity that *portly* connotes. Therefore, *portly* is the best word choice to describe Gage's father.

Strategies for Building Vocabulary

When you read and write, you need to be aware of both the implied meanings of words and the literal meanings of words. An awareness of connotations leads to deeper understanding in your reading and to better word choice in your writing.

❶ **Go Beyond the Literal Meaning** Be sensitive to any emotional meanings of words a writer might have intended. Writers often bring a particular attitude, or **tone,** to their stories; this is conveyed in their choice of words. The connotations of a word can reveal the writer's opinion or reveal what a character thinks. In the following example, consider how the narrator's impressions of Mrs. O'Brien are revealed by his choice of the word *saucy* to describe her manner of speaking.

> **"Why, then indeed I do, and more along with it," she added in the same saucy tone, though the meaning of what she said was not clear to me.**
> —Frank O'Connor, "The Study of History"

Saucy connotes an "exceeding of the limits of good manners, but in an entertaining way" and characterizes Mrs. O'Brien as good-naturedly irreverent.

❷ **Consider the Connotation** In your own writing, when you are trying to choose the best word to use from among various synonyms, think about their connotations. The differences in implied meanings among synonyms can be subtle. The emotions that synonyms evoke can range from positive to negative. Study the chart below, which shows synonyms of *reveal* and their connotations.

Synonyms for *reveal*

Positive Connotation	Neutral Connotation	Negative Connotation
enlighten	tell	unmask
impart	disclose	expose

❸ **Consider the Connotation** A dictionary can sometimes help you weigh the connotative differences between synonyms so that you can choose the word that fits your intentions. The dictionary excerpt below explains the connotations of synonyms of the word *anger*.

> **SYNONYMS: *Anger,* the most general, is strong displeasure. . . . *Rage* and *fury* are closely related in the sense of intense, explosive, often destructive emotion. . . . *Resentment* refers to ill will and smoldering anger generated by a sense of grievance. . . . *Indignation* is righteous anger at something regarded as being wrongful, unjust, or evil.**
> —*The American Heritage Dictionary of the English Language*

EXERCISE From the selections you read in this unit, choose one word that has several synonyms with different connotations (such as *old* or *powerful*). Make a chart like the one above for your word.

AFRO-AMERICAN FRAGMENT

LANGSTON HUGHES

Langston Hughes was among the foremost figures in 20th-century African-American literature. In this poem, Hughes reflects upon the continuing power of an African heritage from which he is far removed.

So long,
So far away
Is Africa.
Not even memories alive
Save those that history books create,
Save those that songs
Beat back into the blood—
Beat out of blood with words sad-sung
In strange un-Negro tongue—
So long,
So far away
Is Africa.

Subdued and time-lost
Are the drums—and yet
Through some vast mist of race
There comes this song
I do not understand,
This song of atavistic[1] land,
Of bitter yearnings lost
Without a place—
So long,
So far away
Is Africa's
Dark face.

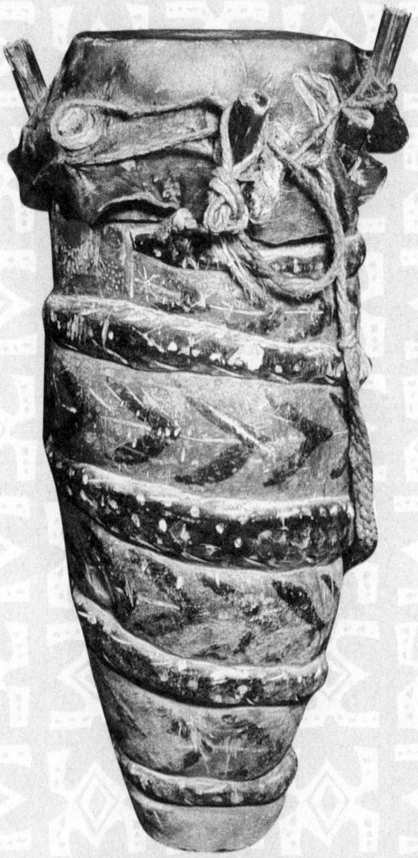

Haitian drum (1940s), artist unknown. Wood and goat skin, 43 × 24 × 24 inches. Collection of Virgil Young.

1. **atavistic** (ăt′ə-vĭs′tĭk): showing a recurrence of characteristics possessed by remote ancestors.

ON YOUR OWN

Possible Objectives

You can use these poems to achieve one or more of the following objectives:

- enjoy silent sustained reading (Option One)
- read and analyze literature with a group (Option Two)
- use the Reader's Notebook to formulate questions about literature (Option Three)
- write in response to literature (Option Three)

Summary

In "Afro-American Fragment," Langston Hughes laments being disconnected from his African heritage.

Judith Wright's "Bora Ring" recognizes Aboriginal heritage as still powerful, even though progress has all but eradicated this culture from Australia.

Reading the Selection

Option One
Silent Sustained Reading

You might set aside time each week for independent reading. During this time, you and all of your students would read for enjoyment. "Afro-American Fragment" and "Bora Ring" will appeal to many students and can be read independently in about ten minutes. If you want to encourage students to read for pleasure, you might forego assignments related to the poems. Should you want to make assignments, Options Two and Three offer suggestions.

Option Two
Shared Reading Groups

You may assign students to groups or allow them to choose their own. Students can read the poems together, alternately reading stanzas aloud, or they can read independently and meet to cooperate in a project that examines some element of the poems.

Possible Projects

- Students can participate in a choral or a dramatic reading of the poems. Suggest to students that they pay special attention to the repetition and the rhythm in each poem.
- Students can use a sketch pad to illustrate the vivid imagery depicted in each poem.

BORA RING

JUDITH WRIGHT

Before the English began to colonize Australia at the end of the 18th century, the Australian aborigines (ăb'ə-rĭj'ə-nēz)*—the native peoples of the continent—probably numbered around 300,000. Seminomadic and dependent on the natural environment for survival, they felt a deep spiritual connection to the land and marked life's passages—such as birth, maturity, marriage, and death—with sacred rituals and ceremonies. The bora ritual, performed in a "bora ring," celebrated a boy's entry into manhood.*

English colonization greatly reduced the number of Australian aborigines and destroyed much of their way of life. Bloodshed, disease, forced resettlement, agricultural expansion, and urbanization all contributed to the destruction of their traditional culture.

The song is gone; the dance
is secret with the dancers in the earth,
the ritual useless, and the tribal story
lost in an alien tale.

Only the grass stands up
to mark the dancing-ring: the apple-gums
posture and mime a past corroboree,
murmur a broken chant.

The hunter is gone: the spear
is splintered underground; the painted bodies
a dream the world breathed sleeping and forgot.
The nomad feet are still.

Only the rider's heart
halts at a sightless shadow, an unsaid word
that fastens in the blood the ancient curse,
the fear as old as Cain.

6 apple-gums: eucalyptus trees, native to Australia.

7 corroboree (kə-rŏb′ə-rē): a nighttime festival in which the Australian aborigines celebrate important events with songs and symbolic dances.

16 Cain (kān): the eldest son of Adam and Eve, who was condemned to be a fugitive after he murdered his brother Abel out of jealousy.

Rock engravings done by aborigines in eastern Australia. Superstock.

497

Option Three
Reader's Notebook

Provide the following direction to students before they read:

Summarize the theme in "Afro-American Fragment" and "Bora Ring."

Tell students to read the poem, pausing at the end of "Afro-American Fragment." At that point, students should summarize the poem's theme in their Reader's Notebook. Have them identify poetic devices, such as figurative language, alliteration, and rhyme or rhythm. Students should repeat this exercise after reading "Bora Ring."

After reading both poems, students will return to their summaries. Ask students to note similarities and differences between the poems. Have them choose the poem they prefer and support their opinion using details from the poem.

After Reading

Possible Activities

Independent Activities

- Invite students to write their own poems in response to "Afro-American Fragment." Suggest that they begin by analyzing the poem for themes and poetic devices they would like to use.
- Assign students to choose and research aspects of Australian Aboriginal culture. Possible topics include
  - **a.** family and tribal relationships
  - **b.** bark and stone painting
  - **c.** "Dreaming" religious beliefs
  - **d.** the purpose of body painting
- Have students review the Learning the Language of Literature and Active Reader, pages 452–454. They can note which skills and strategies they used while reading the selections.

Discussion Activities

- Use the thematic summaries formulated by students as the start of a discussion about these poignant poems.
- Ask students why they think Hughes uses repetition in "Afro-American Fragment."
- Invite students to think about the concluding stanza of "Bora Ring." Ask them how the story of Cain and Abel applies to the poem.

Assessment Opportunities

- You can assess student comprehension of each poem by evaluating the summaries students formulate in their Reader's Notebooks.
- You can use any of the discussion questions as essay questions.
- You can have students turn any one of their Reader's Notebook entries into an essay.

Langston Hughes
1902–1967

Other Works
The Big Sea
The Dream Keeper and Other Poems
I Wonder As I Wander

Early Success Born in Joplin, Missouri, James Langston Hughes was the son of a schoolteacher mother and a businessman father who separated soon after his birth. Until he was 12, he was raised principally by his grandmother. After her death, he lived with his mother and stepfather, eventually settling in Cleveland, Ohio. At the age of 19, Hughes published the poem "The Negro Speaks of Rivers" in a prestigious magazine. During the same year, he moved to New York City, where he briefly attended Columbia University.

Seizing the Moment Hughes next held a series of varied jobs that took him to Africa and Europe as a sailor and to Paris, where he worked as a cook. On returning to the United States, he took a job as a busboy at a Washington, D.C., hotel, where one night he served the famous American poet Vachel Lindsay. Hughes daringly dropped a few of his poems beside Lindsay's plate; Lindsay was so impressed that he read them aloud at a poetry recital he attended that very night. Soon afterward, Hughes had his poetry published in the African-American journal *Opportunity* and in a now-famous volume, *The Weary Blues* (1926).

Renaissance Years Settling in Harlem, the New York City neighborhood that was a mecca for African-American artists in the 1920s, Hughes began a long and influential career marked by achievements in virtually every form of literature—plays, novels, short stories, essays, biographies, and, of course, poetry. He also championed the careers of younger black writers and edited several anthologies of African and African-American literature.

Judith Wright
1915–

Other Works
Woman to Man
The Generations of Men
Because I Was Invited
The Double Tree

Australian Upbringing The acclaimed poet Judith Wright is a descendant of English settlers who arrived on the continent of Australia in 1828. She grew up in a small farming town in the New England district of the Australian state of New South Wales. Educated at home until she was 13, she spent much of her childhood out of doors, on horseback. "The country was deep in my bones," she recalls, "and I loved to look at it."

Recurrent Themes Wright attended the University of Sydney and then traveled in Europe for a year before returning to Australia and embarking on a literary career. "Bora Ring" appeared in Wright's first volume of poetry, *The Moving Image,* which was published in 1946. The poems in this collection and in *Woman to Man,* which followed in 1949, concern the plight of Australian aborigines, the role of women, and the need to protect Australia's natural landscape. These themes have continued to concern the poet throughout her writing career, during which she has produced more than a dozen volumes of verse, as well as short stories, essays, children's books, and plays.

Active Environmentalist Wright helped found a wildlife preservation society in Queensland, Australia, and she has fought to preserve Australia's Great Barrier Reef, to establish national parks, and to protect the land from deforestation. "Four generations of my forebears spent a lot of their time battling against Australian trees," she once observed; ". . . I spend a good deal of my time in the reverse process, battling *for* trees."

Author Study

ALICE WALKER

OVERVIEW

"A fine human being saving her soul through good deeds and extraordinary writing"

—Derrick Bell

A Life of Activism and Writing

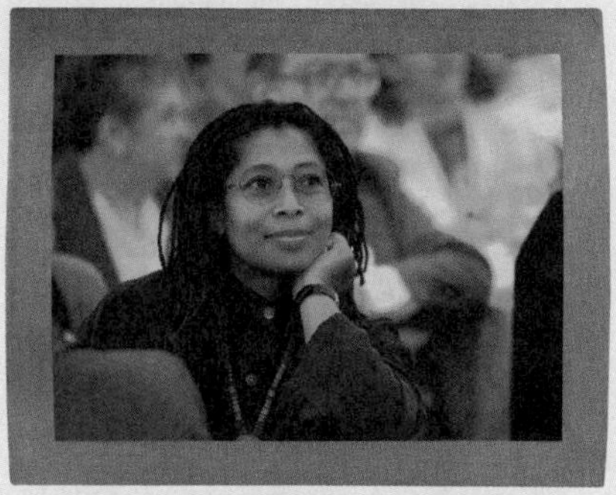

1944–

Alice Walker has used her writing and her fame to fight against social injustices. In her poetry, fiction, and nonfiction, she often focuses on African-American women's struggle to survive in the face of poverty, racism, and sexism. But she also affirms the richness and the deeply spiritual traditions in the black community and the belief that people can change their lives despite seemingly overwhelming obstacles.

(A) A TIME OF HARDSHIP AND UNITY Alice Walker was born in Eatonton, Georgia, in 1944, a time of legal segregation and organized violence against African-Americans. She was the last of eight children in a family of sharecroppers. Despite the dual oppressions of racism and poverty, the young Walker grew up in a black community that nurtured and protected its children. As an adult, Walker recognized this supportive environment as an important part of her heritage.

HER LIFE

1944 **Is born in Eatonton, Georgia**

1952 **Loses sight in one eye in childhood accident and is temporarily disfigured**

1945 1950 1955

HER TIMES

1941 **The United States enters World War II after Pearl Harbor is attacked.**

1950 **Poet Gwendolyn Brooks is first African American to win Pulitzer Prize.**

1954 **In *Brown* v. *Board of Education*, Supreme Court declares segregated schools unconstitutional.**

Linda Brown

499

Author Study

OVERVIEW

Objectives

- appreciate the craft of one of America's premiere African-American authors
- recognize distinctive characteristics of Walker's culture through reading
- connect to Walker's experiences through reading her selections
- gain information about Walker by reading nonfiction

Presenting the Author

The Author Study offers a unique opportunity for students to focus on the work of a major writer. In addition, students can gather information about the life of Alice Walker, gaining insight into the real person behind her famous literary works.

PREVIEW

Using Text Organizers

Have students preview the article noting the basic text organizers: title, subheads, images and captions, and time line. Ask students to describe the information they would expect to find in each section. Have students use the subheads to create an outline or graphic organizer. As they read, suggest they categorize information from the article under the appropriate heading. Remind them that they should use similar text organizers to help them locate and categorize information as they do independent research.

Flannery O'Connor

(A) Alice Walker and her family lived in a sharecropper's shack on the Eatonton-to-Milledgeville Road in rural Georgia, near the home of Flannery O'Connor. In 1974, Walker and her mother visited O'Connor's home outside of Milledgeville. In an essay from *In Search of Our Mothers' Gardens,* Walker angrily compares O'Connor's estate to the rotting four-room tenant shack where Walker's family had lived. In her fiction, O'Connor portrayed white Southern characters as grotesque and bigoted. She used violence and humor to communicate the theme of redemption through God's grace. Most importantly for Walker, O'Connor wrote honestly about the South. O'Connor died of lupus in 1964, about the time Walker discovered O'Connor's work at Sarah Lawrence College.

LIFE AND TIMES

Higher Education

A Spelman College was founded in 1881 by Sophia B. Packard and Harriet E. Giles as Atlanta Baptist Female Seminary. Packard and Giles had formed the school for African-American girls in 1870. This date marked the end of the Freedman's Bureau, which laid the foundation of an educational system for ex-slaves. Early in its life, the school received the patronage of John D. Rockefeller. In honor of Mrs. Rockefeller's parents, Packard and Giles changed the school's name in 1884 to Spelman Seminary. Spelman's primary purpose was to provide training for teachers and church workers, and later, for nurses. The school held its first graduation in 1887.

Social Protest

B African-American college students staged a sit-in in Greensboro, North Carolina. The tactic spread quickly with demonstrations organized by the newly formed Student Nonviolent Coordinating Committee. College students in Atlanta began to sit in at segregated lunch counters and those that refused to serve African Americans. Students started their demonstrations with ads in two of Atlanta's newspapers appealing for human rights. Lunch counters would often close rather than serve the protesters, so organizers would direct students to sit in at another store's lunch counter. The leaders of the Atlanta sit-ins synchronized demonstrations and reported to one another on walkie-talkies. The sit-in movement proved to be successful in desegregating public accommodations.

LITERARY *Contributions*

Poetry Alice Walker first made her name as a poet, and her reputation has grown with the following works:

- ***Once: Poems*** (1968)
- ***Revolutionary Petunias and Other Poems*** (1973)
- ***Horses Make a Landscape Look More Beautiful*** (1984)
- ***Her Blue Body Everything We Know: Earthling Poems 1965–1990*** (1991)

Fiction Walker is probably best known for her novels and short stories:

- ***The Third Life of Grange Copeland*** (1970)
- ***In Love and Trouble: Stories of Black Women*** (1973)
- ***The Color Purple*** (1982)
- ***The Temple of My Familiar*** (1989)
- ***Possessing the Secret of Joy*** (1992)

Nonfiction Walker has written about her life and her vision in nonfiction:

- ***In Search of Our Mothers' Gardens: Womanist Prose*** (1983)
- ***The Same River Twice: Honoring the Difficult*** (1996)
- ***Anything We Love Can Be Saved: A Writer's Activism*** (1997)

Within this setting, the greatest influence in Walker's life was her mother, Minnie Tallulah Grant Walker. From her mother, Walker became aware of the inner strength of African-American women, who, despite their lack of choices, maintained their independence and fought for a better future for their children. Walker has claimed that her own assurance and strength come from her mother and her aunts: "It is because of them, I know women can do anything."

PERSONAL STRUGGLE AND GROWTH When Walker was eight years old, one of her brothers accidentally shot her in the eye with a BB gun. She lost sight in one eye and had a disfiguring scar, which made her intensely self-conscious. "For six years I do not stare at anyone, because I do not raise my head," she explained later. It was at this time that she started to write poems and to notice the importance of relationships in her life. When she was 14, a simple operation removed the physical scar, but the effects of being an outcast remained.

Thanks to money raised by her community and a scholarship from the state of Georgia, Walker enrolled **A** at Spelman College in Atlanta in 1961. At Spelman, the oldest college for African-American women in the United States, Walker embraced the civil rights movement that was sweeping through the South. She **B** described herself and her fellow protesters as "young and bursting with fear and determination to change our world."

1961 **Enters Spelman College in Atlanta**

1964 **Travels to Uganda as exchange student**

1965 **Graduates from Sarah Lawrence College**

1967 **Marries Melvyn Leventhal**

1969 **Daughter, Rebecca, is born**

1960 — 1965 — 1970

Rosa Parks

1955 **Black riders boycott buses in Montgomery, Alabama, to protest segregated seating.**

1961 **Freedom Riders try to desegregate public transportation in the South.**

1963 **Martin Luther King, Jr., leads March on Washington; publication of Betty Friedan's *The Feminine Mystique* launches the modern feminist movement in the United States.**

1968 **Martin Luther King, Jr., is assassinated in Memphis.**

1970 **Maya Angelou publishes *I Know Why the Caged Bird Sings*.**

After two years at Spelman, Walker transferred to Sarah Lawrence College in New York. There Walker discovered feminism and realized that sexism was as great a barrier for African-American women as racism. During her senior year, Walker experienced a period of loneliness and despair. Supported emotionally by her college friends and thoughts of her family and community back home, Walker gradually emerged from her depression and feverishly began to write a series of poems. These poems were eventually published, starting Walker on the road to health and a career in writing.

A Life of Activism and Writing

Shortly after college graduation, Walker returned to the South to work in voter-registration drives. Here she met and eventually married Melvyn Leventhal, a civil rights lawyer, in 1967. Her first book, *Once: Poems*, was published in 1968, and the birth (C) of her daughter, Rebecca, followed in 1969. Her first novel, *The Third Life of Grange Copeland*, came out in 1970. Throughout the 1970s, Walker regularly published stories and poems and taught at various colleges and universities.

(D) In 1976, Walker divorced her husband and eventually moved to San Francisco with her daughter. It was during this time that she began writing *The Color Purple*, the novel that would make her famous. By 1985, with the release of the film version of (E) *The Color Purple* directed by Steven Spielberg, Alice Walker had become a household name.

Scenes from *The Color Purple* (1985)

With fame, however, came controversy. Walker was one of the first African-American women to publicly take up the cause of feminism. Some civil rights activists felt that Walker's attack on sexism in the black community amounted to a betrayal of the fight against racism. Then, after the popular movie version of *The Color Purple* came out, Walker was criticized in the media for her negative portrayals of male characters and for

1973
Receives National Book Award nomination for *Revolutionary Petunias and Other Poems*

1979
Moves to San Francisco

1983
***The Color Purple* wins the Pulitzer Prize.**

1985
Film version of *The Color Purple* is released.

1975 — 1980 — 1985

1977
Record numbers of viewers watch TV adaptation of Alex Haley's *Roots*.

1981
Sandra Day O'Connor becomes first female Supreme Court Justice.

1982
Equal Rights Amendment fails to win ratification.

1984
President Ronald Reagan is reelected.

Mentor

(C) As Walker's creative energy bloomed, she took her poems and pushed them under the door of her teacher and mentor, Muriel Rukeyser, a poet whose work was politically and socially charged. Rukeyser's poems covered the eras of the Depression, World War II, McCarthyism, the Civil Rights Movement, the anti-Vietnam War Movement, and the Women's Liberation Movement. Rukeyser was interested in using the techniques of film for structuring her poetry. She sent Walker's poetry to her editor, and Walker's first book was published in 1968.

Journalism

(D) In 1976, Walker and her husband moved to Brooklyn. Although Walker sometimes taught college, she wrote and edited at *Ms.* magazine, which grew out of the Women's Liberation Movement. At a time when feminists were changing the social structure of American families, workplaces, and government, some women journalists felt that feminist issues needed a national voice. *Ms.* began in 1972 as the first national feminist monthly magazine. Gloria Steinem and Pat Carbine founded *Ms.,* although numerous other women contributed to its development, including newspaper publisher Katherine Graham, Congresswoman Bella Abzug, and writer Jane O'Reilly.

Cinema

(E) The film version of Walker's book, *The Color Purple,* was directed by Steven Spielberg. Despite the director's great success with films such as *Jaws, Raiders of the Lost Ark,* and *E. T.,* some critics expressed concern over the film's important subject matter and Spielberg's race and gender. They were afraid that he might not have the sensitivity to authentically tell a story about a black woman's oppression. The film, however, proceeded with Walker's participation, starring Whoopi Goldberg, Oprah Winfrey, and Danny Glover. It received 11 Academy Award nominations.

LIFE AND TIMES 501

Politics

A The first African-American woman elected to Congress was Shirley Chisholm of Brooklyn in 1968. A Democratic Party activist for many years before that, Chisholm suggested that, in politics, being a woman was more of a handicap than being African American. Her election was part of the change in consciousness about women's roles in society, especially in politics. In 1972, she became the first African-American woman to be nominated as a presidential candidate.

letting a white male director bring her novel to the screen. Throughout these sometimes vicious attacks, Walker stood her ground, insisting that racism and sexism stunted the lives of not only black women but also all men and women, black and white alike.

Today, Alice Walker is one of the most widely respected American writers. Fundamental to her writing is what one critic has called her "vision of survival." Although most of her characters are poor, uneducated, black, and female, they dramatize the capacity to blossom with spiritual vitality and inner beauty. In her works, Walker remains essentially an optimist, as she explains: "Every one of these writings represents my struggle not simply to survive the past and remain nurtured by it but to embrace the present and fight for the future."

More Online: Author Link
www.mcdougallittell.com

LaserLinks: Background for Reading
Historical Connection
Cultural Connection

A Compelling Presence

Like many people of her generation, Alice Walker was deeply affected by the civil rights movement. In a 1966 essay, she describes an intense moment of revelation that determined a new direction in her life.

According to Walker, she had been watching her mother's soap operas on their new television when the image of Dr. Martin Luther King, Jr., appeared on screen. She was immediately captivated by the impassioned figure who led an army of people in nonviolent demonstrations. Watching King being ushered into a police van as if he were a criminal caused such a stir in Walker that she was immediately drawn to the civil rights movement and to the individual who would become, for so many, the icon of the movement. As of that moment, Walker's search for a hero and role model was complete.

1992
Publishes *Possessing the Secret of Joy*

1996
Publishes *The Same River Twice*, her account of the controversy surrounding the movie, *The Color Purple;* declines White House invitation in protest of continuing U.S. embargo of Cuba

1990 **1995** **2000**

1988
George Bush is elected president.

1993
Novelist Toni Morrison is first African American to win Nobel Prize in literature.

1995
The Million Man March in Washington, D.C., addresses role of black men in their communities.

1996
Madeleine Albright is first woman nominated to be secretary of state. **A**

PREPARING to *Read*

Everyday Use

Short Story by ALICE WALKER

"She'd probably be backward enough to put [the quilts] to everyday use."

Connect to Your Life

Family Heritage What aspects of your family heritage are especially important to you? Create a chart like the one shown, in which you note some examples of your heritage under each heading. For example, under *Customs,* you might write down things your family always does on holidays, birthdays, and other important times.

Heritage	
Family Treasures	Traditional Foods
Customs	Language

Build Background

Black Pride This story is set in the rural South during the 1960s when many African Americans were discovering their heritage. The "black pride" movement, which grew out of the civil rights campaigns, called upon African Americans to recognize and celebrate their African roots and to affirm their cultural identity. Many adopted African names and styles of dress; some studied African languages. The advocates of black pride were often young, rebellious, and impatient with the older generation, who they felt was too accommodating to whites. This movement helped to spur renewed interest in black history, literature, art, and fashion.

WORDS TO KNOW
Vocabulary Preview
deliberately, oppress, doctrine, sidle, furtive

Focus Your Reading

LITERARY ANALYSIS CONFLICT / RESOLUTION **Conflict** is the struggle between opposing forces in a story and the basis of the plot. The main conflict in "Everyday Use" centers around two sisters, Dee and Maggie, and their mother, who narrates the story. Conflicts in literature, as in life, are complex and not easily resolved. Although the main conflict may be technically resolved at the end of the story to provide the story's **resolution,** or **falling action,** other conflicts may linger unresolved for the reader to think about.

ACTIVE READING DRAWING CONCLUSIONS In reading this story, you will need to use clues in the two sisters' actions and dialogue to **draw conclusions** about their characters. Especially helpful are the thoughts and feelings of their mother, who gives important background information that will help you understand the conflicts in the story.

READER'S NOTEBOOK As you read, jot down important clues about the three women and their conflicts. Pay particular attention to what each character considers as her heritage and why. Write down any conclusions you come to as you think about the characters.

VIDEODISC **LaserLinks: Background for Reading**
Historical Connection

OVERVIEW

This selection is included in the **Grade 10 InterActive Reader.**

Objectives

1. understand and appreciate a **short story (Literary Analysis)**
2. identify **conflict and resolution (Literary Analysis)**
3. **draw conclusions (Active Reading)**

Summary

A mother and her younger daughter, Maggie, anxiously await the visit of Dee, the sophisticated older daughter. Dee arrives dressed in African-inspired clothing, which contrasts with the simple garments of her sister and her mother. During her visit, Dee shows an interest in household items that reflect African-American heritage, and she wants to take two special family quilts. Her mother hesitates, saying that the quilts are for Maggie, but Dee points out that Maggie will subject the quilts to "everyday use" rather than treat them as art objects. The mother realizes that Maggie values the quilts more than Dee does and decides to give them to her younger daughter.

Thematic Link

A mother realizes that her two daughters have very different ideas about the **power of heritage.**

5-Minute Warm-Up

Daily Language SkillBuilder

Have students **proofread** the display sentences on page 381k and write them correctly. The sentences also appear on Transparency 16 of **Grammar Transparencies and Copymasters.**

Mini Lesson Preteaching Vocabulary

If you would like to preteach the WORDS TO KNOW for this selection, use the Mini Lesson, pp. 506–507.

LESSON RESOURCES

UNIT THREE RESOURCE BOOK, pp. 58–63

ASSESSMENT RESOURCES
Formal Assessment, pp. 83–84
Teacher's Guide to Assessment and Portfolio Use
Test Generator

SKILLS TRANSPARENCIES AND COPYMASTERS
Literary Analysis
- Plot: Conflict, T12 (for Paired Activity, p. 513)

Reading and Critical Thinking
- Drawing Conclusions, T4 (for Think Critically, item 4, p. 513)

Grammar
- Active and Passive Voice, C135 (for Mini Lesson, p. 514)

Vocabulary
- Context Clues, C56 (for Mini Lesson, p. 506)
- Analogies, C57 (for Mini Lesson, p. 510)

Writing
- Levels of Language, T12 (for Writing Option 1, p. 514)
- Effective Language, T13 (for Writing Option 2, p. 514)

Communications
- Interviewing, T9 (for Activities and Explorations 3, p. 514)
- Dramatic Reading, T12 (for Activities & Explorations 2, p. 514)

INTEGRATED TECHNOLOGY
Audio Library
Net Activities
LaserLinks
- Historical Connection: The Black Pride Movement
- Cultural Connection: Quilt Pattern

See **Teacher's SourceBook,** p. 30.
Visit our website: www.mcdougallittell.com

TEACHING THE LITERATURE

Reading and Analyzing

Reading Skills and Strategies: PREVIEW

Briefly summarize the story, emphasizing the interaction of the characters. Discuss the Build Background feature on black pride as well as the image on the opening page.

Active Reading DRAWING CONCLUSIONS

Have students consider Maggie's reaction to Dee's impending visit, and the mother's dream about being reunited with Dee on television. By observing the reactions of Maggie and her mother to Dee, students can draw conclusions about the characters' relationship.

Use **Unit Three Resource Book,** p. 59 for more practice.

Literary Analysis CONFLICT

Sometimes the narrator of a story will point out tensions between characters. These tensions may grow into the major conflicts of the story. Point out that Mrs. Johnson's comment about Maggie's nervousness over her sister's visit suggests previous tension and conflict.

Use **Unit Three Resource Book,** p. 60 for more practice.

ACTIVE READING

A EVALUATE Dee is removed from her family. She has always been successful.

EVERYDAY USE

Alice Walker

I will wait for her in the yard that Maggie and I made so clean and wavy yesterday afternoon. A yard like this is more comfortable than most people know. It is not just a yard. It is like an extended living room.

Working Woman (1947), Elizabeth Catlett. Oil on canvas, courtesy of the Barnett-Aden Collection, Museum of African American Art, Tampa, Florida.

504

Teaching Options

Mini Lesson Viewing and Representing

Working Woman **by Elizabeth Catlett**

ART APPRECIATION The elongated shapes and oval-shaped faces in Catlett's oil painting show the influence of modernist artists such as the Italian Amedeo Modigliani, who borrowed from patterns found in the tribal sculpture of cultures of West Africa. In this painting, Catlett emphasizes the strength of an African-American woman.

Instruction Point out the woman's muscular forearms and large hands, and how the shape of her body is framed by the door. Ask students what the woman's large body implies about her.

Possible Response: The woman's muscular arms and hands and the way her body and head reach beyond and above the framing of the door imply strength and physical power.

Application Ask students what connection they make between the painting and the characters in the story.

Possible Response: Mrs. Johnson, the narrator of "Everyday Use," describes herself as a "large, big-boned woman with rough man-working hands," similar to the woman in the painting.

When the hard clay is swept clean as a floor and the fine sand around the edges lined with tiny, irregular grooves, anyone can come and sit and look up into the elm tree and wait for the breezes that never come inside the house.

Maggie will be nervous until after her sister goes: she will stand hopelessly in corners, homely and ashamed of the burn scars down her arms and legs, eying her sister with a mixture of envy and awe. She thinks her sister has held life always in the palm of one hand, that "no" is a word the world never learned to say to her.

You've no doubt seen those TV shows where the child who has "made it" is confronted, as a surprise, by her own mother and father, tottering in weakly from backstage. (A pleasant surprise, of course: What would they do if parent and child came on the show only to curse out and insult each other?) On TV mother and child embrace and smile into each other's faces. Sometimes the mother and father weep, the child wraps them in her arms and leans across the table to tell how she would not have made it without their help. I have seen these programs.

Sometimes I dream a dream in which Dee and I are suddenly brought together on a TV program of this sort. Out of a dark and soft-seated limousine I am ushered into a bright room filled with many people. There I meet a smiling, gray, sporty man like Johnny Carson who shakes my hand and tells me what a fine girl I have. Then we are on the stage and Dee is embracing me with tears in her eyes. She pins on my dress a large orchid, even though she has told me once that she thinks orchids are tacky flowers.

ACTIVE READING

A **EVALUATE** What impression have you formed of Dee so far?

In real life I am a large, big-boned woman with rough, man-working hands. In the winter I wear flannel nightgowns to bed and overalls during the day. I can kill and clean a hog as mercilessly as a man. My fat keeps me hot in zero weather. I can work outside all day, breaking ice to get water for washing; I can eat pork liver cooked over the open fire minutes after it comes steaming from the hog. One winter I knocked a bull calf straight in the brain between the eyes with a sledge hammer and had the meat hung up to chill before nightfall. But of course all this does not show on television. I am the way my daughter would want me to be: a hundred pounds lighter, my skin like an uncooked barley pancake. My hair glistens in the hot bright lights. Johnny Carson has much to do to keep up with my quick and witty tongue.

But that is a mistake. I know even before I wake up. Who ever knew a Johnson with a quick tongue? Who can even imagine me looking a strange white man in the eye? It seems to me I have talked to them always with one foot raised in flight, with my head turned in whichever way is farthest from them. Dee, though. She would always look anyone in the eye. Hesitation was no part of her nature.

"How do I look, Mama?" Maggie says, showing just enough of her thin body enveloped in pink skirt and red blouse for me to know she's there, almost hidden by the door.

"Come out into the yard," I say.

Have you ever seen a lame animal, perhaps a dog run over by some careless person rich enough to own a car, sidle up to someone who is ignorant enough to be kind to him? That is the way my Maggie walks. She has been like this, chin on chest, eyes on ground, feet in shuffle, ever since the fire that burned the other house to the ground.

WORDS TO KNOW

sidle (sīd'l) *v.* to move sideways, especially in a shy or sneaky way

Customizing Instruction

Less Proficient Readers

Set a Purpose Ask students to discuss people they admire. How do students feel when these people visit? Then have them read to find out how Maggie reacts when her sister Dee arrives.

Students Acquiring English

Explain to students that *everyday* does not necessarily mean literally "every day." It means "common" or "ordinary." Ask students what "everyday use" might mean.

Use **Spanish Study Guide** for additional support, pp. 110–112.

Gifted and Talented

Encourage students to find out more about the black pride movement—its origins, aims, and accomplishments. Students should connect their findings to the story's conflict of values.

BLOCK SCHEDULING: MANAGING TIME

If your schedule requires that you cover the lesson objectives in a shorter time, use . . .
- Preparing to Read, p. 503
- Thinking Through the Literature, p. 513
- Vocabulary in Action, p. 515
- Grammar in Context, p. 515

If you want to take advantage of longer class time, use . . .
- TE Teaching Options: Preteaching Vocabulary, pp. 506–507; Viewing and Representing, pp. 504, 508; Cross Curricular Links, p. 509; Vocabulary Strategy, pp. 510–511; Standardized Test Practice, p. 512;
- Choices & Challenges, pp. 514–515

Reading and Analyzing

Literary Analysis: CHARACTER

A Ask students to contrast Maggie's and Dee's reactions to the fire, as described in this paragraph.
Possible Responses: Dee is delighted; Maggie is horrified. Dee escapes; Maggie is badly burned.

Ask students what they have learned so far about the different personalities of the two sisters.
Possible Response: Dee is confident and forceful, while Maggie is humble and shy.

Literary Analysis CONFLICT

B Ask students to identify the conflict suggested by Dee's reading habits and her desire for "nice things." What does Dee appear unwilling to accept?
Possible Response: Dee conflicts with her mother's and sister's way of life. She reads to her mother and sister as if she could create new lives for them from her books.

Active Reading

DRAWING CONCLUSIONS ABOUT CHARACTERS

C Ask students what conclusions they can draw about Dee from Maggie's statement, "Mama, when did Dee ever *have* any friends?" and from the friendships her mother describes.
Possible Response: Dee is too overbearing to have real friends; she needs to impress people, perhaps because she is insecure.

ACTIVE READING

D **DRAW CONCLUSIONS** They live simple, rural lives; they are somewhat intimidated by Dee.

A Dee is lighter than Maggie, with nicer hair and a fuller figure. She's a woman now, though sometimes I forget. How long ago was it that the other house burned? Ten, twelve years? Sometimes I can still hear the flames and feel Maggie's arms sticking to me, her hair smoking and her dress falling off her in little black papery flakes. Her eyes seemed stretched open, blazed open by the flames reflected in them. And Dee. I see her standing off under the sweet gum tree she used to dig gum out of; a look of concentration on her face as she watched the last dingy gray board of the house fall in toward the red-hot brick chimney. Why don't you do a dance around the ashes? I'd wanted to ask her. She had hated the house that much.

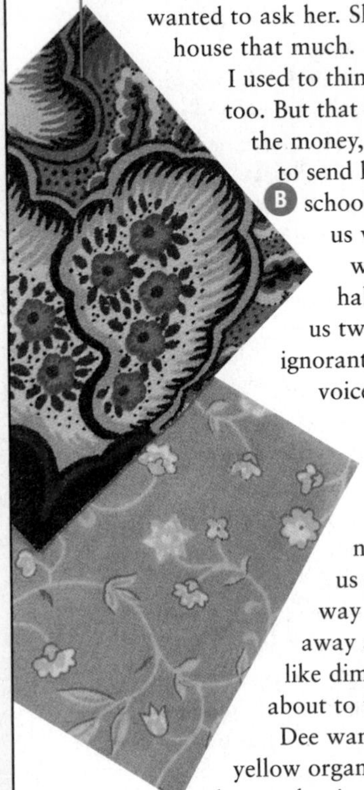

I used to think she hated Maggie, too. But that was before we raised the money, the church and me, to send her to Augusta[1] to **B** school. She used to read to us without pity; forcing words, lies, other folks' habits, whole lives upon us two, sitting trapped and ignorant underneath her voice. She washed us in a river of make-believe, burned us with a lot of knowledge we didn't necessarily need to know. Pressed us to her with the serious way she read, to shove us away at just the moment, like dimwits, we seemed about to understand.

Dee wanted nice things. A yellow organdy dress to wear to her graduation from high school; black pumps to match a green suit she'd made from an old suit somebody gave me. She was determined to stare down any disaster in her efforts. Her eyelids would not flicker for minutes at a time. Often I fought off the temptation to shake her. At sixteen she had a style of her own: and knew what style was.

I never had an education myself. After second grade the school was closed down. Don't ask me why: in 1927 colored asked fewer questions than they do now. Sometimes Maggie reads to me. She stumbles along good-naturedly but can't see well. She knows she is not bright. Like good looks and money, quickness passed her by. She will marry John Thomas (who has mossy teeth in an earnest face) and then I'll be free to sit here and I guess just sing church songs to myself. Although I never was a good singer. Never could carry a tune. I was always better at a man's job. I used to love to milk till I was hooked in the side in '49. Cows are soothing and slow and don't bother you, unless you try to milk them the wrong way.

> ACTIVE READING
> **DRAW CONCLUSIONS** **D** What conclusions have you drawn so far about the narrator and Maggie?

I have deliberately turned my back on the house. It is three rooms, just like the one that burned, except the roof is tin; they don't make shingle roofs any more. There are no real windows, just some holes cut in the sides, like the portholes in a ship, but not round and not square, with rawhide holding the shutters up on the outside. This house is in a pasture, too, like the other one. No doubt when Dee sees it she will want to tear it down. She wrote me once that no matter where we "choose" to live, she will manage to come see us.

1. **Augusta:** a city in Georgia.

WORDS TO KNOW
deliberately (dĭ-lĭb′ər-ĭt-lē) *adv.* as a result of careful thought

Teaching Options

Mini Lesson Preteaching Vocabulary

USING CONTEXT CLUES Call students' attention to the list of WORDS TO KNOW. Remind them that sometimes they can understand the meaning of an unfamiliar word by examining the context in which the word is used. Use the model sentence to demonstrate the strategy of using context clues that provide inferences to word meanings.

1. You *deliberately* made me late to band practice by choosing to let me oversleep.

Instruction
Write the model sentence on the chalkboard.
- Ask a volunteer to summarize the meaning of the sentence.
- Have students use the meaning of the sentence to infer meanings for the word *deliberately*.
- Ask a volunteer to use the word *deliberately* in a sentence.

But she will never bring her friends. Maggie and I thought about this and Maggie asked me, C "Mama, when did Dee ever *have* any friends?"

She had a few. Furtive boys in pink shirts hanging about on washday after school. Nervous girls who never laughed. Impressed with her they worshiped the well-turned phrase, the 1 cute shape, the scalding humor that erupted like bubbles in lye. She read to them.

> HER FEET WERE ALWAYS NEAT-LOOKING, AS IF GOD HIMSELF HAD SHAPED THEM.

When she was courting Jimmy T she didn't have much time to pay to us, but turned all her faultfinding power on him. He *flew* to marry a cheap city girl from a family of ignorant flashy people. She hardly had time to recompose herself.

When she comes I will meet—but there they are!

Maggie attempts to make a dash for the house, in her shuffling way, but I stay her with my hand. "Come back here," I say. And she stops and tries to dig a well in the sand with her toe.

It is hard to see them clearly through the strong sun. But even the first glimpse of leg out of the car tells me it is Dee. Her feet were always neat-looking, as if God himself had shaped them with a certain style. From the other side of the car comes a short, stocky man. Hair is all over his head a foot long and hanging from his chin like a kinky mule tail. I hear Maggie suck in her breath. "Uhnnnh," is what it sounds like. Like when you see the wriggling end of a snake just in front of your foot on the road. "Uhnnnh."

Dee next. A dress down to the ground, in this hot weather. A dress so loud it hurts my eyes. There are yellows and oranges enough to throw back the light of the sun. I feel my whole face warming from the heat waves it throws out. Earrings gold, too, and hanging down to her shoulders. Bracelets dangling and making noises when she moves her arm up to shake the folds of the dress out of her armpits. The dress is loose and flows, and as she walks closer, I like it. I hear Maggie go "Uhnnnh" again. It is her sister's hair. It stands straight up like the wool on a sheep. It is black as night and around the edges are two long pigtails that rope about like small lizards disappearing behind her ears.

"Wa-su-zo-Tean-o!" she says, coming on in that gliding way the dress makes her move. The short stocky fellow with the hair to his navel is all grinning and he follows up with "Asalamalakim,[2] my mother and sister!" He moves to hug Maggie but she falls back, right up against the back of my chair. I feel her trembling there and when I look up I see the perspiration falling off her chin.

"Don't get up," says Dee. Since I am stout it takes something of a push. You can see me trying to move a second or two before I make it. She turns, showing white heels through her sandals, and goes back to the car. Out she peeks next with a Polaroid. She stoops down quickly and lines up picture after picture of me sitting there in front of the house with Maggie cowering behind me. She never takes a shot without

2. **Wa-su-zo-Tean-o!** (wä-so͞o′zō-tē′nō) . . . **Asalamalakim!** (ə-săl′ə-mə-lăk′əm): greetings used by members of the Black Muslims.

WORDS TO KNOW

furtive (fûr′tĭv) *adj.* sneaky, shifty, or secretive

Customizing Instruction

Less Proficient Readers

1 Ask students to explain the phrase "scalding humor" that is used to describe Dee's personality.

Possible Response: Her humor hurts people, like scalding water.

Exercises Read the following sentences. Ask students to use context clues to determine the meanings of italicized terms.

1. Because of her *furtive* movements down the tree-lined path, she took us by complete surprise when she arrived at the campsite.
2. You were so shy that you would *sidle* down the row of lockers until you reached the classroom door.
3. What legal *doctrine* is included in the Bill of Rights of the U.S. Constitution?
4. Even after the death of the dictator, the government continued to *oppress* the peasants and the workers.

Use **Unit Three Resource Book,** p. 61 for more exercises.

A lesson on context clues appears on p. 56 in the Pupil's Edition.

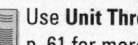

Reading and Analyzing

Reading Skills and Strategies: CLARIFYING

The narrator lists relatives named Dee in response to Dee's rejection of the name. Ask students what the narrator is trying to make clear.

Possible Response: The narrator is trying to tell Dee that she is not named after her "oppressors" but after treasured family members.

Literary Concept: THEME

Invite students to discuss Walker's message about the power of heritage.

Possible Response: Students may feel that Walker says that you don't have to go to extremes to celebrate your heritage, but it is important to recognize that your identity is rooted in your heritage.

508

Nia: Purpose (1991), Varnette Honeywood. Monoprint, collection of Karen Kennedy. Copyright © Varnette P. Honeywood, 1991.

Teaching Options

Mini Lesson Viewing and Representing

Nia: Purpose **by Varnette Honeywood**

ART APPRECIATION Honeywood's monoprint uses many traditional African designs and symbols. The blue-and-white background pattern is representative of African cloth patterns. The figure in the middle represents a helmet mask, or *chi wara*, used by the Bambara peoples of Mali. The four symbols in the corners are often used in patterns on cloth from Ghana.

Application Honeywood's monoprint is filled with symbols of African heritage. What connections might students make between this and the story?

Possible Response: Like the quilts in the story, which are made from clothes of family members, the monoprint patches together many different cultural symbols.

making sure the house is included. When a cow comes nibbling around the edge of the yard she snaps it and me and Maggie *and* the house. Then she puts the Polaroid in the back seat of the car, and comes up and kisses me on the forehead.

Meanwhile Asalamalakim is going through motions with Maggie's hand. Maggie's hand is as limp as a fish, and probably as cold, despite the sweat, and she keeps trying to pull it back. It looks like Asalamalakim wants to shake hands but wants to do it fancy. Or maybe he don't know how people shake hands. Anyhow, he soon gives up on Maggie.

"I COULDN'T BEAR IT ANY LONGER, BEING NAMED AFTER THE PEOPLE WHO OPPRESS ME."

"Well," I say. "Dee."

"No, Mama," she says. "Not 'Dee,' Wangero Leewanika Kemanjo!"[3]

"What happened to 'Dee'?" I wanted to know.

"She's dead," Wangero said. "I couldn't bear it any longer, being named after the people who oppress me."

1 "You know as well as me you was named after your aunt Dicie," I said. Dicie is my sister. She named Dee. We called her "Big Dee" after Dee was born.

"But who was *she* named after?" asked Wangero.

"I guess after Grandma Dee," I said.

"And who was she named after?" asked Wangero.

2 "Her mother," I said, and saw Wangero was getting tired. "That's about as far back as I can trace it," I said. Though, in fact, I probably could have carried it back beyond the Civil War through the branches.

"Well," said Asalamalakim, "there you are."

"Uhnnnh," I heard Maggie say.

"There I was not," I said, "before 'Dicie' cropped up in our family, so why should I try to trace it that far back?"

He just stood there grinning, looking down on me like somebody inspecting a Model A[4] car. Every once in a while he and Wangero sent eye signals over my head.

"How do you pronounce this name?" I asked.

"You don't have to call me by it if you don't want to," said Wangero.

"Why shouldn't I?" I asked. "If that's what you want us to call you, we'll call you."

"I know it might sound awkward at first," said Wangero.

"I'll get used to it," I said. "Ream it out again."

Well, soon we got the name out of the way. Asalamalakim had a name twice as long and three times as hard. After I tripped over it two or three times he told me to just call him Hakim-a-barber.[5] I wanted to ask him was he a barber, but I didn't really think he was, so I didn't ask.

"You must belong to those beef-cattle peoples down the road," I said. They said "Asalamalakim" when they met you, too, but they didn't shake hands. Always too busy: feeding the cattle, fixing the fences, putting up salt-lick shelters, throwing down hay. When the white folks poisoned some of the herd the men stayed up all night with rifles in their hands. I walked a mile and a half just to see the sight.

---

3. **Wangero Leewanika Kemanjo** (wän-gâr′ō lē-wä-nē′kə kĕ-män′jō).
4. **Model A:** an automobile manufactured by Ford from 1927 to 1931.
5. **Hakim-a-barber** (hä-kē′mə-bär′bər).

WORDS TO KNOW

oppress (ə-prĕs′) *v.* to keep down by the cruel or unjust use of power or authority

509

Customizing Instruction

Students Acquiring English

1 Point out to students that "You know as well as me you was named after your aunt Dicie" is in dialect. Help students rephrase the sentence in standard English.

Possible Response: "You know as well as I do that you were named after your aunt Dicie."

Gifted and Talented

2 Identify the conflict implied in the dialogue between the narrator and Wangero, incorporating information about the Black Pride movement.

Cross Curricular Link History

KWANZA Maulana Karenga started the celebration of Kwanza in 1966 as an African-American cultural alternative to Christmas. As the Chairman of the Black Studies Department at the California State University at Long Beach, Karenga was an influential part of the black pride movement of the 1960s. He based Kwanza (a Swahili word meaning "first fruits of the harvest") on African harvest rituals. The holidays are celebrated each year from December 26 through January 1. On each evening, African-American families gather to light a candle on the Kinara, a seven-branched candleholder, and they reflect on the principle associated with the day: December 26, Umoja, or unity; December 27, Kujichagulia, or self-determination; December 28, Ujima, or collective work and responsibility; December 29, Ujamaa, or cooperative economics; December 30, Nia, or purpose; December 31, Kuumba, or creativity; and January 1, Imani, or faith.

Reading and Analyzing

Literary Analysis

CONFLICT AND RESOLUTION

Ask students what larger conflict is indicated by the conflict over the quilts.
Possible Response: The conflict between Dee's concept of heritage as something abstract to be hung on a wall and admired and Maggie's and the narrator's concept of heritage as something immediate and real.

Reading Skills and Strategies:
VISUALIZING

A Ask students to visualize the quilts discussed in this paragraph.
Possible Response: colorful and old, with mismatched colors

Hakim-a-barber said, "I accept some of their doctrines, but farming and raising cattle is not my style." (They didn't tell me, and I didn't ask, whether Wangero (Dee) had really gone and married him.)

We sat down to eat and right away he said he didn't eat collards and pork was unclean. Wangero, though, went on through the chitlins and corn bread, the greens and everything else. She talked a blue streak over the sweet potatoes. Everything delighted her. Even the fact that we still used the benches her daddy made for the table when we couldn't afford to buy chairs.

"Oh, Mama!" she cried. Then turned to Hakim-a-barber. "I never knew how lovely these benches are. You can feel the rump prints," she said, running her hands underneath her and along the bench. Then she gave a sigh and her hand closed over Grandma Dee's butter dish. "That's it!" she said. "I knew there was something I wanted to ask you if I could have." She jumped up from the table and went over in the corner where the churn stood, the milk in it clabber[6] by now. She looked at the churn and looked at it.

"This churn top is what I need," she said. "Didn't Uncle Buddy whittle it out of a tree you all used to have?"

"Yes," I said.

"Uh huh," she said happily. "And I want the dasher,[7] too."

"Uncle Buddy whittle that, too?" asked the barber.

Dee (Wangero) looked up at me.

"Aunt Dee's first husband whittled the dash," said Maggie so low you almost couldn't hear her. "His name was Henry, but they called him Stash."

1 "Maggie's brain is like an elephant's," Wangero said, laughing. "I can use the churn top as a centerpiece for the alcove table," she said, sliding a plate over the churn, "and I'll think of something artistic to do with the dasher."

When she finished wrapping the dasher the handle stuck out. I took it for a moment in my hands. You didn't even have to look close to see where hands pushing the dasher up and down to make butter had left a kind of sink in the wood. In fact, there were a lot of small sinks; you could see where thumbs and fingers had sunk into the wood. It was beautiful light yellow wood, from a tree that grew in the yard where Big Dee and Stash had lived.

After dinner Dee (Wangero) went to the trunk at the foot of my bed and started rifling through it. Maggie hung back in the kitchen over the dishpan. Out came Wangero with two quilts. They had been pieced by Grandma Dee and then Big Dee and me had hung them on the quilt frames on the front porch and quilted them. One was in the Lone Star pattern. The other was Walk Around the Mountain. In both of them were scraps of dresses Grandma Dee had worn fifty and more years ago. Bits and pieces of Grandpa Jarrell's Paisley shirts. And one teeny faded blue piece, about the size of a penny matchbox, that was from Great Grandpa Ezra's uniform that he wore in the Civil War.

"Mama," Wangero said sweet as a bird. "Can I have these old quilts?"

I heard something fall in the kitchen, and a minute later the kitchen door slammed.

"Why don't you take one or two of the others?" I asked. "These old things was just done by me and Big Dee from some tops your grandma pieced before she died."

"No," said Wangero. "I don't want those. They are stitched around the borders by machine."

6. **clabber:** curdled milk.

7. **dasher:** the plunger of a churn, a device formerly used to stir cream or milk to produce butter.

WORDS TO KNOW

doctrine (dŏk'trĭn) *n.* a principle or rule taught by a religious, political, or philosophic group

Teaching Options

Mini Lesson Vocabulary Strategy

UNDERSTANDING ANALOGIES Remind students that sometimes they can understand the meaning of an unfamiliar word by examining its function in an analogy. Use the model analogy to demonstrate the strategy and help students provide inferences to word meaning.

Model Analogy

loud : noisy :: **deliberately** : intentionally

Instruction

- Write the model analogy on the chalkboard.
- Ask a volunteer to summarize the relationship between the first pair of words.
- Have students use the relationship to create the same relationship in the second pair of words.
- Have students infer the meaning of *deliberately* in the second pair of words.

Example: Since *loud* and *noisy* are synonyms, *deliberately* and *intentionally* must be synonyms also. *Intentionally* "on purpose"; therefore, *deliberately* must mean "on purpose," too.

Exercises Read the following analogies. Ask students to use the analogies to determine the meanings of the italicized words.

1. origin : beginning :: *doctrine* : instruction

"That'll make them last better," I said.

"That's not the point," said Wangero. "These are all pieces of dresses Grandma used to wear. She did all this stitching by hand. Imagine!" She held the quilts securely in her arms, stroking them.

"Some of the pieces, like those lavender ones, come from old clothes her mother handed down to her," I said, moving up to touch the quilts. Dee (Wangero) moved back just enough so that I couldn't reach the quilts. They already belonged to her.

"Imagine!" she breathed again, clutching them closely to her bosom.

3 "The truth is," I said, "I promised to give them quilts to Maggie, for when she marries John Thomas."

She gasped like a bee had stung her.

"Maggie can't appreciate these quilts!" she said. "She'd probably be backward enough to put them to everyday use."

4 "I reckon she would," I said. "God knows I been saving 'em for long enough with nobody using 'em. I hope she will!" I didn't want to bring up how I had offered Dee (Wangero) a quilt when she went away to college. Then she had told me they were old-fashioned, out of style.

"But they're *priceless!*" she was saying now, furiously; for she has a temper. "Maggie would put them on the bed and in five years they'd be in rags. Less than that!"

"She can always make some more," I said. "Maggie knows how to quilt."

Customizing Instruction

Students Acquiring English

1 Point out the simile "Maggie's brain is like an elephant's," and discuss Dee's meaning.

Possible Response: Dee compares Maggie's brain to an elephant's because elephants are said to have good memories.

Students Acquiring English

Help students understand the following dialect phrases and terms:

2 Help students rephrase "These old things was just done by me and Big Dee . . ." in standard English.

Possible Response: "These old things were just done by me and Big Dee . . ."

3 Ask students to rephrase "I promised to give them quilts to Maggie . . ." in standard English.

Possible Response: "I promised to give those quilts to Maggie . . ."

4 Explain to students that *'em* is a colloquial, abbreviated form of *them*. Ask them to rephrase ". . . I been saving 'em for long enough . . ." in standard English.

Possible Response: ". . . I have been saving them long enough . . ."

2. obey : subject :: *oppress* : tyrant
3. praise : scold :: forthright : *furtive*
4. kangaroo : hop :: sidewinder : *sidle*

Possible Responses:

1. Since *origin* and *beginning* are synonyms, *doctrine* and *instruction* must be synonyms too. *Instruction* means "something taught"; therefore, *doctrine* must have a meaning similar to "something taught."
2. Since *obey* is what a subject does, *oppress* must be what a tyrant does. Therefore, *oppress* must mean "to use power unjustly."
3. Since *praise* is the opposite of *scold, forthright* must be the antonym of *furtive. Forthright* means "direct"; therefore, *furtive* must mean the opposite of *direct*, or "sly."
4. Since *hop* is the way a kangaroo moves, *sidle* must be the way a sidewinder moves. A sidewinder is a type of snake that moves sideways; therefore, *sidle* must be a type of sideways movement.

Use **Vocabulary Transparencies and Copymasters**, p. 57.

A lesson on analogies appears on p. 263 in the Pupil's Edition.

Reading and Analyzing

Literary Analysis

CONFLICT/RESOLUTION

Remind students that in a story some conflicts are resolved and some remain. Ask students to identify what conflicts remain at the end of the story.

Possible Responses: Dee has not resolved her conflict with her past and her family's poverty; the family has not resolved its members' inability to understand one another.

ACTIVE READING

A QUESTION She means that her mother does not understand her heritage in a broad, abstract sense; she means that her mother does not see her heritage in the same way that she does.

Dee (Wangero) looked at me with hatred. "You just will not understand. The point is *these* quilts, these quilts!"

"Well," I said, stumped. "What would *you* do with them?"

"Hang them," she said. As if that was the only thing you *could* do with quilts.

Maggie by now was standing in the door. I could almost hear the sound her feet made as they scraped over each other.

"She can have them, Mama," she said, like somebody used to never winning anything, or having anything reserved for her. "I can 'member Grandma Dee without the quilts."

I looked at her hard. She had filled her bottom lip with checkerberry snuff and it gave her face a kind of dopey, hangdog look. It was Grandma Dee and Big Dee who taught her how to quilt herself. She stood there with her scarred hands hidden in the folds of her skirt. She looked at her sister with something like fear but she wasn't mad at her. This was Maggie's portion. This was the way she knew God to work.

When I looked at her like that something hit me in the top of my head and ran down to the soles of my feet. Just like when I'm in church and the spirit of God touches me and I get happy and shout. I did something I never had done before: hugged Maggie to me, then dragged her on into the room, snatched the quilts out of Miss Wangero's hands and dumped them into Maggie's lap. Maggie just sat there on my bed with her mouth open.

"Take one or two of the others," I said to Dee.

But she turned without a word and went out to Hakim-a-barber.

"You just don't understand," she said, as Maggie and I came out to the car.

"What don't I understand?" I wanted to know.

"Your heritage," she said. And then she turned to Maggie, kissed her, and said, "You ought to try to make something of yourself, too, Maggie. It's really a new day for us. But from the way you and Mama still live you'd never know it."

ACTIVE READING

QUESTION What does Dee mean when she says that her mother doesn't understand her heritage? **A**

She put on some sunglasses that hide everything above the tip of her nose and her chin.

Maggie smiled; maybe at the sunglasses. But a real smile, not scared. After we watched the car dust settle I asked Maggie to bring me a dip of snuff. And then the two of us sat there just enjoying, until it was time to go in the house and go to bed. ❖

Teaching Options

Assessment Standardized Test Practice

ALTERNATIVE ENDING You can informally assess students' understanding of the selection by having them write an alternative ending to "Everyday Use" in which Mrs. Johnson has given the quilts to Dee rather than Maggie.

RUBRIC

3 **Full Accomplishment** Response reflects a full understanding of the characters and the conflict in the story.

2 **Substantial Accomplishment** Response shows a general understanding of the characters and the conflict in the story.

1 **Little or Partial Accomplishment** Response shows little understanding of the characters and the conflict in the story.

Connect to the Literature

1. **What Do You Think?** Explain which character in the story you liked the best and which you liked the least.

Comprehension Check
- Why did Dee leave home?
- Why does Dee want the quilts?
- Why does the narrator give Maggie the quilts?

Think Critically

2. Do you agree with the narrator's decision to give the quilts to Maggie rather than to Dee? Give reasons for your answer.

3. Who do you think better appreciates her heritage, Dee or Maggie?

THINK ABOUT
- why Dee takes photographs of her family and the house
- which sister knows more about the family's history
- why Dee wants the churn and the quilts
- Maggie's own ability to quilt
- Dee's African clothing, name, and greeting

4. **ACTIVE READING** DRAWING CONCLUSIONS From the notes you took in your READER'S NOTEBOOK as you read, what conclusions can you draw about the three women characters? What positive and negative qualities does each character show? Use evidence from the story to support your conclusion.

Extend Interpretations

5. **Comparing Texts** In an interview, Walker explained that the characters in *The Color Purple* "are all parts of myself, composites and memories and reconstructions." Using what you know about her from the Life and Times section (pages 499–502), explain how the three women in "Everyday Use" are also part of Alice Walker.

6. **Connect to Life** In recent years, many people have come to take an interest in their heritage—both family traditions and the cultural past. What do you think accounts for this interest? What parts of your heritage do you personally relate to?

Literary Analysis

CONFLICT / RESOLUTION The central **conflict** in "Everyday Use" is over the quilts. Both Dee and Maggie want them, but for different reasons. The resolution of this conflict in Maggie's favor essentially concludes the plot of the story and affirms the theme that heritage is something for "everyday use" to enrich people's lives, not something exclusive. But there are other conflicts in the story, some of them left unresolved.

Paired Activity Working with a partner, use a chart like the one below to analyze some of the other conflicts in the story. Two conflicts are listed for you, but add others that you come up with.

Nature of Conflict	Resolved? If so, how?
Dee's conflict with her poverty as a child	
Narrator's conflict with Dee's new life and attitude	

GUIDING STUDENT RESPONSE

Connect to the Literature

1. **What Do You Think?** Students should support their opinion with text evidence.

Comprehension Check
- Dee left home to go to school.
- Dee wants to display the quilts on her wall.
- The narrator gives Maggie the quilts because she realizes that Maggie understands their value.

Use Selection Quiz **Unit Three Resource Book,** p. 63.

Think Critically

2. Students may want to discuss the narrator's decision.
3. Possible Response: Maggie does. She has learned the skills and history of her family and incorporates them into her daily life. To Dee heritage is something outside of herself, to be removed from daily life and put on display.
4. Students should respond using details from the selection.

Extend Interpretations

Comparing Texts The narrator is much like Walker's mother and represents her strength. Walker, like Maggie, was scarred when she was young. Dee went away to college with funds raised by her community, as did Walker.

Connect to Life Allow time for students to share their cultural traditions with their classmates.

Mini Lesson: Analyzing a Performance Review

Instruction Working in small groups, students will write and perform a script for a dramatic presentation of "Everyday Use" by Alice Walker. As the groups present their performances to the class, have the other class members write a review of the performance.

Prepare Tell students the following criteria may be used to analyze a written review of a performance.
- identifies its subject at the beginning
- opens with a general opinion
- includes enough facts, examples, and specifics to support the general opinion
- displays logical organization
- quickly establishes a tone

Present Have several students share their reviews with the class. Then have them compare their responses with those of the other reviewers.

Writing Options

1. **Casting Memo** Students should justify their reasons for selecting the actors they would choose to play the characters.
2. **Story Sequel** Remind students to identify why a character changes dramatically.
3. **Comparison of the Sisters** Have students fill in the chart or create a Venn diagram to organize their response.

Activities & Explorations

1. **Story Quilt** Tell students that their quilt may be representational or abstract, using color, texture, and shape to convey feeling or mood.
2. **Readers Theater** Encourage well-supported interpretations.
3. **Oral History** Encourage students to write out their questions beforehand.
4. **Family Art** Student work could be presented to the class and then put on display.

Inquiry & Research

1. **The Sharecropping System** Students should be encouraged to be creative when they present their findings.
2. **The Black Pride Movement** This assignment lends itself well to cooperative efforts, allowing students with different learning styles to work together to produce the show. Remind students to locate appropriate print and nonprint information using text resources and technical resources including databases and the Internet.

Choices & CHALLENGES

Writing Options

1. Casting Memo If you were going to direct a film of this story, what actors would you choose to play the characters? Write a memo to the producer, describing whom you would like to use as actors and why you think they would interpret Walker's characters well.

2. Story Sequel Write a continuation of "Everyday Use," describing a family reunion held ten years after the events in the story. Before you write, make notes on how each character will have changed and will interact at the reunion.

3. Comparison of the Sisters Write a short essay comparing the two sisters in the story. Use details that support the characterizations of both women as in the following chart.

Writing Handbook See page 1157: Explanatory Writing.

	Dee	Maggie
Physical Appearance		
Mannerisms		
Self-Concept		
Values		

Activities & Explorations

1. Story Quilt Design a story quilt that depicts the important characters, objects, and events from "Everyday Use." Be sure to use colors and designs that help convey the mood and theme of the story. ~ **ART**

2. Readers Theater With a small group, create a dramatic presentation of "Everyday Use." You will need to create a script that fleshes out the physical action and dialogue of the story. ~ **PERFORMING**

3. Oral History Interview one of your relatives or a family friend about life during the 1960s and 1970s. Be sure to find out the person's involvement and/or opinion of the civil rights and women's movements. Transcribe the person's words in an oral history of the period. Place the entry in your **Working Portfolio.** ~ **HISTORY**

4. Family Art Create a collage, mobile, or sculpture using objects you associate with your family. You might include photographs, pieces of cloth, toys, household objects, recipe cards, invitations, and graduation programs. Drawings or magazine photographs of these objects can also be included. ~ **ART**

Inquiry & Research

1. The Sharecropping System With a partner, research the sharecropping system of the rural South. Find out how it developed as an economic system after the Civil War and how it operated in the 20th century to affect Walker's family and the fictional Johnsons in "Everyday Use." Present your findings in an oral report.

2. The Black Pride Movement "I'm Black and I'm Proud" was a popular James Brown song in the late 1960s. Research the black pride movement and the related black power movement of the 1960s and 1970s. Find out who the leaders were, what social programs they initiated, and what problems they had. Also research what became of these leaders in the 1980s and 1990s. Present your findings as a multimedia show, with music, photos, and art, as well as verbal explanations.

Art Connection

Look again at the painting *Working Woman* on page 504. What qualities of this painting are also portrayed in "Everyday Use"?

Teaching Options

Mini Lesson Grammar

ACTIVE AND PASSIVE VOICE

Remind students that the term *voice* suggests the relationship between the action of the verb and subject. In a sentence using active voice, the sentence's subject performs the action, while in passive voice the subject receives the action.

Write the following sentences on the chalkboard.

"Dee <u>went</u> to her mother's in an automobile."

"Dee <u>was taken</u> to her mother's in an automobile."

Underline the verbs as shown. Have students identify the subject of *went* (Dee) in the first sentence. Point out that in the first sentence, the subject, *Dee*, performs the action, and in the second sentence, she receives the action. For this reason, the first sentence is active, and the second sentence is passive.

Vocabulary in Action

EXERCISE Review the Words to Know at the bottom of the selection pages. Then, on your paper, write the word that best completes each sentence.

1. The presence of Dee seemed to _______ Maggie, making it difficult for her to feel comfortable.
2. Dee _______ dressed in clothing that expressed her African heritage.
3. Maggie's _______ expression showed her lack of self-confidence.
4. Maggie would often _______ up to her mother for protection and comfort.
5. The narrator of the story believes in the _______ of hard work and simple living.

Building Vocabulary
Several of the Words to Know in this lesson have interesting origins. For an in-depth lesson on word origins, see page 356.

WORDS TO KNOW			
	deliberately	furtive	sidle
	doctrine	oppress	

Grammar in Context: Active Voice and Passive Voice

In "Everyday Use," the narrator employs both the active voice and the passive voice in telling her story.

ACTIVE VOICE
She washed us in a river of make-believe, burned us with a lot of knowledge we didn't necessarily need to know.

PASSIVE VOICE
After second grade the school was closed down.

Writers use verbs in the **active voice** when they want to emphasize that the subjects are the performers of the actions; they use verbs in the **passive voice** to emphasize that the subjects receive the actions. Writers most often use the active voice, because it makes clear who performed the actions and because it gives their writing a lively tone.

Writers use the passive voice when it is not important who performed an action or when they want to give their writing a more formal, impersonal tone. In the second example above, Alice Walker perhaps used the passive voice because she did not know who was responsible for closing the school.

Usage Tip: Make your writing lively and interesting by using the active voice most of the time.

WRITING EXERCISE Rewrite each sentence, changing the verb's voice to the voice shown in parentheses.

Example: ***Original*** The sun aged the wood. (passive)

Rewritten The wood was aged by the sun.

1. Fire consumed the house. (passive)
2. The sweet gum tree was chosen by Dee as her special place. (active)
3. The other girls were fascinated and impressed with Dee. (active)
4. We made the quilts out of bits and pieces of family clothes. (passive)
5. According to Dee, my heritage was not understood by me. (active)

Connect to the Literature The passive voice can serve different purposes. What is its purpose in the clause "When the hard clay is swept clean . . ." at the beginning of page 505? What is its purpose in the clause "till I was hooked in the side in '49" in the second column on page 506?

Grammar Handbook Active-Passive Voice, p. 1187

Vocabulary in Action

1. oppress
2. deliberately
3. furtive
4. sidle
5. doctrine

Grammar in Context

WRITING EXERCISE

Answers may vary.

1. The house was consumed by fire.
2. Dee chose the sweet gum tree as her special place.
3. Dee fascinated and impressed the other girls.
4. The quilts were made by us out of bits and pieces of family clothes.
5. According to Dee, I did not understand my heritage.

Connect to the Literature

"When the hard clay is swept clean . . ." conveys a sense of working slowly and carefully by hand; "till I was hooked in the side in '49" keeps the focus on "I" rather than on the cows. (Notice, however, that the focus does shift to the cows in the next sentence, reflecting the speaker's train of thought.)

Practice Have students copy the following sentences. Ask them to identify each sentence as being in active or passive voice.

1. Maggie was given the quilts.
   Answer: *passive*
2. Mama gave the quilts to Maggie.
   Answer: *active*
3. Dee chose the items she wanted.
   Answer: *active*
4. Dee's name was changed to Wangero.
   Answer: *passive*
5. Hakim-a-barber shook Maggie's hand.
   Answer: *active*
6. Mama's choice was made.
   Answer: *passive*

Use **Unit Three Resource Book,** p. 62 for additional support.

Use **Grammar Transparencies and Copymasters,** p. 135.

Use McDougal Littell's ***Language Network,*** Chapter 6, for more instruction in active and passive voice.

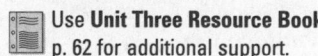

OVERVIEW

Objectives

1. understand and appreciate two contemporary **poems (Literary Analysis)**
2. analyze **diction (Literary Analysis)**
3. understand **denotation and connotation (Active Reading)**

Summary

In "Women," Walker pays tribute to the women of her mother's generation who persevered to make a better life for their children. In "Poem at Thirty-Nine," Walker says she misses her father. From him she learned that saving money was the key to a better life. Her father also taught her to tell the truth, even though she believes many of her truths hurt him. She is much like her father and believes he would be proud of the woman she has become.

Thematic Link

In each of these poems, Walker reflects on her **heritage** and how her parents shaped her into the woman she is today.

5-Minute Warm-Up

Daily Language SkillBuilder

Have students **proofread** the display sentences on page 381k and write them correctly. The sentences also appear on Transparency 17 of **Grammar Transparencies and Copymasters.**

PREPARING to *Read*

"How they knew what we / Must know / Without knowing a page / Of it / Themselves."

Women ❦ Poem at Thirty-Nine

Poetry by ALICE WALKER

Connect to Your Life

Parents You may not often think about your relationship with your parents or guardians. But take a moment now to reflect on this important relationship. Think about two or three good things that a parent or guardian has taught you. What other ways have they helped shape who you are?

Build Background

Life in the South Alice Walker's parents lived in the South at a time when African Americans had very little freedom. Educational opportunities were minimal, and the sharecropping system trapped many black people in a cycle of grueling work and poverty. Qualifying restrictions kept most blacks from voting, while segregation laws kept them separated from whites. In spite of these injustices, Southern blacks developed strong communities and deep family commitments that led them to envision a better life for their children. In these two poems, Alice Walker pays tribute to her parents and to this larger black tradition of which they were a part.

Focus Your Reading

LITERARY ANALYSIS | DICTION **Diction** is a writer's choice of words. In analyzing diction, focus on two things:

- **vocabulary,** or the individual words
- **syntax,** or the arrangement or order of the words

Alice Walker has received critical praise for the clarity and effectiveness of her diction. While reading her poems, pay special attention to the words she has chosen and their arrangement to make your own judgment about her diction.

ACTIVE READING | DENOTATION / CONNOTATION **Denotation** is the literal meaning of a word, the definition you'd find in the dictionary. **Connotation** is the emotional response and mental association evoked by a word. For example, what feelings and associations do you have with the word *hand*? You may have positive feelings and think of holding something, reaching out, or giving help. Now what about the word *fist*? This word may evoke feelings of struggle, as in a fight or in beating down a door.

READER'S NOTEBOOK As you read these poems, notice the connotations as well as the denotations of important words. Write down words that you think have powerful connotations. You might create a chart similar to the one shown.

Word	Denotation	Connotation

LESSON RESOURCES

UNIT THREE RESOURCE BOOK, pp. 64–65

ASSESSMENT RESOURCES
Formal Assessment, pp. 85–86
Teacher's Guide to Assessment and Portfolio Use
Test Generator

SKILLS TRANSPARENCIES AND COPYMASTERS

Literary Analysis
- Style, Voice, Diction, Purpose, T22 (for Cooperative Learning Activity, p. 520)

Reading and Critical Thinking
- Organizational Chart: Horizontal, T51 (for Reader's Notebook, p. 516)

Grammar
- Inactive Verbs: *To Be,* C177 (for Mini Lesson, p. 518)

INTEGRATED TECHNOLOGY
Net Activities
Internet: Research Starter
Visit our website:
www.mcdougallittell.com

Women

Alice Walker

They were women then
My mama's generation
Husky of voice—Stout of
Step
With fists as well as
Hands
How they battered down
Doors
And ironed
Starched white
Shirts
How they led
Armies
Headragged Generals
Across mined
Fields
Booby-trapped
Kitchens
To discover books
Desks
A place for us
How they knew what we
Must know
Without knowing a page
Of it
Themselves.

Three Sisters (1985), Jonathan Green. Oil on masonite, 11″ × 14″. Collection of Ted Carlsen. Photograph by Tim Stamm.

Thinking Through the Literature

1. What **images** from this poem stand out in your mind?
2. What do you think Walker admires most about her mother's generation? Cite evidence from the poem to support your opinion.
3. Why do you think the mothers are described as "Headragged Generals" crossing "mined fields" and "booby-trapped kitchens"?

   THINK ABOUT
   - what the mothers are fighting for
   - what obstacles they had to overcome
4. Point out words in the poem that you think have strong **connotations** or most effectively express Walker's meaning. Explain your choices.

TEACHING THE LITERATURE

Customizing Instruction

Less Proficient Readers

Have students keep these questions in mind as they read both poems:

- Who are the characters in these poems?
  Answers: "Women"—the women of the narrator's mother's generation; "Poem at Thirty-Nine"—the narrator, the narrator's father
- What things have these characters done for the narrator?
  Possible Responses: "Women"—provided educational opportunities; "Poem at Thirty-Nine"—taught to save money, taught to tell the truth

Students Acquiring English

Poetry often uses figurative language; therefore many words and phrases should not be taken literally. For example, "battered down / Doors" (lines 7–8) does not refer to the physical destruction of doors, but to the removal of social barriers.

Use **Spanish Study Guide** for additional support, pp. 113–115.

Thinking Through the Literature

1. Walker's women are as strong and as determined as military generals.
2. Walker admired the vision these women had for the next generation: "How they knew what we / *Must* know . . ."
3. The women Walker describes have been fighting to survive and to improve the lives of their offspring.
4. Words and phrases with strong connotations include "Stout of Step," "battered down," and "Booby-trapped Kitchens."

Reading and Analyzing

Reading Skills and Strategies: PREVIEW

Briefly summarize the poems, pointing out that Walker pays tribute to both genders for different reasons. Discuss the Connect to Your Life and Build Background features before reading the poems.

Active Reading DENOTATION/CONNOTATION

When students finish reading the poems, discuss the connotative interpretation of such words as *hand/fist, pride/vanity,* and *daring/reckless.* Compare these interpretations with the denotations of these words.

Use **Unit Three Resource Book,** p. 64 for additional support.

Literary Analysis DICTION

A poet's diction, or word choice, is a chief tool in creating telling images. Appreciating diction helps us respond to the poem's message. Students may want to jot down any words or images they find particularly effective such as: "Stout of / Step"; "Headragged Generals"; "my brain light"; "voluptuous."

Use **Unit Three Resource Book,** p. 65 for additional support.

Literary Analysis: THEME

A The theme of a poem is the message about life or human nature that the poet shares with the reader. Ask students to think about the theme of this poem. What is the poet trying to say?

Possible Response: The poem specifically pays tribute to her father, but also to the lessons taught by all parents to their offspring. Walker's theme is about the importance of one's roots.

Poem at Thirty-Nine

Alice Walker

How I miss my father.
I wish he had not been
so tired
when I was
born.

Writing deposit slips and checks
I think of him.
He taught me how.
This is the form,
he must have said:
the way it is done.
I learned to see
bits of paper
as a way
to escape
the life he knew
and even in high school
had a savings
account.

He taught me
that telling the truth
did not always mean
a beating;
though many of my truths
1 must have grieved him
before the end.

Teaching Options

Mini Lesson Grammar

INACTIVE VERBS: *TO BE* Overuse of the verb *to be* can make writing seem dull and lifeless. In revising their writing, students should try to replace a form of *to be* with a more active or descriptive verb. This often means rewriting the entire sentence, converting a noun to a verb, or adding information. Remind students that this process is one specific step they can take when they are told to revise their writing.

Write the following sentence on the chalkboard:

Walker's father was a good cook.

Write the following revised sentence on the chalkboard:

Walker's father cooked delicious meals.

Use **Grammar Transparencies and Copymasters,** p. 177.

Use McDougal Littell's ***Language Network,*** Chapter 6, for more instruction in the use of specific verbs.

How I miss my father!
He cooked like a person (A)
dancing
in a yoga meditation
and craved the voluptuous
sharing
of good food.

Now I look and cook just like him:
my brain light;
tossing this and that
into the pot;
seasoning none of my life
the same way twice; happy to feed
whoever strays my way.

He would have grown
to admire
the woman I've become:
cooking, writing, chopping wood,
staring into the fire.

31 voluptuous (və-lŭp'cho͞o-əs): pleasurable to the senses.

Illustration by Raul Colon.

Customizing Instruction

Less Proficient Readers

1 Clarify the meaning of difficult passages such as, "many of my truths / must have grieved him / before the end."

Possible Response: She means that by telling the truth she hurt her father. "Before the end" means before her father died.

Multiple Learning Styles

Visual Learners

Have students summarize each stanza in the poem and write this information in a pictorial series-of-events chain.

Assessment Standardized Test Practice

CHOOSING THE BEST SUMMARY For some standardized tests, students will be asked to choose the best summary of a passage or poem. To provide students with some help in choosing the best summary, read aloud or write on the chalkboard the following question:

Which of the following statements best summarizes Alice Walker's poem "Women"?

A. Women of the speaker's mother's generation worked very hard, but knew little of books.

B. Women of the speaker's mother's generation worked very hard to create opportunities for their children.

C. Women of the speaker's mother's generation were stout with husky voices and fought battles for their children.

Lead students through the process of choosing the best summary. Consider each choice. Point out that while all of the statements contain accurate information about the poem, the best summary should include the most important information. For that reason, **B** is the best choice.

POEM AT THIRTY-NINE **519**

GUIDING STUDENT RESPONSE

Connect to Literature

1. What Do You Think?
Walker's father was strong and taught her how to do life's everyday tasks.

Comprehension Check

- The poet misses her father because she feels they would have a lot in common now and would enjoy each other's company.
- Her father taught her how to handle money, tell the truth, and cook.

Think Critically

2. Possible Response: He would have admired his daughter because she is a strong woman who is a lot like him.
3. Possible Response: No. The poet says in lines 24–26 that she caused her father grief by telling him the truth.
4. Possible Response: The title of the poem could mean that she was 39 years old when she wrote it. Perhaps she remembers her father when he was her age.
5. Generate a class list of words to interpret and ask students to discuss the connotation of the words.

Thinking through the LITERATURE

Connect to the Literature

1. What Do You Think? What impression do you have of Walker's father?

Comprehension Check

- Why does the poet miss her father?
- What specific things does the father teach his daughter?

Think Critically

2. From what you know about the father, why do you think he would have admired the activities the daughter mentions in the last **stanza**?
3. Do you think the father and daughter have always gotten along? Cite evidence in the poem that suggests their past relationship.
4. What do you think the **title** of the poem means?
5. **ACTIVE READING** DENOTATION / CONNOTATION Review the words you wrote down in your READER'S NOTEBOOK as you read this poem. Then, give the **denotative** and **connotative** meanings for each of those words.

Extend Interpretations

6. **Comparing Texts** Compare Walker's memories of her father in "Poem at Thirty-Nine" with her memories of her mother in "Women." What similarities and differences do you find between what each parent taught her?
7. **Connect to Life** How does Walker's relationship with her parents revealed in these two poems compare to your relationship with your parents or guardians? Do you think your views will change as you get older?

Literary Analysis

DICTION **Diction,** or word choice, is an important element in a writer's style and can be described as formal or informal, technical or common, abstract or concrete. For example, Shakespeare's sonnets have very formal diction, with complex syntax and formal vocabulary. You could say that his diction is all dressed-up. His diction also expresses abstract ideas—such as a woman's loveliness, remembrances, and friendship—although he uses fairly common language, at least for his day.

Cooperative Learning Activity With a small group of classmates, analyze the diction of Walker's two poems. Use a chart like the one below to classify examples from the poems. Then draw conclusions about the effects of this diction in her poetry.

Characteristics of Diction (circle one)	Examples from the Poems
formal/informal (informal circled)	They were women then My mama's generation. *from* "Women" Writing deposit slips and checks I think of him. *from* "Poem at Thirty-Nine"
abstract/concrete	
technical/common	

Extend Interpretations

Comparing Texts Both of her parents taught her to be strong and to work hard. Both her mother and father were probably uneducated, and both were sometimes angry. Walker mentions that cooking made her father happy, but she doesn't say what made her mother happy.

Connect to Life Students may prefer to focus on one parent. Remind students to mention concrete images or events as Walker has done in these two poems.

Literary Analysis

Diction Walker's diction can be characterized as informal, concrete, and common. Her simple and direct language reflects the people who are the subjects of her poems. Such language also makes her poetry easily understandable and gives it the touch of common humanity. Student charts should list relevant examples to illustrate Walker's diction.

ON WRITING Poetry

Alice Walker

Preparing to Read

Build Background

In the following excerpt from an interview, Walker explains her process for writing poetry.

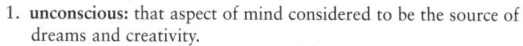

The writing of my poetry is never consciously planned; although I become aware that there are certain emotions I would like to explore. Perhaps my unconscious[1] begins working on poems from these emotions long before I am aware of it. I have learned to wait patiently (sometimes refusing good lines, images, when they come to me, for fear they are not lasting), until a poem is ready to present itself—*all* of itself, if possible. I sometimes feel the urge to write poems way in advance of ever sitting down to write. There is a definite restlessness, a kind of feverish excitement that is tinged[2] with dread. The dread is because after writing each batch of poems I am always convinced that I will never write poems again. I become aware that I am controlled by them, not the other way around. I put off writing as long as I can. Then I lock myself in my study, write lines and lines and lines, then put them away, underneath other papers, without looking at them for a long time. I am afraid that if I read them too soon they will turn into trash; or worse, something so topical[3] and transient[4] as to have no meaning —not even to me—after a few weeks. (This is how my later poetry-writing differs from the way I wrote *Once.*) I also attempt, in this way, to guard against the human tendency to try to make poetry carry the weight of half-truths, of cleverness. I realize that while I am writing poetry, I am so high as to feel invisible, and in that condition it is possible to write anything.

1. **unconscious:** that aspect of mind considered to be the source of dreams and creativity.
2. **tinged** (tĭnjd): affected slightly.
3. **topical** (tŏp′ĭ-kəl): of current interest.
4. **transient** (trăn′shənt): short-lived; temporary.

Thinking Through the Literature

1. What, if anything, surprises you about Walker's way of writing poetry?
2. What do you think Walker means by the phrase "the human tendency to try to make poetry carry the weight of half-truths, of cleverness"?
3. **Comparing Texts** Reread "Women" and "Poem at Thirty-Nine." Does Walker's description here give you additional insight into these poems? Explain.

Teaching Nonfiction

Build Background

Although Walker is best known for her novels, particularly her 1982 book *The Color Purple,* her first published book was a collection of poems, *Once: Poems* (1968). Many of the poems in *Once: Poems* were written during a summer trip to Africa when Walker was a college student. They deal with her feelings and experiences, and have an intimate, personal feel. Even in Walker's later poetry, when she deals with larger issues, particularly sexism and racism, she grounds her views in personal experience. She recounts things she has seen, felt, and heard, and through them attempts to bring out larger truths.

Walker has established Wild Trees Press to publish the works of lesser known writers.

Reading Skills and Strategies: EXAMINING AUTHOR'S PURPOSE

An author's purpose in writing may be to inform, to influence, to express opinions, or to entertain. Although one purpose is usually the most important, a writer can have two or more.

After students read the excerpt from Walker's essay, have them identify her purpose for writing it.

Possible Responses: She probably wanted to inform and explain to readers her philosophy on writing poetry.

Thinking Through the Literature

1. **Possible Response:** that she sometimes doesn't use "good lines" because they may not be "lasting"
2. **Possible Response:** the tendency to concentrate more on the rhythm, rhyme, and form of poetry than on the content or meaning
3. **Possible Response:** It shows how carefully she chooses her words and constructs her sentences. For example, "Headragged Generals" was probably a carefully crafted phrase.

OVERVIEW

Objectives
1. understand and appreciate an **essay (Literary Analysis)**
2. appreciate **author's perspective (Literary Analysis)**
3. determine text's **main idea (Active Reading)**

Summary
In this personal essay, Walker reflects on her mother's life. Her mother, a loving, patient woman who worked very hard, made time to plant ambitious flower gardens. Walker suggests that black women examine their mothers' lives to see how, despite overwhelming oppression, they were able to nurture their creative spirit and pass it on to their daughters. To support her position, Walker refers to the creative efforts of other black women. Guided by her heritage, Walker has found her own *"gardens"* in her writing.

Thematic Link
Walker explores her own **heritage** and the heritage of other black women in this essay. Through her mother's creative example, Walker has learned the power to create in words.

Editor's Note: This selection has been edited slightly to delete material that may be considered objectionable; it is an excerpt from a longer work.

5-Minute Warm-Up

Daily Language SkillBuilder

Have students **proofread** the display sentences on page 381k and write them correctly. The sentences also appear on Transparency 17 of **Grammar Transparencies and Copymasters.**

Mini Lesson
Preteaching Vocabulary
If you would like to preteach the WORDS TO KNOW for this selection, use the Mini Lesson, pp. 524–525.

"In search of my mother's garden, I found my own."

from In Search of Our Mothers' Gardens
Essay by ALICE WALKER

Connect to Your Life

What Is Art? What do you consider art—painting and sculpture in a museum? architecture? literature? Is there such a thing as art in everyday life? Does anyone you know create art? Do you? Write down a definition of art as you understand it and then discuss this issue among your classmates.

Build Background
Women's Art One of the effects of the women's movement in the 1960s and 70s was a reconsideration of art by women. Works by women writers long out of print were being rediscovered and reissued in new editions. Walker herself was responsible for rescuing the literary works of Zora Neale Hurston from oblivion and introducing this talented African-American writer to a new generation of readers.

Women also began to look again at what had traditionally been called the "low arts"—cooking, gardening, sewing, and oral storytelling—often the only activities in which women could express their creativity. Again, Alice Walker was in the vanguard, for she only had to look at her mother to see the art that went unrecognized for so long.

WORDS TO KNOW
Vocabulary Preview
impatient, profusely, ingenious, vibrant, medium

Focus Your Reading
LITERARY ANALYSIS | AUTHOR'S PERSPECTIVE The **author's perspective** is the viewpoint that he or she takes on a subject. It generally reflects the author's feelings and beliefs and so is sometimes called **bias.** Because Walker is both an advocate of civil rights and a feminist, you can expect that her choice of subject matter and what she says about that subject will be influenced by her strong beliefs. Walker is also a very personal writer. She expresses herself sincerely and straightforwardly so that the reader knows exactly what she values and respects. As you read, look for an indication of her values in her diction and in overt statements.

ACTIVE READING | MAIN IDEA A **main idea** is usually a statement that tells not only what a paragraph or passage is about but also what the author says about the topic. Main ideas can be directly stated or implied. **Supporting details** include examples, facts, quotations, and other evidence to reinforce the main idea.

READER'S NOTEBOOK As you read this essay, look for a statement of the main idea. Also, jot down a few of the many details Walker gives to support and develop her idea, using the outline form shown here.

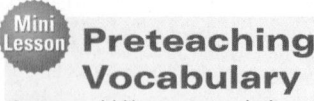

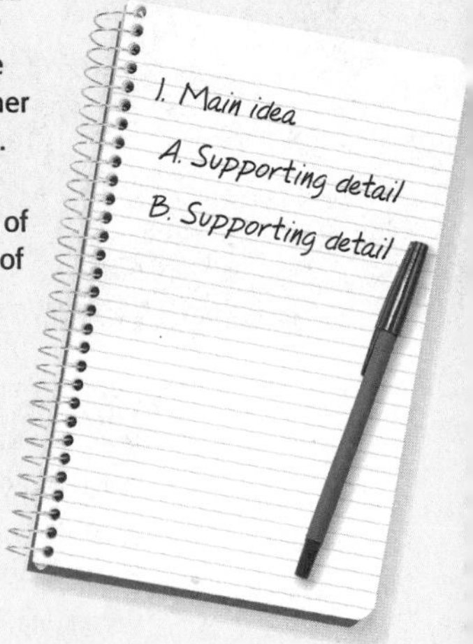

LESSON RESOURCES

UNIT THREE RESOURCE BOOK, pp. 66–70

ASSESSMENT RESOURCES
Formal Assessment, pp. 87–88
Teacher's Guide to Assessment and Portfolio Use
Test Generator

SKILLS TRANSPARENCIES AND COPYMASTERS
Literary Analysis
- Author's Perspective, T13 (for Activity, p. 527)

Reading and Critical Thinking
- Main Idea and Supporting Details, T12 (for Think Critically, item 4, p. 527)

Grammar
- Possessive Nouns, C66 (for Mini Lesson, p. 528)

Vocabulary
- Context Clues, C58 (for Mini Lesson, p. 524)

Writing
- Varying Sentence Openers and Closers, T18 (for Writing Option 1, p. 529)
- Poem, C27 (for Writing Option 2, p. 529)

INTEGRATED TECHNOLOGY
Net Activities
Internet: Research Starter
Visit our website:
www.mcdougallittell.com

from

In Search of Our Mothers' Gardens

Alice Walker

In the late 1920s my mother ran away from home to marry my father. Marriage, if not running away, was expected of seventeen-year-old girls. By the time she was twenty, she had two children and was pregnant with a third. Five children later, I was born. And this is how I came to know my mother: she seemed a large, soft, loving-eyed woman who was rarely impatient in our home. Her quick, violent temper was on view only a few times a year, when she battled with the white landlord who had the misfortune to suggest to her that her children did not need to go to school.

She made all the clothes we wore, even my brothers' overalls. She made all the towels and sheets we used. She spent the summers canning vegetables and fruits. She spent the winter evenings making quilts enough to cover all our beds.

Detail of *Jestina's Garden* (1996), Hyacinth Manning. SuperStock.

WORDS TO KNOW

impatient (ĭm-pā'shənt) *adj.* unable to tolerate irritation

TEACHING THE LITERATURE

Customizing Instruction

Less Proficient Readers

Have students keep these questions in mind as they read:

- How does Walker's mother express her creativity?
- How does Walker express her creativity?
- What is Walker trying to say in this essay?

Students Acquiring English

Help students understand that the image of the gardens is being used as a metaphor.

Students may wish to share other images of creativity from their cultures.

Use **Spanish Study Guide** for additional support, pp. 116–118.

BLOCK SCHEDULING: MANAGING TIME

If your schedule requires that you cover the lesson objectives in a shorter time, use . . .

- Preparing to Read, p. 522
- Thinking Through the Literature, p. 527

If you want to take advantage of longer class time, use . . .

- TE Teaching Options: Preteaching Vocabulary, pp. 524–525; Standardized Test Practice, p. 526
- Choices & Challenges, p. 529

Reading and Analyzing

Reading Skills and Strategies: PREVIEW

Briefly summarize the story emphasizing the metaphor of creativity. Discuss the image on the opening page as well as the title.

Active Reading MAIN IDEA

Help students work with a graphic organizer to identify main ideas and subordinate details.

Use **Unit Three Resource Book** p. 67 for more practice.

Literary Analysis

AUTHOR'S PERSPECTIVE

Suggest that students look for words and details that reveal the author's perspective. For example, word choices such as *muzzled* and *mutilated* are often associated with the treatment of animals. In contrast, she also uses words such as *vibrant* and *creative.* Strong details such as the "anonymous Black woman in Alabama" who made the quilt hanging in the Smithsonian also help the reader understand the author's perspective.

Use **Unit Three Resource Book** p. 68 for more practice.

During the "working" day, she labored beside—not behind—my father in the fields. Her day began before sunup, and did not end until late at night. There was never a moment for her to sit down, undisturbed, to unravel her own private thoughts; never a time free from interruption—by work or the noisy inquiries of her many children. And yet, it is to my mother—and all our mothers who were not famous—that I went in search of the secret of
1 what has fed that muzzled and often mutilated, but vibrant, creative spirit that the black woman has inherited, and that pops out in wild and unlikely places to this day.

But when, you will ask, did my overworked mother have time to know or care about feeding the creative spirit?

The answer is so simple that many of us have spent years discovering it. We have constantly looked high, when we should have looked high—and low.

For example: in the Smithsonian Institution[1] in Washington, D.C., there hangs a quilt unlike any other in the world. In fanciful, inspired, and yet simple and identifiable figures, it portrays the story of the Crucifixion. It is considered rare, beyond price. Though it follows no known pattern of quilt-making, and though it is made of bits and pieces of worthless rags, it is obviously the work of a person of powerful imagination and deep spiritual feeling. Below this quilt I saw a note that says it was made by "an anonymous Black woman in Alabama, a hundred years ago."

If we could locate this "anonymous" black woman from Alabama, she would turn out to be one of our grandmothers—an artist who left her mark in the only materials she could afford, and in the only medium her position in society allowed her to use.

As Virginia Woolf[2] wrote further, in *A Room of One's Own:*

> Yet genius of a sort must have existed among women as it must have existed among the working class. [Change this to "slaves" and "the wives and daughters of sharecroppers."] Now and again an Emily Brontë or a Robert Burns [change this to "a Zora Hurston or a Richard Wright[3]"] blazes out and proves its presence. But certainly it never got itself on to paper. When, however, one reads of a witch being ducked[4], of a woman possessed by devils [or "Sainthood"], of a wise woman selling herbs [our root workers], or even a very remarkable man who had a mother, then I think we are on the track of a lost novelist, a suppressed poet, of some mute and inglorious[5] Jane Austen[6]. . . . Indeed, I would venture to guess that Anon, who wrote so many poems without signing them, was often a woman. . . .

1. **Smithsonian Institution:** a collection of museums in Washington, D.C., founded in 1846, that archives and displays U.S. historical, scientific, and cultural materials.
2. **Virginia Woolf:** British novelist, critic, and essayist of the early 1900s whose works include *To the Lighthouse* and *The Waves.*
3. **Emily Brontë . . . Richard Wright:** The British novelist Emily Brontë was not formally educated (at the time, nearly all those formally educated were males) but became famous for her novel *Wuthering Heights.* Robert Burns, well-known Scottish poet of the late 1700s, wrote in Scottish dialect and grew up in a poor farming family. Zora Neale Hurston (1901–1960) was a U.S. author who wrote novels about African-American life, such as *Jonah's Gourd Vine.* Richard Wright (1908–1960), U.S. author acclaimed for his novel *Native Son,* wrote several works about life as an African American.
4. **witch being ducked:** Some women accused of witchcraft were held under water in the belief that this would prove their guilt or innocence.
5. **inglorious:** unknown; not famous.
6. **Jane Austen:** highly praised English novelist (1775–1817) whose many works included *Sense and Sensibility, Pride and Prejudice,* and *Emma.*

WORDS TO KNOW

vibrant (vī'brənt) *adj.* full of energy and activity
medium (mē'dē-əm) *n.* a specific type of artistic technique or means of expression

524

Teaching Options

Mini Lesson Preteaching Vocabulary

USING CONTEXT CLUES Call students' attention to the list of WORDS TO KNOW. Remind them that sometimes they can understand the meaning of an unfamiliar word by examining the context in which the word is used. Use the model sentence to demonstrate the strategy of using context clues that provide inferences to word meaning.

Model Sentence

After 12 hours of driving in bumper-to-bumper traffic, we were *impatient* to get home.

Instruction

- Write the model sentence on the chalkboard.
- Ask a volunteer to summarize the meaning of the sentence.
- Have students use the meaning of the sentence to infer meanings for the word *impatient.*
- Ask a volunteer to use the word *impatient* in a sentence.

And so our mothers and grandmothers have, more often than not anonymously, handed on the creative spark, the seed of the flower they themselves never hoped to see: or like a sealed letter they could not plainly read.

And so it is, certainly, with my own mother. Unlike "Ma" Rainey's[7] songs, which retained their creator's name even while blasting forth from Bessie Smith's[8] mouth, no song or poem will bear my mother's name. Yet so many of the stories that I write, that we all write, are my mother's stories. Only recently did I fully realize this: that through years of listening to my mother's stories of her life, I have absorbed not only the stories themselves, but something of the manner in which she spoke, something of the urgency that involves the knowledge that her stories—like her life—must be recorded. It is probably for this reason that so much of what I have written is
2 about characters whose counterparts in real life are so much older than I am.

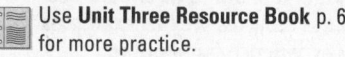

Jestina's Garden (1996), Hyacinth Manning. SuperStock.

But the telling of these stories, which came from my mother's lips as naturally as breathing, was not the only way my mother showed herself as an artist. For stories, too, were subject to being distracted, to dying without conclusion. Dinners must be started, and cotton must be gathered before the big rains. The artist that was and is my mother showed itself to me only after many years. This is what I finally noticed:

Like Mem, a character in *The Third Life of Grange Copeland,* my mother adorned with flowers whatever shabby house we were forced to live in. And not just your typical straggly country stand of zinnias, either. She planted ambitious gardens—and still does—with over fifty different varieties of plants that bloom profusely from early March until late November. Before she left home for the fields, she watered her flowers, chopped up the grass, and laid out new beds. When she returned from the fields she might divide clumps of bulbs, dig a cold pit, uproot and replant roses, or prune branches from her taller bushes or trees—until night came and it was too dark to see.

7. **"Ma" Rainey:** a popular African-American blues singer of the 1920s.

8. **Bessie Smith:** called "Empress of the Blues" for her 1920s recordings in which she sang with famous jazz musicians.

WORDS TO KNOW **profusely** (prə-fyōōs'lē) *adv.* in great abundance

525

Customizing Instruction

Less Proficient Readers

1 Use the following questions to help students understand what Walker is saying about her mother's creative spirit.

- How does Walker's mother inspire her?

  Possible Response: Walker's inspiration came from her mother's stories of her life.

- How can a creative spirit pop out in wild and unlikely places?

  Possible Response: The anonymous black woman in the essay who designs a quilt that is a work of art is an example of how a creative spirit can pop out in wild and unlikely places.

Gifted and Talented

Have students find out more information about Virginia Woolf. Ask students to hypothesize about the connection Walker might have felt to Woolf, a white British writer.

Possible Response: Woolf and Walker are alike in that they were both feminists who wrote about the mothers they cherished. Both challenged the restrictions they encountered as women writers. Their upbringings were quite different, however. Woolf grew up in England and her family was "well-to-do." Walker grew up in poverty in the South.

Students Acquiring English

2 Explain difficult vocabulary such as *counterparts.* The counterparts Walker refers to are the real people on whom her fictional characters are based.

Exercises Read the following sentences. Ask students to use context clues to determine the meanings of the italicized terms.

1. The mouse is an *ingenious* contraption that enables users to move the cursor on the screen without pressing any keys.
2. While Marla often paints with watercolors, oil is her favorite *medium.*
3. She thanked me *profusely* and smothered me with hugs and kisses.
4. My grandmother is a healthy and *vibrant* 87-year-old woman.

Use **Unit Three Resource Book** p. 69 for more practice.

A lesson on context clues appears on p. 56 in the Pupil's Edition.

Reading and Analyzing

Reading Skills and Strategies: VISUALIZING

Have students visualize Walker's mother's garden as they read about it. Ask students for words and phrases that could describe the garden.

Literary Analysis: SYMBOL

A symbol is a person, place, object, or activity that stands for something beyond itself. Certain symbols are commonly used in literature, such as a journey to represent life or night to represent death. Ask students to identify and explain the meaning of the symbols in the following sentence:

"I hear again the praise showered on her because whatever rocky soil she landed on, she turned into a garden."

Possible Response: The rocky soil may symbolize the tough circumstances Walker's mother faced. The garden may symbolize her creativity.

Reading Skills and Strategies: QUESTIONING

Ask students why Walker capitalizes the words *Creator, Beauty,* and *Art.*

Possible Response: Walker capitalizes these words to stress their importance, and because they refer to her mother.

Literary Analysis
AUTHOR'S PERSPECTIVE

(A) The last five lines on p. 526 reiterate the idea stated in the first paragraph on p. 525. Identify other examples of Walker's values in the poem that also appear in the main text of the essay.

Possible Responses: Black women are strong and powerful; education is an important step on the road to equality.

Whatever she planted grew as if by magic, and her fame as a grower of flowers spread over three counties. Because of her creativity with her flowers, even my memories of poverty are seen through a screen of blooms—sunflowers, petunias, roses, dahlias, forsythia, spirea, delphiniums, verbena . . . and on and on.

And I remember people coming to my mother's yard to be given cuttings from her flowers; I hear again the praise showered on her because whatever rocky soil she landed on, she turned into a garden. A garden so brilliant with colors, so original in its design, so magnificent with life and creativity, that to this day people drive by our house in Georgia—perfect strangers and imperfect strangers—and ask to stand or walk among my mother's art.

I notice that it is only when my mother is working in her flowers that she is radiant, almost to the point of being invisible—except as Creator: hand and eye. She is involved in work her soul must have. Ordering the universe in the image of her personal conception of Beauty.

Her face, as she prepares the Art that is her gift, is a legacy of respect she leaves to me, for all that illuminates and cherishes life. She has handed down respect for the possibilities—and the will to grasp them.

For her, so hindered and intruded upon in so many ways, being an artist has still been a daily part of her life. This ability to hold on, even in very simple ways, is work black women have done for a very long time.

This poem is not enough, but it is something, for the woman who literally covered the holes in our walls with sunflowers:

They were women then
My mama's generation
Husky of voice—Stout of
Step
With fists as well as
Hands
How they battered down
Doors
And ironed
Starched white
Shirts
How they led
Armies
Headragged Generals
Across mined
Fields
Booby-trapped
Kitchens
To discover books
Desks
A place for us
How they knew what we
Must know
Without knowing a page (A)
Of it
Themselves.

Guided by my heritage of a love of beauty and a respect for strength—in search of my mother's garden, I found my own.

And perhaps in Africa over two hundred years ago, there was just such a mother; perhaps she painted vivid and daring decorations in oranges and yellows and greens on the walls of her hut; perhaps she sang—in a voice like Roberta Flack's[9]—*sweetly* over the compounds of her village; perhaps she wove the most stunning mats or told the most ingenious stories of all the village storytellers. Perhaps she was herself a poet—though only her daughter's name is signed to the poems that we know.

Perhaps Phillis Wheatley's mother was also an artist.

Perhaps in more than Phillis Wheatley's biological life is her mother's signature made clear. ❖

9. **Roberta Flack:** African-American singer whose vocal styles include soul, light jazz, and rock music.

WORDS TO KNOW **ingenious** (ĭn-jēn′yəs) *adj.* creatively clever

Teaching Options

Assessment Standardized Test Practice

THEME You can informally assess students' understanding of the selection by providing practice in responding to writing prompts. Have them write an essay explaining what Alice Walker means in the following quotation. Students should use examples from the essay as well as examples from their own experience for support.

"Guided by my heritage of a love of beauty and a respect for strength–in search of my mother's garden, I found my own."

RUBRIC

3 **Full Accomplishment** Response reflects a full understanding of the quotation and of the essay. Response is supported by good examples from the essay and from the student's own experience.

2 **Substantial Accomplishment** Response shows a general understanding of the quotation and of the essay. Response is supported by adequate examples from the essay and or the student's own experience.

1 **Little or Partial Accomplishment** Response shows little understanding of the quotation and of the essay. Response lacks adequate support.

Connect to the Literature

1. **What Do You Think?** What impressed you the most about Alice Walker's mother?

Comprehension Check
- What work did Walker's mother do?
- Why were her mother's stories so often incomplete?
- In what ways does Walker say that her mother was an artist?

Think Critically

2. What portrait of Walker's mother do you get from this essay? Think of three or four words to describe her and give examples of her actions to support your description.

3. What does her mother's garden represent, or **symbolize,** to Walker? What does it represent to Walker's mother?

THINK ABOUT
- the variety and abundance of the garden
- how her mother feels when working in the garden
- what Walker means by saying "in search of my mother's garden, I found my own"

4. ACTIVE READING MAIN IDEA Use the details you wrote in your READER'S NOTEBOOK as you read this essay to help you identify the **main idea.** Then summarize the main idea and at least three supporting details in your own words.

Extend Interpretations

5. **What If?** Imagine what Walker's mother said about this essay. Do you think she agreed with her daughter about her own creativity? Explain how you imagine Walker's mother responding.

6. **Critic's Corner** According to one critic, Walker's mother "has given Walker insight not only into the lives of black women but into the essential nature of art as a human process of illuminating and cherishing life." Based on your reading of the excerpt from *In Search of Our Mothers' Gardens* and "Everyday Use," do you agree with this assessment? Summarize what you think is the value of art to Alice Walker.

7. **Connect to Life** Think about your definition of art that you shared in an earlier discussion. After reading the excerpt from *In Search of Our Mothers' Gardens,* would you consider the garden created by Walker's mother to be art? How is this garden similar to or different from a painting, a poem, or a story? Explain.

Literary Analysis

AUTHOR'S PERSPECTIVE

An **author's perspective,** or viewpoint, results from his or her attitudes, beliefs, values, and feelings about issues.

Activity What would you say is Walker's perspective in this essay? Explain how this perspective influences what she writes about, and cite examples from the essay to support your analysis.

ACTIVE READING GENERALIZATIONS

A **generalization** is an idea or statement that emphasizes the general characteristics rather than the specific details of a subject. For example, the sentence, "Alice Walker is a feminist," is a generalization based on statements Walker has made and subjects she has chosen to write about. After having read several selections by Alice Walker, what other generalizations can you make about her beliefs and interests? What specific details led you to make your generalizations? Use a graphic like this one to record your ideas.

Generalizations		Selections	Details
	→		
	→		
	→		

GUIDING STUDENT RESPONSE

Connect to the Literature

1. **What Do You Think?**
Students will admire her for the same reasons Walker does. She has incredible strength and a creative spirit that cannot be suppressed.

Comprehension Check
- She kept house, raised a family, worked in the fields, and maintained a garden.
- She was interrupted by the demands of work and children.
- She told stories and created beautiful gardens.

Use Selection Quiz
Unit Three Resource Book, p. 70.

Think Critically

2. Possible Response: She was loving, patient, creative, and strong. Walker says that her mother was "loving-eyed" and "rarely impatient in our home." Her creativity was evident in her stories and her garden. Her constant hard work and battles for her children's future prove that she was a very strong person, both physically and emotionally.
3. Possible Response: To Walker, her mother's garden symbolizes the creative spirit of all black women, the spirit that was passed on to their daughters even if their daughters did not realize it at first. To Walker's mother, the garden represented beauty and accomplishment.
4. Possible Response: The main idea of this essay is that the spirit of creativity can never be suppressed or denied, as black women have known and demonstrated for generations through their quilts, gardens, stories, and songs. These women have been able to sow the seed of creativity in their offspring.

Extend Interpretations

What If? Most students will say that Walker's mother was proud of this essay and deeply touched by it. Some students may not think that she would agree with Walker about her own creativity; they might imagine that Walker's mother would be humble about her flower garden and not want to acknowledge that a garden could be a work of art.

Critic's Corner Students can refer both to the essay and to the short story in their responses. Most students will agree with this assessment. They may say that Walker believes that art is part of the human spirit.

Connect to Life Students may want to redefine their interpretation of art.

Literary Analysis

Author's Perspective Students will need to have a clear idea about her perspective; discussing her perspective in class could prove helpful in launching the individual search for support.

IN SEARCH OF OUR MOTHERS' GARDENS 527

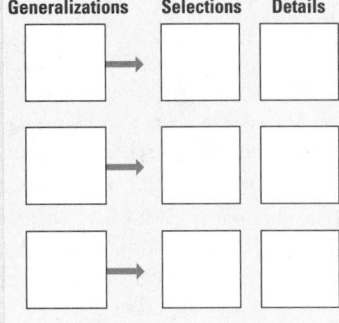

The Author's Style

Beyond the details that appeal to the senses is the consideration of Walker's style, which helps make her African-American experience forceful and poignant.

Analysis of Style

A First activity—**opinions in straightforward diction:** "Everyday Use": The narrator speaks her mind directly, telling her daughter, "The truth is . . . I promised to give them quilts to Maggie"; "In Search of Our Mothers' Gardens": Walker eloquently praises her mother, using fairly simple language, such as, "Whatever she planted grew as if by magic."
concrete details: "Women": "How they battered down / Doors / And ironed / Starched white / Shirts"; "Everyday Use": "Bits and pieces of Grandpa Jarrell's Paisley shirts"
distinctive voices for characters: In "Everyday Use," the narrator's voice expresses her strength and endurance; Maggie's voice, by contrast, is timid and reluctant, while Dee is filled with the self-assurance and smugness of a recently educated youth.
authoritative yet personal voice: Her authority comes from the didacticism of the writing and her use of plural pronouns and verbs of command ("we must"). This last also gives her voice a personal ring.

B Second activity—**other examples:** Walker often writes in the African-American dialect of the South. She also expresses ideas in terms of inheritances, gifts, or history.

C Third activity—In each genre, Walker expresses controversial opinions straightforwardly. Her style is authoritative and personal in each genre as well. What she says often surprises us.

Applications

1. **Speaking and Listening** Have students use the following criteria to critique oral interpretation. The student
   - makes and supports a valid interpretation of how the character might voice those lines
   - uses voice (volume and tone) to establish mood and convey meaning
   - uses movement and gestures to establish mood and convey meaning
   - uses facial expressions to establish mood and convey meaning
2. **Imitating Style** Remind students to revisit the Key Aspects box on the page before beginning their revisions.
3. **Changing Style** Have students go through the entire writing process for this activity—prewriting, drafting, editing, and publishing.

THE AUTHOR'S STYLE

Alice Walker's Passionate Expression

The great stylist E. B. White once wrote, "All writing is communication; creative writing is communication through revelation—it is the Self escaping into the open." Alice Walker would almost certainly agree, for she reveals so much of herself in her writing. Whether speaking through characters in her fiction or as herself in her poetry and nonfiction, Walker's style is to be direct and passionate—to look the reader in the eye and speak her mind.

Key Aspects of Walker's Style

- strong opinions expressed in clear, straightforward diction
- concrete details and images rather than abstract concepts
- a distinctive voice created for each fictional character
- an authoritative, yet personal voice in her essays

Analysis of Style

Study the information above and take a few minutes to review the selections included in this Author Study. Then complete the following activities:

- **A** Find examples of each aspect of Walker's style in one or more of the selections. You might use a chart like the one shown here to organize your work.
- **B** Look for additional aspects of Walker's style that capture your attention. How would you describe them? What examples can you find to illustrate those aspects of style that you identify?
- **C** In a small group, discuss whether Walker's style changes depending on the genre—fiction, nonfiction, poetry. Use the selections in this text—or others by Walker that you have read—to support your opinion.

Aspects of style	Selection(s)	Example(s)
concrete details and images	"Everyday Use"	"large, big-boned woman" "rough, man-working hands"

Applications

1. Speaking and Listening With a small group of classmates, do an oral reading of selected passages from Walker's works included in this Author Study. Try to capture the strong, authoritative voice that comes through loud and clear in all her writing. If you have access to recording equipment, make a recording of the oral readings to share with other literature classes.

2. Imitating Style Review Walker's prose style and look especially at the way she emphasizes ideas that are important to her. Take a sample of your own writing and try adding a bit more passion and energy to your expression. Ask yourself these questions:

- Would someone reading your work recognize how important the topic is to you? In other words, have you chosen to write about something that you really care about?
- Did you use clear, simple diction to express your ideas?
- Does your writing include concrete details that describe characters and events?

3. Changing Style Work with a partner to rewrite a passage from one of the selections you've read, using a different style. For example, you might use more formal diction to rewrite a passage from "Everyday Use." Or you may prefer to try rewriting the ideas expressed in the poem "Women" in prose form. Discuss with a classmate how these changes affect your understanding of Walker's work.

Mini Lesson Grammar

POSSESSIVES An apostrophe and sometimes *s* are used to form possessive nouns. For singular words, add *'s (the girl's books)*. For plural words ending in *s*, add only the apostrophe *(the dogs' kennel)*. For plural words not ending in *s*, add *'s (the children's toys)*. Remember that the apostrophe or apostrophe plus *s* is an addition. Before this addition, always spell the name of the owner or owners without dropping or adding letters *(the Jones's house)*.

Write the following sentence on the chalkboard: "She made all the clothes we wore, even my brothers' overalls."

Underline the possessive as shown. Have students identify that *brothers* is plural because Walker is referring to more than one brother. Therefore, *brothers'* is plural possessive.

Use **Grammar Transparencies and Copymasters,** p. 66.

Use McDougal Littell's ***Language Network,*** Chapter 11, for more instruction in possessives.

Writing Options

1. Personal Response Write a personal essay about Alice Walker explaining your response to her ideas and her art. Be as honest about your opinion as Walker is herself.

2. Praise Poem Pick someone you admire greatly and write a poem about him or her modeled after Walker's poem "Women."

Activities & Explorations

Quilt Display Quilting figures in both "Everyday Use" and the excerpt from *In Search of Our Mothers' Gardens.* Collect images of quilts and quilting patterns that you can display in your class. Feel free to make drawings of quilting patterns. ~ ART

Inquiry & Research

Women's Voices Walker refers to Ma Rainey, Bessie Smith, and Roberta Flack. Find recordings by these singers, and research information about them. Play the recordings for your class, and explain why they provide good examples of Walker's point.

Vocabulary in Action

EXERCISE: MEANING CLUES Decide whether each statement is true or false, based on the meaning of the sentence itself.

1. Impatient people feel as if they have all the time in the world.

2. Alice Walker's mother loved plants that grew profusely.

3. An ingenious story is simple and dull.

4. Alice Walker's story is about the vibrant spirit of African-American women.

5. An artist's medium is used to record financial information.

In the spirit of Alice Walker and her mother, research the art being produced by everyday artists today. Your research can take you around the world or deep into your own community. The point is to celebrate the uncelebrated and explain how art enriches people's lives. Your celebration can take just about any form: for example, you could videotape interviews of local artists and show their works, or you could create an art book that includes biographies of the artists and photos of their works. Be creative—make your product a work of art, too.

Print Sources Look at specialty books about arts and crafts: for example, the history of quilting or the art of regional cooking. You could choose to research ethnic art by particular Asian, African, Native-American, Eastern-European, Latino, African-American, and Anglo-American groups. You don't have to be limited by the visual arts; research music (blues, blue grass, zydeco), dance (pop, jazz), performance art, and literature. Look through the *Reader's Guide* for profiles of artists who work with unusual materials, such as found objects, bottle caps, or uncooked pasta.

Web Sites Try inputting key words about particular art forms, such as art glass, sports art, sculpture, textile art, and oral storytelling.

Leg Work Investigate local artists in your community by attending art fairs, storytelling festivals, and other public exhibitions. Visit the art department of a nearby college or university to get ideas. Attend poetry readings at book stores and coffee houses.

More Online: Research Starter
www.mcdougallittell.com

Author Study Project

CELEBRATING THE CULTURAL ARTS

Students may want to use their cultural research for interdisciplinary projects. Studying successful craft cooperatives of the past is a good way. For example, Appalachian women have practiced quilting for over 200 years. Students may find community craft cooperatives in their areas in addition to researching those of the past.

SOURCES
Most cities and states have an arts commission that channels money to community art groups. These are often good places to find directions to groups of emerging artists. State and local arts commissions can be found in the telephone book or on city and state government Web sites.

MULTIMEDIA PROJECT
Students may want to use the results of their research to create a multimedia project. Students can use photographs, videos, or slides to present their research. If available, computers can also help display Web pages or artwork.

Vocabulary in Action

EXERCISE

1. False
2. True
3. False
4. True
5. False

Writing Options

1. **Personal Response** Students should support their opinions with evidence from the text.
2. **Praise Poem** To help students get started, put a cluster diagram on the board, and brainstorm ideas about someone students admire.

Activities & Explorations

1. **Unsung Heroines** To help students get started, model a process by selecting a heroine and listing her accomplishments on the chalkboard.
2. **Quilt Display** Suggest that students go to a craft store or to the library to find quilt pattern books.

Inquiry & Research

Women's Voices Students should use appropriate print and non-print resources for their research.

Objectives
- write an Oral History
- use a written text as a model for writing
- revise a draft to achieve unity and coherence
- correctly punctuate quoted materials

Introducing the Workshop

A Oral History Students often encounter stories. Historians often interview individuals to reconstruct stories about the past to capture the authenticity of important moments. The interviews we watch on television and read in magazines bring us close to the exciting and significant moments in other people's lives, and they allow us to hear the story in the speaker's own unique voice.

Basics in a Box

B Using the Guidelines & Standards The Guidelines & Standards divide the project into two distinct segments: the interview segment and the presentation of information gathered in the interview, either in writing or orally. Encourage students to set specific goals and standards for each of the two parts.

To engage students visually, use **Power Presentation** 6, Oral History.

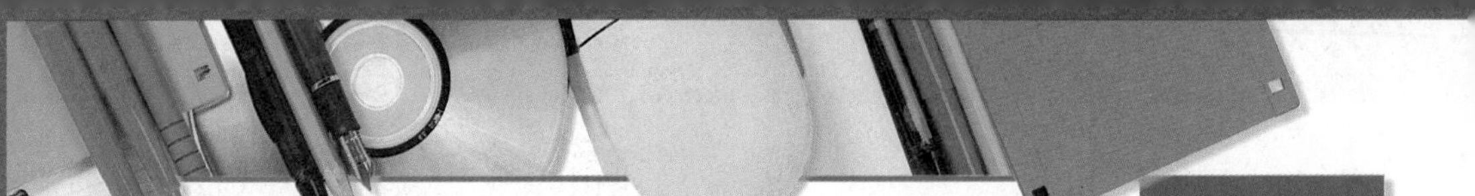

Communication Workshop — Oral History

Retelling a personal history . . .

A **From Reading to Writing** Do you ever wish you knew more about the lives of your parents, grandparents, or friends? Although Rita Dove and Rudolfo Anaya are writers who chose to remember their grandfathers in poetry and prose, some people share memories by creating oral histories. An **oral history** uses a person's own words, gathered from an interview, to record stories and information about that person's life. Counselors, reporters, and anthropologists also use specific types of oral histories in their daily work.

For Your Portfolio

WRITING PROMPT Conduct an interview and write an oral history.

Purpose: To tell someone else's story using that person's own words

Audience: The person you interviewed, others who know that person, patrons of your local library, members of a historical society, or classmates

Basics in a Box

B **GUIDELINES & STANDARDS** Oral History

A successful interview should
- be guided by questions and research about the person, prepared before the interview
- be recorded accurately through notes and a tape recorder, used with the person's permission
- include open-ended and follow-up questions to draw out the person's interests
- last no longer than 90 minutes per interview session

A successful oral history should
- include any necessary background information about the person in an introduction
- feature accurately transcribed quotations
- offer a well-rounded portrait of the person
- present a clear focus and logical organization

LESSON RESOURCES

USING PRINT RESOURCES

Unit Three Resource Book
- Conducting Your Interview, p. 71
- Planning and Drafting, p. 72
- Peer Response, pp. 73–74
- Revising, Editing, and Proofreading, p. 75
- Student Models, p. 76
- Standards for Evaluation, p. 77

USING MEDIA RESOURCES

LaserLinks
Writing Springboards
See Teacher's SourceBook p. 64 for bar codes.

Writing Coach CD-ROM

Visit our website:
www.mcdougallittell.com

Analyzing a Professional Model

by Mary Jo Clark as told to Jack Clark

excerpted from an article in the *Chicago Reader* newspaper

Mary Jo Clark lived in Chicago during the 1930s. Here, she tells her son Jack about leaving school during the Great Depression to work in the office of a manufacturing company.

I did everything in the office. I took dictation. I typed letters. I took phone calls. I wrote out orders—anything they wanted done. I could type 60 words a minute. And take dictation, 125 words a minute. I'd had a course in business law where you learned about checks and that sort of stuff—bills of sale, invoices. So I knew all that stuff, and I wasn't even 16 years old.

But that was because my mother was very smart. She could see the writing on the wall, and she knew that we'd need to go to work to make money to keep the house going.

Well, anyway, orders weren't so good. They weren't making any money, so they asked me if I would go in the factory and wire lamps. Which is probably the only practical thing I ever learned in my whole working life. I can still wire a lamp when I need to.

So I stood at a table and wired lamps. I'd be looking out at this big clock on Union Station, and a clock never moved so slowly. I was insulted that I should be doing factory work. This is at 16.

I always brought my lunch, and at lunchtime I'd eat in a hurry. Then I'd walk all the way down Jackson to Michigan, and then I'd turn around and walk back. I'd never go in a store and look or anything. I just walked. It was strange. And I felt so lost in this great big world out there. I knew nobody, so it was safe to be inside wiring my lamps.

Besides lamps, they also made radio benches. They were sort of kidney shaped, with an upholstered seat. People put them in front of their radio and sat and listened. They also made bookends. "Old Ironsides."

One day I told the boss that I liked those bookends. I said, "They're very nice." And he said, "You can have a pair." He called the factory boy in and said, "Would you paint up a pair of bookends for...." They were metal ships. They painted them black. He said, "Paint up a set of these bookends for Jo to take home. In fact, if you like 'em you can take a set home too."

The kid said, "Oh, I took a set home last night." That finished him. "You're fired," the boss said.

Anyway, you don't take the boss's stuff home without asking, that's for sure.

GUIDELINES IN ACTION

1. The italicized section sets up the selection and gives background information.
2. Captures the subject's first-person voice by keeping her specific word choices and speaking patterns
   Another Option:
   - Include the questions asked, followed by the person's answers.
3. The interviewer draws out his subject's thoughts and feelings to create a well-rounded portrait of the person.
4. Includes specific anecdotes
5. Concludes naturally where the speaker ended this anecdote

Teaching the Lesson

Analyzing the Model

"by Mary Jo Clark as told to Jack Clark"

The professional model recounts the subject's working life in Chicago during the Great Depression when she was sixteen. The article emphasizes a specific incident that taught her an important lesson.

Explain that the events related here formed a significant memory in the subject's life and served to define her identity. She clearly felt insulted at the idea of working in a factory when she was a skilled office worker.

Have students read the professional model, then discuss the Guidelines & Standards. Point out the key words and phrases in the professional model that correspond to the elements mentioned in the second part of the Guidelines & Standards.

1. Point out that students can be more thorough than the model in presenting background information if they need to be. The key is to provide relevant background information.
2. Have students suggest an alternate opening based on the other options listed.
   Possible Response: The writer could put the interview questions in italics and the subject's responses in non italicized type.
3. Point out that follow-up questions in the interview may have resulted in the subject sharing this information. In other words, as the subject is talking, the interviewer responds with natural questions that encourage the subject to share more information or go into greater detail on a specific topic. Explain that details which create a well-rounded portrait often cannot be planned but are the result of a spontaneous, comfortable and natural conversation between interviewer and subject.
4. Ask students how the subject's account suddenly gets focused at this point.
   Possible Response: The subject begins telling of a specific past incident which she shares by creating a scene that includes dialogue.

COMMUNICATION WORKSHOP 531

Guiding Student Writing

Prewriting

Conducting the Interview

If after reading the Idea Bank students are having difficulty choosing people to interview, suggest they try the following:

- Make a list of careers or professions that interest you, then create a list of people in your community who work in those careers and professions.
- Create a list of people who have achieved something you consider admirable, and plan to interview one of them.

Steps for a Successful Interview

1. As a way to begin constructing interview questions, have students freewrite their thoughts and feelings related to the person they plan to interview. They can use these personal responses as a starting point for focusing their interest and for writing questions to pursue those interests.
2. Factual data can be gathered on the Internet, in the library, and from talking with people who know the person to be interviewed. Have students create a "three source" plan in which they consult three different living sources and/or library sources in searching for background information on their subject.
3. Have students formally request an interview, then courteously schedule a convenient date, time, and place. Calling ahead on the day of the appointment to confirm the interview is an additional courtesy. Also, remind students to send a written thank-you note to their interview subject when the assignment is complete.
4. If using a tape recorder, students should take written notes that focus on main ideas. These can provide a source for follow-up questions, following the form "Earlier you said that . . . Could you please elaborate."

Transcribing the Interview

When transcribing a tape-recorded interview, it is important to get the words and phrases exactly right. Explain to students that such accuracy and precision will involve repeated use of the stop, rewind, and play buttons on the tape recorder. Transcribing short phrases that constitute parts of sentences is more efficient than transcribing longer passages. Instead of using the labels "Question" and "Answer" in their transcripts, students may prefer to use their own name and the interview subject's name.

IDEA Bank

1. Your Working Portfolio
Build on one of the **Writing Options** you completed earlier in this unit:

- **Living History Questions,** p. 461
- **Oral History Notes,** p. 492

2. I like to listen to . . .
Make a list of friends, family members, and other people who are special to you. Plan to interview someone from your list.

3. That Must Have Been Something
Make a list of people you know who lived through important events and historical periods such as the 1933 World's Fair and the Great Depression. Contact one of these people to request an interview.

Need help with your interview?

See the **Communications Handbook**
Conducting Interviews, p. 1178

Creating an Oral History

❶ Conducting Your Interview

The first step, of course, is to **choose the person** you want to interview. You might choose someone who lived through an important historical event or who knows about something that interests you. See the **Idea Bank** in the margin for other suggestions. After you pick a person to interview, follow these steps.

Steps for a Successful Interview

1. **Compose your questions.** What do you want to learn about from the person you plan to interview? Prepare a list of questions that focus on a few subjects areas, such as early life, work life, and social life. Avoid questions with *yes/no* answers. Instead, ask questions that begin with words such as *how, what, why, when, where,* or *who.*
2. **Research your subject.** You can learn more about your subject by talking to people who know him or her. If the person you plan to interview is a public person, such as a politician, you can use library resources to learn about the person. Use your research to help you prepare more in-depth questions.
3. **Set up the interview.** Set a date, time, and place for the interview and be sure to show up on time. If you plan to use recording equipment, practice beforehand. Always ask permission before you begin recording.
4. **Listen carefully.** Even if you use a tape recorder, it's important to jot down notes and questions as you listen. You may need to ask follow-up questions later to get more information or to make something clear.

❷ Transcribing the Interview

Transcribe your interview **verbatim**, using the subject's exact words and the questions you asked. You can use parentheses around additional questions you have as you transcribe. Be sure to keep your original notes and recordings in case you need more material or decide to change your focus later. Your transcript may look similar to this example.

Question: *What kind of work did you do as a teenager?*

Answer: . . . I left school early in May (what year?) to take this job at the J Company. Some friends of Ma knew that these men, Mr. Anthony and Mr. Joseph, needed a girl Friday. I took dictation and wrote letters and all that. But after a while they weren't making any money so they asked me if I would go in the factory and wire lamps. Which is probably the only practical thing I ever learned in my whole working career. I can still wire a lamp when I need to.

Question: *It sounds like they expected you to be able to do a lot of things at that job. What else do you remember about working there?*

Answer: The building where I worked was at Clinton Street and Jackson and I'd be looking out at this clock on Union Station. And a clock never moved so slowly. There's a very nice building on that corner now, not like the rickety thing I worked in.

❸ Planning Your Oral History

After you create your transcript, decide how you want to present the oral history. Here are some steps to help you.

Using Your Notes and Transcript

1. **Choose a focus.** Reread the transcript and decide which parts will be the focus of your oral history. For example, if the person you interviewed talked about childhood memories, choose the most interesting memories for your focus.
2. **Structure your material.** How will you present the focus of your oral history? You can structure your oral history as a running narrative, or story, like the Mary Jo Clark history. You can also use the question-and-answer structure of an interview. Use the narrative structure if your oral history focuses on memories told in the order in which they happened. The interview structure works well if your subject talked about memories that are not in sequence, or time order. Be sure to include the questions and the answers if you use this structure.

❹ Drafting

Begin drafting your oral history by editing the transcript. You have already found the sections of the transcript that fit your focus. Now you must decide how much of these sections to use for the **body** of your oral history. Include enough information to make your history interesting to readers.

If you leave out any words, use ellipses (. . .) to show that words were omitted. If you need to add information in your own words, put this added material in brackets [ ].

Introduction

Go back to the beginning and draft an introduction that includes background information about the subject, such as the name and age of the person and the focus of the oral history.

Conclusion

You might end your oral history where your subject finishes telling a story. If this is not possible, write a concluding paragraph that summarizes or restates information from the oral history.

Go back to your subject to fill in any gaps, to add details, and to verify accuracy. Never make up missing details.

Ask Your Peer Reader

- What are the most memorable details about the person I interviewed?
- What did you learn from my interview that you didn't know before?
- What else would you like to know about the person?

Planning the Oral History

Using Your Notes and Transcript

1. A focus marks a center of interest. Have students group their interview subject's ideas and memories by classifying them according to similarities or dominant impressions. From these groupings, they can better see the possibilities for a focus.
2. Have students create a rough outline based on their preliminary analysis of focus possibilities.

Drafting

Deciding what to leave out of an oral history is sometimes a difficult decision. Have students begin the drafting process by writing a sentence stating the tone they want their oral history to convey and the reason why. Then, with this idea for tone clearly in mind, have them reread their transcripts and eliminate all those sections that do not contribute to creating this tone.

COMMUNICATION WORKSHOP 533

Revising

ACHIEVING UNITY AND COHERENCE

As a revision activity, have students go through their drafts and, for each paragraph or for each question-answer exchange, briefly summarize the main point. Then, once main ideas have been identified, they can evaluate the unity and coherence of each section. Remind students that, in addition to moving sections to enhance coherence and unity, they can add transitional words. Students should place any words they add in brackets to signify that these words have been added by the writer.

Editing and Proofreading

PUNCTUATING QUOTED MATERIALS

Remind students that when punctuating quoted materials, end punctuation is usually placed inside the quotation marks. Show students the correct way to punctuate a quotation by writing the following examples on the chalkboard.

"I really couldn't believe that it happened to me."

"Do you know what I mean?"

Reflecting

Ask students to evaluate their reaction to becoming involved in someone else's story. How did they capture the emotion portrayed in the interview? What did this exchange reveal about themselves? Have students add these self-evaluations to their working portfolios.

Need revising help?

Review the **Rubric**, p. 530

Consider **peer reader** comments

Check **Revision Guidelines**, p. 1145

Puzzled by adding punctuation?

See the **Grammar Handbook**

Punctuation Chart, pp. 1203-1204

Publishing IDEAS

- Read your oral history aloud to the class. Play selected passages of the interview tape to convey the person's own voice and words.
- Make a collection of your oral histories. If your school has desktop publishing capabilities, work together to produce and distribute your collection.

More Online: Publishing Options
www.mcdougallittell.com

5 Revising

TARGET SKILL ▶ ACHIEVING UNITY AND COHERENCE Sometimes a person being interviewed gets off the main topic, speaks without making clear transitions, or gives important details out of order. You may need to rearrange some of your material to create a unified and coherent oral history.

So we found out that Providence High School had a two (course) year commercial where you learned typing, shorthand, bookkeeping, and commercial law all in two years. And you got a commercial degree.

In 1927, when Marge was ready to go to high school, my mother said, "You've got to take a two-year commercial course."

6 Editing and Proofreading

TARGET SKILL ▶ PUNCTUATING QUOTED MATERIALS When you transcribed the interview or took notes, you may have skipped quotation marks, commas, and other punctuation. Your final write-up should use punctuation that reflects the speaker's meaning.

So, I left school in early May (what year?) 1930 to take this job at the Jay J Company. Some friends of Ma knew that these men, Mr. Anthony and Mr. Joseph, needed a girl friday. I took dictation and wrote letters and all that. But after a while, they weren't making any money, so they asked me if I would go in the factory and wire lamps.

7 Reflecting

FOR YOUR WORKING PORTFOLIO What did you learn about the person you interviewed? What was it like to listen to and tell someone else's story? Attach your answer to your finished piece. Save your oral history in your **Working Portfolio.**

Assessment Practice Revising & Editing

Read this paragraph from the first draft of a student essay. The underlined sections may include the following kinds of errors:

- **double negatives**
- **punctuation errors**
- **incorrect comparative forms**
- **incorrect possessive forms**

For each underlined section, choose the revision that most improves the writing.

> Mr. Sanchez owns one of our community's <u>successfulest</u> (1) businesses. He offers merchandise <u>you can't get nowhere else</u> (2). When I spoke with him about his achievement, he was very humble. "<u>I have been very lucky" he told me</u> (3). "Every one of my employees has contributed to the success of the store." One key to his prosperity has been attention to our <u>cities</u> (4) population. "<u>We have more young parents in the community now he continued</u> (5). As a result, he offers the <u>better selection</u> (6) of toys of any store in the community.

1. **A.** success
   B. most successfulest
   C. most successful
   D. Correct as is
2. **A.** you could get anywhere else.
   B. you can't hardly get anywhere else.
   C. you can get somewhere else.
   D. you can't get anywhere else.
3. **A.** "I have been very lucky." He told me.
   B. "I have been very lucky he told me.
   C. "I have been very lucky, he told me."
   D. "I have been very lucky," he told me.
4. **A.** cities'
   B. city's
   C. citys'
   D. Correct as is
5. **A.** "We have more young parents in the community now," he continued.
   B. "We have more young parents in the community now." he continued.
   C. We have more young parents in the community now he continued.
   D. Correct as is
6. **A.** more best selection
   B. best selection
   C. most better selection
   D. more better selection

Need extra help?

See the **Grammar Handbook**
Possessive Nouns, p. 1182
Comparison of Modifiers, p. 1188
Punctuation Chart, pp. 1203–1204

Assessment Practice

Before students begin the exercise, you may wish to briefly review the kinds of errors that the passage may contain. Remind students to read all the choices carefully before choosing the correct answer.

Answers:
1. C; **2.** D; **3.** D; **4.** B; **5.** A; **6.** B

Objectives

- reflect on and assess student understanding of the unit
- compare text events with experiences of students and other readers
- provide examples of themes that cross texts
- compare elements such as conflicts and characterization across texts
- assess and build portfolios

Reflecting on Theme

OPTION 1

A successful response will

- create a list of characters and people from Unit 3 who were positively influenced by youthful experiences.
- create a list of characters and people from Unit 3 who were negatively influenced by youthful experiences.
- add the student and partner to the appropriate column on the list.
- discuss reasons for listings.

OPTION 2

A successful response will

- create a proposal nominating a character or person from Unit 3 to speak at a school assembly.
- contain reasons for the nomination of the character or person.
- use persuasive techniques to convince the reader that the character or person nominated should speak at the assembly.

OPTION 3

If students are having trouble choosing identities, assign each student a different character, person, or writer. Give students a little time to get reacquainted with their character, person, or writer and write their monologues.

Self Assessment

Ask students what ideas they had about other people's perceptions of themselves before they read these selections. Ask them to explain how the characters and persons in this unit affected their ideas about identity.

UNIT THREE *Reflect* and Assess

The Search for Identity

Alées Piétonnières (1995), Jean-Pierre Stora.
The Grand Design, Leeds, England/Superstock.

How have your own views about identity been affected by the selections in this unit? How have you developed or improved your skills? Explore these questions by completing one or more of the options in each of the following selections.

Reflecting on Theme

OPTION 1

Classifying Experiences of Youth Draw a horizontal line in the middle of a sheet of paper. On the top half, list characters or real people from this unit who you think have been positively influenced by their youthful experience. On the bottom half, list characters who you think have been negatively affected. Then consider the activity that you completed on page 382, and add yourself and your partner to either category. Compare your lists with those of your classmates, and discuss your reasons for your listings.

OPTION 2

Nominating a Guest Speaker Look at the pie graph you made for the activity on page 451. How do you think this graph would look if it had been made by various characters and real people in this unit? Choose one character or person whose pie graph you think would be especially interesting. Then write an imaginary proposal in which you nominate that character or person to come and speak at a Heritage Day assembly at your school. Cast your nomination with those of your classmates and count them up to see which character from the unit received the most nominations.

OPTION 3

Character Identification This unit begins with a quotation from Lewis Carroll: "Who in the world am I? Ah, that's the great puzzle!" (See page 380.) What do you think the various characters, real people, and writers in this unit would say about themselves in response to that quotation? How would they describe their own identity? Play a game with a small group of classmates in which each group member assumes the identity of a character, real person, or writer from the unit. In your chosen role, without stating your name, deliver a short monologue on the topic of your identity. Other group members must then guess the name of the character, person, or writer you portrayed.

Self ASSESSMENT

READER'S NOTEBOOK

How have your ideas about identity been changed by the selections in this unit? Make a three-column chart. In the first column, record any new insights about how people's heritage influences the development of their identities. In the second column, record your new ideas about how people are shaped by their youthful experiences. In the third column, name the selections that prompted the insights in the first and second columns.

Reviewing Literary Concepts

OPTION 1

Examining Plot Structure Review the definition of plot and its component parts on pages 383–384. While people can usually agree on a story's exposition and rising action, there are often disputes about a story's climax, and some stories do not include falling action. Working with a partner, review the short stories in this unit, identifying the phases of the plot for each story. Compare the results of your analysis with those of your classmates. Discuss any areas of disagreement.

OPTION 2

Analyzing Author's Perspective Review the information about author's perspective on pages 452–453. Then complete a chart like the one shown for the nonfiction selections in this unit. After you complete your chart, identify the piece that had the greatest impact on you. Write a note explaining the reasons for your choice.

Selection	Author's Purpose	Tone	Style	Author's Perspective

Building Your Portfolio

- **Writing Options** Several of the Writing Options in this unit directed you to write a character sketch or personality profile of a character from a selection. Look over your work for these assignments and pick one or two pieces that you think give the most vivid and interesting portrayal of a character. Write a brief cover note in which you explain what you like about these pieces, and add them, along with the note, to your **Presentation Portfolio.**
- **Writing Workshops** In this unit you wrote a Career Search Report exploring options for your own future. You also wrote an Oral History from an interview. Reread these pieces and decide which makes more interesting use of research. Explain your choice in a note attached to the preferred one. Place the piece in your **Presentation Portfolio.**
- **Additional Activities** Think back to any of the assignments you completed under **Activities & Explorations** and **Inquiry & Research.** Keep a record in your portfolio of any assignments that you would like to do further work on in the future.

Self ASSESSMENT

READER'S NOTEBOOK

Copy the following list of literary terms introduced in this unit. Underline the terms that you understand completely. Put questions marks next to any terms that you do not understand fully. Review the terms with question marks by looking them up in the **Glossary of Literary Terms** that begins on page 1124.

plot	style
exposition	imagery
rising action	personification
climax	characterization
falling action	audience
internal conflict	essay
symbol	conflict
narrative nonfiction	narrative poem
form	cultural symbol
author's perspective	literary symbol
tone	resolution
	diction

Self ASSESSMENT

Presentation Portfolio

Consider all the pieces that you now have in your portfolio. Have you changed your opinion about the quality of any of the pieces? Is there an item that no longer represents your ability or interests? You may wish to weed out some pieces and replace them.

Setting GOALS

As you worked through the reading and writing activities in this unit, you probably encountered authors or issues you would like to learn more about. Make a list of subjects you would like to follow up on in your personal reading.

Reviewing Literary Concepts

OPTION 1

Identify the phases of the plot of each short story in Unit 3. Compare with classmates' results and discuss any areas of disagreement.

OPTION 2

Use the Unit 3 Resource Book, page 78, to provide students a ready-made, full-depth chart for recording author's purpose, tone, style, and perspective for nonfiction selections.

Building Your Portfolio

Students will use their Presentation Portfolios to file what they consider their highest quality work—the very best in their Working Portfolios.

For more information on using, writing and assessing portfolios, see the *Teacher's Guide to Assessment and Portfolio Use,* p. 53.

The *Electronic Library* is a CD-ROM that contains additional fiction, nonfiction, poetry, and drama for each unit in *The Language of Literature.*

These are the additional selections found in Unit 3 of the *Electronic Library.*

Czeslaw Milosz
My Faithful Mother Tongue

Henrik Ibsen
A Doll's House

Minfong Ho
The Winter Hibiscus

Emily Brontë
To Imagination

Karel Capek
The Stamp Collection

Lu Xün
My Old Home

Léon Damas
Hiccups

Tru Vu
Who Am I?

Encourage students to choose one of the longer works described as an opportunity to read silently with comprehension over a period of time.

LITERATURE CONNECTIONS

Kaffir Boy

MARK MATHABANE

In this autobiography, Mark Mathabane recalls growing up under apartheid in Johannesburg, South Africa, in the 1960s and 1970s. After Mathabane's father is arrested and subjected to forced labor on a white-owned farm, his mother is determined that her son will get an education. Mathabane excels in school, but it's tennis—and the inspiration of players Arthur Ashe and Stan Smith—that ultimately help him escape apartheid. In this powerful and inspiring memoir, Mathabane demonstrates how the strength of the human spirit endures even in the face of a crushing political system.

These thematically related readings are provided along with *Kaffir Boy:*

***from* Makes Me Wanna Holler**
BY NATHAN MCCALL

The First Day
BY EDWARD P. JONES

***from* Kaffir Boy in America**
BY MARK MATHABANE

The Toilet
BY GCINA MHLOPE

A Message from Nelson Mandela to the Youth of America
BY NELSON MANDELA

A Grandfather's Greatest Gift
BY JEREYLN EDDINGS

Black Hair
BY GARY SOTO

And Even *More* . . .

The Chosen

CHAIM POTOK

Danny Saunders and Reuven Malter are two Jewish boys growing up in Brooklyn. Danny comes from a very strict Hasidic family, his stern father a rabbi. Reuven comes from a family that embraces modern ways while remaining devout. As the boys become best friends, Reuven slowly comes to understand Danny's world. The book is also part of the *Literature Connections* series published by McDougal Littell.

Books

Bless Me, Ultimá
RUDOLFO ANAYA
Tells of the struggles of Antonio, a young boy growing up in a small town in New Mexico, and his touching relationship with the old *curandera*, Ultimá.

The Death of Ivan Ilyich
LEO TOLSTOY
A worldly and accomplished man confronts his own mortality.

The Doll's House
HENRIK IBSEN
In this classic drama, Nora Helmer struggles to free herself from the limiting role she has been cast into by her marriage.

LITERATURE CONNECTIONS

A Separate Peace

JOHN KNOWLES

This critically acclaimed novel, popular since its publication in 1960, explores the deep-rooted conflicts that can warp personalities and destroy relationships. Gene, the narrator, revisits the New Hampshire prep school he attended shortly after the onset of World War II. He remembers Phineas, his roommate and friend who was everything Gene was not—flamboyant, spontaneous, and charismatic. Haunted by the past, Gene recalls the "accident" that crippled Phineas, shattered the summer's peace, and revealed the evil in his own heart.

These thematically related readings are provided along with *A Separate Peace*:

Into My Heart an Air That Kills
BY A. E. HOUSMAN

***from* Growing Up**
BY RUSSELL BAKER

the sonnet-ballad
BY GWENDOLYN BROOKS

Sucker
BY CARSON MCCULLERS

Destiny/Destino
BY ROSARIO CASTELLANOS

A Turn with the Sun
BY JOHN KNOWLES

Initiation
BY SYLVIA PLATH

Alba
BY DEREK WALCOTT

I Know Why the Caged Bird Sings
MAYA ANGELOU
The poet laureate writes a moving account of her early years in Arkansas and California.

The Joy Luck Club
AMY TAN
This book tells the story of four Chinese immigrant women and their relationships with their daughters.

The Outsiders
S.E. HINTON
Teenagers from the wrong side of the tracks find themselves in a dangerous rivalry with the rich kids from the other side of town.

Pygmalion
GEORGE BERNARD SHAW
Language professor Henry Higgins makes a gentlewoman out of flower girl Eliza Dolittle in this play. This play is also part of the *Literature Connections* series published by McDougal Littell.

Other Media

Langston Hughes
James Baldwin and biographer Arnold Rampersad discuss the poet in this part of the *American Poets: Voices and Visions* series. Filmic Archives.
(VIDEOCASSETTE)

The Joy Luck Club
A film version of Amy Tan's novel. Hollywood Pictures Home Video.
(VIDEOCASSETTE)

Kaffir Boy
Read by Howard Rollins. Dove Books on Tape.
(AUDIOCASSETTE)

EXTEND YOUR READING 539

Lessons of History

The selections in Unit Four present students with literary history lessons. Nothing is older than conflicts between people, and such situations can often set up circumstances that reach across the centuries to influence people's current behavior. This unit is divided into three parts to more fully explore the ways in which the past is always with us.

Part 1

Facing the Enemy So often conflicts between people involve large armies engaging in epic battles. However, just as memorable are conflicts involving individuals, sometimes as one-against-many, or one-against-one. For example, in "Cranes," two friends find themselves in opposition due to the conflict of differing political ideologies.

Part 2

Tests of Conviction This part emphasizes the tendency of deeply held beliefs and values to force people into deciding whether defense and preservation of those beliefs and values is worth confrontation with others. For example, in "On the Rainy River," a young man's belief that war is wrong forces him to consider fleeing his country rather than go to war when he is called into service.

Part 3

The Tragedy of Julius Caesar The hunger for power is no less today than it was in the time of Julius Caesar. This part presents the classic Shakespearean play *The Tragedy of Julius Caesar,* which portrays how the pursuit of power affects a leader and those around him.

UNIT FOUR

540

Mini Lesson Viewing and Representing

photograph of ruins of the Roman Forum

ART APPRECIATION

Instruction Through the survival of ruins such as the Forum, we can appreciate today the beautiful architecture of ancient Rome. Resting on low ground between two hills, this public square was built over a 350-year period ending around 150 B.C. The Forum was a place of monuments, temples, statues, courts, and other government buildings. Victorious Roman generals would parade through the Forum. Eventually, earthquakes, fires, and foreign invasions ruined most of it, yet it remains a highly visible presence in the heart of modern-day Rome.

Ask: Judging from the small portion of the Forum ruins seen in this photograph, do you feel this is an appropriate way to preserve the past?

Possible Responses: Yes; there is nothing like a physical reminder of the past to make it seem real. No; such ruins clash with the standards of modern design.

LESSONS OF HISTORY

Fellow citizens,

we cannot

escape

history.

Fellow citizens, we cannot escape history.

ABRAHAM LINCOLN

Roman Forum, Rome, Italy.

Making Connections

To help students explore the connections between the art, the quotation, and the unit theme, have them consider the following questions:

Ask: In what way do you think the lessons of history are important?
Possible Response: History is a record of failures and successes, which, when studied, can teach us who we are now.

The Lincoln quotation is from his second annual message to Congress, delivered on December 1, 1862. Its context is Lincoln's reminding everyone that the actions of Congress and his administration during "the fiery trial through which we pass" will be judged and remembered for all generations to come and bring either lasting "honor or dishonor."

Ask: In what ways is history kept alive?
Possible Response: Reference books preserve details on historical events. People constantly publish new biographies of historical figures and accounts of past events.

Ask: What kinds of stories and experiences might you expect to read about in this unit?
Possible Response: These selections may deal with themes constant through human history, such as conflict between enemies and the desire for power.

PART 1 SKILLS TRACE

Features and Selections	Literary Analysis	Reading and Critical Thinking	Writing Opportunities
Lessons of History **Facing the Enemy**			
Learning the Language of Literature: Irony	Irony, 543		
The Active Reader: Skills and Strategies		Making Inferences and Predictions, 545	
SHORT STORY Two Friends **Difficulty Level:** ***Average*** Literary Link *from* Simple Poetry / Versos Sencillos	Situational Irony, 546, 556 Protagonist / Antagonist, 556	Predicting, 546, 556 Test Practice, 554	Letter, 557 Tale, 557
SHORT STORY The Pit and the Pendulum **Difficulty Level:** ***Challenging***	Suspense, 559, 575 Review: First-Person Point of View, 575	Visualizing, 559, 575 Test Practice, 574	Critical Review, 576 Poe Parody, 576 Inquisition Exposé, 576
POETRY the sonnet-ballad Do not weep, maiden, for war is kind **Difficulty Level:** ***Average*** Building Vocabulary	Verbal Irony, 578, 581 Sonnet Structure, 581	Drawing Conclusions, 578, 579, 581	Mother's Poem, 582 Speaker Comparison, 582 Letter to Author, 582
Real World Link The Remembered War: A Korean War Vet Offers a History Lesson		Magazine Article: Evaluating an Argument, 590	
Comparing Literature: Learning from History		From Analysis to Synthesis, 592	
MEMOIR *from* Night **Difficulty Level:** ***Easy*** Literary Link *from* Nobel Prize Acceptance Speech	Style, 593, 600	Connecting, 593, 600 Test Practice, 598	Holocaust Essay, 601 Interview Questions, 601
MEMOIR *from* Farewell to Manzanar **Difficulty Level:** ***Average***	Memoir, 602, 613	Connecting, 602, 613 Test Practice, 610	Letter, 614 Dialogue, 614 Informal Assess., 612
Comparing Literature: Assessment Practice		Reading the Prompt, 615	Synthesis Essay, 615
Writing Workshop: Persuasive Essay Assessment Practice		Analyzing a Student Model, 617	Persuasive Essay, 619

LEGEND **DLS – Daily Language SkillBuilder**
CCL – Cross Curricular Link
Green type – Teacher's Edition

Speaking and Listening Viewing and Representing	Inquiry and Research	Grammar, Usage, and Mechanics	Vocabulary
		DLS, 546	
Art Appreciation, 540			
Patchwork Design, 557 Performance Piece, 557 Storyboard, 557 Two Fish, 557 Author Activity, 558 Art Appreciation, 547, 550, 553, 555 Interviews, 558	Life Under Siege, 557	Prepositional Phrases, 558 DLS, 546 Prepositional Phrases, 557	Meaning Clues, 557 Using a Dictionary, 548 Word Origins, 552
Illustrated Scene, 576 Radio Soundtrack, 576 Dramatic Reading and Pantomime, 566	Inquisition Report, 576	Appositive Phrases, 577 DLS, 559 Appositives, 572 Appositives and Appositive Phrases, 576	Meaning Clues, 576 Context Clues, 560 Word Origins, 568
War Collage, 582 Art from the Home Front, 582 Interpretive Dance, 582 Art Appreciation, 580 Dramatic Reading, 583	War Through Time, 582 War Journal, 582	DLS, 578 Parallel Compound Predicates, 582	Reference Aids - Foreign Terms, 584
Discussion, 591	Activity Link: Cranes, 591 Inquiry and Research, 591		
Night Report, 601 Film Review, 601 Author Activity, 601 Viewing and Representing, 594		DLS, 593 Modifiers, 601	Context Clues, 601 Analogies, 596
Viewing and Representing, 606, 614	Photo Exhibit, 614 Reparations Bill, 614 Video Viewing, 614 Author Activity, 614	DLS, 602 Comparative and Superlative Modifiers, 608	Suffixes, 604
Picturing Text Structure, 617		Correcting Fragments, 620 Revising and Editing, 621	

UNIT FOUR
PART 2 SKILLS TRACE

Features and Selections	Literary Analysis	Reading and Critical Thinking	Writing Opportunities
Tests of Conviction			
Learning the Language of Literature: Point of View	Point of View, 623		
The Active Reader: Skills and Strategies		Making Judgments, 625	
SHORT STORY On the Rainy River **Difficulty Level:** ***Average*** Literary Link Ghost of a Chance	First-Person Point of View, 626, 642	Making Judgments, 626, 642 Workplace Link, 632	Letter, 643 Definition of Courage, 643 New Ending, 643 Informal Assess., 640
POETRY The Artilleryman's Vision look at this) **Difficulty Level:** ***Challenging***	Tone and Diction, 645, 649	Comparing and Contrasting Speakers, 645, 649	Advice Column, 650 Comparison Essay, 650 Letter, 650 Test Practice, 648
SHORT STORY The Prisoner Who Wore Glasses **Difficulty Level:** ***Average*** Literary Link They Have Not Been Able / No Han Podido	Third-Person Point of View, 652, 660 Review: Setting, 660	Drawing Conclusions, 652, 660 Test Practice, 659 Workplace Link, 661	Letter, 661 Personal Response Essay, 661
Real World Link Nelson Mandela		Magazine Article: Organizing Information Chronologically, 662 Compare and Contrast, 663	
SHORT STORY After the Ball **Difficulty Level:** ***Challenging*** Building Vocabulary	Flashback, 664, 675	Evaluating Characters, 664, 675 Informal Assess., 674	Gossip Column, 676 Father-Daughter Scene, 676 Punishment Proposal, 676

UNIT FOUR
PART 3 SKILLS TRACE

Features and Selections	Literary Analysis	Reading and Critical Thinking	Writing Opportunities
The Tragedy of Julius Caesar Shakespeare's World		Shakespearean Drama, 686	
Learning the Language of Literature: Shakespearean Drama	Shakespearean Drama, 686		
The Active Reader: Skills and Strategies		Reading Shakespearean Drama, 688	
DRAMA The Tragedy of Julius Caesar **Difficulty Level:** ***Challenging***	Blank Verse, 689	Understanding Shakespeare's Plays, 689	
DRAMA Act One **Difficulty Level:** ***Challenging***	Blank Verse, 713	Understanding Shakespeare's Plays, 713 Test Practice, 704	Test Practice, TE 698 Informal Assess., 712

LEGEND **DLS – Daily Language SkillBuilder**
CCL – Cross Curricular Link
Green type – Teacher's Edition

Speaking and Listening Viewing and Representing	Inquiry and Research	Grammar, Usage, and Mechanics	Vocabulary
Discussion, 643 Rainy River Collage, 643 Protest Songs, 643 Art Appreciation, 635, 638, 643	Living History, 643	Gerund Phrases, 644 DLS, 626 Infinitive Phrases, 636 Gerund Phrases, 644	Context Clues, 643 Context Clues, 628 Word Meanings and Spelling, 633
Illustrations of War, 650 Spoken Word, 650 Martial Music, 650 Author Activity, 651	Civil Warfare, 650 Invisible Wounds of War, 650	DLS, 645 Misplaced and Dangling Modifiers, 650	Denotative and Connotative Meanings, 646
Narrative Cartoon, 661 Political Speech, 661 Art Appreciation, 656	From Prisoner to National Leader, 661	DLS, 652 Modifiers, 658	Word Knowledge, 661 Context Clues, 654 Word Origins, 657
	Activity Link: The Prisoner Who Wore Glasses, 663 Inquiry and Research, 663		
Modern Adaptation, 676 Musical Representation, 676 Art Connection, 676 Art Appreciation, 671, 673	Author Activity, 677	Participal Phrases, 677 DLS, 664 Participles, 670 Participial Phrases, 676	Assessment Practice, 676 Words with Multiple Meanings, 678 Context Clues, 666 Analogies, 668
Dramatic Interpretation, 700 Storytelling and Pantomime, 703 Dramatic Reading, 706 Representing the Supernatural, 708		DLS, 689 Double Negatives, 710	Word Origins, 696

PART 3 SKILLS TRACE

Features and Selections	Literary Analysis	Reading and Critical Thinking	Writing Opportunities
DRAMA Act Two **Difficulty Level:** ***Challenging***	Soliloquy / Aside, 735 Review: Figurative Language, 735	Reading Shakespearean Drama, 735 Informal Assess., 726	
DRAMA Act Three **Difficulty Level:** ***Challenging***	Rhetorical Devices, 759 Review: Verbal Irony, 759	Reading Shakespearean Drama, 759 Test Practice, 742	Informal Assess., 746
DRAMA Act Four **Difficulty Level:** ***Challenging***	Dramatic Irony, 777 Test Practice, 768	Reading Shakespearean Drama, 777	Letter, 772
DRAMA Act Five **Difficulty Level:** ***Challenging***	Tragedy, 794 Review: Theme, 794	Reading Shakespearean Drama, 794 Informal Assess., 788	Cause-and-Effect Analysis, 795 Alternative Ending, 795 Essay, 795 Character Evaluation, 795
Real World Link *Review of* Julius Caesar Hail, Caesar		Theater Review: Analyzing a Theater Review, 798	Explanation, 799
Writing Workshop: Cause-and-Effect Essay		Analyzing a Student Model, 801	Cause-and-Effect Essay, 803 Effective Transitions, 804
Reflect and Assess The Lessons of History	Identifying Irony, 807	Analyzing Point of View, 807	Building Your Portfolio, 807
Reading and Writing for Assessment		How to Read a Test Selection, 810 How to Answer Multiple-Choice Questions, 813	How to Respond in Writing, 814

LEGEND **DLS – Daily Language SkillBuilder**
CCL – Cross Curricular Link
Green type – Teacher's Edition

Speaking and Listening Viewing and Representing	Inquiry and Research	Grammar, Usage, and Mechanics	Vocabulary
Interpretive Reading, 715 Viewing and Representing, 718, 734 Representing the Mood, 727		Modifiers, 720	Word Origins, 724
Speaking and Listening, 745 Presenting an Oration, 750 Video, 751 Town Meeting, 754		Modifiers, 756	Archaic Words, 740
Performing a Dramatic Scene, 764		Elliptical Sentences, 770	Word Meanings, 763
Dramatic Scene, 795 Video Viewing, 795 Quotable Collage, 795 Write and Perform a Scene, 784	Roman History, 795 Map Study, 795 Word Derivations, 795 Modern Criticism, 795 Researching Shakespeare's Sources, 786	Prepositional Phrases, 796 Prepositional Phrases, 796	Multiple Meanings and Word Origins, 780
	Activity Link: Julius Caesar, 799 Inquiry and Research, 799		
		Misplaced Modifiers, 804 Revising and Editing, 805 Misplaced Modifiers, 805	
Comparing Foes, 806 Tests of Conviction, 806 The Lessons of Power, 806			
		How to Revise, Edit, and Proofread a Test Selection, 815	

UNIT FOUR
RESOURCE MANAGEMENT GUIDE
PART 1

To introduce the theme/literary period of this unit, use Fine Art Transparencies T26–28 in the Communications Transparencies and Copymasters.

	Unit Resource Book	Assessment	Integrated Technology and Media	Additional Support: Literary Analysis Transparencies
Two Friends *pp. 546–558*	• Summary p. 4 • Active Reading p. 5 • Literary Analysis p. 6 • Words to Know p. 7 • Grammar p. 8 • Selection Quiz p. 9	• Selection Test, Formal Assessment pp. 101–102 Test Generator	Audio Library LaserLinks, Teacher's SourceBook p. 33	• Irony: Situational T14
The Pit and the Pendulum *pp. 559–577*	• Summary p. 10 • Active Reading p. 11 • Literary Analysis p. 12 • Words to Know p. 13 • Grammar p. 14 • Selection Quiz p. 15	• Selection Test, Formal Assessment pp. 103–104 Test Generator	Audio Library	
the sonnet-ballad / **Do not weep, maiden, for war is kind** *pp. 578–583*	• Active Reading p. 16 • Literary Analysis p. 17	• Selection Test, Formal Assessment pp. 105–106 Test Generator	Audio Library Research Starter www.mcdougallittell.com	• Irony: Verbal T16
***from* Night** *pp. 593–601*	• Summary p. 19 • Active Reading p. 20 • Literary Analysis p. 21 • Words to Know p. 22 • Selection Quiz p. 23	• Selection Test, Formal Assessment pp. 107–108 Test Generator	Audio Library LaserLinks, Teacher's SourceBook p. 36	• Style, Voice, Diction, Purpose T22
***from* Farewell to Manzanar** *pp. 602–614*	• Summary p. 24 • Active Reading p. 25 • Literary Analysis p. 26 • Selection Quiz p. 27 • Comparing Literature p. 28	• Selection Test, Formal Assessment pp. 109–110 Test Generator	Video: Literature in Performance, Video Resource Book pp. 17–23	• Types of Nonfiction T4

Writing Workshop: Persuasive Essay

Unit Four Resource Book
- Prewriting p. 29
- Drafting and Elaboration p. 30
- Peer Response Guide pp. 31–32
- Revising, Editing, and Proofreading p. 33
- Student Models pp. 34–39
- Rubric for Evaluation p. 40

Writing Coach

Writing Transparencies and Copymasters T11, T20, C30

Teacher's Guide to Assessment and Portfolio Use

Unit Assessment
- Unit Four, Part 1 Test, Formal Assessment pp. 111–112

Test Generator

- Unit Four Integrated Test, Integrated Assessment pp. 19–24

Unit Technology
ClassZone www.mcdougallittell.com

Electronic Teacher Tools

Electronic Library

T = Transparency C = Copymaster

Reading and Critical Thinking Transparencies	Grammar Transparencies and Copymasters	Vocabulary Transparencies and Copymasters	Writing Transparencies and Copymasters	Communications Transparencies and Copymasters
• Predicting Outcomes T2 • Using Card Catalog/ Computer Catalog T29	• Daily Language SkillBuilder T18 • Function of Prepositional Phrases C96	• Using a Dictionary C59 • Word Origins C60	• Elaboration T10 • Levels of Language T12 • Effective Language T13	• Impromptu Speaking: Dialogue, Role-Play, Debate T13
• Visualizing T8	• Daily Language SkillBuilder T18 • Appositives C98 • Essential and Nonessential Appositives and Appositive Phrases C99	• Context Clues C61 • Word Origins C62	• Writing Process T1, T2 • Writing Structure. T5, T6, T9 • Effective Language T13 • Opinion Statement C25	• Formal Presentations T10
• Drawing Conclusions T4 • Locating Material in the Library I T27	• Daily Language SkillBuilder T19 • Compound Predicates II C87		• Writing Process T1, T2 • Writing Structure T5, T6, T9 • Poem C27	• Dramatic Reading T12
	• Daily Language SkillBuilder T19 • Adjectives and Adverbs C70	• Analogies C63	• Writing Process T1–4 • Writing Structure T6–8, T11 • Persuasive Essay C30	• Evaluation Matrix: Film/Video T7
• Locating Information Using Databases and the Internet T34	• Daily Language SkillBuilder T20 • Comparative and Superlative Modifiers C156	• Suffixes C64	• Writing Structure T6, T9, T11 • Levels of Language T12 • The Uses of Dialogue T24	• Evaluation Matrix: Film/Video T7

STUDENTS ACQUIRING ENGLISH

The **Spanish Study Guide**, pp. 119–136, includes language support for the following pages:

- Family and Community Involvement (per unit)
- Selection Summaries and Vocabulary
- Active Reading
- Literary Analysis

UNIT FOUR
RESOURCE MANAGEMENT GUIDE
PART 2

To introduce the theme/literary period of this unit, use Fine Art Transparencies T23–25 in the Communications Transparencies and Copymasters.

Selection	Unit Resource Book	Assessment	Integrated Technology and Media	Additional Support: Literary Analysis Transparencies
On the Rainy River *pp. 626–644*	• Summary p. 41 • Active Reading p. 42 • Literary Analysis p. 43 • Words to Know p. 44 • Grammar p. 45 • Selection Quiz p. 46	• Selection Test, Formal Assessment pp. 113–114 Test Generator	Audio Library LaserLinks, Teacher's SourceBook pp. 37–39	• Point of View T17
The Artilleryman's Vision look at this) *pp. 645–651*	• Active Reading p. 47 • Literary Analysis p. 48	• Selection Test, Formal Assessment pp. 115–116 Test Generator	Audio Library Research Starter www.mcdougallittell.com	• Style, Voice, Diction, Purpose T22
The Prisoner Who Wore Glasses *pp. 652–661*	• Summary p. 49 • Active Reading p. 50 • Literary Analysis p. 51 • Words to Know p. 52 • Selection Quiz p. 53	• Selection Test, Formal Assessment pp. 117–118 Test Generator	Audio Library LaserLinks, Teacher's SourceBook p. 40	• Point of View T17
After the Ball *pp. 664–677*	• Summary p. 54 • Active Reading p. 55 • Literary Analysis p. 56 • Words to Know p. 57 • Grammar p. 58 • Selection Quiz p. 59	• Selection Test, Formal Assessment pp. 119–120 Test Generator	Audio Library LaserLinks, Teacher's SourceBook p. 41	
		Unit Assessment • Unit Four, Part 2 Test, Formal Assessment pp. 121–122 Test Generator • Unit Four Integrated Test, Integrated Assessment pp. 19–24	***Unit Technology*** ClassZone www.mcdougallittell.com Electronic Teacher Tools Electronic Library	

UNIT FOUR
PART 3

To introduce the theme/literary period of this unit, use Fine Art Transparencies T26–28 in the Communications Transparencies and Copymasters.

Selection	Unit Resource Book	Assessment	Integrated Technology and Media	Additional Support: Literary Analysis Transparencies
The Tragedy of Julius Caesar • Act One *pp. 690–713* • Act Two *pp. 714–735* • Act Three *pp. 736–759* • Act Four *pp. 760–777* • Act Five *pp. 778–797*	• Summary pp. 61, 65, 69, 73, 77 • Active Reading pp. 62, 66, 70, 74, 78 • Literary Analysis pp. 63, 67, 71, 75, 79 • Grammar p. 80 • Selection Quiz pp. 64, 68, 72, 76, 81	• Selection Test, Formal Assessment pp. 123–132 Test Generator	Audio Library Video: Literature in Performance, Video Resource Book pp. 25–30	• Poetry: Sound Devices T8 • Shakespearean Drama I T18 • Shakespearean Drama II T19
		Unit Assessment • Unit Four, Part 3 Test, Formal Assessment pp. 133–134 Test Generator • Unit Four Integrated Test, Integrated Assessment pp. 19–24	***Unit Technology*** ClassZone www.mcdougallittell.com Electronic Teacher Tools Electronic Library	

Writing Workshop: Cause-and-Effect Essay

Unit Four Resource Book
- Prewriting p. 82
- Drafting and Elaboration p. 83
- Peer Response Guide pp. 84–85
- Revising, Editing, and Proofreading p. 86
- Student Models pp. 87–92
- Rubric for Evaluation p. 93

Writing Coach

Writing Transparencies and Copymasters T11, T20, C31–32

Teacher's Guide to Assessment and Portfolio Use

T = Transparency C = Copymaster

	Reading and Critical Thinking Transparencies	Grammar Transparencies and Copymasters	Vocabulary Transparencies and Copymasters	Writing Transparencies and Copymasters	Communications Transparencies and Copymasters
	• Making Judgments T5 • Organizational Chart: Horizontal T51	• Daily Language SkillBuilder T20 • Infinitive Phrases I C100 • Gerund Phrases C106	• Context Clues C65 • Word Meanings and Spellings C66	• Point of View T23 • Identifying Paragraphs T5	• Impromptu Speaking: Dialogue, Role-Play, Debate T13
	• Compare and Contrast T15	• Daily Language SkillBuilder T21 • Avoiding Misplaced and Dangling Modifiers C161	• Denotation and Connotation C67	• Achieving Conciseness T21 • Showing, Not Telling T22	• Dramatic Reading T12
	• Drawing Conclusions T4 • Noting Details T9 • Notetaking T40	• Daily Language SkillBuilder T21 • Comparative Forms C155	• Context Clues C68 • Word Meanings C69	• Point of View T23 • Topic Sentence and Thesis Statements T6	• Impromptu Speaking: Dialogue, Role-Play, Debate T13
	• Organizational Chart: Horizontal T51	• Daily Language SkillBuilder T22 • Participles C102 • Participial Phrases C103	• Context Clues C70 • Analogies C71	• Point of View T23 • The Uses of Dialogue T24 • Persuasive Essay C30	• Dramatic Reading T12 • Impromptu Speaking: Dialogue, Role-Play, Debate T13

STUDENTS ACQUIRING ENGLISH

he **Spanish Study Guide,** pp. 137–148, includes anguage support for the following pages:

- Family and Community Involvement (per unit)
- Selection Summaries and Vocabulary
- Active Reading
- Literary Analysis

	Reading and Critical Thinking Transparencies	Grammar Transparencies and Copymasters	Vocabulary Transparencies and Copymasters	Writing Transparencies and Copymasters	Communications Transparencies and Copymasters
	• Locating Information Using Print References T32 • Locating Information Using Technical Resources T33 • Organizational Chart: Horizontal T51	• Daily Language SkillBuilder T22 • Comparisons Using Prepositional Phrases C97 • Elliptical Clauses C118 • Modifiers: *Good* and *Well* C158 • Modifiers: *Bad* and *Badly* C159 • Double Negatives C160	• Word Origins C73 • Archaic Words and Usage C74 • Word Meanings C75 • Multiple Meanings and Word Origins C76	• Writing Structure T6, T7, T9, T11 • Varying Sentence Openers and Closers T18 • Cause and Effect C32 • Interpretive Essay C33	• Dramatic Reading T12 • Evaluating Roles in Groups T8 • Verbal Strategies T14

STUDENTS ACQUIRING ENGLISH

The **Spanish Study Guide,** pp. 149–163, includes anguage support for the following pages:

- Family and Community Involvement (per unit)
- Selection Summaries and Vocabulary
- Active Reading
- Literary Analysis

DAILY LANGUAGE SKILLBUILDERS

Selection	SkillBuilder Sentences	Suggested Answers
Two Friends	**1.** The fishermen stood ignoring the fish with firmly planted feet. **2.** The woman bought a book from a German bookseller with an extensive table of contents.	**1.** The fishermen **stood with firmly planted feet, ignoring the fish**. **2.** The woman bought **a book with an extensive table of contents from a German bookseller**.
The Pit and the Pendulum	**1.** We brought two dogs tarkington and sam home from the dog pound. **2.** The two best players on the team susan and Leah were both named to the all-conference team.	**1.** We brought two dogs**, T**arkington and **S**am**,** home from the dog pound. **2.** The two best players on the team**, S**usan and **L**eah**,** were both named to the all-conference team.
The sonnet-ballad Do not weep, maiden, for war is kind	**1.** The war effected everyone's attitude she said at the symposium. **2.** Since niether of the two choices are right we chose another alternative.	**1.** **"**The war **affected** everyone's attitude**,"** she said at the symposium. **2.** Since **neither** of the two choices **is** right**,** we chose another alternative.

DAILY LANGUAGE SKILLBUILDERS

Selection	SkillBuilder Sentences	Suggested Answers
from Night	**1.** There votes were tabulated but few people knew who they should vote for in the election. **2.** "Every one is invited" he said. "Keisha, Michael, and her is already coming."	**1.** **Their** votes were tabulated**,** but few people knew **for whom** they should vote in the election. **2.** "**Everyone** is invited**,**" he said. "Keisha, Michael, and **she are** already coming."
from Farewell to Manzanar	**1.** The events greatly effected the author, when she was young. **2.** The ordeal would of been worse without her Mother's strength and her brothers resourcefulness.	**1.** The events greatly **affected** the author when she was young. **2.** The ordeal would **have** been worse without her **m**other's strength and her brothers**'** (or brother**'s**) resourcefulness.
On the Rainy River	**1.** "I enjoyed reading this selection even more than them others said Raymond. Because it had a character I liked." **2.** Did you ever see the film called the deerhunter? Asked Rachel. It was about the war in vietnam too."	**1.** "I enjoyed reading this selection even more than **the** others**,"** said Raymond, **"b**ecause it had a character I liked." **2.** "Did you ever see the film called **The Deerhunter**?" **a**sked Rachel. **"**It was about the war in **V**ietnam**,** too."

DAILY LANGUAGE SKILLBUILDERS

Selection	SkillBuilder Sentences	Suggested Answers
The Artilleryman's Vision look at this)	**1.** Reluctantly, the fish were eaten by the sisters. **2.** Climbing over the hill, a rock fell on my head.	**1.** Reluctantly, **the sisters ate** the fish. **2.** Climbing over the hill, **I was hit on the head by** a rock.
The Prisoner Who Wore Glasses	**1.** The prisoner walks slowly through prison yard, shading his eyes from the sunlight that is more brighter than it's been in weeks. **2.** The warder likes ordering the work crew around because it makes him feel the powerfulest.	**1.** The prisoner walks slowly through **the** prison yard, shading his eyes from the sunlight that is **brighter** than it's been in weeks. **2.** The warder likes ordering the work crew around because it makes him feel the **most powerful**.
After the Ball	**1.** When he was alone at night, Juan was often frighten of the dark. **2.** My father was always the first one home from work, so he start dinner.	**1.** When he was alone at night, Juan was often **frightened** of the dark. **2.** My father was always the first one home from work, so he **started** dinner.
The Tragedy of Julius Caesar	**1.** Julius Caesar wanted to be emperor of Rome although he turned it down in front of the crowds that was at the celebration. **2.** Shakespeare wrote the play Julius Caesar one of my friends think that its the best drama ever wrote.	**1.** Julius Caesar wanted to be emperor of Rome, although he **turned down the honor** in front of the crowds that **were** at the celebration. **2.** Shakespeare wrote the play **Julius Caesar.** **O**ne of my friends **thinks** that **it's** the best drama ever **written**.

INTEGRATING GRAMMAR AND LITERATURE: GRAMMAR PLANNER

Grammar Focus by Unit	Unit One	Unit Two	Unit Three	Unit Four	Unit Five	Unit Six
	Parts of Speech	The Sentence and Its Parts	Verbs and Verbals	Phrases	Clauses	Special Sentence Structures

The Language of Literature offers several options for integrating grammar instruction and literature.

- Each unit has a specific grammar focus. The grammar focus for this unit is highlighted on the planning chart. Categories of grammar skills for this unit are shown in red.
- The Pupil's Edition includes instructive features entitled *Grammar in Context*. The instruction in these features arises from the selections and relates to the grammar focus for each unit.
- The Writing Workshops in the Pupil's Edition include grammar tips that help students produce error-free drafts.
- Mini Lessons in the Teacher's Edition complement the instruction in the *Grammar in Context* features. Additional Mini Lessons relate to the grammar focus for each unit as well as to the literature.
- Daily Language SkillBuilders in the Teacher's Edition provide students with ongoing proofreading practice and reinforce punctuation, spelling, grammar and usage, and capitalization.
- Grammar Copymasters and Transparencies, which may be used independently or in conjunction with Mini Lessons in the Teacher's Edition, present grammar in a traditional, systematic sequence.

PE instruction shown in black
TE Mini Lessons shown in green

Part 1

Parts of Speech
Modifiers: Adjectives and Adverbs
from *Night,* p. 601

Parts of the Sentence
Parallel Compound Predicates
"the sonnet-ballad," "Do not weep, maiden, for war is kind," p. 582

Using Phrases
Prepositional Phrases
"Two Friends," p. 558
Prepositional Phrases: Adjective vs. Adverb
Placement of Prepositional Phrases
"Two Friends," p. 557
Appositives
"The Pit and the Pendulum," p. 577
"The Pit and the Pendulum," pp. 572–573
Essential and Nonessential Appositives and Phrases
"The Pit and the Pendulum," p. 577
"The Pit and the Pendulum," pp. 576–577

Using Clauses
Sentence Fragments
Writing Workshop, p. 621

Using Modifiers
Comparative and Superlative Modifiers
from *Farewell to Manzanar,* pp. 608–609

End Marks and Commas
Commas in Series
Writing Workshop, p. 621

Style
Parallel Structure
Writing Workshop, p. 621

Part 2

Using Phrases
Infinitive Phrases
"On the Rainy River," pp. 636–637
Participles
"After the Ball," p. 670
Participial Phrases
"After the Ball," p. 677
"After the Ball," pp. 676–677
Gerund Phrases
"On the Rainy River," p. 644
"On the Rainy River," p. 644

Using Modifiers
Correct Comparative Forms
"The Prisoner Who Wore Glasses," p. 658
Avoiding Misplaced and Dangling Modifiers
"The Artilleryman's Vision," "look at this)," pp. 650–651

Part 3

Parts of the Sentence
Run-on Sentences
Writing Workshop, p. 805

Using Phrases
Comparisons Using Prepositional Phrases
Julius Caesar, Act Five, p. 796
Julius Caesar, Act Five, pp. 796–797

Using Clauses
Elliptical Sentences
Julius Caesar, Act Four, pp. 770–771

Subject-Verb Agreement
Writing Workshop, p. 805

Using Modifiers
Problems with Modifiers: *Good, Well*
Julius Caesar, Act Two, p. 720
Problems with Modifiers: *Bad* and *Badly*
Julius Caesar, Act Three, pp. 756–757
Avoiding Double Negatives
Julius Caesar, Act One, pp. 710–711
Avoiding Misplaced and Dangling Modifiers
Writing Workshop, p. 805

Style
Parallel Structure
Writing Workshop, p. 805

PART 1 Facing the Enemy

Enemies are as old as human history. Whether facing down an opponent in a personal test of strength or confronting vast forces, such as an army or a government power, human beings are often defined by their struggles against an opponent. Sometimes the enemy is easy to identify. In other situations, the line between foe and friend may be harder to distinguish. In this part of Unit Four, you will read about the struggles that people undergo when facing enemies of different kinds.

ACTIVITY

With several classmates, brainstorm a list of your favorite books, stories, or films. Then, for each work, identify the primary conflict faced by the protagonist. Who or what is the enemy in this work, and what makes the struggle between the protagonist and enemy so compelling? Present your ideas to the class, and compare your responses with those of other classmates.

LEARNING the Language of Literature

Irony is the contrast between what appears to be true (or what is expected) and what turns out to be true. In literature, irony is often used to add a deeper level of meaning—to make the reader stop and think about the nature of life and the surprises it has in store for us all.

Irony is something that's easier to recognize than to define. It's the kind of unexpected reversal that happens, for instance, when the person who needed help with his or her math homework later develops a multimillion-dollar computer company—or when the president of the Science Club grows up to become Hollywood's leading action hero. These unexpected reversals are often amazing, sometimes even thrilling, but they almost always make you stop and think.

Verbal Irony

The most common form of irony is **verbal irony** in which what is said is the opposite of what is meant. For example, when someone comes indoors dripping wet from a thunderstorm and announces, "It's a bit wet out there," you can recognize the irony of the comment. Such an **ironic understatement** de-emphasizes the facts so drastically that the intended meaning is clear. **Sarcasm** is another form of verbal irony, usually a harsher, even meaner form. Siblings often use sarcasm as an insult. For example, one brother may say to another, "Way to go, genius! With your grades, you'll be 85 years old by the time you graduate." Such a statement is personal, scornful, and intended to hurt or insult a person.

Understanding Verbal Irony

This poster is modeled on an original "invitation" that was issued in a town of the Old West. The invitation is, of course, ironic: the Grand Necktie Party is really a hanging. It's unlikely, however, that any criminals showed up. Even if they missed the irony of the necktie party, then surely they understood the irony of their "care and concern" for the town's citizens and stayed away. Probably, that was the sheriff's intent all along—to scare troublemakers away from the town—with irony!

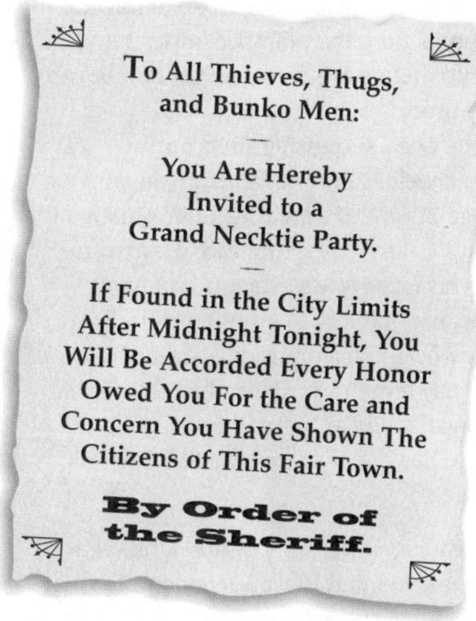

To All Thieves, Thugs, and Bunko Men:
You Are Hereby Invited to a Grand Necktie Party.
If Found in the City Limits After Midnight Tonight, You Will Be Accorded Every Honor Owed You For the Care and Concern You Have Shown The Citizens of This Fair Town.
By Order of the Sheriff.

LEARNING the Language of LITERATURE

OVERVIEW

Objectives
- understand and identify irony in literary works
- identify three types of irony used in literary works: verbal irony, situational irony, and dramatic irony
- analyze the types of irony used in literary works
- analyze the effects of verbal irony, situational irony, and dramatic irony used as literary devices

Teaching the Lesson

This lesson explains and analyzes the types of irony used in literary works and examines how irony affects an audience's response

Introducing the Concepts
Have students recall a surprise they experienced or know of from actual events. Ask them to think about their reactions to the twist of events in which events did not turn out as expected.

Presenting the Concepts
Verbal Irony
Remind students that verbal irony is the simplest form of irony, and the use of verbal irony involves not only understatement but also hyperbole and exaggeration. This creates the humor of ironic comments.

Situational Irony

Suggest to students that situational irony can deeply move readers and audiences because it so closely relates to what people experience in real life.

YOUR TURN

Possible Response: Mrs. Popov wants to remain true to her faithless dead husband so that she can continue to see herself as a faithful, forgiving wife even though the opposite is actually true. Embittered, she is actually harming herself rather than demonstrating virtue.

Dramatic Irony

Remind students of action films in which the excitement and tension are dependent on the audience knowing something that the hero could not possibly know. Ask students to describe their reaction, particularly their physical reaction, to such a film in order to understand the effects of dramatic irony.

YOUR TURN

Possible Response: Gillian and the reader know that the money will go to Miss Hayden even though the lawyers do not know this, and, in fact, think the opposite. This creates both the twist and the surprise ending—and a slightly humorous response in the reader.

Situational Irony

When a character or the reader expects one thing to happen but something else (usually the opposite) happens instead, then the situation is ironic. Watch for situational irony in the stories "Two Friends" (page 546) and "Cranes" (page 585) in this part of the unit.

Anton Chekhov's farce "The Bear" (page 287) is a good example of how situational irony can be used for comic effect. First of all, the title sets the audience up to expect a real bear to appear, but also, practically every situation in the play is ironic. For example, Mrs. Popov buries herself inside her house after her husband dies. The audience expects to find Mrs. Popov deep in grief and to admire her abiding love. But before the first scene is over, the audience finds out that her husband was mean, cruel, and unfaithful to her while he was alive, and that her reasons for secluding herself are not what a person might expect.

SITUATIONAL IRONY

Mrs. Popov (*looking at the snapshot [of her husband]*). Now you shall see how I can love and forgive, Nicholas. My love will only fade when I fade away myself, when this poor heart stops beating. (*laughs, through tears*) Well, aren't you ashamed of yourself? I'm your good, faithful little wifie; I've locked myself up, and I'll be faithful to the grave, while you—aren't you ashamed, you naughty boy? You deceived me, and you used to make scenes and leave me alone for weeks on end.

—Anton Chekhov, *The Bear*

YOUR TURN Read Mrs. Popov's speech from Scene 2 at the right. What is the real motivation for locking herself away after her husband's death? What is ironic about the situation?

Dramatic Irony

The contrast between what a character knows and what the reader or audience knows is called **dramatic irony**. In many of Shakespeare's plays, dramatic irony heightens the suspense, such as when Romeo, thinking Juliet is dead, rushes back to Verona. In fact, much of the sense of tragedy in *Romeo and Juliet* comes from the dramatic irony: the audience knows the truth before the young lovers do but can only watch the tragedy unfold.

Dramatic irony can be used successfully in fiction, nonfiction, and poetry as well as drama. For example, in "One Thousand Dollars" (page 386), O. Henry uses both situational irony and dramatic irony. Gillian's desire for Miss Hayden to have the $50,000 from his late uncle's estate is an ironic situation, for you expect him to want the money himself. At the end of the story, however, O. Henry adds a layer of dramatic irony. As you may remember, Gillian had unselfishly given $1,000 to Miss Hayden. But at the end he tears up the letter explaining what he has done, so that the $50,000 will go directly to Miss Hayden.

DRAMATIC IRONY

Mr. Tolman [the lawyer] reached out for the envelope. Gillian was a little quicker in taking it up. He tore the account and its cover leisurely into strips and dropped them into his pocket.

"It's all right," he said, smiling. "There isn't a bit of need to bother you with this. I don't suppose you'd understand these itemized bets, anyway. I lost the thousand dollars on the races. Good-day to you, gentlemen."

Tolman & Sharp shook their heads mournfully at each other when Gillian left, for they heard him whistling gayly in the hallway as he waited for the elevator.

—O. Henry, "One Thousand Dollars"

YOUR TURN Read the ending of the story at the right. What do Gillian and the reader know that the lawyers do not? What effect does this dramatic irony create?

Suppose you come home from school to find the contents of the overturned garbage container strewn all over the kitchen floor. Your dog looks at you sheepishly from the corner. "Ah ha!" you think, "the guilty party." Then another thought hits you: "I'd better clean this up, or I'll get in trouble." You may not realize it, but you've just made an inference and a prediction. The strategies on this page will help you apply these skills to your reading.

Making Inferences and Predictions

When you make an **inference** while reading, you make a logical guess based on information in a text and your own knowledge or common sense. Think of inferring as reading between the lines, supplying what the author may not have stated directly. Inferring also involves reaching a larger understanding by finding meaning in events and situations that may not be explicitly spelled out for you. A **prediction** is an inference about the future; you use your understanding of clues in a text to make a logical guess about what will happen next.

Both inferring and predicting are essential mental processes for interpreting a literary work, just as they are necessary for interpreting what happens in your own life. What makes you a better reader of literature can also make you a better reader of life.

1 Strategies for Making Inferences

Name of Character	What I Can Infer	Important Details
x		

- Pay attention to details, especially those that reveal important aspects of character, setting, and plot. What do the details add up to? Try keeping track of details in a chart like this one on character.
- **Connect** personally with a selection. Consider what you already know about a subject or how you might act in a similar situation.
- **Question** what a character's actions say about his or her values and beliefs.
- Notice the inferences that an author, a narrator, or a character makes about events and/or other characters. Do you agree with those interpretations? Are those inferences clues to something else?
- **Monitor** your process of inferring as you continue to read. Are you jumping to conclusions? Are there gaps in your logic? You may have to revise what you thought as you get more information.

2 Strategies for Making Predictions

- Analyze a character's motivation to predict what he or she may do next.
- **Evaluate** the behavior and judgment of a character to predict how he or she may react in a given situation.
- Base your predictions on what you've already inferred about the characters or events.
- Expect the unexpected. Imagine what ironic twist could change what you expect to happen.
- **Clarify** your predictions as you go along, revising when appropriate. The aim of prediction is not so much to be right but to stay involved with the reading.

Need More Help?

Remember that active readers use the essential reading strategies explained on page 7: **visualize, predict, clarify, question, connect, evaluate, monitor.**

The Active Reader: Skills and Strategies

OVERVIEW

Objectives

- draw inferences and make predictions that are supported with textual evidence and experience
- use charts to organize information for drawing inferences

Teaching the Lesson

Making Inferences and Predictions

The strategies on this page will help students learn and apply the skills of making inferences and making predictions about characters and events.

Presenting the Strategies

Help students understand how to make inferences by using examples from their daily lives or setting up hypothetical problems for them to infer the answer. Then have them use their initial inferences to make a second inference, or prediction, about what will happen in the future.

1 Strategies for Making Inferences

A sample completion of the chart could look like this:

Name of Character:
Alicia Masson

Important Details:
has acted in plays since 4th grade; both her parents are professional actors

What I Can Infer:
She is likely to win the audition and be cast as the female lead in the spring play.

2 Strategies for Making Predictions

Point out that characters will become more complex as a story progresses. Readers will get more information about the character through an author's direct statements and through a character's own speech and actions. Frequently, our initial judgments about a character or situation must be revised as we gain more information. Encourage students to be attentive to new information and to revise their predictions about both the characters and the situations as necessary.

OVERVIEW

This selection is included in the **Grade 10 InterActive Reader.**

Objectives

1. understand and appreciate a **short story (Literary Analysis)**
2. understand **situational irony (Literary Analysis)**
3. make **predictions** about the plot **(Active Reading)**

Summary

In peacetime, Monsieur Morissot and Monsieur Sauvage went fishing together every Sunday. During the siege of Paris in the Franco-Prussian War, the two friends decide on a whim to go fishing at their old spot, even though it is behind enemy lines. Happily catching fish after fish, the friends ignore the rumbling of distant cannons—until they are captured by the Prussians. The commander tells the captives he will let them go if they will tell him the password needed to get back across French lines; otherwise, he will kill them. He wheedles and makes promises, yet the friends remain silent. The friends bid farewell to one another, then are executed, and the Prussians toss the two bodies into the river.

Thematic Link

Two men on a leisurely fishing trip are confronted by the fatal realities of war. **Facing the enemy** suddenly creates a life-or-death situation for the two friends.

5-Minute Warm-Up

Daily Language SkillBuilder

Have students **proofread** the display sentences on page 541k and write them correctly. The sentences also appear on Transparency 18 of **Grammar Transparencies and Copymasters.**

Mini Lesson: Preteaching Vocabulary

If you would like to preteach the WORDS TO KNOW for this selection, use the Mini Lesson, p. 548.

Two Friends

Short Story by GUY DE MAUPASSANT (gē də mō-pă-sän′)

"Paris was under siege, in the grip of famine, at its last gasp."

Connect to Your Life

Wartime Conditions Think about how it might feel to live in an area that has been at war, with supply lines cut off for some time and your normal activities limited because of danger or lack of goods. Consider how your life under such conditions would contrast with your life in peacetime. What would you miss most? Make a list based on what you have read, experienced, or seen on the news. Then share your ideas in a class discussion.

Build Background

Paris Under Siege

European Nations, 1870

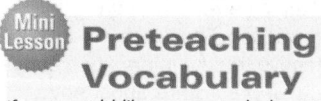

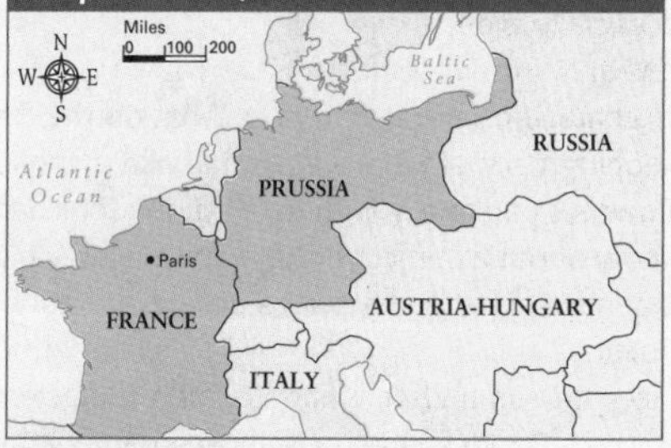

For most of the 1800s, Germany was a collection of separate German-speaking states. Among these, the northern state of Prussia gradually emerged as the most powerful. By 1870, under the leadership of Prussian chancellor Otto von Bismarck, the German states had begun to unite. In July of 1870, fearful of a unified Germany on his borders, Emperor Napoleon III of France began what was called the Franco-Prussian War. By early September, German troops had won several victories and even captured Napoleon III in a battle in northern France. They then laid siege to the French capital of Paris, surrounding the city and trying to starve its citizens into surrender.

In the absence of their emperor, the people of Paris established their own government and raised an army of nearly 600,000 in just a few weeks. For nearly four months, they controlled all movement in and out of the city, using spies and even surprise escapes by balloon to harass and attack the Germans. Still, by January of 1871, Paris was in danger of collapsing under the German siege. The following story takes place at this time in history.

WORDS TO KNOW
Vocabulary Preview

atrocity, fanatical, pensive, rejuvenated, respite

Focus Your Reading

LITERARY ANALYSIS SITUATIONAL IRONY **Irony** is a contrast between what is expected and what actually exists or happens. **Situational irony** is the contrast between what a character or reader expects and what actually happens. As you read the following selection, look for examples of situational irony.

ACTIVE READING PREDICTING

A **prediction** is an attempt to determine what will happen next in a story. When you predict, you combine information from the text with your own prior knowledge to make guesses about how the **plot** will advance. As you read further, you will often come across new information that may cause you to adjust your prediction.

READER'S NOTEBOOK Make an initial prediction after reading the first few paragraphs of "Two Friends." Then adjust your prediction or make new predictions every time you encounter significant new information. Record your predictions and adjustments.

VIDEODISC **LaserLinks: Background for Reading**
Historical Connection

LESSON RESOURCES

UNIT FOUR RESOURCE BOOK, p. 9

ASSESSMENT RESOURCES

Formal Assessment, pp. 101–102

Teacher's Guide to Assessment and Portfolio Use

Test Generator

SKILLS TRANSPARENCIES AND COPYMASTERS

Literary Analysis

- Irony: Situational, T14 (for Paired Activity, p. 556)

Reading and Critical Thinking

- Predicting Outcomes, T2 (for Think Critically, item 2, p. 556)
- Using Card Catalog/Computer Catalog, T29 (for Author Study Project, p. 529)

Grammar

- Function of Prepositional Phrases, C96 (for Mini Lesson, p. 557)

Vocabulary

- Using a Dictionary, C59 (for Mini Lesson, p. 548)
- Word Origins, C60 (for Mini Lesson, p. 552)

Writing

- Elaboration, T10 (for Writing Option 2, p. 557)
- Levels of Language, T12 (for Writing Option 1, p. 557)

Communications

- Impromptu Speaking: Dialogue, Role-Play, Debate, T13 (for Activities & Explorations 2, p. 557)

INTEGRATED TECHNOLOGY

Audio Library

LaserLinks

- Historical Connection: The Franco-Prussian War. See **Teacher's SourceBook,** p. 33.

Visit our website:
www.mcdougallittell.com

Portrait of André Derain (1905), Henri Matisse. Tate Gallery, London/Art Resource, New York. Copyright ©1995 Succession H. Matisse, Paris/Artists Rights Society (ARS), New York.

Two Friends

Guy de Maupassant

TEACHING THE LITERATURE

Customizing Instruction

Less Proficient Readers

To aid students' comprehension, have them ask themselves the following questions as they read:

- Who are the main characters?
  Answer: Monsieur Morissot and Monsieur Sauvage
- What do they decide to do?
  Answer: go fishing
- Why is their plan dangerous?
  Answer: The city is surrounded by enemy soldiers.

Students Acquiring English

Explain to students that the story is set in France, so there are many French place and character names. Tell students not to let the French names interfere with their understanding of the story, as it is not important that students understand exactly what the words mean, just that they understand that each one is the name of a particular place or person.

Use **Spanish Study Guide** for additional support, pp. 122–124.

Mini Lesson Viewing and Representing

Portrait of Andre Derain **by Henri Matisse**

ART APPRECIATION Henri Matisse (1869–1954) was one of the most influential painters of the 20th century. This 1905 portrait shows the profound influence of Paul Cezanne on Matisse's early work. Like Cezanne, Matisse created sculptured effects through his use of color and shadows.

Instruction Point out that this portrait does not intend to flatter its subject by portraying idealized features. Instead, it conveys a strong and somewhat unsettling emotional truth about the subject that borders on uncomfortable. Ask students to share their impressions of the subject in this portrait and the emotion it conveys.

Possible Responses: The surface plane of the subject, disrupted by color and texture, seems disordered rather than calm, suggesting a dimension of the human self hidden beneath the surface and locked deep within the interior. The emotional effect is somber and somewhat unsettling.

Application Ask students to compare the subject in the painting with the human emotions experienced by characters in the opening of the story.

Possible Responses: The emotion conveyed in the painting seems consistent with the emotion conveyed in the story's opening. The painting seems darkly somber while the story relates the grim conditions of war.

Reading and Analyzing

Reading Skills and Strategies: PREVIEW

Have students look through the selection, then ask them what the title, the images, and the called-out quote in the story suggest. Discuss with students the Build Background feature on p. 546, and ask them to jot down questions that they would like to have answered as they read the story. Before students begin reading, give them a brief summary of the selection.

Literary Analysis

SITUATIONAL IRONY

Ask students to find examples of behavior from the two main characters that seem inappropriate under the circumstances, and that therefore create situational irony.

Possible Responses: They comment on the lack of good weather as if that were the greatest hardship they have faced; they decide to go fishing behind enemy lines.

Use **Unit Four Resource Book** p. 6 for more practice.

Active Reading PREDICTING

When students have read to the end of p. 549, ask them to predict how the story will end. As they read, have them continually evaluate and update their prediction.

Use **Unit Four Resource Book** p. 5 for more practice.

ACTIVE READING

EVALUATE **Possible Response:** No. They are very likely to be found and killed.

Paris was under siege,[1] in the grip of famine, at its last gasp. There were few sparrows on the rooftops now, and even the sewers were losing some of their inhabitants. The fact is that people were eating anything they could get their hands on.

One bright January morning Monsieur Morissot[2] was strolling dejectedly along one of the outer boulevards, with an empty stomach and his hands in the pockets of his old army trousers. He was a watchmaker by trade and a man who liked to make the most of his leisure. Suddenly, he came upon one of his close friends, and he stopped short. It was Monsieur Sauvage,[3] whom he had got to know on fishing expeditions.

Every Sunday before the war it was Morissot's custom to set off at the crack of dawn with his bamboo rod in his hand and a tin box slung over his back. He would catch the Argenteuil train and get off at Colombes, from where he would walk to the island of Marante. The minute he reached this land of his dreams he would start to fish—and he would go on fishing till it got dark.

And it was here, every Sunday, that he met a tubby, jolly little man by the name of Sauvage. He was a haberdasher[4] from the Rue Notre-Dame-de-Lorette, and as fanatical an angler[5] as Morissot himself. They often spent half the day sitting side by side, rod in hand, with their feet dangling over the water. And they had become firm friends.

There were some days when they hardly spoke to each other. On other occasions they would chat all the time. But they understood each other perfectly without needing to exchange any words, because their tastes were so alike and their feelings identical.

On spring mornings at about ten o'clock, when the rejuvenated sun sent floating over the river that light mist which moves along with the current, warming the backs of the two enthusiastic fishermen with the welcome glow of a new season, Morissot would say to his neighbor:

"Ah! It's grand here, isn't it?"

And Monsieur Sauvage would reply:

"There's nothing I like better."

This simple exchange of words was all that was needed for them to understand each other and confirm their mutual appreciation.

In the autumn towards the close of day, when the sky was blood-red and the water reflected strange shapes of scarlet clouds which reddened the whole river, and the glowing sun set the distant horizon ablaze, making the two friends look as though they were on fire, and touching with gold the russet leaves which were already trembling with a wintry shudder, Monsieur Sauvage would turn to Morissot with a smile and say:

"What a marvelous sight!"

And Morissot, equally taken up with the wonder of it all, but not taking his eyes off his float, would answer:

"It's better than walking down the boulevards, eh?"

As soon as the two friends had recognized each other, they shook hands warmly, feeling quite emotional over the fact that they had come across each other in such different circumstances. Monsieur Sauvage gave a sigh and remarked:

"What a lot has happened since we last met!"

---

1. **siege** (sēj): the surrounding of a city by an enemy army trying to capture it by cutting off supplies and keeping it under attack.
2. **Monsieur Morissot** (mə-syœ′ mô-rē-sō′)
3. **Sauvage** (sō-väzh′)
4. **haberdasher:** one who sells men's clothing, such as shirts, hats, and gloves.
5. **angler:** fisherman.

WORDS TO KNOW

fanatical (fə-năt′ĭ-kəl) *adj.* extremely enthusiastic

rejuvenated (rĭ-jo͞o′və-nā′tĭd) *adj.* made new or young again **rejuvenate** *v.*

548

Teaching Options

Mini Lesson Preteaching Vocabulary

USING A DICTIONARY Call students' attention to the list of WORDS TO KNOW. Remind them that the most direct way to determine a word's meaning is to simply look it up in the dictionary

Instruction

- For each word, have students guess at its meaning based upon their prior knowledge or on the word's roots.
- Have them write down their guesses on a piece of paper.
- Then have them look up the word in the dictionary and compare their own guess with the true definition or definitions of the word.

Use **Unit Four Resource Book** p. 7 for more practice.

A lesson on using context clues appears on p. 56 in the Pupil's Edition.

Morissot, in mournful tones, lamented:

"And what awful weather we've been having! This is the first fine day of the year."

And, indeed, the sky was a cloudless blue, brilliant with light.

They started to walk on together side by side, pensive and melancholy. Then Morissot said:

"And what about those fishing trips, eh? *There's* something worth remembering!"

"When shall we be able to get back to it?" mused Monsieur Sauvage.

They went into a little café and drank a glass of absinthe.[6] Then they resumed their stroll along the boulevards.

Morissot suddenly stopped and said:

"What about another glass of the green stuff, eh?"

"Just as you wish," consented Monsieur Sauvage, and they went into a second bar.

When they came out they both felt very
1 fuzzy, as people do when they drink alcohol on an empty stomach. The weather was very mild. A gentle breeze caressed their faces.

Monsieur Sauvage, who felt even more fuddled[7] in this warm air, stopped and said:

"What about it, then? Shall we go?"

"Go where?"

"Fishing!"

"But where can we go?"

"To our island, of course. The French frontline is near Colombes. I know the colonel in command—fellow called Dumoulin. I'm sure we'd have no trouble in getting through."

Morissot began to quiver with excitement.

2 "Right!" he said. "I'm your man!"

And the two friends separated and went off to get their fishing tackle.

An hour later they were striding down the main road together. They reached the villa in which the colonel had set up his headquarters. When he heard their request, he smiled at their eccentric enthusiasm but gave them permission. They set off once again, armed with an official pass.

They soon crossed the frontline, then went through Colombes, which had been evacuated, and now found themselves on the fringe of the area of vineyards which rise in terraces above the Seine. It was about eleven o'clock.

ACTIVE READING

EVALUATE Do you think it is a good idea for the two friends to go fishing beyond the frontline? Why or why not?

On the opposite bank they could see the village of Argenteuil, which looked deserted and dead. The hills of Orgemont and Sannois dominated the horizon, and the great plain which stretches as far as Nanterre was empty, completely empty, with nothing to be seen but its leafless cherry trees and gray earth. 3

Pointing towards the high ground Monsieur Sauvage muttered:

"The Prussians are up there."

And as the two friends gazed at the deserted countryside, they felt almost paralyzed by the sense of uneasiness which was creeping through them.

The Prussians! They had never so much as set eyes on them, but for four months now they had been aware of their presence on the outskirts of Paris, occupying part of France, looting, committing atrocities, reducing people to starvation . . . the invisible yet all-powerful Prussians. As they thought of them, a kind of superstitious dread was added to their natural hatred for this unknown, victorious race.

"What if we should happen to run into some of them?" said Morissot nervously.

Monsieur Sauvage gave the sort of reply which showed that cheerful Parisian banter

6. **absinthe:** a syrupy, green alcoholic beverage that has a licorice flavor.

7. **fuddled:** drunk and confused.

WORDS TO KNOW

pensive (pĕn′sĭv) *adj.* thoughtful in a wistful or sad way

atrocity (ə-trŏs′ĭ-tē) *n.* a very cruel or brutal act

Customizing Instruction

Students Acquiring English

1 Help students understand that, in this context, to feel "very fuzzy" means to feel very light-headed.

2 Explain to students that "I'm your man!" in this case means "I'll join you!" or "I'm ready to go along with your plan."

Multiple Learning Styles

Visual Learners

3 Discuss the details of this view and the mood it evokes. Then have students select two colors that would best express this mood. Instruct them to make a two-color (dichromatic) painting of the scene.

Possible Response: The emotion is sadness because the war has taken the life out of the countryside; the colors are gray and brown.

BLOCK SCHEDULING: MANAGING TIME

If your schedule requires that you cover the lesson objectives in a shorter time, use . . .

- Preparing to Read, p. 546
- Thinking Through the Literature, p. 556
- Vocabulary in Action, p. 557
- Grammar in Context, p. 558

If you want to take advantage of longer class time, use . . .

- TE Teaching Options: Preteaching Vocabulary, p. 548; Viewing and Representing, pp. 547, 550, 553, 555; Speaking and Listening, p. 558; Standardized Test Practice, p. 554
- Choices & Challenges and Author Activity, pp. 557–558

Reading and Analyzing

Literary Analysis

SITUATIONAL IRONY

A Ask students what is ironic about the two men calmly fishing and discussing the nature of war while cannons fire above them.

Possible Response: It would make more sense for them to run for cover.

ACTIVE READING

B **PREDICT** **Possible Responses:** The two men will catch many fish, return safely to Paris, and have a feast; the two will be caught and killed by Prussians.

survived in spite of everything.

"Oh, we'll just offer them some nice fish to fry!" **A**

Even so, they were so worried by the silence of the surrounding countryside that they hesitated about going any further.

It was Monsieur Sauvage who finally made up his mind.

"Come on!" he said. "We'll go on—but we must keep a sharp lookout!"

And they scrambled down the slope of one of the vineyards, bent double, crawling on their hands and knees, taking advantage of the cover afforded by the vines, keeping their eyes wide open and their ears on the alert.

All that now separated them from the river-bank was a strip of open ground. They ran across it, and as soon as they reached the river, they crouched amongst the dry rushes.

ACTIVE READING

PREDICT What do you think will happen on the fishing trip? **B**

Morissot pressed his ear to the ground to see if he could detect the sound of marching feet. He could hear nothing. They were alone, completely alone.

They told each other there was nothing to worry about, and started to fish.

Opposite them the deserted island of Marante concealed them from the other bank. The little building which once housed the restaurant was closed and shuttered, and looked as though it had been abandoned for years.

It was Monsieur Sauvage who caught the first fish—a gudgeon. Morissot caught the second, and then, almost without a pause, they jerked up their rods time after time to find a little silvery creature wriggling away on the hook. This really was a miraculous draft of fishes.

They carefully placed each fish into a fine-meshed net which was suspended in the water at their feet. And as they did so they were overcome by a delightful sense of joy, the kind of joy you only experience when you resume something you really love after being deprived of it for a long time.

A kindly sun was shedding its warmth across their backs. They were so absorbed that they no longer heard, or thought, or paid the least attention to the outside world. What did anything matter now? They were fishing! 1

But suddenly, the bank beneath them shook with a dull rumble which seemed to come from underground.

The distant cannon were starting to fire again.

Morissot turned his head, and above the bank, over to the left, he saw the great bulk of Mont Valérien. On the mountainside was a white plume of smoke, showing where the gunpowder had just bellowed out.

Almost immediately another jet of smoke spurted from the fort on the summit, and a few seconds later the rumble of another detonation reached their ears.

Other cannon shots followed, and every now and then the mountain spat out its deadly breath, exhaled its clouds of milky vapor, which rose slowly into the calm sky above.

"There they go again!" said Monsieur Sauvage with a shrug of his shoulders.

Morissot, who was anxiously watching the feather on his float as it bobbed up and down, was suddenly filled with the anger of a peace-loving man for these maniacs who indulge in fighting. 2

"They've got to be really stupid," he growled, "to go on killing each other like that!"

"They're worse than animals," said Monsieur Sauvage.

Morissot, who had just caught another fish, called out:

"And it'll never be any different so long as we have governments!"

"Oh, no," disagreed Monsieur Sauvage. "The

Teaching Options

Mini Lesson: Viewing and Representing

***The Talisman* by Paul Serusier**

ART APPRECIATION Like his contemporary Paul Gauguin, French painter Paul Serusier (1863–1927) filled his canvases with bold strokes and bright colors. On page 551, this 1888 painting contains a human figure in the upper right corner.

Instruction Point out that a talisman is an object that is supposed to act as a charm to avert evil or to bring good luck. Ask students what they think the talisman in this painting is.

Possible Responses: the house; the pond; the painting itself

Application Ask students how the mood of the painting relates to the story.

Possible Responses: The serenity and brightness bring to mind the peace and happiness that the two friends feel as they are fishing.

The Talisman (1888), Paul Serusier. Musée d'Orsay, Paris, Giraudon/Art Resource, New York.

Customizing Instruction

Multiple Learning Styles

Interpersonal Learners

1 Have students describe moments when they have experienced a similar feeling of being so absorbed in an activity that they were no longer aware that the outside world existed. Ask students to discuss both the causes and the consequences of such a state of mind.

Possible Responses: Responses will vary. Causes can be complete fascination and interest. Consequences can be both positive—the satisfaction of deep engagement—and negative—losing track of important occurrences in the surrounding world.

Less Proficient Readers

2 Have students explain why Morissot is angry.

Possible Response: He is angry at the stupidity of war and the fact that it even exists.

Reading and Analyzing

Literary Analysis: PROTAGONIST/ ANTAGONIST

A Remind students that a protagonist is the chief actor in a story and an antagonist frustrates or attempts to frustrate the protagonist's action. Ask students who they think the protagonists and antagonists are at this point in the story. Point out that an antagonist does not have to be a human.
Possible Responses: The protagonists seem to be Morissot and Sauvage; the antagonist seems to be the war itself.

B Ask students who they believe to be the protagonists and antagonists at this point.
Possible Responses: The protagonists are still Morissot and Sauvage; the antagonists are now enemy soldiers.

Reading Skills and Strategies: CLARIFYING

C Ask students why the Prussian officer wants the password.
Possible Response: So that his soldiers can infiltrate the French lines and possibly the city.

Reading Skills and Strategies: PREDICT

D Ask students to predict whether the two men will trade the password for their lives and why or why not.
Possible Responses: Yes, because the two men do not seem particularly interested in either side of the war; no, because to do so would put many French soldiers and civilians in danger.

Republic[8] would never have declared war . . ."

"Look!" interrupted Morissot. "Under kings you have war against other countries. Under republican governments you have civil war."

A And they began to argue, in a calm and friendly way, sorting out all the world's great political problems with the commonsense approach of mild and reasonable men. On one point they were in absolute agreement: mankind would never be free. And as they talked, Mont Valérien went thundering on without respite, demolishing French homes with its cannonades,[9] pounding lives to dust, crushing human beings to pulp, putting an end to so many dreams, to so many long-awaited joys, so much long-expected happiness, tearing into the hearts of all those wives and daughters and mothers with pain and suffering that would never be eased.

"Such is life," said Monsieur Sauvage.

"Better to call it death," laughed Morissot.

But at that moment they both gave a start, scared by the feeling that somebody had been walking just behind them. They looked round and saw standing above them four men, four
1 tall, bearded men, armed to the teeth, dressed like liveried[10] footmen, with flat military caps on their heads—and rifles which they were
B pointing straight at the two friends.

The fishing rods dropped from their hands and went floating down the river.

In a matter of seconds they were seized, tied up, hustled along, thrown into a boat and carried across to the island.

Behind the building which they had thought deserted they saw a group of about twenty German soldiers.

A sort of hairy giant who was sitting astride a chair and smoking a large clay pipe asked them in excellent French:

"Well, messieurs, did the fishing go well?"

One of the soldiers placed at the officer's feet

The fishing rods dropped from their hands and went floating down the river.

the net full of fish which he had been careful to bring along. The Prussian smiled and said:

"Well, well! I can see you didn't do badly at all! . . . But I have to deal with a very different matter. Now, listen to me carefully, and don't get alarmed . . . As far as I am concerned you are a couple of spies sent out here to keep an eye on me. I've caught you and I've every right to shoot you. You were obviously pretending to fish as a cover for your real purposes. It's too bad for you that you've fallen into my hands. But war is war . . . Now, since you've come out here past your own lines, you're bound to have a password so you can get back. Just give me that password and I'll spare your lives." C D

The two friends, ghastly pale, stood there side by side with their hands trembling. They said nothing.

8. **the Republic:** the Second Republic of France (1848–1852), which was France's first truly representative government.
9. **cannonades:** continued firing of cannons.
10. **liveried:** uniformed.

WORDS TO KNOW **respite** (rĕs′pĭt) *n.* a temporary stop; a brief period of rest or relief from activity

552

Teaching Options

Mini Lesson: Vocabulary Strategy

RESEARCHING WORD ORIGINS AS AN AID TO UNDERSTANDING MEANINGS Instruction To help students see how analysis of word origins can help them understand new words, copy the following chart on the chalkboard:

Word	Current Meaning	Original Language	Root Word	Original Meaning
ghastly	terrifying or unpleasant	Old English	*gast*	soul or spirit

Discuss with students the connection between the original Old English and the current meaning.

Possible Response: A soul or spirit might be a terrifying thing to see.

Practice To help students expand their vocabulary, have them complete the chart for five words from the selection, using a dictionary to get their information. Then have the class discuss the connections between the words' current meanings and their origins.

Use **Vocabulary Transparencies and Copymasters,** p. 60.

A lesson on researching word origins appears on p. 356 in the Pupil's Edition.

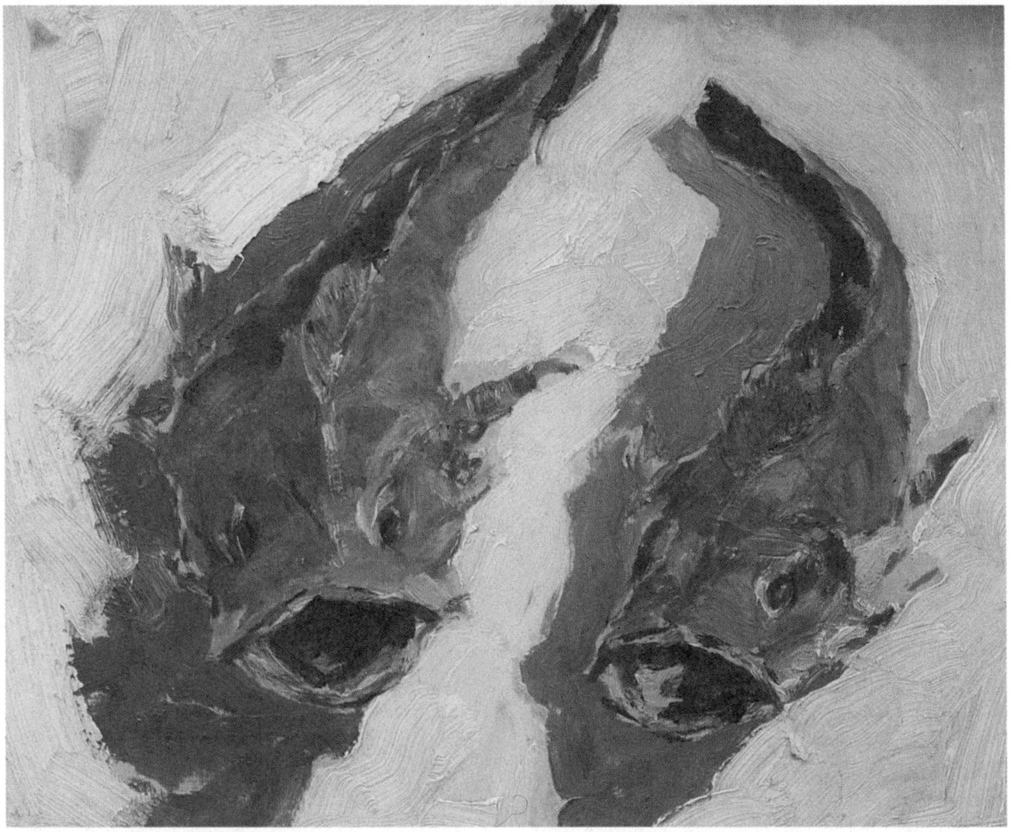

Green Fish (about 1928), Selden Gile. Oil on board, Bedford Gallery, Dean Lesher Regional Center for the Arts, Walnut Creek, California.

"Nobody will ever get to know about it," continued the officer. "You will go back without any trouble, and the secret will go with you . . . If you refuse to cooperate, you'll die—straight away. So take your choice!"

They stood there motionless, keeping their mouths firmly shut.

The Prussian, who was still quite calm, pointed in the direction of the river and said:

"Just think! In five minutes you'll be at the bottom of that river. In five minutes! You must have families. Think of them!"

The rumbling of the cannon was still coming from Mont Valérien.

The two fishermen simply stood there, refusing to speak. The German now gave some orders in his own language. Then he moved his chair some distance away from the prisoners. Twelve men marched up and formed a line twenty yards from them with their rifles at their sides. **2**

Customizing Instruction

Students Acquiring English

1 Explain to students that the expression *armed to the teeth* means "carrying many weapons."

Less Proficient Readers

2 Ask students to summarize the events of the story since the two men began fishing.

Possible Response: They both began to catch many fish. The cannons began firing, and the men got into an argument over the nature of war. Prussian soldiers found them and took them to an officer who asked them for the password to get through the French lines. The two men remained silent, even though the officer threatened them with death.

Mini Lesson: Viewing and Representing

Green Fish by Selden Gile

ART APPRECIATION This painting, which was created around 1928, elicited the following comments from art critic Wayne Thiebaud: *"Green Fish* looks like it's done with thistles—very sticky. Everything is sort of pointed like little bull heads or strange little fish characters. . . ."

Instruction Ask students whether they consider this to be a realistic painting and to discuss details from the painting to support their responses.

Possible Responses: Yes—the fish look like real fish; no—the fish lack fine detail and are more impressionistic than realistic.

Reading and Analyzing

Active Reading PREDICTING

A Ask students to predict what is going to happen to the two men now.
Possible Responses: They will give the officer the password and be set free; they will give the officer the password and be shot anyway; they will give the officer a false password in the hopes of outsmarting him; they will remain silent and be shot.

ACTIVE READING

B CONNECT **Possible Responses:** accept the offer; refuse the offer; give the officer a false password

LITERARY LINK

Ask students whether Morissot and Sauvage would agree with the message of this poem and why or why not.
Possible Response: Yes, they would want to die outside in the sun, as they did, rather than being holed up in the besieged city.

A "I'll give you one minute to make up your minds," called the officer. "And not two seconds more."

Then he jumped to his feet, went up to the two Frenchmen, took Morissot by the arm, and led him to one side. Then he said to him in a very low voice:

1 "Quick! Just let me have that password! Your friend won't know you've told me. I'll make it look as though I've taken pity on you both."

Morissot said nothing.

B ACTIVE READING

CONNECT What would you do in this situation?

The Prussian then dragged Monsieur Sauvage to one side and made the same proposition to him.

Monsieur Sauvage said nothing.

So they were pushed together again, side by side.

It was then that Morissot happened to glance down at the net full of gudgeon which was lying in the grass a few yards away.

A ray of sunlight fell on the heap of glittering fish, which were still quivering with life. As he looked at them he felt a momentary weakness. In spite of his efforts to hold them back, tears filled his eyes.

"Farewell, Monsieur Sauvage," he mumbled.

And Monsieur Sauvage replied:

"Farewell, Monsieur Morissot."

They shook hands, trembling uncontrollably from head to foot.

"Fire!" shouted the officer.

Twelve shots rang out simultaneously.

Monsieur Sauvage fell like a log onto his face. Morissot, who was taller, swayed, spun round, then collapsed on top of his friend, with his face staring up at the sky and the blood welling from where his coat had been burst open across his chest.

The German shouted out more orders. His men went off and came back with some lengths of rope and a few heavy stones which they fastened to the feet of the two bodies. Then they carried them to the riverbank.

All the time Mont Valérien continued to rumble, and now it was capped by a great mountain of smoke.

Two soldiers got hold of Morissot by the head and feet. Two others lifted up Monsieur Sauvage in the same way. The two bodies were swung violently backwards and forwards, then thrown with great force. They curved through the air, then plunged upright into the river, with the stones dragging them down, feet first.

The water spurted up, bubbled, swirled round, then grew calm again, with little waves rippling across to break against the bank. There was just a small amount of blood discoloring the surface.

The officer, still quite unperturbed, said, half aloud:

"Well, now it's the fishes' turn."

As he was going back towards the building, he noticed the net full of gudgeon lying in the grass. He picked it up, looked at the fish, then smiled, and called out:

"Wilhelm!"

A soldier came running up. He was wearing a white apron. The Prussian officer threw across to him the catch made by the two executed fishermen, and gave another order:

"Fry me these little creatures—straight away, while they're still alive. They'll be delicious!"

Then he lit his pipe again. ❖

Translated by Arnold Kellett

Teaching Options

Assessment Standardized Test Practice

OPEN-ENDED QUESTIONS
On standardized tests, students are often required to answer two open-ended reading questions that focus on understanding the effects of literary elements and the ability to analyze and critically evaluate texts. To help students prepare for such assessment, write the following instruction on the board:

Describe an irony present in "Two Friends."

RUBRIC

3 **Full Accomplishment** The response fully accounts for an ironic contrast between what is expected and what actually happens.

2 **Substantial Accomplishment** The response largely accounts for an ironic contrast between what is expected and what actually happens.

1 **Little or Partial Accomplishment** The response contains inaccuracies about expectations or outcomes and fails to recognize ironic contrast.

LITERARY LINK

José Martí

(C) *from* *Simple Poetry*

XXIII

I want to leave this world
By the natural door;
They must carry me off to die
In a cart of green leaves.

Do not put me in the dark
To die like a traitor;
I am good, and so I shall die
With my face to the sun!

Translated by Elinor Randall

from *Versos Sencillos*

XXIII

Yo quiero salir del mundo
Por la puerta natural:
En un carro de hojas verdes
A morir me han de llevar.

No me pongan en lo oscuro
A morir como un traidor:
¡Yo soy bueno, y como bueno
Moriré de cara al sol!

Carving the Spirit of the Flesh (1980), Arnaldo Roche Rabell. Oil pastel on paper, 50″ × 40″, courtesy of the artist and Galeria Botello, Hato Rey, Puerto Rico.

Customizing Instruction

Less Proficient Readers

1 Ask students to paraphrase the offer the officer makes to Morissot.

Possible Response: If you give me the password, I will pretend that you didn't, but that I've decided to let both of you go anyway.

Gifted and Talented

Invite students to discuss how the story might change if it were told from the point of view of someone sympathetic to the Prussian cause.

Mini Lesson: Viewing and Representing

Carving the Spirit of the Flesh **by Arnaldo Roche Rabell**

ART APPRECIATION In this powerful portrait, the Puerto Rican artist Arnaldo Roche Rabell (b. 1955) uses subtle lines and strong shading to reveal the man's features. Notice the direct, almost bold expression of the eyes.

Instruction Ask students what kind of person they think this man is and why.

Possible Responses: brave—the look in his eyes indicates that he will back down from nothing

Application Ask the students how the painting relates to the poem.

Possible Responses: The man does not look afraid of anything and could be contemplating something as serious as what constitutes a "good" death.

GUIDING STUDENT RESPONSE

Connect to the Literature

1. **What Do You Think?**
   Possible Response: outrage—the two men did nothing wrong

Comprehension Check

- Monsieur Morissot and Monsieur Sauvage
- They want to fish at their favorite spot, which is behind enemy lines.
- to give him the password that he can use to penetrate the French line
- They are executed.

Use Selection Quiz in **Unit Four Resource Book**, p. 9.

Think Critically

2. Student responses will vary based on the predictions they made.
3. Possible Responses: They don't take the possible danger seriously; they are tired of the siege, so they take risks to do what they like; they are hungry.
4. Possible Responses: Yes—the two Frenchmen made the right choice; if they had cooperated with the officer and revealed the password, they would have endangered French lives. No, the men should have tried to negotiate with the German officer.
5. Possible Responses: Yes, because each might have had only his own life to risk. It's likely that each was more cautious because he wanted to protect the life of his friend.

Literary Analysis

Situational Irony Help students see that the situational irony here comes from the contrast between the friends' desire to enjoy a peaceful day and their unexpected entrapment in a war they seek to avoid.

Protagonist/Antagonist Possible Response: Morissot and Sauvage are the protagonists of the story; the Prussian officer is the antagonist.

Thinking through the LITERATURE

Connect to the Literature

1. **What Do You Think?** What is your reaction to the way the story ends?

Comprehension Check

- Who are the two friends the title refers to?
- Why do the two friends cross the frontline of the war?
- What does the Prussian commander ask of the captives?
- What happens to the two friends when they don't give the password?

Think Critically

2. ACTIVE READING PREDICTING Refer to the predictions you recorded in your READER'S NOTEBOOK. How accurate were they? How did they change as you made your way through the story?

3. Why do you think Morissot and Sauvage are willing to risk their lives to go fishing?

4. Do you think the Frenchmen do the right thing by refusing to cooperate with the officer?

   THINK ABOUT
   - the officer's promise that "Nobody will ever get to know about it"
   - the values that might have influenced their decision
   - whether you think they know the password

5. Do you think either friend would have acted differently had he been captured alone?

Extend Interpretations

6. **Comparing Texts** What connection can you make between "Two Friends" and the poem by José Martí on page 555? Support your response with details from both selections.

7. **Connect to Life** Recall incidents you have heard about in recent years concerning the treatment of prisoners, the wounded, or civilians during times of war. Which acts do you consider to be morally wrong, and which ones, if any, are acceptable during wartime?

Literary Analysis

SITUATIONAL IRONY **Irony** is a contrast between what is expected and what actually exists or occurs. **Situational irony** occurs when a character or reader expects one thing to happen but something entirely different occurs. In short stories, situational irony often occurs in the form of a surprise ending.

Maupassant is famous for his irony. In "Two Friends," he toys with the reader's expectations—the threat of the enemy looms large and then recedes as the characters relax and begin to enjoy their adventure, until they again become aware of the threat. This cycle repeats itself, lulling the reader into a false sense of security. For this reason, the ironic ending comes to many readers as a great blow.

Paired Activity With a partner, review the comments about war made by Morissot and Sauvage. How does the situational irony of the ending in "Two Friends" contribute to your understanding of the story's theme about war?

PROTAGONIST/ ANTAGONIST

The **protagonist** is the main character involved in the action of the story. Sometimes a story has more than one protagonist. The person or force working against the protagonist is called the **antagonist.** The antagonist can be another character, something in nature or society, or even an internal force within the protagonist.

Activity Who are the protagonists in "Two Friends"? Who or what would you identify as the antagonist? Explain your reasoning.

Extend Interpretations

Comparing Texts Possible Response: The speaker in the poem does not want to die like a traitor, and neither do the two friends in the story.

Connect to Life Responses will vary. Remind students that acts that would be reprehensible in peacetime may be considered acceptable during wartime.

Choices & CHALLENGES

Writing Options

1. Farewell Letter Imagine that the German officer has allowed Morissot or Sauvage to write a final letter to a loved one. Write the letter that one of the two friends might have written.

2. Traitor's Tale Imagine that one of the Frenchmen decided to reveal the password. Write an alternative ending to the story.

Activities & Explorations

1. Patchwork Design Create a paper patchwork quilt or some other design that illustrates with shapes and colors the contrasting feelings associated with war and peace as conveyed by the story. ~ **ART**

2. Performance Piece In a small group, create a multimedia presentation featuring contemporary images of war and peace. Read aloud passages from the story to accompany your images. You may also use music to help establish the mood of your presentation.
~ **SPEAKING AND LISTENING**

3. Short Storyboard Create a storyboard of the events in this story. For each frame of the storyboard, include a sketch of one event. Beneath each frame, write a short statement of what you think the characters are thinking or feeling at that point. Base your work on evidence from the story. ~ **VIEWING AND REPRESENTING**

Inquiry & Research

Life Under Siege Research the siege of Paris during the Franco-Prussian War or another famous siege in history. Find out about the military strategies involved and about the quality of life of the people living under siege. Share your findings in a short research paper.

Art Connection

Two Fish Look at this painting by Selden Gile on page 553. What does it make you think of in the context of this story? Refer to details from the selection in your response.

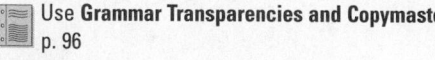

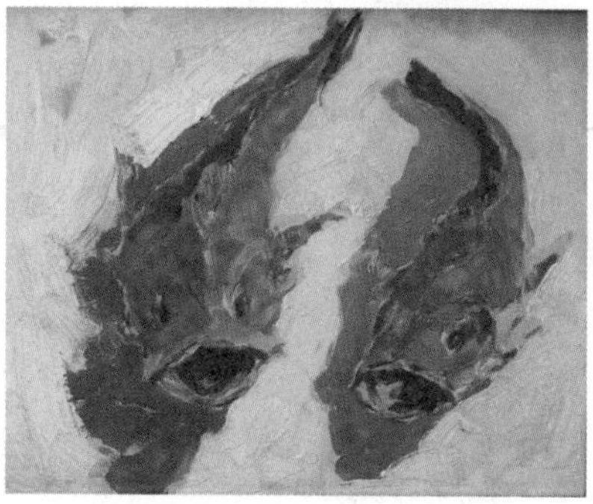

Vocabulary in Action

EXERCISE: MEANING CLUES Read each newspaper headline below, and write the vocabulary word that you would expect to find in an article with that headline.

1. "Crowd of Cheering Fans Mobs Celebrity"
2. "Mass Murders Committed by Rebel Forces"
3. "Vitamin E Shown to Reduce Facial Wrinkles"
4. "Families Reflect on War's Casualties"
5. "Law Requires Short Rest Period for Workers"

WORDS TO KNOW			
	atrocity	pensive	respite
	fanatical	rejuvenated	

Building Vocabulary
For an in-depth lesson using synonym and antonym clues to determine meaning from context, see page 1000.

Writing Options

1. **Farewell Letter** Students should reflect upon how one might feel if one were soon to be executed. Also remind students to make the relationship between the recipient and the friend writing the letter clear.
2. **Traitor's Tale** Students can read their alternative endings out loud and discuss them.

Activities & Explorations

1. **Patchwork Design** Students might have a quilt exhibition, hanging the finished quilts in the classroom and inviting other classes in to view and comment on them.
2. **Performance Piece** Students can look in newspapers and weekly news magazines for their contemporary images. They may also want to listen to music and songs about war and peace to find music that matches the tone they want.
3. **Short Storyboard** Have students divide responsibilities among group members. Some can write caption statements; some can sketch pictures; others can work on layout. Everyone should contribute ideas.

Inquiry & Research

Life Under Siege Encourage students to work in research groups to look for information about famous sieges such as the siege of Vicksburg during the Civil War, the siege of Stalingrad during World War II, or the siege of Sarajevo during the recent Bosnian conflict. Suggest that groups look for details about the siege itself as well as analyses of its effect on that particular war as a whole. Remind them they can locate print and nonprint information using text resources and technical resources including databases and the Internet.

Art Connection

Two Fish Possible Response: The two fish are suggestive of the two friends, at the mercy of the Prussian officer. They are also reminiscent of the fish caught by the friends and then eaten by the officer.

Mini Lesson Grammar

FUNCTION OF PREPOSITIONAL PHRASES
Prepositional phrases function either as adjectives or adverbs. When a prepositional phrase functions as an adjective, it is modifying or limiting the meaning of a noun or pronoun by describing it. Write the following sentence on the board and explain how the prepositional phrase modifies the noun:

The man *in the boat* is my brother.

When a prepositional phrase functions as an adverb, it modifies a verb, an adjective, another adverb, or a whole clause. Often, the phrase will answer the questions *when, where, why, how,* and *to what extent.* Write the following sentence on the board and explain how the prepositional phrase modifies the verb:

The dog bit me *on the ankle*. (*where* the speaker was bitten.)

Practice Have students write a short description of a school activity using at least six prepositional phrases, two that function as adjectives and four that function as adverbs.

Use **Grammar Transparencies and Copymasters,** p. 96

Language Network

Use McDougal Littell's ***Language Network,*** Chapter 3, for more instruction in prepositional phrases.

Author Activity

Tales of Realism Possible Responses: Maupassant offers very precise details of the countryside; he sets the story in his own time, basing it on an actual war; the friends are vividly portrayed, and their dialogue sounds natural; the officer's cruelty seems appropriate to the state of war; the story seems filled with details from ordinary life.

Grammar in Context

WRITING EXERCISE Answers will vary. Possible answers are shown.

1. The two friends know about the Prussian advance, and so the silence of the countryside puzzles them.
2. They crawl through the vineyards on their hands and knees but later run across the open fields.
3. Finally arriving at the stroke of noon, they cast their lines into the water.
4. The sounds of cannon, the smoke from gunpowder, and the rumbling of the earth remind them that a battle is raging nearby.

Vocabulary in Action

EXERCISE: MEANING CLUES

1. fanatical
2. atrocity
3. rejuvenated
4. pensive
5. respite

Grammar in Context: Prepositional Phrases That Add Details

In this excerpt from "Two Friends," notice how prepositional phrases add details referring to the noun *strip* and the verb *crouched.*

> **All that now separated them from the riverbank was a strip of open ground. . . . As soon as they reached the river, they crouched amongst the dry rushes.**

As you may recall, a **prepositional phrase** consists of a preposition, its object, and any modifiers of the object. Prepositional phrases are most frequently used as adverbs and adjectives. In the example above, the prepositional phrases shown in blue help readers to visualize the scene *(strip of open ground)* and to put themselves in the shoes of the two friends *(crouched amongst the dry rushes).*

WRITING EXERCISE Rewrite these sentences, adding prepositional phrases that modify the underlined words. Each prepositional phrase should answer one of the questions in parentheses.

Example: Original Each morning (when?), the two friends go fishing (where?).

Rewritten Each morning at the crack of dawn, the two friends go fishing on the tranquil river.

1. The two friends know (what?), and so the silence (where?) puzzles them.
2. They crawl (where?) (how?) but later run (where?).
3. Finally arriving (when?), they cast their lines (where?).
4. The sounds (from what?), the smoke (from what?), and the rumbling (where?) remind them that a battle is raging nearby.

Grammar Handbook Phrases, p. 1195

Guy de Maupassant
1850–1893

Other Works
The Best Stories of Guy de Maupassant
Selected Short Stories
The Dark Side of Guy de Maupassant

Art and Life Guy de Maupassant is famous for realistic tales based mostly on personal experience. He grew up in Normandy, a region in northwestern France. Several of his stories explore unhappy marriages, no doubt inspired by that of his own parents. His mother and father separated when Guy was 11, and his childhood memories of their bitter quarrels help explain why he himself never married.

Early Influences Maupassant studied law in Paris, but his studies were interrupted by military service in the Franco-Prussian War, which gave him firsthand experience that he would draw on for several more tales. After the war, he resumed his studies and, through his father's influence, obtained a government job. His mother's influence proved even more significant: she asked her friend Gustave Flaubert, the famous French novelist, to keep an eye on her son in Paris. Flaubert became Maupassant's friend and mentor, encouraging the younger man to write and offering him advice.

Maturity and Success During the 1880s, Maupassant enjoyed his most productive years as an author. Although he wrote several novels, his forte was the short story, a form he helped popularize throughout Europe. His financial success allowed him to purchase a fine apartment in Paris as well as a yacht, which he enjoyed sailing. Tragedy came in 1889, however, when his younger brother died of a disease that would soon strike the author. Maupassant, whose final years were marked by mental and physical deterioration, died a month short of his 43rd birthday.

Author Activity

Tales of Realism Guy de Maupassant's tales are pioneering works of realism, the 19th-century literary movement that stressed the need to picture life as it was really lived. With a partner, discuss the aspects of the story that you found true to life.

Teaching Options

Mini Lesson: Speaking and Listening

INTERVIEWS Interviews can reveal facets of ordinary life and major events that have been missed or overlooked in conventional news reports. The interviewer should be willing to allow the interview to flow in unexpected directions.

Application Invite students to interview someone who has lived through a war. Interviewers should be prepared with questions about the war itself and about how it affected people's everyday lives. Some interviewers—with the permission of the subject—may want to use tape recorders. Otherwise, interviewers must take careful notes. The class should discuss what new information or insight each interview brings to light, and how the subject's perspective affects his or her memory of the war.

BLOCK SCHEDULING This lesson is particularly well suited for longer class periods.

PREPARING to *Read*

The Pit and the Pendulum

Short Story by EDGAR ALLAN POE

"I saw clearly the doom which had been prepared for me."

Connect to Your Life

Horror Stories "The Pit and the Pendulum" is a classic horror tale by an American master of the macabre, Edgar Allan Poe. Think of horror stories that you have read in the past or seen at the movies or on television. Which did you find the most terrifying? What was so scary about them? Why do you think people enjoy horror tales? Record your thoughts. Then share your ideas in a class discussion.

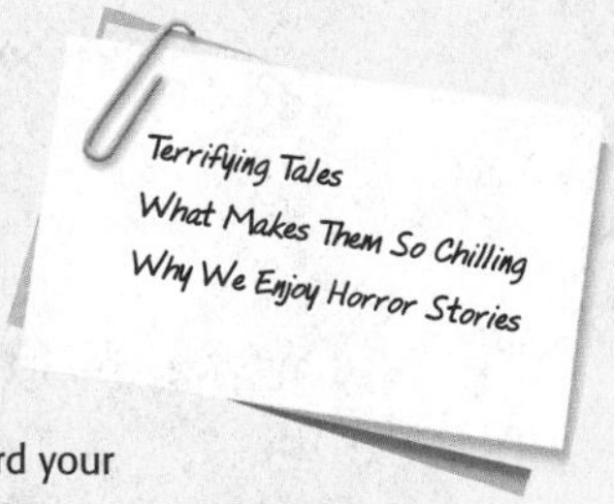

Build Background

Tortured Times "The Pit and the Pendulum" is set in the Spanish city of Toledo during the Spanish Inquisition. The Roman Catholic practice of holding inquisitions began in medieval times to combat heresy, the act of expressing or holding beliefs different from those of the Church. The accused were put on trial and encouraged to confess to heresy. Often they were tortured into confessing and naming fellow heretics. Those found guilty of the worst crimes were sentenced and often executed at an elaborate public ceremony called the auto-da-fé. Under Spain's first grand inquisitor, hundreds of accused heretics were found guilty and burned at the stake. The Spanish Inquisition continued in various forms until 1834.

WORDS TO KNOW
Vocabulary Preview

discordant	lethargy	resolution
eloquent	lucid	stealthily
encompass	pertinacity	supposition
imperceptible	potent	treacherous
insuperable	relapse	voracity

Focus Your Reading

LITERARY ANALYSIS SUSPENSE No horror tale would be effective without **suspense,** which is the excitement or tension that readers feel as they become involved in a story and eager to know the outcome of the **plot.** To create suspense, writers carefully choose the manner in which they reveal critical details. In this passage from "The Pit and the Pendulum," the **narrator** shares with the reader his own suspense and confusion about his surroundings:

> ***So far, I had not opened my eyes. I felt that I lay upon my back, unbound. . . . I strove to imagine where and*** what ***I could be. I longed, yet dared not to employ my vision. I dreaded the first glance at objects around me.***

As you read, pay attention to Poe's methods of creating the suspense.

ACTIVE READING VISUALIZING One way you can better understand a narrative is to **visualize,** or mentally picture, the **characters,** events, and **settings** being described. Here are some guidelines to follow as you read "The Pit and the Pendulum":

- Form a mental picture of where the narrator is at each stage and what is going on around him.
- Try to bring the images into sharper focus by noting precise nouns, verbs, and modifiers used in descriptions, especially those that indicate physical appearance—size, shape, color, and so on.
- Be sure to take note of words and phrases that indicate direction or position—up, down, left, right, at the top, to the north, and so on.

READER'S NOTEBOOK As you read this story, jot down at least ten details that you can vividly picture in your mind.

OVERVIEW

This selection is included in the **Grade 10 InterActive Reader.**

Objectives

1. understand and appreciate a **short story (Literary Analysis)**
2. understand **suspense (Literary Analysis)**
3. **visualize** images of character and setting **(Active Reading)**

Summary

The narrator is a victim of the Spanish Inquisition who has been condemned to death by torture. As he moves around his dark cell, he narrowly escapes falling into a pit that occupies the center of the dungeon. He is drugged and wakes up tied to a wooden frame beneath a pendulum with a sharp blade at the end; the swinging blade gradually drops lower, edging closer and closer to his body. He manages to escape by having rats gnaw through the straps that hold him. When he frees himself, he finds that the burning hot metal walls of the cell are closing in around him. As the walls squeeze closer, he is forced to the edge of the pit where he finally faints as he falls into the rescuing arms of General Lasalle of the French army.

Thematic Link

Imprisoned during the Spanish Inquisition, the narrator **faces the enemy** in the forms of the tortures he endures and his own limitations of mind and strength.

Editor's Note This selection has been edited slightly to delete material that may be considered objectionable.

5-Minute Warm-Up

Daily Language SkillBuilder

Have students **proofread** the display sentences on page 541k and write them correctly. The sentences also appear on Transparency 18 of **Grammar Transparencies and Copymasters.**

LESSON RESOURCES

UNIT FOUR RESOURCE BOOK, pp. 10–15

ASSESSMENT RESOURCES

Formal Assessment, pp. 103–104

Teacher's Guide to Assessment and Portfolio Use

Test Generator

SKILLS TRANSPARENCIES AND COPYMASTERS

Reading and Critical Thinking

- Visualizing, T8 (for Think Critically, item 5, p. 575)

Grammar

- Appositives, C98 (for Mini Lesson, p. 572)
- Essential and Nonessential Appositives and Appositive Phrases, C99 (for Mini Lesson, p. 576)

Vocabulary

- Context Clues, C61 (for Mini Lesson, p. 560)
- Words Origins, C62 (for Mini Lesson, p. 568)

Writing

- Writing Process, T1, T2 (for Writing Options, p. 576)
- Effective Language, T13 (for Writing Option 2, p. 576)
- Opinion Statement, C25 (for Writing Option 1, p. 576)

Communications

- Formal Presentations, T10 (for Activities & Explorations 2, p. 576)

INTEGRATED TECHNOLOGY

Audio Library

Visit our website:
www.mcdougallittell.com

TEACHING THE LITERATURE

Reading and Analyzing

Reading Skills and Strategies: PREVIEW

Have students preview the selection. Ask students what the title, the images, and the called-out quotes in the story suggest. Discuss with students the Build Background feature on page 559. Have students predict how the title and images will come into play as objects of horror. Before students begin reading, give them a brief summary of the selection.

Literary Analysis SUSPENSE

As students read, have them note moments at which they wonder or worry about what will happen next. Ask them to keep a list of the questions these moments produce, and the answers to them that are provided by the text. After they have read the story, have students compare their questions and discuss whether they felt suspenseful at the same points in the story.

Use **Unit Four Resource Book** p. 12 for more practice.

Active Reading VISUALIZING

Remind students that visualizing is an effective technique to use while monitoring and modifying reading strategies. Ask them to visualize what the pit and the pendulum might look like, and how they relate to each other. Have students compare their initial visualization with the images Poe describes.

Possible Response: The pendulum is long and heavy, and swings rapidly in a pit in which a man is trapped.

Use **Unit Four Resource Book** p. 11 for more practice.

The Pit and the

EDGAR ALLAN POE

Impia tortorum longos hic turba furores
Sanguinis innocui, non satiata, aluit.
Sospite nunc patriâ, fracto nunc funeris antro,
Mors ubi dira fuit vita salusque patent.[1]

[Quatrain composed for the gates of a market to be erected upon the site of the Jacobin[2] Club House at Paris.]

1. Impia . . . patent *Latin:* Here the wicked crowd of tormentors, unsated, fed their long-time lusts for innocent blood. Now that our homeland is safe, now that the tomb is broken, life and health appear where once was dread death.
2. Jacobin (jăk′ə-bĭn): belonging to a radical French political group famous for its terrorist policies during the French Revolution.

Teaching Options

Mini Lesson: Preteaching Vocabulary

USING CONTEXT CLUES Call students' attention to the list of WORDS TO KNOW. Remind them that sometimes they can understand the meaning of an unfamiliar word by examining the context in which the word is used. Use the model sentence to demonstrate the strategy of using context clues that provide inferences to word meaning.

Model Sentence

The movement of a clock's hour hand is so slow that it is imperceptible.

Instruction

- Write the model sentence on the board.
- Ask a volunteer to summarize the meaning of the sentence.
- Have students use the meaning of the sentence to infer meanings for the word *imperceptible.*
- Ask a volunteer to use the word *imperceptible* in a sentence.

Use **Unit Four Resource Book** p. 13 for more practice.

A lesson on using context clues appears on p. 56 in the Pupil's Edition.

Customizing Instruction

Less Proficient Readers

Have students keep the following questions in mind as they read:

- Who is telling the story?
  Answer: the main character, a prisoner of the Spanish Inquisition
- What is the story's setting?
  Answer: a dungeon
- What is happening to the narrator?
  Answer: He is being tortured.

Students Acquiring English

Explain to your students that "The Pit and the Pendulum" was written about 150 years ago, and that many of the words Poe uses are difficult even for native English speakers. Remind students to take advantage of the footnotes and the WORDS TO KNOW definitions at the bottom of the page. Encourage them to look up any words they don't know, and to keep a list of these words and their definitions.

Use **Spanish Study Guide** for additional support, pp. 124–125.

Gifted and Talented

Have students read more about the Spanish Inquisition. Encourage them to focus on the Inquisition's methods and instruments. After they have finished the story, have students discuss whether the tortures discussed by Poe might have been used during the Inquisition, and how they compare with other practices of the time.

Reading and Analyzing

Literary Analysis SUSPENSE

A Poe begins to create suspense from the opening paragraph when he refers to the "dread sentence of death." Have students explain how this reference creates suspense.
Possible Response: It creates an anxious tension in readers. We want to know whether and how the narrator will escape the death sentence.

Active Reading VISUALIZING

B The narrator concretely describes two aspects of what he sees in the opening scene: the black-robed judges and seven tall candles. Ask students to close their eyes and visualize the scene as you read it aloud. Have students share and discuss features of their visions.

ACTIVE READING

C QUESTION **Possible Responses:** He is in prison; he is dreaming.

ACTIVE READING

D EVALUATE **Possible Responses:** He is frightened; he is educated, he is in a nightmare.

A I was sick—sick unto death with that long agony; and when they at length unbound me, and I was permitted to sit, I felt that my senses were leaving me. The sentence—the dread sentence of death—was the last of distinct accentuation which reached my ears. After that, the sound of the inquisitorial voices seemed merged in one dreamy indeterminate hum. It conveyed to my soul the idea of revolution—perhaps from its association in fancy with the burr of a millwheel. This only for a brief period; for presently I heard no more. Yet, for a while, I saw; but with how terrible an exaggeration! I saw the lips of the black-robed judges. They appeared to me white—whiter than the sheet upon which I trace these words—and thin even to grotesqueness; thin with the intensity of their expression of firmness—of immoveable resolution—of stern contempt of human torture. I saw that the decrees of what to me was Fate, were still issuing from those lips. I saw them writhe with a deadly locution.[3] I saw them fashion the syllables of my name; and I shuddered because no sound succeeded. I saw, too, for a few moments of delirious horror, the soft and nearly imperceptible waving of the sable draperies which enwrapped the walls of the apartment.[4] And then my vision fell upon the seven tall candles upon the table. At first they wore the aspect of charity, and seemed white slender angels who would save me; but then, all at once, there came a most deadly nausea over B my spirit, and I felt every fiber in my frame thrill as if I had touched the wire of a galvanic[5] battery, while the angel forms became meaningless specters, with heads of flame, and I saw that from them there would be no help. And then there stole into my fancy, like a rich musical note, the thought of what sweet rest there must be in the grave. The thought came gently and stealthily, and it seemed long before it attained full appreciation;[6] but just as my spirit came at length properly to feel and entertain it, the figures of the judges vanished, as if magically, from before me; the tall candles sank into nothingness; their flames went out utterly; the blackness of darkness supervened; all sensations appeared swallowed up in a mad rushing descent as of the soul into Hades. Then silence, and stillness, and night were the universe. C

ACTIVE READING

QUESTION Where is the narrator?

I had swooned; but still will not say that all of consciousness was lost. What of it there remained I will not attempt to define, or even to describe; yet all was not lost. In the deepest slumber—no! In delirium—no! In a swoon—no! In death—no! even in the grave all *is not* lost. Else there is no immortality for man. Arousing from the most profound of slumbers, we break the gossamer web of *some* dream. Yet in a second afterward, (so frail may that web have been) we remember not that we have dreamed. In the return to life from the swoon there are two stages; first, that of the sense of mental or spiritual; secondly, that of the sense of physical, existence. It seems probable that if, upon reaching the second stage, we could recall the impressions of the first, we should find these impressions eloquent in memories of the gulf beyond. And that gulf is—what? How at least shall we distinguish its shadows from those of the tomb? But if the impressions of what I have termed the first stage, are not, at will, recalled, yet, after long interval, do they not come unbidden, while we

3. **locution** (lō-kyo͞o′shən): speech.
4. **apartment:** room.
5. **galvanic** (găl-văn′ĭk): electric.
6. **attained . . . appreciation:** was fully understood.

WORDS TO KNOW

resolution (rĕz′ə-lo͞o′shən) *n.* determination
imperceptible (ĭm′pər-sĕp′tə-bəl) *adj.* impossible to perceive; unnoticeable
stealthily (stĕl′thĭ-lē) *adv.* in a quiet, secretive way
eloquent (ĕl′ə-kwənt) *adj.* vividly expressive

Teaching Options

BLOCK SCHEDULING: MANAGING TIME

If your schedule requires that you cover the lesson objectives in a shorter time, use . . .

- Preparing to Read, p. 559
- Thinking Through the Literature, p. 575
- Vocabulary in Action, p. 576
- Grammar in Context, p. 577

If you want to take advantage of longer class time, use . . .

- TE Teaching Options: Preteaching Vocabulary, p. 560; Speaking and Listening, p. 566; Vocabulary Strategy, p. 568; Standardized Test Practice, p. 574
- Choices & Challenges and Author Activity, pp. 576–577

marvel whence[7] they come? He who has never swooned, is not he who finds strange palaces and wildly familiar faces in coals that glow; is not he who beholds floating in midair the sad visions that the many may not view; is not he who ponders over the perfume of some novel flower—is not he whose brain grows bewildered with the meaning of some musical cadence[8] which has never before arrested his attention.

Amid frequent and thoughtful endeavors to remember; amid earnest struggles to regather some token of the state of seeming nothingness into which my soul had lapsed, there have been moments when I have dreamed of success; there have been brief, very brief periods when I have conjured up remembrances which the lucid reason of a later epoch assures me could have had reference only to that condition of seeming unconsciousness. These shadows of memory tell, indistinctly, of tall figures that lifted and bore me in silence down—down—still down—till a hideous dizziness oppressed me at the mere idea of the interminableness of the descent. They tell also of a vague horror at my heart, on account of that heart's unnatural stillness. Then comes a sense of sudden motionlessness throughout all things; as if those who bore me (a ghastly train!) had outrun, in their descent, the limits of the limitless, and paused from the wearisomeness of their toil. After this I call to mind flatness and dampness; and that all is *madness*—the madness of a memory which busies itself among forbidden things.

ACTIVE READING

EVALUATE What impression do you have of the narrator so far?

Very suddenly there came back to my soul motion and sound—the tumultuous motion of the heart, and, in my ears, the sound of its beating. Then a pause in which all is blank. Then again sound, and motion, and touch—a tingling sensation pervading[9] my frame. Then the mere consciousness of existence, without thought—a condition which lasted long. Then, very suddenly, *thought*, and shuddering terror, and earnest endeavor to comprehend my true state. Then a strong desire to lapse into insensibility. Then a rushing revival of soul and a successful effort to move. And now a full memory of the trial, of the judges, of the sable draperies, of the sentence, of the sickness, of the swoon. Then entire forgetfulness of all that followed; of all that a later day and much earnestness of endeavor have enabled me vaguely to recall.

So far, I had not opened my eyes. I felt that I lay upon my back, unbound. I reached out my hand, and it fell heavily upon something damp and hard. There I suffered[10] it to remain for many minutes, while I strove to imagine where and *what* I could be. I longed, yet dared not to employ my vision. I dreaded the first glance at objects around me. It was not that I feared to look upon things horrible, but that I grew aghast lest there should be *nothing* to see. At length, with a wild desperation at heart, I quickly unclosed my eyes. My worst thoughts, then, were confirmed. The blackness of eternal night encompassed me. I struggled for breath. The intensity of the darkness seemed to oppress and stifle me. The atmosphere was intolerably close. I still lay quietly, and made effort to exercise my reason. I brought to mind the inquisitorial proceedings, and attempted from that point to deduce my real condition. The sentence had passed; and it appeared to me that a very long interval of time had since elapsed.

7. **whence:** from where.
8. **cadence** (kād′ns): series of chords.
9. **pervading:** spreading throughout.
10. **suffered:** allowed.

WORDS TO KNOW
lucid (lo͞o′sĭd) *adj.* clear
encompass (ĕn-kŭm′pəs) *v.* to surround; enclose

Customizing Instruction

Students Acquiring English

1 Explain to students that *swooned* in this context means "fainted."

Less Proficient Readers

To aid students' comprehension, ask them the following questions:

- What punishment have the judges decided on for the narrator?
  Answer: death
- How does the narrator react to the sentence?
  Answer: He faints.
- What does the narrator experience while he is unconscious?
  Answer: He has the sensation of being carried downward and then left on a flat surface.

Reading and Analyzing

Literary Analysis: NARRATOR

A Point out to students that the narrator uses his authority here to express an opinion. Ask students what the narrator thinks of works of fiction in which characters think that they are dead.
Possible Response: They are unrealistic because anyone who is conscious at all is obviously not dead, and will not think that he or she is so.

ACTIVE READING

B VISUALIZE Possible Responses: cold stone walls; shiny green slime; chains and bones

A Yet not for a moment did I suppose myself actually dead. Such a supposition, notwithstanding what we read in fiction, is altogether inconsistent with real existence;—but where and in what state was I? The condemned to death, I knew, perished usually at the *auto-da-fé,*[11] and one of these had been held on the very night of the day of my trial. Had I been remanded to my dungeon, to await the next sacrifice, which would not take place for many months? This I at once saw could not be. Victims had been in immediate demand. Moreover, my dungeon, as well as all the condemned cells at Toledo, had stone floors, and light was not altogether excluded.

A fearful idea now suddenly drove the blood in torrents upon my heart, and for a brief period, I once more relapsed into insensibility. Upon recovering, I at once started to my feet, trembling convulsively in every fiber. I thrust my arms wildly above and around me in all directions. I felt nothing; yet dreaded to move a step, lest I should be impeded by the walls of the *tomb.* Perspiration burst from every pore and stood in cold big beads on my forehead. The agony of suspense grew at length intolerable, and I cautiously moved forward, with my arms extended, and my eyes straining from their sockets, in the hope of catching some faint ray of light. I proceeded for many paces; but still all was blackness and vacancy. I breathed more freely. It seemed evident that mine was not, at least, the most hideous of fates.

And now, as I still continued to step cautiously onward, there came thronging[12] upon my recollection a thousand vague rumors of the horrors of Toledo. Of the dungeons there had been strange things narrated—fables I had always deemed them—but yet strange, and too ghastly to repeat, save in a whisper. Was I left to perish of starvation in the subterranean world of darkness; or what fate, perhaps even more fearful, awaited me? That the result would be death, and a death of more than customary bitterness, I knew too well the character of my judges to doubt. The mode and the hour were all that occupied or distracted me. 1

My outstretched hands at length encountered some solid obstruction. It was a wall, seemingly of stone masonry—very smooth, slimy, and cold. I followed it up! stepping with all the careful distrust with which certain antique narratives had inspired me. This process, however, afforded me no means of ascertaining the dimensions of my dungeon; as I might make its circuit, and return to the point whence I set out, without being aware of the fact; so perfectly uniform seemed the wall. I therefore sought the knife which had been in my pocket, when led into the inquisitorial chamber; but it was gone; my clothes had been exchanged for a wrapper of coarse serge.[13] I had thought of forcing the blade in some minute crevice of the masonry, so as to identify my point of departure. The difficulty, nevertheless, was but trivial; although, in the disorder of my fancy, it seemed at first insuperable. I tore a part of the hem from the robe and placed the fragment at full length, and at right angles to the wall. In groping my way around the prison I could not fail to encounter this rag upon completing the circuit. So, at least I thought: but I had not

ACTIVE READING

VISUALIZE What do you think the narrator would see if there were light in the dungeon?

11. ***auto-da-fé*** (ou'tō-də-fā') *Portuguese:* act of faith—a public execution of people tried by the Inquisition, carried out by the civil authorities.
12. **thronging:** crowding.
13. **serge** (sûrj): a woolen cloth.

WORDS TO KNOW
supposition (sŭp'ə-zĭsh'ən) *n.* an opinion or assumption
relapse (rĭ-lăps') *v.* to fall back into a former state
insuperable (ĭn-sōō'pər-ə-bəl) *adj.* impossible to overcome

Customizing Instruction

Students Acquiring English

1 Explain to students that the narrator says that he is sure that he is going to die. Tell them that mode in this case means "method" or "way" and hour means "time." Ask students what the narrator is still unsure of.

Answer: how and when he will die

2 Help students understand that *ascertaining* the *dimensions* of the dungeon is a formal way of saying "finding out its size."

Less Proficient Readers

To aid students' comprehension, ask them how the narrator plans to measure the room.

Possible Response: He has marked his starting point with a rag. He will walk along the wall, counting his paces, until he returns to his starting point.

Reading and Analyzing

Literary Analysis SUSPENSE

A Point out Poe's technique of withholding information to create suspense. Have students identify why this particular passage is suspenseful.

Possible Responses: The narrator starts to measure the room but falls asleep halfway through, thus postponing the answer to his question and prolonging the tension of suspense.

Active Reading VISUALIZING

B Ask students to imagine the narrator's circumstances by visualizing his physical position. Where is he? How are his face and body positioned? What is he facing? What conclusions can they draw from this information?

Possible Responses: He is facedown with his chin on the floor and his forehead angled down and hanging over a steep-sided pit.

Reading Skills and Strategies: CLARIFYING

C Ask students to consider what it means that the "sudden extinction of life" was not part of the captor's plan.

Possible Responses: It means that the torturers did not intend people to die quickly, but that they wanted their prisoners to suffer a prolonged, agonizing death.

counted upon the extent of the dungeon, or upon my own weakness. The ground was moist and slippery. I staggered onward for some time, (A) when I stumbled and fell. My excessive fatigue induced me to remain prostrate;[14] and sleep soon overtook me as I lay.

Upon awakening, and stretching forth an arm, I found beside me a loaf and a pitcher with water. I was too much exhausted to reflect upon this circumstance, but ate and drank with avidity. Shortly afterward, I resumed my tour around the prison, and with much toil, came at last upon the fragment of the serge. Up to the period when I fell I had counted fifty-two paces, and upon resuming my walk, I counted forty-eight more;—when I arrived at the rag. There were in all, then, a hundred paces; and, admitting two paces to the yard, I presumed the dungeon to be fifty yards in circuit. I had met, however, with many angles in the wall, and thus I could form no guess at the shape of the vault; for vault I could not help supposing it to be.

> AT THE SAME TIME MY FOREHEAD SEEMED BATHED IN A CLAMMY VAPOR, AND THE PECULIAR SMELL OF DECAYED FUNGUS AROSE TO MY NOSTRILS.

I had little object—certainly no hope—in these researches; but a vague curiosity prompted me to continue them. Quitting the wall, I resolved to cross the area of the enclosure. At first I proceeded with extreme caution, for the floor, although seemingly of solid material, was treacherous with slime. At length, however, I took courage, and did not hesitate to step firmly; endeavoring to cross in as direct a line as possible. I had advanced some ten or twelve paces in this manner, when the remnant of the torn hem of my robe became entangled between my legs. I stepped on it, and fell violently on my face.

In the confusion attending my fall, I did not immediately apprehend[15] a somewhat startling circumstance, which yet, in a few seconds afterward, and while I still lay prostrate, arrested my attention. It was this—my chin rested upon the floor of the prison, but my lips and the upper portion of my head, although seemingly at a less elevation than the chin, touched nothing. At the same time my forehead seemed bathed in a clammy vapor, and the peculiar smell of decayed fungus arose to my nostrils. I put forward my arm, and shuddered to find that I had fallen at the very brink of a circular pit, whose extent, of course, I had no means of ascertaining at the moment. Groping (B) about the masonry just below the margin, I succeeded in dislodging a small fragment, and let it fall into the abyss. For many seconds I hearkened to its reverberations[16] as it dashed against the sides of the chasm in its descent; at length there was a sullen plunge into water, succeeded by loud echoes. At the same moment there came a sound resembling the quick opening, and as rapid closing of a door overhead, while a faint gleam of light flashed suddenly through the gloom, and as suddenly faded away.

14. **prostrate** (prŏs′trāt′): lying flat.

15. **apprehend:** become conscious of: perceive.

16. **reverberations** (rĭ-vûr′bə-rā′shənz): echoes.

WORDS TO KNOW **treacherous** (trĕch′ər-əs) *adj.* dangerous

Teaching Options

Mini Lesson Speaking and Listening

DRAMATIC READING AND DRAMATIC PANTOMIME

The story's compelling narrative voice and the strangeness of circumstance and event lend it to dramatic interpretation and reading accompanied by pantomime. Divide the story into scenes and form cooperative groups to work on each scene, with one or more students reading aloud and one or more students performing the pantomime. Discuss important qualities of oral interpretation for readers—tone of voice, pitch, rhythm, volume, speed—and dramatic pantomime for actors: exaggerated body movements, actions coordinated with narrative, bodies frozen in pose until the narrative moves to the next action, and so forth. Students should justify their choice of verbal and nonverbal performance techniques by referring to their interpretation of the text. Let groups select appropriate music to accompany their presentations.

Present Let each group decide how to present its scene. Have audience members pay attention to how dramatic pantomime expresses and correlates with narrative content. Instruct the audience to evaluate how the performance increases their understanding and appreciation of the story.

I saw clearly the doom which had been prepared for me, and congratulated myself upon the timely accident by which I had escaped. Another step before my fall, and the world had seen me no more. And the death just avoided, was of that very character which I had regarded as fabulous and frivolous in the tales respecting the Inquisition. To the victims of its tyranny, there was the choice of death with its direst[17] physical agonies, or death with its most hideous moral horrors. I had been reserved for the latter. By long suffering my nerves had been unstrung, until I trembled at the sound of my own voice, and had become in every respect a fitting subject for the species of torture which awaited me.

Shaking in every limb, I groped my way back to the wall; resolving there to perish rather than risk the terrors of the wells, of which my imagination now pictured many in various positions about the dungeon. In other conditions of mind I might have had courage to end my misery at once by a plunge into one of these abysses; but now I was the veriest of cowards. Neither could I forget what I had read of these pits—that the *sudden* extinction of life formed no part of their most horrible plan.

Agitation of spirit kept me awake for many long hours; but at length I again slumbered. Upon arousing, I found by my side as before, a loaf and a pitcher of water. A burning thirst consumed me, and I emptied the vessel at a draft. It must have been drugged; for scarcely had I drunk, before I became irresistibly drowsy. A deep sleep fell upon me—a sleep like that of death. How long it lasted of course, I know not; but when, once again, I unclosed my eyes, the objects around me were visible. By a wild sulphurous luster,[18] the origin of which I could not at first determine, I was enabled to see the extent and aspect of the prison.

In its size I had been greatly mistaken. The whole circuit of its walls did not exceed twenty-five yards. For some minutes this fact occasioned me a world of vain trouble;[19] vain indeed! for what could be of less importance, under the terrible circumstances which environed me, than the mere dimensions of my dungeon? But my soul took a wild interest in trifles, and I busied myself in endeavors to account for the error I had committed in my measurement. The truth at length flashed upon me. In my first attempt at exploration I had counted fifty-two paces, up to the period when I fell; I must then have been within a pace or two of the fragments of serge; in fact, I had nearly performed the circuit of the vault. I then slept, and upon awaking, I must have returned upon my steps—thus supposing the circuit nearly double what it actually was. My confusion of mind prevented me from observing that I began my tour with the wall to the left, and ended it with the wall to the right. 2

I had been deceived, too, in respect to the shape of the enclosure. In feeling my way around I had found many angles, and thus deduced an idea of great irregularity; so potent is the effect of total darkness upon one arousing from lethargy or sleep! The angles were simply those of a few slight depressions, or niches, at odd intervals. The general shape of the prison was square. What I had taken for masonry seemed now to be iron, or some other metal, in huge plates, whose sutures or joints occasioned the depression. The entire surface of this metallic enclosure was rudely daubed in all the hideous and repulsive devices to which the

17. **direst** (dī′rĭst): most dreadful.

18. **sulphurous** (sŭl′fə-rəs) **luster:** fiery glow.

19. **occasioned . . . trouble:** caused me a great deal of useless worry.

WORDS TO KNOW

potent (pōt′nt) *adj.* powerful
lethargy (lĕth′ər-jē) *n.* sluggishness; unconsciousness

Customizing Instruction

Less Proficient Readers

1 Ask students to consider why the narrator might congratulate himself for tripping and falling.

Possible Response: If he hadn't tripped and fallen, he would have stepped into the pit and died. Tripping saved his life.

2 Ask students to summarize the narrator's reason for his error in computing the distance around the circuit of the walls.

Possible Response: He counted the distance twice—once left and once right—because he fell asleep halfway through and lost track of which direction he was going.

Reading and Analyzing

Reading Skills and Strategies: PREDICT

A Ask students to predict how the rats might figure into the story later.
Possible Responses: They will begin to bite and torment the narrator; he will be reduced to eating them.

Literary Analysis SUSPENSE

B Ask students what about the pendulum's movement heightens suspense.
Possible Responses: It moves downward toward the narrator slowly, in tiny increments.

charnel superstitions[20] of the monks has given rise. The figures of fiends in aspects of menace, with skeleton forms, and other more really fearful images, overspread and disfigured the walls. I observed that the outlines of these monstrosities were sufficiently distinct, but that the colors seemed faded and blurred, as if from the effects of a damp atmosphere. I now noticed the floor, too, which was of stone. In the center yawned the circular pit from whose jaws I had escaped; but it was the only one in the dungeon.

> THE ODOR OF THE SHARP STEEL FORCED ITSELF INTO MY NOSTRILS.

All this I saw distinctly and by much effort: for my personal condition had been greatly changed during slumber. I now lay upon my back, and at full length, on a species of low framework of wood. To this I was securely bound by a long strap resembling a surcingle.[21] It passed in many convolutions about my limbs and body, leaving at liberty only my head, and my left arm to such extent that I could, by dint[22] of much exertion, supply myself with food from an earthen dish which lay by my side on the floor. I saw, to my horror, that the pitcher had been removed. I say to my horror; for I was consumed with intolerable thirst. This thirst it appeared to be the design of my
1 persecutors to stimulate: for the food in the dish was meat pungently seasoned.

Looking upward I surveyed the ceiling of my prison. It was some thirty or forty feet overhead, and constructed much as the side walls. In one of its panels a very singular figure riveted my whole attention. It was the painted figure of Time as he is commonly represented, save that, in lieu of a scythe, he held what, at a casual glance, I supposed to be the pictured image of a huge pendulum such as we see on antique clocks. There was something, however, in the appearance of this machine which caused me to regard it more attentively. While I gazed directly upward at it (for its position was immediately over my own) I fancied that I saw it in motion. In an instant afterward the fancy was confirmed. Its sweep was brief, and of course slow. I watched it for some minutes, somewhat in fear, but more in wonder. Wearied at length with observing its dull movement, I turned my eyes upon the other objects in the cell. 2

A slight noise attracted my notice, and, looking to the floor, I saw several enormous rats traversing it. They had issued from the well, which lay just within view to my right. Even then, while I gazed, they came up in troops, hurriedly, with ravenous eyes, allured by the scent of the meat. From this it required much effort and attention to scare them away. A

It might have been half an hour, perhaps even an hour, (for I could take but imperfect note of time) before I again cast my eyes upward. What I then saw confounded and amazed me. The sweep of the pendulum had increased in extent by nearly a yard. As a natural consequence, its velocity was also much greater. But what mainly disturbed me was the idea that it had perceptibly *descended.* I now observed—with what horror it is needless to say—that its nether extremity was formed of a crescent of glittering steel, about a foot in length from horn to horn; the horns upward, and the under edge evidently

20. **charnel** (chär′nəl) **superstitions:** ghastly irrational beliefs.
21. **surcingle** (sûr′sĭng′gəl): a band used to tie a pack or saddle to a horse.
22. **dint:** force.

Teaching Options

Mini Lesson: Vocabulary Strategy

RESEARCHING WORD ORIGINS AS AN AID TO UNDERSTANDING MEANINGS **Instruction** To help them deal with Poe's challenging vocabulary, have students use a dictionary to trace the etymologies of words on the WORDS TO KNOW list. Show them how to examine the root of a word and look for meanings in the root word that connect to the meaning of the modern word. Write the word *discordant* on the board and explain that it means "conflicting" or "marked by a harsh mixture of sounds." Tell students that the root of *discordant* comes from the Latin word *discordia.* Write *discordia* on the board, and explain that it consists of the prefix *dis-,* which means "apart," and the root *cor,* which means "heart."

Practice Have students choose five words from the WORDS TO KNOW list and trace their etymologies. Instruct them to write the word, define the word, list its etymology, and then write a sentence explaining how the root meaning may connect to the meaning of the word as it is used in Poe's story.

Use **Vocabulary Transparencies and Copymasters,** p. 62.

A lesson on researching word origins appears on p. 356 in the Pupil's Edition.

as keen as that of a razor. Like a razor also, it seemed massy and heavy, tapering from the edge into a solid and broad structure above. It was appended to a weighty rod of brass, and the whole *hissed* as it swung through the air.

I could no longer doubt the doom prepared for me by monkish ingenuity in torture. My cognizance of the pit had become known to the inquisitorial agents—*the pit* whose horrors had been destined for so bold a recusant[23] as myself—*the pit,* typical of hell, and regarded by rumor as the Ultima Thule[24] of all their punishments. The plunge into this pit I had avoided by the merest of accidents, and I knew that surprise, or entrapment into torment, formed an important portion of all the grotesquerie of these dungeon deaths. Having failed to fall, it was no part of the demon plan to hurl me into the abyss; and thus (there being no alternative) a different and a milder destruction awaited me. Milder! I half smiled in my agony as I thought of such application of such a term.

What boots it[25] to tell of the long, long hours of horror more than mortal, during B which I counted the rushing vibrations of the steel! Inch by inch—line by line—with a descent only appreciable at intervals that seemed ages—down and still down it came! Days passed—it might have been that many days passed—ere it swept so closely over me as to fan me with its acrid[26] breath. The odor of the sharp steel forced itself into my nostrils. I prayed—I wearied heaven with my prayer for its more speedy descent. I grew frantically mad, and struggled to force myself upward against the sweep of the fearful scimitar.[27] And then I fell suddenly calm, and lay smiling at the glittering death, as a child at some rare bauble.

There was another interval of utter insensibility; it was brief; for, upon again lapsing into life there had been no perceptible descent in the pendulum. But it might have been long; for I knew there were demons who took note of my swoon, and who could have arrested the vibration at pleasure. Upon my recovery, too, I felt very—oh, inexpressibly sick and weak, as if through long inanition.[28] Even amid the agonies of that period, the human nature craved food. With painful effort I outstretched my left arm as far as my bonds permitted, and took possession of the small remnant which had been spared me by the rats. As I put a portion of it within my lips, there rushed to my mind a half formed thought of joy—of hope. Yet what business had *I* with hope? It was, as I say, a half formed thought—man has many such which are never completed. I felt that it was of joy—of hope; but I felt also that it had perished in its formation. In vain I struggled to perfect—to regain it. Long suffering had nearly annihilated all my ordinary powers of mind. I was an imbecile—an idiot.

The vibration of the pendulum was at right angles to my length. I saw that the crescent was designed to cross the region of the heart. It would fray the serge of my robe—it would return and repeat its operations—again—and again. Notwithstanding its terrifically wide sweep (some thirty feet or more) and the hissing vigor of its descent, sufficient to sunder these very walls of iron, still the fraying of my robe would be all that, for several minutes, it would accomplish. And at this thought I paused. I

---

23. **recusant** (rĕk′yə-zənt): a religious dissenter; heretic.
24. **Ultima Thule** (ŭl′tə-mə tho͞o′lē): according to ancient geographers, the most remote region of the habitable world—here used figuratively to mean "most extreme achievement," "summit."
25. **what boots it:** what good is it.
26. **acrid** (ăk′rĭd): sharp; pungent.
27. **scimitar** (sĭm′ĭ-tər): a curved, single-edged Asian sword.
28. **inanition** (ĭn′ə-nĭsh′ən): wasting away from lack of food.

Customizing Instruction

Students Acquiring English

1 Explain to students that "meat pungently seasoned" would be hot, spicy meat. Have students explain why the missing water pitcher is a problem in this case.

Possible Response: The spicy meat would make the narrator thirsty, and without the pitcher he would be unable to quench his thirst.

Less Proficient Readers

2 Explain that the image of Time referred to is that of an old man with a scythe or sickle.

Multiple Learning Styles

Visual Learners

To help students visualize the setting, have them create a schematic diagram with a top view and a side view indicating the layout. Remind them to include narrator, pit, and pendulum.

THE PIT AND THE PENDULUM 569

Reading and Analyzing

Literary Analysis SUSPENSE

A Point out the way Poe starts three successive paragraphs with the word *down* to create a parallel structure that builds suspense. Ask students to explain how suspense is created here.
Possible Responses: The pendulum steadily progresses downward toward the narrator and readers are repeatedly reminded of that progress by repetition of the word *down.*

Literary Analysis: FIRST-PERSON POINT OF VIEW

Point out that the first-person point of view enables the author to focus intensely on the narrator's thoughts and feelings. Ask students to identify words that indicate focus on thoughts and feelings.
Possible Responses: despair; relief; hope

dared not go farther than this reflection. I dwelt upon it with a pertinacity of attention—as if, in so dwelling, I could arrest *here* the descent of the steel. I forced myself to ponder upon the sound of the crescent as it should pass across the garment—upon the peculiar thrilling sensation which the friction of cloth produces on the nerves. I pondered upon all this frivolity until my teeth were on edge.

> DOWN—STILL UNCEASINGLY—STILL INEVITABLY DOWN! I GASPED AND STRUGGLED AT EACH VIBRATION.

A Down—steadily down it crept. I took a frenzied pleasure in contrasting its downward with its lateral velocity. To the right—to the left—far and wide—with the shriek of a . . . spirit; to my heart with the stealthy pace of the tiger! I alternately laughed and howled as the one or the other idea grew predominant.

A Down—certainly, relentlessly down! It vibrated within three inches of my bosom! I struggled violently, furiously, to free my left arm. This was free only from the elbow to the hand. I could reach the latter, from the platter beside me, to my mouth, with great effort, but no farther. Could I have broken the fastenings above the elbow, I would have seized and attempted to arrest the pendulum. I might as well have attempted to arrest an avalanche!

A Down—still unceasingly—still inevitably down! I gasped and struggled at each vibration. I shrunk convulsively at its every sweep. My eyes followed its outward or upward whirls with the eagerness of the most unmeaning despair; they closed themselves spasmodically at the descent, although death would have been a relief, oh! how unspeakable! Still I quivered in every nerve to think how slight a sinking of the machinery would precipitate that keen, glistening axe upon my bosom. It was *hope* that prompted the nerve to quiver—the frame to shrink. It was *hope*—the hope that triumphs on the rack[29]—that whispers to the death-condemned even in the dungeons of the Inquisition.

I saw that some ten or twelve vibrations would bring the steel in actual contact with my robe, and with this observation there suddenly came over my spirit all the keen, collected calmness of despair. For the first time during many hours—or perhaps days—I *thought.* It now occurred to me that the bandage, or surcingle, which enveloped me, was *unique.* I was tied by no separate cord. 1
The first stroke of the razor-like crescent athwart[30] any portion of the band, would so detach it that it might be unwound from my person by means of my left hand. But how fearful, in that case, the proximity of the steel! The result of the slightest struggle how deadly! Was it likely, moreover, that the minions[31] of the torturer had not foreseen and provided for this possibility! Was it probable that the bandage crossed my bosom in the track of the pendulum? Dreading to find my faint, and, as it seemed, my last hope frustrated, I so far elevated my head as to obtain a distinct view of my breast. The surcingle enveloped my limbs and body close in all directions—*save* 2
in the path of the destroying crescent.

29. **rack:** a device for torturing people by gradually stretching their bodies.
30. **athwart:** across.
31. **minions** (mĭn′yənz): followers; servants.

WORDS TO KNOW **pertinacity** (pûr′tn-ăs′ĭ-tē) *n.* a persistent stubbornness

Customizing Instruction

Students Acquiring English

1 Explain to students that *unique* in this case means "single" or "the only one." Ask them what the narrator is saying about the bandage that ties him down.

Possible Response: It is all one bandage, so that if it were cut anywhere, he could possibly unwind it.

2 Explain to students that *enveloped* in this case means "covered completely" and that *save* in this case means "except." Then ask students to explain what the narrator is saying about the surcingle.

Possible Response: The surcingle covers his entire body except for the path across his chest beneath the pendulum.

Reading and Analyzing

ACTIVE READING

A PREDICT **Possible Responses:** a way to cut the surcingle; a way to escape the surcingle without cutting it; a way to stop the pendulum

Active Reading VISUALIZING

B Although it may not appeal to them, invite students to visualize this moment as the narrator is swarmed by rats. Discuss their emotional responses and the narrator's likely response.

Reading Skills and Strategies: PREDICTING

C Point out that the narrator has just had one success breaking free from the surcingle. Ask students to consider whether it is possible that positive things may now begin to happen. Ask students to predict what might happen next.

Possible Responses: He will be rescued by friends; the Inquisitors will lock him in a cell to contemplate more effective ways to torment him to death.

Literary Analysis SUSPENSE

D Point out that, once again, Poe builds suspense by withholding critical information. He reveals this information slowly. Ask students to explain what they think the line of light is and compare their assumption to what it actually is.

Possible Responses: daylight; moonlight; fire

A ACTIVE READING

PREDICT What do you think the narrator is planning?

Scarcely had I dropped my head back into its original position, when there flashed upon my mind what I cannot better describe than as the unformed half of that idea of deliverance to which I have previously alluded, and of which a moiety[32] only floated indeterminately through my brain when I raised food to my burning lips. The whole thought was now present—feeble, scarcely sane, scarcely definite,—but still entire. I proceeded at once, with the nervous energy of despair, to attempt its execution.

IN THEIR VORACITY THE VERMIN FREQUENTLY FASTENED THEIR SHARP FANGS INTO MY FINGERS.

For many hours the immediate vicinity of the low framework upon which I lay, had been literally swarming with rats. They were wild, bold, ravenous; their red eyes glaring upon me as if they waited but for motionlessness on my part to make me their prey. "To what food," I thought, "have they been accustomed in the well?"

They had devoured, in spite of all my efforts to prevent them, all but a small remnant of the contents of the dish. I had fallen into an

1 habitual see-saw, or wave of the hand about the platter, and, at length, the unconscious uniformity of the movement deprived it of effect. In their voracity the vermin frequently fastened their sharp fangs into my fingers. With the particles of the oily and spicy viand[33] which now remained, I thoroughly rubbed the bandage wherever I could reach it; then, raising my hand from the floor, I lay breathlessly still.

At first the ravenous animals were startled and terrified at the change—at the cessation of movement. They shrank alarmedly back; many sought the well. But this was only for a moment. I had not counted in vain upon their voracity. Observing that I remained without motion, one or two of the boldest leaped upon the framework, and smelt at the surcingle. This seemed the signal for a general rush. Forth from the well they hurried in fresh troops. They clung to the wood—they overran it, and leaped in hundreds upon my person. The measured movement of the pendulum disturbed them not at all. Avoiding its strokes they busied themselves with the anointed bandage. They pressed—they swarmed upon me in ever accumulating heaps. They writhed upon my throat; their cold lips sought my own; I was half stifled by their thronging pressure; disgust, for which the world has no name, swelled my bosom, and chilled, with a heavy clamminess, my heart. Yet one minute, and I felt that the struggle would be over. Plainly I perceived the loosening of the bandage. I knew that in more than one place it must be already severed. With a more than human resolution I lay *still.*

Nor had I erred in my calculations—nor had I endured in vain. I at length felt that I was *free.* The surcingle hung in ribands[34] from my body. But the stroke of the pendulum already pressed upon my bosom. It had divided the serge of the robe. It had cut through the linen beneath.

32. **moiety** (moi′ĭ-tē): half.
33. **viand** (vī′ənd): food.
34. **ribands** (rĭb′əndz): ribbons.

WORDS TO KNOW **voracity** (vô-răs′ĭ-tē) *n.* greed for food; ravenousness

572

Teaching Options

Mini Lesson Grammar

APPOSITIVES Appositives are words or phrases that restate or expand a noun's meaning. Sometimes an appositive is surrounded by commas that set it off from the rest of the sentence. Write the following sentences on the board.

The dungeon, a place where many had perished before me, was green, slimy and damp.

My brother William did not know I had been imprisoned.

Point out to students that in each sentence the word or words that are underlined once restate or expand the meaning of the noun that is underlined twice.

Practice Write the following sentences on the board. Tell students to underline each appositive or appositive phrase once and the noun it modifies twice.

1. The rats, horrible creatures of the underworld, had begun to swarm around me.
2. Above me was a sharp pendulum, the instrument of my impending death.
3. Toledo, the infamous dungeon, held hundreds of tortured prisoners.
4. The *auto-da-fé,* a trial for heretics, had been a grueling experience.
5. The writer Poe was a great teller of horror tales.

Twice again it swung, and a sharp sense of pain shot through every nerve. But the moment of escape had arrived. At a wave of my hand my deliverers hurried tumultuously away. With a
2 steady movement—cautious, sidelong,
C shrinking, and slow—I slid from the embrace of the bandage and beyond the reach of the scimitar. For the moment, at least, *I was free.*

Free!—and in the grasp of the Inquisition! I had scarcely stepped from my wooden bed of horror upon the stone floor of the prison, when the motion of the hellish machine ceased and I beheld it drawn up, by some invisible force, through the ceiling. This was a lesson which I took desperately to heart. My every motion was undoubtedly watched. Free!—I had but escaped death in one form of agony, to be delivered unto worse than death in some other. With that thought I rolled my eyes nervously around the barriers of iron that hemmed me in. Something unusual—some change which at first I could not appreciate distinctly—it was obvious, had taken place in the apartment. For many minutes in a dreamy and trembling abstraction, I busied myself in vain, unconnected conjecture.[35]
D During this period, I became aware, for the first time, of the origin of the sulphurous light which illuminated the cell. It proceeded from a fissure, about half an inch in width, extending entirely around the prison at the base of the walls, which thus appeared, and were, completely separated from the floor. I endeavored, but of course in vain, to look through the aperture.[36]

As I arose from the attempt, the mystery of the alteration in the chamber broke at once upon my understanding. I have observed that, although the outlines of the figures upon the walls were sufficiently distinct, yet the colors seemed blurred and indefinite. These colors had now assumed, and were momentarily assuming, a startling and most intense brilliancy, that gave to the spectral and fiendish portraitures an aspect that might have thrilled even firmer nerves than my own. Demon eyes, of a wild and ghastly vivacity,[37] glared upon me in a thousand directions, where none had been visible before, and gleamed with the lurid luster of a fire that I could not force my imagination to regard as unreal.

Unreal!—Even while I breathed there came to my nostrils the breath of the vapor of heated iron! A suffocating odor pervaded the prison! A deeper glow settled each moment in the eyes that glared at my agonies! A richer tint of crimson diffused itself over the pictured horrors of blood. I panted! I gasped for breath! There could be no doubt of the design of my tormentors—oh! most unrelenting! oh! most demoniac of men! I shrank from the glowing metal to the center of the cell. Amid the thought of the fiery destruction that impended, the idea of the coolness of the well came over my soul like balm.[38] I rushed to its deadly brink. I threw my straining vision below. The glare from the enkindled roof illumined its 3
inmost recesses. Yet, for a wild moment, did my spirit refuse to comprehend the meaning of what I saw. At length it forced—it wrestled its way into my soul—it burned itself in upon my shuddering reason.—Oh! for a voice to speak!—oh! horror!—oh! any horror but this! With a shriek, I rushed from the margin, and buried my face in my hands—weeping bitterly.

The heat rapidly increased, and once again I looked up, shuddering as with a fit of the

35. **conjecture:** guesswork; speculation.
36. **aperture** (ăp′ər-chər): opening.
37. **vivacity** (vĭ-văs′ĭ-tē): liveliness.
38. **balm** (bäm): a soothing ointment.

Customizing Instruction

Less Proficient Readers

1 To aid students' understanding of the story, ask them why the narrator waves his hand over the platter.

Answer: to keep the rats away

Students Acquiring English

2 Explain to students that *deliverers* in this case means "rescuers." Then ask students to whom *deliverers* refers.

Answer: the rats

3 Explain to students that *enkindled* means "burning" and that *illumined* means "lighted." Ask students what the narrator is saying in this sentence.

Possible Response: The light from the burning roof lighted the deepest parts of the pit.

Answers:

1. rat; horrible creatures of the underworld
2. pendulum; the instrument of my impending death
3. Toledo; the infamous dungeon
4. *auto-da-fé*; a trial for heretics
5. writer; Poe

Use **Grammar Transparencies and Copymasters,** p. 98.

Use McDougal Littell's ***Language Network,*** Chapter 3, for more instruction and practice in appositives.

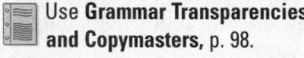

Reading and Analyzing

Active Reading VISUALIZING

A Point out that the narrator is pleading for *any* death except that of the pit. Ask students to visualize what might be in the pit to inspire such horror, then have them share their ideas with the class.

Possible Responses: hundreds of rats; a mound of corpses; sharpened stakes

Literary Analysis SUSPENSE

B Point out to students that the narrator pauses here to ask a series of questions. Ask students why the narrator might do so.

Possible Responses: to slow down the action and delay resolution in order to increase suspense

ague.[39] There had been a second change in the cell—and now the change was obviously in the *form.* As before, it was in vain that I, at first, endeavored to appreciate or understand what was taking place. But not long was I left in doubt. The Inquisitorial vengeance had been hurried by my two-fold escape, and there was to be no more dallying with the King of Terrors. The room had been square. I saw that two of its iron angles were now acute—two, consequently, obtuse. The fearful difference quickly increased with a low rumbling or moaning sound. In an instant the apartment had shifted its form into that of a lozenge. But the alteration stopped not here—I neither hoped nor desired it to stop. I could have clasped the red walls to my bosom as a garment of eternal peace. **A** "Death," I said, "any death but that of the pit!" Fool! might I have not known that *into the pit* it was the object of the burning iron to urge me? Could I resist its glow? **B** or, if even that, could I withstand its pressure? And now, flatter and flatter grew the lozenge, with a rapidity that left me no time for contemplation. Its center, and of course, its greatest width, came just over the yawning gulf. I shrank back—but the closing walls pressed me resistlessly onward. At length for my seared and writhing body there was no longer an inch of foothold on the firm floor of the prison. I struggled no more, but the agony of my soul found vent in one loud, long, and final scream of despair. I felt that I tottered upon the brink—I averted my eyes—

> "DEATH," I SAID, "ANY DEATH BUT THAT OF THE PIT!"

There was a discordant hum of human voices! There was a loud blast of many trumpets! There was a harsh grating as of a thousand thunders! The fiery walls rushed back! An outstretched arm caught my own as I fell, fainting, into the abyss. It was that of General Lasalle. The French army had entered Toledo. The Inquisition was in the hands of its enemies. ❖

39. **the ague** (ā′gyo͞o): a feverish illness.

WORDS TO KNOW **discordant** (dĭ-skôr′dnt) *adj.* marked by a harsh mixture of sounds

Teaching Options

Assessment Standardized Test Practice

OPEN-ENDED QUESTIONS Many standardized tests require students to answer open-ended reading questions that focus on understanding the effects of literary elements and on analyzing and critically evaluating texts. To help students prepare for such assessment, write the following task on the board:

Describe a scene in which Poe creates suspense in "The Pit and the Pendulum."

RUBRIC

3 **Full Accomplishment** The response displays a full understanding of the elements of suspense.

2 **Substantial Accomplishment** The response displays a general understanding of the elements of suspense.

1 **Little or Partial Accomplishment** The response displays little or no understanding of the elements of suspense.

Thinking through the LITERATURE

Connect to the Literature

1. **What Do You Think?** What part of the story did you find most suspenseful? Explain your judgment.

Comprehension Check
- Where is the narrator?
- What are the first two dangers that he faces?
- How does he manage to break free from his bonds?
- Who or what seems to save him at the end?

Think Critically

2. What do you think really happens to the **narrator** at the end of the story?

3. Who do you think shows the greater ingenuity in this story, the narrator or his torturers?

   THINK ABOUT
   - the methods of torture used
   - how the torturers exploit human fears
   - how the narrator saves himself from each torture

4. Which aspect of the narrator's torture—physical or psychological—do you find more horrible? Why?

5. **ACTIVE READING** VISUALIZING Think about the visual details you recorded in your READER'S NOTEBOOK. How did visualizing help you appreciate this story? What, in particular, did it help you to understand better?

Extend Interpretations

6. **What If?** How might your reaction to the tale have been different if the dungeon had not been invaded by General Lasalle at the end?

7. **Critic's Corner** Critic Diane Johnson noted that Poe's "imagination is visual and three-dimensional. . . . If he had been alive today he probably would be a filmmaker." How do you think this story would succeed as a film? Consider what one would have to change in order to translate the story for the screen.

8. **Connect to Life** How do you think this story differs from contemporary tales of horror, whether in fiction or on film? Explain your answer.

Literary Analysis

SUSPENSE **Suspense** is the excitement or tension that readers feel as they become involved in a story and eager to know the outcome. In "The Pit and the Pendulum," Poe builds suspense by using an ominous **setting,** bizarre complications of **plot,** and a **first-person narrator** who gives a vivid description of his mental state at each turn of events. Each time the narrator finds a way to cope with the danger immediately facing him, the reader experiences a temporary release of tension. Each release, however, is followed by a new threat.

Activity Imagine you are creating a soundtrack for a film version of this story. First, identify the moments of greatest suspense, where the music should be the most dramatic. Then create a line graph showing the story events and their level of suspense. An example has been started for you.

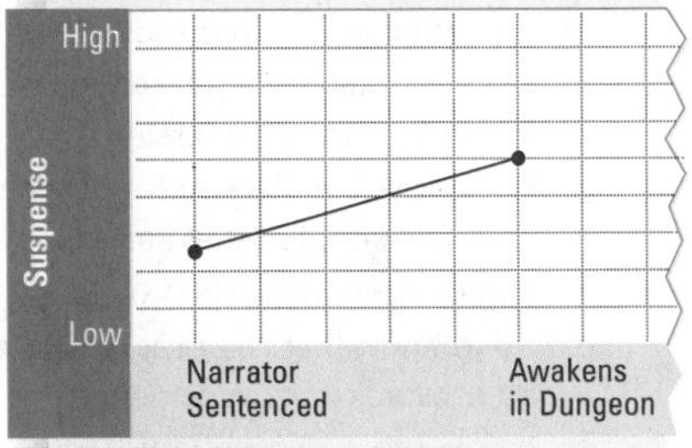

REVIEW FIRST-PERSON POINT OF VIEW

When a character who participates in the action of a story describes it in his or her own words, this is known as **first-person point of view.** Discuss the effects of Poe's use of a first-person **narrator** in "The Pit and the Pendulum." How does it help to build suspense?

GUIDING STUDENT RESPONSE

Connect to the Literature

1. What Do You Think?
Possible Response: The narrator's attempt to have the rats gnaw through his bindings was the most suspenseful because it was unclear whether he would escape without harm.

Comprehension Check
- in a dungeon during the Spanish Inquisition
- a deep pit and a sharp pendulum
- by luring the starving rats to gnaw through the strap that binds him
- General Lasalle and the French army

Use Selection Quiz
Unit Four Resource Book, p. 15.

Think Critically

2. Possible Response: He is rescued and set free.
3. Possible Responses: The torturers are more ingenious because they have a new threat waiting for the narrator each time he escapes; the narrator is more ingenious for having escaped death repeatedly.
4. Possible Responses: physical, because physical pain is difficult to endure; psychological, because the mind can make any situation more intense if it is put under pressure
5. Possible Responses: the physical space in which the story takes place; the appearance and actions of the narrator

Literary Analysis

Suspense If students wish, have them bring in music that they think would be appropriate for the suspenseful moments in the story. Be sure to listen to students' music choices ahead of time to make sure they are suitable for the classroom.

First-Person Point of View Possible Response: Use of first-person point of view contributes greatly to suspense since readers know only what the narrator knows. This technique keeps the reader ignorant of vital information.

Extend Interpretations

What If? Possible Responses: An ending without rescue would have been truer to the predicament; after all the horror the reader has endured, an ending without rescue would be too horrible.

Critic's Corner Possible Response: It would make a brilliant horror film. However, the film would need to provide scenes and events prior to the narrator's imprisonment. Perhaps these could include his so-called "guilty" acts, his capture, and his trial and sentencing. Also, memory flashbacks could be used to help viewers see the narrator's previous life for depth of character and interest.

Connect to Life Possible Response: It is different in the extreme nature of its setting and situation as opposed to the ordinary neighborhood settings portrayed in much modern horror. Also, little blood is actually spilled in this story, unlike most contemporary horror film and fiction.

Writing Options

1. **Critical Review** Criteria may include a terrifying predicament; doom that seems inevitable; vivid, terrifying threats; helpless characters; gripping suspense; and grotesque imagery.
2. **Poe Parody** Comic approaches could include exaggerating everyday occurrences to the point of absurdity.
3. **Inquisition Exposé** Encourage students to study the story looking for factual items to include in their news stories. Present the journalist's questions—who, what, where, when, why, and how—and encourage students to use them to structure their stories.

Activities & Explorations

1. **Illustrated Scene** Encourage students to use color to create a dominant mood for their illustration. When they finish, have students display their work and let class members guess the moment in the narrative being illustrated.
2. **Radio Soundtrack** Have students collaborate in groups of four. Have groups create a story outline that identifies the sequence of scenes. For each scene, they should describe the dominant mood and the level of intensity in the scene and then look for appropriate music. When they finish, have groups share their soundtracks in class.

Inquiry & Research

Inquisition Report You might encourage students to work in research groups to look for information about the Spanish Inquisition. Before students begin their research, have them generate relevant, interesting, and researchable questions. Encourage them to locate appropriate print and nonprint information using text resources and technical resources including on-line databases and the Internet and draw conclusions from the information gathered. As they are conducting their research, remind them to use text organizers, such as overviews, headings, and graphic features, to locate and categorize information.

Writing Options

1. **Critical Review** Write a review of Poe's story in which you evaluate its effectiveness as a horror story. Before you begin to write, decide on criteria that you will use to judge the story's effectiveness. To do so, you might create a series of statements beginning, "A horror story should . . ."
2. **Poe Parody** Write a parody, or comic imitation, of Poe based upon this story. For example, you might create a narrator who is "tortured" by the process of waking up on a school day. Try to imitate Poe's style.
3. **Inquisition Exposé** Imagine that you are a reporter who has followed General Lasalle and his army into Toledo. Write a newspaper story in which you describe the rescue of the narrator and the secret horrors in the dungeons of the Inquisition. Include quotations from Poe's narrator.

Activities & Explorations

1. **Illustrated Scene** Choose one scene from the story and carefully read it again, noting the visual details. Then create your own illustration of that scene. ~ **ART**
2. **Radio Soundtrack** Make a tape of background music and sound effects that you might use for a radio adaptation of "The Pit and the Pendulum." ~ **MUSIC**

Inquiry & Research

Inquisition Report Find out more about the Spanish Inquisition and its victims. Present your findings in an oral report.

An artist's rendering of an *auto-da-fé,* a ritual of the Spanish Inquisition.

Vocabulary in Action

EXERCISE A: MEANING CLUES On your paper, write the Word to Know suggested by each phrase.

1. a firm decision to do something
2. a guess about the reason for a friend's absence
3. a well-worded expression
4. an easy-to-understand explanation
5. an unshakable listlessness

EXERCISE B: SYNONYMS On your paper, write the Word to Know that can best replace the italicized word or words in each sentence.

1. For several centuries the Inquisition was a *very strong* political force in Spain.
2. The prisoner is left alone in a *hazardous* cell.
3. High walls *encircle* the prisoner on all sides.
4. He moves *in a furtive way* around his cell, measuring its dimensions.
5. The movement of the pendulum is almost *invisible* as it descends.
6. The sound of the metal swinging in the air becomes more *jarring* as the pendulum drops.
7. Rats devour his food with *grasping greed.*
8. Several times, the prisoner starts to *sink back* into a deep sleep.
9. For a time, his *persistence* in trying to devise a way of escape keeps him going.
10. Sometimes, his predicament seems *hopeless.*

Building Vocabulary
For an in-depth lesson on using synonyms as context clues, see page 1000.

WORDS TO KNOW					
	discordant	imperceptible	lucid	relapse	supposition
	eloquent	insuperable	pertinacity	resolution	treacherous
	encompass	lethargy	potent	stealthily	voracity

Mini Lesson Grammar

ESSENTIAL AND NONESSENTIAL APPOSITIVES AND APPOSITIVE PHRASES Instruction Explain to students that an essential phrase is one that is necessary to complete the meaning of a sentence, and it is not set off with commas. Write the following sentence on the board:

The novel *Pride and Prejudice* is the one we love.

Point out that the appositive *Pride and Prejudice* is necessary to complete the meaning of the sentence, because it tells which one. Without it, the sentence is complete grammatically, but fails to convey its message.

Explain to students that a nonessential phrase is one unnecessary to complete the meaning of a sentence, and it is set off with commas. Write the following sentence on the board:

Joan O'Brien, the famous child psychologist, used to live down the street from my mother.

Point out that the appositive phrase *the famous child psychologist* is not necessary to complete the meaning of the sentence. Without it, we still know which one.

Grammar in Context: Appositive Phrases

In these excerpts, appositive phrases clarify the narrator's meaning and help to convey a sense of horror.

> **The sentence—the dread sentence of death—was the last of distinct accentuation which reached my ears.**
>
> **Something unusual—some change which at first I could not appreciate distinctly—it was obvious, had taken place in the apartment.**

An **appositive phrase** consists of a noun and its modifiers; it serves to explain or add information about another noun or pronoun. In the examples above, the appositive phrases indicate that "the sentence" refers to a death sentence and that the "something unusual" is a subtle (and perhaps ominous) change in the surroundings.

Punctuation Tip: If an appositive phrase is not essential to the meaning of a sentence, set it off with commas or dashes.

WRITING EXERCISE Combine each pair of sentences by changing the second sentence into an appositive phrase. Underline the appositive phrase.

Example: *Original* I have no doubt of the design of my tormentors. They are unrelenting and demonic men!

Rewritten I have no doubt of the design of my tormentors–those unrelenting and demonic men!

1. Poe's story "The Pit and the Pendulum" is set during the time of the Inquisition. It was a period of religious persecution.
2. He describes the horrors in great detail. There is the pit, the pendulum, thirst, rats, and slime.
3. The figures on the walls seem to mock the narrator. They are fiends with skeletal forms and menacing faces.
4. On the ceiling is a painted image of Time. This figure is usually depicted with a scythe in his hand.

Grammar Handbook Phrases, p. 1195

Edgar Allan Poe
1809–1849

Other Works
"Annabel Lee"
"The Bells"
"The Black Cat"
"The Fall of the House of Usher"
"The Murders in the Rue Morgue"
"The Telltale Heart"

A Troubled Youth The son of traveling actors, Edgar Poe was orphaned at an early age and taken in by John and Frances Allan, a wealthy couple from Richmond, Virginia. A moody adolescent, Poe quarreled with John Allan, who scorned his literary ambitions and wanted him to join the family business. He left the University of Virginia without graduating and was expelled from the U.S. Military Academy at West Point in 1831. He then moved in with his aunt and his cousin Virginia, whom he wed in 1836, when she was just 13 years old.

An Erratic Career Having already published three slim volumes of poetry, Poe began writing reviews and stories for magazines. In 1839 he collected the stories in *Tales of the Grotesque and Arabesque.* Fame came when his mystery tale "The Gold Bug" won first prize in an 1843 contest and especially with the publication, two years later, of his eerie poem "The Raven." By then Virginia was in the throes of the tuberculosis that soon claimed her life. Poe antagonized the literary community by attacking popular writers. He grew ill himself and died on a Baltimore street at age 40.

A Valuable Legacy Although he led an unhappy life shortened by illness, Poe helped to define the modern short story and pioneered the detective mystery. His haunting, sometimes terrifying poems are praised for their brilliant musical sound effects, and his horror tales established him as a master of psychological terror.

Author Activity

Master of Mystery Mystery stories today generally feature a genius detective whose incredible powers of observation and analysis lead him or her to solve a crime that others are unable to solve. Agatha Christie's Miss Marple and Hercule Poirot and Rex Stout's Nero Wolfe are among the more popular of such detectives. In Poe's "The Murders in the Rue Morgue," a mother and daughter are brutally murdered. When the police have no success in finding the murderer, the amateur detective C. Auguste Dupin steps in to solve the mystery. "The Murders in the Rue Morgue" was the first mystery that featured such a detective.

Vocabulary in Action

Exercise A
1. resolution
2. supposition
3. eloquent
4. lucid
5. lethargy

Exercise B
1. potent
2. treacherous
3. encompass
4. stealthily
5. imperceptible
6. discordant
7. voracity
8. relapse
9. pertinacity
10. insuperable

Grammar in Context

WRITING EXERCISE Answers may vary. Possible answers are shown.

1. Poe's story "The Pit and the Pendulum" is set during the time of the Inquisition, a period of religious persecution.
2. He describes the horrors in great detail–the pit, the pendulum, thirst, rats, and slime.
3. The figures on the walls–fiends with skeletal forms and menacing faces–seem to mock the narrator.
4. On the ceiling is a painted image of Time, a figure usually depicted with a scythe in his hand.

Practice Have students working in pairs choose three sentences from the story to rewrite twice, once adding a nonessential appositive or appositive phrase and once adding an essential appositive or appositive phrase. Then have them switch sentences with another pair of students and underline and identify the essential and nonessential appositives and appositive phrases.

Use **Grammar Transparencies and Copymasters,** p. 98, for more practice.

Use McDougal Littell's ***Language Network,*** Chapter 3, for more instruction and practice in appositives.

THE PIT AND THE PENDULUM 577

OVERVIEW

Objectives

1. understand and appreciate **two poems (Literary Analysis)**
2. understand **verbal irony (Literary Analysis)**
3. **draw conclusions** about speaker's attitudes toward war **(Active Reading)**

Summary

In both poems, Gwendolyn Brooks and Stephen Crane write about the cruelties of war. Brooks's "the sonnet-ballad" is a daughter's lament. Speaking to her mother, she anticipates the death of her beloved at war. Crane's ironic poem addresses three people who have lost loved ones in war.

Thematic Link

Gwendolyn Brooks and Stephen Crane effectively use their poetry to show how difficult **facing the enemy** is when war itself is the enemy.

5-Minute Warm-Up

Daily Language SkillBuilder

Have students **proofread** the display sentences on page 541k and write them correctly. The sentences also appear on Transparency 19 of **Grammar Transparencies and Copymasters.**

the sonnet-ballad

Poetry by GWENDOLYN BROOKS

Do not weep, maiden, for war is kind

Poetry by STEPHEN CRANE

Connect to Your Life

The Costs of War Throughout history, humans have waged and endured one war after another; it is a constantly recurring part of the human experience. Do you know anyone who has been involved in a war, either as a participant or a bystander? With your class, discuss the effects of war as you have heard them described or as you imagine them.

Build Background

War Experiences Stephen Crane's "Do not weep, maiden, for war is kind" appeared in a collection of poetry called *War Is Kind* in 1899. Crane never fought in a war, but he served as a special news correspondent in 1898 during Cuba's war for independence from Spain and also covered a war between Greece and Turkey in 1897.

Gwendolyn Brooks belonged to a later generation. She was born during World War I and came of age during World War II. Her poem "the sonnet-ballad" appeared in *Annie Allen,* a collection of poems that was published in 1949.

Focus Your Reading

LITERARY ANALYSIS | **VERBAL IRONY** **Verbal irony** occurs when someone says one thing but means another. The first line of Crane's poem provides an example of such irony:

Do not weep, maiden, for war is kind.

War, by definition, cannot be considered kind. Clearly, the speaker—and poet—mean something quite different than "war is kind." Look for other examples of verbal irony as you read the following poems.

ACTIVE READING | **DRAWING CONCLUSIONS** The process of **drawing conclusions** involves combining information from a text with your own prior knowledge to make logical statements about characters, events, or ideas. In the poems that follow, the poets expect that you already know something about war and what happens to many soldiers who participate. The more you understand about the wartime context for these poems, the more you will appreciate their impact, especially their use of verbal irony.

READER'S NOTEBOOK Read the poems once. Then go back and read them a second time, jotting down words or phrases that serve as clues to figuring out each speaker's attitude toward war. Combine this evidence from the poems with your own prior knowledge to draw conclusions about the speakers and their attitudes toward war.

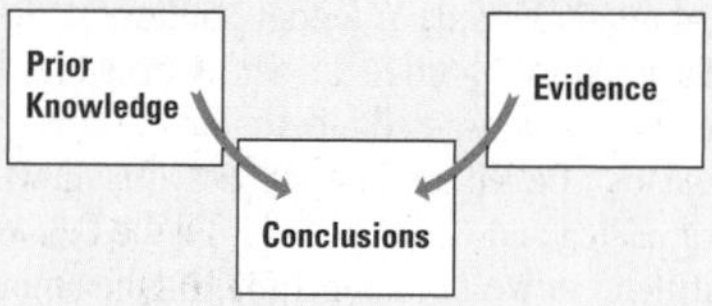

LESSON RESOURCES

UNIT FOUR RESOURCE BOOK, pp. 16–17

ASSESSMENT RESOURCES

Formal Assessment, pp. 105–106

Teacher's Guide to Assessment and Portfolio Use

Test Generator

SKILLS TRANSPARENCIES AND COPYMASTERS

Literary Analysis
- Irony: Verbal, T16 (for Cooperative Learning Activity, p. 581)

Reading and Critical Thinking
- Drawing Conclusions, T4 (for Think Critically, item 2, p. 581)
- Locating Material in the Library I, T27 (for Inquiry & Research 1 and 2, p. 582)

Grammar
- Compound Predicates II, C87 (for Mini Lesson, p. 582)

Writing
- Writing Process, T1, T2 (for Writing Options, p. 582)
- Writing Structure, T5, T6, T9 (for Writing Options, p. 582)
- Poem, C27 (for Writing Option 1, p. 582)

Communications
- Dramatic Reading, T12 (for Mini Lesson, p. 583)

INTEGRATED TECHNOLOGY

Audio Library

Internet: Research Starter

Visit our website: www.mcdougallittell.com

the sonnet-ballad

Gwendolyn Brooks

Oh mother, mother, where is happiness?
They took my lover's tallness off to war,
Left me lamenting. Now I cannot guess
What I can use an empty heart-cup for.
He won't be coming back here any more.
Some day the war will end, but, oh, I knew
When he went walking grandly out that door
That my sweet love would have to be untrue.
Would have to be untrue. Would have to court
Coquettish death, whose impudent and strange
Possessive arms and beauty (of a sort)
Can make a hard man hesitate—and change.
And he will be the one to stammer, "Yes."
Oh mother, mother, where is happiness?

10 **coquettish** (kō-kĕt'ĭsh): behaving like a flirt; **impudent** (ĭm'pyə-dənt): shamelessly bold.

Thinking Through the Literature

1. **Comprehension Check** Where has the speaker's lover gone?
2. ACTIVE READING DRAWING CONCLUSIONS Look at the notes you made in your READER'S NOTEBOOK. What can you conclude about the speaker and her attitude toward war?

   THINK ABOUT
   - the question she asks her mother
   - her fear that her lover will be untrue
   - her description of death
   - how she expects her lover to respond to death
3. The speaker describes death as a rival, calling it "coquettish" and "beautiful." What do you think she means?
4. What kind of answer do you think the mother might give to the question, "where is happiness?"

TEACHING THE LITERATURE

Customizing Instruction

Reading Skills and Strategies: PREVIEW

Remind students that they are expected to establish a purpose for reading. Before students begin reading, give them a brief summary of the selections. Remind them of the importance of reading these poems several times, silently and aloud.

Less Proficient Readers

Point out to students that in both poems, the speakers personify war, speaking of it as if it were a person. Help students identify each instance of personification and explain what the speaker is trying to say about war.

Possible Response: "the sonnet-ballad"—war is described as a woman who tempts men away from those they love; "Do not weep, maiden, for war is kind"—war is described as "kind," an ironic statement indicating just the opposite.

Students Acquiring English

Help students understand the following expressions:

"an empty heart-cup" (p. 579, line 4)

Possible Response: Her lover's leaving has made the speaker feel as though her heart has been emptied, like a cup.

"affrighted" (p. 580, line 3)

Possible Response: terrified

Use **Spanish Study Guide** for additional support, pp. 125–127.

Gifted and Talented

Encourage students to read other poems with different views of war, for instance Tennyson's "The Charge of the Light Brigade." Have students debate the validity of the differing points of view. Which are more realistic? Is realism something we want in war poetry?

BLOCK SCHEDULING: MANAGING TIME

If your schedule requires that you cover the lesson objectives in a shorter time, use . . .
- Preparing to Read, p. 578
- Thinking Through the Literature, p. 581

If you want to take advantage of longer class time, use . . .
- TE Teaching Options: Viewing and Representing, p. 580; Speaking and Listening, p. 583
- Choices & Challenges, pp. 582–583

Thinking Through the Literature

1. He has gone off to fight in the war.
2. Possible Response: She resents war for taking away her love.
3. Possible Response: War lures men away from those they love.
4. Possible Responses: "Happiness is where hope is"; "happiness is with your lover"; or "happiness died in the war."

Reading and Analyzing

Active Reading
DRAWING CONCLUSIONS

Tell students that examining a speaker's tone will help them draw conclusions about what an author is trying to say. For each poem, have students determine the tone that the speaker is using, and then use that tone to draw conclusions about the author's attitude toward war.

Possible Response: The tone of "the sonnet-ballad" is sad and grieving; the author feels that war causes loss and sadness. The tone of "Do not weep, maiden, for war is kind" is bitter and ironic; the author feels that war is brutal and cruel.

Use **Unit Four Resource Book** p. 16 for more practice.

Literary Analysis VERBAL IRONY

Remind students that verbal irony occurs when someone says one thing but means another. Have students list examples of verbal irony from the two poems and explain their meaning.

Possible Responses: "When he went walking grandly out that door" (p.579, line 5)—the speaker does not think it was grand that he left; "coquettish death"—the speaker does not really mean that death is appealing, but that it is unavoidable; "the virtue of slaughter"—the speaker does not think that slaughter is virtuous.

Use **Unit Four Resource Book** p. 17 for more practice.

Do not weep, maiden, for war is kind

Stephen Crane

Do not weep, maiden, for war is kind.
Because your lover threw wild hands toward the sky
And the affrighted steed ran on alone,
Do not weep.
War is kind.

Hoarse, booming drums of the regiment,
Little souls who thirst for fight,
These men were born to drill and die.
The unexplained glory flies above them,
Great is the Battle-God, great, and his Kingdom—
A field where a thousand corpses lie.

Do not weep, babe, for war is kind.
Because your father tumbled in the yellow trenches,
Raged at his breast, gulped and died,
Do not weep.
War is kind.

Swift blazing flag of the regiment,
Eagle with crest of red and gold,
These men were born to drill and die.
Point for them the virtue of slaughter,
Make plain to them the excellence of killing
And a field where a thousand corpses lie.

Mother whose heart hung humble as a button
On the bright splendid shroud of your son,
Do not weep.
War is kind.

We Regret to Inform You (1982), Cleveland R. Wright. Oil on canvas, 36″ × 24″. Courtesy of the artist.

Teaching Options

Mini Lesson: Viewing and Representing

We Regret to Inform You **by Cleveland R. Wright**

ART APPRECIATION

Instruction Direct students' attention to the woman in the picture. What details in the picture help you draw conclusions about what the woman may be feeling?

Possible Responses: The woman appears to be covering her face in shock, sadness, or disbelief. She holds a letter in her hand, which probably brings news of something tragic. She is the only person in the room, which adds to the feeling of isolation.

Application Ask students why this particular painting appears with these two selections.

Possible Response: The painting illustrates the loss of a loved one to war. In particular, this woman might be seen as the "mother whose heart hung humble as a button."

Connect to the Literature

1. **What Do You Think?** What **image** from the poem made the strongest impression on you?

Comprehension Check
- Whom does the **speaker** address in this poem?
- What is lying on the battlefield?
- What has happened to the father of the babe addressed in the third **stanza**?

Think Critically

2. ACTIVE READING DRAWING CONCLUSIONS Refer to the notes you made in your READER'S NOTEBOOK. What can you conclude about the speaker's attitude toward war? On what do you base your conclusion?

THINK ABOUT
- the repetition of the phrase "war is kind"
- the people to whom the poem is addressed
- the poet's use of battle **imagery**

3. Why do you think Crane indents the second and fourth **stanzas**? What sets these stanzas apart from the other three?

Extend Interpretations

4. **Comparing Texts** Compare and contrast the language—including **figures of speech** and **imagery**—that is used to describe war in the two poems.

5. **Comparing Texts** Which poem makes the strongest statement against war? Give evidence from the poems to support your opinion.

6. **Connect to Life** Do you think there are occasions or events that make war appropriate or necessary? Explain your answer.

Literary Analysis

VERBAL IRONY **Irony** is a contrast between what is expected and what actually happens or exists. **Verbal irony** occurs when someone says one thing but means another. In "Do not weep, maiden, for war is kind," Crane uses verbal irony when he says that "war is kind" and when he alludes to the "virtue of slaughter." These statements, taken literally, would be surprising to anyone who knows about the cruelty of war. However, Crane places these statements beside vivid descriptions of war's horrors, such as the "thousand corpses" and the father who "tumbled in the yellow trenches, / Raged at his breast, gulped, and died." This stark contrast highlights the irony and makes it clearer that he is not speaking literally.

Brooks also uses verbal irony in "the sonnet-ballad," as in her description of death as "coquettish" and as a "beauty." In characterizing death as irresistible, Brooks makes the point that death is something many soldiers cannot avoid, no matter how they try.

Cooperative Learning Activity With a group, discuss the use of verbal irony by Crane and Brooks. Why do you think they use this device? Do you think it is fitting to use irony with the topic of war? Why or why not?

REVIEW SONNET STRUCTURE Review the information about **sonnet structure** on pages 233 and 236. What features of the sonnet can you find in "the sonnet-ballad"?

GUIDING STUDENT RESPONSE

Connect to the Literature

1. **What Do You Think?**
Possible Responses: the lover who "threw wild hands toward the sky"; the father who "raged at his breast, gulped and died"

Comprehension Check
- The speaker addresses those left behind by soldiers—a lover, a child, and a mother.
- a thousand corpses
- The father was killed.

Think Critically

2. The speaker hates war. The repetition of the ironic statement "war is kind" and imagery of death create a negative picture of war.
3. Student response should reflect an analysis of text structure, specifically comparison and contrast. Crane indents the second and fourth stanzas to show contrast. He purposely shifts the focus from those left behind to the imagery on the battlefield.

Literary Analysis

Verbal Irony Possible Response: to emphasize the horror of war by comparison to positive things; yes, because it is such a serious matter that it is difficult to approach it directly on in a poem

Sonnet Structure Possible Responses: rhyme scheme; 14 lines; 3 quatrains and 1 couplet

Extend Interpretations

Comparing Texts Possible Response: Similarities in figures of speech and imagery between the two poems include images that suggest that war is wonderful, attractive, and grand. Differences include the sincerity of Brooks's lament and the irony of Crane's praise.

Comparing Texts Possible Responses: Crane's poem gives a more graphic look at the horrors of battle; Brooks's poem deals more with one person's grief.

Connect to Life Remind students to consider instances in which oppressed people are in need of rescue, such as World War II.

Writing Options

1. **Mother's Poem** Good responses should address the daughter's question in a well-thought-out manner. To make this assignment easier, suggest that students pair up and discuss possible responses with a partner. They can place their work in their Working Portfolio.
2. **Speaker Comparison** Student comparisons should include some of the following: both authors use strong imagery; both express strong feelings about the cruelty of war; both describe loved ones leaving for war; both use verbal irony. Differences: Brooks's speaker focuses only on her own loss; Crane's speaker focuses on the losses of others.
3. **Letter to the Author** Have students get into small groups and brainstorm questions they might wish to ask the poets.

Activities & Explorations

1. **War Collage** Remind students that the images do not necessarily have to be of war; any images that represent their feelings about war are appropriate.
2. **Art from the Home Front** Tell students that the art does not necessarily have to be representational. Students may use color, shape, and texture to express feelings.
3. **Interpretive Dance** Screen students' music choices for inappropriate material before they present them. Their original performance must represent a valid interpretation.

Inquiry & Research

1. Encourage students to cover different wars. Have them present their findings to the class in an oral report. Encourage students to discuss the changes in methods of warfare over time.
2. Encourage students to supplement their library research with interviews with veterans they might know. Remind students to write out their questions ahead of time so that they will get all of the information they need.

Choices & CHALLENGES

Writing Options

1. **Mother's Poem** Write a poem from the point of view of the mother in "the sonnet-ballad," written in response to her daughter's question.

2. **Speaker Comparison** In a paragraph, compare and contrast the speakers' attitudes toward war in "Do not weep, maiden, for war is kind" and "the sonnet-ballad." You might want to create a Venn diagram to help clarify your thoughts before writing.

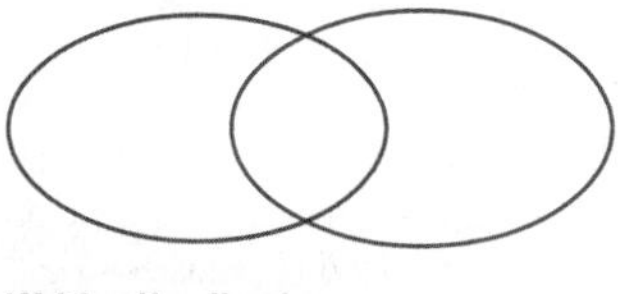

Writing Handbook
See page 1157: Compare and Contrast.

3. **Letter to the Author** Write a letter to Stephen Crane or Gwendolyn Brooks, giving your opinion of his or her poem and asking any questions you might have about it.

Activities & Explorations

1. **War Collage** Find illustrations and photographs in newspapers, magazines, or books, or via the Internet, that reflect your attitude toward war. Assemble these images in a collage. ~ **VIEWING AND REPRESENTING**

2. **Art from the Home Front** Create a sculpture, painting, or drawing that expresses the experience or feelings of someone who has watched a loved one go off to war. ~ **ART**

3. **Interpretive Dance** Working with one of the two poems, choose appropriate music and choreograph a dance that tells the same story or expresses the same ideas and feelings as the poem. Work with a partner if you wish. Perform your dance before the class. ~ **MUSIC AND DANCE**

Inquiry & Research

1. **War Through Time** Crane wrote about wars from the Civil War to the end of the 19th century. Brooks wrote about wars of the 20th century, primarily World War II. How were the methods of warfare of these two periods alike and different? Research one war from each period and write a summary of your findings.

2. **War Journals and Letters** Do research in your library to locate letters and journals written by soldiers during wartime. Prepare an oral report about the soldiers' perspectives on war, using excerpts from the journals and letters to illustrate what you have learned.

More Online: Research Starter
www.mcdougallittell.com

Soldiers relax in the trenches in World War I.

Mini Lesson Grammar

PARALLEL COMPOUND PREDICATES Remind students that compound predicates are predicates joined by a coordinating conjunction. Some examples of coordinating conjunctions are *and, but, or, nor*, and *so*. Tell students that compound predicates must be parallel, or have similar grammatical form, in order for the sentence to make sense. For example, "The boys liked to walk to school and riding their bikes to the library" is not parallel. The sentence would be parallel if rewritten this way: "The boys liked to walk to school and to ride their bikes to the library." *Walk* and *ride* are parallel because they have similar forms. Write the following sentence on the chalkboard:

The war killed many people and corroding our society.

Have students rewrite the sentence to make it parallel.

Use **Grammar Transparencies and Copymasters,** p. 87, for more practice.

Stephen Crane
1871–1900

Other Works
The Black Riders, and Other Lines
The Red Badge of Courage: An Episode of the American Civil War
The Open Boat, and Other Tales of Adventure
War Is Kind

The Classroom of the Streets Stephen Crane was born in Newark, New Jersey. An unremarkable student at Syracuse University, he was known better for his prowess on the baseball field than for anything else. While in school, he supported himself by reporting and writing for his brother's news agency. He had trouble finishing his coursework and finally left school to become a writer. Crane was most interested in writing about the lives of the poor and moved to the Bowery, a rough part of New York, where he could live among the people he wished to write about. When his Civil War novella *The Red Badge of Courage,* published in 1895, achieved enormous critical and popular acclaim, he felt slightly embarrassed to receive so much attention for writing on a topic with which he had so little experience. However, he obliged his readers' demand for more war stories. Around the same time, he began to write poetry, after reading the verse of Emily Dickinson.

War Correspondence Shortly thereafter, Crane began to work as a foreign correspondent, covering wars in Cuba and Greece. He began to learn firsthand about war and its accompanying experiences. Crane was once shipwrecked on his way to Cuba and spent 30 hours at sea in a lifeboat. This experience inspired his famous short story "The Open Boat." He eventually moved to England, where he wrote in the company of such famous British writers as Joseph Conrad. However, Crane suffered from poor health throughout this time until his death of tuberculosis at age 29. Despite his limited years, Crane produced a prodigious number of poems, short stories, and novels. Many have become classics.

Gwendolyn Brooks
1917–2000

Other Works
Annie Allen
The Bean Eaters
Family Pictures
Black Love
Children Coming Home

Chicago Childhood Gwendolyn Brooks has lived most of her life in Chicago. She grew up on the city's south side and has remained strongly attached to her hometown and to the city's African-American community. Brooks began to write poetry as a child, with the encouragement of her parents. A shy teenager, Brooks continued to write and read poetry, some of which she showed to the poet Langston Hughes, who encouraged her as well. In 1950, she won the Pulitzer Prize for poetry for *Annie Allen,* the poetry collection in which "the sonnet-ballad" appeared. She was the first African American to win the award.

Poetic Development In her early poetry, Brooks was strongly influenced by traditional literary forms. As her work evolved, she relied more on free verse, seeking to write poems that would reach out to the African-American people she wrote about. "I've written hundreds . . . of sonnets, and I'll probably never write another one, because I don't feel that this is a sonnet time," she once said of this change. "It seems to me it's a wild, raw, ragged free verse time."

Community Activism Brooks became a spokesperson on racial issues in addition to her work as a poet. One critic observed that Brooks, "more than any other nationally acclaimed writer, has remained in touch with the community she writes about. She lives in the core of Chicago's black community. . . . She is her work." A dedicated educator, Brooks has taught poetry at numerous universities and has received more than 50 honorary doctorates in recognition of her outstanding achievements.

Mini Lesson Speaking and Listening

DRAMATIC READING Prepare Help students prepare a dramatic presentation of each poem. Have them work in cooperative groups to list important elements. Then have them discuss what type of presentation would best portray these elements. Have them consider each speaker's tone, pitch, volume, and speed. They should also consider the speakers' posture and hand gestures. Students should justify their choice of verbal and nonverbal performance techniques by referring to their analysis and interpretation of the poems. Explain that the ironic nature of the poems may mean that the tone and gestures used may not necessarily match the words but rather the intent of the poem.

Present Student groups can decide who presents the dramatic readings and how they will be presented. Students who are audience members should discuss how the performance increases their appreciation and understanding of the poems.

BLOCK SCHEDULING This lesson is particularly well suited for longer class periods.

Building Vocabulary

Objectives

- use reference tools to determine the meaning of foreign terms

EXERCISE

1. *en masse*—all together
2. *coup d'état*—sudden overthrow of a government by a group currently or formerly in power
3. *Zeitgeist*—spirit of the times
4. *alfresco*—in the fresh air; outdoors
5. *carte blanche*—unrestricted power to act at one's own discretion

Understanding Foreign Words

Have you ever made a *faux pas* ("blunder") because you used a foreign phrase that was *malapropos* ("not appropriate")? What do you do when you come across a foreign expression in your reading? What is your *modus operandi* ("method of operating")? For example, how would you find the meaning of *auto-da-fé* in the sentence on the right?

> **The condemned to death, I knew, perished usually at the *auto-da-fé,* and one of these had been held on the very night of the day of my trial.**
>
> —Edgar Allan Poe, "The Pit and the Pendulum"

If you look in a standard English dictionary, you will find something close to this definition of *auto-da-fé*: "the public announcement and execution of sentences on persons tried and found guilty by the Inquisition." Many foreign terms, however, are not included in English dictionaries, so you may need to consult other reference aids when you encounter expressions you don't know.

Strategies for Building Vocabulary

Words move from language to language in a word migration that has been going on for centuries. Some foreign words and phrases have been adopted into the English language, especially when there are no English words to convey certain ideas. At one time the Latin words *capsule* and *habitual*, the Greek word *catastrophe*, and the French word *detail* would have sounded strange to English speakers. Today, however, these words are considered a part of the English vocabulary.

Foreign words are frequently used in literature, and you will likely encounter some that are unfamiliar to you. Learning how to find their meanings in reference aids will help your comprehension.

❶ Use a Dictionary When you need to translate a foreign phrase, you will often find it in an English dictionary by looking for it as one word. For example, even though the French phrase *en route* (meaning "on the way") consists of two words, it is listed in the dictionary among the *enro*-words, right after the verb *enroot*.

❷ Use Other Reference Tools When you can't find a term in an English dictionary, try a foreign-language dictionary; most libraries have such dictionaries. You can also use the Internet to find a translation of a word. Type the name of the foreign language you need and the word "dictionary" in the search engine box (example: French language dictionary). A list of available dictionaries or translation sites will appear. When you go to one of these sites, type the foreign word or phrase, and the English translation will appear.

❸ Learn Foreign Words and Phrases The following list includes some commonly used foreign words and phrases.

Word or Phrase	Meaning
en route (French)	on the way
laissez faire (French)	noninterference
mea culpa (Latin)	my fault
per (Latin)	for, according to
status quo (Latin)	the way things are
aloha (Hawaiian)	hello or goodbye
dolce vita (Italian)	the sweet life
pièce de résistance (French)	an outstanding accomplishment

EXERCISE Use a reference tool to translate the following commonly used foreign words and phrases.

1. en masse
2. coup d'état
3. Zeitgeist
4. alfresco
5. carte blanche

This story takes place during the Korean War, a conflict that often pitted friend against friend and even brother against brother. In 1948, shortly after World War II, the nation of Korea, which occupies a peninsula on the eastern shore of Asia, became officially divided. Two separate governments were established: a Communist government in the north and a non-Communist government in the south. In 1950, North Korea invaded South Korea, beginning a civil war in which other nations, including the United States and China, soon became involved. A truce was signed in 1953, but tension between the two Koreas has continued for decades.

Much of the war took place near the 38th parallel of north latitude, the dividing line between the two countries. This area was the scene of hotly contested battles in which thousands died and the control of villages often shifted back and forth between the North Koreans and the South Koreans. One of these villages is the setting of "Cranes."

CRANES

HWANG SUNWŎN

The northern village lay snug beneath the high, bright autumn sky, near the border at the Thirty-eighth Parallel.

White gourds lay one against the other on the dirt floor of an empty farmhouse. Any village elders who passed by extinguished their bamboo pipes first, and the children, too, turned back some distance off. Their faces were marked with fear.

As a whole, the village showed little damage from the war, but it still did not seem like the same village Sŏngsam[1] had known as a boy.

At the foot of a chestnut grove on the hill behind the village he stopped and climbed a chestnut tree. Somewhere far back in his mind he heard the old man with a wen[2] shout, "You bad boy, climbing up my chestnut tree again!"

The old man must have passed away, for he was not among the few village elders Sŏngsam had met. Holding on to the trunk of the tree, Sŏngsam gazed up at the blue sky for a time. Some chestnuts fell to the ground as the dry clusters opened of their own accord.

A young man stood, his hands bound, before a farmhouse that had been converted into a Public Peace Police office. He seemed to be a stranger, so Sŏngsam went up for a closer look.

1. **Sŏngsam** (səng′säm′).
2. **wen:** a harmless skin tumor.

ON YOUR OWN

Possible Objectives

You can use this selection to achieve one or more of the following objectives:

- enjoy silent sustained reading (Option One)
- read and analyze literature with a group (Option Two)
- use the Reader's Notebook to formulate questions about literature (Option Three)
- write in response to literature (Option Three)

Summary

Sŏngsam returns to his Korean village, which shows little damage from the war but is much changed. When he reaches a farmhouse that has been turned into a Public Peace Police office, he is stunned to find his boyhood friend, Tŏkchae, under arrest for communist activity. Sŏngsam offers to take Tŏkchae to a place where he is to be questioned and shot. He leads Tŏkchae away, outraged that his old friend has become an enemy. As the two men walk, Sŏngsam learns that Tŏkchae, now married, decided to stay on the farm with his ailing father rather than to escape from the enemy army. Sŏngsam reflects upon old times, especially on the time he and Tŏkchae captured a crane and then freed it when its life was endangered. Finally, Sŏngsam tells Tŏkchae to help him hunt a crane by flushing it out. Tŏkchae stares in confusion and then finally understands. He crawls through the weeds to freedom, as nearby cranes soar into the sky.

Intrepreting Historical Context

Have the students read the background paragraphs in italic prior to reading the selection. Then ask them as they read the story to interpret the possible influences of the historical context on this literary work.

CRANES 585

Reading the Selections

Option One
Silent Sustained Reading

You might set aside time each week for independent reading. Remind students that they are expected to establish a purpose for reading (even if their purpose is to read for enjoyment). *Cranes* will appeal to many students and can be read independently in about 20 minutes. If you want to encourage students to read for pleasure, you might forgo assignments related to the selection. Should you want to make assignments, Options Two and Three offer suggestions.

Option Two
Shared Reading Groups

You may assign students to groups or allow them to choose their own. Students can read the selection together, alternately reading sections aloud, or they can read independently and meet to cooperate in a project that portrays some element of the story.

Possible Projects

- Students can create a time line to show the different phases of the relationships between Sŏngsam and his childhood friend. Students should list major events in the relationship and describe the changes in Sŏngsam's attitude toward Tŏkchae. Help students plan their time lines by pointing out that the main action takes place about 1952, at the height of the Korean War, when the two main characters are about 20 years old. The action described on page 586 occurs when the characters were about five or six years old, and the flashback on pages 587–588 occurs when they were twelve.
- Students can photocopy pictures of Korean and other Asian art depicting cranes and use the pictures to create an art exhibit. In a brief presentation, discuss with students the feelings that the artwork evokes and compare these feelings with those evoked by the cranes in the story. Help students with their exhibit by making books of Asian art available to them. Suggest that students also include in their exhibits portions of folklore about cranes or their own original artwork.

He was stunned: this young man was none other than his boyhood playmate, Tŏkchae.[3]

Sŏngsam asked the police officer who had come with him from Ch'ŏnt'ae[4] for an explanation. The prisoner was the vice-chairman of the Farmers' Communist League and had just been flushed[5] out of hiding in his own house, Sŏngsam learned.

Sŏngsam sat down on the dirt floor and lit a cigaret.

Tŏkchae was to be escorted to Ch'ŏngdan[6] by one of the peace police.

After a time, Sŏngsam lit a new cigaret from the first and stood up.

"I'll take him with me."

Tŏkchae averted his face and refused to look at Sŏngsam. The two left the village.

Sŏngsam went on smoking, but the tobacco had no flavor. He just kept drawing the smoke in and blowing it out. Then suddenly he thought that Tŏkchae, too, must want a puff. He thought of the days when they had shared dried gourd leaves behind sheltering walls, hidden from the adults' view. But today, how could he offer a cigaret to a fellow like this?

Once, when they were small, he went with Tŏkchae to steal some chestnuts from the old man with the wen. It was Sŏngsam's turn to climb the tree. Suddenly the old man began shouting. Sŏngsam slipped and fell to the ground. He got chestnut burrs all over his bottom, but he kept on running. Only when the two had reached a safe place where the old man could not overtake them did Sŏngsam turn his bottom to Tŏkchae. The burrs hurt so much as they were plucked out that Sŏngsam could not keep tears from welling up in his eyes. Tŏkchae produced a fistful of chestnuts from his pocket and thrust them into Sŏngsam's . . . Sŏngsam threw away the cigaret he had just lit, and then made up his mind not to light another while he was escorting Tŏkchae.

They reached the pass at the hill where he and Tŏkchae had cut fodder[7] for the cows until Sŏngsam had to move to a spot near Ch'ŏnt'ae, south of the Thirty-eighth Parallel, two years before the liberation.

Sŏngsam felt a sudden surge of anger in spite of himself and shouted, "So how many have you killed?"

For the first time, Tŏkchae cast a quick glance at him and then looked away.

"You! How many have you killed?" he asked again.

Tŏkchae looked at him again and glared. The glare grew intense, and his mouth twitched.

"So you managed to kill quite a few, eh?" Sŏngsam felt his mind becoming clear of itself, as if some obstruction had been removed. "If you were vice-chairman of the Communist League, why didn't you run? You must have been lying low with a secret mission."

Tŏkchae did not reply.

"Speak up. What was your mission?"

Tŏkchae kept walking. Tŏkchae was hiding something, Sŏngsam thought. He wanted to take a good look at him, but Tŏkchae kept his face averted.

Fingering the revolver at his side, Sŏngsam went on: "There's no need to make excuses. You're going to be shot anyway. Why don't you tell the truth here and now?"

"I'm not going to make any excuses. They made me vice-chairman of the League because I was a hardworking farmer and one of the poorest. If that's a capital offense,[8] so be it. I'm still what I used to be—the only thing I'm good at is

3. **Tŏkchae** (tək'jă').
4. **Ch'ŏnt'ae** (chən'tă').
5. **flushed:** driven from hiding.
6. **Ch'ŏngdan** (chəng'dän').
7. **fodder:** coarsely chopped hay or straw used as food for farm animals.
8. **capital offense:** a crime calling for the death penalty.

tilling the soil." After a short pause, he added, "My old man is bedridden at home. He's been ill almost half a year." Tŏkchae's father was a widower, a poor, hardworking farmer who lived only for his son. Seven years before his back had given out, and he had contracted a skin disease.

"Are you married?"

"Yes," Tŏkchae replied after a time.

"To whom?"

"Shorty."

"To Shorty?" How interesting! A woman so small and plump that she knew the earth's vastness, but not the sky's height. Such a cold fish! He and Tŏkchae had teased her and made her cry. And Tŏkchae had married her!

"How many kids?"

"The first is arriving this fall, she says."

Sŏngsam had difficulty swallowing a laugh that he was about to let burst forth in spite of himself. Although he had asked how many children Tŏkchae had, he could not help wanting to break out laughing at the thought of the wife sitting there with her huge stomach, one span around. But he realized that this was no time for joking.

"Anyway, it's strange you didn't run away."

"I tried to escape. They said that once the South invaded, not a man would be spared. So all of us between seventeen and forty were taken to the North. I thought of evacuating, even if I had to carry my father on my back. But Father said no. How could we farmers leave the land behind when the crops were ready for harvesting? He grew old on that farm depending on me as the prop and the mainstay of the family. I wanted to be with him in his last moments so I could close his eyes with my own hand. Besides, where can farmers like us go, when all we know how to do is live on the land?"

Sŏngsam had had to flee the previous June. At night he had broken the news privately to his father. But his father had said the same thing: Where could a farmer go, leaving all the chores behind? So Sŏngsam had left alone. Roaming about the strange streets and villages in the South, Sŏngsam had been haunted by thoughts of his old parents and the young children, who had been left with all the chores. Fortunately, his family had been safe then, as it was now.

They had crossed over a hill. This time Sŏngsam walked with his face averted. The autumn sun was hot on his forehead. This was an ideal day for the harvest, he thought.

When they reached the foot of the hill, Sŏngsam gradually came to a halt. In the middle of a field he espied a group of cranes that resembled men in white, all bent over. This had been the demilitarized zone[9] along the Thirty-eighth Parallel. The cranes were still living here, as before, though the people were all gone.

Once, when Sŏngsam and Tŏkchae were about twelve, they had set a trap here, unbeknown to the adults, and caught a crane, a Tanjŏng crane.[10] They had tied the crane up, even binding its wings, and paid it daily visits, patting its neck and riding on its back. Then one day they overheard the neighbors whispering: someone had come from Seoul[11] with a permit from the governor-general's office to catch cranes as some kind of specimens. Then and there the two boys had dashed off to the field. That they would be found out and punished had no longer mattered; all they cared about was the fate of their crane. Without a moment's delay, still out of breath from running, they untied the crane's feet and wings, but the bird could hardly walk. It must have been weak from having been bound.

The two held the crane up. Then, suddenly, they heard a gunshot. The crane fluttered its wings once or twice and then sank back to the ground.

9. **demilitarized zone:** an area—generally one separating two hostile nations or armies—from which military forces are prohibited.

10. **Tanjŏng** (tän′jəng′) **crane:** a type of crane found in Asia.

11. **Seoul** (sōl): the capital and largest city of South Korea.

Option Three
Reader's Notebook
Provide the following direction to students before they read.

Summarize the setting and the characters in *Cranes.* Ask students to declare which of the two main characters they will focus on as they read and write.

Tell students to read the story, pausing at the end of column one, page 586. At that point, students should summarize the relationship between Sŏngsam and Tŏkchae in their Reader's Notebooks. Have them write any questions they would like to ask either one or both of the characters.

At the end of the story, students will return to their questions. Ask them to note whether any of their questions have been answered and to write down any additional questions they have about Sŏngsam or Tŏkchae.

As they read, students can make a list in their Reader's Notebooks of details from *Cranes* that establish the story's setting. Have them write about how they think the setting influences the actions and attitudes of the characters.

After Reading

Possible Activities

Independent Activities

- Have students create a comparison chart showing the similarities and differences between the lives of Sŏngsam and Tŏkchae. Remind students to review the observations about the characters they wrote in their Reader's Notebooks while they were reading.
- Have students review the Learning the Language of Literature and Active Reader sections, pages 543–545. They can note which skills and strategies they used while reading the selection.

Discussion Activities

- Use the questions formulated by students as the start of a discussion about this story.
- Have students discuss why people at war dehumanize and demonize their enemies. Point out that this process occurs even among people who have much in common—North and South Koreans, Protestants and Catholics in Northern Ireland, Israelis and Arabs in the Middle East. Ask students how people with such historical and geographical ties can become such enemies.
- Have students discuss what they think the significance of the cranes is in the story. Ask students to consider the following before the discussion begins:
- the cranes still living in the demilitarized zone
- the crane that the boys caught and freed
- the last sentence of the story

Assessment Opportunities

- You can assess student comprehension of the story by evaluating the questions they formulate in their Reader's Notebooks.
- You can use any of the discussion questions as essay questions.
- You can have students turn any one of their Reader's Notebook entries into an essay.

Yi Dynasty rank badge (about 1600–1700). Colored silk and gold paper, thread on figured silk, Victoria & Albert Museum, London / Art Resource, New York.

The boys thought their crane had been shot. But the next moment, as another crane from a nearby bush fluttered its wings, the boys' crane stretched its long neck, gave out a whoop, and disappeared into the sky. For a long while the two boys could not tear their eyes away from the blue sky up into which their crane had soared.

"Hey, why don't we stop here for a crane hunt?" Sŏngsam said suddenly.

Tŏkchae was dumbfounded.

"I'll make a trap with this rope; you flush a crane over here."

Sŏngsam had untied Tŏkchae's hands and was already crawling through the weeds.

Tŏkchae's face whitened. "You're sure to be shot anyway"—these words flashed through his mind. Any instant a bullet would come flying from Sŏngsam's direction, Tŏkchae thought.

Some paces away, Sŏngsam quickly turned toward him.

"Hey, how come you're standing there like a dummy? Go flush a crane!"

Only then did Tŏkchae understand. He began crawling through the weeds.

A pair of Tanjŏng cranes soared high into the clear blue autumn sky, flapping their huge wings. ❖

Translated by Peter H. Lee

Hwang Sunwŏn

1915 –

Other Works
Trees on the Cliff
The Book of Masks
Shadows of a Sound

Enemy Tongues For Korea's Hwang Sunwŏn, becoming a published writer in his native tongue was no easy matter. For the first three decades of Hwang's life, Korea was ruled by Japan. The Japanese tried to stamp out Korean nationalism by setting up Japanese-language schools, arresting Korean scholars, and at one point even forcing Koreans to adopt Japanese names. Hwang had to travel to Japan to receive his higher education. However, his years at Waseda University proved stimulating, and he returned to his homeland to publish his first story collection in 1940.

The Interference of War Two years later, his career plans were temporarily blocked when, at the height of World War II, the Japanese banned all Korean-language publications. After the Japanese departed at the war's end, Hwang and his family still faced hardships in the Communist-dominated north where they lived. Luckily, they were able to flee to the south, but invasion by the North Korean forces at the start of the Korean War soon made them refugees once again. Only after the signing of the truce in 1953 was Hwang able to return full-time to his writing. Over the years, Hwang has produced 7 novels and over 100 short stories, which have won him several prestigious awards in his homeland. "Cranes," written in 1953, was the title story of a 1956 collection.

Inquiry & Research

The Korean War lasted just over three years, but almost as many Americans died there as in 10 years in Vietnam. Learn more about the Korean War through personal accounts of soldiers who fought there.

Real World Link
Begin your research by reading the magazine article on page 590.

LaserLinks: Background for Reading
Historical Connection
Cultural Connection

CRANES 589

Real WORLD Link

Magazine Article

Objectives
- evaluate an argument
- identify the main idea in an article
- find detail that supports a main idea

Connecting to the Literature
Hwang Sunwŏn's "Cranes" (p. 585) presents a poignant account of civil war from one Korean soldier's point of view.

Reading for Information

Angus Deming speaks for the service persons who answered America's call to defend South Korea in the "forgotten" war.

1 Deming's main idea is that a war he fought in—the Korean War—has been overlooked and forgotten. Veterans were finally recognized with the dedication of the Korean War Memorial on July 27, 1995. The recognition of their service assuaged the anger and bitterness some veterans felt about the "forgotten war." Deming wants readers to feel outrage and sympathy.

THE REMEMBERED WAR: A Korean War Vet Offers a History Lesson

by Angus Deming

In the United States, the Korean War sometimes is referred to as the "forgotten war." As the writer reminds us, this war was both devastating and momentous, and the soldiers who fought in it were just as dedicated and brave as those who fought in World War II and the Vietnam War.

The weather was almost as perverse[1] as anything we'd known in Korea. Thousands of us—Korean War veterans from all over the country and even overseas—filled the Washington Mall last week. We had come to take part in the dedication of the Korean War Veterans Memorial, honoring those who served in the first of the cold war's hot wars. South Korea's President Kim Young Sam thanked us for helping to save his country from the
❶ communist invaders from the North. Bill Clinton praised our "never surpassed" courage in the face of extreme hardship. Mercifully, both spoke briefly; we were beginning to keel over in the sweltering heat. A thunderstorm washed out the evening's entertainment. But the weather didn't bother us. This was a long overdue celebration. The Korean War—our war—was no longer lost somewhere between World War II and Vietnam. It was no longer the "forgotten war."

The Korean Memorial occupies a grove beneath the Lincoln Memorial, across the reflecting pool from the Vietnam Wall. It's dominated by 19 large, steel statues of infantry-men—a silent patrol moving warily up a slope. They look weary, as though they've been on too many patrols and climbed too many hills. That was us in Korea, the way we were, too. Off to the side there's a granite wall with hundreds of faces etched on it, faces taken from actual photographs of men and women who served in Korea as support troops: truckdrivers, engineers, flight crewmen, nurses, chaplains, sailors. These ghostly faces seem to say, "Don't forget us."

1. **perverse:** wrongly self-willed or stubborn.

Korean War Veterans Memorial, Washington, D.C.

590

Reading for Information

Have you ever built a house of cards with your friends? If so, you know that it doesn't take much to knock it over. Think of a weak argument as a house of cards—easy to knock down. But think of a strong argument as a battleship—virtually indestructible. In this article, the writer constructs an argument about the significance of the Korean War, and the reader must evaluate its strengths and weaknesses.

EVALUATING AN ARGUMENT
An effective argument shows an honest concern about a problem, a grasp of the issues involved, and a respectful attitude toward the audience. In addition, to win over an audience, a writer must establish and maintain credibility, or believability.

YOUR TURN Use the questions and activities below to help you evaluate the writer's argument.

❶ **Identifying the Main Idea** To communicate an argument effectively, a writer generally has to engage both the minds and the emotions of readers. What is Deming's main point in his article? What emotions do you think Deming wants you to feel?

2 We never understood how the Korean War could have been "forgotten" in the first place. It caused such incredible devastation: more than 2 million people dead and more than 2.5 million wounded or injured in just three years. About 54,000 Americans died there, almost as many as in Vietnam in 10 years. More than 8,000 Americans are still listed as missing in action in Korea. Losses on the Communist side were staggering: more than 400,000 Chinese soldiers dead, almost 215,000 North Koreans killed in action. Korea itself—North and South alike—was left in total ruins.

The war ushered in the era of jet fighters and was the first in which helicopters were used in combat. It also was the first (and perhaps last) in which a multinational force fought effectively under the United Nations flag. We did not wear blue helmets, of course; we were in Korea as war makers, not peacekeepers. But Korea was, most of all, a ground war, and "gravel crunchers"—infantry grunts—had a miserable time. The terrain was as much an enemy as the one that was shooting at us. There was always another hill to climb, and the weather seemed to be of two kinds: unbearable heat or unbearable cold. . . .

3 The war lasted three years, one month, and two days. The Marines alone suffered more than 2,000 casualties in the final two months, even as peace talks neared the end. On July 25, 1953, two Chinese battalions attacked a remote Marine outpost on the western front. Sgt. Ambrosio Guillen won a posthumous[2] Congressional Medal of Honor helping repel the assault. The next day the Chinese hit the outpost again, and another Marine sergeant won a posthumous Navy Cross. The following morning the armistice was signed at Panmunjom.

4 In the tight little world of a frontline rifle company, we seldom saw the big picture. We didn't realize then that, as Clinton told us, we had helped South Korea become a free and prosperous nation. Mostly we fought for each other, or to uphold the honor of the Corps—that was what mattered. Most of us escaped the kind of trauma suffered by so many Vietnam vets. It was a different war at a different time, to be sure. But our mindset was also different: we were closer to the World War II generation, and we answered the call simply because our country needed us. Our only anger, really, was that so much bravery, so much uncomplaining devotion to duty, went unrecognized for so long. Now that lingering bitterness has been laid to rest at last.

2. **posthumous** (pŏs′ chə-məs): occurring or continuing after one's death.

2 **Providing Evidence** To show that the argument is well thought out, a writer must provide evidence. Statistical information and facts can strengthen a writer's argument. What facts or statistics does Deming provide to support his main idea? Which of these facts did you find most surprising?

3 Writers also use details to support their general statements and opinions. What details that illustrate the intensity of the fight does the writer provide?

4 **Determining Credibility** In your opinion, does Deming's argument have **credibility?** What do you think is his **motivation** for putting forth this argument? Do you think the fact that he served in Korea strengthens or weakens his argument?

Evaluating the Argument Does the writer provide enough convincing information to support his main idea? On the basis of what you've read, has Deming made a sound, convincing argument? Explain.

Inquiry & Research

Activity Link: "Cranes," p. 589
What added insight about the Korean War did you get from reading this article? Have the facts in the article about the human toll of the war shed new light on Sŏngsam's inner conflict about his duties as a soldier? Discuss your thoughts with a partner.

2 Deming provides statistics about casualties, facts about military technology, and details that relate the devastation suffered in Korea.

3 Details that illustrate the intensity of the fight include the length of time that war lasted (over three years) and the number of casualties suffered by both sides.

4 The facts and statistics Deming presents about the Korean War give his argument credibility. Deming's motivation is to provide insight into the mindset of those who answered the call to duty. That Deming served in Korea strengthens his argument by establishing the credibility of his authentic perspective.

Mini Lesson Inquiry & Research

The Inquiry & Research activity on this page links the article to the Inquiry & Research section following "Cranes," page 589. In that activity, students were asked to interview veterans of the Korean War.

Instruction Oral histories give insight into the effects of historical events on specific persons. Have students compare and contrast facts concerning the human side of the Korean War that were gained from Deming's magazine article with those gained from their oral histories.

Practice With a partner, have students discuss the human toll of war and the possible inner conflicts a soldier might experience. Encourage them to weave the evidence from three sources into their discussion—Deming's article, their oral history of a Korean War veteran, and Sŏngsam's experience in the story "Cranes." Have partners take notes on their discussion and orally report their conclusions to the class.

OVERVIEW

This lesson gives students an opportunity to compare, evaluate, and form opinions about two memoirs. The focus of this comparison is on the injustices experienced by a European Jew and a Japanese American during World War II.

Teaching Option
Because each memoir is accompanied by its own introductory and response pages, teachers have the option of pairing the memoirs or teaching them individually. Used in conjunction with the Comparing Literature: Assessment Practice on page 615, the memoirs may help students prepare for literature-based writing assessments.

What's the Connection?

Have students consider the types of intense personal adversity that an individual might experience during times of war, such as loss of loved ones and family; loss of security in home and community life; denial of freedom; threats to survival; destruction of one's social and economic world; and the adversity of living in constant fear.
Ask: In what ways might one respond to such threatening circumstances?
Possible Responses: One might escape; one might choose to fight against the forces that threaten; one might live carefully and intelligently, seeking to avoid confrontation and survive the best one can; one might courageously help others.

Points of Comparison

Point out that the reactions to injustices students have been discussing assume that the individual has a choice.
Ask: In what ways might a person respond when he or she is trapped in a situation beyond one's control, such as being captured by the enemy?
Possible Response: Perhaps a person never loses control. As Victor Frankl, another survivor of the Nazi concentration camps, has said, his captors controlled his body, but they could not control his mind. In other words, a person can choose to respond in heart and mind in a way that brings inner peace, regardless of external circumstances and outcomes.

Comparing Literature

Learning from History

from Night	*from* Nobel Prize Acceptance Speech	*from* Farewell to Manzanar
Memoir by ELIE WIESEL	*Speech by* ELIE WIESEL	*Memoir by* JEANNE WAKATSUKI HOUSTON AND JAMES HOUSTON

What's the Connection?

Victims of Injustice You are about to read the true stories of people who were victims of terrible injustices. Elie Wiesel, a Jew born in Romania, lived in a concentration camp in Germany as a teenager and lost members of his family to the Holocaust. When Jeanne Wakatsuki was a young girl in the United States, her family was forced to leave their home and live for three years in a California detention camp—all because of fears that Japanese Americans would be disloyal in World War II.

As you will see, human beings find ways of dealing with adversity, even in the worst of circumstances. By reading about what others have lived through, we can at least begin to understand these events. By keeping alive their stories, we can perhaps avoid repeating the injustices of the past.

Japanese Americans being transported to detention camps in World War II.

Points of Comparison

Drawing Lessons from History In this unit so far, you have encountered various characters trapped by the forces of history. The next selections deal with real people who are similarly trapped by forces beyond their control. In the pages that follow, you will be asked to synthesize—a task that involves combining ideas or information to form new ideas—so that you can draw lessons from the experience of these authors.

Critical Thinking: From Analysis to Synthesis
To form a synthesis from two or more works of literature, you first need to analyze the information in each selection. The chart on the right will help you focus on important aspects of each work. Create a separate chart for the two major selections.

READER'S NOTEBOOK You will be asked to fill in your chart at the Points of Comparison in the following selections. Add other categories to your chart as necessary.

Cause of Situation:
↓
How the Author and Other Victims Are Treated:
↓
Psychological Effects on Victims:
↓
How People Try to Cope:
↓
Author's Purpose in Telling About Events:

Critical Thinking: From Analysis to Synthesis
Possible Responses for *Night*
Cause of Situation:
imprisonment of Jews in Nazi concentration camps during World War II
How the Author and Other Victims Are Treated:
like animals: brutal work details; little food, clothing, or medicine; no consideration of personal needs
Psychological Effect on Victims:
Separation from family members and systematic murder of fellow Jews created a psychological effect of unbearable pain and anguish.
How People Try to Cope:
by bonding together as best they could and comforting each other with courage and support; by praying and maintaining their faith
Author's Purpose in Telling About Events:
to make public the effect of these brutal atrocities, to keep the memory alive, and to prevent atrocities from occurring again

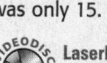

PREPARING to *Read*

from Night

Memoir by ELIE WIESEL (ĕl′ē vē-sĕl′)

"In an hour, we should know the verdict—death or a reprieve."

Connect to Your Life

Jewish Holocaust With a small group of classmates, share what you know about the Holocaust—the slaughter of millions of Jews in Europe during World War II. Where did you learn what you know? How did you react when you first learned about it?

Build Background

Holocaust Origins In the 1920s and 1930s, Germany was in the midst of a major economic depression; millions were unemployed. When Adolf Hitler became chancellor in 1933, he promised people jobs while providing them with a scapegoat for the nation's problems: the Jews. Hitler's Nazi party began its campaign against the Jews by revoking their citizenship, boycotting their businesses, and banning them from certain professions.

Germany's invasion of Poland in 1939 marked the beginning of World War II. Hitler's goal was to expand his empire across Europe and to eliminate the Jews at the same time. In Germany and from each nation Germany occupied, Jews—as well as gypsies, homosexuals, and intellectuals and artists who opposed Hitler—were transported to the concentration camps. Everyone entering the camps was tattooed with a number on the left forearm; the number served to replace one's name. Most of the 6 million Jews who were killed during World War II died in concentration camps. They were put to death in gas chambers, were shot by firing squads, or succumbed to starvation, torture, and disease.

This selection is from the memoir of a survivor who was imprisoned when he was only 15.

WORDS TO KNOW
Vocabulary Preview

din	notorious
emaciated	stature
interminable	

LaserLinks: Background for Reading
Historical Connection

Focus Your Reading

LITERARY ANALYSIS STYLE **Style** is the particular way a piece of literature is written—not *what* is said but *how* it is said. Every writer struggles to find an appropriate style to convey his or her message. Choice of words, length of sentences, and tone all contribute to the style of a writer's work, as illustrated by the following passage from *Night:*

> ***There were only Tibi and Yossi in front of me. They passed. I had time to notice that Mengele had not written their numbers down. Someone pushed me. It was my turn. I ran without looking back.***

As you read this excerpt by Elie Wiesel, pay attention to the manner in which he relates his experiences. Think about why he might have chosen to tell his story in such a simple and straightforward style.

ACTIVE READING CONNECTING When you read anything, you are bound to compare it with what you have previously read, heard about, or experienced yourself. In this way, you are **connecting** with what you are reading. You might also imagine yourself in a situation similar to that of a character or person that you read about. Literature with especially powerful content may provoke strong feelings or reflections about yourself or the world you know.

READER'S NOTEBOOK As you read this excerpt, keep notes of your mental and emotional reactions to the events and conversations related by Wiesel. After you have finished reading, spend a few minutes writing your reflections on the piece itself and on the Holocaust in general.

OVERVIEW

This selection is included in the **Grade 10 InterActive Reader.**

Objectives

1. understand and appreciate a **memoir (Literary Analysis)**
2. recognize how **style** contributes to the effect of the text **(Literary Analysis)**
3. **connect** the text with prior experience or knowledge **(Active Reading)**

Summary

In this excerpt from Elie Wiesel's memoir of life in a concentration camp, he recalls a New Year's Day "selection." Selections were held by the camp to weed out the sick and weak to be killed. On this day, 15-year-old Wiesel escapes the notice of the Nazi doctors, and his father, in another block, thinks he has done so too. A few days later, however, the older Wiesel is ordered to stay in camp while the others go out to work. Elie Wiesel lives that day in dread that he will lose his father. When he returns from the day's work, he finds a miracle in Block 36: his father is still alive!

Thematic Link

Elie Wiesel recounts how he and his father dealt with **facing the enemy** during life in a Nazi concentration camp.

5-Minute Warm-Up

Daily Language SkillBuilder

Have students **proofread** the display sentences on page 541l and write them correctly. The sentences also appear on Transparency 19 of **Grammar Transparencies and Copymasters.**

Mini Lesson **Preteaching Vocabulary**

If you would like to preteach the WORDS TO KNOW for this selection, use the Mini Lesson, p. 596.

LESSON RESOURCES

UNIT FOUR RESOURCE BOOK, pp. 20–21

ASSESSMENT RESOURCES

Formal Assessment, pp. 107–108

Teacher's Guide to Assessment and Portfolio Use

Test Generator

SKILLS TRANSPARENCIES AND COPYMASTERS

Literary Analysis

- Style, Voice, Diction, Purpose, T22 (for Paired Activity, p. 600)

Grammar

- Adjectives and Adverbs, C70 (for Mini Lesson, p. 601)

Vocabulary

- Analogies, C63 (for Mini Lesson, p. 596)

Writing

- Writing Process, T1–4 (for Writing Option 1, p. 601)
- Writing Structure, T6–8, T11 (for Writing Option 2, p. 601)
- Persuasive Essay C30 (for Writing Option 1, p. 601)

Communications

- Evaluation Matrix: Film/Video, T7 (for Inquiry & Research 2, p. 601)

INTEGRATED TECHNOLOGY

Audio Library

LaserLinks

- Historical Connection: The Holocaust. See **Teacher's SourceBook,** p. 36.

Visit our website:
www.mcdougallittell.com

NIGHT **593**

TEACHING THE LITERATURE

Reading and Analyzing

Reading Skills and Strategies: PREVIEW

Remind students that they are expected to establish a purpose for reading. Ask students to consider the title of the story, the called-out quotes, and the image on page 594. Then have them make predictions about how the title will relate to the overall story. Before students begin reading, give them a brief summary of the story.

Literary Analysis STYLE

Every writer has an individual way of communicating ideas, called style. Word choice, use of dialogue, sentence length, and intended audience are a few components that contribute to style. As students read Wiesel's memoir, have them analyze the characteristics of his clearly written text. Have students look at the language in these passages and try to determine what words or techniques made the passages particularly effective.

Use **Unit Four Resource Book,** p. 21 for more practice.

Active Reading CONNECTING

Pair students and have them describe to their partner their concepts of life in a concentration camp.

Use the following questions as prompts:

- What would you eat; where would you sleep; what would you do?
- How might it feel to witness the deaths of friends and relatives?

Be aware that some students may find this piece disturbing, and may feel very upset when discussing it in class.

Use **Unit Four Resource Book,** p. 20 for more practice.

Survivors of a Nazi concentration camp, 1945. The Bettmann Archive.

FROM

NIGHT

Elie Wiesel

The SS[1] gave us a fine New Year's gift.

We had just come back from work. As soon as we had passed through the door of the camp, we sensed something different in the air. Roll call did not take so long as usual. The evening soup was given out with great speed and swallowed down at once in anguish.

1. SS: an elite military unit of the Nazi party that served as Hitler's personal guard and as a special security force.

594

Teaching Options

Mini Lesson Viewing and Representing

Survivors of a Nazi concentration camp, 1945. **The Bettman Archive.**

Explain that this picture was taken in 1945, near the end of World War II, when prisoners were just being released from concentration camps.

Instruction Direct students' attention to the gaunt faces and emaciated bodies of the survivors. Ask students the following questions:

How do their appearances affect the mood of the photograph?

What might their expressions tell you about their feelings?

Possible Responses: The physical appearances of the men create a startling and disturbing mood. The men display a wide range of expressions—joy, sadness, shock, and even blankness—showing the viewer the variety of complex emotions they felt upon release.

Application Ask students to put themselves in the place of the survivors in the photograph. Ask students how the different facial expressions suggest the survivors' views of the future.

Possible Responses: The future might contain mixed emotions. Although the men survived the horrors of the concentration camp during the war, some expressions might be interpreted as hopeful, while others show a lasting sadness at their losses.

I was no longer in the same block as my father. I had been transferred to another unit, the building one, where, twelve hours a day, I had to drag heavy blocks of stone about. The head of my new block was a German Jew, small of stature, with piercing eyes. He told us that evening that no one would be allowed to go out after the evening soup. And soon a terrible word was circulating—selection.

We knew what that meant. An SS man would examine us. Whenever he found a weak one, a *musulman* as we called them, he would write his number down: good for the crematory.

After soup, we gathered together between the beds. The veterans said:

"You're lucky to have been brought here so late. This camp is paradise today, compared with what it was like two years ago. Buna[2] was a real hell then. There was no water, no blankets, less soup and bread. At night we slept almost naked, and it was below thirty degrees. The corpses were collected in hundreds every day. The work was hard. Today, this is a little paradise. The Kapos[3] had orders to kill a certain number of prisoners every day. And every week—selection. A merciless selection. . . . Yes, you're lucky."

"Stop it! Be quiet!" I begged. "You can tell your stories tomorrow or on some other day."

They burst out laughing. They were not veterans for nothing.

"Are you scared? So were we scared. And there was plenty to be scared of in those days."

The old men stayed in their corner, dumb, motionless, haunted. Some were praying.

An hour's delay. In an hour, we should know the verdict—death or a reprieve.

And my father? Suddenly I remembered him. How would he pass the selection? He had aged so much. . . .

The head of our block had never been outside concentration camps since 1933. He had already been through all the slaughterhouses, all the factories of death. At about nine o'clock, he took up his position in our midst:

"Achtung!"[4]

There was instant silence.

"Listen carefully to what I am going to say." (For the first time, I heard his voice quiver.) "In a few moments the selection will begin. You must get completely undressed. Then one by one you go before the SS doctors. I hope you will all succeed in getting through. But you must help your own chances. Before you go into the next room, move about in some way so that you give yourselves a little color. Don't walk slowly, run! Run as if the devil were after you! Don't look at the SS. Run, straight in front of you!"

He broke off for a moment, then added:

"And, the essential thing, don't be afraid!"

Here was a piece of advice we should have liked very much to be able to follow.

I got undressed, leaving my clothes on the bed. There was no danger of anyone stealing them this evening.

Tibi and Yossi, who had changed their unit at the same time as I had, came up to me and said:

"Let's keep together. We shall be stronger."

Yossi was murmuring something between his teeth. He must have been praying. I had never realized that Yossi was a believer. I had even always thought the reverse. Tibi was silent, very pale. All the prisoners in the block stood naked

---

2. **Buna** (bo͞o′nə): a forced-labor camp in Poland, near the Auschwitz concentration camp.
3. **Kapos** (kä′pōz): the prisoners who served as foremen, or heads, of each building or cell block.
4. **Achtung!** (äKH-to͝ong′) *German:* Attention!

WORDS TO KNOW

stature (stăch′ər) *n.* a person's height

Customizing Instruction

Less Proficient Readers

To make sure students understand what kind of place the men are living in, ask them the following questions:

- What is the narrator's life like?

Possible Response: He works hard, gets little to eat, is cold, and lives in constant fear of death.

- What is everyone dreading?

Possible Response: Everyone is dreading a selection, which identifies the weak and ill prisoners who will be sent to the gas chambers.

Students Acquiring English

Students will likely have little difficulty with Wiesel's simple style. However, they may be troubled by the place-names and German and Yiddish words scattered throughout the story. Remind students to use the footnotes to find the meanings of words they do not understand.

Use **Spanish Study Guide** for additional support, pp. 131–133.

Gifted and Talented

In this selection, Elie Wiesel grapples with the ever-present specter of death in a Nazi concentration camp. Ask students to discuss how the constant threat of torture and death might affect a person or a group of people. Interested students may want to read further about the lives of Holocaust survivors. They may also want to read about the symptoms of post-traumatic stress disorder, which is experienced by many who live through wars or other extended catastrophic experiences.

BLOCK SCHEDULING: MANAGING TIME

If your schedule requires that you cover the lesson objectives in a shorter time, use . . .

- Preparing to Read, p. 593
- Thinking Through the Literature, p. 600
- Vocabulary in Action, p. 601

If you want to take advantage of longer class time, use . . .

- TE Teaching Options: Viewing and Representing, p. 594; Preteaching WORDS TO KNOW, pp. 596–597; Standardized Test Practice, p. 598
- Choices and Challenges and Author Activity, p. 601

Reading and Analyzing

Reading Skills and Strategies: COMPARING

Ask students to compare the attitude of the narrator and his friends before the selection and afterward, when they know their numbers weren't written down. Why did their emotions change?
Possible Responses: Wiesel was scared that he would be chosen to die. When he finds out he will live, he is so relieved he is temporarily giddy and happy. However, note that the happiness lasts only until he notices how the doomed men are taking the news.

Literary Analysis STYLE

A Ask students why they think the writer uses repetitive phrases and multiple sets of ellipses in this passage.
Possible Responses: Wiesel is trying to convey his anxious state of mind at the time. He is emphasizing his fears and his weak physical condition, which keep him from thinking clearly in this situation.

Active Reading CONNECTING

B Grief affects people in different ways. Ask students how they reacted to the news that the father's number was, in fact, written down after all. Ask them how they would react to the same news.
Possible Response: They might be frightened and saddened or very angry.

Literary Analysis: DICTION

C Remind students that diction, or word choice, is used by the author to create style. Ask students why Wiesel chooses to start every sentence in this paragraph with "he" or "his."
Possible Responses: He wants to focus on his father's words, and his father's stress and urgency; he wants to keep the focus on his father.

between the beds. This must be how one stands at the last judgment.

"They're coming!"

There were three SS officers standing around the notorious Dr. Mengele,[5] who had received us at Birkenau.[6] The head of the block, with an attempt at a smile, asked us:

"Ready?"

Yes, we were ready. So were the SS doctors. Dr. Mengele was holding a list in his hand: our numbers. He made a sign to the head of the block: "We can begin!" As if this were a game!

The first to go by were the "officials" of the block: *Stubenaelteste,*[7] Kapos, foremen, all in perfect physical condition of course! Then came the ordinary prisoners' turn. Dr. Mengele took stock of them from head to foot. Every now and then, he wrote a number down. One single thought filled my mind: not to let my number be taken; not to show my left arm.

There were only Tibi and Yossi in front of me. They passed. I had time to notice that Mengele had not written their numbers down. Someone pushed me. It was my turn. I ran without looking back. My head was spinning: you're too thin, you're too weak, you're too thin, you're good for the furnace. . . . The race seemed interminable. I thought I had been running for years. . . . You're too thin, you're too weak. . . . At last I had arrived exhausted. When I regained my breath, I questioned Yossi and Tibi: **A**

"Was I written down?"

"No," said Yossi. He added, smiling: "In any case, he couldn't have written you down, you were running too fast. . . ."

I began to laugh. I was glad. I would have liked to kiss him. At that moment, what did the others matter! I hadn't been written down.

Those whose numbers had been noted stood apart, abandoned by the whole world. Some were weeping in silence.

The SS officers went away. The head of the block appeared, his face reflecting the general weariness.

"Everything went off all right. Don't worry. Nothing is going to happen to anyone. To anyone."

Again he tried to smile. A poor, emaciated, dried-up Jew questioned him avidly in a trembling voice:

"But . . . but, *Blockaelteste,*[8] they did write me down!"

The head of the block let his anger break out. What! Did someone refuse to believe him!

"What's the matter now? Am I telling lies then? I tell you once and for all, nothing's going to happen to you! To anyone! You're wallowing in your own despair, you fool!"

The bell rang, a signal that the selection had been completed throughout the camp.

With all my might I began to run to Block 36. I met my father on the way. He came up to me:

"Well? So you passed?"

"Yes. And you?"

"Me too."

How we breathed again, now! My father had brought me a present—half a ration of bread 1
obtained in exchange for a piece of rubber, found

---

5. **Dr. Mengele** (mĕng′ə-lə): Josef Mengele, a German doctor who personally selected nearly half a million prisoners to die in gas chambers at Auschwitz. He also became infamous for his medical experiments on inmates.
6. **Birkenau** (bîr′kə-nou): a large section of the Auschwitz concentration camp.
7. ***Stubenaelteste*** (shtōō′bən-ĕl′tə-stə): a rank of Kapos; literally "elders of the rooms."
8. ***Blockaelteste*** (blôk′ĕl′tə-stə): a rank of Kapos; literally "elders of the building."

WORDS TO KNOW

notorious (nō-tôr′ē-əs) *adj.* having a widely known, usually very bad reputation; infamous
interminable (ĭn-tûr′mə-nə-bəl) *adj.* endless or seemingly endless
emaciated (ĭ-mā′shē-ā-tĭd) *adj.* extremely thin, especially as a result of starvation
emaciate *v.*

596

Teaching Options

Mini Lesson Preteaching Vocabulary

ANALOGIES Call students' attention to the list of WORDS TO KNOW. Remind them that sometimes they can understand the meaning of an unfamiliar word by examining the relationship in which the word is used in an analogy.
Instruction Write the following analogy on the board to demonstrate the strategy of using analogies to determine word meanings:

silence : quiet :: **din** : uproar

Ask a volunteer to summarize the relationship in the first pair of words.
Have students use the relationship from the first pair to infer the meaning of *din* in the second pair of words.
Possible Response: Since *silence* and *quiet* are synonyms, *din* and *uproar* must mean the same thing too. *Uproar* means "loud noise"; therefore, *din* must mean "loud noise" also.

at the warehouse, which would do to sole a shoe.

The bell. Already we must separate, go to bed. Everything was regulated by the bell. It gave me orders, and I automatically obeyed them. I hated it. Whenever I dreamed of a better world, I could only imagine a universe with no bells.

Several days had elapsed. We no longer thought about the selection. We went to work as usual, loading heavy stones into railway wagons. Rations had become more meager: this was the only change.

We had risen before dawn, as on every day. We had received the black coffee, the ration of bread. We were about to set out for the yard as usual. The head of the block arrived, running.

"Silence for a moment. I have a list of numbers here. I'm going to read them to you. Those whose numbers I call won't be going to work this morning; they'll stay behind in the camp."

And, in a soft voice, he read out about ten numbers. We had understood. These were numbers chosen at the selection. Dr. Mengele had not forgotten.

The head of the block went toward his room. Ten prisoners surrounded him, hanging onto his clothes:

"Save us! You promised . . . ! We want to go to the yard. We're strong enough to work. We're good workers. We can . . . we will . . . ."

He tried to calm them to reassure them about their fate, to explain to them that the fact that they were staying behind in the camp did not mean much, had no tragic significance.

"After all, I stay here myself every day," he added.

It was a somewhat feeble argument. He realized it, and without another word went and shut himself up in his room. 2

The bell had just rung.

"Form up!"

It scarcely mattered now that the work was hard. The essential thing was to be as far away as possible from the block, from the crucible of death, from the center of hell.

I saw my father running toward me. I became frightened all of a sudden.

"What's the matter?"

"THOSE WHOSE NUMBERS I CALL WON'T BE GOING TO WORK THIS MORNING; THEY'LL STAY BEHIND IN THE CAMP."

Out of breath, he could hardly open his mouth.

"Me, too . . . me, too . . . ! They told me to stay behind in the camp."

They had written down his number without his being aware of it. B

"What will happen?" I asked in anguish.

But it was he who tried to reassure me.

"It isn't certain yet. There's still a chance of escape. They're going to do another selection today . . . a decisive selection."

I was silent.

He felt that his time was short. He spoke quickly. He would have liked to say so many things. His speech grew confused; his voice choked. He knew that I would have to go in a few moments. He would have to stay behind alone, so very alone. C

"Look, take this knife," he said to me. "I don't need it any longer. It might be useful to you. And take this spoon as well. Don't sell them. Quickly!

Customizing Instruction

Students Acquiring English

1 Ask a volunteer to clarify the sentence "My father had brought me a present . . ."

Possible Response: Wiesel's father found a piece of rubber at the warehouse, and he traded it to another prisoner in exchange for some bread. The other prisoner could use the rubber to make a new sole, or bottom, for a worn shoe.

Less Proficient Readers

2 Ask students why the head of the block shuts himself in his room.

Possible Responses: He feels bad because he can't help the condemned men; he can't face the grief and broken hopes of the men who are going to die.

Exercises Read the following analogies. Ask students to use the relationships in the analogies to determine the meanings of the italicized words.

- heavy : weight :: tall : *stature*
- renowned : Mother Theresa :: *notorious* : Hitler
- *emaciated* : obese :: joy : sorrow
- infinity : *interminable* :: sunshine : bright

Possible Responses: *Heavy* is a characteristic of weight; therefore, *tall* must be a characteristic of stature. *Stature* probably means "height."

Renowned refers to Mother Theresa's positive reputation; therefore, *notorious* must describe Adolf Hitler's negative reputation. *Notorious* probably means "having a bad reputation."

Joy is the opposite of *sorrow,* so *emaciated* must be the opposite of obese. *Obese* means "extremely overweight," so *emaciated* probably means "extremely underweight."

Sunshine is bright, so you would expect that infinity is interminable. Infinity has no end, so *interminable* probably means "without end."

Use **Unit Four Resource Book,** p. 22.

A lesson on analogies appears on p. 263 in the Pupil's Edition.

Reading and Analyzing

Literary Analysis: TONE

A Ask students what contrast they perceive between the author's tone and the words he uses.

Possible Response: His tone is bitter or sorrowful, while his words speak of what is usually a wonderful gift, the gift of an inheritance. An inheritance is usually much more than a knife and a spoon. By referring to these items as an inheritance, the author is showing how few material goods a concentration camp allows its occupants.

Literary Analysis: DIALOGUE

B Ask students why Wiesel chose to use dialogue in this particular part of his speech.

Possible Response: Wiesel uses dialogue to help involve the audience in the story he is telling them. Perhaps he wants them to experience the conversation as if the boy he used to be still exists, so that the boy's experiences are easier to visualize.

Reading Skills and Strategies: QUESTIONING

C Encourage students to question Wiesel's statement, "Because if we forget, we are guilty, we are accomplices." What does the author mean?

Possible Responses: We might forget about those who died and how they died; if we forget, then we have erased their memory and helped the Nazis accomplish their goals; perhaps if we forget, it will make it easier for something like the Holocaust to happen again.

Go on. Take what I'm giving you!"

1 A The inheritance.

"Don't talk like that, Father." (I felt that I would break into sobs.) "I don't want you to say that. Keep the spoon and knife. You need them as much as I do. We shall see each other again this evening, after work."

He looked at me with his tired eyes, veiled with despair. He went on:

"I'm asking this of you. . . . Take them. Do as I ask, my son. We have no time. . . . Do as your father asks."

Our Kapo yelled that we should start.

The unit set out toward the camp gate. Left, right! I bit my lips. My father had stayed by the block, leaning against the wall. Then he began to run, to catch up with us. Perhaps he had forgotten something he wanted to say to me. . . .

But we were marching too quickly . . . Left, right!

We were already at the gate. They counted us, to the din of military music. We were outside.

The whole day, I wandered about as if sleepwalking. Now and then Tibi and Yossi would throw me a brotherly word. The Kapo, too, tried to reassure me. He had given me easier work today. I felt sick at heart. How well they were treating me! Like an orphan! I thought: even now, my father is still helping me.

I did not know myself what I wanted—for the day to pass quickly or not. I was afraid of finding myself alone that night. How good it would be to die here!

At last we began the return journey. How I longed for orders to run!

The military march. The gate. The camp.

I ran to Block 36.

Were there still miracles on this earth? He was alive. He had escaped the second selection. He had been able to prove that he was still useful. . . . I gave him back his knife and spoon. ❖

WERE THERE STILL MIRACLES ON THIS EARTH?

WORDS TO KNOW

din (dĭn) *n.* a jumble of loud noises

598

Teaching Options

Assessment Standardized Test Practice

RECOGNIZING AUTHOR'S PURPOSE

For some standardized tests, students will be asked to recognize the author's point of view and purpose. To provide students with some help in choosing the best purpose, read aloud or write on the board the following question:

Which of the following statements best describes Elie Wiesel's purpose for writing *Night?*

A. He wanted to inform the reader of the number of Jews imprisoned in concentration camps.

B. He wanted to promote the idea of genocide.

C. He wanted to describe the atrocities of the Holocaust in the hope of preventing such events from recurring.

D. He wanted to persuade individuals to lobby for peace in Europe.

Lead students through the process of choosing the best purpose of the selection. Consider each choice. Point out that **B** is incorrect. While **A** and **D** contain accurate information, the best response should include Wiesel's primary reason for writing *Night.* For that reason, **C** is the best choice.

LITERARY LINK

from Nobel Prize Acceptance Speech

Elie Wiesel

It is with a profound sense of humility that I accept the honor you have chosen to bestow upon me. I know: your choice transcends me. This both frightens and pleases me.

It frightens me because I wonder: do I have the right to represent the multitudes who have perished? Do I have the right to accept this great honor on their behalf? I do not. That would be presumptuous. No one may speak for the dead, no one may interpret their mutilated dreams and visions.

It pleases me because I may say that this honor belongs to all the survivors and their children, and through us, to the Jewish people with whose destiny I have always identified.

I remember: it happened yesterday or eternities ago. A young Jewish boy discovered the kingdom of night. I remember his bewilderment, I remember his anguish. It all happened so fast. The ghetto. The deportation. The sealed cattle car. The fiery altar upon which the history of our people and the future of mankind were meant to be sacrificed.

I remember: he asked his father: "Can this be true? This is the 20th century, not the Middle Ages. Who would allow such crimes to be committed? How could the world remain silent?"

And now the boy is turning to me: "Tell me," he asks. "What have you done with my future? What have you done with your life?"

And I tell him that I have tried. That I have tried to keep memory alive, that I have tried to fight those who would forget. Because if we forget, we are guilty, we are accomplices.

And then I explained to him how naive we were, that the world did know and remain silent. And that is why I swore never to be silent whenever and wherever human beings endure suffering and humiliation. We must always take sides. Neutrality helps the oppressor, never the victim. Silence encourages the tormentor, never the tormented.

Customizing Instruction

Less Proficient Readers

Have students describe what happened to the narrator and his father during and after the selections.

Possible Responses: The narrator passes the selection and survives, but his father's number is written down. Several days later his father is told to remain in camp with the rest of the selected men. However, he is not killed because he proves that he is still useful.

Students Acquiring English

1 Explain that an inheritance is property or money received at the bequest of someone who has died. In Europe, a traditional inheritance from one's father would include the family home, savings, and all personal property. Ask students why the narrator refers to the knife and spoon as his inheritance.

Possible Response: It is all that his father, who is probably about to die, has to give him.

GUIDING STUDENT RESPONSE

Connect to the Literature

1. What Do You Think?
Possible Response: a starving, gaunt boy, because the narration is so immediate that it feels as though the boy in the concentration camp is telling the story as it happens.

Comprehension Check

- Camp officials check on the health of the prisoners. Those who are not judged healthy enough to work are held back from work duty and killed.
- The SS doctors assume that anyone who can run fast is healthy and can therefore work.
- His father has survived the second selection and has not been killed.

Use Selection Quiz
Unit Four Resource Book, p. 23.

Think Critically

2. Possible Response: I was saddened and frightened.
3. Possible Responses: The prisoners are starving and frightened, and want the nightmare to end. Friendships and family are still important to them. The camp officials are cold-hearted and mean.
4. Possible Response: The tone moves between sarcastic irony and openly genuine emotion.
5. Possible Responses: Night is dark and frightening; at night, you cannot see what is happening, as many people did not see or believe the atrocities in the concentration camps.

Literary Analysis

Style Encourage students to focus on one paragraph at a time as they analyze their passages.

Thinking through the LITERATURE

Connect to the Literature

1. **What Do You Think?** What mental image did you form of the **narrator** while reading? Explain your thinking.

Comprehension Check

- What occurs at the "selection"?
- Why do the men in the block try to run as fast as they can in front of the SS doctors?
- What does Wiesel learn about his father at the end of the selection?

Think Critically

2. ACTIVE READING CONNECTING Refer to the notes you made in your READER'S NOTEBOOK. How would you describe this selection's effect on you?
3. What are your impressions of the people portrayed in this excerpt?
4. How would you describe Wiesel's **tone**?

   THINK ABOUT
   - his comment that the SS "gave us a fine New Year's gift"
   - his reference to the knife and spoon as his "inheritance"

5. Why do you think Wiesel called his book *Night?*

   THINK ABOUT
   - the circumstances he recounts
   - what the word *night* might symbolize
   - Wiesel's remarks on accepting the Nobel Peace Prize

Extend Interpretations

6. **Comparing Texts** What does the excerpt from Wiesel's Nobel Prize acceptance speech tell you about his motivation for writing *Night?*
7. **Points of Comparison** Fill in the chart that you began on page 592. What do you consider the worst circumstance in this portion of Wiesel's concentration camp experiences? Explain.
8. **Connect to Life** Do you agree with Wiesel's statement from his Nobel Prize acceptance speech that "neutrality helps the oppressor, never the victim"? Support your opinion.

Literary Analysis

STYLE **Style** is the way in which a literary work is written. Style refers not to what is said but to how it is said. Elements that contribute to a writer's personal style include the following: word choice, or **diction;** sentence length, structure, and variety; **tone, imagery,** and **dialogue.** In the following passage, for example, Wiesel relies on short sentences, simple words, and minimal description:

"Look, take this knife," he said to me. "I don't need it any longer. It might be useful to you. And take this spoon as well. Don't sell them. Quickly! Go on. Take what I'm giving you!"

The inheritance.

This simple and direct style heightens the drama of the event.

Paired Activity Choose a passage of five or six paragraphs from this excerpt and analyze it in terms of the elements of style mentioned above. Use a chart like the one started below. When you have finished, discuss how Wiesel's style affects your response to the events described. Why do you think Wiesel chose to tell about his experience in this manner?

Passage beginning	"I was no longer in the same block as my father."
Word choice	simple words; not many adjectives
Sentence length, structure, and variety	Short, simple sentences
Tone	
Imagery	
Dialogue	

Extend Interpretations

Comparing Texts Writing *Night* was a way of calling attention to the suffering and humiliation that occurred in the concentration camps. In his speech, Wiesel says that silence will only encourage the tormentor, and therefore he writes about what he experienced at the hands of the Nazis.

Points of Comparison Possible Response: being uncertain about his father's survival. His father's death would be a fact he could begin to deal with, but the uncertainty leaves him unable to know how to feel.

Connect to Life Yes. If no one calls attention to oppression, then no one will be able to stop it.

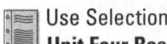

Writing Options

1. Holocaust Essay In recent years, some extremists have argued that the Holocaust never happened. Write a persuasive essay in which you argue against that position, using the excerpts from *Night* and Wiesel's speech as part of your evidence. Add additional factual support as needed. Place the essay in your **Working Portfolio.**

2. Interview Questions Make a list of questions you would ask Wiesel if you had the chance.

Inquiry & Research

1. Night Report Read all of *Night* to find out more about Wiesel's experiences during the Holocaust. Present an oral book report.

2. Film Review Obtain and view a video recording of *Schindler's List,* the 1993 film about a man who enabled more than a thousand Jews to escape the Holocaust. Then locate a review of the movie and compare your response to that of the reviewer. Share your ideas about the movie and its impact in a brief presentation.

Vocabulary in Action

EXERCISE: CONTEXT CLUES On your paper, indicate which of the Words to Know could best replace the italicized word or phrase in each sentence below.

1. To those in concentration camps, the war seemed *as if it would never end.*
2. Auschwitz was *famous in a negative way* for torture and mass murder.
3. Those not killed immediately were fed little and soon grew *incredibly skinny.*
4. Backbreaking labor bent once-tall prisoners to half their *size.*
5. The *clashing background sound* of German patriotic music tore at the prisoners' ears.

WORDS TO KNOW			
	din	interminable	stature
	emaciated	notorious	

Building Vocabulary
For a lesson on affixes, see page 856.

Elie Wiesel

1928–

Other Works
Dawn
The Accident
A Beggar in Jerusalem
Legends of Our Time
A Jew Today

Victim of War Elie Wiesel was born in the town of Sighet (sē′gĕt), Transylvania, an area of Romania that the Germans made part of Hungary when they overran both nations in 1940, during World War II. Cut off by the war from most communication, the 15,000 Jews of Sighet had no idea where they were going when, in the spring of 1944, the Nazis ordered their deportation and shipped them on a cattle train to Auschwitz in Poland. Wiesel's mother and one of his three sisters were murdered there. In 1945, Wiesel and his father were sent to Buchenwald concentration camp in Germany; sadly, Wiesel's father died of starvation and dysentery less than three months before the camp was liberated by the Allies.

Holocaust Survivor After the war, Wiesel settled in France. He studied at the Sorbonne and worked as a writer and journalist, but he made a vow to write nothing about his concentration camp experience for ten years. "I didn't want to use the wrong words," he later explained. Wiesel's 900-page autobiographical account was first written in Yiddish, the language of his childhood, and published in 1956. He condensed the work to just over 100 pages and published it in French as *La Nuit* in 1958. Two years later, the book was published in English as *Night.* A U.S. citizen since 1963, Wiesel has worked tirelessly to call attention to human rights violations in countries around the world, including South Africa, Cambodia, Bangladesh, and Bosnia. He was awarded the Nobel Peace Prize in 1986.

Author Activity

Advocate for Peace Read about Wiesel as a human rights advocate. What were the activities that caused him to be awarded the Nobel Peace Prize? With your classmates, discuss your findings.

Writing Options

1. **Holocaust Essay** Emphasize that supporting opinions and evidence are important in writing such as this. Students should use Wiesel's speech and story as eyewitness support for their arguments.
2. **Interview Questions** Encourage students to ask questions about both his time during the war and the work he has done in more recent years.

Author Activity

Advocate for Peace Encourage students to compare Wiesel's beliefs with his actions. How does he support his belief that people should always oppose injustice?

Vocabulary in Action

1. interminable
2. notorious
3. emaciated
4. stature
5. din

Mini Lesson Grammar

MODIFIERS: ADJECTIVES AND ADVERBS Remind students that modifiers describe or limit other words in a sentence. Adjectives modify nouns and pronouns; adverbs modify verbs, adjectives, and other adverbs. Write the following sentence on the chalkboard.

The boy quickly ran past the notorious doctor.

Underline *ran,* as shown. Have students identify its modifier *(quickly).* Explain that since *ran* is a verb, the word that modifies it is an adverb.

Underline *doctor,* as shown. Have students identify its modifier *(notorious).* Explain that since *doctor* is a noun, the word that modifies it is an adjective.

Use **Grammar Transparencies and Copymasters,** p. 70, for more practice.

Use McDougal Littell's ***Language Network,*** Chapter 9, for more instruction and practice in modifiers.

OVERVIEW

Objectives

1. understand and appreciate a **memoir (Literary Analysis)**
2. **connect** to selection **(Active Reading)**

Summary

The narrator of "Farewell to Manzanar" is part of a Japanese-American family whose father is unjustly imprisoned during World War II. After being relocated for about a month in Boyle Heights, the narrator's family and many others are evacuated to cold, barren, and dust-blown Manzanar. The narrator, who was a young girl at the time, looks back at the daily and continual indignities that camp life brought: unpalatable food, hastily erected and drafty barracks, lack of privacy, inadequate numbers of blankets, and clownish clothing. As she recreates life during those early days at Manzanar, she punctuates her grim tale with the moments of humor and resourcefulness that made life more tolerable and humane. She also recounts in some detail the discomfort and embarrassment—especially for the oldest and most modest of women—of rows of toilets with no walls between them. This was a humiliation that, like all the others, they learned to endure.

Thematic Link

Unjustly perceived as an enemy by a nation at war, this courageous family learned to **face the enemy,** the difficulties inflicted on them by a fearful government.

5-Minute Warm-Up

Daily Language SkillBuilder

Have students **proofread** the display sentences on page 541l and write them correctly. The sentences also appear on Transparency 20 of **Grammar Transparencies and Copymasters.**

PREPARING to *Read*

from Farewell to Manzanar

Memoir by JEANNE WAKATSUKI HOUSTON AND JAMES D. HOUSTON

"We woke early, shivering and coated with dust..."

Connect to Your Life

Civil Rights What do you know about the relocation of Japanese Americans in the United States during World War II? Share your knowledge with your classmates. Why do you think many Japanese Americans were forced to move, while German Americans and Italian Americans did not generally suffer the same consequences?

Build Background

Japanese Internment When Japan's attack on Pearl Harbor drew the United States into World War II in December 1941, people on the West Coast of the United States began to fear that those of Japanese descent living in their communities might secretly aid Japan's war effort. Despite the fact that there was no evidence of Japanese-American espionage or sabotage, and that most of the Japanese had become U.S. citizens or legal residents, racist suspicion fueled public policy.

In February 1942, President Franklin D. Roosevelt signed an order that cleared the way for the removal of Japanese people from their homes. Virtually the entire Japanese-American population of the West Coast—almost 120,000 people—was bused to ten inland "relocation" centers in the western states and Arkansas, where they were interned, or confined, for the duration of the war. With sometimes only 24 hours' notice, they were forced to abandon their homes, farms, and businesses and most of their possessions, most of which they were never able to reclaim.

Jeanne Wakatsuki was seven years old and living in Ocean Park, California, when the United States entered the war. The selection is an excerpt from the memoir that Jeanne Wakatsuki Houston wrote with her husband three decades after the war. At the opening of this selection, her family is living in Los Angeles, after having been forced to move twice by the government.

Focus Your Reading

LITERARY ANALYSIS | MEMOIR A **memoir** is a form of nonfiction in which the writer recalls significant events and people in his or her life. This passage comes from the memoir you are about to read:

> ***I remember my brothers sitting around the table talking very intently about what we were going to do, how we would keep the family together. They had seen how quickly Papa was removed, and they knew now that he would not be back for quite a while.***

As you read the following selection, consider what you learn about the writer's personal perspective of events.

ACTIVE READING | CONNECTING Just as you did with the excerpt from *Night,* pay attention to your own reactions to this selection. Note what comes to your mind as you are reading, and consider how you would respond if you were in a similar situation. The fact that these events occurred here in the United States may cause you to think differently about them than if they had occurred on another continent.

READER'S NOTEBOOK As you read, keep notes of your reactions to this piece, and spend a few minutes afterward writing your general reflections.

LESSON RESOURCES

UNIT FOUR RESOURCE BOOK, pp. 25–26

ASSESSMENT RESOURCES

Formal Assessment, pp. 107–110

Teacher's Guide to Assessment and Portfolio Use

Test Generator

SKILLS TRANSPARENCIES AND COPYMASTERS

Literary Analysis

- Types of Nonfiction, T4 (for Paired Activity, p. 613)

Reading and Critical Thinking

- Locating Information Using Databases and the Internet, T34 (for Inquiry & Research I, p. 614)

Grammar

- Comparative and Superlative Modifiers, C156 (for Mini Lesson, p. 608)

Vocabulary

- Suffixes, C64 (for Mini Lesson, p. 604)

Writing

- Writing Structure, T6, T9, T11 (for Writing Option 1, p. 614)
- Levels of Language, T12 (for Writing Option 2, p. 614)
- The Uses of Dialogue, T24 (for Writing Option 2, p. 614)

Communications

- Evaluation Matrix: Film/Video, T7 (for Inquiry & Research 3, p. 614)

INTEGRATED TECHNOLOGY

Video: Literature in Performance

- *Mitsuye and Nellie.* See **Video Resource Book,** pp. 17–23.

Visit our website:
www.mcdougallittell.com

from
FAREWELL TO MANZANAR

JEANNE WAKATSUKI HOUSTON AND JAMES D. HOUSTON

TEACHING THE LITERATURE

Customizing Instruction

Less Proficient Readers

Tell students to keep in mind that this memoir was written 30 years after the events it describes. Explain that the narrator of the memoir is an adult even though she is describing herself as a child. Help students distinguish between the adult narrator's observations and the memories of a seven-year-old child.

Set a Purpose Have students read to find out what happens to Jeanne and her family at Manzanar.

Students Acquiring English

Students who have experienced the process of immigrating or relocating to this country might want to write about their experiences in their journals. Invite volunteers to share their experiences with the class.

Use **Spanish Study Guide** for additional support, pp. 134–136.

Gifted and Talented

Have students compare the U.S. internment camps for Japanese Americans to Nazi concentration camps or to Russia's Siberian prison camps. How does a country justify jailing specific groups of people? Is this a legitimate defense measure? What do these camps say about the nations that create them? Encourage students to think of alternative ways to ensure national security during times of crisis.

BLOCK SCHEDULING: MANAGING TIME

If your schedule requires that you cover the lesson objectives in a shorter time, use . . .

- Preparing to Read, p. 602
- Thinking Through the Literature, p. 613

If you want to take advantage of longer class time, use . . .

- TE Teaching Options: Vocabulary Strategy, p. 604; Viewing and Representing, pp. 606, 614; Cross Curricular Link, p. 607; Standardized Test Practice, p. 610; Informal Assessment, p. 612
- Choices & Challenges and Author Activity, p. 614

Reading and Analyzing

Reading Skills and Strategies: PREVIEW
Have students preview the selection. Discuss with them the Build Background feature on page 602, and have them make predictions about the memoir's setting and characters. Before students begin reading, give them a brief summary of the memoir. Ask how the selection might be linked to the theme "Facing the Enemy."

Literary Analysis MEMOIR
Encourage students to complete a time line as they read the memoir. Next to each event, have them write the narrator's personal perspective or emotional reaction to the event. Explain that although a memoir is written in the first person, it may be more matter-of-fact than a story. Students may have to infer the narrator's perspective instead of relying on direct statements.

Use **Unit Four Resource Book** p. 26 for more practice.

Active Reading CONNECTING
Lead students in a discussion based on their responses to the Connect to Your Life feature on p. 602 before they begin reading the memoir. Ask them how they would feel if they were forced to move to an internment camp because of their race or national origin.
Possible Responses: angry; sad; betrayed; confused

Use **Unit Four Resource Book** p. 25 for more practice.

★

1 The American Friends Service[1] helped us find a small house in Boyle Heights, another minority ghetto, in downtown Los Angeles, now inhabited briefly by a few hundred Terminal Island refugees. Executive Order 9066 had been signed by President Roosevelt, giving the War Department authority to define military areas in the western states and to exclude from them anyone who might threaten the war effort.
2 There was a lot of talk about internment, or moving inland, or something like that in store for all Japanese Americans. I remember my brothers sitting around the table talking very intently about what we were going to do, how we would keep the family together. They had seen how quickly Papa was removed, and they knew now that he would not be back for quite a while. Just before leaving Terminal Island, Mama had received her first letter, from Bismarck, North Dakota. He had been imprisoned at Fort Lincoln, in an all-male camp for enemy aliens.

3 Papa had been the patriarch.[2] He had always decided everything in the family. With him gone, my brothers, like councilors in the absence of a chief, worried about what should be done. The ironic thing is, there wasn't much left to decide. These were mainly days of quiet, desperate waiting for what seemed at the time to be inevitable. There is a phrase the Japanese use in such situations, when something difficult must be endured.

You would hear the older heads, the Issei,[3] telling others very quietly, *"Shikata ga nai"* (It cannot be helped). *"Shikata ga nai"* (It must be done).

Mama and Woody went to work packing celery for a Japanese produce dealer. Kiyo and my sister May and I enrolled in the local school, and what sticks in my memory from those few weeks is the teacher—not her looks, her remoteness. In Ocean Park my teacher had been a kind, grandmotherly woman who used to sail with us in Papa's boat from time to time and who wept the day we had to leave. In Boyle Heights the teacher felt cold and distant. I was confused by all the moving and was having trouble with the classwork, but she would never help me out. She would have nothing to do with me. 4

This was the first time I had felt outright hostility from a Caucasian. Looking back, it is easy enough to explain. Public attitudes toward the Japanese in California were shifting rapidly. In the first few months of the Pacific war, America was on the run. Tolerance had turned to distrust and irrational fear. The hundred-year-old tradition of anti-Orientalism on the west coast soon resurfaced, more vicious than ever. Its result became clear about a month later, when we were told to make our third and final move.

Tolerance had turned to distrust and irrational fear.

The name Manzanar meant nothing to us when we left Boyle Heights. We didn't know where it was or what it was. We went because the government ordered us to. And, in the case of my older brothers and sisters, we went with a certain amount of relief. They had all heard stories of Japanese homes being attacked, of

1. **American Friends Service:** a Quaker charity often aiding political and religious refugees and other displaced persons.
2. **patriarch** (pā′trē-ärk′): the man who heads his family or clan.
3. **Issei** (ēs′sā′): people born in Japan who immigrate to the United States.

Teaching Options

Mini Lesson Vocabulary Strategy

SUFFIXES Remind students that sometimes they can determine the meaning of an unfamiliar word by examining its parts. Word parts include the root word, or base, and affixes. A suffix is an affix placed after the root to modify the root's meaning. Many suffixes change the part of speech of the root. The suffix has an inherent meaning as well. Write the suffix *-ment* on the chalkboard.

Instruction

- Elicit from students that this suffix changes the root word to a noun.
- Have students think of words with this suffix. List their responses on the chalkboard. Examples include *statement, internment,* and *development.*
- Have students identify the root word for each of the words they thought of. *(state, intern, develop)*
- Then have a student look up *-ment* in a dictionary and read aloud its meanings: 1) concrete result, object, or agent of an action; 2) concrete means or instrument of an action; 3) action or process; 4) place an action occurs; 5) state or condition

beatings in the streets of California towns. They were as frightened of the Caucasians as Caucasians were of us. Moving, under what appeared to be government protection, to an area less directly threatened by the war seemed not such a bad idea at all. For some it actually sounded like a fine adventure.

Our pickup point was a Buddhist church in Los Angeles. It was very early, and misty, when we got there with our luggage. Mama had bought heavy coats for all of us. She grew up in eastern Washington and knew that anywhere inland in early April would be cold. I was proud of my new coat, and I remember sitting on a duffel bag trying to be friendly with the Greyhound driver. I smiled at him. He didn't smile back. He was befriending no one. Someone tied a numbered tag to my collar and to the duffel bag (each family was given a number, and
5 that became our official designation until the camps were closed), someone else passed out box lunches for the trip, and we climbed aboard.

I had never been outside Los Angeles County, never traveled more than ten miles from the coast, had never even ridden on a bus. I was full of excitement, the way any kid would be, and wanted to look out the window. But for the first few hours the shades were drawn. Around me other people played cards, read magazines, dozed, waiting. I settled back, waiting too, and finally fell asleep. The bus felt very secure to me. Almost half its passengers were immediate relatives. Mama and my older brothers had succeeded in keeping most of us together, on the same bus, headed for the same camp. I didn't realize until much later what a job that was. The strategy had been, first, to have everyone living in the same district when the evacuation began, and then to get all of us included under the same family number, even though names had been changed

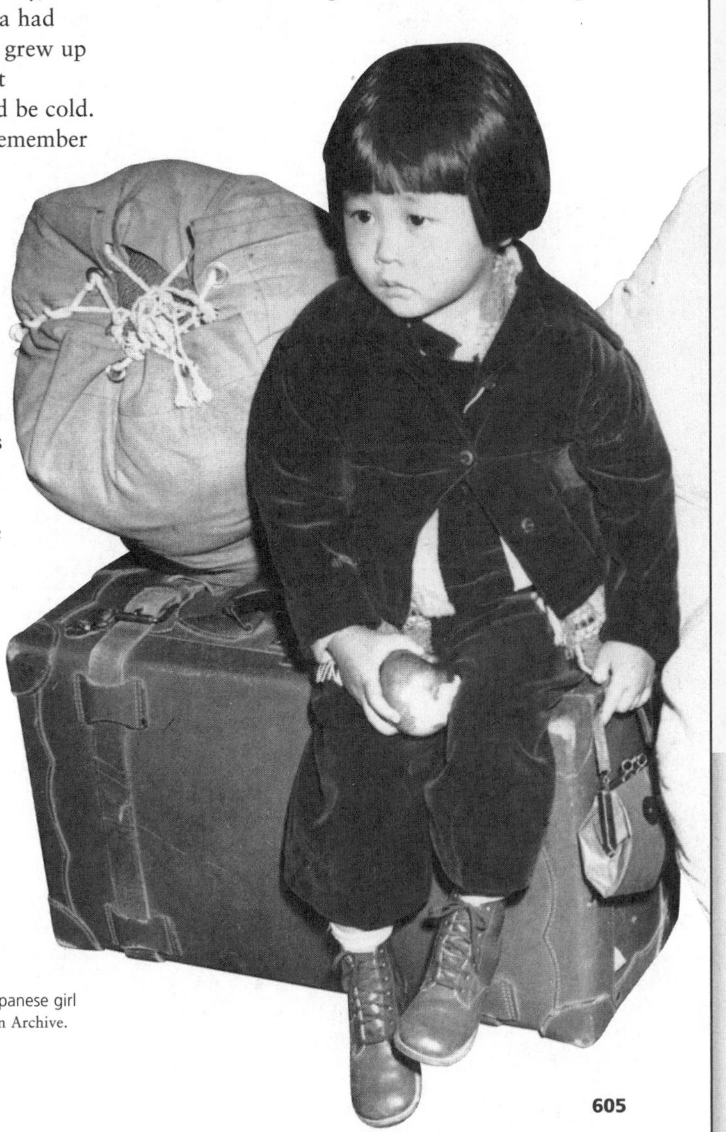

Surrounded by her family's belongings, a young Japanese girl awaits transfer to a relocation center. The Bettmann Archive.

Customizing Instruction

Less Proficient Readers
Have students identify the basic facts of the memoir.

- Who is the memoir about?
  Answer: the Wakatsuki family
- What is the memoir about?
  Answer: the family's relocation from their home to an internment camp
- Where does the action take place?
  Answer: in Boyle Heights, on a bus, in Manzanar
- When does the action take place?
  Answer: during World War II

Students Acquiring English
Help students use context clues to determine the meaning of the following words and phrases:

1 *ghetto*—an inner-city living area, usually with substandard housing

2 *internment*—confinement

3 *councilors*—members of a council, who act as a group in deciding the best advice and direction for the group. Explain to students the difference between *councilors* and *counselors* (those who act alone in giving others advice or direction).

4 *what sticks in my memory*—what I remember

5 *designation*—label or title

Practice Have students use a dictionary to look up the meanings of the following suffixes. Then have them think of at least two words for each suffix.

1. *-ness*
Answer: quality of being
Possible Responses: kindness, happiness, togetherness

2. *-ism*
Answer: act, practice, process, property, or doctrine
Possible Responses: fascism, capitalism, pessimism

3. *-(i)ty*
Answer: act, quality, state, or condition
Possible Responses: reality, frailty, indignity

4. *-ance/-ence*
Answer: act, condition, or fact
Possible Responses: permanence, occurrence, radiance

5. *-tion*
Answer: action, result, or state
Possible Responses: situation, designation, evacuation

Use **Vocabulary Transparencies and Copymasters,** p. 64, for more exercises.

A lesson on suffixes appears on p. 856 in the Pupil's Edition.

Reading and Analyzing

Active Reading CONNECTING

Invite students to tell about the first long trip they can remember when they were younger, perhaps one when they felt uncertain about the destination or outcome. What thoughts did they have about it at the time?

Reading Skills and Strategies: VISUALIZING

A Have students visualize the narrator's arrival at Manzanar. What words does she use to describe this scene?
Possible Responses: "yellow swirl"; "blurred, reddish setting sun"; "billowing flurry of dust and sand"; "rows of black barracks"

Reading Skills and Strategies: CLARIFYING

B Have students reread the paragraph that begins "We rode all day." Ask them what this description of the dust and sand suggests about living conditions in Manzanar.
Possible Responses: Everything will always be covered with dust; Manzanar is in the middle of a desert.

Literary Analysis MEMOIR

C Ask how the narrator's adult perspective of arriving at Manzanar differs from her childhood perspective.
Possible Response: As an adult, she realizes how lucky she was to have come with most of her immediate family to Manzanar; as a child, she took this situation for granted. As an adult, the narrator knows that the dust in Manzanar will be troublesome, but as a child it gives the scene a sense of mystery. The adult narrator understands the silence of the adults on the bus—they are horrified at the sight of the primitive, chaotic camp; as a child, she was happy to have finally arrived and did not recognize the prisonlike appearance of the camp.

The 550-acre Manzanar internment camp was located 200 miles northeast of Los Angeles at the foot of the Sierra Nevada. When the war ended in 1945, the camp's staff buildings and barracks were quickly disassembled and auctioned off. AP/Wide World Photos.

by marriage. Many families weren't as lucky as ours and suffered months of anguish while trying to arrange transfers from one camp to another.

A B 1 We rode all day. By the time we reached our destination, the shades were up. It was late afternoon. The first thing I saw was a yellow swirl across a blurred, reddish setting sun. The bus was being pelted by what sounded like splattering rain. It wasn't rain. This was my first look at something I would soon know very well, a billowing flurry of dust and sand churned up by the wind through Owens Valley.[4] 1

We drove past a barbed-wire fence, through a gate, and into an open space where trunks and sacks and packages had been dumped from the baggage trucks that drove out ahead

4. **Owens Valley:** referring to the valley of the Owens River in south central California west of Death Valley, where Manzanar was built. The once lush and green valley had become dry and deserted in the 1930s after water was diverted to an aquaduct supplying Los Angeles.

Teaching Options

Mini Lesson — Viewing and Representing

Instruction Have students examine the photograph for details. Have them make a list of the different objects in the scene and guess what their uses are.
Possible Responses: Very few of the objects have obvious uses. The metal barrel might hold water, building supplies, or even trash. The wooden barrel farther down the road might be used for the same purposes. The large tank at the left of the photograph could be a propane or other fuel tank. The tall pole is probably for electricity, in which case, the fact that it is bare implies that none of the houses have electric power.
Application Ask students how they would feel if they arrived at the scene in this photograph, knowing that they were going to live there for quite some time.
Possible Responses: horrified; depressed; outraged

of us. I could see a few tents set up, the first rows of black barracks, and beyond them, blurred by sand, rows of barracks that seemed to spread for miles across this plain. 2 People were sitting on cartons or milling around, with their backs to the wind, waiting to see which friends or relatives might be on this bus. As we approached, they turned or stood up, and some moved toward us expectantly. But inside the bus no one stirred. No one waved or spoke. They just stared out the windows, ominously silent. I didn't understand this. Hadn't we finally arrived, our whole family intact? I opened a window, leaned out, and yelled happily. "Hey! This whole bus is full of Wakatsukis!"

Outside, the greeters smiled. Inside there was an explosion of laughter, hysterical, tension-breaking laughter that left my brothers choking and whacking each other across the shoulders. C

We had pulled up just in time for dinner. The mess halls weren't completed yet. An outdoor chow line snaked around a half-finished building that broke a good part of the wind. 3 They issued us army mess kits, the round metal kind that fold over, and plopped in scoops of canned Vienna sausage, canned string beans, steamed rice that had been cooked too long, and on top of the rice a serving of canned apricots. The Caucasian servers were thinking that the fruit poured over rice would make a good dessert. 4 Among the Japanese, of course, rice is never eaten with sweet foods, only with salty or savory foods. Few of us could eat such a mixture. But at this point no one dared protest. It would have been impolite. I was horrified when I saw the apricot syrup seeping through my little mound of rice. I opened my mouth to complain. My mother jabbed me in the back to keep quiet. We moved on through the line and joined the others squatting in the lee[5] of half-raised walls, dabbing courteously at what was, for almost everyone there, an inedible concoction. 5

After dinner we were taken to Block 16, a cluster of fifteen barracks that had just been finished a day or so earlier—although finished was hardly the word for it. 6 The shacks were built of one thickness of pine planking covered with tarpaper. They sat on concrete footings, with

5. lee: the side sheltered from the wind.

Customizing Instruction

Students Acquiring English

1 Have students use context clues to determine that *pelted* means "struck."

2 Help students understand that the idiom *milling around* means "wandering without purpose."

3 Help students understand that a mess hall is like a school cafeteria. Then explain that *chow line* is a slang expression for people waiting in line for food.

4 The people running the camp did not know that Japanese do not like rice served with sweet foods. Ask students to tell about times they have felt that their customs were not known, misunderstood, or blatantly ignored.

5 Have students use context clues to determine that *dabbing* means "poking or patting gently" and that *concoction* means "mixture." Explain that *concoction* carries unpleasant connotations when applied to food.

6 Explain that *barracks* is a term for military housing. Most barracks provide minimal shelter from the elements and have only basic furnishings.

Cross Curricular Link History

ASIANS IN AMERICA The United States has a long history of discriminatory policies toward Asians and Asian Americans. The Chinese Exclusion Act of 1882 prohibited the immigration of Chinese laborers for 10 years. The act was renewed 10 years later, and in 1902 Chinese immigration was suspended indefinitely. (This law was not repealed until 1943.) Other laws prevented Chinese Americans from testifying in court, legalized separate schools for Asians, and sought to keep Asians from owning land. Ironically, in the late 1800s and early 1900s, the United States encouraged Japanese immigration, partly as a way of curtailing Chinese immigration. By 1920, these Japanese immigrants and their descendants controlled more than 10 percent of California's farmland. Some people resented Japanese Americans for this reason, and their resentment was compounded by Japan's alliance with Germany in World War II. Ultimately, this fear and suspicion led to the internment of people of Japanese descent during the war.

FAREWELL TO MANZANAR 607

Reading and Analyzing

Literary Analysis: SETTING

Have students analyze the relevance of the setting to the text's meaning. Ask them to describe the barracks.

Possible Response: The buildings are made of thin pine and covered with tarpaper. Each is divided into six units; each unit has an oil stove and a single light bulb. There are many cracks and knotholes in the buildings that let in cold air, sand, and dust.

Then ask them how the narrator's description of the setting affects their overall impression of the memoir and the narrator.

Possible Response: The vivid description emphasizes that this memoir is about actual events. It also increases the reader's sympathy for the narrator and her family.

Reading Skills and Strategies: QUESTIONING

A Encourage students to ask questions as they read. After they finish reading the section that ends on p. 608, have them write down at least four questions that they have about the events and people described in the memoir.

Possible Responses: How does the family improve their barracks? How many children are in the family? Why were some men sent to prison camps and others sent to the internment camps? How long does Jeanne's family stay in the camp?

Then discuss students' questions as a class. Remind students to look for answers to their questions as they continue reading.

about two feet of open space between the floorboards and the ground. Gaps showed between the planks, and as the weeks passed and the green wood dried out, the gaps widened. Knotholes gaped in the uncovered floor.

Each barracks was divided into six units, sixteen by twenty feet, about the size of a living room, with one bare bulb hanging from the ceiling and an oil stove for heat. We were assigned two of these for the twelve people in our family group; and our official family "number" was enlarged by three digits—16 plus the number of this barracks. We were issued steel army cots, two brown army blankets each, and some mattress covers, which my brothers stuffed with straw.

The first task was to divide up what space we had for sleeping. Bill and Woody contributed a blanket each and partitioned off the first room: one side for Bill and Tomi, one side for Woody and Chizu and their baby girl. Woody also got the stove, for heating formulas.

The people who had it hardest during the first few months were young couples like these, many of whom had married just before the evacuation began, in order not to be separated and sent to different camps. Our two rooms were crowded, but at least it was all in the family. My oldest sister and her husband were shoved into one of those sixteen-by-twenty-foot compartments with six people they had never seen before—two other couples, one recently married like themselves, the other with two teenage boys. Partitioning off a room like that wasn't easy. It was bitter cold when we arrived, and the wind did not abate. All they had to use for room dividers were those army blankets, two of which were barely enough to keep one person warm. They argued over whose blanket should be sacrificed and later argued about noise at night—the parents wanted their boys asleep by 9:00 p.m.—and they continued arguing over matters like that for six months, until my sister and her husband left to harvest sugar beets in Idaho. It was grueling work up there, and wages were pitiful, but when the call came through camp for workers to alleviate the wartime labor shortage, it sounded better than their life at Manzanar. They knew they'd have, if nothing else, a room, perhaps a cabin of their own.

That first night in Block 16, the rest of us squeezed into the second room—Granny; Lillian, age fourteen; Ray, thirteen; May, eleven; Kiyo, ten; Mama; and me. I didn't mind this at all at the time. Being youngest meant I got to sleep with Mama. And before we went to bed I had a great time jumping up and down on the mattress. The boys had stuffed so much straw into hers, we had to flatten it some so we wouldn't slide off. I slept with her every night after that until Papa came back.

We woke early, shivering and coated with dust that had blown up through the knotholes and in through the slits around the doorway. During the night Mama had unpacked all our clothes and heaped them on our beds for warmth. Now our cubicle looked as if a great laundry bag had exploded and then been sprayed with fine dust. A skin of sand covered the floor. I looked over Mama's shoulder at Kiyo, on top of his fat mattress, buried under jeans and overcoats and sweaters. His eyebrows were gray, and he was starting to giggle. He was looking at me, at my gray eyebrows and coated hair, and pretty soon we were both giggling. I looked at Mama's face to see if she thought Kiyo was funny. She lay very still next to me on our mattress, her eyes scanning everything—bare rafters, walls, dusty kids—scanning slowly, and I think the mask of her face would have cracked had not Woody's voice just then come at us through the wall. He was rapping on the planks as if testing to see if they were hollow. **A**

Teaching Options

Mini Lesson Grammar

COMPARATIVE AND SUPERLATIVE MODIFIERS Tell students that in making comparisons, correct modifiers help them to be clear and effective communicators. Remind them that modifiers are either adjectives or adverbs. Review with students the rules for making comparisons with modifiers. Remind them that the comparative form compares two things, while the superlative form compares three or more.

Model

They were <u>quiet</u> at times.
The girl was <u>quieter</u> than her brother.
Her mother was the <u>quietest</u> of all.

Rule

For shorter, commonly used modifiers of one and sometimes two syllables:

- Add *-er* to compare to something else.
- Add *-est* to compare to everything else.

Model

Looking back, some things seem <u>comical.</u>
Her brothers were <u>more comical</u> than she.
She remembers Woody as the <u>most comical</u> of all her brothers.

Rule

For modifiers of two or more syllables:

- Use *more* or *less* to compare to something else.
- Use *most* or *least* to compare to everything else.

"Hey!" he yelled. "You guys fall into the same flour barrel as us?"

"No," Kiyo yelled back. "Ours is full of Japs."

All of us laughed at this.

"Well, tell 'em it's time to get up," Woody said. "If we're gonna live in this place, we better get to work."

He gave us ten minutes to dress, then he
2 came in carrying a broom, a hammer, and a sack full of tin can lids he had scrounged somewhere. Woody would be our leader for a while now, short, stocky, grinning behind his mustache. He had just turned twenty-four. In later years he would tour the country with Mr. Moto, the Japanese tag-team wrestler, as his sinister assistant Suki—karate chops through the ropes from outside the ring, a chunky leg reaching from under his kimono to trip up Mr. Moto's foe. In the ring
3 Woody's smile looked sly and crafty; he hammed it up. Offstage it was whimsical, as if some joke were bursting to be told.

"Hey, brother Ray, Kiyo," he said. "You see these tin can lids?"

"Yeah, yeah," the boys said drowsily, as if going back to sleep. They were both young versions of Woody.

4 "You see all them knotholes in the floor and in the walls?"

They looked around. You could see about a dozen.

Woody said, "You get those covered up before breakfast time. Any more sand comes in here through one of them knotholes, you have to eat it off the floor with ketchup."

"What about sand that comes in through the cracks?" Kiyo said.

Woody stood up very straight, which in itself was funny, since he was only about five-foot-six.

"Don't worry about the cracks," he said. "Different kind of sand comes in through the cracks."

He put his hands on his hips and gave Kiyo a sternly comic look, squinting at him through one eye the way Papa would when he was asserting his authority. Woody mimicked Papa's voice: "And I can tell the difference. So be careful."

During the night Mama had unpacked all our clothes and heaped them on our beds for warmth.

The boys laughed and went to work nailing down lids. May started sweeping out the sand. I was helping Mama fold the clothes we'd used for cover, when Woody came over and put his arms around her shoulder. He was short; she was even shorter, under five feet.

He said softly, "You okay, Mama?"

She didn't look at him, she just kept folding clothes and said, "Can we get the cracks covered too, Woody?"

Outside the sky was clear, but icy gusts of wind were buffeting our barracks every few minutes, sending fresh dust puffs up through the floorboards. May's broom could barely keep up with it, and our oil heater could scarcely hold its own against the drafts.

"We'll get this whole place as tight as a barrel, Mama. I already met a guy who told me where they pile all the scrap lumber."

"Scrap?"

"That's all they got. I mean, they're still building the camp, you know. Sixteen blocks left to go. After that, they say maybe we'll get some stuff to fix the insides a little bit."

Customizing Instruction

Students Acquiring English

1 Have students use context clues to determine the meaning of *alleviate.*
Answer: relieve

2 Explain that *scrounge* means "to collect by foraging."

3 Help students understand that *whimsical* means "fanciful."

Less Proficient Readers

4 Point out Woody's words. Explain that standard English is usually the most acceptable method of written or formal communication. However, people often use nonstandard English in casual conversations. Writers may use nonstandard English in dialogue to make characters seem more realistic. Ask students what words Woody might have used if he were being careful about his choice of words.
Possible Responses: He would say "those knotholes" or "the knotholes" rather than "them knotholes."

Multiple Learning Styles

Visual Learners
To help students understand the setting, have them construct diagrams or dioramas of the barracks.

Model

The conditions were <u>bad</u>.
Some things were <u>worse</u> than others.
The latrines were the <u>worst</u> of all for Mama.

Rule

Some modifiers have irregular forms, including *good* and *bad.*

Adverbs also have comparative and superlative forms. As with longer adjectives, most adverbs form the comparative with *more* or *less* and the superlative with *most* or *least.*

Practice Have the class form eight groups. Assign each group one page of the memoir (consider pages 606 and 607 as one page). Have groups find comparative and superlative modifiers. Tell them to write an additional sentence for each modifier they find in which the other degree of comparison is used and spelled correctly.

Use **Grammar Transparencies and Copymasters,** p. 156, for more practice.

Use McDougal Littell's ***Language Network,*** Chapter 9, for more instruction in comparative and superlative modifiers.

Reading and Analyzing

Literary Analysis: AUTOBIOGRAPHY

Ask students how they think a memoir is both similar to and different from an autobiography.

Possible Response: They are similar in that both are written from the author's personal insights and observations. An autobiography usually encompasses most of the author's life, while a memoir can cover just a short period of time.

Active Reading CONNECTING

A Ask students if they have ever had to wear clothes that did not fit properly. How did they feel? Was it embarrassing? Encourage them to imagine how the people in the camp might have felt about wearing army surplus clothing from World War I—clothing that was almost 30 years old, ugly, and ill-fitting.

Reading Skills and Strategies: EVALUATING

B Ask students why the narrator includes the description of the sanitary arrangements at Manzanar. What does this description add to the memoir?

Possible Response: This description graphically demonstrates the horrible conditions of the camp. It helps readers understand what day-to-day existence was like at Manzanar. It also emphasizes that none of the amenities that most Americans take for granted (food, clothing, shelter, indoor plumbing) were satisfactory in the camps.

Her eyes blazed then, her voice quietly furious. "Woody, we can't live like this. Animals live like this."

It was hard to get Woody down. He'd keep smiling when everybody else was ready to explode. Grief flickered in his eyes. He blinked it away and hugged her tighter. "We'll make it better, Mama. You watch."

We could hear voices in other cubicles now. Beyond the wall Woody's baby girl started to cry.

"I have to go over to the kitchen," he said, "see if those guys got a pot for heating bottles. That oil stove takes too long—something wrong with the fuel line. I'll find out what they're giving us for breakfast."

"Probably hotcakes with soy sauce," Kiyo said, on his hands and knees between the bunks.

"No." Woody grinned, heading out the door. "Rice. With Log Cabin syrup and melted butter."

I don't remember what we ate that first morning. I know we stood for half an hour in cutting wind waiting to get our food. Then we took it back to the cubicle and ate huddled around the stove. Inside, it was warmer than when we left, because Woody was already making good his promise to Mama, tacking up some ends of lath[6] he'd found, stuffing rolled paper around the door frame.

Trouble was, he had almost nothing to work with. Beyond this temporary weather stripping, there was little else he could do. Months went by, in fact, before our "home" changed much at all from what it was the day we moved in—bare floors, blanket partitions, one bulb in each compartment dangling from a roof beam, and open ceilings overhead so that mischievous boys like Ray and Kiyo could climb up into the rafters and peek into anyone's life.

The simple truth is the camp was no more ready for us when we got there than we were ready for it. We had only the dimmest ideas of what to expect. Most of the families, like us, had moved out from southern California with as much luggage as each person could carry. Some old men left Los Angeles wearing Hawaiian shirts and Panama hats and stepped off the bus at an altitude of 4000 feet, with nothing available but sagebrush and tarpaper to stop the April winds pouring down off the back side of the Sierras.[7]

The War Department was in charge of all the camps at this point. They began to issue military surplus from the First World War—olive-drab knit caps, earmuffs, peacoats, canvas leggings. Later on, sewing machines were shipped in, and one barracks was turned into a clothing factory. An old seamstress took a peacoat of mine, tore the lining out, opened and flattened the sleeves, added a collar, put arm holes in and handed me back a beautiful cape. By fall, dozens of seamstresses were working full-time transforming thousands of these old army clothes into capes, slacks, and stylish coats. But until that factory got going and packages from friends outside began to fill out our wardrobes, warmth was more important than style. I couldn't help laughing at Mama walking around in army earmuffs and a pair of wide-cuffed, khaki-colored wool trousers several sizes too big for her. Japanese are generally smaller than Caucasians, and almost all these clothes were oversize. They flopped, they dangled, they hung.

It seems comical, looking back; we were a band of Charlie Chaplins[8] marooned in the 1

6. **lath** (lăth): a thin strip of wood.

7. **Sierras** (sē-ĕr′əz): referring to the Sierra Nevada mountain range in eastern California.

8. **Charlie Chaplins:** referring to actor and director Charlie Chaplin, who portrayed a tramp in baggy clothing in several comedy films of the 1920s and 1930s.

Teaching Options

Assessment Standardized Test Practice

READING COMPREHENSION QUESTIONS On many standardized tests, students are required to answer questions that measure reading comprehension. To help students prepare for such assessment, have them read the excerpt below and choose the answer that best completes the sentence.

"... I'll find out what they're giving us for breakfast."

"Probably hotcakes with soy sauce," Kiyo said, on his hands and knees between the bunks.

"No." Woody grinned, heading out the door. "Rice. With Log Cabin syrup and melted butter."

Woody believes that

A. they will be served rice with syrup and butter for breakfast.

B. it is better to laugh about what they are served than to complain.

C. Caucasians are so stupid they don't know the difference between hotcakes and rice.

D. Kiyo wants to have hotcakes with soy sauce for breakfast.

Lead students through the choices. Remind them that dessert the previous night had been rice with apricots, but the Japanese traditionally serve rice only with salty or savory foods. **A** is not the

California desert. But at the time, it was pure chaos. That's the only way to describe it. The evacuation had been so hurriedly planned, the camps so hastily thrown together, nothing was completed when we got there, and almost nothing worked.

I was sick continually, with stomach cramps and diarrhea. At first it was from the shots they gave us for typhoid, in very heavy doses and in assembly-line fashion: swab, jab, swab, *Move along now,* swab, jab, swab, *Keep it moving.* That knocked all of us younger kids down at once, with fevers and vomiting. Later, it was the food that made us sick, young and old alike. The kitchens were too small and badly ventilated. Food would spoil from being left out too long. That summer, when the heat got fierce, it would spoil faster. The refrigeration kept breaking down. The cooks, in many cases, had never cooked before. Each block had to provide its own volunteers. Some were lucky and had a professional or two in their midst. But the first chef in our block had been a gardener all his life and suddenly found himself preparing three meals a day for 250 people.

The simple truth is the camp was no more ready for us when we got there than we were ready for it.

"The Manzanar runs" became a condition of life, and you only hoped that when you rushed to the latrine, one would be in working order.

3 That first morning, on our way to the chow line, Mama and I tried to use the women's latrine in our block. The smell of it spoiled what little appetite we had. Outside, men were working in an open trench, up to their knees in muck—a common sight in the months to come. Inside, the floor was covered with excrement, and all twelve bowls were erupting like a row of tiny volcanoes.

Mama stopped a kimono-wrapped woman stepping past us with her sleeve pushed up against her nose and asked, "What do you do?"

"Try Block Twelve," the woman said, grimacing. "They have just finished repairing the pipes."

It was about two city blocks away. We followed her over there and found a line of women waiting in the wind outside the latrine. We had no choice but to join the line and wait with them.

Inside it was like all the other latrines. Each block was built to the same design just as each of the ten camps, from California to Arkansas, was built to a common master plan. It was an open room, over a concrete slab. The sink was a long metal trough against one wall, with a row of spigots for hot and cold water. Down the center of the room twelve toilet bowls were arranged in six pairs, back to back, with no partitions. My mother was a very modest person, and this was going to be agony for her, sitting down in public, among strangers.

One old woman had already solved the problem for herself by dragging in a large cardboard carton. She set it up around one of the bowls, like a three-sided screen. OXYDOL was printed in large black letters down the front. I remember this well, because that was the soap we were issued for laundry; later on, the smell of it would permeate these rooms. The upended carton was about four feet high. The old woman behind it wasn't much taller. When she stood, only her head showed over the top.

Customizing Instruction

Students Acquiring English

1 Tell students that *marooned* means "stranded."

Less Proficient Readers

Check students' comprehension with the following questions:

- How does Jeanne's family try to improve their unit in the barracks?
  Answer: They hammer tin can lids over knotholes and stuff lath and rolled-up paper into the cracks. They also hang up blankets to divide the room into two parts.
- Why does Woody have to go to the kitchen?
  Answer: The oil stove in their unit takes too long to heat his baby's formula, so he wants to find a pot for heating bottles.
- What makes the children sick at first?
  Answer: typhoid vaccinations
- What makes everyone sick later?
  Answer: food that has spoiled or been prepared improperly
- How does the elderly woman remain modest while having to use a public latrine?
  Answer: She uses a large cardboard box to make a little wall around her toilet.

Gifted and Talented

Have students brainstorm possible ways to improve the conditions at Manzanar. Remind them that they have limited supplies and money. Arrange students in groups of four and have them work on an improvement plan. Then have each group present its plan to the class. Encourage the use of visual aids.

answer because if Woody really thought that they would be served rice with syrup and butter, he would not be grinning. **C** is not the answer because most Americans are familiar with hotcakes and can distinguish them from rice. Kiyo makes the remark about hotcakes and soy sauce because dessert was so awful, not because he actually wants to eat that; **D** is not the answer. Woody is joking about the food to make Kiyo laugh instead of complain. The correct answer is **B**.

Reading and Analyzing

Active Reading CONNECTING

A Discuss with students how humans can take power away from others. For example, war and slavery are human institutions that create helpless victims. Have students think of a time in which someone made them feel powerless. Encourage them to write about this experience in their journals.

Literary Analysis: CONFLICT

Remind students that internal conflicts occur within a person. External conflicts occur between a person and another person or an outside force. Have students identify at least one conflict in this memoir and tell whether it is internal or external.

Possible Responses: external: the Wakatsuki family vs. nature; internal: Mama's politeness vs. her outrage at the conditions in Manzanar

Literary Analysis MEMOIR

B Ask students what they learn about the writer's perceptions from the last sentence.

Possible Responses: She is much more resentful of her treatment than she has previously revealed; above all else, the lack of privacy was the worst condition at Manzanar.

She was about Granny's age. With great effort she was trying to fold the sides of the screen together. Mama happened to be at the head of the line now. As she approached the vacant bowl, she and the old woman bowed to each other from the waist. Mama then moved to help her with the carton, and the old woman said very graciously, in Japanese, "Would you like to use it?"

Happily, gratefully, Mama bowed again and said, "*Arigato*" (Thank you). "*Arigato gozaimas*" (Thank you very much). "I will return it to your barracks."

"Oh, no. It is not necessary. I will be glad to wait."

The old woman unfolded one side of the cardboard, while Mama opened the other; then she bowed again and scurried out the door.

Those big cartons were a common sight in the spring of 1942. Eventually sturdier partitions appeared, one or two at a time. The first were built of scrap lumber. Word would get around that Block such and such had partitions now, and Mama and my older sisters would walk halfway across the camp to use them. Even after every latrine in camp was screened, this quest for privacy continued. Many would wait in line at night. Ironically, because of this, midnight was often the most crowded time of all.

Like so many of the women there, Mama never did get used to the latrines. It was a humiliation she just learned to endure: *shikata ga nai,* this cannot be helped. She would quickly subordinate her own desires to those of the family or the community, because she knew cooperation was the only way to survive. At the same time, she placed a high premium on personal privacy, respected it in others and insisted upon it for herself. Almost everyone at Manzanar had inherited this pair of traits from the generations before them who had learned to live in a small, crowded country like Japan. Because of the first, they were able to take a desolate stretch of wasteland and gradually make it livable. But the entire situation there, especially in the beginning—the packed sleeping quarters, the communal mess halls, the open toilets—all this was an open insult to that other, private self, a slap in the face you were powerless to challenge. ❖

Teaching Options

Assessment Informal Assessment

You can informally assess students' understanding of the selection by having them write a letter from the narrator to her father. The letter should describe life in Manzanar and give news about the family. Tell students to include as many details from the selection as possible, while keeping in mind the narrator's age and the feelings she describes in the memoir.

RUBRIC

3 **Full Accomplishment** The letters demonstrate a full understanding of the memoir. They are written in a voice appropriate for the narrator and for the audience (the narrator's father) and contain many details from the selection.

2 **Substantial Accomplishment** The letters demonstrate a substantial understanding of the memoir and an awareness of their audience. They contain several details from the selection.

1 **Little or Partial Accomplishment** The letters demonstrate little understanding of the memoir. They contain few or no details from the selection and have an inappropriate narrative voice.

Connect to the Literature

1. **What Do You Think?** What is your impression of the Wakatsuki family?

Comprehension Check
- How did the Wakatsukis get to Manzanar?
- What kind of housing were they given?
- Why did Mama have to borrow the cardboard box?

Think Critically

2. **ACTIVE READING CONNECTING** Look at the notes you made in your READER'S NOTEBOOK. How would you characterize your response to the piece? How do you think you would have reacted if you had been brought to Manzanar?

3. What do you learn about the family from their reactions upon waking up in the dust-covered barracks?

THINK ABOUT
- Mama's reaction
- Woody's reaction
- the family's solution to the problem

4. What do you think was the most difficult aspect of the camp experience for the people there? Cite evidence from the selection when giving your answer.

5. How would you describe the author's **tone** in this excerpt? Cite passages that illustrate that tone. What effect does the tone have on your perception of the family's experience at Manzanar?

6. In the foreword to *Farewell to Manzanar,* Jeanne Wakatsuki Houston says, "It has taken me 25 years to reach the point where I could talk openly about Manzanar." Why do you think it took so long for her to be able to talk about her experience?

Extend Interpretations

7. **Connect to Life** Do you think that a forced internment, like that experienced by the Wakatsuki family, could happen in America today? Why or why not?

8. **Points of Comparison** Fill in the chart you created on page 592 with details from this selection. Then compare this chart with the one you created for *Night.* For each category, jot down notes about the similarities and differences between the two selections and the experiences of the authors.

Literary Analysis

MEMOIR A **memoir** is a form of nonfiction in which a person recalls significant events or people in his or her life. In some cases, *memoir* is simply another word for **autobiography,** a work that tells about the personal experiences of the author. Most memoirs share the following characteristics:

- They are usually structured as first-person narratives in the writer's own voice.
- Though some names may be changed to protect privacy, memoirs are generally true accounts of actual events.
- Despite their personal nature, memoirs may deal with newsworthy events with a significance beyond the writers' own lives.
- Unlike strictly historical accounts, memoirs often include the writers' feelings and opinions about historical events, giving insight into the impact of history on people's lives.

Paired Activity With a partner, review the selection. One of you should write down statements that convey information that might be found in a history book about Japanese relocation. The other should record notes that convey information about the author's personal experience of events. Record your information. Then discuss the following questions: What does a memoir offer that cannot usually be found in a history text? How reliable is a memoir in recording information about events in history?

GUIDING STUDENT RESPONSE

Connect to the Literature

1. **What Do You Think?**
Many students may say that the Wakatsuki family is very brave and resourceful.

Comprehension Check
- The family got to Manzanar on a bus.
- The barracks provided extremely small living areas for several people. They were poorly made and inadequate for the extreme weather.
- The cardboard box gave Mama privacy while she used the public toilet.

Use Selection Quiz in **Unit Four Resource Book,** p. 27.

Think Critically

2. Possible Responses: Some students may say that they were shocked that the United States treated people so terribly and that they would not have reacted as bravely as the Wakatsukis. Other students may say that they would have been able to endure the conditions at Manzanar.
3. Possible Response: They each had different reactions, but all worked together to be resourceful and to improve the conditions. Mama was dejected and almost cried. Woody cracked jokes to make the family feel better.
4. Some students may say that the unsanitary conditions would have been worst, citing the broken latrines and the constant sickness. Others may refer to the lack of privacy, citing the public toilets and newlyweds sharing a room with strangers. Still others might say it was the weather, citing the constant dust and extreme temperatures.
5. Some students may say that the tone is distanced and thoughtful. Others may say that it is quietly angry and resentful, pointing to the closing sentence of the last paragraph. Others may say that it is humorous and light, pointing to the frequent jokes.
6. Possible Response: When it was over, Jeanne wanted to move on with her life and not think about it anymore. She may have been too ashamed and horrified to discuss it.

Extend Interpretations

Connect to Life Some students may say that the civil rights laws passed in the 1960s would prevent such an occurrence in the United States, or that our society today is more accepting and less suspicious of other cultures and would not consider such an action. Others might believe that forced internment is quite possible, even today.

Points of Comparison Similarities include the problems with cold and sickness that existed in both camps. Differences include the ages of the narrators at the time of the experience, the much harsher conditions at Buna, and the more emotional, immediate tone of *Night.*

Literary Analysis

Memoir Student responses should include an evaluation of the credibility of information sources including how the writers' motivation may affect credibility. Student responses should demonstrate an understanding of the fact that memoirs are more personal and subjective than most history texts.

Writing Options

1. **Political Letter** Tell students that a letter to a senator or representative would be a formal letter. Review the parts of a letter with them and emphasize the importance of correct grammar, spelling, and punctuation. Remind students to use objective data as evidence of the conditions.
2. **Manzanar Dialogue** Suggest that students choose a scene that was especially moving or important to them. After students have written their dialogues, have them meet in small groups to read aloud their work. Encourage group members to give each other praise and constructive criticism.

Inquiry & Research

1. **Photo Exhibit** Suggest that students learn more about Dorothea Lange and look up subject entries such as "Japanese Internment" or "World War II and Japanese Americans" in the library catalog or on an Internet browser. You may want to have students complete this activity with a partner.
2. **Reparations Bill** Have students research available government documents, information on Japanese Americans since 1988, and the *Readers' Guide* for information in periodicals. Suggest that they interview members of their communities who had experience with the Reparations Act.
3. **Video Viewing** Have students summarize their understanding of the Wakatsuki family's experience. Then have them describe what the video adds to their understanding.

Author Activity

Encourage students to select different chapters. Have them comment on both the writing style and their personal feelings about the events that are described. Have the reports given in the order that the chapters appear.

Choices & CHALLENGES

Writing Options

1. **Political Letter** Imagine that you are at Manzanar at the same time as the Wakatsukis. Write a persuasive letter to your senator or representative, explaining the circumstances of your relocation and telling him or her what you think should be done about the situation. Place the letter in your **Working Portfolio.**
2. **Manzanar Dialogue** The book *Farewell to Manzanar* was adapted for film. Choose a scene from the selection that you think would translate well into the visual medium of film. Then write a dialogue based upon details from the selection.

Inquiry & Research

1. **Photo Exhibit** Photographer Dorothea Lange took a series of photographs at Manzanar during its operation. Look for her photos and others, both from Manzanar and from other Japanese relocation centers. Photocopy the pictures from books or download them from the Internet and create your own exhibit.
2. **Reparations Bill** In 1988 Congress passed the Civil Liberties Act, which contained an apology to Japanese Americans who had been interned and agreed to pay them $20,000 apiece. Find out more about this bill, the events that led up to it, and the consequent response from Japanese Americans.
3. **Video Viewing** Watch the excerpt from *Mitsuye and Nellie*, a documentary about the experience of Asian immigrants during World War II, which is supplied by McDougal Littell. How does the video add to your understanding of what Jeanne Wakatsuki Houston and her family endured at Manzanar?

VIDEO **Literature in Performance**

Jeanne Wakatsuki Houston

1934–

Other Works
Don't Cry, It's Only Thunder (with Paul G. Hensler)
Beyond Manzanar and Other Views of Asian-American Womanhood

James D. Houston

1933–

Other Works
Between Battles
Gig
Californians: Searching for the Golden State

Coming to Terms The daughter of a Japanese father and a Japanese-American mother, Jeanne Wakatsuki Houston and her mother, brothers, and sisters were among the first to be interned at Manzanar and among the last to be released. In the foreword to her book *Farewell to Manzanar,* Houston says that it took her 25 years to be able to talk about what happened to her and her family in the internment camp. Writing the book, she says, was "a way of coming to terms with the impact these years have had on my entire life." The book, coauthored with her writer husband, James D. Houston, won instant attention and critical praise when it was published in 1973; three years later, the Houstons collaborated on an award-winning screenplay based on the book.

A Writerly Pair The Houstons have spent most of their lives on the West Coast and have written mainly about their home state of California. James Houston served in the U.S. Air Force from 1957 to 1960 and went on to become an award-winning writer of novels and short stories as well as nonfiction.

Author Activity

Read two or three chapters from *Farewell to Manzanar* to find out more about what happened to the Wakatsuki family. Give a brief oral report.

Mini Lesson: Viewing and Representing

Instruction Before showing the video *Mitsuye and Nellie*, write the following questions on the chalkboard:

- How do the characters cope with stressful situations?
- What evidence do you see of both Japanese and American culture?
- How do the characters reflect some of the feelings and attitudes the authors of *Farewell to Manzanar* write about?
- Is the purpose of this video to inform, to entertain, or to advertise?
- What images, sounds, camera angles, and other aspects of filmmaking do the creators use to get their main idea and message across?

Divide the class into five groups. Tell students to take notes during the video in response to the questions. Explain that they will discuss their answers in their groups after viewing the film.

Application After the video is shown, have groups discuss their answers to the questions. Then assign one of the questions to each group. Have group members collaborate on a media presentation that communicates both the question and their answers. Encourage students to use different media in their presentations, including artwork, sound, and video clips.

In writing assessments, you will often be asked to develop your own ideas by synthesizing what you have learned from literary works like *Night* and *Farewell to Manzanar.* You are now going to practice writing an essay with this kind of focus.

PART 1 Reading the Prompt

When you are asked to write in response to a prompt, you should read the entire prompt carefully. Then you should read through it again, looking for key words.

Writing Prompt

In *Night,* Elie Wiesel brought to light the terrible experience of life in a concentration camp. *Farewell to Manzanar* exposed a long-neglected episode from the same time period—the forced internment of Japanese Americans. In an essay that synthesizes what you have learned (1) from your readings, discuss what lessons can be drawn from the injustices exposed by these (2) two works. Why is it important, as Wiesel himself said, "to keep memory alive"? Support (3) your ideas by using examples from both works. (4)

STRATEGIES IN ACTION

1. I will need to **synthesize,** or pull together, what I know, based on my readings.
2. My answer needs to do two things. First, I must **draw lessons** from these works.
3. Second, I need to **connect** the Wiesel quote to the lessons that I draw.
4. I need **examples** or **quotations** from the works to support my opinion.

PART 2 Planning a Synthesis Essay

- Analyze the two selections, paying attention to what they have in common and what sets them apart. (Refer to the charts you completed on pages 600 and 613. You may combine them as shown.)
- Make generalizations based upon what you learned from both works. Come up with your own ideas or insights.
- Clearly show the relationship between your ideas and the selections. Use evidence from the selections as support.

	Night	Farewell to Manzanar
Cause:		
How Victims Are Treated:		
Psychological Effects:		
How People Cope:		
Author's Purpose:		
Lessons Learned:		

PART 3 Drafting Your Essay

Introduction Begin by introducing your topic and summarizing the lessons to be learned. You may use Wiesel's quote here or later in the paper.

Organization Analyze one work at a time to show how it illustrates the lessons that you have identified, or discuss one lesson at a time and explain how both works illustrate it. Use signal words, such as *similarly, also, like, but, unlike,* and *while,* to call attention to similarities and differences between the two selections. Use examples from the works.

Conclusion Wrap up your essay by summing up the lessons you've drawn and emphasizing their importance.

PART 1 Reading the Prompt

Model the process of reading a prompt:

- Read through the entire prompt.
- List key words of the assignment on the board. ("synthesize," "draw lessons," "connect," "examples or quotations")
- Define each key word using Strategies in Action to show how students can restate the prompts in their own words.

PART 2 Planning a Synthesis Essay

- Students can use the charts they have been filling out for the two memoirs (referenced on page 592).
- Suggest that students write Wiesel's quote "to keep the memory alive" above the column of lessons learned. This will help students maintain a focus and reflect on evidence from these two memoirs.
- By adding a column to their graphics for lessons learned, students can articulate conclusions they might use in their essays. Have them highlight and make additional notes about the generalizations they wish to emphasize in their essays.

PART 3 Drafting Your Essay

Introduction Explain to students that opening an essay with a quote can be an effective strategy for an introduction, especially when the topic is highly emotional. Beginning with Wiesel's own words will arouse readers' emotions and engage them with the essay.

Organization Suggest that students create a scratch outline for each of the two organizational strategies described, one in which they focus on the works one at a time and another in which they focus on the lessons one at a time. After seeing how both organizational structures work, students will be in a better position to choose the most effective structure.

Conclusion An effective way to summarize an essay is to generate an emotional response in readers. Suggest that students again use a quote, perhaps this time from the memoir by the Houstons.

Objectives
- write a Persuasive Essay
- use a written text as a model for writing
- revise a draft to write effective introductions
- correct sentence fragments

Introducing the Workshop

A Persuasive Essay Explain to students that persuasive writing influences readers to support a point of view or to take action. This requires supporting an argumentative position with reasons and supporting those reasons with evidence. It also involves acknowledging objections and reasoning to overcome those objections.

Have students name examples of persuasion they have encountered—in political campaigns, on newspaper editorial pages, in school and community politics. What characteristics or patterns can they identify in persuasive discourse? Point out that in writing a persuasive essay, students will present a reasoned argument to persuade readers to accept a point of view on a controversial issue.

Basics in a Box

B Using the Graphic Like the architectural structure in the graphic, a successful persuasive essay consists of a claim that is supported by solid pillars of supporting evidence. The graphic offers suggestions for elements that students can use to draft an effective essay.

C Presenting the Rubric To better understand the assignment, students can refer to the Standards for Writing a Successful Persuasive Essay. You may wish to discuss with them the complete rubric, which describes several levels of proficiency.

Use McDougal Littell's ***Language Network,*** Chapter 22, for more instruction on writing a persuasive essay.

To engage students visually, use **Power Presentation** 7, Persuasive Essay.

Writing Workshop — Persuasive Essay

Presenting a convincing argument . . .

A **From Reading to Writing** The authors of "Night" and "Farewell to Manzanar" describe terrible injustices that they experienced. You, too, may want to take a stand against injustice or express an unpopular opinion that you believe in strongly. One way to convince others that you are right is to write a **persuasive essay** in which you present and defend your position. Many editorials, proposals, petitions, and advertisements also use persuasive techniques to convince their readers.

For Your Portfolio

WRITING PROMPT Write a persuasive essay on an issue you feel strongly about.

Purpose: To persuade
Audience: Classmates, friends, family, or community members

Basics in a Box

B

Persuasive Essay at a Glance

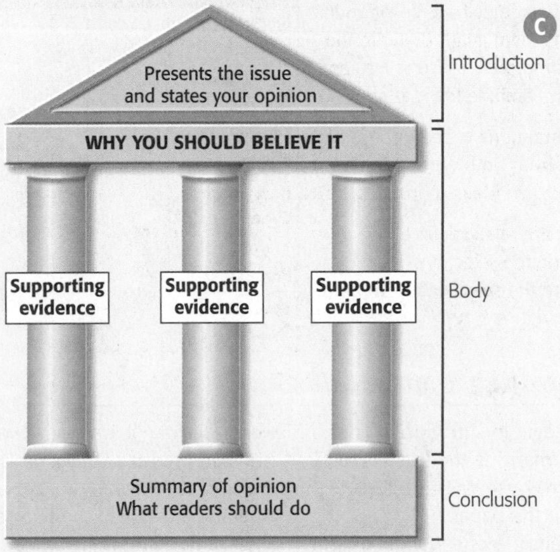

C **RUBRIC Standards for Writing**

A successful persuasive essay should
- state the issue and your position on it clearly in the introduction
- be geared to the audience you're trying to convince
- support your position with facts, statistics, and reasons
- answer possible objections to your position
- show clear reasoning
- conclude with a summary of your position or a call to action

LESSON RESOURCES

USING PRINT RESOURCES
Unit Four Resource Book
- Prewriting, p. 29
- Drafting, p. 30
- Peer Response, pp. 31–32
- Revising, Editing, and Proofreading, p. 33
- Student Models, pp. 34–39
- Rubric, p. 40

Writing Transparencies and Copymasters
- Writing Process Transparencies, pp. 1–4
- Writing Template Copymasters, p. 30

USING MEDIA RESOURCES
LaserLinks
Writing Springboards
See Teacher's SourceBook p. 64 for bar codes.
Writing Coach CD-ROM
Visit our website:
www.mcdougallittell.com

Analyzing a Student Model

Jessica Marie Johnson
Whitney Young High School

RUBRIC IN ACTION

Support School Uniforms

Clothes consciousness is out. School uniforms are in. And, though I know most other students don't agree, I think uniforms are the best thing that could happen to our nation's youth and to the educational system as a whole.

1 States the issue and her position in the introduction

Walking through the halls of some schools used to be like attending a fashion show. Baggy jeans, splashy cropped tops, khaki trousers, and patterned sweaters created a whirlwind of color and styles. Not anymore. School uniforms and uniform dress codes have taken over in many schools and are being considered in many others. A great number of students are rebelling, claiming that wearing a uniform violates their freedom of expression. One student called it "like being in jail," and another complained that "if you wear decent clothes, you shouldn't have to wear uniforms." Some students show their discontent by deliberately dressing sloppily or wearing unapproved colors. I don't think these students have thought the issue through clearly.

D

2 Gives details and quotations to support her statements

I agree that an important goal of education is to foster individuality and creativity, but I don't agree that uniforms limit these qualities. Most schools have a four-day uniform policy that allows students to wear modified uniforms or outfits of their choice on one day—often Friday, as in the business world. In addition, many public schools have adopted a dress code rather than a strict uniform policy. The dress code sets up guidelines for students' clothing choices.

3 Counters objections with facts

In fact, I think that wearing uniforms actually contributes to the development of creativity and individuality. By removing the focus from externals such as clothes, uniforms allow each student to express his or her personality in more important and meaningful ways. Students naturally form cliques in an effort to belong, and students with the same look instinctively seek each other out. With the clothing barrier out of the way, students begin to respond to one another as individuals and to form friendships based on similar outlooks and interests. They begin to get along better.

4 Develops her arguments with clear reasoning

Teaching the Lesson

Analyzing the Model

D "Support School Uniforms"

The student model presents a reasoned argument supporting the claim that schools should adopt a uniform policy.

Explain that the writer is taking a controversial position in addressing her fellow students, an audience that more than likely disagrees with her position.

Have students read the model, then discuss the Rubric in Action. Point out key words and phrases in the student model that correspond to the elements mentioned in the Rubric in Action.

1. Point out that the writer begins by boldly stating her position. Discuss an alternative approach in which she begins first by presenting facts related to the issue before announcing her position.
2. Ask students why they think the writer begins by presenting the opposing view.
   Possible Response: By presenting the opposing view, she is able to set a stage to counter objections logically.
3. Have students state the facts used to counter the opposition's objection.
   Possible Response: A four-day uniform policy preserves individuality.
4. Ask students to explain how the transitional phrase at the start of this paragraph is working.
   Possible Response: The transitional phrase "In fact" indicates that the writer is continuing her previously stated ideas about creativity and individuality.

Mini Lesson: Viewing and Representing

PICTURING TEXT STRUCTURE

Instruction The reasons and facts contained in the persuasive essay are vital in convincing the audience to adopt the writer's argumentative position. However, the way this information is structured and organized is also a necessary component of the essay's effectiveness.

Activity Have students work in pairs to analyze the text structure of the student model by constructing a graphic organizer. The graphic should illustrate how the student writer organized her proposal. Students might begin by rereading the model and jotting down the main idea in each paragraph. From their notes they can construct a graphic organizer that shows how the ideas relate to each other as well as to the whole.

States the writer's position on school uniforms

↓

Presents opposing arguments and refutes them with reasons, statistics, and examples

↓

Presents reasons, quotations, and examples to support writer's position

↓

Summarizes reasons and calls for action

5 Have students suggest an alternative approach for this paragraph based on the other options listed.

Possible Response: The writer could use a quotation from a school administrator or, better yet, a student who supports the claim that school uniforms have had a positive effect.

6 Ask students to describe what other benefits would result from students wearing uniforms.

Possible Response: Positive effects at school would also be reflected at home. Students and parents would also save money since uniforms are more economical than most other clothing students would buy.

As a result, discrimination, jealousy, and even violence and gang activity decrease. According to *Education Week*, in Long Beach, California, the first school district in the nation to establish a uniform code, there was a 34-percent decrease in assault and battery cases, a 5l percent decrease in physical fights, and a 32-percent decrease in suspensions in grades K–8 after the code was established.

> ❺ This writer uses statistics to support her argument.
> **Other Options:**
> • Use quotations.
> • Present an anecdote.

Uniforms will have other beneficial effects on education and on the school as a whole. Wearing the same clothes will encourage students to focus on the reason they are in school in the first place. And that is to learn. When they can no longer compete in the fashion arena, they will begin to concentrate less on their appearance and more on academics.

Uniforms also tend to instill in students a sense of community and pride in their school. A parent at one school said, "When a student wears a uniform, it's her job to be the best student she can possibly be." Wearing neat and businesslike clothing will carry over into students' schoolwork. Uniforms help keep students in line.

In addition to improving the atmosphere at school, uniforms could also have a positive effect at home. Parents often complain about how much money and time their teens spend buying clothes. School uniforms are much less expensive than regular clothes, and they are quick and easy to buy. Most major chain stores now carry uniforms, some even made by brand-name clothing manufacturers. Some schools even make uniforms available to students very cheaply—from $15 to $30 for a pair of pants and a shirt—far less than a typical outfit.

> ❻ Uses transitions to maintain a flow of connected ideas

School uniforms promote personal and social growth and contribute to a healthy learning atmosphere. And they're economical as well. Schools across the nation should implement uniform policies, over students' protests if necessary.

> ❼ Concludes with a summary of her arguments and a call to action

Writing Your Persuasive Essay

❶ Prewriting

Good writers are those who keep the language efficient. That is to say, keep it accurate, keep it clear.

Ezra Pound, poet

Think about issues that are important to you and about which people disagree. Freewrite about events that have affected you strongly. Leafing through newspaper and magazine articles and letters to the editor, and watching news coverage on television, might provide ideas. See the **Idea Bank** in the margin for more suggestions. After you select an issue that you feel strongly about, follow the steps below.

Planning Your Persuasive Essay

1. **Clearly state your position.** What do you believe about the issue? What are your reasons for believing that way?
2. **Consider your audience.** What do your readers know about the issue? What are their opinions on it?
3. **Gather support for your arguments.** Where will you find the information you need? What facts, statistics, examples, anecdotes, and quotations support your position? Which evidence is strongest? What support might people who object to your position present? How can you answer those objections?

❷ Drafting

Drafting is the time to continue exploring and developing your ideas. It's perfectly all right to revise your opinion as you write. Eventually, you will need to state your opinion clearly and support it with convincing evidence, such as facts, statistics, examples, quotations, and anecdotes. You should present a strong case, but beware of using unfair language and faulty reasoning. Avoid these illogical arguments and faulty and deceptive uses of language:

- **circular reasoning**—restating something in other words without offering proof (That's the worst idea I ever heard because it's really stupid.)
- **over-generalization**—making a statement that's too broad to prove (Nobody could possibly believe any other way.)
- **either-or fallacy**—inappropriately stating that there are only two possible alternatives (Either I get an A on the test or my life will be over.)
- **cause-and-effect fallacy**—assuming that because event B followed event A, A caused B (I got chosen for the team because I wore my lucky charm.)

Ask Your Peer Reader

- How would you express my position on this issue?
- What is unclear about the issue or my position?
- What are my most and least convincing arguments?

IDEABank

1. Your Working Portfolio
Look for ideas in the **Writing Options** you completed earlier in this unit:
- **Holocaust Essay**, p. 601
- **Political Letter**, p. 614

2. Change the World
Ask a group of friends or classmates to complete this sentence: "If I could do one thing to change the world, I would. . . ." Develop one of the ideas into a persuasive essay.

3. In This Corner . . .
Think about issues you argue about with your friends and family. Choose one for your topic.

Have a question?

See the **Writing Handbook**
Persuasive Writing
pp. 1161-1162

Guiding Student Writing

Prewriting

Choosing an Issue
If after reading the Idea Bank students are having difficulty choosing an issue, suggest they try the following:
- Consider controversial issues involving the media—film, television, radio, computer games, or the World Wide Web.
- Make a list of issues related to young adults, such as education, crime, dating, or the minimum wage.

Planning the Persuasive Essay
1. Have students create a cluster map by writing their persuasive position or thesis in the center of a sheet of paper and circling it. Instruct students to attach their beliefs and reasons for their beliefs as they relate to this claim.
3. Students may want to bring books, newspapers, or magazines to class to use as references. Besides reading, students may conduct interviews with experts on both sides of the issue.

Drafting

Before students begin drafting, encourage them to find ways to fairly and objectively present the opposition's view. To do this, they might develop an outline before they begin to draft and assign specific segments of the draft to (1) present the opposition's view and (2) refute or concede the opposition's objections. Assigning each of these segments to a separate paragraph may be a good strategy.

Revising

WRITING EFFECTIVE INTRODUCTIONS

To help students see the possibilities for creating effective introductions, have them write three different openings using any three of the suggestions given in the text—a bold statement, an unusual fact, an interesting anecdote, a lively description, a question, or a quotation. When they have written their introductions, put students in pairs to discuss with each other the merits of each introduction and how they might further revise one to effectively "hook" their readers.

Editing and Proofreading

CORRECTING FRAGMENTS

Remind students that sentence fragments occur when either the subject or main verb is missing. A sentence fragment can be confusing to readers because it fails to present a complete idea and leaves readers wondering what the writer's point is. Show students that the primary way to correct sentence fragments is to add the missing element. Also, point out that correcting sentence fragments may result in altering punctuation and capitalization. Encourage students to revise, edit, and proofread carefully to produce error-free writing in the final draft.

Reflecting

Encourage students to evaluate their writing process. Ask them to comment on the prewriting strategies that were most effective. What parts of the process gave them the most difficulty? Have students add these self-evaluations to their working portfolios.

Need revising help?

Review the **Rubric**, p. 616

Consider **peer reader** comments

Check **Revision Guidelines**, p. 1145

❸ Revising

TARGET SKILL ▶ WRITING EFFECTIVE INTRODUCTIONS Your persuasive essay will be most effective if you capture your readers' attention immediately. Try using a bold statement, an unusual fact, an interesting anecdote, a lively description, a question, or a quotation.

> *Clothes consciousness is out* School uniforms are *in.* ~~an issue that I care a lot about.~~ And, though I know most other students don't agree, I think uniforms are *the best thing that could happen to our nation's youth and to the educational system as a whole.* ~~a really good idea.~~

Befuddled by fragments?

See the **Grammar Handbook**

Correcting Fragments, p. 1199

❹ Editing and Proofreading

TARGET SKILL ▶ CORRECTING FRAGMENTS Sentence fragments do not express complete thoughts. For that reason, they make your writing difficult to understand and weaken your arguments. Correct fragments by adding whatever is missing from the sentence—subject, verb, or independent clause.

> In fact, I think that wearing uniforms. Actually contribute*s* to the development of creativity and individuality. By removing the focus from externals such as clothes. *uniforms* Allow each student to express ~~their~~ *his or her* personality. In more important and meaningful ways.

Publishing IDEAS

- Submit your essay as a letter to the editor of your school or local newspaper.
- Present your essay as a speech and have it videotaped.

More Online: Publishing Options www.mcdougallittell.com

❺ Reflecting

FOR YOUR WORKING PORTFOLIO What did you learn about your issue in writing your persuasive essay? What persuasive techniques were most convincing to your audience? Attach your reflections to your finished work. Save your persuasive essay in your **Working Portfolio.**

Option

Managing the Paper Load

Let students who feel confident with their drafts assess each others' work. Spend your time with students who self-select themselves as needing help. Ask them to identify their problem areas as best they can before coming to you. After reviewing their drafts, discuss the major points they should address in revision. Record the advice you give now so that you can key in on the same issues when you grade their final drafts.

Assessment Practice Revising & Editing

Read this paragraph from the first draft of a persuasive essay. The underlined sections may include the following kinds of errors:

- **spelling errors**
- **sentence fragments**
- **lack of parallel structure**
- **comma errors**

For each underlined section, choose the revision that most improves the writing.

> A model United Nations program offers students a chance to be diplomats. They play the roles of ambassedors (1) to the United Nations. They meet in an assembly hall just like the real diplomats and debate (2) current issues. This simulation can help students develop negotiation skills and mediate (3). Debates focus on complex global issues, such as the environment, human rights, and disarmament. (4) Involving students from our entire county. The program could also strengthen inter-school ties. (5) A model United Nations can invigorate, and educate both the participants and spectators (6).

1. **A.** ambassadors
   B. ambasadors
   C. ambassaders
   D. Correct as is

2. **A.** hall, just like the real diplomats and debate
   B. hall just like the real diplomats, and debate
   C. hall, just like the, real, diplomats and debate
   D. Correct as is

3. **A.** mediation skills and negotiate
   B. negotiation skills and mediation
   C. negotiation and mediation skills
   D. Correct as is

4. **A.** issues: such as the environment, human rights, and disarmament.
   B. issues such as the environment, human rights, and, disarmament.
   C. issues such as, the environment, human rights, and disarmament.
   D. Correct as is

5. **A.** By involving students from our entire county, the program could also strengthen inter-school ties.
   B. Involving students from our entire county. The program could also strengthen inter-school ties.
   C. The program could also strengthen inter-school ties. Involving students from the entire country.
   D. Correct as is

6. **A.** invigorate and educate, both the participants and spectators.
   B. invigorate and educate both the participants and spectators.
   C. invigorate, and educate both the participants, and spectators.
   D. Correct as is

Need extra help?

See the **Grammar Handbook**

Correcting Fragments, p. 1199

Punctuation Chart, pp. 1203–1204

Assessment Practice

Briefly review the kinds of errors that students may encounter in the exercise. Remind students to carefully read all of the choices in each question before they select the correct answer.

Answers:
1. A; **2.** D; **3.** C; **4.** D; **5.** A; **6.** B

PART 2 Tests of Conviction

What are some of your most deeply-held values and beliefs? What would you do to defend them? Tests of conviction come in all forms. Sometimes historical circumstances force people to decide where they stand and whether to fight or flee. In other cases, the struggle may be more personal, born in the depths of the human heart. In this part of Unit Four, you will explore different situations in which people's convictions are put to the test.

ACTIVITY

Working with a partner, think of two or three people—perhaps historical figures, contemporary leaders, or others whose actions have gained attention—who have stood up for their convictions in some way. What do they have in common? Were they successful in achieving their goals? How are they different from one another? Tell the class about these people in a brief oral presentation, and compare your examples with those of other pairs of classmates.

Point of view

Point of view refers to the vantage point from which a story is told. Think of it as the lens that a writer chooses for the reader to look through. Point of view determines much about a story—from its overall tone to our opinion of its characters and how much we learn about them. The following passages demonstrate three points of view that writers use most: first-person point of view, third-person omniscient point of view, and third-person limited point of view.

First-Person Point of View

In **first-person point of view,** the narrator is a character in the story, narrating the action as he or she perceives it. A first-person narrator—who may or may not be a major character in the story—speaks directly to the reader, using the pronoun *I* to refer to himself or herself. First-person point of view allows the reader to understand a great deal about the narrator's thoughts and feelings. However, the reader knows only what the narrator is able to know.

Sometimes, a first-person narrator is biased and tells a one-sided story. This kind of narrator is called an **unreliable narrator.** In other cases, the narrator does not fully comprehend what he or she relates. Such a narrator is called a **naive narrator.**

YOUR TURN Read the excerpt at the right. How does this narrative point of view affect your feeling of suspense?

FIRST-PERSON POINT OF VIEW

A fearful idea now suddenly drove the blood in torrents upon my heart, and for a brief period, I once more relapsed into insensibility. Upon recovering, I at once started to my feet, trembling convulsively in every fiber. I thrust my arms wildly above and around me in all directions. I felt nothing; yet dreaded to move a step, lest I should be impeded by the walls of a *tomb.* Perspiration burst from every pore, and stood in cold big beads upon my forehead. The agony of suspense grew at length intolerable, and I cautiously moved forward, with my arms extended, and my eyes straining from their sockets, in the hope of catching some faint ray of light.

—Edgar Allan Poe, "The Pit and the Pendulum"

First Person	ADVANTAGE	• Allows narrator to speak directly to reader, creating a greater sense of intimacy • Allows writer to add depth to story by use of unreliable or naive narrator
	DISADVANTAGE	• Provides only limited knowledge of other characters and events—readers know only what the narrator knows
Third Person Omniscient	ADVANTAGE	• Provides readers with insight into several characters • Allows the writer to develop a more complicated plot or to examine broader issues
	DISADVANTAGE	• May leave readers detached from the story—no obvious character on whom to focus and no character speaking directly to them
Third Person Limited	ADVANTAGE	• Provides readers with a character they can get to know intimately • Allows readers some emotional distance • Allows a writer to withhold information to create suspense or mystery
	DISADVANTAGE	• Limits reader's knowledge of other characters

OVERVIEW

Objectives

- understand the following literary terms:
  - first-person point of view
  - third-person point of view
  - third-person omniscient point of view
  - third-person limited point of view
- analyze how point of view affects suspense, conflict, and characterization in a story
- understand the advantages and limitations of each point of view

Teaching the Lesson

This lesson presents terms related to point of view and explains how narrative point of view affects both the story and the reader.

Introducing the Concepts

Have students retell a personal experience using two different points of view, one in which they speak as a participant and another in which they speak as an outside observer telling the story. Discuss the differences between the two.

Presenting the Concepts

First-Person Point of View

Encourage students to read a first-person narrative aloud in order to hear the narrator's speaking voice.

YOUR TURN

Possible Response: The narrator's precise focus on internal detail and physical activity conveys the intensity of his own fear and anxiety.

Third-Person Point of View

Point out that third-person point of view offers the voice of a nonparticipant telling the story and can provide greater awareness than the limited view of a first-person narrator.

Third-Person Omniscient Point of View

Explain to students that third-person omniscient point of view was a convention widely used by 19th-century writers, but it is almost never used by fiction writers today. To provide insight into all characters' minds is psychologically implausible for anyone.

YOUR TURN

Possible Response: Maupassant possibly used the omniscient point of view because it wouldn't limit his handling the "two friends" subject matter in ways that another point of view might have.

Third-Person Limited Point of View

Explain that a reasonable metaphor for third-person limited point of view might be that of a camera sitting on the shoulder of the viewpoint character, seeing the world as he or she sees it, with the exception that the camera also has access to his or her interior thoughts and feelings.

YOUR TURN

Possible Response: The passage is told from Sŏngsam's vantage point. It offers a close perspective of one side of the conflict.

Third-Person Point of View

Third-person point of view is used when the narrator is not a character in the story but is someone observing from the outside. Such a narrator never uses the pronoun *I* to refer to himself or herself.

Third-Person Omniscient Point of View

In stories that use the **third-person omniscient point of view,** the narrator is all-knowing, or omniscient. Such a narrator has access to the thoughts and feelings of all the characters. Like any third-person narrator, the omniscient storyteller is not a character in the story but rather is an invisible observer. The use of a third-person narrator provides the reader with insight into all the characters and into events that may be occurring simultaneously.

YOUR TURN Read the passage at the right. Why do you think Guy de Maupassant used an omniscient point of view rather than the point of view of one of the two friends?

> There were some days when they hardly spoke to each other. On other occasions they would chat all the time. But they understood each other perfectly without needing to exchange any words, because their tastes were so alike and their feelings identical.
>
> On spring mornings at about ten o'clock, . . . Morissot would say to his neighbor:
>
> "Ah! It's grand here, isn't it?"
>
> And Monsieur Sauvage would reply:
>
> "There's nothing I like better."
>
> This simple exchange of words was all that was needed for them to understand each other and confirm their mutual appreciation.
>
> —Guy de Maupassant, "Two Friends"

Third-Person Limited Point of View

Third-person limited point of view refers to a story in which the third-person narrator has access to the thoughts and feelings of a single character. The other characters' thoughts and feelings are revealed as the point-of-view character discovers them. Third-person limited point of view allows the reader to identify with one character, yet remain somewhat distant. It allows the writer to withhold information to create tension or surprise.

YOUR TURN From whose vantage point is the passage on the right told? How does this help you understand the conflict?

> Sŏngsam felt his mind becoming clear of itself, as if some obstruction had been removed. "If you were vice-chairman of the Communist League, why didn't you run? You must have been lying low with a secret mission."
>
> Tŏkchae did not reply.
>
> "Speak up. What was your mission?"
>
> Tŏkchae kept walking. Tŏkchae was hiding something, Sŏngsam thought. He wanted to take a good look at him, but Tŏkchae kept his face averted.
>
> —Hwang Sunwŏn, "Cranes"

Every day, you make judgments—which movie to see, what toppings you want on your pizza, what clothes to wear. In the same way, readers make judgments about what they read. The strategies here can help you develop good habits of judging.

Making Judgments

When you judge a literary work, you probably evaluate it in light of a few generally accepted standards of what a good work should contain. These standards, or **criteria,** can reflect your own views and interests, but should also be specific to the subject you are judging. For example, if you pick your favorite baseball player based only on the criteria of home runs, you may be overlooking other aspects of the player's game, such as fielding or base running.

Judging a Literary Work Judging a piece of literature calls for the same effort. You may have read many science fiction stories and developed your own standards for what makes a science fiction tale effective. But if you only judge science fiction stories by their otherworldly settings, you might miss the shock of a surprise ending or the intriguing nature of the technology used. The plot, character, setting, and theme–all elements of fiction–usually need to work together for a story to captivate you.

1 Strategies for Using a Graphic to Make Judgments

- Finalize your list of criteria, adding as many criteria as you need. Enter the criteria on a chart like the one begun here for "A Sound of Thunder."
- Find examples from the selection that meet the criteria. Record your ratings.
- On the graphic, rank your criteria in order of their importance in making your judgment.
- Finally, make a judgment about the work that is based on your evaluation.

Selection Criteria

Criteria	Meets	Neutral	Doesn't meet	Order of importance
The reader is transported to another time or place.	✓			2
The use of technology is highly imaginative.		✓		4
Judgment:				

2 Strategies for Making Judgments About Fiction and Nonfiction

As you develop your own criteria for judging a work, consider these questions:

- Does the plot seem realistic? Does the story hold your interest?
- Are the characters believable? Is the narrator reliable?
- Is the theme, or central message, of a story one that conveys something important about the human condition?
- In biography and autobiography, are the subjects and events interesting?
- In historical writing, is the information accurate?
- In an essay, are the opinions convincing? Are they expressed objectively?
- In newspaper or magazine reporting, how well does the news story cover the five W's–*who, what, where, when,* and *why*? Are the sources credible?

Need More Help?

Remember that active readers use the essential reading strategies explained on page 7: **visualize, predict, clarify, question, connect, evaluate, monitor.**

The Active Reader: Skills and Strategies

OVERVIEW

Objectives

- develop and apply criteria for judging fiction and nonfiction
- use a graphic for organizing evaluative criteria and examples from the text necessary to make an evaluation

Teaching the Lesson

The strategies on this page will help students learn and apply the skills of establishing explicit criteria and applying those criteria in order to make evaluative judgments of fiction and nonfiction.

Presenting the Strategies

Help students understand how criteria are implicitly at work in the everyday judgments we make. Cite examples of evaluative judgment from everyday experience, then discuss the implicit evaluative criteria at work by making those criteria explicit.

1 Strategies for Using a Graphic to Make Judgments

Many students are likely to list their criteria in order from most important to least important, producing an "Order of importance" already ranked numerically from top to bottom. The "Neutral" column is provided for instances where students say that an example "sort of" meets their criteria.

2 Strategies for Making Judgments About Fiction and Nonfiction

Encourage students to establish more thorough and comprehensive criteria than those presented here. Have students review appropriate chapters that deal more completely with plot, character, theme, biography, autobiography, history, essay, and news reporting. From those sources, they can add important aspects and elements to their list of criteria.

OVERVIEW

Objectives

1. understand and appreciate a **short story (Literary Analysis)**
2. understand the **first-person point of view (Literary Analysis)**
3. **make judgments (Active Reading)**

Summary

Although the narrator has taken a modest stand against the Vietnam War, he does not feel personally threatened until his draft notice arrives in the summer of 1968. He opens it in disbelief, which turns to rage, self-pity, and numbness. He considers fleeing to Canada to avoid killing and being killed, but he fears exile just as he has feared and hated the war. One morning, he walks away from his factory job and drives north. He stops at the run-down Tip Top Lodge to struggle with his conscience and his fate. On his sixth day there, Elroy Berdahl, the owner of the lodge and a hero to O'Brien, takes the narrator fishing on the Rainy River. As they approach the Canadian border, the narrator sees his past and future and begins to cry. He realizes that he does not have the courage to run away; he will kill and maybe die—because he is embarrassed not to go to war.

Thematic Link

The narrator endures the trials of a tortured conscience and ultimately fails his own **test of conviction**.

5-Minute Warm-Up

Daily Language SkillBuilder

Have students **proofread** the display sentences on page 541l and write them correctly. The sentences also appear on Transparency 20 of **Grammar Transparencies and Copymasters.**

Mini Lesson **Preteaching Vocabulary**

If you would like to preteach the WORDS TO KNOW for this selection, use the Mini Lesson, p. 628.

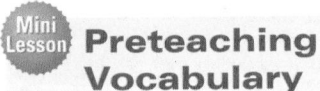

PREPARING to *Read*

On the Rainy River

Short Story by TIM O'BRIEN

"The only certainty that summer was moral confusion."

Connect to Your Life

Life on the Line In this story, a young man must decide whether to fight in a war he opposes. Under what conditions would you be willing to fight in a war? Under what conditions would you be unwilling to fight? Discuss your thoughts with a small group of classmates.

Build Background

Country at War The Vietnam War (1957–1975) was one of the most controversial military conflicts in the history of the United States. The United States entered the war in 1964 in hopes of preventing the spread of communism throughout Southeast Asia. During the course of the war, nearly 3 million Americans were sent overseas to defend the South Vietnamese government against a takeover by Communist North Vietnam and the Viet Cong, a South Vietnamese Communist rebel force.

During the war, nearly 2 million men were drafted into the military. Those who were drafted but who opposed the war faced a difficult decision: whether to risk their lives in a foreign war they couldn't justify or risk imprisonment at home by refusing to serve. Some burned their draft cards as a form of protest; others fled the country, most often by crossing the border into Canada.

WORDS TO KNOW
Vocabulary Preview

acquiescence	platitude
consensus	preoccupied
fathom	pretense
impassive	reticence
imperative	vigil

LaserLinks: Background for Reading
Historical Connection
Geographical Connection

Focus Your Reading

LITERARY ANALYSIS **FIRST-PERSON POINT OF VIEW** "On the Rainy River" is told from the **first-person point of view.** The **narrator** is a **character** in the story and so participates in the events he recounts. Readers see everything through the narrator's eyes. His comments and descriptions convey the difficulty of the momentous decision he faces:

> ***I was bitter, sure. But it was so much more than that. The emotions went from outrage to terror to bewilderment to guilt to sorrow and then back again to outrage.***

In this story, the author blurs the line between fact and fiction by calling his narrator "Tim O'Brien." The story, however, is still a work of fiction. As you read, notice how O'Brien's use of the first-person point of view affects your feelings about the narrator.

ACTIVE READING **MAKING JUDGMENTS** A reader is always processing information. Good readers not only receive information, but they also **make judgments** about it. As you read this story, you will receive considerable information about the narrator and the decision he faces. To make a judgment about a character's decision, you need to think about standards, or criteria for judging. For example, you might consider whether the character has acted honorably or considered the consequences of his decision.

READER'S NOTEBOOK In a chart like the one shown, note the reasons the narrator puts forward in support of each option facing him. What is your judgment of his options and of his ultimate decision? Give reasons to support your judgment.

Going to Vietnam	Going to Canada
Narrator's Views:	Narrator's Views:
My Judgment and Reasons:	My Judgment and Reasons:

LESSON RESOURCES

UNIT FOUR RESOURCE BOOK, pp. 42–43

ASSESSMENT RESOURCES

Formal Assessment, pp. 113–114

Teacher's Guide to Assessment and Portfolio Use

Test Generator

SKILLS TRANSPARENCIES AND COPYMASTERS

Literary Analysis

- Point of View, T17 (for Cooperative Learning Activity, p. 642)

Reading and Critical Thinking

- Making Judgments, T5 (for Think Critically, item 5, p. 642)
- Organizational Chart: Horizontal, T51 (for Reader's Notebook, p. 626)

Grammar

- Infinitive Phrases I, C100 (for Mini Lesson, p. 636)
- Gerund Phrases, C106 (for Mini Lesson, p. 644)

Vocabulary

- Context Clues, C65 (for Mini Lesson, p. 628)
- Word Meaning and Spellings, C66 (for Mini Lesson, p. 633)

Writing

- Identifying Paragraphs, T5 (for Writing Option 2, p. 643)
- Point of View, T23 (for Writing Option 1, p. 643)

Communications

- Impromptu Speaking: Dialogue, Role-Play, Debate, T13 (for Activities & Explorations 1, p. 643)

INTEGRATED TECHNOLOGY

Audio Library

LaserLinks

- Historical Connections
- Geographical Connections

See **Teacher's SourceBook,** pp. 37–39.

Visit our website: www.mcdougallittell.com

On the Rainy River

Tim O'Brien

Portrait of Donald Schrader (1962), Fairfield Porter. The Metropolitan Museum of Art, bequest of Arthur M. Bullowa, 1993 (1993.406.12). Copyright © 1995 The Metropolitan Museum of Art.

This is one story I've never told before. Not to anyone. Not to my parents, not to my brother or sister, not even to my wife. To go into it, I've always thought, would only cause embarrassment for all of us, a sudden need to be elsewhere, which is the natural response to a confession. Even now, I'll admit, the story makes me squirm. For more than twenty years I've had to live with it, feeling the shame, trying to push it away, and so by this act of remembrance, by putting the facts down on paper, I'm hoping to relieve at least some of the pressure on my dreams.

TEACHING THE LITERATURE

Customizing Instruction

Less Proficient Readers

Have students keep these questions in mind as they read:

- Who are the characters in the story? **Answer:** the young man (Tim O'Brien) and Elroy Berdahl
- What are the settings of the story? **Answer:** the young man's midwestern home and the Rainy River, on the U.S.-Canadian border
- What is the main conflict of the story? **Answer:** whether the narrator should answer his draft notice or disobey the law and flee the country

Students Acquiring English

Help students understand the historical and cultural context of the story—the participation of the U.S. in a distant war in a remote part of the world. Invite students to discuss their own experiences with or knowledge of internal conflicts in their countries of origin. Encourage students to voice their feelings about the narrator's actions and thoughts.

Use **Spanish Study Guide** for additional support, pp. 137–139.

Gifted and Talented

Suggest that as they read the story, students note details that reveal the narrator's relationship with his parents. Ask students to summarize their findings.

Multiple Learning Styles

Interpersonal Learners

1 Have students think about the emotions of shame and embarrassment. How do these related emotions govern our lives? How does society use these emotions as measures of control? When and where do we learn to feel shame?

BLOCK SCHEDULING: MANAGING TIME

If your schedule requires that you cover the lesson objectives in a shorter time, use . . .

- Preparing to Read, p. 626
- Thinking Through the Literature, p. 642
- Vocabulary in Action, p. 643
- Grammar in Context, p. 644

If you want to take advantage of longer class time, use . . .

- TE Teaching Options: Preteaching Vocabulary, p. 628; Cross-Curricular Links, pp. 630–631, 634; Workplace Link, p. 632; Multicultural Link, p. 639; Vocabulary Strategy, p. 633; Viewing and Representing, pp. 635, 638; Informal Assessment, p. 640
- Choices & Challenges and Author Activity, pp. 643–644

Reading and Analyzing

Reading Skills and Strategies: PREVIEW
Briefly summarize the story, emphasizing the narrator's internal conflict. To help them understand the historical context, discuss the Build Background feature on page 626. Discuss what information is revealed in the called out quotations.

Active Reading: MAKING JUDGMENTS
Encourage students to think about alternatives the narrator has—from prison to serving as a noncombatant medic in the war. Then, encourage students to make judgments about these alternatives. Prison, of course, is probably a poor alternative, and noncombatant status might be difficult to obtain.

Use **Unit Four Resource Book** p. 42 for more practice.

Literary Analysis
FIRST-PERSON POINT OF VIEW
Remind students that the hallmark of first-person narration is the pronoun *I*. Help students understand the usual distinction between the narrator and the author: the narrator is a *fictional* character through whose eyes we see all action and receive all information. Point out that Tim O'Brien has blurred the line between fact and fiction by naming his narrator after himself.

Use **Unit Four Resource Book** p. 43 for more practice.

ACTIVE READING
A MAKE JUDGMENTS Students may feel that theoretically such a law might discourage war, but the practicality of it would make it unreasonable.

Still, it's a hard story to tell. All of us, I suppose, like to believe that in a moral emergency we will behave like the heroes of our youth, bravely and forthrightly, without thought of personal loss or discredit. Certainly that was my conviction back in the summer of 1968. Tim O'Brien: a 1 secret hero. The Lone Ranger. If the stakes ever became high enough—if the evil were evil enough, if the good were good enough—I would simply tap a secret reservoir of courage that had been accumulating inside me over the years. Courage, I seemed to think, comes to us in finite quantities, like an inheritance, and by being frugal and stashing it away, and letting it earn interest, we steadily increase our moral capital in preparation for that day when the account must be drawn down. It was a comforting theory. It dispensed with all those bothersome little acts of daily courage; it offered hope and grace to the repetitive coward; it justified the past while amortizing the future.

In June of 1968, a month after graduating from Macalester College, I was drafted to fight a war I hated. I was twenty-one years old. Young, yes, and politically naive, but even so the American war in Vietnam seemed to me wrong. Certain blood was being shed for uncertain reasons. I saw no unity of purpose, no consensus on matters of philosophy or history or law. The very facts were shrouded in uncertainty: Was it a civil war? A war of national liberation or simple aggression? Who started it, and when, and why? What really happened to the U.S.S. *Maddox* on that dark night in the Gulf of Tonkin?[1] Was Ho Chi Minh[2] a Communist stooge, or a nationalist savior, or both, or neither? What about the Geneva Accords?[3] What about SEATO[4] and the Cold War?[5] What about dominoes?[6] America was divided on these and a thousand other issues, and the debate had spilled out across the floor of the United States Senate and into the streets, and smart men in pinstripes could not agree on even the most fundamental matters of public policy. The only certainty that summer was moral confusion. It was my view then, and still is, that you don't make war without knowing why. Knowledge, of course, is always imperfect, but it seemed to me that when a nation goes to war it must have reasonable confidence in the justice and imperative of its cause. You can't fix your mistakes. Once people are dead, you can't make them undead.

I was too *good* for this war. Too smart, too compassionate, too everything.

In any case those were my convictions, and back in college I had taken a modest stand against the war. Nothing radical, no hothead stuff, just ringing a few doorbells for Gene

1. **U.S.S. *Maddox* . . . Gulf of Tonkin:** an alleged attack on the U.S. destroyer *Maddox* in the Gulf of Tonkin, off the coast of North Vietnam, in 1964, which provided a basis for expanding U.S. involvement in the Vietnam conflict.
2. **Ho Chi Minh** (hō′ chē′ mĭn′): a political leader who waged a successful fight against French colonial rule and established a Communist government in North Vietnam.
3. **Geneva Accords:** a 1954 peace agreement providing for the temporary division of Vietnam into North and South Vietnam and calling for national elections.
4. **SEATO:** the Southeast Asia Treaty Organization, an alliance of seven nations, including the United States, formed to halt Communist expansion in Southeast Asia after Communist forces defeated France in Indochina.
5. **Cold War:** a term for the post–World War II struggle for influence between Communist and democratic nations.
6. **dominoes:** refers to the domino theory, which holds that if a nation becomes a Communist state, neighboring nations will also become Communist.

WORDS TO KNOW
consensus (kən-sĕn′səs) *n.* general agreement by a group
imperative (ĭm-pĕr′ə-tĭv) *n.* urgent necessity or duty

628

Teaching Options

Mini Lesson: Preteaching Vocabulary

USING CONTEXT CLUES Call students' attention to the list of WORDS TO KNOW. Remind them that sometimes they can understand the meaning of an unfamiliar word by examining the context in which the word is used. Use the model sentence to demonstrate the strategy of using context clues that provide inferences to word meaning.

Model Sentence
After much debate, the students reached a *consensus* on where to hold the school dance.

Instruction
- Write the model sentence on the chalkboard.
- Ask a volunteer to summarize the meaning of the sentence.
- Have students use the meaning of the sentence to infer meanings for the word *consensus.*
- Ask a volunteer to use the word *consensus* in a sentence.

Exercises Read the following sentences aloud. Ask students to use context clues to determine the meanings of the italicized terms.

McCarthy,[7] composing a few tedious, uninspired editorials for the campus newspaper. Oddly, though, it was almost entirely an intellectual activity. I brought some energy to it, of course, but it was the energy that accompanies almost any abstract endeavor; I felt no personal danger; I felt no sense of an impending crisis in my life. Stupidly, with a kind of smug removal that I can't begin to fathom, I assumed that the problems of killing and dying did not fall within my special province.

The draft notice arrived on June 17, 1968. It was a humid afternoon, I remember, cloudy and very quiet, and I'd just come in from a round of golf. My mother and father were having lunch out in the kitchen. I remember opening up the letter, scanning the first few lines, feeling the blood go thick behind my eyes. I remember a sound in my head. It wasn't thinking, it was just a silent howl. A million things all at once—I was too *good* for this war. Too smart, too compassionate, too everything. It couldn't happen. I was above it. I had the world—Phi Beta
2 Kappa and summa cum laude and president of the student body and a full-ride scholarship for grad studies at Harvard. A mistake, maybe—a foul-up in the paperwork. I was no soldier. I
3 hated Boy Scouts. I hated camping out. I hated dirt and tents and mosquitoes. The sight of blood made me queasy, and I couldn't tolerate authority, and I didn't know a rifle from a slingshot. I was a *liberal:* If they needed fresh bodies, why not draft some back-to-the-stone-age hawk? Or some dumb jingo[8] in his hardhat and Bomb Hanoi button? Or one of LBJ's[9] pretty daughters? Or Westmoreland's[10] whole family—nephews and nieces and baby grandson? There should be a law, I thought. If you support a war, if you think it's worth the price, that's fine, but you have to put your own life on the line. You have to head for the front and hook up with an infantry unit and help spill the blood. And you have to bring along your wife, or your kids, or your lover. A *law,* I thought.

ACTIVE READING

MAKE JUDGMENTS How reasonable do you find the kind of law the narrator suggests? (A)

I remember the rage in my stomach. Later it burned down to a smoldering self-pity, then to numbness. At dinner that night my father asked what my plans were.

"Nothing," I said. "Wait."

I spent the summer of 1968 working in an Armour meat-packing plant in my hometown of Worthington, Minnesota. The plant specialized in pork products, and for eight hours a day I stood on a quarter-mile assembly line—more properly, a disassembly line—removing blood clots from the necks of dead pigs. My job title, I believe, was Declotter. After slaughter, the hogs were decapitated, split down the length of the belly, pried open, eviscerated, and strung up by the hind hocks on a high conveyer belt. Then gravity took over. By the time a carcass reached my spot on the line, the fluids had mostly drained out, everything except for thick clots of blood in the neck and upper chest cavity. To remove the stuff, I used a kind of water gun. The machine was heavy, maybe eighty pounds, and was suspended from the ceiling by a heavy rubber cord. There was some bounce to it, an

7. **Gene McCarthy:** Eugene McCarthy, U.S. senator from Minnesota and Vietnam War critic who unsuccessfully sought the 1968 Democratic presidential nomination.
8. **jingo** (jĭng′gō): one who aggressively supports his or her country and favors war as a means of settling political disputes.
9. **LBJ:** Lyndon B. Johnson, U.S. president from 1963 to 1969.
10. **Westmoreland's:** referring to William Westmoreland, American general and the senior commander of U.S. forces in Vietnam from 1964 to 1968.

WORDS TO KNOW

fathom (făth′əm) *v.* to penetrate the meaning or understand the nature of

629

Customizing Instruction

Less Proficient Readers

Set a Purpose Discuss occasions when their views on important issues have differed from those of their families and friends. Suggest that students read to see how the narrator's view of the Vietnam War differs from the views of others in his hometown.

Students Acquiring English

1 Tell students that the Lone Ranger was a cowboy hero who appeared in a television series and in movies. Many people saw him as the ultimate American hero, because his mission was often to correct injustices.

2 Explain that *summa cum laude* is a Latin phrase meaning "with highest honors."

3 Explain that the Boy Scouts is an organization dedicated to building character in boys and young men. Camping and interacting with nature are often considered the primary activities of Boy Scouts.

Gifted and Talented

The narrator names several people who were important figures to Vietnam or during the Vietnam War: Ho Chi Minh, Gene McCarthy, Lyndon Baines Johnson, William Westmoreland, and Bao Dai and Ngo Dinh Diem. Have students research a figure and give a five-minute presentation on how this figure influenced the war.

1. The book was long and complex; students found it difficult to *fathom.*
2. Finding the missing book was an *imperative,* not a choice.
3. Without the mayor's grudging *acquiescence* to our plan, we would have been forced to cancel the parade.
4. The child's *reticence* was so extreme that she could scarcely say hello.
5. My uncle kept a *vigil,* staying with the ailing horse until dawn.
6. Roger dropped all *pretense* of courage and ran out the door.
7. The councilman's speech was full of empty *platitudes* and false promises.
8. I was so *preoccupied* with the club's financial problems that I made a wrong turn.
9. My aunt remained *impassive* throughout the painful ordeal.

Use **Unit Four Resource Book** p. 44 for more exercises.

A lesson on context clues appears on p. 56 in the Pupil's Edition.

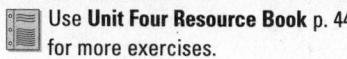

Reading and Analyzing

Literary Analysis

FIRST-PERSON POINT OF VIEW

Point out that, so far, this story has essentially been a long description of the narrator's thoughts and actions. Have students consider how point of view affects a story's style and voice. How would this story be different if it were told from third-person point of view?

Possible Response: A story's point of view largely determines its voice and has a tremendous effect on its style. First-person point of view gives this story an immediacy and intimacy that it would otherwise lack.

Reading Skills and Strategies: QUESTIONING

Encourage students to ask questions about the narrator's actions and anything else that piques their interest. Have students look for answers to these questions as they read.

Possible Responses: Why does the narrator get a job at the meat-packing plant? Where is Winnipeg? Will the narrator really go to Canada?

Literary Analysis: SYMBOLISM

Remind students that symbols are images that stand for broad ideas or concepts. Ask students to think about what the meat-packing plant represents in the story.

Possible Response: It symbolizes the job the narrator feels he'd have to do as a soldier because it involves killing and bloodshed. He pulls a trigger; he wears a uniform; he smells of death.

elastic up-and-down give, and the trick was to maneuver the gun with your whole body, not lifting with the arms, just letting the rubber cord do the work for you. At one end was a trigger; at the muzzle end was a small nozzle and a steel roller brush. As a carcass passed by, you'd lean forward and swing the gun up against the clots and squeeze the trigger, all in one motion, and the brush would whirl and water would come shooting out and you'd hear a quick splattering sound as the clots dissolved into a fine red mist. It was not pleasant work. Goggles were a necessity, and a rubber apron, but even so it was like standing for eight hours a day under a lukewarm blood-shower. At night I'd go home smelling of pig. I couldn't wash it out. Even after a hot bath, scrubbing hard, the stink was always there—like old bacon, or sausage, a dense greasy pig-stink that soaked deep into my skin and hair. Among other things, I remember, it was tough getting dates that summer. I felt isolated; I spent a lot of time alone. And there was also that draft notice tucked away in my wallet.

In the evenings I'd sometimes borrow my father's car and drive aimlessly around town, feeling sorry for myself, thinking about the war and the pig factory and how my life seemed to be collapsing toward slaughter. I felt paralyzed. All around me the options seemed to be narrowing, as if I were hurtling down a huge black funnel, the whole world squeezing in tight. There was no happy way out. The government had ended most graduate school deferments; the waiting lists for the National Guard and Reserves[11] were impossibly long; my health was solid; I didn't qualify for CO[12] status—no religious grounds, no history as a pacifist.[13] Moreover, I could not claim to be opposed to war as a matter of general principle. There were occasions, I believed, when a nation was justified in using military force to achieve its ends, to stop a Hitler or some comparable evil, and I told myself that in such circumstances I would've willingly marched off to the battle. The problem, though, was that a draft board did not let you choose your war.

Beyond all this, or at the very center, was the raw fact of terror. I did not want to die. Not ever. But certainly not then, not there, not in a wrong war. Driving up Main Street, past the courthouse and the Ben Franklin store, I sometimes felt the fear spreading inside me like weeds. I imagined myself dead. I imagined myself doing things I could not do—charging an enemy position, taking aim at another human being.

At some point in mid-July I began thinking seriously about Canada. The border lay a few hundred miles north, an eight-hour drive. Both my conscience and my instincts were telling me to make a break for it, just take off and run like hell and never stop. In the beginning the idea seemed purely abstract, the word Canada printing itself out in my head; but after a time I could see particular shapes and images, the sorry details of my own future—a hotel room in Winnipeg, a battered old suitcase, my father's eyes as I tried to explain myself over the telephone. I could almost hear his voice, and my mother's. Run, I'd think. Then I'd think, Impossible. Then a second later I'd think, *Run.*

11. **National Guard and Reserves:** military reserve units run by each state in the United States. Some men joined these units to avoid service in Vietnam.
12. **CO:** conscientious objector, a person exempted from military service because of strongly held moral or religious beliefs that do not permit participation in war.
13. **pacifist** (păs′ə-fĭst): one who opposes war or other violence as a means of settling disputes.

Teaching Options

Cross Curricular Link History

THE VIETNAM WAR The Vietnam War provoked widespread opposition from a variety of citizens: leftist college students, traditional pacifists, some veterans, even members of Congress. As U.S. involvement grew, so did the opposition. Although by 1968 opposition was sufficiently organized to include candidates in the 1968 Democratic primaries (both Eugene McCarthy and Robert Kennedy opposed the war), not until the early 1970s did public opinion turn resolutely in favor of U.S. withdrawal. By then, antiwar sentiment had discouraged President Lyndon Johnson from seeking a second term in 1968. Richard Nixon, running on a platform that promised quick resolution to the war, faced continued protests as his administration increased bombing over Vietnam and neighboring countries. Thousands of young men refused to register for the draft; many more burned their draft cards in public protests. The late 1960s saw the peak of antiwar demonstrations, including the street violence at the Democratic Convention in Chicago and a huge march on Washington. On college campuses and city streets, protesters chanted antiwar slogans.

It was a kind of schizophrenia.[14] A moral split. I couldn't make up my mind. I feared the war, yes, but I also feared exile. I was afraid of walking away from my own life, my friends and my family, my whole history, everything that mattered to me. I feared losing the respect of my parents. I feared the law. I feared ridicule and censure.[15] My hometown was a conservative little spot on the prairie, a place where tradition counted, and it was easy to imagine people sitting around a table at the old Gobbler Café on Main Street, coffee cups poised, the conversation slowly zeroing in on the young O'Brien kid, how the damned sissy had taken off for Canada. At night, when I couldn't sleep, I'd sometimes carry on fierce arguments with those people. I'd be screaming at them, telling them how much I detested their blind, thoughtless, automatic acquiescence to it all, their simple-minded patriotism, their prideful ignorance, their love-it-or-leave-it platitudes, how they were sending me off to fight a war they didn't understand and didn't want to understand. I held them responsible. By God, yes I *did*. All of them—I held them personally and individually responsible—the polyestered Kiwanis boys, the merchants **1** and farmers, the pious churchgoers, the chatty housewives, the PTA and the Lions club and the Veterans of Foreign Wars and the fine upstanding gentry out at the country club. They didn't know Bao Dai[16] from the man in the moon. They didn't know history. They didn't know the first thing about Diem's[17] tyranny, or the nature of Vietnamese nationalism, or the long colonialism of the French—this was all too damned complicated, it required some reading—but no matter, it was a war to stop the Communists, plain and simple, which was how they liked things, and you were treasonous if you had second thoughts about killing or dying for plain and simple reasons.

I was bitter, sure. But it was so much more than that. The emotions went from outrage to terror to bewilderment to guilt to sorrow and then back again to outrage. I felt a sickness inside me. Real disease.

Most of this I've told before, or at least hinted at, but what I have never told is the full truth. How I cracked. How at work one morning, standing on the pig line, I felt something break open in my chest. I don't know what it was. I'll never know. But it was real. I know that much, it was a physical rupture—a cracking-leaking-popping feeling. I remember dropping my water gun. Quickly, almost without thought, I took off my apron and walked out of the plant and drove home. It was midmorning, I remember, and the house was empty. Down in my chest there was still that leaking sensation, something very warm and precious spilling out, and I was covered with blood and hog-stink, and for a long while I just concentrated on holding myself together. I remember taking a hot shower. I remember packing a suitcase and carrying it out to the kitchen, standing very still for a few minutes, looking carefully at the familiar objects all around me. The old chrome toaster, the telephone, the pink and white Formica on the kitchen counters. The room was full of bright sunshine.

SUPPORT
OUR BOYS
IN
VIETNAM

14. **schizophrenia** (skĭt′sə-frē′nē-ə): a mental disorder. Here, the narrator refers to a split personality.
15. **censure** (sĕn′shər): an expression of strong disapproval or harsh criticism.
16. **Bao Dai** (bou′dī′): the last emperor of Vietnam (1926–1945) and chief of state from 1949 to 1955.
17. **Diem:** Ngo Dinh Diem (nō′ dĭn′ dē-ĕm′), the first president of South Vietnam, who led his country like a brutal dictator. He was murdered by his own generals in 1963.

WORDS TO KNOW

acquiescence (ăk′wē-ĕs′əns) *n.* passive agreement; agreement without protest

platitude (plăt′ĭ-to͞od′) *n.* a trite or unoriginal statement, especially one expressed as if it were original or significant; a cliché

Customizing Instruction

Less Proficient Readers

Make sure students understand the narrator's conflict.

- Compare and contrast the narrator's feelings about the war with the feelings of others in his hometown.
  Possible Response: He thinks the war is wrong, but other people support the war.
- Why is this a problem for him?
  Possible Response: He knows that if he goes to Canada, his family and neighbors will condemn him, and he cares very much about what they think.

Students Acquiring English

1 Explain the clubs such as *Kiwanis* and *Lions* (social and civic groups for men) and *PTA* (Parent and Teacher Association). Discuss the meaning of words such as *polyestered, pious,* and *chatty* so that the students can infer the narrator's attitude toward these groups and other groups.

Multiple Learning Styles

Auditory Learners

Have students read aloud quietly to themselves or to a partner. Remind them to use punctuation marks as a guide to tone and inflection.

The draft, the system of military conscription in the United States, emerged as one of the most controversial aspects of the war. After World War II, the Selective Service System, which governed the draft, expanded the categories to qualify for deferment (including marriage, fatherhood, and registration in college), in addition to the traditional exemptions for disability. Thus, the draft was seen as fundamentally unfair, exempting those who could afford college, but sending poor, uneducated young men to their deaths in an unpopular war. The Draft Act was revised in 1967 to end exemptions for most graduate students. Continued criticism led to the adoption of a lottery system in 1969. In 1973, as troops were withdrawn from Vietnam, the draft was ended, and military service became voluntary. However, all young men still must register with the Selective Service once they turn 18.

Reading and Analyzing

Literary Analysis: SETTING

Have students analyze the relevance of the setting to the text's meaning. Focus on the impact of the story's setting on the main character. Contrast the two settings of the story: the narrator's hometown described on page 631 and the area around Rainy River, on the Canadian border. What images and references paint a picture of the town and the narrator's life there? Why is it important for readers to have a picture of this town in their minds when they think about the remote Rainy River area?

Possible Response: The narrator's drive around his town takes him to Main Street and the courthouse—details that suggest a small town. The description of the town shows why the narrator feels both oppressed by his town and emotionally bound to it. The remote, beautiful Rainy River area represents freedom.

Literary Analysis

FIRST-PERSON POINT OF VIEW

Discuss the impact on the story if it had been told by Elroy Berdahl. What insights would readers lose? What insights might be added?

Possible Responses: Some students may point out that readers might not appreciate the intensity of the young man's feelings if the story were told from Elroy's point of view. Others might say readers would gain a more rational, objective telling of the young man's story, as seen through the eyes of someone who was older and not immediately involved.

ACTIVE READING

A QUESTION Elroy is intelligent, well educated, and spiritual. He sees God in nature and is at peace with himself and his environment.

Everything sparkled. My house, I thought. My life. I'm not sure how long I stood there, but later I scribbled out a short note to my parents.

What it said exactly, I don't recall now. Something vague. Taking off, will call, love Tim.

I drove north.

It was pure flight, fast and mindless. I had no plan. Just hit the border at high speed . . . and keep on running.

It's a blur now, as it was then, and all I remember is a sense of high velocity and the feel of the steering wheel in my hands. I was riding on adrenaline.[18] A giddy feeling, in a way, except there was the dreamy edge of impossibility to it—like running a dead-end maze—no way out—it couldn't come to a happy conclusion and yet I was doing it anyway because it was all I could think to do. It was pure flight, fast and mindless. I had no plan. Just hit the border at high speed and crash through and keep on running. Near dusk I passed through Bemidji, then turned northeast toward International Falls. I spent the night in the car behind a closed-down gas station a half mile from the border. In the morning, after gassing up, I headed straight west along the Rainy River, which separates Minnesota from Canada, and which for me separated one life from another. The land was mostly wilderness. Here and there I passed a motel or bait shop, but otherwise the country unfolded in great sweeps of pine and birch and sumac. Though it was still August, the air already had the smell of October, football season, piles of yellow-red leaves, everything crisp and clean. I remember a huge blue sky. Off to my right was the Rainy River, wide as a lake in places, and beyond the Rainy River was Canada.

1 For a while I just drove, not aiming at anything, then in the late morning I began looking for a place to lie low for a day or two. I was exhausted, and scared sick, and around noon I pulled into an old fishing resort called the Tip Top Lodge. Actually, it was not a lodge at all, just eight or nine tiny yellow cabins clustered on a peninsula that jutted northward into the Rainy River. The place was in sorry shape. There was a dangerous wooden dock, an old minnow tank, a flimsy tar paper boathouse along the shore. The main building, which stood in a cluster of pines on high ground, seemed to lean heavily to one side, like a cripple, the roof sagging toward Canada. Briefly, I thought about turning around, just giving up, but then I got out of the car and walked up to the front porch.

The man who opened the door that day is the hero of my life. How do I say this without sounding sappy? Blurt it out—the man saved 2
me. He offered exactly what I needed, without questions, without any words at all. He took me in. He was there at the critical time—a silent, watchful presence. Six days later, when it ended, I was unable to find a proper way to thank him, and I never have, and so, if nothing else, this story represents a small gesture of gratitude twenty years overdue.

Even after two decades I can close my eyes and return to that porch at the Tip Top Lodge. I can see the old guy staring at me. Elroy Berdahl: eighty-one years old, skinny and shrunken and mostly bald. He wore a flannel shirt and brown work pants. In one hand, I remember, he carried a green apple, a small paring knife in the other. His eyes had the bluish gray color of a razor

18. **adrenaline** (ə-drĕn′ə-lĭn): a hormone that is released into the bloodstream in response to physical or mental stress, such as fear, and that initiates or heightens several physical responses, including an increase in heart rate.

Teaching Options

Workplace Link

READING MAPS The narrator might need to read a map in order to drive from Worthington to the Canadian border. Maps provide a variety of data and are useful in scientific and practical situations. People in the workforce use maps for innumerable tasks: to navigate in a factory, to locate an engineering site, or to correlate anticipated sales with demographic trends. Floor plans and construction blueprints, topographic surveys, and even oceanographic sonar displays are kinds of maps.

Instruction Remind students that reading a road map is useful both on the job and in everyday life. Tell them that to interpret a map, they should look at the key or legend to find out what each symbol represents. Then they can locate their destination and plan their route. Point out that being able to look at a map and orally communicate directions to another person is also a useful skill.

Application Have students work with a partner. Provide each pair with a road map and a list of destinations (courthouse, hospital, shopping mall, stadium, and so forth). One partner should ask how to get to a destination, and the other should read the road map and give directions. Then have students switch roles.

blade, the same polished shine, and as he peered up at me I felt a strange sharpness, almost painful, a cutting sensation, as if his gaze were somehow slicing me open. In part, no doubt, it was my own sense of guilt, but even so I'm absolutely certain that the old man took one look and went right to the heart of things—a kid in trouble. When I asked for a room, Elroy made a little clicking sound with his tongue. He nodded, led me out to one of the cabins, and dropped a key in my hand. I remember smiling at him. I also remember wishing I hadn't. The old man shook his head as if to tell me it wasn't worth the bother.

"Dinner at five-thirty," he said. "You eat fish?"

"Anything," I said.

Elroy grunted and said, "I'll bet."

We spent six days together at the Tip Top Lodge. Just the two of us. Tourist season was over, and there were no boats on the river, and the wilderness seemed to withdraw into a great permanent stillness. Over those six days Elroy Berdahl and I took most of our meals together. In the mornings we sometimes went out on long hikes into the woods, and at night we played Scrabble or listened to records or sat reading in front of his big stone fireplace. At times I felt the awkwardness of an intruder, but Elroy accepted me into his quiet routine without fuss or ceremony. He took my presence for granted, the same way he might've sheltered a stray cat—no wasted sighs or pity—and there was never any talk about it. Just the opposite. What I remember more than anything is the man's willful, almost ferocious silence. In all that time together, all those hours, he never asked the obvious questions: Why was I there? Why alone? Why so <u>preoccupied</u>? If Elroy was curious about any of this, he was careful never to put it into words.

My hunch, though, is that he already knew. At least the basics. After all, it was 1968, and guys were burning draft cards, and Canada was just a boat ride away. Elroy Berdahl was no hick. His bedroom, I remember, was cluttered with books and newspapers. He killed me at the Scrabble board, barely concentrating, and on those occasions when speech was necessary, he had a way of compressing large thoughts into small, cryptic[19] packets of language. One evening, just at sunset, he pointed up at an owl circling over the violet-lighted forest to the west.

"Hey, O'Brien," he said. "There's Jesus."

The man was sharp—he didn't miss much. Those razor eyes. Now and then he'd catch me staring out at the river, at the far shore, and I could almost hear the tumblers clicking in his head. Maybe I'm wrong, but I doubt it. **3**

One thing for certain, he knew I was in desperate trouble. And he knew I couldn't talk about it. The wrong word—or even the right word—and I would've disappeared. I was wired and jittery. My skin felt too tight. After supper one evening I vomited and went back to my cabin and lay down for a few moments and then vomited again; another time, in the middle of the afternoon, I began sweating and couldn't shut it off. I went through whole days feeling dizzy with sorrow. I couldn't sleep; I couldn't lie still. At night I'd toss around in bed, half awake, half dreaming, imagining how I'd sneak down to the beach and quietly push one of the old man's boats out into the river and start paddling

ACTIVE READING

A **QUESTION** What do you think this incident reveals about Elroy?

19. **cryptic** (krĭp'tĭk): having a hidden or mysterious meaning; mystifying.

WORDS TO KNOW **preoccupied** (prē-ŏk'yə-pīd') *adj.* absorbed in one's thoughts; distracted **preoccupy** *v.*

Customizing Instruction

Less Proficient Readers

Use the following questions to guide students to understand the narrator's actions.

- Where does the narrator drive?
  Answer: He drives north, to the Canadian border.
- Why is he driving there?
  Possible Responses: He is trying to escape his anguish; he wants to flee to Canada.
- Where does he finally stop?
  Answer: He stops at Tip Top Lodge.

Students Acquiring English

1 Explain that *a place to lie low* means a place to hide.

2 Help students understand that *sappy* means overly sentimental. It derives from the word *sap,* which refers to the sticky, sweet liquid found in trees.

3 Explain that the phrase *the tumblers clicking in his head* refers to the mechanism of a combination lock. Ask students why the narrator uses this phrase here.
Possible Responses: to show that Elroy is thinking hard; to show that Elroy has "unlocked" the mystery of Tim's presence at the lodge

Multiple Learning Styles

Visual Learners
Have students sketch the Rainy River area from an aerial view, using the description in the story and adding imaginary details where necessary.

Mini Lesson Vocabulary Strategy

WORD MEANINGS AND SPELLING Instruction The meaning of words can help students identify and spell the words correctly. Knowing word meanings can also help them identify prefixes, suffixes, and roots, and identify the word's part of speech. It may also help them tell the difference between two words that sound alike but are spelled differently (homonyms, for example, *altar/alter*).

Practice Have students work in pairs to find the meanings and root word of *preoccupation, occupation*, and *occupancy*. Point out that because the root is *occupy,* the base of all these words is spelled with two *c*'s and one *p*. Then have students find the different meanings of the following homonyms: They may consult a dictionary for precise meaning and usage.

1. cite/sight/site
2. hole/whole
3. pair/pare/pear
4. past/passed
5. there/their/they're
6. to/too/two
7. weather/whether

Use **Vocabulary Transparencies and Copymasters,** p. 66, for more exercises.

A lesson on antonyms appears on p. 1000 in the Pupil's Edition.

Reading and Analyzing

Literary Analysis: CHARACTER

Have students summarize the traits of Elroy Berdahl they have observed.

Possible Response: He is quiet and still like the wilderness, perceptive, well-read, intelligent, insightful, and respectful of others' privacy.

Reading Skills and Strategies: COMPARING

Have students compare the narrator's behavior and personality with Elroy's. What differences exist between the characters? What similarities?

Possible Responses: Students will find numerous differences between the two characters–age, background, maturity, sense of identity. The two characters share traits also: they are both well-read, intelligent men.

Active Reading

MAKING JUDGMENTS

Ask students what they think about the narrator's decision to leave his job and go to the Rainy River.

Possible Responses: It was a good decision because he needed to get away; it was an irresponsible decision because running away is cowardly and never solves anything.

my way toward Canada. There were times when I thought I'd gone off the psychic edge. I couldn't tell up from down, I was just falling, and late in the night I'd lie there watching weird pictures spin through my head. Getting chased by the Border Patrol—helicopters and searchlights and barking dogs—I'd be crashing through the woods, I'd be down on my hands and knees—people shouting out my name—the law closing in on all sides—my hometown draft board and the FBI and the Royal Canadian Mounted Police. It all seemed crazy and impossible. Twenty-one years old, an ordinary kid with all the ordinary dreams and ambitions, and all I wanted was to live the life I was born to—a mainstream life—I loved baseball and hamburgers and cherry Cokes—and now I was off on the margins of exile, leaving my country forever, and it seemed so impossible and terrible and sad.

I'm not sure how I made it through those six days. Most of it I can't remember. On two or three afternoons, to pass some time, I helped Elroy get the place ready for winter, sweeping down the cabins and hauling in the boats, little chores that kept my body moving. The days were cool and bright. The nights were very dark. One morning the old man showed me how to split and stack firewood, and for several hours we just worked in silence out behind his house. At one point, I remember, Elroy put down his maul[20]
1
and looked at me for a long time, his lips drawn as if framing a difficult question, but then he shook his head and went back to work. The man's self-control was amazing. He never pried. He never put me in a position that required lies or denials. To an extent, I supposed, his reticence was typical of that part of Minnesota, where privacy still held value, and even if I'd been walking around with some horrible deformity—four arms and three heads—I'm sure the old man would've talked about everything except those extra arms and heads. Simple politeness was part of it. But even more than that, I think, the man understood that words were insufficient. The problem had gone beyond discussion. During that long summer I'd been over and over the various arguments, all the pros and cons, and it was no longer a question that could be decided by an act of pure reason. Intellect had come up against emotion. My conscience told me to run, but some irrational and powerful force was resisting, like a weight pushing me toward the war. What it came down to, stupidly, was a sense of shame. Hot, stupid shame. I did not want people to think badly of me. Not my parents, not my brother and sister, not even the folks down at the Gobbler Café. I was ashamed to be there at the Tip Top Lodge. I was ashamed of my conscience, ashamed to be doing the right thing.

Some of this Elroy must've understood. Not the details, of course, but the plain fact of crisis.

Although the old man never confronted me about it, there was one occasion when he came close to forcing the whole thing out into the open. It was early evening, and we'd just finished supper, and over coffee and dessert I asked him about my bill, how much I owed so far. For a long while the old man squinted down at the tablecloth.

"Well, the basic rate," he said, "is fifty bucks a night. Not counting meals. This makes four nights, right?"

I nodded. I had three hundred and twelve dollars in my wallet.

Elroy kept his eyes on the tablecloth. "Now that's an on-season price. To be fair, I suppose we should knock it down a peg or two." He leaned back in his chair. "What's a reasonable number, you figure?"

"I don't know," I said. "Forty?"

20. **maul** (môl): heavy, long-handled hammer.

WORDS TO KNOW **reticence** (rĕt′ĭ-səns) *n.* the state or quality of being reserved and keeping one's thoughts to oneself

Teaching Options

Cross Curricular Link History

CROSSING THE BORDER Canada did not refuse entry to those young men who evaded the U.S. draft or deserted the military. In fact, Canada had long opposed the concept of military conscription and regarded U. S. involvement in Vietnam as a terrible mistake. From 1964 to 1973 approximately 10,000 men of draft age fled the country to avoid serving in Vietnam. Some traveled to Sweden, which, like Canada, opposed the war. Many others took advantage of the relative proximity of the Canadian border. After crossing into Canada, they found jobs and adapted to their lives in exile. In 1977, President Carter pardoned most of those who had violated draft laws during that era. However, the pardon did not extend to the estimated 100,000 military deserters.

Sea Air (1987), Douglas Brega. Dry brush on paper, 14″ × 21″, courtesy of the artist.

"Forty's good. Forty a night. Then we tack on food—say another hundred? Two hundred sixty total?"

"I guess."

He raised his eyebrows. "Too much?"

"No, that's fair. It's fine. Tomorrow, though . . . I think I'd better take off tomorrow."

Elroy shrugged and began clearing the table. For a time he fussed with the dishes, whistling to himself as if the subject had been settled. After a second he slapped his hands together.

"You know what we forgot?" he said. "We forgot wages. Those odd jobs you done. What we have to do, we have to figure out what your time's worth. Your last job—how much did you pull in an hour?"

"Not enough," I said.

"A bad one?"

"Yes. Pretty bad."

Slowly then, without intending any long sermon, I told him about my days at the pig plant. It began as a straight recitation of the facts, but before I could stop myself I was talking about the blood clots and the water gun and how the smell had soaked into my skin and how I couldn't wash it away. I went on for a long time. I told him about wild hogs squealing in my dreams, the sounds of butchery, slaughterhouse sounds, and how I'd sometimes wake up with that greasy pig-stink in my throat.

When I was finished, Elroy nodded at me.

"Well, to be honest," he said, "when you first showed up here, I wondered about that. The aroma, I mean. Smelled like you was awful

Customizing Instruction

Less Proficient Readers

Have students explain why Elroy's reticence is so helpful to the narrator.

Possible Response: Elroy's silence allows the narrator to think things out for himself, slowly and without pressure.

Gifted and Talented

1 Students can analyze the diction in this paragraph to explain how it reveals the narrator's disgust for brutality and therefore, his reluctance to join the army.

Mini Lesson Viewing and Representing

Sea Air by Douglas Brega

ART APPRECIATION In this portrait, artist Douglas Brega (1948–) creates unity by repeating lines and textures. He echoes the lines in the man's face with the ribbed cap and jacket zipper. The fur collar and the beard also have related textures. The man's furrowed brow and squinting eye suggest that he is a keen and experienced seaman.

Instruction Point out to students that the lines and textures of the portrait enhance the sense of realism. Ask students what qualities and details in the portrait make the viewer feel that this seaman really exists.

Possible Response: The details of the man's coat and hat and the weathered character of his face make him seem like a real person instead of an artist's creation.

Application Have students compare their impressions of Elroy Berdahl with the subject of Brega's portrait. Is the man in the portrait like Elroy? Why or why not?

Possible Response: Like Elroy, the man in the portrait is older and toughened by his life in nature. Both men seem comfortable with themselves.

Reading and Analyzing

Literary Analysis: CHARACTER

A Ask students what the reader learns (or what is confirmed) about the narrator's personality from the thoughts and descriptions of the fishing trip. Have students discuss whether the narrator seems critical of himself, and, if so, how.

Possible Response: The narrator's indecision, his youthfulness, his fears, and his self-absorption all come across in his description. The description lays open the young man's fears to the reader. He is critical of himself, confessing that he is not the hero he hoped to be.

ACTIVE READING

B **PREDICT** The narrator will flee to Canada; the narrator will make a decision; the narrator will tell Elroy everything.

damned fond of pork chops." The old man almost smiled. He made a snuffling sound, then sat down with a pencil and a piece of
1 paper. "So what'd this crud job pay? Ten bucks an hour? Fifteen?"

"Less."

Elroy shook his head. "Let's make it fifteen. You put in twenty-five hours here, easy. That's three hundred seventy-five bucks total wages. We subtract the two hundred sixty for food and lodging. I still owe you a hundred and fifteen."

He took four fifties out of his shirt pocket and laid them on the table.

"Call it even," he said.

"No."

"Pick it up. Get yourself a haircut."

The money lay on the table for the rest of the evening. It was still there when I went back to my cabin. In the morning though, I found an envelope tacked to my door. Inside were the four fifties and a two-word note that said EMERGENCY FUND.

The man knew.

Looking back after twenty years, I sometimes wonder if the events of that summer didn't happen in some other dimension, a place where your life exists before you've lived it, and where it goes afterward. None of it ever seemed real. During my time at the Tip Top Lodge I had the feeling that I'd slipped out of my own skin, hovering a few feet away while some poor yo-yo with my name and face tried to make his way toward a future he didn't understand and didn't want. Even now I can see myself as I was then. It's like watching an old home movie: I'm young and tan and fit. I've got hair—lots of it. I don't smoke or drink. I'm wearing faded blue jeans and a white polo shirt. I can see myself sitting on Elroy Berdahl's dock near dusk one evening, the sky a bright shimmering pink, and I'm finishing up a letter to my parents that tells what I'm about to do and why I'm doing it and how sorry I am that I've never found the courage to talk to them about it. I ask them not to be angry. I try to explain some of my feelings, but there aren't enough words, and so I just say that it's a thing that has to be done. At the end of the letter I talk about the vacations we used to take up in this north country, at a place called Whitefish Lake, and how the scenery here reminds me of those good times. I tell them I'm fine. I tell them I'll write again from Winnipeg or Montreal or wherever I end up.

On my last full day, the sixth day, **A** the old man took me out fishing on the Rainy River. The afternoon was sunny and cold. A stiff breeze came in from the north, and I remember how the little fourteen-foot boat made sharp rocking motions as we pushed off from the dock. The current was fast. All around us, I remember, there was a vastness to the world, an unpeopled rawness, just the trees and the sky and the water reaching out toward nowhere. The air had the brittle scent of October.

For ten or fifteen minutes Elroy held a course upstream, the river choppy and silver-gray, then he turned straight north and put the engine on full throttle. I felt the bow lift beneath me. I remember the wind in my ears, the sound of the old outboard Evinrude. For a time I didn't pay attention to anything, just feeling the cold spray against my face, but then it occurred to me that at some point we must've passed into Canadian waters, across that dotted line between two different worlds, and I remember a sudden tightness in my chest as I looked up and watched the far shore come at me. This wasn't a daydream. It was tangible and real. As we came in toward land, Elroy cut the engine, letting the boat fishtail lightly about twenty yards off shore. The old man didn't look at me or speak. Bending

ACTIVE READING

B **PREDICT** What do you think will happen on the fishing trip?

Teaching Options

Mini Lesson Grammar

INFINITIVE PHRASES Explain that an infinitive phrase consists of the infinitive form of a verb and its modifiers. An infinitive phrase may function as a noun, an adjective, or an adverb. Write the following sentences on the chalkboard:

To receive a draft notice was every young man's nightmare. (*noun*)

Escaping to Canada was one way to avoid the draft. (*adjective*)

He is proud to have followed his conscience. (*adverb*)

Underline the infinitive phrases as shown. Then discuss with students their functions in the sentences. If possible, help students identify functions by diagramming the sentences.

Practice Have students copy the following sentences. Ask them to underline the infinitive phrases. Work as a class to determine the function of each infinitive phrase.

1. Elroy worked hard to prepare the lodge for winter.
   Answer: infinitive as adverb

down, he opened up his tackle box and busied himself with a bobber and a piece of wire leader, humming to himself, his eyes down.

It struck me then that he must've planned it. I'll never be certain, of course, but I think he meant to bring me up against the realities, to guide me across the river and to take me to the edge and to stand a kind of vigil as I chose a life for myself.

I remember staring at the old man, then at my hands, then at Canada. The shoreline was dense with brush and timber. I could see tiny red berries on the bushes. I could see a squirrel up in one of the birch trees, a big crow looking at me from a boulder along the river. That close—twenty yards—and I could see the delicate latticework of the leaves, the texture of the soil, the browned needles beneath the pines, the configurations of geology and human history. Twenty yards. I could've done it. I could've jumped and started swimming for my life. Inside me, in my chest, I felt a terrible squeezing pressure. Even now, as I write this, I can still feel that tightness. And I want you to feel it—the wind coming off the river, the waves, the silence, the wooded frontier. You're at the bow of a boat on the Rainy River. You're twenty-one years old, you're scared, and there's a hard squeezing pressure in your chest.

What would you do?

Would you jump? Would you feel pity for yourself? Would you think about the family and your childhood and your dreams and all you're leaving behind? Would it hurt? Would it feel like dying? Would you cry, as I did?

I tried to swallow it back. I tried to smile, except I was crying.

Now, perhaps, you can understand why I've never told this story before. It's not just the embarrassment of tears. That's part of it, no doubt, but what embarrasses me much more, and always will, is the paralysis that took my heart. A moral freeze: I couldn't decide, I couldn't act, I couldn't comport myself with even a pretense of modest human dignity.

All I could do was cry. Quietly, not bawling, just the chest-chokes.

At the rear of the boat Elroy Berdahl pretended not to notice. He held a fishing rod in his hands, his head bowed to hide his eyes. He kept humming a soft, monotonous little tune. Everywhere, it seemed, in the trees and water and sky, a great worldwide sadness came pressing down on me, a crushing sorrow, sorrow like I had never known before. And what was so sad, I realized, was that Canada had become a pitiful fantasy. Silly and hopeless. It was no longer a possibility. Right then, with the shore so close, I understood that I would not do what I should do. I would not swim away from my hometown and my country and my life. I would not be brave. That old image of myself as a hero, as a man of conscience and courage, all that was just a threadbare pipe dream.[21] Bobbing there on the Rainy River, looking back at the Minnesota shore, I felt a sudden swell of helplessness come over me, a drowning sensation, as if I had toppled overboard and was being swept away by the sil-

I think he meant to bring me up against the realities . . . to stand a kind of vigil as I chose a life for myself.

21. **pipe dream:** daydream or fantasy that will never happen; vain hope.

WORDS TO KNOW
vigil (vĭj'əl) *n.* a watch kept by a person, especially during normal sleeping hours or to show devotion
pretense (prē'tĕns') *n.* a false outward appearance

Customizing Instruction

Less Proficient Readers

Guide student understanding by asking the following questions:

- Why is the narrator staying at the Tip Top Lodge?
  Possible Response: He drove to the U.S.-Canadian border to get away from his hometown and found the lodge along the river. He doesn't know what to do about his draft notice and was thinking about fleeing to Canada.
- What does the narrator do while he is there?
  Answer: He hikes, does work for Elroy, hangs out with him, and thinks about his situation.

Multiple Learning Styles

Mathematical Learners

1 Have students check Elroy's arithmetic for the bill and the "wages" earned by the narrator (on pages 634–636).

Answer: Elroy inflated the total of the narrator's wages by $30 (the correct total is $345).

Multiple Learning Styles

Visual Learners

2 Encourage students to visualize the anxious narrator against the backdrop of a quiet river scene. What contrasts do the two images suggest?

Possible Response: The narrator is in turmoil, while the river is peaceful. The river is the most important thing in the narrator's life at that moment, while the river is unaffected by the narrator and his inner conflict.

2. The narrator wanted to feel clean.
Answer: infinitive as noun

3. It was a decision to end all decisions.
Answer: infinitive as adjective

4. To avoid embarrassment was Tim's ultimate goal.
Answer: infinitive as noun

5. The Vietnam Memorial in Washington, D.C., is an important place to visit.
Answer: infinitive as adjective

Use **Grammar Transparencies and Copymasters,** p.100, for more exercises.

Use McDougal Littell's ***Language Network,*** Chapter 3, for more instruction in infinitive phrases.

Reading and Analyzing

Reading Skills and Strategies: CLARIFYING

Have students analyze the narrator's hallucination and the "crowd" of onlookers. What does the crowd seem to represent? What does it foreshadow about the narrator's decision?

Possible Response: The crowd represents a cross-section of humanity, including characters from the narrator's future. The narrator even sees a man he would later "kill with a hand grenade"—clearly foreshadowing that he will decide to go to war.

Literary Analysis: DESCRIPTION

Have students discuss the breadth and specificity of the narrator's vision by considering the individual images and their overall effect. Point out the "collage" effect of his description. How do the details help the reader see into the narrator's mind? How does the vision affect the narrator?

Atascadero Dusk (about 1990), Robert Reynolds. Watercolor, 22″ × 15″. *From Painting Nature's Beautiful Places,* published by North Light Books.

638

Teaching Options

Mini Lesson: Viewing and Representing

Atascadero Dusk **by Robert Reynolds**

ART APPRECIATION In this watercolor painting, Reynolds repeats the colors and shadings of the sky and trees in the water reflections. This helps give the painting unity and draws the viewer's eye beyond the boat to the water and the shore behind it.

Instruction Have students focus on the uses of reflection in the painting and how the colors and details create a mood. Ask students to imagine how the mood of the painting would change if the artist had included people in the picture.

Application Ask students whether the mood of the painting matches the mood of the story. Why or why not?

Possible Responses: Some students will see the similarity of settings; others might contrast the reflective, quiet mood of the painting with the inner turmoil of the author.

ver waves. Chunks of my own history flashed by. I saw a seven-year-old boy in a white cowboy hat and a Lone Ranger mask and a pair of holstered six-shooters; I saw a twelve-year-old Little League shortstop pivoting to turn a double play; I saw a sixteen-year-old kid decked out for his first prom, looking spiffy in a white tux and a black bow tie, his hair cut short and flat, his shoes freshly polished. My whole life seemed to spill out into the river, swirling away from me, everything I had ever been or ever wanted to be. I couldn't get my breath; I couldn't stay afloat; I couldn't tell which way to swim. A hallucination, I suppose, but it was as real as anything I would ever feel. I saw my parents calling to me from the far shoreline. I saw my brother and sister, all the townsfolk, the mayor and the entire Chamber of Commerce and all my old teachers and girlfriends and high school buddies. Like some weird sporting event: everybody screaming from the sidelines, rooting me on—a loud stadium roar. Hotdogs and popcorn—stadium smells, stadium heat. A squad of cheerleaders did cartwheels along the banks of the Rainy River; they had megaphones and pompoms and smooth brown thighs. The crowd swayed left and right. A marching band played fight songs. All my aunts and uncles were there, and Abraham Lincoln and Saint George,[22] and a nine-year-old girl named Linda who had died of a brain tumor back in fifth grade, and several members of the United States Senate, and a blind poet scribbling notes, and LBJ, and Huck Finn, and Abbie Hoffman,[23] and all the dead soldiers back from the grave, and the many thousands who were later to die—villagers with terrible burns, little kids without arms or legs—yes, and the Joint Chiefs of Staff[24] were there, and a couple of popes, and a first lieutenant named Jimmy Cross, and the last surviving veteran of the American Civil War, and Jane Fonda dressed up as Barbarella,[25] and an old man sprawled beside a pigpen, and my grandfather, and Gary Cooper,[26] and a kind-faced woman carrying an umbrella and a copy of Plato's *Republic,*[27] and a million ferocious citizens waving flags of all shapes and colors—people in hardhats, people in headbands—they were all whooping and chanting and urging me toward one shore or the other. I saw faces from my distant past and distant future. My wife was there. My unborn daughter waved at me, and my two sons hopped up and down, and a drill sergeant named Blyton sneered and shot up a finger and shook his head. There was a choir in bright purple robes. There was a cabbie from the Bronx. There was a slim young man I would one day kill with a hand grenade along a red clay trail outside the village of My Khe.[28]

The little aluminum boat rocked softly beneath me. There was the wind and the sky.

I tried to will myself overboard.

I gripped the edge of the boat and leaned forward and thought, *Now.*

I did try. It just wasn't possible.

All those eyes on me—the town, the whole universe—and I couldn't risk the embarrassment. It was as if there were an audience to my life, that swirl of faces along the river, and in my

22. **Saint George:** Christian martyr (killed about A.D. 303) and patron saint of England who, according to legend, slew a frightening dragon.
23. **Abbie Hoffman:** social organizer and radical anti–Vietnam War activist known for his humor and politically inspired pranks.
24. **Joint Chiefs of Staff:** the principal military advisors of the U.S. president, including the chiefs of the army, navy, and air force and the commandant of the marines.
25. **Jane Fonda dressed up as Barbarella:** anti–Vietnam War activist and actress Jane Fonda (1937–), dressed as Barbarella, the title character she played in a 1968 science fiction film.
26. **Gary Cooper:** American actor famous for playing strong, quiet heroes.
27. **Plato's *Republic:*** a famous work in which the ancient Greek philosopher Plato describes the ideal state or society.
28. **My Khe** (mē′ kē′).

Customizing Instruction

Less Proficient Readers

Help guide students by asking the following questions:

- What kinds of people take part in the narrator's hallucination?
  Answer: Many different kinds, particularly those the narrator has met or will meet later in life.
- Why are these people watching the narrator?
  Possible Response: They are all affected by his decision or they have influenced his decision in some way.
- How do we know that this scene is imaginary?
  Possible Response: The scene includes people who obviously couldn't be near the Rainy River, especially those who were not yet born.

Students Acquiring English

1 Help students understand idiomatic expressions such as *decked out,* which means "dressed up."

Mini Lesson Multicultural Link

EMIGRATION FROM SOUTHEAST ASIA Following the collapse of South Vietnam's western-backed government at the end of the Vietnam War, large numbers of Vietnamese came to the United States. Just before the fall of Saigon, some 120,000 high-ranking officials from South Vietnam were hastily evacuated. Throughout the late 1970s and early 1980s, more refugees fled economic and political turmoil in Southeast Asia, often escaping in dangerously overcrowded boats. Nearly one million "boat people" settled abroad, with some 750,000 coming to the United States since 1975.

Two groups of immigrants came under special arrangement: mixed-race children of U.S. military personnel and Vietnamese women, and former political prisoners. Many Vietnamese refugees settled in California, Texas, and Virginia.

In addition to Vietnamese immigration, the conflict in Southeast Asia also brought smaller numbers of immigrants from Laos and, after the overthrow of the Khmer Rouge in 1979, from Cambodia. Like other immigrant groups, the refugees from Southeast Asia, while facing language and social barriers, have enriched U.S. culture.

Reading and Analyzing

Active Reading

MAKING JUDGMENTS

Have students discuss their judgments about the narrator's decision. Ask them to review their original views of the narrator's options. Has anything in the story helped change their minds about the narrator's options?

Possible Responses: Some students may feel that the narrator made the right decision based on his circumstances. Others may be disappointed that the narrator did not follow his moral beliefs and flee to Canada.

Literary Analysis: THEME

A story's theme is its central idea or message. Have students identify the theme of this story.

Possible Responses: Making moral decisions can be difficult because of the conflict between an individual's conscience and societal pressures.

Then ask students how the poem by Adrienne Rich helps the reader imagine the narrator's dilemma. Does it have a similar theme?

Possible Response: Rich's description of a fish struggling to breathe air can be applied to the narrator's struggle to make a decision. The poem, like the story, deals with the difficulty of thinking hard without the interference of "the old consolations"–social pressure, cultural norms, and ties to family and friends.

ACTIVE READING

A MAKE JUDGMENTS The narrator is too embarrassed not to go to the war. Students may want to discuss whether this is a sound reason for making a decision, or if the narrator had also considered other reasons.

head I could hear people screaming at me. Traitor! they yelled. Turncoat! I felt myself blush. I couldn't tolerate it. I couldn't endure the mockery, or the disgrace, or the patriotic ridicule. Even in my imagination, the shore just twenty yards away, I couldn't make myself be brave. It had nothing to do with morality. Embarrassment, that's all it was.

And right then I submitted.

I would go to the war—I would kill and maybe die—because I was embarrassed not to.

ACTIVE READING

A **MAKE JUDGMENTS** How do you judge the reason the narrator gives for his decision?

That was the sad thing. And so I sat in the bow of the boat and cried. It was loud now. Loud, hard crying.

Elroy Berdahl remained quiet. He kept fishing. He worked his line with the tips of his fingers, patiently, squinting out at his red and white bobber on the Rainy River. His eyes were flat and impassive. He didn't speak. He was simply there, like the river and the late-summer sun. And yet by his presence, his mute watchfulness, he made it real. He was the true audience. He was a witness, like God, or like the gods, who look on in absolute silence as we live our lives, as we make our choices or fail to make them.

"Ain't biting," he said.

Then after a time the old man pulled in his line and turned the boat back toward Minnesota.

I don't remember saying goodbye. That last night we had dinner together, and I went to bed early, and in the morning Elroy fixed breakfast for me. When I told him I'd be leaving, the old man nodded as if he already knew. He looked down at the table and smiled.

At some point later in the morning it's possible that we shook hands—I just don't remember—but I do know that by the time I'd finished packing the old man had disappeared. Around noon, when I took my suitcase out to the car, I noticed that his old black pickup truck was no longer parked in front of the house. I went inside and waited for a while, but I felt a bone certainty that he wouldn't be back. In a way, I thought, it was appropriate. I washed up the breakfast dishes, left his two hundred dollars on the kitchen counter, got into the car, and drove south toward home.

The day was cloudy. I passed through towns with familiar names, through the pine forests and down to the prairie, and then to Vietnam, where I was a soldier, and then home again. I survived, but it's not a happy ending. I was a coward. I went to the war. ❖

WORDS TO KNOW **impassive** (ĭm-păs′ĭv) *adj.* revealing no emotion; expressionless

Teaching Options

Assessment Informal Assessment

MAKE JUDGMENTS You can informally assess students' understanding of this selection by having them respond to the following statement:

In an interview, writer Tim O'Brien called Elroy "an analogue for conscience . . ."

Have students write an essay explaining how Elroy acts as the narrator's conscience. Evidence from the story or from their own experience can support their explanations.

RUBRIC

3 **Full Accomplishment** Response demonstrates a full understanding of Elroy's role in the story and in the narrator's life. Evidence is thorough and used effectively.

2 **Substantial Accomplishment** Response demonstrates a substantial understanding of Elroy's role in the story and in the narrator's life. Evidence is logical and provides adequate support.

1 **Little or Partial Accomplishment** Response shows little understanding of Elroy's role in the story and in the narrator's life. Evidence is inadequate.

LITERARY LINK

Ghost of a Chance [1]

Adrienne Rich

You see a man
trying to think.

You want to say
to everything:
Keep off! Give him room! [2]
But you only watch,
terrified
the old consolations
will get him at last
like a fish
half-dead from flopping
and almost crawling
across the shingle,
almost breathing
the raw, agonizing
air
till a wave
pulls it back blind into the triumphant
sea.

Customizing Instruction

Less Proficient Readers

Have students answer the following questions:

- How does the narrator react when he finally makes his decision?
  Answer: He cries.
- What does he leave on the kitchen counter?
  Answer: the two hundred dollars that Elroy gave him

Students Acquiring English

[1] Help students understand the meaning of the title of Rich's poem, "Ghost of a Chance." Explain that it means the most remote chance or the smallest opportunity.

[2] Help students understand the meaning of the idiom *give him room* (line 5; let someone have more space, literally and/or figuratively). Discuss the meaning of the phrase *old consolations* (line 8). How might that phrase relate to difficult decisions?

Possible Response: It might mean the easier or less moral decision that someone faced with a dilemma could make.

Gifted and Talented

Have students analyze the imagery in Rich's poem. What has happened to the fish? Why is the fish "almost breathing" (line 14)? Encourage students to compare the water imagery in Tim O'Brien's story with the water imagery in Adrienne Rich's poem.

GUIDING STUDENT RESPONSE

Connect to the Literature

1. What Do You Think?
Some students may feel that the narrator has made the right decision by obeying the law. Others may feel that he should have fled to Canada in order to avoid fighting in a war that he opposes.

Comprehension Check
- He drives to the Canadian border to try to decide what to do about his draft notice.
- Elroy is silent and accepting; he allows the narrator to make up his own mind; finally, on a fishing trip, he takes the narrator to the Canadian border.

Use Selection Quiz
Unit Four Resource Book, p. 46.

Think Critically

2. Some students may agree with the narrator's view, because he cared more for the opinions of others than for his own beliefs. Other students may think that the narrator is being hard on himself and that either decision—avoiding war or going to war—required courage.

3. Elroy provides the narrator with a quiet, supportive place in which to work through his conflicting feelings. By giving the narrator a chance to flee to Canada, Elroy helps him confront his decision; he respects the fact that the narrator has to make his own decision.

4. The description shows the narrator's dislike of killing and blood; it also shows that the narrator is responsible enough to stick to an unpleasant job.

5. Students should be open to discussing the terrible moral predicament that O'Brien confronted.

6. Possible Response: The narrator's conviction that the Vietnam War is wrong is being tested. Another conviction that is tested is his belief that, faced with a crisis, he would draw on heroic reserves of courage and make the moral choice. His conviction that living up to the expectations of his family, his community, and his country is most important.

Thinking through the LITERATURE

Connect to the Literature

1. What Do You Think? What is your reaction to the narrator's final decision?

Comprehension Check
- Why does the narrator drive up near the Canadian border?
- What does Elroy Berdahl do to help the narrator make up his mind?

Think Critically

2. The **narrator** feels he was a coward for fighting in the Vietnam War. Do you share his opinion? Why or why not?

3. What do you think the narrator means when he says that Elroy Berdahl "saved" him?

THINK ABOUT
- the effect of Elroy's silence
- his offer of money to the narrator
- why he takes the narrator fishing

4. The narrator gives a detailed **description** of his summer job in a meat-packing plant. Why do you think this description is included?

5. **ACTIVE READING** MAKING JUDGMENTS Review the chart in your READER'S NOTEBOOK. What judgment did you make about the narrator's final decision? If you had been in his position, would you have chosen to fight in the war or to flee to Canada? Explain your answer.

6. "Tests of Conviction" is the title given to this part of Unit Four. What conviction do you think is being tested in this story? In your opinion, does the narrator "pass" the test? Why or why not?

Extend Interpretations

7. **What If?** What do you think would have happened if the narrator had decided to do the "brave" thing and flee to Canada? How might Elroy have reacted? Would the narrator have regretted his decision? Give reasons to support your answers.

8. **Connect to Life** Should a government be able to compel citizens to fight in wars? Why or why not?

Literary Analysis

POINT OF VIEW In the **first-person point of view,** the **narrator** is a **character** in the story who tells everything in his or her own words. A first-person narrator tends to involve the reader in the story and to communicate a sense of immediacy and personal concern. In the opening of this story, for example, the narrator talks directly to the reader, as if the reader were a close friend or confidant:

This is one story I've never told before. Not to anyone. Not to my parents, not to my brother or sister, not even to my wife.

The first-person point of view can also sometimes make a fictional story seem more true to life.

Cooperative Learning Activity In a small group, choose three or four passages in the story that you think are crucial for understanding the narrator's decision. Take turns reading the passages aloud in a way that communicates the narrator's emotions and state of mind. Based on your readings, discuss how O'Brien's use of first-person point of view affects your feelings about the narrator and your judgment of his action.

Extend Interpretations

What If? If the narrator had decided to flee to Canada, Elroy would have handed him the "emergency fund," said good-bye, and wished him good luck. The narrator would have quickly regretted his decision, because he would hate being exiled from his country. Ultimately, he might also have realized that if he had truly opposed the war, he would have protested more vehemently and earned the status of conscientious objector.

Connect to Life Some students may say that a government must have this power in order to pull together a large enough army to defend itself or its allies against attack. Other students may believe that citizens should have the freedom to choose the causes for which they will fight.

Literary Analysis

Point of View Students may want to share their group's most moving or important passage with the whole class.

Choices & CHALLENGES

Writing Options

1. Elroy's Letter Assume the identity of Elroy in "On the Rainy River" and write a letter to a relative, telling about your unusual week with the boy from Minnesota.

2. Definition of Courage Draft an essay that develops your own definition of courage, showing how your personal definition is similar to or different from the narrator's.

3. New Ending Imagine that when the narrator feels the impulse to jump from the boat and swim toward Canada, he actually does so. Write an alternative ending to the story from this point on.

Writing Handbook
See page 1155: Narrative Writing.

Activities & Explorations

1. Point/Counterpoint Discussion With your entire class, conduct a point/counterpoint discussion that explores both sides of the narrator's conscience. One side of the class should argue in favor of military service; the other side should argue in favor of fleeing to Canada. Use evidence from the story to support your views. ~ **SPEAKING AND LISTENING**

2. Rainy River Collage Create a collage based on the vision the narrator has while he's on the Rainy River (pages 637–640). You may include photos, clippings from newspapers and magazines, and your own drawings of the images that the narrator thinks he sees. ~ **ART**

3. Protest Songs Bring in recordings of folk and rock protest songs from the Vietnam War era and play them for your class. Discuss how these songs express moral and political objections to the conflict. ~ **MUSIC**

Inquiry & Research

Living History Tape-record or videotape interviews with people who lived through the Vietnam War era. Have them describe their feelings about the war and their experiences with the draft, the fighting itself, and the rallies or protests on the home front. Then write a feature story for the school newspaper.

Art Connection

What do you think is the connection between the painting *Portrait of Donald Schrader* on page 627 and the first part of the story?

Vocabulary in Action

EXERCISE: CONTEXT CLUES Choose the word that best completes each of the following sentences.

1. Grandma says that long before Dad was drafted, he was so _______ with the Vietnam War that he couldn't focus on his schoolwork.
2. Dad believed in the _______ of defending one's country, but he didn't understand how the Vietnam War connected to freedom at home.
3. He found the tangled web of Vietnamese politics difficult to _______.
4. In the United States, there was no _______ about the war; hawks said one thing, and doves said another.
5. My grandfather understood Dad's reluctance to fight in that war; he used to say "War is hell," but that was only a _______.
6. After receiving his draft notice, Dad stayed up all night holding a lonely _______.
7. Since Dad was usually so cheerful and talkative in the morning, his _______ at breakfast the next day made my grandfather feel sad.
8. To Grandma he seemed calm, but that was merely _______, for he was troubled.
9. He kept his face _______ so that Grandma could not observe his feelings.
10. When Grandma asked if he would soon be going overseas to fight, he nodded in _______.

WORDS TO KNOW				
acquiescence	fathom	imperative	preoccupied	reticence
consensus	impassive	platitude	pretense	vigil

Building Vocabulary
For an in-depth study on context clues, see page 56.

Writing Options

1. **Elroy's Letter** Elroy was knowledgeable and probably well-read, according to the narrator. Encourage students to include in the letter the thoughts Elroy might have had that he did not share with the narrator.
2. **Definition of Courage** Encourage students to develop definitions of courage through specific illustrations or to narrate a time when they exhibited courage (or failed to exhibit courage).
3. **New Ending** Character analysis will help students imagine how the character would react in an alternative ending. Flight to Canada would have resulted in very definite changes in the narrator's life, especially separation from his parents and home.

Activities & Explorations

1. **Point/Counterpoint Discussion** Encourage teams to anticipate, and plan to counter, the arguments their opponents might use.
2. **Rainy River Collage** Suggest that students refer not only to library sources, but also to friends and family who may have kept magazines and newspapers from the Vietnam War era. If possible, have students work in teams to locate images.
3. **Protest Songs** Well-known antiwar songs include "Where Have All the Flowers Gone" (Pete Seeger), "Blowing in the Wind" (Peter, Paul, and Mary) and "Universal Soldier" (Buffy St. Marie). Bob Dylan, Joan Baez, Judy Collins, and numerous rock groups also sang protest songs.

Inquiry & Research

Living History Good interviewers are good listeners and as a result may modify their questions in the interview process.

Art Connection

The painting shows a young man who, like the narrator, seems to be in a state of indecision and deep thought.

Vocabulary in Action

1. preoccupied
2. imperative
3. fathom
4. consensus
5. platitude
6. vigil
7. reticence
8. pretense
9. impassive
10. acquiescence

Grammar in Action

WRITING EXERCISE Answers may vary. Possible answers are shown.

1. Asking a lot of questions about the war didn't help me find answers.
2. Working in the factory couldn't silence the howls of war in my head.
3. My modest antiwar activities included supporting the campaign of Eugene McCarthy.

Author Activity

Like the story "On the Rainy River," the article jumps back and forth between two different time frames. (Indeed, this effect is much more pronounced in the article, where the time frames are identified by month and year.) Ask students to think about this narrative effect.

Choices & CHALLENGES

Grammar in Context: Gerund Phrases

In this excerpt from "On the Rainy River," the narrator recalls the morning he left home and headed north.

> **I remember** packing a suitcase and carrying it out to the kitchen, standing very still for a few minutes, looking carefully at the familiar objects all around me.

A **gerund phrase** consists of a gerund (a verb form that ends in *-ing* and functions as a noun) along with its modifiers and complements. In the sentence above, the gerund phrases help to convey the vividness, even after 20 years, of the narrator's memory. If the gerunds *packing, carrying, standing,* and *looking* were replaced with verbs in the past tense, the events would seem more distant.

Usage Tip: Gerund phrases can be used as subjects or objects of verbs or as objects of prepositions.

WRITING EXERCISE Rewrite these sentences, changing parts of them into gerund phrases. Underline each gerund phrase.

Example: ***Original*** When I tell the story, it makes me squirm.

Rewritten Telling the story makes me squirm.

1. I asked a lot of questions about the war, but it didn't help me find answers.
2. I worked in the factory; it couldn't silence the howls of war in my head.
3. My modest antiwar activities included support for the campaign of Eugene McCarthy.

Grammar Handbook Verbals, p. 1196

Tim O'Brien

1946–

Other Works
Going After Cacciato
Northern Lights
In the Lake of the Woods

Fact and Fiction Though the events depicted in "On the Rainy River" are fictional, many details in the story match the writer's own experiences. Like the narrator, the real Tim O'Brien grew up in Minnesota and was an exceptional student at Macalester College. He also was drafted into the U.S. Army immediately after graduation. O'Brien, like the narrator, debated fleeing the country but ultimately he decided to serve. "I did not want to be a soldier, not even an observer to war," he later wrote. "But neither did I want to upset a peculiar balance between the order I knew, the people I knew, and my own private world."

"Story Truth" During the Vietnam War, O'Brien was promoted to the rank of sergeant; he also was wounded in combat and awarded the Purple Heart. His first book, *If I Die in a Combat Zone, Box Me Up and Ship Me Home* (1973), is a nonfiction memoir of his tour of duty. O'Brien's novel about Vietnam, *Going After Cacciato,* won two O. Henry Memorial Awards and the 1978 National Book Award. "On the Rainy River" appeared in *The Things They Carried* (1990), a collection of interrelated stories about the Vietnam War and its victims. Despite the presence of a narrator named Tim O'Brien, the stories in the collection are fictional. For O'Brien, whether a story is literally true is less important than the truths it conveys. "I want you to feel what I felt," he once explained. "I want you to know why story truth is truer sometimes than happening truth."

Author Activity

The "Real" Tim O'Brien In a nonfiction article entitled "The Vietnam in Me," published in the *New York Times Magazine* on October 2, 1994, O'Brien writes of his own decision to fight: "I was a coward. I went to Vietnam." Read the article to learn about O'Brien's experience.

VIDEODISC **LaserLinks: Background for Reading**
Historical Connection
Geographical Connection

Teaching Options

Mini Lesson Grammar

GERUND PHRASES Explain that a gerund phrase consists of a gerund and its modifiers.

Write the sentence on the chalkboard.

"Escaping to Canada was one way to avoid the draft."

Underline the gerund phrase as shown. Then discuss its function in the sentence.

Practice Have students copy the following sentences. Ask them to underline the gerund phrases.

1. Going to Canada seemed the most reasonable course of action.
2. Rowing the boat seemed as natural as walking on hard earth.
3. Sitting quietly in a forest is one way to concentrate on a problem.

Use **Grammar Transparencies and Copymasters,** p. 106, for more exercises.

Use McDougal Littell's ***Language Network,*** Chapter 3, for more instruction on gerund phrases.

The Artilleryman's Vision

Poetry by WALT WHITMAN

look at this)

Poetry by E. E. CUMMINGS

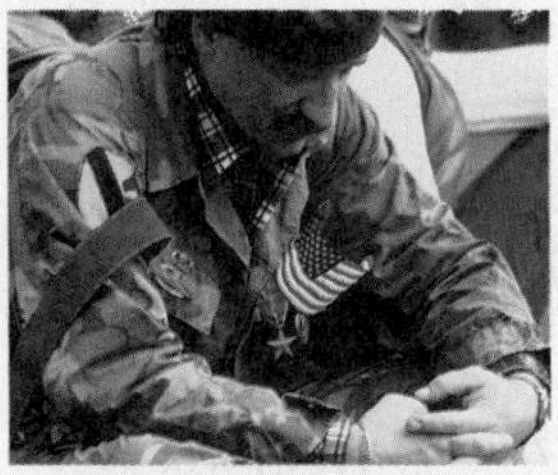

Connect to Your Life

It's War! People react to war in very different ways. Some are fascinated by the decisions of politicians and generals. Others take interest in the latest weaponry. Still others focus on how the war affects ordinary citizens, perhaps taking pity on its innocent victims or protesting against those who initiate war. Think of a war that has occurred during your lifetime or one that you have learned about. What images of the conflict stick in your mind? What are your thoughts and feelings about that war and its effects?

Build Background

Wartime Poets Both Walt Whitman and E. E. Cummings were strongly affected by the experience of war. During the Civil War, Whitman traveled to the war front in Virginia after learning that his younger brother had been wounded. He remained in Washington, D.C., to work as a volunteer nurse, caring for the war's sick and wounded. Drawing on these experiences, he wrote Civil War poems such as "Come Up From the Fields Father," "Memories of President Lincoln," and "The Artilleryman's Vision."

E. E. Cummings volunteered for duty in another war. He served in the Ambulance Corps in France during World War I, joining a volunteer American corps before the United States entered the war. His prose book *The Enormous Room* is considered to be an outstanding literary account of World War I.

Focus Your Reading

LITERARY ANALYSIS TONE AND DICTION The **tone** of a work—the attitude a writer takes toward his or her subject—may be bitter, serious, angry, or detached, among other possibilities. One element that contributes to a work's tone is **diction,** or word choice. Diction consists of **vocabulary** and **syntax,** or the arrangement and order of the words. Cummings's vocabulary and syntax are highly unusual, an effect heightened by the poet's unique use of punctuation and capitalization, as illustrated by the poem's opening:

look at this)
a 75 done
this . . .

By contrast, Whitman's diction helps to portray a battle in vivid detail:

The crashing and smoking, the pride of the men in their pieces . . .

As you read, notice how each poet's use of diction contributes to the work's tone.

ACTIVE READING COMPARING AND CONTRASTING SPEAKERS In poetry, the **speaker** is the voice that "talks" to the reader. The speakers in the following two poems have something in common: both have experienced warfare. In "The Artilleryman's Vision," the speaker recalls the chaos of battle when "the wars are long over." The speaker in "look at this)" reacts to the loss of life in war in a more immediate context, commenting on the recent death of a "buddy." As you read the two poems, continue to **compare** and **contrast** the two speakers and their experiences of war.

READER'S NOTEBOOK While reading each poem, think about the kind of person the speaker seems to be and the attitude he has toward war. Jot down notes to keep track of your observations.

OVERVIEW

These selections are included in the **Grade 10 InterActive Reader.**

Objectives

1. understand and appreciate **two poems (Literary Analysis)**
2. analyze **tone and diction (Literary Analysis)**
3. **compare and contrast speakers** in two poems **(Active Reading)**

Summary

In "The Artilleryman's Vision," the speaker is a veteran of the Civil War who, years after the war has ended, still awakens at night disturbed by horrifying memories. He has a vividly detailed vision of the deadly chaos he once experienced in battle. In "look at this)," the speaker is a soldier who lifts the body of his dead comrade to place him in a pine coffin.

Thematic Link

These two poems show how war is a test of conviction requiring courage and threatens humanity's well-being.

5-Minute Warm-Up

Daily Language SkillBuilder

Have students **proofread** the display sentences on page 541m and write them correctly. The sentences also appear on Transparency 21 of **Grammar Transparencies and Copymasters.**

LESSON RESOURCES

UNIT FOUR RESOURCE BOOK, pp. 47–48

ASSESSMENT RESOURCES

Formal Assessment, pp. 115–116

Teacher's Guide to Assessment and Portfolio Use

Test Generator

SKILLS TRANSPARENCIES AND COPYMASTERS

Literary Analysis
- Style, Voice, Diction, Purpose, T22 (for Paired Activity, p. 649)

Reading and Critical Thinking
- Compare and Contrast, T15 (for Think Critically, item 5, p. 649)

Grammar
- Avoiding Misplaced and Dangling Modifiers, C161 (for Mini Lesson, p. 650)

Vocabulary
- Detonation and Connotation, C67 (for Mini Lesson, p. 646)

Writing
- Achieving Conciseness, T21 (for Writing Option 2, p. 650)
- Showing, Not Telling, T22 (for Writing Option 3, p. 650)

Communications
- Dramatic Reading, T12 (for Activities & Explorations 2, p. 650)

INTEGRATED TECHNOLOGY

Audio Library

Internet: Research Starter

Visit our website: www.mcdougallittell.com

TEACHING THE LITERATURE

Reading and Analyzing

Literary Analysis

ANALYZING TONE AND DICTION

Explain to students that the poet's choice of words helps establish the tone of the poem. Students may want to write down a list of words that evoke a reader response. The tone of each poem will then emerge.

Use **Unit Four Resource Book** p. 48 for more practice.

Active Reading

COMPARING AND CONTRASTING SPEAKERS

The speaker in a poem is the voice that "talks" to the reader, similar to the narrator in fiction. Both speakers write about their war experiences, but one writes with the immediacy of the moment and the other is haunted by memories of war's horror.

Use **Unit Four Resource Book** p. 47 for more practice.

Literary Analysis: SYNTAX

Discuss Whitman's syntax by pointing out that this poem is a single sentence. His use of parentheses (often termed syntactic whispers) is important. Attention should be drawn to the content of these parentheses. Ask students to describe the effect of these devices. **Possible Response:** By making the poem a single long sentence, Whitman creates a relentless speed and rhythm that drives the reader forward. The parenthetical expressions are like special asides to the reader, giving the reader a sense of intimacy with the speaker of the poem.

The Artilleryman's Vision

Walt Whitman

While my wife at my side lies slumbering, and the wars are over long,
And my head on the pillow rests at home, and the vacant midnight passes,
And through the stillness, through the dark, I hear, just hear, the breath of my infant,
1 There in the room as I wake from sleep this vision presses upon me;
The engagement opens there and then in fantasy unreal,
The skirmishers begin, they crawl cautiously ahead, I hear the irregular snap! snap!
I hear the sounds of the different missiles, the short *t-h-t! t-h-t!* of the rifle balls,
I see the shells exploding leaving small white clouds, I hear the great shells shrieking as they pass,
The grape like the hum and whirr of wind through the trees, (tumultuous now the contest rages,)
2 All the scenes at the batteries rise in detail before me again,
The crashing and smoking, the pride of the men in their pieces,
The chief-gunner ranges and sights his piece and selects a fuse of the right time,
After firing I see him lean aside and look eagerly off to note the effect;
Elsewhere I hear the cry of a regiment charging, (the young colonel leads himself this time with brandish'd sword,)
I see the gaps cut by the enemy's volleys, (quickly fill'd up, no delay,)
I breathe the suffocating smoke, then the flat clouds hover low concealing all;
Now a strange lull for a few seconds, not a shot fired on either side,
Then resumed the chaos louder than ever, with eager calls and orders of officers,
While from some distant part of the field the wind wafts to my ears
3 a shout of applause, (some special success,)

5 engagement: battle.

6 skirmishers: soldiers sent out in advance of a main attack.

9 grape: grapeshot—small iron balls shot in a bunch from a cannon.

10 batteries: groups of cannons.

14 brandish'd: raised and waving.

15 volleys: groups of cannonballs fired at the same time.

Teaching Options

Mini Lesson Vocabulary Strategy

DISCRIMINATE BETWEEN DENOTATIVE AND CONNOTATIVE MEANINGS Instruction Explain that a word's connotative meaning carries emotional overtones and associations. Have students think associatively as they read. Write the following sentence on the board and discuss connotations that students associate with the word *patter.*

With the patter of small arms,

While the denotation (literal meaning) of *patter* is a "rapid or mechanical uttering," its connotation (suggested meaning) is associated with the soft sound of rain, or the sound of an infant walking.

Practice Have students write down any unfamiliar words they find in these poems, including words defined in the side notes. Instruct them to use a dictionary to find the denotation.

Use **Vocabulary Transparencies and Copymasters,** p. 67, for more practice.

A lesson on denotation and connotation appears on p. 494 in the Pupil's Edition.

Union soldiers drill in preparation for battle during the Civil War.

And ever the sound of the cannon far or near, (rousing even in
  dreams a devilish exultation and all the old mad joy in the depths
  of my soul,)
And ever the hastening of infantry shifting positions, batteries,
  cavalry, moving hither and thither,
(The falling, dying, I heed not, the wounded dripping and red I heed
  not, some to the rear are hobbling,)
Grime, heat, rush, aide-de-camps galloping by or on a full run,
With the patter of small arms, the warning *s-s-t* of the rifles, (these
  in my vision I hear or see,)
And bombs bursting in air, and at night the vari-color'd rockets.

20 rousing: awakening.

23 aide-de-camps (ăd′dĭ-kămps′): assistants to military commanders.

Thinking Through the Literature

1. **Comprehension Check** Where is the artilleryman when he experiences his "vision," and what time is it?
2. How do you think the **speaker** feels about the incidents he describes? Do you think his feelings have changed since his days as a soldier? Use evidence from the poem to support your answer.
3. Why might the artilleryman have such a vision at this particular moment?
4. Why do you think Whitman chose to end the poem as he did?

Customizing Instruction

Suggest that students break the long clauses in "The Artilleryman's Vision" into individual sentences and read "look at this)" with a partner.

1 Point out that the main subject and predicate of the first sentence do not occur until line 4, when the speaker says, "this vision presses upon me." Everything prior to this is introductory material that sets the scene.

Less Proficient Readers

Encourage students to analyze the syntax of both these poems, locating the beginning and end of complete thoughts.

2 Explain to students that when the speaker says in line 10, "All the scenes . . . rise in detail before me again," he is describing a vision that is appearing here as a flashback.

Students Acquiring English

3 Help students understand that the verb *wafts* (line 19) means "floats" or "drifts."

Use **Spanish Study Guide** for additional support, pp. 140–142.

Thinking Through the Literature

1. Answer: Many years after the war at home in his bed, the artilleryman awakens in the middle of the night.
2. Possible Response: Although it is never stated directly, the speaker's word choices indicate he is tormented by his memories of the war. He seems just as tormented now as he was during his days as a soldier, but also recalls the "mad joy" (line 20) of combat.
3. Possible Response: It is the middle of the night and he cannot sleep. His insomnia brings on a panic attack.
4. Some students might say that it suggests phrases taken from "The Star Spangled Banner." The juxtaposition of the national anthem with the horror of a country viciously killing itself in civil war is bitterly ironic. Others might say that the image of bombs bursting and rockets lighting the sky is a panoramic image that seems to illuminate the battlefield in a way that sets a dramatic "stage" for the speaker's nightmare vision.

Reading and Analyzing

Active Reading

COMPARING AND CONTRASTING SPEAKERS

Ask students to discuss the differences between how the speakers describe the horrors of war. Do we know more about one speaker than we do about the other?

Possible Response: The speaker in the Cummings poem uses few adjectives, and focuses on an action; the speaker in Whitman's poem recalls through sensory images the vision of the war. Students may feel that we understand how tortured the man is in the Whitman poem, and how mechanical the speaker has had to become in the Cummings poem.

Literary Analysis: SYNTAX

Have students discuss the effect of Cummings's unusual syntax and line breaks.

Possible Response: The syntax and line breaks fragment the thoughts in this poem. These devices support the notion that boundaries bleed into each other and that human thought is easily fragmented, particularly during war.

Reading Skills and Strategies: EVALUATING

Have students state their opinions about why the speaker abruptly stops speaking at the end of the poem.

Possible Responses: Placing his friend in a pine coffin is his final gesture, so it is fitting that the poem end at this point.

Literary Analysis: THEME

Cummings's message seems to say that war is full of bitter ironies and strange truths.

look at this)

E. E. Cummings

look at this)
a 75 done
this nobody would
have believed
would they no
kidding this was my particular

pal
funny aint
it we was
buddies
i used to

know
him lift the
poor cuss
tenderly this side up handle

with care
fragile
and send him home

to his old mother in
a new nice pine box

(collect

Teaching Options

Assessment Standardized Test Practice

ALTERNATIVE ENDINGS You can assess students' understanding of the selections by asking them to write alternative endings for the poems. (These endings do not have to be poetry.) Have them write an ending for "The Artilleryman's Vision" in which the wife awakens and, in a moment of dialogue, the artilleryman summarizes what he is feeling about the war. Have students write an ending for "look at this)" in which the speaker does something that vividly expresses his suppressed emotions.

RUBRIC

3 **Full Accomplishment** Response reflects a full understanding of events described in the poems and the speakers' emotional responses to those events.

2 **Substantial Accomplishment** Response shows a general understanding of events but may not fully reflect the speakers' emotional responses.

1 **Little or Partial Accomplishment** Response shows little understanding of events or of the speakers' emotional response.

Connect to the Literature

1. **What Do You Think?** How did you react to the speaker's remark about the pine box at the end of the poem?

Comprehension Check
- What is the situation described in the poem?
- What happened to the speaker's friend?

Think Critically

2. How do you think the **speaker** feels about what happened to his friend?

THINK ABOUT
- the words he uses to describe their relationship
- his instructions to the person he is addressing
- the poem's final image

3. What elements of Cummings's **style** might be considered unusual? In what way do you think this style influences your response to the poem?

4. Which **detail** in each poem do you think you are most likely to remember? Why?

5. ACTIVE READING COMPARING AND CONTRASTING SPEAKERS
What similarities and differences do you see between the speakers of "look at this)" and "The Artilleryman's Vision"? Base your response on the observations you wrote in your READER'S NOTEBOOK.

6. Both of the poems deal with the human cost of warfare. Which poem do you think is more critical of war? Explain your response.

Extend Interpretations

7. **Comparing Texts** How do you think the narrator of "On the Rainy River" would respond to these two poems? Which one comes closest to his own attitude toward war? Cite reasons to support your answer.

8. **Connect to Life** Do you think any of the thoughts expressed in these poems would be relevant to soldiers fighting in wars today? Explain your answer.

Literary Analysis

TONE AND DICTION **Tone** is the attitude a writer takes toward a subject. To identify the tone of these poems, you might find it helpful to read them aloud, as if giving a dramatic reading before an audience. The emotions that you convey in reading should give you hints about the tone of the work.

One way in which writers create tone is through **diction,** or word choice, which includes both **vocabulary** and **syntax,** or word order. For example, in "look at this)," the use of terms such as "this side up" and "handle with care" contributes to a tone of bitterness about the loss of life in warfare.

Paired Activity With a partner, decide which of the following words best describes the tone of each poem. More than one word may apply.

- serious
- proud
- sad
- shocked
- playful
- bitter
- anxious

Review each poem and find examples of ways in which the poet's diction contributes to the tone you have identified.

GUIDING STUDENT RESPONSE

Connect to the Literature

1. What Do You Think?
Students may be uncomfortable with the speaker's apparent lack of emotion as he describes placing his friend in a coffin.

Comprehension Check
- The speaker is lifting the body of a dead comrade to place him in a coffin.
- The speaker's friend was killed in battle.

Think Critically

2. Possible Response: The speaker seems to be in a state of disbelief because his actions seem mechanical. His feelings remain beneath the surface of his words, however, as if he is either afraid—or unable—to confront them completely.
3. Possible Responses: He uses no end punctuation or capitalization to distinguish sentences. His use of the parenthesis at the beginning and the end is also unusual. This helps readers feel the continuous flow of emotion as well as the disjointed nature of the speaker's thoughts.
4. Some students may most remember the language used to describe sending a dead comrade home to his mother as the same as words used for sending an object: ("this side up handle / with care / fragile").
5. The two speakers differ in their distance from the moment. The speaker in Cummings's poem also seems to be less coherent and more fragmented in his response.
6. Both poets criticize war, but in different ways. Cummings is more personal and direct, showing how one soldier becomes dehumanized by his experiences and cannot respond to the death of his friend. Its highly disjointed syntax and fragmented tone and diction emphasize the horrible effect that war has on human emotion. Although Whitman's poem describes the long-term effect of war on the human psyche, the "devilish exultation" and the "mad joy of battle" demonstrate that the immediate effects are evil.

Extend Interpretations

Comparing Texts Most students will say that the speaker in "On the Rainy River" would respond more strongly to "look at this)" because it presents a more horrifying glimpse of war and a stronger antiwar sentiment. Others may say that he would respond positively to both poems, recognizing them as faithful representations of the effects and aftereffects of war.

Connect to Life Soldiers fighting in wars today would probably acknowledge the overwhelming horror of death and destruction that is expressed in both poems.

Literary Analysis

Tone Students may have already accumulated a list of words that will help them describe the tone of the poem.

Writing Options

1. **Advice Column** Advice columns take a "problem/solution" format. The letter addressed to the wife should present a specific proposal for helping her husband or assisting him in finding help.
2. **Comparison Essay** Encourage students to plan their essay's structure and create an informal outline before they begin to write.
3. **Consoling Letter** Because the speaker of Cummings's poem is rather undeveloped, you may want to suggest that students imagine they are writing this letter to the parents of their best friend, who has died in battle.

Activities & Explorations

1. **Illustrations of War** Encourage students to explore both external and internal dimensions of the scene as they produce an image that will capture the speaker's attitude toward war.
2. **Spoken Word** Students should justify their choice of verbal and nonverbal performance techniques by referring to their interpretation of the text.
3. **Martial Music** Encourage students to explore music without lyrics in addition to music with lyrics. Point out the importance of sustaining the emotional tone of the poem.

Inquiry & Research

1. **Civil Warfare** Students can focus their research by rereading the poem and by listing all references to battlefield tactics and weaponry.
2. **Invisible Wounds of War** Encourage students to explore the techniques used to help veterans overcome their battlefield stress.

Choices & CHALLENGES

Writing Options

1. **Advice Column** In Whitman's poem, the artilleryman's wife is shown sleeping peacefully, but she may well be aware of her husband's visions. Imagine that you are an advice columnist who has received a letter from her. Write a response offering suggestions to help her understand and deal with her husband's visions. Place the response in your **Working Portfolio.**

2. **Comparison Essay** Write a brief essay comparing and contrasting the speakers of these poems. Consider their personalities, their attitudes toward war, and the effect that combat has had on them. Use the notes in your **READER'S NOTEBOOK** and your answer to question 5 as a starting point.

Writing Handbook
See page 1157: Compare-Contrast.

3. **Consoling Letter** Write a letter of condolence from the speaker in Cummings's poem to the parents of the dead soldier. Describe your relationship with the soldier and explain the circumstances of his death. Try to capture the personality of the speaker in your letter, although you will probably want to be more tactful than the speaker is in the poem.

Activities & Explorations

1. **Illustrations of War** Draw a picture to illustrate one of the poems, trying to capture the speaker's attitude toward war. After you are finished, explain to your classmates which words or phrases inspired your artwork. ~ **ART**

2. **Spoken Word** In a small group, perform a round-robin reading of "The Artilleryman's Vision." Before reading the poem aloud, decide which lines each student will read and go over the poem together to clarify difficult words and phrases. Think about how you can use the speed and pitch of your voice to suggest the speaker's emotions. ~ **SPEAKING AND LISTENING**

3. **Martial Music** Select a piece of music to accompany one of the poems. As you consider possible music, think about the speaker's emotional reactions as well as the events he describes. After you play the music for the class, explain why you chose it. ~ **MUSIC**

Inquiry & Research

1. **Civil Warfare** In "The Artilleryman's Vision," Whitman offers a vivid description of a Civil War battle. Consult history books about the war for information on battlefield tactics and weaponry used by Union and Confederate soldiers. Write a brief report explaining some of the war imagery in Whitman's poem.

More Online: Research Starter
www.mcdougallittell.com

2. **Invisible Wounds of War** Soldiers from all wars have experienced problems that lingered long after they returned home. Such problems have gone by several names over the years: shell shock, battle fatigue, and post-traumatic stress disorder. Find out more about such problems faced by veterans and report your findings to the class. You might contact a local veterans' organization for information.

An American soldier stares in disbelief after being freed from a Korean prison camp.

Teaching Options

Mini Lesson Grammar

AVOIDING MISPLACED AND DANGLING MODIFIERS Misplaced or dangling modifiers are words or phrases that seem attached to the wrong element or to no specific element in the sentence. Explain to students that they can revise the sentence so that the modifier clearly refers to the proper element. Write the sentences on the chalkboard.

John bought a <u>bicycle</u> from a neighbor <u>with ten speeds</u>.

<u>Hidden under the bed</u>, I found my <u>puppy</u>.

Underline the misplaced and dangling modifiers and the elements they modify as shown. Have students revise the sentences to correct the dangling modifiers.

John bought a bicycle with ten speeds from a neighbor.

I found my puppy, hidden under the bed.

Practice Have students revise the following sentences to correct the misplaced or dangling modifiers.

1. Thumbing quickly through the newsletter, my eyes didn't notice the interesting photographs.

Walt Whitman

1819–1892

Other Works
Leaves of Grass
"When Lilacs Last in the Dooryard Bloom'd"
Specimen Days and Collect

End of Childhood Walt Whitman grew up in a hurry. He left school at age 11, and within a few years he was living on his own in New York City. He drifted from job to job, working as a printer, journalist, and carpenter. He loved to stroll around the city, taking in sights and sounds that he would later use in his poetry.

Leaves of Grass In 1855, Whitman published 12 poems in a volume called *Leaves of Grass.* During the rest of his life, he continually added new poems and revised older ones, putting out nine editions of the book. On one occasion, he compared the finished book to a tree with its successive rings of growth. Upon receiving a copy of the first edition, the poet Ralph Waldo Emerson declared that it was "the most extraordinary piece of wit and wisdom that America has yet contributed"; he went on to say that Whitman was "at the beginning of a great career." However, other distinguished American writers shunned Whitman, who at first was better appreciated in Europe than at home. Most editions of *Leaves of Grass* were published by Whitman himself.

Later Years In 1873, Whitman suffered a stroke that left him partially paralyzed. He spent the rest of his life in Camden, New Jersey. In the decades following his death, Whitman gained recognition as one of the greatest American poets, and today *Leaves of Grass* is regarded as one of the most influential books of American poetry.

Author Activity

Civil War Experiences As you know, Whitman devoted much of his time during the Civil War to caring for wounded and diseased soldiers. Read excerpts from *Specimen Days,* Whitman's prose account of his wartime experiences. Then discuss with classmates how his hospital work might have influenced his poetry.

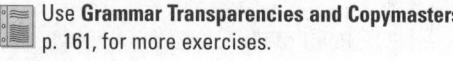

E. E. Cummings

1894–1962

Other Works
Collected Poems
The Enormous Room
Him

A Question of Individuality Edward Estlin Cummings was raised in Cambridge, Massachusetts. He came from a cultured family that encouraged him to pursue artistic interests. His earliest poems were traditional sonnets, but while studying at Harvard University he fell under the influence of modernist poets such as Ezra Pound, and he began to write more experimental verse. In many of his poems, Cummings ignored rules of standard punctuation and capitalization, sometimes creating new words or spellings and running words together. He once remarked, "So far as I am concerned, poetry and every other art was and is and forever will be strictly and distinctly a question of individuality."

Military Service Cummings went overseas in 1917 to serve in the Ambulance Corps in France. With his spontaneity and irreverence, it may have been inevitable that he came into conflict with his superiors. An army censor falsely accused him of treason, and he spent three months in a military prison. He wrote a prose account of this experience, *The Enormous Room,* which made him famous when it was published in 1922.

Growing Popularity After the war ended, Cummings lived for several years in Paris before settling in New York City. He had difficulty getting his work published during the 1930s, but in the last two decades of his life he became increasingly popular. He is now regarded as one of the most important American poets of the 20th century. Besides writing poetry, Cummings was a prolific painter.

Author Activity

Poet at War Read excerpts from *The Enormous Room* and discuss how Cummings's experiences in World War I may have led to his writing poems such as "look at this)."

Author Activity

Civil War Experiences As students read excerpts from *Specimen Days*, instruct them to list details that seem related to Whitman's poem. Alternatively, you could read aloud excerpts from *Specimen Days* and have students take notes as you read.

Poet at War To encourage active listening, instruct students to write down details as you read from *The Enormous Room*. Have them prepare for discussion by writing brief notes that explain how each detail they have listed may have influenced Cummings's poetry.

Possible Response: Thumbing quickly through the newsletter, I didn't notice the interesting photographs.

2. Overcooked and soggy, I could hardly eat the carrots.
   Possible Response: Overcooked and soggy, the carrots could hardly be eaten.
3. As a small girl, her grandfather told her stories about living in the old country.
   Possible Response: As a small girl, she heard her grandfather tell stories about living in the old country.
4. Jumping to conclusions, the votes weren't completely counted before we announced the wrong winner.
   Possible Response: Jumping to conclusions, we announced the wrong winner before the votes were completely counted.
5. Steven saw a bird on the road riding the bus.
   Possible Response: Riding the bus, Steven saw a bird on the road.

Use **Grammar Transparencies and Copymasters,** p. 161, for more exercises.

Use McDougal Littell's ***Language Network,*** Chapter 3, for more instruction on misplaced and dangling modifiers.

OVERVIEW

Objectives

1. understand and appreciate a **short story (Literary Analysis)**
2. understand **third-person point of view (Literary Analysis)**
3. **draw conclusions (Active Reading)**

Summary

Hannetjie, a tough new prison guard, or warder, takes charge of Span One, a closely knit group of black political prisoners in a South African work camp. Hannetjie punishes Brille, the prisoner with glasses, severely for stealing and talking back to him. Eventually, Brille catches Hannetjie stealing fertilizer and uses this as leverage to strike a bargain with him: the prisoners of Span One enjoy privileges that enable them to endure their long, hard confinement and, in turn, they become the hardest workers in the camp, helping Hannetjie steal fertilizer and other items he can use on his farm.

Thematic Link

Within a rigid prison system, prisoners and warder challenge each other as their **convictions** and assumptions about each other are **tested**.

5-Minute Warm-Up

Daily Language SkillBuilder

Have students **proofread** the display sentences on page 541m and write them correctly. The sentences also appear on Transparency 21 of **Grammar Transparencies and Copymasters.**

Editor's Note: This selection has been edited slightly to delete material that may be considered objectionable.

Mini Lesson: Preteaching Vocabulary

If you would like to preteach the WORDS TO KNOW for this selection, use the Mini Lesson, p. 654.

"One of these days we are going to run the country."

The Prisoner Who Wore Glasses

Short Story by BESSIE HEAD

Connect to Your Life

Assert Yourself In a class discussion, tell what you think it means to be assertive. Then discuss the possible advantages and disadvantages of acting assertively. Use examples from various social situations—at home, at school, in your community, and so on.

Build Background

Discrimination by Law From the late 1940s to the early 1990s, black South Africans who tried to be assertive frequently became political prisoners. Some people were imprisoned, for example, simply for speaking out against the government or publicly protesting government policies. South Africa was then ruled by a white minority government whose official policy of apartheid (ə-pärt'hīt') kept the races separate and legally discriminated against the nation's black majority and other people of color. "The Prisoner Who Wore Glasses" is set on a South African prison farm in the years when apartheid was still the law of the land. The two main characters in the story are a black political prisoner and a white prison guard, or warder. The warder is an Afrikaner (ăf'rĭ-kä'nər), a white South African of Dutch descent, who speaks English with a heavy accent.

WORDS TO KNOW
Vocabulary Preview

acute	cower
bedlam	irrelevant
chaos	perpetrate
commodity	ruefully
conviction	tirade

Focus Your Reading

LITERARY ANALYSIS THIRD-PERSON POINT OF VIEW In this story, the author employs **third-person point of view,** the narrative method that occurs when a **narrator** outside the action describes **events** and **characters** without the use of first-person pronouns such as *I, me, we,* and *us.* As you read "The Prisoner Who Wore Glasses," pay attention to the author's use of the third-person point of view. Notice whose thoughts and feelings are revealed to the reader.

ACTIVE READING DRAWING CONCLUSIONS **Drawing conclusions** about a work of fiction involves combining your prior knowledge of the world with your reading of the text in order to make logical statements about elements in a story. As you read this story, combine your knowledge of the political system that existed in South Africa with the story's account of the conditions suffered by one political prisoner.

READER'S NOTEBOOK As you read, record significant details in the story that will help you to draw conclusions about South African society at the time of the story.

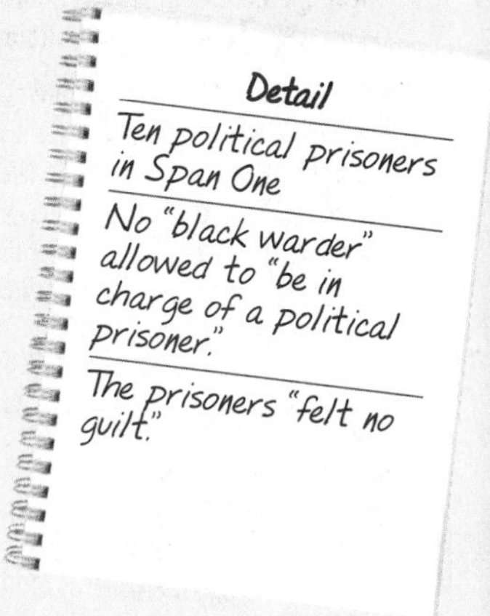

Detail
Ten political prisoners in Span One
No "black warder" allowed to "be in charge of a political prisoner."
The prisoners "felt no guilt."

VIDEODISC **LaserLinks: Background for Reading**
Historical Connection

LESSON RESOURCES

UNIT FOUR RESOURCE BOOK, pp. 50–51

ASSESSMENT RESOURCES
Formal Assessment, pp. 117–118
Teacher's Guide to Assessment and Portfolio Use
Test Generator

SKILLS TRANSPARENCIES AND COPYMASTERS
Literary Analysis
- Point of View, T17 (for Activity, p. 660)

Reading and Critical Thinking
- Drawing Conclusions, T4 (for Think Critically, item 5, p. 660)
- Noting Details, T9 (for Reader's Notebook, p. 652)
- Notetaking, T40 (for Reader's Notebook, p. 652)

Grammar
- Comparative Forms, C155 (for Mini Lesson, p. 658)

Vocabulary
- Context Clues, C68 (for Mini Lesson, p. 654)
- Word Meanings, C69 (for Mini Lesson, p. 657)

Writing
- Point of View, T23 (for Writing Option 1, p. 661)
- Topic Sentences and Thesis Statements, T6 (for Writing Option 2, p. 661)

Communications
- Impromptu Speaking: Dialogue, Role-Play, Debate, T13 (for Activities & Explo]rations 2, p. 661)

INTEGRATED TECHNOLOGY
Audio Library
LaserLinks
- Historical Connection: Apartheid in South Africa, 1948–1991. See **Teacher's SourceBook,** p. 40.

Visit our website:
www.mcdougallittell.com

The Prisoner Who Wore Glasses

Bessie Head

Scarcely a breath of wind disturbed the stillness of the day, and the long rows of cabbages were bright green in the sunlight. Large white clouds drifted slowly across the deep blue sky. Now and then they obscured the sun and caused a chill on the backs of the prisoners who had to work all day long in the cabbage field.

Chain Gang (1939–1940), William H. Johnson. National Museum of American Art, Washington, D.C./Art Resource, New York.

TEACHING THE LITERATURE

Customizing Instruction

Less Proficient Readers
Have the students read the first three paragraphs aloud and then describe the main character. Then ask them to read on to find out more about the main character, Brille, and what happens to him.

Students Acquiring English
Help the students comprehend the warder's dialect by reading aloud specific passages and by explaining the transformations of particular words.

Use **Spanish Study Guide** for additional support, pp. 143–145.

Gifted and Talented
Have students look for textual evidence that shows how Brille's opinion of Hannetjie gradually changes.
Possible Responses: Page 654: At first, Brille is frightened by the warder's brutality ("Because he's not human"); page 657: After Brille discovers Hannetjie's vulnerability, he no longer sees him as a threat and realizes that he can control the warder ("'I saw today that Hannetjie is just a child and stupidly truthful.'"); page 658: Because Hannetjie is so conscientious in meeting the prisoners' needs, Brille begins to see the warder as a decent person (". . . his [Hannetjie's] interpretation of what was good and human often left the prisoners of Span One speechless with surprise").

BLOCK SCHEDULING: MANAGING TIME

If your schedule requires that you cover the lesson objectives in a shorter time, use . . .
- Preparing to Read, p. 652
- Thinking Through the Literature, p. 660
- Vocabulary in Action, p. 661

If you want to take advantage of longer class time, use . . .
- TE Teaching Options: Preteaching Vocabulary, pp. 654–655; Viewing and Representing, p. 656; Vocabulary Strategy, p. 657; Standardized Test Practice, p. 659
- Choices & Challenges, p. 661

Reading and Analyzing

Reading Skills and Strategies: PREVIEW

Remind students that they are expected to establish a purpose for reading. Have students preview the selection. Discuss with them the Build Background feature on page 652, and have them make predictions about the story's setting and characters. Before students begin reading, give them a brief summary of the story.

Active Reading

DRAWING CONCLUSIONS

One way to draw conclusions about a society is to examine the actions and interactions of its members. To this end, encourage students to note how the characters in this story respond to one another.

Use **Unit Four Resource Book** p. 50 for more practice.

Literary Analysis

THIRD-PERSON POINT OF VIEW

The use of a third-person point of view provides the reader with information about all the characters and events.

Use **Unit Four Resource Book** p. 51 for more practice.

Literary Analysis: CHARACTER

A Have students examine Brille's thoughts and draw conclusions about his character.

Possible Response: He seems like an imaginative, sensitive, caring human being.

B Have students contrast the warder's words to Brille's thoughts on page 654 and draw conclusions about his character.

Possible Response: Hannetjie seems like an insensitive, prejudiced human being.

This trick the clouds were playing with the sun eventually caused one of the prisoners who wore glasses to stop work, straighten up and peer shortsightedly at them. He was a thin little fellow with a hollowed-out chest and comic knobbly knees. He also had a lot of fanciful ideas because he smiled at the clouds.

A "Perhaps they want me to send a message to the children," he thought tenderly, noting that the clouds were drifting in the direction of his home some hundred miles away. But before he could frame the message, the warder in charge of his work span[1] shouted:

"Hey, what you tink you're doing, Brille?"[2]

The prisoner swung round, blinking rapidly, yet at the same time sizing up the enemy. He was a new warder, named Jacobus Stephanus Hannetjie.[3] His eyes were the color of the sky but they were frightening. A simple, primitive, brutal soul gazed out of them. The prisoner bent down quickly and a message was quietly passed down the line:

"We're in for trouble this time, comrades."

"Why?" rippled back up the line.

"Because he's not human," the reply rippled down, and yet only the crunching of the spades as they turned over the earth disturbed the stillness.

1 This particular work span was known as Span One. It was composed of ten men, and they were all political prisoners. They were grouped together for convenience, as it was one of the prison regulations that no black warder should be in charge of a political prisoner lest this prisoner convert him to his views. It never seemed to occur to the authorities that this very reasoning was the strength of Span One and a clue to the strange terror they aroused in the warders. As political prisoners they were unlike the other prisoners in the sense that they felt no guilt nor were they outcasts of society. All guilty men instinctively cower, which was why it was the kind of prison where men got knocked out cold with a blow at the back of the head from an iron bar. Up until the arrival of Warder Hannetjie, no warder had dared beat any member of Span One and no warder had lasted more than a week with them. The battle was entirely psychological. Span One was assertive and it was beyond the scope of white warders to handle assertive black men. Thus, Span One had got out of control. They were the best thieves and liars in the camp. They lived all day on raw cabbages. They chatted and smoked tobacco. And since they moved, thought and acted as one, they had perfected every technique of group concealment.

Trouble began that very day between Span One and Warder Hannetjie. It was because of the shortsightedness of Brille. That was the nickname he was given in prison and is the Afrikaans[4] word for someone who wears glasses. Brille could never judge the approach of the prison gates, and on several previous occasions he had munched on cabbages and dropped them almost at the feet of the warder, and all previous warders had overlooked this. Not so Warder Hannetjie.

"Who dropped that cabbage?" he thundered. 2

Brille stepped out of line.

"I did," he said meekly.

"All right," said Hannetjie. "The whole span goes three meals off."

"But I told you I did it," Brille protested.

The blood rushed to Warder Hannetjie's face.

1. **work span:** a work group in the prison.
2. **Brille** (brĭl'ə).
3. **Jacobus Stephanus Hannetjie** (yä-kō'büs stä-fän'üs hä'nĕt-yē).
4. **Afrikaans** (ăf'rĭ-kans'): a language closely related to Dutch and spoken by South Africans of Dutch descent.

WORDS TO KNOW **cower** (kou'ər) *v.* to cringe in fear

Teaching Options

Mini Lesson Preteaching Vocabulary

USING CONTEXT CLUES Call students' attention to the list of WORDS TO KNOW. Remind them that sometimes they can understand the meaning of an unfamiliar word by examining the context in which the word is used. Use the model sentence to demonstrate the strategy of using context clues that provide inferences to word meaning.

Model Sentence

Perhaps the dog *cowers* out of fear that his owner will hit him.

Instruction

- Write the model sentence on the chalkboard.
- Ask a volunteer to summarize the meaning of the sentence.
- Have students use the meaning of the sentence to infer meanings for the word *cowers.*
- Ask a volunteer to use the word *cower* in a sentence.

Exercises Read the following sentences. Ask students to use context clues to determine the meanings of italicized terms.

1. Since the man *perpetrated* the crimes, he had to serve a long prison sentence.

"Look 'ere," he said. "I don't take orders from a kaffir.[5] I don't know what kind of kaffir you tink you are. Why don't you say Baas.[6] I'm your Baas. Why don't you say Baas, hey?"

Brille blinked his eyes rapidly but by contrast his voice was strangely calm.

"I'm twenty years older than you," he said. It was the first thing that came to mind, but the comrades seemed to think it a huge joke. A titter swept up the line. The next thing Warder Hannetjie whipped out a knobkerrie[7] and gave Brille several blows about the head. What surprised his comrades was the speed with which Brille had removed his glasses or else they would have been smashed to pieces on the ground.

> "But I told you I did it," Brille protested. The blood rushed to Warder Hannetjie's face.

That evening in the cell Brille was very apologetic.

"I'm sorry, comrades," he said. "I've put you into a mess."

"Never mind, brother," they said. "What happens to one of us, happens to all."

"I'll try to make up for it, comrades," he said. "I'll steal something so that you don't go hungry."

Privately, Brille was very philosophical about his head wounds. It was the first time an act of violence had been perpetrated against him, but he had long been a witness of extreme, almost unbelievable human brutality. He had twelve children and his mind traveled back that evening through the sixteen years of bedlam in which he had lived. It had all happened in a small drab little three-bedroomed house in a small drab little street in the Eastern Cape,[8] and the children kept coming year after year because neither he nor Martha managed the contraceptives the right way and a teacher's salary never allowed moving to a bigger house and he was always taking exams to improve this salary only to have it all eaten up by hungry mouths. Everything was pretty horrible, especially the way the children fought. They'd get hold of each other's heads and give them a good bashing against the wall. Martha gave up somewhere along the line, so they worked out a thing between them. The bashings, biting and blood were to operate in full swing until he came home. He was to be the bogeyman,[9] and when it worked he never failed to have a sense of godhead[10] at the way in which his presence could change savages into fairly reasonable human beings.

Yet somehow it was this chaos and mismanagement at the center of his life that drove him into politics. It was really an ordered beautiful world with just a few basic slogans to learn along with the rights of mankind. At one stage, before things became very bad, there were conferences to attend, all very far away from home.

"Let's face it," he thought ruefully. "I'm only learning right now what it means to be a politician.

---

5. **kaffir** (kăf'ər): in South Africa, an insulting term for a black.
6. **Baas** (bäs): Afrikaans for *master*. The word has the same Dutch origins as the English *boss*.
7. **knobkerrie** (nŏb'kĕr'ē): a short club with a knobbed end.
8. **the Eastern Cape:** the eastern part of the Cape Province in southern South Africa.
9. **bogeyman** (bŏŏg'ē-măn'): a terrifying figure of fear, dread, or harassment.
10. **godhead:** divinity; the quality or state of being a god.

WORDS TO KNOW

perpetrate (pûr'pĭ-trāt') *v.* to commit
bedlam (bĕd'ləm) *n.* a place or situation of great noise and confusion
chaos (kā'ŏs') *n.* total disorder
ruefully (rōō'fə-lē) *adv.* with regret

Customizing Instruction

Students Acquiring English

1 Clarify what a *political prisoner* is. Ask students to imagine what kinds of "crimes" these ten men might have committed.

Possible Responses: protested apartheid; acted assertively toward whites

Less Proficient Readers

2 Help students understand that by taking responsibility for dropping the cabbage, Brille is requesting that he alone be punished rather than all the comrades in Span One.

Students Acquiring English

3 Explain to students that the phrase *his mind traveled back* means "he thought about the past." It signals a flashback to an earlier time in Brille's life.

Multiple Learning Styles

Linguistic Learners

4 Have students explain, in their own words, why Brille went into politics.

Possible Response: He wanted to escape his overcrowded house and badly behaved children.

Less Proficient Readers

5 Have students examine this passage carefully to explain what "politics . . . [is] an ordered beautiful world" means. Point out the description of Brille's chaotic home in the paragraph above and his rueful comment in the paragraph after.

Possible Response: This description suggests that politics represents an overly simplified world reduced to a few basic beliefs. These clear, simple slogans deny the complexity and chaos of the real world.

2. After we won the state championship, there was so much *chaos* in the locker room that I could barely reach the door.
3. I *ruefully* apologized and took responsibility for my error.
4. The pain in my ankle was so *acute* that I screamed.
5. Since Sharon is totally convinced that she's right, nothing will sway her from her *conviction*.
6. In the middle of my story about surviving the hurricane, Joey asked an *irrelevant* question about the price of bubble gum.
7. I didn't mind getting scolded, but my mother's long *tirade* about my irresponsible nature was more than I could listen to.
8. The new grocery store sold more *commodities* than food.
9. The terrier's pursuit of the cat resulted in *bedlam*—potted plants were overturned, the upholstery was shredded, and Mrs. Pulido's figurine collection was in pieces on the floor.

Use **Unit Four Resource Book** p. 52 for additional support.

A lesson on context clues appears on p. 56 in the Pupil's Edition.

Reading and Analyzing

Active Reading

DRAWING CONCLUSIONS

A "And the pain in his head brought a hard lump to [Brille's] throat." What conclusions has Brille drawn about his own family and his children's behavior?

Possible Response: The warder's brutality makes Brille realize that he was wrong to let his children hit each other. Perhaps Brille is unable to discipline his children because of the oppression that has dominated his life.

Reading Skills and Strategies: EVALUATING

B Have students evaluate the importance of cooperation among the prisoners. How can that same cooperation be applied to the family and ultimately to society?

Possible Response: Cooperation seems to be essential to everyone's well-being.

Reading Skills and Strategies: CONNECTING

Ask students to think about a time in their own lives when someone "told" on them. How did they feel? What happened? Then ask students to think about a time when they "told" on someone else. How did they feel? What happened? Encourage students to put themselves in Warder Hannetjie's place. Why might he have stolen fertilizer? How might he feel about being blackmailed and betrayed by one of his prisoners?

Le nègre Scipion [Black Scipio] (about 1866–1868), Paul Cézanne. Museu de Arte de São Paulo (Brazil) Assis Chateaubriand. Photo by Luiz Hossaka.

All this while I've been running away from Martha and the kids."

A And the pain in his head brought a hard lump to his throat. That was what the children did to each other daily and Martha wasn't managing, and if Warder Hannetjie had not interrupted him that morning, he would have sent the following message:

B "Be good comrades, my children. Cooperate, then life will run smoothly."

The next day Warder Hannetjie caught this old man with twelve children stealing grapes from the farm shed. They were an enormous quantity of grapes in a ten-gallon tin,[11] and for this misdeed the old man spent a week in the isolation cell. In fact, Span One as a whole was in constant trouble. Warder Hannetjie seemed

11. **tin:** the British word for a can, used in South Africa and many other former British colonies.

Teaching Options

Le Nègre Scipion by Paul Cézanne

ART APPRECIATION Known for his use of color and emphasis on forms, French painter Paul Cézanne (1839–1906) greatly influenced many artists of this century. Though Cézanne is famous for his colorful countryside landscapes, early in his career, he used a darker palette. In the painting shown here, he employs somber colors, heavy paint, and brush strokes that give a textural, almost sculptured appearance.

Mini Lesson: Viewing and Representing

Instruction Point out that rather than presenting a familiar "scene" from a recognizable perspective, this painting is composed of forms of color and space. These forms surround a single recognizable object, the human hand. Have students discuss what catches their attention.

Possible Responses: The eye is first drawn to the recognizable object, the hand; then, one's eye moves downward along the angled boundary between white and color.

Application Ask students to connect Cézanne's painting with the situation experienced by characters in the story.

Possible Response: Students may find a deeper meaning in the painting: the dark-skinned hand reaching out of darkness into light could represent the move of people of color from their own societies into white society, or the move of people of color from ignorance to enlightenment.

to have eyes at the back of his head. He uncovered the trick about the cabbages, how they were split in two with the spade and immediately covered with earth and then unearthed again and eaten with split-second timing. He found out how tobacco smoke was beaten into the ground, and he found out how conversations were whispered down the wind.

For about two weeks Span One lived in acute misery. The cabbages, tobacco and conversations had been the pivot of jail life to them. Then one evening they noticed that their good old comrade who wore the glasses was looking rather pleased with himself. He pulled out a four-ounce packet of tobacco by way of explanation, and the comrades fell upon it with great greed. Brille merely smiled. After all, he was the father of many children. But when the last shred had disappeared, it occurred to the comrades that they ought to be puzzled. Someone said:

"I say, brother. We're watched like hawks these days. Where did you get the tobacco?"

"Hannetjie gave it to me," said Brille.

There was a long silence. Into it dropped a quiet bombshell.

"I saw Hannetjie in the shed today," and the failing eyesight blinked rapidly. "I caught him in the act of stealing five bags of fertilizer, and he bribed me to keep my mouth shut."

There was another long silence.

"Prison is an evil life," Brille continued, apparently discussing some irrelevant matter. "It makes a man contemplate all kinds of evil deeds."

He held out his hand and closed it.

"You know, comrades," he said. "I've got Hannetjie. I'll betray him tomorrow."

Everyone began talking at once.

"Forget it, brother. You'll get shot."

Brille laughed.

"I won't," he said. "That is what I mean about evil. I am a father of children, and I saw today that Hannetjie is just a child and stupidly truthful. I'm going to punish him severely because we need a good warder."

The following day, with Brille as witness, Hannetjie confessed to the theft of the fertilizer and was fined a large sum of money. From then on Span One did very much as they pleased while Warder Hannetjie stood by and said nothing. But it was Brille who carried this to extremes. One day, at the close of work Warder Hannetjie said:

"Brille, pick up my jacket and carry it back to the camp."

"But nothing in the regulations says I'm your servant, Hannetjie," Brille replied coolly.

"I've told you not to call me Hannetjie. You must say Baas," but Warder Hannetjie's voice lacked conviction. In turn, Brille squinted up at him. 1

"I'll tell you something about this Baas business, Hannetjie," he said. "One of these days we are going to run the country. You are going to clean my car. Now, I have a fifteen-year-old son, and I'd die of shame if you had to tell him that I ever called you Baas."

Warder Hannetjie went red in the face and picked up his coat.

On another occasion Brille was seen to be walking about the prison yard, openly smoking tobacco. On being taken before the prison commander he claimed to have received the tobacco from Warder Hannetjie. All throughout the tirade from his chief, Warder Hannetjie failed to defend himself, but his nerve broke completely. 2 He called Brille to one side.

"Brille," he said. "This thing between you and me must end. You may not know it, but I

WORDS TO KNOW

acute (ə-kyo͞ot') *adj.* very sharp or severe
irrelevant (ĭ-rĕl'ə-vənt) *adj.* not related to the matter at hand
conviction (kən-vĭk'shən) *n.* certainty; a strong belief
tirade (tī'rād') *n.* a long, angry speech

657

Customizing Instruction

Less Proficient Readers

Check students' understanding of Brille's character by asking the following questions:

- What does the reader learn about Brille's background?
  Possible Response: He worked as a teacher, is the father of twelve children, and went into politics.
- Why is he in prison?
  Possible Response: He is a political prisoner, probably because he opposed South Africa's apartheid laws.
- How do Brille's political views affect his relations with the warder?
  Possible Responses: He refuses to call Hannetjie "Baas"; he risks punishment by speaking openly.

Set a Purpose Have students read on to find out how the relationship between Brille and the warder develops.

Multiple Learning Styles

Auditory Learners

1 Read Brille and Hannetjie's dialogue aloud for students. You may repeat it several times. With each listening, have students focus on details that indicate a change in power in the relationship between the two men.

Students Acquiring English

2 Have students infer from context clues what *his nerve broke completely* means.

Possible Response: The warder became afraid and unsure of himself.

Mini Lesson Vocabulary Strategy

RESEARCH WORD ORIGINS Explain that many words have entered the English language through other languages. To help students see how much of English has been influenced by other languages, have them use a dictionary to research word meanings and trace historical roots. Write the following word on the board and show students how a dictionary shows etymologies that indicate the historical influence of other languages. Explain that the adjective *noisome* has roots going back through Middle English and Old French to Latin.

noisome: adj. 1. offensive to the point of arousing disgust. 2. harmful or dangerous [ME *noisom, noi*] harm (< *anoi*, annoyance < OFr < Latin, *in odio*, hateful)

Practice To help students understand influences on the English language, have them use a college dictionary to research and record the influences of other languages on the WORDS TO KNOW.

Use **Vocabulary Transparencies and Copymasters,** p. 69, for more practice.

A lesson on word origins appears on p. 356 in the Pupil's Edition.

Reading and Analyzing

Literary Analysis: CHARACTER

Have students explain why Brille is respected by other people.

Possible Responses: He has compassion for others, even Hannetjie; he can assess a situation accurately; he has insights into his own feelings and motives; he plans ahead; he conquers his fears.

Literary Analysis: RESOLUTION

Have students explain how the conflict in the story is resolved.

Possible Response: Brille and Hannetjie learn to cooperate. Hannetjie agrees to help the prisoners rather than harassing and brutalizing them. Brille agrees to show Hannetjie respect before his superiors and to help him steal commodities.

Literary Analysis

THIRD-PERSON POINT OF VIEW

In the third-person point of view, the narrator's values, actions, and thoughts come through clearly. Have students describe the values and personality of the narrator of this story.

Possible Response: The narrator thinks apartheid is wrong and recognizes that it is harmful to whites as well as people of color. Despite the serious nature of the story, however, the narrator's wry sense of humor comes through, particularly in the last line of the story.

Reading Skills and Strategies: COMPARING

Have students compare the situation of the speaker of the poem with Brille's situation.

Possible Response: Both are prisoners who appreciate life's daily pleasures and the wonder of nature.

have a wife and children, and you're driving me to suicide."

"Why don't you like your own medicine, Hannetjie?" Brille asked quietly.

"I can give you anything you want," Warder Hannetjie said in desperation.

"It's not only me but the whole of Span One," said Brille cunningly. "The whole of Span One wants something from you."

Warder Hannetjie brightened with relief.

"I tink I can manage if it's tobacco you want," he said.

Brille looked at him, for the first time struck with pity and guilt. He wondered if he had carried the whole business too far. The man was really a child.

"It's not tobacco we want, but you," he said. "We want you on our side. We want a good warder because without a good warder we won't be able to manage the long stretch ahead."

> **Brille looked at him, for the first time struck with pity and guilt.**

Warder Hannetjie interpreted this request in his own fashion, and his interpretation of what was good and human often left the prisoners of Span One speechless with surprise. He had a way of slipping off his revolver and picking up a spade and digging alongside Span One. He had a way of producing unheard-of luxuries like boiled eggs from his farm nearby and things like cigarettes, and Span One responded nobly and got the reputation of being the best work span in the camp. And it wasn't only taken from their side. They were awfully good at stealing commodities like fertilizer which were needed on the farm of Warder Hannetjie. ❖ 1

WORDS TO KNOW

commodity (kə-mŏd'ĭ-tē) *n.* an item—especially a farming or mining product—that can be turned to commercial use or that can provide another advantage

Teaching Options

Mini Lesson Grammar

MODIFIERS: USING CORRECT COMPARATIVE FORMS Explain that the comparative and superlative forms of modifiers are usually expressed in one of the following ways. When the modifier is short (one or two syllables), *-er* or *–est* is added. When the modifier is longer, the words *more* or *most* (*less* or *least*) precede the modifier. Exceptions to these rules include irregular forms such as *good, better, best* and *bad, worse, worst.* Remind students not to double two comparative forms in the same sentence—for example, John was *more happier* than Joe. Write the following adjectives on the chalkboard.

quickly (*more quickly, most quickly*)
round (*rounder, roundest*)
intensely (*more intensely, most intensely*)
dangerous (*more dangerous, most dangerous*)

Have students create the comparative and superlative forms of the modifiers.

Practice Divide the class into groups and have each group search a different page of the story. Have them list all the modifiers they find and then write down the basic, comparative, and superlative form of each. When the groups finish, have them share their results. Guide students away from irregular modifiers and absolutes such as *entirely.*

Use **Grammar Transparencies and Copymasters,** p. 155, for more practice.

Use McDougal Littell's ***Language Network,*** Chapter 9, for more instruction in comparative forms.

LITERARY LINK

They Have Not Been Able

No Han Podido

Armando Valladares
(är-män′dô bä-yä-dä′rĕs)

2 They have not been able to take away
the rain's song
not yet
not even in this cell
but perhaps they'll do it tomorrow
that's why I want to enjoy it now,
to listen to the drops
drumming against
the boarded windows.
And suddenly it comes
through I don't know what crack
through I don't know what opening
that pungent odor
of wet earth
and I inhale deeply
filling myself to the brim
because perhaps they will also
prohibit that tomorrow.

Translated by
Marguerite Guzman Bouvard

No han podido quitarme 3
todavía
en este encierro
el canto de la lluvia
pero quizás lo hagan mañana
por eso quiero ahora disfrutarlo
escuchar las gotas
más allá de mis ojos
y los esperos muros
golpear con insistencia
las ventanas tapiadas.
Y de pronto me llega
no sé por qué ranura
no sé por qué intersticio
ese olor agradable
de la tierra mojada
y la aspiro muy hondo
para llenarme bien
porque quizás también
lo prohiban mañana.

Hombre y su sombra [Man and his shadow] (1971), Rufino Tamayo. Oil on canvas, 50 cm × 40 cm, collection of INBA-Museo de Arte Moderno, Mexico City.

Customizing Instruction

Students Acquiring English

1 Explain the idiom *speechless with surprise.* Relate it to the phrase *his jaw dropped open,* which also indicates that the surprise was so intense (*acute*) that the speaker could form no words.

Less Proficient Readers

2 Help students understand that the end of a line of poetry does not necessarily signal a break in reading. Have them determine the flow of this poem.

Possible Response: A reader should pause after any line that ends with a comma or a period. In the English translation, lines 1 and 2 make more sense if read one right after another. Lines 14 and 15 sound better with a pause between them.

Students Acquiring English

3 Encourage native Spanish speakers to read the original poem aloud for the class. Ask them to explain differences between the Spanish original and the English translation.

Gifted and Talented

Have students discuss the immoral/illegal acts committed in "The Prisoner Who Wore Glasses," including stealing, bribery, and blackmail. What, if anything, about the situation makes this behavior acceptable? How do these acts relate to the development of the story?

Possible Response: Most of these acts seem justified by the circumstances. However, Brille's blackmailing Hannetjie and Hannetjie's offers of bribery are one-sided, twisted efforts at cooperation that ultimately fail. They serve as devices to define the conflict and to advance the plot. It is not until the warder and prisoners achieve a truly cooperative relationship, with give and take on both sides, that the conflict is resolved.

✓ Assessment Standardized Test Practice

SUMMARY One objective tests students' ability to summarize a variety of written texts. To help students prepare for such assessment, have them read Brille's statement to Hannetjie and select the statement that best summarizes the passage.

> "It's not tobacco we want, but you," [Brille] said. "We want you on our side. We want a good warder because without a good warder we won't be able to manage the long stretch ahead."

A. The reason they want him on their side is because a good warder is much better than a bad warder.

B. The reason they want him on their side is because things become easier if they work together.

C. The reason they want him on their side is because they do not want tobacco.

D. The reason they want him on their side is because good warders also make good managers.

The answer must best address the overall situation. **C** is entirely incorrect: the prisoners like tobacco. **A** is true, but trivial compared to the scope of the story. **D** does not relate to the story: management was never an issue. The correct answer is **B**, because not only is it true, but it addresses the overall subject of cooperation between white and black South Africans.

GUIDING STUDENT RESPONSE

Connect to the Literature

1. **What Do You Think?**
   At the beginning of the story Brille and Hannetjie are enemies, but at the end they become comrades.

Comprehension Check
- Brille is in prison for political acts outlawed by the government.
- Hannetjie gives Brille tobacco as a bribe so that Brille won't report that Hannetjie stole fertilizer.
- The prisoners want Hannetjie to consider and treat them as human beings.

Use Selection Quiz in **Unit Four Resource Book,** p. 53.

Think Critically

2. Possible Response: Hannetjie recognizes that in some ways he, like the prisoners, is a victim of the system. For this reason, he understands that he needs to treat the prisoners with more respect.
3. Possible Responses: Brille's message to his children, "Be good comrades, my children. Cooperate, then life will run smoothly," also applies to Hannetjie; Brille comes to realize that violence needs to be replaced with cooperation, whether in the family or in the prison.
4. Possible Response: The story suggests the importance of knowing when and how to cooperate to help advance the individual and improve the system.
5. Possible Responses: South Africa's policy of apartheid hurt not only the individual, but also the whole society; denying the rights of one group ultimately is detrimental to the whole.

Thinking through the LITERATURE

Connect to the Literature

1. **What Do You Think?** How would you describe the relationship between Brille and Hannetjie?

Comprehension Check
- Why is Brille in prison?
- Why does Hannetjie give Brille tobacco?
- What do the prisoners want from Hannetjie?

Think Critically

2. Why do you think Hannetjie becomes such a "good warder" at the end of the story?
3. How does Brille's relationship with his children compare with his relationship with Hannetjie?
4. In your opinion, what is this story's **theme,** or message, about assertiveness and cooperation?

   THINK ABOUT
   - how the different **characters** assert themselves
   - the effectiveness of assertive acts in the story
   - how the men cooperate at the end of the story
5. ACTIVE READING DRAWING CONCLUSIONS Look at the notes in your READER'S NOTEBOOK. What conclusions can you draw about social and political issues in South Africa at the time of the story? Compare your conclusions with those of a classmate and discuss what elements of the story you think support your conclusions.

Extend Interpretations

6. **Comparing Texts** Compare Brille's attitude with that of the speaker in the poem "They Have Not Been Able," on page 659.
7. **Comparing Texts** Compare Brille's means of challenging the system with that of the narrator in "The Thrill of the Grass" by W. P. Kinsella. Which character did you find more clever? Why?
8. **Connect to Life** Consider the hardships endured by Brille and the other prisoners of Span One. What do you think would be the most difficult aspect of life in prison?

Literary Analysis

THIRD-PERSON POINT OF VIEW

Point of view refers to the narrative method used in a literary work. In **first-person point of view,** the narrator is a character in the story who describes the action in his or her own words. In **third-person point of view,** the narrator is not a character but instead stands outside the action, referring to all characters with third-person pronouns such as *he, she,* and *they.* "The Prisoner Who Wore Glasses" uses a third-person point of view. In a **third-person omniscient point of view,** the narrator is omniscient, or all-knowing, and can see into the minds of more than one character. In the **third-person limited point of view,** the narrator describes the thoughts of only one character.

Activity Look back over the story and decide whether the author uses a third-person limited point of view or a third-person omniscient point of view. Why do you think Head tells the story in this way? Why do you think she chose not to have Brille narrate the story?

REVIEW SETTING The **setting** of this story is South Africa at a time when apartheid was still in effect. Why do you think Head set the story in a prison instead of a factory, a slum, or some other place?

Extend Interpretations

Comparing Texts Possible Responses: The speaker in "They Have Not Been Able" has a passive, almost fatalistic, attitude toward prison life; Brille has an active, positive attitude, believing he can better the prison environment; both the speaker and Brille make the best of the present moment.

Comparing Texts Students should support their opinions with specific details from the stories.

Connect to Life Some students may say the lack of freedom would be the most difficult. Others may say that the separation from family and friends would be the most difficult.

Literary Analysis

Third-Person Point of View Students should be able to find passages that reveal the third-person limited point of view.

Review Setting Student responses should reflect an analysis of the relevance of setting to the text's meaning.

Writing Options

1. **Letter to Brille's Children** Assume Brille's identity and write a letter to his children. In it, reveal what you have learned as a result of your experience in prison.
2. **Personal Response Essay** Draft a personal essay in which you compare Brille's response to his warder with your likely response to such a situation.

Activities & Explorations

1. **Narrative Cartoon** Create a narrative cartoon based on this story. ~ ART
2. **Political Speech** Deliver a speech that Brille might have made to political supporters on the day of his release from prison. ~ SPEAKING AND LISTENING

Inquiry & Research

From Prisoner to National Leader In some ways, Brille's situation mirrors the experiences of South Africa's most famous former prisoner, Nelson Mandela. Find out more about Mandela's life and his time as a political prisoner.

Real World Link Begin your research by reading the article on pages 662–663.

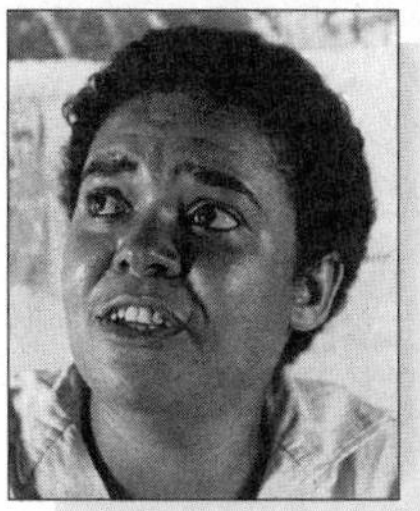

Bessie Head

1937–1986

Other Works
When Rain Clouds Gather
The Collector of Treasures
Serowe: Village of the Rain Wind
Tales of Tenderness and Power

Emigration to Botswana Born in South Africa, Bessie Head experienced firsthand the effects of apartheid. Designated as a "colored" person (part black and part white) under apartheid's rigid classification system, she was denied the full privileges of citizenship in her homeland. Head never knew her parents; she was raised from birth by a child welfare agency and was later placed with foster parents. After training in a missionary school, she worked for several years as a teacher and journalist before emigrating to a small village in Botswana, a neighboring country that was then under British control. Head taught for a few more years, then led a quiet life of writing and farming.

Thoughts of Home Though Head left South Africa physically, its problems were rarely far from her thoughts. While some of her novels and stories explore village life in Botswana, many writings reveal the tragedies and injustices of the land where she was born. Her attitude toward South Africa blended realism and idealism. "It is to be hoped," she once said, "that great leaders will arise there who remember the suffering of racial hatred and out of it formulate a common language of human love for all people." Though she died of hepatitis before reaching her 50th birthday, she left behind an impressive body of work, remarkable for its attentiveness to the lives of ordinary people.

Vocabulary in Action

EXERCISE: WORD KNOWLEDGE For each Word to Know, complete a list like the one shown for the word *assertive.* Use a dictionary or thesaurus if you need help.

Word: assertive
Definition: inclined to bold expression or action
Synonyms: forceful, confident, outspoken, insistent, aggressive
Sentence: The prisoner was assertive when he defied the warder.

WORDS TO KNOW					
	acute	chaos	conviction	irrelevant	ruefully
	bedlam	commodity	cower	perpetrate	tirade

Building Vocabulary
For an in-depth study of connotation and denotation, see page 494.

Workplace Link: Conflict Resolution

Suggest that partners select a conflict they are familiar with, such as where to go on a date or dealing with troublesome classmates, friends, or siblings. Students might then consider Brille's steps toward conflict resolution and apply them to the conflict they are resolving. Steps might be (1) identify the conflict; (2) identify the different viewpoints of the conflicting parties; (3) identify possible solutions including the benefits of compromise; (4) suggest areas of compromise in which each party gives up something in return for gaining something.

Writing Options

1. **Letter to Brille's Children** Help students recall that Brille felt remorse for allowing his children to fight and for acting "the bogeyman" when he returned home. In prison Brille learned to cooperate to gain peace.
2. **Personal Response Essay** Suggest that students recall interactions between Hannetjie and Brille and imagine how their responses might have differed from Brille's. Invite volunteers to read their alternative endings aloud.

Activities & Explorations

1. **Narrative Cartoon** Suggest that students work with a partner to identify three or four important incidents from this story to portray.
2. **Political Speech** Suggest that Brille's release might coincide with the ending of apartheid and that Brille might recount his experiences with Hannetjie to suggest a way in which black and white South Africans can resolve their differences.

Inquiry & Research

From Prisoner to National Leader Nelson Mandela was released from prison in 1990 and later served as the president of South Africa. Encourage them to use the World Wide Web to search for further information.

Vocabulary in Action

EXERCISE
Student sentences will vary.

1. acute; **synonyms:** shrewd, discerning, quick, sharp, keen
2. chaos; **synonyms:** disorder, shambles, confusion, disorganization
3. conviction; **synonyms:** belief, persuasion, faith, opinion, view
4. irrelevant; **synonyms:** inappropriate, unfitting, unrelated, inconsistent
5. ruefully; **synonyms:** sorrowfully, regretfully, dolefully
6. bedlam; **synonyms:** asylum, madhouse, confusion, uproar, turmoil
7. commodity; **synonyms:** goods, article, wares, product
8. cower; **synonyms:** stop, cringe, shrink, crouch
9. perpetrate; **synonyms:** commit, inflict, perform, do, practice
10. tirade; **synonyms:** outpouring, flood, sermon, harangue, diatribe

Real WORLD Link

Magazine Article

Objective
- identify significant events in a biography

Connecting to the Literature
The plot of Bessie Head's short story "The Prisoner Who Wore Glasses" (p. 652) traces events in the life of Brille and other political prisoners in Span One.

Reading for Information

André Brink traces significant events in Nelson Mandela's life.

YOUR TURN

1. Students may find it helpful to use brackets to indicate time spans. For example, the trial extended from 1956 to 1961, but the Sharpeville incident occurred in 1960.
2. Mandela became involved in programs of passive resistance against unjust laws.

Nelson Mandela

by André Brink

President Nelson Mandela and Deputy President F. W. de Klerk

Despite spending nearly 35 years in prison, South Africa's first black president, Nelson Mandela, championed forgiveness and peace. In the following article, André Brink explores the roots of Mandela's moral courage and strength.

❶ Rolihlahla Mandela was born deep in the black homeland of Transkei on July 18, 1918. His first name could be interpreted, prophetically, as "troublemaker." The Nelson was added later, by a primary school teacher. . . . Mandela's boyhood was peaceful enough, spent on cattle herding and other rural pursuits, until the death of his father landed him in the care of a powerful relative. . . . But it was only after he left the missionary College of Fort Hare, where he had become involved in student protests against the white colonial rule of the institution, that he set out on the long walk toward personal and national liberation.

Having run away from his guardian to avoid an arranged marriage, he joined a law firm in Johannesburg as an apprentice. Years of daily exposure to the inhumanities of apartheid, where being black reduced one to the status of a nonperson, kindled in him a kind of absurd courage to change the world. It meant that instead of the easy life in a rural setting he'd been brought up for, or even a modest measure of success as a lawyer, his only future certainties would be sacrifice and suffering. . . .

❷ In these circumstances Mandela opted for nonviolence as a strategy. He joined the Youth League of the African National Congress and became involved in programs of passive resistance against the laws that forced blacks to carry passes and kept them in a position of permanent servility.

Exasperated, the government mounted a massive treason trial against its main opponents, Mandela among them. It dragged on for five years, until 1961, ending in the acquittal of all 156 accused. But by that time the country had been convulsed by the massacre of peaceful black demonstrators at Sharpeville in March 1960, and the government was intent on crushing all opposition. Most liberation movements, including the A.N.C., were banned. . . .

662

Reading for Information

A **biography** is an account of a person's life written by another person. The writer of a biography researches his or her subject to present accurate information that traces the major events in that subject's life.

ORGANIZING INFORMATION CHRONOLOGICALLY

Chronological order is the order in which events occur. The writer uses time order to structure the work.

YOUR TURN To help you trace the momentous events in Nelson Mandela's life that are covered in the article, use these suggestions and activities.

❶ **Creating a Time Line** Begin with the date mentioned here, and create a time line of the significant events and achievements of Mandela's life. What new knowledge about Mandela did you gain from exploring the events chronologically?

❷ Brink states that before Mandela joined the African National Congress (A.N.C.), he "opted for nonviolence as a strategy." What steps did Mandela take to act on his philosophy of nonviolence?

Mini Lesson: Inquiry & Research

The Inquiry & Research activity on this page links this article to the Inquiry & Research section of Choices & Challenges (page 661), in which students are instructed to find out more about Mandela's life.

Instruction Using the information given in Mandela's statement to the court, identify three of Mandela's key character traits. Enter those character traits on a graphic organizer that compares and contrasts Mandela's traits with those of the character Brille.

Practice Have students brainstorm instances of specific actions engaged in by both Mandela and Brille. Then, instruct students to infer a generalization about each man's character based on the actions they have identified

Mandela went underground for more than a year and traveled abroad to enlist support for the A.N.C.

Soon after his return, he was arrested and sentenced to imprisonment on Robben Island for five years. . . . [But within months] Mandela was hauled from prison to face with [the leaders of the A.N.C.] an almost certain death sentence. His statement from the dock was destined to smolder in the homes and servant quarters, the shacks and shebeens and huts and hovels of the oppressed, and to burn in the conscience of the world: "During my lifetime I have dedicated myself to the struggle of the African people. I have fought against white domination, and I have fought against black domination. I have cherished the ideal of a 3 democratic and free society in which all persons live together in harmony and with equal opportunities. It is an ideal which I hope to live for and to achieve. But, if needs be, it is an ideal for which I am prepared to die."

Without any attempt to find a legal way out, Mandela assumed his full responsibility. This conferred a new status of moral dignity on his leadership, which became evident from the moment he was returned to Robben Island.

Even on his first arrival, two years before, he had set an example by refusing to obey an order to jog from the harbor, where the ferry docked, to the prison gates. The warden in charge warned him bluntly that unless he started obeying, he might quite simply be killed. . . . Whereupon Mandela quietly retorted, "If you so much as lay a hand on me, I will take you to the highest court in the land, and when I finish with you, you will be as poor as a church mouse." Amazingly, the warden backed off. . . .

After more than two decades in prison, confident that on some crucial issues a leader must make decisions on his own, Mandela decided on a new approach. And after painstaking preliminaries, the most famous prisoner in the world was escorted, in the greatest secrecy, to the State President's office to start negotiating not only his own release but also the nation's transition from apartheid to democracy. On Feb. 2, 1990, President F. W. de Klerk lifted the ban on the A.N.C. and announced Mandela's imminent release.

Then began the real test. Every inch of the way, Mandela had to win the support of his own followers. More difficult still was the process of allaying[1] white fears. But the patience, the wisdom, the visionary quality Mandela brought to his struggle, and above
4 all the moral integrity with which he set about to unify a divided people, resulted in the country's first democratic elections and his selection as President.

1. **allaying:** reducing the intensity of.

3 Mandela's statement to the court shows his moral stand on the issue of freedom. Identify other events from the article that reveal Mandela's commitment to his cause.

4 Of the events in Mandela's life that you entered on your time line, what do you think was Mandela's most difficult challenge? How did he meet that challenge?

Inquiry & Research

Activity Link: "The Prisoner Who Wore Glasses," p. 661

Use a graphic organizer to compare and contrast the character Brille with Nelson Mandela. If you need more information, check reference sources or other materials.

3 Other events that reveal Mandela's commitment to his cause include the following:
- college protests
- apprenticeship in a law office
- joining the Youth League of the A.N.C. and promoting passive resistance
- going underground to enlist support for A.N.C.
- stating that eliminating apartheid is a cause for which he is prepared to die
- refusing to obey a warden's order
- negotiating the end of apartheid with de Klerk

4 Mandela's most difficult challenge began after his release from prison. He had to win the support of his own followers as well as allay the fears of whites. He succeeded with patience, wisdom, and unwavering commitment to his cause.

OVERVIEW

Objectives

1. understand and appreciate a **short story (Literary Analysis)**
2. understand the use of **flashback (Literary Analysis)**
3. **evaluate characters (Active Reading)**

Summary

Ivan Vassilievich claims that everything in life depends on chance, as he recalls how the direction of his own life changed one night after a ball. He left the ball intoxicated with love after dancing with Varenka, the beautiful daughter of a colonel, most of the night. Unable to sleep, Ivan wandered toward Varenka's home. Near her house, he saw a military procession and heard the sounds of a fife and drum, evil and ominous. A runaway Tartar was being mercilessly beaten under the supervision of Varenka's father. Filled with anguish at what he had witnessed, Ivan questioned what the colonel knew that he did not. Ivan decided not to do any of the things that he had planned to do in the future. His love for Varenka subsided and ultimately came to nothing.

Thematic Link

An older man tells the story of how his life changed because of a chance revelation that **tested his convictions** against the passion of his love.

Editor's Note: This selection has been edited slightly to delete material that may be considered objectionable.

5-Minute Warm-Up

Daily Language SkillBuilder

Have students **proofread** the display sentences on page 541m and write them correctly. The sentences also appear on Transparency 22 of **Grammar Transparencies and Copymasters.**

Mini Lesson: Preteaching Vocabulary

If you would like to preteach the WORDS TO KNOW for this selection, use the Mini Lesson, p. 666.

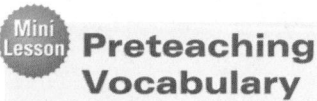

After the Ball

Short Story by LEO TOLSTOY

"The only thing I feared was that something might spoil my happiness."

Connect to Your Life

Good vs. Evil List the qualities and behaviors that you associate with a good person, and then list those that you associate with an evil person. Now think of several famous people you have heard of, and try to classify each as good or evil. Can you always tell whether a person is good or evil?

Build Background

Morality and Society Leo Tolstoy was an important Russian writer, reformer, and moral thinker of the 19th century. For much of his life he was preoccupied with questions of good and evil, the meaning of life, and the structure of society. The major events in "After the Ball" take place in the 1840s. The characters belong to the polite society of the time, for whom lavish dances, or balls, were major social events.

WORDS TO KNOW
Vocabulary Preview

chagrin	majestic
detestable	maliciously
ethereal	perspicacity
imposing	pummel
irate	unassuming

VIDEODISC **LaserLinks: Background for Reading**
Visual Vocabulary

Focus Your Reading

LITERARY ANALYSIS FLASHBACK In this story, the elderly Ivan Vassilievich recounts a significant episode in his life, describing events that helped to shape his world view when he was a young man. Because of this, most of "After the Ball" is told in flashback, an account of events that happened before the beginning of a story.

As you read this story, identify where the flashback begins and ends, and consider what the use of this technique adds to Tolstoy's story.

ACTIVE READING EVALUATING CHARACTERS Ivan tells his tale in order to make a point about people's ability to tell good from evil. As you read Tolstoy's story, be aware of your own evaluation of each character, based on your own standards of right and wrong.

READER'S NOTEBOOK Use a chart like the one below to keep track of the personal qualities and behaviors of the **main characters.** Decide whether you think each quality or behavior is good or evil or a mixture of the two, and record your evaluation in the appropriate box.

Qualities and Behaviors			
Character	**Good**	**Evil**	**Mixture**
Ivan Vassilievich			
Varenka			
Varenka's father, the Colonel			

LESSON RESOURCES

UNIT FOUR RESOURCE BOOK, pp. 55–56

ASSESSMENT RESOURCES
Formal Assessment, pp. 119–120
Teacher's Guide to Assessment and Portfolio Use
Test Generator

SKILLS TRANSPARENCIES AND COPYMASTERS
Reading and Critical Thinking
- Organizational Chart: Horizontal, T51 (for Reader's Notebook, p. 664)

Grammar
- Participles, C102 (for Mini Lesson, p. 670)
- Participial Phrases, C103 (for Mini Lesson, p. 676)

Vocabulary
- Context Clues, C70 (for Mini Lesson, p. 666)
- Analogies, C71 (for Mini Lesson, p. 668)

Writing
- Point of View, T23 (for Writing Option 1, p. 676)
- The Uses of Dialogue, T24 (for Writing Option 2, p. 676)
- Persuasive Essay, C30 (for Writing Option 3, p. 676)

Communications
- Dramatic Reading, T12 (for Activities & Explorations 1, p. 676)
- Impromtu Speaking: Dialogue, Role-Play, Debate, T13 (for Activities & Explorations 1, p. 676)

INTEGRATED TECHNOLOGY
Audio Library
LaserLinks
- Visual Vocabulary
- Author Background: Leo Tolstoy

See **Teacher's SourceBook,** p. 41.
Visit our website:
www.mcdougallittell.com

After the Ball

Leo Tolstoy

"You say a man can't tell good from evil, that everything depends on circumstances, that circumstances determine everything. While I think everything depends on chance. I speak from my own experience."

These were the much-respected Ivan Vassilievich's[1] introductory words following a discussion we had had about the necessity of changing living conditions before people could improve themselves. Strictly speaking, no one had said it was impossible to tell good from evil, but Ivan Vassilievich had a way of answering the thoughts a discussion provoked in his own mind, and then recounting episodes of his own life related to these thoughts. He was often so transported by his story, particularly since he told stories earnestly and honestly, that he completely forgot his reason for telling it. That is what happened this time, too.

"I speak from my own experience. My whole life took one direction instead of another, not because of circumstances, but something completely different."

1. **Ivan Vassilievich** (ĭ-vän′ və-syĭl′yə-vĭch′).

TEACHING THE LITERATURE

Customizing Instruction

Less Proficient Readers

Set a Purpose Read the quotation and elicit that "circumstances" may include such things as where we live, who our parents are, and how much money we have. Then elicit that "chance," on the other hand, includes those unpredictable events that affect us deeply. Have students read on to find out about the circumstances and chance events in the life of young Ivan Vassilievich.

Students Acquiring English

This selection may challenge some students because of its complex sentence structure. You may want to read page 665 aloud to get students into the story. Encourage students to apply reading strategies that have helped them in the past, such as taking notes, rereading, and paraphrasing.

Use **Spanish Study Guide** for additional support, pp. 146–148.

Gifted and Talented

Tell students that Tolstoy first called this story "Daughter and Father." Ask them to keep the original title in mind as they read and to note how it affects their understanding of the story.

BLOCK SCHEDULING: MANAGING TIME

If your schedule requires that you cover the lesson objectives in a shorter time, use . . .

- Preparing to Read, p. 664
- Thinking Through the Literature, p. 675
- Vocabulary in Action, p. 676
- Grammar in Context, p. 677

If you want to take advantage of longer class time, use . . .

- TE Teaching Options: Preteaching Vocabulary, pp. 666–667; Vocabulary Strategy, pp. 668–669; Viewing and Representing, pp. 671, 673; Multicultural Link, p. 672; Informal Assessment, p. 674
- Choices & Challenges and Author Activity, pp. 676–677

AFTER THE BALL **665**

Reading and Analyzing

Reading Skills and Strategies:
PREVIEW

Briefly summarize the selection, emphasizing the structure of flashback. Discuss the title, the images, and the called-out quotations in the story. Before they begin reading, discuss with the students the Build Background on page 664.

Literary Analysis FLASHBACK

A flashback can be identified in a number of ways. The verb tense may shift from past to past perfect; the setting may be different from the present-time setting; the narrator may indicate that he is reflecting on the past as Ivan does: "I speak from my own experience." Students may contribute other ways of indicating a flashback that they have observed.

Use **Unit Four Resource Book** p. 56 for more practice.

Active Reading
EVALUATING CHARACTERS

Evaluating characters is best done by observing their behavior and defining their qualities. To help students evaluate the characters in this selection, have them complete the chart shown on p. 664.

Use **Unit Four Resource Book** p. 55 for more practice.

The Reception (about 1883–1885), James Tissot. Oil on canvas, 56″ × 40″, Albright-Knox Art Gallery, Buffalo, New York, gift of William M. Chase, 1909.

666

Teaching Options

Mini Lesson Preteaching Vocabulary

CONTEXT CLUES: COMPARE OR CONTRAST Call students' attention to the list of WORDS TO KNOW. Explain that sometimes they can understand the meaning of an unfamiliar word by examining the context in which the word appears. Use the model sentence to demonstrate the strategy of using context clues that compare or contrast the unknown word with something known. Signal words for comparisons include *like, as*, and *similar to*. Signal words for contrast include *but, not, although, however*, and *on the other hand*.

Model Sentence

We hardly noticed her presence because she was as *unassuming* as a bashful child.

Instruction

- Write the model sentence on the chalkboard.
- Ask a volunteer to summarize the meaning of the comparison.
- Have students use the meaning of *bashful child* to infer the meaning of the word *unassuming*.
- Ask a volunteer to use the word *unassuming* in a sentence.

Exercises Read the following sentences. Ask students to use context clues to determine the meanings of the italicized terms.

1. His attitude was *detestable*, although he was somewhat agreeable at times.

"What was it then?" we asked.

"Well, that's a long story. To make you understand, I'd have to explain it at length."

"Well, tell us."

Ivan Vassilievich became thoughtful, nodded his head.

"Yes," he said. "My whole life was changed by one night, or rather by one morning."

"But what happened?"

"It happened that I was greatly in love. I had been in love many times, but this was my greatest love. It's past: she has married daughters by now. It was B——,
1 yes, Varenka B—— (Ivan Vassilievich mentioned her surname). At the age of fifteen, she was already a remarkable beauty. As a young girl of eighteen, she was enchanting: tall, well-formed, graceful, majestic—most of all, majestic. She carried herself unusually erect as though she were unable to do otherwise, tipping her head slightly back. Despite her slenderness, even boniness, this posture gave her, with her beauty
2 and her height, a sort of queenly aspect which would have frightened people away from her had it not been for her tenderness, the merry smile on her lips, her enchanting, sparkling eyes, and her whole sweet young self."

"At the age of fifteen, she was already a remarkable beauty. As a young girl of eighteen, she was enchanting: tall, well formed, graceful, majestic—most of all, majestic."

"How well Ivan Vassilievich describes her!"

"No matter how much I described her, I could never make you realize what she was like. But that's beside the point; what I wanted to tell about happened in the forties. I was then a student in a provincial university. Whether it was good or bad I don't know, but at that time we had no clubs or theories in our universities; and we were simply young men, living as young men do: studying and being merry. I was a very gay and venturesome boy, and rich as well. I had a fast trotter and used to take sleigh rides in the hills with the ladies (skates were not yet in fashion) and carouse with my comrades (at that time we drank nothing but champagne; if we had no money, we didn't drink, but we never drank vodka as we do now). Parties and balls were my greatest pleasures. I was a good dancer and not ugly."

"No need to be modest," interrupted one of the ladies. "After all, we've seen your daguerreotype.[2] You weren't just not ugly; you were handsome." 3

"Handsome or not, that's beside the point. The point is that at the time of my greatest love for her, I was at a ball given the last day of Shrovetide[3] by the provincial governor, an affable old man, rich, a generous host, and a nobleman. His wife received equally graciously in a puce velvet dress with her diamond coronet on her head, and her bare, old, plump, white shoulders and throat like the portrait of Elizabeth Petrovna.[4] The ball was marvelous: an excellent 4 ballroom, singers, and musicians—the serfs of a music-loving landowner who were then famous, a magnificent buffet, and a sea of champagne. 5

2. **daguerreotype** (də-gâr′ə-tīp′): an early type of photograph.
3. **the last day of Shrovetide:** Mardi Gras, a day of festivity preceding the fasting and penance of the Christian season of Lent.
4. **Elizabeth Petrovna** (pə-trôv′nə): empress of Russia from 1741 to 1762.

WORDS TO KNOW

majestic (mə-jĕs′tĭk) *adj.* showing lofty dignity or nobility; stately

Customizing Instruction

Less Proficient Readers

1 Point out that Tolstoy only gives the first letter of Varenka's last name. Explain that this was a common device in 19th-century literature. By not revealing the names of certain characters or places, the author creates the illusion that the story is about real people whose "true identities" must be protected. This helps readers get interested and involved in the plot.

2 Ask students why Varenka's *queenly aspect* might have frightened people away.

Possible Response: because they would have thought her snobbish or proud

Gifted and Talented

3 Have students research the photographic technique involved in creating a daguerreotype. Encourage them to develop a class presentation that explains the technique. If possible, bring actual daguerreotypes to class.

Students Acquiring English

4 Define *puce* as "a dark red" and *coronet* as "a small crown."

5 Define *serfs* as "peasants who were owned by a lord and bound to the land."

2. I am not very quick with my hands, but my mental *perspicacity* is remarkable.
3. The golden sunlight made the whole scene appear like an *ethereal* realm on another world.
4. The sheer dimensions of the monument were *imposing*, but not as overwhelming as Mt. Everest.
5. Her posture was as *majestic* as a queen's.
6. The teacher seemed *irate* at first, but then I saw a tiny glimmer of humor in her eye suggesting otherwise.
7. The coach instructed the boxer to *pummel* her opponent, not throw delicate punches.
8. He reacted *maliciously*, like a man angry at having been beaten twice before.
9. I could have felt *chagrin* at losing before such a large crowd, but I decided to disregard other people's negative thoughts.

Use **Unit Four Resource Book** p. 57 for more exercises.

A lesson on context clues appears on p. 56 in the Pupil's Edition.

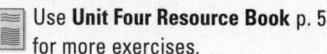

Reading and Analyzing

Reading Skills and Strategies: PREDICTING

Have students predict what will happen in the relationship between Ivan and Varenka.

Possible Responses: Their love will end in marriage and they will be happy together; Varenka is too perfect, making a permanent relationship between Ivan and Varenka impossible.

Literary Analysis FLASHBACK

Tolstoy occasionally interrupts Ivan's flashback and brings the reader back to present time. Students may want to discuss the effect of these interruptions.

Possible Responses: The interruptions add variety to the narrative style; they enable Tolstoy to develop the character traits of both the younger and the older Ivan.

Active Reading

EVALUATING CHARACTERS

Noting the comments of his friends and listeners, students can evaluate the character of the older Ivan. Have them list specific details that support their evaluation.

Possible Response: Ivan seems like a credible narrator and a man of integrity. He is modest; he describes situations well; he is "much respected"; he tells stories "earnestly and honestly." His angry reaction to the listener's comment suggests that he is concerned with purity and has an idealistic attitude toward love.

Although I loved champagne, I did not drink because I was drunk with love without wine, but I danced until exhausted; I danced quadrilles[5] and waltzes and polkas; everything I could, of course, with Varenka. She wore a white dress, a pink sash, and white kid gloves just short of her thin, sharp elbows, and white satin slippers. The detestable Engineer Anisimov[6] beat me to the mazurkas[7]—to this day I haven't forgiven him for that. He had invited her just as she arrived, while I had had to go to the hairdresser's and to fetch a pair of gloves, and was late. So it happened that I danced the mazurka not with her, but with a German girl I had courted a bit before. But I'm afraid I was not very polite to her; I didn't talk to her, didn't look at her; I saw only the tall, well-formed figure in the white dress with the pink sash, her radiant, pink-cheeked, dimpled face and her gentle, kind eyes. I was not alone; everyone looked at her and loved her; men and women loved her, in spite of the fact that she eclipsed them all. It was impossible not to love her.

According to the rules, so to speak, I was not her partner for the mazurkas; but in reality, I danced with her almost all the time. In cotillions,[8] she would cross the whole ballroom straight to me without embarrassment, and I would jump up without waiting for her invitation, and she would thank me for my perspicacity with a smile. When she failed to guess what character trait I had chosen to represent, she would give her hand to someone other than me with a shrug of her thin shoulders and would smile at me as a sign of regret and consolation. When the mazurka featured a waltz, I would waltz with her for a long time, and she, often out of breath, would smile and say *'Encore'*[9] to me. And I would waltz again, feeling completely bodiless."

"Come, how could you feel bodiless! I should think you would feel quite the opposite when you took her by the waist; not only your own body, but hers," said one of the guests.

Ivan Vassilievich suddenly blushed and almost shouted in his anger:

"Yes, that's like you, indeed, today's youth. You see nothing but bodies. In our day it wasn't like that. The more I loved her, the more ethereal she became for me. Now you can see feet, ankles, and still more; you denude the women you love; for me, as Alphonse Karr said—now there was a good writer—the object of my love always wore clothes of bronze. We not only did not denude them but tried to cover up their nakedness, like the good son of Noah. But you wouldn't understand . . . "

"Don't listen to him. What happened next?" said one of us.

"Yes. So I danced some more with her not noticing how time was passing. The musicians had already reached a sort of desperate stage of tiredness, you know, as often happens at the end of a ball; they kept repeating the same mazurka; the papas and mamas had already gotten up from the card tables in the salons and were waiting for supper; the lackeys[10] ran back and forth more and more frequently. It was after two. I had to make use of the last remaining minutes. I chose her once more, and we went across the ballroom for the hundredth time.

5. **quadrilles** (kwŏ-drĭlz′): dances performed by groups of four couples.
6. **Anisimov** (ə-nyĭs′ĭ-môv′).
7. **mazurkas** (mə-zûr′kəz): lively Polish dances similar to the polka.
8. **cotillions** (kō-tĭl′yənz): ballroom dances for couples.
9. ***encore*** (äɴ-kôr′) *French:* again; once more.
10. **lackeys:** servants.

WORDS TO KNOW
detestable (dĭ-tĕs′tə-bəl) *adj.* worthy of scorn; hateful
perspicacity (pûr′spĭ-kăs′ĭ-tē) *n.* keen perception or understanding
ethereal (ĭ-thîr′ē-əl) *adj.* not earthly; heavenly

Teaching Options

Mini Lesson Vocabulary Strategy

UNDERSTANDING ANALOGIES Instruction
Analogies show relationships between words. A typical analogy equation (like those on standardized tests) is similar to the following.

TERRIER : DOG ::
A. fish : pond
B. parakeet : finch
C. auto : van
D. eagle : bird
E. plane : housefly

To solve the analogy equation, students should first determine the relationship between the original pair of words. Then they must state the relationship: *A terrier is a type of dog*. Next, they must find the word pair that expresses the same relationship: *An eagle is a type of bird*. The following relationships are commonly found in analogies: cause and effect, part to whole, object to purpose, item to category, word to synonym, word to antonym.

Practice Have students solve the following analogies. Answers are italicized.

1. IRATE :: LOSER
A. happy :: person
B. police officer :: criminal
C. *joyous :: victor*
D. hungry :: cook

"'Then, after supper, the quadrille is mine?' I asked her, escorting her back to her place.

"'Of course; if they don't take me home,' she said, smiling.

"'I won't give you up,' I said.

"'Give me back my fan, anyway,' she said.

"'It's hard to give it back,' I said, handing back her unassuming, white fan.

"'Then I'll give you something so you won't be sad,' she said and tore off a feather from the fan to give me.

"I took the feather and could only express all my enthusiasm and gratitude with a look. I was not only merry and content, I was happy, blessed; I was pure; I was not I, but a kind of unearthly being, knowing no evil and capable only of good. I hid the feather in my glove and stood there, powerless to leave her.

"'Look, Papa is asking someone to dance,' she said to me, pointing out the tall, dignified figure of her father, a colonel with silver epaulettes,[11] standing at the entrance with the hostess and other ladies.

"'Varenka, come here,' we heard the deep voice of the hostess with her diamond coronet and Elizabethan shoulders say.

"Varenka went to the entrance, and I followed her.

"'Come, *ma chère,*[12] your father will dance with you. Please, now, Piotr Vladislavich.' The hostess turned toward the colonel.

"Varenka's father was a very handsome, imposing, and well-preserved old man. His face was rosy with curled, white mustaches *à la* Nikolai I[13] joining his equally white sideburns with their curls combed forward at the temples.

"The entire ballroom followed the couple's every movement. As for me, I was not just admiring, but was watching them with intense emotion."

His eyes and lips wore the same gentle, joyous smile as his daughter's. He had a handsome build: long, well-formed legs, strong shoulders, and a military chest bearing large, unornate decorations. He was a military commander in the tradition of Nikolai I. 3

"When we reached the entrance, the colonel was protesting, saying he had forgotten how to dance, but just the same, smiling, bending his left hand behind him, he unbuckled his sword, handed it to an obliging young man, and pulling his chamois[14] glove on his right hand—'Must observe the rules,' he said, smiling—he took his daughter's hand and stood in the third row, waiting for the beat.

"At the beginning of the mazurka theme, he nimbly tapped one leg, bent the other, and his tall, robust figure moved around the ballroom, now quietly and smoothly, now noisily and energetically, clicking his feet together. The graceful figure of Varenka swam around him, from time to time imperceptibly shortening or lengthening the steps of her tiny, white satin shoes. The entire ballroom followed the couple's every movement. As for me, I was not just admiring, but was watching them with intense emotion. I was particularly impressed by his boots, drawn tight with straps—fine, calf boots,

11. **epaulettes** (ĕp′ə-lĕts′): ornamental fringed shoulder pads on a military uniform.
12. ***ma chère*** (mä shĕr) *French:* my dear.
13. ***à la* Nikolai** (nyĭk-ə-lī′) **I:** in the style of Nicholas I, czar of Russia from 1825 to 1855.
14. **chamois** (shăm′ē): a soft leather made from the skin of an antelope.

WORDS TO KNOW
unassuming (ŭn′ə-sōō′mĭng) *adj.* not pretentious; modest
imposing (ĭm-pō′zĭng) *adj.* impressive

Customizing Instruction

Multiple Learning Styles

Auditory/Musical Learners

1 Encourage knowledgeable students to describe these musical forms: the quadrille, the waltz, and the polka. They may play music for one of these dances for the class.

Students Acquiring English

2 "I was not I . . . only of good." Ask students to paraphrase Ivan's statement by using context clues.

Possible Response: I did not feel like myself anymore; I was so happy I felt as if I were in heaven.

Less Proficient Readers

Review the first paragraph in the story and ask students to summarize the "circumstances" of young Ivan.

Possible Responses: He is a handsome, rich young man who likes to dance and have fun; he is in love with Varenka.

3 Have students give their impression of Varenka's father.

Possible Response: He is a handsome army colonel who seems to be friendly, kind, and a loving parent.

2. BEHAVIOR :: DETESTABLE
- **A.** *food :: delicious*
- **B.** music :: celebration
- **C.** anger :: cause
- **D.** athletics :: success

3. IMPOSING :: AWESOME
- **A.** funny :: somber
- **B.** ill :: healthy
- **C.** interesting :: dull
- **D.** *faithful :: loyal*

4. LACKEY :: SERVANT
- **A.** athlete :: coach
- **B.** *jockey :: driver*
- **C.** runner :: relay team
- **D.** teacher :: student

5. UNASSUMING :: OBVIOUS
- **A.** hot : hotter
- **B.** *less :: more*
- **C.** captured :: tortured
- **D.** plaster :: concrete

Use **Vocabulary Transparencies and Copymasters,** p. 71, for more exercises.

A lesson on analogies appears on p. 263 in the Pupil's Edition.

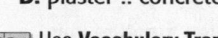

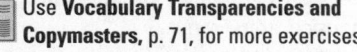

Reading and Analyzing

Active Reading

EVALUATING CHARACTERS

A Have students evaluate Varenka's father based on the description of his boots.

Possible Response: The boots seem to reveal his real character. They are out of place when compared to the rest of the colonel's elegant clothing. The battlefield, not the ballroom, is the true domain of the colonel.

Reading Skills and Strategies: CLARIFYING

B Ask students how this simile helps readers appreciate Ivan's feelings of love.

Possible Response: It helps readers visualize Ivan as being swept away by a love that he cannot contain or control.

Reading Skills and Strategies: PREDICTING

C Remind students that Ivan is about to describe a chance event that changed his life forever. Have volunteers speculate on what might happen in the second half of the story.

Possible Responses: Something terrible will happen to Varenka; Ivan will learn something terrible about Varenka or her father.

Reading Skills and Strategies: EVALUATING

D Have students evaluate the effectiveness of the white feather from the fan as a symbol of Ivan and Varenka's love.

Possible Responses: Some students will feel the symbol is effective because white suggests purity and the feather symbolizes Ivan's soaring feelings while dancing with Varenka. The feather, also insubstantial, could easily float away.

A but unfashionable, ancient ones with square toes and no heels. They were obviously designed as battle boots. 'So his beloved daughter can be well dressed and go out, he wears primitive shoes instead of buying fashionable new ones,' I thought, and those square toes on his boots particularly affected me. It was evident that he had once danced beautifully, but now he was heavy, and his legs were not sufficiently limber for all the elegant, rapid steps he tried to execute. But he completed two turns of the room skillfully, just the same. Everyone burst into loud applause when, quickly spreading his legs apart then joining them together again, he dropped, although somewhat heavily, on one knee, while she, smiling and straightening her skirt, which he had ruffled, turned smoothly around him. Raising himself with some effort, he tenderly and gently placed his hands on his daughter's ears and, kissing her on the forehead, led her back to me on the assumption that I had the next dance. I said that I was not her partner.

"'Well, it doesn't matter; go with her now,' he said, smiling kindly and replacing his sword.

B "It was as though a huge stream had been poured into a bottle which was only one drop short of full—that was how my love for Varenka released all the hidden capacities for love in my heart. I embraced the whole world with my love then. I loved the hostess in her coronet with her Elizabethan bust, and her husband, and her guests, and her lackeys, and even the sulking Engineer Anisimov. Toward her father, with his clumsy boots and his gentle smile so like hers, I felt an intense, tender emotion.

"The mazurka came to an end, and the hostess asked the guests to come to supper, but Colonel B. declined, saying he had to get up early the following day, and he bid the hosts good-by. I was afraid he would take her away, but she stayed with her mother.

"After supper I danced the promised quadrille with her, and although it seemed to me I was already infinitely happy, my happiness kept growing and growing. We never spoke of love. I never even asked either her or myself whether she loved me. It was sufficient for me that I loved her. The only thing I feared was that something might spoil my happiness. 1

When I reached home, undressed and thought of sleep, I realized that sleeping was out of the question. In my hand lay the feather from her fan and the glove she had given me when she got into her carriage, and I had helped seat first her mother, then her. I looked at these things and without closing my eyes saw her before me when, choosing between two partners, she guessed the character trait I was representing; I could hear her sweet voice as she said: 'It's pride. Right?'—and gladly gave me her hand. I saw her, as she sipped a glass of champagne at supper and looked up at me with her tender eyes. But I saw her most clearly as she danced with her father, glided smoothly around him, and glanced with pride and joy at the admiring spectators. And I unconsciously included them both in the same gentle, tender emotion. C D

"At that time, my late brother and I lived alone. My brother did not like society at all and did not go to balls; he was preparing himself for his baccalaureate[15] at that time and led a particularly regulated life. He was asleep. I looked at his head buried in his pillow and half-covered with a flannel blanket, and I felt an affectionate pity for him; pity because he did not know or share my happiness. Our servant, Petrusha, met me with a candle and wanted to help me undress, but I let him go. The sight of his sleepy face and disheveled hair seemed very touching to me. Trying to make no noise, I went to my own room on tiptoe and sat down on the

15. **baccalaureate** (băk′ə-lôr′ē-ĭt): bachelor's degree.

Teaching Options

Mini Lesson Grammar

PARTICIPLES The participle is a verb form used as a modifier. The present participle is the *-ing* form of the verb: *acting, joking, going, seeing.* The past participle of regular verbs ends in *-ed: acted, joked.* Some irregular verbs also have an irregular past participle: *gone, seen.* Write these sentences on the chalkboard:

The students were amused by the joking actress.

Viewers were puzzled by the movie's hidden meaning.

Underline the participles as shown. Guide students to recognize that *joking* and *hidden* function as adjectives.

Practice Have students copy the following sentences. Ask them to underline the participles.

1. Glittering chandeliers hang from the high ceiling of the ballroom.
2. The expensive, gilded furniture was imported from France.
3. The colonel's beaming face shows his pride in his graceful daughter.
4. Varenka smoothes her ruffled skirt and smiles at her father.

Use **Grammar Transparencies and Copymasters,** p. 102, for more exercises.

Use McDougal Littell's ***Language Network,*** Chapter 9, for more instruction and practice in adverbs.

Self-Portrait (about 1865), James Tissot. The Fine Arts Museums of San Francisco, Mildred Anna Williams Collection (1961.16).

Customizing Instruction

Less Proficient Readers

1 Help students understand how the sentence "The only thing I feared was that something might spoil my happiness" foreshadows an event that will spoil Ivan's happiness.

Multiple Learning Styles

Interpersonal Learners

2 Point out how Ivan's awareness of others is expressed in this paragraph. Ask students to explain how Ivan's love for Varenka affects his feelings for the people and things around him.

Possible Response: Ivan is so overcome with love that he views everything around him—including his brother, his servant, and aspects of daily life—with the deepest affection.

Students Acquiring English

3 Explain that *regulated life* refers to the discipline required of a student who is studying for a college degree.

Mini Lesson Viewing and Representing

Self-Portrait by James Tissot

ART APPRECIATION In his day, Tissot was considered a highly successful gentleman-painter, a position greatly admired at the time. He was well groomed and carried himself with reserved elegance. His success, however, caused critics to make jealous and often sarcastic comments about his work. His reputation later came under attack for a variety of reasons. He lost the admiration of French friends and patrons when he joined the Paris Commune; later, he was discredited in England as a result of a scandal in his private life.

Instruction Ask students what his portrait tells them about Tissot. What could he be thinking?

Possible Response: He is young, intellectual, and introspective. The dark brooding colors seem to suggest that he is contemplating an important or painful issue.

Reading and Analyzing

Active Reading

EVALUATING CHARACTERS

Ask students to evaluate the true nature of the colonel by contrasting his behavior as an officer with his behavior as a father.

Possible Response: As a father, he is charming and loving; as the officer in charge of the beating, he is brutal and cruel.

Have students discuss how or why a character could be both good and evil.

Possible Response: Tolstoy could be commenting on the duality of human nature.

Literary Analysis: MOOD

A Have students identify words and phrases in this scene that establish the mood of horror and defeat.

Possible Responses: lurching; dragging; pain-distorted; sobbed; swinging his stick; striped, wet, red; stumbling, shrinking man

Literary Analysis: THEME

Tolstoy seems to be commenting on the paradoxical presence of good and evil in our society and in each individual. He also suggests that each of us must decide, as Ivan has done, which element of our nature will dominate.

bed. No, I was too happy; I could not sleep. Then I began to feel too hot in the heated rooms, and, still dressed, I went quietly out to the entry, put on my overcoat, opened the outer door and went into the street.

"I had left the ball at five o'clock, then gone home and sat there a bit; two hours had gone by, and when I went out it was already light. It was typical Shrovetide weather: fog, water-soaked snow melting on the roads, and water dripping from all the roofs. The B——s then lived at the edge of town, next to a big field with a promenade[16] at one end and a girl's school at the other. I went through our deserted side street and came out onto a big road, where I began to encounter people on foot and others carting firewood on sleds, whose runners scraped the pavement. The horses, rhythmically swinging their wet heads under the glistening shaft bows, and the drivers covered with sacking, splashing in huge boots near their wagons, and the houses looking very tall in the fog—all seemed particularly dear and meaningful to me.

"When I came to the field where her house stood, I saw at the end of it, in the direction of the promenade, something large and black, and I heard the sounds of a fife and drum coming from there. All this time I had continued humming and hearing the theme of the mazurka intermittently. But this was a different, cruel, evil music.

"'What can it be?' I thought, and crossing the middle of the field over a slippery path, I walked in the direction of the sound. After covering a hundred paces, I began to discern a number of black forms through the fog. Soldiers, obviously. 'It must be a drill,' I thought, and along with a blacksmith in his greasy coat and apron, carrying something and walking in front of me,

"I looked in that direction and between the ranks caught sight of something dreadful moving toward me."

I went closer. Soldiers in dark uniforms were drawn up in two ranks facing each other, standing motionless, holding their rifles at their sides. Behind them stood the drummer and the fifer, repeating the same unpleasant, shrill melody without stopping.

"'What are they doing?' I asked the blacksmith, who 1
had stopped next to me.

"'They're whipping a Tartar[17] for running off,' the blacksmith said angrily, glancing at the farthest end of the ranks.

"I looked in that direction and between the ranks caught sight of something dreadful moving toward me. It was a man stripped to the waist, tied to the rifles of two soldiers, who led him. Next to him walked a tall officer in an overcoat and forage cap whose face seemed familiar to me. Resisting with his whole body, his feet splashing in the melting snow, the victim was lurching toward me under the blows falling on
him from both sides; now he keeled over 2
backward—and the sergeants who were dragging him by their rifles shoved him forward; then he fell forward—and the sergeants, preventing him from falling, pulled him back. And never leaving the victim's side, halting and
advancing with a firm tread, was the tall officer. 3
It was her father, with his rosy face and white mustache and sideburns.

"At each blow, the victim, as if surprised, turned his pain-distorted face to the side from which it fell and, disclosing his white teeth, repeated the same words over and over. It was only when he was very close that I heard these words clearly. He sobbed rather than said: 'Brothers, have mercy. Brothers, have mercy.'

16. **promenade:** a public walkway.

17. **Tartar:** a member of a Turkic people of southern Russia.

Teaching Options

Multicultural Link **History**

Since the ball was held the last day of Shrovetide, the next day marks the beginning of Lent. The day of the ball is analogous to Mardi Gras, or Fat Tuesday, with which students may be familiar. Mardi Gras, the last day before Lent, is often an occasion for celebration in Roman Catholic cultures. During Lent, many Christians fast, do penance for their sins, give charity to the poor, and refrain from amusements. Lent originated as a way to prepare spiritually for the Easter observance of Christ's suffering, death, and resurrection. Symbolically, the image of the Tartar tied up and crying out for mercy as he is beaten calls to mind the scourging of Christ before his crucifixion.

The Monument to Peter I on Senate Square in Petersburg (1870), Vasilii Ivanovich Surikov. The State Russian Museum, St. Petersburg, Russia.

But his brothers did not have mercy, and when the procession was even with me, I saw how the soldier standing opposite me stepped forward decisively and, swinging his stick through the air with a swish, brought it down hard on the Tartar's back. The Tartar pulled forward, but the sergeants held him back, and an identical blow fell on him from the other side, and then again from this side, and again from the other side. The colonel walked on, looking now at the victim, now at his own feet, drawing in his breath, blowing out his cheeks, and letting the air out slowly through his puckered mouth. When the procession had passed the spot where I stood, I caught a glimpse of the victim's back between the ranks. It was striped, wet, red; unrecognizable to the point that I could not believe it was the body of a man.

"The procession was moving on, and the blows continued to fall from both sides just as before on the stumbling, shrinking man, and the drum beat as before, and the fife played, and, as before, the tall, dignified figure of the colonel moved with a firm tread next to the victim. Suddenly the colonel stopped and approached one of the soldiers abruptly.

Customizing Instruction

Students Acquiring English

1 Define *blacksmith* as a "person who shapes and forges iron with a hammer and anvil."

2 Help students understand idioms. Explain that *keeled over* means "fell over suddenly."

3 Have students use context clues to determine the meaning of *tread.*
Answer: "step"

Less Proficient Readers

Ask students what Ivan has just learned about Varenka's father.
Possible Responses: He is a brutal disciplinarian; he is inhumane.

Ask students if they can think of other characters in literature or history with two sides to their personality.
Possible Response: Dr. Jekyll/Mr. Hyde

Gifted and Talented

Read aloud the following quotation from A. N. Wilson's biography of Leo Tolstoy.

> Even if no other literature survived from Russia in the first decade of this century except this one, extremely short story ["After the Ball"], we should be able to predict the Revolution, and the subsequent character of Russian life in the twentieth century. It contains all the horrible paradox that a nation which can feel so tenderly has somehow been condemned to policemen and armies and governors of the most ruthless severity.

Have students discuss how this story might "predict" the Communist Revolution of 1917 and the cruelty of Russian leaders such as Joseph Stalin.

Mini Lesson Viewing and Representing

The Monument to Peter I on Senate Square in Petersburg **by Vasilii Ivanovich Surikov**

ART APPRECIATION Descended from a long line of Siberian Cossacks, Surikov (1848–1916) often took trips to Siberia and Crimea. He is best known for his paintings of monuments—in this case, a beautiful historic site on the bank of the Neva River. In the background looms St. Isaac's Cathedral.

Instruction Discuss with students that the power of a painting often lies in the emotions it conveys. Point out the *chiaroscuro* of this painting (distinct contrasts between light and dark) and the highly realistic treatment of textures. Have students analyze how specific details contribute to the painting's mood.

Possible Responses: The fog-shrouded scene conveys a mood of mystery and uncertainty; the snowy, winter scene conveys a cold and somewhat harsh emotion.

Application Have students relate the mood of this painting to the mood of the story.

Possible Response: When Ivan witnesses the beating of the Tartar, the mood of the story is very grim and harsh. The stark contrasts of light and dark in the painting fit very well with the stark contrasts in the colonel's personality and with the rapid change from happiness to horror that Ivan experiences.

Reading and Analyzing

Active Reading

EVALUATING CHARACTERS

Ask students what Ivan's search for an explanation and his subsequent decisions reveal about him.

Possible Responses: He rejects evil and cruelty; he is a good man who has compassion for others. He cannot imagine living a double life.

Literary Analysis FLASHBACK

Invite students to imagine the story as a movie. Ask them how the director might indicate that the narrative is no longer focused on the past.

Possible Response: Some students might say that the director would simply change scenes. Others might suggest a different film technique for the different time frames of the story, such as filming the flashback in black and white or using a hazy camera lens to give the flashback a dreamlike quality.

Reading Skills and Strategies: CLARIFYING

A After students have read to the end of the story, have them examine the importance of this final image of the colonel in the field. If necessary, point out that this image is related to the resolution of Ivan's dilemma.

Possible Responses: Ivan's impression of the colonel makes him feel awkward around Varenka and, consequently, his love for her fades; Ivan wishes to avoid the evil and maliciousness that he sees in the colonel, so he decides not to become a soldier, as he had planned.

"'I'll trounce you,' I heard his irate voice say. 'Will you beat now? Will you?'

"And I saw him pummel the frightened, undersized, frail soldier with his strong, chamois-gloved hand for not having brought his stick down hard enough on the Tartar's red back.

"'Form fresh gauntlets!'[18] he cried and, glancing around, caught sight of me. He pretended he did not know me; he frowned threateningly and maliciously, hurriedly turned around. All the way home I kept hearing first the roll of the drum beating and the whistle of the fife, and then the self-assured, irate voice of the colonel shouting: 'Will you beat now? Will you?' And in my heart there was an almost physical anguish approaching nausea, so strong that I stopped several times, and I felt as though I were about to vomit all the horror with which the spectacle had filled me. I don't remember how I got home and into bed. But as soon as I started to fall asleep, I heard and saw everything again and jumped up.

"'Obviously, he knows something I don't know,' I thought in reference to the colonel. 'If I knew what he knows, I would understand what I saw, and it would not disturb me.' But no matter how much I thought about it, I couldn't figure out what it was the colonel knew, and I went to sleep only toward evening, and then only after visiting a friend and drinking with him until I was completely drunk.

"I suppose you think that I decided then that what I had seen was an evil thing? Not at all. 'If this was done with such conviction and recognized as necessary by all, then it must be that they knew something that I didn't know,' I thought, and I tried to find out what. But no matter how I tried, I could not find out. And not having found out, I could not go into military service, as I had previously wanted to, and not only did I not go into service, but I never served anywhere and, as you see, was never fit for anything."

"Come, we know how you were never fit for anything," said one of us. "But tell us: how many people are really fit for anything, if you're not?"

"Come, that's complete nonsense," Ivan Vassilievich said with sincere chagrin.

"But what about love?" we asked.

"Love? From that day, love went into a decline. When, as frequently happened, she became thoughtful, although still smiling, I would immediately remember the colonel on the field; it became somehow awkward and unpleasant for me, and I began seeing her less frequently. And so love came to nothing. That's how these things happen, and that's what changes and determines a man's whole life. And you say . . . ," and thus he finished. ❖

Translated by Arthur Mendel and Barbara Makanowitzky

18. **gauntlets** (gônt'lĭts): two parallel lines of people who deliver punishment by striking with clubs or other weapons a person forced to run between them.

WORDS TO KNOW

irate (ī-rāt') *adj.* extremely angry; enraged
pummel (pŭm'əl) *v.* to hit repeatedly; beat
maliciously (mə-lĭsh'əs-lē) *adv.* with ill will; spitefully
chagrin (shə-grĭn') *n.* a feeling of humiliation or embarrassment

674

Teaching Options

Assessment Informal Assessment

COMPARE AND CONTRAST Informally assess students' understanding of the selection by having them complete a Venn diagram. Students should compare and contrast the young Ivan and the older Ivan.

RUBRIC

3 **Full Accomplishment** Students identify a full range of traits, including those of young Ivan and the older Ivan as well as those that both share. The traits are clearly based on details in the selection.

2 **Substantial Accomplishment** Students identify at least two traits for both the younger and the older Ivan and at least one trait that they share. The traits are based on details in the selection.

1 **Little or Partial Accomplishment** Students identify no more than one character trait for each part of the diagram. The traits may not be clearly tied to details in the selection.

Connect to Literature

1. **What Do You Think?** What do you consider to be the most memorable aspect of this story?

Comprehension Check
- Why does the elderly Ivan recount what happened during and after the ball?
- What scene does Ivan witness on the morning after the ball?
- How do the events he witnessed affect Ivan's feelings for Varenka?

Think Critically

2. Why do you think the colonel's actions lead to a change in Ivan Vassilievich's feelings for Varenka?

3. Ivan reveals that when the colonel caught sight of him the morning after the ball, "he pretended he did not know me; he frowned threateningly and maliciously, hurriedly turned around." Why do you think Tolstoy includes this **detail** in his story?

4. Do you think Ivan is better off because of what he saw after the ball?

   THINK ABOUT
   - how his friends describe him
   - how the course of his life was changed
   - how he views his life

5. Ivan tells his story to illustrate that everything depends on "chance" rather than "circumstances." Do you think he succeeds? Explain your answer.

6. ACTIVE READING EVALUATING CHARACTERS Compare the chart you made in your READER'S NOTEBOOK with those of your classmates. What is your final **evaluation** of each **character?** Give reasons to support your judgment.

Extend Interpretations

7. **Critic's Corner** The Russian critic Leo Shestov said: "In his youth Tolstoy described life as a fascinating ball; and later, when he was old, it was like the running of the gauntlet." How does this comment apply to "After the Ball" (which, by the way, was written when Tolstoy was in his 70s)?

8. **Connect to Life** In American society, corporal (bodily) punishment is less common than it once was, but it still exists. Drawing on your own ideas and observations and on the depiction of corporal punishment in "After the Ball," comment on whether you think its use is ever justified.

Literary Analysis

FLASHBACK A **flashback** is an account of a conversation, an episode, or an event that happened before the beginning of a story. Often a flashback interrupts the chronological flow to give information that can help readers to understand a character's present situation. "After the Ball" is a story told almost entirely in flashback. The events that happened to Ivan as a young man help readers to understand why he now believes that chance is more important than circumstances in determining the course of a person's life.

Cooperative Learning Activity With three or four classmates, re-create the chronology of events in this story. Then have one person retell the story in strict chronological order, without the use of a flashback. As a whole group, compare the retelling with the original. What does Tolstoy gain or lose by using flashback?

Extend Interpretations

Critic's Corner This comment is very significant in light of the events of the story. At the beginning of "After the Ball," Ivan is literally at a ball. He is giddy with happiness and love and secure in the beauty and goodness of life. Then he witnesses a Tartar running the gauntlet, and his dreams are shattered. Ivan's character experiences in one day what Tolstoy described as a lifetime experience.

Connect to Life Some students may feel that corporal punishment is unjustified because it is cruel or unlikely to change behavior; others may feel that corporal punishment is an effective deterrent for some offenses or for some people.

Literary Analysis

Flashback Students will need to identify the shifts from the present to the past. Review the ways that an author can indicate the shifts in time.

GUIDING STUDENT RESPONSE

Connect to the Literature

1. **What Do You Think?**
   Some students may say that the scene of the soldiers beating the Tartar is most memorable. Other may say that Ivan's character development is most memorable.

Comprehension Check
- Ivan wants to explain how his life was affected by witnessing a cruel event.
- Ivan witnesses the colonel commanding his troops to beat a soldier.
- Ivan's love for Varenka gradually diminishes, because when he sees her, he also thinks of her cruel father.

Use Selection Quiz in **Unit Four Resource Book**, p. 59.

Think Critically

2. Possible Responses: Ivan's love for Varenka fades because he cannot forget her father's cruelty; perhaps Ivan feels that if he marries Varenka he will have to compromise his belief in goodness and compassion.
3. Possible Responses: Tolstoy may have wanted to show that the colonel does not want anyone from a "finer circle" to know about his capacity for cruelty. Thus he rejects Ivan.
4. Possible Responses: Ivan is better off for having learned about the colonel's cruelty before becoming his son-in-law and joining the army; witnessing such cruelty forces Ivan to decide between good and evil.
5. Possible Responses: Some students may agree, pointing out that two major decisions in Ivan's life—his marriage and his career—were changed by one chance event; others may disagree, saying that Ivan's story is just as much about circumstances as about chance.
6. Possible Response: Ivan is a good, sensitive, honest person; Varenka is sweet, charming, and either ignorant of or blind to her father's evil side; the colonel is a study of opposites, cherishing his daughter while acting cruelly and maliciously as a colonel in the army.

Writing Options

1. **Gossip Column** Before students begin to write, discuss the breezy, coy tone typical of a gossip columnist. If possible, read a sample column from a local newspaper.
2. **Father-Daughter Scene** You might suggest that students begin their scenes by having Varenka confront her father about the beating, linking it to Ivan's sudden coolness toward her.
3. **Punishment Proposal** Encourage them to brainstorm alternative solutions with their partner by creating cluster diagrams or by freewriting.

Activities & Explorations

1. **Modern Adaptation** Make sure students divide the responsibilities in their group equally. Once they decide on a contemporary U.S. setting, have them create only a broad outline of the action that is going to occur and then spend time developing ideas for characters. Explain that, in improvisation, an actor should focus on letting the character speak and responding to the other characters.
2. **Musical Representation** Point out that the music needs to convey an appropriate mood but that it does not necessarily have to reflect the time period of the selection.

Art Connection

Students might point out that the figure is young and handsome, like Ivan. Moreover, the expression on his face suggests someone who is sensitive and thoughtful, much like young Ivan.

Vocabulary in Action

EXERCISE A	EXERCISE B
1. d	1. b
2. e	2. b
3. c	3. a
4. d	4. a
5. a	5. c

Choices & CHALLENGES

Writing Options

1. **Gossip Column** Imagine that you are a gossip columnist for a Russian newspaper. Write a newspaper column about the ball. Include descriptions of Varenka, her father, and Ivan, as well as details about romance in the making.

2. **Father-Daughter Scene** Write a dramatic scene in which the colonel explains to his daughter the beating of the Tartar.

3. **Punishment Proposal** With a partner, devise an alternative to the gauntlet as a means of punishing deserters. Write a proposal to the czar in which you explain your idea.

Activities & Explorations

1. **Modern Adaptation** Work with a small group to adapt the plot of "After the Ball" to a contemporary American setting. For example, you might have the events take place at a high school prom, or you might have Varenka's father be a police officer. Perform your adaptation as an improvisation for the class. ~ PERFORMING

2. **Musical Representation** Put together a series of musical recordings that represent the different parts of the story. For example, you might choose a waltz or mazurka to represent the ball; a darker, more serious piece of music might represent Ivan's witnessing the beating. Share your recordings with the class. ~ MUSIC

Art Connection

How does the portrait on page 671 compare with your own mental image of the young Ivan?

Vocabulary in Action

EXERCISE A: ASSESSMENT PRACTICE Determine the relationship between each pair of capitalized words below. On your paper, write the letter of the choice that shows the most similar relationship.

1. QUEEN : **MAJESTIC** :: (a) comedy : tragic (b) sky : dark (c) recreation : sports (d) monster : gruesome (e) education : elementary
2. **CHAGRIN** : EMBARRASSMENT :: (a) ability : musical (b) expense : tax (c) misery : joy (d) sleep : death (e) worry : anxiety
3. BOXERS : **PUMMEL** :: (a) teachers : punish (b) lawyers : win (c) detectives : investigate (d) scholars : cheat (e) collectors : lose
4. HEAVEN : **ETHEREAL** :: (a) grass : dried (b) water : muddy (c) baseball : athletic (d) desert : arid (e) soup : cold
5. **PERSPICACITY** : SHARP :: (a) intelligence : clever (b) fool : wise (c) courage : stupid (d) shyness : sociable (e) sense : visual

EXERCISE B: MEANING CLUES Using your understanding of the boldfaced word, write on your paper the letter of the word or phrase that best completes each sentence below.

1. Tolstoy talked **maliciously** about his wife, Sonya, because he (a) admired her, (b) fought bitterly with her, (c) enjoyed her wit.
2. She became **irate** when he (a) showed her kindness, (b) wanted to give away their wealth, (c) managed their estate wisely.
3. The pilgrims who came to Tolstoy's estate found him **imposing** because of his (a) reputation, (b) forgetfulness, (c) unruly hair.
4. Sonya thought the visitors were **detestable** because they (a) lacked refinement, (b) enjoyed her company, (c) earned her respect.
5. In old age, Tolstoy was **unassuming** about his earlier works; he judged them (a) boldly original, (b) perfect, (c) flawed.

Building Vocabulary
For an in-depth lesson on analogies, see page 263.

Mini Lesson Grammar

PARTICIPIAL PHRASES Explain that participial phrases consist of a participle plus any modifiers, objects, or complements. They always function as adjectives. Use the following sentence as an example: *A car sliding on a slippery highway can be dangerous.* Guide students to recognize that *sliding on a slippery highway* describes the noun *car.* Then explain that participial phrases can be either essential (restrictive) or nonessential (nonrestrictive). Essential phrases are necessary to the meaning of the sentence. Nonessential phrases provide extra information that is not necessary to the meaning of the sentence. Write these sentences on the chalkboard:

Do you see the dog digging in the garbage?

The dog, digging in the garbage, was oblivious to our disapproving gazes.

Underline the participial phrases as shown. Have students identify which phrase is essential to the meaning of the sentence. *(the first one)* Point out that nonessential phrases, like the phrase in the second sentence, are often set off with commas.

Choices & CHALLENGES

Grammar in Context: Participial Phrases

In this excerpt, Leo Tolstoy uses participial phrases to impart a sense of ongoing action to the scene.

> **The colonel walked on,** looking now at the victim, now at his own feet, drawing in his breath, blowing out his cheeks, **and** letting the air out slowly through his puckered mouth.

A **participial phrase** consists of a participle (a verb form that functions as an adjective) along with its modifiers and complements. Besides using participial phrases to provide details, writers use them to create interesting rhythms and to vary their sentence structures. In the sentence above, Tolstoy's use of the participles *looking, drawing, blowing,* and *letting* emphasizes that these actions were ongoing as the colonel walked, not isolated actions that occurred one after the other.

WRITING EXERCISE Rewrite each group of sentences as a single sentence containing one or more participial phrases. Underline each participial phrase.

Punctuation Tip: In many cases, participial phrases should be set off with commas.

Example: ***Original*** The memory has been buried for years. It comes back when he hears her name.

Rewritten The memory, buried for years, comes back when he hears her name.

1. Varenka carries herself unusually erect. She tips her head back in a regal way.
2. He dances every dance with her. He whirls her around. He feels giddy and light as air.
3. The colonel drops to one knee. He inspires the crowd's applause.
4. Near her house he stops. He hears strange, evil music.

Grammar Handbook Verbals, p. 1196

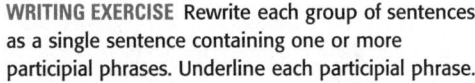

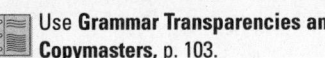

Leo Tolstoy
1828–1910

Other Works
Anna Karenina
War and Peace
The Death of Ivan Ilyich and Other Stories
Master and Man, and Other Stories

From the Army to Literary Fame Nothing about Tolstoy's life, or death, was small. Born into a wealthy, aristocratic family, Tolstoy was orphaned by the age of nine and was raised by aunts. As a young man dissatisfied with his life, he volunteered for the Russian Army. His experience as a soldier in the Crimean War provided material for *Sevastopol Sketches* (1855), a collection of stories that won him literary fame. The next 25 years saw the publication of his two greatest novels, *War and Peace* (1869) and *Anna Karenina* (1877).

Moral Crisis At the height of his creativity, Tolstoy underwent a spiritual crisis that led him to reexamine his life and works. In the last 30 years of his life, he became a kind of prophet, preaching his own gospel for the world's salvation. Though Tolstoy continued literary work, he now believed that literature must teach moral truths. He wrote many books and essays about his beliefs, which included love for humanity, rejection of private property, and suspicion of all forms of government.

Front-Page News Tolstoy's efforts to give up his property led to quarrels with his wife, Sonya, the mother of his 13 children. He eventually decided to leave her, fleeing in the company of his youngest daughter and his doctor. Just days later, the 82-year-old Tolstoy died at a small railroad station, an event that became news around the world.

Author Activity

Philosophical Legacy Research Tolstoy's philosophy of nonviolent resistance and its effects on Martin Luther King, Jr., and Mohandas K. Gandhi. Write a brief report on your findings.

LaserLinks: Background for Reading
Author Background

Grammar in Context

WRITING EXERCISE Answers will vary. Possible answers are shown.

1. Varenka carries herself unusually erect, tipping her head back in a regal way.
2. He dances every dance with her, whirling her around, feeling giddy and light as air.
3. The colonel, dropping to one knee, inspires the crowd's applause.
4. Near her house he stops, hearing strange, evil music.

Author Activity

Philosophical Legacy In addition to looking up the social reformers whose names are listed, encourage students to use a keyword search based on terms such as *nonviolent resistance, nonviolence movement, civil rights movement, peace movements, social reform,* and so forth.

Practice Have students copy the following sentences. Ask them to underline the participial phrases and identify them as essential or nonessential. Then have students meet in cooperative groups to discuss their answers.

1. I was an unearthly being, knowing no evil.
   Answer: nonessential
2. "Oh," began the Engineer Anisimov, "the colonel is the man standing at the entrance with the hostess."
   Answer: essential
3. Straightening her skirt, Varenka turned smoothly around her father.
   Answer: nonessential
4. The soldiers led a man stripped to the waist.
   Answer: essential

Use **Unit Four Resource Book** p. 58 for additional support.

Use **Grammar Transparencies and Copymasters,** p. 103.

Use McDougal Littell's ***Language Network,*** Chapter 3, for more instruction in participial phrases.

Building Vocabulary

Objectives
- identify and select the best meaning for a word
- use context and homonyms to determine a word's meaning

EXERCISE
1. *society:* the rich, privileged, and fashionable social class
2. *frame:* to put into words; to formulate
3. *imperative:* having the power or authority to command or control
4. *execute:* to perform or carry out
5. *presence:* fact of being present in a place

Multiple Personalities of Words

A single word can help readers understand an opinion, or it can cause them confusion. Read the passage on the right and think about how the words *removal* and *province* are used.

Both *removal* and *province* have more than one definition. *Removal* can mean "a psychological distancing," "relocation," or "dismissal." *Province* can mean "a territory," "an area of knowledge," or "the range of one's duties." Which meaning of each word do you think O'Brien intends?

> **I felt no sense of an impending crisis in my life. Stupidly, with a kind of smug removal that I can't begin to fathom, I assumed that the problems of killing and dying did not fall within my special province.**
> —Tim O'Brien, "On the Rainy River"

Strategies for Building Vocabulary

In your writing, make sure readers understand the word meanings you intend. When a word has more than one meaning, make the intended meaning obvious from the context.

❶ Convey Meaning Through Context A word's meaning is often revealed through the sentence or paragraph in which the word appears—its context. Such is the case in the following example.

> **"I've told you not to call me Hannetjie. You must say Baas," but Warder Hannetjie's voice lacked conviction.**
> —Bessie Head, "The Prisoner Who Wore Glasses"

In this context, *conviction* clearly means "a fixed or strong belief," rather than its other meaning, "the act or process of finding or proving guilty."

❷ Watch Out for Homonyms Homonyms are words that have the same pronunciation and often the same spelling, but differ in meaning. Note the use of the homonym *sound* in the following sentence.

> **Surely the only sound foundation for a civilisation is a sound state of mind.**
> —E. M. Forster, "Tolerance"

If you were to look up *sound* in a dictionary, you might find four different entries, each showing a different derivation and different meanings, including "a noise," "having a firm basis," "a body of water," and "to measure depth." Which meaning do you think Forster intended?

❸ Consider a Word's Meanings Writers sometimes purposefully use words that have multiple meanings in order to enrich and extend a statement's meaning. Poets especially use this technique. For example, in "the sonnet-ballad," by Gwendolyn Brooks, the speaker describes the seductive powers death has on soldiers and laments that "Coquettish death . . . Can make a hard man hesitate—and change." In this poem, the word *hard* describes a man who is not only "rugged," but also "strong-minded," and perhaps even "calloused" to the grim realities of war.

EXERCISE Look up each underlined word below in a dictionary and choose the intended meaning or meanings.

1. My brother did not like society at all and did not go to balls. (Leo Tolstoy, "After the Ball")
2. But before he could frame the message, the warder in charge of his work span shouted . . . . (Bessie Head, "The Prisoner Who Wore Glasses")
3. When a nation goes to war it must have reasonable confidence in the justice and imperative of its cause. (Tim O'Brien, "On the Rainy River")
4. His legs were not sufficiently limber for all the elegant, rapid steps he tried to execute. (Leo Tolstoy, "After the Ball")
5. He was there at the critical time—a silent, watchful presence. (Tim O'Brien, "On the Rainy River")

from TOLERANCE

E. M. Forster

Italian Landscape II: Europa (1944), Ben Shahn. Copyright © 1995 Estate of Ben Shahn / Licensed by VAGA, New York.

Great Britain's E. M. Forster ranked tolerance high among the qualities necessary for the world at large. The essay that follows is one of several that Forster broadcast over the radio during or just after World War II (1939–1945) and later collected in his volume Two Cheers for Democracy *(1951). In these essays, Forster often explores the means by which citizens of democracies can counter the spread of the kind of thinking that leads to brutal dictatorships—dictatorships like that of Nazi Germany, Britain's foe during the war. With their claims of racial superiority, their attempts to conquer neighboring nations that they labeled as inferior, and their mass murder of ethnic groups that they branded as undesirable, the Nazis were the supreme example of intolerance.*

Possible Objectives

You can use this selection to achieve one or more of the following objectives:

- enjoy silent sustained reading (Option One)
- read and analyze literature with a group (Option Two)
- use the Reader's Notebook to formulate questions about literature (Option Three)
- write in response to literature (Option Three)

Summary

In the interest of building a sound foundation for civilization, E. M. Forster offers an argument against love and in favor of tolerance. Forster concedes that love is a great force in private life, but he contends that none of us can love what we do not know personally. Citing several failed civilizations to support his view that promoting love does not work, he concludes that what civilization really needs is tolerance, even though it is a dull virtue that consists mainly of not doing things. He states that there are two solutions for dealing with those you dislike: the Nazi solution, which requires killing, banishing, or segregating; or the democratic solution, which requires putting up with people the best you can. Although the democratic solution is just a makeshift one suitable for an overcrowded planet, he writes, it entails imagination and empathy—and offers spiritual exercise as well.

Intrepreting Historical Context

Have students read the background paragraphs in italic prior to reading this selection. Then ask them as they read the story to interpret the possible influences of the historical context on this literary work.

Reading the Selection

Option One
Silent Sustained Reading

You might set aside time each week for independent reading. During this time, you and all of your students would read for enjoyment. The excerpt from *Tolerance* will appeal to many students and can be read independently in about 15 minutes. If you want to encourage students to read for pleasure, you might forgo assignments related to the selection. Should you want to make assignments, Options Two and Three offer suggestions.

Option Two
Shared Reading Groups

You may assign students to groups or allow them to choose their own. Students can read the selection together, alternately reading paragraphs aloud, or they can read independently and meet to cooperate in a project that portrays some element of the story.

Possible Projects

- Have students review a newspaper or news magazine to find an article about a conflict between two groups of people in a community or in the world. Students should analyze the conflict in light of Forster's essay, then list specific steps that might be taken to promote tolerance between the two groups.
- Students can rehearse and deliver Forster's essay as a speech to be broadcast on the radio. Suggest that students listen to tapes of their rehearsals to check the pace and tone.
- Students can design a poster for an ad campaign promoting tolerance. Invite students to come up with some symbols to represent tolerance. Also, students' posters might make use of news photos that portray some tragic results of intolerance.

Surely the only sound foundation for a civilisation is a sound state of mind. Architects, contractors, international commissioners, marketing boards, broadcasting corporations will never, by themselves, build a new world. They must be inspired by the proper spirit, and there must be the proper spirit in the people for whom they are working. . . .

NO ONE HAS EVER WRITTEN AN ODE TO TOLERANCE OR RAISED A STATUE TO HER. YET THIS IS THE QUALITY WHICH WILL BE MOST NEEDED AFTER THE WAR.

What though is the proper spirit? . . . There must be a sound state of mind before diplomacy or economics or trade conferences can function. But what state of mind is sound? Here we may differ. Most people, when asked what spiritual quality is needed to rebuild civilisation, will reply "Love." Men must love one another, they say; nations must do likewise, and then the series of cataclysms[1] which is threatening to destroy us will be checked.

Respectfully but firmly, I disagree. Love is a great force in private life; it is indeed the greatest of all things: but love in public affairs does not work. It has been tried again and again: by the Christian civilisations of the Middle Ages, and also by the French Revolution, a secular movement which reasserted the brotherhood of man.[2] And it has always failed. The idea that nations should love one another, or that business concerns or marketing boards should love one another, or that a man in Portugal should love a man in Peru of whom he has never heard—it is absurd, unreal, dangerous. It leads us into perilous and vague sentimentalism.[3] "Love is what is needed," we chant and then sit back, and the world goes on as before. The fact is we can only love what we know personally. And we cannot know much. In public affairs, in the rebuilding of civilisation, something much less dramatic and emotional is needed, namely, tolerance. Tolerance is a very dull virtue. It is boring. Unlike love, it has always had a bad press. It is negative. It merely means putting up with people, being able to stand things. No one has ever written an ode[4] to tolerance or raised a statue to her. Yet this is the quality which will be most needed after the war. This is the sound state of mind which we are looking for. This is the only force which will enable different races and classes and interests to settle down together to the work of reconstruction.

The world is very full of people—appallingly full; it has never been so full before, and they are all tumbling over each other. Most of these people one doesn't know, and some of them one doesn't like; doesn't like the colour of their skins, say, or the shapes of their noses, or the way they blow them or don't blow them, or the way they talk, or their smell, or their clothes, or their fondness for jazz or their dislike of jazz, and so on. Well, what is one to do? There are two solutions. One of them is the Nazi solution. If you don't like people, kill them, banish them, segregate them, and then strut up and down proclaiming that you are the salt of the earth.[5] The other way is much less thrilling, but it is on the whole the way of the democracies, and I

1. **cataclysms** (kăt′ə-klĭ′zəmz): violent upheavals causing great change and destruction.
2. **French Revolution . . . brotherhood of man:** the French Revolution, which lasted from 1789 to 1799, had the motto "Liberty! Equality! Brotherhood!"
3. **sentimentalism** (sĕn′tə-mĕn′tl-ĭz′əm): a tendency toward too much tender, often shallow emotion.
4. **ode** (ōd): a usually formal poem on a serious subject.
5. **salt of the earth:** the finest or noblest people. The expression derives from a statement in the New Testament of the Bible (Matthew 5:13).

prefer it. If you don't like people, put up with them as well as you can. Don't try to love them: you can't; you'll only strain yourself. But try to tolerate them. On the basis of that tolerance a civilised future may be built. Certainly I can see no other foundation for the postwar world.

For what it will most need is the negative virtues: not being huffy, touchy, irritable, revengeful. I have lost all faith in positive militant ideals; they can so seldom be carried out without thousands of human beings getting maimed or imprisoned. Phrases like "I will purge this nation," "I will clean up this city," terrify and disgust me. They might not have mattered when the world was emptier: they are horrifying now, when one nation is mixed up with another, when one city cannot be organically separated from its neighbours. . . .

I don't then regard tolerance as a great eternally established divine principle, though I might perhaps quote "In my Father's house are many mansions"[6] in support of such a view. It is just a makeshift, suitable for an overcrowded and overheated planet. It carries on when love gives out, and love generally gives out as soon as we move away from our home and our friends and stand among strangers in a queue[7] for potatoes. Tolerance is wanted in the queue; otherwise we think, "Why will people be so slow?"; it is wanted in the tube,[8] or "Why will people be so fat?"; it is wanted at the telephone, or "Why are they so deaf?" or conversely, "Why do they mumble?" It is wanted in the street, in the office, at the factory, and it is wanted above all between classes, races, and nations. It's dull. And yet it entails imagination. For you have all the time to be putting yourself in someone else's place. Which is a desirable spiritual exercise. ❖

6. **"In my Father's house are many mansions":** a quotation from the New Testament (John 14:2).

7. **queue** (kyo͞o): a chiefly British expression for a line of people.

8. **tube:** British term for the Underground, or London subway.

E. M. Forster
1879–1970

Other Works
A Room with a View
A Passage to India
Howards End
Abinger Harvest
Two Cheers for Democracy

Worst Years of His Life Edward Morgan Forster, who was born in London, England, spent the early part of his life hating the private boys' school that he attended, where he was subjected to the taunts of classmates and the severity of teachers. He felt liberated by his subsequent years of study at Cambridge University, which enabled him to expand his intellectual horizons, make close friends, and dedicate himself to the literary life.

Literary Triumph Forster began publishing stories soon after graduation and published his first novel in 1905. There followed a number of acclaimed novels; the best known of these—*A Room with a View* (1908), *Howards End* (1910), and *A Passage to India* (1924)—have recently enjoyed a resurgence of popularity sparked by successful film adaptations.

Farewell to Fiction During the 1920s, Forster achieved prominence as a literary critic, but in the next two decades he turned increasingly to social criticism and virtually gave up writing fiction. Horrified by events in Germany and elsewhere, Forster reacted with lectures and radio broadcasts that stressed the value of goodwill and reason in combating totalitarian thinking.

Author Activity

Literary Virtues Read excerpts from, or watch a film adaptation of, one of Forster's novels. What can you infer from your reading or viewing about the virtues that Forster believed mattered the most?

Option Three
Reader's Notebook

Tell students to try to pin down exactly what Forster means by "tolerance." Students should create a chart in their Reader's Notebooks using the following headings, and record on it brief notes about Forster's intent.

- Words and phrases that describe or define *tolerance*
- Benefits of tolerance
- Why tolerance is needed

Have students write any questions they would like to ask Forster about his essay.

At the end of the selection, students will return to their questions. Ask them to note whether any of their questions have been answered and to write down any additional questions they have about this excerpt from *Tolerance.*

After Reading

Possible Activities
Independent Activity

- Have gifted students write a critical analysis in which they explain the meaning of "In my Father's house are many mansions" and its relevance to Forster's theme.

Discussion Activities

- Use the questions formulated by students as the start of a discussion about this somewhat controversial essay.
- Ask students whether they agree with Forster that tolerance is more useful than love as a foundation of civilization.

Assessment Opportunities

- You can assess student comprehension of the essay by evaluating the questions they formulate in their Reader's Notebooks.
- You can use any of the discussion questions as essay questions.
- You can have students turn any one of their Reader's Notebook entries into an essay.

PART 3 The Tragedy of Julius Caesar

Do you like to have power? Or are you happy to leave it to others? Some people clearly like to be in charge of things, and will go to great lengths to serve their own ambitions, dreams, or ideals. The play you are about to read is one of literature's most famous explorations of power, ambition, and idealism. Add intrigue, deceit, and betrayal, and you have ingredients for a drama that has captivated audiences since the 16th century.

ACTIVITY

With a small group, brainstorm a list of situations in which people can seize power. These situations can fall in the arena of school, family, or government, or any other arena you can think of. Discuss these situations with others in your group, and consider what kind of personal qualities might be found in a person who would seize power in each of the situations. Finally, discuss whether or not you find these qualities admirable.

SHAKESPEARE'S WORLD

SHAKESPEARE'S ENGLAND

Poet and playwright William Shakespeare is considered by many to be the world's greatest writer. Shakespeare lived in England during the Renaissance, the blossoming of European learning that followed the Middle Ages. During the Middle Ages, the European world view had focused on God and the afterlife, but with the Renaissance came a renewal of interest in individual human achievement and in life right here on earth. The new emphasis on personal achievement spurred human beings to expand their horizons in all sorts of ways—scientifically, geographically, commercially, philosophically, artistically. In 1564, when Shakespeare was born, England had already embraced the spirit of Renaissance creativity; in the decades to come, Shakespeare himself would help carry the Renaissance to even greater heights.

Shakespeare's World

Objectives

- apply reading strategies to read nonfiction
- recognize shared and distinctive characteristics of cultures
- make generalizations about a nonfiction article
- interpret the possible influences of historical context on literary works
- identify the main ideas of a nonfiction article

Reading Skills and Strategies:
PREVIEWING

Have students scan the article, noting the heads, illustrations, and captions. Have them determine a purpose for reading. Ask what types of information they expect to encounter in this article.

MAKING COMPARISONS

Have students compare life in the United States today with life in England during medieval times and life in England during the Renaissance. Ask them if they think life today is more like life during medieval times or life during Shakespeare's time.

Possible Response: Today, as in Shakespeare's time, there is a great emphasis on the individual and on freedom of choice. There is also a huge interest today in science, commerce, philosophy, and the arts.

ANALYZING TEXT STRUCTURE

Ask students how the article "Shakespeare's World" is organized. Suggest they use the three subheads to classify the information in the article. They can create a chart or other graphic organizer using the subheads as titles. They can put appropriate details under each head.

MODIFYING PURPOSE FOR READING

As students begin reading the section called "Shakespeare's Theater," have them consider if the subhead suggests that they should modify their purpose for reading.

Possible Response: Instead of finding out about England, a reader is likely to read more about the buildings in which Shakespeare's plays were once performed.

Six years before Shakespeare was born, Elizabeth I became queen of England, and the period of her reign, from 1558 to 1603, is known as the Elizabethan Age. Elizabeth I supported all the arts—literature, painting, sculpture, music, and theater. She was also a frugal and clever leader who, despite frequent political in-fighting and religious turmoil, managed to steer England down a middle road to stability and prosperity. In the first three decades of her reign, the greatest overseas threat to England's interests came from Spain, but in 1588 the English defeated an attempted invasion by the Spanish Armada, a powerful naval fleet. The victory, which was aided by the weather, underscored England's emergence as a major European power.

Elizabeth I

In this golden age of English achievement, London flourished as a great commercial center, not only the capital of the nation but the hub of England's growing overseas empire. It was also the hub of the artistic efforts that Queen Elizabeth championed, drawing talented and ambitious individuals from all over the land. Because a true Renaissance figure was supposed to excel in many fields, Elizabeth's courtiers often dabbled in writing. In fact, some of them, like Sir Walter Raleigh, produced memorable poetry that is still being read today. Topping the list of the era's fine literature, however, was its **verse drama,** plays in which the dialogue consists mostly or entirely of poetry. Several outstanding dramatists appeared, none more notable than William Shakespeare, and by the end of the 16th century, London had more theaters than any other city in Europe.

SHAKESPEARE'S THEATER

From the early 1590s, Shakespeare was affiliated with a theater company known as the Lord Chamberlain's Men, whose chief sponsors were a father and son who served consecutively as England's Lord Chamberlain, an influential

Below, photo of the interior of the New Globe Theatre. *At left,* a drawing of what experts believe the Old Globe Theatre looked like.

member of Elizabeth's court. Not only did Shakespeare write the company's plays; he was also a shareholder, or part owner, and at first even performed occasionally as an actor. In 1599, with the other company shareholders, he became part owner of the Globe Theatre, the new London home of the Lord Chamberlain's Men. Four years later, when Queen Elizabeth died, the company at the Globe acquired a new sponsor, the new King James I, and became known as the King's Men.

The Old Globe Theatre

Located on the banks of the River Thames (tĕmz) in central London, the Globe Theatre was a three-story wooden building that held up to three thousand theatergoers. In the center was an open-air courtyard with a platform stage on which the plays were performed. Those paying the lowest admission charges, known as groundlings, stood in the pit, the part of the courtyard right near the stage. Wealthier theatergoers sat in the building's interior balconies, or galleries, which surrounded all sides of the courtyard except for the part of the building directly behind the stage.

Judging from the success of Shakespeare's company, both classes of theatergoers seem to have enjoyed his plays. That's probably because they included something for everyone—powerful speeches, fancy sword fights, humor, eerie supernatural events, and insightful observations about human nature. Such a mixture was important to Shakespeare. As a playwright, he wanted to explore human behavior, to understand how different people deal with universal problems. Yet he was also part of a commercial venture, writing for an audience that wanted, first and foremost, to be entertained. He made sure that his plays included enough action and excitement to keep just about anyone interested. Audience members in the pit were particularly loud in their appreciation, cheering the heroes, yelling insults at the villains, and laughing loudly at humorous characters and jokes. In fact, by the standards of today's theater, Elizabethan performances were rather rowdy events.

Since the Globe had no artificial lighting or heating, performances were given in daylight in warmer weather. The stage also had no scenery; usually, lines of dialogue told the audience where a scene was taking place. Despite the lack of scenery, productions were by no means drab; costumes could be quite ornate, and props such as swords, shields, and swirling banners added to the colorful display. From behind the stage came sound effects—the chiming of a clock, for instance, or the sound of a cannon. The stage had no curtain. Instead, performers usually walked on and off in full view of the audience.

SHAKESPEARE'S LEGACY

Some of the most familiar lines in the English language come from the plays of Shakespeare: "Friends, Romans, countrymen, lend me your ears" *(Julius Caesar),* "O Romeo, Romeo! wherefore art thou Romeo?" *(Romeo and Juliet),* "To be or not to be" *(Hamlet).* Why do readers and theatergoers continue to enjoy Shakespeare's plays four centuries after they were written? One answer is that Shakespeare thoroughly understood the theater and knew all the tricks of stagecraft: how to move an audience, create an exciting scene, sketch out a setting using only the spoken word. Another answer lies in Shakespeare's language—the beautiful lines and phrases that resound in the minds of all who experience his plays. No other writer, before or since, has developed the potential of the English language to such heights. Still another answer lies in Shakespeare's profound understanding of human psychology, revealed in the unforgettable characters he created. Today, as much as ever, to understand Shakespeare's plays is to understand what is most important about human beings and about life.

CONTRASTING

Ask students what made theater in Shakespeare's time different from theater today.

Possible Response: In Shakespeare's theater, many of the spectators stood in the pit; people cheered, booed, hissed, and sometimes threw things at the players. There was little in the way of scenery, no artificial lighting, and no special effects beyond trumpets, drum rolls, and simulated claps of thunder. Further, women's roles were played by boys, not women.

IDENTIFYING MAIN IDEAS

Ask students to identify the main idea of the section under the subhead "Shakespeare's Legacy." Have them find examples of details that support the main idea.

Possible Response: Main Idea: Shakespeare's legacy includes the plays he wrote, which are still performed today. Supporting Detail: "Why do readers and theatergoers continue to enjoy Shakespeare's plays four centuries after they were written?"

LEARNING the language of LITERATURE

OVERVIEW

Objectives

- understand the following literary terms:
  - tragedy and tragic hero
  - blank verse
  - soliloquy and aside
  - rhetorical devices
  - dramatic irony
- analyze stress patterns to identify iambic pentameter
- infer how soliloquy and asides affect mood
- evaluate the effectiveness of rhetorical devices
- analyze how dramatic irony is created

Teaching the Lesson

This lesson analyzes characteristics of Shakespearean drama and shows how these characteristics are evident in the language and structure of the plays.

Introducing the Concepts

Have students share what they know about the work of William Shakespeare.

Presenting the Concepts

Tragedy and the Tragic Hero

Some critics claim that a tragic hero must be worthy of the viewer's or reader's empathy.

Blank Verse

Have students read blank verse aloud as they tap the rhythm on their desks. Then, direct them to reread the lines, identifying the elements of rhythm that signify iambic pentameter.

YOUR TURN

Possible Responses: The "Yond Cassius" line is perfect iambic pentameter when "Cassius" is read as only two syllables, a stressed followed by an unstressed, which is most common. The second line, however, can better justify a variation. If "dangerous" at the end is pronounced as a stressed syllable followed by the two unstressed ones, then the perfect pattern is broken; alternately, it is possible to read "He thinks too much" as an unstressed syllable followed by three stressed syllables, which also makes the line vary from the perfect.

Shakespeare probably chose to vary the meter to more closely imitate speech patterns.

Shakespearean Drama

Shakespearean Drama generally falls into one of three classifications: **tragedy,** a play that traces the main character's downfall; **comedy,** a play that ends happily and that usually contains many humorous elements; and **history,** a play that chronicles the life of an English monarch. All of these types of plays share the following characteristics: most are written in blank verse and contain soliloquies and asides, rhetorical devices, and dramatic irony. Studying the excerpts from Julius Caesar presented here will help you learn more about these and other characteristics of Shakespearean drama.

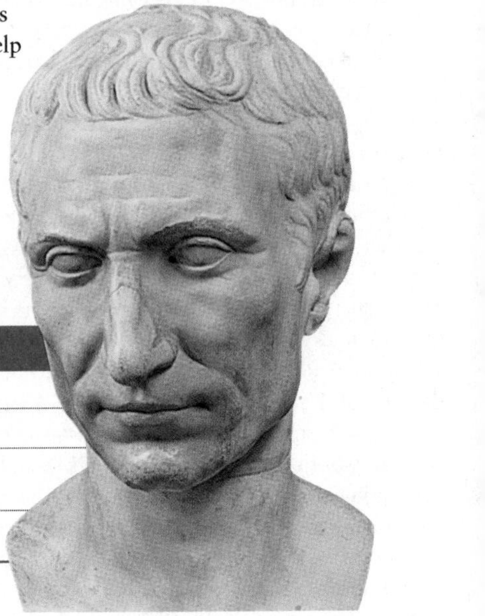

Tragedy and the Tragic Hero

Shakespeare's tragedies are often cited as his greatest plays. A **tragedy** is a work in which a series of actions leads to the downfall of the main character, or **tragic hero**. *Julius Caesar* is a tragedy.

QUALITIES OF A TRAGIC HERO
• Possesses importance or high rank
• Exhibits extraordinary talents
• Displays a tragic flaw—an error in judgment or defect in character—that leads to downfall
• Faces downfall with courage and dignity

Blank Verse

Shakespeare's plays are **verse dramas**, plays in which the dialogue consists almost entirely of poetry. Generally, Shakespeare wrote his verse dramas in **blank verse**, or unrhymed lines of **iambic pentameter**. Iambic pentameter is a fixed pattern of rhythm, or meter, in which most lines contain five unstressed syllables each followed by a stressed syllable.

BLANK VERSE

Let me have men about me that are fat,
Sleek-headed men, and such as sleep o' nights.
Yond Cassius has a lean and hungry look;
He thinks too much, such men are dangerous.

—Act One, Scene 2, Lines 192–195

YOUR TURN The stressed and unstressed syllables in the first two lines in the passage at the right have been marked. Copy the last two lines, and mark the syllables. Which lines seem to vary from perfect iambic pentameter? Why do you think Shakespeare chose to vary the meter?

Soliloquy and Aside

Like all stage plays, Shakespearean drama uses certain devices that an audience is expected to accept even though they are not used in real life. These devices include the soliloquy and the aside.

- A **soliloquy** is a long speech given by a character while alone on stage to reveal his or her private thoughts or intentions.
- An **aside** is a character's quiet remark to the audience or another character that no one else on stage is supposed to hear. A stage direction (often in brackets) indicates an aside.

YOUR TURN What does this aside by Trebonius suggest about his true feelings for Caesar? What mood is created by the aside?

ASIDE TO AUDIENCE

Trebonius. **Caesar, I will. [*Aside*] And so near will I be**
That your best friends shall wish I had been further.

—Act Two, Scene 2, Lines 124–125

Rhetorical Devices

Shakespeare's plays often contain speeches known for their masterful use of **rhetorical**, or persuasive, **devices**. These devices use language and sound to appeal to the audience's emotions and make the speech more convincing and memorable. Among these devices are the following:

- the **repetition** of words and sounds
- **parallelism**, or repeated grammatical structures
- **rhetorical questions**, or questions requiring no answer

YOUR TURN In the examples at the right, which device do you find most effective? Share your ideas with a classmate.

RHETORICAL DEVICES

Repetition:

And do you now put on your best attire?
And do you now cull out a holiday?

—Act One, Scene 1, Lines 50–51

Parallelism:

Not that I loved Caesar less, but that I loved Rome more.

—Act Three, Scene 2, Lines 22–23

Rhetorical question:

Why friends, you go to do you know not what.
Wherein hath Caesar thus deserved your loves?
Alas, you know not!

—Act Three, Scene 2, Lines 238–240

Dramatic Irony

Another powerful tool used by Shakespeare is irony. **Irony** exists when there is a contrast between appearance and reality. In **dramatic irony**, the audience or reader knows something that one or more characters do not know. Because of that knowledge, the audience has a bigger picture of the action.

YOUR TURN In Act Two, Caesar invites Brutus and the other conspirators into his home, even though—as the reader knows—they are plotting his murder. How does the repetition of the word *friends* in this passage emphasize the dramatic irony?

DRAMATIC IRONY

Caesar. **Good friends, go in and taste some wine with me,**
And we (like friends) will straightway go together.

—Act Two, Scene 2, Lines 126–127

Soliloquy and Aside

Unlike fiction, in which the author can present narrative passages that reveal a character's interior thoughts and feelings, drama is limited to presenting a character's actions and speech. Thus, the soliloquy and the aside are conventions for accessing the internal aspects of character.

YOUR TURN

Possible Response: This aside suggests that Trebonius' true feelings for Caesar are less than honorable. The mood is one of tension with a dark feeling of impending confrontation.

Rhetorical Devices

Explain that the poetry of Shakespeare's language is reflected in his use of rhetorical devices.

YOUR TURN

Possible Response: Responses will vary. The example of parallelism is perhaps most memorable to the ear, partly because of the similarities in sound of the words and the depth of meaning.

Dramatic Irony

Help students understand that dramatic irony can have the effect of creating tension in the reader's mind, since the reader knows, in effect, pitfalls of which the character remains unaware.

YOUR TURN

Possible Response: Repetition of the word *friends* in this passage emphasizes Caesar's naiveté concerning the truth about those he calls friends.

LEARNING THE LANGUAGE OF LITERATURE 687

OVERVIEW

Objectives
- interpret characters, setting, and stage directions and apply them to understanding Shakespearean drama
- analyze unusual language and grammatical structures to clarify meaning

Teaching the Lesson

The strategies on this page will help students learn and apply strategies for untangling difficult language and grammatical conventions to enhance their understanding and appreciation of Shakespearean drama.

Presenting the Strategies
To help students understand the archaic grammatical conventions of Renaissance English used by Shakespeare, take everyday expressions from students' lives and convert them into the structure and vocabulary of Shakespearean English.

Strategies for Using Your Reader's Notebook
Encourage students to use their dictionaries and have them define unfamiliar words and terms in their Reader's Notebooks.

1 Strategies for Reading Drama
Point out that not every character listed in the opening cast of characters is of equal importance. Usually, there are two or three major characters, a larger cast of minor characters, and some characters who make an appearance but have no significant role. Instruct students to focus on identifying the major characters and determining the nature of the conflict.

2 Strategies for Understanding Shakespeare's Language
Explain to students that paraphrasing difficult lines and restating them in the idiom of modern English to clarify meaning is extremely helpful in reading Shakespearean drama. Comprehension allows readers to stay focused on the drama that is developing and unfolding. Encourage students to paraphrase and translate difficult lines in their Reader's Notebooks.

The Active Reader: Skills and Strategies

Shakespeare's plays often present challenges to contemporary audiences. Unusual vocabulary, grammar, and word order can be difficult to understand. Even the stage directions and other dramatic conventions can be challenging. The reading strategies explained here can help you enjoy Shakespearean drama.

Reading Shakespearean Drama

Strategies for Using Your READER'S NOTEBOOK
As you read, take notes to
- keep track of the characters and their relationships
- record any dialogue, soliloquies, and asides that interest you
- write down any words or terms that you don't understand

1 Strategies for Reading Drama
- Familiarize yourself with the opening cast of characters.
- Try to **visualize** the setting from any details provided.
- Pay attention to the character labels and stage directions.
- To get a better idea of what the dialogue would sound like, read some of it out loud.
- **Evaluate** a character's speech and actions to help you determine his or her personality, thoughts, and motives.

2 Strategies for Understanding Shakespeare's Language
- Review in the chart shown here the examples from *Julius Caesar* of particular aspects of Shakespeare's use of language.
- Use the sidenotes, context clues, or a dictionary to learn the meaning of unfamiliar vocabulary. Paraphrase lines to **clarify** the meaning.
- Be aware that English spoken in Shakespeare's time contains grammatical forms and structures that are no longer used today.
- Untangle unusual word order so that it conforms to modern usage.
- **Evaluate** puns (jokes that suggest two or more meanings of a word) and allusions (references to well-known people, places, or things) to enrich your understanding of the play. Read sidenotes when they are available, since the wordplay may depend on meanings that are no longer used.

Shakespeare's Language

Unfamiliar Vocabulary	It was mere *foolery*, I did not mark it [*foolery* for *foolishness; mark* for *notice*]
Grammatical Forms	O judgment, *thou art* fled to brutish beasts! [instead of "you are"]
Grammatical Structure	*I denied you not* [instead of "did not deny you"]
Unusual Word Order	Did this *in Caesar seem ambitious*? [instead of "seem ambitious in Caesar"]
Puns	A trade, sir, that I hope I may use with a safe conscience, which is indeed, sir, a mender of bad *soles*. [pun on *souls* and *soles*]
Allusions	Why, man, he doth bestride the narrow world / Like a *Colossus*. [allusion to the giant statue]

Need More Help?
Remember that active readers use the essential reading strategies explained on page 7: **visualize, predict, clarify, question, connect, evaluate, monitor.**

The Tragedy of Julius Caesar

Drama by WILLIAM SHAKESPEARE

"Friends, Romans, countrymen, lend me your ears."

Connect to Your Life

Ambition and Power In *Julius Caesar,* Shakespeare tells a story about the hunger for power, a story based on real people and events from the days when Rome ruled much of the world. Think of stories—fictional or true—that you've read or seen about people who hunger for power. In a group, exchange at least two such stories. Where were they set? Who were the power-hungry individuals? What happened to them? If you're familiar with such stories, you know something about the main theme of *Julius Caesar.*

Like all of Shakespeare's plays, however, *Julius Caesar* deals with many other themes. One of these is friendship. You'll find some interesting views on friendship in the play you're about to read. For example, is it right to persuade a close friend to do something dangerous? This drama also deals with such universal themes as ambition, vanity, envy, and revenge.

Build Background

Roman Politics Julius Caesar was a Roman general and politician who lived from about 100 to 44 B.C. One of the greatest military leaders in Roman history, Caesar conquered most of Gaul, a land that covered the areas now known as France and Belgium. He also brought Roman civilization to the island that eventually came to be Britain and later led his army in a takeover of Egypt.

Caesar gained so much military power that the Roman Senate feared he would try to control the government. To keep that from happening, the Senate ordered him to disband his army around 50 B.C. Caesar refused and led his army into Italy, the peninsula where Rome lay. There he fought a civil war against the armies of his former friend and ally Pompey. The battles spread as far as Spain and Egypt, ending with Caesar's victory in 46 B.C.

Focus Your Reading

LITERARY ANALYSIS BLANK VERSE Blank verse consists of unrhymed lines of **iambic pentameter,** in which a line has five unstressed syllables each followed by a stressed syllable.

You blócks, you stónes, you wórse than sénseless thíngs!

Many people consider iambic pentameter the most natural poetic pattern for English, a language that is based on stressed and unstressed syllables. As you read, decide for yourself by reciting some of Shakespeare's lines aloud. Be sure not to put too much emphasis on the accented syllables.

ACTIVE READING UNDERSTANDING SHAKESPEARE'S PLAYS
Because the English language has changed a great deal since Shakespeare lived, Shakespeare's way of saying things can be difficult for a modern reader to understand. For that reason, virtually every modern edition of a play by Shakespeare includes sidenotes or footnotes that explain unfamiliar language and allusions. In the upcoming text, the sidenotes include questions in blue that will help lead you through the more complex parts of the play.

READER'S NOTEBOOK You may also find the play easier to follow if you keep track of the **characters.** As you read, use a chart like the one shown to list the characters you encounter.

Pro-Caesar	Anti-Caesar	Neutral

OVERVIEW

An excerpt of this selection is included in the **Grade 10 InterActive Reader.**

Objectives

1. understand and appreciate a classic **drama (Literary Analysis)**
2. understand **blank verse (Literary Analysis)**
3. understand Shakespeare's plays **(Active Reading)**

Summary

Julius Caesar opens in 44 B.C. with Caesar, a general and ruler of the Roman Republic, celebrating a great military victory. The citizens are impressed by his success in battle and supportive of his power as dictator of Rome. Many Roman leaders, however, are troubled by his growing ambition and power, and although Caesar thinks them loyal to him, they begin to plot his assassination. Brutus, Cassius, and the conspirators eventually murder Caesar on the Senate floor. Mark Antony, who remains devoted to Caesar, vows to seek revenge for the slain leader and eventually defeats the conspirators' armies, prompting both Cassius and Brutus to commit suicide at the battle of Philippi.

Thematic Link

Julius Caesar, a drama in the classic tradition, raises questions about the nature of friendship, revenge, authority, and ambition and the uses and misuses of persuasion.

5-Minute Warm-Up

Daily Language SkillBuilder

Have students **proofread** the display sentences on page 541m and write them correctly. The sentences also appear on Transparency 22 of **Grammar Transparencies and Copymasters.**

LESSON RESOURCES

UNIT FOUR RESOURCE BOOK, pp. 61–64

ASSESSMENT RESOURCES
Formal Assessment, pp. 123–124
Teacher's Guide to Assessment and Portfolio Use
Test Generator

SKILLS TRANSPARENCIES AND COPYMASTERS
Literary Analysis
- Poetry: Sound Devices, T8 (for Literary Analysis, p. 689)
- Shakespearean Drama I, T18 (for Literary Analysis, p. 713)

Reading and Critical Thinking
- Organizational Chart: Horizontal, T51 (for Reader's Notebook, p. 689)

Grammar
- Double Negatives, C160 (for Mini Lesson, p. 710)

Vocabulary
- Word Origins, C73 (for Mini Lesson, p. 696)

Communications
- Dramatic Reading, T12 (for Mini Lessons, pp. 700, 703, 706)

INTEGRATED TECHNOLOGY
Audio Library
Video: Literature in Performance
- *Julius Caesar.* See **Video Resource Book,** pp. 25–30.

Visit our website:
www.mcdougallittell.com

TEACHING THE LITERATURE

Reading and Analyzing

Reading Skills and Strategies: PREVIEW

Have students preview Act One. Discuss with students that Act One establishes the exposition, outlining the basic situation and introducing the setting, the characters, and the conflict.

Active Reading

UNDERSTANDING SHAKESPEARE'S PLAYS

Remind students that marginal notes are included with the text to help with difficulties in Shakespeare's language and to help clarify the plot. Explain to students that there are two ways to use the side notes: (1) they can read a passage straight through, using as much context as they can to understand its meaning, and then check their understanding by reading the side note; (2) they can read the passage, consulting the side note along the way as they need help. Encourage students to experiment with different strategies for using side notes as they read the play.

Use **Unit Four Resource Book** p. 62 for more practice.

Literary Analysis BLANK VERSE

Review the features of blank verse given on p. 689. Demonstrate the rhythm of iambic pentameter by clapping only the beat (da-DUM, da-DUM, da-DUM, da-DUM, da-DUM). Have students read a passage aloud, paying special attention to the rhythm of the lines. Encourage students to paraphrase the blank verse lines in prose to reinforce their comprehension.

Use **Unit Four Resource Book** p. 63 for more practice.

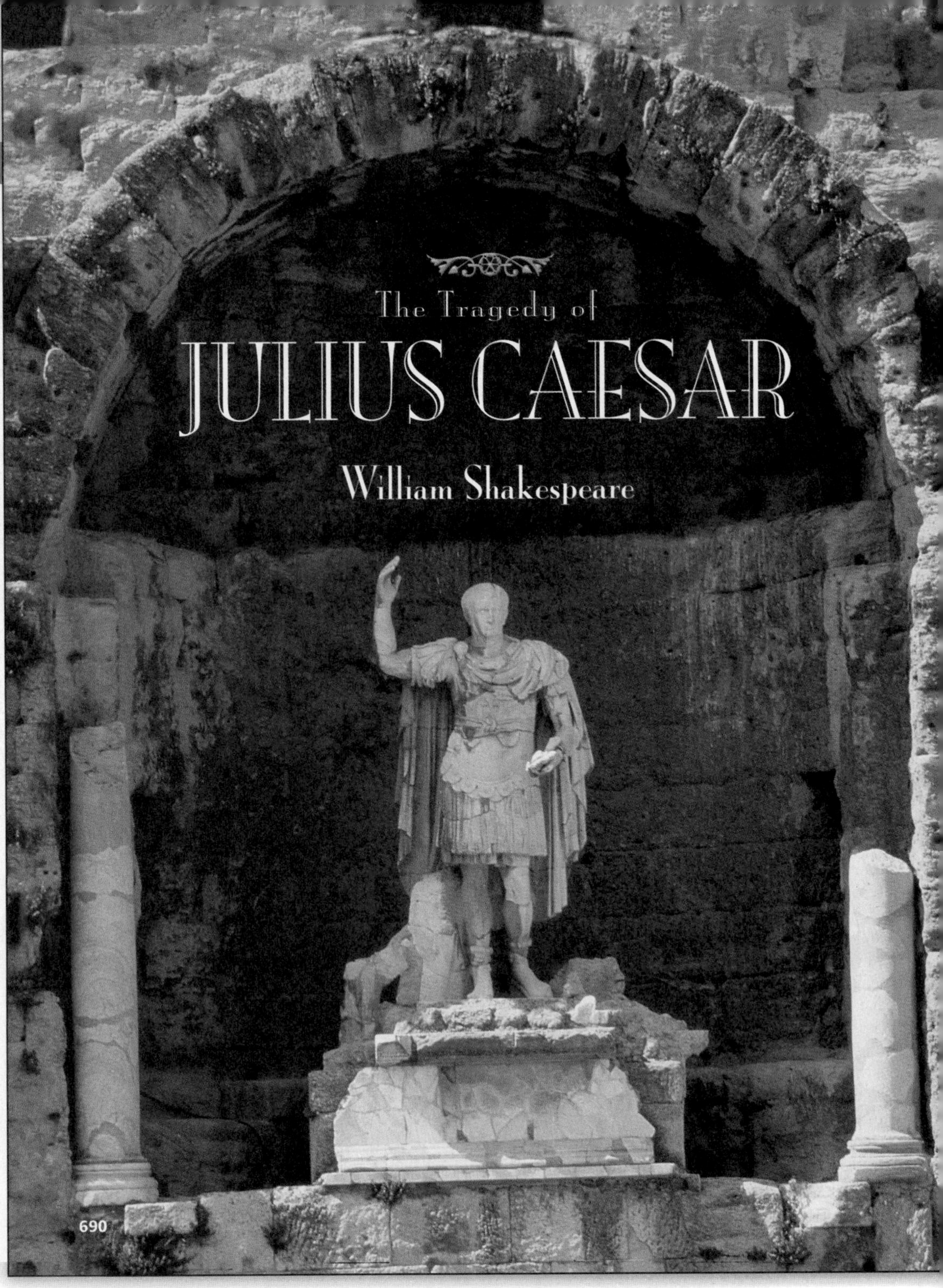

BLOCK SCHEDULING: MANAGING TIME

If your schedule requires that you cover the lesson objectives in a shorter time, use . . .

- Preparing to Read, p. 689
- Thinking Through the Literature, p. 713
- Grammar in Context, p. 796

If you want to take advantage of longer class time, use

- TE Teaching Options: Cross-Curricular Links, pp. 691, 692; Vocabulary Strategy, pp. 696–697; Standardized Test Practice, pp. 698–699, 704; Speaking and Listening, pp. 700, 703, 706; Viewing and Representing, p. 708; Informal Assessment, p. 712

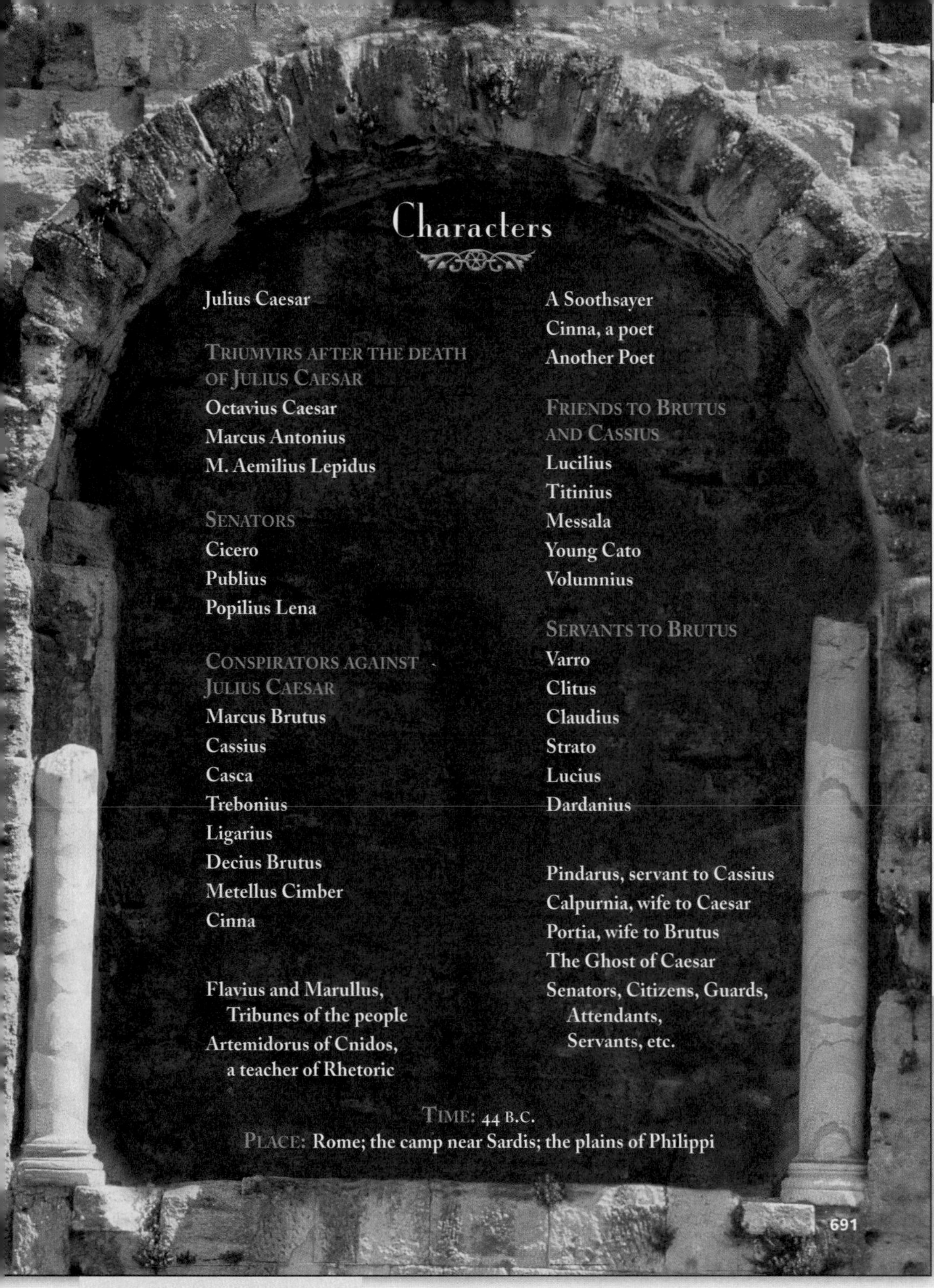

Characters

Julius Caesar

TRIUMVIRS AFTER THE DEATH OF JULIUS CAESAR

Octavius Caesar
Marcus Antonius
M. Aemilius Lepidus

SENATORS

Cicero
Publius
Popilius Lena

CONSPIRATORS AGAINST JULIUS CAESAR

Marcus Brutus
Cassius
Casca
Trebonius
Ligarius
Decius Brutus
Metellus Cimber
Cinna

Flavius and Marullus, Tribunes of the people
Artemidorus of Cnidos, a teacher of Rhetoric

A Soothsayer
Cinna, a poet
Another Poet

FRIENDS TO BRUTUS AND CASSIUS

Lucilius
Titinius
Messala
Young Cato
Volumnius

SERVANTS TO BRUTUS

Varro
Clitus
Claudius
Strato
Lucius
Dardanius

Pindarus, servant to Cassius
Calpurnia, wife to Caesar
Portia, wife to Brutus
The Ghost of Caesar
Senators, Citizens, Guards, Attendants, Servants, etc.

TIME: 44 B.C.
PLACE: Rome; the camp near Sardis; the plains of Philippi

691

Customizing Instruction

Less Proficient Readers

Some students may have difficulties with the large number of characters, especially because the characters have Latin names that may be unfamiliar. Read through the various names with students and make sure they are comfortable pronouncing the Latin names. Encourage students to take notes identifying the characters so they can have a handy reference sheet as they read the play.

Students Acquiring English

The play contains vocabulary that may be difficult for some students. For example, some words are archaic, and Shakespeare's puns depend on recognizing two possible meanings for a single word. Remind students to use the annotations to work through difficult passages. Encourage them to keep lists of unfamiliar words along with their meanings as a reference.

Use **Spanish Study Guide** for additional support, pp. 149–151.

Gifted and Talented

Encourage students to review the characteristics of a tragic hero discussed on p. 686. As they read the play, they should consider whether Julius Caesar possesses these qualities and note their opinions. Have students debate whether Julius Caesar meets the criteria for a tragic hero.

Teaching Options

Cross Curricular Link History

EARLY ROME In Caesar's time, Rome was not yet an empire. Although power in Rome was often seized by military dictators like Caesar, it was still considered a Republic, and its political terminology reflected this attitude. The following political terms were used in Caesar's time:

- Triumvirs: Rulers who share power as a threesome
- Senators: Members of the Roman Senate, a ruling body that had some power but would have been subordinate to Caesar as dictator
- Tribunes of the people: Whereas the Senate represented nobility and landowners, tribunes had limited power and represented the common people.

Reading and Analyzing

Literary Analysis BLANK VERSE

Ⓐ Point out that some of these characters speak in blank verse and some speak in prose. Ask students which characters are speaking in prose, and why they think these characters are given a different form of speech.
Possible Response: The laborers speak in prose. While upper-class characters are given elevated speech to match their position, the commoners are given everyday prose speech to match theirs.

GUIDE FOR READING

Ⓑ **Possible Response:** Flavius' attitude toward the workers seems proud and contemptuous.

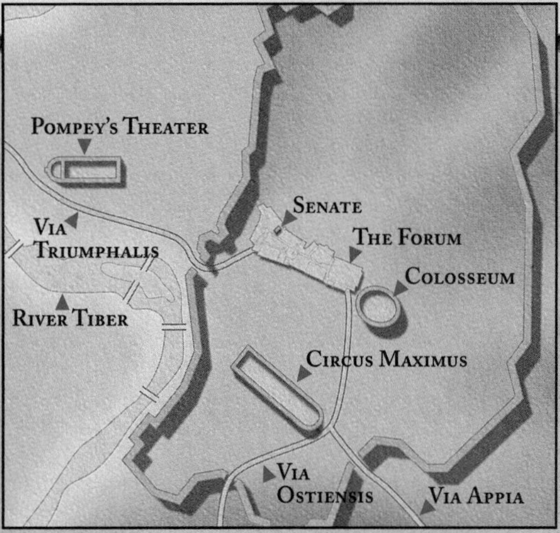

Map of Ancient Rome

The Forum, the seat of the Roman government.

Teaching Options

Cross Curricular Link Architecture

THE ROMAN FORUM The Forum, the name of which is a Latin word referring to any open public space, was the center of business and public life in ancient Rome. Originally, the Forum served as a market and space in which to conduct public business. Later it was used more exclusively for civic business and religious ceremonies. The Forum underwent many changes and additions over the course of about 1,000 years: it was, at different times, a royal palace, several monuments to gods, the Senate house, commercial shops, a public altar, the public treasury, and the building where the assembly met to consider legislation. The Sacred Way, or *Via Sacra*, passed through the Forum and served as a path for victorious generals to parade through the city. Julius Caesar built a new forum (around 46 B.C.) to accommodate the city's population growth, and its chief building was a temple to the god from whom Caesar claimed descent. A temple to Divus Julius, a deified Julius Caesar, was built in 29 B.C.

ACT ONE

SCENE 1 A STREET IN ROME.

The play begins on February 15, the religious feast of Lupercal. Today the people have a particular reason for celebrating. Julius Caesar has just returned to Rome after a long civil war in which he defeated the forces of Pompey, his rival for power. Caesar now has the opportunity to take full control of Rome.

In this opening scene, a group of workmen, in their best clothes, celebrate in the streets. They are joyful over Caesar's victory. The workers meet Flavius and Marullus, two tribunes—government officials—who supported Pompey. The tribunes express their anger at the celebration, and one worker responds with puns. Finally, the two tribunes scatter the crowd.

Flavius. Hence! home, you idle creatures, get you home!
Is this a holiday? What, know you not,
Being mechanical, you ought not walk
Upon a laboring day without the sign
Of your profession? Speak, what trade art thou?

First Commoner. Why, sir, a carpenter.

Marullus. Where is thy leather apron and thy rule?
1 What dost thou with thy best apparel on?
You, sir, what trade are you?

2 **Second Commoner.** Truly sir, in respect of a fine workman I am but, as you would say, a cobbler.

Marullus. But what trade art thou? Answer me directly.

Second Commoner. A trade, sir, that I hope I may use with a safe conscience, which is indeed, sir, a mender of bad soles.

Marullus. What trade, thou knave? Thou naughty knave, what trade?

GUIDE FOR READING

2–5 What, know . . . profession: Since you are workers **(mechanical),** you should be carrying the tools of your trade **(sign / Of your profession).** What is Flavius' attitude toward these workers? B

10–27 In this conversation, the **cobbler** (shoemaker) makes several puns, which all go over the head of Marullus. Imagine the workmen laughing, as Marullus gets angrier and angrier, wondering what's so funny.

16–18 Marullus accuses the commoner of being a wicked, sly person **(naughty knave),** but the commoner begs Marullus not to be angry with him **(be not out with me).**

Customizing Instruction

Less Proficient Readers

1 Point out that line 8 has archaic diction and syntax. Explain that *dost* is a second-person singular form of the verb "to do" and that *thou* and *thy* mean "you" and "your," respectively. Have students paraphrase the line into modern English. Remind them that they may have to change or add words.
Possible Response: "What are you doing with your best apparel on?"

Students Acquiring English

2 Tell students that *cobbler* in Shakespeare's time had two meanings: "a person who makes or repairs shoes" and "clumsy worker." Help students understand how Shakespeare plays with both of these meanings to frustrate and confuse Marullus.
Possible Response: Marullus is thinking of the second meaning, while the workman means the first. Marullus gets flustered and asks the shoemaker again what kind of work he does.

Reading and Analyzing

Reading Skills and Strategies: EVALUATING

A Ask students to evaluate Marullus' speech to discover his feelings about the workers. Why is he upset about their celebrations?

Possible Responses: He is insulting and condescending toward the workers, who are celebrating Pompey's defeat; Marullus is angered because they are celebrating Caesar's triumph over other Romans whom Marullus supports.

Reading Skills and Strategies: CLARIFYING

B Ask students what is being personified in these lines, and then have them explain the personification.

Possible Responses: The river is being personified as a woman who "trembles" as she "hears" the loud sounds of a cheering crowd.

GUIDE FOR READING

C Explain that puns are jokes that depend on two or more meanings of one word or on different words that sound the same.

Literary Analysis: CONFLICT

Explain to students that in an external conflict, a character struggles with an outside force, while a conflict that takes place within a character's mind is an internal conflict. Have students identify the conflict in this opening scene.

Possible Responses: The conflict is between Flavius and Marullus and the workers; the conflict is between supporters of Pompey and supporters of Caesar.

Second Commoner. Nay, I beseech you, sir, be not out with me. Yet if you be out, sir, I can mend you.

Marullus. What mean'st thou by that? Mend me, thou saucy fellow?

Second Commoner. Why, sir, cobble you.

Flavius. Thou art a cobbler, art thou?

Second Commoner. Truly, sir, all that I live by is with the awl. I meddle with no tradesman's matters nor women's matters, but with all. I am indeed, sir, a surgeon to old shoes. When they are in great danger, I recover them. As proper men as ever trod upon neat's leather have gone upon my handiwork.

Flavius. But wherefore art not in thy shop today?
Why dost thou lead these men about the streets?

Second Commoner. Truly, sir, to wear out their shoes, to get myself into more work. But indeed, sir, we make holiday to see Caesar and to rejoice in his triumph.

A **Marullus.** Wherefore rejoice? What conquest brings he home?
What tributaries follow him to Rome
To grace in captive bonds his chariot wheels?
You blocks, you stones, you worse than senseless things!
O you hard hearts, you cruel men of Rome!
Knew you not Pompey? Many a time and oft
Have you climbed up to walls and battlements,
To tow'rs and windows, yea, to chimney tops,
Your infants in your arms, and there have sat
The livelong day, with patient expectation,
To see great Pompey pass the streets of Rome.
And when you saw his chariot but appear,
B Have you not made an universal shout,
That Tiber trembled underneath her banks
To hear the replication of your sounds
Made in her concave shores?
And do you now put on your best attire?
And do you now cull out a holiday?
And do you now strew flowers in his way
That comes in triumph over Pompey's blood?
Be gone!
Run to your houses, fall upon your knees,

---

19 Marullus thinks the cobbler means "I can mend your behavior." He accuses the cobbler of being disrespectful **(saucy)**.

23–24 The cobbler jokes about the similarity of **awl** (a shoemaker's tool) to the word *all*. Do you or any of your friends ever make up puns? **C**

27 neat's leather: calfskin, used to make expensive shoes. The cobbler means that even rich people come to him for shoes.

28 wherefore: why.

35–36 What . . . wheels: What captured prisoners march chained to the wheels of his chariot?

39 Pompey: a former Roman ruler defeated by Caesar in 48 B.C. Pompey was murdered a year after his defeat.

47 Tiber: a river that runs through Rome.

48 replication: echo.

51 cull out: select.

53 Pompey's blood: Caesar is returning to Rome in triumph after defeating Pompey's sons in Spain.

Pray to the gods to intermit the plague
That needs must light on this ingratitude.

Flavius. Go, go, good countrymen, and for this fault
Assemble all the poor men of your sort;
Draw them to Tiber banks, and weep your tears
Into the channel, till the lowest stream
Do kiss the most exalted shores of all.

[*Exeunt all the* Commoners.]

See, whe'r their basest metal be not moved.
They vanish tongue-tied in their guiltiness.
Go you down that way towards the Capitol;
[1] This way will I. Disrobe the images
If you do find them decked with ceremonies.

Marullus. May we do so?
You know it is the feast of Lupercal.

Flavius. It is no matter. Let no images
[2] Be hung with Caesar's trophies. I'll about
And drive away the vulgar from the streets.
So do you too, where you perceive them thick.
These growing feathers plucked from Caesar's wing
Will make him fly an ordinary pitch,
Who else would soar above the view of men
And keep us all in servile fearfulness.

[*Exeunt.*]

56–57 intermit . . . ingratitude: hold back the deadly illness that might be just punishment for your behavior.

60–62 weep . . . of all: weep into the Tiber River until it overflows.

Exeunt (Latin): They leave.

63 Flavius and Marullus are now alone, having shamed the workers into leaving the street. Flavius says that they will now see if they have touched **(moved)** the workers' poor characters **(basest metal).**

66–67 Disrobe . . . ceremonies: Strip the statues of any decorations you find on them.

71–73 I'll about . . . thick: I'll go around and scatter the rest of the commoners. Do the same yourself wherever they are forming a crowd.

74–77 These . . . fearfulness: Flavius compares Caesar to a bird. He hopes that turning away some of Caesar's supporters **(growing feathers)** will prevent him from becoming too powerful.

SCENE 2 A PUBLIC PLACE IN ROME.

As Caesar attends the traditional race at the festival of Lupercal, a soothsayer warns him to beware of the ides of March, or March 15. (The middle day of each month was called the ides.) When Caesar leaves, Cassius and Brutus speak. Cassius tries to turn Brutus against Caesar by using flattery, examples of Caesar's weaknesses, and sarcasm about Caesar's power. Caesar passes by again, expressing his distrust of Cassius. Cassius and Brutus learn of Caesar's rejection of a crown the people of Rome have offered him. They agree to meet again to discuss what must be done about Caesar.

[*A flourish of trumpets announces the approach of Caesar. A large crowd of* Commoners *has assembled; a* Soothsayer *is among them. Enter* Caesar, *his wife* Calpurnia, Portia, Decius, Cicero, Brutus, Cassius, Casca, *and* Antony, *who is stripped for running in the games.*]

Customizing Instruction

Less Proficient Readers

[1] Explain to students that by *ceremonies* and *trophies* Flavius means memorials such as banners and other decorations raised in honor of military victories and that by *images* he means "statues." Have students explain why the tribunes want to remove these memorials from public statues.

Possible Responses: Because they favored Pompey, they want to minimize the celebration of Caesar's victory; they hope that by discouraging the citizens' support of Caesar, they can restrict Caesar's desire for power.

Students Acquiring English

[2] Point out that while *vulgar* is often used as an adjective to mean "common" or "coarse," it can also be used as a noun to refer to "the common people" or the lower classes. Have students identify the part of speech of *vulgar* as it is used in line 72.

Answer: noun

Reading and Analyzing

Reading Skills and Strategies: PREDICTING

A Draw students' attention to the soothsayer's warning to Caesar. Have them try to figure out what will happen based on the soothsayer's caution and Caesar's response.
Possible Response: Because Caesar dismisses the warning, some harm will come to him on the ides of March.

Reading Skills and Strategies: CONNECTING

B Have students discuss superstitions, and point out that Caesar doesn't seem to be very superstitious in this scene. Ask students how they might respond if someone gave them a warning like the one the soothsayer gave Caesar.
Possible Responses: I would ignore it; I would be very careful.

GUIDE FOR READING

C **Possible Response:** Antony is loyal to Caesar and is ready to obey all of Caesar's commands immediately.

Caesar. Calpurnia.
Casca. Peace, ho! Caesar speaks.
Caesar. Calpurnia.
Calpurnia. Here, my lord.
Caesar. Stand you directly in Antonius' way
When he doth run his course. Antonius.
Antony. Caesar, my lord?
Caesar. Forget not in your speed, Antonius,
To touch Calpurnia; for our elders say
The barren, touched in this holy chase,
Shake off their sterile curse.
Antony. I shall remember.
When Caesar says "Do this," it is performed.
Caesar. Set on, and leave no ceremony out.
[*Flourish of trumpets.* Caesar *starts to leave.*]
Soothsayer. Caesar!
Caesar. Ha! Who calls?
Casca. Bid every noise be still. Peace yet again!
Caesar. Who is it in the press that calls on me?
I hear a tongue shriller than all the music
Cry "Caesar!" Speak. Caesar is turned to hear.
Soothsayer. Beware the ides of March.
Caesar. What man is that?
A **Brutus.** A soothsayer bids you beware the ides of March.
1 **Caesar.** Set him before me; let me see his face.
Cassius. Fellow, come from the throng; look upon Caesar.
Caesar. What say'st thou to me now? Speak once again.
Soothsayer. Beware the ides of March.
B **Caesar.** He is a dreamer; let us leave him. Pass.
[*Trumpets sound. Exeunt all but* Brutus *and* Cassius.]
Cassius. Will you go see the order of the course?
Brutus. Not I.
Cassius. I pray you do.
Brutus. I am not gamesome. I do lack some part
Of that quick spirit that is in Antony.
Let me not hinder, Cassius, your desires.
I'll leave you.

3–9 Stand . . . curse: Antony **(Antonius)** is about to run in a race that is part of the Lupercal celebration. Caesar refers to the superstition that a **sterile** woman (one unable to bear children) can become fertile if touched by one of the racers.

9–10 I shall . . . performed: What do these lines tell you about Antony's attitude toward Caesar? C

12–14 Remember that the crowd is cheering constantly. The **soothsayer** (fortuneteller), who calls out Caesar's name can hardly be heard. Casca tells the crowd to quiet down.

15 press: crowd.

18 ides: the middle day of the month.

25–28 Cassius asks if Brutus is going to watch the race **(the order of the course)**, but Brutus says he is not fond of sports **(gamesome)**.

Teaching Options

Mini Lesson: Vocabulary Strategy

RESEARCHING WORD ORIGINS Instruction The ancient Roman setting of *Julius Caesar* is a particularly fitting backdrop to the study of word origins. Much of modern English is derived from words that originate in Latin, the language used by the people of classical Rome. Students can become familiar with the Latin origins of words by using a dictionary, which will help them to understand meanings, spellings, and influences on the English language. *Plebeian, vulgar, patrician, senate,* and *capital* are words important to ancient Roman culture that are also in modern use.

Write the following example on the chalkboard.

Vulgar: Latin *vulgus*—the common people; modern—of or relating to the common people; uneducated

Discuss with students the relationship between the original Latin meaning of the word and its current meaning.

Practice Have students use a dictionary to find the Latin roots of *plebeian, patrician, senate,* and *capital,* and then have them write out a modern definition of each word. Ask them to explain how the two meanings are related, and have them discuss

"Beware the ides of March."

John McMartin as Caesar and Damien Leake as the soothsayer (New York Shakespeare Festival, 1988). Photo by Martha Swope, copyright © Time Inc.

Customizing Instruction

Students Acquiring English

1 Explain to students that when Caesar says, "Set him before me," he does not necessarily mean that his guards should go pick the man up and set him down; he means that the man should come out of the crowd and stand in front of him.

Multiple Learning Styles

Visual or Spatial Learners

Suggest that students draw a diagram or sketch that illustrates how the characters might be positioned on stage for this sequence. Explain that in the theater, arranging the actors in the playing area is called "blocking" and that directors often use diagrams and sketches in rehearsals to block scenes.

how such knowledge of word origins can help them understand the meanings of both familiar and less familiar words.

plebeian: Latin *plebis*—the common people
modern—vulgar; common

patrician: Latin *patres*—fathers or senators
modern—noble, aristocratic

senate: Latin *senis*—old, an old man
modern—a legislative body

capital: Latin *caput*—head
modern—the city that is the seat of government of a state or country; in architecture, the uppermost part of a column

Use **Vocabulary Transparencies and Copymasters,** p. 73, for more exercises.

A lesson on researching word origins appears on p. 356 in the Pupil's Edition.

Reading and Analyzing

Active Reading

UNDERSTANDING SHAKESPEARE'S PLAYS

A Encourage students to use the side notes when reading long or difficult passages by asking them to look for answers to the following questions about Brutus' response to Cassius:

- What do *vexed* and *construe* mean?
  Answer: "troubled" and "interpret"
- At whom has Brutus been frowning?
  Answer: himself
- How has Brutus been acting toward his friends?
  Answers: He has been ignoring his friends.

Literary Analysis: CONFLICT

B Ask students what kind of conflict Brutus encounters at this point in the play, and then ask for the specific line that mentions this conflict.

Answer: Brutus is engaged in an internal conflict, which he mentions when he says "Brutus, with himself at war."

Literary Analysis: CHARACTER

C Ask students to explain what this passage implies about Brutus' most important value in life.

Possible Response: His most important value is honor.

GUIDE FOR READING

D **Possible Responses:** yes, if that person is a close friend; no.

E **Possible Responses:** yes; no

F **Possible Response:** Cassius is trying to tell Brutus that Brutus himself should be the leader of Rome, rather than Caesar.

Cassius. Brutus, I do observe you now of late;
I have not from your eyes that gentleness
And show of love as I was wont to have.
You bear too stubborn and too strange a hand
Over your friend that loves you.

A **Brutus.** Cassius,
Be not deceived. If I have veiled my look,
I turn the trouble of my countenance
Merely upon myself. Vexed I am
Of late with passions of some difference,
Conceptions only proper to myself,
Which give some soil, perhaps, to my behaviors;
But let not therefore my good friends be grieved
(Among which number, Cassius, be you one)
Nor construe any further my neglect
B Than that poor Brutus, with himself at war,
forgets the shows of love to other men.

Cassius. Then, Brutus, I have much mistook your passion,
By means whereof this breast of mine hath buried
Thoughts of great value, worthy cogitations.
Tell me, good Brutus, can you see your face?

Brutus. No, Cassius, for the eye sees not itself
But by reflection, by some other things.

Cassius. 'Tis just.
And it is very much lamented, Brutus,
That you have no such mirrors as will turn
Your hidden worthiness into your eye,
1 That you might see your shadow. I have heard
Where many of the best respect in Rome
(Except immortal Caesar), speaking of Brutus
And groaning underneath this age's yoke,
Have wished that noble Brutus had his eyes.

Brutus. Into what dangers would you lead me, Cassius,
That you would have me seek into myself
For that which is not in me?

Cassius. Therefore, good Brutus, be prepared to hear;
And since you know you cannot see yourself
So well as by reflection, I, your glass,
Will modestly discover to yourself
That of yourself which you yet know not of.
And be not jealous on me, gentle Brutus.

32–34 I do observe . . . to have: Lately I haven't seen the friendliness in your face that I used to see **(was wont to have).** Can you sometimes look into a friend's eyes and tell how he or she is feeling? **D**

38–47 I turn . . . other men: I have been frowning at myself, not at you. I have been troubled **(Vexed)** lately by mixed emotions **(passions of some difference).** They are personal matters that are, perhaps, marring my good manners. I hope my friends won't interpret **(construe)** my actions as anything more than my own private concerns. Do you ever avoid your friends when you have a lot on your mind? **E**

48–50 I have . . . cogitations: I have misunderstood your feelings. As a result, I have kept certain thoughts to myself.

55–62 it is . . . eyes: It is too bad you don't have a mirror that would show you your inner qualities **(hidden worthiness).** In fact, many respected citizens suffering under Caesar's rule **(this age's yoke)** have wished that Brutus could see how much better he is than Caesar. What is Cassius trying to tell Brutus? **F**

66–70 Therefore . . . not of: Listen, Brutus, since you cannot see yourself, I will be your mirror **(glass)** and show you what you truly are.

71 jealous on me: suspicious of me.

Teaching Options

Assessment Standardized Test Practice

WRITING AN EFFECTIVE COMPOSITION For some standardized tests, students will be asked to produce an effective composition that demonstrates a command of the conventions of spelling, capitalization, punctuation, grammar, usage, and sentence structure. To prepare students for exams such as the End-of-Course Examination, ask them to write an effective composition based on the following prompt:

Ralph Waldo Emerson, in his essay "Friendship," first published in 1841, states that "a friend is a person with whom [we] may think aloud. . . . But to most of us society shows not its face and eye, but its side and back." Write an essay in which you discuss how the quote from Emerson's essay applies to Cassius and Brutus and their conversation in lines 32–62.

[2] Were I a common laugher, or did use
To stale with ordinary oaths my love
To every new protester; if you know
That I do fawn on men and hug them hard,
And after scandal them; or if you know
That I profess myself in banqueting
To all the rout, then hold me dangerous.

[*Flourish and shout.*]

Brutus. What means this shouting? I do fear the people
Choose Caesar for their king.

Cassius. Ay, do you fear it?
Then must I think you would not have it so.

Brutus. I would not, Cassius, yet I love him well.
But wherefore do you hold me here so long?
What is it that you would impart to me?
If it be aught toward the general good,
Set honor in one eye and death i' the other,
And I will look on both indifferently;
[C] For let the gods so speed me as I love
The name of honor more than I fear death.

Cassius. I know that virtue to be in you, Brutus,
As well as I do know your outward favor.
Well, honor is the subject of my story.
I cannot tell what you and other men
Think of this life, but for my single self,
I had as lief not be as live to be
In awe of such a thing as I myself.
I was born free as Caesar, so were you;
We both have fed as well, and we can both
Endure the winter's cold as well as he.
For once, upon a raw and gusty day,
The troubled Tiber chafing with her shores,
Caesar said to me, "Dar'st thou, Cassius, now
Leap in with me into this angry flood
And swim to yonder point?" Upon the word,
Accoutered as I was, I plunged in
And bade him follow. So indeed he did.
The torrent roared, and we did buffet it
With lusty sinews, throwing it aside
And stemming it with hearts of controversy.
But ere we could arrive the point proposed,
Caesar cried, "Help me, Cassius, or I sink!"

72–78 Were I . . . dangerous: If you think I am a fool **(common laugher)** or someone who pretends to be the friend of everyone I meet, or if you believe that I show friendship and then talk evil about my friends **(scandal them)** behind their backs, or that I try to win the affections of the common people **(all the rout),** then consider me dangerous and don't trust me.

80–81 do you . . . it so: Imagine Cassius blurting out this line, maybe a little more eagerly than he had intended. He is trying to find a meaning in Brutus' words that may or may not be there.

85–87 If it . . . indifferently: If what you have in mind concerns the good of Rome **(the general good),** I would face either honor or death to do what must be done.

91 outward favor: physical appearance.

95–96 I had . . . I myself: I would rather not live, than to live in awe of someone no better than I am.

101 troubled . . . shores: The Tiber River was rising in the middle of a storm.

105 Accoutered: dressed.

107–109 we did . . . controversy: We fought the tide with strong muscles **(lusty sinews),** conquering it with our spirit of competition **(hearts of controversy).**

110 ere: before.

Customizing Instruction

Less Proficient Readers

1 Help students understand the meaning of "many of the best respect in Rome." Have students attempt a paraphrase of this line.

Possible Response: many of the most respected people in Rome

Students Acquiring English

2 Help students understand that Shakespeare often uses familiar words in unfamiliar ways. *Stale* and *scandal* are usually used in current English as adjectives, but in this passage these words are used as verbs: *stale* means "cheapen," and *scandal* means "slander."

RUBRIC

3 **Full Accomplishment** Composition reflects a full understanding of Emerson's quote and the characterization of Cassius and Brutus.

2 **Substantial Accomplishment** Composition reflects a general understanding of Emerson's quote and the characterization of Cassius and Brutus.

1 **Little or Partial Accomplishment** Composition reflects little understanding of Emerson's quote and the characterization of Cassius and Brutus.

Reading and Analyzing

Reading Skills and Strategies: EVALUATING

A Remind students that tone is the writer's attitude toward his or her subject or audience. Ask students what they think about Shakespeare's tone in Cassius' speech, and have them evaluate how Cassius' words about Caesar reveal Shakespeare's attitude toward Cassius.

Possible Response: Cassius' hostile, petty words about Caesar indicate that Shakespeare sees Cassius as a dismissive, angry, and petulant man.

Reading Skills and Strategies: PREDICTING

Ask students to predict whether Cassius will convince Brutus to join him and the other conspirators against Caesar.

Possible Responses: Brutus will turn against Caesar; his loyalty to Caesar will prevent him from doing Caesar any harm.

GUIDE FOR READING

B Cassius is speaking in an ironic tone.

I, as Aeneas, our great ancestor,
Did from the flames of Troy upon his shoulder
The old Anchises bear, so from the waves of Tiber
Did I the tired Caesar. And this man
Is now become a god, and Cassius is
A wretched creature and must bend his body
If Caesar carelessly but nod on him.
He had a fever when he was in Spain,
And when the fit was on him, I did mark
How he did shake. 'Tis true, this god did shake.
A His coward lips did from their color fly,
And that same eye whose bend doth awe the world
Did lose his luster. I did hear him groan.
Ay, and that tongue of his that bade the Romans
Mark him and write his speeches in their books,
Alas, it cried, "Give me some drink, Titinius,"
As a sick girl! Ye gods! it doth amaze me
A man of such a feeble temper should
So get the start of the majestic world
And bear the palm alone.

[*Shout. Flourish.*]

Brutus. Another general shout?
1 I do believe that these applauses are
For some new honors that are heaped on Caesar.

Cassius. Why, man, he doth bestride the narrow world
Like a Colossus, and we petty men
Walk under his huge legs and peep about
To find ourselves dishonorable graves.
Men at some time are masters of their fates.
The fault, dear Brutus, is not in our stars,
But in ourselves, that we are underlings.
"Brutus," and "Caesar." What should be in that "Caesar"?
Why should that name be sounded more than yours?
Write them together: yours is as fair a name.
Sound them, it doth become the mouth as well.
Weigh them, it is as heavy. Conjure with 'em:
"Brutus" will start a spirit as soon as "Caesar."
Now in the names of all the gods at once,
Upon what meat doth this our Caesar feed
That he is grown so great? Age, thou are shamed!
Rome, thou hast lost the breed of noble bloods!

112–115 I, as Aeneas . . . Caesar: Aeneas (ĭ-nē′ əs), the mythological founder of Rome, carried his father, Anchises (ăn-kī′ sēz), out of the burning city of Troy. Cassius says he did the same for Caesar when Caesar could no longer swim in the raging river.

117 bend his body: bow.

122 His coward . . . fly: His lips turned pale.

123 bend: glance.

125–131 that tongue . . . alone: The same tongue that has led Romans to memorize his speeches cried out in the tone of a sick girl. I'm amazed that such a weak man should get ahead of the rest of the world and appear as the victor **(bear the palm)** all by himself. (A palm leaf was a symbol of victory in war.)

132–134 Another . . . on Caesar: The shouts of the crowd are coming from offstage. Brutus is troubled by this cheering for Caesar, worried about where it might lead.

135–136 he doth . . . Colossus: Cassius compares Caesar to Colossus, the huge statue of the Greek god Apollo at Rhodes. The statue supposedly spanned the entrance to the harbor and was so high that ships could sail through the space between its legs. What is Cassius' tone in these lines? **B**

140–141 The fault . . . underlings: It is not the stars that have determined our fate; we are inferiors through our own fault.

146 Conjure: call up spirits.

150 Age . . . shamed: It is a shameful time **(Age)** in which to be living.

Teaching Options

Mini Lesson Speaking and Listening

DRAMATIC INTERPRETATION Prepare In Scene 2, Cassius sets out to persuade Brutus that Caesar is the wrong man to rule Rome. The dialogue between the two men consists mainly of Cassius' criticisms of Caesar. He is hoping to raise doubts in Brutus' mind about Caesar's growing power and ambition, and he ultimately hopes to persuade Brutus to join the conspirators. Brutus listens to Cassius, but responds cautiously to his harsh critique and dangerous suggestions.

Practice Have students interpret the conversation between Brutus and Cassius (lines 30–190) by rewriting the dialogue into contemporary prose. Students may find it helpful to work in groups, with some group members working on Cassius' lines and others working on Brutus'. They should focus on Cassius' attempts at persuasion as he tries to convince Brutus to see Caesar from the conspirators' point of view. Those rewriting Brutus' lines will want to duplicate his measured answers. Remind students that tone of voice, facial expressions, and body language convey meaning as well as words. Students should justify their choice of verbal and nonverbal performance techniques by referring to their interpretation of the text. Groups should perform their new, updated dialogues for the class.

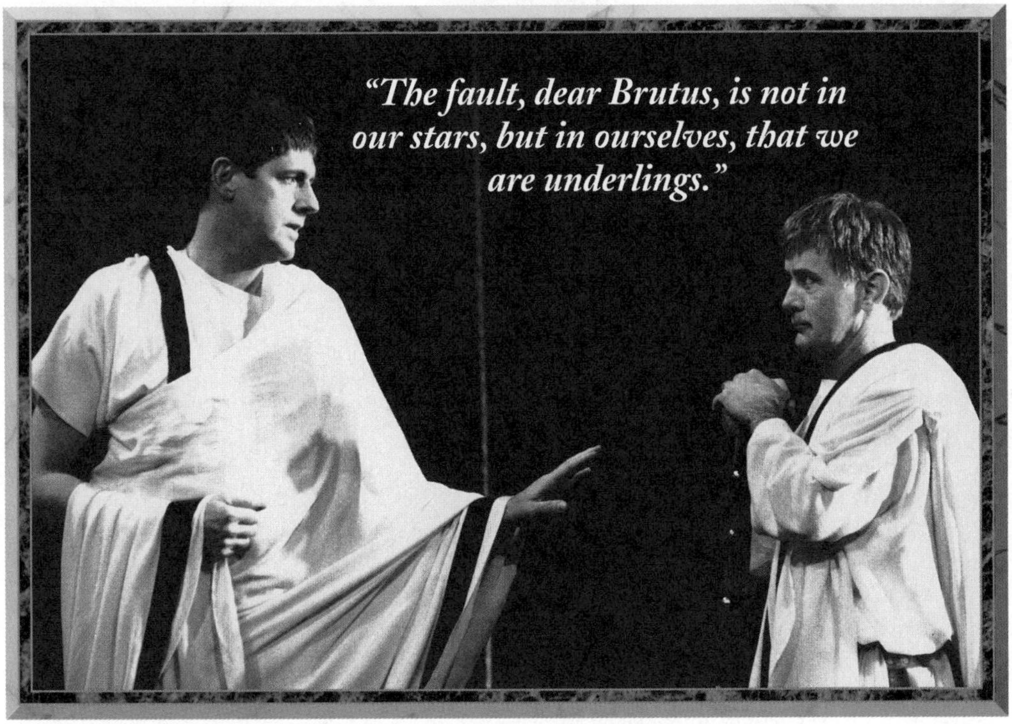
"The fault, dear Brutus, is not in our stars, but in ourselves, that we are underlings."

Edward Herrmann as Cassius and Martin Sheen as Brutus (New York Shakespeare Festival, 1988). Photo copyright © George E. Joseph.

When went there by an age since the great Flood
But it was famed with more than with one man?
When could they say (till now) that talked of Rome
That her wide walls encompassed but one man?
Now is it Rome indeed, and room enough,
When there is in it but one only man!
O, you and I have heard our fathers say
There was a Brutus once that would have brooked
The eternal devil to keep his state in Rome
As easily as a king.

2 **Brutus.** That you do love me I am nothing jealous.
What you would work me to, I have some aim.
How I have thought of this, and of these times,
I shall recount hereafter. For this present,
I would not (so with love I might entreat you)
Be any further moved. What you have said
I will consider; what you have to say

159–161 There was . . . a king: Cassius is referring to an ancestor of Brutus who drove the last of the ancient kings from Rome.

162 am nothing jealous: am sure.

163 have some aim: can guess.

164–167 How I have . . . moved: I will tell you later **(recount hereafter)** my thoughts about this topic. For now, I ask you as a friend not to try to convince me further.

Customizing Instruction

Less Proficient Readers

Cassius claims that although Caesar is treated like a king, he is really just an ordinary man. Ask students what examples of Caesar's mortality Cassius cites.

Possible Responses: Caesar couldn't complete a swim across the Tiber River and was pulled to safety by Cassius; Cassius saw Caesar shaking, groaning, and pale with a fever; Cassius claims Caesar is weak.

Students Acquiring English

1 Point out that *applauses* is used here as a plural noun ("these applauses") rather than as the more familiar singular noun (today we would say "this applause"). Have students offer synonyms for this word in line 133.

Possible Responses: cheers; shouts

Less Proficient Readers

2 Help students understand Brutus' response to Cassius' criticisms of Caesar.

Possible Response: Brutus says that he knows Cassius is his friend, that he has some idea that Cassius is plotting against Caesar, and that he needs time to think about the arguments Cassius has made against their leader.

Reading and Analyzing

Active Reading

UNDERSTANDING SHAKESPEARE'S PLAYS

(A) Draw students' attention to the italicized note that explains how the characters arrange themselves onstage. Make sure they understand that Shakespeare often has multiple conversations occurring at once, and explain that not all conversations are heard by all characters. Ask students why it is important that Antony and Caesar speak privately.

Possible Response: If Cassius were to hear that Caesar is suspicious of him, Cassius would probably treat Caesar differently and perhaps change his plans.

Literary Analysis: CHARACTER

(B) Have students explain how this passage characterizes Caesar, Antony, and Cassius at the same time.

Possible Response: Caesar's words show that he is a shrewd judge of character, while Antony's judgment shows that he is not very perceptive. Cassius is characterized by Caesar as "hungry" and "dangerous." Caesar's speech also reveals that he is extremely self-confident, perhaps even boastful.

Reading Skills and Strategies: QUESTIONING

Ask students to think about why Antony is the one who offered Caesar the crown. Encourage them to articulate any questions they might have about Antony's feelings toward Caesar.

Possible Responses: Why is Antony so loyal to Caesar? Does Antony hope to share in Caesar's power?

GUIDE FOR READING

(C) **Possible Response:** By saying that he would "rather be a villager" than live in Rome, Brutus hints that he might be prepared to take action against Caesar.

(D) Caesar believes that Cassius is a bitter, mocking person who is dangerous because Cassius will never be content as long as he sees a man greater than himself. He feels this way because Cassius does not enjoy entertainments and is lean and unsmiling.

(E) **Answer:** Caesar reveals that he is deaf in one ear.

I will with patience hear, and find a time
Both meet to hear and answer such high things.
Till then, my noble friend, chew upon this:
Brutus had rather be a villager
Than to repute himself a son of Rome
Under these hard conditions as this time
Is like to lay upon us.

Cassius. I am glad
That my weak words have struck but thus much show
Of fire from Brutus.

[*Voices and Music are heard approaching.*]

Brutus. The games are done, and Caesar is returning.

Cassius. As they pass by, pluck Casca by the sleeve,
And he will (after his sour fashion) tell you
What hath proceeded worthy note today.

[*Reenter* Caesar *and his train of followers.*]

1 **Brutus.** I will do so. But look you, Cassius!
The angry spot doth glow on Caesar's brow,
And all the rest look like a chidden train.
Calpurnia's cheek is pale, and Cicero
Looks with such ferret and such fiery eyes
As we have seen him in the Capitol,
Being crossed in conference by some senators.

Cassius. Casca will tell us what the matter is.

(A) [Caesar *looks at* Cassius *and turns to* Antony.]

Caesar. Antonius.

Antony. Caesar?

Caesar. Let me have men about me that are fat,
Sleek-headed men, and such as sleep o' nights.
Yond Cassius has a lean and hungry look;
He thinks too much, such men are dangerous.

Antony. Fear him not, Caesar, he's not dangerous.
He is a noble Roman, and well given.

(B) **Caesar.** Would he were fatter! But I fear him not.
Yet if my name were liable to fear,
I do not know the man I should avoid
So soon as that spare Cassius. He reads much,
He is a great observer, and he looks
Quite through the deeds of men. He loves no plays
As thou dost, Antony; he hears no music.

---

170 meet: appropriate.

173 repute himself: present himself as.

175 What do you think Brutus might be prepared to do? (C)

178 The private conversation is now over. Caesar and his admirers return, with the crowd following close behind.

181 worthy note: worth remembering.

184 chidden train: a group of followers who have been scolded.

185–188 Cicero . . . senators: Cicero was a highly respected senator. Brutus says he has the angry look of a **ferret** (a fierce little animal), the look he gets when other senators disagree with him at the Capitol.

190–214 Brutus and Cassius take Casca aside. The conversation Caesar has with Antony is not heard by any of the other characters around them.

197 well given: Antony says that Cassius, despite his appearance, is a supporter of Caesar.

200–203 I do not . . . of men: Caesar labels Cassius dangerous and, at the same time, one who can see through people and understand their secrets. Caesar makes a boast about himself.

Seldom he smiles, and smiles in such a sort
As if he mocked himself and scorned his spirit
That could be moved to smile at anything.
Such men as he be never at heart's ease
Whiles they behold a greater than themselves,
And therefore are they very dangerous.
I rather tell thee what is to be feared
Than what I fear, for always I am Caesar.
Come on my right hand, for this ear is deaf,
And tell me truly what thou think'st of him.

[*Trumpets sound. Exeunt* Caesar *and all his train except* Casca, *who stays behind.*]

Casca. You pulled me by the cloak. Would you speak with me?

Brutus. Ay, Casca. Tell us what hath chanced today
That Caesar looks so sad.

Casca. Why, you were with him, were you not?

Brutus. I should not then ask Casca what had chanced.

Casca. Why, there was a crown offered him; and being offered him, he put it by with the back of his hand, thus. And then the people fell a-shouting.

Brutus. What was the second noise for?

Casca. Why, for that too.

Cassius. They shouted thrice. What was the last cry for?

Casca. Why, for that too.

Brutus. Was the crown offered him thrice?

2 **Casca.** Ay, marry, was't! and he put it by thrice, every time gentler than other; and at every putting-by mine honest neighbors shouted.

Cassius. Who offered him the crown?

Casca. Why, Antony.

Brutus. Tell us the manner of it, gentle Casca.

Casca. I can as well be hanged as tell the manner of it.
3 It was mere foolery; I did not mark it. I saw Mark Antony offer him a crown—yet 'twas not a crown neither, 'twas one of these coronets—and, as I told you, he put it by once. But for all that, to my thinking, he would fain have had it. Then he offered

210 What is Caesar's opinion of Cassius? Why does he feel this way? **D**

213 What does Caesar reveal about himself in this line? **E**

215 Now only Brutus, Cassius, and Casca remain on stage.

216 hath chanced: has happened.

221 put it by: pushed it aside.

228 Ay, marry, was't: Yes, indeed, it was. *Marry* was a mild oath used in Shakespeare's time (but not in ancient Rome). The word means "by the Virgin Mary."

237 coronets: small crowns made out of laurel branches twisted together. A coronet was less of an honor than the kind of crown a king would wear.

239 fain: gladly.

Customizing Instruction

Students Acquiring English

1 Help students understand that "the angry spot" on Caesar's brow means that he was flushed with anger and his face was red because he was upset. Students might want to discuss whether their own faces ever show anger.

2 Explain that although we now use *gentle* to mean "docile" or "mild," the archaic meaning of *gentle* is "noble" or "well born." It is often used to show respect.

3 Explain that *mark* used in this context does not mean "to put a mark on," but rather "to notice or observe." Thus, Casca is saying that he didn't pay any attention to the "mere foolery" of Antony offering Caesar the crown.

Mini Lesson Speaking and Listening

STORYTELLING AND PANTOMIME Prepare Casca serves as storyteller in this scene when Cassius and Brutus ask him to recount what happened between the crowd and Caesar. Have students consider the times they have retold a story to a group of friends. What kind of gestures, vocal inflections, and expressions did they use?

Practice Have students in groups prepare the scene between Casca, Cassius, and Brutus (lines 215–294), concentrating on Casca's eyewitness account of what happened when Caesar was offered the crown and addressed the crowd. They should concentrate on Casca's version of the story and try to represent how he infuses his story with subjective commentary. Students playing Brutus and Cassius should pay attention to their concerned responses. As an added activity, you might invite the other group members to pantomime the events described here, showing that they understand the meaning of difficult phrases such as "put it by" ("waved it away") and "fell a-shouting" ("began to shout").

BLOCK SCHEDULING This activity is particularly well suited for longer class periods.

Reading and Analyzing

Active Reading

UNDERSTANDING SHAKESPEARE'S PLAYS

Have students note that Casca's speeches in this scene are in prose, whereas Cassius and Brutus speak in verse. Ask students why Shakespeare might have organized the dialogue this way.

Possible Response: Prose in Shakespeare's drama is used primarily for humorous or satirical scenes involving "low" characters; verse is used for loftier characters and themes. Although Casca is not "low-born," prose is still appropriate for his mocking description of the mob; prose also suits Casca's down-to-earth character.

Reading Skills and Strategies: CLARIFY

Ask students why they think Caesar offered to let the crowd cut his throat.

Possible Response: to curry favor with the mob; to dramatize his devotion to the common people.

it to him again; then he put it by again; but to my thinking, he was very loath to lay his fingers off it. And then he offered it the third time. He put it the third time by; and still as he refused it, the rabblement hooted, and clapped their chapped hands, and threw up their sweaty nightcaps, and uttered such a deal of stinking breath because Caesar refused the crown that it had, almost, choked Caesar; for he swounded and fell down at it. And for mine own part, I durst not laugh, for fear of opening my lips and receiving the bad air.

Cassius. But soft, I pray you. What, did Caesar swound?

Casca. He fell down in the market place and foamed at mouth and was speechless.

Brutus. 'Tis very like. He hath the falling sickness.

Cassius. No, Caesar hath not it; but you, and I,
And honest Casca, we have the falling sickness.

Casca. I know not what you mean by that, but I am sure Caesar fell down. If the tag-rag people did not clap him and hiss him, according as he pleased and displeased them, as they use to do the players in the theater, I am no true man.

Brutus. What said he when he came unto himself?

Casca. Marry, before he fell down, when he perceived the common herd was glad he refused the crown, he plucked me ope his doublet and offered them his throat to cut. An I had been a man of any occupation, if I would not have taken him at a word I would I might go to hell among the rogues. And so he fell. When he came to himself again, he said, if he had done or said anything amiss, he desired their worships to think it was his infirmity. Three or four wenches where I stood cried, "Alas, good soul!" and forgave him with all their hearts. But there's no heed to be taken of them. If Caesar had stabbed their mothers, they would have done no less.

Brutus. And after that, he came thus sad away?

Casca. Ay.

Cassius. Did Cicero say anything?

Casca. Ay, he spoke Greek.

241 loath: reluctant.

243 rabblement: unruly crowd.

248 swounded: fainted.

251 soft: Wait a moment.

252–254 There is some historical evidence that Caesar had epilepsy. In Shakespeare's time, this illness was known as the falling sickness (because someone having an epileptic seizure is likely to fall to the floor).

256 Cassius sarcastically uses the phrase **falling sickness** to refer to the tendency to bow down before Caesar.

265 ope his doublet: open his jacket.

266–268 An . . . rogues: If **(An)** I had been a worker with a proper tool, may I go to hell with the sinners **(rogues)** if I would not have done as he asked **(taken him at a word)**.

270 amiss: wrong.

271 infirmity: sickness.

272 wenches: common women.

Teaching Options

Assessment Standardized Test Practice

CHOOSING THE BEST SUMMARY For some standardized tests, students will be asked to choose the best summary of a passage. To provide students with some help in choosing the best summary, read aloud or write on the chalkboard the following question:

Which of the following statements best summarizes Act One, Scene Two?

A. A soothsayer warns Caesar to beware of the ides of March.

B. Mark Antony offers Caesar a crown three times, which Caesar refuses.

C. Cassius tries to persuade Brutus to join a conspiracy against Caesar; Brutus agrees to consider it but does not commit himself.

Lead students through the process of choosing the best summary. Consider each choice. Point out that, while all of the statements contain accurate information about the scene, the best summary should include the most important information. For that reason, **C** is the best choice.

Cassius. To what effect?

Casca. Nay, an I tell you that, I'll ne'er look you i' the face again. But those that understood him smiled at one another and shook their heads; but for mine own part, it was Greek to me. I could tell you more news, too. Marullus and Flavius, for pulling scarfs off Caesar's images, are put to silence. Fare you well. There was more foolery yet, if I could remember it.

Cassius. Will you sup with me tonight, Casca?

Casca. No, I am promised forth.

Cassius. Will you dine with me tomorrow?

1 **Casca.** Ay, if I be alive, and your mind hold, and your dinner worth eating.

Cassius. Good. I will expect you.

Casca. Do so. Farewell both.

[*Exit.*]

Brutus. What a blunt fellow is this grown to be!
He was quick mettle when he went to school.

Cassius. So is he now in execution
Of any bold or noble enterprise,
However he puts on this tardy form.
This rudeness is a sauce to his good wit,
Which gives men stomach to digest his words
With better appetite.

Brutus. And so it is. For this time I will leave you.
Tomorrow, if you please to speak with me,
I will come home to you; or if you will,
Come home to me, and I will wait for you.

Cassius. I will do so. Till then, think of the world.

[*Exit* Brutus.]

Well, Brutus, thou art noble; yet I see
Thy honorable mettle may be wrought
From that it is disposed. Therefore it is meet
That noble minds keep ever with their likes;
For who so firm that cannot be seduced?
Caesar doth bear me hard, but he loves Brutus.
If I were Brutus now and he were Cassius,
He should not humor me. I will this night,
2 In several hands, in at his windows throw,
As if they came from several citizens,
Writings, all tending to the great opinion

286 put to silence: This may mean that the two tribunes have been put to death or that they have been barred from public life.

289 I am promised forth: I have another appointment.

296 quick mettle: clever, intelligent.

297–302 So is . . . appetite: Cassius says that Casca can still be intelligent in carrying out an important project. He only pretends to be slow **(tardy).** His rude manner makes people more willing to accept **(digest)** the things he says.

308–322 Now Cassius is alone on stage. The thoughts he expresses in this speech are thoughts he would not want Brutus to know about.

309–310 Thy . . . disposed: Your honorable nature can be manipulated **(wrought)** into something not quite so honorable.

313 bear me hard: hold a grudge against me.

315 He should . . . me: I wouldn't let him get away with fooling me.

315–319 I will . . . his name: Cassius plans to leave messages at Brutus' home that appear to be from several people.

Customizing Instruction

Students Acquiring English

1 Explain to students that by the phrase "if your mind hold," Casca means "if your intention remains the same."

Less Proficient Readers

2 Draw students' attention to lines 315–319, and explain that this passage in Cassius' soliloquy is particularly difficult because it consists of a series of phrases, some of which disrupt a straightforward subject-verb-object word order. Help students unpack this sentence and rephrase Cassius' line into a more familiar sentence structure. Begin by asking students to pick out the subject ("I"), verb ("will throw"), and direct object ("writing," that is, letters).

Possible Response: Cassius: "I will this night, in several hands, in at his windows throw, as if they came from several citizens, writing, all tending to the great opinion that Rome hold of his name."

Paraphrase: "Tonight, I will throw through Brutus' windows letters that appear to be written by several people and that express the great opinion the people of Rome have of him."

Reading and Analyzing

Literary Analysis: IAMBIC PENTAMETER

A Point out that while the bulk of the dialogue is written in unrhymed iambic pentameter, the closing lines of the scene are rhymed. Shakespeare often used a rhymed couplet to provide a moment of closure and signal the end of a scene. Ask students whether these lines are written in iambic pentameter and have them sound out the accents and meter to check their comprehension.

Answer: Yes. "And **after this** let **Cae**sar **seat** him **sure** / For **we** will **shake** him, **or** worse **days** en**dure**."

Literary Analysis: BLANK VERSE

B Point out that while Casca spoke in prose in the preceding scene, he speaks in blank verse here. Ask students why Shakespeare might have changed Casca's speech from prosaic to poetic, and what impact this change makes on this scene.

Possible Response: Casca spoke in prose when he was engaged in cynical and sometimes humorous conversation; the subjects here—the wildness of nature, the threatening weather, and eventually the plot against Caesar—are more serious, so he uses more formal speech. Casca's tone becomes more sober through his use of blank verse, which contributes to the grave tone of the scene.

GUIDE FOR READING

C **Possible Response:** Cassius might do this to show that he does not fear any danger or any retribution from the gods.

That Rome holds of his name; wherein obscurely
Caesar's ambition shall be glanced at.
A And after this let Caesar seat him sure,
For we will shake him, or worse days endure.
[*Exit.*]

322 **we will . . . endure:** We will remove Caesar from his high position or suffer the consequences.

B SCENE 3 A STREET IN ROME.

It is the night of March 14. Amid violent thunder and lightning, a terrified Casca fears that the storm and other omens predict terrible events to come. Cassius interprets the storm as a sign that Caesar must be overthrown. Cassius and Casca agree that Caesar's rise to power must be stopped by any means. Cinna, another plotter, enters, and they discuss how to persuade Brutus to follow their plan.

[*Thunder and lightning. Enter, from opposite sides,* Casca, *with his sword drawn, and* Cicero.]

Cicero. Good even, Casca. Brought you Caesar home?
Why are you breathless? and why stare you so?

Casca. Are not you moved when all the sway of earth
Shakes like a thing unfirm? O Cicero,
I have seen tempests when the scolding winds
Have rived the knotty oaks, and I have seen
The ambitious ocean swell and rage and foam
To be exalted with the threat'ning clouds;
But never till tonight, never till now,
Did I go through a tempest dropping fire.
Either there is a civil strife in heaven,
Or else the world, too saucy with the gods,
Incenses them to send destruction.

Cicero. Why, saw you anything more wonderful?

Casca. A common slave—you know him well by sight—
Held up his left hand, which did flame and burn
Like twenty torches joined; and yet his hand,
Not sensible of fire, remained unscorched.
Besides—I ha' not since put up my sword—
Against the Capitol I met a lion,
Who glared upon me, and went surly by
1 Without annoying me. And there were drawn
2 Upon a heap a hundred ghastly women,

3 **sway of earth:** the natural order of things.

5 **tempests:** storms.

6 **rived:** torn.

8 **To be exalted with:** to raise themselves to the level of.

11–13 **Either . . . destruction:** Such a terrible storm could be caused by only two things—a civil war **(strife)** in heaven or angry gods destroying the world.

14 **saw . . . wonderful:** Did you see anything else that was strange?

18 **Not sensible of fire:** not feeling the fire.

19–20 **I ha' not . . . lion:** I haven't put my sword back into its scabbard since I saw a lion at the Capitol building.

22–23 **drawn / Upon:** huddled together.

Teaching Options

Mini Lesson: Speaking and Listening

DRAMATIC READING: INSTRUCTION **Prepare** Help students prepare a dramatic presentation based upon Cicero's, Casca's, and Cassius' discussion about how the natural order of things is disturbed. Have students work in cooperative groups to list characteristics of Cicero, Casca, and Cassius and how these characters interpret the storm. Then have students describe the qualities of a presentation that would portray these characteristics and interpretations. Students should consider Casca's voice: its tone, pitch, volume, and speed. Remind them to justify their choice of verbal and nonverbal performance techniques by referring to their interpretation of the text. Have them also consider whether Casca looks Cassius in the eye as he speaks.

Present Student groups can decide how they will present the dramatic reading. Students who are audience members should evaluate how the performance increases their understanding and appreciation of these characters in the play.

BLOCK SCHEDULING This activity is particularly well suited for longer class periods.

Transformed with their fear, who swore they saw
Men, all in fire, walk up and down the streets.
And yesterday the bird of night did sit
Even at noonday upon the market place,
Hooting and shrieking. When these prodigies
Do so conjointly meet, let not men say,
"These are their reasons, they are natural,"
For I believe they are portentous things
Unto the climate that they point upon.

Cicero. Indeed it is a strange-disposed time.
But men may construe things after their fashion,
Clean from the purpose of the things themselves.
Comes Caesar to the Capitol tomorrow?

Casca. He doth, for he did bid Antonius
Send word to you he would be there tomorrow.

Cicero. Good night then, Casca. This disturbed sky
Is not to walk in.

Casca. Farewell, Cicero.

[*Exit* Cicero.]

[*Enter* Cassius.]

Cassius. Who's there?

Casca. A Roman.

Cassius. Casca, by your voice.

Casca. Your ear is good. Cassius, what night is this!

Cassius. A very pleasing night to honest men.

Casca. Who ever knew the heavens menace so?

Cassius. Those that have known the earth so full of faults.
For my part, I have walked about the streets,
Submitting me unto the perilous night,
And, thus unbraced, Casca, as you see,
Have bared my bosom to the thunder-stone;
And when the cross blue lightning seemed to open
The breast of heaven, I did present myself
Even in the aim and very flash of it.

Casca. But wherefore did you so much tempt the heavens?
It is the part of men to fear and tremble
When the most mighty gods by tokens send
Such dreadful heralds to astonish us.

26 bird of night: the owl, usually seen only at night.

28–32 When these . . . upon: When strange events **(prodigies)** like these happen at the same time **(conjointly meet),** no one should say there are natural explanations for them. I believe they are bad omens **(portentous things)** for the place where they happen.

33–35 Indeed . . . themselves: Cicero does not accept Casca's superstitious explanation of events. He agrees that the times are strange. But he says people can interpret events the way they want to, no matter what actually causes the events.

41 Who's there?: Cassius probably has his sword out. Remember, with no light other than moonlight, it could be dangerous to come upon a stranger in the street.

46–52 For my . . . flash of it: Cassius brags that he offered himself to the dangerous night, with his coat open **(unbraced),** exposing his chest to the thunder and lightning. Why might he do this? C

54–56 It is . . . astonish us: Men are supposed to tremble when the gods use signs **(tokens)** to send frightening messengers **(heralds)** to scare us.

Customizing Instruction

Students Acquiring English

1 Tell students that in Shakespeare's time, the word *annoying* had a stronger meaning than it has now; in this context, it means "physically harming."

2 Explain to students that although *ghastly* most commonly means "horrible" or "terrifying," it also means "resembling a ghost" or "white-faced." Ask students what Casca is probably saying about the women.

Possible Response: They are pale with fear.

Less Proficient Readers

Make sure students understand that even though everyone else seems anxious and worried about the weather and unnatural occurrences, Cassius embraces the storm and challenges heaven by baring his chest to the fierce elements. Ask students what they think of Cassius' behavior.

Possible Response: He is tempting Fate by being overconfident and arrogant.

Then ask how Casca responds to Cassius' bold behavior.

Possible Response: Casca advises Cassius to curb his pride and to heed the Gods' warnings.

Reading and Analyzing

Reading Skills and Strategies: EVALUATE

A Ask students how skillful Cassius is in his persuasion of Casca. Have students evaluate Cassius' argument.

Possible Response: Cassius is quite skillful because he plays on Casca's superstitious nature by seeming to agree that the portents are significant; he tries to persuade him, however, that the omens really mean that Caesar must be overthrown.

Literary Analysis: CONFLICT

B Ask students what impending activity becomes representative of Cassius' conflict with Caesar.

Possible Response: Caesar is going to be crowned king and Cassius does not want to be ruled by a king.

GUIDE FOR READING

C **Answer:** Cassius refers to Caesar.

D Most students will say that Cassius seems too hungry for power at this point to commit suicide before Caesar is deposed.

"this dreadful night that thunders, lightens, opens graves, and roars"

Edward Herrmann as Cassius (New York Shakespeare Festival, 1988).
Photo copyright © George E. Joseph.

Teaching Options

Mini Lesson: Viewing and Representing

REPRESENTING THE SUPERNATURAL Prepare Discuss with students the various images presented of the scene on page 709 and have them talk about how Shakespeare creates an atmosphere of foreboding by using such a tumultuous setting. By using the storm and its attendant "unnatural" events, Shakespeare builds suspense as he enlarges the plans of the conspirators.

Practice Have students work in groups and make lists of the different occurrences and images described in this scene, such as the owl that flew in daylight, the slave who suffered no ill effects from his flaming hand, and the lion that walked through the Capitol without attacking anyone. Encourage students to visualize the setting and then have them illustrate this scene using photographs, original drawings and sketches, pictures from magazines, or paintings. Encourage students to try to capture the overall atmosphere of the scene. To that end, they should think about the darkness of the night, the rain and lightning, and the apparently supernatural phenomena. Students might also want to include images that are not specifically mentioned in the play but that fit their interpretation of the setting and feel of the scene.

(A) **Cassius.** You are dull, Casca, and those sparks of life
That should be in a Roman you do want,
Or else you use not. You look pale, and gaze,
And put on fear, and cast yourself in wonder,
To see the strange impatience of the heavens.
But if you would consider the true cause
Why all these fires, why all these gliding ghosts,
Why birds and beasts, from quality and kind;
Why old men fool and children calculate;
[1] Why all these things change from their ordinance,
Their natures, and preformed faculties,
To monstrous quality, why, you shall find
That heaven hath infused them with these spirits
To make them instruments of fear and warning
Unto some monstrous state.
Now could I, Casca, name to thee a man
Most like this dreadful night
That thunders, lightens, opens graves, and roars
As doth the lion in the Capitol;
A man no mightier than thyself or me
In personal action, yet prodigious grown
And fearful, as these strange eruptions are.

Casca. 'Tis Caesar that you mean. Is it not, Cassius?

Cassius. Let it be who it is. For Romans now
[2] Have thews and limbs like to their ancestors.
But woe the while! our fathers' minds are dead,
And we are governed with our mothers' spirits,
Our yoke and sufferance show us womanish.

(B) **Casca.** Indeed, they say the senators tomorrow
Mean to establish Caesar as king,
And he shall wear his crown by sea and land
In every place save here in Italy.

Cassius. I know where I will wear this dagger then;
Cassius from bondage will deliver Cassius.
Therein, ye gods, you make the weak most strong;
Therein, ye gods, you tyrants do defeat.
Nor stony tower, nor walls of beaten brass,
Nor airless dungeon, nor strong links of iron,
[3] Can be retentive to the strength of spirit;
But life, being weary of these worldly bars,
Never lacks power to dismiss itself.
If I know this, know all the world besides,

58 want: lack.

62–71 Cassius insists that heaven has brought about such things as birds and animals that change their natures **(from quality and kind)** and children who predict the future **(calculate)**—all these beings that act unnaturally **(change from their ordinance / Their natures, and preformed faculties).** Heaven has done all this, he says, to warn the Romans of an evil condition that they should correct.

77 prodigious grown: become enormous and threatening. To whom does Cassius refer in lines 72–78? (C)

80–84 Romans . . . womanish: Modern Romans have muscles **(thews)** and limbs like our ancestors, but we have the minds of our mothers, not our fathers. Our acceptance of a dictator **(yoke and sufferance)** shows us to be like women, not like men. (In Shakespeare's time—and in ancient Rome—women were considered weak creatures.)

87–88 he shall . . . Italy: The senators will make Caesar the king of all Roman territories except **(save)** Rome itself **(Italy)**, since Romans would never let their own land be ruled by a king.

89–90 I know . . . deliver Cassius: I will free myself from slavery **(bondage)** by killing myself **(wear this dagger).**

91–97 Cassius shouts these lines toward the sky, trying to be heard over the thunder. Only through suicide, he says angrily, do the gods make the weak strong and able to defeat tyrants. The strong spirit cannot be imprisoned by tower, metal walls, dungeons, or iron chains. The reason is that one can always commit suicide **(life . . . Never lacks power to dismiss itself).** Do you think Cassius would really kill himself? (D)

Customizing Instruction

Students Acquiring English

1 Tell students that *ordinance* in this case means "established order" or "proper function."

2 Explain to students that *thews* means "sinews" or "muscles." Have students try to paraphrase lines 80–81, helping them with the phrase "like to" if they have difficulty.
Possible Response: "For Romans these days have muscles and limbs like their ancestors.'"

3 Help students understand that in current English, the first *nor* in this series would be *neither*. The phrase *can be retentive to* may cause students difficulty; here it means "can imprison."

Reading and Analyzing

Literary Analysis: FIGURATIVE LANGUAGE

A Have students explain the two metaphors in this passage and tell who is compared to what.

Possible Responses: Caesar is compared to a wolf and the Romans to sheep in the first metaphor. In the second, Caesar is compared to a lion and the Romans are compared to female deer. Both metaphors suggest that Caesar preys on the weakness of the Romans.

Literary Analysis: THEME

Remind students that one of the themes of the play is the dilemma of those who have good intentions and convince themselves that noble ideals justify violent means. Ask students why the conspirators are careful to use words such as *noble* and *honorable* when discussing their plot against Caesar, especially when they are speaking to Brutus.

Possible Response: By presenting their plot as a moral and ethical act, they hope to convince Brutus and probably themselves that they are performing a good deed, rather than an act of murderous treason.

GUIDE FOR READING

B **Possible Responses:** Yes, because he has already indicated in the previous scene that he agrees with Cassius; no, because Brutus loves Caesar too much.

C **Possible Responses:** Murder is still murder, whatever the reputation of the person who commits the crime; some murder is justified.

That part of tyranny that I do bear
I can shake off at pleasure.

[*Thunder still.*]

Casca. So can I.
So every bondman in his own hand bears
The power to cancel his captivity.

A **1** **Cassius.** And why should Caesar be a tyrant then?
Poor man! I know he would not be a wolf
But that he sees the Romans are but sheep;
He were no lion, were not Romans hinds.
Those that with haste will make a mighty fire
Begin it with weak straws. What trash is Rome,
What rubbish and what offal, when it serves
For the base matter to illuminate
So vile a thing as Caesar! But, O grief,
Where hast thou led me? I, perhaps, speak this
Before a willing bondman. Then I know
My answer must be made. But I am armed,
And dangers are to me indifferent.

Casca. You speak to Casca, and to such a man
That is no fleering telltale. Hold, my hand.
Be factious for redress of all these griefs,
And I will set this foot of mine as far
As who goes farthest.

Cassius. There's a bargain made.
Now know you, Casca, I have moved already
Some certain of the noblest-minded Romans
To undergo with me an enterprise
Of honorable-dangerous consequence;
And I do know, by this they stay for me
In Pompey's Porch; for now, this fearful night,
There is no stir or walking in the streets,
And the complexion of the element
In favor's like the work we have in hand,
Most bloody, fiery, and most terrible.

[*Enter* Cinna.]

2 **Casca.** Stand close awhile, for here comes one in haste.

Cassius. 'Tis Cinna. I do know him by his gait.
He is a friend. Cinna, where haste you so?

3 **Cinna.** To find out you. Who's that? Metellus Cimber?

Cassius. No, it is Casca, one incorporate

103–111 And why . . . as Caesar: Cassius goes into a tirade about Caesar, saying things for which he could be put to death. He says the only reason for Caesar's strength is the weakness of the Romans. They are **hinds** (female deer) and trash **(offal)** for allowing such a person as Caesar to come to power.

111–113 But, O . . . bondman: Cassius pretends that he did not mean to speak so freely. Maybe, he says, he has been speaking to a happy slave **(willing bondman)** of Caesar.

117 fleering telltale: sneering tattletale.

118–120 Be factious . . . farthest: Form a group, or faction, to correct **(redress)** these wrongs, and I will go as far as any other man.

125–126 by this . . . Porch: Right now, they wait **(stay)** for me at the entrance to the theater Pompey built.

128–130 the complexion . . . terrible: The sky **(element)** looks like the work we have ahead of us—bloody, full of fire, and terrible.

132 gait: manner of walking.

135–136 it is . . . stayed for: This is Casca, who is now part of our plan **(incorporate / To our attempts).** Are they waiting for me?

Teaching Options

Mini Lesson Grammar

AVOIDING DOUBLE NEGATIVES Put the sentence "John doesn't like no bicycles with bells on them" on the chalkboard. Explain that a statement in which a second negative word unnecessarily repeats a negative already in the statement contains a double negative. In addition to *no,* students should look for such words as *not, nothing, nobody,* and *never.* Also remind them not to mix negative adverbs like *hardly, scarcely,* and *barely* with another negative word or phrase. Although sentences that say "no" in two different ways may make sense and be emphatic, they are nonstandard English and should be revised to eliminate the double negative construction.

(Note: Students may find examples of the double negative in Shakespeare or other literature from the Renaissance or earlier. This was not considered incorrect usage at the time; it was not until the 18th century that grammarians began to object to this grammatical form in standard English.)

Practice Have students revise the following sentences to eliminate the double negative constructions. Have students put their revised sentences on the board.

To our attempts. Am I not stayed for, Cinna?

Cinna. I am glad on't. What a fearful night is this!
There's two or three of us have seen strange sights.

Cassius. Am I not stayed for? Tell me.

Cinna. Yes, you are.
O Cassius, if you could
But win the noble Brutus to our party—

Cassius. Be you content. Good Cinna, take this paper
And look you lay it in the praetor's chair,
Where Brutus may but find it, and throw this
In at his window. Set this up with wax
Upon old Brutus' statue. All this done,
Repair to Pompey's Porch, where you shall find us.
4 Is Decius Brutus and Trebonius there?

Cinna. All but Metellus Cimber, and he's gone
To seek you at your house. Well, I will hie
And so bestow these papers as you bade me.

Cassius. That done, repair to Pompey's Theater.

[*Exit* Cinna.]

Come, Casca, you and I will yet ere day
See Brutus at his house. Three parts of him
Is ours already, and the man entire
Upon the next encounter yields him ours.

Casca. O, he sits high in all the people's hearts,
And that which would appear offense in us,
His countenance, like richest alchemy,
Will change to virtue and to worthiness.

Cassius. Him and his worth and our great need of him
You have right well conceited. Let us go,
For it is after midnight, and ere day
We will awake him and be sure of him.

[*Exeunt.*]

142–146 Cassius gives Cinna several notes addressed to Brutus, along with instructions about where each note should be placed.

143 lay it . . . chair: Place this paper in the judge's **(praetor's)** seat.

150–151 I will . . . bade me: I'll hurry **(hie)** to place **(bestow)** these papers as you instructed me.

154–156 Three parts . . . yields him ours: We've already won over three parts of Brutus. The next time we meet him, he will be ours completely. Do you think Brutus will fall for this trick? **B**

157–160 he sits . . . worthiness: The people love Brutus. What would seem offensive if we did it will, like magic **(alchemy)**, become good and worthy because of his involvement. Do you agree with Casca? **C**

162 conceited: judged.

Customizing Instruction

Less Proficient Readers

1 Help students understand that Cassius' comments about Caesar—that he is a wolf among sheep and a lion among deer—are meant as insults to Caesar's power. Have students try to explain why Cassius' metaphors are slurs against Caesar.
Possible Responses: He is saying Caesar's power comes not from Caesar's own strength but from the weakness of those he rules; Cassius' characterization of Caesar cheapens Caesar's power.

Students Acquiring English

2 Explain that *close* here may mean "concealed." Cassius wants Casca to stay hidden until they see who is approaching.

3 Clarify for students that "to find you out" here means "to find you." Modern English often uses this phrase idiomatically to mean "to get to the truth" or even "to catch someone in a lie."

4 Point out to students the lack of subject-verb agreement in lines 148 ("Is Decius Brutus and Trebonius there?") and 154–55 ("Three parts of him is ours already"), and explain that Shakespeare is using what would now be nonstandard usage when he uses singular verbs with plural subjects. Help students recast these lines using current standard English grammar.
Possible Responses: "Are Decius Brutus and Trebonius there?"; "Three parts of him are ours already."

1. Jane couldn't hardly wait to get to the party and see her best friend.
Possible Response: Jane could hardly wait to get to the party and see her best friend.
2. Some dogs don't never bark when the mail arrives.
Possible Response: Some dogs don't ever bark when the mail arrives.
3. John doesn't need nobody to help him with the yard work.
Possible Response: John doesn't need anybody to help him with the yard work.
4. Not nobody can prevent the hurricane from coming ashore.
Possible Response: Nobody can prevent the hurricane from coming ashore.
5. Shelly did not want to buy no dress.
Possible Response: Shelly did not want to buy a dress.

Use **Grammar Transparencies and Copymasters,** p. 160, for more exercises.

Use McDougal Littell's ***Language Network,*** Chapter 9, for more instruction in avoiding double negatives.

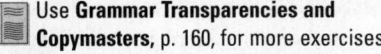

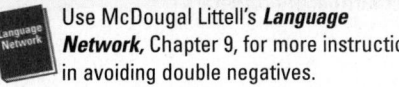

View and Compare

Possible Responses: Jack Medley as Caesar looks very stiff and square, both in his costume and physical bearing. This suggests a very formal and rigid personality. Louis Calhern as Caesar is dressed in flowing robes and looks very regal and proud, aware of his own impressive appearance. This is suggestive of Caesar's great ego and ambition. John McMartin as Caesar has an interesting expression on his face and the photo gives us a close view of his face, making Caesar look more human and natural.

VIEW AND COMPARE

What do these images all suggest about the character of Julius Caesar? What sets them apart? Study the posture, facial expressions, and costuming.

John McMartin as Caesar (New York Shakespeare Festival, 1988). Photo copyright © George E. Joseph.

Louis Calhern as Caesar (MGM film, 1953). Photofest.

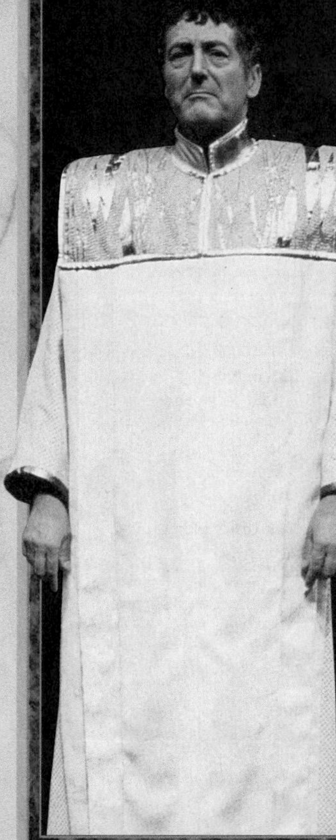

Jack Medley as Caesar (Stratford Festival, 1982). Photo by Robert C. Ragsdale.

Teaching Options

Assessment Informal Assessment

Have students write a summary of Act One in blank verse. Advise students to write their summaries in prose first and then to review the discussion of blank verse and iambic pentameter.

RUBRIC

3 Full Accomplishment Students accurately convey the main idea and supporting details of the first act and produce blank verse in lines of correct iambic pentameter.

2 Substantial Accomplishment Students accurately convey the main idea and some supporting details and produce blank verse lines in generally correct iambic pentameter.

1 Little or Partial Accomplishment Students convey little sense of the main idea and offer few or incorrect supporting details and produce incorrect lines of iambic pentameter.

Connect to the Literature

1. **What Do You Think?** Write one or two adjectives that describe each of these men: Cassius, Brutus, Casca, Antony, and Caesar.

Comprehension Check
- What warning does the Soothsayer give Caesar?
- What does Casca report happened when Mark Antony offered Caesar the crown?
- What does Cassius hope to convince Brutus to do?

Think Critically

2. In Act One, Scene 1, what seems to be tribunes' and commoners' attitudes toward one another? Cite evidence from the scene to support your opinion.
3. What is your opinion of Caesar in this act?

   THINK ABOUT
   - his actions and appearance
   - his remarks about himself and others
   - other characters' remarks about him
4. Why do you think Cassius wants Brutus to join the conspiracy? Do you think Brutus will join? Explain.
5. Who do you think is the most important character in the play so far? Support your answer.
6. What **humor** did you find in Act One? Why do you think Shakespeare included it?
7. ACTIVE READING UNDERSTANDING SHAKESPEARE'S PLAYS
   Review the chart begun in your READER'S NOTEBOOK. In which column did you put the **characters** who appear in Act One, Scene 1? Continue to add to and revise your chart as you read the rest of the play.

Extend Interpretations

8. **Critic's Corner** The editors of the Folger Library edition of *Julius Caesar* point out that Elizabethans "did not have our modern distaste for dictators, . . . and they admired forceful and successful leaders like Caesar." Do you see evidence of this admiration in Act One of the play? Would you say that Shakespeare himself admires Julius Caesar? Cite details from Act One to support your opinions.
9. **Connect to Life** Based on the details in Act One, what do you think Shakespeare's opinion would be of democracy as practiced in America today?

Literary Analysis

BLANK VERSE **Blank verse** is unrhymed lines of poetry written in **iambic pentameter,** meaning that the lines generally contain five unstressed syllables each followed by a stressed syllable. This makes 10 syllables in each line.

Upon what meat doth this our Caesar feed

Playwrights like Shakespeare who wrote their plays in verse chose blank verse because, more than other verse forms, it approximates the sound of spoken English. However, Shakespeare's plays are not completely written in blank verse. Sometimes he has characters speak in prose, and occasionally he uses rhymed lines of iambic pentameter to stress a point or to signal actors that a scene or act is about to end.

Paired Activity With a partner, choose and copy a blank-verse passage from Act One of *Julius Caesar,* marking its unstressed (˘) and stressed (′) syllables to show that it is written in blank verse. How well do you think the passage captures the sound of spoken English?

Now examine the use of prose in Act One, Scene 1. Why do you think Shakespeare had the commoners speak in prose?

GUIDING STUDENT RESPONSE

Connect to the Literature

1. **What Do You Think?**
   Cassius: sarcastic, devious; Brutus: naive, patriotic; Casca: ironic, superstitious; Antony: loyal, noble; Caesar: arrogant, proud

Comprehension Check
- Beware the ides of March.
- Caesar refused three times (and then had an epileptic seizure).
- to join the conspirators in their plot to kill Caesar

Use Selection Quiz
Unit Four Resource Book, p. 64.

Think Critically

2. They don't like each other. The tribunes are scornful of the commoners and their support of Caesar, and they try to squelch the workers' celebration of Caesar's victories. The commoners poke fun at the tribunes, showing little respect for their authority.
3. Possible Response: Caesar is egotistical, overconfident, perceptive, intelligent, hypercritical, superstitious, charismatic, and inspires strong love and hate; he rules like a dictator, but he is shrewd enough not to seem ambitious.
4. Possible Responses: Cassius wants Brutus to join the side of the conspirators because he thinks Brutus' good reputation will lend legitimacy to the assassination. Brutus won't join because he is loyal to Caesar and loves him; Brutus will join because Cassius has planted serious doubts about Caesar's desire to seize power.
5. Possible Responses: Cassius—he has the greatest number of lines in Act One and is the driving force behind the conspiracy against Caesar; Brutus—his support of the conspirators will be critical; Caesar—he is the focus of the action.
6. Possible Responses: The first scene of Act One in which the commoners make puns and tease the tribunes; Shakespeare may have wanted to offer the comic moments as relief from the serious issues in the play.
7. Characters may change their allegiances as the play progresses, so students may need to switch characters to different columns.

Extend Interpretations

Critic's Corner Possible Responses: Caesar looks powerful but not tyrannical, and his refusal of the crown paints him as smart and deferential to the citizens, which are positive qualities; Caesar looks weak and foolish with his fainting, half-deafness and pandering to the crowd.

Connect to Life Possible Response: Shakespeare would approve of our democracy because it prevents leaders from accruing too much power and checks their potential tyrannical impulses; Shakespeare would find our democracy lacking in strong, central leaders who are encouraged to rule with a certain amount of autonomy and power.

Literary Analysis

Blank Verse Encourage students to pick passages they understand and to look up any unfamiliar words or phrases. Have them read the passage aloud to analyze the cadence of the evocative rhythms. The commoners speak in prose, because a more ordinary prosaic style is appropriate to more ordinary, less lofty characters.

Objectives

1. understand **blank verse (Literary Analysis)**
2. understand Shakespeare's plays **(Active Reading)**

TEACHING THE LITERATURE

Reading and Analyzing

Reading Skills and Strategies: PREVIEW

Act Two establishes the rising action or complications of the play. In this act, characters try to resolve the conflict. Have students examine the pictures and consider the called-out quotations. Discuss with students the Build Background feature on p. 689, and ask them to predict how the historical facts about Julius Caesar will be developed in Act Two. Before students begin reading, give them a brief summary of Act Two.

Active Reading

UNDERSTANDING SHAKESPEARE'S PLAYS

A A soliloquy (a speech made by a character when he or she is alone onstage) is a convention, or technique, used to reveal a character's inner thoughts. Discuss with students what Brutus reveals in this soliloquy.

Possible Response: Brutus reveals that although Caesar has not been too tyrannical up to this point, he is worried that Caesar may become a tyrant if he is made king.

Literary Analysis

UNDERSTANDING BLANK VERSE

One of the qualities that makes blank verse such a versatile form is its suitability for run-on lines—lines that do not hold a complete thought, but run over into the next line and perhaps others. Using this method, the poet can employ a more complex sentence structure and unify portions of the verse. Have students find examples of run-on lines in Act Two.

Possible Responses: (Scene 1, lines 15–17); (Scene 1, lines 18–19).

GUIDE FOR READING

B **Possible Response:** Brutus thinks that Caesar may forget lowly people and abuse his power. Caesar may scorn the "base degrees" once he is made king.

ACT TWO

SCENE 1 BRUTUS' ORCHARD IN ROME.

It is a few hours before dawn on March 15—the ides of March. Brutus, unable to sleep, walks in his garden. He faces a crucial decision: either to continue living under the tyranny of Caesar or to kill Caesar and thus end his rule. While considering the problem, Brutus receives an anonymous letter (from Cassius) suggesting that Brutus take action against Caesar. Shortly after, Cassius and the conspirators visit Brutus, and they all agree to assassinate Caesar that day.

Brutus. What, Lucius, ho!
I cannot by the progress of the stars
Give guess how near to day. Lucius, I say!
I would it were my fault to sleep so soundly.
When, Lucius, when? Awake, I say! What, Lucius!

[*Enter* Lucius *from the house.*]

Lucius. Called you, my lord?

Brutus. Get me a taper in my study, Lucius.
When it is lighted, come and call me here.

Lucius. I will, my lord.

[*Exit.*]

[Brutus *returns to his brooding.*]

Brutus. It must be by his death; and for my part,
I know no personal cause to spurn at him,
But for the general. He would be crowned.
How that might change his nature, there's the question.
A It is the bright day that brings forth the adder,
And that craves wary walking. Crown him that,
1 And then I grant we put a sting in him
That at his will he may do danger with.

2–3 I cannot . . . day: There are no stars in the sky to tell me how near it is to morning.

4 I would . . . soundly: I wish I could sleep so soundly.

7 taper: candle.

10–34 Brutus, alone again, thinks out loud about the problem of Caesar. In general, Brutus fears that Caesar will become too powerful.

10–12 It must . . . general: It can only be solved by Caesar's death. I have no personal grudge against him; I'm thinking only of the general welfare.

14–15 It is . . . walking: Sunshine brings out the poisonous snake **(adder),** so walk carefully.

LESSON RESOURCES

UNIT FOUR RESOURCE BOOK, pp. 65–68

ASSESSMENT RESOURCES

Formal Assessment, pp. 125–126

Teacher's Guide to Assessment and Portfolio Use

Test Generator

SKILLS TRANSPARENCIES AND COPYMASTERS

Literary Analysis
- Shakespearean Drama I and II, T18, T19 (for Activity, p. 735)

Reading and Critical Thinking
- Organizational Chart: Horizontal, T51 (for Reader's Notebook, p. 735)

Grammar
- Modifiers: *Good* and *Well,* C158 (for Mini Lesson, p. 720)

Vocabulary
- Word Origins, C73 (for Mini Lesson, p. 724)

Communications
- Dramatic Reading, T12 (for Mini Lesson, p. 715)
- Verbal Strategies, T14 (for Mini Lesson, p. 715)

INTEGRATED TECHNOLOGY

Video: Literature in Performance
- *Julius Caesar.* See **Video Resource Book**, pp. 25–30.

Visit our website: www.mcdougallittell.com

The abuse of greatness is when it disjoins
Remorse from power. And to speak truth of Caesar,
I have not known when his affections swayed
More than his reason. But 'tis a common proof
That lowliness is young ambition's ladder,
Whereto the climber-upward turns his face;
But when he once attains the upmost round,
He then unto the ladder turns his back,
Looks in the clouds, scorning the base degrees
By which he did ascend. So Caesar may.
Then lest he may, prevent. And since the quarrel
Will bear no color for the thing he is,
Fashion it thus: that what he is, augmented,
Would run to these and these extremities;
And therefore think him as a serpent's egg,
Which, hatched, would as his kind grow mischievous,
And kill him in the shell.

[*Reenter* Lucius *with a letter.*]

Lucius. The taper burneth in your closet, sir.
Searching the window for a flint, I found
This paper, thus sealed up, and I am sure
It did not lie there when I went to bed.

[*Gives him the letter.*]

Brutus. Get you to bed again; it is not day.
Is not tomorrow, boy, the ides of March?

Lucius. I know not, sir.

Brutus. Look in the calendar and bring me word.

Lucius. I will, sir.

[*Exit.*]

Brutus. The exhalations, whizzing in the air,
Give so much light that I may read by them.

[*Opens the letter and reads.*]

"Brutus, thou sleep'st. Awake, and see thyself!
Shall Rome, etc. Speak, strike, redress!"
"Brutus, thou sleep'st. Awake!"
Such instigations have been often dropped
Where I have took them up.
"Shall Rome, etc." Thus must I piece it out:
Shall Rome stand under one man's awe? What,
Rome?
My ancestors did from the streets of Rome

18–27 The abuse . . . may: Greatness is misused when it separates pity **(disjoins / Remorse)** from power. I have never known Caesar to be ruled by his heart rather than his head. What does Brutus think Caesar will do if he gets to the top of **ambition's ladder?** What will Caesar's attitude be toward those at the ladder's lower rungs **(base degrees)?**

28–34 lest . . . shell: Rather than let Caesar do that, I should take steps to prevent it. Since our case against Caesar is weak **(Will bear no color)** at present, we must shape **(Fashion)** our argument against him in the following way: We know what kind of person Caesar is now. If his true nature were allowed to develop **(augmented),** it would reach terrible extremes. So we must treat him as a serpent's egg and kill him before he hatches.

35 closet: private room.

44 exhalations: meteors.

47 etc.: and so forth; **redress:** right a wrong. The letter is meant to suggest certain things to Brutus, without actually spelling them out.

49 instigations: suggestions.

51 Thus . . . out: I must guess the rest of the sentence.

52 Shall . . . awe: Should Rome have such fear and respect for just one man?

Customizing Instruction

Less Proficient Readers

1 The figurative language used in this passage communicates meaning beyond the literal meaning of the words. Brutus is comparing Caesar to an adder, which is a poisonous snake that comes out of its hole on sunny days. Brutus compares such a day to the act of crowning Caesar. Ask students what Brutus is saying the crowning of Caesar might cause.

Possible Response: Just as a bright day brings out the dangerous adder, so a coronation might bring out a dangerous part of Caesar.

Students Acquiring English

2 Explain to students that a flint is a stone that is struck to produce sparks in order to start a fire. Lucius was looking for a flint to light the candles in Brutus' room.

Use **Spanish Study Guide** for additional support, pp. 152–154.

Gifted and Talented

Encourage students to read more about the historical plot to assassinate Caesar. Have them consider how well the historical facts agree with the events of the play. Are all of the characters historically based? If so, do their roles represent their historical roles? Have students present and discuss their findings.

Mini Lesson Speaking and Listening

INTERPRETIVE READING In a play, the story is told primarily through dialogue, which is conversation among characters. A soliloquy, however, is a specialized form of dialogue, because it is a conversation a character has with himself or herself. For example, Brutus speaks aloud to himself when he is alone onstage at the beginning of the first scene of Act Two, weighing the arguments for and against allowing Caesar to remain in power.

Practice As readers of plays, we must imagine how dialogue and soliloquies sound as we read. To help clarify the difference between lines spoken in conversation and lines spoken to oneself, have students read aloud Brutus' opening lines and the soliloquy in Act Two. Have someone read Lucius' lines as well, so that the actor presenting Brutus can focus on observing the punctuation and varying the tone and volume to indicate the points at which Brutus calls to his servant and where he speaks to himself. Remind students to justify their choice of verbal and nonverbal performance techniques by referring to their interpretation of the text. Students should present their interpretive readings to the class for discussion.

Reading and Analyzing

Reading Skills and Strategies: PREDICT

A Tell students that the fifteenth of March is the ides of March. Ask students to predict what might happen on the ides of March.

Possible Responses: Caesar will be killed; Caesar will be crowned.

Reading Skills and Strategies: CONNECT

B Brutus hasn't slept since he first thought about turning against Caesar, observing that the time between conceiving a horrible act and the execution of that act is a nightmare; in other words, the waiting is the hardest part. Ask them if they have ever had to wait before doing something they did not want to do.

Possible Responses: Yes, before breaking up with someone; yes, before taking a major test.

Literary Analysis: CHARACTER

In a drama, there are usually minor characters who are less important to the story, but who help advance the plot. Brutus' servant Lucius is a minor character. Ask students what actions he performs that help the plot unfold.

Possible Responses: He finds the anonymous note from Cassius and takes it to Brutus; he provides information about the ides of March; he describes the hidden faces of the conspirators as they knock at the door, which prompts Brutus to remark on the potential shamefulness of the plot.

Guide for Reading

C **Possible Response:** Brutus is divided between his personal love for and loyalty to Caesar and his fear that Caesar may become tyrannical and destroy the state.

"Shall Rome
stand under one
man's awe?"

Martin Sheen as Brutus (New York Shakespeare Festival, 1988). Photo copyright © George E. Joseph.

The Tarquin drive when he was called a king.
"Speak, strike, redress!" Am I entreated
To speak and strike? O Rome, I make thee promise,
If the redress will follow, thou receivest
Thy full petition at the hand of Brutus!

[*Reenter* Lucius.]

A **Lucius.** Sir, March is wasted fifteen days.

[*Knocking within.*]

Brutus. 'Tis good. Go to the gate, somebody knocks.

[*Exit* Lucius.]

Since Cassius first did whet me against Caesar,
I have not slept.
B Between the acting of a dreadful thing
And the first motion, all the interim is
Like a phantasma or a hideous dream.
The genius and the mortal instruments

53–54 My ancestors . . . king: Brutus refers to his ancestor who drove out Rome's last king. After that, rule by the Senate was established.

56–58 I make . . . Brutus: I promise you, Rome, if a remedy for our troubles can follow from my action, you will get what you need from Brutus.

61 whet me: sharpen my appetite.

63–69 Between . . . insurrection: The time between the earliest thought of a terrible act and the actual performance of it is a nightmare. The soul **(genius)** and body **(mortal instruments)** debate the subject, while the man himself feels like a kingdom undergoing a civil war. What is Brutus' internal conflict? **C**

Teaching Options

Cross Curricular Link History

LUCIUS JUNIUS BRUTUS King Tarquin, called "the Proud" because of his lawlessness and arrogance, murdered his father-in-law in the sixth century B.C. to gain the throne. Eventually, the Romans, led by Brutus' ancestor Lucius Junius Brutus, rebelled against Tarquin and drove him out. Lucius Brutus and another Roman, Collatinus, were named the first two consuls of the new Roman Republic; thus, Lucius Brutus was popularly held to be the founder of the Republic, and he was revered for his unflinching devotion to republican principles. He eventually had his colleague removed from the consulship on the grounds that he was related to the Tarquins, and he then passed a law exiling all the Tarquins. When his own sons plotted to restore the monarchy, Lucius Brutus had them executed. While Brutus is hailed as a hero for supporting republican liberties in the face of tyranny, he can also be seen as a driven and ruthless leader himself.

Are then in council, and the state of man,
Like to a little kingdom, suffers then
The nature of an insurrection.

[*Reenter* Lucius.]

Lucius. Sir, 'tis your brother Cassius at the door,
Who doth desire to see you.

Brutus. Is he alone?

Lucius. No, sir, there are more with him.

Brutus. Do you know them?

Lucius. No, sir. Their hats are plucked about their ears
And half their faces buried in their cloaks,
That by no means I may discover them
By any mark of favor.

1 **Brutus.** Let 'em enter.

[*Exit* Lucius.]

They are the faction. O conspiracy,
Sham'st thou to show thy dang'rous brow by night,
When evils are most free? O, then by day
Where wilt thou find a cavern dark enough
To mask thy monstrous visage? Seek none, conspiracy,
Hide it in smiles and affability!
For if thou path, thy native semblance on,
No Erebus itself were dim enough
To hide thee from prevention.

[*Enter the conspirators,* Cassius, Casca, Decius, Cinna, Metellus Cimber, *and* Trebonius.]

Cassius. I think we are too bold upon your rest.
Good morrow, Brutus. Do we trouble you?

Brutus. I have been up this hour, awake all night.
Know I these men that come along with you?

Cassius. Yes, every man of them; and no man here
But honors you; and every one doth wish
You had but that opinion of yourself
Which every noble Roman bears of you.
This is Trebonius.

Brutus. He is welcome hither.

Cassius. This, Decius Brutus.

Brutus. He is welcome too.

Cassius. This, Casca; this, Cinna; and this, Metellus Cimber.

70 brother: Cassius, the husband of Brutus' sister, is his brother-in-law.

75–76 by no . . . favor: There is no way I can tell who they are.

77–85 O conspiracy . . . prevention: If these plotters are afraid to be seen at night, how will they keep these terrible plans from showing on their faces during the day? They must smile and show friendliness **(affability).** If they go out showing their true natures **(native semblance),** even the dark gateway to hell (**Erebus** ĕr′ ə bəs) couldn't hide them.

86 I think . . . rest: I think we may have come too early.

Customizing Instruction

Students Acquiring English

1 Explain to students that *'em* is a shortened, nonstandard form of *them.*

Less Proficient Readers

To make sure students understand the play so far, ask them the following questions:

- Why are Cassius and the others opposed to Caesar?

Possible Response: They think he is becoming too powerful.

- Why is Brutus having trouble deciding what to do?

Possible Response: He has personal attachments to Caesar, but he knows that Caesar is bad for the Republic.

BLOCK SCHEDULING: MANAGING TIME

If your schedule requires that you cover the lesson objectives in a shorter time, use . . .

- Preparing to Read, p. 689
- Thinking Through the Literature, p. 735
- Grammar in Context, p. 796

If you want to take advantage of longer class time, use . . .

- TE Teaching Options: Viewing and Representing, pp. 718, 727, 734; Speaking and Listening, pp. 715; Vocabulary Strategy, p. 724; Cross Curricular Links, pp. 716, 722, 728; Multicultural Link, pp. 730–731; Informal Assessment, p. 726
- Choices & Challenges, p. 795 and Author Activity, p. 797

Reading and Analyzing

Active Reading

UNDERSTANDING SHAKESPEARE'S PLAYS

A Remind students to pay attention to the stage directions, which are usually in italics and enclosed in brackets, as well as to the dialogue, for a clearer picture of how the actors move and speak onstage. The stage directions indicate that Brutus and Cassius whisper together, and the subsequent stage directions clarify that they have stepped away from the group by noting when they "rejoin the others." Ask students why they think Cassius draws Brutus aside for a private conversation.
Possible Responses: He wants to know Brutus' final decision; he wants Brutus to feel that he can speak freely.

GUIDE FOR READING

B **Possible Response:** Brutus believes that the urgency of the conspirators' cause—ridding Rome of a potential tyrant—is stronger than any oath.

Brutus. They are all welcome.
What watchful cares do interpose themselves
Betwixt your eyes and night?

Cassius. Shall I entreat a word?

[*They whisper.*]

Decius. Here lies the east. Doth not the day break
here?

Casca. No.

Cinna. O, pardon, sir, it doth; and yon grey lines
That fret the clouds are messengers of day.

Casca. You shall confess that you are both deceived.
Here, as I point my sword, the sun arises,
Which is a great way growing on the south,
Weighing the youthful season of the year.
Some two months hence, up higher toward the north
He first presents his fire; and the high east
Stands as the Capitol, directly here.

[Brutus *and* Cassius *rejoin the others.*]

Brutus. Give me your hands all over, one by one.

Cassius. And let us swear our resolution.

Brutus. No, not on oath. If not the face of men,
The sufferance of our souls, the time's abuse—
If these be motives weak, break off betimes,
And every man hence to his idle bed.
So let high-sighted tyranny range on
Till each man drop by lottery. But if these
(As I am sure they do) bear fire enough
To kindle cowards and to steel with valor
The melting spirits of women, then, countrymen,
What need we any spur but our own cause
To prick us to redress? what other bond
Than secret Romans that have spoke the word
And will not palter? and what other oath
Than honesty to honesty engaged
That this shall be, or we will fall for it?
Swear priests and cowards and men cautelous,
Old feeble carrions and such suffering souls
That welcome wrongs; unto bad causes swear
Such creatures as men doubt; but do not stain
The even virtue of our enterprise,

98–99 What watchful . . . night: What troubles keep you awake at night?

100 Shall I entreat a word?: Cassius asks Brutus to step aside and talk privately with him. While they talk, the others chatter about the sky (lines 99–108), pretending to be not at all interested in what Cassius and Brutus are discussing.

104 fret: stripe.

107–108 Which is . . . year: from a southerly direction, since it is still early in the year.

114–119 If not . . . lottery: We do not need to swear our loyalty to one another. The sadness of people's faces, our own suffering, and the awful time we live in—if these aren't strong enough to hold us together, then let us all go back to bed. In that case, let tyranny live, while we die off, one at a time, by chance **(by lottery).**

123–128 What does Brutus believe is even stronger than any oath the men could take together? Do you agree?

126 palter: go back on our word.

Teaching Options

Mini Lesson: Viewing and Representing

Students may try to recreate these different versions of the scene in performance. They would have to interpret these photographs, deciding whether Brutus is portrayed as sympathetic, or antagonistic, to the conspirators; they would need to focus on how meaning is conveyed through body language and the physical arrangement of the actors onstage. They could present their interpretations.

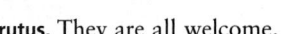

View and Compare

Blocking—where characters stand in relation to each other and the set—is a crucial part of a director's job. Compare and contrast what these images suggest about the relationship between Brutus and the conspirators.

James Mason (*left*) as Brutus (MGM film, 1953). Photofest.

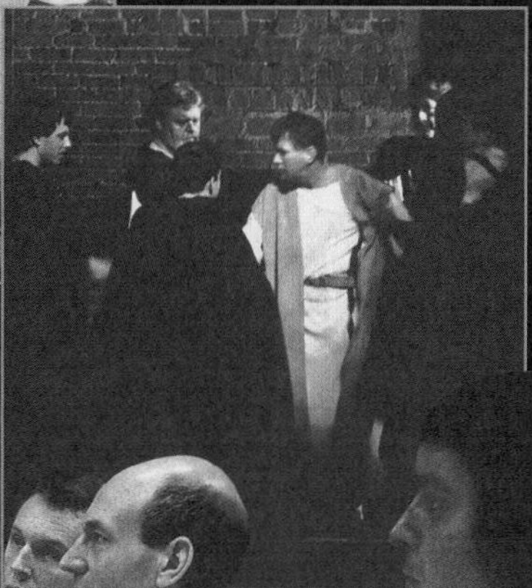

Martin Sheen (*in white*) as Brutus (New York Shakespeare Festival, 1988). Photo copyright © George E. Joseph.

John Wood (*center*) as Brutus (Royal Shakespeare Company, 1972). Photo copyright © Reg Wilson.

Customizing Instruction

Multiple Learning Styles

Visual and Interpersonal Learners

1 Have students sketch this part of the scene (lines 100–117) to illustrate how the characters are initially positioned onstage and how they rearrange themselves when Cassius and Brutus move to speak privately. Students might also stage a reading of this section to work out the physical movements of the characters.

Students Acquiring English

2 Explain to students that *cautelous* means "deceitful," and point out that Shakespeare uses nonstandard syntax in these lines when he places the adjective after the noun it modifies and when he places the verb (*swear*) at the beginning of the sentence. Go on to explain that while *carrion* means "dead and putrefying flesh," Shakespeare uses the word metaphorically here to mean men who are inactive. Help students paraphrase the clause in lines 129–131 by having them first pick out the compound subject and then follow it with the verb.

Possible Response: "Priests and cowards and deceitful men, old feeble inactive men and such suffering souls that welcome wrongs swear."

View and Compare

Possible Response: He is separated from the group to show his role as leader.

Reading and Analyzing

Literary Analysis: CONFLICT

A There are a number of external conflicts between the conspirators, primarily about who should be involved in the plot, who should be killed, and how to orchestrate the assassination. Ask students to explain Cassius' reasons for wanting to kill Caesar and Mark Antony, as well as Brutus' reasons for sparing him.

Possible Response: Cassius argues that Mark Antony is Caesar's supporter and very clever and will therefore cause trouble after the assassination. Brutus argues that killing Caesar is already more than enough blood shed and that Antony without Caesar is harmless.

Literary Analysis: FIGURATIVE LANGUAGE

B What does Brutus mean when he says that Antony "can do no more than Caesar's arm / when Caesar's head is off."

Possible Response: Without Caesar to tell him what to do, Antony is harmless.

GUIDE FOR READING

C Possible Responses: Yes—they seem to put the welfare of Rome first; no—they seem more interested in preserving their own power than in protecting Rome.

D Possible Response: Brutus' line implies that he thinks of the conspiracy as a sacred task, while Cassius sees it as a practical matter.

E Yes, considering Brutus' remarks about Antony's irresponsibility and general dependence on Caesar; no, Cassius' suspicions about Antony's shrewdness and his "ingrafted love" of Caesar.

Nor the insuppressive mettle of our spirits,
To think that or our cause or our performance
Did need an oath when every drop of blood
That every Roman bears, and nobly bears,
Is guilty of a several bastardy
If he do break the smallest particle
Of any promise that hath passed from him.

Cassius. But what of Cicero? Shall we sound him?
I think he will stand very strong with us.

Casca. Let us not leave him out.

Cinna. No, by no means.

Metellus. O, let us have him! for his silver hairs
Will purchase us a good opinion
And buy men's voices to commend our deeds.
It shall be said his judgment ruled our hands;
Our youths and wildness shall no whit appear,
But all be buried in his gravity.

Brutus. O, name him not! Let us not break with him,
For he will never follow anything
That other men begin.

Cassius. Then leave him out.

Casca. Indeed he is not fit.

Decius. Shall no man else be touched but only Caesar?

1 A **Cassius.** Decius, well urged. I think it is not meet
Mark Antony, so well beloved of Caesar,
Should outlive Caesar. We shall find of him
A shrewd contriver; and you know, his means,
If he improve them, may well stretch so far
As to annoy us all; which to prevent,
Let Antony and Caesar fall together.

Brutus. Our course will seem too bloody, Caius Cassius,
To cut the head off and then hack the limbs,
Like wrath in death and envy afterwards;
For Antony is but a limb of Caesar.
Let us be sacrificers, but not butchers, Caius.
We all stand up against the spirit of Caesar,
And in the spirit of men there is no blood.
O that we then could come by Caesar's spirit
And not dismember Caesar! But, alas,
Caesar must bleed for it! And, gentle friends,

129–140 Swear . . . from him: Swearing oaths is for priests, cowards, crafty **(cautelous)** men, old dying men **(feeble carrions),** and unhappy people who enjoy lying. Such people do not have our unfailing courage **(insuppressive mettle).** What we believe or what we are about to do **(or our cause or our performance)** does not need oaths, since our blood would not be truly Roman (would be **guilty of a several bastardy)** if any of us were to break his word. Brutus seems to believe that the other conspirators are as honorable as he is. Do you agree with him?

141 sound him: see what he thinks of the matter.

144–149 let us . . . gravity: Let us get Cicero to join us. His age **(silver hairs)** will win us popular support. People will say our youth and wildness were ruled by his sound judgment. So let us tell him of our plan.

155–161 I think . . . together: Shall we also kill Mark Antony, Caesar's good friend? He is a clever plotter **(shrewd contriver),** and if he had more power **(his means / If he improve them),** he could be trouble for us.

166 How does this line reveal a contrast between Brutus' and Cassius' attitudes toward the plot?

169–170 O that . . . Caesar: Brutus wishes they could remove Caesar's soul without having to destroy his body.

Teaching Options

Mini Lesson Grammar

SPECIAL PROBLEMS WITH MODIFIERS: ***good/well***

Among the trickiest modifiers are *good* and *well*. Explain that *good* is always an adjective; adjectives modify only nouns and pronouns. *Well* can be used as an adjective, but it is usually an adverb; adverbs modify verbs, adjectives, or other adverbs. Give students the following brief guidelines for using *good* and *well*:

- Use *good* after a linking verb when you want to link the modifier to the subject. (*Jane looks good.*)
- Use *well* after the linking verb when you are referring to someone's health. (*Bob will feel well soon.*)
- Use *well*, not *good*, to modify a verb. (*The machine doesn't run well.*)

Practice Ask students to choose and explain the appropriate adverb or adjective.

1. Her report card is (good/well).
2. Her brother felt (good/well) enough to leave the hospital.
3. Most jobs in law offices pay (good/well).
4. The plants in the backyard are growing (good/well).
5. Her birthday cake is (good/well).

Use **Grammar Transparencies and Copymasters,** p. 158, for more exercises.

Use McDougal Littell's ***Language Network,*** Chapter 9, for more instruction on adverbs.

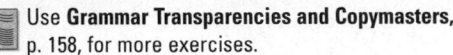

Let's kill him boldly, but not wrathfully;
Let's carve him as a dish fit for the gods,
Not hew him as a carcass fit for hounds.
And let our hearts, as subtle masters do,
Stir up their servants to an act of rage
And after seem to chide 'em. This shall make
Our purpose necessary, and not envious;
Which so appearing to the common eyes,
We shall be called purgers, not murderers.
B And for Mark Antony, think not of him;
For he can do no more than Caesar's arm
When Caesar's head is off.

Cassius. Yet I fear him,
For in the ingrafted love he bears to Caesar—

Brutus. Alas, good Cassius, do not think of him!
If he love Caesar, all that he can do
Is to himself—take thought, and die for Caesar.
And that were much he should; for he is given
To sports, to wildness, and much company.

Trebonius. There is no fear in him. Let him not die,
For he will live and laugh at this hereafter.

[*Clock strikes.*]

Brutus. Peace! Count the clock.

Cassius. The clock hath stricken three.

Trebonius. 'Tis time to part.

Cassius. But it is doubtful yet 2
Whether Caesar will come forth today or no;
For he is superstitious grown of late,
Quite from the main opinion he held once
Of fantasy, of dreams, and ceremonies.
It may be these apparent prodigies, 3
The unaccustomed terror of this night,
And the persuasion of his augurers
May hold him from the Capitol today.

Decius. Never fear that. If he be so resolved,
I can o'ersway him; for he loves to hear
That unicorns may be betrayed with trees
And bears with glasses, elephants with holes,
Lions with toils, and men with flatterers;
But when I tell him he hates flatterers,
He says he does, being then most flattered.

174 Not . . . hounds: Let's not chop him up like the body of an animal to be fed to dogs.

175–180 let our hearts . . . murderers: Let our hearts treat our hands **(servants)** the way sly masters do; we will let our hands do our dirty work, then later scold **(chide)** them for what they have done. This attitude will make us seem to the public **(common eyes)** to be healers **(purgers)** instead of murderers.

184 ingrafted: deep-rooted.

188–189 And that . . . company: Mark Antony isn't likely to kill himself; he loves sports, wildness, and socializing too much to do such a thing.

190 There is no fear in him: We have nothing to fear from Antony. Do you agree? E

193–201 But it is . . . Capitol today: We don't know if Caesar will leave his house **(come forth)** today. Lately he has become superstitious, in contrast to the strong views **(main opinion)** he once had of such beliefs. The cause may be these strange events and the arguments of his fortunetellers **(augurers).** These things may keep him from coming to the Capitol today.

203 o'ersway him: change his mind.

204–208 That unicorns . . . flattered: Decius tells of ways to trap shrewd animals. He says that Caesar, who loves to hear such stories, can also be trapped—by flattery.

Customizing Instruction

Less Proficient Readers

1 Explain to students that *meet,* in this context, is an adjective meaning "appropriate" or "proper."

2 Have students review Cassius' speech and discuss what reasons Cassius gives for why Caesar might fail to appear at the Capitol.

Possible Responses: He says that Caesar has grown superstitious and may be frightened by the unusual omens of that night; he adds that Caesar's fortune-tellers ("augurers") might persuade him to stay home.

Students Acquiring English

3 Explain to students that *prodigies,* in this context, means "strange or rare things."

JULIUS CAESAR ACT TWO 721

Reading and Analyzing

Literary Analysis: IAMBIC PENTAMETER

A Lines written in iambic pentameter have five pairs of unstressed-stressed syllables. Point out that Shakespeare uses a contraction ("upon's") to make this line fit into correct iambic pentameter. Explain that having the extra syllable ("us") would throw off the meter. Have students look for other examples of contractions Shakespeare has used to preserve the meter.

Possible Responses: "Y'have" (Act Two, Scene 1, line 237); "Ne'er" (Act Two, Scene 2, line 11)

Literary Analysis: FIGURATIVE LANGUAGE

B Ask students why Brutus compares the conspirators to actors.

Possible Response: Brutus thinks the conspirators should be like actors on the ancient Roman stage, who hide their true feelings as they play their assigned parts. Brutus uses this suggestive comparison because he doesn't want the conspirators to betray their assassination plot.

Literary Analysis: EVALUATE

C Ask students to evaluate Brutus' greeting to Portia. Do they think that Brutus is sincerely concerned about Portia's health in this passage, or do they think he is apprehensive that Portia may have overheard some of the details of the conspiracy?

Guide for Reading

D Possible Response: Brutus probably lies because he fears that Portia may convince him to change his mind or may worry about his involvement in the conspiracy.

Let me work,
For I can give his humor the true bent,
And I will bring him to the Capitol.

Cassius. Nay, we will all of us be there to fetch him.

Brutus. By the eighth hour. Is that the uttermost?

Cinna. Be that the uttermost, and fail not then.

Metellus. Caius Ligarius doth bear Caesar hard,
Who rated him for speaking well of Pompey.
I wonder none of you have thought of him.

Brutus. Now, good Metellus, go along by him.
He loves me well, and I have given him reasons.
Send him but hither, and I'll fashion him.

Cassius. The morning comes upon's. We'll leave you, Brutus.
And, friends, disperse yourselves; but all remember
What you have said and show yourselves true Romans.

Brutus. Good gentlemen, look fresh and merrily.
Let not our looks put on our purposes,
But bear it as our Roman actors do,
With untired spirits and formal constancy.
And so good morrow to you every one.

[*Exeunt all but* Brutus.]

Boy! Lucius! Fast asleep? It is no matter.
Enjoy the honey-heavy dew of slumber.
Thou hast no figures nor no fantasies
Which busy care draws in the brains of men;
Therefore thou sleep'st so sound.

[*Enter* Portia, *Brutus' wife.*]

Portia. Brutus, my lord!

Brutus. Portia! What mean you? Wherefore rise you now?
It is not for your health thus to commit
Your weak condition to the raw cold morning.

Portia. Nor for yours neither. Y'have ungently, Brutus,
Stole from my bed. And yesternight at supper
You suddenly arose and walked about,
Musing and sighing with your arms across;
And when I asked you what the matter was,
You stared upon me with ungentle looks.
I urged you further, then you scratched your head

210 I can give . . . true bent: I can get him into the right mood.

213 By the . . . uttermost: By eight o'clock. Do we all agree that eight is the latest we will be there?

215–217 Caius . . . of him: Caius Ligarius has a grudge against Caesar, who criticized him for supporting Pompey. I don't know why you haven't asked him to join our plot.

220 fashion: persuade.

225 Let not . . . purposes: Let's not let our appearances give away **(put on)** what we are planning to do.

228 All the other conspirators leave, and Brutus is once again alone in his garden.

233 As you read the conversation between Brutus and his wife, think about the kind of relationship they have.

Teaching Options

Cross Curricular Link History

FAMILIES IN ROMAN SOCIETY The Roman family was governed by the principle of *patria potestas* or "right of the father." Under this principle, a father had complete control over his children. Any property they had was legally his, and the father could punish his children for any offense in any way he saw fit, including capital punishment. A son could only escape *patria potestas* if his father died or voluntarily emancipated him. A daughter ceased to be under her father's *potestas* if she entered a marriage with *manus. Manus* transferred the autocratic power of a woman's father to her husband. Divorce could be initiated only by the husband. By Caesar's time, however, *manus* was rapidly dying out, and most marriages were without it, in which case a husband's and wife's property remained separate, and either party could initiate divorce.

And too impatiently stamped with your foot.
Yet I insisted, yet you answered not,
But with an angry wafture of your hand
Gave sign for me to leave you. So I did,
Fearing to strengthen that impatience
Which seemed too much enkindled, and withal
Hoping it was but an effect of humor,
Which sometime hath his hour with every man.
It will not let you eat nor talk nor sleep,
And could it work so much upon your shape
As it hath much prevailed on your condition,
I should not know you Brutus. Dear my lord,
Make me acquainted with your cause of grief.

Brutus. I am not well in health, and that is all.

Portia. Brutus is wise and, were he not in health,
He would embrace the means to come by it.

Brutus. Why, so I do. Good Portia, go to bed.

Portia. Is Brutus sick, and is it physical
To walk unbraced and suck up the humors
Of the dank morning? What, is Brutus sick,
And will he steal out of his wholesome bed
2 To dare the vile contagion of the night,
And tempt the rheumy and unpurgéd air,
To add unto his sickness? No, my Brutus.
You have some sick offense within your mind,
Which by the right and virtue of my place
I ought to know of; and upon my knees
I charm you, by my once commended beauty,
By all your vows of love, and that great vow
Which did incorporate and make us one,
That you unfold to me, yourself, your half,
Why you are heavy, and what men tonight
Have had resort to you; for here have been
Some six or seven, who did hide their faces
Even from darkness.

Brutus. Kneel not, gentle Portia.

Portia. I should not need if you were gentle Brutus.
Within the bond of marriage, tell me, Brutus,
Is it excepted I should know no secrets
That appertain to you? Am I yourself
But, as it were, in sort or limitation?
To keep with you at meals, comfort your bed,

245 Yet: still.

246 wafture: gesture.

249 withal: also.

250 humor: mood.

253–255 And could . . . you Brutus: If a mood like that could change your appearance **(shape)** the way it changes your personality **(condition),** I would not recognize you.

257 Why do you think Brutus lies to Portia? **D**

261–267 Is Brutus . . . sickness: Do you expect me to believe that you're sick? Is it healthy to walk without a coat **(unbraced)** and breathe the air of a damp morning or the unhealthy night air that is not yet cleansed **(unpurged)** by the sun?

268–270 You have . . . know of: You have a sickness of the mind; as your wife, I have a right to know what it is.

275 heavy: sad.

282 appertain: relate.

283 in sort or limitation: only in part.

Customizing Instruction

Students Acquiring English

1 Encourage students to be on the lookout for unusual vocabulary when they are reading Shakespeare. Make sure students remember that *wherefore* means "why" in Renaissance English. Have students paraphrase "Wherefore rise you now?"

Possible Response: "Why are you up now?"

Students Acquiring English

2 Explain to students that *rheumy* means, in this context, "unhealthy."

Reading and Analyzing

Literary Analysis: FIGURATIVE LANGUAGE

A Point out to students that this figure of speech involves what seems to be a strikingly modern word, *suburbs*. Ask students what *suburbs* are, and then ask them what Portia means in this line.

Possible Response: Suburbs are the outlying parts of a city or town. Portia means that, as Brutus' wife, she should be allowed access to his deepest thoughts and feelings, and not kept on the fringes.

Literary Analysis: CHARACTER

B Portia defines herself largely in terms of the men in her life, namely, her husband and her father. Ask students what Portia's self-characterization might suggest about the position of women in ancient Rome.

Possible Response: When Portia says, "I grant that I am a woman," she acknowledges that women are viewed as inferior. Her attempt to bolster her authority through her connections to respected and powerful men shows that women were not highly regarded on their own, but could gain honor through their connections to men.

GUIDE FOR READING

C **Possible Responses:** Brutus should take Portia into his confidence, treating her as an equal; Brutus should keep the secret, as telling it to anyone could jeopardize the plot.

"Tell me your counsels;
I will not disclose 'em."

Martin Sheen as Brutus and Joan MacIntosh as Portia (New York Shakespeare Festival, 1988). Photo by Martha Swope, copyright © Time Inc.

Teaching Options

Mini Lesson Vocabulary Strategy

RESEARCHING WORD ORIGINS: *nobilis*

Instruction The word *noble* is based upon the Latin root *nobilis*, which means "knowable, known, famous." When Brutus says that Portia is noble, he is not only acknowledging her moral character, but he is also commenting on her famous hereditary rank as the daughter of Cato, a respected Roman. Other words based on the same root include *nobility, nobly, nobleman,* and *noblewoman.*

Practice Have students work in pairs to research the origins of *nobility, nobly, nobleman,* and *noblewoman.* Have them apply the meaning of the root to determine the precise meaning of each word. Ask them to use each word in a sentence. Ask students how they can use knowledge of the root word *nobilis* to remember the meanings of these words.

Use **Vocabulary Transparencies and Copymasters,** p. 73, for more instruction.

A lesson on idioms appears on p. 419 in the Pupil's Edition.

And talk to you sometimes? Dwell I but in the suburbs
Of your good pleasure? If it be no more, **A**
Portia is Brutus' harlot, not his wife.

Brutus. You are my true and honorable wife,
As dear to me as are the ruddy drops
That visit my sad heart.

289–290 the ruddy . . . heart: my blood.

Portia. If this were true, then should I know this secret.
I grant I am a woman, but withal
A woman that Lord Brutus took to wife.
I grant that I am a woman, but withal
A woman well reputed, Cato's daughter.
Think you I am no stronger than my sex, **B**
Being so fathered and so husbanded?
Tell me your counsels; I will not disclose 'em.
I have made strong proof of my constancy,
Giving myself a voluntary wound
Here, in the thigh. Can I bear that with patience,
And not my husband's secrets?

296–302 Think you . . . secrets: How can you consider me merely a typical woman, when I am the daughter of Cato (a highly respected Roman) and the wife of Brutus? So tell me your secret. I have proven my strength by wounding myself here in the thigh. If I can put up with that pain, I can certainly deal with my husband's secrets. Should Brutus tell Portia his secret? **C**

Brutus. O ye gods,
Render me worthy of this noble wife!
[*Knocking within.*]
Hark, hark! one knocks. Portia, go in awhile,
And by-and-by thy bosom shall partake
The secrets of my heart.
All my engagements I will construe to thee,
All the charactery of my sad brows.
Leave me with haste.
[*Exit* Portia.]
Lucius, who's that knocks?

307–308 All may . . . brows: I will explain all my dealings and the reason for my sad looks.

[*Reenter* Lucius *with* Caius Ligarius.]

Lucius. Here is a sick man that would speak with you.

1 **Brutus.** Caius Ligarius, that Metellus spake of.
Boy, stand aside. Caius Ligarius, how?

Caius. Vouchsafe good morrow from a feeble tongue.

313 Vouchsafe . . . tongue: Accept a good morning from a sick man.

Brutus. O, what a time have you chose out, brave Caius,
To wear a kerchief! Would you were not sick!

315 kerchief: a covering to protect the head during sickness.

Caius. I am not sick if Brutus have in hand
Any exploit worthy the name of honor.

Customizing Instruction

Less Proficient Readers

To help students understand the play, ask them the following questions:

- What does Portia want Brutus to do?
  Answer: Tell her his secret
- What is Brutus' secret?
  Answer: He is involved in a plot to murder Caesar.

Students Acquiring English

1 Explain that Shakespeare uses an abbreviated form of greeting here: "How?" means "How are you?"

Reading and Analyzing

GUIDE FOR READING

A Possible Response: Caius means that there are some men who are well who must be made to suffer.

Literary Analysis: CHARACTER

B Sometimes we learn about a character by observing how other people respond to him or her. Ask students what they can learn about Brutus from Caius' declaration of allegiance to him.
Possible Response: Brutus must be a trustworthy person who has a reputation for acting honorably, since Caius has faith in whatever Brutus will do.

Active Reading

UNDERSTANDING SHAKESPEARE'S PLAYS

C Dramatic irony refers to the contrast between what a character knows and what the reader or audience knows. Ask students how Caesar's words reveal dramatic irony in light of the action in the preceding scene.
Possible Response: Because readers or audience members have just seen the conspirators plotting his assassination, they know that his words are truer than he thinks.

Literary Analysis: CHARACTER

D After reading lines 10–12, ask students what they can infer about Caesar's character.
Possible Response: Caesar is courageous, boastful, and overconfident.

Brutus. Such an exploit have I in hand, Ligarius,
Had you a healthful ear to hear of it.

Caius. By all the gods that Romans bow before,
I here discard my sickness! Soul of Rome!
Brave son, derived from honorable loins!
Thou like an exorcist has conjured up
My mortified spirit. Now bid me run,
And I will strive with things impossible;
Yea, get the better of them. What's to do?

Brutus. A piece of work that will make sick men whole.

Caius. But are not some whole that we must make sick?

Brutus. That must we also. What it is, my Caius,
I shall unfold to thee as we are going
To whom it must be done.

B

Caius. Set on your foot,
And with a heart new-fired I follow you,
To do I know not what; but it sufficeth
That Brutus leads me on.

[*Thunder.*]

Brutus. Follow me then.

[*Exeunt.*]

318 exploit: deed.

321 I here discard my sickness!: I declare myself cured.

322 derived . . . loins: descended from noble Romans.

323 exorcist: someone who can call up spirits.

328 What does Caius mean? **A**

331 Set on your foot: Lead the way.

333 it sufficeth: It is enough.

SCENE 2 CAESAR'S HOUSE IN ROME.

It is now past dawn on March 15. Like everyone else in Rome, Caesar and his wife have slept badly because of the storm. There is still some lightning and thunder. Caesar prepares to go to the Capitol, but because of the many threatening omens, his wife Calpurnia insists that he stay home. Caesar agrees, for Calpurnia's sake. He changes his mind when Decius, one of the conspirators, persuades him that he must not seem swayed by his wife's superstitions. Although Caesar doesn't know it, the other conspirators are on their way to his house to make sure he does not decide to stay at home.

[*Enter* Caesar *in his nightgown.*]

C

Caesar. Nor heaven nor earth have been at peace tonight.
Thrice hath Calpurnia in her sleep cried out

Teaching Options

Assessment Informal Assessment

Check students' comprehension by having them respond to the following questions:

1. At the beginning of the scene, Brutus asks his servant whether the ides of March is upon them. Why is Brutus concerned about the date?
2. Think of the letter Brutus receives and the effect it has on him. What does this tell you about Brutus?
3. Recall that friendship is an important theme in this play. Do you think Brutus and Cassius are truly friends? Explain.

Possible Responses:

1. Brutus is concerned about the date because the ides of March is the day that harm is supposed to come to Caesar. Because Brutus is struggling with whether to join the faction that will strike against Caesar on March 15, he realizes that his time for deliberating is running out.
2. Brutus' reaction shows that he is extremely patriotic and highly conscious of the role his ancestors played in freeing the city from a tyrannical king; he is naive and gullible.
3. Cassius and Brutus are not friends because they have such different conceptions of what friendship means: Brutus is idealistic and honest, whereas Cassius is practical and manipulative; Cassius and Brutus are friends because they trust and rely on one another.

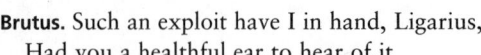

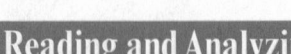

"Help, ho! They murder Caesar!" Who's within? C
[*Enter a* Servant.]

Servant. My lord?

1 **Caesar.** Go bid the priests do present sacrifice,
And bring me their opinions of success.

Servant. I will, my lord.

[*Exit.*]

[*Enter Caesar's wife,* Calpurnia, *alarmed.*]

Calpurnia. What mean you, Caesar? Think you to
walk forth?
You shall not stir out of your house today.

D **Caesar.** Caesar shall forth. The things that threatened me
Ne'er looked but on my back. When they shall see
The face of Caesar, they are vanished.

Calpurnia. Caesar, I never stood on ceremonies,
Yet now they fright me. There is one within,
Besides the things that we have heard and seen,
Recounts most horrid sights seen by the watch.
A lioness hath whelped in the streets,
And graves have yawned and yielded up their dead.
Fierce fiery warriors fought upon the clouds
In ranks and squadrons and right form of war,
Which drizzled blood upon the Capitol.
The noise of battle hurtled in the air,
Horses did neigh, and dying men did groan,
And ghosts did shriek and squeal about the streets.
O Caesar, these things are beyond all use,
And I do fear them!

Caesar. What can be avoided
Whose end is purposed by the mighty gods?
Yet Caesar shall go forth, for these predictions
Are to the world in general as to Caesar.

Calpurnia. When beggars die there are no comets seen;
The heavens themselves blaze forth the death of
princes.

Caesar. Cowards die many times before their deaths;
The valiant never taste of death but once.
Of all the wonders that I yet have heard,
It seems to me most strange that men should fear,
Seeing that death, a necessary end,
Will come when it will come.

5–6 Go bid . . . success: Roman priests would kill an animal as a sacrifice to the gods. Then they would cut the animal open and examine its internal organs for signs of future events.

10–56 As you read this conversation, think about Caesar's view of himself. Remember the way he talked of himself to Antony in Act One. Look for new evidence of Caesar's view of his own importance and his power.

10–12 The things . . . vanished: When I turn to face the things that threaten me, they disappear.

13–26 Caesar, I never . . . fear them: Calpurnia tells Caesar that she has never before believed in omens **(stood on ceremonies),** but now she is frightened. She describes the terrible things she has heard of from the men who were on guard during the night.

25 beyond all use: unlike anything we are accustomed to.

26–29 Caesar insists that, if these are omens and if the gods have destined that certain things will happen, no one can avoid them. He will go out, since the predictions, he believes, apply to the whole world, not only to Caesar.

Customizing Instruction

Students Acquiring English

1 Explain to students that *success* means "outcome," whether good or bad. Caesar wants the priests' opinions on the meaning of the sacrifice, whether it bodes well or ill for him.

Mini Lesson Viewing and Representing

REPRESENTING THE MOOD Instruction Remind students that mood is the feeling, or atmosphere, a writer creates for the reader. Many factors contribute to the mood of the story, such as the writer's use of imagery and figurative language, the setting, characters' motives and actions, and the story's events.

Practice Have students reread Calpurnia's speech describing the strange phenomena she has heard about from the watchmen (lines 13–26), and have them describe these images in their own words. Discuss how both the images and Calpurnia's reaction to them influence the mood of the play at this point. Then have students draw them or represent them artistically in some other way, such as constructing a collage of photographs or pictures. After students have shared their work, have them discuss why Shakespeare has Calpurnia recount these stories, making sure they understand the mood of supernatural horror created here.

Reading and Analyzing

Literary Analysis: CONFLICT

A Ask students what struggles Caesar encounters at this point in the scene. Encourage them to identify both internal and external conflicts.

Possible Responses: Internal conflict: Caesar's desire to go to the Senate House in order to look brave versus his desire to heed the warnings of the bad omens surrounding him; external conflicts: Caesar versus Calpurnia; Caesar versus Decius Brutus.

Reading Skills and Strategies: PREDICT

B Ask students to predict whether Caesar will keep his promise not to go to the Senate House.

Possible Responses: Caesar will not keep his promise because he is too proud; Caesar will remain firm in his decision because he is such a strong-minded person.

Literary Analysis: CHARACTER

C Have students comment on what lines 65–73 reveal about Caesar's personality and about his feelings toward the Senate.

Possible Response: These lines reveal that Caesar is arrogant and holds the Senate in contempt.

GUIDE FOR READING

D **Possible Response:** An actor might use a proud and slightly contemptuous tone.

[*Reenter* Servant.]

What say the augurers?

Servant. They would not have you to stir forth today.
Plucking the entrails of an offering forth,
They could not find a heart within the beast.

Caesar. The gods do this in shame of cowardice.
Caesar should be a beast without a heart
If he should stay at home today for fear.
No, Caesar shall not. Danger knows full well
1 That Caesar is more dangerous than he.
A We are two lions littered in one day,
And I the elder and more terrible,
And Caesar shall go forth.

Calpurnia. Alas, my lord!
Your wisdom is consumed in confidence.
Do not go forth today. Call it my fear
That keeps you in the house and not your own.
We'll send Mark Antony to the Senate House,
And he shall say you are not well today.
Let me upon my knee prevail in this.

B **Caesar.** Mark Antony shall say I am not well,
And for thy humor I will stay at home.
[*Enter* Decius.]
Here's Decius Brutus, he shall tell them so.

Decius. Caesar, all hail! Good morrow, worthy Caesar!
I come to fetch you to the Senate House.

2 **Caesar.** And you are come in very happy time
To bear my greetings to the senators
And tell them that I will not come today.
Cannot, is false; and that I dare not, falser.
I will not come today. Tell them so, Decius.

Calpurnia. Say he is sick.

Caesar. Shall Caesar send a lie?
Have I in conquest stretched mine arm so far
To be afeard to tell greybeards the truth?
3 Decius, go tell them Caesar will not come.

C **Decius.** Most mighty Caesar, let me know some cause,
Lest I be laughed at when I tell them so.

Caesar. The cause is in my will: I will not come.
That is enough to satisfy the Senate;
But for your private satisfaction,

46 littered in one day: born at the same time.

65–68 Shall . . . not come: Caesar is appalled by his wife's suggestion that he lie to a bunch of old men **(greybeards)** about his reason for not going to the Senate. How might an actor say these lines? D

Teaching Options

Cross Curricular Link History

OMENS The ancient historian Plutarch, whose *Lives of the Noble Greeks and Romans* served as one of Shakespeare's sources, reports numerous omens on the evening before Caesar's assassination. The Roman profession of augury was widely respected and exceedingly complex. Fundamentally, it involved foretelling the future by two methods: observation of the flights of birds and a kind of "autopsy" performed on the remains of sacrificial animals. A beast without a heart would be considered a major omen of bad fortune.

"Cowards die many times before their deaths; The valiant never taste of death but once."

John McMartin as Caesar and Harriet Harris as Calpurnia (New York Shakespeare Festival, 1988). Photo by Martha Swope, copyright © Time Inc.

Customizing Instruction

Students Acquiring English

Help students understand the following unusual usage and vocabulary:

1 *littered* (line 46): "born"

2 *happy* (line 60): "opportune" or "convenient"

3 *afeard* (line 67): an archaic form of "afraid"

Reading and Analyzing

Reading Skills and Strategies: EVALUATE

A Have students evaluate Decius' arguments and decide which one(s) seem most instrumental in changing Caesar's mind.

Possible Responses: Because Caesar becomes dismissive of and derisive toward Calpurnia, the argument that Caesar is ruled too much by his wife is the most influential of Decius' reasons; Caesar is most worried about looking cowardly, and so is most affected by Decius' last point.

GUIDE FOR READING

B **Possible Responses:** Decius argues that the Senate may change its mind about crowning Caesar; he says that some senators may mock Caesar for being overly influenced by a superstitious wife; he adds that some people may accuse Caesar of cowardice.

C **Possible Response:** Brutus is saying that his friendship with Caesar has grown to be hypocritical, since, despite appearances, he has joined the conspiracy.

Because I love you, I will let you know.
Calpurnia here, my wife, stays me at home.
She dreamt tonight she saw my statue,
Which, like a fountain with an hundred spouts,
Did run pure blood, and many lusty Romans
Came smiling and did bathe their hands in it.
And these does she apply for warnings and portents
And evils imminent, and on her knee
Hath begged that I will stay at home today.

Decius. This dream is all amiss interpreted;
It was a vision fair and fortunate.
Your statue spouting blood in many pipes,
In which so many smiling Romans bathed,
Signifies that from you great Rome shall suck
Reviving blood, and that great men shall press
For tinctures, stains, relics, and cognizance.
This by Calpurnia's dream is signified.

Caesar. And this way have you well expounded it.

Decius. I have, when you have heard what I can say:
And know it now, the Senate have concluded
To give this day a crown to mighty Caesar.
If you shall send them word you will not come,
Their minds may change. Besides, it were a mock
Apt to be rendered, for some one to say
"Break up the Senate till another time,
When Caesar's wife shall meet with better dreams."
If Caesar hide himself, shall they not whisper
"Lo, Caesar is afraid"?
Pardon me, Caesar, for my dear dear love
A 1 To your proceeding bids me tell you this,
And reason to my love is liable.

Caesar. How foolish do your fears seem now,
Calpurnia!
I am ashamed I did yield to them.
Give me my robe, for I will go.

[*Enter* Brutus, Ligarius, Metellus, Casca, Trebonius, Cinna, *and* Publius.]

And look where Publius is come to fetch me.

Publius. Good morrow, Caesar.

Caesar. Welcome Publius.
What Brutus, are you stirred so early too?
Good morrow, Casca. Caius Ligarius,

80 portents: signs of evil to come.

83–90 Decius has to think fast. He promised the others that he could flatter Caesar into believing anything. Now he must give Caesar a new interpretation of Calpurnia's dream, one that will get him out of the house.

83 amiss: wrongly.

88–89 great men . . . cognizance: Great men will come to you for honors and souvenirs to remember you by.

96–97 it were . . . rendered: It's likely that someone will make a sarcastic comment.

102–104 my dear . . . liable: My sincere interest in your career **(proceeding)** makes me tell you this. My feeling for you overtakes my intelligence **(reason).** What arguments does Decius use to change Caesar's mind? **B**

Teaching Options

Mini Lesson Multicultural Link

DIVINATION The practice of predicting the future and revealing information through supernatural means is known as divination. Although augury, which generally refers to interpreting the flights of birds for knowledge about future events, is mentioned in the play, there are reports of various forms of divination throughout history and all over the world. For example, haruspication—inspecting the entrails of sacrificial animals for clues about the future—is the practice ordered by Caesar in the play. Also, the ancient Greeks placed great importance on the proclamations of oracles, especially the oracle of Apollo at Delphi. Dream interpretation and astrology played an important role in the lives of ancient Babylonians, and many people today closely follow astrological systems for insight into their future. North American Indians have practiced scapulimancy, which is the practice of examining the cracks on a burned animal's shoulder blades.

Caesar was ne'er so much your enemy
As that same ague which hath made you lean.
What is't o'clock?

Brutus. Caesar, 'tis strucken eight.

Caesar. I thank you for your pains and courtesy.

[*Enter* Antony.]

See! Antony, that revels long o'nights,
Is notwithstanding up. Good morrow, Antony.

Antony. So to most noble Caesar.

Caesar. Bid them prepare within.
I am to blame to be thus waited for.
Now, Cinna, now, Metellus. What, Trebonius!
I have an hour's talk in store for you;
Remember that you call on me today;
Be near me, that I may remember you.

Trebonius. Caesar, I will. [*Aside.*] And so near will I be
That your best friends shall wish I had been further.

Caesar. Good friends, go in and taste some wine with me,
And we (like friends) will straightway go together.

Brutus. [*Aside.*] That every like is not the same, O Caesar,
The heart of Brutus yearns to think upon.

[*Exeunt.*]

113 ague: sickness.

116–117 Antony . . . up: Even Antony, who parties **(revels)** late into the night, is up early today.

124 Aside: privately, in a way that keeps the other characters from hearing what is said. Think of it as a whisper that the audience happens to overhear.

128–129 That every . . . upon: The fact that we behave like friends doesn't mean we are friends. My heart grieves **(yearns)** to think of it. What is Brutus saying about his friendship with Caesar?

C

SCENE 3 A STREET IN ROME NEAR THE CAPITOL.

In this brief scene, Caesar has still another chance to avoid the path that leads to his death. Artemidorus, a supporter of Caesar, has learned about the plot. He reads a letter he has written to warn Caesar. Then he waits in the street for Caesar to pass by on his way to the Capitol.

2 [*Enter* Artemidorus, *reading a paper.*]

Artemidorus. "Caesar, beware of Brutus; take heed of
Cassius; come not near Casca; have an eye to Cinna;
trust not Trebonius; mark well Metellus Cimber;
Decius Brutus loves thee not; thou hast wronged Caius
Ligarius. There is but one mind in all these men,

Customizing Instruction

Students Acquiring English

1 Explain to students that *liable* here means "under the influence." Decius is saying that his love for Caesar influences his thoughts.

Less Proficient Readers

2 Point out that Shakespeare's presentation of Artemidorus reading the petition builds suspense, because the audience is now aware that news of the plot has leaked, which means that Caesar has a better chance of discovering the danger that surrounds him.

Set a Purpose Have students read on to find out whether Artemidorus successfully warns Caesar of the conspiracy against him.

The technique of using supernatural phenomena or natural objects to make predictions is another way of purportedly gaining divine knowledge and is exhibited in *Julius Caesar*. For example, comets and eclipses were usually seen as omens, and in both ancient Rome and Elizabethan England, portents and prodigies were taken seriously. The practice of divination might stem from the human need to find explanations of mysterious, indeed, often threatening, events, and to seek help in times of trouble or perplexity.

Reading and Analyzing

Active Reading

UNDERSTANDING SHAKESPEARE'S PLAYS

A The manner or style in which the dialogue is spoken is often as important as the words themselves. Have students reread Portia's lines and note how choppy the dialogue is here, as she first addresses Lucius, then calls on "constancy" as she talks to herself, and finally calls again to the servant. What do these abrupt changes in the dialogue convey about Portia in this scene?

Possible Response: Portia's erratic dialogue shows that she is nervous and feels that she is in a race with the clock.

GUIDE FOR READING

B **Possible Response:** This statement plays on the old stereotype of women as excessively chatty and talkative.

Reading Skills and Strategies: VISUALIZE

C Urge students to try to visualize the soothsayer's description of the crowded street along which Caesar will pass. Ask what kind of event might furnish a modern parallel to this scene.

Possible Response: a presidential motorcade or a parade for a championship sports team

Reading Skills and Strategies: CONNECT

D Encourage students to read this passage aloud, altering their volume, tone, and expression in order to understand Portia's distracted agitation. Ask students whether they can relate to Portia's frame of mind as she worries about her husband and Caesar, and have them talk about whether they have ever personally experienced the kind of flustered anxiety she displays here.

and it is bent against Caesar. If thou beest not
immortal, look about you. Security gives way to
conspiracy. The mighty gods defend thee!
"Thy Lover,
"ARTEMIDORUS."

Here will I stand till Caesar pass along
And as a suitor will I give him this.
My heart laments that virtue cannot live
1 Out of the teeth of emulation.
If thou read this, O Caesar, thou mayst live;
If not, the Fates with traitors do contrive.
[*Exit.*]

9 Lover: devoted friend.

13–14 My heart . . . emulation: My heart is sad that Caesar's greatness cannot escape jealousy **(the teeth of emulation).**

16 contrive: plot.

SCENE 4 In front of Brutus' house.

Shakespeare continues to build suspense with another short scene. This one involves Brutus' wife, Portia, who feels anxious about the conspiracy. Portia nervously orders the servant Lucius to go and see what is happening at the Capitol. She next meets the Soothsayer, who makes her even more anxious as he continues to predict danger for Caesar.

[*Enter* Portia *and* Lucius.]

Portia. I prithee, boy, run to the Senate House.
Stay not to answer me, but get thee gone!
Why dost thou stay?

Lucius. To know my errand, madam.

Portia. I would have had thee there and here again
Ere I can tell thee what thou shouldst do there.
O constancy, be strong upon my side,
A Set a huge mountain 'tween my heart and tongue!
I have a man's mind, but a woman's might.
How hard it is for women to keep counsel!
Art thou here yet?

Lucius. Madam, what should I do?
Run to the Capitol and nothing else?
And so return to you and nothing else?

Portia. Yes, bring me word, boy, if thy lord look well,
For he went sickly forth; and take good note
What Caesar doth, what suitors press to him.
Hark, boy! What noise is that?

4–5 I would have . . . do there: I would have had you travel there and back without telling you what I wanted you to do. (Portia is upset with herself for acting foolishly.)

9 keep counsel: keep a secret. What do you think of Portia's (or Shakespeare's) statement that it is hard for a woman to keep a secret? **B**

15 what suitors press to him: what people stand near him.

Lucius. I hear none, madam.

Portia. Prithee, listen well.
I heard a bustling rumor like a fray,
And the wind brings it from the Capitol.

Lucius. Sooth, madam, I hear nothing.

[*Enter the* Soothsayer.]

Portia. Come hither, fellow. Which way hast thou been?

Soothsayer. At mine own house, good lady.

Portia. What is't o'clock?

Soothsayer. About the ninth hour, lady.

Portia. Is Caesar yet gone to the Capitol?

Soothsayer. Madam, not yet. I go to take my stand,
To see him pass on to the Capitol.

Portia. Thou hast some suit to Caesar, hast thou not?

Soothsayer. That I have, lady. If it will please Caesar
To be so good to Caesar as to hear me,
I shall beseech him to befriend himself.

Portia. Why, know'st thou any harm's intended towards him?

Soothsayer. None that I know will be, much that I fear may chance.
Good morrow to you. Here the street is narrow.
The throng that follows Caesar at the heels,
Of senators, of praetors, common suitors,
Will crowd a feeble man almost to death.
I'll get me to a place more void and there
Speak to great Caesar as he comes along.

C

[*Exit.*]

Portia. I must go in. Ay me, how weak a thing
The heart of woman is! O Brutus,
The heavens speed thee in thine enterprise—
Sure the boy heard me.—Brutus hath a suit
That Caesar will not grant.—O, I grow faint.—
Run, Lucius, and commend me to my Lord;
Say I am merry. Come to me again
And bring me word what he doth say to thee.

D

[*Exeunt severally.*]

18 I heard . . . fray: Portia imagines that she has heard a noise like a battle **(fray).**

20 Sooth: truthfully.

21 The Soothsayer is the same fortuneteller who warned Caesar to beware the ides of March. He is now on his way to the street near the Capitol building where he usually sits.

27 Thou hast . . . Caesar: Have you some favor to ask of Caesar?

32 None . . . chance: I'm not sure of any danger, but I fear that some may chance to happen.

42–43 Brutus hath . . . not grant: Brutus has a favor to ask that Caesar will not give him.

44 commend . . . Lord: Give my husband my good wishes.

severally: in different directions.

Customizing Instruction

Less Proficient Readers

1 Explain to students that *emulation* means "the desire to equal or surpass."

Less Proficient Readers

Help students understand the play by asking them the following questions:

- Why does Calpurnia want Caesar to stay at home?
  Possible Response: She had a dream that indicated danger for Caesar.
- Does Caesar stay home?
  Answer: No. He goes to the Senate House.
- What does Artemidorus intend to give Caesar?
  Answer: a note warning of the assassination attempt
- What does the soothsayer intend to do?
  Answer: warn Caesar that he is in danger as Caesar passes him on the way to the Senate House

View and Compare

Possible Response: She is a perceptive, intelligent woman who senses her husband's desperation. She seems very concerned about Brutus' state and the events that are unfolding.

VIEW AND COMPARE

What do these photos suggest about Portia and her relationship to Brutus? Which one comes closest to your own understanding of their relationship?

James Mason as Brutus and Deborah Kerr as Portia (MGM film, 1953). Hulton Getty/Liaison Agency.

Marti Maraden as Portia and Brian Bedford as Brutus (Stratford Festival, 1990). Photo by David Cooper.

Joan MacIntosh as Portia and Martin Sheen as Brutus (New York Shakespeare Festival, 1988). Photo copyright © George E. Joseph.

Teaching Options

Mini Lesson Viewing and Representing

Encourage students to write brief character sketches based on the actors' expressions and physical positions. Students might also discuss their ideas about marriage, or by extension, loyalty, and their ideas about how Brutus and Portia relate to each other. They can then decide which of their interpretations of the photos fits their sense of Brutus' and Portia's relationship.

Thinking through the LITERATURE

Connect to the Literature

1. **What Do You Think?** Whom do you side with at this point, Caesar or the conspirators? Why?

Comprehension Check
- What does Brutus decide in the orchard?
- What does Brutus promise Portia?
- What omens does Calpurnia mention to Caesar in an effort to warn him?

Think Critically

2. Think about Brutus' reasoning, set forth in Act Two, Scene 1, about why Caesar must die. Do you find his argument convincing? Explain your opinion.
3. Do the **details** in Act Two cause you to change your opinion of Caesar? Why or why not?

THINK ABOUT
- his actions and appearance
- his remarks about himself and others
- other **characters'** remarks about him

4. Who do you think would make a better replacement for Caesar as leader of Rome, Brutus or Cassius? Support your opinion.
5. Contrast the relationship between Caesar and Calpurnia with the relationship between Brutus and Portia. What do the differences suggest about the character of the two men?
6. How would you describe Portia's emotional state in Act Two, Scene 4? What effect might it be intended to have on the **audience**?
7. **ACTIVE READING** READING SHAKESPEAREAN DRAMA
Revisit your chart in your READER'S NOTEBOOK. What changes or additions did you make—or would you now like to make—based on your reading of Act Two?

Extend Interpretations

8. **Critic's Corner** Try to visualize Act Two as it might be performed on stage. What special effects do you imagine? How do you think the audience would react to them?
9. **Connect to Life** Imagine that you are Portia. What advice would you have for Brutus?

Literary Analysis

SOLILOQUY/ASIDE In real life, people don't usually make speeches when no one is listening or whisper loudly and expect not to be heard. On stage, however, an audience needs to accept certain conventions as realistic, even though they are not the way real people behave. A **soliloquy** is a long speech that a **character** makes while alone on stage or when no one on stage is supposed to be listening. An **aside** is a remark that a character says in an undertone to the audience or to another character but that everyone else on stage is not supposed to hear. Shakespeare uses both devices to reveal characters' thoughts to the audience.

Activity Identify the soliloquies and asides in Act Two. Also explain what each soliloquy or aside reveals about the character who speaks it. You might want to make use of a chart similar to the following to organize the information.

Scene and Line Nos.	
Character Who Speaks It	
Soliloquy or Aside?	
What It Reveals About the Character	

REVIEW FIGURATIVE LANGUAGE
In Act Two, Scene 2, Caesar says, "Cowards die many times before their deaths; / The valiant never taste of death but once." What do you think this remark means? Do you agree with it? Explain.

Extend Interpretations

Critic's Corner Students may mention gloomy darkness with lightning flashes and sounds of thunder to capture the bad weather; the sounds of the clock referred to in Scene 1; and eerie background music or sounds when Calpurnia reports her dream and in Scene 4 with Portia.

Connect to Life Students may say that he should think before he acts; that violence begets more violence; that everyone should wait and see if Caesar is in fact a tyrant.

Literary Analysis

Soliloquy/Aside This activity can help guide the students as they read this Act; in addition students can discuss or infer what the passages suggest about a particular character.

GUIDING STUDENT RESPONSE

Connect to the Literature

1. **What Do You Think?**
Possible Responses: Caesar—there is little evidence to prove he is a tyrant; the conspirators—Caesar's arrogance and egotism mark him as a potential tyrant.

Comprehension Check
- to join the conspiracy; that Caesar's power represents a danger
- to confide in her; to share his problems with her
- the violent weather and a dream she had about Caesar's murder

Use Selection Quiz
Unit Four Resource Book, p. 68.

Think Critically

2. Possible Responses: convincing, since he knows Caesar's personality and temperament; not persuasive because, without proof, Brutus tries to rationalize an assassination based on what he thinks Caesar may do.
3. Possible Responses: Students may think Caesar's responses to the predictions of evil show that he is rational and courageous; others may say that since Decius is able to persuade Caesar to go to the Senate House that he is afraid of being called cowardly or subservient to his wife. His conversation with the conspirators shows that he suspects nothing.
4. Possible Responses: Brutus, since he is motivated by the general good; Cassius, since he appears to be more practical and clever
5. Possible Response: Brutus is evasive and at first lies to Portia, but he later shows respect for her argument. Caesar is more open with his wife and is initially persuaded by her warnings, but later changes his mind. Brutus seems more protective, while Caesar seems prouder and more self-centered.
6. Possible Response: Portia's confused words and flustered behavior suggest that she is apprehensive about the plot which helps build suspense.
7. Students may want to chart Brutus' internal conflict as he alternately seems to support and to criticize Caesar before deciding to join the conspirators.

Objectives

1. understand **blank verse**
2. understand Shakespeare's plays **(Active Reading)**

TEACHING THE LITERATURE

Reading and Analyzing

Reading Skills and Strategies: PREVIEW

Have students preview Act Three. Discuss with students that Act Three of the play includes the final complications that lead to the climax or turning point in the play, the point at which the conflict is resolved. Encourage students to examine the pictures and consider the called-out quotes throughout Act Three. Have students review the historical facts about Julius Caesar in the Build Background feature on p. 689, and ask them to predict how these historical facts will be developed in Act Three. Before students begin reading, give them a brief summary of Act Three.

Active Reading

UNDERSTANDING SHAKESPEARE'S PLAYS

Inform students that in Shakespeare's plays, Act Three contains the climax, in which the chief conflict of the play so far is resolved, and the play takes a different direction. Ask students to predict what the climax will be and what direction the action will take afterward.

Possible Responses: The conspirators kill Caesar and then begin to struggle for power among themselves; the conspirators kill Caesar and then face the opposition of Mark Antony.

Literary Analysis BLANK VERSE

Point out to students that Shakespeare will sometimes split a line of blank verse between two or more speakers. Draw their attention to line 14, which is split between Cassius and Popilius. Have students find other examples of such split lines.

Possible Responses: line 55; line 74; line 75

ACT THREE

SCENE 1 THE CAPITOL IN ROME.

Outside the Capitol, Caesar refuses to look at Artemidorus' letter of warning. Caesar next moves into the Capitol. There, the conspirators surround him, pretending to plead a case. Suddenly, they stab him to death. Mark Antony flees, but Brutus persuades the conspirators to let him live. Brutus himself promises to explain the killing and its reasons to the Roman people. Antony returns and pretends to be an ally of the conspirators. Secretly, however, he plans to strike back with help from Octavius Caesar, who is now on his way to Rome.

[*The Senate sits on a higher level, waiting for* Caesar *to appear.* Artemidorus *and the* Soothsayer *are among the crowd. A flourish of trumpets. Enter* Caesar, Brutus, Cassius, Casca, Decius, Metellus, Trebonius, Cinna, Antony, Lepidus, Popilius, *and others.* Caesar *stops in front of the* Soothsayer.]

Caesar. The ides of March are come.

Soothsayer. Ay, Caesar, but not gone.

[Artemidorus *steps up to* Caesar *with his warning.*]

Artemidorus. Hail, Caesar! Read this schedule.

[Decius *steps up quickly with another paper.*]

Decius. Trebonius doth desire you to o'erread
(At your best leisure) this his humble suit.

Artemidorus. O Caesar, read mine first, for mine's a suit
That touches Caesar nearer. Read it, great Caesar!

Caesar. What touches us ourself shall be last served.

[Caesar *pushes the paper aside and turns away.*]

Artemidorus. Delay not, Caesar! Read it instantly!

Caesar. What, is the fellow mad?

Publius. Sirrah, give place.

3 schedule: document.
4–13 Artemidorus is the man who has prepared a written warning for Caesar to read **(o'erread)** about the men plotting against him. The conspirators suspect this and do not want him to get to Caesar. Decius steps in front of Artemidorus and offers a written request from someone else. Then Publius (who is not a conspirator) and Cassius push Artemidorus aside.
10 Sirrah: a form of address used toward a servant or inferior, often to express anger or disrespect; **give place:** get out of the way.

LESSON RESOURCES

UNIT FOUR RESOURCE BOOK, pp. 69–72

ASSESSMENT RESOURCES

Formal Assessment, pp. 127–128

Teacher's Guide to Assessment and Portfolio Use

Test Generator

SKILLS TRANSPARENCIES AND COPYMASTERS

Literary Analysis

- Shakespearean Drama I and II, T18, T19 (for Cooperative Learning Activity, p. 759)

Grammar

- Modifiers: *Bad* and *Badly,* C159 (for Mini Lesson, p. 756)

Vocabulary

- Archaic Words and Usage, C74 (for Mini Lesson, p. 740)

Communications

- Evaluating Roles in Groups, T8 (for Mini Lesson, p. 745)
- Verbal Strategies, T14 (for Mini Lesson, p. 750)

INTEGRATED TECHNOLOGY

Audio Library

Video: Literature in Performance

- *Julius Caesar.* See **Video Resource Book**, pp. 25–30.

Visit our website: www.mcdougallittell.com

[Publius *and the conspirators force* Artemidorus *away from* Caesar.]

Cassius. What, urge you your petitions in the street?
Come to the Capitol.

[Caesar *goes into the Senate House, the rest following.* Popilius *speaks to* Cassius *in a low voice.*]

Popilius. I wish your enterprise today may thrive.

Cassius. What enterprise, Popilius?

Popilius. Fare you well.

[*Advances to* Caesar.]

Brutus. What said Popilius Lena?

Cassius. He wished today our enterprise might thrive.
I fear our purpose is discovered.

Brutus. Look how he makes to Caesar. Mark him.

Cassius. Casca, be sudden, for we fear prevention.
Brutus, what shall be done? If this be known,
Cassius or Caesar never shall turn back,
For I will slay myself.

Brutus. Cassius, be constant.
Popilius Lena speaks not of our purposes,
For look, he smiles, and Caesar doth not change.

Cassius. Trebonius knows his time, for look you, Brutus,
He draws Mark Antony out of the way.

[*Exeunt* Antony *and* Trebonius.]

Decius. Where is Metellus Cimber? Let him go
And presently prefer his suit to Caesar.

Brutus. He is addressed. Press near and second him.

Cinna. Casca, you are the first that rears your hand.

[Caesar *seats himself in his high Senate chair.*]

Caesar. Are we all ready? What is now amiss
That Caesar and his Senate must redress?

Metellus. Most high, most mighty, and most puissant
Caesar,
Metellus Cimber throws before thy seat
An humble heart.

[*Kneeling.*]

Caesar. I must prevent thee, Cimber.
These couchings and these lowly courtesies
Might fire the blood of ordinary men

13 I wish . . . thrive: I hope your venture is successful.

18–24 Look how . . . change: Brutus and Cassius watch Popilius Lena talk privately with Caesar. They fear he is telling Caesar of their plot. Then, seeing Popilius Lena smile, they know they were mistaken.

28 prefer . . . Caesar: ask his favor of Caesar.

29 Press . . . him: Get near him (Metellus Cimber) and back up his request.

33 puissant: powerful.

Customizing Instruction

Less Proficient Readers

Remind students that they must pay particular attention to stage directions in such a congested scene as this one. Students should understand that there is a great deal of confusion in and around the Senate House and that many of the characters represented in this scene are nervous and skittish as the tension surrounding the conspirators' plot is dramatically heightened.

Students Acquiring English

Explain to students that the phrase "be sudden" in line 19 means "be swift," that is, "be ready to act quickly if the plans are forestalled." Explain to students that in this scene people are nervous and anxious about the plot to kill Caesar.

Use **Spanish Study Guide** for additional support, pp. 155–157.

Gifted and Talented

Point out to students that an important part of Act Three is Antony's stirring funeral speech for Caesar. Have students find a historical speech of consequence and compare and contrast its motive, techniques, language, and effectiveness with Antony's speech. Encourage students to share with the class the speeches they have analyzed and their analyses of them. Discuss what makes a speech effective and whether effective oration is a good enough reason to take someone seriously.

BLOCK SCHEDULING: MANAGING TIME

If your schedule requires that you cover the lesson objectives in a shorter time, use . . .

- Preparing to Read, p. 689
- Thinking Through the Literature, p. 759
- Grammar in Context, p. 796

If you want to take advantage of longer class time, use . . .

- TE Teaching Options: Vocabulary Strategy, pp. 740–741; Cross Curricular Links, pp. 738, 744, 748; Standardized Test Practice, pp. 742–743; Informal Assessment, p. 746; Speaking and Listening, pp. 745, 750
- Choices & Challenges and Author Activity, pp. 795, 797

Reading and Analyzing

GUIDE FOR READING

A Possible Response: No. Caesar's evaluation of his own personality conflicts with the fact that he was swayed by Decius Brutus' arguments and flattery in Act Two, Scene 2.

B Possible Response: Yes. Caesar is making outrageous claims about his own firmness and constancy.

Literary Analysis: THEME

C Ask students how Caesar's last words relate to the theme of friendship in the play.

Possible Response: Caesar's last words imply that Brutus' betrayal of his friendship is the blow that finally kills Caesar.

And turn preordinance and first decree
Into the law of children. Be not fond
To think that Caesar bears such rebel blood
That will be thawed from the true quality
With that which melteth fools—I mean, sweet words,
Low-crookèd curtsies, and base spaniel fawning.
Thy brother by decree is banishèd.
If thou dost bend and pray and fawn for him,
I spurn thee like a cur out of my way.
Know, Caesar doth not wrong, nor without cause
Will he be satisfied.

Metellus. Is there no voice more worthy than my own,
To sound more sweetly in great Caesar's ear
For the repealing of my banished brother?

Brutus. I kiss thy hand, but not in flattery, Caesar,
Desiring thee that Publius Cimber may
Have an immediate freedom of repeal.

Caesar. What, Brutus?

Cassius. Pardon, Caesar! Caesar, pardon!
As low as to thy foot doth Cassius fall
To beg enfranchisement for Publius Cimber.

Caesar. I could be well moved, if I were as you;
If I could pray to move, prayers would move me;
But I am constant as the Northern Star,
Of whose true-fixed and resting quality
There is no fellow in the firmament.
The skies are painted with unnumbered sparks,
They are all fire, and every one doth shine;
But there's but one in all doth hold his place.
So in the world: 'tis furnished well with men.
And men are flesh and blood, and apprehensive,
Yet in the number I do not know but one
That unassailable holds on his rank,
Unshaked of motion; and that I am he,
Let me a little show it, even in this,
That I was constant Cimber should be banished
And constant do remain to keep him so.

Cinna. O Caesar!

1 **Caesar.** Hence! Wilt thou lift up Olympus?

Decius. Great Caesar!

Caesar. Doth not Brutus bootless kneel?

Casca. Speak hands for me!

35–48 I must prevent . . . satisfied: Caesar claims that, unlike ordinary men, he cannot be moved by bowing and scraping. He will not let such things change the laws of the country **(preordinance and first decree).** His heart cannot be melted by sweet words, bowing **(curtsies),** and behavior fit for a dog **(base spaniel fawning).** Metellus Cimber's brother, Caesar says, has been banished by law. Begging won't change that. Does Caesar evaluate his own personality correctly?

54 freedom of repeal: the right to return to Rome from exile.

55–57 Caesar is surprised that Brutus would beg for freedom **(enfranchisement)** for Publius Cimber. Actually, Brutus, like the rest of the conspirators, is only looking for an excuse to carry out their plan.

58–74 I could be . . . Olympus: Caesar says he is too strong to be moved by begging, even when it comes from these respected men. He compares himself to the North Star, which sailors use for direction because it always appears at the same place in the sky. Like that star, Caesar says, which has no equal in the sky **(fellow in the firmament),** he cannot be moved. They might as well try to lift Mount Olympus (the mountain where the Greek gods were believed to live). Is Caesar bragging?

75 Doth not . . . kneel: Can't you see that even Brutus' kneeling doesn't sway me? **Bootless** means "without any effect," like a kick from a foot that has no boot.

Teaching Options

Cross Curricular Link Current Events

ASSASSINATION The issue of political assassination is key in *Julius Caesar*. The conspirators justify their deed by claiming that Caesar is such a potentially dangerous—and popular—tyrant that assassination is the only way to prevent dictatorship. Political assassinations often have far-reaching repercussions. The murder of Julius Caesar led to civil war in Rome, but assassinations can even have a global impact. For example, the assassination in 1914 of Archduke Francis Ferdinand, the heir to the Austrian throne, triggered World War I. The modern history of the United States is full of political assassinations: President John F. Kennedy in 1963, his brother Senator Robert Kennedy and the Reverend Martin Luther King, Jr., in 1968. Ronald Reagan, president of the United States from 1981 to 1989, was injured in an assassination attempt in 1981.

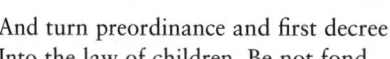

[*They stab* Caesar. Casca, *the others in turn, then* Brutus.]

C **Caesar.** *Et tu, Brute?*—Then fall Caesar!

[*Dies.*]

Cinna. Liberty! Freedom! Tyranny is dead!
Run hence, proclaim, cry it about the streets!

2 **Cassius.** Some to the common pulpits and cry out
"Liberty, freedom, and enfranchisement!"

Brutus. People and Senators, be not affrighted.
Fly not; stand still. Ambition's debt is paid.

Casca. Go to the pulpit, Brutus.

Decius. And Cassius, too.

Brutus. Where's Publius?

Cinna. Here, quite confounded with this mutiny.

3 **Metellus.** Stand fast together, lest some friend of Caesar's
Should chance—

77 *Et tu, Brute?*: Even you, Brutus?

80 Some . . . pulpits: Some of you go to the speakers' platforms. The scene is now chaos—people yelling, screaming, and running in fear. Cassius and Brutus are trying to avoid a riot.

"Liberty, freedom, and enfranchisement!"

Edward Herrmann as Cassius (New York Shakespeare Festival, 1988).
Photo copyright © George E. Joseph.

Customizing Instruction

Students Acquiring English

1 Tell students that *hence* here means "Go away!" Explain to students that *wilt thou* means "will you," and that Olympus is the name of a mountain in Greece.

2 Tell students that *enfranchisement* here means "a voice in government."

Less Proficient Readers

3 Draw students' attention to Metellus' lines after the assassination: he urges the conspirators to "stand fast together," that is, to stick together and make a stand. His words are cut short by Brutus. Ask students what they think Metellus is worried about.

Possible Response: He is worried that Caesar's friends will retaliate against the conspirators.

Reading and Analyzing

Reading Skills and Strategies: EVALUATE

A Ask students how they evaluate Brutus' comment here about having released Caesar from the fear of death; is Brutus sincere?

Possible Response: No. The comment is a rationalization to excuse the murder, since Caesar says in Act Two that he doesn't fear death.

Then ask students what their evaluations reveal about Brutus' character.

Possible Response: He has a desperate need to believe that he is right and that he is not hurting anyone, even the man he has killed.

Literary Analysis: SETTING

B Ask students why Shakespeare chose to have Caesar lie at the base of Pompey's statue. How is this setting relevant to the text's meaning?

Possible Response: The play opened with news of Caesar's defeat of Pompey, Caesar's greatest enemy. It is ironic that Caesar should be lying dead at the base of the statue of the enemy he defeated in battle.

GUIDE FOR READING

C **Possible Responses:** to underline the historic importance of the events portrayed in the play; to make an ironic, self-referential acknowledgment that this is, in fact, a play

D **Possible Responses:** Antony will not be harmed and the conspirators will account for the murder.

E **Possible Responses:** Since this is the second time that Cassius has expressed misgivings about Antony, Shakespeare may be hinting that Cassius is correct to distrust him.

F **Possible Response:** Antony may be honest in that he is so loyal to Caesar that he wishes to die, though it is doubtful that he considers these men great.

Brutus. Talk not of standing! Publius, good cheer.
There is no harm intended to your person
Nor to no Roman else. So tell them, Publius.

Cassius. And leave us, Publius, lest that the people,
Rushing on us, should do your age some mischief.

Brutus. Do so, and let no man abide this deed
But we the doers.

[*Reenter* Trebonius.]

Cassius. Where is Antony?

Trebonius. Fled to his house amazed.
Men, wives, and children stare, cry out, and run,
As it were doomsday.

Brutus. Fates, we will know your pleasures.
That we shall die, we know; 'tis but the time,
And drawing days out, that men stand upon.

A **Cassius.** Why, he that cuts off twenty years of life
Cuts off so many years of fearing death.

Brutus. Grant that, and then is death a benefit.
So are we Caesar's friends, that have abridged
His time of fearing death. Stoop, Romans, stoop,
And let us bathe our hands in Caesar's blood
Up to the elbows and besmear our swords.
Then walk we forth, even to the market place,
And waving our red weapons o'er our heads,
1 Let's all cry, "Peace, freedom, and liberty!"

Cassius. Stoop then and wash. How many ages hence
Shall this our lofty scene be acted over
In states unborn and accents yet unknown!

Brutus. How many times shall Caesar bleed in sport,
B That now on Pompey's basis lies along
No worthier than the dust!

Cassius. So oft as that shall be.
So often shall the knot of us be called
The men that gave their country liberty.

Decius. What, shall we forth?

Cassius. Ay, every man away.
Brutus shall lead, and we will grace his heels
With the most boldest and best hearts of Rome.

[*Enter a* Servant.]

Brutus. Soft! who comes here? A friend of Antony's.

92–93 leave . . . mischief: Cassius wants Publius, an old man, to leave before he gets hurt by the crowd.
94 abide: suffer for.

105–110 Brutus leads the others in covering themselves with Caesar's blood. He wants the Romans to think of their act as a public one, an act they are not trying to hide.

111–114 How many . . . sport: This scene will often be performed as a play in the future in countries and languages that don't even exist now. Why do you think Shakespeare added this line? **C**

115 Pompey's basis: the foot of Pompey's statue.

Teaching Options

Mini Lesson **Vocabulary Strategy**

ARCHAIC WORDS AND USAGE Instruction Language is fluid and changes significantly over time, which is why Shakespeare's language from the 16th century may be difficult to understand at times. Shakespeare often uses words that are by now either entirely outmoded or recognizable to us but with meanings in Renaissance English that differ from modern usage. Such words are termed *archaic,* which means "no longer current." Shakespeare uses many words that are now archaic or have archaic meanings, although often Shakespeare's words hover between an older meaning and a newer one.

Practice Have students work in groups and use dictionaries to find both the archaic and modern meanings of the following words. At the end of the exercise, discuss with students the possible relationships between the words' archaic meanings and their current meanings.

Servant. Thus, Brutus, did my master bid me kneel;
Thus did Mark Antony bid me fall down;
And being prostrate, thus he bade me say:
Brutus is noble, wise, valiant, and honest;
Caesar was mighty, bold, royal, and loving.
Say I love Brutus and I honor him;
Say I feared Caesar, honored him, and loved him.
If Brutus will vouchsafe that Antony
May safely come to him and be resolved
How Caesar hath deserved to lie in death,
Mark Antony shall not love Caesar dead
So well as Brutus living, but will follow
The fortunes and affairs of noble Brutus
Through the hazards of this untrod state
With all true faith. So says my master Antony.

Brutus. Thy master is a wise and valiant Roman.
I never thought him worse.
Tell him, so please him come unto this place,
He shall be satisfied and, by my honor,
Depart untouched.

Servant. I'll fetch him presently.

[*Exit.*]

Brutus. I know that we shall have him well to friend.

Cassius. I wish we may. But yet have I a mind
That fears him much; and my misgiving still
Falls shrewdly to the purpose.

[*Reenter* Antony.]

Brutus. But here comes Antony. Welcome, Mark Antony.

Antony. O mighty Caesar! Dost thou lie so low?
Are all thy conquests, glories, triumphs, spoils,
Shrunk to this little measure? Fare thee well.
I know not, gentlemen, what you intend,
Who else must be let blood, who else is rank.
If I myself, there is no hour so fit
As Caesar's death's hour; nor no instrument
Of half that worth as those your swords, made rich
With the most noble blood of all this world.
I do beseech ye, if you bear me hard,
Now, whilst your purpled hands do reek and smoke,
Fulfill your pleasure. Live a thousand years,
I shall not find myself so apt to die;

123–136 Fearful for his own life, Antony sends a message with his servant. Lying face down on the floor **(being prostrate)**, the servant begs for assurance that Brutus will promise **(vouchsafe)** Antony's safety so that he may come and be given an explanation **(be resolved)** for Caesar's murder. Then Antony will agree to follow Brutus through the dangers of this new, untried government **(the hazards of this untrod state)**.

140–142 What promise does Brutus tell the servant to relay to Antony? **D**

142 presently: immediately.

144–146 But yet . . . purpose: Unlike Brutus, Cassius doesn't trust Antony. He adds that his doubts **(misgiving)** in matters like this are usually accurate. Who do you think is right, Cassius or Brutus? **E**

148–163 The sight of Caesar's body causes Antony to break down. Keep in mind that he truly loved Caesar, almost as a son loves his father.

152–163 Who else . . . this age: Who else is so diseased **(rank)** that he must be "cured" by the knives of the men who just killed Caesar? Antony says he would be honored to be killed at the same time, with the same weapons, and by the same blood-stained **(purpled)** hands that killed Caesar. He adds that the honor would come partly from being killed by such great men **(the choice and master spirits of this age)**. Do you believe that Antony is being honest here? **F**

Customizing Instruction

Less Proficient Readers

Use the following questions to help students understand various characters' reactions to Caesar's death:

- What does Antony do immediately after Caesar is stabbed?
  Answer: He flees.
- What does Brutus encourage the conspirators to do before they walk through the city?
  Possible Response: to bathe their hands and weapons in Caesar's blood
- Whom does Cassius want at the head of the group as the conspirators prepare to leave the Senate?
  Answer: Brutus

Less Proficient Readers

1 Help students understand that Brutus' cry of "Peace, freedom, liberty!" is his subjective interpretation of the assassination. Other Romans might raise a different cry if they were supporters of Caesar. Ask students what alternate cries might be uttered from those with feelings different from Brutus'.
Possible Response: "Chaos, treason, murder!"

Archaic words and usages common to Shakespeare:
prevention
Possible Response: archaic—discovery
modern—hindrance, determent
bondman
Possible Response: archaic—slave, unpaid servant
no common modern usage
fond
Possible Response: archaic—foolish
modern—affectionate
entertain
Possible Response: archaic—to receive into service
modern—to have guests, to amuse
conceit
Possible Response: archaic—idea, imagination
modern—vanity
grief
Possible Response: archaic—grievance, complaint
modern—sadness
presently
Possible Response: archaic—immediately
modern—in the near future, soon

Use **Grammar Transparencies and Copymasters** for more instruction.

Reading and Analyzing

Reading Skills and Strategies: PREDICT

A Ask students to predict whether Antony's speech will support the conspirators or condemn them and to explain why.

Possible Responses: He will condemn them because they killed his friend; he will support them because he fears they will kill him otherwise.

Literary Analysis: THEME

B Ask students what they think of Antony's mention of friendship.

Possible Responses: Seen against his repeated laments for Caesar, Antony's mention of friendship with the assassins may suggest that he is being hypocritical, that he is torn with indecision, or that he is trying to fool them into trusting him so he has more time to plot his revenge.

Active Reading

UNDERSTANDING SHAKESPEARE'S PLAYS

C Explain that an aside is often a character's quiet remark to the audience, but that here Brutus and Cassius speak in asides to each other so that the audience may hear what other characters are not supposed to hear. Ask students why Cassius and Brutus are having this conversation aside.

Possible Response: Cassius does not want Antony to hear him express doubts about him.

No place will please me so, no mean of death,
As here by Caesar, and by you cut off,
The choice and master spirits of this age.

Brutus. O Antony, beg not your death of us!
Though now we must appear bloody and cruel,
As by our hands and this our present act
You see we do, yet see you but our hands
And this the bleeding business they have done.
Our hearts you see not. They are pitiful;
And pity to the general wrong of Rome
(As fire drives out fire, so pity pity)
Hath done this deed on Caesar. For your part,
To you our swords have leaden points, Mark Antony.
Our arms in strength of malice, and our hearts
Of brothers' temper, do receive you in
With all kind of love, good thoughts, and reverence.

Cassius. Your voice shall be as strong as any man's
In the disposing of new dignities.

Brutus. Only be patient till we have appeased
The multitude, beside themselves with fear,
And then we will deliver you the cause
Why I, that did love Caesar when I struck him,
Have thus proceeded.

Antony. I doubt not of your wisdom.
Let each man render me his bloody hand.
First, Marcus Brutus, will I shake with you;
Next, Caius Cassius, do I take your hand;
Now, Decius Brutus, yours; now yours, Metellus;
Yours, Cinna; and, my valiant Casca, yours.
Though last, not least in love, yours, good
Trebonius.
Gentlemen all—Alas, what shall I say?
A My credit now stands on such slippery ground
That one of two bad ways you must conceit me,
Either a coward or a flatterer.
That I did love thee, Caesar, O, 'tis true!
If then thy spirit look upon us now,
Shall it not grieve thee dearer than thy death
To see thy Antony making his peace,
Shaking the bloody fingers of thy foes,
Most noble! in the presence of thy corse?
Had I as many eyes as thou hast wounds,

171 As fire . . . pity: As one fire consumes another, our sorrow for Rome became greater than our sorrow for Caesar.

173–178 To you . . . dignities: As far as you're concerned, Antony, our swords are harmless **(have leaden points).** Our arms, even though they seem cruel **(in strength of malice),** and our hearts, full of brotherly feeling, welcome you. You will have as much to say as anyone in handing out honors from the new government.

191 credit: reputation.

192 conceit: think of.

195–210 These lines are addressed to the corpse **(corse)** of Caesar. Antony is so upset that he temporarily forgets who is with him.

Teaching Options

Assessment Standardized Test Practice

UNDERSTANDING CULTURALLY DIVERSE WRITTEN TEXTS For some standardized tests, students will be asked to display a basic understanding of culturally diverse written texts. Help students develop their readings skills by asking the following questions about the first 160 lines of Act Three of *Julius Caesar*. Students should choose the correct response.

1. How does Artemidorus attempt to warn Caesar of the conspirators' plot?
   A. He holds up a sign with a warning printed on it.
   B. He tries to give Caesar a letter.
   C. He loudly yells the warning to Caesar.
   D. He tries to tell Antony to warn Caesar.
   Answer: B
2. The reader can tell from the play that Caesar
   A. is worried about being assassinated
   B. is afraid to have his friends around him
   C. is completely unaware of the assassins' plot
   D. takes the soothsayer's warning seriously
   Answer: C
3. When Caesar realizes that Brutus is among those who stab him, he feels
   A. peaceful **C.** vengeful
   B. shocked **D.** understanding
   Answer: B

Weeping as fast as they stream forth thy blood,
It would become me better than to close
In terms of friendship with thine enemies.
Pardon me, Julius! Here wast thou bayed, brave hart;
A Here didst thou fall; and here thy hunters stand,
Signed in thy spoil, and crimsoned in thy lethe.
O world, thou wast the forest to his hart;
And this indeed, O world, the heart of thee!
How like a deer, strucken by many princes,
Dost thou here lie!

Cassius. Mark Antony—

Antony. Pardon me, Caius Cassius.
The enemies of Caesar shall say this;
Then, in a friend, it is cold modesty.

Cassius. I blame you not for praising Caesar so;
1 But what compact mean you have with us?
Will you be pricked in number of our friends,
Or shall we on, and not depend on you?

Antony. Therefore I took your hands; but was indeed
Swayed from the point by looking down on Caesar.
B Friends am I with you all, and love you all,
Upon this hope, that you shall give me reasons
Why and wherein Caesar was dangerous.

Brutus. Or else were this a savage spectacle.
Our reasons are so full of good regard
That were you, Antony, the son of Caesar,
You should be satisfied.

Antony. That's all I seek;
And am moreover suitor that I may
Produce his body to the market place
And in the pulpit, as becomes a friend,
Speak in the order of his funeral.

Brutus. You shall, Mark Antony.

Cassius. Brutus, a word with you.

C [*Aside to* Brutus.]
You know not what you do. Do not consent.
That Antony speak in his funeral.
Know you how much the people may be moved
By that which he will utter?

Brutus. By your pardon,

[*Aside to* Cassius.]

204 Here . . . hart: This is the place where you were trapped **(bayed)** like a hunted deer **(hart).**

206 Signed . . . lethe: Marked with your blood **(spoil)** and red in your death. At this point, Antony is probably having difficulty speaking through his tears.

211–213 With these lines, Antony regains control of himself. He points out that even Caesar's enemies will say such things as he has just said.

215 compact: agreement.

216 pricked: listed; marked by punching a hole in a wax tablet.

218 Therefore . . . hands: That is why I shook hands with all of you (because I intend to be counted as an ally of yours).

223 Or else . . . spectacle: If we could not give you reasons for what we have done, it would be nothing but an uncivilized show.

226–235 That's all . . . utter: Antony asks permission to carry Caesar's body outside and make a funeral speech in his honor. Brutus agrees, but Cassius fears that Antony's words might incite the people in Caesar's favor.

Customizing Instruction

Less Proficient Readers

1 Encourage students to use the sidenotes for help with unfamiliar vocabulary in lines 214–217. Then help students understand this passage by pointing out the unusual syntax that is often created when Shakespeare omits a word that would be included in a more modern sentence pattern. Help students put each of the following sentences into more familiar syntax, adding words when necessary.

- "I blame you not for praising Caesar so . . ."

Possible Response: "I do not blame you for praising Caesar so . . ."

- "But what compact mean you have with us?"

Possible Response: "But what agreement do you mean to have with us?"

- "Will you be pricked in number of our friends . . ."

Possible Response: "Will you be counted in the number of our friends . . ."

- "Or shall we on, and not depend on you?"

Possible Response: "Or shall we go on, and not depend on you?"

4. Antony comes back to talk to the conspirators because
A. he wants to congratulate them
B. he wants to fight them in the street
C. he wants them to explain their actions to him
D. he thinks they might let him rule Rome
Answer: C

Help students choose the correct answers. Ask them to give details of the plot and characters. Explain that by reading carefully and taking notes, they can keep track of information and clarify important points, which will enhance their comprehension of the story.

Reading and Analyzing

Literary Analysis: FIGURATIVE LANGUAGE

A Explain that an apostrophe is a figure of speech in which an object, abstract quality, or absent person is addressed directly as if present and able to understand. Antony's speech begins with an apostrophe; have students identify what Antony addresses in lines 254–257.

Possible Response: Antony addresses Caesar's corpse—"thou bleeding piece of earth"—as though it were able to hear and understand him.

Active Reading

UNDERSTANDING SHAKESPEARE'S PLAYS

B Explain that although Antony is technically not alone onstage—Caesar's body is still there, too—Antony's speech can be considered a soliloquy, because he reveals his private thoughts about the assassination only to the corpse and to the audience. Ask students to summarize Antony's main points.

Possible Response: Antony apologizes to the corpse for being civil to the murderers and predicts that a terrible civil war will result from the murder.

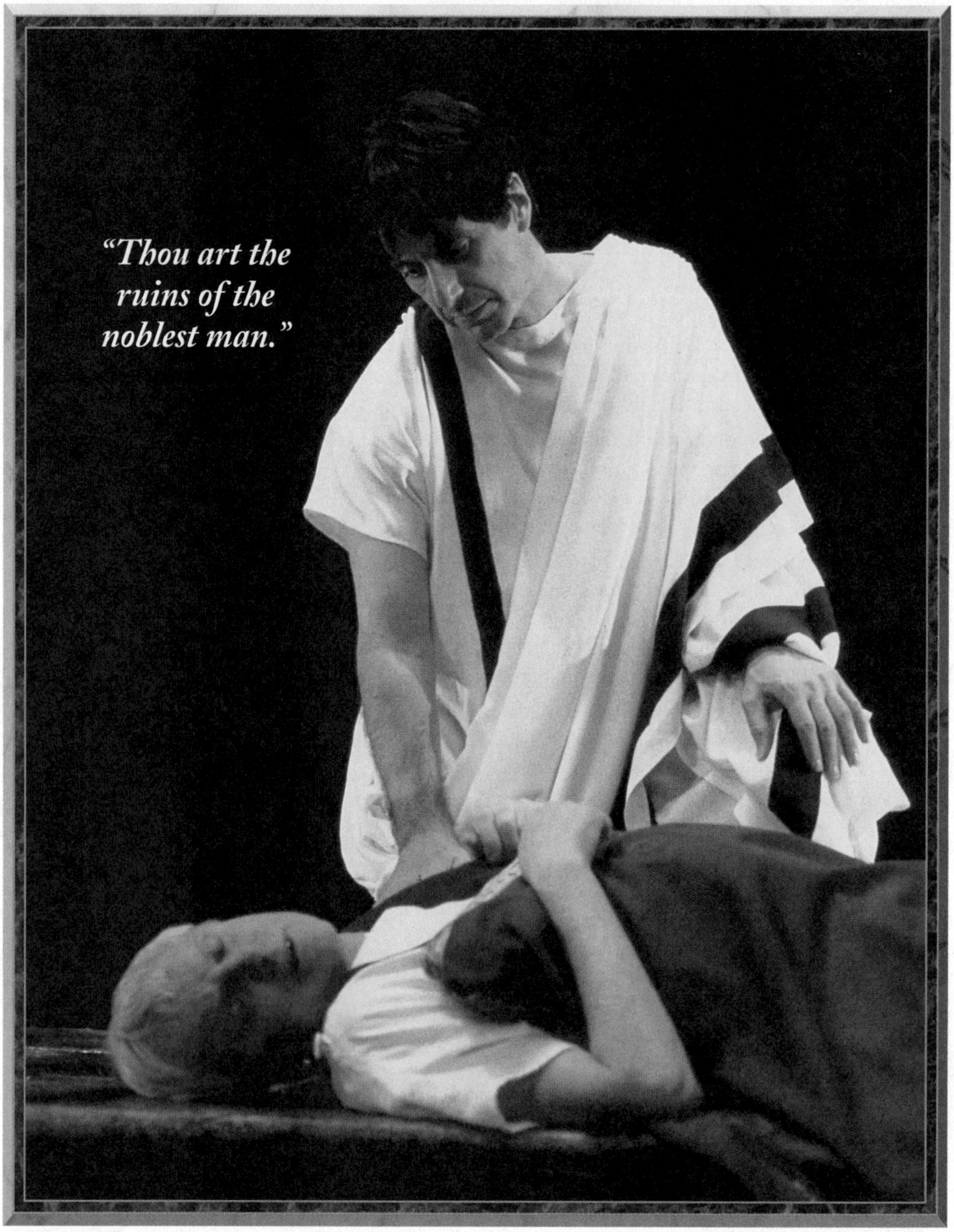
"Thou art the ruins of the noblest man."

Al Pacino as Antony and John McMartin as Caesar (New York Shakespeare Festival, 1988).
Photo by Martha Swope, copyright © Time Inc.

Teaching Options

Cross Curricular Link Theater History

SHAKESPEARE Today Shakespeare is one of the most recognized emblems of high culture and serious literature, but Shakespeare's plays include many characteristics that bear more resemblance to the action movies of Hollywood than the lofty poetry of Renaissance artists. For example, *Julius Caesar* is a story drawn from history, has a plot based on intrigue and suspense, a bloody murder scene, a showdown on a battlefield, and even moments of broad comedy. Theater in Shakespeare's time occupied a place in Elizabethan society similar to the place that the movies occupy in our society today. Much like the audience of a television program or film, the audiences who attended Shakespeare's theater came from a variety of social classes, and Shakespeare's plays were varied enough to appeal to almost everyone. Different plays were offered on different days so that audiences would have variety in their entertainment.

I will myself into the pulpit first
And show the reason of our Caesar's death.
What Antony shall speak, I will protest
He speaks by leave and by permission,
And that we are contented Caesar shall
Have all true rites and lawful ceremonies.
It shall advantage more than do us wrong.

Cassius.
[*Aside to* Brutus.]
I know not what may fall. I like it not.

Brutus. Mark Antony, here, take you Caesar's body.
You shall not in your funeral speech blame us,
But speak all good you can devise of Caesar,
And say you do't by our permission.
Else shall you not have any hand at all
About his funeral. And you shall speak
In the same pulpit whereto I am going,
After my speech is ended.

Antony. Be it so.
I do desire no more.

Brutus. Prepare the body then, and follow us.

[*Exeunt all but* Antony, *who looks down at* Caesar's *body.*]

Antony. O, pardon me, thou bleeding piece of earth,
A That I am meek and gentle with these butchers!
Thou art the ruins of the noblest man
B That ever lived in the tide of times.
Woe to the hand that shed this costly blood!
Over thy wounds now do I prophesy
1 (Which, like dumb mouths, do ope their ruby lips
To beg the voice and utterance of my tongue),
A curse shall light upon the limbs of men;
Domestic fury and fierce civil strife
Shall cumber all the parts of Italy;
Blood and destruction shall be so in use
And dreadful objects so familiar
That mothers shall but smile when they behold
Their infants quartered with the hands of war,
All pity choked with custom of fell deeds;
2 And Caesar's spirit, ranging for revenge,
With Até by his side come hot from hell,
Shall in these confines with a monarch's voice
Cry "Havoc!" and let slip the dogs of war,

238 protest: explain.

242 It shall . . . wrong: His speech will do us more good **(advantage more)** than harm.

254–275 Now that Antony is alone with Caesar's corpse, he speaks truthfully. His speech shows what he really thinks of the men who have just left and what he intends to do about the murder.

257 in the tide of times: in all of history.

263–269 Domestic fury . . . deeds: Rome **(Italy)** will be torn by civil war. People will become so accustomed to horrible sights that mothers will simply smile when they see their children cut into pieces **(quartered).** Pity will disappear among so much cruelty.

271 Até (ā′ tē): the Greek goddess of revenge.

273 "Havoc!": a battle cry signaling mass killings.

Customizing Instruction

Students Acquiring English

1 Explain to students that *dumb* in this context means "not able to speak" and *ope* means "open."

Explain to students that Antony compares Caesar's wounds to mouths that cannot speak and require him to speak on their behalf.

Less Proficient Readers

Encourage students to break Antony's speech into smaller sections as a way of understanding longer, more difficult passages. Have students reread the speech and note the different topics addressed by Antony. Ask students what subjects Antony covers in this soliloquy.

Possible Response: Antony first addresses the body directly ("pardon me, thou bleeding piece of earth"); then he discusses the potential consequences of the murder ("a curse shall light upon the limbs of men"); and he ends with predicting the revenge of Caesar's spirit ("Caesar's spirit . . . come hot from hell").

Students Acquiring English

2 Explain to students that *fell* is used here as an adjective that means "cruel, terrible, or deadly" and that *ranging* means "roving around"; Antony predicts that Caesar's spirit will rove around looking for revenge.

Mini Lesson Speaking and Listening

Instruction Antony finally reveals his true thoughts about Caesar's death when he is alone onstage with the corpse. He begins his speech by speaking directly to Caesar's body and goes on to use vivid images of horror as he describes the curse that he fears will fall on the country as a result of the murder. Antony speaks with great emotion and anger to his dead friend.

Practice Have students work in pairs to turn this soliloquy into a dialogue between Caesar's ghost and Antony. Students may paraphrase Antony's descriptions of chaos and have Caesar offer his opinion about their potential to come true. Students should also pay attention to the end of the passage in which Antony describes Caesar's revenge on the conspirators, and write dialogue that has Caesar articulating what he would do to avenge his death, or what he would have Antony do for him. Groups might also have Caesar express his feelings toward the assassins.

Present Have pairs of students present their interpretations to the class. Students who are audience members should listen and respond appropriately with questions and comments.

BLOCK SCHEDULING This activity is particularly well suited for longer class periods.

Reading and Analyzing

Literary Analysis: SETTING

Remind students that readers of dramatic literature must keep clear visual images of the characters and setting in mind since plays are usually meant to be seen in performance. Remind students that throughout most of this scene, Caesar's corpse has been onstage. Ask students what emotional effect might be produced by such a setting.

Possible Responses: Keeping Caesar's body onstage reinforces the physical consequences of the conspirators' plot—someone has been stabbed to death in public; displaying the body heightens the gravity of the event and might influence the audience's emotions in Antony's favor.

Reading Skills and Strategies: EVALUATE

A **Possible Response:** Antony will skillfully play on the crowd's emotions.

B Have students evaluate what the exclamations of the citizens and orders of Brutus imply about the mood of the people as the scene opens.

Possible Response: The people are angry and threatening; they are suspicious of the conspirators.

GUIDE FOR READING

C **Possible Response:** Yes—he refers to his love of Caesar and of Rome. He honestly feels that the killing was justified.

That this foul deed shall smell above the earth
With carrion men, groaning for burial.

[*Enter* Octavius' Servant.]

You serve Octavius Caesar, do you not?

Servant. I do, Mark Antony.

Antony. Caesar did write for him to come to Rome.

Servant. He did receive his letters and is coming,
And bid me say to you by word of mouth—
O Caesar!

Antony. Thy heart is big. Get thee apart and weep.
Passion, I see, is catching, for mine eyes,
Seeing those beads of sorrow stand in thine,
Began to water. Is thy master coming?

Servant. He lies tonight within seven leagues of Rome.

Antony. Post back with speed and tell him what hath chanced.
Here is a mourning Rome, a dangerous Rome,
No Rome of safety for Octavius yet.
Hie hence and tell him so. Yet stay awhile.
Thou shalt not back till I have borne this corse
1 Into the market place. There shall I try
In my oration how the people take
The cruel issue of these bloody men,
According to the which thou shall discourse
To young Octavius of the state of things.
Lend me your hand.

[*Exeunt with* Caesar's *body.*]

275 With carrion . . . burial: like rotting corpses begging to be buried.

276 Antony is interrupted by a servant of Octavius, an ally of Caesar. The servant begins to relay a message, then sees the bleeding corpse on the floor.

286 He lies . . . Rome: Octavius will set up camp tonight about twenty-one miles **(seven leagues)** outside Rome.

287–297 Post back . . . your hand: Antony tells the servant to hurry back and tell Octavius what has happened. Then he tells the servant to wait. He wants the servant to listen to his funeral speech and report to Octavius how the crowd responds to it. What do you think Antony's funeral speech will be like?

Teaching Options

Assessment Informal Assessment

NEWSPAPER REPORT Have students imagine that they are journalists from the local Roman newspaper who have been covering Caesar's return to the city after his defeat of Pompey. They also will have witnessed the events leading up to the attack on Caesar on the ides of March. Ask each student to write a newspaper report of the assassination, providing brief background information about the days before the conspirators' strike and an account of the activity before, during, and after the murder.

RUBRIC

3 **Full Accomplishment** Students thoroughly report background material, the assassination, and events after the murder.

2 **Substantial Accomplishment** Students adequately report background material, the assassination, and events after the murder.

1 **Little or Partial Accomplishment** Students report little or no background material, show little or no comprehension of the assassination, and show little or no comprehension of the events after the murder.

SCENE 2 The Forum in Rome.

Brutus speaks before a group of "citizens," or common people of Rome. He explains why Caesar had to be slain for the good of Rome. Then, Brutus leaves and Antony speaks to the citizens. A far better judge of human nature than Brutus, Antony cleverly manages to turn the crowd against the conspirators by telling them of Caesar's good works and his concern for the people, as proven by the slain ruler's will. He has left all his wealth to the people. As Antony stirs the citizens to pursue the assassins and kill them, he learns that Octavius has arrived in Rome and that Brutus and Cassius have fled.

B [*Enter* Brutus *and* Cassius *and a throng of* Citizens, *disturbed by the death of Caesar.*]

Citizens. We will be satisfied! Let us be satisfied!

Brutus. Then follow me and give me audience, friends.
Cassius, go you into the other street
And part the numbers.
Those that will hear me speak, let 'em stay here;
Those that will follow Cassius, go with him;
And public reasons shall be rendered
Of Caesar's death.

First Citizen. I will hear Brutus speak.

Second Citizen. I will hear Cassius, and compare their
reasons when severally we hear them rendered.

[*Exit* Cassius, *with some of the* Citizens. Brutus *goes into the pulpit.*]

Third Citizen. The noble Brutus is ascended. Silence!

2 **Brutus.** Be patient till the last.
Romans, countrymen, and lovers, hear me for my cause, and be silent, that you may hear. Believe me for mine honor, and have respect to mine honor, that you may believe. Censure me in your wisdom, and awake your senses, that you may the better judge. If there be any in this assembly, any dear friend of Caesar's, to him I say that Brutus' love to Caesar was no less than his. If then that friend demand why Brutus rose against Caesar, this is my answer: Not that I loved Caesar less, but that I loved Rome more. Had you rather Caesar were living, and die all slaves, than that Caesar were dead, to live all

2–8 give me audience: Listen to me. Brutus is shouting, trying to get the crowd to quiet down so he can speak. He asks Cassius to divide the crowd **(part the numbers)** and speak to another group. We will tell the people our reasons **(public reasons shall be rendered)** for killing Caesar, he says.

13–41 As you read Brutus' speech, think about the kinds of arguments he uses to persuade the crowd. Does he try to appeal to their emotions? Do you think he truly believes that the killing was justified? **C**

13 lovers: friends.

16 Censure me: Judge me.

Customizing Instruction

Students Acquiring English

1 Explain to students that here *try* means "to test."

Less Proficient Readers

Set a Purpose Have students read on to find out which side—Brutus' or Antony's—the crowd decides to support.

2 Ask the following questions to check students' comprehension of the first part of Brutus' speech.

- What does Brutus want the citizens to do as they listen to his speech?

Possible Response: Brutus wants the crowd to be silent and pay attention, believe him, and judge his reasons.

- What reason does Brutus give for rising up against Caesar?

Possible Responses: Although Brutus loved Caesar, he loved Rome more; Caesar would have made slaves of all of them.

Reading and Analyzing

Literary Analysis: THEME

A Ask students what the reaction of the crowd to Brutus' speech suggests about the crowd's loyalty.
Possible Response: The crowd's frenzied approval suggests that they change loyalties easily.

GUIDE FOR READING

B **Possible Response:** frenziedly supportive; worshipful

Literary Analysis BLANK VERSE

C Point out to students that Brutus' speech to the crowd has been in prose, but his response to their approval is in blank verse. Encourage them to speculate about the reasons for this shift.
Possible Response: Brutus' appeal was dull, plodding, and reasonable, but his relief at the crowd's approval sends him into poetry—his emotions are more sincere at this point than when he was struggling to rationalize his actions and persuade the crowd.

GUIDE FOR READING

D **Possible Response:** Given the warnings of Cassius, Brutus may not be wise to depart so soon.

E **Possible Response:** Antony will say that Caesar was not, in fact, a tyrant, but rather a just, heroic, and generous ruler.

"Not that I loved Caesar less, but that I loved Rome more."

Martin Sheen as Brutus and Al Pacino as Antony (New York Shakespeare Festival, 1988). Photo by Martha Swope, copyright © Time Inc.

freemen? As Caesar loved me, I weep for him; as he was fortunate, I rejoice at it; as he was valiant, I honor him; but—as he was ambitious, I slew him. There is tears for his love; joy for his fortune; honor for his valor; and death for his ambition. Who is here so base that would be a bondman? If any, speak, for him have I offended. Who is here so rude that would not be a Roman? If any, speak, for him have I offended. Who is here so vile that will not love his country? If any, speak, for him have I offended. I pause for a reply.

All. None, Brutus, none!

Brutus. Then none have I offended. I have done no more to Caesar than you shall do to Brutus. The question of his death is enrolled in the Capitol; his glory not extenuated, wherein he was worthy, nor his offenses enforced, for which he suffered death.

29–30 Who is . . . bondman: Which of you is so low that you would prefer to be a slave?

31 rude: uncivilized.

38–41 The question . . . death: The reasons for his death are on record in the Capitol. We have not belittled **(extenuated)** his accomplishments or overemphasized **(enforced)** the failings for which he was killed.

Teaching Options

Cross Curricular Link History

JULIUS CAESAR'S ACCOMPLISHMENTS Although he had many political enemies, Julius Caesar was extremely popular with the people of the Roman Republic, and with good reason. Caesar accomplished a great deal of good for the people. He passed an agrarian law that provided land for poor citizens and protected poor tenants in Rome from landlords, established full citizenship as a reward for military service, limited the provincial governors' terms of office to one or two years to protect the provincials from exploitation, and safeguarded the frontiers.

Although Caesar's attempts to organize the empire into a more organic whole with a strong centralized government probably would have been good for Rome in the long run, the aristocracy suspected him of aspiring to kingship and of curtailing their privileges.

[*Enter* Antony *and others, with* Caesar*'s body.*]

Here comes his body, mourned by Mark Antony, who though he had no hand in his death, shall receive the benefit of his dying, a place in the commonwealth, as which of you shall not? With this I depart, that, as I slew my best lover for the good of Rome, I have the same dagger for myself when it shall please my country to need my death.

A **All.** Live, Brutus! live, live!

First Citizen. Bring him with triumph home unto his house.

Second Citizen. Give him a statue with his ancestors.

Third Citizen. Let him be Caesar.

Fourth Citizen. Caesar's better parts
1 Shall be crowned in Brutus.

First Citizen. We'll bring him to his house with shouts and clamors.

Brutus. My countrymen—

Second Citizen. Peace! silence! Brutus speaks.

First Citizen. Peace ho!

Brutus. Good countrymen, let me depart alone,
And, for my sake, stay here with Antony.
Do grace to Caesar's corpse, and grace his speech
Tending to Caesar's glories which Mark Antony,
By our permission, is allowed to make.
I do entreat you, not a man depart,
Save I alone, till Antony have spoke.

[*Exit*]

First Citizen. Stay, ho! and let us hear Mark Antony.

Third Citizen. Let him go up into the public chair.
We'll hear him. Noble Antony, go up.

Antony. For Brutus' sake I am beholding to you.

[*Goes into the pulpit.*]

Fourth Citizen. What does he say of Brutus?

Third Citizen. He says for Brutus'
Sake he finds himself beholding to us all.

Fourth Citizen. 'Twere best he speak no harm of Brutus here!

First Citizen. This Caesar was a tyrant.

49–55 What is the mood of the crowd as Brutus finishes his speech? B

59 grace his speech: Listen to him respectfully.

63 Save: except.

64 Is Brutus wise to depart before Antony makes his speech? D

65 public chair: speaker's platform.

67 beholding: indebted.

68–72 Notice what the people are now saying about Caesar, only minutes after they were crying for him. Antony hears all this. How do you think he will respond? E

Customizing Instruction

Less Proficient Readers

To help students understand the play so far, ask them the following questions:

- When Brutus first speaks to the crowd, what is the crowd's mood?

Possible Responses: angry; upset

- How does Brutus change the crowd's mood?

Possible Responses: He tells them that he killed Caesar to keep them from becoming slaves.

Students Acquiring English

1 Explain to students that *parts* here means "qualities."

Reading and Analyzing

Literary Analysis BLANK VERSE

A Ask students to identify the contrast in form between Antony's oration and Brutus'.

Possible Response: Brutus' speech is in prose, while Antony's speech is in verse.

Have students speculate about the possible effects of this verse speech on the crowd.

Possible Response: Since Shakespeare generally uses verse for serious or lofty themes, Antony's speech may have the more powerful effect on the crowd.

Literary Analysis: RHETORICAL DEVICES

Remind students that rhetorical devices are persuasive techniques used to make a speech more convincing and memorable. Tell students that three such devices that Shakespeare uses are repetition, parallelism, and rhetorical questions. Students should recognize the deceptive modes of persuasion. Have students find examples of each technique in Antony's speech. If they need additional help or examples, refer them to the Rhetorical Devices feature on p. 687.

Possible Responses: repetition: "honorable" (lines 84, 85, 89, 101); parallelism: "It will inflame you, it will make you mad" (line 146); rhetorical question: "Was this ambition?" (line 99)

GUIDE FOR READING

B **Possible Response:** Antony may want to gauge the crowd's reaction, collect his thoughts, or frame a strategy for the second part of his speech.

Third Citizen. Nay, that's certain.
We are blest that Rome is rid of him.

Second Citizen. Peace! Let us hear what Antony can say.

Antony. You gentle Romans—

All. Peace, ho! Let us hear him.

Antony. Friends, Romans, countrymen, lend me your ears;
I come to bury Caesar, not to praise him.
The evil that men do lives after them;
The good is oft interred with their bones.
So let it be with Caesar. The noble Brutus
Hath told you Caesar was ambitious.
If it were so, it was a grievous fault,
And grievously hath Caesar answered it.
Here, under leave of Brutus and the rest
(For Brutus is an honorable man;
So are they all, all honorable men),
Come I to speak in Caesar's funeral.
He was my friend, faithful and just to me;
But Brutus says he was ambitious,
And Brutus is an honorable man.
He hath brought many captives home to Rome,
Whose ransoms did the general coffers fill.
Did this in Caesar seem ambitious?
When that the poor have cried, Caesar hath wept;
Ambition should be made of sterner stuff.
Yet Brutus says he was ambitious;
And Brutus is an honorable man.
You all did see that on the Lupercal
I thrice presented him a kingly crown,
Which he did thrice refuse. Was this ambition?
Yet Brutus says he was ambitious;
And sure he is an honorable man.
I speak not to disprove what Brutus spoke,
But here I am to speak what I do know.
You all did love him once, not without cause.
What cause withholds you then to mourn for him?
O judgment, thou art fled to brutish beasts,
And men have lost their reason! Bear with me,
My heart is in the coffin there with Caesar,
And I must pause till it come back to me.

First Citizen. Methinks there is much reason in his sayings.

75–139 Antony's words at Caesar's funeral make up one of the most famous speeches in all of Shakespeare's plays. Remember that Antony wants to stir the people into a civil war. He must work on them gradually, since they are now supporters of Brutus. One gradual change is in his use of the word *honorable.* As the speech goes on, the word becomes more and more sarcastic.

77–79 The evil . . . Caesar: Let Caesar's good deeds die with him; let him be remembered by his faults.

78 interred: buried.

81 grievous: serious.

83 under leave of: with the permission of.

91 general coffers: the Roman government's treasury.

98 thrice: three times.

107–109 Bear with . . . to me: Antony stops speaking and turns to the corpse. He says he is overcome with grief **(My heart is in the coffin)** and needs to pause for a while. What other reasons might Antony have for pausing at this point in his speech?

Teaching Options

Mini Lesson Speaking and Listening

PRESENTING AN ORATION Instruction Explain that Antony is very skilled as an orator—a person distinguished for speaking well in public. Although he remarks in the play that he is a "plain blunt man," in fact, he possesses great rhetorical skill. Antony's funeral oration for Caesar is one of Shakespeare's most famous speeches, and it most fully reveals its power and cleverness when spoken aloud.

Practice Have students prepare Antony's speech for presentation to the class. First, students should study the text of the speech; have them work in groups, and encourage them to break the speech into smaller sections, paraphrasing passages that are unclear and defining any unfamiliar words. Next, have students mark the text of the speech with cues for expression. For example, do they want to speak forcefully, emotionally, ironically, or angrily at various points in their performance? Remind students to justify their choices of verbal and nonverbal performance techniques by referring to their analysis and interpretation of the speech. Finally, have students practice delivering the speech aloud, perhaps first to their groups and then to the class as a whole. Students who are adept at memorization may want to try to deliver the speech without consulting their notes, but encourage students to use their annotated copies of the text if they need to.

Second Citizen. If thou consider rightly of the matter,
Caesar has had great wrong.

Third Citizen. Has he, masters?
I fear there will a worse come in his place.

Fourth Citizen. Marked ye his words? He would not take the crown;
Therefore 'tis certain he was not ambitious.

First Citizen. If it be found so, some will dear abide it.

Second Citizen. Poor soul! his eyes are red as fire with weeping.

Third Citizen. There's not a nobler man in Rome than Antony.

Fourth Citizen. Now mark him. He begins again to speak.

Antony. But yesterday the word of Caesar might
Have stood against the world. Now lies he there,
And none so poor to do him reverence.
O masters! If I were disposed to stir
Your hearts and minds to mutiny and rage,
I should do Brutus wrong, and Cassius wrong,
Who, you all know, are honorable men.
I will not do them wrong. I rather choose
To wrong the dead, to wrong myself and you,
Than I will wrong such honorable men.
But here's a parchment with the seal of Caesar.
I found it in his closet; 'tis his will.
Let but the commons hear this testament,
Which (pardon me) I do not mean to read,
And they would go and kiss dead Caesar's wounds
And dip their napkins in his sacred blood;
Yea, beg a hair of him for memory,
And dying, mention it within their wills,
Bequeathing it as a rich legacy
Unto their issue.

Fourth Citizen. We'll hear the will! Read it, Mark Antony.

All. The will, the will! We will hear Caesar's will!

Antony. Have patience, gentle friends, I must not read it.
It is not meet you know how Caesar loved you.
You are not wood, you are not stones, but men;
And being men, hearing the will of Caesar,

116 some will dear abide it: Some will pay dearly for it.

120 But: only.

126 honorable men: By this point, Antony is using the term more as an insult than a compliment. He spits it out angrily, wanting the crowd to know that he doesn't believe for a second that it describes the assassins.

130 parchment: document.

133 Which . . . read: Mark Antony is manipulating the crowd here. He has every intention of reading the will, but wants the crowd to force him to do so.

135 napkins: handkerchiefs.

138–139 Bequeathing . . . issue: People would leave it (a hair from Caesar's head) in their wills for their children **(issue).**

143 meet: proper.

Customizing Instruction

Students Acquiring English

1 Explain to students that in this context *answered* means "paid the penalty for." Antony is saying that if Caesar was ambitious, he has paid the penalty for that ambition.

2 Draw students' attention to line 86, and explain that *in* is not the usual preposition in this context. In current English, the phrase would be "at Caesar's funeral."

Less Proficient Readers

Set a Purpose Have students read to discover whether the crowd continues to support Antony.

Mini Lesson Viewing and Representing

Video: Literature in Performance
Have students view and listen critically to Charlton Heston's interpretation of Mark Antony's oration. Encourage students to listen to the speech without looking at a copy of the text, and have them analyze the following elements in Heston's performance:

- facial expression
- tone of voice
- emotional connection
- emphasis on words and phrases
- speed and rhythm of delivery

Have students write a review of the performance and share their responses with the class. Have students talk about their responses to Heston's interpretation of this speech. Did their feelings about Antony or the conspirators change after hearing this performance? Encourage students to be specific about what they did or did not like about Heston's delivery.

Reading and Analyzing

Literary Analysis: VERBAL IRONY

A Point out that Antony uses verbal irony when describing the conspirators. Ask students to explain Antony's use of irony in this passage.

Possible Response: Antony says the opposite of what he means when he says he's worried that he's wronged honorable men. Antony is able to imply ironically that "honorable men" would not have stabbed Caesar.

GUIDE FOR READING

B **Possible Response:** Antony pretends to be at the mercy of the crowd in order to imply that he is their servant, rather than a spokesperson for a dictator. Antony wants to appear democratic, and he wants Caesar's memory, by association, to appear democratic as well.

VIEW AND COMPARE

What do these images suggest about Antony's emotional response to Caesar's death? How is emotion conveyed by each image?

Marlon Brando as Antony (MGM film, 1953). Photofest.

Al Pacino as Antony and John McMartin as Caesar (New York Shakespeare Festival, 1988). Photo copyright © George E. Joseph.

It will inflame you, it will make you mad.
'Tis good you know not that you are his heirs,
For if you should, O, what would come of it?

Fourth Citizen. Read the will! We'll hear it, Antony!
You shall read us the will, Caesar's will!

Antony. Will you be patient? Will you stay awhile?
I have o'ershot myself to tell you of it.
I fear I wrong the honorable men
Whose daggers have stabbed Caesar; I do fear it.

Fourth Citizen. They were traitors. Honorable men!

All. The will! the testament!

Second Citizen. They were villains, murderers! The will!
Read the will!

Antony. You will compel me then to read the will?
Then make a ring about the corpse of Caesar
And let me show you him that made the will.
Shall I descend? and will you give me leave?

All. Come down.

Second Citizen. Descend.

Third Citizen. You shall have leave.

[Antony *comes down.*]

Fourth Citizen. A ring! Stand round.

First Citizen. Stand from the hearse! Stand from the
body!

Second Citizen. Room for Antony, most noble Antony!

Antony. Nay, press not so upon me. Stand far off.

All. Stand back! Room! Bear back!

Antony. If you have tears, prepare to shed them now.
You all do know this mantle. I remember
The first time ever Caesar put it on.
'Twas on a summer's evening in his tent,
That day he overcame the Nervii.
Look, in this place ran Cassius' dagger through.
See what a rent the envious Casca made.
Through this the well-beloved Brutus stabbed;
And as he plucked his cursed steel away,
Mark how the blood of Caesar followed it,
As rushing out of doors to be resolved
If Brutus so unkindly knocked or no;
For Brutus, as you know, was Caesar's angel.

152 I have . . . of it: I have gone too far in even mentioning it to you.

162 Shall I . . . leave: Will you give me permission to come down? Antony pretends to be at the mercy of the crowd. Why do you think he does this?

173 mantle: Caesar's toga.

176 the Nervii: a Belgian tribe that Caesar defeated thirteen years earlier.

178 rent: tear, hole.

181 Mark: notice.

182–183 As rushing . . . or no: Antony says Caesar's blood rushed out of that opening to find out if it really was Brutus who had made the wound.

Customizing Instruction

View and Compare

Possible Response: With his hand outstretched, Marlon Brando as Mark Antony looks like he is feeling very strong emotions, but trying to contain them. Al Pacino, with the palms of his hands turned out at his side, looks vulnerable and even pleading. In each case, Antony appears to be exposing himself and his emotions before a great crowd, a sign of vulnerability calculated to win the crowd's sympathy.

Less Proficient Readers

Help students understand the play by asking them the following questions:

- What is the crowd's mood when Antony begins his speech?

Possible Responses: hostile; anti-Caesar

- What is the crowd's mood by the time Antony shows them the will?

Possible Responses: pro-Caesar; hostile toward the conspirators

Students Acquiring English

1 Explain to students *hearse* here means "the frame or platform on which a coffin or corpse is placed."

Reading and Analyzing

Reading Skills and Strategies: VISUALIZING

A Have students visualize Antony's dramatic gestures as he pulls the cloak off Caesar's body. Ask students whether it would be more effective in a stage production of the play to show the body or to show only the crowd's response to the body as they press around the corpse and keep it from the audience's view.

Possible Response: It would be more effective for the audience to see the wounded body; the power of suggestion is stronger than a physical image. The audience might imagine a scene more horrific than the one staged.

Literary Analysis: CONFLICT

B Ask students what conflict is building as a result of Antony's oration.

Possible Response: a conflict between the conspirators and those who want to punish them and avenge Caesar's death

GUIDE FOR READING

C **Possible Response:** Antony probably says this to make the crowd believe that he is a straightforward, honest man like any of them. He wants to avoid seeming "political," particularly now, when he is at his most political and manipulative.

Judge, O you gods, how dearly Caesar loved him!
This was the most unkindest cut of all;
For when the noble Caesar saw him stab,
Ingratitude, more strong than traitors' arms,
Quite vanquished him. Then burst his mighty heart;
And in his mantle muffling up his face,
Even at the base of Pompey's statue
(Which all the while ran blood) great Caesar fell.
O, what a fall was there, my countrymen!
Then I, and you, and all of us fell down,
Whilst bloody treason flourished over us.
O, now you weep, and I perceive you feel
The dint of pity. These are gracious drops.
Kind souls, what, weep you when you but behold
Our Caesar's vesture wounded? Look you here!
Here is himself, marred, as you see, with traitors.

A [*Pulls the cloak off* Caesar's *body.*]

First Citizen. O piteous spectacle!

Second Citizen. O noble Caesar!

Third Citizen. O woeful day!

Fourth Citizen. O traitors, villains!

First Citizen. O most bloody sight!

Second Citizen. We will be revenged.

B **All.** Revenge! About! Seek! Burn! Fire! Kill! Slay!
Let not a traitor live!

Antony. Stay, countrymen.

First Citizen. Peace there! Hear the noble Antony.

Second Citizen. We'll hear him, we'll follow him,
we'll die with him!

Antony. Good friends, sweet friends, let me not stir you up
To such a sudden flood of mutiny.
They that have done this deed are honorable.
1 What private griefs they have, alas, I know not,
That made them do it. They are wise and honorable,
And will no doubt with reasons answer you.
I come not, friends, to steal away your hearts.
I am no orator, as Brutus is,
But (as you know me all) a plain blunt man
2 That love my friend; and that they know full well
That gave me public leave to speak of him.
For I have neither wit, nor words, nor worth,

189 vanquished: defeated.

197 dint: force.

198–200 weep you . . . traitors: Do you cry when you look only at his wounded clothing **(vesture)**? Here, look at his body! (Antony pulls Caesar's toga aside and reveals the knife wounds.) The people find the sight repulsive, and it makes them angry.

220–222 I am no . . . friend: This is another speaker's trick. Antony has just shown himself to be a much better speaker **(orator)** than Brutus. Why, then, does he say he is "no orator"?

224 wit: intelligence.

Teaching Options

Mini Lesson: Speaking and Listening

TOWN MEETING Instruction Invite students to discuss the crowd's presence in this scene. Point out that "the crowd" as a whole functions as a minor character by providing reactions and opinions that make an impact on the development of the plot. Also, point out that the crowd's feelings change during this scene as they are swayed by the arguments first of Brutus and then of Antony.

Practice Have students elaborate on the crowd's responses by organizing a town meeting at which various factions discuss the pros and cons of Brutus' and Antony's positions in this scene. Have students pick a mediator for the meeting who will keep order and make decisions about who will speak. There should be students representing Brutus' argument in favor of the murder and others who are supporting Antony's position. Other citizens should attend the meeting to ask questions and debate the issues as a way of sorting out whom to follow. At the end of the meeting, have the mediator take a vote on whether Brutus or Antony is more persuasive.

BLOCK SCHEDULING This activity is particularly well suited for longer class periods.

Al Pacino (*center*) as Antony (New York Shakespeare Festival, 1988).
Photo by Martha Swope, copyright © Time Inc.

Action, nor utterance, nor the power of speech
To stir men's blood. I only speak right on.
I tell you that which you yourselves do know,
Show you sweet Caesar's wounds, poor poor dumb mouths,
And bid them speak for me. But were I Brutus,
And Brutus Antony, there were an Antony
Would ruffle up your spirits, and put a tongue
In every wound of Caesar that should move
The stones of Rome to rise and mutiny.

All. We'll mutiny.

First Citizen. We'll burn the house of Brutus.

Third Citizen. Away then! Come, seek the conspirators.

Antony. Yet hear me, countrymen. Yet hear me speak.

All. Peace, ho! Hear Antony, most noble Antony!

Antony. Why, friends, you go to do you know not what.
Wherein hath Caesar thus deserved your loves?
Alas, you know not! I must tell you then.

Customizing Instruction

Students Acquiring English

1 Explain to students that here *griefs* means "grievances" or "causes for complaint," not "sadness."

2 Explain to students that *public leave to speak* means "permission to speak in public."

JULIUS CAESAR ACT THREE 755

Reading and Analyzing

Literary Analysis: CHARACTER

A Ask students what attitude Antony displays after he sees the fury he has stirred up in the crowd.
Possible Response: He seems smug and vengeful, ready for whatever might happen.

Then ask whether Antony displays any ambition for power at the end of this scene.
Possible Response: Although Antony reveals that he is aware of his power to influence the people, he does not hint that he wants to rule Rome.

Literary Analysis: PLOT

Have students analyze and describe the development of the play's plot. Explain that the climax is the turning point in the action of the play, and the falling action consists of events that occur after the climax. Shakespeare presents a challenging question in *Julius Caesar*: Is the climax of the play the murder of Caesar or Antony's speech? Encourage students to discuss both options. Ask them to note whether the direction of the play's action seems to turn after the assassination or after Antony's funeral oration.
Possible Responses: The assassination is the climax because that event sets all other actions, including the funeral speeches, into motion; the falling action—the fight between the conspirators' and Antony's forces—begins when the crowd's support turns in favor of Antony, making that moment the climax of the play.

You have forgot the will I told you of.
All. Most true! The will! Let's stay and hear the will.
Antony. Here is the will, under Caesar's seal.
To every Roman citizen he gives,
1 To every several man, seventy-five drachmas.

245 drachmas: silver coins, worth quite a bit to poor people such as those in the crowd.

Second Citizen. Most noble Caesar! We'll revenge his death!
Third Citizen. O royal Caesar!
Antony. Hear me with patience.
All. Peace, ho!
Antony. Moreover, he hath left you all his walks,
His private arbors, and new-planted orchards,
On this side Tiber; he hath left them you,
And to your heirs for ever—common pleasures,
To walk abroad and recreate yourselves.
Here was a Caesar! When comes such another?

250–254 Reading from the will, Antony tells the crowd that Caesar has left all his private parks and gardens on this side of the Tiber River to be used by the public.

"Here is the will, under Caesar's seal."

Al Pacino as Antony holds the will (New York Shakespeare Festival, 1988). Photo copyright © George E. Joseph.

Teaching Options

Mini Lesson Grammar

SPECIAL PROBLEMS WITH MODIFIERS: *bad/badly*
Alert students that certain adjectives and adverbs can be confusing. *Bad* and *badly* are often used incorrectly. Remind students that *bad* is an adjective describing what something is like; it can modify a noun or pronoun. When it is used after a linking verb, it modifies the subject. *Badly* is an adverb explaining how something is done; it modifies action verbs.

Put the following sentences on the board and explain the correct use of the modifiers.

- Jane felt bad. (*Bad* is an adjective that follows the linking verb *felt*; it modifies the subject *Jane.*)
- The lawn mower rolled badly. (*Badly* is an adverb that modifies the action verb *rolled.*)

2 **First Citizen.** Never, never! Come, away, away!
We'll burn his body in the holy place
And with the brands the traitors' houses.
Take up the body.

Second Citizen. Go fetch fire!

Third Citizen. Pluck down benches!

Fourth Citizen. Pluck down forms, windows, anything!

[*Exeunt* Citizens *with the body.*]

A **Antony.** Now let it work. Mischief, thou art afoot,
Take thou what course thou wilt.
[*Enter a* Servant.]
How now, fellow?

Servant. Sir, Octavius is already come to Rome.

Antony. Where is he?

Servant. He and Lepidus are at Caesar's house.

Antony. And thither will I straight to visit him.
He comes upon a wish. Fortune is merry,
And in this mood will give us anything.

Servant. I heard him say Brutus and Cassius
Are rid like madmen through the gates of Rome.

Antony. Belike they had some notice of the people,
How I had moved them. Bring me to Octavius.

[*Exeunt.*]

258 brands: pieces of burning wood.

263–264 Now let . . . wilt: Alone, Antony gloats over what he has just accomplished. Let things take their course, he says. Whatever happens, happens.

268 thither . . . him: I will go right there to see him.

269–270 He comes . . . anything: Octavius has arrived just as Antony hoped; Antony believes that Fortune, the goddess of fate, is on his side.

272 Are rid: have ridden.

273 Belike: probably.

SCENE 3 A STREET IN ROME.

This scene involves a famous Roman poet named Cinna. (He is not the same Cinna who took part in the assassination.) The angry Roman mob comes upon the poet, believing he is Cinna the conspirator. Soon, they realize this is the wrong man, yet they are so enraged that they slay him anyway. Then, they rush through the city after the true killers of Caesar.

[*Enter* Cinna, *the poet, and after him the* Citizens, *armed with sticks, spears, and swords.*]

Cinna. I dreamt tonight that I did feast with Caesar,
And things unluckily charge my fantasy.
I have no will to wander forth of doors,
Yet something leads me forth.

2 things . . . fantasy: Recent events have caused me to imagine awful things.

Customizing Instruction

Students Acquiring English

1 Explain to students that here *several* means "individual."

2 Explain to students that "we'll burn"—from the preceding line—is the implied subject-verb here. Have students paraphrase this line.
Possible Response: "And with the brands we'll burn the traitors' houses."

Less Proficient Readers

Monitor students' comprehension by asking these questions about the end of the scene.

- Where have Brutus and Cassius gone?
Possible Response: They have fled Rome.
- Why have they left town?
Possible Response: They have left because they have heard that Antony has influenced the people against them.

Practice Have students choose *bad* or *badly* to complete the following sentences. Students should identify whether they've chosen an adjective or adverb and should explain the reason for their choices.

1. Doris felt ________ about losing.
Answer: *bad:* adjective; modifies subject *Doris* after linking verb *felt*
2. The future of the space program looked ________.
Answer: *bad:* adjective; modifies subject *future* after linking verb *looked*
3. The team played ________ for the rest of the game.
Answer: *badly:* adverb; modifies action verb *played*
4. I smelled ________ after cleaning the barn.
Answer: *bad:* adjective; modifies subject *I* after linking verb *smelled*
5. Paul ran ________ with his foot in a cast.
Answer: *badly:* adverb; modifies action verb *ran*

Use **Grammar Transparencies and Copymasters,** p. 159, for more exercises.

Use McDougal Littell's ***Language Network,*** Chapter 9, for more instruction in modifiers.

Reading and Analyzing

Literary Analysis BLANK VERSE

Point out that this brief scene is not in blank verse. Ask students how the short lines of prose contribute to the atmosphere of this chaotic encounter.

Possible Response: The order inspired by the regular rhythm of blank verse is missing; the less predictable form of prose reflects the unpredictable temper of the crowd.

Literary Analysis: THEME

Ask students how this scene relates to the play's theme of the consequences of a breakdown in legitimate authority.

Possible Response: Within hours of Caesar's assassination, Rome has been plunged into social chaos, many of its leaders—the conspirators—have left the city, and the crowd displays a mob mentality as it tears apart an innocent man.

GUIDE FOR READING

A Possible Responses: political protests; unruly sporting events

First Citizen. What is your name?

Second Citizen. Whither are you going?

Third Citizen. Where do you dwell?

Fourth Citizen. Are you a married man or a bachelor?

Second Citizen. Answer every man directly.

First Citizen. Ay, and briefly.

Fourth Citizen. Ay, and wisely.

Third Citizen. Ay, and truly, you were best.

Cinna. What is my name? Whither am I going? Where do I dwell? Am I a married man or a bachelor? Then, to answer every man directly and briefly, wisely and truly: wisely I say, I am a bachelor.

Second Citizen. That's as much to say they are fools that marry. You'll bear me a bang for that, I fear. Proceed—directly.

Cinna. Directly I am going to Caesar's funeral.

First Citizen. As a friend or an enemy?

Cinna. As a friend.

Second Citizen. That matter is answered directly.

Fourth Citizen. For your dwelling—briefly.

Cinna. Briefly, I dwell by the Capitol.

Third Citizen. Your name, sir, truly.

Cinna. Truly, my name is Cinna.

First Citizen. Tear him to pieces! He's a conspirator.

Cinna. I am Cinna the poet! I am Cinna the poet!

Fourth Citizen. Tear him for his bad verses! Tear him for his bad verses!

Cinna. I am not Cinna the conspirator.

Fourth Citizen. It is no matter; his name's Cinna! Pluck but his name out of his heart, and turn him going.

Third Citizen. Tear him, tear him!

[*They attack* Cinna.]

Come, brands, ho! To Brutus', to Cassius'! Burn all! Some to Decius' house and some to Casca's; some to Ligarius'! Away, go!

[*Exeunt all the* Citizens.]

6 Whither: where.

17–18 That's . . . fear: This response shows that Cinna is in danger. The citizen threatens to beat him **(You'll bear me a bang)**, even though Cinna's comment was not meant to be insulting.

34–35 Pluck . . . going: Let's just tear the name out of his heart and send him away.

36 The citizens murder Cinna the poet. Can you think of other examples—from real life or literature—of crowds that have gotten out of control? **A**

Connect to the Literature

1. **What Do You Think?** What is your impression of Antony? Discuss it with your classmates.

Comprehension Check
- Where is Caesar assassinated?
- As he is killed, what does Caesar say about Brutus?
- What effect do Brutus' and Mark Antony's speeches have on the crowd?

Think Critically

2. What do the conspirators believe they have accomplished by killing Caesar? Do you agree? Explain your answer.
3. **ACTIVE READING** **READING SHAKESPEAREAN DRAMA** For a better understanding of Brutus' and Mark Antony's famous funeral speeches, reread Scene 2, lines 13–63 and 75–255. Untangle any unusual word order, and use the sidenotes to decipher the meaning of unfamiliar terms. Then contrast the two speeches. Why is Antony's speech more effective at manipulating the crowd than Brutus' speech?
4. What might Shakespeare be suggesting through his portrayal of the crowd of Roman citizens in Act Three?
5. What is your response to the statement, "Brutus is an honorable man"?

THINK ABOUT
- Caesar's final words to Brutus, and Antony's description of Brutus' act as "the most unkindest cut of all"
- Brutus' treatment of Antony after the assassination
- Brutus' explanation of why he killed Caesar
- other actions that might affect your view of Brutus

Extend Interpretations

6. **What If?** What might have happened if Brutus had listened to Cassius and killed Antony? Support your answer.
7. **Comparing Texts** Compare and contrast the view of friendship presented in the play thus far with the view presented in other works in your text that explore this theme, such as "Two Friends" by Guy de Maupassant or "Cranes" by Hwang Sunwŏn.
8. **Connect to Life** Can public opinion today be as easily swayed as in Shakespeare's portrayal? Cite examples.

Literary Analysis

RHETORICAL DEVICES
The funeral speeches by Brutus and Antony are famous examples of **rhetoric,** or persuasion. Both make use of the following **rhetorical devices** to persuade their audience:
- **Repetition** of words and sounds

Believe me for mine honor, and have respect to mine honor, that you may believe.

- **Parallelism,** or repeated grammatical structures

As Caesar loved me, I weep for him; as he was fortunate, I rejoice at it; as he was valiant, I honor him; but —as he was ambitious, I slew him.

- **Rhetorical questions,** or questions requiring no answer because the answer seems obvious

Had you rather Caesar were living, and die all slaves, than that Caesar were dead, to live all freemen?

Cooperative Learning Activity
Working in a small group, list examples of repetition, parallelism, and rhetorical questions in Mark Antony's famous funeral speech (Act Three, Scene 2, lines 75–255). Then take turns showing how you would give the speech to make its rhetorical devices seem as persuasive as possible.

REVIEW **VERBAL IRONY**
In **verbal irony,** words that seem to say one thing actually mean the opposite. Where in Scene 2 do you think Mark Antony uses verbal irony?

GUIDING STUDENT RESPONSE

Connect to the Literature

1. **What Do You Think?**
Possible Responses: loyal; manipulative; quick-witted

Comprehension Check
- in the Senate House
- *"Et tu, Brute?"* ("Even you, Brutus?")
- Brutus calms the crowd and persuades the people that the assassination was justified, but then Mark Antony excites and angers them, so that they come to hate the conspirators.

Use Selection Quiz
Unit Four Resource Book, p. 72.

Think Critically

2. Possible Responses: The conspirators believe they have delivered Rome from bondage to a tyrant. They have done so, as evidenced by Caesar's arrogance and ambition; they have not, as there is no firm evidence that Caesar would become a tyrant.
3. Possible Responses: Antony speaks in stirring verse, while Brutus speaks in pedestrian prose. Brutus' speech is idealistic, and he tries to justify the conspirators' actions and calm the crowd; Antony, on the other hand, is a master manipulator and wants to incite the people to mutiny.
4. Possible Responses: Shakespeare is suggesting that the crowd is fickle. It wants justice, but is easily swayed by emotion.
5. Possible Responses: Brutus is honorable because he believes he is doing the right thing for his country when he kills Caesar; Brutus is not honorable, because he betrays Caesar's trust by joining the conspirators.

Literary Analysis

Rhetorical Devices Encourage students to construct a chart to keep track of the rhetorical devices used in Antony's speech. Have them use their chart to analyze the text structure.
Verbal Irony Direct students to Antony's funeral oration in Scene 2 for striking examples of his verbal irony.

Extend Interpretations

What If? Encourage students to think about the critical results of Antony's funeral speech. Antony's oration turns the crowd—which is in favor of Caesar's death after hearing Brutus' speech—against the conspirators. If Antony had been killed, he would not have spoken at Caesar's funeral, and the masses would not have turned against the conspirators.
Comparing Texts As students consider the theme of friendship, remind them to keep the related issues of loyalty and betrayal in mind as they examine these works.

Connect to Life Encourage students to think of contemporary politics and the emphasis many politicians, journalists, and campaign contributors place on public opinion polls. Point out that the media coverage of a political event or current issue often influences public opinion, and that polls often show dramatic, frequent shifts in opinion from one side to another.

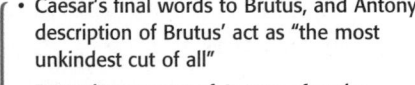

Objectives

1. understand and appreciate **blank verse (Literary Analysis)**
2. understand Shakespeare's plays **(Active Reading)**

TEACHING THE LITERATURE

Reading and Analyzing

Reading Skills and Strategies: PREVIEW

Act Four of the play establishes the falling action and shows the effects of the climax. Review with students historical facts about Julius Caesar, and predict how those facts will be developed in Act Four.

Active Reading

UNDERSTANDING SHAKESPEARE'S PLAYS

Review the characteristics of a tragic hero from p. 686. Ask students to think about who might be the tragic hero of *Julius Caesar*. Remind them that the title character is already dead, and three prominent figures have emerged: Antony, Brutus, and Cassius. Ask students to follow these characters carefully throughout the remaining two acts to determine which one is the tragic hero.

Literary Analysis BLANK VERSE

Shakespeare's iambic pentameter is not always regular. Sometimes the emphasis falls on the wrong syllables, or an extra, unaccented syllable appears at the end of a line. Have students find examples of irregular lines in the remainder of the play and decide whether these irregularities detract from the play's readability.

Possible Response: "He shall not live. Look, with a spot I damn him" (Act 4, Scene 1, line 6). The irregular lines add to the readability of the play, keeping the dialogue from being singsong and too artificial.

Guide for Reading

A Possible Response: A new, cynical side of Antony's character is revealed here. Antony used Caesar's will to get the crowd on his side in Act Three; now he is trying to cheat the people by changing the terms of the will.

B Possible Response: These lines suggest that Octavius is distrustful and apprehensive.

ACT FOUR

SCENE 1 AT A TABLE IN ANTONY'S HOUSE IN ROME.

Antony, Octavius, and Lepidus now rule Rome as a triumvirate—a committee of three. The scene opens on the triumvirate, meeting to draw up a list of their enemies who must be killed. They also discuss changing Caesar's will. As Lepidus goes to fetch the will, Antony expresses his low opinion of Lepidus as a leader. Then, Antony and Octavius begin to discuss how to defeat the armies of Brutus and Cassius.

[*Enter* Antony, Octavius, *and* Lepidus.]

Antony. These many, then, shall die; their names are pricked.

Octavius. Your brother too must die. Consent you, Lepidus?

Lepidus. I do consent.

Octavius. Prick him down, Antony.

Lepidus. Upon condition Publius shall not live,
Who is your sister's son, Mark Antony.

Antony. He shall not live. Look, with a spot I damn him.
But Lepidus, go you to Caesar's house.
Fetch the will hither, and we shall determine
How to cut off some charge in legacies.

Lepidus. What? shall I find you here?

Octavius. Or here or at the Capitol.

[*Exit* Lepidus.]

Antony. This is a slight unmeritable man,
Meet to be sent on errands. Is it fit,
The threefold world divided, he should stand
One of the three to share it?

Octavius. So you thought him,
And took his voice who should be pricked to die

6 with a spot . . . him: I condemn him by marking him on this list.

8–9 Fetch . . . legacies: Bring Caesar's will here, so we can decide how to alter the amounts the people get. Does this statement change your opinion of Antony? Explain. **A**

12–27 This is . . . commons: Now that Antony and Octavius are alone, Antony says what he really thinks of Lepidus. He does not believe Lepidus is worthy of being one of three men in control of Rome's lands in Europe, Asia, and Africa **(The threefold world).** Lepidus, he says, is fit **(Meet)** for running errands. Antony admits that they have accepted Lepidus' opinion about who should be put on the list of those who will die **(black sentence and proscription),** but they have done that only so he will take the blame for the many unpopular things **(divers sland'rous loads)** they plan to do.

LESSON RESOURCES

UNIT FOUR RESOURCE BOOK, pp. 73–76

ASSESSMENT RESOURCES

Formal Assessment, pp. 129–130

Teacher's Guide to Assessment and Portfolio Use

Test Generator

SKILLS TRANSPARENCIES AND COPYMASTERS

Literary Analysis

- Shakespearean Drama I and II, T18, T19 (for Cooperative Learning Activity, p. 777)

Grammar

- Elliptical Clauses, C118 (for Mini Lesson, p. 770)

Vocabulary

- Word Meanings, C75 (for Mini Lesson, p. 763)

Communications

- Dramatic Reading, T12 (for Mini Lesson, p. 764)

INTEGRATED TECHNOLOGY

Video: Literature in Performance

- *Julius Caesar.* See **Video Resource Book**, pp. 25–30.

Visit our website: www.mcdougallittell.com

In our black sentence and proscription.

Antony. Octavius, I have seen more days than you;
And though we lay these honors on this man
To ease ourselves of divers sland'rous loads,
He shall but bear them as the ass bears gold,
To groan and sweat under the business,
Either led or driven as we point the way;
And having brought our treasure where we will,
Then take we down his load, and turn him off
(Like to the empty ass) to shake his ears
And graze in commons.

Octavius. You may do your will;
But he's a tried and valiant soldier.

Antony. So is my horse, Octavius, and for that
I do appoint him store of provender.
It is a creature that I teach to fight,
To wind, to stop, to run directly on,
His corporal motion governed by my spirit.
And, in some taste is Lepidus but so.
He must be taught, and trained, and bid go forth:
A barren-spirited fellow; one that feeds
On objects, arts and imitations
Which, out of use and staled by other men,
Begin his fashion. Do not talk of him,
But as a property. And now, Octavius,
Listen great things. Brutus and Cassius
Are levying powers. We must straight make head.
Therefore let our alliance be combined,
Our best friends made, and our best means stretched
out;
And let us presently go sit in council
How covert matters may be best disclosed
And open perils surest answered.

Octavius. Let us do so; for we are at the stake
And bayed about with many enemies;
And some that smile have in their hearts, I fear,
Millions of mischiefs.

[*Exeunt.*]

29–40 So is my . . . property: Antony compares Lepidus to a horse who is given food **(provender)** and taught how to behave. Antony also says that Lepidus is interested in **(feeds / On)** unimportant things **(objects, arts and imitations)** that he learns of from other people, and these things attract his attention **(Begin his fashion)** after others have lost interest in them.

41–42 Listen . . . head: Listen to important **(great)** matters. Brutus and Cassius are raising an army **(levying powers).** We must move fast **(straight make head)** to build up our own army.

45–47 let us . . . answered: Let us decide the best way to uncover hidden **(covert)** dangers and to deal with the threats we know about.

48–51 for we are . . . mischiefs: We are like a bear tied to a stake and taunted by barking dogs. Some of the people who smile at us may have evil intentions **(mischiefs)** in mind for us. What do these lines tell you about Octavius' state of mind? B

Customizing Instruction

Less Proficient Readers

Explain that the conflict between Antony and the conspirators is escalating as both sides are raising armies and discussing strategies.

Set a Purpose Have students predict the outcome of this military planning.

Students Acquiring English

Explain that Antony now leads one army and Brutus and Cassius lead another. All of Act Four takes place as the characters are preparing for war between Antony's forces on one side and Brutus and Cassius' forces on the other. Tell them to keep this situation in mind as they read Act Four.

Use **Spanish Study Guide** for additional support, pp. 157–159.

Gifted and Talented

Have students discuss the irony of Antony making a list of men marked for assassination. Encourage them to debate whether Caesar's assassination is more justified than the assassinations Antony proposes.

BLOCK SCHEDULING: MANAGING TIME

If your schedule requires that you cover the lesson objectives in a shorter time, use . . .
- Preparing to Read, p. 689
- Thinking Through the Literature, p. 777
- Grammar in Context, p. 796

If you want to take advantage of longer class time, use . . .
- TE Teaching Options: Vocabulary Strategy, p. 763; Speaking and Listening, p. 764; Cross Curricular Links, pp. 766–767, 774; Standardized Test Practice, pp. 768–769; Informal Assessment, p. 772
- Choices & Challenges, p. 795 and Author Activity, p. 797

Reading and Analyzing

Literary Analysis: SETTING

A Have students analyze the relevance of the setting to the text's meaning. Ask students how the setting of this scene presents a contrast with the setting of the first three acts of the play and with the first scene of Act Four.
Possible Response: The setting has shifted to a location far away from Rome and from the civic, public world. Now the play is set in the military world. The sound of drums, the brisk military orders, and the tents reinforce the setting of a military camp.

Literary Analysis: THEME

B Ask students to paraphrase Brutus' observation about friendship in lines 18–27; then ask whether they think his observation is sound.
Possible Response: Brutus says that friends who are growing apart start to make a formal, polite show of friendship to each other. People often use excessive politeness to mask feelings of indifference or distaste.

GUIDE FOR READING

C **Possible Response:** Brutus probably thinks that his officer's report can furnish reliable clues about Cassius' true state of mind and intentions.

VIEW AND COMPARE

What do each of the following images suggest about the character of Brutus? Which image comes closest to your own interpretation of his character?

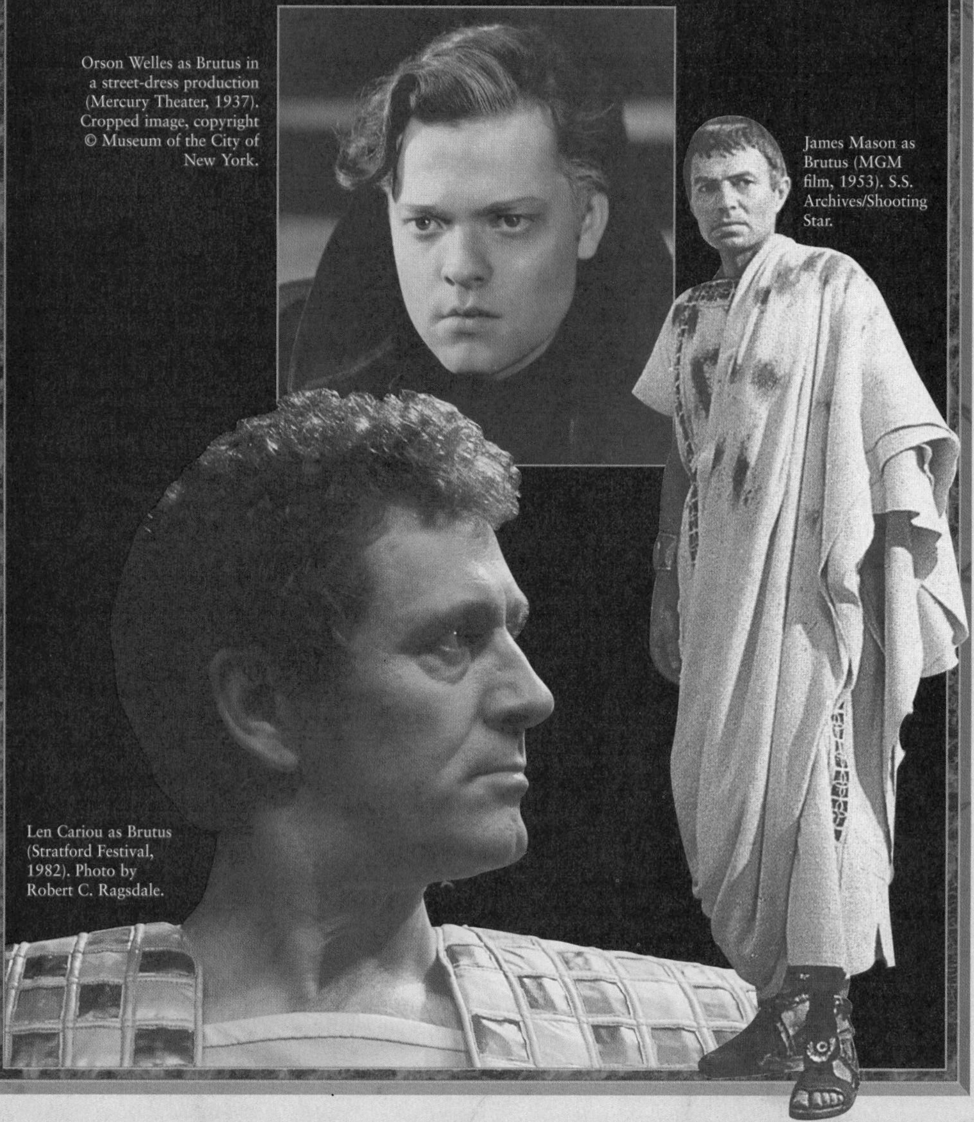

Orson Welles as Brutus in a street-dress production (Mercury Theater, 1937). Cropped image, copyright © Museum of the City of New York.

James Mason as Brutus (MGM film, 1953). S.S. Archives/Shooting Star.

Len Cariou as Brutus (Stratford Festival, 1982). Photo by Robert C. Ragsdale.

SCENE 2

A MILITARY CAMP NEAR SARDIS. IN FRONT OF BRUTUS' TENT.

Brutus seems displeased at the way events are developing, and he tells his servant about Cassius' new cold and distant attitude. Cassius arrives, and he and Brutus go into the tent to talk about their disagreements.

[*Sound of drums. Enter* Brutus, Lucilius, Lucius, *and* Soldiers. Titinius *and* Pindarus, *from Cassius' army, meet them.*] **A**

Brutus. Stand ho!

Lucilius. Give the word, ho! and stand!

Brutus. What now, Lucilius? Is Cassius near?

Lucilius. He is at hand, and Pindarus is come
To do you salutation from his master.

Brutus. He greets me well. Your master, Pindarus,
In his own change, or by ill officers,
Hath given me some worthy cause to wish
Things done undone; but if he be at hand,
I shall be satisfied.

Pindarus. I do not doubt
But that my noble master will appear
Such as he is, full of regard and honor.

Brutus. He is not doubted. A word, Lucilius,
How he received you. Let me be resolved.

Lucilius. With courtesy and with respect enough,
But not with such familiar instances
Nor with such free and friendly conference **1**
As he hath used of old.

Brutus. Thou has described
A hot friend cooling. Ever note, Lucilius,
When love begins to sicken and decay
It useth an enforced ceremony.
There are no tricks in plain and simple faith;
But hollow men, like horses hot at hand,
Make gallant show and promise of their mettle; **B**
[*Low march within.*]
But when they should endure the bloody spur,
They fall their crests, and like deceitful jades
Sink in the trial. Comes his army on?

Lucilius. They mean this night in Sardis to be quartered.

5 do you salutation: bring you greetings.

6–10 He greets . . . satisfied: Cassius sends a good man to greet me. Pindarus, your master has either had a change of heart or is surrounded by incompetent **(ill)** officers. Whatever the reason, he has made me wish that certain things had never happened **(Things done undone).** But if he is here **(at hand),** I will find out for myself **(be satisfied).**

13–14 A word . . . resolved: Brutus takes his officer aside and asks him privately how he was treated when he met Cassius. Why does Brutus want to know this? **C**

17 conference: conversation.

19–27 Ever note . . . trial: Brutus tells Lucilius never to forget **(Ever note)** that when affection begins to cool, it turns into awkward politeness **(enforced ceremony).** Honest relationships, he says, do not involve tricks. Insincere **(hollow)** men, like eager horses, make a great show of courage **(mettle).** But when they get the signal **(spur)** to fight, they drop their heads **(fall their crests)** and fail, like worn-out horses **(jades).**

28 They . . . quartered: Cassius and his army intend to stay here (in Sardis) tonight.

Customizing Instruction

Students Acquiring English

1 Explain to students that the term *familiar instances* here means "friendly acts."

View and Compare

Possible Responses: Each image suggests that Brutus is an intense and serious leader, one that would immediately command respect. Students may be drawn to each of the photos for different reasons. Students may want to list the criteria for judging a character based on appearance. Criteria could include posture, costume, and facial expression.

Mini Lesson Vocabulary Strategy

WORD MEANINGS: *avenge/revenge* Antony's desire to right the wrongs that have been inflicted on Caesar plays an important part in the play. *Avenge* and *revenge* are two words often used to describe the action of seeking punishment for another. Although these words have similar meanings and are often used interchangeably, they have subtle semantic differences.

Instruction Have students use a dictionary to define these words and to clarify their parts of speech. Explain that both words can function as verbs, but only *revenge* can be used as a noun to mean "an act of retaliation." To *avenge* means "to inflict punishment for the sake of vindication or just retribution." To *revenge* means "to inflict pain or injury in resentful or malicious retaliation." Thus, *avenge* involves a desire to correct a wrong because someone has been unfairly harmed. *Revenge*, however, conveys an attitude of ill will and a desire to act with wicked or even unlawful intent.

Practice Discuss which term they would use to describe Antony's actions against the conspirators. For example, Antony would probably claim that he will *avenge* Caesar's death: Antony wants to punish the assassins because he thinks Caesar was a good and noble leader who was judged unfairly and wrongfully murdered.

Use **Vocabulary Transparencies and Copymasters,** p. 75, or more practice.

A lesson on idioms appears on p. 419 in the Pupil's Edition.

Reading and Analyzing

GUIDE FOR READING

A **Possible Response:** Brutus probably feels that it would be undignified for the commanders to argue openly. Such open conflict also might lessen their status in the eyes of the troops.

Reading Skills and Strategies: EVALUATE

B Ask students to summarize and then evaluate the two sides of this argument. Ask students whether they think Brutus or Cassius is more justified in his complaint.

Possible Response: Cassius claims that Brutus should not have punished Pella for taking bribes, since Cassius had supported him and since it was a minor offense. Brutus argues that both Pella and Cassius were guilty of greed. Brutus' point that they must be careful not to commit the same abuses that caused them to kill Caesar is a winning argument.

Reading Skills and Strategies: QUESTION

C Encourage students to question why Cassius allows Brutus to make such critical remarks about him.

Possible Response: Cassius may allow Brutus to say such things about him because he has a real need for Brutus' friendship; on the other hand, he may allow Brutus such liberties because he knows he needs Brutus' support to fight their enemies.

The greater part, the horse in general,
Are come with Cassius.

Brutus. Hark! He is arrived.
March gently on to meet him.

[*Enter* Cassius *and his army.*]

Cassius. Stand, ho!

Brutus. Stand, ho! Speak the word along.

First Soldier. Stand!

Second Soldier. Stand!

Third Soldier. Stand!

Cassius. Most noble brother, you have done me wrong.

Brutus. Judge me, you gods! wrong I mine enemies?
And if not so, how should I wrong a brother?

Cassius. Brutus, this sober form of yours hides wrongs,
And when you do them—

Brutus. Cassius, be content.
Speak your griefs softly. I do know you well.
Before the eyes of both our armies here
(Which should perceive nothing but love from us)
Let us not wrangle. Bid them move away.
Then in my tent, Cassius, enlarge your griefs,
And I will give you audience.

Cassius. Pindarus,
Bid our commanders lead their charges off
A little from this ground.

Brutus. Lucilius, do you the like, and let no man
Come to our tent till we have done our conference.
Let Lucius and Titinius guard our door.

[*Exeunt.*]

29 horse in general: entire cavalry.

34–36 The soldiers are passing the order to stop marching **(Stand)** along the lengthy column that has followed Cassius into camp.

40 sober form: serious manner.

41–47 be content . . . audience: Brutus tells Cassius to stay calm and keep his voice down. He says they should not argue **(wrangle)** in front of their soldiers. Then he invites Cassius into his tent, where he will listen to him **(give you audience).** Why does Brutus want to hide his and Cassius' disagreements from the soldiers? **A**

Teaching Options

Mini Lesson: Speaking and Listening

PERFORMING A DRAMATIC SCENE **Prepare** In Scene 3, Brutus and Cassius reveal another side to their characters when they become petulant and argumentative with each other. They sound very much like friends or siblings fighting with each other. Encourage students to read ahead and to discuss the argument. Have them consider why Brutus and Cassius are on edge.

Practice Have students work in pairs and consider how this scene could be performed. As a way of making this conflict realistic to students, have them choose a part of the scene and paraphrase it using contemporary language. Students may even want to include colloquial phrases within reason. Remind them that they are responsible for accurately interpreting and representing both the content (What are Brutus and Cassius arguing about? How is the plot developing?) and the tone (angry, sarcastic, apologetic, etc.) of the scene. Students should be able to justify their choice of verbal and nonverbal performance techniques by referring to their analysis and interpretation of the scene. Have them perform their paraphrased excerpts for the class.

BLOCK SCHEDULING This activity is particularly well suited for longer class periods.

SCENE 3 Inside Brutus' tent at Sardis.

Brutus and Cassius argue angrily, as Brutus accuses Cassius of corruption and greed. After a while, though, they calm down and become friendly once again. Brutus informs Cassius of Portia's death. Soon after, Massala enters. He tells of all the killings in Rome and of Antony and Octavius approaching with their armies. Brutus persuades Cassius that their forces must meet the enemy at Philippi in Greece. Later, as Brutus reads, the ghost of Caesar appears and promises to see Brutus at Philippi.

[*Enter* Brutus *and* Cassius.]

Cassius. That you have wronged me doth appear in this:
You have condemned and noted Lucius Pella (B)
For taking bribes here of the Sardians;
Wherein my letters, praying on his side,
Because I knew the man, were slighted off.

Brutus. You wronged yourself to write in such a case.

Cassius. In such a time as this it is not meet
That every nice offense should bear his comment.

Brutus. Let me tell you, Cassius, you yourself
Are much condemned to have an itching palm, (C)
To sell and mart your offices for gold
To undeservers.

Cassius. I an itching palm?
You know that you are Brutus that speaks this,
Or, by the gods, this speech were else your last! [1]

Brutus. The name of Cassius honors this corruption,
And chastisement doth therefore hide his head.

Cassius. Chastisement?

Brutus. Remember March; the ides of March remember.
Did not great Julius bleed for justice' sake?
What villain touched his body that did stab
And not for justice? What, shall one of us,
That struck the foremost man of all this world
But for supporting robbers—shall we now [2]
Contaminate our fingers with base bribes,
And sell the mighty space of our large honors
For so much trash as may be grasped thus?
I had rather be a dog and bay the moon
Than such a Roman.

Cassius. Brutus, bait not me!

2 noted: publicly disgraced.

5 slighted off: ignored.

7–8 it is not . . . comment: It is not appropriate for every tiny **(nice)** offense to be criticized.

10 to have an itching palm: to be always looking for bribes.

11 mart: market.

12–14 I an . . . last: Cassius is almost speechless at the insult Brutus has just hurled at him. If anyone other than Brutus said such a thing to me, Cassius says, I would kill him on the spot.

15–16 The name . . . head: Because Cassius' name is linked to the bribery **(corruption),** no one dares talk about punishment **(chastisement)** for those who accept the bribes.

23 But for supporting robbers: because he (Caesar) protected robbers from punishment. This is not one of the charges the conspirators originally made against Caesar.

27 bay: howl at.

Customizing Instruction

Students Acquiring English

1 Point out the unusual syntax in this line and help students understand that a paraphrase into current standard English would be "Or else, by the gods, this speech would be your last!"

Less Proficient Readers

2 Remind students that when Brutus asks rhetorical questions, he does not really expect or want answers. Have students rephrase Brutus' questions as statements.

Possible Response: "Julius died for the sake of justice"; "Anyone who stabbed Caesar for reasons other than justice is a villain"; "None of us who killed Caesar for supporting robbers should now take bribes and sell our honor for money."

Reading and Analyzing

Literary Analysis: FIGURATIVE LANGUAGE

A Have students explain Brutus' metaphor in this passage. Help them by pointing out that Cassius' anger is one part of the comparison.

Possible Response: Brutus compares Cassius' anger to a poisonous liquid that Cassius will have to swallow.

Reading Skills and Strategies: CONNECT

B Have students consider the pattern and tone of the argument between Cassius and Brutus. Ask students whether they have had disagreements with a close friend or relative, and encourage them to discuss how such problems occur.

Possible Response: Stress, fear, or anxiety about an impending event could cause such a quarrel.

GUIDE FOR READING

C He challenges Cassius to prove his boast that he is the better soldier by fighting.

Literary Analysis: CHARACTER

D Have students explain Brutus' metaphor here. Then ask them how this passage affects their sense of Brutus' character.

Possible Responses: Brutus compares his heart to a mint, and the drops of blood from his heart are compared to coins. Brutus says he would rather coin his heart than get money illicitly from hardworking peasants. Brutus sounds honest and willing to sacrifice himself to do the right thing; he's melodramatic and a bit self-righteous.

I'll not endure it. You forget yourself
To hedge me in. I am a soldier, I,
Older in practice, abler than yourself
To make conditions.

Brutus. Go to! You are not, Cassius.

Cassius. I am.

Brutus. I say you are not.

1 **Cassius.** Urge me no more! I shall forget myself.
Have mind upon your health, tempt me no farther.

Brutus. Away, slight man!

Cassius. Is't possible?

Brutus. Hear me, for I will speak.
Must I give way and room to your rash choler?
Shall I be frighted when a madman stares?

Cassius. O ye gods, ye gods! Must I endure all this?

A **Brutus.** All this? Ay, more! Fret till your proud heart break.
Go show your slaves how choleric you are
And make your bondmen tremble. Must I budge?
Must I observe you? Must I stand and crouch
Under your testy humor? By the gods,
You shall digest the venom of your spleen,
Though it do split you; for from this day forth
I'll use you for my mirth, yea, for my laughter,
When you are waspish.

Cassius. Is it come to this?

B **Brutus.** You say you are a better soldier;
Let it appear so. Make your vaunting true,
And it shall please me well. For mine own part,
I shall be glad to learn of noble men.

Cassius. You wrong me every way! You wrong me, Brutus!
I said an elder soldier, not a better.
Did I say "better"?

Brutus. If you did, I care not.

Cassius. When Caesar lived he durst not thus have moved me.

Brutus. Peace, peace! You durst not so have tempted him.

Cassius. I durst not?

28–32 bait not me . . . conditions: Do not try to provoke **(bait)** me into fighting. I will not put up with **(endure)** it. Since I am the more experienced soldier, I should be the one to make decisions **(conditions).**

39–47 Must . . . spleen: Brutus refers to Cassius' quick temper **(rash choler),** to the fact that he is so angry **(choleric),** and to his irritable mood **(testy humor).** You can swallow the poison of your own anger **(spleen),** he says. (People once believed that the spleen, an organ near the stomach, was the source of certain emotions, such as anger and spite.)

50 waspish: ill-tempered.

52 vaunting: bragging. What challenge does Brutus make? **C**

55–56 You wrong . . . better: Cassius now controls his anger and tries to soften some of the things he said earlier. He will soon become angry again, though, since Brutus does not stop insulting him.

58 he durst . . . me: Even Caesar would not have dared to provoke me this way.

Teaching Options

Cross Curricular Link History

ROMAN WARFARE Ancient Rome is known for its skilled and successful armies, which included both infantry and cavalry. The earliest Roman armies followed the pattern of Greek fighting forces. Hoplites, the standard military fighting men so called because of the circular shield—*hoplon*—they carried into battle, were organized into a phalanx, which was a company of soldiers consisting of twelve rows of eight men who advanced as a group. As men were killed or wounded in the front line, those behind merely stepped over the bodies and kept marching. Military men were divided into six classes based on their individual wealth, and, thus, on their ability to provide equipment for battle: those in the higher classes had more weapons and body armor. The group of citizens below the lowest designated class was called the *capite censi* and owned no property of their own. These men were disqualified from military service.

The organization and composition of the Roman army underwent a number of changes in the years leading up to Caesar's rule. By the time Antony and Brutus marched into battle, the

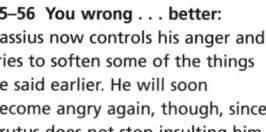

Martin Sheen as Brutus and Edward Herrmann as Cassius (New York Shakespeare Festival, 1988).
Photo by Martha Swope, copyright © Time Inc.

Brutus. No.

Cassius. What, durst not tempt him?

Brutus. For your life you durst not. **B**

Cassius. Do not presume too much upon my love.
I may do that I shall be sorry for.

Brutus. You have done that you should be sorry for. **2**
There is no terror, Cassius, in your threats;
For I am armed so strong in honesty
That they pass by me as the idle wind,
Which I respect not. I did send to you
For certain sums of gold, which you denied me,
For I can raise no money by vile means—
By heaven, I had rather coin my heart
And drop my blood for drachmas than to wring
From the hard hands of peasants their vile trash **D**
By any indirection. I did send
To you for gold to pay my legions,

71–75 For I can . . . indirection: I cannot raise money by dishonest **(vile)** methods. I would rather make coins out of my heart and blood than steal money from peasants by lying **(indirection).**

76 legions: armies.

Customizing Instruction

Students Acquiring English

1 Explain that *urge* here means "bully" or "provoke." Explain that "Have mind upon" here means "Have regard for" or "Think about." Ask students to explain what Cassius is telling Brutus.
Possible Response: Cassius is telling Brutus to stop provoking him or Cassius will lose his temper. He warns Brutus to consider his own safety.

2 Explain to students that "You have done that you should be sorry for" can be rendered into current standard English by simply replacing *that* with *what:* "You have done what you should be sorry for."

phalanx, which maneuvered as a single compact body, was no longer the formation of choice for the Roman army. When Caesar defeated Pompey, and Brutus and Antony rode into battle against each other, they used a looser battle formation with distinct subgroups capable of more independent fighting. These subgroups, called cohorts, were formed into legions of about 5,000 men, and when Caesar expanded his number of legions from four to twelve, he was in charge of a huge fighting machine. By this time, the *capite censi* were also required to fight, and the tour of duty for an average soldier was a minimum of six and no more than sixteen years. Weapons now included not only the slingshot, javelin, and bow of earlier years, but also the massive catapult, which was capable of launching an eight-pound stone a distance of roughly 500 yards. Although Rome's military history tells the story of successful strategies, battles, and weapons, it is important to remember that throughout the Roman Republic, the soldiers fighting for Rome were her own citizens, who considered defense of the state an obligation and an honor.

Reading and Analyzing

Reading Skills and Strategies: CLARIFY

A Ask students what Cassius' purpose is in this dramatic speech.

Possible Response: gain sympathy for himself

Literary Analysis: CONFLICT

B Review this passage so students can describe some of the internal conflicts that seem to plague Cassius.

Possible Response: Cassius seems to want Brutus' friendship desperately, but he fears that Brutus despises him. His melodramatic offer to kill himself might spring from mixed feelings of shame, anger, and pride. He might also have an envious suspicion that Brutus will never be as close to him as he was to Caesar.

Literary Analysis: HUMOR

C Draw students' attention to Brutus' mild joke and to the entrance of the poet who delivers his uninspired verse. Ask students why Shakespeare would include these moments of humor at this point.

Possible Response: He might want to give Cassius and Brutus a chance to become at ease with each other again before they turn their attention back to more serious matters. Shakespeare also might be providing some comic relief for the audience after the strain of the argument.

GUIDE FOR READING

D **Possible Response:** The argument and its ending are believable. The two friends are at first on edge, then flare up against each other. Cassius' plea for the restoration of their friendship touches Brutus. The argument then subsides.

Which you denied me. Was that done like Cassius?
Should I have answered Caius Cassius so?
When Marcus Brutus grows so covetous
To lock such rascal counters from his friends,
Be ready, gods, with all your thunderbolts,
Dash him to pieces!

Cassius. I denied you not.

Brutus. You did.

Cassius. I did not. He was but a fool that brought
My answer back. Brutus hath rived my heart.
A friend should bear his friend's infirmities,
But Brutus makes mine greater than they are.

Brutus. I do not, till you practice them on me.

Cassius. You love me not.

Brutus. I do not like your faults.

Cassius. A friendly eye could never see such faults.

Brutus. A flatterer's would not, though they do appear
As huge as high Olympus.

A **B** **Cassius.** Come, Antony, and young Octavius, come!
Revenge yourselves alone on Cassius.
For Cassius is aweary of the world:
Hated by one he loves; braved by his brother;
Checked like a bondman, all his faults observed,
Set in a notebook, learned and conned by rote
To cast into my teeth. O, I could weep
My spirit from mine eyes! There is my dagger,
And here my naked breast; within, a heart
Dearer than Pluto's mine, richer than gold:
If that thou be'st a Roman, take it forth.
I, that denied thee gold, will give my heart.
Strike as thou didst at Caesar; for I know,
When thou didst hate him worst, thou lov'dst him better
Than ever thou lov'dst Cassius.

Brutus. Sheathe your dagger.
Be angry when you will; it shall have scope.
Do what you will; dishonor shall be humor.
O Cassius, you are yoked with a lamb
That carries anger as the flint bears fire;
Who, much enforced, shows a hasty spark,
And straight is cold again.

78–82 Should . . . pieces: Would I have answered a request from you in the same way? When I become such a miser **(so covetous)** as to deny cheap coins **(rascal counters)** to my friends, may the gods destroy me.

85 rived: torn apart.

86 infirmities: shortcomings.

93–107 Come . . . lov'dst Cassius: Cassius speaks these lines loudly, as though calling to Antony and Octavius, who are far away. He says they might as well kill him. He has been bullied **(braved)** by his true friend **(brother)** and scolded **(Checked)** like a slave; his faults have been written in a notebook and memorized **(conned by rote)** to be thrown into his face **(cast into my teeth).** Cassius then turns to Brutus and offers Cassius' knife to plunge into his own heart.

107–113 Sheathe . . . cold again: Put away **(Sheathe)** your knife. Let your anger run free **(have scope).** Your insults **(dishonor)** will be taken as coming from a bad mood **(humor).** Cassius, you are tied to **(yoked with)** a mild man **(lamb);** anger to me is like the flint to fire. Strike it hard, and it will produce sparks; then it will cool immediately.

Teaching Options

Assessment Standardized Test Practice

DESCRIBE PLOT, SETTING, CHARACTER, AND MOOD

For some standardized tests, students will be asked to identify elements of plot, setting, character, and mood in literary selections. Help students understand these literary features by reading aloud or writing on the chalkboard the following questions. Students should choose the most accurate response for each.

1. Where does Scene 3 take place?
   A. at Caesar's house
   B. at Antony's house
   C. at Brutus' military camp
   D. on the battlefield
   Answer: C
2. The exchange between Brutus and Cassius at the beginning of this scene can be described as
   A. celebratory
   B. argumentative
   C. friendly
   D. subdued
   Answer: B

Cassius. Hath Cassius lived
To be but mirth and laughter to his Brutus
When grief and blood ill-tempered vexeth him?

Brutus. When I spoke that, I was ill-tempered too.

Cassius. Do you confess so much? Give me your hand.

Brutus. And my heart too.

Cassius. O Brutus!

Brutus. What's the matter?

Cassius. Have you not love enough to bear with me
When that rash humor which my mother gave me
Makes me forgetful?

Brutus. Yes, Cassius, and from henceforth,
When you are over-earnest with your Brutus,
He'll think your mother chides, and leave you so.

[*Enter a* Poet *followed by* Lucilius, Titinius, *and* Lucius.] C

Poet. Let me go in to see the generals!
There is some grudge between 'em. 'Tis not meet
They be alone.

Lucilius. You shall not come to them.

Poet. Nothing but death shall stay me.

Cassius. How now? What's the matter?

Poet. For shame, you generals! What do you mean?
Love and be friends, as two such men should be,
For I have seen more years, I'm sure, than ye.

Cassius. Ha, ha! How vilely doth this cynic rhyme!

Brutus. Get you hence, sirrah! Saucy fellow, hence!

Cassius. Bear with him, Brutus. 'Tis his fashion.

Brutus. I'll know his humor when he knows his time.
What should the wars do with these jigging fools?
Companion, hence! 1

Cassius. Away, away, be gone!

[*Exit* Poet.]

Brutus. Lucilius and Titinius, bid the commanders
Prepare to lodge their companies tonight.

Cassius. And come yourselves, and bring Messala with you
Immediately to us.

[*Exeunt* Lucilius *and* Titinius.]

113–115 Hath Cassius . . . him: Have I lived so long only to become a joke to you when sadness and sickness trouble **(vexeth)** you?

118 The two men embrace in friendship, glad to be over their anger with each other.

119–121 Have you . . . forgetful: Don't you love me enough to put up with me when I lose control because of that bad temper I inherited from my mother?

123 He'll think . . . so: I will say it is your mother, not you, showing bad temper, and will forget about it. Do you find Shakespeare's portrayal of this argument and its ending believable? Explain. D

124–138 The two men are briefly interrupted by a poet, who comes to persuade them to end their arguments and insists that nothing will stop **(stay)** him. These lines show that the tension between Brutus and Cassius is now completely gone. They joke about what a terrible poet this rude fellow **(cynic)** is and finally send him away. Once the silly poet is gone, Brutus and Cassius—friends once again—become serious.

Customizing Instruction

Students Acquiring English

1 Explain the following words to students:
know—here, "understand" or "accept"
humor—here, "personality" or "mood"
jigging—here, "singing" or "rhyming"
hence—here, "go away" or "get out"
Help students paraphrase Brutus' remarks in lines 136–138.

Possible Response: I'll understand his mood when he understands the appropriate time for it. What use are those rhyming fools to the war? Companion, get out!

3. For what event do Brutus and Cassius prepare in Scene 3?
A. a battle with Antony
B. an attack on Rome
C. Caesar's burial
D. a reconciliation with Antony
Answer: A

4. As the scene opens, Brutus accuses Cassius of
A. staying out too late
B. making too much noise
C. stealing his sword
D. bribery and greed
Answer: D

Lead students through the process of considering each choice. Point out that their responses should be based on specific information about the setting, plot, character, and mood of the scene. Remind students to pay attention to the stage directions and set descriptions for help in answering these kinds of questions about a play.

Reading and Analyzing

Reading Skills and Strategies: EVALUATE

A Have students evaluate Cassius' response to Portia's death. Ask what it reveals about him.

Possible Response: Cassius appears sensitive and unselfish.

In light of this moment, have students reevaluate the men's friendship.

Possible Response: The men's friendship is stronger than it first appeared, considering the unusual strain Brutus is under when they are arguing.

Active Reading

UNDERSTANDING SHAKESPEARE'S PLAYS

B Students may question this exchange between Brutus and Messala. Have them explain why it seems odd and confusing.

Possible Response: It makes no sense that Messala brings news of Portia's death when Brutus has just informed Cassius of her suicide.

This scene has puzzled critics and commentators for years. Some readers argue that Brutus is deliberately shown to react to tragic news in two contexts, first privately and sadly, and then publicly in a way that shows him being stoic. Other commentators think that Shakespeare revised this scene and merely forgot to remove one of the exchanges.

GUIDE FOR READING

C **Possible Response:** If our enemies are forced to come to us, they will suffer from lack of provisions and fatigue; we, however, will be rested and prepared for the battle.

Brutus. Lucius, a bowl of wine.

[*Exit* Lucius.]

Cassius. I did not think you could have been so angry.

Brutus. O Cassius, I am sick of many griefs.

Cassius. Of your philosophy you make no use
If you give place to accidental evils.

Brutus. No man bears sorrow better. Portia is dead.

Cassius. Ha! Portia?

Brutus. She is dead.

Cassius. How scaped I killing when I crossed you so?
O insupportable and touching loss!
1 Upon what sickness?

Brutus. Impatient of my absence,
And grief that young Octavius with Mark Antony
Have made themselves so strong—for with her death
That tidings came—with this she fell distract,
And (her attendants absent) swallowed fire.

Cassius. And died so?

A **Brutus.** Even so.

Cassius. O ye immortal gods!

[*Reenter* Lucius, *with wine and tapers.*]

Brutus. Speak no more of her. Give me a bowl of wine.
In this I bury all unkindness, Cassius.

[*Drinks.*]

Cassius. My heart is thirsty for that noble pledge.
Fill, Lucius, till the wine o'erswell the cup.
I cannot drink too much of Brutus' love.

[*Drinks. Exit* Lucius.]

[*Reenter* Titinius, *with* Messala.]

Brutus. Come in, Titinius! Welcome, good Messala.
Now sit we close about this taper here
And call in question our necessities.

Cassius. Portia, art thou gone?

Brutus. No more, I pray you.
Messala, I have here received letters
That young Octavius and Mark Antony
Come down upon us with a mighty power,
Bending their expedition toward Philippi.

Messala. Myself have letters of the selfsame tenure.

145–146 Of your . . . evils: You aren't making use of your philosophy if you let chance happenings get you down. (Brutus was a Stoic, one who believed that pain and suffering should be endured calmly and that self-control was all-important.)

148 Ha: Cassius is not laughing but is so shocked by the news of Portia's death that he gasps.

150 How . . . so: How did I escape being killed when I angered you, with such a terrible thing on your mind?

152–156 Impatient . . . fire: She was worried about my absence and about the armies of Antony and Octavius. These things made her depressed **(she fell distract).** When her servants were not around, she swallowed a hot coal and choked.

161 o'erswell: overflow.

164–165 Now sit . . . necessities: Let's sit around this candle and talk about what we must do.

166 Cassius is distracted from the business that has to be discussed. He is having trouble believing that Portia is dead. Brutus asks him to stop talking about the painful topic.

170 Bending . . . Philippi: leading their armies to Philippi (a city in northern Greece).

171 Myself . . . tenure: I have received letters that say the same thing.

Teaching Options

Mini Lesson Grammar

ELLIPTICAL SENTENCES Shakespeare's irregular sentence structure often causes difficulty for modern readers. One unusual sentence structure that Shakespeare uses is elliptical sentence structure—the omission of words that are assumed to be understood. When a reader encounters an elliptical sentence, he or she must be able to infer what is missing and supply the appropriate word or words to complete the line. Write this line on the chalkboard.

"A word, Lucilius, how he received you."

Point out that the verb is not stated. Ask students to rephrase this sentence.

Possible Response: "**Give me** a word, Lucilius, **about** how he received you."

Practice Have students copy the following elliptical sentences. Ask them to supply words to form grammatically complete sentences.

1. "And let us presently go sit in council / How covert matters may be best disclosed / And open perils surest answered."
   Possible Response: And let us presently go sit in council to decide how covert matters may be best disclosed and how open perils may be surest answered.

Brutus. With what addition?

Messala. That by proscription and bills of outlawry
Octavius, Antony, and Lepidus
Have put to death an hundred senators.

Brutus. Therein our letters do not well agree.
Mine speak of seventy senators that died
By their proscriptions, Cicero being one.

Cassius. Cicero one?

Messala. Cicero is dead,
And by that order of proscription.
Had you your letters from your wife, my lord?

Brutus. No, Messala.

Messala. Nor nothing in your letters writ of her?

Brutus. Nothing, Messala.

Messala. That methinks is strange.

Brutus. Why ask you? Hear you aught of her in yours?

Messala. No, my lord.

Brutus. Now as you are a Roman, tell me true.

Messala. Then like a Roman bear the truth I tell,
For certain she is dead, and by strange manner.

Brutus. Why, farewell, Portia. We must die, Messala.
With meditating that she must die once,
I have the patience to endure it now.

Messala. Even so great men great losses should endure. **B**

Cassius. I have as much of this in art as you,
But yet my nature could not bear it so.

Brutus. Well, to our work alive. What do you think
Of marching to Philippi presently?

Cassius. I do not think it good.

Brutus. Your reason?

Cassius. This it is:
'Tis better that the enemy seek us.
So shall he waste his means, weary his soldiers,
Doing himself offense, whilst we, lying still,
Are full of rest, defense, and nimbleness.

Brutus. Good reasons must of force give place to better.
The people 'twixt Philippi and this ground
Do stand but in a forced affection,
For they have grudged us contribution.

173 proscription . . . outlawry: official statements that declare certain acts to be criminal.

194 in art: in theory, in my beliefs.

199–202 How would you rephrase Cassius' reasons for not wanting to attack the armies of Antony and Octavius? **C**

203–212 Good . . . our back: Good reasons have to give way to better ones. The people between **('twixt)** here and Philippi are friendly only because they have to be **(stand but in a forced affection).** They have given us aid grudgingly. If the enemy marches through, they will find recruits. If we face them at Philippi, we'll eliminate this advantage and keep these unfriendly people behind us.

Customizing Instruction

Students Acquiring English

1 Explain that *Upon* here means "As a result of"; thus, Cassius is asking, "Portia died as a result of what sickness?"

Less Proficient Readers

Help students understand the play so far by asking them the following questions:

- Why are Brutus and Cassius arguing?
  Possible Response: Cassius tried to protect a man whom Brutus punished for bribery. Cassius takes offense that Brutus punished the man anyway. Brutus accuses Cassius of bribery.
- How does the argument end?
  Possible Response: The two friends make up.
- What bad news does Brutus receive?
  Answer: His wife is dead.

2. "And now, Octavius, / Listen great things."
   Possible Response: And now, Octavius, listen to great things.
3. "We'll along ourselves and meet them at Philippi."
   Possible Response: We'll move along ourselves and meet them at Philippi.
4. "Is not the leaf turned down / Where I left reading?"
   Possible Response: Is not the leaf turned down where I left off reading?

Use **Grammar Transparencies and Copymasters,** p. 118, for more exercises.

Reading and Analyzing

Literary Analysis: SETTING

A Ask students how a night setting affects the mood of the scene.

Possible Response: It enhances the sense of confusion and exhaustion. It also helps build suspense, as the time for planning has passed and the armies wait for daylight.

GUIDE FOR READING

B **Possible Responses:** Cassius, because his argument is more practical; Brutus, because his arguments deal with more immediate, urgent concerns

The enemy, marching along by them,
By them shall make a fuller number up,
Come on refreshed, new-added, and encouraged;
From which advantage we cut him off
If at Philippi we do face him there,
These people at our back.

Cassius. Hear me, good brother.

Brutus. Under your pardon. You must note beside
That we have tried the utmost of our friends,
Our legions are brimful, our cause is ripe.
The enemy increaseth every day;
We, at the height, are ready to decline.
There is a tide in the affairs of men
Which, taken at the flood, leads on to fortune;
Omitted, all the voyage of their life
Is bound in shallows and in miseries.
On such a full sea are we now afloat,
And we must take the current when it serves
Or lose our ventures. **1**

Cassius. Then, with your will, go on.
We'll along ourselves and meet them at Philippi.

Brutus. The deep of night is crept upon our talk
And nature must obey necessity,
Which we will niggard with a little rest. **A**
There is no more to say?

Cassius. No more. Good night.
Early tomorrow will we rise and hence.

Brutus. Lucius!
[*Reenter* Lucius.]
My gown.
[*Exit* Lucius.]
Farewell, good Messala.
Good night, Titinius. Noble, noble Cassius,
Good night and good repose!

Cassius. O my dear brother,
This was an ill beginning of the night!
Never come such division 'tween our souls!
Let it not, Brutus.

[*Reenter* Lucius, *with the gown.*]

Brutus. Everything is well.

Cassius. Good night, my lord.

213–217 Under . . . decline: Brutus cuts Cassius off and insists on his own position. Their army, he says, is as good as it is ever going to get, while the enemy is getting stronger every day. Do you agree with Brutus or Cassius? Why? **B**

214 tried the utmost: received all we can expect.

218–224 There is . . . ventures: Brutus compares life to a voyage on a ship. Following the high tide can lead to good fortune. Those who do not follow the tide might spend the rest of their lives in shallow water and misery. Our tide comes now, he insists, and we must act now.

228 Which . . . rest: We will reluctantly satisfy **(niggard)** nature by getting a little bit of rest.

232 gown: nightgown.

Teaching Options

Assessment Informal Assessment

WRITING A LETTER HOME Have students monitor their comprehension of the scene thus far by imagining that they are Lucius. As Brutus' servant, Lucius is probably aware of the conversations and activities that occur in this scene. Ask each student to write a letter from Lucius to his family relating the events he has observed.

RUBRIC

3 **Full Accomplishment** Students accurately convey complete details of the argument between Cassius and Brutus, the news of Portia's death, and the plans for attacking the enemy.

2 **Substantial Accomplishment** Students convey adequate details of the argument, Portia's suicide, and the strategic plans.

1 **Little or Partial Accomplishment** Students convey few concrete details about the argument, suicide, and battle plans, or students mention only one or two of the events.

"There is a tide in the affairs of men which, taken at the flood, leads on to fortune."

Martin Sheen as Brutus and Edward Herrmann as Cassius (New York Shakespeare Festival, 1988).

Customizing Options

Students Acquiring English

1 Explain to students the following terms:

- "bound in": "limited to"
- "serves": "serves us"
- "with your will" : "as you wish"
- "We'll along ourselves" : "We'll go along"

Reading and Analyzing

Literary Analysis: CHARACTER

A Ask students to discuss what Brutus reveals about himself in these lines.

Possible Response: Brutus appears solicitous of others here, as he invites his subordinates to share his tent and worries that Lucius has grown too tired.

Reading Skills and Strategies: VISUALIZE

B Have students visualize Brutus' reactions as he sees Caesar's ghost. Ask them to suggest various ways Brutus might respond.

Possible Responses: Brutus might approach the ghost suspiciously and speak with barely repressed fear; he might be so agitated that he shouts at the spirit; he might shrink away and address the apparition in tones of quiet dread.

GUIDE FOR READING

C **Possible Response:** Shakespeare may have added the ghost as a foreshadowing of death and doom, as a reminder of Brutus' feelings of guilt, or as a device to excite and interest his audience.

D **Possible Response:** Brutus wants to know whether they have seen the ghost but does not want to admit that he saw anything.

Brutus. Good night, good brother.

Titinius and Messala. Good night, Lord Brutus.

Brutus. Farewell every one.

[*Exeunt all but* Brutus *and* Lucius.]

Give me the gown. Where is thy instrument?

Lucius. Here in the tent.

A **Brutus.** What, thou speak'st drowsily?
Poor knave, I blame thee not, thou art o'erwatched.
Call Claudius and some other of my men;
I'll have them sleep on cushions in my tent.

Lucius. Varro and Claudius!

[*Enter* Varro *and* Claudius.]

Varro. Calls my lord?

Brutus. I pray you, sirs, lie in my tent and sleep.
It may be I shall raise you by-and-by
On business to my brother Cassius.

Varro. So please you, we will stand and watch your pleasure.

Brutus. I will not have it so. Lie down, good sirs.
It may be I shall otherwise bethink me.

[Varro *and* Claudius *lie down.*]

Look, Lucius, here's the book I sought for so;
I put it in the pocket of my gown.

1 **Lucius.** I was sure your lordship did not give it me.

Brutus. Bear with me, good boy, I am much forgetful.
Canst thou hold up by thy heavy eyes awhile,
And touch thy instrument a strain or two?

2 **Lucius.** Ay, my lord, an't please you.

Brutus. It does, my boy.
I trouble thee too much, but thou art willing.

Lucius. It is my duty, sir.

Brutus. I should not urge thy duty past thy might.
I know young bloods look for a time of rest.

Lucius. I have slept, my lord, already.

Brutus. It was well done; and thou shalt sleep again;
I will not hold thee long. If I do live,
I will be good to thee.

[*Music, and a song.* Lucius *falls asleep as he sings.*]

241 Where is thy instrument?: One of Lucius' duties as a personal servant is to play music that will help Brutus get to sleep.

242–243 What . . . o'erwatched: I see you're sleepy. It's no wonder, since you've been watching and waiting for so long.

249–253 It may . . . bethink me: Brutus wants them to be handy in case he needs to send a message to Cassius. Varro offers to stand guard all night. Brutus insists the men sleep, not stand guard. He says he may change his mind **(otherwise bethink me)** about sending messages to Cassius.

774 UNIT FOUR PART 3: THE TRAGEDY OF JULIUS CAESAR

Teaching Options

Cross Curricular Link Music

ROMAN MUSIC According to most music historians, music occupied an important place in Roman culture. Music was prominent in theatrical productions and religious rituals; often, Roman music is characterized as "utilitarian." Whether among family, at funerals, or in the military, music was considered an integral part of civic life rather than a fine art. Julius Caesar is said to have been an enthusiastic music supporter, and one story relates that Roman musicians threw their elaborate professional garments onto the fire at Caesar's cremation.

Music teachers were paid well, and true talent was recognized and cultivated regardless of a person's class. Highborn Romans in the early Republican period (some several hundred years before Julius Caesar) considered the practice of music beneath them and left musical endeavors to their slaves. This attitude gradually changed as an appreciation of music became more widespread. Soon music was taught in public schools, and both boys and girls participated. The music curriculum included playing the lyre, singing, and dancing. The army generally favored brass instruments, and the Romans developed a number of huge instruments that were coarse and less refined. For example, some lyres were the size of coaches and required two people to play them.

This is a sleepy tune. O murd'rous slumber!
Layest thou thy leaden mace upon my boy,
That plays thee music? Gentle knave, good night.
I will not do thee so much wrong to wake thee.
If thou dost nod, thou break'st thy instrument;
I'll take it from thee; and, good boy, good night.
Let me see, let me see. Is not the leaf turned down
Where I left reading? Here it is, I think.

[*Sits.*]

[*Enter the* Ghost of Caesar.]

How ill this taper burns! Ha! Who comes here?
I think it is the weakness of mine eyes
That shapes this monstrous apparition.
It comes upon me. Art thou anything?
Art thou some god, some angel, or some devil,
That mak'st my blood cold and my hair to stare?
Speak to me what thou art. **B**

Ghost. Thy evil spirit, Brutus.

Brutus. Why com'st thou?

Ghost. To tell thee thou shalt see me at Philippi.

Brutus. Well; then I shall see thee again?

Ghost. Ay, at Philippi.

Brutus. Why, I will see thee at Philippi then.

[*Exit* Ghost.]

Now I have taken heart thou vanishest.
Ill spirit, I would hold more talk with thee.
Boy! Lucius! Varro! Claudius! Sirs! Awake!
Claudius!

Lucius. The strings, my lord, are false.

Brutus. He thinks he still is at his instrument.
Lucius, awake!

Lucius. My lord?

Brutus. Didst thou dream, Lucius, that thou so criedst out?

Lucius. My lord, I do not know that I did cry.

Brutus. Yes, that thou didst. Didst thou see anything?

Lucius. Nothing, my lord.

Brutus. Sleep again, Lucius. Sirrah Claudius!

[*To* Varro.]

Fellow thou, awake!

270 mace: a rod used as a symbol of authority. Brutus is addressing slumber as though it were an officer of the law who has arrested Lucius.

277 How . . . burns: How poorly this candle burns. Everyone in the tent is asleep, except Brutus. At first he thinks the thing he sees is only the result of poor eyesight. Then he realizes that something is really there.

289 Now . . . vanishest: Now that I have my courage back, you disappear. What might have been Shakespeare's purpose in adding a ghost to this play? **C**

293 false: out of tune. Lucius, only half awake, thinks he is playing the instrument that Brutus took from him earlier. Why does Brutus accuse Lucius, Claudius, and Varro of crying out in their sleep? **D**

Customizing Instruction

Students Acquiring English

1 Point out that this line is elliptical. Ask students whether they can figure out which word is missing.

Answer: "I was sure your lordship did not give it **to** me."

2 Explain to students the following words:

- *touch*: "play on"
- *strain*: "tune"
- *an't*: "if it"

Reading and Analyzing

Reading Skills and Strategies:
EVALUATING

A Brutus' purpose here is to test the men to discover whether they, too, have seen a ghost. Have students evaluate the effect their denials might have on Brutus.

Possible Responses: He may doubt the existence of the ghost; he may doubt his sanity; he may conclude that the ghost's message was meant for him alone.

Reading Skills and Strategies:
CONNECTING

B Have students think about whether they have ever been in Brutus' position. Have they ever wondered about the validity of their opinions or observations and tried to find someone to legitimize their position?

"Didst thou dream,
Lucius, that thou so
criedst out?"

Wade Raley as Lucius and Martin Sheen as Brutus (New York Shakespeare Festival, 1988). Photo copyright © George E. Joseph.

Varro. My lord?
Claudius. My lord?
Brutus. Why did you so cry out, sirs, in your sleep?
Both. Did we, my lord?
Brutus. Ay. Saw you anything?
Varro. No, my lord, I saw nothing.
Claudius. Nor I, my lord.
Brutus. Go and commend me to my brother Cassius.
Bid him set on his pow'rs betimes before,
And we will follow.
Both. It shall be done, my lord.
[*Exeunt.*]

308 commend me: give my respects to.

309 Bid . . . before: Tell him to get his army **(pow'rs)** moving early in the morning.

Connect to the Literature

1. **What Do You Think?** Were you surprised by the current state of the relationship between Brutus and Cassius? between Antony, Octavius, and Lepidus? Why or why not?

Comprehension Check
- Who are Rome's present rulers, and whom do they agree to kill?
- What has strained the relationship between Brutus and Cassius?
- Where does Caesar's ghost say he will see Brutus next time?

Think Critically

2. How would you describe Mark Antony after reading Act Four, Scene 1? Do you think he has changed since Act Three? Cite details to explain your opinions.
3. Do the Romans seem better or worse off under their new rulers than they were under Julius Caesar?

THINK ABOUT
- the leadership of Julius Caesar
- the behavior of Mark Antony in the opening scene of Act Four
- Antony's plans regarding Julius Caesar's will
- the looming warfare between the triumvirate and the conspirators

4. Would you say that Brutus himself has changed since the murder of Caesar? Cite evidence to support your opinion.
5. What new **ironies** do you see emerging in Act Four?
6. How would you describe the **mood** at the end of Act Four?
7. **ACTIVE READING** READING SHAKESPEAREAN DRAMA Using the sidenotes to help you, restate in contemporary English Brutus' speech to Cassius in Scene 3, lines 213–224. Compare your "translation" with that of another classmate.

Extend Interpretations

8. **Critic's Corner** Many people think that Cassius becomes a more likable character than Brutus by Scene 3. Do you agree or disagree? Provide support with details from the scene.
9. **Connect to Life** Consider Brutus' often-quoted speech that begins "There is a tide in the affairs of men . . ." (Scene 3, lines 218–221). Share an incident from real life that either illustrates or refutes the opinion expressed in this speech.

Literary Analysis

DRAMATIC IRONY Readers or audiences experience **irony** when they notice a contrast or discrepancy between appearance and reality, between the way things seem and the way they really are. In **dramatic irony,** the reader or audience knows something that one or more **characters** do not know, so that what appears true to the character or characters is not what the audience or reader knows to be true. For example, in the opening incident of Act Three, when Caesar confidently tells the Soothsayer that the ides of March are come, we recognize the irony of his confidence, since we know that he is to be assassinated that very day.

Cooperative Learning Activity Form a group of four and have each person go back through one of the four acts read thus far, looking for incidents that create dramatic irony. Each incident identified should then be included in a chart similar to the following:

Act/Scene/ Line Nos.	What Character(s) Thinks	What Reader/Audience Knows

Then come together again as a group and share your findings. Discuss the role that dramatic irony plays in your overall enjoyment of the play.

Extend Interpretations

Critic's Corner Possible Response: Cassius is more likable—he is sincere and less priggish, especially when trying to comfort Brutus; Brutus is more likable—he is sadder, more mature, and less melodramatic.

Connect to Life Some students may respond with anecdotes that illustrate a time when they took advantage of an opportunity and benefited from it, while others may have missed an opportunity and felt no consequences.

Literary Analysis

Dramatic Irony Possible Response: Scene 4, Act 3, lines 297–300. Lucius thinks his master heard him cry out. The reader knows that Brutus saw a ghost and is trying to confirm his sighting.

GUIDING STUDENT RESPONSE

Connect to the Literature

1. **What Do You Think?**
Possible Responses: Yes—allies should not fight among themselves; no—it is not surprising that powerful people would have a clash of wills and egos.

Comprehension Check
- a triumvirate of Mark Antony, Octavius, and Lepidus; Lepidus' brother and Antony's nephew
- Brutus has condemned Lucius Pella for taking bribes, even though Cassius' letters defended Pella
- at Philippi

Use Selection Quiz
Unit Four Resource Book, p. 76.

Think Critically

2. Possible Responses: Students may point out that Antony kills with no remorse; he cynically prepares to cheat the people of their inheritance under Caesar's will, which he used to draw them to his side in Act Three. Others may think he was highly manipulative even in Act Three and seemed perfectly willing to create a riot.
3. Possible Response: If Antony arrogantly alters Caesar's will, the Romans will be worse off.
4. Possible Response: Brutus seems haunted by a guilty conscience. His comparison of false friends to unreliable horses is particularly harsh.
5. Possible Responses: The conspirators murder Caesar to bring peace and stability to Rome; Antony used Caesar's will to arouse the people and avenge Caesar's death; since the conspirators decided not to ask Cicero to join their cause, it is ironic that he is killed by the triumvirate for being a suspected conspirator; Cassius gives way to Brutus on every issue when his own views are more sensible and practical.
6. Citing the argument between the two generals and the ominous appearance of Caesar's ghost, students may feel that the mood is one of apprehension and foreboding.
7. Remind students to identify the main ideas in Brutus' speech by breaking the speech into smaller sections.

Objectives

1. understand **blank verse (Literary Analysis)**
2. understand Shakespeare's plays **(Active Reading)**

TEACHING THE LITERATURE

Reading and Analyzing

Reading Skills and Strategies: PREVIEW

Have students preview Act Five. Discuss with students that Act Five of the play contains the resolution and tells how the struggles end; it ties up the loose ends of the plot elements. Encourage students to examine the pictures and consider the called-out quotes throughout Act Five. Have students predict how the play will end based on everything they now know about the previous four acts and the characters involved. Before students begin reading, give them a brief summary of Act Five.

Literary Analysis

UNDERSTANDING BLANK VERSE

Tell students that one advantage of blank verse is that it allows the writer to signal important words. Sudden breaks or shifts in the rhythm are jarring, and they make the reader pay special attention to the words that cause the shift. As students read Act Five, have them note shifts or irregularities in the rhythm and what words they emphasize.

Possible Response: "Words before blows" (Act Five, Scene 3, line 28); *Words* is emphasized.

Active Reading

UNDERSTANDING SHAKESPEARE'S PLAYS

Remind students that a tragedy is a work in which a series of actions leads to the downfall of the main character. Have students decide who they think the main character is and trace the actions that have led that character to the situation at the beginning of Act Five. Then, as students read Act Five, have them trace the continuing actions that lead to that character's downfall.

Possible Response: Brutus: agrees to join conspiracy; allows Antony to live; allows Antony to speak; sent Cassius' forces to Philippi, where they are routed; sends own forces to where they are least needed; commits suicide

GUIDE FOR READING

(A) **Possible Response:** Octavius wins this argument.

ACT FIVE

SCENE 1 THE PLAINS OF PHILIPPI IN GREECE.

Antony and Octavius enter the battlefield with their army. Brutus and Cassius enter with their forces. The four leaders meet, but they only exchange insults and taunts. Antony and Octavius leave to prepare for battle. Cassius expresses his fears to Messala. Finally, Brutus and Cassius say their final farewells, in case they should die in battle.

[*Enter* Octavius, Antony, *and their Army.*]

Octavius. Now Antony, our hopes are answered.
You said the enemy would not come down
But keep the hills and upper regions.
It proves not so, their battles are at hand.
They mean to warn us at Philippi here,
[1] Answering before we do demand of them.

[2] **Antony.** Tut! I am in their bosoms and I know
Wherefore they do it. They could be content
To visit other places, and come down
With fearful bravery, thinking by this face
To fasten in our thoughts that they have courage.
But 'tis not so.

[*Enter a* Messenger.]

Messenger. Prepare you, generals,
The enemy comes on in gallant show;
Their bloody sign of battle is hung out,
And something to be done immediately.

Antony. Octavius, lead your battle softly on
Upon the left hand of the even field.

Octavius. Upon the right hand I. Keep thou the left.

Antony. Why do you cross me in this exigent?

Octavius. I do not cross you; but I will do so.

3 keep . . . regions: stay in the higher areas (where they could defend themselves more easily).

5 warn: challenge.

7–11 I am . . . courage: I know their secrets **(am in their bosoms)** and why they have done this. They would rather be in other places, not here fighting us. They come down with a show of bravery, thinking they will convince us they have courage.

14 sign of battle: a red flag symbolizing readiness for battle.

16–20 Antony and Octavius have a small argument about whose soldiers will fight on each side of the field. Who wins this argument? (A)

19 exigent: moment of crisis.

LESSON RESOURCES

UNIT FOUR RESOURCE BOOK, pp. 77–81

ASSESSMENT RESOURCES

Formal Assessment, pp. 131–132

Teacher's Guide to Assessment and Portfolio Use

Test Generator

SKILLS TRANSPARENCIES AND COPYMASTERS

Literary Analysis

- Shakespearean Drama I and II, T18, T19 (for Cooperative Learning Activity, p. 794)

Reading and Critical Thinking

- Locating Information Using Print References, T32 (for Inquiry & Research 1–4, p. 795)
- Locating Information Using Technical Resources, T33 (for Inquiry & Research 1–4, p. 795)

Grammar

- Comparisons Using Prepositional Phrases, C97 (for Mini Lesson, p. 796)

Vocabulary

- Multiple Meanings and Word Origins, C76 (for Mini Lesson, p. 780)

Writing

- Cause and Effect, C32 (for Writing Option 1, p. 795)
- Interpretive Essay, C33 (for Writing Option 3, p. 795)

INTEGRATED TECHNOLOGY

Audio Library

Video: Literature in Performance

- *Julius Caesar.* See **Video Resource Book**, pp. 25–30.

Visit our website: www.mcdougallittell.com

VIEW AND COMPARE

What does each image suggest about Antony's attitude toward battle and his role as military leader? Which image comes closest to your own understanding of Antony?

Charlton Heston as Antony (Commonwealth United film, 1970). S.S. Archives/Shooting Star.

Marlon Brando as Antony (MGM film, 1953). Photofest.

Customizing Instruction

Students Acquiring English

1 Help students understand this phrase by offering this paraphrase: "Appearing against us before we have forced them to fight."

Explain that Octavius and Antony thought that Brutus' armies would not attack first.

2 Students may be confused by some of the words and phrases used here. Help them understand Shakespeare's language by clarifying the following lines.

- "wherefore" (line 8): why
- "fearful bravery" (line 10): false courage
- "face" (line 10): appearance

Use **Spanish Study Guide** pp. 161–163 for additional support.

Less Proficient Readers

Help students understand the events of the play by having them answer the following questions as they read:

- What happens to Cassius?
  Possible Response: He kills himself, thinking he has sent his friend to his death.
- Who wins the war?
  Answer: Antony and Octavius
- What happens to Brutus?
  Answer: He kills himself.

View and Compare

Possible Response: The first image (with Charlton Heston) shows Antony with other soldiers, emphasizing his position as a leader of a group and suggesting some kind of teamwork. The second image (with Marlon Brando) shows Antony alone, brandishing a sword, emphasizing his individual might rather than membership in or leadership of a group. Students' own understandings of Antony will vary.

BLOCK SCHEDULING: MANAGING TIME

If your schedule requires that you cover the lesson objectives in a shorter time, use . . .

- Preparing to Read, p. 689
- Thinking Through the Literature, p. 794
- Grammar in Context, p. 796

If you want to take advantage of longer class time, use . . .

- TE Teaching Options: Vocabulary Strategy, p. 780; Cross Curricular Links, pp. 782, 790; Speaking and Listening, p. 784; Inquiry and Research, p. 786; Informal Assessment, p. 788
- Choices & Challenges and Author Activity, pp. 795, 797

Reading and Analyzing

Reading Skills and Strategies: QUESTIONING

A Have students question why Octavius responds the way he does to Brutus and Cassius. What might his response reveal about his character?
Possible Responses: He is eager to fight because he genuinely wants to avenge Julius Caesar; he is a rash and overzealous youth who eagerly seeks power without thinking through the repercussions of war.

Reading Skills and Strategies: CLARIFYING

Encourage students to consult the side notes on the next page to help clarify Cassius' characterization of Antony. Explain further that *masker* is a reference to someone who attends masquerades; *reveller* refers to someone who celebrates in a riotous manner. Ask students why Cassius would want to describe Antony with these terms.
Possible Response: Cassius wants to insult Antony and perhaps discredit his military skills by implying that he is nothing more than a wild partygoer.

[*March.*]

[*Drum. Enter* Brutus, Cassius, *and their Army;* Lucilius, Titinius, Messala, *and others.*]

Brutus. They stand and would have parley.

Cassius. Stand fast, Titinius. We must out and talk.

Octavius. Mark Antony, shall we give sign of battle?

Antony. No, Caesar, we will answer on their charge.
Make forth. The generals would have some words.

Octavius. Stir not until the signal.

[Brutus, Cassius, Octavius, *and* Antony *meet in the center of the stage.*]

Brutus. Words before blows. Is it so, countrymen?

Octavius. Not that we love words better, as you do.

Brutus. Good words are better than bad strokes, Octavius.

Antony. In your bad strokes, Brutus, you give good words;
Witness the hole you made in Caesar's heart,
Crying "Long live! Hail, Caesar!"

Cassius. Antony,
The posture of your blows are yet unknown;
But for your words, they rob the Hybla bees,
And leave them honeyless.

Antony. Not stingless too.

Brutus. O yes, and soundless too!
For you have stol'n their buzzing, Antony,
And very wisely threat before you sting.

Antony. Villains! you did not so when your vile daggers
Hacked one another in the sides of Caesar.
You showed your teeth like apes, and fawned like hounds,
And bowed like bondmen, kissing Caesar's feet;
Whilst damned Casca, like a cur, behind
Struck Caesar on the neck. O you flatterers!

Cassius. Flatterers? Now, Brutus, thank yourself!
This tongue had not offended so today
If Cassius might have ruled.

Octavius. Come, come, the cause! If arguing make us sweat,
The proof of it will turn to redder drops.

21 They . . . parley: They are standing and waiting for a conference.

24 answer on their charge: respond to their attack.

33–35 The posture . . . honeyless: We don't know yet how effective you'll be as a soldier, but your words are sweeter than honey. (Hybla is a mountain in Sicily known for its sweet honey.)

39–44 you did not so . . . neck: You didn't give warning before you killed Caesar. Instead, you acted like loving pets and slaves while Casca, like a dog **(cur),** stabbed Caesar in the neck.

45–47 Now . . . ruled: Cassius angrily tells Brutus that they wouldn't be listening to these insults if he had had his way **(Cassius might have ruled)** when arguing that Antony should be killed.

48–49 Come . . . drops: Get to the point **(cause).** Arguing is tiresome. We will settle it by shedding blood.

Teaching Options

Mini Lesson Vocabulary Strategy

MULTIPLE MEANINGS AND WORD ORIGINS

Instruction Many words, over time, accumulate multiple meanings. Often definitions of the same word are related, share the same origin, and are listed under the same entry in a dictionary. Arrangements of definitions in a dictionary generally use the following order: most frequently encountered meaning; more specialized uses; rare, obsolete, or archaic meanings. Some words, however, may be spelled the same, but have different meanings *and* different origins. These words with different origins have separate entries in a dictionary.

Practice Have students use a dictionary to look up each of the following words. Students should copy the word's origin or origins and two different meanings. If the word has two different origins, make sure each meaning is related to a different origin.

1. *arm*
Possible Response: origins: 1. *armus*: shoulder; 2. *arma*: weapons
meanings: 1. body part between the shoulder and wrist; 2. to furnish with weapons

"*I draw a sword against conspirators.*"

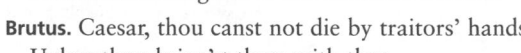

Martin Sheen as Brutus and Robert Curtis-Brown as Octavius (New York Shakespeare Festival, 1988). Photo copyright © George E. Joseph.

Customizing Instruction

Students Acquiring English

1 Point out the following two sentences and help students supply the words necessary to transform the lines into current standard English.

- "We must out and talk."
 Possible Response: "We must **go** out and talk **to them**."
- "The generals would have some words."
 Possible Response: "The generals would **like to** have some words **with us**."

2 Explain to students that "make forth" means "go forward."

Students Acquiring English

3 Help students understand this specialized phrase referring to Octavius' weapon. "The sword goes up again" means "the sword **is put away** again" or "the sword goes **into its sheath** again."

50 Look,
 I draw a sword against conspirators.
 When think you that the sword goes up again? **3** **A**
 Never, till Caesar's three-and-thirty wounds
 Be well avenged, or till another Caesar
55 Have added slaughter to the sword of traitors.

Brutus. Caesar, thou canst not die by traitors' hands
 Unless thou bring'st them with thee.

Octavius. So I hope.
 I was not born to die on Brutus' sword.

Brutus. Oh, if thou wert the noblest of thy strain,
60 Young man, thou couldst not die more honorable.

Cassius. A peevish schoolboy, worthless of such honor,
 Joined with a masker and a reveller!

54–55 or till . . . traitors: or until a second Caesar (that is, Octavius himself—Caesar's grandnephew and adopted son) has been killed by the traitors.

56–57 Caesar . . . with thee: Brutus here refers to Octavius, who took that name. The only way you'll die from a traitor's hands is if you kill yourself, Brutus insists.

2. *tall*
 Possible Response: origin: *getœl*: quick
 meanings: 1. high in stature; 2. brave
 (obsolete)
3. *brave*
 Possible Response: origin: *bravo*: courageous
 meanings: 1. having courage; 2. to face or
 endure
4. *quick*
 Possible Response: origin: *vivus*: living
 meanings: 1. capable of acting with speed;
 2. living, alive (archaic)

5. *humor*
 Possible Response: origin: *humere*: to be
 moist
 meanings: 1. something that is designed to be
 amusing; 2. temperament or disposition

Use **Vocabulary Transparencies and Copymasters,**
p. 76, for more exercises.

**A lesson on multiple meanings and word origins
appears on p. 356 in the Pupil's Edition.**

Reading and Analyzing

GUIDE FOR READING

A **Possible Response:** The bitter insults between the leaders of the opposing sides seems believable, but the meeting accomplishes nothing.

B **Possible Response:** Cassius is unhappy that this one battle will determine the fate of the conspirators' cause.

Literary Analysis: FORESHADOWING

C Have students reread Cassius' speech here. Remind students that foreshadowing is a hint or clue about what is to happen later. Ask students what the omens Cassius mentions might foreshadow.
Possible Response: Brutus' and Cassius' army will be defeated and slaughtered.

Reading Skills and Strategies: PREDICTING

D In light of the preceding dialogue between Cassius and Brutus, have students predict what they think will happen in the battle.
Possible Response: Brutus and Cassius will be defeated, and perhaps Brutus will be faced with deciding whether to commit suicide.

Reading Skills and Strategies: CONNECTING

E Have students think about Brutus' desire to know how things will end before they've begun. Ask students whether they ever wish they knew, at the start of a day, how that day will end and why or why not.
Possible Response: Yes, to experience a sense of control; no, to keep life unpredictable

---

Antony. Old Cassius still.
Octavius. Come, Antony. Away!
Defiance, traitor, hurl we in your teeth.
If you dare fight today, come to the field;
If not, when you have stomachs.
[*Exeunt* Octavius, Antony, *and their Army.*]
Cassius. Why, now blow wind, swell billow, and swim bark!
The storm is up, and all is on the hazard.
Brutus. Ho, Lucilius! Hark, a word with you.
[Lucilius *and* Messala *stand forth.*]
Lucilius. My lord?
[Brutus *and* Lucilius *converse apart.*]
Cassius. Messala.
Messala. What says my general?
Cassius. Messala,
This is my birthday; as this very day
Was Cassius born. Give me thy hand, Messala.
Be thou my witness that against my will
(As Pompey was) am I compelled to set
Upon one battle all our liberties.
You know that I held Epicurus strong
And his opinion. Now I change my mind
And partly credit things that do presage.
Coming from Sardis, on our former ensign
Two mighty eagles fell, and there they perched,
Gorging and feeding from our soldiers' hands,
Who to Philippi here consorted us.
This morning are they fled away and gone,
And in their steads do ravens, crows, and kites
Fly o'er our heads and downward look on us
As we were sickly prey. Their shadows seem
A canopy most fatal, under which
Our army lies, ready to give up the ghost.
Messala. Believe not so.
Cassius. I but believe it partly,
For I am fresh of spirit and resolved
To meet all perils very constantly.
Brutus. Even so, Lucilius.
Cassius. Now, most noble Brutus,

62–63 masker . . . still: Cassius is insulting Antony by calling him a party-goer and a playboy. Same old Cassius **(Old Cassius still),** Antony replies.

66 stomachs: enough nerve. Does the prebattle meeting seem believable? Has anything been accomplished? **A**

68 all . . . hazard: Everything is at stake.

73–75 against . . . liberties: I am forced to gamble the freedom of Rome on one battle. What does he mean? **B**

76–88 I held . . . give up the ghost: Epicurus was a philosopher who did not believe omens. Cassius says that he once was a follower of this philosophy, but now he sometimes believes in things that predict the future **(credit things that do presage).** Cassius then tells Messala of two eagles that accompanied the army from Sardis to Philippi. The eagles have been replaced by ravens, crows, and hawks **(kites)**—birds that symbolize death.

79 former ensign: the flag that was carried at the head of the army's march.

91 constantly: with determination.

Teaching Options

Cross Curricular Link History

DEFEAT IN ANCIENT ROME When a Roman general won a significant victory, he often had a truimphal procession through Rome. On such occasions, the defeated enemy leaders who had been taken alive were paraded through the streets so the crowds could jeer at them. Rather than face this humiliation, defeated leaders would sometimes commit suicide.

The gods today stand friendly, that we may,
Lovers in peace, lead on our days to age!
But since the affairs of men rest still incertain,
Let's reason with the worst that may befall.
If we do lose this battle, then is this
The very last time we shall speak together.
What are you then determined to do?

Brutus. Even by the rule of that philosophy
By which I did blame Cato for the death
Which he did give himself—I know not how,
But I do find it cowardly and vile,
For fear of what might fall, so to prevent
The time of life—arming myself with patience
To stay the providence of some high powers
That govern us below.

Cassius. Then, if we lose this battle,
You are contented to be led in triumph
Through the streets of Rome.

Brutus. No, Cassius, no. Think not, thou noble Roman,
That ever Brutus will go bound to Rome.
He bears too great a mind. But this same day
Must end that work the ides of March begun,
And whether we shall meet again I know not.
Therefore our everlasting farewell take.
For ever and for ever farewell, Cassius!
If we do meet again, why, we shall smile;
If not, why then this parting was well made.

Cassius. For ever and for ever farewell, Brutus!
If we do meet again, we'll smile indeed;
If not, 'tis true this parting was well made.

Brutus. Why then, lead on. O that a man might know
The end of this day's business ere it come!
But it sufficeth that the day will end,
And then the end is known. Come, ho! Away!

[*Exeunt.*]

96 Let's . . . befall: Let's think about the worst that might happen to us.

100–107 Even . . . govern us below: According to the Stoic philosophy that Brutus follows, people should endure their troubles. Brutus therefore finds suicide to be dishonorable **(cowardly and vile).** He mentions Cato, a famous Roman who killed himself after Pompey lost to Caesar.

115 our . . . take: Let's make a final farewell to each other.

Customizing Instruction

Less Proficient Readers

1 Have students list the omens seen by Cassius that cause him to think death is near.

Possible Response: The eagles following the army flew away, and birds symbolizing death (ravens, crows, kites) took their place.

Students Acquiring English

Help students understand the following phrases.

2 "lovers": here, devoted friends

3 "still incertain": always in doubt

4 "time of life": "the rest or remainder of life"

5 "to stay the providence": to endure the ordained fate

Reading and Analyzing

Literary Analysis: CHARACTER

A Have students think about the development of Cassius' character. What does he reveal about himself in this incident?

Possible Response: He reveals that he can become so desperate that he would kill one of his own soldiers; he shows that his willingness to kill is not peculiar to Caesar's assassination—it is a recurring feature of his character.

GUIDE FOR READING

B **Possible Response:** Brutus, who has perceived some weakness among Octavius' troops, seems to feel confident at this point.

C **Possible Response:** angry and dismayed

D **Possible Response:** kill himself

E **Possible Response:** He thinks that his best friend, Titinius, has been captured by the enemy.

SCENE 2 THE BATTLEFIELD.

Brutus sends Messala with orders for the forces across the field.

[*Alarum. Enter* Brutus *and* Messala.]

Brutus. Ride, ride, Messala, ride, and give these bills
Unto the legions on the other side.

[*Loud alarum.*]

Let them set on at once; for I perceive
But cold demeanor in Octavius' wing,
And sudden push gives them the overthrow.
Ride, ride, Messala! Let them all come down.

[*Exeunt.*]

1–2 give . . . side: Give these orders to our soldiers on that side of the field.

4 cold demeanor: lack of courage. How does Brutus feel about the battle at this point? **B**

SCENE 3 ANOTHER PART OF THE BATTLEFIELD.

Cassius retreats, losing the battle to Antony's forces. He sends Titinius to see if nearby forces are friend or enemy. From a hill, Pindarus believes he sees Titinius killed. Completely discouraged, Cassius asks Pindarus to kill him. Titinius returns to find Cassius' body and kills himself. Brutus and others arrive, having defeated Octavius's army. Messala has brought them to see the body of Cassius. Now they see that Titinius is also dead. Brutus mourns the two, but also looks to a second battle with his enemies.

[*Enter* Cassius *and* Titinius.]

A

Cassius. O, look, Titinius, look! The villains fly!
Myself have to mine own turned enemy.
This ensign here of mine was turning back;
I slew the coward and did take it from him.

1

Titinius. O Cassius, Brutus gave the word too early,
Who, having some advantage on Octavius,
Took it too eagerly. His soldiers fell to spoil,
Whilst we by Antony are all enclosed.

[*Enter* Pindarus.]

Pindarus. Fly further off, my lord! fly further off!
Mark Antony is in your tents, my lord.
Fly, therefore, noble Cassius, fly far off!

Cassius. This hill is far enough. Look, look, Titinius!

1–4 The villains . . . him: Cassius is watching his men run away **(fly)** from the battle. He killed his own flag-bearer (the dead **ensign** lying on the ground near him) when he saw the man running away. How does Cassius seem to feel about the battle? **C**

7 His . . . spoil: Brutus' soldiers began looting (instead of fighting the enemy).

Teaching Options

Mini Lesson Speaking and Listening

WRITE AND PERFORM A SCENE

Instruction Point out to students that the scene between Cassius and Pindarus actually contains a scene-within-a-scene. The audience sees Cassius and his servant, who describes a scene that is taking place in the distance, in which Titinius encounters approaching soldiers. The audience must follow the dialogue between Cassius and Pindarus, and at the same time, they must imagine the exchange between Titinius and the unidentified horsemen.

Practice Have students work in groups to write a scene in which they dramatize the encounter between Titinius and the soldiers. They should carefully reread the dialogue between Cassius and Pindarus for clues about what happens to Titinius. Remind students that, based on the actions Pindarus reports, Cassius thinks Titinius has been captured. Have students read ahead to discover that Titinius, in fact, meets friendly troops, not enemies. Students should designate parts for Titinius and the horsemen, and should be sure to include the shouts of joy reported by Pindarus. Have groups stage their scenes for the class, which should listen and comment on the creativity and believability of the scripts.

BLOCK SCHEDULING This activity is particularly well suited for longer class periods.

Are those my tents where I perceive the fire?

Titinius. They are, my lord.

Cassius. Titinius, if thou lovest me,
Mount thou my horse and hide thy spurs in him
Till he have brought thee up to yonder troops
And here again, that I may rest assured
Whether yond troops are friend or enemy.

Titinius. I will be here again even with a thought.

[*Exit.*]

Cassius. Go, Pindarus, get higher on that hill.
My sight was ever thick. Regard Titinius, [2]
And tell me what thou not'st about the field.

[Pindarus *ascends the hill.*]

This day I breathed first. Time is come round,
And where I did begin, there shall I end.
My life is run his compass. Sirrah, what news?

Pindarus.

[*Above.*]

O my lord!

Cassius. What news?

Pindarus.

[*Above.*]

Titinius is enclosed round about
With horsemen that make to him on the spur.
Yet he spurs on. Now they are almost on him.
Now, Titinius!
Now some light. O, he lights too! He's ta'en. [3]

[*Shout.*]

And hark!
They shout for joy.

Cassius. Come down; behold no more.
O coward that I am to live so long
To see my best friend ta'en before my face!

[*Enter* Pindarus *from above.*]

Come hither, sirrah.
In Parthia did I take thee prisoner,
And then I swore thee, saving of thy life,
That whatsoever I did bid thee do,
Thou shouldst attempt it. Come now, keep thine oath.

15–18 Mount . . . enemy: Ride my horse to those troops over there, and come back to tell me if they are friend or enemy.

19 even with a thought: as fast as you can think of it.

25 is run his compass: has come full circle (that is, my life is complete). What is Cassius planning to do? **D**

28–34 From a distance, Pindarus describes the capture of Titinius.

32 ta'en: taken (captured).

38–46 In Parthia . . . the sword: When I saved your life in Parthia (an ancient Asian land), you swore to do whatever I asked. Now keep your oath and become a free man. I'll cover my face as you stab me **(search this bosom)** with the same knife that killed Caesar. Don't argue **(Stand not to answer).** Why does Cassius finally decide to kill himself? **E**

Customizing Instruction

Less Proficient Readers

1 Ask students what Titinius reports to Cassius about Brutus' position in the battle.

Possible Response: He says that Brutus had the advantage over Octavius but attacked too early.

- Have students explain what Brutus' soldiers allegedly do after they think they have beaten Octavius.
  Possible Response: They begin looting the enemy camp instead of seeking other enemy troops to fight.
- Ask students to explain Antony's position relative to Cassius at this point.
  Possible Response: Antony's troops have Cassius' camp surrounded.

2 Explain to students that *thick* here means "dim"; thus, Cassius is saying he has always had poor eyesight. Ask students why Cassius' vision is an issue in this scene.

Possible Response: Because he does not see well at a distance, he must rely on his servant to report on what happens to Titinius as he rides out to determine whether the approaching troops are friend or foe. The servant misinterprets what he sees.

Students Acquiring English

3 Explain to students that in this context *lights* means to "dismount from a horse." Then explain that *ta'en* is a contraction of *taken*. Ask students what Pindarus is reporting.

Possible Response: Cassius thinks Titinius has been captured by enemy soldiers because they all get down off their horses.

Reading and Analyzing

Literary Analysis: CHARACTER

A Point out that although Caesar is killed halfway through the play, he remains an influential character. Ask how Cassius reinforces Caesar's presence here.

Possible Response: He addresses Caesar just as he kills himself and refers to the assassination that put the events of the second half of the play into motion. Cassius states that Caesar has revenge for the assassination.

Reading Skills and Strategies: PREDICTING

B In light of Messala's remarks, ask students to predict how Brutus will take the news of Cassius' suicide.

Possible Response: Brutus will probably be upset and depressed, but he will probably try to endure his friend's death stoically. Students may recall his reaction to news of his wife's death when considering their response.

Now be a freeman, and with this good sword,
That ran through Caesar's bowels, search this bosom.
Stand not to answer. Here, take thou the hilts,
And when my face is covered, as 'tis now,
Guide thou the sword.

[Pindarus *stabs him.*]

A —Caesar, thou are revenged
Even with the sword that killed thee.

[*Dies.*]

1 **Pindarus.** So, I am free, yet would not so have been,
Durst I have done my will. O Cassius!
Far from this country Pindarus shall run,
Where never Roman shall take note of him.

[*Exit.*]

48–49 So . . . will: I am free; but I wouldn't have been if I had done what I wanted (that is, refused to kill Cassius).

Jack Stehlin as Titinius waves a flag over Edward Herrmann as Cassius (New York Shakespeare Festival, 1988). Photo copyright © George E. Joseph.

Teaching Options

Mini Lesson Inquiry and Research

RESEARCHING SHAKESPEARE'S SOURCES

Instruction Students might be interested to know that Shakespeare wrote two other Roman history plays in addition to *Julius Caesar–The Tragedy of Coriolanus* and *The Tragedy of Antony and Cleopatra*. Explain that Shakespeare had to consult references for information about the historical Roman characters in order to dramatize their lives and create the plots of his plays.

Practice Invite students to work on one of Shakespeare's Roman plays and research the sources from which he drew material for his plays. Explain that they will be conducting research on Shakespeare's research. Students might want to work in groups arranged according to the play; students working on *Coriolanus* or *Antony and Cleopatra* might find group support particularly beneficial, especially for help with reading the play. Students should begin their research by generating a list of relevant and researchable questions and using the library to find books and technical resources dealing with Shakespeare's sources. Because there are many books on Shakespeare's plays, students must learn how to

[*Reenter* Titinius *with* Messala.]

Messala. It is but change, Titinius; for Octavius
Is overthrown by noble Brutus' power,
As Cassius' legions are by Antony.

Titinius. These tidings will well comfort Cassius.

Messala. Where did you leave him?

Titinius. All disconsolate,
With Pindarus his bondman, on this hill.

Messala. Is not that he that lies upon the ground?

Titinius. He lies not like the living. O my heart!

Messala. Is not that he?

Titinius. No, this was he, Messala,
But Cassius is no more. O setting sun,
As in thy red rays thou does sink to night
So in his red blood Cassius' day is set!
The sun of Rome is set. Our day is gone;
Clouds, dews, and dangers come; our deeds are done!
Mistrust of my success hath done this deed.

Messala. Mistrust of good success hath done this deed.
O hateful Error, Melancholy's child,
Why dost thou show to the apt thoughts of men
The things that are not? O Error, soon conceived,
Thou never com'st unto a happy birth,
But kill'st the mother that engend'red thee!

Titinius. What, Pindarus! Where art thou, Pindarus?

Messala. Seek him, Titinius, whilst I go to meet
The noble Brutus, thrusting this report
Into his ears. I may say "thrusting" it;
For piercing steel and darts envenomed
Shall be as welcome to the ears of Brutus
As tidings of this sight.

B

Titinius. Hie you, Messala,
And I will seek for Pindarus the while.

[*Exit* Messala.]

[Titinius *looks at* Cassius.]

Why didst thou send me forth, brave Cassius?
Did I not meet thy friends, and did not they
Put on my brows this wreath of victory
And bid me give it thee? Didst thou not hear their shouts?

52–54 It is . . . Antony: It's an even exchange. Just as Antony has defeated Cassius, Brutus has defeated Octavius.

56 disconsolate: extremely sad.

68–72 O hateful . . . thee: Why do mistaken beliefs, which come from sadness **(Melancholy's child),** always seem so true when they are false? A mistake is easily born but always kills its mother at birth.

77 darts envenomed: poisoned darts.

79 Hie you: Hurry.

Customizing Instruction

Less Proficient Readers

1 Make sure students understand what Pindarus is saying here. Because he was Cassius' slave, Pindarus is free now that his master is dead. Ask students what Pindarus thinks of his freedom.

Possible Response: Pindarus would rather have Cassius alive than be free.

narrow their choices to books with information relevant to their topic and play. Encourage students to meet in their groups to form a research plan that might include gathering information about the material Shakespeare consulted (such as Plutarch's *Lives of the Noble Greeks and Romans*). Encourage students to use text organizers to locate and categorize information as they conduct their research organizing that information into categories (such as "Most Important Source"), and asking questions about how closely Shakespeare's plays adhere to the historical accounts. Students may present their findings in an oral report, a visual display such as a chart, or a written report that is distributed to the class.

Reading and Analyzing

Literary Analysis: IRONY

A Ask whether, in addition to the ironic mistake Titinius describes here, there is a broader, unintentional irony in his words, "Alas, thou hast misconstrued everything."
Possible Response: These words could be applied to Cassius' motives for killing Caesar. He misjudged the repercussions of the assassination. Instead of bringing stability to the country, the assassination brought chaos and destruction to Rome.

GUIDE FOR READING

B **Possible Response:** Cassius mistakenly thought that Titinius had been captured by enemy troops.

C **Possible Response:** He thinks he has been indirectly responsible for Cassius' death.

Literary Analysis: CHARACTER

D Have students think about Brutus' lines, "I owe more tears / To this dead man than you shall see me pay," and his subsequent shift from Cassius to preparations for battle. Ask students whether they think this behavior is consistent with his personality, and why or why not.
Possible Response: It is consistent because he responds in a similar fashion when he hears of Portia's death. He tends to keep his grief and mourning private and to act in a way that is best for the common good.

GUIDE FOR READING

E **Possible Response:** Yes—in Scene 1 Brutus declares he will never "go bound to Rome"; no—Brutus is critical of suicide.

A
Alas, thou hast misconstrued everything!
But hold thee, take this garland on thy brow.
Thy Brutus bid me give it thee, and I
Will do his bidding. Brutus, come apace
And see how I regarded Caius Cassius.
By your leave, gods. This is a Roman's part.
Come, Cassius' sword, and find Titinius' heart.

[*Dies.*]

[*Alarum. Enter* Brutus, Messala, Young Cato, Strato, Volumnius, *and* Lucilius.]

Brutus. Where, where, Messala, doth his body lie?

Messala. Lo, yonder, and Titinius mourning it.

Brutus. Titinius' face is upward.

Cato. He is slain.

Brutus. O Julius Caesar, thou art mighty yet!
Thy spirit walks abroad and turns our swords
1 In our own proper entrails.

[*Low alarums.*]

Cato. Brave Titinius!
Look whe'r he have not crowned dead Cassius.

Brutus. Are yet two Romans living such as these?
The last of all the Romans, fare thee well!
It is impossible that ever Rome
Should breed thy fellow. Friends, I owe more tears
To this dead man than you shall see me pay.
I shall find time, Cassius; I shall find time.
Come therefore, and to Thasos send his body.
His funerals shall not be in our camp,
Lest it discomfort us. Lucilius, come;
And come, young Cato. Let us to the field.
Labeo and Flavius set our battles on.
'Tis three o'clock; and, Romans, yet ere night
We shall try fortune in a second fight.

D

[*Exeunt.*]

85 misconstrued: misunderstood. B What was the mistake that led to Cassius' suicide?

86 Titinius removes the laurel wreath his friends put on his head to symbolize his victory. In his grief, he puts the wreath on Cassius' head.

88 apace: quickly.

90 This . . . part: This (killing myself) is the proper thing for a brave Roman to do. C Why does Titinius believe this is the right thing to do?

98 whe'r: whether.

99–102 Are yet . . . fellow: Are there two Romans still living who are as good as these two? I bid you both farewell. Rome will never see your equal **(breed thy fellow).**

105 Thasos (thä′ säs′): an island near Philippi.

111 We shall . . . fight: We'll try our luck in a second battle.

Teaching Options

Assessment Informal Assessment

Have students assess their comprehension by answering the following questions.

1. What do Antony, Octavius, Brutus, and Cassius talk about when they meet before the battle begins?
   Possible Response: They insult and belittle each other.
2. Why is Cassius worried about his side's chances for success as he prepares to join the fighting?
   Possible Response: He thinks he has seen omens in nature that predict the conspirators' doom.
3. How do Cassius and Brutus feel as they say good-bye to each before the battle begins?
   Possible Response: They express their fondness for each other and appear deeply saddened that they may never see each other again.
4. How are Cassius' and Titinius' suicides related?
   Possible Response: Cassius kills himself because he thinks Titinius has been taken by the enemy; Titinius kills himself when he learns of Cassius' suicide.

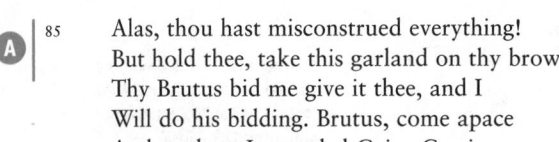

SCENE 4 ANOTHER PART OF THE BATTLEFIELD.

During the battle, Young Cato is killed and Lucilius taken prisoner. Brought to Antony, Lucilius insists that Brutus will never be taken alive.

[*Alarum. Enter* Brutus, Messala, Young Cato, Lucilius, *and* Flavius.]

Brutus. Yet, countrymen, O, yet hold up your heads!

Cato. What fellow doth not? Who will go with me?
I will proclaim my name about the field.
I am the son of Marcus Cato, ho!
A foe to tyrants, and my country's friend.
I am the son of Marcus Cato, ho!

[*Enter* Soldiers *and fight.*]

Brutus. And I am Brutus, Marcus Brutus I!
Brutus, my country's friend! Know me for Brutus!

[*Exit.*]

[Young Cato *falls.*]

Lucilius. O young and noble Cato, art thou down?
Why, now thou diest as bravely as Titinius,
And mayst be honored, being Cato's son.

First Soldier. Yield, or thou diest.

Lucilius. Only I yield to die.

[*Offering money.*]

There is so much that thou wilt kill me straight.
Kill Brutus, and be honored in his death.

First Soldier. We must not. A noble prisoner!

[*Enter* Antony.]

Second Soldier. Room ho! Tell Antony Brutus is ta'en.

First Soldier. I'll tell the news. Here comes the general.
Brutus is ta'en! Brutus, is ta'en, my lord!

Antony. Where is he?

Lucilius. Safe, Antony; Brutus is safe enough.
I dare assure thee that no enemy
Shall ever take alive the noble Brutus.
The gods defend him from so great a shame!
When you do find him, or alive or dead,
He will be found like Brutus, like himself.

4 Marcus Cato: Portia's father, a greatly respected Roman.

12 Yield: surrender.

13–14 There is . . . death: This money is for you, if you will kill me immediately **(straight).** If you kill Brutus, you will win honor for it. Lucilius pretends to be Brutus and fools the soldier.

20–22 Do you agree with Lucilius that Brutus will never be taken alive? E

Customizing Instruction

Students Acquiring English

1 Explain to students that *proper* here means "naturally belonging" or "individual."

Reading and Analyzing

Active Reading

UNDERSTANDING SHAKESPEARE'S PLAYS

Point out that Shakespeare uses stage directions to create suspense even in the last pages of the play. Ask students to clarify how the stage directions here are organized to contribute to the suspense of the final scene.

Possible Response: The whispering that is indicated in the stage directions and the gaps in conversation keep the audience from knowing what Brutus is whispering.

GUIDE FOR READING

A Possible Response: He hopes to make Lucilius an ally.

B Possible Response: Brutus feels that the battle is lost.

C Possible Response: He believes that everyone else is as honorable and devoted to the general good as he is.

Antony. This is not Brutus, friend; but, I assure you,
A prize no less in worth. Keep this man safe;
Give him all kindness. I had rather have
Such men my friends than enemies. Go on,
And see whe'r Brutus be alive or dead;
And bring us word unto Octavius' tent
How everything is chanced.

[*Exeunt.*]

26–28 Why do you think Antony is being so merciful to Lucilius? **A**

SCENE 5 ANOTHER PART OF THE BATTLEFIELD.

Facing defeat, Brutus' forces rest. Brutus feels that all is lost. He asks three men to kill him, but each refuses. Finally, Strato agrees to hold the sword as Brutus kills himself on it. Antony, Octavius, and others arrive. Antony mourns Brutus, calling him the "noblest Roman." Octavius promises him a noble funeral as the play ends.

[*Enter* Brutus, Dardanius, Clitus, Strato, *and* Volumnius.]

Brutus. Come, poor remains of friends, rest on this rock.

Clitus. Statilius showed the torchlight but, my lord,
He came not back. He is or ta'en or slain.

Brutus. Sit thee down, Clitus. Slaying is the word.
It is a deed in fashion. Hark thee, Clitus.

[*Whispers.*]

Clitus. What, I, my lord? No, not for all the world!

Brutus. Peace then. No words.

Clitus. I'll rather kill myself.

Brutus. Hark thee, Dardanius.

[*Whispers.*]

Dardanius. Shall I do such a deed?

Clitus. O Dardanius!

Dardanius. O Clitus!

Clitus. What ill request did Brutus make to thee?

Dardanius. To kill him, Clitus. Look he meditates.

1 **Clitus.** Now is that noble vessel full of grief,
That it runs over even at his eyes.

Brutus. Come hither, good Volumnius. List a word.

2–3 Statilius . . . slain: Statilius (our scout) signaled with his torch that all was well at our camp. But since he hasn't come back, he has been either captured or killed.

4–8 Brutus says that it has become fashionable to kill, not to capture. Then he whispers something to Clitus, who seems shocked by what Brutus has asked him to do. Brutus whispers the same request to Dardanius, who reacts the same way. After this, Brutus walks away from the two men.

15 List: listen to.

Teaching Options

Cross Curricular Link History

MARK ANTONY Antony was a successful general and politician in his own right and shared military and political power with Caesar until Caesar's death. After his famous funeral oration and subsequent victory over the conspirators, Antony served with Octavius as part of the Second Triumvirate, ruling Rome for the better part of the next decade. But it is the personal side of Antony's life that usually sparks the most interest, and his name is seldom mentioned without reference to his famous lover, Cleopatra. In 41 B.C., Antony met the queen of Egypt and began an affair and political alliance that would ultimately lead to his downfall.

Although Antony married Octavius' sister, Octavia, in 40 B.C., he continued his affair with Cleopatra in Egypt. His indulgent affair with the Egyptian queen, his treatment of Octavia, his reputation as a reveler, and his apparent disregard for the affairs of Rome prompted Octavius to declare war on Cleopatra. In 31 B.C., Octavius defeated the Egyptian fleet, which included Antony's forces, at Actium; when Cleopatra fled, Antony followed her. His navy surrendered to Octavius. Antony was unable to keep Octavius out of Egypt, and he killed himself. Rather than go to Rome as a prisoner, Cleopatra committed suicide as well.

Volumnius. What says my lord?

Brutus. Why this, Volumnius.
The ghost of Caesar hath appeared to me
Two several times by night—at Sardis once, **2**
And this last night here in Philippi fields.
I know my hour is come.

Volumnius. Not so, my lord.

Brutus. Nay, I am sure it is, Volumnius.
Thou seest the world, Volumnius, how it goes.
Our enemies have beat us to the pit.

[*Low alarums.*]

It is more worthy to leap in ourselves
Than tarry till they push us. Good Volumnius,
Thou know'st that we two went to school together.
Even for that our love of old, I prithee
Hold thou my sword-hilts whilst I run on it.

Volumnius. That's not an office for a friend, my lord.

[*Alarum still.*]

Clitus. Fly, fly, my lord! There is no tarrying here.

Brutus. Farewell to you; and you; and you, Volumnius.
Strato, thou hast been all this while asleep.
Farewell to thee too, Strato. Countrymen,
My heart doth joy that yet in all my life
I found no man but he was true to me.
I shall have glory by this losing day
More than Octavius and Mark Antony
By this vile conquest shall attain unto.
So fare you well at once, for Brutus' tongue
Hath almost ended his life's history.
Night hangs upon mine eyes; my bones would rest,
That have but labored to attain this hour.

[*Alarum. Cry within:* Fly, fly, fly!]

Clitus. Fly, my lord, fly!

Brutus. Hence! I will follow.

[*Exeunt* Clitus, Dardanius, *and* Volumnius.]

I prithee, Strato, stay thou by thy lord.
Thou art a fellow of a good respect;
Thy life hath had some smatch of honor in it.
Hold then my sword, and turn away thy face
While I do run upon it. Wilt thou, Strato?

Strato. Give me your hand first. Fare you well, my lord.

18 Two several times: twice.

23 pit: a hole into which hunted animals are forced. How does Brutus seem to feel about the battle now? **B**

25 tarry: wait.

27–28 I prithee . . . on it: I beg you to hold my sword (on the ground, with the blade pointing up) while I fall onto it.

29 That's . . . friend: That's no duty for a friend to perform.

34–35 Think about how Brutus sums up his life in these two lines. Then think about the way Cassius manipulated him in Act One, and the way Antony fooled him into letting Antony speak to the crowd. What can you conclude about Brutus' understanding of people? **C**

41–42 my bones . . . hour: My tired bones have worked to bring me to this final hour of rest.

46 smatch: little bit.

Customizing Options

Students Acquiring English

1 Explain to students that a *vessel* is a container. The word is used figuratively to refer to Brutus. The liquid that runs over from the vessel is Brutus' tears.

Less Proficient Readers

2 Be sure students understand that Caesar's ghost has appeared to Brutus twice, even though he only appears once in the actual play. Ask students how Brutus might feel about these apparitions.

Possible response: Brutus might feel guilty, frightened, or resigned that his time of punishment for the assassination has finally come.

Reading and Analyzing

Literary Analysis: TRAGEDY

A Have students review the Qualities of a Tragic Hero chart on p. 686. Ask students whether Brutus qualifies as a tragic hero.

Possible Responses: Yes, since he is portrayed as basically good but disastrously mistaken in his decision to join the conspiracy; no, because his mistakes reveal a trivial and naive nature, not a noble one.

Literary Analysis: CHARACTER

B Ask students what opinion they have of Antony as he speaks these lines about Brutus.

Possible Responses: Antony genuinely admires Brutus and is saddened by the death of such a noble man; Antony is merely lapsing into his rhetorical mode with less than true feeling for Brutus.

GUIDE FOR READING

C **Possible Response:** Antony says that Brutus was not motivated by envy, but rather by what he believed to be the general good; he was a gentle man who displayed all the balanced qualities that a true man should possess.

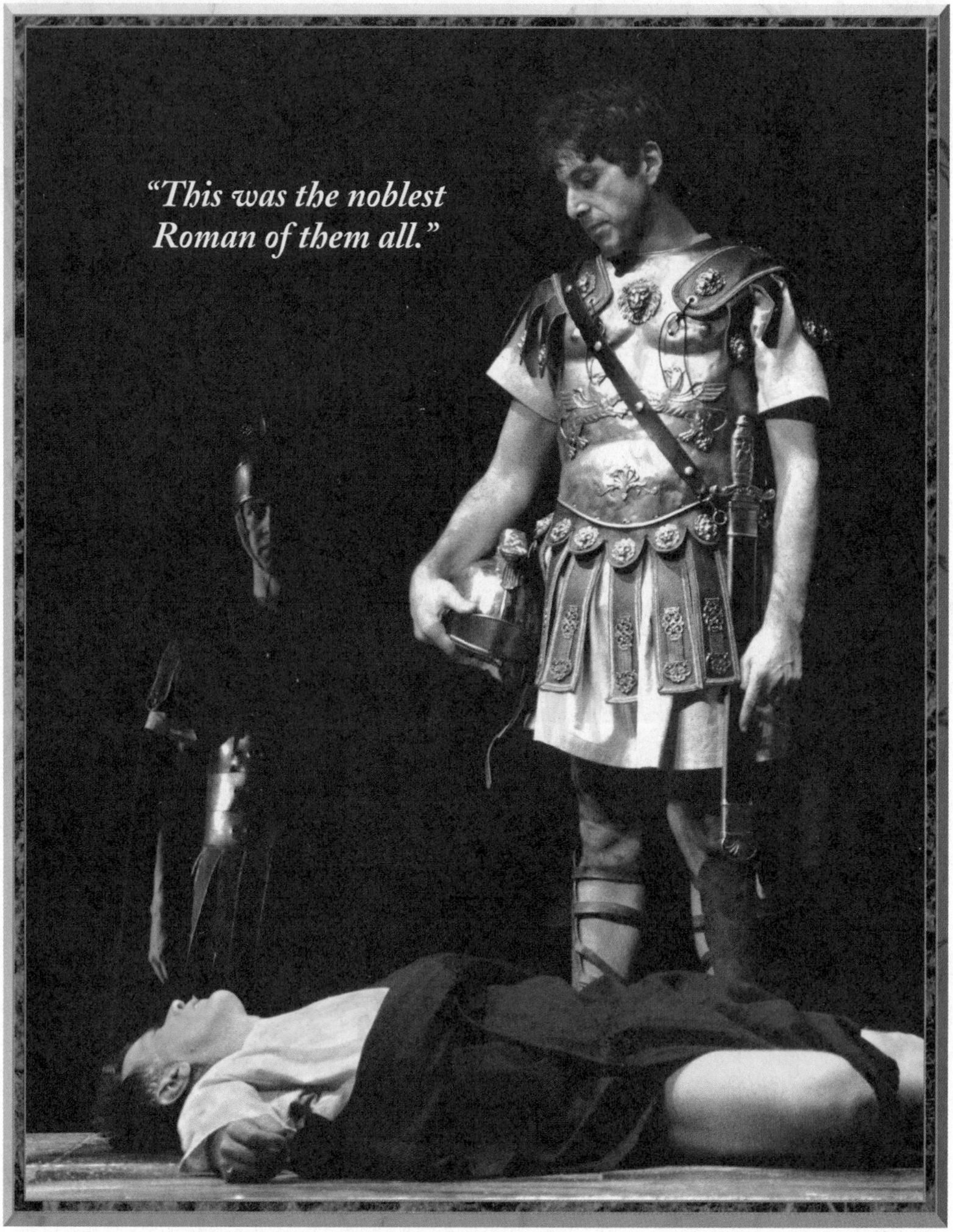
"This was the noblest
Roman of them all."

Al Pacino as Antony and Martin Sheen as Brutus (New York Shakespeare Festival, 1988).
Photo copyright © George E. Joseph.

Brutus. Farewell, good Strato. Caesar, now be still.
I killed not thee with half so good a will. A

[*Dies.*]

[*Alarum. Retreat. Enter* Octavius, Antony, Messala, Lucilius, *and the Army.*]

Octavius. What man is that?

Messala. My master's man. Strato, where is thy master?

Strato. Free from the bondage you are in, Messala.
The conquerors can but make a fire of him;
For Brutus only overcame himself,
And no man else hath honor by his death.

Lucilius. So Brutus should be found. I thank thee, Brutus,
That thou hast proved Lucilius' saying true.

Octavius. All that served Brutus, I will entertain them. 1
Fellow, wilt thou bestow thy time with me?

Strato. Ay, if Messala will prefer me to you.

Octavius. Do so, good Messala.

Messala. How died my master, Strato?

Strato. I held the sword, and he did run on it.

Messala. Octavius, then take him to follow thee,
That did the latest service to my master.

Antony. This was the noblest Roman of them all.
All the conspirators save only he
Did that they did in envy of great Caesar;
He, only in a general honest thought
And common good to all, made one of them.
His life was gentle, and the elements
So mixed in him that Nature might stand up
And say to all the world, "This was a man!" B

Octavius. According to his virtue let us use him,
With all respect and rites of burial.
Within my tent his bones tonight shall lie,
Most like a soldier, ordered honorably. 2
So call the field to rest, and let's away
To part the glories of this happy day.

[*Exeunt.*]

51 I killed . . . will: I didn't kill you (Caesar) half as willingly as I kill myself.

52 man: servant.

58–59 So Brutus . . . true: That is just how Brutus should be found. Thank you, Brutus, for proving me correct (in saying you would never be taken alive).

60–61 All . . . me: All those who served Brutus will now be welcome in my army. Strato **(Fellow),** will you join me?

62 prefer: recommend.

66–67 Octavius . . . master: Octavius, I recommend him for your army; he performed the last favor for Brutus **(my master).**

68–75 Now that the war is won, Antony pays a final tribute to Brutus. What good qualities of Brutus does Antony mention in this tribute? C

69 save: except.

72 made one of them: joined the conspirators.

76 According . . . him: Let us treat him as he deserves.

81 part: divide up.

Customizing Instruction

Less Proficient Readers

1 Explain to students that *entertain* here means "to receive into service."

Students Acquiring English

2 Help students understand the phrase "ordered honorably" by explaining that it means "treated with honor." Octavius plans to treat Brutus with all the marks of respect due a noble soldier.

GUIDING STUDENT RESPONSE

Connect to the Literature

1. **What Do You Think?**
   Possible Responses: It is tragic; the conspirators' demise is justified.

Comprehension Check
- They commit suicide.
- He sees Caesar's ghost.
- Brutus

Use Selection Quiz
Unit Four Resource Book, p. 81.

Think Critically

2. Possible Responses: Antony realizes that Brutus was an honorable man, and so pays him a sincere tribute; Antony is using his rhetorical skill in order to win over Brutus' remaining forces.
3. The conspirators are doomed to be defeated because they acted immorally when they killed Caesar.
4. Possible Response: The issue of Rome's freedom seems irrelevant to both sides. Antony and Octavius are interested in gaining power, while Cassius and Brutus are in a defensive position, fighting for survival.
5. Possible Responses: Brutus, who naively followed a dangerous man and contributed to the chaos and civil war; Cassius, who organized the conspirators who murdered Caesar; Caesar, whose arrogance and overconfidence led to his death and a national crisis; Antony, who manipulated the crowd into supporting his desire for war against the conspirators and power for himself
6. Possible Responses: Brutus would probably appear weary and move slowly; Antony would perhaps address Brutus' body and speak in subdued tones with great feeling.

Thinking through the LITERATURE

Connect to the Literature

1. **What Do You Think?** What is your reaction to the play's ending?

Comprehension Check
- How do both Cassius and Brutus die?
- What supernatural event makes Brutus so certain that it is time for him to die?
- Whom does Antony call "the noblest Roman of them all"?

Think Critically

2. What do you make of Antony's final remarks about Brutus?
3. What would you say is the main reason the conspirators are defeated?

   THINK ABOUT
   - the role of fate or chance in determining events
   - the moral rightness of the conspirators' cause or methods
   - **character traits** of Brutus and Cassius
   - character traits of Antony and Octavius
4. In your estimation, are the leaders of the two armies concerned more for Rome's freedom or for their own power? Explain.
5. In your opinion, who has done the most harm to the state of Rome: Brutus, Cassius, Caesar, or Antony? Support your view with evidence from the play.
6. ACTIVE READING READING SHAKESPEAREAN DRAMA
   Some playwrights give detailed information in their **stage directions** about how characters should move and speak, but Shakespeare does not. Try to envision the final scene of Act Five as it might appear on stage. What do you think Brutus' body language would be like? How do you imagine Mark Antony would speak his famous final lines (lines 68–75)?

Extend Interpretations

7. **Critic's Corner** The 19th-century English critic and historian Thomas Carlyle once observed, "It is in what I called portrait-painting, delineating of men and things, especially of men, that Shakespeare is great." Based on your reading of *Julius Caesar,* do you agree that Shakespeare's strength lies in his **characterization**? Cite evidence to support your evaluation.
8. **Connect to Life** Which characters, if any, in *Julius Caesar* do you think would make the best leaders today? Why?

Literary Analysis

TRAGEDY A **tragedy** is a work in which a series of events leads to the hero's downfall. The **tragic hero,** or **protagonist,** is usually an otherwise admirable figure who nevertheless has a tragic flaw that causes his own downfall or **catastrophe.** Sometimes there is also an **antagonist,** an outside force or another character that helps cause the catastrophe. In most tragedies, the hero faces his or her downfall courageously, so that while the catastrophe horrifies and saddens us, the hero's courage reaffirms our faith in the human spirit.

Cooperative Learning Activity Hold a discussion that focuses on the following questions:
- Who might be considered the tragic hero in *Julius Caesar?*
- What would you say is the hero's tragic flaw? Why?
- Is there another character who might qualify as hero? If so, who, and what is that person's flaw?
- Would you say there is an antagonist in the play? Explain.
- Based on the definition of *tragedy* given above, can an argument be made that *Julius Caesar* is not really a tragedy? Explain.

REVIEW THEME A **theme** is a central idea or message about life conveyed by a work of literature. What themes do you think *Julius Caesar* expresses? Consider what it has to say about these human values and experiences:
- fate
- freedom vs. political stability
- friendship and loyalty
- greed
- group or mob psychology
- political power
- violence and its outcome

Extend Interpretations

Critic's Corner Possible Responses: In *Julius Caesar*, the plot develops in a fairly simple fashion. The characters, however, are complicated and undergo many changes throughout the play.

Connect to Life Possible Responses: Antony, because he displays such skilled rhetoric in his political speeches; Brutus, because he seems most interested in the good of the country

Literary Analysis

Tragedy Possible Response:
- Brutus
- poor judgment; leads him to kill Caesar, make bad military decisions
- Caesar; ambition
- Mark Antony; frustrates Brutus' plans
- Yes; no central hero drives the action throughout the play.

Theme Have students work in groups to consider these ideas, each of which could be considered a Thematic Link in the play. For example, the idea that violence begets violence could be considered one of the central ideas of the play.

Choices & CHALLENGES

Writing Options

1. **Cause-and-Effect Analysis** Write two or three news articles covering different key events in the play, such as the assassination of Caesar or the defeat of Brutus. Explain the causes of the events you chose to report. Place the articles in your **Working Portfolio.**

2. **Alternative Ending** Suppose that Caesar had read Artemidorus' letter and realized that there was a conspiracy against him. How might events have turned out differently for Caesar and the conspirators? Write a new scene to replace Act Two, Scene 3.

3. **Essay on Style** Shakespeare is famous for his poetic style, which includes these elements:
   - precise **diction,** or word choice
   - vivid **imagery** that often appeals to more than one of the five senses
   - **figures of speech,** including similes, metaphors, and personification

   Write an essay exploring these elements of Shakespeare's style as illustrated in *Julius Caesar.*

4. **Character Evaluation** Choose a major character in *Julius Caesar,* and then write a compare-and-contrast essay in which you evaluate the character's positive and negative qualities. You might consider whether Caesar is, on balance, an admirable leader or a tyrannical dictator; whether Brutus is an honorable patriot or a traitorous conspirator; or whether Mark Antony is a loyal friend or a ruthless opportunist.

Writing Handbook
See page 1157: Compare-Contrast.

Activities & Explorations

1. **Dramatic Scene** Working with other students, choose one scene in *Julius Caesar* to rehearse and perform for classmates. As in Shakespeare's time, keep your scenery simple, but feel free to use props and costumes. Afterwards, give justification for the performance techniques you chose. ~ **SPEAKING AND LISTENING**

2. **Video Viewing** View the video excerpt of *Julius Caesar* provided with this program, or rent a film version of the play from your local video store. Then hold a discussion in which you compare the production to the mental images you formed while reading the play. ~ **VIEWING AND REPRESENTING**

   VIDEO **Literature in Performance**

3. **Quotable Collage** Combine three of the following famous lines from *Julius Caesar* with images from magazines and newspapers to create a collage that reflects your interpretation of these quotes:
   - *The fault, dear Brutus, is not in our stars, But in ourselves. . . .*
   - *Cowards die many times before their deaths; The valiant never taste of death but once.*
   - *Et tu, Brute?*
   - *Friends, Romans, countrymen, lend me your ears . . .*
   - *Ambition should be made of sterner stuff.*
   - *There is a tide in the affairs of men Which taken at the flood, leads on to fortune . . .*

Inquiry & Research

1. **Roman History** Do research to find out more about an aspect of ancient Rome or about real people such as Julius Caesar, Calpurnia, Brutus, Mark Antony, or Octavius. For example, you might find out more about the establishment of a Roman republic, Roman social structure, the role of women, Caesar's conquest of Gaul or crossing of the Rubicon, Brutus' famous ancestors, or the life and achievements of Antony or Octavius after the events of the play. Share your findings in an oral report.

2. **Map Study** Using print and technical resources, create a map that reflects the extent of the Roman Empire during Julius Caesar's reign. In an oral presentation to the class, compare it with a current map of the world.

3. **Word Derivations** Find out about the origins of the month name *July* and the words *czar* and *kaiser.* How are these related to Julius Caesar? Present your findings as dictionary entries that show each word's history.

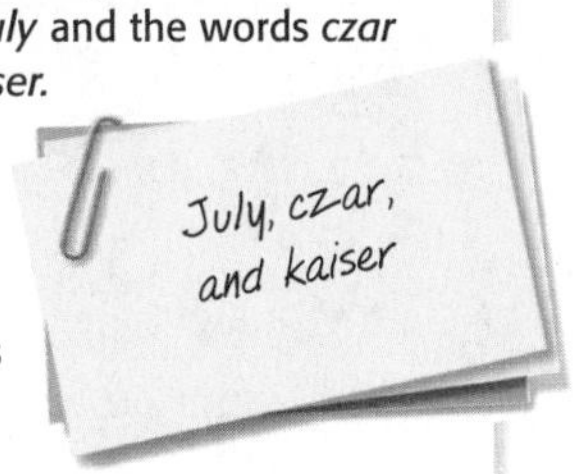

4. **Modern Criticism** *Julius Caesar* is still performed today in countries around the world. What have critics thought about some of these modern-day interpretations?

   Real World Link Begin your investigation by reading the conflicting theater reviews on pages 798–799.

Writing Options

1. **Cause-and-Effect Analysis** Encourage students to consult articles in their daily newspaper for models of journalistic style. Encourage them to pay attention to the supposed tone of objectivity in news articles.
2. **Alternative Ending** Remind students to consider what Caesar might have done to the conspirators (banished them, imprisoned them, executed them) and how the ruling party of Rome might have changed after the treason of some of its leading officials was discovered.
3. **Essay on Style** Students might want to focus on particularly powerful scenes for their essays, such as the storm scene in Act One; the funeral orations in Act Three; and the meeting of Brutus, Cassius, Antony, and Octavius at the beginning of Act Five.
4. **Character Evaluation** After students choose the character about whom they will write, encourage them to make a chart that displays the character traits they want to analyze.

Activities & Explorations

1. **Dramatic Scene** Have students concentrate on blocking the scene and to make careful notes of the vocal tone and expression they want to use to deliver their lines.
2. **Video Viewing** Before students view the video, have them discuss what elements of production they want to follow. For example, they may want to pay attention to speech delivery, special effects, or costumes.
3. **Quotable Collage** Before students collect images, have them paraphrase each quote and jot down ideas about images to portray the quote.

Inquiry & Research

1. **Roman History** Have students first consult general sources, such as encyclopedias and comprehensive books on Roman history, before narrowing their subjects into more specific subtopics.
2. **Map Study** Encourage students to note the date each area was acquired by Rome.
3. **Word Derivations** *July* is derived from *Julius, czar* is Russian, derived from *Caesar; kaiser* is German, derived from *Caesar.*
4. **Modern Criticism** Have students start their research in the *Reader's Guide to Periodical Literature.* If it is available at your school or local libraries, encourage them to look for articles on the topic in a database of dramatic literature.

Choices & CHALLENGES

Grammar in Context: Using Prepositional Phrases to Make Comparisons

In this excerpt from *Julius Caesar,* Mark Antony tells Cassius and Brutus what he thinks of their treachery.

> **You showed your teeth like apes, and fawned like hounds,**
> **And bowed like bondmen, kissing Caesar's feet;**
> **Whilst damned Casca, like a cur, behind**
> **Struck Caesar on the neck. O you flatterers!"**
> **—Act 5, Scene 1**

You may recall that a **prepositional phrase** consists of a preposition, its object (a noun or pronoun), and any modifiers of the object. As the excerpt above illustrates, prepositional phrases beginning with *like* (or *as*) can be used to compare things for dramatic effect. Antony compares the assassins to animals and slaves, emphasizing the baseness of their actions.

Usage Tip: Prepositional phrases beginning with *like* usually modify verbs. Phrases beginning with *as* often modify adjectives that are preceded by the adverb *as.*

Apply to Your Writing Using prepositional phrases to make comparisons can help you

- add powerful images to your writing
- express emotions in a dramatic way

WRITING EXERCISE Create dramatic comparisons by completing these sentences with prepositional phrases that begin with *like* or *as.*

Example: Right up to the moment they stab Caesar, the assassins behave ________.

Right up to the moment they stab Caesar, the assassins behave like loyal pets and servants.

1. To Cassius, Caesar seems to stand over the world ________ while lesser people hover around his feet.
2. On the other hand, Cassius knows that Caesar would not be as wild ________ if the Romans were not as tame ________.
3. Brutus believes that Caesar is ________, harmless now but dangerous if allowed to hatch.
4. Courage is important to Caesar; without it, he would be as empty ________.
5. Calpurnia dreams that a statue of Caesar is bleeding ________.

Connect to the Literature Look at Act Three, Scene 1, lines 148–163 ("O mighty Caesar! . . ."). In this speech, Mark Antony reacts to the sight of Caesar's slain body. Find the prepositional phrases introduced by *as* in the speech. What do they indicate about Antony's feelings at this moment?

Grammar Handbook Phrases, p. 1195

Grammar in Context

WRITING EXERCISE Answers will vary. Possible answers are shown.

1. To Cassius, Caesar seems to stand over the world like a giant while lesser people hover around his feet.
2. On the other hand, Cassius knows that Caesar would not be wild like a wolf if the Romans were not tame like sheep.
3. Brutus believes that Caesar is like a snake's egg, harmless now but dangerous if allowed to hatch.
4. Courage is important to Caesar; without it, he would be like a hollow reed.
5. Calpurnia dreams that a statue of Caesar is bleeding like a fountain.

Connect to the Literature

Comparative prepositional phrases using *as* in Antony's speech, lines 148–163.

Lines 152–154:

"Who else must be let blood, who else is rank.
If I myself, there is not hour so fit
As Caesar's death's hour; nor no instrument
Of half that worth **as** those your swords, . . ."

Lines 161–162:

"No place will please me so, no mean of death,
As here by Caesar, and by you cut off, . . ."

Possible Response: Antony says that if he must die or be injured, there is no better time than at the time of Caesar's death, by the same sword that killed Caesar. By saying this, he is comparing himself to Caesar and showing his alliance with the slain leader. Antony is suggesting that if Caesar must die, he himself will gladly do the same.

Teaching Options

Mini Lesson Grammar

COMPARISONS USING PREPOSITIONAL PHRASES
The combination of a preposition, a noun or pronoun, and modifiers is called a prepositional phrase. Prepositional phrases, which point out many basic relationships, are often used to indicate a comparison between things or people. A common comparative preposition is *like.* This preposition (and the prepositional phrases that contain it) can be difficult to use correctly when we want to show comparisons.

Instruction Explain that many readers object to *like* used to introduce groups of words that have a subject and a verb. *As, as if,* and *as though* are preferred in situations in which a comparison involves a subject and verb. *Like* is acceptable, however, when it introduces a prepositional phrase (a group of words that lacks either a subject or a verb). Write the following examples on the chalkboard, and explain the correct use of the comparative preposition.

Wrong: Betty is strong, *like* you would expect an athlete to be. (*like* is incorrectly used to introduce a clause of comparison)

Correct: Betty is strong, *as* you would expect an athlete to be. (*as* is correctly used to introduce a clause of comparison)

Correct: My dog looks *like* her dog. (*like* is correctly used to introduce a prepositional phrase)

William Shakespeare
1564–1616

Other Works
As You Like It
Hamlet
King Lear
Macbeth
The Merchant of Venice
A Midsummer Night's Dream
Othello
Richard II
Romeo and Juliet
The Taming of the Shrew
The Tempest
Twelfth Night

Mystery Man Though the works of William Shakespeare have probably been seen or read by more people worldwide than works by any other author, the man himself remains something of a mystery. This is particularly true of his early life, before he became a famous playwright. Unlike most Elizabethan authors, who came from prominent noble families and attended England's leading universities, Shakespeare was a son of the middle class, one whose formal education apparently ended with grammar school. What we know of his early life and family background comes from scanty documentary evidence: church records and property deeds, for example.

A Small-Town Boy According to those records, an infant named William Shakespeare was baptized in April 1564 in the local church in Stratford-upon-Avon, a bustling town on the River Avon, northwest of London. His father was a tanner and glove-maker and also served as a local politician. It is likely that Shakespeare attended Stratford's grammar school, where he would have studied Latin, the language of ancient Rome, and classical literature written in Latin and translated from ancient Greek. It is here that he would have been introduced to the writings of the ancient Greek biographer Plutarch, whose *Parallel Lives* provides the historical basis for the events of *Julius Caesar.*

Off to London Records further tell us that in 1582, William Shakespeare married one Anne Hathaway, probably the daughter of a well-to-do Stratford farm family, and that the couple over the next three years had three children, an older daughter named Susanna and twins named Hamnet (a male) and Judith. After the birth of the twins in 1585, nothing is known about Shakespeare for the next several years, after which he turns up again, living in London and working as an actor and playwright. Clearly he was recognized as a promising talent, for he became a shareholder with the Lord Chamberlain's Men, the prestigious acting company with strong ties to Elizabeth's court. Shakespeare's plays helped make the company even more successful, and he was soon allowed—probably even encouraged—to give up acting in order to focus on his writing.

The Years of Fame By 1599, the year in which *Julius Caesar* was first produced, Shakespeare is known to have written 18 of his 38 plays, including early pieces such as his history *Richard III,* his comedy *The Taming of the Shrew,* and his tragedy *Romeo and Juliet.* He was also a rich man. As a shareholder with the Lord Chamberlain's Men, he was now one of the owners of the company's new home, the Globe Theatre. He also made money by having his plays produced and by publishing some of his nondramatic poetry, although his sonnets did not appear in print until 1609.

The Final Years About a year before the sonnets appeared, Shakespeare began curtailing his theater activities. He seems to have spent less time in London and more back in Stratford. He wrote no plays after 1613, when he probably moved back to Stratford permanently. No ones knows for sure just when, where, or how he died, but his gravestone in Stratford's Holy Trinity Church lists the date of his death as April 23, 1616.

Author Activity

Strange Theories Some people have speculated that Shakespeare did not really write the plays and poems attributed to him. Find out more about these theories and the attitude that most Shakespeare scholars take toward them.

Author Activity

Strange Theories For those who think Shakespeare did not write the plays attributed to him, two theories carry the most weight. Some people, known as "Oxfordians," claim that a courtier of Queen Elizabeth I named Edward de Vere, the 17th earl of Oxford, wrote the plays. Another theory, supported by people known as "Baconians," makes a case for the Renaissance philosopher Sir Francis Bacon as the author of Shakespeare's dramas. Students might consult *The Shakespeare Controversy: An Analysis of the Claimants to Authorship, and Their Champions and Detractors* by Warren Hope and Kim Holston, or *Shakespeare—Who Was He?* by Richard F. Whalen, for background information on the authorship question.

Practice Have students copy the following sentences. Ask them to choose the correct term in parentheses to complete each comparison. Have them discuss the reasons for their choices.

1. It looks *(as if/like)* it will rain today.
   Answer: *as if:* introduces clause
2. Her car sounds *(like/as)* a freight train.
   Answer: *like:* introduces prepositional phrase
3. Our team plays *(like/as if)* a contender for the title.
   Answer: *like:* introduces prepositional phrase
4. Mary seems nervous, *(like/as though)* she were afraid to go to the doctor.
   Answer: *as though:* introduces clause
5. The bird looks *(like/as though)* a finch.
   Answer: *like:* introduces prepositional phrase.

Use **Unit Four Resource Book,** p. 80.

Use **Grammar Transparencies and Copymasters,** p. 97, for more exercises.

Language Network
Use McDougal Littell's ***Language Network,*** Chapter 9, for more instruction in comparisons.

Real WORLD Link

Theater Review

Objectives

- identify criteria for evaluating a theater production
- identify the tone used by the writer
- identify a reviewer's credibility

Connecting to the Literature
Each time a classical drama is presented, the director, cast, and crew bring new interpretations to the performance. Responses to the new interpretations may range from appreciation to disappointment.

Reading for Information

Disch begins his review by stating his opinion that *Julius Caesar* is the dullest of Shakespeare's tragedies. Oliver begins her review by comparing this performance of *Julius Caesar* with other performances of that play that she has seen.

1 Disch implies that a play should have dramatic substance, that a play should present a new or fresh interpretation, and that actors should portray characters with subtle complexity. Oliver implies that a play should have solid casting, forceful and complex characters, a handsome and well-lighted stage, and appropriate costumes.

2 Disch's tone may be described as critical, witty, or sarcastic. Oliver's tone may be described as commendatory.

Review of Julius Caesar

by Thomas M. Disch

1 *Julius Caesar* is at once the dullest and the most familiar of Shakespeare's tragedies. It has become the most familiar precisely because it is the dullest, a tale so flensed[1] of dramatic meat that it can be presented to any group of teenagers, however rowdy, without danger of awakening their interest.

2 Given all these liabilities, the best one can hope for from any production of *Julius Caesar* is stateliness, pageantry and music, . . . and these aren't qualities likely to be in large supply at the Public Theater, which undertook *Julius Caesar* as the second production of its six-year assault on the whole oeuvre.[2] It was stoically[3] done. Without the ghost of an idea for making it new, director Stuart Vaughan had his cast trot through their lines as best they could and the devil take the hindmost.[4] The hindmost was indisputably Martin Sheen as Brutus. He declaimed every line in the same hoarse timbre[5] and indicated every statement with alphabet-block simplicity: a thump of his hand to his heart when that organ was mentioned, or a finger pointing to his head, when "thoughts" had to be glossed. He was not left to die entirely by himself, however, but fell upon his sword with careful choreography, and nothing in his role became him like the leaving of it.

Al Pacino as Mark Antony seemed ill. This was an Antony whose protestations of a lack of eloquence can be taken at face value. Had he had to contend against any Brutus but Sheen's, the Romans' preference for him would have been unaccountable. But he did remember all the lines of that long oration, which, you'll recall, is very long indeed. Bravo, Al. Now, my advice to you is get some rest, eat sensibly, exercise, and take Geritol every day.

1. **flensed** (flĕnsd): stripped of the fat or skin; said of an animal.
2. **oeuvre** (œ′vrə): the sum of the lifework of an artist, a writer, or a composer.
3. **stoically** (stō′ĭk-ə-lē): in a manner unaffected by pain or pleasure.
4. **devil take the hindmost:** let others manage as best as they can.
5. **timbre** (tăm′bər): the distinctive tone of an instrument or a voice.

Reading for Information

That play you've heard about has finally come to town. Not wanting to waste time or money, you find a review of the performance before buying a ticket. Knowing how to analyze a review can help you decide whether to see the play.

ANALYZING A THEATER REVIEW

A **theater review** is an opinion of a performance formed by a person who is knowledgeable in the performing arts. In order to analyze a theater review you should look for the following:

- the criteria the reviewer used to judge the performance
- details that support the reviewer's opinion
- the reviewer's tone, or attitude toward his or her subject
- signs of bias

YOUR TURN To analyze two reviews of the same performance of *Julius Caesar*, use the questions and activities below.

1 **Establishing Criteria** An effective theater review usually deals with a list of criteria, or standards, which might begin with a category like the following:

- **Quality of Acting** How well do the actors portray their roles?

Review the article to find criteria the reviewer may have used.

2 The **tone** in a review can vary from humorous to serious to sarcastic. Look for evidence of the tone in **loaded language,** words and phrases that have a strongly positive or negative association. What words would you use to describe the reviewer's tone in this passage?

Mini Lesson — Viewing and Representing

ANALYZING A PERFORMANCE REVIEW

Instruction Show students a film performance of *Julius Caesar.* Have them write a review of the performance.

Prepare Tell students the following criteria may be used to analyze a written review of a performance:

The review:

- identifies its subject at the beginning.
- opens with a general opinion.
- includes enough facts, examples, and details to support the general opinion.
- displays logical organization.
- quickly establishes a tone.

Present Pair students and have them share their reviews with their partners. Together the students may analyze the written reviews using the above criteria. Then have them compare their partner's review with their own responses.

HAIL, CAESAR!

by Edith Oliver

Herewith some impressions of "Julius Caesar," the second entry in the Shakespeare Marathon, at the Public:

This is the first "Caesar" I've ever seen that is dominated by Cassius, in Edward Herrmann's towering performance—towering physically, too, with a lean, but hardly hungry, look. Mr. Herrmann brings an intellectual clarity and force to the character which make him seem the focus of the play, the instigator of the action. And the rest of the casting, as is usual at the Public, is mostly very good. Martin Sheen, a memorable Hamlet there twenty years ago (he recited the "To be, or not to be" soliloquy in a Hispanic accent), now makes the step to Brutus seem inevitable. His Brutus is self-questioning, often melancholy, and virtuous and brave—a man whose honesty, even innocence, makes him an easy mark for more devious types. ③ Which, of course, brings us to Al Pacino's Mark Antony, a devious type if ever there was one, so obviously scheming and sinister right from the start that I doubt he could fool even this Brutus into allowing him to deliver Caesar's funeral oration. (He doesn't fool Cassius.) A sullen, sharp-witted Antony, Mr. Pacino takes the curse of "set piece" off that oration. John McMartin is a surprising but, as it turns out, excellent choice for a Caesar who is aristocratic, cheerful, and friendly—just the sort of ruler to inspire the devotion of Brutus, among others, and perhaps the distrust of Cassius. His very soft "Et tu, Brute!" at the stabbing is indelible. I also admired Joan MacIntosh, in her one passionate, loving scene with Brutus, and, come to think of it, almost everyone else.

④ Under the sensible direction of Stuart Vaughan, the performance as a whole is always absorbing and always clear. If you sense some extra enthusiasm in my praise, you're probably right. It is the fervor of the convert;[6] it took me a long time to enjoy and appreciate the kind of American Shakespeare presented by Joseph Papp at the Public or in the Park. (There have been some lemons, too.) The handsome setting for "Julius Caesar"—a bare stage with a flight of steps at center leading to a platform and surrounded by square, sky-high columns of brick—was designed by Bob Shaw and effectively lighted by Arden Fingerhut; the appropriate costumes were designed by Lindsay W. Davis.

6. **fervor of the convert:** the intensity of emotion experienced by one who has changed one set of beliefs for another.

③ A performance is open to many valid interpretations, so it's important to make sure that opinions are supported with specific examples from the performance. Compare Disch's and Oliver's reviews of actor Al Pacino's portrayal of Mark Antony. Which of the reviewers does a better job supporting his or her opinion?

④ You can judge a reviewer's **credibility**, or believability, by examining the way he or she expresses opinions. The reviewer's viewpoint, or **bias,** can influence his or her choice of what to criticize and how to criticize it. Find evidence of bias in this passage, as well as in the first review. Discuss your findings with a classmate.

Inquiry & Research

Activity Link: *Julius Caesar*, p. 795

Now that you have read and analyzed the reviews, choose the review that you think is more credible. Which one would you rely on to guide you in your decision to see *Julius Caesar?* Write a short explanation of your answer.

3 Oliver does a better job supporting her opinions. Disch states only that Pacino's Antony seemed ill. Oliver describes Pacino's Antony as devious, scheming, and sinister.

4 Oliver states an early bias against Joseph Papp's productions but then overcomes her own bias with a favorable analysis.

Mini Lesson Inquiry & Research

The Inquiry & Research activity on this page links to the Inquiry & Research section of Choices & Challenges on page 795.

Instruction Just as each critic's bias influences the comments in the review, the student's bias will influence the review selected as most credible. Credibility derives from claims that are well supported with reasoning and evidence rather than unsupported.

Practice Students' analyses of the more credible review should include specific references to the printed review. Have students work together in pairs to evaluate the claims of both writers, creating a two-column chart of "Claims Supported with Reasoning and Evidence" and "Claims Not Supported."

Objectives
- write a Cause-and-Effect Essay
- use a written text as a model for writing
- revise for effective transitions
- correct misplaced modifiers

Introducing the Workshop

(A) Cause-and-Effect Essay Remind students that specific events, actions, or trends can trigger a response. The **cause** of an event, action, or trend creates a direct outcome, or **effect.** Cause-and-effect writing allows a writer to examine and analyze an event, action, or trend and its outcome. Scientists, economists, lawyers, and other professionals are always looking at these relationships. For example, do we know what causes an earthquake? How does the employment rate affect consumer costs? Why do people spend less money in January?

Ask students to discuss a specific event from history, for example, the lunar landing. What caused the event? What was the outcome? Encourage students to notice cause-and-effect reporting on television newsmagazine programs.

Point out that writing an effective cause-and-effect essay in their English class will help them sharpen their skills for writing essays in their history, science, and business classes.

Basics in a Box

(B) Using the Graphic The graphic reminds students that they can approach a cause-and-effect essay from one of two directions: examine a cause and its multiple effects, or examine an effect and its multiple causes.

(C) Presenting the Rubric To better understand the assignment, students can refer to the Standards for Writing a Successful Cause-and-Effect Essay. You may also want to share with them the complete rubric, which describes several levels of proficiency.

Use McDougal Littell's ***Language Network,*** Chapter 21, for more instruction on writing a cause-and-effect essay.

To engage students visually, use **Power Presentation** 8, Cause-and-Effect Essay.

Writing Workshop
Cause-and-Effect Essay

Exploring actions and consequences . . .

(A) **From Reading to Writing** Shakespeare's *Julius Caesar* traces the causes and consequences of ambition and hunger for power. Exploring causes and effects is crucial to understanding events in both literature and life. One way of examining these elements is by writing a **cause-and-effect essay.** You can use this type of informative writing to show why something happens, what its consequences are, or how events are connected.

For Your Portfolio

WRITING PROMPT Write an essay that explains the causes and effects of an event.

Purpose: To inform and explain
Audience: Your classmates or other interested readers

Basics in a Box

Cause-and-Effect Essay at a Glance

(B)

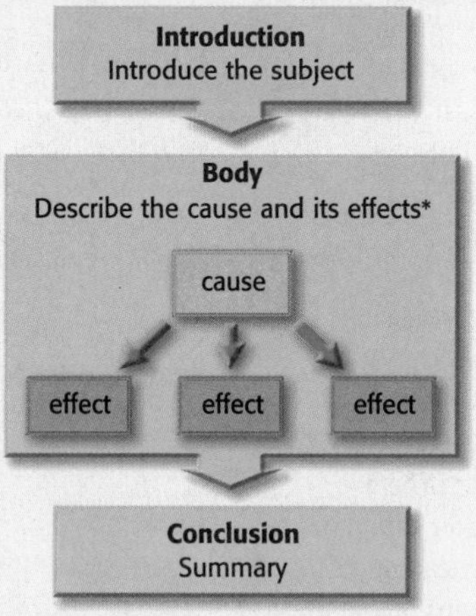

*or may present an effect and then analyze the causes

(C) **RUBRIC Standards for Writing**

A successful cause-and-effect essay should
- clearly identify the cause-and-effect relationship being discussed
- provide any necessary background information
- make the relationship between causes and effects clear
- arrange details logically and include transitions to show relationships between events and causes
- use language and details appropriate to the intended audience
- summarize the cause-and-effect relationship in the conclusion

LESSON RESOURCES

USING PRINT RESOURCES
Unit Four Resource Book
- Prewriting, p. 82
- Drafting, p. 83
- Peer Response, pp. 84–85
- Revising, Editing, and Proofreading, p. 86
- Student Models, pp. 87–92
- Rubric, p. 93

Writing Transparencies and Copymasters
- Writing Process Transparencies, pp. 1–4
- Writing Structure Transparencies, pp. 5–11
- Writing Template Copymasters, pp. 31–32

USING MEDIA RESOURCES
LaserLinks
Writing Springboards
See Teacher's SourceBook p. 64 for bar codes.
Writing Coach CD-ROM
Visit our website:
www.mcdougallittell.com

Analyzing a Student Model

Sheri Fischer
Park Ridge High School

Test Question: Based on information in Shakespeare's Julius Caesar, *write an essay in which you explain the causes of Caesar's assassination. Pay special attention to the motivations of the characters and the effects of events before the assassination.*

Why Julius Caesar Was Assassinated

Why was Julius Caesar assassinated? There are two main reasons, one personal and one political. Some Roman nobles, such as Cassius, were jealous of Caesar's rise to power and wanted to get rid of him because of these personal feelings. Others, such as Brutus, believed that Caesar represented a threat to the Roman republic. They were afraid of what would happen to their country and its people if Caesar became king and turned Rome into a monarchy.

D

At the beginning of the play, Caesar has just returned from a long civil war after defeating Pompey, his rival for power. Crowds have lined the streets to glorify him as a war hero and as the savior of Rome. But some people fear that Caesar, in going against the orders of the Roman Senate in fighting Pompey, wants to take total control of Rome. They have reason for this fear, because Mark Antony, one of Caesar's loyal friends, has offered Caesar the chance to become king. Caesar has refused the offer three times. Many people do not think his refusal is sincere, however. One of those people is Cassius.

Cassius is very jealous of Caesar's rise to power. He says that he and Caesar were equals and that, in fact, he saved Caesar's life. He complains, "And this man is now become a god, and Cassius is a wretched creature and must bend his body if Caesar but carelessly nod on him." Cassius tries to convince Brutus that Caesar is no better than they. "Why, man, he doth bestride the narrow world like a Colossus, and we petty men walk under his huge legs and peep about to find ourselves dishonorable graves." Cassius's desire to kill Caesar is very personal, and very clear.

RUBRIC IN ACTION

1 This writer identifies the effect and its cause by asking a question and giving its answer.

Other Options:
- Begin with an anecdote that illustrates the cause or effect.
- State the cause or effect directly.

2 Provides important background information

3 Begins analysis of first cause of the assassination, providing details and quotations as evidence

Teaching the Lesson

Analyzing the Model

D **"Why Julius Caesar Was Assassinated"** The student model begins with the effect by asking why Julius Caesar was assassinated and identifies the causes as twofold: personal and political.

Have students read the student model, then discuss the Rubric in Action. Point out the key words and phrases in the model that correspond to the elements mentioned in the Rubric in Action.

1 Have students suggest an alternate opening based on the other options listed.
Possible Response: Julius Caesar, Roman dictator and self-proclaimed "Unconquerable God," was assassinated on March 15, 44 B.C. Although the common people loved him, some Roman senators justified the assassination because of their personal jealousy and their fear of what the Roman republic would become under Caesar's rule.

2 Ask students to summarize the important background information.
Possible Response: Caesar has returned from a long civil war after defeating Pompey; crowds have lined the streets to celebrate Caesar's return; Caesar has ignored the orders of the Roman Senate in fighting Pompey; Caesar has refused the offer to become king three times; many people do not think his refusal is sincere.

3 Ask students to identify the first cause of the assassination of Caesar.
Possible Response: Cassius is personally jealous of Caesar's rise to power.

4 Ask students to identify the second cause of the assassination of Caesar. **Possible Response:** Brutus has no personal grudge against Caesar but sees Caesar as a ruler who, when given power, "might turn against his friends and all the citizens of Rome."

5 Ask students to determine whether the underlined transitional words signal cause or effect. **Answer:** *If* signals a cause; *then* signals an effect; *because* signals a cause.

6 Point out that the writer concludes her essay utilizing the same structural strategies with which she began the essay: from effect to causes.

Brutus is not so convinced, however. He has no personal grudge against Caesar, and sees him as a man whose emotions never overrule his reason. Brutus wonders if Caesar might not change as he climbs the ladder of power, though, and think himself above all other men. Brutus compares him to a serpent's egg and is afraid of what will happen if the egg hatches and Caesar is crowned king. Cassius and the other conspirators convince Brutus that if Caesar were given such power, then he might turn against his friends and all the citizens of Rome. The best way to support Caesar, they conclude, is to kill him before he can become so evil and, as a result, save him from himself.

❹ Begins analysis of the second cause of the assassination

This was not an easy decision for Brutus to make, however, and his reasons for agreeing to the assassination are very different from Cassius'. He turns against Caesar not because he didn't love Caesar, but because he loves his country and its way of life more. He asks the Roman citizens, "Had you rather Caesar were living, and die all slaves, than that Caesar were dead, to live all freemen?"

❺ Uses transitional words to show the cause-and-effect relationship

Based on the evidence in the play *Julius Caesar*, there were two main causes of Caesar's assassination. One cause was the personal jealousy and self-interest of those who had once been his friends. These conspirators, led by Cassius, feared Caesar's popularity and worried about their own futures as he became more and more powerful. The other cause was not personal, but political. The spokesman for this point of view was Brutus. He loved Caesar and did not wish him harm. Cassius finally managed to convince Brutus that an all-powerful Caesar was a threat to the Roman republic and way of life, however. So these two causes—the personal and the political—together resulted in Caesar's death.

❻ Concludes by summarizing the effect and its causes

Writing Your Cause-and-Effect Essay

Happy the man who could search out the causes of things.
Virgil, Roman poet

❶ Prewriting

Begin by exploring topics for your essay. What events puzzle you? What consequences would you like to examine before choosing a course of action? **Make a list** of ideas that occur to you. See the **Idea Bank** in the margin for more suggestions. Be sure to choose a topic that truly interests and inspires you. After you select a topic you would like to write about, follow the steps below.

Planning Your Cause-and-Effect Essay

1. **Think about the cause-and effect relationships.** Are the events really linked by cause and effect? An event that follows another in time isn't necessarily caused by it. Does a cause have one effect or many? Is an effect the result of a single cause, or of many causes?
2. **Identify your audience.** What does your audience already know about your subject? What background information will you need to provide?
3. **Gather supporting information.** What kind of information will you need to learn about your topic? Where can you find that information? Possibilities include personal observation and reflection, library research, or interviewing experts.
4. **Sketch out your ideas.** How does the information you have collected fit together? You might create a table or chart to help you organize what you already know and discover what you still need to find out.

❷ Drafting

Use the drafting process to explore your topic and to think more about the cause-and-effect relationships you want to write about. Concentrate on just getting your ideas down on paper. You can revise them later. At some point be sure to clearly state the cause-and-effect relationship you're discussing. Then present **facts, statistics, examples, anecdotes,** or **quotations** to support your statements. You will also need to **organize** your ideas. You might show a single cause leading to multiple effects or multiple causes leading to a single effect.

Cause to Effect

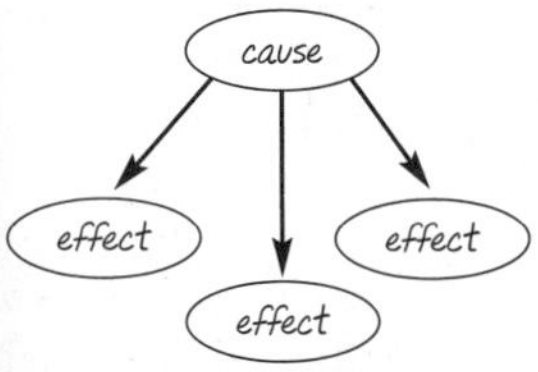

Effect to Cause

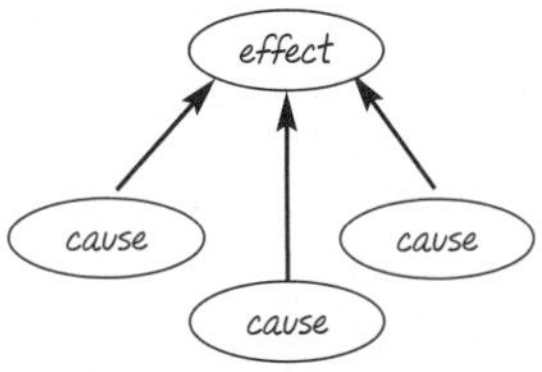

IDEA Bank

1. Your Working Portfolio
Look for ideas in the **Writing Option** you completed earlier in the unit:
<Selection 1>

2. Crystal Ball
Think of the decisions you might have to make about your life. Freewrite about the effects each choice might have on your future.

3. Keys to Success
With a group of classmates, list successful people you know. Brainstorm about the causes of their success.

Have a question?
See the **Writing Handbook** Cause and Effect, p. 1158–1159

Ask Your Peer Reader

- How would you summarize the main cause-and-effect relationship that I wrote about?
- Where was the evidence most convincing? least convincing?
- What parts of the essay were confusing?
- What do you want to know more about?

Guiding Student Writing

Prewriting

Choosing a Topic

If after reading the Idea Bank students are having difficulty choosing their topics, suggest they try the following:

- Watch a news program on television. Write down as many effects of a news event as possible. Try to determine the cause of the event.
- Think about your most recent history lesson. Now make a list of as many topics as you can think of without regard for rational connections. For example, a list of topics might include women's rights, monopoly, capitalism, the Wild West. Topics will then lead to cause-and-effect relationships. Begin with questions such as "How did women gain the right to vote?"(cause); "When women gained the right to vote, how did it change the United States?" (effect).

Planning the Cause-and-Effect Essay

1. Have students work in groups of three to think about the cause-and-effect relationships for the events they have chosen. The first student will have a few minutes to list the event and describe the effect(s) and cause(s) of the event. The other students will help the first student determine whether the effect and the cause are logically linked and whether there are multiple effects and causes. Students will then switch roles.

3. Before students begin gathering supporting information, have them prepare a list of questions they have about the event and a list of possible resources in which to locate that information. Ask them to prepare the kinds of questions that will generate cause-and-effect responses.

4. Have students create a chart with these headings: Known Effects; Known Causes; Possible Effects; Possible Causes; Possible Sources for Further Information. Caution students to avoid limiting their information to what they already know. Encourage them to use their investigative skills to learn more about their topic.

Drafting

Organizing the Draft

The student model represents one approach to writing a cause-and-effect essay. Remind students that they can organize the essay from cause to effect, or from effect to cause; there is no one "right" technique. As students draft their essays, they can refer to the facts, statistics, examples, anecdotes, and quotations that they collected in the prewriting process. Encourage them to continue to gather additional information if necessary.

Revising

EFFECTIVE TRANSITIONS

Point out the first transitional phrase in the example paragraph: *"If Caesar were given such power, then. . . ."* This phrase establishes one possible effect of Caesar's power. The effect is that Caesar might turn against his friends. The second transitional phrase is *"as a result."* This phrase claims that the effect of killing Caesar will be to save him from himself.

As students revise their own essays, encourage them to use transitions that show cause-and-effect relationships between ideas.

Editing and Proofreading

MISPLACED MODIFIERS

Remind students that misplaced modifiers make writing confusing and sometimes absurd. To correct a misplaced modifier, first identify the word being modified, then move the modifier as near as possible to the word it modifies. See the Grammar Mini Lesson on TE 805 for more information on correcting misplaced modifiers. Encourage students to revise, edit, and proofread carefully to produce error-free writing in the final draft.

Reflecting

Have students write a brief response to the questions in the text. They can then attach their written responses to their cause-and-effect essays and place both in their working portfolios.

Need revising help?

Review the **Rubric,** p. 800

Consider **peer reader** comments

Check **Revision Guidelines,** p. 1145

❸ Revising

TARGET SKILL ▶ EFFECTIVE TRANSITIONS One way to be sure your cause-and-effect essay is clear is to use transitions that show the relationships between ideas. Words and phrases such as *therefore, because, as a result of, before,* and *if . . . then* signal causes and effects.

> ~~But~~ Cassius and the other conspirators ~~finally~~ convinced Brutus that *if Caesar were given such power, then he* ~~Caesar~~ might turn against his friends and all the citizens of Rome.
>
> The best way to support Caesar, they conclude, is to kill him before he can become so evil and *as a result,* save him from himself.

Mistified by Modifiers?

See the **Grammar Handbook,**

Misplaced Modifiers, p. 1190

Phrases, p. 1206

❹ Editing and Proofreading

TARGET SKILL ▶ MISPLACED MODIFIERS Misplaced modifiers can make your cause-and-effect writing confusing because they appear to modify something they cannot logically modify. Correct a misplaced modifier by moving it next to the word it actually modifies or by adding a word for it to modify.

> At the beginning of the play, *Caesar has* ~~having~~ just returned from a long civil war after defeating Pompey, his rival for power. Crowds have lined the streets to glorify *him* ~~Caesar~~ as a war hero and as the savior of Rome. In going against the orders of the Roman Senate in fighting Pompey, some people fear that Caesar wants to take control of Rome.

Publishing IDEAS

- Present your essay orally to your class, using visual aids such as charts, photographs, or slides.
- Submit your essay to your school or local newspaper.

More Online: Publishing Options
www.mcdougallittell.com

❺ Reflecting

FOR YOUR WORKING PORTFOLIO What did you learn about the cause-and-effect relationship you wrote about? What techniques did you learn that you can apply to other writing exercises? Attach your reflections to your finished cause-and-effect essay. Save your essay in your **Working Portfolio.**

Assessment Practice Revising & Editing

Read this paragraph from the first draft of a cause-and-effect essay. The underlined sections may include the following kinds of errors:

- **run-on sentences**
- **misplaced modifiers**
- **lack of parallel structure**
- **lack of subject-verb agreement**

For each underlined section, choose the revision that most improves the writing.

Early in Shakespeare's play, Macbeth is drawn toward evil by three weird sisters. They predict Macbeth will become king, as a result, he considers murdering the current king. (1) Lady Macbeth is cunning, devious, and has a strong will. (2) Like her husband, she is anxious to seize the throne. She urges Macbeth to kill King Duncan. Macbeth and his wife wants (3) the reward that the sisters have promised them. Macbeth gives in to the corrupting power of evil his bloodthirsty reign soon begins. (4) Innocent and helpless, Macbeth murders Macduff's family. (5) Macduff feels (6) he is justified in killing Macbeth.

1. **A.** They predict Macbeth will become king. As a result, he considers murdering the current king.
   B. They predict Macbeth will become king as a result, he considers murdering the current king.
   C. They predict Macbeth will become king as a result. He considers murdering the current king.
   D. Correct as is

2. **A.** cunning, devious, and a strong will
   B. cunning, devious, and having a strong will
   C. cunning, devious, and strong-willed
   D. Correct as is

3. **A.** wanting
   B. want
   C. has wanted
   D. Correct as is

4. **A.** Macbeth gives in to the corrupting power of evil, his bloodthirsty reign soon begins.
   B. Macbeth gives in to the corrupting power of evil, and his bloodthirsty reign soon begins.
   C. Macbeth gives in to the corrupting power of evil, his reign begins.
   D. Correct as is

5. **A.** Macduff's family is murdered by Macbeth, innocent and helpless.
   B. Macduff's family is murdered, innocent and helpless, by Macbeth.
   C. Macbeth murders Macduff's innocent and helpless family.
   D. Correct as is

6. **A.** feelings
   B. feel
   C. is feeling
   D. Correct as is

Need extra help?

See the **Grammar Handbook**
Correcting Run-on Sentences, p. 1199
Modifiers, p. 1190,
Subject-Verb Agreement, p. 1200–1202

Assessment Practice

Briefly review the kinds of errors that the passage may contain. Remind students to read the entire passage first before they answer the questions.

Answers:
1. A; **2.** C; **3.** B; **4.** B; **5.** C; **6.** D

Mini Lesson Grammar

MISPLACED MODIFIERS

Instruction A misplaced modifier is a word or group of words that modifies the wrong word. The result is a sentence that is humorous or confusing.

Activity Write the following sentences on the board. Discuss why they are confusing. Then have volunteers correct the sentences.

1. At the age of seven, my grandfather taught me to fish.
2. We waved at our friends skateboarding from our car.
3. The book is still under my bed that I should have returned to the library two weeks ago.

Answers:

1. My grandfather taught me to fish when I was seven years old.
2. From our car, we waved at our friends who were skateboarding.
3. The book that I should have returned to the library two weeks ago is still under my bed.

Objectives

- reflect on and assess student understanding of the unit
- compare text events with experiences of students and other readers
- provide examples of themes that cross texts
- compare across texts elements of texts such as conflicts and characterization
- assess and build portfolios

Reflecting on Theme

OPTION 1

A successful response will
- select the three most threatening or powerful protagonists from Unit Four.
- create a profile of each of the three protagonists.
- explain why the student finds each protagonist particularly formidable.
- discuss what the student would do if faced with one of the protagonists.

OPTION 2

A successful response will
- select from Unit Four four particularly courageous characters who stand up for their beliefs.
- identify what the four characters gained and lost.
- in a short oral report, explain to the class what the four characters gained and lost, providing specific examples.

OPTION 3

A successful response will
- create a two-column chart.
- list on one side of the chart people who seek power for positive reasons.
- list on other side of the chart people who seek power for negative reasons.
- find examples of people who seek power for both positive and negative reasons.

Self-Assessment

Ask students what ideas they had about human nature prior to reading this unit. Did they think it basically good? basically evil? neither? a mix? Then ask them to explain how their perceptions of human nature were affected by the selections in this unit.

Lessons of History

How did the selections in this unit influence your understanding of history and its effects upon people's lives? What progress did you make in your reading and writing skills? Explore these questions as you complete activities in each of the following sections.

Roman Forum, Rome, Italy.

Reflecting on Theme

OPTION 1

Comparing Foes Consider the enemies or opposing forces faced by the protagonists in this unit. Choose the three that, in your judgment, are the most threatening or powerful. Then, as you did in the activity on page 542, consider what makes them so formidable and write a short profile of each enemy or opposing force, explaining the reason for your choice. Finally, choose one of the three and think about what you would do if faced with such an opponent. Discuss your response with your classmates.

OPTION 2

Tests of Conviction Review the activity that you completed on page 622. Based on your responses to this activity, what do you think individuals have to gain from standing up for their convictions? With a partner, look through the selections in this unit for characters who stand up for their beliefs. Choose four that you think are particularly courageous or admirable, and identify what they gained or lost as a result of taking a stand. With your partner, explain your responses to your class in a short oral presentation.

OPTION 3

The Lessons of Power Consider different situations in which people try to seize power, such as those you identified in the activity on page 682. What types of people do you think are most drawn to power? Working in a small group, create a two-column chart. In the first column, list examples—drawn from the selections and your own experience—of people who seek power for positive reasons. In the second column, list examples of people who seek power for negative reasons. Can you think of people who belong in both columns? Discuss your chart with the rest of your classmates.

Self ASSESSMENT

READER'S NOTEBOOK

Now that you have had a chance to reflect on the lessons of history, create a diagram centering on the topic. The three categories should be called "Human Nature," "Human Conflict," and "Human Values." Under each category, list your insights about that topic. Put an X next to any entry that represents an insight prompted by a selection in this unit.

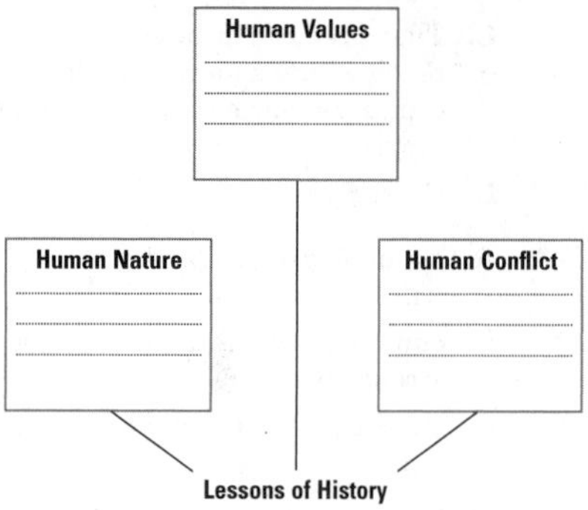

Reviewing Literary Concepts

OPTION 1

Identifying Irony Review the definition of irony on pages 543–544, and identify at least four selections in this unit that contain examples of irony. Then fill out a chart similar to the one shown. For each selection, list one or more examples of irony. Pair up with a classmate and compare charts.

Selection	Situational Irony	Verbal Irony	Dramatic Irony
"Do not weep, maiden, for war is kind"		Speaker says that war is kind but means that war is unkind.	

OPTION 2

Analyzing Point of View The use of point of view in writing fiction may be compared to the use of a camera in making a movie. A close-up shot brings viewers very close to the subject, offering an intimate view. A wide-angle shot, on the other hand, presents a large scene. Which stories in this unit offer the most intimate view of their subjects? Are those stories told from a first-person or a third-person point of view? Review the definition of point of view on pages 623–624. Then discuss how point of view can affect a reader's sense of closeness to a character.

Self ASSESSMENT

READER'S NOTEBOOK

Copy the following list of literary terms introduced or reviewed in this unit. Put a check next to terms that you believe you could easily define in your own words. Underline the terms that you feel are not easy to define. Then get together with a small group of classmates to discuss the meanings of the terms that seem difficult to define.

situational irony
protagonist
antagonist
suspense
first-person point of view
verbal irony
sonnet structure
style
memoir
tone
diction
third-person point of view
setting
flashback
blank verse
soliloquy
aside
figurative language
rhetorical devices
dramatic irony
tragedy
theme

Building Your Portfolio

- **Writing Options** Many of the Writing Options in this unit asked you to write letters for purposes ranging from political to personal. From your letters, choose two that most clearly and powerfully convey your concern for the subject matter. Write a cover note explaining the reason for your choices and attach it to the pieces. Then add the letters and the note to your **Presentation Portfolio.**
- **Writing Workshops** In this unit, you wrote a persuasive essay about an issue you feel strongly about. You also wrote an essay that explains the cause and effect of an event. Reread these pieces and assess the quality of your writing. In which of the pieces do you demonstrate a firmer grasp of your subject matter? Write a note explaining your choice and place it with the piece in your **Presentation Portfolio.**
- **Additional Activities** Think back to the assignments you completed under **Activities & Explorations** and **Inquiry & Research**. Keep a record in your portfolio of any assignments that you think are representative of your best work.

Self ASSESSMENT

Presentation Portfolio

Review the pieces in your portfolio. Which types of writing have proved troublesome? Have your strengths and weaknesses changed during the course of the year?

Setting GOALS

The Reflect and Assess feature at the end of Unit One (pages 218-219) asked you to create a list of skills that you would like to work on. Review that list to judge your progress. Then create an updated list of skills, reflecting your current needs and interests, to work on during the rest of the year.

Reviewing Literary Concepts

OPTION 1

Use the Unit 4 Resource Book, page 94, to provide students a ready-made, full-depth chart for recording their examples of irony.

OPTION 2

A successful response will

- list stories in Unit 4 that offer the most intimate views of their subjects, and offer specific examples for support.
- determine whether each story is told from first-person or third-person point of view.
- discuss how point of view can affect a reader's sense of closeness to a character.

Building Your Portfolio

Students will use their Presentation Portfolios to file what they consider their highest quality work—the very best projects and activities from their Working Portfolios.

For more information on using writing and assessing portfolios, see the *Teacher's Guide to Assessment and Portfolio Use* beginning on page 53.

The *Electronic Library* is a CD-ROM that contains additional fiction, nonfiction, poetry, and drama for each unit in *The Language of Literature.*

These are the additional selections found in Unit 4 of the *Electronic Library.*

Tacitus
The Burning of Rome

Bertolt Brecht
To Posterity

Alphonse Daudet
The Last Lesson

Selma Lagerlöf
The Silver Mine

Miguel Hernández
War

Franz Kafka
A Hunger Artist

Mikhail Zoshchenko
Bees and People

Reading Skills and Strategies
Sustained Silent Reading
Encourage students to select one of the books as an opportunity to read silently with comprehension over a period of time.

UNIT FOUR Extend Your *Reading*

LITERATURE CONNECTIONS

Farewell to Manzanar

JEANNE WAKATSUKI HOUSTON AND JAMES D. HOUSTON

Here is the entire book from which the excerpt on pages 602–614 is taken, a true story of a Japanese-American family's confinement in the Manzanar internment camp in California during World War II. Jeanne Wakatsuki Houston was seven when Japan attacked Pearl Harbor and created the hysteria that forced almost 120,000 Japanese Americans from their homes. She remembers the stress of camp life. She also recalls what she took away from Manzanar after it closed—an odd sense of shame and a fierce determination to be accepted as American.

These thematically related readings are provided along with *Farewell to Manzanar*:

***from* Legends from Camp**
LAWSON FUSAO INADA

Sleep in the Mojave Desert
SYLVIA PLATH

I Remember Pearl Harbor
CHARLES SHIRO INOUYE

Wilshire Bus
HISAYE YAMAMOTO

Trains at Night
ALBERTO ALVARO RÍOS

Visiting Home
KEVIN YOUNG

***from* Unto the Sons**
GAY TALESE

Lectures on How You Never Lived Back Home
M. EVELINA GALANG

And Even *More* . . .

When Rain Clouds Gather

BESSIE HEAD

Fleeing the oppression of South Africa in the mid-1960s, Makhaya crosses the border into Botswana, arriving in a poor rural village. Makhaya becomes involved in political and cultural changes occurring in the village, which reflect those occurring in all of Botswana. This book is also part of the *Literature Connections* series published by McDougal Littell.

Books

Bronzeville Boys and Girls
GWENDOLYN BROOKS
Poems about the experiences of African-American children growing up in a big city.

If Not Now, When?
PRIMO LEVI
This work tells of a personal war against the Nazis that ends with the affirmation of the human spirit.

If I Die in a Combat Zone, Box Me Up and Ship Me Home
TIM O'BRIEN
A memoir of the author's tour of duty in Vietnam.

LITERATURE CONNECTIONS

The Underdogs

MARIANO AZUELA

First published in 1915, this novel offers a classic account of the Mexican Revolution of 1910. Demetrio Macías, the main character, has a ranch in the Juchipila River valley near the chaos and corruption of the revolutionary struggle. In an effort to save his family, the naive and peace-loving Indian joins in the revolution against dictator Porfirio Díaz. Macías becomes a general in the army of Pancho Villa. In the end, the peasant rebels become corrupted by the forces of lawlessness and greed unleashed during the revolution.

These thematically related readings are provided along with *The Underdogs*:

Zapata and ***from* Viva Zapata!**
JOHN STEINBECK

The Festival of Bullets
MARTIN LUIS GUZMÁN

The Dictators
PABLO NERUDA

When Evil-Doing Comes Like Falling Rain
BERTOLT BRECHT

"It's Terrible" or "It's Fine"
MAO ZEDONG

Tienanmen Square: A Soldier's Story
XIAO YE

How Much Land Does a Man Need?
LEO TOLSTOY

All Quiet on the Western Front
ERICH MARIA REMARQUE
Set in the trenches during World War I, this pacifistic novel tells the story of a young German soldier struggling against the hatred of war.

Leaves of Grass
WALT WHITMAN
The collected works of one of America's most influential poets. Whitman's poems celebrate America and the human spirit.

Other Media

Shakespeare: The Man and His Times
Period paintings, prints, and woodcuts show major events of Shakespeare's life. Educational Audio Visual.
(VIDEOCASSETTE)

Julius Caesar
An adaptation of Shakespeare's play starring Charlton Heston, John Gielgud, and others. Republic Pictures.
(VIDEOCASSETTE)

Rappin' with the Bard
Familiar images are used to introduce Shakespearean language and stories. Beacon.
(VIDEOCASSETTE)

Elie Wiesel: Witness to the Holocaust
A portrait of the Nobel Peace Prize recipient. Sunburst Communication.
(VIDEOCASSETTE)

Gwendolyn Brooks
The Pulitzer Prize-winning poet reads her works. Amazon Books.
(AUDIOCASSETTE)

EXTEND YOUR READING 809

OVERVIEW

The Reading and Writing for Assessment feature provides practice in taking standardized tests. As students work through this lesson, they will learn strategies for reading comprehension questions, multiple-choice questions, and essay and short-answer questions. Boxed strategies located alongside the text will help guide students through the activities. These strategies model processes students can use as they take standardized tests.

This feature is based on and will help to prepare students for state assessments, including end-of-course assessments. It will also prepare students for the reading comprehension questions used on such college board examinations as the Scholastic Aptitude Test (SAT) and the American College Test (ACT).

Objectives

- understand and apply strategies for reading a test selection
- recognize literary techniques in a test selection
- understand and apply strategies for answering multiple-choice questions about a test selection
- respond to a writing prompt and present ideas in a logical order
- understand and apply strategies for revising and proofreading a test response

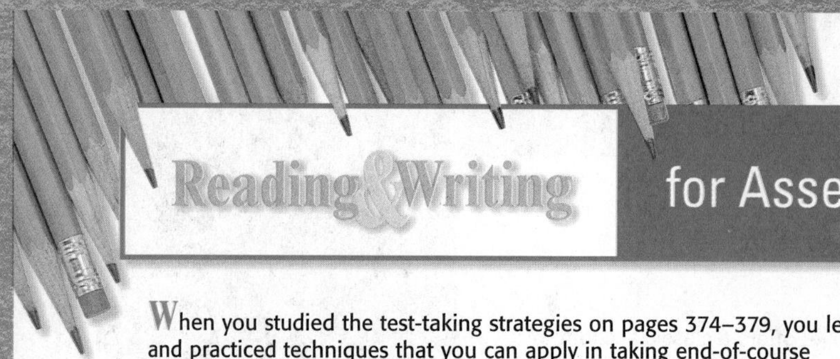

Reading&Writing for Assessment

When you studied the test-taking strategies on pages 374–379, you learned and practiced techniques that you can apply in taking end-of-course examinations, standardized tests, and many other types of assessment.

The following pages will give you more practice using these strategies. Read the explanatory material that follows and then work through each of the models.

PART 1 How to Read the Test Selection

Listed below are the basic reading strategies you studied earlier, along with several new ones geared to a different type of reading selection. Applying these strategies, taking notes, and highlighting or underscoring passages as you read can help you identify the information you will need to answer the test questions.

STRATEGIES FOR READING A TEST SELECTION

- **Before you begin reading, skim the questions that follow the passage.** These can help focus your reading.
- **Think about the title.** What does it suggest about the overall message and tone of the passage?
- **Use active reading strategies such as analyzing, predicting, and questioning.** As you read, constantly ask yourself, "What does this mean, and what are its implications?" If the test directions allow you to mark on the test itself, make notes in the margin.
- **Look for main ideas.** These are often stated at the beginnings or ends of paragraphs. Sometimes they are implied, not stated. After reading each paragraph, summarize what it was about.
- **Note the literary elements and techniques used by the writer.** Consider the tone (writer's attitude toward the subject) and mood (the overall feeling or atmosphere the writer creates). What literary techniques, such as imagery and figurative language, contribute to those effects?
- **Examine the sequence of ideas.** Are the ideas developed in chronological order, presented in order of importance, or organized in some other way? Does the writer examine causes and effects, make comparisons and contrasts, or discuss problems and solutions?
- **Look for expert testimony.** What sources of information does the writer use? Why are these sources appropriate to the subject?
- **Think about the message and the writer's purpose.** What questions does the selection answer? What new questions does it raise? What generalizations can you make about the subject?

Reading Selection

Julius Caesar Takes Control

1 ❶ In 60 B.C., Julius Caesar joined forces with Crassus, a wealthy Roman, and Pompey, a popular general. With their help, Caesar was elected consul in 59 B.C. For the next ten years, these men dominated Rome as a triumvirate, a group of three rulers.

2 Caesar was a strong leader and a genius at military strategy. Abiding by tradition, he served only one year as consul. He then appointed himself governor of Gaul (now France). During 58–50 B.C., Caesar led his legions in a grueling but successful campaign to conquer all of Gaul. Because he shared fully in the hardships of war, he won his men's loyalty and devotion. Here he speaks of rallying his troops in battle:

3 ❷ I had no shield with me but I snatched one from a soldier in the rear ranks and went forward to the front line. Once there, I called to all the centurions by name and shouted encouragement to the rest of the men. . . . My arrival gave the troops fresh hope.

4 The reports of Caesar's successes in Gaul made him very popular with the people of Rome. Pompey, who had become his political rival, feared Caesar's ambitions. In 50 B.C., the senate, at Pompey's urgings, ordered Caesar to disband his legions and return home.

5 Caesar's next move led to civil war. He defied the senate's order. On the night of January 10, 49 B.C., he took his army ❸ across the Rubicon River in Italy, the southern limit of the area he commanded. He marched his army swiftly toward Rome, and Pompey fled. Caesar's troops defeated Pompey's armies in Greece, Asia, Spain, and Egypt. In 46 B.C., Caesar returned to Rome, where he had the support of the army and the masses. That same year, the senate appointed him dictator; in 44 B.C., he was named dictator for life.

6 ❹ **Caesar's Reforms** Caesar governed as an absolute ruler, one who has total power. He made sweeping changes, granting Roman citizenship to many people in the provinces. He expanded the senate, adding friends and supporters from Italy and the provinces. Caesar helped the poor by creating jobs, especially through the construction of new public buildings. He started colonies where the landless could own land and increased pay for soldiers.

7 Many nobles and senators were troubled by Caesar's growing power, success, and popularity. Some feared losing their influence; others considered him a tyrant. A number of important senators,

STRATEGIES IN ACTION

❶ Look for main ideas.

ONE STUDENT'S THOUGHTS

"The selection begins by explaining how Julius Caesar came to power. I wonder how long he ruled."

❷ Read actively—analyze.

"This quotation strongly supports the writer's claim that Caesar's men were devoted to him. Caesar might not be very objective about himself, though."

YOUR TURN

What other evidence can you find in the passage to support or contradict Caesar's popularity?

❸ Read actively—make connections.

"I've heard people say they 'crossed the Rubicon' when they did something they couldn't undo. I guess this must be where that expression came from."

❹ Examine the sequence of ideas.

"The writer presents ideas chronologically, using subheadings to separate topics."

YOUR TURN

Why do you think the writer chose to use chronological order?

Teaching the Lesson

Begin by previewing the text. Note the title and identify the subject of the reading selection. Read through the questions and prompts at the end of the text. Ask students what they will need to look for as they read.

1 When looking for the main idea of a paragraph, students should consider how the paragraph relates to its heading or subheading.

Customizing for Less Proficient Readers

2 Reading comprehension tests often assess students' ability to recognize bias in a test selection. Use the following questions to guide less proficient readers to recognize bias.

- Who is the speaker in this paragraph?
  Answer: Caesar
- Whose feelings, besides his own, does the speaker discuss in the paragraph?
  Answer: the troops'
- What reasons might the speaker have for giving a positive description of events?
  Possible Response: Things actually happened that way; he wants to make himself look good.

YOUR TURN Support: He was elected consul, and he had the support of the army and the masses upon his return to Rome; Contradict: The senate ordered Caesar to disband his army.

3 When students read new material, they should look for words, phrases, or ideas that connect to things they have experienced or learned about previously.

4 If subheadings are supplied, they can be an important indicator of the selection's organization.

YOUR TURN **Possible Response:** Since this is a historical report, relating events in the order in which they occurred helps to show how one situation grew out of another.

5 Not only paragraphs but also larger sections of a selection can have main ideas. A subheading, if present, will usually indicate the main idea of a section. A section's main idea will influence the main ideas of the paragraphs within it.

6 As students read, they should look for loaded or judgmental terms that indicate an author's attitude toward his or her subject.

led by Marcus Brutus and Gaius Cassius, plotted his assassination. On March 15, 44 B.C., they stabbed him to death in the senate chamber.

8 ❺ **Beginning of the Empire** After Caesar's death, civil war broke out again and destroyed what was left of the Roman Republic. Three of Caesar's supporters banded together to crush the assassins. Caesar's 18-year-old grandnephew and adopted son, Octavian, joined with an experienced general named Mark Antony and a powerful politician named Lepidus. In 43 B.C., they took control of Rome and ruled for ten years as the Second Triumvirate. Among those killed in the Triumvirate's purge of Caesar's enemies was Cicero, a defender of the republic in the senate.

9 ❻ The Second Triumvirate ended in jealousy and violence. Octavian forced Lepidus to retire, and he and Mark Antony became rivals. While leading troops against Rome's enemies in Anatolia, Mark Antony met Queen Cleopatra of Egypt. He fell in love with her and followed her to Egypt. Octavian accused Antony of plotting to rule Rome from Egypt, and another civil war erupted. Octavian defeated the combined forces of Antony and Cleopatra at the naval battle of Actium in 31 B.C. Later, Antony and Cleopatra committed suicide.

10 Octavian claimed he would restore the republic and, in fact, did retain some of its forms and traditions. The senate, for example, continued to meet, and Octavian consulted it on important matters. However, Octavian became the unchallenged ruler of Rome. Eventually he accepted the title of Augustus, or "exalted one." He also kept the title Imperator, or supreme military commander, a term from which the word *emperor* is derived. Rome had become an empire ruled by one man.

❺ Look for main ideas.

"This section must explain how the Roman Republic became the Roman Empire. The subhead mentions the empire, and, by skipping ahead, I see that the last sentence of paragraph 10 does, too."

❻ Note the writer's tone.

"The writer explains the motives for the various wars and rivalries but doesn't judge the people involved. The passage has a neutral, objective tone."

Check Your Understanding

Have students use the following questions to test their understanding of the selection before they answer the questions in their texts.

- What were the main ideas in the selection?
- How does the writer encourage readers to care about the information he or she presents?
- What structure does the writer use for the selection?
- Did the selection answer all your questions about the subject? If not, what questions remain unanswered?

PART 2 **How to Answer Multiple-Choice Questions**

Use the strategies in the box and notes in the side column to help you answer the questions below and on the following pages.

Based on the selection you have just read, choose the best answer for each of the following questions.

1. This selection describes Rome's transition from
   A. a time of peace to a time of war.
   B. a dictatorship to a democracy.
   C. an empire to a republic.
   D. a republic to an empire.

2. The ideas in this selection are presented in
   A. chronological order.
   B. order of importance.
   C. an order based on the geographic areas mentioned.
   D. none of the above

3. Judging from the selection, which of the following characteristics did a Roman citizen need MOST in order to become a ruler?
   A. relatives in government
   B. popularity with the people
   C. military expertise
   D. eloquence as a speaker

4. Which of the following passages from the selection has the LEAST objective tone?
   A. "Julius Caesar joined forces with Crassus. . . ."
   B. "He then appointed himself governor. . . ."
   C. "Pompey . . . feared Caesar's ambitions."
   D. "Caesar's troops defeated Pompey's armies. . . ."

5. Which of the following is the BEST example of cause and effect?
   A. Caesar was an absolute ruler, so the senators assassinated him.
   B. Caesar crossed the Rubicon to start a war.
   C. Antony went to Egypt, and Octavian defeated him at Actium.
   D. Octavian came to power and made himself emperor.

STRATEGIES FOR ANSWERING MULTIPLE-CHOICE QUESTIONS

- **Ask questions** that help you eliminate some of the choices.
- **Pay attention to choices such as "all of the above" or "none of the above."** To eliminate them, all you need to find is one answer that doesn't fit.
- **Skim your notes.** Details you noticed as you read may provide answers.

STRATEGIES IN ACTION

Skim your notes.

ONE STUDENT'S THOUGHTS

"The selection does not say that either Caesar or Octavian was particularly eloquent. *So I can eliminate choice D.*"

YOUR TURN

What other answer choices were not mentioned in the selection?

Ask questions. Was the event in the second part of each sentence a direct result of the event in the first part?

ONE STUDENT'S THOUGHTS

"Octavian didn't have to make himself emperor just because he came to power. *So I can eliminate choice D.*"

YOUR TURN

Which of the events was definitely caused by the event that preceded it?

Guiding Student Response

Multiple-Choice Questions

1. D
2. A
3. C
4. C
5. B

Short-Answer Question

Caesar governed as dictator for life with absolute rule, setting the precedent for imperial rule. His assassination led to the rise of Octavian, who became the first emperor on the strength of his defeat of Caesar's assassins and then of Caesar's supporter, Mark Antony.

YOUR TURN Those contributions that most directly led to Rome's transformation into an empire are Caesar's total rule as dictator for life and his assassination, which led to Octavian's rise to emperor.

Essay Question

Caesar and Octavian came to power in similar ways but met different fates.

Both were successful military commanders and defeated former allies in order to achieve sole rule of Rome. Each ruled for a time as a member of a triumvirate. Finally, both became supreme rulers of Rome with almost total authority. However, Caesar was never named emperor. He was assassinated for his ambition; Octavian was made emperor for his.

Although both men rose to power in similar ways and shared many traits, the results of their ambition were very different.

YOUR TURN Both men were successful military commanders. Both were members of triumvirates. Both defeated former allies. Both became autocratic rulers of Rome.

PART 3 How To Respond in Writing

You may also be asked to write answers to questions about a reading passage. **Short-answer questions** usually ask you to answer in a sentence or two. **Essay questions** require a fully developed piece of writing.

Short-Answer Question

STRATEGIES FOR RESPONDING TO SHORT-ANSWER QUESTIONS

- **Identify the key words** in the writing prompt that tell you the ideas to discuss. Make sure you know what the key words mean.
- **State your response directly** and to the point.
- **Support your ideas** by using evidence from the selection.
- **Use correct grammar.**

Sample Question

Answer the following question in one or two sentences.

Summarize the role Julius Caesar played in the decline of the republic and the rise of the Roman Empire.

STRATEGIES IN ACTION

Identify the key words.

ONE STUDENT'S THOUGHTS

"The key words are *summarize* and *role.* That means I have to briefly list Caesar's major contributions to Roman history."

YOUR TURN

Which contributions will you include in your answer?

Essay Question

STRATEGIES FOR ANSWERING ESSAY QUESTIONS

- **Look for direction words** in the writing prompt, such as *essay, analyze, describe,* or *compare and contrast,* that tell you how to respond to the prompt.
- **List the points you want to make** before beginning to write.
- **Write an interesting introduction** that presents your main point.
- **Develop your ideas** by using evidence from the selection that supports the statements you make. Present the ideas in a logical order.
- **Write a conclusion** that summarizes your points.
- **Check your work** for correct grammar.

Sample Prompt

Caesar was named dictator of Rome for life. Later, Caesar's grandnephew and adopted son, Octavian, came to rule Rome as Augustus, "exalted one," and imperator, or supreme military commander. Compare and contrast the two leaders' rise to power and their military and social achievements.

Look for direction words.

"The important words are *compare and contrast.* This means that I'll have to show how Caesar and Octavian were alike and different."

YOUR TURN

What evidence of similarities between the two rulers do you find in the selection?

PART 4 How to Revise, Edit, and Proofread a Test Selection

Here is a student's first draft in response to the writing prompt at the bottom of page 814. Read it and answer the multiple-choice questions that follow.

> Both Caesar and Octavian initially joined forces with other leaders to rule Rome. As part of powerful triumvirates. The members of both triumvirates eventually became political rivals. Caesar and Octavian seized power. The writer says that Caesar won the loyalty of his troops and he gives a quotation from him to support this statement. There is no mention in the selection of how Octavian's troops felt about him. They must have been loyal to him, though, because he won many military battles. Both Caesar and Octavian, who was then called Augustus, realized how important the senate was and made it their ally.

1. What is the BEST way to revise lines 1–2 ("Both Caesar . . . powerful triumvirates")?
   - **A.** Both Caesar and Octavian initially joined forces with other leaders to rule Rome as part of powerful triumvirates.
   - **B.** Both Caesar and Octavian initially joined forces, as part of powerful triumvirates, with other leaders to rule Rome.
   - **C.** As part of powerful triumvirates, both Caesar and Octavian initially joined forces with other leaders to rule Rome.
   - **D.** Make no change.
2. What is the BEST way to combine the sentences in lines 2–4 ("The members of both . . . seized power.")?
   - **A.** The members of both triumvirates eventually became political rivals; Caesar and Octavian seized power.
   - **B.** The members of both triumvirates eventually became political rivals, and therefore, Caesar and Octavian seized power.
   - **C.** The members of both triumvirates eventually became political rivals, allowing Caesar and Octavian to seize power.
   - **D.** Make no change.
3. What is the BEST change, if any, to the sentence in lines 4–6 ("The writer says . . . support this statement.")?
   - **A.** The writer says that Caesar won the loyalty of his troops and the writer gives a quotation from him to support this statement.
   - **B.** The writer says that Caesar won the loyalty of his troops and he gives a quotation from Caesar to support this statement.
   - **C.** The writer says that Caesar won the loyalty of his troops and gives a quotation from Caesar to support this statement.
   - **D.** Make no change.

STRATEGIES FOR REVISING, EDITING, AND PROOFREADING

- **Read the passage carefully.**
- **Note the parts that are confusing or don't make sense.** What kinds of errors might cause that confusion?
- **Look for errors** in grammar, usage, spelling, and capitalization. Common errors include:
  - sentence fragments
  - lack of subject-verb agreement
  - unclear pronoun antecedents
  - lack of transition words

Guiding Student Response

Answers:
1. A
2. C
3. C

Check Your Understanding

Have students reread their own responses to the short-answer and essay questions. Then have students use the following questions to guide themselves as they revise and edit their own work.

- Have I responded directly to the direction words in the writing prompt?
- Have I supported my ideas with evidence from the selection?
- Have I presented my ideas in a logical order?
- Have I included an introduction and a conclusion?
- Have I used correct grammar?

Discovering the Truth

In Unit Five students will read selections which explore moments when people achieve an important understanding about life. The unit contains two parts, both of which contribute to the unit theme by describing a variety of characters as they come to important insights about their lives.

Part 1

Simple Truths Selections in Part 1 highlight a variety of characters' realizations about the world around them. For example, in "A White Heron," a lonely child refuses an attractive offer in order to protect a magnificent bird.

Part 2

Appearance vs. Reality Selections in Part 2 highlight a variety of characters' realizations about what is most important to them in life. For example, in "The Watch," David Mamet eventually learns the value of his relationship with his father after receiving a watch for his college graduation instead of the expected convertible.

Mini Lesson Viewing and Representing

Sea Jewels
by Paul Niemiec, Jr.

ART APPRECIATION

Instruction Born in New York City in 1948, Paul Niemiec creates paintings that are grounded in traditional American realism. His life in rural upstate New York is reflected in his work, which consists of rural landscapes, coastal maritime themes, and wildlife paintings. In his painting Niemiec strives to make a statement about the beauty of life and the land that is so often taken for granted.

In the 1995 painting, *Sea Jewels,* Niemiec conveys a sense of open spaces, a bright atmosphere, and timelessness. He wanted to create a place where a person could reflect, contemplate, observe, or dream.

Ask: What aspects of the painting help communicate these ideas?

Possible Response: The light sky, the serene shore, and the solitary figure all give the impression that this is a place where a person can reflect or contemplate.

the TRUTH

Truth resides in the human heart, and one has to search for it there.

Mohandas Gandhi

Sea Jewels (1995), Paul Niemiec, Jr. Watercolor, 18″ × 28″. Collection of Mr. and Mrs. Stephen H. Palmer.

Making Connections

To help students explore the unit theme, have them consider the following questions:

Ask: **Why do you think "Discovering the Truth" might be an important theme to explore?**
Possible Response: Some students might say that reading about other people's realizations can help us discover truths about ourselves. Other students might suggest that characters' insights can point to general truths about the world.

Ask: **How might the truth reside in the human heart? How does the art on this opener suggest people might find the truth?**
Possible Response: The concept of a personal or ambiguous truth may be difficult for some students. Encourage them to describe their understanding of truth and compare it with the statement by Gandhi. The figure gazing at the ocean in solitude suggests that truth might be subjective. Some students may disagree with that view.

Ask: **What kinds of stories and experiences might you expect to read about in this unit?**
Possible Response: These selections may deal with characters who are confronted with something that gives them a greater understanding of themselves, of their personal relationships, or of the world around them.

UNIT FIVE
PART 1 SKILLS TRACE

Features and Selections	Literary Analysis	Reading and Critical Thinking	Writing Opportunities
Discovering the Truth **Simple Truths**			
Learning the Language of Literature: Symbolism and Figurative Language	Symbols, Figurative Language, 819		
The Active Reader: Skills and Strategies		Strategies for Questioning, 821	
SHORT STORY A White Heron **Difficulty Level:** ***Challenging***	Symbol, 822, 833 Review Point of View, 833	Questioning, 822, 833 Test Practice, 832	Picture Book, 834 Sylvia's Haiku, 834 Epilogue to the Story, 834
Real World Link The Mouse That Roared		Magazine Article: Evaluating Opinions, 836	
POETRY Birches **Difficulty Level:** ***Challenging***	Figurative Language, 838, 841 Alliteration, Assonance, Consonance, 841	Analyzing Images, 838, 841 Informal Assess., 842	Impressive Description, 842 Interpretation of Poem, 842
POETRY For the New Year, 1981 Pride **Difficulty Level:** ***Average***	Extended Metaphor, 843, 846 Personification, 846	Making Inferences, 843, 846 Informal Assess., 847	Thesaurus Entries, 847 Abstract Poem, 847
SHORT STORY Like the Sun **Difficulty Level:** ***Average*** Literary Link: Tell all the Truth but tell it slant— Building Vocabulary	Humor, 848, 853 Review: Alliteration, Assonance, and Consonance, 853	Predicting, 848, 853	Headmaster's Notes, 854 Theme Interpretation, 854 Scene Dialogue, 854
Writing Workshop: Interpretive Essay Assessment Practice		Analyzing Two Student Models, 862	Interpretive Essay, 861

UNIT FIVE
PART 2 SKILLS TRACE

Appearance vs. Reality			
Learning the Language of Literature: Realism	Realistic Fiction, 868		
The Active Reader: Skills and Strategies		Strategies for Analyzing Fiction, Nonfiction, and Poetry, 870	

LEGEND DLS – Daily Language SkillBuilder
CCL – Cross Curricular Link
Green type – Teacher's Edition

Speaking and Listening Viewing and Representing	Inquiry and Research	Grammar, Usage, and Mechanics	Vocabulary
Art Appreciation, 816			
Public Speech, 834 Sylvia's Loyalties, 834 Art Appreciation, 825, 828	Fighting for Survival, 834	Adverb Clauses, 835 DLS, 822 Independent and Subordinate Clauses, 830 Adverb Clauses, 834	Context Clues, 834 Using Context Clues, 824 Researching Word Origins, 826
Debate, 837	Activity Link: A White Heron, 837 Inquiry & Research, 837		
Video Viewing, 842 Leafy Scrapbook, 842		DLS, 838 Conjunctive Adverbs, 840	
Images from Nature, 847		DLS, 843 Correlative Conjunctions, 845	
Truth Survey, 854 Art Appreciation, 851, 852	Legacy of Empire, 854	Adjective Clauses, 855 DLS, 848 Adjective Clauses, 854	Context Clues, 854 Analyzing Word Parts—Affixes, 856 Research Word Origins, 850
Picturing Text Structure, 862		Creating Sentence Variety/ Using *That* and *Which* with Clauses, 865 Revising & Editing, 866 Correct Use of *That* and *Which*, 866	

PART 2 SKILLS TRACE

Features and Selections	Literary Analysis	Reading and Critical Thinking	Writing Opportunities
SHORT STORY The Witness for the Prosecution **Difficulty Level:** ***Average***	Dialogue, 871, 890 Review: Point of View, 890	Drawing Conclusions, 871, 890 Test Practice, 889	Solicitor's Script, 891 Breaking News, 891 Cast List, 891
SHORT STORY The Balek Scales **Difficulty Level:** ***Challenging***	Tone, 893, 901	Analyzing Relevance of Setting, 893, 901 Test Practice, 900	Sunday Sermon, 902 Aristocratic Editorial, 902 Autobiographical Tale, 902
POETRY The Street/ La Calle I Am Not I/ Yo No Soy Yo **Difficulty Level:** ***Challenging*** Building Vocabulary	Modern Poetry, 903, 906	Strategies for Reading Modern Poetry, 903, 906 Test Practice, 905	Identity Poem, 907
Real World Link: Volkswagen Television Ad		Advertisement: Evaluating Advertising, 916	
Life and Times		Voice of the Common People, 918	
FICTION The Flood **Difficulty Level:** ***Average*** PHOTOGRAPHS / CAPTIONS Photo Essay **Difficulty Level:** ***Easy***	Social Criticism, 922, 933	Author's Purpose, 922, 933 Test Practice, 934	Letter to the Editor, 934
NONFICTION *from* Travels with Charley **Difficulty Level:** ***Average***	Comic Irony, 935, 939	Word Choice, 935, 939 Test Practice, 940	Dog's-Eye Essay, 940 Persuasive Essay, 940 Incident Report, 940
NONFICTION Letter to Edith Mirrielees *from* Nobel Prize Acceptance Speech **Difficulty Level:** ***Average***	Tone and Audience, 941, 945 Review: Author's Purpose, 945	Monitoring Reading Strategies, 941, 945	Letter in Response, 947 Newspaper Article, 947
The Author's Style Author Study Project	Analysis of Style, 946		Changing Style, 946 Imitating Style, 946
Writing Workshop: Autobiographical Incident Assessment Practice		Analyzing a Student Model, 949	Autobiographical Incident, 948
Reflect and Assess: Discovering the Truth	Reviewing Literary Concepts, 955	Deceptive Appearances, 954 Choosing Guides to Truth, 954	Truths to Live By, 954 Building Your Portfolio, 954

LEGEND DLS – Daily Language SkillBuilder
CCL – Cross Curricular Link
Green type – Teacher's Edition

Speaking and Listening Viewing and Representing	Inquiry and Research	Grammar, Usage, and Mechanics	Vocabulary
Dramatic Role-Play, 891 Courtroom Sketches, 891 Portrait of the Witness From Page to Stage to Screen, 892 Art Appreciation, 872, 881, 885	Scientific Proof, 891	Noun Clauses, 892 Adverb Clauses, 878 Noun Clauses, 892	Finding Synonyms, 873
Art Appreciation, 899		DLS, 893 Sentence Structure, 896	Using Context Clues, 894 Apply Meanings of Root Words, 898
Dramatic Interpretation, 907		DLS, 903 Correlative Conjunctions, 907	Using Context Clues for Specialized Vocabulary, 908
	Activity Link: The Watch, 917 Inquiry & Research, 917		
Monologue, 934 Photo-Essay, 926		Adverb Clauses That Express Conditions, 934 DLS, 922 Semicolons, 928 Adverb Clauses, 930	Context Clues, 924
Brief Introduction, 940 Travel Comics, 940	Animal Defenses, 940	DLS, 935 Subordinating Conjunctions, 936	
Talk Show Skit, 947 Making a Speech, 947	Nobel Lists, 947	DLS, 941 Semicolons, 942 Adverb Clauses, 944	Using Reference Materials, 946
Speaking and Listening, 946	Touring Steinbeck's California, 947		
Picturing Text Structure, 949		Maintaining Consistency of Tone / Punctuating Clauses, 952 Revising & Editing, 953	

UNIT FIVE
RESOURCE MANAGEMENT GUIDE
PART 1

To introduce the theme/literary period of this unit, use Fine Art Transparencies T29–31 in the Communications Transparencies and Copymasters.

	Unit Resource Book	Assessment	Integrated Technology and Media	Additional Support: Literary Analysis Transparencies
A White Heron *pp. 822–835*	• Summary p. 4 • Active Reading p. 5 • Literary Analysis p. 6 • Words to Know p. 7 • Grammar p. 8 • Selection Quiz p. 9	• Selection Test, Formal Assessment pp. 135–136 Test Generator	Audio Library LaserLinks, Teacher's SourceBook p. 43	• Symbols and Figurative Language T21
Birches *pp. 838–842*	• Active Reading p. 10 • Literary Analysis p. 11	• Selection Test, Formal Assessment pp. 137–138 Test Generator	Audio Library Video: Literature in Performance, Video Resource Book pp. 31–34	• Symbols and Figurative Language T21
For the New Year, 1981 **Pride** *pp. 843–847*	• Active Reading p. 12 • Literary Analysis p. 13	• Selection Test, Formal Assessment pp. 139–140 Test Generator	Audio Library	• Symbols and Figurative Language T21
Like the Sun *pp. 848–855*	• Summary p. 14 • Active Reading p. 15 • Literary Analysis p. 16 • Words to Know p. 17 • Grammar p. 18 • Selection Quiz p. 19	• Selection Test, Formal Assessment pp. 141–142 Test Generator	Audio Library LaserLinks, Teacher's SourceBook pp. 44–45 Research Starter www.mcdougallittell.com	

Writing Workshop: Interpretive Essay

Unit Five Resource Book
- Prewriting p. 21
- Drafting and Elaboration p. 22
- Peer Response Guide pp. 23–24
- Revising, Editing, and Proofreading p. 25
- Student Models pp. 26–28
- Rubric for Evaluation p. 29

Writing Coach

Writing Transparencies and Copymasters T11, T20, C33

Teacher's Guide to Assessment and Portfolio Use

Unit Assessment	Unit Technology
• Unit Five, Part 1 Test, Formal Assessment pp. 143–144 Test Generator • Unit Five Integrated Test, Integrated Assessment pp. 25–30	ClassZone www.mcdougallittell.com Electronic Teacher Tools Electronic Library

T = Transparency   C = Copymaster

Reading and Critical Thinking Transparencies	Grammar Transparencies and Copymasters	Vocabulary Transparencies and Copymasters	Writing Transparencies and Copymasters	Communications Transparencies and Copymasters
• Open-ended Question Frame T59	• Daily Language SkillBuilder T23 • Identifying Independent and Subordinate Clauses C109 • Adverb Clauses I C112	• Context Clues C77 • Word Origins C78	• Writing Process T1, T2 • Sensory Word List T14 • Figurative Language and Sound Devices T15	• Formal Presentations T10
• Organizational Chart: Horizontal T51	• Daily Language SkillBuilder T23 • Conjunctive Adverbs C76		• Figurative Language and Sound Devices T15 • Focused Description C26 • Interpretive Essay C33	• Evaluation Matrix: Film/Video T7
• Making Inferences T7	• Daily Language SkillBuilder T24 • Correlative Conjunctions I C78		• Effective Language T13 • Figurative Language and Sound Devices T15 • Poem C27	
• Predicting Outcomes T2	• Daily Language SkillBuilder T24 • Adjective Clauses C111	• Word Origins C79	• Achieving Conciseness T21 • The Uses of Dialogue T24 • Interpretive Essay C33	• Interviewing T9

STUDENTS ACQUIRING ENGLISH

The **Spanish Study Guide,** pp. 164–178, includes language support for the following pages:

- Family and Community Involvement (per unit)
- Selection Summaries and Vocabulary
- Active Reading
- Literary Analysis

UNIT FIVE
RESOURCE MANAGEMENT GUIDE
PART 2

To introduce the theme/literary period of this unit, use Fine Art Transparencies T29–31 in the Communications Transparencies and Copymasters.

	Unit Resource Book	Assessment	Integrated Technology and Media	Additional Support: Literary Analysis Transparencies
The Witness for the Prosecution *pp. 871–892*	• Summary p. 30 • Active Reading p. 31 • Literary Analysis p.32 • Words to Know p. 33 • Grammar p. 34 • Selection Quiz p. 35	• Selection Test, Formal Assessment pp. 145–146 Test Generator	Audio Library Research Starter www.mcdougallittell.com	• Drama: Dialogue T10
The Balek Scales *pp. 893–902*	• Summary p. 36 • Active Reading p. 37 • Literary Analysis p. 38 • Words to Know p. 39 • Selection Quiz p. 40	• Selection Test, Formal Assessment pp. 147–148 Test Generator	Audio Library LaserLinks, Teacher's SourceBook p. 46	• Mood and Tone T20
The Street/La Calle I am Not I/Yo No Soy Yo *pp. 903–907*	• Active Reading p. 41 • Literary Analysis p. 42	• Selection Test, Formal Assessment pp. 149–150 Test Generator	Audio Library LaserLinks, Teacher's SourceBook p. 47	• Poetry: Form T7
The Flood *from* **The Grapes of Wrath** *pp. 922–934*	• Summary p. 44 • Active Reading p. 45 • Literary Analysis p. 46 • Words to Know p. 47 • Grammar p. 48 • Selection Quiz p. 49	• Selection Test, Formal Assessment pp. 151–152 Test Generator	Audio Library NetActivities	
from **Travels with Charley** *pp. 935–940*	• Summary p. 50 • Active Reading p. 51 • Literary Analysis p. 52 • Selection Quiz p. 53	• Selection Test, Formal Assessment pp. 153–154 Test Generator	Audio Library Research Starter www.mcdougallittell.com NetActivities	• Irony: Verbal T16
Letter to Edith Mirrielees *from* **Nobel Prize Acceptance Speech** *pp. 941–947*	• Summary p. 54 • Active Reading p. 55 • Literary Analysis p. 56 • Selection Quiz p. 57	• Selection Test, Formal Assessment pp. 155–156 Test Generator	Research Starter www.mcdougallittell.com NetActivities	• Mood and Tone T20

Writing Workshop: Autobiographical Incident

Unit Five Resource Book
- Prewriting p. 58
- Drafting and Elaboration p. 59
- Peer Response Guide pp. 60–61
- Revising, Editing, and Proofreading p. 62
- Student Models pp. 63–68
- Rubric for Evaluation p. 69

Writing Coach

Writing Transparencies and Copymasters T11, T20, C35

Teacher's Guide to Assessment and Portfolio Use

Unit Assessment
- Unit Five, Part 2 Test, Formal Assessment pp. 157–158
- Test Generator
- Unit Five Integrated Test, Integrated Assessment pp. 25–30

Unit Technology
- ClassZone www.mcdougallittell.com
- Electronic Teacher Tools
- Electronic Library

T = Transparency C = Copymaster

Reading and Critical Thinking Transparencies	Grammar Transparencies and Copymasters	Vocabulary Transparencies and Copymasters	Writing Transparencies and Copymasters	Communications Transparencies and Copymasters
	• Daily Language SkillBuilder T25 • Adverb Clauses II C113 • Noun Clauses C116	• Synonyms C80 • Antonyms C81	• Effective Language T13	• Impromptu Speaking: Dialogue, Role-Play, Debate T13
	• Daily Language SkillBuilder T25 • Sentence Structure C120	• Context Clues C82 • Meanings of Roots C83	• Opinion Statement C25 • Autobiographical Incident C34	
	• Daily Language SkillBuilder T25 • Correlative Conjunctions II C79		• Sensory Word List T14 • Poem C27	• Impromptu Speaking: Dialogue, Role-Play, Debate T13
• Determining Author's Purpose and Audience T19 • Organizational Chart: Horizontal T51	• Daily Language SkillBuilder T26 • Adverb Clauses III C114 • Semicolons I C167	• Context Clues C84	• Effective Language T13 • Achieving Conciseness T21	• Dramatic Reading T12 • Verbal Strategies T14 • Nonverbal Strategies T15
• Noting Details T9 • Locating Information Using Print References T32 • Locating Information Using Databases and the Internet T34	• Daily Language SkillBuilder T26 • Subordinating Conjunctions C80		• Varying Sentence Openers and Closers T18 • Point of View T23 • Persuasive Essay C30	• Impromptu Speaking: Dialogue, Role-Play, Debate T13
	• Daily Language SkillBuilder T26 • Adverb Clauses IV C115 • Semicolons II C168		• Levels of Language T12 • Achieving Conciseness T21	• Interviewing T9 • Formal Presentations T10

STUDENTS ACQUIRING ENGLISH

The **Spanish Study Guide,** pp. 179–198, includes language support for the following pages:

- Family and Community Involvement (per unit)
- Selection Summaries and Vocabulary
- Active Reading
- Literary Analysis

Selection	SkillBuilder Sentences	Suggested Answers
A White Heron	**1.** The woods in june is filled with shadows from the glimmering sun set. **2.** Being very shy, the bold handsome young man frightens sylvia.	**1.** The woods in **J**une **are** filled with shadows from the glimmering **sunset**. **2.** Being very shy, **Sylvia is frightened by** the bold**,** handsome young man.
Birches	**1.** The narrator remember his self, as a child. **2.** When living in Western Massachusetts, the dark forests made me think that monsters living their.	**1.** The narrator **remembers himself** as a child. **2.** When **I lived** in **w**estern Massachusetts, the dark forests made me think that monsters **lived there**.
For the New Year, 1981 Pride	**1.** Wait a minute I got to run get my checkbook out the car so's I can pay you. **2.** There's two main conflicts in this story, the war between the Irish and the English, and the main characters struggle with poverty.	**1.** Wait a minute**.** I **have** to run **and** get my checkbook out **of** the car **so that** I can pay you. **2.** **There are** two main conflicts in this story**:** the war between the Irish and the English, and the main character**'s** struggle with poverty.

Selection	SkillBuilder Sentences	Suggested Answers
Like the Sun	**1.** Telling the truth can be real difficult if you think it might effect you're relationships. **2.** How would the day been different if Sekhar had announced his purpose to people as soon as he saw them so, that they all knew what was he doing?	**1.** Telling the truth can be **very** difficult if you think it might **affect your** relationships. **2.** How would the day **have** been different if Sekhar had announced his purpose to people as soon as he saw them, so that they all knew what **he was** doing?
The Witness for the Prosecution	**1.** Does she skip ahead in mystery storys to see whom is guilty, or do she wait to find out? **2.** I was frightened by the Mystery story I slept with all the lights on	**1.** Does she skip ahead in mystery stor**ies** to see **who** is guilty, or **does** she wait to find out? **2.** I was frightened by the **m**ystery story**.** I slept with all the lights on**.**
The Balek Scales	**1.** Heinrich Böll who was German won a nobel prize. **2.** One of Bölls novels "The Train Was On Time" is about a young, German, soldier.	**1.** Heinrich Böll**,** who was German**,** won a **N**obel **P**rize. **2.** One of Böll**'s** novels, **<u>The Train Was On Time</u>,** is about a young German soldier.
The Street/La Calle I Am Not I/Yo No Soy Yo	**1.** The basketball game starts and my brother still wasn't in his seat. **2.** Our team was suppose to lose but we came back at the end and won.	**1.** The basketball game **started,** and my brother still wasn't in his seat. **2.** Our team was **supposed** to lose**,** but we came back at the end and won.

DAILY LANGUAGE SKILLBUILDERS

Selection	SkillBuilder Sentences	Suggested Answers
The Flood	**1.** The ice cream, because Ramon was still hungry after dinner, tasted delicious. **2.** Diane was eager to learn how to fly an airplane she loved flying	**1. Because Ramon was still hungry after dinner, t**he ice cream tasted delicious. **2.** Diane was eager to learn how to fly an airplane**. S**he loved flying.
from Travels with Charley	**1.** The shoes that I bought last week, they don't fit very good. **2.** Although, my grandfather is over seventy years old. He still goes to work everyday.	**1.** The shoes that I bought last **week don't** fit very **well**. **2.** Although my grandfather is over seventy years old**, h**e still goes to work **every day**.
Letter to Edith Mirrielees *from* Nobel Prize Acceptance Speech	**1.** John loves apples, however; he hates apple pie. **2.** We waited patiently for the fish to start biting, unfortunately; we never catched any.	**1.** John loves apples; however, he hates apple pie. **2.** We waited patiently for the fish to start biting**. U**nfortunately, we never **caught** any.

INTEGRATING GRAMMAR AND LITERATURE: GRAMMAR PLANNER

Grammar Focus by Unit	Unit One	Unit Two	Unit Three	Unit Four	Unit Five	Unit Six
	Parts of Speech	The Sentence and Its Parts	Verbs and Verbals	Phrases	Clauses	Special Sentence Structures

The Language of Literature offers several options for integrating grammar instruction and literature.

- Each unit has a specific grammar focus. The grammar focus for this unit is highlighted on the planning chart. Categories of grammar skills for this unit are shown in red.
- The Pupil's Edition includes instructive features entitled *Grammar in Context*. The instruction in these features arises from the selections and relates to the grammar focus for each unit.
- The Writing Workshops in the Pupil's Edition include grammar tips that help students produce error-free drafts.
- Mini Lessons in the Teacher's Edition complement the instruction in the *Grammar in Context* features. Additional Mini Lessons relate to the grammar focus for each unit as well as to the literature.
- Daily Language SkillBuilders in the Teacher's Edition provide students with ongoing proofreading practice and reinforce punctuation, spelling, grammar and usage, and capitalization.
- Grammar Copymasters and Transparencies, which may be used independently or in conjunction with Mini Lessons in the Teacher's Edition, present grammar in a traditional, systematic sequence.

PE instruction shown in black
TE Mini Lessons shown in green

Part 1

Parts of Speech

Conjunctive Adverbs
"Birches," p. 840

Correlative Conjunctions
"For the New Year, 1981," "Pride," p. 845

Using Clauses

Independent vs. Subordinate Clauses
"A White Heron," p. 830

Relative Clauses
Writing Workshop, p. 866

Adjective Clauses
"Like the Sun," p. 855
"Like the Sun," pp. 854–855

Adverb Clauses
"A White Heron," p. 835
"A White Heron," p. 834

End Marks and Commas

Commas with Nonessential Clauses and Phrases
Writing Workshop, p. 866

Style

Varying Sentence Structure
Writing Workshop, p. 866

Part 2

Parts of Speech

Correlative Conjunctions
"The Street/La Calle," "I Am Not I/ Yo No Soy Yo," p. 907

Subordinating Conjunctions
from *Travels with Charley,* p. 936

Parts of the Sentence

Run-on Sentences
Writing Workshop, p. 953

Using Clauses

Adverb Clauses
"The Flood," p. 934
"The Flood," p. 930
"The Witness for the Prosecution," p. 878
Letter to Edith Mirrielees, from *Nobel Prize Acceptance Speech,* p. 944

Noun Clauses
"The Witness for the Prosecution," p. 892
"The Witness for the Prosecution," p. 892

Sentence Structure
"The Balek Scales," pp. 896–897

Verb Usage

Verb Tenses
Writing Workshop, p. 953

Using Modifiers

Avoiding Double Negatives
Writing Workshop, p. 953

End Marks and Commas

Other Uses of Commas
Writing Workshop, p. 953

Other Punctuation

Semicolons
"The Flood," p. 928
Letter to Edith Mirrielees, from *Nobel Prize Acceptance Speech,* p. 942

PART 1 Simple Truths

What comes to mind when you hear the phrase *simple truths*? Perhaps you think of childhood, of innocent times and carefree play. Or perhaps you think of those who shared their wisdom with you, easing your path along the roads of life. If you have a skeptical turn of mind, you may even doubt that any truth is simple. In this part of Unit Five, you will encounter a variety of "truths," some of which are not as simple as they may appear.

ACTIVITY

In writing, describe a time when you discovered an important truth about a situation, another person, or yourself. How did the discovery affect you, and what were its consequences?

818

Symbolism and figurative language

make it possible for human beings to think and communicate beyond the limitations of language. Without the ability to convey meanings other than the literal definitions of words, we humans could not express the complexity or range that our minds are capable of. Moreover, our world would not be as meaningful. What would a ring, a rose, a flag, or a trophy be without its symbolic meaning? All of us—from scientists to priests, politicians to cheerleaders—use symbols and figurative language to help formulate what we want to say.

Symbols: When Less Says More

A **symbol** is a person, place, or object that stands for something beyond itself. The word *symbol* comes from a Greek word that means "to throw together," suggesting the power of a symbol to bring together different meanings, to evoke emotions as well as to express ideas. Most **cultural**, or **conventional**, **symbols**–national symbols (such as the U.S. flag), religious symbols, and symbols for peace (a dove)–usually have standard interpretations. But these symbols also tend to have a personal significance as well as a cultural one.

A **literary symbol** takes its meaning from the context of a literary work. For example, in the story "Initiation" (page 397), Sylvia Plath used sparrows–"pale gray-brown birds in a flock, one like the other, all exactly alike"–to symbolize the conformity of the sorority girls. In contrast, the heather birds–"strong and proud in their freedom"–represent the freedom that Millicent, the main character, comes to respect. Ironically, the sorority initiation becomes the means by which Millicent discovers the importance of her individuality. The initiation thus becomes a symbolic act that changes in meaning from representing Millicent's entry into an exclusive group to symbolizing the beginning of her independence.

YOUR TURN In the story "A White Heron," Sarah Orne Jewett describes a great pine tree as a symbol of unspoiled nature. Study the passage at the right. What details help you interpret the tree's symbolism?

SYMBOLISM

Half a mile from home, at the farther edge of the woods, where the land was highest, a great pine tree stood, the last of its generation. Whether it was left for a boundary mark, or for what reason, no one could say; the woodchoppers who had felled its mates were dead and gone long ago, and a whole forest of sturdy trees, pines and oaks and maples, had grown again. But the stately head of this old pine towered above them all and made a landmark for sea and shore miles and miles away. Sylvia knew it well. She had always believed that whoever climbed to the top of it could see the ocean; and the little girl had often laid her hand on the great rough trunk and looked wistfully at those dark boughs that the wind always stirred, no matter how hot and still the air might be below. Now she thought of the tree with a new excitement, for why, if one climbed it at break of day, could not one see all the world? . . .

—Sarah Orne Jewett, "A White Heron"

LEARNING the Language of LITERATURE

OVERVIEW

Objectives

- understand the uses of symbolism and figurative language in literary works
- identify literary symbols and interpret their meanings
- identify types of figurative language: simile, metaphor, and personification
- analyze the meanings of similes, metaphors, and personification used in a literary work

Teaching the Lesson

This lesson identifies terms related to symbolism and figurative language and analyzes their uses in literary works.

Introducing the Concepts

Have students mention examples of symbolism and figurative language they have encountered in their daily lives, such as flags, colors, shapes of street signs, and advertisements and billboards.

Presenting the Concepts

Symbolism

Have students recall the use of symbolism in one of the literary works they have read so far. What associations did they connect to the symbol in the story? Ask students how their associations affected their responses to the story. Remind them that since a symbol can take on many associations for each reader, a literary symbol also will take on many meanings.

YOUR TURN

Details such as the tree's location on high land at the forest's edge, its status as a boundary landmark, the mystery and length of its survival, and its height above the more recently planted trees help the reader to see the tree as a symbol for unspoiled nature.

Figurative Language: A Few Good Words

Simile

Caution students that for a simile to be effective and give the overall sense of the idea the figure of speech represents, the comparison must be apt. The unlike things the simile compares have to be comparable to allow the reader to visualize or sense the meaning.

Metaphor

Remind students that, since a metaphor can be implied or suggested, the metaphor can be in the form of an adjective, and one half of the comparison can be left out.

Personification

Remind students that since neither personification nor metaphor uses the words *like* or *as* for its comparisons, these figures of speech can be hard to tell apart at first glance. Alert students that personification can refer to human physical characteristics and parts of the body as well as human emotions and actions.

YOUR TURN

In Poe's "The Pit and the Pendulum," the simile communicates that the narrator's sense of anticipation or expectation feels like an electric shock. It creates a sensory image because the reader knows what an electric shock feels like and can relate this to the writer's words.

Shakespeare's personification communicates how the hot sun is similar to an eye in the sky staring down at human beings and gives the sense that humans are under the scrutiny of heaven.

Atwood uses an implied metaphor comparing the U. S.-Canadian Border to a one-way mirror to suggest that Canadians stupidly compare themselves to and take their lead from Americans, who in turn pay no attention or are unaware of Canada and Canadians.

O'Brien uses a simile, comparing the transfer of courage to the inheritance of money, and then extends the metaphor by comparing courage to the inheritance which is invested, saved in a bank account, and spent. The extended simile therefore compares courage and wealth.

Figurative Language: A Few Good Words

The difference between **literal** and **figurative language** is similar to the difference between the **denotation**, or the dictionary definition, of a word and its **connotation**, or mental associations. For example, think about the expression "caught between a rock and a hard place." Taken literally, the phrase doesn't mean much. It only makes sense as a way of expressing what it feels like to be stuck in a bad situation. Like symbols, **figures of speech** (another term for figurative language) say a lot with a few well-chosen words. Here are some common figures of speech:

- A **simile** makes a comparison between two unlike things using the word *like* or *as*. For example, R. K. Narayan's story "Like the Sun" (page 849) opens with a simile: "Truth, Sekhar reflected, is like the sun." The simile compares an abstract concept (truth) to a concrete one (sun), thus helping readers understand not only that truth is difficult to face but why.
- A **metaphor** is a comparison between two unlike things that have something in common. A metaphor does not use the word *like* or *as*. Carl Sandburg's poem "Moon Rondeau" (page 258) begins with a metaphor: "'Love is a door we shall open together.'" Sometimes a metaphor does not make a direct comparison but instead merely suggests one.
- A **personification** attributes human qualities to an object, animal, or idea. In "Tonight I Can Write" (page 352), Pablo Neruda personifies the wind in this line: "The night wind revolves in the sky and sings." This personification appears to make the wind a temporary companion to the poet in his sadness and in his solitary act of creating.

YOUR TURN Study the quotations at the right. Identify whether each is a simile, metaphor, or personification. Then analyze what the figure of speech communicates, and how.

FIGURATIVE LANGUAGE

I felt every fiber in my frame thrill as if I had touched the wire of a galvanic battery.

—Edgar Allan Poe, "The Pit and the Pendulum"

Sometime too hot the eye of heaven shines,

And often is his gold complexion dimmed;

—William Shakespeare, "Sonnet 18"

The noses of a great many Canadians resemble Porky Pig's. This comes from spending so much time pressing them against the longest undefended one-way mirror in the world.

—Margaret Atwood, "Through the One-Way Mirror"

Courage, I seemed to think, comes to us in finite quantities, like an inheritance, and by being frugal and stashing it away, and letting it earn interest, we steadily increase our moral capital in preparation for that day when the account must be drawn down.

—Tim O'Brien, "On the Rainy River"

You can't go through life without asking questions. Questions help guide your thinking in specific ways. Sometimes a good question is worth more than the answer because it directs you to think about important issues. The strategies on this page can help you ask questions about what you read.

Questioning

Asking questions about a literary work focuses your concentration while you're reading and keeps you alert to important changes. You also feel more involved with what you read when you look for reasons behind events or motives for a character's feelings and actions. How did that happen? Why does the character make that choice? What does this word mean? How can the character possibly get out of this situation? These are the kinds of questions that you need to ask as you read.

1 Strategies for Asking Questions About a Literary Work

- Pay attention to all questions that naturally occur to you as you read. Trust your instincts.
- **Question** your own response to what you read: Why was I surprised by that? Why don't I like this character? Why am I confused here? Questions such as these can pinpoint key aspects of a work or help **clarify** what you may have missed.
- If you are confused, ask yourself what is confusing you. Is it the sequence of events, the character's motivation, the wording of a sentence? Then you can narrow your question to address the exact source of your confusion.
- Keep track of your questions as you read, and supply the answers when you find them. Sometimes the answers to one question can lead to a new, perhaps more important, question.

2 Strategies for Asking Questions About Symbols

- Look for references to concrete objects, and **question** whether they could be symbols.
- Notice objects or places that are emphasized by lengthy descriptions, repetition, or special placement in a work.
- **Question** whether a place, object, or minor character is essential to the theme of a literary work. If so, then chances are it is a symbol.

"On the Rainy River"

Questions	Answers
Why is the narrator so ashamed to tell this story?	because he thinks he's a coward for not running away to Canada
Why is he giving all these details about the meatpacking plant?	because it makes him (and me) think about killing and war

3 Strategies for Asking Questions about Figurative Language

- Ask yourself what connotations you have for the words in the figure of speech. What feelings does the phrase evoke?
- **Question** why the author chose a particular comparison and not another.
- **Visualize** the image that the figurative phrase evokes. What does this picture tell you about the meaning of the phrase?

Need More Help?

Remember that active readers use the essential reading strategies explained on page 7: **visualize, predict, clarify, question, connect, evaluate, monitor.**

The Active Reader: Skills and Strategies

OVERVIEW

Objectives

- ask detailed, focused questions and answer them with textual evidence and experience
- use questions to develop a challenging, analytical reading experience

Teaching the Lesson

The strategies on this page will help students learn and apply specific skills for questioning a literary work, symbols, and figurative language.

Presenting the Strategies

Make sure students understand how to question critically by using an example from their everyday life or a hypothetical situation.

1 Asking Questions About a Literary Work

Help students focus their questions by creating simple cause-and-effect charts, characterization charts, and plot flow charts.

2 Asking Questions About Symbols

Encourage students to use their questioning techniques to examine the author's choice of symbols as well as the symbols' meanings. Ask students whether the symbols are traditional and archetypal or convey a more individualized meaning.

3 Asking Questions About Figurative Language

Have students jot down their initial impressions of a figurative phrase, then have them connect those impressions to traditional metaphors and similes. Ask students whether the second set of connections evokes a different series of questions or answers their previous ones.

OVERVIEW

This selection is included in the **Grade 10 Interactive Reader.**

Objectives

1. understand and appreciate a **short story (Literary Analysis)**
2. understand **symbol** as a literary device **(Literary Analysis)**
3. ask **questions** about a story **(Active Reading)**

Summary

While walking home to her grandmother's New England farm, nine-year-old Sylvia encounters a friendly young man who is hunting rare birds to add to his collection of stuffed birds. The young man spends the night at the farm and tells Sylvia and her grandmother that he is looking for a white heron he has glimpsed in the area. He offers ten dollars to anyone who will help him find the bird. Sylvia has seen the bird, and she knows that her grandmother could use the money. She spends the next day helping the young man search the woods. Early the following morning, Sylvia climbs a towering pine at the edge of the woods because she wants to discover the heron's nest, surprise the man with its location, and collect the reward as well as the man's gratitude. She locates the heron's nest in the marsh, but when she returns to her grandmother's house, she decides not to tell the man about her discovery. He departs without killing the bird.

Thematic Link

Sylvia discovers that **simple truths**, like the living beauty of a rare white heron, matter more than money.

5-Minute Warm-Up

Daily Language SkillBuilder

Have students **proofread** the display sentences on page 817i and write them correctly. The sentences also appear on Transparency 23 of **Grammar Transparencies and Copymasters.**

Mini Lesson: Preteaching Vocabulary

If you would like to preteach the WORDS TO KNOW for this selection, use the Mini Lesson, p. 824.

A White Heron

Short Story by SARAH ORNE JEWETT

"I can't think of anything I should like so much as to find that heron's nest."

Connect to Your Life

What Matters Most Where do your loyalties lie? Identify some of the people, places, ideals, or values to which you are most committed. Then create a bar graph, like the one shown, to rate the strength of your loyalties.

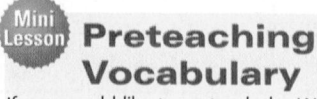

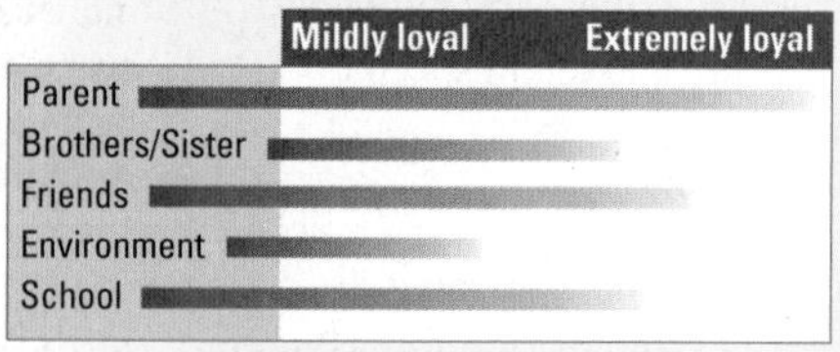

Build Background

Water Bird In the story you are about to read, a white heron plays a prominent role in the test of a young girl's loyalty. Herons are graceful birds with sticklike legs, narrow heads, and long, slender necks. They live near water and hunt for their food by wading in streams, marshes, and swamps. Shy of human populations, they usually live in isolated areas, and they build their nests in tall bushes or in trees to help protect their young from predators. Seeing these large birds hunched in their treetop perches is a remarkable, often startling experience.

Sarah Orne Jewett, the author of "A White Heron," grew up in an environment much like the one described in this story, which is set in rural Maine in the late 1800s. In her writing, Jewett was able to catch the essence of a particular time and place in America by re-creating the life and landscape that she loved as a child.

WORDS TO KNOW
Vocabulary Preview

discreetly, elusive, ponderous, squalor, traverse

Focus Your Reading

LITERARY ANALYSIS | SYMBOL Sylvia, the main **character** in the story, loves her outdoor life on her grandmother's farm. When she thinks of her former life in a crowded manufacturing town, Sylvia envisions a single flower:

> ***She thought often with wistful compassion of a wretched geranium that belonged to a town neighbor.***

In this passage the geranium is a **symbol,** something that represents an idea beyond itself. The symbol of the geranium represents how Sylvia felt about life in town. As you read the story, look out for other symbols from the world of nature.

ACTIVE READING | QUESTIONING Being an active reader involves making observations and asking questions about a story. Searching for reasons behind events and characters' feelings can help you understand a work. Questions you might ask yourself as you read include the following:

- Why do the **characters** behave as they do?
- What is the central **conflict** in the story?
- What is the significance of events in the story?
- Does any object, place, or event have a **symbolic** meaning?

Think of each of your answers as a hypothesis, which further reading of the text will help to prove or disprove.

READER'S NOTEBOOK As you read, jot down questions whenever you reach a point in the story that you find unclear or noteworthy. As you continue reading, make further notes of anything in the text that helps to answer your questions.

VIDEODISC **LaserLinks: Background for Reading**
Science Connection

LESSON RESOURCES

UNIT FIVE RESOURCE BOOK, pp. 5–6

ASSESSMENT RESOURCES

Formal Assessment, pp. 135–136

Teacher's Guide to Assessment and Portfolio Use

Test Generator

SKILLS TRANSPARENCIES AND COPYMASTERS

Literary Analysis

- Symbols and Figurative Language, T21 (for Cooperative Learning Activity, p. 833)

Reading and Critical Thinking

- Open-Ended Question Frame, T59 (for Reader's Notebook, p. 822)

Grammar

- Identifying Independent and Subordinate Clauses, C109 (for Mini Lesson, p. 830)
- Adverb Clauses I, C112 (for Mini Lesson, p. 834)

Vocabulary

- Context Clues, C77 (for Mini Lesson, p. 824)
- Word Origins, C78 (for Mini Lesson, p. 826)

Writing

- Writing Process, T1, T2 (for Writing Option 1, p. 834)
- Sensory Word List, T14 (for Writing Option 2, p. 834)
- Figurative Language and Sound Devices, T15 (for Writing Option 2, p. 834)

Communications

- Formal Presentations, T10 (for Activities & Explorations 1, p. 834)

INTEGRATED TECHNOLOGY

Audio Library

LaserLinks

- Science Connection: Herons and Maine. See **Teacher's SourceBook,** p. 43.

Visit our website:
www.mcdougallittell.com

A White Heron

Sarah Orne Jewett

The woods were already filled with shadows one June evening, just before eight o'clock, though a bright sunset still glimmered faintly among the trunks of the trees. A little girl was driving home her cow, a plodding, dilatory,[1] provoking creature in her behavior, but a valued companion for all that. They were going away from whatever light there was, and striking deep into the woods, but their feet were familiar with the path, and it was no matter whether their eyes could see it or not.

There was hardly a night the summer through when the old cow could be found waiting at the pasture bars; on the contrary, it was her greatest pleasure to hide herself away among the high huckleberry bushes, and though she wore a loud bell she had made the discovery that if one stood perfectly still it would not ring. So Sylvia had to hunt for her until she found her, and call Co'! Co'!

1. **dilatory** (dĭl′ə-tôr′ē): tending to postpone or delay.

Customizing Instruction

Less Proficient Readers

Have students ask themselves the following questions as they read the story:

- Who are the main characters?
  Answer: Sylvia, her grandmother, and a young man hunting birds
- What is the young man hoping to do?
  Answer: kill a white heron for his bird collection
- What decision does Sylvia finally make about the heron?
  Answer: not to tell the young man where to find it

Students Acquiring English

Students may have trouble with the story's many ornate and difficult sentences. Read the first four paragraphs aloud, making sure students understand who Sylvia is, where she comes from, and why she loves nature.

Use **Spanish Study Guide** for additional support, pp. 167–169.

Gifted and Talented

As they read the selection, have students watch for specific passages that show how the author establishes Sylvia's unique relationship with the forest.

Possible Responses:

- page 824—"She was not often in the woods so late as this, and it made her feel as if she were a part of the gray shadows and moving leaves."
- page 826—"Suddenly this little woods-girl is horror-stricken."
- page 831—". . . the least twigs held themselves to advantage this light, weak creature on her way! The old pine must have loved his new dependent."

BLOCK SCHEDULING: MANAGING TIME

If your schedule requires that you cover the lesson objectives in a shorter time, use . . .

- Preparing to Read, p. 822
- Thinking Through the Literature, p. 833
- Vocabulary in Action, p. 834
- Grammar in Context, p. 835

If you want to take advantage of longer class time, use . . .

- TE Teaching Options: Preteaching WORDS TO KNOW, p. 824; Viewing and Representing, pp. 825, 828; Vocabulary Strategies, p. 826; Cross Curricular Link, p. 827; Standardized Test Practice, p. 832
- Choices & Challenges and Author Activity, pp. 834–835

Reading and Analyzing

Reading Skills and Strategies: PREVIEWING

Have students look through the story, paying close attention to the vocabulary at the bottom of each page. If necessary, discuss the Build Background feature on water birds on p. 822. Before students begin reading, give them a brief summary of the story.

Active Reading QUESTIONING

As students read the selection, have them write down questions about events and characters. Encourage students to find answers while they read the selection. After reading the story, ask students whether they were able to locate the answers to their questions. Discuss any questions for which students have not found answers.

Use **Unit Five Resource Book,** p. 5 for additional support.

Literary Analysis SYMBOL

A symbol is something that stands for an idea or thing beyond itself. As they read the selection, invite students to jot down in their Reader's Notebooks any objects or characters that seem to represent something other than themselves.

Use **Unit Five Resource Book,** p. 6 for additional support.

with never an answering Moo, until her childish patience was quite spent. If the creature had not given good milk and plenty of it, the case would have seemed very different to her owners. Besides, Sylvia had all the time there was, and very little use to make of it. Sometimes in pleasant weather it was a consolation to look upon the cow's pranks as an intelligent attempt to play hide-and-seek, and as the child had no playmates she lent herself to this amusement with a good deal of zest. Though this chase had been so long that the wary animal herself had given an unusual signal of her whereabouts, Sylvia had only laughed when she came upon Mistress Moolly at the swamp-side, and urged her affectionately homeward with a twig of birch leaves. The old cow was not inclined to wander farther; she even turned in the right direction for once as they left the pasture, and stepped along the road at a good pace. She was quite ready to be milked now, and seldom stopped to browse. Sylvia wondered what her grandmother would say because they were so late. It was a great while since she had left home at half past five o'clock, but everybody knew the difficulty of making this errand a short one. Mrs. Tilley had chased the hornéd torment too many summer evenings herself to blame anyone else for lingering, and was only thankful as she waited that she had Sylvia, nowadays, to give such valuable assistance. The good woman suspected that Sylvia loitered occasionally on her own account; there never was such a child for straying about out-of-doors since the world was made! Everybody said that it was a good change for a little maid who had tried to grow for eight years in a crowded manufacturing town, but, as for Sylvia herself, it seemed as if she never had been alive at all before she came to live at the farm. She thought often with wistful compassion of a wretched geranium that belonged to a town neighbor.

"'Afraid of folks,'" old Mrs. Tilley said to herself with a smile after she had made the unlikely choice of Sylvia from her daughter's houseful of children and was returning to the farm. "'Afraid of folks,' they said! I guess she
won't be troubled no great with 'em up to the old 1
place!" When they reached the door of the lonely house and stopped to unlock it, and the cat came to purr loudly and rub against them, a deserted pussy, indeed, but fat with young robins, Sylvia whispered that this was a beautiful place to live in, and she never should wish to go home.

The companions followed the shady wood-road, the cow taking slow steps and the child very fast ones. The cow stopped long at the brook to drink, as if the pasture were not half a swamp, and Sylvia stood still and waited, letting her bare feet cool themselves in the shoal[2] water, while the great twilight moths struck softly against her. She waded on through the brook as the cow moved away, and listened to the thrushes with a heart that beat fast with pleasure. There was a stirring in the great boughs overhead. They were full of little birds and beasts that seemed to be wide-awake, and going about their world, or else saying good night to each other in sleepy twitters. Sylvia herself felt sleepy as she walked along. However, it was not much farther to the house, and the air was soft and sweet. She was not often in the woods so late as this, and it made her feel as if she were a part of the gray shadows and the moving leaves. She was just thinking how long it seemed since she first came to the farm a year ago, and wondering if everything went on in the noisy town just the same as when she was there; the thought of the great red-faced boy who used to chase and frighten her made her hurry along the path to escape from the shadow of the trees.

2. **shoal** (shōl): shallow.

Teaching Options

Mini Lesson Preteaching Vocabulary

USING CONTEXT CLUES Call students' attention to the list of WORDS TO KNOW. Remind students that often they can infer the meaning of an unfamiliar word from the context in which the word is used. Use the model sentence to demonstrate the strategy of using context clues that provide inferences to word meaning.

MODEL SENTENCE:

The <u>ponderous</u> boulder was nearly impossible to move.

Instruction

- Write the model sentence on the chalkboard.
- Ask a volunteer to summarize the meaning of the sentence.
- Have students use the meaning of the sentence to infer the meanings of the word *ponderous.*
- Ask a volunteer to use the word *ponderous* in a sentence.

Use **Unit Five Resource Book,** p. 7 for additional support.

A lesson on using context clues appears on p. 56 in the Pupil's Edition.

Springtime (1885), Lionel Percy Smythe. Watercolor, 20¾″ × 15¼″, private collection. Photo by Christopher Newall.

Customizing Instruction

Students Acquiring English

1 Explain to students that the characters in this story speak in a nonstandard dialect of English. Tell students that *'em* means "them." Help students rephrase Mrs. Tilley's remarks in standard English.

Possible Response: "'Afraid of people,' they said! I guess she will not be greatly troubled by them at the old place!"

Mini Lesson Viewing and Representing

Springtime **by Lionel Percy Smythe**

ART APPRECIATION Like many late Victorians who were distressed by the crowded and competitive life in the cities, watercolorist Lionel Percy Smythe (1839–1918) focused on the beautiful and serene life of nature.

Application Have students consider similarities between the girl in the painting and Sylvia. Ask them how Smythe's watercolor complements Jewett's story.

Possible Responses: The girl in the painting, like Sylvia, seems at home in a natural setting. Jewett tells a story of the beauty of nature. Smythe, too, focuses on the beautiful and serene life of nature.

Reading and Analyzing

ACTIVE READING

A CLARIFY Possible Response: Before moving to her grandmother's, Sylvia lived in a crowded manufacturing town and was unhappy. At her grandmother's, Sylvia has freedom and solitude and is happy.

Reading Skills and Strategies: CLARIFYING

B Ask students why the hunter hopes that Sylvia has seen the bird.

Possible Response: He wants Sylvia to lead him to it so that he can shoot it and add it to his collection.

Literary Analysis: NARRATOR

Ask students whether the narrator speaks from a first-person point of view or a third-person point of view.

Answer: third-person point of view

Ask students how the story might be different if Sylvia were narrating in first person.

Possible Response: We would not have access to the hunter's thoughts and feelings and would have to infer them from Sylvia's observations.

ACTIVE READING

A **CLARIFY** How would you describe Sylvia's life before and after moving to her grandmother's farm?

Suddenly this little woods-girl is horror-stricken to hear a clear whistle not very far away. Not a bird's whistle, which would have a sort of friendliness, but a boy's whistle, determined, and somewhat aggressive. Sylvia left the cow to whatever sad fate might await her, and stepped discreetly aside into the bushes, but she was just too late. The enemy had discovered her, and called out in a very cheerful and persuasive tone, "Halloa, little girl, how far is
1 it to the road?" and trembling Sylvia answered almost inaudibly, "A good ways."

She did not dare to look boldly at the tall young man, who carried a gun over his shoulder, but she came out of her bush and again followed the cow, while he walked alongside.

"I have been hunting for some birds," the stranger said kindly, "and I have lost my way and need a friend very much. Don't be afraid," he added gallantly. "Speak up and tell me what your name is, and whether you think I can spend the night at your house, and go out gunning early in the morning."

Sylvia was more alarmed than before. Would not her grandmother consider her much to blame? But who could have foreseen such an accident as this? It did not seem to be her fault, and she hung her head as if the stem of it were broken, but managed to answer "Sylvy" with much effort when her companion again asked her name.

Mrs. Tilley was standing in the doorway when the trio came into view. The cow gave a loud moo by way of explanation.

"Yes, you'd better speak up for yourself, you old trial! Where'd she tucked herself away this time, Sylvy?" But Sylvia kept an awed silence; she knew by instinct that her grandmother did not comprehend the gravity[3] of the situation. She must be mistaking the stranger for one of the farmer lads of the region.

The young man stood his gun beside the door, and dropped a lumpy game bag beside it; then he bade Mrs. Tilley good evening, and repeated his wayfarer's story, and asked if he could have a night's lodging.

"Put me anywhere you like," he said. "I must be off early in the morning, before day; but I am very hungry, indeed. You can give me some milk at any rate, that's plain."

"Dear sakes, yes," responded the hostess, whose long slumbering hospitality seemed to be easily awakened. "You might fare better if you went out to the main road a mile or so, but you're welcome to what we've got. I'll milk right off, and you make yourself at home. You can sleep on husks or feathers," she proffered 2
graciously. "I raised them all myself. There's good pasturing for geese just below here toward the ma'sh.[4] Now step round and set a plate for the gentleman, Sylvy!" And Sylvia promptly stepped. She was glad to have something to do, and she was hungry herself.

It was a surprise to find so clean and comfortable a little dwelling in this New England wilderness. The young man had known the horrors of its most primitive housekeeping and the dreary squalor of that level of society which does not rebel at the companionship of hens. This was the best thrift of an old-fashioned farmstead, though on such a small scale that it seemed like a hermitage.[5] He listened eagerly to the old woman's quaint talk, he watched Sylvia's pale face and shining gray eyes with ever-growing enthusiasm, and insisted that this was the best supper he had eaten for a month, and afterward,

3. **gravity:** seriousness or importance.
4. **ma'sh:** dialect for *marsh,* a low-lying wetland.
5. **hermitage:** place where a hermit, or recluse, lives.

WORDS TO KNOW

discreetly (dĭ-skrēt'lē) *adv.* in a manner showing good judgment; cautiously
squalor (skwŏl'ər) *n.* a filthy and wretched condition

Teaching Options

Mini Lesson Vocabulary Strategy

RESEARCHING WORD ORIGINS: *DISCERNERE*

Instruction Remind students that they are expected to research word origins to understand meanings and extend their vocabulary. The word *discreet* is derived from the Latin word *discernere,* which means "to separate." Discuss with students the relationship between *discreet's* current meaning of "careful or prudent; showing good judgment in what one says or does" and the meaning of *discernere.*

Possible Response: Judgment is the ability to separate the good from the bad.

Practice Inform students that *discern, discrete,* and *discriminate* are all derived from *discernere.* Have students find these words' meanings in a dictionary, and then discuss the relationship of each word's meaning to the meaning of *discernere.*

Application As they read, have students use reference materials to research and record the word origins of at least five words from the selection. Where applicable, they should list words related with a common root.

Use **Vocabulary Transparencies and Copymasters,** p. 78, for more practice.

A lesson on researching word origins appears on p. 356 in the Pupil's Edition.

the new-made friends sat down in the doorway together while the moon came up.

Soon it would be berry time, and Sylvia was a great help at picking. The cow was a good milker, though a plaguy[6] thing to keep track of, the hostess gossiped frankly, adding presently that she had buried four children, so Sylvia's mother and a son (who might be dead) in California were all the children she had left. "Dan, my boy, was a great hand to go gunning," she explained sadly. "I never wanted for pa'tridges or gray squer'ls while he was to home. He's been a great wand'rer, I expect, and he's no hand to write letters. There, I don't blame him; I'd ha' seen the world myself if it had been so I could.

"Sylvia takes after him," the grandmother continued affectionately, after a minute's pause. "There ain't a foot o' ground she don't know her way over, and the wild creatur's counts her one o' themselves. Squer'ls she'll tame to come an' feed right out o' her hands, and all sorts o' birds. Last winter she got the jaybirds to bangeing[7] here, and I believe she'd 'a' scanted herself of her own meals to have plenty to throw out amongst 'em if I hadn't kep' watch. Anything but crows, I tell her, I'm willin' to help support—though Dan he had a tamed one o' them that did seem to have reason same as folks. It was round here a good spell after he went away. Dan an' his father they didn't hitch[8]—but he never held up his head ag'in after Dan had dared him an' gone off."

The guest did not notice this hint of family sorrows in his eager interest in something else.

"So Sylvy knows all about birds, does she?" he exclaimed, as he looked round at the little girl who sat, very demure but increasingly sleepy, in the moonlight. "I am making a collection of birds myself. I have been at it ever since I was a boy." (Mrs. Tilley smiled.) "There are two or three very rare ones I have been hunting for these five years. I mean to get them on my own ground if they can be found."

"Do you cage 'em up?" asked Mrs. Tilley doubtfully, in response to this enthusiastic announcement.

"Oh no, they're stuffed and preserved, dozens and dozens of them," said the ornithologist,[9] "and I have shot or snared every one myself. I caught a glimpse of a white heron a few miles from here on Saturday, and I have followed it in this direction. They have never been found in this district at all. The little white heron, it is," and he turned again to look at Sylvia with the hope of discovering that the rare bird was one of her acquaintances. **B**

But Sylvia was watching a hop-toad in the narrow footpath.

> "A queer tall white bird with soft feathers and long thin legs."

"You would know the heron if you saw it," the stranger continued eagerly. "A queer tall white bird with soft feathers and long thin legs. And it would have a nest perhaps in the top of a high tree, made of sticks, something like a hawk's nest."

Sylvia's heart gave a wild beat; she knew that strange white bird, and had once stolen softly near where it stood in some bright green swamp grass, away over at the other side of the woods. There was an open place where the sunshine always seemed strangely yellow and hot, where tall, nodding rushes grew, and her grandmother had warned her that she might sink in the soft

---

6. **plaguy** (plā′gē): annoying; bothersome.
7. **bangeing** (băn′jĭng): New England colloquial term meaning gathering or lounging about in groups.
8. **didn't hitch:** didn't get along.
9. **ornithologist** (ôr′nə-thŏl′ə-jĭst): one who studies birds.

Customizing Instruction

Less Proficient Readers

1 Ask students why Sylvia is so startled to meet this young man.

Possible Response: Sylvia had thought she was alone; she's afraid of strangers.

Students Acquiring English

2 Explain that husks are the leafy coverings of an ear of corn that are removed when the corn is prepared as food or seed.

Cross Curricular Link Science

ORNITHOLOGY Ornithology is the scientific study of birds. It had its beginnings in ancient times, and many accurate scientific observations relating to birds are found in the writings of Aristotle. The recognition of ornithology as a separate branch of science is rather recent. John James Audubon (1785–1851) and John Gould (1804–1881) are two well-known ornithologists.

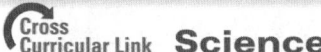

Reading and Analyzing

Literary Analysis: CHARACTERIZATION

Inform students that the name *Sylvia* comes from the Latin word *silva,* meaning "forest." Ask students how this name fits Sylvia.

Possible Response: Sylvia loves the forest and all the creatures that inhabit it. She prefers living in the forest to living in the city.

Active Reading QUESTIONING

A Ask students why the author mentions that Sylvia lives just a few miles from the sea but has never seen it.

Possible Response: The author reveals that Sylvia leads a very sheltered and local life.

ACTIVE READING

B QUESTION Possible Response: He charms her; he leads her away from nature and toward human society.

black mud underneath and never be heard of more. Not far beyond were the salt marshes, and just this side the sea itself, which Sylvia wondered and dreamed much about, but never had seen, whose great voice could sometimes be heard above the noise of the woods on stormy nights. **A**

"I can't think of anything I should like so much as to find that heron's nest," the handsome stranger was saying. "I would give ten dollars to anybody who could show it to me," he added desperately, "and I mean to spend my whole vacation hunting for it if need be. Perhaps it was only migrating, or had been chased out of its own region by some bird of prey."

"I can't think of anything I should like so much as to find that heron's nest," the handsome stranger was saying.

Mrs. Tilley gave amazed attention to all this, but Sylvia still watched the toad, not divining,[10] as she might have done at some calmer time, that the creature wished to get to its hole under the doorstep, and was much hindered by the unusual spectators at that hour of the evening. **B** No amount of thought, that night, could decide how many wished-for treasures the ten dollars, so lightly spoken of, would buy.

The next day the young sportsman hovered about the woods, and Sylvia kept him company, having lost her first fear of the friendly lad, who proved to be most kind and sympathetic. He told her many things about the birds and what they knew and where they lived and what they did with themselves. And he gave her a jack-knife, which she thought as great a treasure as if she were a desert islander. All day long he did not once make her troubled or afraid except when he brought down some unsuspecting singing creature from its bough. Sylvia would have liked him vastly better without his gun; she could not understand why he killed the very birds he seemed to like so much. But as the day waned, Sylvia still watched the young man with loving admiration. She had never seen anybody so charming and delightful; the woman's heart, asleep in the child, was vaguely thrilled by a dream of love. Some premonition[11] of that great power stirred and swayed these young creatures 1
who traversed the solemn woodlands with soft-footed silent care. They stopped to listen to a bird's song; they pressed forward again eagerly, parting the branches—speaking to each other rarely and in whispers; the young man going first and Sylvia following, fascinated, a few steps behind, with her gray eyes dark with excitement.

She grieved because the longed-for white heron was elusive, but she did not lead the guest, she only followed, and there was no such thing as speaking first. The sound of her own unquestioned voice would have terrified her—it was hard enough to answer yes or no when there was need of that. At last evening

ACTIVE READING

B QUESTION What effect does the hunter seem to have on Sylvia?

10. **divining** (dĭ-vī′nĭng): guessing.
11. **premonition:** a sense that something will happen; forewarning

WORDS TO KNOW
traverse (trə-vûrs′) *v.* to travel or pass across, over, or through
elusive (ĭ-lo͞o′sĭv) *adj.* hard to catch or discover

Teaching Options

Mini Lesson: Viewing and Representing

Cosmos (formerly called *The Mountains*)
by Marsden Hartley

ART APPRECIATION Marsden Hartley (1877–1943) began painting the mountains of his native Maine in 1908. Note how he distorts shapes and uses broken patterns of color. Later in his life, Hartley's landscapes were strongly influenced by the French artist Cézanne. Hartley always returned to these Maine mountains as the subject of his work.

Instruction Ask students to note the colors Hartley uses in his portrayal of Maine. Ask students how his choice of colors and his style show contrast in the painting.

Possible Response: Hartley creates contrast through the use of both warm and cool colors. His impressionistic style creates a soft view of the landscape, which contrasts to the way the landscape would appear naturally.

Application Have students discuss how this particular painting captures the feelings Sylvia has about her natural surroundings.

Possible Response: The warm colors and soft, rounded shapes give a feeling of comfort. Sylvia takes great comfort in her natural surroundings.

Cosmos (1908–1909), Marsden Hartley. Oil on canvas, 30″ × 30⅛″, Columbus (Ohio) Museum of Art, gift of Ferdinand Howald (31.179).

Customizing Instruction

Less Proficient Readers
Ask students why Sylvia wants to help the young man.
Possible Responses: Sylvia wants to receive the money and help her grandmother; Sylvia likes the man because he is kind and he gave her his jackknife.

Students Acquiring English
1 Point out to students that the "young creatures" Jewett mentions refer to Sylvia and the young man, not the animals they encounter in the forest.

Reading and Analyzing

Literary Analysis: SETTING

Ask students how the setting adds to the suspense of the sequence in which Sylvia climbs the tree.

Possible Response: The seclusion makes it unlikely that anyone will be nearby to help her if she is in trouble.

Literary Analysis SYMBOL

Ask students what Sylvia's difficult and perilous climb up the tree might symbolize.

Possible Response: the different tasks and situations she will have to endure as she grows up and leans to form human relationships

ACTIVE READING

A PREDICT **Possible Response:** She will see the heron; she won't see the heron; she'll fall from the tree.

began to fall, and they drove the cow home together, and Sylvia smiled with pleasure when they came to the place where she heard the whistle and was afraid only the night before.

Half a mile from home, at the farther edge of the woods, where the land was highest, a great pine tree stood, the last of its generation. Whether it was left for a boundary mark, or for what reason, no one could say; the woodchoppers who had felled its mates were dead and gone long ago, and a whole forest of sturdy trees, pines and oaks and maples, had grown again. But the stately head of this old pine towered above them all and made a landmark for sea and shore miles and miles away. Sylvia knew it well. She had always believed that whoever climbed to the top of it could see the ocean; and the little girl had often laid her hand on the great rough trunk and looked up wistfully at those dark boughs that the wind always stirred, no matter how hot and still the air might be below. Now she thought of the tree with a new excitement, for why, if one climbed it at break of day, could not one see all the world, and easily discover whence the white heron flew, and mark the place, and find the hidden nest?

What a spirit of adventure, what wild ambition! What fancied triumph and delight and glory for the later morning when she could make known the secret! It was almost too real and too great for the childish heart to bear.

All night the door of the little house stood (A) open and the whippoorwills came and sang upon the very step. The young sportsman and his old hostess were sound asleep, but Sylvia's great design[12] kept her broad awake and watching. She forgot to think of sleep. The short summer night seemed as long as the winter darkness, and at last, when the whippoorwills ceased, and she was afraid the morning would after all come too soon, she stole out of the house and followed the pasture path through the woods, hastening toward the open ground beyond, listening with a sense of comfort and companionship to the drowsy twitter of a half-awakened bird, whose perch she had jarred in passing. Alas, if the great wave of human interest which flooded for the first time this dull little life should sweep away the satisfactions of an existence heart to heart with nature and the dumb life of the forest!

There was the huge tree asleep yet in the paling moonlight, and small and silly Sylvia began with utmost bravery to mount to the top of it, with tingling, eager blood coursing the channels of her whole frame, with her bare feet and fingers, that pinched and held like bird's claws to the monstrous ladder reaching up, up, 1
almost to the sky itself. First she must mount the white oak tree that grew alongside, where she was almost lost among the dark branches and the green leaves heavy and wet with dew; a bird fluttered off its nest, and a red squirrel ran to and fro and scolded pettishly[13] at the harmless housebreaker. Sylvia felt her way easily. She had often climbed there, and knew that higher still one of the oak's upper branches chafed against the pine trunk, just where its lower boughs were set close together. There, when she made the dangerous pass from one tree to the other, the great enterprise would really begin.

ACTIVE READING

PREDICT What do you think will happen when Sylvia climbs the tree?

She crept out along the swaying oak limb at last, and took the daring step across into the old pine tree. The way was harder than she thought; she must reach far and hold fast, the sharp dry twigs caught and held her and scratched her like angry talons, the pitch made her thin little fingers clumsy and stiff as she went round and

12. **design:** plan or secretive scheme.

13. **pettishly:** crossly; irritably.

Teaching Options

Mini Lesson Grammar

INDEPENDENT AND SUBORDINATE CLAUSES

Remind students that there are two kinds of clauses: independent clauses and subordinate clauses. Both types of clauses must contain a subject and a predicate, but they differ in an important way. An independent clause, or main clause, can stand alone as a complete sentence. However, a subordinate clause cannot stand alone; it depends on an independent clause to form a complete sentence. Subordinate clauses often begin with subordinating conjunctions such as *after, because, since,* and *when* and relative pronouns such as *who, whom, whose, which,* and *that.* Write the following sentences on the chalkboard:

"In 1908, Marsden Hartley began painting the mountains of Maine."

Sylvia liked the country because it was quiet.

The bird was saved from the hunter who sought it.

Underline the clauses as shown. Have students identify the independent clause and the subordinate clauses. Point out that the underlined clause in the first sentence can stand alone; therefore, it is an independent clause. In the second and third sentences, however, the underlined clauses are subordinate; they cannot stand alone.

Practice Have students copy the following sentences. Ask them to identify the underlined clauses as independent or subordinate.

round the tree's great stem, higher and higher upward. The sparrows and robins in the woods below were beginning to wake and twitter to the dawn, yet it seemed much lighter there aloft in the pine tree, and the child knew she must hurry if her project were to be of any use.

The tree seemed to lengthen itself out as she went up, and to reach farther and farther upward. It was like a great mainmast to the voyaging earth; it must truly have been amazed that morning through all its ponderous frame as it felt this determined spark of human spirit wending its way from higher branch to branch. Who knows how steadily the least twigs held themselves to advantage this light, weak creature on her way! The old pine must have loved his new dependent. More than all the hawks, and bats, and moths, and even the sweet-voiced thrushes, was the brave, beating heart of the solitary gray-eyed child. And the tree stood still and frowned away the winds that June morning while the dawn grew bright in the east.

Look, look! a white spot of him like a single floating feather comes up from the dead hemlock and grows larger.

Sylvia's face was like a pale star, if one had seen it from the ground, when the last thorny bough was past, and she stood trembling and tired but wholly triumphant, high in the treetop. Yes, there was the sea with the dawning sun making a golden dazzle over it, and toward that glorious east flew two hawks with slow-moving pinions.[14] How low they looked in the air from that height when one had only seen them before far up, and dark against the blue sky. Their gray feathers were as soft as moths; they seemed only a little way from the tree, and Sylvia felt as if she too could go flying away among the clouds. Westward, the woodlands and farms reached miles and miles into the distance; here and there were church steeples, and white villages; truly it was a vast and awesome world!

The birds sang louder and louder. At last the sun came up bewilderingly bright. Sylvia could see the white sails of ships out at sea, and the clouds that were purple and rose-colored and yellow at first began to fade away. Where was the white heron's nest in the sea of green branches, and was this wonderful sight and pageant of the world the only reward for having climbed to such a giddy height? Now look down again, Sylvia, where the green marsh is set among the shining birches and dark hemlocks; there where you saw the white heron once you will see him again; look, look! a white spot of him like a single floating feather comes up from the dead hemlock and grows larger, and rises, and comes close at last, and goes by the landmark pine with steady sweep of wing and outstretched slender neck and crested head. And wait! wait! do not move a foot or a finger, little girl, do not send an arrow of light and consciousness from your two eager eyes, for the heron has perched on a pine bough not far beyond yours, and cries back to his mate on the nest and plumes his feathers[15] for the new day!

14. **pinions** (pĭn′yənz): a bird's wings.

15. **plumes his feathers:** cleans and smoothes his feathers with his bill; preens.

WORDS TO KNOW

ponderous (pŏn′dər-əs) *adj.* very heavy; bulky

Customizing Instruction

Less Proficient Readers

1 The first limb of the pine tree is too high for Sylvia to reach. Ask how she is able to get to the limbs of the pine tree.

Possible Response: She climbs an oak tree and then climbs from one of its limbs onto the pine tree.

Set a Purpose Have students read to find out what Sylvia sees from the top of the pine tree.

1. The great white heron, which was thought to be a separate species, is a white phase of the great blue heron.
   Answer: subordinate
2. Because wetlands are vanishing rapidly, herons have a limited habitat.
   Answer: subordinate
3. Most of the time, the heron stalks small fish and frogs in marshes and streams.
   Answer: independent
4. Except during breeding season, many herons are solitary.
   Answer: independent
5. The nests, which are platforms of sticks, can be found in high trees.
   Answer: subordinate

Use **Grammar Transparencies and Copymasters,** p. 109.

Use McDougal Littell's ***Language Network,*** Chapter 4, for more instruction and practice in independent and subordinate clauses.

Reading and Analyzing

Reading Skills and Strategies: EVALUATING

A Ask students to evaluate the grandmother's reaction to Sylvia's silence. Given Sylvia's age, her disappearance, and her disheveled appearance, is the grandmother's rebuke appropriate?

Possible Responses: Yes—Sylvia has caused undue worry by disappearing, and she is also withholding valuable information; no—the grandmother should be showing more concern for Sylvia's welfare and less for the money.

Literary Analysis SYMBOL

Ask students what they think the heron symbolizes for Sylvia.

Possible Response: the quiet, happy world she has found since she moved to the country

The child gives a long sigh a minute later when a company of shouting catbirds comes also to the tree, and vexed by their fluttering and lawlessness, the solemn heron goes away. She knows his secret now, the wild, light, slender bird that floats and wavers, and goes back like an arrow presently to his home in the green world beneath. Then Sylvia, well satisfied, makes her perilous way down again, not daring to look far below the branch she stands on, ready to cry sometimes because her fingers ache and her lamed feet slip. Wondering over and over again what the stranger would say to her, and what he would think when she told him how to find his way straight to the heron's nest.

"Sylvy, Sylvy!" called the busy old grandmother again and again, but nobody answered, and the small husk bed was empty, and Sylvia had disappeared.

The guest waked from a dream, and remembering his day's pleasure hurried to dress himself that it might sooner begin. He was sure from the way the shy little girl looked once or twice yesterday that she had at least seen the white heron, and now she must really be made to tell. Here she comes now, paler than ever, and her worn old frock is torn and tattered, and smeared with pine pitch. The grandmother and the sportsman stand in the door together and question her, and the splendid moment has come to speak of the dead hemlock tree by the green marsh.

But Sylvia does not speak after all, though the old grandmother fretfully rebukes her, and the young man's kind, appealing eyes are looking straight in her own. He can make them rich with money; he has promised it, and they are poor now. He is so well worth making happy, and he waits to hear the story she can tell.

No, she must keep silence! What is it that suddenly forbids her and makes her dumb? Has she been nine years growing and now, when the great world for the first time puts out a hand to her, must she thrust it aside for a bird's sake? The murmur of the pine's green branches is in her ears, she remembers how the white heron came flying through the golden air and how they watched the sea and the morning together, and Sylvia cannot speak; she cannot tell the heron's secret and give its life away.

Dear loyalty, that suffered a sharp pang as the guest went away disappointed later in the day, that could have served and followed him and loved him as a dog loves! Many a night Sylvia heard the echo of his whistle haunting the pasture path as she came home with the loitering cow. She forgot even her sorrow at the sharp report[16] of his gun and the sight of thrushes and sparrows dropping silent to the ground, their songs hushed and their pretty feathers stained and wet with blood. Were the birds better friends than their hunter might have been—who can tell? Whatever treasures were lost to her, woodlands and summertime, remember! Bring your gifts and graces and tell your secrets to this lonely country child! ❖

16. **report:** explosive noise.

Teaching Options

Standardized Test Practice

ALTERNATIVE ENDING You can assess students' understanding of the selection by having them write an alternative ending in which the heron is killed by the young man.

RUBRIC

3 Full Accomplishment Response reflects a full understanding of the events and characters in the story.

2 Substantial Accomplishment Response shows a general understanding of the events and characters in the story.

1 Little or Partial Accomplishment Response shows little understanding of the events and characters in the story.

Connect to the Literature

1. **What Do You Think?** What is your judgment of Sylvia's decision at the end of the story? Explain your reasoning.

Comprehension Check
- Why is the stranger looking for the heron?
- Why does Sylvia climb the pine tree?
- What does she tell the man about the heron's location?

Think Critically

2. How would you describe Sylvia's relationship with the stranger?
3. **ACTIVE READING** QUESTIONING With a classmate, discuss the questions and answers you wrote in your READER'S NOTEBOOK. Which of your questions seem most relevant or important to your understanding of the story? Explain your response.
4. Sylvia, her grandmother, and the stranger all seem to have feelings for nature. How are their attitudes similar, and how are they different?
5. At the end of the story, the **narrator** asks, "Were the birds better friends than their hunter might have been—who can tell?" How do you predict Sylvia will answer this question in ten years, when she is 19?

Extend Interpretations

6. **The Writer's Style** Like many 19th-century writers, Jewett wrote **realistic fiction.** She made use of vivid descriptions in her stories and incorporated her knowledge of local customs and regional **dialect** that conveyed village and rural life in New England. Do you think Jewett was successful in conveying the local color of rural southeastern Maine in "A White Heron"? Explain your point of view, citing evidence from the story.
7. **Comparing Texts** Which of the **characters** in the selections you've read would be most sympathetic to Sylvia and supportive of her choice? Who would have the hardest time understanding or appreciating her dilemma?
8. **Connect to Life** Are the various attitudes toward nature represented in the story still evident today? Discuss.

Literary Analysis

SYMBOL A **symbol** is a person, place, or object that represents something beyond itself. Symbols have the power to communicate complicated, emotionally rich ideas.

Cooperative Learning Activity How do you interpret the following symbols from nature in "A White Heron"?
- the white heron
- the old pine tree

How effective do you find Jewett's use of symbols? Discuss your thoughts with a small group of classmates. Support your answers with evidence from the text.

REVIEW POINT OF VIEW
Point of view refers to the narrative method, or the kind of **narrator,** used in a literary work. In the **third-person point of view,** the narrator is outside the action of the story. Sometimes this narrator is **omniscient,** or all-knowing, and can see into the minds of more than one character, reporting the thoughts, feelings, and experiences of these characters. Cite evidence from the story to show that "A White Heron" has an omniscient narrator. What effect does the narrator have on your impressions of Sylvia, the grandmother, and the stranger?

GUIDING STUDENT RESPONSE

Connect to the Literature

1. **What Do You Think?**
Some students will feel that she did the right thing in not forsaking the nature that she loves. Others may feel that she has regressed by retreating back into nature and away from human company.

Comprehension Check
- He wants to shoot it so that he can add it to his bird collection.
- to be able to spot the heron's nest
- nothing

UseSelection Quiz **Unit Five Resource Book,** p. 9 for additional support.

Think Critically

2. Possible Response: She is attracted to this man and wants to please him. If she were older, she might describe her feelings as "being in love."
3. Student questions will vary, but should reflect an understanding of which points are critical to the story's plot and meaning.
4. Possible Response: They all depend on nature. Nevertheless, their needs are different: The grandmother depends on nature for survival; the man takes a scientific interest in nature; Sylvia has a spiritual and aesthetic connection to nature.
5. As a 19-year old woman, Sylvia might fall in love with the young man, or at least prefer his company to that of the birds.

Extend Interpretations

The Writer's Style Students may say yes, citing the story's minute descriptions of the surroundings and its use of dialect. Students may say that they are unfamiliar with rural southeastern Maine and cannot judge the story's realism.

Comparing Texts Student responses should be well supported and demonstrate an understanding of Sylvia's sensitive, reclusive nature.

Connect to Life Student responses will vary. They may discuss conflicts between environmentalists and real estate developers, or battles between hunters and animal rights activists, for example.

Writing Options

1. **Picture Book Rewrite** Student responses should contain simple language and descriptions. Have students imagine that they are telling the story to a five-year-old.
2. **Sylvia's Haiku** Remind students that a haiku is a three-line poem, with five syllables in the first and third lines and seven in the second.
3. **Epilogue to the Story** Remind students Sylvia will probably have changed more than the stranger has, because she has moved from childhood to adulthood. Students might have Sylvia explain why she kept the heron's nest site a secret, and how this decision has affected her.

Activities & Explorations

1. **Public Speech** Have students think of the various approaches Sylvia might use to persuade her audience. She can appeal to them from an ecological, aesthetic, or humane position.
2. **Sylvia's Loyalties** To extend the activity, have some groups create the bar graph suggested and others create a bar graph for Sylvia at age nineteen. Then compare and contrast the graphs.

Inquiry & Research

Encourage students to begin their research by looking in text resources such as nature conservation magazines as well as on the Internet.

Vocabulary in Action

1. squalor
2. traverse
3. ponderous
4. elusive
5. discreetly

Choices & CHALLENGES

Writing Options

1. **Picture Book** Rewrite "A White Heron" as a children's book. Include both text and color illustrations, using watercolors, crayons, or pastels.

2. **Sylvia's Haiku** Try to imagine how Sylvia feels at the end of the story. Capture these feelings in a haiku poem for publication in your school's literary magazine or for display on a class bulletin board.

3. **Epilogue to the Story** Imagine that Sylvia and the stranger meet again, ten years later. Draft an epilogue to the story, describing the encounter. Include information about what has happened to the two characters and about the kind of life each one is now leading.

Activities & Explorations

1. **Public Speech** Imagine that a real estate developer is seeking approval from the town council to build homes on the land where the old pine tree now stands. Give the speech Sylvia would give at a public hearing, arguing why the tree—and the heron's natural habitat—should be preserved. ~ **SPEAKING AND LISTENING**

2. **Sylvia's Loyalties** Working in a small group, create a bar graph like the one you created for the Connect to Your Life activity on page 822, this one showing Sylvia's loyalties. Consider the people, places, and creatures that Sylvia values and what the narrator says in the last three paragraphs. ~ **VIEWING AND REPRESENTING**

Inquiry & Research

Fighting for Survival Find out more about a species in the United States whose habitat is threatened by the progress of humanity.

Real World Link Begin your research by reading the article on pages 836–837.

The manatee, an aquatic mammal, is threatened by boat propellers and the decline of its food sources.

Vocabulary in Action

EXERCISE A: CONTEXT CLUES Write the Word to Know that best completes each sentence.

1. Whether one lives in splendor or in ________, there is something about the sight of a great white heron that lifts the heart.
2. It flies slowly despite its nearly six-foot wing span, which means that a person lucky enough to see one ________ its habitat may be able to keep it in view for a while.
3. Large as this bird is, it appears anything but ________ in flight.
4. Silent and motionless in the water, the heron may seem asleep until its bill moves, like lightning, to spear the fish too ________ for slower hunters.
5. The hopeful heron-watcher must behave as ________ as the bird, for rash and careless actions will guarantee this graceful creature's quick departure.

EXERCISE B Make a quick sketch or use watercolors to depict the meaning of *traverse, elusive,* or *discreetly.* You might consider illustrating the word's use in Exercise A. Then exchange your artwork with a classmate; each of you should judge whether the other has successfully communicated the meaning of the word.

WORDS TO KNOW			
	discreetly	ponderous	traverse
	elusive	squalor	

Building Vocabulary
For an in-depth study of context clues, see page 1000.

Mini Lesson Grammar

ADVERB CLAUSES Remind students that an adverb clause is a type of subordinate clause that modifies a verb, an adjective, or an adverb. Point out that an adverb clause always begins with a subordinating conjunction. Write the sentence on the chalkboard:

"Jewett began writing when she was 14 years old."

Underline the adverb clause as shown. Point out that the word *when* is the subordinating conjunction that begins the adverb clause. Reiterate that "Jewett began writing" can stand alone as a sentence, but the clause "when she was 14 years old" cannot. The clause is an adverb clause because it modifies the verb *began.*

Practice Write the following sentences on the chalkboard. Have students copy them. Ask them to underline the adverb clause in each sentence and underline the subordinating conjunction twice.

Grammar in Context: Adverb Clauses

At the end of the first sentence of "A White Heron," an adverb clause provides additional information about the time of day.

> **The woods were already filled with shadows one June evening, just before eight o'clock, though a bright sunset still glimmered faintly among the trunks of the trees.**

An **adverb clause** is a subordinate clause that functions as an adverb—that is, it modifies a verb, an adjective, or another adverb. In the example above, the adverb clause shown in blue modifies the verb phrase *were filled.* Notice how the adverb clause helps you visualize the setting, bringing into focus a time of day that figures prominently in the story.

Adverb clauses are introduced by subordinating conjunctions, like the word *though* in the example above. Other subordinating conjunctions include *after, although, as, as if, because, before, even though, if, until, when,* and *while.*

WRITING EXERCISE Add an adverb clause to each sentence, in the place indicated by a caret. Begin the clause with the subordinating conjunction shown in parentheses.

Usage Tip: An adverb clause must contain both a subject and a verb.

Example: ***Original*** ^ She felt at home walking by herself through the woods. *(even though)*

Rewritten Even though Sylvia was easily frightened, she felt at home walking by herself through the woods.

1. ^ She finds the cow near the swamp. *(after)*
2. ^ She compares her surroundings with her former home in town. *(while)*
3. Even the dim light of evening does not bother her; she feels secure ^. *(as if)*
4. Walking along with the young man makes Sylvia uneasy ^. *(until)*
5. Sylvia would like the young man more ^. *(if)*

Grammar Handbook Clauses, p. 1197

Sarah Orne Jewett
1849–1909

Other Works
Country By-Ways
A Country Doctor
A White Heron and Other Stories
The Country of the Pointed Firs

Outdoor Education Sarah Orne Jewett was born and raised in South Berwick, Maine, a town she loved and often wrote about in her fiction. The daughter of a respected Maine physician, she often traveled the countryside with him as he visited his patients; later she said that the best of her education was received in her father's buggy and the places to which it carried her. Jewett enjoyed her father's extensive library, and by the age of 14, she was writing her own poetry and stories.

Regional Writer A few years later, Jewett submitted one of her stories to a children's magazine. Following the publication of this story, Jewett became a frequent contributor to a number of periodicals. When she was 19, the prestigious New England magazine *Atlantic Monthly* published one of her stories. Impressed by her tales of Deephaven, a Maine town modeled on South Berwick, *Atlantic Monthly* editor William Dean Howells encouraged her to pursue the then popular genre of regional fiction, novels and stories that realistically depict the local color of a particular area. The result was her first book, *Deephaven,* published in 1877.

Achievement and Tragedy In 1901 Jewett became the first woman to receive an honorary doctorate from Maine's Bowdoin College, where her father had received his own education and had also taught medicine. On her 53rd birthday, Jewett was thrown from a carriage and suffered head and spinal injuries, putting an end to her writing career and leaving her an invalid.

Grammar in Context

WRITING EXERCISE Answers will vary. Possible answers are shown.

1. After Sylvia hunts in the bushes for a long time, she finds the cow near the swamp.
2. While she walks along, she compares her surroundings with her former home in town.
3. Even the dim light of evening does not bother her; she feels secure, as if she belongs in the woods.
4. Walking along with the young man makes Sylvia uneasy until they arrive at Mrs. Tilley's house.
5. Sylvia would like the young man more if he did not have a gun.

1. The young man offered a cash reward because he desperately wanted to find the heron.
2. Sylvia befriended the young man when she spent time with him in the woods.
3. Sylvia's conflict was resolved when she made her decision to keep quiet about the heron.
4. If Sylvia had remained in the city, she would not have encountered the white heron.
5. Although her grandmother could have used the money, Sylvia knew that the protection of the white heron was the right decision.

Use **Grammar Transparencies and Copymasters,** p. 112.

Use McDougal Littell's ***Language Network,*** Chapter 4, for more instruction and practice in adverb clauses.

Objectives
- evaluate controversial opinions
- recognize underlying factors that may influence a person's opinion

Connecting to the Literature
In Sarah Orne Jewett's short story "A White Heron," nine-year-old Sylvia chooses to remain silent in order to save the heron's life.

Evaluating Opinions
Remind students to evaluate the credibility of information sources, including how the writer's motivation may affect credibility.

Reading for Information
Environmentalists, land owners, lawyers, developers, and legislators may have differing opinions regarding endangered species.

1 Banks, an environmental consultant, focuses on the environment but also has a sensitivity to the needs and desires of the business community. His job might lead him to a balanced opinion on the issue.
2 Since Carlton is director of the Biodiversity Legal Foundation, his comments reflect the environmentalists' point of view. This suggests his alignment on the side of the mouse.

The Mouse That ROARED

by Richard Woodbury

The Endangered Species Act restricts human activities that damage the habitat of any species in danger of becoming extinct. This law has often been a point of conflict between people who want to keep the environment unchanged and those who want economic development. As you read this article, focus on the opinions, or arguments, people put forth to support their particular viewpoints.

Up and down the front range of the Rockies, one of the nation's hottest growth zones, a tiny, obscure rodent named the Preble's meadow jumping mouse is upsetting land planning, forcing developers to alter construction schedules, and snarling highway and utilities projects.

Not bad for a creature hardly anyone has seen.

All the fuss has come about not because the little mouse with the 5-inch tail is an officially endangered species—it isn't—but because it might soon be declared so. On that presumption, federal and local regulators are requiring developers to make elaborate surveys in wetland areas where the mouse allegedly thrives. ❶ Paul Banks, a bemused environmental consultant in Denver, says the elusive jumping mouse may be doing as much to curb Colorado's rampant development as all the slow-growth confabs and environmentalists' lawsuits put together.

If the U.S. Fish and Wildlife Service moves ahead and formally lists Preble's as endangered, as it's expected to do shortly, the obstacles to building will be stronger. And if the government fails to act, mouse advocates vow legal action to force listing. At issue as much as the rodent are the shrub-lined meadows and grassy marshes that abut the streams and creeks lacing the 170 miles from Cheyenne, Wyoming, to Colorado Springs. That stretch of land at the foothills of the Rockies is aswarm with housing and commercial development; three counties on the Front Range are among the Census Bureau's 10 fastest growing. ❷ "We're talking about critical habitat that's almost gone," says Jasper Carlton, director of the Biodiversity Legal Foundation. "We shouldn't be building in these areas anyway. Protecting the mouse saves the environment for all of us."

The little mouse is a reclusive character. Very few scientists have laid eyes on the buff-colored, black-striped mammal, which . . . measures barely 2 inches. Named for a Colorado naturalist . . . ,

Reading for Information

Do we need more houses and malls and the jobs and profits that they create? Or do we need to preserve open space, wetlands, and wilderness? Controversial issues like this one can generate many different opinions.

EVALUATING OPINIONS

This article presents opinions from individuals involved in an economy-versus-environment controversy. Readers need to be able to **evaluate** these **opinions** in order to form their own. Here are some questions to ask when evaluating an opinion:

- How might a person's profession impact his or her opinion?
- Does the person have sufficient education or experience that validates his or her opinion?
- Might the person have motives that could lead him or her to favor one side or the other?

YOUR TURN Use the questions and activities below to help you evaluate the different opinions in this article.

❶ Paul Banks is an environmental consultant—a person who helps developers and manufacturers comply with environmental laws. How might his job affect his opinion about the issue?

❷ Jasper Carlton works for a legal foundation that uses the law to support the case for biodiversity. How does knowing that information affect your reaction to his opinion?

the mouse hibernates for nine months. In summer it emerges only at night, when it commences to bound 4 feet at a leap through the tall grass, aided by . . . long hind legs and an outsize tail that helps stabilize it in flight. "There could be thousands out there, and there could be far fewer; we just don't know," concedes Fish and Wildlife biologist Peter Plage, who has rarely seen the rodent in the wild.

A researcher holds a Preble's meadow jumping mouse.

That's precisely the problem, says Linda Lacy, developer of an 18,000-acre project in Jefferson County, where wildlife agents set traps last summer seeking jumping mice. They caught no Preble's but did get 218 other mice and one rattlesnake. "It's ridiculous to protect the animal when no one can even seem to find it," says Lacy. . . . ❸

With the certainty of greater disruption if the animal wins federal protection, Colorado officials have organized a 200-member coalition to draft the state's own protection plan, which may include finding the mice and relocating some of them into sanctuaries. "It's in the interest of both mouse and man to avoid drastic measures," says Congressman David Skaggs of Boulder, a Democrat who secured a $400,000 appropriation to fund the project. . . .

Environmentalist Carlton, whose lawsuit prodded the government to move on the mouse, says what the state may be scheming is "an end-run around the law to subvert restoring the ecosystem. You might have to move a golf course or road 100 feet or so, but protection isn't going to do in anybody. There's a lot of fearmongering going on." The Fish and Wildlife Service, apparently agreeing, contends that in 95% of cases only minimal disruption occurs when species are listed as endangered.

❹ In Washington, Colorado Senator Ben Nighthorse Campbell isn't waiting for studies. Denouncing the jumping mouse as a "killer" of jobs and economic growth, he says the federal government should be tossing animals and plants off the endangered list rather than putting them on. But the public feels otherwise. A *Denver Post* poll in March showed that 81% support protecting the little mouse that's seldom seen. "Their habitat is shrinking fast," warns Boulder mammalogist Carron Meaney. "We might find the mouse in 100 places now, but in 10 years 95 of those will be under concrete."

❸ What opinions are expressed up to this point? What are the backgrounds of the sources?

❹ **Statistical Evidence** In these paragraphs, an opinion is followed by factual information that either supports it or contradicts it. Why do you think the reporter included this information? If it had not been included, how might your reaction to the opinions in these paragraphs be different?

Constructing a Graphic Review each opinion expressed in the article, using a chart like the one shown here. Compare your chart with that of a classmate, and discuss the opinion you've formed about the Preble's mouse and its future.

Opinion	Background of Source	My Evaluation

Inquiry & Research

Activity Link: "A White Heron," p. 834

On the basis of this article, where do you stand on the conflict between protecting the environment and promoting economic progress? Take part in an informal debate on the topic.

3 The opinions of environmentalists and wildlife officials have been expressed up to this point. The backgrounds of these sources are those of highly educated professionals trained in fish and wildlife management and environmental law.

4 The statistical evidence offers concrete support included to lend credibility to the reporter's claims. Reactions might have been less thoughtful and more emotional without such factual support.

Mini Lesson: Inquiry & Research

The Inquiry & Research activity on this page links this article to the Inquiry & Research section of Choices and Challenges (p. 834).

Instruction Students may recognize parallels between concerns expressed in this article and local environmental issues. Point out that the issue pits two opposing camps: the developers interested in growth and profit, and the environmentalists interested in protection.

Practice Have students collect articles about local environmental issues and select one issue that concerns them. Ask them to formulate a list of specific actions they could take to address their concerns.

Possible Responses: Students may decide to write an article and submit it to a magazine; some students might volunteer for a community organization that is involved with the issue; writing a letter to a government official is another possible response.

OVERVIEW

This selection is included in the **Grade 10 InterActive Reader.**

Objectives

1. understand and appreciate a **poem** **(Literary Analysis)**
2. understand **figurative language** **(Literary Analysis)**
3. **analyze images (Active Reading)**

Summary

Robert Frost uses figurative language in his poem "Birches" to describe the significance of the birch trees common to his native New England. He observes how birches, bent by the harsh realities of a winter ice storm, never right themselves, while those bent by the whim of a young boy rise again. He recalls how a youth could bend and conquer each tree and enjoy climbing to its uppermost branches; so the speaker, "weary of considerations," wishes he could swing from the birch branches as he once did to "get away from earth awhile."

Thematic Link

The birches remind the speaker of life's simple joys and most profound truths.

5-Minute Warm-Up

Daily Language SkillBuilder

Have students **proofread** the display sentences on page 817i and write them correctly. The sentences also appear on Transparency 23 of **Grammar Transparencies and Copymasters.**

"So was I once myself a swinger of birches."

Birches

Poetry by ROBERT FROST

Connect to Your Life

Tree Climbers Did you ever try to climb a tree? Perhaps, as a child, you hoisted yourself up to the lowest branches of a tree in your yard or a nearby park, or maybe you climbed up the trunk all the way to the top. Why do you think tree-climbing has such a strong appeal to children? Why do you think people generally lose interest in this type of activity as they grow older? Share your thoughts and experiences with classmates.

Build Background

Frost's Birches In many of his poems, Robert Frost describes scenes from rural New England, where he lived as a child and later worked on his own farm. In "Birches," one of his most famous poems, Frost paints a vivid picture of the white birch trees that adorn much of the New England countryside. The white birch is a tall, delicate tree with a slender white trunk that can bend quite easily in a moderate wind or under the footsteps of a young tree climber.

Focus Your Reading

LITERARY ANALYSIS | FIGURATIVE LANGUAGE The poem "Birches" is rich in **figurative language,** which conveys ideas beyond the literal meanings of words. The general term *figurative language* includes specific **figures of speech,** such as **similes** and **metaphors,** which make comparisons between two unlike things that have at least one thing in common. Similes use the word *like* or *as,* while metaphors do not. In "Birches," the poet describes life with the following simile:

And life is too much like a pathless wood

Look for other examples of figurative language throughout the poem.

ACTIVE READING | ANALYZING IMAGES Frost uses **images** to create sensory experiences for the reader. The images in "Birches" convey in vivid detail two very different scenes, the birches after an ice storm and a boy swinging on the trees. The last third of the poem is more reflective but still contains powerful imagery.

READER'S NOTEBOOK As you read, try to see, hear, and feel what is described by the poem. Record your observations in a chart like the one shown.

Birches	Images of Sight	Images of Sound or Touch
Line		
1–20		
21–40		
41–59		

LESSON RESOURCES

UNIT FIVE RESOURCE BOOK, pp. 10–11

ASSESSMENT RESOURCES

Formal Assessment, pp. 137–138

Teacher's Guide to Assessment and Portfolio Use

Test Generator

SKILLS TRANSPARENCIES AND COPYMASTERS

Literary Analysis

- Symbols and Figurative Language, T21 (for Paired Activity, p. 841)

Reading and Critical Thinking

- Organizational Chart: Horizontal, T51 (for Reader's Notebook, p. 838)

Grammar

- Conjunctive Adverbs, C76 (for Mini Lesson, p. 840)

Writing

- Figurative Language and Sound Devices, T15 (for Writing Option 1, p. 842)
- Interpretive Essay C33 (for Writing Option 2, p. 842)

Communications

- Evaluation Matrix: Film/Video, T7 (for Activities & Explorations 1, p. 842)

INTEGRATED TECHNOLOGY

Audio Library

Video: Literature in Performance

- "Desert Places" and "Birches." See **Video Resource Book,** pp 31–34.

Visit our website: www.mcdougallittell.com

Birches

Robert Frost

When I see birches bend to left and right
Across the lines of straighter darker trees,
I like to think some boy's been swinging them.
But swinging doesn't bend them down to stay
As ice-storms do. Often you must have seen them
Loaded with ice a sunny winter morning
After a rain. They click upon themselves
As the breeze rises, and turn many-colored
As the stir cracks and crazes their enamel.
Soon the sun's warmth makes them shed crystal shells
Shattering and avalanching on the snow-crust—
Such heaps of broken glass to sweep away
You'd think the inner dome of heaven had fallen.
They are dragged to the withered bracken by the load,
And they seem not to break; though once they are bowed
So low for long, they never right themselves:
You may see their trunks arching in the woods
Years afterwards, trailing their leaves on the ground
Like girls on hands and knees that throw their hair
Before them over their heads to dry in the sun.
But I was going to say when Truth broke in
With all her matter-of-fact about the ice-storm
I should prefer to have some boy bend them
As he went out and in to fetch the cows—
Some boy too far from town to learn baseball,
Whose only play was what he found himself,
Summer or winter, and could play alone.
One by one he subdued his father's trees
By riding them down over and over again

Great Horned Owl, Rod Frederick. Copyright © 1986 Rod Frederick/The Greenwich Workshop®, Inc. Courtesy of The Greenwich Workshop, Inc., Shelton, Connecticut.

TEACHING THE LITERATURE

Customizing Instruction

Less Proficient Readers

Have students keep these questions in mind when reading and rereading the poem:

- Who is the poem's speaker?
  Possible Response: A man who reflects on his boyhood
- Where is he from?
  Possible Response: rural New England
- What would it feel like to grow up on an isolated farm in the early part of this century?
  Possible Response: A boy might invent his own games to amuse himself; he might be close to nature and observe the seasonal changes.

Students Acquiring English

Examine passages where the speaker draws parallels between the trees bent by an ice storm and trees bent by the play of a boy.

Possible Response: In line 5, the speaker changes from describing a boy swinging on the trees to discussing the effects of ice storms. In line 22 he prefers his imaginative explanation to the Truth.

Use **Spanish Study Guide** for additional support, pp. 170–172.

Gifted and Talented

When he departed for England at the age of 40, Frost's works had not been published. Students may want to investigate why Frost encountered such difficulties in the U.S., while he was successful in England.

BIRCHES **839**

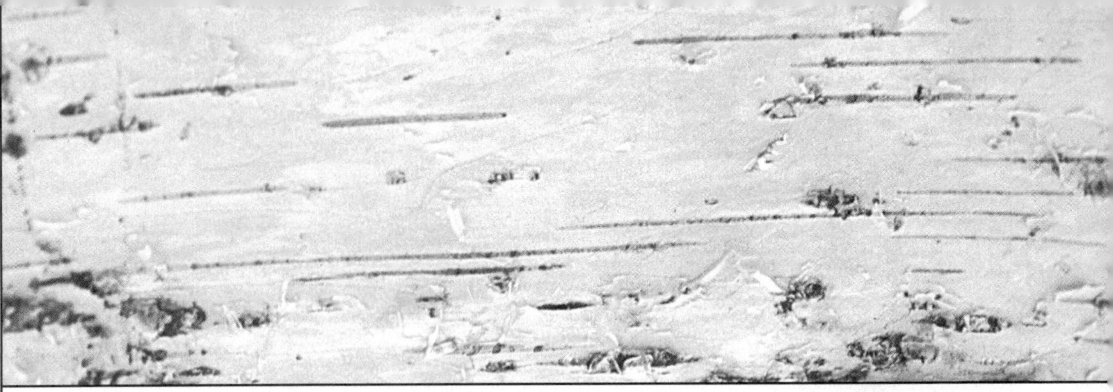

Reading and Analyzing

Reading Skills and Strategies: PREVIEW

Discuss the highlighted quotation on the opening page as well as the title of the poem. The Build Background material also could help students visualize the setting. As they read, have students pay particular attention to the figurative language Frost uses to describe the birch trees.

Active Reading ANALYZING IMAGES

A poet uses imagery to help the reader experience the poem more profoundly. For example, poets often use onomatopoeia to describe certain sounds such as "crack" and "click." Discuss how the sensory appeals in lines 7–9 enhance the description of the birches after an ice storm.

Use **Unit Five Resource Book** p. 10 for more practice.

Literary Analysis
FIGURATIVE LANGUAGE

Similes make comparisons using the words *like* or *as,* while metaphors make comparisons directly. Ask students to write down the comparisons Frost uses as they read the selection. Invite them to share what they have found and offer their interpretations.

Use **Unit Five Resource Book** p. 11 for more practice.

Until he took the stiffness out of them,
And not one but hung limp, not one was left
For him to conquer. He learned all there was
To learn about not launching out too soon
And so not carrying the tree away
Clear to the ground. He always kept his poise
To the top branches, climbing carefully
With the same pains you use to fill a cup
Up to the brim, and even above the brim.
Then he flung outward, feet first, with a swish,
Kicking his way down through the air to the ground.
So was I once myself a swinger of birches.
And so I dream of going back to be.
It's when I'm weary of considerations,
And life is too much like a pathless wood
Where your face burns and tickles with the cobwebs
Broken across it, and one eye is weeping
From a twig's having lashed across it open.
I'd like to get away from earth awhile
And then come back to it and begin over.
May no fate willfully misunderstand me
And half grant what I wish and snatch me away
Not to return. Earth's the right place for love:
I don't know where it's likely to go better.
I'd like to go by climbing a birch tree,
And climb black branches up a snow-white trunk
Toward heaven, till the tree could bear no more,
But dipped its top and set me down again.
That would be good both going and coming back.
One could do worse than be a swinger of birches.

Teaching Options

Mini Lesson Grammar

CONJUNCTIVE ADVERBS Conjunctive adverbs—words like *however, furthermore, nevertheless, consequently,* and *therefore*—can function as both conjunctions and adverbs because they can tie together one independent clause with another. In addition, conjunctive adverbs can modify the second clause. A conjunctive adverb is usually preceded by a semicolon and followed by a comma. Write this sentence on the chalkboard:

Robert Frost was influenced by life in New England; consequently, his poems reflect his upbringing.

Practice Have students identify the conjunctive adverb and punctuate each sentence correctly.

Exercises

1. The ice storm caused severe damage to the trees consequently many branches will need to be pruned.
   Answer: The ice storm caused severe damage to the trees; consequently, many branches will need to be pruned.
2. I want to climb trees however my fear of heights keeps me firmly grounded.
   Answer: I want to climb trees; however, my fear of heights keeps me firmly grounded.

Use **Grammar Transparencies and Copymasters,** p. 76.

Use McDougal Littell's ***Language Network,*** Chapter 1, for more instruction in conjunctive adverbs.

Thinking through the LITERATURE

Connect to the Literature

1. **What Do You Think?** What memories or thoughts did this poem trigger in your mind?

Comprehension Check

- What two explanations does the speaker give for the bent birches?
- According to the speaker, which explanation is more likely?
- How could birches help the speaker to "get away from earth awhile"?

Think Critically

2. What kind of person do you imagine the speaker to be? Give details from the poem to support your answer.
3. What are the differences between the way branches bend from an ice storm and the way they bend from a boy swinging on them? Why are these differences so important to the speaker?
4. What do you think being a "swinger of birches" means to the speaker?

THINK ABOUT

- why swinging on birches is important to the boy in lines 25–40
- why the speaker "dreams" of again becoming a swinger of birches in lines 42–47
- why going up to heaven and coming back to earth are both considered

5. How do you think the statement "Earth's the right place for love: / I don't know where it's likely to go better" relates to the rest of the poem?
6. **ACTIVE READING** INTERPRETING IMAGES Review the chart in your READER'S NOTEBOOK. What do you think is the most vivid or memorable **image** in each section of your chart? How do these images help you to imagine the scenes described by the **speaker?**

Extend Interpretations

7. **Critic's Corner** One critic has said that Frost's "poems often sound . . . much like talk." Read some lines from "Birches" aloud. Do you think this poem resembles "talk"? Why or why not?
8. **Connect to Life** The speaker in this poem would like to leave the earth awhile but then return. One solution is to become a "swinger of birches." In what other ways do people temporarily retreat from the complications and worries of daily life?

Literary Analysis

FIGURATIVE LANGUAGE

Language that communicates ideas beyond the literal meaning of the words is called **figurative language.** Specific types of figurative language, called **figures of speech,** include **similes** and **metaphors.** A simile is a comparison between two things using the words *like* or *as.* Frost makes use of the following simile to compare the tree trunks to young girls:

You may see their trunks arching
in the woods . . .
Like girls on hands and knees that
throw their hair
Before them over their heads to
dry in the sun.

A metaphor makes a comparison without using the words *like* or *as.* Frost uses a metaphor that compares the ice falling from trees to "heaps of broken glass."

Paired Activity Create a metaphor and a simile to add to Frost's description of the wintry scene. Compare your figures of speech with those of your classmates.

ALLITERATION, ASSONANCE, AND CONSONANCE

Alliteration is the repetition of a consonant sound at the beginnings of words, as in "Soon the sun's warmth makes them shed crystal shells." **Assonance** is the repetition of vowel sounds within words, such as "When I see the birches bend to left and right." **Consonance** is the repetition of a consonant sound within and at the ends of words, as illustrated by "girls on hands and knees." Find two more examples each of alliteration, assonance, and consonance in this poem.

GUIDING STUDENT RESPONSE

Connect to the Literature

1. **What Do You Think?**
Students may remember significant moments when they connected with nature.

Comprehension Check

- The two explanations are ice storms and a boy swinging on them.
- The more likely explanation is the weight of ice storms.
- By climbing the birch trees, the speaker could literally get off the earth, and figuratively, rise above his troubles.

Think Critically

2. The speaker seems reflective and weary; gazing at the birches, he realizes that he would like to rise above the troubles of life, even temporarily.
3. When the ice storm bends the branches, the branches don't recover, but when the boy bends the branches, the birches recover their shape. These differences reveal how Frost views life's challenges.
4. The birches represent friends to the boy too far from town; they represent freedom and rejuvenation to the adult speaker; from the top branches one can get a different view of the earth and feel as if one has gotten away.
5. Despite life's troubles and the wish to escape them, Frost knows that love makes life worth living.
6. Remind students that images can be auditory as well as visual. Encourage them to analyze the melodies of the literary language including the use of evocative words and rhythms. Students may notice that Frost uses both genders to create images; in addition, he personifies truth and creates the simile "life is too much like a pathless wood."

Extend Interpretations

Critic's Corner Frost evokes the scene relying on familiar concrete nouns; he also seems to speak to the reader, using the second-person pronoun.

Connect to Life Student answers will probably range from video games to reading, from sports to meditation.

Literary Analysis

Figurative Language Some students may feel more confident rewriting one of Frost's similes or metaphors; others may want to create their own.

Writing Options

1. **Impressive Description** Student responses should contain vivid descriptions of natural scenes using similes and metaphors that appeal to the senses.
2. **Interpretation of Poem** Students should understand Frost's message by interpreting the descriptions of the bent birch trees; the figurative imagery used to describe them seems to symbolize the weariness and anxiety in the speaker's life. Students can place their work in their Working Portfolio.

Activities & Explorations

1. **Video Viewing** After viewing the video, ask students how different oral interpretations affect the poem's meaning.
2. **Leafy Scrapbook** The scrapbook could contain illustrations of trees from the local area. Some students may want to add real leaves to create a collage.

Author Activity

Presidential Inauguration Frost recited "The Gift Outright" at the 1961 presidential inauguration of John F. Kennedy.

Writing Options

1. Impressive Description Think of a natural scene—a tree, a patch of flowers, a waterfall, or some other aspect of the natural world—that impresses you. Then, in one or two paragraphs, write a description of this scene, using figurative language to convey your impressions. You might begin by using a word web to explore your own reactions to the scene you plan to describe.

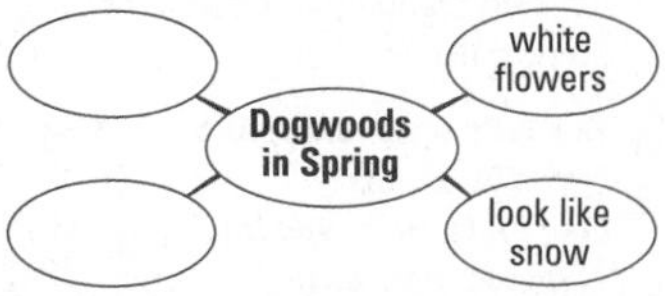

Writing Handbook
See page 1153: Descriptive Writing.

2. Interpretation of Poem Write an essay interpreting the meaning of this poem and the speaker's attitude toward life. Defend your position with evidence from the poem. Place the essay in your **Working Portfolio.**

Activities & Explorations

1. Video Viewing With classmates, watch the video of a dramatic reading of "Birches." Discuss how the actor's reading affects your understanding of the poem. Decide whether you would read the poem in the same way. ~ **VIEWING AND REPRESENTING**

VIDEO **Literature in Performance**

2. Leafy Scrapbook Create a scrapbook of different tree pictures to illustrate why you think trees are so irresistible to young climbers. You could use photographs, magazine illustrations, your own drawings, or a combination of sources to capture various angles and types of trees. ~ **ART**

Robert Frost

1874–1963

Other Works
"The Road Not Taken"
"Mending Wall"
North of Boston
New Hampshire

Unruly Years Although Robert Frost was born in San Francisco, his ancestors were New Englanders. At age 11, shortly after his father's death, Frost moved with his mother and sister to Massachusetts. His mother was a teacher, but Frost was an undisciplined child who frequently skipped school. He did not become interested in books until high school. He then began studying, wrote poems for the school magazine, and was named co-valedictorian of his senior class, an honor he shared with his future wife.

Farmer-Poet Frost attended college briefly and then worked at a variety of jobs, including mill work and teaching. Between 1900 and 1909, he wrote many of his famous poems while living and working on a farm near Derry, New Hampshire. A few were published in magazines, but Frost was almost 40 before his first book was published, in England. He had moved to England in 1912, and by the time he returned to the United States three years later, he was rapidly becoming a distinguished poet.

Honors and Achievements During his lifetime, Frost was awarded 44 honorary college degrees and was invited to teach at numerous colleges and universities, including Dartmouth and Harvard. Ironically, he had once attended and dropped out of both universities. Frost's other honors include four Pulitzer Prizes and a Congressional Gold Medal. He published his last book of poetry, *In the Clearing*, at age 88.

Author Activity

Presidential Inauguration Frost was asked to read a poem at the inauguration of a United States president. He wrote a new poem for the occasion but, in the sun's glare, could not see to read it. Instead, he recited another poem from memory. Find out the name of the president and the name of the poem that Frost read.

Assessment Informal Assessment

You can assess students' understanding of the poem by having students write from Frost's point of view, giving reasons for writing "Birches."

RUBRIC

3 **Full Accomplishment** Response reflects a full understanding of Frost's poem and the influences of his life on the poem.

2 **Substantial Accomplishment** Response reflects a general understanding of Frost's poem and the influences of his life on the poem.

1 **Little or Partial Accomplishment** Response reflects little understanding of Frost's poem and the influences of his life on the poem.

For the New Year, 1981

Poetry by DENISE LEVERTOV

Pride

Poetry by DAHLIA RAVIKOVITCH
(dăl'yə rə-vē'kə-vĭch)

Connect to Your Life

Word Associations What comes to mind when you hear the word *hope?* What about *pride?* For each of these terms, make a word web like the one shown. Write down whatever words or phrases you associate with hope and pride, and then share your webs with a classmate.

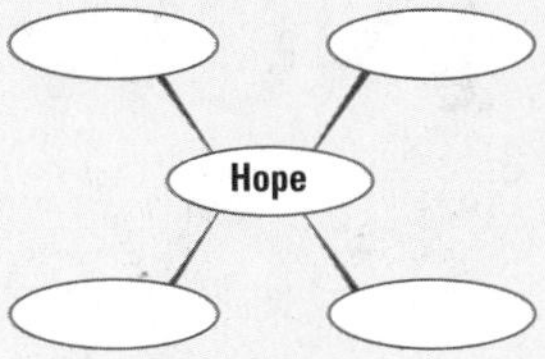

Build Background

Images of Nature Hope and pride are the subjects of the next two poems, both of which were written by contemporary women poets. The speaker in Denise Levertov's "For the New Year, 1981" draws upon images from nature to convey her thoughts about hope. Toward the end of the poem, she makes a comparison to irises, popular perennial plants with orchidlike flowers. Like all perennials, irises can live and bloom for many years; however, they will do so only if they are dug up and divided when they get too crowded. Because the roots of irises are actually thick, gnarled underground stems called rhizomes, dividing the plants can be a difficult chore for a gardener.

The speaker in Dahlia Ravikovitch's "Pride" also uses images from the natural world—rocks at the edge of the sea. To the naked eye, rocks often appear changeless. Geologists tell us, however, that rocks, like all elements of the natural world, are subject to an aging process brought about by weathering and erosion.

Focus Your Reading

LITERARY ANALYSIS | EXTENDED METAPHOR As you know, a **metaphor** is a form of **figurative language** that makes comparisons between two things that have something in common. Unlike a **simile,** a metaphor does not use the words *like* or *as.* In an **extended metaphor,** two unlike things are compared in several ways. As you read the following poems, look for the extended metaphor in each one and consider how they make abstract concepts more concrete.

ACTIVE READING | MAKING INFERENCES Although the **speakers** in the poems that follow do not directly state their ideas about hope and pride, readers can use clues in the texts to **make inferences,** or logical guesses, about the speakers' ideas. For example, consider what the following request in Levertov's poem reveals about the speaker's idea of hope:

Please take
this grain of a grain of hope
so that mine won't shrink.

READER'S NOTEBOOK As you read the poems, try to "read between the lines" and infer the speakers' ideas about their subjects. Note any words, phrases, or lines that contribute to your understanding of what the speakers mean by *hope* and *pride* respectively.

OVERVIEW

Objectives

1. understand and appreciate two **poems (Literary Analysis)**
2. interpret and appreciate an **extended metaphor (Literary Analysis)**
3. **make inferences (Active Reading)**

Summary

In "For the New Year, 1981," Ravikovitch writes about spreading hope from person to person, saying that it grows and blooms when it is well-rooted and shared. In "Pride," the speaker compares pride to rocks that appear solid for ages, but actually have deep fissures and cracks.

Thematic Link

Spreading hope and understanding the effects of pride are **simple truths** in human society. One can help spread hope if one is not too proud to accept a small grain of hope when it is offered.

5-Minute Warm-Up

Daily Language SkillBuilder

Have students **proofread** the display sentences on page 817i and write them correctly. The sentences also appear on Transparency 24 of **Grammar Transparencies and Copymasters.**

LESSON RESOURCES

UNIT FIVE RESOURCE BOOK, pp. 12–13

ASSESSMENT RESOURCES

Formal Assessment, pp. 139–140

Teacher's Guide to Assessment and Portfolio Use

Test Generator

SKILLS TRANSPARENCIES AND COPYMASTERS

Literary Analysis
- Symbols and Figurative Language, T21 (for Activity, p. 846)

Reading and Critical Thinking
- Making Inferences, T7 (for Think Critically, item 3, p. 846)

Grammar
- Correlative Conjunctions I, C78 (for Mini Lesson, p. 845)

Writing
- Effective Language, T13 (for Writing Option 1, p. 847)
- Figurative Language and Sound Devices, T15 (for Writing Option 2, p. 847)
- Poem, C27 (for Writing Option 2, p. 847)

INTEGRATED TECHNOLOGY

Audio Library

Visit our website:
www.mcdougallittell.com

TEACHING THE LITERATURE

Reading and Analyzing

Reading Skills and Strategies: PREVIEW

Have students look through the story. Discuss the information on word associations on p. 843 in Connect to Your Life. Have students share their word web images from the word association activity and compare them to those shared by the authors.

Active Reading MAKING INFERENCES

To understand why the poet compares hope to a grain, ask students what comes to mind when they think of grains. Ask students to list different kinds of grains in their Reader's Notebooks. Remind students that these clues will help them to read between the lines. Ask students what they can infer from these concepts.

Possible Responses: Grains include rice, wheat, and barley, which suggest nourishment, wholeness, and vast quantities. They might also infer that a tiny grain of sand can be part of the creation of vast beaches when it joins forces with other grains. Students might infer that grains of hope represent basic human needs.

Use the **Unit Five Resource Book** p. 12 for additional support.

Literary Analysis
EXTENDED METAPHOR

In "For the New Year, 1981," Levertov compares hope to a grain of crystal which must be divided and shared if it is to grow. Point out to students that the poet spreads this comparison over seven stanzas of unequal length. Ask students to examine the extended metaphor and suggest reasons why it is appropriate for the subject matter.

Possible Responses: Students might note that the length of the extended metaphor and the form and division of the stanzas support the poet's description of hope's growth when one divides and shares it.

Use **Unit Five Resource Book,** p. 13 for more practice.

For the New Year, 1981

Denise Levertov

I have a small grain of hope—
one small crystal that gleams
clear colors out of transparency.

I need more.

I break off a fragment
to send you.

Please take
this grain of a grain of hope
so that mine won't shrink.

Please share your fragment
so that yours will grow.

Only so, by division,
will hope increase,

like a clump of irises, which will cease to flower
unless you distribute
the clustered roots, unlikely source—
clumsy and earth-covered—
of grace.

Thinking Through the Literature

1. **Comprehension Check** What does the **speaker** want to have happen?
2. ACTIVE READING MAKING INFERENCES Review what you wrote in your READER'S NOTEBOOK. What did you **infer** about the meaning of hope to the **speaker?**

   THINK ABOUT
   - the speaker's comparison of hope to a grain, "one small crystal that gleams / clear colors out of transparency" (lines 2–3)
   - the speaker's remark "I need more" (line 4)
   - the reason the speaker gives for sharing hope (lines 5–13)
3. Why do you think the speaker compares hope to irises?
4. What might be the relationship between the speaker and the person addressed?

Thinking Through the Literature

1. Possible Response: The speaker wants to increase hope by sharing it with other people.
2. Possible Response: Hope means faith in one's fellow human being, in life, and in the future, adding grace and beauty to life.
3. The speaker compares hope to irises because, as with the grain, the roots of irises must be divided and spread about regularly if the irises are to increase and bloom.
4. The relationship between the speaker and the person addressed is probably close, perhaps a friend, but the person can also be assumed to represent humanity.

Tidal Flats, Deer Isle, Sunset (1978), A. Robert Birmelin. Acrylic on canvas, 50″ × 57½″, private collection.

Pride

Dahlia Ravikovitch

I tell you, even rocks crack,
and not because of age.
For years they lie on their backs
in the heat and the cold,
so many years,
it almost seems peaceful.
They don't move, so the cracks stay hidden.
A kind of pride.
Years pass over them, waiting there.
Whoever is going to shatter them
hasn't come yet.
And so the moss flourishes, the seaweed
whips around,
the sea pushes through and rolls back—
the rocks seem motionless.
Till a little seal comes to rub against them,
comes and goes away.
And suddenly the rock has an open wound.
I told you, when rocks break, it happens by surprise.
And people, too.

Translated by Chana and Ariel Bloch

Customizing Instruction

Less Proficient Readers

So that students can understand the meaning of the extended metaphor in the poem "Pride," have students make a list of things that the rocks *do* in the poem. Then help them understand the relationship between the rocks and human pride.

Possible Responses: rocks lie on their backs, unmoving; develop cracks; are passed over by years; become covered with moss; are washed by the sea, rubbed by a seal; receive wounds

Then lead students in a discussion of the similarities between rocks and pride, as suggested in the poem.

Students Acquiring English

Students might have difficulty understanding the contradiction between needing more hope and the act of sharing hope. Explain that the speaker will be more hopeful when others are more hopeful, so sharing the hope will expand it. Invite students to visualize the images in the poem to aid their understanding.

Use **Spanish Study Guide** for additional support, pp. 173–175.

Gifted and Talented

Dahlia Ravikovitch is active in the Israeli peace movement. Suggest that students research the history and goals of the peace movement in Israel. Have them apply this knowledge to the poem in order to widen the scope of the poet's meaning.

Mini Lesson Grammar

CORRELATIVE CONJUNCTIONS Instruction Remind students that conjunctions are parts of speech used to tie together or connect words, phrases, and clauses. Different types of conjunctions used in English have different functions. Explain that one kind, correlative conjunctions, is always used in pairs and connects parts of speech (nouns, verbs, etc.) and grammatical structures (phrases, etc.) that are equivalent. Examples of correlative conjunctions are "not only . . . but also," "either . . . or," and "neither . . . nor." When correlative conjunctions tie together nouns or noun phrases used as the subject of a sentence, they can use either a singular or a plural verb form.

Use **Grammar Transparencies and Copymasters,** p. 78.

Use McDougal Littell's ***Language Network,*** Chapter 1, for more instruction in correlative conjunctions.

GUIDING STUDENT RESPONSE

Connect to the Literature

1. What Do You Think?
Accept all reasonable responses, but make sure students mention the specific parts from the poem that generated their visual images.

Comprehension Check
- In Ravikovitch's poem, pride is represented by rocks.
- When the seal rubs against the rock, gentleness breaks through where other forces failed to conquer.

Think Critically

2. Possible Response: The speaker in the poem views pride as a hard, rough rock, successfully hiding its cracks, until the brush of a gentle, innocent touch wounds the hard surface of the rock. In the same way, pride can harden people's sensitivities, keeping them isolated and cold toward others. A soft human touch, however, can break it down.
3. Possible Response: Negative, because the poem personifies pride as a hard rock, seemingly unaffected by its surroundings, hiding the cracks on its back; positive, because a gentle, innocent touch can sometimes break through the hard front that pride projects.
4. Accept all reasonable alternative titles. Have students review the list and evaluate each one in terms of what it contributes to the poem.
5. Possible Response: Both poems are optimistic in tone: "For the New Year, 1981" is a gentle plea to spread hope. In "Pride," the last five lines show the stoic rock opening up after gentle, innocent contact.

Thinking through the LITERATURE

Connect to the Literature

1. **What Do You Think?** What did you picture in your mind as you read "Pride"? Share your thoughts with a classmate.

Comprehension Check
- What is used to represent pride in this poem?
- What happens when the seal rubs against the rocks?

Think Critically

2. Why do you think the **speaker** compares people to rocks?

THINK ABOUT
- what qualities you associate with rocks
- what aspects of human nature the speaker might be comparing to the cracks in a rock
- how the natural forces that act upon a rock might be compared to human experiences
- what an "open wound" might mean

3. ACTIVE READING | MAKING INFERENCES Look back at the words, phrases, and lines you wrote down in your READER'S NOTEBOOK. Do you **infer** that the **speaker** of this poem views pride as positive or negative? Support your opinion with details from the poem.
4. Evaluate the **title** in terms of what it contributes to your understanding of the poem. Then, working with a classmate, brainstorm a list of alternative titles.
5. Compare the **tone** of "For the New Year, 1981" with that of "Pride."

Extend Interpretations

6. **Comparing Texts** What fictional character or real person from the selections you have read might represent the type of hope that is described in "For the New Year, 1981"? Who might represent the type of pride described in "Pride"?
7. **Connect to Life** Review the word web for *pride* that you created for the Connect to Your Life activity on page 843. Then compare your notions of pride with the speaker's.

Literary Analysis

EXTENDED METAPHOR An **extended metaphor** is a metaphor in which two unlike things are compared in more than one way. In "Pride," the rocks at the seaside are the basis for an extended metaphor that is carried out through the entire poem. The first comparison in "For the New Year, 1981," in which hope is called a "small grain," can also be considered an extended metaphor because it is continued across a number of stanzas.

Activity Analyze the extended metaphor in "For the New Year, 1981" by answering the following questions:
- What are the physical qualities of the small grain?
- What does the speaker do with the grain?
- Why does the speaker need to share the grain?
- Why do you think the speaker compares hope to a small grain?

Now compare the use of extended metaphors in both poems. Which extended metaphor do you think is more interesting?

PERSONIFICATION Another form of figurative language is **personification,** a figure of speech in which human qualities are attributed to something nonhuman, such as an object, an animal, or an idea. "The wind sighed" is an example of personification, since it suggests that a nonhuman force, the wind, can engage in the human act of sighing. With a partner, identify examples of personification in "Pride" and explain what human qualities are being personified.

Extend Interpretations

Comparing Texts Responses will vary, but should include specific traits of the person or character that resemble the traits of hope or pride as described by these poems.

Connect to Life Ask students if their notions of pride changed after reading the poem.

Literary Analysis

Extended Metaphor Answers could include the fact that the grain is crystal-like. Like a prism, it turns transparency into the spectrum of colors; it is breakable and dividable; and it can grow and increase almost miraculously by division. The speaker divides the grain and offers a piece of it to another, encouraging the person to share the piece of grain with others so that hope, including her own, will grow. Comparisons and evaluations will vary.

Writing Options

1. Thesaurus Entries Write thesaurus entries for the terms *pride* and *hope* on the basis of the views presented in the two poems. For each entry, include several synonyms and antonyms as well as a brief definition of the term.

2. Abstract Poem Write a poem about pride, hope, or another abstract human attitude or value that you associate with these ideas. The word webs you created for the Connect to Your Life activity on page 843 may help you get started. Try using images from nature to make the abstract attitude or value more concrete.

Activities & Explorations

Images from Nature Choose other images from nature that could be used to communicate the same insights conveyed by the two poems. Find photographs, illustrations, or fine art—or create your own depictions—to suggest those insights. Present your findings to the class, and explain what is suggested by each image.
~ **VIEWING AND REPRESENTING**

Denise Levertov

1923–1997

Other Works
Collected Earlier Poems 1940–1960
New and Selected Essays
Candles in Babylon
Evening Train

A Poet's Destiny Denise Levertov was born and raised in a suburb of London, England. She was educated by her parents at home and inherited her mother's love of nature. As a teenager, Levertov studied ballet and enjoyed painting; she loved traveling alone around London and spending time in the city's many museums and galleries. "Being a poet was, however, from my earliest childhood, what I never had any doubts about," Levertov said. "There is nothing I would ever for a moment prefer to have been." Indeed, Levertov published about two dozen volumes of poetry and received numerous honors and awards—including a Guggenheim Fellowship—for her work.

Political Activist Levertov moved to the United States in 1948 and became a U.S. citizen in 1955. After that time, she worked as the poetry editor of such magazines as *The Nation* and *Mother Jones* and taught at a number of colleges and universities. A pacifist, Levertov was active in antiwar and antinuclear movements over several decades; some of her poems reflect these political convictions.

Dahlia Ravikovitch

1936–

Other Works
A Dress of Fire
The Window: New and Selected Poems

Israeli Poet Dahlia Ravikovitch is among the foremost poets writing in modern Hebrew, the language of Israel. She was born in a town called Ramat Gan, near Tel Aviv, and was raised on Kibbutz Geva, one of the country's many collective farms and settlements. After studying literature at Hebrew University in Jerusalem, she began publishing poetry in the noted journal *Orlogin.* From 1959 to 1963, she taught high school; then she left teaching to devote herself to writing. In addition to several volumes of verse, she has published short stories, children's books, and English-to-Hebrew translations of a number of works. Ravikovitch has also been active in the Israeli peace movement and in programs that teach adults to write poetry.

Writing Options

1. **Thesaurus Entries** Student entries should demonstrate an understanding of hope and pride as characterized by these poems.
2. **Abstract Poem** Remind students to start by referring to their word webs.

Activities & Explorations

Images from Nature If your class has access to the Internet, encourage students to try a picture search, entering keywords describing objects or scenes they think appropriate to the activity.

Assessment Informal Assessment

Ask students to evaluate the title of each poem in terms of its contribution to the reader's understanding of the poem. Suggest that students brainstorm alternative titles. Finally, ask them to write a paragraph about the title's contribution, ending with suggestions for alternative titles.

RUBRIC

3 Full Accomplishment Students' written evaluations and titles show full awareness of the themes and content of the poems.

2 Substantial Accomplishment Students' written evaluations and titles show some understanding of the poems.

1 Little or Partial Accomplishment Students' written evaluations and titles suggest a lack of understanding of the works.

OVERVIEW

Objectives

1. understand and appreciate a **short story (Literary Analysis)**
2. understand sources of **humor (Literary Analysis)**
3. **predict (Active Reading)**

Summary

Sekhar, a teacher in India, decides to spend a day uttering only the absolute truth. At breakfast, he criticizes his wife's cooking. At school, he speaks ill of a man who has just died. Then the headmaster invites Sekhar, known for his musical taste, to judge his singing, in return for which the headmaster grants Sekhar extra time to grade a hundred test papers. After listening for two hours, Sekhar tells the truth: The singing is not good. The next morning, the headmaster thanks Sekhar for the useful advice, but demands to have the hundred papers graded within twenty-four hours. Sekhar decides that spending a sleepless night grading papers is a small price to pay for the luxury of truth.

Thematic Link

Sekhar pays the price for telling the **simple truth**.

5-Minute Warm-Up

Daily Language SkillBuilder

Have students **proofread** the display sentences on page 817j and write them correctly. The sentences also appear on Transparency 24 of **Grammar Transparencies and Copymasters.**

Mini Lesson

Preteaching Vocabulary

If you would like to preteach the WORDS TO KNOW for this selection, use the Mini Lesson, pp. 850–851.

"Truth, he reflected, required as much strength to give as to receive."

Like the Sun

Short Story by R. K. NARAYAN (nə-rī′yən)

Connect to Your Life

Tough Truths Imagine that a friend has purchased a new outfit or has gotten a new haircut that you find unattractive. Your friend seems unsure about his or her appearance and looks to you for approval. Would you express your true feelings? Working in pairs, role-play the different conversations that you and your friend might have. Then discuss with your class whether it's always better to tell the absolute truth or whether truth needs to be tempered in order to spare people's feelings.

Build Background

School Life in India Issues of truth are important to Sekhar, the main character in "Like the Sun." Sekhar is a teacher in India, where schools are modeled on the British educational system. Students begin upper primary school at age 11 and then secondary school at 14 or 15. For seven years they progress through forms, the equivalent of grades in the United States. Sekhar teaches the third form, or ninth grade; the principal of his school is called a headmaster. Sekhar is also a music critic in the small town in which he lives. In the story, he is asked to judge a performance of well-known traditional songs that reflect India's centuries-old musical heritage.

WORDS TO KNOW
Vocabulary Preview
essence
incessantly
shirk
stupefied
tempering

Focus Your Reading

LITERARY ANALYSIS HUMOR The decision made by Sekhar at the beginning of the story sets the stage for the **humor** that will follow:

> ***This day he set apart as a unique day—at least one day in the year we must give and take absolute Truth whatever may happen.***

As you read, note the sources of the story's humor. Does it arise from exaggerated situations, exaggerated **characters,** or humorous language?

ACTIVE READING PREDICTING During his day of absolute truth, Sekhar has a series of encounters with his wife, his colleagues, and his boss, the headmaster of the school where he works. Consider what humorous consequences may arise from Sekhar's decision. At the beginning of each encounter, try to **predict** what is going to happen.

READER'S NOTEBOOK Record your predictions for each of Sekhar's encounters in a chart like the one shown. In the third column, note what actually happens.

Event	Prediction	Outcome
breakfast with his wife		

VIDEODISC **LaserLinks: Background for Reading**
Cultural Connection

LESSON RESOURCES

UNIT FIVE RESOURCE BOOK, pp. 15–16

ASSESSMENT RESOURCES

Formal Assessment, pp. 141–142

Teacher's Guide to Assessment and Portfolio Use

Test Generator

SKILLS TRANSPARENCIES AND COPYMASTERS

Reading and Critical Thinking
- Predicting Outcomes, T2 (for Think Critically, item 4, p. 853)

Grammar
- Adjective Clauses, C111 (for Mini Lesson, p. 854)

Vocabulary
- Word Origins, C79 (for Mini Lesson, p. 850)

Writing
- Achieving Conciseness, T21 (for Writing Options 1, 2, p. 854)
- The Uses of Dialogue, T24 (for Writing Option 3, p. 854)

Communications
- Interviewing, T9 (for Activities & Explorations, p. 854)

INTEGRATED TECHNOLOGY

Audio Library

LaserLinks
- Cultural Connections: Images of India; Scenes of India. See **Teacher's SourceBook,** p. 44.

Internet: Research Starter

Visit our website:
www.mcdougallittell.com

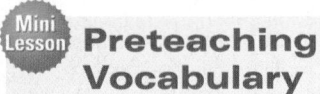

Like the Sun

R. K. Narayan

Truth, Sekhar reflected, is like the sun. I suppose no human being can ever look it straight in the face without blinking or being dazed. He realized that, morning till night, the essence of human relationships consisted in tempering truth so that it might not shock. This day he set apart as a unique day—at least one day in the year we must give and take absolute Truth whatever may happen. Otherwise life is not worth living. The day ahead seemed to him full of possibilities. He told no one of his experiment. It was a quiet resolve, a secret pact between him and eternity.

The very first test came while his wife served him his morning meal. He showed hesitation over a titbit, which she had thought was her culinary[1] masterpiece. She asked, "Why, isn't it good?" At other times he would have said, considering her feelings in the matter, "I feel full up, that's all." But today he said, "It isn't good. I'm unable to swallow it." He saw her wince and said to himself, Can't be helped. Truth is like the sun.

His next trial was in the common room when one of his colleagues came up and said, "Did you hear of the death of so-and-so? Don't you think it a pity?"

"No," Sekhar answered. "He was such a fine man—" the other began. But Sekhar cut him short with: "Far from it. He always struck me as a mean and selfish brute."

During the last period when he was teaching geography for Third Form A, Sekhar received a note from the headmaster: "Please see me before you go home." Sekhar said to himself: It must be about these horrible test papers. A hundred papers in the boys' scrawls; he had shirked this work for weeks, feeling all the time as if a sword were hanging over his head.

The bell rang, and the boys burst out of the class.

Sekhar paused for a moment outside the headmaster's room to button up his coat; that was another subject the headmaster always sermonized about.

He stepped in with a very polite "Good evening, sir."

1. **culinary** (kyo͞o′lə-nĕr′ē): having to do with cooking or the kitchen.

WORDS TO KNOW
essence (ĕs′əns) *n.* the crucial element or basis
tempering (tĕm′pə-rĭng) *n.* modifying or adjusting **temper** *v.*
shirk (shûrk) *v.* to neglect or avoid

TEACHING THE LITERATURE

Customizing Instruction

Less Proficient Readers

Have students read the first paragraph of the story, in which Sekhar vows to tell the absolute truth for one day. Discuss what problems he might encounter.

Set a Purpose Have students read on to see what tests Sekhar faces as a result of his vow.

Students Acquiring English

Discuss with students how people from their home culture deal with telling the truth. Ask whether telling the whole truth, partial truths or lies is allowed or even considered necessary or polite at times. Invite students to give specific examples.

Use **Spanish Study Guide** pp. 175–177.

Gifted and Talented

Have students think of other selections in which the truth is a crucial issue. You might point them to "The Witness for the Prosecution" (p. 871) and "A White Heron" (p. 822). Encourage students to discuss the main characters' approaches to the truth in "Like the Sun" and the other works they have thought of. Ask them to evaluate the characters' use of the truth.

TEACHING THE LITERATURE

Reading and Analyzing

Reading Skills and Strategies: PREVIEW

Have students look over the selection. Ask students to think about how the title, the called-out quotations on p. 848, the art and the title of the Literary Link on p. 852 are related to one another. Have them read the Build Background and Connect to Your Life features on p. 848. Then give them a brief summary of the story.

Active Reading PREDICTING

As students read the story and fill in their prediction charts, have them look for hints the writer inserts in the story to prepare readers for what is to come.

Use **Unit Five Resource Book** p. 15 for more practice.

Literary Analysis HUMOR

Remind students that the perception of humor is subjective and that each writer's method of humorous writing is unique. Students may want to discuss which aspect of Narayan's story (situations, characters, language) they find most successful and amusing.

Use **Unit Five Resource Book** p. 16 for more practice.

The headmaster looked up at him in a very friendly manner and asked, "Are you free this evening?"

Sekhar replied, "Just some outing which I have promised the children at home—"

"Well, you can take them out another day. Come home with me now."

"Oh . . . yes, sir, certainly . . ." And then he added timidly, "Anything special, sir?"

"Yes," replied the headmaster, smiling to himself . . . "You didn't know my weakness for music?"

"Oh, yes, sir . . ."

"I've been learning and practicing secretly, and now I want you to hear me this evening. I've engaged a drummer and a violinist to accompany me—this is the first time I'm doing it full-dress,[2] and I want your opinion. I know it will be valuable."

Sekhar's taste in music was well-known. He was one of the most dreaded music critics in the town. But he never anticipated his musical inclinations would lead him to this trial. . . .

1 "Rather a surprise for you, isn't it?" asked the headmaster. "I've spent a fortune on it behind closed doors. . . ." They started for the headmaster's house. "God hasn't given me a child, but at least let him not deny me the consolation of music," the headmaster said, pathetically, as they walked. He incessantly chattered about music: how he began one day out of sheer boredom; how his teacher at first laughed at him and then gave him hope; how his ambition in life was to forget himself in music.

At home the headmaster proved very ingratiating. He sat Sekhar on a red silk carpet, set before him several dishes of delicacies, and fussed over him as if he were a son-in-law of the house. He even said, "Well, you must listen with a free mind. Don't worry about these test papers." He added half humorously, "I will give you a week's time."

"Make it ten days, sir," Sekhar pleaded.

"All right, granted," the headmaster said generously. Sekhar felt really relieved now—he would attack them at the rate of ten a day and get rid of the nuisance.

The headmaster lighted incense sticks. "Just to create the right atmosphere," he explained. A drummer and a violinist, already seated on a Rangoon mat, were waiting for him. The headmaster sat down between them like a professional at a concert, cleared his throat, and began an alapana,[3] and paused to ask, "Isn't it good Kalyani?"[4] Sekhar pretended not to have heard the question. The headmaster went on to sing a full song composed by Thyagaraja[5] and followed it with two more. All the time the headmaster was singing, Sekhar went on commenting within himself, He croaks like a dozen frogs. He is bellowing like a buffalo. Now he sounds like loose window shutters in a storm.

The incense sticks burnt low. Sekhar's head throbbed with the medley of sounds that had assailed his eardrums for a couple of hours now. He felt half stupefied. The headmaster had gone nearly hoarse, when he paused to ask, "Shall I go on?" Sekhar replied, "Please don't, sir; I think this will do. . . ." The headmaster looked stunned. His face was beaded with perspiration. Sekhar felt the greatest pity for him. But he felt he could not help it. No judge delivering a sentence felt more pained and helpless. Sekhar noticed that the headmaster's wife peeped in from the kitchen, with eager curiosity. The drummer and the violinist put away their burdens with an air of relief. The headmaster removed his spectacles, mopped his brow, and

2. **full-dress:** complete in every respect.
3. **alapana:** improvisational Indian music in the classical style.
4. **Kalyani:** traditional Indian folk songs.
5. **Thyagaraja** (1767–1847): famous Indian composer.

WORDS TO KNOW
incessantly (ĭn-sĕs′ənt-lē) *adv.* endlessly; constantly
stupefied (sto͞o′pə-fīd′) *adj.* dazed; stunned

Teaching Options

Mini Lesson Preteaching Vocabulary

RESEARCH WORD ORIGINS Call students' attention to the list of WORDS TO KNOW. Remind them that sometimes they can better understand the meaning of an unfamiliar word by researching its origins. Use the word *stupefied* to model.

Instruction Model the process of discovering the word origin for students: First, find the uninflected form of the word: *stupefy*. Then look up this form in a dictionary. You will find that it comes from Latin *stupere* "to be astonished" and *facere* "to make or do." Ask a volunteer to apply this meaning in the story context.

Possible Response: Sekhar has been rendered astonished by the long, tedious, incompetent performance.

Exercises For each of the remaining WORDS TO KNOW, have students look up the word origins in a dictionary. Then ask students to identify how the word origin applies to the word as it is used in the story.

Use **Unit Five Resource Book** p. 17 for more practice.

A lesson on word origins appears on p. 356 in the Pupil's Edition.

Detail of *The Dance of Krishna* (about 1650, Mewar, Rajasthan, India). From a manuscript of the Sur-Sagar, opaque watercolor on paper, 11″ × 8⅝″, Collection Gopi Krishna Kanoria, Patna, India.

asked, "Now, come out with your opinion."

"Can't I give it tomorrow, sir?" Sekhar asked tentatively.

"No. I want it immediately—your frank opinion. Was it good?"

"No, sir . . ." Sekhar replied.

"Oh! . . . Is there any use continuing my lessons?"

"Absolutely none, sir . . ." Sekhar said with his voice trembling. He felt very unhappy that he could not speak more soothingly. Truth, he reflected, required as much strength to give as to receive.

All the way home he felt worried. He felt that his official life was not going to be smooth sailing hereafter. There were questions of increment and confirmation[6] and so on, all depending upon the headmaster's goodwill. All kinds of worries seemed to be in store for him. . . . Did not Harischandra[7] lose his throne,

6. **increment and confirmation:** salary increases and job security.

7. **Harischandra:** a legendary Hindu king and the subject of many Indian stories. His name has come to symbolize truth and integrity.

Customizing Instruction

Less Proficient Readers
Make sure students understand the trials Sekhar faces.

- What truth has Sekhar told his wife?
  Possible Response: Her cooking is bad.
- What request has the headmaster made?
  Possible Response: He has asked Sekhar to evaluate his singing.
- Why is this request a problem for Sekhar?
  Possible Response: If the head master sings badly, Sekhar will have to break his vow or risk offending his boss.

Set a Purpose Have students read to see how Sekhar's dilemma is resolved.

Students Acquiring English

1 Explain to students that "behind closed doors" means "in secret" or "in private."

Mini Lesson Viewing and Representing

Detail of *The Dance of Krishna* by unknown artist

ART APPRECIATION This detail comes from a larger painting, which depicts an important Hindu god, Krishna, playing the flute and dancing. The musicians shown here are accompanying the enchanted music of Krishna, who is known for his love of humanity and is seen in the lower left corner of the detail.

Application Ask students how the mood of the painting compares with the mood of the scene in which Sekhar hears the headmaster's recital. Do the figures in the painting seem to have the same attitudes as Sekhar and the musicians in the story?

Reading and Analyzing

Literary Analysis: CHARACTERIZATION

Ask students how they would characterize the headmaster.

Possible Response: He respects Sekhar's judgment as a music critic, but he is resentful and embarrassed—this is why he insists that the test papers be done by the following day.

Literary Analysis: THEME

Have students state the message of the story in their own words.

Possible Response: Absolute truth may need to be tempered by the situation and by other people's feelings.

Literary Link

Ask students how the message of the Dickinson poem relates to the message of "Like the Sun."

Possible Response: Both works express the idea that the truth is too harsh for most people.

wife, child, because he would speak nothing less than the absolute Truth whatever happened?

At home his wife served him with a sullen face. He knew she was still angry with him for his remark of the morning. Two casualties for today, Sekhar said to himself. If I practice it for a week, I don't think I shall have a single friend left.

He received a call from the headmaster in his classroom next day. He went up apprehensively.

"Your suggestion was useful. I have paid off the music master. No one would tell me the truth about my music all these days. Why such antics at my age! Thank you. By the way, what about those test papers?"

"You gave me ten days, sir, for correcting them."

"Oh, I've reconsidered it. I must positively have them here tomorrow. . . ." A hundred papers in a day! That meant all night's sitting up! "Give me a couple of days, sir . . ."

"No. I must have them tomorrow morning. And remember, every paper must be thoroughly scrutinized."

"Yes, sir," Sekhar said, feeling that sitting up all night with a hundred test papers was a small price to pay for the luxury of practicing Truth. ❖

L I T E R A R Y   L I N K

Tell all the Truth but tell it slant—

Emily Dickinson

Tell all the Truth but tell it slant—
Success in Circuit lies
Too bright for our infirm Delight
The Truth's superb surprise
As Lightning to the Children eased
With explanation kind
The Truth must dazzle gradually
Or every man be blind—

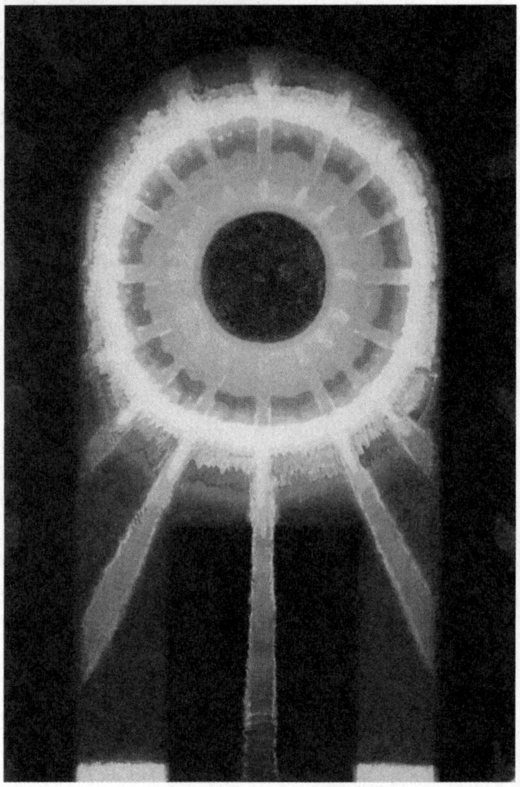

June '70 (1970), Biren De. Oil on canvas, 72″ × 48″, National Gallery of Modern Art, New Delhi, India.

Teaching Options

Mini Lesson Viewing and Representing

***June '70* by Biren De**

ART APPRECIATION This painting by Biren De (1926–) illustrates how abstract techniques that originated among European painters have been adapted to the cultural traditions of India.

Instruction Point out the artist's use of light and darkness in this image of the sun. Ask students why the painter chose to put a dark circle in the middle of the sun.

Possible Response: The circle may represent the dark afterimage created immediately by the intense brightness of the sun on the naked eye.

Application Ask students how they think the painting relates to Sekhar's ideas about truth.

Possible Response: The image of the sun is striking and powerful, corresponding to Sekhar's thought that truth is powerful and dazzling like the sun. The dark spot in its center might represent people's inability to face the truth directly.

Connect to the Literature

1. **What Do You Think?** Did you like the **character** Sekhar? Share what you think with your classmates.

Comprehension Check
- What does Sekhar decide to do for one day?
- How do Sekhar's wife and the headmaster react to his behavior?
- Why must Sekhar stay up all night?

Think Critically

2. What kind of person is Sekhar? Use examples from the text to support your opinion.

THINK ABOUT
- his actions on the day of truth compared with those on other days
- his relationships with other people
- his attitude toward his work
- his reputation as a music critic

3. Why do you think that telling the absolute truth at least one day a year is so important to Sekhar?
4. ACTIVE READING PREDICTING Review the **predictions** you made in your READER'S NOTEBOOK. How closely did your predictions match the events in the story? To what extent did your ability to predict events add to your enjoyment of the story? Explain your answer.
5. Is Sekhar's "experiment" one that you would like to repeat? Why or why not?

Extend Interpretations

6. **Comparing Texts** Does the Literary Link poem "Tell all the Truth but tell it slant—" (page 852) help you to understand Sekhar's observations about truth? Explain your answer.
7. **Critic's Corner** According to critic Perry D. Westbrook, much of Narayan's work conveys this **theme:** "Human beings are human beings, not gods. Men and women can make flights toward godhood, but they always fall a bit short." How do you think this statement applies to "Like the Sun"?
8. **Connect to Life** Do you agree with Sekhar that truth generally requires "as much strength to give as to receive"? Why or why not?

Literary Analysis

HUMOR In literature there are three basic types of **humor,** all of which may involve exaggeration or **irony.**

- **Humor of situation** is derived from the plot of a work. It usually involves exaggerated events or **situational irony,** which occurs when something happens that is different from what one expected.
- **Humor of character** is often based on exaggerated personalities or on characters who fail to recognize their own flaws, a form of **dramatic irony.**
- **Humor of language** may include **sarcasm,** exaggeration, **puns,** or **verbal irony,** which occurs when what is said is not what is meant.

Activity Do you think the humor in "Like the Sun" derives mainly from situation, character, or language? Cite details from the story to support your opinion.

REVIEW ALLITERATION, ASSONANCE, AND CONSONANCE
Review the definitions of alliteration, assonance, and consonance on page 841. Work with a partner to decide which of these sound devices are employed by Emily Dickinson in "Tell all the Truth but tell it slant—"on page 852. Then practice reading the poem aloud to see if you can determine how such repetition contributes to the meaning and effect of the poem.

GUIDING STUDENT RESPONSE

Connect to the Literature

1. **What Do You Think?**
Students may have varying opinions based on their appreciation of the humor.

Comprehension Check
- tell the absolute truth, no matter what
- His wife is hurt and resentful; the headmaster pretends to be grateful but is actually embarrassed.
- He must grade the 100 test papers that he had been putting off.

Use Selection Quiz **Unit Five Resource Book**, p. 19.

Think Critically

2. Possible Responses: Sekhar is weary of telling polite lies every day; he is intelligent and well educated; he has the courage to keep his vow despite challenging circumstances.
3. Possible Responses: Sekhar wants to transcend everyday life; he believes life is not worth living without truth; he wants to experience absolute truth.
4. Sharing their predictions will probably reveal similar results.
5. Students should compare the text events with their own or others' experiences. Students may be able to share their attempts at being completely truthful, and therefore, react to Sekhar's experiment based on a personal connection.

Extend Interpretations

Comparing Texts A discussion could be launched by establishing what it might mean to tell the truth considering Dickinson's terms "slant" and "in Circuit."

Critic's Corner Telling the absolute truth is a difficult goal that most people cannot reach.

Connect to Life Students will probably be able to respond to this question based on personal experiences.

Literary Analysis

Humor Students may respond differently; some may say that humor draws from several sources.

Writing Options

1. **Headmaster's Notes** Remind students that they should decide whether they will "temper" their notes to avoid unnecessary pain or hard feelings.
2. **Theme Interpretation** Thematic statements should draw on support from the story or from personal experiences.
3. **Scene Dialogue** Encourage students to review the details of Sekhar's behavior on p. 849.

Activities & Explorations

Truth Survey Students should be alert to the difficulty of answering questionnaires dealing with moral issues. Explain that the more specific their questions are, the easier it will be for students to make a judgment about how they would behave. Students should compile the results in a single form and make a report to the class. Modeling appropriate questions could be helpful to students.

Inquiry & Research

Legacy of Empire Encourage students to focus their research specifically on the political and economic system. Encourage them to locate appropriate print and nonprint information using text resources and technical resources including on-line databases and the Internet.

Vocabulary in Action

1. lazy
2. someone with an ability to see what's most important
3. hoarse
4. amazement
5. moderating

Choices & CHALLENGES

Writing Options

1. **Headmaster's Notes** As the headmaster of Sekhar's school, write two notes, one to your music master and one to Sekhar. Tell the music master why you are ending your lessons. Then tell Sekhar what you think of his honest evaluation of your performance.
2. **Theme Interpretation** Write a brief interpretation of the theme of the story. What do you think the author is trying to say about truth and personal relationships? Place the interpretation in your **Working Portfolio.**
3. **Scene Dialogue** If this day of "absolute truth" had been like any day of "tempered truth," how might Sekhar have responded to the questions asked by his colleague and by his boss? Rewrite Sekhar's two conversations. Temper the truth about what Sekhar really thinks so that he avoids hurting anyone's feelings.

Activities & Explorations

Truth Survey Take a survey of at least six friends or classmates on the subject of truth. Create a series of questions based on situations from everyday life that are similar to those that Sekhar faced. For example, you might ask, "If a friend who lacked musical talent wanted your opinion about his or her performance, how truthful would you be?" Have participants rate their truthfulness on a scale of 1 to 5, with 1 being "not truthful at all" and 5 being "completely truthful." If you have a graphics program on your computer, use it to design your questionnaire.
~ **SPEAKING AND LISTENING**

Inquiry & Research

Legacy of Empire As you know, the Indian school system described in the story is modeled on the British educational system. Find out more about the British colonization of India. In what other ways can the effects of the British Empire be felt in India? Share your findings with the class in an oral report.

More Online: Research Starter
www.mcdougallittell.com

The British game of cricket is still played in India.

Vocabulary in Action

EXERCISE: CONTEXT CLUES On your paper, answer the questions that follow.

1. Are people who normally **shirk** their work likely to be lazy, efficient, or exhausted?
2. Is a person who can easily identify the **essence** of a problem someone with a sharp sense of smell, someone with an ability to see what's most important, or someone with a taste for the extraordinary?
3. Would a lecturer who spoke **incessantly** most likely find himself or herself applauded, arrested, or hoarse?
4. Does a person become **stupefied** by amusement, amazement, or annoyance?
5. Which of the following is the best synonym for ***tempering:*** *opposing, insisting,* or *moderating?*

Building Vocabulary
Several Words to Know in this lesson have interesting origins. For an in-depth study of word origins, see page 356.

Mini Lesson Grammar

ADJECTIVE CLAUSES An adjective clause is a clause that modifies a noun or pronoun. Adjective clauses often begin with a relative pronoun: *who, whom, which,* or *that.* They may also begin with *whose, where,* or *when.*

Write the following sentence on the chalkboard:

On his truth-telling day, Sekhar was a man who stuck strictly to the truth.

Underline the adjective clause as shown. Have students identify the noun that the adjective clause modifies.

Answer: man

Practice Have students copy the following sentences. Ask them to underline the adjective clauses and identify the nouns or pronouns they modify.

1. Sekhar refuses to eat the food that his wife has prepared.
   Answer: that his wife has prepared (food)
2. According to Sekhar, the man who had died was mean and selfish.
   Answer: who had died (man)

Grammar in Context: Adjective Clauses

In the following sentence, R. K. Narayan uses an adjective clause to help create a humorous description.

> **Sekhar's head throbbed with the medley of sounds that had assailed his eardrums for a couple of hours now.**

An **adjective clause** is a subordinate clause that functions as an adjective—that is, it modifies a noun or pronoun. In the example above, the adjective clause shown in blue modifies the noun phrase *medley of sounds.* The clause helps explain why the main character's head throbbed.

Most adjective clauses begin with relative pronouns, such as *that, which, who, whom,* and *whose. That* is usually used in an essential clause (a clause containing information that is part of the main idea of a sentence). *Which* is usually used in a nonessential clause (a clause adding information that is not part of a sentence's main idea). A nonessential clause is set off with commas; an essential clause is not.

Who is used when the relative pronoun functions as the subject of a verb in the clause. *Whom* is used when it functions as the object of a verb or preposition in the clause. *Who* and *whom* are used in both essential and nonessential clauses.

WRITING EXERCISE Rewrite each sentence, adding an adjective clause that modifies the underlined noun. Begin the adjective clause with the relative pronoun shown in parentheses.

Example: ***Original*** Sekhar makes a decision. (that)

Rewritten Sekhar makes a decision that he will be absolutely honest.

1. Sekhar will tell the truth to anyone. *(who)*
2. Also, he will ignore the test papers. *(that)*
3. He complains about his morning meal. *(which)*
4. He hesitates before announcing his opinion of the music. *(which)*
5. The headmaster gives a difficult task to Sekhar. *(who)*

Grammar Handbook Clauses, p. 1197

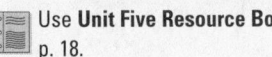

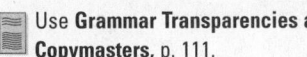

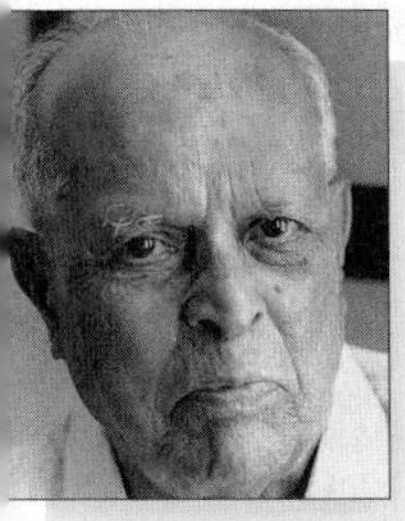

R. K. Narayan

1906–

Other Works
The Guide
Malgudi Days
The English Teacher
My Days: A Memoir
Under the Banyan Tree

A Second Career Born in Madras, India, R. K. Narayan is widely regarded as one of India's greatest authors. For his novel *The Guide* (1958), he won the National Prize of the Indian Literary Academy, his country's highest literary honor. Ironically, he turned to writing after he failed at teaching, having held two different jobs for a total of two days.

Fictional Setting Narayan sets most of his works in a fictional Indian town named Malgudi, a place that resembles both the city of his birth and the city of Mysore, where he has spent most of his life. He created Malgudi for his first novel, *Swami and Friends.* "As I sat in a room nibbling my pen and wondering what to write," he recalls, "Malgudi with its little railway station swam into view."

English Narratives Although Narayan knows the Indian language of Tamil, he always writes in English. Many of his stories were originally published in *Hindu,* one of India's English-language newspapers.

Author Activity

Epic Tradition In addition to writing fiction, Narayan has translated into English certain Indian epics, including the *Ramayana.* Find out more about this great Indian epic, written by the poet Valmiki. Report your findings to your classmates.

Grammar in Context

WRITING EXERCISE Answers will vary. Possible answers are shown.

1. Sekhar will tell the truth to anyone who asks his opinion.
2. Also, he will ignore the test papers that he has avoided correcting for weeks.
3. He complains about his morning meal, which his wife has prepared.
4. He hesitates before announcing his opinion of the music, which hurt his ears.
5. The headmaster gives a difficult task to Sekhar, who doesn't mind.

Author Activity

The *Ramayana* and the *Mahabharata* are considered the two greatest Indian epic poems. The *Ramayana* tells the story of Rama, the king's son who is exiled through the connivance of his stepmother. The epic details Rama's adventures during his years of wandering, including the rescue of his wife, Sita, from Ravana, a Titan who had kidnapped her.

3. Sekhar is a man whose musical taste is admired.
   Answer: whose musical taste is admired (man)
4. In a musical performance, the tanam, which is composed of meaningless words, follows the alapana.
   Answer: which is composed of meaningless words (tanam)
5. The school where Sekhar teaches is governed by a headmaster.
   Answer: where Sekhar teaches (school)

Use **Unit Five Resource Book,** p. 18.

Use **Grammar Transparencies and Copymasters,** p. 111.

Use McDougal Littell's ***Language Network,*** Chapter 4, for more instruction in adjective clauses.

Building Vocabulary

Objectives

- build vocabulary through analyzing prefixes and suffixes
- analyze words into constituent parts
- use new words in a sentence

When students have completed the exercises, have them read their sentences aloud. After they have listened to the sentences, ask students to discuss whether the words are used correctly.

EXERCISE

1. ante/meridian: before noon
   Fish bite best in the antemeridian part of the day.
2. post/operat/ive: after an operation
   The postoperative procedure always involves letting the patient rest extensively.
3. affect/ion/ate/ly: in a manner which shows emotion or caring
   The little girl affectionately hugged her puppy.
4. im/mobile: not mobile or movable
   I was completely immobile the day after skiing.
5. giant/ism: the condition of being great in size
   When I finally stopped growing, my mother was relieved of her fears that I was suffering from giantism.

The Structure of Words

> **Nature had got inexcusably carried away on the summer question and let the whole thing get to be rather much. By duration alone, for instance, a summer's day seemed maddeningly excessive. . . .**
> —Lorraine Hansberry, "On Summer"

The English language has an amazingly rich vocabulary—a lexicon of hundreds of thousands of words. Moreover, the language is constantly growing. All the words in the language, though, have one thing in common. They are made up of various combinations of base words, roots, and **affixes,** or word parts. For example, in the passage on the right, consider the structure of the word *inexcusably*.

Inexcusably consists of the base word *excuse*, which means "to forgive," and two affixes. The affix *in-*, meaning "not," changes the meaning of the base word to its opposite—"not to forgive." The affix *-ably* changes the part of speech of *excuse* from verb to adverb. Understanding how an affix can affect a word's meaning or its part of speech is an essential skill for building vocabulary.

Strategies for Building Vocabulary

An affix may be either a **prefix,** which is attached to the beginning of a word, or a **suffix,** which is attached to the end of a word. Affixes may be added to base words and to roots. Learning the meanings of affixes can help you figure out unfamiliar words.

❶ Learn Prefixes When a prefix is added, it alters the meaning of a base word or root. For example, consider the word *imperfection*. When *im-* is added to *perfection*, it negates, or reverses, the meaning, making a word that means "flaw," or "not perfect." The chart below shows two categories of prefixes.

Prefixes Expressing Size	Meaning	Examples
micro-	small	microcircuit, microscope
mini-	short, small	miniskirt, miniseries

Prefixes Expressing Time	Meaning	Examples
ante-	before	antebellum, antedate
post-	after	postdate, postscript

❷ Learn Suffixes One or more suffixes can be added to the end of a base word or root to alter its meaning. There are two kinds of suffixes—derivational suffixes and inflectional suffixes.

A Derivational Suffix . . .	
Changes the part of speech of a word	immigrate + *-ant* = immigrant

An Inflectional Suffix . . .	
Changes a word from singular to plural	birch + *-es* = birches
Changes the tense of a verb	walk + *-ed* = walked
Changes a word's degree of comparison	great + *-est* = greatest

Knowing suffixes will help you analyze the parts of words and decipher meaning. Study the following chart to learn three types of derivational suffixes.

Noun Suffixes	Meaning	Examples
-ness	state or quality of being	lawlessness, miserliness
-ism	system or theory; the condition of	capitalism, realism

Adjective Suffixes	Meaning	Examples
-ate	Characterized by	passionate
-ive	inclined to	excessive

Adverb Suffixes	Meaning	Examples
-ly	in such a manner	slowly
-wise	like	clockwise

EXERCISE Break each word into its parts and give a definition of the word. If necessary, use a dictionary to help you find the meanings of the word parts. Then write a sentence using each word.

1. antemeridian
2. postoperative
3. affectionately
4. immobile
5. giantism

Lorraine Hansberry was raised in Chicago, where summers can be hot and humid. When Hansberry was a child in the 1930s and 1940s, air conditioning was almost unheard of, so staying comfortable during the summers was nearly impossible. In this autobiographical selection, Hansberry tells about her experiences with the heat of the Chicago summer and why she finally came to "any measure of respect" for the season.

On Summer

Lorraine Hansberry

It has taken me a good number of years to come to any measure of respect for summer. I was, being May-born, literally an "infant of the spring" and, during the later childhood years, tended, for some reason or other, to rather worship the cold aloofness of winter. The adolescence, admittedly lingering still, brought the traditional passionate commitment to melancholy[1] autumn—and all that. For the longest kind of time I simply thought that *summer* was a mistake.

In fact, my earliest memory of anything at all is of waking up in a darkened room where I had been put to bed for a nap on a summer's afternoon, and feeling very, very hot. I acutely disliked the feeling then and retained the bias for years. It had originally been a matter of the heat but, over the years, I came actively to associate displeasure with most of the usually celebrated natural features and social by-products of the season: the too-grainy texture of sand; the too-cold coldness of the various waters we constantly try to escape into; and the icky-perspiry feeling of bathing caps.

It also seemed to me, esthetically[2] speaking, that nature had got inexcusably carried away on the summer question and let the whole thing get to be rather much. By duration alone, for instance, a summer's day seemed maddeningly excessive; an utter overstatement. Except for those few hours at either end of it, objects always appeared in too sharp a relief against backgrounds; shadows too pronounced and light too blinding. It always gave me the feeling of walking around in a motion picture which had been too artsily-craftsily exposed. Sound also had a way of coming to the ear without that

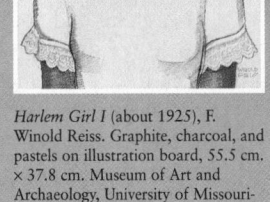

Harlem Girl I (about 1925), F. Winold Reiss. Graphite, charcoal, and pastels on illustration board, 55.5 cm. × 37.8 cm. Museum of Art and Archaeology, University of Missouri-Columbia. Gift of Mr. W. Tjark Reiss.

1. **melancholy** (mĕl′ən-kŏl′ē): sad.
2. **esthetically** (ĕs-thĕt′ĭk-lē): in a way that involves the level of good taste or artistic value.

ON YOUR OWN

Possible Objectives

You can use this selection to achieve one or more of the following objectives:

- enjoy silent sustained reading (Option One)
- read and analyze literature with a group (Option Two)
- use the Reader's Notebook to formulate questions about literature (Option Three)
- write in response to literature (Option Three)

Summary

Lorraine Hansberry recalls the unbearably hot and uncomfortable summers of her childhood in Chicago. She describes in detail how the heat affected her childhood sensibility and how she remembers sleeping with her family on blankets in the cool grass of the park at night. Lying under the stars, she listened to stories told by adults about their childhoods. One summer, the family traveled to her mother's birthplace in Tennessee, and she recalls her mother telling secret stories of the treacheries experienced by her kin while they sought to escape the bondage of slavery. Hansberry describes the subsequent experiences that lead to her gradual awareness of beauty in the summer season. Her mature understanding of summer culminates in the memorable discoveries brought to her through friendship with a woman who is dying of cancer one summer on Cape Cod. The woman's steadfast strength and faith in the genius of humankind to confront and defeat any obstacle provides her with lasting inspiration. This experience leads Hansberry to see, for the first time, the true meaning of summer as a precious time in life when human beings are fully alive.

ON SUMMER 857

Option One
Silent Sustained Reading

You might set aside time each week for independent reading. During this time, you and your students would read for enjoyment. "On Summer" can be read independently in about 20 minutes. If you want to encourage students to read for pleasure, you might forego assignments related to the selection. Should you want to make assignments, Options Two and Three offer suggestions.

Option Two
Shared Reading Groups

You may assign students to groups or allow them to choose their own. Students can read the selection together, alternately reading sections aloud, or they can read independently and meet to cooperate in a project that portrays some element of the essay.

Possible Projects

- Students can access descriptions from the text to create the summer settings portrayed by Hansberry. Have them note how the narrator's attitude toward those settings changes as the selection develops.
- Students can write a statement describing the possibilities of youth that might have been written by the woman dying of cancer on Cape Cod.
- Students can create a monologue in which the woman dying of cancer delivers her inspiring words about the "genius of man."

Shadow and Sunlight (1941), Allan Rohan Crite. National Museum of American Art, Smithsonian Institution, Washington, D.C./Art Resource, New York.

muting influence, marvelously common to winter, across patios or beaches or through the woods. I suppose I found it too stark and yet too intimate a season.

My childhood Southside[3] summers were the ordinary city kind, full of the street games which the other rememberers have turned into fine ballets these days and rhymes that anticipated what some people insist on calling modern poetry:

Oh, Mary Mack, Mack, Mack
With the silver buttons, buttons, buttons
All down her back, back, back
She asked her mother, mother, mother
For fifteen cents, cents, cents
To see the elephant, elephant, elephant
Jump the fence, fence, fence
Well, he jumped so high, high, high
'Til he touched the sky, sky, sky
And he didn't come back, back, back
'Til the Fourth of Ju-ly, ly, ly!

Evenings were spent mainly on the back porches where screen doors slammed in the darkness with those really very special summertime sounds. And, sometimes, when Chicago nights got too steamy, the whole family got into the car and went to the park and slept out in the open on blankets. Those were, of course, the best times of all because the grownups were invariably reminded of having been children in rural parts of the country and told the best stories then. And it was also cool and sweet to be on the grass and there was usually the scent of freshly cut lemons or melons in the air. And Daddy would lie on his back, as fathers must, and explain about how men thought the stars above us came to be and how far away they were. I never did learn to believe that anything could be as far away as *that*. Especially the stars.

3. **Southside:** the part of Chicago that lies south of the downtown area.

My mother first took us south to visit her Tennessee birthplace one summer when I was seven or eight, I think. I woke up on the back seat of the car while we were still driving through some place called Kentucky and my mother was pointing out to the beautiful hills on both sides of the highway and telling my brothers and my sister about how her father had run away and hidden from his master in those very hills when he was a little boy. She said that his mother had wandered among the wooded slopes in the moonlight and left food for him in secret places. They were very beautiful hills and I looked out at them for miles and miles after that wondering who and what a *master* might be.

I remember being startled when I first saw my grandmother rocking away on her porch. All my life I had heard that she was a great beauty and no one had ever remarked that they meant a half century before. The woman that I met was as wrinkled as a prune and could hardly hear and barely see and always seemed to be thinking of other times. But she could still rock and talk and even make wonderful cupcakes which were like cornbread, only sweet. She was captivated by automobiles and, even though it was well into the Thirties, I don't think she had ever been in one before we came down and took her driving. She was a little afraid of them and could not seem to negotiate the windows, but she loved driving. She died the next summer and that is all that I remember about her, except that she was born in slavery and had memories of it and they didn't sound anything like *Gone with the Wind.*[4]

Like everyone else, I have spent whole or bits of summers in many different kinds of places since then: camps and resorts in the Middle West and New York State; on an island; in a tiny Mexican village; Cape Cod,[5] perched atop the Truro bluffs at Longnook Beach that Millay[6] wrote about; or simply strolling the streets of Provincetown[7] before the hours when the parties begin.

And, lastly, I do not think that I will forget days spent, a few summers ago, at a beautiful lodge built right into the rocky cliffs of a bay on the Maine coast. We met a woman there who had lived a purposeful and courageous life and who was then dying of cancer. She had, characteristically, just written a book and taken up painting. She had also been of radical viewpoint all her life; one of those people who energetically believe that the world *can* be changed for the better and spend their lives trying to do just that. And that was the way she thought of cancer; she absolutely refused to award it the stature of tragedy, a devastating instance of the brooding doom and inexplicability of the absurdity of human destiny, etc., etc. The kind of characterization given, lately, as we all know, to far less formidable foes in life than cancer.

But for this remarkable woman it was a matter of nature in imperfection, implying, as always, work for man to do. It was an *enemy,* but a palpable[8] one with shape and effect and source; and if it existed, it could be destroyed. She saluted it accordingly, without despondency, but with a lively, beautiful and delightfully ribald[9] anger. There was one thing, she felt, which would prove equal to its relentless ravages and that was the genius of man. Not his mysticism,[10] but man with tubes and slides and the stubborn human notion that the stars are very much within our reach.

4. ***Gone with the Wind:*** epic novel by Margaret Mitchell, published in 1936 and romanticizing plantation life in the South during the Civil War era; the novel was made into an enormously popular movie.
5. **Cape Cod:** a peninsula in southeastern Massachusetts on the Atlantic Ocean.
6. **Millay** (mĭ-lā′): Edna St. Vincent Millay, an American poet of the 1900s.
7. **Provincetown:** a town at the northern tip of Cape Cod, famous as an artists' community and for its social life.
8. **palpable** (păl′pə-bəl): capable of being touched and felt.
9. **ribald** (rĭb′əld): coarse; vulgar.
10. **mysticism** (mĭs′tĭ-sĭz′əm): experience of interacting with divine forces.

Option Three
Reader's Notebook

Provide the following direction to students before they read.

Tell students to read the selection, pausing at the end of column one on page 858. Then, have students summarize Hansberry's attitude toward summer in their Reader's Notebook. Tell students to finish reading the selection, taking note of how Hansberry shifts her focus from these initial childhood summers to a subsequent variety of summers that she experienced as she grew older. For each shift to a different summer, ask students to note the new place as well as the new memory and deeper attitude that accompanies it.

At the end of the essay, instruct students to return to their notes and seek to discern and describe a pattern of development in Hansberry's attitude and growing understanding of the meaning of summer. Why did she change her attitude?

Have students write a paragraph in their Reader's Notebook describing this development.

Possible Activities

Independent Activities

- Have students review the essay for details concerning the narrator's family. Ask them to write in their Reader's Notebook how the trip to Tennessee was a turning point for Hansberry.
- Have students review the Learning the Language of Literature and Active Reader on pages 819–821. They can note which skills and strategies they used while reading the selection.

Discussion Activities

- Discuss how each summer experience in her childhood seems to lead Hansberry to a deeper awareness, closeness, and understanding of her parents. Discuss the extent to which the older dying woman at the end plays a parental role of wise elder in her life.
- Discuss what Hansberry means by the phrase "life at the apex" as she uses it at the end of the selection and how such a phrase can be associated with a woman who is dying.

Assessment Opportunities

- You can assess student comprehension of the selection by evaluating descriptions of the shifts to different summers and the attitudes that accompany them as students formulated those descriptions in their Reader's Notebook.
- You can use any of the discussion questions as essay questions.
- You can have students develop any one of their Reader's Notebook entries into an essay.

The last time I saw her she was sitting surrounded by her paintings with her manuscript laid out for me to read, because, she said, she wanted to know what a *young person* would think of her thinking; one must always keep up with what *young people* thought about things because, after all, they were *change*.

Every now and then her jaw set in anger as we spoke of things people should be angry about. And then, for relief, she would look out at the lovely bay at a mellow sunset settling on the water. Her face softened with love of all that beauty and, watching her, I wished with all my power what I knew that she was wishing: that she might live to see at least one more *summer*. Through her eyes I finally gained the sense of what it might mean; more than the coming autumn with its pretentious[11] melancholy; more than an austere[12] and silent winter which must shut dying people in for precious months; more even than the frivolous spring, too full of too many false promises, would be the gift of another summer with its stark and intimate assertion of neither birth nor death but life at the apex;[13] with the gentlest nights and, above all, the longest days.

I heard later that she did live to see another summer. And I have retained my respect for the noblest of the seasons. ❖

11. **pretentious** (prĭ-tĕn′shəs): showing off in an extravagant way.
12. **austere** (ô-stîr′): severe.
13. **apex** (ā′pĕks): peak; highest point

Lorraine Hansberry
1930–1965

Other Works
A Raisin in the Sun
To Be Young, Gifted and Black: Lorraine Hansberry in Her Own Words

Challenges of Childhood When Lorraine Hansberry was a child, her father, a leading member of the African-American community in Chicago, moved his family into an all-white neighborhood. The family's experience—they were threatened and even had rocks thrown at them—may have led Hansberry later to describe ignorance as the "prime ancient and persistent enemy of man." When a court upheld local housing restrictions and ordered the Hansberrys to move, her father pursued their rights to the United States Supreme Court, where he won an important test case on integrated housing.

A Talent for Drama In high school, Hansberry became interested in the theater, an interest that flowered in college at the University of Wisconsin. In 1950, she moved to New York to become a writer. Hansberry's first and greatest success was *A Raisin in the Sun*. When it was performed in 1959, it was the first play ever written by an African-American woman to be performed on Broadway. It ran for 530 performances and won the New York Drama Critics Circle Award. In 1964, Hansberry's health began to fail, and she died of cancer at age 34. Robert Nemiroff, Hansberry's ex-husband, published her remaining writings in *To Be Young, Gifted and Black: Lorraine Hansberry in Her Own Words.*

Author Activity

Life and Literature View the film version of *A Raisin in the Sun* with your classmates. Then find a review of the film and compare the reviewer's responses to your own.

Writing Workshop

Interpretive Essay

Discovering the hidden truths in literature . . .

A **From Reading to Writing** In stories like Heinrich Böll's "The Balek Scales" and Agatha Christie's "The Witness for the Prosecution," readers must go beyond the obvious to find the deeper meanings. These stories, like most good literature, contain various levels of meanings beyond their surface appearances. In an **interpretive essay,** you have an opportunity to explore and explain the underlying meanings of stories, poems, and other works of art.

For Your Portfolio

WRITING PROMPT Write an interpretive essay about a work of literature that caused you to respond strongly.

Purpose: To explain your interpretation
Audience: Your teacher and classmates, others who are familiar with the work

Basics in a Box

Interpretive Essay at a Glance

Introduction
Introduces the literary work and includes a clear thesis statement that introduces the interpretation

B **Body**
Supports the interpretation with evidence from the literary work

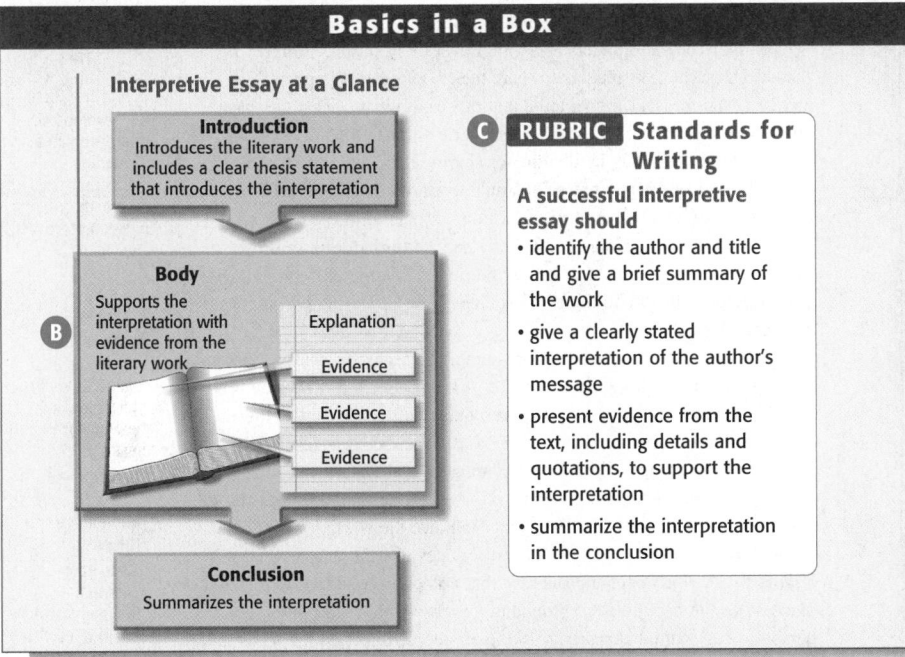

Explanation
Evidence
Evidence
Evidence

Conclusion
Summarizes the interpretation

C **RUBRIC Standards for Writing**

A successful interpretive essay should
- identify the author and title and give a brief summary of the work
- give a clearly stated interpretation of the author's message
- present evidence from the text, including details and quotations, to support the interpretation
- summarize the interpretation in the conclusion

Objectives
- write an Interpretive Essay
- use written texts as models for writing
- revise sentences to create variety
- use correct relative pronouns to introduce clauses

Introducing the Workshop

A Interpretive Essay Remind students that to interpret means to clarify the meaning or significance of a topic. Interpretive essays in the English classroom can indicate how strongly a student responds to a work of literature. Interpretation is different from analysis. Analysis is looking at the separate parts of something to better understand the whole. Interpretation usually follows analysis and explains the significance of the analyzed parts. Conclusions are drawn from analysis and interpretation.

Ask students where they might find an interpretive essay and how interpretive essays are helpful. Have students search for interpretive essays in anthologies, in literary magazines, or on the Internet.

Point out that through writing an interpretive essay, students will be able to introduce their classmates to fascinating works of literature. Establish some criteria for what makes a work of literature fascinating to someone. Students may be interested in literature that reflects their cultural heritage, their common experiences, or a topic that they want to know more about.

Basics in a Box

B Using the Graphic The graphic reminds students that the interpretive essay, like all well-crafted essays, includes an introduction, body paragraphs, and a conclusion. Point out that the evidence to support their interpretation, including details and quotations, must come from the literary work.

C Presenting the Rubric To better understand the assignment, students can refer to the Standards for Writing a Successful Interpretive Essay. You may also want to share with them the complete rubric, which describes several levels of proficiency. Tell students that their essays will be assessed according to these standards.

LESSON RESOURCES

USING PRINT RESOURCES

Unit Five Resource Book
- Prewriting, p. 21
- Drafting, p. 22
- Peer Response, pp. 23–24
- Revising, Editing, and Proofreading, p. 25
- Student Models, pp. 26–28
- Rubric, p. 29

Writing Transparencies and Copymasters
- Writing Process Transparencies, pp. 1–4
- Writing Style Transparencies, pp. 12–24
- Writing Template Copymasters, p. 33

USING MEDIA RESOURCES

LaserLinks
Writing Springboards
See Teacher's SourceBook p. 64 for bar codes.

Writing Coach CD-ROM

Visit our website:
www.mcdougallittell.com

Teaching the Lesson

Analyzing the Models

"What Humanity Can Learn from Denise Levertov"

D The student model interprets a poem by analyzing imagery, using direct quotes, and analyzing the poem's title. Have students read the student models, then discuss the Rubrics in Action. Point out key words and phrases in the student models that correspond to elements mentioned in the Rubrics in Action.

1. Ask students to define a thesis statement and to identify the thesis statement in the student model.
   Possible Response: The thesis statement explains the main idea. The thesis statement in this essay identifies the poem's message: "People need hope."
2. Remind students that metaphors compare two unlike things without using a connective word such as *like* or *as.* Point out that the student writer weaves in the quotation from the poem and makes the quotation a natural part of his sentence.
5. Emphasize that a student's feelings are an important component of an interpretive essay. Remind students to be honest in expressing their feelings.

Use McDougal Littell's ***Language Network,*** Chapter 20, for more instruction on writing a literary interpretation.

To engage students visually, use **Power Presentation** 9, Interpretive Essay.

Analyzing Two Student Models

Rafi Ginsburg
Evanston Township High School

What Humanity Can Learn from Denise Levertov

At first glance, the poem "For the New Year, 1981" by Denise Levertov seems to be saying something that everyone knows—that people need hope. However, its message is really much more complicated.

To understand the poem, we must look for the message beneath the literal meanings of the words. In the first stanza, Levertov describes hope as "one small crystal that gleams / clear colors out of transparency." What she is saying is not really about colors at all. She is using a metaphor to tell readers that hope can take nothing at all (transparency) and make it into everything (clear colors).

The next two stanzas, however, seem to be saying something that is self-contradictory and doesn't make sense in the real world. Levertov first says that she needs more hope, but adds "I break off a fragment / to send you." How can she get more hope by giving it away? She goes on to explain that she must give away a little hope so that it doesn't disappear. Once again, this doesn't seem to make sense.

D

We finally begin to understand what Levertov is getting at in the fifth stanza. There she asks readers to share their hope so that hope can increase. The message seems to be that one can increase what one has, not by holding on to it, but by sharing it. She emphasizes this message by saying directly that only by dividing or sharing hope can it grow.

Levertov then offers a powerful simile to clarify her message. She compares hope to a bunch of irises, which only bloom if the roots are divided. She then takes the comparison one step further. She says that the roots are surprising sources of beauty because they are dirty and gnarled. The message is that good things—like hope—are often found in the least expected places.

The body of the poem conveys this main message of Levertov's poem. However, the title adds another level of meaning. Because Levertov uses the pronouns *I* and *you* in the poem, it seems that the message is meant for just one other person. However, the title, "For the New Year, 1981," brings to mind groups of people celebrating and thinking about their hopes for the new year. Her message is for everyone to understand and to act on: Share your hope with each other to make the world a better place.

In "For the New Year, 1981," Levertov states that the only way to gain hope is by sharing hope, and she says that it is often found in unexpected places. Despite her choice of pronouns, Levertov is not talking to one person in her poem, but rather is asking all people to act on her ideas in order to save humanity.

RUBRIC IN ACTION

1. Identifies the author and title and provides a thesis statement about the message of the poem
2. States his interpretation and supports it with a quotation from the poem
3. Uses a personal reaction to help analyze the poem's message
4. Develops his interpretation by examining evidence from the poem
5. This writer ends by summarizing his interpretation of the writer's message.
   Other Options:
   - End with a quotation from the work.
   - State your personal feelings about the writer's message.

Mini Lesson Viewing and Representing

PICTURING TEXT STRUCTURE

Instruction The interpretation of the author's message and evidence from the text are important to the success of an interpretive essay. However, the structure of that essay–the way in which the interpretation and the evidence are organized–also adds to the effectiveness. Encourage students to select a work of literature that causes them to respond strongly.

Activity Have students analyze the text structure of either student model by constructing a graphic organizer. The graphic students create should illustrate how the student writer has organized the model. Students might begin by rereading the model and jotting down the main idea in each paragraph. From their notes they can construct a graphic organizer that shows how the ideas relate to each other as well as to the whole.

- Title of work and author
- Thesis: The message is more complicated.

→ Only by dividing or sharing hope can it grow.

→ Simile: compares hope to a bunch of irises

→
- Image of people thinking about their hopes for the New Year
- Message: share your hope with one another

→ Summary of interpretation

Dyan Gunther
Senn High School

Understanding "Pride"

Before reading "Pride" by Dahlia Ravikovitch, I would never have thought that human beings and inanimate objects like rocks have anything in common. Now I'm not so sure.

When I first read the title of the poem, I got an image in my mind of a person standing tall and still with her head held high. Then I read the first line of the poem, "I tell you, even rocks crack," and became confused. How do rocks cracking relate to pride, an emotion that only human beings feel?

The next lines of the poem provide a clue. Ravikovitch says that rocks just lie without moving for so many years that "it almost seems peaceful." But, then she says that the peace is only on the surface. There are cracks under the surface, but "the cracks stay hidden" waiting for "whoever is going to shatter them." These images personify rocks, giving them certain human characteristics. But the real message is not that rocks are like people, but that people are like rocks. They, too, have hidden cracks, or weak places.

Ravikovitch goes on to say that rocks don't seem to move or react, no matter what happens to them or around them. "The moss flourishes, the seaweed / whips around, / the sea pushes through and rolls back" and the rocks just sit there. I think she is saying here that some people don't seem to be affected by anything that happens to them; they just keep a stony face. But the important word that Ravikovitch uses is *seem.* Even though rocks—and people—don't appear to be affected by what happens to them, that doesn't mean that everything is calm and peaceful.

The rocks crack open, she says, when "a little seal comes to rub against them, / comes and goes away." How can this be? A seal is soft and gentle, and, as Ravikovitch says, it just brushes against the rocks and then leaves. I think what she really means is that once the rock or person is cracked, it only takes a little thing to shatter it.

The final lines of the poem support this interpretation. Ravikovitch confirms that what causes rocks to crack open is a minor thing, something that "happens by surprise." In the very last line, "And people, too," she makes it clear that she has actually been talking about people all along and has just been using rocks as a metaphor.

So Ravikovitch's message in "Pride" seems to be that people who are too proud are like rocks. They might have a smooth, calm surface and think that nothing can affect them, but they have cracks underneath. Eventually, something will cause people to break open. I think she means that this is a good thing, because it proves they, unlike rocks, are human.

RUBRIC IN ACTION

❶ Identifies the author and title and suggests the main point of her interpretation

❷ This writer develops her interpretation as she works through the poem.

Another Option:
- State the interpretation at the beginning and then show how you arrived at it.

❸ Uses quotations from the poem to support her interpretation

❹ This writer concludes by stating her overall interpretation of the poem.

Another Option:
- State the interpretation at the beginning and restate it in the conclusion.

"Understanding 'Pride'"

2. Have students suggest an alternate organizational strategy by stating the interpretation at the beginning and then showing how they arrived at it.
   Possible Response: The author's real message is not that rocks are like people, but that people are like rocks. They, too, have hidden cracks, or weak places. (The student should then point out how he or she arrived at this interpretation.)
3. Remind students that when they quote poetry, unless they are using block quotes, they must use quotation marks at the beginning and end of the extract. Point out that a slash should be used to indicate where each line breaks in the actual poem; for example, "The moss flourishes, the seaweed / whips around . . ."

WRITING WORKSHOP 863

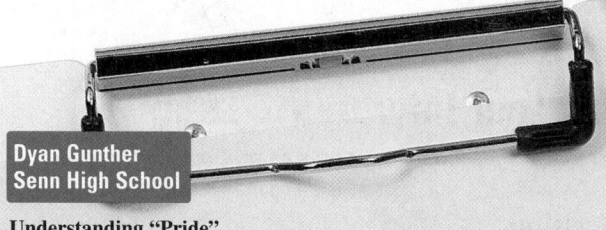

Guiding Student Writing

Prewriting

Choosing a Work to Interpret

If after reading the Idea Bank students are having difficulty choosing their work of literature, suggest they try the following:

- Have students conduct a search for a work of literature in the library. They can use the card catalog, the computerized on-line catalog, or electronic databases to access information about sources.
- Browse through the literature section of your favorite bookstore. Look for works by your favorite authors.

Planning the Interpretive Essay

1. Encourage students to be active readers as they read their selected works of literature. As students read their source material, have them use text organizers, such as overviews, headings, and other graphic features of the work to locate and categorize information as they take notes. Suggest that they take notes on a separate sheet of paper or mark the pages with different slips of color-coded paper. If the book belongs to the student, he or she may want to underline, highlight, and write in the margins.
2. Point out to students the need to freewrite or brainstorm about their interpretation of the author's message in the work of literature. Students may also paraphrase the work of literature as a part of their interpretive strategy. They may also want to keep a chart or list of quotations and details from the work that support their interpretation.
3. Before students begin to share their interpretation with another student, encourage them to bring all of their freewriting and other notes to the discussion. Remind them that the easiest interpretation to support is the one that has the strongest evidence from the literature.

Drafting

Organizing the Draft

The student models represent two approaches to writing an interpretive essay. Have students create their own structure for their essays. Some students may wish to first make an outline or other graphic organizer. Others may feel comfortable drafting with just the notes and quotations they collected earlier during the prewriting process.

Writing Your Interpretive Essay

What I like in a good writer is not what he says, but what he whispers.

Logan Pearsall Smith, British writer

IDEABank

1. Your Working Portfolio
Look for ideas in the **Writing Options** you completed earlier in this unit:

- **Interpretation of Poem**, p. 842
- **Theme Interpretation**, p. 854

2. What Do You Think?
Talk with friends about works they particularly liked, disliked, or didn't understand. Which would you like to write about?

3. Title Search
Browse through the titles of your own books or of selections in your literature textbook. Which titles didn't you understand until you read the work? Choose one of those works for your interpretive essay.

1 Prewriting

Begin by **recalling** poems or stories you have read that confused, surprised, or moved you. Looking through your READER'S NOTEBOOK can help you remember your response to various works in greater detail. See the **Idea Bank** in the margin for more suggestions. After you choose a work to interpret, follow the steps below.

Planning Your Interpretive Essay

1. **Reread the work several times.** Which passages, ideas, or events confused you? Which became clearer as you read the work for a second or third time? Which parts still do not make sense?
2. **Explore your interpretation of the author's message.** Freewrite about your interpretation. Which quotations and details from the work support your interpretation? Which details contradict it?
3. **Discuss your interpretation with others who have read the work.** How do your interpretations compare? Which interpretation seems to be the strongest and the easiest to support?

2 Drafting

Try to write your first draft without stopping to make changes. The important thing is to keep writing, even if you contradict yourself or change your mind. You can sort your ideas out later. Start by writing a **thesis statement** in which you present your main point—the point the rest of your essay will need to support. If you need help getting started, try filling in the blanks in this sentence: "The main message of (name of work) by (name of author) is____________."

In the main **body** of your essay, you will need to offer **supporting evidence** for your interpretation in the form of **details** and **quotations** from the work. You may also wish to explain key passages in your own words. At some point you will need to give a brief summary of the entire text. Sum up your interpretation in the **conclusion.**

Ask Your Peer Reader

- What is my main point about the work?
- What evidence most strongly supports this point?
- What other points should I include to clarify my interpretations?
- What do you disagree with or want to know more about?

❸ Revising

TARGET SKILL ▶ CREATING SENTENCE VARIETY To hold your readers' interest, include a variety of sentence types in your interpretation. Consider using questions and look for ways to combine simple sentences into compound or complex sentences.

> The final lines of the poem support this interpretation. Ravikovitch confirms that what causes rocks to crack open is a minor thing, ~~It is~~ something that "happens by surprise." In the very last line, "And people, too," she makes it clear that ~~She~~ she has actually been talking about people all along, and ~~She~~ has just been using rocks as a metaphor.

Need revising help?

Review the **Rubric**, p. 861

Consider **peer reader** comments

Check **Revision Guidelines**, p. 1145

❹ Editing and Proofreading

TARGET SKILL ▶ USING *THAT* AND *WHICH* WITH CLAUSES To avoid confusing your readers, introduce dependent clauses correctly. Use *that* if the clause is needed for the sentence to make sense. Use *which* if the sentence would make sense without the clause. Remember to use commas to set off a clause beginning with *which*. If a clause is unnecessary, consider deleting it entirely.

> At first glance, the poem "For the New Year, 1981" by Denise Levertov seems to be saying something ~~, which~~ that everyone knows—that people need hope. However, its message ~~, which I will explain in this paper,~~ is really much more complicated.

❺ Reflecting

FOR YOUR WORKING PORTFOLIO What did you learn about the literary work from writing your interpretation? How did your interpretation change as you wrote? Attach your reflections to your interpretive essay. Save your interpretive essay in your **Working Portfolio.**

Publishing IDEAS

- Submit your work to a literary magazine or periodical that publishes literary reviews.
- Get together with classmates who wrote interpretive essays about the same work of literature. Compare your classmates' interpretations with your own.

More Online: Publishing Options
www.mcdougallittell.com

Revising

CREATING SENTENCE VARIETY

Have students look at their drafts and identify sentences that begin with the subject. Then have students reword a few of these sentences by beginning them with a prepositional phrase. Next, have students look for simple sentences in their drafts and look for ways to combine some of them. They should try to vary sentence length as well as sentence style.

Editing and Proofreading

USING *THAT* AND *WHICH* WITH CLAUSES

Point out to students that *that* and *which* are **relative pronouns** because they "relate" an adjective clause to the word the clause modifies. To avoid confusing readers, students must introduce dependent adjective clauses correctly. See the Grammar Mini Lesson on TE p. 866 for more information on correct use of *that* and *which.* Encourage students to revise, edit, and proofread carefully to produce error-free writing in the final draft.

Reflecting

Encourage students to recognize and evaluate what they learned about the interpretive essay. What techniques did they learn that they can apply to other writing exercises? Have students consider the effectiveness of their prewriting and draft. Did a graphic organizer help? Did peer assistance help? Have them add these self-evaluations to their working portfolios.

Assessment Practice

Remind students to carefully read the entire passage before they begin answering the questions.

Answers:
1. A; **2.** C; **3.** A; **4.** C; **5.** A; **6.** B

Assessment Practice Revising & Editing

Read this paragraph from the first draft of an interpretive essay. The underlined sections may include the following kinds of errors:

- **correctly written sentences that should be combined**
- **incorrect use of *that* and *which***
- **spelling errors**
- **incorrect use of suffixes**

For each underlined section, choose the revision that most improves the writing.

I read a story last night. I had a strong reaction to it. It was called "The Tell-Tale Heart." (1) The story which was written by Edgar Allan Poe, still creates (2) a claustrophobic, somberly (3) mood. It is about a man whose sense of guilt compels him to confess to a murder. I think that the narrater (4) is clearly mad. His imagination is strong. It's probably too strong. It may have caused him to make up the murder. (5) Perhaps he is confessing to a crime that never occured. (6)

1. **A.** Last night I read the story "The Tell-Tale Heart" and had a strong reaction to it.
   B. The story "The Tell-Tale Heart" was one I read last night and had a strong reaction to.
   C. I read the story "The Tell-Tale Heart," and, last night, had a strong reaction to it.
   D. Correct as is

2. **A.** The story, that was written by Edgar Allan Poe, still creates
   B. The story which was written by Edgar Allan Poe still creates
   C. The story, which was written by Edgar Allan Poe, still creates
   D. Correct as is

3. **A.** claustrophobic, somber
   B. claustrophobically, somberly
   C. claustrophobic, somberness
   D. Correct as is

4. **A.** narator
   B. narrature
   C. narrator
   D. Correct as is

5. **A.** His imagination is so strong that it may have caused him to make up the murder.
   B. His imagination is so strong. He made up the murder.
   C. The murder may have caused his strong imagination.
   D. Correct as is

6. **A.** ocured
   B. occurred
   C. ocurred
   D. Correct as is

Need extra help?

See the **Grammar Handbook**
The Structure of Sentences, p. 1198

Mini Lesson Grammar

CORRECT USE OF *THAT* AND *WHICH*

Instruction To avoid confusion, writers should introduce dependent clauses correctly. Use *that* if the clause is essential, or necessary to complete the meaning of the sentence; use *which* if the clause is nonessential, or not necessary to complete the meaning of the sentence. Use commas to set off a nonessential clause beginning with *which*.

Activity Write the following sentences on the chalkboard. Have volunteers supply the correct relative pronoun for each blank and identify the clause as essential or nonessential.

1. The novel ___________ I wrote was on the bestseller list for more than 72 weeks.
2. The Women's Literary Society, _________ was founded in 1897, organized the first book club.
3. John's interpretive essay on *A Separate Peace* by John Knowles, _________ I read yesterday, won first prize.
4. The skills _______ John learned about how to write an interpretive essay helped him craft a winning essay.
5. The money ___________ John won will be saved for his college expenses.

Answers:
1. *that;* essential; 2. *which;* nonessential; 3. *which;* nonessential; 4. *that;* essential; 5. *that;* essential

PART 2 Appearance vs. Reality

As magicians know so well, things are seldom the way they appear. Indeed, appearances often hide as much as they reveal. In this part of Unit Five, you will encounter a variety of situations—from a criminal investigation to a poet's meditations—in which appearances are deceiving. As you read, look beyond what meets the eye to see if you can discern the underlying truth.

ACTIVITY

Describe a time when you were fooled or misled by appearances. What led your perception or judgment astray—in other words, why were you fooled? What did you learn as a result of your experience? Record your memory of the event in writing, or tell your classmates about it.

867

OVERVIEW

Objectives

- understand realism as a historical movement in the arts and literature
- identify the characteristics of realistic fiction
- analyze realistic fiction by relying on characteristics
- identify differences between realistic actions of characters in nonrealistic works and characters presented using the methods of realistic fiction

Teaching the Lesson

This lesson analyzes realism as a historical movement and identifies the methods used in realistic fiction.

Introducing the Concepts

Have students suggest movies or television shows they consider unrealistic. Have them compare the unrealistic aspects of these shows to literary realism and the methods of realistic fiction.

Presenting the Concepts

A Short History of Realism

Students may have difficulty understanding types of art as historical movements, so ask them to identify traits of literature or popular music contemporary to them, and then suggest that these are aspects of artistic movements such as multiculturalism, postmodernism, and alternative or punk rock.

YOUR TURN

Possible Response: The passage is about ordinary people—soldiers and villagers—in an unpleasant and morally challenging but ordinary situation.

LEARNING the Language of Literature

Realism as a general term refers to any effort to offer an accurate and detailed portrayal of actual life. The transforming heroes of comic books, the fiery explosions of action movies, the fantastic worlds of science fiction, and the menacing world of horror fiction are not realistic. Neither are Homer's *Odyssey* and the impressionistic stories of Edgar Allan Poe. But stories, novels, plays, and movies that dramatize ordinary human relationships or re-create actual historical events are considered realistic.

Realism is usually something you recognize when you see it. For instance, when you read a story such as Tim O'Brien's "On the Rainy River" (page 626), you immediately recognize the authenticity of time, place, and character. The narrator represents not only a real person but an ordinary one. He's no superhero, and that's the point.

The Winnowers (1855), Gustave Courbet. Oil on canvas, 131 cm × 167 cm. Musée des Beaux-Arts, Nantes, France/Giraudon/Art Resource, New York.

A Short History of Realism

Realism as an artistic movement and later an artistic method is a relatively new historical development. It started around the middle of the 19th century, when writers and artists decided to stop portraying ancient or idealized worlds and to start giving a truthful, objective depiction of the world they lived in. Thus, ordinary people—shopkeepers, workers, farmers—going about their daily affairs began to replace kings, nobles, heroes, and religious figures as the subjects of painting and literature. Some of the great realistic writers of the period include Leo Tolstoy in Russia, Honoré de Balzac in France, George Eliot in England, and Mark Twain in America.

By the end of the 19th century and into the 20th century, other artistic movements—such as naturalism, symbolism, surrealism, and modernism—sprang up to challenge the dominance of realism. But realism has remained very much alive as an artistic method, as you can see from most of the stories and art in this textbook.

YOUR TURN In your opinion, what is realistic about the passage at the right?

"I looked in that direction and between the ranks caught sight of something dreadful moving toward me. It was a man stripped to the waist, tied to the rifles of two soldiers, who led him. Next to him walked a tall officer in an overcoat and forage cap whose face seemed familiar to me. Resisting with his whole body, his feet splashing in the melting snow, the victim was lurching toward me under the blows falling on him from both sides; . . . And never leaving the victim's side, halting and advancing with a firm tread, was the tall officer. It was her father, with his rosy face and white mustache and sideburns."

—Leo Tolstoy, "After the Ball"

Characteristics of Realistic Fiction

To some extent, realism has always been a significant element in literature. After all, epic heroes, such as Odysseus, do act in recognizably human ways. But the realism that developed in the mid-19th century marked a change in the nature and purpose of literature. Here are some characteristics that define the realist method.

Subject Matter from Ordinary Life The rise of realism corresponded to the spread of revolution and democracy in Europe and North America, and so it is not surprising that realistic writers chose subject matter from the middle and lower classes. Details of setting became especially important to creating a convincing portrait of people's lives in a specific time and place. Dialect was increasingly used to characterize economic and regional differences.

An Emphasis on Character With democracy came a belief in the individual; with realism came the importance of character. For the realists, a character's destiny was no longer in the hands of fate but an outgrowth of his or her own actions. Thus, character rather than plot became the center of a realistic story. Think of the many stories you've read in which a character's choice drives the plot, as in "Initiation" and "On the Rainy River," for example. Think of other stories in which the plot is determined by a character's important discovery, such as in "The Prisoner Who Wore Glasses" and "After the Ball."

Concern with Ethical Issues Most literature addresses moral issues. For realistic writers, the situation from which an ethical issue arose had to be presented accurately and honestly. Otherwise, the morality of a story would have seemed too preachy or artificial. Thus, you have Sylvy in "A White Heron" (page 822) making the right decision only after long thought.

YOUR TURN Study the passages at the right, and identify what characteristics of realism are illustrated by each passage.

This day he set apart as a unique day—at least one day in the year we must give and take absolute Truth whatever may happen. Otherwise life is not worth living. The day ahead seemed to him full of possibilities. He told no one of his experiment. It was a quiet resolve, a secret pact between him and eternity.

—R. K. Narayan, "Like the Sun"

Still the young man looked at him in the same dazed, hopeless fashion. To Mr. Mayherne the case had seemed black enough, and the guilt of the prisoner assured. Now, for the first time, he felt a doubt.

"You think I'm guilty," said Leonard Vole, in a low voice. "But, by God, I swear I'm not! It looks pretty black against me; I know that. I'm like a man caught in a net—the meshes of it all round me, entangling me whichever way I turn. But I didn't do it, Mr. Mayherne; I didn't do it!"

—Agatha Christie, "The Witness for the Prosecution"

Then some went to the relief offices, and they came sadly back to their own people.

They's rules—you got to be here a year before you can git relief. They say the gov'-ment is gonna help. They don' know when.

And gradually the greatest terror of all come along.

They ain't gonna be no kinda work for three months.

In the barns, the people sat huddled together; and the terror came over them, and their faces were gray with terror. The children cried with hunger, and there was no food.

—John Steinbeck,
"The Flood" *from* The Grapes of Wrath

Characteristics of Realistic Fiction

Subject Matter from Ordinary Life

Remind students that what they learn in their world history and civics classes can be used to study literature. Ask them to suggest aspects of democracy and events in United States and world history that might have contributed to the rise of realistic fiction.

An Emphasis on Character

Remind students of character types: round and flat, dynamic and static. Suggest they compare the definitions of round and dynamic character types to the definition of realism and the methods of realistic fiction. Suggest that the psychological development and growth that make a character round and dynamic also are aspects of character that contribute to an accurate portrayal of a character in realistic fiction.

Concern with Ethical Issues

Ask students to suggest the morals found in particular fairy tales or the heavily didactic messages of parables found in many religious traditions and political ideologies. Have them compare these with the ways moral issues are developed in realistic fiction.

YOUR TURN

In the excerpt from "Like the Sun," the reader knows the unnamed character through his psychological deliberations and the accurate depiction of his ethical decision making.

The excerpt from "The Witness for the Prosecution" emphasizes characters from everyday life involved in an ethical dilemma. The way the character speaks suggests a particular dialect.

The excerpt by John Steinbeck honestly portrays the hardships of characters from a low economic class and accurately presents a moral crisis for Depression-era readers of Steinbeck's work.

The Active Reader: Skills and Strategies

OVERVIEW

Objective

- examine parts of a literary work to compile an analysis

Teaching the Lesson

The strategies on this page will help students learn and apply specific skills for analyzing fiction, nonfiction, and poetry.

Presenting the Strategies
Help students understand the process of analysis by applying it to a fairy tale or nursery rhyme they are familiar with, or a literary work they have read previously in class.

1 Analyzing Fiction
Explain to students that examination of the main elements of fiction—characterization, setting, and sequence of events—contributes to a reader's overall comprehension. These elements react with each other to determine the work of fiction's success. Have students analyze a literary work they have read previously in class to determine how the main literary elements strengthen and weaken each other.

2 Analyzing Nonfiction
Remind students to read nonfiction critically, noting the author's tone and biases. Have students determine the author's purpose. Then ask them whether the author achieves his or her purpose in the piece. Discuss with students whether a piece they have read previously in class would be more or less effective if written in a different style.

3 Analyzing Poetry
Have students examine the various elements of a poem they have previously read in class. After their initial reading of the poem, have students read the poem aloud or listen to a professional recording of the poem. Then ask students whether their analyses of the poem have changed.

The Active Reader: Skills and Strategies

Legend has it that the American mathematician and astronomer Benjamin Banneker once took a clock apart and put it back together again just to see how it worked. Although literature may not be as complicated as a clock, the same process Banneker used can help you understand how literature works. The strategies on this page can show you how.

Analyzing

To **analyze** something is to separate it into parts for careful study. Analyzing is important to the study of literature because sometimes only by studying the parts of a literary work can you understand the whole. Use these general strategies to help you analyze different genres of literature.

1 Strategies for Analyzing Fiction

- Examine characters closely to identify their strengths and weaknesses. Use such character analysis to understand how and why a character changes, or what he or she has learned. Try using a chart like the one shown:

Name of Character	
Strengths	Weaknesses
How does he/she change? (or what has he/she learned?)	

- **Visualize** the setting. Look for clues in the detailed descriptions that might have an impact on the story. Consider whether the setting has a symbolic meaning.
- Study the sequence of events in the plot and identify conflict and the climax, or turning point. **Question** whether events could have turned out differently, and if so, how.

2 Strategies for Analyzing Nonfiction

- Determine whether the work is narrative (such as biography and autobiography), persuasive (such as a review or an essay), or expository (such as an essay or article).
- In a narrative, watch for bias in a writer's presentation and judgment.
- In a persuasive or expository piece, find the thesis and supporting points. **Evaluate** how well the supporting points prove the argument or clarify the explanation.

3 Strategies for Analyzing Poetry

- Read the whole poem through at least once, then study each stanza or grouping of lines separately to understand the impression or idea that they're building up to.
- Break down figures of speech into their component parts to **clarify** the comparison. What ideas or feelings does the figurative language convey?
- Look for objects, places, people, or actions that may have symbolic meaning.
- **Visualize** images and **evaluate** what purpose they serve.

Need More Help?

Remember that active readers use the essential reading strategies explained on page 7: **visualize, predict, clarify, question, connect, evaluate, monitor.**

PREPARING to *Read*

The Witness for the Prosecution

Short Story by AGATHA CHRISTIE

"But I didn't do it, Mr. Mayherne; I didn't do it!"

Connect to Your Life

Lie Detector How do you decide whether someone is telling you the truth when all you have to go on is the speaker's word? Do you watch the expression on the speaker's face or listen to the tone of voice? With a classmate, talk about the kinds of clues you look for when you need to make a judgment about the truth of what someone tells you. Then share your ideas with the entire class.

Build Background

The Defender In the selection you are about to read, a British lawyer seeks the truth about a murder case that is coming to trial. There are two kinds of lawyers in Britain: solicitors, who conduct legal work outside the court, and barristers, who actually try the cases in court. Defendants who are about to go on trial hire a solicitor to handle their case. The solicitor conducts most of the background work, such as researching evidence and interviewing witnesses. Then the solicitor hires a barrister to appear in court and question witnesses on the client's behalf. In the following mystery by British author Agatha Christie, a solicitor named Mr. Mayherne collects the evidence for his client and then turns it over to a barrister named Sir Charles.

WORDS TO KNOW **Vocabulary Preview**

amicable	churlish	infernal
animosity	cultivate	insolence
assiduously	dastardly	quell
averse	impotently	unfathomable
cajole	infatuated	vindicate

Focus Your Reading

LITERARY ANALYSIS DIALOGUE **Dialogue** is written conversation between two or more characters. Writers use dialogue to bring characters to life and to make their stories richer and more believable. As you read, consider how the dialogue contributes to your understanding of the characters and the plot.

ACTIVE READING DRAWING CONCLUSIONS Many people read mystery stories because they like to try to solve the mystery on their own, before the solution is revealed by the author. This process involves gathering clues and **drawing conclusions,** or making logical guesses based on those clues.

READER'S NOTEBOOK As you read "The Witness for the Prosecution," look for clues that point to the truth about the guilt or innocence of Mr. Mayherne's client. List the clues on a chart like the one shown, with clues indicating guilt on one side and those indicating innocence on the other. Then, just before the trial begins in the last section of the story, pause to weigh the clues and conclude what your verdict would be. Finish reading the story to see if you guessed right.

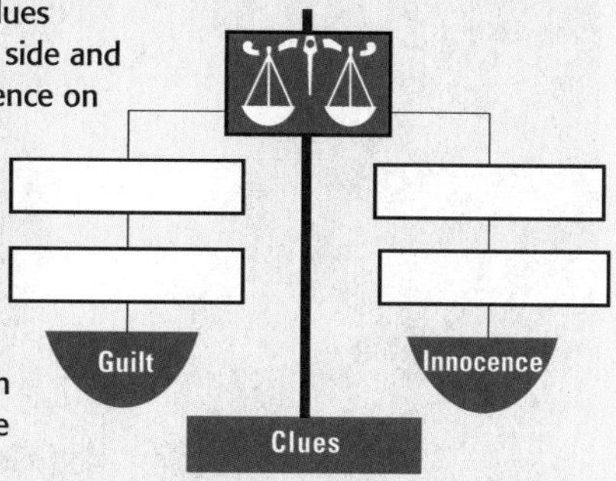

OVERVIEW

Objectives

1. understand and enjoy a **classic mystery (Literary Analysis)**
2. understand the importance of **dialogue (Literary Analysis)**
3. **draw conclusions** based on text evidence **(Active Reading)**

Summary

Though charged with the murder of Miss Emily French, Mr. Vole swears his innocence. He tells his lawyer, Mr. Mayherne, that his devoted wife will be able to give him an alibi. Convinced of his client's innocence, Mayherne goes to see Vole's wife, Romaine. Romaine declares that she hates Vole, that he is not her legal husband, and that she would like to see him hanged by the neck. Mayherne receives a letter from a Mrs. Mogson. He visits the old woman at her slum, and she reveals letters that show Romaine's intention to incriminate her husband. At court, Mayherne exposes Romaine's evil intent. The case against Vole collapses, and he goes free. Only after the trial does Mayherne realize that Romaine herself played the part of Mrs. Mogson—and that Mr. Vole is indeed guilty.

Thematic Link

Mr. Vole, Romaine, and Mrs. Mogson are not who they **appear** to be.

5-Minute Warm-Up

Daily Language SkillBuilder

Have students **proofread** the display sentences on page 817j and write them correctly. The sentences also appear on Transparency 25 of **Grammar Transparencies and Copymasters.**

Mini Lesson Preteaching Vocabulary

If you would like to preteach the WORDS TO KNOW for this selection, use the Mini Lesson, p. 873.

LESSON RESOURCES

UNIT FIVE RESOURCE BOOK, pp. 30–35

ASSESSMENT RESOURCES

Formal Assessment, pp. 145–146

Teacher's Guide to Assessment and Portfolio Use

Test Generator

SKILLS TRANSPARENCIES AND COPYMASTERS

Literary Analysis
- Drama: Dialogue, T10 (for Cooperative Learning Activity, p. 890)

Grammar
- Adverb Clauses II, C113 (for Mini Lesson, p. 878)
- Noun Clauses, C116 (for Mini Lesson, p. 892)

Vocabulary
- Synonyms, C80 (for Mini Lesson, p. 873)
- Antonyms, C81 (for Mini Lesson, p. 886)

Writing
- Point of View, T23 (for Writing Option 1, p. 891)
- Effective Language, T13 (for Writing Option 2, p. 891)

Communications
- Impromptu Speaking: Dialogue, Role-Play, Debate, T13 (for Activities & Explorations 1, p. 891)

INTEGRATED TECHNOLOGY

Audio Library

Internet: Research Starter

Visit our website:
www.mcdougallittell.com

TEACHING THE LITERATURE

Reading and Analyzing

Reading Skills and Strategies:
PREVIEW

Ask students to pay attention to the title, the art, and the highlighted quotations. Have them read the Connect to Your Life feature on p. 871. Before students read, give them a brief summary of the story. Since this is a mystery, you might want to keep the ending a secret.

Literary Analysis DIALOGUE

Point out to students that Mr. Mayherne is the only character whose thoughts the reader may examine. Therefore, the reader must guess what the other characters are thinking from their dialogue. As they read dialogue, have students jot down what they believe the characters are thinking.

Use **Unit Five Resource Book,** p. 32 for additional support.

Active Reading
DRAWING CONCLUSIONS

Have students read the description of Mr. Mayherne on p. 873 to decide whether they would trust Mr. Mayherne's judgment about Mr. Vole's guilt or innocence. Have students explain what details in the description caused them to make their decision about Mr. Mayherne.
Possible Responses: Yes, because Mr. Mayherne is described as shrewd and of very good reputation; no, because his primness indicates that he might put too much emphasis on appearances.

Use **Unit Five Resource Book,** p. 31 for additional support.

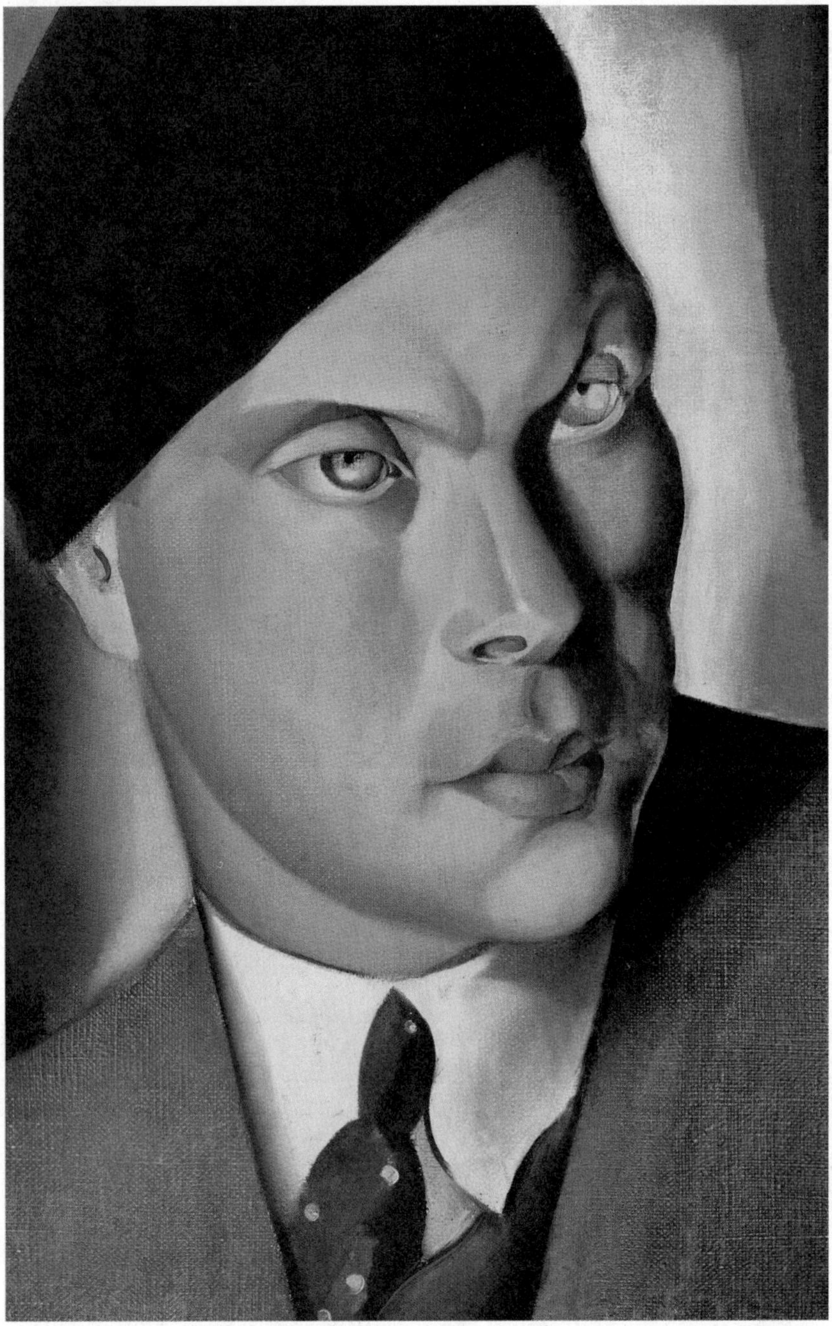

Portrait of Count Fürstenberg-Herdringen (1924), Tamara de Lempicka. Oil on canvas, 16⅛″ × 10¾″, courtesy of Barry Friedman Ltd., New York. Copyright © 1996 Artists Rights Society (ARS), New York/SPADEM, Paris.

Teaching Options

Mini Lesson: Viewing and Representing

***Portrait of Count Furstenberg Herdringen* by Tamara de Lempicka**

ART APPRECIATION Tamara de Lempicka studied in Paris under Cubist painter André Lhote. Her powerful portraits are admired for their striking poses, bright, contrasting colors, and minimal details.
Instruction Point out the use of space in this painting. Ask students what effect they think is obtained by having the subject fill the canvas.
Possible Response: Having the subject fill the canvas makes him seem bold, forceful, commanding, and important.

Application An artist's feelings about the subject influence the choices he or she makes about space, line, and color. These choices determine how we see the subject. How is the influence of an artist's point of view on our perceptions similar to the influence of a narrator's point of view in a story?
Possible Response: Through a narrator, a writer chooses what facts to tell the reader and how to describe events and characters. Because we rely on a narrator to describe characters and events for us, a narrator controls our perception as much as a painter does.

The Witness for the Prosecution

Agatha Christie

Mr. Mayherne adjusted his pince-nez[1] and cleared his throat with a little dry-as-dust cough that was wholly typical of him. Then he looked again at the man opposite him, the man charged with willful murder.[2]

Mr. Mayherne was a small man, precise in manner, neatly, not to say foppishly[3] dressed, with a pair of very shrewd and piercing gray eyes. By no means a fool. Indeed, as a solicitor, Mr. Mayherne's reputation stood very high. His voice, when he spoke to his client, was dry but not unsympathetic.

"I must impress upon you again that you are in very grave danger, and that the utmost frankness is necessary."

Leonard Vole, who had been staring in a dazed fashion at the blank wall in front of him, transferred his glance to the solicitor.

"I know," he said hopelessly. "You keep telling me so. But I can't seem to realize yet that I'm

1. **pince-nez** (păns′nā′): eyeglasses without side pieces, kept in place by a spring gripping the bridge of the nose.
2. **willful murder:** deliberate, not accidental, murder. In law, the term *willful* is used synonymously with *premeditated* (planned beforehand). Willful murder is a more serious crime than murder that is unplanned, accidental, or committed in self-defense.
3. **foppishly:** in the manner of a vain man who pays too much attention to his clothes and appearance.

Customizing Instruction

Less Proficient Readers

To aid their understanding of the story, have students ask themselves the following questions as they read:

- Who are Mr. Vole, Mr. Mayherne, and Romaine?
  Answer: the man accused of murdering Miss Emily French; Mr. Vole's lawyer; Mr. Vole's wife
- What is Mr. Vole's alibi?
  Answer: He was with Romaine at the time of the murder.
- Why is his alibi useless?
  Answer: Romaine will not support it.

Students Acquiring English

Tell students about these basic tenets of British law: the defendant is assumed innocent until proven guilty; the defendant is entitled to be defended by an attorney; the prosecution must prove guilt beyond a reasonable doubt; the case is judged by a jury of the defendant's peers.

Use **Spanish Study Guide** for additional support, pp. 179–181.

Gifted and Talented

Invite students to discuss the dilemma that defense lawyers face: they must defend even a clearly guilty client. Ask students what internal conflicts this might cause for lawyers and how they might deal with this dilemma.

Possible Responses: The lawyer might feel guilty about setting free a guilty person. He or she might see it as his or her duty to provide the best defense possible, no matter what; he or she might, deliberately or unconsciously, provide an inadequate defense.

Mini Lesson: Preteaching Vocabulary

FINDING SYNONYMS Instruction Remind students that synonyms are words with the same or similar meanings. Write the following sentence on the chalkboard.

The <u>fiendish</u> copy machine kept destroying the originals.

Ask students to find the WORD TO KNOW with a meaning the same as or similar to the underlined word.

Answer: infernal

Exercises Have students identify the WORD TO KNOW that is a synonym to the underlined word in each of the following sentences.

1. He was unable to <u>quiet</u> the baby's crying. *(quell)*
2. The child was <u>opposed</u> to calming down. *(averse)*
3. No one could <u>coax</u> the child into peace. *(cajole)*
4. A <u>friendly</u> uncle tried a hand puppet. *(amicable)*

Use **Unit Five Resource Book,** p. 33 for additional support.

A lesson on synonyms appears on p. 1000 in the Pupil's Edition.

Reading and Analyzing

Reading Skills and Strategies: QUESTIONING

Have students think of questions they would like to ask Mr. Vole if they were preparing his defense.

Possible Responses: Can anyone place you somewhere other than the scene of the crime at the time of the crime? Can you think of anyone else who might have committed the crime?

charged with murder—*murder.* And such a dastardly crime too."

Mr. Mayherne was practical, not emotional. He coughed again, took off his pince-nez, polished them carefully, and replaced them on his nose. Then he said:

"Yes, yes, yes. Now, my dear Mr. Vole, we're going to make a determined effort to get you off—and we shall succeed—we shall succeed. But I must have all
1 the facts. I must know just how damaging the case against you is likely to be.
2 Then we can fix upon the best line of defense."

"I DIDN'T DO IT, MR. MAYHERNE; I DIDN'T DO IT!"

Still the young man looked at him in the same dazed, hopeless
3 fashion. To Mr. Mayherne the case had seemed black enough, and the guilt of the prisoner assured. Now, for the first time, he felt a doubt.

"You think I'm guilty," said Leonard Vole, in a low voice. "But, by God, I swear I'm not! It looks pretty black against me; I know that. I'm like a man caught in a net—the meshes of it all round me, entangling me whichever way I turn. But I didn't do it, Mr. Mayherne; I didn't do it!"

In such a position a man was bound to protest his innocence. Mr. Mayherne knew that. Yet, in spite of himself, he was impressed. It might be, after all, that Leonard Vole was innocent.

"You are right, Mr. Vole," he said gravely. "The case does look very black against you. Nevertheless, I accept your assurance. Now, let us get to facts. I want you to tell me in your own words exactly how you came to make the acquaintance of Miss Emily French."

"It was one day in Oxford Street. I saw an elderly lady crossing the road. She was carrying a lot of parcels. In the middle of the street she dropped them, tried to recover them, found a bus was almost on top of her and just managed to reach the curb safely, dazed and bewildered by people having shouted at her. I recovered her parcels, wiped the mud off them as best I could, retied the string of one, and returned them to her."

"There was no question of your having saved her life?"

"Oh, dear me, no! All I did was to perform a common act of courtesy. She was extremely grateful, thanked me warmly, and said something about my manners not being those of most of the younger generation—I can't remember the exact words. Then I lifted my hat and went on. I never expected to see her again. But life is full of coincidences. That very evening I came across her at a party at a friend's house. She recognized me at once and asked that I should be introduced to her. I then found out that she was a Miss Emily French and that she lived at Cricklewood. I talked to her for some time. She was, I imagine, an old lady who took sudden and violent fancies to people. She took one to me on the strength of a perfectly simple action which anyone might have performed. On leaving, she shook me

WORDS TO KNOW **dastardly** (dăs′tərd-lē) *adj.* mean and cowardly

874

Teaching Options

BLOCK SCHEDULING: MANAGING TIME

If your schedule requires that you cover the lesson objectives in a shorter time, use . . .

- Preparing to Read, p. 871
- Thinking Through the Literature, p. 890
- Vocabulary in Action, p. 891
- Grammar in Context, p. 892

If you want to take advantage of longer class time, use . . .

- TE Teaching Options: Viewing and Representing, pp. 872, 880, 884; Preteaching WORDS TO KNOW, p. 873; Cross-Curricular Link, p. 882,; Vocabulary Strategy, p. 886; Standardized Test Practice, p. 888
- Choices & Challenges and Author Activity, pp. 891–892

warmly by the hand, and asked me to come and see her. I replied, of course, that I should be very pleased to do so, and she then urged me to name a day. I did not want particularly to go, but it would have seemed churlish to refuse, so I fixed on the following Saturday. After she had gone, I learned something about her from my friends. That she was rich, eccentric, lived alone with one maid and owned no less than eight cats."

"I see," said Mr. Mayherne. "The question of her being well off came up as early as that?"

"If you mean that I inquired—" began Leonard Vole hotly, but Mr. Mayherne stilled him with a gesture.

"I have to look at the case as it will be presented by the other side. An ordinary observer would not have supposed Miss French to be a lady of means. She lived poorly, almost humbly. Unless you had been told the contrary, you would in all probability have considered her to be in poor circumstances[4]—at any rate to begin with. Who was it exactly who told you that she was well off?"

"My friend, George Harvey, at whose house the party took place."

"Is he likely to remember having done so?"

"I really don't know. Of course it is some time ago now."

"Quite so, Mr. Vole. You see, the first aim of the prosecution will be to establish that you were in low water financially—that is true, is it not?"

Leonard Vole flushed.

"Yes," he said, in a low voice. "I'd been having a run of infernal bad luck just then."

"Quite so," said Mr. Mayherne again. "That being, as I say, in low water financially, you met this rich old lady and cultivated her acquaintance assiduously. Now if we are in a position to say that you had no idea she was well off, and that you visited her out of pure kindness of heart—"

"Which is the case."

"I daresay. I am not disputing the point. I am looking at it from the outside point of view. A great deal depends on the memory of Mr. Harvey. Is he likely to remember that conversation, or is he not? Could he be confused by counsel into believing that it took place later?"

Leonard Vole reflected for some minutes. Then he said steadily enough, but with a rather paler face:

"I do not think that that line would be successful, Mr. Mayherne. Several of those present heard his remark, and one or two of them chaffed[5] me about my conquest of a rich old lady."

The solicitor endeavored to hide his disappointment with a wave of the hand.

"Unfortunate," he said. "But I congratulate you upon your plain speaking, Mr. Vole. It is to you I look to guide me. Your judgment is quite right. To persist in the line I spoke of would have been disastrous. We must leave that point. You made the acquaintance of Miss French; you called upon her; the acquaintanceship progressed. We want a clear reason for all this. Why did you, a young man of thirty-three, good-looking, fond of sport, popular with your friends, devote so much of your time to an elderly woman with whom you could hardly have anything in common?"

Leonard Vole flung out his hands in a nervous gesture.

"I can't tell you—I really can't tell you. After the first visit, she pressed me to come again, spoke of being lonely and unhappy. She made it difficult for me to refuse. She showed so plainly her fondness and affection for me that I was placed in an awkward position. You see, Mr.

4. **circumstances:** financial condition.

5. **chaffed:** teased in a good-natured way.

WORDS TO KNOW

churlish (chûr'lĭsh) *adj.* rude or ill-tempered
infernal (ĭn-fûr'nəl) *adj.* fit to have come from hell; outrageous
cultivate (kŭl'tə-vāt') *v.* to seek to become familiar with
assiduously (ə-sĭj'o͞o-əs-lē) *adv.* in a way that shows steady and careful attention

Customizing Instruction

Students Acquiring English

Explain to students the following phrases:

1 "how damaging the case is"
Answer: how much evidence there is against Vole

2 "line of defense"
Answer: strategy for proving Vole innocent

3 "the case had seemed black enough"
Answer: the evidence seemed to prove Vole's guilt

Less Proficient Readers

Ask students how Mr. Vole and Miss French met.
Answer: Mr. Vole helped her with some parcels she had dropped.

Ask students how the two came to see each other again.
Answer: They were both at the same party.

Multiple Learning Styles:
Kinesthetic, Auditory, and Interpersonal

Suggest that students act out Vole's first meeting with Miss French when he picks up her packages, and suggest that a different group of students act out their second meeting. Both groups should improvise dialogue. Have the class comment on how realistic and probable the scenes seem.

Reading and Analyzing

ACTIVE READING

(A) EVALUATE **Possible Response:** Yes—he seems a sincere man; no—the circumstances are condemning

Literary Analysis: CHARACTERIZATION

(B) Direct students' attention to the description Mr. Vole gives of the maid, Janet Mackenzie. Ask students whether they think Vole's characterization of her is plausible and why or why not.
Possible Responses: Yes—it is reasonable to imagine that Janet is suspicious by nature and easily confused; no—if Janet didn't like Vole, it was probably for a good reason.

Literary Analysis: CONFLICT

Remind students that conflict is what makes the plot of a short story progress and that conflict may be internal or external. Ask students to list the conflicts in the story so far.
Possible Responses: Vole vs. the courts; Vole vs. Janet Mackenzie; Mr. Mayherne vs. the evidence against Vole

Active Reading

DRAWING CONCLUSIONS

Tell students that mystery stories often present facts in such a way that it is possible to draw two or more different conclusions. Ask students to draw at least two different conclusions from the fact that Vole and Janet Mackenzie disagree about Miss French's knowledge of her own financial affairs, as well as Vole's own knowledge of Miss French's intention to leave him her money.
Possible Responses: Vole is being framed by Janet Mackenzie; Vole is lying.

Mayherne, I've got a weak nature—I drift—I'm one of those people who can't say 'No.' And believe me or not, as you like, after the third or fourth visit I paid her I found myself getting genuinely fond of the old thing. My mother died when I was young, an aunt brought me up, and she too died before I was fifteen. If I told you that I genuinely enjoyed being mothered and pampered, I daresay you'd only laugh."

Mr. Mayherne did not laugh. Instead he took off his pince-nez again and polished them, a sign with him that he was thinking deeply.

"I accept your explanation, Mr. Vole," he said at last. "I believe it to be psychologically probable. Whether a jury would take that view of it is another matter. Please continue your narrative. When was it that Miss French first asked you to look into her business affairs?"

"After my third or fourth visit to her. She understood very little of money matters and was worried about some investments."

Mr. Mayherne looked up sharply.

"Be careful, Mr. Vole. The maid, Janet Mackenzie, declares that her mistress was a good woman of business and transacted all her own affairs, and this is borne out by the testimony of her bankers."

"I can't help that," said Vole earnestly. "That's what she said to me."

ACTIVE READING

(A) EVALUATE Do you think Leonard Vole is telling the truth?

Mr. Mayherne looked at him for a moment or two in silence. Though he had no intention of saying so, his belief in Leonard Vole's innocence was at that moment strengthened. He knew something of the mentality of elderly ladies. He saw Miss French, infatuated with the good-looking young man, hunting about for pretexts that would bring him to the house. What more likely than that she should plead ignorance of business and beg him to help her with her money affairs? She was enough of a woman of the world to realize that any man is slightly flattered by such an admission of his superiority. Leonard Vole had been flattered. Perhaps, too, she had not been averse to letting this young man know that she was wealthy. Emily French had been a strong-willed old woman, willing to pay her price for what she wanted. All this passed rapidly through Mr. Mayherne's mind, but he gave no indication of it and asked instead a further question.

"And you did handle her affairs for her at her request?"

"I did."

"Mr. Vole," said the solicitor, "I am going to ask you a very serious question, and one to which it is vital I should have a truthful answer. You were in low water financially. You had the handling of an old lady's affairs—an old lady who, according to her own statement, knew little or nothing of business. Did you at any time, or in any manner, convert to your own use the securities[6] which you handled? Did you engage in any transaction for your own pecuniary[7] advantage which will not bear the light of day?" He quelled the other's response. "Wait a minute before you answer. There are two courses open to us. Either we can make a feature of your probity[8] and honesty in conducting her affairs whilst pointing out how unlikely it is that you would commit murder to obtain money which you might have obtained by such infinitely easier means. If, on the other hand, there is anything in your dealings which the prosecution will get hold of—if, to put it baldly, it can be proved that you

6. **securities:** stock certificates or bonds.

7. **pecuniary** (pĭ-kyo͞o'nē-ĕr'ē): involving money; financial.

8. **probity** (prō'bĭ-tē): the holding of the highest principles and ideals; integrity.

WORDS TO KNOW

infatuated (ĭn-făch'o͞o-ā'tĭd) *adj.* completely carried away by foolish or shallow love or attraction **infatuate** *v.*
averse (ə-vûrs') *adj.* unwilling; deeply reluctant
quell (kwĕl) *v.* to crush; put an end to; quiet

swindled the old lady in any way—we must take the line that you had no motive for the murder, since she was already a profitable source of income to you. You perceive the distinction. Now, I beg of you, take your time before you reply."

But Leonard Vole took no time at all.

"My dealings with Miss French's affairs were all perfectly fair and aboveboard. I acted for her interests to the very best of my ability, as anyone will find who looks into the matter."

"MY DEALINGS WITH MISS FRENCH'S AFFAIRS WERE ALL PERFECTLY FAIR AND ABOVEBOARD."

"Thank you," said Mr. Mayherne. "You relieve my mind very much. I pay you the compliment of believing that you are far too clever to lie to me over such an important matter."

"Surely," said Vole eagerly, "the strongest point in my favor is the lack of motive. Granted that I cultivated the acquaintanceship of a rich old lady in the hopes 1 of getting money out of her—that, I gather, is the substance of what you have been saying—surely her death frustrates all my hopes?"

The solicitor looked at him steadily. Then, very deliberately, he repeated his unconscious trick with his pince-nez. It was not until they were firmly replaced on his nose that he spoke.

"Are you not aware, Mr. Vole, that Miss French left a will under which you are the principal beneficiary?"[9]

"What?" The prisoner sprang to his feet. His dismay was obvious and unforced. "My God! What are you saying? She left her money to me?"

Mr. Mayherne nodded slowly. Vole sank down again, his head in his hands.

"You pretend you know nothing of this will?"

"Pretend? There's no pretense about it. I knew nothing about it."

"What would you say if I told you that the maid, Janet Mackenzie, swears that you *did* know? That her mistress told her distinctly that she had consulted you in the matter and told you of her intentions?"

"Say? That she's lying! No, I go too fast. Janet is an elderly woman. She was a faithful watchdog to her B mistress, and she didn't like me. She was jealous and suspicious. I should say that Miss French confided her intentions to Janet, and that Janet either mistook something she said or else was convinced in her own mind that I had persuaded the old lady into doing it. I daresay that she herself believes now that Miss French actually told her so."

"You don't think she dislikes you enough to lie deliberately about the matter?"

Leonard Vole looked shocked and startled.

"No, indeed! Why should she?"

"I don't know," said Mr. Mayherne thoughtfully. "But she's very bitter against you."

The wretched young man groaned again.

"I'm beginning to see," he muttered. "It's

9. **beneficiary** (bĕn′ə-fĭsh′ē-ĕr′ē): person named in a will to receive money or goods.

Customizing Instruction

Students Acquiring English

1 Explain to students that in this context *granted* means "if we assume" and *frustrates* means "makes difficult" or "puts an end to." Then ask students to restate Vole's argument in their own words.

Possible Response: If we assume that I made friends with a rich old lady to get money from her, wouldn't her death put an end to my hopes?

Reading and Analyzing

Literary Analysis: THIRD-PERSON LIMITED POINT OF VIEW

Remind students that "limited" in third-person limited point of view means that the narrator is limited to seeing through the eyes of one character. She can tell the reader only the thoughts and perceptions of that character, and she cannot tell the reader anything the character does not know. Ask students to which character's point of view the story is limited.

Answer: Mr. Mayherne's

Discuss with students whether the story could be written successfully from Vole's point of view.

Possible Responses: No, because then the reader would know right away whether Vole is guilty, and there would be no suspense; yes, but then the point of the story would be not whether Vole is guilty, but whether he will be convicted.

Reading Skills and Strategies: PREDICT

Ask students to use the information on these pages to predict what will happen when Mr. Mayherne talks with Mrs. Vole.

Possible Response: Mrs. Vole will confirm that Vole returned home by half past nine.

Have students read to find out whether their prediction is correct.

frightful. I made up to her, that's what they'll say, I got her to make a will leaving her money to me, and then I go there that night, and there's nobody in the house—they find her the next day—oh! my God, it's awful!"

"You are wrong about there being nobody in the house," said Mr. Mayherne. "Janet, as you remember, was to go out for the evening. She went, but about half past nine she returned to fetch the pattern of a blouse sleeve which she had promised to a friend. She let herself in by the back door, went upstairs and fetched it, and went out again. She heard voices in the sitting room, though she could not distinguish what they said, but she will swear that one of them was Miss French's and one was a man's."

"At half past nine," said Leonard Vole. "At half past nine . . ." He sprang to his feet. "But then I'm saved—saved—"

"What do you mean, saved?" cried Mr. Mayherne, astonished.

"By half past nine I was at home again! My wife can prove that. I left Miss French about five minutes to nine. I arrived home about twenty past nine. My wife was there waiting for me. Oh, thank God—thank God! And bless Janet Mackenzie's sleeve pattern."

In his exuberance, he hardly noticed that the grave expression on the solicitor's face had not altered. But the latter's words brought him down to earth with a bump.

"Who, then, in your opinion, murdered Miss French?"

"Why, a burglar, of course, as was thought at first. The window was forced, you remember. She was killed with a heavy blow from a crowbar, and the crowbar was found lying on the floor beside the body. And several articles were missing. But for Janet's absurd suspicions and dislike of me, the police would never have swerved from the right track."

"That will hardly do, Mr. Vole," said the solicitor. "The things that were missing were mere trifles of no value, taken as a blind. And the marks on the window were not at all conclusive. Besides, think for yourself. You say you were no longer in the house by half past nine. Who, then, was the man Janet heard talking to Miss French in the sitting room? She would hardly be having an amicable conversation with a burglar!"

"No," said Vole. "No—" He looked puzzled and discouraged. "But, anyway," he added with reviving spirit, "it lets me out. I've got an alibi. You must see Romaine—my wife—at once."

"Certainly," acquiesced the lawyer. "I should already have seen Mrs. Vole but for her being absent when you were arrested. I wired to Scotland at once, and I understand that she arrives back tonight. I am going to call upon her immediately I leave here."

Vole nodded, a great expression of satisfaction settling down over his face.

"Yes, Romaine will tell you. My God! it's a lucky chance that."

"Excuse me, Mr. Vole, but you are very fond of your wife?"

"Of course."

"And she of you?"

"Romaine is devoted to me. She'd do anything in the world for me."

He spoke enthusiastically, but the solicitor's heart sank a little lower. The testimony of a devoted wife—would it gain credence?

"Was there anyone else who saw you return at nine-twenty? A maid, for instance?"

"We have no maid."

"Did you meet anyone in the street on the way back?"

"Nobody I knew. I rode part of the way in a bus. The conductor might remember." 1

Mr. Mayherne shook his head doubtfully.

WORDS TO KNOW

amicable (ăm'ĭ-kə-bəl) *adj.* having or showing a friendly attitude

878

Teaching Options

Mini Lesson Grammar

ADVERB CLAUSES

Instruction Remind students that an adverb clause is a kind of clause that is used to modify a verb, an adjective, or an adverb. Tell them that every adverb clause begins with a subordinating conjunction, such as *after, although, as, as if, as long as, as though, because, before, if, in order that, provided that, since, so, so that, though, till, unless, until, when, where, whereas,* and *while.*

Write the following sentence on the chalkboard.

The dog barked because it was startled.

Underline the adverb clause and then point out to students the subordinating conjunction because. Explain that the addition of "because" to "it was startled" creates an adverb clause that modifies the verb *barked*.

"There is no one, then, who can confirm your wife's testimony?"

"No. But it isn't necessary, surely?"

"I daresay not. I daresay not," said Mr. Mayherne hastily. "Now there's just one thing more. Did Miss French know that you were a married man?"

"Oh, yes."

"Yet you never took your wife to see her. Why was that?"

For the first time, Leonard Vole's answer came halting and uncertain.

"Well—I don't know."

"Are you aware that Janet Mackenzie says her mistress believed you to be single and contemplated marrying you in the future?"

Vole laughed.

"Absurd! There was forty years' difference in age between us."

"It has been done," said the solicitor dryly. "The fact remains. Your wife never met Miss French?"

"No—" Again the constraint.

"You will permit me to say," said the lawyer, "that I hardly understand your attitude in the matter."

Vole flushed, hesitated, and then spoke.

"I'll make a clean breast of it. I was hard up, as you know. I hoped that Miss French might lend me some money. She was fond of me, but she wasn't at all interested in the struggles of a young couple. Early on, I found that she had taken it for granted that my wife and I didn't get on—were living apart. Mr. Mayherne—I wanted the money—for Romaine's sake. I said nothing, and allowed the old lady to think what she chose. She spoke of my being an adopted son to her. There was never any question of marriage—that must be just Janet's imagination."

"And that is all?"

"Yes—that is all."

"SURELY," SAID VOLE EAGERLY, "THE STRONGEST POINT IN MY FAVOR IS THE LACK OF MOTIVE."

Was there just a shade of hesitation in the words? The lawyer fancied so. He rose and held out his hand.

"Good-bye, Mr. Vole." He looked into the haggard young face and spoke with an unusual impulse. "I believe in your innocence in spite of the multitude of facts arrayed against you. I hope to prove it and vindicate you completely."

Vole smiled back at him.

"You'll find the alibi is all right," he said cheerfully.

Again he hardly noticed that the other did not respond.

"The whole thing hinges a good deal on the testimony of Janet Mackenzie," said Mr. Mayherne. "She hates you. That much is clear."

"She can hardly hate me," protested the young man.

The solicitor shook his head as he went out.

"Now for Mrs. Vole," he said to himself.

He was seriously disturbed by the way the thing was shaping.

WORDS TO KNOW **vindicate** (vĭn′dĭ-kāt′) *v.* to clear of blame or suspicion

Customizing Instruction

Less Proficient Readers

1 Tell students that the conductor on the London bus had the same responsibilities as a train conductor: to accept passengers' fares and to ensure that they got off at the right stop. In the United States, buses do not carry conductors; passengers pay fares to the driver. Ask students why they think Mr. Mayherne doesn't believe the bus conductor will be able to help Vole's case.

Possible Response: Mr. Mayherne doesn't believe the conductor would remember.

Gifted and Talented

Invite students to discuss whether Vole's admission about letting Miss French believe he and his wife didn't get along makes him more or less believable. Whom do students generally believe more readily, those who insist on their complete innocence or those who make damaging admissions about themselves?

Possible Response: People who admit their own flaws are probably being more honest, and are therefore more believable.

Exercises Have students copy the following sentences. Have them underline each adverb clause and double underline the subordinating conjunction.

1. The tree was planted before the flowers were put in.
   Answer: before the flowers were put in
2. Until his uncle told him to stop, Mark kicked the chair leg rhythmically.
   Answer: Until his uncle told him to stop
3. He was told that he could snorkel, provided that he supplied his own gear.
   Answer: provided that he supplied his own gear
4. The cars could not move until the truck finished unloading.
   Answer: until the truck finished unloading
5. Although her shinguard fell off, she kept playing.
   Answer: Although her shinguard fell off

Use **Grammar Transparencies and Copymasters,** p. 113, for more exercises.

Use McDougal Littell's ***Language Network,*** Chapter 4, for more instruction in adverb clauses.

Reading and Analyzing

Literary Analysis DIALOGUE

Show students that writers can use dialogue to reveal the thoughts of their characters, but they can also use dialogue to conceal. Ask students what Romaine's words reveal and what they might conceal.

Possible Responses: Her words reveal that she is not English, that she is concerned with whether the jury will believe her testimony, and that she is not an emotional woman; her words conceal how she feels about her husband's trouble.

Active Reading
DRAWING CONCLUSIONS

A Ask students whether Romaine's statements lead them to believe that Vole is guilty or innocent.

Possible Responses: innocent—Romaine is anxious to know whether she can help her husband escape prosecution; guilty—Romaine does not confirm that Vole came in at twenty minutes past nine.

ACTIVE READING

B **EVALUATE** **Possible Response:** She is exotic, intimidating, forceful, credible, and arrogant.

The Voles lived in a small shabby house near Paddington Green. It was to this house that Mr. Mayherne went.

1 In answer to his ring, a big slatternly woman, obviously a charwoman, answered the door.

"Mrs. Vole? Has she returned yet?"

"Got back an hour ago. But I dunno if you can see her."

"If you will take my card to her," said Mr. Mayherne quietly, "I am quite sure that she will do so."

The woman looked at him doubtfully, wiped her hand on her apron and took the card. Then she closed the door in his face and left him on the step outside.

In a few minutes, however, she returned with a slightly altered manner.

"Come inside, please."

She ushered him into a tiny drawing room. Mr. Mayherne, examining a drawing on the wall, started up suddenly to face a tall, pale woman who had entered so quietly that he had not heard her.

"Mr. Mayherne? You are my husband's solicitor, are you not? You have come from him? Will you please sit down?"

"I MUST KNOW EVERYTHING. DO NOT THINK TO SPARE ME."

Until she spoke, he had not realized that she was not English. Now, observing her more closely, he noticed the high cheekbones, the dense blue-black of the hair, and an occasional very slight movement of the hands that was distinctly foreign. A strange woman, very quiet. So quiet as to make one uneasy. From the very first Mr. Mayherne was conscious that he was up against something that he did not understand.

"Now, my dear Mrs. Vole," he began, "you must not give way—"

He stopped. It was so very obvious that Romaine Vole had not the slightest intention of giving way. She was perfectly calm and composed.

"Will you please tell me about it?" she said. "I must know everything. Do not think to spare me. I want to know the worst." She hesitated, then repeated in a lower tone, with a curious emphasis which the lawyer did not understand: "I want to know the worst."

Mr. Mayherne went over his interview with Leonard Vole. She listened attentively, nodding her head now and then.

"I see," she said, when he had finished. "He wants me to say that he came in at twenty minutes past nine that night?"

"He did come in at that time?" said Mr. Mayherne sharply.

"That is not the point," she said coldly. "Will my saying so acquit him? Will they believe me?" **A**

Mr. Mayherne was taken aback. She had gone so quickly to the core of the matter.

"That is what I want to know," she said. "Will it be enough? Is there anyone else who can support my evidence?"

B There was a suppressed eagerness in her manner that made him vaguely uneasy.

ACTIVE READING

EVALUATE What is your impression of Romaine Vole?

Teaching Options

Mini Lesson Viewing and Representing

Portrait de Madame M. **by Tamara de Lempicka**

ART APPRECIATION The vivid colors, bold lines, and angular style of Tamara de Lempicka's painting on page 881 are characteristic of the art deco movement, which enjoyed its heyday during the 1920s and 1930s.

Instruction Point out the use of light and shadow in this painting. Ask students why they think the artist chose to use such dark shadows.

Possible Responses: to bring out the folds of the woman's dress and the symmetry of her face; to make the subject look more dramatic than she did in real life

Application Ask students whether the subject looks similar to their mental image of Romaine and why or why not.

Possible Responses: No—because the woman is less graceful-looking than Romaine seems to be; yes—because they are both exotic and haughty.

Portrait de Madame M., Tamara de Lempicka (1898–1980). Oil on canvas, 99 cm × 65 cm, private collection, Paris. Copyright © 1996 Artists Rights Society (ARS), New York/ SPADEM, Paris.

Customizing Instruction

Students Acquiring English

1 Explain to students that *slatternly* means "dirty" or "untidy" and that *charwoman* means "cleaning woman." Ask students to describe the woman in their own words.

Possible Responses: She is large, messy, unfriendly, and wearing an apron.

Less Proficient Readers

To aid their comprehension, ask students the following questions:

- Why is Mr. Mayherne going to speak to Romaine?
  Answer: He needs her to testify that Mr. Vole was with her at the time of the murder.
- Why is her testimony so important?
  Possible Responses: No one else can corroborate Mr. Vole's story; she is the sole witness for Mr. Vole's alibi.

Multiple Learning Styles

Visual Learners

Suggest that students make a drawing of Romaine or find a magazine photo that reminds them of her. Ask students to think about how the scene would be different if Romaine were more ordinary.

Possible Responses: Mr. Mayherne would not be so uncomfortable; the reader might feel he or she could tell what Romaine was thinking.

Reading and Analyzing

Literary Analysis: CONFLICT

A Ask students what new conflict is introduced here and how it complicates the plot.

Possible Response: The new conflict is between Romaine and Vole; it complicates the plot by making enemies of characters who were to be allies and by removing the one witness for Vole's defense.

ACTIVE READING

B **PREDICT** **Possible Response:** She will testify against Vole.

"So far there is no one else," he said reluctantly.

"I see," said Romaine Vole.

She sat for a minute or two perfectly still. A little smile played over her lips.

The lawyer's feeling of alarm grew stronger and stronger.

"Mrs. Vole—" he began. "I know what you must feel—"

"Do you?" she asked. "I wonder."

"In the circumstances—"

"In the circumstances—I intend to play a lone hand."

He looked at her in dismay.

"But, my dear Mrs. Vole—you are overwrought. Being so devoted to your husband—"

"I beg your pardon?"

The sharpness of her voice made him start. He repeated in a hesitating manner:

"Being so devoted to your husband—"

Romaine Vole nodded slowly, the same strange smile on her lips.

"Did he tell you that I was devoted to him?" she asked softly. "Ah! yes, I can see he did. How stupid men are! Stupid—stupid—stupid—"

She rose suddenly to her feet. All the intense emotion that the lawyer had been conscious of in the atmosphere was now concentrated in her tone.

A "I hate him, I tell you! I hate him. I hate him. I hate him! I would like to see him hanged by the neck till he is dead."

The lawyer recoiled before her and the smoldering passion in her eyes.

She advanced a step nearer and continued vehemently:

"Perhaps I shall see it. Supposing I tell you that he did not come in that night at twenty past nine, but at twenty past ten? You say that he tells you he knew nothing about the money coming to him. Supposing I tell you he knew all about it, and counted on it, and committed murder to get it? Supposing I tell you that he admitted to me that night when he came in what he had done? That there was blood on his coat? What then? Supposing that I stand up in court and say all these things?"

Her eyes seemed to challenge him. With an effort, he concealed his growing dismay, and endeavored to speak in a rational tone.

"You cannot be asked to give evidence against your husband—" **1**

"He is not my husband!" The words came out so quickly that he fancied he had misunderstood her.

"I beg your pardon? I—"

"He is not my husband."

The silence was so intense that you could have heard a pin drop.

"I was an actress in Vienna. My husband is alive but in a madhouse. So we could not marry. I am glad now."

She nodded defiantly.

"I should like you to tell me one thing," said Mr. Mayherne. He contrived to appear as cool and unemotional as ever. "Why are you so bitter against Leonard Vole?"

She shook her head, smiling a little.

"Yes, you would like to know. But I shall not tell you. I will keep my secret. . . ."

Mr. Mayherne gave his dry little cough and rose.

"DID HE TELL YOU THAT I WAS DEVOTED TO HIM?"

Teaching Options

Cross Curricular Link History

THE DEATH PENALTY IN ENGLAND Until England abolished the death penalty in 1965, condemned criminals were executed. In the mid-1800s, the hanging of a condemned prisoner was done publicly, and crowds gathered to watch. However, public opinion turned against the idea of executions as spectacles, and by 1868 all hangings were carried out privately in prisons.

"There seems no point in prolonging this interview," he remarked. "You will hear from me again after I have communicated with my client."

She came closer to him, looking into his eyes with her own wonderful dark ones.

"Tell me," she said, "did you believe—honestly—that he was innocent when you came here today?"

"I did," said Mr. Mayherne.

"You poor little man," she laughed.

"And I believe so still," finished the lawyer. "Good evening, madam."

He went out of the room, taking with him the memory of her startled face.

"This is going to be the devil of a business," said Mr. Mayherne to himself as he strode along the street.

Extraordinary, the whole thing. An extraordinary woman. A very dangerous woman. Women were the devil when they got their knife into you.

ACTIVE READING

3 **PREDICT** What role do you think Romaine will play in the trial?

What was to be done? That wretched young man hadn't a leg to stand upon. Of course, possibly he did commit the crime. . . .

"No," said Mr. Mayherne to himself. "No—there's almost too much evidence against him. I don't believe this woman. She was trumping up the whole story. But she'll never bring it into court."

He wished he felt more conviction on the point.

The police court proceedings were brief and dramatic. The principal witnesses for the prosecution were Janet Mackenzie, maid to the dead woman, and Romaine Heilger, Austrian subject, the mistress of the prisoner.

2 Mr. Mayherne sat in court and listened to the damning story that the latter told. It was on the lines she had indicated to him in their interview.

The prisoner reserved his defense and was committed for trial.

Mr. Mayherne was at his wits' end. The case against Leonard Vole was black beyond words. Even the famous K.C.[10] who was engaged for the defense held out little hope.

"If we can shake that Austrian woman's testimony, we might do something," he said dubiously. "But it's a bad business."

Mr. Mayherne had concentrated his energies on one single point. Assuming Leonard Vole to be speaking the truth, and to have left the murdered woman's house at nine o'clock, who was the man Janet heard talking to Miss French at half past nine?

The only ray of light was in the shape of a scapegrace[11] nephew who had in bygone days cajoled and threatened his aunt out of various sums of money. Janet Mackenzie, the solicitor learned, had always been attached to this young man and had never ceased urging his claims upon her mistress. It certainly seemed possible that it was this nephew who had been with Miss French after Leonard Vole left, especially as he was not to be found in any of his old haunts.[12]

In all other directions, the lawyer's researches had been negative in their result. No one had seen Leonard Vole entering his own house, or leaving that of Miss French. No one had seen any other man enter or leave the house in Cricklewood. All inquiries drew blank.

It was the eve of the trial when Mr. Mayherne received the letter which was to lead his thoughts in an entirely new direction.

It came by the six o'clock post. An illiterate

10. **K.C.:** King's Counsel, a barrister appointed as legal counsel to the British crown. The term refers to a leading or senior barrister.

11. **scapegrace:** scoundrel.

12. **haunts:** places one frequently goes; hangouts.

WORDS TO KNOW **cajole** (kə-jōl') *v.* to persuade by pleasant words, flattery, or false promises

Customizing Instruction

Less Proficient Readers

1 Explain to students that in England at the time of this story, it was illegal for a woman to testify against her husband in a criminal case. Ask students why, then, it is significant that Mr. Vole and Romaine are not married.

Answer: If they are not married, she can testify against him.

Students Acquiring English

2 Tell students that *the latter* means "the second thing or person mentioned." Ask students who is "the latter" here.

Answer: Romaine

Reading and Analyzing

Literary Analysis: SETTING

A Remind students that setting not only makes an impression on the reader, but it also often makes an impression on the characters. Ask students what impression the setting of this scene makes on Mr. Mayherne.

Possible Response: Mr. Mayherne is repulsed by the poverty and dirtiness of the woman's room. It makes him anxious to leave.

Active Reading

DRAWING CONCLUSIONS

Ask students to use the information on this page to infer Mrs. Mogson's motive for giving Mr. Mayherne evidence that would clear Vole.

Possible Response: Because she says, "I'll be even with 'em," we can infer that she is helping Vole in order to get revenge on some person.

scrawl, written on common paper and enclosed in a dirty envelope with the stamp stuck on crooked.

Mr. Mayherne read it through once or twice before he grasped its meaning.

"Dear Mister:

"Youre the lawyer chap wot acts for the young feller. If you want that painted foreign hussy showd up for wot she is an her pack of lies you come to 16 Shaw's Rents Stepney to-night It ull cawst you 2 hundred quid[13] *Arsk for Misses Mogson."*

1 The solicitor read and reread this strange epistle. It might, of course, be a hoax, but when he thought it over, he became increasingly convinced that it was genuine, and also convinced that it was the one hope for the prisoner. The evidence of Romaine Heilger damned him completely, and the line the defense meant to pursue, the line that the evidence of a woman who had admittedly lived an immoral life was not to be trusted, was at best a weak one.

Mr. Mayherne's mind was made up. It was his duty to save his client at all costs. He must go to Shaw's Rents.

He had some difficulty in finding the place, a ramshackle building in an evil-smelling slum, but at last he did so, and on inquiry for Mrs. Mogson was sent up to a room on the third floor. On this door he knocked and, getting no answer, knocked again.

At this second knock, he heard a shuffling sound inside, and presently the door was opened cautiously half an inch, and a bent figure peered out.

Suddenly the woman, for it was a woman, gave a chuckle and opened the door wider.

"So it's you, dearie," she said, in a wheezy voice. "Nobody with you, is there? No playing tricks? That's right. You can come in—you can come in."

With some reluctance the lawyer stepped across the threshold into the small dirty room, with its flickering gas jet.[14] There was an untidy unmade bed in a corner, a plain deal table[15] and two rickety chairs. For the first time Mr. Mayherne had a full view of the tenant of this unsavory apartment. She was a woman of middle age, bent in figure, with a mass of untidy gray hair and a scarf wound tightly round her face. She saw him looking at this and laughed again, the same curious, toneless chuckle.

"Wondering why I hide my beauty, dear? He, he, he. Afraid it may tempt you, eh? But you shall see—you shall see."

She drew aside the scarf, and the lawyer recoiled involuntarily before the almost formless blur of scarlet. She replaced the scarf again.

"So you're not wanting to kiss me, dearie? He, he, I don't wonder. And yet I was a pretty girl once—not so long ago as you'd think, either. Vitriol,[16] dearie, vitriol—that's what did that. Ah! but I'll be even with 'em—"

She burst into a hideous torrent of profanity which Mr. Mayherne tried vainly to quell. She fell silent at last, her hands clenching and unclenching themselves nervously.

"Enough of that," said the lawyer sternly. "I've come here because I have reason to believe you can give me information which will clear my client, Leonard Vole. Is that the case?"

Her eyes leered at him cunningly.

"What about the money, dearie?" she wheezed. "Two hundred quid, you remember."

"It is your duty to give evidence, and you can be called upon to do so."

13. **quid:** in England, slang for the basic monetary unit, the pound.
14. **gas jet:** natural gas flame used to light a room.
15. **deal table:** table made of fir or pine planks.
16. **vitriol:** a strong acid.

Teaching Options

Mini Lesson: Viewing and Representing

Der Rote Turm in Halle II (The red tower in Halle II) **by Lyonel Feininger**

ART APPRECIATION This Bauhaus artist (1871–1956) employed Cubist principles to create elegant architectural landscapes. His dynamic use of straight lines results in compelling, multifaceted structures.

Application Ask students why the artist might have chosen to paint such a narrow view of the tower, hemmed in by buildings on either side.

Possible Responses: The artist wanted the tower to seem remote and inviting; the artist wanted to give a sense of the tower's setting in the middle of the city; the artist wanted the tower to seem mysterious.

Application What connection do students see between the painting and this story?

Possible Responses: The mysterious, crowded quality of the buildings in this setting is similar to the close, dark quarters of the slum where Mayherne visits Mrs. Mogson.

Der Rote Turm in Halle II [The red tower in Halle II] (1930), Lyonel Feininger. 100 cm × 85 cm, Kunstmuseum Mülheimander Ruhr sammlung ziegler.

Customizing Instruction

Students Acquiring English

1 Explain to students that epistle means "letter" and hoax means "trick."

Multiple Learning Styles

Visual and Kinesthetic

Ask students to draw a picture or make a small model of Mrs. Mogson's room. Make sure students use details from the story in their drawings or models. Display the drawings or models in the classroom.

Reading and Analyzing

Literary Analysis DIALOGUE

Ask students what effect the author's decision to write Mrs. Mogson's portion of the dialogue in dialect has on the reader and on Mr. Mayherne.

Possible Response: The use of dialect gives the reader and Mr. Mayherne the impression that Mrs. Mogson is an uneducated, lower-class woman.

Active Reading

DRAWING CONCLUSIONS

A Ask students what conclusions they can draw about the contents of the "top" letter.

Possible Response: It contains statements that contradict Romaine's testimony.

Reading Skills and Strategies: CLARIFYING

Ask students to explain in their own words what happened that made Mrs. Mogson hate Romaine.

Possible Response: Romaine stole Mrs. Mogson's lover and laughed when he threw acid in Mrs. Mogson's face.

"That won't do, dearie. I'm an old woman, and I know nothing. But you give me two hundred quid, and perhaps I can give you a hint or two. See?"

"What kind of hint?"

"What should you say to a letter? A letter from *her.* Never mind how I got hold of it. That's my business. It'll do the trick. But I want my two hundred quid."

Mr. Mayherne looked at her coldly and made up his mind.

"I'll give you ten pounds, nothing more. And only that if this letter is what you say it is."

"Ten pounds?" She screamed and raved at him.

"Twenty," said Mr. Mayherne, "and that's my last word."

He rose as if to go. Then, watching her closely, he drew out a pocketbook and counted out twenty one-pound notes.

"You see," he said. "That is all I have with me. You can take it or leave it."

"SHE'LL SUFFER FOR THIS, WON'T SHE, MR. LAWYER? SHE'LL SUFFER?"

But already he knew that the sight of the money was too much for her. She cursed and raved impotently, but at last she gave in. Going over to the bed, she drew something out from beneath the tattered mattress.

"Here you are, damn you!" she snarled. "It's the top one you want."

It was a bundle of letters that she threw to him, and Mr. Mayherne untied them and scanned them in his usual cool, methodical manner. The woman, watching him eagerly, could gain no clue from his impassive face.

He read each letter through, then returned again to the top one and read it a second time. Then he tied the whole bundle up again carefully.

They were love letters, written by Romaine Heilger, and the man they were written to was not Leonard Vole. The top letter was dated the day of the latter's arrest.

"I spoke true, dearie, didn't I?" whined the woman. "It'll do for her, that letter?"

Mr. Mayherne put the letters in his pocket, then he asked a question.

"How did you get hold of this correspondence?"

"That's telling," she said with a leer. "But I know something more. I heard in court what that hussy said. Find out where she was at twenty past ten, the time she says she was at home. Ask at the Lion Road Cinema. They'll remember—a fine upstanding girl like that—curse her!"

"Who is the man?" asked Mr. Mayherne. "There's only a Christian name here."

The other's voice grew thick and hoarse, her hands clenched and unclenched. Finally she lifted one to her face.

"He's the man that did this to me. Many years ago now. She took him away from me—a chit[17] of a girl she was then. And when I went after him—and went for him too—he threw the cursed

17. **chit:** discourteous young woman.

WORDS TO KNOW **impotently** (ĭm′pə-tənt-lē) *adv.* helplessly; powerlessly

886

Teaching Options

Mini Lesson **Vocabulary Strategy**

ANTONYMS Ask students to match the following words with the WORDS TO KNOW that have opposite meanings.

1. indifferent
2. willing
3. incite
4. politeness
5. understandable

Answers: **1.** infatuated; **2.** averse; **3.** quell; **4.** insolence; **5.** unfathomable

Use **Vocabulary Transparencies and Copymasters,** p. 81, for more exercises.

For more instruction on antonyms, see page 1000 in the Pupil's Edition.

stuff at me! And she laughed—damn her! I've had it in for her for years. Followed her, I have, spied upon her. And now I've got her! She'll suffer for this, won't she, Mr. Lawyer? She'll suffer?"

"She will probably be sentenced to a term of imprisonment for perjury,"[18] said Mr. Mayherne quietly.

"Shut away—that's what I want. You're going, are you? Where's my money? Where's that good money?"

Without a word, Mr. Mayherne put down the notes on the table. Then, drawing a deep breath, he turned and left the squalid room. Looking back, he saw the old woman crooning over the money.

He wasted no time. He found the cinema in Lion Road easily enough, and, shown a photograph of Romaine Heilger, the commissionaire[19] recognized her at once. She had arrived at the cinema with a man some time after ten o'clock on the evening in question. He had not noticed her escort particularly, but he remembered the lady who had spoken to him about the picture that was showing. They stayed until the end, about an hour later.

Mr. Mayherne was satisfied. Romaine Heilger's evidence was a tissue of lies from beginning to end. She had evolved it out of her passionate hatred. The lawyer wondered whether he would ever know what lay behind that hatred. What had Leonard Vole done to her? He had seemed dumbfounded when the solicitor had reported her attitude to him. He had declared earnestly that such a thing was incredible—yet it had seemed to Mr. Mayherne that after the first astonishment his protests had lacked sincerity.

He did know. Mr. Mayherne was convinced of it. He knew, but he had no intention of revealing the fact. The secret between those two remained a secret. Mr. Mayherne wondered if someday he should come to learn what it was.

The solicitor glanced at his watch. It was late, but time was everything. He hailed a taxi and gave an address.

"Sir Charles must know of this at once," he murmured to himself as he got in.

The trial of Leonard Vole for the murder of Emily French aroused widespread interest. In the first place the prisoner was young and good-looking, then he was accused of a particularly dastardly crime, and there was the further interest of Romaine Heilger, the principal witness for the prosecution. There had been pictures of her in many papers, and several fictitious stories as to her origin and history.

The proceedings opened quietly enough. Various technical evidence came first. Then Janet Mackenzie was called. She told substantially the same story as before. In cross-examination counsel for the defense succeeded in getting her to contradict herself once or twice over her account of Vole's association with Miss French; he emphasized the fact that though she had heard a man's voice in the sitting room that night, there was nothing to show that it was Vole who was there, and he managed to drive home a feeling that jealousy and dislike of the prisoner were at the bottom of a good deal of her evidence.

Then the next witness was called.

"Your name is Romaine Heilger?"

"Yes."

"You are an Austrian subject?"

"Yes."

"For the last three years you have lived with the prisoner and passed yourself off as his wife?"

Just for a moment Romaine Heilger's eyes met those of the man in the dock. Her expression held something curious and unfathomable.

18. **perjury:** the deliberate giving of false testimony under oath in court.

19. **commissionaire:** usher.

WORDS TO KNOW
unfathomable (ŭn-făth′ə-mə-bəl) *adj.* too mysterious to be understood

Customizing Instruction

Students Acquiring English

1 Explain to students that the phrase "I've had it in for her" means "I've wanted to cause her harm."

Less Proficient Readers

To make sure students understand the importance of Mrs. Mogson's evidence, ask them the following questions:

- What does Mrs. Mogson give Mr. Mayherne?
  Answer: love letters written by Romaine to her lover, someone other than Leonard Vole; the letters show that she intends to frame Vole for the murder
- Why might these letters be useful to Mr. Mayherne?
  Possible Responses: The letters might contradict Romaine's testimony; they could provide evidence of a motive for Romaine's framing Vole.

Set a Purpose Have students read to find out how the love letters will influence the trial.

Reading and Analyzing

Literary Analysis: PLOT

A Remind students that most plots include the following stages: exposition, rising action, climax, and falling action. Ask students to which stage of the plot the reading of the letter belongs and why.

Possible Response: It is the climax. Romaine Heilger's letter acquits Mr. Vole.

ACTIVE READING

B **DRAW CONCLUSIONS** **Possible Response:** Romaine; both Romaine and the woman have a hand twitch; Romaine, being an actress, could pass herself off as another person.

Literary Analysis: CHARACTERIZATION

C Ask students what they think of Romaine at the end of the story. Have their ideas about what sort of person she is changed?

Possible Responses: She no longer seems cold and ruthless because she has sacrificed herself for Vole's sake; she seems as ruthless as ever because she is shielding a coldblooded murderer.

"Yes."

The questions went on. Word by word the damning facts came out. On the night in question the prisoner had taken out a crowbar with him. He had returned at twenty minutes past ten and had confessed to having killed the old lady. His cuffs had been stained with blood, and he had burned them in the kitchen stove. He had terrorized her into silence by means of threats.

As the story proceeded, the feeling of the court which had, to begin with, been slightly favorable to the prisoner, now set dead against him. He himself sat with downcast head and moody air, as though he knew he were doomed.

Yet it might have been noted that her own counsel sought to restrain Romaine's animosity. He would have preferred her to be more unbiased.

Formidable and ponderous, counsel for the defense arose.

He put it to her that her story was a malicious fabrication[20] from start to finish, that she had not even been in her own house at the time in question, that she was in love with another man and was deliberately seeking to send Vole to his death for a crime he did not commit.

Romaine denied these allegations with superb insolence.

Then came the surprising denouement,[21] the production of the letter. It was read aloud in court in the midst of a breathless stillness.

"Max, beloved, the Fates have delivered him into our hands! He has been arrested for murder—but, yes, the murder of an old lady! Leonard, who would not hurt a fly! At last I shall have my revenge. The poor chicken! I shall say that he came in that night with blood upon him—that he confessed to me. I shall hang him, Max—and when he hangs he will know and realize that it was Romaine who sent him to his death. And then—happiness, Beloved! Happiness at last!" A 2

"AT LAST I SHALL HAVE MY REVENGE."

There were experts present ready to swear that the handwriting was that of Romaine Heilger, but they were not needed. Confronted with the letter, Romaine broke down utterly and confessed everything. Leonard Vole had returned to the house at the time he said, twenty past nine. She had invented the whole story to ruin him.

With the collapse of Romaine Heilger, the case for the Crown collapsed also. Sir Charles

20. **malicious fabrication:** a lie intended to do harm or injury.

21. **denouement** (dā′no͞o-mäɴ′): final revelation.

WORDS TO KNOW

animosity (ăn′ə-mŏs′ĭ-tē) *n.* active dislike; hatred

insolence (ĭn′sə-ləns) *n.* bold rudeness; insulting behavior

Teaching Options

Standardized Test Practice

ALTERNATIVE ENDING You can assess students' understanding of the selection by having them imagine an alternative ending in which Vole is not acquitted but is found guilty of the murder. Students' writing could begin with the trial and focus on the evidence that condemns Vole.

RUBRIC

3 **Full Accomplishment** Response reflects a full understanding of the events in the story.

2 **Substantial Accomplishment** Response shows a general understanding of the events in the story.

1 **Little or Partial Accomplishment** Response shows little understanding of the events in the story.

called his few witnesses; the prisoner himself went into the box and told his story in a manly straightforward manner, unshaken by cross-examination.

The prosecution endeavored to rally, but without great success. The judge's summing up was not wholly favorable to the prisoner, but a reaction had set in, and the jury needed little time to consider their verdict.

"We find the prisoner not guilty."

Leonard Vole was free!

Little Mr. Mayherne hurried from his seat. He must congratulate his client.

1 He found himself polishing his pince-nez vigorously and checked himself. His wife had told him only the night before that he was getting a habit of it. Curious things, habits. People themselves never knew they had them.

An interesting case—a very interesting case. That woman, now, Romaine Heilger.

The case was dominated for him still by the exotic figure of Romaine Heilger. She had seemed a pale, quiet woman in the house at Paddington, but in court she had flamed out against the sober background, flaunting herself like a tropical flower.

If he closed his eyes, he could see her now, tall and vehement, her exquisite body bent forward a little, her right hand clenching and unclenching itself unconsciously all the time.

Curious things, habits. That gesture of hers with the hand was her habit, he supposed. Yet he had seen someone else do it quite lately. Who was it now? Quite lately—

ACTIVE READING

B **DRAW CONCLUSIONS**
Who was the woman in Shaw's Rents? Support your conclusion with evidence.

He drew in his breath with a gasp as it came back to him. The woman in Shaw's Rents . . .

He stood still, his head whirling. It was impossible—impossible— Yet, Romaine Heilger was an actress.

The K.C. came up behind him and clapped him on the shoulder.

"Congratulated our man yet? He's had a narrow shave, you know. Come along and see him."

But the little lawyer shook off the other's hand.

He wanted one thing only—to see Romaine Heilger face to face.

He did not see her until some time later, and the place of their meeting is not relevant.

"So you guessed," she said, when he had told her all that was in his mind. "The face? Oh! that was easy enough, and the light of that gas jet was too bad for you to see the makeup."

"But why—why—"

"Why did I play a lone hand?" She smiled a little, remembering the last time she had used the words.

"Such an elaborate comedy!"

"My friend—I had to save him. The evidence of a woman devoted to him would not have been enough—you hinted as much yourself. But I know something of the psychology of crowds. Let my evidence be wrung from me, as an admission, damning me in the eyes of the law, and a reaction in favor of the prisoner would immediately set in." 3

"And the bundle of letters?"

"One alone, the vital one, might have seemed like a—what do you call it?—put-up job."

"Then the man called Max?"

"Never existed, my friend."

"I still think," said little Mr. Mayherne, in an aggrieved manner, "that we could have got him off by the—er—normal procedure."

"I dared not risk it. You see, you thought he was innocent—"

"And you knew it? I see," said little Mr. Mayherne.

"My dear Mr. Mayherne," said Romaine, "you do not see at all. I knew—he was guilty!" ❖ C

Customizing Instruction

Students Acquiring English

1 Explain to students that *checked himself* means "restrained or controlled himself."

Less Proficient Readers

2 Ask students how the love letter helped Vole go free.

Answer: It showed that Romaine was trying to frame her husband.

3 Have students summarize Romaine's final revelation.

Possible Response: She knew Vole was guilty, so she did whatever she could to help him go free.

GUIDING STUDENT RESPONSE

Connect to the Literature

1. **What Do You Think?**
   Some students will take pleasure in the surprise ending and find that it offers an ingenious conclusion; others may feel that the ending is too implausible to be satisfying.

Comprehension Check
- the murder of Emily French
- by testifying in court that he killed Miss French
- a letter from Romaine to her lover saying that she plans to frame Vole for the murder

Use Selection Quiz
Unit Five Resource Book, p. 35.

Think Critically

2. Clues to Vole's guilt include his need for money, Miss French's wealth, his involvement in her business, her will, Janet Mackenzie's testimony, Mrs. Vole's belief in his guilt, and Romaine Heilger's testimony. His innocence is suggested by his apparent honesty with Mr. Mayherne and Romaine Heilger's love letter to Max.
3. Possible Responses: She is clever and calculating; she is so devoted to her husband that she will do anything for him; she is a consummate actress; she is an unconventional woman.
4. Possible Responses: yes, because he works very hard to defend his clients; no, because he is too easily taken in by others
5. Possible Response: No, it is unlikely that the whole court could have been taken in by Romaine's trick.

Literary Analysis

Dialogue Encourage students to develop distinctive voices for their characters, taking into consideration age, social position, nationality, etc.

Point of View Possible Response: Mr. Mayherne's opinions and perceptions tend to become the reader's own.

Thinking through the LITERATURE

Connect to the Literature

1. **What Do You Think?**
   Did you find the end of the story satisfying? Why or why not?

Comprehension Check
- With what crime is Leonard Vole charged?
- How does Romaine try to discredit Vole?
- What piece of evidence helps Leonard go free?

Think Critically

2. **ACTIVE READING** **DRAWING CONCLUSIONS** Review the chart you made in your **READER'S NOTEBOOK.** In drawing your own conclusion about Vole's guilt or innocence, what evidence did you think mattered the most? Compare your own conclusions about Vole with what you learn about him at the end of the story.

3. What is your opinion of Romaine Heilger?

   THINK ABOUT
   - her physical appearance and demeanor
   - the details of her background
   - her first interview with Mayherne
   - her final revelations

4. Do you think Mr. Mayherne is good at his work? Why or why not?

5. Do you think the **plot** of the story is believable? Use evidence from the story to support your judgment.

Extend Interpretations

6. **Critic's Corner** Commenting on Christie's popularity, H. R. F. Keating said, "She never tried to be clever in her writing, only ingenious in her plots." Do you think that "The Witness for the Prosecution" illustrates this distinction? Explain your view.

7. **Writer's Style** Many of Agatha Christie's mysteries have been adapted for dramatic presentation. Christie herself turned "The Witness for the Prosecution" into a stage play, which then became the basis of a popular 1957 movie; later, there was also a television production. Based on the style of this story, why do you think Christie's fiction lends itself to dramatic adaptation?

8. **Connect to Life** Based on this selection and on cases you may have seen in the news, how effective do you think courts are in finding out the truth?

Literary Analysis

DIALOGUE Written conversation between two or more characters is called **dialogue.** Realistic, well-placed dialogue enlivens a narrative and often helps to advance the **plot.** Dialogue provides the reader with insights into **characters'** personalities and relationships with one another. Dialogue can also show something about the **setting** of a piece, reflecting the language and concerns of a particular place or time period. This lends richness and believability to a literary work.

Cooperative Learning Activity With a group, perform a dramatic reading of several scenes from this story. One member of the group can play the part of the narrator, reading all of the non-dialogue text. The other members can perform the parts of the story's characters, reading the dialogue as they would in a play. After you have performed the reading, discuss how details in the story influenced your oral performance. How does the dialogue contribute to your understanding of the plot, characters, and setting?

REVIEW **POINT OF VIEW** Although the story is narrated from the **third-person point of view,** the reader can only see into the mind of Mr. Mayherne. How does this use of **third-person limited point of view** affect your sympathies or views toward the characters?

Extend Interpretations

Critic's Corner Possible Responses: Yes, the plain writing and surprise ending of this story show the lack of clever writing and the clearness of her plots; no, the plot is predictable, not ingenious.

Writer's Style Possible Response: Christie's stories focus on external rather than internal conflicts, which makes them easier to dramatize.

Connect to Life Possible Responses: Courts must rely too much on humans, who make mistakes and lie; in general, the courts manage to get past emotional or false testimony and find the truth.

Choices & CHALLENGES

Writing Options

1. Solicitor's Script Write a script for the conversation Mr. Mayherne might have had with Leonard Vole after learning the truth from Romaine Heilger.

2. Breaking News Write a newspaper article that might have appeared just after the murder, just after the pretrial (police court) hearing, or the day after Vole was found not guilty.

Writing Handbook
See page 1155: Narrative Writing.

3. Cast List What current movie stars would you cast in the roles of the characters in a modern film version of "The Witness for the Prosecution"? Make a cast list of characters showing which star you would cast in each role. Briefly explain your reasons for each casting decision.

Activities & Explorations

1. Dramatic Role-Play Working with a classmate, role-play the prosecution's examination or the defense's cross-examination of Romaine Heilger. To prepare, review this scene in the story for details that may be helpful for both the verbal and nonverbal aspects of your performance.
~ **PERFORMING**

2. Courtroom Sketches Draw sketches of the defendant, the lawyers, and the witnesses. ~ **ART**

Inquiry & Research

Scientific Proof What current scientific techniques for gathering evidence would make it harder for Vole to conceal his guilt today? Research these techniques, and record your findings in a written report.

More Online: Research Starter
www.mcdougallittell.com

Art Connection

Portrait of the Witness How well does the woman in the painting *Portrait de Madame M.* on page 881 match the way you pictured Romaine Heilger as you read the story?

Vocabulary in Action

EXERCISE A: SYNONYMS For each phrase on the left, write the letter of the synonymous phrase on the right. The Words to Know are boldfaced.

1. **impotently** scream	a. **infernal** colonel
2. notice **insolence**	b. **infatuated** rosiness
3. **churlish** driver	c. observe nerve
4. **amicable** serf	d. opposed to practice
5. sweet-talk the filly	e. crabby cabbie
6. **averse** to rehearsal	f. **cajole** the foal
7. blushes from crushes	g. pleasant peasant
8. quiet the riot	h. **quell** the crowd
9. intolerable officer	i. befriend Ben
10. **cultivate** comrade	j. weakly shriek

EXERCISE B: ASSESSMENT PRACTICE For each group of words below, write the letter of the word that is the best antonym for the boldfaced word.

1. **dastardly** (a) admirable, (b) effective, (c) clever
2. **animosity** (a) jealousy, (b) sophistication, (c) friendliness
3. **vindicate** (a) accuse, (b) retrieve, (c) honor
4. **unfathomable** (a) encouraging, (b) likable, (c) clear
5. **assiduously** (a) respectfully, (b) lazily, (c) heavily

Building Vocabulary
For an in-depth lesson on context clues, focusing on synonym clues and antonym clues, see page 1000.

Writing Options

1. **Solicitor's Script** Remind students to use proper script format.
2. **Breaking News** Discuss the fact that most newspaper articles try to answer the questions *who, what, where, when, why,* and *how.* Suggest that before beginning their articles, students write six questions they should try to answer, one beginning with each word.
3. **Cast List** Invite students to share their ideas, discuss them, and consolidate their choices in a final list.

Activities & Explorations

1. **Dramatic Role-Play** As they role-play the characters, remind them that they should be able to justify their choice of verbal and non-verbal performance techniques by referring to their analysis of the text. Encourage students to think carefully about their characters' motivations.
2. **Courtroom Sketches** Point out that courtroom artists provide newspaper readers and TV viewers with sketches of the principals in a trial. Discuss the fact that a good courtroom sketch focuses on the face and tries to capture facial features and expressions.

Inquiry & Research

Scientific Proof Encourage students to form research groups. Students can work collaboratively to organize the research: researchers can look for information and recorders can create and edit the final report. Groups might interview local police homicide squads or criminal lawyers.

Art Connection

Students should support their opinions with details from both the painting and the story.

Vocabulary in Action

EXERCISE A

1. j	**6.** d
2. c	**7.** b
3. e	**8.** h
4. g	**9.** a
5. f	**10.** i

EXERCISE B

1. a
2. c
3. a
4. c
5. b

Grammar in Context

WRITING EXERCISE Answers will vary. Possible answers are shown.

1. Mr. Mayherne thinks about who would want to kill Emily French.
2. He needs to know when Leonard Vole left Emily French's house on the night of the murder.
3. He seems determined to learn what Romaine Heilger's secret is.
4. Romaine reveals which man committed the crime.

Author Activity

From Page to Stage to Screen As they make their comparisons, encourage students to pay particular attention to the portrayal of the main characters and to the film's ending. You might put the students in small groups to share their film reviews. Group members should compare the others reviews with their own responses.

Grammar in Context: Noun Clauses

In "The Witness for the Prosecution," the following two sentences contain noun clauses:

> **"I want you to tell me in your own words exactly how you came to make the acquaintance of Miss Emily French."**
>
> **"Whether a jury would take that view of it is another matter."**

A **noun clause** is a subordinate clause that functions as a noun—it can be a subject, an object, or a predicate nominative. In the first sentence above, the noun clause shown in blue is the direct object of the verb *tell.* In the second sentence, the noun clause is the subject of the sentence.

Usage Tip: Noun clauses can be introduced by a variety of words. Among these are *what, that, who, which, how, when,* and *where.*

WRITING EXERCISE Rewrite each sentence, adding a noun clause introduced by the underlined word.

Example: ***Original*** Mr. Mayherne tries to figure out how.

Rewritten Mr. Mayherne tries to figure out how he can prove Leonard Vole's innocence.

1. Mr. Mayherne thinks about who.
2. He needs to know when.
3. He seems determined to learn what.
4. Romaine reveals which.

Grammar Handbook Clauses, p. 1197

Agatha Christie

1890–1976

Other Works

Murder on the Orient Express
And Then There Were None
Three Blind Mice and Other Stories
Hickory, Dickory, Death

The Queen of British Mystery Agatha Christie is one of the world's most popular writers of detective fiction. Her books have been translated into more than 100 languages, and probably more copies of her books have been sold than have those of any other writer in the 20th century. Christie's eccentric detective Hercule Poirot appeared on a Nicaraguan postage stamp. Several of her other detectives, including Miss Jane Marple, are still featured regularly in televised versions of her mysteries.

The Path to Success Christie grew up in Torquay, Devonshire, a small resort in the English countryside. Her father, an American, died when she was very young, and she was raised by her British mother. In 1914, after the outbreak of World War I, Christie was married. During the war, she worked as a hospital nurse and thereby gained, among other things, a knowledge of poisons. A challenge from her sister prompted Christie to write her first detective novel, *The Mysterious Affair at Styles,* which was published in 1920. In the next six years, she published six more books, including *The Murder of Roger Ackroyd* (1926), often hailed as her most ingenious mystery. Soon afterward came the famous mystery in Christie's own life: the celebrated author disappeared, and she was discovered, after a nationwide hunt, apparently suffering from amnesia. She subsequently divorced her first husband and married Max Mallowan, an archaeologist, with whom she later made frequent visits to the Middle East. These travels prompted several mysteries, including *Death on the Nile* (1937) and *Death Comes as the End* (1944).

Author Activity

From Page to Stage to Screen Read the dramatic adaptation of this story or watch a video of the 1957 film version, which was based on the play. Then write a review in which you compare the short story with the play or the film version. Be sure to mention which you prefer and why.

Teaching Options

Mini Lesson Grammar

NOUN CLAUSES A noun clause is a clause which may stand in for a noun as a subject, direct object, or other sentence part. Noun clauses often begin with words such as *that, what, whatever, which, who, when, where, whether,* and *why.* Use the following example from the story to illustrate the noun clause:

We are in a position to say that you had no idea she was well off, (clause 1)
that you visited her out of pure (clause 2)

Practice Ask students to make up three sentences using noun clauses as follows:

- as the subject and beginning with *what*

Possible Response: What I'm doing is making a sandwich.

- as the direct object and beginning with *that*

Possible Response: He admitted that he was making a sandwich.

Use **Unit Five Resource Book,** p. 48 for additional support.
Use **Grammar Transparencies and Copymasters,** p. 116.

Use McDougal Littell's ***Language Network,*** Chapter 4, for more instruction and practice in noun clauses.

The Balek Scales

Short Story by HEINRICH BÖLL (hīn′rĭk bœl)

"The justice of this earth, O Lord, hath put Thee to death."

Connect to Your Life

The Scales of Justice What does the word *justice* mean to you? Explore the meaning of the word and its associations by creating a word web to answer the questions that are shown.

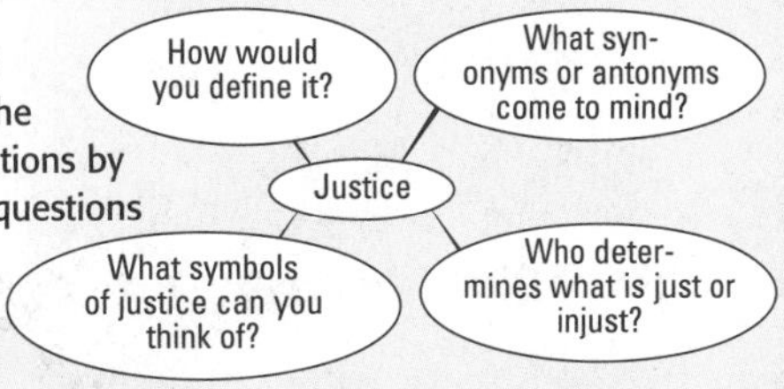

How would you define it?
What synonyms or antonyms come to mind?
Justice
What symbols of justice can you think of?
Who determines what is just or injust?

Build Background

European Social Order This story takes place in central Europe around 1900. In that era, much of Europe was characterized by a strict social hierarchy in which a person's social position was largely determined by birth. At the top of the social ladder were such royal figures as kings or emperors, followed by counts and barons and other members of the aristocracy who passed their titles down to their children. Ranking below the aristocracy were wealthy landowners who had no titles but who often hoped to acquire them as a reward for service or influence. At the bottom of the social ladder were the common people.

In the story you are about to read, the Baleks, a wealthy family, have controlled the lives of the common people for five generations, even to the point of creating laws to control the system of justice. The Baleks live in an elegant chateau (shă-tō′), or country house, and own much of the land in the area.

VIDEODISC

LaserLinks: Background for Reading
Historical Connection

WORDS TO KNOW
Vocabulary Preview
antiquated
flout
forlorn
meager
preside

Focus Your Reading

LITERARY ANALYSIS TONE **Tone** is the attitude a writer or narrator takes toward a subject. A writer's use of language and details helps to create the tone, which might be serious, humorous, ironic, or detached, among other possibilities. As you read, pay attention to the story's tone and how it affects your reaction to the story.

ACTIVE READING ANALYZING RELEVANCE OF SETTING In "The Balek Scales," Böll opens the story by introducing its **setting**—the time and place in which the action occurs—and describing the work that the people do. This description also tells you something about the power of the Balek family and the hardships faced by the working people:

> ***Where my grandfather came from, most of the people lived by working in the flax sheds. For five generations they had been breathing in the dust which rose from the crushed flax stalks, letting themselves be killed off by slow degrees.***

READER'S NOTEBOOK In order to **analyze** a story's setting, you must first break it down into parts. As you read this story, fill in a chart like the one started here. Identify key places in the setting, and give short descriptions of each place and what happens there.

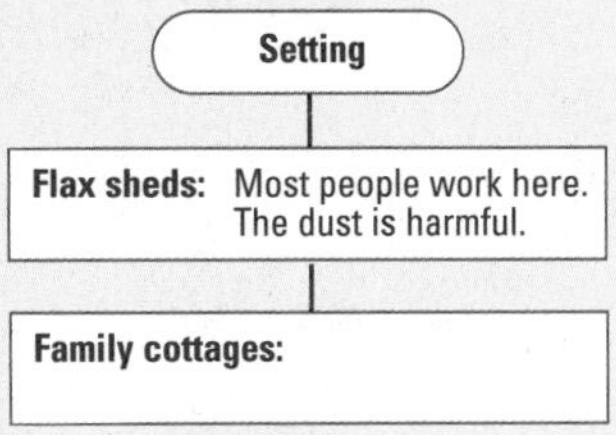

Setting
Flax sheds: Most people work here. The dust is harmful.
Family cottages:

OVERVIEW

Objectives

1. understand and appreciate a **short story (Literary Analysis)**
2. recognize and understand the author's **tone (Literary Analysis)**
3. analyze relevance of setting **(Active Reading)**

Summary

The narrator recalls the small village where his grandfather and most everyone else worked in flax sheds. When the children were not in school, they picked mushrooms, herbs, and hayflowers on the Balek family's land and sold them to the Balek family. The narrator notes that only the Baleks were allowed to own a scale. Raised to the aristocracy on the first day of 1900, the Baleks showed their graciousness by giving a quarter pound of prepackaged coffee to each family on New Year's Eve. The grandfather, who was still a boy at the time, had the opportunity to test the accuracy of the scales using the coffee, and discovered that they were off by 55 grams in favor of the Baleks. When he shared the news, the villagers rebelled and stole the scales and logbook to calculate how much money they were owed. Gendarmes appeared, shooting and stabbing those who stood in their way and threatening the people with prison. Several villagers were killed and the grandfather's family was forced to leave the village. They became basket weavers, traveling the country roads and telling their tale of injustice to the few who would listen.

Thematic Link

Revealing an injustice does not always mean that justice will be served.

5-Minute Warm-Up

Daily Language SkillBuilder

Have students **proofread** the display sentences on page 817j and write them correctly. The sentences also appear on Transparency 25 of **Grammar Transparencies and Copymasters.**

LESSON RESOURCES

UNIT FIVE RESOURCE BOOK, pp. 37–38

ASSESSMENT RESOURCES
Formal Assessment, pp. 147–148
Teacher's Guide to Assessment and Portfolio Use
Test Generator

SKILLS TRANSPARENCIES AND COPYMASTERS
Literary Analysis
- Mood and Tone, T20 (for Cooperative Learning Activity, p. 901)

Grammar
- Sentence Structure, C120 (for Mini Lesson, p. 896)

Vocabulary
- Context Clues, C82 (for Mini Lesson, p. 894)
- Meanings of Roots, C83 (for Mini Lesson, p. 898)

Writing
- Opinion Statement, C25 (for Writing Option 1, p. 902)
- Autobiographical Incident, C34 (for Writing Option 3, p. 902)

INTEGRATED TECHNOLOGY
Audio Library
LaserLinks
- Historical Connection: Rich and Poor in Europe Around 1900. See **Teacher's SourceBook,** p. 46.

Visit our website:
www.mcdougallittell.com

TEACHING THE LITERATURE

Reading and Analyzing

Reading Skills and Strategies: PREVIEW

Summarize the story emphasizing the importance of the settings. The Build Background p. 893 will help students understand the social–economic order that extended over much of Europe during the 1800s.

Active Reading

ANALYZING RELEVANCE OF SETTING

Discuss how the setting can impact the events of the plot, the characters' actions, and the theme of the selection. Students should note important elements of the setting as they are revealed.

Use **Unit Five Resource Book,** p. 37 for additional support.

Literary Analysis TONE

The tone is the author's attitude toward the subject, which must be interpreted through the narrator's attitudes. Ask students to keep a list of details that help to create the tone of the story and to note the places in the story where the tone changes or heightens.

Use **Unit Five Resource Book,** p. 38 for additional support.

ACTIVE READING

ANALYZE **Possible Response:** The people in the village were separated from the poor folks in the countryside and had little idea of or interest in their plight.

The Balek Scales

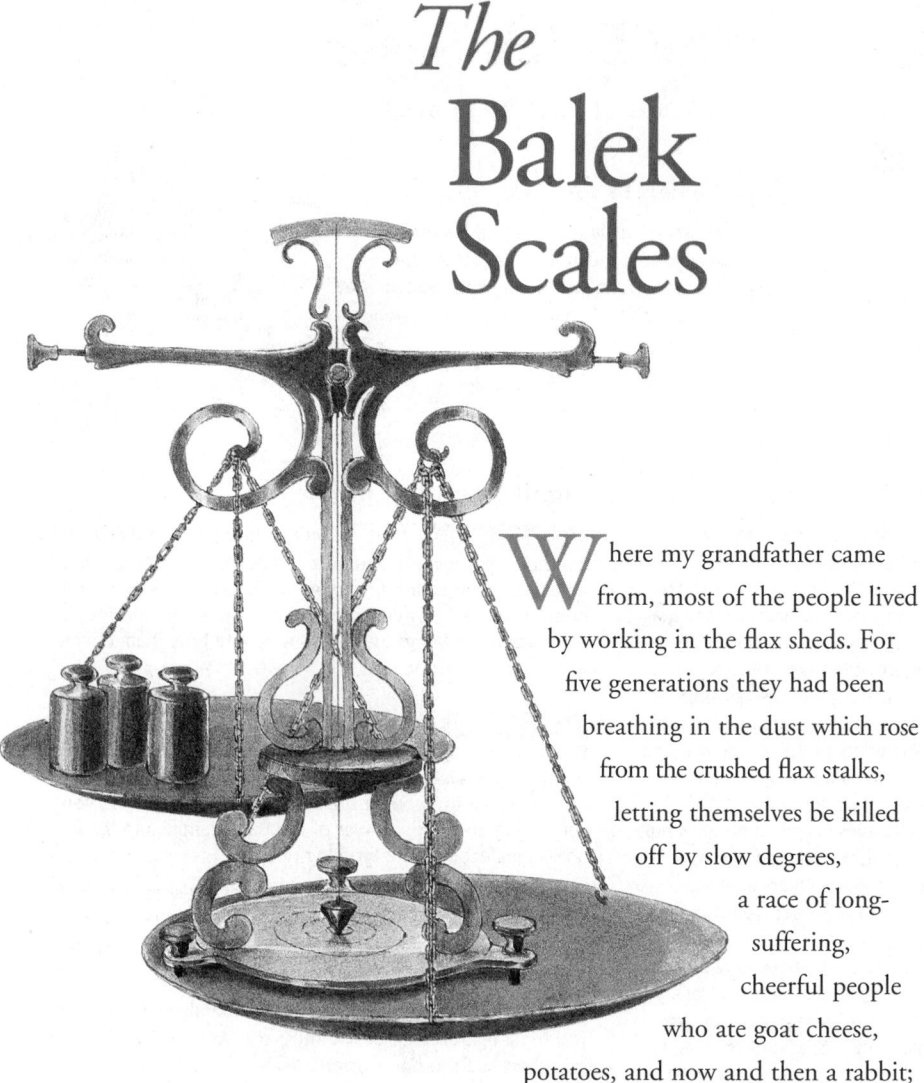

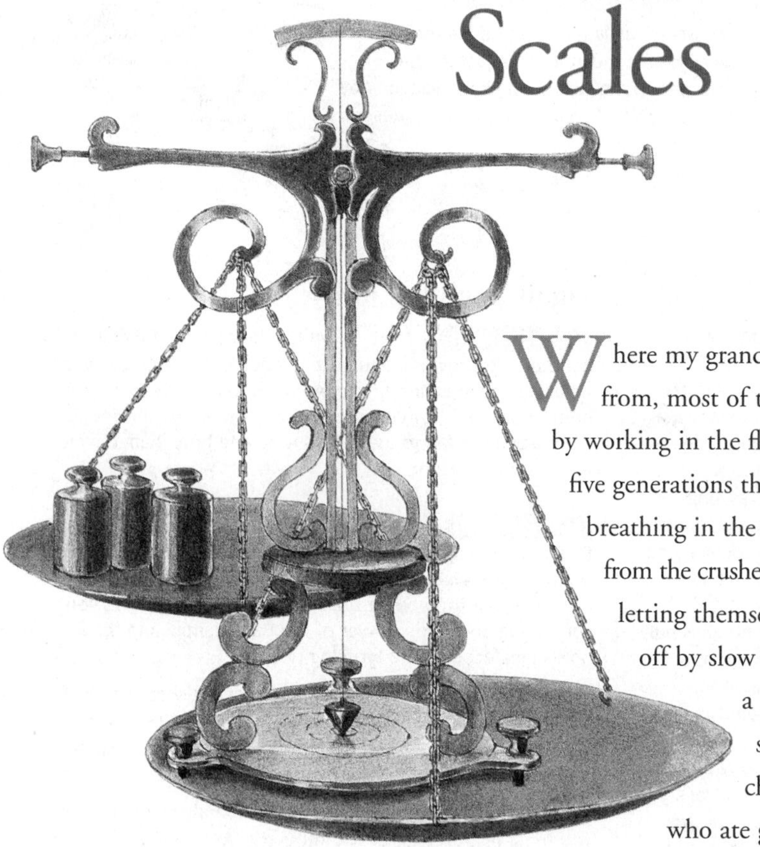

Heinrich Böll

Where my grandfather came from, most of the people lived by working in the flax sheds. For five generations they had been breathing in the dust which rose from the crushed flax stalks, letting themselves be killed off by slow degrees, a race of long-suffering, cheerful people who ate goat cheese, potatoes, and now and then a rabbit; in the evening they would sit at home spinning and knitting; they sang, drank mint tea and were happy.

Teaching Options

Mini Lesson: Preteaching Vocabulary

USING CONTEXT CLUES Call students' attention to the list of WORDS TO KNOW. Remind them that they can sometimes understand the meaning of an unfamiliar word by examining the context in which the word is used.

Model Sentence

Nick, always a rebel, *flouted* his employer's conservative dress code by wearing leather pants to work.

Instruction

- Write the model sentence on the chalkboard, and have a volunteer paraphrase the meaning.
- Have students use the paraphrase to guess meanings for the word *flouted,* and ask a volunteer to use *flout* in a sentence.

Exercises Ask students to use context clues to infer the meanings of the italicized terms in the following sentences.

1. My *meager* breakfast of dry toast and tea wasn't enough to keep me going until lunch.
2. With new software programs coming out every year, computers just ten years old are *antiquated.*
3. My dog Dusty was *forlorn* because we left him at home all alone all day.

Use **Unit Five Resource Book,** p. 39 for additional support.

A lesson on synonyms appears on p. 1000 in the Pupil's Edition.

During the day they would carry the flax stalks to the antiquated machines, with no protection from the dust and at the mercy of the heat which came pouring out of the drying kilns.[1] Each cottage contained only one bed, standing against the wall like a closet and reserved for the parents, while the children slept all around the room on benches. In the morning the room would be filled with the odor of thin soup; on Sundays there was stew, and on feast days[2] the children's faces would light up with pleasure as they watched the black acorn coffee turning paler and paler from the milk their smiling mother poured into their coffee mugs.

The parents went off early to the flax sheds, the housework was left to the children: they would sweep the room, tidy up, wash the dishes and peel the potatoes, precious pale-yellow fruit whose thin peel had to be produced afterwards to dispel any suspicion of extravagance or carelessness.

As soon as the children were out of school, they had to go off into the woods and, depending on the season, gather mushrooms and herbs: woodruff and thyme, caraway, mint and foxglove, and in summer, when they had brought in the hay from their meager fields, they gathered hayflowers. A kilo[3] of hayflowers was worth one pfennig,[4] and they were sold by the apothecaries[5] in town for twenty pfennigs a kilo to highly strung ladies. The mushrooms were highly prized: they fetched twenty pfennigs a kilo and were sold in the shops in town for one mark twenty.[6] The children would crawl deep into the green darkness of the forest during the autumn when dampness drove the mushrooms out of the soil, and almost every family had its own places where it gathered mushrooms, places which were handed down in whispers from generation to generation.

ACTIVE READING

ANALYZE How does this description of setting influence your understanding of the people in the village?

The woods belonged to the Baleks, as well as the flax sheds, and in my grandfather's village the Baleks had a chateau, and the wife of the head of the family had a little room next to the dairy where mushrooms, herbs and hayflowers were weighed and paid for. There on the table stood the great Balek scales, an old-fashioned, ornate bronze-gilt[7] contraption, which my grandfather's grandparents had already faced when they were children, their grubby hands holding their little baskets of mushrooms, their paper bags of hayflowers, breathlessly watching the number of weights Frau[8] Balek had to throw on the scale before the swinging pointer came to rest exactly over the black line, that thin line of justice which had to be redrawn every year. Then Frau Balek would take the big book covered in brown leather, write down the weight, and pay out the money, pfennigs or ten-pfennig pieces and very, very occasionally, a mark. And when my grandfather was a child,

1. **kilns** (kĭlnz): ovens, used here to dry the flax.
2. **feast days:** holidays, especially religious holidays honoring saints.
3. **kilo** (kē′lō): short for *kilogram,* a metric measure equal to 1,000 grams, or about 2.2 pounds.
4. **pfennig** (fĕn′ĭg): a coin equal to a hundredth of a mark, the basic unit of German currency. The word *pfennig* is related to the English *penny.*
5. **apothecaries** (ə-pŏth′ĭ-kĕr′ēz): pharmacists; druggists.
6. **one mark twenty:** one mark and twenty pfennigs.
7. **bronze-gilt:** covered with a thin layer of bronze.
8. **Frau** (frou): a German title indicating a married woman.

WORDS TO KNOW

antiquated (ăn′tĭ-kwā′tĭd) *adj.* old-fashioned; outmoded

meager (mē′gər) *adj.* lacking quantity, fullness, strength, or fertility; feeble; scanty

Customizing Instruction

Less Proficient Readers

Make sure students understand that the Baleks own the flax sheds as well as the woods and fields. Have students read to discover how the Baleks administer their land and their tenants.

Students Acquiring English

This selection contains many long compound and complex sentences which may prove difficult for students to interpret. Suggest that students view each long sentence as a series of short ones joined together by a comma and the word and or by semicolons or colons. You may want to read certain sentences aloud to help students work their way through them.

Use **Spanish Study Guide** for additional support, pp. 181–183.

Gifted and Talented

Have students identify details that Böll uses throughout the story to describe the social and political system under which the villagers live.

Possible Responses:

- Working conditions in the flax sheds. *(The villagers are exploited by their employers.)*
- Description of the cottages and the food the families eat. *(The people are very poor.)*
- The unjust scales. *(The rich often cheat the poor.)*
- How the rebellion is put down. *(The rich control the police and use force to maintain the status quo.)*

BLOCK SCHEDULING: MANAGING TIME

If your schedule requires that you cover the lesson objectives in a shorter time, use . . .

- Preparing to Read, p. 893
- Thinking Through the Literature, p. 901
- Vocabulary in Action, p. 902

If you want to take advantage of longer class time, use . . .

- TE Teaching Options: Preteaching Vocabulary, p. 894; Vocabulary Strategy, p. 898; Viewing and Representing, p. 899; Standardized Test Practice, p. 900
- Choices & Challenges, p. 902

Reading and Analyzing

ACTIVE READING

A PREDICT Possible Response: Maybe they wanted a monopoly on buying and selling. Maybe their scales were rigged in order to cheat people.

Literary Analysis: SETTING

B Have students discuss why they think the author sets these events on the first day of a new century.
Possible Response: Some students may say that this momentous date adds importance to the boy's discovery; others may say that the new century suggests the possibility of a new beginning.

Literary Analysis TONE

C Ask students to describe the tone of this passage about the New Year's preparations and festivities.
Possible Response: Some students may say the tone is festive and full of good cheer. Others may say it reflects the Baleks' sense of their own importance.

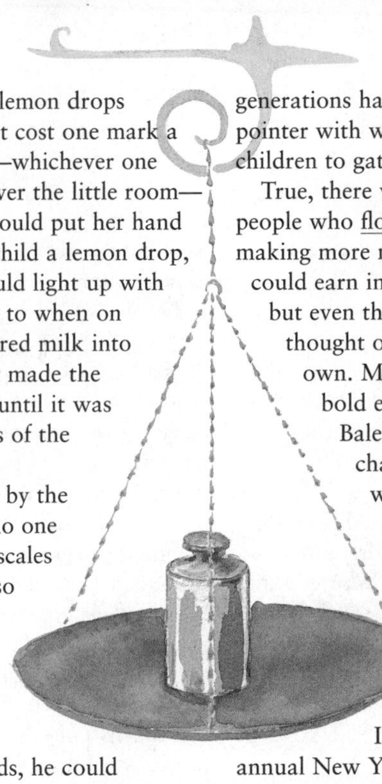

there was a big glass jar of lemon drops standing there, the kind that cost one mark a kilo, and when Frau Balek—whichever one happened to be presiding over the little room—was in a good mood, she would put her hand into this jar and give each child a lemon drop, and the children's faces would light up with pleasure, the way they used to when on feast days their mother poured milk into their coffee mugs, milk that made the coffee turn paler and paler until it was as pale as the flaxen pigtails of the little girls.

One of the laws imposed by the Baleks on the village was: no one was permitted to have any scales in the house. The law was so ancient that nobody gave a thought as to when and how it had arisen, and it had to be obeyed, for anyone who broke it was dismissed from the flax sheds, he could not sell his mushrooms or his thyme or his hayflowers, and the power of the Baleks was so far-reaching that no one in the neighboring villages would give him work either or buy his forest herbs. But since the days when my grandfather's parents had gone out as small children to gather mushrooms and sell them in order that they might season the meat of the rich people of Prague[9] or be baked into game pies, it had never occurred to anyone to break this law: flour could be measured in cups, eggs could be counted, what they had spun could be measured by the yard, and besides, the old-fashioned bronze-gilt, ornate Balek scales did not look as if there was anything wrong with them, and five generations had entrusted the swinging black pointer with what they had gone out as eager children to gather from the woods.

ACTIVE READING

A **PREDICT** Why do you think the Baleks outlawed the ownership of the scales?

True, there were some among those quiet people who flouted the law, poachers bent on making more money in one night than they could earn in a whole month in the flax sheds, but even these people apparently never thought of buying scales or making their own. My grandfather was the first person bold enough to test the justice of the Baleks, the family who lived in the chateau and drove two carriages, who always maintained one boy from the village while he studied theology at the seminary[10] in Prague, the family with whom the priest played taroc[11] every Wednesday, on whom the local reeve,[12] in his carriage emblazoned with the Imperial coat of arms, made an annual New Year's Day call and on whom the Emperor conferred a title on the first day of the year 1900.

My grandfather was hard-working and smart: he crawled further into the woods than the children of his clan had crawled before him, he penetrated as far as the thicket where, according to legend, Bilgan the Giant was supposed to dwell, guarding a treasure. But my

---

9. **Prague** (präg): the capital of the present-day Czech (chĕk) Republic, which borders southeastern Germany. At the time of the story, Prague was ruled by German-speaking Austria and was home to many German merchants as well as native Czechs.
10. **studied theology at the seminary:** studied religious philosophy at the school for training members of the clergy.
11. **taroc** (tăr′ək): a European card game played with a 78-card pack; also spelled *tarok*.
12. **reeve** (rēv): a local authority, here representing the emperor's government.

WORDS TO KNOW

preside (prĭ-zīd′) *v.* to hold the chief position of authority or control
flout (flout) *v.* to show contempt for; to scorn

Teaching Options

Mini Lesson Grammar

SENTENCE STRUCTURE Review with students the terms used to identify different sentence types.

- A **simple** sentence has one independent clause and no subordinate clauses.
- A **compound** sentence has two or more independent clauses and no subordinate clauses.
- A **complex** sentence has one independent clause and one or more subordinate clauses.
- A **compound-complex** sentence has two or more independent clauses and one or more subordinate clauses.

When two independent clauses are joined to form a compound sentence, a **coordinating conjunction** (such as *and* or *but*) is usually used. If no coordinating conjunction is used, a semicolon is used. Subordinate clauses are usually preceded by a **subordinating conjunction** (such as *before, if, when,* etc.) or a **relative pronoun** (such as *that, which, who,* etc.).

Practice Ask students to identify each sentence type, underline the independent clauses, and draw parentheses around the subordinate clauses.

1. While Frau Gertrud, who was the Baleks' maid, was getting another kilo of lemon drops, young Franz Brücher decided to test the accuracy of the scales.

grandfather was not afraid of Bilgan: he worked his way deep into the thicket, even when he was quite little, and brought out great quantities of mushrooms; he even found truffles,[13] for which Frau Balek paid thirty pfennigs a pound. Everything my grandfather took to the Baleks he entered on the back of a torn-off calendar page: every pound of mushrooms, every gram of thyme, and on the right-hand side, in his childish handwriting, he entered the amount he received for each item; he scrawled in every pfennig, from the age of seven to the age of twelve, and by the time he was twelve the year 1900 had arrived, and because the Baleks had been raised to the aristocracy by the Emperor, they gave every family in the village a quarter of a pound of real coffee, the Brazilian kind; there was also free beer and tobacco for the men, and at the chateau there was a great banquet; many carriages stood in the avenue of poplars leading from the entrance gates to the chateau.

But the day before the banquet the coffee was distributed in the little room which had housed the Balek scales for almost a hundred years, and the Balek family was now called Balek von Bilgan
1 because, according to legend, Bilgan the Giant used to have a great castle on the site of the present Balek estate.

My grandfather often used to tell me how he went there after school to fetch the coffee for four families: the Cechs, the Weidlers, the Vohlas[14] and his own, the Brüchers.[15] It was the afternoon of New Year's Eve: there were the front rooms to be decorated, the baking to be done, and the families did not want to spare four boys and have each of them go all the way to the chateau to bring back a quarter of a pound of coffee.

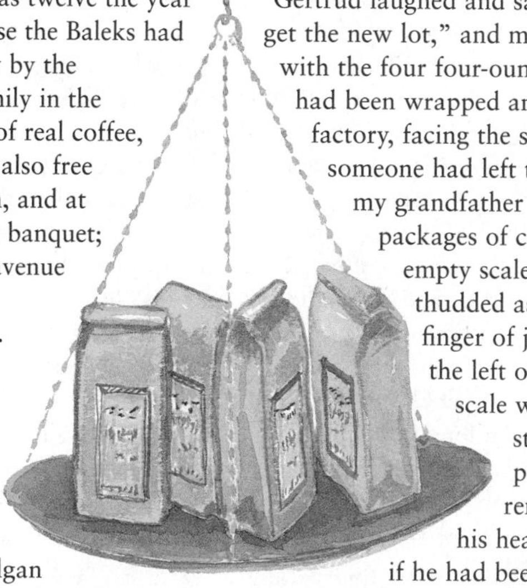

And so my grandfather sat on the narrow wooden bench in the little room while Gertrud the maid counted out the wrapped four-ounce packages of coffee, four of them, and he looked at the scales and saw that the pound weight was still lying on the left-hand scale; Frau Balek von Bilgan was busy with preparations for the banquet. And when Gertrud was about to put her hand into the jar with the lemon drops to give my grandfather one, she discovered it was empty: it was refilled once a year and held one kilo of the kind that cost a mark.

Gertrud laughed and said: "Wait here while I get the new lot," and my grandfather waited with the four four-ounce packages which had been wrapped and sealed in the factory, facing the scales on which someone had left the pound weight, and my grandfather took the four packages of coffee, put them on the empty scale, and his heart thudded as he watched the black finger of justice come to rest on the left of the black line: the scale with the pound weight stayed down, and the pound of coffee remained up in the air; his heart thudded more than if he had been lying behind a bush in the forest waiting for Bilgan the Giant, and he felt in his pocket for the pebbles he always carried with him so he could use his catapult[16] to shoot the sparrows which pecked away at his mother's cabbage plants—he had to put three, four, five pebbles beside the packages of coffee

13. **truffles** (trŭf'əlz): edible fungi that resemble mushrooms but are far rarer and are considered a great delicacy.
14. **the Cechs** (chĕks), **the Weidlers** (vīd'lərz), **the Vohlas** (vō'läz).
15. **Brüchers** (brü'KHərz): The name *Brücher* derives from the German words for "to break" and "to breach."
16. **catapult** (kăt'ə-pŭlt'): here, a slingshot.

Customizing Instruction

Less Proficient Readers

Use these questions to check students' understanding of the prevalent social and economic system:

- Who are the Baleks?
  Answer: A wealthy family that owns the land and the flax sheds where people work
- How do the Baleks use their scales?
  Answer: To weigh flowers, herbs, and mushrooms that children gather and sell to them
- What is special about the Balek scales?
  Answer: They are the only scales in the village; no one else is allowed to own scales.

Set a Purpose Have the students read on to find out what the narrator's grandfather discovers about the Balek scales.

Students Acquiring English

1 Explain to students that at this time in history the aristocracy is a group of people who own most of the land and enjoy high social status and certain privileges denied to common people. When the Baleks become aristocrats, their name is lengthened to reflect their new status—they have a "title."

2. The villagers in Heinrich Böll's story are oppressed by the wealthy Balek family.
3. A kilo of hay flowers was worth one pfennig; they were sold by the apothecaries in town for twenty pfennigs to highly strung young ladies.
4. When Franz Brücher discovered that the Balek scales were inaccurate, he spent the evening determining how much money the Baleks owed him, and then he told his parents of his discovery.

ANSWERS

1. (While Frau Gertrud, (who was the Baleks' maid), was getting another kilo of lemon drops), young Franz Brücher decided to test the accuracy of the scales. **Complex**
2. The villagers in Heinrich Böll's story are oppressed by the wealthy Balek family. **Simple**
3. A kilo of hay flowers was worth one pfennig; they were sold by the apothecaries in town for twenty pfennigs to highly strung young ladies. **Compound**
4. (When Franz Brücher discovered that the Balek scales were inaccurate), he spent the evening determining how much money the Baleks owed him, and then he told his parents of his discovery. **Compound-Complex**

Use **Grammar Transparencies and Copymasters,** p. 120, for more exercises.

Use McDougal Littell's ***Language Network,*** Chapter 4, for more instruction in sentence structure.

Reading and Analyzing

Reading Skills and Strategies: ANALYZING

A Ask students how they account for the behavior of the narrator's grandfather when Gertrud returned.

Possible Response: He didn't take the coffee and stepped on the lemon drop because he knew that his family had been cheated; he didn't want to accept a gift from the people who were taking advantage of his family.

ACTIVE READING

B **CLARIFY** **Possible Response:** He has discovered that the scale is inaccurate. By using scales weighted in their favor, the Baleks have been cheating the villagers.

Literary Analysis: SYMBOL

C Have the students discuss why a giant might be an appropriate symbol for the Baleks.

Possible Responses: Giants are usually powerful and often portrayed as the antagonist.

Reading Skills and Strategies: PREDICT

Ask students to predict what might happen when the other villagers and the Baleks learn about Franz's discovery.

before the scale with the pound weight rose and the pointer at last came to rest over the black line. My grandfather took the coffee from the scale, wrapped the five pebbles in his kerchief, and when Gertrud came back with the big kilo bag of lemon drops which had to last for another whole year in order to make the children's faces light up with pleasure, when Gertrud let the lemon drops rattle into the glass jar, the pale little fellow was still standing there, and nothing seemed to have changed. My grandfather only took three of the packages, then Gertrud looked in startled surprise at the white-faced child who threw the lemon drop onto the floor, ground it under his heel, and said: "I want to see Frau Balek." **A**

"Balek von Bilgan, if you please," said Gertrud.

"All right, Frau Balek von Bilgan," but Gertrud only laughed at him, and he walked back to the village in the dark, took the Cechs, the Weidlers and the Vohlas their coffee, and said he had to go and see the priest.

ACTIVE READING

B **CLARIFY** What has the grandfather discovered?

Instead he went out into the dark night with his five pebbles in his kerchief. He had to walk a long way before he found someone who had scales, who was permitted to have them; no one in the villages of Blaugau and Bernau[17] had any, he knew that, and he went straight through them till, after two hours' walking, he reached the little town of Dielheim[18] where Honig[19] the apothecary lived. From Honig's house came the smell of fresh pancakes, and Honig's breath, when he opened the door to the half-frozen boy, already smelled of punch, there was a moist cigar between his narrow lips, and he clasped the boy's cold hands firmly for a moment, saying: "What's the matter, has your father's lung got worse?"

"No, I haven't come for medicine, I wanted . . . " My grandfather undid his kerchief, took out the five pebbles, held them out to Honig and said: "I wanted to have these weighed." He glanced anxiously into Honig's face, but when Honig said nothing and did not get angry, or even ask him anything, my grandfather said: "It is the amount that is short of justice," and now, as he went into the warm room, my grandfather realized how wet his feet were. The snow had soaked through his cheap shoes, and in the forest the branches had showered him with snow which was now melting, and he was tired and hungry and suddenly began to cry because he thought of the quantities of mushrooms, the herbs, the flowers, which had been weighed on the scales which were short five pebbles' worth of justice. And when Honig, shaking his head and holding the five pebbles, called his wife, my grandfather thought of the generations of his parents, his grandparents, who had all had to have their mushrooms, their flowers, weighed on the scales, and he was overwhelmed by a great wave of injustice and began to sob louder than ever, and, without waiting to be asked, he sat down on a chair, ignoring the pancakes, the cup of hot coffee which nice plump Frau Honig put in front of him, and did not stop crying till Honig himself came out from the shop at the back and, rattling the pebbles in his hand, said in a low voice to his wife: "Fifty-five grams, exactly."

My grandfather walked the two hours home through the forest, got a beating at home, said nothing, not a single word, when he was asked about the coffee, spent the whole evening doing sums on the piece of paper on which he had written down everything he had sold to Frau Balek, and when midnight struck, and the cannon could be heard

17. **Blaugau** (blou′gou′) **and Bernau** (bĕr′nou).
18. **Dielheim** (dēl′hīm′).
19. **Honig** (hô′nĭKH).

Teaching Options

Mini Lesson: Vocabulary Strategy

APPLY MEANINGS OF ROOT WORDS Instruction Students can often guess the meaning of an unfamiliar word by thinking of the meaning of the root word and looking at the context. Use the word *antiquated* in the following sentence from the story to demonstrate the strategy:

During the day they would carry the flax stalks to the antiquated machines, with no protection from the dust and at the mercy of the heat which came pouring out of the drying kilns.

The word *antiquated* has as its root the word *antique,* a word most students will be familiar with. From the context, they know that the working conditions are very bad, which helps to confirm the idea that the machines the workers have to use might be old or outdated.

Practice Using their knowledge of the word *antique* ask them to define the italicized words.

1. Some of the statues in the archeology museum are of great *antiquity.*
2. I wanted to learn more about this old chair, which once belonged to my great-grandfather, so I took it to an *antiquarian.* She told me that it was made in France in the 18th century.
3. I *antiqued* this table with just a can of paint and some special brushes. Now no one can tell that it's actually brand new!

Use **Vocabulary Transparencies and Copymasters,** p. 83, for more exercises.

A lesson on root words appears on p. 183 in the Pupil's Edition.

Une Battue en Campine [Beating the bushes in Campine] (about 1882–1885), Théodor Verstræte. Oil on canvas, 41 ¼″ × 71″, collection of Crédit Communal, Brussels, Belgium.

from the chateau, and the whole village rang with shouting and laughter and the noise of rattles, when the family kissed and embraced all around, he said into the New Year silence: "The Baleks owe me eighteen marks and thirty-two pfennigs." And again he thought of all the children there were in the village, of his brother Fritz who had gathered so many mushrooms, of his sister Ludmilla; he thought of the many hundreds of children who had all gathered mushrooms for the Baleks, and herbs and flowers, and this time he did not cry but told his parents and brothers and sisters of his discovery.

When the Baleks von Bilgan went to High Mass on New Year's Day, their new coat of arms—a giant crouching under a fir tree—already emblazoned in blue and gold on their carriage, they saw the hard, pale faces of the people all staring at them. They had expected garlands in the village, a song in their honor, cheers and hurrahs, but the village was completely deserted as they drove through it, and in church the pale faces of the people were turned toward them, mute and hostile, and when the priest mounted the pulpit to deliver his New Year's sermon, he sensed the chill in those otherwise quiet and peaceful faces, and he stumbled painfully through his sermon and went back to the altar drenched in sweat. And as the Baleks von Bilgan left the church after Mass, they walked through a lane of mute, pale faces. But young Frau Balek von Bilgan stopped in front of the children's pews, sought out my grandfather's face, pale little Franz Brücher, and

Customizing Instruction

Less Proficient Students

1 Use these questions to check students' understanding of what the boy discovered.

- How did the boy test the scales?
  Answer: He put a pound of coffee on the scale, then used five pebbles to gauge how much the scales were off.
- Why is the boy so upset?
  Answer: The Baleks have been cheating his people for generations.

Set a Purpose Have students read to see what the villagers do when they learn about the fraud.

Students Acquiring English

2 Show students an example of a *coat of arms* and explain that each noble family displayed its own coat of arms on its possessions. Ask what implied comparison Böll is making between the Baleks and Bilgan.

Answer: They are both cruel oppressors.

Gifted and Talented

Have students find and research the meanings behind various symbols of justice, including that of Athena holding a balance scale. Ask students to work in groups to create an original symbol for either justice or injustice. Invite a volunteer from each group to explain their symbol to the class.

Mini Lesson: Viewing and Representing

***Une Battue en Campine (Beating the Bushes in Campine)* by Theodor Verstraete**

ART APPRECIATION Verstraete's painting clearly shows the influence of impressionism, an artistic movement that came to the fore in France in the 1870s, with the works of Manet, Monet, and Renoir. Impressionists concentrated on conveying the general impression produced by a scene or object rather than on a detailed, photographic representation. They were devoted to studying the effects of light using unmixed primary colors and short brushstrokes.

Instruction During the period when Verstraete painted (the time of the story), peasant children were often assigned the task of beating the bushes to drive game animals towards the waiting hunters, who were wealthy landowners or aristocrats enjoying a sport.

Application Ask students how the scene depicted here is related to the theme of the story.

Possible Response: In both the painting and the story, one of the tasks of the peasants is to work so that the wealthy can enjoy life. In the story, peasant children gather herbs and mushrooms for the tables of the wealthy; in the painting they work to ensure that the wealthy will have a successful hunt.

Reading and Analyzing

Reading Skills and Strategies: ANALYZING

A Point out that the Baleks force the priest to defend them. Ask students what they can infer about the priest's feelings about the Baleks' dishonesty, and the possible reasons why the priest does not defy the Baleks.

Possible Response: Because they have to force him, it seems likely that he is sympathetic to the poor villagers and that he does not approve of the fraud. However, he is perhaps unable to defy them because they are more powerful than he.

ACTIVE READING

B PREDICT **Possible Response:** The Baleks wanted to prevent possible future abuses.

Reading Skills and Strategies: QUESTIONING

C Ask students to respond to the thought that "everywhere the finger of justice (swings) falsely" and to explain their responses.

Literary Analysis: THEME

Ask students to identify the theme of the story in their own words, and to support their answers with evidence from the text.

Possible Responses: Some students may focus on the hopelessness of fighting injustice, and say that the rich will always exploit the poor and get away with it; others may focus on the valiant fight Franz and his family put up, and say it is important to fight for your rights.

asked him, right there in the church: "Why didn't you take the coffee for your mother?" And my grandfather stood up and said: "Because you owe me as much money as five kilos of coffee would cost." And he pulled the five pebbles from his pocket, held them out to the young woman and said: "This much, fifty-five grams, is short in every pound of your justice"; and before the woman could say anything the men and women in the church lifted up their voices and sang: "The justice of this earth, O Lord, hath put Thee to death. . . ."

While the Baleks were at church, Wilhelm Vohla, the poacher, had broken into the little room, stolen the scales and the big fat leather-bound book in which had been entered every kilo of mushrooms, every kilo of hayflowers, everything bought by the Baleks in the village, and all afternoon of that New Year's Day the men of the village sat in my great-grandparents' front room and calculated, calculated one tenth of everything that had been bought—but when they had calculated many thousands of talers[20] and had still not come to an end, the reeve's gendarmes[21] arrived, made their way into my great-grandfather's front room, shooting and stabbing as they came, and removed the scales and the book by force. My grandfather's little sister Ludmilla lost her life, a few men were wounded, and one of the gendarmes was stabbed to death by Wilhelm Vohla the poacher.

Our village was not the only one to rebel: Blaugau and Bernau did too, and for almost a week no work was done in the flax sheds. But a **A** great many gendarmes appeared, and the men and women were threatened with prison, and the Baleks forced the priest to display the scales publicly in the school and demonstrate that the finger of justice swung to and fro accurately. And the men and women went back to the flax sheds—but no one went to the school to watch the priest: he stood there all alone, helpless and forlorn with his weights, scales, and packages of coffee.

And the children went back to gathering mushrooms, to gathering thyme, flowers and foxglove, but every Sunday, as soon as the Baleks entered the church, the hymn was struck up: "The justice of this earth, O Lord, hath put Thee to death," until the reeve ordered it proclaimed in every village that the singing of this hymn was forbidden.

ACTIVE READING

B **EVALUATE** Why do you think the Baleks were able to return to business as usual?

My grandfather's parents had to leave the village and the new grave of their little daughter; they became basket weavers but did not stay long anywhere because it pained them to see how everywhere the finger of justice swung falsely. **C** They walked along behind their cart, which crept slowly over the country roads, taking their thin goat with them, and passers-by could sometimes hear a voice from the cart singing: "The justice of this earth, O Lord, hath put Thee to death." And those who wanted to listen could hear the tale of the Baleks von Bilgan, whose justice lacked a tenth part. But there were few who listened. ❖

Translated by Leila Vennewitz

20. **talers** (tä'lərz): silver coins used in central Europe until around 1900.
21. **gendarmes** (zhän'därmz'): police officers.

WORDS TO KNOW

forlorn (fər-lôrn') *adj.* appearing sad or lonely because one has been left alone

Teaching Options

Assessment Standardized Test Practice

CHOOSING THE BEST SUMMARY For some standardized tests, students will be asked to choose the best summary of a work. To help students select the best summary, read aloud or write on the chalkboard the following question:

Which of the following statements best summarizes the reaction of the Baleks to the rebellion of the townspeople?

A. The Baleks force the priest to "prove" the accuracy of the scales, and the grandfather's family leaves the village in disgust.

B. The Baleks send the gendarmes to take back the scales and brutally crush the rebellion, then banish the grandfather's family without ever admitting that the scales were inaccurate.

C. After fighting with the villagers, the Baleks finally agree to repair the scales but they banish the grandfather's family.

D. The Baleks threaten the villagers with prison and ban the singing of the villagers' favorite hymn.

Lead students through the process of choosing the best summary. Consider each choice. Point out that while all of the statements contain some accurate information about the story, A and C also contain information that is false, and D is incomplete. The best answer should include the most accurate and complete information. For that reason, the best answer is B.

Connect to Literature

1. **What Do You Think?** What were your reactions to the final outcome of the villagers' protests?

Comprehension Check
- Who are the Baleks?
- What does the narrator's grandfather learn about the Baleks from their scale?
- What happens when the people rebel?

Think Critically

2. How would you describe the **narrator's** grandfather as a boy? Support your answer with details from the story.
3. Consider the thoughts about justice that you explored in Connect to Your Life on page 893. In your opinion, what is the worst injustice in this story? Explain your position.
4. How would you explain the **theme** about justice that is communicated in this story?

THINK ABOUT
- what the Balek scales **symbolize**
- why it took so long for the inaccuracy of the scales to be discovered
- why the narrator's grandfather and his family found that "the finger of justice swung falsely" everywhere they went
- the hymn sung by villagers when the Baleks enter church

5. ACTIVE READING ANALYZING RELEVANCE OF SETTING
Look at the **setting** analysis you completed in your READER'S NOTEBOOK. How does each element of the setting help you to understand the power of the Baleks? Could this same story take place in a different setting or in a different time period? Why or why not?

Extend Interpretations

6. **Critic's Corner** Editor Ralph Ley described Böll as "the humane and incorruptible conscience of his country." What does this story reveal about Böll's conscience?
7. **Connect to Life** The Baleks seem to control nearly every aspect of life in the village, from the weighing of mushrooms to the activities of the police and clergy. Do you think wealthy people in the United States today exert a similar kind of power? Explain your reasoning.

Literary Analysis

TONE **Tone** is the attitude a writer or narrator takes toward a subject. The language and details a writer chooses help to create the tone, which might be playful, serious, bitter, angry, or detached, among other possibilities. To identify the tone of a work, you might find it helpful to read the work aloud, as if giving a dramatic reading. The emotions that you convey in reading should give you hints as to the tone of the work.

In "The Balek Scales," Böll tells a tale of great injustice, with an unhappy and even violent ending. The story's tone, however, is surprisingly calm and detached. Böll's use of descriptive detail and long sentences and paragraphs create a sense of remoteness and an unhurried pace. The contrast between this remote slowness and the power of the story's tragic events lends an ominous quality to the narrative.

Cooperative Learning Activity With a small group of classmates, read aloud the opening and closing paragraphs of "The Balek Scales." Think of words or phrases that describe the tone of these paragraphs. Then analyze the language of the paragraphs to determine exactly how the author has created this tone. Compare your descriptions and analyses with those of other groups.

GUIDING STUDENT RESPONSE

Connect to the Literature

1. **What Do You Think?**
Students may express their disappointment that true justice did not prevail; others may think that the villagers should have protested more forcefully.

Comprehension Check
- a powerful family that controls the local land and economy
- They are cheating the villagers and likely have done so for generations.
- Gendarmes put down the rebellion.

Use Selection Quiz in **Unit Five Resource Book,** p. 40.

Think Critically

2. Possible Responses: He was intelligent in finding a way to test the scales; he was brave in confronting the Baleks; he stood up for justice.
3. Possible Responses: The worst injustice may have been that the socio-economic system was controlled by a small group of powerful people who were not interested in equality nor in justice.
4. Disenfranchised people suffer from injustices inflicted on them by the very system they are forced to sustain. The cycle of injustice is difficult to break because the powerful few have no desire to share their powers.
5. Each element of the setting helps the reader understand that the Baleks' power penetrates every aspect of the villagers' life. The story of injustice can take place any time in any place for a variety of similar reasons. Students may wish to discuss incidents currently in the news.

Extend Interpretations

Critic's Corner Students will probably see that the narrator's grandfather is the conscience of this story, and that Böll probably identified with him. They may note that the grandfather is not a wild-eyed revolutionary intent on overthrowing a social order and obtaining justice on a grand scale, but merely a boy who wants his people to be treated fairly. They may surmise that Böll is mindful of the injustices that still exist today.

Connect to Life Some students may reason that wealthy people in the United States have more control over our society than the average worker. Others may argue that a free press, a democratic constitution, public investigations, and the legal system curb abuses of power.

Literary Analysis

Tone Before working cooperatively, students may benefit from a full class discussion in which they examine a particular passage, describe the tone, and then focus on the details that establish the tone.

Writing Options

1. **Sunday Sermon** Remind students that a sermon, in addition to making moral judgments about events that have already happened, prescribes guidelines for appropriate conduct in similar situations in the future. Also, students could be given the option of having their new priest be either a harsh critic or a defender of the prevailing social order.
2. **Aristocratic Editorial** Students could imagine and describe a bold and generous gesture that the Baleks might make, sincerely or insincerely, to win the villagers' approval, although the Baleks would no doubt deny that the scales were inaccurate.
3. **Autobiographical Tale** As students prepare to write, encourage them to consider the tone they wish to use in their writing.

Vocabulary in Action

1. antiquated
2. meager
3. flout
4. preside
5. forlorn

Choices & CHALLENGES

Writing Options

1. **Sunday Sermon** Imagine that a new priest is assigned to the village and learns about the events related to the scales. Write a sermon in which the priest offers his moral judgment of these events.

2. **Aristocratic Editorial** Write a guest editorial that the Balek family might have placed in the local paper in which they attempt to win back the favor of the villagers.

Writing Handbook
See page 1161: Persuasive Writing.

3. **Autobiographical Tale** Think of a tale from your own youth that you might one day tell your grandchildren. Write the story, describing the events as you recall them. Place the story in your **Working Portfolio.**

Vocabulary in Action

EXERCISE: MEANING CLUES On your paper, match each example below with the appropriate vocabulary word.

1. The machines used for drying the flax were so old that no one could remember when they had first been used.
2. Most of the people had very little to eat; even milk was considered a treat.
3. By refusing the coffee, the grandfather ridiculed the authority of the Baleks.
4. In the next generation, another Frau Balek would be in control of the room with the scales.
5. The grandfather and his family must have felt lonely as they moved from town to town.

Building Vocabulary
For an in-depth study of roots and base words, see page 183.

WORDS TO KNOW: antiquated, flout, forlorn, meager, preside

Heinrich Böll
1917–1985

Other Works
Eighteen Stories
The Stories of Heinrich Böll
What's to Become of the Boy?

Soldier and Critic Heinrich Böll grew up in Cologne (kə-lōn'), Germany, the descendant of English Catholics who centuries before had fled to the Continent to escape religious persecution. Raised in a tolerant household at a time when many Germans were practicing great intolerance, Böll watched in growing horror as the Nazis rose to power. During World War II, he was forced to join the German army; he was wounded four times and was captured and imprisoned by American forces. After the war, he began to publish novels and short stories. His early novels were harshly critical of warfare, which the Nazis had glorified. In *The Train Was on Time* (1949), he traced the despair of a sensitive young German soldier, not unlike himself. In *Adam, Where Art Thou?* (1951), he compared warfare to a contagious and deadly disease.

Champion for Justice With time, Böll broadened his themes, though he remained a social critic. The corruption of power, the victimization of the innocent by those in power, and the dehumanizing effects of modern life are often treated in his novels and short stories. Böll also championed the rights of oppressed fellow writers, providing lodgings for Russian author Aleksandr Solzhenitsyn (ăl'ĭk-săn'dər sōl'zhə-nēt'sĭn) when he was forced to leave his then-Communist homeland. Over the years, Böll produced nearly 40 books and was honored with a Nobel Prize in literature. "The Balek Scales," one of his most widely read stories, was first published in German in 1955.

PREPARING to *Read*

The Street / La Calle

Poetry by OCTAVIO PAZ
(ôk-tä′vē-ô päs)

I Am Not I / Yo No Soy Yo

Poetry by JUAN RAMÓN JIMÉNEZ
(wän rä-môn′ hē-mĕ′nĕs)

Connect to Your Life

Who Are You? If someone asked you to define your identity, how would you respond? Would you be one who looks inward, tapping the depths of the private self hidden from public view? Or would you look outward, defining yourself by your own unique place in the world? In writing, describe how you define your identity.

Build Background

Who Am I? The mysteries of identity are key concerns of the two poems that follow. Both poems are by eminent Spanish-language poets whose achievements were honored with the Nobel Prize in literature. The poetry of Octavio Paz often contains elements of **surrealism,** in which dreamlike images from the unconscious mind are captured in writing. Juan Ramón Jiménez, who preceded Paz by a generation, is responsible in many respects for introducing modernism to Spanish poetry. "The Street" and "I Am Not I" both explore the hidden territories of the self and its relation to the rest of the world.

Focus Your Reading

LITERARY ANALYSIS MODERN POETRY Modern poets have often used their art to explore their own identity. These poets have had more freedom than their predecessors. Compared to poetry prior to the 20th century, **modern poetry** has few, if any, restraints on subject matter, form, or use of poetic language. As you read, think about how the following poems vary from more traditional poetry.

ACTIVE READING STRATEGIES FOR READING MODERN POETRY **Modern poetry,** like other forms of modern art, can be difficult to understand. Readers encounter ambiguity, or unclear meaning, as well as **symbolism** that may be difficult to decipher. When reading such poetry, it is important to realize that you won't understand it all at once.

While the following strategies can be useful in getting the most out of any poem, they are especially helpful for modern poetry:

1. Read through the poem once to get a general idea of what it is about, using clues from the **title** to identify the topic.
2. Notice how **physical arrangement** and punctuation mark units of thought.
3. Consider the **literal meaning** of the situation described. What is going on, and who is involved?
4. Think about the associations that the words, **imagery,** and **figurative language** bring to mind. How do these associations influence understanding?
5. Identify the parts of the poem that puzzle you. Can you use the parts that are clear to you to help explain other parts that are less clear?
6. Consider different ways of interpreting the poem. Which interpretation explains the most?
7. Read the poem aloud, or read it so that you "hear" the poem in your head.

READER'S NOTEBOOK As you read the following poems, jot down observations or questions that come to mind.

OVERVIEW

Objectives

1. understand and appreciate **modern poetry (Literary Analysis)**
2. monitor and modify strategies for reading **modern poetry (Active Reading)**

Summary

Both Octavio Paz and Juan Ramón Jiménez write about the mysteries of identity. In "The Street," the speaker describes a haunting, dreamlike situation in which he encounters an unknown dimension of himself that at first pursues and then is pursued by his conscious-speaking self. In "I Am Not I," the speaker explores the mirrorlike duality of his nature.

Thematic Link

The poems contemplate the inner self and outer self in an effort to distinguish between **appearance** and **reality**.

5-Minute Warm-Up

Daily Language SkillBuilder

Have students **proofread** the display sentences on page 817j and write them correctly. The sentences also appear on Transparency 25 of **Grammar Transparencies and Copymasters.**

LESSON RESOURCES

UNIT FIVE RESOURCE BOOK, pp. 41–42

ASSESSMENT RESOURCES

Formal Assessment, pp. 149–150

Teacher's Guide to Assessment and Portfolio Use

Test Generator

SKILLS TRANSPARENCIES AND COPYMASTERS

Literary Analysis
- Poetry: Form, T7 (for Cooperative Learning Activity, p. 906)

Grammar
- Correlative Conjunctions II, C79 (for Mini Lesson, p. 907)

Writing
- Sensory Word List, T14 (for Writing Options, p. 907)
- Poem, C27 (for Writing Options, p. 907)

Communications
- Impromptu Speaking: Dialogue, Role-Play, Debate, T13 (for Activities & Explorations, p. 907)

INTEGRATED TECHNOLOGY

Audio Library

LaserLinks
- Art Gallery: Studies of the Self. See **Teacher's SourceBook,** p. 47.

Visit our website:
www.mcdougallittell.com

TEACHING THE LITERATURE

Reading and Analyzing

Active Reading: PREVIEW

Have students look over the two poems. Discuss the titles and the picture, focusing on how they seem to relate to each other. If necessary, discuss the Build Background and Connect to Your Life features on p. 903. Before reading the poems, students should review the strategies for reading modern poetry.

Literary Analysis MODERN POETRY

Modern poetry has few restraints on language, form, or subject matter. Students may discuss whether they think these poems would have been more effective if they had been written in a more formal style. Have students name any formal techniques (rhyme, meter, etc.) that they think would have improved the poems.

Use **Unit Five Resource Book,** p. 42 for additional support.

Active Reading

STRATEGIES FOR READING MODERN POETRY

As they read the following poems, have students jot down questions or observations that come to mind in their Reader's Notebooks. Point out that the following clues can be particularly helpful in understanding modern poetry:

- title
- physical arrangement
- literal meaning
- imagery/figurative language

Discuss how each clue aids in understanding the poems.

Use **Unit Five Resource Book,** p. 41 for additional support.

Octavio Paz

The Street

A long and silent street.
I walk in blackness and I stumble and fall
and rise, and I walk blind, my feet
stepping on silent stones and dry leaves.
Someone behind me also stepping on stones, leaves:
if I slow down, he slows;
if I run, he runs. I turn: nobody.
Everything dark and doorless.
Turning and turning among these corners
which lead forever to the street
where nobody waits for, nobody follows me,
where I pursue a man who stumbles
and rises and says when he sees me: nobody.

Translated by Muriel Rukeyser

La Calle

Es una calle larga y silenciosa.
Ando en tinieblas y tropiezo y caigo
y me levanto y piso con pies ciegos
las piedras mudas y las hojas secas
y alguien detrás de mí también las pisa:
si me detengo, se detiene;
si corro, corre. Vuelvo el rostro: nadie.
Todo está oscuro y sin salida,
y doy vueltas y vueltas en esquinas
que dan siempre a la calle
donde nadie me espera ni me sigue,
donde yo sigo a un hombre que tropieza
y se levanta y dice al verme: nadie.

Thinking Through the Literature

1. What **images** came to your mind while you were reading "The Street"?
2. Do you think the **speaker** is describing a real or imagined event?

   THINK ABOUT
   - details about the speaker's surroundings
   - why the speaker feels that someone is following him
   - what the speaker realizes when he turns and sees "nobody"
   - who or what the speaker might be pursuing
3. How do you think the speaker views his own life?

   THINK ABOUT
   - how the speaker feels about the events he describes
   - what the street might **symbolize**
   - why the speaker keeps repeating the word "nobody"

Thinking Through the Literature

1. The images should reflect the ominous and mysterious mood of the poem; they may be based upon the dark and silent street, the sound of another person following the speaker, the invisibility of the follower, or the speaker's pursuit of another.
2. Students may be perplexed by the ambiguity of the poem; the poem seems to be describing an actual event; more insightful readers will probably recognize that the events described are a product of the poet's imagination.
3. Possible Responses: The speaker may feel isolated and threatened; he may be searching for a larger meaning in his life; he may feel uncertain of his own identity.

Juan Ramón Jiménez

"I Am Not I"

I am not I.
I am this one
walking beside me whom I do not see,
whom at times I manage to visit,
and whom at other times I forget;
who remains calm and silent while I talk,
and forgives, gently, when I hate,
who walks where I am not,
who will remain standing when I die.

Translated by Robert Bly

Yo No Soy Yo

Yo no soy yo.
Soy este
que va a mi lado sin yo verlo;
que, a veces, voy a ver,
y que, a veces, olvido.
El que calla, sereno, cuando hablo,
el que perdona, dulce, cuando odio,
el que pasea por donde no estoy,
el que quedará en pie cuando yo muera.

La reproduction interdite (Portrait d'Edward James) [Not to be reproduced (Portrait of Edward James)] (1937), René Magritte. Oil on canvas, 81.3 cm × 65 cm, Museum Boymans–van Beuningen, Rotterdam, the Netherlands, Giraudon/Art Resource, New York. Copyright © 1996 Artists Rights Society (ARS), New York.

Customizing Instruction

Gifted and Talented

Invite students to bring in examples of poems that illustrate one or more of the four techniques explained in the Active Reading, p. 903.

Students Acquiring English

The level of abstraction in these two poems may prove daunting to students. Advise students that both poems describe literal situations that suggest deeper symbolic meanings, which may not be easily identified. Ask students to identify the source of conflict each speaker has.

Use **Spanish Study Guide** for additional support, pp. 185–187.

Less Proficient Readers

Set a Purpose Have students read to appreciate each poem's use of figurative language.

Assessment Standardized Test Practice

For some standardized tests, students will be asked to describe the conflict of a passage. To provide students with some help in choosing the best answer, read aloud or write on the chalkboard the following question:

In each poem, how does the narrator describe the conflict?

A. as occurring within himself
B. as occurring with a friend
C. as occurring with a stranger
D. as occurring with nature

Lead students through the process of choosing the best answer. Consider each choice. Point out that all statements contain inaccurate information, except the first statement. For that reason, **A** is the best choice.

GUIDING STUDENT RESPONSE

Connect to the Literature

1. **What Do You Think?**
Most students will admit to confusion while reading the poem; it is difficult to realize that the speaker is talking about two different versions of himself; students may have imagined other identities for either "I" addressed in the poem.

Think Critically

2. Possible Response: One self is the physical self that changes, has faults, and will die, while the other, the spiritual self, is virtuous and eternal.
3. Possible Response: The speaker suggests that the self "walking beside me" is the better self; the other self is an ordinary, flawed human being.
4. Students may express a number of questions, ranging from issues of symbolic meaning to reasons for writing in such an obscure and indirect manner. Students' understanding of the two poems will vary; accept all responses that indicate a basic understanding of the chosen poem.

Extend Interpretations

Comparing Texts Possible Response: They see themselves as people who have been able to perceive the duality of their nature.

Connect to Life Students will be able to respond to this question quite readily using examples of their peers' behavior.

Literary Analysis

Modern Poetry For each poem, have each group create a five-column chart with the poetic techniques as column heads. Using these techniques, students should explain how each affected their understanding of the poems.

Connect to the Literature

1. **What Do You Think?** What went through your mind as you were reading "I Am Not I"? Describe your reaction.

Think Critically

2. How would you describe the **speaker's** two different selves?

THINK ABOUT
- why the speaker visits his other self only some of the time
- the contrasts in lines 6–8
- your interpretation of the last line

3. How does the speaker seem to evaluate his two different selves?

4. ACTIVE READING | STRATEGIES FOR READING MODERN POETRY Look back at the observations you recorded for "The Street" and "I Am Not I" in your READER'S NOTEBOOK. What questions, if any, do you still have about the two poems? Of the two poems, do you feel that you understand one better than the other? Explain.

Extend Interpretations

5. **Comparing Texts** How do you think the speakers in "The Street" and "I Am Not I" see themselves in relation to the rest of the world?

6. **Connect to Life** Do you think that all people have an inner self that is different from the self they show the world? Explain your opinion.

Literary Analysis

MODERN POETRY Compared to poetry prior to the 20th century, **modern poetry** is free of many traditional forms and conventions of subject matter and language. While many people find this liberating, some find it frustrating or confusing. To understand modern poetry, you should know about the following poetic techniques:

Free Verse Most modern poems are written in free verse, which has no meter and no fixed stanzas or fixed line lengths. Instead, the poet decides where the lines should break, based on where a pause is required or on how the poem will look on the page. The line breaks, punctuation, and spacing help convey the mood and the meaning of each poem.

Literal and Symbolic Meanings Modern poets often rely on situations drawn from everyday life, which are often charged with symbolic meaning to convey a message about life or human nature.

Diction In contrast to the poetry of long ago, notable for its formal language, modern poetry often makes use of informal language drawn from everyday speech.

Imagery and Figurative Language Like all poets, modern poets use imagery and figurative language to convey underlying ideas and emotions.

Cooperative Learning Activity Reread "The Street" and "I Am Not I," identifying the techniques of modern poetry described above. With a group of classmates, discuss how these techniques affect your understanding of both poems.

Choices & CHALLENGES

Writing Options

Identity Poem Write a poem about who you are. You may draw upon the Connect to Your Life questions on page 903.

Activities & Explorations

Dramatic Interpretation With a classmate, prepare a dramatic scene of a situation in the life of the speaker of "I Am Not I." Decide on a situation to enact. Then, using clues from the poem, show how each "I" would react in that situation. ~ **SPEAKING AND LISTENING**

Octavio Paz
1914–1998

Other Works
Configurations
The Collected Poems of Octavio Paz, 1957–1987

A Precocious Youth Octavio Paz, a poet, essayist, and literary scholar, is one of modern Mexico's best-known literary figures. Paz grew up outside Mexico City. He loved books and often devised games based on *Robinson Crusoe* and other popular adventure tales he read. At 17, Paz founded the first of many literary journals that he would establish; at 19, he published his first book of poetry, *Forest Moon* (1933). Like many young writers of the 1930s, he journeyed to Spain to support the Loyalists in the Spanish Civil War.

Bard of Mexico Paz's political convictions and his fascination with the interaction of native Indian and conquering Spanish elements in Mexican history are strong themes in his writing. His highly acclaimed prose work *The Labyrinth of Solitude* (1950) is a major study of Mexican culture. Mexico's early history also inspired his 1957 epic poem *Sun Stone,* whose title refers to the famous calendar stone of the Aztecs.

Poet of the World From 1945 until 1968, Paz served in the Mexican diplomatic corps. While stationed in Japan and India, he developed an interest in Asian arts and philosophy, which is reflected in some of his poems. After 1968, Paz continued to write, and he taught and lectured in Europe and the United States. His receipt of the 1990 Nobel Prize in literature was considered by many critics to be long overdue.

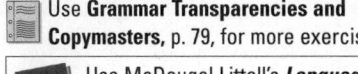

Juan Ramón Jiménez
1881–1958

Other Works
Three Hundred Poems: 1903–1953

A Literary Leader Juan Ramón Jiménez's short and intensely personal poems were an inspiration to a generation of Spanish writers in the 1920s and 1930s. Born in Spain, Jiménez briefly studied law at the University of Seville, but he eventually quit to devote himself to writing. He published his first two volumes of verse in 1900.

Spanish Classics From 1912 until 1916, Jiménez lived in Madrid, where he wrote *Platero and I* (1914), prose poems about walks with a donkey. The book became a beloved Spanish classic. Also during this time, Jiménez met American-born Zenobia Camprubí Aymar, who was visiting in Spain. Jiménez's voyage to the United States to marry Camprubí inspired one of his most successful collections, *Diary of a Newlywed Poet* (1917).

A Poet Abroad After the couple returned to Spain, Jiménez continued to devote himself to poetry. At the outbreak of the Spanish Civil War in 1936, he was sent to the United States as a representative of Spain. Eventually, Jiménez took a position at the University of Puerto Rico. The couple were in San Juan when they received word that Jiménez had won the 1956 Nobel Prize in literature.

VIDEODISC **LaserLinks: Background for Reading**
Art Gallery

Writing Options

Identity Poem Suggest that students review the poetic techniques explained in the Strategies for Reading Modern Poetry on p. 903 and in the Literary Analysis on p. 906 before they begin composing their poems.

Activities & Explorations

Dramatic Interpretation Suggest that students choose a situation that will reveal the two sides of the speaker's identity. You might suggest situations such as responding to an insult, overhearing gossip, or dealing with a difficult person. Make sure that students realize that they need to show two different responses to the same situation. Remind students that their dramatic scene will involve dialogue that they must imagine and create.

Mini Lesson Grammar

CORRELATIVE CONJUNCTIONS Correlative conjunctions function like coordinating conjunctions, but they are always used in pairs: *both . . . and; neither . . . nor; whether . . . or; either . . . or; not only . . . but (also).*

Write the following sentence on the chalkboard.

Both Paz and Jiménez are Spanish poets who won Nobel Prizes.

Ask students to analyze the relationship between the two linked elements.

Practice Ask students to add the appropriate correlative conjunctions in the following sentences.

1. We enjoy ———— Octavio Paz's poetry ———— his essays. *(both; and)*
2. ———— you write a poem ———— a short story, drawing on your life experiences is essential. *(Whether; or)*
3. Jimenez lived ———— in Spain ———— in Puerto Rico. *(not only; but also)*
4. We can ———— do our poetry project in class, ———— we can work on it at home. *(either; or)*

Use **Grammar Transparencies and Copymasters,** p. 79, for more exercises.

Use McDougal Littell's ***Language Network,*** Chapter 1, for more instruction in correlative conjunctions.

Objectives

- understand that jargon is specialized vocabulary
- examine the context of a word to deduce its meaning
- use specialized words in a sentence

VOCABULARY EXERCISE

1. premeditated: planned out ahead of time, not accidental
   My decision to ask the boss for a raise was entirely premeditated on my part.
2. benign: harmless, not malignant or threatening
   The dog barked loudly, but his personality was entirely benign.
3. perjury: lying under oath in a court of law
   The suspect was found guilty of perjury when evidence showed that he was lying.
4. congenital: inherited, since birth
   Since my father and my sister are both extremely smart, some people say my sister's genius is congenital.
5. acquitted: to be found by a court to be not guilty of a crime
   The truth of his innocence was shown when the jury acquitted him.

On-the-Job Language

If you've ever watched a courtroom drama on television or in the movies, you may be familiar with language like this:

> **The police court proceedings were brief and dramatic. The principal witnesses for the prosecution were Janet Mackenzie, maid to the dead woman, and Romaine Heilger, Austrian subject.**
> —Agatha Christie, "The Witness for the Prosecution"

Words like *court proceedings, witnesses,* and *prosecution* belong to a specialized vocabulary used by members of the legal profession. Every trade or profession—for example, medicine, journalism, banking, or cinematography—has its specialized vocabulary, or **jargon.** This vocabulary consists of words and phrases that have special meanings to those on the inside but may sound like a foreign language to outsiders. To a cartoonist, for example, terms such as *thought balloons, idea balloons,* and *maladicta balloons* are part of his or her lingo on the job—easily understood by other cartoonists, but puzzling to those outside the field.

Strategies for Building Vocabulary

When you come upon specialized terms in your reading, use these strategies to figure out their meanings.

❶ **Look at the Context** Sometimes you can find clues to the meaning of a term by examining its context, or surrounding words. For example, the passage below provides clues to the meaning of *prosecution* and *verdict.*

> **The prosecution endeavored to rally, but without great success . . . and the jury needed little time to consider their verdict.**
> **"We find the prisoner not guilty."**
> —Agatha Christie, "The Witness for the Prosecution"

You can infer that *prosecution* refers to those striving to convict the prisoner. The sentence "We find the prisoner not guilty" states the jury's final decision—its *verdict.*

❷ **Use a Glossary** A **glossary** is an alphabetical list of specialized terms that pertain to a particular subject. This list usually appears at the end of a book or an article. For example, at the back of this literature anthology, you will find a glossary that lists and defines such terms as *alliteration, protagonist, foil,* and *foreshadowing*—terms important to the study of literature. If you cannot find a specialized term in a dictionary, try looking it up in the glossary to a particular book about the subject.

EXERCISE Use the context to deduce the meaning of each underlined word. Then write another sentence using each word.

1. The lawyer tried to convince the jury that the victim's death was not accidental, but premeditated.
2. Dr. Morris was relieved to find that the patient's tumor was benign.
3. A witness who lies under oath commits perjury.
4. Because the child had the illness since birth as did some of his older relatives, the pathologist concluded that it was congenital.
5. The defendant felt relief when the jury acquitted him, setting him free.

ON YOUR OWN

In this short autobiographical selection, David Mamet tells a story involving his father and family expectations. His father was a lawyer who gave his son encouragement and support in pursuing his education as an actor and a playwright.

THE WATCH

David Mamet

The Chicago in which I wanted to participate was a workers' town. It was, and, in my memory, is, the various districts and the jobs that I did there: factories out in Cicero or down in Blue Island—the Inland Steel plant in East Chicago; Yellow Cab Unit Thirteen on Halsted.

I grew up on Dreiser and Frank Norris and Sherwood Anderson,[1] and I felt, following what I took to be their lead, that the bourgeoisie[2] was not the fit subject of literature.

1. **Dreiser . . . Anderson:** Theodore Dreiser, American novelist whose work exposed the seamier side of American life; Frank Norris, American author whose work attacked the greed and violence in American commerce; Sherwood Anderson, American author whose work described the frustrations of life in small Midwestern towns.
2. **bourgeoisie** (bo͞or′zhwä-zē′): the middle class.

ON YOUR OWN

Possible Objectives

You can use this selection to achieve one or more of the following objectives:

- enjoy silent sustained reading (Option One)
- read and analyze literature with a group (Option Two)
- use the Reader's Notebook to formulate questions about literature (Option Three)
- write in response to literature (Option Three)

Summary

David Mamet tells about growing up in Chicago in a middle-class family that promised him throughout his childhood that he would receive a new convertible car as a college graduation gift. During his final year in college, Mamet receives a call from his father urging him to come home for the holidays because he wishes to present him with a gift. Mamet returns home, believing that the gift must indeed be the mythical automobile. He recounts the night he flew home, telling how he arrives in Chicago, how he enters his parents' building, and how he notices a new convertible parked on the street. Immediately, he imagines it to be the long-promised gift and begins planning how he will feign surprise so as not to spoil the special moment for his father.

As he goes upstairs, he thinks deeply about his father's wishes and intentions. He is shocked when his father presents him with a railroadman's pocket watch and not the car. Even though the gift is deeply felt and meaningful to his father, Mamet is confused and disappointed. He continues to imagine that the watch is somehow a setup and that the convertible is still forthcoming.

A short time later, he pawns the watch in order to survive, and, years later, regains possession of it because the pawnbroker was a friend of his father and never sold it. Mamet subsequently buys a convertible for himself and, when he drives it, warmly remembers his deceased father.

THE WATCH 909

Reading the Selection

Option One
Silent Sustained Reading

You might set aside time each week for independent reading. During this time, you and your students would read for enjoyment. "The Watch" can be read independently in about 30 to 45 minutes. If you want to encourage students to read for pleasure, you might forego assignments related to the selection. Should you want to make assignments, Options Two and Three offer suggestions.

Option Two
Shared Reading Groups

You may assign students to groups or allow them to choose their own. Students can read the selection together, alternately reading sections aloud, or they can read independently and meet to cooperate in a project that portrays some element of the story.

Possible Projects

- Students can use the narrator's descriptions in the text to create a portrait of his father.
- Students can write the dialogue of the scene in which Mamet is presented with the watch. Have students focus on conveying both the father's pride and the son's surprise and suspicion.
- Have students draw a sketch of the convertible that Mamet eventually buys himself. In addition, have them design a personalized license plate for the car that honors the depth of Mamet's feeling for his father.

So the various jobs paid my rent, and showed me something of life, and they were irrefutable evidence of my escape from the literarily unworthy middle class. For not only was I a son of the middle class, I was, and perhaps I still am, the *ne plus ultra*[3] of that breed: a Nice Jewish Boy. And, as that Nice Jewish Boy, I went to college.

I went to college in the East, at a countercultural[4] institution, a year-round camp, really, where I and those of my class griped about the war and took ourselves quite seriously.

The college was in the very lovely midst of nowhere in New England. It was ten miles from the nearest town; those who did not possess either an auto or a good friend with an auto were under a *de facto*[5] house arrest on the college grounds.

I did not have an auto. My father was the child of immigrants, born right off the boat. He had sent his first-born son, in effect, to finishing school, and it never would have occurred to him to compound this enormity by supplying that son with the sybaritic[6] indulgence of a car.

Neither would it have occurred to me to expect the same. However, I had been told, from what seems to me to've been my earliest youth, that, on my graduation from college, I'd be given a convertible.

It was not any car that I'd receive, it was *the convertible*. How this notion got started, I don't know. But my grandmother said it, and my father said it, and I looked forward to it as a fixed point in my life.

Was it a bribe, was it to be a reward? I don't know. It was an out-of-character assurance on my father's part; for he was capable of generosity, and, indeed, on occasion, of real lavishness, but both, in my memory, were much more likely to stem from impulse than from a thought-out plan. However, he had promised it, and not only had the family heard it, but we joked about it and it became, it seemed, part of our family phrase book; e.g., "Study hard, or you won't get into college, and then you know what you aren't going to get."

So much that I forgot about it. It was nothing to long for, or even, truly, to anticipate. The one event would bring about the other, as retirement, the agreed-upon pension—not a subject for anticipation, or, even, on receipt, for gratitude, but the correct conclusion of an agreement.

It was my final year at college. Graduation was to come in May, and in the preceding November I would turn twenty-one. In three and a half years at college I had learned not a . . . thing. I had no skills, nor demonstrable talents. Upon graduation I would be out in the world with no money, nor prospects, nor plan. Not only did I not care, I had given it no thought at all; and I believe I assumed that some happy force would intervene and allow me to spend the rest of my life in school.

Just before the Thanksgiving break my father called. He told me he was looking forward to my return to Chicago for the holiday. Now, this was news to me, as we had not discussed my coming to Chicago, and I'd made plans to spend the long weekend with friends in the East. But, no, he said, the holiday fell two days from my birthday, and it was important for him that I be back home.

I tried to beg off, and he persevered. He pressed me to come home, and told me that it

3. ***ne plus ultra*** (nā′ plo͝os o͝ol′trä) *Latin:* the ultimate.
4. **countercultural:** having to do with the alternative culture that developed in the 1960s, a culture that drew on the bohemian values of 19th-century artists' communities: pacifism, socialism, and freedom of expression.
5. ***de facto*** (dā făk′tō) *Latin:* a legal term referring to what is actually the case rather than what is occurring in a legal sense.
6. **sybaritic** (sĭb′ə-rĭt′ĭk): pleasure loving.

was essential, as he *had* something for me. He was sending me a ticket, and I had to come.

Well. There I was. It was *the convertible,* and my father had remembered his promise, and was calling to tell me that he was about to make good on his pledge.

I left the phone booth smiling, and quite touched. I told my friends I would be flying to Chicago, but I would be driving back. I flew to O'Hare[7] and took a bus downtown, and took a city bus to the North Side.

On the plane and on the buses I rehearsed both my gratitude and my surprise. Surprise, I knew, was difficult to counterfeit, and this troubled me. I would hate to disappoint my father, or to give him less than what he might consider his just due for the award of a magnificent gift.

IT WAS NOT ANY CAR THAT I'D RECEIVE, IT WAS THE CONVERTIBLE.

But no, I thought, no. The moment boded well to sweep us up in sentiment free of hypocrisy on either of our parts. For was he not the child of immigrants? And was he not raised in poverty, in the Depression, by his mother, my beloved grandmother, and had we not heard countless times, my sister and I, of their poverty, and our ingratitude? And here before us was a ceremony of abundance . . . a ceremony, finally, of manhood. It was my twenty-first birthday; I was graduating from college.

I got off the Broadway bus, and walked down the side street, rehearsing all the while, and there, across from his building, was the car.

No. I had doubted. I realized that as I saw the car. No, I would admit it. To my shame. I'd doubted him. How could I have doubted? What other reason would he have had for his insistence, his almost pleading that I come back home? Of course it was the car; and I was ashamed I had doubted him. I looked at the car from across the street.

It was a Volkswagen convertible. It was a tricked-out model called the Super Beetle. It had outsized bubble skirts and wheels, and it was painted with broad racing stripes. I seem to remember a metallic black, with stripes of yellow and orange. I chuckled. I'm not sure what sort of a vehicle I'd expected—perhaps I'd thought he'd take me shopping, down on Western Avenue, and we'd be buyers together, at the horse fair.[8] I don't know what I expected from him, but when I saw that Beetle, I was moved. It was, I thought, a choice both touching and naïve.[9] It seemed that he had tried to put himself in the place of his son. It was as if he'd thought, What sort of car would the youth of today desire? And there was his answer, across the street.

I thought, No, that's not my style, and then reproached myself. And I was worthy of reproach. For the gift was magnificent, and,

---

7. **O'Hare:** Chicago's largest airport.
8. **the horse fair:** refers to the era when horses were a major form of transportation and were periodically sold at large fairs, held solely for that purpose.
9. **naïve** (nä-ēv′): innocent; unaware.

Option Three
Reader's Notebook

Provide the following direction to students before they read.

Read the first section of the story, pausing at the break in column two on page 910. Draw students' attention to the broad background for what is to follow. Summarize the nature of Mamet's expectation and the conditions that his family established for his receiving a new convertible. Ask students to declare whether they think the car is a bribe or a reward.

After they finish reading the story, tell students to analyze their initial judgment about the car as a bribe or a reward and to develop their ideas further. Have them write in their Reader's Notebook any additional comments or ideas that support their analysis.

Then, ask students to evaluate whether they think it was fair that Mamet did not receive the gift he'd been promised. Instruct them to write reasons supporting their conclusion and to develop each of their reasons with evidence and explanation. Have students debate their position in a class discussion.

THE WATCH **911**

After Reading

Possible Activities

Independent Activities

- Have students jot details from the story in their Reader's Notebook to use for writing an explanation of Mamet's understanding of his father. What details indicate the depth of his respect for his father?
- Have students review the Learning the Language of Literature and Active Reader on pages 868–870. They can note which skills and strategies they used while reading the selection.

Discussion Activities

- Discuss the question of fairness and whether students feel it was fair for the narrator's parents not to give him the convertible they had promised him. Does the outcome seem to have had any influence on the relationship between parents and child?
- Discuss whether students feel—as Mamet did—that all along the convertible was inevitable. Discuss at what point, if any, they began to doubt that the narrator would receive the gift.

Assessment Opportunities

- You can assess student comprehension of the story by asking students to explain Mamet's understanding of the agreement his parents made with him and whether they think his feelings were justified at the end.
- You can use any of the discussion questions as essay questions.
- You can have students develop any one of their Reader's Notebook entries into an essay.

with the gift, his effort to understand me—*that* was the gift, the magnificent gift. Rather than insist that I be like him, he'd tried to make himself like me. And if my chums thought that the car was somewhat obvious, well, . . . I was not some kid in the schoolyard who could be embarrassed by his parents; I was a man, and the owner of a valuable possession. The car could take me to work, it could take me from one city to the next, and finally, my father'd given it to me.

As I walked close to it I saw the error of my momentary reluctance to appreciate its decoration. It was truly beautiful. That such a car would not have been my first choice spoke to the defects not of the car, but of my taste.

I remember the new car sticker on the window, and I remember thinking that my dad must have expected me to come into the building by the other door, or he wouldn't have left the gift out here so prominently. Or did he mean me to see it? That was my question, as I rode the elevator up.

He met me at the door. There was the table, laid out for a party in the living room beyond. Did he look wary? No. I wondered whether to say which route I had taken home, but, no, if he'd wanted to test me, he would ask. No. It was clear that I wasn't supposed to've seen the car.

But why would he have chanced my spotting it? Well, I thought, it's obvious. They'd delivered the car from the showroom, and he'd, carefully, as he did all things, instructed them on where it should be parked, and the car salesman had failed him. I saw that this could present a problem: if we came out of the building on the side opposite from where the car was parked—if we began what he would, doubtless, refer to as a simple walk, and could not *find* the car (which, after all, would not be parked where he'd directed it should be), would it be my place to reveal I'd *seen* it?

No. For he'd be angry then, at the car salesman. It would be wiser to be ignorant, and not be part of that confluence[10] which spoiled his surprise. I could steer our progress back into the building by the other door. Aha. Yes. That is what I'd do.

There was another possibility: that we would leave the building by the door *near* the car, and that he'd come across it in the unexpected place, and be off-guard. But that need not be feared, as, if I stayed oblivious to his confusion for the scantest second, he would realize that my surprise would in no way be mitigated by the car's location. He would improvise, and say, "Look here!" That he'd surely have words with the car dealership later was not my responsibility.

We sat down to dinner. My father, my stepmother, my half-siblings, and several aunts. After the meal my father made a speech about my becoming a man. He told the table how he'd, in effect, demanded my return as he had something to give me. Then he reached in the lapel pocket of his jacket, draped over the back of his chair, and brought out a small case. Yes, I thought, this is as it should be. There's the key.

Some further words were said. I took the case, and fought down an impulse to confess that I knew what it contained, et cetera, thus finessing[11] the question of whether or not to feign[12] surprise. I thanked him and opened the case, inside of which there was a pocket watch.

I looked at the watch, and at the case beneath the watch, where the key would be found. There was no key. I understood that this gift would be in two parts, that *this* was the element of the trip that was the surprise. I'd

10. **confluence:** stream of events.
11. **finessing:** cleverly dealing with.
12. **feign** (fān): pretend.

THE WATCH 913

underestimated my father. How could I have thought that he would let an opportunity for patriarchal[13] drama drift by unexploited.

No mention had been made of the car. It was possible, though unlikely, that he thought I'd forgotten that the car was owing to me; but in *any* case, and even if, as was most likely, I had returned to Chicago expecting the car, such hopes would indeed be dashed before they would be realized. He would make me the present of the watch, and, then, the party would go on, and at some point, he'd say, "Oh, by the way . . ." and draw my attention to the key, secreted in the lining of the watch case, or he'd suggest we go for a walk.

Once again, he would keep control. Well, that was as it should be, I thought. And a brand-new car—*any* car—was not the sort of present that should be given or accepted lightly, and if he chose to present the gift in his own way, it came not primarily from desire for control, but from a sense on his part of drama, which is to say, of what was fitting. I thought that that was fine.

That I had, accidentally, discovered the real present parked outside was to my advantage. It allowed me to feign, no, not to feign, to *feel* true gratitude for the watch he had given me. For, in truth, it was magnificent.

It was an Illinois pocket watch. In a gold Hunter case. The case was covered with scrollwork, and, in a small crest, it had my initials. The back of the case had a small diamond set in it. There was a quite heavy gold chain. In all, it was a superb and an obviously quite expensive present.

I thanked him for it. He explained that it was a railroad watch, that is, a watch made to the stringent standards called for by the railroads in the last century. The railroads, in the days before the radio, relied exclusively upon the accuracy of the railroaders' watches to ensure safety. Yes. I understood. I admired the watch at length, and tried it in various of my pockets, and said that, had I known, I would have worn a vest.

As the party wound down, I excused myself from the table, and took the watch and the case into a back room, where I pried up the lining of the case to find the key.

But there was no key, and there was, of course, no car; and, to one not emotionally involved, the presence of a convertible with a new-car sticker on the street is not worthy of note.

I pawned the watch many times; and once I sold it outright to the pawnbroker under the El[14] on Van Buren Street.

He was a man who knew my father, and, several years after I'd sold it, I ran into him and he asked if I'd like my watch back. I asked why such a fine watch had lain unsold in his store, and he said that he'd never put it out, he'd kept it for me, as he thought someday I'd like it back. So I redeemed it for what I had sold it for.

13. **patriarchal** (pä′trē-är′kəl): relating to a father or father figure.

14. **El:** elevated train, a form of public transportation that travels above street level.

I wore it now and then, over the years, with a tuxedo; but, most of the time, it stayed in a box in my desk. I had it appraised at one point, and found it was, as it looked, valuable. Over the years I thought of selling it, but never did.

I had another fantasy. I thought, or *felt,* perhaps, that the watch was in fact a token in code from my father, and that the token would be redeemed after his death.

I thought that, *after his death,* at the reading of his will, it would be shown that he'd never forgotten the convertible, and that the watch was merely a test; that if I would *present* the watch to his executors[15]—my continued possession of it a sign that I had never broken faith with him—I would receive a fitting legacy.[16]

My father died a year ago, may he rest in peace.

Like him I have turned, I'm afraid, into something of a patriarch, and something of a burgher.[17] Like him I am, I think, overfond of the few difficulties I enjoyed on my travels toward substantiality. Like him I will, doubtless, subject my children, in some degree, to my personality, and my affection for my youth.

I still have the watch, which I still don't like; and, several years ago I bought myself a convertible, which, I think, I never drive without enjoyment. ❖

15. **executors** (ĭg-zĕk′yə-tərz): people appointed to carry out the instructions of a will.

16. **legacy:** money or property bequeathed to someone by will.

17. **burgher** (bûr′gər): a solid, middle-class citizen.

David Mamet

1947–

Other Works
American Buffalo
Glengarry Glen Ross
Speed-the-Plow
The Untouchables

Language Playwright David Mamet has been called a "language playwright" because of his skillful use of realistic dialogue and his ear for the sound and rhythm of language. He began early to develop these skills. He went to high school in Chicago, where he worked as a busboy at a comedy club and backstage at another theater. While on the job he absorbed the rhythms of stage dialogue and action. After high school, Mamet studied literature and drama at Goddard College in Vermont and took acting classes in New York. He briefly tried acting but then turned to writing and directing as a career.

Mamet on Stage Mamet's success was not immediate. While continuing to write, he earned a living as teacher, factory worker, taxi driver, and short-order cook. In the early 1970s, he made his breakthrough with two short plays. Since then, he has become one of America's most successful playwrights. He has received New York Drama Critics Circle Awards for *American Buffalo* and *Glengarry Glen Ross.* He was nominated for an Academy Award for the screenplay *The Verdict* and received a Pulitzer Prize for *Glengarry Glen Ross.*

Inquiry & Research

Find out more about the reasons for the popularity of the Volkswagen in the 1960s and 1970s. How did the company establish its image?

Real World Link
Begin your research by reading the television ad on page 916.

THE WATCH 915

Real WORLD Link

Advertisement

Objectives
- analyze an advertisement
- identify persuasive techniques used in an advertisement
- identify the messenger or main idea in an advertisement

Connecting to the Literature
In his short autobiographical selection "The Watch" (p. 909), David Mamet tells how he expected a convertible as a gift from his family upon graduation from college.

Reading for Information

A storyboard for a television advertisement presents visual images along with printed dialogue for each frame.

1 A funeral procession with limousines is an unusual image for a Volkswagen advertisement.

2 The droll humor indicates that the will contains unusual bequests. The juxtaposition of sadness and humor creates an irony that grabs the reader's attention. The value of money is important to the narrator.

Volkswagen Television Ad

Created by Doyle Dane Bernbach, Inc.

During the 1950s, the trend in American automobiles was toward big cars that consumed large amounts of gasoline. Designs would change every year to entice owners to trade in their old cars for the latest model. In the 1960s and 1970s, Volkswagen worked against that trend. Its advertisements boasted of a simple, reliable, and inexpensive car that changed only to improve performance, not to make earlier models look obsolete.

1

```
Open on funeral procession of limousines
each containing the benefactors of a will.

MVO [male voice-over]:
I, Maxwell E. Snavely, being of sound mind
and body do bequeath the following:
```

2

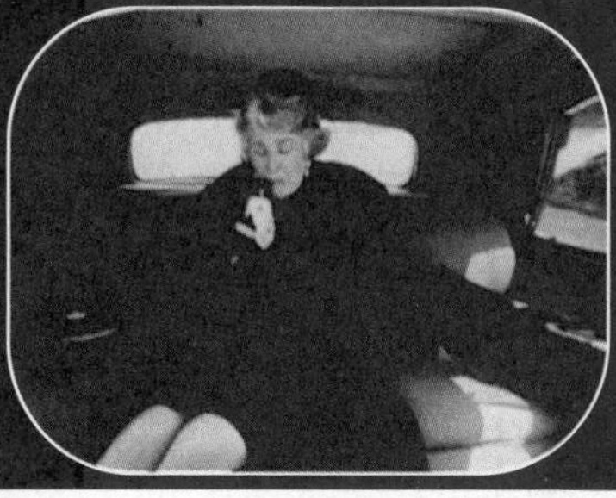

```
To my wife Rose, who spent money like there was
no tomorrow, I leave $100 and a calendar . . .

To my sons Rodney and Victor, who spent every
dime I ever gave them on fancy cars and fast
women . . . . I leave $50 in dimes . . .
```

Reading for Information

Have you ever taken the time to examine the advertisements you see on television? Many of them don't directly sell a product. Instead, they create an appealing image of the buyer, hoping the image will attract customers. Being able to analyze ads allows you to understand the persuasive techniques that manufacturers use to create a market for their products.

EVALUATING ADVERTISING

These pages show a **storyboard**—a visual outline that presents the basic images and scripted dialogue—for a television ad for Volkswagen automobiles. When you read or view an **advertisement,** be aware of the commercial's basic message as well as the impression the advertiser is trying to create.

YOUR TURN Use the questions and activities that follow to help you evaluate this advertisement.

❶ **Setting the Scene** Considering the kind of product being advertised, what strikes you as unusual about the opening image and narration of the commercial?

❷ In this frame, the ad begins to introduce humor. What effect does having a sad image paired with humorous narration have on the viewer? What do you think is important to the narrator?

3

To my business partner, Jules, whose motto was "spend, spend, spend" I leave nothing, nothing, nothing.

And to my other friends and relatives who also never learned the value of a dollar, I leave . . . a dollar

4

Finally, to my nephew, Harold, who oft time said: "A penny saved is a penny earned." And who also oft time said "Gee, Uncle Max, it sure pays to own a Volkswagen."

I leave my entire fortune of one hundred billion dollars.

3 Think about the narrator's attitude toward money as revealed in his will so far. What seems to be the narrator's values? What do you think the advertisers are trying to say about how consumers should choose to spend their money?

4 Notice that this last frame is your first view of the product that's for sale. Why do you think the advertisers chose to delay the presentation of the image? Overall, what do you find humorous or surprising about this ad? Why do you think the ad was effective?

Identifying Main Ideas In an ad, the images and narration combine to convey an important message or **main idea.** What image of a Volkswagen owner do you think the advertisers have conveyed? What message was this ad communicating about Volkswagens?

Inquiry & Research

Activity Link: "The Watch," p. 915

In "The Watch," David Mamet is moved by the appearance of the popular Volkswagen convertible. Do you think that Mamet and other young people of the time would have felt that this Volkswagen ad captured the appeal of the car?

3 The narrator values prudence and frugality. The advertisers are suggesting that consumers should spend their money wisely rather than frivolously.

4 The advertisement delays presentation of the product because the prudence it symbolizes must first be "set up" by excessive frivolity. Humor lies in the exaggerated caricatures. The ad is effective because it shows that people who spend their money wisely will benefit, and, according to the ad, spending money wisely means buying a Volkswagen.

Identifying Main Ideas

The advertisement implies that because Volkswagen owners manage their money wisely, they are wise and prefer a practical, inexpensive car. In the last frame, the advertisement suggests a literal interpretation of the slogan "It pays to own a Volkswagen."

Mini Lesson Inquiry & Research

The Inquiry & Research activity on this page links this advertisement to "The Watch" by David Mamet (p. 909).

Instruction Discuss trends that entice consumers to choose a more expensive item when a less costly choice is available. Have students name examples of popular economical alternatives to expensive consumer products. Then discuss young people as consumers and their motives for buying products. What factors determine their choice of products, especially cars?

Practice Participate in a discussion about the influence of advertisements on making economic decisions.

OVERVIEW

Objectives
- appreciate the craft of one of America's great writers of the 20th century
- interpret the possible influences of historical context on the writings of John Steinbeck
- gain information about Steinbeck by reading nonfiction

This Author Study offers a unique opportunity for students to focus on the work of a major writer. In addition, students can gather information about the life of Steinbeck, gaining insight into the real person behind his now famous literary works.

Preview
Have students preview the Life and Times essay, noting the basic text organizers: title, subheads, images and captions, and time line. Ask students to describe what information they would expect to locate in each section. As they read, have students use the subheads to make an outline or graphic organizer. Have them categorize information from the article with the appropriate heading. Remind them to use text organizers to locate and categorize information as they do independent research.

Hometown
(A) Salinas, California, a prosperous town of about 2,500 people at the time of Steinbeck's birth, consisted of a main street, a downtown of brick stores and saloons, and several residential neighborhoods. At the turn of the century, the Salinas Valley was a difficult area to farm (the land was not yet irrigated), and many farmers went bankrupt. When an earthquake devastated San Francisco in 1906, its aftershocks shook Salinas as well. The destruction caused by this earthquake formed Steinbeck's earliest memory.

Author Study

John Steinbeck

OVERVIEW

"A good writer always works at the impossible."

—John Steinbeck

Voice of the Common People

John Steinbeck was a Nobel Prize-winning writer whose work confronts the range of contrasts in 20th-century American life. In a land of plenty, he chronicled the lives of those displaced during the Great Depression. In a modern-day world that could boast glittering examples of human progress, he found and celebrated the raw, untamed power of nature.

1902–1968

"DAZZLED AND SWEPT UP" John Steinbeck, who believed that a writer's first duty was to "set down his time as nearly as he can understand it," managed perhaps better than anyone else to tell the stories of ordinary people caught up in the Great Depression of the 1930s. His masterpiece, *The Grapes of Wrath*, has been compared to *Uncle Tom's Cabin* for the way that it influenced and shed light on a critical time in the nation's history.

Steinbeck was born on February 27, 1902, in Salinas, (A) California, in one of the nation's most productive farming regions. He was a shy young man who enjoyed spending time alone by the seashore in Monterey where his parents had a

HIS LIFE
HIS TIMES

Family home in Salinas

1902 **Is born February 27 in Salinas, California**

1906 **Views damage of earthquake's aftershocks**

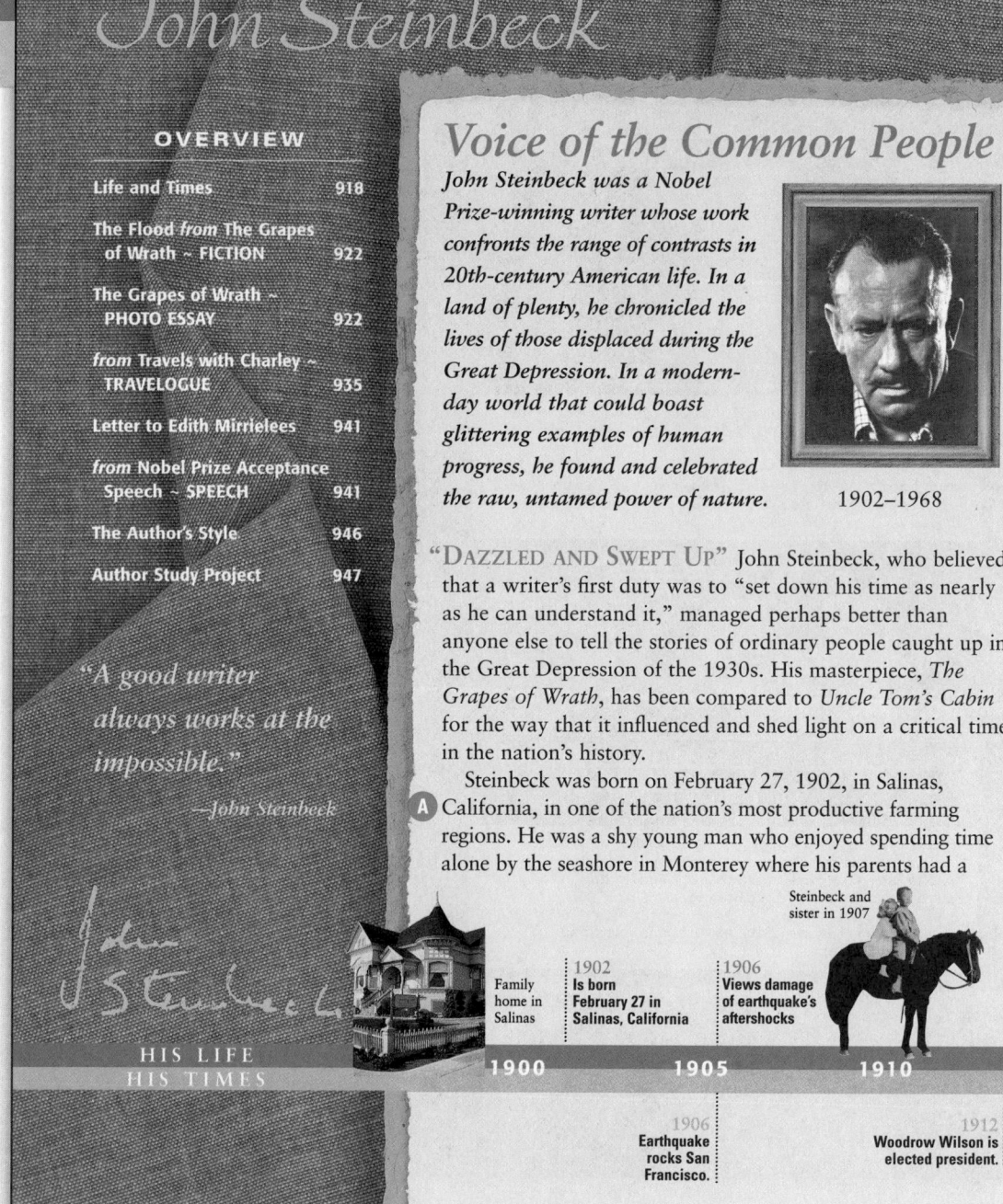

Steinbeck and sister in 1907

1900 — 1905 — 1910

1906 **Earthquake rocks San Francisco.**

1912 **Woodrow Wilson is elected president.**

918

cottage. For adventure, he turned to literature. In particular, he felt "dazzled and swept up" by the legends of King Arthur in Sir Thomas Malory's *Le Morte D'Arthur*.

"A Certain Literary Versatility" The summer after graduating from high school, Steinbeck took a job as a laborer dredging a canal, saving his wages to help pay for college. Unlike him, his fellow workers were for B the most part illiterate migrants from other areas of the United States and other countries. Young Steinbeck was often angered by the biased reports in newspapers that portrayed these migrants as untrustworthy, even dangerous. The teenager's sense of social injustice and appreciation of the decency of the common person would one day be the guiding forces behind his work.

Steinbeck majored in English at Stanford University. His biggest influence was short story teacher Edith Mirrielees, who taught him that "Writing can never be other than a lonely business." Steinbeck left college without a degree in 1925 and, in an effort to start a writing career, made his way to New York City. He was unable to make a living as a writer there but claimed that his brief experience in newspaper work gave him "a certain literary versatility." Steinbeck returned to California. The variety of odd jobs he held during these years—fruit picker, house painter, lab assistant—may explain why his future writings would show such sympathy toward working people.

LITERARY *Contributions*

In a career spanning four decades, John Steinbeck produced short stories, dramas, screenplays, and travel journals.

Novelist Steinbeck's novels include:
- ***Tortilla Flat*** (1935)
- ***In Dubious Battle*** (1936)
- ***Of Mice and Men*** (1937)
- ***The Red Pony*** (1937); (revised, 1945)
- ***The Grapes of Wrath*** (1939)
- ***Cannery Row*** (1945)
- ***The Pearl*** (1947)
- ***East of Eden*** (1952)
- ***The Winter of Our Discontent*** (1961)

Dramatist Steinbeck adapted several of his novels as plays, including
- ***Of Mice and Men,*** with George S. Kaufman (1937)
- ***The Moon Is Down*** (1942)
- ***Burning Bright*** (1950)

Screenwriter The following directors crafted films from Steinbeck's screenplays:
- ***Lifeboat,*** Alfred Hitchcock (1944)
- ***The Pearl,*** Emilio Fernandez (1948)
- ***The Red Pony,*** Lewis Milestone (1949)
- ***Viva Zapata!*** Elia Kazan (1952)

Travel Journalist Steinbeck produced works based on his travels. They are:
- ***Sea of Cortez: A Leisurely Journal of Travel and Research*** with Edward F. Ricketts (1941)
- ***The Log from the Sea of Cortez*** (1951)
- ***Travels with Charley: In Search of America*** (1962)
- ***America and Americans*** (1966)

1919 **Enters Stanford University**

1925 **Travels from Los Angeles to New York City; works as a reporter, laborer**

1929 **Publication of first novel, *Cup of Gold***

1920 **1925** **1930**

1917 **Congress passes 18th amendment, outlawing alcohol.**

1927 **Charles Lindbergh makes the first solo Atlantic flight.**

1929 **Great Depression begins.**

1933 **Franklin D. Roosevelt is inaugurated as president.**

1934 **Drought seizes the Midwest; thousands of homeless families leave the Great Plains.**

LIFE AND TIMES

Migrant Workers

B The struggle of Depression-era farm workers to earn better wages came to a halt, like the Depression itself, with the entry of the United States into World War II. Congressional recommendations that farm workers be covered by the National Labor Relations Act came after most migrant farm workers had entered the army or were working in the shipping or defense industries. To compensate for this lost labor, the U. S. government instituted the Bracero program, which brought hundreds of thousands of Mexican citizens to work in U. S. fields. The Bracero program lasted until 1964, long after the war's end. In 1965, César Chávez led migrant farm workers in California to form a union.

LIFE AND TIMES 919

Critical and Popular Reception

A Although critical reception of *The Grapes of Wrath* was largely favorable, popular reaction was more divided. Some readers simply didn't believe Steinbeck's descriptions of the conditions in which farm workers lived. In addition, he was venomously attacked by ranchers, bankers, and agricultural business interests. The book was banned in schools in New York, Illinois, and California. Steinbeck was denounced in Congress and was labeled a Communist. Finally, both Eleanor and Franklin Roosevelt began recommending the book in the press, and Eleanor verified its accuracy after visiting migrant labor camps in California in 1940.

World War II

B Three months after the bombing of Pearl Harbor, Steinbeck published his first contribution to the Allied propaganda effort, *The Moon Is Down.* This novel concerns the resistance of a small, democratic nation (much like Norway) against occupation by a totalitarian nation (similar to Nazi Germany). Critics questioned Steinbeck's patriotism because he depicted the Nazi-like invaders as human beings rather than as stereotypes. However, the novel had its intended effect among the resistance forces of Denmark, France, and particularly Norway. The novel was translated and smuggled into those countries, reportedly increasing morale among the population. Steinbeck received thousands of letters thanking him for the encouragement that the novel offered. After the end of the war, the Norwegian government awarded Steinbeck its Haakon VII Cross for writing *The Moon Is Down.*

Science

C Steinbeck met Ricketts in 1930, and he would become one of Steinbeck's best friends and form the basis for seven central characters in Steinbeck's novels and stories. In 1940, Steinbeck and Ricketts took a scientific voyage up the inward coast of Baja California to study the marine life of the Gulf of California. Steinbeck's observations would be published as *The Sea of Cortez* (and later, in a more intimate form, as The *Log from the "Sea of Cortez").* To a certain extent, this voyage gave Steinbeck an understanding of the behavior of marine animals that he carried over to his descriptions of human group behavior in his novels. *The Log from the "Sea of Cortez"* became a classic of nature writing.

Author Study: *John Steinbeck*

Exposing Harsh Realities Steinbeck pursued interests in both farm labor reform and marine biology but continued to write. He gained his first success in 1935 with *Tortilla Flat*. This novel is a warm, sentimental treatment of poor but carefree *paisanos*, the Mexican Americans of Monterey. In 1937, he published both a collection of interconnected stories called *The Red Pony* and the tragic novel about the bond between two homeless drifters, *Of Mice and Men*.

That same year President Franklin D. Roosevelt sadly related in a speech, "I see one third of a nation ill-housed, ill-clad, ill-nourished." These realities were brought to life in Steinbeck's 1939 novel, *The Grapes of* **A** *Wrath*. The novel depicts the struggles of an Oklahoma farm family that abandons their drought-plagued land and migrates to California in a desperate search for work. Scornfully labeled as "Okies," the Joad family is hounded by police, abused by the farm-labor system, haunted by starvation, and drawn into the violence of a strike. Steinbeck portrays how the human spirit shines through even the worst of situations. "We ain't gonna die out," Ma Joad declares. "People is goin' on—changin' a little, maybe, but goin' right on." In 1940, *The Grapes of Wrath* won both the National Book Award and the Pulitzer Prize.

The Last Row (about 1935), Art Landy. Watercolor on paper, 14″ × 21″. Courtesy of Jojie Santos. From the Inaugural Exhibition at the National Steinbeck Center *This Side of Eden*, 2000. Courtesy of Hauk Arts, Pacific Grove, California

In Pursuit of Lifelong Interests During World War II, Steinbeck worked as a war correspondent for the *New York Herald Tribune* and even wrote training manuals for the U.S. Army. He continued writing novels **B** but also produced works that reflected his lifelong interests. In 1941, he collaborated with Edward F. Ricketts, a distinguished marine biologist, to produce a book on sea **C** life titled *Sea of Cortez*. Another of Steinbeck's friends was Eugene Vinaver, a literary historian, who shared the writer's fascination with the legends of King Arthur and the Knights of the Round Table. He felt compelled to re-create

1935 **Publication of *Tortilla Flat***

1937 **Publication of *Of Mice and Men* as a play and a novel; publication of *The Red Pony***

1939 **Publication of *The Grapes of Wrath;* in 1940, receives the National Book Award and the Pulitzer Prize**

1941 **Publication of *The Log from the Sea of Cortez***

1944 **First child is born; in 1945, publication of *Cannery Row***

Steinbeck with sons, Thom and John IV

1952 **Publication of *East of Eden***

1935 — 1940 — 1945 — 1950

1935 **The Labor Relations Act allows labor to organize freely; in 1937, unions begin sit-down strikes.**

1938 **Fair Labor Standards Act fixes minimum wage.**

1939 **Start of World War II**

1941 **Japan attacks Pearl Harbor.**

1945 **U.S. drops atomic bomb on Japan.**

1947 **Congress passes anti-union Taft-Hartley Act.**

E *In 1940,* Of Mice and Men *and* The Grapes of Wrath *were made into motion pictures. Each is regarded today as a classic in its own right. In their day, the films were so popular that they helped to boost the sale of Steinbeck's books. Recent stage productions of* The Grapes of Wrath *have also been successful.*

Poster for the film *Of Mice and Men,* 1940

Poster for *The Grapes of Wrath* movie, 1940

***Of Mice and Men,* 1992**

Stage production of *The Grapes of Wrath,* 1988

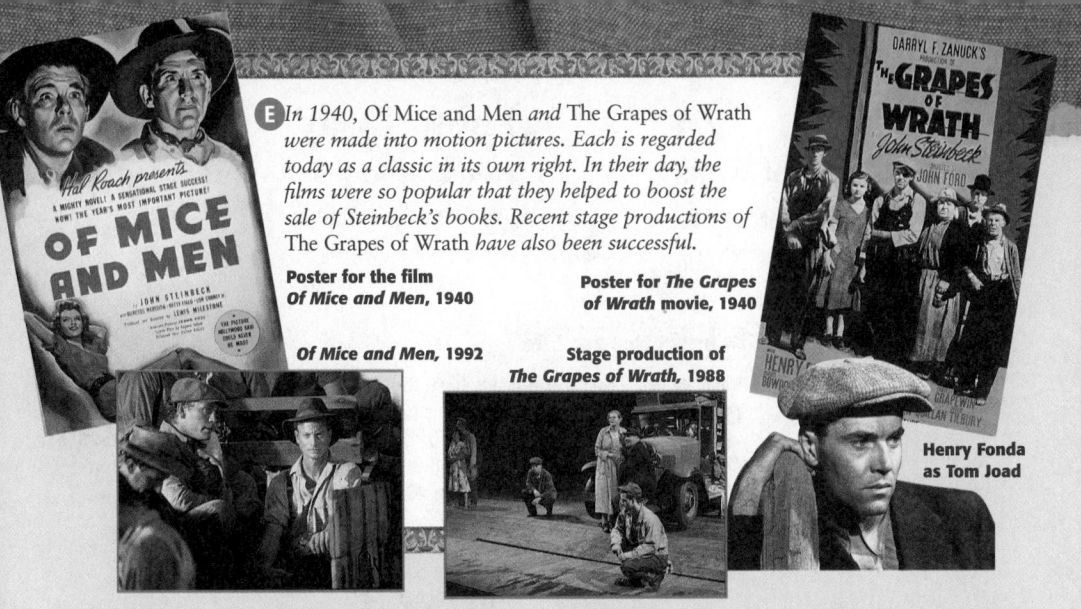

Henry Fonda as Tom Joad

the legends in a version that would delight his sons. In 1956, he began writing *The Acts of King Arthur and His Noble Knights.* (An excerpt focusing on Sir Lancelot and Queen Guinevere appears in Unit Six on page 1090). Steinbeck spent much time researching and writing the tales but never completed the project.

"A KEEN SOCIAL PERCEPTION" From the 1940s into the 1950s, Steinbeck wrote stage plays and screenplays, several of which were adaptations of his own novels. The best-known works of these years are probably the serious stories *Cannery Row* (1945), *The* **D** *Pearl* (1947), and *East of Eden* (1952).

Steinbeck has been variously called a mystic, a primitive, and a naturalist, but one characteristic was constant: he was always a good storyteller. His travels across the United States in 1960 with his pet poodle, Charley, resulted in the travel journal *Travels with Charley* (1962). This was also the year Steinbeck was awarded the Nobel Prize for Literature "for his realistic as well as his imaginative writings, distinguished by a sympathetic humor and a keen social perception." He continued to write until his death in 1968.

More Online: Author Link
www.mcdougallittell.com

VIDEODISC **More Online: Author Background**
Author Background

- 1955 **Meets writer William Faulkner**
- 1960 **Tours U.S. with poodle, Charley**
- 1962 **Is awarded the Nobel Prize for Literature**
- 1964 **Is awarded the United States Medal of Freedom**
- 1968 **Dies December 20 in New York**

1955 — 1960 — 1965

- 1954 **Supreme Court rules against racial segregation in public schools.**
- 1957 **Congress passes first federal civil rights legislation since 1860s.**
- 1962 **Rachel Carson's *Silent Spring* ignites concern about the environment.**
- 1965-1973 **Students protest the Vietnam War.**

Cannery Row

D Cannery Row, a street near the ocean in Monterey, California, housed the major sardine canning factories in the United States from 1900 until 1950. In 1902, the first cannery was built by the Monterey Fishing and Canning Company. Sardine canning reached its most profitable level during World War I and continued as a major industry in Monterey through World War II. In the 1940s, however, the sardine population in Monterey Bay dropped severely, probably because of overharvesting. As the sardine harvest diminished, the canning industry closed down. Today, Cannery Row is the site of the Monterey Bay Aquarium.

Cinema

E A number of Steinbeck's novels and stories were made into popular, sometimes classic, films with Steinbeck's support. The most prominent, *The Grapes of Wrath,* starred Henry Fonda and was directed by John Ford. The film's producers employed Tom Collins, the migrant camp director to whom Steinbeck had dedicated *The Grapes of Wrath,* as a technical adviser to ensure the film's accuracy. Perhaps Steinbeck's most important contribution to film was his screenplay for *Viva Zapata* in 1952. Thematically related to *The Grapes of Wrath,* the film was directed by Elia Kazan and starred Marlon Brando as a Mexican revolutionary who relinquishes political power to return to the people. Over the years, the film has become a cult classic, largely due to Steinbeck's screenplay.

LIFE AND TIMES 921

OVERVIEW

Objectives

1. understand and appreciate **fiction (Literary Analysis)**
2. understand literature as a tool for **social criticism (Literary Analysis)**
3. determine **author's purpose (Active Reading)**

Summary

"The Flood," an excerpt from John Steinbeck's novel *The Grapes of Wrath,* describes the effects of terrible flooding that takes place in California and causes further misery for the poverty-stricken migrant farm workers, refugees from the devastation of the Dust Bowl in Oklahoma. When the rains begin, the migrants can do nothing but huddle in their tents and wait for the rain to stop. Eventually the migrants begin to sicken and starve, faced with unemployment and indifference from local neighbors and authorities. The photo-essay "The Grapes of Wrath" captures the 1930s plight of the same people Steinbeck described in his novel. Steinbeck himself wrote the captions for these photos.

Thematic Link

John Steinbeck offers sharp social criticism and reveals his compassion as both a writer and a human being by immersing himself in the **simple truths** of the migrant families who sought salvation from their problems in California in the 1930s.

5-Minute Warm-Up

Daily Language SkillBuilder

Have students **proofread** the display sentences on page 817k and write them correctly. The sentences also appear on Transparency 26 of **Grammar Transparencies and Copymasters.**

Mini Lesson **Preteaching Vocabulary**

If you would like to preteach the WORDS TO KNOW for this selection, use the Mini Lesson, p. 924.

PREPARING to *Read*

The Flood
from The Grapes of Wrath
Fiction by JOHN STEINBECK

Photo Essay
Photographs by HORACE BRISTOL
Captions by JOHN STEINBECK

"In California the migrants found no promised land."

Connect to Your Life

Promised Land Many Americans have thought of their country as a kind of "promised land." Some see its promise in its good land, bountiful harvests and stable weather conditions. Some see its promise in terms of democratic processes. Still others are dazzled by the opportunities provided by a system of free enterprise. What is your idea of a "promised land"? Share your thoughts with classmates.

Build Background

Damaged Lands In the mid-1930s, a severe drought swept across the Great Plains, affecting the region stretching from Texas to Montana. Thousands of bankrupt farmers left behind ruined farms in what came to be called the Dust Bowl. The farmers migrated west, bound for work in California, a "promised land" of fertile crops. In 1938, the migrants at this destination experienced a cruel twist of fate—a disaster in the form of a flood that poured into California's Salinas Valley.

The two upcoming selections portray that flood in very different ways. John Steinbeck had been closely observing the trek of migrants into Salinas Valley. At the time of the 1938 flood, he helped with rescue efforts. "The Flood" is an excerpt from his 1939 novel *The Grapes of Wrath,* Steinbeck's best-known work. The excerpt is followed by a photo essay that first appeared in *Life* magazine in 1939, when *The Grapes of Wrath* was gaining national attention.

WORDS TO KNOW
Vocabulary Preview

frantic, migrant, penetrate, smolder, sodden

Focus Your Reading

LITERARY ANALYSIS SOCIAL CRITICISM **Social criticism** is a term used to describe literature that addresses real-life issues. The issues might be political, social, religious, or economic. A writer might make comments directly, through statements about an issue, or indirectly, through portrayals of imaginary characters' situations. Notice how Steinbeck portrays the social forces that opposed migrant workers during the flood in the Salinas Valley:

> ***The sheriffs swore in new deputies and ordered new rifles; and the comfortable people in the tight houses felt pity at first, and then distaste, and finally hatred for the migrant people.***

As you explore the selections, look for examples of social criticism.

ACTIVE READING AUTHOR'S PURPOSE **Author's purpose** refers to the reasons an author has for writing something. Usually, an author has one of these four basic purposes in mind:

- to entertain
- to persuade or influence
- to inform or explain
- to express emotions, thoughts, or ideas

As you read and examine the images in the selections, look for clues to the purposes of both the authors and the photographer. Keep in mind that a work may have more than one purpose.

READER'S NOTEBOOK Use a chart like the one below to record any clues you notice about the author's purpose.

	Author's Purpose(s)	Clues
"The Flood"		

LESSON RESOURCES

UNIT FIVE RESOURCE BOOK, pp. 46–47

ASSESSMENT RESOURCES

Formal Assessment, pp. 151–152

Teacher's Guide to Assessment and Portfolio Use

Test Generator

SKILLS TRANSPARENCIES AND COPYMASTERS

Reading and Critical Thinking
- Determining Author's Purpose and Audience, T19 (for Think Critically, item 3, p. 933)
- Organizational Chart: Horizontal, T51 (for Reader's Notebook, p. 922)

Grammar
- Adverb Clauses III, C114 (for Mini Lesson, p. 930)
- Semicolons I, C167 (for Mini Lesson, p. 928)

Vocabulary
- Context Clues, C84 (for Mini Lesson, p. 924)

Writing
- Effective Language, T13 (for Writing Options, p. 934)
- Achieving Conciseness, T21 (for Writing Options, p. 934)

Communications
- Dramatic Reading, T12 (for Activities & Explorations, p. 934)
- Verbal Strategies, T14 (for Activities & Explorations, p. 934)
- Nonverbal Strategies, T15 (for Activities & Explorations, p. 934)

INTEGRATED TECHNOLOGY

Audio Library

Net Activities

Visit our website: www.mcdougallittell.com

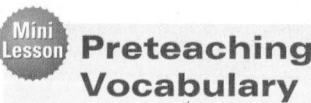

The Flood

from *The Grapes of Wrath,* by John Steinbeck

Over the high coast mountains and over the valleys the gray clouds marched in from the ocean. The wind blew fiercely and silently, high in the air, and it swished in the brush, and it roared in the forests. The clouds came in brokenly, in puffs, in folds, in gray crags; and they piled in together and settled low over the west. And then the wind stopped and left the clouds deep and solid. The rain began with gusty showers, pauses and downpours; and then gradually it settled to a single tempo, small drops and a steady beat, rain that was gray to see through, rain that cut midday light to evening. And at first the dry earth sucked the moisture down and blackened. For two days the earth drank the rain, until the earth was full. Then puddles formed, and in the low places little lakes formed in the fields. The muddy lakes rose higher, and the steady rain whipped the shining water. At last the mountains were full, and the hillsides spilled into the streams, built them to freshets,[1] and sent them roaring down the canyons into the valleys. The rain beat on steadily. And the streams and the little rivers edged up to the bank sides and worked at willows and tree roots, bent the willows deep in the current, cut out the roots of cottonwoods and brought down the trees. The muddy water whirled along the bank sides and crept up the banks until at last it spilled over, into the fields, into the orchards, into the cotton patches where the black stems stood. Level fields became lakes, broad and gray, and the rain whipped up the surfaces. Then the water poured over the highways, and cars moved slowly, cutting the water ahead, and leaving a boiling muddy wake behind. The earth whispered under the beat of the rain, and the streams thundered under the churning freshets.

When the first rain started, the migrant people huddled in their tents, saying, It'll

1. **freshets** (frĕsh′ĭts): streams swollen to overflowing with water from heavy rains or melting snow.

WORDS TO KNOW **migrant** (mī′grənt) *adj.* moving from one area to settle in another

TEACHING THE LITERATURE

Customizing Instruction

Less Proficient Readers

Setting a Purpose Have students keep these questions in mind as they read:

- What is the trouble described in this text?
  Answer: a flood
- Who suffers?
  Answer: migrant farm workers
- How do the people try to solve their problems?
  Possible Responses: They sit on boxes; they take shelter in barns; they beg and steal.

Students Acquiring English

Point out that the selection contains many footnoted words and expressions, in addition to the WORDS TO KNOW. Remind students to break up the reading into more manageable pieces to increase comprehension and to note the words at the bottom of the pages.

Use **Spanish Study Guide** for additional support, pp. 188–191.

BLOCK SCHEDULING: MANAGING TIME

If your schedule requires that you cover the lesson objectives in a shorter time, use . . .

- Preparing to Read, p. 922
- Thinking Through the Literature, p. 933
- Vocabulary in Action, p. 934
- Grammar in Context, p. 934

If you want to take advantage of longer class time, use . . .

- TE Teaching Options: Preteaching WORDS TO KNOW, p. 924; Viewing and Representing, p. 926; Standardized Test Practice, p. 934
- Choices & Challenges, p. 934

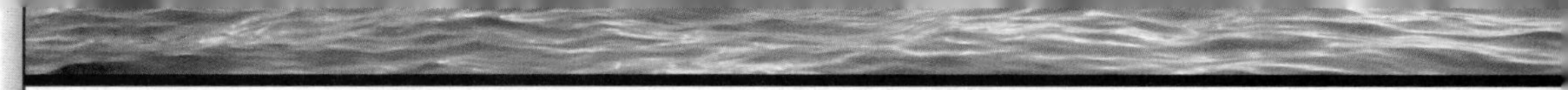

Reading and Analyzing

Reading Skills and Strategies: PREVIEW

Have students look through the photographs in the selection. If necessary, discuss the Build Background material on page 922. Ask students to interpret the possible influences of the historical context on these selections. Remind students that the first selection is fiction although it addresses real-life issues. The second selection is a nonfiction photo-essay.

Active Reading AUTHOR'S PURPOSE

Remind students that an author may have more than one purpose in writing. Ask them to keep in mind Steinbeck's main purpose and to look for evidence in the text that supports their answers. Have students jot down clues in their Reader's Notebooks.

Possible Responses: Some students may say that Steinbeck's main purpose is to arouse the reader's sympathy for the plight of the migrants. Others may say his main purpose is to criticize the government's and the other people's failure to help the migrants.

Use the **Unit Five Resource Book** p. 45 for more practice.

Literary Analysis SOCIAL CRITICISM

Point out that in addition to the government, Steinbeck also criticized the general population's attitude toward the migrants. As they read, have students note passages that seem to condemn people's attitudes.

Possible Response: Students may point to "the comfortable people" who hate the migrants or to the passage showing that horses were treated better than the migrants were.

Use the **Unit Five Resource Book** p. 46 for more practice.

soon be over, and asking, How long's it likely to go on?

And when the puddles formed, the men went out in the rain with shovels and built little dikes around the tents. The beating rain worked at the canvas until it penetrated and sent streams down. And then the little dikes washed out and the water came inside, and the streams wet the beds and the blankets. The people sat in wet clothes. They set up boxes and put planks on the boxes. Then, day and night, they sat on the planks.

Beside the tents the old cars stood, and water fouled the ignition wires and water fouled the carburetors. The little gray tents stood in lakes. And at last the people had to move. Then the cars wouldn't start because the wires were shorted; and if the engines would run, deep mud engulfed the wheels. And the people waded away, carrying their wet blankets in their arms. They splashed along, carrying the children, carrying the very old, in their arms. And if a barn stood on high ground, it was filled with people, shivering and hopeless.

Then some went to the relief offices, and they came sadly back to their own people.

1 They's rules—you got to be here a year before you can git relief. They say the gov'ment is gonna help. They don't know when.

And gradually the greatest terror of all came along.

They ain't gonna be no kinda work for three months.

In the barns, the people sat huddled together; and the terror came over them, and their faces were gray with terror. The children cried with hunger, and there was no food.

Then the sickness came, pneumonia, and measles that went to the eyes and to the mastoids.[2]

And the rain fell steadily, and the water flowed over the highways, for the culverts[3] could not carry the water.

Then from the tents, from the crowded barns, groups of sodden men went out, their clothes slopping rags, their shoes muddy pulp. They splashed out through the water, to the towns, to the country stores, to the relief offices, to beg for food, to cringe and beg for food, to beg for relief, to try to steal, to lie. And under the begging, and under the cringing, a hopeless anger began to smolder. And in the little towns pity for the sodden men changed to anger, and anger at the hungry people changed to fear of them. Then sheriffs swore in deputies in droves, and orders were rushed for rifles, for tear gas, for ammunition. Then the hungry men crowded the alleys behind the stores to beg for bread, to beg for rotting vegetables, to steal when they could.

Frantic men pounded on the doors of the doctors; and the doctors were busy. And sad men left word at country stores for the coroner[4] to send a car. The coroners were not too busy. The coroners' wagons backed up through the mud and took out the dead.

And the rain pattered relentlessly down, and the streams broke their banks and spread out over the country.

2. **mastoids:** parts of the skull that project behind the ears and contain air pockets that can become infected.
3. **culverts:** drains crossing beneath roads.
4. **coroner** (kôr′ə-nər): an official whose job is to investigate deaths in order to determine their causes.

WORDS TO KNOW

penetrate (pĕn′ĭ-trāt′) *v.* to enter, especially by forcing a way in
sodden (sŏd′n) *adj.* thoroughly wet; soaked
smolder (smōl′dər) *v.* to burn without flame; to exist in a concealed form, ready to break out
frantic (frăn′tĭk) *adj.* emotionally out of control

Teaching Options

Mini Lesson: Preteaching Vocabulary

CONTEXT CLUES Call students' attention to the list of WORDS TO KNOW. Remind them that context clues can sometimes help them understand the meaning of an unfamiliar word. Use the model sentence to demonstrate the strategy of using context clues that provide inferences to word meaning.

Model Sentence

Already ten minutes late for work, I continued my *frantic* search for my missing car keys.

Instruction

- Write the model sentence on the chalkboard.
- Ask a volunteer to paraphrase the meaning of the sentence.
- Have students use the meaning of the sentence to infer the meaning of the word *frantic.*
- Ask a volunteer to use the word *frantic* in a sentence.

Use the **Unit Five Resource Book** p. 47.

A lesson on context clues appears on p. 56 in the Pupil's Edition.

Huddled under sheds, lying in wet hay, the hunger and the fear bred anger. Then boys went out, not to beg, but to steal; and men went out weakly, to try to steal.

The sheriffs swore in new deputies and ordered new rifles; and the comfortable people in tight houses felt pity at first, and then distaste, and finally hatred for the migrant people.

In the wet hay of leaking barns

babies were born to women who panted with pneumonia. And old people curled up in corners and died that way, so that the coroners could not straighten them. At night the frantic men walked boldly to hen roosts and carried off the squawking chickens. If they were shot at, they did not run, but splashed sullenly away; and if they were hit, they sank tiredly in the mud.

The rain stopped. On the fields the water stood, reflecting the gray sky, and the land whispered with moving water. And the men came out of the barns, out of the sheds. They squatted on their hams and looked out over the flooded land. And they were silent. And sometimes they talked very quietly.

No work till spring. No work.

And if no work—no money, no food.

Fella had a team of horses, had to use 'em to plow an' cultivate an' mow, wouldn' think a turnin' 'em out to starve when they wasn't workin'.

Them's horses—we're men.

The women watched the men, watched to see whether the break had come at last. The women stood silently and watched. And where a number of men gathered together, the fear went from their faces, and anger took its place. And the women sighed with relief, for they knew it was all right—the break had not come; and the break would never come as long as fear could turn to wrath.

Tiny points of grass came through the earth, and in a few days the hills were pale green with the beginning year. ❖

Thinking Through the Literature

1. **Comprehension Check** As the flood worsens, what actions do the migrant workers take?
2. What comments about human nature might Steinbeck be making?

   THINK ABOUT
   - the actions of the "sodden men"
   - the actions of the sheriffs
   - how "people in tight houses" treat the migrants
3. What reactions to the migrant workers' situation do you think Steinbeck wanted to stir by portraying the effects of a real-life flood?

Customizing Instruction

Less Proficient Readers

Point out to students that Steinbeck does not always use quotation marks when writing speech, and help them determine which lines are speech.

Students Acquiring English

1 Help students understand the different meanings of the word *relief.* A "relief office" is a government office that helps poor people; when the women "sigh with relief," they stop worrying.

Thinking Through the Literature

1. At first, the migrants huddled in their tents; later they built dikes around their tents; then they "set up boxes and put planks on the boxes" where they sat. Finally, they had to move.
2. Students may notice various comments about human nature, from the persistence of those in desperate circumstances to the inherent conflicts between the "haves" and "have-nots." The sheriffs act in fear to control the migrants; the migrants move from fear to anger about their circumstances. People in "tight houses" turn against the migrants.
3. Possible Responses: Steinbeck wanted to make readers angry about the living conditions of the migrants; he hoped to change the way the government responded to the needs of the poor; he wanted people to realize the humanity of the migrant workers.

Reading and Analyzing

Reading Skills and Strategies: **EVALUATING**

Have students consider the impact of the photos and of the descriptions in "The Flood." Ask them which, in their view, more effectively conveys the misery and desperation of the migrants' lives.

Possible Responses: The photos are more immediate and real; the story gets us involved and makes us feel what the migrants are feeling.

Literary Analysis: **DIRECT COMMENTARY**

Discuss the direct commentary about the migrants' situation in the text. Ask students to contrast this with the indirect commentary Steinbeck presents in "The Flood" and to describe the different ways each might affect the reader.

Possible Responses: The indirect commentary in "The Flood" may seem more powerful because it affects the reader on an emotional level. Some readers, however, may be more swayed by the direct commentary in the photo-essay because it states clear, indisputable facts.

Reading Skills and Strategies: **CLARIFYING**

A Ask students how easy it will be for the woman to get ten dollars based on what they read in "The Flood."

Possible Response: It will be very difficult, because there are so few jobs and so many workers to fill them. Also, ten dollars in 1939 was worth a lot more than it is today.

Teaching Options

Mini Lesson Viewing and Representing

Photo-Essay **by Horace Bristol**

ART APPRECIATION Assign a group of students to investigate the source of these Depression-era photographs, particularly photographer Horace Bristol. Research should disclose that the photographs on pages 926–932 were taken by *Life* magazine photographer Horace Bristol. In the late 1930s, the U.S. Department of Agriculture commissioned him and other photographers to record the struggles of Depression-era farmers. Horace Bristol's brutally honest black-and-white photographs of migrant workers in California were taken in 1939, after the rest of the country was well on its way to economic recovery.

Instruction Point out that this photo project was intended to collect and record information about how these people lived. Thus, rather than being purely artistic images, these photographs also constitute a cultural record.

Application Ask students to analyze the photograph of the woman on p. 926. Have them create a list of physical details from which they can draw conclusions about the woman's social and economic circumstances.

Possible Responses: She appears to be a poor working woman who is used to hard physical farm work. Details supporting this conclusion: her dress appears worn and frayed; she has dirt under her fingernails; her fingers are callused; her face and hair are unadorned; her expression is sad and serious.

The Grapes of Wrath

Photographs by **HORACE BRISTOL**
Captions by **JOHN STEINBECK**

The expression "a picture is worth a thousand words" acquired a new shade of meaning in the 1930s, when the Department of Agriculture commissioned photographers to cover the struggles of Depression-era farmers. Because the moments captured in black and white were true-to-life, startlingly realistic portraits emerged. The images in this 1939 photo essay, taken by *Life* magazine photographer Horace Bristol, are examples of what came to be called documentary photography.

"I always kept 'em together and kept 'em fed. I planned for 'em. I can buy this house
A *for ten dollars. I'll have a garden along there. Ducks can swim in the irrigation ditch. I got to get ten dollars."*

In 1934, when the rest of the U.S. began to rise out of Depression, dust began to blow in Oklahoma and Montana, Arkansas and the Dakotas. Thousands of bewildered farmers and farm hands lost their holdings or their jobs and began to drift West. By the time the dust stopped blowing, the banks and the land companies found that mechanized farming over huge areas could make the land pay when individual farmers could not. The drift Westward continued and grew. Lured by assurances of green land and good money, the farmers sold their old tools and older houses, their livestock and furniture for anything they would bring. They used the money to buy shaky old cars, sawing off the bodies to make sedans into flimsy trucks. Along Route 66,[1] through the Texas Panhandle, New Mexico and Arizona, they squeaked and rattled by tens of thousands, a bedraggled leaderless horde, camping beside the creeks and prairie villages, headed for California as a promised land. 1

In California the migrants found no promised land. Instead, they found that thousands of their own kind had already glutted the market for cheap itinerant[2] labor. Furthermore, scrabbling about the State to look for work, fighting each other for jobs, they learned that California hated them because they were hungry and desperate. Because most of them came from Oklahoma, they were scornfully called "Okies," harried along between scarce jobs. Migrants are still in California, squatting[3] in hideous poverty and squalor[4] on the thin margins of the world's richest land. Of the one-third of a nation which is ill-housed, ill-clad, ill-nourished these are the bitterest dregs.[5]

1. **Route 66:** a highway formerly extending from Illinois to California, heavily traveled during the mid-1900s.
2. **itinerant** (ī-tĭn′ər-ənt): traveling from place to place.
3. **squatting:** settling on unoccupied land without legal claim.
4. **squalor** (skwŏl′ər): dirty wretchedness and misery.
5. **dregs:** the poorest parts.

Customizing Instruction

Less Proficient Readers

1 Use a map of the United States to orient students to the geography of this situation. Have them trace the route taken by the migrants.

Have students identify elements in the photos that they recognize from "The Flood" to reinforce their appreciation of the connection between the two.

Possible Response: Students should point out such things as tents, mud, flooding, hungry-looking people, and rusty, old cars.

Students Acquiring English

Help students understand the nonstandard English in the photo captions. Explain that Steinbeck is imitating the way these people talked, and that the speech was typical of rural, poorly educated people at the time.

THE GRAPES OF WRATH: PHOTO ESSAY 927

Reading and Analyzing

Active Reading

AUTHOR'S PURPOSE

Have students discuss similarities and differences between Steinbeck's purpose in "The Flood" and the purpose of the photo-essay.

Possible Response: Both try to increase public awareness of the plight of the migrants and to produce an emotional response in people; however, the photo-essay does this in a much more straightforward, immediate manner. It could also be argued that as a piece of literature, "The Flood" is meant to entertain.

Reading Skills and Strategies:
EVALUATING

Remind students that at the end of "The Flood," the women wonder if "the break" had come—whether the men's spirits had broken and they had lost all hope. Have students examine the photos and discuss which, if any, depict people who have "broken."

Possible Responses: None appear to have "broken"—they are all still able to go on; the woman who was injured by a falling crate seems to have given up.

Reading Skills and Strategies:
CLARIFYING

A Ask students to consider why the writer considers the success of *The Grapes of Wrath* a sign that there is hope for a solution to the problem.

Possible Response: The popularity of the book means that people are becoming more aware of and sympathetic to the Okies' problem. This might mean that people will want to do something to help them.

"Lettuce crate fell on my head. They give me fourteen dollars compensation. I'm the lucky one. I'm gonna die pretty soon now. I wish he didn't feel so bad about it."

"It's the kids. . . . A man can get hungry and it ain't so bad. A man gets sick when the kids are hungry."

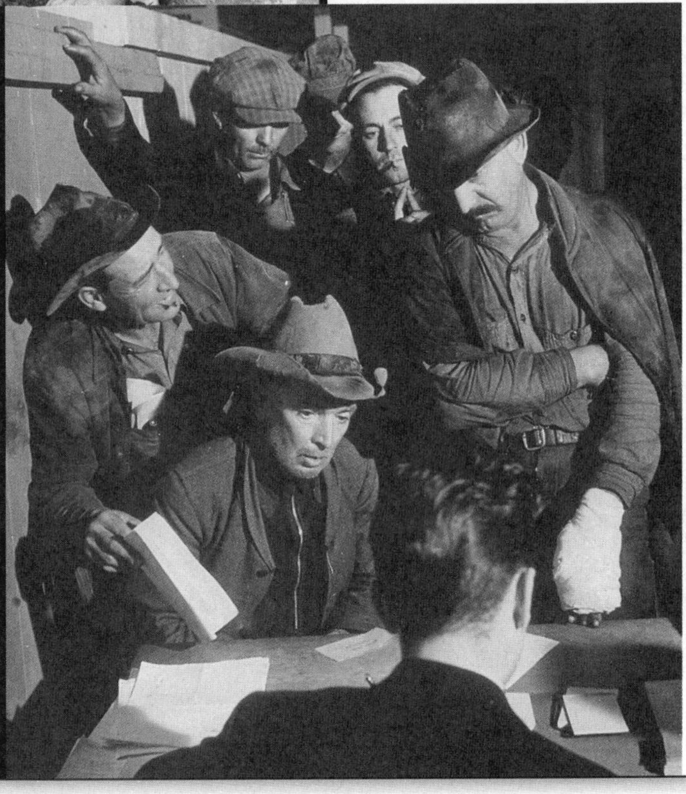

Teaching Options

Mini Lesson Grammar

SEMICOLONS Instruction Remind students that semicolons are used to join independent clauses that are not joined by a coordinating conjunction. If necessary, review independent clauses (subject, predicate, free-standing) and coordinating conjunctions (*and, but, or, for, nor, so, yet*). Write the following sentences on the board, and demonstrate how the punctuation is used correctly and incorrectly:

Correct: The police officer directed traffic; the sheriff's deputy investigated the accident.

Incorrect: My sister won the race; and my brother finished third.

Incorrect: Some say Kyle is a great guy, I say he's just charming when it suits him.

Practice Have students correct the punctuation errors in the following sentences:

1. We ate pizza at my brother's birthday party; and it was delicious.
2. It's an unusual situation, no one is sure what to do about it.

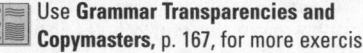

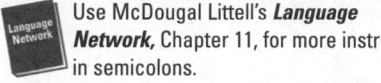

"We just got in. Gonna work in the peas. Got a han'bill that says they's good wages pickin' peas."

The problem of the Okies, though grim, is not insoluble. Some hope of a solution is suggested by the fact that an American writer can not only write about the Okies but that the result can be hailed by U.S. critics as the book of the decade. In *The Grapes of Wrath* (The Viking Press, $2.75), John Steinbeck (*Of Mice and Men*) presents the Okies in all their stink and misery, their courage and confusion. His 600-page novel, which may become a 20th Century *Uncle Tom's Cabin,*[6] is now a nationwide best-seller. Last week, Producer Darryl Zanuck paid $75,000 for the right to make it into a movie. A 1

6. **Uncle Tom's Cabin:** a novel by Harriet Beecher Stowe—first published in 1851–1852—that fueled opposition to slavery and became one of the most widely read novels of the 19th century.

Customizing Instruction

Less Proficient Readers

1 Explain that when the writer says *The Grapes of Wrath* might become another *Uncle Tom's Cabin*, he means that, like the earlier novel, Steinbeck's novel might help to bring about real changes in social conditions in the United States.

Gifted and Talented

Point out that when they were published in the 1930s, both *The Grapes of Wrath* and the photo-essay highlighted a social problem of that time. Today, the photo-essay has largely been forgotten by the public, but *The Grapes of Wrath* continues to enjoy its reputation as a modern classic. Have students discuss the reasons for this difference.

Possible Response: The photo-essay was meant as news and has since lost its immediacy and relevance. It remains remarkable and interesting, but only as a historical record now. The novel stands on its own as a work of great literature; there are other reasons to read it besides to simply become informed of the migrants' living conditions.

3. I don't want to see them build a house in that vacant lot; because we used to play football there.
4. My uncle says he wants a new car and; my sister does, too.
5. High school students should take more academic courses, they will be better prepared for the future.

Answers

1. We ate pizza at my brother's birthday party; it was delicious.
2. It's an unusual situation; no one is sure what to do about it.
3. I don't want to see them build a house in that vacant lot; we used to play football there.
4. My uncle says he wants a new car; my sister does, too.
5. High school students should take more academic courses; they will be better prepared for the future.

Use **Grammar Transparencies and Copymasters,** p. 167, for more exercises.

Use McDougal Littell's ***Language Network,*** Chapter 11, for more instruction in semicolons.

Reading and Analyzing

Reading Skills and Strategies: VISUALIZING

Ask students to visualize what is happening inside the houses shown in the photograph. Have them share their visualizations in discussion.

Possible Responses: The house is empty, because everyone has fled; parents are inside with younger children; a baby is sleeping inside; people are sitting up on boxes, trying to keep dry.

Teaching Options

Mini Lesson Grammar

ADVERB CLAUSES Remind students that adverb clauses modify verbs, adjectives, and other adverbs. An adverb clause begins with a subordinating conjunction and, as with all clauses, has a subject and predicate. Use the model sentence to identify the subject, predicate, and subordinating conjunction that introduces the adverb clause.

Model Sentence

If you look in the night sky, you will see the moon.

Subject/Predicate: *you/will see*

Adverb Clause: *If you look in the night sky,*

Subordinating Conjunction: *If*

Point out that the adverb clause starting with "if" modifies the verb will see.

"We got to have a house when the rains come . . . jus' so's it's got a roof and a floor. Just to keep the little fellas off'n the groun'."

"The company lets us live in 'em when we're pickin' cotton. When we ain't workin', we pay rent. Water's comin' up in 'em now."

The pictures on these pages are not simply types which resemble those described in *The Grapes of Wrath*. They are the people of whom Author Steinbeck wrote. Before starting his book, he lived in California's migratory labor camps. *Life* Photographer Horace Bristol accompanied him. The woman on page 926 might well be Ma Joad, Author Steinbeck's heroine. The man with the double-edged ax (page 932) is a counterpart of his hero, Tom Joad. Captions for their pictures and all others on these pages were written by Steinbeck. Some are excerpts from his book. Others were written especially for *Life*'s photographs. ❖ 1

Customizing Instruction

Less Proficient Readers

1 Explain that Ma and Tom Joad are the main characters in Steinbeck's *The Grapes of Wrath.*

Practice Write the following sentences on the board, and ask students to underline the adverb clauses. Then ask them to double-underline the subordinating conjunction and bracket the word that the adverb clause is modifying.

1. Margaret [ran] as quickly as she could to the next town.
2. She breathed [harder] than she ever had before.
3. If the flood reached the farm, they [would] all [be] in trouble.
4. She wanted to [warn] them before it was too late.

Use **Unit Five Resource Book,** p. 48.

Use **Grammar Transparencies and Copymasters,** p. 114, for more exercises.

Use McDougal Littell's ***Language Network,*** Chapter 4, for more instruction in adverb clauses.

Reading and Analyzing

Reading Skills and Strategies: SUMMARIZING

A Ask students to summarize the speaker's statement in this passage.
Possible Responses: He is saying that there is no logic to explain why this problem remains unsolved when the solution is so obvious. Essentially, he is asking why people can't both work and be fed when there is work to do and food to eat.

"The whole thing's nuts. There's work to do and people to do it, but them two can't get together. There's food to eat and people to eat it, and them two can't get together neither." **A**

"She's awful pretty. An' she been to high school. She could help a man with figuring and stuff like that."

Connect to the Literature

1. **What Do You Think?** Which photograph do you think best depicts the migrants' desperation? Explain.

Comprehension Check
- Why had the farmers of the photo essay migrated to California?
- What hardships did they find there?
- How is John Steinbeck associated with the *Life* magazine piece?

Think Critically

2. How do you think *Life* magazine readers of the 1930s might have reacted to the photo essay?

THINK ABOUT
- the misconceptions many readers might have had about migrant workers
- the depictions of the flood's effects
- the people quoted in Steinbeck's captions

3. **ACTIVE READING** AUTHOR'S PURPOSE What purpose or purposes do you think the writer and photographer of the photo essay had in mind? To support your response, refer to the chart you made in your READER'S NOTEBOOK.

4. What personal qualities do you think are displayed by the migrants in both selections? List them in a web like this one.

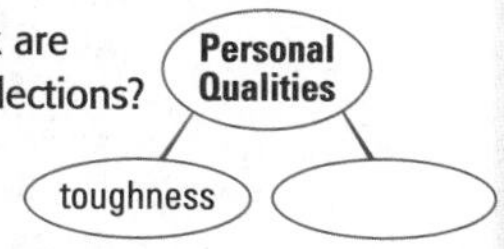

Extend Interpretations

5. **Critic's Corner** Literary critic Daniel Aaron, in his review of *The Grapes of Wrath,* said that the novel "unfolds cinematically almost as if Steinbeck had conceived of it as a documentary film." On the basis of the novel excerpt "The Flood" and Steinbeck's connection with *Life* photographer Horace Bristol, do you think Aaron's view is an accurate one? Why or why not?

6. **Different Perspectives** Consider how *Life* magazine chose to combine its photographs with captions written by a novelist. Take a more critical look at the essay, and choose an example of a paired photograph and caption that you think fit together especially well. Explain your choice.

7. **Connect to Life** Recall the ideas of the promised land that you discussed before exploring the selections. In your opinion, is a "promised land" more within the reach of today's poor people than it was for migrant workers in the 1930s? Discuss your views with other students.

Literary Analysis

SOCIAL CRITICISM Writers of **social criticism** call people's attention to the conditions in society that require change. A writer may use **direct commentary,** by openly stating his or her views about a matter. Or the writer may use **indirect commentary,** which is more common in fiction, to show characters caught up in the issues of the larger world. In "The Flood," in passages such as this one, John Steinbeck draws attention to the unfair restrictions placed on newly arrived migrant workers through the workers' own words:

They's rules—you got to be here a year before you can git relief. They say the gov'ment is gonna help. They don't know when.

Throughout the selection, Steinbeck uses indirect commentary to give dramatic weight to experiences that reflect the hardships faced by real-life migrants in the 1930s.

Cooperative Learning Activity Divide into two groups. One group should look for evidence of social criticism in "The Flood." The other group should examine the evidence of social criticism in the photo essay. Later, combine the groups and share your findings. Determine what elements of social criticism the selections have in common.

Extend Interpretations

Critic's Corner Some may claim that Aaron's view is accurate because of the neutral, camera-like perspective that Steinbeck uses in "The Flood." In addition, Steinbeck's purpose is the same as a documentary filmmaker's: to make people aware of a real-life situation.

Different Perspectives Students should give detailed, supported explanations for their choices.

Connect to Life Some students will point to the recent prosperity in this country and contrast it with the hard times of the Great Depression. Others will point to the growing gap between the rich and poor as evidence of the fact that poverty is still a major obstacle for many in this country. Students' own socioeconomic background will probably influence their ideas on the matter.

GUIDING STUDENT RESPONSE

Connect to the Literature

1. **What Do You Think?**
Accept all reasonable responses, but make sure students justify choices by giving examples from the photo of the migrants' desperation.

Comprehension Check
- to escape the drought that destroyed their farms in Oklahoma and because they heard that there was plenty of farm work in California
- The hardships they found included unfavorable weather conditions and too many migrant workers, which led to unemployment, which in turn led to hunger and disease.
- Steinbeck wrote the captions for the photographs.

Use Selection Quiz
Unit Five Resource Book, p. 49.

Think Critically

2. Acceptable answers will vary, but it is likely that they were surprised to see how bad conditions really were, and that they felt sorry for the migrants.
3. Responses will vary. Students may say that their purpose was to expose the conditions under which the migrants lived, bringing awareness and an eventual solution to the problems experienced by the migrants.
4. Responses will vary. Encourage students to list negative qualities, such as *angry,* as well as positive qualities, such as *hardworking*.

Literary Analysis

Social Criticism Both selections vividly portray human suffering that, it seems, is being ignored by others. "The Flood" more clearly portrays the unsympathetic response to this suffering, while the photo-essay puts more emphasis on the suffering itself.

Writing Options

1. **Letter to the Editor** Explain to students that "Letters to the Editor" is a forum for readers to express personal feelings about issues, offer criticism, or propose a solution to a problem.

Activities & Explorations

Monologue As a way to brainstorm ideas for their monologues, students could pair up to improvise a conversation between the characters they have chosen.

Grammar in Context

WRITING EXERCISE

1. If the fields become flooded, the migrants will not have any work.
2. The sheriff will swear in more deputies if the desperate migrants begin stealing.
3. If the migrants need help, the only person they can rely on is the coroner.
4. The migrants will have work in the spring if they find a way to survive until then.

Vocabulary in Action

1. penetrate
2. migrant
3. sodden
4. frantic
5. smolder

Choices & CHALLENGES

Writing Options

Letter to the Editor Imagine you were a subscriber to *Life* magazine in 1939. Write a letter to the editor about the conditions described in the photo essay.

Activities & Explorations

Monologue Take the part of one of the persons pictured in "The Grapes of Wrath: Photo Essay." Deliver a monologue that begins with the caption and extends it. Refer to the captions and images to help you interpret the migrants' emotions—for example, the despair, weariness, or hopefulness. Rehearse by trying different interpretations until you discover the one that seems the most appropriate. Focus on those emotions as you perform your monologue. ~ **PERFORMING**

Grammar in Context: Adverb Clauses That Express Conditions

In these two excerpts from "The Flood," John Steinbeck uses adverb clauses to show conditional relationships.

> **Then the cars wouldn't start because the wires were shorted; and if the engines would run, deep mud engulfed the wheels.**

> **If they were shot at, they did not run, but splashed sullenly away; and if they were hit, they sank tiredly in the mud.**

An **adverb clause** modifies a verb, an adjective, or another adverb, answering a question such as *how, when, where, why, to what extent,* or *under what circumstances.* In the excerpts above, the adverb clauses shown in blue express conditions, telling under what circumstances things happen. Steinbeck uses the adverb clauses to help him express the hopelessness of the workers' situation: no matter what they do during the flood, something unpleasant happens.

WRITING EXERCISE Combine each pair of sentences by changing one of them into an adverb clause that expresses a condition. Omit italicized words.

Punctuation Tip: A conditional clause at the start of a sentence should be followed by a comma. No comma is needed before one at the end of a sentence.

Example: *Original* The valley floods with water. *It does this whenever* it rains hard for more than two days.

Rewritten The valley floods with water if it rains hard for more than two days.

1. The fields *may* become flooded. *This would mean* the migrants will not have any work.
2. The sheriff will swear in more deputies. *He does this whenever* the desperate migrants begin stealing.
3. The migrants need help. *In such a situation,* the only person they can rely on is the coroner.
4. The migrants will have work in the spring. *But* they *will have to* find a way to survive until then.

Grammar Handbook Clauses, p. 1197

Vocabulary in Action

EXERCISE: MEANING CLUES Read the book titles listed below. Then, on your paper, write the Word to Know suggested by each title.

1. *How to Hammer a Nail Properly*
2. *Working My Way Across America*
3. *Soaked to the Skin*
4. *Frenzy in the Emergency Room*
5. *The Consequences of Repressed Rage*

WORDS TO KNOW frantic, migrant, penetrate, smolder, sodden

Building Vocabulary
Several Words to Know in this lesson have multiple meanings. For an in-depth lesson on words with multiple meanings, see page 678.

Teaching Options

Assessment Standardized Test Practice

CHOOSING THE BEST SUMMARY For some standardized tests, students will be asked to choose the best summary of a passage. To provide students with some help in choosing the best summary, read aloud or write on the chalkboard the following question:

Which of the following statements best summarizes the two-paragraph description on page 927?

A. When farmers in the Midwest lost their farms, they moved to California to look for work.

B. Migrant farm workers, forced to leave their farms in the Midwest, thought they would find a better life in California, but instead found poverty and rejection.

C. Native Californians hated the poor migrants who came to find a better life.

Lead students through the process of choosing the best summary. Consider each choice. Point out that, while all of the statements contain accurate information, the best summary should include the most important information. For that reason, **B** is the best choice.

from Travels with Charley

Nonfiction by JOHN STEINBECK

"I wonder why we think the thoughts and emotions of animals are simple."

Connect to Your Life

Pet Personalities We often attribute human qualities to our pets. Think of the pets you have known and how you would describe their behavior, or "personalities." Jot down your thoughts in a chart similar to the one shown.

Pet Name	Type of Animal	General Behavior	Humanlike Traits

Build Background

Charley Dog In 1960, John Steinbeck decided to take an extended road trip across America, saying, "I'm going to learn about my own country. I've lost the flavor and taste and sound of it." His only companion was an "old French gentleman poodle" he and his wife called Charley Dog. Although bringing Charley was a last minute decision, it gave the travel journal that Steinbeck would write its focus. Charley served as a kind of ambassador for Steinbeck, reaching out to people along the way, providing a natural conversation starter for the author.

Focus Your Reading

LITERARY ANALYSIS | COMIC IRONY **Irony** is a technique that contrasts appearance and reality. **Comic irony** humorously contrasts what is expected to happen with what actually happens. In the excerpt from *Travels with Charley,* Steinbeck uses comic irony as he makes observations about his dog's behavior or about certain aspects of their trip. For example, when warned that Charley should be attached to a leash in a national park because of possible encounters with bears, Steinbeck replies:

> ***I suggest that the greatest danger to your bears will be pique [anger] at being ignored by Charley.***

ACTIVE READING | WORD CHOICE **Word choice,** or **diction,** involves a writer's selection of language. Through careful word choice, good writers, including Steinbeck, are able to capture on paper their own ideas, feelings, and experiences. Note the following sentence:

> ***I must confess to a laxness in the matter of National Parks.***

The word *laxness* suggests both physical laziness and moral failing. Through this word choice, Steinbeck creates a humorous tone, suggesting that by not appreciating national parks he might be out of the ordinary, even unpatriotic.

READER'S NOTEBOOK Jot down any words that you think Steinbeck has specially chosen to communicate his thoughts about his experience.

OVERVIEW

Objectives

1. understand and appreciate **autobiographical incident (Literary Analysis)**
2. understand **comic irony (Literary Analysis)**
3. analyze **word choice (Active Reading)**

Summary

John Steinbeck tells the story of his reluctant visit to Yellowstone National Park, where he makes a surprising discovery about his dog and traveling companion, Charley. When told by the park ranger that dogs must be leashed because of the bears, Steinbeck replies that Charley is completely peace-loving and wouldn't dream of attacking another animal. However, when Steinbeck and Charley encounter a number of bears in the park, Charley reacts in a snarling rage that is completely out of character. Steinbeck is astonished at his dog's behavior and at a loss for an explanation.

Thematic Link

Because his dog Charley always **appeared** to be a gentle, peaceful creature, John Steinbeck is surprised to discover that, in **reality,** his dog also has a vicious side.

5-Minute Warm-Up

Daily Language SkillBuilder

Have students **proofread** the display sentences on page 817k and write them correctly. The sentences also appear on Transparency 26 of **Grammar Transparencies and Copymasters.**

LESSON RESOURCES

UNIT FIVE RESOURCE BOOK, pp. 51–52

ASSESSMENT RESOURCES

Formal Assessment, pp. 153–154

Teacher's Guide to Assessment and Portfolio Use

Test Generator

SKILLS TRANSPARENCIES AND COPYMASTERS

Literary Analysis
- Irony: Verbal, T16 (for Activity, p. 939)

Reading and Critical Thinking
- Noting Details, T9 (for Connect to Your Life, p. 935)
- Locating Information Using Print References, T32 (for Inquiry & Research, p. 940)
- Locating Information Using Databases and the Internet, T34 (for Inquiry & Research, p. 940

Grammar
- Subordinating Conjunctions, C80 (for Mini Lesson, p. 936)

Writing
- Varying Sentence Openers and Closers, T18 (for Writing Options, p. 940)
- Point of View T23 (for Writing Options 1, 3, p. 940)
- Persuasive Essay, C30 (for Writing Option 2, p. 940)

Communications
- Impromptu Speaking: Dialogue, Role-Play, Debate, T13 (for Activities & Explorations 2, p. 940)

INTEGRATED TECHNOLOGY

Audio Library

Net Activities

Internet: Research Starter

Visit our website: www.mcdougallittell.com

TEACHING THE LITERATURE

Reading and Analyzing

Reading Skills and Strategies: PREVIEW

Have students look at the highlighted quotation on pp. 935, 937, and 938. Have them consider the title, the photographs, and the Build Background feature. Before students read the selection, give them a brief summary.

Literary Analysis COMIC IRONY

Steinbeck uses different kinds of irony in this story for comic effect. He uses both verbal irony, which involves a contrast between what is said and what is meant, and situational irony, which occurs when what actually happens is different from what is expected. As students read, have them identify examples of both kinds of irony.

Possible Responses Verbal irony: "He turns his steps rather than disturb an earnest caterpillar." This is an exaggeration; situational irony: Steinbeck expects his dog to ignore the bears, but instead the dog hates them.

Use **Unit Five Resource Book,** p. 52 for more practice.

Active Reading WORD CHOICE

Remind students to analyze the characteristics of clearly written text, specifically word choice. Steinbeck chooses words for their humorous effect. Have students identify sentences that contain words and phrases they find humorous. Then ask them to paraphrase those sentences, and to note whether the paraphrases retain the humor of the original sentences.

Use **Unit Five Resource Book,** p. 51 for more practice.

FROM TRAVELS WITH

I must confess to a laxness[1] in the matter of National Parks. I haven't visited many of them. Perhaps this is because they enclose the unique, the spectacular, the astounding—the greatest waterfall, the deepest canyon, the highest cliff, the most stupendous works of man or nature. And I would rather see a good Brady[2] photograph than Mount Rushmore. For it is my opinion that we enclose and celebrate the freaks of our nation and of our civilization. Yellowstone National Park is no more representative of America than is Disneyland.

This being my natural attitude, I don't know what made me turn sharply south and cross a state line to take a look at Yellowstone. Perhaps it was a fear of my neighbors. I could hear them say, "You mean you were that near to Yellowstone and didn't go? You must be crazy."

Again it might have been the American tendency in travel. One goes, not so much to see but to tell afterward. Whatever my purpose in going to Yellowstone, I'm glad I went because I discovered something about Charley I might never have known.

Teaching Options

Mini Lesson Grammar

SUBORDINATING CONJUNCTIONS Subordinating conjunctions such as *after, although, as, because, if, since, when, where,* and *while* are sometimes used to relate subordinate (dependent) clauses to independent clauses. The subordinating conjunction introduces the subordinate clause and shows the relationship between the two clauses.

Write the following sentence on the chalkboard:

> John never missed basketball practice <u>because</u> he loved playing basketball.

Underline the subordinating conjunction as shown. Have students identify the subject and verb in both the subordinate and main clause and then discuss the relationship between the two clauses.

CHARLEY

JOHN STEINBECK

A pleasant-looking National Park man checked me in and then he said, "How about that dog? They aren't permitted in except on leash."

"Why?" I asked.

"Because of the bears."

"Sir," I said, "this is an unique dog. He does not live by tooth or fang. He respects the right of cats to be cats although he doesn't admire them. He turns his steps rather than disturb an earnest caterpillar. His greatest fear is that someone will point out a rabbit and suggest that he chase it. This is a dog of peace and tranquility. I suggest that the greatest danger to your bears will be pique[3] at being ignored by Charley."

The young man laughed. "I wasn't so much worried about the bears," he said. "But our bears have developed an intolerance for dogs. One of them might demonstrate his prejudice with a clip on the chin, and then—no dog."

"I'll lock him in the back, sir. I promise you Charley will cause no ripple in the bear world, and as an old bear-looker, neither will I."

"I just have to warn you," he said. "I have no doubt your dog has the best of intentions. On the other hand, our bears have the worst. Don't leave food about. Not only do they steal but they are critical of anyone who tries to reform them. In a word, don't believe their sweet faces or you might get clobbered. And don't let the dog wander. Bears don't argue."

LESS THAN A MILE FROM THE ENTRANCE I SAW A BEAR BESIDE THE ROAD, AND IT AMBLED OUT AS THOUGH TO FLAG ME DOWN.

We went on our way into the wonderland of nature gone nuts, and you will have to believe what happened. The only way I can prove it would be to get a bear.

Less than a mile from the entrance I saw a bear beside the road, and it ambled out as though to flag me down. Instantly a change came over Charley. He shrieked with rage. His lips flared, showing wicked teeth that have some trouble with a dog biscuit. He screeched insults at the bear, which hearing, the bear reared up and seemed to me to overtop Rocinante.[4] Frantically I rolled the windows shut and, swinging quickly to the left, grazed the animal, then scuttled on while Charley raved and ranted beside me, describing in detail what he would do to that bear if he could get at him. I was never so astonished in my life. To the best of my knowledge Charley had never seen a bear, and in his whole history had showed great tolerance for every living thing. Besides all this, Charley is a coward, so deep-seated a coward that he has developed a technique for concealing it. And yet he showed every evidence of wanting to get out 1

1. **laxness:** inattention to duty; slackness.
2. **Brady:** Mathew B. Brady, a famous Civil War photographer.
3. **pique** (pēk): a feeling of wounded pride; vexation.
4. **Rocinante** (rô-sē-nön'tĕ): the camper in which Steinbeck traveled, named for the broken-down horse ridden by Don Quixote in Miguel de Cervantes's satiric novel *Don Quixote*.

Customizing Instruction

Less Proficient Readers

Have students keep the following questions in mind as they read:

- What does the narrator assume to be true about his dog?
  Answer: He is peace-loving and gentle.
- What does the narrator discover?
  Answer: His dog becomes violent and savage when it sees bears.
- How does the narrator feel about this discovery?
  Possible Response: surprised and disturbed

Students Acquiring English

Explain to students that a national park is an area of particular natural beauty or scientific interest set aside and maintained by the federal government.

Use **Spanish Study Guide** for additional support, pp. 192–194.

Gifted and Talented

1 The reference to Rocinante comes from the satiric masterpiece *Don Quixote* written by Miguel Cervantes in the early 17th century. Have students look up a synopsis of the work and find reference to the primary traits of the character Don Quixote. Then ask students to explain the humor in Steinbeck's reference to Don Quixote's horse.

Possible Response: In Cervantes's novel, Don Quixote is on a quest to right the world's wrongs. As the prototypical idealist, he lives by his own vision of the world rather than the factual realities of that world. In calling his trailer Rocinante, Steinbeck establishes himself as a Quixotic character whose assumptions about reality are somewhat idealized and unrealistic.

Practice Have students complete the following sentences by supplying a subordinate clause appropriate for the conjunction provided.

1. Nina got a good grade on her test although ______.
   Possible Response: she did not study for it
2. I'll accept that job offer if ______.
   Possible Response: it pays well enough
3. Rick is going to take a vacation when ______.
   Possible Response: he finishes school
4. We went to a movie while ______.
   Possible Response: the others went shopping
5. Lindsey didn't have much free time before ______.
   Possible Response: school started

Accept any reasonable responses, making sure that the relationship between the clauses is appropriate for the conjunction.

Use **Grammar Transparencies and Copymasters**, p. 80, for more practice.

Use McDougal Littell's ***Language Network***, Chapter 4, for more instruction in subordinating conjunctions.

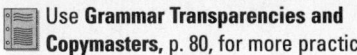

Reading and Analyzing

Reading Skills and Strategies: VISUALIZING

A Have students visualize the back of the camper both before and after Charley is locked in the back.

Possible Response: The camper is probably very tidy before, with the food arranged neatly. Afterward, the food and other objects are probably strewn about, and the table and windows are scratched or broken.

Literary Analysis: HYPERBOLE

B Explain to students that hyperbole is the use of exaggeration to create an effect. Have students explain the hyperbole in "Heretofore he has been a little tenderhearted toward an underdone steak."

Possible Response: Steinbeck emphasizes Charley's peaceful nature by implying that Charley might feel sorry for eating an underdone steak. In reality, Charley would probably gobble it up without thinking about it.

Literary Analysis: PLOT

Point out that a plot is considered resolved when all of the conflicts are settled. Ask students to identify the point at which they think the plot of this story is resolved.

Possible Responses: The conflicts are resolved when Charley is locked away and Steinbeck leaves the park; resolution occurs when Steinbeck accepts that animals are more complex than we think.

and murder a bear that outweighed him a thousand to one. I don't understand it.

A little farther along two bears showed up, and the effect was doubled. Charley became a maniac. He leaped all over me, he cursed and growled, snarled and screamed. I didn't know he had the ability to snarl. Where did he learn it? Bears were in good supply, and the road became a nightmare. For the first time in his life Charley resisted reason, even resisted a cuff on the ear. He became a primitive killer lusting for the blood of his enemy, and up to this moment he had had no enemies. In a bearless stretch, I opened the cab, took Charley by the collar, and locked him in the house. But that did no good. When we passed other bears he leaped on the table and scratched at the windows trying to get out at them. I could hear canned goods crashing as he struggled in his mania. Bears simply brought out the Hyde in my Jekyll-headed dog.[5] What could have caused it? Was it a pre-breed memory of a time when the wolf was in him? I know him well. Once in a while he tries a bluff, but it is a palpable lie.[6] I swear that this was no lie. I am certain that if he were released he would have charged every bear we passed and found victory or death.

BEARS SIMPLY BROUGHT OUT THE HYDE IN MY JEKYLL-HEADED DOG.

It was too nerve-wracking, a shocking spectacle, like seeing an old, calm friend go insane. No amount of natural wonders, of rigid cliffs and belching waters, of smoking springs could even engage my attention while that pandemonium went on. After about the fifth encounter I gave up, turned Rocinante about, and retraced my way. If I had stopped the night and bears had gathered to my cooking, I dare not think what would have happened.

At the gate the park guard checked me out. "You didn't stay long. Where's the dog?"

"Locked up back there. And I owe you an apology. That dog has the heart and soul of a bear-killer and I didn't know it. Heretofore he has been a little tenderhearted toward an underdone steak."

"Yeah!" he said. "That happens sometimes. That's why I warned you. A bear dog would know his chances, but I've seen a Pomeranian[7] go up like a puff of smoke. You know, a well-favored bear can bat a dog like a tennis ball."

I moved fast, back the way I had come, and I was reluctant to camp for fear there might be some unofficial non-government bears about. That night I spent in a pretty auto court near Livingston. I had my dinner in a restaurant, and when I had settled in with a drink and a comfortable chair and my bathed bare feet on a carpet with red roses, I inspected Charley. He was dazed. His eyes held a faraway look and he was totally exhausted, emotionally no doubt. Mostly he reminded me of a man coming out of a long, hard drunk—worn out, depleted, collapsed. He couldn't eat his dinner, he refused the evening walk, and once we were in he collapsed on the floor and went to sleep. In the night I heard him whining and yapping, and when I turned on the light his feet were making running gestures and his body jerked and his eyes were wide open, but it was only a night bear. I awakened him and gave him some water. This time he went to sleep and didn't stir all night. In the morning he was still tired. I wonder why we think the thoughts and emotions of animals are simple. ❖

5. **brought out . . . dog:** brought out the viciousness in my mild-mannered dog. (In Robert Louis Stevenson's *The Strange Case of Dr. Jekyll and Mr. Hyde,* Dr. Jekyll (jĕ′kəl) develops a drug that releases the evil side of his personality, turning him into the murderous Mr. Hyde.)
6. **palpable** (păl′pə-bəl): obvious.
7. **Pomeranian** (pŏm′ə-rā′nē-ən): a small breed of dog with long, silky hair.

Connect to the Literature

1. **What Do You Think?** What is your explanation of Charley's behavior?

Comprehension Check
- Why has Steinbeck normally avoided national parks?
- How does he assume Charley will react to bears?
- How does Charley actually react?

Think Critically

2. What are your impressions of John Steinbeck as the narrator of this selection?

THINK ABOUT
- his observations about national parks
- the concerns he expresses about Charley's reactions
- his conversations with the Yellowstone guard

3. ACTIVE READING ANALYZING WORD CHOICE Review the list of unusual words you jotted down in your READER'S NOTEBOOK. Point out to a partner a word or phrase that you found to be particularly effective in this humorous account.

4. At the start of his park visit, Steinbeck promises, "Charley will cause no ripple in the bear world." In your opinion, was Steinbeck more shaken by Charley's behavior or by his discovery that he hadn't really known his dog as well as he had thought? Support your opinion with evidence from the selection.

Extend Interpretations

5. **The Writer's Style** The author and the National Park guard exchange pleasantries about the personalities of animals by referring to them as if they were humans: "He [Charley] respects the rights of cats to be cats," says Steinbeck. About bears, the guard warns, "Not only do they steal, but they are critical of anyone who tries to reform them." Find other examples of animals described in humanlike terms.

6. **Connect to Life** Think back to the chart of pet personality traits that you filled in earlier. In your opinion, do pets really have personalities, or do pet owners merely interpret pet behavior in familiar human terms? Give reasons for your opinion.

Literary Analysis

COMIC IRONY **Comic irony** is a humorous contrast between appearance and reality. A writer usually creates this type of irony by stating one thing when he or she means another, commenting on a topic that is amusing or intriguing. One example of comic irony in the excerpt from *Travels with Charley* is the unexpected idea that a poodle, a breed of dog associated with very civilized behavior, could, in the right setting, behave as a wild animal. Steinbeck achieves comic irony through the use of two very different techniques.

- **Understatement** is the technique of deliberately saying less about a subject in order to emphasize it. For example, in the excerpt, the Yellowstone guard warns, "Bears don't argue," meaning in fact that bears can be ferociously deadly.
- **Hyperbole** is the technique of exaggerating the truth. Steinbeck uses hyperbole to describe Charley's reaction to the bear: ". . . he showed every evidence of wanting to get out and murder a bear that outweighed him a thousand to one."

Activity Review the selection to find two or three other examples of comic irony. Explain why each is ironic. Pay particular attention to the use of understatement and hyperbole.

GUIDING STUDENT RESPONSE

Connect to the Literature

1. **What Do You Think?**
Students might suggest instinct or a lack of understanding of the danger of the bears.

Comprehension Check
- because they highlight the extraordinary rather than the common elements of the American experience
- He assumes Charley will react to bears as he reacts to all other animals, that is, with a calm disregard.
- Charley goes berserk.

Use Selection Quiz **Unit Five Resource Book,** p. 53.

Think Critically

2. Possible Responses: Steinbeck narrates the story with a sense of humor; he seems like an intelligent and compassionate person who loves his dog.
3. Students may point out any number of words and phrases that they find interesting or unusual in this context, such as "pique," "intolerance," "cause no ripple in the bear world," "best of intentions," "argue," "nature gone nuts," and "screeched insults."
4. Possible Response: He seems most shaken that he didn't know Charley as well as he thought. He says, "I discovered something about Charley I might never have known." He says, "I was never so astonished in my life" and then describes in detail what he thought Charley's personality to be.

Literary Analysis

Comic Irony Possible Responses: "His greatest fear is that someone will point out a rabbit and suggest that he chase it." This hyperbole exaggerates Charlie's lack of ferocity. "One of them might demonstrate his prejudice with a clip on the chin . . ." understates the danger of a bear's attack.

Extend Interpretations

The Writer's Style Possible Responses: A bear "might demonstrate his prejudice"; "bears don't argue"; Charley "screeched insults"; Charley ranted, "describing in detail what he would do to that bear."

Connect to Life Those students who say that pets have personalities will probably base their argument on their own experience; others may note that owners tend to exaggerate the human characteristics of their pets.

Writing Options

1. **Dog's-Eye Essay** Encourage students to approach this essay with the same comic irony that Steinbeck uses. By attributing language to Charley, they also give him a higher intelligence, perhaps one from which he looks down on his master and the ranger for their simple-minded thinking. They could also create a dialogue in which the bear and Charley are arguing a point or perhaps disagreeing about something trivial.
2. **Persuasive Essay** Students who do not own a pet may want to begin by interviewing someone who does.
3. **Incident Report** Encourage students to use comic irony. Remind them that this is probably not the first time that someone entering the park has ignored the ranger's warning.

Activities & Explorations

1. **Brief Introduction** Have students consider the tone of their introduction. Is the episode being presented as a warning to dog owners planning a trip to Yellowstone or as an example of a humorous travel mishap?
2. **Travel Comics** Remind students that hyperbole can add humor to a story, and that similarly, their drawings can include humorous exaggerations.

Inquiry & Research

Animal Defenses First discuss a system for classifying various types of animal defense systems: built-in defensive armor, playing dead, hiding, fighting, and escaping. Then let students decide whether they would like to research the defense system of one animal or whether they would like to research how different animals use one type of defense system.

Choices & CHALLENGES

Writing Options

1. **Dog's-Eye Essay** In a short essay, relate the incident from the perspective of Charley. Exactly how does he view his master? the park guard? the bears?

Writing Handbook
See pages 1155–1156: Narrative Writing.

2. **Persuasive Essay** Near the beginning of the account of Charley's encounters, Steinbeck states, "Whatever my purpose in going to Yellowstone, I'm glad I went because I discovered something about Charley I might never have known." Do you think it's often possible to learn a life lesson through an experience with a pet? In a persuasive essay, express your opinions. Support your position with evidence from the excerpt or from your own life.

3. **Incident Report** Create the entry about Charley that the park guard might have recorded in a daily logbook.

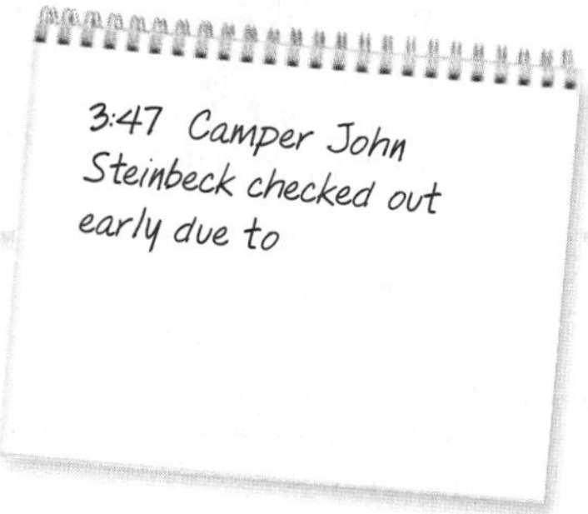
3:47 Camper John
Steinbeck checked out
early due to

Activities & Explorations

1. **Brief Introduction** In the role of a television host, introduce the excerpt as if it had been adapted as an episode of a travel show.
~ **PERFORMING**

2. **Travel Comics** In small groups, share any humorous experiences you've had traveling. Then convey your experiences in the form of comic-strip drawings.
~ **SPEAKING AND LISTENING/ART**

Inquiry & Research

Animal Defenses Refer to Web sites, encyclopedias, and other reference sources to investigate the ways different animals protect themselves or to explore dog behavior. How closely does tame house dogs' behavior match that of their counterparts in the wild—wolves?

More Online: Research Starter
www.mcdougallittell.com

Assessment Standardized Test Practice

IDENTIFYING A TEXT'S MAIN IDEA On some standardized tests, students will be asked to pick a sentence that best describes the main idea of a text. Have students discuss the following question:

Which of the following best describes the main idea of this excerpt from *Travels with Charley*?

A. While visiting Yellowstone, Steinbeck's dog wants to fight the bears.
B. While visiting Yellowstone, Steinbeck discovers that he really does not know his dog very well.
C. While visiting Yellowstone, Steinbeck is amazed to learn that his seemingly peace-loving dog possesses a violent side.

Lead students through the process of choosing the best answer. Consider each choice and point out that while all of the statements contain some accurate information, the best answer should include the most important information. For that reason, **C** is the best choice.

"Literature is as old as speech."

Letter to Edith Mirrielees
from Nobel Prize Acceptance Speech

Nonfiction by JOHN STEINBECK

Connect to Your Life

Earning Recognition The letter and speech you are about to read each involve a form of recognition. Think about qualities or actions that you have been recognized for in your life. Were you competing with others? What feelings did the recognition stir in you? Record your experiences in a diagram like the one shown.

Build Background

Nobel Prize In March of 1962, John Steinbeck wrote a letter to Edith Mirrielees, his short-story teacher at Stanford University, in recognition of the instruction he had received.

In October of the same year, Steinbeck was awarded the Nobel Prize for literature. Nobel laureates, or honorees, are generally regarded as among the most talented and worthy people of their generation. However, by the time Steinbeck had received the Nobel Prize, his work had fallen out of favor with some literary critics. One writer had declared, "Any critic knows it is no longer legal to praise John Steinbeck."

Nevertheless, when Steinbeck heard that a woman in Denmark had rowed eight miles to exchange two of her chickens for a copy of one of his books, he said: "That is what you write for. That is as good a prize as you can get."

Focus Your Reading

LITERARY ANALYSIS TONE AND AUDIENCE **Tone** is the attitude a writer takes toward a subject. Writers adopt different tones for different audiences. For example, in this passage from his acceptance speech, Steinbeck uses a formal tone:

> ***In my heart there may be doubt that I deserve the Nobel Award over other men of letters whom I hold in respect and reverence—but there is no question of my pleasure and pride in having it for myself.***

ACTIVE READING MONITORING READING STRATEGIES Understanding what you read involves being aware both of *what* you are reading and *how* you are reading. It's often necessary to **monitor** how you're reading in order to keep on track. Changing the pace of reading can be a particularly useful technique when reading nonfiction material. When unfamiliar information is conveyed, or when unfamiliar words or terms appear, slow down, as a bicyclist or driver would slow down over a difficult patch of road.

READER'S NOTEBOOK As you read Steinbeck's letter and speech, jot down references to passages that caused you to slow down and read more carefully.

OVERVIEW

Objectives

1. understand and appreciate **a letter** and a **speech (Literary Analysis)**
2. analyze **tone** and **audience (Literary Analysis)**
3. monitor reading strategies **(Active Reading)**

Summary

In his "Letter to Edith Mirrielees," his writing teacher at Stanford University, John Steinbeck recalls the lessons about short story writing that she had taught him. He thanks her for showing him that there is no "recipe" for writing a good short story. Instead, the only rule is that a short story must convey something powerful to the reader in order to be effective. In his "Nobel Prize Acceptance Speech," Steinbeck thanks the Swedish Academy for honoring him and comments on the duties and responsibilities of the writer. He states his belief that writers are not separate from the rest of humanity and that the writer's purpose is not only to celebrate human greatness, but also to expose human faults and failures. Above all, he insists, the writer must believe in human perfectibility.

Thematic Link

In these selections, John Steinbeck acknowledges his struggles as a writer and articulates what he believes to be the larger purposes and goals of the writer. In both selections, he recognizes the dedication one must have to achieve these purposes.

5-Minute Warm-Up

Daily Language SkillBuilder

Have students **proofread** the display sentences on page 817k and write them correctly. The sentences also appear on Transparency 26 of **Grammar Transparencies and Copymasters.**

LESSON RESOURCES

UNIT FIVE RESOURCE BOOK, pp. 55–56

ASSESSMENT RESOURCES

Formal Assessment, pp. 155–1567

Teacher's Guide to Assessment and Portfolio Use

Test Generator

SKILLS TRANSPARENCIES AND COPYMASTERS

Literary Analysis
- Mood and Tone, T20 (for Activity, p. 945)

Grammar
- Adverb Clauses IV, C115 (for Mini Lesson, p. 944)
- Semicolons II, C168 (for Mini Lesson, p. 942)

Writing
- Levels of Language, T12 (for Writing Option 2, p. 947)
- Achieving Conciseness, T21 (for Writing Option 1, p. 947)

Communications
- Interviewing, T9 (for Activities & Explorations 1, p. 947)
- Formal Presentations, T10 (for Activities & Explorations 2, p. 947)

INTEGRATED TECHNOLOGY

Audio Library

Net Activities

Internet: Research Starter

Visit our website:
www.mcdougallittell.com

TEACHING THE LITERATURE

Reading and Analyzing

Reading Skills and Strategies: PREVIEW

Have students study the title of the selection and the images presented to predict possible connections. Have students read the Build Background feature on p. 941 before giving them a brief summary of the selection.

Active Reading

MONITOR READING STRATEGIES

Suggest that students quickly read through the works to make note of Steinbeck's main ideas. Then students can read through the works again, this time at a much slower and careful pace to note details and use context to understand unfamiliar words.

Use **Unit Five Resource Book** p. 55 for additional support.

Literary Analysis

TONE AND AUDIENCE

The writer's relationship to the audience can bring subtle changes in emotion that cause changes in tone. As students read, have them imagine the audience of each work. Discuss how Steinbeck adjusts his tone for his audience.

Use **Unit Five Resource Book** p. 56 for additional support.

Letter to Edith Mirrielees

John Steinbeck

Dear Edith Mirrielees:

Although it must be a thousand years ago that I sat in your class in story writing at Stanford, I remember the experience very clearly. I was bright-eyed and bushy-brained and prepared to absorb from you the secret formula for writing good short stories, even great short stories. You canceled this illusion very quickly. The only way to write a good short story, you said, is to write a good short story. Only after it is written can it be taken apart to see how it was done. It is a most difficult form, you told us, and the proof lies in how very few great short stories there are in the world.

The basic rule you gave us was simple and heartbreaking. A story to be effective had to convey something from writer to reader, and the power of its offering was the measure of its excellence. Outside of that, you said, there were no rules. A story could be about anything and could use any means and any technique at all—so long as it was effective. As a subhead[1] to this rule, you maintained that it seemed to be necessary for the writer to know what he wanted to say, in short, what he was talking about. As an exercise we were to try reducing the meat of a story to one sentence, for only then could we know it well enough to enlarge it to three or six or ten thousand words. 1

So there went the magic formula, the secret ingredient. With no more than that you set us on the desolate, lonely path of the writer. And we must have turned in some abysmally[2] bad stories. If I had expected to be discovered in a full bloom of excellence, the grades you gave my efforts quickly disillusioned me. And if I felt unjustly criticized, the judgments of editors for many years afterwards upheld your side, not mine. The low grades on my college stories were echoed in the rejection slips, in the hundreds of rejection slips.

It seemed unfair. I could read a fine story and could even know how it was done, thanks to your training. Why could I not then do it myself? Well, I couldn't, and maybe it's because no two stories dare be alike. Over the years I have written a great many stories and I still don't know how to go about it except to write it and take my chances.

If there is a magic in story writing, and I am convinced that there is, no one has ever been able to reduce it to a recipe that can be passed from one person to another. The formula seems to lie solely in the aching urge of the writer to convey something he feels important to the reader. If the writer has that urge, he may sometimes but by no means always find the way to do it. And if your

1. **subhead:** secondary idea.
2. **abysmally** (ə-bĭz′mə-lē): terribly.

Teaching Options

Mini Lesson Grammar

SEMICOLONS Semicolons are used to link independent clauses that are closely related in thought. They can sometimes be used in place of conjunctions. Write the following sentence on the chalkboard:

> Everyone in town was eager to try the new restaurant; on opening day, customers were lined up at the door waiting to get in.

Discuss the close relationship between the ideas in the clauses that makes the use of the semicolon appropriate.

Practice Ask students to create a new sentence that uses a semicolon.

1. It's no surprise that regions with warm climates are popular. Sports such as golf and tennis can be played year-round.
2. I will never forget my trip to Mexico. I got run over by a herd of goats!

Use **Grammar Transparencies and Copymasters,** p. 168, for more practice.

Use McDougal Littell's ***Language Network,*** Chapter 11, for more instruction in semicolons.

book, Edith, does nothing more, it will teach many readers to perceive the excellence that makes a good story good or the errors that make a bad story. For a bad story is only an ineffective story.

It is not so very hard to judge a story after it is written, but, after many years, to start a story still scares me to death. I will go so far as to say that the writer who is not scared is happily unaware of the remote and tantalizing majesty of the medium.

I wonder whether you will remember one last piece of advice you gave me. It was during the exuberance of the rich and frantic 'twenties, and I was going out into that world to try to be a writer.

You said, "It's going to take a long time, and you haven't any money. Maybe it would be better if you could go to Europe."

"Why?" I asked.

"Because in Europe poverty is a misfortune, but in America it is shameful. I wonder whether or not you can stand the shame of being poor."

It wasn't too long afterward that the depression came down. Then everyone was poor and it was no shame any more. And so I will never know whether or not I could have stood it. But surely you were right about one thing, Edith. It took a long time—a very long time. And it is still going on, and it has never got easier. You told me it wouldn't.

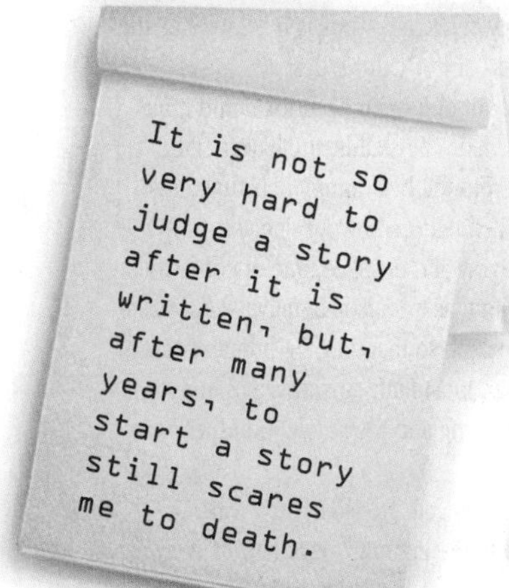
It is not so very hard to judge a story after it is written, but, after many years, to start a story still scares me to death.

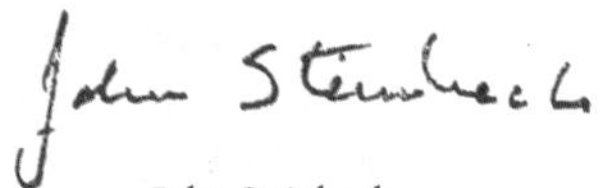

John Steinbeck
March 8, 1962

Thinking Through the Literature

1. After reading Steinbeck's letter, what two or three words would you use to describe him?
2. What do you think were Edith Mirrielees's thoughts after reading the letter?
3. What do you think motivated Steinbeck to write to his teacher so many years after his time at Stanford?

Customizing Instruction

Less Proficient Readers

Set a Purpose Have students keep in mind the following questions as they read:

- What is Steinbeck's purpose in writing this letter?
  Answer: to thank his former teacher
- What did Edith Mirrielees teach him about the difficulty of learning to write?
  Possible Response: "A story had to be effective to convey something from writer to reader, and the power of its offering was the measure of its excellence."
- Why does he thank her for this?
  Possible Response: Steinbeck realizes she was right; he has learned the primary secret of writing from her.

Students Acquiring English

1 Explain to students that "reducing the meat of a story to one sentence" means summarizing the story in a single sentence.

Use **Spanish Study Guide** for additional support, pp. 195–198.

Gifted and Talented

Steinbeck recounts the advice he received from Edith Mirrielees about the difficulties of becoming a writer. Have students research what other writers have said on this subject and hold a conference called "The Writer and the Writing Life," in which they present and discuss the views of writers they have researched.

Thinking Through the Literature

1. Word choices may reflect Steinbeck's dedication to writing, his affection for and gratitude to his teacher, his admission of his own fears about writing, or his memories of youthful innocence and idealism.
2. Students will probably assume that she would be thrilled to receive a thank-you letter from a former student, especially one so acclaimed as Steinbeck. Others may wonder if Mirrielees shared her student's preoccupation with the passing of time.
3. Some students may view the letter as a product of Steinbeck's own self-assessment of his career in writing. Because Steinbeck's reputation had declined, he may have felt a need to get in touch with his own roots in writing. Others may note that a sense of gratitude can come to a person long after an experience.

Reading and Analyzing

Literary Analysis: ALLITERATION

Alliteration is sometimes a feature of formal prose and can be used for emphasis. Have students identify examples of alliteration in Steinbeck's speech.

Possible Responses: "respect and reverence"; "pleasure and pride"; "pride in my profession and in the great and good men who have practiced it"; "faults and failures, with dredging up to the light our dark and dangerous dreams"

Literary Analysis

TONE AND AUDIENCE

Ask students what elements of this speech contribute to its formal tone and what conclusions they can draw about Steinbeck's audience.

Possible Responses: The vocabulary, the subject matter, the use of alliteration, and the complex sentence structures combine to create a formal tone. The audience probably consists of highly educated people, many of whom are also writers.

Reading Skills and Strategies: QUESTIONING

A Ask students to consider why Steinbeck seems to be so adamant about the point that writers are "not separate and exclusive."

Possible Responses: Steinbeck is critical of writers who are not deeply connected to the rest of humanity. He feels that it is a writer's duty to try to improve people and that to do so, the writer cannot be "separate and exclusive."

from NOBEL PRIZE ACCEPTANCE SPEECH

John Steinbeck

I thank the Swedish Academy for finding my work worthy of this highest honor. In my heart there may be doubt that I deserve the Nobel Award over other men of letters whom I hold in respect and reverence—but there is no question of my pleasure and pride in having it for myself.

Steinbeck, receiving his award in Stockholm, Sweden.

It is customary for the recipient of this award to offer scholarly or personal comment on the nature and the direction of literature. However, I think it would be well at this particular time to consider the high duties and the responsibilities of the makers of literature.

Such is the prestige of the Nobel Award and of this place where I stand that I am impelled, not to squeak like a grateful and apologetic mouse, but to roar like a lion out of pride in my profession and in the great and good men who have practiced it through the ages.

Literature was not promulgated[1] by a pale and emasculated[2] critical priesthood singing their litanies[3] in empty churches—nor is it a game for the cloistered elect,[4] the tin-horn mendicants[5] of low-calorie despair.

Literature is as old as speech. It grew out of human need for it and it has not changed except to become more needed. The skalds, the bards,[6] the writers are not separate and exclusive. From the beginning, their functions, their duties, their responsibilities have been decreed by our species. **A**

Humanity has been passing through a gray and desolate time of confusion. My great predecessor, William Faulkner,[7] speaking here, referred to it as a tragedy of universal physical fear, so long sustained that there were no longer problems of the spirit, so that only the human heart in conflict with itself seemed worth writing about. Faulkner, more than most men, was aware of human strength as well as of human weakness. He knew that the understanding and the resolution of fear are a large part of the writer's reason for being.

This is not new. The ancient commission of the writer has not changed. He is charged with exposing our many grievous faults and failures, with dredging up to the light our dark and dangerous dreams for the purpose of improvement.

Furthermore, the writer is delegated to declare and to celebrate man's proven capacity for greatness of heart and spirit—for gallantry in defeat, for courage, compassion and love. In the endless war against weakness and despair, these are the bright rally flags of hope and of emulation.[8] I hold that a writer who does not passionately believe in the perfectibility of man has no dedication nor any membership in literature.

1. **promulgated** (prŏm′əl-gā′tĭd): put into circulation.
2. **emasculated** (ĭ-măs′kyə-lā′tĭd): lacking manly strength.
3. **litanies** (lĭt′n-ēz): prayers.
4. **cloistered elect:** protected group of privileged people.
5. **tin-horn mendicants** (mĕn′dĭ-kənts): pretentious beggars.
6. **skalds . . . bards:** ancient Scandinavian and Celtic poets.
7. **William Faulkner:** a Nobel Prize-winning American novelist whose writings draw on the history, legends, and social problems of his native South.
8. **emulation** (ĕm′yə-lā′shən): a striving to imitate the accomplishments of others.

Teaching Options

Mini Lesson Grammar

ADVERB CLAUSES An adverb clause is used to modify a verb, an adjective, or another adverb and begins with a subordinating conjunction, such as *after, although, because, before, if, since, unless, until, when, where,* and *while*. If an adverb clause is used to introduce the sentence, it is followed by a comma. If it follows the word it modifies, a comma is not necessary. Write the following sentences on the board. Underline the adverb clause and circle the word that the clause modifies.

John (shouted) in frustration <u>because he thought he would never find his way home.</u>

<u>Because he thought he would never find his way home</u>, John (shouted) in frustration.

Practice On the chalkboard, write the subordinating conjunctions listed at the left. Have students work in pairs to write three sentences that use an adverb clause using a subordinating conjunction from the list. Then have pairs exchange sentences and ask them to underline the adverb clauses and circle the word that each clause modifies.

Use **Unit Five Resource Book,** p. 57 for additional support.

Use McDougal Littell's ***Language Network,*** Chapter 9, for more instruction and practice in adverbs.

Connect to the Literature

1. **What Do You Think?** Which of Steinbeck's statements about literature is most memorable to you?

Comprehension Check
- What does Steinbeck say is the customary thing to talk about in such a speech?
- Why does he praise William Faulkner?
- What kind of writers does Steinbeck scorn?

Think Critically

2. **ACTIVE READING MONITORING READING STRATEGIES** Look back over any notes you may have recorded in your READER'S NOTEBOOK about difficult passages. What thought or statement expressed by Steinbeck did you understand better once you slowed down?

3. What do you think was Steinbeck's basic view of prizes and recognition?

   THINK ABOUT
   - his statement about receiving the prize
   - his statements about the role of writers
   - his thoughts about Faulkner and other writers

4. Both "Letter to Edith Mirrielees" and the "Nobel Prize Acceptance Speech" were written when Steinbeck was in the later stage of his writing career. On the basis of the views he expressed in both the letter and speech, what advice do you think he would have given to a beginning writer at that time?

Extend Interpretations

5. **Critic's Corner** A biographer of Steinbeck's once said that whatever we read of his work "almost invariably strikes us as genuine." Think about the Steinbeck pieces you've encountered in this Author Study. Explain why you agree or disagree with that observation.

6. **Comparing Texts** Although Steinbeck's **tone** differs between the two selections, are his statements about the role of the writer consistent? Cite evidence from the selections to support your response.

7. **Connect to Life** Refer to the diagram in which you recorded details about an experience of earning recognition. Trophies, ribbons, medals, and certificates are common symbols of achievement. When do you think an award is most meaningful? Share your thoughts with others in your class.

Literary Analysis

TONE AND AUDIENCE Writers convey different **tones,** or attitudes, towards their subjects, often depending on the audience and the form of the writing. In "Letter to Edith Mirrielees," for example, Steinbeck's basic tone is personal and conversational:

I could read a fine story and could even know how it was done, thanks to your training.

However, in the "Nobel Prize Acceptance Speech," he uses a formal, elevated tone:

Such is the prestige of the Nobel Award . . . that I am impelled, not to squeak like a grateful and apologetic mouse, but to roar like a lion.

Steinbeck also presents a more elevated tone in parts of the letter through rhythmic phrases that use **alliteration** to emphasize important words:

the remote and tantalizing majesty of the medium . . .

Activity Select other passages from both the letter and the speech, and identify what kind of tone Steinbeck has used. Be aware that there is a wider range of tone used in "Letter to Edith Mirrielees."

REVIEW **Author's Purpose** Authors write for one or more purposes: to inform, to express an opinion, to entertain, or to persuade. What would you identify as Steinbeck's purpose for writing both the letter and the speech? Cite details to support your response.

Extend Interpretations

Critic's Corner Some students may agree, citing Steinbeck's honest recognition of people's fears, struggles, and limitations. Others may claim that Steinbeck exaggerates people's weaknesses and, conversely, their strengths.

Comparing Texts Possible Response: Steinbeck's statements are consistent. In the "Letter," he refers to "the aching urge of the writer to convey something he feels important to the reader." In the "Speech," he says the writer is charged with "dredging up to the light our dark and dangerous dreams for the purpose of improvement." He believes a writer must be sincere and passionate.

Connect to Life Praise from a mentor or a feeling of self-worth after completing a difficult task are other awards.

GUIDING STUDENT RESPONSE

Connect to the Literature

1. **What Do You Think?**
   Possible Response: Some students may be drawn to statements about the problems of modern life; others may appreciate Steinbeck's views about the timeless role of the writer.

Comprehension Check
- Steinbeck says it is customary to talk about the nature and direction of literature.
- He praises Faulkner because Faulkner, more than most men, recognized human strengths and weaknesses.
- He scorns writers who do not believe in the perfectibility of humanity.

Use Selection Quiz **Unit Five Resource Book,** p. 57 for additional support.

Think Critically

2. Ask students to verbalize how they knew where they needed to slow down in their reading and perhaps reread passages. Suggest that they point out any passages that are still unclear to them.
3. Possible Response: Although he acknowledges his pleasure in the recognition, he feels that the most important goal for a writer is to understand and improve humanity.
4. Possible Responses: Steinbeck might have advised beginning writers not to shut themselves off from society, but to stay involved with humanity, observing and learning from its failures and triumphs. Only by truly understanding people can a writer hope to be inspiring and effective.

Literary Analysis

Tone and Audience For example, in the "Letter," Steinbeck writes, "It is not so very hard to judge a story after it is written, but, after many years, to start a story still scares me to death." The first half of this sentence has a formal tone, while the last half is more informal and personal. In the "Speech," he writes, "Literature was not promulgated by a pale and emasculated priesthood singing their litanies in empty churches—nor is it a game for the cloistered elect, the tin-horn mendicants of low-calorie despair." This sentence has a very formal and elevated tone.

The Author's Style

Students will be made aware of Steinbeck's style through the "Key Aspects of Steinbeck's Style" chart and then find examples of the five points in the excerpts in the right margin.

Analysis of Style

Point out to students that these questions will help them analyze the characteristics of clearly written text; including patterns of organization, syntax, and word choice.

A First activity

Biblical rhythms and structures: "At last the mountains were full, and the hillsides spilled into the streams"

Repeated use of the word *and:* "The sheriffs swore in new deputies and ordered new rifles; and the comfortable people . . . felt pity at first, and then distaste, and finally hatred for the migrant people."

Figurative language: Personification: "At last the mountains were full, and the hillsides spilled into the streams"

Humor through irony: "The only way I can prove it would be to get a bear." Steinbeck is describing something so strange that people would not believe unless it happened to them. In "Letter to Edith Mirrielees," Steinbeck uses irony to demonstrate modesty about his writing.

Dialect: "nature gone nuts"

B Second activity

In "The Flood" from *The Grapes of Wrath,* the style is heightened and grand because Steinbeck imitates Biblical rhythms. In *Travels with Charley,* however, Steinbeck's style is much more informal and conversational.

C Third activity

There are many examples of the Key Aspects of Steinbeck's style throughout this unit. For example, in *Travels with Charley,* Steinbeck uses irony to describe how his peaceful dog became ferocious at the sight of a bear.

The Author's Style

Steinbeck's Stirring Descriptions

Although John Steinbeck was an experimenter, writing in different genres and expressing a range of moods, he was generally praised for his descriptive abilities.

Key Aspects of Steinbeck's Style

- use of biblical rhythms and structures that add an air of significance to events ("For two days the earth drank the rain, until the earth was full.")
- repeated use of the word *and* to emphasize the building up of events and of characters' emotions
- use of figurative language ("The earth whispered under the beat of the rain.")
- use of humor through irony
- use of dialect reflecting the speech of ordinary people

Analysis of Style

At the right are four excerpts from Steinbeck's work. Study the chart above, and then complete the following activities:

- **A** Identify examples of different aspects of Steinbeck's style.
- **B** Compare the style of Steinbeck's fiction with that of his nonfiction writings.
- **C** Review the selections in this Author Study to find other examples of these key aspects of Steinbeck's style.

Applications

1. Speaking and Listening With a partner, take turns reading aloud the passage from "The Flood" at the top right. One reader should place a stress on the content words; the other should read by placing stress only on the word *and.* After reading, compare the dramatic effects of these two interpretations.

2. Changing Style Discuss how differently a passage from the "Nobel Prize Acceptance Speech" might read if it had originally appeared as part of the "Letter to Edith Mirrielees." Rewrite a passage from the speech as if it were a passage in the letter.

3. Imitating Style In the style of "The Flood," write a page of description of a storm or any weather-related event you have witnessed. Use phrases that suggest the rhythmic flow of events.

***from* "The Flood"**

At last the mountains were full, and the hillsides spilled into the streams, built them to freshets, and sent them roaring down the canyons into the valleys.

***from* Travels with Charley**

We went on our way into the wonderland of nature gone nuts, and you will have to believe what happened. The only way I can prove it would be to get a bear.

***from* "Letter to Edith Mirrielees"**

Over the years I have written a great many stories and I still don't know how to go about it except to write it and take my chances.

***from* "The Flood"**

The sheriffs swore in new deputies and ordered new rifles; and the comfortable people in tight houses felt pity at first, and then distaste, and finally hatred for the migrant people.

Applications

1. **Speaking and Listening** Have students use the following criteria to critique oral interpretation. The student
   - makes and supports a valid interpretation of how the character might voice those lines
   - uses voice (volume and tone) to establish mood and convey meaning
   - uses movement and gestures to establish mood and convey meaning
   - uses facial expressions to establish mood and convey meaning
2. **Changing Style** Have students go through the entire writing process for this activity—prewriting, drafting, editing, and publishing.
3. **Imitating Style** Remind students to revisit the Key Aspects box on the page before beginning their paragraphs.

Choices & CHALLENGES

Writing Options

1. Letter in Response Put yourself in the place of Edith Mirrielees, having just received John Steinbeck's letter. Write back to him about any of the points he has made concerning literature. Assume that the timing of your response is after he has received the Nobel Prize for literature so that you can respond to his thoughts in that speech as well.

2. Newspaper Article Write an article for a literary newspaper reporting on Steinbeck's Nobel speech.

Activities & Explorations

1. Talk Show Skit Using this Author Study as a resource, prepare a skit about "prepping" a talk show host who has never read Steinbeck but is about to interview a biographer of the author. Provide the host with a set of questions that would convince the author that the host is fascinated with Steinbeck's life and works. Also supply the host with the likely responses he or she will receive from the guest. ~ **PERFORMING**

2. Making the Speech Perform Steinbeck's acceptance speech in front of a group. Look for words or phrases within the speech that suggest what emotions to express and what ideas to emphasize. Choose the appropriate nonverbal gestures as well. How does the experience of reading it aloud, or listening to it, differ from reading the words silently? ~ **SPEAKING AND LISTENING**

Inquiry & Research

Nobel Lists John Steinbeck was a much recognized writer, having won the Pulitzer Prize and the National Book Award as well as the Nobel Prize. Using this text and technical resources, find listings of the Nobel laureates, or honorees, for literature. Make your own list of laureates whose works you've read or would like to read.

Much of Steinbeck's work centers around the 50 or so miles that surround his birthplace in California—its fertile farmland, rolling hills, and wondrous sea life. In small groups, investigate these lands Steinbeck loved, discovering what works these lands inspired and what themes the author used the settings to emphasize. Your guided tour might take the form of a travel brochure, a slide show, an oral interpretation of descriptions of Steinbeck settings, or some combination of these. To get started, research the following topics.

Salinas Valley Steinbeck was born and raised in this section of northern California. Locate photographic essays about this area (one example is the book *Steinbeck Country* by Steve Crouch). Skim the stories of Steinbeck's *The Red Pony* to find descriptions of settings. These stories also provide details about the nature of farm life in the region.

Monterey Bay Long before environmental writing became a popular literary form, Steinbeck wrote about the wonders of sea life. Using the book *Sea of Cortez* as one source, find out about his study of the sea, centering on the Great Tide Pool, an area on the tip of the Monterey Peninsula. Discover how Steinbeck's study of the sea helped to shape his philosophy of life and his views about the human condition. You might also skim a copy of *Travels with Charley* to find Steinbeck's comments about Monterey.

More Online: Research Starter
www.mcdougallittell.com

Writing Options

1. **Letter in Response** Before students compose their letters, have them summarize the points that Steinbeck makes about literature. Then select those to which they would like to respond.
2. **Newspaper Article** Point out that a news report should include a summary of the speech that Steinbeck delivered as well as details of Steinbeck's personal history and professional background.

Activities & Explorations

1. **Talk Show Skit** Discuss examples of "open-ended" questions, which require extended explanations, as opposed to "closed" questions, which can be answered in a few words. Students could pair up to challenge each other to answer the questions they have prepared.
2. **Making the Speech** Remind students that the occasion for this speech was a formal one; thus, the speech should be delivered with a serious, somber tone. The speaker should have a podium and wear a suit jacket.

Inquiry & Research

Nobel Lists Students who do not often read on their own could be encouraged to try reading short stories by the authors they have listed.

Author Study Project

TOURING STEINBECK'S CALIFORNIA

The language of a travel brochure must be informative, but at the same time, appeal to the senses. You may want to bring travel brochures to class from a local travel agent so students can get an idea of the language used in them. Tell students that most writing for travel brochures is done as a team. If students intend to produce a travel brochure, suggest that they work in small groups.

SOURCES ON THE WORLD WIDE WEB
The Monterey Bay Aquarium is located on the site of Cannery Row, about which Steinbeck wrote. The marine life of the tidal pools described in *The Sea of Cortez* are on display here. Students can visit the Aquarium's Web site and print out the pictures it displays. Students can also check out California travel books from the library to obtain information on these places.

MULTIMEDIA PROJECT
Students can turn their research into a multimedia project by creating and videotaping an episode of a travel show. Students can work in small groups of six or seven, with one student acting as director, one as tour guide or host, one or more as writers, one as cameraperson, and one as locator of appropriate photographs.

Objectives
- write an Autobiographical Incident
- use a written text as a model for writing
- revise a draft to maintain consistency of tone
- use commas after introductory clauses and between independent clauses

Introducing the Workshop

A Autobiographical Incident An autobiographical incident is a different type of a narrative in that the story is about the writer's experience. In such accounts, people relate true experiences that reveal something important about themselves and their lives. People can often be seen sharing stories of their experiences on television programs and in magazines. Autobiographical stories are popular because they allow readers and viewers to share the exciting, dramatic, and meaningful moments in people's lives.

Ask students to name people whose autobiographical stories they have read or heard. Do the kinds of stories and incidents they've read or heard show any particular patterns? Point out that through writing an autobiographical incident, students will be able to share one of their own significant experiences with readers.

Basics in a Box

B Using the Graphic Like the divisions shown in the graphic, an autobiographical incident has a narrative structure with a beginning, middle, and end. As the graphic suggests, students can isolate these parts of their narrative and give special attention to the elements described therein.

C Presenting the Rubric To better understand the assignment, students can refer to the Standards for Writing a Successful Autobiographical Incident. You may wish to discuss with them the complete rubric, which describes several levels of proficiency.

Use McDougal Littell's ***Language Network,*** Chapter 18, for more instruction on writing an autobiographical narrative.

To engage students visually, use **Power Presentation** 10, Autobiographical Incident.

Writing Workshop

Autobiographical Incident

Describing a turning point. . .

A **From Reading to Writing** In "A White Heron," Sylvia is unable to betray the location of the heron to a hunter: "She cannot tell the heron's secret and give its life away." Just as such a turning point can reveal character in a story, similar incidents can reveal some aspect of your own attitude or personality. Writers include such **autobiographical incidents** in their memoirs and essays.

For Your Portfolio

WRITING PROMPT Write an essay describing a turning point or change in your life that was important to you.

Purpose: To share and explain
Audience: Family members and friends

Basics in a Box

B

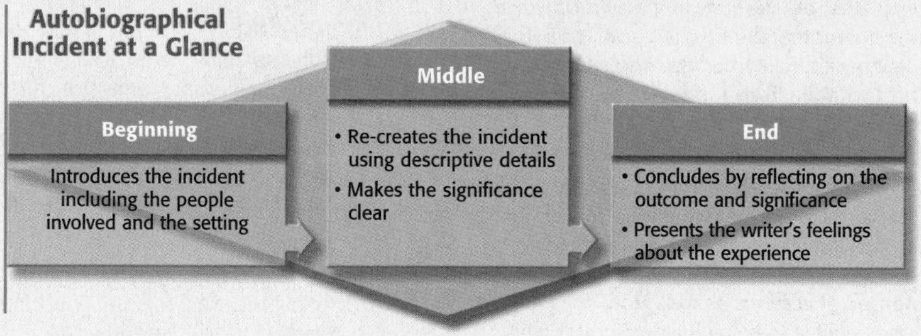

Autobiographical Incident at a Glance
Beginning
Introduces the incident including the people involved and the setting
Middle
• Re-creates the incident using descriptive details
• Makes the significance clear
End
• Concludes by reflecting on the outcome and significance
• Presents the writer's feelings about the experience

C **RUBRIC Standards for Writing**

A successful autobiographical incident should
- focus on a well-defined incident or series of related incidents
- provide background information for the incident
- use elements such as plot, character, and setting as appropriate
- make the order of events clear
- use description or dialogue as appropriate
- include precise language and specific details
- show why the experience was significant
- maintain a consistent tone and point of view

LESSON RESOURCES

USING PRINT RESOURCES

Unit Five Resource Book
- Prewriting, p. 58
- Drafting, p. 59
- Peer Response, pp. 60–61
- Revising, Editing, and Proofreading, p. 62
- Student Models, pp. 63–68
- Rubric, p. 69

Writing Transparencies and Copymasters
- Writing Process Transparencies, pp. 1–4
- Writing Template Copymasters, p. 34

USING MEDIA RESOURCES

LaserLinks
Writing Springboards
See Teacher's SourceBook p. 64 for bar codes.

Writing Coach CD-ROM

Visit our website:
www.mcdougallittell.com

Analyzing a Student Model

Bisco Hill
Southern Hills School

I Am Kwakkoli

A few months after my tenth birthday, my dad began to talk to me about receiving my Indian name. He said this had to be done in a ceremony by a medicine person or an elder in our tribe. My older sister, Megan, had received her Indian name, Maquegquay (Woman of the Woods), when she was only three. At that time my family lived on the Oneida Reservation just outside of Green Bay, Wisconsin.

My family moved from Wisconsin to Colorado three years before I was born. My grandfather died when I was only two and a half, and both of these major events delayed my Naming Ceremony. My dad talked about naming me for several years. Because of the sacred and traditional aspects of this, it is not like anyone can just call and order a Naming Ceremony, like ordering a pizza! As it happened, my Uncle Rick became the chairman of the tribe when I was ten, and he was able to talk to the right people and select the time. The right time was the summer solstice, near June 20, and it was also the time of the annual Strawberry Ceremony.

There are many traditions connected to the Naming Ceremony. For one thing, there are a limited number of names among the Oneida people. When a person dies, his or her name returns to the "pool" of available names and can be given to someone else. The medicine person decides whose energy fits which available name, or a person may ask for a certain name. In my case, I was named after my grandfather through my Anglo name, but I also wanted to take his Indian name. I felt that if I had both of his names, it made a full circle and I was wholly connected to him and to my family. The name that was his is "Kwakkoli," or "Whippoorwill" in English.

A few days before the ceremony in June of 1990, my parents and I flew to the Oneida Reservation. Oneida is very small and different from any other city I have known. My dad and his brother knew the names of everyone. They knew who was married to whom and who everyone's grandparents and parents were. They remembered all kinds of funny stories and laughed a lot. I thought it must be nice to live in a small town where everyone knows everyone for all those years. It is also a place where everyone is connected by common heritage, customs, and beliefs.

The night before the ceremony, I got very nervous. My stomach hurt as if I had the flu, but I think it was just butterflies. I finally fell asleep at about 3:30 in the morning. I don't know what I was afraid of—maybe just not knowing what was going to happen or what I would have to do.

RUBRIC IN ACTION

1. This writer begins by giving the background for the incident.
   Other Options:
   - Start with dialogue.
   - Begin with the incident itself.
2. Establishes the significance of the incident
3. Establishes the time and setting of the incident
4. Uses a transitional phrase to show the order of events

Teaching the Lesson

Analyzing the Model

"I Am Kwakkoli"

D The student model tells the story of how Kwakkoli attended the Naming Ceremony of the Oneida people and was granted the gift of his grandfather's name.

Explain that this event is immensely significant in the life of an Oneida boy, reflecting the deep layers of connection to self-identity and tribal heritage that are transmitted in the naming ritual.

Have students read the model, then discuss the Rubric in Action. Point out key words and phrases in the student model that correspond to the elements mentioned in the Rubric in Action.

1. Have students suggest an alternate opening based on the other options listed.
   Possible Response: The writer could open with a dialogue between the narrator and his father concerning the significance of the Naming Ceremony or the name itself.
2. Ask students what the boy's attitude toward his grandfather's names tells readers about the character of the boy.
   Possible Response: It shows that the boy holds deep respect for his elders and the tribal traditions of his people.
3. Point out how the narrative has suddenly shifted from background information to a specific focus on action that constitutes the climactic moments of the incident.
4. Ask students how the focus in the incident tightens at this point.
   Possible Responses: It establishes the specific, heightened moment of the event and leads us to expect that the action will grow more intense.

Mini Lesson Viewing and Representing

PICTURING TEXT STRUCTURE

Instruction An autobiographical incident has a temporal structure that involves movement through time. Events can be presented in chronological order, using transitional words, such as *first, then, next,* and *finally.* Within this structure, the incident builds toward a climax that usually is delivered near the end.

Activity Have students map the temporal structure of the student model by marking changes in time, including any "flashback" moments that move from the present to recall an earlier moment.

Bisco Hill's 10th birthday approaches → Flashback • family moves to Colorado • Bisco's grandfather dies → Naming ceremony planned when Bisco is ten → Night before naming ceremony → Naming ceremony

5. Ask students how this shift in tone heightens the narrative focus.
Possible Response: It serves to increase tension by bringing emotions to the surface.
6. Have students describe how the writer focuses this paragraph with specific details to create the feel of a "present moment."
Possible Response: The writer uses dialogue to create a feeling of the present and, in addition, describes the actions that surround the exchange of speech.
7. Have students compare the opening and closing paragraphs in the model.
Possible Response: The opening paragraph provides background information; the closing paragraph states the significance of the incident in the writer's life.

After getting about four hours of sleep, I woke up to the sound of a shower running. I quickly put on my ribbon shirt, a pair of black pants, and moccasins. The ceremony was set for 9:30 that morning, so we had to hurry.

On our short drive to the reservation, my stomach felt like it was going to explode! I had to at least get those butterflies flying in formation! I was pretty anxious but really excited about getting my Indian name. We arrived at the longhouse a little early, and I sat with my dad and one of his friends while other people finished setting up tables and chairs.

❺ Maintains an excited, hopeful tone

The ceremony finally began. The Faithkeeper called up the three clans of the Oneida Tribe: the Bear, the Turtle, and the Wolf. I am in the Turtle Clan, so I would be named in the second group. The Faithkeeper named all the children in the Bear Clan, then moved on to the Turtles. He named two people, then stepped in front of me. He spoke to me in Oneida. It is a language with unusual sounds like no other language I have ever heard. Most of the words were not understandable to me. He later translated them as, "You must try to learn the Oneida language and our ways. I would like you to come to some of the other ceremonies and events. You now have an Oneida name, 'Kwakkoli,' and the Creator will know you by that name." I was proud to have both of my grandfather's names because he was an important man in our tribe.

❻ This writer uses dialogue to illustrate the significance of the event.

Another Option:
- Describe actions that reveal significance.

The Faithkeeper named the others, and we all sat down as the Chief said a few more prayers. After about an hour, we all danced to Indian songs and drum music.

Next, we ate and drank. One of the drinks was a kind of strawberry juice. It is sacred and is part of the ceremony because the Creator gave this gift of the strawberry to the Oneida people. The drink was very good.

When it was time to go, we thanked the Faithkeeper and the Chief and gave them gifts. The gift that I received, and will be mine for life, is a very special name that runs through my family and connects me to my grandfather, whom I barely knew. My name also reminds me of the many traditions and beliefs that are part of my heritage and about which I have a lot to learn and understand. I look forward to visiting my reservation as I grow up.

❼ Emphasizes why the experience was meaningful

Writing Your Autobiographical Incident

❶ Prewriting

Begin by choosing the incident you will write about. You may choose to focus on something that happened to you, or you may decide to write about an event you witnessed but did not participate in.

You might make a list with three columns: *People, Places, Things*. Then list all the things that come to mind in each category that represent something important to you. You might also remember meaningful events in your past by using the phrase, "I remember when. . . ," then jotting down the thoughts that come to mind. See the **Idea Bank** in the margin for other suggestions. When you have chosen the event you want to write about, follow the steps below.

Planning Your Autobiographical Incident

1. **Test your topic.** Do you remember the incident well enough to write about it? Why is this memory important? Will you be comfortable sharing the memory? Will writing about it show what you learned from the event or what impact it had on you?
2. **Think about your purpose and audience.** How can you show readers how and why the incident affected you?
3. **Choose some of your building blocks.** What other people took part in the incident? Is the time or place important? What are some of the key events?

❷ Drafting

Get your memory down on paper. Don't worry about how it comes out. You can make improvements later. If you find yourself losing interest in the incident or have trouble telling it, choose another memory. As you draft, consider the following hints:

- Use some or all of the story elements—**plot, character,** and **setting.** Include any background information that the reader needs to know.
- Use **dialogue** when you can.
- Use language that appeals to the **senses.**
- **Organize** your incident. Usually **chronological order** is the clearest method of organization, but you might decide you can make a greater impact by starting in the middle of the incident. In that case, you can use a **flashback** to fill in all the missing parts.

After you finish your first draft, let it sit for a while. Then reread it. Ask your peer readers for reactions, too.

Ask Your Peer Reader

- Why do you think this experience was important to me?
- Which part of the incident is described most vividly?
- What parts are unnecessary or need more explanation?

IDEA Bank

1. Your Working Portfolio
Build on the **Writing Option** you completed earlier in this unit:
- **Autobiographical Tale**, p. 902

2. Life Map
To jog your memory, make a road map of your life. Start with your birth, and draw figures or symbols for important events. Choose one event to write about.

3. Special Days
Try recalling memorable things that happened on birthdays, holidays, or vacations. Make short notes about the events. Then write about one of them.

Need help with your autobiographical incident?

See the **Writing Handbook**
Narrative Writing, pp. 1155–1156

Guiding Student Writing

Prewriting

Choosing an Incident

If after reading the Idea Bank students are having difficulty choosing an incident, suggest they try the following:

- Make a list of humorous situations you've experienced. Ask others who shared the incident how they remembered it.
- Make a list of "firsts" that you've experienced, including the first time you accomplished something or the first time you realized you had a particular skill or quality.
- Browse through photographs or keepsakes of your past to jog your memory for interesting incidents. A souvenir, such as a shell or ticket stub, can often trigger a powerful memory.

Planning an Autobiographical Incident

1. As a way to explore the event's significance, have students freewrite about their feelings at the moment the event took place, and then have them freewrite about their feelings now as they look back on the event from a more distant perspective.
3. Have students create two lists to help them explore specific aspects of the event: a list of "Key People" who played a role in the incident; a list of "Key Moments or Scenes" involved in the incident.

Drafting

One approach to drafting a narrative incident is to first develop the dialogue independently of the narrative. Students should have participants speak to each other on paper without adding any other narrative information. Once students have written the dialogue, have them pull out specific passages that work effectively and incorporate them into the draft or use them as the foundation around which to build scenes.

When drafting an autobiographical incident, students will have to decide on an organizational plan for relating the incident. More experienced writers may want to incorporate a flashback. Encourage students to leave out details and events that stray away from the main incident. The details in this narrative should unfold in a way that leads to a climactic moment. Finally, the writer should conclude with a summary reflection on the event's significance.

WRITING WORKSHOP 951

Revising

MAINTAINING CONSISTENCY OF TONE

Have students begin the revision process by writing a sentence in which they state the tone they want to establish in their essay and the reason why. Then, with the idea for tone clearly in mind, instruct them to highlight words, phrases, or events in their autobiographical incident that are inconsistent. You may also encourage students to reread their drafts aloud in order to better hear the tone their language creates and to better hear the "glitches" where their tone is off.

Editing and Proofreading

PUNCTUATING CLAUSES

Remind students that two independent clauses can be joined by a comma and a coordinating conjunction—*and, but, so, or, for, nor, yet.*

One kind of common error involves leaving the comma out of the sentence. Another kind of comma error involves putting the comma after the coordinating conjunction instead of before. Show students the correct way to punctuate a compound sentence by placing the comma before the coordinating conjunction.

Correct: John likes picnics, but Susan prefers movies.

Incorrect: Sarah enjoys fishing and Bill likes hiking.

Incorrect: David wants sunshine so, Mary hopes for rain.

Encourage students to revise, edit, and proofread carefully to produce error-free writing in the final draft.

Reflecting

Ask students to take stock of their self-awareness as a result of writing this essay. In what ways do they feel the essay led them to greater self-awareness? Do they feel they know themselves better now than before? In what respects? Did writing the essay put them in touch with a part of themselves they'd forgotten? Have students add these self-evaluations to their working portfolios.

Need revising help?

Review the **Rubric**, p. 948

Consider **peer reader** comments

Check **Revision Guidelines**, p. 1145

Puzzled by punctuating clauses?

See the **Grammar Handbook**

Independent and Subordinate Clauses p. 1197

Publishing IDEAS

- Gather a group of classmates and read your works aloud to each other.
- Read your work to your family. Ask whether they remember the events the same way as you wrote about them.

More Online: Publishing Options
www.mcdougallittell.com

❸ Revising

I can't write five words but that I change seven.

Dorothy Parker, writer and humorist

TARGET SKILL ▶ MAINTAINING CONSISTENCY OF TONE Your autobiographical incident will have more impact if the tone is the same throughout. A humorous piece that unintentionally turns serious or a serious piece that suddenly becomes sarcastic will likely confuse the reader.

will be mine for life,
The gift that I received, and ~~I'll have to live with forever~~
is a very special
~~whether I want to or not, is (get this!) Kwakkoli~~ a name
runs through *and connects me to*
that my family ~~is stuck with. It's from~~ my grandfather,
whom I barely knew.

❹ Editing and Proofreading

TARGET SKILL ▶ PUNCTUATING CLAUSES Your incident will have more impact if you vary the sentences you use to tell about it. To avoid too many short, choppy sentences, writers combine ideas into one sentence with two or more clauses. Using commas after introductory clauses and between independent clauses helps to make the meaning clear.

a
As it happened, my uncle Rick became the chairmen of
and
the tribe when I was ten, He was able to talk to the right
people and select the time.

❺ Reflecting

FOR YOUR WORKING PORTFOLIO What did you remember about your life that you had forgotten? What details became clearer as you wrote? How important does this incident seem now? Attach your reflections to your finished essay. Save your autobiographical incident in your **Working Portfolio.**

Assessment Practice Revising & Editing

Read this paragraph from the first draft of an autobiographical essay. The underlined sections may include the following kinds of errors:

- **double negatives**
- **comma errors**
- **run-on sentences**
- **incorrect verb tenses**

For each underlined section, choose the revision that most improves the writing.

When I was ten years old, my family and I were on a cruise ship that sank. Even at the start of our voyage, there is trouble (1). As we set out to sea fuel oil (2) in the cargo hold caught fire. By the time we were miles from shore, the lower decks of the ship were burning no one could put the fire out (3). We couldn't hardly believe (4) what was happening. The captain radioed for help, and we all got into (5) the lifeboats and rowed away from the burning ship. A few hours later, a Greek freighter rescued us. From the deck of the freighter, we watch (6) our ship sink into the ocean. What an experience that was!

1. **A.** there has been trouble
B. there may be trouble
C. there was trouble
D. Correct as is

2. **A.** As we set out to sea fuel, oil
B. As we set out to sea, fuel oil
C. As we set out, to sea fuel oil
D. Correct as is

3. **A.** the lower decks of the ship were burning. No one could put the fire out.
B. the lower decks of the ship were burning and couldn't put the fire out.
C. the lower decks of the ship were burning, which no one could put out.
D. Correct as is

4. **A.** couldn't scarcely
B. could hardly
C. couldn't barely
D. Correct as is

5. **A.** radioed for help and we all got into
B. radioed for help: and we all got into
C. radioed for help and we, all, got into
D. Correct as is

6. **A.** are watching
B. have watched
C. watched
D. Correct as is

Need extra help?

See the **Grammar Handbook**

Correcting Run-on Sentences, p. 1199

Punctuation Chart, pp. 1203–1204

Subject-Verb Agreement, p. 1200

Assessment Practice

Answers:
1. C; **2.** B; **3.** A; **4.** B; **5.** D; **6.** C

Objectives
- reflect on and assess student understanding of the unit
- compare text events with experiences of students and other readers
- provide examples of themes that cross texts
- compare across texts elements of texts such as conflicts and characterization
- assess and build portfolios

Reflecting on Theme

OPTION 1

A successful response will
- select four selections from Unit 5 in which truths are discovered or communicated.
- write a brief explanation of each of these truths.
- explain which of the truths is most relevant to the student's life, and why.

OPTION 2

A successful response will
- select characters from Unit 5 who would have the most sympathy for a student who was fooled by appearances.
- select characters from Unit 5 with the greatest understanding of human gullibility and weakness.
- explain choices, based on the understanding that "sympathy" and "understanding" are different, if sometimes overlapping, qualities.

OPTION 3

A successful response will
- select a character from Unit 5 who would make a desirable guide on a journey to find truth.
- select a character from Unit 5 who would make an undesirable guide on a journey to find truth.
- explain in writing each choice, using specific examples from the unit selections.

Self Assessment
Ask students what aspects of truth were most important to them before they read the selections in this unit: honesty? loyalty? fairness? Then ask them how the selections in this unit have affected their appreciation of truth. Has a new aspect of it achieved greater importance? Is truth more important to students than it was before?

Discovering the Truth

How have your feelings or views about truth been affected by the selections in this unit? How would you rate your development as a reader and a writer during your work on the unit? Explore these questions by completing one or more of the options in each of the following sections.

Sea Jewels (1995), Paul Niemiec, Jr. Watercolor, 18″ × 28″. Collection of Mr. and Mrs. Stephen H. Palmer.

Reflecting on Theme

OPTION 1

Truths to Live By Review the activity on page 818, which asked you to describe your own discovery of truth. Then choose four selections from this unit in which truths are discovered or communicated to the reader. For each selection, write a brief explanation of the truth that is conveyed. Finally, answer the following question in writing: Which of these truths do you think is most relevant to your own life?

OPTION 2

Deceptive Appearances On page 867, you were asked to describe a time when you were fooled by appearances. Which of the characters or writers in this unit do you think would have the most sympathy for what you experienced? Which characters or writers seem to have the greatest understanding of human gullibility and weakness? Explain your choices in writing, keeping in mind that "sympathy" and "understanding" are two different qualities.

OPTION 3

Choosing Guides to Truth Many classic works of literature feature characters who embark on great journeys to find truth. Often the main character is guided by a person who serves as both guide and mentor. If you were to embark on such a journey, which character or writer from this unit would you most want as a guide? Who do you think would be the least trustworthy or desirable as guide? Explain your choices in writing.

Self ASSESSMENT

READER'S NOTEBOOK

Create a tree diagram to show the different meanings that truth has for you. On each major branch, write a word or phrase that conveys one aspect of truth, such as *honesty* or *loyalty.* On the smaller branches, list titles of selections that relate to the word or phrase on the major branch, as well as your own elaboration of its meaning.

Reviewing Literary Concepts

OPTION 1

Understanding Imagery Some images depend upon the literal meanings of words, presenting the evidence of the senses directly. Others rely on figurative language, requiring readers to use their imagination. Create a chart like the one shown. Find at least seven striking images in the unit selections, and place each in the appropriate category. Compare your chart with those of your classmates.

Selection	Literal Image	Figurative Image
"Birches"	"When I see birches bend to left and right Across the lines of straighter darker trees"	"Such heaps of broken glass to sweep away You'd think the inner dome of heaven had fallen."

OPTION 2

Defining Modern Poetry Review the information about modern poetry on page 906. Then work with a partner to make your own extended definition of modern poetry. Which poems in this unit best illustrate your definition? Are there any poems that your definition doesn't seem to fit? Present the results of your work in a brief oral report.

Self ASSESSMENT

READER'S NOTEBOOK

The following literary terms were presented in this unit. Create categories for the terms, putting similar ones together. For example, one category might be "Sound Effects." The terms can be categorized in a number of ways; you just need to explain your reasoning. If there are terms you do not understand, refer to the **Glossary of Literary Terms** (page 1124). Compare your categories with those of classmates.

symbol
point of view
figurative language
alliteration
assonance
consonance
extended metaphor
personification
humor
realism
dialogue
tone
modern poetry
social criticism
author's purpose
comic irony
word choice
tone and audience

Building Your Portfolio

- **Writing Options** A number of the Writing Options in this unit asked you to write essays in response to the selections. Look over your work for these assignments and pick two pieces that you think show the most insight into the literature. Write a note explaining your choices, then add the pieces and the note to your **Presentation Portfolio.**
- **Writing Workshops** In this unit, you wrote an Interpretive Essay (based on your response to a literary work) and an Autobiographical Incident. Reread these pieces and judge their use of details and elaboration. Would you like to keep one or both of these compositions? If so, attach a note indicating how well you made use of details. Place the piece or pieces in your **Presentation Portfolio.**
- **Additional Activities** Think about any of the assignments you completed under **Activities & Explorations** and **Inquiry & Research**. Which of these assignments helped you to make a new discovery about your skills, abilities, or interests? Keep a record in your portfolio of any assignment that brought out hidden talents or interests.

Self ASSESSMENT

Presentation Portfolio

Compare the recent additions to your portfolio with pieces that you included earlier in the year. How satisfied are you with your progress? Write an evaluation of your development as a writer and reader up to this point in the year.

Setting GOALS

Make a list of things that you would like to change about yourself as a reader and writer. Circle the changes that seem achievable by the end of the year. Use the circled items as goals for your work.

Reviewing Literary Concepts

OPTION 1

Use the Unit 5 Resource Book, page 70, to provide students a ready-made, full-depth chart for recording their images.

OPTION 2

A successful response will
- create an extended definition of modern poetry.
- list those poems from Unit 5 that best illustrate this definition.
- list those poems from Unit 5 that the definition does not fit.
- give a brief oral report that provides the definition, lists the poems that best illustrate the definition, and lists the poems that the definition does not fit.

Building Your Portfolio

Students will use their Presentation Portfolios to file what they consider their highest quality work—the very best in their Working Portfolios.

For more information on using writing and assessing portfolios, see the *Teacher's Guide to Assessment and Portfolio Use,* p. 53.

REFLECT AND ASSESS 955

The *Electronic Library* is a CD-ROM that contains additional fiction, nonfiction, poetry, and drama for each unit in *The Language of Literature.*

These are the additional selections found in Unit 5 of the *Electronic Library.*

Selma Lagerlöf
The Rat Trap

E. T. A. Hoffman
The Sandman

Junichiro Tanizaki
The Thief

Moliére
Tartuffe

Anatole France
Putois

Nathaniel Hawthorne
The Birthmark

Elizabeth Jolley
Mr. Parker's Valentine

Jesus del Corral
Cross Over, Sawyer!

Encourage students to select one of the books as an opportunity to read silently with comprehension over a period of time.

UNIT FIVE Extend Your *Reading*

LITERATURE CONNECTIONS

Great Expectations

CHARLES DICKENS

Set in 19th-century England, this novel depicts the rags-to-riches story of the orphan Pip. After his contact with a wealthy eccentric, Pip dreams of becoming a gentleman. One day he learns that a secret patron has arranged for this to happen. Pip moves to London to fulfill his "great expectations," where he will learn eventually the true measures of nobility and love.

These thematically related readings are provided along with *Great Expectations*:

The Duke's Children
FRANK O'CONNOR

***from* Silent Dancing**
JUDITH ORTIZ COFER

You Are a Part of Me
FRANK YERBY

Time Does Not Bring Relief
EDNA ST. VINCENT MILLAY

The Peasant Marey
FYODOR DOSTOEVSKY

The Spinster's Day/ Jornada de la Soltera
ROSARIO CASTELLANOS
TRANSLATED BY MAGDA BOGIN

The Jilting of Granny Weatherall
KATHERINE ANNE PORTER

The House on the Hill
EDWARD ARLINGTON ROBINSON

And Even *More* . . .

The Chocolate War

ROBERT CORMIER

Freshman Jerry Renault is trying to make his way at Trinity High. Jerry finds himself in a struggle between two leaders on an unlikely battlefield—the school's annual chocolate sale. When Jerry dares to disturb the order of things, the consequences are shocking. This book is also part of the *Literature Connections* series published by McDougal Littell.

Books

Siddhartha
HERMANN HESSE
A restless young man searches for a truth that will guide him through life.

A Raisin in the Sun
LORRAINE HANSBERRY
An African-American family pursuing the American dream of their own home encounters racism and obstacles of their own making. This book is also part of the *Literature Connections* series published by McDougal Littell.

LITERATURE CONNECTIONS

A Place Where the Sea Remembers

SANDRA BENÍTEZ

This best-selling novel, published in 1993, is set in Santiago, Mexico, and consists of short interrelated narratives, each one focused on a single character. Benítez's work depicts the triumphs and tragedies of common people—a flower seller, a healer, a fisherman, a teacher, a midwife—whose lives are interwoven by fate and passion. The characters struggle to survive and prevail in a difficult and mysterious world, one that is edged by the rhythms, power, and beauty of the sea.

These thematically related readings are provided along with *A Place Where the Sea Remembers*:

Night
LOUISE BOGAN

All day I hear the noise of waters
JAMES JOYCE

Talking to the Dead
JUDITH ORTIZ COFER

Paciencia
JUDITH ORTIZ COFER

Death of a Young Son by Drowning
MARGARET ATWOOD

Sophistication
SHERWOOD ANDERSON

An Astrologer's Day
R. K. NARAYAN

The Seekers
DANIEL J. BOORSTIN
A famous historian offers a sweeping account of humanity's search for truth, ranging from prophets such as Moses to modern scientists such as Einstein.

Of Mice and Men
JOHN STEINBECK
The tragic story of two ranch hands, George and Lennie, who dream of one day owning a place of their own.

Other Media

The Grapes of Wrath
John Ford's classic 1940 movie based on John Steinbeck's novel about the lives of migrant workers in the Depression. Filmic Archives.
(VIDEOCASSETTE)

Of Mice and Men
A 1992 film adaptation of Steinbeck's novel, starring John Malkovich and Gary Sinise. Filmic Archives.
(VIDEOCASSETTE)

Robert Frost
A biographical sketch of the famous poet, with a dramatic reading of "Mending Wall" by Leonard Nimoy. Part of the *Poetry by Americans* series. Filmic Archives.
(VIDEOCASSETTE)

Emily Dickinson
A look into the life and work of the mysterious and complex Emily Dickinson. Part of the *American Poets: Voices and Visions* series.
(VIDEOCASSETTE)

EXTEND YOUR READING 957

The Making of Heroes

In Unit Six, students will encounter many kinds of heroes from ancient and contemporary times. This unit has two parts: Part 1, "Unsung Heroes," and Part 2, "The Heroic Tradition." Selections in both parts contribute to the unit theme by examining the qualities and circumstances that make people heroes.

Part 1

Unsung Heroes Selections in Part 1 emphasize the mostly unrecognized, but heroic qualities within everyday human beings. For example, in "The Man in the Water," an ordinary man gives up his chance of surviving a plane crash to help other victims to safety.

Part 2

The Heroic Tradition Part 2 includes classic works that feature larger-than-life heroes. For example, in "Sir Launcelot du Lake" from *Le Morte d'Arthur,* a knight wins a victory over his enemies by using his superior strength and intelligence.

UNIT SIX

Detail of *Arming and Departure of the Knights* (1895–1896), Sir Edward Coley Burne-Jones. From the *Holy Grail Tapestry Series.* Birmingham City Council Museums and Art Gallery, England.

958

Mini Lesson Viewing and Representing

detail of *Arming and Departure of the Knights*
by Sir Edward Coley Burne-Jones

ART APPRECIATION

Instruction English artist Sir Edward Burne-Jones (1833–1898) is famous for his paintings of medieval lore. He also designed tapestry, and an example is reproduced here. *Arming and Departure of the Knights* is one of six panels he envisioned for a wool-and-silk tapestry depicting knights preparing for a Grail Quest, the seeking out of the Holy Grail. According to legend, the Grail is a magical cup or dish, supposedly used by Christ at The Last Supper, that was said in the Middle Ages to reside somewhere in Britain. It was eagerly sought by King Arthur's knights.

Ask: What elements of contrast and of sameness do you find in the tapestry?

Possible Response: Contrast is achieved by showing the heroic knights in darker battle gear and the female attendants in pastel, flowing

THE MAKING OF
HEROES

THE HERO IN ONE AGE WILL BE A HERO IN ANOTHER.

CHARLOTTE LENNOX

Making Connections

To help students explore the connections between the art, the quotation, and the unit theme, have them consider the following questions:

Ask: **Why do you think heroism has been such a popular theme of literature through the ages?**
Possible Response: Some students might say many people would like to think of themselves as being capable of heroic acts if necessary. Others might say stories about heroism are exciting and full of adventure.

Ask: **How would you paraphrase Lennox's statement about heroes?**
Possible Responses: Some may say a true hero will transcend the passage of time and retain his or her heroic status; others might say that the qualities that make people heroes are enduring and will always be important, admired qualities in a person.

Ask: **How do the quotation and painting work together on the subject of heroes?**
Possible Responses: The quotation claims that the heroes of the past remain heroes in the present, and the painting's subject is of knights of the middle ages—figures that have retained their heroic image into present times.

Ask: **What kinds of stories and experiences might you expect to read about in his unit?**
Possible Responses: adventure stories; stories with brave characters in dangerous situations; stories about people who, in one way or another, stand out as heroes.

Have you ever had a particular experience that has helped you understand the meaning of heroism?
Responses will vary.

robes. Sameness comes from the expressions and pleasing physical features of the men and of the women, emphasizing the romance of the legend.

UNIT SIX
PART 1 SKILLS TRACE

Features and Selections	Literary Analysis	Reading and Critical Thinking	Writing Opportunities
The Making of Heroes **Unsung Heroes**			
Learning the Language of Literature: Style	Style, 961		
The Active Reader: Skills and Strategies		Strategies for Clarifying	
SHORT STORY A Chip of Glass Ruby **Difficulty Level:** ***Average***	Dialogue, 964, 974	Clarifying, 964, 974 Informal Assess., 972	Interpretive Essay, 975 Diary of a Daughter, 975 Title Analysis, 975 Stage Scene, 975
ESSAY The Man in the Water **Difficulty Level:** ***Average***	Tone, 977, 981	Summarizing, 977, 981 Test Practice, 980	Hero's Tribute, 982
SHORT STORY And of Clay Are We Created **Difficulty Level:** ***Challenging***	Style, 983, 995 Review: Dialogue, 995	Clarifying, 983, 995 Informal Assess., 996	Television Commentary, 996 Love Letter, 996
Real World Link: Girl Trapped in Water for 55 Hours Dies Despite Rescue Attempts **Building Vocabulary**		News Article: Comparing Factual and Fictional Versions, 998 Comparing and Contrasting, 999	
Communication Workshop: **Multimedia Presentation** **Assessment Practice**		Analyzing a Multimedia Presentation, 1009	Multimedia Presentation, 1008

UNIT SIX
PART 2 SKILLS TRACE

Features and Selections	Literary Analysis	Reading and Critical Thinking	Writing Opportunities
The Heroic Tradition			
Learning the Language of Literature: Myths and Legends	Myths and Legends, 1015		
The Active Reader Skills and Strategies		Strategies for Reading Myths and Legends, 1017	

LEGEND **DLS – Daily Language SkillBuilder**
CCL – Cross Curricular Link
Green type – Teacher's Edition

Speaking and Listening Viewing and Representing	Inquiry and Research	Grammar, Usage, and Mechanics	Vocabulary
Art Appreciation, 958			
Interior Illustration, 975 Interview with an Activist, 975 Art Appreciation, 967, 971	The Fight Against Apartheid, 975	Compound-Complex Sentences, 976 DLS, 964 Compound-Complex Sentences, 976 Identifying Inverted Subjects, 970	Using Context Clues, 965
Television Report, 982 Viewing and Representing, 978	Plane Crashes, 982	DLS, 977	Preteaching Vocabulary, 979
Azucena's Eulogy, 996 Volcanic Poster, 996 In Swirling Water, 996 Telephone Conversation, 988 Art Appreciation, 994	Inquiry & Research, 996	Using Parallel Structures, 997 DLS, 983 Parallel Structure, 992 Parallel Structure, 997	Identifying Synonyms, 984 Using Reference Materials, 990
	Activity Link: "And of Clay Are We Created," 999 Inquiry & Research, 999		Context Clues, 1000
		Varying Your Material/ Consistent Form, 1012 Revising and Editing, 1013	

PART 2 SKILLS TRACE

Features and Selections	Literary Analysis	Reading and Critical Thinking	Writing Opportunities
DRAMA Antigone **Difficulty Level:** ***Challenging***	Classical Drama, 1019, 1061 Review: Dramatic Irony, 1061	Strategies for Reading Classical Drama, 1019, 1061 Test Practice, 1040, 1046 Informal Assess., 1060	Letter to a Character, 1062 Diary Entry, 1062 Report on Athenian Women, 1062
ROMANCE The Crowning of Arthur Sir Launcelot du Lake **Difficulty Level:** ***Challenging***	Romance, 1064, 1080	Making Judgments, 1064, 1080 Review: Summarizing, 1080 Informal Assess., 1068 Test Practice, 1079	Day-in-the-Life Article, 1081 Editorial About Chivalry, 1081 Arthurian Guidebook, 1081
The Mists of Avalon **Difficulty Level:** ***Average***	First-Person Point of View, 1083, 1086	Analyzing Characters, 1083, 1086 Comparing and Contrasting, 1086 Test Practice, 1084	Another View, 1087
ROMANCE **Real World Link:** The Once and Future Merlin		Magazine Article: Summarizing, 1088	
ROMANCE *from* The Acts of King Arthur and His Noble Knights **Difficulty Level:** ***Average*** **Building Vocabulary**	Style, 1090, 1099	Making Inferences, 1090, 1099 Test Practice, 1098	Castle News, 1100 Lancelot Interview, 1100 Arthurian Soap-Opera, 1100
Writing Workshop: **Research Report** **Assessment Practice**		Analyzing a Student Model, 1106	Research Report, 1105
Reflect and Assess: The Making of Heroes	Reviewing Literary Concepts, 1115	The Invention of a Hero, 1114	Assessing Heroism, 1114 Portfolio Building, 1115

LEGEND **DLS – Daily Language SkillBuilder**
CCL – Cross Curricular Link
Green type – Teacher's Edition

Speaking and Listening Viewing and Representing	Inquiry and Research	Grammar, Usage, and Mechanics	Vocabulary
Readers Theater, 1062 Tragedy Mask, 1062 Antigone on Film, 1062 Viewing and Representing, 1019, 1032, 1034, 1036, 1048 Dramatic Scene, 1038 Art Appreciation, 1041 Press Conference, 1044 Debate, 1050	Comparing Translations, 1062	Inverted Sentences, 1063 DLS, 1018 Direct and Indirect Objects, 1030 Inverted Sentences, 1062	Using Context Clues, 1020 Word Origins, 1054
Arthur in the Movies, 1081 Knightly Images, 1081 Movie Commercial, 1081 Art Connection, 1081 Art Appreciation, 1066, 1070, 1072, 1076 Dramatic Reading, 1069 Speech, 1074 Analyze a Film Review, 1081	Medieval Tournaments, 1081	Creating Subject-Verb Splits. 1082 DLS, 1064 Subject-Verb Split, 1082	Assessment Practice, 1081 Using Context Clues, 1065 Applying Meanings of Roots, 1073
Igraine's Monologue, 1087 Comic Strip, 1087	Mysterious Wizard, 1087	DLS, 1083 Objective Complements, 1087	
Class Chart, 1089	Activity Link: *from* The Mists of Avalon, 1089 Inquiry & Research, 1089		
Dramatized Interview, 1100 Walk the Walk, 1100 Art Appreciation, 1095	Medieval Castles, 1100	Making Compound Predicates Parallel, 1101 DLS, 1090 Making Compound Predicates Parallel, 1100	Context Clues, 1100 Using Context Clues, 1092 Prefixes, 1094 Developing a Stronger Vocabulary, 1102
		Elaborating with Facts and Statistics/ Parallelism, 1112 Revising and Editing, 1113	
"The Hero in One Age. . . ." 1114			

RESOURCE MANAGEMENT GUIDE PART 1

To introduce the theme/literary period of this unit, use Fine Art Transparencies T32–34 in the Communications Transparencies and Copymasters.

	Unit Resource Book	Assessment	Integrated Technology and Media	Additional Support: Literary Analysis Transparencies
A Chip of Glass Ruby *pp. 964–976*	• Summary p. 4 • Active Reading p. 5 • Literary Analysis p. 6 • Words to Know p. 7 • Grammar p. 8 • Selection Quiz p. 9	• Selection Test, Formal Assessment pp. 159–160 Test Generator	Audio Library LaserLinks, Teacher's SourceBook p. 50 Research Starter www.mcdougallittell.com	• Drama: Dialogue T10
The Man in the Water *pp. 977–982*	• Summary p. 10 • Active Reading p. 11 • Literary Analysis p. 12 • Words to Know p. 13 • Selection Quiz p. 14	• Selection Test, Formal Assessment pp. 161–162 Test Generator	Audio Library LaserLinks, Teacher's SourceBook p. 51	• Mood and Tone T20
And of Clay Are We Created *pp. 983–997*	• Summary p. 15 • Active Reading p. 16 • Literary Analysis p. 17 • Words to Know p. 18 • Grammar p. 19 • Selection Quiz p. 20	• Selection Test, Formal Assessment pp. 163–164 Test Generator	Audio Library LaserLinks, Teacher's SourceBook p. 52	• Style, Voice, Diction, Purpose T22

Communication Workshop: Multimedia Presentation

Unit Six Resource Book
- Planning Your Presentation p. 20
- Developing, Planning, and Presenting p. 23
- Peer Response Guide pp. 24–25
- Revising, Editing, and Proofreading p. 26
- Standards for Evaluation p. 27

Unit Assessment
- Unit Six, Part 1 Test, Formal Assessment pp. 165–166

Test Generator
- Unit Six Integrated Test, Integrated Assessment pp. 31–36

Unit Technology

ClassZone www.mcdougallittell.com

Electronic Teacher Tools

Electronic Library

T = Transparency C = Copymaster

Reading and Critical Thinking Transparencies	Grammar Transparencies and Copymasters	Vocabulary Transparencies and Copymasters	Writing Transparencies and Copymasters	Communications Transparencies and Copymasters
• Locating Information Using Print References T32 • Organizational Chart: Horizontal T51	• Daily Language SkillBuilder T27 • Identifying Subjects in Inverted Sentences C90 • Compound-Complex Sentences C125	• Context Clues C86	• Extending Sentences T19 • The Uses of Dialogue T24 • Interpretive Essay C33	• Interviewing T9 • Formal Presentations T10
• Paraphrasing and Summarizing T41	• Daily Language SkillBuilder T27	• Context Clues C87	• Effective Language T13 • Showing, Not Telling T22	• Impromptu Speaking: Dialogue, Role-Play, Debate T13
• Organizational Chart: Horizontal T51	• Daily Language SkillBuilder T27 • Dependent Clauses: Parallelism C178 • Parallel Structures C179	• Synonyms C88 • Using Reference Materials C89	• Effective Language T13 • Sensory Word List T14	• Impromptu Speaking: Dialogue, Role-Play, Debate T13 • Verbal Strategies T14

STUDENTS ACQUIRING ENGLISH

The **Spanish Study Guide,** pp. 199–210, includes language support for the following pages:

- Family and Community Involvement (per unit)
- Selection Summaries and Vocabulary
- Active Reading
- Literary Analysis

UNIT SIX
RESOURCE MANAGEMENT GUIDE
PART 2

To introduce the theme/literary period of this unit, use Fine Art Transparencies T32–34 in the Communications Transparencies and Copymasters.

	Unit Resource Book	Assessment	Integrated Technology and Media	*Additional Support* Literary Analysis Transparencies
Antigone *pp. 1018–1063*	• Summary p. 28 • Active Reading p. 29 • Literary Analysis p. 30 • Words to Know p. 31 • Grammar p. 32 • Selection Quiz p. 33	• Selection Test, Formal Assessment pp. 167–168 Test Generator	Audio Library LaserLinks, Teacher's SourceBook pp. 54–55 Video: Literature in Performance, Video Resource Book pp. 35-42	• Myths and Legends I T23 • Myths and Legends II T24
from **Le Morte d'Arthur** *pp. 1064–1082*	• Summary p. 34 • Active Reading p. 35 • Literary Analysis p. 36 • Words to Know p. 37 • Grammar p. 38 • Selection Quiz p. 39	• Selection Test, Formal Assessment pp. 169–170 Test Generator	Audio Library LaserLinks, Teacher's SourceBook p. 56 Research Starter www.mcdougallittell.com	
from **The Mists of Avalon** *pp. 1083–1087*	• Summary p. 40 • Active Reading p. 41 • Literary Analysis p. 42 • Selection Quiz p. 43	• Selection Test, Formal Assessment pp. 171–172 Test Generator	Audio Library	• Point of View T17
from **The Acts of King Arthur and His Noble Knights** *pp. 1090–1101*	• Summary p. 44 • Active Reading p. 45 • Literary Analysis p. 46 • Words to Know p. 47 • Grammar p. 48 • Selection Quiz p. 49	• Selection Test, Formal Assessment pp. 173–174 Test Generator	Audio Library LaserLinks, Teacher's SourceBook pp. 57–59	• Style, Voice, Diction, Purpose T22

Writing Workshop: Research Report		*Unit Assessment*	*Unit Technology*
Unit Six Resource Book • Prewriting p. 51 • Drafting and Elaboration p. 52 • Peer Response Guide pp. 53–54 • Revising, Editing, and Proofreading p. 55 • Student Models pp. 56–61 • Rubric for Evaluation p. 62	**Writing Coach** **Writing Transparencies and Copymasters** T11, T20, C35 **Teacher's Guide to Assessment and Portfolio Use**	• Unit Six, Part 2 Test, Formal Assessment pp. 175–176 • End-of-Year Test, Formal Assessment pp. 177–188 Test Generator • Unit Six Integrated Test, Integrated Assessment pp. 31–36 • End-of-Year Integrated Assessment pp. 37–60	ClassZone www.mcdougallittell.com Electronic Teacher Tools Electronic Library

	Reading and Critical Thinking Transparencies	Grammar Transparencies and Copymasters	Vocabulary Transparencies and Copymasters	Writing Transparencies and Copymasters	Communications Transparencies and Copymasters
	• Visualizing T8 • Reading for Details T16	• Daily Language SkillBuilder T28 • Direct and Indirect Objects C91 • Inverted Sentences C146	• Context Clues C90 • Word Origins C91, C92	• Writing Structure T5-8, T11 • Research Report T35	• Dramatic Reading T12 • Evaluation Matrix: Film/Video T7
	• Making Judgments T5 • Summarizing T10 • Organizational Chart: Horizontal T51	• Daily Language SkillBuilder T28 • Subject-Verb Split C140	• Context Clues C93 • Word Origins C94	• Writing Structure T6, T8-10 • Effective Language T13	• Evaluation Matrix: Commercial T6 • Evaluation Matrix: Film/Video T7
	• Cluster Diagram T48	• Daily Language SkillBuilder T28 • Objective Complements C92		• Showing, Not Telling T22 • Point of View T23	• Impromptu Speaking: Dialogue, Role-Play, Debate T13 • Giving and Using Feedback to Improve Performance T16
	• Making Inferences T7	• Daily Language SkillBuilder T29 • Making Compound Predicates Parallel I C88 • Making Compound Predicates Parallel II C89	• Context Clues C95 • Prefixes C96	• Levels of Language T12 • The Uses of Dialogue T24	• Interviewing T9 • Impromptu Speaking: Dialogue, Role-Play, Debate T13

STUDENTS ACQUIRING ENGLISH

The **Spanish Study Guide,** pp. 211-220, includes language support for the following pages:

- Family and Community Involvement (per unit)
- Selection Summaries and Vocabulary
- Active Reading
- Literary Analysis

Selection	SkillBuilder Sentences	Suggested Answers
A Chip of Glass Ruby	**1.** Martin Luther King Jr who struggle against racism and segregation was influenced by Indian leader Mohandas Gandhi	**1.** Martin Luther King, Jr., who struggl**ed** against racism and segregation, was influenced by Indian leader Mohandas Gandhi.
	2. Gandhi who believed that injustice could be overcome thru nonviolent protest was in turn influenced by Henry David Thoreau the American who wrote the essay civil disobedience.	**2.** Gandhi, who believed that injustice could be overcome **through** nonviolent protest, was in turn influenced by Henry David Thoreau, the American who wrote the essay "**C**ivil **D**isobedience."
The Man in the Water	**1.** My oldest brothers guitar teacher agreed with many students opinions that learning music should be fun.	**1.** My oldest brother**'s** guitar teacher agreed with many studen**ts'** opinions that learning music should be fun.
	2. The players seats on the team bus were occupied by the coaches children.	**2.** The player**s'** seats on the team bus were occupied by the coache**s'** (or coach**'s**) children.
And of Clay Are We Created	**1.** As a child Isabel Allende wrote in her notebook and draw on her bedroom wall.	**1.** As a child, Isabel Allende wrote in her notebook and **drew** on her bedroom wall.
	2. As a journalist, she found objectivity difficult, she wanted to twist reality, and put herself into news stories she covered.	**2.** As a journalist, she found objectivity difficult; she wanted to twist reality and put herself into news stories she covered.

Selection	SkillBuilder Sentences	Suggested Answers
Antigone	**1.** According to some tales, Teiresias the blind Prophet, lived for seven generacions. **2.** His mother the nimph, chariclo, told him the secrets of the Gods, as a result the Gods struck him blind.	**1.** According to some tales, Teiresias**,** the blind **p**rophet, lived for seven **generations**. **2.** His mother**,** the **nymph C**hariclo, told him the secrets of the **g**ods**;** as a result**,** the **g**ods struck him blind.
from Le Morte d'Arthur	**1.** "It must of been hard to be a good knight said Ellen." Having to follow the code of chivalry. **2.** "I dont think so responded Harris. What's so hard about being Loyal and Courteous."	**1.** "It must **have** been hard to be a good knight**,"** said Ellen**, "h**aving to follow the code of chivalry**."** **2.** "I don**'**t think so**,"** responded Harris. **"**What's so hard about being **l**oyal and **c**ourteous**?"**
from The Mists of Avalon	**1.** "When you really think about it." It would be hard to be a Prince or a Princess, Dahlia said. **2.** "I know," said Leroy. Sounds to me like it means growing up with constant competition and distraction.	**1.** "When you really think about it**, i**t would be hard to be a **p**rince or a **p**rincess**,"** Dahlia said. **2.** "I know," said Leroy. **"It s**ounds to me **as if** it means growing up with constant competition and distraction**."**

DAILY LANGUAGE SKILLBUILDERS

Selection	SkillBuilder Sentences	Suggested Answers
from The Acts of King Arthur and His Noble Knights	**1.** Donna sighed. "I'll bet Guinevere and Lancelot were unhappy cause they couldnt never be together.	**1.** Donna sighed. "I'll bet Guinevere and Lancelot were unhappy **because** they **could never** be together."
	2. "I agree, said Dwayne. Its to bad, but it make's a good story."	**2.** "I agree," said Dwayne. **"It's too** bad, but it **makes** a good story."

	Unit One	Unit Two	Unit Three	Unit Four	Unit Five	Unit Six
Grammar Focus by Unit	Parts of Speech	The Sentence and Its Parts	Verbs and Verbals	Phrases	Clauses	Special Sentence Structures

The Language of Literature offers several options for integrating grammar instruction and literature.

- Each unit has a specific grammar focus. The grammar focus for this unit is highlighted on the planning chart. Categories of grammar skills for this unit are shown in red.
- The Pupil's Edition includes instructive features entitled *Grammar in Context*. The instruction in these features arises from the selections and relates to the grammar focus for each unit.
- The Writing Workshops in the Pupil's Edition include grammar tips that help students produce error-free drafts.
- Mini Lessons in the Teacher's Edition complement the instruction in the *Grammar in Context* features. Additional Mini Lessons relate to the grammar focus for each unit as well as to the literature.
- Daily Language SkillBuilders in the Teacher's Edition provide students with ongoing proofreading practice and reinforce punctuation, spelling, grammar and usage, and capitalization.
- Grammar Copymasters and Transparencies, which may be used independently or in conjunction with Mini Lessons in the Teacher's Edition, present grammar in a traditional, systematic sequence.

PE instruction shown in black
TE Mini Lessons shown in green

Part 1

Parts of the Sentence

Identifying Inverted Subjects
"A Chip of Glass Ruby," p. 970

Using Clauses

Compound-Complex Sentences
"A Chip of Glass Ruby," p. 976
"A Chip of Glass Ruby," p. 976

Sentence Fragments
Communication Workshop, p. 1013

Capitalization

Communication Workshop, p. 1013

End Marks and Commas

Commas in Series
Communication Workshop, p. 1013

Commas with Nonessential Clauses and Phrases
Communication Workshop, p. 1013

Style

Parallel Structure
"And of Clay Are We Created," p. 997
"And of Clay Are We Created," pp. 992–993
"And of Clay Are We Created," p. 997

Part 2

Parts of the Sentence

Run-on Sentences
Writing Workshop, p. 1113

Making Compound Predicates Parallel
from *The Acts of King Arthur and His Noble Knights,* p. 1101
from *The Acts of King Arthur and His Noble Knights,* p. 1101

Direct and Indirect Objects
Antigone, pp. 1030–1031

Objective Complements
from *The Mists of Avalon,* p. 1087

Subject-Verb Agreement

Subject-Verb Agreement
Writing Workshop, p. 1113

Subject-Verb Split
from *Le Morte d'Arthur,* p. 1082
from *Le Morte d'Arthur,* p. 1082

Inverted Sentences
Antigone, p. 1063
Antigone, p. 1062–1063

Style

Parallel Structure
Writing Workshop, p. 1113

PART 1 Unsung Heroes

Are you a strong person? In times of trial, can you find the strength to do what needs to be done—to overcome obstacles, to withstand opposition, even to face danger? Often, people never know what they are capable of doing until circumstances push them to the limit. In this part of Unit Six, you will encounter a number of ordinary people who must confront extraordinary challenges. As you will see, such challenges can produce unexpected heroes.

ACTIVITY

List the names of three people whom you regard as heroes. These may be figures from history, people in the news, or personal acquaintances. Write a brief explanation of what makes each of these people heroic. Then compare your list with those of your classmates and discuss what you regard as the essential ingredients of heroism.

LEARNING the Language of *Literature*

Style, in general, is the particular way something is expressed. Almost everything has a style—from haircuts to shoes, architecture to music. People also express their individuality through their personal style of dressing, talking, and acting. Style as a literary term refers to the way a work is written. Just as your personal style expresses your individuality, a writer's literary style is a unique signature, expressing his or her personal way of writing.

Style in Diction

n essential element of literary style is **diction**, or writer's choice of words. When Agatha Christie escribed Mr. Mayherne's voice in "The Witness for he Prosecution" (page 871), she chose the word *ry* to characterize the reserved lawyer. Generally, hristie's diction is spare but telling. She gives eaders just enough information to keep them uessing. Christie's reserved diction contrasts with arah Orne Jewett's more expressive diction in "A White Heron" (page 822). Jewett's purpose is quite ifferent from Christie's, of course. She is not writing mystery story but a story full of emotion and elicate beauty.

DICTION AND SENTENCE STRUCTURE

Mr. Mayherne adjusted his pince-nez and cleared his throat with a little dry-as-dust cough that was wholly typical of him. Then he looked again at the man opposite him, the man charged with willful murder.

Mr. Mayherne was a small man, precise in manner, neatly, not to say foppishly dressed, with a pair of very shrewd and piercing gray eyes. By no means a fool. Indeed, as a solicitor, Mr. Mayherne's reputation stood very high. His voice, when he spoke to his client, was dry but not unsympathetic.

—Agatha Christie, "The Witness for the Prosecution"

Style in Sentence Structure

entence structure includes both sentence length nd kind of sentence (simple, compound, complex, r compound-complex). Choices about sentence tructure have a subtle influence on style. For example, hristie frequently used short, simple sentences, which re good vehicles for conveying details and giving a ast-paced rhythm to her story—key elements of a good nystery.

Sarah Orne Jewett, on the other hand, was more nterested in the mystery of the human heart and the najesty of nature. She used long sentences in her tory to express complicated feelings and to draw mportant connections between her characters and ature.

OUR TURN Analyze the two passages at the right in erms of diction and sentence structure. Point to xamples of differences between the two authors.

The woods were already filled with shadows one June evening, just before eight o'clock, though a bright sunset still glimmered faintly among the trunks of the trees. A little girl was driving home her cow, a plodding, dilatory, provoking creature in her behavior. . . .

There was hardly a night the summer through when the old cow could be found waiting at the pasture bars; on the contrary, it was her greatest pleasure to hide herself away among the high huckleberry bushes, and though she wore a loud bell she had made the discovery that if one stood perfectly still it would not ring. So Sylvia had to hunt for her until she found her, and call Co'! Co'! with never an answering Moo, until her childish patience was quite spent.

—Sarah Orne Jewett, "A White Heron"

LEARNING the Language of LITERATURE

OVERVIEW

Objectives

- understand the following literary terms:
  - style in diction
  - style in sentence structure
  - dialogue
  - imagery
  - tone
- analyze how diction and sentence structure affect style
- analyze how imagery and tone affect style

Teaching the Lesson

This lesson analyzes terms related to style and illustrates how choices in style reflect an author's individuality.

Introducing the Concepts

Have students mention authors they have read whose styles are distinct and memorable. Ask them what features make the writing of these authors stand out.

Presenting the Concepts

Style in Diction

Explain to students that a dimension of a writer's style is not just choice of diction but also the quantity of words. Some writers use few words and some writers use many words, depending on their purpose and subject matter.

Style in Sentence Structure

Point out that compound-complex sentence structures, in addition to being longer than simple sentences, also have greater complexity because they show the logical relations between ideas. Words such as *because, otherwise,* and *although* signal explanation and reasoning that indicate logical relations.

YOUR TURN Possible Response: Christie uses shorter sentences with a precise and formal-sounding rhythm. Her diction is objective, clear, and direct. Jewett uses longer sentences, on the other hand, with a lilting, smooth rhythm. Her diction is more subjective and emotional.

Making Connections

Dialogue
The use of dialogue as opposed to narration emphasizes an author's decision to give an impression of objectivity.

Imagery
Explain that images generally have a dominant visual dimension but may also include appeals to hearing, smell, touch, and taste.

Tone
Point out that tone can be established through the primary traits of a viewpoint character and not just through word choice or sentence structure.

YOUR TURN Possible Response: The tone of Christie's passage is somewhat reserved, accumulated through images of the untidy apartment filtered through Mr. Mayherne's fact-gathering perspective. The tone of Jewett's passage is innocent in its description of nature from a child's perspective.

Dialogue

Another important aspect of a writer's style is the use of **dialogue**, or the written conversation between two or more characters. Dialogue is a major feature of Christie's story: the facts of the case are primarily revealed through what the characters say. Characters also reveal and conceal aspects of themselves through their dialogue. Jewett relies less on dialogue and more on the comments of an omniscient narrator to express the rich inner life of her main character.

Imagery

Imagery, or descriptive words and phrases that create sensory experiences for the reader, is perhaps the most recognizable aspect of a writer's style. In Christie's story, only a few telling images create a scene or distinguish a character, whereas Jewett's story is almost completely constructed with images. From the opening scene with the plodding cow to the climax of Sylvia at the top of the majestic pine tree, the reader is immersed in a lush woodland of fragrant pines and twittering birds. Images of light and dark help to evoke awe at nature's simple marvels and instill in the reader the sense of secrecy that Sylvia herself feels.

Tone

Tone, the attitude a writer takes toward a subject, might be playful, serious, bitter, angry, or detached. Jewett's sympathetic tone in "A White Heron" comes mostly from the comments of the omniscient narrator. But the narrator's sympathy for Sylvia depends on the supporting imagery of nature to justify it. Mr. Mayherne's manner sets the tone in Christie's story, as he diligently searches dark corners for the truth.

YOUR TURN Analyze the imagery in the two passages at the right. Then identify the tone of each passage and explain how the imagery and tone are related.

IMAGERY AND TONE

With some reluctance the lawyer stepped across the threshold into the small dirty room, with its flickering gas jet. There was an untidy unmade bed in a corner, a plain deal table and two rickety chairs. For the first time Mr. Mayherne had a full view of the tenant of this unsavory apartment. She was a woman of middle age, bent in figure, with a mass of untidy gray hair and a scarf wound tightly round her face. She saw him looking at this and laughed again, the same curious, toneless chuckle.

"Wondering why I hide my beauty, dear? He, he, he. Afraid it may tempt you, eh? But you shall see—you shall see."

She drew aside the scarf, and the lawyer recoiled involuntarily before the almost formless blur of scarlet. She replaced the scarf again.

—Agatha Christie, "The Witness for the Prosecution"

There was the huge tree asleep yet in the paling moonlight, and small and silly Sylvia began with utmost bravery to mount to the top of it, . . .

She crept out along the swaying oak limb at last, and took the daring step across into the old pine tree. The way was harder than she thought; she must reach far and hold fast, the sharp dry twigs caught and held her and scratched her like angry talons, the pitch made her thin little fingers clumsy and stiff as she went round and round the tree's great stem, higher and higher upward. The sparrows and robins in the woods below were beginning to wake and twitter to the dawn, yet it seemed much lighter there aloft in the pine tree, and the child knew she must hurry if her project were to be of any use.

—Sarah Orne Jewett, "A White Heron"

"What do you mean by that?" "Would you repeat the question?" "Let me see if I have this right: you're saying that . . ." These are expressions that you might use in your everyday life to clear up a confusion or a misunderstanding. The strategies on this page will help you apply this same skill to your reading.

Clarifying

Clarifying can help you fully comprehend what you read. Basically, **clarifying** means stopping occasionally during your reading to review what you understand so far. Clarifying not only helps you find answers to questions you had before, but it can also signal when you're confused and need to reread a passage. Periodically clarifying your understanding helps you stay alert and follow the developments in a literary work—the twists and turns of a story, for instance, or the line of argument in an essay.

1 Strategies for Clarifying in Fiction

- **Question** the characters' feelings, attitudes, and behavior so that you can **clarify** their motivations. As you read, try to answer the five W's *(Who, What, When, Where,* and *Why)* about the characters and plot of the story.
- **Visualize** descriptions of character and setting. Is the setting real or imaginary? Think about the time and place of the story. Is the setting important to the plot? **Evaluate** how the setting might affect the characters. Are the two closely related?
- Use a chart like this to keep track of important events and details as you read.
- Stop periodically to review conflicts in a story and changes within a character.
- At the end, state the theme, or main idea.

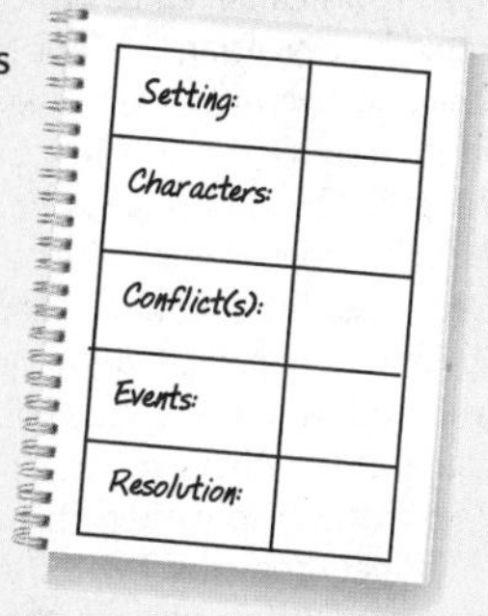

2 Strategies for Clarifying in Nonfiction

- Before you read, skim the selection: read the headline, the first and last paragraphs, the first sentence of other paragraphs, and any graphics, including maps, timelines, charts, and diagrams.
- **Clarify** your understanding by periodically summarizing main ideas as you read.
- Identify the writer's purpose. Is he or she entertaining, informing or explaining, persuading, or expressing ideas and feelings?
- Separate facts from opinions. Remember that a fact can be proved or disproved. An opinion expresses beliefs or attitudes about which people can disagree.

3 Strategies for Clarifying in Poetry

- **Visualize** all images and figurative language, and ask yourself why the poet chose those descriptions and comparisons.
- **Connect** personally with ideas, situations, and feelings in the poem.
- Read the poem at least three times, paraphrasing complex thoughts and feelings.

Need More Help?

Remember that active readers use the essential reading strategies explained on page 7: **visualize, predict, clarify, question, connect, evaluate, monitor.**

The Active Reader: Skills and Strategies

OVERVIEW

Objectives

- apply strategies to clarify meaning and monitor comprehension of fiction, nonfiction, and poetry
- organize details into different forms, such as charts, to clarify and keep track of significant information

Teaching the Lesson

The strategies on this page will help students learn and apply skills that enhance their ability to understand the meaning of the fiction, nonfiction, and poetry they read.

Presenting the Strategies

Help students understand how meaning can be clarified by acting out an example of giving directions and showing how a simple strategy such as pausing to question specific words, phrases, and sentences can help clarify the meaning of the whole message.

1 Strategies for Clarifying in Fiction

Point out that clarifying strategies requires readers to make a slight extra effort to pause and step outside the flow of reading to engage in a dialogue with themselves. These brief reflective pauses, however, allow readers to simplify complexities and thus gain more control over their reading process. Taking notes and pausing periodically to review those notes can lead to observations students might otherwise have missed.

2 Strategies for Clarifying in Nonfiction

Encourage students to first skim a nonfiction selection and then write a prediction in their Reader's Notebook of what the piece is about. This initial prediction helps readers focus their reading.

3 Strategies for Clarifying in Poetry

Encourage students to pause and summarize or respond to important elements at the end of each stanza of a poem. Explain that the overall meaning of a poem is built from the meanings of its smaller, successive parts.

OVERVIEW

Objectives

1. understand and appreciate a **short story (Literary Analysis)**
2. analyze **dialogue (Literary Analysis)**
3. **clarify** characters' attitudes and behaviors **(Active Reading)**

Summary

Zanip Bamjee, an Indian woman living in South Africa, runs off political leaflets on a duplicating machine in her kitchen and holds secret antiapartheid meetings with prominent Indian leaders. Her husband, Yusuf, does not share in or understand his wife's political activities. At three o'clock in the morning, the police come to arrest Zanip, leaving her nine children in Yusuf's care. Gradually, the children help Yusuf to understand their mother's deep commitment to the antiapartheid movement. When Zanip sends his stepdaughter over to celebrate Yusuf's birthday, he realizes that it is his wife's very humanity and concern for others that made him love her in the first place.

Thematic Link

A husband comes to understand his wife as an **unsung hero** for her commitment to an important political cause.

5-Minute Warm-Up

Daily Language SkillBuilder

Have students **proofread** the display sentences on page 959i and write them correctly. The sentences also appear on Transparency 27 of **Grammar Transparencies and Copymasters.**

PREPARING to *Read*

A Chip of Glass Ruby

Short Story by NADINE GORDIMER

"...but then his wife was not like other people, in a way he could not put his finger on."

Connect to Your Life

Active Involvement Think of a household where one parent is heavily involved in political or charitable activities outside the home. With a small group of classmates, discuss how the family might be affected by such activities. List the positive and negative effects that such involvement might have on the family.

Build Background

Life Under Apartheid In this story, an Indian woman living in South Africa juggles the responsibilities of family life with her work as a political activist. The story takes place during the time of apartheid (ə-pärt'hīt'), a system of racial segregation. Under apartheid, every citizen was classified as either white, colored (mixed race), Asian (of East Indian ancestry), or Bantu (native black). Complex laws set limits on the lives of those who were not white. For example, the Group Areas Act, mentioned in this story, forced nonwhites to live in certain areas. Pass laws required that black South Africans carry passes identifying where they lived and what areas they could visit. While Asians did not have to carry passes, their movements also were restricted.

For decades, many South Africans struggled against apartheid, despite the threat of being jailed. Among the most influential groups was the African National Congress (ANC), called simply "Congress" in the story.

WORDS TO KNOW
Vocabulary Preview

disarm, presumption, morose, sallow, patronize

VIDEODISC **LaserLinks: Background for Reading**
Historical Connection

Focus Your Reading

LITERARY ANALYSIS DIALOGUE **Dialogue** is written conversation between two or more characters. Used in most fictional narratives, dialogue adds life to a story, moves the **plot** along, and provides the reader with insights into the **characters** and their relationships with one another.

As you read this story, pay attention to the dialogue and what it tells you about the characters.

ACTIVE READING CLARIFYING When you read, it is helpful to stop occasionally and review what you understand so far. "A Chip of Glass Ruby" is a story about a family, focusing primarily on the differences between a husband and wife. In order to understand the story, it will help you to stop and **clarify** the attitudes and behaviors of these two **characters.**

READER'S NOTEBOOK As you read the following story, stop at each major event. Pay attention to how Bamjee and Mrs. Bamjee, the husband and wife in the story, respond to that event. Record your observations in a chart like the one shown, noting their attitudes and behaviors. As you move through the story, be prepared for new ideas or perceptions. Be aware that your understanding may change as you read.

Event	Attitude/Behavior	
	Bamjee	Mrs. Bamjee
Duplicating machine arrives		

LESSON RESOURCES

UNIT SIX RESOURCE BOOK, pp. 4–9

ASSESSMENT RESOURCES

Formal Assessment, pp. 159–160

Teacher's Guide to Assessment and Portfolio Use

Test Generator

SKILLS TRANSPARENCIES AND COPYMASTERS

Literary Analysis

- Drama Dialogue, T10 (for Paired Activity, p. 974)

Reading and Critical Thinking

- Locating Information Using Print References, T32
- Organizational Chart: Horizontal, T51(Reader's Notebook, p. 964)

Grammar

- Identifying Subjects in Inverted Sentences, C90 (for Mini Lesson, p. 970)
- Compound-Complex Sentences, C125 (for Mini Lesson, p. 976)

Vocabulary

- Context Clues, C86 (for Mini Lesson, p. 965)

Writing

- Extending Sentences, T19 (for Writing Option 3, p. 975)
- The Uses of Dialogue, T24 (for Writing Option 4, p. 975)
- Interpretive Essay, C33 (for Writing Option 1, p. 975)

Communications

- Interviewing, T9 (for Activities & Explorations 2, p. 975)
- Formal Presentations, T10 (for Inquiry & Research, p. 975)

INTEGRATED TECHNOLOGY

Audio Library

LaserLinks

- Historical Connection: A Struggle for Freedom
- Author Background: Nadine Gordimer. See **Teacher's SourceBook,** p. 50.

Internet: Research Starter

Visit our website:
www.mcdougallittell.com

A Chip of Glass Ruby

Nadine Gordimer

When the duplicating machine was brought into the house, Bamjee said, "Isn't it enough that you've got the Indians' troubles on your back?" Mrs. Bamjee said, with a smile that showed the gap of a missing tooth but was confident all the same, "What's the difference, Yusuf? We've all got the same troubles."

"Don't tell me that. We don't have to carry passes; let the natives protest against passes on their own; there are millions of them. Let them go ahead with it."

TEACHING THE LITERATURE

Customizing Instruction

Less Proficient Readers
Refer to the Build Background feature on the previous page, making sure that students understand what apartheid is and how it affected the different racial groups in South Africa.

Students Acquiring English
Have students answer the following questions as they read:

- Who are the main characters?
  Answer: Zanip Bamjee and Yusuf Bamjee
- Why is Mrs. Bamjee arrested?
  Answer: She is arrested for printing antiapartheid leaflets.
- What does Mrs. Bamjee remember about Yusuf that Yusuf has forgotten?
  Answer: his birthday

Use **Spanish Study Guide** for additional support, pp. 202–204.

Gifted and Talented
Have students research the history of Indians in South Africa. In particular, have them note similarities and differences in how Asian and black South Africans were treated under the apartheid laws.

Mini Lesson Preteaching Vocabulary

USING CONTEXT CLUES

Instruction Call students' attention to the list of WORDS TO KNOW. Remind them that sometimes they can understand the meaning of an unfamiliar word by examining the context in which the word is used. Use the model sentence to demonstrate the strategy:

Model Sentence
Although initially the lost little boy was frightened by Officer Rodriguez's badge and gun, the policeman's smile and kind words so *disarmed* the boy that he relaxed and told the officer where he lived.

- Write the sentence on the board.
- Ask a volunteer to summarize the meaning of the sentence.
- Have students use the context clues in the sentence to infer the meaning of the word *disarmed.*
- Ask a volunteer to use *disarmed* in a sentence.

Use **Unit Six Resource Book** p. 7 for more practice.

A lesson on using context clues appears on p. 56 in the Pupil's Edition.

Reading and Analyzing

Reading Skills and Strategies: PREVIEW

Remind students that they are expected to establish a purpose for reading. Ask students what the title, the images, and the highlighted quotes suggest to them. Discuss with students the Build Background feature on page 964.

Active Reading CLARIFYING

Ask students to answer the following questions about the story as they read:

- What is the primary conflict in the story?
  Possible Response: Yusuf's conflict with his wife because of her political activities
- What is the story's setting?
  Possible Response: South Africa in the time of apartheid

Use **Unit Six Resource Book** p. 5 for more practice.

Literary Analysis DIALOGUE

Remind students that dialogue between characters often reveals the nature of the characters' relationship with one another. As students read the story, ask them to take note of what the dialogue between Zanip, Yusuf, and the children reveals about their relationships with one another.

ACTIVE READING

A CLARIFY Possible Responses: He feels that if he doesn't know what is in the pamphlets, he can't be held responsible; he will only become angrier if he knows; he is afraid of finding out what his wife is really involved in.

Use **Unit Six Resource Book** p. 6 for more practice.

The nine Bamjee and Pahad children were present at this exchange as they were always; in the small house that held them all there was no room for privacy for the discussion of matters they were too young to hear, and so they had never been too young to hear anything. Only their sister and half-sister, Girlie, was missing; she was the eldest, and married. The children looked expectantly, unalarmed and interested, at Bamjee, who had neither left the room nor settled down again to the task of rolling his own cigarettes, which had been interrupted by the arrival of the duplicator. He had looked at the thing that had come hidden in a washbasket and conveyed in a black man's taxi, and the children turned on it too, their black eyes surrounded by thick lashes like those still, open flowers with hairy tentacles that close on whatever touches them.

"A fine thing to have on the table where we eat," was all he said at last. They smelled the machine among them; a smell of cold black grease. He went out, heavily on tiptoe, in his troubled way.

"It's going to go nicely on the sideboard!" Mrs. Bamjee was busy making a place by removing the two pink glass vases filled with plastic carnations and the hand-painted velvet runner with the picture of the Taj Mahal.[1]

After supper she began to run off leaflets on the machine. The family lived in that room—the three other rooms in the house were full of beds—and they were all there. The older children shared a bottle of ink while they did their homework, and the two little ones pushed a couple of empty milk bottles in and out the chair legs. The three-year-old fell asleep and was carted away by one of the girls. They all drifted off to bed eventually; Bamjee himself went before the older children—he was a fruit-and-vegetable hawker[2] and was up at half past four every morning to get to the market by five. "Not long now," said Mrs. Bamjee. The older children looked up and smiled at him. He turned his back on her. She still wore the traditional clothing of a Moslem woman, and her body, which was scraggy and unimportant as a dress on a peg when it was not host to a child, was wrapped in the trailing rags of a cheap sari,[3] and her thin black plait[4] was greased. When she was a girl, in the Transvaal[5] town where they lived still, her mother fixed a chip of glass ruby in her nostril; but she had abandoned that adornment as too old-style, even for her, long ago.

She was up until long after midnight, turning out leaflets. She did it as if she might have been pounding chilies.

Bamjee did not have to ask what the leaflets were. He had read the papers. All the past week Africans had been destroying their passes and then presenting
themselves for arrest. Their leaders were jailed 1
on charges of incitement,[6] campaign offices were raided—someone must be helping the few minor leaders who were left to keep the campaign going without offices or equipment. What was it the leaflets would say—"Don't go to work tomorrow," "Day of Protest," "Burn Your Pass for Freedom"? He didn't want to see.

ACTIVE READING

CLARIFY Why doesn't Bamjee want to see the leaflets? **A**

He was used to coming home and finding his wife sitting at the table deep in discussion with strangers or people whose names

1. **Taj Mahal** (täzh′ mə-häl′): a beautiful white marble building in India, built in the seventeenth century by Shah Jahan as a tomb for his wife and himself.
2. **hawker:** a peddler who sells goods by calling out.
3. **sari** (sä′rē): a garment worn by East Indian women and girls, consisting of a long cloth wrapped around the body, with one end draped over the shoulder.
4. **plait** (plāt): a braid of hair.
5. **Transvaal** (trăns-väl′): a province in northeast South Africa.
6. **incitement** (ĭn-sīt′mənt): a rousing, stirring up, or calling to action.

BLOCK SCHEDULING: MANAGING TIME

If your schedule requires that you cover the lesson objectives in a shorter time, use . . .

- Preparing to Read, p. 964
- Thinking Through the Literature, p. 974
- Vocabulary in Action, p. 975
- Grammar in Context, p. 976

If you want to take advantage of longer class time, use . . .

- TE Teaching Options: Preteaching WORDS TO KNOW, p. 965; Viewing and Representing, pp. 967, 971; Informal Assessment, p. 972
- Choices & Challenges, p. 975

News from the Gulf (about 1991), Robert A. Wade. Watercolor, 19″ × 29″, private collection.

were familiar by repute.[7] Some were prominent Indians, like the lawyer, Dr. Abdul Mohammed Khan, or the big businessman, Mr. Moonsamy Patel, and he was flattered, in a suspicious way, to meet them in his house. As he came home from work next day, he met Dr. Khan coming out of the house, and Dr. Khan—a highly educated man—said to him, "A wonderful woman." But Bamjee had never caught his wife out in any presumption; she behaved properly, as any Moslem woman should, and once her business with such gentlemen was over would never, for instance, have sat down to eat with them. He found her now back in the kitchen, setting about the preparation of dinner and carrying on a conversation on several different wavelengths with the children. "It's really a shame if you're tired of lentils, Jimmy, because that's what you're getting—Amina, hurry up, get a pot of water going—don't worry, I'll mend that in a minute; just bring the yellow cotton, and there's a needle in the cigarette box on the sideboard."

"Was that Dr. Khan leaving?" said Bamjee.

"Yes, there's going to be a stay-at-home on Monday. Desai's ill, and he's got to get the word around by himself. Bob Jali was up all last night **2**

7. **repute** (rĭ-pyo͞ot′): reputation; fame.

WORDS TO KNOW

presumption (prĭ-zŭmp′shən) *n.* behavior or language that is boldly arrogant or offensive

Customizing Instruction

Less Proficient Readers

1 Ask students to explain what Zanip has been doing with the duplicator.

Possible Responses: She uses the duplicator to produce leaflets urging black South Africans to oppose apartheid.

Students Acquiring English

2 Explain to students that a "stay-at-home" is a form of protest in which people refuse to go to work and remain in their homes.

Gifted and Talented

Ask students to analyze the role that Moslem tradition plays in Zanip's life.

Possible Responses: Zanip is both a traditional and a modern Moslem woman. She is traditional enough to wear the Moslem sari, but she deems the glass ruby in her nostril as too old-fashioned. She runs the household as would be expected in a Moslem community; however, her deep commitment to her political cause seems to be a departure from Moslem tradition. The fact that she conducts business with non-Moslem men shows her modern side; however, her husband knows that her sense of tradition is strong enough that she would never socialize with them.

Teaching Options

Mini Lesson: Viewing and Representing

News from the Gulf **by Robert A. Wade**

ART APPRECIATION This watercolor about the Gulf War is the result of a technique Wade calls "visioneering." It is compiled from two different sketchbook drawings. In the painting, women at home in Iraq listen to news of loved ones away at war. *News from the Gulf* dates from about 1991.

Application Why do you think this painting was chosen to illustrate this story? Use details from the story and the painting to explain your opinion.

Possible Responses: The people in the painting are in traditional Moslem dress, and they are conferring in the shadows on a serious political topic. This subject recalls the secret meetings of the anti-apartheid activists, some of whom are traditional Moslems as well.

Reading and Analyzing

Literary Analysis DIALOGUE

A Ask students what inferences they can make about Zanip based on her response to Yusuf's concerns.

Possible Responses: Zanip seems unafraid. She laughs and she changes the topic at the end of the conversation, indicating that for her, the topic of apartheid is as much a part of her everyday life as family gossip. This does not mean, however, that Zanip does not appreciate the seriousness of apartheid. She points out that apartheid has hit close to home, that it has affected Indians, and that people they know have lost their homes. For her, there is no choice but to fight back.

ACTIVE READING

B **CLARIFY Possible Response:** Yusuf has mixed feelings about his wife. On the one hand, her behavior, which is not like that of a typical Indian woman, sometimes upsets him. On the other hand, he seems proud that she is different from most women.

Literary Analysis: CHARACTER

C Ask students to compare Yusuf's response to his wife's arrest with Jimmy's response. Ask them to explain what their responses reveal about their characters.

Possible Responses: Yusuf is distraught about his wife's arrest and responds by blaming her for bringing on the arrest. Jimmy, however, is calm. He responds by helping his mother to prepare for her departure. Yusuf is an emotional man who doesn't handle stress well. Jimmy, still a child, is more mature in some ways than his stepfather.

printing leaflets, but he's gone to have a tooth out." She had always treated Bamjee as if it were only a mannerism that made him appear uninterested in politics, the way some woman will persist in interpreting her husband's bad temper as an endearing gruffness hiding boundless goodwill, and she talked to him of these things just as she passed on to him neighbors' or family gossip.

"What for do you want to get mixed up with these killings and stonings and I don't know what? Congress should keep out of it. Isn't it enough with the Group Areas?"

A She laughed. "Now, Yusuf, you know you don't believe that. Look how you said the same thing when the Group Areas started in Natal. You said we should begin to worry when we get moved out of our own houses here in the Transvaal. And then your own mother lost her house in Noorddorp,[8] and there you are; you saw that nobody's safe. Oh, Girlie was here this afternoon; she says Ismail's brother's engaged—that's nice, isn't it? His mother will be pleased; she was worried."

"Why was she worried?" asked Jimmy, who was fifteen, and old enough to patronize his mother.

"Well, she wanted to see him settled. There's a party on Sunday week at Ismail's place—you'd better give me your suit to give to the cleaners tomorrow, Yusuf."

One of the girls presented herself at once. "I'll have nothing to wear, Ma."

Mrs. Bamjee scratched her sallow face. "Perhaps Girlie will lend you her pink, eh? Run over to Girlie's place now and say I say will she lend it to you."

The sound of commonplaces often does service as security, and Bamjee, going to sit in the armchair with the shiny armrests that was wedged between the table and the sideboard, lapsed into an unthinking doze that, like all times of dreamlike ordinariness during those weeks, was filled with uneasy jerks and starts back into reality. The next morning, as soon as he got to market, he heard that Dr. Khan had been arrested. But that night Mrs. Bamjee sat up making a new dress for her daughter; the sight disarmed Bamjee, reassured him again, against his will, so that the resentment he had been making ready all day faded into a morose and accusing silence. Heaven knew, of course, who came and went in the house during the day. Twice in that week of riots, raids, and arrests, he found black women in the house when he came home; plain ordinary native women in doeks,[9] drinking tea. This was not a thing other Indian women would have in their homes, he thought bitterly; but then his wife was not like other

ACTIVE READING

CLARIFY What seems to be Bamjee's attitude toward his wife? B

This was not a thing other Indian women would have in their homes, he thought bitterly.

8. **Natal** (nə-tăl') . . . **Noorddorp** (nōrt'dôrp): provinces in South Africa.

9. **doeks** (düks): cloth head coverings.

WORDS TO KNOW

patronize (pā'trə-nīz) *v.* to behave in a manner that shows feelings of superiority
sallow (săl'ō) *adj.* of a sickly, yellowish color or complexion
disarm (dĭs-ärm') *v.* to overcome or reduce the intensity of suspicion or hostility; to win the confidence of
morose (mə-rōs') *adj.* gloomy; sullen

968

people, in a way he could not put his finger on, except to say what it was not: not scandalous, not punishable, not rebellious. It was, like the attraction that had led him to marry her, Pahad's widow with five children, something he could not see clearly.

When the Special Branch[10] knocked steadily on the door in the small hours of Thursday morning, he did not wake up, for his return to consciousness was always set in his mind to half past four, and that was more than an hour away. Mrs. Bamjee got up herself, struggled into Jimmy's raincoat which was hanging over a chair, and went to the front door. The clock on the wall—a wedding present when she married Pahad—showed three o'clock when she snapped on the light, and she knew at once who it was on the other side of the door. Although she was not surprised, her hands shook like a very old person's as she undid the locks and the complicated catch on the wire burglar-proofing. And then she opened the door and they were there—two colored policemen in plain clothes. "Zanip Bamjee?"

"Yes."

As they talked, Bamjee woke up in the sudden terror of having overslept. Then he became conscious of men's voices. He heaved himself out of bed in the dark and went to the window, which, like the front door, was covered with a heavy mesh of thick wire against intruders from the dingy lane it looked upon. Bewildered, he appeared in the room, where the policemen were searching through a soapbox of papers beside the duplicating machine. "Yusuf, it's for me," Mrs. Bamjee said.

At once, the snap of a trap, realization came. He stood there in an old shirt before the two policemen, and the woman was going off to prison because of the natives. "There you are!" he shouted, standing away from her. "That's what you've got for it. Didn't I tell you? Didn't I? That's the end of it now. That's the finish. That's what it's come to." She listened with her head at the slightest tilt to one side, as if to ward off a blow, or in compassion.

Jimmy, Pahad's son, appeared at the door with a suitcase; two or three of the girls were behind him. "Here, Ma, you take my green jersey." "I've found your clean blouse." Bamjee had to keep moving out of their way as they helped their mother to make ready. It was like the preparation for one of the family festivals his wife made such a fuss over; wherever he put himself, they bumped into him. Even the two policemen mumbled, "Excuse me," and pushed past into the rest of the house to continue their search. They took with them a tome[11] that Nehru[12] had written in prison; it had been bought from a persevering traveling salesman and kept, for years, on the mantelpiece. "Oh, don't take that, please," Mrs. Bamjee said suddenly, clinging to the arm of the man who had picked it up.

The man held it away from her.

"What does it matter, Ma?"

It was true that no one in the house had ever read it; but she said, "It's for my children."

"Ma, leave it." Jimmy, who was squat and plump, looked like a merchant advising a client against a roll of silk she had set her heart on. She went into the bedroom and got dressed. When she came out in her old yellow sari with a brown coat over it, the faces of the children were behind her like faces on the platform at a railway station. They kissed her goodbye. The policemen did not hurry her, but she seemed to be in a hurry just the same.

"What am I going to do?" Bamjee accused them all.

The policemen looked away patiently.

"It'll be all right. Girlie will help. The big

10. **Special Branch:** the South African secret police.
11. **tome:** a book, especially a large or scholarly one.
12. **Nehru** (nā′ro͞o): Jawaharlal (jə-wä′hər-läl′) Nehru, nationalist leader in India's movement for self-governance and the first prime minister of independent India.

Customizing Instruction

Students Acquiring English

1 Explain to students that *commonplaces* here refers to ordinary, common things.

2 A *sideboard* is a piece of dining-room furniture for keeping tableware, linens, etc.

Reading and Analyzing

Literary Analysis: NARRATIVE PROSE

A great deal of activity and interaction takes place when the Special Branch comes for Zanip. Gordimer's narrative can easily be converted into stage directions. Lead students in a discussion of how they would script this "scene" for a play, including stage directions and nonverbal instructions (Yusuf becomes angry; Jimmy is calm and quiet; and so forth). At the conclusion of this discussion, ask students how well Gordimer describes both the actions and the emotions of the characters.

ACTIVE READING

A CLARIFY **Possible Responses:** Yusuf is too self-centered to pay attention to his wife's activities; he thinks that his wife should spend all of her time taking care of him and the family; he resents his wife's involvement; because she is so traditional in most other aspects of her life, he does not recognize those parts of her life that are contrary to tradition.

Active Reading CLARIFYING

B Ask students why they think Yusuf does not speak of his wife for weeks after she is arrested.

Possible Responses: Yusuf is angry with his wife for putting herself in the position to be arrested and for leaving him with the care of their nine children; he is so distraught over his wife's absence that he cannot bear to speak of her.

children can manage. And Yusuf—" The children crowded in around her; two of the younger ones had awakened and appeared, asking shrill questions.

"Come on," said the policemen.

"I want to speak to my husband." She broke away and came back to him, and the movement of her sari hid them from the rest of the room for a moment. His face hardened in suspicious anticipation against the request to give some message to the next fool who would take up her pamphleteering until he, too, was arrested. "On Sunday," she said. "Take them on Sunday." He did not know what she was talking about. "The engagement party," she whispered, low and urgent. "They shouldn't miss it. Ismail will be offended."

They listened to the car drive away. Jimmy bolted and barred the front door and then at once opened it again; he put on the raincoat that his mother had taken off. "Going to tell Girlie," he said. The children went back to bed. Their father did not say a word to any of them; their talk, the crying of the younger ones and the argumentative voices of the older, went on in the bedrooms. He found himself alone; he felt the night all around him. And then he happened to meet the clock face and saw with a terrible sense of unfamiliarity that this was not the secret night but an hour he should have recognized: the time he always got up. He pulled on his trousers and his dirty white hawker's coat and wound his grey muffler up to the stubble on his chin and went to work.

The duplicating machine was gone from the sideboard. The policemen had taken it with them, along with the pamphlets and the conference reports and the stack of old newspapers that had collected on top of the wardrobe in the bedroom—not the thick dailies of the white men but the thin, impermanent-looking papers that spoke up, sometimes interrupted by suppression or lack of money, for the rest. It was all gone. When he had married her and moved in with her and her five children, into what had been the Pahad and became the Bamjee house, he had not recognized the humble, harmless, and apparently useless routine tasks—the minutes of meetings being written up on the dining-room table at night, the government blue books that were read while the latest baby was suckled, the employment of the fingers of the older children in the fashioning of crinkle-paper Congress rosettes—as activity intended to move mountains. For years and years he had not noticed it, and now it was gone.

ACTIVE READING

EVALUATE Why do you think Bamjee hadn't paid attention to his wife's political activities? **A**

The house was quiet. The children kept to their lairs, crowded on the beds with the doors shut. He sat and looked at the sideboard, where the plastic carnations and the mat with the picture of the Taj Mahal were in place. For the first few weeks he never spoke of her. There was the feeling, in the house, that he had wept and raged at her, that boulders of reproach had thundered down upon her absence, and yet he had said not one word. He had not been to inquire where she was; Jimmy and Girlie had gone to Mohammed Ebrahim, the lawyer, and when he found out that their mother had been taken—when she was arrested, at least—to a prison in the next town, they had stood about outside the big prison door for hours while they waited to be told where she had been moved from there. At last they had discovered that she was fifty miles away, in Pretoria.[13] Jimmy asked Bamjee for five shillings to help Girlie pay the train fare to Pretoria, once she had been interviewed by the police and had been given a permit to visit her mother; he put three two-shilling pieces on the

13. **Pretoria** (prĭ-tôr′ē-ə): the administrative capital of South Africa.

Teaching Options

Mini Lesson Grammar

IDENTIFYING INVERTED SUBJECTS

Instruction Although the subject of the sentence usually comes before the verb, sometimes the verb precedes the subject. This inverted order occurs in sentences that begin with *here* or *there* and in interrogative statements.

Here are the new leaflets.

Why are you aiding the antiapartheid movement?

In the first sentence, the subject is *leaflets.* In the second, the subject *you* is sandwiched between the helping verb *are* and the main verb *aiding.* Sometimes a writer switches the standard word order to emphasize something other than the grammatical subject of the sentence.

Brave is the person who will stand up for what he or she believes.

In this sentence, the subject is *person;* however, the writer wishes to emphasize the person's bravery.

Use **Grammar Transparencies and Copymasters,** p. 90.

Use McDougal Littell's ***Language Network,*** Chapter 2, for more instruction in inverted subjects.

Light in the Souk, (about 1991), Robert A. Wade. Watercolor, 19″ × 29″, private collection.
 From *Painting Your Vision in Watercolor,* North Light Books.

table for Jimmy to pick up, and the boy, looking at him keenly, did not know whether the extra shilling meant anything, or whether it was merely that Bamjee had no change.

It was only when relations and neighbors came to the house that Bamjee would suddenly begin to talk. He had never been so expansive in his life as he was in the company of these visitors, many of them come on a polite call rather in the nature of a visit of condolence. "Ah, yes, yes, you can see how I am—you see what has been done to me. Nine children, and I am on the cart all day. I get home at seven or eight. What are you to do? What can people like us do?"

"Poor Mrs. Bamjee. Such a kind lady."

"Well, you see for yourself. They walk in here in the middle of the night and leave a houseful of children. I'm out on the cart all day; I've got a living to earn." Standing about in his shirt-sleeves, he became quite animated; he would call for the girls to bring fruit drinks for the visitors. When they were gone, it was as if he, who was orthodox[14] if not devout and never drank liquor, had been drunk and abruptly sobered up; he looked dazed and could not have gone over in his mind what he had been saying. And as he cooled, the lump of resentment and wrongedness stopped his throat again.

14. **orthodox:** conforming to established religious rules or principles.

Customizing Instruction

Less Proficient Readers

Make sure that students are following the events of the story. Ask the following questions:

- How would you describe life in the Bamjee household since Zanip has been arrested?

  Possible Responses: It has been very quiet, with Yusuf and the children keeping to themselves; a number of visitors have come to pay condolences.

- How has his wife's arrest affected Yusuf?

  Possible Responses: He seems lonely and lost without her presence and resents her for causing this trouble; he complains about his fate to visitors.

Mini Lesson: Viewing and Representing

Light in the Souk **by Robert A. Wade**

ART APPRECIATION This watercolor, also produced by the "visioneering" method, portrays the market in Marrakesh, Morocco.

Application Have students describe how the mood of the painting reflects the mood in "A Chip of Glass Ruby."

Possible Responses: The shadowy figures suggest secrecy and mystery. To the South African government, Zanip Bamjee is a shadowy figure. To the Bamjees, the South African government lurks in the shadows as it attempts to catch antiapartheid activists.

Reading and Analyzing

Literary Analysis DIALOGUE

A Ask students to explain what Yusuf's response to Ahmed's school problems reveals about him.
Possible Response: Yusuf is angry and wishes to blame someone. When he learns that the teacher has humiliated Ahmed because his mother is in jail, he blames his wife.

Literary Analysis: CONFLICT

B Jimmy explains why Ahmed's teacher has "made an example of him." Ask students whether this type of conflict is something Zanip should have anticipated and prevented.
Possible Responses: Zanip should have been more concerned for her family; Zanip showed her concern for her family by looking out for their future, rather than worrying about short-term consequences.

ACTIVE READING

C **CLARIFY** **Possible Response:** He feels as though he has been victimized by his wife's activism; he feels that his life has been rendered incomprehensible.

1 Bamjee found one of the little boys the center of a self-important group of championing brothers and sisters in the room one evening. "They've been cruel to Ahmed."

"What has he done?" said the father.

"Nothing! Nothing!" The little girl stood twisting her handkerchief excitedly.

An older one, thin as her mother, took over, silencing the others with a gesture of her skinny hand. "They did it at school today. They made an example of him."

A "What is an example?" said Bamjee impatiently.

"The teacher made him come up and stand in front of the whole class, and he told them, 'You see this boy? His mother's in jail because she likes the natives so much. She wants the Indians to be the same as natives.' "

"It's terrible," he said. His hands fell to his sides. "Did she ever think of this?"

He had a sudden vision of her at the duplicating machine.

"That's why Ma's *there,*" said Jimmy, putting aside his comic and emptying out his schoolbooks upon the table. "That's all the kids need to know. Ma's there because things like this happen. Petersen's a colored teacher, and it's his black blood that's brought him trouble all his life, I suppose. He hates anyone who says everybody's the same because that takes away from him his bit of whiteness that's all he's got. What d'you expect? It's nothing to make too much fuss about."

"Of course, you are fifteen and you know everything," Bamjee mumbled at him.

"I don't say that. But I know Ma, anyway." The boy laughed.

There was a hunger strike among the political prisoners, and Bamjee could not bring himself to ask Girlie if her mother was starving herself too. He would not ask; and yet he saw in the young woman's face the gradual weakening of her mother. When the strike had gone on for nearly a week, one of the elder children burst into tears at the table and could not eat. Bamjee pushed his own plate away in rage.

Sometimes he spoke out loud to himself while he was driving the vegetable lorry.[15] "What for?" Again and again: "What for?" She was not a modern woman who cut her hair and wore short skirts. He had married a good plain Moslem woman who bore children and stamped her own chilies. He had a sudden vision of her at the duplicating machine, that night just before she was taken away, and he felt himself maddened, baffled, and hopeless. He had become the ghost of a victim, hanging about the scene of a crime whose motive he could not understand and had not had time to learn.

ACTIVE READING

C **CLARIFY** How does Bamjee feel about his life?

15. **lorry:** a truck.

Teaching Options

Assessment **Informal Assessment**

SELF-ASSESSMENT You can help students assess their understanding of the selection and the characters by having them write a dialogue that might occur between Yusuf and Zanip after she is released from prison. Students should have each character ask the other questions and discuss the events that occurred during their long separation. The dialogue should also take into account Yusuf's realization about his wife at the end of the story.

To help students assess their own work, have them respond to the following questions:

- Is my dialogue consistent with the characters as they are portrayed in the story?
- Are the details in my dialogue consistent with the events described in the story?

The hunger strike at the prison went into the second week. Alone in the rattling cab of his lorry, he said things that he heard as if spoken by someone else, and his heart burned in fierce agreement with them. "For a crowd of natives who'll smash our shops and kill us in our houses when their time comes." "She will starve herself to death there." "She will die there." "Devils who will burn and kill us." He fell into bed each night like a stone and dragged himself up in the mornings as a beast of burden is beaten to its feet.

One of these mornings, Girlie appeared very early, while he was wolfing bread and strong tea—alternate sensations of dry solidity and stinging heat—at the kitchen table. Her real name was Fatima, of course, but she had adopted the silly modern name along with the clothes of the young factory girls among whom she worked. She was expecting her first baby in a week or two, and her small face, her cut and curled hair, and the sooty arches drawn over her eyebrows did not seem to belong to her thrust-out body under a clean smock. She wore mauve lipstick and was smiling her cocky little white girl's smile, foolish and bold, not like an Indian girl's at all.

"What's the matter?" he said.

She smiled again. "Don't you know? I told Bobby he must get me up in time this morning. I wanted to be sure I wouldn't miss you today."

"I don't know what you're talking about."

She came over and put her arm up around his unwilling neck and kissed the grey bristles at the side of his mouth. "Many happy returns! Don't you know it's your birthday?"

"No," he said. "I didn't know, didn't think—" He broke the pause by swiftly picking up the bread and giving his attention desperately to eating and drinking. His mouth was busy, but his eyes looked at her, intensely black. She said nothing but stood there with him. She would not speak, and at last he said, swallowing a piece of bread that tore at his throat as it went down, "I don't remember these things."

The girl nodded, the Woolworth baubles in her ears swinging. "That's the first thing she told me when I saw her yesterday—don't forget it's Bajie's birthday tomorrow." **2**

He shrugged over it. "It means a lot to children. But that's how she is. Whether it's one of the old cousins or the neighbor's grandmother, she always knows when the birthday is. What importance is my birthday, while she's sitting there in a prison? I don't understand how she can do the things she does when her mind is always full of woman's nonsense at the same time—that's what I don't understand with her."

"Oh, but don't you see?" the girl said. "It's because she doesn't want anybody to be left out. It's because she always remembers; remembers everything—people without somewhere to live, hungry kids, boys who can't get educated—remembers all the time. That's how Ma is."

"Nobody else is like that." It was half a complaint.

"No, nobody else," said his stepdaughter.

She sat herself down at the table, resting her belly. He put his head in his hands. "I'm getting old"—but he was overcome by something much more curious, by an answer. He knew why he had desired her, the ugly widow with five children; he knew what way it was in which she was not like the others; it was there, like the fact of the belly that lay between him and her daughter. ❖

Customizing Instruction

Students Acquiring English

1 Ask students what they think the expression *championing brothers and sisters* means. Have them look up the word *champion* in the dictionary and ask them to pay attention to the definition of the verb form of the word. Help them understand that the children are defending and supporting their brother.

Less Proficient Readers

2 Ask students why Girlie has come to see Yusuf.

Answer: Zanip has reminded her that it is Yusuf's birthday.

GUIDING STUDENT RESPONSE

Connect to the Literature

1. **What Do You Think?**
   Possible Responses: Zanip, because she is caring; Yusuf, because he faces the very real hardship of having to care for nine children on his own

Comprehension Check

- working for the antiapartheid movement and caring for her family
- He doesn't understand why his wife would risk her own life for the native black South Africans.
- The government has her arrested.
- Zanip wishes her husband a happy birthday.

Use Selection Quiz
Unit Six Resource Book, p. 9.

Think Critically

2. Possible Response: Yes. She knows that she will one day be arrested, yet she continues working for the anti-apartheid movement. She goes bravely and calmly to jail.
3. Possible Responses: Yusuf has conflicting feelings about his wife's political activities; he is both irritated with her and proud of her. Despite her involvement in politics, Zanip takes good care of her family. Yusuf is a responsible breadwinner. At home, however, he takes a passive role with his wife and children.
4. Possible Response: Positive effects—she has taught her children to recognize injustice and stand up for people in need. Negative effects—her involvement leads to her arrest, leaving Yusuf to care for nine children on his own.
5. Possible Response: Mrs. Bamjee doesn't change much. Yusuf, however, becomes more sympathetic when he realizes why he loves his wife.
6. Student discussions should include an analysis of the characteristics of clearly written text, specifically patterns of organization, syntax, and word choice.

Thinking through the LITERATURE

Connect to the Literature

1. **What Do You Think?** With which **character** did you sympathize more, Bamjee or Mrs. Bamjee? Share your response with a partner.

Comprehension Check

- What activities occupy Mrs. Bamjee's time and energy?
- How does Bamjee feel about his wife's activities?
- How does the government react to Mrs. Bamjee's activities?
- What message does Mrs. Bamjee send her husband from prison?

Think Critically

2. Do you think that Mrs. Bamjee is a heroic character? Cite details from the story to support your opinion.
3. How would you describe the relationship between the husband and wife?

   THINK ABOUT
   - what Bamjee realizes at the story's conclusion about "why he had desired her"
   - how he feels about his wife's political involvement
   - how each of them handles the responsibilities of marriage and parenthood

4. In your judgment, what are the positive and negative effects of Mrs. Bamjee's political activities on her family?
5. ACTIVE READING CLARIFYING Refer to the observations in your READER'S NOTEBOOK. Did your understanding of Bamjee and Mrs. Bamjee change during the course of the story? Explain why or why not.

Extend Interpretations

6. **The Writer's Style** Read aloud the description of Mrs. Bamjee's late-night arrest. After completing your oral reading, discuss Gordimer's **style.** Consider her **word choice,** her **tone,** her handling of **dialogue,** her use of **description,** and any other aspects of style that you notice.
7. **Critic's Corner** The critic Brigitte Weeks wrote that "Gordimer insists that her readers face South African life as she does: with affection and horror." How do you think this statement applies to "A Chip of Glass Ruby"?
8. **Connect to Life** In what ways might this story be relevant to people living in the United States?

Literary Analysis

DIALOGUE **Dialogue** is written conversation between two or more characters. Dialogue is used in most forms of prose writing, especially in fiction. It enlivens **narrative** prose and often serves to move the **plot** along. Writers often use dialogue as a method of developing **characters** and revealing their relationships with one another.

Paired Activity Working with a partner, choose three characters from this story whom you would like to focus on. Then review the story to find examples of dialogue that reveal those characters' traits. Create three diagrams like the one shown to record your findings.

Jimmy	
Dialogue	**Traits Revealed**
"Ma's there because things like this happen"	—respect for mother —concern for social injustice

Extend Interpretations

The Writer's Style Students will probably note that Gordimer's use of verbs such as *struggled, snapped, heaved,* and *shouted* emphasizes the tension and conflict of the situation. The dialogue occurs in short bursts, not set apart by paragraph breaks. This and the occurrence of many small events in a short time convey the frenzied quality of the scene, although Mrs. Bamjee's speech shows her to be calm, despite the fact that she is being arrested.

Critic's Corner Possible Response: In the Bamjee family, we see simple people who do not need a lot of material goods to be happy. Their lives, however, are not without horror. And of course, apartheid—which involves "killings and stonings"—affects all.

Connect to Life Students may remark that the struggle against apartheid is similar to the struggle of minorities, particularly African Americans, against racism in the United States.

Literary Analysis

Dialogue Yusuf's dialogue reveals an angry, confused, irritable, worried man. Zanip's dialogue reveals a calm, capable woman who controls her emotions. Jimmy's dialogue reveals a mature young man who respects his mother. Girlie's dialogue reveals a happy, confident young woman who is proud of her mother.

Choices & CHALLENGES

Writing Options

1. Interpretive Essay A character in one of Gordimer's novels says, "The real definition of loneliness... is to live without social responsibility." Draft an essay explaining how Yusuf and Zanip Bamjee would respond to such a statement and how they would define their own responsibilities.

2. Diary of a Daughter Write the diary entry that Girlie might have written soon after Mrs. Bamjee's arrest.

3. Title Analysis Write a literary analysis in which you offer your own explanation of the significance of this story's title.

Writing Handbook
See page 1159: Analysis.

4. Stage Scene Rewrite an episode from the story as a dramatic scene with stage directions and dialogue.

Activities & Explorations

1. Interior Illustration Create an illustration that shows an interior scene of the Bamjee household, based on details in the story. You may work in any medium that you like. Try to portray the household as you visualized it while reading. ~ **ART**

2. Interview with an Activist Conduct an interview with someone who is involved in political or charitable activities in your community. Determine why he or she is involved in this work and what—if anything—he or she has sacrificed to provide time for such a commitment.
~ **SPEAKING AND LISTENING**

Inquiry & Research

The Fight Against Apartheid Find out more about antiapartheid protests led by the African National Congress or about earlier protests in South Africa led by India's Mohandas Gandhi. Use magazines, newspapers, and other print media, as well as the Internet. Share your findings with your class in an oral report.

More Online: Research Starter
www.mcdougallittell.com

Mohandas Gandhi (1869–1948), Indian leader famous for his philosophy of nonviolent protest.

Vocabulary in Action

EXERCISE: MEANING CLUES Answer the following questions.

1. Would people be most likely to **patronize** someone they fear, look up to, or look down on?
2. Would a person with a **sallow** appearance be most likely to look as if he or she has spent a lot of time indoors, out in the sun, or at the gym lifting weights?
3. Does a **morose** person typically act conceited, depressed, or frightened?
4. Is a **presumption** an act that is usually seen as being humorous, bashful, or rude?
5. If you were trying to **disarm** someone, would you be most likely to behave in a friendly, bossy, or insulting manner?

Building Vocabulary
Several Words to Know in this lesson have multiple meanings. For an in-depth lesson on multiple meanings, see page 678.

WORDS TO KNOW			
	disarm	patronize	sallow
	morose	presumption	

Writing Options

1. **Interpretive Essay** Students might write that Zanip would agree. Zanip believes in taking care of people, and her concern extends beyond her immediate family. Yusuf might be more inclined to disagree. He might feel that taking responsibility for society leads to taking on other people's problems. However, if he truly thinks about the statement, he might come to agree with it. His wife's sense of social responsibility is what made him love her in the first place.
2. **Diary of a Daughter** The diary entry should show Girlie's respect for her mother and her values, and her concern over her father's struggles. It might also reflect Girlie's differences with her mother regarding clothing and makeup.
3. **Title Analysis** Some students may say that Zanip Bamjee does not wear the ruby because she is humble; she is content to work behind the scenes against apartheid. Other students might see the title as a statement about tradition. Zanip is both traditional and modern, wearing the sari and running the household, but not wearing the ruby because she deems it too old-fashioned.
4. **Stage Scene** Accept all dramatic scenes that use appropriate stage directions (both for actions and emotions) and that depict characters using appropriate dialogue.

Activities & Explorations

1. **Interior Illustration** Encourage students to pick two or three predominant colors that reflect the mood of the scene.
2. **Interview with an Activist** Remind students to call or write the interviewee to arrange an interview time and to write out their interview questions ahead of time.

Inquiry & Research

The Fight Against Apartheid Some students might research Nelson Mandela. Others might research the status of apartheid in South Africa today, and how nonwhites acted when they acquired political power.

Vocabulary in Action

1. look down on
2. indoors
3. depressed
4. rude
5. friendly

A CHIP OF GLASS RUBY 975

Grammar in Context

WRITING EXERCISE Answers will vary. Possible answers are shown.

1. When Bamjee gets home from work, he sometimes sees important Indians coming out of his house, and this flatters him.
2. One week there are riots, and native women twice arrive at the Bamjees' house while Bamjee is working.
3. Early one morning the secret police knock at the Bamjees' door, and Mrs. Bamjee is taken away because the government wants to stop her political activities.

Choices & CHALLENGES

Grammar in Context: Compound-Complex Sentences

In "A Chip of Glass Ruby," a compound-complex sentence describes events involving Bamjee.

> **As he came home from work next day, he met Dr. Khan coming out of the house, and Dr. Khan—a highly educated man—said to him, "A wonderful woman."**

A **compound-complex sentence** consists of two or more independent clauses along with at least one subordinate clause. You may recall that an independent clause can stand alone as a sentence and a subordinate clause cannot. In the sentence above, the subordinate clause is shown in red type, and the two independent clauses are shown in blue and green type. Nadine Gordimer uses many long sentences to convey the complex relationships within South African society during apartheid.

WRITING EXERCISE Change each compound sentence into a compound-complex sentence by adding a subordinate clause in the place indicated by the caret. Begin the clause with the word in parentheses.

Example: ***Original*** ^ Mrs. Bamjee begins making leaflets, and Bamjee shows his displeasure. *(after)*

Rewritten After the duplicating machine is brought into the house, Mrs. Bamjee begins making leaflets, and Bamjee shows his displeasure.

1. ^ He sometimes sees important Indians coming out of his house, and this flatters him. *(when)*
2. One week there are riots, and native women twice arrive at the Bamjees' house ^. *(while)*
3. Early one morning the secret police knock at the Bamjees' door, and Mrs. Bamjee is taken away ^. *(because)*

Grammar Handbook The Structure of Sentences, p. 1198

Nadine Gordimer
1923–

Other Works
Selected Stories
Six Feet of the Country
My Son's Story
Jump and Other Stories

Upbringing and Discovery Nadine Gordimer was born and raised in Springs, South Africa, a small mining town near Johannesburg, the country's largest city. She attended an all-white school and spent much of her free time reading at the local library. Gordimer realized early on that she had little in common with her peers, however, and she began questioning the racial attitudes of white South Africa. She discovered, in her words, that she "was not merely part of a suburban white life aping Europe" but "lived with and among a variety of colors and kinds of people."

Success in Writing Gordimer knew she would be a writer when, at the age of 15, she had her first short story published; her first story collection, *The Soft Voice of the Serpent,* appeared in 1952. She was recognized almost immediately as a serious and talented artist, and she gained an American audience by publishing her stories in such magazines as *The New Yorker* and *Harper's.*

Social Critic Much of Gordimer's writing has focused on the theme of the destructive influence of apartheid on relationships among South Africans of all colors; as a result, several of her books were banned in her homeland for many years. Although she has said that she's not by nature a political person, she joined the African National Congress (ANC) and also helped found the Congress of South African Writers. "The real influence of politics on my writing is the influence of politics on people," she said. "Their lives, and I believe their very personalities, are changed by the extreme political circumstances one lives under in South Africa." On learning that she had won the 1991 Nobel Prize for literature, she called the event the second greatest thrill of recent years; the first, she said, was the release of ANC leader Nelson Mandela after 27 years as a political prisoner.

VIDEODISC **LaserLinks: Background for Reading**
Author Background

Teaching Options

Mini Lesson Grammar

COMPOUND-COMPLEX SENTENCES

Instruction A compound-complex sentence contains two or more independent clauses and one or more dependent clauses. Tell students that they will probably not use compound-complex sentences as frequently as they use other types; however, the compound-complex sentence can be useful for expressing a complicated thought in a precise way. Write the following sentences on the board:

> Before he left the house, he checked all the rooms; everything was fine.
>
> While she printed the pamphlets, her husband dozed, and her children played.

Explain that each sentence contains one dependent clause and two independent clauses. In the first sentence, the two independent clauses are separated by a semicolon. In the second, the independent clauses are separated by a comma and a coordinating conjunction. Either method is acceptable.

Use **Unit Six Resource Book,** p. 8.
Use **Grammar Transparencies and Copymasters,** p. 125.

Use McDougal Littell's ***Language Network,*** Chapter 4, for more instruction in compound-complex sentences.

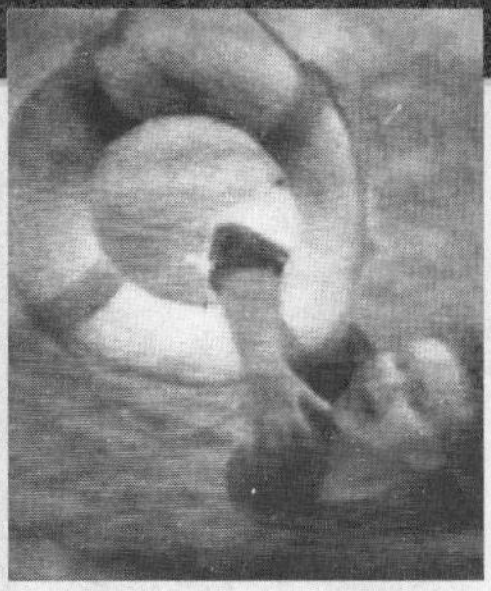

PREPARING to *Read*

The Man in the Water

Essay by ROGER ROSENBLATT

Connect to Your Life

Act Fast! In a disaster—such as an earthquake, a flood, a tornado, or a plane crash—people react in many different ways. With your classmates, discuss how such disasters can bring out the best—or worst—in people. Draw upon your own knowledge for examples.

Build Background

The Crash of Flight 90 One of the most publicized disasters of its time occurred on January 13, 1982, when a passenger jet crashed in Washington, D.C., during the evening rush hour. The jet was taking off in freezing rain and failed to gain enough altitude. Crashing onto the 14th Street Bridge, which crosses the Potomac River, the plane broke in two and fell into the icy river. Seventy-eight people died in the disaster—some of them in the plane, some in their cars on the bridge, and some in the frigid waters of the Potomac.

Following the crash of Flight 90, news reports on television and in newspapers provided extensive details of the tragedy. This essay, which appeared in *Time* magazine shortly after the crash occurred, offers more than a news report. It presents the author's viewpoints on the meaning of the events that took place immediately following the crash. In particular, the author looks at how one passenger behaved in those confusing, terrifying moments and considers what his behavior says about all of us.

WORDS TO KNOW
Vocabulary Preview
abiding, flail, chaotic, anonymity, implacable

LaserLinks: Background for Reading
Historical Connection

Focus Your Reading

LITERARY ANALYSIS TONE **Tone** is the attitude a writer takes toward a subject. Through word choice and use of details, a writer can create a tone that is playful, angry, persuasive, or reverent, to name a few possibilities. In nonfiction a writer's tone is influenced by his or her purpose for writing, as well as the writing format. As you read "The Man in the Water," think about how you would describe the essay's tone.

ACTIVE READING SUMMARIZING When you **summarize** a text, you tell about it in your own words, leaving out all but the most important information. A summary is an objective recounting of information, identifying the text's main idea and supporting details. It does not include the opinions or ideas of the person writing the summary.

Summarizing can be helpful in that it requires you to understand and remember what you have read. It can also help you share what you have read with others. Sometimes it is desirable to summarize particular aspects of a text's contents for purposes of discussion.

READER'S NOTEBOOK Create a two-column chart like the one shown. As you read, list in each column words and phrases (supporting details) from the essay that convey Rosenblatt's views about nature and human nature. Your notes will later help you to summarize his main points.

Nature	Human Nature

OVERVIEW

Objectives

1. understand and appreciate an **essay (Literary Analysis)**
2. analyze author's **tone (Literary Analysis)**
3. summarize information **(Active Reading)**

Summary

Journalist Roger Rosenblatt writes about the events following a plane crash in Washington, D.C., in 1982. He praises the heroic actions of a helicopter team and a concerned passerby. Then he considers "the man in the water" who repeatedly passed a lifeline to other passengers, sacrificing his own life in the process. Rosenblatt muses that this man had been an ordinary passenger, probably desperate to live, yet he sacrificed himself to save others. By his actions, he reflected the classic struggle between man and nature. Rosenblatt notes that the man lost his own fight against nature but won the fight for others. Although the man in the water could not defeat death, he could—and did—use charity and his own natural powers to hold death to a standoff.

Thematic Link

In this essay, an **unknown** man finds the strength within himself to be a **hero**.

5-Minute Warm-Up

Daily Language SkillBuilder

Have students **proofread** the display sentences on page 959i and write them correctly. The sentences also appear on Transparency 27 of **Grammar Transparencies and Copymasters.**

LESSON RESOURCES

UNIT SIX RESOURCE BOOK, pp. 10–14

ASSESSMENT RESOURCES

Formal Assessment, pp. 161–162

Teacher's Guide to Assessment and Portfolio Use

Test Generator

SKILLS TRANSPARENCIES AND COPYMASTERS

Literary Analysis
- Mood and Tone, T20 (for Activity, p. 981)

Reading and Critical Thinking
- Paraphrasing and Summarizing, T41 (for Think Critically, item 4, p. 981)

Vocabulary
- Context Clues, C87 (for Mini Lesson, p. 979)

Writing
- Effective Language, T13 (for Writing Options, p. 982)
- Showing, Not Telling, T22 (for Writing Options, p. 982)

Communications
- Impromptu Speaking: Dialogue, Role-Play, Debate, T13 (for Activities & Explorations, p. 982)

INTEGRATED TECHNOLOGY

Audio Library

LaserLinks
- Historical Connection: The Crash of Air Florida Flight 90. See **Teacher's SourceBook,** p. 51.

Visit our website:
www.mcdougallittell.com

Mini Lesson **Preteaching Vocabulary**

If you would like to preteach the WORDS TO KNOW for this selection, use the Mini Lesson, p. 979.

TEACHING THE LITERATURE

Reading and Analyzing

Literary Analysis: PREVIEW

Have students preview the selection and discuss what is taking place in the photographs. Discuss with students the Build Background feature on p. 977.

Active Reading SUMMARIZING

When summarizing, students should craft an opening sentence that clearly states the main idea of the selection. To this end, have students read the selection and complete their charts from the Active Reading: SUMMARIZING feature on p. 977.

Use **Unit Six Resource Book** p. 11 for more practice.

Literary Analysis TONE

Tone is the attitude a writer takes toward a subject. It reflects the author's feelings and may also contribute to the mood, or the emotional response of the reader to a work. Ask students to find passages from the selection that reveal the author's tone.

Use **Unit Six Resource Book** p. 12 for more practice.

The Man in the Water

Roger Rosenblatt

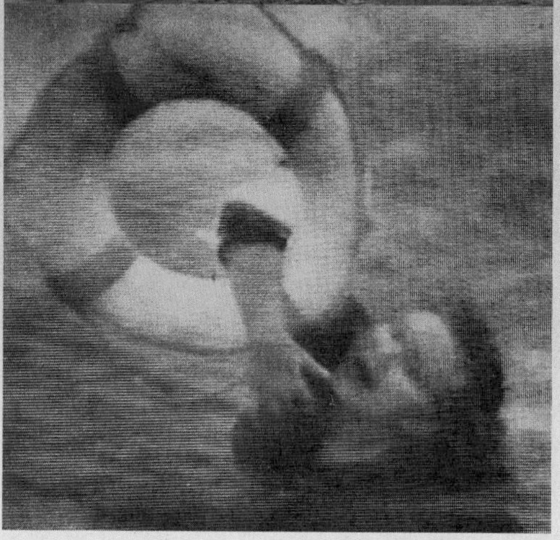

A paramedic pulls a woman from the Potomac River following the crash of Air Florida Flight 90. AP / Wide World Photos.

A woman holds on to a safety ring as she is pulled from the Potomac River. AP / Wide World Photos.

As disasters go, this one was terrible, but not unique, certainly not among the worst on the roster of U.S. air crashes. There was the unusual element of the bridge, of course, and the fact that the plane clipped it at a moment of high traffic, one routine thus intersecting another and disrupting both. Then, too, there was the location of the event. Washington, the city of form and regulations, turned chaotic, deregulated, by a blast of real winter and a single slap of metal on metal. The jets from Washington National Airport that normally swoop around the presidential monuments like famished gulls are, for the moment, emblemized by the one that fell; so there is that detail. And there was the aesthetic[1] clash as well—blue-and-green Air Florida, the name a flying garden, sunk down among gray chunks in a black river. All that was worth noticing, to be sure. Still, there was nothing very special in any of it, except death, which, while always special, does not necessarily bring millions to tears or to attention. Why, then, the shock here?

Perhaps because the nation saw in this disaster something more than a mechanical failure. Perhaps because people saw in it no

1. **aesthetic** (ĕs-thĕt′ĭk): relating to that which is beautiful or pleasing to the senses.

WORDS TO KNOW **chaotic** (kā-ŏt′ĭk) *adj.* extremely confused or disordered

978

Teaching Options

Mini Lesson: Viewing and Representing

Photographs, pp. 978 and 980.

Instruction Point out the feeling of confusion and drama expressed by these two photographs. Ask the students to describe what they see and how they interpret each object as they perceive it. What emotions are being highlighted at each moment of perception?

Possible Responses: The helicopter creates a sense of relief as it rescues the man. The ice floes make the scene more urgent, suggesting the discomfort and danger the man must be experiencing. The life ring creates a sense of safety, but the expression on the woman's face indicates fear.

failure at all, but rather something successful about their makeup. Here, after all, were two forms of nature in collision: the elements and human character. Last Wednesday, the elements, indifferent as ever, brought down Flight 90. And on that same afternoon, human nature—groping and flailing in mysteries of its own—rose to the occasion.

Of the four acknowledged heroes of the event, three are able to account for their behavior. Donald Usher and Eugene Windsor, a park police helicopter team, risked their lives every time they dipped the skids into the water to pick up survivors. On television, side by side in bright blue jumpsuits, they described their courage as all in the line of duty. Lenny Skutnik, a twenty-eight-year-old employee of the Congressional Budget Office, said: "It's something I never thought I would do"—referring to his jumping into the water to drag an injured woman to shore. Skutnik added that "somebody had to go in the water," delivering every hero's line that is no less admirable for its repetitions. In fact, nobody had to go into the water. That somebody actually did so is part of the reason this particular tragedy sticks in the mind.

But the person most responsible for the emotional impact of the disaster is the one known at first simply as "the man in the water." (Balding, probably in his fifties, an extravagant mustache.) He was seen clinging with five other survivors to the tail section of the airplane. This man was described by Usher and Windsor as appearing alert and in control. Every time they lowered a lifeline and flotation ring to him, he passed it on to another of the passengers. "In a mass casualty, you'll find people like him," said Windsor. "But I've never seen one with that commitment." When the helicopter came back for him, the man had gone under. His selflessness was one reason the story held national attention; his anonymity another. The fact that he went unidentified invested him with a universal character. For a while he was Everyman, and thus proof (as if one needed it) that no man is ordinary.

Still, he could never have imagined such a capacity in himself. Only minutes before his character was tested, he was sitting in the ordinary plane among the ordinary passengers, dutifully listening to the stewardess telling him to fasten his seat belt and saying something about the "no smoking sign." So our man relaxed with the others, some of whom would owe their lives to him. Perhaps he started to read, or to doze, or to regret some harsh remark made in the office that morning. Then suddenly he knew that the trip would not be ordinary. Like every other person on that flight, he was desperate to live, which makes his final act so stunning.

For at some moment in the water he must have realized that he would not live if he continued to hand over the rope and ring to others. He *had* to know it, no matter how gradual the effect of the cold. In his judgment he had no choice. When the helicopter took off with what was to be the last survivor, he watched everything in the world move away from him, and he deliberately let it happen.

Yet there was something else about the man that kept our thoughts on him, and which

WORDS TO KNOW

flail (flāl) *v.* to wave or swing vigorously; thrash

anonymity (ăn'ə-nĭm'ĭ-tē) *n.* the state of being unknown or unidentified

Customizing Instruction

Less Proficient Readers

Have students keep these questions in mind as they read:

- What were the circumstances surrounding the crash of Flight 90?
  Answer: There was freezing rain, and the jet crashed into a bridge.
- What heroic acts are described?
  Answer: helicopter team risking their lives to save people; Lenny Skutnik diving into the water to save an injured woman; an unknown man in the water handing lifeline to others
- What was unusual about this man?
  Answer: He kept handing the life ring to others and never tried to save himself.

Students Acquiring English

Make two lists on the board to help students understand the contrast between the forces of nature and humans. Review the meanings of the words *distinctions, principles,* and *faith* and show how these elements are part of the makeup of humans, but not of nature.

Use **Spanish Study Guide** for additional support, pp. 205–207.

Gifted and Talented

Have students recall well-known heroes from literature and history and then compare and contrast these heroes with the man in the water from this essay. Students may determine which qualities are most important in a hero, and who most nearly embodies them: the traditional, famous heroes or the unknown man of the essay.

Mini Lesson Preteaching Vocabulary

USING CONTEXT CLUES

Instruction One kind of context clue is restatement, in which a concept is described again in different terms, or restated as in the example below.

The airport was completely chaotic, filled with disorder and confusion, when nine flights all unloaded at once.

Discuss how "disorder and confusion" suggests the meaning of the word *chaotic.*

Exercises Write the following words on the board. Have students look up the definition of each word in a dictionary and then write a sentence using restatement to suggest the meaning of the word.

1. abiding
2. anonymity
3. flail
4. implacable

Possible Sentences for *abiding* and *anonymity*

1. The abiding wonder of the story, which will endure when all other questions are answered, is why the man made the choice he did.
2. His anonymity–the fact that he went unidentified–makes him a universal character.

Use **Unit Six Resource Book** p. 13 for more exercises.

A lesson on context clues appears on p. 56 in the Pupil's Edition.

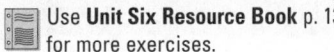

Reading and Analyzing

Reading Skills and Strategies: VISUALIZING

Rosenblatt describes the struggle between the unknown man and nature. Ask students to visualize this struggle and suggest details that dramatize it.

Possible Responses: Ice floes float in the water; people's teeth chatter and their extremities turn blue; the man hands the rope to another person, who is lifted into a helicopter.

Reading Skills and Strategies: EVALUATING

A Ask students to evaluate the author's claim that "we do not even really believe that the man in the water lost his fight."

Possible Responses: Some students may feel that it is accurate if we accept the author's premise that the ability to act selflessly is a victorious part of human nature; no, it is not accurate if we look purely at the fact that, in the end, the man died.

Literary Analysis: ESSAY

An essay is a short work of nonfiction that deals with a single subject. Ask students to state the purpose of this essay. Is its purpose to express ideas or feelings? analyze a topic? inform? entertain? persuade?

Possible Responses: The purpose of this essay is to express ideas and feelings by analyzing a topic. The author expresses his ideas about human nature by showing and analyzing the elements of a particular crisis.

keeps our thoughts on him still. He was *there,* in the essential, classic circumstance. Man in nature. The man in the water. For its part, nature cared nothing about the five passengers. Our man, on the other hand, cared totally. So the timeless battle commenced in the Potomac. For as long as that man could last, they went at each other, nature and man: the one making no distinctions of good and evil, acting on no principles, offering no lifelines; the other acting wholly on distinctions, principles, and, one supposes, on faith.

Since it was he who lost the fight, we ought to come again to the conclusion that people are powerless in the world. In reality, we believe the reverse, and it takes the act of the man in the water to remind us of our true feelings in this matter. It is not to say that everyone would have acted as he did, or as Usher, Windsor, and Skutnik. Yet whatever moved these men to challenge death on behalf of their fellows is not peculiar to them. Everyone feels the possibility in himself. That is the abiding wonder of the story. That is why we would not let go of it. If the man in the water gave a lifeline to the people gasping for survival, he was likewise giving a lifeline to those who observed him.

A The odd thing is that we do not even really believe that the man in the water lost his fight. "Everything in Nature contains all the powers of Nature," said Emerson. Exactly. So the man in the water had his own natural powers. He could not make ice storms, or freeze the water until it froze the blood. But he could hand life over to a stranger, and that is a power of nature too. The man in the water pitted himself against an implacable, impersonal enemy; he fought it with charity; and he held it to a standoff. He was the best we can do. ❖

January 25, 1982

Two more survivors are pulled from the icy water. UPI/Bettmann.

A section of the plane's fuselage is hoisted from the river several days after the crash. UPI/Bettmann.

WORDS TO KNOW

abiding (ə-bī′dĭng) *adj.* lasting or enduring **abide** *v.*
implacable (ĭm-plăk′ə-bəl) *adj.* impossible to appease or satisfy; relentless

Teaching Options

Assessment Standardized Test Practice

OPEN-ENDED QUESTIONS On many standardized tests, students are required to answer two open-ended reading questions that focus on the ability to analyze and critically evaluate texts. To help students prepare for such assessment, write the following assignment on the board:

Give examples from the essay that help define heroic behavior.

RUBRIC

3 **Full Accomplishment** The response thoroughly presents examples that help explain heroic behavior.

2 **Substantial Accomplishment** The response shows some examples that help explain heroic behavior.

1 **Little or Partial Accomplishment** The response contains inaccuracies about the examples or fails to offer an explanation of heroic behavior.

Connect to the Literature

1. **What Do You Think?** What do you think about the behavior of the man in the water?

Comprehension Check
- What disaster happened on January 13, 1982?
- What did the man in the water do?
- What finally happened to him?
- Whom does the author think the man represents?

Think Critically

2. Why do you think Rosenblatt chose to focus on the anonymous man in the water rather than on one of the other three acknowledged heroes of the tragedy?

3. Rosenblatt concludes that "we do not even really believe that the man in the water lost his fight" with nature. Do you agree or disagree?

   THINK ABOUT
   - Rosenblatt's view of nature
   - the lessons that Rosenblatt draws from the man's sacrifice
   - the power that enabled the man to "hand life over to a stranger"

4. **ACTIVE READING** **SUMMARIZING** Refer to the chart you made in your READER'S NOTEBOOK. Based on the information you recorded, summarize Rosenblatt's view of nature and his view of human nature. How do Rosenblatt's views compare to your own?

5. What does the essay's final statement—"He was the best we can do"—mean to you? Explain your response.

Extend Interpretations

6. **Connect to Life** Do you think that everyone is capable of acting as heroically as the man in the water? Give reasons for your response.

Literary Analysis

TONE Tone is the attitude a writer takes toward a subject, exhibited through word choice and use of details. Writing in newspapers and magazines may exhibit a variety of tones. For example, the tone of an informative newspaper article is typically detached and objective. In contrast, the tone of an editorial may be angry or pleading, urging readers to action, while a personal narrative may have a nostalgic tone, appropriate to the recollection of one's past. The **essay,** common in magazines, is often different in tone from the forms named above.

Activity Read aloud several paragraphs of "The Man in the Water." What word or words would you use to describe Roger Rosenblatt's tone? How might the tone be related to Rosenblatt's purpose for writing the essay?

GUIDING STUDENT RESPONSE

Connect to the Literature

1. **What Do You Think?**
   Possible Responses: Some students may find it difficult to understand why someone would sacrifice his life for strangers. Others may argue that his act was one of pure love.

Comprehension Check
- A passenger plane crashed into a bridge in Washington, D.C.
- He saved the lives of five people.
- He drowned.
- The author believes that everyone feels the possibility in himself or herself to act heroically.

Use Selection Quiz
Unit Six Resource Book, p. 14.

Think Critically

2. Possible Responses: The anonymous man in the water could have been anyone; his actions were more heroic since he sacrificed his life.
3. Possible Responses: Students may need help understanding Rosenblatt's premise that man is connected to nature. Some students will feel that in losing his life, he lost his fight; others may say that he demonstrated his own natural powers, giving life to others. This is the victory.
4. Possible Response: Rosenblatt feels nature is impersonal and implacable while human nature at its best is self-sacrificing.
5. Possible Responses: This man's heroic self-sacrifice exemplified the best that human beings can do in the face of tragedy; he set an ideal that people should aspire to; he was the best we can do because he saved others rather than himself.

Extend Interpretations

Connect to Life Students may want to discuss specific examples of heroism that support their opinion. Yes, everyone has heroic potential that can come out in a crisis; no, most people are too self-centered and too concerned with self-preservation.

Literary Analysis

Tone Possible Response: Rosenblatt's tone is philosophic, respectful, and serious since his main purpose for writing the essay is to draw a lesson from a tragic, yet heroic, event.

Writing Options

Hero's Tribute Remind students that tributes on plaques are generally short and formal. Students may wish to create an appropriate quotation to include in their tribute.

Activities & Explorations

Television Report Remind students that news reports should answer the questions *who, what, why, when, where,* and *how* and should reflect multiple viewpoints.

Inquiry & Research

Encourage students to achieve a balance between researched written text and visual material.

Vocabulary in Action

1. flail
2. abiding
3. chaotic
4. anonymity
5. implacable

Writing Options

Hero's Tribute Write a tribute to the man in the water that would be appropriate for a memorial plaque to be placed on the 14th Street Bridge. Place your work in your **Working Portfolio.**

Activities & Explorations

Television Report Stage a television report from the scene of the airplane crash. A reporter can interview people on the scene, such as Lenny Skutnik, a rescued person, and a witness to the disaster. If possible, videotape the report and show the tape to other classes. ~ **SPEAKING AND LISTENING**

Inquiry & Research

Do research to learn about the role that weather can play in plane crashes. For example, you might investigate wind shear or the effects of ice on a plane's wings. Present your findings in a bulletin-board display in your classroom or in your school's library.

Vocabulary in Action

EXERCISE: MEANING CLUES Write the word that applies to each description below.

1. Tree limbs may do this during a windstorm.
2. A crush will not be this, but true love is supposed to be.
3. Riots, wild scenes, rowdy classrooms, and some children's bedrooms are this.
4. Beloved movie stars often wish for this when they go out in public.
5. Nothing is good enough for this kind of person, and apologies to him or her may be met with stony silence.

Building Vocabulary

Several Words to Know in this lesson have interesting roots. For an in-depth lesson on roots and base words, see page 183.

WORDS TO KNOW			
	abiding	chaotic	implacable
	anonymity	flail	

Roger Rosenblatt

1940–

Other Works

Black Fiction
Children of War
The Man in the Water: Essays and Stories
Witness: The World Since Hiroshima

A Well-Rounded Journalist A journalist and essayist who has won many awards for his writing, Roger Rosenblatt is a New York City native with a Ph.D. from Harvard University. After teaching literature at Harvard, he served for two years as the director of education for the National Endowment for the Humanities. In 1975 he turned to journalism, working first as the literary editor of the Washington-based magazine *The New Republic* and then as an editorial writer for the *Washington Post.* He has also been a senior writer for *Time* and *U.S. News and World Report* and has regularly contributed oral essays to the TV news show *The Newshour with Jim Lehrer.*

Investigative Author Known for his sensitivity and literary flair, Rosenblatt has won praise for several nonfiction books on controversial topics, including *Witness: The World Since Hiroshima,* which examines the impact of the atomic bomb on different aspects of modern life. Perhaps the best known of Rosenblatt's books is *Children of War* (1983), an investigation into the lives of children in war-torn Ireland, Israel, Lebanon, Cambodia, and Vietnam.

"The sky is weeping,' Azucena murmured, and she, too, began to cry."

And of Clay Are We Created

Short Story by ISABEL ALLENDE (ä-yĕn′dā)

Connect to Your Life

From Fact to Fiction Think about the novels or stories you have read that are based upon actual events, such as wars, natural disasters, or other thought-provoking occurrences. Why do you think certain fiction writers choose to use factual events in their writing, often altering details to suit their stories? Do you enjoy reading such fictionalized accounts? Or would you rather read a nonfiction account of those events? As a class, discuss your experience in reading fiction that is based upon fact. Then discuss your views about the relationship between fact and imagination in storytelling.

Build Background

Volcanic Disasters In this story, which is based on an actual disaster, a reporter becomes involved in rescue efforts following a deadly volcanic eruption. When a volcano erupts, it releases lava, hot gases, rock fragments, and ash. Some volcanoes, such as the one in this story, emit early warning signals of an eruption. Small earthquakes and clouds of gas signal that the pressure within the volcano is building.

On November 13, 1985, the Nevado del Ruiz (dĕl rōō-ēz′) volcano in Colombia, South America, erupted. The intense heat from the eruption melted the mountain's icecap and sent a torrent of water, ash, mud, and rocks into the valley below. The liquid avalanche buried the town of Armero, killing more than 20,000 people.

WORDS TO KNOW
Vocabulary Preview

embody	stupor
equanimity	tenacity
fortitude	tribulation
irreparably	visceral
pandemonium	vulnerable

LaserLinks: Background for Reading
Historical Connection

Focus Your Reading

LITERARY ANALYSIS STYLE **Style** refers to the way a piece of literature is written. Note, for example, the vivid **imagery** in the following passage from the story you are about to read, which contributes to Allende's distinctive style:

> ***They discovered the girl's head protruding from the mud pit, eyes wide open, calling soundlessly. She had a First Communion name, Azucena. Lily... The television cameras transmitted so often the unbearable image of the head budding like a black squash from the clay that there was no one who did not recognize her and know her name.***

As you read the story, be aware of the author's style.

ACTIVE READING CLARIFYING Stories that are very rich or complex often require you to stop and **clarify** what you have read so far, to review what has happened in order to be sure that you understand the story and its characters.

READER'S NOTEBOOK As you read this story, stop at the sentences given in the chart shown (all of which are at the beginning of paragraphs). At each point, write down what you understand so far about Rolf Carlé, one of the main **characters.** Be prepared for your understanding of Rolf to change as you read further in the story.

Stopping Point	Understanding of Rolf Carlé
"'What's your name?' he asked the girl..."	
"Many miles away..."	
"The third day in the valley of the cataclysm began..."	
"You are back with me, but you are not the same man."	

LESSON RESOURCES

UNIT SIX RESOURCE BOOK, pp. 16–17

ASSESSMENT RESOURCES

Formal Assessment, pp. 163–164

Teacher's Guide to Assessment and Portfolio Use

Test Generator

SKILLS TRANSPARENCIES AND COPYMASTERS

Literary Analysis
- Style, Voice, Diction, Purpose, T22 (for Cooperative Learning Activity, p. 995)

Reading and Critical Thinking
- Organizational Chart: Horizontal, T51 (for Reader's Notebook, p. 983)

Grammar
- Dependent Clauses: Parallelism, C173 (for Mini Lesson, p. 992)
- Parallel Structures, C179 (for Mini Lesson, p. 997)

Vocabulary
- Synonyms, C88 (for Mini Lesson, p. 984)
- Using Reference Materials, C89 (for Mini Lesson, p. 990)

Writing
- Effective Language, T13 (for Writing Option 1, p. 996)
- Sensory Word List, T14 (for Writing Option 2, p. 996)

Communications
- Impromptu Speaking: Dialogue, Role-Play, Debate, T13 (for Activities & Explorations 1, p. 996)
- Verbal Strategies, T14 (for Activities & Explorations 1, p. 996)

INTEGRATED TECHNOLOGY

Audio Library

LaserLinks
- Historical Connection: The Eruption of Nevado del Ruiz. See **Teacher's SourceBook,** p. 52.

Visit our website:
www.mcdougallittell.com

OVERVIEW

Objectives
1. understand and appreciate a **short story (Literary Analysis)**
2. analyze author's **style (Literary Analysis)**
3. **clarify** understanding **(Active Reading)**

Summary
An unnamed narrator tells about the aftermath of a volcanic eruption in South America, when a girl named Azucena is discovered alive but almost completely buried in mud. Rolf Carlé, a news reporter, is the first to reach Azucena. He struggles valiantly to free her, but she is trapped by both the rubble and her dead siblings, who cling to her legs. As Rolf reassures the girl, the narrator, watching on television, feels her love for Rolf grow. He radios for a water pump, but none is available so he stays with Azucena and waits for help. During the second night while giving encouragement to the girl, Rolf faces the pain of his own life for the first time. He relives unspeakable memories from his childhood. The next day he assures Azucena, who claims that no boy has ever loved her, that she is loved—that he loves her more than he's ever loved anyone. That night he holds her gaze until she dies, then closes her eyes and lets her sink.

Thematic Link
Rolf and Azucena act heroically despite life-threatening circumstances.

5-Minute Warm-Up

Daily Language SkillBuilder

Have students **proofread** the display sentences on page 959i and write them correctly. The sentences also appear on Transparency 27 of **Grammar Transparencies and Copymasters.**

TEACHING THE LITERATURE

Reading and Analyzing

Reading Skills and Strategies: PREVIEW

Have students read the Build Background feature on p. 983 and then the first paragraph of the story. Students may wish to discuss the significance of the title and the images.

Active Reading CLARIFYING

Clarifying, or reviewing portions of a text, can often be done by using the organizational pattern of the selection. For example, the chronology of daily events in this short story offers the reader frequent opportunities to question and clarify. Encourage students to locate words that signal the sequence of events and to use these points to review what they have read.

Use **Unit Six Resource Book** p. 16 for more practice.

Literary Analysis STYLE

(A) Understanding an author's style requires readers to consider elements such as word choice, syntax, and figurative language. In the passage marked, students may notice that Allende prefers lengthy sentences packed with description and imaginative images.

Use **Unit Six Resource Book** p. 17 for more practice.

And of Clay Are We Created

Isabel Allende

They discovered the girl's head protruding from the mud pit, eyes wide open, calling soundlessly. She had a First Communion name,[1] Azucena.[2] Lily. In that vast cemetery where the odor of death was already attracting vultures from far away, and where the weeping of orphans and wails of the injured filled the air, the little girl obstinately clinging to life became the symbol of the tragedy. The television (A)

1. **First Communion name:** a name traditionally given to a Roman Catholic child at the time of the child's first participation in the rite of Holy Communion.
2. **Azucena** (ä′zo͞o-kĕ′nä).

Teaching Options

Mini Lesson: Preteaching Vocabulary

IDENTIFYING SYNONYMS

Instruction Remind students that synonyms are words with the same or nearly the same meaning. Write the following sentence on the chalkboard:

His bravery enabled him to face the results of the disaster calmly.

Ask students to identify the WORD TO KNOW that has the same or nearly the same meaning as the underlined word.

Answer: fortitude

Application In the following sentences, have students identify the WORD TO KNOW that is a synonym for each of the underlined words.

1. The ruckus caused by the rescue efforts kept everyone from sleeping. *(pandemonium)*
2. The irremediably damaged buildings were abandoned. *(irreparably)*
3. The people walked around aimlessly, in a daze. *(stupor)*
4. They hoped for relief from their ordeal. *(tribulation)*

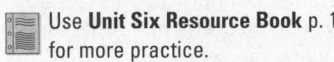

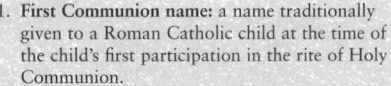

cameras transmitted so often the unbearable image of the head budding like a black squash from the clay that there was no one who did not recognize her and know her name. And every time we saw her on the screen, right behind her was Rolf Carlé,[3] who had gone there on assignment, never suspecting that he would find a fragment of his past, lost thirty years before.

First a subterranean[4] sob rocked the cotton fields, curling them like waves of foam. Geologists had set up their seismographs[5] weeks before and knew that the mountain had awakened again. For some time they had predicted that the heat of the eruption could detach the eternal ice from the slopes of the volcano, but no one heeded their warnings; they sounded like the tales of frightened old women. The towns in the valley went about their daily life, deaf to the moaning of the earth, until that fateful Wednesday night in November when a prolonged roar announced the end of the world, and walls of snow broke loose, rolling in an avalanche of clay, stones, and water that descended on the villages and buried them beneath unfathomable meters of telluric[6] vomit. As soon as the survivors emerged from the paralysis of that first awful terror, they could see that houses, plazas, churches, white cotton plantations, dark coffee forests, cattle pastures—all had disappeared. Much later, after soldiers and volunteers had arrived to rescue the living and try to assess the magnitude of the cataclysm,[7] it was calculated that beneath the mud lay more than twenty thousand human beings and an indefinite number of animals putrefying in a viscous soup.[8] Forests and rivers had also been swept away, and there was nothing to be seen but an immense desert of mire.

When the station called before dawn, Rolf Carlé and I were together. I crawled out of bed, dazed with sleep, and went to prepare coffee while he hurriedly dressed. He stuffed his gear in the green canvas backpack he always carried, and we said goodbye, as we had so many times before. I had no presentiments.[9] I sat in the kitchen, sipping my coffee and planning the long hours without him, sure that he would be back the next day.

He was one of the first to reach the scene, because while other reporters were fighting their way to the edges of that morass in jeeps, bicycles, or on foot, each getting there however he could, Rolf Carlé had the advantage of the television helicopter, which flew him over the avalanche. We watched on our screens the footage captured by his assistant's camera, in which he was up to his knees in muck, a microphone in his hand, in the midst of a bedlam of lost children, wounded survivors, corpses, and devastation. The story came to us in his calm voice. For years he had been a familiar figure in newscasts, reporting live at the scene of battles and catastrophes with awesome <u>tenacity</u>. Nothing could stop him, and I was always amazed at his <u>equanimity</u> in the face of danger and suffer-

3. **Rolf Carlé** (rälf kär-lĕ′).
4. **subterranean** (sŭb′tə-rā′nē-ən): underground.
5. **seismographs** (sīz′mə-grăfs): instruments that record the intensity and duration of earthquakes and other tremors.
6. **telluric** (tĕ-lo͝or′ĭk): relating to the earth.
7. **cataclysm** (kăt′ə-klĭz′əm): a violent and sudden change in the earth's crust; upheaval that destroys.
8. **putrefying** (pyo͞o′trə-fī′ĭng) . . . **soup:** rotting in a thick soup.
9. **presentiments** (prĭ-zĕn′tə-mənts): feelings that something is about to happen; forebodings.

WORDS TO KNOW

tenacity (tə-năs′ĭ-tē) *n.* the state or quality of holding persistently to something; firm determination

equanimity (ē′kwə-nĭm′ĭ-tē) *n.* the quality of being calm and even-tempered; composure

Customizing Instruction

Less Proficient Readers

Set a Purpose Invite students to share true stories they know that they think would be good to fictionalize. Then have students read to discover what happens in this fictionalized account of a volcanic eruption.

Students Acquiring English

Define the following words for students, and have them write down the words and their definitions for reference as they read.

- *avalanche:* a sliding of a large amount of snow, rocks, or other material down a mountainside
- *crater:* a bowl-shaped depression or pit, usually made by an explosion
- *icecap:* a large cover of ice or snow
- *rubble:* loose fragments of rock or building materials

Use **Spanish Study Guide** for additional support, pp. 208–210.

Gifted and Talented

Have students work in pairs to list attributes that describe Isabel Allende's writing style. Then suggest that each pair read a different story from *The Stories of Eva Luna* to explore her writing style further.

5. Despite the reports of the scientists, the villagers had an <u>instinctive</u> fear of another eruption. *(visceral)*
6. The first eruption left them feeling <u>unprotected</u>. *(vulnerable)*
7. For them, the volcano seemed to <u>personify</u> evil. *(embody)*
8. Only their <u>persistence</u> allowed them to rebuild their lives. *(tenacity)*
9. After such a disaster, though, it was difficult for them to keep their <u>composure</u>. *(equanimity)*

Use **Unit Six Resource Book** p. 18 for more exercises.

A lesson on synonyms appears on p. 1000 in the Pupil's Edition.

Reading and Analyzing

Reading Skills and Strategies: QUESTIONING

A Encourage students to formulate questions about the narrator's comments regarding the effect of a camera's lens on Rolf.

Possible Responses: What cowardly behavior does he display when he is not in front of the camera? From what emotions does he need protection?

Literary Analysis STYLE

B Ask students to note the length of sentences in this paragraph. Ask students why Allende might have chosen to begin the paragraph with a relatively short sentence and then continue with long, complicated sentences.

Possible Response: The first sentence merely states Rolf's involvement. The subsequent sentences discuss the detailed process of his involvement; the subject matter invites more detailed and therefore longer sentences.

ing; it seemed as if nothing could shake his fortitude or deter his curiosity. Fear seemed never to touch him, although he had confessed to me that he was not a courageous man, far from it. I believe that the lens of a camera had a strange effect on him; it was as if it transported him to a different time from which he could watch events without actually participating in them. When I knew him better, I came to realize that this fictive[10] distance seemed to protect him from his own emotions.

Rolf Carlé was in on the story of Azucena from the beginning. He filmed the volunteers who discovered her, and the first persons who tried to reach her; his camera zoomed in on the girl, her dark face, her large desolate eyes, the plastered-down tangle of her hair. The mud was like quicksand around her, and anyone attempting to reach her was in danger of sinking. They threw a rope to her that she made no effort to grasp until they shouted to her to catch it; then she pulled a hand from the mire and tried to move but immediately sank a little deeper. Rolf threw down his knapsack and the rest of his equipment and waded into the quagmire, commenting for his assistant's microphone that it was cold and that one could begin to smell the stench of corpses.

"What's your name?" he asked the girl, and she told him her flower name. "Don't move, Azucena," Rolf Carlé directed, and kept talking to her, without a thought for what he was saying, just to distract her, while slowly he worked his way forward in mud up to his waist. The air around him seemed as murky as the mud.

It was impossible to reach her from the approach he was attempting, so he retreated and circled around where there seemed to be firmer footing. When finally he was close enough, he took the rope and tied it beneath her arms, so they could pull her out. He smiled at her with that smile that crinkles his eyes and makes him look like a little boy; he told her that everything was fine, that he was here with her now, that soon they would have her out. He signaled the others to pull, but as soon as the cord tensed, the girl screamed. They tried again, and her shoulders and arms appeared, but they could move her no farther; she was trapped. Someone suggested that her legs might be caught in the collapsed walls of her house, but

10. **fictive** (fĭk'tĭv): imaginary or fictional.

WORDS TO KNOW **fortitude** (fôr'tĭ-to͞od') *n.* strength of mind to endure misfortune or pain with courage

986

Teaching Options

BLOCK SCHEDULING: MANAGING TIME

If your schedule requires that you cover the lesson objectives in a shorter time, use . . .
- Preparing to Read, p. 983
- Thinking Through the Literature, p. 995
- Vocabulary in Action, p. 996
- Grammar in Context, p. 997

If you want to take advantage of longer class time, use . . .
- TE Teaching Options: Preteaching Vocabulary, p. 984–985; Cross Curricular Links, p. 987; Speaking and Listening, p. 988; Viewing and Representing, p. 994; Informal Assessment, p. 996
- Choices & Challenges, p. 996

Copyright © Ernst Haas / Tony Stone Images.

she said it was not just rubble, that she was also held by the bodies of her brothers and sisters clinging to her legs.

2 "Don't worry, we'll get you out of here," Rolf promised. Despite the quality of the transmission, I could hear his voice break, and I loved him more than ever. Azucena looked at him but said nothing.

During those first hours Rolf Carlé exhausted all the resources of his ingenuity to rescue her. He struggled with poles and ropes, but every tug was an intolerable torture for the imprisoned girl. It occurred to him to use one of the poles as a lever but got no result and had to abandon the idea. He talked a couple of soldiers into working with him for a while, but they had to leave because so many other victims were calling for help. The girl could not move, she barely could breathe, but she did not seem desperate, as if an ancestral resignation allowed her to accept her fate. The reporter,

Customizing Instruction

Students Acquiring English

1 Invite a volunteer to explain the characteristics of quicksand, including the fact that if a person caught in quicksand struggles to get out, he or she is pulled deeper into the mud and is eventually pulled under completely.

Less Proficient Readers

2 Point out that the expression "exhausted all the resources of his ingenuity" means that Rolf tried every possible thing he could think of.

Cross Curricular Link History

MOUNT VESUVIUS Perhaps the most famous volcanic eruption in the Western world occurred in what is now Italy in A.D. 79 when Mount Vesuvius erupted, burying the cities of Pompeii, Herculaneum, and Stabiae. The mud and ash from the eruption encased much of what was in its destructive path. This effectively preserved many of the towns' sites, giving modern archaeologists invaluable information about Mediterranean life during that time period.

AND OF CLAY ARE WE CREATED 987

Reading and Analyzing

Literary Analysis: TONE

A Ask students what the phrase "premature optimism" suggests about the author's tone.

Possible Response: The author is sympathetic to Rolf's efforts, but is pessimistic about the results.

Reading Skills and Strategies: PREDICTING

B Ask students to predict what will happen if a pump does not arrive.

Possible Responses: The young girl will not be rescued, or the rescuers will devise some other way of extracting her from the mud.

Reading Skills and Strategies: VISUALIZING

Ask students to visualize and describe the scene so that listeners might be motivated to donate equipment or money.

Possible Responses: people trying to salvage their belongings; the doctor struggling to help survivors; children looking for their parents

on the other hand, was determined to snatch her from death. Someone brought him a tire, which he placed beneath her arms like a life buoy, and then laid a plank near the hole to hold his weight and allow him to stay closer to her. As it was impossible to remove the rubble blindly, he tried once or twice to dive toward her feet but emerged frustrated, covered with mud, and spitting gravel. He concluded that he would have to have a pump to drain the water, and radioed a request for one but received in return a message that there was no available transport and it could not be sent until the next morning.

"We can't wait that long!" Rolf Carlé shouted, but in the pandemonium no one stopped to commiserate. Many more hours would go by before he accepted that time had stagnated[11] and reality had been irreparably distorted.

A military doctor came to examine the girl and observed that her heart was functioning well and that if she did not get too cold she could survive the night.

"Hang on, Azucena, we'll have the pump tomorrow," Rolf Carlé tried to console her.

"Don't leave me alone," she begged.

"No, of course I won't leave you."

Someone brought him coffee, and he helped the girl drink it, sip by sip. The warm liquid revived her, and she began telling him about her small life, about her family and her school, about how things were in that little bit of world before the volcano erupted. She was thirteen, and she had never been outside her village. **A** Rolf Carlé, buoyed by a premature optimism, was convinced that everything would end well: the pump would arrive, they would drain the water, move the rubble, and Azucena would be transported by helicopter to a hospital where she would recover rapidly and where he could visit her and bring her gifts. He thought, She's already too old for dolls, and I don't know what would please her; maybe a dress. I don't know much about women, he concluded, amused, reflecting that although he had known many women in his lifetime, none had taught him these details. To pass the hours he began to tell Azucena about his travels and adventures as a news hound, and when he exhausted his memory, he called upon imagination, inventing things he thought might entertain her. From time to time she dozed, but he kept talking in the darkness, to assure her that he was still there and to overcome the menace of uncertainty.

That was a long night. **B**

Many miles away, I watched Rolf Carlé and the girl on a television screen. I could not bear the wait at home, so I went to National Television, where I often spent entire nights with Rolf editing programs. There, I was near his world, and I could at least get a feeling of what he lived through during those three decisive days. I called all the important people in the city, senators, commanders of the armed forces, the North American ambassador, and the president of National Petroleum, begging them for a pump to remove the silt, but obtained only vague promises. I began to ask for urgent help on radio and television, to see if there wasn't *someone* who could help us. Between calls I would run to the newsroom to monitor the satellite transmissions that periodically brought new details of the catastrophe. While reporters selected scenes with most impact for the news report, I searched for footage that featured Azucena's mud pit. The screen reduced the disaster to a single plane and accentuated the tremendous distance that separated me from Rolf Carlé; nonetheless, I was there with him. The child's every suffering hurt me as it did him; I felt his frustration, his

11. **stagnated:** stopped moving.

WORDS TO KNOW

pandemonium (păn′də-mō′nē-əm) *n.* a wild uproar or noise

irreparably (ĭ-rĕp′ər-ə-blē) *adv.* in a way that is impossible to repair or correct

Teaching Options

Mini Lesson: Speaking and Listening

TELEPHONE CONVERSATION

Prepare The narrator makes a number of frantic calls to seek help for Azucena. People often miss vital information on the telephone because they fail to listen attentively. Ask students to share examples from their own experience in which mistakes were made due to inattentive telephone listening.

Present Invite a pair of students to role-play their interpretation of one of the telephone conversations that the narrator might have had. One student can assume the role of the narrator, and the other should take the part of an official who might be able to send help to rescue Azucena.

Encourage students to get a map of Colombia, find the volcano, and locate the nearest airport, then brainstorm additional information about the pump. As a result of the telephone conversation, the student who is the important official should repeat back to the narrator the requests that he or she has understood. Then have the participants and the rest of the class discuss exactly what was said and how well the responses fit the requests. If possible, record the conversation and play back the recording to check understanding.

BLOCK SCHEDULING This activity is particularly well suited for longer class periods.

impotence.[12] Faced with the impossibility of communicating with him, the fantastic idea came to me that if I tried, I could reach him by force of mind and in that way give him encouragement. I concentrated until I was dizzy—a frenzied and futile activity. At times I would be overcome with compassion and burst out crying; at other times, I was so drained I felt as if I were staring through a telescope at the light of a star dead for a million years.

I watched that hell on the first morning broadcast, cadavers[13] of people and animals awash in the current of new rivers formed overnight from the melted snow. Above the mud rose the tops of trees and the bell towers of a church where several people had taken refuge and were patiently awaiting rescue teams. Hundreds of soldiers and volunteers from the civil defense were clawing through rubble searching for survivors, while long rows of ragged specters[14] awaited their turn for a cup of hot broth. Radio networks announced that their phones were jammed with calls from families offering shelter to orphaned children. Drinking water was in scarce supply, along with gasoline and food. Doctors, resigned to amputating arms and legs without anesthesia, pled that at least they be sent serum and painkillers and antibiotics; most of the roads, however, were impassable, and worse were the bureaucratic obstacles that stood in the way. To top it all, the clay contaminated by decomposing bodies threatened the living with an outbreak of epidemics.

Azucena was shivering inside the tire that held her above the surface. Immobility and tension had greatly weakened her, but she was conscious and could still be heard when a microphone was held out to her. Her tone was humble, as if apologizing for all the fuss. Rolf Carlé had a growth of beard, and dark circles beneath his eyes; he looked near exhaustion. Even from that enormous distance I could sense the quality of his weariness, so different from the fatigue of other adventures. He had completely forgotten the camera; he could not look at the girl through a lens any longer. The pictures we were receiving were not his assistant's but those of other reporters who had appropriated Azucena, bestowing on her the pathetic responsibility of embodying the horror of what had happened in that place. With the first light Rolf tried again to dislodge the obstacles that held the girl in her tomb, but he had only his hands to work with; he did not dare use a tool for fear of injuring her. He fed Azucena a cup of the cornmeal mush and bananas the army was distributing, but she immediately vomited it up. A doctor stated that she had a fever but added that there was little he could do: antibiotics were being reserved for cases of gangrene.[15] A priest also passed by and blessed her, hanging a medal of the Virgin around her neck. By evening a gentle, persistent drizzle began to fall.

"The sky is weeping," Azucena murmured, and she, too, began to cry.

"Don't be afraid," Rolf begged. "You have to keep your strength up and be calm. Everything will be fine. I'm with you, and I'll get you out somehow."

Reporters returned to photograph Azucena and ask her the same questions, which she no longer tried to answer. In the meanwhile, more television and movie teams arrived with spools of cable, tapes, film, videos, precision lenses, recorders, sound consoles, lights, reflecting screens, auxiliary motors, cartons of supplies, electricians, sound

12. **impotence:** powerlessness.
13. **cadavers** (kə-dăv′ərz): dead bodies.
14. **specters:** ghosts or ghostlike visions.
15. **gangrene:** death and decay of body tissue, usually resulting from injury or disease.

WORDS TO KNOW **embody** (ĕm-bŏd′ē) *v.* to give a concrete shape to; personify or represent

Customizing Instruction

Less Proficient Readers

Make sure students understand the situation to this point.

- What is Azucena's condition?
  Possible Response: She continues to hang on, but she is losing strength.
- What is your view of Rolf Carlé as a reporter?
  Possible Response: He seems more concerned with rescuing the young girl and offering her comfort than with reporting about the disaster.

Multiple Learning Styles

Visual Learners

Have students collect pictures, illustrations, diagrams, or photographs of erupting volcanoes and their aftermath. Then invite students to draw illustrations for this selection.

Reading and Analyzing

Literary Analysis: RHYTHM

A Ask students to reread the sentences in the passage, thinking about each one's rhythmic effect. Have them analyze what creates rhythm in each sentence.

Possible Response: a recurring pattern in the subject-verb structure

Literary Analysis STYLE

B Ask students to identify words and phrases that appeal to the senses in this passage and comment on the effectiveness of the sensory language. Ask students to describe the emotional effect this sensory language has on readers.

Possible Responses: The description of the clinging appeals to the sense of touch and creates the feel of desperation; the description of the smells recreates an impression of the home that contrasts with the children's fear.

technicians, and cameramen: Azucena's face was beamed to millions of screens around the world. And all the while Rolf Carlé kept pleading for a pump. The improved technical facilities bore results, and National Television began receiving sharper pictures and clearer sound, the distance seemed suddenly compressed, and I had the horrible sensation that Azucena and Rolf were by my side, separated from me by impenetrable glass. I was able to follow events hour by hour; I knew everything my love did to wrest the girl from her prison and help her endure her suffering; I overheard fragments of what they said to
A one another and could guess the rest; I was present when she taught Rolf to pray and when he distracted her with the stories I had told him in a thousand and one nights beneath the white mosquito netting of our bed.

When darkness came on the second day, Rolf tried to sing Azucena to sleep with old Austrian folk songs he had learned from his mother, but she was far beyond sleep. They spent most of the
B night talking, each in a stupor of exhaustion and hunger and shaking with cold. That night, imper-
1 ceptibly, the unyielding floodgates that had contained Rolf Carlé's past for so many years began to open, and the torrent of all that had lain hidden in the deepest and most secret layers of memory poured out, leveling before it the obstacles that had blocked his consciousness for so long. He could not tell it all to Azucena; she perhaps did not know there was a world beyond the sea or time previous to her own; she was not capable of imagining Europe in the years of the war. So he could not tell her of defeat, nor of the afternoon the Russians had led them to the concentration camp to bury prisoners dead from starvation. Why should he describe to her how the naked bodies piled like a mountain of firewood resembled fragile china? How could he tell
2 this dying child about ovens and gallows? Nor did he mention the night that he had seen his mother naked, shod in stiletto-heeled red boots, sobbing with humiliation. There was much he did not tell, but in those hours he relived for the first time all the things his mind had tried to erase. Azucena had surrendered her fear to him and so, without wishing it, had obliged Rolf to confront his own. There, beside that hellhole of mud, it was impossible for Rolf to flee from himself any longer, and the visceral terror he had lived as a boy suddenly invaded him. He reverted to the years when he was the age of Azucena and younger, and, like her, found himself trapped in a pit without escape, buried in life, his head barely above ground; he saw before his eyes the boots and legs of his father, who had removed his belt and was whipping it in the air with the never-forgotten hiss of a viper coiled to strike. Sorrow flooded through him, intact and precise, as if it had lain always in his mind, waiting. He was once again in the armoire[16] where his father locked him to punish him for imagined misbehavior, there where for eternal hours he had crouched with his eyes closed, not to see the darkness, with his hands over his ears to shut out the beating of his heart, trembling, huddled like a cornered animal. Wandering in the mist of his memories he found his sister, Katharina, a sweet, retarded child who spent her life hiding, with the hope that her father would forget the disgrace of her having been born. With Katharina, Rolf crawled beneath the dining room table, and with her hid there under the long white tablecloth, two children forever embraced, alert to footsteps and voices. Katharina's scent melded with his own sweat, with aromas of cooking, garlic, soup, freshly baked bread, and the unexpected odor of putrescent[17] clay. His sister's hand in his, her frightened breathing, her silk hair against his

16. **armoire** (ärm-wär′): a large, ornate wardrobe or cabinet.

17. **putrescent** (pyo͞o-trĕs′ənt): rotting and foul smelling.

WORDS TO KNOW

stupor (sto͞o′pər) *n.* a state of mental numbness, as from shock

visceral (vĭs′ər-əl) *adj.* instinctive or emotional rather than intellectual

Teaching Options

Mini Lesson Vocabulary Strategy

USING REFERENCE MATERIALS TO DETERMINE PRECISE WORD MEANINGS

Instruction Some of the WORDS TO KNOW in this lesson contain suffixes. As the word *tenacity* is displayed for the class, have one or more students locate the word in a dictionary and identify and define the root and suffix. Then, students should apply the meaning of the suffix to understand the word.

Possible Response:
Root: *tenēre,* "to hold firmly"
Suffix: *-ity,* state or quality

Application Have students work in pairs, following the procedure described above, to learn more about these words:

1. *fortitude*
   Possible Response: *fortis,* "strong"; *-tude,* "state, condition, quality, degree"
2. *tribulation*
   Possible Response: *trībulāre,* "to cause distress or suffering"; *-ation,* "action or process"
3. *vulnerable*
   Possible Response: *vulnus,* "wound"; *-able,* "capable of"

Use **Vocabulary Transparencies and Copymasters,** p. 89.

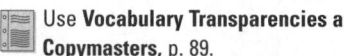

Illustration by David Loew / ARTCO.

Customizing Instruction

Students Acquiring English

1 Explain to students that *floodgates* are gates that are used to control the flow of water. Tell them that the term is used metaphorically here.

2 Explain to students that a *gallows* is the support for the rope used in a hanging.

Reading and Analyzing

Active Reading CLARIFYING

A Ask students to discuss why Rolf is finally able to weep for his sister's death.

Possible Response: Rolf has made himself numb in response to the tragedies in his childhood. He did not allow himself to fully feel the loss of his sister because of the guilt he felt for having abandoned her. Because of his experience with Azucena, he can now release his true feelings.

Literary Analysis: WORD CHOICE

B Point out the repetition of *you* in the last paragraph—how it is much like a poem. Point out that the narrative is addressed directly to Rolf. Ask what the narrator might be trying to accomplish with the repetition of *you.*

Possible Response: The repetition of *you,* coupled with the shift in address directly to Rolf, emphasizes that this story is about Rolf and his pain.

Reading Skills and Strategies: COMPARING

Guide students in comparing this story with "The Man in the Water." Ask them the following question:

What do Rolf and the man in the water have in common?

Possible Response: They both are committed to saving others, against all odds. Both realize that man's fight against nature is often futile.

cheek, the candid gaze of her eyes. Katharina . . . Katharina materialized before him, floating on the air like a flag, clothed in the white tablecloth, now a winding sheet, and at last he could weep for her death and for the guilt of having abandoned her. He understood then that all his exploits as a reporter, the feats that had won him such recognition and fame, were merely an attempt to keep his most ancient fears at bay, a stratagem for taking refuge behind a lens to test whether reality was more tolerable from that perspective. He took excessive risks as an exercise of courage, training by day to conquer the monsters that tormented him by night. But he had to come face to face with the moment of truth; he could not continue to escape his past. He *was* Azucena; he was buried in the clayey mud; his terror was not the distant emotion of an almost forgotten childhood, it was a claw sunk in his throat. In the flush of his tears he saw his mother, dressed in black and clutching her imitation-crocodile pocketbook to her bosom, just as he had last seen her on the dock when she had come to put him on the boat to South America. She had not come to dry his tears, but to tell him to pick up a shovel: the war was over and now they must bury the dead. **A**

"Don't cry. I don't hurt anymore. I'm fine," Azucena said when dawn came.

"I'm not crying for you," Rolf Carlé smiled. "I'm crying for myself. I hurt all over."

The third day in the valley of the cataclysm began with a pale light filtering through storm clouds. The president of the republic visited the area in his tailored safari jacket to confirm that this was the worst catastrophe of the century; the country was in mourning; sister nations had offered aid; he had ordered a state of siege; the armed forces would be merciless; anyone caught stealing or committing other offenses would be shot on sight. He added that it was impossible to remove all the corpses or count the thousands who had disappeared; the entire valley would be declared holy ground, and bishops would come to celebrate a solemn mass for the souls of the victims. He went to the army field tents to offer relief in the form of vague promises to crowds of the rescued, then to the improvised hospital to offer a word of encouragement to doctors and nurses worn down from so many hours of tribulations. Then he asked to be taken to see Azucena, the little girl the whole world had seen. He waved to her with a limp statesman's hand, and microphones recorded his emotional voice and paternal tone as he told her that her courage had served as an example to the nation. Rolf Carlé interrupted to ask for a pump, and the president assured him that he personally would attend to the matter. I caught a glimpse of Rolf for a few seconds kneeling beside the mud pit. On the evening news broadcast, he was still in the same position; and I, glued to the screen like a fortuneteller to her crystal ball, could tell that something fundamental had changed in him. I knew somehow that during the night his defenses had crumbled and he had given in to grief; finally he was vulnerable. The girl had touched a part of him that he himself had no access to, a part he had never shared with me. Rolf had wanted to console her, but it was Azucena who had given him consolation.

I recognized the precise moment at which Rolf gave up the fight and surrendered to the torture of watching the girl die. I was with them, three days and two nights, spying on them from the other side of life. I was there

WORDS TO KNOW

tribulation (trĭb'yə-lā'shən) *n.* great distress or suffering

vulnerable (vŭl'nər-ə-bəl) *adj.* unprotected and easily hurt; sensitive

Teaching Options

Mini Lesson Grammar

PARALLEL STRUCTURE

Instruction Tell students that words, phrases, and clauses that serve the same function in a sentence should have the same structure, or be *parallel.* Display the following sentence:

After high school, I will continue my schooling so that I can get a good job, so that I can continue to learn, and so that I can help my family.

Point out the underlined dependent clauses in the display sentence all display similar structure, making them parallel. Then display the following sentence:

After high school, I will continue my schooling so that I can get a good job, continue to learn, and help my family.

Point out to students that the underlined phrases all display similar structure, making them parallel. Then display the following sentence:

After high school, I will continue my schooling so that I can get a good job, continue to learn, and I can help my family.

Point out to students that the underlined elements do not display similar structure, making them not parallel.

when she told him that in all her thirteen years no boy had ever loved her and that it was a pity to leave this world without knowing love. Rolf assured her that he loved her more than he could ever love anyone, more than he loved his mother, more than his sister, more than all the women who had slept in his arms, more than he loved me, his life companion, who would have given anything to be trapped in that well in her place, who would have exchanged her life for Azucena's, and I watched as he leaned down to kiss her poor forehead, consumed by a sweet, sad emotion he could not name. I felt how in that instant both were saved from despair, how they were freed from the clay, how they rose above the vultures and helicopters, how together they flew above the vast swamp of corruption and laments. How, finally, they were able to accept death. Rolf Carlé prayed in silence that she would die quickly, because such pain cannot be borne.

By then I had obtained a pump and was in touch with a general who had agreed to ship it the next morning on a military cargo plane. But on the night of that third day, beneath the unblinking focus of quartz lamps and the lens of a hundred cameras, Azucena gave up, her eyes locked with those of the friend who had sustained her to the end. Rolf Carlé removed the life buoy, closed her eyelids, held her to his chest for a few moments, and then let her go. She sank slowly, a flower in the mud.

You are back with me, but you are not the same man. I often accompany you to the station, and we watch the videos of Azucena again; you study them intently, looking for something you could have done to save her, something you did not think of in time. Or maybe you study them to see yourself as if in a mirror, naked. Your cameras lie forgotten in a closet; you do not write or sing; you sit long hours before the window, staring at the mountains. Beside you, I wait for you to complete the voyage into yourself, for the old wounds to heal. I know that when you return from your nightmares, we shall again walk hand in hand, as before. ❖ **B** **2**

Translated by Margaret Sayers Peden

Customizing Instruction

Less Proficient Readers

1 Ask students the following questions:

- What does Rolf tell Azucena after she reveals that no boy ever loved her?
  Answer: He tells her that he loves her.

2 How does the narrator view Rolf at the end of the story?
Answer: She thinks that he has been profoundly changed by his experience because he has been able to confront his painful war memories.

Exercises Students should correct sentences with faulty parallel structure.

1. My brother ran to the bank, to the store, and to the school. *(No changes)*
2. The dog whimpered, howled, and she wailed. *(The dog whimpered, howled, and wailed.)*
3. To write her report, Agnes needed pens, paper, and she needed reference books. *(To write her report, Agnes needed pens, paper, and reference books.)*
4. Nubar wanted to run, jump, and scream. *(No changes)*
5. A job requires that you arrive on time, and you must avoid using the phone. *(A job requires that you arrive on time and that you avoid using the phone.)*

Use **Unit Six Resource Book,** p. 19.

Use **Grammar Transparencies and Copymasters,** p. 178.

Use McDougal Littell's ***Language Network,*** Chapter 16, for more instruction on parallel structure.

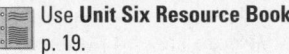

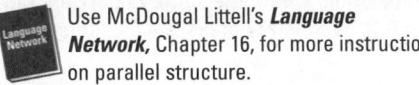

LITERARY LINK

Reading and Analyzing

Literary Analysis: THEME

Have students state the main idea that the poet conveys in this poem. In discussing the message of this poem, students may also notice thematic connections to the Allende selection.

Possible Responses: Life is fleeting; we do not fully understand our reason for living; the line between dream and reality is a blurred one.

Literary Analysis: MOOD

Ask students to describe the mood of this poem.

Possible Response: sad, resigned, wistful

Reading Skills and Strategies: EVALUATING

Ask students to evaluate the speaker's attitude toward life.

Possible Responses: The speaker realizes that life is brief and often mysterious, a bit like a dream from which we awaken just briefly. Encourage students to respond to the speaker's thoughts.

LITERARY LINK

Nocturne

Nocturno

Rosario Castellanos

Time is too long for life;
for knowledge not enough.

What have we come for, night, heart
of night?

All we can do is dream, or die,
dream that we do not die
and, at times, for a moment, wake.

Translated by Magda Bogin

Para vivir es demasiado el tiempo;
para saber no es nada.

¿A qué vinimos, noche, corazón de la
noche?

No es posible sino soñar, morir,
soñar que no morimos
y, a veces, un instante, despertar.

Nocturnal Landscape (1947), Diego Rivera. Oil on canvas, 111 cm × 91 cm, courtesy of Museo de Arte Moderno (INBA), Mexico City. Photo Copyright © 1995, Dirk Bakker/The Detroit Institute of Arts.

Teaching Options

Mini Lesson Viewing and Representing

Nocturnal Landscape **by Diego Rivera**

ART APPRECIATION Diego Rivera (1886–1957) was a Mexican artist who held radical political beliefs and became a controversial figure in Mexican politics. His most famous works are murals that represent Mexican life and Mexican people before the Spanish conquest.

Instruction Point out that the artist alternates darker and lighter areas. Ask students whether the tree trunk would create the same impact if it did not contrast with darker areas, such as those on the branches and limbs. Point out the twisted limbs that look as though they have struggled in order to continue growing. Encourage students to hypothesize why the human figures are perched on the branches of the tree.

Possible Response: The tree has both lighter and darker areas, just as nature has lighter and darker aspects. It is an organic form that follows its own course in a twisted and unpredictable way, just like nature and many people's lives. The people, perched like chickens roosting for the night, seem anonymous and powerless.

Connect to the Literature

1. **What Do You Think?** How did you react to the outcome of the story? Jot down a few words and phrases that best describe your response.

Comprehension Check
- How is the narrator made aware of what Rolf is doing?
- What piece of equipment does Rolf need to rescue Azucena?
- What hidden memories does Rolf unlock during his time with Azucena?

Think Critically

2. How would you describe the relationship that develops between Rolf and Azucena?

THINK ABOUT
- what they learn from each other
- the painful childhood memories he is able to recall
- why he tells Azucena that he loves her more than he could ever love anyone

3. **ACTIVE READING** CLARIFYING Look back at the notes you made in your READER'S NOTEBOOK. How did your understanding of Rolf change as you moved through the story? Cite details from the story to illustrate the changes in your understanding.

4. How do you think Rolf's experience with Azucena will affect him in the future?

5. According to the **narrator,** the name Azucena means "lily." Why do you think the author might have given her this name?

6. Describe the narrator's feelings about the events she relates and her relationship with Rolf.

Extend Interpretations

7. **Comparing Texts** What connection do you see between the poem "Nocturne" on page 994 and Allende's story?

8. **Critic's Corner** After reading this story, student reviewer Quoleshna Elbert wrote, "The story got under my skin; that's what makes a good story." Do you feel the same way about this story? What makes a good story for you?

9. **Connect to Life** Azucena died partly because no one transported a pump to the disaster site. Could a similar situation happen in this country? Why or why not?

Literary Analysis

STYLE **Style** refers to the way a piece of literature is written. It refers not to what is said but to how something is said. Elements such as **tone, imagery, sensory language, repetition, rhythm, syntax,** and **sentence length** all contribute to a writer's individual style. Allende's style is full of imagery and evocative description that appeal to the senses of sight, sound, and smell. She also writes long sentences and makes use of listing and repetition, as in the following passage:

He smiled at her with that smile that crinkles his eyes and makes him look like a little boy; he told her that everything was fine, that he was here with her now, that soon they would have her out.

Cooperative Learning Activity In a small group, choose one paragraph from the story that is typical of Allende's style and illustrates at least four of the elements described above. Designate one group member to read the paragraph aloud. In a group discussion, analyze how Allende's style influences each group member's response to the story.

REVIEW DIALOGUE With a partner, review the dialogue in Allende's story. How does the dialogue contribute to your understanding of the characters? Read aloud passages to support your opinion.

GUIDING STUDENT RESPONSE

Connect to the Literature

1. **What Do You Think?**
Possible Responses: saddened by Azucena's death; impressed by the care and love given by Rolf; angry with bureaucratic inefficiency; glad that Rolf was able to confront his painful childhood

Comprehension Check
- She watches him on TV.
- He needs a pump.
- painful childhood memories involving his father, his sister, his mother, and a concentration camp

Use Selection Quiz
Unit Six Resource Book, p. 20.

Think Critically

2. Possible Response: Rolf and Azucena become very close, each sensing the pain in the other. They are both needy, but for different reasons. Their understanding and love for each other are magnified by the present situation and by Rolf's past.
3. Rolf is objective, just doing his job at first, then he becomes involved in the rescue efforts. He commits himself totally to directing the efforts to save Azucena, developing a close bond with her.
4. Perhaps he will confront life more directly and not hide behind his camera as much. He may dedicate himself to helping others by reporting on their plight.
5. It implies that she is beautiful and delicate, like a flower; a lily will grow beautifully even in muddy, contaminated waters. The whiteness of a lily symbolizes purity.
6. The narrator loves Rolf. She is deeply touched by the rescue attempts that she witnesses on live television. Her love for him grows even though she feels she may never share with him a bond as strong as the one he shares with Azucena.

Extend Interpretations

Comparing Texts The speaker of the poem believes that life doesn't last long enough for us to learn and experience everything we want to know. Azucena never experiences life beyond her small village.
Critic's Corner Possible Response: A good story makes you empathize with the protagonists, allowing you to share their emotional experiences.
Connect to Life Possible Responses: Yes, because people are detached and distant from the plight of others; No, because there are many people who would help and because there is better transportation in this country, and finding a pump would be less difficult.

Literary Analysis

Style Suggest to students that each group member become a "specialist" in one element of Allende's style represented in the group's passage. Each specialist should be given time to thoroughly examine all examples of the stylistic element found in the paragraph.

Writing Options

1. **Television Commentary** Student monologues should review the details of the disaster and then give Rolf's reactions to it; they should consider how he has been affected by his experience.
2. **Love Letter** Suggest that students go back through the story and look for details that give clues to the narrator's state of mind and her feelings toward Rolf. Encourage them to imitate the style of her narrative voice in the letter.

Activities & Explorations

1. **Azucena's Eulogy** A eulogy is a speech given at a funeral ceremony, focusing on the praiseworthy characteristics of the deceased person. Students can gather details about Azucena's character that are worthy of praise.
2. **Volcanic Poster** Encourage students to explore the effects of volcanic eruptions on local populations. Their poster can give information and statistics about the effects of major volcanic eruptions throughout history.

Inquiry & Research

Encourage students to look for print information in issues of *Time, Newsweek,* and *U.S. News and World Report* from the week of November 25, 1985. They can also locate nonprint information by searching the Internet.

Art Connection

In Swirling Water The illustration portrays a desperate moment, while a note of hope is introduced with the image of the butterflies released from the drowning hands. They seem to suggest the love and final liberation that Rolf and Azucena experience.

Vocabulary in Action

1. antonyms
2. synonyms
3. antonyms
4. antonyms
5. synonyms
6. synonyms
7. antonyms
8. antonyms
9. synonyms
10. antonyms

Choices & CHALLENGES

Writing Options

1. **Television Commentary** Write the monologue that Rolf might give in a retrospective television broadcast one year after the tragic destruction of the town.
2. **Love Letter** Write a love letter that the narrator might write to Rolf in the months following the disaster.

Activities & Explorations

1. **Azucena's Eulogy** Assume the identity of Rolf or the narrator and deliver a eulogy for Azucena. ~ **SPEAKING AND LISTENING**
2. **Volcanic Poster** Read about the inner workings of a volcano and what happens when one erupts. Illustrate your findings on a poster to display for your class. ~ **EARTH SCIENCE**

Inquiry & Research

Find out more about what really happened to Omaira Sanchez, the girl this story was based on, when the Nevado del Ruiz volcano erupted.

Real World Link Begin your research by reading the newspaper article on page 998.

Art Connection

In Swirling Water What is your interpretation of the illustration on page 991? Why do you think it was chosen to accompany this story?

Vocabulary in Action

EXERCISE A: ASSESSMENT PRACTICE Identify each pair of words as synonyms or antonyms.

1. **visceral**—logical
2. **fortitude**—endurance
3. **tenacity**—doubt
4. **equanimity**—hysteria
5. **stupor**—daze
6. **pandemonium**—disturbance
7. **vulnerable**—immune
8. **tribulation**—blessing
9. **embody**—symbolize
10 **irreparable**—correctable

EXERCISE B: WORD KNOWLEDGE In a small group, tell a "round robin" story using the Words to Know. One person should begin a story and continue to speak until he or she has used one of the words in a sentence. Then the next person picks up the story where the first person left off, continuing until another of the words is used. Continue this process until all ten words are used and the story is brought to a conclusion.

Building Vocabulary

Most of the Words to Know in this lesson contain prefixes or suffixes. For an in-depth study of word parts, see page 856.

WORDS TO KNOW					
	embody	fortitude	pandemonium	tenacity	visceral
	equanimity	irreparably	stupor	tribulation	vulnerable

Informal Assessment

Informally assess students' understanding of the selection by having them write two entries from Rolf Carlé's diary, the first dated the day he discovers Azucena, the second dated the morning after she dies. Encourage students to review the story for details about Azucena's effect on Rolf Carlé and the repressed memories she forces him to confront.

RUBRIC

3 **Full Accomplishment** Student diary entries show a full understanding of Rolf's character.

2 **Substantial Accomplishment** Student diary entries show a general understanding of Rolf's character.

1 **Little or Partial Accomplishment** Student diary entries show little or no understanding of Rolf's character.

nmar in Context: Using Parallel Structures

following sentence, Isabel Allende uses parallel
res to describe how Rolf Carlé reassures
a.

e smiled at her with that smile that crinkles his
es and makes him look like a little boy; he
ld her that everything was fine, that he was
re with her now, that soon they would have
er out.

elism is a repetition of similar grammatical
res within a sentence or paragraph. In the
ce above, the parallel elements shown in blue
e noun clauses. Notice how Allende's use of
lism creates a nice rhythm and helps her
Rolf's concern for the young woman.

WRITING EXERCISE Fill in each blank with a word, phrase, or clause that is parallel to the other items in the series.

Example: Rolf gets dressed, packs his bags, and ________.

Rolf gets dressed, packs his bags, and says goodbye.

1. The eruption looses a torrent of rocks, ash, and ________, which destroys the valley below.
2. The camera zooms in on the young girl, with ________, her large helpless eyes, and her tangled hair.
3. When Rolf is finally close enough to Azucena, he takes the rope, ties it around her, and ________.
4. Azucena's pulse weakens, her eyes lock with those of Rolf, and ________.

Isabel Allende

1942–

Other Works
Of Love and Shadows
Eva Luna
The Stories of Eva Luna
Paula
The Infinite Plan

Creative Childhood Born in Lima, Peru, Isabel Allende moved with her mother to Santiago, Chile, when she was three years old and grew up in the home of her maternal grandparents. Her mother nurtured her creativity from the time she was very young, encouraging her to record her thoughts in a notebook and to draw anything she wanted on a bedroom wall. After graduating from high school, Allende worked for many years as a journalist and television interviewer. "My love for words induced me to work as a journalist since I was 17, but my vicious imagination was a great handicap," she said. "I could never be objective, I exaggerated and twisted reality, I would put myself in the middle of every feature."

Forced Exile Isabel Allende's uncle and godfather, Salvador Allende, became president of Chile in 1970 but was murdered when the military seized power in 1973. As a result, Isabel Allende and her family—along with many Chilean artists and intellectuals—went into exile, moving first to Venezuela and later to the United States. In her words, she felt "like a Christmas tree, cut off from all roots" after fleeing from her homeland, and for several years she was unable to write or to find work as a journalist.

Writing to Remember After receiving word in 1981 that her nearly 100-year-old grandfather was dying, however, she began writing a long letter to him. Her grandfather believed that people died only when you forgot them, and Allende says she wanted to prove to him that she had forgotten nothing, "that his spirit was going to live with us forever." Allende's letter became her first novel, *The House of the Spirits.* Written in the style of magical realism, the novel is based on her own family history and the political upheaval in modern Chile. The work became an international bestseller, hailed by critics as a powerful and original piece of historical fiction. Allende writes her novels and short stories in Spanish, then has her work translated.

Grammar in Context

WRITING EXERCISE Answers will vary. Possible answers are shown.

1. The eruption looses a torrent of rocks, ash, and mud, which destroys the valley below.
2. The camera zooms in on the young girl, with her muddy face, her large helpless eyes, and her tangled hair.
3. When Rolf is finally close enough to Azucena, he takes the rope, ties it around her, and tries to pull her out of the mud.
4. Azucena's pulse weakens, her eyes lock with those of Rolf, and she dies.

Mini Lesson Grammar

PARALLEL STRUCTURES

Instruction Like clauses and phrases, verbs can also have parallel structure. Explain that verbs that refer to the same subject should be consistent in tense and number. Illustrate by displaying the following sentence. Ask students to identify and correct the errors in parallelism.

Our music teacher always lectured, sings and is dancing during our music class.

Possible Response: Our music teacher always lectures, sings, and dances during our music class.

Practice Working in pairs, have students create a "quiz" containing three to five sentences with errors in parallel verb structure. They should also create an "answer key" that shows the errors corrected. When they finish, have them exchange quizzes with another pair of students.

Use **Unit Six Resource Book,** p. 19.

Use **Grammar Transparencies and Copymasters,** p. 179.

Use McDougal Littell's ***Language Network,*** Chapter 16, for more instruction in parallel structure.

Real WORLD Link

Internet Feature Article

Objectives

- identify features of a factual report
- identify features of a fictional account
- evaluate and compare the effects of a factual and fictional account of the same event

Connecting to the Literature

Isabel Allende's short story "And of Clay Are We Created" is based on the events described in Julia Preston's news article.

Reading for Information

Julia Preston's news article tells of the prolonged tragic death of Omaira Sanchez.

1 All of the five W's are answered in the first paragraph. The questions *why* or *how* this happened will be the focus of the following paragraphs.

2 **Possible Responses** She is trapped by a cement slab, by the body of her aunt, and by chilling waters. Allende might have changed this to increase the dramatic and emotional effect.

Girl Trapped in Water for 55 Hours Dies Despite Rescue Attempts

BY JULIA PRESTON

In November 1985, a sudden volcanic eruption buried the town of Armero, Colombia, killing thousands of people. Isabel Allende drew on news reports of this disaster for her story, "And of Clay Are We Created." As you read the following news account, compare its facts with the details Allende uses in her story.

❶ **Armero, Colombia**—Omaira Sanchez, a 13-year-old girl trapped up to her neck for more than 55 hours in flood-water, died yesterday morning despite rescuers' frantic efforts to free her.

❷ Omaira's legs were pinned in the ruins of what was once her home by a cement slab and by the body of an aunt who drowned in the avalanche of mud that rolled over Armero Wednesday night.

Trapped in the chilly water the little girl shivered violently and her hands turned a deathly white. Finally her blood pressure dropped so low she suffered a heart attack, according to Alejandro Jimenez, 23, a medical student volunteer at the disaster site who attended the child.

❸ "You can imagine how I feel," said Jimenez, looking drawn and exhausted yesterday morning. "We stayed up all night trying to save her."

About a dozen rescuers from the Colombian Air Force, the Red Cross, and fire departments of towns near Armero radioed increasingly desperate pleas since Thursday for an electric pump to keep the fetid waters from rising above the girl's chin. They called for picks, shovels, and winches to clear away rubble trapping her.

Reading for Information

Newspaper reporters generally write about real events, while fiction writers create their own plots. However, sometimes fiction writers draw inspiration from actual news accounts, as in the case of Allende and her story.

COMPARING FACTUAL AND FICTIONAL VERSIONS

Comparing factual and fictional accounts of the same real-life event can provide readers with two kinds o insight. First, a **fictional** account of a event often enhances the drama of the event by revealing the personal details and emotional impact that a factual version might not offer. On the other hand, a **factual** account focuses on details that give readers a fuller understanding of the reality of an event.

YOUR TURN Use the following activities to help you explore how a news account differs from a story based on the same event.

❶ A news account usually gives details that answer the questions *who, what, when, where,* and *why.* Which of these questions are answered in the first paragraph? What questions do you expect will be the focus of the paragraphs to follow?

❷ **Comparing Texts** Recall how in the Allende story, the child is trapped by "the bodies of her brothers and sisters clinging to her legs." What is she trapped by in the article? Why do you think Allende might have made this change?

Rescue efforts to save Omaira Sanchez, the Colombian teenaged girl who inspired this story.

At 2 P.M. yesterday, four hours after Omaira died, a Colombian radio station announced that 18 pumps had just arrived in a town 45 miles from Armero. To the end, rescue workers dug with their bare hands at the cement slab leaning on Omaira's numb legs, and bailed the water with a tin can.

4 Someone stretched a dirty blue-and-white checkered tablecloth over the scene of the tragedy, a scene that, displayed in newspapers around the world yesterday, came to represent the horror of the disaster.

Aftermath of disaster caused by Nevado del Ruiz eruption.

3 The news account quotes a rescue worker named Alejandro Jimenez, who fills a role similar to that of Rolf Carlé in the story. Why do you think Allende gives this character so much more emphasis than Jimenez receives in the original news account?

4 In what way are the details in the last paragraph of the news report similar to details you might find in a fictional account?

Inquiry & Research

Activity Link: "And of Clay Are We Created," p. 996

Compare and contrast facts about the real event with those portrayed in the story. You may wish to present your findings in chart form.

3 **Possible Response** Jimenez is a medical volunteer at the scene. Carlé is a television newscaster. Allende's focus on Carlé opens up his emotional interior and gives readers a primary emotional perspective on the event.

4 Fictional writing often contains imagery and symbolism. The dirty blue-and-white checkered tablecloth is a vivid image suggesting that even innocent families are subject to disaster and tragedy.

Mini Lesson Inquiry & Research

The Inquiry & Research activity on this page links to the Inquiry & Research section of Choices & Challenges on page 996.

Instruction On the chalkboard, list facts about the event presented in the news article. In a separate column, list the "facts" about the event presented in Allende's story. Then compare and contrast the real-life events with the events portrayed in the story. Ask students to identify the embellishments on fact as well as details and additional events that were added to the story.

Practice In a class discussion, have students take notes as you focus discussion on the question of how the fictional embellishments influence the reader's experience. Discuss the overall effect these embellishments have on the story. What insights or effects does their presence create?

Objectives
- identify synonyms, definitions, and antonyms for words in context
- use context clues to determine and understand word meanings
- use new words in a sentence

EXERCISE

Possible Responses

1. tenacity: firm determination
   clue: synonym
   The dog had such tenacity that he wouldn't let go of the ball.
2. seismographs: instruments for recording the intensity and the duration of the earth's tremors
   clue: definition
   The seismograph in the lab recorded the precise time that the earthquake struck.
3. pandemonium: chaos or upset
   clue: synonym
   If an earthquake strikes, you can expect complete pandemonium in cities, towns, and villages.
4. visceral: in the body
   clue: definition
   His visceral response to the earthquake was so overwhelming that he stood stiff with fright as if frozen.
5. stupor: a state of being dazed
   clue: definition
   I couldn't concentrate on anything; I was in a stupor all day.

Tackling New Words

Learning new words requires a variety of strategies. The more strategies you have for figuring them out, the better reader you will be.

In Unit One (page 56) you learned to look for context clues that help to clarify word meaning. This lesson presents three additional context clues. One is illustrated on the right. Read the example and try to determine the meaning of *fortitude*.

> **It seemed as if nothing could shake his fortitude or deter his curiosity. Fear seemed never to touch him.**
> —Isabel Allende, "And of Clay Are We Created"

The words "fear seemed never to touch him" suggest that *fortitude* means the opposite of *fear*. The words are an antonym clue to the meaning of *fortitude*—"courage."

Strategies for Building Vocabulary

Three types of context clues are synonyms, definitions, and antonyms. A **synonym** is a word that has the same or almost the same meaning as another word. A **definition** refers to an explanation of the meaning of a word. An **antonym** is a word with a meaning opposite to that of another word.

❶ **Find Synonym Clues** Use a synonym clue to figure out the meaning of *anonymity* in this passage.

> **His selflessness was one reason the story held national attention; his anonymity another. The fact that he went unidentified invested him with a universal character.**
> —Roger Rosenblatt, "The Man in the Water"

The word *unidentified* in the phrase "the fact that he went unidentified" suggests that *anonymity* means "the state of not being known."

❷ **Note Definition Clues** Sometimes a word's meaning may be clarified with a definition rather than a synonym. In the following example, the word *doeks* is explained by the definition that follows it.

> **Bamjee resented the people who were showing up in his house, plain ordinary native women in doeks, or cloth head coverings.**

Definition clues are often signaled by punctuation and by key words and phrases, such as *which is, that is, or,* and *in other words.*

❸ **Look for Antonym Clues** Sometimes you can identify words that are opposite in meaning to an unfamiliar word. What words seem to contrast with the word *chaotic* in the following sentence?

> **Washington, the city of form and regulations, turned chaotic, deregulated, by a blast of real winter and a single slap of metal on metal.**
> —Roger Rosenblatt, "The Man in the Water"

The phrase "city of form and regulations" describes what Washington was like before experiencing a sudden change; therefore *chaotic* must mean something opposite to *form* and *regulations,* like "disorderly" or "confusing."

EXERCISE Define the underlined words in these sentences. In each case, tell what kind of context clue helped you understand the word's meaning. Then write a sentence of your own for each word.

1. With firm determination, he held onto his hope of saving the child—a tenacity that made him a hero in the eyes of the world.
2. Some geologists had predicted trouble, based on the data from their seismographs, instruments that record the intensity and duration of earth tremors.
3. At the base of the mountain, the villagers pursued their peaceful lives. They received no warning of the coming pandemonium.
4. His reaction to the disaster was not intellectual but visceral.
5. They stared at the dark green sky in a stupor, too dazed to speak or think.

The Leap

Louise Erdrich

This story focuses on the life of a woman who took great physical risks as a blindfolded trapeze performer. Although trapeze acts often appear to be foolhardy stunts, the risks are well calculated by the trained performer, who may spend several years perfecting a single maneuver. Working on the trapeze requires not only tremendous strength, precise timing, and delicate balance but also considerable mental effort. Alfred Codona, one of the world's greatest trapeze artists, repeatedly emphasized the importance of "brain coordination" in aerial routines, warning other performers that any lack of mental clarity could result in death.

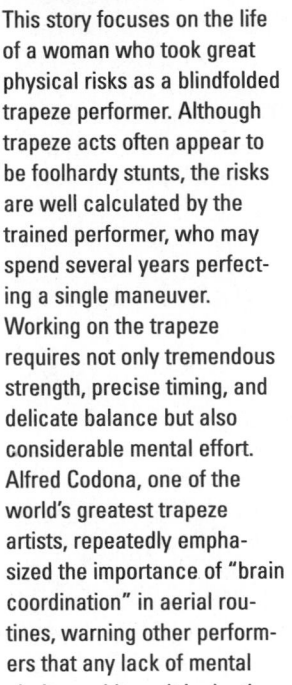

Illustration by Sarah Figlio.

My mother is the surviving half of a blindfold trapeze act, not a fact I think about much even now that she is sightless, the result of encroaching and stubborn cataracts.[1] She walks slowly through her house here in New Hampshire, lightly touching her way along walls and running her hands over knickknacks, books, the drift of a grown child's belongings and castoffs. She has never upset an object or as much as brushed a magazine onto the floor. She has never lost her balance or bumped into a closet door left carelessly open.

1. **encroaching . . . cataracts:** Cataracts are clouded areas on the lens of the eye. When they encroach, or advance beyond previous limits, they can cause total blindness.

ON YOUR OWN

Possible Objectives

You can use this selection to achieve one or more of the following objectives:

- enjoy silent sustained reading (Option One)
- read and analyze literature with a group (Option Two)
- use the Reader's Notebook to formulate questions about literature (Option Three)
- write in response to literature (Option Three)

Summary

The narrator explains how she owes her existence to her mother three times. In the first instance, which occurred before the narrator's birth, her mother was performing a blindfolded-trapeze act when lightning struck a tent pole and sent her hurling toward nothing. Her mother managed to pull off her blindfold, twist in midair, and hang on to a hot-braided wire. She survived, but her first husband, who was also in the act, did not. The second instance took place in the local hospital, where her mother met her father and the two fell in love as he taught her to read and write. In the third instance, the family home caught on fire. The narrator, seven years old, was trapped in her upstairs bedroom. Her mother climbed a nearby tree, lowered herself into the bedroom, scooped the girl up, and jumped with her to the safety of the firefighter's net. The narrator realizes that what her mother claims is true: "As you fall, there is time to think."

THE LEAP 1001

Reading the Selection

Option One
Silent Sustained Reading

You might set aside time each week for independent reading. During this time, you and all of your students would read for enjoyment. "The Leap" can be read independently in about 25 minutes. If you want to encourage students to read for pleasure, you might forgo assignments related to the selection. Should you want to make assignments, Options Two and Three offer suggestions.

Option Two
Shared Reading Groups

You may assign students to groups or allow them to choose their own. Students can read the selection together, alternately reading sections aloud, or they can read independently and meet to cooperate in a project that portrays some element of the story.

Possible Projects

- Students can learn more about the flying trapeze act—how it has changed since it was invented in 1859, the kinds of stunts a trapeze act includes, and the famous families who have popularized the act. Students might want to consider turning their research into a bulletin board display or an oral report.
- Students can make a collage of the most powerful images in "The Leap." Have students use clippings from magazines and their own artwork to piece together a visual portrait of the story. Remind students that they can include words as well as images in their collages, but the words should be presented artistically and be visually interesting.

It has occurred to me that the catlike precision of her movements in old age might be the result of her early training, but she shows so little of the drama or flair one might expect from a performer that I tend to forget the Flying Avalons. She has kept no sequined costume, no photographs, no fliers or posters from that part of her youth. I would, in fact, tend to think that all memory of double somersaults and heart-stopping catches had left her arms and legs were it not for the fact that sometimes, as I sit sewing in the room of the rebuilt house in which I slept as a child, I hear the crackle, catch a whiff of smoke from the stove downstairs, and suddenly the room goes dark, the stitches burn beneath my fingers, and I am sewing with a needle of hot silver, a thread of fire.

> It is from those old newspapers, now historical records, that I get my information.

I owe her my existence three times. The first was when she saved herself. In the town square a replica tent pole, cracked and splintered, now stands cast in concrete. It commemorates the disaster that put our town smack on the front page of the Boston and New York tabloids.[2] It is from those old newspapers, now historical records, that I get my information. Not from my mother, Anna of the Flying Avalons, nor from any of her in-laws, nor certainly from the other half of her particular act, Harold Avalon, her first husband. In one news account it says, "The day was mildly overcast, but nothing in the air or temperature gave any hint of the sudden force with which the deadly gale would strike."

I have lived in the West, where you can see the weather coming for miles, and it is true that out here we are at something of a disadvantage. When extremes of temperature collide, a hot and cold front, winds generate instantaneously behind a hill and crash upon you without warning. That, I think, was the likely situation on that day in June. People probably commented on the pleasant air, grateful that no hot sun beat upon the striped tent that stretched over the entire center green. They bought their tickets and surrendered them in anticipation. They sat. They ate caramelized popcorn and roasted peanuts. There was time, before the storm, for three acts. The White Arabians of Ali-Khazar rose on their hind legs and waltzed. The Mysterious Bernie folded himself into a painted cracker tin, and the Lady of the Mists made herself appear and disappear in surprising places. As the clouds gathered outside, unnoticed, the ringmaster cracked his whip, shouted his introduction, and pointed to the ceiling of the tent, where the Flying Avalons were perched.

They loved to drop gracefully from nowhere, like two sparkling birds, and blow kisses as they threw off their plumed helmets and high-collared capes. They laughed and flirted openly as they beat their way up again on the trapeze bars. In the final vignette[3] of their act, they actually would kiss in midair, pausing, almost hovering as they swooped past one another. On the ground, between bows, Harry Avalon would skip quickly to the front rows and point out the smear of my mother's lipstick, just off the edge of his mouth. They made a romantic pair all right, especially in the blindfold sequence.

That afternoon, as the anticipation increased, as Mr. and Mrs. Avalon tied sparkling strips of cloth onto each other's face and as they puckered their lips in mock kisses, lips destined

2. **tabloids:** newspapers containing short and often sensational articles.
3. **vignette** (vĭn-yĕt′): a short sketch or scene.

"never again to meet," as one long breathless article put it, the wind rose, miles off, wrapped itself into a cone, and howled. There came a rumble of electrical energy, drowned out by the sudden roll of drums. One detail not mentioned by the press, perhaps unknown—Anna was pregnant at the time, seven months and hardly showing, her stomach muscles were that strong. It seems incredible that she would work high above the ground when any fall could be so dangerous, but the explanation—I know from watching her go blind—is that my mother lives comfortably in extreme elements. She is one with the constant dark now, just as the air was her home, familiar to her, safe, before the storm that afternoon.

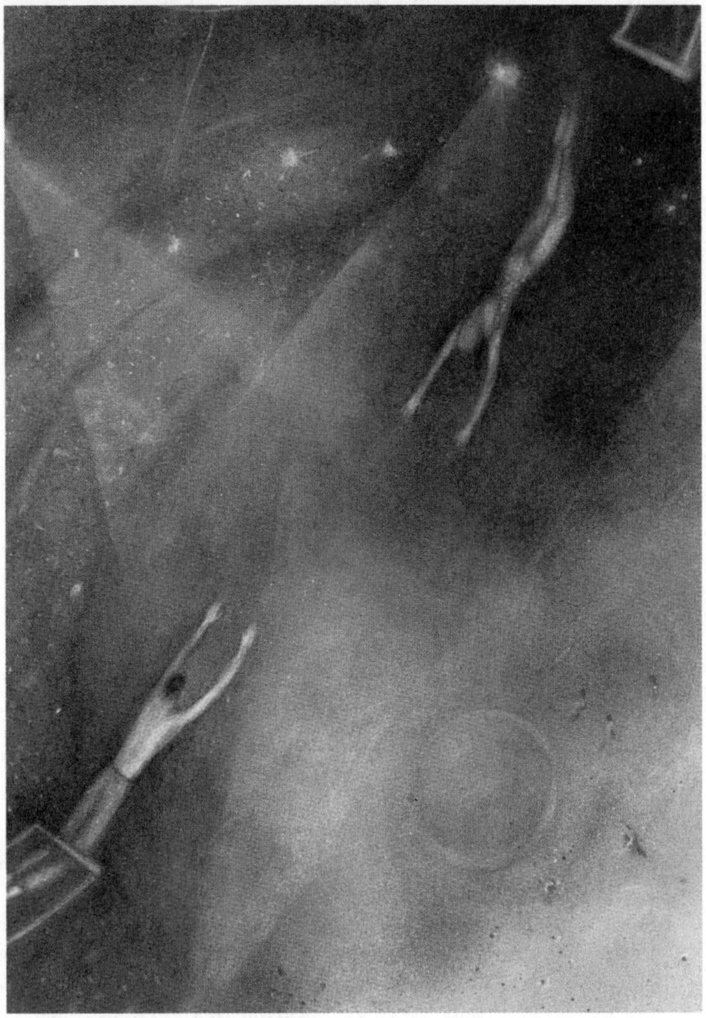

From opposite ends of the tent they waved, blind and smiling, to the crowd below. The ringmaster removed his hat and called for silence, so that the two above could concentrate. They rubbed their hands in chalky powder, then Harry launched himself and swung, once, twice, in huge calibrated[4] beats across space. He hung from his knees and on the third swing stretched wide his arms, held his hands out to receive his pregnant wife as she dove from her shining bar.

It was while the two were in midair, their hands about to meet, that lightning struck the main pole and sizzled down the guy wires, filling the air with a blue radiance that Harry Avalon must certainly have seen through the cloth of his blindfold as the tent buckled and the edifice[5] toppled him forward, the swing continuing and not returning in its sweep, and Harry going down, down into the crowd with

4. **calibrated:** measured.

5. **edifice** (ĕd′ə-fĭs): structure; building.

Option Three
Reader's Notebook

Provide the following direction to students before they read:

Have students read the text under the title. Then ask them to reflect in their Reader's Notebook on the following quote: "As you fall, there is time to think."

Have students read the selection, pausing at the break in column one, page 1005. Have them write any questions they would like to ask the narrator's mother in their Reader's Notebook. How does the narrator feel about the sister she never had?

At the end of the story, students will return to their questions. Ask them to note whether any of their questions have been answered. Have students describe the relationship the narrator has with her mother.

Have students analyze the story's theme, or message, in their Reader's Notebooks. Ask students to write how the theme of "The Leap" relates to the title.

After Reading

Possible Activities

Independent Activities

- Have students write the tabloid article that might have appeared after the lightning struck the circus tent. Students should use information presented in "The Leap" but should also feel free to embellish details.
- Have students create an annotated time line of the events in "The Leap." They should add as many details from the story as possible, including information about the mother's early life. Remind students that the flashbacks disrupt the chronology; they will have to read carefully to determine the chronological order of the story's events.

Discussion Activities

- Use the questions formulated by students as the start of a discussion about this story.
- Discuss how the narrator's use of imagery on page 1006 mirrors the circus disaster.
- Ask students what, in their opinion, are the mother's most admirable qualities. Have them consider the following before the discussion begins:
  - how she saves herself after the lightning strikes
  - what she does in the years following the aerial accident
  - the risk she takes to save her daughter's life
  - how she manages with her present blindness

Assessment Opportunities

- You can assess student comprehension of the story by evaluating the questions students formulate in their Reader's Notebooks.
- You can use any of the discussion questions as essay questions.
- You can have students turn any one of their Reader's Notebook entries into an essay.

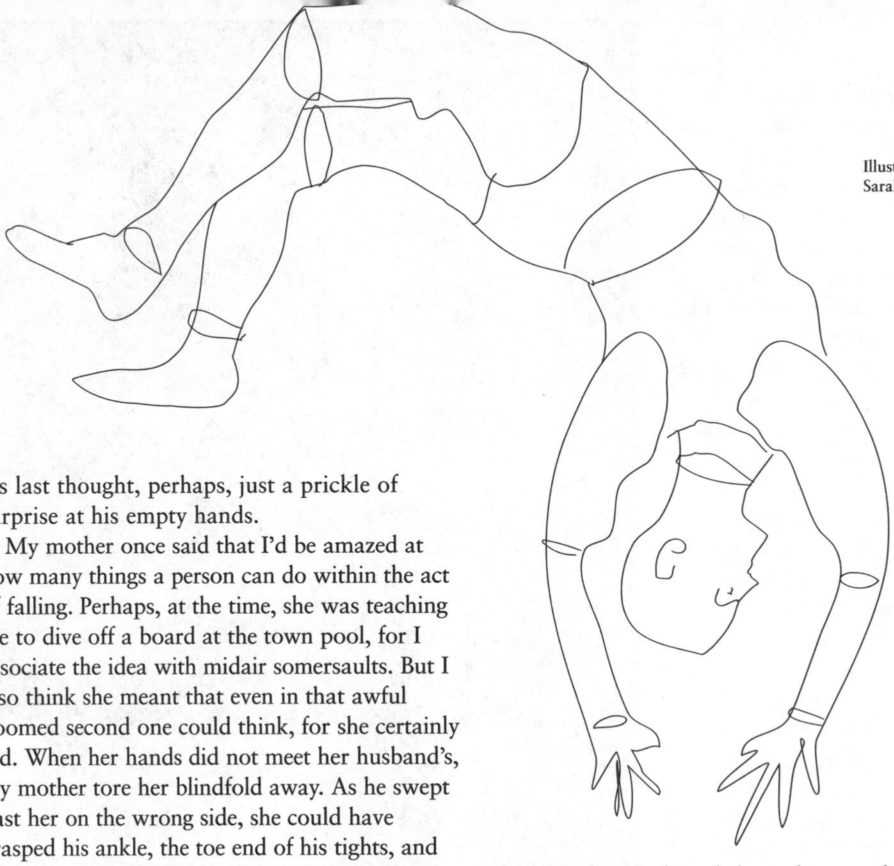

Illustration by Sarah Figlio.

his last thought, perhaps, just a prickle of surprise at his empty hands.

My mother once said that I'd be amazed at how many things a person can do within the act of falling. Perhaps, at the time, she was teaching me to dive off a board at the town pool, for I associate the idea with midair somersaults. But I also think she meant that even in that awful doomed second one could think, for she certainly did. When her hands did not meet her husband's, my mother tore her blindfold away. As he swept past her on the wrong side, she could have grasped his ankle, the toe end of his tights, and gone down clutching him. Instead, she changed direction. Her body twisted toward a heavy wire, and she managed to hang on to the braided metal, still hot from the lightning strike. Her palms were burned so terribly that once healed they bore no lines, only the blank scar tissue of a quieter future. She was lowered, gently, to the sawdust ring just underneath the dome of the canvas roof, which did not entirely settle but was held up on one end and jabbed through, torn, and still on fire in places from the giant spark, though rain and men's jackets soon put that out.

Three people died, but except for her hands my mother was not seriously harmed until an overeager rescuer broke her arm in extricating her and also, in the process, collapsed a portion of the tent bearing a huge buckle that knocked her unconscious. She was taken to the town hospital, and there she must have hemorrhaged,[6] for they kept her, confined to her bed, a month and a half before her baby was born without life.

Harry Avalon had wanted to be buried in the circus cemetery next to the original Avalon, his uncle, so she sent him back with his brothers. The child, however, is buried around the corner, beyond this house and just down the highway. Sometimes I used to walk there just to sit. She was a girl, but I rarely thought of her as a sister or even as a separate person really. I suppose you could call it the egocentrism[7] of a child, of

6. **hemorrhaged** (hĕm′ər-ĭjd): bled heavily from a blood vessel.

7. **egocentrism:** self-centeredness; the belief that everything revolves around oneself.

all young children, but I considered her a less finished version of myself.

When the snow falls, throwing shadows among the stones, I can easily pick hers out from the road, for it is bigger than the others and in the shape of a lamb at rest, its legs curled beneath. The carved lamb looms larger as the years pass, though it is probably only my eyes, the vision shifting, as what is close to me blurs and distances sharpen. In odd moments, I think it is the edge drawing near, the edge of everything, the unseen horizon we do not really speak of in the eastern woods. And it also seems to me, although this is probably an idle fantasy, that the statue is growing more sharply etched, as if, instead of weathering itself into a porous mass, it is hardening on the hillside with each snowfall, perfecting itself.

It was during her confinement in the hospital that my mother met my father. He was called in to look at the set of her arm, which was complicated. He stayed, sitting at her bedside, for he was something of an armchair traveler and had spent his war quietly, at an air force training grounds, where he became a specialist in arms and legs broken during parachute training exercises. Anna Avalon had been to many of the places he longed to visit—Venice, Rome, Mexico, all through France and Spain. She had no family of her own and was taken in by the Avalons, trained to perform from a very young age. They toured Europe before the war, then based themselves in New York. She was illiterate.

It was in the hospital that she finally learned to read and write, as a way of overcoming the boredom and depression of those weeks, and it was my father who insisted on teaching her. In return for stories of her adventures, he graded her first exercises. He bought her her first book, and over her bold letters, which the pale guides of the penmanship pads could not contain, they fell in love.

I wonder if my father calculated the exchange he offered: one form of flight for another. For after that, and for as long as I can remember, my mother has never been without a book. Until now, that is, and it remains the greatest difficulty of her blindness. Since my father's recent death, there is no one to read to her, which is why I returned, in fact, from my failed life where the land is flat. I came home to read to my mother, to read out loud, to read long into the dark if I must, to read all night.

Once my father and mother married, they moved onto the old farm he had inherited but didn't care much for. Though he'd been thinking of moving to a larger city, he settled down and broadened his practice in this valley. It still seems odd to me, when they could have gone anywhere else, that they chose to stay in the town where the disaster had occurred, and which my father in the first place had found so constricting. It was my mother who insisted upon it, after her child did not survive. And then, too, she loved the sagging farmhouse with its scrap of what was left of a vast acreage of woods and hidden hay fields that stretched to the game park.

I owe my existence, the second time then, to the two of them and the hospital that brought them together. That is the debt we take for granted since none of us asks for life. It is only once we have it that we hang on so dearly.

I was seven the year the house caught fire, probably from standing ash. It can rekindle, and my father, forgetful around the house and perpetually exhausted from night hours on call, often emptied what he thought were ashes from cold stoves into wooden or cardboard containers. The fire could have started from a flaming box, or perhaps a buildup of creosote[8] inside the chimney was the culprit. It started

8. **creosote** (krē′ə-sōt′): an oily tar deposit from burned wood, which collects in a chimney.

THE LEAP **1005**

right around the stove, and the heart of the house was gutted. The baby sitter, fallen asleep in my father's den on the first floor, woke to find the stairway to my upstairs room cut off by flames. She used the phone, then ran outside to stand beneath my window.

When my parents arrived, the town volunteers had drawn water from the fire pond and were spraying the outside of the house, preparing to go inside after me, not knowing at the time that there was only one staircase and that it was lost. On the other side of the house, the superannuated[9] extension ladder broke in half. Perhaps the clatter of it falling against the walls woke me, for I'd been asleep up to that point.

As soon as I awakened, in the small room that I now use for sewing, I smelled the smoke. I followed things by the letter then, was good at memorizing instructions, and so I did exactly what was taught in the second-grade home fire drill. I got up; I touched the back of my door before opening it. Finding it hot, I left it closed and stuffed my rolled-up rug beneath the crack. I did not hide under my bed or crawl into my closet. I put on my flannel robe, and then I sat down to wait.

Outside, my mother stood below my dark window and saw clearly that there was no rescue. Flames had pierced one side wall, and the glare of the fire lighted the massive limbs and trunk of the vigorous old elm that had probably been planted the year the house was built, a hundred years ago at least. No leaf touched the wall, and just one thin branch scraped the roof. From below, it looked as though even a squirrel would have had trouble jumping from the tree onto the house, for the breadth of that small branch was no bigger than my mother's wrist.

From below, it looked as though even a squirrel would have had trouble jumping from the tree onto the house . . .

Standing there, beside Father, who was preparing to rush back around to the front of the house, my mother asked him to unzip her dress. When he wouldn't be bothered, she made him understand. He couldn't make his hands work, so she finally tore it off and stood there in her pearls and stockings. She directed one of the men to lean the broken half of the extension ladder up against the trunk of the tree. In surprise, he complied. She ascended. She vanished. Then she could be seen among the leafless branches of late November as she made her way up and, along her stomach, inched the length of a bough that curved above the branch that brushed the roof.

Once there, swaying, she stood and balanced. There were plenty of people in the crowd and many who still remember, or think they do, my mother's leap through the ice-dark air toward that thinnest extension, and how she broke the branch falling so that it cracked in her hands, cracked louder than the flames as she vaulted with it toward the edge of the roof, and how it hurtled down end over end without her, and their eyes went up, again, to see where she had flown.

I didn't see her leap through air, only heard the sudden thump and looked out my window. She was hanging by the backs of her heels from the new gutter we had put in that year, and she was smiling. I was not surprised to see her, she was so matter-of-fact. She tapped on the window. I remember how she did it, too. It was the friendliest tap, a bit tentative, as if she was afraid she had arrived too early at a friend's house. Then she gestured at the latch, and when

9. **superannuated** (so͞o′pər-ăn′yo͞o-ā′tĭd): too old or worn for further work or service.

I opened the window, she told me to raise it wider and prop it up with the stick so it wouldn't crush her fingers. She swung down, caught the ledge, and crawled through the opening. Once she was in my room, I realized she had on only underclothing, a bra of the heavy stitched cotton women used to wear and step-in, lace-trimmed drawers. I remember feeling light-headed, of course, terribly relieved, and then embarrassed for her to be seen by the crowd undressed.

I was still embarrassed as we flew out the window, toward earth, me in her lap, her toes pointed as we skimmed toward the painted target of the fire fighter's net.

I know that she's right. I knew it even then. As you fall, there is time to think. Curled as I was, against her stomach, I was not startled by the cries of the crowd or the looming faces. The wind roared and beat its hot breath at our back; the flames whistled. I slowly wondered what would happen if we missed the circle or bounced out of it. Then I wrapped my hands around my mother's hands. I felt the brush of her lips and heard the beat of her heart in my ears, loud as thunder, long as the roll of drums. ❖

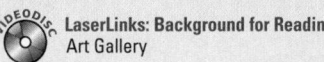

Louise Erdrich
1954–

Other Works
Jacklight
Baptism of Desire
The Beet Queen
Tracks
The Bingo Palace

A Child of Teachers Chippewa on her mother's side and German on her father's, Louise Erdrich was born in Little Falls, Minnesota, and grew up in the small town of Wahpeton, North Dakota, near the Minnesota border. Both of her parents taught at the Bureau of Indian Affairs boarding school in Wahpeton, and her grandfather was a tribal leader of the nearby Turtle Mountain Reservation. Her childhood love of writing was encouraged by both her father, who gave her a nickel for every story she wrote, and her mother, who stapled the tales into construction paper covers. "So at an early age," Erdrich humorously notes, "I felt myself to be a published author earning substantial royalties."

New Directions Erdrich enrolled in Dartmouth in 1972, the first year in which the New Hampshire college admitted women. There she took courses in the new Native American studies department—chaired by anthropologist Michael Dorris—and began coming to terms with the importance of her Native American heritage. After working at several jobs and obtaining a master's degree, she returned to Dartmouth as a writer-in-residence and began a close professional friendship with Dorris, who was also part Native American. They married in 1981.

The Step to Success Erdrich's first novel, *Love Medicine,* grew out of a short story that she and Dorris worked on together. Winner of the 1984 National Book Critics Circle Award, *Love Medicine* traces the lives of several Native American families in a series of interconnected stories. Many of the characters in *Love Medicine* appear in three of Erdrich's subsequent novels. "My characters choose me," she once said, "and once they do it's like standing in a field and hearing echoes. All I can do is trace their passage."

Additional Works Erdrich and Dorris continued to work in unusually close collaboration until Dorris's death in 1997. They read and revised each other's drafts, and even jointly published one novel, *The Crown of Columbus.* Erdrich has published two highly regarded volumes of poetry and a number of prize-winning short stories. Her first major work of nonfiction, *The Blue Jay's Dance: A Birth Year,* was published in 1995.

VIDEODISC **LaserLinks: Background for Reading**
Art Gallery

THE LEAP **1007**

Objectives
- create a Multimedia Presentation
- use a multimedia presentation as a model
- use effective presentation techniques
- refine a presentation to vary material
- edit and proofread for consistent form

Introducing the Workshop

A Multimedia Presentation Remind students that the prefix *multi-* means "more than one." Therefore, a multimedia presentation involves more than one method of communication. Through the combination of sound, visuals, and text, multimedia presentations have more of an impact on an individual or group because of the multisensory approach. Ask students to discuss their impressions of multimedia techniques or products such as political advertising on television, foreign films with subtitles, CD-ROM encyclopedias, and video games. Ask students to give specific examples and discuss why these techniques are effective. Explain that by creating their own mulitmedia presentations, students will be able to acquaint others in their community with unsung heroes.

Initiate a discussion about heroes. Ask students to identify their heroes and answer the following questions: What are the hero's most admirable qualities? How does the hero demonstrate heroism? How does a hero today differ from a hero of the past?

Remind students how writers reveal a character's personality. A writer can provide direct statements, describe the character, let the character speak, reveal the character's thoughts, reveal what others say or think about the character, and show a character's actions. Encourage them to consider the same types of techniques to discuss their hero.

Basics in a Box

B Using the Guidelines & Standards Point out to students that a successful multimedia presentation involves two aspects: content and delivery. Ask students who are involved in drama, debate, or speech classes to share their ideas about effective content and delivery.

Communication Workshop Multimedia Presentation

Using media to present ideas . . .

A **From Reading to Presenting** Heroes come in many forms, from the housewife in "A Chip of Glass Ruby" to the unnamed rescuer in "The Man in the Water." Some heroes do their good deeds in the public eye, while others act quietly behind the scenes. However, even quiet deeds can make for an inspiring story, especially when shared in an effective presentation. One way to inspire or inform others is with a **multimedia presentation,** which combines sound, visuals, and text. Politicians and businesspeople often use multimedia presentations to convey their messages at rallies, trade shows, and meetings of all kinds.

For Your Portfolio

WRITING PROMPT Create a multimedia presentation about an unsung hero in your life or community.

Purpose: To inform
Audience: Classmates, the student body, members of the community

Basics in a Box

B **GUIDELINES & STANDARDS** Multimedia Presentation

Content

A successful multimedia presentation should
- capture the audience's attention with a strong beginning
- clearly, directly, and logically present information
- use media appropriate to the content
- end by stating the importance of the topic, summarizing the points made, or drawing a conclusion about the topic

Delivery

An effective presenter should
- have good posture and maintain eye contact with the audience
- vary his or her pacing as well as the pitch, tone, and volume of his or her voice
- use gestures and body language to enhance the presentation
- smoothly incorporate the media components into the presentation

LESSON RESOURCES

USING PRINT RESOURCES

Unit Six Resource Book
- Planning Your Presentation, p. 22
- Developing, Practicing, and Presenting, p. 23
- Peer Response, pp. 24–25
- Refining, Editing, and Proofreading, p. 26
- Standards for Evaluation, p. 27

USING MEDIA RESOURCES

LaserLinks
Writing Springboards
See Teacher's SourceBook p. 64 for bar codes.

Writing Coach CD-ROM

Visit our website:
www.mcdougallittell.com

Analyzing a Multimedia Presentation

GUIDELINES IN ACTION

<show first visual: Lee Chavez>
How would you like to spend your summer outside in 90° weather, mowing lawns and painting porches? Doesn't sound like much fun, does it? But it was for 20 Kelley High School students.

❶ Script includes notes about when to present visuals.

❷ Introduces topic with a provocative question

<show second visual: newspaper clipping>
It all started last spring when tenth grader Lee Chavez read a newspaper article about an elderly woman named Virginia Wilson. Apparently, town authorities had decided her house was an eyesore, but Mrs. Wilson couldn't afford to repair it. Lee brought the article to his English class, and his classmates got interested in Mrs. Wilson's story.

❸ Covers ideas in chronological order

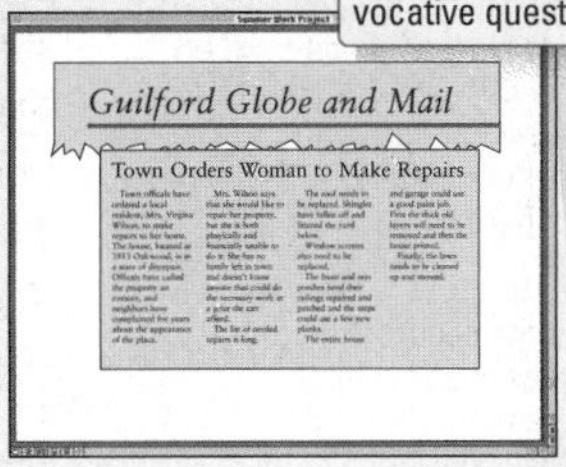

Guilford Globe and Mail
Town Orders Woman to Make Repairs

<show third visual: list of repairs>

Six students visited Mrs. Wilson at her home to see if they could help. Together, they made a list of the repairs her house needed. The students also attended city council meetings to learn about zoning laws and building permits.

❹ Visuals summarize information.

<show fourth visual: pie chart>
Next, the students visited local businesses to ask for donations in the form of cash, supplies, or skilled labor. Several employees at a local building and supply company offered their time and expertise to the project.

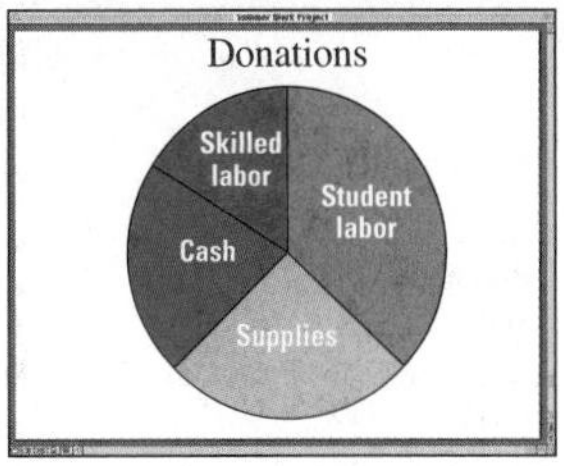

<show fifth visual: girl working>
As news of the project spread, more and more people got involved. By mid-June, the group had grown to 20 students and 8 adults. They finished repairing Mrs. Wilson's house in early July and began work on four more houses in the neighborhood. The project kept growing—over 200 people are involved now—and the group will work on six more homes next spring.

You may wonder, Why would these students give up their free time to help repair other people's houses? Listen to them tell why they did it, in their own words.

<play cued tape cassette of students' voices>

These students may see themselves as average teens, but to me and to many others, they are unsung heroes.

❺ Includes an audio recording to personalize presentation

❻ This writer ends by drawing a conclusion about the topic.

Another Option:
• Summarize the points made.

Use McDougal Littell's ***Language Network***, Chapter 30, for more instruction on creating multimedia products.

To engage students visually, use **Power Presentation** 11, Multimedia Presentation.

Teaching the Lesson

Analyzing a Multimedia Presentation

C The student model illustrates how an oral presentation incorporates media components. The presentation about student involvement in the community uses various visuals and an audio recording.

1. Point out to students that notes about when to present visuals are similar to the stage directions in a play or camera directions for a movie or TV script. Bracketed notes will help students remember how they want to sequence their presentation.
2. Remind students that if they use a rhetorical question, they should not expect an answer from the audience. Tell students that they can also use an anecdote, a startling fact, or a powerful quotation to grab the audience's interest at the beginning.
3. Presenting the details in chronological order helps the audience follow the presentation. Tell students that some content may lend itself to other options such as cause and effect or comparison-and-contrast order.
4. Point out that visuals in a multimedia presentation broaden and enhance the message. Examples of visuals include charts, graphs, maps, cartoon strips, photographs, newspaper and magazine articles, print ads, etc. Remind students that visuals that have words should be large enough for a viewer in the back of the room to see clearly.
5. Music is another option in multimedia presentations. Music can help set a desired mood and can help pace a particular segment of the presentation. Students can experiment with all types of music. Remind them that music with lyrics should not be overpowering.
6. Ask students to summarize the points that have been made.
   Possible Response: Tenth-grader Lee Chavez read a newspaper article about a woman, Mrs. Wilson, who could not afford to repair her house. Lee took the article to his English class, enlisting the help of six other students. They made a list of repairs, attended city council meetings, and visited local businesses. As the news spread, more volunteers got involved and began work on additional homes.

Planning the Presentation

Choosing a Topic

If after reading the Idea Bank students are having difficulty choosing a topic for their presentation, suggest they try the following:

- Research possible heroes in the library or use the Internet.
- Interview neighbors, teachers, or members of local community groups for ideas on possible heroes.

Planning the Multimedia Presentation

1. Have students take notes when they conduct their research or interviews. They can use note cards or tape-record the interview for transcription at a later time. Remind them that they must ask permission to tape-record the interview. Tell students to write out their questions in advance, but to be ready to ask questions off-the-cuff. Questions should elicit more than a "yes" or "no" response. Good interviewers not only listen to what the subject says, but they also observe the subject's actions during the interview.
2. Remind students that their intended audience will help them decide the kind of script they will write. If the audience is familiar with the subject, the presenter will have to present ideas in a new and refreshing way. If the audience knows very little about the subject, the student will need to pay particular attention to accuracy of facts and details.
4. Students may want to create a storyboard using a large poster to outline their ideas, including where the visuals and audio segments will be placed.
5. Students should use their creativity and also rely on resources such as their school librarian or technology consultant for assistance.

IDEABank

1. Your Working Portfolio
Look at the **Writing Option** you completed earlier in this unit:
- **Hero's Tribute,** p. 982

2. Read All About It
Read local and neighborhood newspapers for stories about heroic acts performed by ordinary people. You also might use the Internet to look for online newspapers. Scan some recent back issues for stories about heroes.

3. Write It Out
Freewrite about the qualities and acts that make a hero. Consider everyday acts of courage and kindness as well as life-and-death ones. Then list people who exhibit those qualities.

Have a question?

See the **Communication Handbook**
Giving a Speech, pp. 1176-1177
Conducting Interviews, p. 1178
Using Visual Representations, p. 1179

Creating Your Multimedia Presentation

❶ Planning Your Presentation

To find a topic for your presentation, try brainstorming with your classmates about people whose work you admire. You also might talk with your family about relatives who have done something heroic. See the **Idea Bank** in the margin for more ideas. After you have chosen your topic, follow the steps below.

Steps for Planning Your Multimedia Presentation

1. **Gather information about your hero.** What heroic act did the person perform? What was his or her motivation? What were the effects of his or her actions? Conduct research or interviews to collect answers to these and other questions you generate.
2. **Think about your audience.** What do they already know about the person? What do you *want* them to know? What background information will you need to provide?
3. **Evaluate your information.** Although your presentation may make an emotional appeal, be sure your facts are accurate. If necessary, use additional sources.
4. **Organize your information.** What is the best order in which to present your information? Where will you incorporate media elements?
5. **Decide which media to use in your presentation.** What types of resources are available? Which will help you get your point across most effectively? Here are some options to consider:
   - **Audiotapes and CDs** allow you to present sound effects, including music and voices.
   - **Flip charts, posters, photos, slides, charts, and graphs** allow you to present visuals in a variety of formats and don't necessarily require the use of a computer.
   - **Videos** allow you to present both sound and visual material.
   - **Computer presentation software** allows you to incorporate sound and visuals and to produce graphs, charts, and drawings; you can even project a slide show from a computer.

❷ Developing Your Presentation

Once you have gathered the information you want to include in your multimedia presentation, you can begin organizing it and creating the text and multimedia components.

Steps for Developing Your Multimedia Presentation

1. **Create an outline of the points you will make.** If you wish, you can write out your script word for word. Be sure to indicate where you will include your media elements. Remember that you may need to introduce and explain the audio and visual materials you present.
2. **Create a strong introduction and conclusion.** Use a question, an anecdote, a startling fact, or a powerful quotation to grab your audience's interest right away. End with a clear, powerful statement to leave a memorable impression.
3. **Gather or create your media components.** Make sure that all images and text in your visuals are large enough to be seen at the back of the presentation area. Check audio materials to ensure that the sound can be heard clearly.
4. **Evaluate your materials.** Look critically at your materials to see whether you have used the various media—including your oral delivery of the text—as effectively as possible. Large amounts of detailed material, for example, are often best presented in charts or graphs rather than in words. Presenting people's recorded voices can be more powerful than describing what they said.

❸ Practicing and Presenting

Practice your presentation several times to become comfortable with speaking from your script or outline and handling your media elements. Keep the following points in mind as you rehearse.

- **Use your voice effectively.** Speak loudly enough to be heard, but vary the tone and pitch of your voice to keep your audience's attention. Use changes in volume and pace to emphasize particular points.
- **Maintain eye contact and use appropriate gestures and facial expressions.** Keep your audience with you by looking directly at them and using gestures and expressions to maintain their interest and emphasize your points.
- **Weave the media elements smoothly into your presentation.** Make sure you know how to operate the equipment you will be using. Become completely familiar with the content of your visuals and audio materials so that you can talk about them knowledgeably.

When you feel confident in your work, you might want to invite several friends or family members to review your presentation. If necessary, modify your presentation on the basis of their feedback.

Ask Your Peer Reviewer

- What did you learn from my presentation?
- What elements were most effective?
- What information was unclear or confusing?
- How did my media choices help or distract you?
- What would you like to know more about?

TECHTool

To create a multimedia presentation on a computer, you will need software programs for creating, editing, and combining text, graphics, sound, and videos. For help, ask your school's technology advisor or use tutorials and other aids such as slide-show templates. You can find templates and tutorials in many computer programs and on the Internet.

Developing the Multimedia Presentation

Point out that each student's presentation will be unique and that they can bring their own special touches to the product. Remind them to be objective about all aspects of the presentation and to pretend that they are an audience member. They should ask themselves questions: What is the best way to convey the factual information? What kind of an introduction would be most memorable? Are my media components compelling? Are these the appropriate materials to effectively convey my message?

Practicing and Presenting

Remind students that being well prepared is a way to ward off nervousness. There are also other techniques that they can use to avoid the jitters:

- Keep time restraints in mind. Practicing ahead of time will allow you to edit and revise to meet your allotted time.
- Tape-record the presentation so that you can hear your voice in the way that your audience will. Practice varying the pitch and tone to keep the audience's attention.
- Have someone videotape your presentation and evaluate it.
- Pretend that you are a famous reporter or television talk show host as you practice.
- Take slow, deep breaths before you begin the actual presentation.
- Practice, practice, practice.

Refining the Presentation

VARYING YOUR MATERIAL

As a quick review, ask students to identify and define the four types of sentences. Volunteers should write an example of each on the board.

Answers: declarative (makes a statement); interrogative (asks a question); imperative (gives an order or makes a request); and exclamatory (shows strong feelings)

Explain that sentences are also classified by their structure—by the number and kinds of clauses they have. A simple sentence has one independent clause and no subordinate clauses. A compound sentence has two or more independent clauses joined together. A complex sentence has one independent clause and at least one subordinate clause. A compound-complex sentence has two or more independent clauses and one or more subordinate clauses. Have volunteers write an example of each on the board.

Editing and Proofreading

CONSISTENT FORM

Items in a sentence or list should be expressed in parallel or similar forms: nouns should be paralleled by nouns; adjectives by adjectives; action verbs by action verbs, etc. If a list begins with a noun, subsequent items should begin with a noun. Point out how the model visual was edited so that all repairs begin with a present-tense verb. Remind students that, although they are creating a visual, it is important that they produce an error-free final draft of their text. They should be careful as they revise, edit, and proofread.

Reflecting

Encourage students to recognize and evaluate what they learned about the multimedia presentation. What techniques did they learn that they can apply to other assignments? Ask students to consider the effectiveness of their planning and practicing. Have them add these reflections to their presentation script. Save their script in their Working Portfolio.

Need Revising help?

Review the **Rubric**, p. 1008

Consider **peer reviewer** comments.

Check **Revision Guidelines**, p. 1145

4 Refining Your Presentation

TARGET SKILL ▶ VARYING YOUR MATERIAL To maintain your audience's interest in your presentation, vary the types and structures of your sentences. For instance, asking a question can get your listeners' attention, but asking several questions may confuse or bore your audience.

> How ~~W~~would you like to spend your summer outside in 90° weather~~?~~ ~~Would you like to~~ mow*ing* lawns and paint*ing* porches? Doesn't sound like much fun, does it? *But it was for* ~~How do you think~~ 20 Kelley High School students ~~felt about it?~~ .

5 Editing and Proofreading

TARGET SKILL ▶ CONSISTENT FORM Because visuals frequently present a great deal of information in a small space, it is important that they be clear and easy to read. Using correct and consistent capitalization can help you get your message across effectively.

> Repairs needed on Mrs. Wilson's House
>
> • ~~R~~repair roof
>
> • replace windows ~~and~~ screens
>
> • *fix* porch railing and *steps* ~~screens~~
>
> • paint~~ing~~ house
>
> • clean up and mow lawn

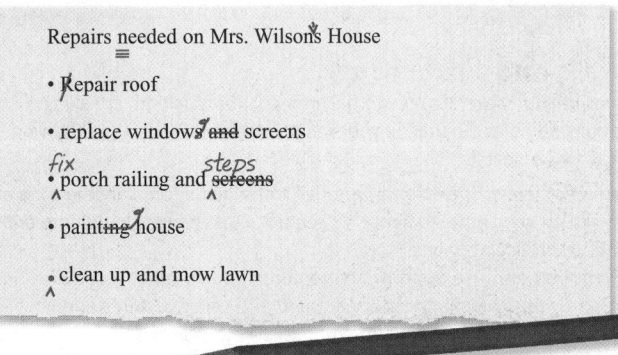

Publishing IDEAS

- Have someone videotape your presentation, and show it to other classes.
- Make your presentation to community members or other people interested in your hero.

More Online: Publishing Options
www.mcdougallittell.com

6 Reflecting

FOR YOUR WORKING PORTFOLIO What conclusions did you draw about your unsung hero? What did you learn about media while creating and presenting your multimedia presentation? Attach your reflections to your presentation script. Save your script in your **Working Portfolio.**

Assessment Practice Revising & Editing

Read this paragraph from the first draft of a student essay. The underlined sections may include the following kinds of errors.

- **sentence fragments**
- **correctly written sentences that should be combined**
- **capitalization errors**
- **comma errors**

For each underlined section, choose the revision that most improves the writing.

> Mr. Wilkinson is the Hero of Grove street. (1) He made it his responsibility. To clean up Grove Street. (2) All year long, Mr. Wilkinson works to make the street look nice. He paints the rusty light poles. He also paints the benches. Finally, he picks up litter. (3) Other shop keepers have been inspired by Mr. Wilkinson's work. They have begun to take better care of the areas. Around their stores. (4) You will see them planting, sweeping, and painting (5) in front of their stores. Jan Lewis our mayor recently (6) awarded Mr. Wilkinson the Clean Streets Award for the third year in a row.

1. **A.** Mr. Wilkinson is the hero of Grove street.
B. Mr. Wilkinson is the Hero of grove street.
C. Mr. Wilkinson is the hero of Grove Street.
D. Correct as is

2. **A.** He made it his responsibility, to clean up Grove Street.
B. He made it his responsibility to clean up Grove Street.
C. He made it his responsibility: to clean up Grove Street.
D. Correct as is

3. **A.** He paints the rusty light poles and the benches and picks up litter.
B. He paints the rusty light poles, the benches, and picks up litter.
C. He paints the rusty light poles. Also the benches, and picks up litter.
D. Correct as is

4. **A.** They have begun to take better care of the areas around their stores.
B. They have begun to take better care of the areas, around their stores.
C. They have begun to take better care of the areas and around their stores.
D. Correct as is

5. **A.** planting sweeping, and painting
B. planting sweeping and painting
C. planting, sweeping, and, painting
D. Correct as is

6. **A.** Jan Lewis, our mayor recently
B. Jan Lewis our mayor, recently
C. Jan Lewis, our mayor, recently
D. Correct as is

Need extra help?

See the **Grammar Handbook**
Capitalization Chart, p. 1205
Correcting Fragments, p. 1199
Punctuation Chart, pp. 1203–1204

Assessment Practice

Briefly review the kinds of errors that students may encounter in the passage. Remind students to carefully read all of the choices before they select the correct answer. You may wish to demonstrate how to eliminate incorrect choices for the first question.

A. This choice is incorrect because *street* is part of a proper noun and should be capitalized.
B. This choice is incorrect because *hero* should not be capitalized but *Grove Street* should.
D. This choice in incorrect because *hero* should not be capitalized but *street* should.
C. This is correct because *Grove Street* is capitalized and *hero* is not.

Answers:
1. C; **2.** B; **3.** A; **4.** A; **5.** D; **6.** C

PART 2 The Heroic Tradition

Can a hero exist without someone to tell his or her story? When you think about it, heroes and storytelling go hand in hand. From ancient times to the present, people have shared stories about great deeds, and each generation learns about the heroes of old. Often, these heroes represent qualities or character traits that are valued by the entire culture. As you will see in this part of Unit Six, stories of heroes can be kept alive for centuries.

ACTIVITY

Create a list of your own childhood heroes. Then describe one of those heroes to a small group of classmates, explaining what you found interesting about him or her. After every person in the group has described a hero, discuss how these heroes reflect qualities and character traits that are valued by cultures.

1014

LEARNING the Language of Literature

Myths and legends are stories that have survived the test of time. **Myths** are traditional stories, often concerning supernatural beings or events, that were told to explain natural processes or phenomena. For many ancient peoples, myths were both a kind of science and a religion, allowing humans to make sense of birth, death, and the origins of the universe. Classical mythology, the myths that have had the most influence on Western literature, took root in ancient Greece. Our earliest written example of Greek mythology is the *Iliad*, Homer's epic poem about gods and warriors that dates back approximately 3,000 years.

Legends are stories handed down from the past that are often believed to be based on actual historical events. Unlike myths, legends do not always incorporate supernatural events, although legendary heroes are often presented as "larger than life." The stories of Robin Hood and King Arthur are examples of legends.

The Olympians: The Major Players

The ancient Greeks believed that powerful gods ruled the world from the top of Mount Olympus, the highest mountain in Greece. As Rome became an empire and conquered Greece, it adopted and adapted the gods of Greek mythology, often renaming them. Greek and Roman myths often portrayed the remarkable abilities of the gods and the brave deeds of heroes. The gods possessed both supernatural and humanlike qualities, as well as the very human weaknesses of stubbornness and jealousy. Yet despite their flaws, the gods controlled the destinies of mortals, including, for example, the heroes of Homer's *Iliad* (and later the *Odyssey*). At the right and below are a few of the most important Olympians.

YOUR TURN What myths and characters can you recall from Greek or Roman mythology? Which of these gods have you seen portrayed in movies or on TV? In your opinion, which gods have the most interesting roles?

ZEUS
Roman Name: Jupiter
Role: Ruler of the gods
Controls Fate of: Hercules, Perseus

HERA
Roman Name: Juno
Role: Goddess of marriage
Controls Fate of: Paris, Echo, Orion

ATHENA
Roman Name: Minerva
Role: Goddess of crafts, war, wisdom
Controls Fate of: Odysseus, Arachne

APOLLO
Roman Name: Apollo
Role: God of light, medicine, poetry
Controls Fate of: Cassandra, Paris, Achilles

LEARNING the Language of LITERATURE

OVERVIEW

Objectives

- understand the following literary terms:
  - myth
  - legend
  - dramatic irony
  - romance
- understand historical threads of mythology and legend from ancient Greece through medieval England
- identify elements of mythology and explain their appeal

Teaching the Lesson

This lesson defines mythology and legend, explains prominent features of both, and describes their historical roots.

PREVIEW

Using Text Organizers

Have students preview the article, noting the basic text organizers: titles, subheads, images and captions. Ask students to describe the information they would expect to locate in each section. Have students use the subheads to make an outline or graphic organizer. As they read, have them categorize information from the article with the appropriate heading. Remind students that when they do independent research, similar attention to text organizers will help them locate and categorize information.

Introducing the Concepts

Have students name myths and legends they have encountered in books, television, and film. Ask them to describe the most memorable features of the characters of mythology and legend.

Presenting the Concepts

The Olympians: The Major Players

Point out the anthropomorphic nature of Greek gods and goddesses; their characters often seem as much human as they are divine.

YOUR TURN

Possible Response: Student responses will vary depending on the movies or television programs they are familiar with.

Making Connections

Greek Drama's Golden Age
Gods and goddesses have an indirect presence in Greek plays and, even though they may not be directly present, are often referred to.

Arthur Through the Ages
As they read, encourage students to note the distinct absence of focus on the interior psychology of characters in Malory's version of Arthur, putting it in sharp contrast to modern versions of the Arthurian legends.

YOUR TURN
Possible Response: The passage expresses a romantic sense of daring adventure, intrigue, and suspense.

Greek Drama's Golden Age

One important literary source of classical mythology is ancient Greek drama. Writing 25 centuries ago, Sophocles and fellow dramatists drew from classical myths and legends to produce these dramas. For example, Sophocles' drama *Antigone* (page 1018) combines references to the gods with semi-historical legends of kings and queens. These myths and legends were familiar to the audience—and believed by many.

While the audience knew the story behind a play, the characters, of course, did not. This play device, known today as **dramatic irony**, has been used by playwrights across time. The lines at the right appear in the first scene from Sophocles' *Antigone*. The speaker is Creon, the new ruler of Thebes, who issues this command before other major characters are aware and are able to react.

> **Polyneices, I say, is to have no burial: no man is to touch him or say the least prayer for him; he shall lie on the plain, unburied; and the birds and the scavenging dogs can do with him whatever they like.**
>
> **This is my command, and you can see the wisdom behind it.**
>
> —Sophocles, *Antigone*

Arthur Through the Ages

During the Middle Ages, traveling poets told long, glowing tales about legendary figures such as Arthur, a glorious king of medieval Britain. Some modern-day scholars suggest that the tales are based on a 6th-century high king. The legend of King Arthur and his knights of the Round Table has been told repeatedly through the ages. The term for Arthurian legends, **romance,** refers to any imaginative story concerned with noble heroes, codes of honor, passionate love, daring deeds, and supernatural events.

As with most oral literature, romances came to be written down, and probably the most famous version is Sir Thomas Malory's *Le Morte d'Arthur*. In this part of Unit 6, you will read two excerpts from Malory's work as well as excerpts from two modern retellings of the legend. Each retelling brings the tools of modern fiction to bear on the legend, exploring the motivations and personalities of characters.

> **"My good fellow, if you know the forest hereabouts, could you tell me in which direction I am most likely to meet with adventure?"**
>
> **"Sir, I can tell you: less than a mile from here stands a well-moated castle. On the left of the entrance you will find a ford where you can water your horse, and across from the ford a large tree from which hang the shields of many famous knights. Below the shields hangs a caldron, of copper and brass: strike it three times with your spear, and then surely you will meet with adventure—such, indeed, that if you survive it, you will prove yourself the foremost knight in these parts for many years."**
>
> —Sir Thomas Malory, *from* Le Morte d'Arthur

YOUR TURN Read the excerpt at right from *Le Morte d'Arthur*. What elements do you think it contains that show the lasting appeal of Arthurian legends?

Myths and legends still possess the power to captivate and inspire. Unlike listeners or readers of the distant past, you probably don't have complete knowledge of most myths and legends. The reading strategies explained here can help you to appreciate these classic retellings.

Reading Myths and Legends

Strategies for Using Your READER'S NOTEBOOK

As you read, take notes to

- **connect** your personal experiences to what you read about the heroes, their qualities, and their quests
- record any phrases, passages, or ideas you find particularly exciting
- write down questions you may have about the plot, character, setting, or theme of a myth or legend

1 Strategies for Understanding Myths and Legends

- **Consider** the source of what you're reading. Was a myth written at a time when the audience believed in the beings and events described? Is the myth a retelling from a later time?
- Do not read legends as history. Try to get a sense of the truth behind a legend but enjoy the adventurous elements.
- Suspend your disbelief. Myths and legends do not try to be as lifelike as modern "realistic" fiction.
- **Visualize** the wondrous characters and events.
- Don't be thrown by unfamiliar twists. There are numerous versions of many myths and legends.

2 Strategies for Exploring the Cultures Behind Myths and Legends

- Consider the purpose the tale may have had for those who created it. Was it meant to provide moral instruction? as an explanation of nature? Use a chart like this one to analyze cultural connections.

Myth or Legend	Origin	Possible Purpose

- **Evaluate** the source of a retold myth or legend. Look for what new perspectives and insights a modern reteller brings to a tale.

3 Strategies for Recognizing the Themes of Myths and Legends

- Fill in a diagram like the one at the right as you follow a hero's quest. It may be that a hero's actions or attitudes are connected to an important message. After reading, analyze the message.
- Try to separate what is universal—elements that deal with values common to all people—from elements specific to a particular time or culture.
- Ask yourself what views or beliefs of a different time or culture are evident in the tale. For example, do gods exist? Is magic possible?

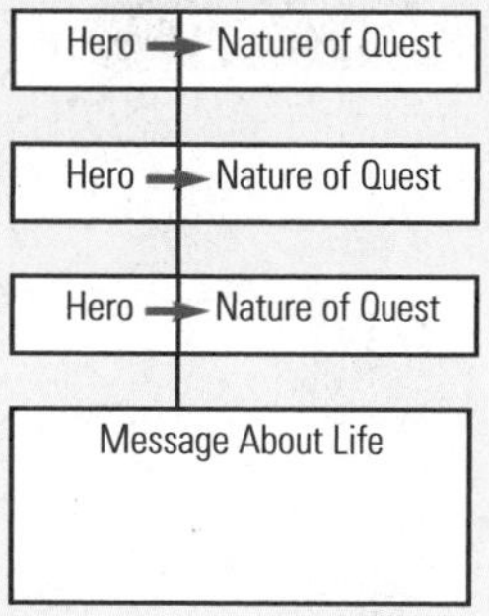

Need More Help?

Remember that active readers use the essential reading strategies explained on page 7: **visualize, predict, clarify, question, connect, evaluate, monitor.**

3 Strategies for Recognizing the Themes of Myths and Legends

A sample completion of the chart could look like this:

Hero: Odysseus

Nature of Quest: to defy temptation and return to his faithful wife

Hero: Odysseus

Nature of Quest: to defy treachery and remain alive

Hero: Odysseus

Nature of Quest: to defy suitors and regain his wife

Message About Life: Commitment can overcome even the most treacherous opposition.

The Active Reader: Skills and Strategies

OVERVIEW

Objectives

- apply strategies that enhance understanding and appreciation of myths and legends from the distant past
- use charts and diagrams to clarify cultural connections and analyze themes

Teaching the Lesson

The strategies on this page will help students learn and apply skills to critically evaluate the literary elements in myths and legends and to explore the larger cultural sources of those myths and legends.

Presenting the Strategies

Make sure students understand that a story need not be realistic in order to be meaningful. Even though myths may contain fantastical and unrealistic elements, they often convey emotional truths that are realistic and significant to readers today. Use an example such as "Jack and the Beanstalk" to illustrate how the fantastical can nevertheless be meaningful.

Strategies for Using Your Reader's Notebook

When connecting personal experiences to myths and legends, encourage students to identify with the human elements in the mythical characters that offer a personal point of connection.

1 Strategies for Understanding Myths and Legends

Encourage students to keep a list in their Reader's Notebook that includes all the points where a willing suspension of disbelief must be exercised. Have them use this list to observe patterns.

2 Strategies for Exploring the Cultures Behind Myths and Legends

A sample completion of the chart could look like this:

Myth or Legend:

Legend: King Arthur and the Knights of the Roundtable

Origin:

Medieval England

Possible Purpose:

to provide a heroic model of a mighty warrior who is a generous and just ruler

OVERVIEW

An excerpt of this selection is included in the **Grade 10 InterActive Reader.**

Objectives

1. understand and appreciate a **classical drama (Literary Analysis)**
2. apply **strategies for reading classical drama (Active Reading)**

Summary

In the battle for the throne of Thebes, Antigone's brother Eteocles has died defending the city, while her brother Polyneices has died attacking it. Creon, the king of Thebes, has sworn that although Eteocles has been given a soldier's funeral, Polyneices' body will remain unburied. Antigone defies the decree and buries her brother, even though her sister, Ismene, refuses to help her. Creon then condemns both Antigone and Ismene to death. He changes his mind about Ismene, but locks Antigone away in a stone vault. Later, after the blind prophet Teiresias predicts doom, Creon decides to free Antigone, only to find that she has committed suicide. Antigone's death leads to the suicide of Creon's son, Haemon, who was betrothed to her, and then to the suicide of Creon's wife, Eurydice.

Thematic Link

The tragic clash between moral and civil law forms the basis of this **heroic** tragedy.

5-Minute Warm-Up

Daily Language SkillBuilder

Have students **proofread** the display sentences on page 959j and write them correctly. The sentences also appear on Transparency 28 of **Grammar Transparencies and Copymasters.**

Mini Lesson: Preteaching Vocabulary

If you would like to preteach the WORDS TO KNOW for this selection, use the Mini Lesson, p. 1020.

PREPARING to *Read*

Antigone (ăn-tĭg′ə-nē)

Drama by SOPHOCLES (sŏf′ ə-klēz′)
Translated by DUDLEY FITTS *and* ROBERT FITZGERALD

"There is no guilt in reverence for the dead."

Connect to Your Life

A Matter of Principle Consider the principles listed to the right, and rank them in the order of their importance to you. Discuss your ranking and your reasoning with the class. Which of the principles might you be willing to fight for—or willing to uphold if it meant making a sacrifice?

- loyalty or obligation to family
- obedience to civil law
- observance of religious law
- protection of personal dignity
- freedom
- protection of community or nation

Build Background

Basis in Legend Sophocles was one of the great dramatists of ancient Greece, and his play *Antigone* is regarded as one of the finest examples of classical Greek tragedy. The main characters in this play come into conflict because they stand firmly behind their principles—principles that are contradictory.

Most Greek tragedies are based on legends or myths that the audience of ancient Greece was very familiar with. *Antigone* is based on the legend of the family of Oedipus (ĕd′ə-pəs), the doomed king of Thebes. As the play begins, Antigone and her sister, Ismene (ĭs-mē′nē), recall their dead father, Oedipus, who unknowingly killed his father and then married his own mother. Upon discovering the truth, Oedipus blinded himself and went into exile, where he was cared for by his two daughters until his death. After his death, his sons, Eteocles (ē-tē′ə-klēz′) and Polyneices (pŏl′ĭ-nī′sēz), agreed to share the kingship of Thebes, ruling in alternate years. However, when Eteocles had served his first term as king, he banished Polyneices from Thebes and refused to relinquish the throne to him, claiming that Polyneices was unfit to rule. Polyneices then enlisted an army from Argos, a powerful city-state and a long-standing enemy of Thebes, to fight his brother. In the course of battle, the brothers killed each other. Their uncle, Creon, has become king and faces the task of restoring order in Thebes. As the new king, he plans to honor one corpse and insult the other.

WORDS TO KNOW
Vocabulary Preview

auspicious	lamentation
compulsive	lithe
defile	perverse
dirge	sated
edict	transgress

VIDEODISC **LaserLinks: Background for Reading**
Reading Connection

LESSON RESOURCES

UNIT SIX RESOURCE BOOK, pp. 28–33

ASSESSMENT RESOURCES

Formal Assessment, pp. 167–168

Teacher's Guide to Assessment and Portfolio Use

Test Generator

SKILLS TRANSPARENCIES AND COPYMASTERS

Literary Analysis
- Myths and Legends I and II, T23, T24 (for Extend Interpretations 6, p. 1061)

Reading and Critical Thinking
- Visualizing, T8 (for Reading Skills and Strategies, p. 988)
- Reading for Details, T16 (for Think Critically, item 3, p. 995)

Grammar
- Direct and Indirect Objects, C91 (for Mini Lesson, p. 1030)
- Inverted Sentences, C146 (for Mini Lesson, p. 1062)

Vocabulary
- Context Clues, C90 (for Mini Lesson, p. 1020)

Word Origins, C91, C92 (for Mini Lesson, p. 1054)

Writing
- Writing Structure, T5–8, T11 (for Writing Option 2, p. 1062)
- Research Report, T35 (for Writing Option 3, p. 1062)

Communications
- Dramatic Reading, T12 (for Mini Lesson, p. 1038, and Activities & Explorations 1, p. 1062)
- Evaluation Matrix: Film/Video, T7 (for Mini Lesson, p. 1019, and Activities & Explorations 3, p. 1062)

INTEGRATED TECHNOLOGY

Audio Library

LaserLinks
- Reading Connection: Classical Drama.
- Cultural Connection: The World of Sophocles

See **Teacher's SourceBook,** pp. 54–55.

Video: Literature in Performance
- *Antigone.* See **Video Resource Book,** pp. 35–42

Visit our website:
www.mcdougallittell.com

Focus Your Reading

LITERARY ANALYSIS CLASSICAL DRAMA **Classical drama** arose in Athens, Greece, from religious celebrations in honor of Dionysus (dī'ə-nī'səs), the god of wine and fertility. These celebrations included ritual chants and songs performed by a group called a chorus. Drama evolved from these celebrations during the sixth century B.C., when individual actors began entering into dialogue with the chorus to tell a story.

The Theater Greek drama was filled with the spectacle and pageantry of a religious festival. Attended by thousands, plays were performed during the day in an outdoor theater with seats built into a hillside. The action of each play was presented at the foot of the hill, often on a raised platform. A long building, called the **skene,** served as a backdrop for the action and as a dressing room. A spacious circular floor, the **orchestra,** was located between the skene and the audience.

Actors and Chorus The actors—all men—wore elegant robes, huge masks, and often elevated shoes, all of which added to the grandeur of the spectacle. Sophocles used three actors in his plays; between scenes, they changed costumes and masks when they needed to portray different characters. The **chorus**—a group of about 15—commented on the action, and the leader of the chorus, the **choragus** (kə-rā'gəs), participated in the dialogue. Between scenes, the chorus sang and danced to musical accompaniment in the orchestra, giving insights into the message of the play. The chorus is often considered a kind of ideal spectator, representing the response of ordinary citizens to the tragic events unfolding in the play.

Tragedy and the Tragic Hero During Sophocles' lifetime, three playwrights were chosen each year to enter a theatrical competition in the festival of Dionysus. Each playwright would produce three tragedies, along with a satyr (sā'tər) play, a short comic interlude. A **tragedy** is a drama that recounts the downfall of a dignified, superior character who is involved in historically or socially significant events.

The **protagonist,** or **tragic hero,** of the work is in conflict with an opposing character or force, the **antagonist.** The action builds from one event to the next and finally to a **catastrophe** that leads to a disastrous conclusion. Twists of fate play a key role in the hero's destruction.

Aristotle's Theory of the Tragic Flaw

According to the Greek philosopher Aristotle, a tragic hero possesses a defect, or **tragic flaw,** that brings about or contributes to his or her downfall. This flaw may be poor judgment, pride, weakness, or an excess of an admirable quality. The tragic hero, noted Aristotle, recognizes his or her flaw and its consequences, but only after it is too late to change the course of events.

ACTIVE READING STRATEGIES FOR READING CLASSICAL DRAMA Use the following strategies to help you read classical drama.

- Imagine the spectacle of the play as staged, **visualizing** as you read.
- Try to understand the hero's **motivations** and the qualities that make him or her a noble figure.
- Pay close attention to the causes of the **conflict** between the hero and his or her antagonist.
- Determine the circumstances or flaws that lead to the hero's downfall.
- Consider how the words and actions of **minor characters** help you to understand the **main characters.**
- Notice how the comments of the chorus interpret the action and point to universal **themes.**
- Monitor your own reading strategies. Modify them when your understanding breaks down by rereading, using resources, and questioning.

READER'S NOTEBOOK As you read *Antigone,* record your answers to the questions printed in blue alongside the play. Apply the strategies listed above, and note any other thoughts, questions, and comments that you have.

FOCUS YOUR READING

Literary Analysis CLASSICAL DRAMA

Students may read aloud the information about classical drama. Each of the elements can be examined by using the following suggestions.

- **The Theater** Have students turn to pp. 1020–1021 and look at the picture of the ancient theater. Ask them to identify the orchestra and the skene.
- **Actors and Chorus** Invite students to discuss shows they may have seen in which an actor portrayed several different characters. Ask students to explain how the actor achieved each transformation—with changes in voice, costume, and/or props.
- **Tragedy and Tragic Hero** Have students discuss other tragedies with which they are familiar, such as *Romeo and Juliet* or *Julius Caesar.* Encourage students to name movies that could qualify as tragedies, such as *Titanic.* Have students name the protagonist(s), antagonist(s), and catastrophe in each tragedy.

Active Reading

STRATEGIES FOR READING CLASSICAL DRAMA

Students will see how using the reading strategies increases their comprehension of a long or difficult text. In turn, these strategies can also be used to structure class discussions of the selection. It may be helpful to assign specific strategies for reading particular scenes.

Mini Lesson Viewing and Representing

Instruction Have students view the video clip of the opening scene of the play before they begin reading. The clip comes from the 1961 film version of *Antigone* starring Irene Papas.

Application Encourage students to discuss how the cinematic techniques or visual components of the scene contribute to the historical setting and tone of the play. Ask them how the clip grabbed their attention and motivated them to want to see the rest of the film.

TEACHING THE LITERATURE

Reading and Analyzing

Literary Analysis CLASSICAL DRAMA

Students should keep the following points in mind as they read:

- Like any narrative, a tragedy moves from exposition through the rising action and climax to the falling action. Have students analyze and describe the development of the plot. Identifying each stage of the plot can be very helpful in understanding character and theme.
- Focus closely on dialogue; be prepared to discuss the hidden meaning behind the characters' conversations.

Use **Unit Six Resource Book** p. 30 for more practice.

Active Reading

STRATEGIES FOR READING CLASSICAL DRAMA

Help students visualize the staging. A student might want to sketch the scene for the class. Students should be prepared to define the early conflict as it unfolds in the prologue.

Use **Unit Six Resource Book** p. 29 for more practice.

ANTIGONE

1020

Teaching Options

Mini Lesson Preteaching Vocabulary

USING CONTEXT CLUES

Instruction Call students' attention to the list of WORDS TO KNOW. Remind them that sometimes they can understand the meaning of an unfamiliar word by examining the context in which the word is used. Use the following sentence to demonstrate the strategy of locating synonyms or antonyms that provide clues to word meaning:

After pigeons *defiled* the statue of the university's founder, the sanitation crew had the unpleasant job of cleaning it.

- Write the model sentence on the chalkboard.
- Ask a volunteer to locate an antonym for *defiled*.
- Have students use the meaning of the antonym *clean* to determine the meaning of the word *defile*.
- Ask a volunteer to use the word *defile* in a sentence.

CAST OF CHARACTERS

Antigone / **Ismene** } daughters of Oedipus, former king of Thebes

Creon (krē′ŏn′), king of Thebes, uncle of Antigone and Ismene

Haemon (hē′mŏn′), Creon's son, engaged to Antigone

Eurydice (yo͝o-rĭd′ĭ-sē), wife of Creon

Teiresias (tī-rē′sē-əs), a blind prophet

Chorus, made up of about 15 elders of Thebes

Choragus, leader of the chorus

a Sentry

a Messenger

Bust of Sophocles. Museo Lateranense, Vatican Museums, Vatican City, Alinari / Art Resource, New York.

Antigone contemplates her fate. Culver Pictures.

Ruins of ancient theater at Epidaurus, Greece. Copyright © 1993 Barbara Ries / Photo Researchers, Inc.

SOPHOCLES

Customizing Instruction

Less Proficient Readers

To help students distinguish between the characters and understand their motivations, have them copy the cast of characters in their notebooks or journals, leaving ample space between each name. Have students write notes and details about each character.

Students Acquiring English

Classical drama was written as poetry. Most likely, students will find the long speeches and the choral odes difficult to read. Ask them to pay special attention to the punctuation marks—commas, periods, colons, semicolons, etc.—as guides for reading. They should also use the annotations at the side of the text.

Use **Spanish Study Guide** for additional support, pp. 211–213.

Gifted and Talented

Challenge students to make inferences from *Antigone* about the qualities the ancient Greeks prized in their heroes. Remind them to support their inferences with text evidence.

Exercises Read the following sentences. Have students use context clues to determine the meaning of the italicized terms.

1. The composer sat down to write a *dirge*, but all that came to mind were cheerful ditties.
2. The *edict* was posted in the town square, where everyone could see the sheriff's ruling.
3. Although Ian had no intention of *transgressing,* he seemed unable to obey his parents' rules.
4. Instead of the *lamentation* the reporter expected after the senator's defeat, she found his team celebrating.
5. My little brother is a *perverse,* contrary creature.
6. A salmon's *compulsive* need to swim upstream to spawn is similar to our cat's pressing desire to sharpen his claws on the furniture.
7. The shaman considered a shooting star an *auspicious* sign and searched for that fortunate omen.
8. The *lithe* yoga instructor encouraged her students to become as flexible as she by practicing daily.
9. The *sated* lioness, stuffed full of her kill, licked her whiskers.

Use **Unit Six Resource Book** p. 31 for more exercises.

A lesson on synonyms appears on p. 1000 in the Pupil's Edition.

ANTIGONE **1021**

Reading and Analyzing

Reading Skills and Strategies: ANALYZING

A Ask students what Antigone's opening speech reveals about her feelings for her sister, Ismene.
Possible Response: Antigone's use of the phrase "dear sister" and her reference to their shared tragic past suggest that she feels close to her sister and believes they share a common outlook.

Reading Skills and Strategies: MAKING JUDGMENTS

B Ask students whether they agree with Antigone or Ismene. Would they break the law to bury a loved one, or would they obey the law and leave the family member unburied?
Possible Responses: Some students will say moral law supersedes civil law, while others may think civil law is supreme because it protects everyone against anarchy.

GUIDE FOR READING

C **Possible Response:** Antigone is resolute and determined, and she follows her own sense of morality; Ismene is fearful of authority.

D **Possible Response:** Antigone loved her brother deeply and is willing to die to uphold the god's laws.

Scene: *Before the palace of Creon, king of Thebes. A central double door, and two doors at the side. A platform extends the length of the stage, and from this platform three steps lead down into the orchestra, or chorus ground.*

Time: *Dawn of the day after the repulse of the Argive army from the assault on Thebes*

GUIDE FOR READING

repulse: an act of turning away or beating back.

PROLOGUE

(Antigone *and* Ismene *enter from the central door of the palace.*)

A
Antigone. Ismene, dear sister,
You would think that we had already suffered enough
For the curse on Oedipus:
I cannot imagine any grief
That you and I have not gone through. And now—
Have they told you the new decree of our king Creon?

Ismene. I have heard nothing: I know
That two sisters lost two brothers, a double death
In a single hour; and I know that the Argive army
Fled in the night; but beyond this, nothing.

Antigone. I thought so. And that is why I wanted you
To come out here with me. There is something we must do.

Ismene. Why do you speak so strangely?

Antigone. Listen, Ismene:
Creon buried our brother Eteocles
With military honors, gave him a soldier's funeral,
And it was right that he should; but Polyneices,
Who fought as bravely and died as miserably—
They say that Creon has sworn
No one shall bury him, no one mourn for him,
But his body must lie in the fields, a sweet treasure
For carrion birds to find as they search for food.
That is what they say, and our good Creon is coming here
To announce it publicly; and the penalty—
1 Stoning to death in the public square!
There it is,
And now you can prove what you are:
A true sister, or a traitor to your family.

B
Ismene. Antigone, you are mad! What could I possibly do?

Antigone. You must decide whether you will help me or not.

Ismene. I do not understand you. Help you in what?

Antigone. Ismene, I am going to bury him. Will you come?

9 Argive: of Argos.

20–22 The obligation to bury the dead with appropriate burial rites was considered a sacred law among the ancient Greeks. They believed that the soul of someone left unburied would never find peace.

28–35 What contrast between Antigone and Ismene is suggested by the conversation between them? **C**

BLOCK SCHEDULING: MANAGING TIME

If your schedule requires that you cover the lesson objectives in a shorter time, use . . .
- Preparing to Read, pp. 1018–1019
- Thinking Through the Literature, p. 1061
- Vocabulary in Action, p. 1062
- Grammar in Context, p. 1063

If you want to take advantage of longer class time, use . . .
- TE Teaching Options: Preteaching Vocabulary, pp. 1020–1021; Multicultural Links, pp. 1024, 1028, 1052; Cross-Curricular Links, pp. 1026, 1042, 1056; Viewing and Representing, pp. 1032, 1034, 1036, 1041, 1048; Standardized Test Practice, pp. 1040, 1046; Speaking and Listening, pp. 1038, 1044, 1050; Vocabulary Strategy, pp. 1054–1055; Informal Assessment, p. 1060
- Choices & Challenges and Author Activity, pp. 1062–1063

Ismene. Bury him! You have just said the new law forbids it.

Antigone. He is my brother. And he is your brother, too.

Ismene. But think of the danger! Think what Creon will do!

Antigone. Creon is not strong enough to stand in my way.

Ismene. Ah sister!
Oedipus died, everyone hating him
For what his own search brought to light, his eyes
Ripped out by his own hand; and Jocasta died,
His mother and wife at once: she twisted the cords 2
That strangled her life; and our two brothers died,
Each killed by the other's sword. And we are left:
But oh, Antigone,
Think how much more terrible than these
Our own death would be if we should go against Creon
And do what he has forbidden! We are only women;
We cannot fight with men, Antigone!
The law is strong, we must give in to the law
In this thing, and in worse. I beg the dead
To forgive me, but I am helpless: I must yield
To those in authority. And I think it is dangerous business
To be always meddling.

Antigone. If that is what you think,
I should not want you, even if you asked to come.
You have made your choice; you can be what you want to be.
But I will bury him; and if I must die,
I say that this crime is holy: I shall lie down
With him in death, and I shall be as dear
To him as he to me.
It is the dead,
Not the living, who make the longest demands: 3
We die forever. . . .
You may do as you like,
Since apparently the laws of the gods mean nothing to you.

Ismene. They mean a great deal to me; but I have no strength
To break laws that were made for the public good.

Antigone. That must be your excuse, I suppose. But as for me,
I will bury the brother I love.

Ismene. Antigone,
I am so afraid for you!

Antigone. You need not be:
You have yourself to consider, after all.

39 Jocasta, the mother of Antigone and Ismene, hanged herself when she realized the truth about her relationship with Oedipus.

55–61 What do these lines reveal about Antigone's feelings for her brother and the gods' laws? D

Customizing Instruction

Students Learning English

1 Help students understand that stoning, a punishment that was rather common in ancient Mediterranean cultures, occurred when a group of people threw stones at someone until that person was dead.

2 Explain to students that these lines have two likely meanings: that Jocasta tied the knot in the noose that strangled her, or that she hanged herself with yarn that she had spun.

Less Proficient Readers

3 Ask students the meaning of line 60. Elicit that Antigone means that death is an ongoing, eternal process. Until his corpse receives a proper burial, Polyneices will be doomed to a restless, wretched afterlife.

Multiple Learning Styles

Spatial or Graphic Learners

Have students sketch the scene, based on the stage directions. Invite volunteers to share their completed sketches with the rest of the class.

Gifted and Talented

Tell students that during Sophocles' day it was illegal to bury a traitor in land that was part of the Athenian city-state. However, the body could be carried beyond the border and given funeral rites. Ask students how they interpret Creon's decree, based on this fact.

ANTIGONE **1023**

Reading and Analyzing

Active Reading

STRATEGIES FOR READING CLASSICAL DRAMA

A Have students consider how the works and actions of Ismene, a minor character, help them understand the main character, Antigone.

Possible Response: Ismene's phrase "So fiery!" implies that Antigone is furious about Ismene's response to her request. Antigone's fierce emotions are also suggested by her use of exclamatory sentences.

Literary Analysis **CLASSICAL DRAMA**

B Make sure students read the side note explaining that the parodos marks the entry of the chorus. Ask students to describe the connection between the parodos and Antigone and Ismene's conversation.

Possible Response: The parodos helps to explain the sisters' conversation. Its rejoicing tone serves as a contrast to the grim topic of the conversation. The final verse of the chorus is ironic and also foreshadows the tragic events to come.

GUIDE FOR READING

C **Possible Response:** Zeus was punishing arrogance and overweening pride.

Ismene. But no one must hear of this; you must tell no one!
I will keep it a secret, I promise!

Antigone. Oh tell it! Tell everyone!
Think how they'll hate you when it all comes out
If they learn that you knew about it all the time!

Ismene. So fiery! You should be cold with fear.

Antigone. Perhaps. But I am doing only what I must.

Ismene. But can you do it? I say that you cannot.

Antigone. Very well: when my strength gives out, I shall do no more.

Ismene. Impossible things should not be tried at all.

Antigone. Go away, Ismene:
I shall be hating you soon, and the dead will too,
For your words are hateful. Leave me my foolish plan:
I am not afraid of the danger; if it means death,
It will not be the worst of deaths—death without honor.

Ismene. Go then, if you feel that you must.
You are unwise,
But a loyal friend indeed to those who love you.

(*Exit into the palace.* Antigone *goes off, left. Enters the* Chorus, *with* Choragus.)

B PARODOS

Chorus. Now the long blade of the sun, lying
Level east to west, touches with glory
Thebes of the Seven Gates. Open, unlidded
Eye of golden day! O marching light
Across the eddy and rush of Dirce's stream,
Striking the white shields of the enemy
Thrown headlong backward from the blaze of morning!

Choragus. Polyneices their commander
Roused them with windy phrases,
He the wild eagle screaming
Insults above our land,
His wings their shields of snow,
His crest their marshaled helms.

Chorus. Against our seven gates in a yawning ring
The famished spears came onward in the night;
But before his jaws were sated with our blood,

PARODOS: The parodos is a song that marks the entry of the chorus, which represents the leading citizens of Thebes.

5 Dirce's (dûr'sēz) **stream:** a stream flowing past Thebes. The stream is named after a murdered queen who was thrown into it.

14–15 Thebes had seven gates, which the Argives attacked all at once.

WORDS TO KNOW

sated (sā'tĭd) *adj.* satisfied fully **sate** *v.*

Teaching Options

Mini Lesson **Multicultural Link**

PLAYWRIGHTS Sophocles' dramatic portrayal of Antigone's tragic story has influenced playwrights as well as readers around the world. One of the most famous dramatic adaptations of the play came from the 20th-century French playwright Jean Anouilh. In 1942, during the German occupation of France in World War II, Anouilh wrote his adaptation of the Greek legend of the daughter of Oedipus. He produced his play in February 1944, with his wife in the title role. Although Anouilh's Creon is less rigid than his Sophoclean counterpart, his *Antigone* provides a forceful condemnation of the abuse of state power. Anouilh's own sympathies were with Antigone, who represented the anti-Nazi forces of the French Resistance. During its initial run, the play was an inspiration to the patriotic French.

Other famous versions of the Antigone story include Athol Fugard's play *The Island* (1973), which incorporates a production of *Antigone* as a play-within-a-play performed by convicts in a South African prison, and Polish playwright Janusz Glowacki's drama *Antigone in New York*, about a homeless Puerto Rican woman's attempt to bury a homeless man in the park. *Antigone*'s themes have appealed to dramatists and performers from many cultures for thousands of years.

Or pine fire took the garland of our towers,
He was thrown back; and as he turned, great Thebes—
No tender victim for his noisy power—
Rose like a dragon behind him, shouting war.

Choragus. For God hates utterly
The bray of bragging tongues; 4
And when he beheld their smiling,
Their swagger of golden helms,
The frown of his thunder blasted
Their first man from our walls.

Chorus. We heard his shout of triumph high in the air
Turn to a scream; far out in a flaming arc
He fell with his windy torch, and the earth struck him.
And others storming in fury no less than his
Found shock of death in the dusty joy of battle.

Choragus. Seven captains at seven gates
Yielded their clanging arms to the god
That bends the battle line and breaks it.
These two only, brothers in blood,
Face to face in matchless rage,
Mirroring each the other's death,
Clashed in long combat.

Chorus. But now in the beautiful morning of victory
Let Thebes of the many chariots sing for joy!
With hearts for dancing we'll take leave of war:
Our temples shall be sweet with hymns of praise,
And the long night shall echo with our chorus.

21–26 Zeus, the king of the gods, threw a thunderbolt, which killed the first Argive attacker. What type of conduct was Zeus punishing? C

32–34 When the seven captains were killed, their armor was offered as a sacrifice to Ares (âr′ēz), the god of war.

Customizing Instruction

Students Acquiring English

Help students understand the figurative language in the parodos.

1 The description of the sun as a "long blade" tells the reader that it is dawn. The chorus asks the sun to rise high and shine on the fallen enemy.

2 The phrase "shields of snow" refers to the enemy's white shields, and the term "marshaled" means that the soldiers are marching in an orderly fashion.

3 This metaphor compares the invading force to a gaping mouth eager for blood.

4 Explain that *bray* is often used to describe the sound that a donkey makes. Make sure students understand that the soldiers, not the helmets, are swaggering.

Less Proficient Readers

- Why does Antigone decide to bury her brother Polyneices? What punishment does she face for this act?
  Answers: to give her brother's soul peace; death
- Who does Antigone ask to help her bury Polyneices? Why?
  Answers: her sister, Ismene; because they are sisters
- How are Antigone and Ismene alike? How are they different?
  Answer: They are both ancient Greek women and sisters; Antigone is heroic and motivated by a strong moral sense; Ismene is more timid and fearful of authority.

Set a Purpose Have students read to discover if Antigone carries out her plan to bury her brother Polyneices.

Reading and Analyzing

Literary Analysis: FIGURATIVE LANGUAGE

A Ask students to explain the metaphor of the ship.
Possible Response: The metaphor compares the ship to the government, suggesting that both have successfully navigated dangerous waters.

Reading Skills and Strategies: PREDICTING

B Ask students what they can predict about Creon's future actions as a ruler from his speech.
Possible Response: He will be inflexible and exceedingly rigid.

GUIDE FOR READING

C **Possible Response:** Creon feels that allegiance to the state deserves the highest loyalty. Students who place the public good above private needs will agree; those who place the private over the public will disagree.

D **Possible Responses:** Students who place moral law above civil law will disagree with Creon's ruling; other students will support him. He seeks to assert his leadership and establish his power.

Choral scene from a contemporary staging of a Greek tragedy at Guthrie Theater, Minneapolis, Minnesota. Copyright © 1992 Michal Daniel.

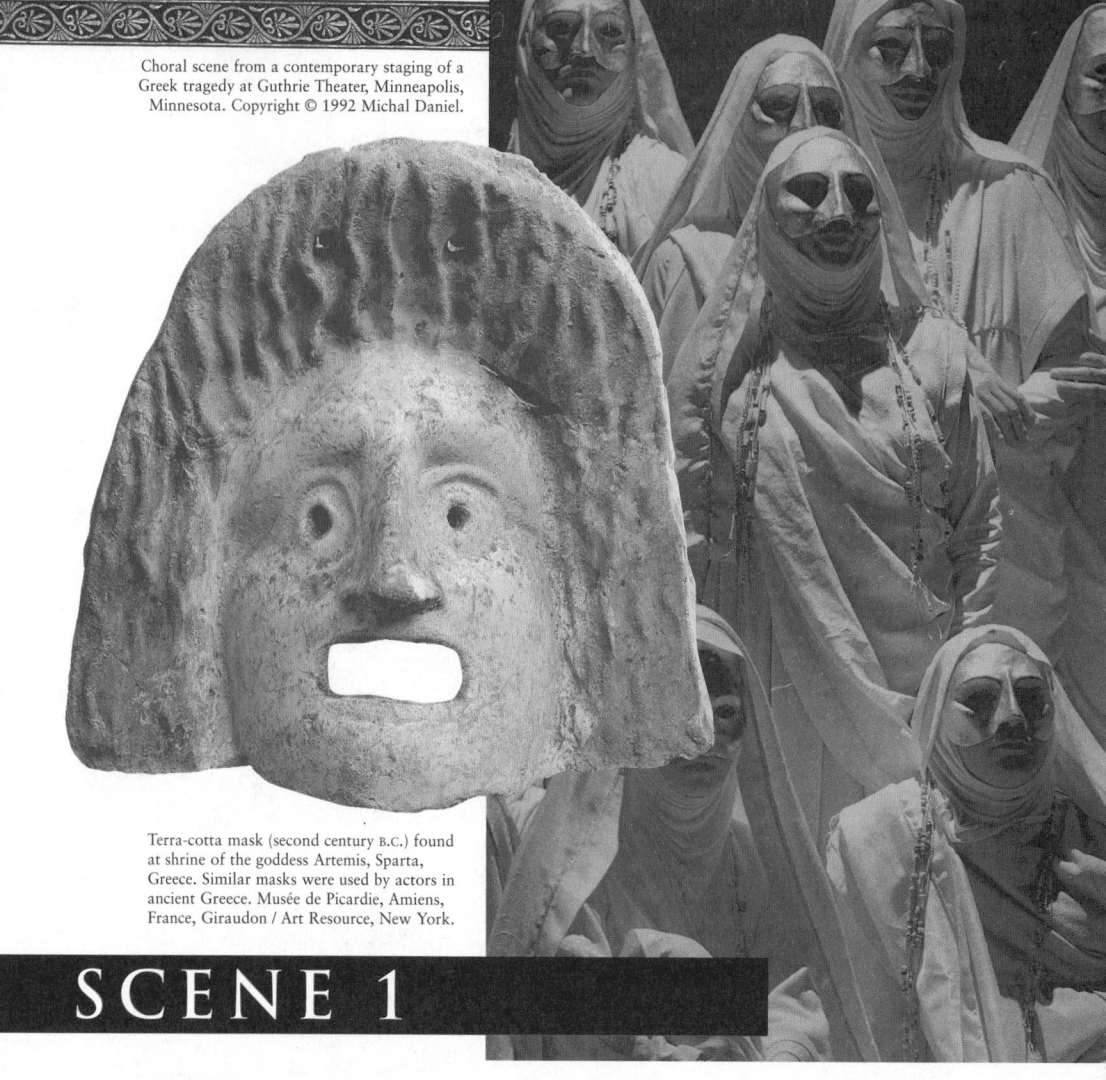

Terra-cotta mask (second century B.C.) found at shrine of the goddess Artemis, Sparta, Greece. Similar masks were used by actors in ancient Greece. Musée de Picardie, Amiens, France, Giraudon / Art Resource, New York.

SCENE 1

Choragus. But now at last our new king is coming:
Creon of Thebes, Menoeceus' son.
In this auspicious dawn of his reign
What are the new complexities
That shifting Fate has woven for him?
What is his counsel? Why has he summoned
The old men to hear him?

(*Enter* Creon *from the palace. He addresses the* Chorus *from the top step.*)

2 Menoeceus (mə-nē′syo͞os).

5 The Greeks believed that human destiny was controlled by three sisters called the Fates: Clotho (klō′thō), who spun the thread of human life; Lachesis (lăk′ĭ-sĭs), who determined its length; and Atropos (ăt′rə-pŏs′), who cut the thread.

WORDS TO KNOW **auspicious** (ô-spĭsh′əs) *adj.* promising success; favorable

Teaching Options

Cross Curricular Link History

ANCIENT GREECE Thebes was one of the most celebrated cities in ancient Greece. Among its myths are stories of the twin brothers Amphion and Zethus, said to have ruled Thebes and built its walls; the tragic fate of King Oedipus and his children; the return of the nature god Dionysus; and the birth and exploits of the famous hero Hercules. It was the greatest city-state in the area known as Boeotia, which it nominally controlled. When the Persians tried to take over Greece in the fifth century B.C. (less than 40 years before Sophocles wrote *Antigone*), Thebes joined Athens's great enemy, the Persians. In the fourth century, Thebes rebelled against Alexander the Great after a rumor spread that he had died. Alexander responded by destroying everything in the city except the house of the great poet Pindar. Today, the modern city of Thevai lies on the ruins of ancient Thebes.

Creon. Gentlemen: I have the honor to inform you that our ship of state, which recent storms have threatened to destroy, has come safely to harbor at last, guided by the merciful wisdom of heaven. I have summoned you here this morning because I know that I can depend upon you: your devotion to King Laius was absolute; you never hesitated in your duty to our late ruler Oedipus; and when Oedipus died, your loyalty was transferred to his children. Unfortunately, as you know, his two sons, the princes Eteocles and Polyneices, have killed each other in battle; and I, as the next in blood, have succeeded to the full power of the throne.

I am aware, of course, that no ruler can expect complete loyalty from his subjects until he has been tested in office. Nevertheless, I say to you at the very outset that I have nothing but contempt for the kind of governor who is afraid, for whatever reason, to follow the course that he knows is best for the state; and as for the man who sets private friendship above the public welfare—I have no use for him, either. I call God to witness that if I saw my country headed for ruin, I should not be afraid to speak out plainly; and I need hardly remind you that I would never have any dealings with an enemy of the people. No one values friendship more highly than I; but we must remember that friends made at the risk of wrecking our ship are not real friends at all.

These are my principles, at any rate, and that is why I have made the following decision concerning the sons of Oedipus: Eteocles, who died as a man should die, fighting for his country, is to be buried with full military honors, with all the ceremony that is usual when the greatest heroes die; but his brother Polyneices, who broke his exile to come back with fire and sword against his native city and the shrines of his fathers' gods, whose one idea was to spill the blood of his blood and sell his own people into slavery—Polyneices, I say, is to have no burial: no man is to touch him or say the least prayer for him; he shall lie on the plain, unburied; and the birds and the scavenging dogs can do with him whatever they like.

This is my command, and you can see the wisdom behind it. As long as I am king, no traitor is going to be honored with the loyal man. But whoever shows by word and deed that he is on the side of the state—he shall have my respect while he is living, and my reverence when he is dead.

Choragus. If that is your will, Creon son of Menoeceus,
You have the right to enforce it: we are yours.

Creon. That is my will. Take care that you do your part.

12 Laius (lā'əs): father of Oedipus.

18–30 According to Creon, what deserves the highest loyalty? How do you feel about Creon's principles?

31–42 Do you think Creon is justified in treating Polyneices' corpse in this way? What do you think his motive is?

Customizing Instruction

Students Acquiring English

1 Have students use punctuation marks to help them decide where to break the long sentences into shorter ones. Use lines 11–14 as an example, replacing the colon and semicolons with periods.

2 Make sure students understand that this reference to a ship refers to the metaphor at the beginning of the speech.

3 Have students use context clues to infer that *broke his exile* means "came back from abroad."

Gifted and Talented

Explain that the ancient Greeks placed great emphasis on a virtue they called *sophrosyne*. This word meant various things at different times, but it is most often translated as *temperance*. *Sophrosyne* can also mean self-restraint, contentment, and self-knowledge. Have students look for examples of *sophrosyne* or the lack of it in the characters of this play.

Reading and Analyzing

Reading Skills and Strategies: MAKING INFERENCES

A Have students explain what the sentry's behavior suggests about Creon's reputation.

Possible Responses: Creon is greatly feared; he expects his orders to be carried out completely.

Literary Analysis: PLOT

B The rising action of a play involves the revelation of complications that cause difficulties for the main characters. Ask students what the sentry has discovered.

Answer: Someone has buried Polyneices' body, defying Creon's decree.

Ask students how this discovery heightens the conflict.

Possible Response: Creon will be looking for the rebel. This creates suspense because the audience thinks that Antigone buried Polyneices.

Reading Skills and Strategies: ANALYZING

C Discuss Creon's scornful reaction to the chorus's suggestion that the gods buried the body. Remind them that, at this point, there is no evidence that Antigone has buried the body. Analyze Creon's response.

Possible Response: Students should conclude that Creon is arrogant and brash because he presumes to know what the gods are thinking.

Literary Analysis: TRAGIC FLAW

D Challenge students to explain what they think Creon's tragic flaw might be.

Possible Responses: pride; inflexibility; arrogance; rashness

---

Choragus. We are old men: let the younger ones carry it out.

Creon. I do not mean that: the sentries have been appointed.

Choragus. Then what is it that you would have us do?

Creon. You will give no support to whoever breaks this law.

Choragus. Only a crazy man is in love with death!

Creon. And death it is; yet money talks, and the wisest
Have sometimes been known to count a few coins too many.

(*Enter* Sentry.)

A

Sentry. I'll not say that I'm out of breath from running, King, because every time I stopped to think about what I have to tell you, I felt like going back. And all the time a voice kept saying, "You fool, don't you know you're walking straight into trouble?"; and then another voice: "Yes, but if you let somebody else get the news to Creon first, it will be even worse than that for you!" But good sense won out, at least I hope it was good sense, and here I am with a story that makes no sense at all; but I'll tell it anyhow, because, as they say, what's going to happen's going to happen, and—

Creon. Come to the point. What have you to say?

Sentry. I did not do it. I did not see who did it. You must not punish me for what someone else has done.

1

Creon. A comprehensive defense! More effective, perhaps,
If I knew its purpose. Come: what is it?

Sentry. A dreadful thing . . . I don't know how to put it—

Creon. Out with it!

B

Sentry. Well, then;
The dead man—
Polyneices—

(*Pause. The* Sentry *is overcome, fumbles for words.* Creon *waits impassively.*)

out there—
someone—
New dust on the slimy flesh!

(*Pause. No sign from* Creon.)

2

Someone has given it burial that way, and
Gone. . . .

(*Long pause.* Creon *finally speaks with deadly control.*)

Creon. And the man who dared do this?

Sentry. I swear I
Do not know! You must believe me!

78 Note that Creon assumes it is a man who has tried to bury the body.

Teaching Options

Mini Lesson Multicultural Link

RELIGION Honoring the dead through proper burial is important across cultures. Christians, Jews, and Muslims traditionally bury the bodies of their dead. In Islamic countries, the body is interred with its right side toward Mecca, the holy city of Islam. Among the Kansa, a Native American people, the women of the tribe paint the face of the corpse and cover it with bark and a buffalo robe. The body is buried under rock slabs with clothing, food, and important possessions. Buddhists and Hindus practice cremation. In Hinduism, after the body is cremated, the remains are gathered and often deposited in sacred rivers. Eastern followers of the ancient Persian religion of Zoroastrianism place the corpses of their dead on high, exposed platforms known as Towers of Silence. The bodies are quickly eaten by vultures.

Listen:
The ground was dry, not a sign of digging, no,
Not a wheel track in the dust, no trace of anyone.
It was when they relieved us this morning: and one of them,
The corporal, pointed to it.
There it was,
The strangest—
Look:
The body, just mounded over with light dust: you see?
Not buried really, but as if they'd covered it
Just enough for the ghost's peace. And no sign
Of dogs or any wild animal that had been there.

And then what a scene there was! Every man of us
Accusing the other: we all proved the other man did it;
We all had proof that we could not have done it.
We were ready to take hot iron in our hands,
Walk through fire, swear by all the gods,
It was not I!
I do not know who it was, but it was not I!

(Creon*'s rage has been mounting steadily, but the* Sentry *is too intent upon his story to notice it.*)

And then, when this came to nothing, someone said
A thing that silenced us and made us stare
Down at the ground: you had to be told the news,
And one of us had to do it! We threw the dice,
And the bad luck fell to me. So here I am,
No happier to be here than you are to have me:
Nobody likes the man who brings bad news.

Choragus. I have been wondering, King: can it be that the gods have done this?

Creon (*furiously*). Stop!
Must you doddering wrecks
Go out of your heads entirely? "The gods!"
Intolerable!
C The gods favor this corpse? Why? How had he served them?
Tried to loot their temples, burn their images,
Yes, and the whole state, and its laws with it!
Is it your senile opinion that the gods love to honor bad men?
A pious thought!—
No, from the very beginning
D There have been those who have whispered together,
Stiff-necked anarchists, putting their heads together,

85–88 Notice that the burial of Polyneices is symbolic and ritualistic rather than actual.

104–109 Note how quickly Creon rejects a reasonable question posed by the choragus. Creon is convinced that he knows how the gods think.

114 anarchists (ăn′ər-kĭsts): persons favoring the overthrow of government.

Customizing Instruction

Students Acquiring English

1 Have students paraphrase Creon's reaction in simple, everyday English.

Possible Response: You are doing a good job of excusing yourself, but it would help if I knew what you were talking about.

Less Proficient Readers

2 Ask students what has happened to Polyneices' body.

Answer: It has been buried under a light covering of dust.

Is there any evidence at the scene of the "crime" to suggest who may have done this deed?

Answer: No; the dry ground yielded neither wheel track nor footprint, and there were no signs of dogs or other wild animals around the body.

Multiple Learning Styles

Bodily-Kinesthetic Learners

Invite a pair of students to pantomime the scene between Creon and the sentry. Encourage them to use body language, including posture, facial expressions, and gestures to convey Creon's fury and the sentry's terror.

ANTIGONE **1029**

Reading and Analyzing

Literary Analysis: DRAMATIC IRONY

A Dramatic irony occurs when the audience knows or recognizes something that the characters onstage do not. Ask students what could be ironic about Creon's outburst.

Possible Response: Although Creon assumes that a man was paid to bury Polyneices, it was actually Antigone, a woman, who buried her brother out of love and piety.

GUIDE FOR READING

B **Possible Response:** He assumes that the people who buried Polyneices have defied him for money.

Literary Analysis: FIGURATIVE LANGUAGE

C Invite volunteers to point out the figures of speech in this passage and evaluate their effectiveness.

Possible Response: Metaphor (example: man's "mind" is compared to a "net") and personification (example: birds and beasts "cling to cover") are used throughout the lyrical hymn to illustrate man's power over nature.

Literary Analysis: THEME

D The comments of the chorus often point to the themes of the tragedy. Ask them what themes they find in this ode.

Possible Responses: Humans have accomplished much, but they cannot avoid death; a civilization can only exist if its laws are obeyed and enforced; anarchy is the ultimate evil.

GUIDE FOR READING

E **Possible Response:** Humans can achieve greatness when they stay within the laws; humans can suffer tragedy when they transgress those laws.

Scheming against me in alleys. These are the men,
And they have bribed my own guard to do this thing.
(*sententiously*) Money!
There's nothing in the world so demoralizing as money.
Down go your cities,
Homes gone, men gone, honest hearts corrupted,
Crookedness of all kinds, and all for money!
(*to* Sentry) But you—!
I swear by God and by the throne of God, **A**
The man who has done this thing shall pay for it!
Find that man; bring him here to me, or your death
Will be the least of your problems: I'll string you up
1 Alive, and there will be certain ways to make you
Discover your employer before you die;
And the process may teach you a lesson you seem to have missed:
The dearest profit is sometimes all too dear.
That depends on the source. Do you understand me?
A fortune won is often misfortune.

Sentry. King, may I speak?

Creon. Your very voice distresses me.

Sentry. Are you sure that it is my voice, and not your conscience?

Creon. By God, he wants to analyze me now!

Sentry. It is not what I say, but what has been done, that hurts you.

Creon. You talk too much.

Sentry. Maybe; but I've done nothing.

2 **Creon.** Sold your soul for some silver: that's all you've done.

Sentry. How dreadful it is when the right judge judges wrong!

Creon. Your figures of speech
May entertain you now; but unless you bring me the man,
You will get little profit from them in the end.

(*Exit* Creon *into the palace.*)

Sentry. "Bring me the man"—!
I'd like nothing better than bringing him the man!
But bring him or not, you have seen the last of me here.
At any rate, I am safe!

(*Exit* Sentry.)

117 sententiously (sĕn-tĕn′shəs-lē): in a pompous, moralizing manner.

117–121 What does Creon assume about the motives of those who have disobeyed him? **B**

Teaching Options

Mini Lesson Grammar

DIRECT AND INDIRECT OBJECTS

Instruction A predicate can contain complements called direct and indirect objects. A direct or an indirect object is a noun or pronoun and its modifiers. As their names suggest, a direct object is directly acted upon by the verb while an indirect object receives action indirectly. Remind students that the preposition *to* or *for* can generally be placed before an indirect object without changing the meaning of the sentence. Point out that an indirect object almost always appears with a direct object. Then write the following sentence on the chalkboard:

At the end of the play, the chorus gives Creon advice.

Underline the objects as shown. Have students identify the direct object *(advice)* and the indirect object *(Creon)* of *gives*. Explain that the direct object of *gives* is *advice* because that is the focus of the chorus's action. By receiving the advice, Creon is *indirectly* affected by the action.

Exercises In the following sentences ask students to underline the direct objects once and the indirect objects twice.

ODE 1

Chorus. Numberless are the world's wonders, but none **3** **4**
More wonderful than man; the storm-grey sea
Yields to his prows; the huge crests bear him high;
Earth, holy and inexhaustible, is graven
With shining furrows where his plows have gone
Year after year, the timeless labor of stallions.

The light-boned birds and beasts that cling to cover,
The lithe fish lighting their reaches of dim water,
All are taken, tamed in the net of his mind;
The lion on the hill, the wild horse windy-maned,
Resign to him; and his blunt yoke has broken
The sultry shoulders of the mountain bull. **C**

Words also, and thought as rapid as air,
He fashions to his good use; statecraft is his,
And his the skill that deflects the arrows of snow,
The spears of winter rain: from every wind
He has made himself secure—from all but one:
In the late wind of death he cannot stand.

O clear intelligence, force beyond all measure!
O fate of man, working both good and evil!
When the laws are kept, how proudly his city stands!
When the laws are broken, what of his city then?
Never may the anarchic man find rest at my hearth,
Never be it said that my thoughts are his thoughts. **D**

ODE: An ode is a song chanted by the chorus.

4 graven: carved; engraved.

24 What does this ode convey about human greatness and tragic limitation? **E**

WORDS TO KNOW **lithe** (līth) *adj.* limber; physically flexible

1031

Customizing Instruction

Less Proficient Readers

1 Point out the lines "I'll string you up / Alive, and there will be certain ways to make you / Discover your employer before you die." Make sure students understand that Creon is threatening the sentry with torture.

2 Who has defied Creon and buried Polyneices?

Answer: Antigone

- What principles does Creon live by?
  Possible Response: He sets public interest above private concerns.
- What is the sentry's attitude toward Creon?
  Answer: He fears Creon greatly.
- What does Creon ask the sentry to do?
  Answer: bring to him the man who has buried Polyneices

Set a Purpose Have students read Scene 2 to find out if Creon captures Antigone.

Students Acquiring English

3 Have students restate the opening clause of the ode in everyday English.

Possible Response: The world's wonders are numberless.

Explain that this is an example of inverted word order, in which the subject of a verb follows the verb instead of preceding it.

4 Students may be interested to know that the Greek word *deima,* which has been translated as *wonder* in this ode, can also mean "terror." Ask students how the meaning of the ode changes when they substitute *terrors* and *terrible* for *wonders* and *wonderful* in the first two lines. Invite students to share their experiences with the problems of translating concepts from one language to another.

1. Antigone buried her brother's body.
2. Ismene did not offer Antigone her help.
3. Creon thought the sentry was telling him lies.
4. Creon's anger frightened the sentry.
5. Antigone faced death bravely.
6. Oedipus bequeathed his children the curse.

Use **Grammar Transparencies and Copymasters,** p. 91.

Use McDougal Littell's ***Language Network,*** Chapter 2, for more instruction in direct and indirect objects.

Reading and Analyzing

Literary Analysis CLASSICAL DRAMA

A Ask students what purpose the choragus's lines serve at the beginning of this scene. Remind them that the choragus is the only member of the chorus who interacts with the characters in the play.

Possible Responses: His lines instantly let the audience know the situation in this scene: that the sentry has captured Antigone and that Creon is coming from the house. Because the characters could be identified only by the actors' changes of mask and costume, the choragus reminds the audience of the characters' identities by calling them by name.

B Point out that the beginning of this scene has a number of entrances. The skene was the long building on the platform of the stage through which characters entered and exited the playing area. Ask students how the skene is used here to add suspense to the plot.

Possible Response: The skene allows Creon to remain offstage until the sentry and Antigone appear. The audience is kept waiting to see what Creon's reaction will be when he discovers she is the one who has defied him.

GUIDE FOR READING

C **Possible Response:** Creon should learn from the sentry that nothing in life is certain. He needs to be more flexible and open-minded in making decisions.

D **Possible Response:** The sentry's comparison of Antigone to a mother bird returning to a stripped nest creates sympathy.

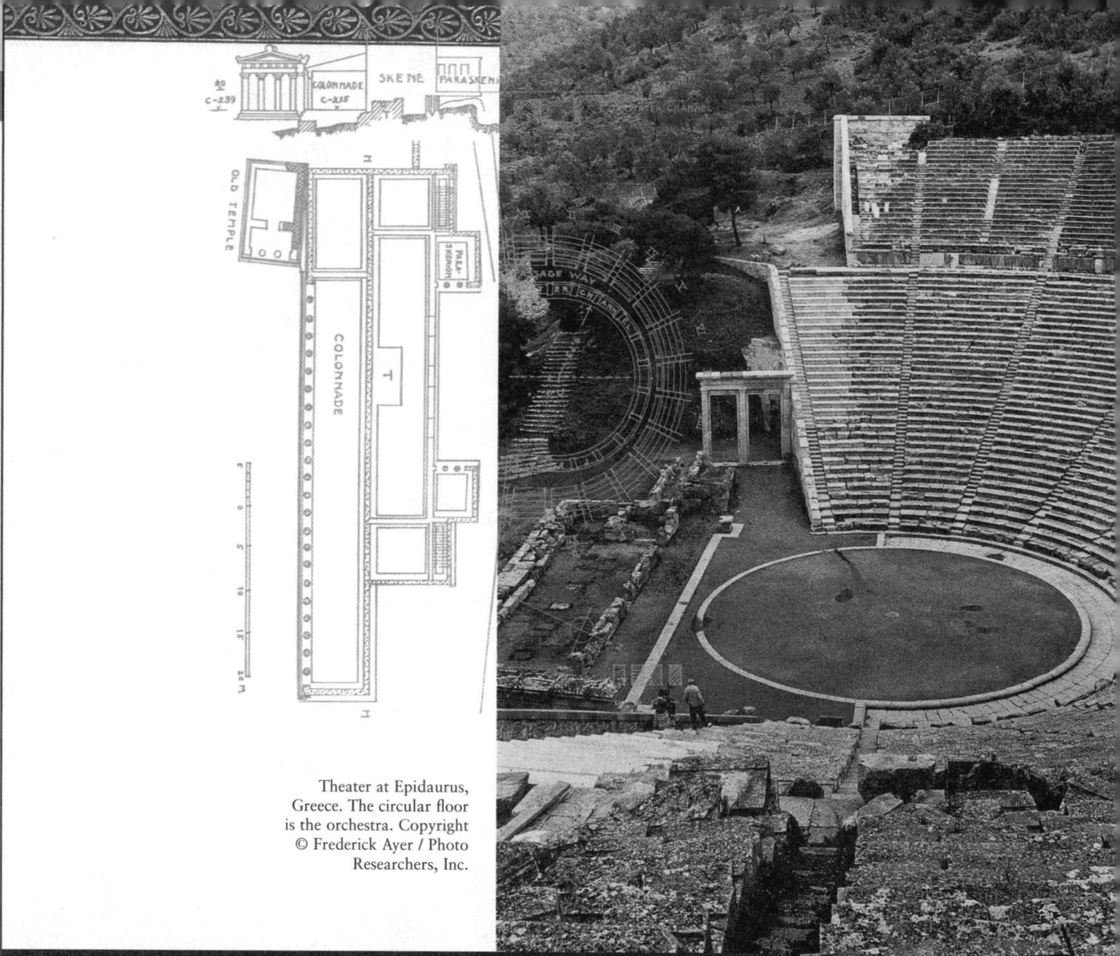

Theater at Epidaurus, Greece. The circular floor is the orchestra. Copyright © Frederick Ayer / Photo Researchers, Inc.

SCENE 2

(*Reenter* Sentry *leading* Antigone.)

Choragus. What does this mean? Surely this captive woman
Is the princess, Antigone. Why should she be taken?

Sentry. Here is the one who did it! We caught her
In the very act of burying him. Where is Creon?

Choragus. Just coming from the house.

(*Enter* Creon, *center.*)

Creon. What has happened?
Why have you come back so soon?

Teaching Options

Mini Lesson: Viewing and Representing

Theater at Epidarus, Greece

Instruction Have students study the photograph of the theater at Epidaurus and the diagram to the left of the photograph. Permanent stone theaters such as this one were not built until the 4th century B.C., years after Sophocles was alive. Then tell students that the theater in which *Antigone* was first performed would have been similar, although the structures would probably have been wooden.

Application Encourage students to visualize how the theater at Epidaurus would have looked before it was ruined, with the colonnade, skene, and paraskene behind the orchestra and the seats full of spectators. Have students sketch the façade of the colonnade and skene and then draw the sentry, Antigone, and Creon as they might have appeared in this scene.

Sentry (*expansively*). O King,
A man should never be too sure of anything:
I would have sworn
That you'd not see me here again: your anger
Frightened me so, and the things you threatened me with;
But how could I tell then
That I'd be able to solve the case so soon?
No dice throwing this time: I was only too glad to come!
Here is this woman. She is the guilty one:
We found her trying to bury him.
Take her, then; question her; judge her as you will.
I am through with the whole thing now, and glad of it.

Creon. But this is Antigone! Why have you brought her here?

Sentry. She was burying him, I tell you!

Creon (*severely*). Is this the truth?

Sentry. I saw her with my own eyes. Can I say more?

Creon. The details: come, tell me quickly!

Sentry. It was like this:
After those terrible threats of yours, King,
We went back and brushed the dust away from the body.
2 The flesh was soft by now, and stinking,
So we sat on a hill to windward and kept guard.
No napping this time! We kept each other awake.
3 But nothing happened until the white round sun
Whirled in the center of the round sky over us:
Then, suddenly,
A storm of dust roared up from the earth, and the sky
4 Went out, the plain vanished with all its trees
In the stinging dark. We closed our eyes and endured it.
The whirlwind lasted a long time, but it passed;
And then we looked, and there was Antigone!
I have seen
A mother bird come back to a stripped nest, heard
Her crying bitterly a broken note or two
For the young ones stolen. Just so, when this girl
Found the bare corpse, and all her love's work wasted,
She wept, and cried on heaven to damn the hands
That had done this thing.
And then she brought more dust
And sprinkled wine three times for her brother's ghost.
We ran and took her at once. She was not afraid,

7–13 Note the change in attitude on the part of the sentry. How might his statement "A man should never be too sure of anything" apply to Creon? **C**

35–45 How does the sentry's speech create sympathy for Antigone? **D**

Customizing Instruction

Less Proficient Readers

1 Ask students to whom *him* in line 4 refers.

Answer: Polyneices

Students Acquiring English

2 Model for students the use of the cause-and-effect type of context clue. Point out that because the body was now stinking, the sentries wanted to avoid the smell. From this clue, students can infer that *windward* means "upwind."

Less Proficient Readers

3 Ask students at what time of day the sentries see Antigone trying to bury Polyneices' body. How do they know?

Answer: about noon; "the white round sun / Whirled in the center of the round sky over us"

4 Ask students what could have caused the dust storm.

Possible Responses: An act of nature or the gods could have caused the storm.

ANTIGONE 1033

Reading and Analyzing

Literary Analysis:
PROTAGONIST/ANTAGONIST

Remind students that the protagonist is the central character in a play or story. He or she often changes during the course of the work; sometimes, there can be more than one protagonist. The antagonist is the character or force in a play or story against which the protagonist is pitted. The antagonist may be another character, an aspect of society or nature, or an internal force within the protagonist. Ask students who they think the protagonist and the antagonist are in this play.

Have students keep their answer in mind as they read the remainder of the play.

GUIDE FOR READING

A Possible Response: Antigone recognizes God's law as the supreme one.

B Possible Responses: She calmly accepts death as inevitable; she does not fear death.

1034

Teaching Options

Mini Lesson Viewing and Representing

Antigone (film still)

Instruction Discuss the staging of this scene with students. Point out that a vertical hierarchy exists, with the corpse at the bottom, Antigone in the middle, and the soldiers at the top. Ask students what they think this arrangement means.

Possible Response: The state has the most power in this setting, but Antigone still has enough power to show honor to the body of her brother.

Application Have students reread the sentry's account of this scene on the preceding page. Then have them sketch the scene that the sentry describes. They can base their drawings on the film still or create their own arrangement. Students may want to dress the characters in modern clothing.

Not even when we charged her with what she had done.
She denied nothing.
And this was a comfort to me,
And some uneasiness: for it is a good thing
To escape from death, but it is no great pleasure
To bring death to a friend.
Yet I always say
There is nothing so comfortable as your own safe skin!

Creon (*slowly, dangerously*). And you, Antigone,
You with your head hanging—do you confess this thing?

Antigone. I do. I deny nothing.

Creon (*to* Sentry). You may go.

(*Exit* Sentry.)

(*to* Antigone) Tell me, tell me briefly:
Had you heard my proclamation touching this matter?

Antigone. It was public. Could I help hearing it?

Creon. And yet you dared defy the law.

Antigone. I dared.
It was not God's proclamation. That final Justice
That rules the world below makes no such laws.
Your edict, King, was strong,
But all your strength is weakness itself against
The immortal unrecorded laws of God.
They are not merely now: they were, and shall be,
Operative forever, beyond man utterly.
1 I knew I must die, even without your decree:
I am only mortal. And if I must die
Now, before it is my time to die,
Surely this is no hardship: can anyone
Living, as I live, with evil all about me,
Think Death less than a friend? This death of mine
Is of no importance; but if I had left my brother
Lying in death unburied, I should have suffered.
Now I do not.

57–63 What law does Antigone recognize as the supreme one? **A**

64–70 What is Antigone's attitude toward death? **B**

Film still from the 1960 movie *Antigone*. Antigone is about to be taken prisoner after sprinkling dust and wine over her brother's corpse. Culver Pictures.

WORDS TO KNOW
edict (ē′dĭkt′) *n.* an order put out by a person in authority

Customizing Instruction

Multiple Learning Styles

Auditory Learners

1 Suggest that students read Antigone's speech aloud after they read it silently. Discuss the impact of each method.

Possible Responses: Most students will probably think that reading the speech aloud fosters more emotional connections to Antigone and will find the oral presentation more moving than their silent reading.

Less Proficient Readers

Suggest that students break the long sentences in Antigone's speech into shorter sentences, using punctuation marks as guides.

Possible Response: "Your edict, King, was strong. All your strength, however, is weakness itself against the immortal unrecorded laws of God."

Reading and Analyzing

Literary Analysis: DRAMATIC IRONY

A Ask students to explain the dramatic irony in the comments the choragus and Creon make. Then explore how the irony in this scene adds to the tragedy.
Possible Response: The audience recognizes that the dual comments about stubbornness apply to Creon as much as they do to Antigone. Creon's lack of self-knowledge helps the play build to its climax and reinforces the inevitability of the tragedy.

Active Reading

STRATEGIES FOR READING CLASSICAL DRAMA

Have students monitor and evaluate how well their reading strategies have been working. Remind them to make modifications, such as rereading, when understanding breaks down. Remind students that a key aspect to understanding a play is understanding its characters. Then have them briefly describe Ismene, Antigone, and Creon.
Possible Responses: Ismene is a timid, sweet girl. Antigone is self-righteous and stubborn; she hates injustice and reveres the laws of the gods. Creon values his power as the king and thinks his own civil law is more important than the laws of the gods. He has a bad temper and is both stubborn and inflexible.

GUIDE FOR READING

B **Possible Response:** Antigone assumes that the members of the chorus agree with her but they are too afraid of Creon to voice their true feelings. She is probably right.

1
You smile at me. Ah Creon,
Think me a fool, if you like; but it may well be
That a fool convicts me of folly.

Choragus. Like father, like daughter: both headstrong, deaf to
reason!
She has never learned to yield.

Creon. She has much to learn.
The inflexible heart breaks first, the toughest iron
Cracks first, and the wildest horses bend their necks
At the pull of the smallest curb.
Pride? In a slave?
This girl is guilty of a double insolence,
Breaking the given laws and boasting of it.
A Who is the man here,
She or I, if this crime goes unpunished?
Sister's child, or more than sister's child,
Or closer yet in blood—she and her sister
Win bitter death for this!
(*to servants*) Go, some of you,
Arrest Ismene. I accuse her equally.
Bring her: you will find her sniffling in the house there.

Her mind's a traitor: crimes kept in the dark
Cry for light, and the guardian brain shudders;
2 But how much worse than this
Is brazen boasting of barefaced anarchy!

Antigone. Creon, what more do you want than my death?

Creon. Nothing.
That gives me everything.

Antigone. Then I beg you: kill me.
This talking is a great weariness: your words
Are distasteful to me, and I am sure that mine
Seem so to you. And yet they should not seem so:
I should have praise and honor for what I have done.
All these men here would praise me
Were their lips not frozen shut with fear of you.
(*bitterly*) Ah the good fortune of kings,
Licensed to say and do whatever they please!

Creon. You are alone here in that opinion.

Antigone. No, they are with me. But they keep their tongues in leash.

Creon. Maybe. But you are guilty, and they are not.

Antigone. There is no guilt in reverence for the dead.

82–83 Think about how Creon's perception of Antigone as a threat to his manhood heightens the conflict.

99–104 What does Antigone assume about the attitude of the chorus? Do you think she is right? **B**

Confrontation between Antigone and Creon in the 1960 film. Photofest.

Teaching Options

Mini Lesson: Viewing and Representing

Antigone (film still)

Instruction When *Antigone* was originally performed, the stage was limited to an open area (orchestra) and a permanent backdrop (skene), which may have had steps in front of it or a feature that could be used as a balcony. Ask students how the set in this film still is similar to an ancient Greek stage.
Possible Response: The set is very simple, consisting of a temple structure and steps. This would have been easy to stage even in an ancient amphitheater.
Application Ask students how this picture suggests that Creon has much greater power than Antigone. Encourage them to examine the arrangement of the figures, the characters' costumes, and the props for clues.
Possible Response: This scene takes place in a public arena, suggesting that those with political and social power will be stronger than those with personal or religious power. Creon is standing on a higher step than Antigone, making manifest his greater public power. Antigone is unarmed, carrying only a shawl, whereas the soldiers have spears and shields and the members of the chorus carry shepherd's crooks. Creon is wearing formal attire and a crown, which emphasize his importance.

Customizing Instruction

Less Proficient Readers

Have students monitor their comprehension by asking the following questions:

- What is the primary conflict in the play?
  Possible Responses: the conflict between moral law and social law, which is embodied in the conflict between Antigone and Creon
- What has Antigone done since the play began?
  Possible Response: She has asked Ismene to help her bury Polyneices' body. She then buried the body once or possibly twice. She was captured by the sentries guarding Polyneices' body, and she has now been brought before Creon to answer for her crime.

Students Acquiring English

1 Point out that the words *fool* and *folly* are related. Ask students to think of a synonym for *folly*.

Possible Response: *foolishness*

2 Help students understand what Creon means by "the guardian brain shudders." Discuss possible interpretations of this line.

Possible Response: Creon is contrasting the mind and the brain, the soul and the intellect, emotions and reason. He means that the intellect hates treachery even if the soul demands it. The word *shudders* conveys the strain that the brain feels at keeping silent when it knows that it should speak.

Reading and Analyzing

Literary Analysis: FIGURATIVE LANGUAGE

A Have students identify and explain the metaphors and personification in this passage. Then explore with the class how the figurative language helps readers visualize the characters and understand their motivation.

Possible Responses: "The cloud / That shadows her eyes rains down gentle sorrow" is a metaphor comparing tears to rain; it is also personification, giving human qualities to rain. The phrase "snake in my ordered house, sucking my blood" is a metaphor, comparing Ismene's supposed betrayal to a snake's treachery. The first figure of speech portrays Ismene as compassionate and helpless; the second shows Creon as irrationally suspicious.

Reading Skills and Strategies: QUESTIONING

B Have students question why Ismene now wants to accept equal blame for the crime of burying Polyneices.

Possible Responses: She realizes that she made a mistake; she loves her sister and wants to share in her punishment.

Guide for Reading

C **Possible Responses:** Some students may agree that it is justified; others may argue that Antigone is too hard on Ismene.

D **Possible Response:** Creon feels that personal feelings, such as the bond between lovers, take second place to allegiance to the state.

Creon. But Eteocles—was he not your brother too?
Antigone. My brother too.
Creon. And you insult his memory?
Antigone (*softly*). The dead man would not say that I insult it.
Creon. He would: for you honor a traitor as much as him.
Antigone. His own brother, traitor or not, and equal in blood.
Creon. He made war on his country. Eteocles defended it.
Antigone. Nevertheless, there are honors due all the dead.
Creon. But not the same for the wicked as for the just.
Antigone. Ah Creon, Creon,
Which of us can say what the gods hold wicked?
Creon. An enemy is an enemy, even dead.
Antigone. It is my nature to join in love, not hate.
Creon (*finally losing patience*). Go join them, then; if you must have your love,
Find it in hell!
Choragus. But see, Ismene comes:
(*Enter* Ismene, *guarded.*)
A Those tears are sisterly; the cloud
That shadows her eyes rains down gentle sorrow.
Creon. You too, Ismene,
1 Snake in my ordered house, sucking my blood
Stealthily—and all the time I never knew
That these two sisters were aiming at my throne!
Ismene,
Do you confess your share in this crime or deny it?
Answer me.
B **Ismene.** Yes, if she will let me say so. I am guilty.
Antigone (*coldly*). No, Ismene. You have no right to say so.
You would not help me, and I will not have you help me.
Ismene. But now I know what you meant; and I am here
To join you, to take my share of punishment.
2 **Antigone.** The dead man and the gods who rule the dead
Know whose act this was. Words are not friends.
Ismene. Do you refuse me, Antigone? I want to die with you:
I too have a duty that I must discharge to the dead.
Antigone. You shall not lessen my death by sharing it.
Ismene. What do I care for life when you are dead?
Antigone. Ask Creon. You're always hanging on his opinions.

115–116 Unlike Creon, Antigone holds that humans cannot understand the thinking of the gods.

131–143 What do you think of Antigone's treatment of her sister? **C**

Teaching Options

Mini Lesson: Speaking and Listening

DRAMATIC SCENE

Prepare Encourage students to reread this scene between Creon, Antigone, and Ismene. Have them take notes on stage directions and internal clues that dictate how the lines should be delivered: "softly"; "finally losing patience"; "coldly"; "you are laughing at me"; "a joyless laughter." Invite students to experiment with other expressions that would be appropriate for various lines in this scene.

Present Divide students into groups and have them prepare this scene for performance, paying special attention to their vocal expression, as well as to their body language and gestures. Students should justify their choice of verbal and nonverbal performance techniques by referring to their interpretation of the scene. Remind them that they must pay close attention to their partners "onstage" so that they may respond with the appropriate tone and emotion. If students have trouble memorizing their lines, have them photocopy the text and make performance notes to aid them during their presentation.

BLOCK SCHEDULING This activity is particularly well suited for longer class periods.

Ismene. You are laughing at me. Why, Antigone?

Antigone. It's a joyless laughter, Ismene.

Ismene. But can I do nothing?

Antigone. Yes. Save yourself. I shall not envy you.
There are those who will praise you; I shall have honor, too.

Ismene. But we are equally guilty!

Antigone. No, more, Ismene.
You are alive, but I belong to Death.

Creon (*to the* Chorus). Gentlemen, I beg you to observe these girls:
One has just now lost her mind; the other,
It seems, has never had a mind at all.

Ismene. Grief teaches the steadiest minds to waver, King.

Creon. Yours certainly did, when you assumed guilt with the guilty!

Ismene. But how could I go on living without her?

Creon. You are.
She is already dead.

Ismene. But your own son's bride!

Creon. There are places enough for him to push his plow.
I want no wicked women for my sons!

Ismene. O dearest Haemon, how your father wrongs you!

Creon. I've had enough of your childish talk of marriage!

Choragus. Do you really intend to steal this girl from your son?

Creon. No; Death will do that for me.

Choragus. Then she must die?

Creon. You dazzle me.
—But enough of this talk! **3**
(*to guards*) You, there, take them away and guard them well:
For they are but women, and even brave men run
When they see Death coming. **4**

(*Exeunt* Ismene, Antigone, *and guards.*)

154 Ismene's line reveals a complication in the plot: Creon's son, Haemon, is engaged to Antigone. Creon's love for his immediate family is now an issue in his conflict with Antigone.

155–156 How does Creon feel about the bond between Haemon and Antigone? **D**

ODE 2

Chorus. Fortunate is the man who has never tasted God's vengeance!
Where once the anger of heaven has struck, that house is shaken
Forever: damnation rises behind each child
Like a wave cresting out of the black northeast,
When the long darkness under sea roars up
And bursts drumming death upon the wind-whipped sand.

Customizing Instruction

Students Acquiring English

1 Explain that the word *house* is used here as a metonymy. Metonymy is the substitution of one term for another with which it is closely related. In this case, *house* refers to an entire family, generation after generation. Explain that this word probably became metonymic because, in earlier times, a house was bequeathed by one generation to the next and came to stand for the family that lived there. Then ask students to which family the chorus is referring.

Answer: The chorus is referring to the family of Oedipus, which includes his parents, his descendants, and, because Jocasta was both Oedipus's mother and wife, her relatives.

Less Proficient Readers

2 Ask students what Antigone means when she says, "Words are not friends."

Possible Response: She means that Ismene's words do not prove her friendship. Antigone believes that only actions have real meaning.

3 Ask students what tone Creon might use when he says, "You dazzle me." Elicit that he is being sarcastic to the choragus.

4 Ask students what they can infer from these two lines.

Possible Response: Creon believes that Antigone and Ismene will try to escape.

Multiple Learning Styles

Auditory Learners

Between scenes the chorus sang and danced. Invite students to write or find music that captures the mood of this scene.

Reading and Analyzing

Literary Analysis: ODE

A Explain that an ode is an exalted, complex lyric that develops a serious and dignified theme. Odes appeal to both the imagination and the intellect. Have students identify the theme of this ode.

Possible Responses: the power of the gods, the eternal nature of the gods' wrath, the weakness of humankind, and the inevitability of fate

Then have students contrast this ode to Ode 1.

Possible Response: Ode 1 praises the accomplishments of humans and emphasizes their power over nature and their ability to make laws and establish cities. Ode 1 suggests that humans have something to be proud of. Ode 2, in contrast, suggests that pride will be the downfall of humankind. This ode puts humans in their place, subordinating them to the gods and to fate and pointing out their weakness and ignorance.

GUIDE FOR READING

B **Possible Responses:** Yes, because the pleasure Creon takes in punishing Antigone will be the cause of his destruction; no, because Creon does not seem to take pleasure in anything.

I have seen this gathering sorrow from time long past
Loom upon Oedipus' children: generation from generation
Takes the compulsive rage of the enemy god. **A**
So lately this last flower of Oedipus' line
Drank the sunlight! but now a passionate word
And a handful of dust have closed up all its beauty.

What mortal arrogance
Transcends the wrath of Zeus?
Sleep cannot lull him, nor the effortless long months
Of the timeless gods: but he is young forever,
And his house is the shining day of high Olympus.
All that is and shall be,
And all the past, is his.
No pride on earth is free of the curse of heaven.

The straying dreams of men
May bring them ghosts of joy:
But as they drowse, the waking embers burn them;
Or they walk with fixed eyes, as blind men walk.
But the ancient wisdom speaks for our own time:
Fate works most for woe
With Folly's fairest show.
Man's little pleasure is the spring of sorrow.

17 Olympus: a mountain in northern Greece, home of the gods and goddesses.

28 Do you think this line could apply to Creon? **B**

WORDS TO KNOW

compulsive (kəm-pŭl′sĭv) *adj.* having the ability to compel or force

Teaching Options

Assessment **Standardized Test Practice**

CHOOSING THE BEST SUMMARY For some standardized tests, students will be asked to choose the best summary of a passage. To provide students with some help in choosing the best summary, read aloud or write on the chalkboard the following question:

Which of the following statements best summarizes the conversation between Antigone and Creon at the beginning of Scene 2?

A. Antigone calls Creon a fool, and Creon sentences her to death.

B. Creon asks whether Antigone heard his decree, and she answers that she heard it but decided to bury Polyneices anyway.

C. Antigone asserts that the unwritten laws of the gods are supreme, and Creon responds that she is guilty of breaking his law and honoring a wicked traitor.

Lead students through the process of choosing the best summary. Consider each choice. Point out that while all the statements contain accurate information about the conversation, the best summary should include the most important information. For that reason, **C** is the best choice.

Painting on wine cup, showing the god Dionysus, the patron of theater, in his ship (540 B.C.), Exekias. Greek pottery often featured scenes from mythology. Antikensammlung, Munich, Germany. Photo Copyright © Erich Lessing / Art Resource, New York.

Theatrical masks on a fragment of a Greek bowl, about 410 B.C. The Granger Collection, New York.

SCENE 3

Choragus. But here is Haemon, King, the last of all your sons.
Is it grief for Antigone that brings him here,
And bitterness at being robbed of his bride?

(*Enter* Haemon.)

Creon. We shall soon see, and no need of diviners.
—Son,
You have heard my final judgment on that girl:
Have you come here hating me, or have you come
With deference and with love, whatever I do?

Haemon. I am your son, Father. You are my guide.
You make things clear for me, and I obey you.

4 diviners: those who predict the future.

Customizing Instruction

Less Proficient Readers

- What happens to Antigone in Scene 2?
  Answer: Creon captures her and sentences her to death.
- How did the sentry discover that Antigone had buried Polyneices?
  Answer: He and his men caught her trying to bury the body.
- Why do you think Antigone did not try to deny her crime?
  Possible Responses: There was too much evidence against her; she was proud of what she did; she realized that denial would not help her.
- How does the art on these pages add to your understanding of the tragedy?
  Possible Response: It helps the reader visualize events.

Set a Purpose Have students read Scene 3 to discover how Creon's son Haemon reacts to Antigone's death sentence.

Mini Lesson Viewing and Representing

Ancient Greek Pottery

ART APPRECIATION Vase painting was an important ancient Greek art form. About 675 B.C., Corinthian vase painters began to decorate their vases with simple black, silhouetted figures. Around 550 B.C., the style changed to include elaborate mythical creatures. Soon painters began signing their names to their creations. A new style of vase painting, distinguished by a sophisticated conception of space, developed around 540 B.C. The artists created three-dimensional figures by using shading and a brown wash over the drawings.

Instruction Point out the eyes on the prow of the ship. Explain that ancient Greeks believed that painting eyes on the front of the ship would help keep them and the ship safe. Discuss the differences between the two paintings, focusing on the scene and the quality of the artistry. Ask students which creation they prefer.

Application Remind students that scenes on vases often illustrated important events, people, or ideas. Have students sketch a vase painting that captures the main idea of *Antigone* and explain what it represents.

ANTIGONE 1041

Reading and Analyzing

GUIDE FOR READING

A Possible Response: Creon's words suggest that he sees his son as subservient, existing only to honor and serve his father.

B Possible Response: Creon sees government as controlling every aspect of his subjects' lives. To Creon, kings must be obeyed without question.

Literary Analysis: CHARACTERIZATION

C Ask students to explain what Haemon reveals about himself in his speech.
Possible Response: Haemon's words reveal that he is a loving son, intelligent and perceptive. He speaks to his father in an honest, forthright manner and understands his father's strong and weak points.

Reading Skills and Strategies: QUESTIONING

Ask students what questions come to mind as they read Creon's and Haemon's long speeches on pages 1042 and 1043.
Possible Responses: Would Creon have sentenced Haemon to death if he had broken the law? Is Haemon being sincere, or is he just flattering his father in the hope of persuading him? How will Creon react to Haemon's speech? Remind students to look for answers as they read the rest of the play.

GUIDE FOR READING

D Possible Response: Haemon talks about humanity's ability to reason, suggesting that people have the ability to participate in their own government and decide their own fates.

No marriage means more to me than your continuing wisdom.

Creon. Good. That is the way to behave: subordinate
Everything else, my son, to your father's will.
This is what a man prays for, that he may get
Sons attentive and dutiful in his house,
Each one hating his father's enemies,
Honoring his father's friends. But if his sons
Fail him, if they turn out unprofitably,
What has he fathered but trouble for himself
And amusement for the malicious?
So you are right
1 Not to lose your head over this woman.
Your pleasure with her would soon grow cold, Haemon,
And then you'd have a hellcat in bed and elsewhere.
Let her find her husband in hell!
Of all the people in this city, only she
Has had contempt for my law and broken it.

Do you want me to show myself weak before the people?
Or to break my sworn word? No, and I will not.
The woman dies.
2 I suppose she'll plead "family ties." Well, let her.
If I permit my own family to rebel,
3 How shall I earn the world's obedience?
Show me the man who keeps his house in hand,
He's fit for public authority.
I'll have no dealings
With lawbreakers, critics of the government:
Whoever is chosen to govern should be obeyed—
Must be obeyed, in all things, great and small,
Just and unjust! O Haemon,
The man who knows how to obey, and that man only,
Knows how to give commands when the time comes.
You can depend on him, no matter how fast
The spears come: he's a good soldier; he'll stick it out.
4 Anarchy, anarchy! Show me a greater evil!
This is why cities tumble and the great houses rain down;
This is what scatters armies!
No, no: good lives are made so by discipline.
We keep the laws then, and the lawmakers,
And no woman shall seduce us. If we must lose,
Let's lose to a man, at least! Is a woman stronger than we?

Choragus. Unless time has rusted my wits,

11–19 What do Creon's words suggest about his relationship with his son? **A**

26–44 What do Creon's words tell you about his views of government and his role as king? **B**

47–48 Again Creon hints that he feels his manhood is threatened.

Teaching Options

Cross Curricular Link Government

GREEK DEMOCRACY Unlike the Thebes depicted in *Antigone,* Athens was a democracy when Sophocles was writing plays. *Democracy* comes from the Greek words *demos,* "people," and *kratia,* "rule." Democracy evolved from the Greek city-states around the 7th century B.C. Athens overthrew its aristocracy in the 6th century and established a constitution that gave supreme power to the *ecclesia,* a citizens' assembly. Only freeborn male citizens—about 40,000 out of 400,000—could vote. Women, slaves, and immigrants were excluded. Sophocles served in government as president of the Hellenotamiae, the treasury board that managed tribute payments.

What you say, King, is said with point and dignity.

Haemon (*boyishly earnest*). Father:
Reason is God's crowning gift to man, and you are right
To warn me against losing mine. I cannot say—
I hope that I shall never want to say!—that you
Have reasoned badly. Yet there are other men
Who can reason, too; and their opinions might be helpful.
You are not in a position to know everything
That people say or do, or what they feel:
Your temper terrifies them—everyone
Will tell you only what you like to hear.
But I, at any rate, can listen; and I have heard them
Muttering and whispering in the dark about this girl.
They say no woman has ever, so unreasonably,
Died so shameful a death for a generous act:
"She covered her brother's body. Is this indecent?
She kept him from dogs and vultures. Is this a crime?
Death? She should have all the honor that we can give her!"

This is the way they talk out there in the city.

C

You must believe me:
Nothing is closer to me than your happiness.
What could be closer? Must not any son
Value his father's fortune as his father does his?
I beg you, do not be unchangeable:
Do not believe that you alone can be right.
The man who thinks that,
The man who maintains that only he has the power
To reason correctly, the gift to speak, the soul—
A man like that, when you know him, turns out empty.

It is not reason never to yield to reason!

In flood time you can see how some trees bend,
And because they bend, even their twigs are safe,
While stubborn trees are torn up, roots and all.
And the same thing happens in sailing:
Make your sheet fast, never slacken—and over you go, **5**
Head over heels and under: and there's your voyage.
Forget you are angry! Let yourself be moved!
I know I am young; but please let me say this:
The ideal condition
Would be, I admit, that men should be right by instinct;
But since we are all too likely to go astray,
The reasonable thing is to learn from those who can teach.

51–60 In what ways does Haemon's speech reflect the ideals of democracy? D

61–68 Haemon suggests that Creon is causing the very thing he most wants to prevent—anarchy.

79–85 Compare Haemon's words to Creon with Creon's words to Antigone in Scene 2, beginning "The inflexible heart breaks first . . ." (line 77, page 1036).

Customizing Instruction

Students Acquiring English

1 Help students understand that the idiom *lose your head* means "become irrational," to "lose your ability to think logically."

2 Explain that *family ties* are the connections that bind a family together. Ask students how Creon and Antigone are related.

Answer: Creon is Antigone's uncle.

3 Help students understand the idiom *keep his house in hand.* Remind students that *house* can stand for *family.* Explain that *in hand* can mean "in check" or "under control." Then have students restate the idiom in everyday English.

Possible Response: keep his family under control

Less Proficient Readers

4 Have students analyze the break before "No, no" at the end of Creon's speech. Has his tone changed? Is he responding to Haemon or the choragus?

Possible Response: This break signals a change in tone. Creon was very agitated at the end of the previous passage, but now he is calmer as he summarizes his views and tries to become more rational.

Students Acquiring English

5 Make sure students understand the unusual uses of *sheet* and *fast* in this line. Have students use context clues to determine the meaning of *sheet.*

Answer: sail

Then explain that, in this context, *fast* means "tight" or "secure." This meaning is most often used to refer to knots and connections or joints.

ANTIGONE 1043

Reading and Analyzing

Reading Skills and Strategies: CONNECTING

A Ask students how the conflict between Haemon and Creon illustrates a typical conflict between a parent and a child.

Possible Response: Creon wants his son to defer to his age, experience, and authority; Haemon does not want to be treated like a child; he wants his father to listen to his reasons.

Reading Skills and Strategies: ANALYZING

B Have students analyze Haemon's comment.

Possible Responses: The state needs to listen to its citizens; rigid governmental control can be destructive.

Literary Analysis CLASSICAL DRAMA

C Through dialogue the plot evolves, the characters are revealed, and conflicts occur. In order to discuss these elements, have students closely examine the dialogue between Creon and Haemon.

Possible Response: Haemon implies that if Antigone dies, he will commit suicide. Creon mistakenly interprets Haemon's remark as a threat on his (Creon's) life.

Guide for Reading

D **Possible Response:** Creon's decision is both ironic and cruel.

Choragus. You will do well to listen to him, King,
If what he says is sensible. And you, Haemon,
Must listen to your father. Both speak well.

Creon. You consider it right for a man of my years and experience
To go to school to a boy?

Haemon. It is not right
If I am wrong. But if I am young, and right,
What does my age matter? A

Creon. You think it right to stand up for an anarchist?

Haemon. Not at all. I pay no respect to criminals.

Creon. Then she is not a criminal?

Haemon. The city would deny it, to a man.

Creon. And the city proposes to teach me how to rule?

Haemon. Ah. Who is it that's talking like a boy now?

Creon. My voice is the one voice giving orders in this city!

Haemon. It is no city if it takes orders from one voice. B

Creon. The state is the king!

Haemon. Yes, if the state is a desert.

(*Pause*)

Creon. This boy, it seems, has sold out to a woman. 1

Haemon. If you are a woman: my concern is only for you.

Creon. So? Your "concern"! In a public brawl with your father!

Haemon. How about you, in a public brawl with justice?

Creon. With justice, when all that I do is within my rights?

Haemon. You have no right to trample on God's right.

Creon (*completely out of control*). Fool, adolescent fool! Taken in by a woman!

Haemon. You'll never see me taken in by anything vile. 2

Creon. Every word you say is for her!

Haemon (*quietly, darkly*). And for you.
And for me. And for the gods under the earth.

Creon. You'll never marry her while she lives.

Haemon. Then she must die. But her death will cause another.

Creon. Another?
Have you lost your senses? Is this an open threat? C

Haemon. There is no threat in speaking to emptiness.

Creon. I swear you'll regret this superior tone of yours!

Teaching Options

Mini Lesson Speaking and Listening

PRESS CONFERENCE

Prepare A press conference conveys information about an individual or an organization to the media. Usually, a press conference consists of a prepared statement followed by a question-and-answer session. An official speaker at a press conference often attempts to recast embarrassing incidents in a more flattering light. Reporters, in contrast, usually try to ask questions that reveal the truth about the incident.

Present Invite students to work in small groups to hold a press conference explaining Creon's decision to sentence Antigone to death. Half of the students in each group should be Creon's representatives; the rest should be reporters asking questions. Guide the court representatives to recast Creon's decision in the best possible light, and encourage the reporters to press for the full story. You may wish to videotape the press conference.

BLOCK SCHEDULING This activity is particularly well suited for longer class periods.

You are the empty one!

Haemon. If you were not my father,
I'd say you were perverse.

Creon. You girl-struck fool, don't play at words with me!

Haemon. I am sorry. You prefer silence.

Creon. Now, by God—!
I swear, by all the gods in heaven above us,
You'll watch it; I swear you shall!
(*to the servants*) Bring her out!
Bring the woman out! Let her die before his eyes,
Here, this instant, with her bridegroom beside her!

Haemon. Not here, no; she will not die here, King.
And you will never see my face again.
Go on raving as long as you've a friend to endure you.

(*Exit* Haemon.)

Choragus. Gone, gone.
Creon, a young man in a rage is dangerous!

Creon. Let him do, or dream to do, more than a man can.
He shall not save these girls from death.

Choragus. These girls?
You have sentenced them both?

Creon. No, you are right.
I will not kill the one whose hands are clean.

Choragus. But Antigone?

Creon (*somberly*). I will carry her far away,
Out there in the wilderness, and lock her
Living in a vault of stone. She shall have food,
As the custom is, to absolve the state of her death.
And there let her pray to the gods of hell:
They are her only gods:
Perhaps they will show her an escape from death,
Or she may learn,
though late,
That piety shown the dead is pity in vain. 3

(*Exit* Creon.)

141–149 What do you make of Creon's decision to bury a person who is still alive when he has steadfastly refused to bury a dead one? D

WORDS TO KNOW **perverse** (pər-vûrs') *adj.* willfully determined to go against what is expected or desired

Customizing Instruction

Multiple Learning Styles

Kinesthetic Learners

Have students act out the conversation between Creon and Haemon. Encourage them to use gestures and body language to bring the characters to life.

Students Acquiring English

1 Help students understand that the idiom *sold out* means "betrayed one's principles." In this case, Creon is accusing Haemon of turning against his father and his father's values for the sake of Antigone and his love for her.

2 Make sure students understand that *vile* means "disgusting" or "evil."

3 Help students see the clever way that the translators have rendered this line. Point out that the words *piety* and *pity* are a slant rhyme, which means that the rhyme is not exact but approximate. The line also looks balanced because the words are spelled almost the same way. Then read the line aloud so that students can hear the compelling rhythm. Have students discuss the difficulty of evoking the same level of poetry and elegance in a translation as in the original.

Reading and Analyzing

Reading Skills and Strategies: ANALYZING

A Ask students what the chorus believes has prompted the confrontation between Haemon and Creon.
Possible Responses: The chorus blames everything on the power of Haemon's love for Antigone; the chorus blames Aphrodite, the goddess of love.

Literary Analysis: THEME

B After students read Ode 3, have them discuss emerging themes in *Antigone.* Direct them to look for themes especially in the odes. One theme that appears in both Ode 2 and Ode 3 is that of the fleeting nature of human life. Another theme that appears in both odes is that of the awesome, inevitable, and sometimes arbitrary power of the gods. Then ask students how these themes are revealed in the play.

Literary Analysis CLASSICAL DRAMA

C Review with students the concept of catastrophe as it occurs in a classical drama, returning to page 1019 if necessary. With only two scenes remaining ask students to predict what the catastrophe might be.
Possible Responses: Antigone's death; Haemon's death; Creon's death

ODE 3

Chorus. Love, unconquerable
Waster of rich men, keeper
Of warm lights and all-night vigil
In the soft face of a girl: **1**
(A) Sea wanderer, forest visitor!
Even the pure immortals cannot escape you,
(B) And mortal man, in his one day's dusk,
Trembles before your glory.

Surely you swerve upon ruin
The just man's consenting heart,
As here you have made bright anger
Strike between father and son—
And none has conquered but Love!
A girl's glance working the will of heaven:
Pleasure to her alone who mocks us, **2**
(C) Merciless Aphrodite.

16 Aphrodite (ăf′rə-dī′tē): goddess of love and beauty.

Teaching Options

Standardized Test Practice

For some tests, students will be asked to produce an effective composition for a specific purpose. Have students write a brief essay in which they agree or disagree with the following statement:

> Antigone and Creon are both tragic heroes of Sophocles' classical drama *Antigone.*

They must support their position with evidence from the play and demonstrate a command of the conventions of spelling, capitalization, punctuation, grammar, usage, and sentence structure.

RUBRIC

3 **Full Accomplishment** Essay maintains a clear, consistent position that is well supported by evidence from the play. Essay demonstrates a command of the conventions of spelling, capitalization, punctuation, grammar, usage, and sentence structure.

2 **Substantial Accomplishment** Essay maintains a consistent position that is supported by some evidence from the play. Essay demonstrates an awareness of the conventions of spelling, capitalization, punctuation, grammar, usage, and sentence structure.

1 **Little or Partial Accomplishment** Essay does not maintain or support a position. Essay fails to demonstrate a command of the conventions of spelling, capitalization, punctuation, grammar, usage, and sentence structure.

Coins used by Greek citizens to gain admission to the theater. Each letter marks a different section of seats. Andromeda Oxford Ltd.

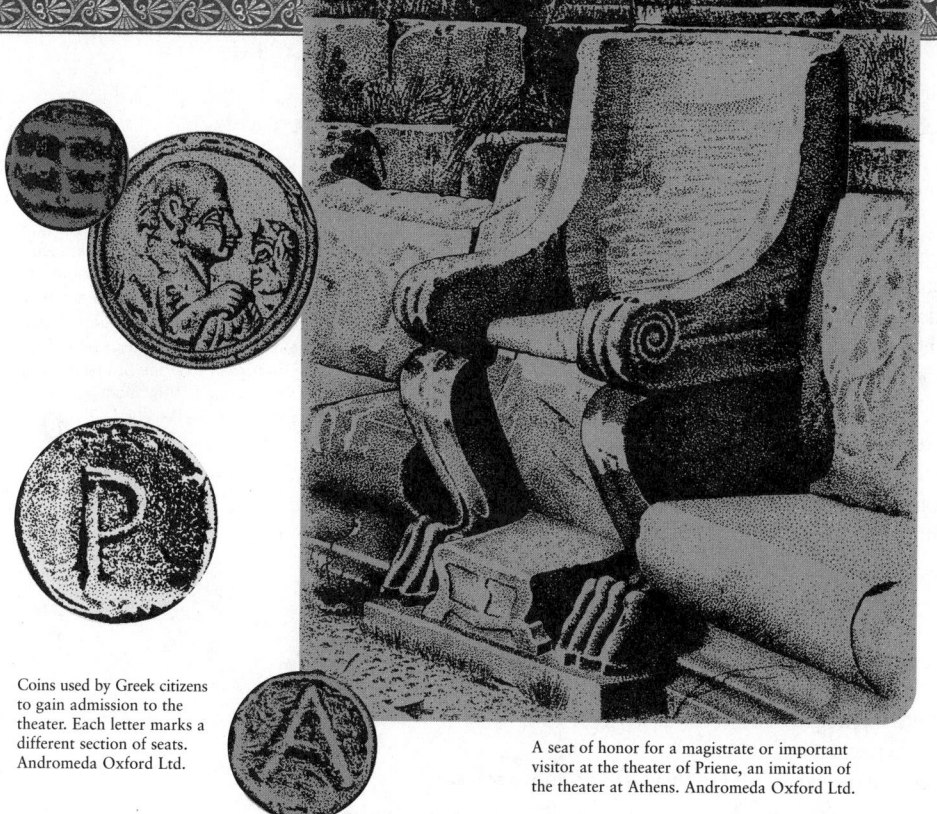

A seat of honor for a magistrate or important visitor at the theater of Priene, an imitation of the theater at Athens. Andromeda Oxford Ltd.

SCENE 4

Choragus (*as* Antigone *enters, guarded*). But I can no longer stand
in awe of this,
Nor, seeing what I see, keep back my tears.
Here is Antigone, passing to that chamber
Where all find sleep at last.

Antigone. Look upon me, friends, and pity me
Turning back at the night's edge to say
Good-bye to the sun that shines for me no longer;
Now sleepy Death
Summons me down to Acheron, that cold shore:

9 Acheron (ăk'ə-rŏn'): in Greek mythology, one of the rivers bordering the underworld, the place inhabited by the souls of the dead.

Customizing Instruction

Less Proficient Readers

- What does Haemon want Creon to do in Scene 3?
  Answer: Haemon wants Creon to spare Antigone's life and to reconsider his approach to government.
- What is Haemon's attitude toward his father at the beginning of their meeting?
  Answer: Haemon is respectful and polite.
- What reasons does Creon give for condemning Antigone to death?
  Answer: Creon says that she deserves death because she broke the law; to not kill her would show he is weak and cannot keep his word.
- How are Creon and Haemon the same? How are they different?
  Possible Response: Both are intelligent, strong men. Creon is despotic and inflexible; Haemon is democratic and reasonable.

Set a Purpose As students read Scene 4, direct them to see how Antigone faces the prospect of death.

Students Acquiring English

1 Help students understand the figurative language in Ode 3. Explain that *keeper* in line 2 belongs with both the phrases in line 3: ". . . keeper / Of warm lights and [keeper of] all-night vigil." Make sure students understand that *vigil* means "watch" or "wait."

2 Ask students to whom her refers in line 15.
Answer: Aphrodite

ANTIGONE **1047**

Reading and Analyzing

Literary Analysis CLASSICAL DRAMA

A Critics disagree about the exact purpose of the chorus. Some believe the chorus's responses are meant to serve as a model for proper behavior. Others believe that the chorus's responses are meant to simulate those of the average person and are not meant as a moral guide. Have students discuss the chorus's attitude toward Antigone. How might this group's attitude affect the audience?

Possible Response: In contrast to the choragus, who feels great sympathy for Antigone and her unjust plight, the chorus seems rather severe and distant in its responses. This attitude heightens the suspense of the moment, keeping the audience on edge as the action builds to the tragic climax.

GUIDE FOR READING

B Possible Response: The stone that will entomb Antigone reminds her of Niobe. Both women feel enormous sadness and loneliness, having lost loved ones to a cruel fate.

There is no bride song there, nor any music.

A **Chorus.** Yet not unpraised, not without a kind of honor,
You walk at last into the underworld;
Untouched by sickness, broken by no sword.
What woman has ever found your way to death?

Antigone. How often I have heard the story of Niobe,
Tantalus' wretched daughter, how the stone
Clung fast about her, ivy-close: and they say
The rain falls endlessly
And sifting soft snow; her tears are never done.
I feel the loneliness of her death in mine.

1 **Chorus.** But she was born of heaven, and you
Are woman, woman-born. If her death is yours,
A mortal woman's, is this not for you
Glory in our world and in the world beyond?

Antigone. You laugh at me. Ah, friends, friends,
Can you not wait until I am dead? O Thebes,
O men many-charioted, in love with Fortune,
Dear springs of Dirce, sacred Theban grove,
Be witnesses for me, denied all pity,
Unjustly judged! and think a word of love
For her whose path turns
Under dark earth, where there are no more tears.

Chorus. You have passed beyond human daring and come at last
Into a place of stone where Justice sits.
I cannot tell
What shape of your father's guilt appears in this.

Antigone. You have touched it at last: that bridal bed
Unspeakable, horror of son and mother mingling:
Their crime, infection of all our family!
O Oedipus, father and brother!
Your marriage strikes from the grave to murder mine.
I have been a stranger here in my own land:
All my life
The blasphemy of my birth has followed me.

2 **Chorus.** Reverence is a virtue, but strength
Lives in established law: that must prevail.
You have made your choice;
Your death is the doing of your conscious hand.

Antigone. Then let me go, since all your words are bitter,
And the very light of the sun is cold to me.

15–20 Niobe (nī'ə-bē) was a queen of Thebes whose children were killed by the gods because she had boasted that she was greater than a goddess. After their deaths, she was turned to stone but continued to shed tears. Why might Antigone compare herself to Niobe? **B**

44 blasphemy of my birth: Antigone is referring to her father's marriage to his own mother, an incestuous relationship that resulted in her birth. This type of relationship was considered a sin against the gods.

Irene Papas playing the title role in the 1960 movie. Culver Pictures.

Teaching Options

Mini Lesson Viewing and Representing

Antigone (film still)

Instruction Discuss the film shot on page 1049 with students. Elicit that the director has chosen a close-up shot that throws Antigone into sharp focus and leaves the background blurred. Ask students why the director chose to show Antigone looking back over her shoulder rather than a full-front view.

Possible Response: By showing Antigone like this, the director can emphasize her isolation. She is almost turned away from the audience. She appears remote, defended only by the shrouding shawl she wears.

Application Have students describe how Antigone looks in this photograph.

Possible Responses: Antigone looks courageous and proud because, although her face is rather sad, she is standing straight and proceeding toward her destiny; Antigone looks stubborn and arrogant because her chin is set and lifted high, as if in defiance.

Customizing Instruction

Less Proficient Readers

1 Have students restate this sentence in modern, everyday English.

Possible Response: But she was the daughter of a god (or goddess), and you are a mortal woman, the daughter of a mortal woman. If you are comparing your death to Niobe's, isn't your death glorious both in this world and the next?

2 Ask students what the chorus means in these two lines.

Possible Response: Antigone's burial of her brother showed her reverence for the gods, which is a virtue. However, established law (Creon's law) is stronger than virtue and will always prevail.

Gifted and Talented

Ask students if they have ever heard the word *hubris.* Explain that hubris is the opposite of *sophrosyne* (review p. 1027). Instead of temperance and self-restraint, a person demonstrating hubris will act excessively or unacceptably. Although Creon has hardly seemed self-restrained thus far, tell students that some critics have argued that Antigone suffers from hubris while Creon demonstrates *sophrosyne.* Have students discuss this interpretation in light of Antigone's words on page 1048.

Reading and Analyzing

Literary Analysis: PROTAGONIST/ ANTAGONIST

Students may want to discuss who they think is the progtagonist and who they think is the antagonist. A class poll can be taken. Students may explain their thinking or changes in their opinion, based on the events in the play.

Possible Response: To many students, Antigone is the protagonist because the play opens with her, she has the most tragic fate, and she is the title character. Many students will say that they have always thought Creon was the antagonist because he is clearly Antigone's enemy and he has many negative qualities.

Reading Skills and Strategies: CLARIFYING

(A) Ask students what Antigone is asking the gods to do.

Possible Response: She is asking that Creon be punished by death if he was, in fact, wrong to condemn her to death.

GUIDE FOR READING

(B) **Possible Response:** These lines suggest that Antigone most values the laws of the gods, the moral laws.

Lead me to my vigil, where I must have
Neither love nor lamentation; no song, but silence.

(Creon *interrupts impatiently.*)

Creon. If dirges and planned lamentations could put off death,
Men would be singing forever.
(*to the servants*) Take her, go!
You know your orders: take her to the vault
And leave her alone there. And if she lives or dies,
That's her affair, not ours: our hands are clean.

1

Antigone. O tomb, vaulted bride-bed in eternal rock,
Soon I shall be with my own again
Where Persephone welcomes the thin ghosts underground:
And I shall see my father again, and you, Mother,
And dearest Polyneices—
dearest indeed
To me, since it was my hand
That washed him clean and poured the ritual wine:
And my reward is death before my time!
And yet, as men's hearts know, I have done no wrong;
I have not sinned before God. Or if I have,
I shall know the truth in death. But if the guilt
Lies upon Creon who judged me, then, I pray,
May his punishment equal my own.

(A)

60 Persephone (pər-sĕf′ə-nē): wife of Hades (hā′dēz) and queen of the underworld.

Choragus. O passionate heart,
Unyielding, tormented still by the same winds!

Creon. Her guards shall have good cause to regret their delaying.

Antigone. Ah! That voice is like the voice of death!

Creon. I can give you no reason to think you are mistaken.

Antigone. Thebes, and you my fathers' gods,
And rulers of Thebes, you see me now, the last
Unhappy daughter of a line of kings,
Your kings, led away to death. You will remember
What things I suffer, and at what men's hands,
Because I would not transgress the laws of heaven.
(*to the guards, simply*) Come: let us wait no longer.

75–80 What do these lines suggest about what Antigone values most? (B)

(*Exit* Antigone, *left, guarded.*)

WORDS TO KNOW
lamentation (lăm′ən-tā′shən) *n.* an expression of grief
dirge (dûrj) *n.* a slow, mournful piece of music; a funeral hymn
transgress (trăns-grĕs′) *v.* to violate or break a law, command, or moral code

1050

Teaching Options

Mini Lesson

Speaking and Listening

DEBATE

Prepare Explain that a debate is a controlled event in which two sides argue a specific point of view, supporting their case with evidence. The debate teams also use persuasive techniques to convince listeners that their position is the correct one. Invite students to discuss any debates that they have witnessed or in which they have participated. Ask them what sorts of persuasive techniques the debaters used.

Present Divide the class into two teams. Have one team defend Antigone's statement that she has been "unjustly judged" (p. 1048, line 30) and the other team argue against her statement. Set time limits for the teams' opening arguments and rebuttals.

BLOCK SCHEDULING This activity is particularly well suited for longer class periods.

ODE 4

Chorus. All Danae's beauty was locked away
In a brazen cell where the sunlight could not come:
A small room, still as any grave, enclosed her.
Yet she was a princess too,
And Zeus in a rain of gold poured love upon her.
O child, child,
No power in wealth or war
Or tough sea-blackened ships
Can prevail against untiring Destiny!

And Dryas' son also, that furious king,
Bore the god's prisoning anger for his pride:
Sealed up by Dionysus in deaf stone,
His madness died among echoes.
So at the last he learned what dreadful power
His tongue had mocked:
For he had profaned the revels
And fired the wrath of the nine
Implacable sisters that love the sound of the flute.

And old men tell a half-remembered tale
Of horror done where a dark ledge splits the sea
And a double surf beats on the grey shores:
How a king's new woman, sick
With hatred for the queen he had imprisoned,
Ripped out his two sons' eyes with her bloody hands
2 While grinning Ares watched the shuttle plunge
Four times: four blind wounds crying for revenge,

Crying, tears and blood mingled. Piteously born,
Those sons whose mother was of heavenly birth!
Her father was the god of the north wind,
And she was cradled by gales;
She raced with young colts on the glittering hills
And walked untrammeled in the open light:
But in her marriage deathless Fate found means
To build a tomb like yours for all her joy.

1–5 Danae (dăn'ə-ē') was a princess who was imprisoned by her father because it had been predicted that her son would one day kill him. After Zeus visited Danae in the form of a shower of gold, she gave birth to his son Perseus, who eventually did kill his grandfather.

10–18 King Lycurgus (lĭ-kûr'gəs), son of Dryas (drī'əs), was driven mad and imprisoned in stone for objecting to the worship of Dionysus. The nine implacable sisters are the Muses, the goddesses who presided over literature, the arts, and the sciences. Once offended, they were impossible to appease.

19–34 These lines refer to the myth of King Phineus (fĭn'yo͞os), who imprisoned his first wife, the daughter of the north wind, and allowed his new wife to blind his sons from his first marriage.

Customizing Instruction

Students Acquiring English

1 Be sure that students understand that the idiom *our hands are clean* means "we are not guilty." Then invite students to share examples of idioms that might have similar meaning from their own language.

2 Explain that a *shuttle* is an instrument used in weaving. A shuttle is usually sharply pointed at both ends.

Gifted and Talented

Explain that another virtue admired by the Greeks was *arete,* which meant "excellence" or "heroism." Ask students whether Antigone's actions exhibit *sophrosyne,* hubris, or *arete,* and why.

Less Proficient Readers

- What words describe Antigone in this scene?
  Possible Responses: courageous; defiant
- Why does the chorus recount tales of horror?
  Possible Responses: These tragic tales hint at the play's catastrophic ending; the chorus feels that terrible things are going to happen.

Set a Purpose Have students read the final scene to find out what happens to Antigone.

ANTIGONE 1051

Reading and Analyzing

Reading Skills and Strategies: PREDICTING

(A) Have students read the side note for lines 1–7. Then invite students to predict what Teiresias will say to Creon.
Possible Response: The prophet will warn Creon about the consequences of his actions.

Literary Analysis CLASSICAL DRAMA

(B) Ancient Greeks believed that prophets were the instruments of the gods and could see the future or make sound judgments. Ask students how Teiresias' long speech affects the audience's view of the play's action and characters. How are the gods involved in the plot?
Possible Response: This speech lets the audience know that the gods are displeased with Creon's actions. Until Teiresias spoke, it was unclear whether Antigone or Creon was right. The speech casts Creon in a negative light and elevates Antigone to the position of heroine. The gods are no longer distant abstractions, but prime movers in the plot and in the lives of the characters.

GUIDE FOR READING

(C) **Possible Response:** These lines suggest that the gods are very displeased with Creon's refusal to allow Polyneices to be buried.

(D) **Possible Response:** These lines suggest that Creon has placed himself above the gods. This is the classic tragic flaw of *hubris,* or overweening pride.

Two views of Sophocles, who was regarded by his Greek admirers as "the perfect man." *Left,* Museo Gregoriano Profano, Vatican Museums, Vatican State, Alinari / Art Resource, New York. *Right,* Museo Lateranense, Vatican Museums, Vatican City, Alinari / Art Resource, New York.

SCENE 5

(*Enter blind* Teiresias, *led by a boy. The opening speeches of* Teiresias *should be in singsong contrast to the realistic lines of* Creon.)

Teiresias. This is the way the blind man comes, princes, princes,
Lock step, two heads lit by the eyes of one.

Creon. What new thing have you to tell us, old Teiresias?

Teiresias. I have much to tell you: listen to the prophet, Creon.

Creon. I am not aware that I have ever failed to listen.

Teiresias. Then you have done wisely, King, and ruled well.

Creon. I admit my debt to you. But what have you to say?

1–7 The blind Teiresias is physically blind but spiritually sighted. As a prophet, he is an agent of the gods in their dealings with humans. His revelation of the truth to Oedipus led Oedipus to leave Thebes, which indirectly helped Creon to become king. (A)

Teaching Options

Multicultural Link: Augury

Augury is the prediction of the future based on the observation of natural phenomena. These phenomena vary greatly. Observing the behavior of birds and other animals is one method. Other methods include "reading" the entrails or other parts of a sacrificed animal or divining the signs of atmospheric conditions, fire, or smoke. Still other sources of augury include cards and dice.

For millennia, the *I Ching* has been an important source of guidance for Chinese people about to make an important decision. This book interprets the figure created by the tossing of yarrow stalks.

The practice of augury is mentioned in the Bible as well as in ancient Greco-Roman sources. Augury was particularly important in ancient Rome. Cicero wrote a treatise on Roman augury in about 44 B.C. called *De divinatione (Concerning Divination).*

Official augurs determined whether a proposed course of action was approved by the gods. Augurs watched the sky for signs such as thunder, lightning, and the flight of birds. They also listened for the cries of particular birds and watched the pecking behavior of sacred chickens.

Teiresias. This, Creon: you stand once more on the edge of fate.

Creon. What do you mean? Your words are a kind of dread.

Teiresias. Listen, Creon:
I was sitting in my chair of augury, at the place
1 Where the birds gather about me. They were all a-chatter,
As is their habit, when suddenly I heard
A strange note in their jangling, a scream, a
Whirring fury; I knew that they were fighting,
B Tearing each other, dying
In a whirlwind of wings clashing. And I was afraid.
I began the rites of burnt offering at the altar,
But Hephaestus failed me: instead of bright flame,
There was only the sputtering slime of the fat thigh-flesh
Melting: the entrails dissolved in grey smoke;
2 The bare bone burst from the welter. And no blaze!

This was a sign from heaven. My boy described it,
Seeing for me as I see for others.

I tell you, Creon, you yourself have brought
3 This new calamity upon us. Our hearths and altars
Are stained with the corruption of dogs and carrion birds
That glut themselves on the corpse of Oedipus' son.
The gods are deaf when we pray to them; their fire
Recoils from our offering; their birds of omen
Have no cry of comfort, for they are gorged
With the thick blood of the dead.
O my son,
These are no trifles! Think: all men make mistakes,
But a good man yields when he knows his course is wrong,
And repairs the evil. The only crime is pride.

4 Give in to the dead man, then: do not fight with a corpse—
What glory is it to kill a man who is dead?
Think, I beg you:
It is for your own good that I speak as I do.
You should be able to yield for your own good.

Creon. It seems that prophets have made me their especial province.
All my life long
I have been a kind of butt for the dull arrows
Of doddering fortunetellers!
No, Teiresias:
5 If your birds—if the great eagles of God himself—
Should carry him stinking bit by bit to heaven,
I would not yield. I am not afraid of pollution:

11–17 The chair of augury is the place where Teiresias sits to hear the birds, whose sounds reveal the future to him. The fighting among the birds suggests that the anarchy infecting Thebes has spread even to the world of nature.

19 Hephaestus (hĭ-fĕs'təs): god of fire.

18–32 According to Teiresias, the birds and dogs that have eaten the corpse of Polyneices have become corrupt, causing the gods to reject the Thebans' offerings and prayers. What do these lines suggest about how the gods view Creon's refusal to allow Polyneices to be buried? C

44–48 What do these lines suggest about Creon's view of himself and the gods? D

Customizing Instruction

Students Acquiring English

1 Explain that *all a-chatter* means "all chattering." Although this construction is uncommon in formal English, students may encounter it in dialect and in fiction.

2 Help students understand that *welter* means "turmoil, jumble."

3 Guide students to infer from context clues the meaning of *calamity.*
Answer: catastrophe, disaster

Less Proficient Readers

4 Read lines 36 and 37 aloud to the class. Ask students what they think Teiresias means. In what ways is Creon killing a man who is already dead?
Possible Response: Help students understand that Teiresias believes that the gods want Creon to allow Polyneices a decent burial. Creon should honor the corpse, not fight against it.

Gifted and Talented

5 Explain that the eagle was the special symbol of Zeus, the king of the gods. Eagles are birds of prey, hunting and killing for food, not carrion birds that feed on dead animals. Have students give their own interpretations of these lines.
Possible Response: In these lines, Creon converts Zeus's sacred eagles into carrion birds. This sacrilegious comparison shows that Creon scorns the gods; it also reveals his arrogance.

ANTIGONE 1053

Reading and Analyzing

Literary Analysis: IRONY

(A) Have students explain the irony in Teiresias' comment to Creon about the cost of Teiresias' words.

Possible Response: Teiresias' words do not cost money, but the truth will be costly for Creon because it will cause him great anguish.

GUIDE FOR READING

(B) **Possible Response:** Creon assumes that Teiresias is motivated by a desire for personal profit.

(C) **Possible Response:** Creon will end up being punished by the Furies.

Literary Analysis: CHARACTERIZATION

(D) Explore with students how Creon displays great self-knowledge here. Then ask the class what Creon's self-knowledge adds to our perception of his character.

Possible Response: Creon's self-knowledge and awareness of his pride helps us to sympathize with him, perhaps for the first time in the play.

Reading Skills and Strategies: PREDICTING

(E) Have students predict whether Creon will arrive in time to rescue Antigone.

Possible Response: Many students will probably be pessimistic about Creon's chances of arriving in time to save Antigone, because they have been given clues to the approaching catastrophe.

No man can defile the gods.
Do what you will;
Go into business, make money, speculate
In India gold or that synthetic gold from Sardis,
Get rich otherwise than by my consent to bury him.
Teiresias, it is a sorry thing when a wise man
Sells his wisdom, lets out his words for hire!

Teiresias. Ah Creon! Is there no man left in the world—

Creon. To do what? Come, let's have the aphorism!

Teiresias. No man who knows that wisdom outweighs any wealth?

Creon. As surely as bribes are baser than any baseness.

Teiresias. You are sick, Creon! You are deathly sick!

Creon. As you say: it is not my place to challenge a prophet.

Teiresias. Yet you have said my prophecy is for sale.

Creon. The generation of prophets has always loved gold.

1 **Teiresias.** The generation of kings has always loved brass.

Creon. You forget yourself! You are speaking to your king.

Teiresias. I know it. You are a king because of me.

Creon. You have a certain skill; but you have sold out.

Teiresias. King, you will drive me to words that—

Creon. Say them, say them!
Only remember: I will not pay you for them.

Teiresias. No, you will find them too costly.

Creon. No doubt. Speak:
Whatever you say, you will not change my will.

(A)

Teiresias. Then take this, and take it to heart!
The time is not far off when you shall pay back
Corpse for corpse, flesh of your own flesh.
You have thrust the child of this world into living night;
You have kept from the gods below the child that is theirs:
The one in a grave before her death, the other,
Dead, denied the grave. This is your crime:
And the Furies and the dark gods of hell
Are swift with terrible punishment for you.
Do you want to buy me now, Creon?
Not many days,
And your house will be full of men and women weeping,
And curses will be hurled at you from far

49–53 What does Creon assume is the motive behind Teiresias' prophecies? (B)

50 Sardis (sär′dĭs): the capital of ancient Lydia, where metal coins were first produced.

77–78 Furies: three goddesses who avenge crimes, especially those that violate family ties. How might this prophecy be fulfilled? (C)

WORDS TO KNOW **defile** (dĭ-fīl′) *v.* to make foul, dirty, unclean, or impure

1054

Teaching Options

Mini Lesson Vocabulary Strategy

WORD ORIGINS

Instruction The word *protagonist* derives from the Greek root *agōn*, which means "contest." The protagonist in a play is participating in a contest with the antagonist. Other words that share the same root are *antagonist, agony,* and *agonize.* Explain that the Greek language has had a tremendous influence on English. Discuss with students how words of Greek origin could have come into English. Remind students that the first scientists, scholars, and playwrights in the West were Greek. Early versions of parts of the Bible appeared in Greek. Many of the Greek terms for areas of study are in use today. For example, the word *drama* has its roots in Greek, as does almost every word ending in *–logy* and *-metry*. These Greek suffixes mean, respectively, "word" or "study," and "measure."

2 Cities grieving for sons unburied, left to rot before the walls of Thebes.

These are my arrows, Creon: they are all for you.

A (*to boy*) But come, child: lead me home.
Let him waste his fine anger upon younger men.
Maybe he will learn at last
To control a wiser tongue in a better head.

(*Exit* Teiresias.)

Choragus. The old man has gone, King, but his words
Remain to plague us. I am old, too,
But I cannot remember that he was ever false.

D **Creon.** That is true. . . . It troubles me.
Oh it is hard to give in! but it is worse
To risk everything for stubborn pride.

Choragus. Creon: take my advice.

Creon. What shall I do?

Choragus. Go quickly: free Antigone from her vault
And build a tomb for the body of Polyneices.

Creon. You would have me do this?

Choragus. Creon, yes!
And it must be done at once: God moves
Swiftly to cancel the folly of stubborn men.

Creon. It is hard to deny the heart! But I
Will do it: I will not fight with destiny.

Choragus. You must go yourself; you cannot leave it to others.

Creon. I will go.
—Bring axes, servants:
Come with me to the tomb. I buried her; I
Will set her free.
Oh quickly!
My mind misgives—
The laws of the gods are mighty, and a man must serve them
E To the last day of his life!

(*Exit* Creon.)

Customizing Instruction

Less Proficient Readers

1 Ask students what they think Teiresias means in this line.
Possible Response: He means that kings have always loved things that look like gold but are actually less expensive.

2 Tell students to visualize Teiresias' description of the future. Then ask them what he is predicting.
Possible Response: His description of young men left to rot before the walls of Thebes means that Thebes will come under attack from cities far away. The soldiers will die where they fall and remain unburied.

Application Have students research the origins of the following words and use each word in an original sentence. Then have them find other words that share the same root and apply the meaning of the root to help them understand the word.

1. anthropology
   Root: *anthrōpos,* human being; **Possible Responses:** philanthropist, misanthrope
2. astronomy
   Root: *astēr,* star; **Possible Responses:** astrology, asteroid, asterisk
3. astigmatism
   Root: *stigma,* spot or mark; **Possible Responses:** stigma, stigmata, stigmatize
4. athlete
   Root: *athlos,* prize or contest; **Possible Responses:** triathlon, decathlon, athletic
5. police
   Root: *polis,* city; **Possible Responses:** policy, politics, metropolis, Naples, Constantinople

Use **Vocabulary Transparencies and Copymasters,** pp. 91–92.

A lesson on word origins appear on p. 356 in the Pupil's Edition.

Reading and Analyzing

Literary Analysis CLASSICAL DRAMA

A Understanding the allusions to myths and legends can help students deepen their appreciation of the play's story. Have students analyze the allusions in this paean to explain how they impact the main idea.

Possible Response: The allusions show the power of Dionysus and his special relationship to Thebes. The chorus is desperately calling for divine intervention, realizing that humans cannot resolve this dilemma.

Literary Analysis: THEME

B Be sure students understand that a theme is a perception about life or human nature shared with the reader. Then invite students to analyze these lines to find one of the play's themes.

Possible Responses: A person's future is determined by fate, not by his or her own efforts; people cannot predict or control the future because it is in the hands of a higher authority.

Active Reading

STRATEGIES FOR READING CLASSICAL DRAMA

C Encourage students to reread and visualize the descriptive passages. Invite students to read the paean aloud to emphasize the rhythm of the hymn.

GUIDE FOR READING

D **Possible Response:** This messenger is deadly serious, in contrast to the almost playful tone of the previous messenger.

PAEAN

Choragus. God of many names
Chorus. O Iacchus
son
of Cadmean Semele
O born of the thunder!
guardian of the West
regent
of Eleusis' plain
O prince of maenad Thebes
and the Dragon Field by rippling Ismenus:

Choragus. God of many names
Chorus. the flame of torches
flares on our hills
the nymphs of Iacchus
dance at the spring of Castalia:
from the vine-close mountain
come ah come in ivy:
Evohé evohé! sings through the streets of Thebes

Choragus. God of many names
Chorus. Iacchus of Thebes
heavenly child
of Semele bride of the Thunderer!
The shadow of plague is upon us:
come
with clement feet
oh come from Parnassus
down the long slopes
across the lamenting water

Choragus. Io Fire! Chorister of the throbbing stars!
O purest among the voices of the night!
Thou son of God, blaze for us!
Chorus. Come with choric rapture of circling Maenads
Who cry *Io Iacche!*
God of many names!

PAEAN: A paean (pē′ən) is a hymn appealing to the gods for assistance. In this paean, the chorus praises Dionysus, or Iacchus (yä′kəs), and calls on him to come to Thebes to show mercy and drive out evil.

2 Cadmus was the legendary founder of Thebes. Dionysus was the son of Cadmus' daughter Semele (sə-mē′lē) and Zeus, who is referred to here as thunder.

4–5 These lines name locations near Athens and Thebes. The maenads (mē′nădz′) were priestesses of Dionysus.

8–9 The spring of Castalia is on the sacred mountain Parnassus. Grape vines and ivy were symbols of Dionysus.

10 evohé: hallelujah.

Teaching Options

Cross Curricular Link Fine Arts

THEATER Modern drama has its roots in classical drama. The basic structure of the theater is the same, and many of the terms that describe plays (including the words *tragedy* and *comedy*) come from Greek. Then, as now, the theater had patrons who helped defray the costs of production. Each play had its own patron, or *choregus,* who paid the chorus and provided costumes and props. However, there are significant differences between an ancient Greek production and a modern one. The festivals at which the plays were presented were sponsored by the state. The state also paid the actors and selected which plays would be presented. Many of the speeches were sung, not spoken, but the music has not survived. Most importantly, thousands of people watched a Greek tragedy, and a significant portion of the population participated in the festivities surrounding the production, as well as in the drama itself. Since the days of ancient Greece, only in Shakespeare's era have plays been intended for and watched by such a broad audience.

EXODOS

(*Enter* Messenger.)

Messenger. Men of the line of Cadmus, you who live
Near Amphion's citadel:
I cannot say
Of any condition of human life, "This is fixed,
This is clearly good, or bad." Fate raises up,
And Fate casts down the happy and unhappy alike:
No man can foretell his fate.
Take the case of Creon:
Creon was happy once, as I count happiness:
Victorious in battle, sole governor of the land,
Fortunate father of children nobly born.
And now it has all gone from him! Who can say
That a man is still alive when his life's joy fails?
He is a walking dead man. Grant him rich;
Let him live like a king in his great house:
If his pleasure is gone, I would not give
So much as the shadow of smoke for all he owns.

Choragus. Your words hint at sorrow: what is your news for us?

Messenger. They are dead. The living are guilty of their death.

Choragus. Who is guilty? Who is dead? Speak!

Messenger. Haemon.
1 Haemon is dead; and the hand that killed him
Is his own hand.

Choragus. His father's? or his own?

Messenger. His own, driven mad by the murder his father had done.

Choragus. Teiresias, Teiresias, how clearly you saw it all!

Messenger. This is my news: you must draw what conclusions you can from it.

Choragus. But look: Eurydice, our queen:
Has she overheard us?

(*Enter* Eurydice *from the palace, center.*)

Eurydice. I have heard something, friends:
As I was unlocking the gate of Pallas' shrine,
For I needed her help today, I heard a voice
Telling of some new sorrow. And I fainted
There at the temple with all my maidens about me.
But speak again: whatever it is, I can bear it:
Grief and I are no strangers.

EXODOS: The exodos is the last episode in the play. It is followed by a final speech made by the choragus and addressed directly to the audience.

2 Amphion: Niobe's husband, who built a wall around Thebes by charming the stones into place with music.

15 How does the messenger compare with the sentry who appeared in Scenes 1 and 2? D

27 Pallas: Athena, the goddess of wisdom.

32 Megareus (mə-găr'ē-əs), the older son of Eurydice and Creon, had died in the battle for Thebes.

Customizing Instruction

Multiple Learning Styles

Auditory and Kinesthetic Learners

Choose one student to play the part of the choragus; the rest of the class can be divided into two sections. Explain to students that the Greek chorus often broke into two groups while dancing and singing. Then help students prepare a choral reading of the paean. The first section of students can read the first and third choral parts of the paean; the second section of students can read the second and fourth parts. Have students chant their lines and accompany them with simple movements.

Students Acquiring English

Model the pronunciation of the Greek names in the paean. Make sure students read the side notes carefully and look up any words they do not know. Students might make a chart of the Greek names and places mentioned here with brief defining notes.

Less Proficient Readers

1 Make sure students understand that Haemon killed himself, driven mad by his father's cruelty. Then ask them who else might have died along with Haemon.

Possible Response: Antigone

Reading and Analyzing

Reading Skills and Strategies: CLARIFYING

A Ask students why they think Creon decided to give the remains of Polyneices' body a proper burial.

Possible Responses: Creon realized that he had been wrong in refusing Antigone's request, and he wanted to make amends for his error; Creon was afraid of displeasing the gods.

Literary Analysis: CHARACTERIZATION

B Have students explain why they think Antigone killed herself. Explore with the class what this action reveals about Antigone's character.

Possible Responses: Antigone perhaps believed that she would not be rescued and wanted to die an honorable death by her own hand; she had lost all hope and succumbed to despair.

Reading Skills and Strategies: MAKING JUDGMENTS

C Ask students if they think Haemon's act of spitting in his father's face is justified.

Possible Responses: Haemon's action is justified because Creon is responsible for the chain of events that led to this tragedy; Haemon's anger is misplaced because Antigone's death was a result of fate, not of human action.

Reading Skills and Strategies: PREDICTING

D Have students predict what they think Eurydice's silent departure means.

Possible Responses: Eurydice's silence is a bad omen, suggesting that she will kill herself.

Messenger. Dearest lady,
I will tell you plainly all that I have seen.
I shall not try to comfort you: what is the use,
Since comfort could lie only in what is not true?
The truth is always best.
I went with Creon
To the outer plain where Polyneices was lying,
No friend to pity him, his body shredded by dogs.
We made our prayers in that place to Hecate
And Pluto, that they would be merciful. And we bathed
The corpse with holy water, and we brought
Fresh-broken branches to burn what was left of it,
And upon the urn we heaped up a towering barrow
Of the earth of his own land.
When we were done, we ran
To the vault where Antigone lay on her couch of stone.
One of the servants had gone ahead,
And while he was yet far off he heard a voice
Grieving within the chamber, and he came back
And told Creon. And as the king went closer,
The air was full of wailing, the words lost,
And he begged us to make all haste. "Am I a prophet?"
He said, weeping. "And must I walk this road,
The saddest of all that I have gone before?
My son's voice calls me on. Oh quickly, quickly!
Look through the crevice there, and tell me
If it is Haemon, or some deception of the gods!"

We obeyed; and in the cavern's farthest corner
We saw her lying:
She had made a noose of her fine linen veil
And hanged herself. Haemon lay beside her,
His arms about her waist, lamenting her,
His love lost underground, crying out
That his father had stolen her away from him.
When Creon saw him, the tears rushed to his eyes,
And he called to him: "What have you done, child? Speak to me.
What are you thinking that makes your eyes so strange?
O my son, my son, I come to you on my knees!"
But Haemon spat in his face. He said not a word,
Staring—
and suddenly drew his sword
And lunged. Creon shrank back; the blade missed, and the boy,
Desperate against himself, drove it half its length

39–40 Hecate (hĕk'ə-tē) **and Pluto:** other names for Persephone and Hades, the goddess and god of the underworld.

43–44 Note the contrast between the barrow, or burial mound, erected by Creon and the handful of dirt used by Antigone to cover her brother.

60 Note that this is the same way in which Jocasta, Antigone's mother, killed herself.

Teaching Options

Cross Curricular Link History

THE CITY DIONYSIA The City Dionysia, which was held between December and April in ancient Athens, is the name of the most prominent of the four religious festivals honoring Dionysus. It is the festival at which the theatrical competitions occurred and was designated the "City" Dionysia to differentiate it from the festivals held in rural areas. Although the City Dionysia was primarily a religious celebration, the festival also included events that went well beyond religious worship and emphasized the pride Athenians took in their government and civic institutions. Taking place over several days, the City Dionysia opened with a lavish parade of religious and civic leaders and dramatic performers. Religious sacrifices and offerings then took place within the theater itself at an altar to Dionysus that was situated on the stage. After the religious observances, Athens received its annual tribute of goods, money, and slaves from territories under its control, and treaties were often negotiated and cemented. Before the main dramatic contest began, two days of the festival were devoted to the songs and dances of choral groups comprised of 100 men and boys drawn from each of the ten major Athenian social groups, called "tribes." The Greek theater was a public spectacle and provided the citizens an opportunity to show their religious devotion, artistic talent, and civic development.

Into his own side and fell. And as he died,
He gathered Antigone close in his arms again,
Choking, his blood bright red on her white cheek.
And now he lies dead with the dead, and she is his
At last, his bride in the houses of the dead.

(*Exit* Eurydice *into the palace.*)

D **Choragus.** She has left us without a word. What can this mean?

Messenger. It troubles me, too; yet she knows what is best;
Her grief is too great for public lamentation,
And doubtless she has gone to her chamber to weep
For her dead son, leading her maidens in his dirge.

Choragus. It may be so: but I fear this deep silence.

(*Pause*)

Messenger. I will see what she is doing. I will go in.

(*Exit* Messenger *into the palace. Enter* Creon *with attendants, bearing* Haemon*'s body.*)

1 **Choragus.** But here is the king himself: oh look at him,
Bearing his own damnation in his arms.

Creon. Nothing you say can touch me any more.
My own blind heart has brought me
From darkness to final darkness. Here you see
The father murdering, the murdered son—
And all my civic wisdom!
Haemon my son, so young, so young to die,
I was the fool, not you; and you died for me.

Choragus. That is the truth; but you were late in learning it.

Creon. This truth is hard to bear. Surely a god
Has crushed me beneath the hugest weight of heaven,
And driven me headlong a barbaric way
To trample out the thing I held most dear.

The pains that men will take to come to pain!

(*Enter* Messenger *from the palace.*)

Messenger. The burden you carry in your hands is heavy,
But it is not all: you will find more in your house.

Creon. What burden worse than this shall I find there?

Messenger. The queen is dead.

Creon. O port of death, deaf world,
Is there no pity for me? And you, angel of evil,
I was dead, and your words are death again.

Customizing Instruction

Less Proficient Readers

1 Ask students what Creon is carrying, based on the choragus's comment that he is "bearing his own damnation in his arms."

Answer: Haemon's body

Then ask students how Haemon's death could be Creon's condemnation. Refer them to lines 76–78 on page 1054.

Possible Response: The Furies will punish those who violate family ties. The choragus suggests that because Creon caused Haemon's death by condemning Antigone, the Furies will punish him.

Less Proficient Readers

- What happens in this scene?
  Answer: Antigone hangs herself; Haemon and his mother stab themselves to death.
- At the beginning of the scene, why does Teiresias come to see Creon?
  Answer: The prophet comes to warn Creon that his own actions will bring tragedy to his land.
- How does Creon treat Teiresias?
  Possible Response: with contempt, accusing the prophet of selling out

Gifted and Talented

Students may want to write a final scene for the play that resolves specific issues such as what becomes of Ismene, the only surviving child of Oedipus and Jocasta and what happens to Creon and the city of Thebes.

ANTIGONE 1059

Reading and Analyzing

Literary Analysis: PLOT

A plot's climax is the turning point of the action, the moment when interest and intensity reach their peak. Have students identify the climax of this play.
Possible Response: The climax occurs here, when Creon realizes that he has lost everything that matters to him.

Reading Skills and Strategies: ANALYZING

Ask students why they think Sophocles ends the play with Creon's comments.
Possible Response: Creon's self-knowledge reinforces the tragedy and the senseless waste of human potential and life.

Literary Analysis CLASSICAL DRAMA

After students have read the conclusion of *Antigone,* lead them in a discussion about the differences between classical drama and more modern plays they have read or seen. Use the following questions as discussion prompts:

- How does this play compare to *Julius Caesar*?
- Did you find the chorus effective or distracting? Why?
- How does the language in *Antigone* compare to the dialogue in other plays?
- Was it difficult to visualize the action of this play? Why or why not?
- Did you find the characters realistic and sympathetic? How do they compare to the main characters in other plays?

Is it true, boy? Can it be true?
Is my wife dead? Has death bred death?

Messenger. You can see for yourself.

(*The doors are opened, and the body of* Eurydice *is disclosed within.*)

Creon. Oh pity!
All true, all true, and more than I can bear!
O my wife, my son!

Messenger. She stood before the altar, and her heart
Welcomed the knife her own hand guided,
And a great cry burst from her lips for Megareus dead,
And for Haemon dead, her sons; and her last breath
Was a curse for their father, the murderer of her sons.
And she fell, and the dark flowed in through her closing eyes.

Creon. O God, I am sick with fear.
Are there no swords here? Has no one a blow for me?

Messenger. Her curse is upon you for the deaths of both.

Creon. It is right that it should be. I alone am guilty.
I know it, and I say it. Lead me in,
Quickly, friends.
I have neither life nor substance. Lead me in.

Choragus. You are right, if there can be right in so much wrong.
The briefest way is best in a world of sorrow.

Creon. Let it come;
Let death come quickly and be kind to me.
I would not ever see the sun again.

Choragus. All that will come when it will; but we, meanwhile,
Have much to do. Leave the future to itself.

Creon. All my heart was in that prayer!

Choragus. Then do not pray any more: the sky is deaf.

Creon. Lead me away. I have been rash and foolish.
I have killed my son and my wife.
I look for comfort; my comfort lies here dead.
Whatever my hands have touched has come to nothing.
Fate has brought all my pride to a thought of dust.

(*As* Creon *is being led into the house, the* Choragus *advances and speaks directly to the audience.*)

Choragus. There is no happiness where there is no wisdom;
No wisdom but in submission to the gods.
Big words are always punished,
And proud men in old age learn to be wise.

Teaching Options

Informal Assessment

To help students assess their understanding of *Antigone,* have them respond to the following questions in writing or in brief oral reports:

1. Which character do you admire the most in the play? Why?
2. If you were Antigone, what would you have done in her situation? Why?
3. This play was written centuries ago. What do you think it can teach people about life today? Explain your answer.

RUBRIC

3 Full Accomplishment Responses indicate a full understanding of the play. Responses are logical and well supported by evidence from the text and from students' own experiences.

2 Substantial Accomplishment Responses indicate a substantial understanding of the play. Responses are reasonable and supported by some evidence from the text and/or from students' own experiences.

1 Little or Partial Accomplishment Responses indicate little or no understanding of the play. Responses are not reasonable and/or are unsupported by evidence.

Connect to the Literature

1. **What Do You Think?** How did you react to what happens at the end of this play? Share your thoughts with a classmate.

Comprehension Check
- What does Antigone do against Creon's wishes?
- How does Creon punish Antigone?
- How does Antigone die?

Think Critically

2. How much do you think Creon is to blame for the suicides of Antigone, Haemon, and Eurydice?

THINK ABOUT
- Creon's judgment of himself at the end
- how Haemon and Eurydice feel about Creon at the moment of death
- Creon's failed effort to rescue Antigone

3. What do you think is the main reason that Creon and Antigone cannot resolve their **conflict**?

THINK ABOUT
- the principles that motivate each character
- the attitude of each character toward the gods
- any flaws or defects exhibited by each character

4. How do the **minor characters**—such as Ismene, Teiresias, Haemon, and Eurydice—help you to understand and evaluate the actions of Antigone and Creon?

5. ACTIVE READING | STRATEGIES FOR READING CLASSICAL DRAMA Compare the notes in your READER'S NOTEBOOK with those of a classmate. Discuss which of the strategies listed on page 1019 were most useful. How did you modify your reading strategies when your understanding broke down?

Extend Interpretations

6. **The Writer's Style** Throughout *Antigone*, Sophocles makes **allusions** to myths that his original audience would have been familiar with. With a partner, research the full story of one of these myths. Then write an explanation of how the myth relates to the story of Antigone and why you think Sophocles included the allusion.

7. **Connect to Life** Which of the **themes,** or messages, conveyed by Sophocles do you think is most relevant today?

Literary Analysis

CLASSICAL DRAMA Two aspects of **classical drama,** or the theater of ancient Greece, that are frequently still debated today are the role of the **chorus** and the concept of the **tragic hero.** Often, critics and scholars disagree with one another about how to interpret the comments of the chorus. Disagreement also arises about how to apply the concept of the tragic hero.

Paired Activity Review the information about classical drama on page 1019. Then discuss the following questions:
- Who do you think best fits the definition of a tragic hero, Antigone or Creon?
- How do the chorus and its leader, the **choragus,** influence your understanding of Antigone and Creon?
- How do the choral **odes** contribute to your understanding of the play's **themes?**

Use evidence from the text to support your answer.

REVIEW DRAMATIC IRONY **Dramatic irony** occurs when readers or viewers are aware of information that a character is unaware of. For example, Creon tells Antigone, "That [her death] gives me everything." Once you know the outcome of the play, you realize that Antigone's death will take from Creon all that is meaningful in his life. This contrast between Creon's limited knowledge and your fuller understanding generates dramatic irony.

With a small group of classmates, find and explain other examples of dramatic irony in *Antigone*.

GUIDING STUDENT RESPONSE

Connect to the Literature

1. What Do You Think?

Although students may not be surprised by the death of Antigone, they may be unprepared for the deaths of Haemon and Eurydice. Some students may be troubled that Creon, whose behavior seems to cause much of the destruction, survives at the end of the play.

Comprehension Check
- She buries the body of her brother Polyneices.
- He sentences her to death and shuts her inside a vault.
- She hangs herself with her veil.

Use Selection Quiz
Unit Six Resource Book, p. 33.

Think Critically

2. Possible Responses: Creon is completely to blame because he passed the decree that placed civil law above moral law; Creon is only partially to blame because the fate of people is determined by the gods.
3. Possible Responses: Each is motivated by different principles; each suffers from the tragic flaw of excessive pride.
4. Possible Responses: Each of these characters reinforces an important trait in one of the main characters; they all comment on the action.
5. Encourage students to point out specific passages that the use of their reading strategies helped to clarify. They might also elaborate on any strategies that were useful in one context but not in another.

Extend Interpretations

The Writer's Style Guide students to use a standard book of myths, such as *The Age of Fable* by Bullfinch. Allusions in *Antigone* include the myths of Niobe, Danäe, King Lycurgus, and King Phineus. Students may want to include illustrations to draw further parallels between *Antigone* and the original myths.

Connect to Life Possible themes include
- the inevitability of fate
- the supremacy of divine law over civil law
- the dangers of pride and stubbornness

To make this question easier, provide students with one of the themes and then ask them to explain why it is still relevant today.

Literary Analysis

Classical Drama Students can share their responses in a full class discussion, as part of a culminating activity.

Review Dramatic Irony After students have suggested examples of dramatic irony, have them discuss why Sophocles used this technique.

Writing Options

1. **Letter to a Character** Have students prewrite by clustering, freewriting, or outlining.
2. **Diary Entry** A diary entry is written in the first person. Before students choose a minor character, have them list the character traits of each one. Guide students to capture the voice and feelings of their character.
3. **Report on Athenian Women** Sources on ancient Greece abound, but students may discover that historians have recently begun to have different ideas about the roles and lives of Athenian women. Encourage students to present both interpretations in their reports.

Activities & Explorations

1. **Readers Theater** Explain that in a Readers Theater, actors do not use props, scenery, or costumes. Point out that some scenes are more appropriate for a formal presentation and some are more appropriate for a contemporary style.
2. **Tragedy Mask** Encourage students to use different media for their masks, such as papier-mâché, clay, plaster, or wood.
3. **Antigone on Film** Students might consider how the style of this production compares to the descriptions of ancient Greek theater given at the beginning of this selection. Encourage interested students to view the entire film.

Inquiry & Research

Comparing Translations Students will probably need to go to a public library to find a good selection of translations. Make sure students check out a translation of Sophocles' play and not a translation or an adaptation of Jean Anouilh's *Antigone.*

Choices & CHALLENGES

Writing Options

1. **Letter to a Character** Compare the way you ranked the principles listed in the Connect to Your Life activity on page 1018 with the way you think Antigone, Creon, or some other character in the play would rank them. Then write a letter to that character, either in support of or in opposition to his or her decisions and behavior.

2. **Diary Entry** Think about how one of the minor characters—such as Ismene, the sentry, or Teiresias—might have viewed what happened to Antigone. Write a diary entry expressing the thoughts and feelings of this character.

3. **Report on Athenian Women** At various times in *Antigone,* Creon's remarks show his attitude toward having his authority challenged by a woman. With a partner, research the typical role of noblewomen in Athens during the fifth century B.C. Working collaboratively, write a short report on this topic. Place the report in your **Working Portfolio.**

Activities & Explorations

1. **Readers Theater** With a group of classmates, perform a Readers Theater production of a scene from this play. Sit in chairs at the front of the classroom and take turns reading the parts. Choose whether you want to present the scene in the formal manner of the ancient Greek theater or in a more contemporary style. ~ **PERFORMING**

2. **Tragedy Mask** Create a mask to be worn in a production of *Antigone.* You may research the masks worn in ancient Greek productions or create your own original version. ~ **ART**

3. **Antigone on Film** Watch the video clip of the opening scene of the play. How does the setting compare with the way you visualized the palace as you read? Do Antigone and Ismene play their roles as you imagined? Discuss your views with a small group of classmates. ~ **VIEWING AND REPRESENTING**

VIDEO **Side by Side: Literature in Performance**

Inquiry & Research

Comparing Translations Locate one or two other translations of *Antigone.* Choose a passage from the play, and compare the different versions. With a small group of classmates, discuss which translation you find most effective and why.

Vocabulary in Action

EXERCISE: MEANING CLUES Answer the questions that follow.

1. Is a **dirge** a piece of music that is sad, joyful, or complicated?
2. Are people who **transgress** a law those who make it, break it, or enforce it?
3. Would a person's appetite be **sated** by the smell of food, a light snack, or a large meal?
4. Is an **edict** a request, a command, or a question?
5. Would **lamentation** be most expected after a tragedy, a dinner party, or a graduation?
6. Does a person **defile** a lake by photographing it, polluting it, or stocking it with fish?
7. When is it most important to be **lithe**—while competing in a spelling bee, lifting weights, or performing gymnastics?
8. If people demonstrate **compulsive** behavior, is what they do rude, sympathetic, or beyond their control?
9. Is a person most likely to respond to **auspicious** events by feeling encouraged, frightened, or exhausted?
10. If a child was described to you as being **perverse,** would you expect the child to be angelic, disobedient, or shy?

Building Vocabulary
For an in-depth lesson on connotation and denotation, see page 494.

Mini Lesson Grammar

INVERTED SENTENCES

Instruction For use with Grammar in Context, page 1063. Remind students that the natural word order in English sentences is *subject, verb, object:* Mary *(subject)* had *(verb)* a little lamb *(object)*. Explain that some sentences invert this word order. In these sentences, the subject appears after the verb. Inverted statements are rare in modern English and occur mostly in literature and in formal writing. You may want to tell students that many questions use inverted word order: Did *(verb)* Mary *(subject)* have *(verb)* a little lamb *(object)*? Point out that *did have* is the complete verb. Write the following sentence on the chalkboard:

"Swift <u>is</u> an arrow from Cupid's bow."

Underline the verb as shown. Have students identify the subject of the verb *is (an arrow).* Point out that the word *swift* is an adjective and that an adjective alone cannot be the subject of a sentence.

Grammar in Context: Inverted Sentences

Notice where the translator of *Antigone* places the subject and its verb in each of these excerpts.

> **Chorus.** Numberless are the world's wonders,
> but none
> More wonderful than man; . . .
>
> **Chorus.** Fortunate is the man who has never
> tasted God's vengeance!

One way in which expert writers vary their sentences to make their writing more interesting is by changing the order of subjects and verbs. In most sentences subjects come before verbs, but in the sentences above, the verbs (in blue type) are placed before the subjects (in red type). Sentences like these are called **inverted sentences.** They can give a formal tone to writing and can be used to create poetic effects.

WRITING EXERCISE Rewrite each sentence, placing the main verb before the subject.

Usage Tip: When writing an inverted sentence, make sure the subject agrees in number with the verb.

Example: ***Original*** Creon is merciless in dealing with his dead nephew Polyneices.

Rewritten Merciless is Creon in dealing with his dead nephew Polyneices.

1. Antigone pleads passionately with Ismene for help in burying their dead brother.
2. Creon, king of Thebes, is cruel.
3. The sentry who found Polyneices buried is frightened.
4. Antigone speaks eloquently when she is brought before Creon.

Grammar Handbook Subject-Verb Agreement, p. 1200

Sophocles

496?–406 B.C.

Other Works
Ajax
Oedipus the King
Electra
Oedipus at Colonus
Trachinian Women
Philoctetes

Chorus Leader Born near Athens in the village of Colonus, Sophocles was the son of a wealthy manufacturer of armor. In his youth, he received a fine education and was said to be skilled in wrestling, dancing, and playing the lyre. These skills and a handsome appearance apparently led to his being chosen to lead a chorus in a celebration of the Greek victory over the Persians at the Battle of Salamis.

Festival Winner In 468 B.C., Sophocles defeated his teacher, the great playwright Aeschylus (ĕs′kə-ləs), in the Dionysian dramatic festival, an annual competition. That first-place award was followed by as many as 23 other victories, more than any other Greek playwright. Sophocles also was active in the political life of Athens. He was elected several times to the body of high executives commanding the military and was one of ten commissioners in charge of helping Athens recover after a severe military defeat in Sicily. In 406 B.C., the year of his death, he led a chorus of public mourners in honor of Euripides (yo͞o-rĭp′ĭ-dēz′), a younger playwright who had often been his rival at the annual drama festivals.

Missing Work Sophocles wrote more than 100 plays, although only 7 of them survive today. *Antigone,* which rivals *Oedipus the King* as his best-known play, was probably first performed in 442 or 441 B.C. *Oedipus at Colonus,* which shows the playwright's affection for his native village, was written when Sophocles was around 90.

Author Activity

Classical Age Sophocles lived during a period often described as the pinnacle of ancient Athens. Research why this is the case, and find out what fate befell the city the year after Sophocles' death.

LaserLinks: Background for Reading
Cultural Connection

Vocabulary in Action

1. sad
2. break it
3. a large meal
4. a command
5. tragedy
6. polluting it
7. performing gymnastics
8. beyond their control
9. encouraged
10. disobedient

Grammar in Context

WRITING EXERCISE

1. Passionately pleads Antigone with Ismene for help in burying their dead brother.
2. Cruel is Creon, king of Thebes.
3. Frightened is the sentry who found Polyneices buried.
4. Eloquently speaks Antigone when she is brought before Creon.

Author Activity

Classical Age Fifth-century Athens was a center of learning, art, and architecture. The city was led by Pericles, who is considered one of the greatest statesmen who ever lived. The Parthenon, one of the great wonders of the ancient and modern world, was built, and Socrates was teaching philosophy. After Sophocles died, however, the Peloponnesian War between Athens and Sparta ended with the defeat of Athens in 404 B.C.

Exercises Have students copy the following sentences. Ask them to underline the verb once, the subject twice, and tell whether the sentence is inverted. Have students meet in cooperative groups to discuss their answers.

1. The sentry told his story hesitantly.
2. Joyously sang the maenads in the streets of Thebes.
   Answer: inverted
3. Outraged, Creon sentenced Antigone to death.
4. From the marble halls of the house came the cry of a grieving woman.
   Answer: inverted
5. Blessed are the ignorant.
   Answer: inverted

Use **Unit Six Resource Book,** p. 32.
Use **Grammar Transparencies and Copymasters,** p. 146.

Use McDougal Littell's ***Language Network,*** Chapter 2, for more instruction in inverted sentences.

OVERVIEW

Objectives

1. understand and appreciate a medieval **romance (Literary Analysis)**
2. **make judgments (Active Reading)**

Summary

In "The Crowning of Arthur," King Uther Pendragon, ruler of all Britain, falls in love with Igraine, the wife of the Duke of Tintagil. Merlin the Prophet promises to unite Uther and Igraine if the king agrees to give him the child of their union. Merlin enables the king to impersonate the duke and to fool Igraine, who conceives Arthur. When King Uther dies, Arthur is revealed as the true heir to the throne of Britain, because he alone is able to remove a sword from an anvil embedded in a stone, thus fulfilling a prophecy. In "Sir Launcelot du Lake," Launcelot, the finest of the knights of the Round Table, sets out in search of adventure with his nephew Sir Lyonel. While Launcelot is napping one day, Lyonel is taken prisoner by Sir Tarquine. Sir Ector, who is following Launcelot, is also taken prisoner by Tarquine. Four queens find the sleeping Launcelot and demand that he choose one of them or die. He chooses death, but a woman helps him escape in exchange for his promise to fight for her father, King Bagdemagus, in a tournament. Launcelot wins the tournament for Bagdemagus and then goes to Tarquine's castle, kills Tarquine, and frees the prisoners.

Thematic Link

Arthur and Launcelot embody **the heroic tradition**—they seek adventure and fulfill their destinies, all while subscribing to the chivalric code.

5-Minute Warm-Up

Daily Language SkillBuilder

Have students **proofread** the display sentences on page 959j and write them correctly. The sentences also appear on Transparency 28 of **Grammar Transparencies and Copymasters.**

"Your child is destined for glory."

PREPARING to *Read*

from Le Morte d'Arthur

The Crowning of Arthur
Sir Launcelot du Lake

Romance by SIR THOMAS MALORY
Retold by KEITH BAINES

Connect to Your Life

Round Table Discussion In a small-group discussion, share what you know about the legend of King Arthur and his knights of the Round Table. What types of actions do you associate with Arthurian knights? What do you know about their ideals and motives? What personal qualities do they exhibit?

Build Background

Legendary King According to legend, Arthur became king of England and established his court at Camelot. He then gathered the best knights of the realm to join with him in the fellowship of the Round Table. These knights lived according to a specific code of behavior—the chivalric code—which stressed, among other things, loyalty to the king, courage, personal honor, and defending those who could not defend themselves. The most famous model of chivalry was Sir Launcelot, Arthur's friend and the greatest knight of the Round Table.

The earliest tales of Arthur come from Welsh literature of the 6th through 12th centuries. Most English-speaking readers know of the Arthurian legend through Sir Thomas Malory's *Le Morte d'Arthur* ("The Death of Arthur"), completed about 1470, or one of its many adaptations. The excerpts you are about to read are from Keith Baines's modern retelling of *Le Morte d'Arthur.*

WORDS TO KNOW
Vocabulary Preview
adversary, champion, fidelity, prowess, recompense

Focus Your Reading

LITERARY ANALYSIS **ROMANCE** In the Middle Ages in Europe, wandering storytellers would retell adventurous tales of knights and other noble heroes. Such tales were known as **romances,** and, by Malory's time, they had moved from the oral tradition into written versions. Like other medieval romances, *Le Morte d'Arthur* recounts the heroic deeds of noble knights and celebrates the chivalric code of honor.

ACTIVE READING **MAKING JUDGMENTS** The chivalric code is of great importance in the world Malory describes. For example, the code states that knights must be courteous to their opponents. This principle leads Sir Tarquine to pay the following compliment to his opponent in a joust:

"That was a fine stroke; now let us try again."

However, some characters live up to the ideals of the code better than others.

READER'S NOTEBOOK As you read, **make judgments** about the **main characters** on the basis of how well you think they follow the chivalric code of honor. Record your thoughts about each character in a chart like the one shown. Mark with a check whether you think the character lives up to, or falls short of, each aspect of the code listed.

Chivalric Code	Character: Uther	
	Lives up to code	Falls short of code
Honorable		
Chaste		
Loyal		
Courageous		
Truthful		
Courteous		

LESSON RESOURCES

UNIT SIX RESOURCE BOOK, pp. 34–39

ASSESSMENT RESOURCES
Formal Assessment, pp. 169–170
Teacher's Guide to Assessment and Portfolio Use
Test Generator

SKILLS TRANSPARENCIES AND COPYMASTERS
Reading and Critical Thinking
- Making Judgments, T5 (for Think Critically, item 5, p. 1080)
- Summarizing, T10 (for Summarizing, p. 1080)
- Organizational Chart: Horizontal, T51 (for Reader's Notebook, p. 1064)

Grammar
- Subject-Verb Split, C140 (for Mini Lesson, p. 1082)

Vocabulary
- Context Clues, C93 (for Mini Lesson, p. 1065)
- Word Origins, C94 (for Mini Lesson, p. 1073)

Writing
- Writing Structure, T6, T8–10 (for Writing Options, p. 1081)
- Effective Language, T13 (for Writing Options, p. 1081)

Communications
- Evaluation Matrix: Commercial, T6 (for Activities & Explorations 3, p. 1081)
- Evaluation Matrix: Film/Video, T7 (for Activities & Explorations 1, p. 1081)

INTEGRATED TECHNOLOGY
Audio Library
LaserLinks
- Art Gallery: Art of the Arthurian Legends. See **Teacher's SourceBook,** p. 56.

Internet: Research Starter
Visit our website:
www.mcdougallittell.com

The Crowning of Arthur

from Le Morte d'Arthur
Sir Thomas Malory

King Uther Pendragon,[1] ruler of all Britain, had been at war for many years with the Duke of Tintagil in Cornwall when he was told of the beauty of Lady Igraine,[2] the duke's wife. Thereupon he called a truce and invited the duke and Igraine to his court, where he prepared a feast for them, and where, as soon as they arrived, he was formally reconciled to the duke through the good offices[3] of his courtiers.

In the course of the feast, King Uther grew passionately desirous of Igraine and, when it was over, begged her to become his paramour.[4] Igraine, however, being as naturally loyal as she was beautiful, refused him.

1. **Uther Pendragon** (ōō′thər pĕn-drăg′ən): *Pendragon* was a title used in ancient Britain to refer to a supreme chief or leader.
2. **Igraine** (ē-grān′).
3. **offices:** services.
4. **paramour** (păr′ə-mŏŏr′): lover or mistress.

TEACHING THE LITERATURE

Customizing Instruction

Less Proficient Readers
To help students become interested in the selection, have them draw a sketch of King Arthur or Sir Launcelot, suggesting the character's heroic qualities. Then have them read on to find out more about the qualities these heroes display.

Students Acquiring English
To help clarify the rank of the characters in these stories, list these various titles on the board and discuss what each terms means: *king* (the male ruler of a country), *queen* (the female ruler of a country or the wife of a king), *duke* (a nobleman of the highest rank), *duchess* (a noblewoman of the highest rank), *knight* (a member of a medieval warrior class), *archbishop* (a bishop of the highest rank). Point out to students that important men and women are addressed as *Sir* and *Lady*.

Use **Spanish Study Guide** for additional support, pp. 214–217.

Gifted and Talented
Have students form small discussion groups to discuss the following questions as they read the selection:

- What values does the author seem to be espousing?
- How are these values similar to or different from those in our society today?
- What deeds described in these two stories seem to you to be heroic?

Mini Lesson: Preteaching Vocabulary

USING CONTEXT CLUES

Instruction Remind students that sometimes they can understand the meaning of an unfamiliar word by examining the context. Use the model sentence to demonstrate the strategy:

The football player demonstrated his <u>prowess</u> by making three touchdowns in a row.

- Write the model sentence on the board and ask a volunteer to summarize the meaning.
- Have students infer the meaning of *prowess*.
- Ask a volunteer to use the word *prowess* in a sentence.

Exercises Ask students to use context clues to determine the meanings of the underlined words.

1. His <u>adversary</u> put up a tremendous fight.
2. The knight agreed to <u>champion</u> the cause because it seemed noble to him.
3. No one questioned the knight's <u>fidelity</u>, as he had always been faithful before.

Use **Unit Six Resource Book,** p. 37 for more practice.

A lesson on context clues appears on p. 56 in the Pupil's Edition.

Reading and Analyzing

Reading Skills and Strategies: PREVIEW

Discuss with students the Build Background feature on p. 1064, and then discuss with them what they know about Arthurian legends. Then have students look at the images throughout the selection and make predictions about how the images will connect to what they already know about these legends. Remind students that they are expected to establish a purpose for reading.

Active Reading MAKING JUDGMENTS

As they read, have students set up their own chart like the one on p. 1064, only with their own criteria for honorable behavior in the left column. Then have the students pick a character and chart how well he or she lives up to the new code.

Possible criteria: kind; forgiving; brave; generous; responsible; hardworking

Use **Unit Six Resource Book,** p. 35 for more practice.

Literary Analysis ROMANCE

Romantic elements, which include the chivalric code and noble deeds performed by knights and other heroes, persist in modern literature. Have students give several examples of romances from modern movies and books.

Possible Responses: Some examples of movies are *Brian's Song, The Fisher King, Batman*, and *Star Wars*. Examples of books include Ursula LeGuin's *Earthsea* trilogy and Tolkien's *The Lord of the Rings*.

Use **Unit Six Resource Book,** p. 36 for more practice.

The Granger Collection, New York.

Teaching Options

Mini Lesson Viewing and Representing

King Arthur Drawing Forth the Sword
by Howard Pyle

ART APPRECIATION Howard Pyle (1853–1911) was born in Wilmington, Delaware. He gained renown first as a magazine illustrator and then as an author and illustrator of children's books. His style is noted for its clear, firm lines and careful composition.

Instruction Point out that the painting has two parts. Ask students to draw an imaginary line from the upper right corner to the lower left corner of the painting. Ask how the two parts of the painting are different.

Possible Response: The lower right half of the painting is dominated by the stone, and the upper left half of the painting is dominated by people.

Application Ask students to identify details that show the solemnity and importance of this occasion.

Possible Responses: The royalty are seated in a lavish hall, wearing their finery. All, except for Merlin, are at a distance from Arthur. All faces, especially Arthur's, are expressionless, indicating concentration.

"I suppose," said Igraine to her husband, the duke, when this had happened, "that the king arranged this truce only because he wanted to make me his mistress. I suggest that we leave at once, without warning, and ride overnight to our castle." The duke agreed with her, and they left the court secretly.

The king was enraged by Igraine's flight and summoned his privy council.[5] They advised him to command the fugitives' return under threat of renewing the war; but when this was done, the duke and Igraine defied his summons. He then warned them that they could expect to be dragged from their castle within six weeks.

The duke manned and provisioned[6] his two strongest castles: Tintagil for Igraine, and Terrabyl, which was useful for its many sally ports,[7] for himself. Soon King Uther arrived with a huge army and laid siege to Terrabyl; but despite the ferocity of the fighting, and the
1 numerous casualties suffered by both sides, neither was able to gain a decisive victory.

Still enraged, and now despairing, King Uther fell sick. His friend Sir Ulfius came to him and asked what the trouble was. "Igraine has broken my heart," the king replied, "and unless I can win her, I shall never recover."

"Sire," said Sir Ulfius, "surely Merlin the Prophet could find some means to help you? I will go in search of him."

Sir Ulfius had not ridden far when he was accosted by a hideous beggar. "For whom are you searching?" asked the beggar; but Sir Ulfius ignored him.

"Very well," said the beggar, "I will tell you: you are searching for Merlin, and you need look no further, for I am he. Now go to King Uther and tell him that I will make Igraine his if he will reward me as I ask; and even that will be more to his benefit than to mine."

"I am sure," said Sir Ulfius, "that the king will refuse you nothing reasonable."

"Then go, and I shall follow you," said Merlin.

Well pleased, Sir Ulfius galloped back to the king and delivered Merlin's message, which he had hardly completed when Merlin himself appeared at the entrance to the pavilion. The king bade him welcome.

"Sire," said Merlin, "I know that you are in love with Igraine; will you swear, as an anointed[8] king, to give into my care the child that she bears you, if I make her yours?"

The king swore on the gospel that he would do so, and Merlin continued: "Tonight you shall appear before Igraine at Tintagil in the likeness of her husband, the duke. Sir Ulfius and I will appear as two of the duke's knights: Sir Brastius and Sir Jordanus. Do not question either Igraine or her men, but say that you are sick and retire to bed. I will fetch you early in the morning, and do not rise until I come; fortunately Tintagil is only ten miles from here."

The plan succeeded: Igraine was completely deceived by the king's impersonation of the duke, and gave herself to him, and conceived Arthur. The king left her at dawn as soon as Merlin appeared, after giving her a farewell kiss. But the duke had seen King Uther ride out from the siege on the previous night and, in the course of making a surprise attack on the king's army, had been killed. When Igraine realized that the duke had died three hours before he had appeared to her, she was greatly disturbed in mind; however, she confided in no one.

Once it was known that the duke was dead, the king's nobles urged him to be reconciled to Igraine, and this task the king gladly entrusted to Sir Ulfius, by whose eloquence it was soon accomplished. "And now," said Sir Ulfius to his fellow nobles, "why should not the king marry the beautiful Igraine? Surely it would be as well for us all."

5. **privy** (prĭv'ē) **council:** a group of advisors who serve a ruler.
6. **provisioned:** supplied.
7. **sally ports:** gates or passages in the walls of fortifications, from which troops can make a sudden attack.
8. **anointed:** chosen as if by divine intervention.

Customizing Instruction

Less Proficient Readers

Use the following questions to help students understand some of the basic plot elements of the tale.

- Why do Igraine and the duke flee the court?
  Answer: King Uther has asked Igraine to be his mistress.
- What deal does Merlin make with King Uther?
  Answer: That he will unite Igraine and Uther if Uther promises to give him the child of their union.
- What happens to the duke?
  Answer: He is killed in battle.

Set a Purpose Have students read on to discover whether King Uther will keep the promise he has made to Merlin.

Students Acquiring English

1 Explain to students the following terms:
ferocity: ferocious or savage nature
casualties: people wounded or killed
decisive victory: a victory that brings an end to the dispute

Multiple Learning Styles

Interpersonal Learners

Ask students to think about the way in which Igraine is deceived. Lead a class discussion about whether the end—in this case, conceiving the future king—justifies the means.

BLOCK SCHEDULING: MANAGING TIME

If your schedule requires that you cover the lesson objectives in a shorter time, use . . .

- Preparing to Read, p. 1064
- Thinking Through the Literature, p. 1080
- Vocabulary in Action, p. 1081
- Grammar in Context, p. 1082

If you want to take advantage of longer class time, use . . .

- TE Teaching Options: Preteaching Vocabulary, p. 1065; Viewing and Representing, pp. 1066, 1070, 1072, 1076; Informal Assessment, p. 1068; Speaking and Listening, pp. 1069, 1074; Vocabulary Strategy, p. 1073; Standardized Test Practice, p. 1079
- Choices & Challenges, pp. 1081–1082

THE CROWNING OF ARTHUR 1067

Reading and Analyzing

Active Reading MAKING JUDGMENTS

A Women in the Middle Ages were relatively powerless. Ask students to keep this in mind and explain whether they think Igraine's reaction to Uther is appropriate.

Possible Responses: She should have defied Uther and refused him, even if it cost her life, because he killed her husband; she made the best of a bad situation and did well in accepting Uther's proposal; she was actually fortunate to "trade up" for a more powerful husband.

Literary Analysis ROMANCE

B Hidden identity is often an important element of romance tales. Ask students why Merlin wants to keep the child's identity a secret.

Possible Responses: He may think the child, as heir to the throne, would be in danger or that others might exert undesirable influence on the child; he may want the child to grow up without all the trappings of a royal childhood.

Literary Analysis: SETTING

C Students should analyze the relevance of the setting and time frame to the text's meaning. Have students explain the significance of the day on which Arthur pulls the sword from the stone.

Possible Response: It is New Year's Day, possibly signifying a new beginning for Britain.

The marriage of King Uther and Igraine was celebrated joyously thirteen days later; and then, at the king's request, Igraine's sisters were also married: Margawse, who later bore Sir Gawain, to King Lot of Lowthean and Orkney; Elayne, to King Nentres of Garlot. Igraine's daughter, Morgan le Fay, was put to school in a nunnery; in after years she was to become a witch, and to be married to King Uryens of Gore, and give birth to Sir Uwayne of the Fair Hands.

A A few months later it was seen that Igraine was with child, and one night, as she lay in bed with King Uther, he asked her who the father might be. Igraine was greatly abashed.

"Do not look so dismayed," said the king, "but tell me the truth, and I swear I shall love you the better for it."

"The truth is," said Igraine, "that the night the duke died, about three hours after his death, a man appeared in my castle—the exact image of the duke. With him came two others who appeared to be Sir Brastius and Sir Jordanus. Naturally I gave myself to this man as I would have to the duke, and that night, I swear, this child was conceived."

"Well spoken," said the king; "it was I who impersonated the duke, so the child is mine." He then told Igraine the story of how Merlin had arranged it, and Igraine was overjoyed to discover that the father of her child was now her husband.

Sometime later, Merlin appeared before the king. "Sire," he said, "you know that you must provide for the upbringing of your child?"

"I will do as you advise," the king replied.

B "That is good," said Merlin, "because it is my reward for having arranged your impersonation of the duke. Your child is destined for glory, and I want him brought to me for his baptism. I shall then give him into the care of foster parents who can be trusted not to reveal his identity before the proper time. Sir Ector would be suitable: he is extremely loyal, owns good estates, and his wife has just borne him a child. She could give her child into the care of another woman, and herself look after yours."

Sir Ector was summoned and gladly agreed to the king's request, who then rewarded him handsomely. When the child was born, he was at once wrapped in a gold cloth and taken by two knights and two ladies to Merlin, who stood waiting at the rear entrance to the castle in his beggar's disguise. Merlin took the child to a priest, who baptized him with the name of Arthur, and thence to Sir Ector, whose wife fed him at her breast.

Two years later King Uther fell sick, and his enemies once more overran his kingdom, inflicting heavy losses on him as they advanced. Merlin prophesied that they could be checked only by the presence of the king himself on the battlefield, and suggested that he should be conveyed there on a horse litter.[9] King Uther's army met the invader on the plain at St. Albans, and the king duly appeared on the horse litter. Inspired by his presence, and by the lively leadership of Sir Brastius and Sir Jordanus, his army quickly defeated the enemy, and the battle finished in a rout. The king returned to London to celebrate the victory.

But his sickness grew worse, and after he had lain speechless for three days and three nights, Merlin summoned the nobles to attend the king in his chamber on the following morning. "By the grace of God," he said, "I hope to make him speak."

In the morning, when all the nobles were assembled, Merlin addressed the king: "Sire, is it your will that Arthur shall succeed to the throne, together with all its prerogatives?"[10]

The king stirred in his bed and then spoke so that all could hear: "I bestow on Arthur God's blessing and my own, and Arthur shall succeed to the throne on pain of forfeiting my blessing."

9. **horse litter:** a stretcher fastened to a horse.

10. **prerogatives:** rights or privileges held by a person or group.

Teaching Options

Assessment Informal Assessment

ALTERNATIVE ENDING/CAUSE AND EFFECT You can informally assess students' understanding of the selection thus far by having them imagine a different ending in which Arthur does *not* have the opportunity to remove the sword from the stone. Students could consider all the factors leading to Arthur's success and imagine the consequences if any of these events had not occurred.

RUBRIC

3 **Full Accomplishment** Response shows a full understanding of cause and effect in the story.

2 **Substantial Accomplishment** Response shows a general understanding of cause and effect in the story.

1 **Little or Partial Accomplishment** Response shows little understanding of cause and effect in the story.

Then King Uther gave up the ghost. He was buried and mourned the next day, as befitted his rank, by Igraine and the nobility of Britain.

During the years that followed the death of King Uther, while Arthur was still a child, the ambi-
1 tious barons fought one another for the throne, and the whole of Britain stood in jeopardy. Finally the day came when the Archbishop of Canterbury, on the advice of Merlin, summoned the nobility to London for Christmas morning. In his message the archbishop promised that the true succession to the British throne would be miraculously revealed. Many of the nobles purified themselves during their journey, in the hope that it would be to them that the succession would fall.

WHOSO PULLETH OUTE THIS SWERD OF THIS STONE AND ANVYLD IS RIGHTWYS KYNGE BORNE OF ALL BRYTAYGNE

The archbishop held his service in the city's greatest church (St. Paul's), and when matins[11] were done, the congregation filed out to the yard. They were confronted by a marble block into which had been thrust a beautiful sword. The block was four feet square, and the sword passed through a steel anvil which had been struck in the stone, and which projected a foot from it. The anvil had been inscribed with letters of gold:

2 WHOSO PULLETH OUTE THIS SWERD OF THIS STONE AND ANVYLD IS RIGHTWYS KYNGE BORNE OF ALL BRYTAYGNE

The congregation was awed by this miraculous sight, but the archbishop forbade anyone to touch the sword before mass had been heard. After mass, many of the nobles tried to pull the sword out of the stone, but none was able to, so a watch of ten knights was set over the
C sword, and a tournament proclaimed for New Year's Day, to provide men of noble blood with the opportunity of proving their right to the succession.

Sir Ector, who had been living on an estate near London, rode to the tournament with Arthur and his own son Sir Kay, who had been recently knighted. When they arrived at the tournament, Sir Kay found to his annoyance that his sword was missing from its sheath, so he begged Arthur to ride back and fetch it from their lodging.

Arthur found the door of the lodging locked and bolted, the landlord and his wife having left for the tournament. In order not to disappoint his brother, he rode on to St. Paul's, determined to get for him the sword which was lodged in the stone. The yard was empty, the guard also having slipped off to see the tournament, so Arthur strode up to the sword, and, without troubling to read the inscription, tugged it free. He then rode straight back to Sir Kay and presented him with it.

Sir Kay recognized the sword and, taking it to Sir Ector, said, "Father, the succession falls to me, for I have here the sword that was lodged in the stone." But Sir Ector insisted that they should all ride to the churchyard, and once there bound Sir Kay by oath to tell how he had come by the sword. Sir Kay then admitted that Arthur had given it to him. Sir Ector turned to Arthur and said, "Was the sword not guarded?"

"It was not," Arthur replied.

"Would you please thrust it into the stone again?" said Sir Ector. Arthur did so, and first Sir Ector and then Sir Kay tried to remove it, but both were unable to. Then Arthur, for the second time, pulled it out. Sir Ector and Sir Kay both knelt before him.

"Why," said Arthur, "do you both kneel before me?"

"My lord," Sir Ector replied, "there is only

11. **matins** (măt′nz): morning prayers.

Customizing Instruction

Less Proficient Readers

Use the following questions to guide students to understand Arthur's status as a hero:

- Who is Arthur's true father?
  Answer: King Uther
- What is the significance of Arthur's ability to pull the sword from the stone?
  Answer: It shows he is the true heir (inheritor) to the throne of Britain.

Students Acquiring English

1 Explain that the phrase *stood in jeopardy* in this sentence means "was in danger."

2 Tell students that the inscription is written in an archaic form of English. Encourage them to look at each word and help them in translation: "Whoever pulls out this sword from this stone and anvil is rightfully born king of all Britain."

Mini Lesson Speaking and Listening

DRAMATIC READING

Prepare Help students prepare a dramatic presentation based on the scene in which Arthur draws the sword from the stone. Have them work in cooperative groups to list the elements they want to include in their interpretation. Encourage them to write a script complete with dialogue and notes on costumes, props, sets, sound effects, music, and lighting. Ask them to pay special attention to the character of Arthur. As a romantic hero, how should he be portrayed? What posture, gestures, tone of voice, and diction are especially appropriate for his character? Students should justify their choice of verbal and nonverbal performance techniques by referring to their interpretation of this scene.

Present Student groups can decide how they will perform the dramatic presentation. After the performance, students who are audience members should discuss how the performance increases their understanding of the characters in Malory's tale.

BLOCK SCHEDULING This activity is particularly well suited for longer class periods.

Reading and Analyzing

Literary Analysis: TONE

A Ask students to describe the tone of the concluding paragraphs of this chapter.

Possible Response: The tone is solemn and dignified, which is appropriate for the formal recognition of the prophesied king of Britain.

The Granger Collection, New York.

Teaching Options

Mini Lesson Viewing and Representing

Arthur as King **by Howard Pyle**

ART APPRECIATION This portrait of Arthur is another illustration from Pyle's four-volume retelling of the Arthurian legends.

Application Ask students what details indicate royalty. How would students describe the attitude of the king in this image?

Possible Responses: His crown, staff, and royal blue robe all indicate royalty, as does the orb he holds. He is serious and self-assured; he is aware of his responsibilities.

one man living who can draw the sword from the stone, and he is the true-born King of Britain." Sir Ector then told Arthur the story of his birth and upbringing.

"My dear father," said Arthur, "for so I shall always think of you—if, as you say, I am to be king, please know that any request you have to make is already granted."

Sir Ector asked that Sir Kay should be made Royal Seneschal,[12] and Arthur declared that while they both lived it should be so. Then the three of them visited the archbishop and told him what had taken place.

All those dukes and barons with ambitions to rule were present at the tournament on New Year's Day. But when all of them had failed, and Arthur alone had succeeded in drawing the sword from the stone, they protested against one so young, and of ignoble[13] blood, succeeding to the throne.

The secret of Arthur's birth was known only to a few of the nobles surviving from the days of King Uther. The archbishop urged them to make Arthur's cause their own; but their support proved ineffective. The tournament was repeated at Candlemas and at Easter, and with the same outcome as before.

Finally at Pentecost, when once more Arthur alone had been able to remove the sword, the commoners arose with a tumultuous cry and demanded that Arthur should at once be made king. The nobles, knowing in their hearts that the commoners were right, all knelt before Arthur and begged forgiveness for having delayed his succession for so long. Arthur forgave them and then, offering his sword at the high altar, was dubbed first knight of the realm. The coronation took place a few days later, when Arthur swore to rule justly, and the nobles swore him their allegiance. ❖ (A)

12. **Royal Seneschal** (sĕn′ə-shəl): the representative of a king in judicial and domestic matters.

13. **ignoble:** not noble; common.

Customizing Instruction

Students Acquiring English

Explain to students the following terms:

- *tumultuous:* noisy and wild
- *dubbed:* made someone a knight
- *swore him their allegiance:* swore to be faithful to him

Multiple Learning Styles

Interpersonal Learners

Have students discuss a situation in which an underdog bested someone in a competition. They may have had this experience personally, know someone who had it, or recall such a situation from a TV show, book, or movie. Ask them how Arthur must have felt to suddenly learn he should be king, while at the same time encountering the jealousy and resistance of those he needed to support him.

Thinking Through the Literature

1. **Comprehension Check** How does Arthur become king?
2. How much control would you say the **characters** have over their lives?

   THINK ABOUT
   - Uther's passion for Igraine and the way he makes her his wife
   - what happens to Igraine's sister and daughter after her wedding
   - Merlin's comment that Arthur is "destined for glory" and the instructions he gives for Arthur's care
   - Arthur's discovery that he is heir to the throne
3. In your opinion, does Arthur deserve to be king?

   THINK ABOUT
   - the sacrifices other people must make to bring him to power
   - the support he receives from the common people
   - the kind of person he seems to be
4. What do you think it would be like to live in the world depicted in this selection? Explain.

Thinking Through the Literature

1. by removing the sword from the stone
2. Possible Response: The characters seem controlled by fate and their own passions. Uther wages war because he is captivated by Igraine's beauty. Arthur's entire life seems dictated by Merlin's prophecy. The women seem dependent on the good will of men.
3. Possible Responses: Arthur seems worthy to be king. He is beloved by the commoners, loyal to Sir Ector, and kind; Arthur is not worthy of the kingship. He has no experience or training in ruling.
4. Some will desire the pageantry and glory of this heroic age. Others will note that it has few, if any, of today's "necessities" and conveniences.

Reading and Analyzing

Literary Analysis ROMANCE

Launcelot's relationship to Queen Gwynevere is governed by courtly love, a medieval concept of love with a demanding set of rules. A knight chooses one lady to serve faithfully, performing noble deeds for her sake. Ideal courtly love is chaste, and a knight's chosen lady is often married and therefore unattainable. Ask students whether they can think of a modern equivalent to this romantic ideal.

Possible Response: people who are fervent, faithful admirers of celebrities they can never hope to meet

Reading Skills and Strategies: CONNECTING

Ask students whether they think the chivalric qualities—honor, chastity, loyalty, courage, honesty, and courtesy—should be important to people today. Why or why not?

Possible Responses: Yes—they make someone a better person; no—they handicap someone in today's highly competitive environment.

For those who are inclined to dismiss the chivalric qualities, rephrase the question—are these qualities the ones they would want in their friends? in their husbands or wives?

Tournament in King Arthur's court. MS Douce 383, fol. 16r. The Bodleian Library, Oxford, England.

Teaching Options

Mini Lesson: Viewing and Representing

Tournament in King Arthur's Court **Unknown Artist**

ART APPRECIATION This is an illustration from a medieval French manuscript. Manuscripts with these elaborate illustrations and decorations are called "illuminated" because of their shiny gold leaf. Tell students that the text in Gothic lettering is in Old French and that the title of the manuscript is, in English, "Guiron the Courtier."

Application Ask students to describe the various elements of the illustration. In what ways does this illustration portray the chivalric ideals?

Possible Responses: The jousting knights, the lances on the ground, the knights sitting to the right, the standing soldiers in the back left, the musicians, and the observers in the stands illustrate the chivalric ideal—brave knights in solo combat, noble ladies looking on attentively, with stirring romantic music playing in the background.

Sir Launcelot du Lake

from Le Morte d'Arthur
Sir Thomas Malory

When King Arthur returned from Rome, he settled his court at Camelot, and there gathered about him his knights of the Round Table, who diverted themselves with jousting and tournaments. Of all his knights one was supreme, both in prowess at arms and in nobility of bearing, and this was Sir Launcelot, who was also the favorite of Queen Gwynevere, to whom he had sworn oaths of fidelity.

One day Sir Launcelot, feeling weary of his life at the court, and of only playing at arms, decided to set forth in search of adventure. He asked his nephew Sir Lyonel to accompany him, and when both were suitably armed and mounted, they rode off together through the forest.

At noon they started across a plain, but the intensity of the sun made Sir Launcelot feel sleepy, so Sir Lyonel suggested that they should rest

WORDS TO KNOW
prowess (prou'ĭs) *n.* superior strength, courage, or daring, especially in battle
fidelity (fĭ-dĕl'ĭ-tē) *n.* faithfulness to duties and obligations; devotion; loyalty

Customizing Instruction

Less Proficient Readers

Explain to students that between Arthur's coronation and the beginning of this chapter, Arthur has put down a rebellion of princes and married the beautiful Gwynevere. At the castle Camelot in southern England, Arthur has established the Knights of the Round Table, a brotherhood of knights selected for their bravery, skill, and moral purity—their chivalry. Lead a class discussion about King Arthur's Round Table. Ask them what purposes such a brotherhood might serve.

Possible Responses: They might protect the kingdom from invaders; they might serve as a police force; they might serve as an example and inspiration to other knights.

Students Acquiring English

Explain to students the following terms:
- *jousting:* "fighting on horseback, using lances"
- *bearing:* "manner of conducting oneself"
- *arms:* here, "weapons"
- *armed:* "carrying weapons"

Mini Lesson: Vocabulary Strategy

APPLYING MEANINGS OF ROOTS

Instruction The word *fidelity* is based upon the Latin *fides*, which means "faith." When Launcelot swears an oath of fidelity to Queen Gwynevere, he is promising that he will defend her and be her champion. Other words based on the same root are *infidelity* and *infidel*.

Practice Have students work in pairs to apply the meaning of the root to the meaning of the words *infidelity* and *infidel*. Ask them to use each word in a sentence. Ask students to describe how they can use knowledge of the root word *fides* to remember the meanings of these words.

Use **Vocabulary Transparencies and Copymasters,** p. 29, for more practice.

A lesson on word origins appears on p. 356 in the Pupil's Edition.

Reading and Analyzing

Reading Skills and Strategies: CLARIFYING

A Ask students why Sir Ector, who is looking for Sir Launcelot, asks the forester where he would most likely meet adventure.

Possible Response: That sort of place is the most likely in which to find Launcelot.

Active Reading MAKING JUDGMENTS

B Ask students to determine what Launcelot's response to the four queens' ultimatum reveals about his character.

Possible Responses: He is chaste and loyal; he is courageous and will stand up for his beliefs.

1 beneath the shade of an apple tree that grew by a hedge not far from the road. They dismounted, tethered their horses, and settled down.

"Not for seven years have I felt so sleepy," said Sir Launcelot, and with that fell fast asleep, while Sir Lyonel watched over him.

Soon three knights came galloping past, and Sir Lyonel noticed that they were being pursued by a fourth knight, who was one of the most powerful he had yet seen. The pursuing knight overtook each of the others in turn and, as he did so, knocked each off his horse with a thrust of his spear. When all three lay stunned, he dismounted, bound them securely to their horses with the reins, and led them away.

Without waking Sir Launcelot, Sir Lyonel mounted his horse and rode after the knight and, as soon as he had drawn close enough, shouted his challenge. The knight turned about, and they charged at each other, with the result that Sir Lyonel was likewise flung from his horse, bound, and led away a prisoner.

The victorious knight, whose name was Sir Tarquine,[1] led his prisoners to his castle and there threw them on the ground, stripped them naked, and beat them with thorn twigs. After that he locked them in a dungeon where many other prisoners, who had received like treatment, were complaining dismally.

Meanwhile, Sir Ector de Marys,[2] who liked to accompany Sir Launcelot on his adventures, and finding him gone, decided to ride after him. Before long he came upon a forester.

A "My good fellow, if you know the forest hereabouts, could you tell me in which direction I am most likely to meet with adventure?"

"Sir, I can tell you: less than a mile from here stands a well-moated castle. On the left of the entrance you will find a ford where you can water your horse, and across from the ford a large tree from which hang the shields of many famous knights. Below the shields hangs a caldron, of copper and brass: strike it three times with your spear, and then surely you will meet with adventure—such, indeed, that if you survive it, you will prove yourself the foremost knight in these parts for many years."

"May God reward you!" Sir Ector replied.

The castle was exactly as the forester had described it, and among the shields Sir Ector recognized several as belonging to knights of the Round Table. After watering his horse, he knocked on the caldron, and Sir Tarquine, whose castle it was, appeared.

They jousted, and at the first encounter Sir Ector sent his opponent's horse spinning twice about before he could recover.

"That was a fine stroke; now let us try again," said Sir Tarquine.

This time Sir Tarquine caught Sir Ector just below the right arm and, having impaled him on his spear, lifted him clean out of the saddle and rode with him into the castle, where he threw him on the ground.

"Sir," said Sir Tarquine, "you have fought better than any knight I have encountered in the last twelve years; therefore, if you wish, I will demand no more of you than your parole[3] as my prisoner."

"Sir, that I will never give."

"Then I am sorry for you," said Sir Tarquine, and with that he stripped and beat him and locked him in the dungeon with the other prisoners. There Sir Ector saw Sir Lyonel.

"Alas, Sir Lyonel, we are in a sorry plight. But tell me, what has happened to Sir Launcelot? for he surely is the one knight who could save us."

"I left him sleeping beneath an apple tree, and what has befallen him since I do not know," Sir Lyonel replied; and then all the unhappy prisoners once more bewailed their lot.

While Sir Launcelot still slept beneath the

1. **Tarquine** (tär'kwĭn).
2. **Sir Ector de Marys** (măr'əs): brother of Launcelot.
3. **parole:** the promise of a prisoner to abide by certain conditions in exchange for full or partial freedom.

Teaching Options

Mini Lesson Speaking and Listening

SPEECH

Prepare Help students prepare speeches to deliver to the class, based on some aspect of medieval life and values portrayed in the selection. Their speeches may be designed to entertain, inform, or persuade. After students have written their speeches, ask them to think about how to use movements, gestures, and tone of voice to keep the audience's interest and to accomplish their objective.

Present Students should practice and then deliver their speeches to the class. Students who are audience members should then discuss the effect of each speech—were they entertained? informed? persuaded?

BLOCK SCHEDULING This activity is particularly well suited for longer class periods.

apple tree, four queens started across the plain. They were riding white mules and accompanied by four knights who held above them, at the tips of their spears, a green silk canopy, to protect them from the sun. The party was startled by the neighing of Sir Launcelot's horse and, changing direction, rode up to the apple tree, where they discovered the sleeping knight. And as each of the queens gazed at the handsome Sir Launcelot, so each wanted him for her own.

"Let us not quarrel," said Morgan le Fay. "Instead, I will cast a spell over him so that he remains asleep while we take him to my castle and make him our prisoner. We can then oblige him to choose one of us for his paramour."

Sir Launcelot was laid on his shield and borne by two of the knights to the Castle Charyot, which was Morgan le Fay's stronghold. He awoke to find himself in a cold cell, where a young noblewoman was serving him supper.

"What cheer?"[4] she asked.

"My lady, I hardly know, except that I must have been brought here by means of an enchantment."

"Sir, if you are the knight you appear to be, you will learn your fate at dawn tomorrow." And with that the young noblewoman left him. Sir Launcelot spent an uncomfortable night, but at dawn the four queens presented themselves and Morgan le Fay spoke to him:

"Sir Launcelot, I know that Queen Gwynevere loves you, and you her. But now you are my prisoner, and you will have to choose: either to take one of us for your paramour, or to die miserably in this cell—just as you please. Now I will tell you who we are: I am Morgan le Fay, Queen of Gore; my companions are the queens of North Galys, of Estelonde, and of the Outer Isles. So make your choice."

B "A hard choice! Understand that I choose none of you, lewd sorceresses that you are; rather will I die in this cell. But were I free, I would take pleasure in proving it against any who would champion you that Queen Gwynevere is the finest lady of this land."

"So, you refuse us?" asked Morgan le Fay.

"On my life, I do," Sir Launcelot said finally, and so the queens departed.

Sometime later, the young noblewoman who had served Sir Launcelot's supper reappeared.

"What news?" she asked.

"It is the end," Sir Launcelot replied.

"Sir Launcelot, I know that you have refused the four queens, and that they wish to kill you out of spite. But if you will be ruled by me, I can save you. I ask that you will champion my father at a tournament next Tuesday, when he has to combat the King of North Galys, and three knights of the Round Table, who last Tuesday defeated him ignominiously."

"My lady, pray tell me, what is your father's name?"

"King Bagdemagus."[5]

"Excellent, my lady; I know him for a good king and a true knight, so I shall be happy to serve him."

"May God reward you! And tomorrow at dawn I will release you and direct you to an abbey which is ten miles from here, and where the good monks will care for you while I fetch my father."

"I am at your service, my lady."

As promised, the young noblewoman released Sir Launcelot at dawn. When she had led him through the twelve doors to the castle entrance, she gave him his horse and armor, and directions for finding the abbey.

"God bless you, my lady; and when the time comes, I promise I shall not fail you."

Sir Launcelot rode through the forest in search of the abbey but at dusk had still failed to find it

---

4. **What cheer?:** How are you?

5. **Bagdemagus** (băg′də-măg′əs).

WORDS TO KNOW **champion** (chăm′pē-ən) *v.* to fight for; defend

Customizing Instruction

Students Acquiring English

1 Explain to students the following terms:

- *dismounted:* "got down from a horse"
- *tethered:* "fastened a rope, chain, or cord to an animal to keep it from wandering"

Reading and Analyzing

Reading Skills and Strategies: COMPARING

A Ask students to compare this scene with the scene in which Igraine is deceived by King Uther. What different effects do these scenes have?

Possible Response: Both Igraine and Sir Belleus believe they are with someone else. In the first scene, the effect is one of anxiety; in the second scene, with Sir Belleus mistaking Launcelot for a paramour, the effect is largely humorous.

Explain to students that although Sir Belleus is gravely wounded as a result of this comical misunderstanding, in the heroic tradition, wounds are usually not important, and wouldn't detract from the humor of the situation for Mallory's contemporaries.

and, coming upon a red silk pavilion, apparently unoccupied, decided to rest there overnight and continue his search in the morning.

He had not been asleep for more than an hour, however, when the knight who owned the 1 pavilion returned and got straight into bed with him. Having made an assignation[6] with his 2 paramour, the knight supposed at first that Sir Launcelot was she and, taking him into his arms, started kissing him. Sir Launcelot awoke with a start and, seizing his sword, leaped out of bed and out of the pavilion, pursued closely by the other knight. Once in the open they set to with their swords, and before long Sir Launcelot had wounded his unknown adversary A so seriously that he was obliged to yield.

The knight, whose name was Sir Belleus, now asked Sir Launcelot how he came to be sleeping in his bed and then explained how he had an assignation with his lover, adding:

"But now I am so sorely wounded that I shall consider myself fortunate to escape with my life."

"Sir, please forgive me for wounding you; but lately I escaped from an enchantment, and I was afraid that once more I had been betrayed. Let us go into the pavilion, and I will staunch your wound."

Sir Launcelot had just finished binding the wound when the young noblewoman who was Sir Belleus's paramour arrived and, seeing the wound, at once rounded in fury on Sir Launcelot.

"Peace, my love," said Sir Belleus. "This is a noble knight, and as soon as I yielded to him, he treated my wound with the greatest care." Sir Belleus then described the events which had led up to the duel.

"Sir, pray tell me your name, and whose knight you are," the young noblewoman asked Sir Launcelot.

"My lady, I am called Sir Launcelot du Lake."

"As I guessed, both from your appearance and from your speech; and indeed I know you better than you realize. But I ask you, in recompense for the injury you have done my lord, and out of the courtesy for which you are famous, to recommend Sir Belleus to King Arthur, and suggest that he be made one of the knights of the Round Table. I can assure you that my lord deserves it, being only less than yourself as a man-at-arms, and sovereign of many of the Outer Isles." 3

"My lady, let Sir Belleus come to Arthur's court at the next Pentecost. Make sure that you come

Lancelot rescuing Guinevere by crossing the sword bridge (about 1300). From *Le Roman de Lancelot du Lac,* M. 806, f. 166, The Pierpont Morgan Library, New York/Art Resource, New York.

6. **assignation** (ăs′ĭg-nā′shən): an appointment for a meeting between lovers.

WORDS TO KNOW

adversary (ăd′vər-sĕr′ē) *n.* an opponent; enemy

recompense (rĕk′əm-pĕns′) *n.* amends made, as for damage or loss; payment in return for something, such as a service

Teaching Options

Mini Lesson: Viewing and Representing

Lancelot rescuing Guinevere by crossing the sword bridge **from *Le Roman de Lancelot du Lac***

ART APPRECIATION This illustration is from a French collection of tales about Launcelot, published around 1300. Note that this illustration contains more than one scene.

Application Ask students whether they think this illustration captures the heroic spirit of Launcelot. Why or why not?

Possible Responses: Yes, it captures the spirit of Launcelot because it shows he is willing to endure sliced hands and feet to rescue his lady; no, it doesn't capture Launcelot's spirit because his facial expressions suggest he's weak—not at all heroic.

with him, and I promise I will do what I can for him; and if he is as good a man-at-arms as you say he is, I am sure Arthur will accept him."

As soon as it was daylight, Sir Launcelot armed, mounted, and rode away in search of the abbey, which he found in less than two hours. King Bagdemagus's daughter was waiting for him and, as soon as she heard his horse's footsteps in the yard, ran to the window and, seeing that it was Sir Launcelot, herself ordered the servants to stable his horse. She then led him to her chamber, disarmed him, and gave him a long gown to wear, welcoming him warmly as she did so.

King Bagdemagus's castle was twelve miles away, and his daughter sent for him as soon as she had settled Sir Launcelot. The king arrived with his retinue[7] and embraced Sir Launcelot, who then described his recent enchantment, and the great obligation he was under to his daughter for releasing him.

"Sir, you will fight for me on Tuesday next?"

"Sire, I shall not fail you; but please tell me the names of the three Round Table knights whom I shall be fighting."

"Sir Modred, Sir Madore de la Porte, and Sir Gahalantyne. I must admit that last Tuesday they defeated me and my knights completely."

"Sire, I hear that the tournament is to be fought within three miles of the abbey. Could you send me three of your most trustworthy knights, clad in plain armor, and with no device,[8] and a fourth suit of armor which I

7. **retinue** (rĕt′n-o͞o): attendants.

8. **device:** a design, often a motto, on a coat of arms.

Customizing Instruction

Less Proficient Readers

Make sure students understand the episodic nature of this romance. Ask the following questions:

- What is the first adventure Sir Launcelot encounters?
  Answer: He is taken prisoner by the four queens.
- How does Launcelot repay the young noblewoman who releases him from the four queens?
  Answer: He promises to help her father, King Bagdemagus.

Set a Purpose Have students continue reading to learn about more of Launcelot's adventures.

Students Acquiring English

Explain to students the following terms:

1 *pavilion:* "tent"

2 *paramour:* "lover"

3 *man-at-arms:* "soldier"

Reading and Analyzing

Active Reading MAKING JUDGMENTS

Ask students to compare Launcelot's courteous behavior to ladies and to other knights with his violent behavior in the tournament. Have them give their opinions of Launcelot's code of conduct.

Possible Response: Since Launcelot holds strictly to the chivalric code, it seems that his violence must be acceptable within that code. Considering the specific aspects of this code—honor, chastity, loyalty, courage, honesty, and courtesy—one can see that restraint from violence is not a required quality. In fact, the violence he exhibits on these two pages *helps* him display several of the chivalric qualities, including honor, loyalty, and courage. Help students realize that even though the chivalric code requires many worthy qualities, it does not necessarily embrace all of the qualities that are considered worthy today.

Literary Analysis: TONE

A Have students describe Launcelot's tone in the final paragraph of this section. Is it appropriate for his character?

Possible Response: The tone is both imperious and courteous, fitting for an honorable and courteous knight of chivalry.

myself shall wear? We will take up our position just outside the tournament field and watch while you and the King of North Galys enter into combat with your followers; and then, as soon as you are in difficulties, we will come to your rescue and show your opponents what kind of knights you command."

This was arranged on Sunday, and on the following Tuesday Sir Launcelot and the three knights of King Bagdemagus waited in a copse,[9] not far from the pavilion which had been erected for the lords and ladies who were to judge the tournament and award the prizes.

The King of North Galys was the first on the field, with a company of ninescore knights; he was followed by King Bagdemagus with fourscore[10] knights, and then by the three knights of the Round Table, who remained apart from both companies. At the first encounter King Bagdemagus lost twelve knights, all killed, and the King of North Galys six.

With that, Sir Launcelot galloped on to the field, and with his first spear unhorsed five of the King of North Galys's knights, breaking the backs of four of them. With his next spear he charged the king and wounded him deeply in the thigh.

"That was a shrewd blow," commented Sir Madore and galloped onto the field to challenge Sir Launcelot. But he too was tumbled from his horse, and with such violence that his shoulder was broken.

Sir Modred was the next to challenge Sir Launcelot, and he was sent spinning over his horse's tail. He landed headfirst, his helmet became buried in the soil, and he nearly broke his neck, and for a long time lay stunned.

Finally Sir Gahalantyne tried; at the first encounter both he and Sir Launcelot broke their spears, so both drew their swords and hacked vehemently at each other. But Sir Launcelot, with mounting wrath, soon struck his opponent a blow on the helmet which brought the blood streaming from eyes, ears, and mouth. Sir Gahalantyne slumped forward in the saddle, his horse panicked, and he was thrown to the ground, useless for further combat.

Sir Launcelot took another spear and unhorsed sixteen more of the King of North Galys's knights and, with his next, unhorsed another twelve; and in each case with such violence that none of the knights ever fully recovered. The King of North Galys was forced to admit defeat, and the prize was awarded to King Bagdemagus.

That night Sir Launcelot was entertained as the guest of honor by King Bagdemagus and his daughter at their castle and before leaving was loaded with gifts.

"My lady, please, if ever again you should need my services, remember that I shall not fail you."

The next day Sir Launcelot rode once more through the forest and by chance came to the apple tree where he had previously slept. This time he met a young noblewoman riding a white palfrey.[11]

"My lady, I am riding in search of adventure; pray tell me if you know of any I might find hereabouts."

"Sir, there are adventures hereabouts if you believe that you are equal to them; but please tell me, what is your name?"

"Sir Launcelot du Lake."

"Very well, Sir Launcelot, you appear to be a sturdy enough knight, so I will tell you. Not far away stands the castle of Sir Tarquine, a knight who in fair combat has overcome more than sixty opponents whom he now holds prisoner. Many are from the court of King Arthur, and if you can rescue them, I will then ask you to deliver me and my companions from a knight who distresses us daily, either by robbery or by other kinds of outrage."

"My lady, please first lead me to Sir

9. **copse** (kŏps): a thicket of small trees.
10. **ninescore . . . fourscore:** a score is a set of 20; thus, ninescore is 180 and fourscore is 80.
11. **palfrey:** a gentle riding-horse.

Tarquine; then I will most happily challenge this miscreant knight of yours."

When they arrived at the castle, Sir Launcelot watered his horse at the ford and then beat the caldron until the bottom fell out. However, none came to answer the challenge, so they waited by the castle gate for half an hour or so. Then Sir Tarquine appeared, riding toward the castle with a wounded prisoner slung over his horse, whom Sir Launcelot recognized as Sir Gaheris, Sir Gawain's brother and a knight of the Round Table.

"Good knight," said Sir Launcelot, "it is known to me that you have put to shame many of the knights of the Round Table. Pray allow your prisoner, who I see is wounded, to recover, while I vindicate the honor of the knights whom you have defeated."

"I defy you, and all your fellowship of the Round Table," Sir Tarquine replied.

"You boast!" said Sir Launcelot.

At the first charge the backs of the horses were broken and both knights stunned. But they soon recovered and set to with their swords, and both struck so lustily that neither shield nor armor could resist, and within two hours they were cutting each other's flesh, from which the blood flowed liberally. Finally they paused for a moment, resting on their shields.

"Worthy knight," said Sir Tarquine, "pray hold your hand for a while and, if you will, answer my question."

"Sir, speak on."

"You are the most powerful knight I have fought yet, but I fear you may be the one whom in the whole world I most hate. If you are not, for the love of you I will release all my prisoners and swear eternal friendship."

"What is the name of the knight you hate above all others?"

"Sir Launcelot du Lake; for it was he who slew my brother, Sir Carados of the Dolorous Tower, and it is because of him that I have killed a hundred knights and maimed as many more, apart from the sixty-four I still hold prisoner. And so, if you are Sir Launcelot, speak up, for we must then fight to the death."

"Sir, I see now that I might go in peace and good fellowship or otherwise fight to the death; but being the knight I am, I must tell you: I am Sir Launcelot du Lake, son of King Ban of Benwick, of Arthur's court, and a knight of the Round Table. So defend yourself!"

"Ah! this is most welcome."

Now the two knights hurled themselves at each other like two wild bulls; swords and shields clashed together, and often their swords drove into the flesh. Then sometimes one, sometimes the other, would stagger and fall, only to recover immediately and resume the contest. At last, however, Sir Tarquine grew faint and unwittingly lowered his shield. Sir Launcelot was swift to follow up his advantage and, dragging the other down to his knees, unlaced his helmet and beheaded him.

Sir Launcelot then strode over to the young noblewoman: "My lady, now I am at your service, but first I must find a horse."

Then the wounded Sir Gaheris spoke up: "Sir, please take my horse. Today you have overcome the most formidable knight, excepting only yourself, and by so doing have saved us all. But before leaving, please tell me your name."

"Sir Launcelot du Lake. Today I have fought to vindicate the honor of the knights of the Round Table, and I know that among Sir Tarquine's prisoners are two of my brethren, Sir Lyonel and Sir Ector, also your own brother, Sir Gawain. According to the shields there are also Sir Brandiles, Sir Galyhuddis,[12] Sir Kay, Sir Alydukis,[13] Sir Marhaus, and many others. Please release the prisoners and ask them to help themselves to the castle treasure. Give them all my greetings and say I will see them at the next Pentecost. And please request Sir Ector and Sir Lyonel to go straight to the court and await me there." ❖ 1 A

12. **Galyhuddis** (găl′ĭ-hŏŏd′əs).

13. **Alydukis** (ăl′ĭ-dōō′kəs).

Customizing Instruction

Students Acquiring English

1 Explain to students that *vindicate* means "to clear of blame" or "to prove the value of."

Assessment Standardized Test Practice

CHOOSING THE BEST SUMMARY For some standardized tests, students will be asked to choose the best summary of a passage. To provide students with help in choosing the best summary, read aloud or write on the board the following question:

Which of the following statements best summarizes Launcelot's adventures?

A. Launcelot falls asleep. When he wakes up, he has to rescue some knights and help a woman who is distressed. He kills some knights and rescues some prisoners.

B. As Launcelot sleeps, Lyonel and Ector are both taken captive by Sir Tarquine. Launcelot is discovered by four queens, who threaten death if he does not choose one of them. He escapes through the aid of a noblewoman, champions her father in a tournament, and eventually defeats Sir Tarquine and liberates Lyonel, Ector, and the other prisoners.

C. Launcelot grows sleepy and rests beneath an apple tree. Lyonel and Ector are imprisoned. Sir Tarquine eventually appears, and Launcelot defeats him.

Lead students through the process of choosing the best summary. Point out that a summary should contain the most important information. Therefore, **B** is the best choice.

GUIDING STUDENT RESPONSE

Connect to the Literature

1. **What Do You Think?**
   Possible Response: The Launcelot in this selection is more cruel. He beheads Sir Tarquine after rendering him helpless and severely injures many knights at the tournament.

Comprehension Check
- by fighting for her father at a tournament and winning
- to rescue the knights Tarquine has imprisoned

Use Selection Quiz
Unit Six Resource Book, p. 39.

Think Critically

2. Possible Response: The knights are held to a strict code of honor, loyalty, bravery, honesty, and courtesy.
3. Possible Responses: Yes—he will face any odds to do what he thinks is right; no—he is completely unable to think for himself and follows his code blindly, even if it requires brutality of him.
4. Possible Responses: The female characters are more interesting than the men. Since they can't use force to get what they want, they use more varied methods. For example, the young noblewoman who helps Launcelot and the paramour who gets Sir Belleus a recommendation for a seat at the Round Table.
5. Suggest that students examine each character's motives when making judgments.

Vocabulary in Action

1. d
2. b
3. a
4. a
5. c

Connect to the Literature

1. **What Do You Think?** How does the Launcelot depicted in this selection compare with your own **image** of Arthur's most famous knight? Explain.

Comprehension Check
- How does Launcelot repay the noblewoman who releases him from the four queens?
- Why does Launcelot fight Tarquine?

Think Critically

2. Judging from the behavior of Sir Launcelot and the other knights in this selection, how would you describe the chivalric code that they live by?

   THINK ABOUT
   - the reasons the knights fight
   - Sir Launcelot's reaction to the four queens' proposal
   - Sir Tarquine's reaction to the fighting skills of Sir Ector and Sir Launcelot
   - Sir Launcelot's answer to Sir Tarquine's question about his identity

3. Do you think that Sir Launcelot is truly heroic? Support your opinion with details from the selection.
4. What is your opinion of the female **characters** in this story? Use **details** from the story to support your answer.
5. ACTIVE READING **MAKING JUDGMENTS** Which character in the two excerpts do you think best lives up to the chivalric code? Discuss your **judgments** with a classmate, using the charts you completed in your READER'S NOTEBOOK to support your opinions.

Extend Interpretations

6. **Comparing Texts** Think about the way Uther Pendragon, Launcelot, and other characters in these excerpts view war and fighting. What differences do you see between their views and those expressed by the characters in "On the Rainy River" (page 626) and other selections in this book?
7. **Connect to Life** Do you think leaders and heroes with qualities like those of Uther, Arthur, and Launcelot still exist in today's world? Explain your opinion.

Literary Analysis

ROMANCE The term **romance** refers to any imaginative story concerned with noble heroes, chivalric codes of honor, passionate love, daring deeds, and supernatural events. Writers of romances tend to idealize their heroes as well as the eras in which the heroes live. Medieval romances, such as *Le Morte d'Arthur,* are stories of kings, knights, and ladies, who are motivated by love, religious faith, or simply a desire for adventure. Such romances are comparatively lighthearted in **tone** and loose in **structure,** containing many episodes. Usually the main **character** has a series of adventures while on a quest to accomplish some goal.

Cooperative Learning Activity In a small group, talk about ways in which these excerpts from *Le Morte d'Arthur* illustrate the characteristics of a romance. Then discuss romantic elements in modern forms of entertainment, such as soap operas, romance novels, Westerns, and adventure films.

ACTIVE READING **SUMMARIZING**
Review the information about summarizing on page 977. Then, working with a partner, create a written summary of "The Crowning of Arthur" (pages 1065–1071). Compare your summary to those of your classmates, and choose the one that provides the best summary of the selection.

Extend Interpretations

Comparing Texts Possible Response: Most other main characters in this book recognize the horrors of war and the consequences of killing. Malory's characters seem to see only the honor that an enemy's death brings to the hero.

Connect to Life Possible Response: Uther's warlike behavior parallels the belligerent nature of many current leaders. As far as Arthur and Launcelot are concerned, their professed adherence to honor and their readiness to enter into skirmishes are relatively common qualities of modern leaders.

Literary Analysis

Romance Encourage students to make lists of the romantic characteristics of each of the entertainments listed. Have students determine which genre embodies the greatest number of romance characteristics before they begin their discussions. (Students may be surprised by the Westerns.)

Writing Options

1. **Day-in-the-Life Article** Write a magazine article about a typical day in the life of Sir Launcelot. Incorporate details about his habitual fighting, his relationships with women, and his friendships and rivalries with other knights.

2. **Editorial About Chivalry** In an editorial, persuade fellow students that society would either improve or worsen if people tried to live up to chivalric ideals as presented in these selections.

Writing Handbook
See page 000: Persuasive Writing.

3. **Arthurian Guidebook** Write a guidebook for tourists visiting the Arthurian world. Include descriptions and pictures of the people, their residences, and their activities, noting the distinctive features of life in this world. Also offer advice about how to behave.

Activities & Explorations

1. **Arthur in the Movies** Watch a videotape of *Camelot* or another film about the legend of Arthur. In an oral movie review, compare the view of the Arthurian world shown in the movie with the impression you get from these selections. ~ **VIEWING AND REPRESENTING**

2. **Knightly Images** Create a drawing or painting of your favorite scenes or characters from these selections. For inspiration, examine some of the artwork in this part of the unit or in illustrated volumes of Arthurian legends. ~ **ART**

3. **Movie Commercial** With a partner, create a television commercial for a new movie or television series about Launcelot's glorious deeds. You may wish to include a dramatization, a catchy theme song, or an interview with the leading man. ~ **PERFORMING**

Inquiry & Research

Medieval Tournaments Research medieval tournaments—their purpose, the equipment used, the participants, the contests or events held, and the way winners were determined. Then create a program for such a tournament, describing the events in which the knights of the Round Table might have participated.

More Online: Research Starter
www.mcdougallittell.com

Art Connection

How does the picture *King Arthur Drawing Forth the Sword* (page 1066) affect your view of the young Arthur and his suitability for kingship?

Vocabulary in Action

EXERCISE: ASSESSMENT PRACTICE Write the letter of the word pair that best expresses a relationship similar to that of the first pair.

1. TIP : **RECOMPENSE** :: (a) arm : body, (b) prediction : recollection, (c) disk : computer, (d) memo : correspondence
2. DOG : **FIDELITY** :: (a) chicken : egg, (b) fox : cleverness, (c) wolf : timidity, (d) whale : mammal
3. **PROWESS** : GLADIATOR :: (a) tact : diplomat, (b) honesty : thief, (c) wisdom : fool, (d) humility : actor
4. **CHAMPION** : PROTECTOR :: (a) teach : instructor, (b) cure : patient, (c) referee : competitor, (d) arrest : judge
5. **ADVERSARY** : FRIEND :: (a) cat : pet, (b) hunter : trapper, (c) servant : ruler, (d) member : club

Building Vocabulary
For an in-depth lesson on analogies, see page 263.

Writing Options

1. **Day-in-the-Life Article** Remind students to focus on the journalistic questions *who, what, where, when, why,* and *how*. Have students review celebrity profiles in magazines for examples of style and content.
2. **Editorial About Chivalry** Have students review the editorial page of a local newspaper to find models for their editorials. Remind students that they may make emotional and logical appeals, and help them find examples of each in the newspaper.
3. **Arthurian Guidebook** Have students look at published guidebooks for examples of style and content.

Activities & Explorations

1. **Arthur in the Movies** Students should give specific examples of details that are compared. Encourage students to focus on the physical circumstances of life during the Middle Ages.
2. **Knightly Images** A more challenging task would be to portray a single character's face, illustrating the character's qualities and emotions.
3. **Movie Commercial** Remind students that a commercial must capture the viewer's attention right away. Encourage them to focus on the most exciting details or situations.

Inquiry & Research

Medieval Tournaments As they create their tournament program, remind your students to include details of the personal feuds between the participants.

Art Connection

Tell students to think about what qualities Arthur is displaying in this painting. Have them consider his pose, the task he is performing, and the expressions of the onlookers.

Mini Lesson: Viewing and Representing

ANALYZE A FILM REVIEW

Instruction Show students the film *Camelot* or another film about the legend of Arthur. Have them write a review of the film.

Prepare Tell students the following criteria may be used to analyze a written review of a film.

- identifies its subject at the beginning
- opens with a general opinion
- includes enough facts, examples, and specifics to support the general opinion
- displays logical organization
- quickly establishes a tone

Present Pair students and have them share their reviews with their partners. Together the students may analyze the written reviews using the above criteria. Then have them compare their partner's review with their own responses.

Grammar in Context

WRITING EXERCISE

1. Lady Igraine's beauty, which many people admire, is brought to the attention of King Uther.
2. Merlin, after he gets Uther to pledge him a child, makes the king look like the Duke of Tintagil.
3. Young Arthur, having removed the sword from the stone, is declared to be the rightful heir to the throne.

Grammar in Context: Creating Subject-Verb Splits

In this sentence from *Le Morte d'Arthur,* a descriptive element appears between the subject and the verb.

> subject
> **One day Sir Launcelot, feeling weary of his life at the court, and of only playing at arms, decided to**
> verb
> **set forth in search of adventure.**

Expert writers sometimes make their writing more interesting by adding descriptive details to the beginning, middle, or end of simple sentences. When a descriptive element is inserted between the subject and the verb of a sentence, the sentence is said to contain a **subject-verb split.** In the example above, the subject and verb are separated by a participial phrase (shown in blue) that indicates why Sir Launcelot went off in search of adventure. Participial phrases are not, however, the only grammatical structures that can come between subjects and verbs; others include appositive phrases, adjective clauses, and adverb clauses.

Punctuation Tip: In a sentence containing a subject-verb split, the element that comes between the subject and the verb is usually set off with commas.

WRITING EXERCISE Rewrite each sentence, creating a subject-verb split by correctly inserting the words in parentheses between the subject and the verb.

Example: ***Original*** King Uther Pendragon has been at war for many years. (ruler of all Britain)

Rewritten King Uther Pendragon, ruler of all Britain, has been at war for many years.

1. Lady Igraine's beauty is brought to the attention of King Uther. (which many people admire)
2. Merlin makes the king look like the Duke of Tintagil. (after he gets Uther to pledge him a child)
3. Young Arthur is declared to be the rightful heir to the throne. (having removed the sword from the stone)

Grammar Handbook Punctuation, p. 1203

Sir Thomas Malory

1405?–1471

A Knight Himself The man who wrote *Le Morte d'Arthur* called himself "Syr Thomas Maleore, knyght." He also indicated that he completed this work in the ninth year of Edward IV's reign (1469 or 1470), and he added a prayer that he be safely delivered from prison. Although his precise identity remains uncertain, most scholars feel that he is Sir Thomas Malory (1405?–1471), a knight from the English county of Warwickshire who led a life of adventure at the end of the Middle Ages.

Behind Bars As a youth, Malory served bravely in battle under the Earl of Warwick, fighting for England during the final years of the Hundred Years' War with France. He inherited his father's estates in 1433 or 1434 and about a decade later represented Warwickshire in Parliament. In 1451, however, he was arrested and jailed for violently entering and robbing an abbey. Malory was imprisoned several more times in the next decade, accused of crimes such as cattle theft, highway robbery, and attempted murder, though the charges may have been politically motivated. Twice he escaped from prison but was recaptured. In 1462 he joined rebels opposing King Edward IV in the civil war known as the Wars of the Roses. Imprisoned for treason in 1468, he was specifically excluded from the pardons Edward granted to many of the other rebels. He spent the remainder of his life in London's Newgate Prison, where he apparently occupied his time by writing *Le Morte d'Arthur.* The work was published in 1485, 14 years after his death.

VIDEODISC **LaserLinks: Background for Reading** Art Gallery

Teaching Options

Mini Lesson Grammar

SUBJECT-VERB SPLIT

Instruction For use with Grammar in Context, p. 1082. Remind students that, although verbs often directly follow their subjects, sometimes they are "split" from the subject by a descriptive phrase. Write the following sentence on the board:

> Launcelot, certain of victory, challenged the evil knight to a duel.

Have students identify the subject of the sentence *(Launcelot)* and the verb *(challenged).* The phrase "certain of victory" gives more information about the subject and separates it and its verb.

Exercises Have students underline once the subject and verb and underline twice the interrupting word or phrase.

1. Launcelot, exhausted, fell asleep under a tree.
   Answer: Launcelot; exhausted; fell asleep
2. The four queens, sure that Launcelot was in their power, insisted that he choose among them.

Answer: queens; sure that Launcelot was in their power; insisted

Use **Grammar Transparencies and Copymasters,** p. 140.
Use **Unit Six Resource Book,** p. 38.

Use McDougal Littell's ***Language Network,*** Chapter 7, for more instruction on the subject-verb split.

"This is your little brother and you must love him and care for him."

from The Mists of Avalon

Romance by MARION ZIMMER BRADLEY

Connect to Your Life

New Arrivals What effect can the arrival of a baby brother or sister have on an older sibling? Imagine how you would react if such a circumstance occurred. If you actually have a younger brother or sister, recall how you reacted when he or she was born. Share your thoughts with a classmate.

Build Background

Morgan le Fay The character Morgaine in Bradley's novel *The Mists of Avalon* is based on Morgan le Fay, one of the more mysterious figures in the Arthurian legends. Her name comes from the Irish word *morrigain,* which means "great queen," and the French words *le fée,* which mean "the fairy." She probably originated in several myths about pagan goddesses. Some legends portray Morgan as a benevolent healer, but others portray her as a sorceress who plots against King Arthur and his wife. In the tradition that Bradley follows, she is Arthur's half-sister. Their mother, Igraine, (ē-grān'), married Arthur's father, Uther Pendragon (o͞o' thər pĕn-drăg' ən), after the death of her first husband, Gorlois (gôr-loiz').

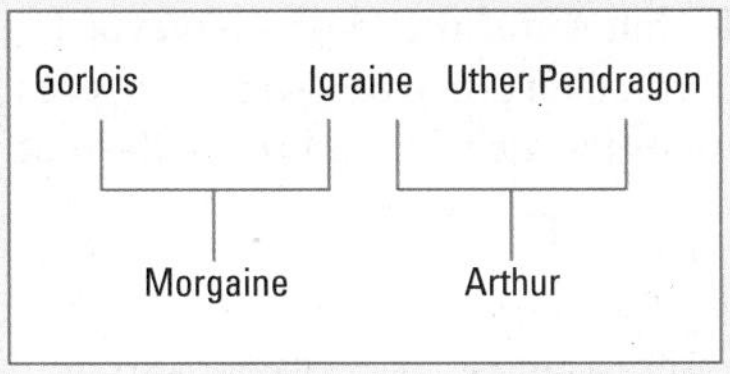

Focus Your Reading

LITERARY ANALYSIS **FIRST-PERSON POINT OF VIEW** When a character who participates in a story also narrates the action, the writer is using the **first-person point of view.** The events in this excerpt are told by the character Morgaine:

> ***I think that my first real memory is of my mother's wedding to Uther Pendragon. I remember my father only a little.***

A first-person **narrator** is able to give the reader an eyewitness account of the events in a story. As you read this selection, notice how Morgaine expresses her feelings about each of the characters.

ACTIVE READING **ANALYZING CHARACTERS** Bradley's modern retelling of Arthurian legend involves revision of traditional versions of the story, presenting views of Arthurian characters that are quite different from those in previous versions. As you read, be aware of what you learn about each character, including the narrator. Remember that since Morgaine narrates this selection, all of our information is colored by her judgment.

READER'S NOTEBOOK Create a word web, like the one shown, for each of these characters: Uther, Arthur, Igraine, and the narrator. Use the web to analyze what you learn about each character and Morgaine's feelings about him or her. In the case of Morgaine herself, include information about how she views herself.

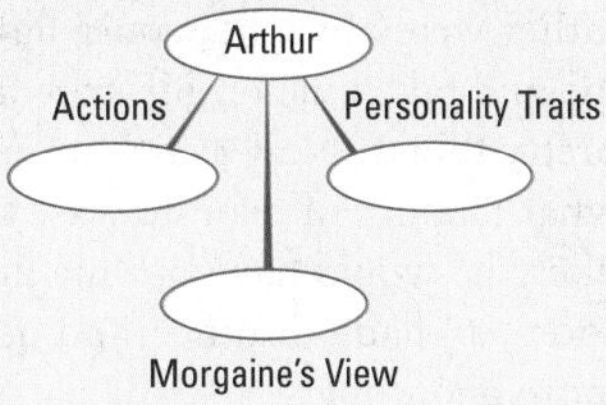

OVERVIEW

Objectives

1. enjoy an excerpt from a modern version of an **Arthurian legend (Literary Analysis)**
2. understand the **first-person point of view (Literary Analysis)**
3. analyze **characters (Active Reading)**

Summary

Morgaine, the stepdaughter of Uther Pendragon and the daughter of Igraine, describes the jealousy she felt toward those who stole her mother's attention—first King Uther and then her brother, Arthur.

Thematic Link

In an unusual perspective on **the heroic tradition**, the great King Arthur is seen as a little child, vulnerable and dependent on his older sister.

5-Minute Warm-Up

Daily Language SkillBuilder

Have students **proofread** the display sentences on page 959j and write them correctly. The sentences also appear on Transparency 28 of **Grammar Transparencies and Copymasters.**

LESSON RESOURCES

UNIT SIX RESOURCE BOOK, pp. 40–43

ASSESSMENT RESOURCES

Formal Assessment, pp. 171–172

Teacher's Guide to Assessment and Portfolio Use

Test Generator

SKILLS TRANSPARENCIES AND COPYMASTERS

Literary Analysis
- Point of View, T17 (for Paired Activity, p. 1086)

Reading and Critical Thinking
- Cluster Diagram, T48 (for Reader's Notebook, p. 1083)

Grammar
- Objective Complements, C92 (for Mini Lesson, p. 1087)

Writing
- Showing, Not Telling, T22 (for Writing Options, p. 1087)
- Point of View, T23 (for Writing Options, p. 1087)

Communications
- Impromptu Speaking: Dialogue, Role-Play, Debate, T13 (for Activities & Explorations 1, p. 1087)
- Giving and Using Feedback to Improve Performance, T16 (for Activities & Explorations 1, p. 1087)

INTEGRATED TECHNOLOGY

Audio Library

Visit our website: www.mcdougallittell.com

Reading and Analyzing

Active Reading

ANALYZING CHARACTERS

Encourage students to analyze Morgaine's descriptions of herself and other characters to form their own opinion of her. Have students ask themselves the following questions as they read:

- What is Morgaine's attitude toward others?
  Possible Response: She resents anyone who takes attention away from her.
- What seems to be her main concern?
  Possible Response: gaining her mother's attention
- How does her age affect your perception of her?
  Possible Response: It makes plain that her emotions are normal and reasonable for a child her age.

Use **Unit Six Resource Book,** p. 41 for more practice.

Literary Analysis

FIRST-PERSON POINT OF VIEW

The first-person narrator involves the reader in the story because the character describes the action as a participant. Encourage students to analyze the benefits and limitations of this point of view. Students may want to discuss how this excerpt would be different if it had been narrated from the point of view of Uther or Igraine.

Use **Unit Six Resource Book,** p. 42 for more practice.

from

THE MISTS OF AVALON

MARION ZIMMER BRADLEY

Morgan Le Fay, Aubrey Beardsley. Courtesy of the Newberry Library, Chicago.

Morgaine speaks . . .

I think that my first real memory is of my mother's wedding to Uther Pendragon. I remember my father only a little. When I was unhappy as a little girl, I seemed to remember him, a heavyset man with a dark beard and dark hair; I remember playing with a chain he wore about his neck. I remember that as a little maiden when I was unhappy, when I was chidden[1] by my mother or my teachers, or when Uther—rarely—noticed me to disapprove of me, I used to comfort myself by thinking that if my own father were alive, he would have been fond of me and taken me on his knee and brought me pretty things. Now that I am older and know what manner of man he was, I think it more
1 likely he would have put me into a nunnery as soon as I had a brother, and never thought more about me.

Not that Uther was ever unkind to me; it was simply that he had no particular interest in a girl child. My mother was always at the center of his heart, and he at hers, and so I resented that—that I had lost my mother to this great fair-haired, boorish[2] man. When Uther was away in battle—and there was battle a good deal of the time when I was a maiden—my mother Igraine cherished me and petted me, and taught me to spin with her own hands and to weave in colors. But when Uther's men were sighted, then I went back into my rooms and was forgotten until he went away again. Is it any wonder I hated him and resented, with all my heart, the sight of the dragon banner on any horsemen approaching Tintagel?[3]

And when my brother was born it was worse. For there was this crying thing, all pink and white, at my mother's breast; and it was worse that she expected me to care as much for him as she did. "This is your little brother," she said, "take good care of him, Morgaine, and love him." Love him? I hated him with all my heart, for now when I came near her she would pull away and tell me that I was a big girl, too big to be sitting in her lap, too big to bring my ribbons to her for tying, too big to come and lay my head on her knees for comfort. I would have pinched him, except that she would have hated me for it. I sometimes thought she hated me anyhow. And Uther made much of my brother. But I think he always hoped for another son. I was never told, but somehow I knew—maybe I heard the women talking, maybe I was gifted even then with more of the Sight[4] than I realized—that

1. **chidden:** scolded.
2. **boorish:** rude; ill-mannered.
3. **Tintagel** (tĭn-tăj′əl): a castle in Wales—the legendary birthplace of King Arthur.
4. **the Sight:** a supernatural ability to see future, past, or faraway events.

Teaching Options

Assessment Standardized Test Practice

CHOOSING THE BEST SUMMARY For some standardized tests, students will be asked to choose the best summary of a passage. To provide students with some help in choosing the best summary, read aloud or write on the board the following question:

Which of the following statements best summarizes Morgaine's relationship with her brother Arthur?

A. Morgaine doesn't like Arthur.

B. Morgaine tells the story of her life. When Arthur is born, she is jealous because she doesn't get attention from her mother anymore.

C. When Arthur is first born, Morgaine is jealous, believing that he has taken away the affection and attention of her mother. She comes to realize, though, that their mother would rather be with her husband than with either of her children, and so she becomes protective of Arthur.

Lead students through the process of choosing the best summary. Consider each choice. Point out that while all of the statements contain accurate information about Morgaine's relationship with Arthur, **A** has no detail and **B** has extraneous detail. **C** gives the best information, with no unnecessary details, and thus is the best choice.

he had first lain with my mother when she was still wedded to Gorlois, and there were still those who believed that this son was not Uther's but the son of the Duke of Cornwall.

How they could believe that, I could not then understand, for Gorlois, they said, was dark and aquiline,[5] and my brother was like Uther, fair-haired, with grey eyes.

Even during the lifetime of my brother, who was crowned king as Arthur, I heard all kinds of tales about how he came by his name. Even the tale that it was from Arth-Uther, Uther's bear; but it was not so. When he was a babe, he was called Gwydion[6]—bright one—because of his shining hair; the same name his son bore later—but that is another story. The facts are simple: when Gwydion was six years old he was
2 sent to be fostered by Ectorius, one of Uther's vassals[7] in the North country near Eboracum,[8] and Uther would have it that my brother should be baptized as a Christian. And so he was given the name of Arthur.

But from his birth until he was six years old, he was forever at my heels; as soon as he was weaned, my mother, Igraine, handed him over to me and said, "This is your little brother and you must love him and care for him." And I would have killed the crying thing and thrown him over the cliffs, and run after my mother begging that she should be all mine again, except that my mother cared what happened to him.

Once, when Uther came and she decked herself in her best gown, as she always did, with her amber and moonstone necklaces, and looked down on me with a careless kiss for me and one for my little brother, ready to run down to Uther, I looked at her glowing cheeks—heightened with color, her breathing quickened with delight that her man had come—and hated both Uther and my brother. And while I stood weeping at the top of the stairs, waiting for our nurse to come and take us away, he began to toddle down after her, crying out, "Mother, Mother"—he could hardly talk, then—and fell and cut his chin on the stair. I screamed for my mother, but she was on her way to the King, and she called back angrily, "Morgaine, I told you, look after the baby," and hurried on.

I picked him up, bawling, and wiped his chin with my veil. He had cut his lip on his tooth—I think he had only eight or ten, then—and he kept on wailing and calling out for my mother, but when she did not come, I sat down on the step with him in my lap, and he put up his little arms around my neck and buried his face in my tunic[9] and after a time he sobbed himself to sleep there. He was heavy on my lap, and his hair felt soft and damp; he was damp elsewhere, too, but I found I did not mind much, and in the way he clung to me I realized that in his sleep he had forgotten he was not in his mother's arms. I thought, *Igraine has forgotten both of us, abandoned him as she abandoned me. Now I must be his mother, I suppose.*

And so I shook him a little, and when he woke, he put up his little arms around my neck to be carried, and I slung him across my hip as I had seen my nurse do.

"Don't cry," I said, "I'll take you to nurse."

"Mother," he whimpered.

"Mother's gone, she's with the King," I said, "but I'll take care of you, brother." And with his chubby hand in mine I knew what Igraine meant; I was too big a girl to cry or whimper for my mother, because I had a little one to look after now.

I think I was all of seven years old. ❖

5. **aquiline** (ăk′wə-līn′): having a prominent nose, like an eagle's beak.
6. **Gwydion** (gwĭd′ē-ən).
7. **vassals** (văs′əlz): nobles subject to a king or lord.
8. **Eboracum** (ĭ-bôr′ə-kəm): the ancient Roman name for the city of York in England.
9. **tunic:** a loose-fitting garment, with or without sleeves, that extends to the knees.

Customizing Instruction

Less Proficient Readers

Have students keep these questions in mind as they read:

- Who is telling the story?
  Answer: Morgaine
- What is the narrator's relationship with the other characters?
  Answer: Igraine's daughter, Uther's stepdaughter, Arthur's half-sister
- What is the setting of the story?
  Answer: Morgaine's home, a castle

Students Acquiring English

Explain to students the following terms:

1 *nunnery*: a convent; a place where nuns live

2 *fostered:* raised, especially by someone other than one's parents

Use **Spanish Study Guide** for additional support, pp. 218–220.

Gifted and Talented

Encourage students to find out more about the lives of aristocratic women during the Middle Ages and to discuss how their findings compare with the portrayal of Igraine's life given in this excerpt. Useful books are *The Ties That Bound* by Barbara Hanawalt and *A Distant Mirror* by Barbara Tuchman.

GUIDING STUDENT RESPONSE

Connect to the Literature

1. What Do You Think?
Possible Response: Morgaine is the most sympathetic because she does, in fact, take good care of her brother even though at first she resents him very much.

Comprehension Check
- Uther is Morgaine's stepfather; Arthur is her half-brother.
- Morgaine is largely ignored by her mother, Igraine; Morgaine is expected to take care of the child.
- Possible Response: In a sense, they have both been abandoned by their parents.

Use Selection Quiz
Unit Six Resource Book, p. 43.

Think Critically

2. Students will probably note that, seen through Morgaine's eyes, the other characters in the story appear rather cold and self-absorbed. The first-person narration allows us to understand her emotions and needs.
3. Possible Response: Morgaine is a dynamic character. She learns to stop depending on her mother and to take care of Arthur.
4. Possible Responses: She might feel that it is time for the little girl to take on new responsibilities; Igraine might identify Morgaine with her previous marriage and want to distance herself from that life.
5. Possible Response: By today's standards both parents seem selfish and distant from their children, giving them attention when it is convenient.

Thinking through the LITERATURE

Connect to the Literature

1. **What Do You Think?** Which **character** do you find most sympathetic? Give reasons for your choice.

Comprehension Check
- How is Morgaine related to Uther and Arthur?
- What changes occur in Morgaine's life after Arthur is born?
- What does Morgaine feel she has in common with Arthur?

Think Critically

2. **ACTIVE READING** **ANALYZING CHARACTERS** Based on the information provided by Morgaine, what opinions did you form of Arthur, Uther, Igraine, and the narrator herself? Use the character webs in your **READER'S NOTEBOOK** to support your **analysis** of each **character.** Consider how your opinion was influenced by Morgaine's judgment.

3. Do you consider Morgaine a **static** or **dynamic character**? Explain your answer.

   THINK ABOUT
   - her behavior toward Arthur
   - her thoughts about herself
   - her relationship with her mother

4. Why do you think that Igraine begins to pull away whenever Morgaine approaches her?

5. What do you think of the way Igraine and Uther treat their children? Explain your answer.

Extend Interpretations

6. **Comparing Texts** This selection describes many of the events recounted in "The Crowning of Arthur." What differences do you see between the two selections?

7. **Critic's Corner** Critic Charlotte Spivack maintains that *The Mists of Avalon* is "probably the most ambitious retelling of the Arthurian legend in the 20th century." Why do you think so many modern writers return to Arthurian legend for their stories?

8. **Connect to Life** Based on your reading of this selection, what modern concerns do you think Bradley has in mind in her retelling of the Arthurian legend?

Literary Analysis

FIRST-PERSON POINT OF VIEW

In the **first-person point of view,** a character within the story relates the action as a participant. Because of this, the **narrator** cannot describe with certainty the thoughts and feelings of other characters. In this selection, Morgaine often expresses confusion about her mother's feelings, as in the following example:

I would have pinched him [Arthur], except that she would have hated me for it. I sometimes thought she hated me anyhow.

Readers sometimes have to be skeptical about a first-person narrator's remarks because he or she may lack objectivity or understanding.

Paired Activity With a partner, write down a list of incidents that the narrator describes. Discuss whether the narrator is objective about each of the incidents and whether she has a good understanding of the events. Use elements from the text to defend your response.

ACTIVE READING **COMPARING AND CONTRASTING**

When the same character appears in two different versions of a story, we can often gain insight into the writers' views by **comparing** and **contrasting** how that character is portrayed in each work. With a partner, discuss the similarities and differences between the portrayals of Uther Pendragon in *Le Morte d'Arthur* and *The Mists of Avalon.* To guide your discussion, go back over each selection and consider the following:
- the character's traits
- the character's actions
- the narrator's attitude

Extend Interpretations

Comparing Texts *The Mists of Avalon* gives a much more personal view. They used different points of view.

Critic's Corner The material is inherently interesting, filled with romantic events and characters larger than life; the characters and stories are well known, so a writer can offer new perspectives on events and characters with which the reader is already familiar.

Connect to Life the relationships between children and their parents and between siblings, as well as gender roles

Literary Analysis

First-Person Point of View Discuss with students whether a first-person narrator can tell the "truth" about anything other than his or her feelings.

Comparing and Contrasting When students have discussed the comparisons and contrasts, ask them why the two different authors might have used these two different interpretations of the same character.

Writing Options

Another View Using Igraine, Uther, or Arthur as the narrator, retell one of the incidents described by Morgaine. Before you begin, consider your narrator's personality traits and how he or she feels about the other characters.

Activities & Explorations

1. Igraine's Monologue Think about how Morgaine's mother might explain her actions and her relationship with her daughter. Review the selection, paying attention to how Igraine might interpret the events portrayed. Then perform a monologue in which you give her side of the story. After your performance, ask for audience feedback on the verbal and nonverbal aspects of your monologue.
~ **PERFORMING**

2. Comic Strip Create a four-panel comic strip about Morgaine's experiences growing up in Uther's household. Your comic strip may refer to incidents described in the selection or to incidents you have imagined.
~ **VIEWING AND REPRESENTING**

Inquiry & Research

Mysterious Wizard Every retelling of Arthurian legend includes Merlin, but the ways in which the wizard is portrayed vary greatly. Find out more about this legendary character and the different ways he has been characterized.

Real World Link Start your research by reading the magazine article by Bradley on page 1088.

Marion Zimmer Bradley
1930–

Other Works
The Shattered Chain
The Firebrand
Lady of Avalon

From Fan to Writer Marion Zimmer Bradley grew up on a farm in upstate New York. Her mother, a historian, encouraged her love for reading. Bradley wrote science fiction and fantasy stories as a teenager. In 1949 she married a fellow science-fiction fan named Robert Bradley. Soon afterward she started writing professionally to help support her family.

Exploring Other Worlds Bradley has published over 50 books in the science fiction and fantasy genres. Her career took off in the early 1960s with a series of novels set on "Darkover," a harsh, cold planet settled by colonists from Earth. The Darkover books are so popular that they have inspired story collections in which other writers set their tales on Bradley's fictional planet. In addition to writing fiction, Bradley has edited anthologies and magazines.

Arthurian Legends *The Mists of Avalon* was Bradley's first mainstream bestseller. Her fascination with the Arthurian legends goes back to her childhood, when she was introduced to them in a comic book series called Prince Valiant. She says that "the legends were a lot more interesting than the farming community where we lived." Bradley has written other books focusing on the Arthurian female characters.

Writing Options

Another View Encourage two or more students to examine the characters' perceptions of one another.

Activities & Explorations

1. **Igraine's Monologue** Remind students that people usually see their actions and attitudes as appropriate. Have them think of reasons that Igraine might think are very important for behaving as she does. Students should be able to justify their choice of verbal and nonverbal performance techniques by referring to their interpretation of the text.
2. **Comic Strip** Remind students that the facial expressions of the characters are very important. Such things as the details of the actual events are easier to draw, but the faces can reveal the characters' thoughts.

Inquiry & Research

Mysterious Wizard Inform students that a visit to the science fiction/fantasy section of a bookstore or library will supply them with many different versions of Merlin. T. H. White and Mary Stewart have written noteworthy books on the subject.

Mini Lesson Grammar

OBJECTIVE COMPLEMENTS Remind students that a complement is a word or group of words that completes a verb's meaning. Explain to students that an objective complement is a complement that does not refer to the subject. Objective complements never follow linking verbs.

Igraine ignored Morgaine.

Point out to students that *Morgaine* completes the verb's meaning, but does not refer to the subject. Tell students that both direct objects (objects that receive the action of a verb) and indirect objects (objects that tell *to whom* or *for whom*) are objective complements.

Igraine showed Morgaine the baby.

Point out to students that both the indirect object, *Morgaine,* and the direct object, *baby,* are objective complements.

Practice Have students copy the following sentences. Ask them to underline the objective complements of each sentence.

1. Morgaine gave Arthur reassurance.
2. At first, Arthur annoyed Morgaine.
3. Uther denied Morgaine attention.

Use **Grammar Transparencies and Copymasters,** p. 92, for more practice.

Use McDougal Littell's ***Language Network,*** Chapter 2, for more instruction in objective complements.

Internet Feature Article

Objectives
- identify main ideas (R2.0)
- paraphrase main ideas (R2.4)
- summarize an article (R2.0)

Connecting to the Literature
The excerpt from Marion Zimmer Bradley's *The Mists of Avalon* (page 1083) introduces the reader to Morgaine. She, like Merlin, is old even when young. Without the care of both Morgaine and Merlin, Arthur would not have survived.

Reading for Information

Unlike most classical characters, Merlin is portrayed in various ways.

1 Arthur and Merlin are immortal and mysterious.

2 Merlin is always there, in the background. Without Merlin's presence, Arthur would not be the legendary king that he is.

3 One can never be sure of Merlin's goals, actions, or beliefs. Trickery and magic are part of his job.

THE ONCE AND FUTURE *Merlin*

by Marion Zimmer Bradley

When the miniseries Merlin *brought the Arthurian legend to television, Marion Zimmer Bradley wrote this background article for* TV Guide. *The article describes Merlin as a split character—both good and not so good—who has a role outside of literature in the popular culture.*

1 Of all the characters in the Arthurian saga, only Arthur and Merlin are immortal in any sense other than the literary. Arthur, of course, is the warrior, the king who was and who will be, who lies in enchanted slumber until Britain has need of him again. Merlin is something else entirely, something much more mysterious.

2 Over the centuries the story has been told and retold and told again, often with a widely varying cast of characters. Knights, priests and priestesses, kings and queens, and various users of magic come and go, but always there is Arthur, the sun around which all else revolves: his faithless wife (Guinevere), his equally faithless best friend (Lancelot), the illegitimate son (Mordred) who becomes his bane[1]—and Merlin. Whatever his role, Merlin is always there, and it is always clear that Arthur could not have existed, survived, or become king without him. But Merlin's role is mostly in the background. He's visible, but no one is quite certain exactly what he has done or is doing. If Arthur is the sun, perhaps Merlin is gravity, keeping the dance of the spheres in place and at tempo, or trying to do so and occasionally failing in spots—after all, it's such a great task.

3 When the story starts, Arthur is the new character, the simple, straightforward young boy, young man, warrior and king. All of his roles are well defined. He is the light and the Christian, the champion of the New Religion. . . . Merlin is the old one—even as a young man—the magic, the enigma. . . . Merlin works by dark and in secret; even when you see him, you never know what he's up to. He's a wizard, and trickery is part of his job. He may have been created to save the Old Religion, but if he saved any of it, it was only a small part hidden away somewhere—in an oak tree, perhaps? One is never sure of Merlin's goals, let alone his actions or beliefs.

1. **bane:** a cause of death or destruction.

Reading for Information

This article falls into an unusual category of written work: it is a nonfiction piece about a famous fictional literary figure. When reading any nonfictional material that is complex or for which you have a limited background, it is helpful to stop at times to put what you are reading into your own words.

SUMMARIZING

A **summary,** a shortened version of a text put into the reader's own words, helps you to better understand the content, because you only restate the most important points.

YOUR TURN Use the questions that follow to help you summarize the writer's ideas.

1. **Identifying the Main Idea** In the first paragraph, Bradley introduces the topic of her article. Identify the **main idea** of the paragraph.
2. **Paraphrasing** In summarizing nonfiction, you zero in on major points and leave out unimportant ones. Bradley uses details in this paragraph to support the main idea. Paraphrase the most important point she makes about Merlin here.
3. In this section, Bradley contrasts her view of Merlin with the accepted views of Arthur. She states that "Merlin is the old one—even as a young man—the magic, the enigma [mystery]." Identify other specific details that support the main idea.

Merlin was the man (assuming he was a man) who came from a place no one knew, whose parentage was unknown, who had no kin in a society in which kinship was very important. . . .

So many things come from Merlin's decisions and actions; he is the point at which the paths diverge. Merlin is a set of contradictions, and each person who tells the story must find a way to deal with him (one writer even did it by having him live backward!).

When I started to write *The Mists of Avalon*, my version of the Matter of Britain, I had been incubating the work in my head for almost 40 years. Some characters were easy. . . . But when I came to Merlin and tried to create or envision a character who could do all the things he did in the story, I couldn't do it. His actions were not only mysterious; they were so inconsistent and contradictory that I could not reconcile them in a single person.

So my solution was to make "The Merlin" a title, a sort of arch-druid,[2] and use two different characters. The "old Merlin" (Taliesin) was responsible for Arthur's existence and ascension to the throne, while the "young Merlin" (Kevin) was the one who betrayed Avalon. . . . One Merlin built up Arthur and Camelot, the other helped bring them down. . . .

The story always ends with Arthur dead or otherwise out
4 of action (in his enchanted slumber), the New Religion superseding[3] the Old and Merlin somewhere out of sight.

But like Arthur, although in a different way, Merlin is immortal. Even in my version, where Kevin is killed, there would be a new Merlin to follow him. Even separate from the world, Avalon and its magic live on. And in many other versions, Merlin is shut up in a tree, which can hardly be expected to hold him forever. . . .

Perhaps Merlin has been free and wandering about, quietly working his magic behind the scenes for centuries (that was quite a storm the Spanish Armada ran into in 1588, wasn't it?), or perhaps he is still drowsing in a tree somewhere, waiting until we really need him, for whatever it is we need him for. It's clear we need him for something, but I'm still not certain just quite what it is. And I don't think we'll be comfortable with it if we get it; the comfort of the people around him was never part of Merlin's job.

2. **arch-druid:** a chief or principal priest of ancient Ireland or England who appears in literature as a prophet with magical abilities.

3. **superseding:** taking the place of or replacing.

4 Paraphrase Bradley's comments about the role of Merlin in her retelling.

Summarizing With a partner, compare your paraphrasings of the article. If necessary, revise any paraphrase that now seems incomplete. Then summarize the entire article.

MERLIN
IMAGINE A WORLD WHERE DREAMS COME TRUE... AND MAGIC IS REAL.

Advertisement for the television miniseries on Merlin.

Inquiry & Research

Activity Link: *from* The Mists of Avalon, p. 1087

Use the information in this article as well as any additional materials you've encountered about Merlin to contribute to a class chart of Merlin portrayals.

4 She creates two Merlins to represent the contradiction in his character: one who builds up Arthur and one who brings him down.

Mini Lesson Inquiry & Research

The Inquiry & Research activity on this page links to the Inquiry & Research section of Choices & Challenges on page 1087.

Instruction With students, brainstorm on the chalkboard a list of Merlin's characteristics as Bradley describes them. Add other characteristics students find in their research. Discuss generalizations about Merlin's character that can be drawn from these specific traits.

Practice In small groups, have students create charts illustrating the ways Merlin is portrayed. Instruct them to organize their charts using the generalizations they've reached about his character as a guide. Possible generalizations could include "cunning, unpredictable, magical, supportive."

OVERVIEW

This selection is included in the **Grade 10 InterActive Reader.**

Objectives

1. appreciate an excerpt from a modern version of an Arthurian **romance tale (Literary Analysis)**
2. appreciate author's **style (Literary Analysis)**
3. **make inferences (Active Reading)**

Summary

At the Whitsun banquet hosted by King Arthur, Sir Lancelot's victorious deeds are praised to the point of exaggeration. Embarrassed by the recitation of his exploits and preoccupied with his own thoughts, Lancelot leaves and shortly joins Arthur and Guinevere in the tower room, where they recall the evening's events. Lancelot confesses that he does not remember doing the deeds that people claim he has done. Guinevere inquires about his rescue of damsels, but Lancelot assures the queen that he has kept his oath of chivalrous devotion to her. Soon after Guinevere leaves them, Lancelot bids Arthur good night. On the way to his room, he meets Guinevere on the stairs. After a brief passionate moment, Lancelot breaks free and leaves, weeping bitterly.

Thematic Link

Lancelot's heroism is tested by his passionate love for his best friend's wife.

5-Minute Warm-Up

Daily Language SkillBuilder

Have students **proofread** the display sentences on page 959k and write them correctly. The sentences also appear on Transparency 29 of **Grammar Transparencies and Copymasters.**

Mini Lesson

Preteaching Vocabulary

If you would like to preteach the WORDS TO KNOW for this selection, use the Mini Lesson, pp. 1092–1093.

from The Acts of King Arthur and His Noble Knights

Romance by JOHN STEINBECK

"When she was gone, the room was bleak, and the glory was gone from it."

Connect to Your Life

Fame for a Day Think of a famous person you admire. Make notes on what it would be like to live the life of this person for one day, including both positive and negative aspects. Then discuss your ideas with classmates, comparing your views of fame with theirs.

Build Background

Steinbeck and Arthur In this selection, modern novelist John Steinbeck portrays what it might be like to be Lancelot (also spelled *Launcelot*), the most famous knight of the Round Table. From childhood, Steinbeck was fascinated by the Arthurian legend, and as an adult he attempted to set down a retelling that his own sons could enjoy. He researched the legend in England and Italy, studying rare manuscripts, and wrote in a room he named Joyous Garde, after Lancelot's castle. Unfortunately, Steinbeck never completed his version of the legend; in 1976, several years after his death, his unfinished work was published as *The Acts of King Arthur and His Noble Knights.* The excerpt you are about to read offers a new perspective on some of the events from Malory's tale of Sir Launcelot.

WORDS TO KNOW
Vocabulary Preview

carriage	haggard
decorous	intemperate
disparagement	penitence
exalt	reprisal
fallible	vagrant

Focus Your Reading

LITERARY ANALYSIS STYLE In his introduction to *The Acts of King Arthur and His Noble Knights,* Steinbeck states his aim to set down the story of Arthur in "plain present-day speech," avoiding the archaic language of Malory's version. As you read the excerpt, notice the distinctive aspects of the author's **style.** Consider how Steinbeck's style adds to his retelling of Arthurian legend.

ACTIVE READING MAKING INFERENCES **Inferences** are logical guesses based on information in the text, common sense, and your own experience. To get the most out of this story, which presents a day in the life of the famed Lancelot, you will need to make **inferences,** or logical guesses, about Lancelot's feelings and behavior. For example, when Queen Guinevere (also spelled *Gwynevere*) asks Lancelot whether he has really encountered fair queen enchantresses, he looks away nervously and does not answer her directly. The reader can infer that he did meet such women and that he does not want to tell Guinevere about his encounters. As you read, look for other clues to help you understand Lancelot.

READER'S NOTEBOOK Keep track of your inferences by making a chart like the one shown. Consider both the evidence in the text and your own experience when making your inferences.

Inferences About Lancelot

	Clues	Inferences
His Attitude Toward His Fame		
His Feelings About Guinevere		
Other Aspects of His Life		

VIDEODISC **LaserLinks: Background for Reading** Cultural Connection

LESSON RESOURCES

UNIT SIX RESOURCE BOOK, pp. 44–49

ASSESSMENT RESOURCES

Formal Assessment, pp. 173–174

Teacher's Guide to Assessment and Portfolio Use

Test Generator

SKILLS TRANSPARENCIES AND COPYMASTERS

Literary Analysis

- Style, Voice, Diction, Purpose, T22 (for Literary Analysis, p. 1099)

Reading and Critical Thinking

- Making Inferences, T7 (for Think Critically, item 2, p. 1099)

Grammar

- Making Compound Predicates Parallel I, C88 (for Mini Lesson, p. 1100)
- Making Compound Predicates Parallel II, C89 (for Mini Lesson, p. 1100)

Vocabulary

- Context Clues, C95 (for Mini Lesson, p. 1092)
- Prefixes, C96 (for Mini Lesson, p. 1094)

Writing

- Levels of Language, T12 (for Writing Options 1 and 2, p. 1100)
- The Uses of Dialogue, T24 (for Writing Option 3, p. 1100)

Communications

- Interviewing, T9 (for Activities & Explorations 1, p. 1100)
- Impromptu Speaking: Dialogue, Role-Play, Debate, T13 (for Activities & Explorations 2, p. 1100)

INTEGRATED TECHNOLOGY

Audio Library

LaserLinks

- Cultural Connection: Castle Life
- Author Background: John Steinbeck
- Historical Connection: The Castles of England

See **Teacher's SourceBook,** p. 57

Visit our website: www.mcdougallittell.com

from THE ACTS *of* KING ARTHUR *and* HIS NOBLE KNIGHTS

JOHN STEINBECK

TEACHING THE LITERATURE

Customizing Instruction

Less Proficient Readers
Have students keep these questions in mind as they read:

- What is the setting of the story?
  Answer: A royal banquet and the royal quarters in Winchester.
- What is the main conflict in the story?
  Possible Response: The conflict between Lancelot's devotion to Arthur and his devotion to Guinevere.

Set a Purpose Ask students to read to find out how Lancelot and Queen Guinevere feel about each other.

Gifted and Talented
In his introduction to *The Acts of King Arthur*, Steinbeck writes: "In no sense do I wish to rewrite Malory, or reduce him, or change him, or soften or sentimentalize him." Have students work in pairs to analyze Lancelot's personality in episodes of Malory's account and debate whether Steinbeck has softened or sentimentalized Malory's portrayal of Lancelot.

BLOCK SCHEDULING: MANAGING TIME

If your schedule requires that you cover the lesson objectives in a shorter time, use . . .

- Preparing to Read, p. 1090
- Thinking Through the Literature, p. 1099
- Vocabulary in Action, p. 1100
- Grammar in Context, p. 1101

If you want to take advantage of longer class time, use . . .

- TE Teaching Options: Preteaching Vocabulary, pp. 1092–1093; Viewing and Representing, p. 1095; Standardized Test Practice, p. 1098
- Choices & Challenges, pp.1100–1101

Reading and Analyzing

Reading Skills and Strategies: PREVIEW

Have students preview the selection. Ask them to study the portraits on pages 1093 and 1095, and read the Build Background feature on page 1090. Encourage students to predict how Steinbeck's portrayal of Arthur and Lancelot may differ from Malory's (and Bradley's). Before students begin reading, give them a brief summary of the selection.

Active Reading MAKING INFERENCES

Students make inferences all the time when they make logical guesses based on common sense and available information. For example, students can make inferences that may explain why Lancelot bowed his head and dozed during the testimony to his greatness.

Use **Unit Six Resource Book,** p. 45 for more practice.

Literary Analysis STYLE

Important elements that contribute to the author's style are word choice (or diction), tone, syntax, and figures of speech. In this selection, Steinbeck uses elevated diction and complex sentences. As students read the first few paragraphs, have them find examples of these elements. Discuss why Steinbeck chooses this particular style for his retelling of the Arthurian story.

Use **Unit Six Resource Book,** p. 46 for more practice.

King Arthur held Whitsun[1] court at Winchester, that ancient royal town favored by God and His clergy as well as the seat and tomb of many kings. The roads were clogged with eager people, knights returning to stamp in court the record of their deeds, of bishops, clergy, monks, of the defeated fettered to their paroles,[2] the prisoners of honor. And on Itchen water, pathway from Solent[3] and the sea, the little
1 ships brought succulents, lampreys, eels and
2 oysters, plaice and sea trout, while barges loaded with casks of whale oil and casks of wine came tide borne. Bellowing oxen walked to the spits on their own four hooves, while geese and swans, sheep and swine, waited their turn in hurdle pens. Every householder with a strip of colored cloth, a ribbon, any textile gaiety, hung it from a window to flap its small festival, and those in lack tied boughs of pine and laurel over their doors.

In the great hall of the castle on the hill the king sat high, and next below the fair elite company of the Round Table, noble and decorous as kings themselves, while at the long trestle boards the people were as fitted as toes in a tight shoe.

Then while the glistening meat dripped down the tables, it was the custom for the defeated to celebrate the deeds of those who had overcome them, while the victor dipped his head in disparagement of his greatness and fended off the compliments with small defensive gestures of his hands. And as at public penitence sins are given stature they do not deserve, little sins grow up and baby sins are born, so those knights who lately claimed mercy perchance might raise the exploits of the brave and merciful beyond reasonable gratitude for their lives and in anticipation of some small notice of value.

This no one said of Lancelot, sitting with bowed head in his golden-lettered seat at the Round Table. Some said he nodded and perhaps dozed, for the testimony to his greatness was long and the monotony of his victories continued for many hours. Lancelot's immaculate fame had grown so great that men took pride in being unhorsed by him—even this notice was an honor. And since he had won many victories, it is possible that knights he had never seen claimed to have been overthrown by him. It was a way to claim attention for a moment. And as he dozed and wished to be otherwhere, he heard his deeds exalted beyond his recognition, and some mighty exploits once attributed to other men were brought bright-painted out and laid on the shining pile of his achievements. There is a seat of worth beyond the reach of envy whose occupant ceases to be a man and becomes the receptacle of the wishful longings of the world, a seat most often reserved for the dead, from whom neither reprisal nor reward may be expected, but at this time Sir Lancelot was its unchallenged tenant. And he vaguely heard his strength favorably compared with elephants, his ferocity with lions, his agility with deer, his cleverness with foxes, his beauty with the stars, his justice with Solon,[4] his stern probity[5] with St. Michael, his humility with newborn lambs; his military

1. **Whitsun:** another name for Pentecost, a Christian festival celebrated on the seventh Sunday after Easter.
2. **fettered to their paroles:** bound by their word of honor to lay down arms.
3. **Itchen . . . Solent:** waterways in southern England.
4. **Solon:** Athenian statesman and lawgiver who lived in the sixth century B.C.
5. **probity:** uprightness; honesty.

WORDS TO KNOW

decorous (dĕk′ər-əs) *adj.* behaving in a manner appropriate to the occasion; proper
disparagement (dĭ-spăr′ĭj-mənt) *n.* belittlement
penitence (pĕn′ĭ-təns) *n.* expression of regret for sins or wrongdoing
exalt (ĭg-zôlt′) *v.* to glorify, praise, or honor
reprisal (rĭ-prī′zəl) *n.* retaliation in the form of harm or injury similar to that received; revenge

Teaching Options

Mini Lesson Preteaching Vocabulary

USING CONTEXT CLUES Call students' attention to the list of WORDS TO KNOW. Remind them that sometimes they can understand the meaning of an unfamiliar word by examining the context in which the word is used. Use the following sentence to demonstrate the strategy of using context clues to determine word meaning:

Many people who strive for perfection are dismayed to discover they are *fallible*.

Instruction

- Write the sentence on the board.
- Ask a volunteer to summarize the meaning of the sentence.
- Have students use the context clues in the sentence to infer the meaning of the word *fallible*.
- Ask a volunteer to use the word *fallible* in a sentence.

Exercise Read the following sentences. Ask students to use context clues to determine the meaning of the italicized terms.

1. Unlike her cousin, who kept talking with her mouth full at the table, Elaine acted in a *decorous* manner.

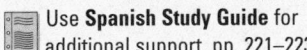

Study for Lancelot (1893), Sir Edward Burne-Jones. From *Drawings of Sir Edward Burne-Jones*, published by Charles Scribner's Sons, New York. Photo by Hollyer.

Customizing Instruction

Less Proficient Readers

Have students ask themselves the following questions in order to understand the character of Lancelot:

- How does Lancelot respond as he is being praised?
  Answer: He ducks his head and wishes to be elsewhere.
- Why do knights brag about being defeated by Lancelot?
  Possible Response: It is a way of sharing in Lancelot's fame.
- Does Lancelot seem happy?
  Answer: No

Students Acquiring English

Explain to students the following terms:

1 *succulents:* juicy plants or animals

2 *plaice:* a flounder, a type of fish

Use **Spanish Study Guide** for additional support, pp. 221–223.

2. Because of the *disparagement* he received the first time he tried, Lee was afraid to ask another girl to the dance.
3. If you have done something wrong, an act of *penitence* might make you feel better.
4. Kyle *exalts* his teacher by putting her on a pedestal.
5. Being robbed is an appropriate *reprisal* for a thief.
6. My grandmother led a *vagrant* lifestyle, moving from one city to another until she finally met my grandfather and settled down.
7. When he moved across the stage, the ballet dancer's *carriage* was graceful.
8. Overeating is *intemperate* behavior.
9. Yvonne looked *haggard* after staying up all night to study for the test.

Use **Unit Six Resource Book,** p. 47 for more exercises.

A lesson on synonyms appears on p. 1000 in the Pupil's Edition.

Reading and Analyzing

ACTIVE READING

A EVALUATE **Possible Responses:** The knights sincerely admire Lancelot and his bravery; Lancelot has become a mythic hero, even in his own day; in addition, anything they can say about him draws them closer to him, reflecting glory on them, as well.

Literary Analysis STYLE

B Note Steinbeck's word choice in describing the three characters who are ill at ease. Discuss how Steinbeck's diction makes the characters' state so vivid that the reader also senses their discomfort.
Possible Responses: Steinbeck uses simple, succinct descriptions such as "sat very still and did not fiddle with his bread," "still as a painted statue," and "studied the open pages of his hands," to portray the awkward feelings of the characters.

Literary Analysis: DESCRIPTIVE DETAIL

C Guide students to analyze the details in this passage to explain what they reveal about the society Steinbeck is portraying.
Possible Response: It is a highly ordered society bound by strict rules and codes of conduct. There is a great division between the nobility and the commoners. The "painted wire" reveals that it can also be a cruel, confining world where transgressions are harshly punished.

ACTIVE READING

D QUESTION **Possible Responses:** They are embarrassed by the excessive praise; they are tired and bored.

---

niche would have caused the Archangel Gabriel[6] to raise his head. Sometimes the guests paused in their chewing the better to hear, and a man who slopped his metheglin[7] drew frowns.

> ACTIVE READING
> **A** **EVALUATE** Why do you think the knights are so extravagant in their praise of Lancelot?

Arthur on his dais[8] sat very still and did not fiddle with his bread, and beside him sat lovely Guinevere, still as a painted statue of herself. **B** Only her inward eyes confessed her vagrant thoughts. And Lancelot studied the open pages of his hands—not large hands, but delicate where they were not knobby and scarred with old wounds. His hands were fine-textured—soft of skin and very white, protected by the pliant leather lining of his gauntlets. **1**

The great hall was not still, not all upturned listening. Everywhere was movement as people came and went, some serving huge planks of meat and baskets of bread, round and flat like a plate. And there were restless ones who could not sit still, while everyone under burden of half-chewed meat and the floods and freshets of mead and beer found necessity for repeated departures and returns.

Lancelot exhausted the theme of his hands and squinted down the long hall and watched the movement with eyes so nearly closed that he could not see faces. And he thought how he knew everyone by carriage. The knights in long full floor-brushing robes walked lightly or thought their feet barely touched the ground because their bodies were released from their crushing boxes of iron. **C** Their feet were long and slender because, being horsemen, they had never widened and flattened their feet with walking. The ladies, full-skirted, moved like water, but this was schooled and designed, taught to little girls with the help of whips on raw ankles, while their shoulders were bound back with nail-studded harnesses and their heads held high and rigid by painful collars of woven willow or, for the forgetful, by supports of painted wire, for to learn the high proud head on a swan's neck, to learn to flow like water, is not easy for a little girl as she becomes a gentlewoman. But knights and ladies both matched their movements to their garments; the sweep and rhythm of a long gown informs the manner of its moving. It is not necessary to inspect a serf or a slave, his shoulder wide and sloping from burdens, legs short and thick and crooked, feet splayed and widespread, the whole frame slowly crushed by weights. In the great hall the serving people walked under burdens with the slow weight of oxen and scuttled like crabs, crooked and nervous when the weight was gone.

A pause in the recital of his virtues drew Lancelot's attention. The knight who had tried to kill him in a tree had finished, and among the benches Sir Kay was rising to his feet. Lancelot could hear his voice before he spoke, reciting deeds like leaves and bags and barrels. Before his friend could reach the center of the hall, Sir Lancelot wriggled to his feet and approached the dais. "My lord king," he said, "forgive me if I ask leave to go. An old wound has broken open."

Arthur smiled down on him. "I have the same old wound," he said. "We'll go together. Perhaps you will come to the tower room when we have attended to our wounds." **D** And he signed the trumpets to end the gathering, and the bodyguards to clear the hall.

> ACTIVE READING
> **QUESTION** Why do you think Lancelot and Arthur suddenly leave the hall?

6. **St. Michael . . . Archangel Gabriel:** In several religious traditions, Michael and Gabriel are archangels, the chief messengers of God. Both are celebrated as warriors against evil.
7. **metheglin** (mə-thĕg′lĭn): a liquor made from honey.
8. **dais** (dā′ĭs): a raised platform used for a seat of honor.

WORDS TO KNOW
vagrant (vā′grənt) *adj.* wandering
carriage (kăr′ĭj) *n.* manner of moving one's body

1094

Teaching Options

Mini Lesson Vocabulary Strategy

PREFIXES Instruction Many prefixes—word parts found at the beginnings of some words—are based upon Greek or Latin roots. Tell students that learning the meanings of prefixes will help them determine the meanings of unfamiliar words. The word *intemperate*, for instance, begins with the prefix *in-*, which means "not." *Intemperate*, therefore, means "not temperate," or "extreme." Other prefixes with the same or similar meaning are *il-*, *ir-*, *non-*, *un-*, and *dis-*.

Practice Have students work in pairs to find the meanings of five other words with these prefixes that they find in the selection. (Using a dictionary will help them learn the meanings of different prefixes.) Have the students apply the meaning of the prefix to determine the word's meaning. Ask them to use each word in a sentence. Finally, ask students to describe how they can use knowledge of prefixes to remember the meanings of these words.

Use **Vocabulary Transparencies and Copymasters,** p. 96, for more practice.

A lesson on prefixes appears on p. 856 in the Pupil's Edition.

Study on Brown Paper (1895), Sir Edward Burne-Jones. From *Drawings of Sir Edward Burne-Jones*, published by Charles Scribner's Sons, New York. Photo by Hollyer.

1095

Customizing Instruction

Students Acquiring English

Explain to students the following words:

1 *pliant:* easily bent; flexible

2 *serf:* a person bound to the land and under the landowner's control

Less Proficient Readers

3 Discuss the interchange between Lancelot and Arthur when they talk about their wounds. Ask students whether Lancelot really has a reopened wound and what Arthur means when he says that he had the same wound.

Possible Response: No. Lancelot is just looking for an excuse to escape his discomfort. Arthur means that he is also uncomfortable and ready to leave.

Multiple Learning Styles

Kinesthetic Learners

Students might enjoy pantomiming Lancelot's body language during the long recitations of his virtues.

Mini Lesson: Viewing and Representing

Study on Brown Paper **by Sir Edward Burne-Jones**

ART APPRECIATION This study exemplifies the Pre-Raphaelites' concern for purity of form, stylization, and high moral tone, qualities they perceived in medieval painting and design. Burne-Jones was a key figure in the revival of medieval arts led by his Oxford friend William Morris, a noted poet and artist. Burne-Jones designed stained-glass windows, tapestries, and mosaics in the medieval mode.

Application Ask students what similarities and differences they see between this picture and Burne-Jones's study of Lancelot on page 1093. How do these qualities affect their perceptions of the main characters in this selection?

Possible Responses: Both are dressed in a simple style, suggesting they are not pretentious. Neither character is facing the artist—both appear to be pensive. However, Lancelot's brow is furrowed, and he is looking downward, not out. Both of these latter features suggest that his thoughts are more intense or troubling than Guinevere's.

Reading and Analyzing

Reading Skills and Strategies: VISUALIZE

A Have students visualize the castle, noting the location of the keep, the strongest, most secure part of a medieval castle. Point out that King Arthur invites Lancelot to the keep, and ask students what this reveals about the relationship between the king and his knight.

Possible Responses: Welcoming Lancelot into the keep—the heart of his home—reveals that the king trusts Lancelot with his life.

Literary Analysis STYLE

B Call attention to the use of dialogue in this passage. Invite volunteers to analyze the diction, sentence structure, and tone to discover what they reveal about Lancelot. Then ask students if this is how they would expect Lancelot to speak.

Possible Response: The commonplace words, simple sentences, and humble tone reveal a modest, self-effacing man—the ideal heroic character. Judging from his reaction to the praise in the hall, this is not a surprising way for Lancelot to speak.

ACTIVE READING

C **INFER** **Possible Response:** Lancelot loves Guinevere deeply and passionately. However, he realizes that his love can only be offered from a distance.

The stone stairway to the king's room was in the thickness of the wall of the round tower of the keep. At short intervals a deep embrasure[9] and a long, beveled[10] arrow slit commanded some aspect of the town below.

No armed men guarded this stairway. They were below and had passed Sir Lancelot in. The king's room was round, a horizontal slice of the tower, windowless save for the arrow slits, entered by a narrow arched door. It was a sparsely furnished room, carpeted with rushes. A wide bed, and at its foot a carved oaken chest, a bench before the fireplace, and several stools completed the furnishing. But the raw stone of the tower was plastered over and painted with solemn figures of men and angels walking hand in hand. Two candles and the reeky fire gave the only light.

When Lancelot entered, the queen stood up from the bench before the fire, saying, "I will retire, my lords."

"No, stay," said Arthur.

"Stay," said Lancelot.

The king was stretched comfortably in the bed. His bare feet projecting from his long saffron[11] robe caressed each other, the toes curled downward.

The queen was lovely in the firelight, all lean, down-flowing lines of green samite.[12] She wore her little mouth-corner smile of concealed amusement, and her bold golden eyes were the same color as her hair, and odd it was that her lashes and slender brows were dark, an oddity contrived with kohl[13] brought in a small enameled pot from an outland by a far-wandering knight.

"How are you holding up?" Arthur asked.

"Not well, my lord. It's harder than the quest."

"Did you really do all the things they said you did?"

Lancelot chuckled. "Truthfully, I don't know. It sounds different when they tell about it. And most of them feel it necessary to add a little. When I remember leaping eight feet, they tell it at fifty, and frankly I don't recall several of those giants at all."

The queen made room for him on the fire bench, and he took his seat, back to the fire.

Guinevere said, "The damsel—what's her name—talked about fair queen enchantresses,[14] but she was so excited that her words tumbled over each other. I couldn't make out what happened."

Lancelot looked nervously away. "You know how excitable young girls are," he said. "A little back-country necromancy[15] in a pasture."

"But she spoke particularly of queens."

"My lady, I think everyone is a queen to her. It's like the giants—makes the story richer."

"Then they were not queens?"

"Well, for that matter, when you get into the field of enchantment, everyone is a queen, or thinks she is. Next time she tells it, the little damsel will be a queen. I do think, my lord, there's too much of that kind of thing going on. It's a bad sign, a kind of restlessness, when people go in for fortunetelling and all such things. Maybe there should be a law about it."

"There is," said Arthur. "But it's not in secular hands. The Church is supposed to take care of that."

"Yes, but some of the nunneries are going in for it."

"Well, I'll put a bug in the archbishop's ear."

The queen observed, "I gather you rescued damsels by the dozen." She put her fingers on

---

9. **embrasure** (ĕm-brā′zhər): opening in a wall, through which cannons are fired.
10. **beveled:** having a sloping edge.
11. **saffron:** golden yellow, named for the spice that has that color.
12. **samite:** a heavy silk fabric.
13. **kohl:** a cosmetic preparation used as eye makeup.
14. **fair queen enchantresses:** Morgan le Fay and three other queens, the four of whom, as related in "Sir Launcelot du Lake," imprisoned Lancelot, demanding that he take one of them as his lover.
15. **necromancy:** magic.

his arm and a searing shock ran through his body, and his mouth opened in amazement at a hollow ache that pressed upward against his ribs and shortened his breath.

After a moment she said, "How many damsels did you rescue?"

His mouth was dry. "Of course there were a few, madame. There always are."

"And all of them made love to you?"

"That they did not, madame. There you protect me."

"I?"

"Yes. Since with my lord's permission I swore to serve you all my life and gave my knightly courtly love to you, I am sheltered from damsels by your name."

"And do you want to be sheltered?"

ACTIVE READING

INFER How does Lancelot feel about Guinevere?

"Yes, my lady. I am a fighting man. I have neither time nor inclination for any other kind of love. I hope this pleases you, my lady. I sent many prisoners to ask your mercy."

"I never saw such a crop of them," Arthur said. "You must have swept some counties clean."

Guinevere touched him on the arm again and with side-glancing golden eyes saw the spasm that shook him. "While we are on this subject, I want to mention one lady you did not save. When I saw her, she was a headless corpse and not in good condition, and the man who brought her in was half crazed."[16]

"I am ashamed of that," said Lancelot. "She was under my protection, and I failed her. I suppose it was my shame that made me force the man to do it. I'm sorry. I hope you released him from the burden."

"Not at all," she said. "I wanted him away before the feast reeked up the heavens. I sent him with his burden to the Pope. His friend will not improve on the way. And if his loss of interest in ladies continues, he may turn out to be a very holy man, a hermit or something of that nature, if he isn't a maniac first."

The king rose on his elbow. "We will have to work out some system," he said. "The rules of errantry[17] are too loose, and the quests overlap. Besides, I wonder how long we can leave justice in the hands of men who are themselves unstable. I don't mean you, my friend. But there may come a time when order and organization from the crown will be necessary."

The queen stood up. "My lords, will you grant me permission to leave you now? I know you will wish to speak of great things foreign and perhaps tiresome to a lady's ears."

The king said, "Surely, my lady. Go to your rest."

"No, sire—not rest. If I do not lay out the designs for the needlepoint, my ladies will have no work tomorrow."

"But these are feast days, my dear."

"I like to give them something every day, my lord. They're lazy things and some of them so woolly in the mind that they forget how to thread a needle from day to day. Forgive me, my lords."

She swept from the room with proud and powerful steps, and the little breeze she made in the still air carried a strange scent to Lancelot, a perfume which sent a shivering excitement coursing through his body. It was an odor he did not, could not, know, for it was the smell of Guinevere distilled by her own skin. And as she passed through the door and descended the steps, he saw himself leap up and follow her, although he did not move. And when she was gone, the room was bleak, and the glory was gone from it, and Sir Lancelot was dog-weary, tired almost to weeping.

"What a queen she is," said King Arthur softly.

16. **When I saw her . . . half crazed:** Guinevere is referring to a woman Lancelot was unable to save—a woman who was beheaded by her jealous husband. As punishment, Lancelot commanded the husband to take the woman's body to Guinevere and to throw himself on her mercy.

17. **errantry** (ĕr′ən-trē): the knightly pursuit of adventure.

Customizing Instruction

Less Proficient Readers

To help students understand the relationship between Lancelot and Guinevere, ask them the following questions:

- Why do you think Guinevere questions Lancelot about the damsels he rescued?
  Possible Response: She is jealous.
- Why does Lancelot feel so lonely?
  Possible Response: He loves Guinevere but she is Arthur's wife and therefore unattainable.

Set a Purpose Have students read on to find out what will happen between Lancelot and Guinevere.

Students Acquiring English

1 Explain to students that "How are you holding up?" means "How are you doing?"

Gifted and Talented

Have students read more of *The Acts of King Arthur and His Noble Knights*. Suggest that they compare an episode from Steinbeck's version to a similar one in Malory's version.

Reading and Analyzing

Literary Analysis STYLE

Ask students to describe Lancelot's tone when he speaks with Arthur. **Possible Response:** His tone is restrained, humble, and somewhat dispirited.

ACTIVE READING

A EVALUATE Possible Responses: Arthur is right to marry the woman he loved; Merlin is right to warn him that he would be hurt.

"And what a woman equally. Merlin was with me when I chose her. He tried to dissuade me with his usual doomful prophecies. That was one of the few times I differed with him. Well, my choice has proved him fallible. She has shown the world what a queen should be. All other women lose their sheen when she is present."

ACTIVE READING

A EVALUATE Who do you think is right about Arthur's marriage, Merlin or Arthur?

Lancelot said, "Yes, my lord," and for no reason he knew, except perhaps the intemperate dullness of the feast, he felt lost, and a cold knife of loneliness pressed against his heart.

The king was chuckling. "It is the device of ladies that their lords have great matters to discuss, when if the truth were told, we bore them. And I hope the truth is never told. Why, you look haggard, my friend. Are you feverish? Did you mean that about an old wound opening?"

"No. The wound was what you thought it was, my lord. But it is true that I can fight, travel, live on berries, fight again, go without sleeping, and come out fresh and fierce, but sitting still at Whitsun feast has wearied me to death."

Arthur said, "I can see it. We'll discuss the realm's health another time. Go to your bed now. Have you your old quarters?"

"No—better ones. Sir Kay has cleared five knights from the lovely lordly rooms over the north gate. He did it in memory of an adventure which we, God help us, will have to listen to tomorrow. I accept your dismissal, my lord."

And Lancelot knelt down and took the king's beloved hand in both of his and kissed it. "Good night, my liege[18] lord, my liege friend," he said and then stumbled blindly from the room and felt his way down the curving stone steps past the arrow slits.

As he came to the level of the next landing, Guinevere issued silently from a darkened entrance. He could see her in the thin light from the arrow slit. She took his arm and led him to her dark chamber and closed the oaken door.

"A strange thing happened," she said softly. "When I left you, I thought you followed me. I was so sure of it I did not even look around to verify it. You were there behind me. And when I came to my own door, I said good night to you, so certain I was that you were there."

He could see her outline in the dark and smell the scent which was herself. "My lady," he said, "when you left the room, I saw myself follow you as though I were another person looking on."

Their bodies locked together as though a trap had sprung. Their mouths met, and each devoured the other. Each frantic heartbeat at the walls of ribs trying to get to the other until their held breaths burst out and Lancelot, dizzied, found the door and blundered down the stairs. And he was weeping bitterly. ❖

18. **liege** (lēj): under feudal law, entitled to the service or allegiance of subjects.

WORDS TO KNOW
fallible (făl′ə-bəl) *adj.* capable of being wrong or mistaken
intemperate (ĭn-tĕm′pər-ĭt) *adj.* extreme
haggard (hăg′ərd) *adj.* appearing worn and exhausted

Teaching Options

Standardized Test Practice

ALTERNATIVE ENDING You can informally assess students' understanding of the selection by having them imagine a different ending in which Lancelot does *not* betray Arthur by giving in to his feelings for Guinevere. Ask them to think of what might replace the inevitable tragic ending of the story which is to come. Have them write a paragraph (about 100 words) describing this different ending.

RUBRIC

3 **Full Accomplishment** Response reflects a full understanding of circumstances of the story.

2 **Substantial Accomplishment** Response shows a general understanding of the circumstances of the story.

1 **Little or Partial Accomplishment** Response shows little or no understanding of the circumstances of the story.

Connect to the Literature

1. **What Do You Think?** Were you surprised by Lancelot's actions at the end of this selection? Why or why not?

Comprehension Check
- Why is Lancelot praised at the feast?
- What reason does he give for leaving the feast?
- What happens in Guinevere's room?

Think Critically

2. **ACTIVE READING** MAKING INFERENCES What **inferences** did you make about Lancelot as you were reading? Explain your views, making use of the chart that you created in your READER'S NOTEBOOK.

3. The knights' tributes to Lancelot imply that he is a "winner." Do you think Lancelot would agree?

THINK ABOUT
- his fame and his achievements
- his relationships with Arthur and Guinevere
- why Lancelot weeps as he goes down the stairs

4. How does the view of fame presented in this selection compare with the views about fame expressed in your discussion for the Connect to Your Life activity on page 1090?

5. Do you think the amount of **detail** Steinbeck includes adds to or detracts from the story? Explain your opinion.

THINK ABOUT
- the description of the town and of Arthur's great hall during the feast
- Lancelot's observations about the carriage of different groups in society
- the physical descriptions of Lancelot, Arthur, and Guinevere

Extend Interpretations

6. **Comparing Texts** Based on the excerpts from *Le Morte d'Arthur* and *The Acts of King Arthur and His Noble Knights,* what generalizations can you make about the character of Arthur?

7. **Connect to Life** Consider this statement in Steinbeck's tale: "There is a seat of worth beyond the reach of envy whose occupant ceases to be a man and becomes the receptacle of the wishful longings of the world." What modern-day figures, male or female, might you apply this statement to?

Literary Analysis

STYLE **Style** is the particular way in which a piece of literature is written. Style refers not so much to what is said but to how it is said. **Descriptive detail, dialogue,** depth of **characterization, diction** (word choice), and **tone** all contribute to a writer's style. Though both Steinbeck and Baines (author of "The Crowning of Arthur" and "Sir Launcelot du Lake" on page 1064) rely on the same sources for their versions of the Arthurian legend, each writer retells the legend in his own distinctive style. Baines, for instance, in trying to render Malory's work, includes much less descriptive detail than Steinbeck does.

Paired Activity Working with a partner, compare the styles of Baines and Steinbeck. Complete a chart like the one shown, noting key aspects of each author's style. After completing your chart, write a sentence for each author, summing up his style.

Style	Baines	Steinbeck
Descriptive Detail		
Dialogue		
Characterization		
Diction		
Tone		

GUIDING STUDENT RESPONSE

Connect to the Literature

1. **What Do You Think?**
Possible Responses: No—there are details that show the strong attraction between the two; yes—given Lancelot's role as a knight and his professed values, we might expect him to resist his feelings for Guinevere.

Comprehension Check
- He is praised for his great prowess as a knight.
- An old wound is giving him trouble.
- Lancelot and Guinevere share a passionate, breathless embrace, then Lancelot flees.

Use Selection Quiz **Unit Six Resource Book,** p. 49.

Think Critically

2. Lancelot is a flawed human being, not a mythic figure. He may be struggling to live up to his image; he professes not to remember his good deeds. In fact, Lancelot becomes bored and maybe uncomfortable listening to people praise him. The final scene, in which he briefly succumbs to desire and then runs away, shows a deep moral conflict.
3. Possible Responses: Yes—he knows the truth of what he has accomplished; no—he feels ashamed by some of his actions.
4. Students may realize that living up to a reputation, especially one larger than life, can be a tremendous burden or an ongoing struggle.
5. Possible Responses: The amount of detail creates a strong picture of the setting, the times, and the characters; it detracts from the story because a story of great mythic figures should not focus on minutiae.

Extend Interpretations

Comparing Texts Possible Response: Arthur is a great king, embodying the values and virtues of his followers, the Knights of the Round Table. He is loyal to his knights and to Guinevere, but a mighty foe to his enemies.

Connect to Life Students will come up with various names and roles. The list might include sports stars, religious leaders, political leaders such as the president, leaders in areas such as the military, civil rights and women's rights, and even entertainers.

Literary Analysis

Style To make valid comparisons, students must analyze the characteristics of clearly written texts including patterns of organization, syntax, and word choices. When the pairs have finished their charts and summary sentences, have them compare results. Encourage them to discuss any differences in their results, explaining their reasoning.

Writing Options

1. **Castle News** Bring in newspapers so that students can study the society column as an example. Remind them not to forget to describe the food, the entertainment, and the famous people in attendance.
2. **Lancelot Interview** Have students look at interviews in entertainment magazines to get ideas for format and content.
3. **Arthurian Soap Opera** Encourage students to use the clichéd dialogue popular on soap operas.

Activities & Explorations

1. **Dramatized Interview** Remind students that Arthur and his court would certainly want to make a good impression and would therefore present their values and ideals in a positive way.
2. **Walk the Walk** It might be fun to include an element of guessing in the demonstration, to see if the audience can correctly identify each character that the "walkers" imitate.

Inquiry & Research

Medieval Castles Your students will likely notice that, although the castle was home to the aristocrats, it had fewer comforts and conveniences than a modest modern-day house. Its primary purpose, of course, was defense, and their diagrams should reflect this.

Vocabulary in Action

1. exalt
2. haggard
3. intemperate
4. carriage
5. vagrant
6. decorous
7. penitence
8. disparagement
9. reprisal
10. fallible

Choices & CHALLENGES

Writing Options

1. **Castle News** Pretend you are a society reporter covering the feast at the castle. Write a brief feature article describing the event.
2. **Lancelot Interview** In an interview to be published in a celebrity magazine, have Lancelot discuss his views about fame.
3. **Arthurian Soap-Opera** Write a soap-opera scene in which Guinevere discusses her plight with one of her ladies-in-waiting.

Activities & Explorations

1. **Dramatized Interview** Imagine that a foreign visitor has come to Winchester to interview Arthur, Guinevere, and Lancelot about their values and ideals. In a small group, create a dramatization of that interview. ~ **SPEAKING AND LISTENING**
2. **Walk the Walk** Lancelot believes he can identify people by their gait, or way of walking. Reread the description of the gaits of knights, ladies, and serfs, beginning on page 1094. With two classmates, present a demonstration of each gait for the class. After your demonstration, offer an oral explanation of your analysis and interpretation of the text. ~ **PERFORMING**

Inquiry & Research

Medieval Castles Research the design and construction of medieval English castles. Then create a diagram of Arthur's castle, using the information that you find as well as details from the selection. Place your notes and diagram in your **Working Portfolio.**

Vocabulary in Action

EXERCISE: CONTEXT CLUES Fill in each blank with the Word to Know that best completes the sentence.

1. Although medieval romances often ________ knights and their gallantry, nonfiction accounts of the times are generally more critical.
2. Most people were poor, had inadequate diets, worked constantly, and slept on thin straw mats, leaving them ________ and in poor health.
3. Even nobles were uncomfortable, for castles were freezing cold in the winter, hot and stuffy in the summer—in short, miserable places in any ________ weather.
4. The ladies who walked so elegantly learned that graceful ________ through harsh, even cruel, training in their youth.
5. Most knights served a single lord; some, however, lived a more _____ life, moving from place to place, serving one lord and then another.
6. Good manners were critical for a knight, for ________ behavior was important to the upper class.
7. However, acts of cruelty toward women and peasants were common, and because such behavior was not considered wicked, it required no ________.
8. Knights expected great praise for their bravery and reacted negatively to insults or any form of ________.
9. Because tempers were short and law enforcement was lacking, insults or injuries were likely to be met by acts of ________.
10. Legal disputes were often decided by combat because people believed that while humans were ________ and might misjudge a situation, God would cause the guilty party to be defeated.

Building Vocabulary
For an in-depth lesson on context clues, see page 1000.

WORDS TO KNOW				
carriage	disparagement	fallible	intemperate	reprisal
decorous	exalt	haggard	penitence	vagrant

Teaching Options

Mini Lesson Grammar

MAKING COMPOUND PREDICATES PARALLEL For use with Grammar in Context, p. 1101. Remind students that a predicate tells what a subject did or what happened to the subject. A compound predicate occurs when the subject is followed by two or more predicates. Write the following sentence on the board:

> Lancelot clenched his fists and choked back his sorrow.

Have students identify the compound predicate of the sentence ("clenched his fists," "choked back his sorrow"). Point out that the predicate includes the verbs and other modifiers. Explain that all parts of the predicate should be parallel with each other, as in the example above.

Practice Have students copy the following sentences. Ask them to identify the compound predicate of each sentence. If there is faulty parallelism, have them make corrections.

1. Lancelot leaves the king, sees Guinevere, and then he is passionately embracing her.
   Answer: Lancelot leaves the king, sees Guinevere, and then passionately embraces her.

Grammar in Context: Making Compound Predicates Parallel

In the following sentence, John Steinbeck uses a compound predicate to enrich a description of servants.

> **In the great hall the serving people walked under burdens with the slow weight of oxen and scuttled like crabs, crooked and nervous when the weight was gone.**

You may recall that a sentence's **predicate** tells what the subject did or what happened to the subject. When a subject is followed by a series of two or more predicates, the sentence is said to contain a **compound predicate.** In the example above, notice how the parts of the compound predicate (shown in blue) create a vivid picture of the movements of servants with and without food.

The parts of a compound predicate should be grammatically and logically parallel. Each part should make sense when read separately after the shared subject, and there should be no unnecessary shifts in verb tense.

Punctuation Tip: When a compound predicate consists of only two parts, do not separate them with a comma.

WRITING EXERCISE Rewrite these sentences, correcting errors in parallelism. Be sure that the verbs in each compound predicate refer to the same subject and that verb tenses are used consistently. If a sentence has no errors, write *Correct.*

Example: ***Original*** The knights stuff their faces with meat, slurp metheglin, and they listen to tales.

Rewritten The knights stuff their faces with meat, slurp metheglin, and listen to tales.

1. A knight tells a story about Lancelot, exaggerates the events, and Lancelot shakes his head.
2. A servant picks up a plank loaded with goose meat, staggers down the aisle, and plunks the meat down at the head table.
3. The knights gaze up at Guinevere, admire her beauty, and sighed with contentment.
4. Arthur listens to Lancelot's comment, he looks at the trumpet players, and signals them to end the feast.
5. When Lancelot enters the tower room, Guinevere rose to leave but stays at the men's request.

Connect to the Literature In the first column on page 1094, find a sentence that contains a three-part compound predicate. What idea is conveyed by the compound predicate?

Grammar Handbook The Sentence and Its Parts, p. 1192

John Steinbeck

1902–1968

A biography of John Steinbeck appears on page 918.

LaserLinks: Background for Reading
Historical Connection
Author Background

Grammar in Context

WRITING EXERCISE Answers will vary. Possible answers are shown.

1. A knight tells a story about Lancelot, exaggerates the events, and causes Lancelot to shake his head.
2. Correct
3. The knights gaze up at Guinevere, admire her beauty, and sigh with contentment.
4. Arthur listens to Lancelot's comment, looks at the trumpet players, and signals them to end the feast.
5. When Lancelot enters the tower room, Guinevere rises to leave but stays at the men's request.

Connect to the Literature Possible Response: "Lancelot exhausted the theme of his hands and squinted down the long hall and watched the movement with eyes so nearly closed that he could not see faces."

Possible Response: The compound predicate (with "and" rather than commas) suggests an unbroken sequence, as Lancelot tries to find something to do to occupy himself.

2. When the knights are praising Lancelot, he seems bored and is looking at his hands.
   Answer: When the knights are praising Lancelot, he seems bored and looks at his hands.
3. Guinevere gets up to leave the room, bids the men good night, and Arthur kisses her on the hand.
   Answer: Guinevere gets up to leave the room, bids the men good night, and receives a kiss from Arthur on the hand.

Use **Grammar Transparencies and Copymasters,** p. 88, for more practice.

Use McDougal Littell's ***Language Network,*** Chapter 16, for more instruction in making compound predicates parallel.

Objectives

- create a semantic map for specific words
- use a semantic map strategy for determining word meanings

EXERCISE

Responses will vary depending on the words students select.

Building Word Meanings

A map can be a big help when you're figuring out how to travel from one place to another. Often a map will show you several ways to get to your destination, and then you must choose the best route. Similarly, finding your way to the meaning of an unfamiliar word involves a process of working through several routes. What steps would you take to figure out the meaning of the word *decisive* in the excerpt on the right from *Le Morte d'Arthur?*

> **Soon King Uther arrived with a huge army and laid siege to Terrabyl; but despite the ferocity of the fighting, and the numerous casualties suffered by both sides, neither was able to gain a decisive victory.**
> —Sir Thomas Malory, from *Le Morte d'Arthur*

The word *decisive* and the context in which it appears may remind you of the words *decide* and *decision.* You might also recognize the Latin root *cise* (to cut) and the prefix *de-* (from). Together with context clues, such as "but despite," "suffered by both sides," and "neither was able to gain," you might infer that *decisive* probably means "conclusive" or "crucial."

Strategies for Building Vocabulary

Semantics is the study of word meanings. Use the strategies below and the semantic map on the right to learn one method for understanding and remembering a word.

❶ **Map Out the Meaning** Note the word *testimony* as you read the excerpt below. Then follow the analysis of the meaning of the word *testimony.*

> **It was the custom for the defeated to celebrate the deeds of those who had overcome them. . . . Some said [Lancelot] nodded and perhaps dozed, for the testimony to his greatness was long and the monotony of his victories continued for many hours.**
> —John Steinbeck, from *The Acts of King Arthur and His Noble Knights*

Steps	Example
1. Consider the Context	Details like "to celebrate the deeds," "to his greatness," "long," and "monotony of his victories" imply that a testimony is a kind of celebratory speech.
2. Think of Similar Words	*Testimony* resembles the legal words *testament* and *testify,* which refer to giving evidence.
3. Identify Word Parts	All three words are based on the Latin *testis,* which means "witness."
4. Develop a Meaning	I think a testimony might be a speech that gives witness to something.
5. Check a Dictionary	*Testimony* is defined as "a statement in support of a given truth, fact, or claim." It also means "proof" or "evidence in support of an assertion."

Semantic Map

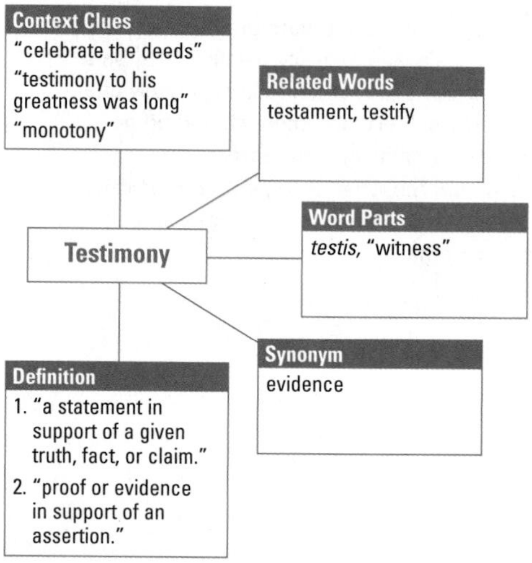

❷ **Record and Use the Word** To make the word a part of your permanent vocabulary, write it down and use it in conversation or in your writing for several days or weeks.

EXERCISE Choose five unfamiliar words from the selections in this part of the unit, and apply the strategies outlined above to each word to create a semantic map.

THE KNIGHT

ADRIENNE RICH

Millefleurs tapestry with horseman and arms of Jean de Daillon (late 1400s), unknown Flemish artist. National Trust Photographic Library.

A knight rides into the noon,
and his helmet points to the sun,
and a thousand splintered suns
are the gaiety of his mail.
The soles of his feet glitter
and his palms flash in reply,
and under his crackling banner
he rides like a ship in sail.

A knight rides into the noon,
and only his eye is living,
a lump of bitter jelly
set in a metal mask,
betraying rags and tatters
that cling to the flesh beneath
and wear his nerves to ribbons
under the radiant casque.

ON YOUR OWN

Possible Objectives

You can use this selection to achieve one or more of the following objectives:

- enjoy silent sustained reading (Option One)
- read and analyze literature with a group (Option Two)
- use the Reader's Notebook to formulate questions about literature (Option Three)
- write in response to literature (Option Three)

Summary

The knight rides out to battle in his brilliantly shining armor during the first stanza. The second stanza describes the only part of the knight that is visible—his eye—as bitter and reveals that his clothes under his armor are tattered and ragged. The third stanza discusses the knight's future downfall in battle, which will free him of his oppressive suit of armour.

Reading the Selection

Option One
Silent Sustained Reading

You might set aside time each week for independent reading. During this time, you and all of your students would read for enjoyment. "The Knight" will appeal to many students and can be read independently. If you want to encourage students to read for pleasure, you might forgo assignments related to the selection. Should you want to make assignments, Options Two and Three offer suggestions.

Option Two
Shared Reading Groups

You may assign students to groups or allow them to choose their own. Students can read the selection together, alternately reading stanzas aloud, or they can read independently and meet to cooperate in a project that portrays some element of the story.

Possible Projects

- Students can write an extension of the poem loosely following Rich's rhyming pattern—ABCDEFGD—and including an alternate ending.
- Students can apply a different viewpoint to their readings. Have students imagine the main character in "The Knight" as a woman trapped by a different type of armor. Ask students how this shift in perspective affects their reactions to the poem.

Option Three
Readers Notebook

Provide the following direction to students before they read:

Give students a brief summary of the poem. Describe the setting of the poem (medieval Europe, outdoors on horseback, a battlefield).

Tell students to read the poem, pausing at the end of the first stanza. At that point, students should summarize this stanza in their Reader's Notebooks. Have them write any questions they would like the knight to answer. Have students repeat this exercise when they pause after the second stanza.

At the end of the selection, students will return to their questions. Ask them to note whether any of their questions have been answered and to write down any additional questions they have about "The Knight."

Have students imagine the knight defeated in battle and temporarily held prisoner. Students can write a possible conversation between the knight and his conqueror in their Reader's Notebooks.

After Reading

Possible Activities
Independent Activity

- Have gifted students skim over the poem, jotting down details and descriptions about the knight's armor. Ask them to write in their Reader's Notebooks why the author chose to describe the armor as vividly and grotesquely as she did.

Discussion Activities
- Use the questions formulated by students as the start of a discussion about this poignant poem.
- Discuss why the author chose to title her poem *The Knight* instead of *The Armor.*
- Have students compare and contrast the stanzas' portrayals of the knight.

Assessment Opportunities
- You can assess student comprehension of the poem by evaluating the questions they formulate in their Reader's Notebooks.
- You can use any of the discussion questions as essay questions.
- You can have students turn any one of their Reader's Notebooks entries into an essay.

Who will unhorse this rider
and free him from between
the walls of iron, the emblems
crushing his chest with their weight?
Will they defeat him gently,
or leave him hurled on the green,
his rags and wounds still hidden
under the great breastplate?

Adrienne Rich
1929–

Other Works
Diving into the Wreck
The Dream of a Common Language
An Atlas of the Difficult World

Times of Change Over the years, Adrienne Rich has moved from the acceptance of traditional women's roles to a more critical feminist stance. In her first volume of poetry, *A Change of World* (1951), she was influenced primarily by male poets, such as W. H. Auden. Her book *The Diamond Cutters,* appeared in 1955, the same year she gave birth to the first of three sons. The demands of family life left Rich with little time or energy for writing, and her next book did not appear until eight years later. In 1966 she moved to New York City, where she began a teaching career at the City College of the City University of New York and became involved in radical and feminist politics. Her poems increasingly came to reflect feminist concerns, as seen in her 1973 collection *Diving into the Wreck,* which won a National Book Award. Among the prose that Rich has published is *Of Woman Born: Motherhood as Experience and Institution,* which critically examines traditional women's roles.

One of the Best Rich has received a number of prestigious awards for her poetry. For many years she continued to balance teaching with writing at universities such as Rutgers and Stanford. Many of Rich's poems are noted for their bold and intense statements about personal experiences and political and social issues. Author Margaret Atwood has noted, "Adrienne Rich is not just one of America's best feminist poets, or one of America's best woman poets, she is one of America's best poets."

Writing Workshop

Research Report

Exploring a topic in depth . . .

A **From Reading to Writing** The drama *Antigone* was written and performed 2,500 years ago in a society that was very different from ours. You probably have many questions about that society. How much influence did the gods have in the daily lives of people in ancient Greece? Who was the audience for the plays? How were the plays staged? A **research report** can help you find the answers to questions like these. Research can help you not only to understand literature but also to investigate a science problem, understand a historical event, or choose a career.

For Your Portfolio

WRITING PROMPT Write a research report about a literary topic or another topic that interests you.

Purpose: To share information and draw a conclusion about your topic

Audience: Your classmates, teacher, and other people who share your interest in the topic

Basics in a Box

Research Report at a Glance

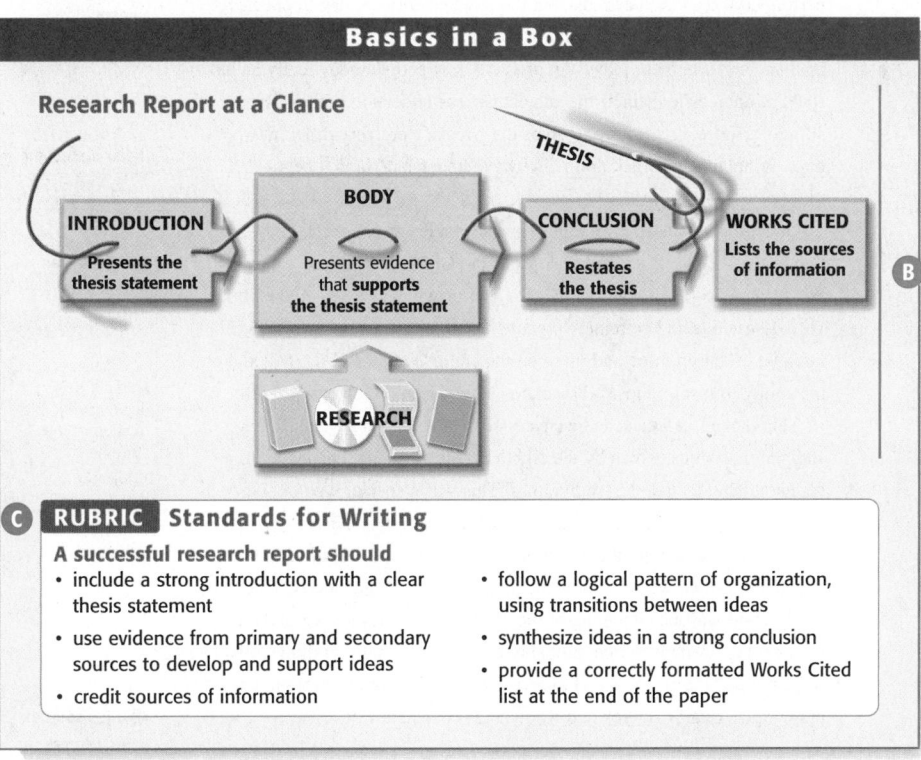

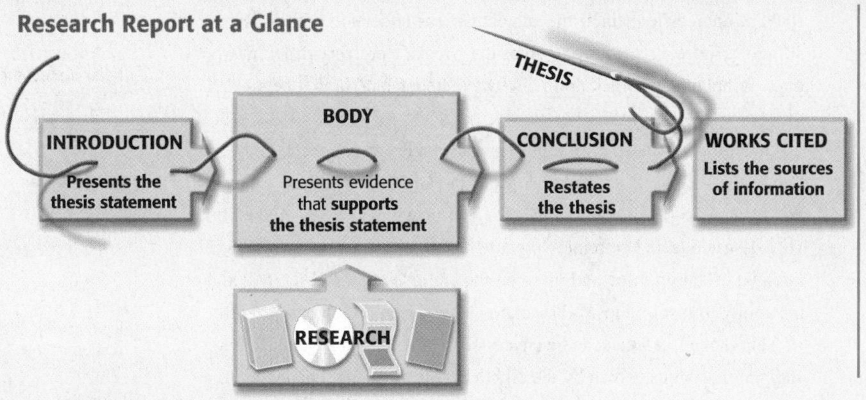

B

C **RUBRIC** Standards for Writing

A successful research report should

- include a strong introduction with a clear thesis statement
- use evidence from primary and secondary sources to develop and support ideas
- credit sources of information
- follow a logical pattern of organization, using transitions between ideas
- synthesize ideas in a strong conclusion
- provide a correctly formatted Works Cited list at the end of the paper

LESSON RESOURCES

USING PRINT RESOURCES

Unit Six Resource Book
- Prewriting, p. 51
- Drafting, p. 52
- Peer Response, pp. 53–54
- Revising, Editing, and Proofreading, p. 55
- Student Models, pp. 56–61
- Rubric, p. 62

Writing Transparencies and Copymasters
- Writing Process Transparencies, pp. 1–4
- Writing Structure Transparencies, pp. 5–11
- Writing Template Copymasters, p. 35

USING MEDIA RESOURCES

LaserLinks
Writing Springboards
See Teacher's SourceBook p. 64 for bar codes.

Writing Coach CD-ROM

Visit our website:
www.mcdougallittell.com

Objectives
- write a Research Report
- use a written text as a model for writing
- revise a draft to elaborate with facts and statistics
- maintain parallelism

Introducing the Workshop

A Research Report Explain to students that research reports require the writer to pull together information from many diverse sources. Such a synthesis of material is frequently required in many jobs and professions. Lawyers, teachers, social workers, psychologists, business people, and company managers all engage in writing tasks that require them to find sources that will support their claims and develop new ideas. Citing your sources of information in your report is important to establishing your credibility and also to giving readers factual information to support your claims. Ask students to name situations in which people draw on outside sources for information to support their point. Is there any recognizable pattern in the kinds of sources that are commonly cited?

Point out that writing a research report will enable students to make and support a point by citing outside sources of information. Establish some criteria for what makes a claim believable and gives it authority. The credibility of the source, including its expertise, knowledge, credentials, objectivity, and character, may influence the validity of a claim.

Basics in a Box

B Using the Graphic As the graphic suggests, the items in a research report must be closely interlinked to create a solid, well-supported report. The graphic offers suggestions for pieces that students can use to draft an effective research report.

C Presenting the Rubric To better understand the assignment, students can refer to the Standards for Writing a Successful Research Report. You may wish to discuss with them the complete rubric, which describes several levels of proficiency.

Teaching the Lesson

Analyzing the Model

D "Greek Theater in Its Own Time" The student model states that to appreciate ancient Greek drama, one must understand the religious origins of Greek theater rooted in the worship of Dionysus.

Have students read the model, then discuss the Rubric in Action. Point out key words and phrases in the student model that correspond to the elements mentioned in the Rubric in Action.

1. Have students suggest an alternate opening based on the other options listed.
   Possible Response: The writer could open with the statement that early Greek drama was thought to be religious worship.
2. Ask students to analyze the purpose of this thesis statement—to inform, to persuade, or both?
   Possible Response: Its purpose is primarily to inform. To support this thesis, the writer must present factual information about the society from which Greek theater sprang.
4. Point out that the writer here moves from the more general claim that Dionysus was thought to be inspirational to the more specific claims concerning the special forms of poetry that Dionysus inspired.

Use McDougal Littell's ***Language Network,*** Chapter 25, for more instruction on writing a research report.

Power Presentation

To engage students visually, use Power Presentation 12, Research Report.

Analyzing a Student Model

April Sykes
Mr. Lynch
English II
26 April

Sykes 1

Greek Theater in Its Own Time

Slowly a large crowd gathered in the amphitheater and found places to sit on the bare stone. They were there to worship the great god Dionysus with songs and poetry and with music and dance. The greatest poets of the world had also gathered for this celebration, and they would present their new works of drama as gifts to the god.

This celebration took place 2,500 years ago in Athens, Greece, the birthplace of modern drama (Cheney 37–38). Most of the plays that were performed there have been lost, but the few that survive, like Sophocles' *Antigone,* are among the great literature of Western civilization. We still read and perform these plays, but probably few people today really understand or appreciate them as the ancient Greeks understood them. <u>The culture, science, arts, and religion of the Greeks were very different from ours. To appreciate Greek drama, we must understand how it began and the society that created it.</u>

Greek theater came from religious ceremonies to honor the god Dionysus, a son of Zeus, the greatest of the Greek gods (Nardo, <u>Greek and Roman</u> 16–17). Dionysus was the god of wine, and he could be both very destructive and extremely creative. As time passed, the worship of Dionysus focused more and more on the creative aspect of the god and on his ability to inspire those who acknowledged him (Hamilton 71–74).

This change in focus can be clearly seen in the religious rituals worshipping Dionysus, which by the eighth century B.C. had changed into a ceremony that included a "dithyramb." This was a special type of poetry that told the story of Dionysus or that honored him in some way. With the passage of time, the dithyrambs evolved further into a kind of drama in which a priest led worshipers in chanting and singing the poetry. This group chant was the beginning of the chorus found in *Antigone* and other Greek plays. Certain people, probably priests, began writing dithyrambs to be performed during the worship ceremonies. These priests were the first playwrights (Nardo, <u>Greek and Roman</u> 15–16; Cheney 36–37).

RUBRIC IN ACTION

1. This writer opens with an interesting description.
   Other Options:
   - Present an intriguing fact or statistic.
   - Start with a quote.
   - Relate an anecdote.
2. Presents the thesis statement
3. Cites a secondary source of information
4. This writer uses an example to support the statement.
   Other Options:
   - Cite a fact.
   - Provide a quotation.
5. Cites sources

1106 UNIT SIX PART 2: THE HEROIC TRADITION

Sykes 2

In about 535 B.C., the worship of Dionysus became really dramatic when the city of Athens began to sponsor an annual festival for the god. The festival took place once a year in the spring and lasted five days. It didn't take place in a temple, but in a theater. Dionysus was thought to be present. His priest was the guest of honor, and the greatest poets of the period wrote plays to read and have performed at the festival. Prizes were awarded for the best play. The entire festival was an act of religious worship. The actors, poets, and spectators were all servants of Dionysus (Hamilton 73–74; Cheney 38–39).

> ❻ This writer develops ideas in chronological order.
>
> **Other Options:**
> - Present ideas in order of importance.
> - Use cause-and-effect order.

Sykes 11

Works Cited

Butler, James H. The Theatre and Drama of Greece and Rome. San Francisco: Chandler, 1972.

Cheney, Sheldon. The Theatre: Three Thousand Years of Drama, Acting and Stagecraft. New York: McKay, 1972.

Didaskalia: Ancient Theater Today. U of Warwick. 20 April 1998 <http://www.warwick.ac–uk/didaskalia/>.

Goetsch, Sallie. "Playing Against the Text." Drama Review 38 (1994): 75–95.

Goodman, Randolph. Drama on Stage. New York: Holt, 1978.

Hamilton, Edith. Mythology. Boston: Little, 1942.

Nardo, Don. Greek and Roman Theater. San Diego: Lucent, 1995.

---, ed. Readings on Sophocles. San Diego: Greenhaven, 1997.

Novick, Julius. "Drama." World Book Multimedia Encyclopedia. 1997 ed. CD-ROM. Chicago: World Book, 1997.

Sophocles. Antigone. Trans. Dudley Fitts and Robert Fitzgerald. Greek Plays in Modern Translation. Ed. Dudley Fitts. New York: Dial, 1974. 455–499.

> **Works Cited**
> - Identifies sources of information used in researching a paper
> - Organizes resources alphabetically by author's last name or article title
> - Gives complete publication information
> - Punctuates entries correctly
> - Double spaces entire list
> - Follows a preferred style

Need help with Works Cited?

See pages 1166–1168 in the **Writing Handbook.**

6. Have students suggest an alternate order based on the other options listed.

Possible Response: The writer could use an "order of importance" structure and begin by talking about how the festival was an act of religious worship. She could then continue by explaining what this means.

Works Cited

Explain to students that each entry on the Works Cited list has three parts—author information, title information, and publication information. Point out that each part ends with a period. This is the reason for all the periods in a Works Cited entry.

Show students how to key the sources listed in the student model with those listed on the Works Cited page.

WRITING WORKSHOP 1107

Guiding Student Writing

Prewriting

Choosing a Topic

If after reading the Idea Bank students are having difficulty choosing their topics, suggest they try the following:

- Skim newspapers and news magazines in search of problems and controversies at the local, national, and international level. Use these controversies as the starting point to develop a report whose purpose is to inform readers about particular social or political problems.
- List questions that interest or puzzle you and for which you would like to find answers. Conducting research for the purpose of answering a question is a solid foundation for a research project.

Planning the Research Report

1. Have students explore their topic by creating a cluster map. Then ask them to "interrogate" each branch of their map by asking the journalist's questions–who? what? when? where? why? how?

3. Explain to students that, generally, research reports are written with the goal of informing or persuading an audience. Have students consider how their approach might differ depending on which goal they choose to pursue.

4. Once they decide on their thesis, have students write it on a 3X5 card and tape it in their notebook or on their computer screen to help them keep their writing in focus. As students get involved in their research, they may find it necessary to revise their thesis statements.

Researching

Have students review the Works Cited list for the student model to see the kinds of sources that can be used in research. Encyclopedia articles are good places to begin a research project because they provide a broad overview of the subject as well as key words that can be used to guide further research. However, students should attempt to locate current publications to support their claims. A reference librarian can provide instruction on how to conduct key word searches in the card or computer catalog and on the Internet.

IDEA Bank

1. Your Working Portfolio
Look for ideas in the **Writing Option** you completed earlier in this unit:
- **Report on Athenian Women,** p. 1062

2. Freewriting
Begin with a general topic and freewrite about it for three minutes. Then pick an interesting idea that's emerged and write about it for three more minutes. Keep writing until you hit on a topic you like.

3. Listing Questions
To explore a topic, ask the questions *who, what, when, why, where,* and *how.* Choose an interesting idea, and ask more questions until you find a topic.

Writing Your Research Report

❶ Prewriting and Exploring

You might begin by brainstorming topics that interest you. Then, put your unique spin on the subject by creating a cluster diagram with the topic in the center. What related ideas come up? Try narrowing some of the related topics even further. See the **Idea Bank** for more suggestions on finding a topic.

Planning your Research Report

1. **Evaluate your topic.** Is your topic broad enough that you can find enough information? Is it narrow enough that you can cover it adequately? You might do preliminary research to answer these questions. Making a cluster diagram can help you either broaden or narrow your focus.

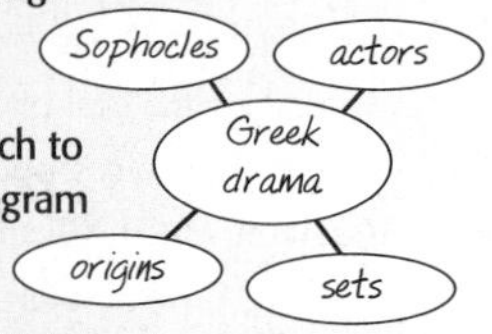

2. **Establish a goal.** What do you want to accomplish in your report? Do you want to analyze the topic? inform your readers?
3. **Identify your audience.** Who will read your report? What does your audience already know about the topic? What do they need to know?
4. **Consider your purpose.** How can you express your purpose in a single sentence? That statement can help you stay on target as you do research. Later on, you can revise it and make it your thesis statement.

❷ Researching

Researching is gathering information from reliable sources. Make a list of questions you have about your topic based on the purpose of your report and what your audience needs to know. Begin your search in the library. Look for both **primary sources**, which give eyewitness accounts of events, and **secondary sources**, which present information compiled from or based on other sources. Primary sources include letters, journals, historical documents, and original works of fiction. Secondary sources include works of criticism and commentary and most newspaper and magazine articles.

Evaluate Your Sources

These guidelines can help you evaluate the reliability of your sources.

- **How up-to-date is the source?** Use the most recent secondary sources you can find. Certain fields, such as science, technology, and medicine, change especially rapidly.
- **How reliable is the source?** Look for sources whose authors are from respected universities, businesses, or other institutions. Poor sources of information include tabloid newspapers and some personal Web sites.
- **What are the author's biases?** Consider how the author's gender, ethnic background, and political position influence his or her viewpoint. Be sure to read material from several viewpoints to get a balanced picture.

Research TIP

Secondary sources are valuable for explaining ideas and interpreting information. Try to use primary sources to illustrate or prove the points you make.

More Online: Research Starter
www.mcdougallittell.com

Evaluate the Sources

A good indicator of the thoroughness and reliability of a source lies in its bibliography. Does the source that students are evaluating have a Works Cited list? The presence of a Works Cited list can provide clues about the writer's objectivity, up-to-date status, and reliability. The publication date may also make a difference, especially with scientific claims.

Create Source Cards

Make a source card for each source you use. Record complete publishing information on index cards like those at the right. Number the cards so that you can easily refer to them as you take notes and prepare your Works Cited page. Follow the format shown for each type of resource. For library books, list the call number as well.

Take Notes

Record the information you gather on index cards like the one below. Write one idea on each card so you can easily reorder your cards as you organize your report. Label each card with the number of the source card and the page number in the source.

Paraphrase. Unless you are quoting material directly, paraphrase what you read: that is, write it in your own words. That way, you will be less likely to accidentally **plagiarize**, or use someone else's material without permission, and you can reduce the information to fewer words.

Quotation. If you quote a source, use quotation marks and double-check the accuracy of your quotation. Quote material that is particularly well stated or that helps you emphasize a point.

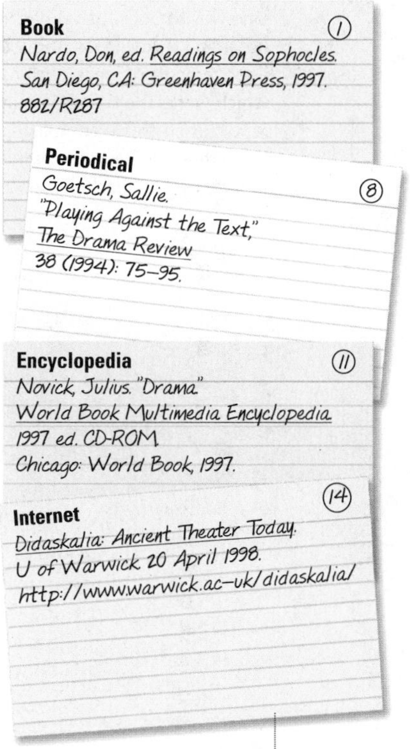

Book
1
Nardo, Don, ed. Readings on Sophocles.
San Diego, CA: Greenhaven Press, 1997.
882/R287
Periodical
8
Goetsch, Sallie.
"Playing Against the Text,"
The Drama Review
38 (1994): 75–95.
Encyclopedia
11
Novick, Julius. "Drama."
World Book Multimedia Encyclopedia.
1997 ed. CD-ROM.
Chicago: World Book, 1997.
Internet
14
Didaskalia: Ancient Theater Today.
U of Warwick 20 April 1998.
http://www.warwick.ac-uk/didaskalia/

Paraphrase. Restate ideas in your own words to summarize them and to avoid plagiarism.

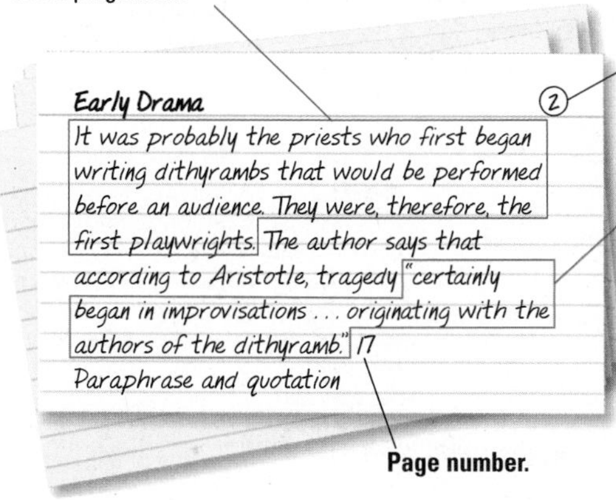

Early Drama
2
It was probably the priests who first began writing dithyrambs that would be performed before an audience. They were, therefore, the first playwrights. The author says that according to Aristotle, tragedy "certainly began in improvisations . . . originating with the authors of the dithyramb." 17
Paraphrase and quotation

Source number.

Quotation. Write the quotation exactly as it appears in the source. Use quotation marks to show where the quotation begins and ends.

Page number.

INTERNET Sources

Evaluate all information obtained from Internet sites. Information from some sites, such as those from universities (.edu) and the government (.gov), should be reliable. Personal Web sites may be less reliable. Use your judgment and double-check your facts.

Create Source Cards

Place examples of each type of source card in the classroom. Explain to students that accuracy is of the utmost importance. Encourage students to take the time to record all the information needed for a Works Cited list entry on every source card. Then, when they later complete their Works Cited list, they won't face the uncertainties and potential error of not having accurate entries.

Take Notes

As students read and take notes on their source material, remind them to use text organizers, such as tables of contents, overviews, headings and graphics to locate and categorize information.

On each note card, have students indicate the source number, the main idea, the page number, and the type of note—paraphrase or quotation. When students complete their research and notetaking, it will be easier to sort and group note cards if they have key words to indicate how a note card might be relevant or might fit into the logical flow of the report.

WRITING WORKSHOP **1109**

Organize the Material

Spend extra time giving feedback to students at this stage of the project. Students will need feedback on the logic of their outline and report. Conferring with students individually can be useful here. Have students provide you with a topic outline for you to preview before the conference.

Need help with your research report?

See the **Writing Handbook,** pp. 1163–1168

Organize Your Material

One way to begin organizing your research information is to group your note cards according to key ideas. This will help you see how the information is related. Try several arrangements of ideas, such as **chronological** and **cause-and-effect** order to see which works the best. You may want to use different orders in different parts of your report. Then create an outline, using the key ideas as the main headings of the outline. Label these with Roman numerals. Subheadings, which summarize smaller groupings of note cards in each group, are labeled with capital letters.

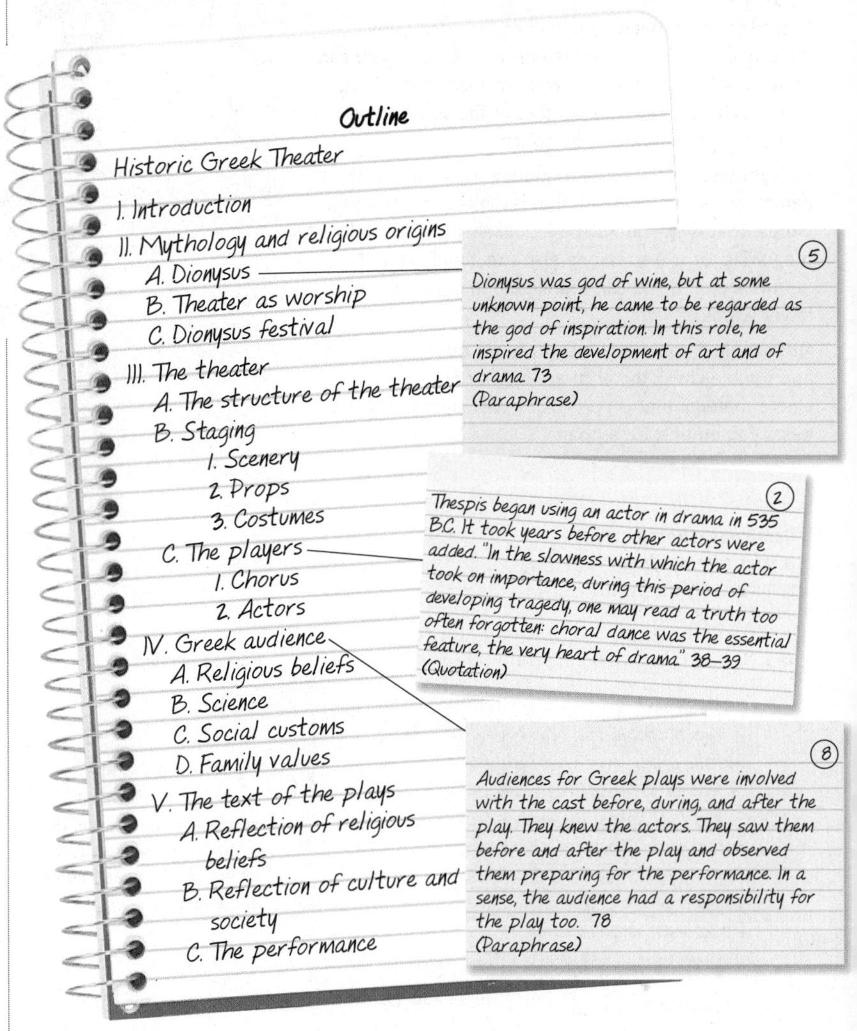
Outline
Historic Greek Theater
I. Introduction
II. Mythology and religious origins
A. Dionysus
B. Theater as worship
C. Dionysus festival
III. The theater
A. The structure of the theater
B. Staging
1. Scenery
2. Props
3. Costumes
C. The players
1. Chorus
2. Actors
IV. Greek audience
A. Religious beliefs
B. Science
C. Social customs
D. Family values
V. The text of the plays
A. Reflection of religious beliefs
B. Reflection of culture and society
C. The performance
5
Dionysus was god of wine, but at some unknown point, he came to be regarded as the god of inspiration. In this role, he inspired the development of art and of drama. 73
(Paraphrase)
2
Thespis began using an actor in drama in 535 B.C. It took years before other actors were added. "In the slowness with which the actor took on importance, during this period of developing tragedy, one may read a truth too often forgotten: choral dance was the essential feature, the very heart of drama." 38–39
(Quotation)
8
Audiences for Greek plays were involved with the cast before, during, and after the play. They knew the actors. They saw them before and after the play and observed them preparing for the performance. In a sense, the audience had a responsibility for the play too. 78
(Paraphrase)

Research TIP

Ask your librarian about specialized reference sources relating to your topic.

❸ Drafting

As you begin writing, keep in mind that your goal in drafting is to get your ideas down on paper in a reasonably organized manner. Use your outline as a guide and write from your note cards. At some point, write a **thesis statement** that expresses the main idea of your report. You will support your thesis with the information gathered in your research.

Choose Writing Strategies

You may want to use some of these strategies for developing your ideas.

- **Narration.** Presenting material as a narrative can add interest and drama to your report.
- **Definition.** Identify and define terms or concepts that your audience may not know.
- **Description.** You might imagine what an eyewitness would see and describe this using sensory details to help draw your audience into the event or setting.
- **Classification.** Discuss the characteristics of your topic by comparing it to similar topics or by breaking it into logical parts and examining each one.

Organize Your Report

Think of your report as having three parts: introduction, body, and conclusion. The **introduction** should include a hook that captures your readers' interest and should clearly state your thesis. The **body** should present the information that supports your thesis. Some information might be organized in chronological order, other information in order of importance, spatial order, or cause-and-effect order, for example. End your report with a memorable **conclusion** that summarizes your thesis, draws a conclusion, or points out topics that need further examination.

Document Your Sources

Document each quotation, paraphrase, or summary of information in your report by citing the author and page number of the source in parentheses. Your readers can refer to your Works Cited list for full information.

Evaluate Your Draft

Think about these questions as you review your draft.

- How can I rework my report to better achieve my purpose and goals for writing?
- Does all of my information support my thesis statement? What information should I add? What information should I delete?
- What facts, quotations, and other information do I need to check and document?
- How can I better communicate my interest in this topic?
- How can I improve the organization of my report?

Drafting TIP

Although a research report is a formal paper, it doesn't have to be dry or dull. Spice it up with interesting details, narratives, and descriptions. Be sure your interest shows in your tone.

Need help documenting sources?

See the **Writing Handbook,** p. 1166–1168

Ask Your Peer Reader

- What did you like most about my report?
- What did you like least about my report?
- What is the main point I'm making?
- What additional information do you need or want to know about the topic?
- What parts were confusing?

Drafting

Rather than getting lost in the forest of such a large, multiphase project as this, encourage students to set realistic goals focused on one step at a time.

Point out that the thesis statement is the main claim or assertion of the report. It should convey the essential "point" the writer wishes to make and should also suggest or forecast the direction the report will take. Have students work in groups of three to trade thesis statements, discuss, and revise them for precision and clarity.

Organize the Report

One effective drafting strategy is to have students write a "ten minute draft" in which you give them ten minutes to write the entire draft. The idea is to use the "ten minute draft" as a sketchy beginning point that needs to be fleshed out, developed, and documented.

Document the Sources

Remind students that the Works Cited list contains only sources that have actually been cited—that is, quoted, paraphrased, or summarized. If they've read or consulted a work but did not specifically cite it in the text, then it should not appear on the Works Cited list.

Evaluate the Draft

Have students work in pairs and use the questions listed in the text to examine and evaluate each other's drafts. Then have them share their responses in discussion.

Revising

ELABORATING WITH FACTS AND STATISTICS

One strategy for helping students locate statements that might benefit from elaboration is to have them read their drafts with the phrase "Define Your Terms" in mind for each sentence. As students confront each sentence, have them apply the phrase "Define Your Terms" to help them locate places where factual elaboration would help specify or clarify the meaning of a phrase or sentence.

Editing and Proofreading

PARALLELISM

Explain that parallelism involves expressing related ideas or items in similar grammatical forms and structural patterns. Parallelism can appear at the level of words, phrases, clauses, sentences, and even paragraphs. Write the following sentences on the chalkboard and discuss their parallel structure.

Parallel verbs: The boy was singing, dancing, and whistling. (three *-ing* verbs)

Parallel clauses: John was older; Jim was younger. (two independent clauses)

Parallel sentences: The boy was singing, dancing, and whistling. His sister was running, skipping, and jumping. (two sentences using a series of *-ing* verbs)

Remind students as they revise, edit, and proofread that they should produce an error-free final draft.

Making a Works Cited List

Remind students that the items on the Works Cited list should be arranged alphabetically by the author's last name or, if there is no author listed, by the first word of the title. Arranging the source cards in alphabetical order prior to typing will alleviate some of the frustration students have with the Works Cited page.

Reflecting

Encourage students to evaluate their performance on this writing assignment by discussing the parts that gave them the most trouble as well as the parts that gave them the least trouble. Adding these self-evaluations to their portfolios can help them gain a clearer sense of where they stand as writers and where they need to improve.

Need revising help?

Review the **Rubric,** p. 1105

Consider **peer reader** comments

Check **Revision Guidelines,** p. 1145

❹ Revising

TARGET SKILL ▶ ELABORATING WITH FACTS AND STATISTICS As you revise, look for opportunities to elaborate on your ideas by adding facts and statistics. A fact is a statement that can be proved either by the use of reference materials or by firsthand observation. Statistics are facts expressed in numbers.

> called the Theater of Dionysus. Located on the side of a hill near the Acropolis
>
> The plays were performed in a large theater ^ in Athens. It was shaped like a stadium with rows of seats stretching halfway around a central stage. [called the orchestra] [the theater held about 14,000 people.]

❺ Editing and Proofreading

TARGET SKILL ▶ PARALLELISM When parts of a sentence have parallel functions, the structure of the sentence parts should also be parallel. For example, when connecting two or more similar ideas, use the same part of speech for both.

> At the annual festival of Dionysus, prizes were awarded for ~~performing on stage~~ acting and ~~having sung in the~~ chor~~us~~al singing for both comedy and tragedy. Having a play performed and ~~to~~ earn^ing^ a prize were great honors given to Aeschylus, Sophocles, Euripides, and other Greek playwrights.

Publishing IDEAS

- Share your paper with the class as an oral presentation.
- Post your paper on your school's Web site.

More Online: Publishing Options
www.mcdougallittell.com

❻ Making a Works Cited List

When you have finished revising, editing, and proofreading your report, make a **Works Cited list** and attach it to the end of your paper. See pages 1166–1168 in the **Writing Handbook** for the correct format.

❼ Reflecting

FOR YOUR PORTFOLIO Now that you know more about your topic, what new questions do you have about it? Make a list of questions you could use to further research your topic. Keep your list with your research report in your **Working Portfolio.**

Assessment Practice Revising & Editing

Read this paragraph from the first draft of a report. The underlined sections may include the following kinds of errors:

- **spelling errors**
- **run-on sentences**
- **lack of parallel structure**
- **lack of subject-verb agreement**

For each underlined section, choose the revision that most improves the writing.

Tragedy and comedy are two forms of dramatic literiture (1). Both forms grew out of early Greek celebrations in honor of the god Dionysus. Comedy uses humor to entertain, tragedy evokes strong emotions and sympathies (2). A classical Greek tragedy show (3) a noble hero in a struggle he is certain to lose. The flawed hero is usually struggling with fate. Characters in a comedy are usually ordinary people. They are not noble, courageous, or having to struggle (4). Modern tragedy and comedy come (5) from these ancent (6) forms.

1. **A.** literature
   B. litereture
   C. litarature
   D. Correct as is

2. **A.** Comedy uses humor to entertain tragedy evokes strong emotions and sympathies.
   B. Comedy uses humor to entertain, and, tragedy evokes strong emotions and sympathies.
   C. Comedy uses humor to entertain. Tragedy evokes strong emotions and sympathies.
   D. Correct as is

3. **A.** shown
   B. shows
   C. showing
   D. Correct as is

4. **A.** They are not noble, courageous, or struggling.
   B. They are not noble, forced to be courageous, having to struggle.
   C. They do not have courage or to struggle.
   D. Correct as is

5. **A.** comes
   B. had come
   C. coming
   D. Correct as is

6. **A.** ainchent
   B. anchent
   C. ancient
   D. Correct as is

Need extra help?

See the **Grammar Handbook**

Correcting Run-on Sentences, p. 1199

Subject-Verb Agreement, pp. 1200-1201

Assessment Practice

Briefly explain the kinds of errors the passage may contain. Encourage students to carefully read all the choices before they answer each question.

Answers:
1. A; **2.** C; **3.** B; **4.** A; **5.** D; **6.** C

Objectives
- reflect on and assess student understanding of the unit
- compare text events with experiences of students and other readers
- provide examples of themes that cross texts
- compare across texts elements of texts such as conflicts and characterization
- assess and build portfolios

Reflecting on Theme

OPTION 1

A successful response will
- review the list the heroes created for the Part 1 contents page and revisit the discussion of the essential ingredients of heroism
- review the selection in the unit
- list the heroic qualities the student would value in his or her own life.

OPTION 2

A successful response will
- create a profile of a hero for contemporary society
- include traits a contemporary hero should have
- reflect contemporary cultural values

OPTION 3

A successful response will
- select four characters or real people who will still be regarded as heroic far into the future.
- list qualities that a hero needs in order to last for centuries.

Self-Assessment
Ask students to think about their idea of a hero before they read the selections in this unit. Have them explain how the selections in this unit affected their idea of heroism. Did they confirm it? alter it? contradict it?

The Making of Heroes

How have your thoughts and feelings about heroism been affected by the selections in this unit? At this stage in the school year, how do you rate yourself as a reader and as a writer? Explore these questions by completing one or more of the options in each of the following sections.

Detail of Arming and Departure of the Knights (1895–1896), Sir Edward Coley Burne-Jones. From the *Holy Grail Tapestry Series.* Birmingham City Council Museums and Art Gallery, England.

Reflecting on the Unit

OPTION 1

Assessing Heroism What qualities and accomplishments would you need in order to consider yourself a hero? Review the list of heroes that you created for the activity on page 960, and consider your discussion of the essential ingredients of heroism. Then review the selections in the unit. Make a list of the heroic qualities and accomplishments they present that you would value in your own life.

OPTION 2

The Invention of a Hero As you have seen, heroes often reflect the values of their culture, from the physical courage of Lancelot to the religious principles of Antigone. With a partner, create a profile of a hero for our own contemporary society. What traits does your hero need to possess? How will your hero reflect cultural values? To create your profile, reflect upon the various traits of the heroes in this unit, as well as the listing of childhood heroes that you created for the activity on page 1014.

OPTION 3

"The Hero in One Age. . . ." This unit began with a quote from the British novelist Charlotte Lennox, who said, "The hero in one age will be a hero in another." In a small group, examine each of the heroes presented in the unit selections. Choose four characters or real people who, in your judgment, will still be regarded as heroic in distant generations. What qualities are needed to make a hero that can last for centuries?

Self ASSESSMENT

READER'S NOTEBOOK

Which of the selections in this unit gave you the deepest insights into the concept of heroism or influenced your thinking the most? Write a paragraph in which you explain your choice.

Reviewing Literary Concepts

OPTION 1

Appreciating Style Review the information about style presented on pages 961–962, 995, and 1099. In a small group, choose four selections from the unit that represent different kinds of style. Fill out a chart like the one shown to record your observations about the style of each of the selections.

Title	Distinctive Characteristics of Style	Figurative Language

OPTION 2

Distinguishing Myth and Legend With a partner, create working definitions of *myth* and *legend*, based upon the information on pages 1015–1016. Then apply your definitions to the selections in the unit. Which selections contain elements of myth? Which contain elements of legend? Create a Venn diagram to record your findings, with the overlapping area showing selections that contain elements of both.

Self ASSESSMENT

READER'S NOTEBOOK

On a sheet of paper, copy the following literary terms presented in this unit. For each term, find an example from outside this unit that illustrates its meaning. To illustrate the concept of tone, for example, you might write a brief description of the tone of an essay in a previous unit. For some concepts, you will need to go outside this textbook. Consult the **Glossary of Literary Terms** (page 1124) as needed.

style	tone
sentence structure	myth
diction	legend
dialogue	classical drama
imagery	dramatic irony
	romance

Building Your Portfolio

- **Writing Options** Review the Writing Options that you completed for this unit, and choose one or two that could profit from trimming and tightening. Revise them and include your revisions in your **Presentation Portfolio.** Attach a note that explains the reasoning behind your revisions.
- **Writing Workshops** In this unit you wrote a Research Report and created a Multimedia Presentation about a heroic person. Review your works and decide which one does a better job of presenting information. Explain your choice and place a record of your preferred work in your **Presentation Portfolio.**
- **Additional Activities** Reflect upon the assignments that you completed under **Activities & Explorations** and **Inquiry & Research.** Which work did you regard as the most successful? Write a note explaining your choice, and include it in your portfolio.

Self ASSESSMENT

Presentation Portfolio. At this stage, your writing portfolio should represent the work of an entire year. Review the pieces in your portfolio and choose three of your best works—one done in the fall, one in the winter, and one in the spring. Write a note explaining what these works reveal about your progress and abilities as a writer.

Setting GOALS

Reflect on all the goals that you set for yourself during the course of the year. Which goals did you reach? Which goals seem nearly within your reach? Which ones still seem far away? Write an evaluation of your progress this year, and identify three goals for the next school year.

Reviewing Literary Concepts

OPTION 1

Use the Unit 6 Resource Book, page 63, to provide students a ready-made, full-depth chart for recording the styles of their selections.

OPTION 2

A successful response will
- create working definitions of *myth* and *legend,* using the information on pages 1015–1016.
- determine which selections from Unit 6, according to these definitions, contain elements of myth and which contain elements of legend.
- create a Venn diagram to indicate which selections contain elements of myth, which contain elements of legend, and which contain elements of both.

Building Your Portfolio

Students will use their Presentation Portfolios to file what they consider their highest quality work–the very best projects and activities from their Working Portfolios.

For more information on using writing and assessing portfolios, see the *Teacher's Guide to Assessment and Portfolio Use* beginning on page 53.

REFLECT AND ASSESS 1115

The *Electronic Library* is a CD-ROM that contains additional fiction, nonfiction, poetry, and drama for each unit in *The Language of Literature.*

These are the additional selections found in Unit 6 of the *Electronic Library.*

Albert Camus
The Myth of Sisyphus

Émile Zola
The Attack on the Mill

Virgil
from the **Aeneid**

Plato
from **The Apology**

Ursula K. Le Guin
The Lady of More

Edgar Allan Poe
Eldorado

Johann Wolfgang von Goethe
Prometheus

Thucydides
Funeral Oration of Pericles

Encourage students to use one of the selections described as an opportunity to read silently with comprehension over time.

UNIT SIX Extend Your *Reading*

LITERATURE CONNECTIONS

West with the Night

BERYL MARKHAM

A famous aviator reveals her heroic and adventurous spirit in this poetic memoir of her life. Born in England in 1902, Markham grew up in East Africa—a land of spectacular beauty and diversity. In her 20s she became an aviator, flying a small plane into remote parts of Africa. In 1936 Markham became the first person to fly solo across the Atlantic Ocean from east to west.

These thematically related readings are provided along with *West with the Night*:

I Saw a Man
STEPHEN CRANE

***from* Queen Bess, Daredevil Aviator**
DORIS L. RICH

The Campers at Kitty Hawk
JOHN DOS PASSOS

***from* The Flame Trees of Thika**
ELSPETH HUXLEY

African Song
RICHARD RIVE

How the People Hunted the Moose
JOSEPH BRUCHAC

Africa
MAYA ANGELOU

And Even *More* . . .

A Lesson Before Dying

ERNEST GAINES

Grant Wiggins has decided to return to his Louisiana roots, only to come face to face with the injustice of 1940s segregation. The young African-American teacher is tempted to flee the state until his aunt asks him to take on the greatest challenge of his life. Will he teach the death-row convict, Jefferson, how to die with dignity and pride? Together, the two men heroically strive to resist the inevitable.

Books

Oedipus Rex
SOPHOCLES
A confident Oedipus seeks the truth that will save his subjects from the plague—only to learn his own tragic fate.

The Crystal Cave
MARY STEWART
Merlin is not simply a wizard in this Arthurian saga; he is a believable and compelling human being with extraordinary powers.

Profiles in Courage
JOHN F. KENNEDY
A Pulitzer Prize–winning book that profiles American political leaders who dared to stand apart from the crowd.

LITERATURE CONNECTIONS

A Tale of Two Cities

CHARLES DICKENS

In this Victorian novel, set against the background of the French Revolution, love and self-sacrifice prove to be the virtues of the true hero. One of Dickens's most popular novels, *A Tale of Two Cities* was published serially in 1859 in a magazine that Dickens himself edited. The action of the story alternates between England and France. Drawing on the history of the Revolution, Dickens portrays the excesses that culminate at the guillotine. As in his other novels, Dickens includes vivid characters from every rung of the social ladder.

These thematically related readings are provided along with *A Tale of Two Cities*:

A Short "History" of the French Revolution

***from* Hind Swarj or Indian Rule**
MOHANDAS K. GANDHI

***from* Guillotine: Its Legend and Lore**
DANIEL GEROULD

Five Men
ZBIGNIEW HERBERT

The Pit and the Pendulum
EDGAR ALLAN POE

***from* Darkness at Noon**
SIDNEY KINGSLEY

The Strike
TILLIE OLSEN

Other Media

Heroines: Remarkable and Inspiring Women
MARGE PIERCY
A richly illustrated anthology of short biographies about women who overcame adversity to become leaders in their fields.

Once Upon a Time When We Were Colored
CLIFTON L. TAULBERT
The inspiring story of Taulbert's coming of age in the segregated South.

Joseph Campbell and The Power of Myth
In this six-part series, Bill Moyers interviews Joseph Campbell and explores the power of mythology to guide our lives. Filmic Archives.
(VIDEOCASSETTE)

Antigone
This Greek film, with English subtitles, presents Sophocles' masterpiece in its native setting. With Irene Pappas. Filmic Archives.
(VIDEOCASSETTE)

A Chip of Glass Ruby
Films for the Humanities & Sciences.
(VIDEOCASSETTE)

Louise Erdrich Reads
American Audio Prose Library.
(AUDIOCASSETTE)

EXTEND YOUR READING 1117

EMILY DICKINSON
AMY TAN
WALT WHITMAN
EDNA ST. VINCENT MILLAY
MAYA ANGEL
ROBERT FROST
KURT VONNEGUT, JR.
O. HENRY
LEO TOLSTOY
GABRIELA MISTRAL
SIR THOMAS MALOR
ALICE WALKER
CORETTA SCOTT KING
AGATHA CHRISTIE
LANGSTON HUGHES
STEPHEN CRANE
SANDRA CISNEROS
ISABEL ALLENDE
CHINUA ACHEBE
MARK TWAIN
GUY DE MAUPASSANT
CARL SANDBURG
NIKKI GIOVANNI
TIM O'BRIEN
RAY BRADBURY
EDGAR ALLAN POE
ANTON CHEKH
PABLO NERUDA
1118
WILLIAM SHAKESPEA

Student *Resource Bank*

1119

Reading for Different Purposes

You read for many different reasons. In a single day, you might read a short story for fun, a textbook for information to help you pass a test, and a weather map to find out if it will rain. For every type of reading, there are specific strategies that can help you understand and remember the material. This handbook will help you become a better reader in school, at home, and on the job.

Reading Literature

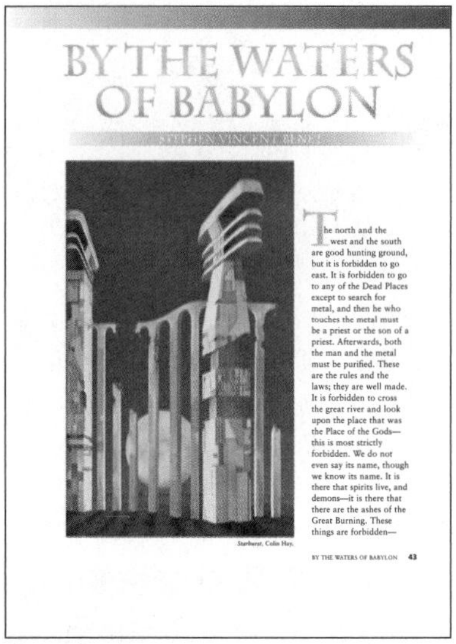
BY THE WATERS OF BABYLON

STEPHEN VINCENT BENÉT

The north and the west and the south are good hunting ground, but it is forbidden to go east. It is forbidden to go to any of the Dead Places except to search for metal, and then he who touches the metal must be a priest or the son of a priest. Afterwards, both the man and the metal must be purified. These are the rules and the laws; they are well made. It is forbidden to cross the great river and look upon the place that was the Place of the Gods—this is most strictly forbidden. We do not even say its name, though we know its name. It is there that spirits live, and demons—it is there that there are the ashes of the Great Burning. These things are forbidden—

Starburst, Colin Hay.

BY THE WATERS OF BABYLON 43

Before Reading

- **Set a purpose** for reading. What do you want to learn? Are you reading as part of an assignment or for fun? Establishing a purpose will help you focus.
- **Preview** the work by looking at the title and any images and captions. Try to **predict** what the work will be about.
- Ask yourself if you can **connect** the subject matter with what you already know.

During Reading

- **Check your understanding** of what you read. Can you restate the plot in your own words?
- Try to **connect** what you're reading to your own life. Have you experienced similar events or emotions?
- **Question** what's happening. You may wonder about events and characters' feelings.
- **Visualize,** or create a mental picture of, what the author describes.
- **Pause** from time to time to **predict** what will happen next.

After Reading

- **Review** your predictions. Were they correct?
- Try to **summarize** the work, expressing the **main idea** or the basic plot.
- **Reflect on** and evaluate what you have read. Did the reading fulfill your purpose?
- To **clarify** your understanding, write down opinions or thoughts about the work, or discuss it with someone.

Reading for Information

Is "youth sports rage" on the rise?

Parents become violent and abusive during kids' games

by Belinda Liu

The news stories are frightening. In Virginia, the mother of a soccer player assaults a 14-year-old referee and is fined. In Pennsylvania, a "midget league" football game results in a brawl involving about 100 players and spectators. Accounts of "youth sports rage" are reported in Britain, Canada, Australia, and New Zealand.

Are spectators at youth sports becoming more violent? Some observers believe they are.

"There have always been problem parents" in kids' sports, explains soccer coach Larry Fiore. "But the vast majority of parents, coaches, and athletes act appropriately."

However, some factors are making the problem worse, be-lieves sports psychologist Theresa Mathelier. "Sports are getting more expensive for parents in terms of equipment, traveling, and coaching," she explains. "The tendency now is to start kids in organized sports earlier and to get them to specialize in one sport."

As a result, Mathelier says, "a few parents get unrealistic ideas about college scholarships and professional careers in sports. They start to live through their kids, and if something goes wrong, they blow up."

Fiore and Mathelier both say that it is rarely the athletes who cause the problems. Serena Terell, a 15-year-old soccer player, agrees.

"It's so embarrassing when the parents yell and curse," Serena explains, adding that her parents always behave themselves. "Their kids just want them to stop. After all, it's only a game, and parents should be role models."

"Parents should be role models."

Stopping sports rage

Here are steps that some groups have taken to prevent youth sports rage.

- The National Youth Sports Safety Foundation has created a Sport Parent Code of. Penalties range from a verbal warning to a season suspension for parents.
- Many soccer leagues designate one day as "Silent Sunday." Spectators are not allowed to cheer or even talk until the game is over.
- Some coaches choose one parent to be in charge of crowd control. This parent patrols the bleachers or sidelines, making sure that fans of his or her team behave.

1120 READING HANDBOOK

Set a Purpose for Reading
- Decide why you are reading the material—to study for a test, to do research, or to find out more about a topic that interests you.
- Use your **purpose** to determine how detailed your **notes** will be.

Look at Design Features
- Look at the **title** and **subheads,** and at **boldfaced words or phrases, boxed text,** and any other text that is highlighted in some way.
- Use these **text organizers** for help in previewing the text and identifying the main ideas.
- Study photographs, maps, charts, and captions.

Notice Text Structures and Patterns
- Does the text make **comparisons?** Does it describe **causes** and **effects?** Is there a **sequence** of events?
- Look for **signal words** such as *same, different, because, first,* and *then*. They can reveal the material's organizational pattern.

Read Slowly and Carefully
- **Take notes** on the main ideas. State the information in your own words.
- Map the information by using a word web or another **graphic organizer.**
- Notice **unfamiliar words.** These are sometimes defined in the text.
- If there are **questions** accompanying the text, be sure that you can answer them.

Evaluate the Information
- Think about what you have read. Does the text make sense? Is it complete?
- **Summarize** the information—state the main points in just a few words.

Functional Reading

Setting the Sleep Timer

1. Press the MENU key. The Setup menu will appear on your television.
2. Select the Timer Setup on your screen by using the UP/DOWN arrows on your remote control.
3. Now press the RIGHT/LEFT arrows. A menu of the Timer Setup will appear on the screen.
4. Sleep Timer: Use the RIGHT/LEFT arrows to program the length of time until the TV shuts down. You can select any time from ten minutes to four hours. Press ENTER to return to TV viewing.

Setting the On/Off Timer

5. Follow steps 1 and 2 above to get to the Timer Setup menu. Using the UP/DOWN arrows on the remote control, select On Time on your screen.
6. Press the RIGHT or LEFT arrow to adjust the time your television will turn on automatically.
7. Press the TIMER button to choose either A.M. or P.M.
8. Repeat steps 5 through 7 to set Off Time. Use the UP/DOWN arrows to select the On/Off Timer, and activate the timer by pressing a RIGHT/LEFT arrow.

WARNING: The On/Off timer will not work until the clock on your television has been set.

Identify the Audience, Source, and Purpose
- Look for clues that tell you whom the document is for. Is there an address or a title? Does the information in the document affect you?
- Look for clues that tell you who created the document. Is the **source** likely to be reliable?
- Think about the **purpose** of the document. Is it to show you how to do something? to warn you about something? to tell you about community events?

Read Carefully
- Notice **headings** or **rules** that separate one section from another.
- Look for numbers or letters that signal steps in a **sequence.** If you are reading directions, read them all the way through at least once before performing the steps.
- Examine any charts, photographs, or other **visuals** and their captions.
- **Reread** complex instructions if necessary.

Evaluate the Information
- Think about whether you have found the information you need.
- Look for telephone numbers, street addresses, or e-mail addresses of places where you could find more information.

READING HANDBOOK 1121

Reading Different Genres

Reading an autobiography and reading a poem require different skills. Here are some tips to help you get the most out of the different genres, or types, of literature you read. The graphic organizers shown are just suggestions—use the note-taking method that works best for you.

Reading a Short Story

Strategies for Reading

- Keep track of events as they happen. Creating a chart like this one may help you.

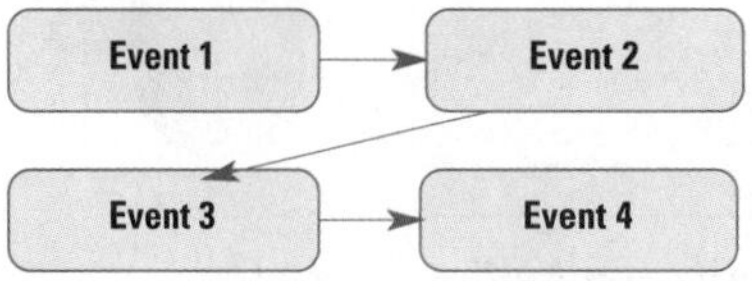

- From the details the writer provides, **visualize** the characters. **Predict** what they might do next.
- Look for specific adjectives that help you visualize the **setting**—the time and place in which events occur.

Reading a Poem

Strategies for Reading

- Notice the **form** of the poem, or the number of its lines and their shape on the page.
- Read the poem aloud a few times. Listen for **rhymes** and **rhythms.**
- **Visualize** the images and comparisons.
- **Connect** with the poem by asking yourself what message the poet is trying to send.
- Create a word web or other **graphic organizer** to record your reactions and questions.

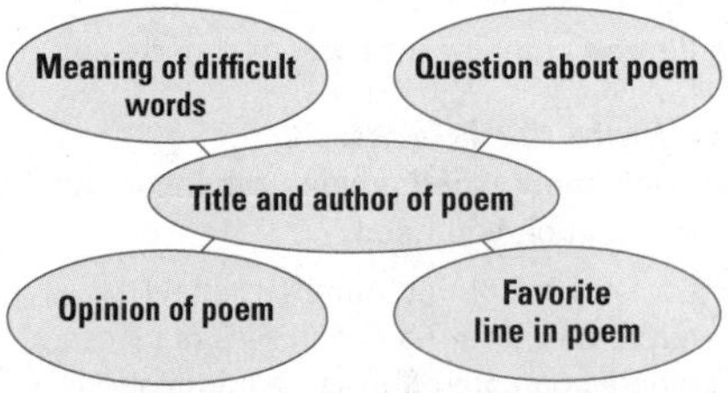

Reading a Play

Strategies for Reading

- Read the stage directions to help you **visualize** the setting and characters.
- **Question** what the title means and why the playwright chose it.
- Identify the main conflict (struggle or problem) in the play. To **clarify** the conflict, make a chart that shows what the conflict is and how it is resolved.
- **Evaluate** the characters. What do they want? How do they change during the play? You may want to make a chart that lists each character's name, appearance, mannerisms, and other information.

Reading Nonfiction

Strategies for Reading

- If you are reading a biography or autobiography, keep track of the people who are mentioned. You may want to sketch a family tree or a word web.
- When reading an essay, **evaluate** the writer's ideas and reasoning. Does the writer support opinions with facts?
- When reading an article or interview, **skim** it first to learn what its subject is. Look at any **headings** or **captions.** Then read slowly, looking for the **main idea.** Use a chart like this one to help you.

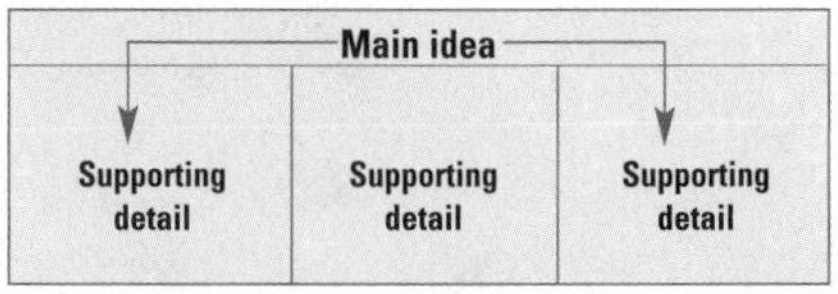

1122 READING HANDBOOK

Reading Different Formats

These strategies will help you when you need to do research, learn about current events, or just find out more about a topic that interests you.

Reading Online Text

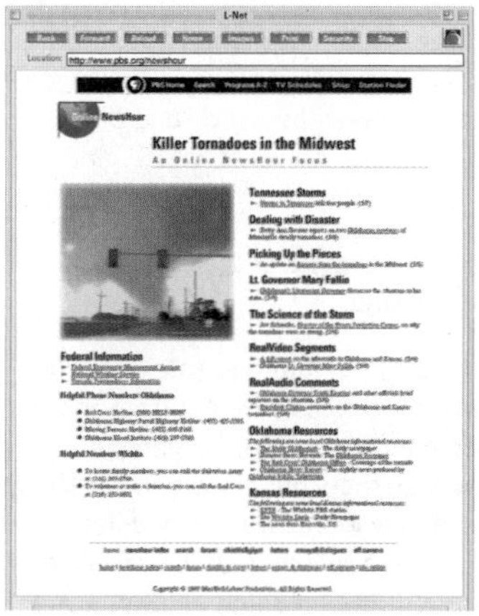

Strategies for Reading

- Notice the page's **Web address,** sometimes called a URL. You may want to make a note of it if you will need to return to that page. Most Web addresses begin with the coding http://www.
- Read the **title** of the page to get a general idea of what topics the page covers.
- Notice **links** to related pages. Links are often "buttons" or underlined words. Clicking on a link will take you to a different page—one that may or may not have been created by the same person or organization.
- Look for a **menu bar** along the top, bottom, or side of the page. This gives you links to other parts of the Web site.
- Notice any **source citations.** Some sites tell you where their information is from, enabling you to judge its reliability.
- Write down **important ideas** and **details.** Try to restate the text in your own words. Then decide whether you need to check other sources.

Reading a Newspaper or Magazine Article

Strategies for Reading

- Read the **headline** and any **subheads** to learn what the article is about and how it is organized.
- Notice any photographs, charts, graphs, or other **visuals.** Read their **captions.** Be sure you understand how the visuals and the main text are related.
- Notice any **quotations.** Think about whether the people who are quoted are likely to be reliable authorities on the topic.

Reading an Encyclopedia Article

Strategies for Reading

- Read the **headline** and any **subheads** to make sure that the article covers the topic of interest to you.
- Look at **visuals** and read their **captions.** Some online or CD-ROM encyclopedias also include sound files, animated maps, and short movies.
- Pay attention to how the article is organized. You may want to **skim** the article, or read it quickly, as you look for **key words** related to your topic. Once you find the information you need, read slowly and carefully.
- Watch for a **"see also"** or **"related articles"** section or—if the encyclopedia is online—for highlighted links. These features direct you to additional articles that may include information on your subject.

READING HANDBOOK 1123

Enriching Your Vocabulary

Context Clues

One way to figure out the meaning of a word you don't know is by using context clues. The context of a word consists of the punctuation marks, other words, sentences, and paragraphs that surround the word.

General Context Sometimes you need to read all the information in the sentence or paragraph in order to infer the meaning of an unfamiliar word.

> When Mike felt the paint and found it was still **tacky,** he looked at the directions to see how long it should take to dry.

> The gray, gloomy day made Ann feel weepy and **melancholy.**

Definition Clues Often a difficult word will be followed by its definition. Commas, dashes, or other punctuation marks may signal a definition.

> **Permafrost**—a layer of permanently frozen ground—is underneath about one-fifth of Earth's land surfaces.

Restatement Clues Sometimes a writer restates a word or term in easier language. Commas, dashes, or other punctuation as well as expressions such as *that is, in other words,* and *or,* may signal restatement clues.

> The film critic complained that *My Only Love* was too **sentimental;** in other words, it was mushy and overly emotional.

Example Clues Sometimes writers suggest the meanings of words with one or two examples.

> The hero of the novel faced many **imperilments,** including poisonous snakes, hungry tigers, and huge deserts.

Comparison Clues Sometimes a word's meaning is suggested by a comparison to something similar. *Like* and *as* are words that signal comparison clues.

> At night our house is as **frigid** as the North Pole.

Contrast Clues Sometimes writers point out differences between things or ideas. Contrast clues are often signaled by words and phrases such as *although, but, however, unlike,* and *in contrast to*.

> The swimmer was **agile** in the water but clumsy on dry land.

Idioms and Slang An idiom is an expression whose overall meaning is different from the meaning of the individual words. Slang is informal language that comprises both made-up words and ordinary words that carry different meanings than in formal English. Use context clues to figure out the meaning of idioms and slang.

> None of us finished our homework, so we are **all in the same boat.** (idiom)

> Stop **bugging out!** We'll make it to the concert on time. (slang)

TIP One way to clarify your understanding of a word is to write a sentence using that word. Even better, use one of the context-clue strategies in your sentence. For example, include a restatement or definition clue.

For more about context clues, see pages 56, 908, and 1000; for more about idioms and slang, see page 419.

1124 READING HANDBOOK

Word Parts

If you know base words, roots, and affixes—that is, prefixes and suffixes—you can figure out the meanings of many new words.

Base Words A **base word** is a word that can stand alone. Other words or word parts can be added to base words to form new words.

Roots Many English words contain roots that come from older languages, such as Greek, Latin, and Old English. A **root** is a word part that contains the core meaning of the word. Knowing the meaning of a word's root or roots can help you figure out the word's meaning.

Root	Meaning	Examples
dynam (Greek)	power, force	dynamic, dynamo
paleo (Greek)	ancient, early, prehistoric	paleobiology, paleolithic
cent (Latin)	one hundred	century, percent
gress (Latin)	step	progress, regressive
port (Latin)	carry	portable, transport
lor(e)n (Old English)	lost	forlorn, lovelorn
mer(e) (Old English)	sea, pool	mermaid, merman

Prefixes A **prefix** is a word part that appears at the beginning of a base word or another word part. Attaching a prefix to an existing word usually changes the meaning of that word. Familiarizing yourself with the meanings of common prefixes can help you be prepared to figure out the meanings of unfamiliar words.

Prefix	Meaning	Examples
hyper-	over, excessive	hyperactive, hypersensitive
inter-	among, between	interactive, Internet
re-	again	renew, replace, refinish
tele-	distant	television, telescope
un-	not	uncomfortable, unlike

Suffixes A **suffix** is a word part attached to the end of a base word or another word part. Attaching a suffix to an existing word may alter the word's meaning. However, a suffix does not change a word's meaning when it is added as follows:

- to a noun to change the number
- to a verb to change the tense
- to an adjective to change the degree of comparison
- to an adverb to show how

Suffix	Purpose	Examples
-s, -es	to change the number of a noun	sock + *s*, socks
-ed, -ing	to change verb tense	jump + *ed*, jumped jump + *ing*, jumping
-er, -est	to change the degree of comparison in modifiers	young + *er*, younger young + *est*, youngest
-ly	to show how	wild + *ly*, wildly

Other suffixes are added to a base word or root to change the word's meaning. These suffixes can also be used to change the word's part of speech.

Suffix	Meaning	Examples
-ist	one who is or does	artist, florist, terrorist
-ish	of, relating to, being	boyish, selfish
-ize	to make	energize, dramatize

To infer the meaning of an unfamiliar word from its parts, follow these steps.

- Divide the word into parts. Think of other words you know that share the same root(s) or base word.
- Ask, Do these other words all have the same or similar meanings?
- Consider the meanings of any prefixes or suffixes in the word.
- From the meanings of the unfamiliar word's parts, predict what the word means.
- Check the context and consult a dictionary or glossary to find out whether your prediction is correct.

For more about roots, prefixes, and suffixes, see pages 183 and 356.

READING HANDBOOK 1125

Word Origins

When you study a word's history and origin, you find out when, where, and how the word came to be. A complete dictionary entry includes each word's history.

dra•ma (drä′mə) *n.* **1.** A work that is meant to be performed by actors. **2.** Theatrical works of a certain type or period in history. [Late Latin *drāma, drāmat-*, from Greek *drān*, to do or perform.]

This entry shows you that the earliest form of the word *drama* was the Greek word *drān*.

Word Families Words that have the same root have related meanings. Such words make up a word family. The charts below show common Greek and Latin roots. Notice how the meanings of the English words are related to the meanings of their roots.

Greek Root:	***soph,*** wise
English:	**sophomore** "wise fool"; a student in the second year of high school or college
	sophisticated worldly, refined, or complex
	philosophy "love of wisdom"; the study of logic and basic truths

Latin Root:	***circum,*** around or about
English:	**circumference** the boundary line of a circle
	circumnavigation the act of moving completely around
	circumstance a condition or fact surrounding an event

Latin Root:	***fin,*** to end
English:	**final** forming or occurring at the end
	finish to bring to an end
	finite having bounds; limited

Latin Root:	***struct,*** to build
English:	**construct** to build
	destructive causing the ruin or elimination of something
	structure a building

TIP Once you recognize a root in one English word, you will notice the same root in other words—members of the same word family. Because these words developed from the same root, they are similar in meaning.

Foreign Words Some words that enter the English language keep their original form.

Dutch	French	Italian	Japanese
aloof	boutique	graffiti	judo
cookie	chauffeur	paparazzi	kimono
gruesome	espionage	soprano	origami
knack	mirage	spaghetti	samurai
maelstrom	sabotage	staccato	tsunami
sloop	vague	virtuoso	soy

For more about word families, see pages 183 and 356; for more about foreign words, see page 584.

Synonyms and Antonyms

When you read, pay attention to the precise words a writer uses.

Synonyms A **synonym** is a word that has the same or almost the same meaning as another word. Read each set of synonyms listed below.

happen/occur
plagiarize/cheat
woods/forest
lukewarm/mild
pact/agreement
considerate/thoughtful
rarely/seldom
gently/lightly

TIP You can find synonyms in a thesaurus or dictionary. In a dictionary, synonyms are often given following the definition of a word.

1126 READING HANDBOOK

Antonyms An **antonym** is a word with a meaning opposite of that of another word. Read each set of antonyms listed below:

idle/busy
early/late
generous/stingy
comfort/irritate
hard/soft
hurry/dawdle
before/after
rough/smooth

Some antonyms are formed by adding one of the negative prefixes *anti-*, *in-*, and *un-* to a word, as in the chart below.

Word	Prefix	Antonym
bacterial	*anti-*	antibacterial
thesis	*anti-*	antithesis
accurate	*in-*	inaccurate
consistent	*in-*	inconsistent
true	*un-*	untrue
usual	*un-*	unusual

TIP You can find antonyms in dictionaries of synonyms and antonyms, as well as in some thesauruses.

TIP Some dictionaries contain notes that discuss synonyms and antonyms. These notes often include sentences that illustrate the relationships among the words.

For more about synonyms and antonyms, see page 1000.

Denotative and Connotative Meaning

Good writers choose just the right word to communicate a specific meaning.

Denotative Meaning A word's dictionary meaning is called its **denotation.** The denotation of the word *thin*, for example, is "having little flesh; spare; lean."

Connotative Meaning The images or feelings you connect to a word are called **connotations**. Connotative meaning stretches beyond a word's dictionary definition. Writers rely on connotations of words to communicate shades of meaning, as well as positive or negative feelings. For example, which of these sentences gives you a positive mental picture, and which gives you a negative mental picture?

A season on the track team left Xavier looking **lean** and **slender.**

A season on the track team left Xavier looking **skinny** and **scrawny.**

Examples of similar words with different connotations are listed below.

Positive Connotations	Negative Connotations
aroma	stench
assertive	bossy
bold	reckless
casual	sloppy
caution	cowardice
gaze	glare
inquisitive	nosy
popular	commonplace
slender	scrawny

TIP Some dictionaries contain notes that discuss connotative meanings of the entry word and other related words.

For more information about denotative and connotative meanings, see page 494.

READING HANDBOOK 1127

Homonyms, Multiple-Meaning Words, and Homophones

Homonyms, multiple-meaning words, and homophones can be confusing to readers and can plague writers.

Homonyms Words that have the same spelling and pronunciation but different meanings and, in most cases, different origins are called **homonyms**. Consider this example:

> The city's oldest **bank** was on the **bank** of the Charles River.

Bank can mean "a place or organization where money is kept, loaned, or invested," but it can also mean "the land alongside a river, creek, or pond."

Words with Multiple Meanings Multiple-meaning words are those that have over time acquired additional meanings based on the original meaning. Consider these examples:

> I hurt my **back** and neck last Friday.
>
> We were playing stickball in **back** of the convenience store.

Back clearly has multiple meanings, but all of the additional meanings have developed from the same original meaning. You will find all the meanings for *back* under one entry in the dictionary.

Homophones Words that sound alike but have different meanings and spellings are called homophones. Consider these examples:

> The birds **soar** gracefully in the air.
>
> Kristin's legs were **sore** after she ran a marathon.

Many common words with Anglo-Saxon origins have homophones *(there, their; write, right).* Check your writing to make sure you have used the right word and not its homophone.

For more about homonyms and multiple-meaning words, see page 678.

Analogies

Analogy An **analogy** is a comparison between two things that are similar in some way. Analogies often appear on tests, usually in a format like this:

BRANCH : TREE :: A) floral : pattern
B) toe : foot
C) autumn : season
D) limb : arm
E) tree : limb

To choose the correct answer, follow these steps:

- Read the part in capital letters as "*Branch* is to *tree* as . . . "
- Read the answer choices as "*floral* is to *pattern*," "*toe* is to *foot*," "*autumn* is to *season*," and so on.
- Ask yourself how the first two words, *branch* and *tree*, are related. (A branch is a part of a tree. So *branch* and *tree* have a part-to-whole relationship.)
- Then look for the answer that best shows the same relationship. (Of these possible answers, only item B shows the relationship of a part to a whole. The trickiest answer is E, because it shows a whole-to-part relationship, which is close to, but not exactly, the same relationship.)

Types of Analogies Here are some common relationships that are often expressed in analogies:

Relationship	Example
Part to whole	BRANCH : TREE
Synonyms	EASY : SIMPLE
Antonyms	BOILING : FREEZING
Degree of intensity	HAPPY : ECSTATIC
Characteristics to object	SMOOTHNESS : SILK
Item to category	TRACTOR : VEHICLE

For more about analogies, see page 263.

1128 READING HANDBOOK

Specialized Vocabulary

Professionals who work in fields such as law, science, or sports use their own technical or specialized vocabulary.

The high court **reversed** and **remanded** the case, ordering the lower-court judge to reexamine her faulty reasoning.

Use these strategies to help you figure out the meanings of specialized vocabulary.

Use Context Clues Often the surrounding text gives clues that help you infer the meaning of an unfamiliar term.

The computer-generated **special effects** in the movie are incredibly realistic.

Use Reference Tools Textbooks often define a special term when it is first introduced. Look for definitions or restatement clues in parentheses. Also you can try to find definitions in footnotes, a glossary, or a dictionary. If you need more information, refer to a specialized reference, such as one of the following:

- an encyclopedia
- a field guide
- an atlas
- a user's manual
- a technical dictionary

Decoding Multisyllabic Words

Many words that are familiar to you when you speak or hear them may be unfamiliar to you when you see them in print. When you come across a word unfamiliar in print, first try to pronounce it to see if you recognize it. The following syllabication generalizations can help you figure out a word's pronunciation:

Generalization 1: VCCV
When there are two consonants between two vowels, divide between the two consonants, unless they are a blend or a digraph.

lum/ber   shat/ter   broth/er

Generalization 2: VCCCV
When there are three consonants between two vowels, divide between the blend or the digraph and the other consonant.

an/gler   mer/chant   tum/bler

Generalization 3: VCCV
When there are two consonants between two vowels, divide between the consonants, unless they are a blend or a digraph, the first syllable is a closed syllable, and the vowel is short.

traf/fic   ush/er   sum/mer

Generalization 4: Common Vowel Clusters
Do not split common vowel clusters, such as long vowel digraphs, *r*-controlled vowels, and vowel diphthongs.

gar/den   pain/ful   gar/age

Generalization 5: VCV
When you see a VCV pattern in the middle of a word, divide the word either before or after the consonant. If you divide the word after the consonant, pronounce the first vowel sound as short. If you divide the word before the consonant, pronounce the first vowel sound as long.

lev/er   o/boe   spi/der

Generalization 6: Compound Words
Divide compound words between the individual words.

bath/tub   some/one

Generalization 7: Affixes
When a word includes an affix, divide between the base word and the affix.

like/ness   uni/form

Reading for Information

Reading informational materials—such as textbooks, magazines, newspapers, and Web pages—requires the use of special strategies. For example, you need to study text organizers, such as headings and special type, to learn the main ideas, facts, terms, and names that are of importance. You also need to identify patterns of organization in the text. Using such strategies will help you to read informational materials with ease and quickly gain a clear understanding of their contents.

Reading a Textbook

Look for headings, large or dark type, pictures, and drawings that signal the most important information on the page. These special features, called **text organizers,** help you understand and remember what you read.

Strategies for Reading

- **A** First, look at the **title** and any **subheads.** These will tell you the main ideas.
- **B** Many textbooks include a list of **objectives** or **key terms** at the start of each lesson. Keep these in mind as you read. They will help you focus on the most important facts and details.
- **C** **Key terms** are often boldfaced or underlined where they first appear in the text. Be sure that you understand what they mean.
- **D** Notice any **special features,** such as sidebar articles or extended quotations. These provide important details and can help you visualize the information.
- **E** Look at the **visuals**—charts, maps, time lines, photographs, illustrations—and read any **captions** or **questions** that accompany them. Visuals often present information that is not in the main text.

3 Napoleon Forges an Empire (A)

(B) TERMS &
- Napoleo
- coup d'ét
- plebiscit
- lycée
- concorda
- Napoleo
- Battle of

MAIN IDEA	WHY IT MATTERS NOW
A military genius, Napoleon Bonaparte, seized power in France and made himself emperor.	In times of political turmoil, military dictators often seize control of nations, as in Haiti in 1991.

SETTING THE STAGE Napoleon was a short man (five feet three inches tall) who cast a long shadow over the history of modern times. He would come to be recognized as one of the world's greatest military geniuses, along with Alexander the Great of Macedonia, Hannibal of Carthage, and Julius Caesar of Rome. In only four years (1795–1799), Napoleon rose from relative obscurity to become master of France.

(A) Napoleon Grasps the Power

Napoleon Bonaparte was born in 1769 on the Mediterranean island of Corsica. When he was nine years old, his parents sent him to a military school in northern France. In 1785, at the age of 16, he finished school and became a lieutenant in the artillery. When the Revolution broke out, Napoleon joined the army of the new government.

Hero of the Hour In October 1795, fate handed the young officer a chance for glory. When royalist rebels marched on the National Convention, a government official told Napoleon to defend the delegates. Napoleon and his gunners greeted the thousands of royalists with a cannonade. Within minutes, the attackers fled in panic and confusion. Napoleon Bonaparte became the hero of the hour and was hailed throughout Paris as the savior of the French republic.

In 1796, the Directory appointed Napoleon to lead a French army against the forces of Austria and the Kingdom of Sardinia. Crossing the Alps, the young general swept into Italy and won a series of remarkable victories, which crushed the Austrian troops' threat to France. Next, in an attempt to protect French trade interests and to disrupt British trade with India, Napoleon led an expedition to Egypt. Unfortunately, his luck did not hold. His army was pinned down in Egypt, and his naval forces were defeated by the British admiral Horatio Nelson. However, he managed to keep the reports of his defeat out of the press, so that by 1799 the words "the general" could mean only one man to the French—Napoleon.

Coup d'État By 1799, the Directory had lost control of the political situation and the confidence of the French people. Only the directors' control of the army kept them in power. Upon Napoleon's return from Egypt, the Abbé Sieyès urged him to seize political power. Napoleon and Josephine, his lovely socialite wife, set a plan in motion. Napoleon met with influential persons to discuss his role in the Directory, while Josephine used her connections with the wealthy directors to influence their decisions. The action began on November 9, 1799, when Napoleon was put in charge of the military. It ended the next day when his troops drove out the members of one chamber of the

Vocab
cann
bardm
artiller

(D) **HISTORY MAKERS**

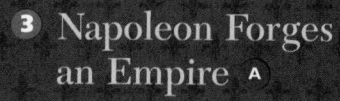

Napoleon Bonaparte 1769–1821

Napoleon Bonaparte had a magnetism that attracted the admiration of his men. His speeches were designed to inspire his troops to valorous feats. In one speech, he told soldiers, "If the victory is for a moment uncertain, you shall see your Emperor place himself on the front line."

Bonaparte was generous in his rewards to the troops. Many received the Legion of Honor—a medal for bravery. Sometimes Napoleon would take the medal from his own chest to present it to a soldier. (He kept a few spares in his pocket for these occasions.) A cavalry commander, Auguste de Colbert, wrote, "He awakened in my soul the desire for glory."

584 Chapter 23

1130 READING HANDBOOK

More Strategies for Reading Textbooks

- Before you begin the text, read any **questions** that appear at the end of the lesson or chapter. These will help you focus your reading.
- Read slowly and carefully. If you see an unfamiliar word and can't find a definition in the text or in a marginal note, check the **glossary** or a dictionary. Look for **pronunciation guides** as you read.
- Take **notes** as you read. These will help you understand new ideas and terms. Review your notes before a test to jog your memory.
- You may want to take notes in the form of a **graphic organizer,** such as a cause-and-effect chart, or a comparison-and-contrast chart.

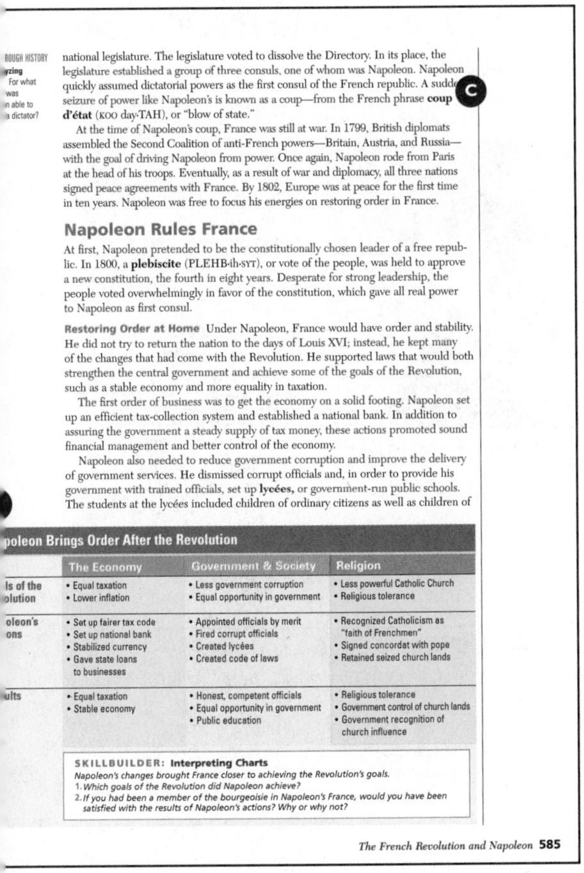

ROUGH HISTORY
yzing
For what
was
n able to
a dictator?

national legislature. The legislature voted to dissolve the Directory. In its place, the legislature established a group of three consuls, one of whom was Napoleon. Napoleon quickly assumed dictatorial powers as the first consul of the French republic. A sudde[n] seizure of power like Napoleon's is known as a coup—from the French phrase **coup d'état** (KOO day·TAH), or "blow of state."

C

At the time of Napoleon's coup, France was still at war. In 1799, British diplomats assembled the Second Coalition of anti-French powers—Britain, Austria, and Russia—with the goal of driving Napoleon from power. Once again, Napoleon rode from Paris at the head of his troops. Eventually, as a result of war and diplomacy, all three nations signed peace agreements with France. By 1802, Europe was at peace for the first time in ten years. Napoleon was free to focus his energies on restoring order in France.

Napoleon Rules France

At first, Napoleon pretended to be the constitutionally chosen leader of a free republic. In 1800, a **plebiscite** (PLEHB·ih·SYT), or vote of the people, was held to approve a new constitution, the fourth in eight years. Desperate for strong leadership, the people voted overwhelmingly in favor of the constitution, which gave all real power to Napoleon as first consul.

Restoring Order at Home Under Napoleon, France would have order and stability. He did not try to return the nation to the days of Louis XVI; instead, he kept many of the changes that had come with the Revolution. He supported laws that would both strengthen the central government and achieve some of the goals of the Revolution, such as a stable economy and more equality in taxation.

The first order of business was to get the economy on a solid footing. Napoleon set up an efficient tax-collection system and established a national bank. In addition to assuring the government a steady supply of tax money, these actions promoted sound financial management and better control of the economy.

Napoleon also needed to reduce government corruption and improve the delivery of government services. He dismissed corrupt officials and, in order to provide his government with trained officials, set up **lycées,** or government-run public schools. The students at the lycées included children of ordinary citizens as well as children of

poleon Brings Order After the Revolution

	The Economy	Government & Society	Religion
ls of the olution	• Equal taxation • Lower inflation	• Less government corruption • Equal opportunity in government	• Less powerful Catholic Church • Religious tolerance
oleon's ons	• Set up fairer tax code • Set up national bank • Stabilized currency • Gave state loans to businesses	• Appointed officials by merit • Fired corrupt officials • Created lycées • Created code of laws	• Recognized Catholicism as "faith of Frenchmen" • Signed concordat with pope • Retained seized church lands
ults	• Equal taxation • Stable economy	• Honest, competent officials • Equal opportunity in government • Public education	• Religious tolerance • Government control of church lands • Government recognition of church influence

SKILLBUILDER: Interpreting Charts
Napoleon's changes brought France closer to achieving the Revolution's goals.
1. *Which goals of the Revolution did Napoleon achieve?*
2. *If you had been a member of the bourgeoisie in Napoleon's France, would you have been satisfied with the results of Napoleon's actions? Why or why not?*

The French Revolution and Napoleon **585**

More Examples

To examine the structural features of other kinds of informational materials, see the pages listed below.

For an example of a **newspaper article,** see page 998.

For examples of **magazine articles,** see pages 181, 276, 482, 590, 662, 836, 1088, and 1132.

READING HANDBOOK 1131

Reading Handbook

Reading a Magazine Article

Strategies for Reading

A Read the **title** and any other **headings** to get an idea of what the article is about and how it is organized.

B As you read the main text, notice any **quotations.** Who is quoted? Is the person a reliable authority on the subject?

C Notice text that is set off in some way, such as a passage in a **different typeface.** A quotation or statistic that sums up the article is sometimes presented in this way. A **sidebar article** can present more information.

D Study **visuals,** such as photographs, graphs, charts, and maps. Read their captions and make sure you know how they relate to the main text.

D

A

Is "youth sports rage" on the rise?

Parents become violent and abusive during kids' games

by Belinda Liu

The news stories are frightening. In Virginia, the mother of a soccer player assaults a 14-year-old referee and is fined. In Pennsylvania, a "midget league" football game results in a brawl involving about 100 players and spectators. Accounts of "youth sports rage" are reported in Britain, Canada, Australia, and New Zealand.

D

Are spectators at youth sports becoming more violent? Some observers believe they are.

B "There have always been problem parents in kids' sports," explains soccer coach Larry Fiore. "But the vast majority of parents, coaches, and athletes act appropriately."

However, some factors are making the problem worse, believes sports psychologist Theresa Mathelier. "Sports are getting more expensive for parents in terms of equipment, traveling, and coaching," she explains. "The tendency now is to start kids in organized sports earlier and to get them to specialize in one sport."

As a result, Mathelier says, "a few parents get unrealistic ideas about college scholarships and professional careers in sports. They start to live through their kids, and if something goes wrong, they blow up."

Fiore and Mathelier both say that it is rarely the athletes who cause the problems. Serena Terell, a 15-year-old soccer player, agrees. "It's so embarrassing when the parents yell and curse," Serena explains, adding that her parents always behave themselves. "Their kids just want them to stop. After all, it's only a game, and parents should be role models."

C *"Parents should be role models."*

Stopping sports rage **C**

Here are steps that some groups have taken to prevent youth sports rage.

- The National Youth Sports Safety Foundation has created a Sport Parent Code of Conduct. Penalties range from a verbal warning to a season suspension for parents.
- Some soccer leagues designate one day as "Silent Sunday." Spectators are not allowed to cheer or even talk until the game is over.
- Some coaches choose one parent to be in charge of crowd control. This parent patrols the bleachers or sidelines, making sure that fans of his or her team behave.

1132 READING HANDBOOK

Reading a Web Page

Strategies for Reading

A Look for the page's **Web address,** sometimes called a URL. You may want to write down the Web address if you think you will need to return to the page.

B Read the **title** of the page to find out what topics the page covers.

C Look for a **menu bar** along the top, bottom, or side of the page. This tells you about other parts of the site.

D Notice any **links** to related pages. Links are often "buttons" or underlined words.

E Some sites have **interactive areas** where you can communicate with experts or with other users of the site. This site allows users to participate in a forum with other users.

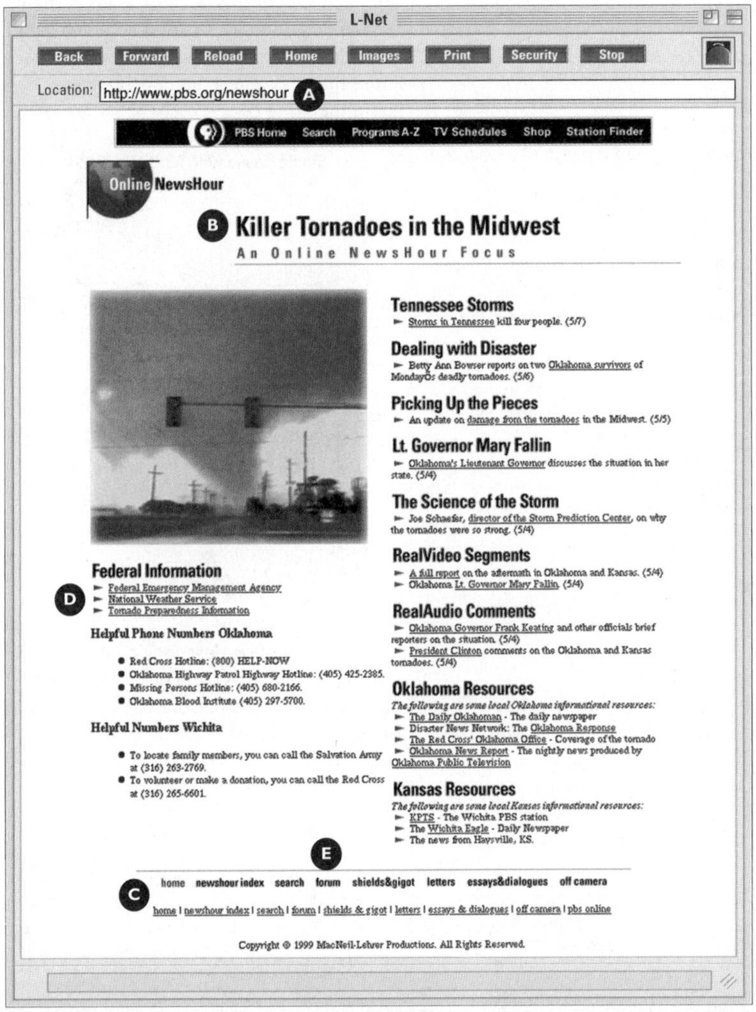

READING HANDBOOK 1133

Patterns of Organization

Reading any type of writing is easier if you understand how it is organized. A writer organizes ideas in a structure, or pattern, that helps the reader see how the ideas are related. Five important structures are the following:

- main idea and supporting details
- chronological order
- comparison and contrast
- cause and effect
- problem-solution

This page contains an overview of the five structures, which you will learn about in more detail on pages 1135–1139. Each type has been represented graphically to help you see how the ideas are organized in it.

Main Idea and Supporting Details

The main idea of a paragraph or a longer piece of writing is its most important point. Supporting details give more information about the main idea.

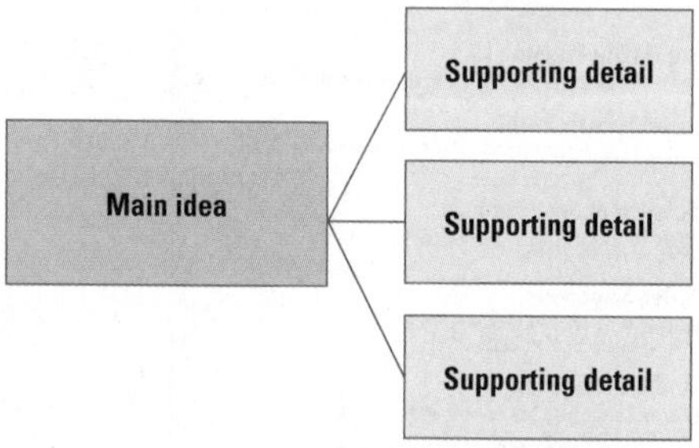

Chronological Order

Writing that is organized in chronological order presents events in the order in which they occur.

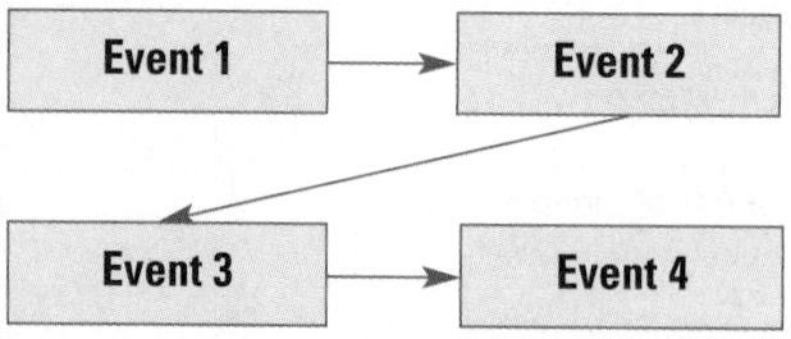

Comparison and Contrast

Comparison-and-contrast writing explains how two or more subjects are similar and how they are different.

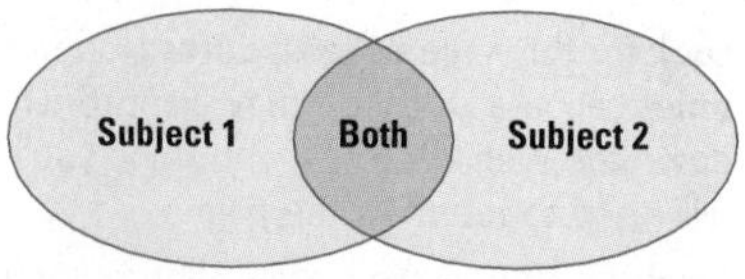

Cause and Effect

Cause-and-effect writing explains the relationship between events. A cause is an event, or a condition, that gives rise to another event or a condition, called an effect. A cause may have more than one effect, and an effect may have more than one cause.

Single Cause with Multiple Effects

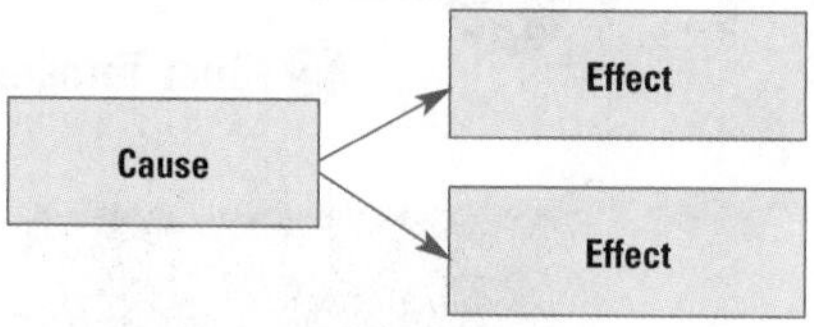

Multiple Causes with Single Effect

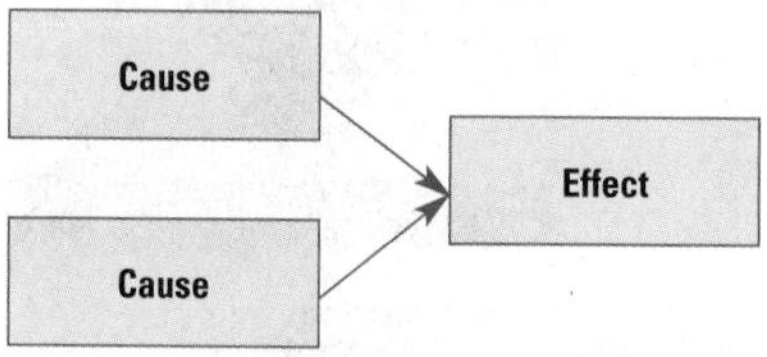

Problem-Solution

This type of writing describes a difficult issue and suggests at least one way of dealing with it. The writer provides reasons to support his or her suggestion.

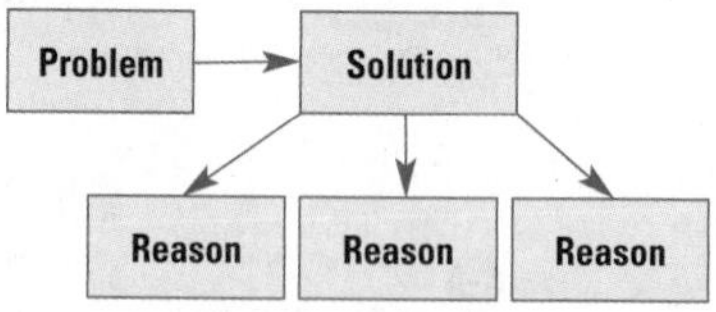

1134 READING HANDBOOK

Main Idea and Supporting Details

The **main idea** of a paragraph is the basic point the writer is making in that paragraph. The **supporting details** give you additional information about the main idea. A main idea may be stated directly, or it may be implied. If it is stated, it may appear anywhere in the paragraph. Often it appears in the first or the last sentence. An implied main idea is suggested through the details that are provided.

Strategies for Reading

- To find the **main idea,** ask, What is this paragraph about?
- To find **supporting details,** ask, What else do I learn about the main idea?

MODEL

Main Idea in the First Sentence

Main idea

Supporting details

Under Queen Elizabeth I, who ruled from 1558 to 1603, the Protestant faith again became England's official religion. In 1559, Parliament passed the Act of Supremacy. The Act made the queen the sole head of the Church of England. Also, English replaced Latin as the main language of the church and clergy were allowed to marry. Elizabeth further strengthened the Church of England by personally appointing all but one of the bishops.

MODEL

Main Idea in the Last Sentence

Supporting details

Main idea

The Renaissance in England was also called the Elizabethan Age, after Elizabeth I. During this time, nearly all English landowners and merchants could read and write. The Elizabethan Age was also an era of school-building and educational funding. The queen was well-educated and knew French, Italian, Latin, and Greek. Elizabeth wrote poetry, and she financed and encouraged artists and writers. During the Elizabethan Age, England experienced a revolution in arts and culture.

MODEL

Implied Main Idea

Implied main idea: Elizabeth I was greatly admired and celebrated by her subjects.

Artists and poets celebrated Elizabeth I in a variety of mythological disguises. She was portrayed as Diana, the goddess of the moon, and as Gloriana, the queen of the fairies. Portraits of Elizabeth were very popular. They usually showed the queen in her youth, wearing priceless pearls, rich furs, and pure white lace. Soon after her death, the English people began to long for the rule of Elizabeth, often called "Good Queen Bess."

PRACTICE AND APPLY

Queen Mary I died on November 17, 1558. When Mary's sister, Elizabeth, inherited the English throne, she quickly began making changes within the country. Elizabeth reduced the size of the Privy Council to make it more efficient as an advisory body. She also reorganized the large royal household and assembled a group of experienced advisers. Furthermore, England was soon restored to the Protestantism it had known under Henry VIII, Mary and Elizabeth's father.

Read the paragraph above and then do the following activities:

1. Identify the main idea of the model.
2. Is the main idea stated or implied? If it is stated, where does it appear in the model?
3. List at least three details that support or give evidence for the main idea.

PRACTICE AND APPLY ANSWERS

1. When Mary's sister, Elizabeth, inherited the English throne, she quickly began making changes within the country.
2. Stated; second sentence
3. Possible answers: Elizabeth reduced the size of the Privy Council; she reorganized the royal household; she assembled a group of advisers; England was restored to Protestantism.

READING HANDBOOK 1135

Chronological Order

Events discussed in **chronological order,** or time order, are treated in the order they happen. Historical events are usually presented in chronological order. The steps of a process may also be presented this way.

Strategies for Reading

- Look for the **individual events** or **steps in the sequence.**
- Look for words or phrases that identify **time,** such as *in a year, three hours earlier, in 202 B.C.,* and *later.*
- Look for words that signal **order,** such as *first, afterward, then, before, finally,* and *next.*

MODEL

Events

Time phrases

Order words and phrases

Napoleon Bonaparte was born in 1769 on the Mediterranean island of Corsica. As a boy, he was sent to boarding school in France. When Napoleon turned 16, he joined the French army. This marked the beginning of his military career.

After becoming a soldier, Napoleon was gradually given more important military duties, including the defense of a revolutionary convention in 1795 against royalist rebels. A few years later and after many military successes, Napoleon was given complete control of the military on November 9, 1799. The next day, Napoleon drove out members of the legislature and seized power. By 1802, after failing to defeat Napoleon, the nations of Britain, Austria, and Russia had signed a peace agreement with France. For the first time in 10 years, Europe was at peace.

Next, Napoleon began to restore order to France. He set up an efficient tax-collecting system, established a national bank, introduced a code of law, and reduced government corruption. In 1804, Napoleon crowned himself emperor.

Napoleon controlled the largest European empire since the time of the Romans. However, unlike the Roman Empire, Napoleon's empire lasted only 10 years. Napoleon's failed attempt to invade Russia in 1812 weakened the French military. His enemies were quick to take advantage of his weakness. By March 1814, the Russian czar and the Prussian king led their troops in a parade through Paris.

In April, Napoleon gave up his throne and was exiled to the island of Elba, off the coast of Italy. After an escape from Elba and a brief return to power in 1815, Napoleon was defeated at the Battle of Waterloo on June 15, 1815. He was again banished, this time to the island of St. Helena, in the South Atlantic. He died in 1821.

Historians recognize Napoleon as a military genius. However, his most lasting accomplishments were acts that did not require military force, such as his law code and some of his other reforms.

PRACTICE AND APPLY

Reread the model and then do the following activities:

1. List at least eight words or phrases the writer uses to indicate time or order.
2. Create a time line that begins with Napoleon's birth and ends with his death. List the events described in the model.

PRACTICE AND APPLY ANSWERS

1. Possible answers: in 1769; As a boy; When Napoleon turned 16; This marked the beginning; After; gradually; in 1795; A few years later; after; on November 9, 1799; The next day; By 1802; after; For the first time in 10 years; Next; In 1804; since the time of the Romans; only 10 years; in 1812; By March 1814; In April; After; in 1815; again; in 1821
2. 1769—Napoleon born; 1785—joins army; 1795—defends revolutionary convention; 1799—is given control of military and seizes power; 1802—other nations sign peace agreement with France; 1804—crowns self Emperor; 1812—fails in attempt to invade Russia; 1814—enemies parade through Paris and Napoleon is exiled; 1815—escapes, returns to power, is defeated at Waterloo, and is exiled again; 1821—dies

Comparison and Contrast

Comparison-and-contrast writing explains how two subjects are alike and different. This type of writing is usually organized by subject or by feature. In **subject organization,** the writer discusses first one subject, then the other. In **feature organization,** the writer compares a feature of one subject with the same feature of the other, then compares another feature of both, and so on.

Strategies for Reading

- Look for words and phrases that signal **comparisons,** such as *like, similar, similarly, both,* and *in the same way.*
- Look for words and phrases that signal **contrasts,** such as *unlike, in contrast, differ,* and *different.*

MODEL

The pyramid is perhaps the most well-known accomplishment of ancient peoples. When most people think of these amazing structures, they think of Egypt. However, Egypt was not the only place where pyramids were built. Pyramids were also constructed in the Americas, mainly in Central and South America.

Subjects

Most pyramid construction in Egypt took place between 2686 and 2345 B.C. In contrast, most Central and South American pyramids were built much later. So far, only one pyramid of the Americas has been found to be similar in age to the Egyptian pyramids. A pyramid in Caral, Peru, has been dated to 2627 B.C.

Contrast words and phrases

Comparison words and phrases

Both the Pyramid of the Sun at Teotihuacán, Mexico, and the Great Pyramid at Giza, Egypt, measure nearly the same at their base. Egyptian pyramids are taller, however. The Great Pyramid originally reached a height of 481 feet, while the tallest pyramid in the Americas is 216 feet high. Even the pyramid at Caral is only one-eighth the height of the Great Pyramid.

Pyramids in Egypt and the Americas have major structural differences as well. Pyramids in the Americas have receding steps that resemble the layers of a cake. Egyptian pyramids, on the other hand, have smooth sides that connect in a point at the top.

Egyptian pyramids were always part of a larger collection of buildings, including temples and houses. Similarly, American pyramids were built in the middle of cities. However, pyramids in the Americas typically served as temples and were the sites of human and animal sacrifices. In contrast, all Egyptian pyramids were built to be royal burial chambers.

Modern scientists are still amazed at the size and durability of these structures. Many pyramids took as long as 20 years to build, using millions of stone blocks and thousands of laborers. Pyramids in Egypt and in the Americas were both outstanding accomplishments for the civilizations that created them.

PRACTICE AND APPLY

Reread the model and then answer the following questions:

1. Is the model organized by subject or by feature?
2. List at least three features that the writer compares and contrasts.
3. List at least five words or phrases the writer uses to signal comparison or contrast.

Reading Handbook

PRACTICE AND APPLY ANSWERS

1. by feature
2. Possible responses: location, age, base size, height, structural differences, nearness to other buildings, purpose, general size, durability, time needed to build, materials and people needed to build
3. Possible responses: however, also, In contrast, similar, Both, while, differences, on the other hand, Similarly

PRACTICE AND APPLY ANSWERS

1. The American wood stork, an endangered bird, is disappearing from Florida swamps.
2. Possible answers: swamplands drained for people to use, drought, changing water levels
3. Possible answers: as a result, cause, because, reason, consequently

Reading Handbook

Cause and Effect

A **cause** is an event or a condition that brings about an **effect**. An **effect** is something that happens as a result of a cause or causes. **Cause-and-effect** writing explains the relationship between causes and effects. Such writing is usually organized in one of three ways:

1. as a description of the cause(s) followed by an explanation of the effect(s)
2. as a descripton of the effect(s) followed by an explanation of the cause(s)
3. as a chain of causes and effects

Strategies for Reading

- To find the **effect** or **effects,** ask, What happened?
- To find the **cause** or **causes,** ask, Why did it happen?
- Look for words and phrases that signal **relationships between events,** such as *because, as a result, for that reason, so, consequently,* and *since.*

MODEL

Effect

The endangered American wood stork is disappearing from its native Florida swamps, changing the delicate ecological balance in southern Florida wildlife sanctuaries. Researchers have found that the storks have been migrating north to Georgia and South Carolina during mating season. Commercial development of swamplands, changes in weather conditions, and varying water levels have all contributed to the storks' migration.

Cause

Signal words and phrases

Since 1900, Florida swamplands have been drained to make room for homes, farms, golf courses, and roads. As a result, the wood storks and other wildlife that had lived in the swamps have had to find other places to feed.

Drought is also a cause of the wood stork's migration north. Wood storks prefer somewhat dry weather because fish become concentrated in small pools of water and are easy to find. Too much drought, however, brings water down to a level where even wood storks have to fly elsewhere for food. Dry spells also often force the U.S. Army Corps of Engineers to drain swamps to provide running water for Floridians. This process continues the destruction of swamps, including protected areas such as the Everglades.

Unusually wet weather can also be a reason for wood stork migration. Water is pumped into the Everglades during wet years to keep cities and farms safe and dry. High water levels cause fish and other food sources to spread out. Consequently, birds must fly long distances for food.

Flying north is not a perfect solution for the wood stork because it puts storks and their young in danger of cold spells. Luckily, plans to restore the Florida swamps and better manage swamp water are being developed. If these plans succeed, the wood stork might return to nest in Florida. John Ogden, a biologist from the South Florida Water Management District, has this message for northern states: "We're going to get those South Carolina and Georgia wood storks back!"

PRACTICE AND APPLY

Reread the model and then do the following activities:

1. Identify the main effect the writer describes.
2. Identify at least two causes of that main effect.
3. List at least three words or phrases that the writer uses to signal causes or effects.

1138 READING HANDBOOK

Problem-Solution

Problem-solution writing describes a difficult issue or problem and offers a solution for it. Logical arguments are used to convince readers that the proposed solution will solve the problem.

Strategies for Reading

- To find the **problem,** ask, What is this writing about?
- To find the **solution,** ask, What suggestion does the writer offer to remedy the problem?
- Look for the **reasons** the writer gives to support the solution. Is the thinking behind them logical? Is the evidence presented strong and convincing?

MODEL

It's midnight, and you're trying to go to sleep. A car alarm goes off outside your window. Then a street sweeper drives by. Then a neighbor turns on a stereo. If you have ever found yourself in this situation, then you are a victim of one of today's most common problems: noise pollution. **Problem**

People who live in cities, suburbs, or rural areas may have trouble with excessive noise. Traffic, lawn mowers, leaf blowers, airplanes, snowmobiles, and loud parties are some common sources. Forming a community anti-noise group can be useful in the battle for peace and quiet. **Solution**

To get started, ask neighbors if they feel the same way that you do about noise. Encourage them to ask their friends if they have troubles with noise pollution. Then invite people who are interested to a meeting at your home or at a community center. You are well on your way to fighting excessive noise!

Your anti-noise group should educate your community. According to hearing experts, noise in excess of 85 decibels can cause hearing loss if exposure is long enough. Hair dryers and lawn mowers commonly reach levels of 90 decibels. A personal CD player turned up all the way is 112 decibels, and an ambulance siren is 120 decibels. Noise pollution is not just an annoyance—it can actually be dangerous. **Reason**

Your group must also research your community's laws about noise levels. Most areas have daytime and nighttime limits. Some communities restrict or ban the use of leaf blowers and other noisy equipment. Make sure that your complaints are supported by the law.

You can increase awareness about noise pollution by printing fliers, giving presentations to other local groups, and meeting with local politicians. Once people in your community are aware of the problems and dangers of noise pollution, they will be more likely to take action. People will also be less embarrassed or scared to complain about noise pollution if they know that their neighbors will support them.

Make sure that your group sets a good example for the community by being responsible, considerate citizens. Just because you live in a modern world does not mean that you have to put up with excessive noise levels.

PRACTICE AND APPLY

Reread the model and then answer the following questions:

1. According to the model, why is it important to control noise pollution?
2. What are three steps the writer recommends a community anti-noise group should take?

Reading Handbook

PRACTICE AND APPLY ANSWERS

1. It is annoying and may be dangerous.
2. *Possible answers:* ask neighbors whether noise is a problem; hold meetings; educate the community; research local laws; increase awareness through publicity and meeting with others in the community; set a good example

PRACTICE AND APPLY ANSWERS

1. to make part of a graph bigger
2. Press the number that is to the left of the item, or press the down arrow key until the item number is highlighted and then press the Enter key.
3. the number 2
4. the Window key

Reading Handbook

Functional Reading

Functional reading is reading to discover such information as instruction in how to do something. When you read a map, a technical manual, a job application, or a recipe, you are engaged in functional reading. These guidelines show how you can improve your functional-reading skills.

Technical Directions

Strategies for Reading

A Read the **title** to learn what material the page covers. This page is from the manual for a graphing calculator.

B Notice any **introductory text** to find general information.

C Look for **numbered steps** or a **bulleted list** to learn how to perform a particular task. Some manuals present the steps of a process in paragraph form, with signal words such as *first, next, then,* and *finally.*

D Examine **pictures** or other **graphics** that illustrate the steps. If you are having trouble completing the process, pictures can help you pinpoint where you are going wrong.

PRACTICE AND APPLY

Reread the page from the manual and then answer the following questions:

1. What does this page explain how to do?
2. According to the instructions, how do you select a menu item?
3. What key should you press to zoom in?
4. What key should you press to display the new window settings?

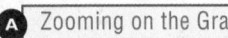

A Zooming on the Graph

B You can magnify the viewing **WINDOW** around a specific location using the **ZOOM** instructions to help identify maximums, minimums, roots, and intersections of functions.

C 1. Press [ZOOM] to display the ZOOM menu.

This menu is typical of TI-82 menus. To select an item, you may either press the number to the left of the item, or you may press [▼] until the item number is highlighted and then press [ENTER].

ZOOM MEMORY
1:ZBox
2:Zoom In
3:Zoom Out
4:ZDecimal
5:ZSquare
6:ZStandard
7↓ZTrig

2. To zoom in, press **2**. The graph is displayed again. The cursor has changed to indicate that you are using a ZOOM instruction.

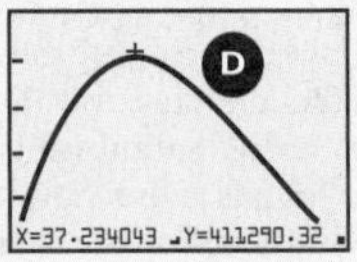

3. Use [◄], [▲], [►], and [▼] to position the cursor near the maximum value on the function and press [ENTER].

The new viewing WINDOW is displayed. It has been adjusted in both the X and Y directions by factors of 4, the values for ZOOM factors.

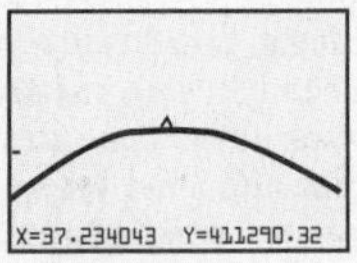

4. Press [WINDOW] to display the new WINDOW settings.

WINDOW FORMAT
Xmin=24.734042...
Xmax=49.734042...
Xscl=10
Ymin=348790.32...
Ymax=473790.32...
Yscl=100000

Recipe

Reading Handbook

Strategies for Reading

A Read the entire recipe at least once before beginning. Look at the **list of ingredients** to make sure that you have everything you need. Some recipes also include a list of kitchen equipment.

B Watch for notations of **preparation time** and **cooking time.** Does this recipe need to be made hours or days before it is served? Do you have enough time to prepare it?

C Notice the **number of servings** the recipe makes. You may need to double or halve the recipe to feed the right number of people.

D Read the **cooking directions** carefully. Follow the steps in the order they are given. Some recipes are not written in complete sentences.

E If you don't understand certain **terms** in the recipe, check a dictionary. Some cookbooks include a **glossary** of difficult words at the back of the book.

PRACTICE AND APPLY

Reread the recipe and answer the questions:

1. What does this recipe tell you how to make?
2. How much cheese does the recipe require?
3. About how much time should you set aside to prepare and cook this dish?
4. If you needed to feed six people, would you double or halve the recipe?
5. What does "sauté" mean? (Use context clues, a dictionary, or a cookbook glossary to figure this out.)

Vegetable Pizza Supreme

A You will need:

1 loaf of French bread (about 1 pound)
1/4 cup red bell pepper, chopped
1/4 cup mushrooms, cleaned and sliced
1/4 cup whole black olives (optional)
1/4 cup white or red onion, peeled and chopped
Cooking spray or 1 tablespoon olive oil
1/2 cup of your favorite bottled spaghetti sauce or pizza sauce
1 cup mozzarella cheese, shredded
a sprinkle of ground black pepper (for seasoning)

102

B Preparation time: about 20 minutes
Cooking time: about 18 minutes
Serves: 2 to 3 **C**

D
1. Preheat the oven to 450 degrees.
2. Slice the bread lengthwise. Scoop out the soft bread center from the bottom half. Set aside the top half—you won't need it for this recipe.
3. Line a cookie sheet with aluminum foil. Place the bottom half of the bread on it and bake for 3 to 5 minutes. Remove from oven, turn over, and bake for 3 to 5 minutes on the other side.
4. As the bread is browning, heat the oil or cooking spray in the frying pan. Sauté **E** the chopped onions and peppers for about 5 minutes, until they begin to soften.
5. Take bread out of oven. Spread cut side with sauce. Sprinkle with cheese and top with onions, peppers, mushrooms, and olives.
6. Return to oven and bake 6 to 8 minutes or until cheese is bubbly.
7. Remove from oven. To slice, press a large, sharp knife into the pizza at about three-inch intervals. Do not use a sawing motion, as this will remove the cheese.
8. Top with black pepper and serve!

103

PRACTICE AND APPLY ANSWERS

1. Vegetable Pizza Supreme
2. 1 cup
3. about 28 minutes
4. double
5. fry in a pan

PRACTICE AND APPLY ANSWERS

1. how to search the World Wide Web using LookQuick
2. simple, AND, OR, NOT, NEAR, and quotation searches
3. more than one billion
4. Possible answers: Lincoln AND Nebraska; Lincoln NOT Abraham; Lincoln NEAR Nebraska; "Lincoln, Nebraska"

Web Search Guide

Strategies for Reading

A Read the **title** to learn what process the guide explains.

B Notice any **subheads** or **categories.** You may not need to read the entire guide to get the information you need.

C Look for **instructions** on what steps to take and in what order.

D Pay attention to **hints, tips,** and **examples.** Hints and tips can help you avoid common mistakes. Examples give you a clearer understanding of the material.

PRACTICE AND APPLY

Reread the guide and then answer the following questions:

1. What task does this guide explain?
2. List the six types of searches mentioned in the guide.
3. How many Web pages does the search engine cover?
4. You type in "Lincoln" to search for Web pages about Lincoln, Nebraska, but you keep finding information about Abraham Lincoln. What are some ways that you could refine your search?

L-Net

Back | Forward | Reload | Home | Images | Print | Security | Stop

Location: http://www. lookquick.net/websearch/htm

A Using LookQuick to Search the World Wide Web

B Simple Searches

If you enter a term that you would like to find out about, the search engine will search more than one billion Web pages for that term.

Examples: Shakespeare, typhoons, Bolivia

Hint: Make sure that your search term is spelled correctly.

C AND/OR/NOT/NEAR Searches

Sometimes you may need to use more than one term to perform a precise search.

- Using AND tells the engine to search for both terms.
  Examples: Shakespeare AND sonnets, science AND fiction
- Using OR tells the engine to search for either term.
  Examples: movie OR film, Kwanza OR Kwanzaa
- Using NOT tells the engine to search for one term but not the other.
  Examples: Apollo NOT rocket, amazon NOT river
- Using NEAR tells the engine to search for two terms that occur within 10 words of each other.
  Examples: Senate NEAR budget, art NEAR modernism

Quotation Searches

If you enter a word or phrase in quotation marks, the engine will search for that exact word or phrase.

Example: "I have not yet begun to fight"

D ***Hint:*** If you are uncertain of the capitalization or word order of the phrase, try an AND or NEAR search that uses two or three of the key words that you are seeking, such as *yet AND begun AND fight.*

Broadening Your Search

If your search results in too few items:

- Reduce the number of keywords.
- Make the keywords more general *(dog* rather than *Dalmatian).*
- Double-check your spelling of each keyword.
- Try a different search engine.

Narrowing Your Search

If your search results in too many items:

- Add keywords.
- Make the keywords more specific.
- Use the NOT command to exclude certain terms.
- Try a different search engine.

Home | Questions | Guest Book | Privacy Policy

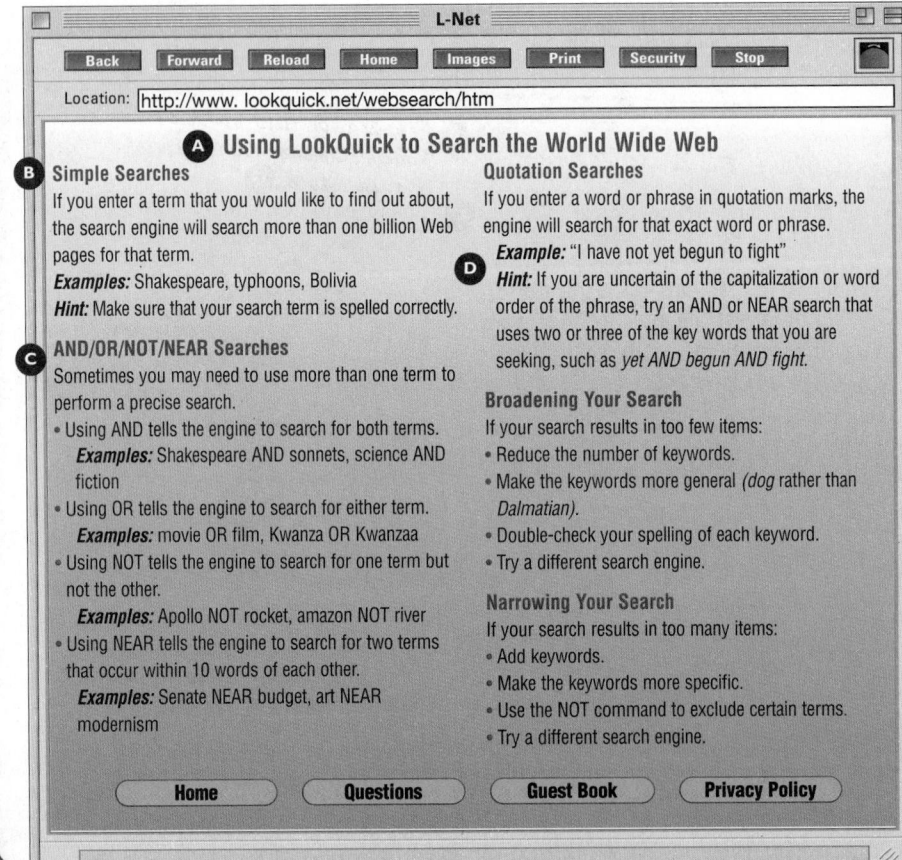

Instruction Manual

Strategies for Reading

A Read the **title** to learn what process the directions explain. This page is from the manual for a television remote control.

B Look for **numbers** or **letters** that indicate what steps to follow. Read all the steps in order at least once before you begin.

C Match the numbers or letters to the **diagram** or other visual, if there is one.

D Look for **words that explain what to do,** such as *press, select, set,* or *turn.*

E Pay close attention to **warnings** or **notes** that describe potential problems.

PRACTICE AND APPLY

Reread the page from the instruction manual and then answer the following questions:

1. What do these directions explain how to do?
2. According to the directions, what happens when the ENTER button is pressed?
3. What button allows the user to select A.M. or P.M.?
4. What does the warning tell you?

A Setting the Sleep Timer

1. Press the MENU key. The Setup menu will appear on your television.
2. Select the Timer Setup on your screen by using the UP/DOWN arrows on your remote control.
3. **B** Now press the RIGHT/LEFT arrows. A menu of the Timer Setup will appear on the screen.
4. Sleep Timer: Use the RIGHT/LEFT arrows to program the length of time until the TV shuts down. You can select any time from ten minutes to four hours. Press ENTER to return to TV viewing.

Setting On/Off Timer

5. Follow steps 1 and 2 above to get to the Timer Setup menu. Using the UP/DOWN arrows on the remote control, select On Time on your screen.
6. **D** Press the RIGHT or LEFT arrow to adjust the time your television will turn on automatically.
7. Press the TIMER button to choose either A.M. or P.M.
8. Repeat steps 5 through 7 to set Off Time. Use the UP/DOWN arrows to select the On/Off Timer, and activate the timer by pressing a RIGHT/LEFT arrow.

E WARNING: The On/Off timer will not work until the clock on your television has been set.

C

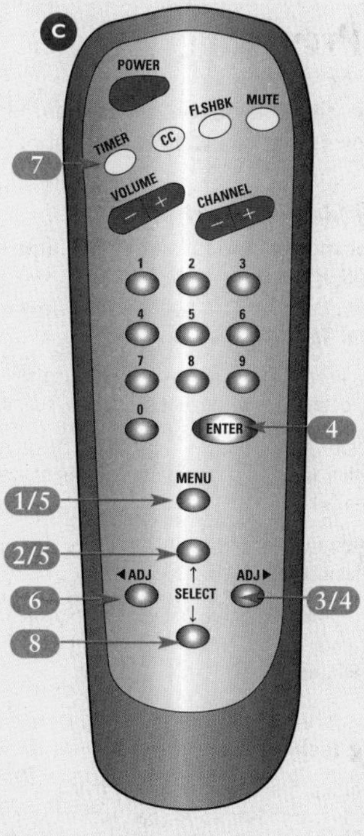

PRACTICE AND APPLY ANSWERS

1. set a sleep timer using a television remote control
2. lets the user return to television viewing
3. the TIMER button
4. The On/Off timer will not work until the clock on the television has been set.

Writing Handbook

1 The Writing Process

Different writers use different processes. Try out different strategies and figure out what works best for you. For some assignments, it is best to start by figuring out what you need to end up with, make a plan or outline, and stick to it. Other writing assignments may be more successful if you start by writing everything you know about the topic, allow things to get messy, and then reshape and revise the writing so it fits the assignment. Try both approaches and get to know yourself as a writer.

Also consider whether the assignment is high-stakes or low-stakes writing. When the success of the piece is very important, such as in a test, you might choose to focus on meeting the requirements or criteria of the assignment. When the purpose of the writing is to develop your ideas, there is more opportunity to experiment and take risks. Take into account the time factor as well. In a timed writing test, you may not have time to explore and revise.

Correct grammar and spelling are very important in your final product. You don't need to focus on these as you shape your ideas and draft your piece, but be sure you allow time for a careful edit before turning in your final piece.

1.1 Prewriting

In the prewriting stage, you explore your ideas and discover what you want to write about.

Finding Ideas for Writing

Try one or more of the following techniques to help you find a writing topic.

Personal Techniques

- Practice imaging, or trying to remember mainly sensory details about a subject—its look, sound, feel, taste, and smell.
- Complete a knowledge inventory to discover what you already know about a subject.
- Browse through magazines, newspapers, and on-line bulletin boards for ideas.
- Start a clip file of articles that you want to save for future reference. Be sure to label each clip with source information.

Sharing Techniques

- With a group, brainstorm a topic by trying to come up with as many ideas as you can without stopping to critique or examine them.
- Interview someone who knows a great deal about your topic.

Writing Techniques

- After freewriting on a topic, try looping, or choosing your best idea for more freewriting. Repeat the loop at least once.
- Make a list to help you organize ideas, examine them, or identify areas for further research.

Graphic Techniques

- Create a pro-and-con chart to compare the positive and negative aspects of an idea or a course of action.
- Use a cluster map or tree diagram to explore subordinate ideas that relate to your general topic or central idea.

Determining Your Purpose

Your purpose for writing may be to express yourself, to entertain, to describe, to explain, to analyze, or to persuade. To clarify it, ask questions like these:

- Why did I choose to write about my topic?
- What aspects of the topic mean the most to me?
- What do I want others to think or feel after they read my writing?

1144 WRITING HANDBOOK

LINK TO LITERATURE One purpose for writing is to clarify a subject. For example, W.P. Kinsella wrote "The Thrill of the Grass," page 57, to clarify the reasons he feels some changes have hurt the game of baseball.

Identifying Your Audience

Knowing who will read your writing can help you focus your topic and choose relevant details. As you think about your readers, ask yourself questions like these:

- What does my audience already know about my topic?
- What will they be most interested in?
- What language is most appropriate for this audience?

1.2 Drafting

In the drafting stage, you put your ideas on paper and allow them to develop and change as you write.

Two broad approaches in this stage are discovery drafting and planned drafting.

Discovery drafting is a good approach when you are not quite sure what you think about your subject. You just plunge into your draft and let your feelings and ideas lead you where they will. After finishing a discovery draft, you may decide to start another draft, do more prewriting, or revise your first draft.

Planned drafting may work better for research reports, critical reviews, and other kinds of formal writing. Try making a writing plan or a scratch outline before you begin drafting. Then, as you write, you can fill in the details.

LINK TO LITERATURE Rarely does a successful writer achieve a final manuscript without several attempts and rewrites. E.B. White, who wrote "Once More to the Lake," page 112, revised a book on writing style and added his own chapter. In *The Elements of Style* White admits that he has repeatedly used unnecessary words like *the fact that* in first drafts, having to delete them for the final copy.

1.3 Revising, Editing, and Proofreading

The changes you make in your writing during this stage usually fall into three categories: revising for content, revising for structure, and proofreading to correct mistakes in mechanics.

Use the questions that follow to assess problems and determine what changes would improve your work.

Revising for Content

- Does my writing have a main idea or central focus? Is my thesis clear?
- Have I incorporated adequate detail? Where might I include a telling detail, revealing statistic, or vivid example?
- Is any material unnecessary, irrelevant, or confusing?

WRITING TIP Be sure to consider the needs of your audience as you answer the questions under Revising for Content and Revising for Structure. For example, before you can determine whether any of your material is unnecessary or irrelevant, you need to identify what your audience already knows.

Revising for Structure

- Is my writing unified? Do all ideas and supporting details pertain to my main idea or advance my thesis?
- Is my writing clear and coherent? Is the flow of sentences and paragraphs smooth and logical?
- Do I need to add transitional words, phrases, or sentences to make the relationships among ideas clearer?
- Are my sentences well constructed? What sentences might I combine to improve the grace and rhythm of my writing?

Proofreading to Correct Mistakes in Grammar, Usage, and Mechanics

When you are satisfied with your revision, proofread your paper, looking for mistakes in grammar, usage, and mechanics. You may want

WRITING HANDBOOK 1145

to do this several times, looking for different types of mistakes each time. The following checklist may help.

Sentence Structure and Agreement

- Are there any run-on sentences or sentence fragments?
- Do all verbs agree with their subjects?
- Do all pronouns agree with their antecedents?
- Are verb tenses correct and consistent?

Forms of Words

- Do adverbs and adjectives modify the appropriate words?
- Are all forms of *be* and other irregular verbs used correctly?
- Are pronouns used correctly?
- Are comparative and superlative forms of adjectives correct?

Capitalization, Punctuation, and Spelling

- Is any punctuation mark missing or not needed?
- Are all words spelled correctly?
- Are all proper nouns and all proper adjectives capitalized?

WRITING TIP For help identifying and correcting problems that are listed in the Proofreading Checklist, see the Grammar Handbook, pages 1181–1216.

You might wish to mark changes on your paper by using the proofreading symbols shown in the chart below.

Proofreading Symbols

∧	Add letters or words.	/	Make a capital letter lowercase.
⊙	Add a period.	¶	Begin a new paragraph.
≡	Capitalize a letter.	↖	Delete letters or words.
⊂	Close up space.	∿	Switch the positions of letters or words.
∧	Add a comma.		

1.4 Publishing and Reflecting

Always consider sharing your finished writing with a wider audience. Reflecting on your writing is another good way to bring closure to a project.

Creative Publishing Ideas

Following are some ideas for publishing and sharing your writing.

- Post your writing on an electronic bulletin board or send it to others via e-mail.
- Create a multimedia presentation and share it with classmates.
- Publish your writing in a school newspaper or literary magazine.
- Present your work orally in a report, a speech, a reading, or a dramatic performance.
- Submit your writing to a local newspaper or a magazine that publishes student writing.
- Form a writing exchange group with other students.

WRITING TIP You might work with other students to publish an anthology of class writing. Then exchange your anthology with another class or another school. Reading the work of other student writers will help you get ideas for new writing projects and find ways to improve your work.

Reflecting on Your Writing

Think about your writing process and whether you would like to add what you have written to your portfolio. You might attach a note in which you answer questions like these:

- What did I learn about myself and my subject through this writing project?
- Which parts of the writing process did I most and least enjoy?
- As I wrote, what was my biggest problem? How did I solve it?
- What did I learn that I can use the next time I write?

1146 WRITING HANDBOOK

1.5 Using Peer Response

Peer response consists of the suggestions and comments your peers or classmates make about your writing.

You can ask a peer reader for help at any point in the writing process. For example, your peers can help you develop a topic, narrow your focus, discover confusing passages, or organize your writing.

Questions for Your Peer Readers

You can help your peer readers provide you with the most useful kinds of feedback by following these guidelines:

- Tell readers where you are in the writing process. Are you still trying out ideas, or have you completed a draft?
- Ask questions that will help you get specific information about your writing. Open-ended questions that require more than yes-or-no answers are more likely to give you information you can use as you revise.
- Give your readers plenty of time to respond thoughtfully to your writing.
- Encourage your readers to be honest when they respond to your work. It's OK if you don't agree with them—you always get to decide which changes to make.

Tips for Being a Peer Reader

Follow these guidelines when you respond to someone else's work:

- Respect the writer's feelings.
- Make sure you understand what kind of feedback the writer is looking for, and then respond accordingly.
- Use "I" statements, such as "I like . . . ," "I think . . . ," or "It would help me if . . . ." Remember that your impressions and opinions may not be the same as someone else's.

WRITING TIP Writers are better able to absorb criticism of their work if they first receive positive feedback. When you act as a peer reader, try to start your review by telling something you like about the piece.

The chart below explains different peer-response techniques to use when you are ready to share your work.

Peer-Response Techniques

Sharing Use this when you are just exploring ideas or when you want to celebrate the completion of a piece of writing.

- *Will you please read or listen to my writing without criticizing or making suggestions afterward?*

Summarizing Use this when you want to know if your main idea or goals are clear.

- *What do you think I'm saying? What's my main idea or message?*

Replying Use this strategy when you want to make your writing richer by adding new ideas.

- *What are your ideas about my topic? What do you think about what I have said in my piece?*

Responding to Specific Features Use this when you want a quick overview of the strengths and weaknesses of your writing.

- *Are the ideas supported with enough examples? Did I persuade you? Is the organization clear enough for you to follow the ideas?*

Telling Use this to find out which parts of your writing are affecting readers the way you want and which parts are confusing.

- *What did you think or feel as you read my words? Would you show me which passage you were reading when you had that response?*

WRITING HANDBOOK 1147

2 Building Blocks of Good Writing

Whatever your purpose in writing, you need to capture your readers' interest, organize your ideas well, and present your thoughts clearly. Giving special attention to some particular parts of a story or an essay can make your writing more enjoyable and more effective.

2.1 Introductions

When you flip through a magazine trying to decide which articles to read, the opening paragraph is often critical. If it does not grab your attention, you are likely to turn the page.

Kinds of Introductions

Here are some introduction techniques that can capture a reader's interest.

- Make a surprising statement
- Provide a description
- Pose a question
- Relate an anecdote
- Address the reader directly
- Begin with a thesis statement

Make a Surprising Statement Beginning with a startling statement or an interesting fact can capture your reader's curiosity about the subject, as in the model below.

MODEL

September should be the seventh month, and October should be the eighth. Any Latin student knows that the root *septem* is "seven" and *octo* is "eight." Where did the calendar makers go wrong? The truth is that when the months acquired their names, during Roman times, the year started in March.

Provide a Description A vivid description sets a mood and brings a scene to life for your reader. Here, details about a lion observing possible prey set the tone for an essay on survival in the wild.

MODEL

Cool and cunning eyes followed the impala herd from a sturdy low-slung tree branch. The young female lion watched hungrily to see whether any of the impalas might be sickly or slower than the others. She kept every muscle quiet, though tense and ready to spring if an opportunity arose.

Pose a Question Beginning with a question can make your reader want to read on to find the answer. The following introduction asks questions about the incredible persistence of racial segregation.

MODEL

How is it possible that as late as the mid-twentieth century in the United States of America, "the land of the free," riders on public buses were segregated by race? How is it possible that even today there are segregated social events, schools, and towns, no longer segregated by law but with effects just as real and damaging?

Relate an Anecdote Beginning with a brief anecdote, or story, can hook readers and help you make a point in a dramatic way. The anecdote below introduces an essay about the downside of self-closing shoe straps.

MODEL

My five-year old nephew, Ali, has never tied a shoelace. All his shoes have self-closing straps. Little boys already suffer because they are encouraged to develop large muscles by throwing and climbing, while little girls gain dexterity by dressing dolls and coloring in coloring books. Ali's younger sister, who has learned to tie bows on her doll clothes, may well have to stick around to tie the bows on Ali's gift packages and tie his bow tie for his tuxedo.

1148 WRITING HANDBOOK

Address the Reader Directly Speaking directly to readers establishes a friendly, informal tone and involves them in your topic.

MODEL
If you've ever wondered how to avoid using pesticides in your garden, you can find answers from Natural Gardens, Inc. It's easy to protect the environment and have pest-free plants.

Begin with a Thesis Statement A thesis statement expressing a paper's main idea may be woven into both the beginning and the end of nonfiction writing. The following is a thesis statement that introduces an essay on the relationship of caring for pets and children.

MODEL
Pet owners who are casual about their pet's health and safety are likely to be the same ones who are casual about the health and safety of their children.

WRITING TIP In order to write the best introduction for your paper, you may want to try more than one of the methods and then decide which is the most effective for your purpose and audience.

2.2 Paragraphs

A paragraph is made up of sentences that work together to develop an idea or accomplish a purpose. Whether or not it contains a topic sentence stating the main idea, a good paragraph must have unity and coherence.

Unity

A paragraph has unity when all the sentences support and develop one stated or implied idea. Use the following techniques to create unity in your paragraphs.

Write a Topic Sentence A topic sentence states the main ideas of the paragraph; all other sentences in the paragraph provide supporting details. A topic sentence is often the first sentence in a paragraph. However, it may also appear later in the paragraph or at the end, to summarize or reinforce the main idea, as shown in the model that follows.

MODEL
Plastic that does not rust, rot, or shatter is useful, of course, but does add to the ever-increasing problems of waste disposal. It is possible to add chemicals to plastic that make it dissolvable by other chemicals. There are plastics that slowly disintegrate in sunlight. Biodegradable plastic is available and should be preferred over non-biodegradable plastic.

Relate All Sentences to an Implied Main Idea A paragraph can be unified without a topic sentence as long as every sentence supports the implied, or unstated, main idea. In the example below, all the sentences work together to create a unified impression of a swim meet.

MODEL
The swimmers were lined up along the edge of the pool. Toes curled over the edge, arms swung back in the ready position, and bodies leaned forward. The swimmers' eyes looked straight ahead. Their ears were alert for the starting signal.

Coherence

A paragraph is coherent when all its sentences are related to one another and flow logically from one to the next. The following techniques will help you achieve coherence in paragraphs.

- Present your ideas in the most logical order.
- Use pronouns, synonyms, and repeated words to connect ideas.
- Use transitional devices to show the relationships among ideas.

In the model below, the writer used some of these techniques to create a unified paragraph.

MODEL
As we experience day and night repeatedly, it is hard to imagine the enormous significance of that change. We have day and night because our planet rotates on its axis. We have seasons because Earth revolves around our solar system's star, the sun. Our solar system, along with many others, rotates with the Milky Way Galaxy. The universe is a gigantic structure of which our daily experiences of day and night, summer and winter are tiny parts.

WRITING HANDBOOK 1149

2.3 Transitions

Transitions are words and phrases that show the connections between details. Clear transitions help show how your ideas relate to each other.

Kinds of Transitions

Transitions can help readers understand several kinds of relationships:

- Time or sequence
- Spatial relationships
- Degree of importance
- Compare and contrast
- Cause and effect

Time or Sequence Some transitions help to clarify the sequence of events over time. When you are telling a story or describing a process, you can connect ideas with such transitional words as *first, second, always, then, next, later, soon, before, finally, after, earlier, afterward,* and *tomorrow.*

MODEL
Teaching a puppy to come when called takes patience from the owner and the puppy. First tie a lightweight rope to the dog's collar and go to a large play area. Play with the pup a while and then call to it. At the same time pull gently on the rope. Always praise the puppy for coming when called. Next allow the puppy to play again. Carry out this exercise several times a day.

Spatial Relationships Transitional words and phrases such as *in front, behind, next to, along, nearest, lowest, above, below, underneath, on the left,* and *in the middle* can help readers visualize a scene.

MODEL
On the porch, wicker chairs stand in casual disorder along the red wall of the house. Next to the red-and-white porch railing, orange day lilies nod in the breeze. Overhead, a flycatcher perches on a bare branch, alert for her next meal. Beyond the lawn, a small stream flows from beneath an arched stone bridge.

Degree of Importance Transitional words such as *mainly, strongest, weakest, first, second, most important, least important, worst,* and *best* may be used to rank ideas or to show degree of importance, complexity, or familiarity.

MODEL
The Repertory Theater performed six plays last year. All the plays were exciting, but the most outstanding one was *Master Class.*

Compare and Contrast Words and phrases such as *similarly, likewise, also, like, as, neither . . . nor,* and *either . . . or* show similarity between details. *However, by contrast, yet, but, unlike, instead, whereas,* and *while* show difference. Note the use of both types of transitions in the model below.

MODEL
Dr. Herriot was a successful veterinarian. Mrs. Donovan also took care of sick animals. He cured his patients with medical treatments and laboratory medications. Mrs. Donovan, by contrast, used home remedies and constant affection.

WRITING TIP Both *but* and *however* may be used to join two independent clauses. When *but* is used as a coordinating conjunction, it is preceded by a comma. When *however* is used as a conjunctive adverb, it is preceded by a semicolon and followed by a comma.

Cause and Effect When you are writing about a cause-and-effect relationship, use transitional words and phrases such as *since, because, thus, therefore, so, due to, for this reason,* and *as a result* to help clarify that relationship and to make your writing coherent.

MODEL
Because we never feed our dog from the table, she doesn't beg for food while we are eating. We are happy to take credit for her one good habit.

1150 WRITING HANDBOOK

2.4 Conclusions

A conclusion should leave readers with a strong final impression. Try any of these approaches.

Kinds of Conclusions

Here are some effective methods for bringing your writing to a conclusion:

- Restate your thesis
- Ask a question
- Make a recommendation
- Make a prediction
- Summarize your information

Restate Your Thesis A good way to conclude an essay is by restating your thesis, or main idea, in different words. The conclusion below restates the thesis introduced on page 1149.

> MODEL
> **Although each pet has a personality of its own just as each child does, there are many ways of encouraging the best behavior in each. Love, persistence, patience, and consistency make all the difference in training pets as well as in raising children.**

Ask a Question Try asking a question that sums up what you have said and gives readers something new to think about. The question below concludes an appeal to support a local politician.

> MODEL
> **Have you noticed that the roads are in better repair and that there are more safe playgrounds and parks since Mayor Ballwin has been in office?**

Make a Recommendation When you are persuading your audience to take a position on an issue, you can conclude by recommending a specific course of action.

> MODEL
> **Today's youth are at risk of damaging their hearing by listening to very loud music. Consider turning down the bass and turning down the volume on your headphones.**

Make a Prediction Readers are concerned about matters that may affect them and therefore are moved by a conclusion that predicts the future.

> MODEL
> **If the government continues to spend money from Social Security taxes for current operations, we will create a disastrous burden of debt for future generations.**

Summarize Your Information Summarizing reinforces the writer's main ideas, leaving a strong, lasting impression. The model below concludes with a statement that summarizes a film review.

> MODEL
> **The movie *The Postman* shows the tremendous influence of the Chilean poet Pablo Neruda on a young Italian man—not only in his love life but also in his acquired self-confidence and his dedication to a cause.**

2.5 Elaboration

Elaboration is the process of developing a writing idea by providing specific supporting details that are relevant and appropriate to the purpose and form of your writing.

- **Facts and Statistics** A fact is a statement that can be verified, while a statistic is a fact stated in numbers. Make sure the facts and statistics you supply are from a reliable, up-to-date source. As in the model below, the facts and statistics you use should strongly support the statements you make.

> MODEL
> **Our entire solar system speeds through the Milky Way Galaxy at a speed of 180 miles a second. One could worry about the ability of any of us to stay in place with our feet on the ground. Or one could marvel at the magnificence of a universe that keeps everything whirling with such constancy.**

WRITING HANDBOOK 1151

- **Sensory Details** Details that show how something looks, sounds, tastes, smells, or feels can enliven a description, making readers feel they are actually experiencing what you are describing. Which senses does the writer appeal to in this paragraph?

MODEL
The campers lay as quiet as mice inside their tent as they considered the power of the massive beast they'd glimpsed through the tent flap. Snuffling and crackling brought news that the black bear had found something delectable inside the garbage can, probably leftover corncobs and pork-chop bones. The campfire smoke lingered, and the campers fervently hoped that the odors of grease and butter wouldn't bring the animal even closer to the tent.

- **Incidents** From our earliest years, we are interested in hearing "stories." One way to illustrate a point powerfully is to relate an incident or tell a story, as shown in the example below.

MODEL
January 24, 1848, began one of the most colorful periods of United States history. On that day James Marshall found gold at Sutter's Mill in California. That discovery brought on massive immigration of European Americans to the West. It also brought many new images and words—*gold rush, gold miners,* and *forty-niners,* to name a few.

- **Examples** An example can help make an abstract or a complex idea concrete or can provide evidence to clarify a point for readers.

MODEL
The mere mention of the names of some writers causes distinct reactions, even from those who have not read the writers' works. For example, the mention of William Shakespeare causes many people to take in a sharp breath of admiration and others to think of something long and tedious. On the other hand, the name Edgar Allan Poe brings an involuntary shiver to almost everyone.

- **Quotations** Choose quotations that clearly support your points, and be sure that you copy each quotation word for word. Remember always to credit the source.

MODEL
In her book *How to Talk to Your Cat,* Patricia Moyes replies to certain authorities who claim that cats cannot smile: "I can only presume that these people have never owned a cat in the true sense of the word." She goes on to describe the cat's smile as a "relaxed upward tilting of the corners of the mouth" that occurs when the cat is feeling peaceful or pleased, perhaps while being stroked or while having happy dreams.

2.6 Using Language Effectively

Effective use of language can help readers to recognize the significance of an issue, to visualize a scene, or to understand a character. The specific words and phrases that you use have everything to do with how effectively you communicate meaning. This is true of all kinds of writing, from novels to office memos. Keep these particular points in mind.

- **Specific Nouns** Nouns are specific when they refer to individual or particular things. If you refer to a *city*, you are being general. If you refer to *London*, you are being specific. Specific nouns help readers identify the *who, what,* and *where* of your message.
- **Specific Verbs** Verbs are the most powerful words in sentences. They convey the action, the movement, and sometimes the drama of thoughts and observations. Verbs such as *trudged, skipped,* and *sauntered* provide a more vivid picture of the action than the verb *walked*.
- **Specific Modifiers** Use modifiers sparingly, but when you use them, make them count. Is the building *big* or *towering*? Are your poodle's paws *small* or *petite*? Once again, it is the more specific word that carries the greater impact.

1152 WRITING HANDBOOK

3 Descriptive Writing

Descriptive writing allows you to paint word pictures about anything and everything in the world, from events of global importance to the most personal feelings. It is an essential part of almost every piece of writing, including essays, poems, letters, field notes, newspaper reports, and videos.

RUBRIC **Standards for Writing**

A successful description should

- have a clear focus and sense of purpose.
- use sensory details and precise words to create a vivid image, establish a mood, or express emotion.
- present details in a logical order.

3.1 Key Techniques

Consider Your Goals What do you want to accomplish in writing your description? Do you want to show why something is important to you? Do you want to make a person or scene more memorable? Do you want to explain an event?

Identify Your Audience Who will read your description? How familiar are they with your subject? What background information will they need? Which details will they find most interesting?

Think Figuratively What figures of speech might help make your description vivid and interesting? What simile or metaphor comes to mind? What imaginative comparisons can you make? What living thing does an inanimate object remind you of?

MODEL

After the 10-mile hike, we pounced on the buffet table like starving lions. Some of us stuffed pieces of bread and morsels of roast beef into our mouths before we'd even finished filling our plates. By the time we flopped into chairs, we looked even more like scavenging carnivores, with our dripping hands and greasy mouths. But the predatory look in our eyes had abated somewhat.

Gather Sensory Details Which sights, smells, tastes, sounds, and textures make your subject come alive? Which details stick in your mind when you observe or recall your subject? Which senses does it most strongly affect?

MODEL

Light snowflakes brushed her cheek as she poised at the top of the mountain. After an admiring glance at the spots of bright color on the slope, she lifted both ski poles and crouched in preparation for the leap forward to start her fifth run through the powdery snow.

You might want to use a chart like the one shown here to collect sensory details about your subject.

Sights	Sounds	Textures	Smells	Tastes

Create a Mood What feelings do you want to evoke in your readers? Do you want to soothe them with comforting images? Do you want to build tension with ominous details? Do you want to evoke sadness or joy?

MODEL

It was always difficult to see the dangerous rocks just below the surface of the lake, but in the dark and without the light it was impossible. If only Guy had remembered the backup batteries. Although he had only been on this lake twice before, he had been confident he could run this fishing trip without incident. Now, as gray clouds gathered to cover even the faint light of the new moon, Guy worried not just about his summer job but also about the safety of his first paying customers.

WRITING HANDBOOK 1153

3.2 Options for Organization

Spatial Order Choose one of these options to show the spatial order of a scene.

EXAMPLE 1

Top → Bottom

EXAMPLE 2

Left → Right

EXAMPLE 3

Outside / Inside

EXAMPLE 4

Near → Far

MODEL

Thunder's nostrils quivered as he was led into the barn. How would this be as a place to spend nights from now on? In the stall to the left, the straw smelled fresh. Beyond that stall a saddle hung from rough boards. To the right of his stall was another, from which a mare looked at him curiously. So far, so good. From the far right, beyond two empty stalls, strode the barn cat.

WRITING TIP Use transitions that help the reader picture the relationship among the objects you describe. Some useful transitions for showing spatial relationships are *behind, below, here, in the distance, on the left, over,* and *on top.*

Order of Impression Order of impression is how you notice details.

What first catches your attention → What you notice next → What you see after that → What you focus on last

MODEL

As her foot slipped on the pebbles, her first thought was of whether she would sprain an ankle sliding into the surf. Her heart began a dangerous thumping, but soon the soft sand provided a comfortable seat so that her body responded by calming down. She realized that the water was shallow and warm. Her hat would shade her eyes and prevent sunburn. By the time she remembered she had on dry-clean-only shorts, she'd decided that sitting in the surf while her friends gathered shells was a perfectly fine way to enjoy the beach.

WRITING TIP Use transitions that help readers understand the order of the impressions you are describing. Some useful transitions are *after, next, during, first, before, finally,* and *then.*

Order of Importance You might want to use order of importance as the organizing structure for your description.

Least Important → More Important → Most Important

MODEL

Annaliese tried to imprint on her memory everything about the accident. She remembered unimportant details, like the song that was playing on her radio before the truck loomed up ahead. She remembered her panic as she steered into the guard rail. Gradually she recalled more important information—her conservative speed, the fact that the truck was on the wrong side of the road coming toward her, the driver's long beard. Finally, when she closed her eyes and really concentrated, she could remember the license plate number at eye level as the truck zoomed on by.

WRITING TIP Use transitions that help the reader understand the order of importance that you attach to the elements of your description. Some useful transitions are *first, second, mainly, more important, less important,* and *least important.*

1154 WRITING HANDBOOK

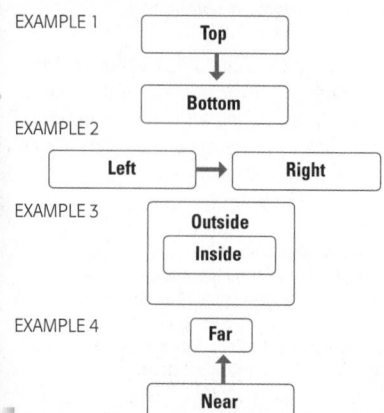

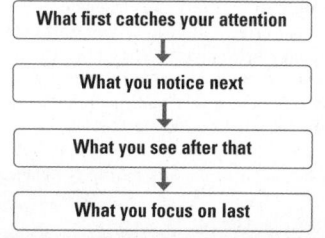

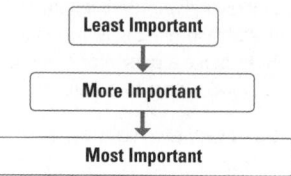

4 Narrative Writing

Narrative writing tells a story. If you write a story from your imagination, it is a fictional narrative. A true story about actual events is a nonfictional narrative. Narrative writing can be found in short stories, novels, news articles, and biographies.

RUBRIC **Standards for Writing**

A successful narrative should

- include descriptive details and dialogue to develop the characters, setting, and plot.
- have a clear beginning, middle, and end.
- have a logical organization, with clues and transitions to help the reader understand the order of events.
- maintain a consistent tone and point of view.
- use language that is appropriate for the audience.
- demonstrate the significance of events or ideas.

4.1 Key Techniques

Identify the Main Events What are the most important events in your narrative? Is each event part of the chain of events needed to tell the story? In a fictional narrative, this series of events is the story's plot.

MODEL

Event 1 **A railroad porter notices a woman boarding the train and pulling along a young child.**

Event 2 **Because the porter has the sense the child is frightened, he finds several excuses to appear at their compartment door.**

Event 3 **When he hears the child crying, he goes to the compartment and sees the glint of gunmetal inside a partially open market basket.**

Event 4 **The porter begins to plan how to identify the woman and child and to separate the child from the woman.**

Describe the Setting When do the events occur? Where do they take place? How can you use setting to create mood and to set the stage for the characters and their actions?

MODEL

Bright spring sunshine highlighted the auburn hair of the child being pulled along by the matronly woman carrying a market basket. Joshua helped her up the steps onto the train. He stooped to lift the little girl at the same moment the woman jerked the small arm, so that the child stumbled up the stairs on her own.

Depict Characters Vividly What do your characters look like? What do they think and say? How do they act? What vivid details can show readers what the characters are like?

MODEL

Joshua hardly noticed the other passengers as his eyes followed the woman and child. His instincts warned him that something was wrong here.

WRITING TIP Dialogue is an effective way of developing characters in a narrative. As you write dialogue, choose words that express your characters' personalities and show how the characters feel about one another and about the events in the plot.

MODEL

"Hello, ma'am. I'm Joshua, and I'll be in soon to get your compartment ready for the night."

The woman's whisper sent chills down Joshua's spine. "Yeah, OK."

"Are you having a nice ride?" he asked the thin little girl.

"She likes the train," answered the woman.

WRITING HANDBOOK 1155

Writing Handbook

4.2 Options for Organization

Option 1: Chronological Order One way to organize a piece of narrative writing is to arrange the events in chronological order, as shown below.

MODEL

Introduction *characters and setting*

It is the middle of March, the beginning of the year in Rome, and the first time in a while that young Marius has been able to go into the center of the city near the senate house and capitol.

Event 1

A crowd gathers to watch the senators arrive. There is a rumor that the emperor will also come. Marius hurries toward the front of the crowd.

Event 2

The crowd thickens, and Marius can barely make out the laurel-wreath head-covering indicating that indeed the emperor has arrived. There is great commotion, with shouts and screams.

End *perhaps show the significance of the events*

Marius witnesses the assassination of Julius Caesar and hears the speeches condemning Caesar. He then goes home with the sad news of the murder and a premonition that there are bad times ahead for Rome.

Option 2: Flashback It is also possible in narrative writing to arrange the order of events by starting with an event that happened before the beginning of the story.

Flashback
Begin with a key event that happened before the time in which the story takes place.

↓

Introduce characters and setting.

↓

Describe the events leading up to the conflict.

Option 3: Focus on Conflict When the telling of a fictional narrative focuses on a central conflict, the story's plot may follow the model shown below.

MODEL

Describe the main characters and setting.

The brothers arrive at the school gym long before the rest of the basketball team. Although the twins are physically identical, their personalities couldn't be more different. Mark is outgoing and impulsive, while Matt is thoughtful and shy.

Present the conflict.

Matt realizes his brother is missing shots on purpose and believes they will lose the championship.

Relate the events that make the conflict complex and cause the characters to change.

- Matt has a chance at a basketball scholarship if they win the championship.
- Mark needs money to buy a car.
- Matt and Mark have stood by each other no matter what.

Present the resolution or outcome of the conflict.

Matt retells a family story in which their grandfather chose honor and integrity over easy money. Mark plays to win.

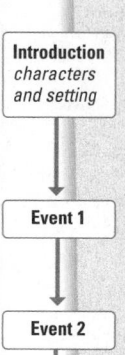

5 Explanatory Writing

Explanatory writing informs and explains. For example, you can use it to evaluate the effects of a new law, to compare two movies, to analyze a piece of literature, or to examine the problem of greenhouse gases in the atmosphere.

5.1 Types of Explanatory Writing

There are many types of explanatory writing. Think about your topic and select the type that presents the information most clearly.

Compare and Contrast How are two or more subjects alike? How are they different?

> MODEL
> **As Isaac Asimov points out, both dial and digital clocks show the time, but only dial clocks show at a glance the relationship of the hours to one another.**

Cause and Effect How does one event cause something else to happen? Why do certain conditions exist? What are the results of an action or a condition?

> MODEL
> **Because Charley did not want his brother to appear "country" carrying a brown paper bag through a fancy hotel lobby, he pretended he was taking the sweet potato pie home with him.**

Analysis How does something work? How can it be defined? What are its parts?

> MODEL
> **Some contributions of dial clocks that Asimov fears will be lost if the clocks disappear are concepts of clockwise and counterclockwise and of establishing location by referring to position, such as pointing out an object "at the two o'clock position."**

Problem-Solution How can you identify and state a problem? How would you analyze the problem and its causes? How can it be solved?

> MODEL
> **The narrator, Shanshan, in "Love Must Not Be Forgotten" has some questions about marrying her fiancé; she decides that it will be better to be single than to marry without love.**

5.2 Compare and Contrast

Compare-and-contrast writing examines the similarities and differences between two or more subjects. You might, for example, compare and contrast two short stories, the main characters in a novel, or two movies.

RUBRIC **Standards for Writing**

Successful compare-and-contrast writing should

- clearly identify the subjects that are being compared and contrasted.
- include specific, relevant details.
- follow a clear plan of organization, dealing with the same features of both subjects under discussion.
- use language and details appropriate to the audience.
- use transitional words and phrases to clarify similarities and differences.

Options for Organization

Compare-and-contrast writing can be organized in different ways. The examples that follow demonstrate feature-by-feature organization and subject-by-subject organization.

WRITING HANDBOOK 1157

Option 1: Feature-by-Feature Organization

MODEL

Feature 1 I. Response to social pressure to marry
- Subject A. Zhong Yu: married man she did not really love
- Subject B. Shanshan: engaged to man she isn't sure she loves

Feature 2 II. Response to need for romantic love
- Subject A. Zhong Yu: after her divorce, feels love for a man she admires from a distance
- Subject B. Shanshan: decides not to marry a man she doesn't really love

Option 2: Subject-by-Subject Organization

MODEL

Subject A I. Zhong Yu
- Feature 1. Response to social pressure to marry: married man she did not really love
- Feature 2. Response to need for romantic love: after her divorce, feels love for a man she admires from a distance

Subject B II. Shanshan:
- Feature 1. Response to social pressure to marry: engaged to man she isn't sure she loves
- Feature 2. Response to need for romantic love: decides not to marry a man she doesn't really love

WRITING TIP Remember your purpose for comparing and contrasting your subjects, and support your purpose with expressive language and specific details.

5.3 Cause and Effect

Cause-and-effect writing explains why something happened, why certain conditions exist, or what resulted from an action or a condition. You might use cause-and-effect writing to explain a character's actions, the progress of a disease, or the outcome of a war.

RUBRIC Standards for Writing

Successful cause-and-effect writing should
- clearly state the cause-and-effect relationship.
- show clear connections between causes and effects.
- present causes and effects in a logical order and use transitions effectively.
- use facts, examples, and other details to illustrate each cause and effect.
- use language and details appropriate to the audience.

Options for Organization

Your organization will depend on your topic and purpose for writing.

- If you want to explain the causes of an event such as the closing of a factory, you might first state the effect and then examine its causes.

Option 1: Effect to Cause Organization

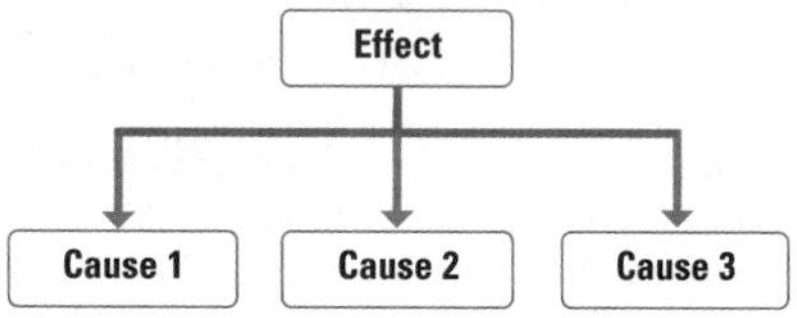

- If your focus is on explaining the effects of an event, such as the passage of a law, you might first state the cause and then explain the effects.

Option 2: Cause to Effect Organization

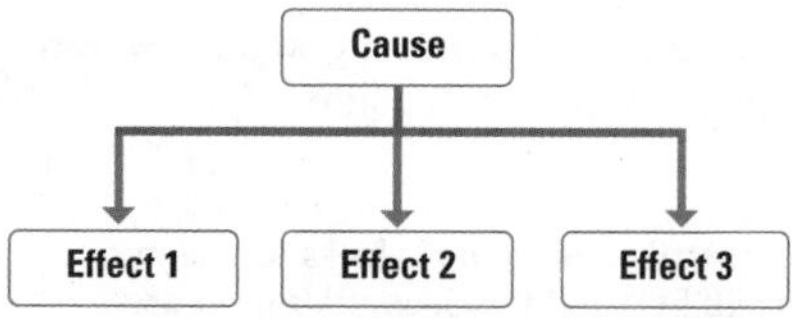

- Sometimes you'll want to describe a chain of cause-and-effect relationships to explore a topic such as the disappearance of tropical rain forests or the development of home computers.

1158 WRITING HANDBOOK

Option 3: Cause-and-Effect Chain Organization

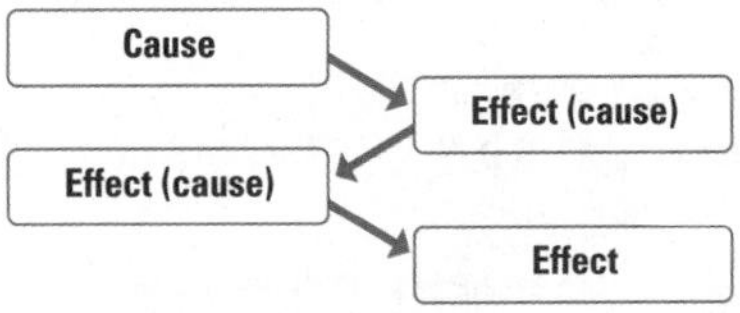

WRITING TIP Don't assume that a cause-and-effect relationship exists just because one event follows another. Look for evidence that the later event could not have happened if the first event had not caused it.

5.4 Problem-Solution

Problem-solution writing clearly states a problem, analyzes the problem, and proposes a solution to the problem. It can be used to identify and solve a conflict between characters, analyze a chemistry experiment, or explain why the home team keeps losing.

RUBRIC **Standards for Writing**

Successful problem-solution writing should

- identify the problem and help the reader understand the issues involved.
- analyze the causes and effects of the problem.
- integrate quotations, facts, and statistics into the text.
- explore possible solutions to the problem and recommend the best one(s).
- use language, tone, and details appropriate to the audience.

Options for Organization

Your organization will depend on the goal of your problem-solution piece, your intended audience, and the specific problem you choose to address. The organizational methods that follow are effective for different kinds of problem-solution writing.

Option 1: Simple Problem-Solution

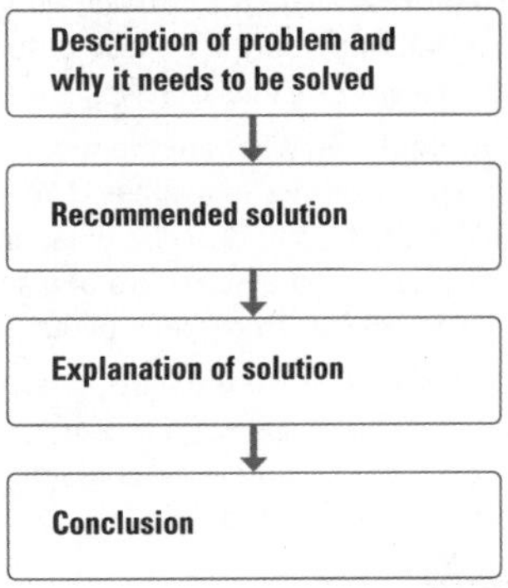

Option 2: Deciding Between Solutions

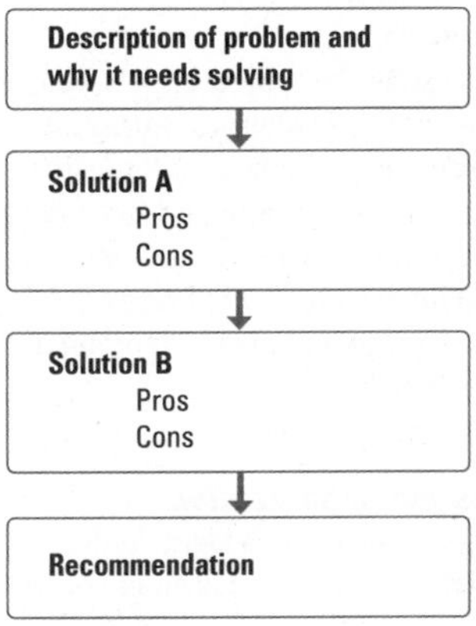

WRITING TIP Have a classmate read and respond to your problem-solution writing. Ask your peer reader: Is the problem clearly stated? Is the organization easy to follow? Do the proposed solutions seem logical?

5.5 Analysis

In writing an analysis, you explain how something works, how it is defined, or what its parts are. The details you include will depend upon the kind of analysis you write.

Process Analysis What are the major steps or stages in a process? What background information does the reader need to know—such as definitions of terms or a list of needed equipment—to understand the analysis? You might use process analysis to explain how to program a VCR or prepare for a test, or to explain the stages of an insect's life.

Definition Analysis What are the most important characteristics of a subject? You might use definition analysis to describe what an insect is, explain the characteristics of a sonnet, or outline the skills of an airplane pilot.

Parts Analysis What are the parts, groups, or types that make up a subject? Parts analysis could be used to explain the parts of an insect's body or the mechanics of an airplane.

RUBRIC **Standards for Writing**

A successful analysis should
- hook the readers' attention with a strong introduction.
- clearly state the subject and its parts.
- use a specific organizing structure to provide a logical flow of information.
- show connections among facts and ideas through subordinate clauses and transitional words and phrases.
- use language and details appropriate for the audience.

Options for Organization

Organize your details in a logical order appropriate for the kind of analysis you're writing.

Option 1: Process Analysis A process analysis is usually organized chronologically, with steps or stages in the order they occur.

MODEL

Introduction	**Insect metamorphosis**
Background	**Many insects grow through a four-step life cycle.**
Explain Steps	**Step 1 egg** **Step 2 larva** **Step 3 pupa** **Step 4 adult**

Option 2: Definition Analysis You can organize the details in a definition or parts analysis in order of importance or impression.

MODEL

Introduce Term	**What is an insect?**
General Definition	**An insect is a small animal with an external skeleton, three body segments, and three pairs of legs.**
Explain Features	**Feature 1: external skeleton** **Feature 2: three body segments** **Feature 3: three pairs of legs**

Option 3: Parts Analysis The following parts analysis describes the major parts of an insect's body.

MODEL

Introduce Subject	**An insect's body is divided into three main parts.**
Explain Parts	**Part 1: The head includes eyes, mouth, and antennae.** **Part 2: The thorax has the legs and wings attached to it.** **Part 3: The abdomen contains organs for digesting food, eliminating waste, and reproducing.**

WRITING TIP Try to capture your readers' interest in your introduction. You might begin with a vivid description or an interesting fact, detail, or quotation. For example, an exciting excerpt from the narrative could open the process analysis.

An effective way to conclude an analysis is to return to your thesis and restate it in different words.

1160 WRITING HANDBOOK

6 Persuasive Writing

Persuasive writing allows you to use the power of language to inform and influence others. It can take many forms, including speeches, newspaper editorials, billboards, advertisements, and critical reviews.

RUBRIC **Standards for Writing**

Successful persuasion should

- state the issue and the writer's position.
- give opinions and support them with facts or reasons.
- have a reasonable and respectful tone.
- answer opposing views.
- use sound logic and effective language.
- conclude by summing up reasons or calling for action.

6.1 Key Techniques

Clarify Your Position What do you believe about the issue? How can you express your opinion most clearly?

MODEL
Our city needs to find ways to decrease pollution, especially during the work week.

Know Your Audience Who will read your writing? What do they already know and believe about the issue? What objections to your position might they have? What additional information might they need? What tone and approach would be most effective?

MODEL
Everyone wants to breathe clean air, at least cleaner than what we've had in our city lately. The smog is heavier during the work week, when more people drive to work, more buses run, and businesses burn more fuel to heat or cool buildings.

Support Your Opinion Why do you feel the way you do about the issue? What facts, statistics, examples, quotations, anecdotes, or opinions of authorities support your view? What reasons will convince your readers? What evidence can answer their objections?

MODEL
Climate geographers from Arizona State University report that 45 statistical analyses have shown that along the eastern seaboard rainfall is highest on Saturdays, with an average of 658 millimeters per year, and lowest on Mondays, with an average of 538 millimeters per year. The researchers have found that pollution is also highest on Saturdays and lowest on Mondays.

Begin and End with a Bang How can you hook your readers and make a lasting impression? What memorable quotation, anecdote, or statistic will catch their attention at the beginning or stick in their minds at the end? What strong summary or call to action can you conclude with?

Ways to Support Your Argument	
Statistics	Facts that are stated in numbers
Examples	Specific instances that explain your point
Observations	Events or situations you yourself have seen
Anecdotes	Brief stories that illustrate your point
Quotations	Direct statements from authorities

BEGINNING
A recent research report finds there is more rain on weekends than during the week. Scientists attribute this to the extra work week pollution that builds throughout the week.

CONCLUSION
We need to plan for more car-pooling, efficient heating and cooling, and consolidation of some bus schedules to improve our air quality—and provide better weekend weather.

WRITING HANDBOOK 1161

6.2 Options for Organization

In a two-sided persuasive essay, you want to show the weaknesses of other opinions as you explain the strengths of your own.

The example below demonstrates one method of organizing your persuasive essay to convince your audience.

Option 1: Reasons for Your Opinion

- Introduction includes the issue and your position on it
- ↓ Reason 1 with evidence and support
- ↓ Reason 2 with evidence and support
- ↓ Reason 3 with evidence and support
- ↓ Objections to whole argument
- ↓ Response to objections
- ↓ Conclusion includes restatement of your position and recommended action

Option 2: Point-by-Point Basis

In the organization that follows, each reason and its objections are examined on a point-by-point basis.

- Introduction includes the issue and your position on it
- ↓ Reason 1 with evidence and support
- ↓ Objections and responses to Reason 1
- ↓ Reason 2 with evidence and support
- ↓ Objections and responses to Reason 2
- ↓ Reason 3 with evidence and support
- ↓ Objections and responses to Reason 3
- ↓ Conclusion includes a restatement of your position and recommended action

Beware of Illogical Arguments Be careful about using illogical arguments. Opponents can easily attack your argument if you present illogical material.

Circular reasoning—trying to prove a statement by just repeating it in different words

> Precipitation is heavier on weekends because of higher rainfall then.

Either-or fallacy—stating that there are only two alternatives when there are many

> Either we cut weekday car travel by fifty percent or pollution will make our city unlivable.

Overgeneralization—making a statement that is too broad to prove

> Nobody is doing anything to reduce air pollution.

Cause-and-effect fallacy—falsely assuming that because one event follows another, the first event caused the second

> The growing population of our region has caused the increase in air pollution.

1162 WRITING HANDBOOK

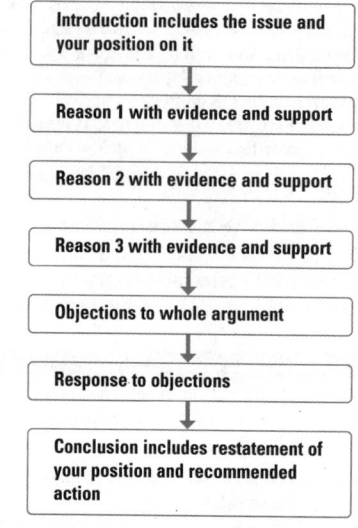

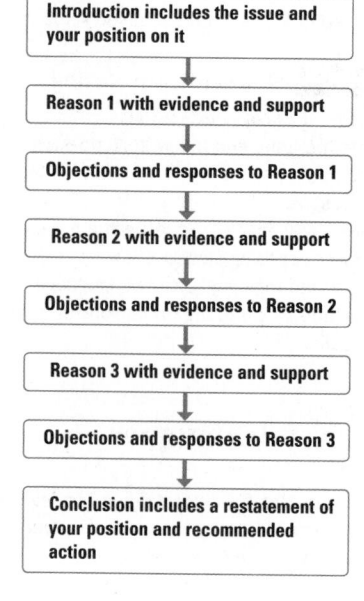

7 Research Report Writing

A research report explores a topic in depth, incorporating information from a variety of sources.

RUBRIC **Standards for Writing**

An effective research report should

- clearly state the purpose of the report in a thesis statement.
- use evidence and details from a variety of sources to support the thesis.
- contain only accurate and relevant information.
- document sources correctly.
- develop the topic logically and include appropriate transitions.
- include a properly formatted Works Cited list.

7.1 Key Techniques

Develop Relevant, Interesting, and Researchable Questions Asking thoughtful questions is an ongoing part of research. Begin with a list of basic questions that are relevant to your topic. Focus on getting basic facts that answer the *who, what, where, when,* and *why* of your topic. If you were researching the civil rights movement you might develop a set of questions like these.

MODEL
What wrongs did the civil rights movement hope to correct?

How did African Americans live when they were denied the right to vote?

As you become more familiar with your topic, think of questions that might provide an interesting perspective that makes readers think.

.MODEL
What groups of people have been denied equal rights in the United States?

Check that your questions are researchable. Ask questions that will uncover facts, statistics, case studies, and other documentable evidence.

Clarify Your Thesis A thesis statement is one or two sentences clearly stating the main idea that you will develop in your report. A thesis may also indicate the organizational pattern you will follow and reflect your tone and point of view.

MODEL
The struggle for civil rights in the United States has been a series of peaks and valleys for those struggling for their rights.

Document Your Sources You need to document, or credit, the sources where you find your evidence. In the example below, the writer uses and documents a quotation from an essay.

MODEL
In a 1967 essay, "The Civil Rights Movement: What Good Was It?" Alice Walker states that the civil rights movement "is dead for the white man because it no longer interests him" (121).

Support Your Ideas You should support your ideas with relevant evidence–facts, anecdotes, and statistics–from reliable sources. In the example below the writer includes a fact about racial discrimination in the armed forces.

MODEL
By executive order issued July 30, 1948, President Truman banned segregation and racial discrimination in the United States armed forces (Morris and Morris 498).

WRITING HANDBOOK 1163

7.2 Gathering Information: Sources

You will use a range of sources to collect the information you need to develop your research paper. These will include both print and electronic resources.

General Reference Works To clarify your thesis and begin your research, consult reference works that give quick, general overviews on a subject. General reference works include encyclopedias, almanacs and yearbooks, atlases, and dictionaries.

Specialized Reference Works Once you have a good idea of your specific topic, you are ready to look for detailed information in specialized reference works. In the library's reference section, specialized dictionaries and encyclopedias can be found for almost any field. For example, in the field of literature, you will find specialized reference sources such as *Contemporary Authors* and *Twentieth-Century Literary Criticism.*

Periodicals Journals and periodicals are a good source for detailed, up-to-date information. Periodical indexes, found in print and on-line catalogs in the library, will help you find articles on a topic. The *Readers' Guide to Periodical Literature* indexes many popular magazines. More specialized indexes include the *Humanities Index* and the *Social Sciences Index.*

Electronic Resources **Commercial information services** offer access to reference works such as dictionaries and encyclopedias, databases, and periodicals.

The **Internet** is a vast network of computer networks. News services, libraries, universities, researchers, organizations, and government agencies use the Internet to communicate and to distribute information. The Internet gives you access to the World Wide Web, which provides information on particular topics and links you to related topics and resources.

A **CD-ROM** is a research aid that stores information on a compact disk. Reference works on CD-ROMs may include text, sound, images, and video.

Databases are large collections of related information stored electronically. You can scan the information or search for specific facts.

RESEARCH TIP To find books on a specific topic, check the library's on-line catalog. Be sure to copy the correct call numbers of books that sound promising. Also look at books shelved nearby. They may relate to your topic.

7.3 Gathering Information: Validity of Sources

When you find source material, you must determine whether it is useful and accurate.

Credibility of Authorship Check whether an author has written several books or articles on the subject and has published in a well-respected newspaper or journal.

Objectivity Decide whether the information is fact, opinion, or propaganda. Reputable sources credit other sources of information.

Currency Check the publication date of the source to see whether the information is current.

Credibility of Publisher Seek information from a respected newspaper or journal, not from a tabloid newspaper or popular-interest magazine.

WEB TIP Be especially skeptical of information you locate on the Internet since virtually anyone can post anything there. Read the URL, or Internet address. Sites sponsored by a government agency (*.gov*) or an educational institution (*.edu*) are generally more reliable.

7.4 Taking Notes

As you find useful information, record the bibliographic information of each source on a separate index card. Then you are ready to take notes on your sources. You will probably use these three methods of note-taking.

1164 WRITING HANDBOOK

Paraphrase, or restate in your own words, the main ideas and supporting details of the passage.

Summarize, or rephrase in fewer words, the original materials, trying to capture the key ideas.

Quote, or copy word for word, the original text, if you think the author's own words best clarify a particular point. Use quotation marks to signal the beginning and the end of the quotation.

For more details on making source cards and taking notes, see the Research Report Workshop on pages 1105–1112.

7.5 Options for Organization

Begin by reading over your note cards and sorting them into groups. The main-idea headings may help you find connections among the notes. Then arrange the groups of related note cards so that the ideas flow logically from one group to the next.

Option 1: Topic Outline

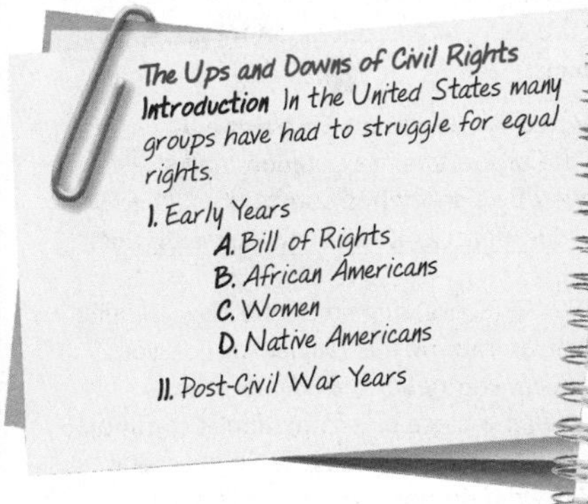
The Ups and Downs of Civil Rights
Introduction In the United States many groups have had to struggle for equal rights.
I. Early Years
A. Bill of Rights
B. African Americans
C. Women
D. Native Americans
II. Post-Civil War Years

Like other forms of writing, research reports can be organized in several different ways. Some subjects may fit in chronological order. For other subjects, you may want to compare and contrast two topics. Other possibilities are a cause-and-effect organization or least-important to most-important evidence. If your material does not lend itself to any of the above organizations, try a general-to-specific approach.

Whatever your organizational pattern, making an outline can help guide the drafting process. The subtopics that you located in sorting your note cards will be the major topics of your outline, preceded by Roman numerals. Make sure that items of the same importance are parallel in form. For example, in the Option 1 Topic Outline below, topics I and II are both phrases. So are subtopics A and B.

A second kind of outline, shown below in Option 2, uses complete sentences instead of phrases for topics and subtopics.

Option 2: Sentence Outline

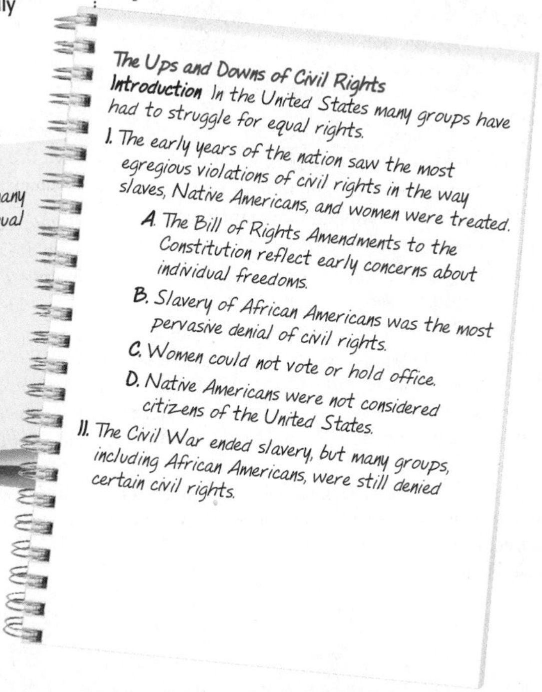
The Ups and Downs of Civil Rights
Introduction In the United States many groups have had to struggle for equal rights.
I. The early years of the nation saw the most egregious violations of civil rights in the way slaves, Native Americans, and women were treated.
A. The Bill of Rights Amendments to the Constitution reflect early concerns about individual freedoms.
B. Slavery of African Americans was the most pervasive denial of civil rights.
C. Women could not vote or hold office.
D. Native Americans were not considered citizens of the United States.
II. The Civil War ended slavery, but many groups, including African Americans, were still denied certain civil rights.

WRITING HANDBOOK 1165

Writing Handbook

7.6 Documenting Sources

When you quote, paraphrase, or summarize information from a source, you need to credit that source. Parenthetical documentation is the accepted method for crediting sources. You may choose to name the author in parentheses following the information, along with the page number on which the information is found.

> MODEL
> **Slaves had fought with the Continental Army for American independence, and when they were denied basic human rights by the new nation, many were ready to take up arms to overthrow slavery (McKissack and McKissack 6).**

In parenthetical documentation, you may also use the author's name in the sentence, along with the information. If so, enclose, in parentheses after the sentence, only the page number on which the information is found.

> MODEL
> **As Eve Merriam points out, "English law had discriminated severely against women; the colonies carried on that tradition" (9).**

In either case, your reader can find out more about the source by turning to your Works Cited page, which lists complete bibliographical information for each source.

PUNCTUATION TIP When only the author and page number appear in parentheses, there is no punctuation between the two items. Also notice that the parenthetical citation comes after the closing quotation marks of a quotation, if there is one, and before the end punctuation of the sentence.

The examples above show citations for books with one author. The list that follows shows the correct way to write parenthetical citations for several kinds of sources.

Guidelines for Parenthetical Documentation

Work by One Author
Put the author's last name and the page reference in parentheses: **(Walker 120).**

If you mention the author's name in the sentence, put only the page reference in parentheses: **(120).**

Work by Two or Three Authors
Put the authors' last names and the page reference in parentheses: **(McKissack and McKissack 6).**

Work by More Than Three Authors
Give the first author's last name followed by *et al.* and the page reference: **(Armento et al. 127).**

Work with No Author Given
Give the title or a shortened version and (if appropriate) the page reference: **("The Factory Girl" 305).**

One of Two or More Works by Same Author
Give the author's last name, the title or a shortened version, and the page reference: **(Walker, Living 41).**

Selection from a Book of Collected Essays
Give the name of the author of the essay and the page reference: **(Irwin 33).**

Dictionary Definition
Give the entry title in quotation marks: **("feminist").**

Unsigned Article in an Encyclopedia
Give the article title in quotation marks, followed by a shortened source title: **("Uncle Tom," Encyclopedia of Word and Phrase Origins).**

WRITING TIP Presenting someone else's writing or ideas as your own is plagiarism. To avoid plagiarism, you need to credit sources. However, if a piece of information is common knowledge—information available in several sources—you do not need to credit a source.

1166 WRITING HANDBOOK

Writing Handbook

7.7 Following MLA Manuscript Guidelines

The final copy of your report should follow the Modern Language Association (MLA) guidelines for manuscript preparation.

- The heading in the upper left-hand corner of the first page should include your name, your teacher's name, the course name, and the date, each on a separate line.
- Below the heading, center the title on the page.
- Number all the pages consecutively in the upper right-hand corner, one-half inch from the top. On the second and suceeding pages, include your last name before the page number.
- Double-space the entire paper.
- Except for the margins above the page numbers, leave one-inch margins on all sides of every page.

The Works Cited page at the end of your report is an alphabetized list of the sources you have used and documented. In each entry all lines after the first are indented an additional one-half inch.

WRITING TIP When your report includes a quotation that is longer than four lines, set it off from the rest of the text by indenting the entire quotation one inch from the left margin. In this case, you should not use quotation marks.

Works Cited
Models for Works Cited entries

Works Cited

Armento, Beverly J., et al. A More Perfect Union. Boston: Houghton, 1991.

Irwin, Inez Haynes. "Why I Earn My Own Living." These Modern Women: Autobiographical Essays from the Twenties. Ed. Elaine Showalter. Old Westbury: Feminist, 1978.

McKissack, Patricia, and Fredrick McKissack. Rebels Against Slavery: American Slave Revolts. New York: Scholastic, 1996.

---. The Civil Rights Movement in America from 1865 to the Present. Chicago: Childrens, 1987.

Merriam, Eve, ed. Growing Up Female in America: Ten Lives. Garden City: Doubleday, 1971.

Mitchell, Michael Dan. "Acculturation Problems Among the Plains Indians." The Chronicles of Oklahoma 3 (1966): 281-289.

Walker, Alice. In Search of Our Mother's Gardens. Orlando: Harcourt, 1983.

1. Book with more than three authors; note that publishers' names are shortened.
2. Selection from a book of collected essays
3. Book with two authors
4. Second work by same author
5. Book with editor but no single author
6. Article in scholarly journal
7. Book with one author

WRITING HANDBOOK 1167

7.8 MLA Documentation: Electronic Sources

As with print sources, information from electronic sources such as CD-ROMs or the Internet must be documented on your Works Cited page. You may find a reference to a source on the Internet and then use the print version of the article. If so, document it as you do other printed works. However, if you read or print out an article directly off the Internet, document it as shown below for an electronic source. Although electronic sources are shown separately below, they should be included on the Works Cited page with print sources.

Internet Sources Works Cited entries for Internet sources include the same kind of information as that for print sources. They also include the date you accessed the information and the electronic address of the source. Some of the information about the source may be unavailable. Include as much as you can. For more information on how to write Works Cited entries for Internet sources, see the MLA guidelines posted on the Internet or access this document through the McDougal Littell Website.

More Online: Style Guidelines
www.mcdougallittell.com

CD-ROMs Entries for CD-ROMs include the publication medium (CD-ROM), the distributor, and the date of publication. Some of the information shown may not always be available. Include as much as you can.

Works Cited

Models for Works Cited entries for electronic sources

Works Cited

"Civil Rights." Grolier Multimedia Encyclopedia. 1998 ed. CD-ROM. Danbury: Grolier Interactive.

❶ Encyclopedia article from CD-ROM version

Lien, Pei-te. "An Examination of Policy Opinions Among Asian Americans." Asian American Policy Review 7 (1997). Abstract. 10 Sept. 1998 <http://www.ksg.harvard.edu/~aapr/Volume7.html#Lien>.

❷ Abstract of an article in a scholarly journal, available on the Internet; includes access date

Park, Maud Wood. Lucy Stone: A Chronicle Play. Boston: Baker, 1938. Votes for Women: Selections from the National American Woman Suffrage Association Collection, 1848–1921. 17 Aug. 1998 <http://lcweb2.loc.gov/cgi-bin/query/r?ammem/naw:@field(FLD001+38008512+):@@@REF>.

❸ Complete text of a play, available on the Internet; includes access date

"Reconstruction." Britannica Online. Vers. 98.2. Apr. 1998. Encyclopaedia Britannica. 24 Sept. 1998 <http://www.eb.com.180>.

❹ Encyclopedia entry from online version

U.S. Department of Justice Home Page. 10 Sept. 1998 <http://www.usdoj.gov>.

❺ Home page; shows date you accessed it

1168 WRITING HANDBOOK

8 Business Writing

The ability to write clearly and succinctly is an essential skill in the business world. As you prepare to enter the job market, you will need to know how to create letters, memos, and résumés.

Writing Handbook

RUBRIC

Standards for Writing

Successful business writing should

- have a tone and language geared to the appropriate audience.
- state the purpose clearly in the opening sentences or paragraph.
- use precise words and avoid jargon.
- present only essential information.
- present details in a logical order.
- conclude with a summary of important points.

8.1 Key Techniques

Think About Your Purpose Why are you doing this writing? Do you want to "sell" yourself to a college admissions committee or a job interviewer? Do you want to order or complain about a product? Do you want to set up a meeting or respond to someone's ideas?

Identify Your Audience Who will read your writing? What background information will they need? What questions might they have? What tone or language is appropriate?

Support Your Points What specific details clarify your ideas? What reasons do you have for your statements? What points most strongly support them?

Finish Strongly How can you best sum up your statements? What is your main point? What action do you want others to take?

8.2 Options

Model 1: Letter

#1 Andover Lane
Sunnydale, CA 93933
July 16, ____

Heading *Where the letter comes from and when*

Inside Address *To whom the letter is being sent*

Customer Service Representative
Bionic Bikes, Inc.
12558 Industrial Drive
Schaumburg, IL 60193

Salutation *Greeting*

Dear Customer Service Representative:

Body *Text of the message*

I was really pleased to get a Bionic Bike for my birthday in March. I've ridden it every day—to school, to the rec center, and everywhere.

The bike is great, but the handlebars are not comfortable. I think you should raise the angle of the hand grips about two inches so that riders can hold them comfortably while looking straight ahead.

Thank you for considering my suggestion.

Sincerely yours,
Marisa LaPorta

Closing

WRITING HANDBOOK 1169

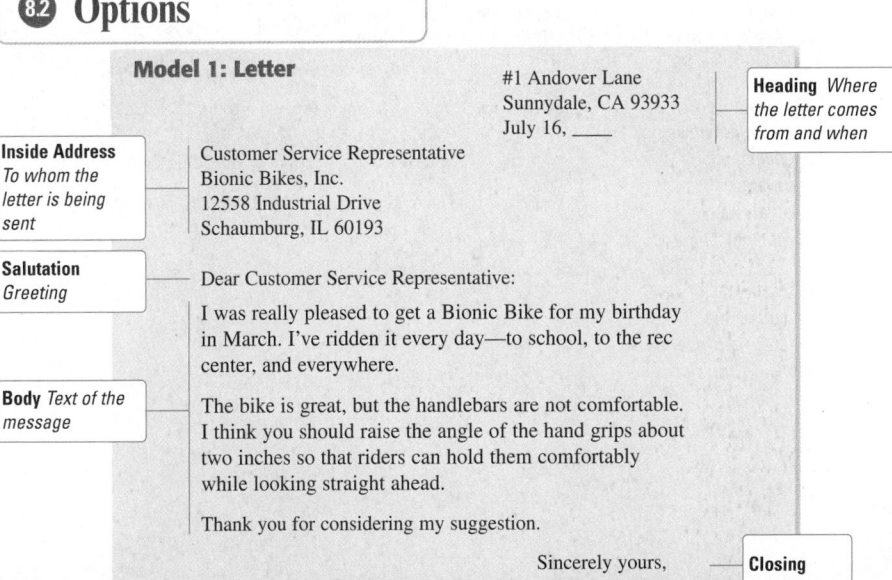

Model 2: Memo

Heading *Whom the memo is to and from, what it's about, and when it's being sent*

To: Jeff Kniffen
From: LaDonna Ford
Re: customer letter
Date: 8/15/__

Body

Jeff, please send a brief note to this customer thanking her for her suggestion. Enclose a brochure explaining the structure of the handlebars.

Also, please forward the suggestion to the engineers.

Thanks.

Model 3: Résumé A well-written résumé is invaluable when you apply for a part-time or full-time job or to college. It should highlight your skills, accomplishments, and experience. Proofread your résumé carefully to make sure it is clear and accurate and free of errors in grammar and spelling. It is a good idea to save a copy of your résumé on your computer or on a disk so that you can easily update it.

State your purpose. *This résumé is for a job application. A modified style can be used for a college application.*

List your previous employment experience *in reverse chronological order.*

Extracurricular activities and hobbies *can give a fuller picture of you and point out special job-related skills.*

JENNIFER RUDY
P.O. Box 2211
White Horse, TX 79801

Objective	Part-time position at veterinary clinic
Qualifications	Love of animals Owner of three dogs and one cat Serious, hard worker
Work Experience	1998—Junior counselor at Camp Wanabe, White Horse, TX 1997–Present—Partner in pet-sitting service
Education	Currently a sophomore at White Horse High School
Extracurricular Activities	Science Club, varsity cheerleader, Honor Society
Hobbies	Pet-sitting, reading, swimming
References	Available upon request

1170 WRITING HANDBOOK

1 Inquiry and Research

In this age of seemingly unlimited information, the ability to locate and evaluate resources efficiently can spell the difference between success and failure—in both the academic and the business worlds. Make use of print and nonprint information sources.

1.1 Finding Sources

Good research involves using the wealth of resources available to answer your questions and raise new questions. Knowing where to go and how to access information can lead you to interesting and valuable sources.

Reference Works

Reference works are print and nonprint sources of information that provide quick access to both general overviews and specific facts about a subject. These include

Dictionaries—word definitions, pronunciations, and origins

Thesauruses—lists of synonyms and antonyms for each entry

Glossaries—collections of specialized terms, such as those pertaining to literature, with definitions

Encyclopedias—detailed information on nearly every subject, arranged alphabetically (*Encyclopaedia Britannica*). Specialized encyclopedias deal with specific subjects, such as music, economics, and science (*Encyclopedia of Economics*).

Almanacs and Yearbooks—current facts and statistics (*World Almanac, Statistical Abstract of the United States*)

Atlases—maps and information about weather, agricultural and industrial production, and other geographical topics (*National Geographic Atlas of the World*)

Specialized Reference Works—biographical data (*Who's Who, Current Biography*), literary information (*Contemporary Authors, Book Review Digest, Cyclopedia of Literary Characters, The Oxford Companion to English Literature*), and quotations (*Bartlett's Familiar Quotations*)

Electronic Sources—Many of these reference works and databases are available on CD-ROMs, which may include text, sound, photographs, and video. CD-ROMs can be used on a home or library computer. You can subscribe to services that offer access to these sources on-line.

Periodicals and Indexes

One kind of specialized reference is a periodical.

- Some periodicals, such as *Atlantic Monthly* and *Psychology Today,* are intended for a general audience. They are indexed in the *Readers' Guide to Periodical Literature.*
- Many other periodicals, or journals, are intended for specialized or academic audiences. These include titles and subject matter as diverse as *American Psychologist* and *Studies in Short Fiction.* These are indexed in the *Humanities Index* and the *Social Sciences Index.* In addition, most fields have their own indexes. For example, articles on literature are indexed in the *MLA International Bibliography.*
- Many indexes are available in print, CD-ROM, and on-line forms.

Internet

The Internet is a vast network of computers. News services, libraries, universities, researchers, organizations, and government agencies use the Internet to distribute information and to communicate. The Internet can provide links to library catalogs, newspapers, government sources, and many of the reference sources described above. The Internet includes two key features:

World Wide Web—source of information on specific subjects and links to related topics

Electronic mail (e-mail)—communications link to other e-mail users worldwide

COMMUNICATION HANDBOOK 1171

Other Resources

In addition to reference works found in the library and over the Internet, you can get information from the following sources: corporate publications, lectures, correspondence, and media such as films, television programs, and recordings. You can also observe directly, conduct your own interviews, and collect data from polls or questionnaires that you create yourself.

1.2 Evaluating Sources

Not all information is equal. You need to be a discriminating consumer of information and evaluate the credibility of the source, the reliability of the specific information included, and its value in answering your research needs.

Credibility of Sources

You must determine the credibility and appropriateness of each source in order to write an effective report or speech. Ask yourself the following questions:

Is the writer an authority? A writer who has written several books on a subject or whose name is included in many bibliographies may be considered an authoritative source.

Is the source reliable and unbiased? What is the author's motivation? For example, a defense of an industry in which the author has a financial interest may be biased. A profile of a writer or scientist written by a close relative may also be biased.

WEB TIP Be especially skeptical of information you locate on the Internet, since virtually anyone can post anything there. Read the URL, or Internet address. Sites sponsored by a government agency (*.gov*) or an educational institution (*.edu*) are generally more reliable.

Is the source up-to-date? It is important to consult the most recent material, especially in fields such as medicine and technology that undergo constant research and development. Some authoritative sources have withstood the test of time, however, and should not be overlooked.

Is the source appropriate? What audience is the material written for? In general, look for information directed at the educated reader. Material geared to experts or to popular audiences may be too technical or too simplified and therefore not appropriate for most research projects.

Distinguishing Fact from Opinion

As you gather information, it is important to recognize facts and opinions. A **fact** can be proven to be true or false. You could verify the statement "Congress rejected the bill" by checking newspapers, magazines, or the *Congressional Record.* An **opinion** is a judgment based on facts. The statement "Congress should not have rejected the bill" is an opinion. To evaluate an opinion, check for evidence presented logically and validly to support it.

Recognizing Bias

A writer may have a particular bias. This does not automatically make his or her point of view unreliable. However, recognizing an author's bias can help you evaluate a source. Recognizing that the author of an article about immigration is a Chinese immigrant will help you understand that author's bias. In addition, an author may have a hidden agenda that makes him or her less than objective about a topic. To avoid relying on information that may be biased, check an author's background and gather a variety of viewpoints.

1.3 Collecting Information

People use a variety of techniques to collect information during the research process. Try out several of those suggested below and decide which ones work best for you.

Paraphrasing and Summarizing

You can adapt material from other sources by quoting it directly or by paraphrasing or summarizing it. A paraphrase involves restating the information in your own words. It is often a simpler version but not necessarily a shorter

1172 COMMUNICATION HANDBOOK

version. A summary involves extracting the main ideas and supporting details and writing a shorter version of the information.

Remember to credit the source when you paraphrase or summarize. See the Writing Handbook–Research Report, pp. 1163–1168.

Strategies for Paraphrasing
1. Select the portion of the article you want to record.
2. Read it carefully and think about those ideas you find most interesting and useful to your research. Often these will be the main ideas.
3. Retell the information in your own words.

Strategies for Summarizing
1. Read the article carefully. Determine the main ideas.
2. In your own words, write a shortened version of these main ideas.

Avoiding Plagiarism

Plagiarism is copying someone else's ideas or words and using them as if they were your own. This can happen inadvertently if you are sloppy about collecting information and documenting your sources. Plagiarism is intellectual stealing and can have serious consequences.

How to Avoid Plagiarism

1. When you paraphrase or summarize, be sure to change entirely the wording of the original by using your own words.
2. Both in notes and on your final report, enclose in quotation marks any material copied directly from other sources.
3. Indicate in your final report the sources of any ideas that are not general knowledge—including those in the visuals—that you have paraphrased or summarized.
4. Include a list of Works Cited with your finished report. See the Writing Handbook–Research Report, pp. 1163–1168.

2 Study Skills and Strategies

As you read an assignment for the first time, review material for a test, or search for information for a research report, you use different methods of reading and studying.

2.1 Skimming

When you run your eyes quickly over a text, paying attention to overviews, headings, topic sentences, highlighted words, and graphic features, you are skimming.

Skimming is a good technique for previewing material in a textbook or other source that you must read for an assignment. It is also useful when you are researching a self-selected topic. Skimming a source helps you determine whether it has pertinent information. For example, suppose you are writing a research report on Mark Twain. Skimming an essay on the literature of the frontier can help you quickly determine whether any part of it deals with your topic.

2.2 Scanning

To find a specific piece of information in a text, use scanning. To scan, place a card under the first line of a page and move it down slowly. Look for key words and phrases that signal the information you are looking for.

Scanning is useful in reviewing for a test or in finding a specific piece of information for a paper. Suppose you are looking for a discussion of Twain's relationship with his family for your research report. You can scan a book chapter or an essay, looking for the key names *Olivia, Susy, Clara,* and *Jean Clemens.*

COMMUNICATION HANDBOOK 1173

2.3 In-Depth Reading

When you must thoroughly understand the material in a text, you use in-depth reading.

In-depth reading involves asking questions, taking notes, looking for main ideas, and drawing conclusions as you read slowly and carefully. For example, in researching your report on Twain, you may find an essay on how Twain's point of view changed in his later literature. Since this is closely related to your topic, you will read it in depth and take notes. You also should use in-depth reading for reading textbooks and literary works.

2.4 Outlining

Outlining is an efficient way of organizing ideas and is useful in taking notes.

Outlining helps you retain information as you read in depth. For example, you might outline a chapter in a history textbook, listing the main subtopics and the ideas or details that support them. An outline can also be useful for taking notes for a research report or in reading a piece of literature. The following is an example of a topic outline that summarizes, in short phrases, part of a chapter.

MAIN IDEA: **Mark Twain as a mirror of American culture.**

I. Early Years
- **A. Humorous newspaper accounts**
- **B. Successful lecture tour**

II. Hartford Years
- **A. Successful humorous books**
- **B. Satiric criticisms of some American behavior**

III. Later Years
- **A. Personal tragedy, business problems**
- **B. Works emphasize gloomy view of human selfishness**

IV. Evaluations of Twain
- **A. Distinctly American voice**
- **B. Outstanding humorist**
- **C. More than a humorist**

2.5 Identifying Main Ideas

To understand and remember any material you read, identify its main idea.

In informative material, the main idea is often stated. The thesis statement of an essay or article and the topic sentence of each paragraph often state the main idea. In other material, especially literary works, the main idea is implied. After reading the piece carefully, analyze the important parts, such as characters and plot. Then try to sum up in one sentence the general point that the story makes.

2.6 Taking Notes

As you listen or read in depth, take notes to help you understand the material. Look and listen for key words that point to main ideas.

One way to help you summarize the main idea and supporting details is to take notes in modified outline form. In using a modified outline form, you do not need to use numerals and letters. Unlike a formal outline, a modified outline does not require two or more points under each heading, and headings do not need to be parallel grammatically. Yet, like a formal outline, a modified outline organizes a text's main ideas and related details. The following modified outline describes methods of communication:

Preliterate Methods
- **storytelling**
- **messengers**
- **smoke signals**
- **drums**

Literate Methods
- **writing**
- **printing press**

Electronic Methods
- **telegram**
- **telephone**
- **movies**
- **television**
- **Internet**

Use abbreviations and symbols to make note taking more efficient. Following are some commonly used abbreviations for note taking.

w/	with	re	regarding
w/o	without	=	is, equals
#	number	*	important
&, +	and	def	definition
>	more than	Amer	America
<	less than	tho	although

1174 COMMUNICATION HANDBOOK

3 Critical Thinking

Critical thinking includes the ability to analyze, evaluate, and synthesize ideas and information. Critical thinking goes beyond simply understanding something. It involves making informed judgments based on sound reasoning skills.

3.1 Avoiding Faulty Reasoning

When you write or speak for a persuasive purpose, you must make sure your logic is valid. Avoid these mistakes in reasoning, called **logical fallacies.**

Overgeneralization

Conclusions reached on the basis of too little evidence result in the fallacy called overgeneralization. A person who saw three cyclists riding bicycles without helmets might conclude, "Nobody wears bicycle helmets." That conclusion would be an overgeneralization.

Circular Reasoning

When you support an opinion by simply repeating it in different terms, you are using circular reasoning. For example, "Sport utility vehicles are popular because more people buy them than any other category of new cars." This is an illogical statement because the second part of the sentence simply uses different words to restate the first part of the sentence.

Either-Or Fallacy

Assuming that a complex question has only two possible answers is called the either-or fallacy. "Either we raise the legal driving age or accidents caused by teenage drivers will continue to increase" is an example of the either-or fallacy. The statement ignores other ways of decreasing the automobile accident rate of teenagers.

Cause-and-Effect Fallacy

The cause-and-effect fallacy occurs when you say that event B was caused by event A just because event B occurred after event A. A person might conclude that because a city's air quality worsened two months after a new factory began operation, the new factory caused the air pollution. However, this cause-and-effect relationship would have to be supported by more specific evidence.

3.2 Identifying Modes of Persuasion

Understanding persuasive techniques can help you evaluate information, make informed decisions, and avoid persuasive techniques intended to deceive you. Some modes of persuasion appeal to your various emotions.

Loaded Language

Loaded language is words or phrases chosen to appeal to the emotions. It is often used in place of facts to shape opinion or to evoke a positive or negative reaction. For example, you might feel positive about a politician who has a *plan.* You might, however, feel negative about a politician who has a *scheme*.

Bandwagon

Bandwagon taps into the human desire to belong. This technique suggests that "everybody" is doing it, or buying it, or believing it. Phrases such as "Don't be the only one . . ." and "Everybody is . . . " signal the bandwagon appeal.

Testimonials

Testimonials present well-known people or satisfied customers who promote and endorse a product or idea. This technique taps into the appeal of celebrities or into people's need to identify with others just like themselves.

COMMUNICATION HANDBOOK 1175

3.3 Logical Thinking

Persuasive writing and speaking require good reasoning skills. Two ways of creating logical arguments are deductive reasoning and inductive reasoning.

Deductive Arguments

A deductive argument begins with a generalization, or premise, and then advances with facts and evidence that lead to a conclusion. The conclusion is the logical outcome of the premise. A false premise leads to a false conclusion; a valid premise leads to a valid conclusion provided that the specific facts are correct and the reasoning is correct.

Generalization — We need to reduce our dependence on fossil fuels.
↓
Specific fact — Cars that get very high mileage from using a mixture of gasoline and electric power are now available in some countries.
↓
Conclusion — Congress should provide tax incentives for manufacturers and consumers to use cars that use gasoline/electric power.

You may use deductive reasoning when writing a persuasive paper or speech. Your conclusion is the thesis of your paper. Facts in your paper supporting your premise should lead logically to that conclusion.

Inductive Arguments

An inductive argument begins with specific evidence that leads to a general conclusion.

Specific fact — Dorothea Dix led the drive to improve the treatment of the mentally ill.
↓
Specific fact — Dix also campaigned for more humane treatment of prisoners.
↓
Specific fact — She was superintendent of the United States Army nurses during the Civil War.
↓
General Conclusion — Dorothea Dix was a strong presence on behalf of the helpless.

The conclusion of an inductive argument often includes a qualifying term such as *some, often,* or *most.* This usage helps to avoid the fallacy of overgeneralization.

4 Speaking and Listening

Good speakers and listeners do more than just talk and hear. They use specific techniques to present their ideas effectively, and they are attentive and critical listeners.

4.1 Giving a Speech

In school, in business, and in community life, giving a speech is one of the most effective ways of communicating. Whether to persuade, to inform, or to entertain, you may often speak before an audience.

Analyzing Audience and Purpose

In order to speak effectively, you need to know to whom you are speaking and why you are speaking. When preparing a speech, think about how much knowledge and interest your audience has in your subject. A speech has one of two main purposes: to inform or to persuade. A third purpose, to entertain, is often considered closely related to these two purposes.

A speech **to inform** gives the audience new information, provides a better understanding of information, or enables people to use information in a new way. An informative speech is presented in an objective way.

In a speech **to persuade,** a speaker tries to change the actions or beliefs of an audience.

1176 COMMUNICATION HANDBOOK

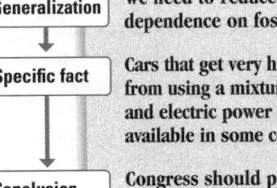

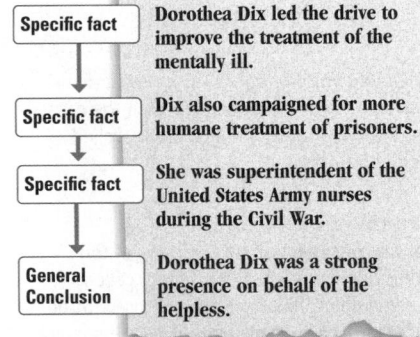

Preparing and Delivering a Speech

There are four main methods of preparing and delivering a speech:

Manuscript When you speak from **manuscript,** you prepare a complete script of your speech in advance and use it to deliver your speech.

Memory When you speak from **memory,** you prepare a written text in advance and then memorize it so you can deliver it word for word.

Impromptu When you speak **impromptu,** you speak on the spur of the moment without any special preparation.

Extemporaneous When you give an **extemporaneous** speech, you research and prepare your speech and then deliver it with the help of notes.

Points for Effective Speech Delivery
• Avoid speaking either too fast or too slow. Vary your **speaking rate** depending on your material. Slow down for difficult concepts. Speed up to convince your audience that you are knowledgeable about your subject.
• Speak loud enough to be heard clearly, but not so loud that your voice is overwhelming.
• Use a **conversational tone.**
• Use a change of **pitch,** or inflection, to help make your tone and meaning clear.
• Let your **facial expression** reflect your message.
• Make **eye contact** with as many audience members as possible.
• Use **gestures** to emphasize your words. Don't make your gestures too small to be seen. On the other hand, don't gesture too frequently or wildly.
• Use **good posture**—not too relaxed and not too rigid. Avoid nervous mannerisms.

4.2 Analyzing, Evaluating and Critiquing a Speech

Evaluating speeches helps you make informed judgments about the ideas presented in a speech. It also helps you learn what makes an effective speech and delivery. Use these criteria to help you analyze, evaluate, and critique speeches.

CRITERIA **How to Evaluate a Persuasive Speech**

- Did the speaker have a clear goal or argument?
- Did the speaker take the audience's biases into account?
- Did the speaker support the argument with convincing facts?
- Did the speaker use sound logic in developing the argument?
- Did the speaker use voice, facial expression, gestures, and posture effectively?
- Did the speaker hold the audience's interest?

CRITERIA **How to Evaluate an Informative Speech**

- Did the speaker have a specific, clearly focused topic?
- Did the speaker take the audience's previous knowledge into consideration?
- Did the speaker cite sources for the information?
- Did the speaker communicate the information objectively?
- Did the speaker present the information in an organized manner?
- Did the speaker use visual aids effectively?
- Did the speaker use voice, facial expression, gestures, and posture effectively?

COMMUNICATION HANDBOOK 1177

4.3 Using Active Listening Strategies

Listeners play an active part in the communication process. A listener has a responsibility just as a speaker does. Listening, unlike hearing, is a learned skill.

As you listen to a public speaker, use the following active listening strategies:

- Determine the **speaker's purpose.**
- Listen for the **main idea** of the message and not simply the individual details.
- **Anticipate the points** that will be made based on the speaker's purpose and main idea.
- Listen with an open mind, but **identify faulty logic, unsupported facts,** and **emotional appeals.**

4.4 Conducting Interviews

Conducting a personal interview can be an effective way to get information.

Preparing for the Interview

- Read any articles by or about the person you will interview. This background information will help you get to the point during the interview.
- Prepare a list of questions. Think of more questions than you will need. Include some yes/no questions and some open-ended questions. Order your questions from most important to least important.

Participating in the Interview

- Listen interactively. Be prepared to follow up on a response you find interesting.
- Avoid arguments. Be tactful and polite.

Following Up on the Interview

- Summarize your notes while they are still fresh in your mind.
- Send a thank-you note to the interviewee.

5 Viewing and Representing

In our media-saturated world, we are immersed in visual messages that convey ideas, information, and attitudes. To understand and use visual representations effectively, you need to be aware of the techniques and the range of visuals that are commonly used.

5.1 Understanding Visual Messages

Information is communicated not only with words but with graphic devices. A **graphic device** is a visual representation of data and ideas and the relations among them.

Reading Charts and Graphs

A chart organizes information by arranging it in rows and columns. It is helpful in showing complex information clearly. When interpreting a chart, first read the title. Then analyze how the information is presented. Charts can take many different forms. The following chart shows comparison and contrast in Ray Bradbury's description of a Tyrannosaurus Rex in "A Sound of Thunder."

Comparison and Contrast in a Description of a Dinosaur

Massive	Delicate
thirty feet above trees	delicate watchmaker's claws
each thigh a ton of meat	two delicate arms
head a ton of sculptured stone	gliding ballet step

There are several different types of **graphs,** visual aids that are often used to display numerical information.

1178 COMMUNICATION HANDBOOK

- A **circle graph** shows proportions of the whole.
- A **line graph** shows the change in data over a period of time. The following line graph shows the change in the area of the United States during the 19th century.

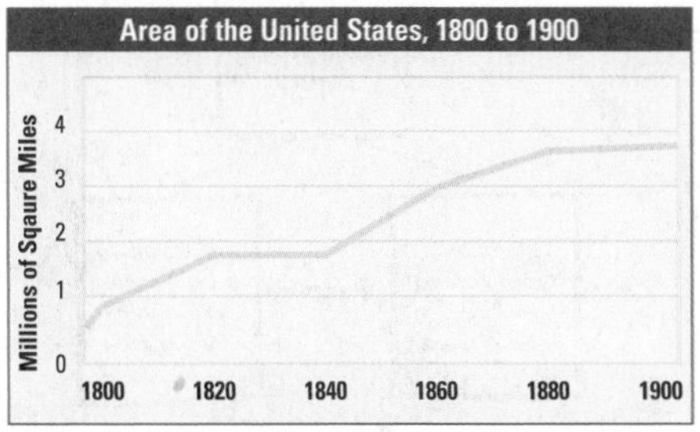

- A **bar graph** compares amounts. The following bar graph shows how many books Twain wrote in each period of his writing career.

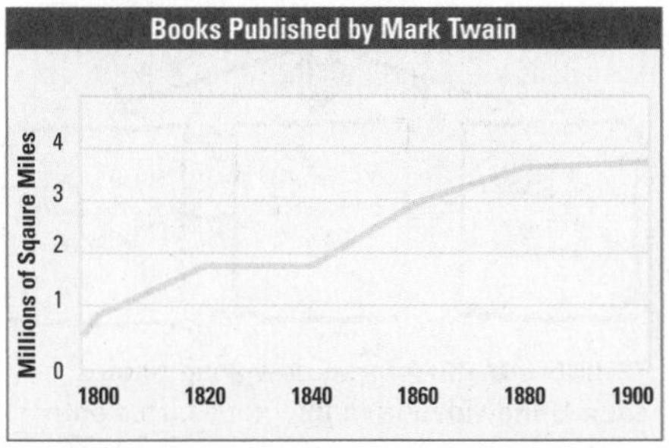

Interpreting Images

Speakers and writers often use visual aids to inform or persuade their audiences. These aids can be invaluable in helping you understand the information being communicated. However, you must interpret visual aids critically, as you do written material.

- **Examine photographs critically.** Does the camera angle or the background in the photo intentionally evoke a positive or negative response? Has the image been altered or manipulated?
- **Evaluate carefully the data presented in charts and graphs.** Some charts and graphs may exaggerate the facts. For example, a circle graph representing a sample of only ten people may be misleading if the speaker suggests that this data represents a trend.

5.2 Evaluating Visual Messages

When you view images, whether they are cartoons, advertising art, photographs, or paintings, there are certain elements to look for.

CRITERIA **How to Analyze Images**

- Is color used realistically? Is it used to emphasize certain objects? to evoke a specific response?
- What tone is created by color and by light and dark in the picture?
- Do the background images intentionally evoke a positive or negative response?
- What is noticeable about the picture's composition, that is, the arrangement of lines, colors, and forms? Does the composition emphasize certain objects or elements in the picture?
- For graphs and charts, does the visual accurately represent the data?

5.3 Using Visual Representations

Tables, graphs, diagrams, pictures, and animations often communicate information more effectively than words alone do.

Use visuals with written reports to illustrate complex concepts and processes or to make a page look more interesting. Computer programs, CD-ROMs, and on-line services can help you generate

- **graphs** that present numerical information
- **charts** and **tables** that allow easy comparison of information
- **logos** and **graphic devices** that highlight important information
- **borders** and **tints** that signal different kinds of information
- **clip art** that adds useful pictures
- **interactive animations** that illustrate difficult concepts

You might want to explore ways of displaying data in more than one visual format before deciding which will work best for you.

COMMUNICATION HANDBOOK 1179

5.4 Making Multimedia Presentations

A multimedia presentation is an electronically prepared combination of text, sound, and visuals such as photographs, videos, and animation. Your audience reads, hears, and sees your presentation at a computer, following different "paths" you create to lead the user through the information you have gathered.

Planning Presentations

To create a multimedia presentation, first choose your topic and decide what you want to include. Then plan how you want your user to move through your presentation. For a multimedia presentation on the role of the setting in literature, you might include the following items:

- text defining setting and discussing elements of settings
- taped reading from "The Son from America" describing the hut and village accompanied by photo of a painting of a simple place
- taped reading from "A White Heron" accompanied by a sequence of slides showing scenes similar to those described
- chart comparing two descriptions of a family farm setting, one positive, one negative
- video interview with an author on the role of the setting in his or her work
- video of Mississippi River as seen from a river pilot's seat, voice-over discussing Twain's *Life on the Mississippi*
- series of short film clips showing spooky settings from horror movies

You can choose one of the following ways to organize your presentation:

step by step, with only one path, or order, in which the user can see and hear the information

a branching path that allows users to make some choices about what they will see and hear, and in what order

A flow chart can help you figure out the paths a user can take through your presentation. Each box in the flow chart that follows represents something about setting for the user to read, see, or hear. The arrows on the flow chart show the possible paths the user can follow.

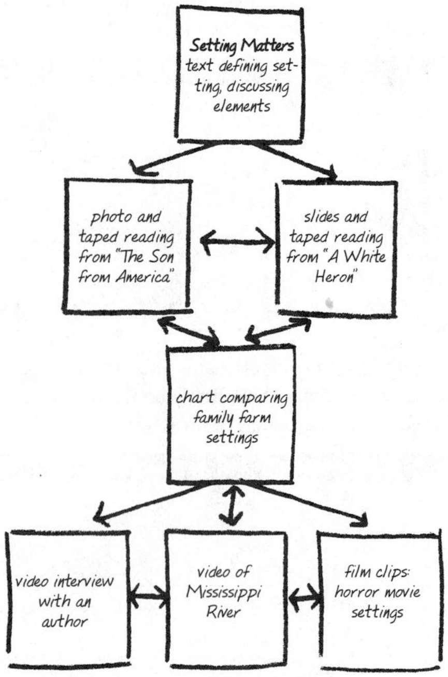

TECHNOLOGY TIP You can download photos, sound, and video from Internet sources onto your computer. This process lets you add to your presentation elements that would usually require complex editing equipment.

Guiding Your User

Your user will need directions to follow the path you have planned for your multimedia presentation.

Most multimedia authoring programs allow you to create screens that include text or audio directions that guide the user from one part of your presentation to the next.

If you need help creating your multimedia presentation, ask your school's technology adviser. You may also be able to get help from your classmates or your software manual.

1180 COMMUNICATION HANDBOOK

Grammar Handbook

1 Quick Reference: Parts of Speech

Part of Speech	Definition	Examples
Noun	Names a person, place, thing, idea, quality, or action.	Margaret, Texas, knuckles, nature, beauty, beginning
Pronoun	Takes the place of a noun or another pronoun.	
Personal	Refers to the one speaking, spoken to, or spoken about.	I, me, my, mine, we, us, our, ours, you, your, yours, she, he, it, her, him, hers, his, its, they, them, their, theirs
Reflexive	Follows a verb or preposition and refers to a preceding noun or pronoun.	myself, yourself, herself, himself, itself, ourselves, yourselves, themselves
Intensive	Emphasizes a noun or another pronoun.	(Same as reflexives)
Demonstrative	Points to specific persons or things.	this, that, these, those
Interrogative	Signals questions.	who, whom, whose, which, what
Indefinite	Refers to person(s) or thing(s) not specifically mentioned.	both, all, most, many, anyone, everybody, several, none, some
Relative	Introduces subordinate clauses and relates them to words in the main clause.	who, whom, whose, which, that
Verb	Expresses action, condition, or state of being.	
Action	Tells what the subject does or did, physically or mentally.	run, reaches, listened, consider, decides, dreamt
Linking	Connects subjects to that which identifies or describes them.	am, is, are, was, were, sound, taste, appear, feel, become, remain, seem
Auxiliary	Precedes and introduces main verbs.	be, have, do, can, could, will, would, may, might
Adjective	Modifies nouns or pronouns.	**strong** women, **two** epics, **enough** time
Adverb	Modifies verbs, adjectives, or other adverbs.	walked **out**, **really** funny, **far** away
Preposition	Relates one word to another (following) word.	at, by, for, from, in, of, on, to, with
Conjunction	Joins words or word groups.	
Coordinating	Joins words or word groups used the same way.	and, but, or, for, so, yet, nor
Correlative	Join words or word groups used the same way and are used in pairs.	both . . . and, either . . . or, neither . . . nor
Subordinating	Joins word groups not used the same way.	although, after, as, before, because, when, if, unless
Interjection	Expresses emotion.	wow, ouch, hurrah

GRAMMAR HANDBOOK 1181

2 Nouns

A noun is a word used to name a person, place, thing, idea, quality, or action. Nouns can be classified in several ways. All nouns can be placed in at least two classifications. They are either common or proper. All are also either abstract or concrete. Some nouns can be classified as compound, collective, and possessive as well.

2.1 ***Common Nouns*** are general names, common to an entire group.

EXAMPLES: *motor, tree, time, children*

2.2 ***Proper Nouns*** name specific, one-of-a-kind things. (See Capitalization, page 1205.)

EXAMPLES: *Bradbury, Eastern Standard Time, Maine*

2.3 ***Concrete Nouns*** name things that can be perceived by the senses.

EXAMPLES: *stadium, jacket, St. Louis, Wrigley Field*

2.4 ***Abstract Nouns*** name things that cannot be observed by the senses.

EXAMPLES: *intelligence, fear, joy, loneliness*

	Common	Proper
Abstract	beauty	Age of Enlightenment
Concrete	planet	Mars

2.5 ***Compound Nouns*** are formed from two or more words but express a single idea. They are written as single words, as separate words, or with hyphens. Use a dictionary to check the correct spelling of a compound noun.

EXAMPLES: *sunshine, call waiting, job-sharing*

2.6 ***Collective Nouns*** are singular nouns that refer to groups of people or things. (See Collective Nouns as Subjects, page 1202.)

EXAMPLES: *army, flock, class, species*

2.7 ***Possessive Nouns*** show who or what owns something. Consult the chart below for the proper use of the possessive apostrophe.

Possessive Nouns

Category	Rule	Examples
All singular nouns	Add apostrophe plus *-s*	Lily's, bass's, pitcher's, daughter-in-law's
Plural nouns not ending in *-s*	Add apostrophe plus *-s*	children's women's people's
Plural nouns ending in *-s*	Add apostrophe only	witnesses' churches' males' Johnsons'

GRAMMAR PRACTICE

A. For each underlined noun, first tell whether it is common or proper. Then tell whether it is concrete or abstract.

1. Atwood says many Canadians seem to be looking through a one-way mirror.
2. Canadian society has been accused of having an identity crisis.
3. Sometimes Canadians think it is their job to explain the Yanks to the rest of the world.
4. There are some disputes about minor issues such as fish.
5. She thinks both superpowers suffer from arrogance.
6. Pat Mora misses the language sounds of El Paso and the Southwest where she grew up.
7. She misses the pleasure of weaving in and out of Spanish and English.
8. Sounds burst forth from the radio broadcast like confetti.
9. She reads poetry in Spanish.
10. The sky fills her with energy and reveals the glare of truth.

B. 11–15. From the sentences above, write three compound nouns and two collective nouns.

C. Write the possessive form of the following nouns.

16. Margaret Atwood	**21.** Southwest
17. Pat Mora	**22.** humans
18. fish	**23.** hearts
19. thorns	**24.** crisis
20. culture	**25.** businessmen

GRAMMAR PRACTICE ANSWERS

1. proper, concrete; proper, concrete
2. common, abstract; common, abstract
3. common, concrete; proper, concrete
4. common, concrete
5. common, concrete; common, abstract
6. proper, concrete; proper, concrete
7. common, abstract
8. common, concrete; common, concrete
9. common, concrete; proper, concrete
10. common, abstract

11–15. compound: El Paso, Southwest, broadcast; collective: society, poetry

16. Margaret Atwood's
17. Pat Mora's
18. fish's
19. thorns'
20. culture's
21. Southwest's
22. humans'
23. hearts'
24. crisis's
25. businessmen's

1182 GRAMMAR HANDBOOK

3 Pronouns

A pronoun is a word that is used in place of a noun or another pronoun. The word or word group to which the pronoun refers is called its antecedent.

3.1 ***Personal Pronouns*** are pronouns that change their form to express person, number, gender, and case. The forms of these pronouns are shown in the chart that follows.

	Nominative	Objective	Possessive
Singular			
First Person	I	me	my, mine
Second Person	you	you	your, yours
Third Person	she, he, it	her, him, it	her, hers, his, its
Plural			
First Person	we	us	our, ours
Second Person	you	you	your, yours
Third Person	they	them	their, theirs

3.2 ***Pronoun Agreement*** Pronouns should agree with their antecedents in number and person. Singular pronouns are used to replace singular nouns. Plural pronouns are used to replace plural nouns. Pronouns must also match the gender (masculine, feminine, or neuter) of the nouns they replace.

3.3 ***Pronoun Case*** Personal pronouns change form to show how they function in a sentence. This change of form is called *case.* The three cases are **nominative, objective,** and **possessive.**

A nominative pronoun is used as the subject or the predicate nominative of a sentence.

An objective pronoun is used as the direct or indirect object of a sentence or as the object of a preposition.

SUBJECT OBJECT

He will lead them to us.

OBJECT OF PREPOSITION

A possessive pronoun shows ownership. The pronouns *mine, yours, hers, his, its, ours,* and *theirs* can be used in place of nouns.

EXAMPLE: *This horse is mine.*

The pronouns *my, your, her, his, its, our,* and *their* are used before nouns.

EXAMPLE: *This is my horse.*

USAGE TIP To decide which pronoun to use in a comparison, such as *He tells better tales than (I* or *me),* fill in the missing words: *He tells better tales than I tell.*

WATCH OUT! Many spelling errors can be avoided if you watch out for *its* and *their.* Don't confuse the possessive pronoun *its* with the contraction *it's,* meaning *it is* or *it has.* The homonyms *they're* (contraction for *they are*) and *there* (a place or an expletive) are often mistakenly used for *their.*

3.4 ***Reflexive and Intensive Pronouns***
These pronouns are formed by adding *-self* or *-selves* to certain personal pronouns. Their forms are the same, and they differ only in how they are used.

Reflexive pronouns follow verbs or prepositions and reflect back on an earlier noun or pronoun.

EXAMPLES: *He likes himself too much. She is now herself again.*

Intensive pronouns intensify or emphasize the nouns or pronouns to which they refer.

EXAMPLES: *They themselves will educate their children. You did it yourselves.*

GRAMMAR HANDBOOK 1183

GRAMMAR PRACTICE ANSWERS

1. him = he
2. hisself = himself
3. he = him
4. them = those
5. were = was

Grammar Handbook

Singular	
First Person	myself
Second Person	yourself
Third Person	herself, himself, itself
Plural	
First Person	ourselves
Second Person	yourselves
Third Person	themselves

WATCH OUT! Avoid using *hisself* or *theirselves.* Standard English does not include these forms.

NONSTANDARD: *The children sang theirselves to sleep.*
STANDARD: *The children sang themselves to sleep.*

USAGE TIP Reflexive and intensive pronouns should never be used without antecedents.

INCORRECT: *Read a tale to my brother and myself.*
CORRECT: *Read a tale to my brother and me.*

3.5 ***Demonstrative Pronouns*** point out things and persons near and far.

	Singular	Plural
Near	this	these
Far	that	those

WATCH OUT! Avoid using the objective pronoun *them* in place of the demonstrative *those.*

INCORRECT: *Let's dramatize one of them tales.*
CORRECT: *Let's dramatize one of those tales.*

3.6 ***Indefinite Pronouns*** do not refer to specific persons or things and usually have no antecedents. The chart shows some commonly used indefinite pronouns:

Singular	Plural	Singular or Plural	
each	both	all	half
either	few	any	plenty
neither	many	more	none
another	several	most	some

Here is another set of indefinite pronouns, all of which are singular. Notice that, with one exception, they are spelled as one word:

anyone	everyone	no one	someone
anybody	everybody	nobody	somebody
anything	everything	nothing	something

USAGE TIP Since all these are singular, pronouns referring to them should be singular.

INCORRECT: *Did everybody play their part well?*
CORRECT: *Did everybody play his or her part well?*

If the antecedent of the pronoun is both male and female, *his or her* may be used as an alternative, or the sentence may be recast:

EXAMPLES: *Did everybody play his or her part well?*
Did all the students play their parts well?

GRAMMAR PRACTICE

Write the correct form of all incorrect pronouns in the sentences below.

1. In "By the Waters of Babylon," him who touches the metal in the Dead Places must be a priest or son of a priest.
2. The narrator's father hisself questioned him.
3. He feared that the swift current would carry the raft and he out into the Bitter Water.
4. When John saw a heap of broken stones, he cautiously approached them stones.
5. Each of the god roads John saw were in constant motion.

3.7 ***Interrogative Pronouns*** tell a reader or listener that a question is coming. The interrogative pronouns are *who, whom, whose, which,* and *what.*

EXAMPLES: *Who is going to rehearse with you?*
From whom did you receive the script?

USAGE TIP *Who* is used for subjects, *whom* for objects. To find out which pronoun you need to use in a question, change the question to a statement:

QUESTION: *(Who/Whom?) did you meet there?*
STATEMENT: *You met (?) there.*

Since the verb has a subject *(you)*, the needed word must be the object form, *whom.*

EXAMPLE: *Whom did you meet there?*

WATCH OUT! A special problem arises when you use an interrupter such as *do you think* within a sentence:

EXAMPLE: *(Who/Whom) do you think will win?*

If you eliminate the interrupter, it is clear that the word you need is *who.*

3.8 *Relative Pronouns* relate, or connect, clauses to the words they modify in sentences. The noun or pronoun that the clause modifies is the antecedent of the relative pronoun. Here are the relative pronouns and their uses:

Replacing:	Subject	Object	Possessive
Persons	who	whom	whose
Things	which	which	whose
Things/Persons*	that	that	whose

* *That* generally will not replace specific names, such as *Nikki Giovanni.*

Often short sentences with related ideas can be combined using relative pronouns to create a more effective sentence.

SHORT SENTENCE: *Amy Tan won a writing contest at the age of eight.*
RELATED SENTENCE: *Amy Tan did not plan to have a literary career.*
COMBINED SENTENCE: *Amy Tan, who won a writing contest at the age of eight, did not plan to have a literary career.*

GRAMMAR PRACTICE

Choose the appropriate interrogative or relative pronoun from the words in parentheses.

1. The narrator thinks people gossip and say, "(Who/Whom) does she think she is, to be so choosy?"
2. Qiao Lin, (who/whom) she is considering marrying, is athletic and handsome.
3. She thinks it would be sad to marry a man (who/whom) she doesn't love.
4. Law and morality are factors (that/who) bind a married couple.
5. Her nurse, (who/whom) is shrewd but uneducated, is critical of the narrator's reluctance to marry.
6. Her mother had told her about her father, (who/whom) was a fine handsome fellow.
7. The narrator wonders whether her mother was miserable, being deprived of a man to (who/whom) she was devoted.

4 Verbs

A verb is a word that expresses an action, a condition, or a state of being. There are two main kinds of verbs: action and linking. Other verbs, called auxiliary verbs, are sometimes used with action verbs and linking verbs.

4.1 *Action Verbs* tell what action someone or something is performing, physically or mentally.

PHYSICAL ACTION: *You hit the target.*
MENTAL ACTION: *She dreamed of me.*

4.2 *Linking Verbs* do not express action. Linking verbs link subjects to complements that identify or describe them. Linking verbs may be divided into two groups:

FORMS OF *TO BE*: *She is our queen.*
VERBS THAT EXPRESS CONDITION: *The writer looked thoughtful.*

4.3 *Auxiliary Verbs,* sometimes called helping verbs, precede action or linking verbs and modify their meanings in special ways. The most commonly used auxiliary verbs are parts of the verbs *be, have,* and *do.*

Be: *am, is, are, was, were, be, being, been*
Have: *have, has, had*
Do: *do, does, did*

Other common auxiliary verbs are *can, could, will, would, shall, should, may, might,* and *must.*

EXAMPLES: *I always have admired her.*
You must listen to me.

4.4 *Transitive and Intransitive Verbs* Action verbs can be either transitive or intransitive. A transitive verb directs the action towards someone or something. The transitive verb has an object. An intransitive verb does not direct the action towards someone or something. It does not have an object. Since linking verbs convey no action, they are always intransitive.

Transitive: *The storm sank the ship.*
Intransitive: *The ship sank.*

GRAMMAR PRACTICE ANSWERS

1. Who
2. whom
3. whom
4. that
5. who
6. who
7. whom

GRAMMAR HANDBOOK 1185

4.5 *Principal Parts* Action and linking verbs typically have four principal parts, which are used to form verb tenses. The principal parts are the *present*, the *present participle*, the *past*, and the *past participle*.

If the verb is a regular verb, the past and past participle are formed by adding the ending *-d* or *-ed* to the present part. Here is a chart showing four regular verbs:

Present	Present Participle	Past	Past Participle
risk	(is) risking	risked	(have) risked
solve	(is) solving	solved	(have) solved
drop	(is) dropping	dropped	(have) dropped
carry	(is) carrying	carried	(have) carried

Note that the present participle and past participle forms are preceded by a form of *be* or *have*. These forms cannot be used alone as main verbs and always need an auxiliary verb.

EXAMPLES: *She once thought her mother was wasting her time.*

Now she has stopped trying to be like everyone else.

The past and past participle of irregular verbs are not formed by adding *-d* or *-ed* to the present; they are formed in irregular ways.

Present	Present Participle	Past	Past Participle
begin	(is) beginning	began	(have) begun
break	(is) breaking	broke	(have) broken
bring	(is) bringing	brought	(have) brought
choose	(is) choosing	chose	(have) chosen
go	(is) going	went	(have) gone
lose	(is) losing	lost	(have) lost
see	(is) seeing	saw	(have) seen
swim	(is) swimming	swam	(have) swum
write	(is) writing	wrote	(have) written

4.6 *Verb Tense* The tense of a verb tells the time of the action or the state of being. An action or state of being can occur in the present, the past, or the future. There are six tenses, each expressing a different range of time.

Present tense expresses an action that is happening at the present time, occurs regularly, or is constant or generally true. Use the present part.

EXAMPLES

NOW: *This soup tastes delicious.*

REGULAR: *I make vegetable soup often.*

GENERAL: *Crops require sun, rain, and rich soil.*

Past tense expresses an action that began and ended in the past. Use the past part.

EXAMPLE: *The storyteller finished his tale.*

Future tense expresses an action (or state of being) that will occur. Use *shall* or *will* with the present part.

EXAMPLE: *They will attend the next festival.*

Present perfect tense expresses action (1) that was completed at an indefinite time in the past or (2) that began in the past and continues into the present. Use *have* or *has* with the past participle.

EXAMPLE: *Poetry has inspired readers throughout the ages.*

Past perfect tense shows an action in the past that came before another action in the past. Use *had* before the past participle.

EXAMPLE: *Before we left, we had asked him to find a place to stay.*

Future perfect tense shows an action in the future that will be completed before another action in the future. Use *shall have* or *will have* before the past participle.

EXAMPLE: *They will have finished the novel before seeing the movie version of the tale.*

4.7 *Progressive Forms* The progressive forms of the six tenses show ongoing action. Use a form of *be* with the present participle of a verb.

PRESENT PROGRESSIVE: *She is rehearsing her lines.*

PAST PROGRESSIVE: *She was rehearsing her lines.*

FUTURE PROGRESSIVE: *She will be rehearsing her lines.*

1186 GRAMMAR HANDBOOK

PRESENT PERFECT PROGRESSIVE: *She has been rehearsing her lines.*
PAST PERFECT PROGRESSIVE: *She had been rehearsing her lines.*
FUTURE PERFECT PROGRESSIVE: *She will have been rehearsing her lines.*

WATCH OUT! Do not shift tense needlessly. Watch out for these special cases.

- In most compound sentences and in sentences with compound predicates, keep the tenses the same.

  INCORRECT: *I keyed in the password, but I get an error message.*
  CORRECT: *I keyed in the password, but I got an error message.*

- If one past action happens before another, do shift tenses—from the past to the past perfect:

  INCORRECT: *They wished they started earlier.*
  CORRECT: *They wished they had started earlier.*

GRAMMAR PRACTICE

Identify the tense of the verb(s) in each of the following sentences. If you find an unnecessary tense shift, correct it.

1. Plath's story "Initiation" is about a high school sorority initiation.
2. No one who joined the sorority fails to get through initiation.
3. Millicent tells Tracy they still will be best friends after the initiation.
4. She thought, "This is getting serious."
5. When Millicent made her decision, she remembers the reply of the man on the bus.

4.8 *Active and Passive Voice*

The voice of a verb tells whether the subject of a sentence performs or receives the action expressed by the verb. When the subject performs the action, the verb is in the active voice. When the subject is the receiver of the action, the verb is in the passive voice.

Compare these two sentences:

ACTIVE: *Her sunglasses hid most of her face.*
PASSIVE: *Most of her face was hidden by her sunglasses.*

To form the passive voice use a form of *be* with the past participle of the main verb.

WATCH OUT! Use the passive voice sparingly. It tends to make writing less forceful and less direct. It can also make the writing awkward.

AWKWARD: *She was given the handmade quilts by her mother.*
CORRECT: *Her mother gave her the handmade quilts.*

There are occasions when you will choose to use the passive voice because

- you want to emphasize the receiver: *The king was shot.*
- the doer is unknown: *My books were stolen.*
- the doer is unimportant: *French is spoken here.*

4.9 *Mood*

The mood identifies the manner in which the verb expresses an idea. There are three moods.

The indicative mood states a fact or asks a question. You use this mood most often.

EXAMPLE: *His trust was shattered by the betrayal.*

The imperative mood is used to give a command or make a request.

EXAMPLE: *Be there by eight o'clock sharp.*

The subjunctive mood is used to express a wish or a condition that is contrary to fact.

EXAMPLE: *If I were you, I wouldn't get my hopes up.*

GRAMMAR PRACTICE

For the first five items below, identify the boldfaced verbs as active or passive.

1. In her stories, Alice Walker **has shown** the dignity of people who are her subjects.
2. The story "Everyday Use" **was written** by Alice Walker.
3. The mother in the story **knows** both her daughters very well.
4. The yard in front of the house **was swept** clean as a floor.
5. Their other house **had been burned** down.

GRAMMAR PRACTICE ANSWERS

Column 1

1. is = present tense
2. joined = past tense
   fails = present
   fails > failed
3. tells = present tense
   will be = future tense
4. thought = past tense
   is getting = present progressive tense
5. made = past tense
   remembers = present
   remembers > remembered

Column 2

1. has shown = active
2. was written = passive
3. knows = active
4. was swept = passive
5. had been burned = passive

GRAMMAR HANDBOOK 1187

GRAMMAR PRACTICE ANSWERS
6. indicative
7. subjunctive
8. indicative
9. indicative
10. subjunctive

Grammar Handbook

For the following items, identify the boldfaced verbs as indicative or subjunctive in mood.

6. The story **shows** how the mother respects the everyday use of the quilts.
7. If Dee **were** more like Maggie, she would understand the value of the quilts in a different way.
8. Dee **wanted** to hang the quilts on the wall because of their beauty and their history.
9. Maggie and her mother **were planning** to use the quilts as bedcovers.
10. If Walker **were** not such a good writer, she might have made the story seem commonplace.

5 Modifiers

Modifiers are words or groups of words that change or limit the meanings of other words. The two kinds of modifiers are adjectives and adverbs.

5.1 ***Adjectives*** An adjective is a word that modifies a noun or pronoun by telling *which one, what kind, how many,* or *how much.*

WHICH ONE: *this, that, these, those*
EXAMPLE: *These tomatoes have grown quickly.*

WHAT KIND: *tiny, impressive, bold, rotten*
EXAMPLE: *The bold officer stood in front of the crowd.*

HOW MANY: *some, few, thirty, none, both, each*
EXAMPLE: *Some of us had three helpings of sweet potatoes.*

HOW MUCH: *more, less, enough, scarce*
EXAMPLE: *There was enough chicken to serve everyone.*

The **articles** *a, an,* and *the* are usually classified as adjectives. These are the most common adjectives that you will use.

EXAMPLES: *The bridge was burned before the attack.*
A group of peasants led the procession in the town.

5.2 ***Predicate Adjectives*** Most adjectives come before the nouns they modify, as in the examples above. Predicate adjectives, however, follow linking verbs and describe the subject.

EXAMPLE: *My friends are very intelligent.*

Be especially careful to use adjectives (not adverbs) after such linking verbs as *look, feel, grow, taste,* and *smell.*

EXAMPLE: *The weather grows cold.*

5.3 ***Adverbs*** modify verbs, adjectives, or other adverbs by telling *where, when, how,* or *to what extent.*

WHERE: *The children played outside.*
WHEN: *The author spoke yesterday.*
HOW: *We walked slowly behind the leader.*
TO WHAT EXTENT: *He worked very hard.*

Unlike adjectives, adverbs tend to be mobile words; they may occur in many places in sentences.

EXAMPLES: *Suddenly the wind shifted. The wind suddenly shifted. The wind shifted suddenly.*

Changing the position of adverbs within sentences can vary the rhythm in your writing.

5.4 ***Adjective or Adverb*** Many adverbs are formed by adding *-ly* to adjectives.

EXAMPLES: *sweet, sweetly; gentle, gently*

However, *-ly* added to a noun will usually yield an adjective.

EXAMPLES: *friend, friendly; woman, womanly*

5.5 ***Comparison of Modifiers*** The form of an adjective or adverb indicates the degree of comparison that the modifier expresses. Both adjectives and adverbs have three forms, or degrees: the positive, comparative, and superlative.

The positive form is used to describe individual things, groups, or actions.

EXAMPLES: *The emperor's chariots are fast.*
Cassius's speech was effective.

The comparative form is used to compare two things, groups, or actions.

EXAMPLES: *The emperor's chariots are faster than the senators' chariots.*
Brutus's speech was more effective than Cassius's speech.

The superlative form is used to compare more than two things, groups, or actions.

EXAMPLES: *The emperor's chariots are the fastest in the empire.*
Antony's speech was the most effective of all.

5.6 *Regular Comparisons* One-syllable and some two-syllable adjectives and adverbs form their comparative and superlative forms by adding *-er* or *-est.* All three-syllable and most two-syllable modifiers form their comparative and superlative by using *more* or *most.*

Positive	Comparative	Superlative
small	smaller	smallest
thin	thinner	thinnest
sleepy	sleepier	sleepiest
useless	more useless	most useless
precisely	more precisely	most precisely

WATCH OUT! Note that spelling changes must sometimes be made to form the comparative and superlative of modifiers.

EXAMPLES: *friendly, friendlier* (change *y* to *i* and add the ending)
sad, sadder (double the final consonant and add the ending)

5.7 *Irregular Comparisons* Some commonly used modifiers have irregular comparative and superlative forms. You may wish to memorize them.

Positive	Comparative	Superlative
good	better	best
bad	worse	worst
far	farther or further	farthest or furthest
little	less or lesser	least
many	more	most
well	better	best
much	more	most

5.8 *Using Modifiers Correctly* Study the tips that follow to avoid common mistakes.

Farther and Further *Farther* is used for distances; use *further* for everything else.

Avoiding double comparisons You make a comparison by using *-er/-est* or by using *more/most.* Using *-er* with *more* or using *-est* with *most* is incorrect.

INCORRECT: *I like her more better than she likes me.*
CORRECT: *I like her better than she likes me.*

Avoiding illogical comparisons An illogical or confusing comparison results if two unrelated things are compared or if something is compared with itself. The word *other* or the word *else* should be used in a comparison of an individual member with the rest of the group.

ILLOGICAL: *Shakespeare's plays are more popular than those of any Elizabethan writer.* (Was Shakespeare an Elizabethan writer?)
LOGICAL: *Shakespeare's plays are more popular than those of any other Elizabethan writer.*

Bad vs. Badly *Bad,* always an adjective, is used before nouns or after linking verbs to describe the subject. *Badly,* always an adverb, never modifies a noun. Be sure to use the right form after a linking verb.

INCORRECT: *Ed felt badly after his team lost.*
CORRECT: *Ed felt bad after his team lost.*

Good vs. Well *Good* is always an adjective. It is used before nouns or after a linking verb to modify the subject. *Well* is often an adverb meaning "expertly" or "properly." *Well* can also be used as an adjective after a linking verb, when it means "in good health."

INCORRECT: *Helen writes very good.*
CORRECT: *Helen writes very well.*
CORRECT: *Yesterday I felt bad; today I feel well.*

GRAMMAR HANDBOOK 1189

GRAMMAR PRACTICE ANSWERS

1. more popular
2. most powerful
3. any
4. could
5. well
6. any
7. best
8. better
9. bad
10. anyone

Grammar Handbook

Double negatives If you add a negative word to a sentence that is already negative, the result will be an error known as a double negative. When using *not* or *-n't* with a verb, use "*any-*" words, such as *anybody* or *anything,* rather than "*no-*" words, such as *nobody* or *nothing,* later in the sentence.

INCORRECT: *I don't have no money.*
CORRECT: *I don't have any money.*

INCORRECT: *We haven't seen nobody.*
CORRECT: *We haven't seen anybody.*

Using *hardly, barely,* or *scarcely* after a negative word is also incorrect.

INCORRECT: *They couldn't barely see two feet ahead.*
CORRECT: *They could barely see two feet ahead.*

Misplaced modifiers A misplaced modifier is one placed so far away from the word it modifies that the intended meaning of the sentence is unclear. Place modifiers as close as possible to the words they modify.

MISPLACED: *We found the child in the park who was missing.* (The child was missing, not the park.)

CLEARER: *We found the child who was missing in the park.*

GRAMMAR PRACTICE

Choose the correct word from each pair in parentheses.

1. Shakespeare's plays are (popularer/more popular) than those of any other playwright.
2. The play *Julius Caesar* is about the death of the (powerfulest, most powerful) emperor of Roman times.
3. The emperor didn't pay (no/any) attention to the soothsayer who warned him about the ides of March.
4. Caesar (could/couldn't) hardly know what lay in store for him.
5. He thought Brutus loved him (well/good).
6. He didn't have (any/no) fear of his friends.
7. Some Romans thought that Caesar was the (most good/best) leader they would ever have.
8. Between Antony and Brutus, Brutus was supposed to be the (better/best) public speaker.
9. In this scene, we learn that Mark Antony felt (bad/badly) that Caesar was killed.
10. Antony didn't want (anyone/no one) to know his plans.

6 Prepositions, Conjunctions, and Interjections

6.1 ***Prepositions*** A preposition is a word used to show the relationship between a noun or a pronoun and another word in the sentence.

Commonly Used Prepositions

above	down	near	through
at	for	of	to
before	from	on	up
below	in	out	with
by	into	over	without

The preposition is always followed by a word or group of words that serve as its object. The preposition, its object, and modifiers of the object are called the **prepositional phrase.** In each example below, the prepositional phrase is underlined and the object of the preposition is in boldface type.

EXAMPLES
*The future of the entire **kingdom** is uncertain.*
*We searched through the deepest **woods.***

Prepositional phrases may be used as adjectives or as adverbs. The phrase in the first example is used as an adjective modifying the noun *future.* In the second example, the phrase is used as an adverb modifying the verb *searched.*

WATCH OUT! Prepositional phrases must be as close as possible to the word they modify.

MISPLACED: *We have clothes for leisure wear of many colors.*
CLEARER: *We have clothes of many colors for leisure wear.*

1190 GRAMMAR HANDBOOK

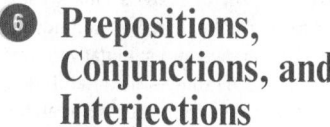

Grammar Handbook

6.2 *Conjunctions* A conjunction is a word used to connect words, phrases, or sentences. There are three kinds of conjunctions: **coordinating conjunctions, correlative conjunctions,** and **subordinating conjunctions.**

Coordinating conjunctions connect words or word groups that have the same function in a sentence. These include *and, but, or, for, so, yet,* and *nor.*

Coordinating conjunctions can join nouns, pronouns, verbs, adjectives, adverbs, prepositional phrases, and clauses in a sentence.

These examples show coordinating conjunctions joining words of the same function:

EXAMPLES

I have many friends but few enemies. (two noun objects)

We ran out the door and into the street. (two prepositional phrases)

They are pleasant yet seem aloof. (two predicates)

We have to go now, or we will be late. (two clauses)

Correlative conjunctions are similar to coordinating conjunctions. However, correlative conjunctions are always used in pairs.

Correlative Conjunctions		
both . . . and	neither . . . nor	whether . . . or
either . . . or	not only . . . but also	

Subordinating conjunctions introduce subordinate clauses—clauses that cannot stand by themselves as complete sentences. The subordinating conjunction shows how the subordinate clause relates to the rest of the sentence. The relationships include time, manner, place, cause, comparison, condition, and purpose.

SUBORDINATING CONJUNCTIONS	
TIME	*after, as, as long as, as soon as, before, since, until, when, whenever, while*
MANNER	*as, as if*
PLACE	*where, wherever*
CAUSE	*because, since*
COMPARISON	*as, as much as, than*
CONDITION	*although, as long as, even if, even though, if, provided that, though, unless, while*
PURPOSE	*in order that, so that, that*

In the example below, the boldface word is the conjunction, and the underlined words are called a subordinate clause:

EXAMPLE: *We sing **because** we are happy.*

We sing is an independent clause because it can stand alone as a complete sentence. *Because we are happy* cannot stand alone as a complete sentence; it is a subordinate clause.

Conjunctive adverbs are used to connect clauses that can stand by themselves as sentences. Conjunctive adverbs include *also, besides, finally, however, moreover, nevertheless, otherwise,* and *then.*

EXAMPLE: *She loved the fall; however, she also enjoyed winter.*

6.3 *Interjections* are words used to show strong emotion, such as *wow* and *cool.* Often followed by an exclamation point, they have no grammatical relationship to the rest of a sentence.

EXAMPLE: *You've written a poem? Great!*

GRAMMAR PRACTICE

Label each of the boldfaced words as a preposition, conjunction, or interjection.

1. Carl Sandburg was a writer **and** lecturer.
2. He is well-known **for** his poetry, **but** he also won prizes **for** his biographies.
3. **In** Sandburg's poem "Moon Rondeau," the lovers feel that they own the moon. **Wonderful!**
4. They felt this way **because** they were in love.
5. They thought the moon looked like a silver button **as well as** a plaque of gold.
6. They looked at the moon one evening **when** they could smell leaves and roses.
7. The lovers talk together of love, **yet** they notice the way things look and smell.
8. They looked long **at** the moon and talked about it as if it were special just for them. **Terrific!**
9. Is it spring **because** there is the smell of "the beginnings of roses **and** potatoes"?
10. They sat together until late **in** the evening.

GRAMMAR PRACTICE ANSWERS

1. and = conjunction
2. for = preposition
   but = conjunction
   for = preposition
3. in = preposition
   wonderful = interjection
4. because = conjunction
5. as well as = conjunction
6. when = conjunction
7. yet = conjunction
8. at = preposition
   terrific = interjection
9. because = conjunction
   and = conjunction
10. in = preposition

7 Quick Reference: The Sentence and Its Parts

The diagrams that follow will give you a brief review of the essentials of the sentence–subjects and predicates–and of some of its parts.

The writer's **pen** **hit** the floor.

The **complete subject** includes all the words that identify the person, place, thing, or idea that the sentence is about.

The **complete predicate** includes all the words that tell or ask something about the subject.

pen

hit

The **simple subject** tells exactly whom or what the sentence is about. It may be one word or a group of words, but it does not include modifiers.

The **simple predicate,** or **verb,** tells what the subject does or is. It may be one word or several, but it does not include modifiers.

For his graduation, the family **had given** the young **Buddy** money.

A **prepositional phrase** consists of a preposition, its object, and any modifiers of the object. In this phrase, *for* is the preposition and *graduation* is its object.

subject

Verbs often have more than one part. They may be made up of a **main verb,** like *given,* and one or more **auxiliary,** or **helping, verbs,** like *had.*

An **indirect object** is a word or a group of words that tells *to whom* or *for whom* or *to what* or *for what* about the verb. A sentence can have an indirect object only if it has a direct object. The indirect object always comes before the direct object in a sentence.

A **direct object** is a word or group of words that tells who or what receives the action of the verb in the sentence.

8 The Sentence and Its Parts

A sentence is a group of words used to express a complete thought. A complete sentence has a subject and predicate.

8.1 *Kinds of Sentences* Sentences make statements, ask questions, give commands, and show feelings. There are four basic types of sentences.

Type	Definition	Example
Declarative	states a fact, wish, intent, or feeling	I read White's essay last night.
Interrogative	asks a question	Did you like the essay?
Imperative	gives a command, direction	Read this paragraph aloud.
Exclamatory	expresses strong feeling or excitement	I wish I had thought of that!

WRITING TIP One way to vary your writing is to employ a variety of different types of sentences. In the first example below, each sentence is declarative. Notice how much more interesting the revised paragraph is.

> **SAMPLE PARAGRAPH:** *You have to see Niagara Falls in person. You can truly appreciate their awesome power in no other way. You should visit them on your next vacation. They are a spectacular sight.*
>
> **REVISED PARAGRAPH:** *Have you ever seen Niagara Falls in person? You can truly appreciate their awesome power in no other way. Visit them on your next vacation. What a spectacular sight they are!*

WATCH OUT! Conversation frequently includes parts of sentences, or **fragments.** In formal writing, however, you need to be sure that every sentence is a complete thought and includes a subject and predicate. (See Correcting Fragments, page 1199.)

8.2 *Complete Subjects and Predicates*

A sentence has two parts: a subject and a predicate. The complete subject includes all the words that identify the person, place, thing, or idea that the sentence is about. The complete predicate includes all the words that tell what the subject did or what happened to the subject.

Complete Subject	Complete Predicate
The poets of the time	wrote about nature.
This new approach	was extraordinary.

8.3 *Simple Subjects and Predicates*

The simple subject is the key word in the complete subject. The simple predicate is the key word in the complete predicate. In the examples that follow they are underlined.

Simple Subject	Simple Predicate
The <u>poets</u> of the time	<u>wrote</u> about nature.
This new <u>approach</u>	<u>was</u> extraordinary.

8.4 *Compound Subjects and Predicates* A compound subject consists of two or more subjects that share the same verb. They are typically joined by the coordinating conjunction *and* or *or.*

> **EXAMPLE:** *<u>Lawrence and Hayden</u> write about families.*

A compound predicate consists of two or more predicates that share the same subject. They, too, are usually joined by the coordinating conjunction *and, but,* or *or.*

> **EXAMPLE:** *The father in "Those Winter Sundays" <u>got up early and dressed in the dark.</u>*

8.5 *Subjects and Predicates in Questions* In many interrogative sentences, the subject may appear after the verb or between parts of a verb phrase.

> **INTERROGATIVE:** *Did <u>Father</u> get up early?*
> **INTERROGATIVE:** *Why has that <u>book</u> sold so well?*

Grammar Handbook

GRAMMAR HANDBOOK 1193

GRAMMAR PRACTICE ANSWERS

1. Eugenia Collier wrote the short story "Sweet Potato Pie."
2. The narrator recounts events from his childhood and from that afternoon.
3. There are two flashbacks in the story.
4. Lil and Charley took care of the younger children in the family.
5. Now Charley drives a cab in New York City.
6. In the afternoon, Buddy left his meeting and headed uptown.
7. Bea gave Buddy fried fish and cornbread for dinner.
8. All evening they talked and remembered their past lives.
9. Why didn't Charley want Buddy to take the sweet potato pie?
10. None of the people in the lobby carried a paper bag.

8.6 *Subjects and Predicates in Imperative Sentences* Imperative sentences give commands, requests, or directions. The subject of an imperative sentence is the person spoken to, or *you*. While it is not stated, it is understood to be *you*.

EXAMPLE: *(You) Please tell me what you're thinking.*

8.7 *Subjects in Sentences That Begin with* There *and* Here When a sentence begins with *there* or *here*, the subject usually follows the verb. Remember that *there* and *here* are never the subjects of a sentence. The simple subjects in the example sentences are underlined.

EXAMPLES

Here is the solution to the mystery.

There is no time to waste now.

There were too many passengers on the boat.

GRAMMAR PRACTICE

Copy each of the following sentences. Then draw one line under the complete subject and two lines under the complete predicate.

1. Eugenia Collier wrote the short story "Sweet Potato Pie."
2. The narrator recounts events from his childhood and from that afternoon.
3. There are two flashbacks in the story.
4. Lil and Charley took care of the younger children in the family.
5. Now Charley drives a cab in New York City.
6. In the afternoon, Buddy left his meeting and headed uptown.
7. Bea gave Buddy fried fish and cornbread for dinner.
8. All evening they talked and remembered their past lives.
9. Why didn't Charley want Buddy to take the sweet potato pie?
10. None of the people in the lobby carried a paper bag.

8.8 *Complements* A complement is a word or group of words that completes the meaning of the sentence. Some sentences contain only a subject and a verb. Most sentences, however, require additional words placed after the verb to complete the meaning of the sentence. There are three kinds of complements: **direct objects, indirect objects,** and **subject complements.**

Direct objects are words or word groups that receive the action of action verbs. A direct object answers the question *what?* or *whom?* In the examples that follow the direct objects are underlined.

EXAMPLES

The students asked many questions. (asked what?)

The teacher quickly answered them. (answered what?)

The school accepted girls and boys. (accepted whom?)

Indirect objects tell *to* or *for whom* or *what* the action of the verb is performed. Indirect objects come before direct objects. In the examples that follow the indirect objects are underlined.

EXAMPLES

My sister usually gave her friends good advice. (gave to whom?)

Her brother sent the post office a heavy package. (sent to what?)

His kind grandfather mailed him a new tie. (mailed to whom?)

Subject complements come after linking verbs and identify or describe the subject. Subject complements that name or identify the subject of the sentence are called **predicate nominatives.** These include **predicate nouns** and **predicate pronouns.** In the examples that follow the subject complements are underlined.

EXAMPLES

My friends are very hard workers.

The best writer in the class is she.

Other subject complements describe the subject of the sentence. These are called **predicate adjectives.**

EXAMPLE: *The pianist appeared very energetic.*

GRAMMAR PRACTICE

Write all of the complements in the following sentences and label them as direct objects, indirect objects, predicate nouns, predicate pronouns, or predicate adjectives.

1. The playwright Sophocles was famous in ancient Greece.
2. He gave the world many important dramas.
3. *Antigone* is a respected example of Greek tragedy.
4. Two of the main characters in the play are Antigone and Ismene.
5. Without the king's consent, Antigone buries her brother.
6. Polyneices had attacked Thebes during the war.
7. Creon condemns Antigone and Ismene.
8. The Greek chorus represents the ordinary citizens.
9. The final victim of Creon's pride is he himself.
10. Fate dealt Creon great misfortune.

9 Phrases

A phrase is a group of related words that does not have a subject and predicate and functions in a sentence as a single part of speech.

9.1 *Prepositional Phrases* A prepositional phrase is a phrase that consists of a preposition, its object, and any modifiers of the object. Prepositional phrases that modify nouns or pronouns are called **adjective phrases.** Prepositional phrases that modify a verb, an adjective, or another adverb are **adverb phrases.**

ADJECTIVE PHRASE: *The central character of the story is a wicked villain.*
ADVERB PHRASE: *He reveals his nature in the first scene.*

9.2 *Appositives and Appositive Phrases* An appositive is a noun or pronoun that usually comes directly after another noun or pronoun and identifies or provides further information about that word. An appositive phrase includes the appositive and all its modifiers. In the following examples, the appositive phrases are underlined.

EXAMPLES
This poem was written by Walt Whitman, a great poet.
He wrote this poem, a sad remembrance of war, about an artilleryman.

Occasionally, an appositive phrase may precede the noun it tells about.

EXAMPLE: *A great poet, Walt Whitman wrote many of the poems we are studying.*

10 Verbals and Verbal Phrases

A verbal is a verb form that is used as a noun, an adjective, or an adverb. A verbal phrase consists of a verbal, all its modifiers, and all its complements. There are three kinds of verbals: infinitives, participles, and gerunds.

10.1 *Infinitives and Infinitive Phrases*

An infinitive is a verb form that usually begins with *to* and functions as a noun, adjective, or adverb. The infinitive and its modifiers constitute an infinitive phrase. The examples that follow show several uses of infinitives and infinitive phrases. Each infinitive phrase is underlined.

NOUN: *To know her is my only desire.* (subject)

She wrote to voice her opinions. (direct object)

Her goal was to promote women's rights. (predicate nominative)

ADJECTIVE: *We saw his need to be loved.* (adjective modifying *need*)
ADVERB: *I'm planning to walk with you.* (adverb modifying *wrote*)

Grammar Handbook

GRAMMAR PRACTICE ANSWERS

1. famous–predicate adjective
2. world–indirect object
   dramas–direct object
3. example–predicate noun
4. Antigone and Ismene–predicate nouns
5. brother–direct object
6. Thebes–direct object
7. Antigone and Ismene–direct objects
8. citizens–direct object
9. he–predicate pronoun
10. Creon–indirect object
    misfortune–direct object

Like verbs themselves, infinitives can take objects (*her* in the first noun example), be made passive (*to be loved* in the adjective example), and take modifiers (*with you* in the adverb example).

Because *to*, the sign of the infinitive, precedes infinitives, it is usually easy to recognize them. However, sometimes *to* may be omitted.

EXAMPLE: *Let no one dare [to] enter this shrine.*

10.2 Participles and Participial Phrases

A participle is a verb form that functions as an adjective. Like adjectives, participles modify nouns and pronouns. Most participles use the present participle form, ending in *-ing*, or the past participle form, ending in *-ed* or *-en*. In the examples below the participles are underlined.

MODIFYING A NOUN: *The dying man had a smile on his face.*
MODIFYING A PRONOUN: *Frustrated, everyone abandoned the cause.*

Participial phrases are participles with all their modifiers and complements.

MODIFYING A NOUN: *The dogs searching for survivors are well trained.*
MODIFYING A PRONOUN: *Having approved your proposal, we are ready to act.*

10.3 Dangling and Misplaced Participles

A participle or participial phrase should be placed as close as possible to the word that it modifies. Otherwise the meaning of the sentence may not be clear.

MISPLACED: *The boys were looking for squirrels searching the trees.*
CLEARER: *The boys searching the trees were looking for squirrels.*

A participle or participial phrase that does not clearly modify anything in a sentence is called a **dangling participle.** A dangling participle causes confusion because it appears to modify a word that it cannot sensibly modify.

Correct a dangling participle by providing a word for the participle to modify.

CONFUSING: *Running like the wind, my hat fell off.* (The hat wasn't running.)
CLEARER: *Running like the wind, I lost my hat.*

10.4 Gerunds and Gerund Phrases

A gerund is a verb form ending in *-ing* that functions as a noun. Gerunds may perform any function nouns perform.

SUBJECT: *Running is my favorite pastime.*
DIRECT OBJECT: *I truly love running.*
SUBJECT COMPLEMENT: *My deepest passion is running.*
OBJECT OF PREPOSITION: *Her love of running keeps her strong.*

Gerund phrases are gerunds with all their modifiers and complements. The gerund phrases are underlined in the following examples.

SUBJECT: *Wishing on a star never got me far.*
OBJECT OF PREPOSITION: *I will finish before leaving the office.*
APPOSITIVE: *Her avocation, flying airplanes, finally led to full-time employment.*

GRAMMAR PRACTICE

Identify the underlined phrases as appositive phrases, infinitive phrases, participial phrases, or gerund phrases.

1. Born into an aristocratic family, Tolstoy was orphaned by the age of nine.
2. *War and Peace,* Tolstoy's longest novel, was published in 1869.
3. His attempt to get rid of his property brought about disagreements with his wife.
4. Dancing with Varenka made Ivan indescribably happy.
5. Ivan gradually lost interest in Varenka, his former sweetheart.

GRAMMAR PRACTICE ANSWERS

1. participial phrase
2. appositive phrase
3. infinitive phrase
4. gerund phrase
5. appositive phrase

1196 GRAMMAR HANDBOOK

11 Clauses

A clause is a group of words that contains a subject and a verb. There are two kinds of clauses: independent clauses and subordinate clauses.

11.1 ***Independent and Subordinate Clauses*** An independent clause can stand alone as a sentence, as the word *independent* suggests.

INDEPENDENT CLAUSE: *Emily Dickinson did not wish her poems to be published.*

A sentence may contain more than one independent clause.

EXAMPLE: *Emily Dickinson did not wish her poems to be published, but seven were published during her lifetime.*

In the example above the coordinating conjunction *but* joins the two independent clauses.

A subordinate clause cannot stand alone as a sentence. It is subordinate to, or dependent on, the main clause.

EXAMPLE: *Emily Dickinson did not wish her poems to be published, although she shared them with friends.*

Although she shared them with friends cannot stand by itself.

11.2 ***Adjective Clauses*** An adjective clause is a subordinate clause used as an adjective. It usually follows the noun or pronoun it modifies.

EXAMPLE: *Robert Frost wrote about birch tree branches that boys swing on.*

Adjective clauses are typically introduced by the relative pronouns *who, whom, whose, which,* and *that* (see Relative Pronouns, page 1185). In the examples that follow, the adjective clauses are underlined.

EXAMPLES

One song that we like became our theme song.

Emily Dickinson, whose poems have touched many, lived a very quiet life.

The candidate whom we selected promised to serve us well.

WATCH OUT! The relative pronouns *whom, which,* and *that* may sometimes be omitted when they are objects of their own clauses.

EXAMPLE: *Robert Frost is a poet [whom/that] many have read.*

11.3 ***Adverb Clauses*** An adverb clause is a subordinate clause that is used as an adverb to modify a verb, an adjective, or another adverb. It is introduced by a subordinating conjunction (see Subordinating Conjunctions, page 1191).

Adverb clauses typically occur at the beginning or end of sentences. The clauses are underlined in these examples.

MODIFYING A VERB: *When we need you, we will call.*

MODIFYING AN ADVERB: *I'll stay here where there is shelter from the rain.*

MODIFYING AN ADJECTIVE: *Roman felt good when he finished his essay.*

11.4 ***Noun Clauses*** A noun clause is a subordinate clause that is used in a sentence as a noun. A noun clause may be used as a subject, a direct object, an indirect object, a predicate nominative, or an object of a preposition. Noun clauses are often introduced by pronouns such as *that, what, who, whoever, which,* and *whose,* and by subordinating conjunctions, such as *how, when, where, why,* and *whether*. (See Subordinating Conjunctions, page 1191.)

USAGE TIP Because the same words may introduce adjective and noun clauses, you need to consider how the clause functions within its sentence.

To determine if a clause is a noun clause, try substituting *something* or *someone* for the clause. If you can do it, it is probably a noun clause.

EXAMPLES: *I know whose woods these are.* ("I know something." The clause is a noun clause, direct object of the verb *know.*)

Give a copy to whoever wants one. ("Give a copy to someone." The clause is a noun clause, object of the preposition *to.*)

GRAMMAR HANDBOOK 1197

GRAMMAR PRACTICE ANSWERS

1. adjective clause
2. noun clause
3. adverb clause
4. noun clause
5. adjective clause

Grammar Handbook

GRAMMAR PRACTICE

Identify each underlined clause as an adjective clause, an adverb clause, or a noun clause.

1. R.K. Narayan, who is regarded as one of India's greatest writers, was a teacher very briefly.
2. The teacher in Narayan's "Like the Sun" thought that telling the absolute truth was important.
3. When he told his wife the meal wasn't very good, he made her angry.
4. He seemed not to question whether he really should tell exactly what he thought.
5. His decision, which would last one day, might have cost him his job.

12 The Structure of Sentences

When classified by their structure, there are four kinds of sentences: simple, compound, complex, and compound-complex.

12.1 *Simple Sentences* A simple sentence is a sentence that has one independent clause and no subordinate clauses. The fact that such sentences are called "simple" does not mean that they are uncomplicated. Various parts of simple sentences may be compound, and they may contain grammatical structures such as appositives and verbals.

EXAMPLES

Mark Twain, an unsuccessful gold miner, wrote many successful satires and tall tales. (appositive and compound direct object)

Pablo Neruda, drawn to writing poetry at an early age, won celebrity at age 20. (participial and gerund phrases)

12.2 *Compound Sentences* A compound sentence has two or more independent clauses. The clauses are joined together with a comma and a coordinating conjunction (*and, but, or, nor, yet, for, so*), a semicolon, or a conjunctive adverb with a semicolon. Like simple sentences, compound sentences do not contain any dependent clauses.

EXAMPLES

The main character in "Lalla" happily goes to London, but she eventually returns to rural Cornwall.

Amy Lowell's poem "The Taxi" has powerful images; however, it does not use the word taxi *anywhere in it.*

WATCH OUT! Do not confuse compound sentences with simple sentences that have compound parts.

EXAMPLE: *A subcommittee drafted a document and immediately presented it to the entire group.* (here *and* signals a compound predicate, not a compound sentence)

12.3 *Complex Sentences* A complex sentence has one independent clause and one or more subordinate clauses. Each subordinate clause can be used as a noun or as a modifier. If it is used as a modifier, a subordinate clause usually modifies a word in the main clause and the main clause can stand alone. However, when a subordinate clause is a noun clause, it is a part of the independent clause; the two cannot be separated.

MODIFIER: *One should not complain, unless she or he has a better solution.*

NOUN CLAUSE: *We sketched pictures of whomever we wished.* (noun clause is the object of the preposition *of* and cannot be separated from the rest of the sentence)

12.4 *Compound-Complex Sentences* A compound-complex sentence has two or more independent clauses and one or more subordinate clauses. Compound-complex sentences are, simply, both compound and complex. If you start with a compound sentence, all you need to do to form a compound-complex sentence is add a subordinate clause.

COMPOUND: *All the students knew the answer, yet they were too shy to volunteer.*

COMPOUND-COMPLEX: *All the students knew the answer that their teacher expected, yet they were too shy to volunteer.*

1198 GRAMMAR HANDBOOK

GRAMMAR PRACTICE

Tell whether each sentence is a simple sentence, a compound sentence, a complex sentence, or a compound-complex sentence.

1. Born in Massachusetts, Mary Lavin has spent most of her life in Ireland.
2. Owen wants Brigid to live close by, but his wife wants to send Brigid to a care home.
3. Owen's wife thinks that her daughters cannot be happy with Brigid nearby.
4. After Owen died, his wife felt that she had failed him.
5. The neighbors thought that she would send Brigid away, but Owen's wife invited Brigid to live with her.

13 Writing Complete Sentences

A sentence is a group of words that expresses a complete thought. In writing that you wish to share with a reader, try to avoid both sentence fragments and run-on sentences.

13.1 *Correcting Fragments* A sentence fragment is a group of words that is only part of a sentence. It does not express a complete thought and may be confusing to the reader or the listener. A sentence fragment may be lacking a subject, a predicate, or both.

FRAGMENT: *waited for the boat to arrive* (no subject)
CORRECTED: *We waited for the boat to arrive.*
FRAGMENT: *people of various races, ages, and creeds* (no predicate)
CORRECTED: *People of various races, ages, and creeds gathered together.*
FRAGMENT: *near the old cottage* (neither subject nor predicate)
CORRECTED: *The burial ground is near the old cottage.*

In your own writing, fragments are usually the result of haste or incorrect punctuation. Sometimes fixing a fragment will be a matter of attaching it to a preceding or following sentence.

FRAGMENT: *We saw the two girls. Waiting for the bus to arrive.*
CORRECTED: *We saw the two girls waiting for the bus to arrive.*
FRAGMENT: *Newspapers appeal to a wide audience. Including people of various races, ages, and creeds.*
CORRECTED: *Newspapers appeal to a wide audience, including people of various races, ages, and creeds.*

13.2 *Correcting Run-on Sentences* A run-on sentence is made up of two or more sentences written as though they were one. Some run-ons have no punctuation within them. Others may use only a comma where a conjunction or stronger punctuation is necessary. Use your judgment in correcting run-on sentences, as you have choices. You can make two sentences if the thoughts are not closely connected. If the thoughts are closely related, you can keep the run-on as one sentence by adding a semicolon or a conjunction.

RUN-ON: *We found a place by a small pond for the picnic it is three miles from the village.*
MAKE TWO SENTENCES: *We found a place by a small pond for the picnic. It is three miles from the village.*
RUN-ON: *We found a place by a small pond for the picnic it was perfect.*
USE A SEMICOLON: *We found a place by a small pond for the picnic; it was perfect.*
ADD A CONJUNCTION: *We found a place by a small pond for the picnic, and it was perfect.*

WATCH OUT! When you add a conjunction, make sure you use appropriate punctuation before it: a comma for a coordinating conjunction, a semicolon for a conjunctive adverb. (See Conjunctions, page 1191.) A very common mistake is to use a comma instead of a conjunction or an end mark. This error is called a **comma splice**.

INCORRECT: *He finished the apprenticeship, then he left the village.*
CORRECT: *He finished the apprenticeship, and then he left the village.*

GRAMMAR PRACTICE ANSWERS
1. simple sentence
2. compound sentence
3. complex sentence
4. complex sentence
5. compound-complex sentence

GRAMMAR PRACTICE ANSWERS

Anton Chekhov was born in the south of Russia to a poor family. To support his family, he began writing comical sketches. He sold them to newspapers and journals. Chekhov had a medical degree, but he practiced medicine only occasionally. *The Seagull* received very poor reviews for the first production; this discouraged Chekhov so much he almost quit writing. Now, however, he is known as one of Russia's greatest authors. He is best remembered for *Uncle Vanya, The Three Sisters,* and *The Cherry Orchard.*

Grammar Handbook

GRAMMAR PRACTICE

Rewrite the following paragraph, correcting all fragments and run-ons.

Anton Chekhov was born in the south of Russia. To a poor family. To support his family, he began writing comical sketches he sold them to newspapers and journals. Chekhov had a medical degree he practiced medicine only occasionally. *The Seagull* received very poor reviews for the first production this discouraged Chekhov so much he almost quit writing. Now, however, known as one of Russia's greatest authors. Best remembered for *Uncle Vanya, The Three Sisters,* and *The Cherry Orchard.*

14 Subject-Verb Agreement

The subject and verb of a sentence must agree in number. Agreement means that when the subject is singular, the verb must be singular; when the subject is plural, the verb must be plural.

14.1 *Basic Agreement* Fortunately, agreement between subject and verb in English is simple. Most verbs show the difference between singular and plural only in the third person present tense. The present tense of the third person singular ends in *-s*.

Present Tense Verb Forms

Singular	Plural
I sleep	we sleep
you sleep	you sleep
she, he, it sleeps	they sleep

14.2 *Agreement with Be* The verb *be* presents special problems in agreement because this verb does not follow the usual verb patterns.

Forms of *Be*

Present Tense Singular	Present Tense Plural	Past Tense Singular	Past Tense Plural
I am	we are	I was	we were
you are	you are	you were	you were
she, he, it is	they are	she, he, it was	they were

14.3 *Words Between Subject and Verb* A verb agrees only with its subject. When words come between a subject and its verb, ignore them when considering proper agreement. Identify the subject and make sure the verb agrees with it.

EXAMPLES

A story in the newspapers tells about the 1890s.

Dad as well as Mom reads the paper daily.

14.4 *Agreement with Compound Subjects* Use a plural verb with most compound subjects joined by the word *and.*

EXAMPLE: *My father and his friends (they) read the paper daily.*

You could substitute the plural pronoun *they* for *my father and his friends*. This shows that you need a plural verb.

If the compound subject is thought of as a unit, you use the singular verb. Test this by substituting the singular pronoun *it.*

EXAMPLE: *Peanut butter and jelly [it] is my brother's favorite sandwich.*

Use a singular verb with a compound subject that is preceded by *each, every,* or *many a*.

EXAMPLE: *Each novel and short story seems grounded in personal experience.*

With *or, nor*, and the correlative conjunctions *either . . . or* and *neither . . . nor*, make the verb agree with the noun or pronoun nearest the verb.

EXAMPLES

Cookies or ice cream is my favorite dessert.

Either Cheryl or her friends are being invited.

Neither ice storms nor snow is predicted today.

14.5 *Personal Pronouns as Subjects* When using a personal pronoun as a subject, make sure to match it with the correct form of the verb *be*. (See the chart in 14.2.) Note especially that the pronoun *you* takes the verbs *are* and *were*, regardless of whether it is referring to the singular *you* or to the plural *you*.

1200 GRAMMAR HANDBOOK

WATCH OUT! *You is* and *you was* are nonstandard forms and should be avoided in writing and speaking. *We was* and *they was* are also forms to be avoided.

INCORRECT: *You was helping me. They was hoping for this.*

CORRECT: *You were helping me. They were hoping for this.*

14.6 *Indefinite Pronouns as Subjects*

Some indefinite pronouns are always singular; some are always plural. Others may be either singular or plural.

Singular Indefinite Pronouns			
another	either	neither	other
anybody	everybody	nobody	somebody
anyone	everyone	no one	someone
anything	everything	nothing	something
each	much	one	

EXAMPLES

Each of the writers was given an award.
Somebody in the room upstairs is sleeping.

The indefinite pronouns that are always plural include *both, few, many*, and *several*. These take plural verbs.

EXAMPLES

Many of the books in our library are not in circulation.

Few have been returned recently.

Still other indefinite pronouns may be either singular or plural.

Singular or Plural Indefinite Pronouns			
all	enough	most	plenty
any	more	none	some

The number of the indefinite pronouns *any* and *none* depends on the intended meaning.

EXAMPLES

Any of these topics has potential for a good article. (any one topic)

Any of these topics have potential for a good article. (all of the many topics)

The indefinite pronouns *all, some, more, most*, and *none* are singular when they refer to a quantity or part of something. They are plural when they refer to a number of individual things. Context will usually give a clue.

EXAMPLES

All of the flour is gone. (referring to a quantity)

All of the flowers are gone. (referring to individual items)

14.7 *Inverted Sentences*

Problems in agreement often occur in inverted sentences beginning with *here* or *there*; in questions beginning with *why, where*, and *what*; and in inverted sentences beginning with a phrase. Identify the subject—wherever it is—before deciding on the verb.

EXAMPLES

There clearly are far too many cooks in this kitchen.

What is the correct ingredient for this stew?

Far from the embroiled cooks stands the master chef.

GRAMMAR PRACTICE

Locate the subject of each sentence. Then choose the correct verb.

1. Most scholars (think/thinks) the author of *Le Morte d'Arthur* is Sir Thomas Malory.
2. (Is/Are) the author "Syr Thomas Maleore, knyght," the same as "Sir Thomas Malory"?
3. Sir Thomas himself, who lived during the Middle Ages, (was/were) a knight.
4. There (is/are) many knights and ladies in the tales of King Arthur.
5. One of the greatest prose works in the English language, *Le Morte d'Arthur* (was/were) based on French versions that were told earlier.
6. Many legends of King Arthur (was/were) also preserved in Wales.
7. Nearly everyone reading these tales (enjoy/enjoys) the adventures of the knights and ladies.
8. Several times Malory (was/were) put in prison.
9. He spent the last three years of his life in prison; he wrote *Le Morte d'Arthur* while he (was/were) there.
10. These tales featuring King Arthur (was/were) published after Malory's death.

GRAMMAR PRACTICE ANSWERS

1. subject: scholars
   verb: think
2. subject: author
   verb: Is
3. subject: Sir Thomas
   verb: was
4. subject: knights and ladies
   verb: are
5. subject: *Le Morte d'Arthur*
   verb: was
6. subject: legends
   verb: were
7. subject: everyone
   verb: enjoys
8. subject: Malory
   verb: was
9. subject: he
   verb: was
10. subject: tales
    verb: were

Grammar Handbook

14.8 *Sentences with Predicate Nominatives*

When a predicate nominative serves as a complement in a sentence, use a verb that agrees with the subject, not the complement.

EXAMPLES

The tales of King Arthur are a great work of literature. (*Tales* is the subject—not *King Arthur*—and it takes the plural verb *are*.)

A great work of literature is the tales of King Arthur. (The subject is the singular noun *work*.)

14.9 Don't *and* Doesn't *as Auxiliary Verbs*

The auxiliary verb *doesn't* is used with singular subjects and with the personal pronouns *she, he*, and *it*. The auxiliary verb *don't* is used with plural subjects and with the personal pronouns *I, we, you*, and *they*.

SINGULAR

She doesn't want to be without her cane.

Doesn't the school provide help?

PLURAL

They don't know what it's like to be hungry.

Bees don't like these flowers by the door.

14.10 *Collective Nouns as Subjects*

Collective nouns are singular nouns that name a group of persons or things. *Team*, for example, is the collective name of a group of individuals. A collective noun takes a singular verb when the group acts as a single unit. It takes a plural verb when the members of the group act separately.

EXAMPLES

Our team usually wins. (the team as a whole wins)

Our team vote differently on most issues. (the individual members vote)

14.11 *Relative Pronouns as Subjects*

When a relative pronoun is used as a subject of its clause—*who, which*, and *that* can serve as subjects—the verb of the clause must agree in number with the antecedent of the pronoun.

SINGULAR: *Have you selected one of the poems that is meaningful to you?*

The antecedent of the relative pronoun *that* is the singular *one;* therefore, *that* is singular and must take the singular verb *is.*

PLURAL: *The younger redwoods, which grow in a circle around an older tree, are also very tall.*

The antecedent of the relative pronoun *which* is the plural *redwoods.* Therefore, *which* is plural, and it takes the plural verb *grow.*

GRAMMAR PRACTICE

Choose the correct verb for each of the following sentences.

1. "A Sound of Thunder" (involves/involve) time travel.
2. A group of travelers (go/goes) on a safari into the past.
3. In the travel office there (was/were) lots of colors and sounds.
4. The destination of the safari, 60 million years in the past, (was/were) in the time of dinosaurs.
5. The leader explains that the government (doesn't/don't) approve of the trip.
6. He also reminds the group that none of the famous leaders of later times (exists/exist) at the time of the safari.
7. A huge dinosaur, its flesh glittering like thousands of coins, (rises/rise) up in front of the hunters.
8. One of the characters (do/does) not obey orders to stay on the path.
9. This character who changed the future by his actions (finds/find) things very much different back in the present.
10. What do you think Bradbury (is/are) saying through this story?

GRAMMAR PRACTICE ANSWERS

1. involves
2. goes
3. were
4. was
5. doesn't
6. exists
7. rises
8. does
9. finds
10. is

Quick Reference: Punctuation

Punctuation	Function	Examples
End Marks period, question mark, exclamation point	to end sentences	The games begin today. Who is your favorite contestant? What a play Jamie made!
	initials and other abbreviations	Prof. Ted Bakerman, D. H. Lawrence, Houghton Mifflin Co., P.M., A.D., oz., ft., Blvd., St.
	items in outlines	I. Volcanoes A. Central-vent 1. Shield
	exception: P.O. states	NE (Nebraska), NV (Nevada)
Commas	before conjunction in compound sentence	I have never disliked poetry, but now I really love it.
	items in a series	She is brave, loyal, and kind. The slow, easy route is best.
	words of address	Oh wind, if winter comes. . . . Come to the front, children.
	parenthetical expressions	Well, just suppose that we can't? Hard workers, as you know, don't quit. I'm not a quitter, believe me.
	introductory phrases and clauses	In the beginning of the day, I feel fresh. While she was out, I was here. Having finished my chores, I went out.
	nonessential phrases and clauses	Ed Pawn, captain of the chess team, won. Ed Pawn, who is the captain, won. The two leading runners, sprinting toward the finish line, ended in a tie.
	in dates and addresses	August 18, 1999. Send it by August 18, 1999, to Cherry Jubilee, Inc., 21 Vernona St., Oakland, Minnesota.
	in letter parts	Dear Jim, Sincerely yours,
	for clarity, or to avoid confusion	By noon, time had run out. What the minister does, does matter. While cooking, Jim burned his hand.
Semicolons	in compound sentences that are not joined by coordinators *and,* etc.	The last shall be first; the first shall be last. I read the Bible; however, I have not memorized it.
	with items in series that contain commas	We invited my sister, Jan; her friend, Don; my uncle Jack; and Mary Dodd.
	in compound sentences that contain commas	After I ran out of money, I called my parents; but only my sister was home, unfortunately.

Grammar Handbook

GRAMMAR HANDBOOK 1203

Punctuation	Function	Examples
Colons	to introduce lists	**Correct:** Those we wrote were the following: Dana, John, and Will. **Incorrect:** Those we wrote were: Dana, John, and Will.
	before a long quotation	Susan B. Anthony said: "Woman must not depend upon the protection of man. . . ."
	after the salutation of a business letter	To Whom It May Concern: Dear Ms. Costa:
	with certain numbers	1:28 P.M., Genesis: 2:5
Dashes	to indicate an abrupt break in thought	I was thinking of my mother—who is arriving tomorrow—just as you walked in.
Parentheses	to enclose less important material	Throughout her life (though some might think otherwise), she worked hard. The temperature on this July day (Would you believe it?) is 65 degrees!
Hyphens	with a compound adjective before nouns	She lives in a first-floor apartment.
	in compounds with *all-, ex-, self-, -elect*	The president-elect is a well-respected woman.
	in compound numbers (to *ninety-nine*)	Today, I turn twenty-one.
	in fractions used as adjectives	My cup is one-third full.
	between prefixes and words beginning with capital letters	Is this a pre-Bronze Age artifact? Caesar had a bad day in mid-March.
	when dividing words at the end of a line	Finding the right title has been a chal-lenge for the committee.
Apostrophes	to form possessives of nouns and indefinite pronouns	my friend's book, my friends' book, anyone's guess, somebody else's problem
	for omitted letters in contractions or numbers in dates	don't (omitted **o**); he'd (omitted **woul**) the class of '99 (omitted **19**)
	to form plurals of letters and numbers	I had two A's and no 2's on my report card.
Quotation Marks	to set off a speaker's exact words	Sara said, "I'm finally ready." "I'm ready," Sara said, "finally." Did Sara say, "I'm ready"? Sara said, "I'm ready!"
	for titles of stories, short poems, essays, songs, book chapters	We read Hansberry's "On Summer" and Alvarez's "Exile." My eyes watered when I heard "The Star-Spangled Banner."
Ellipses	for material omitted from a quotation	"Neither slavery nor involuntary servitude . . . shall exist within the United States . . . ."
Italics	for titles of books, plays, magazines, long poems, operas, films, TV series, recordings	*The Mists of Avalon, Julius Caesar, Newsweek, Paradise Lost, La Bohème, ET, The Cosby Show, The Three Tenors in Concert*

1204 GRAMMAR HANDBOOK

Quick Reference: Capitalization

Category/Rule	Examples
People and Titles	
Names and initials of people	Alice Walker, E. B. White
Titles used with or in place of names	Professor Holmes, Senator Long, The President has arrived.
Deities and members of religious groups	Jesus, Allah, the Buddha, Zeus, Baptists, Roman Catholics
Names of ethnic and national groups	Hispanics, Jews, African Americans
Geographical Names	
Cities, states, countries, continents	Charleston, Nevada, France, Asia
Regions, bodies of water, mountains	the Midwest, Lake Michigan, Mount McKinley
Geographic features, parks	Continental Divide, Everglades, Yellowstone
Streets and roads, planets	361 South Twenty-third Street, Miller Avenue, Jupiter, Saturn
Organizations and Events	
Companies, organizations, teams	Monsanto, the Elks, Chicago Bulls
Buildings, bridges, monuments	the Alamo, Golden Gate Bridge, Lincoln Memorial
Documents, awards	the Constitution, World Cup
Special named events	Super Bowl, World Series
Governmental bodies, historical periods and events	the Supreme Court, Congress, the Middle Ages, Boston Tea Party
Days and months, holidays	Tuesday, October, Thanksgiving, Valentine's Day
Specific cars, boats, trains, planes	Cadillac, *Titanic, Orient Express*
Proper Adjectives	
Adjectives formed from proper nouns	Doppler effect, Mexican music, Elizabethan age, Gulf coast
First Words and the Pronoun *I*	
The first word in a sentence or quote	This is it. He said, "Let's go."
Complete sentence in parentheses	(Consult the previous chapter.)
Salutation and closing of letters	Dear Madam, Very truly yours,
First lines of most poetry The personal pronoun *I*	Then am I A happy fly If I live Or if I die.
First, last, and all important words in titles	*A Tale of Two Cities,* "The World Is Too Much with Us"

GRAMMAR HANDBOOK 1205

Grammar Handbook

Little Rules That Make A Big Difference

Sentences

Avoid sentence fragments. Make sure all your sentences express complete thoughts.

A sentence fragment is a group of words that does not express a grammatically complete thought. It may lack a subject, a predicate, or both. Fragments may be corrected by adding the missing element(s) or by changing the punctuation to make the fragment part of another sentence.

FRAGMENT: *One of my heroes is Barbara Jordan. A Texas senator who had an impressive record and great dedication to justice.*

COMPLETE: *One of my heroes is Barbara Jordan. She was a Texas senator who had an impressive record and great dedication to justice.* (adding a subject and a predicate)

COMPLETE: *One of my heroes is Barbara Jordan, a Texas senator who had an impressive record and great dedication to justice.* (changing the punctuation)

Avoid run-on sentences. Make sure all clauses in a sentence have the proper punctuation and/or conjunctions between them.

A run-on sentence consists of two or more sentences written as though they were one or separated only by a comma. Correct run-ons by making two separate sentences, using a semicolon, adding a conjunction, or rewriting the sentence.

RUN-ON: *James Galway is a great musician, he plays the flute.*

CORRECT: *James Galway is a great musician. He plays the flute.*

CORRECT: *James Galway is a great musician; he plays the flute.*

CORRECT: *James Galway, who plays the flute, is a great musician.*

Use end marks correctly. Use a period, not a question mark, at the end of an indirect question.

An indirect question is a question that does not use the exact words of the original speaker. Note the difference between the following sentences, and observe that the second sentence ends in a period, not a question mark.

DIRECT: *Lou asked, "What is that?"*

INDIRECT: *Lou asked what it was.*

Do not use quotation marks with indirect quotations within a sentence.

A direct quotation uses the speaker's exact words. An indirect quotation puts the speaker's words in other words. Compare these sentences:

DIRECT: *Jean said, "I'm going to be up all night writing my essay."* (quotation marks appropriate)

INDIRECT: *Jean said that she was going to be up all night writing her essay.* (no quotation marks)

Phrases

Place participial and prepositional phrases as close as possible to the words they modify. Participial and prepositional phrases are modifiers; that is, they tell about some other word in a sentence. To avoid confusion, they should be placed as close as possible to the word that they modify.

INCORRECT: *Tiny microphones are planted by agents called bugs.*

CORRECT: *Tiny microphones called bugs are planted by agents.*

Avoid dangling participles. Make sure a participial phrase does modify a word in the sentence.

INCORRECT: *Disappointed in love, a hermit's life seemed attractive.* (Who was disappointed?)

CORRECT: *Disappointed in love, the man became a hermit.*

Clauses

Use commas to set off nonessential adjective clauses.

Do you need the clause in order to indicate precisely who or what is meant? If not, it is nonessential and should be set off by commas.

USE COMMAS: *Jim's dogs, who had barked from morning until night, were suddenly quiet.*
NO COMMAS: *The dogs who had barked from morning until night were suddenly quiet.*

Verbs

Don't use past tense forms with an auxiliary verb or past participle forms without an auxiliary verb. (See Auxiliary Verbs, page 1185.)

INCORRECT: *I have saw her somewhere before.* (*saw* is past tense and shouldn't be used with *have*)

CORRECT: *I have seen her somewhere before.*

INCORRECT: *I seen her somewhere before.* (*seen* is a past participle and shouldn't be used without an auxiliary)

Shift tense only when necessary.

Usually, when you are writing in present tense, you should stay in present tense; when you are writing in past tense, you should stay in past tense.

INCORRECT: *When Cosby spoke at the fair, we all pay attention.*

CORRECT: *When Cosby spoke at the fair, we all paid attention.*

Sometimes a shift in tense is necessary to show a logical sequence of actions or the relationship of one action to another.

CORRECT: *After he had told his story, everybody went to sleep.*

Subject-Verb Agreement

Make sure subjects and verbs agree in number.

INCORRECT: *Several plays of Sophocles is based on the legend of Oedipus.*

CORRECT: *Several plays of Sophocles are based on the legend of Oedipus.*

INCORRECT: *Antigone as well as others in the play are in the family.*

CORRECT: *Antigone as well as others in the play is in the family.*

INCORRECT: *Antigone and Ismene was daughters of Oedipus.*

CORRECT: *Antigone and Ismene were daughters of Oedipus.*

Use a singular verb with nouns that look plural but have singular meaning.

Some nouns that end in *-s* are singular, even though they look plural. Examples are *measles, news, Wales,* and the names ending in *-ics* when they refer to a school subject, science, or general practice.

EXAMPLES: *Has headquarters heard from you yet?*
Physics is available to everyone who qualifies to take it.

Use a singular verb with titles.

EXAMPLE: The Mists of Avalon *is on my summer reading list.*
"The Interlopers" was written by Saki.

Use a singular verb with words of weight, time, and measure.

EXAMPLES: *Forty pounds is what my niece weighs now.*
One hundred dollars is the price of the new equipment.

Pronouns

Use personal pronouns correctly in compounds.

Don't be confused about case when *and* joins a noun and a personal pronoun; the case of the pronoun still depends upon its function.

GRAMMAR HANDBOOK 1207

INCORRECT: *Marlene and her will conduct the interview.*

CORRECT: *Marlene and she will conduct the interview.*

INCORRECT: *She asked Sunny and I to wait for her.*

CORRECT: *She asked Sunny and me to wait for her.*

INCORRECT: *Show Anne and they how to work the video recorder.*

CORRECT: *Show Anne and them how to work the video recorder.*

Usually, if you remove the noun and *and,* the correct pronoun will be obvious.

Use *we* and *us* correctly with nouns.

When a noun directly follows *we* or *us*, the case of the pronoun depends upon its function.

INCORRECT: *Us cheerleaders have many new cheers.*

CORRECT: *We cheerleaders have many new cheers.* (*we* is the subject)

INCORRECT: *It makes a big difference to we players.*

CORRECT: *It makes a big difference to us players.* (*us* is the object of *to*)

Avoid unclear pronoun reference.

The reference of a pronoun is ambiguous when the reader cannot tell which of two preceding nouns is its antecedent. The reference is indefinite when the idea to which the pronoun refers is only weakly or vaguely expressed.

AMBIGUOUS: *Mary Oliver, not Adrienne Rich, wrote "The Sun," and she* [who?] *also wrote "Wild Geese."*

CLEARER: *Mary Oliver, not Adrienne Rich, wrote "The Sun," and Oliver also wrote "Wild Geese."*

INDEFINITE: *Oliver won a National Book Award in 1992, which is a prestigious award for writers.*

CLEARER: *In 1992, Oliver won a National Book Award, which is a prestigious award for writers.*

Avoid change of person.

If you are writing in third person—using pronouns such as *she, he, it, they, them, his, her, its*—do not shift to second person—*you*.

INCORRECT: *The feudal laborer had to obey his lord, and you needed to obey the king as well.*

CORRECT: *The feudal laborer had to obey his lord, and he needed to obey the king as well.*

Use correct pronouns in elliptical comparisons.

An elliptical comparison is a comparison from which words have been omitted. In order to choose the proper pronoun, fill in the missing words. Note the difference below:

EXAMPLES: *I like Carlos better than* (I like) *her.*
I like Carlos better than she (likes Carlos).

Don't confuse pronouns and contractions.

Personal pronouns are made possessive without the use of an apostrophe, as is the relative pronoun *whose*. Whenever you are unsure whether to write *it's* or *its*, *who's* or *whose*, ask if you mean *it is/has* or *who is/has*. If you do, write the contraction. Do the same for *you're* and *your*, *they're* and *their*, except that the contraction in this case is for the verb *are*.

Modifiers

Avoid double comparisons.

A double comparison is a comparison made twice. In general, if you use *-er* or *-est* on the end of a modifier, you would not also use *more* or *most* in front of it.

INCORRECT: *Juan cooks more better since he's taken the chef's course.*

CORRECT: *Juan cooks better since he's taken the chef's course.*

INCORRECT: *Now he's the most greatest cook in the class.*

CORRECT: *Now he's the greatest cook in the class.*

Avoid illogical comparisons.

Can you tell what is wrong with the following sentence?

Plays are more entertaining than any kind of performance art.

This sentence is difficult to understand. To avoid such illogical comparisons, use *other* when comparing an individual member with the rest of the group.

Plays are more entertaining than any other kind of performance art.

To avoid another kind of illogical comparison, use *than* or *as* after the first member in a compound comparison.

ILLOGICAL: *Sophocles wrote as many great plays if not more than Aeschylus.* (Did he write as many plays or as many great plays?)

CLEARER: *Sophocles wrote as many great plays as Aeschylus, if not more.*

Avoid misplacing modifiers.

Modifiers of all kinds must be placed as close as possible to the words they modify. If you place them elsewhere, you risk being misunderstood.

MISPLACED: *Flying from the hemlock tree, Sylvia sees the white heron.*

CLEARER: *Sylvia sees the white heron flying from the hemlock tree.*

Sylvia isn't flying—the heron is.

Words Not to Capitalize

Do not capitalize *north, south, east,* and *west* when they are used to tell direction.

EXAMPLE: *London is east of New York City. Charleston is the capital of West Virginia.* (Here *West* is part of a proper name.)

Do not capitalize *sun* and *moon,* and capitalize *earth* only when it is used with the names of other planets.

EXAMPLES: *The sun and the moon are heavenly bodies in a solar system that includes Mars, Jupiter, and the Earth.*

We now live on the earth, not in heaven.

Do not capitalize the names of seasons.

EXAMPLE: *The winter snows have nearly disappeared.*

Do not capitalize the names of most school subjects.

School subjects are capitalized only when they name a specific course, such as World History I. Otherwise, they are not capitalized.

EXAMPLE: *I'm taking physics, social studies, and a foreign language this year.*

Note: English and the names of other languages are always capitalized.

EXAMPLE: *Everybody takes English and either Spanish or French.*

GRAMMAR PRACTICE

Rewrite each sentence correctly.

1. Mrs. Kulpinsky asked Trish and I to help with the decorations.
2. Let's keep this information between we girls.
3. An award-winning collection of poems, Mary Oliver wrote *Dream Work.*
4. Babe Ruth who played for the New York Yankees hit 60 home runs in one season.
5. *The Producers,* starring Zero Mostel and Gene Wilder, are a funny movie.
6. We wanted to know what the speaker means.
7. In Harrison Bergeron's time everyone was equal, and you had to wear clumsy weights if you were graceful.
8. I like Frank O'Connor more better than Nicholas Gage.
9. Preserving nature, a major concern of most citizens.
10. Stumbling forward at the finish line, the race was barely won by the shortest runner.

GRAMMAR PRACTICE ANSWERS

1. Mrs. Kulpinsky asked Trish and me to help with the decorations.
2. Let's keep this information between us girls.
3. Mary Oliver wrote *Dream Work,* an award-winning collection of poems.
4. Babe Ruth, who played for the New York Yankees, hit 60 home runs in one season.
5. *The Producers,* starring Zero Mostel and Gene Wilder, is a funny movie.
6. We wanted to know what the speaker meant.
7. In Harrison Bergeron's time everyone was equal, and people had to wear clumsy weights if they were graceful.
8. I like Frank O'Connor better than Nicholas Gage.
9. Preserving nature should be a major concern of most citizens.
10. Stumbling forward at the finish line, the shortest runner barely won the race.

Commonly Confused Words

accept/except	The verb *accept* means "to receive or believe"; *except* is usually a preposition meaning "excluding."	The teams accept everyone except those who don't have at least a C average.
advice/advise	*Advise* is a verb; *advice* is a noun naming that which an *adviser* gives.	How did the soothsayer advise Julius Caesar? Was Caesar given good advice?
affect/effect	As a verb, *affect* means "to influence." *Effect* as a verb means "to cause." If you want a noun, you will almost always want *effect*.	How did Antony's speech affect the crowd? Did it effect a change in their attitude? The effect was dramatic.
all ready/already	*All ready* is an adjective meaning "fully ready." *Already* is an adverb meaning "before or by this time."	Before Antony's speech, they were all ready to praise Brutus. One citizen had already talked of crowning Brutus.
allusion/illusion	An *allusion* is an indirect reference to something. An *illusion* is a false picture or idea.	Modern literature has many allusions to the works of Shakespeare. The world's apparent flatness is an illusion.
among/between	*Between* is used when you are speaking of only two things. *Among* is used for three or more.	There is respect between Dove and Angelou. "Birches" is among my favorite Frost poems.
bring/take	*Bring* is used to denote motion toward a speaker or place. *Take* is used to denote motion away from such a person or place.	Bring the books over here, and I will take them to the library.
fewer/less	*Fewer* refers to the number of separate, countable units. *Less* refers to bulk quantity.	We have less literature and fewer selections in this year's curriculum.
leave/let	*Leave* means "to allow something to remain behind." *Let* means "to permit."	The librarian will leave some books on display but will not let us borrow any.
lie/lay	To *lie* is "to rest or recline." It does not take an object. *Lay* always takes an object.	Dogs love to lie in the sun. We always lay some bones next to him.
loose/lose	*Loose* (lo͞os) means "free, not restrained"; *lose* (lo͞oz) means "to misplace or fail to find."	Who turned the horses loose? I hope we won't lose any of them.
precede/proceed	*Precede* means "to go or come before." Use *proceed* for other meanings.	The drum major preceded the other band members. The band director proceeded to direct the national anthem.
than/then	Use *than* in making comparisons; use *then* on all other occasions.	I like Asimov better than Bradbury. We read one, then the other.
two/too/to	*Two* is the number. *Too* is an adverb meaning "also" or "very." Use *to* before a verb or as a preposition.	Meg had to go to town, too. We had too much reading to do. Two chapters is too much.

Grammar Glossary

This glossary contains various terms you need to understand when you use the Grammar Handbook. Used as a reference source, this glossary will help you explore grammar concepts and the ways they relate to one another.

A

Abbreviation An abbreviation is a shortened form of a word or word group; it is often made up of initials. (B.C., A.M., *Maj.*)

Active voice. *See* **Voice.**

Adjective An adjective modifies, or describes, a noun or pronoun. (*happy* camper, she is *small*)

A ***predicate adjective*** follows a linking verb and describes the subject. (The day seemed *long.*)

A ***proper adjective*** is formed from a proper noun. (*Jewish* temple, *Alaskan* husky)

The ***comparative*** form of an adjective compares two things. (*more alert, thicker*)

The ***superlative*** form of an adjective compares more than two things. (*most abundant, weakest*)

What Adjectives Tell	Examples
How many	*some* writers *much* joy
What kind	*grand* plans *wider* streets
Which one(s)	*these* flowers *that* star

Adjective phrase. See **Phrase.**

Adverb An adverb modifies a verb, an adjective, or another adverb. (Clare sang *loudly.*)

The ***comparative*** form of an adverb compares two actions. (*more generously, faster*)

The ***superlative*** form of an adverb compares more than two actions. (*most sharply, closest*)

What Adverbs Tell	Examples
How	climb *carefully* chuckle *merrily*
When	arrived *late* left *early*
Where	climbed *up* moved *away*
To what extent	*extremely* upset *hardly* visible

Adverb, conjunctive. *See* **Conjunctive adverb.**

Adverb phrase. *See* **Phrase.**

Agreement Sentence parts that correspond with one another are said to be in agreement.

In ***pronoun-antecedent agreement,*** a pronoun and the word it refers to are the same in number, gender, and person. (*Bill* mailed *his* application. The *students* ate *their* lunches.)

In ***subject-verb agreement,*** the subject and verb in a sentence are the same in number. (*A child cries* for help. *They cry* aloud.)

Ambiguous reference An ambiguous reference occurs when a pronoun may refer to more than one word. (Bud asked his brother if *he* had any mail.)

Antecedent An antecedent is the noun or pronoun to which a pronoun refers. (If *Adam* forgets *his* raincoat, *he* will be late for school. *She* learned *her* lesson.)

Appositive An appositive is a noun or phrase that explains one or more words in a sentence. (Cary Grant, *an Englishman,* spent most of his adult life in America.)

An ***essential appositive*** is needed to make the sense of a sentence complete. (A comic strip inspired the musical *Annie.*)

A ***nonessential appositive*** is one that adds information to a sentence but is not necessary to its sense. (O. Henry, *a short-story writer,* spent time in prison.)

Article Articles are the special adjectives *a, an,* and *the.* (*the* day, *a* fly)

The ***definite article*** (the word *the*) is one that refers to a particular thing. (*the* cabin)

An ***indefinite article*** is used with a noun that is not unique but refers to one of many of its kind. (*a* dish, *an* otter)

Auxiliary verb. *See* **Verb.**

C

Clause A clause is a group of words that contains a verb and its subject. (*they slept*)

An ***adjective clause*** is a subordinate clause that modifies a noun or pronoun. (Hugh bought the sweater *that he had admired.*)

An ***adverb clause*** is a subordinate clause used to modify a verb, an adjective, or an adverb. (Ring the bell *when it is time for class to begin.*)

Grammar Handbook

GRAMMAR HANDBOOK 1211

A ***noun clause*** is a subordinate clause that is used as a noun. (*Whatever you say* interests me.)

An ***elliptical clause*** is a clause from which a word or words have been omitted. (We are not as lucky as *they.*)

A ***main (independent) clause*** can stand by itself as a sentence. (*the flashlight flickered*)

A ***subordinate (dependent) clause*** does not express a complete thought and cannot stand by itself. (*while the nation watched*)

Clause	Example
Main (independent)	The hurricane struck
Subordinate (dependent)	while we were preparing to leave.

Collective noun. *See* **Noun.**

Comma splice A comma splice is an error caused when two sentences are separated with a comma instead of a correct end mark. (*The band played a medley of show tunes, everyone enjoyed the show.*)

Common noun. *See* **Noun.**

Comparative. *See* **Adjective; Adverb.**

Complement A complement is a word or group of words that completes the meaning of a verb. (The kitten finished the *milk.*) *See also* **Direct object; Indirect object.**

An ***objective complement*** is a word or a group of words that follows a direct object and renames or describes that object. (The parents of the rescued child declared Gus a *hero.*)

A ***subject complement*** follows a linking verb and renames or describes the subject. (The coach seemed *anxious.*) *See also* **Noun (predicate noun); Adjective, (predicate adjective).**

Complete predicate The complete predicate of a sentence consists of the main verb plus any words that modify or complete the verb's meaning. (The student *produces work of high caliber.*)

Complete subject The complete subject of a sentence consists of the simple subject plus any words that modify or describe the simple subject. (*Students of history* believe that wars can be avoided.)

Sentence Part	Example
Complete subject	The man in the ten-gallon hat
Complete predicate	wore a pair of silver spurs.

Compound sentence part A sentence element that consists of two or more subjects, verbs, objects, or other parts is compound. (*Lou* and *Jay* helped. Laura *makes* and *models* scarves. Jill sings *opera* and *popular music.*)

Conjunction A conjunction is a word that links other words or groups of words.

A ***coordinating conjunction*** connects related words, groups of words, or sentences. (*and, but, or*)

A ***correlative conjunction*** is one of a pair of conjunctions that work together to connect sentence parts. (*either . . . or, neither . . . nor, not only . . . but also, whether . . . or, both . . . and*)

A ***subordinating conjunction*** introduces a subordinate clause. (*after, although, as, as if, as long as, as though, because, before, if, in order that, since, so that, than, though, till, unless, until, whatever, when, where, while*)

Conjunctive adverb A conjunctive adverb joins the clauses of a compound sentence. (*however, therefore, yet*)

Contraction A contraction is formed by joining two words and substituting an apostrophe for a letter or letters left out of one of the words. (*didn't, we've*)

Coordinating conjunction. *See* **Conjunction.**

Correlative conjunction. *See* **Conjunction.**

D

Dangling modifier A dangling modifier is one that does not clearly modify any word in the sentence. (*Dashing for the train,* the barriers got in the way.)

Demonstrative pronoun. *See* **Pronoun.**

Dependent clause. *See* **Clause.**

Direct object A direct object receives the action of a verb. Direct objects follow transitive verbs. (Jude planned the *party.*)

Direct quotation. *See* **Quotation.**

Divided quotation. *See* **Quotation.**

Double negative A double negative is the incorrect use of two negative words when only one is needed. (*Nobody didn't care.*)

E

End mark An end mark is one of several punctuation marks that can end a sentence. See the punctuation chart on page 1203.

1212 GRAMMAR HANDBOOK

F

Fragment. *See* **Sentence fragment.**

Future tense. *See* **Verb tense.**

G

Gender The gender of a personal pronoun indicates whether the person or thing referred to is male, female, or neuter. (My cousin plays the tuba; *he* often performs in school concerts.)

Gerund A gerund is a verbal that ends in *-ing* and functions as a noun. (*Making* pottery takes patience.)

H

Helping verb. *See* **Verb (auxiliary verb).**

I

Illogical comparison An illogical comparison is a comparison that does not make sense because words are missing or illogical. (My computer is *newer than Kay.*)

Indefinite pronoun. *See* **Pronoun.**

Indefinite reference Indefinite reference occurs when a pronoun is used without a clear antecedent. (My aunt hugged me in front of my friends, and *it* was embarrassing.)

Independent clause. *See* **Clause.**

Indirect object An indirect object tells to whom or for whom (sometimes to what or for what) something is done. (Arthur wrote *Kerry* a letter.)

Indirect question An indirect question tells what someone asked without using the person's exact words. (*My friend asked me if I could go with her to the dentist.*)

Indirect quotation. *See* **Quotation.**

Infinitive An infinitive is a verbal beginning with *to* that functions as a noun, an adjective, or an adverb. (He wanted *to go* to the play.)

Intensive pronoun. *See* **Pronoun.**

Interjection An interjection is a word or phrase used to express strong feeling. (*Wow! Good grief!*)

Interrogative pronoun. *See* **Pronoun.**

Intransitive verb. *See* **Verb.**

Inverted sentence An inverted sentence is one in which the subject comes after the verb. (*How was the movie? Here come the clowns.*)

Irregular verb. *See* **Verb.**

L

Linking verb. *See* **Verb.**

M

Main clause. *See* **Clause.**

Main verb. *See* **Verb.**

Modifier A modifier makes another word more precise. Modifiers most often are adjectives or adverbs; they may also be phrases, verbals, or clauses that function as adjectives or adverbs. (*small* box, smiled *broadly,* house *by the sea,* dog *barking loudly*)

An ***essential modifier*** is one that is necessary to the meaning of a sentence. (Everybody *who has a free pass* should enter now. None *of the passengers* got on the train.)

A ***nonessential modifier*** is one that merely adds more information to a sentence that is clear without the addition. (We will use the new dishes, *which are stored in the closet.*)

N

Noun A noun names a person, a place, a thing, or an idea. (*auditor, shelf, book, goodness*)

An ***abstract noun*** names an idea, a quality, or a feeling. (*joy*)

A ***collective noun*** names a group of things. (*bevy*)

A ***common noun*** is a general name of a person, a place, a thing, or an idea. (*valet, hill, bread, amazement*)

A ***compound noun*** contains two or more words. (*hometown, pay-as-you-go, screen test*)

A ***noun of direct address*** is the name of a person being directly spoken to. (*Lee,* do you have the package? No, *Suki,* your letter did not arrive.)

A ***possessive noun*** shows who or what owns or is associated with something. (*Lil's* ring, a *day's* pay)

A ***predicate noun*** follows a linking verb and renames the subject. (Karen is a *writer.*)

A ***proper noun*** names a particular person, place, or thing. (*John Smith, Ohio, Sears Tower, Congress*)

Number A word is **singular** in number if it refers to just one person, place, thing, idea, or action, and **plural** in number if it refers to more than one person, place, thing, idea, or action. (The words *he, waiter,* and *is* are singular. The words *they, waiters,* and *are* are plural.)

O

Object of a preposition The object of a preposition is the noun or pronoun that follows a preposition. (The athletes cycled along the *route.* Jane baked a cake for *her.*)

GRAMMAR HANDBOOK 1213

Grammar Handbook

Object of a verb The object of a verb receives the action of the verb. (Sid told *stories.*)

P

Participle A participle is often used as part of a verb phrase. (had *written*) It can also be used as a verbal that functions as an adjective. (the *leaping* deer, the medicine *taken* for a fever)

The ***present participle*** is formed by adding *-ing* to the present form of a verb. (*Walking* rapidly, we reached the general store.)

The ***past participle*** of a regular verb is formed by adding *-d* or *-ed* to the present form. The past participles of irregular verbs do not follow this pattern. (*Startled,* they ran from the house. *Spun* glass is delicate. A *broken* cup lay there.)

Passive voice. *See* **Voice.**

Past tense. *See* **Verb tense.**

Perfect tenses. *See* **Verb tense.**

Person Person is a means of classifying pronouns.

A ***first-person*** pronoun refers to the person speaking. (*We* came.)

A ***second-person*** pronoun refers to the person spoken to. (*You* ask.)

A ***third-person*** pronoun refers to some other person(s) or thing(s) being spoken of. (*They* played.)

Personal pronoun. *See* **Pronoun.**

Phrase A phrase is a group of related words that does not contain a verb and its subject. (*noticing everything, under a chair*)

An ***adjective phrase*** modifies a noun or a pronoun. (The label *on the bottle* has faded.)

An ***adverb phrase*** modifies a verb, an adjective, or an adverb. (Come *to the fair.*)

An ***appositive phrase*** explains one or more words in a sentence. (Mary, *a champion gymnast,* won gold medals at the Olympics.)

A ***gerund phrase*** consists of a gerund and its modifiers and complements. (*Fixing the leak* will take only a few minutes.)

An ***infinitive phrase*** consists of an infinitive, its modifiers, and its complements. (*To prepare for a test,* study in a quiet place.)

A ***participial phrase*** consists of a participle and its modifiers and complements. (*Straggling to the finish line,* the last runners arrived.)

A ***prepositional phrase*** consists of a preposition, its object, and the object's modifiers. (The Saint Bernard does rescue work *in the Swiss Alps.*)

A ***verb phrase*** consists of a main verb and one or more helping verbs. (*might have ordered*)

Possessive A noun or pronoun that is possessive shows ownership or relationship. (*Dan's* story, *my* doctor)

Possessive noun. *See* **Noun.**

Possessive pronoun. *See* **Pronoun.**

Predicate The predicate of a sentence tells what the subject is or does. (The van *runs well even in winter.* The job *seems too complicated.*) *See also* **Complete predicate; Simple predicate.**

Predicate adjective. *See* **Adjective.**

Predicate nominative A predicate nominative is a noun or pronoun that follows a linking verb and renames or explains the subject. (Joan is a computer *operator.* The winner of the prize was *he.*)

Predicate pronoun. *See* **Pronoun.**

Preposition A preposition is a word that relates its object to another part of the sentence or to the sentence as a whole. (Alfredo leaped *onto* the stage.)

Prepositional phrase. *See* **Phrase.**

Present tense. *See* **Verb tense.**

Pronoun A pronoun replaces a noun or another pronoun. Some pronouns allow a writer or speaker to avoid repeating a proper noun. Other pronouns let a writer refer to an unknown or unidentified person or thing.

A ***demonstrative pronoun*** singles out one or more persons or things. (*This* is the letter.)

An ***indefinite pronoun*** refers to an unidentified person or thing. (*Everyone* stayed home. Will you hire *anybody?*)

An ***intensive pronoun*** emphasizes a noun or pronoun. (The teacher *himself* sold tickets.)

An ***interrogative pronoun*** asks a question. (*What* happened to you?)

A ***personal pronoun*** shows a distinction of person. (*I* came. *You* see. *He* knows.)

A ***possessive pronoun*** shows ownership. (*My* spaghetti is always good. Are *your* parents coming to the play?)

1214 GRAMMAR HANDBOOK

A ***predicate pronoun*** follows a linking verb and renames the subject. (The owners of the store were *they.*)

A ***reflexive pronoun*** reflects an action back on the subject of the sentence. (Joe helped *himself.*)

A ***relative pronoun*** relates a subordinate clause to the word it modifies. (The draperies, *which* had been made by hand, were ruined in the fire.)

Pronoun-antecedent agreement. *See* **Agreement.**

Pronoun forms

The ***subject form*** of a pronoun is used when the pronoun is the subject of a sentence or follows a linking verb as a predicate pronoun. (*She* fell. The star was *she.*)

The ***object form*** of a pronoun is used when the pronoun is the direct or indirect object of a verb or verbal or the object of a preposition. (We sent *him* the bill. We ordered food for *them.*)

Proper adjective. *See* **Adjective.**

Proper noun. *See* **Noun.**

Punctuation Punctuation clarifies the structure of sentences. See the punctuation chart below.

Q

Quotation A quotation consists of words from another speaker or writer.

A ***direct quotation*** is the exact words of a speaker or writer. (Martin said, *"The homecoming game has been postponed."*)

A ***divided quotation*** is a quotation separated by words that identify the speaker. (*"The homecoming game,"* said Martin, *"has been postponed."*)

An ***indirect quotation*** reports what a person said without giving the exact words. (*Martin said that the homecoming game had been postponed.*)

R

Reflexive pronoun. *See* **Pronoun.**

Regular verb. *See* **Verb.**

Relative pronoun. *See* **Pronoun.**

Run-on sentence A run-on sentence consists of two or more sentences written incorrectly as one. (*The sunset was beautiful its brilliant colors lasted only a short time.*)

S

Sentence A sentence expresses a complete thought. The chart at the top of the next page shows the four kinds of sentences.

A ***complex sentence*** contains one main clause and one or

Punctuation	Uses	Examples
Apostrophe (')	Shows possession	Lou's garage Alva's script
	Indicates a contraction	I'll help you. The baby's tired.
Colon (:)	Introduces a list or quotation	three colors: red, green, and yellow
	Divides some compound sentences	This was the problem: we had to find our own way home.
Comma (,)	Separates ideas	The glass broke, and the juice spilled all over.
	Separates modifiers	The lively, talented cheerleaders energized the team.
	Separates items in series	We visited London, Rome, and Paris.
Exclamation point (!)	Ends an exclamatory sentence	Have a wonderful time!
Hyphen (-)	Joins parts of some compound words	daughter-in-law, great-grandson
Period (.)	Ends a declarative sentence	Swallows return to Capistrano in spring.
	Indicates most abbreviations	min. qt. Blvd. Gen. Jan.
Question mark (?)	Ends an interrogative sentence	Where are you going?
Semicolon (;)	Divides some compound sentences	Marie is an expert dancer; she teaches a class in tap.
	Separates items in series that contain commas	Jerry visited Syracuse, New York; Athens, Georgia; and Tampa, Florida.

GRAMMAR HANDBOOK 1215

more subordinate clauses. (*Open the windows before you go to bed. If she falls, I'll help her up.*)

A ***compound sentence*** is made up of two or more independent clauses joined by a conjunction, a colon, or a semicolon. (*The ship finally docked, and the passengers quickly left.*)

Kind of Sentence	Example
Declarative (statement)	Our team won.
Exclamatory (strong feeling)	I had a great time!
Imperative (request, command)	Take the next exit.
Interrogative (question)	Who owns the car?

A ***simple sentence*** consists of only one main clause. (*My friend volunteers at a nursing home.*)

Sentence fragment A sentence fragment is a group of words that is only part of a sentence. (*When he arrived. Merrily yodeling.*)

Simple predicate A simple predicate is the verb in the predicate. (John *collects* foreign stamps.)

Simple subject A simple subject is the key noun or pronoun in the subject. (The new *house* is empty.)

Split infinitive A split infinitive occurs when a modifier is placed between the word *to* and the verb in an infinitive. (*to quickly speak*)

Subject The subject is the part of a sentence that tells whom or what the sentence is about. (*Lou* swam.) *See* **Complete subject; Simple subject.**

Subject-verb agreement. *See* **Agreement.**

Subordinate clause. *See* **Clause.**

Subordinating conjunction. *See* **Conjunction.**

Superlative. *See* **Adjective; Adverb.**

T

Transitive verb. *See* **Verb.**

U

Unidentified reference An unidentified reference usually occurs when the word *it, they, this, which,* or *that* is used. (In California *they* have good weather most of the time.)

V

Verb A verb expresses an action, a condition, or a state of being.

An ***action verb*** tells what the subject does, has done, or will do. The action may be physical or mental. (Susan *trains* guide dogs.)

An ***auxiliary verb*** is added to a main verb to express tense, add emphasis, or otherwise affect the meaning of the verb. Together the auxiliary and main verb make up a verb phrase. (*will* intend, *could have* gone)

A ***linking verb*** expresses a state of being or connects the subject with a word or words that describe the subject. (The ice *feels* cold.) Linking verbs include *appear, be* (*am, are, is, was, were, been, being*), *become, feel, grow, look, remain, seem, smell, sound,* and *taste.*

A ***main verb*** expresses action or state of being; it appears with one or more auxiliary verbs. (will be *staying*)

The ***progressive form*** of a verb shows continuing action. (She *is knitting.*)

The past tense and past participle of a ***regular verb*** are formed by adding *-d* or *-ed.* (*open, opened*) An ***irregular verb*** does not follow this pattern. (*throw, threw, thrown; shrink, shrank, shrunk*)

The action of a ***transitive verb*** is directed toward someone or something, called the object of the verb. (Leo *washed* the windows.) An ***intransitive verb*** has no object. (The leaves *scattered.*)

Verb phrase. *See* **Phrase.**

Verb tense Verb tense shows the time of an action or the time of a state of being.

The ***present tense*** places an action or condition in the present. (Jan *takes* piano lessons.)

The ***past tense*** places an action or condition in the past. (We *came* to the party.)

The ***future tense*** places an action or condition in the future. (You *will understand.*)

The ***present perfect tense*** describes an action in an indefinite past time or an action that began in the past and continues in the present. (*has called, have known*)

The ***past perfect tense*** describes one action that happened before another action in the past. (*had scattered, had mentioned*)

The ***future perfect tense*** describes an event that will be finished before another future action begins. (*will have taught, shall have appeared*)

1216 GRAMMAR HANDBOOK

Verbal A verbal is formed from a verb and acts as another part of speech, such as a noun, an adjective, or an adverb.

Verbal	Example
Gerund (used as a noun)	Lamont enjoys *swimming.*
Infinitive (used as an adjective, an adverb, or a noun)	Everyone wants *to help.*
Participle (used as an adjective)	The leaves *covering the drive* made it slippery.

Voice The voice of a verb depends on whether the subject performs or receives the action of the verb.

In the ***active voice*** the subject of the sentence performs the verb's action. (We *knew* the answer.)

In the ***passive voice*** the subject of the sentence receives the action of the verb. (The team *has been eliminated.*)

GRAMMAR HANDBOOK 1217

Glossary of Literary Terms

Act An act is a major unit of action in a play. Acts are sometimes divided into scenes; each scene is limited to a single time and place.

Examples: Shakespeare's plays, such as *Julius Caesar,* all have five acts. Contemporary plays usually have two or three acts, although some only have one act. Anton Chekhov's *The Bear* is an example of a one-act play.

Alliteration Alliteration is the repetition of initial consonant sounds. Alliteration occurs in everyday speech and in all forms of literature. Poets, in particular, use alliteration to emphasize certain words, to create mood, to underscore meaning, and to enhance rhythm. Notice the repeated *h* and *s* sounds in the following lines:

> **Mother whose heart hung humble as a button**
> **On the bright splendid shroud of your son,**
>
> **—Stephen Crane,**
> **from "Do not weep, maiden, for war is kind"**

See pages 225, 841, 853.
See also **Assonance; Consonance.**

Allusion An allusion is an indirect reference to a historical or literary person, place, thing, or event with which the reader is assumed to be familiar.

Example: The title of Stephen Vincent Benét's "By the Waters of Babylon" is an allusion to the beginning of Psalm 137 in the Bible: "By the rivers of Babylon, there we sat down, yea, we wept, when we remembered Zion."

Analogy An analogy is a point-by-point comparison between two things that are alike in some respect. Often, analogies are used in nonfiction, when an unfamiliar subject or idea is explained in terms of a familiar one. In the following analogy, the border between the United States and Canada is compared to a one-way mirror:

> **The noses of a great many Canadians resemble Porky Pig's. This comes from spending so much time pressing them against the longest undefended one-way mirror in the world. The Canadians looking through this mirror behave the way people on the hidden side of such mirrors usually do: they observe, analyze, ponder, snoop and wonder what all the activity on the other side means. . . .**
>
> **—Margaret Atwood,**
> **from "Through the One-Way Mirror"**

See also **Extended Metaphor; Metaphor; Simile.**

Antagonist The antagonist in a work of literature is the character or force against which the main character, or protagonist, is pitted. The antagonist may be another character, something in nature or society, or even an internal force within the protagonist.

Examples: In Guy de Maupassant's "Two Friends," the German officer who encounters the fishermen is the main antagonist. In Isabel Allende's "And of Clay Are We Created," the destructive force unleashed by the volcano may be considered an antagonist.

See page 556.
See also **Conflict; Protagonist.**

Aside In drama, an aside is a remark spoken in an undertone by one character either to the audience or to another character, which the remaining characters supposedly do not hear. The aside is a traditional dramatic convention, a device that the audience accepts even though it is obviously unrealistic. The aside can be used to express a character's feelings, opinions, and reactions, and thus functions as a method of characterization. In the following example, the aside reveals Trebonius' murderous intentions after Caesar has asked him to stand near him in the Forum:

1218 GLOSSARY OF LITERARY TERMS

> Trebonius. Caesar, I will. [*Aside*] And so near will I be
> That your best friends shall wish I had been further.
> —William Shakespeare, from *Julius Caesar*

See page 735.

Assonance Assonance is the repetition of a vowel sound within nonrhyming words. *Helter-skelter, sweet dreams,* and *high and mighty* are examples of assonance. Writers of both poetry and prose use assonance to give their work a musical quality and unify stanzas and passages. Robert Frost uses assonance in this line from "Birches": "With the same pains you use to fill a cup. . . ." Notice also the long *a* assonance in the following lines:

> then with cracked hands that ached
> from labor in the weekday weather made
> banked fires blaze. . . .
> —Robert Hayden,
> from "Those Winter Sundays"

See pages 225, 841, 853.
See also **Alliteration; Consonance.**

Atmosphere. *See* **Mood.**

Audience The audience for a piece of writing is the person or persons intended to read it. Every writer has an audience in mind when he or she is writing. The intended audience of a work influences a writer's choice of form, style, tone, and the details included.

Example: Nicholas Gage wrote his essay "The Teacher Who Changed My Life" for a general magazine audience, choosing information and details that would make his story clear to that audience. For a different audience—for instance, a group of young children—he may have presented different details and written in a simpler style.

See pages 491, 945.

Author's Perspective An author's perspective is the set of beliefs, feelings, and attitudes that he or she brings to a piece of writing. Sometimes an author's perspective is recognizable through the tone of a piece, or the attitude the writer displays toward the subject matter.

An author's perspective is more likely to be visible in nonfiction than in fiction. Often a writer will conceal personal attitudes and beliefs when creating fictional characters.

Example: Alice Walker, who is both a feminist and a civil-rights advocate, seems to be guided by her feminist perspective in *In Search of Our Mothers' Gardens.*

See pages 452–453, 460.
See also **Tone.**

Author's Purpose Authors write for one or more of the following purposes: to inform, to express an opinion, to entertain, or to persuade. For instance, the purpose of a news report is to inform; the purpose of an editorial is to persuade the readers or audience to do or believe something.

Example: Elie Wiesel wrote *Night* to inform readers about the horrors of concentration camps and to persuade them to resist evil that made these horrors possible.

See page 945.

Autobiography An autobiography is a writer's account of his or her own life and is, in almost every case, told from the first-person point of view. Generally, an autobiography focuses on the most significant events and people in the writer's life over a period of time and on the ways in which those events and people affected the writer. Shorter autobiographical narratives include such private writings as **journals, diaries,** and **letters.** An autobiographical essay, another type of short autobiographical work, focuses on a single person or event in the writer's life, as illustrated by Lorraine Hansberry's "On Summer" and David Mamet's "The Watch." A **memoir** is a form of autobiography that may also deal with historical events affecting the writer. In "Montgomery Boycott," Coretta Scott King shares her

GLOSSARY OF LITERARY TERMS 1219

recollections of how the boycott led to her husband's becoming a leader of the protest movement. The excerpt from *Farewell to Manzanar* recounts Jeanne Wakatsuki Houston's memories of life in a World War II internment camp.

See pages 104, 121, 613.

Ballad A ballad is a narrative poem that was originally meant to be sung. Ballads usually begin abruptly, focus on a single tragic incident, contain dialogue and repetition, and imply more than they actually tell. Traditional ballads are written in four-line stanzas with regular rhythm and rhyme. The rhythm often alternates between four-stress and three-stress lines, and the rhyme scheme usually is *abcb* or *aabb.*

Folk ballads were composed orally and handed down by word of mouth. These ballads usually tell about ordinary people who have had unusual adventures or have performed daring deeds. The literary ballad is a poem written by a poet who imitates the form and content of the folk ballad.

The following anonymous ballad was popular during the Civil War. Each line has four stresses, and the rhyme scheme is *abcb.*

"Mother, is the battle over?
Thousands have been slain, they say.
Is my father come? and tell me,
Has the army gained the day?
"Is he well, or is he wounded?
Mother, do you think he's slain?
If he is, pray will you tell me.
Will my father come again?
"Mother, I see you always sighing
Since that paper last you read;
Tell me why you are crying:
Is my dearest father dead?"
"Yes, my boy, your noble father
Is one numbered with the slain;
Though he loves me very dearly,
Ne'er on earth we'll meet again."

See also **Meter; Narrative Poem; Rhyme.**

Biography A biography is an account of a person's life written by another person. The writer of a biography, or biographer, often researches his or her subject in order to present accurate information. A biographer may also draw upon personal knowledge of his or her subject. Although a biographer—by necessity and by inclination—presents a subject from a certain point of view, a skilled biographer strives for a balanced treatment, highlighting weaknesses as well as strengths, failures as well as achievements.

Example: André Brink's biographical essay "Nelson Mandela" gives a brief account of the South African leader's life and the hardships that he had to overcome.

See pages 104, 121.

Blank Verse Blank verse is unrhymed poetry written in iambic pentameter. Each line has five metrical feet, and each foot has an unstressed syllable followed by a stressed syllable.

Much of *Julius Caesar* is written in blank verse. The following lines, spoken by the conspirator Casca, describe one of the wonders Casca observed during the storm on the night before Caesar was assassinated. Note the iambic pentameter and the lack of end rhyme:

A common slave—you know him well by sight—
Held up his left hand, which did flame and burn
Like twenty torches joined; and yet his hand,
Not sensible of fire, remained unscorched.
—William Shakespeare, from *Julius Caesar*

See page 713.
See also **Meter; Rhythm.**

Character Characters are the individuals who participate in the action of a literary work. The most important characters are called **main characters.** Less prominent characters are known as **minor characters.** In Joan Aiken's "Searching for Summer," Tom and Lily are main

1220 GLOSSARY OF LITERARY TERMS

characters; William Hatching is a minor character.

Whereas some characters are two-dimensional, with only one or two dominant traits, a fully developed character possesses many traits, mirroring the psychological complexity of a real person. In longer works of fiction, main characters often undergo change as the plot unfolds. Such characters are called **dynamic characters,** as opposed to **static characters,** who remain the same. In Doris Lessing's "No Witchcraft for Sale," Gideon is a dynamic character because his attitude about his duty to the Farquars changes; on the other hand, the Farquars are static characters.

See pages 17, 39, 101, 156, 284.
See also **Antagonist; Characterization; Foil; Protagonist.**

Characterization Characterization refers to the techniques writers use to develop characters. There are four basic methods of characterization:

1. The writer may use physical description. In "Sweet Potato Pie," author Eugenia Collier presents a picture of "Charley's slender, dark hands whittling a toy from a chunk of wood, his face thin and intense, brown as the loaves Lil baked when there was flour."
2. The character's own speech, thoughts, feelings, or actions may be presented. In Collier's story, Charley's opinion of himself is revealed when he says, ""I didn't want your students to know your brother wasn't nothing but a cab driver.'"
3. The speech, thoughts, feelings, or actions of other characters provide another means of developing a character. In the scene in Charley's apartment, it is clear that his wife and children have an easy, loving relationship with him.
4. The narrator's own direct comments also serve to develop a character. The narrator says that "Charley never had any childhood at all," that within the family Charley was "somehow the protector of them all."

See pages 252, 326, 479.
See also **Character; Narrator; Point of View.**

Chorus In the theater of ancient Greece, the chorus was a group of actors who commented on the action of the play. Between scenes the chorus sang and danced to musical accompaniment in the orchestra—the circular floor between the stage and the audience—giving insights into the message of the play. The chorus is often considered a kind of ideal spectator, representing the response of ordinary citizens to the tragic events unfolding in the play. In Sophocles' *Antigone,* the chorus represents the leading citizens of Thebes.

See page 1019.
See also **Drama.**

Climax In dramatic or narrative literature, the climax is the moment when the interest and emotional intensity reach their highest point. This moment is also called the **turning point,** since it usually determines how the conflict of the story will be resolved.

Example: In Stephen Vincent Benét's "By the Waters of Babylon," John's discovery of the dead "god" can be considered the climax of the story. As a result of his discovery, John realizes the truth about the past and the destruction of a way of life.

See pages 384, 394, 407.
See also **Falling Action; Plot; Rising Action.**

Comedy A comedy is a dramatic work that is light and often humorous in tone, usually ending happily with a peaceful resolution of the main conflict. A comedy differs from farce by having a more believable plot, more realistic characters, and less boisterous behavior.

See also **Drama; Farce.**

Comic Relief Comic relief is a humorous scene, incident, or speech that is included in a serious drama to break the tension and allow the audience to prepare emotionally for events to come. In many of Shakespeare's plays, comic relief is provided by a fool or through scenes with servants or common folk.

Conflict Conflict is the struggle between opposing forces and is the basis of plot in dramatic and narrative literature. **External conflict** occurs when a character is pitted against an outside force, such as another

GLOSSARY OF LITERARY TERMS 1221

character, a physical obstacle, or an aspect of nature or society. **Internal conflict** occurs when the struggle takes place within a character.

Examples: In Mary Lavin's "Brigid," Owen's wife experiences internal conflict when she struggles with her feelings of guilt over letting Owen down. The main source of the external conflict between Owen and his wife is Brigid herself. In some stories, as in Chinua Achebe's "Marriage Is a Private Affair," the source of the conflict is cultural; that is, it arises from differences in beliefs and values.

See pages 194, 326, 407.
See **Antagonist; Plot; Rising Action.**

Connotation Connotation is the emotional response evoked by a word, in contrast to its **denotation,** which is its literal or dictionary meaning. *Kitten,* for example, is defined as a "young cat." However, the word also suggests, or connotes, images of softness, warmth, and playfulness.

Example: In W. P. Kinsella's "The Thrill of the Grass," the narrator describes baseball players who "recall sprawling in the lush outfields of childhood." The word *sprawling* connotes the joy and ease of childhood.

Consonance Consonance is the repetition of consonant sounds within and at the ends of words. "Last but not least" and a "stroke of luck" contain examples of consonance. Consonance, assonance, alliteration, and rhyme give writing a musical quality and contribute to the **melodies of literary language.** Such devices may be used to unify poems and passages of prose writing. Notice the repetition of internal and final consonant *s* sounds in the following lines:

> **But in another wilderness,**
> **the possibilities,**
> **the loneliness,**
> **can strangulate like jungle vines.**
>
> **—Cathy Song, from "Lost Sister"**

See pages 225, 841, 853.
See also **Alliteration; Assonance.**

Couplet *See* **Sonnet.**

Denotation *See* **Connotation.**

Dénouement *See* **Falling Action.**

Description Description is writing that appeals to the senses. Good descriptive writing helps the reader to see, hear, smell, taste, or feel the subject that is described and usually relies on precise adjectives, adverbs, nouns, and verbs, as well as on vivid, original phrases. Figurative language, such as simile, metaphor, and personification, is also an important tool in description. The following passage illustrates the use of vivid descriptive language:

> **He came to a cloverleaf intersection which stood silent where two main highways crossed the town. During the day it was a thunderous surge of cars, the gas stations open, a great insect rustling and a ceaseless jockeying for position as the scarab-beetles, a faint incense puttering from their exhausts, skimmed homeward to the far directions. But now these highways, too, were like streams in a dry season, all stone and bed and moon radiance.**
>
> **—Ray Bradbury, from "The Pedestrian"**

See page 101.
See also **Connotation; Imagery; Style.**

Dialect A dialect is the particular variety of a language spoken in a definite place by a distinct group of people. Dialects vary in pronunciation, vocabulary, colloquial expressions, sentence structure, and grammatical constructions. Writers use dialect to establish setting, to provide local color, and to develop characters.

Example: In Eugenia Collier's "Sweet Potato Pie," all the characters in the narrator's family speak in an African-American dialect. Here is Charley speaking to his brother: "Buddy, you ain pressed out them pants right. . . . Can't you git a better shine on them shoes? . . . Lord, you done messed up that tie!"

See page 252.

1222 GLOSSARY OF LITERARY TERMS

Dialogue Dialogue is written conversation between two or more characters. Dialogue is used in most forms of prose writing and also in narrative poetry. In drama the dialogue carries the story line. Realistic, well-placed dialogue enlivens narrative, descriptive, and expository prose and provides the reader with insights into characters' personalities and relationships with one another. The dialogue can also reflect the time and place in which the action takes place, giving a richness and believability to the literary work.

See pages 284, 300, 890, 962, 974, 995.
See also **Characterization; Drama.**

Diary A diary is a writer's personal day-to-day account of his or her experiences and impressions. Most diaries are private and not intended to be shared. Some, however, have been published because they are well written and provide useful perspectives on historical events or on the everyday life of particular eras. Anne Frank's *The Diary of a Young Girl* is an example of a famous diary. Though Elie Wiesel's *Night* is actually a memoir, its day-to-day retellings of what happened in the concentration camp make it sound like a diary.

See also **Autobiography.**

Diction Diction is a writer's choice of words. Diction encompasses both vocabulary (individual words) and syntax (the order or arrangement of words). Diction can be described in terms such as formal or informal, technical or common, abstract or concrete, literal or figurative.

The writer of a scientific essay on thunderstorms, for example, would use formal, technical, and abstract words with precise denotative meanings. In the following essay, however, a more informal language is used, relying on words that are common and concrete, as shown by this figurative description of a thunderstorm at a lake:

> **Then the kettledrum, then the snare, then the bass drum and cymbals, then crackling light against the dark, and the gods grinning and licking their chops in the hills. Afterward the calm, the rain steadily rustling in the calm lake. . . .**
>
> **—E. B. White, from "Once More to the Lake"**

See pages 600, 649, 906, 961.

Drama Drama is literature that develops plot and character through dialogue and action; in other words, drama is literature in play form. Dramas are meant to be performed by actors and actresses who appear on a stage, before radio microphones, or in front of television or movie cameras.

Unlike other forms of literature, such as fiction and poetry, a work of drama requires the collaboration of many people in order to come to life. In an important sense, a drama in printed form is an incomplete work of art. It is a skeleton that must be fleshed out by a director, actors, set designers, and others who interpret the work and stage a performance. When an audience becomes caught up in a drama and forgets to a degree the artificiality of a play, the process is called the "suspension of disbelief."

Most plays are divided into acts, with each act having an emotional peak, or climax, of its own. The acts sometimes are divided into scenes; each scene is limited to a single time and place. Shakespeare's plays, such as *Julius Caesar,* all have five acts. Contemporary plays usually have two or three acts, although some have only one act. Anton Chekhov's *The Bear* is an example of a one-act play.

See pages 284–285, 300, 1019.
See also **Act; Chorus; Dialogue; Props; Scene; Stage Directions.**

Dramatic Irony *See* **Irony.**

Dramatic Monologue A dramatic monologue is a lyric poem in which a speaker addresses a silent or absent listener in a moment of high intensity or deep emotion, as if engaged in private conversation. To increase the dramatic impact of the poem, the poet often reveals the motivations as well as the feelings, personality, and circumstances of the speaker. "Exile" by Julia Alvarez is a dramatic monologue.

GLOSSARY OF LITERARY TERMS 1223

Epic An epic is a long narrative poem on a serious subject, presented in an elevated or formal style. In most epics, the hero is a figure of high social status and often of great historical or legendary importance. Homer's *Iliad* and *Odyssey* are famous epics in the Western tradition. The *Ramayana* is a great epic of India.

Essay An essay is a brief nonfiction composition on a single subject, usually presenting the personal views of the writer. An essay may seek to persuade, as does E. M. Forster's "Tolerance." An essay may offer a personal reflection on an episode in the writer's life, in the manner of E. B. White's "Once More to the Lake." Other essays, such as Roger Rosenblatt's "The Man in the Water," are reflections on current events. Essays may also be expository, explaining topics as well as providing writers' opinions about them, as illustrated by Isaac Asimov's "Dial Versus Digital."

Some essays are formal and impersonal, and the major argument is developed systematically. Other essays are informal, personal, and less rigidly organized. The informal essay often includes anecdotes and humor.

See pages 105, 110, 121.

Exposition Exposition is the part of a literary work that provides the background information necessary to understand characters and their actions. Exposition typically occurs at the beginning of a work and introduces the characters, describes the setting, and summarizes significant events that took place before the action begins.

Examples: In Stephen Vincent Benét's "By the Waters of Babylon," the exposition introduces the narrator and his priest-father and establishes the primitive setting. The exposition in Joan Aiken's "Searching for Summer" introduces the main characters Lily and Tom on their wedding day, tells about the bombs that permanently darkened the sky, and announces the newlyweds' intention to find the sun.

See pages 383, 394.
See also **Plot; Rising Action.**

Extended Metaphor In an extended metaphor two unlike things are compared in several ways. Sometimes the comparison is carried throughout a paragraph, a stanza, or an entire selection. The whole text of Dahlia Ravikovitch's "Pride" is an extended metaphor comparing people and their pride with rocks. Shakespeare makes a comparison between ambition and a ladder in this extended metaphor:

> **That lowliness is young ambition's ladder,**
> **Whereto the climber-upward turns his face;**
> **But when he once attains the upmost round,**
> **He then unto the ladder turns his back,**
> **Looks in the clouds, scorning the base degrees**
> **By which he did ascend.**
>
> **—William Shakespeare, from *Julius Caesar***

See page 846.
See also **Analogy; Figurative Language; Metaphor; Simile.**

External Conflict *See* **Conflict.**

Falling Action In a dramatic or narrative work, the falling action occurs after the climax, or high point of intensity or interest. The falling action shows the results of the major events and resolves loose ends in the plot. The final resolution or clarification of the plot is sometimes called the **dénouement.**

Example: In Stephen Vincent Benét's "By the Waters of Babylon," the falling action occurs after the main character, John, has discovered the dead "god." During the falling action, John realizes the truth about the past and the destruction of a way of life.

See pages 384, 394.
See also **Climax; Plot; Rising Action.**

Fantasy The term *fantasy* is applied to a work of fiction characterized by extravagant imagination and disregard for the restraints of reality. The aim of a fantasy may be purely to delight or may be to make a serious comment on reality. One type of fantasy is represented by *Alice's Adventures in Wonderland,* in which Lewis Carroll creates a nonexistent, unreal, imaginary world. A less extreme form of fantasy, such as Joan Aiken's "Searching for Summer,"

1224 GLOSSARY OF LITERARY TERMS

portrays realistic characters within a world that marginally oversteps the bounds of reality. Finally, science fiction is a form of fantasy, for it extends scientific principles to new realms of time or place. An example is Ray Bradbury's "A Sound of Thunder," which is set in both the distant future and the distant past.

See page 39.
See also **Science Fiction.**

Farce A farce is a play that prompts laughter through ridiculous situations, exaggerated behavior and language, and physical comedy. Characters are often stereotypes; that is, they conform to a fixed pattern or are defined by a single trait. In Anton Chekhov's *The Bear,* for example, Luke might be seen as a stereotype of a loyal but critical servant who tells the lady of the house more than she wants to hear.

See pages 287, 300.
See also **Comedy; Stereotype.**

Fiction A work of fiction is a narrative that springs from the imagination of the writer, though it may be based on actual events and real people. The writer shapes his or her narrative to capture the reader's interest and to achieve desired effects. The two major types of fiction are novels and short stories. The basic elements of fiction are character, setting, plot, and theme.

See pages 17–18.
See also **Novel; Short Story.**

Figure of Speech. *See* **Figurative Language; Hyperbole; Metaphor; Personification; Simile; Understatement.**

Figurative Language Figurative language is language that communicates ideas beyond the literal meanings of the words. Although what is said is not literally true, it stimulates vivid pictures or concepts in the mind of the reader. Figurative language appears in poetry and prose as well as in spoken language. The general term *figurative language* includes specific figures of speech, such as simile, metaphor, personification, and hyperbole.

Example: The narrator in Alice Walker's "Everyday Use" says of Dee's hair, "It stands straight up like the wool on a sheep. It is black as night and around the edges are two long pigtails that rope around like small lizards disappearing behind her ears." Obviously, Dee's pigtails do not literally move like lizards, but the passage vividly suggests the look of Dee's hair.

See pages 226, 260, 349, 354, 735, 841.
See also **Hyperbole; Metaphor; Personification; Simile; Understatement.**

First-Person Point of View *See* **Point of View.**

Flashback A flashback is an account of a conversation, an episode, or an event that happened before the beginning of a story. Often a flashback interrupts the chronological flow of a story to give information that can help readers to understand a character's present situation.

Examples: Tolstoy's "After the Ball" is a story told almost entirely in flashback. The events that happened to the main character, Ivan, as a young man help readers to understand his present situation and beliefs. Similarly, flashbacks play a vital role in Louise Erdrich's "The Leap," in which the narrator recounts her memories of her mother.

See page 675.

Foil A foil is a character who provides a striking contrast to another character. By using a foil, a writer calls attention to certain traits possessed by a main character or simply enhances a character by contrast. In Anton Chekhov's *The Bear,* for example, Luke, the dutiful servant, is a foil for Smirnov, the loud, rude, and quarrelsome visitor.

Foreshadowing Foreshadowing is a writer's use of hints or clues to indicate events that will occur later in a narrative. This technique often creates suspense and prepares the reader for what is to come.

Examples: Ray Bradbury's "A Sound of Thunder" and Mark Twain's "The Californian's Tale" both contain elements of foreshadowing. In Bradbury's story, the discussion of Deutscher

GLOSSARY OF LITERARY TERMS 1225

as a leader who would create the "worst kind of dictatorship" and the constant warnings about staying on the path both foreshadow what will happen at the end of the story.

See pages 82, 311.

Form At its simplest, the word *form* refers to the physical arrangement of words in a poem—the length and placement of the lines and the grouping of lines into stanzas. The term can also be used to refer to other types of patterning in poetry, anything from rhythm and other sound patterns to the design of a traditional poetic type, such as a sonnet or dramatic monologue. Finally, *form* can be used as a synonym for genre, which refers to literary categories ranging from the broad (short story, novel) to the narrowly defined (sonnet, dramatic monologue). William Shakespeare's "Sonnet 18" and Edna St. Vincent Millay's "Sonnet 30" illustrate the use of sonnet form. "Exile" by Julia Alvarez is an example of a dramatic monologue.

See pages 225, 233, 236.

Frame Story A frame story exists when a story is told within a narrative setting or frame—hence, there is a story within a story. This storytelling technique has been used for over one thousand years and was employed in famous works such as *One Thousand and One Arabian Nights* and Geoffrey Chaucer's *The Canterbury Tales.*

Free Verse Free verse is poetry that does not contain regular patterns of rhyme and meter. The lines in free verse often flow more naturally than do rhymed, metrical lines and thus achieve a rhythm more like everyday human speech. Much of the poetry written in the 20th century is free verse. Notice the natural flow of these free-verse lines:

> **What did we say to each other**
> **that now we are as the deer**
> **who walk in single file**
> **with heads high . . .**
> **—N. Scott Momaday, from "Simile"**

See pages 260, 906.

Hero The word *hero* has come to mean the main character in a literary work. A traditional hero possesses good qualities that enable him or her to triumph over an antagonist who is evil or bad in some way.

The term **tragic hero,** first used by the Greek philosopher Aristotle, refers to a central character in a drama who is dignified or noble. According to Aristotle, a tragic hero possesses a defect, or **tragic flaw,** that brings about or contributes to his or her downfall. This flaw may be poor judgment, pride, weakness, or an excess of an admirable quality. The tragic hero, noted Aristotle, recognizes his or her own flaw and its consequences, but only after it is too late to change the course of events. Brutus is often considered the tragic hero of *Julius Caesar.*

The term **cultural hero** refers to a hero who represents the values of his or her culture. King Arthur, for example, represents the physical courage, moral leadership, and loyalty that were valued in Anglo-Saxon society. Antigone can also be considered a cultural hero because her sense of duty to family and the gods, as well as her courage, reflects the values of ancient Greece.

See pages 794, 1019, 1061.
See also **Tragedy.**

Humor In literature there are three basic types of humor, all of which may involve exaggeration or irony. **Humor of situation** is derived from the plot of a work. It usually involves exaggerated events or situational irony, which occurs when something happens that is different from what is expected. **Humor of character** is often based on exaggerated personalities or on characters who fail to recognize their own flaws, a form of dramatic irony. **Humor of language** may include sarcasm, exaggeration, puns, or verbal irony, which occurs when what is said is not what is meant. R. K. Narayan's "Like the Sun" contains, to varying degrees, all three types of humor. So does Anton Chekhov's *The Bear.*

See page 853.

1226 GLOSSARY OF LITERARY TERMS

Hyperbole Hyperbole is a figure of speech in which the truth is exaggerated for emphasis or for humorous effect. The expression "I'm so hungry I could eat a horse" is an example of hyperbole. The following lines describing the meekness of John Steinbeck's dog illustrate hyperbole:

> **He turns his steps rather than disturb an earnest caterpillar. His greatest fear is that someone will point out a rabbit and suggest that he chase it.**
>
> **—John Steinbeck, from *Travels with Charley***

Iambic Pentameter *See* **Meter.**

Imagery Imagery describes words and phrases that re-create vivid sensory experiences for the reader. Because sight is the most highly developed sense, the majority of images are visual. Imagery may also appeal to the senses of smell, hearing, taste, and touch. Effective writers of both prose and poetry frequently use imagery that appeals to more than one sense simultaneously.

Examples: In D. H. Lawrence's "Piano," the phrase "the boom of the tingling strings" appeals to the senses of hearing and touch. The expression "with eyes the color of caterpillar," from Sandra Cisneros's "Salvador Late or Early," appeals to the sense of sight.

See pages 231, 466, 906, 962.

Internal Conflict *See* **Conflict.**

Irony Irony is a contrast between what is expected and what actually exists or happens. There are three basic types of irony.

Situational irony occurs when a character or the reader expects one thing to happen but something entirely different occurs. In Guy de Maupassant's "Two Friends," the reader expects the Frenchmen to eat the fish they have caught. However, it is the German officer who eats the fish, after he executes the men. In John Steinbeck's *Travels with Charley,* the narrator expects his dog to behave meekly when he encounters bears. In actuality, however, bears cause Charley to become aggressive. This second example shows how situational irony can have comic results.

Verbal irony occurs when someone says one thing but means another. The speaker in Stephen Crane's poem continually repeats that "war is kind" while presenting images that suggest just the opposite. The father who "tumbled in the yellow trenches. . . gulped and died" and the "bright splendid shroud" of a dead soldier communicate the horror of war.

Dramatic irony refers to the contrast between what a character knows and what the reader or audience knows. For example, Julius Caesar goes to the Senate on the Ides of March in the belief that he may receive a crown. The audience knows, however, that the conspirators are planning his assassination.

See pages 543–544, 556, 581, 777, 853, 939.
See also **Hyperbole; Understatement.**

Legend A legend is a story handed down from the past, especially one that is popularly believed to be based on historical events. The story of the rise and fall of King Arthur is a famous example of a legend. Though legends often incorporate supernatural elements and magical deeds, they claim to be the story of a real human being and are often set in a particular time and place. These characteristics separate a legend from a myth.

See page 1015–1016.
See also **Myth.**

Lyric Poem In ancient Greece, the lyre was a musical instrument, and the lyric became the name for a song accompanied by music. In ordinary speech, the words of songs are still called lyrics. In literature, a lyric poem is any short poem that presents a single speaker who expresses his or her innermost thoughts and feelings. In a love lyric, such as Amy Lowell's "The Taxi" or Carl Sandburg's "Moon Rondeau," the speaker expresses romantic love. In other lyrics, a speaker may meditate on nature or explore personal issues, such as those addressed by Juan Ramón Jiménez's "I Am Not I" and José Martí's *Simple Poetry.*

GLOSSARY OF LITERARY TERMS 1227

Magical Realism Magical realism refers to a style of writing that often includes exaggeration, unusual humor, magical and bizarre events, dreams that come true, and superstitions that prove warranted. Magical realism differs from pure fantasy in combining fantastic elements with realistic elements such as recognizable characters, believable dialogue, a true-to-life setting, a matter-of-fact tone, and a plot that sometimes contains historic events. A famous example of magical realism is Gabriel García Márquez's novel, *One Hundred Years of Solitude.*

Melodies of Literary Language *See* **Alliteration; Assonance; Consonance; Meter; Rhythm.**

Memoir *See* **Autobiography.**

Metaphor A metaphor is a form of figurative language that makes a comparison between two things that have something in common. Unlike a simile, a metaphor does not use the word *like* or *as.* The first line of Carl Sandburg's "Moon Rondeau" is a metaphor: "Love is a door we shall open together."

The comparison in a metaphor is often suggested rather than directly expressed. In the following lines, the loved one is indirectly compared to a bird in flight:

> **Suddenly I've felt you flying through my soul**
> **in quick, lofty flight,**
> **—Luis Lloréns Torres, from "Love Without Love"**

See pages 226, 260, 349, 354.
See also **Extended Metaphor; Figurative Language; Simile.**

Meter Meter is the repetition of a regular rhythmic unit in a line of poetry. The meter of a poem is like the beat of a song; it establishes a predictable means of emphasis.

Each unit of meter is known as a **foot,** with each foot having one stressed and one or two unstressed syllables. The four basic types of metrical feet are the **iamb,** an unstressed syllable followed by a stressed syllable (˘ ´); the **trochee,** a stressed syllable followed by an unstressed syllable (´ ˘); the **anapest,** two unstressed syllables followed by a stressed syllable (˘ ˘ ´); and the **dactyl,** a stressed syllable followed by two unstressed syllables (´˘˘).

A line of poetry is named not only for the type of meter but also for the number of feet in the line. The most common metrical names are **trimeter,** a three-foot line; **tetrameter,** a four-foot line; **pentameter,** a five-foot line; and **hexameter,** a six-foot line.These lines illustrate iambic pentameter, the most common form of meter in the English language:

> **Nor yet a floating spar to men that sink**
> **And rise and sink and rise and sink again;**
> **—Edna St. Vincent Millay, from "Sonnet 30"**

See pages 226, 236, 713.

Minor Characters *See* **Character.**

Monologue *See* **Soliloquy.**

Mood Mood is the feeling, or atmosphere, that a writer creates for the reader. The writer's use of connotation, imagery, and figurative language, as well as sound and rhythm, can all help to develop mood. Notice how the author makes use of all of these techniques to create a tense mood in the following passage, where the narrator's grandfather begins to realize that he has been cheated:

> **. . . my grandfather took the four packages of coffee, put them on the empty scale, and his heart thudded as he watched the black finger of justice come to rest on the left of the black line: the scale with the pound weight stayed down, and the pound of coffee remained up in the air; his heart thudded more than if he had been lying behind a bush in the forest waiting for Bilgan the Giant. . . .**
> **—Heinrich Böll, from "The Balek Scales"**

See also **Connotation; Diction; Figurative Language; Imagery; Style.**

1228 GLOSSARY OF LITERARY TERMS

Myth A myth is a traditional story, usually concerning some supernatural being or unlikely event. Frequently, myths attempt to explain natural phenomena, such as solar and lunar eclipses and the cycle of the seasons. For some peoples, myths were both a kind of science and a religion. In addition, myths served as literature and entertainment, just as they do for modern-day audiences.

Some of the most famous myths in the Western tradition, such as the stories of Theseus and Hercules, originated among the ancient Greeks and Romans. Norse mythology, consisting of myths from Scandinavia and Germany, is also important classical literature. Native Americans have produced fascinating myths of various kinds, as have the peoples of Africa, Asia, and Latin America.

Many Greek dramas were based on myths that would have been familiar to the audience. The origins of *Antigone,* for example, can be traced to myths about the family of King Oedipus.

See pages 1015–1016.
See also **Legend.**

Narrative A narrative is any type of writing that is primarily concerned with relating an event or a series of events. A narrative can be imaginary, as is a short story or novel, or it can be factual, as is a newspaper account or a work of history. Maya Angelou's "Getting a Job" is an example of narrative nonfiction.

See pages 384, 417.
See also **Fiction; Nonfiction; Novel; Plot; Short Story.**

Narrative Poem A narrative poem tells a story. Like a short story, a narrative poem has characters, a setting, a plot, and a point of view, all of which combine to develop a theme.

Examples: Epics, such as Homer's *Iliad* and Virgil's *Aeneid,* are narrative poems, as are ballads. "Exile," by Julia Alvarez, is an example of a contemporary narrative poem; it tells the story of her family's move from the Dominican Republic to the United States.

See page 437.

Narrator The narrator is the character or voice from whose point of view events are told. In "The Leap" by Louise Erdrich, the narrator is the daughter of the main character in the story. In James Herriot's nonfictional "A Case of Cruelty," the narrator is the author himself.

See page 343.
See also **Point of View; Speaker.**

Nonfiction Nonfiction is prose writing that is about real people, places, and events. Unlike fiction, nonfiction is largely concerned with factual information, although the writer shapes the information according to his or her purpose and viewpoint. Nonfiction includes an amazingly diverse range of writing; newspaper articles, cookbooks, letters, movie reviews, editorials, speeches, true-life adventure stories—all are considered nonfiction. E. B. White's "Once More to the Lake," Margaret Atwood's "Through the One-Way Mirror," Maya Angelou's "Getting a Job" and Elie Wiesel's "Nobel Prize Acceptance Speech" are some examples of nonfiction.

See pages 104, 178.
See also **Autobiography; Biography; Diary; Essay; Fiction.**

Novel The novel is an extended work of fiction. Like a short story, a novel is essentially the product of a writer's imagination. The most obvious difference between a novel and a short story is length. Because the novel is considerably longer, a novelist can develop a wider range of characters and a more complex plot. George Orwell's *Animal Farm* is an example of a novel.

Onomatopoeia The word *onomatopoeia* literally means "name-making." It is the process of creating or using words that imitate sounds. The *buzz* of the bee, the *honk* of the car horn, the *peep* of the chick are onomatopoetic, or echoic, words. Onomatopoeia as a literary technique goes beyond the use of simple echoic words. Writers, particularly poets, choose words whose sounds suggest their denotative and connotative meanings: for example, *whisper, kick, gargle, gnash,* and *clatter.* In D. H. Lawrence's poem "Piano," examples of

GLOSSARY OF LITERARY TERMS 1229

onomatopoeia include "the boom" of the strings and "the tinkling piano."

See page 225.

Paradox A paradox is a seemingly contradictory or absurd statement that may nonetheless suggest an important truth.

Examples: Shakespeare employed a paradox in these lines from *Julius Caesar:* "Cowards die many times before their deaths; / The valiant never taste of death but once." The statement suggests the fearful and constant anticipation of death is worse than death itself. Juan Ramón Jiménez's poem "I Am Not I" reflects upon the paradox expressed in the title, which suggests that the speaker feels separated from himself.

Parallelism Parallelism is the use of similar grammatical constructions to express ideas that are related or equal in importance. The parallel elements may be words, phrases, sentences, or paragraphs. Parallelism occurs in the following lines:

So long as men can breathe, or eyes can see,
So long lives this, and this gives life to thee.
—William Shakespeare from "Sonnet 18"

Parody A parody imitates or mocks another serious work or type of literature. Like caricature in art, parody in literature mimics a subject or a style. The purpose of a parody may be to ridicule through broad humor. On the other hand, a parody may broaden understanding or add insight to the original work. Some parodies are even written in tribute to a work of literature. Mark Twain's book *A Connecticut Yankee in King Arthur's Court,* in which a time traveler from Twain's era tries to make sense of what he encounters in the Arthurian Age, parodies the legend of King Arthur.

Personification Personification is a figure of speech in which human qualities are attributed to an object, animal, or idea. Writers use personification to make images and feelings concrete for the reader.

Examples: In Pablo Neruda's "Tonight I Can Write . . . ," human physical attributes are given to stars in the phrase "the blue stars shiver." In Dahlia Ravikovitch's "Pride," rocks "lie on their backs" and "the rock has an open wound."

See pages 226, 354, 466, 846.
See also **Figurative Language; Imagery; Metaphor; Simile.**

Persuasion Persuasion is a technique used by speakers or writers to convince an audience to adopt an opinion, perform an action, or both. Effective persuasion appeals to both the emotions and the intellect. Persuasion is often used in essays; essayists try to convince readers to accept their views. E. M. Forster's "Tolerance" is an example.

Plot The word *plot* refers to the chain of related events that take place in a story. The plot is the writer's blueprint for what happens, when it happens, and to whom it happens. Usually, the events of a plot progress because of a **conflict,** or struggle between opposing forces. Although there are many types of plots, most include the following stages:

1. **Exposition** The exposition lays the groundwork for the plot and provides the reader with essential background information. Characters are introduced, the setting is described, and the plot begins to unfold. Although the exposition generally appears at the opening of a story, it may also occur later in the narrative. In Stephen Vincent Benét's "By the Waters of Babylon," the exposition introduces the narrator and his priest-father and establishes the primitive setting, particularly the characters' fear of the Place of the Gods.
2. **Rising Action** As the story progresses, complications usually arise, causing difficulties for the main characters and making the conflict more difficult to resolve. As the characters struggle to find solutions to the conflict, suspense builds. In "By the Waters of Babylon" the rising action begins as the narrator sets off on his journey.
3. **Climax** The climax is the turning point of the action, the moment when interest and intensity reach their peak. The climax of a story usually involves an important event, decision, or discovery that affects the final outcome. In

1230 GLOSSARY OF LITERARY TERMS

"By the Waters of Babylon" the climax comes when John goes to the Place of the Gods and discovers the dead "god"—a man.

4. **Falling Action** The falling action consists of the events that occur after the climax. Often, the conflict is resolved, and the intensity of the action subsides. Sometimes this phase of the plot is called the **dénouement** (dā′no͞o-mäɴ′), from a French word that means "untying." In the dénouement, also known as the **resolution,** the tangles of the plot are untied and mysteries are solved. In "By the Waters of Babylon" the falling action comes as John realizes the truth about the past and what it means to his own people.

See pages 17, 53, 167, 285, 383, 394.
See also **Climax; Conflict; Falling Action; Rising Action.**

Poetry Poetry is language arranged in lines. Like other forms of literature, poetry attempts to re-create emotions and experiences. Poetry, however, is usually more condensed and suggestive than prose. Because poetry frequently does not include the kind of detail and explanation found in prose, poetry tends to leave more to the reader's imagination. Poetry also may require more work on the reader's part to unlock meaning.

Poems often are divided into stanzas, or groups of lines. The stanzas in a poem may contain the same number of lines or they may vary in length. Some poems have definite patterns of meter and rhyme. Others rely more on the sounds of words and less on fixed rhythms and rhyme schemes. The use of figurative language is also common in poetry.

See also **Figurative Language; Form; Free Verse; Meter; Repetition; Rhyme; Rhythm.**

Point of View Point of view refers to the narrative method used in a short story, novel, or nonfiction selection. The two basic points of view are first-person and third-person.

When a character within a selection describes the action as a participant, in his or her own words, the writer is using the **first-person point of view.** A first-person narrator tends to involve the reader in the story and to communicate a sense of immediacy and personal concern. Tim O'Brien's "On the Rainy River" and Rosamund Pilcher's "Lalla" are examples of the first-person point of view. The excerpt from Marion Zimmer Bradley's *The Mists of Avalon* shows how the use of first-person narration can bring a legendary character to life.

Third-person point of view occurs when a narrator outside the action describes events and characters. In **third-person omniscient point of view,** the narrator is omniscient, or all-knowing, and can see into the minds of more than one character. The use of a third-person narrator gives the writer tremendous flexibility and provides the reader with access to all the characters and to events that may be occurring simultaneously. Sarah Orne Jewett's "A White Heron" is told from a third-person omniscient point of view. In this story, the reader has access to the thoughts and feelings not only of Sylvia, but also to some extent of the grandmother and the stranger. We learn, for example, about the stranger's thoughts upon awakening, which are occurring at approximately the same time as which Sylvia is out spotting the heron.

In the **third-person limited point of view** events are related through the eyes of one character. The narrator describes only that character's feelings and the events that he or she witnesses. Bessie Head's "The Prisoner Who Wore Glasses" is an example of the third-person limited point of view. In this story, we know only the thoughts of Brille, and everything is filtered through the perspective of this character.

See pages 18, 53, 93, 343, 575, 623–624, 642, 660, 833, 890, 1086.

Props The word *prop,* an abbreviation of *property,* refers to the physical objects that are used in a stage production. In Anton Chekhov's *The Bear,* the props include a snapshot of Mrs. Popov's late husband and the pistols to be used in her duel with Smirnov. Props help to establish the setting for a play.

See also **Drama.**

Protagonist The central character in a story or play is called the protagonist. The protagonist is always involved in the central conflict of the

GLOSSARY OF LITERARY TERMS 1231

plot and often changes during the course of the work. Sometimes more than one character can be the protagonist of a story.

Examples: The protagonist in R. K. Narayan's "Like the Sun" is the character Sekhar, who encounters problems while seeking to tell the truth. The protagonist in Doris Lessing's "No Witchcraft for Sale" is Gideon, the servant who displays his knowledge of medicinal herbs.

See page 556.
See also **Antagonist.**

Quatrain A quatrain is a four-line stanza, or unit of poetry. The most common stanza in English poetry, the quatrain can display a variety of meters and rhyme schemes. Quatrains are often used in sonnets, as in these lines from William Shakespeare's "Sonnet 18." The rhyme scheme in this quatrain is *abab.*

> **Shall I compare thee to a summer's day?** *a*
> **Thou art more lovely and more temperate:** *b*
> **Rough winds do shake the darling buds of May,** *a*
> **And summer's lease hath all too short a date:** *b*
> **—William Shakespeare, from "Sonnet 18"**

See also **Meter; Poetry; Rhyme; Sonnet; Stanza.**

Realism In literature, realism has both a general meaning and a special meaning. As a general term, *realism* refers to any effort to offer an accurate and detailed portrayal of actual life. Thus, critics talk about Shakespeare's realistic portrayals of his characters and praise the medieval poet Chaucer for his realistic descriptions of people from different social classes.

More specifically, realism refers to a literary method developed in the 19th century. The realists based their writing on careful observations of their contemporary life, often focusing on the middle or lower classes. They attempted to present life objectively and honestly, without the sentimentality or idealism that had characterized earlier literature. Typically, realists developed their settings in great detail in an effort to re-create a specific time and place for the reader. Guy de Maupassant, Leo Tolstoy, Mark Twain, and Sarah Orne Jewett are all considered realists.

Repetition Repetition is a literary technique in which a sound, word, phrase, or line is repeated for emphasis. Note the use of repetition in the following lines:

> **Love is not all: it is not meat nor drink**
> **Nor slumber nor a roof against the rain;**
> **Nor yet a floating spar to men that sink**
> **And rise and sink and rise and sink again;**
> **—Edna St. Vincent Millay, from "Sonnet 30"**

See pages 225, 354, 759.

Resolution *See* **Falling Action.**

Rhyme Words rhyme when the sound of their accented vowels and all succeeding sounds are identical, as in *tether* and *together.* For **true rhyme,** the consonants that precede the vowels must be different, as in Shakespeare's rhyming of *day* and *May* in "Sonnet 18." Rhyme that occurs at the ends of lines of poetry is called **end rhyme.** End rhyme that is not exact but approximate is called **off rhyme,** as in *other* and *bother.* Rhyme that occurs within a single line, as in the following example, is called **internal rhyme:**

> **Once upon a midnight dreary, while I pondered weak and weary,**
> **Over many a quaint and curious volume of forgotten lore—**
> **While I nodded, nearly napping, suddenly there came a tapping,**
> **As of someone gently rapping, rapping at my chamber door.**
> **—Edgar Allan Poe, from "The Raven"**

See pages 225, 233.

Rhyme Scheme A rhyme scheme is the pattern of end rhyme in a poem. The pattern is charted by assigning a letter of the alphabet, beginning with the letter *a,* to each line. Lines that rhyme are given the same letter. The following example has an *abab* rhyme scheme:

1232 GLOSSARY OF LITERARY TERMS

But thy eternal summer shall not fade, *a*
Nor lose possession of that fair thou owest; *b*
Nor shall Death brag thou wander'st in
his shade, *a*
When in eternal lines to time thou growest: *b*
—William Shakespeare, from "Sonnet 18"

See pages 225, 233.

Rhythm Rhythm refers to the pattern or beat of stressed and unstressed syllables in a line of poetry. Poets use rhythm to bring out the musical quality of language, to emphasize ideas, to create mood, and to reinforce subject matter.

See pages 226, 236.
See also **Meter.**

Rising Action Rising action refers to the part of the plot in which complications develop and the conflict intensifies, building to the climax, or highest point of interest and intensity in the plot. The rising action in Anton Chekhov's *The Bear* describes the growing conflict between Smirnov and Mrs. Popov.

See pages 384, 394.
See also **Climax; Falling Action; Plot.**

Romance A romance refers to any imaginative story concerned with noble heroes, chivalric codes of honor, passionate love, daring deeds, and supernatural events. Writers of romances tend to idealize their heroes as well as the eras in which the heroes live. Medieval romances, such as Malory's *Le Morte d'Arthur,* are stories of kings, knights, and ladies who are motivated by love, religious faith, or simply a desire for adventure. Such romances are comparatively lighthearted in tone and loose in structure, containing many episodes. Usually the main character has a series of adventures while on a quest to accomplish some goal.

See page 1080.

Satire Satire is a literary technique in which ideas, customs, behaviors, or institutions are ridiculed for the purpose of improving society. Satire may be gently witty, mildly abrasive, or bitterly critical, and it often uses exaggeration to force readers to see something in a more critical light.

Example: Kurt Vonnegut Jr.'s "Harrison Bergeron" is a satire that criticizes those who pursue an ideal at the expense of common sense. Vonnegut depicts a future society that has gone to ridiculous lengths to ensure complete equality among its citizens, rewarding mediocrity and penalizing individual talent.

Scene A scene is a subdivision of an act in drama. Each scene usually establishes a different time or place. In Shakespeare's *Julius Caesar,* for example, the first scene of Act One takes place at a public celebration on a street in Rome. The last scene in Act Five takes place on a battlefield.

Science Fiction Science fiction is prose writing that presents the possibilities of the future, using known scientific data and theories as well as the creative imagination of the writer. Most science fiction comments on present-day society through the writer's fictional conception of a future society.

Examples: Ray Bradbury's "A Sound of Thunder" presents a vision of the future in order to show how all aspects of nature are interrelated and that human interference with the ecological cycle can lead to disaster. Bradbury's "The Pedestrian" portrays a future in which human beings are rendered completely passive by television.

See pages 27, 82.

Setting Setting is the time and place of the action of a short story, novel, play, narrative poem, or narrative nonfiction work. In addition to place and time, however, setting may include the larger historical and cultural contexts that form the background for a narrative. Setting is one of the main elements in fiction and often plays an important role in what happens and why.

Examples: In Ray Bradbury's "There Will Come Soft Rains," the house setting is essential to what happens in the story; it functions almost as a character. The desolate frontier setting of

GLOSSARY OF LITERARY TERMS 1233

Mark Twain's "The Californian's Tale" provides a historical context that helps to explain Henry's actions. The setting of Zhang Jie's "Love Must Not Be Forgotten" includes information about the cultural environment that enables the reader to understand the actions of the characters.

See pages 18, 93, 209, 311, 660.

Shakespearean Sonnet *See* **Sonnet.**

Short Story A short story is a work of fiction that can be read in one sitting. Generally, a short story develops one major conflict. The four basic elements of a short story are setting, character, plot, and theme.

A short story must be unified; all the elements must work together to produce a total effect. This unity of effect is reinforced through an appropriate title and through the use of literary devices, such as symbolism and irony.

See also **Character; Conflict; Plot; Setting; Theme.**

Simile A simile is a stated comparison between two things that are actually unlike but that have something in common. Like metaphors, similes are figures of speech, but whereas a metaphor implies a comparison, a simile expresses the comparison clearly by the use of the word *like* or *as.*

Example: In W. P. Kinsella's "The Thrill of the Grass," the narrator describes his shadow as being "black as an umbrella." This simile links the shadow and the umbrella by their common color.

See pages 226, 260, 349, 354.
See also **Figurative Language; Metaphor.**

Situational Irony *See* **Irony.**

Soliloquy In a dramatic work, a soliloquy is a speech in which a character speaks his or her private thoughts aloud. The character is usually on stage alone and generally appears to be unaware of the presence of an audience. Soliloquies are characteristic of Shakepeare's plays; *Julius Caesar* has several soliloquies. Casca begins plotting how to win over Brutus in a soliloquy that begins with these lines:

> **Well, Brutus, thou art noble; yet I see**
> **Thy honorable mettle may be wrought**
> **From that it is disposed.**
> **—William Shakespeare, from *Julius Caesar***

See page 735.

Sonnet A sonnet is a lyric poem of 14 lines, commonly written in iambic pentameter. For centuries the sonnet has been a popular form, for it is long enough to permit development of a complex idea yet short and structured enough to challenge any poet's artistic skills.

The **Shakespearean,** or **English, sonnet** is sometimes also called the **Elizabethan sonnet.** It consists of three quatrains, or four-line units, and a final **couplet,** or two-line unit, which reflect the logical organization of the poem. The typical rhyme scheme is *abab cdcd efef gg.* In the English sonnet, the rhymed couplet at the end of the sonnet provides a final commentary on the subject developed in the preceding three quatrains. The poems by William Shakespeare and Edna St. Vincent Millay included in this text are sonnets.

Some poets have written a series of related sonnets that have the same subject. These are called **sonnet sequences,** or **sonnet cycles.** Toward the end of the 16th century, writing sonnets became fashionable, with a common subject being love for a beautiful but unattainable woman. Shakespeare's sonnets are the most famous of all sonnet sequences.

See pages 233, 236, 581.
See also **Meter; Poetry; Quatrain; Rhyme; Rhythm.**

Sound Devices *See* **Alliteration; Assonance; Consonance; Onomatopoeia; Meter; Repetition; Rhyme.**

Speaker The speaker in a poem is the voice that "talks" to the reader, similar to the narrator in fiction. Speaker and poet are not necessarily synonymous. Often a poet creates a speaker with a distinct identity in order to achieve a particular effect.

Example: In Stephen Crane's "Do not weep, maiden, for war is kind," the speaker is an ironic observer of war's tragedy.

See page 231.

1234 GLOSSARY OF LITERARY TERMS

Stage Directions The stage directions in a dramatic script serve as a kind of instructional manual for the director, actors, and stage crew as well as for the general reader. Often the stage directions are printed in italic type, and they may be enclosed in parentheses or brackets.

Stage directions serve a number of important functions. They may describe the scenery, or setting, as well as lighting, costumes, props, music, sound effects, or, in the case of film productions, camera angles and shots. Most important, the stage directions usually provide hints to the performers on how the characters look, move, and speak.

Example: In Chekhov's *The Bear,* the stage directions give information about the actions and expressions of the characters, as well details about the props and Mrs. Popov's drawing room, where the action takes place.

See page 285, 300.
See also **Props.**

Stanza A stanza is a group of lines that form a unit of poetry. The stanza is roughly comparable to the paragraph in prose. In traditional poems, the stanzas usually have the same number of lines and often have the same rhyme scheme and meter as well. In the 20th century, poets have experimented more freely with stanza form than did earlier poets, sometimes writing poems that have no stanza breaks at all.

Stereotype In literature, simplified or stock characters who conform to a fixed pattern or are defined by a single trait are called stereotypes. Such characters do not usually demonstrate the complexities of real people.

Examples: Familiar stereotypes in popular literature include the absent-minded professor, the dumb athlete, and the busybody. In Chekhov's *The Bear,* the servant Luke might be seen as a stereotype of a loyal but critical servant who tells the lady of the house more than she wants to hear.

See page 300.
See also **Farce.**

Structure Structure is the way in which the parts of a work of literature are put together. In poetry, structure refers to the arrangement of words and lines to produce a desired effect. A common structural unit in poetry is the stanza, of which there are numerous types. In prose, structure is the arrangement of larger units or parts of a selection. Paragraphs, for example, are a basic unit in prose, as are chapters in novels and acts in plays. The structure of a poem, short story, novel, play, or nonfiction selection usually emphasizes certain important aspects of content.

See pages 233, 236.
See also **Act; Stanza.**

Style Style is the way in which a piece of literature is written. Style refers not to what is said but to how it is said. Elements such as word choice, sentence length, tone, imagery, figurative language, use of dialogue, and point of view contribute to a writer's personal style.

Examples: Sarah Orne Jewett's style in "A White Heron" might be described as a blend of the poetic and realistic. Through her use of sensory details, regional dialect, and a sensitive narrator, she creates both an accurate and an admiring picture of the main character and her world. Frank O'Connor's style in "The Study of History" might be described as matter-of-fact and humorously understated, reflecting the engaging personality of its youthful narrator.

See pages 460, 600, 995, 1099.

Surprise Ending A surprise ending is an unexpected twist in plot at the conclusion of a story. The conclusion of Guy de Maupassant's "Two Friends" surprises the reader because earlier events in the story had suggested a different outcome.

Suspense Suspense is the tension or excitement felt by the reader as he or she becomes involved in a story and eager to know the outcome of the conflict. Suspense is created when a writer purposely leaves readers uncertain or apprehensive about what will happen.

Example: In Edgar Allan Poe's "The Pit and the

GLOSSARY OF LITERARY TERMS 1235

Pendulum," the reader wants to know if the narrator can possibly escape from his situation. The tension is maintained as the narrator finds a way to cope with each threat that he encounters, only to be faced with a new and even greater threat.

See page 575.

Symbol A symbol is a person, place, or object that represents something beyond itself. For instance, a star on a door represents fame; a star pinned to the shirt of a sheriff stands for authority and power. Symbols can succinctly communicate complicated, emotionally rich ideas. A flag, for example, can symbolize patriotism and a national heritage.

Examples: The cranes in Hwang Sunwŏn's story of the same name symbolize the childhood friendship of the two main characters, as well as peace and tranquillity. The medicinal plant in Doris Lessing's "No Witchcraft for Sale" symbolizes native African culture.

See pages 407, 833, 906.

Tall Tale A tall tale is a humorously exaggerated story about impossible events, often relating the supernatural abilities of the main character. The tales about folk heroes such as Paul Bunyan and Davy Crockett are typical tall tales.

Theme The theme is the central idea or message in a work of literature. Theme should not be confused with subject, or what the work is about. Rather, theme is a perception about life or human nature shared with the reader. Sometimes the theme is directly stated within a work; at other times it is implied, and the reader must infer the theme. For example, Kurt Vonnegut, Jr., in "Harrison Bergeron" never directly states his criticism of the society and government. The reader needs to put details and events together to identify his theme about the damage that can be done when people go to extremes in service of equality.

One way to discover the theme of a work of literature is to think about what happens to the central characters. The importance of those events, stated in terms that apply to all human beings, is often the theme. For example, in Doris Lessing's "No Witchcraft for Sale," the misunderstanding and distrust between Gideon and Mrs. Farquar suggests the more general theme that lack of understanding between races and cultures can create tension. Several other selections in this book have themes that involve the need for people to accept one another by dealing with differences in their culture.

See pages 18, 27, 156, 167, 178, 794.

Third-Person Narration *See* **Point of View.**

Title The title of a literary work introduces the readers to the piece and usually reveals something about its subject or theme. Some titles are deliberately straightforward, stating exactly what the reader can expect to discover in the work. Others suggest possibilities, perhaps hinting at the subject and forcing the reader to search for interpretations.

Example: The title of Nadine Gordimer's "A Chip of Glass Ruby" refers to a traditional Indian adornment. When Mrs. Bamjee was a girl, her mother had fixed a glass ruby in her daughter's nostril, "but she [Mrs. Bamjee] had abandoned that adornment . . . long ago." On one hand, the title suggests her rejection of a narrowly defined traditional role. On the other hand, the title suggests the husband's frustrated desire for a wife solely focused on traditional duties.

Tone Tone is the attitude a writer takes toward a subject. The language and details a writer chooses help to create the tone, which might be playful, serious, bitter, angry, or detached, among other possibilities. To identify the tone of a work of literature, you might find it helpful to read the work aloud, as if giving a dramatic reading before an audience. The emotions that you convey in reading should give you hints as to the tone of the work.

Unlike mood, which refers to the emotional response of the reader to a work, tone reflects the feelings of the writer.

Examples: Rudolfo A. Anaya uses an admiring, respectful tone to describe his grandfather in "A Celebration of Grandfathers." Roger Rosenblatt's "The Man in the Water" exhibits a philosophic,

1236 GLOSSARY OF LITERARY TERMS

somber tone, reflecting the author's efforts to draw a lesson from a tragic yet heroic event.

See pages 452, 460, 649, 901, 945, 962, 981.
See also **Connotation; Diction; Mood; Style.**

Tragedy In broad terms, tragedy is literature, especially drama, in which actions and events turn out disastrously for the main character or characters. In tragedy the main characters, and sometimes other involved characters and innocent bystanders as well, are destroyed. Usually the destruction is death, as in Shakespeare's *Julius Caesar* or Sophocles' *Antigone.* In some tragedies, however, the main characters are alive at the end but are devastated. Tragic heroes evoke both pity and fear in readers or viewers—pity because they feel sorry for the characters and fear because they realize that the problems and struggles faced by the characters are perhaps a necessary part of human life. At the end of a tragedy, a reader or viewer generally feels a sense of waste, because humans who were in some way superior have been destroyed.

See pages 794, 1019, 1061.
See also **Hero.**

Tragic Flaw *See* **Hero.**

Tragic Hero *See* **Hero.**

Turning Point *See* **Climax.**

Understatement Understatement is the technique of creating emphasis by saying less than is actually or literally true. As such, it is the opposite of exaggeration, or hyperbole. The statement made by the park guide in John Steinbeck's *Travels with Charley,* "Bears don't argue," is an example of understatement. It suggests that even though bears don't talk, they know of more aggressive ways to express their wants. Understatement can be a biting form of sarcasm or verbal irony. Jonathan Swift, the 18th-century English writer best known for *Gulliver's Travels,* often used understatement as a satiric weapon. For example, Swift wrote, "Last week I saw a woman flayed [skinned alive], and you will hardly believe how much it altered her appearance for the worse."

See page 939.
See also **Hyperbole; Irony.**

Verbal Irony *See* **Irony.**

Voice The term *voice* refers to a writer's unique use of language that allows a reader to "hear" a human personality in his or her writing. The elements of style that determine a writer's voice include sentence structure, diction, and tone. For example, some writers are noted for their reliance on short, simple sentences, while others make use of long, complicated ones. Certain writers use concrete words, such as *lake* or *cold,* which name things that you can see, hear, feel, taste, or smell. Others prefer abstract terms like *memory,* which name things that cannot be perceived with the senses. A writer's tone also leaves its imprint on his or her personal voice.

The term can also be applied to the narrator of a selection. In Alice Walker's "Everyday Use," the narrator establishes her personality through her manner of narration. She emerges as a strong, down-to-earth character with a gift for descriptive language.

Word Choice *See* **Diction.**

GLOSSARY OF LITERARY TERMS 1237

Glossary of Words to Know

Glossary of Words to Know

In English and Spanish

A

abdicate (ăb'dĭ-kāt') *v.* to give up an office or position
abdicar *v.* renunciar a un cargo

abiding (ə-bī'dĭng) *adj.* lasting or enduring **abide** *v.*
duradero *adj.* perdurable; resistente **durar** *v.*

acquaint (ə-kwānt') *v.* to inform; familiarize
conocer *v.* informar; familiarizarse

acquiescence (ăk'wē-ĕs'əns) *n.* passive agreement; agreement without protest
consentimiento *s.* aceptación pasiva; aceptación sin protestar

acute (ə-kyo͞ot') *adj.* very sharp or severe
agudo *adj.* grave o severo

adamant (ăd'ə-mənt) *adj.* remaining firm despite the pleas or reasoning of others; stubbornly unyielding
obstinado *adj.* que permanece firme a pesar de ruegos o razonamientos; testarudo; inflexible

adversary (ăd'vər-sĕr'ē) *n.* an opponent; enemy
adversario *s.* opositor; enemigo

amicable (ăm'ĭ-kə-bəl) *adj.* having or showing a friendly attitude
amigable *adj.* que tiene una actitud amistosa

analyze (ăn'ə-līz') *v.* to study carefully by separating into parts
analizar *v.* estudiar cuidadosamente, separando en partes

anecdote (ăn'ĭk-dōt') *n.* a short account of an interesting or humorous incident
anécdota *s.* narración breve de un incidente interesante o chistoso

animosity (ăn'ə-mŏs'ĭ-tē) *n.* active dislike; hatred
animosidad *s.* desagrado fuerte; odio

annihilate (ə-nī'ə-lāt') *v.* to destroy completely; wipe out
aniquilar *v.* destruir completamente; desbaratar; eliminar

annul (ə-nŭl') *v.* to do away with or make invalid; cancel
anular *v.* abolir; invalidar; cancelar

anonymity (ăn'ə-nĭm'ĭ-tē) *n.* the state of being unknown or unidentified
anonimato *s.* estado en que no se es reconocido o identificado

antiquated (ăn'tĭ-kwā'tĭd) *adj.* old-fashioned; outmoded
anticuado *adj.* a la antigua; pasado de moda

ardent (är'dnt) *adj.* displaying great warmth of feeling; passionate
ardiente *adj.* de sentimientos muy cálidos; apasionado

ascend (ə-sĕnd') *v.* to rise; climb
ascender *v.* subir; trepar

assiduously (ə-sĭj'o͞o-əs-lē) *adv.* in a way that shows steady and careful attention
asiduamente *adv.* con constancia y perseverancia

astutely (ə-sto͞ot'lē) *adv.* with keen perceptiveness; wisely
astutamente *adv.* con perspicacia; inteligentemente

atonement (ə-tōn'mənt) *n.* the act of making up for a serious error, sin, or wrong
expiación *s.* acto de reparar un error, un pecado o un mal

atrocity (ə-trŏs′ĭ-tē) *n.* a very cruel or brutal act
atrocidad *s.* acto muy cruel o brutal

auspicious (ô-spĭsh′əs) *adj.* promising success; favorable
propicio *adj.* que promete éxito; favorable

authoritarian (ə-thôr′ĭ-târ′ē-ən′) *adj.* expecting or demanding absolute obedience
autoritario *adj.* que espera o demanda obediencia absoluta

averse (ə-vûrs′) *adj.* unwilling; deeply reluctant
adverso *adj.* opuesto; muy reacio

aversion (ə-vûr′zhən) *n.* a strong, definite dislike
aversión *s.* antipatía clara y fuerte

B

balmy (bä′mē) *adj.* soothingly fragrant; mild and pleasant
suave *adj.* de fragancia tranquilizante; delicado y placentero

bedlam (bĕd′ləm) *n.* a place or situation of great noise and confusion
jaleo *s.* situación de mucho ruido y confusión

benediction (bĕn′ĭ-dĭk′shən) *n.* a blessing
bendición *s.* acto de bendecir; don o favor

benign (bĭ-nīn′) *adj.* mild; gentle
benigno *adj.* suave; benévolo

bereft (bĭ-rĕft′) *adj.* suffering the death of a loved one; deprived of someone or something important
privado (de) *adj.* desolado; que sufre por la muerte de un ser querido; que ha perdido alguien o algo importante

biased (bī′əst) *adj.* marked by an unfair preference; prejudiced
tendencioso *adj.* caracterizado por una preferencia injusta; prejuiciado

boding (bō′dĭng) *n.* a warning or omen about the future, especially of evil **bode** *v.*
presagio *s.* pronóstico o advertencia acerca del futuro, especialmente de algo malo **presagiar** *v.*

boisterous (boi′stər-əs) *adj.* loud, noisy, and unrestrained
escandaloso *adj.* alborotado, ruidoso y sin control

brooding (bro͞od′ĭng) *adj.* having a moody or depressed disposition **brood** *v.*
decaído *adj.* que tiene una disposición melancólica o deprimida **decaer** *v.*

C

cajole (kə-jōl′) *v.* to persuade by pleasant words, flattery, or false promises
engatusar *v.* persuadir con bellas palabras; convencer con halagos o falsas promesas

calculating (kăl′kyə-lā′tĭng) *adj.* crafty; cunning
calculador *adj.* mañoso; hábil

calibrated (kăl′ə-brā′tĭd) *adj.* marked with measurements **calibrate** *v.*
calibrado *adj.* marcado con medidas **calibrar** *v.*

callousness (kăl′əs-nĭs) *n.* emotional hardness; lack of feeling
insensibilidad *s.* dureza emocional; indiferencia

carriage (kăr′ĭj) *n.* manner of moving one's body
porte *s.* modo de andar

catalyst (kăt′l-ĭ) *n.*something that causes change or action
catalizador *s.* algo que causa un cambio o acción

censure (sĕn′shər) *v.* to criticize severely; to blame
censurar *v.* criticar severamente; culpar

chagrin (shə-grĭn′) *n.* a feeling of humiliation or embarrassment
disgusto *s.* sentimiento de humillación o vergüenza

champion (chăm′pē-ən) *v.* to fight for; defend
abogar *v.* defender una causa o persona; apoyar

chaos (kā′ŏs′) *n.* total disorder
caos *s.* desorden total

GLOSSARY OF WORDS TO KNOW 1239

chaotic (kā-ŏt'ĭk) *adj.* extremely confused or disordered
caótico *adj.* extremadamente confuso o desordenado

charade (shə-rād') *n.* an ill-disguised pretense
charada *s.* farsa o payasada; acertijo

churlish (chûr'lĭsh) *adj.* rude or ill-tempered
grosero *adj.* rudo o insolente

coercion (kō-ûr'zhən) *n.* the use of power or threats to force someone to do something
coerción *s.* uso de poder o amenazas para obligar a actuar

coherently (kō-hîr'ənt-lē) *adv.* in a manner that shows clear thinking and makes sense
coherentemente *adv.* con claridad, constancia y sensatez

commiserate (kə-mĭz'ə-rāt') *v.* to express sorrow or pity for another's trouble
conmiserarse *v.* expresar dolor o piedad por los problemas de otro

commodity (kə-mŏd'ĭ-tē) *n.* an item—especially a farming or mining product—that can be turned to commercial use or that can provide another advantage
mercancía *s.* producto —especialmente agrícola o minero— que puede tener uso comercial u otras ventajas

complacently (kəm-plā'sənt-lē) *adv.* in a contented, unconcerned manner
complacientemente *adv.* en forma bonachona o tolerante

comprehend (kŏm'prĭ-hĕnd') *v.* to understand
comprender *v.* entender

compulsive (kəm-pŭl'sĭv) *adj.* having the ability to compel or force
compulsivo *adj.* que obliga o fuerza

comradeship (kŏm'răd-shĭp') *n.* companionship
camaradería *s.* compañerismo

conclusively (kən-klo͞o'sĭv-lē) *adv.* unquestionably; decisively
concluyentemente *adv.* de modo terminante; incuestionablemente

consensus (kən-sĕn'səs) *n.* general agreement by a group
consenso *s.* acuerdo general de grupo

consternation (kŏn'stər-nā'shən) *n.* a confused amazement or fear
consternación *s.* aflicción y temor; pesadumbre

construe (kən-stro͞o') *v.* to interpret
interpretar *v.* explicar

contemptuously (kən-tĕmp'cho͞o-əs-lē) *adv.* in a way that shows one's low opinion of someone or something; scornfully
desdeñosamente *adv.* con desprecio; burlonamente

contour (kŏn'to͝or') *n.* an outline of a shape
contorno *s.* borde de una figura

convalescence (kŏn'və-lĕs'əns) *n.* the gradual return to health and strength after an illness or an injury
convalecencia *s.* retorno gradual de la salud y la fuerza después de una enfermedad o herida

conviction (kən-vĭk'shən) *n.* certainty; a strong belief
convicción *s.* seguridad; creencia firme

coquettishly (kō-kĕt'ĭsh-lē) *adv.* in a flirtatious manner
coquetamente *adv.* de forma seductora

cosmopolitan (kŏz'mə-pŏl'ĭ-tn) *adj.* worldly; sophisticated
cosmopolita *adj.* mundano; sofisticado

cower (kou'ər) *v.* to cringe in fear
agazaparse *v.* esconderse u ocultarse con miedo

coyness (coi'nĭs) *n.* the pretense of being more modest and innocent than one really is
gazmoñería *s.* apariencia de modestia o inocencia

cultivate (kŭl'tə-vāt') *v.* to seek to become familiar with
cultivar *v.* hacer lo necesario para mejorar un conocimiento o una relación

1240 GLOSSARY OF WORDS TO KNOW

D

dastardly (dăs′tərd-lē) *adj.* mean and cowardly
vil *adj.* cruel y cobarde

decipher (dĭ-sī′fər) *v.* to read or interpret something unclear; to figure out
descifrar *v.* leer o interpretar algo que no está claro; explicar

decorous (dĕk′ər-əs) *adj.* behaving in a manner appropriate to the occasion; proper
decoroso *adj.* que se comporta de manera apropiada a la ocasión; correcto

deference (dĕf′ər-əns) *n.* courteous regard or respect
deferencia *s.* atención o respeto cortés

defile (dĭ-fīl′) *v.* to make foul, dirty, unclean, or impure
profanar *v.* ensuciar o deshonrar; quitarle su pureza

degrading (dĭ-grā′dĭng) *adj.* tending to lower one's dignity; insulting **degrade** *v.*
degradante *adj.* que quita dignidad; insultante **degradar** *v.*

deliberately (dĭ-lĭb′ər-ĭt-lē) *adv.* as a result of careful thought
deliberadamente *adv.* con cuidadoy premeditación

desolation (dĕs′ə-lā′shən) *n.* the state of being empty, deserted, or forlorn; barrenness; loneliness
desolación *s.* sensación de vacío, abandono o aislamiento; aridez; soledad

detestable (dĭ-tĕs′tə-bəl) *adj.* worthy of scorn; hateful
detestable *adj.* despreciable y abominable; odioso

devoid (dĭ-void′) *adj.* completely lacking; empty
desprovisto *adj.* despojado; vacío

dexterous (dĕk′stər-əs) *adj.* skillful; clever
diestro *adj.* hábil; ingenioso

diametrically (dī′ə-mĕt′rĭ-klē) *adv.* in complete opposition
diametralmente *adv.* en completa oposición

din (dĭn) *n.* a jumble of loud noises
estruendo *s.* mezcla de ruidos fuertes

dirge (dûrj) *n.* a slow, mournful piece of music; a funeral hymn
canto fúnebre *s.* pieza musical lenta y dolida

disarm (dĭs-ärm′) *v.* to overcome or reduce the intensity of suspicion or hostility; to win the confidence of
desarmar *v.* vencer o reducir sospecha u hostilidad; ganarse la confianza

discordant (dĭ-skôr′dnt) *adj.* marked by a harsh mixture of sounds
discordante *adj.* caracterizado por una mezcla desagradable de sonidos

discreetly (dĭ-skrēt′lē) *adv.* in a manner showing good judgment; cautiously
discretamente *adv.* con buen juicio; cautelosamente

disinherited (dĭs′ĭn-hĕr′ĭ-tĭd) *adj.* deprived of a rightful inheritance **disinherit** *v.*
desheredado *adj.* privado de su herencia **desheredar** *v.*

disparagement (dĭ-spăr′ĭj-mənt) *n.* belittlement
desprecio *s.* menosprecio

disreputable (dĭs-rĕp′yə-tə-bəl) *adj.* having a bad reputation; not respectable
desprestigiado *adj.* que tiene mala reputación; que no es respetable

dissuasion (dĭ-swā′zhən) *n.* the persuading of someone not to perform an action
disuasión *s.* acto de persuadir o convencer de no hacer algo

distasteful (dĭs-tāst′fəl) *adj.* unpleasant; disagreeable
desagradable *adj.* fastidioso; de mal gusto

doctrine (dŏk′trĭn) *n.* a principle or rule taught by a religious, political or philosophic group
doctrina *s.* principio o regla de un grupo religioso, político o filosófico

E

edict (ē′dĭkt′) *n.* an order put out by a person in authority
edicto *s.* orden de una persona de autoridad

edifice (ĕd′ə-fĭs) *n.* building; structure
edificio *s.* construcción; estructura

GLOSSARY OF WORDS TO KNOW 1241

Glossary of Words to Know

efficacy (ĕf'ĭ-kə-sē) *n.* the power to produce a desired effect; effectiveness
eficacia *s.* capacidad para producir un efecto deseado; habilidad

eloquent (ĕl'ə-kwənt) *adj.* vividly expressive
elocuente *adj.* que se expresa de modo eficaz

elusive (ĭ-lo͞o'sĭv) *adj.* hard to catch or discover
elusivo *adj.* difícil de descubrir o de interpretar

emaciated (ĭ-mā'shē-ā-tĭd) *adj.* extremely thin, especially as a result of starvation **emaciate** *v.*
emaciado *adj.* en los huesos; muydelgado por pasar hambre **emaciarse** *v.*

emancipation (ĭ-măn'sə-pā'shən) *n.* a setting free from restraint or controls
emancipación *s.* liberación; independencia

embody (ĕm-bŏd'ē) *v.* to give a concrete shape to; personify or represent
encarnar *v.* dar forma concreta; personificar o representar

emphatically (ĕm-făt'ĭ-klē) *adv.* forcefully; strongly
enfáticamente *adv.* con énfasis; con fuerza

encompass (ĕn-kŭm'pəs) *v.* to surround; enclose
abarcar *v.* rodear; encerrar

encumber (ĕn-kŭm'bər) *v.* to burden
estorbar *v.* recargar; molestar

enmity (ĕn'mĭ-tē) *n.* the hatred between enemies; antagonism; hostility
enemistad *s.* odio entre enemigos; antagonismo; hostilidad

entity (ĕn'tĭ-tē) *n.* a being
entidad *s.* ente; ser

equanimity (ē'kwə-nĭm'ĭ-tē) *n.* the quality of being calm and even-tempered; composure
ecuanimidad *s.* capacidad de mantener la calma sin cambios de ánimo;compostura

essence (ĕs'əns) *n.* the crucial element or basis
esencia *s.* elemento crucial o básico

ethereal (ĭ-thîr'ē-əl) *adj.* not earthly; heavenly
etéreo *adj.* irreal; celestial

exalt (ĭg-zôlt') *v.* to glorify, praise, or honor
exaltar *v.* glorificar, alabar u honrar

exaltation (ĕg'zôl-tā'shən) *n.* the act of glorifying, praising, or honoring
exaltación *s.* acto de glorificar, alabar u honrar

exasperated (ĭg-zăs'pə-rā'tĭd) *adj.* made impatient or angry; annoyed **exasperate** *v.*
exasperado *adj.* impaciente o enojado; irritado **exasperar** *v.*

exclusive (ĭk-sklo͞o'sĭv) *adj.* tending to exclude others; select
exclusivo *adj.* que excluye a otros; selecto

expendable (ĭk-spĕn'də-bəl) *adj.* dispensable; unnecessary
dispensable *adj.* que sale sobrando; innecesario

expenditure (ĭk-spĕn'də-chər) *n.* an act of spending
gasto *s.* acto de gastar

exposé (ĕk'spō-zā') *n.* an account that reveals something negative to the public
exposé *s.* relato que revela algo negativo al público

F

fallible (făl'ə-bəl) *adj.* capable of being wrong or mistaken
falible *adj.* capaz de equivocarse o de cometer errores

fanatical (fə-năt'ĭ-kəl) *adj.* extremely enthusiastic
fanático *adj.* extremadamente entusiasta

fanfare (făn'fâr') *n.* showy display or celebration
fanfarria *s.* demostración deslumbrante o celebración

fathom (făth'əm) *v.* to penetrate the meaning or understand the nature of
descifrar *v.* penetrar en el significado o entender la naturaleza de algo

fidelity (fĭ-dĕl'ĭ-tē) *n.* faithfulness to duties and obligations; devotion; loyalty
fidelidad *s.* responsabilidad hacia tareas y obligaciones; dedicación; lealtad

1242 GLOSSARY OF WORDS TO KNOW

flail (flāl) *v.* to wave or swing vigorously; thrash
sacudir *v.* mover vigorosamente; zarandear

flax (flăks) *n.* a plant that is the source of the fibers used to make linen
lino *s.* planta que produce las fibras con que se fabrica la tela de lino

flout (flout) *v.* to show contempt for; to scorn
mofarse *v.* mostrar desprecio; humillar

forlorn (fər-lôrn′) *adj.* appearing sad or lonely because one has been left alone
abandonado *adj.* con aspecto triste o desolado por la soledad

formidable (fôr′mĭ-də-bəl) *adj.* inspiring awe, fear, or wonder
formidable *adj.* que inspira admiración, miedo o asombro

forsaken (fôr-sā′kən) *adj.* abandoned
forsake *v.*
desamparado *adj.* abandonado **desamparar** *v.*

fortitude (fôr′tĭ-to͞od′) *n.* strength of mind to endure misfortune or pain with courage
fortaleza *s.* fuerza emocional para soportar desgracias o dolor con valentía

frantic (frăn′tĭk) *adj.* emotionally out of control
frenético *adj.* sin control emocional

furtive (fûr′tĭv) *adj.* shifty; having a hidden motive or purpose
furtivo *adj.* solapado; que tiene un motivo o propósito oculto

futile (fyo͞ot′l) *adj.* serving no useful purpose
fútil *adj.* inútil; de poca importancia

G

gaunt (gônt) *adj.* thin and bony
flaco *adj.* delgado y huesudo

genially (jēn′yə-lē) *adv.* in a friendly manner
cordialmente *adv.* de manera amable

gnome (nōm) *n.* an imaginary dwarflike creature that lives underground
gnomo *s.* enano imaginario que vive bajo la tierra

grizzled (grĭz′əld) *adj.* streaked with or partly gray
grisáceo *adj.* con tintes grises o parcialmente gris

H

haggard (hăg′ərd) *adj.* appearing worn and exhausted
ojeroso *adj.* de aspecto cansado y exhausto

haphazardly (hăp-hăz′ərd-lē) *adv.* in an aimless or random manner
fortuitamente *adv.* de cualquier modo; al azar

haughty (hô′tē) *adj.* proud; arrogant
altivo *adj.* orgulloso; arrogante

haunt (hônt) *n.* a place visited frequently
lugar predilecto *s.* lugar visitado con frecuencia

heretic (hĕr′ĭ-tĭk) *n.* a person who holds controversial opinions that do not conform to the prevailing opinions of a society, religion, or group
hereje *s.* persona de opiniones polémicas que no están de acuerdo con las opiniones generales de una sociedad, religión o grupo

hindrance (hĭn′drəns) *n.* something that interferes with an activity; obstacle
impedimento *s.* algo que interfiere con una actividad; obstáculo

hinterland (hĭn′tər-lănd′) *n.* a region far from large cities
interior *s.* región alejada de las grandes ciudades

homily (hŏm′ə-lē) *n.* a tedious, moralizing lecture; sermon
homilía *s.* sermón aburrido

hone (hōn) *v.* to sharpen
afilar *v.* afinar

hypocrisy (hĭ-pŏk′rĭ-sē) *n.* a pretense of being what one is not; falsehood
hipocresía *s.* apariencia distinta de lo que se es; falsedad

I

illegible (ĭ-lĕj′ə-bəl) *adj.* unreadable
ilegible *adj.* que no puede leerse

GLOSSARY OF WORDS TO KNOW 1243

impassive (ĭm-păs'ĭv) *adj.* revealing no emotion; expressionless
impasible *adj.* que no muestra emociones; inexpresivo

impatient (ĭm-pā'shənt) *adj.* unable to tolerate irritation
impaciente *adj.* incapaz de tolerar algo irritante

impeccably (ĭm-pĕk'ə-blē) *adv.* flawlessly; perfectly
impecablemente *adv.* sin falla; perfectamente

impenetrable (ĭm-pĕn'ĭ-trə-bəl) *adj.* impossible to understand; incapable of being pierced
impenetrable *adj.* imposible de entender; que no puede ser perforado

imperative (ĭm-pĕr'ə-tĭv) *n.* urgent necessity or duty
imperativo *s.* necesidad u obligación urgente

imperceptible (ĭm'pər-sĕp'tə-bəl) *adj.* impossible to perceive; unnoticeable
imperceptible *adj.* que no se puede percibir; inadvertido

impersonal (ĭm-pûr'sə-nəl) *adj.* showing no emotion or signs of personality
impersonal *adj.* que no muestra emoción o indicios de personalidad

impertinent (ĭm-pûr'tn-ənt) *adj.* rude; insolent
impertinente *adj.* rudo; insolente

implacable (ĭm-plăk'ə-bəl) *adj.* impossible to appease or satisfy; relentless
implacable *adj.* imposible de apaciguar o satisfacer; despiadado

imploring (ĭm-plôr'ĭng) *adj.* begging; making an urgent appeal **implore** *v.*
implorante *adj.* suplicante; que hace un ruego urgente **implorar** *v.*

imposing (ĭm-pō'zĭng) *adj.* impressive
imponente *adj.* impresionante

impotently (ĭm'pə-tənt-lē) *adv.* helplessly; powerlessly
impotentemente *adv.* inútilmente; sin poder

impudent (ĭm'pyə-dənt) *adj.* bold and shameless
impúdico *adj.* atrevido y desvergonzado

incessantly (ĭn-sĕs'ənt-lē) *adv.* endlessly; constantly
incesantemente *adv.* sin final; constantemente

incredulously (ĭn-krĕj'ə-ləs-lē) *adv.* in a manner expressing skepticism or disbelief
incrédulamente *adv.* con escepticismo o desconfianza

indelible (ĭn-dĕl'ə-bəl) *adj.* impossible to remove or eliminate; permanent
indeleble *adj.* imposible de quitar o eliminar; permanente

indifferently (ĭn-dĭf'ər-ənt-lē) *adv.* in a way showing no particular interest or concern
indiferentemente *adv.* sin interés o preocupación

indignation (ĭn'dĭg-nā'shən) *n.* anger aroused by something unjust, mean, or unworthy
indignación *s.* ira causada por injusticia o crueldad

indomitable (ĭn-dŏm'ĭ-tə-bəl) *adj.* not easily discouraged, defeated, or subdued
indomable *adj.* que no es fácilmente desalentado, derrotado o sometido

infatuated (ĭn-făch'o͞o-ā'tĭd) *adj.* completely carried away by foolish or shallow love or attraction **infatuate** *v.*
encaprichado *adj.* enamorado tonta o superficialmente **encapricharse** *v.*

infernal (ĭn-fûr'nəl) *adj.* fit to have come from hell; outrageous
infernal *adj.* como salido del infierno; escandaloso

infinitesimally (ĭn'fĭn-ĭ-tĕs'ə-mə-lē) *adv.* in steps so small as to be immeasurable or incalculable
infinitesimalmente *adv.* en tramos o pasos tan pequeños que no puede ser medido; incalculable

ingenious (ĭn-jēn'yəs) *adj.* creatively clever
ingenioso *adj.* ocurrente; de inteligencia creativa

insolence (ĭn'sə-ləns) *n.* bold rudeness; insulting behavior
insolencia *s.* rudeza descarada; conducta ofensiva

1244 GLOSSARY OF WORDS TO KNOW

insuperable (ĭn-so͞o'pər-ə-bəl) *adj.* impossible to overcome
insuperable *adj.* imposible de vencer

intemperate (ĭn-tĕm'pər-ĭt) *adj.* extreme
inmoderado *adj.* extremado; desmedido

interminable (ĭn-tûr'mə-nə-bəl) *adj.* endless or seemingly endless
interminable *adj.* que no tiene final o parece no tener fin

irate (ī-rāt') *adj.* extremely angry; enraged
iracundo *adj.* muy enojado; furioso

irrelevant (ĭ-rĕl'ə-vənt) *adj.* not related to the matter at hand
irrelevante *adj.* que no tiene relación con el tema o la situación

irreparably (ĭ-rĕp'ər-ə-blē) *adv.* in a way that is impossible to repair or correct
irreparablemente *adv.* de forma que es imposible de reparar o corregir

L

lamentation (lăm'ən-tā'shən) *n.* an expression of grief
lamentación *s.* expresión de dolor

languidly (lăng'gwĭd-lē) *adv.* without vigor or energy; listlessly
lánguidamente *adv.* sin vigor o energía; débilmente

languish (lăng'gwĭsh) *v.* to suffer with longing
languidecer *v.* sufrir abatimiento o debilidad

lethargy (lĕth'ər-jē) *n.* slugishness; unconsciousness
letargo *s.* sopor; inconsciencia

liberty (lĭb'ər-tē) *n.* an action that is too bold or forward
libertades *s.* manera de tratar demasiado atrevida

lithe (līth) *adj.* limber; physically flexible
ágil *adj.* ligero; flexible

lucid (lo͞o'sĭd) *adj.* clear
lúcido *adj.* claro

ludicrous (lo͞o'dĭ-krəs) *adj.* laughably absurd; ridiculous
risible *adj.* tan absurdo que causa risa; ridículo

luminous (lo͞o'mə-nəs) *adj.* bright; brilliant
luminoso *adj.*resplandesciente; brillante

M

majestic (mə-jĕs'tĭk) *adj.* showing lofty dignity or nobility; stately
majestuoso *adj.* que muestra dignidad o nobleza; señorial

maliciously (mə-lĭsh'əs-lē) *adv.* with ill will; spitefully
maliciosamente *adv.* con mala voluntad; perversamente

meager (mē'gər) *adj.* lacking quantity, fullness, strength, or fertility; feeble; scanty
magro *adj.* de poca cantidad, fuerza o fertilidad; débil; escaso

medium (mē'dē-əm) *n.* a specific type of artistic technique or means of expression
medio *s.* tipo específico de técnica artística o de expresión

mentor (mĕn'tôr') *n.* a wise and trusted teacher
mentor *s.* maestro sabio y de confianza

migrant (mī'grənt) *adj.* moving from one area to settle in another
migrante *adj.* que se muda de un lugar para vivir en otro

militant (mĭl'ĭ-tənt) *adj.* showing a fighting spirit; aggressive
militante *adj.* de espíritu de lucha; agresivo

morose (mə-rōs') *adj.* gloomy; sullen
moroso *adj.* lento; triste

mortify (môr'tə-fī') *v.* to cause to feel shame or humiliation
mortificar *v.* causar vergüenza o humillación

muse (myo͞oz) *n.* guiding spirit or source of inspiration
musa *s.* espíritu que guía; fuente de inspiración

GLOSSARY OF WORDS TO KNOW 1245

myopia (mī-ō'pē-ə) *n.* nearsightedness
miopía *s.* cortedad de vista

mystic (mĭs'tĭk) *adj.* showing supernatural powers; spiritual; inspiring mystery or wonder
místico *adj.* que muestra poderes sobrenaturales; espiritual; que inspira misterio o asombro

N

naiveté (nä'ēv-tā') *n.* lack of sophistication; childlike innocence
ingenuidad *s.* falta de sofisticación; inocencia infantil

notorious (nō-tôr'ē-əs) *adj.* having a widely known, usually very badreputation; infamous
notorio *adj.* de mala reputación; tristemente célebre

nuance (no͞o'äns') *n.* subtle or slight variation
matiz *s.* variación sutil o ligera

O

omen (ō'mən) *n.* a thing or event supposed to foretell good or evil; a sign
presagio *s.* cosa o suceso que supuestamente anuncia algo bueno o malo; señal

oppress (ə-prĕs') *v.* to keep down by the cruel or unjust use of power or authority
oprimir *v.* someter mediante poder o autoridad cruel o injusta

oppression (ə-prĕsh'ən) *n.* unjust or cruel exercise of power or authority
opresión *s.* ejercicio injusto o cruel del poder o de la autoridad

ordained (ôr-dānd') *adj.* established by authority or fate **ordain** *v.*
ordenado *adj.* establecido por la autoridad o el destino **ordenar** *v.*

ostensibly (ŏ-stĕn'sə-blē) *adv.* apparently; supposedly
ostensiblemente *adv.* visiblemente; aparentemente; supuestamente

P

pandemonium (păn'də-mō'nē-əm) *n.* a wild uproar or noise
pandemonio *s.* alboroto o escándalo incontrolable

panorama (păn'ə-răm'ə) *n.* an unobstructed view of a wide area
panorama *s.* vista amplia de un lugar; vista sin obstáculos

parry (păr'ē) *v.* to turn aside or avoid (a question) with a clever reply
esquivar *v.* hacerse a un lado; evitar una pregunta con una respuesta ingeniosa

patronize (pā'trə-nīz) *v.* to behave in a manner that shows feelings of superiority
condescender *v.* actuar con superioridad

pendant (pĕn'dənt) *n.* a piece of jewelry made to hang from a necklace or bracelet
dije *s.* pieza de joyería hecha para colgar de un collar o pulsera

penetrate (pĕn'ĭ-trāt') *v.* to enter, especially by forcing a way in
penetrar *v.* entrar, especialmente por medio de la fuerza

penitence (pĕn'ĭ-təns) *n.* expression of regret for sins or wrongdoing
penitencia *s.* expresión de arrepentimiento por pecados o males

pensive (pĕn'sĭv) *adj.* thoughtful in a wistful or sad way
pensativo *adj.* meditabundo; triste o preocupado

perfunctorily (pər-fŭngk'tə-rĭ-lē) *adv.* in a careless, uninterested way
superficialmente *adv.* de manera descuidada; sin interés

perpetrate (pûr'pĭ-trāt') *v.* to commit
perpetrar *v.* cometer

perpetuation (pər-pĕch'o͞o-ā'shən) *n.* a long-lasting continuation
perpetuación *s.* continuación a largo plazo

1246 GLOSSARY OF WORDS TO KNOW

persevere (pûr'sə-vîr') *v.* to persist in the face of difficulties
perseverar *v.* persistir; seguir adelante a pesar de dificultades

perspicacity (pûr'spĭ-kăs'ĭ-tē) *n.* keen perception or understanding
perspicacia *s.* percepción o comprensión aguda o acertada

pertinacity (pûr'tn-ăs'ĭ-tē) *n.* a persistent stubbornness
pertinacia *s.* terquedad; persistencia

perverse (pər-vûrs') *adj.* willfully determined to go against what is expected or desired
perverso *adj.* que actúa con mala intención y se divierte haciendo daño

petulant (pĕch'ə-lənt) *adj.* showing unreasonable annoyance over little things
petulante *adj.* que se molesta en exceso por cosas pequeñas

placidly (plăs'ĭd-lē) *adv.* in an undisturbed manner; quietly; calmly
plácidamente *adv.* de manera tranquila; serenamente; apaciblemente

platitude (plăt'ĭ-to͞od') *n.* a trite or unoriginal statement, especially one expressed as if it were original or significant; a cliché
trivialidad *s.* declaración superficial o poco original, especialmente cuando se expresa como si fuera original o importante; lugar común

ponderous (pŏn'dər-əs) *adj.* very heavy; bulky
pesado *adj.* corpulento; abultado

potent (pōt'nt) *adj.* powerful
potente *adj.* poderoso

precariousness (prĭ-kâr'ē-əs-nĭs) *n.* insecurity; uncertainty
precariedad *s.* inseguridad; incertidumbre

predecessor (prĕd'ĭ-sĕs'ər) *n.* someone who came before and has been succeeded or replaced by another
predecesor *s.* persona anterior o que ocupó un cargo y fue sucedida o reemplazada por otra

preoccupied (prē-ŏk'yə-pīd') *adj.* absorbed in one's thoughts; distracted **preoccupy** *v.*
preocupado *adj.* absorto en sus pensamientos; distraído **preocupar** *v.*

preside (prĭ-zīd') *v.* hold the chief position of authority or control
presidir *v.* ocupar la principal posición de autoridad o control

prestige (prĕ-stēzh') *n.* high status; esteem
prestigio *s.* fama; reconocimiento

presumption (prĭ-zŭmp'shən) *n.* behavior or language that is boldly arrogant or offensive
presunción *s.* conducta o lenguaje arrogante u ofensivo

pretense (prē'tĕns') *n.* a false outward appearance
pretensión *s.* fingimiento; apariencia falsa

prevalent (prĕv'ə-lənt) *adj.* widespread; common
predominante *adj.* ampliamente extendido; frecuente; común

primeval (prī-mē'vəl) *adj.* belonging to the earliest times or ages
primitivo *adj.* que pertenece a las épocas o edades más antiguas

profusely (prə-fyo͞os'lē) *adv.* in great abundance
profusamente *adv.* con mucha abundancia

prowess (prou'ĭs) *n.* superior strength, courage, or daring, especially in battle
valor *s.* gran fuerza, valentía y arrojo, especialmente en la batalla

proximity (prŏk-sĭm'ĭ-tē) *n.* closeness
proximidad *s.* cercanía

prudent (pro͞od'nt) *adj.* caracterized by good judgment
prudente *adj.* caracterizado por el buen juicio

pummel (pŭm'əl) *v.* to hit repeatedly; beat
aporrear *v.* golpear repetidamente; dar puñetazos

Q

quell (kwĕl) *v.* to crush; put an end to; quiet
sofocar *v.* aplastar; poner fin; aquietar

GLOSSARY OF WORDS TO KNOW 1247

R

radiant (rā'dē-ənt) *adj.* bright; glowing
radiante *adj.* brillante; resplandeciente

rank (răngk) *adj.* growing abundantly or excessively
frondoso *adj.* que crece abundante o excesivamente

raspingly (răs'pĭng-lē) *adv.* in a harsh manner; gratingly
ásperamente *adv.* con tono áspero o irritante

raucous (rô'kəs) *adj.* loud and disorderly; boisterous
estridente *adj.* chillón y desordenado; escandaloso

recite (rĭ-sīt') *v.* to say out loud something memorized
recitar *v.* decir en voz alta algo que ha sido memorizado

recompense (rĕk'əm-pĕns') *n.* amends made, as for damage or loss; payment in return for something, such as a service
recompensa *s.* pago como premio o a cambio de un servicio

rejuvenated (rĭ-jo͞o'və-nā'tĭd) *adj.* made new or young again **rejuvenate** *v*
rejuvenecido *adj.* que ha recuperado la juventud **rejuvenecer** *v.*

relapse (rĭ-lăps') *v.* to fall back into a former state
recaer *v.* regresar a un estado anterior

reminiscence (rĕm'ə-nĭs'əns) *n.* pleasant memory or recollection
reminiscencia *s.* recuerdo o evocación placentera

remorse (rĭ-môrs') *n.* a deep sense of guilt over a wrong one has done
remordimiento *s.* profundo sentimiento de culpa por un mal cometido

renounce (rĭ-nouns) *v.* to give up, especially as a matter of principle
renunciar *v.* dejar, especialmente cuando se hace por principios

reprisal (rĭ-prī'zəl) *n.* retaliation in the form of harm or injury similar to that received; revenge
revancha *s.* represalia con daños o heridas similares a los recibidos; venganza

resignation (rĕz'ĭg-nā'shən) *n.* the act of giving up; submission
renuncia *s.* acto de dejar; sumisión

resilient (rĭ-zĭl'yənt) *adj.* capable of bouncing or springing back to an original shape after being stretched, bent, or compressed
elástico *adj.* capaz de regresar a su estado o forma original después de haber sido estirado, doblado o comprimido

resolution (rĕz'ə-lo͞o'shən) *n.* determination
resolución *s.* determinación

respite (rĕs'pĭt) *n.* a temporary stop; a brief period of rest or relief from activity
respiro *s.* tregua; alto temporal; período breve de descanso o alivio

reticence (rĕt'ĭ-səns) *n.* the state or quality of being reserved and keeping one's thoughts to oneself
reticencia *s.* reserva; prudencia y discreción

reverently (rĕv'ər-ənt-lē) *adv.* with great respect
reverentemente *adv.* con gran respeto

revoke (rĭ-vōk') *v.* to cancel or withdraw
revocar *v.* cancelar o retirar

ruefully (ro͞o'fə-lē) *adv.* with regret
tristemente *adv.* con pena o dolor

S

sallow (săl'ō) *adj.* of a sickly, yellowish color or complexion
cetrino *adj.* amarillento y enfermizo

sated (sā'tĭd) *adj.* satisfied fully **sate** *v.*
saciado *adj.* satisfecho por completo **satisfacer** *v.*

saucy (sô'sē) *adj.* disrespectful in a bold or high-spirited way; pert
fresco *adj.* descarado; desfachatado; impertinente

1248 GLOSSARY OF WORDS TO KNOW

sedate (sĭ-dāt′) *adj.* serenely deliberate, composed, and dignified
sereno *adj.* deliberadamente tranquilo, compuesto y digno

sever (sĕv′ər) *v.* to cut or break off
cortar *v.* separar o dividir; romper

sheathed (shēthd) *adj.* enclosed in a protective covering **sheathe** *v.*
enfundado *adj.* envuelto en una cubierta protectora **enfundar** *v.*

shirk (shûrk) *v.* to neglect or avoid
rehuir *v.* ignorar o evitar

sidle (sīd′l) *v.* to move sideways, especially in a shy or sneaky way
escurrirse *v.* moverse de lado con sigilo

smolder (smōl′dər) *v.* to burn without flame; to exist in a concealed form, ready to break out
arder en rescoldo *v.* arder sin llama; estar latente o a la espera

sniveling (snĭv′əl-ĭng) *adj.* whining
llorón *adj.* que lloriquea o gimotea

sodden (sŏd′n) *adj.* thoroughly wet; soaked
empapado *adj.* totalmente mojado; bañado

spontaneous (spŏn-tā′nē-əs) *adj.* occurring or acting without a plan; impulsive
espontáneo *adj.* que ocurre o actúa sin un plan; impulsivo

squalor (skwŏl′ər) *n.* a filthy and wretched condition
escualidez *s.* miseria y suciedad

stature (stăch′ər) *n.* a person's height
estatura *s.* altura de una persona

stealthily (stĕl′thĭ-lē) *adv.* in a quiet, secretive way
furtivamente *adv.* de manera callada y secreta

stipulate (stĭp′yə-lāt′) *v.* to state as a condition; specify
estipular *v.* poner como condición; especificar

stupefied (sto͞o′pə-fīd′) *adj.* dazed; stunned
estupefacto *adj.* asombrado; atónito

stupor (sto͞o′pər) *n.* a state of mental numbness, as from shock
estupor *s.* pasmo; profundo asombro

subliminal (sŭb-lĭm′ə-nəl) *adj.* below the threshold of conscious perception; subconscious
subliminal *adj.* por debajo del umbral de la percepción consciente; subconsciente

sultry (sŭl′trē) *adj.* warm and humid
bochornoso *adj.* caliente y húmedo

supplicating (sŭp′lĭ-kāt′ĭng) *adj.* humbly or sincerely asking, begging, or praying **supplicate** *v.*
suplicante *adj.* que pide, ruega o reza con humildad y sinceridad **suplicar** *v.*

supposition (sŭp′ə-zĭsh′ən) *n.* an opinion or assumption
suposición *s.* opinión o creencia

symmetry (sĭm′ĭ-trē) *n.* a similarity between the two sides of something; balance
simetría *s.* similitud entre los dos lados de algo; equilibrio

synchronizing (sĭng′krə-nī′zĭng) *n.* matching the timing of **synchronize** *v.*
sincronización *s.* operación que se realiza para que dos cosas ocurran al mismo tiempo **sincronizar** *v.*

T

tact (tăkt) *n.* the sensitivity to say and do what is appropriate when dealing with other people
tacto *s.* sensibilidad para tratar a otras personas con delicadeza

taint (tānt) *n.* a trace of something that harms, spoils, or corrupts
mancha *s.* huella de algo que daña, arruina o corrompe

tempering (tĕm′pə-rĭng) *n.* modifying or adjusting **temper** *v.*
modificación *s.* ajuste **modificar** *v.*

tenacity (tə-năs′ĭ-tē) *n.* the state or quality of holding persistently to something; firm determination
tenacidad *s.* tesón y constancia; obstinación

tentatively (tĕn′tə-tĭv-lē) *adv.* hesitantly; uncertainly
tentativamente *adv.* dudosamente; inciertamente

GLOSSARY OF WORDS TO KNOW 1249

Glossary of Words to Know

terse (tûrs) *adj.* brief; concise
seco *adj.* cortante; breve; conciso

thatched (thăcht) *adj.* covered with plant stalks or leaves **thatch** *v.*
techado de paja *adj.* cubierto con ramas u hojas **techar con paja** *v.*

theological (thē'ə-lŏj'ĭ-kəl) *adj.* having to do with the study of God and religion
teológico *adj.* relacionado con el estudio de Dios y la religión

tirade (tī'răd') *n.* a long, angry speech
perorata *s.* discurso largo y con ira

transcend (trăn-sĕnd') *v.* to move above and beyond; to be greater than expected or desired
trascender *v.* rebasar; ser mejor de lo esperado o deseado

transgress (trăns-grĕs') *v.* to violate or break a law, command, or moral code
transgredir *v.* violar una ley, una orden o un código moral

traverse (trə-vûrs') *v.* to travel or pass across, over, or through
atravesar *v.* viajar de un lado a otro de un lugar o de una cosa

treacherous (trĕch'ər-əs) *adj.* dangerous
peligroso *adj.* inseguro; traicionero

trepidation (trĕp'ĭ-dā'shən) *n.* a state of alarm or dread; apprehension; anxiety
trepidación *s.* estado de alarma o miedo; aprensión; ansiedad

tribulation (trĭb'yə-lā'shən) *n.* great distress or suffering
tribulación *s.* gran sufrimiento o preocupación

U

unassuming (ŭn'ə-so͞o'mĭng) *adj.* not pretentious; modest
modesto *adj.* sin pretensiones; humilde

unavailing (ŭn'ə-vā'lĭng) *adj.* useless; ineffective
inservible *adj.* inútil; ineficaz

uncanny (ŭn-kăn'ē) *adj.* strange; eerie; weird
extraordinario *adj.* extraño; misterioso; raro

undulate (ŭn'jə-lāt') *v.* to move in waves or in a smooth, wavelike motion
ondular *v.* mover en forma de ondas; mover suavemente como las olas

unfathomable (ŭn-făth'ə-mə-bəl) *adj.* too mysterious to be understood
insondable *adj.* inexplicable; misterioso

unnervingly (ŭn-nûrv'ĭng-lē) *adv.* in a way that causes someone to become nervous or upset; disturbingly
desconcertantemente *adv.* de manera que causa nerviosismo o alteración; inquietantemente

V

vacillating (văs'ə-lāt'ĭng) *adj.* swinging indecisively from one course of action or opinion to another **vacillate** *v.*
vacilante *adj.* indeciso; que cambia de parecer **vacilar** *v.*

vagrant (vā'grənt) *adj.* wandering
vagabundo *adj.* que va de un lado al otro sin rumbo fijo

vague (vāg) *adj.* unclear; hazy
vago *adj.* confuso; impreciso

venerable (vĕn'ər-ə-bəl) *adj.* worthy of respect by virtue of age or dignity
venerable *adj.* que merece respeto por su edad o dignidad

versatility (vûr'sə-tĭl'ĭ-tē) *n.* an ability to do many things well
versatilidad *s.* capacidad para hacer muchas cosas bien

vibrant (vī'brənt) *adj.* full of energy and activity
vibrante *adj.* lleno de energía y actividad

vigil (vĭj'əl) *n.* a watch kept by a person, especially during normal sleeping hours or to show devotion
vigilia *s.* vela; desvelo; acción de mantenerse despierto de noche o como señal de devoción

vigilance (vĭj'ə-ləns) *n.* alert attention; watchfulness
vigilancia *s.* atención alerta; cuidado

1250 GLOSSARY OF WORDS TO KNOW

vindicate (vĭn'dĭ-kāt') *v.* to clear of blame or suspicion
vindicar *v.* justificar; retirar culpa o sospecha

visceral (vĭs'ər-əl) *adj.* instinctive or emotional rather than intellectual
visceral *adj.* instintivo; más emocional que intelectual

vivacious (vĭ-vā'shəs) *adj.* lively; spirited
vivaz *adj.* animado; vital; lleno de vida

void (void) *n.* a feeling of loss; emptiness
desolación *s.* sentimiento de pérdida; vacío

voluble (vŏl'yə-bəl) *adj.* in or with a long flow of words; talkative
locuaz *adj.* hablador; charlatán

voracity (vô-răs'ĭ-tē) *n.* greed for food; ravenousness
voracidad *s.* apetito ansioso; hambre intensa

vulnerable (vŭl'nər-ə-bəl) *adj.* unprotected and easily hurt; sensitive
vulnerable *adj.* desprotegido y fácil de lastimar; delicado

W

wince (wĭns) *v.* to shrink or flinch involuntarily, especially in pain
estremecerse *v.* encogerse o contraerse involuntariamente por dolor

wistful (wĭst'fəl) *adj.* full of wishful longing; sad
melancólico *adj.* lleno de nostalgia; triste

withered (wĭth'ərd) *adj.* shriveled or shrunken, as if from lack of water or food
marchito *adj.* seco encogido por falta de agua o de comida

GLOSSARY OF WORDS TO KNOW 1251

Glossary of Words to Know

Pronunciation Key

Symbol	Examples	Symbol	Examples	Symbol	Examples
ă	at, gas	m	man, seem	v	van, save
ā	ape, day	n	night, mitten	w	web, twice
ä	father, barn	ng	sing, anger	y	yard, lawyer
âr	fair, dare	ŏ	odd, not	z	zoo, reason
b	bell, table	ō	open, road, grow	zh	treasure, garage
ch	chin, lunch	ô	awful, bought, horse	ə	awake, even, pencil, pilot, focus
d	dig, bored	oi	coin, boy	ər	perform, letter
ĕ	egg, ten	o͝o	look, full		
ē	evil, see, meal	o͞o	root, glue, through		
f	fall, laugh, phrase	ou	out, cow		
g	gold, big	p	pig, cap		
h	hit, inhale	r	rose, star		
hw	white, everywhere	s	sit, face		
ĭ	inch, fit	sh	she, mash		
ī	idle, my, tried	t	tap, hopped		
îr	dear, here	th	thing, with		
j	jar, gem, badge	*th*	then, other		
k	keep, cat, luck	ŭ	up, nut		
l	load, rattle	ûr	fur, earn, bird, worm		

Sounds in Foreign Words

KH	*German* ich, auch; *Scottish* loch
N	*French* entre, bon, fin
œ	*French* feu, cœur; *German* schön
ü	*French* utile, rue; *German* grün

Stress Marks

ʹ This mark indicates that the preceding syllable receives the primary stress. For example, in the word *language,* the first syllable is stressed: lăngʹgwĭj.

ʹ This mark is used only in words in which more than one syllable is stressed. It indicates that the preceding syllable is stressed, but somewhat more weakly than the syllable receiving the primary stress. In the word *literature,* for example, the first syllable receives the primary stress, and the last syllable receives a weaker stress: lĭtʹər-ə-cho͝orʹ.

1252 GLOSSARY OF WORDS TO KNOW

Index of Fine Art

INDEX OF FINE ART **1253**

1254 INDEX OF FINE ART

INDEX OF FINE ART **1255**

Index of Skills

Literary Concepts

1256 INDEX OF SKILLS

INDEX OF SKILLS 1257

Reading and Critical Thinking Skills

1258 INDEX OF SKILLS

INDEX OF SKILLS **1259**

1260 INDEX OF SKILLS

Vocabulary Skills

Grammar, Usage, and Mechanics

INDEX OF SKILLS 1261

1262 INDEX OF SKILLS

INDEX OF SKILLS **1263**

Writing Skills, Modes, and Formats

1264 INDEX OF SKILLS

INDEX OF SKILLS **1265**

Inquiry and Research

1266 INDEX OF SKILLS

INDEX OF SKILLS **1267**

1268 INDEX OF SKILLS

Speaking and Listening

Viewing and Representing

INDEX OF SKILLS 1269

Assessment

1270 INDEX OF SKILLS

Index of Titles and Authors

Page numbers that appear in italics refer to biographical information.

INDEX OF TITLES AND AUTHORS **1271**

1272 INDEX OF TITLES AND AUTHORS

INDEX OF TITLES AND AUTHORS **1273**

Acknowledgments *(continued)*

Unit One

Don Congdon Associates: "A Sound of Thunder" by Ray Bradbury. First published in *Collier's,* 28 June 1952. Copyright © 1952 by Crowell-Collier Publishing, renewed 1980 by Ray Bradbury. Reprinted by permission of Don Congdon Associates, Inc.

Excerpt from "An Interview with Ray Bradbury" by Frank Filosa, from *On Being a Writer* (Cincinnati: Writer's Digest Books, 1989). Copyright © 1989 by Writer's Digest Books. Reprinted by permission of Don Congdon Associates, Inc.

"There Will Come Soft Rains" by Ray Bradbury. First Published in *Collier's,* 6 May 1950. Copyright © 1950 by Crowell-Collier Publishing, renewed 1977 by Ray Bradbury. Reprinted by permission of Don Congdon Associates, Inc.

"The Pedestrian" by Ray Bradbury. First published in *The Reporter,* 7 August 1951. Copyright © 1951 by The Fortnightly Publishing Company, renewed 1979 by Ray Bradbury. Reprinted by permission of Don Congdon Associates, Inc.

Ralph M. Vicinanza, Ltd.: "Dial Versus Digital," from *The Dangers of Intelligence and Other Scientific Essays* by Isaac Asimov. Copyright © 1986 by Isaac Asimov. Published by permission of the Estate of Isaac Asimov, c/o Ralph M. Vicinanza, Ltd.

Tilbury House: "Once More to the Lake," from *One Man's Meat* by E. B. White. Text copyright © 1941 by E. B. White, renewed 1998 by Joel White. Reprinted by permission of Tilbury House, Publishers, Gardiner, Maine.

E. B. White Estate: Excerpt from "A Letter from E. B. White" by E. B. White (*The Norton Sampler,* 1985). Reprinted by permission of Allene M. White on behalf of the E. B. White Estate.

Henry Holt & Company: "Montgomery Boycott," from *My Life with Martin Luther King, Jr.* (rev. ed.) by Coretta Scott King. Copyright © 1969, 1993 by Coretta Scott King. Reprinted by permission of Henry Holt & Company, Inc.

University of Georgia Press: "Sit-Ins," from *This Is My Century: New and Collected Poems* by Margaret Walker Alexander. Copyright © 1989 by Margaret Walker Alexander. Reprinted by permission of the University of Georgia Press.

Simon & Schuster and Jonathan Clowes Ltd.: "No Witchcraft for Sale," from *African Stories* by Doris Lessing. Copyright © 1951, 1953, 1954, 1957, 1958, 1962, 1963, 1964, 1965, 1972, 1981 by Doris Lessing. Reprinted with the permission of Simon & Schuster and Jonathan Clowes Ltd., London, on behalf of Doris Lessing.

Farrar, Straus & Giroux: "The Son from America," from *A Crown of Feathers and Other Stories* by Isaac Bashevis Singer. Copyright © 1973 by Isaac Bashevis Singer. Reprinted by permission of Farrar, Straus & Giroux, Inc.

W. W. Norton & Company: "Grudnow," from *The Imperfect Paradise* by Linda Pastan. Copyright © 1988 by Linda Pastan. Reprinted by permission of W. W. Norton & Company, Inc.

Phoebe Larmore Literary Agency: "Through the One-Way Mirror" by Margaret Atwood, *The Nation,* 22 March 1986. Reprinted by permission of Phoebe Larmore Literary Agency on behalf of the author.

University of New Mexico Press: "The Border: A Glare of Truth," from *Nepantla: Essays from the Land in the Middle* by Pat Mora. Copyright © 1993 by University of New Mexico Press. Reprinted by permission of the University of New Mexico Press.

U.S. News & World Report: Excerpt from "To Make a Nation: How Immigrants Are Changing America" by Penny Loeb, Dorian Friedman, and Mary C. Lord, with Dan

McGraw and Kukula Glastris, *U.S. News & World Report,* 4 October 1993. Copyright © October 4, 1993, U.S. News & World Report. Reprinted by permission.

Sandra Dijkstra Literary Agency: "Fish Cheeks" by Amy Tan. First appeared in the *Seventeen Magazine.* Copyright © 1987 by Amy Tan. Reprinted by permission of Amy Tan and the Sandra Dijkstra Literary Agency.

Doubleday and Harold Ober Associates: "Marriage Is a Private Affair," from *Girls at War and Other Stories* by Chinua Achebe. Copyright © 1972, 1973 by Chinua Achebe. Used by permission of Doubleday, a division of Bantam Doubleday Dell Publishing Group, Inc., and Harold Ober Associates Incorporated.

Chinese Literature Press: "Love Must Not Be Forgotten" by Zhang Jie, from *Seven Contemporary Chinese Women Writers* (Panda Books, 1982). Published by Chinese Literature Press, Beijing, China. Copyright © 1983 by Chinese Literature Press. Reprinted by permission of Chinese Literature Press.

Katie Eskra: Adaptation of "A Momentary Sadness" by Katie Eskra. Copyright © 1995 by Katie Eskra. Reprinted by permission of the author.

Unit Two

Viking Penguin: "Piano" by D. H. Lawrence, from *The Complete Poems of D. H. Lawrence,* edited by V. de Sola Pinto and F. W. Roberts. Copyright © 1964, 1971 by Angelo Ravagli and C. M. Weekley, Executors of the Estate of Frieda Lawrence Ravagli. Used by permission of Viking Penguin, a division of Penguin Putnam Inc.

Liveright Publishing Corporation: "Those Winter Sundays," from *Angle of Ascent: New and Selected Poems* by Robert Hayden. Copyright © 1966 by Robert Hayden. Reprinted by permission of Liveright Publishing Corporation.

Elizabeth Barnett, Literary Executor: Sonnet XXX of *Fatal Interview,* from *Collected Poems* by Edna St. Vincent Millay (HarperCollins). Copyright © 1931, 1958 by Edna St. Vincent Millay and Norma Millay Ellis. All rights reserved. Reprinted by permission of Elizabeth Barnett, Literary Executor.

Eugenia Collier: "Sweet Potato Pie" by Eugenia Collier, from *Black World* magazine, 1969. Copyright © 1969 by Eugenia W. Collier. Reprinted by permission of the author.

Susan Bergholz Literary Services: "Salvador Late or Early," from *Woman Hollering Creek and Other Stories* by Sandra Cisneros. Copyright © 1991 by Sandra Cisneros. Published by Vintage Books, a division of Random House, Inc., and originally in hardcover by Random House, Inc. Reprinted by permission of Susan Bergholz Literary Services, New York. All rights reserved.

N. Scott Momaday: "Simile," from *Angle of Geese and Other Poems* by N. Scott Momaday. Copyright © 1974 by N. Scott Momaday. Reprinted by permission of the author.

Harcourt Brace & Company: "Moon Rondeau," from *Honey and Salt* by Carl Sandburg. Copyright © 1958 by Carl Sandburg and renewed 1986 by Margaret Sandburg, Helga Sandburg Crile, and Janet Sandburg. Reprinted by permission of Harcourt Brace & Company.

William Morrow & Company: "Woman," from *Cotton Candy on a Rainy Day* by Nikki Giovanni. Copyright © 1978 by Nikki Giovanni. Reprinted by permission of William Morrow & Company, Inc.

St. Martin's Press and Harold Ober Associates: "A Case of Cruelty," from *All Things Bright and Beautiful* by James Herriot. Copyright © 1973, 1974 by James Herriot. Reprinted by permission of St. Martin's Press, Incorporated and Harold Ober Associates Incorporated.

Joan Daves Agency: "Ocho Perritos"/"Eight Puppies" by Gabriela Mistral, from *Selected Poems of Gabriela Mistral,* translated by Doris Dana. Copyright © 1971 by Doris

ACKNOWLEDGMENTS **1275**

Dana. Reprinted by arrangement with Doris Dana, c/o Joan Daves Agency as agent for the proprietor.

Time Inc.: "An Angry Public Backs Champ," *People Weekly,* 21 May 1990. Copyright © 1990 Time Inc. Reprinted by permission.

Sheila Schmitt: "Through Whispers in the Wind" by Sheila Schmitt. Copyright © 1997 by Sheila Schmitt. Reprinted by permission of the author.

The Apprentice Writer: "Perspective" by Nathan Fellman, *The Apprentice Writer* 14 (1997). Reprinted by permission of *The Apprentice Writer,* Susquehanna University, Selinsgrove, Pennsylvania.

Hanging Loose Press: "In the Steel City" by Mara Noëlle Scanlon, from *Bullseye: Stories and Poems by Outstanding High School Writers,* edited by Mark Pawlak and Dick Lourie. Copyright © 1995 by Hanging Loose Press. Reprinted by permission.

Sterling Lord Literistic: *The Bear* by Anton Chekhov, translated by Ronald Hingley. Copyright © 1968 by Ronald Hingley. Reprinted by permission of Sterling Lord Literistic, Inc.

American Heritage Magazine: "Gold Is Found and a Nation Goes Wild," from *The American Heritage Book of the Pioneer Spirit.* Copyright © Forbes, Inc. Reprinted by permission of American Heritage Magazine, a division of Forbes, Inc.

Elizabeth Walsh Peavoy, Literary Executor: "Brigid," from *Collected Stories* by Mary Lavin (Boston: Houghton Mifflin, 1971). Copyright © 1971 by Mary Lavin. Reprinted by permission of Elizabeth Walsh Peavoy, Literary Executor.

Felicity Bryan: "Lalla," from *Love Stories* by Rosamunde Pilcher. Copyright © Rosamunde Pilcher. Reprinted by permission of Felicity Bryan, Oxford, England.

Editorial Cordillera: "Love Without Love" ("Amor sin amor") by Luis Lloréns Torres. Copyright © 1967 by Editorial Cordillera. Reprinted by permission of Editorial Cordillera, San Juan, Puerto Rico.

Random House UK: "Puedo Escribir Los Versos"/"Tonight I Can Write . . . ," from *Selected Poems* by Pablo Neruda, translated by W. S. Merwin. Originally published by Jonathan Cape Ltd. Reprinted by permission of Random House UK Ltd.

Doubleday: Excerpt from *Love & Marriage* by Bill Cosby. Copyright © 1989 by Bill Cosby. Used by permission of Doubleday, a division of Bantam Doubleday Dell Publishing Group, Inc.

Unit Three

HarperCollins Publishers: "Initiation," from *Johnny Panic and the Bible of Dreams* by Sylvia Plath. Copyright © 1952, 1953, 1954, 1955, 1956, 1957, 1960, 1961, 1962, 1963 by Sylvia Plath. Copyright © 1977, 1979 by Ted Hughes. Reprinted by permission of HarperCollins Publishers, Inc.

Letter, October 6, 1952, by Sylvia Plath, from *Letters Home by Sylvia Plath: Correspondence, 1950–1963* by Aurelia Schober Plath. Copyright © 1975 by Aurelia Schober Plath. Reprinted by permission of HarperCollins Publishers, Inc.

Random House: Excerpt from *I Know Why the Caged Bird Sings* by Maya Angelou. Copyright © 1969 and renewed 1997 by Maya Angelou. Reprinted by permission of Random House, Inc.

Academy Chicago Publishers: "The Opportunity" by John Cheever, from *Thirteen Uncollected Stories by John Cheever,* edited by Franklin H. Dennis. Copyright © 1994 by Academy Chicago Publishers. Reprinted by arrangement with Academy Chicago Publishers, Ltd..

Susan Bergholz Literary Services: "Exile," from *The Other Side/El Otro Lado* by Julia Alvarez, published by Dutton, a division of Penguin USA. Copyright © 1995 by

1276 ACKNOWLEDGMENTS

Julia Alvarez. Reprinted by permission of Susan Bergholz Literary Services, New York. All rights reserved.

Excerpt from "A Celebration of Grandfathers" by Rudolfo Anaya. First published in *New Mexico Magazine,* March 1983. Copyright © 1983 by Rudolfo Anaya. Reprinted by permission of Susan Bergholz Literary Services, New York. All rights reserved.

Yale University Press: "Lost Sister," from *Picture Bride* by Cathy Song. Copyright © 1983 by Cathy Song. Reprinted by permission of Yale University Press.

W. W. Norton & Company: "Fifth Grade Autobiography," from *Grace Notes* by Rita Dove. Copyright © 1989 by Rita Dove. Reprinted by permission of the author and W. W. Norton & Company, Inc.

Naomi Shihab Nye: "Remembered," from *Words Under the Words: Selected Poems* by Naomi Shihab Nye. Copyright © 1980, 1982, 1986, 1995 by Naomi Shihab Nye. Reprinted by permission of the author.

Alfred A. Knopf and Joan Daves Agency: "The Study of History," from *Collected Stories* by Frank O'Connor. Originally appeared in *The New Yorker.* Copyright © 1957 by Frank O'Connor. Copyright © 1981 by Harriet O'Donovan Sheehy, Executrix of the Estate of Frank O'Connor. Reprinted by permission of Alfred A. Knopf, Inc., and by arrangement with Harriet O'Donovan Sheehy, Executrix of the Estate of Frank O'Connor, c/o Joan Daves Agency as agent for the proprietor.

Time Inc.: Excerpt from "Were You Born That Way?" by George Howe Colt, *Life,* April 1998. Copyright © 1998 Time Inc. Reprinted by permission.

Nicholas Gage: "The Teacher Who Changed My Life" by Nicholas Gage, *Parade,* 17 December 1989. Copyright © 1989 by Nicholas Gage. Reprinted by permission of the author.

Alfred A. Knopf: "Afro-American Fragment," from *Collected Poems* by Langston Hughes. Copyright © 1994 by the Estate of Langston Hughes. Reprinted by permission of Alfred A. Knopf, Inc.

Carcanet Press: "Bora Ring," from *Collected Poems, 1942–1985* by Judith Wright. Copyright © 1994 Judith Wright. Reprinted by permission of Carcanet Press Limited.

Harcourt Brace & Company: "Everyday Use," from *In Love & Trouble: Stories of Black Women* by Alice Walker. Copyright © 1973 by Alice Walker. Reprinted by permission of Harcourt Brace & Company.

"Women," from *Revolutionary Petunias & Other Poems* by Alice Walker. Copyright © 1970 by Alice Walker. Reprinted by permission of Harcourt Brace & Company.

"Poem at Thirty-Nine," from *Horses Make a Landscape Look More Beautiful* by Alice Walker. Copyright © 1983 by Alice Walker. Reprinted by permission of Harcourt Brace & Company.

Excerpt from "In Search of Our Mothers' Gardens," from *In Search of Our Mothers' Gardens: Womanist Prose* by Alice Walker. Copyright © 1974 by Alice Walker. Reprinted by permission of Harcourt Brace & Company.

Wendy Weil Agency: "On Writing Poetry" by Alice Walker, excerpt from *Interviews with Black Writers* by John O'Brien. Copyright © 1973 by Alice Walker. Reprinted by permission of the Wendy Weil Agency on behalf of Alice Walker.

Jack Clark: Excerpt from "West Side Stories" by Mary Jo Clark as told to Jack Clark, *Reader* [Chicago], 26 June 1998. Copyright © 1998 by Jack Clark and Mary Jo Clark. Reprinted by permission of Jack Clark.

Unit Four

Carroll & Graf Publishers: "Two Friends" by Guy de Maupassant, from *The Dark Side of Guy de Maupassant,* translated by Arnold Kellett. Copyright © 1972, 1976, 1989 by Arnold Kellett. Reprinted by permission of Carroll & Graf Publishers Inc.

ACKNOWLEDGMENTS **1277**

Holmes & Meier Publishers: Poem XXIII of *Versos Sencillos/Simple Poetry* by José Martí, from *José Martí: Major Poems, a Bilingual Edition,* translated by Elinor Randall and edited by Philip S. Foner (New York: Holmes & Meier, 1982). Copyright © 1982 by Holmes & Meier Publishers, Inc. Reproduced with the permission of the publisher.

Gwendolyn Brooks: "The Sonnet-Ballad," from *Blacks* by Gwendolyn Brooks (Chicago: Third World Press, 1991). Copyright © 1991 by Gwendolyn Brooks. Reprinted by permission of the author.

Peter H. Lee: "Cranes" by Hwang Sunwŏn, translated by Peter H. Lee, from *Flowers of Fire: Twentieth-Century Korean Stories,* edited by Peter H. Lee. Reprinted by permission of Peter H. Lee.

Newsweek: Excerpt from "The Remembered War: A Korean War Vet Offers a History Lesson" by Angus Deming, *Newsweek,* 7 August 1995. Copyright © 1995 Newsweek, Inc. All rights reserved. Reprinted by permission.

Hill and Wang: Excerpt from *Night* by Elie Wiesel. Copyright © 1960 by MacGibbon & Kee. Copyright renewed © 1988 by The Collins Publishing Group. Reprinted by permission of Hill and Wang, a division of Farrar, Straus & Giroux, Inc.

Nobel Foundation: Excerpt from Nobel Prize acceptance speech by Elie Wiesel. Copyright © 1962 The Nobel Foundation. Reprinted by permission of The Nobel Foundation.

Houghton Mifflin Company: Excerpt from *Farewell to Manzanar* by James D. Houston and Jeanne Wakatsuki Houston. Copyright © 1973 by James D. Houston. Reprinted by permission of Houghton Mifflin Company. All rights reserved.

Houghton Mifflin Company/Seymour Lawrence: "On the Rainy River," from *The Things They Carried* by Tim O'Brien. Copyright © 1990 by Tim O'Brien. Reprinted by permission of Houghton Mifflin Company/Seymour Lawrence. All rights reserved.

W. W. Norton & Company: "Ghost of a Chance," from *Collected Early Poems, 1950–1970* by Adrienne Rich. Copyright © 1993, 1967, 1963 by Adrienne Rich. Reprinted by permission of the author and W. W. Norton & Company, Inc.

Liveright Publishing Corporation: "look at this)," from *Complete Poems, 1904–1962* by E. E. Cummings, edited by George J. Firmage. Copyright 1926, 1954, © 1991 by the Trustees for the E. E. Cummings Trust. Copyright © 1985 by George J. Firmage. Reprinted by permission of Liveright Publishing Corporation.

John Johnson Ltd.: "The Prisoner Who Wore Glasses," from *Tales of Tenderness and Power* by Bessie Head, published by Heinemann International in the African Writers Series. Copyright © 1989 The Estate of Bessie Head. Reprinted by permission of John Johnson Ltd. on behalf of the Estate of Bessie Head.

Georges Borchardt, Inc.: Excerpt from "Nelson Mandela" by André Brink, *Time,* 13 April 1998. Copyright © 1998 Time Inc. Reprinted by permission.

Harcourt Brace & Company; the Provost and Scholars of King's College, Cambridge; and The Society of Authors: Excerpt from "Tolerance," from *Two Cheers for Democracy* by E. M. Forster. Copyright © 1951 by E. M. Forster and renewed 1979 by Donald Parry. Reprinted by permission of Harcourt Brace & Company; the Provost and Scholars of King's College, Cambridge; and The Society of Authors as literary representatives of the E. M. Forster Estate.

The Nation: Excerpt from "Julius Caesar" by Thomas M. Disch. Reprinted with permission from the April 23, 1988, issue of *The Nation.*

The New Yorker: "Hail, Caesar!" by Edith Oliver. Originally published in *The New Yorker,* 28 March 1988. Copyright © 1988 Edith Oliver. Reprinted by permission. All rights reserved.

1278 ACKNOWLEDGMENTS

Unit Five

Time Inc.: "The Mouse That Roared" by Richard Woodbury, *Time,* 4 May 1998. Copyright © 1998 Time Inc. Reprinted by permission.

"The Grapes of Wrath: Photo Essay," *Life,* 5 June 1939. Copyright 1939 Time Inc. Reprinted with permission.

Henry Holt & Company: "Birches" by Robert Frost, from *The Poetry of Robert Frost,* edited by Edward Connery Lathem. Copyright © 1944 by Robert Frost. Copyright 1916, © 1969 by Henry Holt & Company. Reprinted by permission of Henry Holt and Company, Inc.

New Directions Publishing Corporation: "For the New Year, 1981," from *Candles in Babylon* by Denise Levertov. Copyright © 1982 by Denise Levertov. Reprinted by permission of New Directions Publishing Corp.

"La calle"/"The Street" by Octavio Paz, from *Early Poems of Octavio Paz,* translated by Muriel Rukeyser. Copyright © 1973 by Octavio Paz and Muriel Rukeyser. Reprinted by permission of New Directions Publishing Corp.

Chana Bloch: "Pride," from *The Window: New and Selected Poems* by Dahlia Ravikovitch, translated and edited by Chana Bloch and Ariel Bloch. Copyright © 1989 by Chana Bloch and Ariel Bloch. Reprinted by permission of Chana Bloch.

Viking Penguin: "Like the Sun," from *Under the Banyan Tree* by R. K. Narayan. Copyright © 1985 by R. K. Narayan. Used by permission of Viking Penguin, a division of Penguin Putnam Inc.

"The Flood," from *The Grapes of Wrath* by John Steinbeck. Copyright 1939, renewed © 1967 by John Steinbeck. Used by permission of Viking Penguin, a division of Penguin Putnam Inc.

Excerpts from *The Grapes of Wrath* by John Steinbeck. Copyright 1939, renewed © 1967 by John Steinbeck. Used by permission of Viking Penguin, a division of Penguin Putnam Inc.

Excerpt from *Travels with Charley* by John Steinbeck. Copyright © 1961, 1962 by The Curtis Publishing Co., © 1962 by John Steinbeck, renewed © 1990 by Elaine Steinbeck, Thom Steinbeck, and John Steinbeck IV. Used by permission of Viking Penguin, a division of Penguin Putnam Inc.

"Nobel Prize Acceptance Speech," from *The Portable Steinbeck* by John Steinbeck, introduction by Pascal Covici. Copyright 1943, renewed © 1971 by The Viking Press, introduction. Used by permission of Viking Penguin, a division of Penguin Putnam Inc.

Estate of Robert Nemiroff: "On Summer" by Lorraine Hansberry. Copyright © 1960 by Robert Nemiroff as Executor of the Estate of Lorraine Hansberry, © 1988 Robert Nemiroff. All rights reserved. Used by permission of the Estate of Robert Nemiroff.

Putnam Berkley and Harold Ober Associates: "The Witness for the Prosecution," from *Witness for the Prosecution and Other Stories* by Agatha Christie. Copyright 1924 by Agatha Christie, renewed. Used by permission of Putnam Berkley, a division of Penguin Putnam Inc., and Harold Ober Associates Incorporated.

Joan Daves Agency and Leila Vennewitz: "The Balek Scales," from *Eighteen Stories* by Heinrich Böll, translated by Leila Vennewitz. Copyright © 1966 by Heinrich Böll. Reprinted by permission of Verlag Kiepenheuer & Witsch, c/o the Joan Daves Agency as agent for the proprietor, and Leila Vennewitz.

Robert Bly: "I Am Not I" by Juan Ramón Jiménez, from *Lorca and Jiménez: Selected Poems,* translated by Robert Bly (Boston: Beacon Press, 1973, 1997). Copyright © 1973, 1997 by Robert Bly. Reprinted by permission of Robert Bly.

Carmen Hernández-Pinzón: "Yo No Soy Yo" by Juan Ramón Jiménez, from *Lorca and Jiménez: Selected Poems,* chosen and translated by Robert Bly (Boston: Beacon Press, 1973, 1997). Copyright © 1973, Herederos de Juan Ramón Jiménez, Madrid, España. Reprinted by permission of Carmen Hernández-Pinzón on behalf of the Estate of Juan Ramón Jiménez.

ACKNOWLEDGMENTS **1279**

Random House: "The Watch," from *The Cabin* by David Mamet. Copyright © 1992 by David Mamet. Reprinted by permission of Random House, Inc.

McIntosh & Otis: "Letter to Edith Mirrielees" by John Steinbeck, from *John Steinbeck: A Study of the Short Fiction,* edited by R. S. Hughes (Boston: Twayne Publishers, 1989). Copyright © 1989 by John Steinbeck. Reprinted by permission of McIntosh & Otis, Inc.

Merlyn's Pen Publishing: "I Am Kwakkoli" by Bisco Hill. First appeared in *Merlyn's Pen* magazine. Copyright © Merlyn's Pen, Inc. All rights reserved. Reprinted by permission of Merlyn's Pen Publishing.

Unit Six

Viking Penguin: "A Chip of Glass Ruby," from *Selected Stories* by Nadine Gordimer. Copyright © 1961 by Nadine Gordimer. Used by permission of Viking Penguin, a division of Penguin Putnam Inc.

Time Inc.: "The Man in the Water" by Roger Rosenblatt, *Time,* 25 January 1982. Copyright © 1982 Time Inc. Reprinted by permission.

Scribner: "And of Clay Are We Created," from *The Stories of Eva Luna* by Isabel Allende, translated from the Spanish by Margaret Sayers Peden. Copyright © 1989 by Isabel Allende. English translation copyright © 1991 by Macmillan Publishing Company. Reprinted with the permission of Scribner, a division of Simon & Schuster.

Magda Bogin: "Nocturne" by Rosario Castellanos, from *The Selected Poems of Rosario Castellanos,* translated by Magda Bogin. Translation copyright © 1988 by Magda Bogin. Reprinted by permission of Magda Bogin.

Fondo de Cultura Económica: "Nocturno" by Rosario Castellanos, from *The Selected Poems of Rosario Castellanos,* edited by Cecilia Vicuña and Magda Bogin. Copyright © 1988 by the Estate of Rosario Castellanos. Reprinted by permission of Fondo de Cultura Económica.

Boston Globe: "Girl Trapped in Water for 55 Hours Dies Despite Rescue Attempts" by Julia Preston, *The Boston Globe,* 16 November 1985. Reprinted courtesy of The Boston Globe.

Harper's Magazine: "The Leap" by Louise Erdrich, *Harper's Magazine,* March 1990. Copyright © 1990 by Harper's Magazine. All rights reserved. Reproduced from the March 1990 issue by special permission.

Harcourt Brace & Company: *Antigone,* from *Sophocles: The Oedipus Cycle, An English Version* by Dudley Fitts and Robert Fitzgerald. Copyright 1939 by Harcourt Brace & Company and renewed © 1967 by Dudley Fitts and Robert Fitzgerald. Reprinted by permission of the publisher. CAUTION: All rights, including professional, amateur, motion picture, recitation, lecturing, performance, public reading, radio broadcasting, and television, are strictly reserved. Inquiries on all rights should be addressed to Harcourt Brace & Company, Permissions Department, Orlando, FL 32887-6777.

Clarkson N. Potter: Excerpts from *Le Morte D'Arthur* by Sir Thomas Malory, translated by Keith Baines. Copyright © 1967 by Keith Baines. Reprinted by permission of Clarkson N. Potter, Inc., a division of Crown Publishers, Inc.

Scovil Chichak Galen Literary Agency: Excerpt from *The Mists of Avalon* by Marion Zimmer Bradley. Copyright © 1982 by Marion Zimmer Bradley. Reprinted by permission of the author and the author's agents, Scovil Chichak Galen Literary Agency, Inc.

Excerpt from "The Once and Future Merlin" by Marion Zimmer Bradley, *TV Guide,* 25 April 1998. Reprinted by permission of the author and the author's agents, Scovil Chichak Galen Literary Agency, Inc.

1280 ACKNOWLEDGMENTS

Farrar, Straus & Giroux: Excerpt from *The Acts of King Arthur and His Noble Knights* by John Steinbeck. Copyright © 1976 by Elaine Steinbeck. Reprinted by permission of Farrar, Straus & Giroux, Inc.

W. W. Norton & Company: "The Knight," from *Collected Early Poems, 1950–1970* by Adrienne Rich. Copyright © 1993, 1967, 1963 by Adrienne Rich. Reprinted by permission of the author and W. W. Norton & Company, Inc.

The editors have made every effort to trace the ownership of all copyrighted material found in this book and to make full acknowledgment for its use. Omissions brought to our attention will be corrected in a subsequent edition.

Reading Handbook

Texas Instruments: Excerpt from *TI-82 Guidebook*. Copyright © 1993, 2000, 2001 Texas Instruments. Reproduced by permission.

Art Credits

Cover, Frontispiece

Illustration copyright © 1998 Lee Christiansen.

Front Matter

x *left, The Spirit of Our Time* (about 1921), Raoul Hausmann. Assemblage with wigmaker's dummy head, 12¾″ high. Collections Musée National d'Art Moderne, Centre Georges Pompidou, Paris; *right, Chicago Tribune* photo by Heather Stone. Copyright © 1998 Chicago Tribune. World rights reserved; **xi** *top* AP/Wide World Photos; *bottom, Girl with Tear III* (1977), Roy Lichtenstein. Oil and magna on canvas, 46″ × 40″. Copyright © Estate of Roy Lichtenstein/Leo Castelli Gallery, New York; **xii** *Red Peonies* (1929), Ch'i Pai-Shih. Ink and colors on paper, 53½″ × 12⅞″. Courtesy of the Arthur M. Sackler Museum, Harvard University Art Museums, loan from the family of F. Y. Chang (321.1985). Copyright © President and Fellows, Harvard College, Harvard University Art Museums; **xiii** *The Lovers (Somali Friends)* (1950), Lois Mailou Jones. Casein on canvas. The Evans-Tibbs Collection, Washington, D.C.; **xv** *Allées Piétonnières* [Pedestrian walkways] (1995), Jean-Pierre Stora. Oil on canvas, 61″× 50″. The Grand Design, Leeds, England/SuperStock; **xvi** *left* Copyright © Ilene Perlman/Impact Visuals/PNI; *right* Haitian drum (1940s), unknown artist. Wood and goat skin, 43″ × 24″ × 24″. Collection of Virgil Young; **xvii** Copyright © Michael Yamashita; **xviii** *bottom, Hombre y su sombra* [Man and his shadow] (1971), Rufino Tamayo. Oil on canvas, 50 cm × 40 cm. Collection of INBA–Museo de Arte Moderno, Mexico City; **xix** Martha Swope. Copyright © Time Inc.; **xx** *Sea Jewels* (1995), Paul Niemiec, Jr. Watercolor, 18″ × 28″. Collection of Mr. and Mrs. Stephen H. Palmer; **xxi** Copyright © Archive Photos/PNI; **xxii** *right* Musée de Picardie, Amiens, France/Giraudon/Art Resource, New York; **xxiii** Antikensammlung, Munich, Germany/Erich Lessing/Art Resource, New York; **2** *right* Photofest; **3** *left* Copyright © Hallmark Entertainment/Shooting Star. All rights reserved; *right* Illustration by Arthur Rackham. Christie's Images, New York; **6–7** Copyright © 1993 Jay Ullah/Stern/Black Star.

Unit One

29 AP/Wide World Photos; **40** Copyright © Sovfoto/Eastfoto/PNI; **42** *Toto* (1988), Jimmy Lee Sudduth. Paint with mud on wood, 31¾″ × 24″. From *American Self-Taught* by Frank Maresca and Roger Ricco, published by Knopf, 1993; **55** National Archives; **57** *background* Copyright © Michael W. Thomas/Stock South/PNI; **60, 64, 65** Copyright © 1997 PhotoDisc; **66** Canapress Photo Service; **67–71** *border* Photo by Sharon Hoogstraten; **67** *portrait* AP/Wide World Photos; *frame* Photo by Sharon Hoogstraten; **68** *top* Courtesy of Bantam Doubleday Books; *bottom* Sovfoto/Eastfoto; **69** NASA; **70** *top, center left* Photofest; *center right* Copyright © 1988 PhotoDisc; *bottom right* Copyright © 1990

ACKNOWLEDGMENTS **1281**

Chicago Sun-Times. Reprinted with permission; **71** Copyright © 1996 Glenn Dean; **72–73, 74, 79** *ferns* Photo by Sharon Hoogstraten; **72, 74, 76–77, 78, 79** *patterned background* Copyright © 1995 PhotoDisc; **81, 82–83** *border,* **83** Photos by Sharon Hoogstraten; **84, 85** Copyright © 1986 Jay Kay Klein; **86** *Girl with Tear III* (1977), Roy Lichtenstein. Oil and magna on canvas, 46″× 40″. Copyright © Estate of Roy Lichtenstein/Leo Castelli Gallery, New York; **93–95** *border* Photo by Sharon Hoogstraten; **95** *Flying Man with Briefcase No. 2816932* (1983), Jonathan Borofsky. Painted Gatorfoam, 94½″ × 24½″ × 1″. Copyright © 1983 Jonathan Borofsky/Gemini G.E.L., Los Angeles, California; **101–103** *border* Photo by Sharon Hoogstraten; **102, 103** *portraits* Copyright © 1986 Jay Kay Klein; **111** AP/Wide World Photos; **112** *Morning of Life* (1907), David Ericson. Oil on canvas, 27″ × 22¼″. Collection of Tweed Museum of Art, University of Minnesota, Duluth, gift of Mrs. E. L. Tuohy; **113, 118** *backgrounds* Illustration by Gary Head; **122** Photo courtesy of Maria Mariottini; **123** The Granger Collection, New York; **134** Copyright © 1965 Bob Adelman/Magnum Photos; **135** Globe Photos; **136** UPI/Corbis-Bettmann; **138–142** Photos by Sharon Hoogstraten; **148** Detail of *The Ukimwi Road* (1994), John Harris; **157** H. Armstrong Roberts; **158** Globe Photos; **159, 163, 165** Photos by Sharon Hoogstraten; **168** Copyright © Bill Aron/PhotoEdit; **169** AP/Wide World Photos; **171** *left, right* Copyright © 1997 PhotoDisc; *center* Copyright © Warner Brothers/Shooting Star; **173** Photofest; **174–175** R. Krubner/H. Armstrong Roberts; **176, 177** *top* Photos by Sharon Hoogstraten; **177** *bottom* Corbis; **180** *left* Photo by Anthony Loew; *right* Arte Público Press; **186** *portrait* AP/Wide World Photos; **187** Corbis; **188** *Wooing* (1984), Varnette Honeywood. Collage. Copyright © 1984 Varnette P. Honeywood; **195** The Schomburg Center for Research in Black Culture, The New York Public Library, Astor, Lenox and Tilden Foundations; **197** *Red Peonies* (1929), Ch'i Pai-Shih. Ink and colors on paper, 53½″ × 12⅞″. Courtesy of the Arthur M. Sackler Museum, Harvard University Art Museums, loan from the family of F. Y. Chang (321.1985). Copyright © President and Fellows, Harvard College, Harvard University Art Museums; **210** *top, New Look of a Village* (about 1970), Niutung People's Commune Spare-Time Art Group; *bottom* Copyright © Dennis Cox/China Stock; **212–216** Photos by Sharon Hoogstraten.

Unit Two

228 Detail of *Sunday Morning Breakfast* (1943), Horace Pippin. Private collection, courtesy Galerie St. Etienne, New York; **232** *left* The Granger Collection, New York; **233, 234** Copyright © Eiji Vanagi/Photonica; **238** *left* North Wind Picture Archive; *right* The Bettmann Archive; **239, 240** *top left,* **242, 244, 246, 247** J. Graham/H. Armstrong Roberts; **250** Detail of *Street Corner Shop,* Colin Middleton. Christie's Images, New York; **253** *Spring Planting* (1988), Jonathan Green. Oil on masonite, 24″ × 32″. Collection of Shigeki Masui. Photograph by Tim Stamm; **256** Details of *Corn Maiden* (1982) David Dawangyumptewa. Photo copyright © 1987 by Jerry Jacka; **261** *left* AP/Wide World Photos; *right, White Breeze* (1995), Jonathan Green. Oil on canvas, 48″ × 60″. Collection of Gilbert and Elizabeth Ney. Photograph by Tim Stamm; **262** *left* The Granger Collection, New York; *right* Copyright © Nancy Crampton; **264–265** Copyright © Masakazu Kure/Photonica; **273** AP/Wide World Photos; **277–281** Photos by Sharon Hoogstraten; **283** Copyright © Uniphoto; **285** Mander & Mitchenson, Kent, England; **287, 288** Photo by Sharon Hoogstraten; **301, 302** Sovfoto; **303** Photo courtesy of Carmine Fantasia; **304, 305** *backgrounds* Courtesy of the Economics and Public Affairs Division, The New York Public Library, Astor, Lenox and Tilden Foundations; **306** Photo courtesy of Carmine Fantasia; *frame* Photo by Sharon Hoogstraten; **307** *background* Courtesy of the Economics and Public Affairs Division, The New York Public Library, Astor, Lenox and Tilden Foundations; **312, 314** Corbis-Bettmann; **327** Sean Sexton Collection/Corbis; **328** Drawing by Sean O'Sullivan; **329** *top* Illustration by

1282 ACKNOWLEDGMENTS

Robbin Gourley; **335, 341** *backgrounds* Photo by Sharon Hoogstraten; **344** Leo de Wys, Inc./ de Wys/D & J Heaton; **346, 347** *foreground* Copyright © Uniphoto; **347** *background* Copyright © David Rigg/Tony Stone Images; **350** By permission of the Houghton Library, Harvard University; **352–353** Illustration by Sarah Figlio; **355** *left* Globe Photos; **355** *right,* **359** Photos by Sharon Hoogstraten; **361** Copyright © SuperStock; **362** Photo from European Picture Service/FPG International; **363** AP/Wide World Photos; **364–368** Photos by Sharon Hoogstraten; **370** Detail of *The Lovers (Somali Friends)* (1950), Lois Mailou Jones. Casein on canvas. The Evans-Tibbs Collection, Washington, D.C.; **374–376** Photos by Sharon Hoogstraten.

Unit Three

386 Courtesy Cluett, Peabody & Co., Inc.; **395** The Granger Collection, New York; **396** Stock Montage; **397** Illustration by Emma Baron. Copyright © Stock Illustration Source; **409** Courtesy the Lilly Library, Indiana University, Bloomington, Indiana; **410** Photo first appeared in *Letters Home.* Copyright © 1975. Reprinted with permission from Aurelia Schober Plath. All rights reserved; **414–415** Corbis; **418** Corbis-Bettmann; **431** Globe Photos; **432** Copyright © Culver Pictures; **433** Illustration by Meredith Nemirov; **438** Copyright © 1995 Bill Eichner; **439** *Portrait of Miss Jen Sun-ch'ang* (1934), William McGregor Paxton. Pastel on dark tan paper, 18″ × 14″. Courtesy of Robert Douglas Hunter; **443** *top* Photo by Sharon Hoogstraten; *bottom* Lynette Tom; **445–449** Photos by Sharon Hoogstraten; **455** *Campesino* [Farmer] (1976), Daniel DeSiga. Oil on canvas, 50½″ x 58½″. Collection of Alfredo Aragón, courtesy UCLA at the Armand Hammer Museum of Art and Cultural Center, Los Angeles, California; **467** *left* Photo by Fred Viebahn; *right* Photo by Michael Nye; **468** *Jimmy O'D* (about 1925), Robert Henri. Oil on canvas, 24″ × 20″. Collection of the Montclair (New Jersey) Art Museum, museum purchase, Picture Buying Fund (26.1); **480** AP/Wide World Photos; **481** Copyright © G. Paul Bishop; **482** Corbis; **485** *background,* Photo by Sharon Hoogstraten; **492** *right* Corbis; **493** AP/Wide World Photos; **496–497, 498** *photographic backgrounds* Copyright © H. Franca/SuperStock; **498** *left* The Granger Collection, New York; *right* Coward of Canberra; **499–503** *border* Photo by Sharon Hoogstraten; **499** *top* Copyright © Ilene Perlman/Impact Visuals/PNI; *frame* Photo by Sharon Hoogstraten; *bottom* Carl Iwasaki/*Life* magazine. Copyright © 1953 Time, Inc.; **500** *left* UPI/Corbis-Bettmann; *right* Courtesy of Spelman College, Atlanta, Georgia; **501** *bottom left* Copyright © 1990 TIB/West/J .P. Pieuchot; *top right (three images)* Photofest; **502** *top* Copyright © 1963 Bob Adelman/Magnum Photos; *television* Copyright © PhotoDisc; *bottom* Copyright © James Keyser/Contact Press Images/PNI; **503, 506** Photo by Sharon Hoogstraten; **507, 509** Details of *Nia: Purpose* (1991), Varnette Honeywood. Monoprint. Collection of Karen Kennedy. Copyright © 1991 Varnette P. Honeywood; **510–511, 512** Photos by Sharon Hoogstraten; **513–516** *border* Photo by Sharon Hoogstraten; **514** *Working Woman* (1947), Elizabeth Catlett. Oil on canvas. Courtesy of the Barnett-Aden Collection, Museum of African American Art, Tampa, Florida; **519** From *Always My Dad* by Sharon Dennis, illustrated by Raul Colon. Illustrations copyright © 1994 Raul Colon. Reprinted by permission of Alfred A. Knopf, Inc.; **520** *border* Photo by Sharon Hoogstraten; **521** Copyright © Anthony Barboza/Shooting Star; **522, 527–529** *border* Photo by Sharon Hoogstraten; **528** Copyright © Ilene Perlman/Impact Visuals/PNI; **529** Copyright © Frank Capri/Saga/Archive Photos/PNI; **530–534** Photos by Sharon Hoogstraten.

Unit Four

546 *Portrait of André Derain* (1905), Henri Matisse. Tate Gallery, London/Art Resource, New York. Copyright © 1995 Succesion H. Matisse, Paris/Artists Rights Society (ARS), New York; **557** *Green Fish* (about 1928), Selden Gile. Oil on board. Bedford Gallery, Dean Lesher Regional Center for the Arts, Walnut Creek, California; **558** The Granger Collection,

ACKNOWLEDGMENTS **1283**

New York; **559, 561, 565, 571** Illustrations from *Tales of Edgar Allan Poe,* illustrated by Barry Moser, one of the Books of Wonder Series. Illustrations copyright © 1991 Pennyroyal Press. By permission of Morrow Junior Books, a division of William Morrow & Company, Inc.; **576** *Detail of Auto de Fe in the Plaza Mayor, Madrid, 30 June 1680,* Francisco Rizi. Museo del Prado, Madrid, Spain/Art Resource, New York; **577** From the collections of the Library of Congress; **582** Imperial War Museum, London; **583** *left* The Granger Collection, New York; *right* Howard Simmons; **585** Illustration by Lee Steadman; **590** Peter Finger/Corbis; **592** National Archives; **593** The Bettmann Archive; **594–599** *barbed wire* Photo by Sharon Hoogstraten; **599** The Bettmann Archive; **601** Erich Hartmann/Magnum Photos; **602** The Bettmann Archive; **603** From the collections of the Library of Congress; **614** Howard Ikemoto; **616–620** Photos by Sharon Hoogstraten; **644** Copyright © Jerry Bauer; **645** Copyright © 1998 Medford Taylor/Black Star; **647** From the collections of the Library of Congress; **648** Copyright © 1998 Medford Taylor/Black Star; **650** Michael Rougier/*Life* magazine. Copyright © Time, Inc.; **651** *left* National Archives; *right* By permission of the Houghton Library, Harvard University; **661** Globe Photos; **662** AP/Wide World Photos; **664** Detail of *The Monument to Peter I on Senate Square in Petersburg* (1870), Vasilii Ivanovich Surikov.The State Russian Museum, St. Petersburg, Russia; **665, 666–667** *background* Photo by Sharon Hoogstraten; **676** *Self-Portrait* (about 1865), James Tissot. The Fine Arts Museums of San Francisco, Mildred Anna Williams Collection (1961.16); **677** Itar-Tass/Sovfoto; **681** Culver Pictures; **682** Photofest; **683** *portrait* The Granger Collection, New York; *frame* Image Farm; **684** *top* The Granger Collection, New York; *bottom left* Drawing by C. Walter Hodges; *bottom right* Photo by Chantal Schütz, courtesy of Shakespeare's Globe, London; **685** The Granger Collection, New York; **686** Museo Pio Clementino, Vatican Museums, Vatican State/Scala/Art Resource, New York; **690–691** Copyright © Antonio Attini/White Star; **692** *reconstruction of Forum* Soprintendenza alle Antichità, Rome/Scala/Art Resource, New York; *inset* Map by Bill Graham/Koralik Associates; **762** *top center* Museum of the City of New York Theatre Collection, gift of Mrs. Barry Sommers (53.215.45); **797** North Wind Picture Archive; **798, 800–804, 810–812** Photos by Sharon Hoogstraten.

Unit Five

834 Amos Nachoum/Corbis; **835** The Granger Collection, New York; **837** Photo by Marcia Booth Murdock, courtesy of Rocky Flats Photography Department; **842** National Archives; **847** *left* The Luce Studio; *center* Copyright © Jan Kanter; *right* Copyright © Layle Silbert; **849** Detail of Jain ceremonial scroll *(Surya Pragnapti).* Spencer Collection, The New York Public Library, Astor, Lenox and Tilden Foundations (Indian MS 69); **854** Catherine Karnow/Corbis; **855** Globe Photos; **860** AP/Wide World Photos; **861–865** Photos by Sharon Hoogstraten; **871** *Portrait of Count Fürstenberg-Herdringen* (1924), Tamara de Lempicka. Oil on canvas, 16⅛″ × 10¾″. Courtesy of Barry Friedman Ltd., New York. Copyright © 1996 Artists Rights Society (ARS), New York/SPADEM, Paris; **891** *Portrait de Madame M.,* Tamara de Lempicka. Oil on canvas, 99 cm × 65 cm. Private collection, Paris. Copyright © 1996 Artists Rights Society (ARS), New York/SPADEM, Paris; **892** The Granger Collection, New York; **893, 894** *Scales* (about 1968–1977), Mitsumasa Anno. From *The Unique World of Mitsumasa Anno,* published by Kodansha Ltd., Tokyo; **896, 897** Illustrations by Rebecca McClellan; **902** German Information Service; **903** *La reproduction interdite (Portrait d'Edward James)* [Not to be reproduced (Portrait of Edward James)] (1937), René Magritte. Oil on canvas, 81.3 cm × 65 cm. Museum Boymans–van Beuningen, Rotterdam, Netherlands/Giraudon/Art Resource, New York. Copyright © 1996 Artists Rights Society (ARS), New York; **907** *left* Neil Libbert/Camera Press/Globe Photos; *right* UPI/Bettmann; **909, 911** Photo by Sharon Hoogstraten; **913** Copyright © 1990 Ron Kimball; **914** Photo by Sharon

1284 ACKNOWLEDGMENTS

Hoogstraten; **915** AP/Wide World Photos; **918–922** *border* Photo by Sharon Hoogstraten; **918** *signature* The Granger Collection, New York; *top right* Copyright © Archive Photos/PNI; *bottom left* Copyright © Myrleen Ferguson/PhotoEdit; *bottom right* Courtesy of The Steinbeck House, Salinas, California; **920** *right* Courtesy of The Steinbeck House, Salinas, California; **921** *counterclockwise from left* Photofest; Photofest; Photo by Michael Brosilow, courtesy of Steppenwolf Theater, Chicago; Photofest; S.S. Archives/Shooting Star International; **926, 928** *bottom* Horace Bristol/Corbis; **928** *top,* **929, 930, 931** Copyright © Horace Bristol; **932** *top, bottom* Horace Bristol/Corbis; **933–935** *border* Photo by Sharon Hoogstraten; **935, 936** UPI/Corbis-Bettmann; **939–941** *border* Photo by Sharon Hoogstraten; **940** D. Robert Franz/Corbis; **943** *signature* The Granger Collection, New York; **944** AP/Wide World Photos; **945–947** *border* Photo by Sharon Hoogstraten; **946** UPI/Corbis-Bettmann; **947** Copyright © Archive Photos/PNI; **948–952** Photos by Sharon Hoogstraten.

Unit Six
964 Detail of *News from the Gulf* (about 1991), Robert A. Wade. Watercolor, 19″ × 29″. Private collection. Copyright © Robert A. Wade. From *Painting Your Vision in Watercolor* (North Light Books); **965, 967** *background,* **968, 971** *background,* **972** Photos by Sharon Hoogstraten; **975** Corbis-Bettmann; **976** Reuters/Bettmann; **977** AP/Wide World Photos; **996** Illustration by David Loew/ARTCO; **997** AP/Wide World Photos; **999** *top* Carraro/Rex USA Ltd.; *bottom* Reuters/Bettmann; **1001** *left* Copyright © 1989 Michelle Barnes/The Image Bank; **1007** Michael Dorris; **1008** Photo by Sharon Hoogstraten; **1009** *top* Copyright © Mary Kate Denny/PhotoEdit; *bottom* Copyright © Monkmeyer Press/Shackman; **1012** Photo by Sharon Hoogstraten; **1018** Copyright © 1992 Michal Daniel; **1032** *theater diagram* From *The History of the Greek and Roman Theater* by Margarete Bieber, published by Princeton University Press, 1939; **1063** The Granger Collection, New York; **1064** Detail of illumination showing Lancelot rescuing Guinevere by crossing the sword bridge (about 1300), from a manuscript of *Le Roman de Lancelot du Lac* (M. 806, fol. 166). The Pierpont Morgan Library, New York/Art Resource, New York; **1081** The Granger Collection, New York; **1087** *left* Copyright © 1978 Jay Kay Klein; *right* Stock Montage; **1089** Copyright © Hallmark Entertainment/Shooting Star. All rights reserved; **1101** AP/Wide World Photos; **1104** *top* Detail of millefleurs tapestry with horseman and arms of Jean de Daillon (late 1400s), unknown Flemish artist. National Trust Photographic Library; *bottom* Annie F. Valva; **1105–1112** Photos by Sharon Hoogstraten.

Reading Handbook
1120 *bottom inset left* Copyright © Paul Simcock/Brand X Pictures/PictureQuest; *bottom inset center* Copyright © PhotoDisc/Getty Images; *bottom inset right* Copyright © Paul Simcock/Brand X Pictures/PictureQuest; **1132** *left* Copyright © Paul Simcock/Brand X Pictures/PictureQuest; *center* Copyright © PhotoDisc/Getty Images; *right* Copyright © Paul Simcock/Brand X Pictures/PictureQuest; **1141** Copyright © PhotoDisc/Getty Images.

Multicultural Advisory Board *(continued)*

Noreen M. Rodriguez, Trainer for Hillsborough County School District's Staff Development Division, independent consultant, Gaither High School, Tampa, Florida

Olga Y. Sanmaniego, English Department Chairperson, Burges High School, El Paso, Texas

Liz Sawyer-Cunningham, Los Angeles Senior High School, Los Angeles, California

Michelle Dixon Thompson, Seabreeze High School, Daytona Beach, Florida

ACKNOWLEDGMENTS **1285**

Teacher Review Panels *(continued)*

CALIFORNIA (continued)

Karen Buxton, English Department Chairperson, Winston Churchill Middle School, San Juan School District

Bonnie Garrett, Davis Middle School, Compton School District

Sally Jackson, Madrona Middle School, Torrance Unified School District

Sharon Kerson, Los Angeles Center for Enriched Studies, Los Angeles Unified School District

Gail Kidd, Center Middle School, Azusa School District

Corey Lay, ESL Department Chairperson, Chester Nimitz Middle School, Los Angeles Unified School District

Myra LeBendig, Forshay Learning Center, Los Angeles Unified School District

Dan Manske, Elmhurst Middle School, Oakland Unified School District

Joe Olague, Language Arts Department Chairperson, Alder Middle School, Fontana School District

Pat Salo, 6th Grade Village Leader, Hidden Valley Middle School, Escondido Elementary School District

FLORIDA

Judith H. Briant, English Department Chairperson, Armwood High School, Hillsborough County School District

Beth Johnson, Polk County English Supervisor, Polk County School District

Sharon Johnston, Learning Resource Specialist, Evans High School, Orange County School District

Eileen Jones, English Department Chairperson, Spanish River High School, Palm Beach County School District

Jan McClure, Winter Park High School, Orange County School District

Wanza Murray, English Department Chairperson (retired), Vero Beach Senior High School, Indian River City School District

Shirley Nichols, Language Arts Curriculum Specialist Supervisor, Marion County School District

Debbie Nostro, Ocoee Middle School, Orange County School District

Barbara Quinaz, Assistant Principal, Horace Mann Middle School, Dade County School District

OHIO

Glyndon Butler, English Department Chairperson, Glenville High School, Cleveland City School District

Ellen Geisler, English/Language Arts Department Chairperson, Mentor Senior High School, Mentor School District

Dr. Paulette Goll, English Department Chairperson, Lincoln West High School, Cleveland City School District

Loraine Hammack, Executive Teacher of the English Department, Beachwood High School, Beachwood City School District

Marguerite Joyce, English Department Chairperson, Woodridge High School, Woodridge Local School District

Sue Nelson, Shaw High School, East Cleveland School District

Dee Phillips, Hudson High School, Hudson Local School District

Carol Steiner, English Department Chairperson, Buchtel High School, Akron City School District

1286 ACKNOWLEDGMENTS

Nancy Strauch, English Department Chairperson, Nordonia High School, Nordonia Hills City School Dictrict

Ruth Vukovich, Hubbard High School, Hubbard Exempted Village School District

TEXAS

Dana Davis, English Department Chairperson, Irving High School, Irving Independent School District

Susan Fratcher, Cypress Creek High School, Cypress Fairbanks School District

Yolanda Garcia, Abilene High School, Abilene Independent School District

Patricia Helm, Lee Freshman High School, Midland Independent School District

Joanna Huckabee, Moody High School, Corpus Christi Independent School District

Josie Kinard, English Department Chairperson, Del Valle High School, Ysleta Independent School District

Mary McFarland, Amarillo High School, Amarillo Independent School District

Gwen Rutledge, English Department Chairperson, Scarborough High School, Houston Independent School District

Bunny Schmaltz, Assistant Principal, Ozen High School, Beaumont Independent School District

Michael Urick, A. N. McCallum High School, Austin Independent School District

Manuscript Reviewers *(continued)*

Kathleen M. Anderson-Knight, United Township High School, East Moline, Illinois

Anita Arnold, Thomas Jefferson High School, San Antonio, Texas

Cassandra L. Asberry, Dean of Instruction, Carter High School, Dallas, Texas

Jolene Auderer, Pine Tree High School, Longview, Texas

Don Baker, English Department Chairperson, Peoria High School, Peoria, Illinois

Beverly Ann Barge, Wasilla High School, Wasilla, Alaska

Louann Bohman, Wilbur Cross High School, New Haven, Connecticut

Rose Mary Bolden, J. F. Kimball High School, Dallas, Texas

Lydia C. Bowden, Boca Ciega High School, St. Petersburg, Florida

Angela Boyd, Andrews High School, Andrews, Texas

Judith H. Briant, Armwood High School, Seffner, Florida

Hugh Delle Broadway, McCullough High School, The Woodlands, Texas

Stephan P. Clarke, Spencerport High School, Spencerport, New York

Kathleen D. Crapo, South Fremont High School, St. Anthony, Idaho

Dr. Shawn Eric DeNight, Miami Edison High School, Miami, Florida

JoAnna R. Exacoustas, La Serna High School, Whittier, California

Linda Ferguson, English Department Head, Tyee High School, Seattle, Washington

Ellen Geisler, Mentor Senior High School, Mentor, Ohio

Ricardo Godoy, English Department Chairman, Moody High School, Corpus Christi, Texas

Meredith Gunn, Secondary Language Arts Instructional Specialist, Katy, Texas

Judy Hammack, English Department Chairperson, Milton High School, Alpharetta, Georgia

Robert Henderson, West Muskingum High School, Zanesville, Ohio

Martha Watt Hosenfeld, English Department Chairperson, Churchville-Chili High School, Churchville, New York

Janice M. Johnson, Assistant Principal, Union High School, Grand Rapids, Michigan

Eileen S. Jones, English Department Chair, Spanish River Community High School, Boca Raton, Florida

ACKNOWLEDGMENTS **1287**

Paula S. L'Homme, West Orange High School, Winter Garden, Florida
Bonnie J. Mansell, Downey Adult School, Downey, California
Linda Maxwell, MacArthur High School, Houston, Texas
Ruth McClain, Paint Valley High School, Bainbridge, Ohio
Rebecca Miller, Taft High School, San Antonio, Texas
Deborah Lynn Moeller, Western High School, Fort Lauderdale, Florida
Bobbi Darrell Montgomery, Batavia High School, Batavia, Ohio
Bettie Moody, Leesburg High School, Leesburg, Florida
Margaret L. Mortenson, English Department Chairperson, Timpanogos High School, Orem, Utah
Marjorie M. Nolan, Language Arts Department Head, William M. Raines Sr. High School, Jacksonville, Florida
Julia Pferdehirt, freelance writer, former Special Education teacher, Middleton, Wisconsin
Cindy Rogers, MacArthur High School, Houston, Texas
Pauline Sahakian, English Department Chairperson, San Marcos High School, San Marcos, Texas
Jacqueline Y. Schmidt, Department Chairperson and Coordinator of English, San Marcos High School, San Marcos, Texas
David D. Schultz, East Aurora High School, East Aurora, New York
Milinda Schwab, Judson High School, Converse, Texas
John Sferro, Butler High School, Vandalia, Ohio
Brad R. Smedley, English Department Chairperson, Hudtloff Middle School, Lakewood, Washington
Faye S. Spangler, Versailles High School, Versailles, Ohio
Rita Stecich, Evergreen Park Community High School, Evergreen Park, Illinois
GayleAnn Turnage, Abiline High School, Abiline, Texas
Ruth Vukovich, Hubbard High School, Hubbard, Ohio
Kevin J. Walsh, Dondero High School, Royal Oak, Michigan
Charlotte Washington, Westwood Middle School, Grand Rapids, Michigan
Tom Watson, Westbridge Academy, Grand Rapids, Michigan
Linda Weatherby, Deerfield High School, Deerfield, Illinois

1288 ACKNOWLEDGMENTS